The Scots
Dialect Dictionary

The Scots Dialect Dictionary

serving as a glossary for Ramsay, Fergusson, Burns, Scott, Galt, minor poets, kailyard novelists, and a host of other writers of the Scottish tongue

COMPILED BY

ALEXANDER WARRACK, M.A.

with a new Foreword and Introduction by

BETTY KIRKPATRICK, M.A.

NEW ORCHARD EDITIONS
POOLE   DORSET

Originally published in 1911
This 1988 edition published by
Tantallon Books
17 Abercorn Court
Edinburgh EH8 7LP

Copyright © 1988 New Orchard Editions Ltd.

ISBN 1-85079-129-5

Printed in Austria

CONTENTS

INTRODUCTION
By BETTY KIRKPATRICK

It is likely that most people will use this dictionary to find the meanings of words encountered either in the course of their reading or in the speech of their acquaintances. Many, particularly those of an older generation will use it to reacquaint themselves with old friends – words familiar to them in childhood but now scarcely remembered. Relatively few will use it to teach themselves Scots. For the sake of those brave mortals, and others who will find it helpful, some guidance is necessary on how to pronounce some of the words listed in the dictionary.

Without making the dictionary too large it is impossible to include a pronounciation guide for each word. However, this is not really a handicap for users. If some patterns of words are committed to memory, then no specialised knowledge of pronunciation is necessary. A remarkable number of people, including many Scots themselves have a hazy notion of what constitutes the Scots language. It is even common to regard it as a dialectal form of standard English, and a debased, ungrammatical form at that. This attitude is simply a reflection on how important the South of England has become in almost every aspect of our lives. Because it boasts the seat of British government and throne, not to mention many major institutions, its language has become the standard method of communication throughout the United Kingdom. But it is quite wrong if not verging on the criminal to regard Scots simply as an offshoot of English. In fact it developed as a separate language, albeit alongside the language of Scotland's close neighbours, and as such has a vocabulary, spelling, pronunciation and etymology all its own. Because standard English has long been the official language of education, many Scots are nervous of pronouncing words in their native tongue. The traditional bilingual Scots pupil with one language for the classroom and one for the playground and home was left with the virtually indelible impression that his/her unofficial language was an inferior and uneducated one.

It is difficult to give a guide to Scots pronunciation which is at once comprehensive and concise. There are too many regional variations for this to be practical. Both pronunciation and vocabulary can change quite dramatically from the Borders to the North East and the North East to the islands of Orkney and Shetland.

For example Scots speakers in the area around Aberdeen substitute **f** for **wh** at the beginning of certain words as in **fit** for **what** a **fa** for **who**. Vowel variations are common also with the Scots equivalent of the English **call** being pronounced **caw** in some areas and **cah** in others. All of this can seem very confusing particularly to people totally unused to the Scots language. A few minutes concentrating on the main points of distinction between Scots and English pronunciation, will provide a way through the maze, at least for those who have a working knowledge of English.

PRONUNCIATION GUIDE

VOWELS

Scots a	as in warm	pronounced like a	in English arm
,, ai ,,	,, sair (= sore)	,, ,, a ,,	,, bare
,, au ,,	,, staun (= stand)	,, ,, aw ,,	,, lawn
,, ei ,,	,, cheip (= chirp)	,, ,, ee ,,	,, weep
,, ie ,,	,, chiel (= man)	,, ,, ee ,,	,, weep
,, e ,,	,, leme (= gleam)	,, ,, ee ,,	,, weep
,, eu ,,	,, neuk (= nook)	,, ,, yoo ,,	,, you
,, ey ,,	,, gey (= very)	,, ,, i ,,	,, mine
,, ou ,,	,, broun (= brown)	,, ,, oo ,,	,, moon
,, ow ,,	,, howe (= hollow)	,, ,, ow ,,	,, down
,, ui ,,	,, guid (= good)	,, ,, i ,,	,, lid
,, ue ,,	,, spune (= spoon)	,, ,, u	in French plume
,, ui ,,	,, puir (= poor)	,, ,, a	in English pair
,, ch ,,	,, loch	,, ,, German ich, (gluttural	
	nicht (= night)	sound with no English equivalent)	
,, ch ,,	,, chitter (= shiver)	,, ,, ch	in English charm
,, ch ,,	,, streetch (= stretch)	,, ,, ch ,,	,, stretch
,, ng ,,	,, finger	(pronounced with the g silent like the	
		English singer)	

There are two general points to remember about the pronunciation of Scots. One is that the "r" sound is pronounced with much more emphasis than in English. The other is the famous or infamous glottal stop. This occurs in the Scots equivalent of English words such as **butter** and **patter** where many Scots ignore both "t's". Likewise Scots tend not to pronounce the hard consonant in words such as **tumble**, **fumble** and **handle** which became **tuml**, **fuml** etc. This is frequently reflected in the Scots spelling **tummle**, **haunle** etc.

Many lovers of words, Scots or otherwise, are particularly interested in the origins of words and phrases. Sadly although Scots is rich in its historical associations, many words, particularly those of Scandinavian or French origin, being absent from its English cousin, word origins have had to be left out because of pressure of space. In any case etymology, the science of dealing with the origin of words, is almost by definition one of the least precise sciences. Origins inevitably get confused or even lost by the passage of time. Word family trees are even more difficult to compile than those of people. Many words therefore end up being designated either "etymology unknown" or "origin uncertain". Yet more are the subject of heated dispute as one person's inspired guess becomes someone else's rejected theory. Folk etymology is almost as common as folk tales. Giving all the conjectured details of the pros and cons is therefore space consuming and beyond the scope of this book. Those who are particularly interested in this aspect of Scots should consult either the Scottish National Dictionary or the Dictionary of the Older Scottish Tongue. Both of these excellent many volumed works of scholarship also make absorbing further reading for those whose linguistic appetites have been whetted by the present volume. Those who find themselves short of the valuable commodity time or who simply want an introduction to the seeming mysteries of Scots will find the present volume ideally suited at a price they can afford!

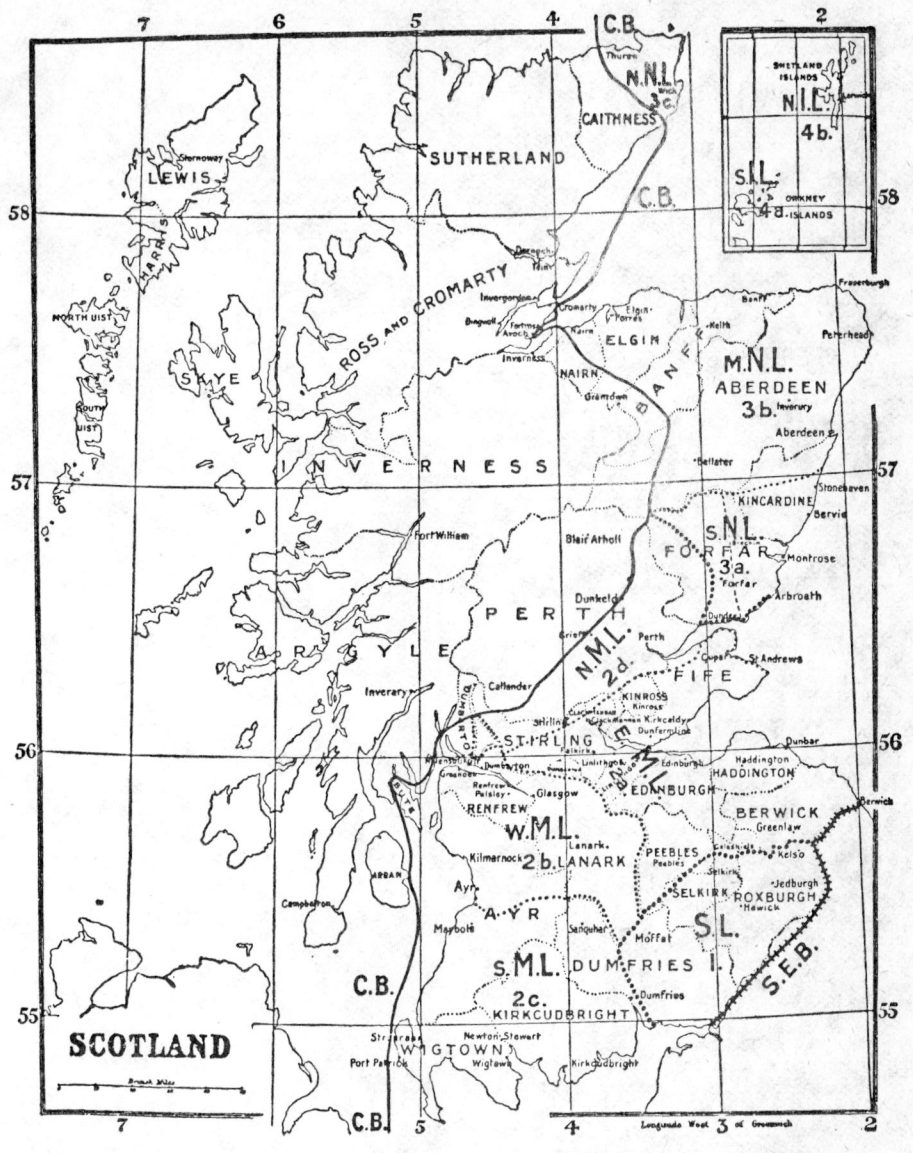

SCOTLAND

C.B.	Celtic Border	**N.**	North(ern)	**S.**	South(ern)
S.E.B.	Scottish-English Border	**E.**	Eastern	**W.**	Western
L.	Lowland	**M.**	Mid	**I.**	Insular

The figures, as 2a., 2b., 2c., 2d., etc., show sub-divisions of a dialect region.

NEW FOREWORD
By BETTY KIRKPATRICK M.A.

One of the most encouraging things to happen in Scotland in recent times is the increase in interest in the Scots language. At last we seem to have been made aware of the richness of our linguistic heritage – and not before time.

It is difficult to know whether this interest has been aroused by the recent spate of Scots language reference books or whether the books were published in response to the interest. Which was the chicken and which was the egg?

In either event this particular volume, first published long before the renaissance of the interest in Scots, has stood the test of time and is as relevant today as it was on its publication date. Unlike the English language the Scots language is not subject to regular wholesale change, perhaps because not enough of us use it on a day-to-day basis.

Apart from the inevitable development of urban Scots slang there have been relatively few additions to the Scots language in recent years. When innovation was necessary we have tended to opt for the English word. Hence, unlike its English counterparts, the vocabulary list of a Scots dictionary does not vary significantly from year to year.

One of the most useful features of this particular volume is the number of spelling variants it includes. Partly because Scots has been for so long a secondary, or even a dying language, partly because it has been very much based on an oral tradition, it lacks a standard spelling scheme of the kind enjoyed by the English language.

This makes the compilation of a Scots dictionary something of a problem. Does the compiler select almost at random one possible spelling and hope that the user finds it? Or does he try to allow for the most common variants and increase the length of the book – but make it more user-friendly?

Those involved in the present work opted for ease of use at the expense of some repetition. Thus the Scots for a fir-cone is entered both at *ewe* and *jow*, muddy at *jummlie* and *jumly*, a clock at *knock* and *nock*, reluctant at *sweired* and *sweert*, worn out at *forfochen* and *forfouchen* and so on.

The dictionary is not only an aid to reading Scots literature or understanding what Scots speakers are saying but a wonderful book to browse through. It reveals all kinds of linguistic treasures, some half-remembered, some never known.

Most households have at least one English dictionary, however out-of-date, but even now too few have any form of Scots dictionary. This is particularly sad from the point of view of children who are in danger of losing contact with Scots. Think how hard it is for it to compete with the language of the television set.

A reliable Scots dictionary would at least go some way in combating this influence. If children can be shown in black and white that the strange words used by their parents, or even more so by their grandparents, are not just personal idiosyncracies, they might take them more seriously.

Moreover, it might just encourage them to start using such words themselves. After all it is to them that our linguistic heritage must be handed on. Otherwise it will die. Do we really want to take the responsibility for that?

EDINBURGH
JULY 1988

LIST OF ABBREVIATIONS USED IN THIS DICTIONARY.

adj.	. . .	adjective.	*pl.*	. . .	plural.
adv.	. . .	adverb.	*poss.*	. .	possessive.
aux.	. . .	auxiliary.	*ppl.*	. .	participle.
Cf.	. . .	compare.	*ppl. adj.*	. .	participial adjective.
comb.	. .	combination.	*pref.*	. .	prefix.
conj.	. . .	conjunction.	*prep.*	. .	preposition.
excl.	. . .	exclamation.	*pret.*	. .	preterite, perfect tense.
int.	. . .	interjection.	*pron.*	. .	pronoun.
n.	. . .	noun.	*refl. pron.*	.	reflexive pronoun.
neg.	. . .	negative.	*suff.*	. .	suffix.
phr., phrs.	.	phrase, phrases.	*v.*	. . .	verb.

The † prefixed in the text indicates words apparently not of Scottish parentage
but imported from abroad.

SCOTS DIALECT DICTIONARY

A, *prep.* in *comp.* on.
A, *v.* have.
A, *pron.* I. Cf. Aw.
A, *int.* ah ! eh !
A', *adj.* all ; every. Cf. Aw.
A, Aa, *n.* an island. Cf. Ey.
Aa, *ppl.* owning ; possessed of.
Aa, *v.* to owe.
Aad, *v. pret.* owed.
Aal, *adj.* old. Cf. Auld.
Aan, Aand, *ppl.* owing.
Aar, *n.* the alder. Cf. Arn.
Aar, *n.* a scar. Cf. Arr.
Aaron's beard, *n.* St John's wort ; the *Linaria cymbalaria* ; the *Orchis mascula.*
Aaron's rod, *n.* mullein.
Aava, *int.* an excl. of banter or contradiction. Cf. Awa.
Aave, *n.* a spoon-net, or 'scummer,' used in herring-fishing. Cf Haave.
Aback, *adv.* aloof ; away ; of time : ago.— *v.* to keep or hold back.
Abaid, *v. pret.* abode.
†Abaisin, Abasin, *n.* ill-treatment by word or deed.
†Abaisit, *ppl.* abashed ; confounded ; ill-treated.
Abaw, *v.* to suffer for. Cf. Aby.
Abb, *n.* the weft.
Abbey-laird, *n.* a bankrupt who fled for sanctuary to Holyrood precincts.
Abee, *adv. phr.* 'let-abee,' to let alone ; not to mention.—*n.* forbearance.
Abeech, *adv.* at a distance ; aloof. Cf. Abeigh.
Abeen, *adv.* and *prep.* above. Cf. Aboon.
Abefoir, *adv.* formerly.
Abeigh, *adv.* aloof ; at a distance.
Abeis, *prep.* in comparison with.
Aben, *adv.* in the parlour ; in the 'ben.' Cf. Ben.
Aberdeen-awa, *adv.* in or near Aberdeen.— *adj.* native of, or hailing from, Aberdeen.
Abidden, *ppl.* of abide ; dwelt.
A-bie', *adv.* in shelter.
Abies, *prep.* in comparison with. Cf. Abeis.

†Abigent, *n.* forcible driving away in theft.
Ability, *n.* wealth.
Abin, *adv.* and *prep.* above. Cf. Aboon.
Abit, *conj. phr.* yes ! but——.
Ablach, Ablack, *n.* a dwarf ; an insignificant, worthless person ; a particle, fragment.— *adj.* incapable.
Able, *adj.* substantial ; well-to-do ; fit ; liable.
Able, Ables, *adv.* perhaps ; possibly. Cf. Ablins.
Ableeze, *adv.* ablaze.
Able-sea, *adv.* it may be so.
Ablich, *n.* a dwarf. Cf. Ablach.
Ablins, *adv.* possibly ; perhaps.
Ablow, *prep.* below.
A'body, *n.* everybody.
Aboil, *adv.* in or to a boiling state.
Abok, *n.* a talkative, forward child. Cf. Yabbock.
Aboon, *adv.* above ; overhead.—*prep.* beyond ; superior to ; more than.
Aboot, *adv.* into the bargain ; to boot.
Aboot, *prep.* about.—*adv.* alternately ; about ; out of the way.
Aboot with, *phr.* upsides with.
Aboulziement, *n.* dress. Cf. Abuliement.
Above, *prep.* in addition to ; after.
Abraid, *adv.* abroad.
Abraidit, *ppl. adj.* used of a carpenter's whetstone too smooth to sharpen tools.
Abrede, Abreed, Abreid, *v.* to publish ; to spread abroad.—*adv.* in breadth ; in pieces ; asunder ; to the winds ; abroad.
Abroad, *adv.* out of doors ; away from home.
Absent, *n.* an absentee.
Abstinence, *n.* a truce ; cessation of hostilities ; a fast ; a time of fasting.
†Abstract, *adj.* apart ; withdrawn from.—*v.* to withdraw a person ; to withdraw from considering ; to withhold.
Abstractness, *n.* aloofness.
Abstraklous, *adj.* cross-grained ; bad-tempered ; obstreperous.
Abuliement, *n.* dress ; cloth ; habiliment.
Abune, *adv.* and *prep.* above. Cf. Aboon.

Aby, *v.* to pay smartly for ; to suffer for ; to expiate ; to atone.

Abye, *adv.* ago ; past.

Acamie, Acamy, *adj.* small, diminutive.—*n.* anything diminutive.

Acause, *conj.* because.

†**Accable,** *v.* to overthrow.

†**Accedent,** *n.* an accession ; a casual payment.

Accept, *v.* to welcome.

Access, *n.* accession ; being accessory to.

†**Accidence,** *n.* an accident ; a slip, as of memory.

Accidently, *adv.* accidentally.

Acclame, *v.* to claim, put in a claim.

Accomie, Accumie, *n.* latten ; a mixed metal ; a trumpet made of 'accomie.'

Accomie-pen, *n.* a metallic pencil for writing on a tablet.

Accomie-spoons, *n.* spoons made of 'accomie.'

Accompt, *n.* and *v.* account.

Accost, *v.* to court, pay addresses.

Ace, *n.* ashes. Cf. Ase.

Ace, *n.* the smallest division of a thing ; a particle.

Achan, *n.* a special kind of pear. Cf. Auchan.

Ache, *v.* to cause to ache.

Achen, *n.* a marine bivalve used for bait.

Acher, *n.* an ear of corn. Cf. Icker.

Acherspire, *v.* to germinate.—*n.* the sprouting of malt.

Ack, *n.* an act.—*v.* to act ; to enact.

Ackadent, *n.* whisky ; an ardent spirit resembling rum.

Ackavity, *n.* whisky. Cf. Aqua.

Acker, Ackre, *n.* an acre.—*v.* to pay at a fixed rate per acre ; to pay at this rate harvest labourers.

Acker-dale, *adj.* divided into single acres or small portions.

Ackran, Ackrin, *n.* the harvesting of grain-crops at so much per acre.

Ackrer, *n.* one who harvests crops at so much per acre.

Ackward, *adj.* backward ; back-handed.

A-clatter, *adv.* on to talking or gossiping.

Aclite, Aclyte, *adv.* awry ; to one side ; out of joint.

Acquaintancy, *n.* acquaintance.

†**Acquant, Acquaint,** *ppl. adj.* acquainted.

Acqueesh, *prep.* between. Cf. Atweesh.

†**Acquent,** *ppl. adj.* acquainted. Cf. Acquant.

Acquit, *ppl. adj.* acquitted.

Acre, *v.* to reap at a fixed rate per acre. Cf. Acker.

Acre-braid, *n.* an acre.

Acrer, *n.* a very small proprietor.

Acrerer, *n.* an 'acrer.'

Act, *v.* with *one's self*, to come under legal obligation to do or not do certain things ; to enter in a court-book.

Action-sermon, *n.* the sermon preceding the celebration of the Lord's Supper, intended to stir up thanksgiving.

Actual, *adj.* of a minister : in full orders.

Adaes, *n.* difficulties. Cf. Ado.

†**Addebted,** *ppl.* indebted.

†**Addebtor,** *n.* a debtor.

Adder-bead, *n.* a stone supposed to be formed by adders.

Adder-bell, *n.* the dragon-fly.

Adder-cap, *n.* the dragon-fly.

Adder-stane, *n.* an ' adder-bead.'

Addikit, *ppl.* addicted.

Addiscinse, *n.* attention ; audience. Cf. Audiscence.

Addle, *n.* foul and putrid water ; the urine of cattle.—*adj.* rotten ; putrid ; foul.—*v.* to water plants with liquid manure from a byre.

Addle-dub, *n.* a pool of putrid water.

Adee, *n.* ado ; a difficulty. Cf. Ado.

Adew, *adj.* gone ; departed.

Adhibit, *v.* used of faith : to place it in one.

Adidst, *prep.* on this side of. Cf. Adist.

Adience, *n.* room ; space ; scope.

Adiest, *prep.* on this side of. Cf. Adist.

Adill, *n.* putrid water. Cf. Addle.

Adist, *prep.* on this side of.

Adjournal, *n.* the record of sentences passed in a law-court.

Adminicle, *n.* a writing, &c., tending to establish the existence or terms of a lost deed ; collateral proof.

Adminiculate, *v.* to support by 'adminicle.'

Admirality, *n.* Admiralty.

Admiration, *n.* a wonder, marvel.

Admire, *v.* to wonder, marvel.

Ado, *v.* to do.—*n.* stir ; excitement ; in *pl.* difficulties ; a pretence.

Adone, *int.* cease ; leave off.

Adow, *adj.* worth. Cf. Dow.

Adrad, *ppl. adj.* afraid ; in dread.

Adreich, *adv.* behind ; at a distance.

Adulterate, *ppl. adj.* used of money : forged, false.

Advent, *n.* interest or other money payable in advance.

Advertish, *v.* to advertise ; to warn.

Advise, *v.* to deliberate judicially with a view to judgment ; to seek advice ; to purpose, be of a mind to.

Advisement, *n.* advice ; counsel.

Advocate, *v.* to order or allow an appeal from an inferior to a superior court.

Advocation, *n.* the granting of such an appeal.

Adwang, *adj.* tiresome ; oppressive. Cf. Dwang.

Adzoons, *int.* an excl. of surprise, &c.

Ae, a'e, *adj.* one ; only ; used intensively superlatives.

Ae ae, *adj. phr.* one only.

Ae-beast-tree, *n.* a swingle-tree for a single horse ploughing.

Aefald, Aefauld, *n.* a single fold.—*adj.* guileless ; honest ; simple ; sincere.

Aefaldness, *n.* singleness of heart ; uprightness ; sincerity.

Ae-fur, *adj.* having all the soil turned one way by the plough.

Ae-fur-land, *n.* steep land ploughed only in one direction.

Ae-haun't, *adj.* single-handed ; with one hand.

Aem, *n.* vapour ; hot air ; warm glow from a fire. Cf. Oam.

Aen, *adj.* one. Cf. Ane.

Ae-pointit-girse, *n.* sedge grass.

Aesome, *adj.* single ; solitary ; lonely ; used of husband and wife : in harmony, at one.

Aesomeness, *n.* loneliness.

Afald, *adj.* honest ; sincere. Cf. Aefald.

Afeared, *adj.* afraid.

Aff, *adv.* off ; past ; beyond.—*prep.* out of ; from ; from the direction of.—*adj.* deranged mentally.—*v.* to go or run off.

Aff-book, *adv.* extempore ; without notes or book.

Aff-brack, *n.* a break-off ; any part disrupted from the whole.

Aff-cast, *n.* a castaway ; anything cast off.

Aff-come, *n.* issue ; escape ; an evasion ; an apology ; excuse.

Affect, *v.* used of lands : to burden them.

†**Affeiring,** *ppl.* appertaining to ; proportionate. Cf. Effeir.

Aff-fa'in', *n.* a scrap ; a dropping ; a perquisite ; a decline ; a falling off ; a person or thing that falls off or away from ; off-scouring.

Aff-fall, *n.* a scrap ; a piece fallen off.

Aff-fend, *v.* to ward off.

Aff-gäin', *n.* outset. Cf. Aff-going.

Aff-gang, *n.* outlet ; an ' off-go.'

Aff-ganging, *adj.* used of a tenant : leaving his farm.—*n.* the proportion of crop due to such a tenant by his successor.

Aff-gate, *n.* an outlet or market for goods.

Aff-go, *n.* a start ; beginning.

Aff-going, *n.* outset ; departure ; death.

Aff-han', *adv.* instantly ; on the spur of the moment ; extempore.—*adj.* plain-spoken ; blunt ; plain.

Aff-handit, *adj.* written or done on the spur of the moment.

†**Affidat,** *ppl. adj.* affianced.

Affin-hand, *adj.* and *adv.* 'aff-han'.'

Aff-lat, *n.* an outlet ; any outlet for water at a roadside ; a great show-off ; a temporary respite from work ; a short holiday.

Aff-loof, -lufe, *adv.* off-hand ; extempore ; without premeditation ; from memory ; without book or notes.

Affordell, *adj.* alive ; yet remaining. Cf. Fordel.

Aff-put, Aff-pit, *n.* delay ; an evasion ; pretence for delay ; a makeshift ; one who delays.

Aff-putting, *ppl. adj.* loitering ; trifling ; procrastinating.

Affront, *v.* to disgrace, put to shame.—*n.* disgrace ; shame.

Affrontedly, *adv.* with a bold, shameless front ; shamelessly.

Affrontless, *adj.* shameless ; past feeling.

Aff-set, *n.* dismission ; dismissal ; an excuse ; pretence ; what 'sets-off' or becomes a person or thing ; an ornament ; recommendation ; outset ; delay ; hindrance ; illness.

Aff-side, *n.* the farther side ; the off-side.

Aff-tak, *n.* a piece of waggery ; 'chaff' ; a wag ; mimic ; one who turns another to ridicule.

Aff-takin', *ppl. adj.* poking fun ; taking-off in ridicule.

Affward, *adv.* away ; off.

Afiel', *adv.* abroad ; in the fields ; from home.

Afire, *adv.* on fire.

Afit, *adv.* afoot.

Aflat, *adv.* flat.

Aflaught, *adv.* lying flat.

Afley, *v.* to dismay ; discomfit ; to frighten.

Aflocht, Aflought, *ppl.* agitated ; fluttered ; flustered.

Afoord, *v.* to afford.

Afore, *adv.* in front.—*prep.* before.—*conj.* ere.

Afore-fit, *adv.* indiscriminately ; without any exception.

Afore-hand, *adv.* beforehand.

Afore-lang, *adv.* shortly, erelong

Afore-syne, *adv.* formerly ; previously.

Afore-the-stern, *n.* a large sleeping-bunk in a fishing-boat.

Afouth, *adv.* enough ; in plenty ; in numbers. Cf. Fouth.

Afrist, *adv.* on credit ; in a state of delay. Cf. Frist.

Aft, *adv.* oft ; often.

Aft-crap, *n.* stubble-grass ; aftermath.

Aft-crap, *v.* to take two successive similar crops from the same field.

Aften, *adv.* often.

After, *prep.* courting ; in pursuit of ; past.—*adv.* afterwards ; left over ; with *ppl.* denotes an action just about to take place, or one that has just taken place.

After ane, *adj.* alike ; uniform.—*adv.* similarly.

Aftercast, *n.* consequence ; result.

Afterclap, *n.* disastrous result ; evil issue.

Aftercome, *n.* consequence.

Aftergait, *adj.* proper ; seemly ; moderate ; tolerable.

Aftergang, *v.* to follow ; to go after.

Afterheid, *n.* grass in the stubble after harvest.

Afterhin', Afterhend, *adv.* afterwards ; behind.

Afterings, *n.* the remainder; surplus; the last milk drawn from a cow; consequences.

After ither, *adj.* resembling each other.—*v.* to follow each other in succession.

Afternoon, *n.* afternoon refreshment.

Aftershot, *n.* the last whisky that comes from the still.

Afterstang, *n.* the pain that follows certain pleasures.

Aftersupper, *n.* the time between supper and bedtime.

Afterwald, *n.* the 'outfield' part of a farm.

Aftwhiles, *adv.* often; ofttimes.

Afward, *adv.* off; away from. Cf. Affward.

Again, *prep.* against; averse or opposed to; before; in time for.—*adv.* at another indefinite time.—*conj.* by the time that; until.

Again-call, *v.* to recall; gainsay.

Again-calling, *n.* revocation.

Again-give, *v.* to restore.

Again-say, *v.* to recall.

Against, *conj.* in readiness for; before.

Agait, *adv.* astir; afoot; on the road; away; at a distance; astray; at a loss.

Agaitward, *adv.* on the way; on the road; on the way towards.

Agate, *n.* a glass marble of variegated colour.

Agate, *adv.* astir; afoot. Cf. Agait.

A' gates, *adv.* everywhere; in all directions; all ways.

Agatting, *ppl.* gathering together.

Agee, *adj.* awry; crooked; ajar; off one's balance.—*adv.* aside.

Agent, *n.* one's lawyer, solicitor, &c.—*v.* to act as such; to manage.

Agenter, *n.* an agent; solicitor.

†Aggrege, Aggrage, *v.* to aggravate; to enhance; to increase.

Agitate, *v.* to discuss thoroughly.

Agitation, *n.* a heated discussion; a debate.

Aglee, Agley, Aglie, Agly, *adv.* off the straight; obliquely; amiss; in an immoral direction; unsuccessfully after all scheming.

Agog, *adv.* adrift; loose, 'to the winds.'

Agone, *adv.* ago.

Agonizing, *ppl.* suffering the death-throes.

Agree, *v.* agree with; agree to; with *with*, to like an article of food, to partake of it without subsequent discomfort; to settle business; to reconcile. Cf. Gree.

Agreeable, *adj.* willing; compliant; kind; obliging; with *to*, in accordance with.

Agreeance, *n.* agreement; harmony. Cf. Greeance.

Agroof, Agrouf, Agrufe, *adv.* on one's belly; prone; grovelling. Cf. Grouf.

Agrue, *adv.* in a shudder. Cf. Grue.

Agyaun, *ppl.* agoing.

Ahame, *adv.* at home; within doors.

Ahan, *n.* a horse; a cow a year old.

Ahechie, *int.* an excl. of ludicrous contempt. Cf. Hech.

Ahin, Ahint, Ahent, *prep.* behind; after; at the back of.—*adv.* late; behind in time; behindhand; backward; in error; in debt; in arrear.

A-hishi-baw, *n.* a lullaby. Cf. Hushie-ba.

Ahomel, *adv.* bottom upwards; upside-down. Cf. Awhummel.

Ah-wa, *int.* an excl. of surprise, contempt, &c.

Aiblach, *n.* a dwarf; a worthless person. Cf. Ablach.

Aiblins, *adv.* perhaps; possibly. Cf. Ablins.

Aich, *n.* an echo.—*v.* to echo.

Aichan, *n.* a small marine bivalve used for bait. Cf. Achen.

Aicher, *n.* an ear of barley; a head of oats or barley. Cf. Icker.

Aicherd, *ppl. adj.* used of grain: eared.

Aicht, *ppl.* possessed of. Cf. Aucht.

Aichus, *n.* a heavy fall causing strong respiration. Cf. Haiches.

Aidle, *n.* the urine of cattle. Cf. Addle.

Aidle-hole, *n.* a hole to receive 'aidle.'

Aifer, *n.* ground exhalations on a warm day.

Aifrins, *n.* the last milk drawn from a cow; 'afterings.'

Aiftland, *n.* the 'infield' part of a farm, made to bear oats after barley without fresh manure. Cf. Aith.

Aig, *v.* to work persistently and eagerly.

Aigar, Aiger, *n.* grain dried very much in a pot before being ground in a hand-mill.

Aigar-brose, *n.* 'brose' made with 'aigar-meal.'

Aigar-meal, *n.* the meal of 'aigar'; a mixture of oatmeal and peasemeal.

Aigh, *v.* to owe.

Aighins, *n.* debt; correction for faults.

Aight, *v.* to own; to owe. Cf. Aucht.

†Aiglet, *n.* a tagged bootlace; a jewel in a cap.

†Aigre, *adj.* sour.

Aik, *n.* an oak.

Aiken, *adj.* oaken.

Aiken, *n.* a small marine bivalve, used for bait. Cf. Aichan.

Aiken Drum, *n.* the name of an unprepossessing but beneficent 'brownie.'

Aiker, *n.* an acre. Cf. Acker.

Aiker, *n.* the break or movement made in the water by a fish swimming rapidly.

Aiker-braid, *n.* the breadth of an acre.

Aikerit, *ppl. adj.* of grain: eared. Cf. Aicherd.

Aikie guineas, *n.* children's name for small flat pieces of shells bleached by the sea.

Aikle, *n.* a molar tooth.

Aikraw, *n.* the pitted, warty lichen.

Aik-snag, *n.* the broken bough of an oak.

Ail, *v.* to affect with pain; to be unwell or suffering in body; to have something amiss;

with *at*, to be dissatisfied with; to hinder, prevent.—*n.* an illness, ailment.

†**Aile**, *n.* an aisle. Cf. Aisle.

Ailickey, *n.* the bridegroom's man and messenger at a wedding. Cf. Allekay.

Ailing, *n.* sickness; ailment.

Ailis, Ailiss, *n.* a large glowing fire.

Ailsa-cock, -parrot, *n.* the puffin.

Aim, *n.* a blast of hot air; vapour. Cf. Oam.

Ain, *adj.* own.

Ain, *v.* to own; to acknowledge.

Aince, Aincin, *adv.* once.

Ainlie, *adj.* familiar; friendly.

Ains, Ainse, *adv.* once.

Ainsel', *n.* own self.

Air, *n.* a small quantity of anything; a pinch of snuff; a whiff; a taste.—*v.* to taste.

Air, *n.* a sandbank; a beach.

Air, *n.* an oar.

Air, *adj.* early.—*adv.* long since. Cf. Ear, Ere.

Air, *v.* to fan; to take off the chill, &c.

Air, Aire, *n.* an itinerant court of justice.

Airch, *n.* an arch; an aim.—*v.* to aim; to *let* fly a missile.

Airch, *adj.* timorous; hesitating; undecided; scanty; insufficient. — *adv.* scantily; insufficiently; scarcely. Cf. Argh.

Aircher, *n.* a marksman.

Air-cock, *n.* a weathercock.

Airel, *n.* a pipe made from a reed; a wind instrument; in *pl.* musical tones of any kind.

Airgh, *adj.* hollow, needing to be made up to level. Cf. Argh.

Airgh, *v.* to hesitate; to be reluctant. Cf. Argh.

Air-goat, *n.* the snipe.

Airie, *n.* hill pasture; an opening in the hills; a summer residence for a herdsman; a 'sheilin.'

Airish, *adj.* chilly.

Airle, Airl-penny, *n.* earnest - money; an earnest. Cf. Arles-penny.

Airles, *n.* earnest-money. Cf. Arles.

Airn, *n.* iron; in *pl.* fetters.—*v.* to iron.

Airness, *n.* earliness.

Airny, *adj.* hard or strong as iron.

Air-oe, *n.* a great-grandchild. Cf. Ier-oe.

Air-up, *adj.* early up.

Airt, *n.* the quarter of the heavens; point of compass; the direction of the wind; a direction; way.—*v.* used of the wind: to blow from a certain quarter; to urge onward; to incite to mischief; to irritate; to point out the way to a place; to direct; to turn in a certain direction; to tend towards; to aim at; to find out, discover.

Airt, *n.* art.

Airtan, *n.* direction; the placing towards a point of the compass.

Airt-an'-pairt, *adj.* accessory to; aiding and abetting.

Airter, *n.* an inciter.

Airth, *n.* point of the compass. Cf. Airt.

Airtie, *adj.* artful; dexterous; ingenious.

Airtily, *adv.* artfully.

Airtiness, *n.* artfulness.

Airy, *adj.* showy; pretentious; conceited.

Air-yesterday, *n.* the day before yesterday. Cf. Ere-yesterday.

Air-yestreen, *n.* the night before last. Cf. Ere-yestreen.

Aise, *n.* ashes. Cf. Ase.

Aise-backet, *n.* a wooden box for holding or carrying ashes.

Aishan, *n.* stock; brood; family; a term of contempt.

Aishin, Aisin, *n.* the eaves of a house. Cf. Easing.

Aislar, *n.* ashlar.

Aislar-bank, *n.* a reddish bank, with projecting rocks in a perpendicular form, resembling ashlar-work.

†**Aisle**, *n.* a passage between pews; a projection from the body of a church; a wing of a transept; an enclosed and covered burial-place adjoining a church, but not part of it; a mausoleum.

Aisle, *v.* to dry in the sun; to dry on the surface.—*n.* drying by the sun; the first process of drying linen. Cf. Haisle.

Aisle-tooth, *n.* a molar tooth.

Ait, *n.* a custom; a bad habit. Cf. Ett.

Ait, *n.* an eating; a feed; a feast.

Aiten, *adj.* oaten.

Aiten, *n.* a partridge.

Aiten, *n.* a giant; a hobgoblin. Cf. Ettin.

Aiten, *n.* the juniper.

Ait-farle, *n.* the quarter of a circular oatcake.

Aith, *n.* an oath.

Aith, *n.* the 'infield' part of a farm, made to bear oats after barley without fresh manure.

Aith, *adj.* easy. Cf. Eith.

Aither, *v.* to weave straw or coir ropes on the thatch of a stack or roof. Cf. Ether.

Aither, *n.* an adder. Cf. Ether, Edder.

Aither, *adj. pron.* and *conj.* either.

Aitherens, *adv.* and *conj.* either Cf. Eitherins.

Aitherins, *n.* ropes woven crosswise on thatch. Cf. Etherins.

Aitherns, *conj.* either; rather. Cf. Eitherens.

Aitliff-crap, *n.* the crop after barley.

Aitnach, *n.* the juniper; in *pl.* juniper berries.

Aitseed, *n.* oat-sowing and its season.

Aiver, *n.* a gelded he-goat. Cf. Aver.

Aiver, *n.* an old horse. Cf. Aver.

†**Aiverie**, *adj.* very hungry.

Aiverin, *n.* the cloudberry. Cf. Averin.

Aivering, *ppl. adj.* eager for, hungering.

Aivrin, *n.* the larboard.

Aixies, *n.* the access of an ague; hysterics. Cf. Exies.

Aix-tree, *n.* an axle-tree.
Aize, *n.* a large glowing fire. Cf. Auze.
Aizle, *n.* a hot ember; a live coal. Cf. Eyzle.
Aizle-tooth, *n.* a molar tooth. Cf. Aisle-tooth.
Ajee, *adj.* awry. Cf. Agee.
Alabast-beer, *n.* a superior kind of beer.
Alacampine, *n.* elecampane; a coarse candy.
Alagust, *n.* suspicion. Cf. Allagust.
Alaigh, *adv.* below, as to situation relative to another place.
Alakanee, *int.* alas!
Alake, Alacke, *int.* alas!
†**Alamod,** *n.* a fashionable kind of cloth.
Alane, *adj.* alone.
Alanerlie, *adv.* only; solely.—*adj.* only; sole. Cf. Allanerly.
Alang, *adv.* and *prep.* along.
†**Alavolee,** *adv.* at random. Cf. Allavolie.
Albuist, *conj.* though; albeit.
Ald, *adj.* old. Cf. Auld.
Ale-brewin, *n.* in *phr.* 'a sma' ale-brewin,' courting with a view to marriage.
Alee, *adv.* to the leeward.
Aleen, *adj.* alone.
Alenth, *adv.* in the direction of the length.
Ale-saps, *n.* wheaten bread boiled in beer.
Aless, *conj.* unless.
Algates, *adv.* in every way; by all means; however; at all events.
Alicht, *v.* to alight.
Alicreesh, *n.* liquorice; 'black sugar.'
Aliftin, *adj.* unable to rise from weakness.
Alikay, *n.* the bridegroom's man. Cf. Allekay.
Aliment, *n.* parochial relief to paupers; sum given by law for support of a wife or child in cases of separation, &c., or of an illegitimate child in cases of affiliation.—*v.* to pay such aliment; to maintain, support.
Alis, *int.* a sudden cry of pain.
Alist, *adv.* in *phr.* to 'come alist,' to recover from faintness or decay; to revive; to recover from a swoon.—*adj.* alive.
Alkin', *adj.* of every kind.
Allagrugous, *adj.* grim; ghastly; discontented-looking.
†**Allagust,** *n.* suspicion.
Allakey, *n.* the bridegroom's man. Cf. Allekay.
Allanerly, *adj.* sole; alone.—*adv.* solely; exclusively; quite alone.
Allanhawk, *n.* the great northern diver; Richardson's skua.
Allar, *n.* the alder.
Allars, *n.* garden walks; alleys like garden walks.
†**Allavolie, Alle-volie,** *adj.* giddy; volatile.—*adv.* at random.
Allege, *v.* to confirm.

Allegiance, *n.* allegation.
†**Allekay,** *n.* the bridegroom's man and messenger at a wedding.
†**Allemand,** *v.* to conduct or escort in a formal manner.
Aller, *n.* the alder.
Allerish, *adj.* weird; uncanny; surly; of weather: chilly; of a sore or wound: painful; fretted. Cf. Eldritch.
Alleviation, *n.* palliation of an offence.
All-heal, *n.* the mistletoe.
Allicomgreenyie, *n.* a girls' game, like 'drop handkerchief.'
Allister, *adj.* sane; *compos mentis;* all astir.
Allo, *adv.* and *prep.* below. Cf. Alow.
Allocate, *v.* to apportion the sums due by each landholder in a parish in an augmentation of a parish minister's stipend; to assign seats in a parish church.
All one's lane, *phr.* quite alone.
Alloo, *v.* to allow; to order.
All out, *adv.* in a great degree: beyond comparison.
All out, *adj.* mistaken; disappointed.—*adv.* too late.
All over, *prep.* over and above.
†**Allow,** *v.* to order; to approve of; to oblige.—*n.* the way in which trees were made to fall when cut down.
†**Allowance,** *n.* approbation.
Allure, *n.* a lure; an attraction; an inducement.
Allutterly, Alluterlie, *adv.* wholly; completely.
Allycriesh, *n.* liquorice. Cf. Alicreesh.
Alm, *n.* alum. Cf. Aum.
†**Almanie-whistle,** *n.* a small flageolet used by children.
Almery, *n.* a cupboard. Cf. Aumrie.
Almous, *n.* alms; a dole; a meritorious act.
Almous-dish, *n.* a beggar's dish for alms.
Alona, *n.* a term of endearment.
Alonely, *adv.* only; solely.
Alow, *adv.* and *prep.* below.
Alow, Alowe, *adv.* on fire; ablaze.
Alpuist, *conj.* although. Cf. Albuist.
Alrich, Alrisch, *adj.* weird; unearthly. Cf. Eldritch.
Alry, *adj.* weird; unearthly. Cf. Eldritch.
Alse, *adv.* else.
Alshin, Alson, *n.* a shoemaker's awl. Cf. Elsin.
Alshinder, *n.* the horse-parsley.
Alter, *n.* a change; a change of weather.
Alterchange, *v.* to exchange.
Alunt, *adv.* ablaze, aflame.
Alutterly, *adv.* wholly. Cf. Allutterly.
†**Alvertly,** *adv.* utterly.
Always, *adv.* still.
Always, *conj.* notwithstanding.

Amains o', in *phr.* 'teen amains o',' taken in hand; apprehended and dealt with.

Amaist, *adv.* almost.

Amand, *n.* a penalty.

Amang, *prep.* among; in; into; together with.

Amang hands, *phr.* 'in the meantime'; 'at hand'; 'in process'; 'among other things.'

Amaton, *n.* a thin, bony person; an opprobrious term.

Ambry, *n.* a chest; a cupboard; a pantry. Cf. Aumrie.

†Amel, *n.* enamel.

Amerciate, *v.* to amerce.

Amers, *n.* embers.

Amind, *adj.* of a mind.

†Amission, *n.* loss; forfeiture.

†Amit, *v.* to lose; a legal term, to forfeit.

Amitan, *n.* a weak, foolish person; one given to excess of anger.

Ammel, *n.* a swingle-tree.

Ammer-goose, *n.* the great northern diver or ember-goose.

Amo', *prep.* among.

Amond, Amon't, *phr.* 'among it.'

†Amove, Amow, *v.* to vex; to move to anger; to rouse.

Amplefeyst, *n.* a fit of the sulks or spleen; needless talk.

Amplush, *v.* to nonplus in argument.

†Amry, *n.* a cupboard; a plate-rack placed on the top of a kitchen-dresser. Cf. Aumrie.

Amshach, *n.* an accident; a misfortune.

Amshack, *n.* a noose; a fastening.

Amuve, *v.* to vex; to rouse. Cf. Amove.

An, *adj.* equal; the same.

An, *prep.* before; ere; by the time of.

An', *conj.* and.

An, *conj.* if; although.

'An, *conj.* than.

An' a', *phr.* 'et cetera'; and everything else; also.

Ana, Anay, *n.* a river-island, a holm; an 'ey' or 'ae.'

Analie, *v.* to alienate property.

Analier, *n.* one who alienates property.

Anam, *n.* a spectre; a ghost.

Anan, *int.* an interrogative excl.: 'What did you say?'

Anatomy, *n.* a skeleton; a thin, bony person; a term of contempt for a man.

Ance, *adv.* once.

Anchor-stock, *n.* a large, long rye-loaf. Cf. Anker-stock.

Ancient, *adj.* used of children, staid; demure; precocious.

Ancientry, *n.* antiquity; precociousness in children.

Anciety, *n.* antiquity.

Ancleth, *n.* an ankle.

And, *conj.* if. Cf. An.

Andirmess, Andirmas, *n.* St Andrew's Day. Nov. 30.

†Andlet, *n.* a very small ring; a mail.

Andrea Ferrara, *n.* a basket-hilted Highland broadsword.

Ane, *adj.* one.—*n.* a single person or thing.

Aneath, *prep.* and *adv.* beneath; under.

Anee, *int.* an excl. of sorrow.

Anent, *prep.* opposite to; in front of; over against; side by side with; about; concerning; in competition with.

Anerly, *adv.* alone; singly.—*adj.* single; solitary; given to solitude.

Anermas, *n.* St Andrew's Day. Cf. Andirmess.

Anery, *n.* a children's term in a counting-out game. Cf. Onerie.

Anes, *adv.* once.

Ane's errand, *n.* an exclusive errand; express purpose. Cf. End's errand.

Aneth, *prep.* and *adv.* beneath; under. Cf. Aneath.

Aneuch, Aneugh, *adj.* enough, used of quantity.—*adv.* sufficiently.

Anevval, *adj.* lying on the back. Cf. Neval.

Anew, *adj.* enough, used of numbers.

Anew, *prep.* and *adv.* below; beneath.

Anger, *v.* to become angry; to grieve.—*n.* grief.

Angersome, *adj.* annoying; provoking; vexatious.

Angleberry, *n.* an excrescence on the feet of sheep and cattle.

Angry, *adj.* used of a sore: inflamed.

Angry teeth, *n.* the fragment of a rainbow appearing on the horizon, and when seen on the north or east indicating bad weather.

Anie, *n.* a little one.

Aniest, *prep.* near; next to.

Aniest, *prep.* on this side of.

Animose, *adj.* hearty; spontaneous.

Animositie, *n.* hardihood; firmness; courage.

Anist, *prep.* near to. Cf. Aniest.

Anist, *prep.* on this side of. Cf. Aniest.

Anither, *adj.* and *pron.* another.

†Anker, *n.* a liquid measure of about four gallons used by smugglers for convenience of carriage on horseback; a dry measure, like the 'firlot,' for measuring potatoes.

Ankerly, *adv.* unwillingly.

Ankerstock, *n.* a large, oblong rye loaf; sometimes one of wheat.

Ann, *n.* a half-year's stipend legally due to a deceased parish minister's heirs, over and above what was due to him at the date of his death in his incumbency.

Annal, *n.* yearly income, produce, or ground-rent.

Annat, *n.* half-year's stipend due as 'ann.'

Anno, *v.* to keep a boat's head to the wind while fishing with rod or line.

Annosman, *n.* the man who 'annos' a boat.

†**Annoy**, *n.* annoyance.

Annual, *n.* annual feu-duty; annual income or interest.

Annual-rent, *n.* yearly interest.

Annuity, *n.* yearly house-rent.

Anonder, Anoner, *prep.* under.—*adv.* beneath. Cf. Anunder.

Anower, *prep.* in or into and over.—*adv.* within.; under. Cf. Inower.

Anse, *conj.* else; otherwise. Cf. Ense.

Answer, *v.* to supply with sufficient funds from a distance; of a colour: to suit, become.

Anter, *v.* to venture; to chance; to wander; to saunter.

Antercast, *n.* a misfortune; an accident; mischance.

Anterin, *ppl. adj.* wandering; occasional; meeting occasionally. — *n.* an occasional meeting or thing, &c.

Anthony-over, *n.* the game of throwing a ball over a house from the one party to the other.

Antic, *n.* an oddity; an eccentric person; 'a spectacle'; in *pl.* odd ways, dress, tricks.

Anti-lifters, *n.* a name given to those who objected to the minister at the Communion lifting the bread before the thanksgiving. Cf. Lifter.

Antle, *v.* to keep harping on a grievance; to go on fault-finding, complaining, or grumbling.

Antonmas, *n.* St Anthony's Day, Jan. 17 N.S., Jan. 29 O.S.

Antrin, *ppl. adj.* occasional. Cf. Anterin.

Anunder, *adv.* beneath.—*prep.* underneath.

Anwell, *n.* annual feu-duty, income, or interest. Cf. Annual.

A'oot, *adj.* mistaken.—*adv.* too late. Cf. All out.

A'owre, *prep.* over and above. Cf. All over.

Apen, *v.* to open.—*adj.* open.

Apen-furth, *n.* the free air; an open exposure.

Apenin, *n.* a gap; opening.

Apenly, *adv.* openly.

†**Apert**, *adj.* open; manifest; avowed.

Apery, *n.* scandalous imitation of what is sacred.

Apiece, Apiest, *conj.* although. Cf. Alpuist.

Aplace, *adv.* in this place; here.

Aploch, *n.* a dwarf; carrion; a remnant; in *pl.* corners of corn-fields or of meadows left unmowed for the supposed benefit of the warlocks, to keep their favour. Cf. Ablach.

Apo', Apon, *prep.* upon.

Apotheck, *n.* a lot; collection; concern. Cf. Hypothec.

Appeal, *v.* to challenge to a duel.

Appell, *v.* to cease to rain. Cf. Uppal.

Appety, *n.* appetite.

Apple-glory, *n.* apple-blossom.

Apple-ringie, *n.* southernwood.

Apple-rose, *n. Rosa villosa.*

†**Apport**, *v.* to bring; to conduce.

Approve, *v.* to bring proof.

Approven, *ppl. adj.* approved.

Appryse, *v.* to value for distraint.

Apprysing, *n.* the act of valuing for distraint; such valuation.

April-gowk, *n.* April fool.

Apron, *n.* the abdomen of a crab.

Apurpose, *adv.* intentionally; expressly.

†**Aqua, Aquavitæ**, *n.* whisky; spirits.

Aqueesh, *prep.* between. Cf. Atweesh.

Ar, *adj.* early. Cf. Air.

Arage, *n.* servitude due by tenants in men and horses to their landlords. Cf. Average.

†**Arbres**, *n.* an arrangement of trees marking distances in the game of the mall.

†**Arch**, *v.* to aim.—*n.* an aim. Cf. Airch.

Arch, *adj.* timorous; hesitating; scanty.—*v.* to hesitate. Cf. Argh.

Archer, *n.* one who throws.

Archilagh, Archilowe, *n.* the return which a guest who has been treated makes to the tavern company who were hosts.

Archness, *n.* shyness; timidity; reluctance. Cf. Arghness.

Ardent, *n.* whisky.

Are, *adj.* early. Cf. Air.

†**Ared**, *v.* to erase, remove.

Arend, *v.* used of a horse: to rear.

Argh, *adj.* timorous; apprehensive; hesitating; reluctant; scanty; insufficient.—*adv.* scarcely; insufficiently.—*v.* to be timid; to hesitate.

Arghness, *n.* shyness; timidity; awe; reluctance.

Argie, *v.* to argue; to wrangle.—*n.* an assertion in a dispute.

Argie-bargie, *n.* a contention; a quarrel.—*v.* to contend.

Argie-bargiement, *n.* wrangling; contention.

Argie-, Argey-reerie, *n.* a wrangle; a scolding.

Argle-bargle, *v.* to bandy words, cavil, dispute.

Argle-bargler, *n.* a caviller, a contentious person.

Argle-bargling, -barging, *n.* cavilling, contention.

Argol-bargol, *v.* to 'argle-bargle.'

Argol-bargolous, *adj.* quarrelsome; contentious about trifles.

Argoseen, *n.* the lamprey.

Argufy, *v.* to argue; to signify, matter.

Argument, *n.* the subject of a Latin version or piece of English dictated at school to be turned into Latin.

Arguy-barguy, *v.* to 'argie-bargie.'

Arguy-barguying, *n.* contention.

Aricht, *adv.* rightly; aright.

Ark, *n.* a large wooden chest for holding meal, flour, &c.

Ark, *n.* the masonry in which the water-wheel of a mill moves.

Ark, *n.* a formation of clouds supposed to resemble Noah's ark.

Ark-bane, *n.* the bone called the *os pubis*.

Arle, *v.* to give an earnest of any kind; to pay money to confirm a bargain; to engage for service by payment of a coin as earnest of wages; to beat severely.

Arles, *n.* money paid as an earnest; money given to a servant on engagement; one's deserts; a thrashing.

Arles-penny, Arle-penny, *n.* an earnest; the pledge-token; a coin given on engaging a servant.

Arlich, Arlitsh, *adj.* sore; fretted; painful.

Arling, *n.* the giving of arles.

Arm, *v.* to give one's arm to; to walk arm-in-arm.

Armless, *adj.* unarmed.

Arn, *n.* the alder.

Arn, *n.* the awn of wheat or barley.

Arnet, Arnit, Arnot, *n.* a shrimp.

Arnot, Arnut, *n.* the pig-nut or earth-nut.—*phr.* 'lea arnot,' a stone lying in a field.

A-road, *adv.* here and there; in disorder.

Aron, *n.* the *Arum maculatum* or wake-robin, cuckoo's pint.

Arr, *n.* a scar left by a wound or sore; the mark of smallpox; a grudge; ill-feeling.

Arrage, *n.* service of tenants to landlords in men, horses, &c. Cf. Average.

Arran-ake, *n.* the red-throated diver.

†Arras, Arres, *n.* the angular edge of anything, of a stone; the tips of the little ridges laid by the plough.

Arrayed, *ppl. adj.* used of a mare in season.

Arred, *ppl. adj.* marked by smallpox; scarred.

Arrisat, *n.* an ancient dress of Hebridean women.

Arrow, *adj.* shy; timid; reluctant. Cf. Argh.

Arse, *n.* the fundament of a person; the rump of an animal; the bottom or hinder part of anything.—*v.* to move backwards; push back; to balk, defeat; to back out of a promise, engagement, &c.; to shuffle.

Arse-bare, *adj.* with bare buttocks.

Arse-burd, *n.* the backboard of a cart; a tailboard.

Arse-cockle, *n.* a hot pimple on any part of the body. Cf. Esscock.

Arselins, *adv.* backwards.

Arselins-coup, *n.* the act of falling backwards on the hams.

Arset, Arset-back, *adv.* backwards.

Arsé-versé, *n.* a spell on the side of a house to ward off fire.

Arsin, *n.* shuffling.

Art and part, *phr.* 'aiding and abetting.'

Artful, *adj.* skilled in one's art or craft; expert.

Artificial, *n.* artificial manure in contrast to farm-dung.

Artval-, Arvil-supper, *n.* the supper given after a funeral.

Arty, *adj.* artful; dexterous; ingenious.

As, *adv.* how.

As, *conj.* than; as if; used to express the superlative degree, when occurring between an *adj.* and its immediate repetition.

Asclent, *adv.* obliquely. Cf. Asklent.

Ascrive, *v.* to ascribe.

Ase, *n.* ashes.

Ase-backet, *n.* a wooden box for removing ashes.

Ase-hole, *n.* a hole beneath or in front of the grate or out-of-doors to receive ashes.

Ase-midden, *n.* an ash-heap.

Ase-packad, *n.* a box to contain ashes.

Ase-pit, *n.* an ash-pit.

Ase-puckle, *n.* a spark from the fire.

Ashad, *n.* an 'ashet.'

Ashen, *adj.* belonging to, or consisting of, ash-trees.

†Ashet, *n.* a large, flat, oval dish on which a joint is placed on the table.

Ash-gray, *adj.* gray as ashes.

Ashie-pattle, *n.* a neglected child; a dirty child or animal that lies about the hearth.

Ashie-pet, *n.* an 'ashie-pattle'; an idle slattern; a kitchen drudge.

Ashiler, *n.* ashlar.

Ash-, Ashen-keys, *n.* the seed-vessels of the ash.

Aside, *prep.* beside; near to; compared with.

Asil, *n.* a molar tooth. Cf. Aisle-tooth.

Ask, *n.* a newt.

Ask, *n.* a chain for fastening cattle in the stall; the stake to which they are fastened.

Ask, *v.* to publish the banns of marriage; with *out*, used of a child: to ask permission to leave school for a few minutes.

Asking, *n.* a petition, request; the price asked.

Asklent, *adv.* aslant; obliquely; dishonourably.—*prep.* across.

Askoy, *adv.* asquint; askew.

Asled, *adv.* aslant.

A-slew, *adv.* aslant.

Aslin-tooth, *n.* a molar tooth. Cf. Aisle-tooth.

Asloap, *adv.* aslant; on the slope.

A-slype, *adv.* aslant.

Asol, *v.* to dry in the sun. Cf. Aisle.

Asoond, *adv.* in a swoon. Cf. Aswoon.

Aspait, *adv.* in flood; in a 'spate.'

†Aspar, *adv.* wide apart; in a state of opposition.

Ass, *n.* ashes. Cf. Ase.

Assal-, Assle-tooth, *n.* a molar tooth. Cf. Aisle-tooth.

†**Assassinat, Assassinite,** *n.* an assassin.

Asseer, *v.* to assure.

Assie, *adj.* abounding in ashes.

Assie-pet, *n.* an idle slattern. Cf. Ashie-pet.

Assignay, *n.* an assignee.

Assilag, *n.* the storm-petrel.

Assil-tree, *n.* an axle-tree.

Assize, *v.* to try by jury.—*n.* a jury; a tax; a measure of fourteen gallons.

Assize-fish, *n.* so many fish from each boat for liberty of anchorage, &c.

Assize-herring, *n.* herring-duty; a royalty on herring-fishing.

Assizer, *n.* a juryman.

†**Assoilyie, Assoilzie,** *v.* to acquit, absolve.

Assort, *v.* to dress up; to overdress.

†**Assuess,** *v.* to accustom.

Assy-pet, Assy-pod, *n.* a dirty little creature; a slatternly woman. Cf. Ashie-pet.

Assyth, *v.* to make compensation; to satisfy for injury.

Assythement, *n.* legal compensation; atonement.

Asteep, *adv.* in steep; in a soaking condition.

Asteer, *adv.* astir; in confusion or bustle out of doors.

Asterne, *adj.* austere in looks. Cf. Austern.

Astid, *adv.* instead of.

†**Astit, Astid,** *adv.* as soon; rather; as well as.

Astraying, *ppl. adj.* straying; wandering.

Astren, *adj.* austere in looks; ghastly in appearance. Cf. Austern.

Astrick, *v.* to astrict.

†**Astrologian,** *n.* an astronomer.

†**Astruct,** *v.* to prove or confirm by investigation.

Aswaip, *adv.* aslant.

Aswim, *adv.* afloat; covered with water; in a swim.

Aswoon, *adv.* in a swoon.

Asyle, *n.* an asylum; a sanctuary.

At, *prep.* used of feeling towards a person; with; towards; with *himself,* in full possession of one's mind, &c.

At, *pron.* who; whom; which; that; with a *poss. pron.* whose.

'**At,** *conj.* that.

At a will, *phr.* 'to one's utmost wish.'

Atchison, *n.* a copper coin washed with silver, worth eight pennies Scots, or two-thirds of an English penny.

Ate-meat, *n.* an idler who lives upon others.

Ather, *adj. and conj.* either.

Ather, *n.* an adder.

Ather-bill, *n.* the dragon-fly. Cf. Adder-bell.

†**Ather-cap,** *n.* the dragon-fly. Cf. Adder-cap.

Athil, *n.* a noble; a prince.

Athin, *prep. and adv.* within.

A'thing, *phr.* used in playing marbles: a claim for every advantage.

Athis'd, *adv.* on this side.

Athol-brose, *n.* a mixture of whisky and honey.

Athoot, *prep.* without.—*adv.* outside.—*conj.* unless.

Athort, *adv.* across; far and wide; abroad.— *prep.* across; over; through; athwart; along.

Athraw, *adv.* awry; off the straight; acrosswise.

A-tift, *adv.* on the alert.

Ation, *n.* family; stock; brood; used contemptuously. Cf. Etion.

Atomie, Atomy, *n.* a skeleton; a term of contempt. Cf. Anatomy.

Atour, At-ower, *prep.* across; over; 'outover'; in spite of.—*adv.* over and above; besides; moreover; at a distance away. Cf. Outower.

Atry, *adj.* purulent; fretful; virulent. Cf. Attery.

Attact, *v.* to attack.

Attamie, *n.* a skeleton. Cf. Anatomy.

Atter, *n.* poison; purulent matter; proud flesh; ill-nature.

Attercap, *n.* a spider; an irascible person. Cf. Ettercap.

Attery, *adj.* purulent; fretful; irascible; grim; virulent; quarrelsome; irritable.

Attle, *v.* to intend; to aim at.—*n.* an aim; an attempt. Cf. Ettle.

Attour, *adv.* out of the way; over and above. —*v.* to get out of the way. Cf. Atour.

Attrie, *adj.* purulent; irascible. Cf. Attery.

Atwa, *adv.* in two.

Atweel, *adv.* indeed; truly; of course.

Atween, *prep.* between.

Atweesh, Atweesht, *prep.* between.

Atwixt, *prep.* between; betwixt.

Auch, *adj.* timorous. Cf. Argh.

Auchan, *n.* a species of pear.

Auchimuty, *adj.* mean; paltry.

Auchindoras, *n.* a large thorn-tree at the end of a house.

Auchlet, *n.* a measure of meal, the eighth-part of a boll.

Aucht, *num. adj.* eight.

Aucht, *v.* ought.

Aucht, Aught, *v.* to own; to possess; to owe; to be indebted to.

Aucht, Aught, *ppl.* possessed of.

Aucht, Aught, *n.* property; possession; applied often contemptuously to persons; opinion; judgment; 'eyes.'

Aucht, *n.* duty; place; office.

Aucht, *pron.* anything. — *n.* importance; moment.

Aucht-day, *n.* a common daily occurrence.

Auchtigen, Auchtikin, *n.* the eighth-part of a barrel or half a 'firkin.'

Auchtlins, Aughtlins, *adv.* in any or the least degree.

Auchtsome, *adj.* consisting of eight persons, &c.

Audie, *n.* a careless or stupid fellow; a simpleton.

Audiscence, *n.* audience; hearing; attention.

Augh, *int.* an excl. of disgust or impatience.

Aughimuty, *adj.* mean; paltry. Cf. Auchimuty.

Auld, Aul', *adj.* old; eldest; stale; in arrears; usual; unreasonable; great; fine; used jocularly of the devil with the following names: A' Ill Thing; Ane; Bobby; Bogie; Bo-ho; Boy; Carle; Chap; Chiel; Clootie; Donald; Fellow; Hangie; Harry; Hornie; Mahoun; Man; Neil; Nick; Nickey; Nickie Ben; Roughy; Sandy; Saunders; Smith; Sooty; Thief; Waghorn; Whaup-neb.

Auld-aunty, *n.* a grand-aunt.

Auld-boy, *n.* an old man with youthful propensities, &c.

Auld-day, *n.* an idle day after feasting or hard drinking.

Auld-fangle, *adj.* old-fashioned.

Auld-farrant, *adj.* old-fashioned; precocious. —*n.* an old head on young shoulders.

Auld-fashiontness, *n.* childish precocity.

Auld-father, *n.* a grandfather.

Auld fowk, *adj.* elderly people; the parents of bride and bridegroom.

Auld Gibbie, *n.* the common cod.

Auld-headed, *adj.* sagacious; shrewd.

Auld Kirk, *n.* the Established Church of Scotland; whisky.

Auld Langsyne, *n.* old days of long ago; old friendship.

Auld Licht, *adj.* conservative in theology and church practices.—*n.* a member of the 'Secession' Church.

Auldlike, *adj.* old-looking.

Auld-man's-beard, *n.* the wild clematis.

Auld-man's-bell, *n.* the blue-bell.

Auld-man's-fauld, *n.* a portion of ground set apart for the devil.

Auld-man's-milk, *n.* a potation of milk and whisky or rum.

Auld-mither, *n.* a grandmother.

Auld-mou'd, *adj.* sagacious in speech.

Auldness, *n.* oldness; age.

Auldrife, Auldruff, *adj.* of the old style.

Auld shanks, -shanky, *n.* death.

Auld son, *n.* the eldest son.

Auld sough, *n.* an habitual cant or whine.

Auld threep, *n.* a legend; tradition; an old superstition.

Auld-uncle, *n.* a granduncle.

Auld-warld, -wardle, *adj.* ancient; old-fashioned.

Auld wecht, *n.* more than one's fair share of brains.

Auld wife, *n.* an old woman, a great talker; a chimney-cowl.

Auld wife's necessary, *n.* a tinder-box.

Auld woman, *n.* a chimney-cowl.

Auld word, *n.* a proverb, saw.

Auld-young, *adj.* middle-aged.

Auld-Yule, *n.* Christmas O.S.

Aum, *n.* alum.—*v.* to dress leather or paper with alum; to thrash or beat soundly.

Auman, *n.* a sound thrashing.

Aumer, *n.* an ember.

Aumeril, *n.* a stupid, unmethodical person; a mongrel dog.

Aumitant, *n.* an opprobrious term. Cf. Amaton.

Aum-leather, *n.* white leather.

Aumous, *n.* alms; a kind deed. Cf. Almous.

Aum-paper, *n.* paper soaked in a solution of alum and water, and used as tinder.

†**Aumrie,** *n.* a cupboard; a pantry; a stupid person.

Aumus, *n.* alms. Cf. Almous.

Aun, *n.* due.—*ppl. adj.* owing.

Aunch, *adj.* empty.

Auncient, *adj.* ancient; precocious. Cf. Ancient.

Auner, *n.* an owner.

Aunter, *v.* to venture; to saunter, stroll. Cf. Anter.

Aunterens, *adv.* occasionally; perhaps.

Auntern, *adj.* occasional. Cf. Anterin.

Aunterous, *adj.* adventurous.

Aunty, *n.* an aunt; a loose woman; a female brothel-keeper; the 'bottle'; a debauch.

Aur, *n.* a scar. Cf. Arr.

Aurea, *n.* area.

Aurgle-bargle, *v.* to wrangle. Cf. Argle-bargle.

Aurnit, *n.* a pig-nut. Cf. Arnot.

Aurrie, *n.* a passage in a church; the unseated 'area' in a church before the introduction of fixed pews.

Ause, *n.* ashes. Cf. Ase.

Austern, *adj.* austere in looks; frightful or ghastly in appearance.

Austrous, *adj.* frightful; ghastly.

Author, *n.* ancestor; predecessor; one who transfers property to another; an informant; authority for a statement.

Auwis-bore, *n.* a knot-hole in a board. Cf. Navus-bore.

Aux, *v.* to ask. Cf. Ax.

Aux-bit, *n.* a V-shaped nick, cut out of the hinder part of a sheep's ear.

Auze, *n.* a blazing, glowing fire.

Ava, *adv.* at all; of all.

Ava, *int.* an excl. of banter, ridicule, &c. Cf. Awa.

Avail, *n.* value; worth; property; means.

Aval, *n.* helplessness; a helpless condition; prostration.—*adj.* helpless; prostrate; lying on the back and unable to move.—*adv.* helplessly; in a helpless condition. Cf. Awald.

Aval, *n.* the second of two crops of corn, in the rotation of crops. Cf. Awald.

Aval-broth, *n.* second day's broth.

Aval-land, *n.* land laid down to be cropped.

Aval-moon, *n.* the moon lying on its back.

Aval-thrawn, *adj.* overthrown; cast prostrate.

†**Avant curriers**, *n.* the advanced guard of an army.

Ave, *n.* the bucket of a mill-wheel. Cf. Awes.

Avel, *adj.* of a sheep: lying on its back and unable to move. Cf. Awald.

Aver, *n.* a beast of burden; a cart-horse; an old, outworn, worthless animal; a stupid person.

Aver, *n.* a gelded goat.

Average, *n.* service of tenants to landlords in men, horses, and carts.

†**Averile**, *n.* April.

Averin, Averan, *n.* the cloudberry.

Avil, *n.* the second of two crops of corn. Cf. Awald.

†**Avise**, *n.* advice; counsel.—*v.* to inform, make aware; to deliberate judicially with a view to giving a decision.

Avizandum, *n.* judicial consideration before giving judgment.

†**Avoke**, *v.* to call away; to keep off.

Avow, *int.* an excl. of sorrow; alas!

Avowe, *n.* a declaration; a discovery; an avowal.

Aw, *adj.* all.

Aw, *pron.* I.

Aw, *ppl. adj.* owning; owing.

Awa, *int.* excl. of banter or contradiction.

Awa', *adv.* away; along; forward; off; in the state of death; 'departed'; in a reduced state of health; in a decline; in a swoon.

Awa-gain, -gaun, *adj.* outgoing; departing. —*n.* departure; death.

Awald, Awal, *n.* the second of two crops of corn; a field lying the second year without being cropped; lea of the second year that has not been sown with artificial grasses.— *adj.* belonging to the second crop after lea; of land laid down to be cropped.

Awald, Awalt, *adj.* used of a sheep or other animal: lying on its back and unable to rise.

Awald-, Awal-aits, *n.* the second crop of oats after grass.

Awald-, Awal-crap, *n.* the second crop after grass.

Awald-, Awal-infield, *n.* the second crop after bear.

Awald-, Awal-land, *n.* ground under a second crop.

Award, Awart, *adj.* of an animal: lying on its back and unable to rise. Cf. Awald.

Award-crap, *n.* a crop of corn after several others in succession.

Awastle, *adv.* to the westward of; at a distance.

Awat, *adv.* indeed; truly.

Awat, *n.* the second of two crops after corn; ground ploughed after the first crop from grass. Cf. Awald.

Awat-crap, *n.* the crop produced from ground so ploughed.

Away-taking, *n.* abduction.

Aw-bund, Awbun', *adj.* under restraint; submissive to authority; reverential.

Awe, *v.* to own; to owe.

Awe-band, *n.* a band or rope for fastening cattle to the stake; a person who inspires reverence; a check; restraint.—*v.* to bind with an 'awe-band.'

Aweel, *int.* ah well! well then! well, well!

Aweers, *adv.* on the point of; about to; within a little of.

Awelt, Awelled, *adj.* lying on the back and unable to rise. Cf. Awald.

Awerin, *n.* harvesting at so much per acre.

Awes, *n.* used of a windmill: the sails or shafts; of a mill-wheel: the buckets or floats.

Awesome, *adj.* awful; awe-inspiring; appalling.—*adv.* very; extremely.

Awfall, *adj.* simple; sincere; honest. Cf. Aefald.

Awfulsome, *adj.* awful; dreadful.

A'where, *adv.* everywhere.

A-whilt, *adv.* in a state of perturbation.

A-whummel, *adv.* upside-down; bottom upwards.

A-wid, *adj.* eager; anxious; longing for.

A-will, *adv.* of one's own accord; of itself.

Awin, *adj.* own; proper.

Awin, *ppl.* owing.

Awis, *adv.* certainly.

Awittens, *adv.* unwittingly.

Awkart, *prep.* athwart.

Awkir, *n.* a bit; piece; fragment.

Awkward-crap, *n.* a crop of corn after several others in succession. Cf. Award-crap.

Awl, *n.* in *phr.* 'to pack one's awls,' 'to stick one's awls in the wall'; to give anything up as a bad business.

Awm, *n.* alum. Cf. Aum.

Awmous, *n.* alms. Cf. Almous.

Awmrie, *n.* a cupboard, pantry; a fool. Cf. Aumrie.

Awn, *ppl.* owing.

Awn, *v.* to own, acknowledge.

Awn, *adj.* own. Cf. Ain.

Awner, *n.* owner.

Awnie, *adj.* used of barley or wheat: having awns or beards.

Awowe, *int.* an excl. of sorrow. Cf. Avow.

Awp, *n.* the curlew, 'whaup.'

Awrige, *n.* the angular points, above the level of a ploughed field, into which the seed falls; the edge of a stone, beam; the edge of anything. Cf. Arras.

Aws, *n.* the buckets of a mill-wheel driven by water; the sails of a windmill. Cf. Awes.

Awsk, *n.* a newt. Cf. Ask.

Awsum, *adj.* frightful.

Awte, *n.* the direction in which a stone or piece of wood splits; the grain; a flaw in a stone.

Awtus, *n.* a dwarf; anything diminutive.

Awytens, *adv.* unwittingly. Cf. Awittens.

Ax, *v.* to ask.

Axes, *n.* business with; a right to meddle with.

Axes, *n.* an ague-fit; aches; pains; hysterics. Cf. Exies.

Axle-tooth, *n.* a molar tooth. Cf. Aisle-tooth.

Ax-tree, *n.* an axle-tree; an axle.

Ay, *int.* an excl. of surprise or wonder.

Ay-de-mi, *int.* an excl. of regret, pity, sorrow, &c.

Aye, *adv.* always; continually; still.

Aye, *adv.* yea; yes.

Ayen, *n.* a beast of the herd of one year old; a year-old child.

Aye sure, *adv.* surely.

Aynd, *n.* breath.—*v.* to whisper. Cf. Eind.

Ayoke, *adv.* in the yoke for ploughing, carting, &c.

Ayon, *prep.* beyond.

A' yonner, *phr.* 'quite sane,' '*compos mentis.*'

Ayont, *prep.* beyond; in excess of; after; later than.—*adv.* farther, beyond.

Ba', *n.* a ball.

Baa, *v.* to cry like a calf; to bleat like a sheep.—*n.* a calf's cry; a sheep's bleat. Cf. Bae.

Baa, *v.* to lull asleep. Cf. Baw.

Baach, *adj.* disagreeable to the taste; shy; tired. Cf. Bauch.

Baachle, *n.* an old shoe; a clumsy person.— *v.* to shamble. Cf. Bauchle.

Baak, *n.* the first two furrows in ploughing a field, laid facing each other. Cf. Balk.

Baak-ropes, *n.* the ropes on the upper edge of a drift-net.

Baal, *adj.* bold.

Baal-fire, *n.* any large fire; a bonfire. Cf. Bale-fire.

Baass, *adj.* used of potatoes: hollow in the heart. Cf. Boss.

Bab, *n.* a nosegay; a tassel; a knot of ribbons; a bunch of grass, corn, &c., growing above the rest.—*v.* to grow in luxuriant patches.

Bab, *n.* a slight blow; a taunt; gibe.

Bab, *n.* the smartest and sprightliest lad or lass in a company.

Bab, *v.* to bob; to dance; to pop in and out; to curtsey; to move quickly.—*n.* a dance; a quick motion; a curtsey; a bow.

Bab, *v.* to close, shut.

Bab, *v.* to fish for eels with worsted.

Ba'-baises, *n.* a particular game at ball; ? base-ball. Cf. Ball-baises.

Bab-at-the-bowster, *n.* an old Scottish dance, winding up festive gatherings; a children's singing-game, played with a cushion or handkerchief.

Babbanqua, *n.* a quaking bog.

Babber, *n.* a fishing-float; a poacher catching salmon with the illegal bob-net; the hook

used in fly-fishing, as distinguished from the 'trailer.' Cf. Bobber.

Babbis, *v.* to scoff, gibe.

Babbity-bowster, *n.* an old Scottish dance. Cf. Bab-at-the-bowster.

Babble, *adj.* half-witted.—*n.* in *pl.* foolish nonsense; nonsense that may be truth in reality.

Babbs, *n.* particles of loose skin on the face when the beard has not been shaved for two or three days.

Babby, *n.* a baby.

Babie, *n.* a halfpenny.

Babie-clouts, *n.* baby's napkins or clothes.

Babie-pickle, *n.* the small grain lying in the bosom of a lower one, at the top of a stalk of oats.

Babret, *n.* a kneading-trough. Cf. Back-bread.

Bacchus' oil, *n.* spirituous liquor.

Bach, *int.* an excl. of disgust.

Bachelor-coal, *n.* dead coal which does not burn, but only turns white.

Bachie, *n.* a bachelor. Cf. Batchie.

Bachille, Bachelle, *n.* a pendicle or small piece of arable land.

Bachle, *n.* an old, worn, or twisted shoe; a person or thing of no account; a bungle; a butt; a clumsy person—*v.* to distort; to shamble; to wear shoes out of shape; to walk loosely or in slippers. Cf. Bauchle.

Bachram, Bachrim, *n.* an adhesive spot of dirt; cow-dung, used as fuel or left to dry where it fell.

Back, *n.* a wooden vessel for carrying peat, coal, &c.; a brewer's large cooling-vat; a vessel or board for kneading dough.

Back, *n.* an instrument for toasting bread.

Back, *n.* back premises or yard; the outermost board from a sawn tree; a body of supporters; a backing; used of one who has changed his occupation or mode of living, or has seen better days; also of anything worn out; a refusal; repulse.

Back, *v.* to mount a horse; to carry on one's back; to address a letter; to endorse a bill; to place at the back of.

Back, *adj.* of crops: late; backward.—*adv.* behindhand; late.

Back-aboot, *adj.* lonely; out-of-the-way; remote.

Back-an'-face, *adv.* completely.

Back-an'-fore, -forrit, *adv.* backwards and forwards.

Back-at-the-wa', *phr.* unfortunate; in trouble; at extremity.

Back-band, *n.* the chain or strap passing over the cart or carriage saddle, and holding up the shafts.

Back-band, *n.* a bond that nullifies or modifies a former one entered into for a special and temporary purpose.

Back-bid, *v.* to bid at a sale simply to raise the price.

Back-bind, *n.* the 'back-band' of a cart-saddle, &c.

Back-birn, *n.* a load on the back.

Back-bit, *n.* a nick on the back part of a sheep's ear.

Back-bond, *n.* a bond modifying one entered into temporarily. Cf. Back-band.

Back-bone-links, *n.* the vertebræ; the spine.

Back-bread, *n.* a baking or kneading trough.

Back-breed, -breeth, *n.* the breadth of the back; a fall or throw on the back.

Back-burd, *n.* the larboard of a boat.

Back-burd, *n.* the hind-board of a cart.

Back-burden, *n.* a burden on the back.—*v.* to burden the back, weigh down.

Back-ca', *n.* a recall; a relapse; a driving back; a misfortune.

Back-cast, *n.* a retrospect; a review; a relapse; a misfortune.—*adj.* retrospective.

Back-chap, *n.* a back-stroke.

Back-come, *n.* a return.—*v.* to return; used of food: to repeat in eructation.

Back-coming, *n.* return.

Back-creel, *n.* a fishwife's 'creel.'

Back-door, *n.* the movable hinder-board of a cart, &c.

Back-door-trot, *n.* diarrhœa.

Back-draught, *n.* the convulsive gasp of a child with whooping-cough.

Back-drawer, *n.* an apostate; one who recedes from his former profession or course.

Backend, *n.* the close of a season or of the year, autumn, winter; the outlying part of a parish or district; the place where mine rubbish is cast.

†**Backet,** *n.* a box or trough of wood to carry fuel, ashes, &c.; a small wooden box with a perforated sloping lid, kept near the kitchen fireplace, for holding salt.

Backet-stane, *n.* a stone on which the 'saut-backet' rested.

Back-fa', *n.* the side-sluice of a mill-lade or pond where the water runs off when a mill is not going; a fall backwards; a relapse.

Back-faulds, *n.* fields at the back of, or at a distance from, a farmhouse.

Back-fear, *n.* an object of fear from behind.

Back-feast, *n.* the groomsman's return-feast for the wedding-feast given by the bride's friends.

Back-friend, *n.* one who seconds or abets another; a secret enemy; a place of strength behind an army.

Backfu', *n.* as much as can be carried on the back.

Back-gäin, *n.* a relapse; decline; consumption.—*ppl. adj.* receding; not healthy or prosperous.

Backgane, *ppl. adj.* ill-grown; not thriven in health or business.

Back-gangin', *ppl. adj.* back-going; not thriving.

Back-gate, *n.* a back-road; cunning; immoral conduct.

Back-half, *n.* the worse or latter half of an article.

Backhander, *n.* a blow with the back of the hand; a sarcastic retort; an indirect snub.

Back-hap, *v.* to draw back from an agreement.

Back-hash, *n.* ill-natured, abusive talk.—*v.* to scold vigorously.

Back-hicht, *n.* high excitement, great anger. —*adv.* as high as the ceiling. Cf. Balk-height.

Backie, *n.* a lift or hoist on the back.

Backie, *n.* the bat.

Backie, *n.* a square wooden vessel for holding food for cattle, fuel, ashes, &c.

Backie, *n.* the stake of a tether. Cf. Baikie.

Backie-bird, *n.* the bat.

Backin, *n.* the day after a wedding.

Backin', *n.* a body of followers; support.

Backin', *n.* the direction on a letter.

Backins, *n.* the refuse of flax, wool, &c., used for coarser stuffs. Cf. Backs.

Backin'-turf, *n.* the turf laid on a low cottage-fire at bedtime, to keep it alive till morning; one placed against the back of the fireplace, in putting on a new turf-fire, to support the side-turfs.

Backit-dyke, *n.* a stone fence backed up with earth on the inner side.

Back-jar, *n.* a sly, ill-natured objection or opposition; an artful evasion; a reverse.

Back-jaw, *n.* mutual bad language; altercation.—*v.* to retort abusive language ; to altercate.

Back-land, *n.* a house or building lying back from the street.

Back-letter, *n.* a letter which virtually qualifies one previously given that was written to serve a purpose.

Back-lick, *n.* a back-blow.

Backlins, *adv.* backwards ; back.

Back-load, -loaden, *v.* to overload a cart or a horse ; to burden heavily.

Back-look, *n.* a retrospect, review ; the act of reviewing ; a record of the past.

Back-lying, *adj.* in arrear.—*n.* in *pl.* arrears of rent, &c.

Backman, *n.* a follower in war ; a henchman.

Back-out-owre, *adv.* backwards ; back to a place in order to return thence ; back ; away from.

Back-owre, *adv.* behind ; far back.—*prep.* from the back of.

Back-rans, *adv.* backwards.

Back-rape, *n.* the band over the horse's back in the plough, supporting the traces.

Back-rent, *n.* a mode of fixing the rent of a farm, by which the tenant was always three terms in arrears.

Back-roup, *v.* to bid at an auction simply to raise prices.

Backs, *n.* the refuse of flax, wool, &c. Cf. Backins.

Back-seam, *n.* a seam up the back.

Backset, *n.* a check, a reverse, a relapse ; a sub-lease ; compensation ; a 'set-off.'

Backset, *v.* to weary, to disgust.

Back-sey, *n.* the sirloin. Cf. Sey.

Backside, *n.* the rear ; the side of an object which is farthest from the speaker ; back premises of house, &c. ; the posteriors, buttocks.

Backspang, *n.* an unsettling, underhand trick ; a retreat from a bargain ; a reverse, a recoil ; a back-current ; a retort on a person after a contested affair has seemed settled.

Back-spare, -spaiver, *n.* the back cleft or opening of breeches.

Back-spaul, -spauld, *n.* the back of the shoulder ; the hindleg.

Back-speir, -speer, -spear, *v.* to trace back a report to its source, if possible ; to cross-examine, cross-question.

Back-speirer, -spearer, *n.* a cross-examiner.

Back-spoken, *adj.* contradictory, gainsaying.

Back-sprent, *n.* the backbone ; a spring or catch.

Back-stane, *n.* a stone at the back of a fireplace.

Back-stool, *n.* a stool with a back ; a rough chair made of rungs.

Back-talk, *n.* contradiction ; saucy replies to a superior.

Back-trace, *v.* to investigate past events.

Back-tread, *n.* retrogression.

Back-trees, *n.* the joists in a cothouse, &c. Cf. Balk.

Back-turn, *n.* a relapse.

Backwardlies, *adv.* backwards.

Back-water, *n.* too much water in a mill-lade, hindering the revolution of the mill-wheel ; tears.

Back-widdie, -woodie, *n.* the band or chain over a cart-saddle, supporting the shafts.

Backwuth, *adv.* backwards.

Back-yett, *n.* a back-gate.

Bacon-ham, *n.* the ham of a pig, as distinguished from a 'mutton'-ham.

Bad, *adj.* nl ; sick.

Bad, *v. pret.* bade ; did bid.

Bad bread, *n.* in *phr.* to 'be in bad bread' ; to be in danger or poverty ; to be at enmity with.

Badder, *v.* to bother.—*n.* trouble. Cf. Bather.

Badderlocks, *n.* an edible seaweed resembling the hart's-tongue fern.

Badders, Baddords, *n.* low raillery.

Baddock, *n.* the fry of the coal-fish.

Bade, *v. pret.* did bide.

Badge, *n.* a large, ill-shaped bundle.

Badger, *v.* to beat.

Badgeran, *n.* a beating.

Badger-reeshil, *n.* a severe blow.

Badling, *n.* a worthless person.

Badlins, *adj.* out of health ; poorly.

Badly, *adj.* sick ; unwell.

Badman, *n.* a child's name for the devil.

Badminnie, Bad money, *n.* the baldmoney ; gentian.

Badock, *n.* the common skua ; the Arctic gull.

Bad place, *n.* a child's name for hell.

Badrons, Badrans, *n.* a cat. Cf. Baudrons.

Bad use, *v.* to use badly, abuse.

Bae, *v.* to bleat like a sheep ; to cry like a calf.—*n.* a sheep's bleat ; a calf's cry.

Bae-wae, *adj.* out of sorts ; not very well.

Baff, *n.* a blow, a buffet ; a shot ; a thud ; a jog with the elbow.—*v.* to beat ; to buffet ; to strike the ground with the sole of the club-head in playing golf.

Baffin, *n.* a soft, stupid person. Cf. Beffan.

Baffle, *n.* a trifle ; a thing of no value ; nonsense ; a sheet of scroll-paper on which schoolboys sketched mathematical diagrams or mensuration plans ; a portfolio.

Baffy, *adj.* chubby. Cf. Buffie.

Bafle, *n.* a check ; a snub.

Bag, *n.* a sack ; the stomach ; a playful or reproachful designation of a child.—*v.* to swell, bulge ; to cram the stomach ; to dismiss from employment ; to jilt in love.

Bagaty, *n.* the female of the lump or sea-owl.

Bagenin, *n.* rough, and sometimes indecent, horseplay at harvest-time.

†**Baggage,** *n.* rubbish.

†**Baggage,** *n.* a strumpet; an opprobrious epithet applied to women and children.

Bagged, *ppl. adj.* having a big belly; pregnant; corpulent.

Baggie, *n.* the belly; a corpulent person.

Baggie, *n.* the purple-top Swedish turnip. Cf. Baigie.

Baggie, *n.* a large minnow.

Baggie-mennon, *n.* a large minnow. Cf. Bag-mennon.

Bagging-time, *n.* baiting-time.

Baggit, *n.* a contemptuous name for a child; an insignificant little person; a feeble sheep.

Baggit, *ppl. adj.* corpulent. Cf. Bagged.

Baggity, *adj.* greedy.

Baggy, *adj.* blistered.

Baghash, *n.* abuse with the tongue.—*v.* to scold vigorously; to vituperate. Cf. Backhash.

Baglin, *n.* a misgrown child; a puny child with a big belly; a term of abuse.

Bag-mennon, *n.* a large minnow.

Bagnet, Bagonet, *n.* a bayonet.

Bag-rape, *n.* a straw rope used in fastening the thatch of a roof or stack.

Bagrel, *n.* a minnow; a person or animal corpulent and misgrown otherwise; a child; a silly person.—*adj.* puny and plump.

Bagrie, *n.* trash.

Bags, *n.* the entrails.

Bagwame, *n.* a silly, gluttonous fellow.

Bai, *n.* the cry of a calf.—*v.* to cry as a calf. Cf. Bae.

Baible, *v.* to tipple; to drink carelessly so as to spill; to drink as a child.

Baich, Baichie, *n.* a child, used with some contempt.

Baichie, *v.* to cough. Cf. Beigh.

Baid, *v. pret.* did bide.

Baigie, *n.* the purple-top Swedish turnip.

Baigle, *n.* an odd figure; a 'sight'; a 'fright.'

Baigle, *v.* to run or walk with short steps, as a child; to walk slowly, as if weary.

Baiglet, *n.* an under-waistcoat. Cf. Baiklet.

Baignet, Baiginet, *n.* a bayonet. Cf. Bagnet.

Baik, *n.* a biscuit. Cf. Bake.

Baik-bred, -brod, *n.* a kneading-trough. Cf. Back-bread.

Baiken, *n.* a burden (of skins); a sort of flap.

Baikie, *n.* the stake to which cattle are bound in the stall; a piece of wood with rope attached, to tie up cattle to the stake; the stake or peg of a tether.

Baikie, *n.* a square wooden vessel used for carrying fuel, ashes, &c., feeding cattle, and washing dishes. Cf. Backie.

Baikiefu', *n.* the fill of a 'baikie.'

Baikins, *n.* a beating; drubbing.

Baiklet, *n.* an under waistcoat or flannel shirt worn next the skin; a 'semmit'; a 'binder'; a piece of dress, linen or woollen, formerly worn above a young child's shirt.

Bail, *v.* with *up*, to tie up.—*n.* a call to cows to stand still.

Bail, *v.* to guarantee, warrant.

Bailch, *n.* a fat person breathless from corpulence; used contemptuously of a child; a 'brat.' Cf. Bilch.

†**Bailie, Baillie,** *n.* a farm-steward; a man or boy in charge of the cows on a farm; a city magistrate.

Bailierie, Bailliary, *n.* the office of a bailiff of a lord of regality; the extent of his jurisdiction in a barony.

Ba'in', *n.* a football match.

Bain, *n.* a bone.

Baingle, *n.* an abusive term applied to a woman.

Bainie, *adj.* bony.

Baird, *v.* to caparison.

Baird, *n.* a beard.—*v.* to rub with the beard.

Bairdie, *n.* the loach.

Bairdie, *n.* the whitethroat.

Bairdie, *n.* the three-spined stickleback.

Bairdie, *n.* a large jar; a 'graybeard' for holding spirits, &c.

Bairdie-loach, -lowrie, *n.* the loach.

Bairge, *n.* the voice loudly used; one who uses his voice loudly.—*v.* to raise the voice loudly; to scold, abuse, bully.

Bairge, *n.* an affected, bobbing walk.—*v.* to walk with a jerking spring upwards; to strut.

Bairge-board, *n.* a barge-board; a board at the gable of a building, hiding the timbers of the roof.

Bairn, *n.* a child; a weak-minded or childish person, irrespective of age.

Bairn-clouts, *n.* dolls' clothes.

Bairned, *ppl. adj.* in a state of dotage.

Bairn-folk, *n.* children.

Bairnie, *n.* a little child.—*adj.* childish; silly.

Bairnie o' the e'e, *n. phr.* the pupil of the eye.

Bairnish, *adj.* childish; silly.

Bairnless, *adj.* childless.

Bairnlike, *adj.* like a child; childish; weak-minded.

Bairnliness, *n.* childishness.

Bairnly, *adj.* childish.

Bairnly-like, *adj.* childish.

Bairn's bairn, *n.* a grandchild.

Bairn's bargain, *n.* a bargain that may be easily broken; a mutual agreement to overlook anything unpleasant in the past between two persons or parties.

Bairn's-fee, *n.* a nursemaid's wages.

Bairn's pan, *n.* a small pan for preparing a child's food.

Bairns'-part o' gear, *n. phr.* that part of a man's personal estate to which his children succeed.

Bairn's-piece, *n.* biscuit, cake, cheese, &c., given in connection with the birth or baptism of an infant.

Bairns'-play, *n.* children's sports; a matter easily performed.

Bairn-stooth, -stowth, *n.* the stealing of children by fairies.

Bairn's-woman, *n.* a dry-nurse.

Bairn-time, -teme, *n.* the time during which a woman bears children; a woman's whole birth of children; childhood.

Baise, *n.* haste; expedition.—*v.* to move or walk with energy.

Baise, *v.* to persuade, to coax.

Baise, *v.* to sew slightly. Cf. Baiss.

Baise, Baiss, *adj.* ashamed; sad; sorrowful.

Baisler, *n.* a bachelor of arts.

Baiss, *v.* to beat, drub; to baste.

Baiss, *v.* to sew slightly; to sew with long stitches, or in a loose, careless manner; to baste in sewing.

Baissie, *n.* a basin for holding meal, &c. Cf. Bassie.

Baissing, *n.* a drubbing.

Baissing, *n.* a slight sewing.

Baissing-thread, *n.* basting-thread.

Baist, *adj.* great.

Baist, *ppl. adj.* apprehensive; afraid.

Baist, *v.* to beat, strike; to baste; to defeat, overcome.—*n.* one who is struck by others, especially in children's play; one who is defeated.

Baistin, *n.* a drubbing.

Bait, *n.* the grain or cleavage of wood or stone.

Bait, *n.* the lye in which skins are steeped.—*v.* to steep and soften skins in a lye of hens' or pigeons' dung, in order to clean them before tanning.

Bait, *v. pret.* bit; did bite.

Baitchil, *v.* to beat soundly.

Baiten, *ppl.* bitten; eaten.

Baith, *adj.* and *pron.* both.

Baitie-bummil, *n.* a petty fumbler; an actionless fellow. Cf. Batie-bum.

Bait-pick, *n.* a spud for removing limpets for bait.

Bait-pot, *n.* a large pot for cooking food for horses, &c.

Baittle, *adj.* of pasture: short, close, and rich. Cf. Battle.

Bait-troch, *n.* a trough in a stall for feeding horses.

Bait-yaud, *n.* a woman who gathers bait for fishermen.

Baivee, *n.* a large fire. Cf. Bevie.

Baivee, *n.* a kind of whiting.

Baivenjar, *n.* a ragamuffin; tatterdemalion.

Baiver, *v.* to gad about; to run after shows, &c.

Baiver, *v.* to quiver; to tremble. Cf. Bever.

Baivie, *n.* a bevy; a large collection; a large family; a covey of partridges.

Baivie, *n.* a large fire. Cf. Baivee.

†Bajan, *n.* a first year's student at Aberdeen University. Cf. Bejan.

Bake, *n.* a small biscuit.—*v.* to knead dough or paste.

Bake-brod, *n.* a kneading-board.

Bakement, *n.* bakemeat.

Baken, *ppl.* baked.

Baker-legs, *n.* knock-knees.

Bakie, *n.* a kind of peat, kneaded or baked from the wet 'dross' or dust of peats.

Bakie, *n.* a stake. Cf. Baikie.

Bakie-bird, *n.* the bat. Cf. Backie.

Baking-case, *n.* a kneading-trough.

Bakin-lotch, *n.* a species of bread.

Bakster, *n.* the one of two bakers who kneads dough. Cf. Baxter.

Balaloo, *n.* a lullaby; sleep.

Bala-pat, *n.* a pot in a farmhouse for the family, but not for the reapers, in harvest.

Balax, *n.* a hatchet.

Bald, *adj.* bold; pungent to taste or smell; keen; biting; used of a fire: big, great; of the moon: bright. Cf. Bauld.

Balderry, Baldeirie, Baldberry, *n.* the female handed orchid, *O. maculata;* the *O. latifolia,* formerly used in love-potions.

Baldie-worrie, *n.* an artichoke. Cf. Worry-baldie.

Bale, *n.* a blaze; a bonfire.

†Baleen, Balene, *n.* whalebone.

Bale-fire, *n.* any large fire; a bonfire.

Balillalee, *n.* a lullaby. Cf. Balaloo.

Balk, *n.* a ridge in ploughing; a pathway through a corn-field; the first two furrows in ploughing a field, laid facing each other; a strip of ground untilled, serving as a boundary; a beam or rafter; the beam of a pair of scales; a henroost; in *pl.* the gallery of a church.

Balk, *v.* to miss accidentally a strip of ground in ploughing, sowing, or reaping; to secure a cow's head during milking; to shy at an obstacle; to be restive.

Balk and burral, *n.* a ridge raised very high by the plough and a barren space of nearly the same extent alternately.

Balk-height, *adv.* as high as the 'balk' or ceiling.

Balkie, *n.* a narrow strip of land separating two farms.

Balkie, *n.* a head-stake to fasten a cow at milking-time. Cf. Baikie.

Balksome, *adj.* used of a horse: restive; given to shying.

Ball, *n.* the calf of the leg; the palm of the hand; a globular sweetmeat.

Ball, *n.* a bustle; disturbance; uproar.—*v.* to behave in a disorderly way.

Ball, *n.* a 'spree.'

Ball, *n.* a parcel; bundle; bale.

Ball, *v.* to pelt, throw at.

Ball, *v.* to play at football.

Ball, *v.* used of snow: to gather in lumps; to stick to the feet.

Ballan, Ballant, *n.* a ballad; a song.

Ballant-bodice, *n.* a leather bodice formerly worn by ladies.

Ball-baises, *n.* a game of ball.

Ball-clay, *n.* very adhesive clay; 'pell-clay.' Cf. Pell-clay.

Ballerny, *n.* exaggeration in narrative; 'drawing the long-bow.'

Ball-fire, *n.* a bonfire; signal-fire. Cf. Balefire.

Ballfuff, *n.* in *phr.* 'back o' Ballfuff,' an unknown distance.

Ballillilly, -loo, -low, *n.* a lullaby. Cf. Balaloo.

Balling, *n.* pelting.

Balling, *n.* frequenting balls.

Ballion, *n.* a knapsack; a tinker's tool-box; any box that can be borne on the back.

Ballion, *n.* a supernumerary reaper who assists any that fall behind on their 'rig.'

Ballish, *n.* ballast.

Balloch, *adj.* slow; unwilling; strong; plump. —*n.* a short, plump person.

Balloch, *n.* a narrow mountain-pass.

Ballop, Ballup, *n.* the old-fashioned flap in the forepart of trousers.

Bally, *n.* a milk-pail.

Bally-cog, *n.* a milk-pail with a handle.

Balm, *v.* to soothe, ease, assuage.

†Balne, *n.* a bath.

Balow, Baloo, *int.* a nursery excl. hush!— *n.* a lullaby.

Balter, *n.* a sudden bolt or start upwards.

Bam, *n.* a joke; trick; a hoax.—*v.* to hoax, play a trick.

Bambaze, *v.* to confuse, puzzle; to bamboozle. Cf. Bumbaze.

Bambling, *ppl. adj.* awkwardly made; clumsy.

Bamboozle, *v.* to handle roughly; to affront.

Bamf, *v.* to stump; to toss or stumble about.

Bamling, Bammeling, *ppl. adj.* awkward; 'bambling.'

Ba'-money, *n.* money demanded from a wedding party to buy a football.

Bamullo, *n.* in *phr.* to 'gar ane lauch, sing,' or 'dance Bamullo,' to make one change one's mirth into sorrow.

Ban', *n.* a band. Cf. Band.

Ban, *v.* to curse, swear; to abuse, scold; to use the devil's name as an intensive or expletive.

Band, *n.* twine; a rope or chain for tying cattle; a straw or hay rope for tying thatch; twisted straw for tying sheaves; a hinge; a narrow, flat strip of iron with a loop at the end, fixed in a door, to receive an iron hook fixed on the door-post; the hair-band once worn by women; a choir; a bond; covenant; agreement; a binding-stone inserted in a wall; a brace or couple of things; a number of things fixed on a string; the bond of marriage.

Band, *n.* the ridge of a small hill.

Band, *v. pret.* bound.

†Bandaher, *n.* a bandoleer.

Bander, *n.* one who enters into a bond or covenant.

Bandie, *n.* the stickleback.

Bandless, *adj.* without bonds; altogether abandoned to evil.

Bandlessly, *adv.* regardlessly.

Bandlessness, *n.* abandonment to evil.

Bandrums, *n.* a cat. Cf. Baudrons.

Bandsman, *n.* a binder of sheaves.

Bandstane, *n.* a large binding-stone in a wall, used for stability.

Bandster, *n.* a binder of sheaves.

Band-string, *n.* a string across the breast for ornamental tying; a kind of long-shaped confection.

Bandwin, *n.* a band of six or eight reapers served by one 'bandster.'

Bandwin-rig, *n.* a ridge wide enough to contain a 'bandwin.'

Bandy, *adj.* impudent; obstinate.

Bane, *n.* in *phr.* 'King of Bane,' or 'King of the Bean,' a character in the Christmas gambols, the person who got that part of a divided cake which contained a bean.

Bane, *n.* bone; in *pl.* the substantial portion of anything; the mechanism; a skeleton. —*adj.* made of bone.

Bane, *adj.* ready; prepared.

Bane, *n.* poison; envy; malice.

Baned, *ppl. adj.* evil-disposed; envious.

Bane-dry, *adj.* thoroughly dry.

Bane-dyke, *n.* in *phr.* 'gane to the bane-dyke,' reduced to skin and bone; fit only for the 'dyke' where the bones of dead horses lie.

Banefire, *n.* a bonfire.

Bane-idle, *adj.* thoroughly idle; 'bone-lazy.'

Baneless, *adj.* insipid: without pith.

Bane-mill, *n.* a mill for crushing or grinding bones.

Bane-prickle, *n.* the stickleback.

Banes-breaking, *n.* a bloody quarrel.

Banff-baillies, *n.* white, snowy-looking clouds on the horizon, betokening foul weather.

Bang, *n.* a blow ; onslaught ; an act of haste ; impetuosity ; a fit of temper ; a 'huff.'

Bang, *n.* a crowd ; a large number.

Bang, *v.* to change places with impetus ; to beat, knock ; to throw or thrust violently ; to overcome ; to excel, outdo, surpass ; to push off with salmon-fishing boats without having seen fish in the river.

Bang, *adj.* vehement ; agile ; strong.—*adv.* quite ; suddenly.

Bang-beggar, -the-beggar, *n.* a constable ; a cudgel.

Bang-dollop, *n.* the whole number.

Banged, *ppl. adj.* under the influence of drink.

Bangie, *n.* a policeman.

Bangie, *adj.* huffy ; irritable.

Banging, *n.* a beating ; a defeat.

Bangister-swipe, *v.* to cozen artfully. Cf. Bangster.

Bangistry, *n.* violence. Cf. Bangstrie.

Bangnue, *n.* much ado about nothing.

Bang-rape, *n.* a rope with noose, used by thieves to carry off corn or hay.

Bangrel, Bangree, *n.* an ill-natured, ungovernable woman.

Bangsome, *adj.* quarrelsome.

Bangster, *n.* a bully ; a braggart ; a victor ; a loose woman.—*adj.* rough ; violent.

Bangstership, *n.* force ; violence.

Bangstrie, *n.* violence to person or property.

Bangyal, *n.* a bundle ; a slovenly fellow ; a crowd of people.—*v.* to crowd ; to move in a confused crowd. Cf. Banyel.

Bangyalin', *n.* the act of crowding.

Banjie, *n.* a great number ; a disorderly mob.

Bank, *n.* the place in a peat-moss whence peats are cut ; the part of a mine above ground.

Bank, *n.* a public proclamation.

Bank, *v.* to save and put by money.

Bank-dollar, *n.* a species of dollar, ten of which equalled ten ordinary dollars *plus* £1 Scots.

Banker, *n.* the bench or table on which a mason rests the stone he is working.—*v.* to place a stone in position on the 'banker.'

Banker, *n.* a bench-cloth or carpet.

Banker, *n.* one who buys corn sold by auction.

Bankerup, *adj.* bankrupt.

Banking-crop, *n.* corn bought or sold by auction.

Bank-rape, *v.* to become bankrupt.

†Bankrout, *n.* a bankrupt.

Banks, *n.* precipitous rocks or crags near the sea ; the seashore.

Bankset, *adj.* full of little eminences.

Bankster, *n.* a bully. Cf. Bangster.

Bankstership, *n.* force ; violence.

Bannag, *n.* a white trout ; a sea-trout.

Banna-rack, *n.* the frame before which

bannocks are put to be toasted when taken off the 'girdle.'

Bannet, *n.* a bonnet ; a man's cap.

Bannet-fire, *n.* a punishment inflicted by boys on a companion with their caps, similar to running the gauntlet.

Bannet-fluke, *n.* the turbot. Cf. Bannock-fluke.

Banniel, *n.* a bundle. Cf. Banyel.

Bannock, *n.* a thick, round, flat cake, generally of oatmeal, baked on a 'girdle'; a small quantity of oatmeal, as a perquisite, due to the servants of a mill, owing to 'thirlage.'

Bannock-chower, *n.* a bannock-eater.

Bannock-even, *n.* Shrove-Tuesday.

Bannock-fed, *adj.* fed chiefly on bannocks.

Bannock-fluke, *n.* the turbot.

Bannock-hive, *n.* corpulence owing to plentiful eating ; a corpulent person.

Bannock-stick, *n.* a rolling-pin for bannocks.

†Banquier, *n.* a banker.

Bansel, *n.* what is given for good luck ; 'hansel.'

Banstickle, *n.* the stickleback or minnow.

Banters, *n.* rebukes ; admonitions.

Bantin, Banton, *n.* a bantam.

Banty, *n.* a bantam.

Banty, *n.* a stickleback or minnow. Cf. Bandie.

Banyel, *v.* to bandy to and fro ; to crowd ; to move in a confused crowd.—*n.* a bundle ; a slovenly, idle fellow ; a crowd. Cf. Bangyal.

Bap, *n.* a small, flat, diamond-shaped breakfast roll ; a thick cake of bread baked in an oven.

Bapper, *n.* a baker.

Bapp-nose, *n.* ? a nose threatening to meet the chin.

Bapteeze, *v.* to baptize.

Bapteezement, *n.* baptism.

Bar, *n.* a flail ; the 'swing' of a flail ; a toll-bar ; an obstacle.

Bar, *n.* an infant's flannel waistcoat. Cf. Barrie.

Bar, *n.* a joke ; a game ; a matter of joking.

Bar, *n.* four-rowed barley. Cf. Bear.

Bar, *v.* to swing a flail ; to thresh. Cf. Barry.

Bar, *v.* to exclude, shut out ; to except.

Bar-bannock, *n.* a barley-meal bannock.

†Barbar, *n.* a barbarian.

Barbarize, Barbaze, *v.* to act as a barber.

Barber, *n.* what is best or excellent of its kind.

Barber-eel, *n.* the viviparous blenny.

Barbet, *n.* an arrow.

Barbour, Barbourize, *v.* to act as a barber.

Bar-bread, *n.* barley-bread.

†Barbulyie, Barbulzie, *n.* perplexity ; quandary.—*v.* to perplex.

Barchan's Day, *n.* June 21.

Bard, *n.* a scold ; a bold, noisy woman.

Bard, *v.* to caparison.

Bardach, Bardoch, *adj.* bold; fearless.

Bardie, *n.* a gelded cat.

Bardie, *n.* a minor poet; a humble bard.

Bardily, *adv.* boldly; fearlessly; pertly.

Bardiness, *n.* forwardness; pertness in conversation.

Bardish, *adj.* rude; insolent.

Bardizan, *n.* a bartisan.

Bard's croft, *n.* the piece of land on the property of a chief hereditarily appropriated to the family bard.

Bardy, *adj.* bold; fierce; turbulent; pert; shameless; insolent.—*v.* to vituperate; to bandy words with.

Bare, *adj.* plain; unadorned; mere; meagre; 'hard up'; poor.—*v.* to remove surface soil for what lies beneath.

Bare-back, *n.* a species of fluke.

Barefit, *adj.* barefooted.

Barefit-broth, -kail, *n.* broth made with butter and vegetables without meat.

Barelies, *adv.* barely; scarcely; hardly.

Bareman, *n.* a bankrupt who has given all up to his creditors.

Bare-powed, *adj.* bareheaded.

Barescrape, *n.* very poor land yielding little return for labour.

Bar-for-bar, *n.* a rhyming game.

Bargane, Bargain, *n.* contention; controversy. —*v.* to contend, fight.

Bargain-gud, *n.* a kind of pear.

Bargain-tacker, *n.* a foreman undertaking work in a section of a lead-mine.

Bargle, *n.* a squabble.—*v.* to wrangle; to bandy words.

Bark, *n.* the skin; cuticle.—*v.* to excoriate; to strip a tree of bark; to tan leather, nets, &c.; to clot; to besmear; to encrust on the skin.

Bark, *v.* to give a hard, rapid cough.

Barken, *v.* to become clotted, encrusted, or hardened on the skin, &c.; to tan; to stiffen anything, as with blood, mire, &c.

Barker, *n.* a tanner.

Barking and fleeing, *phr.* said of property prodigally wasted, so as to lead to bankruptcy.

Barla-fummil, *n.* a cry for truce by one who has fallen in fighting or wrestling.

Barley, *int.* a cry for truce in a children's game.

Barley-bing, *n.* a heap of barley.

Barley-box, *n.* a small cylindrical box formerly used by farmers to carry samples of grain; a toy for children.

Barley-breaks, Barla-bracks, *n.* a stackyard game of 'tig.'

Barley-bree, -brie, -broo, *n.* malt liquor; whisky.

Barley-corn, *n.* a species of grain. Cf. John Barleycorn.

Barley-doons, *n.* the place for playing at 'barley-breaks.'

Barley-fetterer, *n.* an implement for removing the awns of barley.

Barley-fever, *n.* illness owing to hard drinking.

Barley-hood, *n.* a fit of drunken, angry passion.

Barley-joice, *n.* malt liquor; whisky.

Barley-kail, *n.* barley-broth.

Barley-, Barlaw-men, *n.* a court of neighbours for settling local affairs, disputes, &c. Cf. Burlaw.

Barley-oats, *n.* early white oats with short grains.

Barley-pickle, *n.* a grain of barley; the topmost grain on an ear of barley.

Barley-sick, *adj.* sick from excessive drinking.

Barley-unction, *n.* malt liquor; whisky.

Barlic-, Barlik-hood, *n.* a fit of drunken anger. Cf. Barley-hood.

Barm, *n.* a peculiar kind of dance.

Barm, *n.* yeast; froth; nonsense; foolish talk. —*v.* used of the mind: to work; to fret; to mix wort with barley to cause fermentation; used of money: to grow with interest.

Barman, *n.* a thresher; a user of a flail.

Barming, *n.* interest accruing.

†Barmkin, *n.* a barbican; the outermost fortification of a wall.

Barmskin, *n.* a leathern apron worn by tanners and curriers.

Barmy, *adj.* volatile; flighty; passionate; irascible.

Barmy-brained, *adj.* foolish; giddy.

Barmy-faced, *adj.* wearing a silly expression.

Barmy scones, *n.* 'scones' levigated with 'barm.'

Barnacles, *n.* spectacles; eyeglasses.

†Barnage, *n.* a military company; army followers.

Barn-bole, *n.* an aperture in a barn-wall.

Barne, *n.* a child. Cf. Bairn.

Barn-fan, *n.* a winnowing-fan.

Barnheid, *n.* childhood.

Barnman, *n.* one who labours in the barn; a thresher with a flail.

Barnman's jig, *n.* a thresher's dance.

Barn's-breaking, *n.* a mischievous action; an idle frolic.

Barnyard, *n.* a stackyard adjoining the barn.

Barnyard-beauty, *n.* a buxom rustic beauty.

Baron-bailie, *n.* the deputy of the baron in a burgh of barony.

Barr, *n.* a kind of fishing-fly.

Barr, *n.* a ridge of a hill; a large hill.

Barrace, Barras, *n.* tournament-lists.

Barragon, *n.* a cloth used for cloaks; a rich cloth imported from Italy. Cf. Paragon.

Barras, *n.* a wire fireguard.

Barras-door, *n.* a door made of equidistant bars of wood.

Bar-reet, *n.* a crop of oats after bear. Cf. Bear-reet.

†**Barreis**, *n.* tournament-lists ; a cockpit. Cf. Barrace.

Barrel, *n.* the belly of a horse ; the barrel-shaped part of a loom.

Barrel-briestit, *adj.* corpulent.

Barrel-fevers, *n.* disorders of the body through excessive drinking.

Barrel-gird, *n.* the hoop of a barrel ; the name given to a thin horse with projecting ribs.

Barrelled, *ppl. adj.* of a cow : having its belly filled with grass, and like a barrel.

Barrie, *n.* an infant's flannel swaddling-cloth ; a woman's petticoat.

Barrier, *n.* a thresher.

Barrow, *v.* to carry in a wheelbarrow or in a sedan-chair.

Barrow, *v.* to borrow.

Barrowman, *n.* a mason's labourer who carries stone, mortar, &c. on a hand-barrow ; a lame beggar, formerly carried from farm to farm in a barrow.

Barrow-steel, *n.* equal co-operation ; drawing well together.

Barrow-tram, *n.* the shaft of a wheelbarrow ; a raw-boned, awkward-looking person ; a muscular arm or leg.

Barry, Barrie, *v.* to thresh corn. Cf. Bar.

Barry, *n.* a barrow.

Bars, *n.* a grate.

Bars, *n.* a schoolboys' game ; prisoner's base.

Bar-seed, *n.* the time of sowing bear. Cf. Bear-seed.

Barsk, *adj.* harsh ; husky. Cf. Bask.

Barst, *v. pret.* burst.

Bar-stane, *n.* one of the upright stones in a fireplace, to which the bars of a grate are fixed.

Bartice, *n.* a brattice.

Bartle Day, *n.* St Bartholomew's Day, Aug. 24.

Bartle-fair, *n.* a fair held on St. Bartholomew's Day.

Bash, *n.* a heavy blow ; a dint.—*v.* to beat ; to crush, smash ; to bruise, dint ; with *up*, to bend the point of an iron instrument inwards.

Bash, *v.* to abash.

Bash, *n.* a term of contempt.

Bash-hat, *n.* a soft hat.

Bashle, *v.* to shamble. Cf. Bauchle.

Bashle-bands, *n.* bands to keep up shoe-heels.

Ba'-siller, *n.* pence given to children at a wedding. Cf. Ba'-money.

Bask, *adj.* dry ; withering ; bitter ; harsh to the taste.

Basket-hinger, *n.* the gold-crested wren.

Basle, *v.* to talk ignorantly or at random.—*n.* idle talking. Cf. Besle.

†**Basnet**, *n.* a helmet.

Ba' speil, *n.* a game of football.

Bass, *n.* a door-mat ; the soft fibres composing a bird's nest ; a workman's tool-basket ; a straw horse-collar ; a table-mat to protect a table from hot dishes ; the bast or inner bark of a tree.

Bass-bottomed, *adj.* used of chairs : having the seat made of rushes or of ' bass.'

Bass-cock, *n.* the puffin.

†**Bassen'd, Bassand, Bassent**, *adj.* white-faced. Cf. Bausand.

Basser-, Bass-goose, *n.* the gannet.

Bassie, *n.* an old horse. Cf. Bawsie.

Bassie, *n.* a large wooden basin or bowl, frequently used for carrying and mixing oatmeal in baking.

Bassin, *n.* a church offertory-plate ; a 'kirk-basin.'

Bassle, *v.* to struggle ; to wallow.

Bastardrie, *n.* illegitimacy.

Bastardy, *n.* the property of a bastard.

Basties, Bastish, *adj.* coarse, hard, bound, as applied to soil ; obstinate of temper.

†**Bastile, Bastle**, *n.* a fortress, principally used for prisoners.

†**Bastiment**, *n.* a building ; pile ; structure.

Bastle-house, *n.* a fortified house.

†**Bastoun**, *n.* a cudgel. Cf. Batton.

Bastous, *adj.* coarse ; hard. Cf. Basties.

Bat, *conj.* but.

Bat, *n.* a staple or loop of iron.

Bat, *n.* a smart blow ; a stroke of work ; condition ; state of health.

Bat, *n.* a bundle of straw or rushes.

Bat, *n.* a holm ; a river-island ; low-lying land overflowed at spring-tides and floods.

Bat, *v.* to hit ; to press or beat down with a spade; to thresh by striking sheaves against a stone, &c. ; used of mistletoe, ivy, &c. : to cling to a tree, grow on a tree.

Batch, *n.* a bachelor.

Batch, *n.* a crew ; a gang ; a set number ; a baking ; a clump.

Batch-bread, *n.* bread made of common flour.

Batch-day, *n.* baking-day.

Batchie, *n.* a bachelor.

Batchie, *n.* a card-game ; the male loser in the game.

Batch-loaf, *n.* a loaf of ' batch-bread.'

Bate, *v.* to cease ; to reduce the price.

Bate, *v. pret.* did beat.

Bate, *v. pret.* did bite.

Bath, *v.* to give or take a bath.

Bather, *v.* to bother, pester.—*n.* a bother ; a troublesome person.

Batherlocks, *n.* a seaweed like the hart's-tongue fern. Cf. Badderlocks.

Batherment, *n.* bother; trouble.
Bathie, *n.* a booth; hovel; a 'bothie.' Cf. Bothie.
†Batie, *n.* a large dog of any species; a hare; a term of contempt for a man. Cf. Bawty.
Batie, *adj.* round; plump.
Batie-bum, -bummil, *n.* a simpleton; a fool.
Bating, *prep.* excepting; except.
Baton, *n.* an instrument for beating mortar.
Batridge, *n.* the lace or band for tying up the fold of a cocked hat.
Batrons, *n.* a cat. Cf. Baudrons.
Bats, Batts, *n.* botts, a disease in horses or dogs caused by small worms or the bot-fly; the colic.
Batt, *n.* in *phr.* to 'keep one at the batt,' to keep one steady.
Batted, *ppl. adj.* hardened.
Batter, *n.* paste; weaver's and shoemaker's paste.—*v.* to fasten with or apply adhesive paste; with *up*, to clout, patch shoes, &c.
Batter, *n.* a heavy blow.—*v.* to give repeated blows.
Batter, *n.* the slope or inclination of a wall, embankment, &c.; a spree or drinking-bout.—*v.* to build a sloping wall, &c.
Batter, *n.* the cover of a book.
Battered, *ppl. adj.* of a book: provided with 'batters,' covers, or boards.
Battered, *ppl. adj.* pasted and posted on a board or wall.
Batter-horn, *n.* a horn for holding shoemaker's paste.
Battle, *adj.* fat; thickset; used of soil: rich, fertile. Cf. Baittle.
Battle, *n.* a bundle or bottle of straw.—*v.* to put straw into bottles.
Battock, *n.* a tuft of grass; a spot of gravel or ground of any kind surrounded by water; flat ground by a river-side.
Batton, *v.* to cudgel.
Battoon, *n.* a general's baton.
Baub, *n.* beat of drum.
Baubee, *n.* a halfpenny. Cf. Bawbee.
Bauch, *adj.* disagreeable to the taste, &c.; not good; insufficient; incapable; in-different; timid; sheepish; shy; tired-out; of ice: partially thawing.—*v.* to make one look sheepish.
Bauch, *v.* to speak loudly and noisily.
Bauchle, *v.* to shamble; to wear shoes out of shape; to distort; to treat contemptuously; to make of little or no account; to jilt.—*n.* an old shoe; a slipper down-at-heels; a person or thing of nought; a laughing-stock; a clumsy person.
Bauchle, *n.* the upright front of a peat-barrow; one of two pieces of wood fixed on the sides of a cart to extend the surface.
Bauchling, *n.* scorning; rallying; taunting.

Bauchly, *adv.* sorrily; indifferently.
Bauchness, *n.* slowness from timidity; want; defect of every kind.
Bauckie, *n.* the bat. Cf. Backie.
Baud, *n.* a mass of furze, broom, &c. growing thickly together.
Baudminnie, *n.* a plant with the medicinal virtue of savin.
Baudrons, *n.* a kindly designation of a cat; puss.
Bauf, *v.* to make a clattering noise with shoes or clogs in walking.
Baugh, *v.* to look or be confused, sheepish, put out.
Baugh, *adj.* unpleasant to the taste; sheepish. Cf. Bauch.
Baughed, *ppl. adj.* confounded; made to look sheepish.
Baughle, *v.* to wear shoes out of shape.—*n.* an old shoe. Cf. Bauchle.
Baughling, *n.* taunting. Cf. Bauchling.
Bauk, *n.* a strip of untilled land.—*v.* to miss furrows, &c., in sowing; to balk; to dis-appoint. Cf. Balk.
Bauk, Baulk, *n.* the cross-beam of a house; the beam of a pair of scales. Cf. Balk.
Bauken, *n.* the bat.
Bauk-heicht, *adv.* as high as the rafters or ceiling. Cf. Balk-height.
Baukie, *n.* a tether-stake. Cf. Baikie.
Baukie, *n.* the razor-bill or auk; the black guillemot.
Baukie, *n.* the bat.
Baukie, Baukie-up, *n.* a hoist up on one's back.—*v.* to raise a person on one's shoulders. Cf. Backie.
Baukin, *n.* a hobgoblin; a supernatural appearance.
Bauld, *adj.* bold; keen; pungent; fiery-tempered; harsh; stormy; used of a fire: great, strong.—*v.* to kindle or blow up a fire. Cf. Bald.
Bauld, *adj.* bald.
Bauld-daur, *adj.* bold and daring.
Baulkie, *n.* a narrow strip of land separating two farms. Cf. Balkie.
Baumy, *adj.* balmy.
Baun, *n.* a band. Cf. Band.
Baur, *n.* a joke. Cf. Bar.
Baurdy, *adj.* bold; shameless. Cf. Bardy.
†Bausand, Bausent, Bauson, Bausond, *adj* used of animals: having a white spot or streak on the face.
Bausand-faced, *adj.* streaked with white on the face.
Bausy, *adj.* large; corpulent; coarse.—*n.* a big, fat person or animal.
Bauthrin, *ppl.* bustling; fluttering.
Bauthrin, *n.* a cat. Cf. Baudrons.
Bautie, *adj.* guileful.

Bauty, *n.* a name given to a dog. Cf. Batie.

Bavard, *adj.* worn-out ; bankrupt.

Bavarie, Bavarra, *n.* a greatcoat ; a disguise.

Baver, *v.* to shake ; to tremble. Cf. Bever.

Baw, *n.* a ball ; the ball of the leg.

Baw, *v.* to lull asleep.—*n.* in *phr.* 'beddie baw,' a child's cradle or bed.

Bawaw, *n.* a scornful side-glance.

Bawaw, *n.* a ludicrous term for a child.

Bawbee, *n.* a halfpenny ; in *pl.* money ; a dowry.

Bawbee-dragon, *n.* a boy's cheap kite.

Bawbee-elder, *n.* an elder who merely takes up church collections.

Bawbee-jo, *n.* a lover hired to walk with a girl for a shilling or so.

Bawbee-kirk, *n.* the Free Church of Scotland.

Bawbee-row, *n.* a halfpenny roll.

Bawbee-whistle, *n.* a halfpenny whistle.

Bawb-net, *n.* a 'bob-net,' now illegal in salmon-fishing.

Bawbreck, *n.* a kneading-trough ; a baking-board. Cf. Back-bread.

Bawbrie, *n.* a broil ; great noise.

Bawburd, *n.* a baking-board. Cf. Bake-brod.

Bawd, *n.* a hare.

Bawd-bree, *n.* hare-soup.

Bawk, *n.* a strip of untilled land.—*v.* to miss in ploughing, &c. Cf. Balk.

Bawk, *n.* a cross-beam ; a henroost. Cf. Balk.

Bawsie, *n.* a horse with white on its face ; an old horse.

†Bawsint, *adj.* streaked white on the face. Cf. Bausand.

Bawsy-broon, *n.* a 'brownie' ; a hobgoblin.

†Bawty, *n.* a dog ; a hare. Cf. Batie, Bawd.

Baxter, *n.* a baker.

Baxter-chap, *n.* a baker's man or boy.

Bay, *v.* to weep loudly ; to raise the voice loudly.—*n.* the voice raised loudly.

Bay, *n.* an unseemly mass.

Bay, *n.* the sound of birds' notes.

Bayed, *ppl.* bent or giving way in the middle.

Baze, Baize, *n.* a state of bewilderment.—*v.* to bewilder ; to daze.

Bazed, *ppl.* stung by insects ; stupefied ; stupid.

†Bazil, *n.* a drunkard ; a sot.

Bazzle, *v.* to rush about ; to bustle.

Be, *v.* pay for ; be at the cost of.

Be, *prep.* by ; in comparison with ; towards. —*conj.* than. Cf. By.

Bead, *n.* a ring of people hastily formed on any pressing business.—*v.* to form such a ring of people.

Bead, *n.* a glass of spirits.

Bead-house, *n.* an almshouse.

Bead-lambs, *n.* part of the mounting of a silk-loom.

Beagle, *n.* a sheriff's officer.

Beagle, *n.* an oddly dressed figure ; a person bespattered with mud.

Beagle, *n.* a duck.

Beak, *v.* to cry loudly ; to roar, bellow like a bull.

Beak, *n.* the nose ; the face.—*v.* to kiss ; to bill ; to attack with the bill.

Beak, *v.* to warm. Cf. Beek.

Beal, *v.* to fester, suppurate ; to swell with pain or remorse Cf. Beil.

Beal, *n.* a narrow mountain-pass.

Bealing, *n.* a festering sore ; a boil.—*ppl. adj.* festering, suppurating.

Beam, *v.* to warm a teapot before use.

Beam, *v.* to soak the staves of a leaking tub, barrel, &c. in order to stop leakage.

Beam, *n.* the chief support of a plough.

Beamfill, *v.* to fill up spaces in the walls of a house after the beams are placed ; to fill up completely.

Beamfilling, *n.* chips of brick and stone used to 'beamfill' the walls of a house.

Beamfilt, *adj.* indulged.

Beamfull, *adj.* full to overflowing.

Beam-shin'd, *adj.* having the shinbone rising with a curve.

Beam-traddle, *n.* the treadle of a weaver's beam.

Bean, *adj.* snug ; well-to-do. Cf. Bein.

Bean, *n.* advantage.

Bean-hool, *n.* a bean-pod.

Bean-shaup, *n.* an empty bean-pod.

Bean-swaup, *n.* a bean-pod ; a thing or person of no value or strength.

Bear, *n.* four-rowed barley, big.

Bear, *v.* to go to a length.

Bear-barrel, *n.* whisky ; a festival celebrating the 'stooking' of the bear.

Bear-buntling, *n.* a bird like a thrush, haunting especially growing bear.

Bear-curn, *n.* a hand-mill or 'quern' for husking bear.

Beard, *v.* to rub with the beard. Cf. Baird.

Bearder, *n.* one who rubs with the beard.

Beardie, *n.* rubbing a man's beard on a child's face in sport.

Beardie, *n.* a large 'graybeard' jar. Cf. Bairdie.

Beardie, *n.* the three-spined stickleback ; the loach.

Beardie, *n.* the whitethroat.

Beardie-lotch, -lowrie, *n.* the loach.

Beardly, *adj.* stalwart. Cf. Buirdly.

Beardoc, *n.* the loach.

Bear-feys, *n.* land set apart for barley.

Bearge, *v.* to persist in clamorous repetition. Cf. Bairge.

Bear-land, *n.* land set apart for barley.

Bear-lave, *n.* ground the first year after a crop of barley.

Bear-meal-raik, *n.* a fruitless errand.

Bear-meal-wife, *n.* a woman who cannot pay her debts.

Bear-mell, *n.* an implement for beating the husks off barley.

Bear-pundlar, *n.* an instrument for weighing barley.

Bear-reet, *n.* land that has borne a crop of barley in the previous year; the first crop after bear.

Bear's-ears, *n.* the auricula.

Bear-seed, *n.* barley; the time of sowing barley or of preparing the ground for it.

Bear-seed-bird, *n.* the yellow wagtail.

Bear-stane, *n.* a hollow stone anciently used for husking bear or barley.

Beast, *v.* to vanquish.—*n.* a puzzle; what beats one to discover. Cf. Baist.

Beast, *n.* a horse, cow, ox, or sheep; a louse; the devil; any animal but man.

Beastie, *n.* diminutive of beast: used to express sympathy or affection.

Beastie-milk, *n.* the milk of a newly calved cow. Cf. Beest-milk.

Beastie-milk-cheese, *n.* a cheese made of 'beastie-milk.'

Beat, *n.* a stroke, blow, contusion; what beats or puzzles one.

Beat, *n.* a small bundle of flax or hemp.—*v.* to tie up flax in bundles. Cf. Beet.

Beat, *v.* to bruise the feet in walking.—*n.* a bruise.

Beat-the-badger, *n.* an old game used in Fife.

Beat-to-chucks, *phr.* to surpass utterly.

Beattocks, *n.* mashed potatoes.

Beautiful, *adj.* delicious.

Beaver, *n.* a top-hat.

Beb, *v.* to drink immoderately; to swill. Cf. Bib.

Bebbing-full, *adj.* used of the tide: high, full.

Bebble, *v.* to sip; to tipple; to drink carelessly.

Bebbs, *n.* small bits of skin on a chin unshaved for some days. Cf. Babbs.

Beblacken, Beblaiken, *n.* to calumniate boldly.

Becam, *v. pret.* became.

Because, *n.* a cause.

Bechance, *v.* to happen by chance.

Bechle, *n.* a settled cough.—*v.* to cough.

Becht, *n.* a bight; a loop on cord or rope.—*v.* to put a loop on a rope. Cf. Bicht.

Becht, *ppl.* tied.

Beck, *n.* a brook.

Beck, *n.* the call of the grouse.

Beck, *n.* a curtsey; obeisance.—*v.* to curtsey; to cringe; to do obeisance; used of a horse: to jerk the head.

Becklet, *n.* an under-waistcoat; a flannel shirt. Cf. Baiklet.

Bed, *n.* a woman's confinement; litter for animals.—*v.* to go or put to bed; to give litter to animals; to lay a stone evenly; to plant in flower-beds.

Bed-board, *n.* the board in front of a 'box-bed.'

Bed-bound, *adj.* bedridden.

Bed-cronie, *n.* a bedfellow.

Beddal, *n.* a bedridden person.

Beddall, Beddell, *n.* a licensed beggar.

Beddie, *n.* a small bed.

Beddie-ba', *n.* a child's cradle or cot.

Bedding, *n.* litter for horses or cattle; an old wedding-custom of putting bride and bridegroom to bed.

Beddit, *ppl.* gone to bed; put to bed.

Beddle, *n.* a bedridden person.

Beddle, *n.* a beadle.

Beddy, *adj.* greedy; covetous of trifles; conceited; self-sufficient.

Bedeen, Bedien, *adv.* immediately; forthwith; often used as an expletive or as a rhyme-word to eke out a line.

Bede-house, *n.* an almshouse.

Bedeman, *n.* a resident in an almshouse; a pauper who formerly received the king's annual bounty, with a blue coat and badge.

Bederal, *n.* a church beadle. Cf. Bedral.

Bed-evil, *n.* sickness confining one to bed.

Bedfast, *adj.* bedridden.

Bedfellow, *n.* a spouse.

Bedgown, *n.* a woman's short, cotton, working jacket.

Bedink, *v.* to dress out smartly; to bedizen.

Bedirtin, *ppl. adj.* soiled with excrement.

Bedler, *n.* a beadle.

Bedoitrify, *v.* to stupefy.

Bedown, *prep.* down.—*adj.* downwards.

Bed-plaid, *n.* a blanket.

Bedraigle, *v.* to bedraggle.

Bedral, Bedrel, *n.* a church beadle, bellman, and sexton in one.

Bedrel, Bedral, *n.* a bedridden person; a helpless cripple.—*adj.* bedridden.

Bedrite, *v.* to soil with excrement; to bedirt.

Bedritten, *ppl. adj.* soiled with excrement. Cf. Bedirtin.

Beds, *n.* the game of hop-scotch.

Bedshank, *n.* buttermilk.

Bedstock, *n.* the front bar of wood in a bed.

Bed-stone, *n.* the nether millstone; the piece of stone or slate used in the game of 'beds.'

Bedunder, *v.* to stupefy; confound.

Bee, *n.* a metal ring; a ferrule for implements, axles, &c.

Bee, *n.* the hollow between the ribs and hip bone of a horse.

Bee-ale, *n.* mead made from refuse honey.

Be-east, *adv.* eastwards.

Bee-baw-babbety, *n.* a game.

Bee-bike, *n.* a wild bees' nest.

Bee-bread, *n.* a mixture of pollen and honey, the food of the bees' larvæ.

Beed, *n.* delay.

Beed, *v. pret.* must ; had to, used of moral or logical necessity. Cf. Bood.

Beef-boat, *n.* a pickling tub or barrel.

Beef-brewis, *n.* beef-broth.

Beef-brose, *n.* 'brose' made with the skimmings of beef-broth.

Beefer, *n.* an ox or cow fed for the butcher.

Beefy, *adj.* fat ; pursy ; short and stout ; used of oxen : yielding good and abundant beef. —*n.* a nickname for a short and stout person.

Beegle, *n.* a beagle ; a sheriff's officer. Cf. Beagle.

Bee-headit, *adj.* harebrained ; flighty ; eccentric ; excitable.

Bee-in-the-bonnet, *n.* an eccentric ; a flighty person.

Beek, *v.* to warm before the fire ; to make warm ; to bask in the sun or warmth of a fire ; of the sun : to shine brightly ; to add fuel to fire.—*n.* what warms ; basking in the sun or warmth of a fire.

Beek, *v.* to bathe, foment.

Beel, *v.* used of cattle : to collect them at night to a spot suitable for their spending the night in the open.—*n.* a place where they are so collected.

Beel, *n.* a shelter. Cf. Bield.

Beel, *v.* to fester ; to swell with pain or remorse. Cf. Beal.

Beeld, *n.* an image.

Beeld, *v.* to shelter. Cf. Bield.

Beeldy, *adj.* giving shelter. Cf. Bieldy.

Beem, *v.* to steep tubs, &c., in order to make them watertight. Cf. Beam.

Been, *n.* a bone. Cf. Bane.

Beene, *v.* to steep a tub when its staves have shrunk.

Beenge, *v.* to bow ; to cringe, fawn.

Beenmost, *adj.* uppermost. Cf. Bunemost.

Beeny, *adj.* bony ; full of bones.

Beer, *n.* a drinking-bout.

Beerach, *n.* a cord fastening a cow's tail to her leg during milking. Cf. Bourach.

Beeran, *n.* a small trout.

Beerlin, *n.* a half-decked galley. Cf. Berlin.

Beer-mell, *n.* a 'mell' for pounding barley.

Bees, *n.* a state of confusion ; muddle ; lightheadedness ; fuddle.

Bee-scap, -skep, *n.* a beehive.

Beesnin, *n.* the milk drawn from a cow newly calved.

Beest, *v.* had to ; was compelled to. Cf. Beed, Bood, Beet.

Beest, *n.* the milk of a cow newly calved.

Beest-, Beesting-cheese, *n.* cheese made of coagulated 'beest.'

Beest-milk, *n.* the milk of a cow newly calved.

Bee-stone, *n.* the stone on which a hive rests.

Bee's-wisp, *n.* a wild bee's nest on the surface of the ground.

Beet, *v.* to tie up flax in sheaves or bundles.— *n.* a sheaf or bundle of flax prepared for the mill.

Beet, *v.* to kindle or mend a fire ; to rouse or kindle a passion ; to repair ; to praise ; to blazon ; to supply ; to prevent waste by addition ; to soothe, mitigate.—*n.* an addition ; a supply ; in *pl.* needful things.

Beet, *n.* a boot.

Beet, *v.* had to ; was compelled. Cf. Beest, Bood.

Beetikin, *n.* a hobnailed boot.

Beetin-band, *n.* the strap which binds a bundle of flax.

Beetle, *v.* to beat with a beetle ; to pound ; to mash.—*n.* a flat piece of wood used by dyers and washerwomen.

Beetle, *v.* to project ; to grow long and sharp.

Beetle, *v.* to amend ; used of crops : to recover. Cf. Bietle.

Beetle-bee, *n.* a flying beetle ; a humming beetle.

Beetle-hicht, *n.* the height of a beetle.

Beetling-stone, *n.* the stone on which clothes are 'beetled.'

Beetl't-taties, -praties, *n.* mashed potatoes.

Beet-master, -mister, *n.* a person or thing helpful in emergency.

Beeton, *n.* in *phr.* 'burdie-beeton,' a fondling term for a little child.

†Beetraw, *n.* beetroot.

Beff, *n.* a stupid person.

Beff, *v.* to strike ; to beat.—*n.* a stroke. Cf. Baff.

Beffam, Beffin, *n.* a soft, stupid person.

Beflum, *v.* to befool by cajolery.—*n.* idle, nonsensical, wheedling talk.

Befong, *n.* a kind of handkerchief, and its material.

Before, *adv.* of a watch or clock : fast.—*conj.* rather than.

Beft, *v.* to beat ; to strike.

Befyle, *v.* to soil, defile.

Begairied, *ppl. adj.* bespattered ; bedaubed ; variegated.

Begairies, *n.* ornamental stripes of cloth on garments.

†Begarie, Begarrie, *v.* to variegate ; to be spatter, besmear.

Begarred, *ppl. adj.* variegated ; covered with filth ; bespattered with mud.

Begeck, Begeik, *v.* to deceive ; to jilt ; to disappoint.—*n.* a trick ; disappointment.

Beges, *adv.* by chance ; at random.

Begg, *n.* barley ; bigg.

Beggar, *v.* used as a quasi-imprecation.—*n.* a term of reproach or familiar address.

Beggar-bolts, *n.* darts ; missiles of stone.

Beggar's-bed, *n.* a bed allotted to beggars in the barn.

Beggar's-brown, *n.* light-brown snuff made from tobacco-stems.

Beggar's-plaits, *n.* wrinkles or creases in garments as if slept in.

Begin| *v.* to say grace before a meal.

Begink, *v.* to cheat ; to jilt.—*n.* a cheat ; a jilting. Cf. Begunk.

Beglammer, *v.* to bewitch ; to deceive ; to hoodwink.

Beglaum, *v.* to bewitch.

Begnet, *n.* a bayonet. Cf. Bagnet.

Bego, *int.* used as an expletive or oath.

Begoud, Begouth, *v. pret.* began.

Begowk, Begouk, *v.* to trick, befool ; to jilt. —*n.* a trick ; jilting.

Begowker, *n.* a deceiver.

Begoyt, *adj.* foolish.

Begrat, Begratten, Begritten, *ppl. adj.* tear-stained ; disfigured with weeping.

Begrudge, *v.* to regret ; to ill-wish.—*n.* suspicion.

Begrutten, *ppl. adj.* tear-stained. Cf. Begrat.

Beguid, *v. pret.* began. Cf. Begoud.

Beguile, *v.* to deprive by a trick ; to lead into error ; to disappoint.—*n.* a trick ; disappointment.

Begullion, *n.* a glamour deceiving the eyes.

Begunk, *n.* a trick ; misfortune ; unlooked-for disappointment ; jilting.—*v.* to cheat ; to jilt ; to play a trick ; to disappoint.

Behad, *v.* to stop, wait ; to hold, maintain, hold as certain. Cf. Behald.

Behadden, Behadin, *ppl.* held or kept back ; indebted ; obliged.

Behald, Behauld, *v.* to behold ; to wait ; to delay ; to permit ; to connive at ; to watch ; to scrutinize ; to view with jealousy or suspicion ; to recognize.—*n.* recognition ; notice.

Behand, *adv.* in *phr.* 'to come weel behand,' to manage well.

Behauden, *ppl.* under obligation ; indebted. Cf. Behadden.

Behinds, *n.* the posteriors.

Behint, Behin', *adv.* late ; too late ; in arrears of work, payment, or fulfilment ; used of a clock or watch : slow.—*prep.* behind.

Beho, *n.* a laughing-stock. Cf. Boho.

Behold, *v.* to scrutinize ; to take no notice of, connive at ; to hold back. Cf. Behald.

Beholden, *ppl.* indebted.

Behoove, Behove, *v.* to be obliged.—*n.* behoof.

Beigh, *v.* to cough.

Beik, *n.* trifles ; a nest of wild bees ; a gathering. Cf. Bike.

Beik, *v.* to warm ; to bask in the sun. Cf. Beek.

Beik, *n.* a cant word for a person ; a man's mouth, face, &c. Cf. Beak.

Beikat, *n.* a male salmon. Cf. Bykat, Bukat.

Beil, Beill, *v.* to fester ; to give pain or trouble to. Cf. Beal.

Beild, *n.* an image. Cf. Beeld.

Beild, *n.* a shelter. Cf. Bield.

Beildless, *adj.* unsheltered.

Beiling, *n.* suppuration.

Bein, *n.* a bone. Cf. Bane, Been.

Bein, *adj.* well-to-do ; comfortable ; eager ; used of a house or cask : thoroughly dry, watertight.—*adv.* comfortably. Cf. Bien.

Beine, *v.* to 'beam' or warm a *t*eapot before using it. Cf. Beene.

Being, *n.* livelihood ; means of subsistence.

Being, *n.* the beach of the seashore.

Beinge, *v.* to bow ; to cringe. Cf. Beenge.

Beinless, *adj.* comfortless.

Bein-like, *adj.* in apparent comfort and well-being.

Beinly, *adv.* comfortably ; happily ; prosperously.

Beinness, *n.* comfort ; prosperity ; moderate wealth.

Beir-tree, *n.* the bier on which a corpse is carried to the grave.

Beis, *prep.* in comparison with ; in addition to.

Beis, *v.* 3*rd per. sing. pres. subj. of* be.

Beisand, *adj.* quite at a loss ; stupefied ; benumbed.

Beist-, Beistie-milk, *n.* the first milk of a cow after calving. Cf. Beest.

Beit, *v.* to kindle ; to add fuel ; to supply. Cf. Beet.

Beiting-band, *n.* the bandage of a sheaf of flax or lint. Cf. Beetin-band.

Beizless, *adj.* extreme.—*adv.* extremely.

†Bejan, *n.* a first year's student at a Scottish university.—*v.* to initiate a new shearer in the harvest-field by bumping his posteriors on a stone.

Beke, *v.* to warm ; to bask. Cf. Beek.

Belaired, *ppl. adj.* stuck fast in mud, &c.

Belaubir, *v.* to belabour.

Belay, *v.* to overcome.

Belbevar, *v.* to puzzle ; to perplex ; to be unable to decide.

Belch, *n.* a very fat person or animal ; a brat of a child. Cf. Bilch.

Beld, *adj.* bald.—*v.* to make bald ; to become bald.

Beldness, *n.* baldness.

Belicket, *n.* in *phr.* 'deil-belicket,' 'fient-belicket,' absolutely nothing.

Belike, *adj.* probable ; likely.—*adv.* probably.

Belie, *adv.* speedily ; soon. Cf. Belyve.

Belirt, *v.* to jilt ; to beguile, deceive. Cf. Lirt.

Belive, *adv.* speedily; immediately; soon. Cf. Belyve.

Belks, *n.* the stems of seaweed, formerly used in making kelp.

Bell, *n.* the top of a hill; the highest part of a slope; a bellman; a town-crier with a bell.—*v.* to advertise by means of a bellman.

Bell, *n.* a bubble.—*v.* to bubble; to swell out.

Bell, *n.* a blaze or white mark on a horse's face.

Bell, *n.* the blossom of a plant.

Bell, *adj.* bald. Cf. Beld.

Bella, *n.* a bonfire. Cf. Bale.

Bellam, *n.* a stroke. Cf. Bellum.

Bellandine, *n.* a broil, squabble.

Beller, *v.* to bubble up.

Bell-heather, *n.* the cross-leaved heather.

Bell-house, *n.* a church-tower, belfry.

Belli-bucht, *n.* a hollow in a hill transverse to the slope.

Bellicon, *n.* a blusterer.

Bellie-mantie, *n.* blindman's buff.

Belli-hooin', *n.* riotousness.

†Bellisand, *adj.* elegant; of imposing appearance.

Bell-kite, *n.* the bald coot.

Bell-money, *n.* money demanded by children at a house in which there is a wedding. Cf. Ba'-money.

Belloch, *v.* to bellow; to cry loudly, roar.—*n.* a roar, bellow.

Belloch, *n.* a narrow mountain-pass. Cf. Balloch.

Bellonie, *n.* a brawling, noisy woman.

Bell-penny, *n.* money laid past to provide for one's funeral.

Bell-pow, *n.* a bald head.

Bellraive, *v.* to rove about; to be unsteady; to act on impulse.

Bell-ringer, *n.* the long-tailed titmouse.

Bell't, *adj.* bald. Cf. Beld.

Bell'tness, *n.* baldness.

Bellum, *n.* force; impetus; a stroke; a blow; a blast.

Bellums, *n.* a boys' game.

Bellware, *n.* seaweed, of which kelp was made.

Bellwaver, *v.* to straggle; to stroll; used of the mind: to fluctuate, be inconstant; to tell a story incoherently.

Bellwavering, *n.* fluttering; rambling.

Bell-weed, *n.* 'bellware.'

Belly, *v.* to eat or drink voraciously; to stuff the belly.

Belly, *v.* to bellow; to weep loudly.

Belly-blind, *adj.* quite blind.—*n.* blindman's buff.

Belly-flaught, *adv.* headlong; hastily; face-down; flat-forward; overhead in skinning an animal.

Belly-flaughtered, *ppl. adj.* thrown flat on the ground.

Belly-god, *n.* a glutton.

Belly-gourdon, -gut, -hudroun, *n.* a glutton.

Belly-rack, *n.* gormandizing.

Belly-rive, *n.* a great feast; a social gathering.

Belly-thraw, *n.* a colic.

Belly-timber, *n.* food; provisions.

Below, *v.* to demean.

Belsh, *n.* a very fat person. Cf. Belch.

Belshach, *n.* a contemptuous designation of a child; a brat. Cf. Belch.

Belshie, *adj.* short and fat. Cf. Belch.

Belstracht, *adv.* headlong, prostrate.

Belt, *n.* the bolt of a door.

Belt, *n.* a narrow plantation.

Belt, *v.* to flog; to scourge.

Belt, *v.* to come forward with a sudden spring.

Belt, *v.* to gird as an honorary distinction.

Beltane, *n.* the 1st of May O.S. and N.S.; sometimes the 3rd of May, and Whitsunday; a festival formerly kept by herds and young people on May 1 and June 21.

Belted plaid, *n.* a Highlander's full military dress plaid.

Belter, *n.* a heavy blow, a succession of blows; bickering.

Beltie, *n.* a small, narrow plantation.

Beltie, *n.* a water-hen.

Belting, *n.* 'Beltane.'

Bely, *v.* to besiege.

Belyve, *adj.* immediately; by-and-by.

Bemang, *v.* to hurt, injure; to maul.

Bemean, *v.* to degrade, to lower one's self.

Bement, *v.* to render demented.

Bemmle, *n.* an ill-made man; an ungainly walker.

Ben, *n.* a hill, mountain.

Ben, *n.* the supply of empty coal-tubs.

Ben, *n.* a small species of salmon.

Ben, *adv.* in, inside, within; in or into the parlour; in toward the speaker.—*prep.* in, within.—*n.* an inner room, a parlour.

Ben-a-hoose, *adj.* belonging to the parlour or the best room.—*adv.* in the parlour.

Ben-a-hoose-breakfast, *n. phr.* breakfast for the farmer's family in the parlour.

Ben-a-hoose-breid, *n. phr.* an oatcake of finer quality for use in a farmer's parlour.

Ben-a-hoose-woman, -umman, *n. phr.* a parlour-maid.

Bench, *n.* a plate-rack.

Bend, *n.* strong, thick leather for the soles of boots or shoes.

Bend, *n.* a piece of bent iron-plate going over the back of the last horse at plough; in *pl.* the complete furniture of a peat-horse. —*v.* to adjust on a horse the harness for panniers.

Bend, *n.* a foolish, foppish fellow; a 'booser;'

a draught of liquor.—*v.* to drink hard or greedily ; to ' boose.'

Bend, *n.* a bound, spring, leap. — *v.* to bound, spring.

Bend, *n.* a muffler ; a kerchief ; a cowl.

Bend, *v.* to cock a gun.

Bend, *v.* with *up,* to embolden.

Bend, *adj.* bold.—*adv.* bravely.

Bender, *n.* a silly fellow ; a hard drinker. Cf. Bend.

Bendit, *ppl. adj.* crouching, ready to spring.

Bend-leather, *n.* thick leather for soling boots and shoes.

Bene, *adj.* well-to-do. Cf. Bein.

Benefit, *n.* farm servants' wages so far as paid in kind.

Benefit-man, *n.* a farm-servant paid partly in kind.

Ben-end, *n.* the better room in a two-roomed house ; the best part of anything.

Benew, *adv.* beneath.

Bengie, *n.* a penalty exacted by harvesters from a visitor to the field, either in money or in the infliction of 'bumping' on the stubble. —*v.* to inflict the penalty of 'bumping.'

Bengiel, *n.* a heap ; a large quantity. Cf. Bangyal.

Ben-hoose, *n.* the inner or principal room.

Ben-inno, *adv.* to within ; towards the speaker in a room.

†Benjamine, *n.* benzoin.

Benjel, *n.* a heap. Cf. Bangyal.

Benk, *n.* a bench ; a plate-rack. Cf. Bink.

Benlin, *n.* a long, light stone, slung in the loops of straw-ropes on a thatched or turfed roof.

Benlins, *adv.* towards the interior of a house.

Benmost, *adj.* inmost, farthest 'ben.'

Benn, *n.* a sash ; a kerchief. Cf. Bend.

Bennel, *n.* long, reedy grass, growing in stagnant waters ; in *pl.* mats made of 'bennel,' and used as cottage partitions and ceilings ; dry, withered weeds gathered for burning.

Bennels, *n.* the seed of flax.

Benner, *adj.* inner.

Benner gowan, *n.* the mountain daisy ; the garden fever-few.

Bennermost, *adj.* innermost.

Benorth, *adv.* to the northward of.

Bense, *n.* a violent movement ; a blow, spring, strong push ; vigour, energy.—*v.* to walk or move violently ; to bounce.— *adv.* violently.

Benshee, *n.* a 'banshee.'

Bensie, *v.* to strike vigorously.

Bensil, Bensell, *v.* to beat ; to bang.—*n.* a heavy blow ; a violent or sudden movement ; violence of storm, &c. ; a severe rebuke ; a place exposed to the violence of the storm.

Bensing, *n.* the showing of great vigour in walking, working, &c.—*ppl. adj.* bouncing, vigorous ; used of a bow : full bent.

Bensome, *adj.* quarrelsome.

Bent, *n.* coarse grass growing near the sea or on moorland ; common hair-grass ; the open field ; a sandy knoll covered with 'bent' ; the slope or hollow of a hill.

Bent-dues, *n.* a levy formerly exacted from scholars for playing on the links on half-holidays.

Ben-the-hoose, *adv.* in the parlour.—*n.* the best or inner part of a house. Cf. Ben-a-hoose.

Bentiness, *n.* the state of being covered with ' bent.'

Bent-moss, *n.* soil composed of hard moss covered thickly with 'bent.'

Bent-silver, *n.* ? 'blessed money,' claimed on a saint's day.

Benty, *adj.* covered with bent-grass.

Benty bows, *n.* ? bandy-legs.

Benward, *adv.* inward, forward.

Benweed, Benwood, *n.* the common ragwort.

Benwuth, *adv.* 'benward.'

Benzel, *n.* a heap. Cf. Benjel.

Beowld, *ppl. adj.* distorted. Cf. Beuld.

Berge, *v.* to scold ; to storm. Cf. Bairge.

Berlin, *n.* a sort of galley, a half-decked rowing-boat.

Bern-windlin, *n.* a kiss given in the corner of a barn.

Berry, *n.* the grain of corn ; a gooseberry.

Berry, *n.* in *phr.* 'no' the berry,' a bad character, 'not the thing.'

Berry, *v.* to beat, to cudgel ; to thresh corn. Cf. Barry.

Berry-barn, *n.* the third finger.

Berry-heather, *n.* the crowberry.

Berthinsek, *n.* a law by which no man was to be capitally punished for stealing a calf or sheep, or so much meat as he could carry on his back in a sack.

Bervie, Bervie-haddock, *n.* a haddock split and smoke-dried.

Besaunt, *v.* to canonise ; to repute as very holy.

Beseek, Beseik, *v.* to beseech.

Beseene, *ppl. adj.* conversant with ; skilled in ; provided, furnished with.

Beset, *v.* to 'set,' become.

Besetment, *n.* a besetting weakness, trouble, or sin.

Beshachil, *v.* to crook ; to deviate from the straight.

Beshacht, *ppl.* not straight ; tattered, dirty.

Besides, *prep.* in comparison with.

Beslabber, *v.* to eat slovenly ; to besmear in eating or drinking.

Besle, *v.* to talk much at random and ignorantly.—*n.* idle talk.

Besmarten, v. to make smart, neat.

Besmiacher, v. to besmear.

Besmotter, v. to smear or daub with mud, &c. ; to bespatter, foul.

Besna, v. *neg.* be not.

Besnang, v. to crush, batter, beat in.

Besom, *n.* a loose or slovenly woman; a 'gipsy,' a term of contempt applied to a woman.

Besom-clean, *adj.* clean only on the surface ; clean by sweeping though not by washing.

Besom-shank, *n.* the handle of a besom.

Besouth, *adv.* to the southward of.

Bess, v. to sew slackly ; to baste. **Cf.** Baiss.

Bessy, *n.* an ill-mannered, romping, or bad-tempered woman or girl; a light-headed girl.

Bessy-lorch, *n.* the loach.

Best, v. to excel, to get the better of one. **Cf.** Beast, Baist.

Best, *adj.* better.

Best, *n.* a beast.

Best-aucht, *n.* the best thing of a kind that one possesses.

Best-cheip, -cheap, *adj.* the best for the money.

†**Bestial,** *n.* the live-stock on a farm.

Best like, *adj.* best-looking.

Best maid, *n.* a bridesmaid.

Best man, *n.* a bridegroom's supporter.

Best respects, *n.* intimate friends.

Besturted, *ppl.* startled, alarmed.

Besweik, Beswik, v. to allure ; to cheat, deceive. **Cf.** Swick.

Bet, v. to beat ; to defeat.—v. *pret.* did beat.

Bet, v. to assuage, mitigate. **Cf.** Beet.

Betake, Betack, v. to inflict ; to hand over ; to resort ; to recover ; to take over.

Betaucht, v. *pret.* and *ppl.* committed, delivered up. **Cf.** Beteach.

Betchell, v. to beat.

Betchellin', *n.* a drubbing.

Beteach, v. to deliver up ; to entrust ; to recommend to.

Beteach us, *phr.* have a care of us ; give us understanding.

Bethank, *n.* thanks ; indebtedness.

Bethankit, *int.* God be thanked !—*n.* grace after meat.

Betheikit, *ppl.* thatched.

Betheral, Bethral, *n.* beadle and sexton. **Cf.** Bedral.

Bethout, *pret.* and *adv.* without.

Betid, Beted, v. *pret.* befell.

Betimes, *adv.* occasionally, at times; by-and-by.

Bet-lick, *n.* the conquering blow.

Betoggit, *ppl. adj.* covered ; burdened.

Betooch, Betootch, v. to commit, entrust. **Cf.** Beteach.

Betooch-us-to, *int.* alas ! commend us to (God) ! have a care of us !

Better, v. to improve in health.—*n.* the best.

—*adj.* greater, more, higher in price ; recovered from illness. — *adv.* repeatedly ; with renewed efforts.

Better-cheap, *adv.* cheaper, at a less price.

Better-gates, *adv.* in a better way or manner.

Better-like, *adj.* better-looking ; looking better (in health, &c.).

Betterlins, *adv.* better.

Betterness, *n.* improvement in health.

Betters, *n.* in *phr.* 'ten betters,' ten times better.

Better side, *n.* what is more or older than.

Better sort, *n.* the upper classes.

Bettle, *n.* a blow, a stroke.

Between-hands, *adv.* at intervals.

Between-the-lights, *phr.* twilight.

Between two minds, *phr.* undecided.

Betweesh, *prep.* between. **Cf.** Atweesh.

Betwixt and between, *phr.* neither one thing nor another ; intermediate.

Beuch, *n.* the bow of a boat or ship ; a person, an individual person.

Beuchel, v. to shamble ; to walk feebly with short steps.—*n.* a little, weak, crooked creature.

Beugle-backit, *adj.* crook-backed.

Beuk, *n.* a book ; a Bible.—v. to register for proclamation of banns of marriage.

Beuk, v. *pret.* baked.

Beuk, v. used of cattle: to grow fat, take on flesh. **Cf.** Bouk.

Beukin'-nicht, *n.* the evening when names are 'beukit' for marriage-banns.

Beuk-lare, -lear, *n.* knowledge gained from books ; schooling.

Beuk-lared, -lear'd, *adj.* learned ; educated.

Beuk-worm, *n.* a bookworm.

Beuld, *adj.* bow-legged.

Beust, *n.* grass two years old ; grass withered from standing through the winter.

Beusty, *adj.* dry ; half-withered, used of grass.

Beuter, *n.* the bittern. **Cf.** Bewter.

Bevel, *n.* a strong thrust ; a heavy blow.

Bever, v. to shake, quiver ; to tremble from age, infirmity, fright, or cold.

Beverage, Beveridge, *n.* a fine in money, kisses, or drink, demanded of any one on the first wearing of new clothes ; the first kiss given to a newly-married bride by the bridegroom ; a 'hansel.'—v. to 'hansel.'

Bevie, *n.* a large fire.

Bevie, *n.* a jog, push. **Cf.** Bevel.

Bevil, v. to manage, arrange.

Bevil-edge, *n.* the edge of a sharp tool, sloping towards the point.

Bevir-horse, *n.* a lean horse, one worn-out with age or hard work.

Bevver, v. to quiver. **Cf.** Bever.

Bewave, v. to lay wait for ; to overcome by mean stratagem.

Bewest, *adv.* to the west of.

Bewiddied, *ppl. adj.* bewildered.

Bewill, *v.* to cause to go astray.

Bewith, *n.* a temporary substitute or makeshift.

Bewk, *v. pret.* baked.

Bewter, *n.* the bittern.

Bey, *n.* a room of a cottage or house.

Beyont, *adv.* yonder, beyond; beyond all things; over and above.—*prep.* beyond.— *n.* a place or district supposed to be beyond ken.

Beyon'-the-beyont, *phr.* quite incredible; quite out of the way.

Beysand, *adj.* quite at a loss; benumbed; stupefied. Cf. Beisand.

Beyzless, *adj.* extreme.—*adv.* extremely. Cf. Beizless.

Bezle, *v.* to talk ignorantly or at random. Cf. Besle.

Biach, *n.* a familiar term of address, often used to children.

Bias, *adv.* very. Cf. Byous.

Bib, *n.* the stomach.

Bib, Bibble, *v.* to tipple.

Bibble, *v.* to snivel. Cf. Bubble.

Bibble, *n.* nonsense.

Bibbles, *n.* nasal mucus.

Bibblie, *adj.* snotty; blubbering. Cf. Bubbly.

Bibblie-gauger, *n.* the nose.

Bible, *n.* a book of any kind; a large quarto or folio volume.

†Bibliothecar, *n.* a librarian.

†Bibliotheck, *n.* a library.

Bicht, *n.* anything folded or doubled, the loop in a rope; a measure of the length of a coil of fishing-line; a bay, creek. Cf. Becht.

Bick, *v.* in *phr.* 'bick and birr,' to cry as grouse.

Bick, *n.* bitch; a sluttish woman.

Bicker, *v.* to pelt with stones; to strike repeatedly; to move quickly and noisily; to ripple; to indulge in rough or indelicate horseplay.—*n.* a scrimmage; a stone-fight; a rapid and noisy movement; a rough, stupid, and noisy person.

Bicker, *n.* a wooden beaker or drinking-cup; a porridge-dish; a bowl; a small wooden vessel, with one of the staves prolonged as a handle.

Bicker-cut, *n.* hair-cutting by means of a bowl placed on the head.

Bickerfu', *n.* a bowlful.

Bickerin', *n.* indelicate toying; quarrelling.

Bicker-raid, *n.* a harvest frolic in which a young man threw down a girl, and the other harvesters covered them with their 'bickers.'

Bid, *v.* to desire, wish; to invite to a wedding or funeral.

Biddableness, *n.* docility, compliance.

Biddably, *adv.* obediently, meekly.

Biddenable, *adj.* obedient, docile.

Bidding, *n.* an invitation.

Bide, *v.* used of persons: to wait, remain, tarry; dwell, live; of things: to remain, continue; to await; to tolerate; to be the better of, receive, require.—*n.* pain, suffering.

Bide by, *v.* to adhere to, maintain.

Biding, *n.* endurance, enduring; in *pl.* sufferings.

Biel', Bield, *n.* image, figure, form. Cf. Beeld.

Bield, Biel, *v.* to shelter, protect; to take shelter.—*n.* a shelter, refuge, a home, house; anything that shelters or shades.

Bielding, *n.* shelter; protection.

Bieldy, Biely, *adj.* furnishing shelter; snug.

Bien, *adj.* thriving; prosperous; comfortable. Cf. Bein.

Bier, *v.* to roar as a bull.—*n.* a shout; a complaint.

Bier, *n.* twenty threads in the breadth of a web.

Bierling, *n.* a galley. Cf. Berlin.

Bierly, *adj.* big, burly, 'buirdly.'

Biets, *n.* the milk of a newly-calved cow. Cf. Beest.

Bietle, *v.* to amend, recover health; used of a crop: to improve.

Biffy, *n.* a nickname for a short, pursy fellow. Cf. Beefy.

Big, *adj.* pregnant, gravid; haughty, consequential.

Big, Bigg, *v.* to build; to build a nest.

Big coat, *n.* a greatcoat.

Big end, *n.* the greater part.

†Bigent, *n.* a first year's student at St Andrews University. Cf. Bejan.

Bigger, *n.* a builder.

Biggie, Biggin, *n.* a linen cap or coif.

Biggin, *n.* a building; a house; a cottage; the act of building.

Biggit, *ppl. adj.* built; grown; wealthy.

Biggit-land, *n.* land built on.

Biggit-wa's, *n.* buildings; houses.

Biggle, *v.* to separate grain from the straw by shaking it.

Biggonet, *n.* a linen cap or coif.

Bighornie, *n.* the devil, the 'muckle deil.'

Bightsom, *adj.* having an air of ease combined with activity.

Bigly, *adj.* pleasant; commodious.

Big mavis, *n.* the missel-thrush.

Big miss, *n.* a great loss by death, or by the departure of a friend.

Bigness, *n.* size, bulk.

Bignet, *n.* a bayonet. Cf. Bagnet.

Big on, -upon, *v.* to fall upon, attack.

Big-ox-eye, *n.* the great titmouse.

Bigsie, *adj.* rather large; proud, conceited; used contemptuously.

Big up, *v.* to confirm in an opinion; to devote one's self to an opinion, idea, purpose, or person.

Bike, *n.* a nest of wild bees; a swarm; a habitation; an assembly of people; a windfall, unexpected luck; an erection shaped like a bee-hive for preserving grain.—*v.* to swarm like bees; to assemble, crowd.

Bike, *n.* the hook of the crook from which pots hang over a fire in cooking.

Biking, *n.* a hive, a swarm.

Bikker, *n.* a smuggling-vessel. Cf. Bukker.

Bilbie, *n.* a residence; shelter.

Bilch, *n.* a fat, short person or animal; a monster; a 'brat'; a little, crooked, insignificant person.

Bilch, *v.* to limp, halt.

Bilcher, *n.* one who limps.

Bilder, *n.* a scab.

Bile, *n.* a boil; in *phr.* a 'bile in the stomach,' a bilious attack.

Bile, *n.* the heating of corn-stacks.—*v.* to boil.

Bilf, *n.* a contemptuous designation of a pursy person; a monster.

Bilf, *n.* a blunt stroke.

Bilgate, *n.* a 'bout,' a 'go.'

Bilget, *n.* a projection to support a shelf, &c. —*adj.* bulging, jutting out.

Bill, *n.* a letter, a missive.

Bill, *v.* to register; to indict.

Bill, *n.* a bull.

Billatory, *n.* a restless bull.

Bill-blo, *n.* a bull.

Billibue, *n.* a hullabaloo.

Billie, *n.* a brother; a comrade. Cf. Billy.

Bill-jock, *n.* a bull.

Billseag, *n.* an old, castrated bull.

Bill-sweater, *n.* a money-lender.

Billy, *n.* a young fellow; a comrade; a brother; a lover; a boy.

Billy, *n.* the golden warbler.

Billy, *v.* to bellow; to low. Cf. Belly.

Billy-bentie, *n.* a smart, roguish boy.

Billy-blin, *n.* a benevolent sprite, a 'brownie.'

Billy-blind, *n.* blindman's buff; the person blindfolded in the game.

Billy-blinder, *n.* the person who hoodwinks another in the game of blindman's buff; an imposture, a 'blind.'

Billy-fairplay, *n.* a game of chance, common at village fairs.

Billy-hood, *n.* brotherhood.

Billy-play-fair tummlin' tams, *n. phr.* riddles for riddling coals.

Billy-whitethroat, *n.* the golden warbler.

Bilsh, *n.* a short, plump person; a thriving, stout person or animal. Cf. Belch.

Bilshie, *adj.* short and stout; plump and thriving.

Bilt, *n.* a short, thickset person.

Bilt, *n.* a blow.

Bilt, *n.* a limp.—*v.* to limp; to walk with crutches.

Bilter, *n.* a child.

Biltie, *adj.* thickset; clubbish; clumsy.

Biltieness, *n.* clumsiness.

Bilting, *ppl.* moving like a short, thickset person.

Bim, *n.* to hum, to buzz.—*n.* the act of humming or buzzing.

Bimmer, *n.* anything that hums or buzzes.

Bin, *n.* a hill; a mountain. Cf. Ben.

Bin, *n.* key, mood, humour, 'pin.'

Bin, Binn, *v.* to bind.

Bin, *v.* to move or run swiftly.

Bin, *v.* to curse; *imperative* used as an imprecation.

Bind, *n.* capacity, ability, sense.

Bind, *v.* to tie sheaves in harvesting; to restrain.

Binder, *n.* one who ties sheaves at harvest; a strip of cloth put round cheese when taken from the 'chessel'; the bandage wound round a new-born child; the bandage wound round a woman after parturition; a large stone built in a wall to give solidity.

Binding-bouse, *n.* a treat at the signing by master and man of the engagement for service.

Bindle, *n.* a cord or rope of hemp or straw, for tying or binding.

Bind-pock, *n.* a niggard.

Bindweed, *n.* the ragwort.

Bindwood, *n.* ivy.

Bine, *n.* a tub. Cf. Boyne.

Bing, *n.* a crowd; a heap, pile.—*v.* to pile; to accumulate.

Bing, *v.* to go.

Bing, *n.* a bin or box for corn, wine, &c.

Bing, *n.* the sea-beach. Cf. Being.

Binge, *v.* to sneak, cringe, fawn; to bow. Cf. Beenge.

Bingly, *adv.* comfortably.

Binjel, *n.* a bundle of hay, &c. Cf. Bunjel, Banyel.

Bink, *n.* a large shelf; a plate-rack; a bench; a bank; a ledge in a cliff; a peat-bank; a wasps' or wild bees' nest; a small heap of clay, mortar, &c.

Bink, *n.* a crease, a fold.

Bink, *v.* to bend down; to lean forward awkwardly; to curtsy; to press down; to destroy the shape of shoes.—*n.* a bending movement.

Binkart, *n.* a pile of stones, dirt, &c. Cf. Binker.

Binked shoes, *n.* shoes full of creases and bends; shoes down at the heels.

Binker, v. to pile up in a heap.—n. a heap of stones, dirt, &c.

Binkie, adj. gaudy, trimly dressed.

Bink-side, n. the side of a long seat near the fire in a country-house.

Binn, n. strength; excellence. Cf. Bind.

Binn, n. the reapers in a harvest-field. Cf. Boon.

Binna, v. be not.

Binna, Binnae, prep. except, save.

Binne, n. a temporary enclosure for preserving grain.

Binner, adj. more comfortable. Cf. Bein.

Binner, v. to move swiftly; to rush; to work with a dash; to cause a whirring or humming sound, to buzz.—n. a quick movement, noisy dash; a sounding blow; a quantity of work done; the boiling-point. —adv. noisily and forcibly.

Binnins, n. the chains, &c., by which cattle are tied up in the 'byre.'

Binster, n. one who ties sheaves in harvesting; a 'bandster.'

Bir, n. force, impetus. Cf. Birr.

Birbeck, n. the call of the moorcock or grouse.

Bird, n. a young bird; a damsel; offspring of quadrupeds, in particular of the fox; a grouse; a partridge; also applied to man or woman in ironic familiarity.

Bird-and-joe, adv. cheek-by-jowl, like Darby and Joan.

Bird-mouthed, -mou'd, adj. unwilling to speak out; mealy-mouthed; tender in finding fault.

Bird's-nest, n. the wild carrot.

Birk, n. a piece of round timber laid horizontally in roof-making, over which the rafters were laid loose.

Birk, n. the birch-tree.

Birk, n. a smart youth. Cf. Birkie.

Birk, v. to give a tart answer; to converse in a lively or cutting way; with up, to brisk up, cheer up.

Birken, adj. abounding in birches; made of birch.—n. a birch-tree.

Birkenshaw, n. a small wood of birch-trees, &c.

Birkie, adj. abounding in birches.

Birkie, n. a lively, smart youth; a designation of a person of any age.—adj. lively, smart; spirited in speech and action.

Birkie, n. the card-game 'beggar-my-neighbour.'

Birk-knowe, n. a knoll covered with birches.

Birl, v. to revolve with a whirring sound; to twirl round; to spin; to cause to sound; to move quickly, hurry along; to spend money freely in drink or gaming; to pour out liquor; to ply with drink; to drink hard; to carouse.—n. a brisk dance; a whirring sound.

Birley-oats, n. a species of oats. Cf. Barley-oats.

Birlie, Birlin, n. a loaf of bread; a small cake of barley or oatmeal.

Birlie-, Birlaw-court, n. a court of country neighbours to settle local concerns, &c. Cf. Burlaw.

Birlie-man, n. a member of the 'birlie-court.' Cf. Barley-men.

Birlin, n. a half-decked galley or rowing-boat. Cf. Berlin.

Birling, n. a feast, a carousal; a drinking-match, in which the drink is clubbed for; a whirring noise; a noisy, rapid revolution of a wheel.

Birn, n. a burden; a load carried on the back.

Birn, n. the labia pudenda of a cow.

Birn, n. a burnt mark; a burnt mark on a sheep's nose for identification; a scorched stem of burnt heather.—v. to burn.—phr. 'skin and birn,' the whole of anything or any number.

Birn, n. dry, heathery pasture for summering of lambs after weaning.—v. to put lambs on a poor, dry pasture.

Birney, adj. ? sturdy, rough, muscular, brawny.

Birnman, n. the man who carried grain to a mill and carried back the meal.

Birny, adj. covered with charred stems of heather; having rough or stunted stems; ? of the temper: crusty, sour, irascible.

Birr, n. force; impetus, energy; violence; passion; a rapid, whirling motion; a whirring noise.—v. to move rapidly, bustle; to act with energy; to whir; to be in a turmoil or confusion.

Birrel, n. a ring for a staff. Cf. Virl.

Birringly, adv. with vigour, energetically.

Birrit, Birritie, n. the hedge-sparrow; the willow-warbler.

Birr up, v. to prick up the ears.

Birs, n. the gadfly.

Birse, n. a bristle; hair; a plume of hair or bristles; a bristle attached to the end of shoemakers' or saddlers' waxed thread; temper, anger.—v. to bristle, to get suddenly angry.

Birse, n. a bruise, contusion; pressure, a squeeze.—v. to bruise, crush, squeeze, force, press.

Birsie, adj. pushing, forward; bristly; hot-tempered, passionate; keen, sharp.—n. a pert, forward child. Cf. Birsy.

Birsk, n. gristle, cartilage.

Birsle, v. to scorch, toast, parch; to crackle with heat.—n. a thorough warming.

Birslin', ppl. adj. drying, scorching.—n. a scorching.

Birst, n. a small, impudent person.

Birst, *n.* a difficulty, emergency, battle; brunt; burst; over-exertion causing injury; convulsive weeping. - *v.* to over-exert injuriously; to burst; to burst into tears.

Birstle, *v.* to scorch. Cf. Birsle.

Birstle, *n.* a bristle.

Birsy, *adj.* rough, bristly; easily irritated; keen, bleak. Cf. Birsie.

Birsy, *n.* a nickname for a pig.

Birth, *n.* a berth, office, situation.

Birth-brief, *n.* evidence of birth, a birth-certificate.

Birthy, *adj.* prolific, productive.

Birze, *v.* to bruise; to press. Cf. Birse.

Biscuit, *n.* a small round cake of flour.

Bishop, *n.* a cantankerous, ill-natured boy; the great northern diver; a second-hand horseshoe; an implement for packing and pressing soil round a post, or levelling a causeway.—*v.* to beat down soil or stones with a 'bishop.'

Bishop's foot, *n.* a taste of burning in food.

Bishop-weed, *n.* the gout-weed.

Bisket, *n.* brisket, the breast.

Bisse, *v.* to buzz, to make a hissing noise.—*n.* a buzz; a hissing noise; a bustle.

Bissom, *n.* a lewd, worthless woman. Cf. Besom.

Bit, *n.* a morsel of food; food; a piece of money; a place, position, station; a short distance or time; a crisis, point; the nick of time; the hinge of an argument, the conclusion aimed at or reached; an ear-mark for sheep or cattle.—*v.* to cut an ear-mark.—*adj.* small; puny; used contemptuously or endearingly.

Bit, *v.* had to. Cf. Beet.

Bit, *n.* a blow, a stroke.

Bitch, *n.* a term of contempt applied to a man.

Bitch, *n.* the cheating of a landlord by a moonlight 'flittin'.'

Bitch-fou, -fu', *adj.* beastly drunk.

Bite, *n.* a mouthful; a little food; pasturage; a hoax; a taunt, scoff; a disappointment in love.—*v.* to smart, tingle; to sting; to take food. Cf. Bit.

Bite and brat, *n.* food and clothing.

Bite and buffet, *phr.* food and blows.

Bite and drap, *phr.* something to eat and drink.

Bite and soup, sup, *phr.* something to eat and drink.

Bitle, *v.* to beat with a beetle. Cf. Beetle, Bittle.

Bittag, *n.* a small bit, a 'bittock.'

Bitter, *adj.* spiteful.

Bitter-bank, Bitterie, *n.* the sand-martin.

Bitterness, *n.* bitter, stormy weather.

Bittie, *n.* a little bit.

Bittle, *n.* a beetle; a leg.—*v.* to beat with a beetle.

Bittlins, *n.* the battlements of any old building.

Bittock, *n.* a little bit, a short distance.

Bizz, *v.* to hiss, as water on hot iron; to hiss like an adder; to buzz; to frizzle; to fuss about.—*n.* a buzz; a bustle; a state of 'tousled' hair; the 'startling' or 'pricking' of cattle in hot weather; the hissing noise of water on hot iron.

Bizzan, *n.* a multitude, a confused crowd.

Bizzard-gled, *n.* a hawk.

Bizzel, *n.* a hoop or ring round the end of any tube.

Bizzie, *n.* a stall in a cattle-shed.

Bizzy, *adj.* busy; bustling; officious, meddling.

Blaad, *v.* to sully, soil; to strike.—*n.* a blow. Cf. Blad.

Blaadin, *n.* a blow.

Blaadit, *ppl. adj.* weakly.

Blaathrie, *adj.* wet, muddy. Cf. Blawthirie.

Blaavin, *ppl.* blowing, puffing; boasting.

Blab, *n.* a drop of moisture; a blister; the honey-bag of a bee.—*v.* to blot, smear; to bubble; to rob a bee of its honey-bag; to plunder.

Blab, *n.* a gossip; a tell-tale.

Blab, *v.* to tipple; to slobber in drinking.—*n.* a quantity of liquor; a gurgling noise in drinking or taking semi-liquid food.

Blabban, *n.* the act of drinking with a gurgling noise.

Blabber, *n.* a tippler.

Blabber, *v.* to babble; to speak indistinctly.

Blabber, *v.* to drink much and often; to make a gurgling noise in drinking or supping.—*n.* a quantity of strong drink; a gurgling noise with the lips in drinking or supping.

Blabberin, *n.* the act of making a gurgling noise in drinking, &c.

Black, *v.* to blacken; to put a thing in black and white by writing it; to grow black; to scold; to defame, slander.—*n.* a scoundrel, blackguard; smut in wheat; a mild imprecation.—*adj.* dark in complexion; grimy; used of the weather: overcast, foul; sad, melancholy; extreme, dead.—*adv.* quite, thoroughly.

Black airn, *n.* malleable iron, in contrast to tin.

Black-aviced, -avized, *adj.* of dark, swarthy complexion.

Blackball, *v.* to scold, abuse.

Black-bean, *adj.* unlucky.

Black-belickit, *n.* absolutely nothing.

Blackberry, *n.* the crowberry.

Black-bide, *n.* a blackberry. Cf. Blackboyd.

Black-bitch, *n.* a bag clandestinely attached to a hole in the mill-spout to abstract some of the meal running down the spout.

Black-blutter, *n.* a blackberry, a bramble.

Black-bonnet, *n.* an elder of the Church ; the black-headed bunting.

Black-boo, *n.* a nursery bogy.

Blackbcyd, *n.* a blackberry.

Black-burning, *adj.* causing intense blushing or shame.

Black-cap, *n.* the cole-tit.

Black-clock, *n.* a cockroach ; a black-beetle.

Black-coaly-head, *n.* the reed-bunting.

Blackcoat, *n.* a minister of religion.

Blackcock, *n.* in *phr.* 'to make a blackcock of one,' to shoot one.

Black-cork, *n.* porter.

Black cow, *n.* a misfortune. Cf. Black ox.

Black-crap, *n.* a crop of beans or peas ; a crop which is always green.

Black-doctor, *n.* a leech.

Black-doggie, *n.* a variety of the game, 'drop the handkerchief.'

Black-dooker, *n.* the cormorant.

Blackening, *n.* the black that affects iron-moulders injuriously.

Black-fasting, *adj.* practising severe fasting.

Black-fish, *n.* newly-spawned fish ; a salmon after spawning.

Black-fisher, *n.* a night-poacher of fish ; a fisher of 'black-fish.'

Black-fishing, *n.* fishing illegally for salmon at night, or for 'black-fish.'

Blackfit, *n.* a lovers' go-between.

Black frost, *n.* hard frost without rime or snow.

Black-fyse, *adj.* of swarthy complexion. Cf. Black-aviced.

Blackgang, *adj.* blackguardly.

Blackguard, *n.* 'black-rappee' snuff, 'Irish blackguard.'

Blackhead, *n.* the laughing gull.

Black-headed tomtit, *n.* the great tit.

Black hole, *n.* prison ; police cell.

Black hudie, *n.* the black-headed bunting ; the cole-head or reed-bunting.

Blackie, *n.* a blackbird.

Blackie, *n.* a bee ; a kind of wild bee.

Black-jack, *n.* a dark-coloured sweetmeat made of sugar or treacle and spice.

Black-keel, *n.* plumbago.

Blackleg, *n.* a workman who works for a master whose men are on strike.

Blackleg, *n.* a disease of cattle.

Blackleg, *n.* a match-maker, a lovers' go-between. Cf. Blackfit.

Blacklie, *adj.* ill-coloured ; dirty ; badly washed ; dark with threatening clouds.

Blackman, *n.* a nursery bogy ; liquorice or 'black-sugar.'

Black martin, *n.* the swift.

Blackmill, *n.* a water-mill with one wheel.

Black money, *n.* forged copper coinage.

Blackneb, *n.* a person disaffected toward Government ; a carrion crow ; a 'blackleg' workman.

Black-nebbit, *adj.* having a black bill ; disaffected toward Government.

Blacknebbit crow, *n.* the carrion crow.

Black oil, *n.* oil made from the haddock and other fish.

Black o' the e'e, *n. phr.* the apple of the eye.

Black ox, *n.* a misfortune ; a bereavement ; a great calamity.

Black ox-eye, *n.* the cole titmouse.

Black Peter, *n.* a portmanteau ; a lamp in which the pith of rushes served as the wick.

Black pishminnie, *n.* a black ant.

Black quarter, *n.* a disease of cattle.

Black rappee, *n.* a kind of snuff.

Blacks, *n.* black clothes ; mourning garments.

Black saxpence, *n.* the devil's sixpence, supposed to be received as pledge of engagement to be his, soul and body, and reputed, if kept constantly in the pocket, to have always another sixpence along with it, however much be spent.

Black-sole, *n.* a lovers' go-between. Cf. Blackfit, Blackleg.

Black spats, *n.* irons on the legs.

Black-spaul, -spauld, *n.* pleurisy in cattle, and especially calves.

Black starling, *n.* the starling.

Black-stool, *n.* the 'stool of repentance' for offenders doing public penance. Cf. Stool.

Black-strap, *n.* weak treacle-beer ; a contemptuous name for porter.

Black swift, *n.* the swift.

Black-tang, *n.* the ore-weed, seaweed.

Black-toed gull, *n.* Richardson's skua.

Black victual, *n.* peas and beans.

Black ward, *n.* servitude to a servant.

Black weather, *n.* rainy weather.

Black wet, *n.* rain as distinguished from snow.

Black wine, *n.* dark-coloured, in contrast to white wine.

Black winter, *n.* the last cartload of grain brought from the harvest-field.

Blad, *v.* to take long steps, treading heavily. —*n.* a long and heavy step in walking ; a person walking with long and heavy step.

Blad, *n.* a large portion of anything ; a leaf ; a specimen ; a fragment ; a portfolio ; a blotting-pad.

Blad, *n.* a person of weak, soft constitution, from rapid overgrowth.

Blad, *n.* a slap, blow ; a squall ; a heavy fall of rain ; a dirty spot ; a discoloration.—*v.* to slap, strike, thrust violently ; used of wind and rain : to beat against, to drive in gusts ; to spoil, to injure ; to soil ; to abuse, defame.

Bladderdash, *n.* nonsense.

Bladderskate, *n.* a foolish, noisy talker. Cf. Blatherskite.

Bladdin, *ppl. adj.* breezy, gusty.—*n.* a spoiling, destruction.

Bladdo, Bladdoch, *n.* buttermilk. Cf. Bleddoch.

Bladdy, *adj.* gusty, unsettled.

Blade, *v.* to slap ; to spoil. Cf. Blad.

Blade, *n.* a cabbage or 'kail' leaf.—*v.* to take the outer leaves off cabbages.

Blad haet, *n.* absolutely nothing.

Bladie, *adj.* full of large, broad leaves growing from the stem.

Bladrock, *n.* a talkative, silly fellow.

Bladry, *n.* trumpery ; foolishness, deception. Cf. Blaidry.

Blads and dawds, *n. phr.* large leaves of greens boiled whole in broth.

Blae, *adj.* bluish ; livid ; lead-coloured ; disappointed ; blank as with disappointment ; bleak, cold.—*v.* to numb.

Blae, *v.* to bleat as a lamb ; to cry as a child.—*n.* a loud bleat.

Blae, *n.* a hard blue clay ; in *pl.* laminæ of this clay. Cf. Blaze.

Blae, *n.* in *pl.* the rough parts of wood left in consequence of boring or sawing.

Blaeberry, *n.* the bilberry.

Blae-bows, *n.* the flower of the flax.

Blaeflummery, *n.* nonsense, vain imaginations. Cf. Bleflummery.

Blaelike, *adj.* livid, pale.

Blaeness, *n.* lividness.

Blaese, *n.* the bilberry.

Blaewort, *n.* the blue corn-flower ; the round-leaved bell-flower.

Blaff, *n.* a blow.—*v.* to 'bang.'

Blaffart, *n.* a blow.

Blaffen, *n.* loose flakes or laminæ of a stone.

Blaflum, *n.* nonsense, idle talk, a hoax ; a pompous, empty-headed person.—*v.* to coax, cajole, deceive, play upon.

Blaick, *n.* a scoundrel. Cf. Black.

Blaick, Blaik, *v.* to puzzle, mystify, baffle.—*n.* a puzzle. Cf. Bleck.

Blaidry, *n.* nonsense, foolish talk, 'blethers': phlegm coughed up ; empty parade ; unmerited applause.

Blaids, *n.* a disease attended with pustular eruptions.

Blain, *n.* a fault ; a blemish ; a scar ; discoloration of skin after a sore. Cf. Blane.

Blain, *n.* a bare place in a field where grain has not sprung ; a blank, a vacancy.—*v.* used of a field : to be covered with blank spaces ; of grain : to have no kernel.

Blainag, *n.* a small pustule, a pimple.

Blainch, *v.* to cleanse.

Blaink, *n.* a 'blink,' a passing gleam. Cf. Blink.

Blains, *n.* empty grain.

Blair, *v.* to dry by exposure to drought.—*n.* that part of flax which is used in manufacture, after being steeped and laid out to dry.

Blair, *v.* to make a noise ; to cry aloud ; to bleat as a sheep.—*n.* a loud sound, a cry ; the bleat of a sheep. Cf. Blare.

Blair, *v.* to blear. Cf. Blear.

Blairin, *n.* the ground on which flax is dried, or where peats are spread to dry.

Blais'd, *ppl. adj.* soured ; used of milk : spoiled. Cf. Bleeze, Blased.

Blaise, *n.* the particles of wood scooped out by a wimble in boring. Cf. Blae.

Blaister, *v.* to blow with violence.

Blait, *adj.* naked, bare.

Blait, *adj.* shy, sheepish ; modest, retiring ; stupid, easily imposed on ; dull, not brisk ; backward in growth. Cf. Blate.

Blaith, *adj.* blithe, glad.

Blaitie-bum, *n.* a lazy fellow, a simpleton, a sheepish fellow.

Blaitly, *adv.* bashfully.

Blait-mouit, *adj.* bashful, sheepish ; shy in speaking.

Blaize, *n.* a blow.

Blakwak, *n.* the bittern.

Blamefull, *adj.* blameworthy.

Blan, *v. pret.* ceased, caused to cease. Cf. Blin.

Blanch, *n.* a flash or sudden blaze.

Blanded-bear, *n.* barley and common bear sown together. Cf. Blendit-bear.

Blander, *v.* to scatter sparingly ; to sow thinly ; to babble, spread a report or calumny ; to exaggerate or misstate.

Bland-hoe, *n.* the rabbit-fish. Cf. Blind-hoe.

Blandish, *n.* the grain left uncut by careless reapers in the furrows during a 'kemp,' or struggle to be first done.

Blandish, *n.* flattery.

Blandrin, *n.* a scanty diffusion, a withholding of sufficient seed.

Blane, *n.* the mark left by a wound. Cf. Blain.

Blanket, *n.* a form of the game 'hie-spy.'

Blanket-bay, *n.* bed.

Blanket-heezie, *n.* one who tosses another in a blanket. Cf. Heezy.

Blardit, *ppl. adj.* short-winded, broken-winded.

Blare, *v.* to bleat ; to cry out.—*n.* the bleat of a sheep or goat ; a cry ; noisy scolding.

Blart, *v.* to fall flat in the mud.—*n.* the sound of such a fall.

Blased, *ppl. adj.* used of milk : turned sour. Cf. Bleezed.

Blash, *n.* a splash or dash of liquid, mud, &c. ; a heavy shower of rain ; too much water for the purpose of diluting; a deluge.—*v.* to drench, soak, deluge; to splash liquid or mud about, by spilling it or treading in it; to rain heavily and noisily; to drink to excess.

Blashy, *adj.* rainy, wet, gusty; weak, watery.

Blasnit, *adj.* ? hairless.

Blast, *n.* a whiff of the pipe; a sudden illness; a chill; a stroke; a brag, boast.—*v.* to pant; to smoke tobacco; to play the bagpipe; to brag; to use big words or strong language; to have a stroke of paralysis.

Blaster, *n.* a boaster; one who exaggerates; one who blasts stones.

Blastie, *n.* a shrivelled, dwarfish person; an ill-tempered or unmanageable child; a term of contempt.

Blastie, *adj.* gusty, blustering; puffing, panting.

Blasting, *n.* the 'cow-quake,' or inflated stomach of cows; the cold easterly wind that causes the disease.

Blatant, *ppl. adj.* bellowing like a calf.

Blate, *adj.* shy; sheepish; bashful; timid; simple; dull, unpromising; of crops: backward.

Blately, *adj.* used of rain: soft, gentle.—*adv.* bashfully.

Blateness, *n.* shyness.

Blather, *n.* a bladder; the bladder.—*v.* to talk nonsense. Cf. Blether.

Blatherskite, *n.* a babbler; a foolish talker; nonsense.

Blatherumskite, *n.* a 'blatherskite.'

Blathrie, *adj.* nonsensical, foolish.

Blatter, *v.* to rattle; to make a rattling sound; to beat on with force and noise like hail; to dash noisily; to make a disturbance; to talk loudly and noisily.—*n.* a rattling sound; a hailstorm; a noisy dash or blast; loud, forcible, noisy talk.

Blatter, *v.* of breath or life: to flutter, flicker.

Blaud, *v.* to slap; to blow in gusts; to injure. Cf. Blad.

Blaud, *n.* a large piece or fragment; a large leaf of cabbage or 'kail'; a portfolio. Cf. Blad.

Blaudie, *adj.* full of large, broad leaves. Cf. Bladie.

Blaugh, *adj.* bluish or sickly in colour, 'blae.'

Blaver, *n.* the harebell; the corn bluebottle. Cf. Blawort.

Blaw, *n.* a blow, a stroke.

Blaw, *v.* to blow; to breathe; to publish; to brag; to exaggerate from ostentation; to whisper in the ear, flatter, coax, wheedle; to puff-up; to 'huff' in the game of draughts; to scold; to pull at a drinking-vessel; to smoke a pipe; to play the bagpipe, &c.—*n.* a blast, gust; the direction of

the wind; a tune on any wind-instrument; a boast; a lie from ostentation; a smoke; a whiff of a pipe; a pull at a drinking-vessel, a jorum of liquor.

Blaw, *n.* a blossom, a bloom.—*v.* to blossom, to flower.

Blawart, *n.* the harebell; the corn bluebottle. Cf. Blawort.

Blawerts, *n.* a blacksmith's bellows.

Blawflum, *n.* a pompous, empty person; a flattering delusion; a gewgaw; a mere deception. Cf. Blaflum.

Blaw-i'-my-lug, *n. phr.* flattery; a flatterer.

Blawing-girss, *n.* the blue mountain-grass.

Blawn-cod, *n.* a split cod, half-dried.

Blawn-drink, *n.* the remainder of drink in a glass of which one or more have partaken, and which has frequently been breathed on.

Blawort, Blawirt, *n.* the harebell; the corn bluebottle.

Blaw-out, *n.* a good meal; a drinking-bout; a great display or feast.

Blawp, *v.* to belch, heave up water.—*n.* watery matter gathered under the skin.

Blawstick, *n.* a tube used as a bellows.

Blawthir, *n.* wet weather.

Blawthirie, *adj.* very wet.

Blay, *n.* in *pl.* the rough parts of wood left in consequence of boring or sawing. Cf. Blae.

Blaze, *v.* to vilify, calumniate; to spread reports; to bluster; to brag. Cf. Bleeze.

Blaze, *n.* alum ore; a substance lying above coal. Cf. Blae.

Blaze, *n.* the torch used in salmon-spearing; a sudden blast of dry wind. Cf. Bleeze.

Blazed, *ppl. adj.* in a state in which liquor begins to tell. Cf. Bleezed.

Blazing-fou', *adj.* uproariously drunk.

Blaznicks, *n.* large and showy ornaments.

Bleach, *v.* to strike; to fall flat.—*n.* a blow; a fall.—*adv.* violently; with a heavy blow.

Bleacher, *n.* a severe blow.

Bleaching, *n.* a beating; a beating about.

Bleak-bleak, *n.* the cry of the hare.

Blear, *n.* anything dimming the sight; in *pl.* tears or their causes.—*v.* to dim the vision; to deceive by flattery.

Bleared, *ppl. adj.* of milk, &c.: thin and bluish in colour; skimmed.

Blearie, *adj.* dim of sight; watery-eyed.

Bleart, *ppl. adj.* 'blearie.'

Bleat, *adj.* shy, timid. Cf. Blate.

Bleater, *n.* the cocksnipe. Cf. Blitter.

Bleatly, *adv.* timidly.

Bleb, *n.* a bubble; a small blister or pustule; a drop; in *pl.* a children's skin eruption.—*v.* to spot; to slobber; to sip; to tipple. Cf. Blab.

Blebber, *n.* a tippler.—*v.* to drink hard and often. Cf. Blabber.

Blebbit, *ppl. adj.* blurred ; besmeared.

Bleck, *n.* a challenge to a feat ; a baffle at any feat ; a nonplus in an argument or examination ; as a school term, thus : 'if A be below B in the class, and during B's absence gets farther up in the class than B, B is said to have a " bleck " upon A, and takes place of him when he gets next to him.'—*v.* to baffle ; to surpass ; to nonplus or overcome in an argument ; to puzzle.

Bleck, *adj.* black.—*n.* blacking ; smut.—*v.* to blacken ; to apply blacking ; to defame. Cf. Black.

Bledd, *n.* a blade ; a leaf. Cf. Blade.

Bledder, *n.* a bladder.

Bledder, *v.* to talk idly or foolishly. Cf. Blether.

Bleddoch, *n.* buttermilk.

Blee, *n.* complexion.

Bleech, *v.* to strike ; to fall flat.—*n.* a blow ; a fall. Cf. Bleach.

Bleech, *v.* to blanch ; to bleach.

Bleed, *n.* blood.—*v.* to shed blood ; used of corn : to yield well when threshed.

Bleeder, *n.* corn yielding well when threshed.

Bleed-raing, *v.* to become bloodshot.

Bleedy, *adj.* bloody.

Bleem, *n.* the potato-plant ; its stalk.

Bleer, *v.* to blear ; to make the eyes water ; to bedim the eyes with rheum or tears.—*n.* what dims the sight ; a trace of weeping. Cf. Blear.

Bleerit, *ppl. adj.* dim-sighted.

Bleery, *adj.* dim-sighted ; watery-eyed.

Bleery, *adj.* used of liquor : weak, thin.—*n.* thin, poor gruel, soup, &c. ; boiled oatmeal and buttermilk, with the addition of a piece of butter.

Bleet, *v.* to bellow.

Bleetly, *adv.* modestly. Cf. Blately.

Bleevit, *n.* a blow.

Bleeze, *n.* the rough parts of wood left after boring or sawing. Cf. Blae, Blaise.

Bleeze, *n.* a smart blow with the fist.

Bleeze, *v.* to turn slightly sour.

Bleeze, Bleese, *v.* to blaze ; to flare up ; to get angry ; to spread news or scandal ; to defame ; to boast ; to bluster. — *n.* a rage, passion ; a rapid growth ; a fire of furze, straw, &c. ; a sudden blast of dry wind.

Bleezed, *ppl. adj.* fuddled ; at the state of intoxication when the face reddens or is flushed ; ruffled ; fretted.

Bleeze-money, *n.* a gratuity formerly given by scholars to their master at Candlemas, when the one who gave most was proclaimed King or Queen, and had to entertain the whole school.

Bleezie, *n.* a small blaze.

Bleffart, *n.* a squall, storm, hurricane ; a sudden and violent snowstorm ; the blow of a calamity ; a stroke.—*v.* to bluster, as the wind.

Bleflum, *n.* a sham, an illusion, what has no reality in it. Cf. Blaflum.

Bleflummery, *n.* vain imaginations.

Bleib, *n.* a pustule, blister ; in *pl.* a pustular eruption in children. Cf. Bleb.

Bleid, *n.* blood.

Bleir, *v.* to asperse, calumniate.

Bleirie, *n.* a lie, a fabrication.

Bleirie, *n.* oatmeal and buttermilk boiled thicker than gruel, and enriched with butter ; water-gruel. —*adj.* of liquor : thin, weak. Cf. Bleery.

Bleis, *n.* the river-fish bleak, *Leuciscus alburnus.*

Bleize, *v.* to blaze. Cf. Bleeze.

Blellum, *n.* an idle, talking fellow.

Blenched, *ppl. adj.* used of milk : a little sour.

†**Blench-lippit**, *ppl. adj.* having a white mouth.

Blendit-bear, *n.* bear or big mixed with barley.

Blenk, *v.* to shine ; to glimmer ; to wink.— *n.* a glance. Cf. Blink.

†**Blenshaw**, *n.* a drink composed of meal, milk, water, &c.

Blent, *v.* used of the sun : to shine after the sky has been overcast ; of fire : to flash.

Blenter, *n.* a boisterous, intermittent wind ; a gust ; a flat stroke, a strong, sharp blow. —*v.* to rush, make haste ; to strike with a strong, sharp blow. Cf. Blinter.

Blentering, *ppl. adj.* near-sighted ; blundering. Cf. Blintering.

Blephum, *n.* a sham. Cf. Blaflum.

Blet, *n.* a large fragment. Cf. Blad.

Blether, *v.* to speak indistinctly ; to stammer ; to talk nonsense ; to prattle, chatter.—*n.* nonsense, foolish talk ; a 'wind-bag.'

Blether, *n.* a bladder.

Bletheration, *n.* foolish talk.

Bletherbag, *n.* a fluent, foolish talker.

Bletherer, *n.* a foolish talker.

Blether-headed, *adj.* foolish ; noisy.

Bletherie, *n.* foolishness ; deception ; 'blethers.'

Bletherin, *n.* loud, foolish talking ; stammering.

Blett, *v. pret.* bleated.

Bleuchan, *n.* a small salt-water fish of some kind. Cf. Bluchan.

Blevit, *n.* a blow. Cf. Bleevit.

Blewder, *n.* a hurricane. Cf. Blouter.

Blewdery, *adj.* tempestuous.

Blib, *n.* used of tea, &c. : a weak, watery portion.

Blibbans, *n.* strips of soft, slimy matter, seaweed on rocks at ebb-tide ; large shreds of greens or cabbage put into broth.

Blibe, *n.* a stroke ; the mark of a blow.

Blicham, *n.* a contemptuous designation of a person.

Blichan, Blichen, *n.* a small person; a lean, worn-out animal; a lively, showy youth; a harum-scarum fellow; a worthless person; a term of contempt.

Blicher, *n.* a spare portion.

Blicht, *v.* to blight.—*n.* a blight.

Blichtnin', *ppl. adj.* blighting.

Blide, *adj.* blithe, glad.

Bliers, *n.* the eyelashes.

Bliffart, Bliffert, *n.* a squall, a gust; a short and sudden fall of snow; a stroke, a buffet.—*v.* to bluster, as the wind. Cf. Bleffart.

Blighan, *n.* a small person; a term of contempt. Cf. Blichan.

Blighten, *v.* to blight. Cf. Blichtnin'.

Blin, Blind, *v.* to cease, desist; to stop, cause to stop.—*n.* delay, hindrance; deceit.

Blin', *adj.* blind.—*v.* to blind; to close the eyes in sleep.—*n.* a little sleep.

Blind-barnie, *n.* blindman's buff.

Blind-bell, *n.* a game in which all the players were blindfolded except one who bore a bell, which he rang while endeavouring to escape being caught by the others.

Blind-bitch, *n.* a bag formerly used by millers. Cf. Black-bitch.

Blind-brose, *n.* 'brose' without butter.

Blind-champ, *n.* a cruel pastime of boys, who, when blindfolded, turn round and try to crush eggs from a harried bird's-nest laid on the ground.

Blind coal, *n.* a kind of coal that gives no flame.

Blind dorbie, *n.* the purple sandpiper.

Blind-, Blin'-drift, *n.* heavily driving snow; a blinding, drifting snow.

Blind-, Blin'-drunk, *adj.* unable to see properly from drink.

Blind-fair, *adj.* ? like an albino.

Blind-fish, *n.* the lesser spotted dogfish.

Blind-, Blin'-fou, *adj.* unable to see properly from drink.

Blind Harry, *n.* blindman's buff.

Blind-hoe, *n.* the rabbit-fish.

Blindlins, *adv.* blindly, blindfolded.

Blind lump, *n.* a boil that does not come to a head.

Blindman's-ball, -bellows, -e'en, *n.* the common puff-ball or devil's snuff-box.

Blind-palmie, -pawmie, *n.* blindman's buff.

Blinds, *n.* the pogge or miller's thumb.

Blind-staff, -stam, *n.* the boys' game of 'blind-champ.'

Blindstam, *n.* a method of sewing a patch on a boot-upper; used figuratively for blind, captious, or arbitrary criticism.

Blind-tam, *n.* a bundle of rags made up as a child, carried by beggars.

Blind-window, *n.* an imitation window in a wall.

Blink, *n.* a gleam, a ray; the least glimmer; a glance, a glimpse, a wink; a moment; sunshine between two showers; a jilting, 'the slip.'

Blink, *v.* to shine, gleam; to twinkle, glimmer, flicker; to take a hasty glance; to wink, cause to wink; to look with pleasure or fondness; to ignore, evade; to jilt, deceive; to bewitch, 'overlook,' exercise an evil influence; to turn anything sour; to spoil.

Blinker, *n.* a smart, attractive girl; used also contemptuously; a star; a poser, 'settler': the eye; a blear-eyed person; a person blind of one eye; a near-sighted person; in *pl.* eyelids.

Blinkit, *ppl. adj.* bewitched; soured, spoiled; half-drunk.

Blinkit milk, *n.* sour milk.

Blinlins, *adv.* blindly. Cf. Blindlins.

Blinner, *v.* to move the eyelids like one with weak sight.

Blint, *v.* to shed a feeble or glimmering light.

Blinter, *v.* to shine with a feeble, unsteady light; to flicker; to 'blink'; to look at with weak eyes; to see obscurely.—*n.* a feeble light; a person with weak eyes.

Blinter, *v.* to rush, hasten; to strike a sharp, stout blow.—*n.* a gust of wind; a strong, sharp blow.

Blinteran, *n.* a beating.

Blinteran, *n.* the act of looking with the eyelids nearly closed.

Blinterer, *n.* a person with weak eyes.

Blinterin', *ppl. adj.* having weak eyes; near-sighted; blundering.

Blipe, *n.* a stroke, a blow.

Blipe, *n.* a shred of skin when it peels off.

Blirt, *v.* to burst into tears, to weep; to rain or snow.—*n.* a burst of weeping; a storm of wind and rain; a cold drift of snow.—*adj.* bleared; pale with fear; on the verge of tears.

Blirted, *ppl. adj.* tear-stained; swollen with weeping.

Blirtie, *adj.* of weather: changeable, squally; cheerless.

Blirty-eild, *n.* extreme old age, in which tears trickle as if one were weeping.

Bliry, *n.* the exterior of a mare's uterus.

Blissing, *n.* increase of property.

Blithe, *adj.* cheerful, merry, glad. — *adv.* cheerfully, merrily.

Blithely, *adv.* cheerfully; gladly.

Blithemeat, *n.* food, bread and cheese, partaken of by visitors at the birth of a child.

Blithen, *v.* to gladden.

Blitheness, *n.* gladness, gaiety, cheerfulness.

Blithesome, *adj.* merry, cheerful, happy, jolly.

Blitter, *n.* the snipe. Cf. Bleater.

Blitter-blatter, *n.* a rattling, irregular noise.

Blizzen, *v.* to parch, dry-up and wither.

Blob, *n.* a bubble; a blister; a drop or splash of liquid; a small patch of colour; a blur; the honey-bag of a bee; a large gooseberry. —*v.* to gather in drops; to weep; to bubble; to blister; to rob a bee of its honey-bag; to plunder; to blot; to blur. Cf. Blab.

Blobby, *adj.* containing or causing bubbles; very rainy.

Blocher, *v.* to make a rough noise in coughing from phlegm.

Block, *v.* to bargain; to exchange; to plan, to devise.—*n.* a scheme; a bargain; an exchange; an agreement; a honorarium.

Blockan, *n.* the young coal-fish.

Block, hammer, and nails, *n. phr.* a boys' rough game of 'bumping.'

Blockie, *n.* a small cod.

Blockin'-ale, *n.* drink taken at the conclusion of a bargain.

Bloichum, *n.* a person troubled by a cough.

Bloik, *n.* mischief.

Bloisent, *ppl. adj.* bloated; used of the face : red, swollen, whether by weather or intemperance.

Bloit, *n.* diarrhœa.

Blood, *v.* to bleed; to let blood.—*n.* bloodshed; effusion of blood. Cf. Bleed.

Blood-friend, *n.* a blood-relation.

Blood-grass, *n.* a disease of cattle, bloody urine.

Blood-run, *adj.* bloodshot. Cf. Bleed-raing.

Blood-tongue, *n.* the goose-grass.

Blood-wit, -wyte, *n.* a fine formerly paid for the violent effusion of blood.

Bloody-bells, -fingers, *n.* the foxglove.

Bloody-jaudie, *n.* a 'bloody-pudding.'

Bloody-pudding, *n.* a 'black-pudding' of blood, suet, onions, and pepper in part of a sheep or ox gut.

Bloody-scones, *n.* scones made with the blood which formerly was drawn from farm cattle.

Bloom, *n.* the efflorescent crystallisation on the outside of thoroughly dried fishes.

Bloomer, *n.* a schoolgirl's head-dress or bonnet.

Bloom-fell, *n.* yellow clover, the bird's trefoil. Cf. Fell-bloom.

Blort, *v.* used of a horse : to snort.

Bloss, *n.* a term of endearment applied to a buxom young woman.

Blost, *v.* to blow up; to pant; to boast.—*n.* an explosion; a whiff of a pipe; a brag, a boast.

Blot, *v.* to nonplus, to puzzle.

Blots, *n.* water for washing clothes; soapsuds, dirty water.

Blot-sheet, *n.* blotting-paper.

Blotty O, *n.* a schoolboy's slate-game.

Bloust, *n.* a brag, a boasting narration; an ostentatious person.—*v.* to brag, boast; to bluster. Cf. Blost.

Blout, *n.* the bursting of a storm : a sudden fall of rain, snow, or hail, with wind; a sudden and noisy eruption of liquid matter; foul water thrown from washing-tubs.—*v.* used of liquids : to belch or rush out with force.

Blouter, *n.* a blast of wind. Cf. Blewder.

Bloutering, *ppl.* boasting, bragging.

Blow, *v.* to divulge; to rate; to boast.—*n.* one's fling. Cf. Blaw.

Blower, *n.* a boaster, exaggerator.

Blowing, *n.* flattery; boasting.

Blown, *ppl. adj.* used of fish : dried by wind without salt.

Blown-cod, *n.* a split cod half-dried.

Blown-fish, *n.* fish wind-dried without salt.

Blown-skate, *n.* skate dried without salt by pressure and exposure to the wind.

Blow-out, *n.* a great display; a festive occasion; a drinking-bout.

Blowt, *v.* to belch forth.—*n.* in *phr.* 'windy blowts,' flatus. Cf. Blout.

Blowthir, *v.* used of a large body : to plunge with great force; to blunder.—*n.* the plunge of a heavy body; a blow; a big, stupid person; a sudden gust of wind; exposure to a storm.

Blowthirin, *n.* the act of plunging.—*ppl. adj.* blundering, stupid; gusty, stormy.

Blow-up, *v.* to mislead, delude; used of a cow : to swell with flatus.

Blowy, *adj.* gusty, blustering, windy.

Blub, *v.* to cry, weep. Cf. Blob.

Blubbert, Blubbit, *ppl. adj.* tear-stained, disfigured by weeping.

Bluchan, *n.* some kind of small salt-water fish.

Bluchtan, Bluchton, *n.* a piece of the hollow stem of the mugwort, used as a pop-gun.

Bludder, *v.* to make a noise in the mouth or throat in swallowing any liquid.

Bludder, *v.* to blot or disfigure any writing; to disfigure the face in any way; to besmear with blood, mud, tears; to disfigure in a moral sense; to exhibit in an unfair point of view.—*n.* mud; any dirty or disgusting liquid or semi-liquid substance; wet weather; a spell of foul weather.

Blude, *n.* blood. Cf. Bleed, Blood.

Bludker cake, *n.* a cake mixed with hog's blood, eaten on Easter Sunday, called also a redemption or ransom cake.

Blue, *n.* whisky.

Blue, *adj.* used of the weather: chill, frosty.—*adv.* used as an intensive.

Blue-bannet, *n.* the blue titmouse.

Blue-bell, *n.* the harebell.

Blue blanket, *n.* the banner of the Edinburgh craftsmen.

Blue-blaver, *n.* the bell-flower or wild blue campanula.

Blue-bonnet, *n.* the devil's bit, the flower of *Scabiosa succisa;* the mountain centaury.

Blue-bonnet, *n.* a man's blue cap; a Scotsman.

Blue bore, *n.* a rift or opening in the clouds.

Blue-cap, *n.* the blue titmouse.

Blue-day, *n.* a day which is bleak and frosty; a day of uproar or disturbance.

Blue-fly, *n.* a bluebottle; a flesh-fly.

Blue-gled, *n.* the hen-harrier.

Blue-gown, *n.* a king's pensioner, who wore a blue gown with a badge on it, and was licensed to beg.

Blue-grass, *n.* the name given to various sedges, especially the carnation grass.

Blue-hap, *n.* the blue titmouse.

Blue-hawk, *n.* the sparrow-hawk; the hen-harrier.

Blue-jay, *n.* the jay.

Blue-kite, *n.* the hen-harrier.

Blue-lit, *n.* blue dye.

Blue-maa, *n.* the common gull.

Blue-merlin, *n.* the sparrow-hawk.

Blue mogganer, *n.* a jocular designation of a native of Peterhead, from the wearing of coarse blue stockings over boots.

Blue-mooled, *adj.* used of cheese: blue-mouldy.

Blue nappy, *n.* whisky.

Blue ox-eye, *n.* the blue titmouse.

Blues, *n.* delirium tremens, 'blue devils.'

Blue seggin, *n.* the blue flower-de-luce; the stinking iris.

Blue sickness, *n.* a kind of rot in sheep.

Blue sleeves, *n.* the hen-harrier.

Blue spald, *n.* a disease of cattle. Cf. Black-spaul.

Blue sparrow, *n.* the hedge-sparrow.

Bluester, *n.* a blusterer; one who uses bullying speech.

Bluestone, *n.* sulphate of copper.

Blue thread, *n.* whisky.

Blue tom, *n.* the hedge-sparrow.

Blue yaup, *n.* the fieldfare.

Bluff, *n.* a credulous person; a trick, cheat.

Bluffert, *v.* to bluster, as the wind.—*n.* the blast sustained in meeting a rough wind or squall; a blow, a buffet. Cf. Bleffart.

Bluffet, *n.* a blow, a buffet.

Bluffle-headed, *adj.* having a large head; stupid-looking.

Bluid, *n.* blood.—*v.* to bleed. Cf. Bleed, Blood.

Bluid-run, *adj.* bloodshot.

Bluid-wyte, *n.* a fine paid for effusion of blood.

Bluidy, *adj.* bloody.

Bluidy-fingers, *n.* the foxglove.

Bluist, *v.* to boast. Cf. Bloust.

Bluiter, *n.* a coarse, clumsy, inconsiderate, blundering fellow; a rumbling noise.—*v.* to blurt; to make a rumbling noise; to obliterate; to work clumsily; to spoil work in the doing of it; to overdilute with water; to splutter.

Bluiter, *n.* mud; any dirty stuff.—*v.* to besmear with mud, &c. Cf. Bludder.

Bluiter, *v.* to talk foolishly.—*n.* a great talker. Cf. Blether.

Bluiterin, *ppl. adj.* clumsy.

Blume, *v.* to blossom.

Blumf, *n.* a dull, stupid fellow.

Blunk, *n.* coarse cotton or linen for printing.

Blunk, *n.* a small block of wood or stone; a dull, lifeless person.

Blunk, *v.* to bungle; to spoil a thing; to mismanage; to injure mischievously.

Blunkart, *n.* a small block of wood or stone; a thickset person; a stupid person.

Blunker, *n.* one who prints cloth.

Blunker, *n.* a bungler.

Blunkit, *ppl. adj.* pale.

Blunner, *v.* to blunder. Cf. Blunther.

Blunnerboar, *n.* a blundering fool.

Blunt, *n.* a stupid fellow.

Blunther, *v.* to blunder; to move clumsily and noisily; to stumble; to make a noise. —*n.* a loud noise, as of stumbling.

Bluntie, *n.* a stupid fellow; a sniveller.

Blunyierd, *n.* an old gun; any old rusty weapon.

Blup, *n.* a misfortune or mistake owing to want of foresight; one who makes an awkward appearance.

Blupt, *ppl. adj.* suffering misfortune from want of foresight.

Blush, *v.* to chafe the skin so as to cause a tumour or blister, to blister.—*n.* a blister; a boil.

Blushin, Blushion, Blushon, *n.* a blister or boil on hands or feet; a pustule full of matter.

Bluster, *v.* to disfigure in writing.

Blusterous, *adj.* used of the weather: boisterous, blustering.

Blute, *n.* a bad or foolish action.

Blute, *n.* a sudden burst of sound.

Bluther, *v.* to blot; to disfigure; to soil. Cf. Bludder.

Bluther, *v.* to make a noise in swallowing; to make an inarticulate sound; to raise wind-bells in water. Cf. Bludder.

Bluthrie, *adj.* wet, stormy.

Bluthrie, *n.* phlegm; frothy, incoherent, flatulent discourse.

Bluthrie, *n.* thin porridge; water-gruel.

Blutter, *v.* to make a noise in swallowing. Cf. Bludder

Blutter, *n.* a dirty, clumsy, slovenly person. Cf. Bluiter.

Blutter, *v.* to talk foolishly. Cf. Bluiter.

Blutter, *n.* a term of reproach; one who has not the power of retention.

Blyave, Blyaave, *v.* to blow, pant; to fire a gun; to boast. Cf. Blaw.

Blybe, *v.* to drink much and often.—*n.* a large quantity of liquor; a drunkard. Cf. Bleb.

Blybe, *n.* a stroke, a blow. Cf. Blibe.

Blyber, *v.* to drink hard. Cf. Blebber.

Blyberin, *n.* hard drinking.

Blybin, *n.* the act of drinking spirits.

Blype, *n.* a stroke, a blow. Cf. Blipe.

Blype, *n.* a shred of skin when it peels off; a lump. Cf. Blipe.

Blyte, *n.* a flying shower.

Blyter, *v.* to besmear. Cf. Bluiter.

Blythe, *adj.* glad; merry. Cf. Blithe.

Bo, *n.* a louse.

Bo, *n.* a submerged rock.

Bo, *n.* a hobgoblin.

Bo, *int.* an excl. meant to frighten or surprise.

Bo, *v.* to talk noisily; used of cattle: to low. Cf. Boo.

Boag, *v.* used of a shoemaker: to go out to work in the house of his customers.

Boak, *v.* to retch; to vomit. Cf. Boke.

Boakie, *n.* a hobgoblin; a scarecrow; an oddly-dressed person; dried nasal mucus.

Boal, *n.* a small square aperture in a wall for light or air; a similar recess in a wall for holding small articles; a small doorless cupboard. Cf. Bole.

Board, *n.* a table; a tailor's table; a parochial board; parish relief.

Board, *v.* to become intimate with.

Board-cloth, *n.* a tablecloth.

Board-end, *n.* the table-end.

Board-head, *n.* the head of the table.

Board-trees, *n.* the plank on which a corpse is stretched.

Board-wages, *n.* the money paid by a person for his board.

Boar's-ears, *n.* the auricula.

Boas, *adj.* hollow. Cf. Boss.

Boast, *v.* to threaten.—*n.* a threat, a scolding.

Boat, *v.* to take boat; to carry in a boat.—*n.* a barrel or tub to hold meal or meat; a pickling-tub; a small vessel for serving melted butter; a wooden skimming-dish.

Boatie, *n.* a yawl, small boat; a ferryman.

Boat's-draw, *n.* the furrow made by a boat's keel when launched or drawn ashore.

Boat-stick, *n.* the pole of a boat; the mast of a small sailing-boat.

Boatswain, *n.* a sailor's name for the skua and other birds with pointed tails.

Bob, Bobb, *n.* a bunch; a nosegay; a tuft of grass growing above the rest; a tassel; a knot of ribbons; an ornamental knob.—*v.* to grow luxuriantly in patches. Cf. Bab.

Bob, *n.* a gust, blast. Cf. Bub.

Bob, *n.* a slight blow, slap; a mark, butt; a taunt, gibe; a scolding; a curtain-lecture.

Bob, *v.* to move up and down quickly; to dance; to curtsy, bow low.—*n.* a dance; a curtsy, obeisance, nod. Cf. Bab.

Bob, *n.* the best-dressed or best-looking lad or lass in a company. Cf. Bab.

Bob, *n.* a fishing-float.

Bobantilter, *n.* any dangling piece of dress; a pendant; an icicle.

Bobber, *n.* the hook used in fly-fishing as distinguished from the 'trailer,' a fishing-float; a poacher who catches salmon with the illegal bob-net.

Bobbin, *n.* a weaver's quill.

Bobbin, *n.* the seed-pod of birch.

Bobbinjohn, *n.* a tin cylinder perforated at one end, for sowing by hand turnip-seed where it has failed in the drills.

Bobbinqua, *n.* a quaking bog. Cf. Babbanqua.

Bobbins, *n.* the wild arum; the water-lily, *Nymphæa alba*; the bunch of edible ligaments attached to the stalk of the badder-locks seaweed.

Bobbin-wheel, *n.* a wheel used in filling 'bobbins'; the wheel of time with its revolutions and changes.

Bobbit, *ppl. adj.* ornamented with tassels; uneven of surface.

Bobble, *n.* a slovenly fellow.

Bobby, *n.* a grandfather; a policeman.

Bobby, *n.* the robin; the devil. Cf. Auld.

Bob-net, *n.* an illegal fixed fishing-net. Cf. Bawb-net.

Bob-robin, *n.* the robin.

Boch, *n.* a child's plaything; an untidy or disagreeable woman.

Bochars and stars, *n.* the prickly-headed carex.

Bocht, *v. pret.* and *ppl.* bought.

Bock, *v.* to retch; to vomit. Cf. Boke.

Bockie, *n.* a bugbear.

Bo-cow, *n.* a scarecrow; a bugbear. Cf. Boakie.

Bod, *n.* a dwarf; a person of small size, a 'creature,' a 'body.'

Bod, *n.* a personal invitation; a price bidden or asked. Cf. Bode.

Bod, *n.* in *phr.* 'new bod, new shod,' afresh, with renewed effort.

Bodach, *n.* an old man; a spectre, hobgoblin; a diminutive person, a 'body'; a name of the devil.

Bodach, *n.* the small-ringed seal.

Bodden, *ppl. adj.* forced on one. Cf. Bode.

Boddle, *n.* a copper coin, value one-sixth of an English penny, or of two pennies Scots; anything of trifling value.

Boddle-pieces, *n.* small coins.

Boddle-, Bodle-pin, *n.* a large pin for fastening clothes together.

Boddom, *n.* bottom; the seat of the human body, buttocks; the sole of a shoe. Cf. Bottom.

Boddom-lyer, *n.* a large trout that keeps to the bottom of a pool.

Boddom-room, *n.* a sitting for one person in a church pew.

Boddum, *n.* a tub. Cf. Bodom.

Bode, *n.* a portent.—*v.* to foretell, portend; to expect, look for; to desire; to betoken, signify.

Bode, *n.* a bid, a price asked or offered at a sale; an invitation.—*v.* to bid at a sale; to offer a price; to offer with insistence; to promise, proffer.

Bodeable, *adj.* marketable.

Boden, Bodden, *adj.* arrayed, prepared, furnished with.

Bodeword, *n.* a portent, an ominous prediction regarding a person or family.

Bodgel, *n.* a little man.

Bodie, Boddie, *n.* a person. Cf. Body.

Bodily, *adv.* entirely, completely.

Bodin, *adj.* prepared, equipped. Cf. Boden.

Boding, *ppl. adj.* desiring; striving.

Bodle, *n.* a small copper coin. Cf. Boddle.

Bodom, *n.* a tub; a barrel; a ship.

Bodsie, *n.* a nickname given to a short, thick-set person. Cf. Bod.

Bodword, *n.* a 'bodeword.'

Body, *n.* a person, any one; an inferior; a puny person; a term of contempt.

Body-claes, *n.* wearing apparel.

Body-like, *adv.* with the whole bodily faculties complete.

Bofft, *ppl. adj.* of standing grain: suffering from ravages of birds and from a long and wet harvest.

Bog, *v.* to stick in the mire or bog; to confuse, befog, 'dumfounder'; to entangle one's self inextricably in an argument or dispute.

Bog, *n.* a bug.

Bog, *v.* to go out working at so much a day. Cf. Boag.

Bogan, *n.* a boil. Cf. Boggan, Bolgan.

Bog-bean, *n.* the common trefoil. Cf. Buck-bean.

Bog-blitter, -blutter, -bumper, -drum, *n.* the bittern.

Boggan, Boggen, *n.* a boil; a tumour; a large pimple filled with white matter, chiefly appearing between the fingers of children in spring.

Boggart, *n.* a bugbear.

Boggie, *n.* a designation of a displaced priest who married people contrary to canon laws, though not to nature's laws.—*adj.* plotting in secret.

Boggle, *v.* to perplex, baffle; to quake as a bog; to take fright, shy.—*n.* a fright, fear, scruple; a 'bogle.'

Bog-gled, *n.* the moor-buzzard; the marsh-harrier.

Bogglie, *adj.* quaking like a bog.

Bog-hay, *n.* hay grown on marshy, uncultivated ground.

Bog-hyacinth, *n.* the orchis 'Adam and Eve.'

Bogie, *n.* a 'bogle'; a craze, infatuation; a hobby; a name for the devil. Cf. Auld.

Bogie-keek, *n.* bo-peep.

Bogle, *n.* an apparition; a scarecrow; a game of 'hide-and-seek.'

Bogle, *n.* a supper-cake eaten in Shetland on Bogle Day, 29th March.

Bogle, *v.* to bewitch, 'bamboozle'; to terrify.

Bogle-, Bogill-about-the-bush, *n. phr.* the game of 'hide-and-seek'; circumvention.

Bogle-about-the-stacks, *n. phr.* the game of 'hide-and-seek' played in a full stackyard.

Bogle-bo, *n.* a hobgoblin; a pettish humour; any object of terror.

Bogle-catch-the-fairy, *n. phr.* the game of 'hide-and-seek.'

Bogle-day, *n.* the 29th of March.

Bogle-rad, *adj.* afraid of ghosts.

Boglesome, *adj.* shy, skittish.

Bogle wark, *n.* the matter of ghostly action.

Boglie, *adj.* haunted by hobgoblins or 'bogies.'

Bog-nut, *n.* the marsh trefoil.

Bog-reed, *n.* a reed-pipe.

Bog-sclent, *v.* to avoid fighting, to abscond on the day of battle.—*n.* a coward.

Bog-spavin, *n.* wind-gall, a soft swelling on a horse's leg.

Bog-stalker, *n.* an idle, lounging, stupid fellow.

Boguish, *adj.* of land: soft, spongy.

Bog-war, *n.* tangles and other seaweeds with balls or bladders on the fronds.

Boho, *n.* a laughing-stock. Cf. Beho.

Boho, *n.* a name for the devil. Cf. Auld.

Boich, *v.* to cough with difficulty.—*n.* a short, difficult cough. Cf. Beigh.

Boicher, *n.* one having a short, difficult cough.

Boichin, *n.* a continuance of coughing with difficulty.

Boid, *n.* a blackberry.

Boikin, *n.* the piece of beef called the brisket.

Boikin, *n.* a bodkin.

Boil, *n.* the bole or trunk of a tree.

Boil, *n.* meat for boiling in contrast to meat for roasting; the boiling-point.—*v.* to well up; with *out*, to waste in boiling.

Boiler, *n.* a large cast-iron kettle.

Boil-house, *n.* an outhouse where food for cattle is steamed or boiled.

Boiling, *ppl.* in a towering passion.—*n.* enough for boiling at a time; the whole quantity, party, &c.

Boilled, *adj.* profusely decked.

Boin, *n.* a washing-tub; a flat, broad-bottomed wooden milk-vessel. Cf. Boyne.

Boir, *n.* an aperture. Cf. Bore.

Boisert, *n.* a louse.

†Boist, *n.* a box or chest; a coffin. Cf. Buist.

Boist, *v.* to threaten.—*n.* a threat. Cf. Boast.

Boistart, *adj.* boisterous.

Boit, *n.* a cask or tub for pickling beef, &c.; a butt.

Boke, *v.* to retch, vomit, belch; to object to.—*n.* a belch, vomiting; a drinking to the extent of vomiting.

Bokie, *n.* a bogie, hobgoblin, bugbear. Cf. Boakie.

Bokie-blindie, *n.* blindman's buff.

Bold, *adj.* of a fire: great, big; of wind: tempestuous. Cf. Bauld.

Bolden, *v.* to take courage, put on a bold face; to swell with pride, wrath, &c. Cf. Bowden.

Boldie, *n.* the chaffinch.

Boldin, *ppl. adj.* swelled. Cf. Bowden.

Bole, *n.* a small opening in a wall for air or light, or as a press or cupboard for holding odds and ends in daily use. Cf. Boal.

Bole-hole, *n.* a small opening in the wall of a barn, stable, or cowhouse for light and ventilation, &c.

Bolgan, *n.* a swelling that becomes a boil or pimple. Cf. Boggan.

Bolgan-leaves, *n.* the nipple-wort.

Boll, *n.* an old Scotch dry measure, not exceeding six bushels. Cf. Bow.

Boll, *n.* a flash of lightning.

Bolster, *n.* the part of a mill in which the axle-tree moves.

Bomacie, *n.* a thunderstorm.

Bomariskie, *n.* an herb the roots of which taste exactly like liquorice; ? rest-harrow.

Bombard, *n.* a cannon.

Bombard-shot, *n.* cannon-shot.

Bombass, Bombaze, *v.* to confound. Cf. Bumbaze.

Bombell, *v.* to read in a low, indistinct voice; to weep. Cf. Bumble.

Bombell, *v.* to bungle. Cf. Bumble, Bummil.

Bomf, *n.* a bump, shake.

Bomill, *n.* a cooper's tool.

Bommle, *v.* to work confusedly. Cf. Bumble.

Bomulloch, *n.* in *phr.* 'to gar ane lauch bomulloch,' to make one's mirth turn to sorrow. Cf. Bamullo.

Bon, *adj.* gratuitous; begged, borrowed.

†Bon-accord, *n.* amity, agreement; the city of Aberdeen; that city's motto.

Bonage, *n.* 'bondage.' Cf. Bondage.

†Bonally, Bonaillie, *n.* farewell; good-speed; a farewell feast.

†Bona magna, *n.* a kind of plum.

†Bon-criteon, *n.* the pear called *bon Chrétien.*

Bond, *v.* to mortgage.—*n.* a mortgage.—*adj.* conjoined in a bond or written obligation.

Bondage, *n.* the services due by a tenant to a proprietor, or by a cottager to a farmer, on whose farm he dwells.

Bondage-hook, *n.* a tenant bound to reap for his landlord in harvest.

Bondage-peats, *n.* peats which a tenant is bound to supply to his landlord.

Bondager, *n.* a female worker provided by a cottager when he undertakes to work for a farmer.

Bone-dry, *adj.* very dry, as dry as a bone.

Bonefire, *n.* a bonfire.

Bone-lazy, *n.* thoroughly lazy. Cf. Bane-idle.

Boneless, *adj.* without pith or substance; insipid.

Bones-breaking, *n.* a fight, scrimmage; a bloody quarrel.

Bone-shanks, *n.* Death represented as a skeleton with a scythe.

Bone-, Bon-wark, -wrak, *n.* rheumatic pains; aching of the bones.

†Bongrace, *n.* a woman's large linen or cotton bonnet; a large straw bonnet.

Bonnage, *n.* 'bondage.' Cf. Bondage.

Bonnar, *n.* a bond; a mortgagee.

Bonnet, *n.* a man's cap. Cf. Bannet.

Bonnet, *n.* a person who bids for his own goods at a sale; one who is employed by the owner to bid for him.

Bonnet-ba', *n.* a boys' game played with their caps and a ball.

Bonnet-fecht, *n.* a boys' fight with their caps as weapons.

Bonnet-fire, *n.* a penalty inflicted by boys on one who breaks the rules of the game.

Bonnetie, *n.* the game of 'bonnet-ba.'

Bonnetie, *n.* the little grebe.

Bonnet-laird, *n.* a yeoman, one who farms his own land; one who farmed land as tenant, in its natural state and at a nominal rent, for a long lease, sometimes of 99 years.

Bonnet-lug, *n.* the ear which is more visible when the cap is worn on one side of the head.

Bonnet-man, *n.* a ploughman.

Bonnet-piece, *n.* a gold coin of James V., who is represented on it wearing a 'bonnet.'

Bonnilie, *adv.* beautifully.

Bonnivochil, *n.* the great northern diver.

Bonnock, *n.* a sort of cake; a 'bannock.'

Bonny, *n.* a small quantity of anything.

Bonny, Bonnie, *adj.* beautiful, pretty; handsome, fine, attractive; goodly; of a wound:

healthy; also used ironically.—*adv.* prettily, finely, well.

Bonny die, *n.* a trinket, a toy.

Bonny-fyd, *adj.* bonâ-fide.

Bonnylike, *adj.* good to look at, fine to appearance.

Bonnyness, *n.* beauty.

Bonny penny, *n.* a goodly sum of money.

Bonny sair, *n.* a healthy sore.

Bonny-wallies,-wawlies, *n.* gewgaws, trinkets.

Bonny wee, *n.* a good while.

Bonoch, *n.* a binding for a cow's hindleg during milking.

Bonour, *n.* a bond. Cf. Bonnar.

Bonspeil, Bonspiel, *n.* a contest or match, at curling especially; a match at any game on a large scale.

Bonxie, *n.* the common skua.

Boo, *n.* a manor-house; farmhouse; a village. Cf. Bow.

Boo, *n.* an object of terror; a bugbear. Cf. Bo.

Boo, *n.* a bull.

Boo, *v.* to bow, to bend.—*n.* a bow, &c. Cf. Bow.

Boo, *v.* to cry; to roar; to low.—*n.* a crying.

Booby, *n.* the lowest in a class of children at school.

Bood, *v. pret.* had to, behoved. Cf. Beed.

Bood be, *n.* a necessary obligation.

Boodie, *n.* dried nasal mucus.

Boodie, *n.* a ghost, hobgoblin; a small and unattractive person, a dwarf. Cf. Bod.

Boodie-bo, *n.* a bugbear; an object of dread.

Booff, *v.* to strike with the hand, causing a hollow sound.—*n.* the sound thus produced; such a stroke.

Boogers, *n.* rafters or cross-spars of a roof. Cf. Bougars.

Boo-hoo, *int.* an excl. of derision with out-shot lips.—*n.* a cry of derision; an outburst of weeping.—*v.* to show contempt in cries of derision; to weep noisily.

Booin', *n.* disorderly shouting 'Boo!'

Booin', *n.* bowing; cringing.

Booit, *n.* a hand-lantern. Cf. Bouet.

Book, *n.* the Bible.—*v.* to record names of a couple for proclamation of banns of marriage. Cf. Beuk.

Booking, *n.* the act of recording names for proclamation of banns; the feast formerly held on that occasion.

Booking, *n.* a peculiar tenure of lands in Paisley; a holding under this tenure.

Booking-night, *n.* the night on which parties were 'booked' for proclamation of banns of marriage.

Bookit, *ppl.* 'booked' for proclamation of marriage banns.

Book-lare, -lear, *n.* education; knowledge gained from books.

Book-lared, *adj.* educated; learned.

Book-leernt, *adj.* educated; learned.

Bool, *n.* a boy's marble; a large round stone; a bowler's bowl.

Bool, *n.* the curved handle of a bucket, kettle, cup, jug; the bow of a key, scissors, shears; anything curved or circular; a pot-hook; an iron movable handle for lifting a pot by the 'ears' on and off the fire; in *pl.* the rims of spectacles.

Bool, *n.* a term of contempt for an old man; a thickset man or boy.

Bool, *v.* to weep in childish fashion; to drawl in singing.

Boo-lady, *n.* a cow.

Bool-backit, *adj.* round-shouldered; hump-backed.

Bool-bag, *n.* a boy's bag for carrying his marbles.

Booler, *n.* a large marble for throwing.

Bool-fit, *n.* a crooked, deformed foot. Cf. Bowl.

Bool-horned, *adj.* perverse; headstrong.

Boolie, *adj.* crooked, deformed; used of the legs: 'bandy.' Cf. Bowlie.

Boolie-back, *n.* a bent back; a humpback.

Boolie-backit, *adj.* 'bool-backit.'

Boolyie, *n.* a loud, threatening noise, like a bull's bellow.

Boom, *v.* used of a flying beetle: to make a booming sound.

Boo-man, *n.* the cattleman on a large farm. Cf. Bowman.

Boon, *n.* the core and worthless part of a stalk of flax.

Boon, *n.* a band of reapers or turf-cutters. Cf. Binn.

Boon, *adv.* and *prep.* above.

Boon-dinner, *n.* the dinner given in the harvest-field to the reapers.

Booner, *adj.* upper.

Boonermost, *adj.* uppermost.

Boon-hook, *n.* the harvest-work which a tenant was bound to give to his landlord. Cf. Bondage-hook.

Boonmost, *adj.* uppermost.

Boorach, *n.* a band on a cow's legs at milking.

Boord, *v.* to board, to stay with.—*n.* a board.

Boord, *v.* to split a stratified stone.

Boordly, *adj.* stalwart, sturdy, strong, manly. Cf. Buirdly.

Boorichy, *n.* a small cluster, heap, or crowd. Cf. Bourach.

Boorick, *n.* a shepherd's hut; a dwelling; a heap. Cf. Bourach.

Boor-tree, *n.* the elder-tree. Cf. Bour-tree.

Boosam, *adj.* busy, bustling.

Boosan, *n.* moving about, bustling.

Booscht, *n.* a little, talkative person.
Boose, *n.* a cow's stall; a crib.—*v.* to enclose in a stall.
†**Boose**, *n.* force, energy; a bounce.—*v.* to push, to bounce, to bustle about; to be violently active.
Booshty, *n.* a bed; a small bed. Cf. Buisty.
Boosin, *ppl. adj.* active, bouncing.
Boost, *v. pret.* must, ought; used of moral or logical necessity. Cf. Bood.
Boost, *v.* to ' shoo ' off; to guide in a particular direction.
†**Boost**, *n.* a box. Cf. Buist.
Boost, *n.* the tar-mark on a sheep. Cf. Buist.
Boot, *n.* an instrument of torture for the leg, formerly used in Scotland. Cf. Beet.
Boot, *n.* a flour-sieve. Cf. Bout.
Boot, *v.* must; ought. Cf. Bood, Beet.
Boot, *n.* what is given into the bargain or to equalize an exchange.
Boo't, *ppl. adj.* bent.
Boot-catcher, *n.* a servant who removed a person's boots for cleaning.
Boot-dighter, *n.* the boot-cleaner.
Boo-teind, *n.* a tithe of the produce or value of cows.
Booth-meal, -mail, *n.* shop-rent.
Bootikin, *n.* a small boot; in *pl.* the 'boot' as an instrument of torture. Cf. Beetikin.
Booting, *n.* booty, prize.
Bootsna, *v. neg.* matters not.
Booty, *n.* a disease of growing wheat in spring.
Bootyer, *n.* a glutton. Cf. Boutger, Byoutour.
Booze, *n.* intoxicating liquor; a carouse.
Boozer, *n.* a fuddler, a sot.
Boozy, *adj.* bulky; plump; stout.
Boozy, *adj.* tipsy, fond of drink.
Boozy, *adj.* bushy; hairy.
Bor, *n.* a hole. Cf. Bore.
Borag, *n.* a bradawl; a pointed iron heated for boring.
Boral, Borale, *n.* a wimble; a borer, an end of which is placed on the breast.
Boral-hole, *n.* a hole made by a wimble.
Boral-tree, *n.* the handle of a wimble.
Bord, *n.* a broad hem or welt; a ruffle, frill; used of a woman's cap: the border or the band in front -*v.* to provide an edge or border.
†**Bordel, Bordel-house**, *n.* a brothel.
Bore, *n.* a crevice, chink, hole; a break in the clouds; a teat; a 'new leaf' in conduct; in curling: a passage between two guarding stones; in cricket: the passage of the ball between two fielders.—*v.* to sew.
Bore-awl, *n.* a shoemaker's awl.
Bore-iron, *n.* an instrument for boring holes.
Borel, Borell, *n.* a ' boral.'
Boreman, *n.* a smith who wields the sledge-hammer.

Bore's-ears, *n.* the auricula. Cf. Boar's ears.
Bore-staff, *n.* part of a loom which deals with the tension of the web.
Bore-staff-cord, *n.* a smooth cord regulating by pulley and lever the tension of the web.
Bore-tree, *n.* the elder-tree. Cf. Bour-tree.
Borie, *n.* a clear opening of the sky in wet weather. Cf. Bore.
Born-days, *n.* lifetime.
Born-deevil, *n.* a downright blackguard.
Borne-doon, *ppl. adj.* depressed in mind, health, or outward circumstances.
Born-head, *n.* a young precocious fellow; a very foolish person.
Born-head, *adv.* straightforward, impetuously; headlong.—*adj.* furious, impetuous.
Born-mad, *n.* furious.
Boroughmonger, *n.* a rabbit.
Borough-, Borough's-town, *n.* a burgh.
Borra, Borrach, *n.* a heap of stones covering cells; a 'cairn.' Cf. Bourach.
Borrach, *n.* a band round a cow's legs, preventing her from kicking during milking. Cf. Bourach.
Borral, *n.* the elder-tree.
Borrel, *adj.* rough, rude, clownish.
Borrel, *n.* a borer, an instrument for piercing. Cf. Boral.
Borrow, *n.* a burgh or town.
Borrow, *n.* a pledge, a surety; anything borrowed.—*v.* to be surety for; to ransom; to give security to; to urge one to drink, to pledge one in liquor. Cf. Burrows.
Borrow-flag, *n.* the burgh-standard with the town's arms.
Borrowing-days, *n.* the last three days of March, o.s.
Borrow land, *n.* a 'land' or tenement in a burgh.
Borrow-mail, *n.* annual tribute formerly paid to the king by a burgh, in return for certain privileges.
Borrowstoun, *n.* a royal burgh; a 'borough town.'
Bose, *adj.* hollow. Cf. Boss.
Bosie, *n.* the bosom.
Boskill, *n.* an opening in the middle of a stack of corn, made by pieces of wood fastened on the top, a 'boss kiln.'
Bosky, *adj.* the worse for drink; wild, unfrequented.
Bosness, *n.* of stone: friableness, tendency to moulder.
Boss, *n.* a frame of wood on a staddle.
Boss, *n.* anything hollow; a despicable, worthless person. — *adj.* hollow, empty; weak, ignorant; emaciated; poor, despicable, worthless; pretentious; applied to a recess or bay-window.

Boss, *n.* a small cask.

Boss, *n.* a bunch or tuft of grass ; a round projecting mass ; the front of the body from chest to loins.

Bossie, *n.* a large wooden basin, used for oatmeal in baking. Cf. Bassie.

Bossie, *n.* a metal button used in the game of 'buttons,' got from naval or military uniforms or livery-servants' coats.

Bossin, *n.* a ventilating opening in a corn-stack.

Bossness, *n.* hollowness ; emptiness from lack of food.

Bost, *v.* to scold, speak roughly ; to threaten. Cf. Boast.

Bote, *n.* help ; advantage ; compensation.

Botheration, *int.* used as an expletive.

Botherment, *n.* trouble, perplexity.

Bothersome, *adj.* troublesome.

Bothie, Bothy, *n.* a cottage in common for farm-servants.

Bothie-man, *n.* a farm-servant living in a ' bothie.'

Bothier, *n.* a ' bothie-man.'

Bothom, *n.* bottom. Cf. Boddom.

Botion, *n.* botching.

Botkin, *n.* a bodkin.

Bottle, *n.* a bottle of medicine ; the contents of a bottle.

Bottle, *v.* to bundle-up hay or straw for fodder.

Bottle-crony, *n.* a boon-companion.

Bottle-nose, *n.* the ' ca'ing ' whale.

Bottle-screw, *n.* a corkscrew.

Bottling, *n.* a festivity ; a gathering of friends invited to a wedding.

Bottom, *n.* the breech. Cf. Boddom.

Bottomer, *n.* one who attends to the bottom of a pit-shaft.

Bottom-room, *n.* a seat for one in a church-pew ; as much room as a person requires in sitting.

Bottom-runner, *n.* the boards between the stern-boards of a boat.

Bottrel, *adj.* thickset, dwarfish.—*n.* a thickset, dwarfish person.

Bou, *v.* to bow, bend.

Boubie, *n.* the lowest in a class at school. Cf. Booby.

Bouch, *n.* a coward, a sneak.

Boucht, *n.* a curvature, bend ; the hollow of the elbow or knee ; a coil of fishing-line, a fishing-line of 50 to 55 fathoms ; a bay, bight.—*v.* to fold down ; to enclose in a loop.

Boucht, *n.* a fold for sheep or cattle ; a milking-pen for ewes ; a house for folding sheep at night ; a large, square church-pew.—*v.* to fold or pen cattle, &c.; to fence in, enclose for shelter.

Boucht-curd, *n.* sheep-droppings that fall into the milk-pail.

Bouchting-blanket, *n.* a small blanket laid across a feather-bed, with the ends tucked in on both sides.

Bouchting-time, *n.* the time for milking ewes.

Boucht-knot, *n.* a running knot ; one made with doubled cord.

Boucht-seat, *n.* a large, square church-pew ; a pew with a table.

Boud, *v. pret.* had to. Cf. Bood.

Bouden, *ppl. adj.* swollen, inflated. Cf. Bowden.

†**Bouet,** *n.* a hand-lantern. Cf. Bowet.

Bouff, *v.* to strike, buffet. Cf. Booff.

Bouff, *v.* to bark like a large dog ; to cough noisily.—*n.* a loud bark ; a noisy cough ; a dog. Cf. Buff.

Bouff, *n.* a stupid, blundering fellow.

Bouffie, *n.* a dog's short bark.

Bouffin, *n.* continued coughing.—*ppl. adj.* given to barking.

Bouffin, *n.* a big, stout person ; used rather contemptuously.

Boug, *n.* a child's name for the stomach or belly.

Bougars, *n.* the rafters or cross-spars of the roof of a house, on which wattlings were placed. Cf. Bugar.

Bougar-stakes, *n.* the lower part of the rafters, in old houses, resting on the ground.

Bougar-sticks, *n.* strong pieces of wood fixed to the rafters by wooden pins.

Bouger, *n.* the puffin.

Bought, *n.* a curve. Cf. Boucht.

Bought, *n.* a sheepfold. Cf. Boucht.

Boughtie, *n.* a twig.

Bougie, *n.* a sheepskin bag.

Bougil, *n.* cockcrow ; the crow of a cock.

†**Bouguie,** *n.* a posy, nosegay, bouquet.

Bouk, *n.* the whole body ; size, quantity, bulk. —*v.* to make bulk ; to pack in (small) compass.

Bouk, *n.* a lye made of cow-dung and stale urine or soapy water, in which foul linen was steeped in order to its being cleansed or whitened.—*v.* to steep foul linen in such a lye.

Bouk, *v.* to retch, vomit.—*n.* a retching, vomiting. Cf. Boke.

Boukie, *adj.* bulky. Cf. Bouky.

Bouking, *n.* the quantity of clothes steeped for washing at a time.

Bouking-, Boukit-washing, *n.* the great annual washing of family linen by means of the ' bouk ' or lye of cow-dung, &c.

Boukit, *ppl. adj.* large, bulky ; swollen ; corpulent ; pregnant.

Bouksome, *adj.* bulky, of large size ; pregnant ; morally great.

Bouky, *adj.* bulky ; obese ; well-attended ; numerous.

Boul, *n.* a contemptuous expression applied to a person.

Boul, *n.* anything curved. Cf. Bool.

Boulden, *ppl. adj.* swelled ; inflated. Cf. Bowden.

Boulder, *n.* a strong blast of wind. Cf. Bowder.

Boulder-stane, *n.* a paving-stone.

Boule, *n.* a gap, break ; an opening in the clouds betokening fine weather. Cf. Bole.

Boul-horned, *adj.* headstrong. Cf. Bool-horned.

Boullin'-maill, *n.* a charge for playing bowls on a green.

Boult-claith, *n.* a bolting-cloth for sifting flour.

Bouman, *n.* a tenant who takes stock from his landlord and shares with him the profit.

Boun, *v.* to make ready, prepare ; to dress ; to betake one's self to a place ; to go.

Boun, *ppl. adj.* ready, prepared ; bound for.

Bouncer, *n.* a lively person.

Bouncing, *ppl. adj.* lively ; vigorous.

Bouncy, *adj.* 'bouncing.'

Bound, *n.* a district ; a boundary ; limit or size of the body.

Bound, *ppl.* sure, certain.

Bounder, *v.* to limit, set boundaries to.

Bound out, *v.* to swell out, to enlarge.

Bound-road, *n.* a fenced road ; a boundary-road ; a frontier.

Bountie-shoes, *n.* shoes given as part of a servant's wages.

Bountith, Bounteth, *n.* something given in reward for service, over and above wages; a bounty, a bonus.

Boun-tree, Bountry, *n.* the elder-tree. Cf. Bour-tree.

Boun-tree-berries, *n.* elder-berries.

Boun-tree-gun, *n.* an elder-wood pop-gun.

Bourach, *n.* a mound ; a heap of stones ; a small 'cairn'; a confused heap ; a cluster, ring, or crowd of people and things ; a hut of loose stones ; a shepherd's hut ; a house that children build in play ; a knoll ; an enclosure.—*v.* to enclose, encircle ; to crowd together in a mass or ring, or confusedly.

Bourach, *n.* a band put round a cow's hind-legs at milking-time. Cf. Burroch.

Bourbee, *n.* the spotted whistle-fish.

†**Bourd,** *v.* to jest ; to dally.—*n.* a jest, joke ; a scoff.

Bourd, *n.* an encounter, fight. Cf. Bowrad.

Bourding, *n.* jesting.

Bourie, *n.* a rabbit's burrow ; a fox's den.

Bouroch, Bourock, *n.* a house, home. Cf. Bourach.

†**Bourriau, Bourrier,** *n* an executioner.

Bour-tree, *n.* the elder-tree.

Bouse, *n.* intoxicating drink. Cf. Booze.

Bouser, *n.* a sot.

Boushty, *n.* a bed. Cf. Buisty.

Boust, *v.* must. Cf. Buist.

Bousteous, *adj.* boisterous , fierce Cf. Busteous.

Bouster, *n.* a bolster. Cf. Bowster.

Bousterous, *adj.* boisterous.

Bousum, *adj.* merry.

Bousy, *adj.* tipsy ; fond of liquor. Cf. Boozy.

Bousy, *adj.* covered with bushes ; hairy. Cf. Boozy.

Bousy, *adj.* large, bulky, plump. Cf. Boozy.

Bousy-like, *adj.* apparently distended or big.

Bout, *prep.* without. Cf. But.

Bout, *n.* every two turns with the plough ; the extent of land mown by a labourer moving straightforward ; the amount of thread wound on a clew while held in the same position ; the corn and hay cut by a scythe and lying in rows ; a swath of grass ; an attack of illness.

Bout, *v.* to bolt, spring, leap ; to rise quickly from beneath a surface.—*n.* a bolt into or out of a room, &c. ; the act of coming upon by surprise.

Bout, *n.* a roll of cloth, &c., of 28 ells.

Bout, *v.* to sift flour through a fine sieve or cloth.—*n.* a sieve.

Boutch, *v.* to botch, bungle.

Bout-claith, *n.* cloth of a thin texture.

†**Boutefeu,** *n.* an incendiary ; one who 'adds fuel to fire.'

Bout-gang, *n.* the space gone over, or the work done, with one sharpening of a scythe, in harvesting.

Bout-gate, *n.* a 'bout-gang'; a roundabout way ; an underhand means ; a deceitful course.

Boutger, *n.* a glutton. Cf. Bootyer, Byoutour.

Bouting, *n.* a 'bout-gang.'

†**Bouvrage,** *n.* drink, beverage.

Bouzy, *adj.* bushy, wooded ; bushy in appearance ; umbrageous. Cf. Bousy.

Bouzy, *adj.* big, swelling, distended ; fat, overgrown ; of a jolly and good-humoured appearance. Cf. Boozy.

Bow, *n.* a 'boll,' an old Scottish dry measure of not more than six bushels.

Bow, *n.* the boll containing flax-seed.

Bow, *n.* the arch of a bridge ; the curve of a street ; the wooden yoke for attaching oxen to the plough ; a fiddler ; the semicircular handle of a pail, pot, &c. ; in *pl.* sugar-tongs. —*v.* to curve, bend.

Bow, *n.* a field for cows ; a cattle-fold ; a house ; the principal farmhouse on an estate. Cf. Boo.

Bow, *n.* a fisherman's buoy ; the iron which

passes through the lead-stone from which the hooks hang.—*v.* to buoy up; to affix buoys to fishing-lines.

Bow, *v.* in *phr.* 'bow an e'e,' to close an eye, to sleep.

Bowater, *n.* a night-poacher of salmon, who uses a torch or lantern.

Bow-brig, *n.* a one-arched bridge.

Bowd, *n.* a breaker, a billow.

Bow'd, *ppl. adj.* crooked.

Bowden, *v.* to fill; to burden; to create flatulent distention; used of cattle: to swell from overeating; to swell with wrath or courage.

Bowden, *ppl. adj.* swollen, heavy; burdened, provided.

Bowder, *n.* a great squall, blast, a heavy storm of wind and rain. Cf. Boulder.

Bowdie-leggit, *adj.* having 'bow-legs.'

Bowding, *n.* swelling.

Bowel-hive, *n.* an inflammation of the bowels in children.

Bowel-hive grass, *n.* the field ladies' mantle, supposed to be effective in children's 'bowel-hive.'

Bowen, *n.* a broad, shallow dish made of staves, for holding milk, &c.; a washing-tub. Cf. Boin.

Bower, *n.* an inner room, a parlour, a 'boudoir.'

Bower, *n.* a bow-maker.

Bower, *n.* the manager of a dairy on a dairy-farm.

Bowerique, *n.* a small bower or parlour.

Bower-woman, *n.* a lady's-maid.

Bowet, *n.* a hand-lantern; the moon. Cf. Bouet.

Bowet-licht, *n.* lantern-light.

Bowfarts, *n.* in *phr.* 'in the bowfarts,' on the back and unable to rise.

Bowff, *v.* to bark like a dog. Cf. Bouff.

Bowff, *v.* to strike with the hand so as to cause a hollow sound.—*n.* a stroke causing a hollow sound.

Bowfit-steel, *n.* a buffet-stool.

Bowg, *n.* a child's belly.

Bowger, *n.* the puffin.

Bow-han', *n.* a fiddler; style of fiddling; a fiddler's right hand.

Bow-houghed, *adj.* bow-legged; with 'bow-thighs.'

Bow-houghs, *n.* crooked legs or thighs.

Bowie, *n.* a small barrel or cask open at one end; a tub; a milk-pail; a water-bucket or pail with a 'bow-handle'); a wooden vessel with staves and hoops, for holding milk, porridge, 'brose,' broth, &c.

Bowiefu', *n.* the fill of a 'bowie.'

Bowing, *n.* a holding or lease of a grass-farm and its live-stock; the management of a dairy on a dairy-farm.

Bowing-chaffs, *n.* distortion of the face by grimaces.

Bowk, *v.* to retch, vomit.—*n.* a vomiting. Cf. Boke.

Bowk, *n.* body; bulk. Cf. Bouk.

Bow-kail, -caill, *n.* cabbage.

Bow-keg, *n.* a small keg used as a buoy for fishing-lines.

Bowl, *v.* to boil.

Bowl, *v.* to crook. Cf. Bool.

Bowled-like, *adj.* crooked-like; with the appearance of being bowed.

Bow-leggit, *adj.* having bandy legs.

Bowler, *n.* a kettle, a boiler.

Bowlie, *adj.* crooked, bent.—*n.* a contemptuous name for a bow-legged person. Cf. Boolie.

Bowlie-backit, *adj.* round-shouldered; hump-backed.

Bowl-man, *n.* a male hawker of crockery.

Bowlochs, *n.* the ragweed; the mugwort.

Bowltest, *adj.* the most bent or crooked.

Bowl-wife, *n.* a female hawker of crockery.

Bowman, *n.* a cottager, a ploughman, a cattle-man, on a farm.

Bown, *v.* to make ready. Cf. Boun.

Bow-pot, *n.* a nosegay, bouquet.

Bowrach, *n.* a fetter for a cow at milking-time. Cf. Bourach.

Bowrack, Bowrick, Bowrock, *n.* a heap of stones; a cluster. Cf. Bourach.

Bowrad, *n.* a fatal encounter.

Bow-ribbed, *ppl. adj.* bent in the ribs or spars.

Bowrow, *n.* the row of a boat from one buoy to another when a line breaks, and the fisherman seeks to haul it from the other end.

Bows, *n.* a severe punishment; in *phr.* 'through the bows,' said of one who misbehaves and suffers punishment.

Bowsan, *adj.* very big, 'thumping.'

Bow-saw, *n.* a flexible, narrow-bladed saw fixed in a bow-shaped frame, for cutting.

Bowse, *n.* a 'bowsie' for frightening children. Cf. Bowsie.

Bowse, *v.* to rush like the wind.

Bowse, *v.* to bouse, pull hard in tacking.

Bowset, *n.* in *phr.* 'bowset and down the middle,' a country dance.

Bowsey, *n.* nasal excrement.

Bowsie, *adj.* bushy, hairy. Cf. Bousy.

Bowsie, *adj.* curved like a bow.—*n.* a contemptuous name for a crooked person.

Bowsie, *adj.* large. Cf. Bousy.

Bowsie, *n.* a huge, misshapen, hairy monster, used to frighten children.

Bowsprit, *n.* the nose.

Bowster, *n.* a bolster.

Bow-stock, *n.* a cabbage.

Bowt, *n.* a bolt; a thunderbolt; an iron rod.

Bowt, *v.* to spring up or away; to bolt.

Bow't, *ppl. adj.* bowed, bent; crooked.

Bowt, *n.* as much worsted as is wound upon a clew while it is held in one position. Cf. Bout.

Bowt, *n.* a roll of cloth.

Bowting-claith, *n.* cloth of fine texture. Cf. Boult-claith.

Bowt o' nittin, *n. phr.* a roll of tape.

Bow-tow, *n.* a buoy-rope.

Bow-wow, *v.* to scare; to frighten by barking; to bully, cheat.—*n.* a threat.—*adj.* captious, snarling.

Bowze, *v.* to drink hard. Cf. Booze.

Bowzelly, *adj.* bushy, unkempt. Cf. Bousy.

Box, *n.* the poor's fund in each parish, as formerly supplied by church collections, fines, &c.; the fund of a guild, benefit or friendly society; a precentor's desk.

Box, *v.* to panel walls with wood, to wainscot, to wall in with wood.

Box, *v.* used of cattle: to strike, gore, or push with the head.

Box and dice, *n. phr.* the sum total, everything; the whole collection.

Box-barrow, *n.* a wheelbarrow with wooden sides.

Box-bed, *n.* a bed with wooden sides and top, and two sliding or hinged panels for door; a folding-bed in the form of a chest of drawers.

Box-drain, *n.* a drain laid carefully with stones.

Boxed, *ppl. adj.* sheltered, walled in.

Box-feeding, *n.* the method of feeding sheep in sheds, &c.

Boxie-vrack, *n.* the seaweed *Fucus pixidatus.*

Boxing, *n.* wainscotting.

Boxings, *n.* the coarse offal of grain after the bran is taken off.

Box-ladder, *n.* a ladder-shaped staircase, in which each step forms part of a sloping box, as it were.

Box-master, *n.* the treasurer of a town's fund, or of any guild, benefit society, &c.

Box-seat, *n.* a square pew in church.

Boy, *n.* a male person of any age and condition, if unmarried and residing in the parental home; a smart, clever, capable fellow; used in derision as well as praise.

Boyd, *n.* a blackberry. Cf. Boid.

Boyne, Boyen, *n.* a broad, flat dish for holding milk; a tub; a washing-tub. Cf. Boin.

Boynfu', *n.* the fill of a ' boyne.'

Boytach, *n.* a bunch, a bundle; a small, dumpy animal.

Boytoch, *adj.* bad at walking from stoutness.

Bra', *adj.* fine. Cf. Braw.

Bra, *n.* a hill. Cf. Brae.

Braad, *n.* a sharp pull to hook a fish.—*v.* to give such a pull.

Braal, *n.* a fragment.

Brabblach, *n.* refuse.

Brace, *n.* a chimney-piece; a chimney of straw and clay; the projection of the wall into a room, in which the chimney is placed; a bit of wall in the middle of a Caithness kitchen-floor against which the fire was placed.

Bracel, *v.* to advance hastily and noisily. Cf. Brachle.

Brace-piece, *n.* a chimney-piece.

Brachan, *n.* water-gruel with butter. Cf. Brochan.

Brachle, *v.* to advance hastily and noisily.

Brachton, *n.* a term of contempt.

Brack, *v.* to break.—*n.* a break, breach; breaking waves; a large number. Cf. Break.

Brack, *n.* a strip of untilled land lying between two plots of land; a tract of barren ground in or near a township.

Brack, *n.* a sudden fall of earth or snow on a slope; a flood from a thaw; a sudden and heavy fall of rain.

Brack, *n.* very salt liquid or half-liquid food.

Bracken, Brachen, *n.* the female fern.

Bracken-clock, *n.* the small, gay-coloured chafer.

Brackit, *adj.* speckled. Cf. Brockit.

Bracks, *n.* a disease of sheep, ' braxy.'

Bracksy, *n.* of sheep: suffering from ' bracks.'

Brad, *n.* an opprobrious epithet applied to an old man.

Braddan, *n.* a salmon.

Brade, *adj.* broad.—*n.* breadth. Cf. Braid.

Brade, *v.* to resemble, like members of a family or stock. Cf. Breed.

Brae, *n.* a declivity, hillside, steep road; a knoll; a hill; the bank of a river; the upper part of a country.

Brae-face, *n.* the front or slope of a hill.

Brae-hag, -hauld, *n.* the overhanging bank of a stream.

Brae-head, *n.* the top of a ' brae.'

Braeie, *adj.* hilly; sloping.

Brae-laird, *n.* a landowner on the southern slope of the Grampians.

Brae-man, *n.* a dweller on the southern slope of the Grampians.

Braengel, *n.* a confused crowd. Cf. Brangle.

Braeset, *adj.* full of ' braes.'

Brae-shot, *n.* a quantity of earth fallen from a slope; a large sum of money which one unexpectedly inherits.

Braeside, *n.* a hillside.

Brag, *v.* to challenge to a feat; to defy; to reproach.—*n.* a boast.

Braggand, Braggie, Braggy, *adj.* boastful; bombastic.

Braggir, *n.* a coarse seaweed; the broad leaves of marine algæ.

Bragwort, *n.* mead; honey and ale fermented together.

Braichum, *n.* a horse-collar; any untidy or clumsy piece of dress, especially anything wrapped round the neck.

Braichum up, *v.* to wrap up untidily for protection against the weather.—*n.* the act of doing so.

Braid, *n.* the cry of a new-born child.

Braid, *v.* to resemble, to take after; used of members of the same stock or family. Cf. Breed.

Braid, *adj.* broad; having a strong dialect language or accent.—*adv.* broadly; without reserve.—*n.* breadth.

Braid-band, *n.* corn spread out unbound on the 'band.'—*adv.* with *fa'*, said of a woman who does not resist improper toying.

Braidcast, *n.* sowing with the hand.—*ppl. adj.* used of seed: scattered over the whole surface, broadcast.

Braid lining, *n.* a peculiar kind of soft woollen cloth.

Braidness, *n.* breadth.

Braidways, *adv.* broadside, on one's breadth.

Braig, *v.* to brag, boast.

Braiggle, *n.* an old and dangerously rickety article.

Braik, *n.* an instrument for separating hemp or flax from the core; a large, heavy harrow for breaking clods. Cf. Brake.

Braik, *n.* an internal mortification; a disease among sheep, 'braxy.'

Braik, *v.* to retch. Cf. Break.

Braiken, *n.* a 'bracken.'

Braikit, *ppl. adj.* speckled. Cf. Brockit.

Brain, *n.* spirit, mettle; a severe injury.—*adj.* furious raging.—*v.* to hurt severely; to stun by an injury to the head.

Brain-box, *n.* the skull.

Braindge, Brainge, *v.* to plunge rashly forward; to dash carelessly towards; to bustle about noisily in a fit of temper; to use violence, to dash in pieces; to vibrate.—*n.* a forward dash or plunge; bustling, angry haste; a fit of temper.

Brainding, *ppl.* striving to be first on the harvest-field, 'kemping.'

Brainger, *n.* one who rushes forward; a formidable foe.

Brainin, *n.* a severe injury.

Brainish, *adj.* hot-headed; high-spirited; delirious.

Brain-mad, *adj.* determined; keenly bent on; hurried on with the greatest impetuosity; mad.

Brain-pan, *n.* the skull.

Brain-wud, *adj.* mad; acting with fury or intense impetuosity.

Brainy, *adj.* unmanageable, high-mettled; spirited, lively.

Brainyell, Brainzel, *v.* to rush headlong; to break forth violently; to 'brangle,' to storm, to rave.—*n.* the act of rushing forward or doing anything carelessly or violently.

Braird, *n.* the first sprouting of young grain, turnips, &c.; a young, growing fellow.—*v.* to germinate, to sprout above ground.

Brairded-dyke, *n.* a fence made of thorn, furze, &c.

Brairdie, *adj.* abounding with 'braird.'

Brairds, *n.* the coarsest sort of flax; the short 'tow' drawn out straight in carding it; the best part of flax after a second 'heckling.' Cf. Breards.

Braisant, *ppl. adj.* brazened; impudent, bold; hardened, shameless.

Braise, *n.* the roach; a fish of the genus *Pagrus vulgaris.*

Braissil, *v.* to work hurriedly.—*n.* a rush, start; in *pl.* fits and starts.

Braist, *v.* to burst.

Braithel, *n.* a wedding.

Braithel-ale, *n.* ale drunk at a wedding.

Braize, *n.* the 'broose' raced for at a wedding. Cf. Broose.

Brak, *v.* to break; to become bankrupt; to express great sorrow; with *out,* to block out roughly.—*n.* the breaking-up; breach; noise; uproar. Cf. Break.

Brak-back, *n.* the harvest moon as entailing heavy labour.

Brake, *n.* a toothed instrument for dressing flax or hemp; a heavy harrow for clodbreaking.—*v.* to treat land with such a harrow. Cf. Braik.

Brake, *n.* a considerable number.

Brake, *n.* a bracken.

Brake, *v.* to puke, to retch. Cf. Braik.

Brakeseugh, *n.* a disease of sheep. Cf. Braxy.

Brakkins, Braks, *n.* the remains of a feast; broken meats.

Brallion, *n.* an unwieldy person or animal.

Bramlin, Brammel-worm, Brammin, *n.* a red-and-yellow worm found in old dunghills, used as bait for fresh-water fish, the 'stripey.'

Bramskin, *n.* a tanner's leathern apron.

Bran, *n.* the calf of the leg, the 'brawn.'

Brancher, *n.* a young bird unable to fly; a young crow leaving the nest for branches.

Brand, *n.* a glowing cinder; a burning peat; a worthless person.

Brand, *n.* the calf of the leg. Cf. Brawn.

Branded, *adj.* brindled.

Branden, *ppl. adj.* grilled.

Brander, *n.* a gridiron; a trestle, the support of a scaffold; a grating for the mouth of a drain or sewer.—*v.* to broil or bake on a 'brander'; to be broiled; to form a foundation in building, as for a ceiling or a scaffold.

Brander-bannock, *n.* a 'bannock' fired on a 'brander.'

Brandered, *ppl. adj.* cooked on a 'brander'; used of ceilings : having a framework as well as joists.

Brandering, *n.* scaffolding ; framework for panelling ; cooking on a 'brander.'

Brandie, *adj.* brindled.—*n.* a brindled cow.

Brandied, *ppl. adj.* brindled.

Brandling-worm, *n.* a striped worm used in fishing. Cf. Bramlin.

Brandraucht, Brandreth, *n.* a 'brander.'

Brandstickle, *n.* the stickleback.

Brandy-cellars, *n.* underground places for storing smuggled brandy.

Brandy-cleek, *n.* palsy in the leg from hard drinking.

Brandy-holes, *n.* 'brandy-cellars.'

Brandy-wine, *n.* brandy.

Brang, *v. pret.* brought.

Brange, *v.* to dash forward impetuously. Cf. Braindge.

Branglant, *ppl. adj.* brandishing.

†**Brangle,** *v.* to brandish ; to vibrate, shake ; to entangle, confuse ; to throw into doubt ; to cast doubt upon.—*n.* a tangle ; a confused crowd.

Branglement, *n.* confusion ; perplexity.

Brangler, *n.* a quarrelsome, wrangling person.

Brank, *v.* to bridle or restrain.—*n.* a sort of bridle or halter for horses or cows when at grass or tethered ; in *pl.* a bridle for scolds, witches, &c. ; the mumps.

Brank, *v.* to hold the head erect in a constrained or affected manner ; to bridle-up ; to prance ; to trip ; to toss the head ; to deck, dress up.—*n.* a prance ; a toss of the head, a caper.

Brankie, *adj.* finely dressed, gaudy, pranked-up.

Brankin, Branken, *ppl. adj.* lively, gay ; showy, ostentatious ; prancing.

Brankit, *ppl. adj.* vain, puffed-up.

Brankless, *adj.* unrestrained.

Brank-new, *adj.* quite new.

Branks, *v.* to put on the 'branks'; to halter, bridle.

Branlie, Branlin, *n.* the samlet or parr.

Brann, *n.* a boar-pig. Cf. Brawn.

Brannie, *n.* a brindled cow. Cf. Brandie.

Brannit, Bran'it, *ppl. adj.* brindled. Cf. Branded.

Brannock, *n.* a young salmon.

Branstickle, *n.* the three-spined stickleback. Cf. Brandstickle.

Brash, *n.* a sudden gust, shower, or thunder-peal ; a short turn at work ; a short but severe attack of illness ; an effort ; an attack.—*v.* to assault, bruise ; to break bones ; to belch acrid liquid into the mouth.

Brash, *n.* broken bits, fragments, pieces.

Brash, *v.* to rush headlong.

Brash-bread, *n.* bread made from a mixture of oats and rye.

Brashloch, *n.* rubbish ; a mixed crop of oats and rye, or of barley and rye.

Brashnoch, *n.* the wild mustard.

Brashy, *adj.* weak ; of delicate constitution ; subject to frequent ailments.

Brashy, *adj.* noisy ; stormy ; rugged.

Brass, *n.* money ; effrontery.

Brassle, *v.* to work hurriedly.—*n.* a rush, start. Cf. Braissil.

Brassy, *n.* a golf-club shod with brass on the sole.

Brassy, *n.* the fish wrasse or 'old wife.' Cf. Bressie.

Brast, *v. pret.* burst.

Brastle, *n.* a push ; an encounter ; a wrestle.

Brat, *n.* clothing in general ; a child's pinafore ; a coarse kind of apron ; a bib ; a rag ; scum, floatings of whey ; the glazed skin of porridge or flummery.

Brat, *n.* a cloth put on a ewe to prevent copulation.—*v.* to cover the hinder part of a ewe.

Brat, *n.* a child, used in contempt or disparagement.

Bratch, *n.* a bitch-hound.

Bratchel, *n.* a heap of flax-husks set on fire.

Bratchet, Bratchart, *n.* a pert, mischievous child ; a silly person ; a true lover.

Bratchie, *n.* india-rubber.

Brath, *v.* to plait straw-ropes on the thatch of a stack or house.

Brathins, *n.* the cross-ropes on the thatch of a stack or house.

Bratt, *n.* an apron, bib ; scum. Cf. Brat.

Brattice, Brattish, *n.* a wooden partition between rooms.

Brattie, *n.* a small apron : a shepherd's plaid.

Brattie-string, *n.* an apron-string.

Bratting, *ppl.* covering a ewe with a cloth to prevent copulation.

Brattle, *n.* a loud, clattering noise ; the crash of thunder or of a storm ; a sudden start ; a short race ; a noisy fray.—*v.* to make a loud rattling or crashing sound ; to run quickly, to hurry ; used of a stream : to flow tumultuously and noisily ; to peal as thunder.

Bratty, *adj.* ragged.

Braughtin, *n.* green cheese parings or wrought-curd, kneaded with butter or suet, and broiled in the frying-pan. Cf. Brughtin.

Braul, *v.* to shake.

Braun, *n.* a boar-pig. Cf. Brawn.

Brauner, *n.* a gelt pig.

Brauny, *adj.* brindled. Cf. Brandie.

Brave, *adj.* handsome ; goodly, fine ; used also ironically ; considerable, great.—*adv.* capitally, in first-rate style. Cf. Braw.

Brave and, *adv. phr.* very, exceedingly.

Bravelies, *adv.* very well, finely, prosperously.

Bravely, *adv.* very well, satisfactorily, prosperously; in good health.

Braverie, *n.* a bravado; show, splendour; fine clothes, showy dress; fine or ornate language.

Bravity, *n.* courage, bravery; fine show, display, finery.

†Bravoora, *n.* a mad-like degree of irritation or fury in man and beast.

Braw, *adj.* fine, gaily dressed; handsome; pleasant, agreeable; worthy, excellent; very good, surpassing in any respect; stout, able-bodied.—*n.* in *pl.* fine clothes; wedding-clothes.

Braw and, *adv. phr.* very, exceedingly.

Brawchton, *n.* anything weighty or unwieldy.

Brawd, *n.* a large, clumsy article.

Brawl, *v.* to gallop.

Brawlies, Brawlins, *adv.* well, finely; in good health, fairly well.

Brawlins, *n.* the trailing strawberry-tree, or bearberry.

Brawly, *adv.* well, finely; in good health.—*adj.* grand, splendid.

Brawn, *n.* the calf of the leg.

Brawn, *n.* a boar-pig.

Brawn-burdened, *adj.* having sturdy calves or legs.

Brawner, *n.* a gelt boar.

Brawnit, *adj.* brindled.

Brawny, *adj.* brindled.—*n.* a brindled bull, cow, or ox; a name given to such an animal. Cf. Brannie.

Brawsome, *adj.* rather 'braw'; comely.

Braw-warld, *adj.* showy, gaudy.

Braxy, *n.* an internal inflammation in sheep; a sheep that has died of 'braxy' or other natural death; the flesh of such sheep; diseased mutton; food of any kind.

Bray, *v.* to press, squeeze; to shove, push.—*n.* a squeeze.

Bray, *n.* a 'brae,' hill.

Brayie, *adj.* hilly. Cf. Braeie.

Braze, *n.* the roach. Cf. Braise.

Brazed, *ppl. adj.* brazened; hardened to effrontery.

Breach, *n.* broken water on the seashore.

Bread, *n.* a roll; a loaf; oatcake.

Bread, *n.* breadth; a breadth of material. Cf. Braid.

Breadberry, *n.* children's pap.

Bread-kit, *n.* a kit in which fishermen carry provisions to sea.

Breadlings, *adv.* with the flat side of a sword, &c.

Bread-meal, *n.* the flour of peas and barley.

Bread-morning, *n.* bread which a labourer takes with him when going to work in the morning; morning 'piece.'

Bread-spaad, *n.* an iron spattle for turning bread on the gridiron.

Breadth, *n.* a row of potatoes, &c.

Bread-turner, *n.* a wooden spattle for turning bannocks on the gridiron.

Break, *n.* a piece of ground broken up; a division of land on a farm; a furrow in ploughing; a breach; the breaking waves on the shore; a heavy fall of rain or snow; a large harrow; a hollow in a hill; an instrument for taking the rind off flax; the turning-point of a road or hill; failure, bankruptcy.

Break, *n.* a large number, a crowd.

Break, *v.* to prepare land for cultivation or for a particular crop in rotation; to become bankrupt; to cut up, carve; to 'burgle'; to open a full bottle; to begin spending; to change money; to set out or run off briskly; to defeat; to cause a breach of the peace; to begin to use a store of food, &c.; to disappoint, deny, refuse; to sell by retail; to break the skin, abrade; to spread manure; to lower prices or wages; used of milk: to curdle; of sheep or cattle: to break fences or stray; to trample down and destroy crops.

Break an egg, *phr.* to strike one curling-stone with another with just force enough to crack an egg on contact.

Break-back, *n.* the harvest moon, so called by harvest labourers because of the additional work it entails.

Break bread, *v.* to taste food, to breakfast; to deprive one of means of subsistence.

Break breath, *v.* to utter a sound.

Break down, *v.* of the weather: to become wet or stormy.

Breaker, *n.* one who carves a fowl or cuts up a carcass; a retailer, one who sells goods in small quantities; a large, hard marble for throwing; a red-clay marble.

Break-faith, *adj.* perfidious, treacherous.

Break-fur, *v.* to plough roughly so as to lay the upturned furrow over the uncut furrow. —*n.* such rough ploughing.

Break-heart, *n.* heart-break.

Breaking bread on the bride's head, *phr.* breaking the 'infar' cake on the bride's head as she crosses the threshold of her new home.

Breaking of bread, *n.* breakfast; the spoiling of one's prospects.

Breakings, *n.* the remains of a feast, broken meats.

Break-off, *v.* a type-casting term; to discharge wind from the stomach.—*n.* the turning-point of a road or hill.

Break one's day, *phr.* to take a holiday or part of one; to interrupt one's daily work.

Break out, *v.* to bring new ground under cultivation; of the skin: to have a rash, sores, &c.

Break out fine, *phr.* used of the weather: to clear-up.

Breakshough, *n.* the dysentery in sheep. Cf. Braxy.

Break-the-barn, *n.* a child's name for one of the fingers.

Break the ground, *phr.* to open a grave.

Break the weather, *v.* to bring about a change in the weather, said of a cat washing its face with its paws.

Break up, *v.* of the weather: to change; to open an ecclesiastical meeting with a sermon; to break into, as a burglar.

Break upon, *v.* to change money; to draw on one's savings, &c.

Break with the full hand, *phr.* to make a fraudulent bankruptcy.

Breard, *v.* to sprout.—*n.* the first appearance of germination. Cf. Braird.

Breards, *n.* the short flax recovered from the first tow by a second heckling.

Breast, *n.* the front, the forepart; the part of a peat-moss from which peats are cut; a step or layer in a manure-heap; in *phr.* 'in a breast,' abreast, side by side.

Breast, *v.* to mount a horse, wall, &c. by applying one's breast to it; to get up; to spring up or forward; to cut peats horizontally; to overcome a difficulty; to swallow an affront; to believe a wonder; used of a bride and bridegroom: to face the minister at a marriage.

Breast-beam, *n.* a beam in a handloom, reaching up to the weaver's breast.

Breast-bore, *n.* a wimble.

Breast-knot, *n.* a 'knot' of ribbons worn on the breast.

Breast-peat, *n.* a peat formed by a horizontal push of the spade into the perpendicular face of the moss.

Breast-spade, *n.* a peat-spade pushed forward with the breast.

Breast-woodie, *n.* the harness round the breast of a horse.

Breath, *n.* opinion; sentiments, tendency of thought; a moment.

Breath-bellows, *n.* the lungs.

Breathe, *v.* to give a horse time to recover breath.

Breathin', *n.* an instant of time.

Brecham, Brechan, Brechom, *n.* the collar of a working horse; an untidy piece of dress; a wrap for the neck. Cf. Braichum.

Brechan, *n.* a Highland plaid.

Brechin, *n.* the harness round the hinder-part of a horse, the breeching; in *phr.* 'to hang in the brechin,' to lag behind. Cf. Britchin.

Breck, *n.* barren ground in or near a township.

Breck, *v.* to break; to become insolvent.

Breckan, *n.* a brake; a fern.

Brecks, *n.* a piece of cloth sewed across the tail of a ewe, and extending about six inches down the hips on each side.

Breckshaw, *n.* the dysentery in sheep, 'braxy.'

Bred, *n.* a board, plank; the lid of a pot or pan; the board of a book; the offertory-plate.

Breder, *n.* brethren.

Bree, *n.* liquor, whisky, ale, &c.; moisture of any kind; water in which any article of food is boiled, broth, soup, gravy, sauce, juice.— *v.* to pour water on articles of food to be boiled; to drain solids that have been boiled; to brew. Cf. Broo.

Bree, *n.* a disturbance, fuss, hurry; bustle; the brunt.

Bree, *n.* the brow; the eyebrow.

Breears, *n.* the eyelashes.

Breech, *v.* to flog on the breech; to tuck the skirts above the knee, to 'kilt the coats'; to put in trousers. Cf. Breek.

Breed, *v.* to educate, train, bring up.—*n.* a brood, a litter.

Breed, *n.* bread.

Breed, *v.* to resemble, take after. Cf. Braid.

Breed, *n.* breadth.

Breeder, *n.* brethren; brother.

Breeding, *n.* education; good-breeding.

Breeds, *n.* the pancreas.

Breef, *n.* an irresistible spell. Cf. Brief.

Breeghle, *v.* to waddle and bustle about work, like a small person; to do little work with a great fuss.

Breeghlin, *n.* motion with much bustle and little result.

Breeid, *n.* a curch; a fine linen handkerchief worn by married women on their heads with a flap hanging down their backs, peculiar to the Hebrides.

Breeirs, *n.* eyelashes. Cf. Breears.

Breek, *n.* the leg of a trouser; in *pl.* trousers, breeches.—*v.* to put into breeches; to don the trousers; used of female labourers: to tuck up the skirts to facilitate working in rainy weather; to flog.

Breek-band, *v.* to lay hold of the band of the breeches; to wrestle.

Breek-bandit, *n.* a wrestling-match.

Breek-brother, *n.* a rival in love.

Breekens, *n.* breeches.

Breek-folk, *n.* the male sex.

Breekies, *n.* a young boy's breeches.

Breekies, *n.* the half-grown roe of the haddock.

Breek-knees, *n.* knee-breeches.

Breeklan, *ppl. adj.* shabby in appearance, in person, or in dress.

Breekless, *adj.* without breeches, wearing a kilt.

Breek-pouch, *n.* trousers-pocket.

Breekum, *n.* a person of short stature ; in *pl.* knee-breeches ; short ' breeks.'

Breekumstoich, *n.* a short, thick child in ' breeks.'

Breekum trullie, *n.* one whose breeches do not fit him ; a very little boy too young to wear breeches.

Breel, *v.* to move rapidly ; to make a noise ; to reel.

Breelish, *n.* whisky in its strong ale stage.

†Breells, *n.* spectacles ; double-jointed spectacles ; eyeglasses.

Breem, *n.* broom.

Breem, *adj.* keen, fierce, violent, bleak.

Breem, *v.* of a sow : to desire the boar, to copulate. Cf. Brim.

Breenge, *v.* to move impetuously. Cf. Braindge.

Breenging, *n.* a severe beating, an assault.

Breer, Breerd, *v.* to sprint ; to sprout, to spring up, to 'braird.'—*n.* the first sprouting of a crop. Cf. Braird.

Breer, *n.* a briar.

Breerie, *adj.* full of briars ; sharp, smart, clever. Cf. Briary.

Breers, *n.* the eyelashes ; in *phr.* ' to draw the breers owre ane's een,' to hoodwink one.

Brees, *n.* the 'broose' raced for at a wedding. Cf. Broose.

Breese, *n.* sandstone chippings ; crushed sandstone, for strewing on the floor.

†Breese, *v.* to bruise.—*n.* a bruise.

Breese, *v.* to come on in a hurry.—*n.* a broil ; a blow, stroke.

Breese, *n.* brose ; porridge made with various ingredients.

Breeshle, Breesil, *v.* to come on in a hurry ; to rustle.—*n.* a hurried advance ; an onset ; a rapid descent.

Breest, *n.* the breast. Cf. Breast.

Breet, *n.* a brute, contemptuously applied to a person.

Breeth, *n.* breadth.

Breether, *n.* a brother ; brethren.

Breether, *n.* corn in the seed-leaf.—*v.* to germinate.

Breetner, *n.* an energetic worker.

Breeze, *n.* crushed sandstone. Cf. Breese.

Breeze, *v.* to bruise. Cf. Breese.

Breeze, *v.* to come on in a hurry.—*n.* a blow. Cf. Breese.

Breggan, *n.* an iron collar, for the neck of offenders, fastened by a chain to a wall.

Bregwort, *n.* honey and ale fermented together. Cf. Bragwort.

Breid, *n.* bread. Cf. Bread.

Breid, *v.* to educate. Cf. Breed.

Breid, *v.* to resemble, take after. Cf. Braid.

Breid, *adj.* broad.—*n.* breadth ; a breadth. Cf. Braid.

Breif, *n.* a spell, charm. Cf. Brief.

Brein, *v.* to roar. Cf. Brien.

Breinge, *v.* to move impetuously. Cf. Braindge.

Breird, *v.* to sprout. Cf. Braird.

Breird, *n.* the surface ; the top.

Breist, Breistie, *n.* the breast.

Breme, *n.* broom.

Breme-buss, *n.* a simpleton. Cf. Broom-buss.

Brenn, *v.* to burn.

Brent, *v. pret.* and *ppl.* burned.

Brent, *adj.* steep, difficult to ascend ; used of the forehead : lofty, unwrinkled ; straight, direct.—*adv.* directly, clearly.

Brent, *v.* to dart or spring suddenly and violently or fearlessly.—*n.* a sudden spring or bound.—*adv.* with a spring or bound.

Brent, *n.* spring (of the year).—*adj.* relating to the spring.

Brent, *n.* a doorpost.

Brent-brow, *n.* a smooth, high forehead.

Brent-browed, *adj.* forward, impudent.

Brent-fir, *n.* fir or pine dug out of bogs.

Brenth, *n.* breadth.

Brent-new, *adj.* quite new, 'spick and span.'

Brenty, *adj.* smooth, unwrinkled.

Bress, *n.* brass.

Bress, *n.* the chimney-piece ; the back of the fireplace. Cf. Brace.

Bressie, *n.* the fish wrasse or ' old wife.'

Brest, *v.* to burst. Cf. Brast.

Bretchin, *n.* a horse's breeching.

Brether, Brethir, *n.* brothers, brethren.

Breuk, *n.* a kind of boil. Cf. Bruick.

Breuk, *n.* the mark on the knees of a broken-kneed horse.

Breukie, *n.* a cant name for a smith's bellows. Cf. Brookie.

Brevity, *n.* fine show, display. Cf. Bravity.

Brew, *n.* soup, broth. Cf. Bree, Broo.

Brew, *n.* a good opinion. Cf. Broo.

Brew, *v.* to suspect ; to fear future evil ; to meditate mischief.

Brew-creesh, -tallon, -tauch, *n.* a duty paid formerly to a landlord for liberty to brew.

Brewis, *n.* broth, pottage.

Brewster-wife, *n.* a female publican.

Brey, *v.* to frighten.

Briary, *adj.* prickly, thorny ; sharp, clever, bold, restless.

Brichen, *n.* breeches.

Brich'en, *v.* to brighten.

Bricht, *adj.* bright.

Brichten, *v.* to brighten.

Brichtie, Bricht-lintie, *n.* the chaffinch.

Brick, *n.* an oblong loaf of bread of various sizes.

Brick, *n.* a breach ; a distinct portion of land. Cf. Break.

Bricker, *n.* a boy's marble made of brick-clay, a large marble.

Brickit, *ppl. adj.* used of sheep: particoloured. Cf. Brockit.

Brickle, *adj.* brittle, fragile. Cf. Bruckle.

Bridder, *n.* a brother. Cf. Brither.

Bridal-bread, *n.* bread broken over a bride's head, and scrambled for, after the marriage.

Bridal-potion, *n.* a drink formerly given at the 'bedding' of the bride and bridegroom.

Bridal-wife, *n.* a newly-married wife.

Bride-bed, *n.* the bridal-bed.

Bride-bun, *n.* a wedding-cake, formerly broken over the bride's head.

Bride-day, *n.* the wedding-day.

Bride's-knots, *n.* ribbons worn at a wedding.

Bride's-pie, *n.* a pie of which the contents were contributed by neighbours, and which served as a bride-cake at penny-weddings.

Bride-stool, *n.* the pew in the church reserved for those who were to be married.

Bridie, *n.* a beef or mutton pie with gravy in it.

Bridle, *n.* the head of a plough; the piece of iron fastened to the end of the beam of a plough, to which the harness is attached.—*v.* to modify; to rope a stack, thatch a roof.

Bridle-renzie, *n.* a bridle-rein.

Bridling-ropes, *n.* ropes that hold down the thatch of a stack, &c.

Brie, *n.* in *phr.* 'to spoil the brie,' 'to upset the apple-cart.' Cf. Bree.

Brie, *v.* to crush, pound.—*n.* crushed sandstone for floors, &c.

Brie, *n.* the eyebrow. Cf. Bree.

Brief, *n.* a spell, a charm; a certificate, as of birth.

Brief, *adj.* keen, clever, apt; busy, bustling.

Brien, *v.* to roar, bellow.

Brier, *n.* an eyelash.

Brier-blade, *n.* the sprouting blade.

Brierd, Brier, *v.* to sprout.—*n.* the first or sprouting blade. Cf. Braird.

Briest, *v.* to breast.—*n.* a breast. Cf. Breast.

Brie-stone, *n.* sandstone or freestone for rubbing on a door-step, &c. Cf. Brie.

Brig, *n.* a bridge.—*v.* to bridge.

Brigancie, *n.* robbery, spoliation; brigandage.

†Briganer, Brigander, *n.* a robber, brigand; a rough, rude, boisterous person.

Briggie-stones, *n.* a pavement of flagstones.

Bril, *n.* the merry-thought of a fowl.

Brilch, *n.* a short, thickset, impudent person.

Briler, *n.* a particular kind of large marble.

Brim, *v.* of swine: to be in heat, to copulate. —*adj.* in heat.—*n.* a harlot, a trull. Cf. Breem.

Brim, *adj.* bleak, exposed to the weather.

Brime, *n.* brine, pickle; salt.

Brimful, *adj.* full of sorrow or anger.

Brimming, *ppl. adj.* used of a sow: in heat. Cf. Brumming.

Brimstane, *n.* sulphur; a term of abuse.

Brin, Brinn, *n.* a ray, flash, beam.—*v.* to burn. Cf. Brenn.

Brindal, Brindal-brass, Brindle, *n.* cash, money.

Bringle-brangle, *n.* a very confused bustle.

Brink, *n.* a river's bank.

Brinkie, Brinkum, *n.* a comely and lively person.

Brinkie-brow, *n.* a nursery term for the forehead.

Brinnage, *n.* the brunt of a fight.

Brinth, *n.* breadth. Cf. Brenth.

Brise, *v.* to bruise. Cf. Brize.

Brisken, *v.* to refresh, make or become livelier.

Briskie, Brisk-finch, *n.* the chaffinch.

Briss, *v.* to bruise. Cf. Brize.

Brissal, *adj.* brittle.

Brissel-cock, *n.* the turkey-cock.

Brissle, *v.* to broil, scorch. Cf. Birsle.

Bristow, *n.* a white crystal set in a ring; a Bristol diamond.

Brit, *n.* a brute.

Britchin, *n.* the portion of harness that passes round the hinder-part of a horse in shafts.

Brithell, *n.* a bridal, marriage. Cf. Braithel.

Brither, *n.* brother.—*v.* to match, pair; to initiate into a society or guild; with *down*, to accompany in being swallowed. Cf. Brother.

Brither-bairn, *n.* a cousin, an uncle's child.

Brither-dochter, *n.* a niece, a brother's daughter.

Brither-sin, *n.* a nephew, a brother's son.

Brittle, *v.* to render friable.—*adj.* shaky; on the verge of bankruptcy; difficult; ticklish.

Brittle-brattle, *n.* hurried motion with clattering noise. Cf. Brattle.

†Brize, Brizz, *v.* to bruise, crush, squeeze.— *n.* force, pressure. Cf. Birze.

Brizel'd, *ppl. adj.* bruised. Cf. Broizle.

Broach, *n.* a clasp.

Broach, *n.* a flagon or tankard.

Broach, *n.* a spit; the spindle or reel on which newly-spun yarn is wound; yarn so wound; a narrow, pointed iron chisel for hewing stones.—*v.* to rough-hew.

Broad-meal, *n.* barley-meal.

Broadside, *n.* in *phr.* 'at a broadside,' suddenly; unawares.

Broadsome, *adj.* broad.

Broak, *v.* to soil with soot; to streak with black or white. Cf. Brook.

Broakie, *n.* a cow with a black-and-white face; a person whose face is streaked with dirt. Cf. Brookie.

Broakit, *ppl. adj.* with black and white stripes; variegated; grimy. Cf. Brookit.

Broakitness, *n.* the condition of being 'broakit.'

Broath, *v.* to be in a state of perspiration. Cf. Broth.

Broble, *n.* a sharp-pointed piece of wood to keep horses apart in ploughing.

Broch, *n.* a narrow piece of wood or metal to support a stomacher.

Broch, *n.* a prehistoric structure, in shape a circular tower, supposed to be Pictish.

Broch, *n.* a halo round the sun or moon; the circle round the 'tee' in a curling-rink. Cf. Brugh.

Broch, *n.* a burgh, a town; the nearest town. Cf. Brugh.

Broch, *adj.* broken in small pieces. Cf. Brock.

Brochan, *n.* water-gruel, thin porridge made of oatmeal, butter, and honey.

Broch an' haimil, *phr.* proof; legal security. Cf. Brogh and hammel.

Broch-dweller, *n.* a dweller in a 'broch'; a Pict.

†**Broche**, *n.* a spit; a spindle; a mason's sharp-pointed chisel.—*v.* to indent with a 'broche.' Cf. Broach.

Brochle, *adj.* lazy, indolent.—*n.* a lazy fellow.

Brocht, *v. pret.* and *ppl.* brought.

Brock, *n.* a badger; an opprobrious epithet applied to a person.

Brock, *n.* a scrap of food; broken meats; rubbish, refuse, remnants; grass and bits of straw shaken out of corn after threshing. —*v.* to cut or crumble anything to shreds or small pieces.

Brock, *v.* to work unskilfully; to waste cloth in cutting.—*n.* work ill-done; an unskilful workman.

Brockage, *n.* fragments of crockery, biscuits, furniture, &c.

Brockan, *n.* unskilful working; the wasting of cloth in cutting-out.

Brockit, *ppl. adj.* variegated; with black and white stripes or spots. Cf. Brook.

Brocklie, *adj.* brittle. Cf. Bruckle.

Brock-skin, *n.* a badger's skin.

Brod, *n.* a board; a shutter; the lid of a pot or kettle; the cover or board of a book; the offertory-'plate' at the church-door; a piece of wood sprinkled with rough sand, used for whetting a scythe.—*v.* to cover with a lid; to put the lid on a pot, &c.

Brod, *n.* a goad; a short nail, a brad; a thorn, prickle; a stroke, stab, or push with a pointed instrument; a nudge, poke.—*v.* to goad, prick, pierce; to jog; to poke.

Brod, *n.* brood, breed.

Broddit-staff, *n.* a pike-staff; a staff with a sharp point. Cf. Broggit-staff.

Broddy, *adj.* used of a sow with a litter of pigs.

†**Brodequin**, *n.* a half-boot.

Brod-hen, *n.* a brood-hen, a sitting hen.

Brodie, *n.* the fry of the rock-tangle or kettle codling.

Brodmil, *n.* a brood.

Brod-mother, *n.* a brood-hen; the mother of a family.

Brod's-mother, *n.* a brood-hen.

Broe, *n.* broth. Cf. Bree.

Brog, *n.* a coarse shoe, a brogue.

Brog, *n.* a brad-awl; a boring instrument; a thrust with a stick, &c.; a sprig-bit; a poke with a boring instrument.—*v.* to prick, pierce; to goad; to incite.

Brogan, *n.* a coarse, light kind of shoe, made of horse-leather.

Broggit-staff, *n.* a staff with a sharp iron point; a pikestaff.

Broggle, Brogle, *v.* to prick.—*n.* a vain effort to strike with a pointed instrument.

Broggle, Brogle, *v.* to bungle, 'botch'; to cobble shoes, to vamp.—*n.* a bungler.

Broggler, *n.* one who fails to strike with a pointed instrument.

Broggler, *n.* a bad tradesman; a bungler.

Brogh, *n.* a burgh. Cf. Broch.

Brogh and hammel, -hammer, *phr.* proof, evidence; legal security; proof of legal possession.

Brogue, *n.* a trick, an 'off-take.'

Brogue-shod, *adj.* wearing brogues.

Brogwort, *n.* honey and ale fermented together. Cf. Bragwort.

Broigh, Broich, *v.* to pant and sweat profusely. —*n.* a state of violent perspiration and panting.

Broil, *v.* to be very warm and perspire profusely.—*n.* a state of heat and perspiration.

Broilerie, Broillerie, *n.* a state of contention; a struggle, broil.

Broilyie, *v.* to parboil, and then roast on a gridiron.

Broizle, *v.* to press, crush to atoms.

Brok, *n.* broken meat, fragments, rubbish, refuse.—*v.* to cut, crumble, or fritter into shreds or small pieces. Cf. Brock.

Broked, *ppl. adj.* variegated; streaked with black and white. Cf. Brook.

Broken, *ppl. adj.* bankrupt; curdled; churned; outlawed; vagabond.

Broken bottle, *n.* a bottle of which the contents have been broken upon.

Broken men, *n.* outlaws; robbers; men separated from their clans through crime, &c.

Broken-up, *ppl.* begun upon; broken upon.

Broker, *n.* a male flirt.

Broll, *n.* a drinking-pot.

Brollochan, *n.* a bivalve used for bait.

Bron, *n.* a brand or peat for burning, used as a torch or as a signal; a glowing cinder. Cf. Brenn.

Bronse, Bronze, *v.* to overheat one's self in a strong sun or too near a hot fire.

Broo, *n.* broth ; juice ; liquor ; snow-water. Cf. Bree.

Broo, *n.* inclination, liking ; good opinion.

Broo, *n.* the brow ; the part of a moss out of which peats are cut.

Broo-creesh, *n.* custom paid in tallow or kitchen-fee for liberty to brew. Cf. Brew-creesh.

Brood, *n.* a young child ; the youngest child of a family ; a goose that has hatched goslings.

Broody, *adj.* prolific; having a brood; fruitful, fecund.

Broofle, *v.* to be in a great hurry ; to toil and moil ; to be overheated by exertion.—*n.* impetuous haste. Cf. Bruffle.

Brook, *n.* a heap, gathering, or 'drift' of sea-ware, driven ashore.

Brook, *v.* to use, possess, enjoy ; to bear a name ; to grace, become. Cf. Bruik.

Brook, *v.* to soil with soot ; to dirty ; to become spotted, streaked.—*n.* soot adhering to pots, kettles, &c.

Brookable, *adj.* tolerable, bearable.

Brookie, *adj.* smutty, grimy, sooty, dirty.—*n.* a person whose face is smeared with dirt ; a blacksmith ; a cow with white hair on her face ; a child whose face is streaked with dirt.

Brookie-face, *n.* a person with a face streaked with dirt ; a blacksmith.

Brookie-faced, *adj.* sooty, smutty, having a dirty face.

Brookit, Brookt, *ppl. adj.* streaked with grime ; soiled with tears, &c. ; of cattle, sheep, &c. : speckled, streaked with black and white on the face, &c.

Broo-lan', *n.* steep ground.

Broom, *v.* to signal by a broom how many whales are taken.

Broom-buss, *n.* a broom-bush ; a simpleton.

Broom-cow, *n.* a broom or heather bush used to 'sweep' in curling.

Broom-deevil, -dog, *n.* an instrument for grubbing up broom, furze, &c.

Broom-thackit, *adj.* thatched with broom ; covered with broom.

Broon, *adj.* brown.—*n.* porter, ale.

Broonie, *n.* a benevolent household sprite. Cf. Brownie.

Broonie, *n.* a kind of wild bee.

Broo o' maut, *n.* whisky.

Broo-talloun, -tauch, *n.* a tax on brewing. Cf. Brew-creesh.

Broose, *n.* a race on horseback at a country wedding, from the church or the bride's house to the bridegroom's house.

Broost, *n.* a violent forward motion ; a spring.

Broostle, *n.* a state of great bustle ; an impetuous forward movement.—*v.* to be in a great bustle about little, to be in a great hurry.

Brooze, *v.* to browse.

Broozle, *v.* to perspire greatly from exertion.

Broozle, *v.* to press, squeeze, crush. Cf. Broizle.

Brose, *v.* to toil arduously.

Brose, *n.* oatmeal or peasemeal mixed with boiling water, milk, colewort, or the skimmed fat of soup, &c. ; porridge ; any ordinary article of food ; a meal.

Brose-caup, *n.* the wooden cup in which the ploughman made his brose ; the ploughman himself.

Brose-meal, *n.* meal of peas much parched, of which brose was made.

Brose-time, *n.* supper-time.

Brosilie, *adv.* in an inactive manner, sluggishly.

Brosiness, *n.* semi-fluidity ; softness and consequent inactivity.

Brosy, Brosey, *adj.* semi-fluid ; soft, inactive ; bedaubed with brose ; stout ; well-fed.—*n.* a very fat person.

Brosy-airt, *adj.* fat, inactive, heavy.

Brosy-faced, *adj.* having a fat, flaccid face.

Brosy-heidit, *adj.* fat, inactive, stupid.

Brosy-mou'd, *adj.* fat, stupid, slow of speech.

Brot, *n.* a name for the Pleiades.

Brot, *n.* a rag. Cf. Brat.

Brot, *n.* a tangle, muddle, bungle.—*v.* to entangle ; to quilt over ; to cobble ; to darn clumsily.

Brot, Brotach, *n.* a quilted cloth or covering used to keep the back of a horse from being ruffled by the 'shimach,' or straw mat, on which the panniers are hung, being fastened to a pack-saddle.

Brotag, *n.* the caterpillar of the drinker-moth or of the tiger-moth.

Brotch, *v.* to plait straw-ropes round a corn-stack.

Brotch, *n.* a clasp. Cf. Broach.

†Brotekins, *n.* buskins, half-boots. Cf. Brodequin.

Broth, *n.* in *phr.* 'a broth of a sweat,' a violent perspiration.—*v.* to be in a state of perspiration.

Brother, *v.* to inure, accustom, often by rough usage ; to initiate into a guild or citizenship, often by ludicrous means.—*n.* inurement ; rough usage ; exposure to rough weather.

Brotherin, *n.* rough usage ; initiation, proper and formal, or ludicrous.

Brottlet, *n.* a small coverlet.

Brotty, *adj.* ragged.

Brough, *n.* a halo round the sun or moon ; the circle round the 'tee' in a curling-rink. Cf. Brugh.

Brough, *n.* a town, a burgh. Cf. Brugh.
Broughan, *n.* water-gruel; thin porridge. Cf. Brochan.
Brouk, *v.* to soil with soot. Cf. Brook.
Brow, *n.* a hill, a steep slope, a peat-breast. —*v.* to force; to browbeat. Cf. Broo.
Brow, *n.* liking; favourable opinion. Cf. Broo.
Browden, *v.* to be fond of, warmly attached; to be set upon; to pet, pamper.—*adj.* fond of, warmly attached; petted.
Browdened, Browdent, *ppl. adj.* pampered; arrayed, decked.
Browhead, *n.* the forehead.
Browlies, *adj.* well; in good health. Cf. Brawlies.
Brown, *n.* ale or porter.—*adj.* used of soup: rich with animal juice; discontented; indifferent. Cf. Broon.
Brown-bill, *n.* a brown-painted halberd formerly borne by foot-soldiers and watchmen.
Brown cow, *n.* a liquor-jar.
Brown-cow's-lick, *n.* hair on a child's head standing almost erect, and resembling the marks cattle make on their skins by licking them.
Brown gled, *n.* the hen-harrier.
Brownie, *n.* a benevolent household sprite. Cf. Broonie.
Brownie, *n.* a kind of wild bee. Cf. Broonie.
Brownie-bae, *n.* a benevolent 'brownie.'
Brownie's-stone, *n.* an altar dedicated to a 'brownie.'
Brown-janet, *n.* a knapsack; a musket.
Brown-leamer, *n.* a nut ripe and ready to fall from the husk. Cf. Leamer.
Brown-swallow, *n.* the swift.
Brown-yogle, *n.* the short-eared owl.
Browst, *n.* a brewing, what is brewed at a time; an opportunity for drinking; a booze; the consequences of one's own acts; urine.
Browster, *n.* a brewer.
Browster-wife, *n.* an ale-wife.
Browten, *v.* to be fond of. Cf. Browden.
Broylie, *n.* a broil. Cf. Bruilyie.
Broyliement, *n.* a commotion.
Brub, *v.* to check, restrain, oppress.
Bruch, *n.* a halo round the sun or moon; the circle round the 'tee' in a curling-rink. Cf. Brugh.
Bruch, *n.* a town, burgh. Cf. Brugh.
Bruch, *n.* a prehistoric fortified structure credited to the Picts. Cf. Broch.
Brucher, *n.* a curling-stone lying within the circle round the 'tee' in a curling-rink. Cf. Brugher.
Bruchle, *v.* with *up*, to muffle or wrap up a person untidily.—*n.* wrapping up.
Bruchman. *n.* a burgher, citizen.

Bruchty, *adj.* dirty, soot-begrimed. Cf. Brook.
Bruck, *v.* to break in pieces.—*n.* broken meats; bits of wood; refuse; offals of fish, &c. Cf. Brock.
Bruck, *v.* to use, enjoy, possess; to bear a name. Cf. Brook.
Bruck, *v.* to soil with soot; to streak. Cf. Brook.
Bruckie, *adj.* grimy; speckled.—*n.* a blacksmith; a cow streaked with white. Cf. Brookie.
Bruckit, *ppl. adj.* striped; grimy. Cf. Brookit, Brockit.
Bruckle, *adj.* fragile, brittle, friable; uncertain, not to be relied on.—*v.* to crumble away.
Bruckleness, *n.* the state of being 'bruckle.'
Bruckles, *n.* the prickly-head carex; the bent-grass.
Bruckly, *adj.* brittle; used of the weather: uncertain, changeable.—*adv.* in a brittle manner or state.
Brude, *n.* a brood.
Brudy, Bruddy, *adj.* prolific. Cf. Broody.
Brue, *n.* brew; liquor; juice. Cf. Bree.
Bruff, *v.* to clothe thickly.
Bruffle, *v.* to be in a great hurry; to toil and moil; to be overheated by exertion or excitement; to work clumsily.—*n.* impetuous haste; a bungler, botcher. Cf. Broofle.
Brugh, *n.* a halo round the sun or moon; the circle round the 'tee' in a curling-rink.
Brugh, *n.* a town, burgh.
Brugh and hammer, *phr.* proof; legal security. Cf. Brogh and hammel.
Brugher, *n.* a curling-stone lying within the circle round the 'tee.'
Brughle, *v.* to exert one's self violently and be overheated. Cf. Bruffle.
Brughtin, Brughtin-cake, *n.* green cheese parings, or wrought curd, kneaded with butter or suet, broiled in a frying-pan, and eaten with bread.
Brughtins, *n.* an oatcake or bannock toasted, crumbled down, put into a pot over the fire with butter, and made into a sort of porridge, for shepherds at the Lammas Feast.
Bruick, *n.* a boil, a tumour.
Bruick-boil, *n.* a swelling of the glands under the arm.
†Bruik, *v.* to stitch, embroider.
Bruik, Bruick, *v.* to enjoy, possess. Cf. Brook.
†Bruil, Bruillie, *n.* a broil; a quarrel.
†Bruilyie, Bruilzie, *v.* to fight; to get engaged in a broil.—*n.* a quarrel; a disturbance; a broil.
Bruilyie, *v.* to broil; to heat; to be in a ferment.

Bruind, *v.* to emit sparks. Cf. Brund.

Bruise, *v.* to jam, squeeze.

Bruistle, Bruizle, *v.* to bustle about; to crush to atoms.—*n.* a bustle; a keen chase. Cf. Broostle, Broozle.

Bruke, *v.* to soil with soot; to streak with dirt. Cf. Brook.

Bruk-kneed, *adj.* broken-kneed.

Brulie, *v.* to fight. Cf. Bruilyie.

Brulie, Brulye, Brulzie, *v.* to fight.—*n.* disturbance. Cf. Bruilyie.

Brulyie, *v.* to broil; to heat; to be overcome with heat. Cf. Bruilyie.

Brulyiement. *n.* a disturbance, a broil; commotion.

Brumble, *v.* to make a hollow, murmuring sound, as rushing water.

Brume, *n.* the broom.

Brummel, Brummle, n. the blackberry, bramble.

Brummel, *v.* to 'brumble.'

Brummin, *ppl. adj.* of a sow: in heat. Cf. Brim.

Brumple, *n.* the viviparous blenny.

Brumstane, *n.* brimstone.

Brumstane-candle, *n.* a match made of brimstone and paper to suffocate bees.

Brun, *n.* the brow of a hill.

Brund, *n.* a vestige, portion.

Brund, *v.* to flash; to emit sparks; to see 'stars' owing to a heavy blow on the head; used of the eye: to sparkle, to glance; to be angry.—*n.* a brand for burning; a spark of fire.

Brung, *v. pret.* and *ppl.* brought.

Brungle, *n.* a job, trick; a knavish piece of business.

Brunstane, *n.* brimstone. Cf. Brumstane.

Brunstickle, *n.* the stickleback.

Brunt, *v. pret.* burned.—*ppl.* burnt; used of a curling-stone: illegally touched or played; taken-in in a bargain; cheated; tricked. Cf. Burn.

Brunt, *adj.* keen, eager, ardent.

Brunt-crust, *n.* a 'played-out' person.

Bruntie, *n.* a blacksmith.

Bruntlin, *n.* a burnt moor.—*adj.* belonging to a burnt moor.

Bruse, *n.* the race at a wedding.—*v.* to strive in any way. Cf. Broose.

Bruse, *n.* a brew-house.

Brush, *n.* vigorous exercise of any kind; a determined effort for a short time; a struggle, tussle.

Brush, *v.* to beat, thrash.

Brush, *v.* with *up*, to smarten, 'titivate.'

Brushie, *adj.* smartly dressed, fond of dress.

Bruskness, *n.* brusqueness; freedom of speech or manner.

Brussen, *ppl.* burst.

Brussle, *v.* to rush forward in rude or disorderly fashion.—*n.* bustle. Cf. Broostle.

Brust, *v.* to burst. Cf. Brast.

Brusten, *ppl.* burst.

Brustle, *v.* to dry, parch, scorch, to 'birsle.' Cf. Brissle.

Brustle, *v.* to bustle about; to crush to atoms.—*n.* a keen chase. Cf. Broostle.

Brutch, *n.* the spindle or reel on which newly spun yarn is wound. Cf. Broach.

Brutify, *v.* to make a beast of one's self.

Brye, *n.* powdered sandstone, used for scouring. Cf. Brie-stone.

Brylies, *n.* bearberries. Cf. Brawlins.

Bryttle, *v.* to cut up or carve venison.

Bu, *n.* a sound made to cause terror; a bugbear; a hobgoblin. Cf. Bo.

Bu, *n.* a bull. Cf. Boo.

Bu, *v.* to talk noisily; to roar; used of cattle: to low. Cf. Boo.

Buat, *n.* a lantern. Cf. Bouet.

Bub, *n.* a blast, a gust.

Bubbies, Bubies, n. the breasts.

Bubblan, *n.* tippling, toping.

Bubble, *v.* to discharge nasal mucus; to 'snivel,' 'blubber,' weep.—in *pl.* nasal mucus, snot.

Bubbly, *adj.* dirty, tear-stained; snotty.

Bubbly-jock, *n.* a turkey-cock.

Bubbly-nosed, *adj.* having a dirty, snotty nose.

Buccar, *n.* a fast-sailing smuggling craft. Cf. Bikker.

Buchan-sergeant, *n.* a skim-milk cheese.

Buchan-vittal, *n.* meal consisting of two-thirds oats and one-third of barley; a person on whom no reliance can be placed.

Bucharet, *n.* the swift.

Bucht, *n.* a curve, a bend, the curve of elbow or knee; a coil of fishing-lines.—*v.* to fold down. Cf. Boucht.

Bucht, *n.* a sheep- or cattle-fold; a sheep-pen; a house for sheep at night; a square pew in a church.—*v.* to fold or pen sheep. Cf. Boucht.

Buchted, *ppl. adj.* enclosed; sheltered.

Bucht-flake, *n.* a hurdle at the entrance to a sheep-pen.

Buck, *n.* the body; the carcass of an animal. Cf. Bouk.

Buck, *n.* the beech-tree.

Buck, *v.* to butt, push.—*adv.* vigorously, with force.

Buck, *v.* of water: to gush out, pour forth; to gurgle when poured from a strait-necked bottle.

Buck, *n.* lye made from cow-dung, stale urine, or wood-ashes, for washing clothes.—*v.* to wash clothes in lye. Cf. Bouk.

Buck, *n.* the sound made by a stone falling into water.—*v.* to gulp in swallowing.

Buck, *n.* walking over the same ground repeatedly ; crowding.—*v.* to walk on the same ground repeatedly ; to crowd ; to walk with stately step.

Buckalee, *n.* a call to negligent herd-boys, who allow the cows to eat the corn : 'Buckalee, buckalo, buckabonnie, buckabo ; a fine bait among the corn—what for no'?'

Buckan, *n.* the act of walking or crowding.

Buck and crune, *phr.* to show extreme solicitude to possess anything.

Buckartie-boo, *v.* to coo as a pigeon.

Buckaw, *n.* the short game which concludes a curling match or 'bonspiel.'

Buck-bean, *n.* the common trefoil. Cf. Bogbean.

Buck-beard, *n.* a hard, whitish moss found growing on rocks, often in the shape of a wine-glass or inverted cone.

Bucker, *v.* to rustle ; to wear rich, rustling clothes ; to move or work fussily or awkwardly.—*n.* the rustling of paper, silk, &c.; noisy bustle ; annoyance ; an awkward, noisy person.

Bucker, *n.* a name given in the west of Scotland to a species of whale.

Bucker, *n.* a native of Buckie in Banffshire ; a person from the south coast of the Moray Firth ; a boat of a special build used on the Moray Firth coast.

Buckerin, *n.* rustling ; fuss.—*ppl. adj.* fussy, awkward.

Bucket, *n.* a cant name for a glass of spirits.

Bucketie, *n.* weavers' paste.

Buckie, *n.* the sea-snail, or its shell ; any spiral shell ; a periwinkle ; a trifle of no value.

Buckie, *n.* a child's rattle made of rushes.

Buckie, *n.* the fruit of the wild-rose.

Buckie, *n.* a smart blow or push.—*v.* to strike or push roughly ; to walk hurriedly.—*adv.* violently.

Buckie, *n.* a refractory person ; a mischievous boy.

Buckie, *n.* the hind-quarters of a hare.

Buckiean, *n.* the act of striking.—*ppl. adj.* pushing, bouncing.

Buckie-berries, *n.* the fruit of the wild-rose.

Buckie-brier, *n.* the wild-rose.

Buckie-brow, *n.* a projecting or beetling brow.

Buckie-faalie, -faulie, *n.* the primrose.

Buckie-ingram, *n.* the crab.

Buckie-man, *n.* a seller of periwinkles.

Buckie-prin, *n.* a periwinkle.

Buckie-ruff, *n.* a wild, giddy boy ; a romping girl.

Buckie-tyauve, *n.* a struggle ; a good-humoured struggle or wrestling-match.

Bucking, *n.* the sound of water escaping through a narrow neck.

Bucking-basket, *n.* a clothes-basket ; a buck-basket.

Buckise, *n.* a smart stroke.—*v.* to beat with smart strokes.

Buckle, *n.* a tussle, a 'pretended struggle.—*v.* to wrap in or round ; to bandage ; to secure, mend ; to marry ; to join in marriage ; to bend, twist, warp ; to quarrel, struggle, attack, meddle with ; to apply one's self to work.

†**Buckle,** *n.* a curl, curliness.

Buckle-beggar, Buckle-the-beggars, *n.* one who marries persons clandestinely or in irregular fashion ; a hedge-parson ; a Gretna Green parson.

Buckle-horned, *adj.* perverse, headstrong, obstinate.

Buckle-to, *v.* to set to work ; to join in marriage.

Buckle with, *v.* to assail, grapple with ; to have the worst in an argument ; to be engaged in a business so as to be at a loss to finish it.

Bucksturdie, *adj.* obstinate.

Bucky, *n.* the sluice of a mill-pond.

Bud, *n.* a bribe.—*v.* to bribe.

Bud, Bude, *v.* must, had to. Cf. Boost.

Bud-be, *n.* a necessary duty devolving on any one.

Budden, *ppl.* bidden, invited.

Budder, *v.* to trouble, bother.

Buddy, *n.* a pet designation of a little child ; a 'bodie.'

Budget, *n.* a workman's wallet.

Budna, *v.* must not, could not, might not. Cf. Bud.

Bue, *v.* to low as a bull. Cf. Boo.

†**Buff,** *v.* to beat, buffet ; to strike with a soft substance ; to emit a dull, soporific sound ; to thresh corn ; to half-thresh grain ; to lose by a bargain.—*n.* a blow, buffet ; a blow in challenge to fight ; any dull, soporific sound ; the sound of a blow with a soft substance, or of anything that falls. Cf. Boof.

Buff, *v.* to bark gently ; to burst out laughing. —*n.* nonsense.—*int.* an excl. of contempt for what another has said. Cf. Bouff.

Buff, *n.* of time : a while.

Buff, *n.* the skin.

Buff, *v.* used of herrings : to steep salted herrings in water and hang them up.

†**Buff,** *n.* a puff or blast of wind ; a fuss, outcry ; an ado.

Buffer, *n.* a dolt ; a 'fellow'; used half-contemptuously, as 'chap.'

Buffet, *v.* in *phr.* 'buffet the boar,' a boys' game.

†**Buffets,** *n.* a swelling in the glands of the neck, mumps.

Buffet-stool, *n.* a stool with sides, like a square table with leaves folded down.

†**Buffie, Buffle,** *adj.* fat, chubby; pursed; shaggy, dishevelled.

Buffle, *v.* to confuse, perplex; to baffle.

†**Buffle-headit,** *adj.* large-headed; dull of comprehension.

Bufflin', *ppl. adj.* of boys: wandering, unsettled; roving.

Buff nor sty, *phr.* nothing whatever; not the smallest part.

Buft, *ppl. adj.* of standing corn: having the ears eaten by birds, or shaken by wind, or wasted by a prolonged harvest; shorn; half-shorn.

Bug, *v. pret.* built. Cf. Big.

Bug, *n.* in *phr.* 'let bug,' to give sign, to 'let on.'

Bugaboo, *n.* a hobgoblin.

Bugars, *n.* the rafters of a house. Cf. Bougars.

Bugge, *n.* a bogey, bugbear.

Buggen, *ppl.* built. Cf. Big.

Bugger, Buggar, *v.* to imprecate in vile language.—*n.* a contemptuous term used in vile imprecation.

Buggery, *n.* in *phr.* 'to play buggery,' 'to play the mischief.'

Buggle, *n.* a bog, morass.

Bught, *n.* a curve, bend; the hollow of the elbow or knee; a coil of fishing-lines; a ribbon-bow.—*v.* to fold down. Cf. Boucht.

Bught, *n.* a sheep- or cattle-fold; a sheep-pen; a house for sheep at night; a square pew with table in a church; a small bag to hold comfits.—*v.* to fold or pen sheep; to pen ewes for milking. Cf. Boucht.

Bughted-glade, *n.* a winding glade.

Bugle, *v.* of bulls: to bellow; of cocks: to crow.—*n.* a cock's crow.

Buick, *v. pret.* curtsied. Cf. Beck.

Buik, *n.* the body; size. Cf. Bouk.

Buik, *v. pret.* baked. Cf. Beuk.

Buik, *n.* a book; the Bible. Cf. Beuk.

Buik-lare, *n.* learning; schooling.

Buik-leared, *adj.* book-learned, educated.

Build, *v.* to pile or stack sheaves or peats.

†**Builyie,** *n.* a quandary, perplexity.

Buind, *n.* a band of reapers or peat-cutters. Cf. Boon.

Buird, *n.* a board.

Buirdly, *adj.* stalwart, goodly, fine-looking, well-made.

Buise, *n.* a cow's stall; a crib. Cf. Boose.

Buise, *n.* in *phr.* 'to shoot the buise,' ? to 'swing,' to be hanged.

Buist, *n.* a box, chest; a coffin; a large meal-chest; a receptacle; the match for a fire-lock; a thick or gross object; stays; a bodice.—*v.* to enclose.

Buist, *v. pret.* must, had to. Cf. Boost.

Buist, *v.* to mark cattle and sheep with tar, to brand.—*n.* a branding-iron, an instrument for marking sheep; a tar-mark of ownership on sheep or cattle.

Buisting-iron, *n.* the instrument used in marking sheep, &c.

Buist-maker, *n.* a coffin-maker.

Buisty, *n.* a bed; a nest; an animal's lair.

Buit, *n.* a 'buist,' a box; a firelock-match. Cf. Buist.

Buit, *n.* a boot.

Buith, *n.* a booth.

Buittle, *v.* to walk ungracefully, taking short, bouncing steps.

Bukat, *n.* a male salmon. Cf. Bykat.

Buke, *v. pret.* baked.

Buke, *n.* the body; bulk. Cf. Bouk.

Buke, *n.* a book; the Bible.

Bukk, *v.* to incite, instigate.

Bukkar, *n.* a large, heavy-armed lugger used in smuggling. Cf. Bikker.

Bukker, *n.* vexation, annoyance.

Bulb, Bulboch, *n.* a disease of sheep causing them to drink until they swell and burst.

Bulch, *n.* a stout person or animal. Cf. Bilch.

Bulder, *n.* a loud gurgling noise; a bellowing. —*v.* to make a gurgling sound as of water rushing to and fro in the cavity of a rock, or passing through a narrow pipe which emits an echo; to gush out; to bellow.

Bule, *v.* to weep. Cf. Bool.

Bule, *n.* the curved handle of a pot. Cf. Bool.

Bulf, Bulfart, *n.* a fat, pursy person; a fat child.

Bulfie, *adj.* dull, stupid.—*n.* a stout, fat boy; used as a nickname for such a boy.

Bulfin, *n.* a very stout person.

Bulgan's Day, *n.* July 4th, the feast of St Martin. Cf. Bullion's Day.

Bulger, *n.* a boy's large marble.

Bulk, *v.* to play marbles.

Bulker, *n.* the puffin. Cf. Bouger.

Bulkie, *n.* a game in which marbles are placed in a row, and each player has two chances.

Bulkie, *n.* a policeman.

Bulkish, *adj.* bulky.

Bull, *n.* the bar or beam of a harrow.

Bull, *n.* in *phr.* 'the black bull of Norroway,' an imaginary monster.—*v.* to desire the bull; to serve a cow; with *in*, to swallow hastily.

Bulla, *n.* a brother; a comrade. Cf. Billy.

Bullace, *n.* an axe.

Bullament, *n.* odds and ends of any kind. Cf. Bulyiement.

Bullax, *n.* a hatchet.

Bullax-vright, *n.* a clumsy, unskilful wright.

Bull-beef, *n.* in *phr.* 'as proud as bull-beef,' proud, conceited.

Bull-beggar, *n.* a scarecrow.

Bull-daisy, *n.* a wild orchis.
Buller, *v.* to make a gurgling or rattling noise; to stutter in speech; to gush out; to bellow, roar.—*n.* a loud, gurgling noise; a bellowing. Cf. Bulder.
Bullet, *n.* a boulder.
Bullet-stane, *n.* a round stone, used as a bullet for throwing along the highway in the game of 'lang bullet.'
Bull-fit, *n.* a swift; a martin.
Bull-french, *n.* a bullfinch.
Bull-head, *n.* a tadpole.
Bullie, *n.* the bullfinch.
Bullie, *v.* to speak, call, or weep loudly.—*n.* a loud cry, weeping, roaring. Cf. Bool.
Bulliean, *n.* a loud raising of the voice.
Bulligrubs, *n.* a colic.
Bulliheisle, Bulliheizilie, Bulliehislee, *n.* a boys' game, in which it is attempted to throw on the ground all the boys standing close in a line; a scramble; a squabble.
†Bullion's Day, *n.* July 4th, the translation of St Martin.
Bullister, *n.* a sloe-bush; the wild plum, the bullace.
Bulliwan, *n.* the stalk of a dock.
Bull-maill, *n.* fee for the service of a bull.
Bull-neck, *n.* an onion that does not bulb, but grows like a leek.
Bull of the bog, *n.* the bittern.
Bull's bags, *n.* any tuberous orchis supposed to be aphrodisiac.
Bull-seg, *n.* any tuberous orchis.
Bull-seg, *n.* a bulrush; the great cat-tail.
Bull-segg, *n.* a castrated bull.
Bull's grass, *n.* the goose-grass.
Bull's head, *n.* an ancient signal of execution brought in at a feast.
Bull-stirk, *n.* a young bull.
Bullyrag, *v.* to scold vigorously; to hector; to haggle; to wrangle.
Bullyraggle, *n.* a noisy, abusive wrangle.
Bulmie, *n.* any large edible root.
Bulrash, *n.* a bulrush.
Bult, *v.* to push violently, jolt; to butt.
Bultin', *ppl. adj.* used of a cow: apt to butt.
Bulty, *adj.* bulky, large.
Bulwand, *n.* the bulrush; the common mugwort.
Bulwaver, *v.* to go astray. Cf. Bellwaver.
†Bulyiement, *n.* clothing, habiliments; odds and ends. Cf. Habiliments.
†Bulyon, *n.* a crowd, a collection; 'boiling.' Cf. Boiling.
Bum, *n.* the bottom.
Bum, *n.* a term of contempt for a big, dirty, lazy woman.
Bum, *v.* to hum like a top; to buzz like a bee, &c.; to spin a top, to make it hum; to drone, to make a sound like the bagpipe

or big bass fiddle; to be glad; to sing; to read in a droning, indistinct manner; to sing or play badly; to cry, to weep.—*n.* the hum of bees, tops, &c.; the hum of conversation; the noise in a busy street; an indistinct or droning reader; a singer or player without taste or skill.
Bum, *v.* to strike, knock; to throw away carelessly.
Bu-man, *n.* a nursery bogey; a hobgoblin; the devil.
Bumbaze, *v.* to confound, bewilder, stupefy.
Bumbee, *n.* a humble- or bumble-bee.
Bumbee-byke, *n.* a nest of 'bumbees.'
Bumbee-looking, *adj.* looking like a 'bumbee.'
Bumbeleery-buzz, *n.* a sound made by children, when they see cows 'startling,' to incite them to greater speed.
Bumble, *v.* to bungle. Cf. Bummil.
Bumble-kite, *n.* a blackberry.
Bum-bumming, *n.* a continuous humming sound.
Bum-clock, *n.* a humming, flying beetle.
Bumfle, *n.* a large pucker.—*v.* to pucker.
Bum-fly, *n.* a stout, pursy person.
Bum-fodder, *n.* toilet-paper, 'curl-paper.'
Bum-leather, *n.* the skin of the buttocks.
Bumler, Bummeler, *n.* a bungler.
Bumling, *n.* the humming noise of a bee.
Bumlock, Bumlack, *n.* a small, prominent, shapeless stone; anything that endangers one's falling or stumbling.
Bummack, *n.* the brewing of malt to be drunk at once at a merry-making.
Bumman, Bumming, *n.* reading or talking in a drawling, indistinct manner; singing or playing badly.—*ppl. adj.* weeping, given to weeping; chicken-hearted.
Bummer, *n.* a blundering, drawling reader; a bad singer or player on an instrument; a managing, officious person; a head-man, manager; one given to weeping.
Bummer, *n.* a bumble-bee; a bluebottle-fly; any buzzing insect; a great boaster; an empty, foolish talker; a thin piece of serrated wood attached to a string, used by children swinging it to give out a booming sound; a boy's peg-top that 'bums' loudly when spinning.
Bummie, *n.* a stupid fellow, fool; a bumble-bee.
Bummie-bee, *n.* a bumble-bee.
Bummil, Bummle, *v.* to bungle; to read or sing indistinctly and badly; to bustle about, work busily; to weep, 'blubber.'—*n.* a wild bee; a drone; an idle fellow; a bungler; a clumsy, heavy person; clumsy work; low, blundering reading; one who reads, sings, or plays without skill or taste.
Bumming-duff, *n.* a tambourine.

Bummler, *n.* a bungler, blunderer.

Bump, *n.* a stroke; a swelling caused by a blow or fall.—*v.* to initiate into burgess-ship, &c., by bumping a person's buttocks against a stone or post. Cf. Burgess.

Bump, *v.* to boom like a bittern.

Bumper, *v.* to fill to the brim; to drink healths in a bumper.

Bumphle, *v.* to pucker. Cf. Bumfle.

Bum-pipe, *n.* the dandelion.

Bumplefeist, *n.* a sulky humour; a fit of spleen. Cf. Amplefeyst.

Bumpy, *n.* the buttocks.

Bumpy-coat, -jacket, *n.* one reaching only to the buttocks.

Bumshot, *adj.* said of those whose plot gives way with them.

Bum-speal, *n.* a 'speal' of wood, notched on both sides, with a string at the end for whirling round in the air. Cf. Bummer.

Bum-whush, *n.* perdition, ruin; obscurity; annihilation.

Bun, *n.* a cake baked with flour, dried fruits, and spices, used about the New Year, and known also as 'sweetie loaf.'

Bun, *n.* the core of flax, the dry stalky part of flax or hemp. Cf. Boon.

Bun, *n.* a rabbit; the tail of a rabbit; the seat, the posteriors.

Bun, *n.* a large cask in which water is carted from a distance.

Bun, Bund, *v. pret.* and *ppl.* bound.

Bun-briest, *n.* a wooden bed.

Bunce, *n.* a schoolboy's claim to the half of anything he finds; a bonus, dividend.

Bunch, *n.* an awkward-looking woman or girl.

Bunch, *v.* to hobble, walk clumsily, used of squat or corpulent persons. — *n.* a blow, push, punch; the line from which a start in a race is made; the point from which one jumps in 'leap-frog.'

Bunching, *ppl. adj.* showy in dress or manner; of an imposing appearance.

Bunder, *n.* a bang; a sudden, heavy fall; a battering sound.

Bundle, *v.* to sleep together without undressing in the same bed or couch, an old form of courting; to live in concubinage.

Bundling, *n.* the practice of sweethearts sleeping together in their clothes.

Bund-sack, *n.* a person engaged, or under promise of marriage.

Bundweed, Bunweed, *n.* the ragweed.

Bune, *n.* the worthless part of a stalk of flax. Cf. Boon.

Bunemost, *adj.* uppermost. Cf. Boonmost.

Buner, *adj.* upper.

Bunewand, *n.* the cow-parsnip; the dock.

Bung, *adj.* tipsy, fuddled.—*v.* to make tipsy.

Bung, *v.* to throw with force; to get in a

passion; to bang; to walk quickly and proudly; to incur displeasure.—*n.* a blow, crash, bang; bad temper, a pet; offence. Cf. Bang.

Bung, *v.* to emit a booming or twanging sound, as when a stone is slung.—*n.* the sound thus made; the act of slinging a stone.

Bung, *n.* an old, worn-out horse.

Bung, *n.* the instep of a shoe.

Bung-fu', *adj.* quite intoxicated.

Bungie, *adj.* tipsy. Cf. Bungy.

Bung-tap, *n.* a humming-top.

Bungy, *adj.* petulant, testy, 'huffy.'

Bungy, *adj.* tipsy, fuddled; full to the bung.

Bunjel, *n.* a bundle of hay, straw, &c. Cf. Banyel.

Bunk, *n.* a chest which serves for a seat. Cf. Benk.

Bunker, Bunkart, *n.* an earthen seat in the fields; a roadside bank; a large heap of stones, &c.; the desk of a schoolmaster or precentor; an inequality in the surface of ice; a small sand-pit.

Bunker, *n.* a country dance.

Bunkle, *n.* a stranger.

Bunnel, Bunnle, *n.* ragwort; cow-parsnip.

Bunnerts, *n.* cow-parsnip.

Bunnet, *n.* a boy's cap.

Bunshie, *adj.* fat, plump.

Bunsucken, *adj.* used of a farm: bound to have all the corn grown on it ground at a particular mill.

Bunt, *n.* the tail of a horse or rabbit. Cf. Bun.

Bunt, *v.* to hurry, run away; to provide for, look after, attend; to forage.

Buntin, *adj.* short and thick, plump.—*n.* a short, thickset person. Cf. Buntlin.

Buntin-crab, *n.* a crab-apple.

Bunting-lark, *n.* the common or corn bunting.

Buntlin, *n.* the blackbird; the corn bunting.

Buntlin, *adj.* short and thickset, plump.—*n.* a dwarf. Cf. Buntin.

Buntling, *n.* a bantling.

Buntling-lark, *n.* the corn-bunting.

Bunty, *n.* a cock or hen without a tail.

Bunwand, *n.* the cow-parsnip; the dock. Cf. Bunewand.

Bunweed, *n.* ragweed. Cf. Bundweed.

Bunyel, *n.* a beggar's old bags. Cf. Bunjel.

Bunyoch, *n.* diarrhœa.

Buoy, *v.* used of smells: to rise up, swell up.

Bur, *n.* a fir-cone.

†Burble, *v.* to purl; to bubble or boil up, like water from a spring.—*n.* a 'bell' or bubble on water; purling, a purl.

Burble, *n.* perplexity, trouble, disorder.—*v.* to perplex, trouble.

Burble-headed, *adj.* stupid, confused.

Burd. *n.* a table. Cf. Board.

Burd, *n.* a maiden ; a young lady.

Burd, *n.* offspring, in a bad sense ; an un-weaned seal. Cf. Bird.

Burd alane, *adj.* quite alone.—*n.* the only surviving child of a family.

Burden, *n.* the drone of a bagpipe. Cf. Burdoun.

Burdenable, *adj.* burdensome.

Burden-carrier, *n.* a carrier of wood.

Burdenous, *adj.* burdened.

Burdie, *n.* a small bird ; a term of endear-ment or of irony, used to a young man or woman.

Burdiehouse, *n.* in *phr.* 'gang to Burdie-house,' used by old people to those with whose conduct or language they are, or pretend to be, displeased.

Burdinseck, *n.* a law which forbade capital punishment for theft of a calf or sheep, or so much meat as one could carry in a sack on his back. Cf. Berthinsek.

Burdit, *ppl.* used of stones : split into laminæ.

Burdliness, *n.* stateliness.

Burdly, *adj.* stately, stalwart. Cf. Buirdly.

Burd-mou'd, *adj.* unwilling to scold ; gentle in fault-finding.

Burdocken, *n.* the burdock.

†Burdoun, *n.* the drone of a bagpipe.

Bure, *n.* a loose woman.

Bure, *v. pret.* bore.

Bouregh, *v.* to crowd together. Cf. Bourach.

Burgess, *v.* in 'riding the marches' of a burgh, to make burgesses by bumping them on a stone. Cf. Bump.

Burges-thread, *n.* flaxen thread.

Burg-hall, *n.* a town-hall.

Burgher, *n.* a member of the Secession Church who upheld the lawfulness of the burgess oath.

Burg of ice, *n.* whalefishers' name for an ice-field afloat.

Burgonet, *n.* a linen cap or coif. Cf. Biggonet.

Burg-toon, *n.* a burgh.

Burial-boding, *n.* a death-warning.

Burial-bread, *n.* cakes, &c., partaken at a funeral 'service.'

Burian, *n.* a mound, tumulus ; a kind of fortification ; a prehistoric camp.

Buried, *ppl. adj.* obsolete.

†Burio, Burrio, *n.* an executioner. Cf. Bourrier.

Burlaw, *n.* a court of neighbours in a district to settle local disputes, &c. Cf. Birlie.

Burlaw-baillie, *n.* the officer of the 'burlaw'-court.

Burley-bracks, *n.* the game of 'hide-and-seek' played in a stackyard. Cf. Barley-breaks.

Burley-whush, *n.* an obsolete game of ball.

Burlins, *n.* bread burned in the oven in baking.

Burly, *n.* a crowd, a tumult.

Burly, *adj.* thick, rough, strong.

Burly-baillie, *n.* the officer of the 'burlaw'. court.

Burly-headit, *adj.* of rough appearance.

Burly-man, *n.* a member of the 'burlaw'-court. Cf. Burlaw.

Burly-twine, *n.* strong, coarse twine, some-what thicker than packthread.

Burn, *n.* a brook ; water from a fountain or well ; water used in brewing ; the brew itself ; urine.

Burn, *v.* to deceive ; to cheat in a bargain ; to suffer in any effort ; to derange the game of curling by improper interference. Cf. Brunt.

Burn-airn, *n.* a branding-iron.

Burn-becker, *n.* the water-ouzel ; the water-wagtail.

Burn-blade, *n.* a large, broad-leaved plant growing on the banks of 'burns.'

Burnbrae, *n.* a slope with a 'burn' at its foot.

Burnewin, *n.* a blacksmith. Cf. Burn-the-wind.

Burn-grain, *n.* a small 'burn' flowing into a larger one.

Burnie-baker, *n.* the water-ouzel. Cf. Burn-becker.

Burning beauty, *n.* a very beautiful person.

Burning-water, *n.* marine phosphorescence.

Burnist, *v. pret.* and *ppl.* burnished, polished : decorated.

Burn-sae, *n.* a water-butt carried by two persons on a pole resting on their shoulders.

Burnside, *n.* ground at the side of a 'burn.'

Burn-the-water, *phr.* to 'leister' salmon by torchlight.

Burn-the-wind, *n.* a blacksmith.

Burnt-nebbit, -tae'd, *adj.* used of 'tawse': having the ends hardened in the fire.

Burn-wood, *n.* firewood.

Burr, *n.* a stout, strong, thickset person of stubborn temper ; the sea-urchin.

Burr, *n.* the tongue of a shoe ; the edge of the upper leather.

Burr, *v.* to make a whirring sound in the throat in pronouncing the letter 'r.'

Burrach'd, *ppl.* enclosed, encircled. Cf. Bourach.

Burran, *n.* the act of sounding the letter 'r' in the throat.

Burran, *n.* a badger.

Burrel, *n.* a barrel.

Burrel, *n.* a hollow piece of wood used in twisting ropes.

Burrel-ley, -rig, *n.* land of an inferior kind, where there was only a narrow ridge ploughed, and a large strip of barren land lay between every ridge.

Burrian, *n.* the red-throated diver.

Burrie, *v.* to push roughly; to crowd confusedly and violently; to overpower in working or in striving at work.—*n.* crowding; a rough push; a children's game.—*adv.* roughly.

Burroch, *n.* a band put round the hinder-legs of a cow when she is being milked to keep her from kicking.—*v.* to fasten such a band on a cow.

Burrochit, *ppl. adj.* restrained.

Burrochless, *adj.* wild; intractable; without restraint.

Burrow, *n.* a burgh.

Burrows, *n.* security, 'caution.' Cf. Borrow.

†Bursar, *n.* one who holds a scholarship at school or college.

†Bursary, *n.* a scholarship at school or college.

Bursen, *ppl. adj.* dainty about food, as if already surfeited; burst; breathless; panting from overexertion; overpowered by fatigue.

Bursen-belch, *n.* a person breathless from corpulence.

Bursen-kirn, *n.* such a laborious harvest that all the grain is not cut before sunset.

Burss-money, *n.* a 'bursary.'

Burst, *v.* to overfeed; to fill to excess; to be breathless, overheated, and exhausted from great exertion.—*n.* injury from overexertion; an outburst of drinking.

Bursted-churn, *n.* a 'bursen-kirn.'

Bursten, *ppl. adj.* burst; breathless from exertion, overfatigue.

Burstin, *n.* grain dried over the fire.

Burth, *n.* a counter-current in a bay, caused by the tidal current outside.

Burth, *n.* birth.

Burthen, *n.* a stone in curling so retarded by touching another as to become harmless.

Bur-thristle, *n.* the spear-thistle.

Burying, *n.* a funeral.

Bus, *n.* a call to cattle to stand still in the stall.

Buse, *n.* a cow's stall, a crib.—*v.* to enclose cattle in a stall. Cf. Buise.

Buse-airn, *n.* a marking-iron, for sheep. Cf. Boost.

Bush, *v.* to sheathe, to enclose in a metal case; to fit a metal lining to a cylindrical body, to put on an iron ring or 'bush.'—*n.* a ring inserted to prevent the effect of friction.

Bush, *v.* to place bushes on fields to prevent poachers from netting partridges.

Bush, *v.* to burst or gush out.

Bush, *v.* to move about briskly; to tidy up.

Bush, *int.* expressive of a rushing sound, as of water rushing out.

Bushel, *n.* a small pond, a dam made in a gutter to intercept water.

Bushel-breeks, *n.* wide, baggy trousers.

Busheries, *n.* clumps of bushes.

Bush-rope, *n.* the rope to which the nets of a drift are attached.

Busht, *n.* a box. Cf. Boist.

Bushty, *n.* a small bed. Cf. Buisty.

Busk, *v.* to make ready; to dress, deck, adorn; to dress flies for fishing.—*n.* dress, decoration.

Busker, *n.* one who dresses another.

Buskie, *adj.* fond of dress, smart.

Buskie, *adj.* bushy.

Buskin, *n.* dressing.

Buskry, *n.* dress, decoration.

Buss, *n.* a bush; straw, &c., used as litter for animals or material for birds' nests; a sunken rock on which at very low tides seaweed is visible, like a bush; a clump or tussock of rushes, &c.; a pouting or sulking mouth.

Buss, *v.* to dress, 'busk'; to dress hooks.

Buss, *n.* cant name for a 'bursary' or scholarship.

Bussard, *n.* a class of carnations.

Bussie, *adj.* bushy.

Bussin, *n.* a linen cap or hood, worn by old women.

Bussing, *n.* covering.

Bussle, *n.* bustle.

Buss-sparrow, *n.* the hedge-sparrow.

Buss-taps, *n.* in *phr.* to 'gang o'er the buss-taps,' to behave extravagantly.

Bust, *v.* to powder, to dust with flour.

Bust, *v.* to beat.

Bust, *n.* a box, a chest. Cf. Boist.

Bust, *n.* a stall, crib.—*v.* to enclose cattle in a stall. Cf. Boose, Buse.

Bust, *n.* the tar-mark on sheep. Cf. Buist.

Bust, *v.* had to, must. Cf. Boost.

Busteous, *adj.* boisterous, powerful, fierce, terrible.

Bustiam, Bustian, Bustine, Bustin, *n.* fustian; a cotton fabric used for waistcoats.

Bustle, *v.* to toast. Cf. Birsle.

Bustuous, Bustyious, *adj.* boisterous, fierce. Cf. Busteous.

But, *prep.* without, outside.—*adv.* out, outside of, in the outer room or kitchen.—*n.* the outer room or kitchen of a two-roomed cottage.—*adj.* outer, outside; pertaining to the 'but' or kitchen of a cottage.

But, *n.* an impediment; an 'if.'

But, *conj.* unless, nothing but; except, save only.—*adv.* verily, certainly; used redundantly for emphasis.

But, *v.* must, had to. Cf. Bood.

But-a-hoose, *n.* the kitchen-end of a house.

But and, *phr.* besides; as well as; and also.

But and a ben, *n.* a two-roomed cottage.

But and ben, *adv.* from the 'but' to the 'ben,' and *vice versâ*; backwards and forwards.

Butch, *v.* to act as butcher, to be a butcher; to kill for the market.

†Buter, *n.* the bittern.

But gif, But gin, *conj.* but if.

But-hoose, *n.* the kitchen, the outer room.

Butt, *n.* ground set apart for archery ; the distance between a player and the goal or target in playing marbles, &c.

Butt, *n.* a piece of ground which in ploughing does not form a proper ridge, but is excluded as an angle ; a small piece of land disjoined from adjacent lands.

Butt, *n.* the bottom of a sheaf or stack.

Butt, *n.* the part of tanned hides of horses which is under the crupper.

Butt, *v.* used in curling : to drive at one or more stones lying near the 'tee' so as to remove them.

Butten, *prep.* without.

Butter, *v.* to coax, flatter.—*n.* flattery, fulsome praise.

Butter-and-bear-caff, *n. phr.* gross flattery.

Butter-bake, *n.* a biscuit made with butter.

Butter-boat, *n.* a small table-dish for serving melted butter.

Butter-brughtins, *n.* an oatcake or bannock toasted, crumbled down, cooked in a pot with butter, and made into a sort of porridge. Cf. Brughtins.

Butter-clocks, *n.* small pieces of butter floating on the top of milk.

Butter-crock, *n.* a butter-jar.

Butter-dock, *n.* the broad-leaved dock.

Butter-fish, *n.* a species of the blenny.

Butter-groat, *n.* a farmer's wife's perquisite of butter-money.

Butterie, *adj.* used of the tongue : plausible, flattering for selfish ends.

Butter-luck, *n.* an expression used as a charm in butter-making.

Buttermilk-gled, *n.* a bird of the falcon tribe.

Butter-saps, *n.* oatcake or wheaten bread soaked in melted butter and sugar.

Butter-wife, *n.* a woman who sells butter.

Buttery, *n.* a butterfly.

Buttery-fingers, *n.* a person who lets things slip from the fingers.

Buttery-Willie-Collie, *n.* a nickname for an undergraduate of Aberdeen University, especially in his first session, when his scarlet gown is new.

Buttle, *n.* a sheaf, bundle of corn, &c. Cf. Battle.

Buttlins, *n.* the battlements of a tower or steeple. Cf. Bittlins.

Buttock, *n.* the remainder, end ; the bottom.

Buttock-mail, *n.* the fine formerly imposed by a kirk session in a case of fornication.

Button, *n.* in *pl.* the boys' game played with buttons aimed at a 'mote.'

Button-mouse, *n.* small field-mouse.

Buttons and buttonholes, *adv. phr.* entirely, completely.

Buttony, *n.* a children's game in which the

players, with eyes shut and palms open, guess who has received a button from another player who passes along the line in which they stand.

Butt'rie, *n.* a butterfly. Cf. Buttery.

Butts, *n.* used of children : intimate companions.

Butty, *n.* an intimate companion ; a fellow-workman.

Butwards, *adv.* towards the 'but' of a cottage or the outer part of a room.

Bux, *v.* to hurry, bustle.

Buy, *v.* in *phr.* 'to buy a broom,' to take out a warrant.

Buzzard, *n.* a bluebottle.

Buzzard-hawk, *n.* the buzzard.

Buzzle, *v.* used of grain crops : to rustle when touched in the 'stook,' indicating readiness to be carted home.—*n.* the rustling sound emitted by a sheaf ready for the stack.

By, *prep.* beyond ; by the side of ; judging from ; relating to, in comparison with ; from ; against, except ; out of ; besides, over and above.

By, *conj.* by the time that.

By, Bye, *adj.* lonely, out-of-the-way ; in combination with *up, down, in, near, out owre,* denoting locality not far off ; past ; 'done for'; finished off.—*adv.* aside, out of the way.

Byaak, *v.* to bake.

Byach, *int.* a meaningless excl.

Byass, *n.* bias.

Byauch, *n.* any small living creature.

By-bit, *n.* an extra bit ; a 'snack' between meals.

By-blow, *n.* an illegitimate child.

By-board, *n.* a side-table, a sideboard.

By-body, *n.* one who procrastinates.

By-comin', *n.* passing by.

By-common, *adj.* extraordinary, out of the common.—*adv.* extraordinarily.

By-courting, *n.* courting on the sly.

By-east, *adv.* towards the east.

Bye-attour, *conj.* moreover.

Byehand, *adv.* over, past.

Byeless, *adv.* unusually, extraordinarily.

By-end, *n.* a sinister end ; a side-issue.

Byes, *prep.* compared with. Cf. By's.

By-gaein, -ganging, -gawn, *n.* passing by ; with *in,* incidentally.

Bygane, *n.* the past.—*adj.* past, gone by.

By-gate, *n.* a byway.

By-hands, *adj.* casual, accidental ; underhand, devious.—*adv.* finished, settled ; over. Cf. Byehand.

By himself, *phr.* out of his mind.

By-hours, *n.* extra time, odd hours ; time not allotted to regular work ; overtime ; leisure hours.

Bykat, *n.* a male salmon. Cf. Beiket.

Byke, *n.* a bees' or wasps' nest. Cf. Bike.

Byke, *n.* the nose, 'beak.'

Byke, *n.* the hook of the crook by which pots are hung over a fire. Cf. Bike.

Byke, *v.* to weep, whine, sob.

Byle, *n.* a boil.

Bynall, *n.* a tall, lame person.

By-name, *n.* a nickname, sobriquet; 'to-name.'

By-neuk, *n.* an out-of-the-way corner.

By-ocht, *adj.* used of something almost impossible or inconceivable.

By one's sell, *phr.* distracted, demented.

By-ordinar', *adj.* out of the common.—*adv.* extraordinarily.

Byous, *adj.* extraordinary, remarkable.—*adv.* very, in a great degree.

Byouslie, *adv.* uncommonly, extraordinarily, remarkably; very.

Byoutour, *n.* a gormandiser, a glutton. Cf. Bootyer.

Byowtifu', *adj.* beautiful.

Byowty, *n.* beauty.

By-pit, *n.* a makeshift; a slight repast between meal-times; a pretence, an 'off-put'; one who procrastinates; a pretender.

By-pitting, *adj.* procrastinating; pretending.

By random, *adv.* at random.

Byre, *n.* a cowhouse.

Byre-man, *n.* the man who attends to farm cattle.

Byre-time, *n.* the time for bringing cows to the 'byre' for milking, &c.

Byre-woman, *n.* the woman who attends to the cows on a farm.

Byruns, *n.* arrears.

By's, By'se, *prep.* compared with; besides, in addition to. Cf. Beis.

Bysenful, *adj.* disgusting.

Bysenless, *adj.* worthless, shameless.

By-set, *n.* a substitute.

By-shot, *n.* one who is set aside for an old maid.

By-spell, Byspale, *n.* one who has become a byword for anything remarkable; an illegitimate child.—*adv.* exceedingly, remarkably.

Byssum, *n.* contemptuous term for a woman of unworthy character. Cf. Besom.

By-stand, *n.* a stand-by.

By-start, *n.* a bastard.

By-start-born, *adj.* illegitimate.

By-table, *n.* a side-table, a sideboard.

By-time, *n.* extra or leisure time, odd hours.

By token, *phr.* an expression introducing a confirmatory statement.

By-whiles, *adv.* now and then, at times.

By-word, *n.* a proverb, a proverbial saying.

Ca, *n.* a mountain-pass, a defile.

Ca', *n.* quick, oppressive breathing. Cf. Caw.

Ca', *n.* a call; a summons by voice or instrument; a whistle, pipe; occasion, need, obligation; a passing visit; the right to call on the next performer; the sound of the sea before or after a storm; the call to die; an invitation to be minister of a particular congregation.—*v.* to call, name; to abuse, scold, call names; with *again,* to contradict, retort; with *for* or *with,* to pay a visit.

Ca', *v.* to drive cattle, vehicles, tools, machinery, &c.; to hammer, knock; to overturn; to move rapidly; to submit to be driven; with *about,* to spread a report, &c.—*n.* a knock; of water: the motion of waves as driven by the wind; a walk for cattle, a district in which cattle pasture; a drove of sheep; a strip of ground left open for cattle going to a common pasture.

Ca', *v.* to calve.—*n.* a calf; a silly, foolish person.

Caa, *v.* to drive; to hammer. Cf. Ca'.

Caa, *v.* to call; to name. Cf. Ca'.

Caaing, *n.* the driving of whales into shallow water; a drove of whales.

Caaing-whale, *n.* the *Delphinus deductor.*

Caak, *v.* to cackle as a hen; to talk noisily.

Caar, *adj.* left, left-handed. Cf. Car.

Caar-cake, *n.* a cake baked with eggs for Fastern's Eve. Cf. Car-cake.

Caa-tee, *n.* a great disturbance, a driving together, or to and fro, of people.

Cab, *v.* to pilfer; to snatch by underhand means.

Cabal, *n.* a group of drinkers; a violent dispute.—*v.* to dispute; to quarrel; to find fault with. Cf. Cabble.

Cabarr, *n.* a lighter, a 'gabert.'

Cabback, *n.* a cheese. Cf. Kebbock.

Cabbage-daisy, *n.* the globe-flower.

Cabbage-fauld, *n.* a place where cabbage is grown.

Cabber, *n.* an old lean horse. Cf. Cabre.

Cabbie, *n.* a box made of laths, which claps close to a horse's side, and is narrow at the top to prevent the corn in it from being spilled.

Cabble, *n.* a violent dispute.—*v.* to quarrel; to dispute; to find fault with.

Cabbrach, *adj.* rapacious; lean.—*n.* lean meat; meat unfit for use; a disagreeable person as to temper and manners; a big, uncouth, greedy person.

Cabbrach, Cabrach-sweetie, *n.* a box on the ears.

†**Cabelow,** *n.* salted fish. Cf. Kabbelow.

Caber, Cabre, *n.* a large, heavy pole for tossing at athletic contests; a beam; a rafter; a large stick, a 'rung'; in *pl.* the small wood laid on the rafters under the roofing; the transverse beams on a kiln, on which grain is laid for drying; the thinnings of young plantations.

Cabre, *n.* an old, lean, useless animal.

Cabroch, Cabrach, *adj.* lean, meagre; used of meat: unfit to use. Cf. Cabbrach.

Cache, *v.* to shake, knock about.—*n.* a shake, jog. Cf. Cadge.

Cack, *v.* used of children: to void excrement. —*n.* human excrement.

Cacker, *n.* the calker of a horseshoe; the iron shod of a clog or shoe.

Cackie, *v.* to 'cack.'—*n.* in *pl.* human excrement.

Ca'd, *v. pret.* and *ppl.* called.

Ca'd, *v. pret.* drove.—*ppl.* driven.

Caddel, *n.* saudle, a warm drink.

†**Caddie,** *n.* a cadet; an errand-boy; a street-porter; a young fellow; a golfer's attendant.

Caddis, *n.* shreds; rags; cotton-wool; surgeon's lint; a pledget.

Caddle, *n.* a set of four cherry-stones in the game of 'papes'; a couple of cherry-stones. Cf. Castle, Caugle.

Caddle, *v.* to move violently.—*n.* a disordered, broken mass.—*adv.* in a disordered, broken mass.

Cadge, *v.* to shake roughly; to knock about. —*n.* a shake, jog.

Cadge, *v.* to carry.

Cadgell, *v.* to carry roughly.—*n.* a wanton fellow, a rake.

Cadger, *n.* a carrier; a person of disagreeable temper.

Cadger-like, *adj.* like a carrier.

Cadger-pownie, *n.* a huckster's pony.

Cadgie, Cadgey, *adj.* gay, sportive; wanton; in good spirits; kind and hospitable.—*adv.* gaily, happily, cheerfully.

Cadgily, *adv.* gaily, merrily, happily.

Cadgin, *ppl.* having a jolting motion.—*n.* the act of being jolted.

Cadgy, *adj.* jolting.

Cadie, *n.* a cadet; an errand-boy; a street-porter. Cf. Caddie.

Cadie, *n.* a hat.

Cadie, *n.* a tea-caddy.

Cadis, *n.* surgeon's lint.—*v.* to apply lint to a wound. Cf. Caddis.

Caducity, *n.* a legal term: the falling of a 'feu' to a superior in irritancy.

Caern, *n.* a very small quantity, a 'curn.'

Caew, *v.* to knead dough; to mix clay, &c.

Ca'f, *n.* a calf; a simpleton. Cf. Caif.

Caff, *n.* chaff.

Caff, *v.* to purchase. Cf. Caft.

Caff-bed, *n.* a chaff-bed; a mattress filled with chaff.

Cafle, *n.* a lot; a share; fate, destiny. Cf. Cavel.

Ca'f's-lick, *n.* a lock of hair rising up on the head.

Caft, *v. pret.* and *ppl.* bought. Cf. Coft.

Ca'f-ward, *n.* an enclosure for calves.

Cag, *n.* a keg.

Cag, *v.* to annoy, vex, offend, grieve.

Cagey, Cagie, *adj.* merry, cheerful. Cf. Cadgie.

Cagily, *adv.* merrily. Cf. Cadgily.

Cahow, Cahoo, *int.* the call of those who hide themselves to the seeker in the game of 'hide and seek,' to let him know to begin his search.—*n.* the game of 'hide and seek.' Cf. Kee-how.

†**Cahute,** *n.* the cabin of a ship.

Caib, *n.* iron used in making a spade or any such tool.

Caich, *v.* to jolt. Cf. Cadge.

Caidge, *v.* to wanton.

Caidgie, *adj.* cheerful, merry. Cf. Cadgie.

Caidgieness, *n.* wantonness; gaiety; sportiveness; affectionate kindness.

Caif, *adj.* tame; familiar.

Caige, *v.* to wax wanton. Cf. Caidge.

Caigh, *n.* in *phr.* 'caigh and care,' every kind of anxiety.

Caik, *n.* a stitch or sharp pain in the side.

Caikal, *n.* a hungry worm supposed to lodge in the intestine and produce a voracious appetite.

Caikie, *n.* a gawky; a foolish, silly person.

Caikle, *v.* to cackle; to chuckle; to recover one's spirits; to become eager. — *n.* a chuckle; noisy laughter; loud chatter; idle, foolish talk; cackle. Cf. Keckle.

Cail, *n.* colewort. Cf. Kail.

Cailleach, Cailliach, *n.* an old woman.

Caim, *n.* a small peninsula terminating on the beach, and connected with the cliffs by a narrow, low isthmus. Cf. Cam.

Cain, *n.* the cheese made by a farmer during the season; 300 stones of cheese. Cf. Ken.

Cain, *n.* part or whole of a rent paid in kind by a farmer; a penalty. Cf. Kain.

Cain-and-Abel, *n.* the *Orchis latifolia.*

Cain-bairn, *n.* a child supposed to be paid as tribute to the fairies or to the devil.

Cain-cock, -fowl, -hen, *n.* a fowl given in part-payment of rent.

Cain-rent, *n.* the rent or part of it paid in kind.

Caip, *n.* the highest part of anything.—*v.* to put on a copestone or the covering of a roof. Cf. Cape.

Caiper, *v.* to caper.—*n.* a caper.

Caipercaillie, *n.* the wood-grouse or mountain cock. Cf. Capercailzie.

Caipstane, *n.* a copestone.

Cair, *v.* to toss to and fro; to stir about; to mix; to rake from the bottom the thickest of soup, &c.; to try to catch by raking from the bottom; to handle overmuch; to search for among dust, ashes, &c.—*n.* the act of extracting the thickest of soup, &c., at the bottom of a dish; much handling.

Cair, *adj.* left; left-handed. Cf. Car.

Cairban, *n.* the basking shark.

Cair-cleuck, *n.* the left hand. Cf. Carcleugh.

Caird, *n.* a travelling tinker; a gipsy, tramp; a sturdy beggar.

Caird, *n.* a calling-card; a photograph of card-size; a playing-card.

Caird, *v.* to card wool; to scold, abuse.—*n.* a comb for dressing wool, made of wires set in leather; a rude, scolding person.

Cairder, *n.* a card-player.

Cairder, *n.* a wool-carder.

Cairdin'-mill, *n.* a carding-mill.

Cairdy, *n.* a wool-carder.

Cair-handit, *adj.* left-handed.

Cairie, *n.* the motion of the clouds in stormy weather. Cf. Carry.

Cairlin, *n.* an old woman. Cf. Carlin.

Cairn, *n.* a loose pile of stones; a conical heap of stones; a tumulus; a ruined building; a heap of rubbish; a high hill.

Cairn-tangle, *n.* the fingered fucus, 'seagirdle,' 'hangers.'

Cairn-tombed, *adj.* used of a chieftain: buried under a 'cairn.'

Cairny, *adj.* abounding in cairns.

Cairt, *n.* a cart.

Cairt, Cairte, *n.* a card. Cf. Caird.

Cairter, *n.* a carter.

Cairter, *n.* a card-player.

Cairts, *n.* a game of cards.

Cairt-sheuch, *n.* a cart-track or rut.

Cait, *v.* used of cats: to desire the male. Cf. Cate.

Caithie, *n.* a large-headed fish, *Lophius piscatorum.*

†Caition, *n.* security.—*v.* to guarantee; to give security. Cf. Caution.

Caiver, *v.* to waver in mind; to be incoherent.

Cake, *n.* a thin, hard cake of oatmeal; oil-cake for feeding cattle.

Caker, *n.* a stroke on the palm of the hand from the 'tawse.'

Cakker, *n.* the hinder-part of a horseshoe sharpened and turned downwards to prevent slipping; the iron rim or plate on a wooden clog or shoe-heel.

Calamy, Calomy, *n.* calomel.

Calavin, *n.* a lead-pencil. Cf. Keelyvine.

Calaw, *n.* the pintail-duck; the long-tailed duck. Cf. Caloo.

Calchen, *n.* a square wooden frame, like a gridiron, in which 'fir-candles' were dried in the chimney.

Cald, *adj.* cold; dry in manner, unkind, repellent.—*n.* a cold.

Caldrife, *adj.* giving the sensation of cold, chilly; susceptible to cold; indifferent, cool, reserved; used of a sermon or a preacher: not interesting, delivered in a cold fashion, not rousing.

†Calender, *n.* a mangle.

Caley, *n.* gossip, chat.

†Calf, *v.* to stop a hole; to wad a gun; to cram with food.—*n.* the act of stuffing; the material used for stopping a hole. Cf. Colf.

Calf, *n.* a simpleton; a stupid, silly person; a term of ridicule.

Calf-country, -ground, *n.* native place.

Calf-drukken, *adj.* as fond as calves of drinking milk.

Calfin, *n.* wadding for a gun; stuffing for a hole.—*v.* to stuff. Cf. Colfin.

Calf-lea, *n.* infield ground, one year under natural grass.

Calf-reed, *n.* rennet.

Calf-skins, *n.* the sea ruffled by the wind in occasional spots; 'cat's-paws.'

Calf-sod, *n.* sward bearing fine grass.

Calf-stick, *n.* a stick for driving cattle or calves.

Calf-ward, *n.* a small enclosure for feeding calves.

Calimanco, *n.* calamanco.

Calk, *n.* the iron point on a horseshoe to prevent slipping.—*v.* to turn down the ends and toes of horseshoes. Cf. Cauk.

Calker, *n.* a maker of iron heel-plates, &c.; a country blacksmith.

Call, *v.* to invite a minister to the charge of a congregation.—*n.* such an invitation. Cf. Ca'.

Callack, *n.* a young girl.

Callan, Callant, *n.* a stripling, a lad, a term of affection; a girl (rarely).

Calledin-o'-the-blade, *n. phr.* a slight shower which cools and refreshes grass.

Caller, Callour, *adj.* fresh, not stale, newly caught or gathered, in proper season; cool, refreshing, bracing.—*v.* to cool, freshen, refresh.

Callet, *n.* a prostitute, concubine.

†Callet, *n.* a woman's cap, without a border. Cf. Callot.

Callet, *n.* the head.

Callevine, *n.* a lead-pencil. Cf. Keelyvine.

Callion, *n.* anything old and ugly.

Call-me-to-you, *n. phr.* the heart's-ease.

†**Callot,** *n.* a woman's cap, without a border.

Calloused, *ppl. adj.* callous, hard-hearted.

Call-the-guse, *n.* a kind of game.

Calm, *adj.* used of ice : smooth, even.

Calm, *n.* a mould ; a bullet-mould ; a frame ; a 'heddle.' Cf. Caulm.

Calmes, *n.* the small cords through which the warp is passed in the loom.

Calm sough, *n.* silence, quietness, saying little.

Calourie, *n.* cockweed.

Calsay, *n.* the causeway, street.

Calsay-paiker, *n.* a street-walker.

Calse maill, *n.* road-money ; tolls.

Calshes, *n.* a slip-dress buttoned behind, and forming jacket and trousers for young boys, and vest and trousers for older ones. Cf. Kilches.

Calshie, Calshich, *adj.* crabbed, ill-humoured, rude. Cf. Kelshie.

Calumnie, *v.* to calumniate.

Calver, *n.* a cow in calf, or that has calved.

Cam, *n.* a small peninsula terminating on the beach, and connected with the cliff by a narrow, low isthmus.

Cam, *v. pret.* came.

Cam, *n.* 'whitening.'—*v.* to whiten a hearth.

Camack, *n.* hockey, 'shinty.' Cf. Cammock.

Cambie-leaf, *n.* the white water-lily, *Nymphæa alba.*

Camble, *v.* to prate saucily ; to scold, bully.

Camblet, *n.* camlet.

Cambuslang marble, *n.* a calcareous stratum near Rutherglen and Cambuslang.

Camdootshie, *adj.* sagacious.

Camdui, *n.* a species of trout.

Came, *n.* a honeycomb ; a comb. Cf. Kame, Kaim.

Camel's-hair, *n.* the vertebral ligament, the 'fick-fack.'

Cameral, *n.* a spawned haddock.

Cameral, Cameril, *n.* a large, ill-shaped, awkward person.

Camerick, *n.* cambric.

Camester, *n.* a wool-comber.

Camla-like, *adj.* sullen, surly.

Cammag, *n.* a short staff with a crooked head. Cf. Cammock.

Cammas, *n.* a coarse cloth.

Cammel, *n.* a crooked piece of wood used as a hook for hanging things on.

Cammelt, *ppl. adj.* crooked.

Cammeril, *n.* a butcher's gambrel. Cf. Cammel.

Cammock, Cammok, Cammon, *n.* a curved stick used in playing hockey or 'shinty'; the game of 'shinty.'

Camovine, Camowyne, *n.* camomile.

Camp, *n.* a heap of potatoes, turnips, &c. covered with earth through winter.

Camp, *adj.* brisk, active, spirited.—*n.* a romp. —*v.* to play the romp ; to contend ; to strive to outstrip in the harvest-field. Cf. Kemp.

†**Campagne, Campaine,** *adj.* suited or belonging to the country.

Campaine-hat, *n.* a hat for country wear.

Campaine-shoes, *n.* shoes for country wear.

Campaine-wig, *n.* a wig for country wear.

†**Campesce,** *v.* to restrain. Cf. Compesce.

Campruly, *adj.* quarrelsome.

Campsho, *adj.* distorted, crooked. Cf. Camshach.

Campy, *adj.* spirited.—*n.* a smart young fellow.

Camrel, *n.* a butcher's gambrel.

Camshach, *adj.* crooked, distorted ; cross-grained, ill-tempered ; stern-faced ; unlucky.

Camshachle, Camschacle, Camshacle, *v.* to distort, pull askew ; to upset ; disorder.— *adj.* involved, intricate ; confused.

Camshack, *adj.* crooked ; cross-grained ; unlucky. Cf. Camshach.

Camshak-kair, *n.* an unlucky concern.

Camshauchle, Camshaucle, *v.* to distort ; to be angry ; to be difficult to repeat ; to walk inactively or lamely. Cf. Camshachle.

Camsheuch, Camschol, *adj.* stern-faced ; crabbed ; crooked. Cf. Camshach.

Camstane, *n.* common compact limestone ; indurated white clay ; pipeclay, 'whitening'; coarse fuller's earth.

Camstairical, *adj.* 'camstairy.'

Camstairiness, *n.* obstinacy, perversity.

Camstairy, Camstairie, Camstary, Camsteary, Camsteerie, Camsteery, Camsterie, Camstrary, *adj.* wild, unmanageable, obstinate, riotous.—*n.* an obstinate, unmanageable person.

Camstrudgeous, *adj.* wild, unmanageable, 'camstairy.'

Can, *n.* a cup ; a broken piece of earthenware.

Can, *n.* skill, knowledge ; ability ; cleverness.

Canage, *n.* payment of 'cain'-duty.

†**Canailyie, Canalyie,** *n.* a rabble, a mob.

Cancer, *n.* the red campion.

Cancer, *n.* the burying beetle.

Canch, *n.* a breadth of digging land.

Candavaig, *n.* a foul salmon that has lain in fresh water till summer, without going to the sea ; a peculiar species of salmon.

Candel-bend, *n.* very thick sole-leather used for ploughmen's boots, such as was picked and tanned at Kendal.

Candle, Can'le, *n.* in *phr.* 'can'le and castock,' a turnip-lantern, with a face formed by blacking on the outside.

Candle-coal, *n.* parrot coal ; a piece of splint coal put on a cottage fire to give light to spin by.

Candle-doup, *n.* a candle-end

Candle-fir, *n.* bog-fir or moss-fallen fir, split and used for candles.

Candle-futtle, -gullie, *n.* a large knife for splitting up bog-fir for candles.

Candlemas, Can'lemas, *n.* Scottish quarter-day, Feb. 2.

Candlemas-ba', *n.* a football-match played at Candlemas.

Candlemas-bleeze, *n.* a gift formerly made by pupils to their schoolmaster at Candlemas; a bonfire on the evening of Feb. 2. Cf. Bleeze-money.

Candlemas-crown, *n.* a badge of distinction formerly given at some schools to the pupil giving the highest gratuity to the master at Candlemas.

Candlemas-king, -queen, *n.* the boy and the girl giving the highest gratuity to the schoolmaster.

Candlemas-offering, *n.* the gift formerly made by pupils to their teacher at Candlemas.

Candlemas-silver, *n.* the Candlemas offering.

Candle-shears, *n.* a pair of snuffers.

Candle-whittle, *n.* a 'candle-futtle.'

Candy-broad-sugar, *n.* lump-sugar.

Candy-glue, *n.* candy made from treacle, &c., well boiled.

Candy-man, *n.* a seller or hawker of candy.

Candy-rock, *n.* candy in blocks or stalks.

Cane, *n.* rent, or a portion of it, paid in kind. Cf. Cain.

Canech, *n.* the pip in fowls. Cf. Cannagh.

Cangle, *v.* to quarrel, wrangle, haggle, bandy words; to cavil.

Cangler, *n.* a jangler, a caviller.

Cangling, *n.* altercation, quarrelling.

Canker, *v.* to fret, become peevish or ill-humoured; to put into a bad temper; to render cross, to sour; of plants: to be covered with blight; of the weather: to become stormy.—*n.* bad temper; a corroding care.

Canker-nail, *n.* a painful slip of flesh at the base of a finger-nail.

Cankersome, *adj.* cross-grained, bad-tempered.

Cankert, Cankered, *ppl. adj.* cross, ill-humoured, fretful; used of a sore: inflamed, festered; of the weather: threatening, gusty.

Cankert-leukin', *adj.* used of a sore: inflamed, painful; of persons: sour, unkind in expression; of weather: threatening, lowering.

Cankert-like, *adj.* cross-looking; threatening in appearance.

Cankertly, *adv.* ill-naturedly, crossly.

Cankery, *adj.* bad-tempered; eating like a cancer.

Cankling, *ppl. adj.* quarrelsome, wrangling. Cf. Cangle.

Cankrif, *adj.* cankering.

Cank'rous, *adj.* sore, painful

Cankry, *adj.* cross-grained, cantankerous. Cf. Cankery.

Canlie, *n.* a boys' game, of the nature of 'tig.'

Cann, *n.* knowledge; skill, ability. Cf. Can.

Canna, Cannae, *v. neg.* cannot.

Canna, Cannach, *n.* the cotton-grass.

Canna-down, *n.* the cotton-grass.

Cannagh, *n.* the pip in fowls.

Cannalye, *n.* the rabble. Cf. Canailyie.

Cannas, Cannes, *n.* coarse canvas; sailcloth, the sail of a ship; a coarse sheet used for keeping grain from falling to the ground when winnowed in a sieve.

Cannas-braid, *n.* the breadth of such a sheet.

Canneca, *n.* the wood-worm.

Cannel, *n.* the sloping edge of an axe or chisel. —*v.* to bevel the edge of a knife, &c.; to chamfer.

†Cannel, *n.* cinnamon.

Cannel, *n.* a candle. Cf. Candle.

Cannel-water, *n.* cinnamon-water.

Canniburr, Canniber, *n.* the sea-urchin.

Cannie-nail, *n.* the nail that holds the cart-body to the axle.

Cannily, *adv.* cautiously, craftily, skilfully, gently, frugally, quietly, easily.

Canniness, *n.* the possession of 'canny' qualities. Cf. Canny.

Cannon-nail, *n.* the 'cannie-nail.'

Canny, Cannie, *adj.* cautious, prudent, shrewd; artful, crafty, dexterous; careful, frugal, sparing in the use of; moderate in charges, conduct, spirit; not extortionate, hard, or exacting; gentle, useful, beneficial; handy, expert, skilful in midwifery; gentle in using the hands or the tongue; soft, easy, slow in action or motion; safe, not dangerous; composed, deliberate, not flustered; not difficult of execution; snug, comfortable, cosy; fortunate, lucky, of good omen, from a superstitious point of view; favourable; endowed with supposed supernatural know ledge or magical skill; good, worthy, 'douce', convenient, well-fitted; comely, agreeable, pleasant; used as a general term of affection, good-will, and approbation.—*adv.* cautiously; gently.

Cannyca, *n.* the wood-worm. Cf. Canneca.

Canny-moment, *n.* the moment of birth.

Canny Nannie, *n.* a kind of bumble-bee.

Canny noo, *int.* take it easy!

Canny-wife, *n.* a midwife, a 'howdie.'

Canny-wyes, *adv.* 'cannily.'

†Canopy, *n.* a sofa, couch.

Canse, *v.* to speak pertly and conceitedly.

Canshie, *adj.* cross, ill-humoured.

Cansie, *adj.* pert, speaking from self-conceit.

Cant, *v.* to sing; to speak in recitative; to talk cheerfully, gossip.—*n.* gossip, tattle; speaking in recitative.

Cant, *n.* a jerk, a turn to one side.—*v.* to set a stone on edge; to upset.

Cant, *v.* to canter.

Cant, *n.* an illusion.

Cant, *n.* a trick, a bad habit; a custom.

Cant, *n.* a little rise of rocky ground on a highway.

Cantation, *n.* talk, conversation.

Canter, *n.* a plausible beggar.

Cantily, *adv.* cheerfully, merrily.

Canting, *n.* a sale by auction.

Cantle, *n.* a triangular piece; a slice; the leg of a lamb or other young animal; the crown of the head.

Cantle, *v.* to tilt up, to fall over; to set aloft, to perch up; with *up*, to brighten up, to recover health or spirits.

†**Cantlin**, *n.* a corner; the chine of a cask or adze.

†**Canton**, *n.* an angle.—*v.* to divide, distribute.

Cantraip, **Cantrip**, *n.* a magic spell, incantation, charm; witch's trick; any trick, frolic, piece of mischief.—*adj.* magical, witch-like.

Cantraps, *n.* caltrops.

Cant-robin, *n.* the dwarf wild-rose, with white flowers.

Canty, *adj.* lively, pleasant, cheerful; small and neat; in good health.—*adv.* contentedly, merrily.

Canty, *n.* a hole in the game of 'kypes' played with marbles.

Canty-smatchet, *n.* a louse.

Canvas, *v.* to ponder, think over.

Canyel, *v.* to jolt; to cause a jolt.—*n.* a jolt; jolting.

Cap, *n.* the comb of wild bees; the top put on a beehive in order to get the combs.

Cap, *n.* a wooden cup or bowl.

Cap, *v.* to outdo, crown, surpass, 'beat'; to take off the hat or cap in saluting; to confer a degree at a Scottish university.—*n.* the lifting of the cap in saluting.

Cap, *v.* to seize by violence what belongs to another; to act piratically, or as a privateer.

Cap, *v.* to bulge, twist, warp.

Cap-ale, *n.* a beer between table-beer and ale. Cf. Cappie.

Cap-ambry, *n.* a cupboard for holding small wooden cups.

Cap and knee, *phr.* humbly and gratefully.

Cape, *n.* the highest part of anything; coping of a wall or house.—*v.* to put on the cover of a roof or wall.

Cape, *v.* to privateer. Cf. Cap.

Caped, *ppl. adj.* of a ship: taken by a pirate.

Caper, *n.* a captor, one who takes a prize; a privateer, a pirate.

Caper, *n.* a piece of buttered oatcake with a slice of cheese on it.

Caper, *v.* to frisk, dance.

Capercailzie, *n.* the wood-grouse or mountain cock.

Caperer, *n.* bread, butter, and cheese toasted together.

Caperilla, **Caperoilie**, *n.* the heath-pea.

Caper-lintie, *n.* the whitethroat.

Capernoited, *adj.* peevish, irritable; under the influence of drink; imbecile; whimsical.

Capernoitet-looking, *adj.* peevish-looking.

Capernoitetness, *n.* perversity, obstinacy.

Capernoitie, *n.* the head, the 'noddle.'

Capernoitie, *adj.* peevish.

Capernuted, *adj.* 'capernoited.'

Caperonish, *adj.* used of food : good, excellent, first-rate.

Capes, *n.* grains of corn to which the chaff adheres after threshing; grain insufficiently ground, or where the shell remains with part of the grain; flakes of meal which come from the mill when the grain has not been properly dried.

Capestane, *n.* a copestone; a remediless calamity.

Capey-dykey, *n.* a game of marbles.

Cap-full, *n.* the fourth of a peck.

Capidocious, *adj.* capital, first-rate.

Capie-dosie, *n.* a hairy cap.

Capie-hole, *n.* the game of marbles, 'kypes.'

Capilation, *n.* drugget; a cheap and light stuff.

Capilow, *v.* to outdo another in reaping.

Caping, *n.* privateering.

†**Capitane**, *n.* captain.

Cap-neb, *n.* an iron plate on the toe of a boot.

Capon, *n.* in *phr.* 'a Crail capon,' a dried haddock.

Cap out, *v.* to drink to the bottom.—*n.* the act of so drinking.

Capper, *n.* a cup-bearer; a turner of wooden bowls or 'caups.'

Capper, *n.* copper.

Capper, *n.* a spider.

Capper, *n.* part of a shoemaker's tools for toe-caps, &c.

Capper, *v.* to seize ships, privateer; to lay hold of forcibly. — *n.* a privateer. Cf. Caper.

Cappernishious, *adj.* short-tempered; perpetually fault-finding.

Cappid, *ppl. adj.* fickle; flighty; whimsical.

Cappie, *n.* a beer between ale and table-beer, drunk out of 'caups.'

Cappie, *adj.* cup-shaped, hollow.

Cappie, *n.* a small cap; a drinking-cup.

Cappie, *adj.* given to warping like green wood.

Cappie-out, *n.* deep drinking; drinking to the bottom.

Cappilow, *v.* to distance; to outdo another in reaping, &c. Cf. Capilow.

Cappin, *n.* the leather or wood band through which the middle band of a flail passes.

Cappit, *ppl. adj.* twisted, bent, warped.

Cappit, *adj.* crabbed, ill-humoured, quarrelsome; short-tempered.

Caprowsy, *n.* a short cloak with a hood.

Cap-sheaf, *n.* a sheaf covering a 'stook' in wet weather; straw forming the top of a thatched rick or roof; the finishing touch.

Capshon, *n.* a 'catch,' windfall, prize. Cf. Caption.

Capstane, *n.* copestone.

Cap-stride, *v.* to forestall another in drinking as the 'cap' goes round; to cheat.

Captain, *n.* the gray gurnard.

Caption, *n.* arrest, apprehension; in *phr.* 'horning and caption,' an order requiring a debtor to pay his debt on pain of being declared a rebel; a lucky, valuable, or serviceable acquisition; a windfall.

Captivity, *n.* waste, destruction.

Car, *n.* calves.

Car, *n.* a sledge; a cart wanting wheels, ledges, sides, and front.

Car, *adj.* left, left-handed; sinister; fatal.

Carameile, *n.* the root of the heath-pea. Cf. Carmele.

Carb, *v.* to cavil, carp.—*n.* cavilling, carping, dissatisfaction.

Carb, *n.* a raw-boned, loquacious woman.

Carberry, *v.* to wrangle, to argue perversely.

Carbin, *n.* the basking shark. Cf. Cairban.

Carbin, *ppl. adj.* fretful, peevish.

Carble, *v.* to cavil, carp, show dissatisfaction; to be captious.

Carbling, *n.* a wrangling.

Car-, Care-cake, *n.* a small cake, baked with eggs, eaten on Fastern's E'en.

†Carcant, *n.* a garland of flowers for the neck. Cf. Carket.

Carcase, Carcatch, *n.* the trunk of the human body.

Car-cleugh, *n.* the left hand.

Carcudeuch, *n.* intimate, familiar. — *adv.* fondly. Cf. Curcuddoch.

Card, *n.* a photograph. Cf. Cairt.

Card, *v.* to scold. Cf. Caird.

†Cardecue, *n.* a silver coin worth about 1s. 4d. sterling.

Carder, *n.* a card-player.

Carding, *n.* a scolding.

Carding, *n.* card-playing.

Cardow, *v.* used of a tailor: to mend, patch; to botch. Cf. Curdow.

Cardower, *n.* a mender of old clothes.

Cardin, *n.* a rare trout found in Lochleven.

Care, *v.* to rake from the bottom. Cf. Cair.

Care, *v.* to care for, regard; with the *neg.*, to have no objection; with the *neg.* and *by*, to be indifferent, to take no interest in.

Care, *n.* in *phr.* 'care's my case,' woeful is my plight; *phr.* 'to take care of,' to refuse.

Care-bed, *n.* a bed of suffering.

Care-bed-lair, *n.* a bed of suffering; a disconsolate situation.

Careerin, *adv.* swiftly, cheerfully.

Careful, *adj.* careworn.

Care-weeds, *n.* mourning garb.

Carf, *n.* a cut in timber for the insertion of another piece of wood; the incision made by an axe or a saw.

Carfin, *n.* the basking shark. Cf. Carbin.

†Carfuddle, *v.* to discompose; to rumple.

†Carfuffle, *v.* to disarrange; to disorder; to tumble; to crease.—*n.* fuss, excitement, disorder. Cf. Curfuffle.

Carfuffle, *n.* a contemptuous designation of a person.

Carfumish, *n.* to diffuse a very bad smell; to overpower by a bad smell. Cf. Curfumish.

†Cargliff, *n.* any shock to the heart. Cf. Curglaff.

Carhail, *v.* to hail in a bantering manner.

Car-handed, *adj.* left-handed.

Carie, *adj.* soft, lazy; pliable.

Carin', *ppl. adj.* causing care or pain.

Cark, *v.* to fret; to complain peevishly.

Carket, *n.* a garland of flowers worn as a necklace.

Carking, *ppl. adj.* anxious, fretting.

Carl, Carle, *n.* a man; a clown, boor in manners, a churl; an old man.

Carl, Carle, *n.* a carol; a gift to carol-singers at Christmas; a licentious song.

Carl-again, *v.* to resist, to return a stroke, to retort.—*n.* a retort; the return of a stroke; tit for tat.

Carlage, *adj.* churlish. Cf. Carlish.

Carl-and-cavel, *phr.* honest man and rogue; all without distinction.

Carl-cat, *n.* a tom-cat.

Carl-crab, *n.* the male of the black-clawed crab.

Carl-doddy, *n.* a stalk of rib-grass; the greater plantain; a term of endearment. Cf. Curl-doddy.

Carle, *n.* a tall rustic candlestick.

Carled, *ppl.* used of a bitch: served by a dog.

Carl-gropus, *n.* a stupid person.

Carl-hemp, *n.* the largest stalk of hemp; mental vigour, firmness.

Carlie, *n.* a little man; a precocious boy.

Carlin, Carline, *n.* an old woman; a shrew, hag; a witch; a man, an old man; the last handful of corn cut in a field, when it is not shorn before Hallowmas. Cf. Kerlin.

Carling, *n.* the name of a fish, ? the pogge.

Carlin'-heather, *n.* fine-leaved heath, bell-heather.

Carlin's, *n.* brown peas boiled or broiled, eaten on the fifth Sunday in Lent.

Carlin's E'en, *n.* the last night of the year.

Carlin'-spurs, *n.* needle furze or petty whin.

Carlin Sunday, *n.* the fifth Sunday in Lent, Passion Sunday.

Carlin-teuch, *adj.* sturdy, tough as an old wife.

Carlish, Carlitch, *adj.* churlish, boorish; rustic, clownish.

Carl-tangle, *n.* a large, long tangle, with tree-like roots. Cf. Cairn-tangle.

Carl-wife, *n.* a man that meddles with household matters.

†Carmalade, *adj.* sick, diseased.

Carmele, *n.* the root of the heath-pea.

Carmovine, *n.* camomile. Cf. Camovine.

Carmud, *adj.* intimate, comfortable. Cf. Curmud.

Carmudgelt, *ppl. adj.* made soft by lightning.

Carmudgeon, *n.* a curmudgeon; a forward child.

Carnaptious, *adj.* irritable, quarrelsome. Cf. Curnaptious.

Carnawin, *n.* a painful feeling of hunger. Cf. Curnawing.

Carnock-pear, *n.* a kind of pear.

Carn-tangle, *n.* a large, long tangle, with roots like a tree. Cf. Cairn-tangle.

Carnwath, Carnwath-like, *adj.* awkward-looking, boorish, rustic. —*adv.* out of line.

Carol-ewyn, *n.* the last night of the year, when young people go from door to door carol-singing.

Caroline-hat, *n.* a black hat, fashionable towards the end of the 17th century.

Carp, *v.* to talk; to recite as a minstrel, sing.

Car-pawed, *adj.* left-handed.

Carpets, *n.* carpet slippers or shoes.

Carrant, *n.* a running, violent dance; a scolding; a great fuss. Cf. Courant.

Carreen, *v.* to lean to one side.

Carr-gate, *n.* a road across steep rocks.

Carribine, *n.* a carbine.

Carrick, *n.* the game of 'shinty' or hockey; the ball played with.

Carrickin', *n.* a gathering of herd-boys to play 'shinty' at Lammas, Aug. 1.

Carrie, *n.* a two-wheeled barrow.

Carried, *ppl. adj.* light-headed, conceited; delirious.

Carrie-elt, *n.* a thick, badly baked oat-bannock. Cf. Carry.

Carrier, *n.* in *phr.* 'to come back with the blind carrier,' to return, if ever, after a very long time.

Carrion, *n.* a term of reproach to a person.

Carrion-corp, *n.* a dead body.

Carris, *n.* flummery, 'sowens.'

Carritch, *v.* to catechize.—*n.* a catechism; in *pl.* the Shorter Catechism; reproof; scolding.

Carritch'd, *ppl. adj.* taught the Shorter Catechism.

Carrot-pow, *n.* a head of red hair.

Carry, *adj.* left, as opposed to right. Cf. Car.

Carry, *adj.* used of oatmeal: badly baked.

Carry, *v.* used of land: to provide food for farm-stock.—*n.* the bulk or weight of a burden, what is carried; the motion of wind-driven clouds; the sky; the distance anything is carried.

Carry coals, *v. phr.* to submit to indignity.

Carrying on, *n.* unseemly behaviour; undue familiarity.

Carry-my-lady-to-London, *n.* a children's game.

Carry on, *v.* to behave strangely or improperly; to do or to speak anything at a great rate; to flirt; to scold continuously. —*n.* proceedings; flirtation; unbecoming behaviour; fuss.

†Carry-warry, *n.* a 'charivari'; a burlesque serenade.

Carry-wattle, *n.* a general 'scrimmage' or wordy conflict.

Carsackie, *n.* a workman's coarse apron; a woman's bedgown or loose working-dress. Cf. Cursackie.

Car-saddle, *n.* the small saddle on the back of a carriage-horse, to support the shafts.

Carse, *n.* the watercress. Cf. Kerse.

Carse, Carse-land, *n.* a stretch of flat, fertile land near a river.

Carseese, *v.* to examine strictly, catechize; to reprove.—*n.* a reproof; a strict examination. Cf. Curseese.

Car-sham-ye, *int.* an excl. in the game of 'shinty' when one of the players strikes the ball with the club in his left hand.

Carsons, *n.* the lady's mantle.

Carsons, *n. pl.* the watercress.

Carstang, *n.* the shaft of a cart.

Cart, *n.* a map, chart.

Cart-aver, *n.* a cart-horse.

Carte, *n.* a playing-card.

Carters'-play, *n.* a yearly procession of the Carters' Society.

Cart-gate, *n.* a cart-road.

Carthanum, *n.* the carthamine or safflower.

Cartie, *n.* a small cart.

Cartil, *n.* a cartload.

†Cartouch, *n.* a jacket worn by women when working; a little frock for a girl.

Cartow, *n.* a great cannon; a battering-piece.

Cart-piece, *n.* an ancient kind of ordnance.

Cart-tram, *n.* the shaft of a cart.

Carvey, Carvie, *n.* caraway; a confection containing caraway.

Carvey-seed, *n.* caraway-seed.

Carvey-sweetie, *n.* caraway coated with sugar.

Ca's, *v. pres.* calls.

Ca's, *v. pres.* drives.

Case, *n.* shape, repair, size.—*v.* to shut up, confine.

Case, *n. phr.* 'case-alike,' all the same ; 'case be,' lest, in case.

Caseable, Casable, *adj.* natural ; naturally belonging to a particular case ; possible.

Casements, *n.* carpenters' planes called 'hollows' and 'rounds.'

Caserrin, *n.* a crook-handled spade, used by Highlanders ; a kind of foot-plough.

Cashhornie, *n.* a game played with clubs by two opposite parties, who each try to drive a ball into a hole belonging to their antagonists.

Cashie, *adj.* delicate, easily tired ; soft, flabby, spongy ; luxuriant, succulent ; of rapid growth.

Cashie, *adj.* talkative ; forward.

Cashle, *v.* to squabble.—*n.* a squabble.

Cashlick, *adj.* careless, regardless.

Caspicaws, Caspie-laws, Caspitaws, *n.* an obsolete instrument of torture.

†**Cass,** *v.* to annul, make void, repeal ; a legal term.

†**Cassedone,** *n.* chalcedony.

Cassen, *ppl.* cast. Cf. Casten.

Cast, *n.* a twist ; opportunity ; a turn, event ; lot, fate, chance ; a casual lift, ride, or help on a journey ; help, assistance ; the cutting of a certain quantity of peats ; a swarm of bees ; a handful of herrings, haddocks, oysters, &c., four in number ; a district, tract of country ; the direction in which one travels ; appearance, style, slight likeness ; a degree ; touch, little ; a throw of a fishing-line ; the earth thrown up by moles, &c. ; an earthen mound as fence or boundary ; of scales : the turn ; some mental power.

Cast, *v.* to put on, scatter, sprinkle ; to toss the head ; to throw on the back ; to thwart, defeat, condemn in an action at law ; used of clothes : to throw off, discard ; of hair, teeth, &c. : to shed, cast off ; of cows : to abort ; of soil : to bear crops that do not ripen ; of bees : to swarm ; of colour : to fade, become pale ; to vomit ; to dig, or cut, and cast up with a spade ; to add up, compute ; to estimate the quantity of grain in a stack by counting the sheaves ; to ponder, consider ; to warp, twist ; to coat with lime or plaster ; to tie a knot ; used of clouds or sky : to clear after rain or at dawn, to gather, to threaten rain ; to beat-up eggs for puddings, &c., to drop their whites into water for divination ; to foretell events, divine ; with *about*, to plan, look about for, manage, arrange for ; with *at*, to

spurn, object to, find fault with ; with *by*, to make one's self ill ; with *out*, to quarrel ; with *up*, to call to remembrance and upbraid for some past fault, misfortune, &c.; to throw up scum ; to discontinue, renounce ; to occur, to come accidentally in one's way, turn up ; to befall ; to vomit.

Cast, *ppl. adj.* prematurely born, aborted ; rejected as faulty ; worthless, inadmissible.

Castan, *n.* the estimating the quantity of grain in a stack.

Castawa', *n.* a person or thing neglected or rejected as useless.

Cast-by, *n.* what is thrown aside as unserviceable.

Casten, *ppl. adj.* used of meat, &c.: spoilt, worthless ; thrown aside.

Casten-awa', *n.* anything thrown away as worthless.

Caster, *n.* a peat-cutter.

Caster-hat, *n.* a beaver-hat.

Cast-ewe, *n.* a ewe not fit for breeding.

Casting, *ppl. adj.* applied to land on which crops fail to ripen.

Casting, *n.* rough-casting ; the swarming of bees ; a quantity of peats ; the cutting of peats.

Casting-out, *n.* a quarrel.

Castings, *n.* cast-off clothes.

Casting-stone, *n.* the stone by which a set-line is cast into a river.

Casting up, *n.* taunting, recalling the past, reminding unpleasantly.

Castle, *n.* four cherry-stones in the game of 'paips.' Cf. Caddle, Caugle.

Castle-waird, *n.* castle-defence.

Cast-line, *n.* a fishing-line.

Castock, *n.* the stem of colewort or cabbage.

Cast-of-corn, *n.* as many oats as a kiln will dry at a time, ? six bushels.

Cast out, *n.* a quarrel.

Cast up, *n.* a taunt ; an unpleasant reminder ; a reproach.

Cast weeds, *n.* perennial weeds growing on bean-stalks.

Casual, *adj.* accidental from mistake or ignorance.

Casualty, *n.* an incidental payment or duty.

Ca't, *v. pret.* drove.—*ppl.* driven.

Ca't, *v. pret.* and *ppl.* called.

Cat, *n.* a ball or piece of wood used in certain games ; the stick used to strike the 'cat' in such games ; soft clay mixed with straw, used in building mud walls, and thrust between the laths and the walls ; a handful of straw or reaped grain simply laid on the ground ; a small piece of rag rolled up and put between the handle of a pot and the hook which suspends it over the fire, in order to raise the pot a little ; a small lump of manure.—*v.* to toss or strike a ball or 'cat' with the hand or a light bat in certain games.

Cat and clay, *n.* a method of building mud walls, &c., by thrusting soft clay mixed with straw between the laths and the walls, and afterwards daubing or plastering it.

Cat-and-dog, *n.* a boys' game played by three.

Cat-and-dog-hole, *n.* the hole towards which the 'cat' is thrown in the game of 'cat-and-dog.'

Catastrophes, *n.* fragments, pieces.

Cat-band, *n.* an iron bar or band for securing a door or gate, hooked into a staple at one end, and locked at the other; a strong hook fixed to the wall and inside a door or gate, to keep it shut; a chain across a street for defence in war.

Cat-bar, *n.* a bar that fastens that half of a door which does not contain the lock.

Cat-beds, *n.* a children's game, played with pieces of turf.

Catch, *n.* an acquisition; a most eligible husband or wife, a good matrimonial match; a knack, the trick of a thing; a sudden pain or stitch; the 'sneck' of a door, &c.; a stumble; a sudden surprise.

Catched, *v. pret.* and *ppl.* caught.

Catch-honours, *n.* a card game.

Catchie, *adj.* merry, jocund; attracting one's interest, liking, &c.

Catchie, *n.* a mason's small hammer for pinning walls.

Catch-match, *n.* a match of great advantage to one side.

Catch-rogue, *n.* goose-grass.

Catcht, *v. pret.* and *ppl.* caught.

Catch-the-lang-tens, *n.* a card game.

Catch-the-plack, *n.* money-grubbing.

Catch-the-salmon, *n.* a boys' game, played with a piece of rope.

Catch-the-ten, *n.* a card game.

Catch-the-thief, *n.* a constable.

Catchy, *adj.* disposed to take unfair advantage; quick at taking the catch; uncertain, unsettled; irritable; ready to take offence.

Cate, *v.* used of cats: to desire the male.

Catechis, *n.* a catechism; the Shorter Catechism.

Category, *n.* a list or class of accused persons.

Cater, *n.* money, cash.

Cater, *v.* used of cats: to desire the male.

Cateran, *n.* a Highland robber or freebooter.

Cat-fish, *n.* the sea-wolf, the sea-cat.

Cat-gull, *n.* the herring-gull.

Cat-gut, *n.* sea-laces.

Cath, *v.* to drive or toss a ball by striking it with the hand or a light club or bat.

Cat-harrow, *n.* in *phr.* 'to draw the cat-harrow,' used of persons: to quarrel among themselves, thwart each other.

Cathead band, *n.* a coarse ironstone.

Cat-heather, *n.* a species of heather growing in separate upright stalks with flowers at the top.

Cathel, *n.* caudle; a hot-pot of ale, sugar, and eggs.

Cathel-nail, *n.* the nail by which the body of a cart is fixed to the axle.

Ca'-the-shuttle, *n.* a weaver.

Cat-hole, *n.* a loophole or narrow opening in the wall of a barn to give cats admission and exit; a niche in the wall in which small articles are deposited.

Ca' through, *n.* great energy; an uproar.

Cat-hud, *n.* a large stone at the back of the fire on a cottage hearth.

Catill, Cattil, *v.* to thrust the fingers forcibly under the ears, as a cruel punishment.—*n.* the act of inflicting such.

Cat-in-clover, *n.* bird's-foot trefoil. Cf. Catten-clover.

Cat-in-the-barrel, *n.* a barbarous game formerly played at Kelso once a year.

Cat-in-the-hole, *n.* a boys' game.

Cat-kindness, *n.* cupboard-love.

Catling, *n.* catgut, a fiddle-string.

Catloup, *n.* a short distance; a moment of time.

Catmaw, *n.* a somersault; in *phr.* 'tumble the catmaw,' to turn topsy-turvy.—*adv.* used of the eyes: turned upward; heels over head.

Catogle, *n.* the great horned owl.

Catribat, *v.* to contend; to quarrel.

Catrick, *n.* a supposed disease of the roots of the fingers from too frequent handling of cats; a cataract supposed to affect the eyes of the first person that meets a cat which has leapt over a dead body.

Catridge, Catrons, *n.* a diminutive person fond of women.

Cat's-carriage, *n.* a seat formed by two persons crossing their hands, on which to place a third; 'queen's-cushion.'

Cat's-cradle, *n.* a plaything of twine on the fingers of one person transferred to those of another.

Cat's hair, *n.* the down on an unfledged bird; the down on the face of a boy before a beard grows; thin hair growing on the bodies of persons in bad health; the 'cirrus' and 'cirro-stratus' clouds.

Catsherd, *n.* cataract. Cf. Catrick.

Cat siller, *n.* mica.

Cat's-lug, *n. Auricula ursi.*

Cat's-stairs, *n.* a child's toy made of thread, &c., and so disposed by the hand as to fall down like steps of a stair, or twisted into the shape of stairs.

Cats'-tails, *n.* hare's-tail rush, cotton-grass.

Catstanes, *n.* the upright stones which support a grate on either side.

Cat-steps, *n.* the projections of the stones in the slanting part of a gable.

Cat-strand, *n.* a very small stream.

Cat-tails, *n.* cotton-grass. Cf. Cats'-tails.

Catten-clover, *n.* bird's-foot trefoil.

Catter, *n.* money, cash. Cf. Cater.

Catter, *n.* a disease at the roots of the fingers, supposed to arise from the too frequent handling of cats. Cf. Catrick.

Catterbatch, *n.* a broil, quarrel.

Catterbatter, *v.* to wrangle good-humouredly.

Catter-wier, *adj.* snappish; surly; churlish.

Catter-wower, *v.* to caterwaul.—*n.* a caterwaul.

Cattie-and-doggie, *n.* the game of 'cat-and-dog.' Cf. Cat-and-dog.

Cattie-bargle, -bargie, *n.* a noisy, angry quarrel among children.

Cattie-wurrie, *v.* to dispute noisily and violently.—*n.* a violent dispute; a noisy, angry quarrel among children.

Cattie-wurriein, *n.* a continuous violent disputing.—*ppl. adj.* peevish.

Cattle, *n.* lice, fleas, &c.; used contemptuously of persons.

Cattle-close, *n.* a farm cattle-yard.

Cattle-creep, *n.* a low arch or gangway to enable cattle to pass under or over a railway.

Cattleman, *n.* a servant in charge of the cattle on a farm.

Cattle-raik, *n.* a common, or extensive pasturage, where cattle feed at large.

Cat-wa', *n.* a stone wall dividing a cottage into two rooms.

Cat-whins, *n.* the needle furze.

Cat-witted,-wutted, *adj.* harebrained; savage in temper.

Catyogle, *n.* the great horned owl. Cf. Catogle.

†Caudebec-hat, *n.* a woollen French hat.

Cauder, *n.* money. Cf. Cater.

Caudron, *n.* a caldron.

Cauf, *n.* a calf, a fool. Cf. Calf.

Cauf, *n.* chaff.

Cauf-grun, *n.* one's native place.

Caugle, *n.* four cherry-stones in the game of 'paips.' Cf. Caddle, Castle.

Cauk, *n.* chalk.—*v.* to draw with chalk; to mark down a debt.

Cauk, *n.* cark.

Cauk, *n.* the point turned down on a horseshoe.—*v.* to turn down the ends and toes of horseshoes.

Cauker, *n.* the hind-part of a horseshoe sharpened and turned down; the iron rim or plate on a clog or shoe-heel.

Cauker, *n.* a bumper; a drink of spirits.

Caul, Cauld, *n.* a damhead; a weir on a river to divert water into a 'mill-lade.'

Caul, Cauld, *v.* used of a river-bank: to lay a bed of loose stones from the channel of the river backwards, as far as necessary, to defend the land from the inroads of the water.

Caul, Cauld, *n.* a cold.—*adj.* cold.

Caul cap, *n.* an old woman's cap, of triangular shape.

Cauld-bark, *n.* a coffin, grave.

Cauld-casten-tee, *adj.* lifeless, dull; insipid.

Cauld coal, *n.* in *phr.* to 'blaw a cauld coal,' to engage in unpromising work, to undergo failure or loss.

Cauld comfort, *n.* inhospitableness, poor entertainment.

Cauld-kail-het-again, *n. phr.* broth warmed up again; a sermon preached twice to the same audience; a broken-off love affair renewed; an insipid repetition of anything.

Cauld-like, *adj.* used of the weather: likely to be cold.

Cauldness, *n.* coldness.

Cauldrid, *adj.* chilling.

Cauldrife, *adj.* cold, chilly; indifferent; lacking animation in preaching; disaffected. Cf. Caldrife.

Cauld seed, *n.* late peas.

Cauld steer, *n.* sour milk or cold water and meal stirred together.

Cauld straik, *n.* a 'dram' of raw spirits.

Cauld win', *n.* little encouragement.

Cauld winter, *n.* the last load of corn brought from the field to the stackyard.

Cauler, Cauller, *adj.* cool, fresh. Cf. Caller.

Cauliflower, *n.* the head on ale.

Caulk, *n.* chalk. Cf. Cauk.

Caulker, *n.* a drink of spirits.

Caulker, *n.* a calker.

Caulm, *n.* a mould, frame; a bullet-mould; in *pl.* course of framing or construction. Cf. Calm.

Caulm, *adj.* calm; smooth, even. Cf. Calm.

Caulms, *n.* the small cords through which the warp is passed in the loom, the 'heddles.'

Caum, *n.* slate-pencil.—*v.* to whiten a hearth with 'camstane.' Cf. Cam.

Caum, *n.* a mould, frame. Cf. Cam.

Caum, *adj.* calm; smooth.

Caumshell, *n.* a piece of white shell, or bony matter, in shape not unlike a lady's slipper, frequently found on the seashore.

Caumstane, *n.* pipeclay; 'whitening.' Cf. Camstane.

Ca up, *n.* a thorough, overhauling search.

Caup, *n.* blackmail paid by private men to thieves.

Caup, *n.* a wooden drinking-vessel.

Caup, *v.* to twist, bulge, warp. Cf. **Cap.**

Caup, *n.* the shell of a snail.
Cauped, *ppl. adj.* bulging, bending in curves.
Caup-snail, *n.* the snail inhabiting the black shell, common among old gardens and castles.
Caur, Caure, *n.* calves. Cf. Car.
Caur, Caurry, *adj.* left, as opposed to right. Cf. Car.
Caurry-, Caur-handed, *adj.* left-handed.
Cause, *conj.* because.
Cause, *n.* sake; trial in a court; in *phr.* 'hour of cause,' the time of a trial, in inferior courts, formerly from 10 A.M. to 12 noon.
†Causey, Caussey, *n.* a causeway, street.— *v.* to pave.
Causey-clash, *n.* street gossip.
Causey-clothes, *n.* dress in which one may appear in public.
Causey-crown, *n.* the middle or highest part of the road.
Causey-dancer, *n.* a gadabout, one who is continually on the street.
Causeyer, *n.* a pavior, one who makes a 'causey.'
Causey-faced, *adj.* brazen-faced, unashamed.
Causey-raker, *n.* a street-sweeper, a scavenger.
Causey-stanes, *n.* cobble-stones, paving-stones.
Causey-tales, *n.* common news, street news.
Causey-talk, *n.* street gossip.
Causey-webs, *n.* in *phr.* 'to make causey-webs,' to neglect one's work, and idle in the streets.
†Caution, *n.* security, guarantee; a surety.— *v.* to be surety; to wager; to guarantee, warrant.
Cautioner, *n.* a surety for another.
Cautionry, *n.* suretyship.
Cautious, *adj.* unassuming, kindly, obliging, quiet. Cf. Cowshus.
Cauts, *n.* the tremulous appearance near the surface of the ground in hot sunshine.
Cave, *n.* a hen-coop. Cf. Cavie.
Cave, *n.* a deficiency in intelligence.
Cave, *v.* to push; to drive backward and forward; to toss; to toss the head haughtily or awkwardly; to rear and plunge; to topple over; to climb a steep wall, &c.; to walk awkwardly; to tread heavily, as in mud or from fatigue; to separate grain from broken straw, after threshing; to separate corn from chaff.—*n.* a stroke, a push; a toss of the head, forelegs, or hands.
Cavee, *n.* a state of commotion; perturbation of mind. Cf. Cavy.
Cavel, *n.* a low fellow.
Cavel, *v.* to quarrel; to scold. Cf. Cavil.
Cavel, *n.* a lot; a share; lot, fate, destiny; a division or share by lot; a 'rig' of growing

corn on the 'run-rig' system; a rod, pole, long staff.—*v.* to divide by lot.
Cavelling, *n.* the division by lot.
Caver, *n.* a gentle breeze moving the water slightly. Cf. Kever.
Cavie, *n.* a hen-coop; the lower part of an 'aumrie,' or meat-press.
Cavie, *v.* to rear, prance; to toss the head; to walk with an airy or affected step.
Cavied, *ppl.* cooped up.
Cavie-keek-bo'in', *phr.* courting near the 'aumrie-cavie.'
Cavil, *n.* a wrangle, quarrel.—*v.* to argue, quarrel; to scold. Cf. Kevel.
Cavings, *n.* the short, broken straw from which the grain has been separated after threshing. Cf. Kevins.
Cavy, *n.* perturbation of mind; a state or commotion.
Caw, *v.* to drive, impel; to hammer.—*n.* the motion of wind-driven water. Cf. Ca'.
Caw, *v.* to call; to call names. Cf. Ca'.
Caw, *n.* quick, oppressive breathing.
Caw-again, *v.* to contradict.
Cawaw'd, *ppl.* fatigued; wearied to disgust.
Cawdah, *n.* lint.
†Cawdebink-hat, *n.* a woollen French hat. Cf. Caudebec-hat.
†Cawdy, *n.* a cadet; an errand-runner. Cf. Caddie.
Cawer, *n.* a driver.
Cawk, *n.* chalk. Cf. Cauk.
Cawk, *n.* the point turned down on a horse-shoe. Cf. Cauk.
Cawker, *n.* the calker of a horseshoe.
Cawker, *n.* a morning glass of spirits, a 'dram.' Cf. Caulker.
Cawlie, *n.* a boy; a disreputable fellow. Cf. Coulie.
Cawmer, *v.* to calm, quiet.
Cawmril, *n.* a spawned haddock. Cf. Cameral.
Cawnle-licht, *n.* candle-light.
Cawper, *n.* bargain, profit, advantage.
Cawr, *adj.* left, as opposed to right.
Cawsay, Cawsey, *n.* a causeway, street. Cf. Causey.
Cazzie, *n.* a sack or net made of straw twisted and plaited.
Cazzie-chair, *n.* an easy-chair made of straw twisted and plaited.
Cea, *n.* a small tub. Cf. Say.
Cedent, *n.* a legal term: one who cedes or yields to another, or executes a bond of resignation.
Cell, *n.* a chain for fastening a cow in a stall. Cf. Seal.
Censor, *n.* one who calls the roll of students at the University and of the scholars of the Grammar School at Aberdeen.

Censure, *v.* to take toll of.

Cep, Ceps, Cept, *prep.* except, but.—*conj.* except, unless, but.

Cepin, *conj.* excepting.

Cert, *n.* in *phr.* 'for cert,' beyond a doubt.

Certainly, *adv.* accurately, correctly.

Certaint, *adj.* certain, sure.

†**Certes, Certis, Certies, Certie, Certy**, *adv.* of a truth, certainly.—*n.* in *phr.* 'my certie,' by my troth, take my word for it.

Certify, *v.* to warn of legal consequences of disobedience, &c.

Certiorate, *v.* to certify; a legal term.

Cess, *n.* a tax, rate; a local tax; a pest.

Cess-money, *n.* money paid in rates or taxes.

Chack, *n.* a slight and hasty refreshment, a 'snack'; a slight bruise or knock.—*v.* to cut or bruise suddenly; to prick, 'jag'; to cause moral pain; to lay hold of anything quickly, so as to gash it with the teeth.

Chack, *v.* to clack, make a clicking or clinking noise; used of the teeth: to chatter with cold or fright.

Chack, *n.* the wheatear.

Chack, *v.* to check, squeeze.—*n.* a check, squeeze. Cf. Check.

Chack, *n.* a rut in a road; a wheel-track.

Chack, *adj.* of a check pattern.

Chack-a-pudding, *n.* a selfish fellow who always seizes what is best at meals.

Chackart, Chackert, *n.* the stonechat; the whinchat; the wheatear; a term of endearment or of affectionate reproach.

Chackie, *n.* a striped cotton bag for carrying a ploughman's clean clothes, &c.

Chackie, *n.* the stonechat.

Chackie, *adj.* unequal; full of ruts; gravelly.

Chackie, *adj.* ? dimpled.

Chackie-mill, *n.* the death-watch.

Chackit, *ppl.* checkered; of a check-pattern; chequered.

Chack-lowrie, *n.* mashed cabbage mixed with barley-broth.

Chack-reel, *n.* the common reel for winding yarn, with a check, or a clicking noise, when a 'cut' of yarn has been wound on it.

Chad, *n.* compacted gravel; small stones forming a river-bed.

Chaddy, *adj.* gravelly.

Chaet, *v.* to cheat.—*n.* a cheat. Cf. Cheat.

Chaetry, *n.* cheating. Cf. Cheatery.

Cha'fause, *v.* ? to suffer.

Chaff, *v.* to chew; to eat. Cf. Chaft.

Chaff, *v.* to chatter, be loquacious.

Chaff, *v.* to chafe, rub; to fret, be angry.—*n.* a rage; ill-humour.

Chaffer, *n.* the round-lipped whale.

Chaffer, *n.* a chafing-dish.

Chaffie, *n.* the chaffinch.

Chaffle, *v.* to chaffer, higgle.

Chaffrie, *n.* refuse, rubbish.

Chaft, *n.* the jaw, jaw-bone; in *pl.* chops, cheeks.

Chaft-blades, *n.* jaws, jaw-bones.

Chaft-talk, *n.* prattle, idle talk.

Chaft-tooth, *n.* a jaw-tooth, molar.

Chain-drapper, *n.* a cheap jeweller who frequents fairs and professes to give great bargains to his own loss and to the advantage of his customers.

Chainge, *v.* to change. Cf. Change.

†**Chaip**, *v.* to escape. Cf. Chape.

Chaip, *v.* to ask the price of an article on sale.—*n.* purchase, bargain.

Chaipin, *n.* inquiry as to price of an article.

Chair-haffets, *n.* the upright sides of a high-backed easy-chair.

†**Chaistain**, *n.* a chestnut. Cf. Chasten.

Chaistifie, *v.* to chastise. Cf. Chastify.

Chak, *n.* a snack.—*v.* to bite, chew; to cause pain. Cf. Chack.

Chak, *n.* a rut; a wheel-track. Cf. Chack.

Chalder, *n.* a measure of grain, nearly eight quarters.

Challenge, *v.* to rate, scold.—*n.* a call, summons to death.

Chalmer, *n.* a room, chamber; an upper room; a bedroom; the police-court; the magistrate's room.—*v.* to closet; to shut up. Cf. Chamber, Chaumer.

Chalmer-chield, *n.* a valet or groom of the chambers.

Chalmer-glew, *n.* secret wantonness, 'chambering.'

Chalmerie, *n.* a small chamber.

Chalmer o' deis, *n.* a parlour; the best bed-room. Cf. Chambradeese.

Cham, *v.* to chew.

Chamber, *n.* any upper room; a bedroom; the police-court.

Chamber-bed, *n.* the bed in the best bedroom.

Chambered, *ppl. adj.* closeted; shut up.

Chambradeese, *n.* a parlour; the best bed-room.

Chamer, *n.* a chamber.

Chamie, *n.* the game of 'shinty' or hockey.

Chammer, *v.* to silence, settle, 'shut up.'

Champ, *n.* stamp, quality, kind.

Champ, *n.* a mire; ground trodden and mashed by the feet of animals.—*v.* to chop; to mash; to crush, bruise.

†**Champ**, *n.* the figure raised on diaper, silk, &c.; tapestry.

†**Champart**, *n.* field-rent; rent in kind.

Champers, Champies, *n.* mashed potatoes.

Champion, *adj.* first-rate; very good; in fine health.

Champit, *adj.* used of patterns or figures: raised on a ground.

Chance, *v.* to risk; to give the chance.

Chance-bairn, *n.* an illegitimate child.
Chancellor, *n.* the foreman of a jury.
Chancer, *n.* a brass button, gilded and lettered.
Chance-time, *n.* odd times.
Chancler, *n.* a chancellor; foreman of a jury.
†**Chancy**, *adj.* lucky, auspicious, presaging good fortune; fortunate, happy; safe to deal or meddle with; generally with *neg.*
†**Chandler**, *n.* a candlestick.
Chandler-chafts, *n.* lantern-jaws; a meagre visage.
Chandler-pins, *n.* in *phr.* 'to be a' on chandler-pins,' to be particularly precise or nice in speech; to speak 'fine English.'
Chang, *n.* a loud, confused noise, like that of a flock of geese.
Change, *n.* the custom of one who buys from particular persons; a small inn, a tavern, alehouse; in *pl.* underlinen.—*v.* used of milk : to turn sour; of meat, &c. : to decompose; to exchange; to substitute, as fairies were supposed to do with children; with *self*, to change one's clothes.
Change-house, *n.* an alehouse, tavern.
Change-keeper, *n.* a tavern-keeper; the landlord of a petty inn.
Change-seats-the-king-is-coming, *n.* a children's game.
Change-wife, *n.* a female tavern-keeper.
Changy, *adj.* fickle, given to change.
Chanler, *n.* a candlestick. Cf. Chandler.
Channel, *n.* gravel from the channel of a river.—*v.* to play at 'curling'; to cover with gravel, to spread gravel.
Channelly, *adj.* gravelly, 'shingly.'
Channel-stane, *n.* a curling-stone.
Channer, Channers, *n.* gravel.
Channer, *v.* to scold fretfully; to grumble.—*n.* strife; querulousness.
Channery, *adj.* gravelly.
Channery-, Chanry-kirk, *n.* a canonry church, a church of the canons.
Chanrock, *n.* a channel of round stones.
Chant, *v.* to speak much pertly, to speak with a strange accent, or with an English accent.—*n.* pert language; a person given to pert language.
Chanter, *n.* the fingering part of a bagpipe.
Chanter-horn, *n.* a shepherd's pipe or reed.
Chanticleer, *n.* the fish dragonet.
Chantie-beak, *n.* a chatterbox.
Chanting, *ppl. adj.* loquacious, pert.
Chanty, *n.* a chamber-pot; a kind of flat-topped spinning-top.
Chap, *n.* a fellow; a person; used humorously of a woman; with *auld*, the devil.
Chap, *v.* to strike a bargain; to choose, fix upon.—*n.* in *phr.* 'chap and choice,' a great variety to choose from.
Chap, *v.* to knock; to strike; to hammer; to

rap; used of a clock : to strike; to chop, pound, bruise, break in pieces; to step, walk; with *hands*, to clasp in betrothing or bargaining; with *out*, to call a person out by tapping at a window; with *yont*, to get out of the way.—*n.* a knock, stroke, blow with a hammer; a tap; used of drought : a long period; the noise of breaking waves on a pebbly beach.
Chap, *n.* the jaw, the cheek.
Chap, *n.* a shop.
†**Chape**, *v.* to escape.
Chapel-folk, *n.* Episcopalians.
†**Chapin**, *n.* a chopine. Cf. Chappin.
Chapling, *n.* of a guild or craft : the loss of individual votes of members at an election who go with the majority.
Chapman's-drouth, *n.* hunger and thirst.
Chap-mill, *n.* clappers.
Chappan, *n.* tall of stature, clever, lusty, 'chopping.'
Chapper, *n.* a door-knocker.
Chapper, *n.* a blacksmith's man who wields the sledge-hammer.
Chapper, *n.* a 'beetle' for mashing potatoes, &c.
Chappie, *n.* a little fellow.
Chappie, *n.* a name given to a ghost, from its frequent knockings.
†**Chappin**, *n.* a chopine; a dry or liquid measure, nearly an English quart.
Chappin'-hammer, *n.* a stone-breaker's hammer.
Chappin'-knife, *n.* a butcher's knife or cleaver.
Chappin'-stick, *n.* any instrument or weapon used for striking with.
Chaps me, *int.* an excl. when one person claims a share in anything found by two or more persons in company, or when he chooses a particular article.
Chaps ye, *int.* an excl. used by a person at once accepting an offer or bargain.
Chapterly, *adv.* used of the meeting of a presbytery when all the members are present.
Char'd, *n.* a leaning-place.
Chare, *n.* care, charge; a ward, one under a guardian. Cf. Chiel nor chare.
†**Charet**, *n.* a chariot.
Char-filler, *n.* a blast-furnace worker.
Charge, *n.* expense, cost.
Chargeable, *adj.* costly, expensive.
Chariot, *n.* a urinal or chamber-pot.
Charitcher, *n.* the Shorter Catechism.
Chark, *v.* to make a grating noise, as teeth in biting any gritty substance; to make a grinding, grunting noise; to be continually complaining, to be querulous; of a bird : to repeat a melancholy call; to chirp as a cricket.

Charker, *n.* a cricket.

Charlie-mufti, *n.* the whitethroat.

Charnle-, Charnal-pins, *n.* the pins on which the hinges of machinery turn; in *phr.* ' to miss one's charnle-pins,' to be unable to stand straight through intoxication.

Chaser, *n.* a ram with only one testicle.

Chass-window, *n.* a sash-window. Cf. Chess.

†Chasten, *n.* chestnut. Cf. Chaistain.

Chastify, *v.* to chastise, castigate.

Chastise, *v.* to abridge.

Chat, *n.* chatter, talkativeness, pert language.

Chat, *n.* a lunch, slight refreshment.

Chat, *n.* an opprobrious epithet addressed to a child; a chit.

Chat, *n.* the gallows.

Chat, *v.* to bruise slightly; to chafe, rub.

Chat, *n.* a call to swine.

Chat-dinner, *n.* a little bit of dinner.

Chatter, *v.* to divide a thing by causing many fractions; to shatter; to break suddenly into small pieces; to tear, bruise.—*n.* a bruise; the act of shattering.

Chatter, *v.* to rattle.

Chattering-bit, -piece, *n.* a piece of oatcake eaten on leaving the water after bathing in the open air.

Chattle, *v.* to nibble, chew, chew feebly; to eat as a lamb or a young child.

Chatty-puss, *n.* a call to a cat. Cf. Cheetie.

†Chaudmallet, Chaudmellé, *n.* a sudden broil or quarrel; a blow, a beating; homicide in a passion.

Chauffer, *n.* a person of bad disposition.

Chauks, *n.* a sluice.

Chaum, *v.* to chew voraciously; to eat up. Cf. Cham.

Chaumer, *n.* a chamber. Cf. Chalmer, Chamber.

Chaumerie, *n.* a small chamber.

Chauner, *v.* to fret; to grumble. Cf. Channer.

Chaunter, *n.* the pipe of the bagpipe. Cf. Chanter.

Chaup, *v.* to strike a bargain. Cf. Chap.

Chaup, *v.* to knock, strike, hammer; to tap. Cf. Chap.

Chaut, *v.* to chew feebly; to chew with a crackling sound.

Chauther, *n.* a ' chalder,' a grain-measure. Cf. Chalder.

Chauttle, *v.* to nibble. Cf. Chattle.

Chauve, *adj.* used of cattle : having white hair pretty equally mixed with black; of a swarthy person : pale.

Chaveling, *n.* a spokeshave. Cf. Shavelin.

Chaw, *v.* to chew; to fret or cut by attrition; to vex, provoke; to be sulky, feel annoyed. —*n.* a mouthful; a quid of tobacco; a bitter and envious disappointment which shows itself in face and eyes; with *words,*

to speak indistinctly; with *upon,* to brood upon, to think over.

Chawchling, *ppl. adj.* eating like a swine.

Cheap, *adj. phr.* ' cheap o't,' thoroughly deserving of it, ' serves one right.'

Cheap-good, *adj.* cheap.—*n.* a good bargain.

Chearer, *n.* a glass of toddy. Cf. Cheerer.

Cheat, *n.* a call to cats. Cf. Cheet.

Cheat, *v.* to deceive, mistake, used *impersonally* or in *passive.*

Cheatery, Cheatry, *n.* cheating, fraud, deception.—*adj.* fraudful, deceitful, false.

Cheats, *n.* the sweetbread.

Cheat-the-wuddy, *n.* a gallows-knave, one who deserves to be hanged.

Check, *n.* the wheatear. Cf. Chack.

Check, *v.* to bite; to bruise; to clack.—*n.* a slight bruise; a slight refreshment, a ' snack.' Cf. Chack.

Check-reel, *n.* a reel for winding yarn. Cf. Chack-reel.

Check-spail, *n.* a box on the ear or on the cheek.

Check-weigher, *n.* the man who checks the weight of coal on the surface.

Cheek, *v.* with *in with,* to flatter, curry favour; with *up,* to use insolent language; with *up till,* to court, to make love to.—*n.* the side of a place, post, door, or fire; a door-post; a gate-post; the side of a loaf of bread; impertinence.

Cheek-aside, *adv.* on the side of the ' cheek '; beside the ' cheek.'

Cheek-blade, *n.* the cheek-bone.

Cheek-bone, -rack, *n.* the bridle of the twelve-oxen plough.

Cheek-for-chow, *adv.* side by side, close together.

Cheek-haffit, *n.* the side of the face or head.

Cheekie, *adj.* full of cunning; forward; impertinent.

Cheekie-for-chowie, *n.* a dainty made of oatmeal, butter, and sugar.

Cheekie-, Cheek-for-chowie, *adv.* side by side.

Cheek-spool, *n.* a box on the ear; a blow on the cheek. Cf. Check-spail.

Cheel, Cheelie, *n.* a young fellow. Cf. Chield.

Cheemist, *n.* a chemist, druggist.

Cheen, *v.* to chain.—*n.* a chain.

Cheenge, *v.* to change. Cf. Change.

Cheeny, *n.* china; a boys' china marble.

Cheep, *n.* a chirp, cry of a young bird; a creak, faint noise; a soft or light kiss; a word, hint, least mention.—*v.* to chirp, cry like a young bird; to squeak like a mouse or rat, to creak like a shoe or door; to speak feebly or quietly; to make a slight sound; to disclose a secret, tell only a little; of grain : to begin to sprout in malting.

Cheepart, *n.* the meadow-pipit; a small person with a shrill voice.

Cheeper, *n.* a half-fledged bird, a young grouse or partridge; a silent kiss; the cricket; the bog-iris.

Cheer, *n.* a chair.

Cheese, *n.* the receptacle of the thistle, *Carduus lanceolatus;* in *phr.* 'not to say cheese,' to say nothing.

Cheese-breaker, *n.* a curd-crusher.

Cheese-brizer, *n.* a cheese-press.

Cheese-drainer, *n.* a vessel for draining whey from the curd.

Cheese-ford, *n.* a cheese-press. Cf. Chess-ford.

Cheese-hake, -rack, *n.* a frame for drying cheese.

Cheese-loft, *n.* an upper room in a dairy reserved for the storing and 'ripening' of cheese newly made.

Cheese-set, *n.* a cheese-press.

Cheese-stane, *n.* a large, heavy stone, worked with a screw, for pressing cheese.

Cheese-tub, -vat, *n.* a tub for pressing cheese.

Cheet, *n.* a call to cats; a cat.

Cheetie, *n.* a call to cats; pussy.

Cheetie-bautherin, *n.* a cat. Cf. Baudrons.

Cheetle, *v.* to chirp, pipe, warble.

Cheik, *n.* a brass button.

Cheim, *v.* to divide equally; to cut down the backbone of an animal equally.

Cheip, *v.* to chirp; to creak. Cf. Cheep.

Cheir, *v.* to cut, wound.

Cheirs, *n.* scissors, 'shears.'

Cheitle, *v.* to chirp. Cf. Cheetle.

Chenyie, *n.* a chain.

Cherk, *v.* to emit a grating sound; to creak. Cf. Chirk.

Cherry, *n.* a red worsted knob on the top of a man's 'bonnet.'

Chesbow, *n.* the poppy.

†**Chess,** *n.* the sash or frame of a window.

Chess, *n.* the quarter or smaller division of an apple or pear cut regular into pieces; the 'lith' of an orange.

Chessart, Chessirt, *n.* a tub for pressing cheese.

Chessel, Chessil, *n.* a 'chessart.' Cf. Cheswell.

Chessford, *n.* a 'chessart.'

Chest, *n.* a large box for holding meal, bread &c.; a coffin.—*v.* to put into a coffin. Cf. Kist.

Chester-barley, -bear, *n.* a coarse barley with four rows on each head.

Chesting, *n.* the ceremony of putting a corpse into the coffin, the 'coffining.'

Cheswell, *n.* a cheese press or vat.—*v.* to press cheese in a vat.

Chettoun, *n.* the setting of a precious stone.

Cheugh-jean, *n.* a jujube.

Chevalier, *n.* a favourite son.

†**Cheveron,** *n.* a kid glove.

Chew, *v.* to stew.

Chew, *int.* a call to a dog to get out of the way, or of reproof.

Chice, *n.* choice.

Chick, *int.* a call to chickens, &c.

Chick, *n.* a tick; a beat.—*v.* to tick, make a clicking noise.

Chicken, *adv.* cowardly, timid.

Chicken-weed, -wort, *n.* chickweed.

Chicker, *v.* to cluck as a hen.

Chickmarly, *n.* a hen gray and black.

Chickstane, *n.* the wheatear.

Chide, *n.* a chiding, scolding.

Chief, *adj.* intimate, friendly, 'thick.'

Chield, Chiel, *n.* a child; a fellow, a man; a son; a daughter; a young man or woman, a stripling; a valet, a servant; a term of fondness or intimacy.

Chiel nor (or) chare, *phr.* kith nor (or) kin; belongings, relations.

Chier, *v.* to cut, to wound. Cf. Cheir.

Chiff, *v.* to spit, making a noise or puff with the lips.

Chiffer-oot, *n.* one who bears a name tabooed among fishermen of the N.E. of Scotland.

Chilcorn, *n.* a blackhead on the face. Cf. Shillcorn.

Childer, *n.* children.

Chill-cauld, *adj.* nearly frozen.

Chilpy, *adj.* chilly, chilled.

Chim, *v.* to take by small portions.

Chim, *n.* a friend, a 'chum.'

Chimbla, Chimblay, *n.* a chimney. Cf. Chimney.

Chim-cham, *v.* to talk in a long-winded, undecided way.

Chimins, *n.* 'sowens,' furmenty.

Chimla, Chimley, *n.* a chimney. Cf. Chimney.

Chimla-brace, *n.* the mantelpiece; the beam supporting 'cat and clay' chimneys in cottages.

Chimla-can, *n.* a chimney-pot.

Chimla-cheek, *n.* the fireside; the side of the grate; an insertion to lessen the size of the grate.

Chimla-end, *n.* the wall of a room where the fireplace is.

Chimla-heid, *n.* a chimney-top.

Chimla-lug, *n.* the fireside.

Chimla-nook, *n.* the fireside or a corner near it.

Chimla-ribs, *n.* the bars of a grate.

Chimney, *n.* a grate, fireplace; the fire.

Chin, *n.* a primitive knocker, being a metal boss fixed on the door-post, and struck by any one wishing admittance.

China, *n.* a boys' painted china marble. Cf. Cheeny.

Chin-cloth, *n.* a kind of mask for the lower part of the face.

Chine, *n.* that part of the staves of a barrel which projects beyond the head.

Chingle, *n.* gravel free from dirt; sea-gravel, shingle.

Chingly, Chingily, *adj.* gravelly.

Chink, *n.* money, cash.

Chink, *n.* the reed-bunting.

Chinkie, *n.* the chin.

Chinlie, *adj.* gravelly, shingly. Cf. Chingly.

Chintie-chin, *n.* a long chin, a projecting chin.

Chip, *v.* to chop, cut with an axe; used of seeds, buds, &c. : to burst, sprout, germinate ; of young birds : to begin to crack the shell, to prepare for necessary flight ; to be in the early stage of pregnancy ; used of ale : to begin to ferment in the vat.

Chip, *n.* beaver for hats.

Chip-hat, *n.* a beaver-hat.

Chippie-burdie, *n.* a promise made to pacify a child.

Chippit, *ppl. adj.* touched with liquor.

Chirk, *v.* to emit a grating sound ; to creak, squeak ; to grind with the teeth, to gnaw.— *n.* a grating sound, a sound made by the teeth when rubbed together, or by one hard body rubbing against another.

Chirking, *ppl. adj.* shifty, tricky.

Chirkle, *v.* to grind the teeth.

Chirl, *v.* to chirp, warble merrily ; to whistle shrilly ; to emit a low, melancholy sound, as birds do in winter or before a storm ; to laugh immoderately.— *n.* a low, melancholy sound ; chirping.

Chirle, *n.* a double chin ; the wattles or barbs of a cock.

Chirle, Chirlie, *n.* a small piece of anything edible ; a piece of coal of intermediate size between the largest and small coal used in smithies.

Chirlie, *adj.* well-shaped ; of a handy size ; suitable, handy for use.

Chirm, *n.* the note or song of a bird ; a low, murmuring, mournful conversation.—*v.* to chirp, sing ; to make a low, melancholy note, as a bird before a storm ; to warble, 'croon,' hum ; to murmur, fret, complain.

Chirm, *n.* a small or undeveloped thing ; in *pl.* the early shoots of grass.

Chirnells, *n.* small hard swellings in the neck-glands of young people. Cf. Kernel.

Chirper, *n.* the cricket.

Chirple, *v.* to twitter as a swallow.—*n.* a twittering note.

Chirr, *v.* to chirp ; to emit a shrill sound.— *n.* the call of a partridge. Cf. Churr.

Chirt, *v.* to make a grating noise with the teeth. —*n.* a grating noise. Cf. Chirk.

Chirt, *v.* to squirt with the teeth ; to press, squeeze ; to press out ; to act in a gripping manner ; to practise extortion.—*n.* a squeeze ; a squirt ; a small quantity.

Chirt, *v.* to press hard at stool.

Chirt, *v.* to restrain laughter.

†Chirurgeon, *n.* a surgeon.

†Chirurgerie, *n.* surgery.

Chisell, *v.* to press in a cheese-press.—*n.* a cheese-press. Cf. Cheswell.

Chiskin, *n.* the wheatear. Cf. Chickstane.

Chislet, *ppl. adj.* engraved.

Chisp, *n.* a gap in the woof of cloth.

Chissat, *n.* a cheese-press. Cf. Chessart.

Chit, *n.* a small bit of bread or of any kind of food.

Chit, *n.* a call to a cat ; a cat. Cf. Cheet.

Chits, *n.* the sweetbread. Cf. Cheats.

Chitter, *v.* to tremble ; to shiver from cold ; of the teeth : to chatter ; to twitter ; to chirp.—*n.* a fragment ; a piece broken by a fall.

Chitter-chatter, *n.* foolish talk ; the chattering of the teeth from cold.—*v.* to chatter ; to talk foolishly.— *adv.* in a chattering fashion.

Chitterie-chatterie, *n.* a piece of bread eaten immediately after bathing.

Chittering, *n.* talking, chattering.

Chittering-bit, -chow, -piece, *n.* a piece of bread eaten immediately after bathing in the open air.

Chitterling, *n.* an old-fashioned shirt-frill.

Chittery, *n.* small, backward fruit ; small, bad potatoes.

Chittle, *v.* to eat corn from the ear, to pull off the husks with the teeth.

Chittle, *v.* to warble, to chatter, to twitter, chirp.

Chittler, *n.* a small bird of the titmouse species.

Chitty-face, *n.* a thin, pinched, or childish face ; one who has a thin face.

Chiver, *v.* to shiver.

Chivery-, Chivering-chow, *n.* a piece of bread eaten just after bathing.

Chize, *v.* to choose. Cf. Chice.

Chizer, *n.* a chooser.

Chizors, *n.* scissors.

Chizzard, Chizzat, Chizat, *n.* a cheese-press. Cf. Chessart.

Chizzel, *n.* a cheese-press.—*v.* to press cheese. Cf. Cheswell.

Chizzel, *v.* to cheat.

Choak, *v.* to stifle ; to check ; to choke.

Choalt, *n.* a foster-brother.

Chock, *n.* the croup.

Choffer, *n.* a chafing-dish.

Choice, Choise, *v.* to choose.

Choiced, *v. pret.* chose.

Choicen, *ppl.* chosen.

Choke-a-block, *adv.* quite full, chock-full.

Choke-band, *n.* a leather band for fastening the bridle round the jaws of a horse.

Choke-rope, *n.* a rope used to clear the throat of a cow that chokes in eating turnips.

Chol, *n.* the jowl.

Choller, Choler, *n.* a double chin; the flesh covering the jaw of man or beast, when fat and hanging; in *pl.* the gills of a fish. Cf. Chuller.

Choo, *int.* a call to silence a dog. Cf. Chew.

Chookie, *n.* a chicken, hen, &c.—*int.* a call to fowls.

Chool, *n.* the jowl; a whine.—*v.* to distort the face; to whine. Cf. Chowl.

Choop, *n.* the fruit of the wild-briar.

Choosed, *v. pret.* chose.

Choowow, *v.* to grudge, grumble.

Choowowing, *n.* grumbling.

Chop, *n.* a shop.

Chop, *v.* to go on, proceed.

Chop, *n.* a 'chap,' a crack.

Chops me, *int.* an expletive. Cf. Chaps me.

Chore, *n.* a company, a party. Cf. Core.

Chork, *v.* to make a grating noise. Cf. Chirk.

Chorp, *v.* used of shoes: to creak or squeak when there is water in them.

Chouk, *n.* the jaw, cheek, neck; a gland of the throat.

Choup, *n.* the fruit of the briar. Cf. Choop.

Chouskie, *n.* a knave.

Chow, *v.* to chew.—*n.* a chew; a quid of tobacco. Cf. Chaw.

Chow, *n.* the wooden ball used in 'shinty'; the game of 'shinty'; a bullet-head.

Chow, *n.* the jowl. Cf. Chol.

Chow'd mouse, *n.* a worn-out person; one who is 'seedy' after a night's debauch.

Chowks, *n.* the jaws; the throat; the neck-glands. Cf. Chouk.

Chowl, *v.* to distort the face; to whine; to emit a mournful cry.—*n.* a mournful cry; a whine. Cf. Showl.

Chows, *n.* a small coal used in forges.

Chowtle, *v.* to chew feebly, like a child or old person.

Choyse, *v.* to choose. Cf. Choice.

Chraisy, *n.* a cap or bonnet covering the head and the back of a woman's neck. Cf. Crazy.

Christèndie, *n.* Christendom.

Christening-bit, *n.* a 'piece' of bread, of cheese, and of gingerbread given to the first person met, by those carrying the child to be baptized.

Christenmass, *n.* Christmas.

Christmas-flower, *n.* black hellebore.

Chub, *n.* a chubby child.

Chuck, *int.* a call to fowls.—*n.* a fowl, chicken; a term of endearment.

Chuck, *n.* a pebble; a boys' marble; a girls' game played with pebbles or shells.

Chuck, *v.* to toss or throw anything smartly from the hand.

Chucken, *n.* a chicken.

Chucken-heartit, *adj.* faint-hearted.

Chucket, *n.* the blackbird.

Chuckie, *n.* a hen, a chicken.—*int.* a call to fowls.

Chuckie-stane, *n.* a small pebble; a small fragment of quartz, &c., as in the crop of hens; in *pl.* a girls' game with small pebbles.

Chuckle, *v.* to nurse, look after children.

Chuckle-head, *n.* a stupid person, a dolt.

Chucks, *n.* the game of 'chuckie-stanes.'

Chuffie, *adj.* fat, chubby of cheek.

Chuffie-cheekit, *adj.* fat-faced.

Chuffie-cheeks, *n.* a fat-faced child.

Chug, *v.* to tug at an elastic substance; to pull, jerk.

Chuist, *v. pret.* chose.

Chuller, *n.* a double chin; a fat and hanging jaw. Cf. Choller.

Chum, *n.* food, provisions; 'chump.'

Chumla, *n.* a chimney. Cf. Chimla.

Chump, *n.* a short, fat person; a sharp blow; the head.

Chun, *n.* the sprout of grain or potatoes.—*v.* of potatoes: to sprout; to nip off the shoots to prevent sprouting.

Chunner, *v.* to grumble, mutter, murmur. Cf. Channer.

Chunnering, *n.* grumbling.

Church-and-mice, *n.* a children's game.

Churl, *v.* to chirp. Cf. Chirl.

Churm, *v.* to tune, sing; to grumble.—*n.* a low, murmuring conversation. Cf. Chirm.

Churnels, *n.* small, hard swellings in the neck-glands of children. Cf. Kernel.

Churn-staff, *n.* the staff fitted for working in the old-fashioned churn. Cf. Kirn-staff.

Churr, *v.* to chirp, twitter; to coo, to murmur; to call as a moorcock, partridge, &c.—*n.* the call of a partridge, &c.

Churr-muffit, *n.* the whitethroat.

Churr-owl, *n.* the night-jar.

Chuttle, *v.* to chew feebly. Cf. Chowtle.

†Chymy, *n.* chemistry.

Chynge, *v.* to change.

†Ciel, Cielery, *n.* ceiling.

Cinder, *n.* spirits mixed with water, tea, &c.

Circumduce, *v.* a legal term: to declare time elapsed for introducing evidence.

Circumjack, *v.* to enfold closely; to correspond with, agree to.

Cirssen, *v.* to baptize. Cf. Kirsen.

Cit, *n.* the civet.

Civileer, *n.* an inquisitor formerly appointed by the Town Council and the kirk-session of Glasgow to apprehend persons taking a walk on the Sabbath-day.

Civils, *n.* civil matters as distinguished from criminal.

Claaick, *n.* the state of having all the corn on a farm reaped, but not 'led' to the stack-yard ; the harvest-home.

Claaick-sheaf, *n.* the last handful of corn cut down by the reapers.

Claaick-supper, *n.* the feast formerly given on the cutting down of the corn, but latterly when the crop is stacked.

Claams, *n.* a shoemaker's pincers. Cf. Clams.

Claar, *n.* a large wooden vessel.

Clabber, *n.* soft, sticky mud ; mud on a roadway ; mire ; a handful, a dollop.—*v.* to cover with mud or dirt.

Clabby, *adj.* sticky.

Clachan, *n.* a hamlet, village, containing a church ; a village alehouse.

Clachan-howdie, *n.* a village midwife.

Clach-coal, *n.* candle or parrot coal.

Clacher, *v.* to move onwards slowly and with difficulty and clumsily.

Clack, *n.* the clapper of a mill ; the noise made by hens, &c.; noisy talk ; slander or impertinent talk ; gossip ; a female scandal-monger, gossip.—*v.* to cackle like a hen, &c.; to cry incessantly or clamorously ; to clatter, resound, echo ; to chatter, talk gossip or scandal.

Clack, *n.* a kind of toffee or treacle-candy. Cf. Claggie.

Clacken, *n.* a wooden hand-bat or racket, used by the boys of the Edinburgh Academy and High School.

Clacker, *v.* to progress slowly and with difficulty. Cf. Clacher.

Clacking, *n.* talking ; gossip.

Clackrie, *n.* talk, gossip, chatter.

Clad, *ppl. adj.* thickly covered, thronged ; accompanied, attended by.

Cladach, *n.* talk Cf. Cleitach.

Clade, *v.* to clothe.

Claes, *n.* clothes.

Claes-beetle, *n.* a mallet for beating clothes in washing.

Claff, *n.* the cleft or part of a tree where the branches separate.

Claffie, *adj.* disordered, dishevelled.—*n.* a slattern.

Clag, *v.* to clog, cover with mud, glue, &c.; to dirty, bemire.—*n.* clay, mud, &c. adhering to shoes, skirts, &c.; an encumbrance, burden ; fault, imputation of blame ; a mess of food.

Claggie, Claggim, *n.* a sticky sweetmeat made of treacle.

Claggie, *adj.* glutinous ; adhesive ; spotted with mire ; miry.

Clagginess, *n.* adhesiveness in moist, miry soils, substances, &c.

Claggock, *n.* a draggle-tail ; a dirty wench.

Claghan, *n.* a small village. Cf. Clachan.

Clagher, *v.* to move slowly, clumsily, and with difficulty. Cf. Clacker.

Claich, *v.* to besmear ; to work a viscous or semi-liquid stuff in a disgusting fashion ; to walk in mud or wet soil in a disgusting fashion ; to expectorate greatly, to clear one's throat.—*n.* the act of besmearing or working viscous stuff in a dirty way.

Claichie, *adj.* viscous, sticky, 'messy.'

Claiching, *ppl. adj.* untidy, dirty, unskilful, 'messy.'

Claid, *v. pret.* and *ppl.* covered, clothed.

Claik, *n.* the teredo or ship-worm.

Claik, *v.* to bedaub or dirty with any viscous substance.—*n.* a quantity of dirty or adhesive substance. Cf. Claich.

Claik, *v.* to cluck, cackle like a hen ; to cry clamorously ; to talk much in a trivial way ; to tattle, carry tales.—*n.* the cackle of a hen ; an idle or false report ; a woman addicted to talking. Cf. Clack.

Claik, Claik-goose, *n.* the barnacle-goose.

Claik-eaten, *adj.* bored by the ship-worm.

Claikie, *adj.* adhesive, sticky.

Claiking, *ppl.* and *n.* gossiping ; used of crows : cawing.

Claikrie, *n.* tattling, gossiping.

Claip, *n.* the clapper of a mill.

Clair, *v.* to search by raking or scratching.—*adj.* distinct, exact, ready, prepared ; confident, certain. Cf. Clear.

Clairach, *v.* to do any kind of domestic work in a dirty, awkward manner ; to expectorate much ; to sit over the fire lazily, as if unwell ; to make much ado in nursing a person not very ill.—*n.* a mass of liquid or semi-liquid substance ; ill-cooked food. Cf. Clorach.

Clairshach, Clairshoe, *n.* a harp.

Clairt, *v.* to besmear ; to be employed in any dirty or messy work.—*n.* any dirty or defiling substance ; an habitual slattern ; any large, awkward, dirty thing. Cf. Clart.

Claish, *n.* clothes. Cf. Claes.

Claister, *n.* any sticky compound ; a person bedaubed with mud or clay.—*v.* to bedaub, plaster.

Claith, *n.* cloth ; *phr.* 'lang in the claith,' long in the dead-clothes, long dead and buried.

Claithing, *n.* clothes, clothing.

Claith-like, *adj.* comfortably clothed.

Claithman, *n.* a clothier, a woollen draper.

Claiver, *v.* to talk idly or foolishly.—*n.* idle talk, nonsense. Cf. Claver.

Clake, *n.* the barnacle-goose. Cf. Claik.

Clake, *v.* to cackle; to gossip.—*n.* a gossip. Cf. Clack.

Clam, *adj.* mean, low; a schoolboys' word.

Clam, *n.* a scallop-shell. Cf. Clam-shell.

Clam, *v. pret.* climbed.

Clam, *v.* to grope at, grasp ineffectually.—*n.* in *pl.* an instrument for weighing gold, like a forceps; a vice or pincers used by saddlers and shoemakers; nippers used by farriers for castration of animals, and by shipwrights for drawing strong nails.

Clam, *v.* to besmear, daub; to stop a hole with an adhesive substance.—*adj.* moist, clammy, sticky.

Clamb, *v. pret.* climbed.

Clamehewit, Clamiehewit, Clamahouit, *n.* a stroke, blow; a drubbing; a misfortune.

Clamersum, *adj.* clamorous.

Clamjamfry, Clamjamphrey, *n.* a company of people; a mob; a vulgar crowd; the 'riff-raff'; trumpery, odds and ends; nonsensical talk.—*v.* to crowd, to fill with a rabble.

Clammer, *v.* to clamber, climb.

Clammersome, Clamoursome, *adj.* clamorous.

Clammyhewit, *n.* a stroke; a drubbing; a misfortune. Cf. Clamehewit.

Clamp, *n.* a small heap of peats.—*v.* to put peats in 'clamps'; to heap up potatoes, turnips, &c. in a mound.

Clamp, *n.* an iron brace to strengthen masonry.—*v.* to hoop or brace with iron.

Clamp, *n.* a patch. –*v.* to patch clothes.

Clamp, *v.* to make a noise with the shoes in walking; to walk with a heavy and noisy tread; to crowd things together noisily; to walk on ice with 'clamps' on the shoes. —*n.* a noisy blow or stroke; a heavy footstep or noisy tread; a piece of spiked iron fastened to the sole of the shoe by a strap across the instep, worn by curlers on the ice, 'cramp.'

Clamper, *v.* to patch, mend, or make clumsily; to patch up accusations industriously.—*n.* a piece of metal with which a vessel is mended; the vessel thus mended; arguments formerly answered; a patched-up handle for crimination.

Clamper, *v.* to make a clattering noise in walking; to crowd things together noisily. —*n.* a stout, heavy shoe.

Clamper, *v.* to fight a thing out.

Clampers, *n.* claws, pincers used for castrating animals.

Clampet, *n.* a piece of iron worn on the shoes by curlers on the ice; the guard of a sword-handle. Cf. Crampit.

Clamph, *v.* to walk heavily, as in too large shoes. Cf. Clomph.

Clampher, *v.* to litter, strew in confusion.

Clamp-kill, *n.* a kiln built of sods, for burning lime.

Clamsh, *n.* a piece of wood with which a thing is clumsily mended.—*v.* to splice two pieces of wood together.

Clam-shell, *n.* a scallop-shell; in *pl.* wild sounds supposed to be made by goblins in the air.

Clan, *n.* a coterie, group, class, 'set' of people.

Clanch, *n.* an unmannerly person who eats like a pig.

Clanglumshous, *adj.* sulky.

Clanjamph, Clanjamfry, Clanjamphries, *n.* low, worthless people. Cf. Clamjamfry.

Clank, *v.* to strike with noise; to thrash; to seat one's self noisily and violently; to take hold of noisily and violently.—*n.* a hasty catch; a sounding noise; a severe blow; chatter.

Clankum-bell, *n.* a bellman.

Clankum-jankum, *n.* the noisy working of a pump-handle.

Clanter, *n.* the noise made by walking in a house with clogs.

Clap, *v.* to press down; to sit or lie down; to crouch; to lie flat; to place down or on hastily; to pat, fondle; to smooth with a flat implement; to slam; to beat the arms for warmth; to strike with a noise; to adhere; to halt, tarry; with *down*, to write down; with *to*, to shut; with *up*, to imprison.—*n.* a stroke; the tongue of a bell; the clapper of a mill; a heavy fall; the sound of a heavy fall; a watchman's or town-crier's rattle; a night-watchman's pole for rousing sleepers in the morning by knocking on their windows; a moment.

Clapdock breeches, *n.* breeches tightly made round the breech.

Clap-door, *n.* the lower half of a door divided in the middle; a trap-door.

Clapman, *n.* a public crier.

Clap-mill, *n.* 'clappers,' used like castanets.

Clapper, *n.* a wooden rattle for scaring birds; a door-knocker; a watchman's rattle; a talkative person's tongue; a talkative person; a sharp, rattling noise; the contrivance in a mill for shaking the hopper so as to move the grain down to the millstones.—*v.* to make a rattling noise.

Clapper, *n.* a rabbit's hole.

Clapperclash, *n.* gossip.

Clapperclaw, *v.* to strike a blow, as a spider at a fly; to scratch in fighting.

Clappers, *n.* two pieces of wood or bones used like castanets.

Clapper-stick, *n.* the 'clapper' of a mill.

Clappertie-clink, *n.* the sound of a mill-'clapper.'

Clappit, *ppl. adj.* used of a horse : shrunk in the flesh after great fatigue ; flabby.

Clappity, *adj.* talkative.

Clark, *n.* a clerk.—*v.* to act as an amanuensis or clerk ; to write.

Clarried, *ppl. adj.* besmeared with mud.

Clart, *n.* a spot of dirt, mud ; any sticky substance ; a dirty, slovenly woman ; a worthless article or person.—*v.* to daub, smear with mud or dirt ; to work in a sloppy fashion ; to nurse a child to an excessive degree with little good effect.

Clarty, *adj.* dirty, sticky, filthy ; muddy ; miry.—*v.* to dirty, befoul.

Clash, *n.* the sound made by a heavy blow or fall, a blow, slap ; a heavy fall ; a quantity of moist or soft substance thrown at an object ; a heap of any heterogeneous substances, a mess ; a large quantity of anything ; a sudden shock ; a dash ; the throwing of a soft body ; something learned or repeated by rote ; gossip, tittle-tattle ; tale-bearing ; a tale-bearer, a great talker ; news.—*v.* to slam, bang, shut violently ; to slap with the open hand or something soft ; to pelt, throw mud or water, &c. ; to gossip, tattle, tell tales ; with *up*, to cause one object to adhere to another, by mortar, &c. —*adv.* with a clashing sound.

Clash, *n.* a cavity of considerable extent on the acclivity of a hill.

Clashach, *n.* a lump of soft stuff.

Clash-bag, *n.* a tale-bearer, a great talker ; a bundle of scandal, gossip ; a person full of low, mean stories.

Clasher, *n.* a tattler, tale-bearer.

Clashing, *n.* gossip, scandal ; a meeting for gossip.—*ppl. adj.* given to tattling.

Clash-ma-clavers, Clash-ma-claters, *n.* low, idle, scandalous tales ; silly talk.

Clash-market, *n.* a tattler, a scandal-monger ; one greatly given to gossip.

Clash-piet, -pyot, *n.* a tell-tale, scandal-monger.

Claspin, *n.* a clasp, a bracelet.

Clasps, *n.* an inflammation of the termination of the sublingual gland, a disease of horses, caused by eating bearded forage.

Clat, *n.* a clod of earth, turf, &c. ; cow-dung ; moist, wet earth ; a mess, a muddle.—*v.* to bedaub, dirty, make a mess.

Clat, *v.* to prattle, chatter.

Clat, *n.* an instrument for raking together dirt, mud, dung ; for clearing the bars of a furnace of slag, cinders, ashes ; a hoe ; raking together property ; what is scraped together by niggardliness ; dirt, mud, dung, &c. as gathered in heaps ; a gathering of rags.—*v.* to rake together, to scrape, scratch together ; to accumulate by 'gripping' or extortion ; to clean out a dish, pot, or pan with a spoon.

Clatch, *n.* a brood of chickens or ducklings.

Clatch, *n.* a mess, slop ; mire, dung, &c. raked together in heaps ; any soft substance thrown in order to daub ; any work done carelessly, a clumsily made article ; a fat, clumsy woman ; a slut ; a very loquacious woman.—*v.* to daub with lime ; to close up with any adhesive substance ; to finish work carelessly and hurriedly. Cf. Clotch.

Clatch, *n.* a slap with the palm of the hand ; the noise of the collision of soft bodies or of a heavy fall.

Clatch, *n.* a clutch, a sudden grasp at any object. Cf. Clautch.

Clatchin, *n.* a brood of chickens or ducklings ; a 'setting' of eggs.

Clate, *v.* to bedaub ; to dirty. Cf. Clat.

Clats, *n.* layers of 'cat and clay,' the materials of which a mud-walled cottage is constructed.

Clatt, *v.* to dirty ; to bedaub. Cf. Clat.

Clatter, *n.* noisy talk, chatter, familiar conversation ; gossip ; a chatterer, a gossip ; news, idle rumour.—*v.* to work noisily ; to chatter, talk fast or familiarly ; to gossip.

Clatterbags, *n.* a chatterer, a tale-bearer.

Clatter-bane, *n.* a bone supposed humorously to move when one chatters.

Clatter-banes, *n.* bones used as castanets.

Clatterbus, *n.* a gossip.

Clatterer, *n.* a chatterer, a tale-bearer.

Clatter-goose, *n.* the brent-goose.

Clatter-malloch, *n.* meadow trefoil.

Clattern, *n.* a tattler, babbler, a gossip.

Clatter-strap, *n.* a noisy, chattering person.

Clatter-traps, *n.* articles, goods for sale.

Clatter-vengeance, *n.* one who talks with a 'vengeance.'

Clattie, *adj.* nasty, dirty, muddy ; obscene.

Clattilie, *adv.* nastily, dirtily ; obscenely.

Clattiness, *n.* nastiness ; obscenity.

Clatts, *n.* cards for teasing wool. Cf. Clauts.

Clauber, *n.* soft, sticky mud ; a handful, dollop. Cf. Clabber.

Claucher, *v.* to use both hands and feet in rising to stand or walk ; with *up*, to snatch up ; with *to*, to move forward to an object feebly from old age. Cf. Clacher.

Claucht, Claught, *v.* to lay hold of forcibly and suddenly, to clutch.—*v. pret.* clutched, caught.—*n.* a sudden and forcible catch, a clutch, a grasp ; a handful ; a blow in clutching.

Clauer, *v.* to clutch. Cf. Claur.

Clauick, *n.* the harvest-home. Cf. Claaick.

Claum, *v.* to grope at.—*n.* a saddlers' vice. Cf. Clam.

Claum, *v.* to besmear, daub.—*adj.* moist ; of ice: beginning to thaw, Cf. Clam.

Claumy, *adj.* clammy ; viscous.

Claur, *v.* to clutch.

Claurt, *n.* a clutch, grasp, scratch.

Claurt, *v.* to scrape together.—*n.* what is so scraped.

Claut, *n.* a clutch ; a grasping hand ; a handful ; a blow ; a scraper with a long handle ; a rakeful.—*v.* to scratch with the nails, claw ; to rake or scrape together. Cf. Clat.

Clautch, *n.* a clutch, a sudden grasp at anything.

Clautie-scone, *n.* coarse bread made of oatmeal and yeast ; a cake carelessly baked and fired.

Clauts, *n.* cards for teasing wool.

Claver, *n.* clover.

Claver, *v.* to talk idly or foolishly ; to chat, gossip.—*n.* one who talks foolishly ; idle talk, gossip ; generally in *pl.*

Claverer, *n.* a chatterer ; a gossip.

Clavie, *n.* a tar-barrel, within which is fixed a fir prop, surmounted by the staves of a herring-cask, burned at Burghead on New Year's Eve to secure a good year's fishing.

Claw, *n.* finger, hand ; clutch ; a scratch ; an iron spoon for scraping a baking-board.—*v.* to scratch, tear with the claws ; to clutch ; to snatch up ; to paw, handle, fondle ; to scrape ; to hit ; to do anything smartly ; with *aff*, to eat rapidly and voraciously.

Claw, *n.* a clause.

Clawback, *n.* a flatterer.

Claw-hammer coat, *n.* a swallow-tail coat.

Clawscrunt, *n.* an old tree against which cattle rub themselves.

Clay, *v.* to stop a hole with clay or any viscous or adhesive substance ; with *up*, of the eyes: to 'bung up' or blind in boxing.—*n.* a boys' clay marble ; the body, the flesh ; the grave.

Clay-biggin, *n.* a cottage built of clay and wood.

Clay-cauld, *adj.* quite cold, lifeless.

Clayer, *n.* a boys' clay marble.

Clay-hallan, *n.* a thin partition wall in a cottage.

Clayock, *n.* the harvest-home. Cf. Claaick.

Clead, *v.* to clothe. Cf. Cleed.

Cleadfu', *adj.* handsomely dressed.

Cleading, *n.* clothing, clothes. Cf. Cleeding.

Clean, *v.* to clear land of weeds, &c. ; to clear, remove.

Clean, *n.* the after-birth of a cow or sheep.

Clean, *adj.* neat, well-made, shapely ; free from weeds ; of grain : properly winnowed. —*adv.* altogether, entirely.

Clean-fittet, *adj.* having neat feet.

Clean-fung, *adv.* cleverly.

Clean muck, *n.* nothing but 'muck.'

Cleanse, *v.* to acquit, absolve. Cf. Clenge.

Clean-shankit, *adj.* having neat, well-shaped legs.

Cleansing, *n.* the after-birth of cows, sheep, &c.

Clean town, *n.* a farm which all the servants leave together at one term.

Clear, *adj.* certain, sure, determined ; ready, prepared, free from punishment.—*adv.* certainly, confidently.

Clear, *v.* to search by raking or scratching ; to pay off in full.—*n.* with *def. art.* whisky.

Clearer, *n.* a water-insect with two rows of legs, found in quarry-holes.

Clear-headed, *adj.* bald-headed.

Clearing, *n.* a scolding ; a beating ; generally in *pl.*

Clear kelty aff, *v. phr.* to empty one's glass.

Clear-lowing, *adj.* brightly burning.

Clear o' the warld, *phr.* free of debt, able to pay one's way.

Cleary, *adj.* ? shrill, sharp.

Cleave, *v.* with *candles*, to make candles of bog-fir ; with *down*, to plough to the outside and from the middle ridge.

Cleaving, *n.* the 'fork' of the human body.

Cleck, *n.* the barnacle-goose. Cf. Claik.

Cleck, *v.* to hatch, bring forth ; to invent.

Cleck, *v.* to gossip, to be talkative.—*n.* idle, pert chatter.

Clecker, *n.* a sitting hen.

Cleckie, *adj.* prolific.

Cleckin, *ppl. adj.* gossiping, loquacious.

Cleckin, *n.* a brood, litter, family.

Cleckin-brod, -bred, *n.* a board for striking with at hand-ball, a 'baw-board.'

Cleckin-hen, *n.* a sitting hen.

Cleckin-stane, *n.* any stone that separates into small parts by exposure to the atmosphere.

Cleckin-time, *n.* hatching-time ; the time of birth.

Cleckit, *ppl. adj.* hatched, born ; in *phr.* 'ill-cleckit,' misbegotten, base-born.

Cled, *ppl. adj.* clad, clothed.

Cled-bow, *n.* a heaped boll.

Cled-score, *n.* twenty-one to the score.

Cleed, *v.* to clothe ; to cover over with a protection, to shelter, to heap.—*n.* an article of clothing ; dress.

Cleeding, *n.* clothes ; a suit of clothes ; a covering of deal-boards ; the outer casing of a cylinder-pipe or boiler ; the cover of a threshing-mill drum.

Cleek, *v.* to seize with the claws, to clutch ; to grab, to snatch hastily, roughly, or eagerly ; to hook, catch up by a hook, fasten on a hook ; to hook arms, walk arm in arm ; to attach one's self to, unite with, marry ; to cheat.—*n.* a clutch ; the arm ; a hook on which to hang pots over the fire ; a shepherd's crook ; a salmon-gaff ; an inclination to cheat, a fraudulent disposition.

Cleek, *n.* a small catch designed to .fall into the notch of a wheel ; the latch of a door or gate.

Cleek-anchor, *n.* a hook-anchor of a boat.

Cleek-hours, *n.* the keeping horses in the harvest-field yoked for ten hours a day.

Cleek-in-the-back, *n.* lumbago ; rheumatism.

Cleeks, *n.* cramp in the legs of horses.

Cleekum, *n.* a pastoral crook.

Cleeky, *n.* a staff or stick with a crooked end. —*adj.* ready to snatch advantage ; inclined to cheat. Cf. Clicky.

Cleepie, *n.* a severe blow ; a contusion ; a blow on the head.

Cleer, *v.* to clear.—*adj.* bright, shining. Cf. Clear.

Cleesh, *n.* a large mass of any semi-liquid substance.

Cleesh, *v.* to repeat any idle story. Cf. Clish.

Cleeshach, *n.* the soft part of an animal's frame ; the fat or entrails of slaughtered animals ; a stout, unhealthy, dirty-looking woman.

Cleester, *n.* a clyster.

Cleetit, *ppl. adj.* emaciated ; lank ; in a state of decay.

Cleevin, *n.* the 'fork' of the legs.

Cleg, *n.* a gadfly, horsefly ; a prick, sting.

Cleid, *v.* to clothe. Cf. Cleed.

Cleidach, *v.* to talk. -*n.* talk. Cf. Cleitach.

Cleighin, *n.* something comparatively light. Cf. Clichen.

Cleik, *v.* to catch.—*n.* a hook, &c. Cf. Cleek.

Cleik, *adj.* lively, agile, fleet.

Cleiro, *n.* a sharp noise ; a shrill sound.

Cleish, *v.* to whip, lash.—*n.* a whip ; a lash from a whip.

Cleitach, *v.* to talk in a strange language ; to talk inordinately ; to chatter as a child.—*n.* talk, discourse.

Cleitch, *n.* a hard, heavy fall.

Clekan-wittit, *adj.* childish, feeble-minded.

Clekin, *n.* a small wooden bat or racket. Cf. Clacken.

Clem, *adj.* mean, low ; untrustworthy ; curious, singular. Cf. Clam.

Clem, *v.* to stop a hole by compression, or by clay, mortar, &c. Cf. Clam.

Clench, *v.* to limp.—*n.* a limp. Cf. Clinch.

Clench, *v.* to clutch with the hands.

Clenchie-fit, *n.* a club-foot.

Clenge, *v.* to cleanse ; to exculpate, prove innocent.

Clep, *v.* to call, name.—*n.* a citation in criminal cases.

Clep, *n.* an iron hook on which a pot is hung over the fire.

Clep, *v.* to walk or move like a crab.

Clep, *v.* to act as tell-tale or informer ; to chatter, prattle, speak pertly.—*n.* tattle, loquacity. Cf. Clype.

Clepie, *n.* a tattler, chatterbox.—*adj.* pert, talkative. Cf. Clypie.

Clepped, *adj.* web-footed ; with the fingers webbed.

Clepping, *n.* tale-telling.

Clepshears, *n.* an earwig. Cf. Clipshears.

Clerk, *n.* a scholar.—*v.* to write, indite, compose ; to act as an amanuensis.—*adj.* learned, scholarly. Cf. Clark.

Clerk-curate, *n.* a priest.

Clerk-plays, *n.* theatrical representations of scriptural subjects.

Clert, *v.* to soil, dirty. Cf. Clart.

Clet, Clett, *n.* a rock or cliff in the sea broken off from adjoining rocks on the shore.

Cleuch, *adj.* clever, dexterous, light-fingered ; inclined to take advantage ; niggardly.

Cleuch, *n.* a ravine ; a narrow glen ; a deep wooded valley ; a coal-pit.

Cleuch-brae, *n.* a cliff overhanging a ravine ; the slope of a ' cleuch.'

Cleuchten, *n.* a flat-lying ridge. Cf. Scluchten.

Cleugh, *n.* a narrow glen. Cf. Cleuch.

Cleuk, *n.* a hand ; a claw ; a paw ; a clutch, grasp, hold.—*v.* to seize ; to scratch with the claws ; to grip, clutch.

Cleurach, *v.* to do domestic work in a dirty, awkward manner ; to expectorate much ; to sit over the fire, as if in bad health ; to fuss while nursing a person not very ill.—*n.* a mass of liquid or semi-liquid substance ; ill-cooked food. Cf. Clorach.

Clev, *v.* to reel-up a fishing hand-line after use

Clever, *v.* to climb, to scramble ; to hurry, to make haste, look sharp.

Clever, *adj.* good, well-behaved ; eloquent, fluent of speech, able ; quick, speedy.

Cleverality, *n.* ability, cleverness.

Clew, *n.* in *phr.* ' the winding of the clew,' a Hallowe'en ceremony to ascertain one's future spouse ; wealth amassed.

Clew, *v. pret.* clawed.

Clibber, *n.* a wooden saddle, a pack-saddle.

Clichen, *n.* something comparatively very light.

Click, *n.* a moment of time ; a latch of a door or gate ; the tick of a clock.—*v.* to tick as a clock, &c.

Click, *v.* to seize, catch up hastily, grab, steal.

Click-clack, *n.* uninterrupted loquacity.

Clickett-staff, *n.* a hooked staff.

Click-for-clack, *adv.* with ceaseless talk.

Clicking, *n.* ticking.

Clicky, *n.* a shepherd's crook ; a hooked staff. —*adj.* quick at catching ; ready to take advantage of others. Cf. Cleeky.

Clicky-staff, *n.* a hooked staff.

Clidyoch, *n.* the gravel-bed of a river.

Clien, *n.* a small heap of stones.

Cliers, *n.* a disease affecting the throat of a cow ; thick saliva which obstructs the wind-pipe.

Clift, *n.* a cleft ; the 'fork' of the legs; a piece of ground separated from the rest.

Cliftie, *adj.* clever, fleet, applied to a horse of light make and good action ; used of fuel: easily kindled and burning brightly.

Cliftie, *adj.* rugged, with clefts and fissures in ground.

Cliftiness, *n.* the quality of being easily kindled and burning brightly.

Clim, *v.* to climb.—*n.* a climb.

Clime, *n.* in *phr.* 'to heeze up to the climes,' to extol to the skies.

Climmer, *n.* a climber.

Climp, *v.* to hook ; to take hold of suddenly ; to pilfer.

Climp, *v.* to limp, to halt.

Climpet, *n.* a sharp-pointed rock.

Climpie, *n.* a lame person.

Climpy, *adj.* thievish, inclined to purloin.

Clinch, *v.* to limp, to halt ; to feign lameness. —*n.* a halt, a limp.

Clincher, *n.* a lame or halt person.

Cling, *v.* used of vessels made with staves: to shrink with heat, to 'gizzen.'

Cling, *n.* the diarrhœa in sheep.

Cling-and-clang, *n.* the clinking of glasses, &c.

Clink, *n.* a sharp metallic sound or ring ; a chime ; stroke of a bell ; a smart, resound-ing blow ; rhyme, jingling metre ; a woman tell-tale ; money, cash, coin ; an instant, a moment.—*v.* to chink, jingle ; to beat, thrash ; used of verses : to rhyme, go well together, to compose ; to move with a clinking sound, walk briskly ; to do any-thing smartly or unexpectedly ; to spread scandal, to fly as a rumour ; with *up*, to seize forcibly and quickly ; with *off*, to die.

Clink, *v.* to hammer, to weld by hammering, to clinch ; to mend, patch clothes ; to hold to an agreement ; to jot down in writing.

Clink, *adj.* alert.

Clink-and-clank, *n.* the clinking of glasses, &c.

Clinker, *n.* a tell-tale.

Clinker, *n.* anything large or good of its kind.

Clinkers, *n.* broken pieces of rock.

Clinkie, *adj.* noisy.

Clinking, *ppl. adj.* jerking ; used of coin : jingling, chinking ; of verses : rhyming, jingling.

Clinking, *n.* a beating, a thrashing.

Clinkit, *ppl. adj.* struck ; mended, clasped ; riveted.

Clink-knock, *v.* to rhyme easily and readily.

Clink-nail, *n.* a nail that is clinched or riveted.

Clinkum, *n.* a ringer of a church-bell or of a town-bell.

Clinkum-bell, *n.* a church- or town-bell ringer.

Clinkum-clankum, *n.* a rattling sound in which a metallic sound predominates.

Clinkum-jankum, *n.* a creaking, rattling sound, as when water is drawn from a well into a bucket by a pump.

Clinkum-toll, *n.* the ringing of a bell.

Clint, *n.* a rocky cliff ; a projecting rock or ledge ; flinty or hard rock ; a hard, tough stone used in curling, and first played off.

Clinted, *ppl. adj.* used of sheep : caught among cliffs by leaping down to a ledge from which ascent is impossible by leaping back.

Clinter, *n.* the player of a 'clint' in curling.

Clinty, *adj.* hard, flinty.

Clip, *n.* the foal of a mare ; an unbroken colt.

Clip, *n.* a gaff for landing fish ; an instrument for lifting a pot from the fire ; one for carrying a barrel, &c., between two per-sons ; a pincer-shaped wooden implement for weeding out thistles ; an instrument like tongs, with long wooden handles, formerly used to catch dogs intruding into a church. —*v.* to gaff a salmon or other fish ; to catch and hold a dog in a 'clip.'

Clip, *v.* to embrace, clasp with the arms ; used of a musket-ball : to pass quite close to, whiz past almost touching one.

Clip, *v.* to cut horses' rough winter coats ; to shear sheep ; to cut short, curtail, lessen ; to speak indistinctly, to speak fine. *n.* a newly shorn sheep ; the yearly sheep-shear-ing ; the amount of wool shorn yearly ; a smart cuff or blow ; with *the*, the very thing.

Clip, *n.* a wild, romping, pert girl.

Clip-clouts, *n.* a sharp-tongued person.—*v.* to argue or speak snappishly ; to talk sharply about little or nothing.

Clipe, *v.* to scratch with the nails.—*n.* a scratch made by the nails.

Clipe, *v.* to fall. Cf. Clype.

Clipe, *v.* to drudge.—*n.* a drudge. Cf. Clype.

Clipe, *v.* to chatter ; to tell tales.—*n.* a tell-tale. Cf. Clype.

Clipfast, *n.* a pert, impudent girl.

Clip-house, *n.* the house formerly set apart for defacing or clipping false coin.

Clipie, *adj.* talkative ; tattling.—*n.* a talkative, tattling woman. Cf. Clypie.

Clipmalabor, *n.* a girl who does as little work as possible ; an impudent girl. Cf. Slipmalabour.

Clipock, *n.* a fall. Cf. Clypock.

Clippart, *n.* a shorn sheep.

Clippart, *n.* a talkative woman.

Clipper, *n.* a sheep-shearer.

Clipper, *n.* anything first-rate of its kind.

Clipper-clapper, *n.* the sound of a revolving mill-wheel or clapper.

Clipperty-clap, *n.* 'clipper-clapper.'

Clippet, *ppl. adj.* used of language: affected, 'fine'; indistinct from mincing one's words.

Clippie, *n.* a young person wearing too neatly cut clothes; a talkative woman.—*adj.* sharp of speech, snappish, pert.

Clippie, *n.* a shorn sheep.

Clippin', *n.* sheep-shearing.

Clippinet, *n.* an impudent girl, a talkative woman.

Clipping-house, *n.* the house for clipping false coin.

Clippin'-time, *n.* the nick of time.

Clippock, *n.* a sharp-tongued person.

Clips, *n.* shears; snuffers.

Clips, *n.* stories, false tales.

Clipshears, *n.* the earwig.

Clipwit, *adj.* biting or shrewd of speech.—*n.* a sharp-tongued, quick-witted speaker.

Clire, *n.* a gland. Cf. Clyre.

Clired, *ppl. adj.* having tumours in the flesh.

Clish, *v.* to repeat an idle story.

Clish-clash, *n.* idle talk; rumour; scandal.

Clish-for-clash, *n.* ceaseless talking.

Clish-ma-clash, *n.* idle talk; gossip.

Clish-ma-claver, *n.* idle talk; gossip; false or scandalous reports.—*v.* to indulge in idle talk, gossip, &c.

Clite, *v.* to fall heavily and noisily.—*n.* a hard, heavy, and sudden fall; a lump. Cf. Clyte.

Clite, *adj.* splay-footed. Cf. Clyte.

Clitie, *n.* the fall of a child. Cf. Clytie.

Clitter-clatter, *n.* a sharp, clattering noise; a succession of rattling sounds; chatter, idle talk, noisy talk.—*v.* to make a sharp, rattling noise; to walk or run with sharp, noisy steps; to talk a great deal noisily.—*adv.* with a succession of rattling sounds.

Clitter-clatterin', *n.* idle talk; the act of gossiping.—*ppl. adj.* given to gossip.

Clivace, *n.* a hook for catching the buckets in which coals were drawn up from the pit.

Clivver, *n.* clover.

Clivvie, *n.* a cleft in the branch of a tree; an artificial cleft in a piece of wood for holding a rushlight.

Cloa, *n.* coarse woollen cloth, made in the Isle of Skye.

Cloan, *n.* a large, round mass of dirt.

Clobber, *n.* mud, clay, dirt. Cf. Clabber.

Clobber-hoy, *n.* a dirty walker, one who becomes muddy in walking.

Clobbery, *adj.* dirty, muddy.

Clocaleddy, *n.* the ladybird. Cf. Clock-leddie.

Cloch, *v.* to cough frequently and feebly.

Clocharch, *n.* the wheatear.

Clocharet, Clochret, *n.* the stonechat.

Clocher, *v.* to cough with much expectoration, wheeze.—*n.* a wheezing in the throat or chest with much mucus.

Clocherin, *n.* mucous ronchus; the sound of coughing.—*ppl. adj.* wheezing.

Clock, *v.* to cluck; to hatch, sit on eggs; to call chickens together.—*n.* the condition of a hen when she wishes to 'sit'; a hen's call to her chickens.

Clock, *n.* a beetle.

Clock-bee, *n.* a flying beetle.

Clocker, *n.* a sitting hen.

Clockiedow, *n.* the river pearl-oyster or horse-mussel.

Clocking, *n.* the act of hatching or desiring to sit on eggs; the disposition or wish to marry; inclination to wantonness.

Clocking-hen, *n.* a brooding or sitting hen; a woman capable of bearing children; a sum of money at interest in a bank.

Clocking-time, *n.* the time for hatching; the time of child-bearing; pregnancy.

Clock-leddie, *n.* the ladybird.

Clocks, *n.* the refuse of grain.

Clocksie, Clocksey, *adj.* vivacious.

Clod, *v.* used of crows: to dart up and down in flying.

Clod, *n.* a clew of yarn, &c.; a ball of twisted straw-rope.

Clod, *n.* a small halfpenny loaf or 'bap,' made of coarse, brownish flour.

Clod, *n.* a single peat or piece of peat.—*v.* to throw as a clod; to pelt with clods; to fling, dash; to throw or pile up peats in building a stack; to break clods on land.

Cloddan, *n.* flying up and down rapidly.

Clodder, *n.* the person who throws up peats to the builder of the stack.

Cloddoch, *n.* a small heap of stones.

Cloddy, *adj.* full of clods.

Clod-fire, *n.* a peat-fire.

Clod-mell, *n.* a wooden mallet for breaking clods.

Clod-shod, *adj.* used of a ploughman, &c.: having the boots weighted with adhering soil.

Clod-thumper, *n.* a heavy roller for crushing clods on land.

Cloff, *n.* a fissure, crevice; a cleft between two hills; the fork or cleft of a tree where a branch joins the trunk.

Cloffin, *n.* the act of sitting idly by the fire.

Cloffin, *n.* the noise made by a loose shoe on man or beast.

Clog, *n.* a small, short log; a short cut of a tree; a thick piece of timber.—*v.* to burden an estate.

Clogger, *n.* a maker of wooden shoes.

Cloggie, *n.* a wearer of wooden shoes.

Cloich, *n.* a place of shelter; the cavity of a rock where one may elude search.

Cloit, *v.* to fall heavily down suddenly; to bump down smartly; to squat down.—*n.* a hard and sudden fall.—*adv.* suddenly, with a bump. Cf. Clyte.

Cloit, *n.* a heavy burden; a clown; a stupid, inactive fellow.

Cloit, *n.* an afternoon nap, siesta.

Cloiter, *v.* to do dirty work; to handle liquid in a careless or slovenly way.—*n.* the act of working carelessly or dirtily among liquids or wet substances. Cf. Clyter.

Cloitery, *adj.* dirty; messy; sticky.—*n.* dirty, messy work; filth; offal. Cf. Clytrie.

Cloitery-maid, *n.* a female servant whose work it was to carry off filth or rubbish. Cf. Clytrie-maid.

Cloitery-market, *n.* an Edinburgh market where the offal of animals was sold.

Cloitery-wife, *n.* a woman who cleans and sells tripe. &c.

Clokie-doo, *n.* the horse-mussel. Cf. Clockie-dow.

Clok-leddy, *n.* the ladybird. Cf. Clock-leddie.

Clomb, *v. pret.* climbed.

Clomph, *v.* to walk in a dull, heavy manner; to walk in shoes too large or loose.

Cloo, *n.* a scraper of heavy sheet-iron, riveted on to an ox-hoof, used for scraping scalded pigs.

Clook, *n.* a claw.—*v.* to claw, to clutch. Cf. Cleuk.

Cloor, *n.* a tumour; a blow; a dint.—*v.* to strike, indent. Cf. Clour.

Clooster, *n.* a cluster; a group; a collection or bunch of various things; a miscellaneous heap; a mass of wet or sticky stuff, mud, &c.—*v.* to besmear, to clot.

Cloot, *n.* a division of the hoof of cattle, sheep, pigs, &c.; the hoof, foot; in *pl.* the devil.

Cloot, *n.* a patch; a rag; a garment.—*v.* to patch, mend; to dress. Cf. Clout.

Cloot, *v.* to beat, cuff.—*n.* a blow on the head. Cf. Clout.

Clooter, *n.* the noise made by a badly delivered curling-stone. Cf. Clouter.

Clootie, Clootie-ben, *n.* the devil.

Clootie's-craft, *n.* the devil's croft, the 'goodman's field,' a small portion of land set apart for the devil, and left untilled.

Clooty, *adj.* patched.

Clorach, *v.* to do domestic work dirtily and untidily; to expectorate greatly; to sit lazily over a fire, as if in bad health; to coddle a sick child or animal by over-nursing.—*n.* a mass of liquid or semi-liquid substance; ill-cooked or ill-served food.

Clort, *n.* any soft, sticky stuff; a thick bannock; a lazy, ill-dressed woman.—*v.* to dirty, besmear; to bake 'clorts.' Cf. Clart.

Clortin, *n.* a besmearing; with *on*, a thick besmearing.

Clorty, *adj.* dirty, messy.

Close, *n.* enclosed land; a farmyard; a narrow alley; a blind alley.

Close, *adj.* constant; regular; reticent; used of weather: oppressive; of evening: dusky; foggy; of a fog: thick.—*adv.* constantly, regularly.

Close, *v.* to breathe with difficulty from cold, &c.

Close-bed, *n.* a panelled bedstead with wooden hinged or sliding doors, a 'box-bed.'

Close-cart, *n.* a farm-cart; a covered ammunition-cart.

Closeevie, *n.* a collection, lot, number; in *phr.* 'the haill closeevie,' the whole 'hypothec.'

Close-fit, *n.* the lower or inner end of a 'close' or alley.

Close-head, *n.* the entrance or mouth of a close, opening on a street.

Close-mouth, *n.* the principal entrance to a 'close.'

Close-nieved, *adj.* close-fisted.

Closer, *n.* a 'settler'; the act of shutting-up.

Close-sichtit, *adj.* near-sighted; short-sighted.

Close-thonged, *adj.* tightly laced.

Closhach, *n.* a large mass or handful of a semi-liquid substance; a handful; a gathering; money saved; a person lying in a heap; a dead body.

Closing, *n.* a difficulty in breathing from cold, asthma, &c.

Closs, *n.* a 'close'; a lane; a passage through a house.

Clossach, *n.* a 'closhach,' bulk, a body.

Closter, *n.* a cloister.

Clotch, *v.* to walk heavily, move awkwardly. —*n.* a clumsy, awkward person; anything worn-done; a person with broken constitution; a bungler. Cf. Clatch.

Clotch, *v.* to sit lazily.

Clotchy, *adj.* liable to colds.

Clothes-press, *n.* a wardrobe.

Cloth-rund, *n.* a 'washer' of cloth on the spindle of a roving-box, between the lifter-plate and roving.

Clotter, *v.* to clot, congeal.

Cloudberry, *n.* the ground mulberry.

Cloudy, *adj.* threatening, perilous.

Cloughret, *n.* the stonechat. Cf. Clocharet.

Clouk, *v.* to cluck as a hen.

Clouks, *n.* the refuse of grain after sifting in a riddle. Cf. Clocks.

Cloup, *n.* a curve or bend in a stick.

Cloupie, *n.* a walking-stick with the head bent in a semicircle.

Cloupit, *ppl. adj.* used of a walking-stick : having the head curved.

Clour, *v.* to strike, indent, batter, beat.—*n.* a blow ; an indentation ; a lump caused by a blow.

Clouring, *n.* a beating.

Clouse, *n.* a sluice. Cf. Clow.

Clout, *v.* to beat, strike with the hands.—*n.* a blow, slap, box on the ear ; a heavy fall. —*phr.* 'to fa' clout,' to fall on the ground with force.

Clout, *v.* to patch, mend, repair.—*n.* a patch ; a rag, a shred of cloth ; a cloth used for household purposes ; a sail of a boat ; a garment ; an infant's napkin ; in *pl.* clothes, ragged clothes ; *phr.* 'as white 's a clout,' very pale.

Clouted, *ppl.* dressed ; clothed ; patched.

Clouter, *n.* the noise made by a badly delivered curling-stone.

Clouty, *adj.* ragged, patched ; made of cloth-clippings.

Clove, *n.* an instrument used in preparing flax by which those 'shows' are removed which have not been taken off at the 'scutch-mill'; used of a mill : that which removes the bridge-heads ; in *pl.* an implement of wood, closing like a vice, in which carpenters fix their saws to sharpen them.—*v.* to separate lint from the stalk.

Clover-sick, *adj.* used of land on which clover has been grown too often to support it further.

Clow, Clowe, *n.* a clove ; one of the laminæ of a head of garlic ; the clove-pink.

Clow, *v.* to beat down.

Clow, *v.* to eat or sup greedily.

Clow, *n.* a sluice.

Clowg, *n.* a small bar of wood on a screw pivot, fixed to a door to prevent it from being opened.

Clow-July-flower, *n.* the clove-pink, clove-gillyflower.

Clowk, *n.* the gurgling in the neck of a bottle while its contents are being poured out.— *v.* to gurgle when liquid is poured from a full bottle ; to whip up eggs.

Clowns, *n.* the butterwort.

Clowr, *v.* to strike ; to indent.—*n.* a stroke, indentation. Cf. Clour.

Clowse, *n.* a sluice. Cf. Clow.

Clowtter, *v.* to work dirtily ; to do dirty work.

Cloyte, *n.* a hard and heavy sudden fall.—*v.* to fall heavily. Cf. Clyte.

Club, *n.* a golf or 'shinty' club ; a club-shaped knot in which men's hair was formerly dressed ; 'finger and toe' in turnips.—*v.* used of turnips, cabbage, &c. : to be diseased with 'finger and toe,' or bulbous malformation ; to dress or wear the hair in a 'club.'

Clubber, *n.* a wooden saddle ; a pack-saddle. Cf. Clibber.

Clubbish, *adj.* clumsy, heavy, disproportionately made.

Clubbock, *n.* the spotted blenny.

Club-fitted, *ppl. adj.* having the feet turned too much inward ; having deformed feet ; club-footed.

Clubsides you, *int. phr.* used by boys at 'shinty' when a player strikes from the wrong side.

Club-tae'd, *ppl. adj.* club-footed.

Clucking, *n.* the hatching of eggs already laid. Cf. Clocking.

Clud, *n.* a cluster, crowd ; a cloud.

Cluddock, *n.* a dry, shingly bed at the side of a stream.

Cluddy, *adj.* cloudy.

Clud fawer, *n.* a bastard child, one fallen from the clouds.

Clue, *v. pret.* clawed, scratched.

Cluf, *n.* a hoof ; a claw.

Cluff, *v.* to cuff, slap.—*n.* a cuff, slap.

Cluggie, *n.* a person who wears clogs. Cf. Cloggie.

Clugston, *n.* an obsolete amusement among farmers.

Cluif, *n.* a hoof. Cf. Cluf.

Cluik, *v.* to grip ; to scratch.—*n.* the hand ; a claw, paw ; a clutch. Cf. Cleuk.

Cluish, *v. pret.* gossiped ; slapped ; slammed. Cf. Clash.

Cluit, *n.* a hoof. Cf. Cloot.

Cluke, *v.* to grasp.—*n.* a claw, paw. Cf. Cleuk.

Clukny, *n.* a hen ; a term of contempt for a person.

Clum, *ppl.* climbed.

Clumber, *v.* to daub, as with clay.

Clump, *n.* a heavy, unwieldy person ; the noise of a heavy shoe or footfall ; a thud, a heavy blow.—*v.* to walk or tread heavily.

Clumper, *n.* in *pl.* shapeless blocks of stone scattered on the ground ; thick, heavy shoes or clogs.—*v.* to make a noise in walking, as with heavy or loose shoes.

Clumsey, *adj.* used of a meat-bone : having meat adhering to it.

Clunch, *n.* a lump, a mass, a hunch.

Clung, *ppl. adj.* shrunken, empty from want of food, hungry.

Clunk, *v.* to emit a hollow, interrupted sound, like liquid issuing from a bottle or narrow orifice.—*n.* a hollow sound as of a fall ; the sound of a cork being drawn, of a liquid coming from a bottle or narrow orifice, or of a pebble falling perpendicularly from a height into smooth and deep water ; a draught, what is swallowed at a gulp ; the call of a hen to her chickens when she has found food for them.

Clunkart, *n.* a very large piece of anything; a large hump or bump on the body; a stout, dumpy person or child.

Clunker, *n.* a tumour; a bump; a good big glassful; in *pl.* dirt hardened in clots, rendering a road, pavement, or floor uneven; inequalities in a road, &c., caused by frost.

Clunkerd, *adj.* used of a road or floor: overlaid with clots of indurated dirt.

Clunkertonie, *n.* a jelly-fish, medusa.

Cluph, *n.* an idle, trifling creature.

Cluphin, *ppl.* spending time idly and in a slovenly way. Cf. Cloffin.

Clure, *v.* to dint. Cf. Clour.

Clushach, *n.* a handful; a gathering. Cf. Closhach.

Clushan, *n.* cow-dung as it drops in a small heap.

Clushet, *n.* the udder of a cow; the stomach of a sow.

Clushet, *n.* one in charge of a cow-house.

Clute, *n.* the half of the hoof of a cloven-footed animal; the whole hoof; a single beast. Cf. Cloot.

Clute, *n.* a rag, &c. Cf. Clout.

Cluther, *v.* to conceal, to cover, huddle up.

Cluther, *n.* a heap, a crowd. Cf. Clutter.

Clutie, *n.* the devil. Cf. Clootie.

Clutter, *n.* a disorderly heap; a piece of bad stone building; noise, commotion, bustle.— *v.* to do anything in an awkward or dirty way of working.

Clyack, *n.* the last handful of corn cut in the harvest-field. Cf. Claaick.

Clyack-horn, *n.* a drinking-horn used at the harvest-home.

Clydigh, *v.* to talk in a strange tongue, especially Gaelic; to talk inarticulately, chatter as a child.—*n.* talk, discourse. Cf. Cleitach.

Clydyock, *n.* the gravel bed of a river. Cf. Clidyoch.

Clyer, *n.* a gland formed in the fat of beef or mutton; a hard substance formed on the liver or lungs of animals; in *pl.* a disease affecting the throat of a cow. Cf. Clyre.

Clypach, *v.* to work dirtily and in slovenly fashion; to walk in a dirty and ungraceful fashion; to hang wet, loose, and dishevelled; to gossip; to speak much and loudly.—*n.* a large, wet mass of anything semi-liquid; a hanging wet mass; work done dirtily among semi-liquid substances; walking ungracefully; a heavy fall on wet ground; a dirty, uncomely, and disagreeable person; gossip, one who gossips.—*adv.* flatly, heavily, with noise.

Clype, *v.* to tell tales, gossip.—*n.* a tell-tale; idle tales.

Clype, *v.* to walk over wet ground in a slovenly fashion; to act as a drudge.—

n. work done in a dirty manner; a clot, a confused, wet mass; a drudge; an ugly, ill-shaped fellow.

Clype, *v.* to fall.—*n.* a fall.—*adv.* flat, heavily, with noise. Cf. Sklype.

Clyper, *n.* a tell tale.

Clypie, *n.* a tell-tale.—*adj.* gossiping; loquacious; tattling.

Clypit, *ppl. adj.* used of clothes: loose; ill-made; badly fitting.

Clypock, *n.* a fall. Cf. Clypach.

Clyre, *n.* a gland in meat; in *pl.* diseased glands in cattle. Cf. Clyer.

Clystre, *v.* to besmear.—*n.* a mass of semi-liquid stuff. Cf. Claister.

Clytach, *v.* to walk or work dirtily.—*n.* a mass of semi-liquid stuff.

Clytach, *v.* to talk in a strange tongue.—*n.* talk, discourse. Cf. Cleitach.

Clyte, *n.* a mass of liquid or semi-liquid stuff.

Clyte, *v.* to fall suddenly and heavily.—*n.* a sudden fall. Cf. Cloit.

Clyter, *v.* to walk ungracefully; with *over*, to overnurse; to gossip; to speak a strange tongue.—*n.* an ungraceful walk, as over wet ground; gossiping; speaking and speech in a strange tongue. — *adv.* with ungraceful step; with force.

Clyter, *v.* to be engaged in dirty work, &c.—*n.* mess, muddle. Cf. Cloiter.

Clyteran, *n.* the hum of many people speaking; overnursing.

Clytie-lass, *n.* the servant-girl who carries out house filth, &c.

Clytrie, *n.* tripe; animal intestines; house filth, &c. Cf. Cloitery.

Clytrie-maid, *n.* a female servant who carries off filth, rubbish, &c. from a house. Cf. Cloitery-maid.

Clytrie-market, *n.* a tripe-market.

Clytrie-wife, *n.* a woman who cleans and sells tripe.

Co, *n.* a rock-cave, with a narrow entrance, on the seashore. Cf. Cove.

Co, *v. pret.* quoth.

Coach, *v.* to drive in a coach.

Coachbell, *n.* an earwig.

†Coact, *ppl.* forced, constrained.

Coag, *v.* to shear, and so save, the neck-wool of sheep sometime before the regular sheep-shearing.

Coag, *n.* a wooden vessel for holding porridge, milk, &c. Cf. Cog.

Coal, *n.* a red-hot cinder.

Coal-and-candle-light, *n.* the long-tailed duck.

Coal-grieve, *n.* a coal-overseer.

Coal-gum, *n.* coal-dust.

Coal-heugh, *n.* a coal-pit.

Coal-hood, -hoodie, -hooden, *n.* the reed-bunting; the blackcap; the British cole-titmouse.

Coalmie, *n.* the full-grown coal-fish.

Coalsay, *n.* the coal-fish, the saith.

Coal-scoop, *n.* a coal-scuttle.

Coal-stalk, *n.* a vegetable impression found on stones in coal-mines.

Coal-stealer-rake, *n.* a thief, a vagabond.

Coalyer, *n.* a collier.

Coaly-hood, *n.* the British cole-titmouse. Cf. Coal-hood.

Coan, *v.* to cry as a child. Cf. Cown.

†Coarctat, *ppl.* coerced, restrained.

Coarse, *adj.* used of the weather: rough, stormy; rough, brutal.

Coaster, *n.* a resident along the coast of Caithness, south of Wick.

Coat, *n.* a petticoat.

Coat-and-bit, *phr.* clothes and food.

Coatie, *n.* a child's coat; a child's petticoat.

Coats, *n.* refuse of threshed corn, beans, &c. given to horses.

Cob, *v.* to shear the wool off a ewe's udder.

Cob, *n.* the husk of a pea.

Cob, *n.* a coin (? gold) worth about 4s. 6d.

Cob, *v.* to beat one on the backside.—*n.* a blow.

Cobble, *v.* to bungle.—*n.* a tangle, confusion.

Cobbler, *n.* a bungler.

Coble, *n.* a short, flat-bottomed boat, used in salmon-fishings and in ferries; a deckless fishing-boat, with sharp bow, flat, sloping stern, and without a keel, used on N.E. coast.

Coble, *n.* a place for steeping malt.—*v.* to steep malt for brewing.

Coble, *n.* a square pew in a church, or 'table-seat.'

Coble, *n.* a pond for cattle, &c., to drink at.

Coble, *v.* to rock; to undulate, be unsteady; to see-saw.—*n.* a rocking motion; a see-saw; playing at see-saw.

Cobleing, *n.* steeping malt.

Cobletehow-mutch, *n.* ? a cap ironed or dressed fancifully.

Coblie, *adj.* shaky; liable to rock or undulate.

Coblie, *n.* a small pond.

Cob-seibow, *n.* a young shoot from onions of the second year's growth.

Cobworm, *n.* the larva of the cockchafer.

Cochbell, *n.* an earwig. Cf. Coachbell.

Cock, *n.* a brisk, smart fellow; a familiar term of address; a boys' game, 'rexa-boxa-king'; the 'tee' of a curling-rink.

Cock, *n.* a cap, a head-dress; an upward turn or tilt; a brickwork projection in steps to receive a piece of timber.—*v.* to swagger, show off; to hold erect, prick up; to lift up threateningly; to throw up to a high or inaccessible place; to stick a hat or cap jauntily on one side of the head; to mount an offender on another's back for a flogging;

to make a false shot, miss; to go back from a bargain; with *up,* used contemptuously of giving to any one what he does not deserve or can use, or to one who is too ambitious; to indulge, pamper needlessly.

Cock, *adj.* fuddled.

Cock-a-bendy, *n.* a sprightly boy; an instrument for twisting ropes, consisting of a hollow piece of wood, through which runs a pin that, being turned, twists the rope.

Cock-able, *adj.* of age; of the age of puberty.

Cock-a-breekie, *n.* a person of small stature.

Cock-a-hoop, *adj.* 'half-seas over,' intoxicated.—*n.* a bumper.

†Cockalane, Cockaland, *n.* a comic representation; a satire; an imperfect writing; an infamous libel; a pasquinade.

Cock-a-leekie, *n.* soup made of a fowl boiled with leeks.

Cockalorum-like, *adj.* foolish, absurd.

Cock-and-key, *n.* a stopcock.

Cock-and-pail, *n.* a spigot and faucet.

Cockandy, *n.* the puffin.

Cock-a-pentie, *n.* one whose pride makes him live above his income.

Cock-a-ridy, *v.* used of a child: to ride on the shoulders with a leg on each side of the person carrying.

Cock-a-roora-koo, *n.* the sound of cock-crowing.

Cockats, *n.* a scolding.

Cockawinie, *v.* to ride on the shoulders of another.

Cock-bead-plane, *n.* a plane for making a moulding which projects above the common surface of the timber.

Cock-bird-height, *n.* tallness equal to that of a male chicken; infancy; elevation of spirits.

Cock-bird-high, *adj.* youthful, very young.

Cock-brain, *n.* a weak brain.

Cock-bree, *n.* cock-broth, 'cock-a-leekie.'

Cock-crow'n-kail, *n.* broth heated a second time.

Cocked, *ppl.* containing sperm; with *up,* conceited; with *up with,* overindulged.

Cockee, *n.* the circle round the 'tee' towards which curling-stones must be played.

Cocker, *n.* theisperm of an egg.

Cocker, *n.* a dram of whisky, a 'caulker.'

Cocker, *v.* to be tottering, unsteady; to put in an insecure place.

Cocker, *v.* to fondle, indulge, pamper.

Cocker-de-cosie, -de-hoy, *v.* to sit or ride astride on the shoulders of a person.

Cockerie, *adj.* unsteady in position, likely to tumble.

Cockerieness, *n.* insecurity of position; instability.

Cockernonie, *n.* the gathering of a woman's hair into the 'snood' or fillet; anything small, neat, and old-fashioned.

Cockernonied, *ppl.* having the hair dressed in a 'cockernonie.'

Cockersum, *adj.* unsteady, threatening to tumble.

Cockertie-hooie, *n.* carrying a boy astride the neck.

Cockerty, *adj.* unstable, shaky.

Cock-fechtin, *n.* cock-fighting.

Cock-fight, *n.* a boys' game played by two hopping on one leg and butting each other with their shoulders until one lets down his leg.

Cock-head, *n.* the herb all-heal or woundwort.

Cock-headed, *adj.* vain, conceited, whimsical.

Cockie, *adj.* vain; affecting airs of importance.

Cockie-bendie, *n.* the cone of the fir-tree; the large conical bud of the plane-tree.

Cockie-breekie, *adv.* in *phr.* 'to ride cockie-breekie,' to sit or ride astride on the shoulders of a person.

Cockie-dandie, *n.* a bantam cock; a pert, forward youngster.

Cockie-leekie, *n.* soup made from a fowl boiled with leeks.

Cockie-leerie, *n.* a cock, chanticleer; the sound of a cock crowing.

Cockie-loorie, *n.* a children's name for any showy artificial flower or bright-coloured thing with which they play; a knot of ribbon or other bright-coloured thing.

Cockie-ridie-rousie, -rosie, *n.* a game of children in which one rides on another's shoulders; a punishment inflicted by children on each other.

Cockin', *n.* a cock-fight.

Cockin, *n.* the sperm of an egg.

Cock-laird, *n.* a small landholder who cultivates his own estate; a yeoman.

Cockle, *v.* to crow like a cock; to cackle like a hen.

Cockle, *v.* to totter, be unstable.

Cockle, *v.* to cuckold.

Cockle, *v.* to mark the cogs of a mill before cutting off the ends of them, so that the whole may preserve the circular form.—*n.* the instrument used in marking the cogs of a mill.

Cockle, *v.* with *up*, to become better in health or spirits.

Cockle-brained, *adj.* whimsical, eccentric.

Cockle-cutit, *adj.* having bad ankles, so that the feet seem twisted away from them, lying outwards.

Cockle-headed, *adj.* whimsical, 'maggoty,' eccentric.

Cockler, *n.* one who 'cuckolds' a husband.

Cock-loft, -laft, *n.* the space between the uppermost ceiling and the roof; the highest gallery in a church.

Cockman, *n.* a sentinel. Cf. Gockmin.

Cock-melder, *n.* the last 'melder' or grinding of a year's grain.

Cocknee-stones, *n.* the echinus or button-stone.

Cock o' crowdie, *n. phr.* a term of commendation.

Cock o' pluck, *n. phr.* a brave fellow.

Cock o' the midden, *n. phr.* the master, superior, one who has it all his own way; 'cock of the walk.'

Cock o' the North, *n.* a name given to the Dukes of Gordon.

Cock-paddle, *n.* the lump-fish.

Cock-picket, *adj.* pecked or dabbled in by poultry.

Cock-raw, *adj.* sparingly roasted or boiled.

Cockrel, *n.* a cockerel; a young male raven.

Cock-rose, *n.* a wild poppy with a red flower.

Cock's-caim, *n.* meadow-pink or cuckoo-flower.

Cock's-comb, *n.* adder's-tongue.

Cock's-eye, *n.* a halo that appears round the moon and indicates stormy weather.

Cock's-foot, Cock's-foot-grass, *n.* the dew-grass.

Cocksie, *adj.* affecting airs of importance.

Cock's-odin, -hoddin, *n.* a boys' game of 'hide and seek.'

Cock-stool, -stule, *n.* the cuckstool; the pillory.

Cockstride, *n.* a short distance; used figuratively of the lengthening of days; a boys' game.

Cock-up, *n.* a hat or cap turned up in front.

Cocky, *n.* a brisk, smart young fellow; a friendly term of address.—*adj.* pert, saucy; conceited; elated.

Coclico, *adj.* red, purple.

Cod, *n.* a pillow; a cushion; a kind of riding-pad.

Cod, *v.* with *out*, used of grain: to separate easily from the husk.

Cod, *v.* to sham, hoax, humbug.

Cod, *n.* the penis.

Cod, *v.* in *phr.* 'to cod pease,' to pilfer peas; to steal.

Cod-bait, *n.* the straw-worm; the caddis-worm.

Codber, *n.* a pillow-slip.

Cod-crune, -croonin', *n.* a curtain-lecture.

Coddle, *v.* to embrace, 'cuddle.'—*n.* an embrace, a 'cuddle.'

Coddle, *v.* to roast apples before the fire.

Codgebell, *n.* an earwig. Cf. Cochbell.

Codger, *n.* a fellow, a 'character.'

Codgie, *adj.* comfortable, cosy; in fair health.

Cod-hule, *n.* a pillow-slip.

Codle, *v.* to make grain fly out of the husk by a stroke.

Codlick, Codlock, *n.* the spotted gunnel.

Codlins-and-cream, *n.* the great hairy willow-herb.

Codroch, *adj.* rustic, clownish; dirty, slovenly, nasty.

Codrugh, *adj.* chilly, cold, 'cauldrife.'

Codslip, Codware, *n.* a pillow-slip.

Co'er, *v.* to cover.

Cofe, *n.* a bargain, a barter.

Coff, *v.* to buy, barter, to procure, usually in *pret.* and *pa. ppl.*

Coffee, Coffe, *n.* a beating; a *quid pro quo.*

Coffer, *n.* a legacy of wealth, a fortune.

Coff-fronted, *adj.* used of a bed : half-shuttered, comparatively open.

Coffin-clock, *n.* a grandfather's clock.

Coffining, *n.* the ceremony of putting a corpse into the coffin.

Cog, *v.* to steady anything shaky by wedging it; to scotch a wheel.—*n.* a wedge or support for a wheel, &c.

Cog, *n.* a wooden vessel for holding milk, ale, porridge, broth, &c. ; a pail ; a measure, the fourth part of a peck ; liquor.—*v.* to empty into, or fill, a 'cog.'

Cog-and-soup, *n.* some food and drink.

Cog-boine, *n.* a small wooden trough, a tub.

Cog-fu', *n.* the fill of a 'cog.'

Cogg, *n.* a flat surface not lying horizontally.

Coggie, Coggun, *n.* a small 'cog.'

Cogging, *ppl. adj.* given to drink.

Coggle, *v.* to prop, support.

Coggle, *v.* to shake, to move unsteadily.

Cogglety, *adj.* shaky, insecure, not steady.

Cogglety-carry, *n.* the game of 'see-saw.'

Cogglin, *n.* a prop, a support.

Coggly, *adj.* unsteady, unstable; apt to be overset.

Cog-hand, *n.* the left hand.

Coghle, *v.* to wheeze, as from cold or asthma.

Coghling, *ppl. adj.* husky, wheezing.

Cogie, *n.* a small 'cog.'

Cogill, *n.* the fill of a 'cog', the fourth part of a peck.

Coglan-tree, *n.* the 'covin-tree'; the large tree in front of an old Scottish mansion, where the laird met his visitors.

Cogle, *v.* to move unsteadily. Cf. Coggle.

†Cognosce, *v.* a legal term : to inquire, investigate, with a view to judgment; to scrutinize the character of a person, or state of a thing, in order to a decision or regulation of procedure; to pronounce a decision as the result of investigation; to pronounce a person to be an idiot or insane by the verdict of an inquest; to survey lands in order to a division of property.

Cognost, *v.* to sit close together and plan in secrecy some harmless mischief.

Cognostin, *n.* sitting in secret conference.

Cogster, *n.* the person who, in 'swinging flax, first breaks it with a swing-bat, and then throws it to another.

Cogue, *n.* a small wooden dish for holding porridge, &c. Cf. Cog.

Cog-wame, *n.* a protuberant belly.

Cog-wymed, *adj.* corpulent, portly.

Cohow, *n.* the call used in the game of 'hide and seek.' Cf. Cahow.

Coil, *n.* an instrument formerly used in boring for coal.

Coil, *v.* to enfold in a coil ; to ensnare.

Coil, *n.* noisy disturbance, fuss, stir.

Coil, Coile, *n.* a haycock.—*v.* to put hay in cocks.

Coil-heuch, *n.* a coal-pit.

Coinyel, *v.* to agitate, as in churning milk; to injure a liquid by too much shaking.

Coinyelling, *n.* a shaking.

Coist, *n.* dues payable in kind; a servant's rations as distinct from money as wages. Cf. Cost.

Coit, *v.* to play at curling.

†Coject, *v.* to agree ; to fit.

Cokaddy, *n.* a dance performed by children in a crouching posture. Cf. Cookuddy.

Cokeweed, *n.* cockweed.

Col-candle-wick, *n.* the long-tailed duck.

Cold, *adj.* used of land : stiff and holding moisture.—*n.* a cold, a chill. Cf. Cauld.

Colded, *ppl. adj.* suffering from cold.

Coldie, *n.* the long-tailed duck.

Coldingham-packmen, *n.* cumulus clouds in the north or east on fine summer afternoons.

Cole, *n.* a haycock. Cf. Coil.

Cole, *n.* money.

Cole-hood, -hooding, *n.* the blackcap. Cf. Coal-hood.

Cole-hough, -heugh, *n.* a coal-pit.

Colemie, *n.* the coal-fish. Cf. Coalmie.

Colf, *v.* to stuff; to stop a hole; to wad a gun; to caulk a ship.—*n.* wadding for guns; the act of stuffing ; the material used for stuffing a hole. Cf. Calf.

Colfin, *v.* to stuff, to 'colf.'—*n.* wadding for guns, 'colf.' Cf. Calfing.

Colibrand, *n.* a contemptuous name for a blacksmith.

Colin-blackhead, *n.* the reed-bunting.

Colk, *n.* the eider-duck.

Coll, *n.* the 'hog-score' in a curling-rink.

Coll, *v.* to cut ; to clip ; to snuff a candle.

Coll, *n.* a haycock.—*v.* to put hay into cocks. Cf. Coil.

Collady-stone, *n.* quartz.

Collation, *v.* to collate; to partake of a collation.

Colleague, *v.* to conspire; to be in league with. Cf. Collogue.

Colleck, *v.* to collect; to recollect, think.

College, *v.* to educate at a college.

College-fee, *n.* a schoolmaster's fee.

Collegener, Colliginer, *n.* a collegian, a student at college.

Colley, Collie, *n.* a lounger; one who hunts for a dinner; one who dogs another constantly; a great admirer.

Collie, Colley, *v.* to abash; to silence in an argument; to domineer over; to bewilder, entangle; to wrangle, quarrel; to attack.

Collie, Colley, *v.* to yield in a contest; to 'knock under.'

Colliebuction, *n.* a noisy quarrel, a wrangle, disturbance.

Collier, *n.* the black-dolphin, an insect injurious to growing beans.

Collieshangie, *n.* an uproar, squabble; loud, earnest, or gossiping talk; a ring of plaited grass or straw, through which a lappet of a woman's dress, or fold of a man's coat, is clandestinely thrust, to excite ridicule.—*v.* to wrangle, fight.

Collinhood, *n.* wild poppy.

Collocan-gull, *n.* the black-headed gull.

Collogue, *v.* to conspire, plot together for mischief; to talk confidentially.—*n.* collusion; a conversation, a confidential chat. Cf. Killogue.

Colloguin', *ppl. adj.* scheming, plotting.—*n.* a plot, conspiracy.

Colloguy, *v.* to conspire; to plot together for mischief. Cf. Collogue.

Collop, *n.* a portion.

Collop-tongs, *n.* tongs for roasting slices of meat.

Colly, *n.* the 'hog-score' in a curling-rink. Cf. Coll.

Colly-tyke, *n.* a dog of any kind.

Coloured knittings, *n.* red tape, tape used by lawyers.

Colpindach, *n.* a young cow that has never calved.

Colsie, *adj.* comfortable, cosy, snug.

Comamie, *n.* a young coal-fish.

Comb, *n.* a coal-fish of the fifth year.

Comball, *v.* to meet together for amusement; to plot together, cabal.—*n.* a company of plotters, a cabal.

Comble-stane, *n.* the top-stone of a heap.

Comb's Mass, *n.* St Columba's Mass, Whitsunday.

Comburgess, *n.* a fellow-citizen.

Combustion, *n.* a fierce, hot wrangle.

Come, *v.* to sprout, spring, germinate; to sprout at the lower end in the process of malting grain; with *of* or *on*, to become of, happen to.—*n.* growth; the act of vegetation.

Come, *n.* a crook, bend, curve.

Come, *ppl. adj.* born, descended from.

Come about, -about again, *phr.* to recover

from an illness.—*n.* a call to a horse in a stall to move to one side.

Come above, *phr.* to recover, get over.

Come after, *phr.* to woo, court.

Come-again, *n.* a severe scolding; a kiss at the close of a dance.

Come-against, *adj.* repulsive.

Come-and-be-kissed, *n.* a garden flower, ? the *Viola tricolor.*

Come and gang, *phr.* give and take.

Come at, *phr.* come to; to strike, assault.

Come-a'thegither, *adj.* quite sane.

Come-ather, -ether, *n.* a call to a horse to turn to the left.

Come athort, *phr.* to strike across or athwart.

Come away, *phr.* used of seed: to germinate; to come along.

Come back, *phr.* to regain consciousness.

Come by, *phr.* to obtain; to meet with an accident.

Come crack for crack, *phr.* to give a sound whipping.

Come doon, *phr.* to lower a price; to become bankrupt; used of a river: to be in flood.

Come doon upon, *phr.* to scold, reprove.

Come doon with, *phr.* pay down.

Come gude for, *phr.* be security for.

Come hame, *phr.* to be born.

Come in, *phr.* to shrink in size or measurement; to come to be of use.

Come inowre, *phr.* to come in towards the speaker.

Come-keik, *n.* a novelty.

Comeling, *n.* a strange animal that attaches itself to a person or place.

Comely, *adj.* reverent; well-behaved.

Come-of-will, *n.* an illegitimate child; anything that comes or grows accidentally; a new-comer.

Come on, *phr.* to thrive, grow, succeed; to get on, manage, 'fend'; to rain; to follow on.

Come on ahin, *phr.* to retaliate; to interfere with another secretly and unfairly in bargaining; to become surety for.

Come one's ways, *phr.* to come along.

Come out, *phr.* to widen, expand.

Come-out-awa, *n.* a swindler.

Come outowre, *phr.* to strike; to come ou' of; to come toward the speaker.

Come over once, *phr.* to have little experience.

Come owre, *phr.* to cajole, coax successfully; to outwit; to happen; to overtake; to repeat what one has been told in confidence; to strike, to assault.

Come owre, *n.* a call to a horse to move to one side of the stall.

†**Comer, Comere**, *n.* a gossip, a godmother. Cf. Cummer.

Comerade, v. to meet for social gossip.—n. a meeting for social gossip.

Comeradin, n. the habit of visiting, day after day, with little interruption.

Come round, phr. to recover consciousness; to recover from an illness ; to be reconciled; to cajole ; to regain lost temper.

Come speed, phr. to thrive, prosper.

Comestable, adj. eatable ; fit for food.

Come thrift, phr. to thrive, prosper.

Come through, phr. to recover from an illness.

Come time, adv. by-and-by.

Come to, phr. to recover consciousness ; to become reconciled, come up to; to happen; to recover from bad temper ; to yield or agree to a proposal, &c. ; to rise to a state of honour.

Come together, phr. to be married.

Come to milk, phr. used of cows: to give milk after calving.

Come to one's self, phr. to perish, die, become useless.

Come to one's time, phr. used of a woman: to be confined.

Come-to-pass, n. an event that comes to pass.

Come to the bile, phr. to begin to boil.

Come to the door, phr. used of a knock : to sound on the door.

Come to with, phr. to overtake.

Come up, n. a call to a horse to start or to go faster.

Come upon with, phr. to strike, assault, with.

Comfarant-like, adj. decent, becoming.

Comflek, v. to reflect.

Comfort-, Comfer-knit-bane, n. the plant Symphytum tuberosum.

Comical - tommy, n. a game of chance; 'billy-fairplay.'

Cominie, n. a young coal-fish. Cf. Comamie.

Commandement, n. a command, mandate, commandment.

Commanding, ppl. adj. of pain : severe, disabling.

Commands, n. the Decalogue.

Commend, n. commendation.

†Commer, n. a godmother. Cf. Cummer.

Commerce, n. intercourse, communication, dealings with.—v. to have to do with.

Commission, n. the quarterly meeting of the General Assemblies for specific business.

Commodity, n. a measure ; a considerable quantity.

Common, n. an obligation ; indebtedness ; what is common or usual.—v. to arrange ; to agree in bargaining.—adv. commonly. Cf. Commune.

Common corn, n. oats in which each grain hangs singly on the stalk.

Common debtor, n. a legal term : one in whose favour a fund is held by trustees.

Common good, n. the funds of a royal burgh ; a town or village common.

Commonty, n. a common ; the right of common pasturage ; the commonalty.

Commune, v. to arrange ; to agree in a bargain.

Communer, n. a party to an agreement.

Commuve, v. to bring into a state of commotion ; to perturb ; to offend, displease; to move.

Comorade, n. a comrade.

Comp, n. company.

Compack, n. a compact.

Companion, n. a low fellow.

Companionry, n. companionship, fellowship.

Compear, v. to appear before a court in answer to a citation.

Compearance, n. appearance before a court in answer to a citation.

†Compesce, v. to restrain, keep under; to assuage.

Compleen, v. to complain ; to ail ; to feel unwell and express it.

Compleit, v. to pay arrears in full.

Complext, qdj. complex.

Complice, n. an accomplice.

Compliment, n. a present, gift.—v. to make a present of.

Complimental, adj. complimentary ; expressive of courtesy.

Complouther, Complouter, Comploutre, Complowther, Compluther, v. to agree ; to mix ; to work together ; to comply ; to suit, fit, answer an end proposed.—n. a mixture ; a mess, confusion ; an entanglement ; a mistake.

Comply, v. to bring about, accomplish.

Compone, v. to compose ; to settle ; to compound.

Composity, n. composure ; self-possession.

Compost, n. used of a person : a mixed character, compound.

Comprizement, n. the valuation of timber in farm-buildings at a change of tenancy ; the values ascertained in ' comprizing.'

†Compromit, v. to promise jointly; to compromise.—n. a compromise.

Compryse, Comprize, v. to attach for debt legally ; to value the timber in farm-buildings at a change of tenancy.

Compryser, n. the person who attaches the estate of another for debt.

Comprysing, n. attachment for debt.

Compt, n. company.

†Compt, v. to account for; to count; to justify.—r. an account, a reckoning.

†Compt, adj. neat in dress.

Comptable, adj. accountable for.

Comthankfow, adj. thankful, grateful.

Compting, n. counting.

Con, *n.* a squirrel.

Con, *v.* in *phr.* 'to con thanks,' to return thanks.

Conceit, Concait, *n.* a fancy ornament; a knick-knack; neatness; good taste; an opinion; a fancy; a liking; an eccentric or oddly dressed person.—*v.* to imagine, fancy, think.

Conceit-net, *n.* a fixed net enclosing a portion of a river or estuary.

Conceity, *adj.* conceited, vain; witty, appropriate.

Concerns, *n.* relations by blood or affinity.

Conclude, *v.* to decide; to prove valid or sufficient.

Concluding, *ppl. adj.* conclusive.

Concos-mancos, *adj.* of sound mind, *compos mentis.*

Concurrans, *n.* occurrence.

Concurse, *n.* concurrence; co-operation.

Concussion, *n.* coercion; the forcible exaction of money, extortion.

Condemn, *v.* to block up entrance and exit.

Condescend, *v.* a legal term: to state one's case specifically; to particularize; to agree.

Condescendence, *n.* a detailed statement of one's case.

Condiddle, *v.* to make away with, filch.

Condie, *n.* a conduit, a drain. Cf. Cundy.

Conding, *adj.* condign.

Condingly, *adv.* agreeably, lovingly.

†**Conduce,** *v.* to hire; to bargain, deal; to agree, arrange.

Conducer, *n.* a hirer.

Conduction, *n.* hiring; the hiring of troops.

Condumacity, *n.* contumacy.

Confab, *v.* to confabulate.—*n.* a confabulation.

Confabble, *n.* a confabulation.

Confeerin, Confeirin, *ppl. adj.* corresponding to, accordant with. —*conj.* considering.

Confeese, *v.* to confuse.

Confeesed-like, *adj.* looking confused.

Conference, *n.* analogy, agreement.

Confess, *v.* used of a bottle: to be drained to the last drop by pouring or dripping; to bring up the contents of the stomach.

Confident, *adj.* trustworthy.

Confine, *n.* confinement; an enclosure.

Confirm, *v.* to fall in with an agreement.

Confit, *n.* a comfit.

Confloption, *n.* panic, flurry, fluster.

Confoon', *v.* to confound.

†**Conform,** *adj.* conformable.—*adv.* conformably.

Conformity, *n.* a concession, consent.

†**Confort,** *v.* to comfort.—*n.* a comfort.

†**Congee,** *n.* a bow, a flattering obeisance.— *v.* to bow, salute.

†**Congey,** *n.* leave, permission.

Congou-bree, *n.* tea.

Congree, *v.* to agree.

Conjee, *n.* a most polite bow. Cf. Congee.

Conjugality, *n.* conjugal union.

Conjunck, *adj.* conjunct, conjoined.

Conjured, *ppl. adj.* perjured.

Con-kind, *n.* all kinds or sorts. Cf. Kin-kind.

Connach, *n.* a fatal distemper of cows. Cf. Connoch.

Connach, *v.* to waste, destroy, trample on, spoil; to consume carelessly.—*n.* an unskilful worker; a waster of food, &c.; work badly done, spoilt.

Connachin, *n.* overcareful nursing.—*ppl. adj.* lazy, clumsy at work, from fondness for good living.

Connagh, *n.* the pip in fowls. Cf. Cannagh.

Conneck, *v.* to connect.

Connect, *ppl. adj.* connected, consecutive.

Connie, *n.* a rabbit, coney.

Connoch, *n.* a fatal distemper of cows.

Connoch, *v.* to waste, destroy, spoil. Cf. Connach.

Connoch-worm, *n.* a caterpillar lurking in grass and causing disease to cows.

Connyshonie, *n.* a silly, gossiping conversation; a whispered conversation.

†**Conquess, Conquest,** *v.* to acquire otherwise than by inheritance; to conquer.—*n.* acquired possessions, personal acquisition, in contrast to inheritance.

Consate, *n.* knick-knack.—*v.* to fancy, imagine. Cf. Conceit.

Conscienceable, *adj.* conscionable, according to conscience.

Conscious, *adj.* privy to.

Consequentially, *adv.* consequently.

Consolement, *n.* consolation.

Constable, *n.* a large drinking-vessel, to be drained by one in a company who has drunk less than the rest, or otherwise has transgressed the rules of the company.

Constancy, *n.* in *phr.* 'for a constancy,' continually, always.

Constant, *adj.* evident, manifest.

Constitute, *v.* to open an ecclesiastical court with prayer.

Consume, *v.* to nullify, neutralize.

Consuming, *ppl. adj.* wasteful, not economical.

Consumpt, *n.* consumption, phthisis.

Consumption-dyke, *n.* a temporary wall of stones which have been cleared off land.

Cont, *n.* estimation.

Contain, *v.* to restrain one's self.

Conteena, *v.* to continue.

Contend, *v.* to contend for.

Contens, *n.* used as an oath in *phr.* 'by my contens.'

Content, *v.* in *phr.* 'to content and pay,' to satisfy a creditor; to pay up in full.

†**Conter,** *v.* to contradict, thwart, run counter to.—*n.* a reverse of fortune, a cross, trial; in *pl.* a state of opposition.—*prep.* against. —*adv.* in opposition to.—*adj.* contrary, opposite.

Contermashious, *adj.* perverse; contumacious. Cf. Contramashous.

Conter-poison, *n.* an antidote to poison.

Conter-tree, *n.* a cross-bar of wood, or stick attached by a rope to a door, and resting on the wall at each side, in order to keep the door shut from without.

Conthankfow, *adj.* grateful.

Con thanks, *phr.* to return thanks. Cf. Con.

Contingency, *n.* contiguity; close relationship; connection.

Contingent, *n.* one near in blood.

Continuation, *n.* prorogation.

Continue, *v.* to delay, postpone, prorogue.

Contra, *n.* the country.

Contrack, *v.* to contract; to betroth; to give in the names of a couple for the proclamation of their banns.—*n.* a formal betrothal before witnesses; an application to the session-clerk of a parish to register the names of a couple for proclamation of their banns.

Contract-night, *n.* Saturday night, when names were generally given in for proclamation of banns.

Contradict, *v.* to object to.

†**Contrair,** *adj.* contrary, opposite.—*n.* the contrary, the opposite.—*prep.* against.—*v.* to oppose.

Contrairisum, *adj.* perverse, froward.

Contrairy, *adj.* contrary, adverse; perverse, stubborn.—*adv.* in opposition to.

Contramashous, Contramacious, Contramawcious, *adj.* self-willed; obstinate; rebellious. Cf. Contermashious.

†**Contrecoup,** *n.* opposition; a repulse in the pursuit of an object.

Contrepoise, *v.* to counteract.

Contrive, *v.* to design.

Contumace, Contumasse, *v.* to act contumaciously; to pronounce one to be contumacious.

†**Contumax,** *adj.* contumacious.

†**Convell,** *v.* to refute.

Convene, Conveen, *v.* to assemble, meet together; to cite to a court.—*n.* a gathering; a convention.

Convene, Conveane, *v.* to agree.

Convene, *n.* convenience.

Conveniable, *adj.* accessible, convenient.

Conveniency, *n.* expediency.

Convenient, *adj.* near, contiguous.

Conventicular, *n.* an attender of conventicles.

Conversation, Conversation-lozenge, *n.* a flat lozenge of various shapes, printed with a motto or short sentence.

Convey, *v.* to escort, accompany, courteously or in kindness; to confer an office.

Conveyancy, *n.* a legal conveyance.

Convocate, *v.* to call to arms.

Convocation, *n.* an assembly of men to arms.

†**Convoy,** *v.* to escort; to see a person home; to accompany part of the way; to convey; to manage, see a business through.—*n.* a personal escorting; a marriage company going to meet and escort the bride; mode or channel of conveyance; skilful management; painstaking action; successful accomplishment.

Convoyance, *n.* management; finesse.

Coo, *n.* a pigeon's call.

Coo, *n.* a cow.

Cooch, *n.* a dog's kennel.—*v.* to lie down. Cf. Couch.

Coocher, *n.* a coward; in *pl.* the 'cowardly blow,' the blow given to, and submitted to tamely by, a coward. Cf. Coucher.

Cood, *adj.* harebrained. Cf. Cude.

Cood, *n.* the cud.

Coodie, *n.* a small tub; a wooden nursery chamber-pot. Cf. Cootie.

Cooer, *v.* to squat down. Cf. Coor.

Coof, *n.* a fool, simpleton; a man who interferes with domestic work.

Coofish, *adj.* bashful, awkward.

Coog, *n.* a boys' game, the same as 'cahow' or 'keehow.'

Cooie, *n.* a small cow; a hornless cow. Cf. Cowie.

Cook, *v.* to manage, arrange so as to gain one's end.

Cook, *v.* to appear and disappear by fits; to hide one's self.

Cook, *v.* to imitate the call of the cuckoo.

Cooke, *n.* a big draught of liquid; a mouthful.—*v.* to take a long draught of liquid.

Cookie, *n.* a small plain bun; a bath-bun.

Cookie-shine, *n.* a tea-party.

Cook-stool, *n.* a cucking-stool.

Cookuddy, *n.* a dance performed by children in a crouching posture; *phr.* to 'dance cookuddy,' to perform antics. Cf. Cucuddy.

Cool, *n.* a nightcap; a close cap worn within doors. Cf. Cowl.

Coolie, *n.* a raised peak in the centre of the foam on home-brewed ale; a nightcap.

Coolin, *n.* a West Highland New-year's Eve sport; the principal actor in the game.

Cooling-stone, *n.* a large stone, in or near a school, on which a boy who has been breeched is set to cool his posteriors.

Coolriff, *adj.* cool, cold; indifferent. Cf. Cauldrife.

Cool-the-loom, *n.* an indifferent worker; a lazy person.

Cooly, *v.* to flatter; to wheedle; to cheat. Cf. Cully.

Coom, *n.* the wooden frame used in building a bridge; a coffin-lid.

Coom, *n.* coal-dust; peat-dust; very small coal used in smithies; the dust of grain; soot; dirt.—*v.* to blacken, begrime.

Coomb, *n.* the bosom of a hill having a semicircular form; a hollow in a mountain-side.

Coom-ceiled, *adj.* used of a garret: having the ceiling sloping or arched.

Coo-me-doo, *n.* a term of endearment.

Coomy, *adj.* grimy; begrimed with 'coom.'

Coonjer, *v.* to give a drubbing; to frighten.— *n.* in *pl.* a scolding. Cf. Counger.

Coont, *v.* to count; to do sums; to settle accounts.—*n.* in *pl.* sums. Cf. Count.

Coony, *n.* coin, money. Cf. Cunzie.

†Coony, Coonyie, *n.* a corner; a coign.

Coop, *v.* to catch in traps.

Coop, *n.* a cart with closed sides and ends. Cf. Coup.

Coop, *n.* a small heap.

Coop, *v.* to hoop, bind with hoops.

Cooper, *n.* a horse imperfectly gelded.

Cooper, *v.* to tinker up.

Cooperman, *v.* to play into each other's hands unjustly.

Cooper o' Stobo, *phr.* one who excels another in any particular line.

†Coopin, *n.* a shred; clipping. Cf. Cowpon.

Coor, *v.* to cower, squat down; to hide, keep still in a place; to bend, submit; to lower, droop.

Coor, *v.* to cover; to recover.

Coordie, *n.* a coward. Cf. Cowardie.

Coordie, *v.* to surpass in athletics. Cf. Cowardie.

Coordie-lick, *n.* a 'coward's blow,' challenging to fisticuffs.

Coordie-smit, *n.* a 'coward's blow.'

Coorie, *v.* to cower, crouch, stoop down.

Coorse, *adj.* coarse.

Coorse, *n.* course.

Coort, *v.* to court.

Coorter, *n.* a courter.

Cooser, *n.* a stallion; a stout, vulgar fellow; a libertine.

Coo-sharn, *n.* cows' dung.

Coosie, *n.* a challenge to difficult feats, given by boys.

Coost, *n.* condition of body.

Coost, *v. pret.* and *ppl.* cast.

Coosten, *ppl.* cast.

Coot, *n.* the guillemot.

Coot, *n.* the ankle.

Cootcher, *v.* to parcel out.

Cooted, *ppl. adj.* having ankles. Cf. Cuited.

Cooter, *v.* to set on one's feet; to handle tenderly; to restore to health. Cf. Cuiter.

†Cooter, *v.* to sew carelessly.

Cooth, *n.* a young coal-fish.

Cooth, *adj.* pleasant, affable. Cf. Couth.

Coothie, *adj.* pleasant, kind. Cf. Couthie.

Cootie, *n.* a small wooden bowl or basin; a bucket-shaped barrel; a wooden chamber-pot in nursery use.

Cootie, *adj.* used of fowls: having the legs covered with feathers.

Cootikins, *n.* gaiters. Cf. Cuitikins.

Cootle, *v.* to handle carefully; to put to rights; to lay heads together; to fondle, caress, 'cuddle'; to wheedle. Cf. Cuitle.

Cootrie, *n.* the puffin.

Cope, *n.* a coffin.

Cope, *n.* the vault of heaven.

Coper, *n.* a dealer. Cf. Couper.

Cophouse, *n.* a house or room for keeping cups.

Copy, *n.* a copy-book.

Coranich, *n.* a Highland dirge, or a 'coronach.'

Corback, *n.* the roof of a house.

Corban, *n.* a basket.

Corbandie, *n.* in *phr.* 'there comes in corbandie,' used of a plausible hypothesis which is opposed by some great difficulty that occurs.

Corbie, *n.* a raven; a crow.—*v.* to speak in a harsh, guttural manner.

Corbie-aits, *n.* a species of black oats.

Corbie-craw, *n.* a raven; the carrion-crow.

Corbie-messenger, *n.* a messenger who returns either not at all or too late.

Corbie-steps, *n.* the projections on the slanting part of a gable resembling steps. Cf. Craw-steps.

Corcolit, *n.* a purple dye made from a lichen. Cf. Corkie-lit.

Corcuddoch, Corcudoch, *adj.* kindly.—*v.* to whisper together. Cf. Curcuddoch.

Cord, *v.* to accord, be in accord.

Cordet, *ppl. adj.* used of a baking-roller: ridged, as if with cords.

†Cordevan, *n.* sealskin or horseskin, used as leather. Cf. Cordowan.

Cordiner, Cordiwaner, *n.* a cordwainer; a shoemaker.

†Cordisidron, *n.* lemon- or citron-peel.

†Cordon, *n.* a band, wreath.

†Cordowan, *n.* Spanish leather; sealskin used as leather, tanned horseskin.

Cords, *n.* a contraction of the muscles of the neck, a disease of horses.

Cordy, *n.* a familiar designation of a shoemaker.

Core, *n.* the heart.

Core, *n.* a choir, company of singers or musicians; a convivial company; friendly terms.

Corf-house, *n.* a house or shed for curing salmon, &c., and for keeping nets in the close season.

Corft, *ppl. adj.* used of salmon and other fish: cured, salted; boiled with salt and water.

Corianders, *n.* coriander-seeds covered with sugar and used as sweets.

†**Corie,** *v.* to curry leather.

Corier, *n.* a currier.

Cork, *n.* an overseer; a master tradesman; an employer; applied by weavers to the manufacturers' agents, and by journeymen tailors to their masters.

Cork, *v. phr.* 'to cork the bottle,' to throw a pebble up so as to fall perpendicularly into a pond or river with a 'plop.'

Cork-coom, *n.* burnt cork.

Corker, Corker-pin, *n.* a very large pin; a corking-pin.

Corkie, *n.* a species of lichen used for dyeing.

Corkie, *n.* the largest kind of pin; a bodkin-pin; corking-pin.

Corkie-lit, Corklit, *n.* a purple dye made from the lichen 'corkie.'

Corkin-preen, *n.* a corking-pin.

Corkir, *n.* the lichen 'corkie,' used for dyeing.

Cork-swollen, *adj.* beery.

Corky, *adj.* airy, brisk, flighty, frivolous; drunk.

Corky-headit, *adj.* light-headed, giddy.

Corky-noddle, *n.* a light-headed person.

Cormeille, *n.* the bitter vetch.

†**Cormes,** *n.* sorb-apples.

†**Cormundum,** *v.* to confess a fault; to sue for peace; to own one's self vanquished.

Corn, *n.* oats; a single grain of anything, such as sand, pellets, &c.; a small quantity of anything.—*v.* to feed with oats; to exhilarate with liquor; to sprinkle meat with salt, to pickle; used of cereals: to fill out, yield much good grain.

Corn, *n.* a 'quern,' a circular stone for grinding malt, &c.

Corn-ark, *n.* a stable corn-bin.

Corn-baby, *n.* a bunch of oats in the ear, as an ornament.

Corn-cart, *n.* an open-spoked cart.

Corn-cauger, *n.* a corn-carrier.

Corn-clock, *n.* a beetle found among corn.

Corn-craik, -craker, *n.* the landrail; a hand-rattle; a child's rattle.

Corned, *ppl. adj.* fed, provisioned; slightly drunk; salted, pickled.

Cornel, *n.* a colonel.

Corner, *n.* in *phr.* 'to put one to a corner,' to take precedence or authority in a house.

Corner, *v.* used of grain: to fill out.

Corners-change-corners, *n.* a game; *phr.* 'to play corners-change-corners,' to play fast and loose.

†**Cornet,** *n.* a scarf anciently worn by doctors or professors as part of their academical costume.

Corn-fatt, *n.* a corn-chest.

Corn-harp, *n.* a wire implement for freeing grain from seeds of weeds.

Corn-head, *n.* the end-pickle on a stalk of oats.

Cornief, *n.* cats' excrement.

Corning, *n.* a feed of oats; food, provision.

Cornish, *n.* a cornice.

Corn-kist, *n.* a stable corn-bin.

Corn-knot, *n.* the knot of the band which ties up the sheaf.

Corn-loft, *n.* a granary.

Corn-mou, *n.* a stack of corn; the place where corn is stacked.

†**Cornoy,** *n.* sorrow, trouble.

Corn-pickle, *n.* an ear of 'corn,' a very small quantity of 'corn.'

Corn-pipe, *n.* a reed or whistle, with a horn affixed by the tip.

Corn-rig, *n.* a 'ridge' of growing corn.

Corn-scrack, -skraugh, *n.* the landrail.

Corn-stook, *n.* a shock of corn.

Corn-waters, *n.* distilled spirits.

Corny, *adj.* fruitful, prolific, abounding in grain.

Cornyard, *n.* the stackyard.

Corny-skraugh, *n.* the landrail. Cf. Corn-scrack.

Corny-wark, *n.* food made of grain.

Coronoy, *n.* sorrow. Cf. Cornoy.

Corp, *n.* a corpse.

Corp-candle, *n.* a 'will-o'-the-wisp.'

Corphed, *ppl. adj.* of salmon: cured. Cf. Corft.

Corpie, *n.* a child's corpse.

Corplar, *n.* a corporal.

Corp-lifter, *n.* a body-snatcher.

Corpse, *n.* a living body.

Corpse-chesting, *n.* the placing of the corpse in the coffin.

Corpse-sheet, *n.* a shroud, winding-sheet.

Corp-snapper, *n.* a body-snatcher.

†**Corpus,** *n.* the body of a man or animal.

Corrach, Corrack, *n.* a pannier, a basket.

Correck, *adj.* correct; upright, steady, of good character.

Correctory, *adj.* correcting; explanatory.

Correnoy, *n.* a disturbance in the bowels; a rumbling noise in the belly.

Corrie, *v.* with *on*, to hold exclusive intimate correspondence in a low sort of way; to gossip together.

Corrieneuchin, *ppl.* conversing intimately, talking together.

Corrock, *n.* a pannier. Cf. Corrach.

Corruption, *n.* bad temper, 'bile.'

Corrydander, *n.* the coriander plant. Cf. Corianders.

Cors, Corse, Corss, *n.* a cross; a market-place; the signal formerly sent round for assembling the Orcadians; a piece of silver money which bore a cross.—*v.* to cross, pass over; to thwart.

Corsicrown, *n.* a game, with a square figure divided by four lines crossing each other on the crown or centre, played by two with three 'men' each.

Corsy-belly, *n.* a child's first shirt.

Corter, *n.* a quarter; a 'quarter' of oatcake.

Cosey, *n.* a woollen cravat.

Cosh, *adj.* neat, snug, comfortable; quiet, uninterrupted; familiar, friendly, loyal; smart; brisk; vivacious; happy.

Cosh, *adj.* with a hollow beneath, over a hollow.

Coshly, *adv.* neatly, comfortably, briskly.

Cosie, *n.* a straw-basket. Cf. Cazzie.

Coss, *v.* to exchange, barter.—*n.* a bargain, exchange.

Coss a doe, *phr.* to exchange one piece of bread for another.

Cossblade, *n.* a flower of some kind.

Cossnent, *n.* working for wages without victuals; *phr.* 'to work black cossnent,' to work without meat or wages.

Cost, *n.* duty paid in kind, as distinguished from that paid in money; the board, &c., given to a servant instead of money; meal and malt, a feu-duty paid in meal and malt.

Costard, *n.* the head.

Coster, *n.* a piece of arable land.

Cot, *v.* to cohabit; to live together in a small cottage.

Cote, *n.* a house or cottage of humble construction.

Coteral, *n.* an elastic piece of thin split iron, put through a bolt to prevent it from losing hold, as the end opens after passing through the orifice.

Cotham, *v.* to satisfy with food; to eat to excess.

Cothaman, *n.* a surfeit.

Cothie, *adj.* warm, snug, comfortable. Cf. Couthie.

Cothiely, *adv.* snugly.

Cothroch, *v.* to work or to cook in a dirty, disgusting manner; to overnurse; to handle too much.

Cothrochie, *adj.* fond of good eating; making much ado about cooking.

Cothrochin, *ppl. adj.* dirty and unskilful.

Cothrugh, *adj.* rustic, boorish. Cf. Codroch.

Cotlander, *n.* a cottager who keeps a horse to plough his croft.

Cotman, *n.* a farm-cottager.

Cottar, Cotter, *n.* the inhabitant of a cot house or cottage.

Cottar-body, *n.* a cottager.

Cottar-folk, *n.* cottagers.

Cottar-house, *n.* a farm-labourer's house.

Cottar-man, *n.* a cottager.

Cottar's-ha', *n.* a peasant's cottage.

Cottar-toun, *n.* a hamlet inhabited by cottagers dependent for work on the neighbouring farms.

Cottar-wark, *n.* stipulated work done by the cottagers for the farmer on whose ground they dwell.

Cotter, *v.* used of eggs: to fry them with butter, stirring them round until they are cooked.

Cotter, *v.* to grow potatoes by giving seed, manure, and culture for the use of the land.

Cotter, *v.* to potter about.—*n.* unskilful working.

Cotterie, *n.* a cottar's holding; his provision of a house.

Cottie, *n.* a short coat; a petticoat. Cf. Coatie.

Cotton, *v.* to take a liking to; to make one's self agreeable to.

Cottonial, *adj.* cotton-like.

Cotton weavry, *n.* cotton-weaving.

Cotton-winsey, *n.* a material made of cotton and wool.

Couch, *v.* to sleep.—*n.* a dog's kennel.

Coucher, *v.* to bow down, crouch; to do in a trial of strength what another cannot.—*n.* a coward.

Coucher's-blow, *n.* the blow given by a mean and cowardly fellow before he gives up; the last blow to which a coward submits. Cf. Coordie-lick.

Couda, *v.* could have.

Coudie, *adj.* affable, familiar, loving; comfortable; pleasant to the ear; ominous of evil. Cf. Couthie.

Coudle, *v.* to float as a feather, alternately rising and sinking with the waves.

Couf, *n.* a fool. Cf. Coof.

Coug, *n.* a small wooden vessel with hoops, a 'cog.'

Cougher, *v.* to continue coughing. Cf. Cocher.

Couk, *v.* to retch. Cf. Cook.

Couk, *v.* to sort, arrange; to manage dexterously. Cf. Cook

Couk, *v.* to appear and disappear by fits. Cf. Cook.

Coukie, *n.* a small bun. Cf. Cookie.

Coul, Coulie, *n.* a nightcap. Cf. Cowl.

Coulie, *n.* a boy; a contemptuous designation of a man.

Coulter, *n.* a nose; the appendage to a turkey-cock's bill.

Coulter-neb, *n.* the puffin.

Coulter-nebbit, *adj.* long-nosed.

Coum, *n.* dust ; coal-dust. Cf. Coom.

Coumit-bed, *n.* a bed formed of deals on all sides except the front, which is hung with a curtain.

Coummie-edge, *n.* an edge of bad, ill-polished steel.

Coun, *v.* used of children : to cry, weep aloud. Cf. Cown.

Council-house, *n.* the town-hall.

Council-post, *n.* a special messenger, such as formerly bore messages from the Lords of the Council.

Counger, Counjer, *v.* to intimidate ; to give a drubbing. Cf. Coonjer.

Count, *v.* to practise arithmetic ; to settle accounts.—*n.* calculation ; a sum in arithmetic.

Count-book, *n.* an account-book ; a text-book of arithmetic.

Counter, *n.* a person learning arithmetic, an arithmetician.

Counter-check, -check-plane, *n.* a tool for working out the groove which unites the two sashes of a window in the middle.

Counter-coup, *v.* to overcome, surmount ; to repulse ; to overturn ; to destroy.

Counter-louper, *n.* a draper's assistant ; a shopman.

Counting, *n.* arithmetic ; the yearly settlement between landlord and tenant.

Counting-dram, *n.* the dram of spirits given after a settlement of accounts.

Count-kin-with, *phr.* to compare one's pedigree with another's ; to claim blood-relationship with.

Country, *n.* a quarter, region ; the people of a district. Cf. Kintra.

Country-keeper, *n.* one employed in a district to apprehend delinquents.

Coup, *n.* a 'caup,' cup, or bowl.

Coup, *v.* to exchange, barter ; to expose to sale ; to deal, traffic.—*n.* a good bargain ; anything bought below its real value.

Coup, *n.* a company of people ; a quantity of things.

Coup, *v.* to capsize, tilt ; to tumble ; to become bankrupt ; to empty by overturning ; to turn the scale ; to drink off ; to bend, submit.—*n.* a tip-cart ; a fall, upset ; a sudden break in a stratum of coal ; a place for emptying cartloads of earth, ashes, rubbish, &c.

Coup, *n.* a box-cart, with closed ends and sides. Cf. Coop.

Coup aff, *v.* to fall off.

Coupal, *n.* a disease of sheep, causing lameness.

Coup and creel, *phr.* entirely.

Coup-cart, *n.* a box-cart that tilts up.

Coup carts, *phr.* to turn heels over head.

†**Coupe-jarret**, *n.* one who hamstrings another.

Couper, *n.* a dealer ; a horse- or cattle-dealer.

Couper-word, *n.* the first word in demanding 'boot' in a bargain.

†**Coupin**, *n.* a piece cut off ; a shred, slice ; a fragment. Cf. Coupon.

Coupit, *ppl. adj.* confined to bed by illness.

Couple, *n.* a rafter.—*v.* to marry ; to mate.

Couple-baulk, -baak, *n.* a rafter, beam ; the collar-beam of a roof.

Couple-hicht, *adj.* in great excitement or anger.

Couple-nail, *n.* a rafter-nail.

Couple-yill, *n.* a drink given to carpenters on putting up the 'couples' in a new house.

†**Coupon**, *n.* a piece ; a portion of a body that has been quartered.

Coup over, *v.* to fall asleep ; to be confined in childbed.

Coup over the creels, *phr.* to come to grief, make a mess of.

Coup the cart, *phr.* get the better of, be done with.

Coup the crans, *phr.* to overthrow, get the better of.

Coup the creels, *phr.* to fall, turn head over heels ; to die ; to bring forth an illegitimate child.

Coup the harrows, *phr.* to overthrow.

Coup-the-ladle, *n.* the game of 'see-saw.'

Cour, *v.* to stoop, crouch. Cf. Coor.

Cour, *v.* to recover. Cf. Coor.

Courage-bag, *n.* the scrotum.

†**Courant**, *n.* a running and violent dance ; a great fuss ; a scolding.

Courch, *n.* a woman's cap. Cf. Curch.

†**Courchieff**, *n.* a covering for a woman's head.

Courie, *adj.* timid.

Courie, *n.* a small stool. Cf. Currie.

Courple, *n.* a crupper. Cf. Curple.

Court, *n.* the lawn or grass-plot about a house.

Court-day, *n.* rent-day.

Courtin, *n.* a farm straw-yard.

Courtiser, *n.* one who holds property by right of 'courtesy.'

Couser, *n.* a stallion. Cf. Cooser.

Cousin-red, *n.* kinship, consanguinity.

Coust, *n.* duty paid in kind. Cf. Cost.

Cout, *n.* a young horse ; a term of contempt applied to a man.

Cout, *n.* a hard-twisted handkerchief used in the game of 'craw.'

Coutch, *v.* to lay out land in a proper and convenient division among joint proprietors. —*n.* a portion of land held in one lot and not in 'runrig.'

Coutchack, *n.* a blazing fire ; the clearest part of a fire. Cf. Guschach.

Coutcher, *v.* to bow down, crouch.—*n.* a coward. Cf. Coucher.

Couter, *n.* a coulter.

Cout-evil, *n.* strangles in young horses.

Couth, *v. pret.* could.

Couth, *adj.* pleasant, kind, affable; comfortable, snug.—*n.* kindness.

Couthie, *adj.* kind, pleasant, agreeable, affable; tender, sympathetic; snug, comfortable; well-to-do.—*adv.* affectionately.

Couthily, *adv.* kindly.

Couthiness, *n.* friendliness, familiarity.

Coutnless, *adj.* cold, unkind.

Couthy-like, *adj.* having the appearance of kindness.

Coutribat, *n.* a tumult.

Coutter, *n.* a sort of decanter for holding wine. Cf. Cutter.

Coutterthirl, *n.* the vacuity between the coulter and the ploughshare.

Cove, *n.* a cave, cavern; a sea-cave with narrow entrance.

Covenant, *n.* wages without food.

Covenanter, *n.* a whisky-jar.

Cover, *n.* stock, property, &c. convertible into cash.

Cover, *n.* a good crop covering the ground.

Covetise, *n.* covetousness.

Covetta, *n.* a plane used for moulding framed work.

Covine, *n.* fraud, artifice.

Covine, *n.* a company or division of witches, consisting of thirteen.

Covin-tree, *n.* a large tree in front of an old mansion-house, where the laird met his visitors.

Cow, *n.* a twig of a shrub; a bush; a besom of broom; a birch for whipping; fuel for a temporary fire.

Cow, *n.* a goblin, sprite, apparition; scarecrow.

Cow, *v.* to rate, upbraid; to scold an equal or superior; to snub; to surpass, beat, outdo. —*n.* a fright; a coward; a frightful object.

Cow, *v.* to cut, crop, clip short, prune; to crop, browse.—*n.* a clipping, polling; the act of pruning. Cf. Coll.

Cow, *n.* a rude shed over the mouth of a coal-pit.

Cowan, *n.* a fishing-boat.

Cowan, *n.* a mason who builds 'dry-stone dykes' or walls without mortar; a term of contempt for a mason who has not been regularly apprenticed; one who is not a Freemason.

Cowaner, *n.* a 'cowan'-mason.

Cowardie, *v.* to surpass in athletics.

Cowardie, *n.* a coward.

Cowardie-blow, -lick, *n.* a blow given as a challenge to fight.

Cowardie-smit, *n.* a blow given as a challenge to fight.

Cowardly-blow, *n.* a blow given as a challenge to fight.

Cow-baillie, *n.* a cattleman on a farm.

Cow-beast, *n.* a cow, an ox.

Cowble, *v.* used of ice: to undulate; to 'shog. Cf. Coble.

Cow-byre, *n.* a cow-house.

Cow-cakes, *n.* wild parsnip.

Cow-carl, *n.* a bugbear; one who uses intimidation.

Cow-cloos, *n.* the common trefoil.

Cow-clushern, *n.* cow's dung as it drops in a heap.

Cow-couper, *n.* cow-dealer.

Cow-cracker, *n.* the bladder-campion.

Cow-craik, *n.* a mist with an easterly wind, a 'haar.'

Cowd, *v.* to float slowly, moving on slight waves; to swim.—*n.* a gentle, rocking motion; a pleasant sail; a swim.

Cowda, Cowdach, *n.* a small cow; a heifer.

Cowder, *n.* a boat that sails pleasantly.

Cowdie, *adj.* pleasant, kindly, cheerful. Cf. Couthie.

Cowdle, *v.* to float, move with the motion of the waves.

Cow-doctor, *n.* a veterinary surgeon.

Cowdrum, *n.* a beating; a severe scolding.

Cowdy, *n.* a little cow; a hornless cow; a heifer. Cf. Cowda.

Cowe, *n.* a broom; a besom; a bush. Cf. Cow.

Cowe, *v.* to frighten; to snub; to surpass.— *n.* a fright, a coward. Cf. Cow.

Cowe, *v.* to crop; to clip short; to prune; to browse.—*n.* a clipping, polling. Cf. Cow, Coll.

Cowe'en-, Cowen-elders, *n.* cormorants.

Cowen, *n.* a mason who builds walls without mortar. Cf. Cowan.

Cower, *v.* to keep still; to bend, yield to; to lower; to droop.

Cower, *v.* to recover, get well, get over.

Cowery, *v.* to crouch. Cf. Coorie.

Cowey, *n.* the seal. Cf. Cowie.

Cow-feeder, *n.* a dairyman who keeps cows and retails milk.

Cow-fish, *n.* any large, oval shell-fish.

Cow-gang, *n.* a cow's walk.

Cow-grass, *n.* the common purple clover.

Cow-heave, *n.* the colt's-foot.

Cowhow, *n.* a state of excitement, a hubbub, much ado.

Cow-hubby, *n.* a cowherd.

Cowie, *n.* a hornless cow; a small cow; the seal.

Cowie, *adj.* odd, queer.

Cowie, *adv.* very, exceedingly.

Cow-ill, *n.* any disease of cows.

Cowin', *n.* a fright ; an alarm ; a snubbing.

Cowin's, *n.* what is cut or broken off.

Cowit, *ppl. adj.* closely cropped or polled ; with short and thin hair.

Cowk, *v.* to retch, strain, vomit.—*n.* a belch, a vomit.

Cowl, *n.* a nightcap.

Cowlady-stone, *n.* a kind of quartz. Cf. Collady-stone.

Cowl-headed, *adj.* wearing a nightcap.

Cowlick, *n.* a lock of hair that will not lie flat. Cf. Cow's-lick.

Cowlie, *n.* a nightcap.

Cowlie, *n.* a man who picks up a girl on the street ; a rogue, fellow ; a boy ; a term of contempt. Cf. Coulie.

Cowll, *n.* a fellow, 'cowlie.'

Cow-mack, *n.* the bladder-campion.

Cowman, *n.* a name for the devil.

Cown, *v.* used of children : to cry, weep aloud.

Cowp, *n.* a basket for catching fish.

Cowp, *n.* a number, quantity. Cf. Coup.

Cowp, *v.* to barter, deal. Cf. Coup.

Cowp, *v.* to fall, overturn. Cf. Coup.

Cowpendoch, *n.* a young cow. Cf. Colpindach.

Cowper, *n.* a horse-dealer.

Cowper-justice, *n.* trying a man after execution ; 'Jeddart justice.'

Cowpers, *n.* part of the mounting of a weaver's loom.

Cow-plat, *n.* cow-dung dropped in the fields.

†**Cowpon**, *n.* a shred, fragment ; in *pl.* shivers, bits. Cf. Coupon.

Cow-quake, *n.* a cattle-disease caused by cold weather ; the cold easterly wind in May that produces the disease.

Cowr, *v.* to crouch. Cf. Cower.

Cowr, *v.* to recover. Cf. Cower.

Cow's-backrin, *n.* cow-dung dropped in the fields.

Cow's-band, *n.* the band binding the cow to the stake, given in pledge for borrowed money.

Cowschot, Cowshot, *n.* the ringdove. Cf. Cushet.

Cow-sharn, *n.* cow-dung.

Cow-shite, *n.* a contemptible person.

Cowshot, *n.* a kind of marl, brown and gray.

Cowshus, Cowshious, *adj.* cautious.

Cowslem, *n.* the evening star.

Cow's-lick, *n.* an upstanding lock of hair.

Cow's-mouth, *n.* the cowslip.

Cow's-thumb, *n.* a small distance ; a hair's-breadth.

Cowstick, *n.* lunar caustic.

Cowt, *n.* a colt ; a rough, clumsy fellow, lout.

Cowt, *v.* to colt ; to beat, thrash.—*n.* a cudgel, rung, strong stick.

Cow-the-cady, -cuddy, *phr.* to surpass, outdo.

Cow-the-gowan, *phr. n.* a fleet horse.—*v.* to outdo, excel.

Cow-tushlach, *n.* cow-dung.

Cowzie, *adj.* boisterous ; terrific.

Cox, *v.* to coax ; to persuade.

Coxy, *adj.* conceited, coxcombical.

Coxy, *adj.* coaxing.

Coy, *n.* a heifer. Cf. Quey.

Coy-duck, *n.* a decoy.

Cozin, *n.* a cousin.

Crab, *n.* a sour, disagreeable person ; a crab-apple.—*v.* to put out of temper, fret.

Crab, *n.* a kerb.

Crabbit-like, *adj.* looking cross-grained.

Crabbitly, *adv.* crossly ; peevishly ; morosely.

Crabbitness, *n.* crossness ; bad temper.

Crab-craigs, *n.* rocks on which crabs are caught.

Crab-fish, *n.* a crab.

Crab-grained, *adj.* cross-grained, ill-tempered.

Crab-stane, *n.* a kerb-stone.

Crack, *n.* a sudden, loud crash ; a thunderpeal ; an instant ; a blow ; a boast, brag ; conversation, gossip ; a tale, story ; a lie ; a good talker, a gossip.—*v.* to become bankrupt ; to strike a sharp blow ; to strike a match ; to brag, boast ; to chat, gossip ; with *up*, to extol, praise. — *adj.* crack-brained.

Crack a spunk, *phr.* to strike a match.

Cracker, *n.* a boaster ; a great talker ; a gossip ; the small cord at the end of a whip ; a manifest exaggeration ; an astounding statement.

Crackerheads, *n.* the roots of tangles, the vesicles of which crack.

Crackers, *n.* castanets ; bones or pieces of wood used as castanets.

Cracket, *n.* a small wooden stool.

Cracket, *n.* the cricket.

Crack-hemp, *n.* a gallows-bird.

Crackie, Crackie-stool, *n.* a low, three-legged stool with a small hole in the middle of the seat for lifting it.

Crackin-bout, *n.* a bout of gossip.

Cracking of the herrings, *phr.* a loud sound like a pistol-crack, after which the herrings leave a place.

Crackings, *n.* a dish made of the strainings of suet or lard, mixed with oatmeal, and browned over the fire.

Crackling, *n.* tallow-refuse.

Crackling-biscuit, *n.* a biscuit made for dogs of the refuse of fat used in making margarine.

Crackling-cheese, *n.* refuse tallow pressed into the form of cheese, for feeding dogs or poultry.

Crackly, *adj.* brittle.

Crack-massie, *n.* a boaster ; boasting.

Crack-nut, *n.* a hazel-nut.
Cracks, *n.* news.
Cracksie, *adj.* talkative, 'newsy.'
Crack-tryst, *n.* one who fails to keep an engagement to meet.
Cracky, *adj.* talkative; affable.
Cracky, *adj.* silly, cracked, of weak mind.
Cradden, Cradeuch, *n.* a dwarf; a diminutive person.
Cradle, *n.* a frame for carrying glass.—*v.* to iie still in the cradle.
Cradle-chimlay, *n.* a large, oblong cottage-grate, open on all sides.
Cradle-end, *n.* the beginning.
Cradley-ba, *n.* a cradle; a lullaby.
Craem, *n.* a merchant's booth. Cf. **Crame**.
Craft, *n.* a craftsman.
Craft, *n.* a croft.
Craft-crammed, *adj.* stuffed with learning.
Crafter, *n.* a crofter.
Craftily, *adv.* skilfully, cleverly.
Craggin, *n.* a jar, a pitcher. Cf. **Crogan**.
Craich, *n.* a Highland raid. Cf. **Creagh**.
Craickle, *n.* a hoarse, croaking sound.
Craid, *n.* yellow clover.
Craig, *v.* to creak; to make a harsh noise.
Craig, *n.* a crag, a rocky place.
Craig, *n.* the neck, throat.—*v.* to drink, swallow.
Craig-agee, *adj.* wry-necked.
Craig-bane, *n.* the collar-bone.
Craig-cloth, *n.* a neckcloth, cravat.
Craiged, *ppl. adj.* pertaining to the neck or throat.
Craig-fluke, *n.* the rock-flounder.
Craig-herring, *n.* the allice shad.
Craighle, *v.* to cough huskily or hard.—*n.* a short, dry cough. Cf. **Croighle**.
Craigie, *n.* the throat; a long-necked bottle.
Craigie-heron, *n.* the heron.
Craig-lug, *n.* the point of a rock; a sharp-pointed rock.
Craig's close, *n.* the throat.
Craig-sitting, *n.* a seat on the rocks for fishing.
Craigsman, *n.* one who climbs sea-cliffs for sea-fowl or their eggs.
Craigstane, *n.* a seat on the rocks for sea-fishing.
Craigy, *adj.* rocky.
Craik, *n.* the landrail; a child's toy-rattle.
Craik, *v.* to croak; to cry out harshly; to murmur; to whine for anything.—*n.* a croaking cry, grumbling; the cry of a hen after laying.
Craik, *n.* a gossip; ill-natured talk; telling tales.
Craik, *v.* to creak, as a door-hinge.
Craiker *n.* the landrail.
Crail-capon, *n.* a dried haddock.

Craim, *n.* a merchant's stand or shop, a booth. Cf. **Crame**.
Crainroch, *n.* hoar-frost, rime. Cf. **Cranreuch**.
Craise, Craize, *v.* to weaken, shatter; to be ready to fall to pieces; to creak, groan; to sit on a chair tilted up, and move it backwards and forwards; to confuse, muddle.—*n.* a crack, a blow; dotage; wrong-headedness; a foolish fondness. Cf. **Craze**.
Crait, *n.* a crate for holding window-glass.
Craive, *n.* a pig-sty. Cf. **Cruive**.
Crake, *v.* to croak. Cf. **Craik**.
Cram, *v.* to gorge.
†**Cramasie, Cramasye, Cramesye**, *n.* crimson colour; crimson cloth. Cf. **Cramoisie**.
Crambo-clink, -jingle, -jink, *n.* rhyme, doggerel verse.
Crame, *n.* a merchant's booth; a stall for sale of goods in a street or in a market; merchandise.—*v.* to hawk goods.
Cramer, *n.* a pedlar, hawker.
Crame-ware, *n.* articles sold at a stall or booth.
Crame-wife, *n.* a female stall-holder at markets or fairs.
†**Cramoisie, Cramosie**, *n.* crimson; crimson cloth.
Cramp, *n.* an iron sheet, indented to grip the ice, on which the curler stands to throw his stones.—*v.* to contract.—*adj.* confined; difficult to decipher or understand.
Cramp-bit, *n.* a spiked iron strapped to the shoe by curlers to prevent slipping.
Cramp-hand, *n.* a cramped style of handwriting.—*adj.* not easily deciphered.
Crampit, Crampet, *n.* an iron with small spikes, worn on the curler's foot to keep him from slipping; a cramping-iron; the cramp-iron of a scabbard; the guard of a sword-handle; the iron shod of a staff; an iron runner of a sledge; a spike driven into a wall to support something.
Cramp-speech, *n.* a set speech in Latin, formerly made by an advocate on his entry at the Scottish Bar.
Cramp-word, *n.* a word difficult to pronounce or understand.
Cran, *n.* a measure of herrings taken from the net, averaging 750.
Cran, *n.* an iron tripod for supporting a pot on a hearth-fire; an iron instrument, laid across the fire, reaching from the front to the back of the grate, to support a pot or kettle; a bent tap.
Cran, *n.* the crane; the heron; the swift.
Cran, *n.* a carcass, dead body. Cf. **Crang**.
Cranberry, *n.* the cowberry; the bearberry.
Crance, *n.* a crack or chink in a wall, through which wind blows.
Crance, *n.* a chaplet.

Cranch, v. to crush, crunch, grind with the teeth.—n. a crush, a crunch, grinding with the teeth.
Cran-craig, n. one who has a long neck.
Cran-craigie, -craigit, adj. long-necked.
Crancreugh, n. hoar-frost, rime. Cf. Cran-reuch.
Crancrums, n. things hard to be understood.
Crancum, n. a prank, trick.
Crandruch, n. hoar-frost, rime. Cf. Cran-reuch.
Crane, n. the tap of a gaslight or of a barrel.
Craneberry, n. the cranberry.
Cranes, n. stilts.
Crane-swallow, n. the swift.
Crang, n. a carcass, dead body. Cf. Cran.
Cran-hooks, n. the hooks for lifting barrels by their chines.
Cranie, n. a small person. Cf. Crannie.
Cranie-wee, adj. very small.
Crank, n. an iron attached to the feet in curling, to prevent the player from slipping on the ice; a difficult point; an effort to overcome a difficulty.—adj. twisted, distorted; ill-balanced; infirm, sick; impossible to get on with or manage; hard, difficult, curious, not easy to understand.
Crank, n. a harsh, creaking noise; the noise of an ungreased wheel; inharmonious verse.
Crank, v. to shackle a horse.
Crankous, adj. fretful, captious.
Cranky, adj. ailing, sickly; irritable.
Crannach, n. porridge.
Crannie, n. the little finger.
Crannie, n. a square or oblong aperture in the wall of a house; a 'bole,' a 'bore.'
Crannie-bore, -hole, n. a chink, crevice.
Crannied, ppl. adj. pent up.
Crannie-wannie, n. the little finger.
Cranreuch, Cranreuth, n. hoar-frost, rime.
Cranrochie, adj. rimy; abounding with hoar-frost.
Cranshach, Cranshak, Cranshank, n. a cripple; a deformed person.
Crany, Crany-wany, n. the little finger. Cf. Crannie, Crannie-wannie.
Crap, n. a bird's crop; the throat; the stomach; the highest part of anything; of whey: the thick part that rises to the surface; the 'stilts' of a plough; the horizon; the cone of a fir-tree.—v. to top; to keep to the top.
Crap, v. to fill; to stuff.
Crap, v. pret. crept.
Crap, v. to crop; to lop; to gather flowers; to yield a crop; to cut the hair closely.—n. a crop, produce of the fields, of lambs, of wool, &c.; a close cutting of the hair.
Crap, n. the quantity of grain put at one time on a kiln to be dried.

Crap and root, phr. entirely; from top to bottom.
Crapfu', n. a full crop or maw.
Crapin, n. a bird's crop. Cf. Crappin.
Crap-land, n. land under crop.
Crap o' the causey, n. the crown or raised middle of the causeway.
Crap o' the wa', n. the highest part of an inside wall.
Crap o' the water, n. the first water taken from a well after midnight of Dec. 31, supposed to bring good luck for the new year.
Crappet, ppl. adj. crop-eared.
Crappie, adj. used of cereals: bearing well, having large ears.
Crappin, n. a bird's crop; the stomach.
Crappin, n. carping; asking troublesome questions.
Crappin-, Crappit-head, n. the head of a cod or haddock stuffed with a mixture of oatmeal, suet, onions, and pepper.
Crapple-mapple, n. ale.
Craps, n. runches; the seed-pods of runches or wild mustard.
Crasie, n. a woman's cotton sun-bonnet.
Crat, adj. puny, feeble.—n. a weak child; a person of weak stomach.
Crater, n. the centre; the vortex.
Cratur, n. a creature; whisky. Cf. Creature.
Craug, n. the neck; the weasand. Cf. Craig.
Crauk, v. to fret, complain; to croak. Cf. Craik.
Craundroch, n. hoar-frost, rime. Cf. Cran-reuch.
Craup, v. pret. crept.
Crave, v. to demand payment, dun for a debt; to long for food and drink; to go about begging.
Crave, n. a pig-sty. Cf. Cruive.
Craver, n. a creditor, a dun; a note demanding payment of a debt.
Craving, n. dunning; hunger, from want of food or from cold.
Craving-card, n. a begging-letter.
Craving extracts, phr. asking extracts of minutes of an inferior Church court in an appeal to a higher.
Craw, n. the rook; the carrion crow; the hooded crow; a strong craving for drink; a children's game.—v. to caw; to croak.
Craw, n. the crop of a bird.
Craw, n. a pen, a pig-sty. Cf. Crue.
Craw, v. to crow like a cock; to boast, brag.—n. the crow of a cock; a brag, boast; a shout, noise as of children at play.
Craw-berry, -croup, n. the crowberry.
Craw-bogle, -deil, n. a scarecrow.
Craw-day, n. the morning, dawn.
Crawdoun, n. a coward.
Craw-dulse, n. an edible fringed fucus.

Craw-feet, *n.* wrinkles round the eyes. Cf. Craw-foot.

Craw-flee, *n.* a boys' game.

Craw-flower, *n.* the wild hyacinth; the ranunculus. Cf. Craw-tae.

Craw-foot, *n.* the ranunculus, crow-foot.

Craw-foot, *n.* a caltrop.

Craw-head, *n.* the chimney-head.

Crawl, *v.* used of insects : to swarm, infest, abound.

Craw-maa, *n.* the kittiwake.

Craw-mill, *n.* a large rattle for frightening crows.

Craw-plantin, *n.* a rookery.

Craw-pockies, *n.* the eggs of sharks, skate, and dog-fish.

Craw-prod, *n.* a pin fixed on the top of a gable to which the ropes fastening the roof of a cottage are tied.

Craw-road, *n.* the direct way, as the crow flies.

Craws, *n.* in *phr.* 'wae 's my craws!' woe 's my heart!

Craws'-bridal, -court, -marriage, *n.* a large gathering of crows.

Craws' nest, *n.* a robbers' den.

Craw's-purse, *n.* the ovarium of a skate.

Craws'-siller, *n.* mica.

Craw-steppit, *adj.* having 'craw-steps.'

Craw-steps, *n.* a set of projecting steps on the gables of the roofs of old houses. Cf. Corbie-steps.

Craw-Sunday, *n.* the first Sunday in March, on which crows were supposed to begin to build nests.

Craw-tae, *n.* the wild hyacinth; the ranunculus or crowfoot; a wrinkle about the eye.

Crawtaes, *n.* caltrops.

Crawtt, *n.* a small, insignificant person.

Cray, *n.* a hutch, a coop.

Craze, *v.* to weaken, wear out, be ready to fall in pieces; to creak, groan; to distract, to madden.—*n.* a crack, blow; a measure of wrong-headedness, dotage; foolish or inordinate fondness.

Craziness, *n.* physical weakness.

Crazy, *n.* a woman's cotton sun-bonnet. Cf. Chraisy.

Crazy, *adj.* rickety; dilapidated; tumble-down; infirm, weak.

Creagh, *n.* a Highland raid; prey, booty.

Cream, *n.* a merchant's booth, a market-stall; a pack of goods for sale.—*v.* to hawk goods. Cf. Crame.

Creamer, *n.* a pedlar; stall-keeper.

Creamerie, *n.* merchandise; goods sold by a pedlar.

Cream of the well, *n.* the first water drawn from a well on New Year's Day.

Cream-ware, *n.* articles sold from a booth.

Cream-wife, *n.* a female stall-keeper at a fair.

Crear, *n.* a kind of lighter or barque.

Creash, *n.* grease. Cf. Creesh.

Creast, *v.* to worry or tear in pieces with the mouth.

Creature, *n.* whisky; a term of contempt or pity.

Credit, *n.* approbation, approval.

Credulity, *n.* belief.

Cree, *n.* a pen; sty; fold.

Cree, *v.* to meddle with.

Creech, *n.* a declivity encumbered with large stones.

Creed, *n.* a severe rebuke, 'lecture'; 'a bit, of one's mind'; an adage, saying.

Creek, *n.* in *phr.* 'creek o' day,' daybreak.

Creekle, *v.* to tremble, shake in feebleness.

Creeks, *n.* in *phr.* 'creeks and corners,' nooks and corners.

Creeks, *n.* traps, snares.

Creel, *n.* a state of perplexity, stupefaction, or madness; the stomach.—*v.* with *eggs*, to meddle with.

Creel, *adj.* worth preserving; worth house-room.

Creel-fu', *n.* a basketful.

Creelie, *n.* a small creel.

Creeling, *n.* an obsolete marriage custom on the second day of the wedding.

Creen, *v.* to hum, sing in a low, plaintive style, 'croon'; to whine.

Creenge, *v.* to cringe.

Creenie, *adj.* diminutive.—*n.* the little finger. Cf. Crannie.

Creenie-cranie, *n.* the little finger.

Creep, *v.* used of a child: to crawl on all-fours; of the flesh : to shudder or shiver from cold or fear.—*n.* a crawl; a shiver from cold or fear.

Creep-at-even, *n.* one who courts under cloud of night.

Creeper, *n.* a grapnel; in *pl.* dragging-tackle used by smugglers to catch and raise to the surface kegs which had been sunk at the approach of a revenue-cutter; the sensation of creeping or shivering.

Creepie, *n.* a grapnel.—*adj.* having a sensation of creeping.

Creepie, *n.* a bed.

Creepie, Creepie-stool, *n.* a low stool; a child's stool; a milking-stool; any small stool; the 'stool of repentance.'

Creepie-chair, *n.* a low chair; the 'stool of repentance' for public penitents.

Creep-in, *v.* to shorten, to grow short, shrink, contract.

Creeping-bur, *n.* the club-moss.

Creeping-seefer, *n.* the ivy-leaved toad-flax.

Creeping-wheat-grass, *n.* couch-grass.

Creepit, *v. pret.* and *ppl.* crept.

Creep-out, *v.* to lengthen, grow long.

Creep-over, *v.* to swarm with insects, vermin, &c.

Creep together, *v.* to marry.

Creepy, *n.* the hedge-sparrow.

†Creese, *n.* a crisis.

†Creesh, *n.* grease, fat, oil ; a blow, thrashing.—*v.* to grease, lubricate ; to thrash, beat ; with *loof*, to bribe.

Creeshie, *adj.* greasy, oily.—*n.* a greasing ; sometimes used of a big pinch of snuff.

Creeshiness, *n.* greasiness.

Creeshing, *n.* a beating.

Creeshless, *adj.* lean, without fat.

Creest, *v.* to raise the head, crest. Cf. Criest.

Creesty, *adj.* forward, precocious.

†Creeze, *n.* a crisis. Cf. Crise.

Creighle, *v.* to cough huskily.—*n.* a husky cough. Cf. Croighle.

Creil, *n.* a creel. Cf. Creel.

Creish, *n.* grease. Cf. Creesh.

Creist, *n.* a diminutive and loquacious person. Cf. Cryste.

Cresie, Cresie-jean, *n.* a woman's cotton sunbonnet. Cf. Chraisy.

Crespeis, Crespie, *n.* a grampus ; a small whale.

Cress, *v.* to crease ; to rumple.—*n.* a crease ; a rumple.

Cressy, *adj.* abounding in cress.

Crested-doucker, *n.* the great crested-grebe.

Creuk, *n.* a hook on which a gate hangs ; a hook and chain for hanging pots, &c., over a fire ; anything crooked ; a scheme, device ; the turn of a stream ; a misfortune, trial, cross ; a limp, halt.—*adj.* awry, crooked.—*v.* to bend, bow ; to limp. Cf. Crook.

Creuzie, *n.* an obsolete rushlight oil-lamp. Cf. Crusie.

Creuzie, *n.* a flat hat worn by women.

Crevice, Crevise, Crevish, *n.* the rack above the manger in a stable.

†Crevish, *n.* the crayfish.

Cre-waw, *n.* a jackdaw's cry.

Crewe, *n.* a hovel ; a pig-sty. Cf. Croo, Crue.

†Crewells, *n.* scrofula. Cf. Cruels.

Creyst, *n.* a diminutive and talkative person. Cf. Cryste.

Creyt, *n.* a species of polypody fern.

Criauve, *v.* to crow.

Crib, *n.* a bicker of porridge ; food.

Crib, *n.* a reel for winding yarn.

Crib, *n.* a coop, a pen.

Crib, *n.* a curb ; the kerb-stone.—*v.* to curb, check.

Cribbie, *n.* the quantity of yarn reeled on a ' crib.'

Crib-biter, *n.* a horse that gnaws the manger and sucks in wind.

Crib-stane, *n.* a kerb-stone. Cf. Crab-stane.

Crick-crack, *n.* a talk, a chat.

Cricke, *n.* a species of tick, a louse. Cf. Crike.

Cricket, *n.* the grasshopper.

Cricklet, *n.* the smallest of a litter ; the weakest nestling.

Cried-fair, *n.* a market or fair, of which time and place have been proclaimed some time before, and which is therefore well attended.

Criesh, *n.* grease. Cf. Creesh.

Criest, *v.* to rear, raise, erect. Cf. Creest.

Criftens, Crifty, *int.* an excl. of surprise.

Crike, *n.* a species of tick infesting the human body ; a louse.

Crile, *n.* a dwarf ; a child that does not thrive.

Cril't, *ppl. adj.* unthriven, stunted.

Crim, *v.* to purse up the mouth.

Criminals, *n.* criminal matters, in contrast to civil.

Crim-mou't, *adj.* having the mouth pursed up or deeply sunk in the face ; proud, conceited.

Crimp, *adj.* crisp ; hard, difficult.

Crimp, *adj.* short of measure, scarce, ' scrimp.'

Crimp, *v.* to pucker.

Crimpet, *n.* a crumpet.

Crimping-pin, *n.* an instrument for puckering the border of a lady's cap.

Crinch, *v.* to grind with the teeth ; to masticate hard and brittle substances, as biscuits, unboiled vegetables, or unripe fruit.—*n.* a small bit or morsel.

Crine, *v.* to shrivel ; to shrink in cooking : to dry up from exposure ; to grow small through old age, &c.

Cringe, *v.* to tremble for one's safety.

Crinkams, *n.* twists and turns.

Crinkie-winkie, *n.* a contention.

Crinkling, *ppl. adj.* used of a cough : hard, dry, rustling.

Crinky, *n.* an iron rod with a hook at the end.

Crinsh, *v.* to crunch.—*n.* a small piece of anything. Cf. Crinch.

Cripple, *v.* to walk lame ; to hobble ; to struggle lamely.

Cripple-dick, *n.* a lame person.

Cripple-goat, *n.* the last cut handful of corn, sent as a trophy by a farmer to his neighbour who is still busy cutting corn.

Cripple-justice, *n.* a person lame yet proud of personal appearance.

Cripple men, *n.* oatcakes toasted before a fire.

†Crise, *n.* a crisis. Cf. Creese.

Crisp, *v.* to crackle, as ground under the feet in a slight frost.

Cristendie, *n.* Christendom.

Cristing, *n.* a christening.

Crittle, *n.* a broken piece, as of fuel. Cf. Crottle.

Crittly, *adj.* friable, crumbly.

Criv, Crive, *n.* a pen; a pig-sty; an enclosure for hens; a cabin, hovel.—*v.* to shut up, pen up. Cf. Cruive.

Cro, *n.* a cattle-disease affecting the limbs.

Cro, *n.* compensation made for the slaughter of a man, according to his rank. Cf. Croy.

Croachle, *v.* to cough huskily.—*n.* a husky cough. Cf. Croighle.

Croagh, *v.* to strangle.

Croak, *n.* a ewe past breeding. Cf. Crock.

Croak, *v.* to crow like a child; to die.

Crocanition, *n.* shivers; utter destruction; smash. Cf. Crockanition.

Croch, *v.* to make a noise in the throat, as if from cold or weak lungs.

Crochet, *n.* the end of a curb-chain.

Crochle, *n.* in *pl.* a disease in the hindlegs of cattle, rendering them lame.—*v.* to limp, be a cripple.

Crochle-girs, *n.* the self-heal plant, believed to produce the disease of 'crochles.'

Crock, *n.* a large earthenware jar for holding butter, sugar, salt, &c.; a fragment of earthenware.

Crock, Crock-yow, *n.* an old ewe, one too old for breeding.

Crock, *v.* to crouch, cower.

Crock, *v.* to kill.

Crock, *v.* to croak; used of the bowels: to rumble.

Crockanition, *n.* shivers, bits; destruction; smash.

Crockats, *n.* ruffles, neck ornaments; curls, tresses.

Crocker, *n.* a species of boys' marble.

Crockie, *n.* a low stool for children. Cf. Crackie.

Crof, Croft, *n.* a temporary shed variously used during the fishing season. Cf. Corf.

Croft, *n.* in *phr.* 'the goodman's croft,' a small piece of land left untilled, and dedicated to the devil.

Croft, *n.* a crop.

Crofthead, *n.* the end of the croft or small field adjoining the dwelling-house.

Croftie, *n.* a small croft.

Crofting, *n.* the state of land constantly in crop; the land thus cropped.

Croft-land, *n.* land of superior quality, kept constantly manured and under crop.

Croft-rig, *n.* a croft ridge or field.

Crog, *n.* a milk-bowl. Cf. Crock.

Crog, *n.* a paw; a large hand.

Crogan, *n.* paws.

Crogan, *n.* a milk-bowl.

Croichle, *v.* to limp. Cf. Crochle.

Croighle, Croichle, *v.* to cough huskily.—*n.* a short, dry cough.

Croighlin, *n.* dry, hard coughing.

Croil, *n.* a frail person or animal; one broken down from age or use; a dwarf, a stunted person or animal. Cf. Crile.

Crointer, *n.* the gray gurnard.

Croise, *n.* to burn with a mark; to brand with a cross. Cf. Cross.

Croise, *v.* to gossip; to talk much about little; to whine in sympathy; to use flattering talk; to whine.—*n.* flattery; a flatterer. Cf. Crose.

Croishtarish, *n.* the fiery-cross as a war-signal.

Croittoch, *n.* a lameness in cattle's hoofs.

Croittoch'd, *ppl. adj.* suffering from 'croittoch.

Crok, *n.* a dwarf.

Crok, *v.* to suffer decay from age; to die.

Crok, *n.* a ewe past breeding. Cf. Crock.

Crok, *n.* a milk-bowl. Cf. Crog.

Croke, *v.* to croak; to crow like a child; to die.

Crokets, *n.* ruffles. Cf. Crockats.

Crokonition, Crockonition, Crokynition, *n.* shivers; destruction; smash. Cf. Crockanition.

Croll, *n.* a pause; respite; time for reflection.

Crom, *v.* to bend; to double.—*n.* a bend.—*adj.* bent.

Cromack, Cromag, *n.* the hand with the finger-tips and thumb brought together.

Cromag's-fu, *n.* the quantity lifted with the fingers and thumb brought together.

Crombie's-punch, *n.* grog, half-water, half-whisky. Cf. Crummie's-punch.

Cromie, *n.* a cow with crumpled horns. Cf. Crummy.

Cronach, *n.* a Highland dirge, or a 'coronach.'

Cronachie, *n.* a child's name for the little finger.

Cronaching, *ppl.* gossiping, tattling.

Crone, *v.* to use many words in a wheedling way; to sing softly; to make a monotonous sound. Cf. Croon.

Crony, *n.* a potato.

Crony-hill, *n.* a potato-field.

Croo, *n.* satisfaction for accidental death, given by the person who occasioned it. Cf. Croy.

Croo, *v.* to coo, as a pigeon.

Croo, *n.* a hovel; a sty; a small yard; a pen for sheep, &c. Cf. Cruive.

Croo, *v.* to hide by crouching.

Croobacks, *n.* panniers worn by horses in mountainous districts for carrying grain, peat, &c.

Crood, *v.* to coo, as a pigeon; to croak, as a frog; to groan, complain.

Crood, *n.* curd.

Crood, *v.* to crowd.—*n.* a crowd.

Crooding-doo, *n.* a wood-pigeon; a term of endearment.

Croodle, *v.* to huddle together for warmth or protection; to crouch, cower, stoop down. —*n.* a heap, a collection.

Croodle, *v.* to coo like a dove; to purr as a cat; to hum a song.

Croodling-doo, *n.* a wood-pigeon; a term of endearment.

Crook, *v.* to halt in walking.—*n.* a halt, limp.

Crook, *n.* the iron hook on which a gate or door is hung; the iron hook and chain on which pots, kettles, &c. are hung over the fire; the fireside; anything bent; a device; a bend in a river; a trial or cross in one's lot; a mark cut out in a sheep's ear.—*adj.* twisted, awry. —*v.* to bend, to bow, to twist.

Crookal, *adj.* pertaining to a 'crook,' or cooking-vessel.

Crookal-band, *n.* the chain by which the 'crook' is suspended over the fire.

Crook-and-the-links, *n.* pot-hooks or suspenders.

Crooked, *ppl. adj.* deformed, crippled; cross, crabbed.

Crooked-mouth, *n.* a species of flounder.

Crooked-whittle, *n.* a reaping-hook.

Crookie, *n.* a sixpence. Cf. Cruckie.

Crook-liver, *n.* a disease of calves causing inflammation of the intestines.

Crook-saddle, *n.* a saddle for bearing panniers or creels.

Crooks and bands, *n.* the hinges and iron braces of a door.

Crook-shell, *n.* a hook for suspending a pot, &c., over a fire.

Crook-studie, -tree, *n.* a cross-beam or iron bar in a chimney from which the crook hangs.

Croon, *v.* used of cattle: to low; to roar in a menacing tone like an angry bull; to sing softly, hum, murmur; to make a low, monotonous sound; to purr like a cat; to wail, lament; to mutter a prayer; to sing a tune in a low tone; to use many words in a wheedling way; to hobnob.—*n.* the lowing of cattle; a low murmuring sound; the purr of a cat; a mournful song, wail, lament. Cf. Crone.

Croon, *v.* to crown; to top, excel.—*n.* the top of anything; a crown; the top balk in supporting the roof in a coal-pit; the head; that part in deciduous vegetables from which new shoots spring.

Crooner, *n.* the gray gurnard.

Crooning, *n.* the bellowing of a bull; a murmuring sound.

Croon-piece, *n.* the upper of the two main cross-beams which tie the rafters in the timbering of a house-roof.

Croop, *v.* to croak, speak hoarsely; to whine, wheedle, flatter. — *n.* a croak; flattery. Cf. Croup.

Croop, *n.* a berry. Cf. Croup.

Croose, *adj.* bold; eager; brisk; conceited; happy; proud. Cf. Crouse.

Croot, *n.* a puny, feeble child; the smallest pig of a litter; the youngest bird of a brood.

Croot, *v.* to make a croaking noise; used of the intestines: to rumble. Cf. Crout.

Crootles, *n.* a nickname for a small and ill-proportioned person.

Crootlie, *adj.* short-legged in proportion to the body.

Crootling, *ppl.* hunched up, crouching, cowering over. Cf. Croodle.

Croove, *n.* a sort of basket for catching fish.

Croovie, *n.* a little snug hut or den. Cf. Cruive.

Croovie-skool, *n.* a small or snug cottage school-house.

Croozumit, *n.* a puny person; one worn with age; a hermit, one living alone.

Crop, *v.* to pick flowers; to yield a crop.— *n.* the stomach. Cf. Crap.

Crop, *n.* a potato-stem.

Cropen, Croppen, *ppl.* crept; contracted, shrunken.

Cropped-head, *n.* a stuffed cod's head. Cf. Crappin-head.

Cropper, *n.* that which yields a crop.

Cropt, *n.* a crop.

Crose, *v.* to whine in sympathy; to speak in a whining, flattering voice; to gossip; to magnify trifles.—*n.* flattery, expression of sympathy; a flatterer.

Croser, *n.* one given to flattery.

Crosle, *v.* to settle down gently, to 'croodle,' to nestle.

Crospunk, *n.* the Molucca bean, drifted to the shores of some of the western islands.

Cross, *n.* the obverse side of a coin bearing a cross; a pile of stones on a hill-top.—*v.* to brand with the mark of the cross; used of the hand of a clock: to approach a certain point.—*adj.* contrary, untoward, wrong, inconvenient.—*adv.* crossly; untowardly.

†Cross-and-pile, *n.* coin, money.

Cross-braces, *n.* leathern supports for the body of a carriage.

Cross-brath'd, *adj.* braided across.

Cross-fish, -fit, *n.* the star-fish.

Cross-ful, *adj.* cross-tempered.

Crossie-croon-shillin', *phr.* a coin, over which cows were first milked after calving, to protect them from the evil eye and every evil cantrip.

Crosslet, *n.* a crucifix, small cross.

Cross-mark, *n.* a person scarred by burning.

Cross-nook, v. to check, restrain; to sit close into the 'neuks'; to make room for another person at the fire.

†**Cross nor pile,** n. no money whatever.

Cross-roupin', n. a sale by auction at the public cross.

Cross-skeppack, n. the game of 'cross-tig.' Cf. Skeppack.

Cross-speir, v. to cross-examine.

Cross-stick-war, n. cudgelling.

Cross-tig, n. a variety of the game of 'tig.'

Crotal, Crottle, n. a lichen, 'cudbear,' used for dyeing reddish-brown.

Crotal-coat, n. a coat of the colour of 'crotal'; a term of contempt.

Crottle, n. a crumb, fragment of any hard body. Cf. Cruttlins.

Crottlie, adj. covered with lichen.

Crouchie, adj. humped, having a hunch on the back.—n. a hunchback.

Croud, v. to coo; to croak; to groan, complain. Cf. Crood.

Croude, n. a fiddle.

Croudle, v. to coo like a dove. Cf. Croodle.

Crouds, n. curds. Cf. Crud.

Croun, n. crown; head.—v. to crown.

Croun, v. to sing softly; to make a monotonous sound; to bellow like an angry bull.—n. a low, monotone. Cf. Croon.

Croup, v. to croak as a raven, frog, &c.; to speak hoarsely; of the bowels: to rumble from flatulence; to speak in a whining or wheedling way, to flatter.—n. a croak; flattery.

Croup, n. a berry.

Croup, v. to stoop, bend, crouch.—n. the slope of a hill.

Croupie, Croupie-craw, n. the raven.

Croupy, adj. hoarse.

Crouse, adj. brisk, lively, cheerful; bold, keen; conceited, elated; cosy, comfortable. —adv. briskly, proudly, conceitedly.

Crousely, Crously, adv. proudly, confidently, boldly; briskly, merrily, eagerly.

Crouseness, n. boldness, forwardness, conceit, apparent courage.

Crousie, adv. briskly, merrily, eagerly.

Crousy, adj. brisk, 'crouse.'

Crout, v. to croak, make a hoarse noise; to coo; used of the bowels: to rumble.

Crow, v. to boast. Cf. Craw.

Crowder, n. a constant attendant; a diligent frequenter.

Crowdie, n. thick gruel. Cf. Cowdy.

Crowdle, v. to crawl as a crab.

Crowdle, v. to huddle together; to stoop over, crouch.—n. a heap, a collection. Cf. Croodle.

Crowdle, v. to coo; to purr; to hum a song. Cf. Croodle.

Crowdy, n. meal and cold water, forming a gruel; porridge; a mixture of pure curd with butter; food in general.

Crowdy-butter, n. a mixture of curds and butter. Cf. Cruddy-butter.

Crowdy-meal, n. milk and meal boiled together; milk-porridge.

Crowdy-mowdy, n. milk-porridge.

Crowdy-time, n. meal-time.

Crowl, n. a dwarf; a stunted, deformed person or child.

Crowl, v. to crawl, creep.

Crowly, adj. lame; crawling in walk.

Crown, n. the head. Cf. Croon.

Crownary, Crownry, n. the office of 'crowner.'

Crowner, n. the gray gurnard. Cf. Crooner.

Crowner, n. a commander of troops raised in a county; an officer of a 'justice-air.'

Crownfull, n. a certain quality of herrings.

Crowp, v. to croak; to flatter.—n. flattery; a croak.

Croy, n. compensation made by workmen in some factories for the shortcomings of any of their number.

Croy, n. a semicircular pen on a beach, for catching fish; a mound or quay projecting into a river to break the force of the stream.

Croyd, n. yellow clover.

Croydie, adj. covered with clover.

Croyl, n. a dwarf. Cf. Crawl.

Croyn, v. to shrink in; to shrivel. Cf. Crine.

Croze, v. to whine in sympathy; to gossip; to magnify trifles; to flatter; used of an infant: to crow.—n. flattery; a flatterer. Cf. Crose.

Crozie, adj. fawning, wheedling.

Crub, n. a crib for cattle.—v. to curb, restrain, confine.

Crub, n. the curb of a bridle.

Cruban, n. a disease of cows produced by hard grass, scarcity of pasture, and severe sucking of their calves.

Cruban, n. a term of contempt for a tippler.

Cruban, n. a wooden pannier for a horse's back.

Crubbin', n. a snub.

Crubbit, ppl. adj. cribbed, pinched for room, confined.

Crubs, n. the framework within which a millstone revolves.

Cruchlin, n. a dry, husky cough. Cf. Croighle.

Cruck, v. to lame. Cf. Crook.

Cruck, n. a crook; a hook and chain for hanging pots over a fire. Cf. Crook.

Cruckie, n. a crooked sixpence, a sixpence.

Crud, n. curd.

Cruddle, Crudle, v. to coagulate, curdle, congeal.

Cruddy, adj. curdled; containing curds.

Cruddy-butter, n. a preparation of butter and cheese, of each a half. Cf. Crowdy-butter.

Crue, *n.* a sheep-pen, a small fold; a hovel. Cf. Croo, Cruive.

Crue-herring, *n.* the shad.

†Cruels, *n.* scrofula; 'king's evil.'

Cruet, *n.* a water-bottle; a small decanter.

Cruety, *adj.* vinegarish, sour-tempered.

Crufe, *n.* a pen for cattle. Cf. Cruive.

Cruggles, *n.* a disease of young cattle, causing convulsive movements of the limbs. Cf. Crochle.

Cruick, Cruik, *v.* to bend. Cf. Crook.

Cruik-studie, *n.* an anvil with projecting 'horn' for bending horseshoes.

Cruise, Cruisie, *n.* an old-fashioned oil-lamp used with a rush wick. Cf. Crusie.

Cruisken, *n.* a measure of whisky.

Cruit, *n.* the smallest of a litter. Cf. Croot.

Cruive, *n.* a pen for live-stock; a pig-sty; a cabin, hovel; a cottage-garden; an apparatus and method of catching salmon in a river or sea-beach.—*v.* to shut up in a 'cruive'; to shut up.

Cruizey, Cruizie, Cruizy, *n.* an oil-lamp for rushlights, with handles for hanging. Cf. Crusie.

Cruke, *v.* to lame. Cf. Crook.

Cruke, *n.* the winding of a river, the space enclosed on one side by the windings of a river. Cf. Crook.

Crulge, *n.* a confused coalition, conjunction, or heap.—*v.* to contract, draw together, crouch.

Crull, *v.* to contract, draw one's self together; to stoop, cower.—*n.* a confused heap.

Crulzie, *v.* to crouch, cower.

Crum, *n.* a crumb; a small portion of anything, as paper.

Crumby, *n.* a 'crummie,' a cow with crooked horns.

Crumch, *n.* a small piece. Cf. Crinch.

Crumchick, *n.* a very small piece.

Crumchickie, *n.* a very, very small piece.

Crumle, *v.* to crumble.—*n.* a crumb, a broken piece; in *pl.* broken meats.

Crumlick, *n.* a very small piece, a crumb.

Crumlickie, *n.* an extremely small piece.

Crummet, *adj.* with crooked horns.

Crummie, *n.* a cow with crooked horns; a name for a cow.

Crummie's-punch, *n.* 'crombie's punch'; grog, half-water, half-whisky.

Crummie-staff, -stick, *n.* a staff with crooked handle, used by boys herding cattle.

Crummilt, *ppl. adj.* crooked, crumpled; bent spirally, twisted.

Crummock, *n.* a short staff with crooked head; a name for a cow.

Crummock, Crumock, *n.* the plant skirret.

Crummy, *n.* a crumb, a very small portion, a particle.

Crump, *v.* to smack, knock.—*n.* a smart blow.

Crump, *adj.* crisp, brittle; crumbling; friable. —*v.* to crunch with the teeth anything hard or brittle; to emit a crackling sound, like ice or snow when trodden on; to boast noisily, brag.

Crumpie, *n.* a crisp oatcake.—*adj.* of bread : hard, brittle, crisp.

Crumping, *ppl. adj.* crackling, noisy.

Crunch, *n.* a small piece resulting from 'crunching.' Cf. Crinch.

Crune, *v.* to emit a murmuring sound or a menacing sound, as an angry bull.—*n.* a low murmuring sound. Cf. Croon.

Cruner, *n.* the gray gurnard. Cf. Crooner.

Crunkle, *v.* to crease, rumple; to shrivel, contract; to wrinkle with cold.—*n.* a crease, wrinkle; a crackle as of crumpling paper.

Crunkly, *adj.* shrivelled, shrunken; rough, as with frost or ice; rough of character.

Crunt, *n.* a blow with a cudgel; a smart blow on the head.—*v.* to strike the head with a weapon.

Cruppen, *ppl.* crept.

Cruppen thegether, *phr.* used of one bowed by age or shrunken with cold.

Cruppocks, *n.* crisp oatcakes.

Cruse, *adj.* brisk; lively. Cf. Crouse.

Crushie, *n.* a familiar name for a shepherd's dog; a collie.

Crusie, Crusy, Cruzy, *n.* a small, old-fashioned open lamp, in which the pith of rushes was burned with animal oil; a triangular iron candlestick, with one or more sockets to hold candles; a crucible or hollow piece of iron for melting metals.

Crusie-gabbit, *adj.* used of a dog: having a mouth like a 'crusie,' sharp-pointed.

Crusil, *v.* to contract the body in sitting.

Crut, *n.* a short person.

Crutch, *n.* the pommel of a lady's saddle.

Crutch-phrase, *n.* a phrase like 'as it were,' or 'so to say,' which gives a speaker time to think what comes next.

Crute, *n.* a decrepit person. Cf. Croot.

Crutlachin, *ppl.* conversing in a silly, tattling way.

Cruttlins, *n.* the refuse of soft food.

Cruve, *n.* a pen for cattle; a pig-sty; a hovel. Cf. Cruive.

Cry, *n.* a call, summons, shout; a musical sound; in *pl.* the proclamation of banns of marriage.—*v.* to call; to summons; to proclaim, publish in the streets; to publish banns of marriage; used of a woman: to cry in travail; to speak, talk, make a sound.

Cry doon, *phr.* to depreciate, decry.

Cry in, *phr.* to invite to enter; to make a passing call.

Cryin', *n.* proclamation of banns; a woman's

confinement; a feast given to neighbours shortly after a woman's confinement.

Cryin'-bannock, *n.* a special cake eaten at the feast held on the birth of a child.

Cryin'-cheese, -kebbuck, *n.* cheese given to neighbours and visitors on the occasion of the birth of a child.

Cryin'-fever, *n.* a raving, raging fever.

Cryin'-out, *n.* an outcry; misfortune, calamity.

Cryin'-pipes, *n.* little straw-pipes through which children make a noise.

Cryin'-siller, *n.* the fee paid for proclamation of banns.

Cryin'-wife, *n.* a woman in travail.

Cryle, *n.* a dwarf; a deformed person. Cf. Crile.

Cryne, *v.* to shrink in; to shrivel up. Cf. Crine.

Cryste, *n.* a diminutive, talkative person.

Cubb, *n.* a droll fellow.

Cubbag, *n.* a small hand-basket, made of leather, and narrow at the bottom.

Cubbirt, *n.* a cupboard.

Cubby-hole, *n.* a dog-hutch.

†Cubicular, *n.* a page of the bedchamber.

Cuckie, *n.* a small, plain bun, a bath-bun. Cf. Cookie.

Cucking, *n.* the sound made by the cuckoo.

Cuckold, *n.* in *phr.* 'cuckold's-cut,' -'slice,' the first or uppermost slice of a loaf of bread.

Cuckold-carlie, *n.* an old cuckold.

Cuckoo, *v.* to harp on a subject, say the same thing over and over again.

Cuckoo's-meat, Cuckoo-sorrel, *n.* the wood-sorrel.

Cuckoo's-spittens, -spittle, *n.* a froth discharged by the young frog-hoppers or frog-flies.

Cuck-stule, *n.* the cucking-stool; a pillory.

Cucuddy, *n.* a children's game in which they sit on their hams and hop round. Cf. Cur-'cuddie.

Cud, *v.* to chew the cud.

Cud, *n.* a tub; a wooden chamber-pot. Cf. Queed.

Cud, *n.* a cudgel.—*v.* to cudgel.

Cud, *n.* an ass; an inferior.

Cud, *n.* an untruthful young man.

Cud, *v. pret.* could.

Cuddeigh, *n.* a bribe; a present. Cf. Cudeigh.

Cuddem, *v.* to tame, subdue.—*adj.* tame. Cf. Cuddum.

Cudden, *n.* the young of the coal-fish. Cf. Cuddin.

Cudderie, *adj.* chilly; susceptible to cold. Cf. Cutherie.

Cuddie, *n.* a 'cudden.'

Cuddie, *n.* a small basket made of straw.

Cuddie, *n.* a street-gutter; a conduit; an overflow connection between a canal and a river; a 'cundy.'

Cuddie, *n.* a children's game, in which they sit on their hams and hop round. Cf. Cur-cuddie.

Cuddin, *n.* the coal-fish from a year old till full-grown.

Cudding, *n.* the char.

Cuddle, *v.* to nestle for warmth or shelter; to sleep, lie down to sleep; to crouch, to sit over; to approach a person flatteringly; used of lovers: to talk in soft tones, fondle; to coax, entice; of marbles: to get the 'pitcher' to lie as near the 'ring' as possible.—*n.* a very close intimacy; conversation in low or soft tones.

Cuddle-mudllin, Cuddle-muddle, *n.* a low, muttered conversation.

Cuddler, *n.* a bedfellow; a nestling; a fondling.

Cuddlie, *n.* whispering among a number of people.

Cuddlin, *n.* close intimacy; whispered conversation.

Cuddly, *n.* a nursery word for bed.

Cuddoch, Cuddock, *n.* a young cow, heifer. Cf. Cuttoch.

Cuddom, *v.* to accustom; to tame.—*n.* a custom. Cf. Cuddum.

Cud-doos, *n.* eider-ducks, 'St Cuthbert's pigeons.'

Cuddum, *n.* substance; the largest share.

Cuddum, *v.* to tame; to domesticate.—*adj.* tame, broken-in.

Cuddumin'-siller, *n.* money given to a shepherd for special attention to a beast newly joined to his herd or drove.

Cuddy, *n.* a simpleton; a stupid or half-witted person.

Cuddy-and-the-powks, *n.* a boys' game.

Cuddy-block, *n.* a blockhead.

Cuddy-cairt, *n.* a donkey-cart.

Cuddy-door, *n.* the opening in the gable of a 'byre' for carrying out the dung.

Cuddy-heel, *n.* an iron heel on a boot.

Cuddy-loup, *n.* a boys' game.

Cuddy-rung, *n.* a cudgel.

Cuddy-wanter, *n.* one on the outlook for a donkey.

Cude, *n.* the cud.

Cude, *adj.* harebrained; appearing deranged or greatly alarmed. Cf. Keude.

Cude, *n.* a small tub. Cf. Cootie.

Cude, *n.* a face-cloth for a child at baptism.

Cudeigh, Cudeich, *n.* a bribe; a clandestine gift; a present in addition to wages. Cf. Cuddeigh.

Cudger, Cudgie, *n.* a blow given by one boy to another as a challenge to fight. Cf. Coucher's blow.

Cudie, *n.* a small tub. Cf. Cootie.

Cudiegh, *n.* a bribe, present, bonus. Cf. Cudeigh.

Cudroch-chiel, *n.* a timid, worthless youth.
Cudum, *n.* substance; the largest share. Cf. Cuddum.
Cudyuch, *n.* an ass; a sorry animal.
Cue, *v.* to fuddle.
Cue, *n.* humour, temper.
Cuer, *n.* one who intoxicates others.
Cufe, *n.* a simpleton. Cf. Coof.
Cuff, *n.* the scruff of the neck; the nape.
Cuff, *n.* an old man; contemptuous term for one.
Cuff, *v.* to winnow corn, &c., for the first time.
Cuffet, *n.* a blow, buffet; in *pl.* a boys' game.
Cuffie, *adj.* chubby.
Cuffin-riddle, *n.* the riddle used in the first winnowing of cereals.
Cuffock, *n.* a mode of winding up a worsted clew.
Cufie, Cuffie, *v.* to surpass, outstrip.—*n.* the act by which one is surpassed.
Cugg, *v.* to prop up. Cf. Cog.
Cuggly, *adj.* unsteady, shaky.
Cuid, *n.* a child's face-cloth at baptism. Cf. Cude.
Cuide, *adj.* harebrained. Cf. Cude.
Cuif, *n.* a simpleton, fool. Cf. Coof.
Cuil, *adj.* cool.—*v.* to cool.
Cuilzie, *v.* to befool. Cf. Culyie.
Cuinyie, Cuinzie, *n.* a coin; a mint-house.—*v.* to coin. Cf. Cunzie.
Cuinyie-hoose, *n.* the mint-house.
†Cuirie, *n.* a stable, mews.
†Cuisse-madame, *n.* the French jargonelle. Cf. Queez-maddam.
Cuisser, *n.* a stallion. Cf. Cooser.
Cuist, *v. pret.* and *ppl.* cast.
Cuist, *n.* condition. Cf. Coost.
Cuisten, *ppl.* cast.
Cuit, *n.* an ankle. Cf. Coot.
Cuit, *v.* to play at curling. Cf. Cute.
Cuitchen, *ppl.* caught.
Culter, *v.* to talk in a low and confidential tone; to fondle; to coax, wheedle; to cocker, fuss over; to manage one adroitly; to set on one's feet; to restore to health; to patch, mend, put to rights.
Cuiterer, *n.* a coaxer, flatterer.
Cuitie-boyn, *n.* a small tub for washing the feet, and holding as much water as will cover the 'cuits' or ankles.
Cuitikins, *n.* gaiters; leggings.
Cuiting, *n.* a covering, coverlet.
Cuitle, Cuittle, *v.* to wheedle, coax, flatter, to fuss over; to tickle; to flirt; with *in with*, to gain friendship or affection; with *up*, to wheedle successfully.—*adj.* difficult, ticklish; 'kittle.'
Cuitling, *n.* a flatterer, wheedler.
Cuittie, *n.* bowl of liquor; a measure of beer or spirits.

Cule, *v.* to cool.—*adj.* cool.
Cule-an'-sup, *n.* a state of poverty.
†Cules, *n.* the buttocks.
Cule-the-lume, *n.* a person very indolent at his work.
Culf, *v.* to ram, stuff. Cf. Colf.
Cull, *n.* a fool, dupe, stupid fellow.
Cull, *n.* a lump of hard food.
†Cullage, *n.* the distinctive marks of sex.
Culliebuction, *n.* a noisy squabble without mischief. Cf. Colliebuction.
Cullion, *n.* a poltroon; a base fellow; a person of disagreeable temper and manners.
Cullionly, *adv.* rascally.
Cullionry, *n.* cowardice, roguery.
Cullishangy, *n.* a squabble, quarrel, broil. Cf. Collyshangy.
†Culls, *n.* the testicles of the ram.
Cully, *v.* to make a fool of; to cheat; to entice by flattery.—*n.* a flatterer. Cf. Culyie.
Cullyeon, *n.* a poltroon. Cf. Cullion.
Cully-haikie, *n.* the lifting and carrying of a tired child. Cf. Curry-haikie.
Culm, *n.* the slack of anthracite coal used in lime-burning; coal-dust; peat-dust. Cf. Coom.
Culrach, *n.* surety, security.
Culravage, *n.* a disorderly mob. Cf. Gilravage.
Culroun, *n.* a scamp, rascal.
Culsh, *n.* a big, disagreeable person.
Cultie, *n.* a young colt; a nimble-footed animal; in *pl.* the feet.
Culyeon, *n.* a poltroon, a base fellow. Cf. Cullion.
Culyie, Culye, Culzie, *v.* to befool, dupe.—*n.* a flatterer; flattery.
Cum, *v.* to come.
Cum, *n.* a crook, bend, curve.
Cum, Cumb, *n.* a tub; a cistern; a large ladle for bailing out a boat.
Cumallee, *n.* the king's signal in the game of 'king of Cantilene.'
Cumber, *n.* encumbrance, inconvenience. Cf. Cummer.
Cumbered, *ppl. adj.* used of the hands: benumbed, stiff with cold.
Cumbluff, *adj.* stupefied, 'bumbazed.'
Cumlin, *n.* an animal that comes and attaches itself voluntarily to a person or place. Cf. Comeling.
Cummer, *v.* to cumber.—*n.* cumbrance; an encumbrance.
†Cummer, *n.* a gossip, godmother; a midwife; a girl, young woman; a contemptuous designation for a woman, old or young; a supposed witch.—*v.* to meet for a gossip.
Cummer-fialls, *n.* an entertainment formerly given on recovery from childbirth.
Cummerlyke, *adj.* like 'cummers' or gossips.

Cummer-room, *v.* to appear as an intruder.— *n.* an encumbrance.

Cummer-skolls, *n.* entertainment given to visitors on occasion of a child's birth.

Cumming, *n.* a vessel for holding wort. Cf. Cum.

Cummock, *n.* the rest-harrow.

Cummock, *n.* a short staff with curved head. Cf. Cammock.

Cummudge, *adj.* snug, cosy, comfortable. Cf. Curmud.

Cum-out-awa', *n.* a swindler.

Cumplouter, *v.* to agree.—*n.* mixture. Cf. Complouther.

Cumsiled, *ppl. adj.* used of small houses: ceiled with wood, partly on the rafters and collars. Cf. Coom-ceiled.

Cumstroun, *adj.* dangerous.

Cun, *v.* to learn, to know; to taste, to test by tasting.

Cun, *v.* in *phr.* 'to cun thanks,' to give thanks; to feel grateful. Cf. Con.

†Cundy, *n.* a covered drain; a concealed hole, an apartment; the hole covered by a grating for receiving dirty water for the common sewer; a small drain crossing a roadway.

Cundy-hole, *n.* a conduit, as one across a road.

Cungle, *n.* a rumpus, quarrel.

Cuningar, *n.* a rabbit-warren.

Cunjert, *ppl.* overawed, subdued to obedience, &c. Cf. Counger.

Cunnach, *n.* the 'pip' in fowls. Cf. Cannach.

Cunner, *v.* to scold.—*n.* a scolding, reproof.

Cunniack, *n.* a chamber-pot.

Cunning, *adj.* skilful, expert; difficult to find.

Cunster, *n.* a taster, who tested officially the quality of liquor sold in a burgh.

Cuntack, *n.* the fish father-lasher.

†Cunyie, Cunzie, *n.* a corner; coign.

Cunyie-mirk, *n.* a very snug situation.

†Cunzie, Cunyie, *n.* money, coin.—*v.* to coin, to mint.

Cup, *n.* a small thick biscuit, slightly hollow in the middle; a kind of fishing-net or trap.

Cupar, *n.* in *phr.* 'he that will to Cupar maun to Cupar,' a wilful man must have his way.

Cupar-justice, *n.* judgment after execution; 'Jeddart justice.'

Cuplins, *n.* the length between the tops of the shoulder-blades and the tops of the hip-joints.

Cup-moss, *n.* a name given to the lichen *tartareus.*

Cupper, *n.* a toper, tippler.

Cuppil, Cupple, *n.* a rafter. Cf. Couple.

Cupplin, *n.* the lower part of the backbone.

Curach, *n.* a skiff. Cf. Currach.

Curbawdy, *n.* active courtship.

Curch, *n.* a woman's cap or head-dress; a kerchief. Cf. Curshe.

Curch, *v.* to bend, to curtsy.

Curchie, *n.* a curtsy.—*v.* to curtsy.

Curcuddie, Curcuddock, *n.* a children's game in which they sit on their houghs and hop round.

Curcuddock, Curcuddoch, Curcudyuch, Curcoddoch, *adj.* sitting close together in a friendly manner; cordial, intimate, kindly, fond.—*v.* to whisper or talk intimately together; to sit closely and cosily together.

Curdie, *n.* a small bit of curd.

Curdoo, Curdow, *n.* the cooing sound of pigeons.—*v.* to make love.

Curdow, *v.* to patch, mend, sew clumsily.

Curdower, *n.* one who works at any trade within a burgh of which he is not a freeman; a tailor or sempstress who goes from house to house to mend old clothes.

Curdy-butter, *n.* curds broken up and mixed with butter. Cf. Cruddy-butter.

Cureckity coo, *v.* to coo; to make love to.

†Curfuffle, *v.* to rumple, ruffle, dishevel, discompose.—*n.* a ruffling, tremor, fuss, agitation, dishevelment. Cf. Carfuffle.

Curfumish, *v.* to give out a bad smell. Cf. Carfumish.

†Curgellit, *ppl.* shocked by seeing or hearing anything horrible.

†Curglaff, Curgloff, *n.* the shock felt in bathing at the first plunge into cold water.

†Curgloft, *ppl. adj.* panic-stricken.

Curhung, *n.* a slide on ice on one's 'hunkers.'

Curious, *adj.* careful, particular; anxious, eager; fond.

Curiously, *adv.* carefully.

Curjute, *v.* to overwhelm, overthrow; to overcome with strong drink.

Curkling, *n.* the sound emitted by the quail.

Curl-doddy, *n.* the cone of a pine- or fir-tree; curled cabbage; natural clover; ribgrass.

Curled-mill, *n.* a snuff-box made of the tip of a horn.

Curlie-doddie, *n.* blue scabious; the daisy; a kind of sugar-plum.

Curlie-fuffs, *n.* false hair worn by women to make up deficiencies.

Curlies, *n.* curled colewort; 'curly kale.'

Curlie-wurlie, *n.* a fantastic figure or ornament on stone, &c.

Curlippie, *v.* to steal slyly.

Curluns, *n.* the earth-nut, pig-nut.

Curly, *n.* a curly head; a curly-headed boy.

Curly-andrew, *n.* sugared coriander seed.

Curly-head-a-craw, *adv.* topsy-turvy.

Curly-kale, *n.* curled colewort, 'curlies.'

Curly-murchy, *n.* the female nymphæ, &c.

Curly-murchy, *adj.* churlish and ungrateful.

Curly-murly-nightcap, *n.* the monkshood.

Curly-plant, *n.* 'curled kale.'

Curmow, *n.* an accompaniment, a 'convoy' in a walk, escort.

Curmud, *adj.* cordial, intimate, neighbourly; snug, comfortable.—*v.* to sit close, to be very intimate.

Curmudge, *n.* a mean fellow, a curmudgeon.

Curmudgeous, *adj.* mean, niggardly.

Curmudlie, *n.* close contact, pressure. Cf. Curmud.

Curmur, *n.* the purring of a cat.

Curmurrin, *n.* a low, rumbling sound, a murmuring; a source of grumbling.

Curn, *n.* a grain or particle of corn; a quantity of indefinite size or number; a party, band, assembly; a small price.—*adv.* in small pieces.

Curn, *n.* a handmill.—*v.* to grind. Cf. Quern.

Curnab, *v.* to pilfer, seize.

Curnaptious, *adj.* cross, ready to take offence, irritable. Cf. Carnaptious.

Curnawin', *n.* the sensation of hunger.

Curney, *n.* a small quantity of anything. Cf. Curnie.

Curnie, *adj.* full of grains; knotted, candied.

Curnie, *n.* nursery term for the little finger.

Curnie, *n.* a small quantity.

Curnie-wurnie, *n.* the little finger, a nursery term.

Curnoitted, *adj.* peevish.

Curpal, Curple, *n.* a crupper.

Curpin, curpan, curpen, curpon, *n.* a crupper; the back; the backbone; the buttocks; the rump of a fowl.

Curr, *v.* to coo; to purr.—*n.* a whisper; a rumour.

Curr, *v.* to cower, crouch; to squat.

Curr, *v.* to move a thing by touching it slightly with anything pointed; with *at*, to attempt such a movement.—*n.* such a touch.

Currach, Currack, *n.* a wickerwork pannier; a small cart made of twigs.

Currach, *n.* a small boat or skiff.

Currack, *n.* a sea-tangle.

Currack, *n.* a person of stubborn temper.

Currag, *n.* the forefinger.

Curragh, *n.* a small boat. Cf. Currach.

Curran, *n.* a small quantity. Cf. Curn.

Curran, *n.* a currant.

Curran-petris, *n.* the wild carrot.

Currant-bun, *n.* a large Christmas bun, consisting mainly of dried fruits and spices, a 'sweetie-loaf.'

Currbawty, *n.* the art of seeking a quarrel.

Current, *n.* every single peck, as multure for so many ground at a mill, so that the '17th current' is every 17th peck.

Curriched, *adj.* made of wickerwork; covered with hides. Cf. Currach.

Currie, *n.* a small stool.

Currie, *n.* a deep pool or recess in a river, where fishes hide.

Currieboram, *n.* a crowd of living creatures.

Curriebuction, Currybuckshon, *n.* a confused gathering which is quarrelsome or dangerous.

Curriebushel, *n.* a confused crowd of people.

Curriehunkers, *n.* the hams, the hams in a crouching posture.

Curriemudge, Curriemudgel, *v.* to beat good naturedly.

Curriemushel, *n.* a confused crowd of people.

Currie-wirrie, -wurrie, *n.* a violent dispute. —*adv.* violently disputing.—*v.* to dispute violently.

Currie-wurriein', *n.* a prolonged violent dispute.—*adv.* peevish, fretful.

Currit, *v.* used of a vehicle: to run smoothly.

Currivell, *v.* to squabble noisily.—*n.* a noisy squabble.

Curroch, *n.* a wickerwork pannier.

Currock, *n.* a skiff. Cf. Currach.

Currock-cross't, *adj.* bound to a 'currach.'

Curroo, *v.* to coo.

Currough, *n.* a boat, a skiff. Cf. Currach.

Currough, *n.* a cairn, a heap of stones.

Currove, *v.* to coo.

Curry-haikie, *n.* the lifting and carrying of a tired child.

Curry-shang, *n.* a broil, an uproar.

Cursackie, *n.* a long, coarse smock worn by workmen over their clothes.

Cursaddle, *n.* the small saddle on a carriage-horse. Cf. Carsaddle.

Curse, *n.* in *phr.* 'the curse o' Scotland,' the nine of diamonds in a pack of cards.

Curseese, *v.* to catechize, scold, reprove. Cf. Carseese.

Curshe, *n.* a kerchief. Cf. Curch.

Cursour, *n.* a stallion. Cf. Cuisser.

Curst, *ppl. adj.* ill-tempered.

Curstness, *n.* crabbedness, ill-temper.

Curtle, *n.* a sluttish girl.

Curtoush, *n.* a woman's 'short-gown.' Cf. Cartouch.

Curtsey, *n.* a woman's cap, 'curch.'

Curtshy, *v.* to curtsy.

Curunddoch, *n.* a dance-play among children. Cf. Curcuddie.

Curwurring, *n.* a rumbling, murmuring. Cf. Curmurring.

Cush, *int.* an excl. of surprise.

Cushat, Cushet, Cushat-doo, *n.* the wood-pigeon; the wild pigeon; the stock-dove.

Cushie, Cushie-bonnie, *int.* a milkmaid's call to a cow.

Cushie, Cushey, Cushie-, Cushey-doo, Cushy, *n.* a 'cushat.'

Cushineel, *n.* cochineal.

Cushlan, *n.* a gentle sliding down.

Cushle, *v.* to slide down gently.—*n.* a gentle sliding down.

Cushle-mushle, *n.* a hubbub, confused muttering and movement.

Cussels, *n.* the viviparous blenny.

Cusser, *n.* a stallion. Cf. Cooser.

Cussit, *n.* a small chest.

Custen, *ppl.* cast.

Custoc, Custock, *n.* the stem of a cabbage, &c. Cf. Castock.

Customary-weaver, *n.* one who weaves for private customers.

Customer, *n.* the lessee of burgh customs and dues.

Customer-wark, *n.* weaving or work done for private customers.

Custril, *n.* a sort of fool or silly fellow.

Custroune, *n.* a vagabond, cad.—*adj.* caddish; low-born.

Cut, *v.* to castrate; to spay; to thrash with a whip.—*n.* a blow with a whip; appetite; grass, hay, or corn to be reaped; an artificial watercourse; an excavation or cutting; a piece of cloth of varying length, cut from the warp; a measure of yarn, the 12th of a hank; temper, mood.

Cut, *n.* a lot.—*v.* to decide by lot.

Cut, *v.* to run quickly, hasten away.

Cutchack, *n.* the clearest part of a fire. Cf. Coutchack.

Cutcher, *n.* a coward. Cf. Coucher.

Cutchie, *n.* kitchen.

Cutchin, *adj.* cowardly, knocking under.—*n.* a coward.

Cute, *v.* to play at curling. Cf. Cuit.

Cute, *n.* the ankle; the foot. Cf. Coot.

Cutekins, *n.* gaiters. Cf. Cuitikins.

Cuter, *v.* to cocker; to fondle, coax; to mend, patch; to talk confidentially in a low tone, whisper. Cf. Cuiter.

Cuterer, *n.* a flatterer.

Cut-fingered, *adj.* used of gloves: with the fingers cut short; abrupt, curt, giving or getting short answers; leaving a company abruptly.

Cuth, *n.* a coal-fish not fully grown.

Cuthbert's (Saint) beads, *n.* portions of the jointed stems of fossil encrinites common in the mountain limestone.

Cutherie, Cuthrie, *adj.* chilly; susceptible to cold.

Cuthie, *adj.* affable. Cf. Couthie.

Cuthil, *n.* corn carried to another field than that on which it grew. Cf. Cutle.

Cutie-stane, *n.* a curling-stone.

Cutikins, *n.* leggings. Cf. Cuitikins.

Cutit, *ppl. adj.* having ankles.

Cutle, *v.* to carry corn from one position to a more convenient one, from a distant to a nearer field.—*n.* corn carried and set up in another place. Cf. Cuttle.

Cutle, *v.* to coax, wheedle; to manage adroitly. Cf. Cuitle.

Cutling, *n.* a flatterer; flattery.

Cut-luggit, *adj.* crop-eared; used contemptuously.

Cut-lugs, *n.* a crop-eared horse.

Cut-pock, -pyock, *n.* the stomach of a fish or of a person.

Cutt, *n.* a term of reproach.

Cuttay, *n.* a term of reproach for a girl, a 'cutty.'

Cutter, *n.* a mowing-machine; a reaping machine.

Cutter, *n.* a small whisky-bottle. Cf. Coutter.

Cutthroat, *n.* a kind of sweetmeat.

Cut-throat, *n.* a dark-lantern, a 'bowet'; the name formerly given to a piece of ordnance.

Cuttie, *n.* a hare.

Cuttie, *v.* to eat greedily.

Cuttie, *n.* a horse or mare two years old.

Cuttie, *n.* the black guillemot; the razor-bill.

Cuttie, *adj.* cut short; short. Cf. Cutty.

Cuttie-boyn, *n.* a small tub for washing the feet. Cf. Cuitie-boyn.

Cuttie-brown, *n.* a horse crop-eared, or, perhaps, docked in the tail.

Cuttie-clap, *n.* a hare's form.

Cuttie-free, *adj.* able to take food.

Cuttiein, *n.* the act of eating greedily.

Cuttie-rung, *n.* a crupper for a horse wearing a pack-saddle.

Cuttie's fud, *n.* a hare's tail.

Cutting-off, *n.* excommunication.

Cutting-off-piece, *n.* the feast of harvest home.

Cuttings, *n.* encouragement, countenance.

Cuttit, *ppl. adj.* abrupt, rude, snappish; offended; laconic.

Cuttitly, *adv.* abruptly; laconically; tartly.

Cuttle, *v.* to carry reaped corn from low ground to higher for winnowing; to remove corn from a distant field to one near the stack-yard; to wait the earliest opportunity of securing the crop. Cf. Cutle.

Cuttle, *v.* to sharpen.

Cuttle, *v.* to smile or laugh in a suppressed way.

Cuttoch, *n.* a cow between one and two years old. Cf. Cuddoch.

Cuttum-rung, *n.* that part of the piece of wood (which keeps back the 'sunks' used for a saddle) that goes under the horse's tail.

Cutty, *n.* the wren.

Cutty, *adj.* short, cut short; diminutive; short-tempered, hasty.—*n.* a short clay-pipe; a short-handled horn spoon; a small knife; a short, stumpy girl; a worthless woman; a rompish child.—*v.* to sup with a spoon.

Cutty, *n.* a short, three-legged stool.

Cutty, *n.* a small, thick cake of oatmeal, with a hole in the middle.

Cutty-basket, *n.* a basket for holding horn spoons.

Cutty-clay, *n.* a short clay-pipe.

Cutty-full, *n.* a small measure full.

Cutty-glies, -glier, *n.* a short, squat flirt.

Cutty-gun, *n.* a short tobacco-pipe.

Cutty-hunker-dance, *n.* an old burlesque dance, performed by mendicants.

Cutty-knife, *n.* a small knife.

Cutty-mun, *n.* in *phr.* 'Cutty-mun and Tree-ladle,' the supposed name of an old tune; used of one who swings on the gallows.

Cutty-pipe, *n.* a short tobacco-pipe.

Cutty-quean, *n.* a worthless woman.

Cutty-queen, *n.* the wren.

Cutty-sark, *n.* part of a woman's underlinen cut short; a worthless woman.

Cutty-spune, *n.* a short-handled horn spoon.

Cutty-stool, *n.* a short three-legged stool; the 'stool of repentance,' on which offenders formerly sat in church.

Cutty-stoup, *n.* a small drinking-vessel; a quartern measure.

Cutty-wren, *n.* the wren.

Cutwiddie, Cutwuddie, *n.* the bar of a plough or harrow to which the traces are attached.

Cutworm, *n.* a white grub which destroys vegetables by cutting through the stem; a person with destructive tendencies.

Cuz, *adj.* close.—*adv.* closely.

Cwaw, *phr.* come away!

†**Cyclops,** *n.* a name given to a tawse, from its having a large hole or 'eye' in its head.

Cyle, *n.* a beam, rafter. Cf. Sile.

†**Cymar,** *n.* a shroud. Cf. Seymar.

Cypher-man, *n.* a diminutive man; a person good for little; a loafer; a lazy, drunken rascal; a 'cypher.' Cf. Seefer.

Cyprus-cat, *n.* a cat of three colours, black, brown, and white.

Cythe, *v.* to make known; to become known. —*n.* appearance. Cf. Kythe.

Da, *n.* a child's name for father.

Da, Daa, *n.* a sluggard; a slovenly woman, drab. Cf. Daw.

Daach, *n.* a measure of land. Cf. Daugh, Davoch.

Daachter, *n.* a daughter.

Daad, *v.* to strike. Cf. Dad.

Daak, *v.* to doze for a short time; of bad weather: to abate for a short time.—*n.* a lull in bad weather.

Daaken, *v.* to dawn. Cf. Dawken.

Daakenin, *n.* the dawn, the early dawn.

Daar, *adj.* dear.

Daart, *v.* to raise the price of anything. Cf. Dearth.

Daat, *v.* to pet, caress, fondle.—*n.* a darling. Cf. Daut.

Daatie, *n.* a little darling. Cf. Dautie.

Dab, *v.* to give a slight stroke; to strike with a sharp or pointed weapon; to prick; to peck like a bird; to press or put smartly down; to dip into.—*n.* a blow or slap; a thrust, poke, peck; a small quantity of anything.—*adv.* with force, violently, sharply.

Dab, *v.* in *phr.* 'let dab,' to hint, give sign, 'let on.'

Dab, *v.* to daub.

Dab, *n.* an expert, an adept.

Dabach, *v.* to thrust, prod.—*n.* a blow, a thrust.—*adv.* sharply, with force.

Dabach, *n.* an expert, an adept.

Dabber, *v.* to stupefy one with rapid talk; to confound; to jar; to wrangle.—*n.* a wrangle.

Dabberin, *n.* continued wrangling.—*ppl. adj.* quarrelsome.

Dabbies, *n.* in *phr.* 'holy dabbies,' cakes of shortbread, formerly used in Galloway instead of plain bread at the Lord's Supper; a sort of cake baked with butter, called 'petticoat-tails.'

Dabbin, *n.* the act of pecking, pricking, pushing, or pressing.

Dabble, *v.* to trifle.—*n.* a slight washing.

Dabble, *v.* to chew.

Dabble, *v.* to wrangle; to stupefy with talk.

Dabble-dock, *n.* the last candle made at a dipping; a person with wet, dripping clothes.

Daberlick, Daberlack, *n.* a long seaweed, 'bladderlock'; any wet strap of cloth or leather; the hair of the head, hanging in long, lank, tangled locks; a long, lanky person; used contemptuously.

Dablet, *n.* an imp, a little devil.

Dabster, *n.* a proficient, an expert.

Daccle, *v.* to hesitate; to slacken pace. Cf. Dackle.

Dacent, *adj.* decent. Cf. Decent.

Dachan, *n.* a puny, dwarfish creature.

Dacker, *v.* to saunter idly, stroll leisurely, jog; to go about in feeble health; continue on, continue irresolutely; to peddle, barter; to dispose in an orderly way, 'lay out' a dead body; to search, examine; to inquire after stolen or smuggled goods; to wrangle, challenge, engage; to trifle at work.—*n.* a stroll, a short walk; a wrangle, struggle.—

adj. used of the weather : uncertain, unsettled.

Dackle, *v.* to hesitate, to lessen speed.—*n.* a state of suspense, hesitation ; a pause ; the abating of heat as a fire fades.

Dacklie, *adj.* swarthy ; pale, sickly in appearance.

Dacklin, *n.* a slight shower.

Dacklin', *ppl. adj.* in a state of doubt ; slow, dilatory.

Dacre, *v.* to inflict corporal punishment.

Dad, *n.* a pet name for father.

Dad, *n.* a large piece, a lump. Cf. Daud.

Dad, *v.* to strike, thrash ; to dash, drive forcibly ; to bespatter ; to pelt ; to wander about ; to knock ; to abuse ; to fall with force ; with *about*, to dash or drive about a district ; with *aff*, to shake off ; with *down*, to fall down, knock down.—*n.* a dash ; a violent blow ; a sudden thrust with violence ; the clapping of hands in applause ; a heavy fall.

Dad, *ppl. adj.* dashed, knocked about, 'daddit.'

Dad a bit, *phr.* not a bit, devil a bit.

Dadd, *n.* father.

Daddin, *n.* rough usage ; knocking, striking ; knocking about, wandering.—*ppl. adj.* used of wind or rain : beating, driving.

Daddins, *n.* a beating.

Daddit, *ppl. adj.* beaten ; dashed ; knocked about.

Daddle, *v.* to walk slowly ; to work leisurely ; to dawdle, trifle ; to walk with short, feeble, unsteady steps ; to draggle, bemire one's clothes ; to fondle a child. Cf. Daidle.

Daddle, Daddlie, *n.* a pinafore, a large bib. Cf. Daidlie.

Daddy Cloots, *n.* the devil.

Daddy-da, *n.* a child's name for father.

Dadge, *n.* a bannock.

Dadgeon-weaver, -wabster, *n.* a linen-weaver ; one who weaves for private customers.

Dadjell, *v.* to stroll, saunter.

Dadle, *v.* to work slowly ; to dawdle ; to draggle. Cf. Daddle.

Dae, *v.* to do.—*aux. v.* do.

Daevle, *n.* devil.

Daff, *v.* to be foolish ; to sport ; to jest ; to talk nonsense ; to flirt ; to romp ; to toy amorously.

Daffadile, *n.* a daffodil ; a silly, flashy woman ; an effeminate or delicate man.

Daffer, *n.* merriment ; one who 'daffs.'

Daffery, *n.* gaiety ; sportiveness ; folly.

Daffin, *n.* sport ; folly ; idle waste of time in foolish talk ; loose talk ; dallying ; matrimonial intercourse.

Daffing-green, *n.* a village green, where games are played or young people meet to 'daff.'

Daffins, *n.* daffodils.

Daffins, *n.* the small cords by which herring-nets are fastened to the rope on their upper edge.

Daffodil, Daffodilly, *n.* a silly, flashy woman ; an effeminate or delicate man.

Daft, *adj.* mentally deranged ; delirious ; silly, foolish ; giddy, thoughtless ; innocently gay or merry ; excessively gay ; playful ; extremely fond of and eager to obtain ; doting.

Daft-days, *n.* the holidays at Christmas and the New Year.

Daftish, *adj.* rather 'daft' ; mentally slow ; stupid.

Daft-like, *adj.* giddy ; foolish ; thoughtless ; dull-witted ; absurd ; reckless ; mad ; eccentric in appearance.

Daftly, *adv.* foolishly ; merrily ; madly.

Daftness, *n.* foolishness ; fatuousness ; light-headedness.

Daftrie, *n.* gaiety, sportiveness ; folly.

Dafty, *n.* a half-witted person ; a nickname applied to such a person, or to one who is 'queer.'

Dag, *n.* a drizzling rain ; a heavy shower ; a fog, a mist.—*v.* to drizzle, rain gently ; to be foggy.

Dag, Dagg, *v.* to shoot, let fly ; to stab.—*n.* a gun, a pistol.

Dag, *v.* to confound, used as an imprecation.

Dag-daw, *n.* the jackdaw.

Dag-durk, *n.* a dirk for stabbing.

Dage, *n.* a slut, trollop ; a dirty, mismanaging woman.

Dagg, *n.* a cut of earth.

Daggin, *v.* used as an expletive. Cf. Dagone.

Daggined, *ppl.* 'dashed.'—*adv.* used as a very strong intensive.

Daggle, *v.* to fall in torrents ; to drizzle, rain continuously.

Daggle, *v.* to 'knock about,' dangle, trail ; to lounge.

Daggler, *n.* a lounger ; an idler.

Daggy, *adj.* drizzling, misty, rainy.

Dagh, *n.* dough. Cf. Daich.

Dag-head, -man, *n.* the hammer or the dog-head of a gun or pistol.

Dagone, *v.* to confound, dash, used as an imprecation ; to use freely the expletive 'dagone.'

Dagont, *n.* an expletive.—*adv.* used as a very strong intensive. Cf. Dag.

Dahie, *adj.* used of weather : warm, misty, 'muggy.' Cf. Daich.

Dai, *n.* a dairymaid. Cf. Dey.

Daible, *v.* to wash slightly ; to dabble ; to drink in a slovenly fashion.—*n.* a slight washing. Cf. Dabble.

Daible, *v.* to walk like a child ; to go about feebly.

Daich, *adj.* soft, flabby. – *n.* dough ; food for poultry. Cf. Daigh.

Daichy, *adj.* soft. Cf. Daighie.

Daickle, *v.* to hesitate ; to feel reluctant. Cf. Dackle.

Daiddie, *n.* father.

Daidle, *n.* a pinafore, a bib. Cf. Daddle.

Daidle, *v.* to dawdle ; to trifle ; to saunter ; to tipple ; to bedaub one's self in eating or in walking.—*n.* a ramble. Cf. Daddle.

Daidler, *n.* a trifler.

Daidley, *adj.* dawdling.

Daidlie, *n.* a pinafore.

Daidlin, *ppl. adj.* silly ; mean-spirited ; cowardly ; trifling.

Daigh, *n.* dough ; anything made of dough ; hens' meat.

Daighie, *adj.* doughy ; soft, flabby ; spiritless ; cowardly ; childish ; ill-dressed ; used of rich ground : composed of clay and sand properly mixed.

Daighie, *n.* a simpleton.

Daighiness, *n.* flabbiness ; the state of being 'daighie.'

Daigle, *v.* to drizzle ; to rain continuously. Cf. Daggle.

Daik, *v.* to smooth down ; to moisten, soak. —*n.* a smooth down.

†Daiken, *n.* a decade.

Daiker, *v.* to stroll ; to go about feebly ; to hesitate ; to peddle ; to search for stolen or smuggled goods ; to wrangle.—*n.* a stroll ; a wrangle. Cf. Dacker.

†Daiker, *v.* to dress, deck.

Daikins, *int.* an excl. of surprise.

Daikit, *ppl. adj.* used, put to use.

Dail, *n.* a field.

Dail, Daill, *n.* a deal, number of persons ; a part, portion ; value.

Dail, *n.* a deal-board ; a stretching-board for a corpse. Cf. Deal.

Dail, *n.* a ewe fattened for the butcher.

Daill, *n.* interference ; dealing.

Daily-day, *adv.* every day, continually.

Daily-dud, *n.* a dish-clout.

Dailygone, *n.* the twilight. Cf. Dayligaun.

Daime-and-laive, *phr.* great plenty ; wasteful extravagance.

Daimen, *adj.* occasional, rare.—*adv.* now and then.

Daimen icker, *n.* an ear of corn met with occasionally.

Daimis, *v.* to stun. Cf. Dammish.

Daine, *adj.* gentle, modest, lowly.

Dainshoch, *adj.* nice, dainty, squeamish.

Dainta, Daintis, *int.* no matter ! it is of no consequence.

Daintess, *n.* a dainty, a delicacy, a rarity.

Daintie, *n.* affection. Cf. Dent.

Daintith, Dainteth, *n.* a dainty, a delicacy.

Dainty, *adj.* used of things : large ; of children, &c. : plump, thriving ; comely ; pleasant, good-natured ; worthy, excellent ; liberal ; used ironically for scanty.

Dair, *v.* to affect ; to impress. Cf. Dere.

Dair away, *phr.* used of sheep : to wander, roam from their usual pasture.

Dairg, *n.* a day's work. Cf. Darg.

Dairgie, *n.* a dirge ; a funeral feast. Cf. Dirgie.

†Dais, Daiss, *n.* a wooden settle or sofa, convertible into a table, bed, or seat ; a bench of stone or turf at a cottage door ; a bench-seat ; a church-pew.

Daise, *v.* to stun, stupefy with drink ; to benumb ; to wither ; to rot.—*n.* the powder or that part of a stone which is bruised by the stroke of a chisel or pickaxe ; anything that so injures wood, clothes, &c. as to spoil or rot them. Cf. Daze.

Daised, *ppl. adj.* used of wood, plants, &c.: spoiled, withered, rotten.

Daisie, *adj.* used of the weather : cold, damp, raw, sunless, chilling.

Daising, *n.* a disease of sheep, called also 'pining' and 'vanquish.'

Daisy, *adj.* covered with daisies ; remarkable ; darling.

Daiver, *v.* to stun, confound ; used as an imprecation ; to wander aimlessly ; to wander in mind ; to tarry ; to be benumbed, become stiff with cold.—*n.* a stunning blow.

Daivered, *ppl. adj.* fatigued ; stupid ; confused.

Daivilie, *adv.* spiritlessly, listlessly.

Daize, Daizie, *v.* to stun ; to stupefy, to go about stupidly. Cf. Daise.

Dajon-wabster, *n.* one who weaves linen or woollen stuffs for country neighbours or private customers. Cf. Dadgeon-weaver.

Daker, *v.* to search for stolen goods, &c. Cf. Dacker, Daiker.

Daldoo, *n.* a great noise, a hubbub.

Daldrum, *n.* a foolish fancy ; mental confusion.

Dale, *n.* a deal ; a board for measuring a corpse.

Dale, *n.* part interest, management. Cf. Dail, Daill.

Dale, *n.* a goal, a 'dell.'

Dale-land, *n.* the lower and arable ground of a district.

Dale-lander, -man, *n.* an inhabitant of the lower ground or 'dale-land.'

Dalgan, *n.* the stick used in binding sheaves. Cf. Delgin.

Dalk, *n.* varieties of slate clay ; common clay ; a coal-miner's term.

Dall, *n.* a large cake of sawdust and cow-dung, formerly used by the poor as fuel.

Dall, *n.* a sloven.

Dall, *n.* a doll; a dressy, foolish young woman. Cf. Doll.

Dallion, *n.* a person with large, ill-fitting clothes, or with an awkward gait.

Dallish, *adj.* slovenly.

Dalloch, *n.* a flat piece of rich land.

Dallop, *n.* a steep 'shank' or glen, where two haughs are exactly opposite to each other.

Dallow, *v.* to dig with a spade, delve.

Dally, *n.* the stick sometimes used in binding sheaves.

Dally, *n.* a girl's doll; a painted figure or image; a silly, dressy woman.

Dalt, *n.* a foster-child.

Dam, *n.* the water confined by a dam or barrier, a mill-pond; used of children: the quantity of urine discharged at a time; a 'mill-lade.'

†**Dam,** *n.* a mother, woman.

†**Dam** *n.* a piece or 'man' in the game of draughts.

Dam, *n.* the damson plum.

Damack, Damackie, *n.* a girl, a young woman.

Damage, *n.* legal damages; cost, expense.

Damas, *n.* damask.

Damasee, *n.* the damson or damask plum.

Damborded, *adj.* of a checked pattern, crossed like a 'dambrod.'

Dambrod, *n.* a draught-board.—*adj.* checked like a 'dambrod.'

Dam-dyke, *n.* the wall of a mill-pond, &c.

Dame, *n.* the mistress of a house; a farmer's wife; a mother; a young, unmarried woman; a damsel.

Dam-e'e, *n.* the outlet of a mill-pond.

Dam-head, *n.* the upper embankment of a mill-pond.

†**Damishell,** *n.* a damsel.

Dammer, *n.* a miner; one who constructs 'dams.'

Dammer, *v.* to astonish, confuse, astound.

Dammertit, *ppl. adj.* stupid.

Dammin' and lavin', *phr.* fish-poaching, by damming and diverting the course of a stream, and then laving out the water.

Damming and loving, *phr.* preferring a sure though small gain to the prospect of a greater with uncertainty.

Dammish, *v.* to stun, stupefy; to bruise the surface of fruit; to injure, damage; used as an expletive.

Dammishment, *n.* damage, injury.

Dammit, *ppl.* stunned.

Damnage, Dampnage, *n.* injury, damage.

Damnation, *n.* judicial condemnation.

Damnify, *v.* to damage, injure by loss.

Damp, *n.* coal-pit gas.

Damp, *n.* rain.—*adj.* downcast, damped.—*v.* to throw down, fell.

†**Dams,** *n.* the game of draughts.

Damsel, *n.* the damson plum.

Dan, *n.* a respectful term of address.

Dance, *n.* a needless, hurried, or exasperating hunt for a person or thing.

Dance-in-my-lufe, *n.* a very diminutive person.

Dancing, *ppl.* in *phr.* 'to send one dancing,' to send one quickly.

Dancing-mad, *adj.* in a towering passion.

Dandalie, *adj.* celebrated for beauty, spoilt by admiration.—*n.* a woman spoilt by admiration. Cf. Dandillie.

Dander, *n.* temper, anger; spirit.

Dander, *v.* to stroll, saunter; to trifle.—*n.* a stroll.

Danderer, *n.* a saunterer; a habitual saunterer.

Dandering, *ppl.* vibrating, resounding; emitting an unequal sound.

Dandering-Kate, *n.* the stone-bore or stone-orpine.

Danders, *n.* smithy-fire refuse; clinkers, slag.

Dandgell, *n.* a large, thick topcoat; a clumsy person with large, ill-fitting clothes.

Dandiefechun, *n.* a stroke, a hollow blow on any part of the body.

Dandies, Dandie-han'-lin', *n.* a hand-line for catching herring or mackerel from a boat or ship sailing at a moderate rate.

Dandillie, Dandily, *adj.* celebrated for beauty, spoilt by admiration.—*n.* a fondling; a woman who makes too much of herself.

Dandillie-chain, *n.* a chain made by children of dandelion stems for play or ornament.

Dandrum, *n.* a whim, freak.

Dandy, Dandie, *n.* an elegant woman; a distinguished or prominent person.—*adj.* fine, gay; *phr.* 'the dandy,' the very thing, the fashion, 'the ticket.'

Dane, *ppl.* done.

Daner, *v.* to saunter. Cf. Dander.

Dang, *v. pret.* dung, beat, drove. Cf. Ding.

Dang, *v.* to throw violently, knock, bang; to drive.

Dang, *v.* used as an imprecation for 'damn.'

Dangerous, *adj.* dangerously ill.

Dangle, *v.* to swing, vibrate; to throb, tingle; to quiver with pain.

Dank-will, *n.* a will-o'-the-wisp. Cf. Will.

Dannar'd, *ppl. adj.* in a state of stupor. Cf. Donnert.

Danner, *v.* to saunter. Cf. Dander.

Danners, *n.* clinkers; slag from a smithy or foundry; scoriæ. Cf. Danders.

Dannle, *v.* to dangle; to throb or vibrate with pain. Cf. Dangle.

Dant, *v.* to daunt; to be afraid. Cf. Daunt.

Danton, *v.* to daunt · to depress. Cf. Daunton.

Danyel, *v.* to dangle ; to jolt while driving on a rough road.

Dapperpy, *adj.* diapered ; used of variegated woollen cloth.

Dapse, *v.* to choose, fix upon, ' chaps.'

Dardum, *n.* uproar, damage ; ill-humour ; a riotous noise ; a scolding ; a stroke, blow. Cf. Dirdum.

Dare, *v.* to challenge, defy.—*n.* a challenge.

Dare, *v.* to be afraid, shrink in fear ; to crouch, lie hid ; to terrify, stupefy.—*n.* a feeling of fear or awe.

Dare-deviltry, *n.* a dare-devil spirit.

Dare-the-deil, *n.* a dare-devil ; one who fears nothing and will attempt anything.

Darg, Dargue, *n.* a day's work ; work done in a day ; work, whether done in a day or not ; a set task ; a quantity of land.— *v.* to work by the day ; to toil.

Darg, *n.* the noise made by a spade in soft earth.

Darg-days, *n.* days of work given as part of a farmer's or cottager's rent.

Darger, *n.* a day-labourer.

Darging, *n.* a day-labourer's work ; hard, plodding toil.

Dark, *n.* a day's work. Cf. Darg.

Dark, *v.* to grow dark ; to cloud with evil ; to hide, take shelter.

Darken, *v.* in *phr.* to ' darken one's door,' to enter one's house.

Darkening, *n.* twilight, dusk.

Darket, *ppl. adj.* dull, down-hearted.

Darkle, *v.* to darken suddenly in alternation with a gleam of light ; to be momentarily obscured.

Darklins, *adv.* darkly ; in the dark.

Darksome, *adj.* melancholy, dismal.

Darle, *n.* a bit of bread or of anything ; a portion. Cf. Dorle.

Darloch, *n.* a bundle ; a valise ; a sheaf of arrows. Cf. Dorloch.

Darlock, *n.* a large piece of anything solid.

Darn, *v.* to hide, conceal ; to hearken stealthily ; to loiter at work ; to think, muse ; with *behind,* to fall back.

Darn, *v.* used in imprecation for 'damn.'

Darn, *n.* a disease of cattle, supposed to be caused by eating the wood-anemone.

Darn, *v.* to stuff a hole ; to zigzag like a drunk man on a street.

Darna, *v. neg.* dare not. Cf. Daurna.

Darr, *v.* used of a blow : to fall, alight.

Darra, *n.* a hand-line for catching large fish ; the hooks and sinkers attached to the line.

Darra-shaft, *n.* the frame on which the 'darra' is kept ; the 'darra' itself.

Darsna, *v.* durst not.

Dar't, *ppl.* dared.

Dash, *v.* to abash, dismay, confuse ; to show off ;

to flourish in writing ; to erase, strike out ; used in imprecation.—*n.* a display ; a flourish in writing ; of rain : a sudden fall.

Dash, *n.* a hat, a cap.

Dashelled, *ppl. adj.* beaten and wasted by weather, ' tashed.'

Dashie, *adj.* making a great show.

Dashing, *n.* a disappointment.

Dashy-looking, *adj.* smart, well-dressed.

Dask, *n.* a desk ; a precentor's desk.

Dass, *n.* the portion of a haystack cut off with a hay-knife ; the corn left in a barn after part is removed ; a stratum of stones ; a layer in a mass slowly built up ; a small landing-place ; a step.

Datch, *v.* to jog, shake.

Datchel-like, *adj.* having a dangling appearance.

Datchie, *adj.* used of the intellect : penetrating ; sly, cunning, ' cute '; hidden, secret.

Datchle, *v.* to waddle ; to walk carelessly, with ill-fitting clothes.

Date, *n.* in *phr.* 'to gi'e date and gree,' to give the preference.

Daub, *n.* a dash, a sudden stroke. Cf. Dab.

Daub, *n.* an adept, proficient. Cf. Dab.

Dauble, *v.* to thrust, work into, dibble.

Dauch, *n.* a soft, black substance, composed chiefly of clay, mica, and coal-dust.

Dauchle, *v.* to slacken speed. Cf. Dackle.

Dauchy, *adj.* a curling term, used of the ice : wet, sloppy, ' drug,' rendering play difficult.

Daud, *n.* a large piece. Cf. Dad.

Daud, *v.* to strike. Cf. Dad.

Daudnel, *adj.* shabby in appearance.

Daug, *n.* a thick fog. Cf. Dag.

Daugeon, *n.* fellow, person.

Daugh, *n.* a measure of land, estimated to yield 48 bolls.

Daugh, *v. pret.* had ability, was able.

Daugh, *n.* a very heavy dew or drizzling rain.—*v.* to moisten, bedew. Cf. Dawch.

Daught, *v. pret.* was able. Cf. Dow.

Daught, *n.* taste ; effluvium.

Dauk, *adj.* stupid, doltish.

Dauk, *n.* clay used for making fire-bricks.

Dauk, *adj.* dark, murky.

Dauky, *adj.* moist, damp.

Dauler, *n.* a supine, delicate person.

Dault, *n.* a foster-child. Cf. Dalt.

Daumer, *v.* to stun, stupefy ; to knock about ; to bewilder.—*n.* a stunning blow.

Daumert, *ppl. adj.* bewildered, sleepy, silly.

Daunder, Dauner, *v.* to stroll, saunter.—*n.* a drunken frolic ; a saunter. Cf. Dander.

Daunders, *n.* the scoriæ of metals. Cf. Danders.

Daunt, *v.* to break in.—*n.* a check, a discouragement. Cf. Dant.

Daunting, *ppl. adj.* ominous, discouraging.

Dauntingly, *adv.* courageously.

Daunton, *v.* to terrify, subdue; to depress; to awe. Cf. Danton.

Daupet, *ppl. adj.* silly, inactive; stupid, unconcerned; mentally weak.

Daupit-blind, *adj.* stupid and blind.

Daur, *v.* to challenge. Cf. Dare.

Daur, *v.* to fear, stand in awe.—*n.* a feeling of awe. Cf. Dare.

Dauredna, *v. neg.* dared not.

Daurg, Daurk, *n.* a day's work. Cf. Darg.

Daurin', *ppl. adj.* used of beard or whiskers : very big, bushy; bold, venturesome.

Daurken, *v.* to grow dark.

Daurna, *v. neg.* dare not.

Daurnin, *n.* a thrashing, knocking about.

Daurt, *ppl.* dared.

Daur upon, *phr.* to affect, impress.

Daut, *v.* to fondle, dote upon, make much of. —*n.* a caress; a pat fondly given.

Dautie, *n.* a darling; a dear; a sweetheart.

Dauting, *n.* a caress; petting; fondling.

Dautit, *ppl. adj.* fondled, petted; spoiled by overpetting.

Dave, *v.* used of pain : to cease; to assuage. Cf. Deave.

Davel, *v.* to strike with violence; to knock down; to trample.—*n.* a stunning blow. Cf. Devel.

Davelin, *n.* the flat planks on the centres, for supporting the arch-stones of bridges, while building.

Daver, *v.* to stun, stupefy; to benumb; to go out of one's mind. Cf. Daiver.

Davering, *ppl. adj.* riding or walking in a dazed condition.

Daver't, *ppl. adj.* silly, senseless; benumbed.

Davie-drap, *n.* ? the cuckoo-grass or chimney-sweeps.

Daviely, *adv.* listlessly. Cf. Daivilie.

Davoch, *n.* an ancient measure of land, averaging 416 acres.

Davy, *n.* Sir H. Davy's safety-lamp.

Daw, *n.* a lazy, good-for-nothing person; a sluggard; an untidy woman or housewife; a slattern; a trull.

Daw, *n.* fire-clay found on coal; a cake of cow-dung and coal-dust used as fuel.

Daw, *n.* an atom, particle, jot.

Daw, *n.* to dawn.—*v.* to dawn.

Dawch, *v.* to moisten with dew; to damp.— *n.* a heavy dew or drizzling rain. Cf. Dauk.

Dawd, *n.* a lump. Cf. Dad.

Dawd, *v.* to strike.—*n.* a blow. Cf. Dad.

Dawdge, *n.* a tatterdemalion, ragged fellow.

Dawdie, *adj.* slovenly, sluttish, dowdy.

Dawdle, *n.* a lazy, indolent person.—*v.* to be indolent; to mess, bedabble. —*adv.* indolently.

Dawdry, *adj.* slovenly, untidy.

Dawds and blawds, *n.* 'kail-blades' boiled whole and eaten with bannocks; the greatest abundance.

Daw-fish, *n.* the lesser dog-fish.

Dawghie, *adj.* moist, damp.

Dawing, *n.* the dawn.

Dawk, *v.* to drizzle.—*n.* a drizzling rain. Cf. Dauk.

Dawken, *v.* to dawn.

Dawkenin', *n.* the dawn.

Dawkie, *adj.* moist; damp.

Dawless, *adj.* lazy; without energy; feeble. Cf. Dowless.

Dawlie, *adj.* slow of movement.

Dawmer, *v.* to stupefy. Cf. Daumer.

Dawner, *v.* to stroll, saunter. Cf. Dander.

Dawpit, *ppl. adj.* having lost mental vigour.

Dawsie, *adj.* constitutionally stupid or inactive.

Dawt, *v.* to caress; to pet. Cf. Daut.

Dawtie, *n.* a darling, pet.

Day-aboot, *n. phr.* alternate days; an equal footing; 'tit for tat.'

Day an' daily, *phr.* every day.

Day an' way o't, *phr.* self-support; daily payment of one's way.

Day-darger, *n.* a day-labourer.

Day-daw, -dawin, *n.* the dawn.

Day-levcl, *n.* a mine bored to some point lower than the workings, to which the water was carried by gravitation.

Dayligaun, *n.* twilight. Cf. Dailygone.

Day-lily, *n.* the asphodel.

Day-nettle, *n.* the dead-nettle; a whitlow, a gathering on the finger.

Days, *n.* a curling term : in *phr.* 'gi'e him days,' do everything right to keep the stone running.

Day-set, *n.* nightfall.

Day-sky, *n.* daylight; daybreak; the appearance of the sky at daybreak or twilight.

Daze, *v.* to stupefy with drink, bemuddle; to wither, spoil, or rot.—*n.* the powder of stone when bruised by chisel or pickaxe. Cf. Daise.

Dazed, *ppl. adj.* stupid, foolish-looking.

Dazie, *adj.* used of the weather : cold, raw, sunless. Cf. Daisie.

Dazzle, *v.* to daze, stupefy.

Dazzly, *adj.* dazzling.

Deacon, *n.* a head-workman; a master or chairman of a trade-guild; an adept, expert, proficient.

Deaconry, *n.* the office of a 'deacon'; a trade-guild under a 'deacon.'

Dead, *v* to strike. Cf. Dad.

Dead, *adj.* exact; stagnant; flat; stale, unprofitable, yielding no interest; of bowls, quoits, &c. : equidistant from the 'tee.'—*n.* death; the cause of death, a mortal injury or sickness : in *pl.* quoits, bowls, &c. equidistant from the 'tee'; coarse soil from the bottom of a ditch.—*adv.* quite, exceedingly.

Deadal, *n.* death. Cf. Dead-ill.

Dead and gone, *phr.* dead and buried.

Dead-auld, *adj.* extremely old.

Dead-bell, *n.* the passing-bell; the funeral bell; singing in the ears as an omen of death.

Dead-candle, *n.* phosphorescent light, will-o'-the-wisp, as an omen of death.

Dead-chack, *n.* the sound made by a woodworm in houses, regarded as an omen of death.

Dead-chack, *n.* the dinner formerly prepared for the magistrates of a burgh after a public execution.

Dead-chap, *n.* a sharp stroke heard, as an omen of death.

Dead-chest, *n.* a coffin.

Dead-claes, *n.* shroud, winding-sheet.

Dead-days, *n.* the days during which a corpse remained unburied, and no ploughing or opening of the earth was allowed on a farm.

Dead-deaf, *adj.* quite deaf.

Dead-deal, -dale, *n.* the board used for measuring and lifting a corpse.

Dead-dole, *n.* a dole formerly given at a funeral.

Dead-dour, *adj.* utterly immovable.

Dead-drap, *n.* a drop of water falling heavily and at intervals on a floor, as an omen of death.

Dead-gown, *n.* a winding-sheet; a part of the 'dead-clothes.'

Dead-hole, *n.* the grave.

Dead-house, *n.* a mortuary; a grave.

Dead-ill, *n.* a mortal illness; a deadly hurt, a fatal injury.—*adj.* sick with a mortal illness.

Deadily, *n.* a boys' game, when one with clasped hands has to run and catch others.

Dead-kist, *n.* a coffin.

Dead-knack, *n.* a stroke as of a switch upon the door or bed, the cause of which is unknown, as an omen of death.

Dead-knell, *n.* a death-knell.

Dead-licht, *n.* a 'corpse-candle'; phosphorescence, supposed to appear in graveyards; the *ignis-fatuus.*

Dead-lift, *n.* help at a pinch; a difficulty; a dilemma; a crisis.

Dead-looks, *n.* signs on the face of the nearness of death.

Dead-lown, *adj.* used of the atmosphere: in a dead calm, quite still.

Deadly, *adj.* death-like, lifeless.

Deadman's-bell, *n.* the passing-bell.

Deadman's-creesh, *n.* the water-hemlock.

Deadman's-paps, *n.* the star-fish *Alcyonium digitatum.*

Deadman's-sneeshin, *n.* the dust o the common puff-ball.

Deadmen's-bells, *n.* the purple foxglove.

Dead-nip, *n.* a blue mark on the body ascribed to necromancy, and regarded as ominous; a sudden and effectual check to one.

Dead-picture, *n.* an exact likeness.

Dead-rattle, -ruckle, *n.* the sound made by a dying person.

Dead-set, *n.* the fixed expression of the eye in death.—*adj.* quite determined on.

Dead-sheet, -shroud, *n.* a death-shroud.

Dead-spale, *n.* the grease of a candle which falls over the edge in a semicircular form, called 'a winding-sheet,' and is regarded as a premonition of death.

Dead-swap, *n.* a sharp stroke, supposed to be ominous of death.

Dead-sweer, -swear, *adj.* utterly lazy; extremely unwilling.

Dead-thraw, *n.* the death-throes; *phr.* 'in the deid-thraw,' used of fish : not fresh; of things cooked : neither hot nor cold when served.

Dead-watch, *n.* the death-watch, or 'dead-chack,' a ticking thought to presage death.

Deaf, *adj.* used of grain : having lost the power to germinate; of shell and kernelled fruit : empty, without a kernel; of soil: flat.

Deaf-nit, *n.* a woman without money.

Deaister, *n.* a hurricane. Cf. Doister.

Deal, *n.* a periodic dole ; the time at which it is given.

Deal, *n.* a portion of land. Cf. Dail.

Deal, *n.* the stretching-board for a dead body

Deam, *n.* a young woman. Cf. Dame, Deem.

Deamie, *n.* a girl.

Dean, *n.* a deep wooded valley; a small valley; a hollow where the ground slopes on both sides.

Dear be here, Dear keep's, Dear kens, Dear knows, Dear sake, *int.* various excls. of surprise, sorrow, pity, &c.

Dearie, *n.* a sweetheart, a darling.

Dear-meal-cart, *n.* a farmer's vehicle which came into use when high war-prices were got in the early part of the 19th century.

Dearth, *v.* to raise the price of anything.

Dearth-cap, *n.* a name given in the Carse of Gowrie to a fungus resembling a cup, containing a number of seeds, supposed to have got its name from the notion that it gave supply in a time of dearth.

Dearthful, *adj.* expensive, of high price.

Dear year, *n.* a year of great scarcity in the beginning of the 19th century.

†Deas, *n.* a turf seat on the outside, or in the porch of a cottage; a long wooden settle, convertible into a bed, seat, or table ; a pew. Cf. Dais.

Deasie, *adj.* used of the weather: cold, raw, uncomfortable. **Cf. Daisie.**

Deasil, Deasoil, *n.* walk or movement with the sun from east to west.

Death, *n.* in *phr.* 'to be going to death with a thing,' to be quite positive and sure about it. Cf. Dead.

Death-candle, *n.* a corpse-candle.

Death-chap, *n.* a knocking ominous of death.

Death-deal, *n.* a stretching-board for a corpse.

Death-dwam, *n.* a death-swoon or faint.

Death-hamper, *n.* a long basket made of rushes, used for funerals formerly in some parts of the Highlands.

Death-ill, *n.* a mortal illness.

Deathin, *n.* the water-hemlock.

Death-ruckle, *n.* the death-rattle.

Death-sang, *n.* a banshee's song, supposed to portend death.

Death-shank, *n.* a thin leg like that of a dead person.

Death-shut, *adj.* closed in death.

Death's-mailin, *n.* a burial-ground.

Death-sough, *n.* the last breath of a dying person.

Death-swap, *n.* a knock betokening the nearness of death.

Death-trouble, *n.* a mortal illness.

Death-weed, *n.* a shroud.

Death-yirm, *n.* the phlegm that causes the death-rattle.

Deave, *v.* to deafen, stun with noise; to worry, bother.

Deave, *v.* used of pain : to mitigate, lessen, deaden. Cf. Dave.

Deavesome, *adj.* deafening.

Deaving, *n.* deafening noise.

Deaw, *v.* to drizzle.

Debait, *v.* to cease eating after having had enough ; to cease.

Debait, Debate, *n.* a fight, struggle for existence, &c.

Debaitless, *adj.* without spirit or energy to struggle ; 'feckless'; helpless.

Debateable, *adj.* able to shift for one's self ; energetic.

†Debaurd, *n.* departure from the right way. —*v.* to go beyond proper bounds or to excess.

†Debaush, *v.* to debauch or seduce a woman. Cf. Debosh.

Debitor, *n.* debtor.

†Debord, *n.* excess.—*v.* to go beyond bounds or to excess.

Debording, *n.* excess.

†Debosh, *n.* excessive indulgence ; extravagance, waste ; a debauch ; one who over-indulges himself.—*v.* to indulge one's self to excess. Cf. Debaush.

Deboshed, *ppl. adj.* debauched, worthless.

Deboshing, *ppl. adj.* wasteful ; given over to excessive indulgence.

Deboshrie, *n.* a debauch, waste, excessive indulgence.

†Debout, *v.* to thrust from.

Debritch, *n.* debris.

Debt, *n.* in *phr.* 'to come in the debt,' to break, destroy, make an end of.

Debtfull, *adj.* due, indebted.

Debuck, *v.* to prevent any design from being carried through ; used chiefly in the game of 'nine-pins.'

Debuction, *n.* the loss of thirteen to a player at 'nine-pins' if he knocks down more pins than make up the number required in the game.

†Deburse, *v.* to disburse.

Debursing, *n.* disbursement.

†Debush, *n.* excessive indulgence, debauch.— *v.* to indulge to excess. Cf. Debosh.

†Debushens, *n.* dismissal from a situation, &c.

Decanter, *n.* a jug.

Decay, *n.* consumption, 'a decline.'

Decedent, *n.* one who demits an office.

Deceive, *n.* a deception.

Deceiverie, *n.* a habit or course of deception.

Decency, *n.* a respectable way of living.

Decent, *adj.* satisfactory for one's position, &c., tolerable, good enough.

Decern, *v.* to adjudge, decree, determine.

Decerniture, *n.* a decree or judgment of court.

Dech, *v.* to build with turfs. Cf. Deigh.

Dechlit, *ppl.* wearied and wayworn.

Declarator, *n.* a legal or authentic declaration ; an action with that object.

Declinable, *adj.* used of a witness : that may be rejected as incompetent.

Declination, *n.* a courteous refusal.

Declinature, *n.* an act declining the jurisdiction of a judge or court.

Decline, *n.* consumption, phthisis ; the end.

†Decoir, Decore, *v.* to decorate, adorn.

Decorement, Decorament, *n.* decoration.

Decourt, *v.* to dismiss from court.

Decreet, *n.* a decree ; final judicial sentence.

Dede, *n.* death.—*adj.* dead. Cf. Dead.

Dee, *v.* to die.

Dee, *n.* a dairymaid. Cf. Dey.

Dee, *v.* to do.

Deeble, *v.* to dibble.—*n.* a dibble.

Deece, *n.* a long settle used as a bed, &c. Cf. Dais.

Deed, *adj.* dead.

Deed, *n.* in *phr.* 'by' or 'upo' my deed,' surely, certainly.—*int.* an excl. of confirmation or interrogation ; indeed !

Deed-doer, *n.* the doer of a deed ; perpetrator.

Deedin, *v.* to deaden.

Deeding, *n.* the act of making a deed or contract.

Deedle, *n.* 'deid-ill'; mortal injury or sickness. Cf. Dead-ill.

Deedle, *v.* to dandle, as an infant ; to train an infant ; to sing in a low tone, hum an air without the words. Cf. Doodle.

Deedle-doodle, *n.* a meaningless song ; a badly played tune.

Deedley-dumplin', *n.* a term of endearment to an infant.

Deeds, *n.* coarse soil or gravel taken from the bottom of a ditch. Cf. Dead.

Deeds I, -aye, *phr.* yes, indeed !

Deedy, Deedie, *adj.* given to doing ; *gen.* in *phr.* 'ill-deedie,' mischievous.

Dee-er, *n.* a doer.

Deef, *adj.* deaf.

Deefen, *v.* to deafen.

†Deek, *v.* to spy out, descry.

Deem, *n.* a young woman. Cf. Dame.

Deem, *v.* to judge ; to estimate.

Deemer, *n.* one who forms an estimate of another's conduct or intentions.

Deemes, Deemas, *n* a great sum.—*adj.* great. —*adv.* exceedingly. Cf. Dooms.

Deemie, *n.* a young girl. Cf. Deamie.

Deemster, *n.* a judge ; the official of a court who used to proclaim formally its sentence on the prisoner at the bar.

Deen, *adv.* extremely. Cf. Doon.

Deen, *ppl.* done.

Deen out, *adj.* exhausted.—

Deep, *adj.* clever, crafty.—*n.* the deepest part of a river, the channel.

Deep-draucht, *n.* a crafty circumvention.

Deep-drauchtit, *adj.* designing, artful.

Deepen, *v.* to take soundings.

Deepens, *n.* depth.

Deepin, *n.* a fishing-net. Cf. Dipin.

Deepin-weaver, *n.* a net-weaver.

Deeply-sworn, *adj.* solemnly sworn.

Deepooperit, *ppl.* weak, worn-out in body or mind ; impoverished, depauperated.

Deep-sea-buckie, *n.* the *Murex corneus.*

Deep-sea-crab, *n.* the spider-crab.

Deer-, Deer's-hair, *n.* the heath club-moss.

Deester, *n.* a 'doer,' agent.

Dee't, *v. pret.* died.

Deeve, *v.* to deafen. Cf. Deave.

Deeve, *v.* to deaden pain. Cf. Dave.

Deevil, *n.* the devil, a devil. Cf. Deil.

Deevilick, Deeviluck, *n.* a little imp or devil.

Deevilish, *adj.* extraordinary, wonderful, super-natural.—*adv.* used intensively.

Deeze, *v.* to stupefy. Cf. Daise.

Defaisance, *n.* defeasance.

†Defait, Defeat, *ppl. adj.* defeated ; exhausted by sickness or fatigue.

†Defalk, *v.* to resign a claim ; to do without payment ; to deduct.

Defalt, *v.* to adjudge as culpable.

Defame, *v.* to report guilty.

Defeekulty, *n.* difficulty.

Defence, *n.* confidence in possessing the means of defence.

Defend, *v.* to ward off, keep off a blow ; to forbid, prevent.

Defendant, *adj.* in *phr.* 'degrees defendant,' the forbidden degrees.

Defenn, *n.* dirt.

Defett, *ppl. adj.* defeated ; exhausted. Cf. Defait.

Deficient, *adj.* failing in duty.

Deforce, *n.* deforcement ; violent ejection or seizure.

Deforcer, *n.* a ravisher, one who commits rape.

Deform, *n.* a deformed person.

Defraud, *n.* a fraud, the act of defrauding.

Deft, *adj.* bold.

Deftly, *adv.* fitly, properly ; handsomely.

Deg, *v.* to strike smartly with a sharp-pointed weapon ; to pierce or indent with a sharp-pointed instrument.—*n.* a sharp blow or stroke ; the hole or indentation made by a pointed instrument.—*adv.* 'slap,' 'bang.'

Deg, *n.* a pistol. Cf. Dag.

Degener, *v.* to degenerate.

Degger, *n.* one who 'degs.'

Degust, *n.* disgust.

Dei, *n.* a dairymaid. Cf. Dey.

Deid, *n.* death ; pestilence.—*ppl. adj.* dead. Cf. Dead.

Deid's pairt, *n.* that portion of his movable estate which a person deceased had a right to dispose of before his death in whatsoever way he pleased.

Deid-wed, *n.* a mortgage.

Deigh, *v.* to build with turfs.

Deighle, *n.* a simpleton.

Deil, *n.* devil.

Deil a bit, *phr.* nothing at all ; not at all.

Deil a mony, *phr.* not many.

Deil-be-lickit, *phr.* nothing at all.

Deil-blaw-lickit, *phr.* nothing at all.

Deil fitchit, *phr.* an emphatic kind of negation.

Deil gin, *phr.* would to the devil that.

Deil haet, *phr.* nothing at all.

Deil-in-a-bush, *n.* the herb paris.

Deil-in-the-bush, *n.* love-in-a-mist, *Nigella damascena.*

Deil-ma-care, *adj.* utterly careless.—*adv.* no matter.

Deil-mal- matter, *adj.* careless.—*adv.* no matter.

Deil-o'-me, *phr.* not I ; never for my part.

Deil-perlicket, *phr.* nothing at all.

Deilry, *n.* devilry.

Deil's apple-rennie, *n.* the wild camomile.

Deil's apple-trees, *n.* the sun-spurge.

Deil's barley, *n.* the crimson stone-crop.

Deil's beef-tub, *n.* a roaring linn.

Deil's bird, *n.* the magpie.

Deil's bit, *n.* the blue scabious.

Deil's books, *n.* playing-cards.

Deil's buckie, *n.* an imp; a mischievous youth.

Deil's butterfly, *n.* the tortoise-shell butterfly.

Deil's cup, *n.* strong drink.

Deil's darning-needle, *n.* the dragon-fly; the shepherd's needle.

Deil's dirt, *n.* asafœtida.

Deil's dizzen, *n.* thirteen.

Deil's dog, *n.* any strange black dog met at night.

Deil's dung, *n.* asafœtida.

Deil's elshin, *n.* the shepherd's needle.

Deil's-gut, *n.* the wild convolvulus.

Deil's guts, *n.* various species of *Cuscuta.*

Deil's kirnstaff, *n.* the petty spurge, the sun-spurge.

Deil's limb, *n.* an imp; a tiresome or trouble-some youth.

Deil's mark, *n.* marks crescent-wise arranged on the lower part of a pig's foreleg.

Deil's metal, *n.* mercury.

Deil's milk, *n.* the white milky sap of the dandelion and other plants.

Deil's milk-plant, *n.* the dandelion.

Deil speed one, *phr.* a form of imprecation.

Deil's pet, *n.* an imp; a mischievous youth.

Deil's picture-, -painted-books, *n.* playing-cards.

Deil's pots and pans, *n.* holes in the bed of a stream, caused by stones carried down and boiling in flood-time.

Deil's putting-stones, *n.* perched boulders.

Deil's snuff-box, *n.* the common puff-ball.

Deil's sowen-bowie, *n.* a children's game.

Deil's spadefu's, *n.* natural heaps or hummocks of sand or gravel.

Deil's specs, *n.* 'cup and ring' marks.

Deil's spoons, *n.* the water-plantain; the broad-leaved bindweed.

Deil's toddy, *n.* punch made with hot whisky instead of water.

Deil's wind, *n.* a winnowing-machine.

Deil-tak-him, *n.* the yellow-hammer.

Deir, *v.* to be afraid; to terrify. Cf. Dare.

Deis, *n.* a long settle, table, pew, turf seat, &c. Cf. Deas.

Deisheal, *adv.* with the sun, from east to west. Cf. Deasil.

†Dejeune, *n.* breakfast.

Delash, *v.* to discharge, let fly.

†Delator, *n.* an informer, accuser.

Delaverly, *adv.* freely, continuously. Cf. Deliverly.

Deleer, Deleir, Deler, Delier, *v.* to intoxicate, render delirious.

Deleerin', *ppl. adj.* maddening.

Deleerit, *ppl.* gone mad, out of one's senses.

Deleeritness, *n.* madness; delirium.

Delf, *n.* a pit, a quarry; the mark of an animal's foot in soft ground; a sod or cut turf; a large space cut into turfs; a peat-hag.—*v.* to cut mould, clay, &c. in large lumps.

Delf-house, *n.* a pottery.

Delfin, *adj.* made of earthenware.

Delf-ware, *n.* earthenware, crockery.

Delgin, *n.* the stick used in binding sheaves. Cf. Dally.

Delicate, *n.* a delicacy, a luxury, a dainty.

Delichtsome, *adj.* delightful.

†Delict, *n.* a misdemeanour.

Deliverly, *adv.* nimbly; continually. Cf. Delaverly.

Dell, *n.* the goal in boys' games.

Dell, *v.* to dig, labour with a spade, delve.

Delt, *v.* to fondle, treat or spoil with great kindness; to delight in; to toy amorously.

Delting, *ppl.* spoiling with kindness.

Deltit, *ppl. adj.* spoiled with kindness; treated with great care; petted.

Deltit, *ppl. adj.* hid from public view; used of the retired habits of one devoted to a literary life.

Delve, *v.* to hide, insert; to work hard, drudge.

Dem, *v.* to dam water; to stop the inrush of flood-water.

†Demean, Demaine, Demane, Demayne, *v.* to treat any one in a particular way; to ill-treat; to punish by cutting off a hand.

Demeans, *n.* lands, demesnes.

†Demelle, *n.* a rencontre.

†Demellit, *ppl.* hurt, injured.

†Demellitie, *n.* a hurt; the effects of a dispute.

†Demember, *v.* to deprive of a bodily member.

Demembration, *n.* mutilation; the act of 'demembering.'

Dementation, *n.* a state of derangement.

Dementit, *ppl. adj.* distracted, crazy; stupid, nonsensical.

Dem-fow, *adj.* quite full. Cf. Dem.

Demit, *v.* to dismiss, permit to go.

Demmish, *v.* to stun by blow or fall. Cf. Dammish.

Demous, *adj.* great. Cf. Dooms.

Demple, *n.* a potato-dibble.

Dempster, *n.* a judge; an officer of court who pronounces doom. Cf. Deemster.

†Demur, *n.* a plight.

Den, *n.* a glen, dell, ravine; the 'home' in boys' games; the forecastle of a decked fishing-boat; the place where the scythe is laid into the sned.—*v.* to hide, lurk in a den; to run to cover. Cf. Dean.

Den-fire, *n.* the fire in a decked fishing-boat.

Dengle, *v.* to quiver with pain; to throb. Cf. Dangle.

Denk, *adj.* neat, trim; precise, nice; saucy. —*v.* to deck, dress neatly or finely. Cf. Dink.

Denner, *n.* dinner; *phr.* 'little denner,' a repast taken before the usual breakfast by those who rise earlier in the morning than usual.—*v.* to have or give dinner.

Denner-piece, *n.* a workman's lunch, a substitute for dinner at home.

Dennle, *v.* to quiver with pain. Cf. Dengle.

Denrick, *n.* a smoke-board for a chimney.

Densaix, *n.* a Danish axe, a Lochaber axe.

Denshauch, *adj.* hard to please, nice in regard to food.

Den-stair, *n.* the stair in a decked fishing-boat.

Dent, Denta, *n.* affection, regard. Cf. Daintie.

Dent, *n.* a tough clay, soft clay-stone.

Dentelion, *n.* dandelion.

Dentice, *n.* a dainty. Cf. Daintess.

Dentis, *int.* just so; very well; no matter; an expression of indifference. Cf. Dainta.

Denty, *adj.* large; plump; comely; pleasant. Cf. Dainty.

Denty-lion, *n.* dandelion.

Denum, *v.* to confound, used as an imprecation; to stupefy by much talking.

Denumm't, *ppl. adj.* confounded.

Deny, *v.* to refuse, decline.

Depairt, *v.* to die; to part, divide.

Depart, *n.* departure.

Departal, *n.* death; *phr.* 'to take one's departal,' to die.

Departure, *n.* death.

Depauper, *v.* to impoverish. Cf. Deepooperit.

Deplorat, *ppl. adj.* deplorable.

Depone, *v.* to deposit; to depose, give evidence as witness.

Deponent, *n.* a witness.

Depositat, *v.* to lay aside.

Depurse, *v.* to disburse.

Depursement, *n.* disbursement.

Deputation, *n.* the act or deed of appointing a deputy.

Depute, *n.* a deputy.—*adj.* deputed.

†Deray, *n.* disorder, uproar; a festive crowd, boisterous mirth.

Derb, *n.* common marble.

Dere, *v.* to terrify, to fear. Cf. Dare.

Dere, *v.* to affect, make an impression.—*n.* injury.

†Deregles, *n.* loose habits, irregularities; deceptions, fraudulent informations.

Derf, Derff, *adj.* bold, vigorous; unbending, sullen, taciturn; massive, capable of giving a severe blow; hard, cruel.

Derfly, *adv.* boldly, fiercely, vigorously.

Dergy, *n.* a dirge; a funeral feast. Cf. Dirgie.

Derision, *n.* a practical joke.

Derk, *adj.* dark.

Derkening, *n.* twilight.

Derl, *n.* a broken piece of bread, cake, &c.; a rag.

Dern, *v.* to hide; to listen; to loiter at work; to muse, to think; with *behind*, to fall back. —*adj.* secret, obscure; dark, dreary, lonely, dismal.—*n.* darkness, secrecy.

Dern, *adj.* bold, daring; fierce, wild.—*adv.* boldly; fiercely.

Dern, *v.* to darn.

Derril, *n.* a broken piece of bread. Cf. Derl.

Derrin, *n.* a broad, thick cake or loaf of oat- or barley-meal, or of the flour of pease and barley mixed, baked in an oven or on a hearth covered with hot ashes.

Dert, *ppl. adj.* frightened, terrified. Cf. Dare.

Descrive, *v.* to describe.

Descriver, *n.* describer.

Designed, *ppl. adj.* disposed, inclined.

Desk, *n.* a precentor's desk; the name formerly given to that part of a church, near the pulpit, where baptism was administered.

Desperate, *adj.* irreclaimable, very bad; great, excessive.—*adv.* exceedingly, beyond measure.

Desperation, *n.* in *phr.* 'like desperation,' as if in despair.

Despite, *v.* to be filled with indignation.

Dess, *n.* a settle; a turf bench. Cf. Dais.

Destinate, *v.* to design.

Destructionfu', *adj.* destructive; wasteful.

Detfall, *adj.* due; obligatory.

Detort, *v.* to distort; to turn aside in retorting.

Deuch, *n.* a drink, a draught.

Deuch-an-dorach, *n.* a stirrup-cup; stark love and kindness. Cf. Doch-an-dorris.

Deug, *n.* a tall, tough man.

Deugind, *adj.* wilful, obstinate; litigious.

Deugle, *n.* anything long and tough.

Deugs, *n.* rags; shreds. Cf. Dewgs.

Deuk, *v.* a duck.

Deuk, *n.* a cover, shelter.

Deuk-dub, *n.* a duck-pond.

Deuks' faul, *n.* a dilemma.

Deule-weeds, *n.* mourning weeds. Cf. Dool, Dule.

†Devall, Devaill, Devaul, Devawl, Devald, Devalve, Devauld, *v.* to descend, to fall; to halt, cease.—*n.* a sunk fence; an inclined plane for a waterfall; a pause; cessation.

Devalling, Devalving, *n.* cessation, stop.

Devan, *n.* a large piece of turf or sod. Cf. Divan.

Deve, *v.* to deafen. Cf. Deave.

Devel, *v.* to stun with a blow, maul; to fall heavily.—*n.* a stunning blow. Cf. Davel.

Develer, *n.* a first-rate boxer; a dexterous young fellow.

Dever, *n.* a tumble, fall; a severe blow.—*v.* to stun, stupefy; to be stupid. Cf. Daiver.

Devilan, *n.* an insane person.

Devilick, Devilock, *n.* a little devil, an imp. Cf. Deevilick.

Devilish, *adj.* extraordinary. Cf. Deevilish.

Devilment, *n.* wickedness.

Devilry, *n.* communication with the devil.

Deviltry, *n.* mischief, devilry, wickedness; communication with the devil, witchcraft.

Devle, Devvel, *v.* to stun with a blow. Cf. Devel.

Devol, *v.* to deviate.

Dew, *n.* whisky.—*v.* to rain slightly.

Dew-cup, *n.* the ladies' mantle.

Dew-droukit, *adj.* drenched with dew.

Dewgs, *n.* rags, shreds, scraps of cloth.

Dew-piece, *n.* a little food taken early in the morning by a servant or worker before the regular breakfast.

Dew-wat, *adj.* dewy, wet with dew.

Dey, *n.* a dairymaid; a person in charge of a dairy, male or female.

Dey, *n.* a child's name for father.

Deyken, *n.* a deacon; an adept. Cf. Deacon.

Diacle, *n.* the compass used in a fishing-boat.

Diagram, *n.* the scale of working drawn up for each driver or fireman by the railway companies.

Dib, *n.* a small pool of water, a 'dub.'

Dibber-dabber, *n.* an uproar, wrangle.—*v.* to wrangle; to wriggle in argument.

Dibber-derry, *n.* a confused discussion.

Dibble-dabble, *n.* uproar, accompanied with violence.—*v.* to wrangle.

Dibbler, *n.* a large wooden platter.

Diblet, *n.* in *phr.* 'neither dish nor diblet,' no table-dishes whatever.

Dice, *n.* a small square or diamond shape; *phr.* 'box and dice,' the whole concern.— *v.* to sew a wavy pattern near the border of a garment; to weave in figures resembling dice; to do anything quickly and neatly.

Dice-board, *n.* a draught- or chess-board.

Dichel, Dichal, *n.* a bad scrape, 'pickle'; in *pl.* a scolding, drubbing.

Dichens, *n.* a beating, punishment.

Dichling, *n.* a beating, drubbing.

Dicht, *v.* to dress food; to wipe, to clean; to dry by rubbing; to sift grain; to handle a subject; to drub, beat; to dress one's self; to prepare for use; to put in order, tidy.— *n.* a wipe, a clean; a blow, beating.

Dichter, *n.* a winnower of grain.

Dichtings, *n.* refuse; the refuse of grain.

Dichty, *adj.* dirty, foul.

Dickie, *n.* filth, ordure.—*adj.* dirty.

†**Dickies,** *n.* a severe scolding. Cf. Dixie.

Dicky, *n.* the hedge-sparrow.

Dicky, *n.* in *phr.* 'up to dicky,' tip-top, up to date.

Dict, *v.* to dictate.

†**Dictionar,** *n.* a dictionary.

Diddle, *v.* to shake, jog; to move like a dwarf; to keep time with the feet to a tune; to jog up and down; to dance or walk with short, quick steps; to sway to and fro; to dandle, as one does a child.—*n.* a shake, a jog; a jingle of music.

Diddle, *n.* a swindle, fraud.

Diddle, *v.* to sing in a low tone without words.—*n.* a tune in a low key. Cf. Deedle.

Diddle, *v.* to busy one's self with trifles; to show great energy with little result.—*n.* trifling activity; a dawdler.

Diddler, *n.* a trickster, a cheat.

Diddler, *n.* a dawdler.

Diddler, *n.* a person who can hum a tune for others to dance to.

Diddling, *n.* fiddling; keeping time with the feet; dandling.

Diddling, *ppl. adj.* apparently busy; untrustworthy.

Die, *n.* a toy, plaything, gewgaw.

Died, *n.* a meal, diet.

Diel, *n.* devil. Cf. Deil.

Dien-done, *adj.* quite done.

Diet, *n.* an excursion, journey; the meeting of an ecclesiastical assembly; the fixed day for holding a market; the stated time of public worship, &c.

Diet-book, *n.* a diary.

Diet-loaf, *n.* a large sponge-cake.

Diet-time, *n.* meal-time.

Diffame, *v.* to defame. Cf. Defame.

Differ, *v.* to separate, cause difference between.—*n.* difference, a misunderstanding.

Differ, *v.* to defer, yield to.

Difference, *v.* to differentiate.

Differr, *v.* to delay, procrastinate.

†**Difficil,** *adj.* difficult; reluctant.

Difficult, *v.* to perplex; to render difficult.

Diffide, *v.* to distrust.

Digaal, *n.* a bad scrape; an awkward fix. Cf. Dichel.

Dig-for-silver, *n.* a children's singing game.

Diggot, *n.* a contemptuous name given to a child, implying some dishonourable action.

Dight, *adv.* properly, fitly.

Dight, *v.* to winnow corn; to prepare. Cf. Dicht.

Dighter, *n.* a winnower of grain. Cf. Dichter.

†**Digne,** *adj.* worthy.

Dignities, *n.* dignitaries.

†**Dignosce,** *v.* to distinguish.

Dike, *n.* a wall; a vein of whinstone traversing coal-strata; a causeway or track; a fault or fissure in the stratum.—*v.* to dig, to pick with a pick-axe, &c.; to build a 'dike'; to fence in with a 'dike'; *phr.* 'dike inhauld,' to enclose within walls or ramparts.

Dike-end, *n.* a 'dike' built on the ebb-shore, running seaward, to cut off access to the arable land through the ebb, and thus prevent cattle from trespassing.

Dike-hopper, *n.* the wheatear.

Dike-king, *n.* the game of 'rax,' as played by boys.

Dike-louper, *n.* an animal given to leaping fences; an immoral person, a transgressor.

Dike-loupin', *ppl. adj.* fence-breaking, that cannot be kept within fences; loose, immoral.

Dike-queen, *n.* the game of 'rax' as played by girls.

Diker, *n.* a builder of 'dikes.'

Dike-sheugh, *n.* a narrow trench or ditch alongside a 'dike.'

Dike-tip, *n.* the top of a 'dike.'

Dikie, *n.* a low wall, a small ditch; in *phr.* 'to loup the dikie,' to die.

Dilate, *v.* to accuse, delate.

Dilator, *n.* an informer, accuser.

Dilature, *n.* legal postponement, delay.

Dilder, *v.* to shake, jerk; to dribble, ooze, trickle, glide; to trifle, waste time, work carelessly.—*n.* a smart jerk, a jolt.

Dildermot, *n.* an obstacle, a great difficulty.

Diled, *ppl. adj.* stupid; crazed. Cf. Doilt.

Dileer, *v.* to intoxicate. Cf. Deleer.

Dileerious, *adj.* extremely foolish. Cf. Deleer.

†Diligence, *n.* a writ of execution; a warrant to enforce the attendance of witnesses or the production of documents.

Dilip, *n.* a legacy.

Dill, *v.* to conceal; to calm; to assuage, remove; with *down*, to subside, die down.

Dill, *v.* to flap, shake loosely.

Dillagate, *n.* a delicacy, a dainty. Cf. Delicate.

Dillow, *n.* a noisy quarrel.

Dilly, Dilly-castle, *n.* a boys' name for a sand-castle on the beach, on which they stand till it is washed away.

Dilly-dally, *n.* an indolent woman.

Dilly-daw, *n.* one who is slow and slovenly.

Dilmont, *n.* a two-year-old wedder. Cf. Dinmont.

Dilp, *n.* a trollop, a thriftless housewife; a heavy, lumpish person.—*v.* to walk with long steps; to stalk.

Dilse, *n.* dulse, an edible seaweed.

Dilser, *n.* the rock- or field-lark.

Dim, *n.* midsummer twilight between sunset and sunrise.

Dimit, *v.* to pass into; to terminate.

Dimment, *n.* a wedder of the second year, or from the first to the second shearing. Cf. Dinmont.

Dimple, *v.* to indent, make an impression; used of a stream: to ripple, not to flow still or sluggishly.

Din, *n.* report, fame; loud talking.

Din, *adj.* dun, dingy, sallow.—*n.* a dun colour.

Dine, *n.* dinner.

†Ding, *adj.* worthy.

Ding, *v.* to smash, beat to powder; to overcome; to excel; to discourage, vex; to drive; to dash down; to cut bark in short pieces for the tanner; of rain: to fall heavily or continuously.—*n.* a blow.

Ding, *v.* used imprecatively.

Ding-dang, *adv.* in rapid succession; ding-dong; pell-mell, helter-skelter.—*n.* noise, clatter, confusion.

Dinge, *v.* to indent, bruise.—*n.* an indentation, a bruise.

Dinging, *n.* a beating.

Dinging on, *ppl.* raining heavily.

Dingle, *v.* to jingle.

Dingle, *v.* to draw together.—*n.* the state of being drawn together, a group, gathering.

Dingle, *v.* to dangle; to vibrate, resound, tremble; to tingle, thrill.

Dingle-dangle, *adv.* swaying to and fro or from side to side.

Dingle-dousie, -douzie, *n.* a stick ignited at one end, swung about by a child in play; a jack-in-the-box.

Dingle't, *adj.* stupid, stupefied.

Ding-me-yavel, *phr.* lay me flat, used as an expletive.

Dink, *n.* a dint, indentation, bruise.—*v.* to sit down with a bang.

Dink, *adj.* neat, finely dressed; dainty, nice, squeamish.—*v.* to deck, adorn, dress up.

Dinkie, *adj.* neat, trim.

Dinkly, *adv.* neatly.

Dinle, *v.* to shake, vibrate, tremble; to tingle with cold or pain; to cause to shake.—*n.* vibration; a thrilling blow, a tingling sensation; a slight sprain; a vague report; a slight noise.

Dinlin', *ppl. adj.* rattling. — *n.* a tingling sensation.

Din-luggit, *adj.* having dun-coloured ears.

Dinmont, *n.* a wedder from the first to the second shearing.

Dinna, Dinnae, *v. neg.* do not.

Dinna good, *adj.* worthless morally.

Dinna gude, *n.* a disreputable person past all hope of doing good.

Dinnel, Dinnle, *v.* to vibrate; to tingle. Cf. Dinle.

Dinnen-skate, *n.* the young of the fish *Raia batis.*

Dinner, *v.* to dine. Cf. Denner.

Dinness, *n.* sallowness.

Dinnous, *adj.* noisy.

Dint, *n.* a blow, shock, impression; a momentary opportunity. —*v.* used of fairies: to injure cattle, elf-shoot.

Dint, *n.* affection. Cf. Dent.

Dintle, *n.* a thin species of leather.

Diocy, *n.* a diocese.

Dip, *n.* a fluid for dipping sheep to kill vermin.—*v.* to dip sheep in that fluid ; to sit down ; with *in,* to join at intervals in a conversation ; with *upon* or *on,* to deal with, discuss ; to concern, approximate to.

Dipin, *n.* part of a herring-net ; the bag of a salmon-net.

Dippen, *n.* the stairs at a river-side.

Dipper, *n.* a Baptist.

Dipping, *n.* a mixture of boiled oil and grease used by curriers to soften leather.

Dipthaery, *n.* diphtheria.

Dird, *n.* a blow, onslaught, an achievement. —*v.* to beat, thump, dump, dash.—*adv.* with violence, heavily.

Dirder, *n.* a driver, whipper-in, dog-breaker.

Dirdoose, *v.* to hurt, to thump.

Dirdum, Dirdom, Dirdrim, *n.* a tumult ; damage ; passion, ill-humour ; a great noise, a noisy sport ; severe scolding ; blame ; a stroke, blow ; a squabble ; a woman that has been jilted ; in *pl.* ridicule, disgustful slanderings, twinges of conscience.

Dirdum-dardum, *n.* an expression of contempt for an action.

Dirdy-lochrag, *n.* the lizard.

Dirdy-wachle, *n.* the lizard.

Direck, *v.* to direct.—*adv.* directly.

Direction-book, *n.* a book of household recipes for cooking, &c.

†Dirgie, Dirige, *n.* a funeral feast ; a dirge.

Dirk, *adj.* thickset, strongly made. Cf. Durk.

Dirk, *v.* to grope in utter darkness.—*adj.* dark. Cf. Durk.

Dirl, *n.* a tremulous stroke ; a sharp stroke ; a blow ; a vibration ; a vibrating sound ; a thrill ; anxious haste, hurry ; a twinge of conscience ; a thrilling pleasure or pain of body or mind.—*v.* to pierce, drill ; to tingle, thrill ; to emit a tingling sound ; to move with the wind ; to vibrate noisily ; to produce loud vibrations ; to rattle ; to move briskly.

Dirler, *n.* a vibrating stick that strikes the large bolter of a mill.

Dirr, *adj.* torpid, benumbed ; insensible, destitute of physical or moral feeling.—*v.* to be benumbed ; to deaden pain by narcotics.

Dirr, *n.* a loud noise, 'racket.'

Dirray, *n.* disorder. Cf. Deray.

Dirt, *n.* a term of contempt, used for worthless persons or things, or troublesome children.

Dirt-bee, *n.* the yellow fly that haunts dunghills.

Dirten, *ppl.* fouled with excrement ; dirtied ; miry, mean, contemptible.

Dirten-allan, *n.* the Arctic gull, Richardson's skua.

Dirten-gab, *n.* a foul-mouthed person.

Dirtenly, *adv.* in a dirty way.

Dirt-fear, *n.* great, excessive fear affecting the intestines.

Dirt-feared, *adj.* in excessive fear.

Dirt-flee, *n.* the yellow fly that haunts dunghills ; a young woman who, after having long remained single from pride, at last makes a low marriage.

Dirt-fleyed, *adj.* in excessive fear.

Dirt-haste, *n.* extreme haste, as if the power of retention were lost.

Dirt-house, *n.* a close-stool ; a privy.

Dirtrie, *n.* despicable, good-for-nothing people.

Dirty, *adj.* used of weather : wet, stormy ; of land : infested with weeds ; mean, contemptible, paltry.

Dirty-allan, *n.* Richardson's skua.

Dirty-coal, *n.* pure coal mixed with shale, stones, &c.

Dirty-drinker, *n.* one who drinks alone and for the love of drinking.

Dis, *v.* does.

Disabeeze, Disabuse, *v.* to misuse, abuse ; to mar, spoil.—*n.* a stir, disturbance.

Disabil, *n.* dishabille ; untidiness.

Disagreeance, *n.* disagreement.

Disaguise, *v.* to disguise.

Disassent, *v.* to dissent, disapprove.

Disaster, *v.* to injure seriously ; to disgust.—*n.* disgust.

Disbust, *n.* an uproar, broil.

Discerne, *v.* to decree. Cf. Decerne.

Dischairge, *v.* to forbid, prohibit, charge not to do.

Disclamation, *n.* disclaiming one as the superior of lands ; refusing the duty which is the condition of tenure ; repudiation.

Discomfish, *v.* to discomfit, defeat.

Discomfist, *ppl.* overcome.

Discomfit, *v.* to put to inconvenience.

Disconform, Disconformed, *ppl. adj.* not conformable.

Discontigue, *adj.* not contiguous.

Disconvenience, *n.* an inconvenience.—*v.* to inconvenience.

Disconvenient, *adj.* inconvenient.

Discoursy, *adj.* conversable.

Discover, *v.* to uncover ; to take off one's hat.

Discreet, *adj.* civil, obliging, courteous, polite.

Discreetness, *n.* politeness, civility.

Discretion, *n.* courtesy, hospitality.

Discuss, *v.* to fight with a man-of-war.

Disdoing, *adj.* not thriving.

Diseirish, *v.* to disinherit, cast off ; to put in disorder through officious or improper meddling.

Disformed, *adj.* deformed.

Disfriendship, *n.* animosity, disaffection.

Disgeest, Disgest, *n.* digestion.—*v.* to digest.

Disgeester, *n.* digestion ; the stomach.

Disgushle, *v.* to distort by rheumatism, &c.; to warp by the action of heat.

Dish, *v.* to make the spokes of a wheel lie obliquely towards the axle ; used of a horse : to splay the forefeet in running ; to 'do for,' outwit, get the better of; with *out*, to serve a dish.

Dish, *v.* to push or thrust with horns, butt.

Dish, *v.* to rain heavily.

Dishabilitate, *v.* to incapacitate legally.

Dishabilitation, *n.* the act of rendering a child incapable of succeeding to a father's estate, titles, &c.

Dishalago, *n.* the tussilago or colt's-foot. Cf. Dishilago.

Dishaloof, *n.* a game of children and young people, played by placing hand above hand on a table, and removing in succession the lowermost and placing it on the uppermost.

Dishaunt, *v.* to cease to frequent, to forsake.

Dishaunter, *n.* a non-attender ; a non-frequenter of church, &c.

Dish-browed, *adj.* having a flat or hollow brow.

Dish-cloot, *n.* a cloth for washing dishes.

Disheart, *v.* to dishearten.

Disheartsum, *adj.* disheartening, saddening.

Disherys, Disherish, *v.* to disinherit. Cf. Diseirish.

Dish-faced, *adj.* having a flat or hollow face.

Dishilago, *n.* tussilago, colt's-foot.

Dishings, *n.* a beating.

Dishle, *v.* to move, run. Cf. Dissle.

Dish-man, *n.* a male hawker of crockery.

Dish-nap, *n.* a small tub for washing dishes.

Dishort, *n.* a deficiency, loss ; a disappointment ; an inconvenience ; a disadvantage ; mischief.

Dish o' want, *phr.* no food at all.

Dish-wash, *n.* dish-water ; thin, poor soup.

Dishy-lagy, *n.* colt's-foot. Cf. Dishilago.

Disjasket, *ppl. adj.* forlorn, dejected ; broken down ; exhausted.

Disjeest, *n.* digestion.—*v.* to digest.

†**Disjeune, Disjune, Disjoon**, *n.* breakfast. Cf. Dejeune.

Disk, *n.* a half-crown ; a piece of money.

Dislade, *v.* to unload.

Disload, Disloaden, *v.* to unload.

†**Dislock**, *v.* to dislocate.

Disna, *v. neg.* does not.

Disobedient, *n.* a disobedient person.

Disobligation, *n.* a disobliging action.

†**Dispach**, *v.* to drive out of.

†**Disparage**, *n.* disparity of rank.

Dispard, Dispart, Dispert, *adj.* keen ; violent ; incensed ; excessive.—*adv.* excessively.

Disparple, *v.* to scatter ; to be scattered ; to divide.

Displenish, *v.* to disfurnish ; to sell off goods, stock, &c. on leaving a farm.

Displenishing sale, *n.* a sale by auction of stock, implements, &c. on a farm.

Displinis, *n.* a displenishing sale.

Dispone, *v.* to convey to another in legal form ; to dispose ; to dispose of.

Disponee, *n.* the person to whom property is legally conveyed.

Disponer, *n.* the person who 'dispones' property.

Dispose, *n.* disposal.—*v.* with *upon*, to dispose of, deal with.

Disposition, *n.* a legal conveyance, a formal disposal of property ; deposition, forfeiture.

Dispurse, *v.* to disburse.

Dispute, *v.* to refuse.

Disremember, *v.* to forget.

Disrespeckit, *ppl.* unnoticed, neglected.

Dissipate, *v.* to disperse a gathering.

Dissle, *v.* to drizzle.—*n.* a drizzle ; wetness on standing corn, the effect of a slight rain.

Dissle, *n.* an attack.—*v.* to run, move.

Dist, *n.* dust ; the husk of grain, 'sids.'

†**Distan**, *v.* to distinguish.

Distance, *n.* difference, distinction.

Distant, *adj.* distinct.

Distinct, *adj.* definite, not discursive.

Distract, *v.* to go distracted ; to become mad.

Distrenzie, Distrinzie, *v.* to distrain.

Distressed, *ppl.* ill, disordered.

Distriction, *n.* distraint.

Distrubil, *v.* to disturb.

Disty, *adj.* dusty.

Disty-melder, *n.* the last quantity of meal made from a year's crop ; one's last end. Cf. Dusty-melder.

Dit, Ditt, *v.* to indulge, fondle, make much of.

Dit, Ditt, *v.* to close up, shut up ; to shut the mouth.

Ditch, *v.* to clean out a ditch.

Dite, *v.* to indite, compose ; to dictate to an amanuensis ; to point out as duty.

Ditement, *n.* anything indited or dictated by another.

Diting, *n.* composition, inditing, writing.

Dittay, Ditty, *n.* an indictment, legal accusation ; a scolding.

Ditty, *n.* a story.

Div, *v. aux.* do.

Divan, *n.* a large piece of turf or sod ; a big 'divot.'

Divan, *n.* a small wild plum or kind of sloe.

Divauld, *v.* to cease. Cf. Devall.

Dive, *n.* putrid moisture from the mouth, &c., of a person after death.

Dive, *v.* to deafen. Cf. Deave.

Dive, *v.* to plunge, hurry forward.

Diven't, *v. neg.* don't, do not?
Diver, *n.* a debtor, a scamp. Cf. Dyvour.
Diver, *n.* the pochard; the golden-eye.
Divert, *n.* an amusement, diversion, a diverting person.—*v.* to go out of one's way; to separate, live apart; to depart; to amuse.
Divet, *n.* a sod, a large piece of turf. Cf. Divot.
Divider, *n.* a soup-ladle.
Dividual, *adj.* individual, particular, identical, precise.
Divie-goo, *n.* the black-backed gull.
Diving-duck, *n.* the pochard, the golden-eye.
Divna, *v. neg.* do not.
Divnin', *v. neg.* do not?
†**Divor,** *n.* a debtor. Cf. Dyvour.
Divot, *n.* a thin, flat piece of sod, used as thatch; a lump; a clumsy, irregular mass of anything; a short, thick, stout person; a sod used as fuel; a broad, flat necktie.—*v.* to cut 'divots,' to cover with 'divots.'
Divot-cast, *n.* as much land as one 'divot' can be cut on.
Divot-dyke, *n.* a turf 'dike' or wall.
Divoted, *ppl. adj.* made or covered with 'divots.'
Divot-happit, *ppl. adj.* thatched or covered with 'divots.'
Divot-house, -hut, *n.* a turf-covered house or hut.
Divoting, *n.* cutting 'divots.'
Divot-seat, *n.* a seat made of 'divots.'
†**Dixie,** *n.* a severe scolding.—*v.* to scold severely. Cf. Dickies.
Dixie-fixie, *n.* a state of confinement in prison or in the stocks.
Dixiein, *n.* a severe scolding.
Dizen'd, *ppl.* bedizened.
Dizzen, *n.* a dozen; as much yarn as a woman might spin in a day, or a dozen 'cuts.'
Dizzy, *adj.* bemused, fuddled.
Do, *v.* to suffice; to have the effect of, cause. —*n.* a swindle.
Doach, Doagh, *n.* a salmon-weir or cruive.
Doak, *v.* to dock. Cf. Dock.
Doaver, *v.* to sleep lightly; to be half-asleep; to doze; to stun, stupefy.—*n.* a light slumber; semi-consciousness. Cf. Dover.
Dob, *n.* the razor-fish.
Dob, *v.* to peck as a bird; to prick.—*n.* a prick; a bird's peck.
Dobbie, Dobie, *n.* a fool, booby, clown.
Dobbie, *adj.* prickly.
Docas, *n.* a stupid fellow. Cf. Docus.
Doce down, *v.* to pitch down, pay down. Cf. Dossy.
Doch-an-dorris, *n.* the stirrup-cup, parting glass. Cf. Deuch-an-dorach.
Docher, *n.* fatigue, strain; injury; deduction.
Dochle, *n.* a dull, heavy person.

Dochlin, *adj.* soft, silly, foolish.
Docht, *v. pret.* could; availed.—*n.* power, ability. Cf. Douch, Dow.
Dochter, *n.* a daughter.
Dochterlie, *adj.* becoming a daughter.
Dochtless, *adj.* weak; worthless. Cf. Douchtless.
Dochtna, *v. neg.* could not.
Dochty, *adj.* strong; assuming; malapert.
Dochy, *adj.* used of ice: thawing, softening, 'drug.' Cf. Dauchy.
Dock, *v.* to deck, to make one's self look attractive; to shorten a baby's clothes; to abridge; to lessen wages or price; to cut the hair; to flog on the breech; to walk with short steps or in a conceited fashion. —*n.* a cutting of the hair; the breech; the peg of a top.
Docken, *n.* the dock; anything worthless.
Docker, *v.* to toil as in job-work.—*n.* a struggle. Cf. Dacker.
Docketie, *adj.* short, round, and jolly.
Dockie, *n.* a bad humour.
Dockit, *ppl. adj.* used of words: clipt, minced.
Dockle, *v.* to flog on the hips; to punish.
Dockus, *n.* anything very short. Cf. Docus.
Docky, *n.* a neat little person taking short steps.—*v.* to move with short steps.
Docky-doon, *n.* help in descending from a vehicle.
Doctor, *n.* an assistant-master in a high school. —*v.* to kill; to do one's business successfully.
Doctor-student, *n.* a medical student.
Doctory, *n.* doctoring.
Docus, *n.* a stupid fellow.
Docus, *n.* anything very short. Cf. Dockus.
Dod, Dodd, *n.* a slight fit of ill-temper; in *pl.* the sulks.—*v.* to sulk.
Dod, *n.* euphemism for 'God,' in excl.
Dod, *prop. n.* a familiar form of 'George.'
Dod, *n.* a soft, reddish marble.
Dodd, *v.* to be, or be made, hornless.
Dodd, *n.* a bare, round hill or fell.
Dodd, *v.* to jog; to jolt in trotting.
Dodder, *v.* to shake, tremble; to potter about, dawdle.
Doddered, *ppl. adj.* decayed.
Dodderment, *n.* one's deserts, recompense.
Doddle, *v.* to walk feebly, 'toddle'; with *about*, to wag, to move from side to side.
Doddle, *v.* to dandle a child. Cf. Doodle, Deedle.
Doddy, Doddie, *adj.* hornless; bald.—*n.* a hornless cow or ox.
Doddy, *adj.* sulky; surly; peevish; pettish.
Doddy, *prop. n.* a familiar form of 'George.'
Doddy-mitten, *n.* a worsted glove without separate divisions for the four fingers.
Dode, *n.* a slow person.

Dodge, *n.* a large cut or slice of food.

Dodge, *v.* to jog, trudge along.

Dodgel, *v.* to walk infirmly, hobble; to jog on.

Dodgel, *n.* a large piece, a lump; a lumpish person.

Dodgel-hem, *n.* the hem made by sewing down the edges of two pieces of cloth which have been run up in a seam; a 'splay' hem.

Dodger, *n.* a slow, easy-going person.

Dodgie, *adj.* thin-skinned, irritable.

Dodgill-, Dodjell-reepan, *n.* the meadow-rocket, supposed to produce love.

Dodle, *v.* to trouble, bother.

Dod-lip, *n.* a pouting lip.

Dodrum, *n.* a whim, fancy.

Dodsake, *int.* for God's sake.

Doe, *n.* the wooden ball used in 'shinty' or hockey.

Doeler, *n.* anything large; a large marble. Cf. Dollar.

Doer, *n.* a legal agent, steward, factor to a landlord.

Dofart, *adj.* stupid; dull; dismal.—*n.* a stupid, dull fellow. Cf. Dowfart.

Dog, *n.* a sawyer's implement to hold timber together; an iron implement, hook-shaped, for lifting stones; the trigger or hammer of a pistol; a blacksmith's lever used in horse-shoeing, &c.; a name given to various atmospheric appearances; a dog-fish; used in excl. and mild oaths.

Dog, *v.* with *up,* to wrangle, threaten to fight.

Dog-a-bit, *n.* a mild oath.

Dog-dirder, *n.* a caretaker of dogs.

Dog-dirt, *n.* ruin, bankruptcy.

Dog-dollar, *n.* a coin worth £2, 18s. Scots.

Dog-drave, -drive, -driving, *n.* ruin, bankruptcy.

Dog-drug, *n.* ruinous circumstances.

Dog-foolie, *n.* a sea-bird.

Dogger, *n.* a coarse ironstone.

Doggerlone, *n.* wreck, ruin.

Doggie-hillag, *n.* a small hillock with long grass.

Doggies, *n.* a child's feet.

Doggindales, *n.* clouds of mist clinging to hill-sides, betokening southerly winds.

Doggle, Dogle, *n.* a boys' common marble.

Doghead, *n.* the hammer of a firelock; the part of the lock that holds the flint.

Dog-hip, -hippin, *n.* the fruit of the dog-rose.

Dog-hole, *n.* an opening at the foot of a house-wall to give the dogs access.

Dog-hook, *n.* an instrument of sawyers, &c., for holding timber together or moving heavy logs.

Dog-ling, *n.* a young ling or cod.

Dog-luggit, *adj.* dog-eared.

Dog-nashicks, *n.* a species of gall-nut on the leaves of the trailing willow.

Dogont, *n.* a mild oath. Cf. Dagont.

Dog-rowan, *n.* the berry of the red elder.

Dog-rowan-tree, *n.* the red elder.

Dog-rung, *n.* one of the spars connecting the 'stilts' of a plough.

Dog's camovyne, *n.* weak-scented feverfew.

Dog's drift, *n.* ruin.

Dog's gowan, *n.* weak-scented feverfew.

Dog's helper, *n.* a person of mean appearance.

Dog's lug, *n.* a 'dog's-ear' in a book.

Dog's lugs, *n.* the foxglove.

Dogs ont, *n.* a mild oath. Cf. Dagont.

Dog's paise, *n.* the lady's fingers.

Dog's siller, *n.* the yellow rattle or cock's-comb; its seed-vessels.

Dog's tansy, *n.* the silver weed.

Dog-sure, *adj.* quite certain.

Dog's wages, *n.* food alone as wages for service.

Dog-thick, *adj.* very intimate.

Dog-tired, *adj.* very tired.

Dog-trot, *n.* a jog-trot, a steady pace.

Dog-winkle, *n.* the shell-fish *Purpura lapillus.*

Doichle, *n.* a dull, stupid person.—*v.* to walk in a dreamy, stupid state. Cf. Doychle.

Doid, *n.* a fool; a sot. Cf. Doit.

Doighlin, *n.* a drubbing.

Doil, *n.* a piece of anything, as bread.

Doilt, *adj.* stupid; crazed, confused.—*n.* a foolish man.

Doing, *ppl. phr.* 'to be doing,' to maintain the *status quo;* to make no change in one's procedure; to be content with; to bear with.

Doing, *n.* a friendly party or entertainment.

Doingless, *adj.* lazy, inactive.

Doing-off, -up, *n.* a scolding; a clearance of scores.

Doish, Doisht, *n.* a heavy blow, thump.

Doist, *n.* a sudden and noisy fall; the noise made by it.

Doister, *n.* a hurricane; storm from the sea; a strong, steady breeze.

Doistert, *ppl. adj.* confused; overwhelmed with surprise.

Doit, *n.* an obsolete copper coin of the value of one-twelfth of a penny sterling; a trifle, money; a small share or piece; a mite.

Doit, *n.* a species of rye-grass.

Doit, *n.* a fool, a numskull.—*v.* to grow feeble in mind; to walk stupidly, blunder along; to stupefy, puzzle.—*adj.* stupid, mazed.

Doited, *ppl. adj.* foolish, childish; stupefied; in dotage.

Doitelt, *ppl. adj.* enfeebled.

Doiter, *v.* to walk as if stupefied or indolent; to walk feebly or totter from old age; to dote; to become superannuated.

Doitered, *ppl. adj.* confused, stupid, imbecile.

Doitrified, *ppl. adj.* dazed, stupefied.

Doken, *n.* a dock. Cf. Docken.

Dolbert, *n.* a blockhead, a 'dunderhead.' Cf. Dulbart.

Doldie, *n.* a big, fat, clumsy person.

Doldrum, *n.* low spirits and ill-temper; anything very big.

Dole, *n.* fraud; a design to circumvent; malice.

Dole, *n.* misfortune. Cf. Dool.

Dole, *n.* a 'doxy.'

Dole-bread, *n.* bread given as a dole.

Doleful, *adj.* troublesome, vexatious.

Doler, *n.* anything large. Cf. Dollar.

Doless, *adj.* idle; thriftless; incapable; helpless. Cf. Dowless.

Dolf, *adj.* dull, melancholy; frivolous. Cf. Dowf.

Doll, *n.* a smartly dressed young woman; a term of affection; the 'harvest-maiden.' Cf. Maiden.

Doll, *n.* pigeons' dung.

Doll, *n.* a dole; a large lump of anything.

Dollar, *n.* a five-shilling piece; a small, thick biscuit; a boys' large marble, three or four times larger than an ordinary one; in *pl.* money.

Dollar-bake, *n.* a small, thick biscuit of the circumference of a crown-piece.

Doll in, *n. phr.* a call used by children to enter school.

Dollop, *n.* a lump, a large piece; 'the lot.'

Doll-wean, *n.* a doll.

Dolly, *n.* a silly, 'dressy' woman.—*adj.* silly, 'dressy.'

Dolly, *n.* an old-fashioned iron oil-lamp; a 'crusie.'

Dolly, *adj.* dull; spiritless; possessing no power of excitement; failing mentally through age in poetic composition. Cf. Dowie.

Dolly-oil, *n.* oil used for burning in a 'dolly'; oil of any kind.

Dolp, *n.* the posteriors; the end of a thing. Cf. Doup.

Doltard, *n.* a dolt; a dull, stupid fellow.

Dolver, *n.* anything large; a large apple; a large marble.

†Domage, *n.* damage.

Dome, *n.* a dwelling-place of any kind.

Domeror, *n.* a madman.

Domicils, *n.* household articles, excluding clothing.

Dominie, *n.* a slightly contemptuous name for a minister; a schoolmaster.

Don, *n.* an adept, proficient; a favourite; a leading spirit; an intimate acquaintance.

†Don, *n.* a gift.

Do-nae-better, *n.* a substitute, when one can find nothing better.

Do-nae-gude, *n.* one likely to do no good; a thoroughly worthless fellow.

Donal'-blue, *n.* the jelly-fish.

Donald, *n.* a glass of spirits.

Donald, *n.* the last small stack brought from the field to the cornyard.

Donar, *v.* to stupefy. Cf. Donner.

Donator, *n.* one who received an escheat.

Doncie, *n.* a booby, a clown. Cf. Donsie.

Done, *ppl.* and *ppl. adj.* outwitted; exhausted, tired; worn-out with fatigue, illness, old age, &c.

Donel, *n.* a glass of spirits. Cf. Donald.

Donie, *n.* a hare.

Donkey-beast, *n.* a donkey.

Donn'd, *ppl. adj.* fond, greatly attached.

Donner, Donnar, Donnor, *v.* to stupefy, stun.

Donner-bee, *n.* a bumble-bee, drum-bee.

Donnering, *ppl. adj.* walking stupidly.

Donnert, *ppl. adj.* in dotage; stupid, dazed.— *n.* a blockhead, fool.

Donnertness, *n.* stupidity.

Donnery, *n.* a clothes-moth.

Donnot, Donnat, Donot, *n.* a good-for-nothing person.

Donsie, *n.* a stupid, lubberly fellow.—*adj.* unlucky; weak, sickly; dull, stupid, heavy, dunce-like, dreamy; depressed.

Donsie, *adj.* neat, trim; affectedly neat, self-important; saucy, restive, testy.

Donsielie, *adj.* in poor health.

Dontibour, *n.* a courtesan.

Doo, *n.* a dove; a term of endearment.

Doo, *n.* an infant; a child's doll.

Doobie, *n.* a dull, stupid fellow; a dunce. Cf. Dobbie.

Dooble, *adj.* double.

Doocot, *n.* a dovecot.

Doocot-hole, *n.* a pigeon-hole.

Doodle, *v.* to dandle; to lull an infant to sleep.

Doodle, *v.* to drone on the bagpipe.

Doodle, *v.* to hum over a dance-tune when no instrumental music is to be had. Cf. Deedle.

Doodlie, *n.* a nursery name for the little finger.

Doof, *n.* a stupid fellow.—*v.* to render stupid. Cf. Dowff.

Dooff, *n.* a blow with a soft body; a dull, heavy blow; a hollow, sounding fall, like a loaded sack coming to the ground.—*v.* to strike forcibly, fall heavily.

Dooffart, Doofert, *n.* a dull, soft fellow.—*adj.* stupid, feeble, spiritless; dull, melancholy. Cf. Dowfart.

Dook, *n.* a stout peg or wedge driven into a plastered wall to hold a nail, &c.; the bung of a cask.—*v.* to bung a cask; to drive home a 'dook.'

Dook, *n.* an inclined road or 'dip' in a mine Cf. Douk.

Dook, *v.* to duck; to bathe. Cf. Douk.

Dooket, *n.* a dovecot.

Dookie, *n.* a Baptist. Cf. Douk.

Dookin'-pool, *n.* pond for ducking witches, &c.

Dool, *n.* a blow with a flat surface.—*v.* to beat, thrash.

Dool, *n.* the 'den' or goal in a game; a boundary mark in an unenclosed field.—*v.* with *off*, to fix the boundaries.

Dool, *n.* a large piece. Cf. Doll.

Dool, *n.* an iron spike for keeping the joints of boards together in laying a floor.

†Dool, *n.* sorrow, grief, misfortune; mourning weeds; sombre hangings.—*adj.* sorrowful, mournful.

Dool-a-nee, *int.* alas!

Dool-charged, *adj.* sorrow-charged.

Dooless, *adj.* inactive. Cf. Doless.

Doolful, *adj.* sad, sorrowful; troublesome, annoying.

Dool-hill, *n.* a hill formerly occupied by a castle or place of refuge.

Doolie, *adj.* sorrowful, gloomy, solitary.

Doolie, *n.* a hobgoblin, spectre; a scarecrow.

Doolie-doomster, *n.* a spectre.

Doolie-yates, *n.* ghost-haunted gates.

Dool-like, *adj.* having the appearance of sorrow.

Doolloup, *n.* a steep glen in which two 'haughs' are exactly opposite each other.

Doolsome, *adj.* sad, sorrowful.

Dool-string, *n.* a long string worn on the hat as a sign of mourning.

Dool-tree, *n.* a gallows; a tree or post on which evil-doers were hanged in the exercise of the power of 'pit and gallows.'

Dool-tree, *n.* a tree which marks the goal in playing ball.

Dool-weeds, *n.* mourning garb.

Doolzie, *n.* a frolicsome, thoughtless woman.

Doom-hour, *n.* the last hour; the hour of doom.

Doomie, *n.* a mischievous sprite.

Dooming, *n.* sentence, judgment; destiny.

Dooms, *adj.* great.—*adv.* extremely, exceedingly.—*n.* a great sum.

Doomster, *n.* the official who formerly pronounced the death-sentence in a criminal court; a judge.

Doon, *n.* the goal in a game; the place used for playing it.

Doon, *adv.* extremely.

Doon, *ppl. adj.* done, worn-out.

Doon, *prep.* down.—*adj.* down; laid down, sown, fixed down; confined to bed by illness; knocked down; far gone in drinking, drunk.—*adv.* down; in reduction of rent, price; in payment of cash instead of credit.—*v.* to upset; to overthrow; to throw in wrestling; to fell, knock down; with *take*, to dilute spirits, &c., by adding water, &c.

Doona, *v. neg.* do not, 'dinna.'

Doon-bearing, *n.* oppression; the pain or signs of approaching parturition.

Doon-brae, *adv.* downwards.

Doon-broo, *n.* a frown.

Doon-bye, *adv.* down below, down yonder.

Doon-casting, *adj.* grieved, sorrowful, depressing.—*n.* depression.

Doon-come, *n.* a heavy fall of rain, snow; a descent, fall in the market, means, or social position.

Doon-comin', *n.* a heavy fall of rain, &c.

Doon-cryin', *n.* disparagement, depreciation.—*adj.* disparaging, deprecatory.

Doon-ding, *n.* a heavy fall of rain, snow, sleet.

Doon-drag, *n.* what keeps a person down in the world; a dead-weight; a sin or weakness that acts as a drag; a person who is a grief or disgrace to his family.

Doon-draucht, *n.* a gust of wind sending smoke down a chimney; any thing or person that is a reproach or a moral deadweight.

Doon-draw, *n.* a cause of depression, reproach, or disgrace. Cf. Doon-drag.

Doon-draw, *v.* to launch a boat.

Doon-drawin', *n.* a feast at Beltane on launching a fishing-boat for the fishing.

Doon-drug, *n.* a 'doon-drag.'

Doon-efter, *adj.* following downwards.

Dooner, *adj.* lower, nearer the bottom.

Doonermaist, *adj.* lowest, farthest down.

Doonfa', *n.* a fall of rain, snow; a slope; descent of food, &c., in swallowing; low ground at a mountain-foot whither sheep retire in winter; a reverse, misfortune.

Doon-gang, *n.* used of a person who has a very large appetite.

Doon-had, *n.* hindrance, drawback, check; what represses growth, &c.

Doon-hadden, *ppl. adj.* repressed, kept in check, kept down.

Doon-haddin', *ppl. adj.* repressing, oppressive, holding down.

Doon-head, *n.* a grudge, pique.

Doon-head-clock, *n.* the dandelion.

Doon-hill, *n.* a castle or refuge on a hill; a 'dool-hill.'

Doon-lay, *n.* a heavy fall of snow, &c.

Doon-leuk, *n.* a frowning face; disapproval, displeasure.

Doon-leuking, *adj.* supercilious; condescending; morose-looking.

Doon-lie, *n.* a grave, a resting-place.

Doonlins, *adv.* very, in a great degree.

Doon-looking, *adj.* unable or unwilling to look one in the face.

Doon-lying, *n.* a woman's confinement.

Doonmaist, *adj.* lowermost.

Doon-moo't, *adj.* melancholy, in low spirits, 'down in the mouth.'

Doon-pour, *n.* a heavy fall of rain.

Doon-proud, *adj.* very proud.

Doon-richteous, *adj.* downright.

Doons, *adv.* extremely. Cf. Doon.

Doon-seat, *n.* a settlement as to situation.

Doon-set, -sit, *n.* a settlement, provision, especially in marriage; a location, a home in marriage.

Doon-set, *n.* any work that depresses or over-powers; a 'doon-come'; a scolding that silences.

Doon-sett, *n.* a downward stroke.

Doon-setter, *n.* a 'settler'; what settles an argument.

Doon-sinking, *n.* the sun-setting; depression, melancholy.

Doonsins, *adv.* very, exceedingly. Cf. Doon.

Doon-sitting, *n.* a sitting down to drink; a drinking-bout; a sederunt or session of a church court; a settlement; a location; a home or settlement in marriage.

Doon-stroy, *v.* to destroy.

Doon-sway, *n.* a downward impetus or direction.

Doon-tak, *n.* anything enfeebling the body or mind.

Doon-takin, *n.* reduction in price.

Doon-the-brae, *phr.* towards the grave.

Doon-through, *adv.* in the low or flat country.

Doon-throw, *v.* to upset, overthrow.

Doon-toon, *n.* down the village.

Doon-weicht, *n.* overweight.

Doonwith, *adv.* downwards.—*n.* a declivity.—*adj.* downward.

Doon-worth, *n.* a declivity.

Doop, *n.* the end of an egg, candle, or anything; the bottom of a person, animal, or thing; a moment; the end of a day, month, year, &c.—*v.* to bump on the buttocks; to duck down suddenly; of darkness: to descend. Cf. Doup.

Door-band, *n.* a door-hinge; the iron band by which a hinge is fixed to the door.

Door-board, *n.* the panel of a door.

Door-cheek, *n.* a door-post; a threshold.

Door-crook, *n.* a door-hinge.

Door-deaf, *adj.* very deaf, deaf as a door-nail.

Door-drink, *n.* a stirrup-cup.

Door-head, *n.* the lintel of a door.

Doorie, *n.* a game of marbles, played against a wooden door.

Door-land, *n.* a plot of ground near a door.

Door-nail-deafness, *n.* stone-deafness.

Door-neighbour, *n.* a next-door neighbour.

Door-sill, *n.* a threshold.

Door-sneck, *n.* a door-latch.

Door-stane, *n.* the flagstone at the threshold of a door.

Door-step, *n.* the landing-place at a door.

Door-stoop, *n.* a door-post.

Doo's cleckin, *n.* a family of two.

Doose, *adj.* gentle; hospitable; sedate, grave; sober-minded; virtuous, neat, comfortable.—*adv.* gently; soberly. Cf. Douce.

Doosey, *n.* a punishment among men and boys by bumping the posteriors on the ground.

Doosht, *n.* a soft, heavy blow; a heavy fall or throw.—*v.* to strike with a soft, heavy blow; to bump; to throw in a violent, careless manner.

Doosil, *v.* to beat, thump.—*n.* a thump, blow.

Doot, *v.* to doubt.

Dootious, *adj.* cherishing an unpleasant conviction.

Dootsome, *adj.* doubtful, uncertain, apprehensive.

Doozil, *n.* an uncomely woman; a lusty child.

Doozy, *adj.* uncomely, unpleasant.

Dorbel, *n.* anything unseemly in appearance.

Dorbie, *n.* a stone-mason, hewer, or builder.

Dorbie, *adj.* sickly, weakly; soft, sleepy, lazy.

Dorbie, *n.* the red-backed sandpiper, the dunlin.

Dorbie-brither, *n.* a fellow stone-mason.

Dorbie's knock, *n.* a peculiar knock, as a Freemason's signal.

Dordermeat, *n.* a bannock or piece of oatcake formerly given to farm-servants after loosing the plough, between dinner and supper.

Dore-cheek, *n.* a door-post.

Doreneed, *n.* the youngest pig of a litter.

Dore-stane, *n.* a threshold-stone.

Dorlach, Dorloch, *n.* a truss, bundle; a valise; a quiver; a sheaf of arrows.

Dorlach, *n.* a short sword; a dagger.

Dorlack, *n.* a large piece of anything.

Dorle, *n.* a piece of anything; a portion of food.

Dornel, *n.* a horse-dealers' name for the fundament of a horse.

Dornell, *n.* darnel.

Dornick, Dornock, *n.* linen cloth, formerly made at Tournay, for table use; diaper.

Dornicle, *n.* the viviparous blenny.

Dornoch-law, *n.* execution before trial; summary justice.

Dornton, Dorntor, *n.* a slight repast. Cf. Dortor.

Doroty, *n.* a doll, puppet; a very diminutive woman. Cf. Dorrity.

Dorra, *n.* a net fixed to a hoop of wood or iron, used for catching crabs.

Dorrity, *n.* a doll; a tiny woman; the name Dorothy.

Dort, *n.* a pet, sulks.—*v.* to sulk, to become pettish; with *at*, to overnurse.—*adj.* sulky, pettish.

Dortilie, *adv.* saucily, pettishly.

Dorting, *n.* sulkiness.

Dortor, *n.* a slight repast; food taken between meals. Cf. Dordermeat.

†**Dortour, Dortor,** *n.* a bedchamber, dormitory; a sleeping-draught taken at bed-time.

Dorts, *n.* a slight repast.

Dorty, *adj.* spoilt, pettish, proud, haughty, conceited; used of plants: difficult to rear except in certain soils.

Dorty-pouch, *n.* a saucy person.

Dose, *v.* to drug, stupefy.—*n.* a large quantity.

Dose, *v.* to spin a top so rapidly that it seems motionless; to spin rapidly round. Cf. Doze.

Dosen, *v.* to benumb, stupefy, daze; used for 'damn' in imprecation. Cf. Dozen.

Doss, *n.* a tobacco-pouch.

Doss, *v.* with *down,* to throw one's self down; to sit down violently; to pay down smartly. Cf. Dossie.

Doss, *v.* with *about,* to go about one's business properly; to do neatly, exactly; with *up, off,* to trim, adorn.—*n.* an ornament.—*adj.* neat, spruce.

Dossach, *v.* with *with,* to treat, nurse tenderly; to overnurse; to gain, win.—*n.* overtender nursing.

Dossan, *n.* the forelock.

Dossick, *n.* a small truss or bundle.

Dossie, *n.* a small heap.

Dossie, *n.* a neat, well-dressed person.—*adj.* well-dressed.

Dossie, *v.* with *down,* to pay, or throw down money in payment; to toss down.

Dossins, *n.* human ordure.

Dosslie, *adv.* with neatness and simplicity combined.

Dossness, *n.* neatness.

Dost up, *ppl.* neatly dressed.

Dot, *n.* a diminutive person or thing; walking with short, quick steps; a short sleep.—*v.* to walk with short, quick steps; to fall into a short sleep.

Dot and go one, *phr.* the walk of a lame person whose legs are not equal.

Dotch, *v.* to dangle.

Dote, *n.* a 'doit'; next to nothing.

Dote, *n.* a dowry; an endowment.—*v.* to endow; to give as a salary.

Dother, *n.* daughter. Cf. Dochter.

Dotrified, *ppl. adj.* dazed; stupefied. Cf. Doitrified.

Dotter, *v.* to stagger, totter, walk unsteadily or as if paralysed; to become stupid with age, &c.—*n.* a totter, a stagger. Cf. Doiter.

Dottered, *ppl. adj.* doting in old age.

Dotterel, *n.* a silly person, a dotard.

Dottet, *ppl. adj.* stupefied. Cf. Doit.

Dottie, *v.* to 'dotter.'

Dottle, Dottal, Dottel, *n.* a small particle; a plug, a stopper; the unconsumed tobacco remaining in a pipe; the core of a boil.

Dottle, *n.* a fool, a dotard.—*adj.* silly, crazy, in dotage; of weak intellect; stupid from drink.—*v.* to be in dotage, become crazy; to hobble from age and infirmity; to walk with short, quick steps.

Dottle-trot, *n.* the quick, short step of an old man; the old man's walk.

Dotty, *adj.* imbecile, half-witted; in dotage.

Doubie, *n.* a booby. Cf. Dobbie.

Double, *adj.* used of a letter of the alphabet: capital.—*n.* a duplicate, a copy.—*v.* to make a copy; to repeat; to clench the fists.

Double-breasted, *adj.* used of a word: long, not easily understood.

Double-down-come, *n.* a mode of measuring yarn by a 'reel.'

Double-sib, *adj.* related both by father and mother.

Doublet, *n.* a sleeved jacket or waistcoat; in *pl.* clothes in general.

Doubt, *v.* to apprehend or expect with a measure of certainty; to suspect; to have an unpleasant conviction.

Douce, *adj.* gentle, kind, pleasant; sedate, sober-minded, grave; respectable; prudent; modest, virtuous; tidy, neat, soft, soothing; not giddy or frivolous.

Douce, *v.* to strike.—*n.* a blow. Cf. Douse.

Douce-gaun, *adj.* prudent, circumspect.

Douce-like, *adj.* quiet, respectable in appearance.

Douce-looking, *adj.* grave-looking, of quiet, sober appearance.

Doucely, *adv.* sweetly, gently, kindly; quietly, sedately, soberly.

Douceness, *n.* the quality of being 'douce.'

Doucht, *n.* a stroke, a blow; strength, ability, power. Cf. Dought.

Doucht, *v. pret.* was able, could. Cf. Dow.

Douchtless, *adj.* weak, feeble.

Douchty, *adj.* doughty; vigorous of body; used ironically of deeds that promise much and perform little.

Doud, *n.* a woman's cap with a caul.

Doudle, *n.* the root of the common reed-grass.

Doudle, *v.* to dandle. Cf. Doodle.

Doudle, *v.* to drone on the bagpipe; Cf. Doodle.

Doudler, Doudlar, *n.* the roots of the bog-bean.

Douf, *v.* to become dull.—*n.* a dullard. Cf. Dowf.

Douff, *v.* to strike forcibly.—*n.* a dull, heavy blow. Cf. Doof.

Douffert, *n.* a blow.

Douffie, *adj.* shy; backward. Cf. Dowffie.

Doufness, *n.* dullness, melancholy.

Douf on, *v.* to continue in a dull, slumbering state.

Dough, *n.* a dirty, useless untidy person. Cf. Daigh, Duff.

Dought, *n.* strength, might, ability, power; a deed.

Dought, *v. pret.* could; was able.

Doughtless, *adj.* weak, worthless, pithless.

Doughty, *adj.* strong, powerful, stout; malapert, saucy.

Doughy, *adj.* half-baked; 'soft'; foolish; cowardly. Cf. Daighie.

Douhale, *n.* an easy-going fellow, one who does not object to being regarded as a fool.

Douk, *n.* a wooden wedge driven into a wall.

Douk, *v.* to duck; to plunge or dip into water; to bathe; to dive.—*n.* a dive, a bathe; the condition of being drenched with rain; as much ink as a pen takes up.

Douk, *n.* duck, sailcloth.

Douk, *v.* to bow the head or body hastily in obeisance; to incline the head for any purpose in an unseemly way; to duck so as to avoid suddenly; to 'jouk.'

Douker, Doucker, *n.* a diving bird; the tufted duck; the pochard; the golden-eye; the didapper; a bather.

Douket, *n.* a dovecot.

Doukie, *n.* a Baptist.

Doukin, *n.* a ducking, drenching.

Douking-stool, *n.* the cucking-stool.

Doul'd, *ppl. adj.* fatigued.

Doulie, *n.* a hobgoblin; a scarecrow. Cf. Doolie.

Doumineer, *v.* to stupefy, pester with much talk; to weary.

Doun, *adv.* down. Cf. Doon.

Douna, *v. neg.* cannot; dare not.

Doun-draugh, *n.* overburdening weight, oppression.

Douner, *v.* to stupefy; to muddle. Cf. Donner.

Doung, *v.* to dash, 'ding.'

Dounnins, *adv.* a little way downwards.

Dounwith, *adv.* downwards.

Doup, *n.* the bottom or end of anything, as an egg, candle, day, &c.; the breech or buttocks; a moment; a cavity.—*v.* to dump, thump; to thump or bump the posteriors; to stoop, incline the head or body downwards; used of night: to descend; of the weather: to become gloomy.

Doup-scour, *n.* a fall on the buttocks.

Doup-scud, *adv.* with a heavy fall on the buttocks.

Doup-skelper, *n.* one who beats the buttocks; a schoolmaster.

Doup-wark, *n.* work at the bottom of a weaving-machine.

Dour, Doure, *adj.* hard, stern, stiff; sullen, sulky, stubborn, unyielding; used of weather, &c.: severe, hard; of soil: barren, stiff to work: of ice: rough; of a task, &c.: difficult to accomplish; slow in learning, backward.

Dour, *v.* to slumber lightly; to be half-asleep. Cf. Dover.

Dourdon, *n.* appearance.

Dourie, *n.* a dowry.

Dourin, *ppl.* dozing, slumbering, 'dovering.' Cf. Dover.

Dourlach, *n.* a bundle, truss. Cf. Dorlach.

Dourly, *adv.* pertinaciously, stubbornly.

Dourness, *n.* obstinacy, stubbornness; melancholy, gloom; severity.

Dour-seed, *n.* a species of oats, slow in ripening.

Douse, *v.* to strike, knock; to extinguish; to throw down with a bang, to pay down money.—*n.* a blow; a dull, heavy blow; the sound of such a blow.

Douse, *adj.* solid; gentle; sober. Cf. Douce.

†Doush, *n.* a douche; a dash of water.—*v.* to duck, plunge; to dash water.

Dousht, *n.* a heavy blow, &c. Cf. Doosht.

Douss, *v.* to strike. Cf. Douse.

Doussle, *v.* to beat soundly.

Dout, *v.* to doubt.

Dout, *n.* a penny Scots; a 'doit.' Cf. Doit.

Douth, *adj.* dull, dispirited, melancholy; gloomy, causing melancholy.

Douth, *adj.* snug, comfortable, in easy circumstances.

Douth, *n.* shelter.

Doutish, *adj.* doubtful.

Doutless, *adv.* doubtless.

Doutsum, *adj.* hesitating, uncertain. Cf. Dootsome.

Douzie, *n.* a light of any kind, a spark. Cf. Dingle-douzie.

Dove, *v.* to be half-asleep; to be in a doting, foolish state.

Dove-dock, *n.* the tussilago or colt's-foot.

Dovened, *ppl. adj.* benumbed with cold deafened with noise.

Dover, *v.* to fall into a light slumber, be half-asleep, doze; to stun, stupefy, 'daver.'—*n.* a light slumber; semi-consciousness; a faint, swoon.

Dovering, *ppl. adj.* occasional, rare.

Dovie, *adj.* stupid, apparently weak-minded. —*n.* a stupid person, an imbecile.

Dow, *n.* a dove; a term of endearment.

Dow, *v.* to be able to; with *neg.* to be reluctant to do; to thrive, do well.— *n.* worth, value.

Dow, *v.* to betake one's self; to hasten.

Dow, *v.* to wither, decay; to grow stale or putrid; to doze, fall into a sleepy state, 'dover'; to trifle with, perform carelessly. —*adj.* doleful, gloomy.

Dowatty, *n.* a silly, foolish person.

Dowbart, *n.* a stupid fellow. Cf. Dulbart.

Dowbreck, *n.* a species of fish.

Dowcht, *v. pret.* could. Cf. Dow.

Dow-cot, *n.* a dovecot.

Dowd, *n.* a woman's dress-cap with a caul.

Dow'd, *v. pret.* could. Cf. Dow.

Dow'd, *ppl. adj.* not fresh, pithless ; used of water, &c. : flat, dead ; of meat : lukewarm, not properly hot.

Dow'd fish, *n.* fish that has been drying for a day or two.

Dowdie, *adj.* fading, withering.

Dowdies, *n.* a child's feet.

Dowdy, *n.* an old woman.

Dowf, *adj.* melancholy, gloomy ; hollow ; silly ; inactive ; rotten ; dull to the eye, hazy ; unfeeling ; worthless, paltry ; infertile.—*n.* a dull, heavy person, a fool.— *v.* to render stupid ; to become dull. Cf. Douf.

Dowfart, *n.* a dull, stupid fellow, a 'duffer.' —*adj.* dull, stupid, inefficient, spiritless ; dumpish.

Dowff, *v.* to strike a dull, heavy blow.—*n.* a dull, heavy blow.

Dowffie, *adj.* low-spirited, melancholy ; dull, inactive ; stupid ; shy.

Dowffy-hearted, *adj.* lacking courage.

Dowfness, *n.* melancholy, sadness.

Dowie, *adj.* sad, mournful, dismal ; inclined to decay ; languid, weak, ailing.—*adv.* sadly, wearily. Cf. Dolly.

Dowie-like, *adj.* sad-looking, sorrowful.

Dowiely, *adv.* sadly, wearily.

Dowieness, *n.* sadness.

Dowiesome, *adj.* sad, rather melancholy.

Dowiewise, *adj.* sad, sorrowful, rather 'dowie.'

Dowk, *v.* to duck ; to dip ; to bathe. Cf. Douk.

Dowl, *n.* a large piece. Cf. Doll.

Dowl, *v.* to weary, to fatigue ; to depress.

Dowl-cap, *v.* to cover the head by drawing anything over it.

Dowless, *adj.* lazy, helpless, unthrifty, without energy, unprosperous ; unhealthy.

Dowlie-horn, *n.* a horn that hangs down in cattle.

Dowlie-horned, *adj.* with drooping horns.

Dowly, *adv.* dully, sluggishly, feebly ; sadly.

Down, *adj.* sown ; laid down. Cf. Doon.

Downa, *v. neg.* cannot, want inclination. Cf. Dow.

Downa-do, *n.* exhaustion of age.

Downans, *n.* green hillocks.

Down-sinking, *n.* sinking of heart.

Dowp, *n.* the buttocks ; the end of anything. Cf. Doup.

Dowre, *adj.* hard, stern ; stubborn. Cf. Dour.

Dox, *n.* a sweetheart.

Doxie, *adj.* lazy, slow, restive.

Doxy, *n.* a sweetheart ; a wench.

Doyce, Doyse, *v.* to give a dull, heavy blow.

—*n.* a dull, heavy blow ; the flat sound caused by the fall of a heavy body. Cf. Douse.

Doychle, *n.* a dull, stupid person ; a sloven.— *v.* to walk in a dull, dreamy state.

Doyloch, *n.* a crazy person.

Doyst, *v.* to fall with a heavy sound ; to throw down.—*n.* a sudden fall, the noise made by falling. Cf. Doyce.

Doyte, *v.* to walk stupidly, blunder along.-- *n.* a fool.—*adj.* stupid. Cf. Doit.

Doze, *v.* to spin a top so rapidly that it seems motionless ; to spin round rapidly.

Doze, *n.* a dose ; as much as one takes of liquor at a time.

Doze, *v.* used of straw, hay, wood : to become spoiled by fungus growths.

Doze-brown, *adj.* snuff-coloured ; fox-coloured.

Dozed, *ppl. adj.* used of wood : decayed, unsound.

Dozen, *n.* in *phr.* 'baker's dozen,' thirteen ; 'fisher's dozen,' twenty.

Dozen, *v.* to benumb, stupefy, daze ; to become torpid ; to be impotent ; to become spiritless ; used as an imprecation, to 'damn.'

Dozent, *ppl. adj.* benumbed ; stupid ; impotent ; spiritless.

Draa, *v.* to draw.

Draan, *ppl.* drawn.

Draatch, *v.* to be slow in movement or action.

Drabble, Drable, *v.* to make wet or dirty ; to slobber ; to draggle ; to besmear.—*n.* a slattern ; a person of dirty habits ; in *pl.* food dropped on clothes while eating ; spots of dirt.

Drabble, *n.* a small quantity of liquid or semi-liquid stuff : inferior food.

Drabblich, *n* inferior food, 'drabble.'

Drabbly, *adj.* used of the weather : wet ; of soil : muddy ; spotted with 'drabbles.'— *n.* a child's bib.

Drabloch, *n.* refuse, trash, applied to very small potatoes and bad butcher-meat.

Drachle, *n.* one who is slow in action or movement ; a laggard.—*v.* to straggle, drag slowly along ; to splash or soil with mud. Cf. Draggle.

Drachling, *adj.* lazy, easy-going.

Drachted, *ppl.* designing, crafty. Cf. Draucht.

Drack, *v.* to soak, drench. Cf. Drawk.

Draed, *v. pret.* dreaded.

Draff-cheap, *adj.* very low in price.

Draff-pock, *n.* a sack for carrying draff or grain ; an imperfection, a flaw ; a term of reproach.

Draff-sack, *n.* a sack for holding grain or draff ; a lazy glutton.

Draffy, *adj.* used of draff; of inferior quality, applied to liquor brewed from 'draff.'

Draft, *n.* animals selected from a herd, &c.; a picture.—*v.* to select animals from a herd, &c. Cf. Draucht.

Draft-ewe, *n.* a ewe withdrawn from the flock as one of the best, or as past breeding. Cf. Draucht-ewe.

Draft-gimmer, *n.* a gimmer put aside as unfit for breeding.

Drag, *n.* a toil, hindrance, encumbrance.

Draggle, *v.* to soak or soil with rain, &c.; to straggle, drag slowly on; to moisten meal, flour, &c.—*n.* a wet, muddy condition, a soaking with rain or mud; an untidy person; a feeble, ill-conditioned person.

Dragon, *n.* a boys' kite, made generally of paper.

Dragouner, *n.* a dragoon.

Drag-tae, *n.* a 'drag-to' or rake.

Draible, *v.* to draggle; to besmear; to drop food on one's clothes.—*n.* a slattern; a spot of dirt; a drop of food on the clothes. Cf. Drabble.

Draibly, *n.* a child's bib.—*adj.* used of clothes: spotted with dropped food. Cf. Drabbly.

Draich, Draick, *n.* a lazy, lumpish, useless person.

Draicky, *adj.* slow, spiritless, lazy.

Draidgie, *n.* a funeral feast; a burial service. —*adj.* ominous of death; pertaining to a 'draidgie.' Cf. Dirgie.

Draig, *n.* a dirty, low-lying place; an untidy, disordered place.

Draighie, *n.* a lazy, useless person. Cf. Draich.

Draigie, *n.* a funeral feast; a dirge. Cf. Dirgie.

Draigle, *v.* to draggle; to trail in the mud. Cf. Draggle.

Draigle, *n.* a small quantity.

Draigled, Draiglit, *ppl. adj.* dirty, splashed with mud; used of 'stooks': soaked with rain.

Draiglers, *n.* the invaders in the game of 'het rows and butter-baiks.'

Draigle-tail, *n.* a trailing, mud-bespattered skirt.—*adj.* splashed with mud.

Draiglin, *n.* a small quantity.

Draiglin, *n.* a soaking with rain or mud; a wet, dirty condition.

Draigly, *adj.* dragging the feet wearily.

Draigon, *n.* a boys' paper kite. Cf. Dragon.

Draik, *n.* an untidy, disordered condition. Cf. Draig.

Draik, Drake, *v.* to soak, drench. Cf. Drawk.

Drain, *n.* a drop; a small quantity of liquor.

Dram, *n.* a glass of whisky.—*v.* to drink, tipple.

Dram, *adj.* indifferent, cool; melancholy.

Dramach, *n.* raw meal and water. Cf. Drammach.

Dram-drinking, *n.* tippling.

Dram-glass, *n.* a wine-glass used for whisky, &c.

Dram-hearted, *adj.* depressed, melancholy.

Drammach, *n.* a mixture of raw meal and water. Cf. Drammock.

Dramming, *n.* tippling.

Drammlichs, *n.* small pieces of oatmeal leaven adhering to a bowl or kneading-board.

Drammock, *n.* a mixture of raw meal and water.

Dram-shop, *n.* a public-house.

Drandering, *n.* the chorus of a song.

Drangle, *v.* to dawdle, loiter, linger.

Drant, *v.* to drawl; to drone; to pass time slowly.—*n.* a slow, drawling tone.

Drap, *n.* a drop; a small quantity of liquid; a sugar-plum; a small shot; a weight of nearly 10 oz.—*v.* to drop; to fall; to die; to rain slightly; used of animals: to give birth to young.

Drap, *n.* a thick woollen cloth used for cloaks, coats, &c.

Drap awa', *phr.* to die in succession.

Drap-glasses, *phr.* to drop the white of an egg into a glass of water, and from the shape it assumes to predict the future; a custom on Fastern's Eve.

Drap o' dew, *n.* a little whisky.

Drappie, *n.* a little drop or quantity; with *the*, drink, whisky.

Drappikie, *n.* a very small quantity of liquid; the usual modicum of liquor.

Drappit, *ppl. adj.* dropped here and there; occasional.

Drappit-eggs, *n.* eggs dropped into a pan to be cooked or fried.

Drappit-scones, *n.* scones made like pancakes.

Drap-ripe, *adj.* dead-ripe; quite ready.

Drap's bluid, *phr.* related by blood.

†**Draptaberrie**, *n.* cloth made at Berry, in France.

Dratch, *v.* to linger.

Drate, *v. pret.* and *ppl.* voided excrement. Cf. Drite.

Draucht, Draught, *n.* convulsive breathing; a load to be carried or drawn; what is carted at a time; a plan, scheme, policy, design; a lineament of the face; a method of producing a fancy design from plain healds in weaving; light grain blown away in winnowing; the entrails of a wolf or sheep.—*v.* to breathe convulsively.

Draucht, Draught, *n.* a money draft; a sketch; a photograph.—*v.* to draft from a flock; to draw.

Draucht, Draught, *n.* a ditch as a farm boundary; the land enclosed within such a ditch.

Draucht-ewe, *n.* a ewe picked out for fatten ing or selling if fat.

Drauchtiness, *n.* artfulness, craftiness.

Drauchty, *adj.* designing; artful; crafty; capable of artfulness.

Drauk, *v.* to drench.—*n.* damp, wet weather. Cf. Drawk.

Drauky, *adj.* used of the weather : damp, wet.

Draunt, *v.* to drawl ; to drone. Cf. Drant.

Drave, *n.* a drove of sheep or cattle ; a shoal of fishes ; a draught of herrings ; a crowd of people.

Drave, *v. pret.* drove.

Draw, *v.* to drag ; to get on together, agree ; to withdraw ; to cart ; in curling : to make a careful shot ; to select animals from a herd or flock ; to let off water from a mill-pond, &c. ; to extract the entrails of poultry or game ; to draw straw for thatching ; to filter through or ooze ; to infer, conclude.—*n.* a tug, wrench ; a carefully played shot in curling ; a short smoke of tobacco ; a draught of air.

Draw a leg, *phr.* to fool or trick.

Draw aside with, *phr.* to frequent, consort with.

Drawback, *n.* a hindrance, obstruction.

Drawboy, *n.* a boy formerly employed by weavers to pull the cords of their harness.

Draw cuts, *phr.* to cast lots with various lengths of paper slips, &c.

Drawers'-head, *n.* the top of a chest of drawers.

Drawing, *n.* dragging or pulling girls about in a romp ; making a careful shot in curling.

Drawing the sweer-tree, *n.* a 'tug of war' with a swingle-tree.

Drawk, *v.* to drench, soak.—*n.* damp, wet weather.

Drawky, *adj.* used of the weather: wet, drizzly, rainy.

Drawl, *v.* to be slow in action.

Drawlie, *adj.* slow of movement, slovenly.

Draw-ling, *n.* bog-cotton or moss-crop ; the tufted club-rush.

Draw-moss, *n.* bog-cotton, the sheathed cotton-sedge.

Drawnt, *v.* to drawl ; to drone. Cf. Drant.

Draw the table, *phr.* to clear the table.

Draw til, -to, *v.* to come to regard with interest or affection ; to incline to ; to give signs of approaching rain, &c. ; to take a seat at table.

Draw up, *v.* to increase a bid or offer ; to court ; to come together in marriage.

Dread, *v.* to look forward with anxiety; to suspect.—*n.* suspicion.

Dreader, *n.* a suspicious person, one given to suspicion ; terror.—*v.* to fear.

Dreadour, *n.* fear, dread.—*v.* to fear, dread. Cf. Dreddour.

Dreaming-bread, -cake, *n.* bride's cake or christening-cake, pieces of which are laid under the pillow to be dreamt on.

Drean, *n.* the branch of a bramble.

Drear, *n.* dreariness.

Drearisome, *adj.* dreary, wearisome, lonely.

Drearisomeness, *n.* loneliness.

Dreck, *n.* a dirty, low-lying place ; an untidy state. Cf. Draig.

Dreddour, Dreder, *n.* dread, fear.—*v.* to fear.

Dredge, Dredge-box, *n.* a dredger for sprinkling flour, pepper, &c.

Dredgie, *n.* a funeral service ; a funeral feast ; a dirge.—*adj.* ominous of death. Cf. Dirgie.

Dree, *v.* to endure, suffer, undergo ; to bear pain, burden, &c. ; to last, endure ; to suffer from anxiety.—*n.* suffering ; a protracted, tiresome tune or song.

Dreech, *adj.* long, slow, tedious, tiresome ; tardy, dilatory ; continuous ; slow to pay, begin, or move ; dreary, dull. Cf. Dreich.

Dreed, *v.* to dread.—*n.* dread ; what one dreads.

Dreedle, *v.* to dwindle, fade slowly. Cf. Driddle.

Dreeful, *adj.* sad, foreboding.

Dreegh, *n.* a dwarf, pigmy. Cf. Droich.

Dreegh, *adj.* slow. Cf. Dreich.

Dreek, *adj.* slow ; tedious ; protracted. Cf. Dreich.

Dreel, *v.* to drill ; to move or run quickly ; used of a spinning-wheel, &c. : to rotate quickly, to work quickly and smoothly ; to scold, reprove smartly.—*n.* a swift, violent motion ; energy, 'birr,' rapid movement ; work speedily got through ; of wind : a hurricane ; a spell of stormy weather ; a scolding ; a drill.

Dreeling, *n.* swift and smooth motion ; a severe scolding.

Dreen, *ppl.* driven.

Dreep, *v.* to drip, drop slowly ; to cause to drip ; to drain a bottle, &c. ; to drop, descend perpendicularly, to let one's self down ; to walk slowly ; to do anything slowly and dully.—*n.* a dripping condition ; a ditch ; a drip ; dripping from a roast ; the eaves, the spot where eave-drops fall.

Dreep, *n.* a humiliating disappointment.

Dreep, *n.* a term used in the game of marbles ; in *phr.* 'play dreep,' to play for stakes.

Dreepend, *n.* dripping of a roast ; perquisites ; a fat income or living.

Dreepie, *adj.* used of the weather : dripping, wet.

Dreeping, *n.* a dripping, drop, dreg ; drink, liquor.

Dreeping-roast, *n.* a constant good income, a fat living with perquisites.

Dreeping-wet, *adj.* soaked to the skin, very wet.

Dreeple, *v.* to trickle, fall in drops.—*n.* a small quantity of liquid.

Dreeplick, Dreeplickie, *n.* a very small quantity of liquid.

Dreet, *v.* to void excrement. Cf. Drite.

Dreetle, *v.* to fall in drops, or in small quantities.—*n.* a small quantity of anything.

Dreetlick, Dreetlickie, *n.* very small quantity of any liquid.

Dreetling, *ppl. adj.* slow, without energy. Cf. Druttle.

Dreg, *n.* a very small quantity of spirits ; the refuse of the still from distilleries ; brewers' grains.

Dreg, *n.* a drag, brake.—*v.* to drag.

Dreg, *n.* a funeral feast. Cf. Dirgie.

Dreg-boat, *n.* a boat or punt carrying a dredger, or carrying away dredgings ; a track- or canal-boat drawn by a horse.

Dreggle, *v.* to draggle. Cf. Draigle.

Dreggle, *n.* a small drop of any liquid.

Dregg-salt, *n.* refuse salt.

Dreggy, *adj.* consisting of 'dreg'; turbid.

Dregie, Dregy, *n.* a funeral feast. Cf. Dirgie.

Dregle, *v.* to be tardy, to loiter. Cf. Draigle.

Dreg-pot, *n.* a tea-pot, a 'track-pot.'

Dreg-tow, *n.* the rope attached to a dredging-machine.

Dreich, *n.* a stunted, dwarfish person, a 'droich.'

Dreich, Dreigh, *adj.* slow; tedious; persistent, continuous; tardy, dilatory; slow in paying, beginning, ending, moving, &c. ; close-fisted, hard in bargaining ; dreary ; dull ; wearisome ; in *phr.* 'dreich i' the draw,' 'dreich o' drawin',' slow to act.

Dreichlie, *adv.* slowly.

Dreichness, *n.* slowness ; tedium.

Dreik, *n.* excrement.

Dreip, *v.* to drip. Cf. Dreep.

Dreipie, *n.* an inactive female.

Dremur't, *ppl.* downcast ; dejected, rendered demure. Cf. Drummure.

Dress, *v.* to iron linen, clothes ; to scold, thrash ; to manure land ; to clean, rub down a horse ; to winnow grain.

Dresser-head, *n.* the rack or shelf of a kitchen-dresser ; the top of a kitchen-dresser.

Dressing, *n.* weavers' paste ; a scolding, drubbing.

Dret, *v. pret.* voided excrement.

Dretch, *v.* to go heavily and unwillingly ; to loiter, dawdle.

Drib, *n.* a drop, small quantity of liquid ; a drizzling rain ; slaver ; in *pl.* dregs.—*v.* to drip ; to draw the last milk from a cow.

Drib, *v.* to beat, scold, punish ; to drub.

Dribbing, *n.* a beating, a scolding.

Dribbings, *n.* the last milk drawn from a cow.

Dribbit, *n.* a small quantity of anything.

Dribble, *v.* to drizzle ; to tipple.—*n.* a drop, small quantity of liquid ; drizzling rain ; in *pl.* dregs.

Dribble-beards, *n.* long strips of cabbage in broth.

Dribbler, *n.* a tippler.

Dribblick, Dribblickie, *n.* a very small quantity of liquid.

Dribbling, *n.* the dropping of liquid ; in *pl.* the dregs or droppings of a liquid ; the last milk drawn from a cow.

Dribbling, *ppl. adj.* tippling ; drizzling.

Dribloch, *n.* a small quantity of anything ; a trifle ; a thing of no value.

Dridder, *v.* to dread. Cf. Dreddour.

Driddle, *v.* to dawdle, to potter about a thing ; to let fall in small quantities, to spill carelessly ; to urinate in small quantities.

Driddler, *n.* an idler at his work, loiterer.

Driddles, *n.* the buttocks ; the intestines of an animal slain for food.

Driddlins, *n.* meal forming small lumps in water, 'knotted' meal.

Drider, *v.* to dread. Cf. Dreddour.

Drie, *v.* to endure. Cf. Dree.

Driech, *adj.* slow, tedious. Cf. Dreich.

Drieshach, *n.* a bright, blazing fire ; the red glow of a peat-fire.

Drieve, *v. pret.* drove.

Driffle, *n.* a drizzling rain ; a short period of storm ; a scolding ; a large quantity of work done speedily.—*v.* to drizzle.

Driffling, *n.* small rain.

Drift, *n.* a drove of cattle, &c.; a flock of birds ; snow, &c., driven by wind ; a set of fishing-nets ; delay.—*v.* to delay, put off ; to let anything slide gently through the fingers ; used of snow : to be driven by the wind ; *phr.* 'to drift time,' to put off time.

Drifter, *n.* a steam-trawler.

Drift-line, *n.* a rope to which smuggled kegs of spirit were attached and sunk a few feet below the surface of the sea by sufficient weights.

Drifty, *adj.* abounding in driving snow.

Drill, *v.* to move quickly.—*n.* swift, violent motion. Cf. Dreel.

Drily, *adj.* used of the weather : fine, not rainy.

Drimuck, *n.* cold water mixed with meal. Cf. Drammock.

Dring, *v.* to roll, drive forward : to press tightly, to suffocate by strangling.—*n.* a close-fisted person, a miser.

Dring, Dringe, *v.* to linger, loiter ; to sing slowly and lugubriously ; used of a kettle : to sound before boiling.—*n.* the noise of a kettle before boiling.—*adj.* dilatory, slow.

Dringing, *n.* suffocation by strangulation.

Dringing, *ppl. adj.* dawdling.

Dringle, *v.* to be slow, dilatory.

Drink, *v.* with *in*, to shrink, become shorter, used of the shortening day; with *out*, to drink off; with *one*, to drink his health.

Drink, *n.* a lanky, overgrown person.

Drink-siller, *n.* drink-money; a perquisite, 'tip'; used figuratively.

Drinking-sowens, *n.* flummery thin for drinking, generally with treacle or sugar and butter as a relish.

Drins, *n.* drops of water.

Dripple, *v.* to dribble, trickle. Cf. Dreeple.

Drite, *v.* to void excrement.—*n.* excrement.

Drither, *v.* to dread. Cf. Dreddour.

Drive, *v.* used of time : to delay, prolong; to hurry; to throw with force; to pile up in a heap; to float ashore.—*n.* a push, shove; a heavy blow.

Driver, *n.* a curling-stone forcibly driven.

Drizzen, *v.* to low plaintively, as a cow or ox; to grumble, as a sluggard over his work.—*n.* the low, plaintive sound of a cow wanting food.

Drizzle, Drizel, *v.* to let fall slowly in small quantities; to walk slowly.—*n.* the scanty water in a stream that does not seem to run.

Drizzling, *n.* slaver.

Drob, *v.* to prick with a needle, thorn, &c.—*n.* a thorn, prickle.

Droch, *n.* a dwarf, pigmy. Cf. Droich.

Drochle, *v.* to walk with short, uneven steps; to stagger; to dawdle.

Drochle, *n.* a puny person.

Drochlin, *ppl. adj.* puny; lazy; wheezing.—*n.* a staggering.

Drocht, *n.* a drought; thirst; dryness. Cf. Drouth.

Drod, *n.* a short, thick, clubbish person.

Drod, *n.* a rude candle-holder used in visiting farm-offices at night.

Droddum, Drodum, *n.* the breech.

Droddum-skelpin', *n.* and *adj.* whipping on the breech.

Drodge, *v.* to do servile work, drudge.—*n.* a person always behind with his work.

Drodlich, *n.* a useless mass.

Drods, *n.* the pet; ill-humour. Cf. Dort.

†**Drog,** *n.* a drug.—*v.* to drug; to take drugs.

Drog, *n.* a buoy attached to the end of a harpoon-line, when the whale runs it out.

†**Drogat, Drogget, Droggit, Drogit,** *n.* a coarse woollen cloth used for women's gowns; a cloth made of a mixture of flax and wool.

Drogester, *n.* a druggist.

Droggie, Droggist, *n.* a druggist.

Droghle, *v.* to walk with short, uneven steps; to stagger; to dawdle.

Droghlin, *ppl. adj.* puny, lazy; wheezing.

†**Drogue,** *n.* a drug.—*v.* to take drugs. Cf. Drog.

Droich, *n.* a dwarf; a short, unwieldy person.

Droichan, *n.* any small living animal; a term of reproach.

Droichle, *n.* a stout, dumpy person or animal.

Droichy, *adj.* dwarfish.

Droke, *v.* to drench.—*n.* meal mixed with water. Cf. Drouk, Drawk.

Drokin, *n.* a drenching.

Droll, *n.* a droll person; humour, oddity, eccentricity; a droll story or saying.—*v.* to joke.—*adj.* unusual, strange.

Drollity, *n.* a curiosity; a curio; an unusual thing.

Dronach, *n.* penalty.

Drone, *n.* a dull, drawling speaker; the lowest boy in a class at school; the low, plaintive sound made by a hungry cow; the bass pipe of a bagpipe.—*v.* to drawl; to sing in a low, monotonous voice; to play the bagpipe; used of a cow : to moan plaintively.

Drone, *n.* the breech, backside.

Drone-brat, *n.* an apron formerly worn behind.

Droner, *n.* a player on the bagpipe; a bumble-bee.

Drony, *adj.* slow, sluggish. —*v.* to doze, slumber.

Droochle, *v.* to drench.

Droochlet-like, *adj.* looking as if drenched.

Droog, *v.* to tug, drag at.—*n.* a rough pull.

Droog, Droogle, *v.* to do dirty, heavy work.

Drook, *v.* to drench. Cf. Drouk.

Drookit-oxter, *n.* a good dowry.

Drool, *v.* to trill, cry mournfully.

Droon, *v.* to drown.

Droonyie, *v.* to moan, complain mournfully. —*n.* a droning song; the moaning of cattle; the wail of a child when ceasing to cry.

Droopit, *ppl. adj.* weakly, infirm, drooping.

Droop-rumplet, *adj.* used of horses : drooping at the crupper.

Drooth, *n.* drought; thirst. Cf. Drouth.

Dropper, *n.* a sudden disappointment.

Dropping, Droppy, *adj.* used of the weather : showery, wet.

Drop-ripe, *adj.* dead-ripe; quite prepared.

Dross, *n.* coal- or peat-dust.

Drossy, *adj.* of a gross habit, indicating an unwholesome temperament or a bad constitution.

Drotch, *v.* to dangle.

Drotchell, *n.* an idle wench; a sluggard. Cf. Dratchell.

Drotes, *n.* a derisive term for uppish yeomen or 'cock-lairds.'

Drouble, *v.* to bellow, as the hart for the doe.

Droud, *n.* a cod-fish; a heavy, lumpish person; a worthless female; a wattled sort of box for catching herrings.

Drouk, *v.* to drench, soak.—*n.* a drenching, soaking, a soaked condition; oatmeal mixed with water.

Droukitness, *n.* the state of being drenched.

Drouky, *adj.* wet, drenching.

Droul, *n.* in *phr.* 'in dust and droul,' in dust and ashes.

Droup-rumpl't, *adj.* used of horses: drooping at the crupper. Cf. Droop-rumplet.

Drouth, *n.* drought; a period of fine, drying weather; thirst, dryness; a thirsty person, a drunkard, a tippler.

Drouthielie, *adv.* thirstily.

Drouthiesome, *adj.* given to drink.

Drouthiesomeness, *n.* addiction to drink.

Drouthy, *adj.* thirsty; dry, parching; craving for drink.—*n.* a thirsty person; a heavy drinker.

Drove, *v.* to drive cattle and sheep; to come in droves.—*n.* a road used for driving cattle.

Drove, *n.* a broad chisel, the broadest iron used by masons in hewing stones.—*v.* to hew stones for building by means of a 'drove'; to drive horizontal lines on the face of the stone with a 'drove.'

Drove-sail, *n.* a sail hanging under water to hinder the too rapid motion of a 'dogger' when fishing.

Droving, *n.* cattle-driving.

Drow, *n.* a fit of illness; a swoon; a qualm of anxiety.

Drow, *n.* a cold, damp mist; a cloud, shower, squall, a 'haar.'—*v.* with *on*, to gather in a thick, wet mist.

Drow, *n.* a melancholy sound; a wail; the distant noise of breaking waves.

Drow, *n.* a very small quantity of fluid, a drop.

Drowie, *adj.* moist, misty.

Drown, *v.* to dilute with too much water, &c.; to flood; to be drowned; used in expletives or as a strong appeal.

Drowper, *n.* one who gives way to dejection.

Drowsying, *n.* sleepiness, drowsiness.

Drowth, *n.* drought; dryness; thirst; craving for drink; a drunkard.

Drub, *v.* to beat the ground, trudge, tramp.

Drubbly, *adj.* muddy, turbid, dark.

Drucht, *n.* drought; a season of drought.

Druchty, *adj.* used of the weather: droughty, drying.

Drucken, *ppl. adj.* drunk, having drunk.

Drucken, *adj.* drunken.

Drucken-bite, *n.* food of a kind to encourage drinking liquor.

Drucken-groat, *n.* a fine for drunkenness; money paid for drink at a penny-wedding; a tippler's expenditure for drink.

Druckensum, *adj.* drunken; given to drink.

Drudging-box, *n.* a flour-box, dredger. Cf. Dredge.

Druffy, *adj.* dull, downcast: dispirited.

Drug, *n.* a tug, a violent pull.

Drug, *adj.* slow, dull, dragging heavily; used of ice: moist, not keen, making curling-stones go heavily.

Drug-saw, *n.* a 'cross-cut' saw.

Druidle, Druitle, *v.* to idle away time; to move slowly. Cf. Druttle.

Druitlin', *n.* dawdling, wasting time.

Druken, Drukken, *adj.* drunken.

Drule, *n.* the goal which players strive to reach.

Drule, *n.* a sluggard, a lazy person; a stupid person.

Drulie, *adj.* muddy, thick; muddled.

Drulie-heidit, *adj.* thick-headed; muddled in the head.

Drulled, *adj.* stupid.

Drum, *n.* the drum-shaped part of a threshing-mill.—*v.* to repeat monotonously; to pore over wearily.

Drum, *n.* a knoll, ridge, hill.

Drum, *adj.* melancholy. Cf. Dram.

Drumble, Drumle, *v.* to make muddy; to raise disturbance; to confuse; to bedim.—*n.* mud, &c., raised by troubling water, &c.

Drumble, *v.* to move sluggishly; to murmur, to 'maunder.'

Drumbling, *ppl. adj.* muddy, turbid.

Drumlie-droits, -drutshocks, *n.* blackberries.

Drumlieness, *n.* muddiness; confusion; obscurity.

Drumly, *adj.* thick, turbid, muddy; gloomy; confused as to mind; troubled; sullen.

Drumly-voiced, *adj.* rough-, hoarse-voiced.

Drum-major, *n.* a virago, a masculine woman.

Drummel, *v.* to render water muddy; to confuse. Cf. Drumble.

Drummel'd, *ppl. adj.* stupefied, muddled.

Drummock, *n.* a mixture of raw meal and water. Cf. Drammock.

Drummoolich, *adj.* melancholy, in low spirits.

Drummure, *adj.* demure; grave, serious, sad. Cf. Dremur't.

Drummy land, *n.* wet land of gentle curves and with a subsoil of 'till.'

Drums, *n.* curved wet lands.

Drumshorlin, *adj.* sulky, pettish.

Drumster, *n.* a drummer.

Drune, *n.* the murmuring sound made by cattle; a slow, drawling tune; the termination of a child's crying after a whipping.—*v.* to low in a hollow or depressed tone. Cf. Drone.

Drunk, *n.* a drinking-bout; a drunk person.

Drunken, *ppl. adj.* shrunken.

Drunken-fu', *adj.* quite drunk.

Drunkensome, *adj.* given to drinking.

Drunt, *n.* ill-humour, a pet, sulk.—*v.* to sulk.

Drunt, *v.* to drawl ; to pass the time tediously. —*n.* a drawling style of speech or song. Cf. Drant.

Drury, *n.* a dowry.

Druschoch, *n.* any liquid food of a heterogeneous composition and nauseous appearance ; a compound drink ; a mixture of various drugs.

Drush, *n.* dross, scum, refuse ; fragments ; peat-dust ; peat broken small.—*v.* to crush, crumble ; to spoil, go wrong.

Drute, *n.* a lazy, slovenly, unfeeling person.

Druther, *n.* a suspicion, fear, doubt. Cf. Dreddour.

Drutle, *v.* used of a horse or dog: to stop frequently on its way to eject a small quantity of dung.

Druttle, *v.* to be slow in movement ; to dawdle ; to waste time.—*n.* a useless, good-for-nothing person.

Dry, *adj.* thirsty ; used of a cow: having ceased to give milk ; reserved and stiff in manner, not affable.—*n.* a division in a stone where it can be parted ; a flaw.—*v.* to make cows go 'dry.'

Dry-braxy, *n.* inflammation in the bowels of sheep.

Dry-darn, *n.* costiveness in cattle.

Dry-dyke, *n.* a wall built without mortar.

Dry-dyker, *n.* a builder of 'dry-dykes.'

Dry-farrand, *adj.* frigid in manner, not affable.

Dry-gair-flow, *n.* the place where two hills meet and form a bosom.

Dry-goose, *n.* a handful of the finest meal pressed very close together, dipped in water, and then roasted.

Dry-haired, *adj.* cold in manner, not affable.

Dry-handed, *adj.* without weapons.

Drylander, *n.* one who lives on dry land, neither aquatic nor amphibious.

Dry-like, *adv.* with some reserve ; without frankness.

Dryll, *v.* to waste time.

Dry-lodgings, *n.* lodgings without board.

Dry-mou'd, *adj.* not drinking while others drink.

Dry-multures, *n.* corn paid to a mill whether the payer grinds at it or not.

Dryness, *n.* reserve in manner ; want of affection ; a coolness between friends.

Dry-nieves, *n.* bare hands in fisticuffs.

Dry-seat, *n.* a close-stool.

Dry-siller, *n.* hard cash, ready money ; money laid past.

Drysome, *adj.* tasteless ; insipid ; tedious ; uninteresting.

Drystane-dyke, *n.* a wall built without mortar.

Dryster, *n.* one who has charge of drying grain in a kiln or cloth at a bleachfield.

Dry-stool, *n.* a close-stool.

Dry talk, *n.* an agreement made without drinking, and therefore not binding.

Dryte, *v.* to void excrement.

Dryward, *adj.* rather dry ; dull, prosy.

Duan, *n.* the division of a poem, a canto ; poem, song.

Dub, *n.* a small pool of water ; a puddle ; a gutter ; in *pl.* mud.—*v.* to cover with mud, bedaub.

Dubback, *n.* a game at marbles in which the 'pitcher' is forcibly thrown at the others.

Dubbin, *n.* a mixture of tallow and oil for softening leather and preventing boots, &c., from getting wet.

Dubbit, *ppl. adj.* mud-stained.

Dubble, *n.* mud, dirt, &c.

Dubby, *adj.* abounding in puddles ; muddy, wet, dirty.

Dubie, *adj.* doubtful.

Dubish, *adj.* suspicious, jealous. Cf. Jubish.

Dub-skelper, *n.* one who goes his way regardless of mud and puddles ; a rambling fellow ; used ludicrously of a young bank-clerk whose duty it is to run about giving notice that bills are due.

Dub-water, *n.* muddy water, water from a puddle.

Ducadoon, *n.* a ducatoon, worth £3, 10s. Scots.

Duchal, *n.* an act of gormandising.

Duchas, *n.* the ancestral seat ; the holding of land in one's birthplace or family estate.

Ducht, Dught, *v. pret.* could. Cf. Dowcht.

Duchtna, *v. neg.* could not.

Duchty, *adj.* powerful. Cf. Dochty.

Duck, *n.* a term of endearment.

Duck, *n.* a young people's game in which they try to knock off a small stone, or the 'duck,' placed on a larger.

Duck-dub, *n.* a duck-pool.

Ducker, *n.* the cormorant.

Duck-your-head, *n.* a boys' game.

Dud, *n.* a hare.

Dud, *n.* a rag ; a soft, spiritless person ; in *pl.* clothes ; dirty, shabby clothes.

Dudder, *v.* to shake, quiver, as a sail in the wind ; of the wind : to be boisterous.

Dudderon, *n.* a person in rags ; a slut, sloven, lazy person.

Duddie, *n.* a dish turned out of solid wood, with two 'ears,' and generally of octagonal form on the brim.

Duddies, *n.* rags ; garments.

Duddiness, *n.* raggedness.

Duddingston-dinner, *n.* a sheep's head and haggis.

Duddrie, *n.* a quarrel, wrangle.

Duddry, *adj.* disorderly, rough, ill-shaken together.

Duddy, *adj.* ragged.

Duddy, *n.* a hornless ox or cow, a 'doddy.' Cf. Doddy.

Dudgeon, *n.* a short clay-pipe.

Due, *adj.* indebted, owing.—*v.* to owe money.

Dufe, Duff, *v.* to strike with a soft substance. —*n.* a blow with a soft substance; the sound of such a blow. Cf. Dooff.

Dufe, Duff, *n.* dough; the soft or spongy part of a loaf, cheese, turnip, &c.; a soft, spongy peat; a soft, silly fellow; dry, decomposed moss used as litter.

Duffart, Duffer, *n.* a blunt, stupid fellow; dull-burning coal. Cf. Dowfart.

Duffie, *adj.* blunt, round-pointed.

Duffie, *adj.* soft, spongy; foolish; cowardly. Cf. Doughy.

Duffifie, *v.* to lay a bottle on its side for a time, when its contents have been poured out, that it may be drained of what remains.

Duffiness, *n.* sponginess.

Duffing-bout, *n.* a thumping, beating.

Duff-mould, *n.* dry, decomposed peat, used as litter.

Duff's-luck, *n.* some special good fortune.

Duffy, *adj.* powdery, used of coal that crumbles when struck by the poker; soft, spongy; stupid.—*n.* a soft, silly fellow.

Dugget, *n.* cloth thickened and toughened by shrinking.

Dugind, *adj.* wilful, obstinate, 'thrawn.'

Dugon, *n.* contemptuous expression for a poor, weak fellow.

†Duil, *n.* sorrow. Cf. Dool.

Duke, *n.* a duck.

Duke, *v.* to dip; to bathe. Cf. Douk.

Duke-ma-lordie, *n.* a nobleman.

Dukery-packery, *n.* trickery. Cf. Jookery-pawkrie.

Duke's-meat, *n.* the lesser duckweed.

Dulbart, *n.* a heavy, stupid person; a block-head.

Dulder, *n.* anything large.

Dulderdum, *adj.* confused by argument; in a stupor.

Duldie, *n.* anything large; a large piece of bread, meat, &c.

†Dule, *n.* sorrow. Cf. Dool.

Dule, *n.* the goal in a game; a boundary of land.—*v.* to mark out limits, fix a boundary. Cf. Dool.

Dulenee, *int.* alas!

Duless, *adj.* feeble, inert, incapable, lazy. Cf. Dowless.

Dulget, *n.* a small bundle or lump.

Dull, *adj.* deaf, hard of hearing.—*v.* with *down,* to pass out of mind or memory.

Dullion, *n.* a large piece; a large, thick bannock of oat- or barley-meal.

Dullyeart, *adj.* of a dirty, dull colour.

Dulse, *v.* to make dim.—*adj.* dull, heavy.

Dulse-man, -wife, *n.* a male or female seller of dulse.

Dulshet, *n.* a small bundle. Cf. Dulget.

Dult, Dults, *n.* a dolt, dunce.

Dultish, *adj.* stupid, doltish.

Dumb, *adj.* used of windows: built up and painted outside to resemble glazed windows.

Dumbarton-youth, *n.* a person over thirty-six years of age, generally applied to a woman.

Dumb-chaser, *n.* an imperfectly developed ram.

Dumbfounder, Dumfooner, -founer, -funer, *v.* to dumfound, stun, stupefy by a blow or an argument; to amaze.

Dumbfoundered, *ppl. adj.* amazed, perplexed.

Dumbfounderedly, *adv.* amazedly, in perplexity.

Dumbfounderment, *n.* amazement, bewilderment, confusion.

Dumbie, *n.* a dumb person; a deaf-mute. Cf. Dummy.

Dumb-nut, *n.* a 'deaf' nut, a nut with no kernel.

Dumb-swaul, *n.* a long, noiseless sea-swell in calm, windless weather.

Dumfoutter, *v.* to bewilder; to tease, make game of, annoy.

Dummart, *n.* a blockhead.

Dummy, *n.* a dumb person; one who is speechless; a deaf-mute.

Dum-ned, *n.* a hard, continuous step in walking.

Dump, *v.* to set down heavily; to throw down violently; to thump, beat, kick; to walk heavily, stump with short steps; to strike with a marble the knuckles of the loser.—*n.* a game of marbles played with holes in the ground, 'kypes'; a stroke on the knuckles with marbles; a game in which the winner 'dumps' the loser's knuckles; a place in which rubbish, &c., is shot; a blow, a bump; a fit of the dumps.

Dumpage, *adj.* sad, melancholy, dumpish.

Dumpeesed, Dumpest, *adj.* stupid, dull, spiritless.

Dumph, *n.* a dull, stupid person, a 'sumph.' —*adj.* dull, stupid.

Dumpiness, *n.* the state of being short and thick; shortness.

Dumpish, *v.* to depress, make despondent.

Dumple, *n.* a quantity, bundle; a lump.

Dumple, *n.* a breakage. Cf. Dimple.

Dumpling, *n.* a lump of oatmeal and suet boiled in broth.

Dumps, *n.* mournful tunes.

Dumpy, *n.* a short, thickset person.—*adj.* used of cloth: coarse and thick.

Dumscum, *n.* a children's game, like 'beds.'

Dum-Tam, *n.* a bunch of clothes on a beggar's back under his coat.

Dun, *n.* a hill; a hill-fort.

Dun, *v.* to beat, thump; to stun with noise.

Dunbar-wedder, *n.* a salted herring.

Dun-bird, *n.* the female pochard.

Dunch, *v.* to push, jog, bump, knock about; to butt with the head.—*n.* a thrust, nudge, bump; a butt, push, a knock-down blow by a bull.

Dunch, *n.* a bundle or truss of rags, straw, &c.; one who is short and thick.

Dunchin'-bull, *n.* a hornless bull that butts with its head.

Dunchy, *adj.* short, squat.

Dunckle, Duncle, *v.* to dint; to damage. Cf. Dunkle.

Dundee, Dundeerie, *n.* a great noise of people quarrelling in earnest or in fun.

Dunder, *v.* to rumble, give a thundering, reverberating sound.—*n.* a loud noise like thunder; a reverberation. Cf. Dunner.

Dunder-clunk, *n.* a big, stupid person.

Dunderhead, *n.* a blockhead.

Dunderheaded, *adj.* dull, stupid.

Dundiefeckan, *n.* a stunning blow. Cf. Dandiefechan.

Dune, *ppl. adj.* done; exhausted.

Dung, *ppl. adj.* beaten, defeated; overcome with fatigue; dejected. Cf. Ding.

Dung-by, *ppl. adj.* confined by illness.

Dunge, *v.* to nudge; to push; to butt. Cf. Dunch.

Dungel, *n.* a blow, a 'dunt.'

Dungeon, *n.* in *phr.* 'dungeon of wit,' a profound intellect.

Dung-flee, *n.* a fly that feeds on excrement.

Duniwassal, *n.* used contemptuously of the lower class of farmers.

Dunk, *adj.* damp.—*n.* a mouldy dampness.

Dunkle, *n.* a dint caused by a blow or fall; a dimple.—*v.* to indent, make a hollow or depression, to damage by dinting; to injure one's character.

Dunner, *v.* to rumble; to give a loud, thundering noise; to reverberate.—*n.* a loud rumbling noise; a reverberating sound.

Dunnerhead, *n.* a blockhead.

Dunnerheadit, *adj.* stupid.

Dunnerin, *n.* a loud, thundering sound; a reverberating sound.

Dunnerin-brae, *n.* a 'brae' that gives forth a rumbling sound when a vehicle drives over it.

Dunnie, *n.* a mischievous sprite. Cf. Doomie.

Dunniewassal, *n.* a farmer of the lower class. Cf. Duniwassal.

Dunsch, Dunsh, Dunse, *v.* to nudge; to butt. Cf. Dunch.

Dunsch, *n.* a bundle of rags, &c.; a short and thick person. Cf. Dunch.

Dunshach, *n.* a heavy, soft blow; a big, untidy bundle.

Dunsheugh, *n.* a nudge.

Dunshing, *n.* the act of pushing, nudging, butting.

Dunt, *n.* a blow, knock; a blow causing a dull sound; the sound of a hard body falling; a heavy fall; a thump; throb, palpitation of the heart; a gibe; a slanderous lie. —*v.* to beat; to fall heavily; to throb, palpitate; with *out,* to drive out with repeated strokes, to settle a question or dispute; to indent by striking; to shake together the contents of a sack, &c., by striking it on the ground; *phr.* 'done and duntit on,' quite done for.

Dunt, *n.* a large piece of anything.

Dunt-about, *n.* a piece of wood driven about at 'shinty,' or like games; anything knocked about in common use as of little value; a servant who is roughly treated and is driven about from one piece of work to another.

Dunter, *n.* a porpoise.

Dunter, *n.* a fuller of blankets, cloth, &c.

Dunter-goose, *n.* the eider-duck.

Dunting, *n.* a continuous beating, causing a hollow sound.

Dunting-case, *n.* a prostitute.

Dunty, *n.* a 'doxy,' paramour.

Dunyel, *v.* to jolt with a hollow sound.

Dunze, *adv.* extremely. Cf. Doon.

Duplickin, *n.* a duplicate.

Duply, *n.* a defender's rejoinder to a pursuer's reply.—*v.* to make a rejoinder.

Durdam, -den, -don, -drum, -dum, *n.* strife, a row; uproar. Cf. Dirdum.

Dure, *n.* a door.

Dure, *adj.* stern; unyielding. Cf. Dour.

Durg, *n.* a day's work. Cf. Darg.

Durgin, Durgon, *n.* a big, ill-tempered person.

Durgy, *adj.* thick, gross; short, thickset.

Durk, *n.* a dagger, dirk.—*v.* to stab with a dagger; to spoil, ruin.

Durk, *n.* a short, thickset person; anything short, thick, and strong.—*adj.* thickset, strongly made.

Durken on, *v.* to become discouraged.

Durkin, *n.* a short, thickset person; anything short, thick, and strong.

Durnal, *v.* used of the cheeks: to move when a flabby person runs or walks very fast.

Durr, *v.* to deaden pain by narcotics. Cf. Dirr.

Dursie, *adj.* obdurate; hard-hearted.

Dush, *v.* to move with force and speed; to butt, push forcibly, thrust; to strike.—*n.* a blow, push, stroke.

Dushill, *n.* an untidy female worker.—*v.* to disgust with slovenliness.

Dusht, *v.* to strike a heavy blow. Cf. Doosht.

Dusht, *ppl. adj.* struck dumb, silenced; silent.

Dusk, *v.* to dim, shadow, darken.

Dusk-maill, *n.* peat-rent.

Duosie, *adj.* obedient, docile.

Dust, *n.* chaff; husks of oats; blacksmiths' small coal; a disturbance, uproar; money. —*v.* to beat, thrash; to raise a disturbance.

Dustyfoot, Dustifit, *n.* a homeless tramp; a pedlar.

Dusty-melder, -meiller, *n.* the last meal made from the crop of one year; the end of life; the last child born in a family. Cf. Distymelder.

Dusty-miller, *n.* the common auricula.

Dut, *n.* a stupid fellow.

Dutch, *n.* tobacco from Holland.

Dutch admiral, *n.* a kind of garden flower.

Dutch-plaise, *n.* the fish *Pleuronectes platessa*.

Dutch-pound, *n.* a weight of 28 oz.

Dutch-splay, *n.* a hem-seam one side of which alone is sewn.

Dute, Dutt, *v.* to doze, slumber.

Duthe, *adj.* substantial, efficient; nourishing. Cf. Douth.

Duty-multure, *n.* a yearly duty paid to the landlord in money or grain whether the tenant ground his corn at the mill or not.

Duxy, *adj.* slow, lazy. Cf. Doxie.

Dwab, *adj.* feeble.

Dwable, Dwabil, *adj.* flexible, limber; weak, feeble; loose, shaky.—*n.* a weak, overgrown person; anything long, flexible, and so weak.—*v.* to walk feebly or with faltering steps.

Dwably, *adj.* feeble, shaky, infirm.

Dwadle, *v.* to dawdle, lounge; to waste time.

Dwaffil, *adj.* weak, pliable; not stiff or firm.

Dwaible, *adj.* limber; weak. Cf. Dwable.

Dwaibly, *adj.* feeble, shaky. Cf. Dwably.

Dwall, *v.* to dwell.

Dwallion, *n.* a dwelling.

Dwam, Dwalm, *n.* a swoon, qualm, fit of illness.—*v.* to faint, fall ill; to decline in health.

Dwaminess, *n.* faintness.

Dwaming, *n.* the fading of light.

Dwaming-fit, *n.* a fainting-fit.

Dwamish, *adj.* faint, like to faint.

Dwamle, Dwamel, *v.* to faint, to look like fainting.—*n.* a short swoon, a fit of illness.

Dwamlock, *n.* a very sickly person.

Dwamy, *adj.* like to faint; languid, sickly.

Dwamy, *v.* to oppress with labour, harass, overcome; to toil; to bear or draw a load unequally.—*n.* oppressive toil; a rough shake or throw; a large iron lever or turnkey for raising stones or screwing nuts for bolts; a stout bar of wood used by carters for tightening ropes; in *pl.* transverse pieces of wood between joists to strengthen a floor and prevent swinging.

Dwannie, *adj.* weak, sickly. Cf. Dwine.

Dwaub, *n.* a feeble person.

Dwaum, Dwawm, *n.* a swoon. Cf. Dwam.

Dwebble, Dweble, *adj.* limber; weak. Cf. Dwable.

Dweeble, Dwibel, *adj.* limber, weak. Cf. Dwable.

Dwibly, *adj.* feeble; shaky. Cf. Dwably.

Dwine, *v.* to waste away, languish, decline in health; to fade away, decay, gradually dis appear; to cause to consume or dwindle; used in imprecations.—*n.* a decline; the waning of the moon.

Dwingle, *v.* to loiter, tarry.

Dwining, *n.* a wasting illness, consumption; a fading, dwindling; the waning of the moon.

Dwinnil, *v.* to dwindle; to pine away; to waste gradually; to degenerate; with *out*, to cozen, deprive of by cheating, &c.

Dwiny, *adj.* puny, sickly; ill-thriven.

Dwybal, Dwyble, *adj.* limber; weak. Cf. Dwable.

Dwybe, *n.* an overall, slender, feeble person. Cf. Dwaub.

Dwyne, *v.* to waste away. Cf. Dwine.

Dyb, *n.* a puddle, a pool of water. Cf. Dib.

Dyed-i'-the-woo, *phr.* naturally clever.

Dyester, *n.* a dyer. Cf. Dyster.

Dyet, *n.* a meal, diet.

Dyet, *n.* the meeting of an ecclesiastical court on a fixed day; the time appointed for public worship, pastoral catechising, &c. Cf. Diet.

Dyke, *n.* a wall of stone or turf. Cf. Dike.

Dyke-slouch, -sheuch, *n.* a ditch or open drain at the bottom of a 'dyke.'

Dykey, *n.* a game of marbles.

Dyled, Dylt, *ppl. adj.* stupefied; silly. Cf. Doilt.

Dymmond, *n.* a two-year-old wedder. Cf. Dinmont.

Dyn, *n.* din.

Dyoch, *n.* a drink.

Dyod, *int.* a euphemism for 'God.' Cf. Dod.

Dyrll, *v.* to pierce; to tingle, thrill. Cf. Dirl.

Dyse, *int.* used as an imprecation for 'damn.'

Dyst, *n.* a dull, heavy blow; the sound of a heavy body falling. Cf. Doist.

Dyster, *n.* a hurricane, storm from the sea; a strong, steady breeze. Cf. Doister.

Dyster, *n.* a dyer.

Dyte, *v.* to walk with short, sharp steps; to walk crazily, to blunder along stupidly.—*n.* a short, quick step; a person of small stature. Cf. Doit.

Dytit, *ppl. adj.* stupid, 'doited.'

Dytter, *v.* to walk in a stupid way or with tottering steps. Cf. Doiter.

Dyuck, *n.* a duck.

†Dyvour, Dyver, Dyvor, *n.* a debtor, bankrupt; a rascal, 'broken man,' 'ne'er-do-weel'; a restless, troublesome person.—*v.* to impoverish, make bankrupt.

Dyvour's hose, *n.* stockings of different colours, formerly worn by those guilty of fraudulent bankruptcy.

E', *pron.* you.

Ea, *adj.* one. Cf. Ae.

Each, *n.* a horse.

Each, *n.* an adze.

Eag, *v.* to egg; to incite to mischief.

Eak, *n.* natural grease from wool or hair. Cf. Eik.

Ealie, *int.* alas! an excl. of woe.

Ealins, *n.* children of the same age. Cf. Eeldins.

Eam, *n.* a maternal uncle; an intimate friend. Cf. Eme.

Ean, *adj.* one. Cf. Ane.

Ean, *n.* a one-year-old horse.

Eanarnich, *n.* a strong soup; flesh-juice. Cf. Imrigh.

Eance, *adv.* once.

Eand, *v.* to breathe.—*n.* breath. Cf. Aynd.

Ear, *n.* a kidney. Cf. Near.

Ear, *v.* to plough or till land.

Ear, *adv.* early. Cf. Air.

Eard, *n.* earth; unploughed land; one ploughing or furrow.—*v.* to bury; to cover with earth for protection against frost, &c.; to knock violently to the ground. Cf. Yird.

Eard-bark, *n.* the roots of tormentil, used for tanning.

Eard-din, *n.* thunder; thunder in the earth; an earthquake.

Eard-drift, *n.* snow or hail driven off from the surface of the earth by the force of the wind.

Eard-eldin, *n.* fuel of peat or earth.

Eard-fast, *adj.* deep-rooted in the earth.—*n.* a stone or boulder firmly fixed in the earth.

Eard-house, *n.* a subterraneous house of 'dug' stones, roofed with large stones.

Eard-hunger, *n.* eagerness for land; the eagerness for food sometimes shown by the dying.

Eard-hungry, *adj.* ravenously hungry.

Eard-meal, *n.* churchyard soil.

Eard-swine, *n.* a frightful beast supposed to haunt graveyards and batten on corpses.

Eard-titling, *n.* the meadow-pipit.

Earest, *adv.* especially. Cf. Erast.

Earl, *v.* to fix a bargain or engagement by paying an earnest. Cf. Arle.

Earl-duck, *n.* the red-breasted merganser.

Ear-leather, *n.* the loin-strap, passing through the crupper and over the kidneys of a horse.

Ear-leather-pin, *n.* an iron pin for fastening the chain by which a horse draws a cart.

Earm, *v.* to whine, complain fretfully; to chirp as a bird. Cf. Yirm.

Earn, *n.* the eagle.

Earn, *v.* to coagulate; to curdle milk with rennet, &c. Cf. Yearn.

Earn-bleater, -bliter, *n.* the snipe; the curlew.

Earnest, *n.* a game of marbles in which they are staked.

Earning, *n.* rennet.

Earnin'-grass, *n.* the common butterwort.

Ear-nit, *n.* the pig-nut. Cf. Arnot.

Earock, *n.* a hen of the first year.

Earth, *n.* one ploughing of land.—*v.* to protect with earth. Cf. Eard, Yird.

Earthlins, *adv.* earthwards; along the ground.

Ease, *v.* to slacken, abate.—*n.* with *up*, a hoist, a lifting up.

Easedom, *n.* relief from pain, comfort.

Easel, *adv.* eastward.—*adj.* easterly. Cf. Eassel.

Easenent, *n.* a motion of the bowels, an evacuation.

Easening, *adj.* feeling desire. Cf. Eassin.

Easer, *n.* maple-wood. Cf. Ezar.

Easing, *n.* the eaves of a house; the part of a stack where it begins to taper.

Easing-butt, *n.* a water-butt into which the droppings from the 'easing' are led.

Easing-drap, *n.* the projection of a house-roof that carries off the drops; the dropping water from a roof after rain.

Easing-gang, *n.* a course of sheaves projecting a little at the 'easing' of a stack, to keep the rain from getting in.

Easing-water, *n.* water draining from the 'easing' of a house.

Easle, *n.* the eaves of a house.

Eassel, Eassil, Eassilt, *adv.* eastwards, in an easterly direction.—*adj.* easterly.

Easselward, *adv.* towards the east.

Eassin, *v.* used of a cow: to desire the bull; to desire strongly. Cf. Eisin.

Eassint, *ppl.* having taken the bull.

East-bye, *adv.* eastward.

Easter, *adj.* eastern, towards the east.—*n.* the east wind.

Easter-side, *n.* the eastern side.

Eastie-wastie, *n.* a vacillating person.

Eastilt, *adv.* eastward. Cf. Eassel.

Eastin, *v.* to desire the bull. Cf. Eisin.

Eastland, *n.* the countries bordering on the Baltic.—*adj.* belonging to the east.

Eastle, *adv.* eastward. Cf. Eassel.

Eastlin, *adj.* easterly, east.

Eastlins, *adv.* eastward.

Eastning-wort, *n.* scabious.

Easy, *adj.* supple, free from stiffness; moderate in price.—*adv.* easily.

Easy-osy, -ozy, *adj.* easy-going.—*n.* an easy-going person.

Eat, *v.* to taste.—*n.* the act of eating; a feed, a feast; taste.

Eatche, *n.* an adze. Cf. Each.

Eated, Eatit, *v. pret.* ate.

Eaten and spued, *phr.* used of an unhealthy, dyspeptic person.

Eaten corn, *n.* growing corn partly eaten by trespassing domestic animals.

Eather, *n.* heather.

Eatin, *n.* the juniper. Cf. Etnach.

Eattocks, *n.* dainties, sweets.

Eave, *n.* the nave of a cart- or carriage-wheel.

Eazle, *n.* the eaves of a house. Cf. Easle.

Ebb, *adj.* shallow, not deep, applied to vessels and their liquid contents; near the surface, not deep in the ground.—*n.* the foreshore; the part of the beach between high and low tide.

Ebb-bait, *n.* shell-fish used by fishermen as bait.

Ebb-fur, *n.* a shallow furrow; a method of ploughing down rye sown over dung.

Ebb-land, *n.* shallow soil.

Ebb-minded, *adj.* shallow, frivolous.

Ebb-mother, *n.* the last of the ebb-tide.

Ebbness, *n.* shallowness.

Ebb-sleeper, *n.* the dunlin.

Ebb-stone, *n.* a rock exposed at ebb-tide.

Eccle-grass, *n.* the butterwort.

Ech, Echay, *int.* an excl. of wistfulness or longing. Cf. Hech.

Echie nor ochie, *phr.* absolutely nothing. Cf. Eechie.

Ech nor och, *phr.* not the smallest word or sound, neither one thing nor another.

Echo-stone, *n.* a black, hard stone, full of holes, and making them of a sound-returning nature.

Echt, *ppl.* owning, possessed of. Cf. Aught.

Eckle-feckle, *adj.* cheerful, merry; possessing a shrewd judgment.

Edder, *n.* an adder.

Edder, *conj.* either.

Edder, *v.* to twist ropes round a stack. Cf. Ether.

Edder, *n.* an animal's udder; a woman's breast.

Edderin, *n.* a short straw-rope; a cross-rope of the thatch on a house or stack. Cf. Etherin.

Edderin, Edderins, Edderon, *conj.* either; rather.

Eddikat, *ppl. adj.* educated.

Edge, *n.* the ridge of a hill; the summit of a range of hills; the highest part of a large, moorish, and elevated tract of ground which may lie between two streams.

Edgie, *v.* to be alert or quick in action.—*adj.* eager; clever; quick-tempered, easily irritated.

Ediwut, *n.* an idiot, a 'natural'; a simpleton.

Ee, *pron.* you.

E'e, *n.* an eye; an orifice for the passage or outflow of water; an opening into a coal-shaft; a regard, liking; desire, craving; a darling, chief delight.—*v.* to eye; used of liquids: to ooze, well-up.

Eean, *n.* a one-year-old horse. Cf. Ean.

E'ebree, E'ebroo, *n.* the eyebrow.

Eebrek-crap, *n.* the third crop after lea.

Eechie, *n.* in *phr.* 'eechie nor ochie,' 'eechie or nochy,' not a sound, nothing at all. Cf. Echie nor ochie.

Eeck, *n.* an addition.—*v.* to enlarge, add to. Cf. Eik.

Eediwut, *n.* an idiot; a simpleton.

Eedle-deedle, *adj.* easy-going in business, &c. —*n.* a man of little enterprise or energy.

E'e-feast, *n.* a rarity; what excites wonder; a satisfying glance that gratifies curiosity.

Eeghie nor oghie, *phr.* neither one thing nor another. Cf. Eechie.

Eek, *n.* an addition.—*v.* to increase by addition. Cf. Eik.

Eek, *n.* the natural grease oozing from sheep. Cf. Eik.

Eekfow, Eekfull, *adj.* blithe, affable; just, equal.—*n.* a match, an equal.

Eeksy-peeksy, *adj.* equal, exactly equal, alike.

Eel, *adj.* used of cows: ceasing to give milk. Cf. Yeld.

Eel, *n.* in *phr.* 'nine e'ed eel,' the lamprey.

Eel, *n.* oil.

Eel, *n.* Yule, Christmas.

Eelans, *n.* equals in age. Cf. Eeldins.

Eelat, *n.* the fish myxine, or glutinous hag.

Eel-backit, *adj.* used of a horse: having a dark stripe along the back.

Eel-beds, *n.* the water crow-foot.

Eeldins, *n.* equals in age.

Eel-dolly, *n.* an old-fashioned oil-lamp, a crusie.

Eel-drowner, *n.* one who is not clever or capable of performing a difficult task.

Eel-e'en, *n.* Christmas Eve.

Eelie, *v.* to ail; with *away,* to dwindle. Cf. Ely.

Eelie, *adj.* oily.—*n.* oil; a glazed earthenware marble.

Eelie-dolly, *n.* an 'eel-dolly.'

Eelie-lamp, *n.* an oil-lamp.

Eelist, *n.* a desire to possess something not easily obtained.

E'e-list, *n.* an eyesore; defect; a break in a page; a legal imperfection; a flaw, offence; cause of regret.

Eel-pout, *n.* the viviparous blenny.

Eel-tows, *n.* lines laid inshore to catch eels for bait.

Eely, *v.* to disappear gradually; to vanish one by one. Cf. Ely.

Eem, *n.* a maternal uncle; a familiar friend. Cf. Eme.

Eemock, Eemuch, *n.* the ant.

Eemor, *n.* humour.

Eemost, Eemist, *adj.* uppermost.

Een, *adj.* and *n.* one. Cf. Ane.

E'en, *n.* eyes.

Een, *n.* an oven.

E'en, *n.* even, evening.

E'en, *adv.* even, even so; nevertheless.

Eenach, *n.* the natural grease of wool.

E'enbright, *adj.* shining, luminous; bright to the eyes.

Eence, *adv.* once.

E'end, *adj.* even, straight.

Eenerie, *n.* a child's word in counting-out rhymes. Cf. Anery.

E'en-holes, *n.* eye-sockets.

Eenil, *v.* used of a woman: to be jealous of her husband's fidelity. Cf. Eyndill.

Eenkin, *n.* kith and kin.

Eenlins, *n.* equals in age. Cf. Eeldins.

E'enow, E'ennow, E'enoo, *adv.* just now; shortly.

Eens, *adv.* even as.

E'enshanks, *n.* an evening meal.

Eent, *adv.* 'even it,' used for emphasis.

Eer, *n.* colour, tinge; an iron stain on linen. Cf. Ure.

Eeram, *n.* a boat-song; a rowing-song.

Eeran, *n.* an errand. Cf. Errand.

Eerie, *adj.* apprehensive, afraid of ghosts, &c.; dismal, dull, gloomy; weird, uncanny, haunted by ghosts, &c.; awe-inspiring; dreary. Cf. Irie.

Eerieful, *adj.* foreboding evil, uncanny.

Eerielike, *adj.* appearing like what causes fear.

Eeriely, *adv.* dismally, forebodingly.

Eerieness, *n.* fear excited by the idea of an apparition.

Eeries and orries, *phr.* particulars, details; 'ins and outs.'

Eeriesome, *adj.* dull, sad; ghostly, weird.

Eeriesomeness, *n.* apprehensiveness of ghosts, &c.

E'erly, *adv.* continually. Cf. Everly.

Eerock, *n.* a pullet. Cf. Earock.

E'erthestreen, *n.* the night before yesternight.

Eese, *n.* use.—*v.* to use.

E'esicht, *n.* vision, eyesight.

Eesk, *v.* to hiccup; to heave at the stomach; to cough up.—*n.* a hiccup. Cf. Yesk.

E'esome, *adj.* attractive, gratifying to the eye.

E'estane, *n.* a perforated pebble, supposed to heal eye diseases.

E'estick, *n.* something that fixes the eye; a rarity, dainty. Cf. Eistack.

E'e-string, *n.* an eyelid.

Eeswall, *adj.* usual.

E'e-sweet, *adj.* beautiful, acceptable.

Eet, *n.* a custom, a bad habit. Cf. Ett, Ait.

Eeth, *adj.* easy. Cf. Eith.

Eetim, *n.* an item; a puny creature.

Eetion, *n.* a living creature.

Eetnoch, *n.* a moss-grown, precipitous rock.

Eettie, *n.* in *phr.* 'eettie ottie for a tottie, where shall this boy go?' &c., a boys' game.

Eevenoo, *adj.* very hungry.

Eever, *adj.* used of places: upper, higher, over.

Eevery, *adj.* hungry. Cf. Aiverie.

E'e-winkers, *n.* the eyelashes.

Eezin, *n.* the eaves of a house. Cf. Easing.

Efauld, *adj.* upright, honest, guileless. Cf. Aefald.

Eff-crap, *v.* to after-crop, to take two successive crops of the same kind from a field. Cf. Aft-crop.

Eff-, Eft-crop, *n.* stubble-grass; aftermath. Cf. Aft-crop.

Effect, *v.* used of money: to secure, recover payment; of lands: to make them bear the burden of repayment of money with which they have been burdened.—*n. pl.* produce of anything sold or of money invested.

Effeir, *n.* pomp and circumstance; what is fitting; bearing; garb, panoply.

Effeir, *v.* to pertain to; to fall to by right; to proportionate to.

Effrayit, *ppl. adj.* afraid.

Effront, *v.* to affront, put out of countenance.

Efter, *prep.* after.—*adv.* afterwards. Cf. After.

Efter-hend, -hin', *prep.* after.—*adv.* afterwards.

Efterin, *prep.* after.

Efterwal, *n.* leavings, refuse; soil rendered useless for cultivation.

Eft-stool, *n.* a newt- or lizard-stool.

†Egal, *adj.* equal.

Ege, *n.* the ridge of a hill.—*v.* to move gradually to one side. Cf. Edge.

Egg. *v.* to incite.

Egg-bed, *n.* the ovarium of a fowl; used of the brain: where thought arises in the mind.

Egg-doup, *n.* the lower end of an egg; a woman's cap with oval back.

Egg-doupit, *adj.* shaped like the end of an egg.

Egger, Egges, *n.* grain very much dried in a pot, for grinding in a 'quern.' Cf. Aigar.

Eggle, *v.* to 'egg,' to incite to evil.

Egg taggle, *n.* wasting time in bad company ; immodest conduct.

Eghin and owin, *phr.* humming and hawing.

Eght, *ppl.* owning, possessed of. Cf. Aucht.

Egsome, *adj.* pushing, forward.

Egypt-, Egyptian-herring, *n.* the saury pike.

Egyptian, *n.* a gypsy, vagabond ; a sturdy beggar.

Egyptian band, *n.* gypsies.

Eicen, *v.* used of a cow : to desire the bull. Cf. Eassin.

Eidence, *n.* industry ; diligence.

Eident, *adj.* industrious ; diligent ; steady, continuous ; attentive.

Eidently, *adv.* diligently ; attentively.

Eidi-streen, *n.* the night before last night.

Eidi-yesterday, *n.* the day before yesterday.

Eightpence drink, *n.* a very strong ale.

Eightsome, *adj.* consisting of eight persons. —*n.* a company or family of eight.

Eightsome-reel, *n.* a reel with eight dancers.

Eik, *n.* the natural grease of wool ; liniment used in greasing sheep.

Eik, *v.* to add ; to increase, supplement ; to subjoin.—*n.* an addition ; an addition to a glass of whisky, &c. ; an addition to a bee-hive.—*adv.* in addition to, besides, also.

Eikend, *n.* the short chain attaching the traces to the swingle-trees of a plough.

Eik-name, *n.* a 'to-name,' used among fishing-folk to distinguish those who bear the same names ; a nickname.

Eikrie, *n.* an addition to support or prolong anything.

Eild, *adj.* applicable to a cow that has ceased to give milk. Cf. Yeld.

Eild, *n.* age ; old age ; an old person.—*adj.* aged, old.—*v.* to grow old.

Eilden, *n.* fuel. Cf. Elding.

Eildins, Eillins, *n.* equals in age. Cf. Eeldins.

Eildron, *adj.* unearthly, uncanny, weird, 'eldritch.'

Eill, *adj.* used of cows : not giving milk. Cf. Yeld.

Ein', *v.* to end, come to a close.

Ein, Eind, *v.* to breathe ; to whisper ; to devise ; to make an appointment to meet. —*n.* breath. Cf. Aynd.

Eindill, Eindle, *v.* used of a woman : to be jealous of her husband's fidelity.

Eindling, *ppl. adj.* jealous.

Eindown, *adv.* thoroughly. - *adj.* downright ; thoroughly honest ; plain, without reserve. Cf. Evendown.

Einel, *v.* to be jealous. Cf. Eindill.

Eir, *n.* fear.

Eirack, *n.* a hen of the first year. Cf. Earock.

Eird, *n.* earth. Cf. Eard.

Eirne, *n.* the eagle. Cf. Ern.

Eiry, *adj.* uncanny. Cf. Eerie.

Eisin, *v.* to desire the male ; to desire strongly. Cf. Eassin.

Eisin, *n.* the eaves of a house. Cf. Easing.

Eisning, *n.* a strong desire or longing ; the copulation of a cow and a bull.

Eissel, *adv* eastward.—*adj.* easterly. Cf. Eassel.

Eistack, *n.* a dainty. Cf. Eestick.

Eistit, *adv.* rather.

Eitch, *n.* an adze. Cf. Each.

Eith, *adj.* easy.—*adv.* easily.

Eitheren, *n.* a straw-rope for fastening the thatch of a stack, &c. Cf. Etherin.

Eitherens, *conj.* either, rather. Cf. Edderins.

Eith-kent, *adj.* easily known or recognised.

Eithly, *adv.* easily.

Eiz, *n.* the eaves of a house. Cf. Easing.

†**Eizel,** *n.* an ass, a donkey.

Eizel, *n.* a hot ember ; charcoal.

Eizen, *n.* the eaves of a house. Cf. Easing.

Eke, *v.* to 'egg,' to incite ; to incite to mischief.

Eke, *v.* to add.—*n.* an addition. Cf. Eik.

Elbock, Elbuck, *n.* the elbow.—*v.* to raise one's self on the elbows.

Elbow-chair, *n.* an arm-chair.

Elbow-grease, *n.* snuff, brown rappee.

Elbowit-grass, *n.* the fox-tail grass.

Elder, *n.* in *phr.* 'elders o' Cowend' [Colvend], cormorants. Cf. Coween.

Elderen, Elderin, Eldern, *adj.* elderly.

Elder's hours, *phr.* respectable hours.

Elding, *n.* fuel of any kind.

Elding-docken, *n.* the water-dock.

Eldren, Eldrin, *adj.* elderly.

Eldrish, Elrish, *adj.* 'eldritch.'

Eldritch, Eldrich, Eldricht, *adj.* unearthly, ghostly, uncanny ; ghastly, frightful ; of a sore or wound : painful, fretting ; of the weather : chill ; surly in temper and manners.

Eleck, *v.* to elect, choose.

Eleid, *v.* to chide ; to quash. Cf. Elide.

Element, *n.* the sky.

Elenge, *adj.* foreign.

Elevener, *n.* a labourer's luncheon about 11 o'clock A.M.

Eleven-hours, *n.* a slight refreshment about 11 o'clock A.M.

Elf, *n.* a term of contempt or opprobrium.

Elf-bore, *n.* a hole in a piece of wood, out of which a knot has been driven or has dropped.

Elf-cups, *n.* small stones perforated by friction of a waterfall, supposed to be the work of fairies, often nailed over a stable-door to protect horses from being 'elf-shot.'

Elf-door, *n.* the opening in an 'elf-ring' by which the fairies were supposed to enter.

Elfer-stone, *n.* a chipped flint, believed to possess magical properties.

Elf-girse, *n.* grass given to cattle supposed to have been hurt by fairies.

Elf-hill, *n.* a fairy knoll.

Elfin, *n.* an euphemism for 'hell.'

Elf-mill, *n.* the death-watch, or 'chackie-mill.'

Elf-ring, *n.* a fairy circle within which elves were supposed to dance, &c., generally in old pasture.

Elf-shoot, *v.* to bewitch; to shoot with an elf-arrow.

Elf-shot, *n.* a flint arrow-head; a disease or injury to persons or cattle, credited to fairy malice; the lady's mantle.—*ppl. adj.* shot or injured by fairies.

Elf-stone, *n.* a flint arrow-head.

Elf-switches, *n.* elf-locks; tangled locks of hair.

Elgins, *n.* the water-dock. Cf. Eldin-docken.

Elide, *v.* legal term: to quash, annul; to evade the force or authority of.

Ell, *adj.* not giving milk. Cf. Yeld.

Ell, *n.* the 'Scotch'=37·0578 inches; the 'plaiden ell'=38·416 inches.

Ellan, *n.* a very small island in a river.

Eller, *n.* the alder.

Ellerisch, *adj.* unearthly. Cf. Eldritch.

Ellieson, *n.* a shoemaker's awl. Cf. Elsin.

Ellinge, *adj.* foreign. Cf. Elenge.

Ellion, *n.* fuel. Cf. Elding.

Ell-stick, *n.* an ell-measure; a measuring-rod.

Ellwand, *n.* an ell-measure; a measuring-rod; a standard.

Ellwand of stars, *n.* the three stars in the northern constellation of Lyra; the king's or lady's ellwand, the stars of Orion's belt.

Elne, *n.* an ell.

Elocate, *ppl. adj.* legal term, used of a woman: betrothed or wedded.

Elore, *int.* alas! woe is me! Cf. I-lore.

Elrick, Elricht, Elritch, *adj.* unearthly. Cf. Eldritch.

Else, *adv.* otherwise; at another time, already; *phr.* 'or else no,' an expression of contempt.

Elsin, Elshin, *n.* a shoemaker's awl.

Elsin-blade, *n.* an awl.

Elsin-box, *n.* a box for holding awls.

Elsin-heft, *n.* the handle of an awl; a jargonelle pear, as resembling the 'heft' of an awl.

Elson, Elsyn, *n.* an 'elsin.'

Elt, *v.* to mix meal and water; to knead dough; to injure by constant or rough handling; to toil or slave at working the ground; to meddle with; to bemire.—*n.* dough; with *carrie,* a thick, ill-baked cake; with *muckle,* a stout, clumsy woman.

Elvant, Elvint, *n.* a measuring-rod. Cf. Ellwand.

Ely, *v.* to disappear, vanish gradually, or one by one.

Elyer, *n.* an elder.

†**Elymosinar,** *n.* an almoner.

Embase, *v.* to debase money.

Ember, *n.* the great northern diver, or ember-goose.

†**Embezill,** *v.* to injure, to damage. Cf. Imbecille.

†**Embezilment,** *n.* injury, damage.

Eme, *n.* a maternal uncle; a familiar friend.

Emerant, *n.* an emerald.

Emergent, *n.* anything that emerges.

Emerteen, *n.* an ant.

Emm, *n.* an uncle. Cf. Eme.

Emmack, *n.* an ant. Cf. Eemock.

Emmers, *n.* embers, red-hot ashes.

Emmis, *adj.* variable; insecure, unsteady; used of the weather: gloomy.

Emmle-deug, Emmeldyug, *n.* butchers' offal, scrap or paring of carcass; a piece of anything loose and flying; a tatter fluttering from a dress.

Emmock, Emmot, Emock, *n.* an ant. Cf. Eemock.

Emmot-pile, *n.* an ant-heap.

Empanell, *v.* to accuse, charge; to put at the bar, a legal term.

†**Empesch,** *v.* to hinder.

Enact, *v.* to bind one's self; to put one's self under legal obligations.

Enanteen, *n.* an ant. Cf. Emerteen.

Enaunter, *conj.* lest.

End, *v.* to breathe; to whisper.—*n.* breath. Cf. Aynd.

End, *n.* a room in a cottage; a parlour; the end of a room; a shoemaker's waxed thread; the finishing game of a rink contest in curling; a use.—*v.* to set on end; to kill.

Endie, *adj.* attached to one's own interests; selfish; scheming; fertile in expedients; shuffling, shifty.

Ending-stroke, *n.* a death-blow; a finishing-stroke.

Endlang, *prep.* alongside of.—*adv.* at full length, lengthwise, along; from end to end; continuously.—*v.* to harrow a ploughed field from end to end.—*n.* full length.

Endlangin, *n.* harrowing a field along the furrows.

Endlangwyse, *adv.* lengthwise.

Endless, *adj.* long-winded ; pertinacious.

End-pickle, *n.* a head of corn.

Endrift, *n.* snow driven by the wind.

End's errand, *n.* an exclusive errand, express purpose. Cf. Anes errand.

Endurable, *adj.* lasting, enduring.

Endways, *adv.* forward, onward ; well on ; successfully.

Endwye, *n.* headway, progress.

Ene, *n.* eyes. Cf. Een.

Enel-sheet, *n.* a winding-sheet.

Enemy, *n.* the devil ; a person of evil disposition ; an ant.

Eneuch, Eneugh, *n.* and *adj.* enough.

Enew, *adj.* enough. Cf. Enow.

Engage, *v.* to attract.

†Engine, Engyne, *n.* genius, intellect, disposition, character. Cf. Ingine.

English, *n.* English, in contrast to Gaelic.

English and Scots, *n.* a children's game.

Englisher, *n.* an Englishman.

English-weight, *n.* avoirdupois weight.

Engrage, *v.* to irritate ; to 'aggravate' by irony.

†Engross, *v.* to swallow up entire ; to render a woman pregnant.

†Enixe, *adj.* express.

Enkerloch, *adj.* having a difficult temper.

Enlang, *prep.* alongside of. Cf. Endlang.

Enlarger, *n.* an expositor, one who enlarges in preaching.

Enlighten, *v.* to fill or flood with light.

Enner, *adj.* nether ; inferior in place.

Ennermair, *adj.* with greater inferiority in place.

Ennermaist, *adj.* nethermost.

†Enorme, *adj.* enormous ; horrid.

Enow, *adj.* enough ; sufficient in number.

Enow, Enoo, *adv.* just now ; presently, shortly. Cf. Eenow.

Enquire for, *v.* to inquire after.

Ens, Ense, *conj.* else.—*adv.* otherwise.

†Ensigneer, *n.* an ensign (officer).

Entering, *ppl. adj.* favourable for beginning or entering on.

Entertain, *v.* to welcome ; to pay for the support of.

Entitule, *v.* to entitle, to have as a title.

Entramells, *n.* bondage ; prisoners of war.

Entry, *n.* an alley or narrow passage between two houses ; a house lobby.

Entry-mouth, *n.* the entrance of a 'close' or narrow passage.

Enuch, *adj.* enough.

Enveigh, *v.* to inveigh.

Envy-fow, -fu', *adj.* envious ; full of malice.

Enze, *conj.* else. Cf. Ens.

Ephesian, *n.* a pheasant.

Epicacco, *n.* ipecacuanha.

†Epie, *n.* a blow with a sword.

Episcolaupian, Episcopian, *n.* an Episcopalian.

Eppersyand, *n.* the sign &, *et per se,* and.

Equal-aqual, *adj.* equally balanced ; exactly alike or equal ; 'upside with.'—*n.* exact equality.—*v.* to make all equal ; to balance.

Equals-aquals, *adv.* on a strict equality.

Equiable, *adj.* equable.

Equipage, *n.* utensils of all kinds, as of glass, china, earthenware.

Erack, *n.* a pullet. Cf. Earock.

Erch, *adj.* timorous, shy.—*adv.* nearly.—*v.* to hesitate. Cf. Arch.

Erchin, *n.* a hedgehog, 'hurcheon.' Cf. Urchin.

Erd, *n.* earth.—*v.* to bury ; to protect with earth. Cf. Eard.

Erd and stane, *n.* a mode of symbolical investiture with land in ownership.

Ere, *adj.* early.—*prep.* before.—*conj.* previous to ; rather than. Cf. Or.

Ere-fernyear, *n.* the year before last.

Erethestreen, *n.* the evening before last.

Erf, *adj.* shy.—*adv.* scarcely.—*v.* to hesitate. Cf. Arch, Argh.

Ergane, *ppl.* overflowing.

Ergh, *adj.* half-boiled.

Ergh, *adj.* timorous ; scrupulous ; shy.—*adv.* nearly, scarcely.—*v.* to hesitate, to be shy. Cf. Argh.

Erle, *v.* to give an earnest.—*n.* in *pl.* an earnest or instalment of wages for service. Cf. Arle.

Erlish, *adj.* unearthly, uncanny ; ghastly. Cf. Eldritch.

Ermit, *n.* an earwig.

Ern, *v.* used of the eye : to be wet, to water.

Ern, *n.* iron.

Ern, *n.* the eagle, erne.

Ern-bleater, *n.* the snipe.

Ern-fern, *n.* the brake-fern.

Ernistfull, *adj.* eager ; ardent.

Ernit, *n.* the pig-nut. Cf. Arnot.

Ern tings, *n.* iron tongs.

Erock, *n.* a pullet. Cf. Earock.

Erp, *v.* to grumble ; to repine.

Errack, *n.* a pullet. Cf. Earock.

Erran', *n.* an errand ; a message or parcel, &c., for delivery ; in *pl.* marketings, shoppings, and articles then bought.

Errand-bairn, *n.* a child-messenger.

Errie, *adj.* uncanny ; superstitiously gloomy. Cf. Eerie.

Erruction, *n.* a 'rumpus,' a violent outbreak, a 'ruction.'

Erse, *n.* the fundament. Cf. Arse.

Ersit, *adj.* perverse, contrary.

Erst, *adv.* in the first place.

Ert, *v.* to urge on, incite ; to irritate. Cf. Airt.

Erthlins, *adv.* earthward. Cf. Earthlins.

Ertienig, *adj.* ingenious; capable of laying plans.

Erudition, *n.* civility, respect, courtesy.

†Erumption, *n.* an outburst, 'rumpus.'

Ery, Erie, *adj.* weird; ghostly; timorous. Cf. Eerie.

Escape, *n.* an omission, an oversight; an offence.

Esk, *n.* a newt. Cf. Ask.

Esk, *v.* to hiccup; to cough up.—*n.* a hiccup. Cf. Yesk.

Eskdale-souple, *n.* a broadsword, a two-handed sword.

Esplin, *n.* a stripling, a youth.

Ess, Esse, *n.* an S-shaped hook or link for traces, &c.; the ends of a curb-chain.

Essael, *pron.* himself.

Essart, *adj.* perverse, crooked.

Ess-cock, *n.* the dipper.

Esscock, *n.* a hot pimple on any part of the body. Cf. Arse-cockle, Nesscock.

Essel, *n.* a red-hot cinder, an ember. Cf. Aizle.

Essis, *n.* ornaments of jewellery in the shape of the letter S.

†Essonyie, Essoinzie, *v.* to excuse one's self for absence from a law-court.—*n.* such excuse for absence.

Est, *n.* a nest.

Estalment, *n.* an instalment.

†Estit, *adv.* as soon, rather. Cf. Astid.

Estlar, *n.* ashlar; hewn or polished stone. Cf. Aislar.

Estlins, *adv.* rather, 'as lief.'

Eterie, *adj.* used of the weather: keen, bitter; ill-tempered; hot-headed; angry-looking. Cf. Attery.

Eth, *adj.* easy. Cf. Eith.

Ether, *v.* to twist ropes of straw round a stack.—*n.* a twig, switch. Cf. Yether.

Ether, *n.* an adder. Cf. Edder.

Ether, *adj. pron.* and *conj.* either.

Ethercap, *n.* a spider; an ill-humoured person; a hot-tempered person. Cf. Attercap.

Etherins, Etherans, *conj.* either.—*adv.* rather. Cf. Eitherens.

Etherins, Etherans, *n.* the cross-ropes of a thatched roof or stack.

Ether-stane, *n.* an adder-bead.

†Ethik, *adj.* delicate.

Etion, *n.* kindred; genealogy; descent. Cf. Ation.

Etnach, *n.* juniper.—*adj.* of juniper; of juniper-wood. Cf. Aitnach.

Ett, *n.* a custom, habit; generally in a bad sense.

Etten, *ppl.* eaten.

Etter, *v.* to fester.

Ettercap, *n.* a spider; an ant; an irascible, captious, malignant person.

Etterlin, *n.* a cow which has a calf when only two years old. Cf. Otterline.

Ettin, Etin, *n.* a giant.

Ettle, *v.* to intend, purpose; to take aim; to direct one's course towards; to attempt, struggle, make an effort; to make ready; to hanker after, to be eager to do or begin; to suppose, guess, reckon, count on.—*n.* an intent, aim, effort, attempt; chance; a mark.

Ettler, *n.* one who 'ettles.'

Ettling, *n.* effort, endeavour.—*ppl. adj.* ambitious, pushing.

Euk, *v.* to itch. Cf. Yeuk.

Evacuate, *v.* to nullify, set aside, neutralize.

Evanish, *v.* to vanish, disappear quite.

Evasion, *n.* a way or means of escape from danger.

Eveat, *v.* to avoid, shun; to escape. Cf. Evite.

Eve-, Evil-eel, *n.* the conger-eel.

Eveleit, Evelit, *adj.* prompt; ready; cheerful. Cf. Evleit.

Even, *v.* to compare; to level down, demean; to suggest as a suitable person to marry; to impute, hint, charge with; to think entitled to.—*n.* in *pl.* equals, quits.

Even and eyn, *phr.* in good earnest.

Evendoun, *adj.* perpendicular; honest, downright; direct, without reserve or qualification; mere, sheer; habitual, confirmed; of rain: very heavy and straight down.—*adv.* thoroughly, completely.

Even-hands, *adv.* on an equality.—*n.* an equal bargain.

Evenliness, *n.* equanimity, composure.

Evenly, *adj.* of ground, &c.: smooth, level.

Evenner, *n.* a weaver's implement for spreading yarn on the beam.

Even-noo, Eve'noo, *adv.* just now; in a minute. Cf. E'enow.

Even on, *adv.* continuously.

Even out, *adv.* loudly.

Even-up back, *n.* in *phr.* to 'keep an even-up back,' to keep straight.

Ever, *v.* to nauseate.

Ever, *adj.* used of places: upper, over.

Ever alack, *int.* alas!

Ever and on, *adv.* continually.

Everilk, *adj.* each; every.

Everilk-on, -one, *phr.* each single one, every individual one.

Everlasting, *adv.* continually.

Everly, *adv.* continually; perpetually.

Ever now, *adv.* just now.

Everochs, *n.* the cloudberry. Cf. Averin.

Every, *adj.* both, each of two.

Every, *adj.* hungry. Cf. Aiverie.

Eve-, Ever-, Ere-yesterday, *n.* the day before yesterday.

Eve-, Ever-, Ere-yestreen, *n.* the night before yesternight.

Evict, *v.* to dispossess legally of property, used not of the person but of the property.

Evident, *n.* a title-deed; documentary proof.

Evil-headit, *adj.* used of an ox or bull: prone to butt.

Evil-man, *n.* the devil.

Evil-money, *n.* false coin.

†Evite, *v.* to avoid, shun; to evade; to escape.

Evleit, *adj.* prompt, active; ready, willing; sprightly, cheerful; handsome. Cf. Oleit.

Evrie, *adj.* hungry. Cf. Every.

Ewden-drift, *n.* drifted snow. Cf. Youden-drift.

Ewder, *n.* a disagreeable smell; the steam of a boiling pot; the odour of anything burning; dust; the dust of flax; a collection of small particles.

Ewder, *n.* a blaze.

Ewdroch, Ewdruch, *n.* a strong, disagreeable smell. Cf. Ewder.

Ewe, *n.* a stupid, easy-going person; the cone of a fir, larch, &c.

Ewe-bucht, -bught, *n.* a sheep-pen; a place where ewes are milked.

Ewe-gowan, *n.* the common daisy.

Ewe-hogg, *n.* a ewe at the stage next to a lamb's.

E-wel, *int.* indeed! really! Cf. Aweel.

Ewe-milker, *n.* one who milks ewes.

Ewendrie, *n.* the refuse of oats after winnowing; weak grain.

Ewer, *n.* the udder of a cow, sheep, &c. Cf. Ure.

Ewer-locks, *n.* the wool round a sheep's udder, removed near lambing-time.

Ewest, *adj.* most contiguous; nearest.

E-whow, *int.* an excl. of grief, surprise, or alarm. Cf. Avow.

Ewie, *n.* a young ewe; a small fir-cone.

Ewindrift, *n.* snow driven by the wind. Cf. Ewden-drift.

Ewk, *v.* to itch. Cf. Yeuk.

Exack, *v.* to exact.

Exack, *adj.* exact.—*adv.* exactly.

Exact, *adj.* expert.—*adv.* exactly; straitly.

Exactable, *adj.* exigible.

Examine, *n.* an examination.

Excamb, Excambie, *v.* to exchange lands.

Excambion, *n.* an exchange of lands

Exceppins, *prep.* except.

†Excresce, *n.* overpayment; overplus in value.

Excrescence, *n.* a surplus.

†Exeem, Exeme, *v.* to exempt.

Exem, *v.* to examine.

Exemmin, *n.* an examination.—*v.* to examine.

Exemp, *n.* exemption.—*adj.* exempt.

Exemplar, *adj.* exemplary.

Exemplarly, *adv.* for example.

†Exerce, *v.* to exercise.

Exercise, *v.* to conduct family worship; to expound Scripture at a meeting of presbytery.—*n.* family worship; the presbyterial exposition; a part of a divinity student's 'trials' for license to preach; a name for a presbytery.

Exercise and additions, *n.* an exposition, paraphrase, and application of a passage, in the original, of Scripture, delivered by a student of divinity or by members of a presbytery in rotation.

Exercising, *n.* public worship.

†Exheredate, *v.* to disinherit; to deprive of an inheritance, a legal term.

Exhibition, *n.* in *phr.* to 'raise an exhibition,' to call for the production of writs.

Exhort, *n.* an address, exhortation.

Exhoust, *v.* to exhaust.—*ppl. adj.* exhausted.

Exies, *n.* hysterics; an access of ague. Cf. Aixies.

Exigent, *n.* an exigency, an emergency.

Exle, *n.* an axle.

Exoner, *v.* to relieve from a burden; to exonerate from responsibility, trusteeship, &c., a legal term.

Exorbitant, *adj.* extreme; extravagant.

Expectancy, *n.* the state of being an 'expectant.'

Expectant, *n.* a divinity student preparing for license to preach.

†Expede, *v.* to expedite, despatch.

Experimented, *ppl. adj.* experienced.

†Expone, *v.* to explain, expound; to expose; to represent, characterize.

Express, *n.* a special errand.

Extenuate, *v.* used of the body: to become thin, slender.

Exterics, *n.* hysterics.

Extinguish, *v.* used of a debt: to pay off gradually.

Extort, *v.* to practise extortion on one.

Extortion, *n.* an exorbitant price.—*v.* to charge exorbitantly.

Extranean, *adj.* coming from a distance.—*n.* a scholar coming to the higher classes of Aberdeen Grammar School from another school for special drill in classics; an outsider; one not of the family.

Extraordinar, Exterordinar, *adj.* extraordinary.—*n.* in *pl.* unusual occurrences.—*adv.* extraordinarily.

†Extravage, *v.* to wander about; to wander in discourse; to speak incoherently; to enlarge in speaking.

Ey, *n.* an island.

Ey, *adv.* aye, always.
Eydent, *adj.* industrious, diligent.
Eydi-yesterday, *n.* the day before yesterday.
Eydi-yestreen, *n.* the night before yester-night.
Eye-last, -list, *n.* an eyesore; a flaw; a fault; an offence; a cause of regret. Cf. Ee-list.
Eyen, *n.* eyes.
Eye-sweet, *adj.* pleasing to the eye.
Eye-winker, *n.* an eyelid, an eyelash.
Eyn, *n.* an end.—*v.* to end.
Eynd, *v.* to breathe; to whisper.—*n.* a breath. Cf. Aynd.

Eyndill, *v.* used of a woman : to suspect the fidelity of her husband ; to be jealous.
Eyndling, *ppl. adj.* jealous.—*n.* jealousy.
Eyn't, *ppl.* ended.
Eyven, *adv.* even.
Eyzle, *n.* a live coal ; a hot ember. Cf. Aizle.
Eyzly, *adj.* red, fiery.
Eyzly-e'e't, *adj.* fiery-eyed.
Ezar, *n.* maple-wood.—*adj.* of or belonging to the maple.
Ezin, *n.* an eave of a house. Cf. Easing.
Ezle, *n.* a spark of fire ; a hot ember. Cf. Aizle.

Fa, *pron.* who.
Fa, *v.* to become, to suit, used impersonally.
Fa', *n.* a fall ; a fall of rain or snow ; a trap, snare ; a lot, fortune ; a share, portion.—*v.* to fall ; used of the sea : to grow calm ; of lime : to become powdery ; to befall ; to change into ; to become pregnant ; to fall to one's duty ; to excel, win ; to fail ; to put up ; to take in hand.
Faad, *v. pret.* fell.
Faags, *int.* faith ! Cf. Fegs.
Fa' ahint, *v.* to fall behind, into arrears of rent, work, &c.
Faal, *n.* a fold.—*v.* to fold ; to bend.
Fa'an, *ppl.* fallen.
Faang, *n.* an unpleasant person.
Faar'd, *ppl. adj.* favoured, featured. Cf. Faured.
Fa' awa', *v.* to waste away.
Fab, *v.* to trick, cheat.—*n.* a trick, cheat.
Fab, *n.* a fob ; a small pocket ; a tobacco-pouch.
†Fabala, *n.* a trimming of a petticoat ; a flounce, a furbelow.
Fabric, *n.* a person, animal, or thing of big, clumsy appearance.
Fa' by, *v.* to be sick ; to be in childbed.
Fac, *n.* fact ; truth, reality.—*int.* indeed ! Cf. Fack.
Face, *n.* the edge of any sharp instrument.
Faceable, *adj.* fit to be seen, pretty ; likely to be true.
Face o' clay, *phr.* any living person.
Face-plate, *n.* the face.
Face-wise, *adj.* facing.
†Facherie, *n.* trouble, worry. Cf. Fasherie.
Facht, *v.* to fight ; to struggle.—*n.* a fight ; a struggle. Cf. Fecht.
Facie, *adj.* bold, fearless ; insolent, impudent.
Fack, *n.* fact, truth, reality.—*int.* indeed ! really !
Faction, *n.* the name formerly given to a bench in the Aberdeen Grammar School.
Factor, *n.* the manager of a landed property,

who lets farms, collects rents, and pays wages ; a person legally appointed to manage sequestrated property.—*v.* to act as factor.
Factorship, Factory, *n.* the office of 'factor'; agency.
Faddom, *v.* to fathom ; to measure ; to encompass with the arms.
Fade, *n.* a director in sports, &c.
Fader, *n.* father.
Faderil, *n.* the loose end of anything ; in *pl.* apparatus.
Fadge, *n.* a faggot, bundle of sticks.
Fadge, *n.* a fat, clumsy woman ; a short, thickset person.
Fadge, *n.* a large, flat loaf or 'bannock'; a flat wheaten loaf.
Fadle, *v.* to walk clumsily, waddle.
Fadmell, *n.* a weight of lead, 70 lbs. Cf. Fodmell.
Fae, *pron.* who.
Fae, *n.* foe.
Fae, *prep.* from, away from.
Faedom, *n.* witchcraft. Cf. Feydom.
Faegit, *ppl. adj.* fagged.
Fael, *n.* turf. Cf. Fail.
Faem, *n.* foam, froth.—*v.* to foam.
Fa'en, *ppl. adj.* fallen.
Faerdy, *adj.* strong, stout-built. Cf. Feerdy.
Faert, *n.* a ford. Cf. Fierd.
Faert, *ppl. adj.* afraid.
Faffer, *n.* a flapper ; a fan.
Fag, *n.* a sheep-louse or tick ; in *pl.* lousiness in sheep.
Faggald, Fagald, *n.* a bundle of heath or twigs bound with straw-ropes, a faggot.
Faggie, *adj.* fatiguing, tiring.
Fag-ma-fuff, *n.* a garrulous old woman.
Fagot, Faggot, *n.* a slattern.
Fagsum, *adj.* wearisome, tiring.
Fagsumness, *n.* tiresomeness.
Faick, *v.* to lower a price. Cf. Faik.
Faick, Faicks, *int.* faith ! Cf. Faix.
Faid, *n.* a director of sports.

Faidle, *v.* to waddle. Cf. Fadle.

Faighlochs, *n.* sorry workers doing little.

Faigs, *int.* an excl. of surprise, faith !

Faik, *n.* truth.—*int.* in truth !

Faik, *v.* to fondle ; to tuck up ; to caress.— *n.* a plaid ; a fold, ply ; the part of a full sack drawn together for tying ; a stratum of stone in a quarry.

Faik, *v.* to lower a price ; to excuse ; to reduce, abate a claim ; to let go unpunished.

Faik, *v.* to fail from weariness ; to stop, intermit.—*n.* a failure.

Faik, *n.* the strand of a rope. Cf. Fake.

Faik, *n.* the razor-bill. Cf. Falk.

Faikie, *n.* a plaid.

Faikins, Faickens, *n.* truth, used in mild oaths.

Faikit, *ppl. adj.* wearied out.

Faiks, *n.* faith. Cf. Faix.

Fail, Faill, Faile, *n.* a sward; a flat sod of turf ; turf.

Fail, *v.* to break down in health ; to grow weak.—*adj.* frail, weak.—*n.* decline.

Fail-caster, *n.* one who cuts 'fails.'

Fail-delf, *n.* the place from which 'fails' have been dug.

Fail-dyke, *n.* a wall built of 'fails.'

Fail-housie, *n.* a small house built with 'fails.'

Fail-roofed, *adj.* roofed with 'fails.'

Fail-wa', *n.* a house- or hut-wall built of turf.

Failyie, Failzie, *v.* to fail.—*n.* failure, default, penalty for breach of bargain.

Faim, *n.* foam, froth.

Fa' in, *v.* to shrink in ; to subside.

Fain, *adj.* eager, anxious ; fond, affectionate, in love.—*adv.* fondly.

Fain, *adj.* used of grain in the field : not thoroughly dry so as to be stacked ; of meal : of bad quality, made of grain not ripe enough.

Fainfu', *adj.* affectionate, kind, loving.

Fainly, *adj.* pleasant, gladsome, welcome ; amiable, affectionate.—*adv.* gladly, eagerly, excitedly ; fondly, lovingly.

Fainness, *n.* gladness ; desire ; liking ; fondness, love, affection.

Faint, *n.* the devil ; nothing, in excls. Cf. Fient.

Faint, *v.* to enfeeble ; to make faint.

Faintly, *adj.* weak, faint.

Faints, *n.* low wines ; inferior spirits.

Fainty-grund, *n.* ground, in passing over which it is deemed necessary to have a bit of bread in one's pocket to prevent fainting.

Faiple, *n.* anything loose and flaccid hanging from the nose ; a turkey's crest or comb when elated ; the under-lip of men and beasts when it hangs down large and loose.

Fair, *n.* a gift from a fair, a fairing.—*v.* to treat at a fair.

Fair, *adj.* plausible, pleasant ; clean, tidy, set in order ; likely, having a good chance ; complete, utter.—*adv.* quite, completely, thoroughly ;. exactly. — *v.* used of the weather : to become fine, clear up.

Fair, *v.* to travel ; to fare ; to entertain with food. Cf. Fare.

Fair-ba's, *n.* fairplay.

Fair-ca'in, *n.* address, skill, care. — *adj.* plausible, smooth-tongued.

Faird, *n.* stir, bustle ; a violent onset, a wrangle.—*v.* to bustle ; to wrangle.

Faird, *v.* to paint. Cf. Fard.

Fairdie, *adj.* passionate, irascible ; clever, handy.

Fairding, *n.* painting ; embellishment.

Fair fa', *phr.* good-luck to, an expression of good wishes.

Fair-fa', *v.* to wrestle.—*n.* a wrestling-match.

Fair-faced, *adj.* of plausible or deceitful appearance.

Fair-fa'in, *n.* a wrestling.

Fair fa' ma sel', *phr.* used of one who boasts of his success.

Fair-farand, *adj.* good to look at but hurtful.

Fair-fashioned, -fassint, *adj.* apparently, but not really, civil ; fair-seeming, plausible.

Fair-faughlit, *ppl. adj.* worn-out, jaded by fatigue. Cf. Forfaughlit.

Fair fa' ye, *int.* good-luck to you !

Fairfle, *n.* an eruption of the skin.

Fairflitten, *n.* a severe scolding.—*ppl. adj.* severely scolded. Cf. Forflitten.

Fair-flutter, *v.* to discompose.—*n.* agitation. Cf. Forflutter.

Fair folk, *n.* fairies.

Fair-foor-, -foor-, -fuir-days, *n.* broad daylight.

Fair-furth, Fair-furth-the-gate, *phr.* straightforward, honest.

Fair-ga'en, *adj.* used of an invalid : likely to recover.

Fair-grass, *n.* the goose-grass ; the buttercup.

Fair-gude-day, *n.* good-morning.

Fair-gude-e'en, *n.* good-evening.

Fair-hair, *n.* the tendon of the neck of cattle or sheep.

Fair hornie, *n.* fairplay.

Fairin', *n.* a gingerbread fairing ; a present bought at a fair ; a drubbing, deserts ; holding a fair.

Fairin', *n.* food, fare. Cf. Faring.

Fairish, *adj.* tolerably good.—*adv.* fairly.

Fairlaithie, *v.* to loathe ; to disgust. — *n.* a loathing ; a surfeit. Cf. Forlaithie.

Fairleens, Fairlins, *adv.* almost, not quite.

Fairley, *n.* a wonder.—*v.* to wonder, think strange. Cf. Ferly.

Fairly, *adv.* quite ; certainly, surely.
Fairly-fu', *adj.* full of wonder. Cf. Ferly-full.
Fairm, *n.* a farm.—*v.* to farm.
Fairmaist, *adj.* foremost.
Fairney cloots, *n.* the small horny substance above the hoofs, where the pastern of a horse lies, but said to be found only in sheep or goats.
Fairney-, Fairn-tickles, *n.* freckles. Cf. Fern-tickles.
Fairntosh, *n.* 'peat-reek' whisky formerly distilled at Ferintosh in Ross-shire.
Fairn-year, *n.* the past year. Cf. Fern-year.
Fairock, *n.* a mock sun.
Fair-ower, -owre, *adv.* in exact exchange.
Fairscomfisht, *ppl. adj.* overcome by heat or a bad smell. Cf. Forscomfist.
Fair-strae-death, *n.* a natural death in bed.
Fairt, *ppl. adj.* afraid.
Fair-trade, *n.* smuggling.
Fairy-dart, *n.* a flint arrow-head.
Fairy-green, *n.* a small circle of darker green grass in meadows, &c., supposed to be the fairies' dancing-ground.
Fairy-hammer, *n.* a 'celt' or stone-hatchet.
Fairy-hillock, *n.* a verdant knoll, supposed to have been the dwelling- or the dancing-place of fairies.
Fairy-knowe, *n.* a 'fairy-hillock.'
Fairy-rade, *n.* the fairies' expedition to where they held their great annual banquet on May 1.
Fairy-ring, *n.* a 'fairy-green.'
Faise, *v.* to drive ; to disturb ; to put to inconvenience.—*n.* inconvenience. Cf. Fease.
Faise, *v.* to screw, twist ; used of cloth : to fray out ; of a sharp instrument : to have the edge jagged or turned up ; to rub hard ; to work briskly. Cf. Feeze.
Faishochs, *n.* sorry workers who do little. Cf. Faighlochs.
Faisins, *n.* stringy parts of cloth, resembling lint, applied to a wound. Cf. Feeze.
Fait, *adj.* fit ; clever ; neat, tidy.—*n.* an achievement. Cf. Feat.
Fait, *n.* in *phr.* 'to lose fait of,' to lose one's good opinion of.
Faitchen, *ppl.* fetched.
Faith, *int.* an excl. indeed ! truly !
Faitha, *int.* by my faith !
Faith and troth, *phr.* by my faith and truth !
Faither, *n.* father.
Faix, *n.* a mild expletive, faith.—*int.* faith !
Faizart, *n.* a hermaphrodite of the hen-tribe ; a puny young man of feminine appearance ; an impudent or shameless person.
Faize, *v.* to twist ; used of cloth : to unravel, fray out, assume the form of the raw material where there is a rent ; to turn the edge of a razor. Cf. Feeze.

Faizing, *n.* the stringy parts of cloth when the wool is rubbed out from the warp.
Faizle, *v.* to flatter, coax.
Pak, *n.* fact. Cf. Fack.
Fake, *n.* a sight, a vision.
Fake, *n.* the strand of a rope.
Fakes, *n.* an excl. used in mild oaths. Cf. Faix.
†**Falcage,** *n.* the right of mowing.
Fald, *n.* a sheep-fold.—*v.* to enclose in a sheep-fold. Cf. Fauld.
Fald, *n.* a fold.—*v.* to fold ; to bend ; to enfold ; to bow.
Fald-dyke, *n.* a turf wall round a sheep-fold.
Falderal, Faldaral, *n.* a gewgaw, useless ornament ; an idle fancy ; a trifling excuse ; a pedantic, giddy person ; in *pl.* odds and ends, trifles.—*v.* to make trifling excuses ; to behave in a pedantic, giddy way.
Fale, *n.* a flat piece of turf. Cf. Fail.
Falk, *n.* the razor-bill.
Falkland-bred, *adj.* bred at court, courtly, polished.
Fall, *n.* scrap, offal.
Fall, *n.* a trap, a fall-trap. Cf. Fa'.
Fall, *n.* a measure of 6 ells square, a perch.
Fallall, *n.* a superfluous article of dress or part of dress, superficial ornament of women's dress ; a gewgaw, trumpery ornament ; a 'kickshaw,' needless dainty.
†**Fallauge, Falawdge,** *adj.* lavish, profuse. Cf. Volage.
Fall-board, *n.* the hinged wooden shutter of an unglazed window.
Fall-cap, *n.* a stuff cap worn by a child to protect the head in falling.
Fallen-star, *n.* the sea-nettle ; in *pl.* the jelly tremella, a gelatinous plant found in pastures, &c., after rain.
Falling nieve, *n.* a method of cheating at marbles.
Falling-sickness, *n.* epilepsy.
Falloch, *n.* a large lump, heap, piece of eatables or of anything lumpish or weighty.
Fallow, *n.* a fellow ; a match.
Fallow-break, *n.* land under grass for two years, and then ploughed up.
Fallow-chat, *n.* the wheatear.
Falsary, *n.* a liar, cheat, a false witness.
Falser, *n.* a user of false weights, &c.
Falset, *n.* falsehood ; dishonesty.
False-tastedly, *adv.* in false or bad taste.
Falten, *n.* a fillet.
†**Faltive,** *adj.* faulty.
Fame, *n.* common report ; country gossip.
Fame, *n.* a film of anything floating on another ; a rage, passion.—*v.* to be in a rage.
Famh, Famhphear, *n.* a small, noxious beast ; a monster ; a cruel, mischievous person.

Family duty, *n.* family worship.
Famous, *adj.* of good character ; well reported of.
Fan, *adv.* when.
Fan, *n.* fanners for winnowing.
Fan', Fand, *v. pret.* and *ppl.* found.
Fancy, *v.* to care for, fall in love with.—*n.* affection, liking.
Fand, *n.* a bow, knot.
Fane, *adj.* of meal : of bad quality. Cf. Fain.
Fane, *n.* an elf, fairy.
Fanerels, *n.* anything loose or flapping.
Fang, *v.* to clutch, grasp ; to steal ; to fill a pump with water to make it work properly. —*n.* a trap, a 'tight place'; the act of thieving ; spoil, booty, anything stolen ; a catch in buying ; a cheap bargain ; a heavy burden in the hands or arms ; a claw, hook, talon ; a thief, scamp ; a term of contempt ; a lout ; the coil of a rope, the thong of a whip ; the grip or power of suction in a pump ; a large lump or 'whang' cut from something.
Fank, *n.* an enclosure ; a sheep-cot, a pen for cattle at night.—*v.* to fold or pen sheep or cattle.
Fank, *n.* a coil, noose ; a tangle ; a coil of ropes.—*v.* to coil a rope ; to twist ; to entangle the feet ; to hinder.
Fank-day, *n.* the day on which sheep were clipped.
Fankle, *v.* to entangle, twist ; to knot ; to coil, wind ; to disorder, complicate.—*n.* an entanglement.
Fa' o', *v.* to abate.
Fa' o'er, *v.* to fall asleep ; used of a woman : to be confined.
Faple, *n.* the under-lip, especially of a horse. Cf. Faiple.
Far, *adv.* where ; whither. Cf. Whaur.
Far, *adv.* greatly, much.—*n.* a degree ; the greater part.—*adj.* difficult ; in *phr.* 'far to seek,' not easy to find.
Farack, *n.* a small mark on the skin.
Far aff, *adj.* distantly related.
Farand, *adj.* seeming. Cf. Fair-farand.
Farand-man, *n.* a stranger, traveller ; a merchant-stranger.
Far-awa, *adj.* used of relationship : distant ; of time or place : remote, distant.—*n.* abroad, 'foreign parts.'
Far-awa-screed, *n.* a letter or news from abroad.
Far-ben, *adj.* in high favour ; in one's good graces ; intimate ; advanced.
Far-by, *adv.* far past, beyond.—*prep.* quite beyond.
Farcie, *adj.* righteous.
Far-come, *adj.* foreign, at a distance ; distantly related.

†**Farcost,** *n.* a trading-vessel.
Fard, *v.* to paint ; to embellish.—*n.* paint ; embellishment.
Far'd, *ppl. adj.* favoured ; mannered.
Fard, *n.* a bustle, stir ; a violent onset. Cf. Faird.
Fardel, *n.* a quantity, a lot.
Fardel, *n.* progress.—*adj.* ready for future use. —*v.* to store up for the future. Cf. Fordal.
Farder, *adj.* farther.—*adv.* further, farther. —*v.* to further.
Fardest, *adj.* and *adv.* furthermost, farthest.
Farding, *n.* painting ; embellishment.
Fare, *n.* a fair ; a present from a fair. Cf. Fair.
Fare, *v.* to entertain with food ; to serve with food.
Farer, *adj.* further, farther.
Farest, *adj.* furthermost, farthest.
Fareway, *n.* the passage or channel in a river or the sea for a ship, &c.
Fareweel, *n.* farewell.
Far-hie-an-atour, *phr.* at a considerable distance.
Farie, *n.* a stir, bustle ; *phr.* 'fiery-farie,' a great hubbub.
Faring, *n.* food, fare.
Farkage, *n.* a confused bundle of things ; a mass of cordage entangled beyond unravelling.
Far-keeker, *n.* the eye.
Far-kent, *adj.* widely known.
Farle, *n.* a quarter segment of oatcake ; a cake.
Far-leukit, *adj.* far-seeing, prudent, penetrating.
Farley, Farlie, *adj.* strange, unusual. Cf. Ferly.
Farlin, *n.* the box or trough out of which the 'gutters' take the herrings.
Farm, *n.* rent ; part of farm-rent paid in grain or meal.
Farm-meal, *n.* rent paid in oatmeal.
Farm-steading, *n.* a farmstead.
Farm-town, *n.* a farmhouse and buildings.
Farn-year, *n.* the preceding year, last year. Cf. Fernyear.
†**Farouchie,** *adj.* ferocious, savage, cruel.
Far-out, *adj.* distantly related.
Far-ower, *adv.* too, far too.
Farra, *adj.* used of a cow : not with calf. Cf. Farrow.
Farrach, Farrich, Farroch, *n.* force, strength, ability, pith, energy ; managing faculty.
Farrachie, *adj.* strong, able, energetic.
Farran, *adj.* starboard.
Farrand, Farrant, Farren, *adj.* fashioned, seeming, mannered, sagacious ; well-behaved.

Farrel, *n.* a quarter of a circular oatcake. Cf. Farle.

Farrer, *adj.* further, farther.

Farres, *n.* boundaries; ridges marked out by the plough.

Farrest, *adj.* furthermost, farthest.

Farrow, *adj.* used of a cow: not with calf; not yielding milk.

Farry, *v.* to farrow; to bring forth pigs.

Far-seen, *adj.* learned; penetrating; prudent; well-instructed.

Farshach, *n.* the greater black-headed gull.

Farthel, *n.* the quarter of a circular oatcake. Cf. Farle.

Farthing-compliment, *n.* a worthless compliment.

Far-through, *adj.* very weak, near death.

Far to the fore, *phr.* much to be preferred to.

Far-yaud, *n.* a shepherd's cry to his dog.

Fas, *n.* a knot; bunch; a truss of straw, &c. Cf. Fass.

Fa-say, *n.* a sham, pretence.

Fascal, *n.* a straw mat used to screen from draughts.

Fascious, *adj.* troublesome. Cf. Fashious.

†**Fash**, *v.* to trouble, inconvenience, vex, worry with importunity; to weary; to vex one's self, be annoyed.—*n.* trouble, care, annoyance, vexation, labour; a troublesome person; one who molests, &c. — *phr.* to 'fash one's beard,' 'head,' 'noddle,' or 'thumb,' to trouble or vex one's self.

†**Fashery**, *n.* trouble, worry, annoyance, vexation.

Fashion, *n.* in *phr.* 'for the fashion,' for appearance' sake; 'to make a fashion,' to make a show or pretence.

Fashioned, *ppl. adj.* fashionable, in the fashion; conditioned.

Fashionless, *adj.* out of fashion.

†**Fashious, Fashous**, *adj.* troublesome, vexatious; not easily pleased.

Fashiousness, *n.* troublesomeness.

Fashrie, *n.* trouble, worry. Cf. Fashery.

Faskidar, *n.* the northern gull.

Fass, *n.* a knot; bunch; a truss of straw, &c.

Fassag, *n.* a straw hassock as a seat for a child, or, when broad and thin, for backs of horses. Cf. Fass.

Fassint, *ppl. adj.* fashioned.

Fassit, *ppl. adj.* knotted.

†**Fasson, Fassin**, *n.* fashion.

Fast, *adj.* busily engaged with; trustworthy, firm; very near or intimate; forward; irascible.

Fast and snell, *phr.* straightforward, in a straight line, briskly and without deviation.

Fasten-, Fasten's-e'en, *n.* Shrove Tuesday.

Faster-, Fastern's-eve, *n.* Shrove Tuesday.

Fasting-spittle, *n.* a fasting man's saliva, as a supposed cure for ringworm.

Fastren's-eve, *n.* Shrove Tuesday.

Fat, *adj.* what.

Fat, *adj.* thriving, prosperous; used of soil: rich, fertile.

Fat-a-feck, *adj.* used of the weather: favourable, seasonable.

Fatality, *n.* fate; a fatal defect.

Fatch, *v.* to fetch.

Fatch, *v.* to shift horses at the plough.—*n.* exchange. Cf. Fotch.

Fatch, *n.* in *phr.* 'at the fatch,' toiling, drudging.

Fatch-pleugh, *n.* a plough employed for two yokings each day; a plough used for killing weeds in turnip-drills, a 'harrow-plough.' Cf. Fotch-plough.

Father, *n.* in *phr.* 'father and son,' a boys' game.

Father-better, *adj.* surpassing one's father.

Father-brother, *n.* a paternal uncle.

Father-in-law, *n.* a step-father.

Father's-fiddle, *n.* a boys' game.

Father-sister, *n.* a paternal aunt.

Father-waur, *adj.* worse than one's father.

Fathom, *v.* to grasp or hold in one's arms; to measure by the outstretched arms.

Fathoming a 'rick, stack, *phr.* a Hallowe'en ceremony of measuring a stack with outstretched arms thrice against the sun, when the last 'fathom' would show the apparition of the future husband or wife.

Fa' throw, *v.* to bungle; to cease working through sloth or carelessness.

Fa' till, *v.* to attack; to begin to eat.

Fatna, *adj.* what sort of a.

Fat-reck, *int.* who cares?—*conj.* notwithstanding. Cf. Whatreck.

Fat-recks, *int.* an excl. of surprise. Cf. Whatrack.

Fatten, *adj.* what sort of.

Fattenin' and battenin', *phr.* a toast of a child's fattening and thriving, given at its baptism in private, when the bread, cheese, and whisky customary are partaken of.

Fatter, *v.* to thresh the awns of barley.

Fatter, Fattera, *adj.* what sort of.

Fattrils, Fattrels, *n.* folds, puckerings; ribbon-ends; ornaments of a woman's dress.

Fauce, *adj.* false. Cf. Fause.

Fauch, *n.* fallow ground; land ploughed at Martinmas for a green crop the next year.— *adj.* fallow.—*v.* to fallow; to beat soundly; to rub vigorously. Cf. Faugh.

Fauch, *adj.* pale-red; dun; fallow-coloured. Cf. Faugh.

Fauchentulie, *n.* a contentious argument.— *v.* to contend in argument.

Faucht, *n.* a fight, struggle.—*v. pret.* did fight.—*ppl.* fought.

Fauchten, *ppl.* fought.

Fauconless, *adj.* without strength.

Faucumtulies, *n.* fowls, &c., paid as 'cain,' or part of rent, to a landlord.

Faud, *n.* a fold.—*v.* to fold ; to bow ; in *phr.* 'faud the houchs,' to sit down.

Faugh, *adj.* dun ; pale-red.

Faugh, *n.* a furrow from lea ; fallow ground ; a tearing one's character to pieces. —*adj.* fallow.—*v.* to fallow ; to rub vigorously ; to beat soundly ; with *up*, to work with speed.

Faugh-blue, *adj.* bleached blue.

Faughin, *n.* a tearing up, ploughing ; a constant rubbing ; a beating.

Faugh-riggs, *n.* fallow ground.

Faughs, *n.* a division of land, not manured, but prepared for a crop by a slight fallowing.

Faught, *v. pret.* did beat. Cf. Faugh.

Faught, *v. pret.* and *ppl.* fought.—*n.* a fight, struggle.

Faul, *n.* a halo round the moon, indicating a fall of rain.

Faul, Fauld, *n.* a sheep-fold.—*v.* to fold sheep.

Faul, Fauld, *n.* a fold ; a curve.—*v.* to fold.

Fauld, *n.* a section of a farm manured by folding sheep or cattle on it.

Fauld-dyke, *n.* the wall of a sheep-fold.

Faulderall, *n.* a gewgaw.

Faulding, *n.* a sheep-fold.

Faulding-slap, *n.* the gate or opening of a sheep-fold.

Faulies, *n.* the 'faulds' of a farm.

Faulter, *n.* hesitation.

Faun, *v. pret.* found.

Faung, *n.* a big lump, a 'whang.' Cf. Fang.

Faup, *n.* the curlew. Cf. Whaup.

Fa' upon, *v.* to pilfer ; to tamper with.

Faur, *adv.* where ; whither.

Faur, *adj.* and *adv.* far. Cf. Far.

Faured, Faurd, *ppl. adj.* favoured, featured.

Faurer, *adv.* further, farther.

Faurest, *adj.* furthermost, farthest.

Fauron, *adv.* whereupon.

Faur-on, *adj.* nearly drunk ; near death.

Fauschious, *adj.* troublesome. Cf. Fashious.

Fause, *adj.* false.—*v.* to coax, cajole.

Fause-face, *n.* a mask ; a deceitful person ; a hypocrite.

Fause-house, *n.* a vacant space in a stack for ventilation.

Fause-loon, *n.* a traitor.—*adj.* traitorous.

Fause-tail, *n.* a braid of hair.

†Faut, Faute, *n.* a fault ; blame ; injury ; defect, want ; negligence.—*v.* to find fault with, blame ; to reprove.

Faut, *n.* fortune, lot ; what befalls one. Cf. Fa', Faw.

†Fauter, Fautor, *n.* an offender ; a guilty person.

Faut-free, *adj.* blameless ; sound, not defective.

Fautifu', *adj.* fault-finding ; not easy to please.

Fautless, *adj.* faultless.

Fauty, *adj.* faulty ; guilty ; unsound.

Favour, *n.* countenance, complexion, appearance ; in *pl.* favour.—*v.* to resemble in feature or appearance.

Favoured, *ppl. adj.* featured ; fashioned ; mannered. Cf. Faured.

Faw, *v.* to fall ; to befall ; to obtain a share. —*n.* a fall ; a share ; a lot ; a trap.

Faw, *adj.* pale-red, dun. Cf. Fauch.

Fa' wi', *v.* to go to waste or ruin.

Fawn, *n.* a white spot on moorish or mossy ground ; a rough, wet place on a hill.

Fawn, *v.* to caress, fondle ; to fawn upon.

Fawsont, *adj.* honest, becoming, seemly.

†Fay, *n.* faith.

Fay, *adj.* fated to die, near death. Cf. Fey.

Faze, *v.* to inconvenience. Cf. Fease.

Fead, *n.* feud, hatred, quarrel ; a cause of quarrel ; an enemy.

Feake, *n.* that part of a full sack which is drawn together at the top by the cord that ties the sack. Cf. Faik.

†Feal, *adj.* faithful, loyal ; just, fair.

Feal, *n.* turf. Cf. Fail.

Feal, *adj.* cosy ; clean, neat ; smooth, soft. Cf. Feil.

Feam, *v.* to foam with rage, be in a violent passion. Cf. Fame.

Fear, *adj.* strong ; entire. Cf. Fere.

Fear, *n.* a fright.—*v.* to frighten, scare.

Fearder, *adj.* more afraid.

Feared, *ppl. adj.* afraid ; with *for*, afraid of.

Fear-fangit, *adj.* panic-stricken, seized with fear.

Fearfu', *adj.* easily frightened ; of very large quantity or dimension.—*adv.* exceedingly, extraordinarily.

Fearie, *adj.* afraid.

Fearn, *n.* prepared gut ; a fiddle-string. Cf. Fern.

Fear-nothing, *n.* a rough cloth overcoat, a dreadnought.

Fearn-owl, *n.* the night-jar.

Fears, *n.* the prices of grain legally fixed in each county for the current year. Cf. Fiars.

Fearsome, *adj.* terrifying, fearful, awful ; timid, frightened.

Fearsome-like, *adj.* frightful, fearful.

Fearsome-looking, *adj.* frightful-looking, of terrifying appearance.

Fearsomely, *adv.* frightfully, dreadfully.

Feart, *ppl. adj.* afraid ; timorous, cowardly. Cf. Feared.

Feart-like, *adj.* like one afraid, frightened.

Fease, *v.* to drive ; to drive out ; to disturb, annoy.—*n.* annoyance, inconvenience.

Fease, *v.* to screw, twist ; used of cloth : to fray out ; of a sharp instrument : to have the edge turned ; to rub hard ; to work briskly. Cf. Feeze.

Feasible, *adj.* neat, tidy.—*adv.* neatly. Cf. Faceable.

Feat, *adj.* fitting, fitted, suitable ; clever, smart ; dexterous ; tidy, neat, pretty.—*adv.* dexterously ; prettily.—*v.* to dress neatly ; to qualify, prepare.

Feather, *n.* part of a peat-cutting spade at right angles with the broadest part.—*v.* used of a bird : to get feathers, to fly ; to beat, chastise, fall foul of.

Feather-cling, *n.* a disease affecting black cattle.

Feathered, *ppl. adj.* used of cattle : marked with a feather for identification.

Feather-lock, *n.* a lock, the end of whose spring resembles the hairs of a feather.

Feather-wheelie, *n.* the feverfew.

Featless, *adj.* feeble.

Featly, *adv.* cleverly, smartly ; prettily, neatly.

†Featour, *n.* a transgressor, evil-doer.

Feat-peak, *n.* a neat top or finish to a stack, head-dress, &c.

Feauk, *n.* a plaid. Cf. Faik.

Feaze, *v.* to screw ; used of cloth : to fray out ; to turn the edge of a knife, &c. ; to rub hard ; to work briskly. Cf. Feeze.

Feberwarry, Februar, *n.* February.

Fechen, Fechin, *ppl.* fought.

Fechie-lechie, *adj.* insipid, tasteless ; diminutive in size ; inactive.

Fecht, *v.* to fight ; to struggle ; to harass.— *n.* a fight ; a struggle for a living, &c. ; hard work.

Fechter, *n.* a fighter ; in *pl.* stalks of the rib-grass, which children use in a sort of mimic battle as weapons.

Fechtie, *n.* a fighter.

Fechtin'-cock, *n.* a cock trained to cock-fighting.

Feck, *n.* value, worth ; the majority, the bulk ; abundance, quantity.—*adj.* strong, vigorous.

Feck, *v.* to fidget ; to fuss ; to vex. Cf. Fike.

Feck, *n.* familiar intercourse ; affection, esteem.

Feck, *v.* to attain by dishonourable means, to steal.

Fecket, *n.* a waistcoat, under-jacket ; a shirt.

Feck-fack, *n.* a finicking job ; needless bustle.—*v.* to trifle away time. Cf. Fike-fack.

Feck-fow, *adj.* wealthy, of substance.

Feck-fow-like, *adj.* apparently wealthy ; capable-looking.

Feckfu', *adj.* 'feck-fow' ; capable, full of resource ; powerful, able ; stout.

Feckfully, *adv.* efficiently, powerfully.

Feckle, *n.* trouble, anxiety.

Feckless, *adj.* weak, feeble, impotent ; incapable, incompetent, not resourceful ; awkward, unhandy ; spiritless, weak in mind or resolution ; of little or no value, profitless ; trifling, pithless, tasteless ; poor, poverty-stricken.—*n.* the poor, the weak, the unhandy.

Fecklessly, *adv.* weakly, incompetently, irresponsibly.

Fecklessness, *n.* weakness, incompetence ; worthlessness.

Fecklins, *adj.* physically weak ; spiritless ; irresponsible, worthless.

Fecklins, *adv.* mostly, almost, chiefly.

Feckly, *adv.* for the most part, mainly.

Fecks, *int.* faith ! Cf. Faix.

Fecky, *adj.* gaudy.

Fect, *n.* value ; a part, the larger part.—*adj.* strong, vigorous. Cf. Feck.

Fectfully, *adv.* effectively, powerfully, efficiently. Cf. Feckfully.

Fedam, *n.* unusual behaviour as presaging death. Cf. Feydom.

Fedder, *n.* a feather.—*v.* to fly ; to fall foul of, chastise. Cf. Feather.

Fede, *n.* a feud, enmity.

Fed-gang, *n.* a 'foot-gang,' a low, narrow chest, extending along a wooden bed, and serving as a step to enter the bed.

Fedmart, *n.* an ox fattened for killing at Martinmas ; used also figuratively for one whose prosperity paves the way for his destruction.

Fedmel, Fedmal, Fedmill, *adj.* fattened ; gluttonous ; fat and lazy.

Fedmit, *n.* a glutton.—*adj.* gluttonous.

Fee, *adj.* predestined ; on the verge of death ; behaving strangely so as to presage death under a fatality. Cf. Fey.

Fee, *n.* salary ; a servant's wages ; recompense.—*v.* to engage for wages, hire one's self ; to hire servants.

Feech, *int.* an excl. of disgust.

Feechie, *int.* an excl. in games, by which one player holds another to the point. Cf. Feeshie.

Feed, *v.* to supply a mill or machine with material.—*n.* food, fodder, 'keep' for cattle, &c.

Fee'd, *ppl. adj.* engaged for service.

Feeder, *n.* an ox being fattened for the market ; one who supplies a mill or machine with material ; one who supplies balls, cherry-stones, &c. in various games ; one who fattens cattle for the butcher.

Feeding-storm, *n.* an increasing fall of snow which threatens to continue long.

Feedin-mairt, *n.* a bullock fattened for winter provision.

Feedle, *n.* a field.

Feedlie, *n.* a small field.

Feedom, *n.* a presentiment or presage of death ; a fatality. Cf. Feydom.

Feedow, *n.* the store of cherry-stones from which children furnish their 'castles of pips.'

Feegarie, *n.* a gewgaw ; a woman's showy, flaunting attire. Cf. Fleegarie.

Feegh, *int.* an excl. of disgust.

Feegur, *n.* a figure.

Feeing, *n.* engaging as servants.

Feeing-fair, -market, *n.* a hiring-fair or market for farm-servants.

Feek-fike, *n.* a small household job ; needless bustle.—*v.* to trifle away time. Cf. Fike-fack.

Feel, *v.* to smell ; to taste ; to understand, comprehend.

Feel, *n.* a fool.—*adj.* foolish.

Feel, Feele, *adj.* smooth, soft. Cf. Feil.

Feeless, *adj.* without wages or recognized worth.

Feelimageeries, *n.* gewgaws, knick-knacks, useless trifles.

Feelin'-hairted, *adj.* tender- or kind-hearted.

Feelless, *adj.* without feeling or sensation ; insensible.

Feem, *v.* to lie by, in the game of marbles.

Feeneekin, *n.* a small person ; a person of a tart or finical disposition.

Feenichin, *adj.* foppish, fantastical, finical.

Feent, *n.* the devil ; nothing, not ; used in excls. or oaths. Cf. Fient.

Feer, *v.* to draw the first furrow in ploughing ; to mark out the 'riggs' before ploughing the whole field.

Feer, *n.* a standard, a measure ; a tall, lanky person. Cf. Fier.

Feer, *n.* a companion. Cf. Fere.

Feer, *adj.* vigorous, healthy. Cf. Fere.

Feerach, *n.* vigour ; 'go' ; ability ; agility. Cf. Farrach.

Feerach, *n.* a bustle ; a confused, agitated state ; a passion, rage ; a bustling person.— *v.* to hurry, bustle ; to work in a bustling or excited manner. Cf. Foorich.

Feerachin, *ppl. adj.* bustling, agitated.—*n.* a bustling, confused state.

Feerdy, *adj.* strong, able-bodied ; hale and hearty.—*n.* a person of good constitution.

Feerdy-limbed, *adj.* stalwart, having sturdy limbs.

Feer for feer, *phr.* an equal match. Cf. Fere.

Feerich, *n.* strength, ability, energy. Cf. Farrach.

Feerich, *n.* a bustle.—*v.* to bustle. Cf. Foorich.

Feerichin, *ppl. adj.* bustling.

Feerie, *adj.* clever ; active ; nimble.

Feerie, *adj.* in poor health, looking weakly.

Feerilie, *adv.* nimbly, cleverly.

Feering, *n.* the furrow drawn out to mark the ' riggs' before ploughing the whole field.

Feering-furrow, *n.* the 'feering.'

Feerious, *adj.* furious ; exceeding.—*adv.* exceedingly, used intensively.

Feerly, *adj.* vigorously. Cf. Ferely.

Feeroch, *n.* bustle.—*v.* to bustle. Cf. Foorich.

Feeroch, *n.* strength ; force. Cf. Farrach.

Feerochrie, *n.* ability, activity, agility. Cf. Farrach.

Feerochrie, *n.* a state of great anger or passion. Cf. Foorich.

Feerrich, *n.* bustle.—*v.* to bustle. Cf. Foorich.

Feers, *n.* the prices of grain for each county legally settled for the current year. Cf. Fiars.

Feersday, *n.* Thursday.

Feery, *n.* tumult, bustle, confusion ; rage, passion.

Feery-fary, *n.* a great hubbub ; an angry tumult.

Feery o' the feet, *phr.* active in moving the feet.

Feese, *v.* to screw ; to squeak like a screw turning ; to turn, twist ; used of cloth : to fray out. Cf. Feeze.

Feese, *v.* to drive ; to put to inconvenience. —*n.* inconvenience, annoyance. Cf. Fease.

Feese, *v.* to saunter about a spot.

Feesh, *v. pret.* fetched.

Feeshie, *int.* an excl. keeping or bringing an opponent to a point, used in boys' fights and games.

Feess, *v. pret.* fetched.

Feesyhant, *n.* a pheasant. Cf. Ephesian.

Feet, *n.* in curling : an acceleration of a stone by sweeping before it.

Feet-ale, *n.* drink after a cattle-sale, paid by the seller.

Feet-fa'in', *n.* the period of childbirth.

Feeth, Feeth-net, *n.* a fixed net stretching across a river.

Feeties, *n.* a child's feet ; small feet.

Feeting, *n.* running.

Feets, *n.* in *phr.* ' fit-out-o'-the-feets,' a designation given to one who betrays a genuine spirit of contradiction ; one who will not keep his feet out of the 'theets' or traces.

Feetsides, *n.* ropes used for chains, fixed to the 'haims' and to the 'swingle-tree' in ploughing.

Feet up, *int.* a call to a stumbling horse.

Feerich, *n.* a bustle.—*v.* to bustle. Cf. Foorich.

Feerichin, *ppl. adj.* bustling.

Feet-washing, *n.* the custom of washing the feet of a bride or a bridegroom the night before marriage ; the night before marriage.

Feeze, *v.* to screw, twist, turn ; used of a sharp instrument : to have the edge turned ; of cloth : to fray out ; to rub hard ; to work briskly.

Feeze about, *v.* to hang off and on, keep near a place ; to potter or shuffle about ; to turn round.

Feeze into, *v.* to ingratiate one's self, to worm into confidence.

Feeze-nail, *n.* a screw-nail.

Feeze off, *v.* to unscrew.

Feeze on, *v.* to screw.

Feeze-pin, *n.* a screw-pin.

Feeze up, *v.* to flatter ; to work up into a passion.

Feezing, *n.* a continuance of hard rubbing ; briskness in working ; in *pl.* the stringy parts of cloth when the woof is rubbed out from the warp.

Feff, *n.* a stench, bad odour.

Feft, *ppl. adj.* put in legal possession ; claimed by right or long possession.

Feftment, *n.* enfeoffment.

Feg, *n.* a thing of no value ; a fig.

Feg, *v.* to propel a marble with the thumb from the middle of the second finger curved ; to knock off a marble lying close to another.

Feghie-lechie, *adj.* insipid ; diminutive. Cf. Fechie-lechie.

Fegrim, *n.* a whim ; finery.

Fegs, *n.* faith.—*int.* truly ! used in mild oaths and excls. of surprise.

Feich, *int.* an excl. of disgust. Cf. Feigh.

Feid, *n.* feud, enmity ; a cause of quarrel ; an enemy.

Feidom, *n.* enmity.

Feigh, *int.* fie ! an excl. of disgust.

Feighing, *ppl.* uttering excls. of disgust.

Feight, *n.* a fight, struggle.—*v.* to fight. Cf. Fecht.

Feignyie, *v.* to feign, pretend ; to forge.

Feik, *v.* to fidget.—*n.* the fidgets. Cf. Fike.

Feike, *v.* to screw ; to force ; to abate a legal due under pressure.

Feik-fak, *n.* a troublesome job ; needless bustle.—*v.* to trifle away time. Cf. Fike-fack.

Feil, *adj.* comfortable, snug ; soft, smooth ; silky to the touch.

Feil, *adj.* many.

Feil, *n.* a thin piece of turf ; a sod. Cf. Fail.

Feil, *adv.* very ; exceedingly. Cf. Fell.

Feil-beg, *n.* a fillibeg.

Feim, *n.* foam ; a great heat over the body, with violent perspiration. Cf. Fame, Faim.

Feint, Feind, *n.* the devil, used in strong negations. Cf. Fient.

Feinyie, Feinzie, *v.* to feign ; to forge.

Feir, *v.* to draw the first furrow in ploughing. Cf. Feer.

Feir, *n.* a standard of measurement ; a long, lanky person. Cf. Fier.

Feir, *n.* a companion. Cf. Fere.

Feir, *n.* military equipment.

Feirdy, *adj.* strong, sturdy. Cf. Feerdy.

Feirie, *adj.* clever. Cf. Feerie.

Feiroch, *adj.* clever, strong, active. Cf. Farrach.

Feiroch, *n.* a bustle ; a bustling person.—*v.* to hurry, bustle. Cf. Foorich.

Feish, *v. pret.* fetched.

Feist, *n.* a noiseless breaking of wind.

Feist, *v.* to exert one's self with difficulty and little effect.—*n.* exertion with little effect ; a weak person.

Feit, *adj.* clever, dexterous. Cf. Feat.

Feith, *n.* a fixed net stretching out into the bed of a river. Cf. Feeth.

Fek, *n.* plenty. Cf. Feck.

Fell, *n.* the cuticle immediately above the flesh.

Fell, *n.* a fairly level field on the top or side of a hill ; untilled ground, or ground unfit for pasture, lying high.

Fell, *v.* to stun ; to kill ; to injure severely or fatally ; to surpass, beat ; to cast out a net from a boat ; to befall, happen.—*n.* lot, destiny ; a knock-down blow.

†Fell, *adj.* keen, pungent, tasty ; eager, desirous, energetic, sharp, intelligent ; severe, cutting ; strong, valiant, vigorous ; grave, serious, weighty ; strange, unusual ; great, very large. —*adv.* exceedingly, used as an intensive.

Fell, *n.* a thin piece of turf ; a sod. Cf. Fail.

Fell, *n.* a large quantity.

Fell-bloom, *n.* the birds' trefoil, yellow clover. Cf. Bloom-fell.

Fell-down, *n.* a fight, struggle.

Felled, *ppl. adj.* overcome with surprise ; prostrate with illness.

Felled-, Fell't-sick, *adj.* extremely sick, so as to be unable to stir.

Fellenly, *adv.* vigorously ; effectively.

Fellill, Fellin, *n.* a disease affecting the skin of cattle.

Fellin, Fellon, *adv.* pretty ; very ; wonderfully.

Fellon, Felon, *n.* a whitlow.

Fellon-, Fellin-grass, *n.* the plant *Angelica sylvestris*.

Fell-rot, *n.* a disease of sheep, affecting the skin.

Fell well, *adv.* very well.

Felt, *n.* creeping wheat-grass, couch-grass ; a thick growth of weeds.—*v.* to become matted or entangled.

Felt, Feltie, *n.* the missel-thrush.

Felt, *n.* the disease of the stone.

Felter, *v.* to encumber, cling about; to weave cloth faultily; to filter, fall in drops.—*n.* a fault in weaving, a knot.

Felt-, Felty-gravel, *n.* the disease of the sandy gravel.

Feltifare, *n.* the redshank.

Feltiflyer, *n.* the fieldfare.

Felt-marshal, *n.* a provost-marshal.

Femlans, *n.* the remains of a feast.

Femmel, *v.* to select the best, rejecting the remainder as refuse.

Femmil, *adj.* well-knit, athletic; active, agile. —*n.* strength, stamina.

Fen', *v.* to defend; to work hard for a living; to manage to subsist. Cf. Fend.

Fence, *v.* to protect from, defend; to open formally an assembly or law-court; to warn off, debar from the Lord's Table unworthy communicants.—*n.* the act of 'fencing' a court; a prohibition; security.

Fence-fed, *adj.* stall-fed, well-nourished.

Fence-louper, *n.* an animal that leaps over bounds or fences in a field; an intractable person; one who goes beyond bounds.

Fencer, *n.* a pugilist; any one who fights with his fists.

Fencible, *adj.* capable of bearing arms to defend the country.—*n.* in *pl.* militia; persons capable of bearing arms.

Fencing, *n.* the warning addressed to intending communicants before the administration of our Lord's Supper.

Fencing-prayer, *n.* prayer in connection with the 'fencing of the tables.'

Fend, *v.* to defend, shelter, guard; to ward off, turn aside; to work hard for a livelihood, to struggle; to make shift, provide for; to fare, get on; to support life, exist; to manage, provide subsistence.—*n.* a defence, protection; an attempt, endeavour; a struggle for existence; provision, food; a makeshift.

Fend-cauld, *n.* what wards off the cold.

Fend-fou, *adj.* resourceful, good at finding expedients.

Fendie, Fendy, *adj.* economical; resourceful; handy; buoyant; healthy.

Fending, *n.* means of subsistence, livelihood; management, providence.

Fendless, *adj.* shiftless; without energy; weak, without body or flavour.

†Fenester, *n.* a window; a casement.

Fenniegreg, *n.* fenugreek.

Fennin, *n.* means of subsistence; contriving. Cf. Fending.

Fenny, *adj.* clever; resourceful; handy; healthy. Cf. Fendie.

Fensible, *adj.* well fenced.

†Fent, *n.* an opening or slit in a sleeve, shirt, coat, or petticoat; in *pl.* remnants of cloth sewed together.

Fent-piece, *n.* a piece of cloth sewed to the upper end of a 'fent' to prevent its tearing.

Fenwick-twist, *n.* a twist given in delivering a curling-stone, introduced first, and practised more generally, by the curlers of Fenwick in Ayrshire.

Fenzie, *v.* to feign. Cf. Feignyie.

†Fercost, *n.* a barque. Cf. Farcost.

Ferd, *n.* force. Cf. Faird.

Ferdilest, *adj.* strongest, stoutest.

Ferdin, *n.* a farthing. Cf. Fardin.

Ferdy, *adj.* strong, active. Cf. Feerdy.

Fere, *n.* a friend, comrade; a spouse; an equal, match.

Fere, *n.* a company, a troop.

Fere, *n.* a puny, dwarfish person.

Fere, *adj.* strong, sturdy, entire; *phr.* 'hale and fere,' thoroughly healthy, whole and entire.

Ferely, *adv.* vigorously.

Ferie, *adj.* vigorous, active. Cf. Feery.

Ferie-fary, *n.* bustle, stir, disorder.

Feriness, *n.* adhesiveness, consolidation.

Ferintosh, *n.* 'peat-reek' whisky distilled at Ferintosh in Ross-shire.

Feritie, *n.* violence.

Ferkishin, *n.* a crowd; a large quantity.

Ferle, *n.* a quarter of oatcake. Cf. Farle.

Ferly, *adj.* strange, wonderful.—*n.* a wonder; a novelty; a 'curio,' a curiosity; used contemptuously for a 'sight,' spectacle; in *pl.* show-things, the 'lions' of a place.— *v.* to wonder, be surprised at.

Ferly-full, *adj.* astonished; filled with wonder.

Ferly-, Ferlie-troke, *n.* a strange, miscellaneous stock of goods.

Ferm, *n.* prepared gut, 'thairm'; the string of a fiddle, &c. Cf. Fern.

Ferm, Ferme, *n.* a farm; farm-rent.

Ferme-meal, *n.* meal paid as rent.

Fermentated, *ppl. adj.* used of the stomach: distended owing to the fermenting of its contents.

Fern, *n.* a prepared gut as a fiddle-string.

Fernent, *prep.* opposite to.—*adv.* in front. Cf. Forenent.

Ferner, *n.* a remote, indefinite period; a time or date that may never arrive.—*adv.* never. Cf. Fern-year.

Ferniegreg, *n.* fenugreek.

Fer-nothing, *n.* a 'dreadnought' coat. Cf. Fear-nothing.

Fern-storm, *n.* rain caused by the burning of fern or heather.

Fern-tickled, *ppl. adj.* freckled.

Fern-tickles, *n.* freckles.

Ferny-buss, *n.* a clump of ferns.

Fern-year, -yer, *n.* the last or past year; a time that may never come.

Ferny-hirst, *n.* a fern-clad hill.

Ferny-, Ferni-ticle, *n.* a freckle.

Fern-zear, -zeer, -zier, *n.* 'fern-year.'

Ferra, *adj.* used of a cow : not having a calf ; not yielding milk.—*n.* a cow not with calf. Cf. Farrow.

Ferrichie, *adj.* strong, robust. Cf. Feerochrie.

Ferrick, *n.* a mock sun. Cf. Fairock.

Ferrow, *adj.* and *n.* 'ferra.'

Ferry, *v.* to bring forth young.—*adj.* not in calf, farrow.

Ferry-louper, *n.* a settler from Scotland in Orkney ; one not a native of Orkney.

Fersell, Fershell, *adj.* bustling, energetic.—*v.* to fuss about ; to rustle, bustle.

Fersie, *n.* the farcy.

Ferss, Fers, *adj.* fierce.—*adv.* fiercely.

Ferter, *n.* a fairy.

Ferter, Fertor, Fertour, *n.* a casket, a coffin.

Ferter-like, *adj.* seeming ready for the coffin ; death-like.

Ferture, *n.* wrack and ruin.

Ferven', *adv.* eagerly, readily, fervently.

Fesart, *n.* an impudent person. Cf. Faizart.

Fesh, *v.* to fetch.

Fesh, *v.* to trouble. Cf. Fash.

Feshen, *ppl.* fetched.

Fesil, *v.* to rustle. Cf. Fissle.

Fes'n, *v.* to fasten.

Fess, *v.* to fetch.

Fessen, *v.* to fasten.

Fessen, *ppl.* fetched.

Fess't, Fest, *adj.* and *adv.* fast.

Fest, *n.* a feast, festival.

Festen, *v.* to fasten, to bind.

Festeren's-, Festren's-eve, *n.* Shrove Tuesday. Cf. Fasten's-eve.

Festy-cook, *n.* new-ground meal made into a ball, and baked among the burning 'seeds' in a kiln or mill.

Fetch, *v.* to draw a long breath, gasp ; to pull by fits and starts ; to strike a blow ; to arrive at ; to catch sight of.—*n.* a trick, stratagem ; a long, deep breath, as of one dying ; a tug ; a jerk.

Fetching, *n.* a long, deep breath ; a gasping for breath.

Feth, *n.* faith.—*int.* faith !

Fether, *n.* father.

Fetherfewie, *n.* feverfew.

Fethir, *n.* a feather.—*v.* to chastise ; to fly. Cf. Feather.

Fett, *adj.* neat, tidy ; clever. Cf. Feat.

Fettle, *n.* state, condition ; temper, humour ; energy, power ; order, repair ; faculty or capacity of speech, movement, &c.—*v.* to repair, put in good order ; to attend to animals ; to dress, put on clothes ; to trim up ; to beat, 'settle'; to set about or to work ; to manage.—*adj.* trim ; well-made ; in good condition.

Fettle, *n.* a rope or strap by which a creel can be carried on the back, leaving the arms free ; a handle of straw or rope on the side of a large basket or creel.—*v.* to wind a band or rope round anything ; to fasten a 'fettle' to a creel.

Feu, *n.* land held in perpetuity, or for 99 years, generally, in payment of a yearly rent.—*v.* to let out land in 'feu'; to take land in 'feu.'

Feu, *v.* to promise well, make a good beginning. Cf. Few.

Feuach, *n.* a very short, light crop of grass or grain.

Feuar, *n.* one who takes land in 'feu,' generally for building.

Feuch, *int.* an excl. of disgust. Cf. Feegh.

Feuch, *v.* to smoke a pipe.—*n.* a whiff of a pipe, a short smoke.

Feuch, *n.* a sounding blow. — *v.* to work hard. Cf. Feugh.

Feuchin, *ppl.* fought. Cf. Feughen.

Feuchin up, *n.* a sound beating.

Feuchit, *n.* a sounding blow.

Feuchter, *n.* a slight fall of snow.

Feu-duty, -ferme, *n.* the yearly rent of a 'feu.'

Feug, *n.* a sharp and sudden blow.

Feuggil, *n.* a small twisted bundle of hay, straw, rags, &c. for stopping a hole.

Feuggle, *v.* to beat soundly.

Feugglin', *n.* a beating.

Feugh, *v.* to smoke.—*n.* a short smoke. Cf. Feuch.

Feugh, *n.* a sounding blow ; a sharp and sudden blow ; a rush, a rushing sound.— *v.* to work hard ; with *up*, to beat soundly.

Feughen, *ppl.* fought.

Feughin up, *n.* a sound beating.

Feught, *v. pret.* fought.

Feughter, *n.* a sudden, slight fall of snow. Cf. Feuchter.

Fever, *v.* to become excited.

Fever-foullie, *n.* the feverfew.

Fever-largie, -largin, *n.* laziness, idleness.

Fever-wheelie, *n.* the feverfew. Cf. Feather-wheelie.

Few, *adj.* in *phr.* a 'few broth,' &c., a small quantity of broth, &c.

Few, *v.* to show promise or aptitude ; to make a good beginning.

Fewe, *adj.* fallow. Cf. Faugh.

Fews, *n.* the house-leek. Cf. Fouet.

Fey, *n.* a small field or croft.

Fey, *adj.* doomed to calamity or death ; acting unnaturally, as if under doom : of grain : decayed, reduced in substance. — *n.* the warning or predestination, or presage of calamity or doom.—*v.* to be mad ; to act unnaturally, and so presage death.

Fey-crop, *n.* a crop more than usually good, portending the owner's death.

Feydom, *n.* a presentiment of calamity or death.

Feyk, *v.* to fidget. Cf. Fike.

Fey-land, *n.* the portion of a farm formerly getting all the farmyard dung, and being constantly cropped; the best land on the farm.

Fey-like, *adj.* as if 'fey,' or doomed.

Feyness, *n.* the state of being 'fey'; a 'wraith,' a spectral likeness.

Fey-taiken, *n.* a presentiment betokening or presaging death.

Feyther, *n.* father.

Fial, *n.* one who receives wages.

Fial, *n.* one who has the reversion of property; one who holds land in fee.

Fiars, *n.* the prices of grain legally fixed for the year in each county. Cf. Fier.

Fiarter, *n.* a term of disrespect; an untidy person.

Fibsch, *n.* a big person of disagreeable temper.

Ficher, *v.* to work slowly and awkwardly; to fumble, trifle, fidget.—*n.* slow, awkward work; toying, fumbling; a fumbler, a person slow and awkward at work.

Ficherin', *n.* trifling, idling, fidgeting.

Fichil, *n.* a challenge to a difficult feat, a 'brag.'

Fichil-pins, *n.* a game. Cf. Fickle-pins.

Fick-fack, *n.* the ligament running along the vertebræ of the back; the tendon of the neck.

Fick-fack, -fyke, *n.* a troublesome job; needless bustle; in *pl.* silly jargon; trifling sayings; whims; peculiarities of temper.—*v.* to trifle away time; to bustle about needlessly. Cf. Fike-fack.

Fickle, *v.* to puzzle, entangle; to cause to fidget; to do what others cannot do.—*adj.* unsafe; treacherous; ticklish.

Fickle-pins, *n.* a game in which a number of rings are taken off a double wire united at both ends.

Fickly, *adj.* puzzling.

Ficks, *n.* a disease of sheep.

Fid, *v.* to move up and down or from side to side; to wag like a rabbit's tail. Cf. Whid.

Fidder, *conj.* whether. Cf. Fudder.

Fidder, *v.* to move like a hawk when it wishes to remain stationary over a place, or like a bird in the nest over her young.

Fidder, *n.* a large quantity; a cartload; a certain weight of lead. Cf. Fudder.

Fiddle, *v.* to dawdle, trifle.

Fiddle, *n.* the proper or correct thing.

Fiddle-diddle, *n.* the music of the fiddle; the movements of a fiddler's arm in playing.

Fiddle-doup, *n.* a term of contempt.

Fiddle-faddle, *n.* nonsense, fancifulness; whim, trifle.—*v.* to trifle, dawdle.

Fiddle-fike, *n.* a troublesome peculiarity of conduct; an overpunctilious person; a trifler.

Fiddle-ma-fyke, *n.* a silly, fastidious person.

Fiddler, *n.* the common sandpiper.

Fiddler's news, *phr.* stale news.

Fiddltie-fa, *n.* a trifling excuse; hesitancy. —*v.* to hesitate; to make much ado about nothing.

Fidel-didel, *n.* fiddle-playing. Cf. Fiddle-diddle.

Fidge, *v.* to fidget, move restlessly, kick with the feet; to be anxious, to worry; to be eager.—*n.* a fidget, twitch, shrug.

Fidge-fain, -fu' fain, *v.* to be eager with restlessness.

Fidgie, *n.* a fugitive; a coward. Cf. Fugie.

Fidgin, *n.* fidgeting; uneasiness.

Fidgy, *adj.* restless, fidgety.

Fie, *adj.* fated to die. Cf. Fey.

Fiedle, *n.* a field. Cf. Feedle.

Fief, *n.* a stench. Cf. Feff.

Fief-like, *adj.* malodorous.

Fie-gae-to, *n.* a great bustle.

Fiel, *adv.* very. Cf. Fell.

Fiel, *v.* to feel; to understand.

Field, *v.* to sink a margin round a panel of wood.

Fieldert, *adv.* towards the fields, abroad.

Fieldfare, *n.* the missel-thrush.

Field-gear, *n.* gala attire.

Fielding-plane, *n.* the plane used in sinking a margin round a panel of wood.

Field-man, *n.* a peasant.

Fieldwart, *adv.* towards the fields, abroad.

Field-wench, *n.* a female field-worker.

Fieldy, *n.* the hedge-sparrow.

Fien, *n.* a fiend.

Fienden, *n.* the devil. Cf. Fient.

Fient, Fiend, *n.* devil, the fiend; used in negations as an oath or excl. like 'devil a.'

Fient-a-bit, -flee, -gear, -hair, -hait, *phrs.* nothing at all, not at all.

Fient-a-fear, *phr.* no fear!

Fient ane, *phr.* not one.

Fient ane o' me, Fient o' me, *phr.* not I for my part; by no means I.

Fient-ma-care, *phr.* no matter.

Fient-perlicket, *phr.* nothing at all.

Fier, *n.* a standard of any kind; a tall, lanky person.

Fier, *n.* a companion. Cf. Fere.

Fier, *adj.* sound, healthy; active; strong. Cf. Fere.

Fier, *v.* to draw the first furrow in ploughing. Cf. Feer.

Fiercelings, Fiercelins, *adv.* fiercely, with violence, in haste.—*adj.* fierce, violent.

Fiercie, *n.* the farcy.

Fierd, *n.* a ford. Cf. Faert.

Fierdy, *adj.* strong; able-bodied. Cf. Feerdy.

Fieroch, *n.* bustle; rage. Cf. Feeroch.

Fiersday, *n.* Thursday.

Fiery, Fierie, *n.* bustle; confusion; rage. Cf. Feery.

Fiery-bron, *n.* a blazing peat or 'brand,' used for signalling, as a torch.

Fiery-fary, *n.* a hubbub; a show; a pretended bustle. Cf. Feery-fary.

Fiery-flaw, *n.* the sting-ray.

Fiery-stick, *n.* stern reality, dead earnest.

Fiery-tangs, *n.* a crab; a lobster.

Fiery-water, *n.* marine phosphorescence.

Fiery-wud, *adj.* eager, keen; quite mad, 'red-wud.'

Fiese-wilk, *n.* the striated whelk.

Fifer, *n.* a boys' marble, soft, and of a dull brown colour.

Fifish, *adj.* rather eccentric, weak in mind, or deranged.

Fifishness, *n.* eccentricity; lack of saneness.

Fifteen, *n.* in *phr.* 'the Fifteen,' the judges of the Court of Session, before the reduction of their number; the Rebellion of 1715 A.D.

Fig, *n.* a metal vest-button, used in the game of 'buttons'; a thing of little value.

Fige, *v.* to fidget. Cf. Fidge.

Fig-fag, *n.* the tendon of the neck of cattle or sheep. Cf. Fick-fack.

Figgle, *n.* a small twisted bundle or bunch. Cf. Feuggil.

Figgle-faggle, *n.* silly or trifling conduct; ludicrous or unbecoming conduct.

Figgle-faggler, *n.* one who destroys good morals.

Figgleligee, *adj.* finical, foppish; ostentatiously polite.

Fight, *v.* to struggle; to harass.—*n.* effort, struggle. Cf. Fecht, Faught.

Figmalirie, *n.* a whim, a 'whigmaleerie.'

Figure, *v.* to do arithmetic; to 'count.'

Figuring, *n.* arithmetic.

Fike, *v.* to fidget, move restlessly; to fuss over trifles; to vex one's self; to trouble, make uneasy; to flirt, dally with a woman; to shrug.—*n.* a restless motion, a fidget; bustle, fuss; trouble, care, worry; dalliance, flirtation; a whim, freak; a fancy article, a gewgaw.

Fike, *n.* burnt leather.

Fike-fack, *n.* a troublesome, finicking job; needless stir; in *pl.* minute pieces of work, causing great trouble; little troublesome peculiarities of temper; nonsense.—*v.* to trifle away time.

Fike-ma-facks, *n.* nonsense; silly trifling sayings.

Fikery, *n.* fussiness; worry about trifles or troubles.

Fiket, *ppl. adj.* fidgety; difficult to please, fastidious.

Fikiness, *n.* agitation.

Fiking, *n.* trouble, effort.—*ppl. adj.* troublesome, bustling.

Fiking-fain, *adj.* restlessly eager.

Fik-ma-fyke, *n.* a silly, unsettled creature; one busied with nonentities and trifles.

Fiky, *adj.* troublesome, fidgety, fastidious, worrying over trifles, punctilious; itchy; restive.

Filbow, *n.* a thump, a thwack.

Filch, *n.* weeds or grass covering ground, especially under crop. Cf. Filsch.

Filchan, *n.* a confused, dirty mass; in *pl.* rags patched or fastened together; the attire of a travelling beggar.

File, *n.* class or rank in society.

File, *v.* to defile, soil; to disorder; to accuse; to condemn.

File, *conj.* as long as.—*n.* a while; in *pl.* now and then, 'whiles.' Cf. Fill.

Filement, *n.* obloquy; moral filth.

Filie, *n.* a little while.

Filik, *n.* a little while. Cf. Whilock.

Filing, *n.* the act of soiling.

Filjit, *n.* a disreputable vagabond; a tramp.

Filk, *pron.* which. Cf. Whilk.

Fill, *pron.* which.

Fill, *v.* to hold a lease of a farm; to fill bobbins with yarn.—*n.* anything that fills, as a fill of tobacco or of a pipe, &c.

Fill, *adv.* while.—*prep.* until.

Fillad, *n.* a thigh.

Fill and fetch mair, *phr.* riotous prodigality; a continuous bout of drinking.

Filler, *n.* a funnel for filling bottles, &c., with liquid.

Fill-fou, *n.* as much liquor as makes one quite drunk.

Fillibeg, Filabey, Filibeg, Filipeg, Fillabeg, *n.* the short kilt worn by Highlanders.

Fillies, *n.* felloes, fellies.

Fillister, *n.* the plane used for making the outer part of a window-sash fit for receiving glass.

Fillock, *n.* a filly or young mare.

Filly-tails, *n.* fleecy cirrus clouds.

Filock, *n.* a little while. Cf. Whilock.

Filp, *n.* a person of disagreeable temper.

Filp, *n.* a fall off one's feet.

Filrey, *adj.* fussy, troublesome about trifles.

Filsch, Filsh, *n.* grass or weeds covering a field, especially when under crop; a long, lean, lank person or child; a term of contempt, generally applied to a man.

Filsch, *n.* a thump, a blow.

Filsch, Filsh, *adj.* empty, faint, hungry.—*v.* to faint; to flinch.

Filsched-up, *ppl. adj.* 'filschy.'

Filschy, *adj.* used of a sheaf: swelled up with weeds or natural grass.

Filshens, *n.* tattered garments. Cf. Filchan.

Filter, *n.* a fault in weaving.—*v.* to weave any part of a web faultily. Cf. Felter.

Fimmer, *v.* to move the feet quickly in walking or in dancing gracefully.

Fin, *adv.* when.

Fin, *n.* basalt, whinstone.

Fin', *n.* humour, vein; temper; eagerness; anger.

Fin', *v.* to find; to feel, have a sensation of; to feel, grope, search; to provide, supply. —*n.* feel, sensation, feeling.

Findhorn-haddock, *n.* a haddock split, and cured by smoking, so called from Findhorn in Morayshire.

Finding, *n.* searching, feeling, groping.

Findle, *n.* anything found; the act of finding; treasure-trove.

Findon-haddock, *n.* a smoked haddock. Cf. Finnan-haddie.

Findrum, *n.* a smoke-dried haddock. Cf. Findhorn-haddock.

Findrum-speldin', *n.* a small haddock, split, and dried in the sun until hard and tough.

Findsily, *adj.* clever or apt to find.

Findy, *adj.* full, substantial, supporting, solid.

Fine, *adj.* docile, well-behaved, agreeable; very well; in good health or spirits; prosperous.—*adv.* very much; perfectly; finely; prosperously.—*v.* to free wool from the coarse parts.

Fine and, *phr.* very.

Fineer, *v.* to veneer.

Fine-lever, *n.* a levier of fines.

Finely, *adv.* perfectly, quite well; used of convalescence.

Fineries, *n.* delicacies, dainties.

Finever, *adv.* whenever.

Fingauls, *n.* a name formerly given to inhabitants of the south end of Kirkmaiden parish in Wigtownshire.

Finger, *v.* in weaving: to work the flowers on a web.

Finger-and-toe, *n.* a disease of turnips.

Fingerer, *n.* the boy or girl who 'fingers' on a web.

Finger-fed, *adj.* delicately reared, pampered.

Finger-full, *n.* a pinch, very small quantity.

Fingering, *n.* fine worsted, spun from combed wool on the small wheel.

Fingering-breid, *n.* a better quality of oatcake, finely baked and toasted, thin and brittle, for a farmer's own table.

Fingerings, *n.* a coarse, slight, woollen cloth. Cf. Fingroms.

Finger-neb, *n.* a finger-tip.

Finger o' scorn, *phr.* a contemptible fellow.

Fingroms, *n.* 'fingerings.'

Fingted, *n.* a bandaged finger.

Finnack, Finnock, *n.* a white trout, in colour and shape like a salmon.

Finnan-haddie, *n.* a haddock, split, and cured with smoke, so called from the village of Findon in Kincardineshire.

Finner, *n.* a 'finnack.'

Finnie, *n.* a salmon not a year old.

Finnie, *adj.* full, solid, substantial. Cf. Findy.

Finnie, *n.* sensation, the feeling imparted by a thing.

Finnin, *n.* the devil. Cf. Fienden.

Finnisin, Finnison, *n.* anxious expectation; earnest desire.—*adj.* eager, very desirous.

Fin'sily, *adj.* clever at finding. Cf. Findsily.

Fint, *n.* devil, fiend; used as negation in oaths and excls. Cf. Fient.

Fintock, *n.* the cloud-berry, the 'averin.'

Fintram, *n.* a smoke-dried haddock. Cf. Findrum.

Finzach, *n.* the knot-grass.

Fipple, *n.* the under-lip. Cf. Faiple.

Fir, *n.* a pine-torch, 'firwood' used as a candle.

Firach, *n.* a fire; a fluster; a fit of fiery temper.

Fir-candle, *n.* a torch; 'firwood' used as a candle.

Fir-dale, *n.* a plank of fir.

Fire, *n.* fuel; a light to a pipe; a smithy-spark, especially when it strikes the eyeball; marine phosphorescence; carburetted hydrogen in coal-mines; sheet-lightning; the sultriness preceding a thunderstorm.—*v.* to bake or toast bread; to discharge any missile; to cauterize; to inflame or irritate the skin; to warm; to scorch grass or grain by lightning or hot, dry winds; to light up; to brighten up; to spoil milk in sultry weather.

Fire and tow, *phr.* an irascible person.

Fire-bit, -burn, *n.* marine phosphorescence.

Fire-cheek, *n.* the fireside.

Fire-cross, *n.* the fiery cross.

Fired, *ppl. adj.* used of the skin: irritated: of milk: tasting ill from sultry weather.

Fire-dairt, *n.* lightning.

Fire-drum, *n.* a drum beaten as an alarm of fire.

Fire-edge, *n.* the first eagerness or heat.

Fire-en', *n.* the fireplace; the end of a room where the fireplace is.

Fire-engines, *n.* cannon, guns, pistols, &c.

Fire-fang, -fangit, *adj.* used of cheese: spoiled by too much heat before drying; of manure: spoiled by over-fermentation; of food: scorched.

Fire-fanging, *n.* the effect of too much heat on cheese, dung, &c.

Fire-fangitness, *n.* the state of being 'fire-fangit.'

Fire-flaught, *n.* a flash of lightning.

Fire-flaw, *n.* the sting-ray.

Fire-house, *n.* the kitchen of a two-roomed cottage; a house in which there is at least one fireplace.

Fire-hung, *adj.* hanging over the fire.

Fire-kettle, *n.* a pot for holding fire in a fishing-boat.

Fire-kindling, *n.* a 'house-warming' entertainment.

Fire-levin, *n.* lightning.

Fire-lug, *n.* the side of the fireplace.

Fire-penny, *n.* a charge for use of flint and steel, paid in kind.

Fire-room, *n.* the sitting-room of a cotter family; a room with a fireplace.

Fire-shool, *n.* a fire-shovel.

Fire-slaught, *n.* lightning.

Fire-spang, *n.* a quick-tempered person.

Fire-tail, Fire-tail-Bob, *n.* the redstart.

Fir-ewe, *n.* a fir-cone, used as a child's plaything.

Fire-wheel, *n.* a St Catherine's wheel.

Fire-works, *n.* firearms.

Fir-fecket, *n.* a coffin.

Fir-futtle, *n.* a large knife for cutting 'fir-candles.'

Fir-gown, *n.* a coffin.

Firie, *n.* a tumult, bustle. Cf. Feery.

Firie-farry, *n.* confusion; uproar; concern, bustling anxiety. Cf. Feery-fary.

Firing-girdle, *n.* a baking-griddle.

Fir-jacket, *n.* a coffin.

Firk, *v.* to poke, rummage among; to pilfer.

Firl, *v.* to measure corn.

Firlot, *n.* a corn measure of varying capacity; a large quantity; a quarter of a boll.

Firmance, *n.* stability; imprisonment.

Firnackit, *n.* a fillip. Cf. Fornackit.

Firnie, *n.* a quarrel, broil.

Firple, *v.* to whimper.—*n.* the under-lip. Cf. Fipple, Faiple.

Firrating, *n.* a kind of tape, galloon; a shoe-lace.

Firry, *n.* a tumult, bustle. Cf. Feery.

Firrystoich, *n.* a bustle; a broil; a fight.

Firsle, *v.* to bustle about; to rustle. Cf. Fershell, Fissle.

First, *adj.* next, ensuing.

First, *v.* to grant credit. Cf. Frist.

Firsten, *adj.* first.

Firstend, *n.* the first payment of interest, or a due.

First-foot, -fit, *n.* the first person met on certain special occasions: the first person met with on New Year's Day. - *v.* to act as, or be, a 'first-foot.'

First-footer, *n.* a 'first-foot.'

Firstlin', *adj.* first, earliest.

Firstlins, *adv.* first, at first.

Firth, *n.* a place on a moor where peats for fuel could be cut; a small wood. Cf. Frith.

Firtig, *v.* to fatigue.

Firtigesom, *adj.* fatiguing.

Firwood, *n.* bog-wood, formerly used for candles.

Fir-yowe, *n.* a fir-cone. Cf. Fir-ewe.

Fiscal, *n.* the public prosecutor in criminal cases, the Procurator-Fiscal.

Fish, *v.* to strive, try hard.

Fish, *v.* to splice, to fasten a piece of wood on a mast, &c., to strengthen it.

Fish-carle, *n.* a fisherman.

Fish-currie, *n.* any deep hole or recess in a river where fishes hide.

Fisher-land, *n.* land on the seashore used by fishermen to dry fish, spread nets, &c.

Fish-garth, *n.* an enclosure of stakes and wattles for catching fish in a river.

Fish-gouries, *n.* fish-garbage.

Fish-hake, *n.* a weight anchoring a fishing-line or -net; a triangular framework of wood for drying fish before cooking.

Fish-, Fishing-hawk, *n.* the osprey.

Fishick, *n.* the brown whistle-fish.

Fishing-wand, *n.* a fishing-rod.

Fish-rig, *n.* the backbone of a fish.

Fish-staff, *n.* a large iron hook with wooden handle, for striking into the fishes and lifting them into the boat.

†Fisk, *n.* the Exchequer; the Treasury.

Fisle, *v.* to rustle; to whistle. Cf. Fissle.

Fison, *n.* pith; vigour; 'fissen.'

Fissen, *n.* pith; vigour; substance. Cf. Fushion.

Fissenless, *adj.* pithless; tasteless; without 'body' or substance.

Fissle, Fissil, *v.* to rustle; to make a rustling, whistling sound, to whistle; to cause to rustle; to fidget; to bustle about.—*n.* a whistling sound; fussy compliments; a fuss, bustle.

Fissle-fisslin', *n.* a faint rustling sound.

Fissling, *n.* a rustle; a whistling; the sound of wind in the keyhole.

Fist, *v.* to grasp with the hand.

Fist-foundered, *ppl. adj.* knocked down with the fists.

Fistle, *v.* to rustle, to whistle. Cf. Fissle.

Fisty, *n.* a left-handed person.

Fit, *n.* the foot; speed; the lower part; a foot-step.—*v.* to go afoot; to dance; to kick; to put a new foot to a stocking; to add up, balance or adjust accounts.

Fit, *adj.* able; capable; inclined; matching; on the point of, ready; in vigorous health. —*v.* to set up a mast; to become, suit; to provide what is fitting or supply what one wants.

Fit, *n.* a whit; a bit; an action.

Fit, *n.* a custom, habit.

Fit-ba', *n.* a football.

Fit-band, *n.* a halter for the feet ; a company of infantry.

Fit-board, -brod, *n.* a foot-rest, a footstool.

Fit-braid, -breeth, *n.* a foot-breadth.

Fitch, *v.* to move a thing slightly from its place ; to lift and lay down again ; to touch frequently ; used of a louse : to crawl ; to fidget ; to move at the game of draughts.— *n.* a slight change of place ; a move in the game of draughts.

Fit-dint, *n.* a footprint.

Fite, *v.* to cut, whittle. Cf. White.

Fite, *adj.* white. Cf. White.

Fite-breid, *n.* loaf-bread.

Fit-eitch, *n.* a foot-adze.

Fit-fall, *n.* a grown-up lamb.

Fit-feal, *n.* the skin of a lamb between castration and weaning.

Fit-for-fit, *phr.* very exactly ; step for step.

Fit-gang, *n.* as much ground as one can walk on ; a long, narrow chest extending along-side a wooden bed.

Fither, *adv. conj. pron.* whether.

Fithit, *int.* an excl. of confirmation of one's saying.

Fitless, *adj.* feeble on one's feet, apt to stumble.

Fitless-cock, *n.* a cake of lard and oatmeal boiled in broth ; a sodden bannock, usually made at Shrovetide.

Fit-lickin', *adj.* cringing, fawning.

Fitlin, *n.* a loose bar to place the feet against in rowing.

Fit-nowt, *n.* the hindmost pair of a team of oxen.

Fitocks, *n.* large peats or sods, used for 'resting' a fire through the night.

Fit-pad, *n.* a footpath.

Fit-peat, *n.* peat cut with the foot pressing on the peat-spade.

Fit-rig, *n.* the ridge of land at the lower end of a field, on which the horses and plough turn.

Fit-road, *n.* a footpath through enclosed lands.

Fit-rot, *n.* the foot-rot in sheep.

Fits, *n.* in *phr.* 'the fits and the fors o't,' 'the whys and the wherefores of it,' all about it.

Fit-shakin', *n.* a dance, a ball.

Fit-side, *adj.* on an equal footing ; 'upsides with,' revenged upon.—*adv.* step for step. —*n.* in *pl.* ropes, used for chains, attached to the 'haims' and to the 'swingle-tree' in ploughing.

Fit-soam, *n.* an iron chain extending from the muzzle of the plough and fixed to the yoke of the oxen next the plough. Cf. Soam.

Fit-sole, *n.* the foot.

Fit-stap, *n.* a footstep.

Fit-sted, -stead, *n.* a footprint.

Fit-stool, *n.* the face of the earth, God's footstool.

Fitter, *v.* to patter or make a noise with the feet ; to potter about ; to totter in walking ; to injure by frequent treading ; to fumble ; to knock unsteadily.

Fittering, *n.* fidgeting, fumbling.

Fit-the-gutter, *n.* a low, loose slipper.

Fittie, *n.* a term of endearment addressed to a shepherd's dog.

Fittie, *adj.* having good feet, safe enough to walk with.

Fittie, *adj.* expeditious, neat, trim.

Fittie, *n.* a short stocking ; a person with deformed feet ; a mud-stained foot.

Fittie, *n.* an imaginary person of a very useless nature.

Fittie-fies, *n.* quirks, quibbles ; 'whittie-whaws.'

Fittie-lan', *n.* the near horse of the last pair in a plough, which walks on the un-ploughed land.

Fitting, *n.* footing ; the footing of a stocking.

Fitting, *n.* training, preparation.

Fitting-ale, *n.* a feast given by parents when their child begins to walk.

Fittings, *n.* peats set on end to dry ; in *sing.* the setting of peats on end to dry.

Fittininment, *n.* concern, interest ; a good footing with a person.

Fittocks, *n.* the feet of stockings cut off and worn as shoes.

Fit-tree, *n.* the treadle of a spinning-wheel.

Fit-washing, *n.* the custom of washing the feet of a bride and bridegroom on the night before the marriage. Cf. Feet-washing.

Fit-weary, *adj.* with weary feet.

Fit-yoke, *n.* the hindmost pair of a team of oxen.

Fiumart, *n.* a polecat. Cf. Foumart.

Five-sax, *phr.* five or six.

Fivesome, *n.* a set of five, five together.

Fivey, *n.* a game played with five small stones.

Fivver, *n.* a fever.

Fix-fax, *n.* the tendon of the neck of cattle and sheep ; a pillory confining the neck and hands ; the punishment inflicted in such a pillory. Cf. Fick-fack, Fig-fag.

Fixfax, *n.* hurry ; the middle of a business. Cf. Fick-fack.

Fizenwill, *n.* part of a gun belonging to the doghead.

Fizz, *n.* a blaze ; stir, bustle, fuss, commotion.—*v.* to make a spluttering sound ; to fuss, bustle about ; to rage.

†**Fizzen, Fizen,** *n.* food; pith, substance, essence. Cf. Fushion.

Fizzenless, *adj.* without substance or flavour, insipid, not nutritious; useless, feeble in body or mind; ineffectual. Cf. Fushionless.

Fizzer, *n.* any thing or person first-rate or excellent; a puzzling question, a 'poser.'

Flaacht, *n.* a peat-spade.

Flab, *n.* a mushroom.

Flab, *n.* a large, showy article.

Flabby, *adj.* ostentatious, showy, foppish.

Flabrigast, *v.* to 'flabbergast'; to boast, brag.

Flabrigastit, *ppl. adj.* 'flabbergasted'; worn out with exertion, extremely fatigued.

Flach, *v. pret.* did fly, flew. Cf. Flich.

Flachan, *n.* a flake of snow.

Flacht, *n.* a flake of snow; a flash; a handful of wool before it is carded.—*v.* to pare; to weave. Cf. Flaught.

Flacht, *n.* a spreading or flapping of wings; a flight of birds on the wing.—*v.* to flutter. —*adv.* at full length. Cf. Flaught.

Flachter, *v.* to pare turf from the ground. Cf. Flaughter.

Flachter, *v.* to flutter. Cf. Flaughter.

Flachter, *v.* to knock down. Cf. Flaughter.

Flack, *n.* a square plaid.

Flack, *v.* to hang loosely.

Flacket, *n.* a small spirit-flask.

Flad, *n.* a piece, portion, slice.

Fladge, *n.* a flake, a large piece; anything broad; a broad-bottomed person.

Flae, *n.* a skin; what is flayed off.—*v.* to pare land. Cf. Flay.

Flae, *n.* a flea.

Flae, *v.* to frighten. Cf. Fley.

Flaeie, *adj.* abounding in fleas.

Flaesick, *n.* a blazing spark from a woodfire.

Flaff, *v.* to flutter, fly about, flap, wave; to flap the wings; used of the wind : to blow in gusts; to fan, blow up; to go off, as gunpowder, to shoot forth.—*n.* a flutter of the wings; a fop, one who flutters about; a sudden gust of wind, a flash; an instant; a light blow, fillip; a buffet.

Flaffer, *v.* to flutter; to move with a rustling, awkward motion.—*n.* a wing; a fluttering motion; a pound note.

Flaffer, *n.* a duckling, fledged over the body but as yet without quill-feathers.

Flafferie, *adj.* light, easily compressible.

Flaffin', *n.* a fluttering of the wings; a flapping; fluttering of the heart, palpitation; any very light body; a flake of any kind. —*ppl. adj.* puffing, suddenly shooting out.

Flag, *n.* a piece of green sward cut or pared off; a large sod, placed at the back of a fire; in *pl.* a side pavement paved with flagstones.

Flag, *n.* a flake of snow.—*v.* to snow in flakes.

Flag, *n.* a contemptuous name for a woman, a slut.

Flagarie, *n.* a vagary; finery; a gewgaw; a fanciful, fastidious person. Cf. Fleegarie.

Flagartie, *adj.* squally, stormy.

Flagaryin', *n.* busying one's self about trifles of dress.

Flaght, *n.* a flapping of wings. Cf. Flaught.

Flagirt, *n.* a flapping, flaunting thing; used as a term of reproach.

Flagon-bun, *n.* a bun baked in a can among hot water.

Flagrum, *n.* a blow, thump.

Flag-side, *n.* in *phr.* 'the flag-side of a split haddock'; the side without the bone.

Flaich, *n.* a flea.

Flaik, *n.* a square plaid. Cf. Flack.

Flaik-stand, *n.* a refrigerator; the cooling vessel through which the pipes pass in distilling.

Flail, *n.* a tall, ungainly person.—*v.* to beat, thump.

Flailer, *n.* a 'settler,' a 'poser'; a thresher with the flail.

Flain, *n.* an arrow. Cf. Flane.

Flainen, *n.* flannel. Cf. Flannen.

Flaip, *n.* an unbroken fall; a flat fall on soft ground; a blow caused by a fall and producing a dull, flat sound; a flop.—*v.* to strike; to flop. Cf. Flap.

Flaiper, *n.* a heavy fall; a blow.—*v.* to flap; to flop. Cf. Flapper.

Flaiper, *n.* a person foolish in dress and manners.—*v.* to flaunt in foolish clothes.

Flair, *n.* the skate.

Flair, *n.* a floor.

Flair, *v.* to cajole, flatter. — *n.* flattery; boasting. Cf. Flare.

Flairach, *n.* a giddy person who talks much in a shrill voice, and makes a great ado about little.—*v.* to act as a 'flairach.'

Flairdy, *v.* to coax, cajole, wheedle; to flatter.

Flairy, *v.* to coax. Cf. Flare.

Flait, Flaite, Flaitte, *v. pret.* scolded. Cf. Flite.

Flaither, *v.* to use wheedling or fawning language.

Flake, *n.* a hurdle for penning sheep on a turnip-field, or cattle, &c., at a show; a hurdle used as a gate, or to close a gap in a fence; a frame above the chimney-piece for holding a gun; in *pl.* temporary sheeppens.

Flake, *n.* a ray, a flash.

Flaket, *n.* a small flask. Cf. Flacket.

Flam, *n.* a humbug, fabrication; flattery, cajolery.—*v.* to flatter, humbug.

†**Flam,** *n.* pancake. Cf. Flaune.

Flam, *n.* a sudden puff of wind, a gust.—*v.* to be squally ; to blow in gusts ; to fly out and in. Cf. Flan.

†**Flamb, Flam,** *v.* to baste roasting meat ; to besmear one's self while eating.

†**Flamboy,** *n.* a flambeau, a torch.

Flame, *n.* a fit of hot anger ; a species of carnation ; a sweetheart. —*v.* used of a flag : to float gallantly in the wind ; of an author : to become famous.

Flame, Flamm, *v.* to baste roasting meat. Cf. Flamb.

Flamfoo, *n.* a gaudy ornament or frippery in a woman's dress ; a gaudily-dressed woman ; a woman fond of dress.

Flaming, *ppl. adj.* shining out, egregious.

Flamming, *ppl. adj.* used of oars : dipping in and out of the water. Cf. Flam.

Flamp, *adj.* inactive ; in a state of lassitude.

Flan, *adj.* shallow, flat.

Flanch, *v.* to flatter, cajole, wheedle.—*n.* a flatterer.

Flanderkin, *n.* a Fleming, a native of Flanders.

Flane, *n.* an arrow.

Flang, *v. pret.* flung.

Flann, Flan, *n.* a sudden blast of wind off the land ; a sudden down-draught in a chimney.—*v.* to be squally, gusty.

Flannen, *n.* flannel.—*adj.* made of flannel.

Flanninette, *n.* flannelette.—*adj.* made of flannelette.

Flanny, *adj.* gusty, squally.

Flansh, *v.* to flatter, wheedle.—*n.* a flatterer ; a hypocrite. Cf. Flanch.

Flanter, *v.* to waver ; to be slightly delirious ; to quiver in agitation ; to flinch, falter in speaking ; to prevaricate, equivocate.

Flanty, *adj.* eccentric, capricious ; flighty, unsteady.

Flap, *v.* to come or strike upon suddenly ; to flop, fall suddenly ; to fly, to turn inside out.—*n.* a blow caused by a fall and producing a dull, flat sound ; a fall on to a soft substance ; a slice ; a smart blow with anything flat.

Flapdawdron, *n.* a tall, ill-dressed person.

Flapper, *n.* a heavy resounding fall ; a bird just able to fly.—*v.* to flap, flutter.

Flapper-bags, *n.* the burdock.

Flare, *n.* a floor.

Flare, *v.* to coax.—*n.* cajolery, flattery. Cf. Flair.

Flash, *v.* to spend lavishly ; to lash.

Flash, *n.* a depository for timber.

Flashy-fiery, *adj.* flashing like fire.

Flasicks, *n.* atoms, small pieces.

Flass, *n.* a flask.

Flast, *v.* to boast, brag.

Flat, *n.* a saucer ; a cake of cow-dung ; low, level ground.—*v.* to flatten.

Flatch, *v.* to flatten ; to lay over, fold down ; to knock down ; to walk clumsily.

Flate, *v. pret.* scolded. Cf. Flite.

Flate, *n.* a straw mat under a horse's saddle to prevent chafing ; one used as a draught-screen, or as an inner door.

Flate, *n.* a hurdle, a ' flake.'

Flat in the fore, *phr.* having the stomach empty, hungry.

Flatlins, Flatlines, *adv.* flat ; with the flat side of anything.

Flatter, *v.* to float.

Flatterin' Friday, *n.* a fine Friday during a time of wet, supposed to indicate more wet weather.

Flauf, *v.* to flutter ; to flap. Cf. Flaff.

Flaught, Flaucht, Flauch, Flauchten, Flaughen, *n.* a flake of snow ; a lock of hair ; a handful of wool before it is carded ; a roll of wool carded and ready for spinning ; a hide, skin ; a bunch, a piece cut off from a larger portion ; a flash, gleam ; a gust of wind ; a cloud of smoke from a chimney at either end ; a stream of vapour ; used of land : a division, a croft.—*v.* to card wool into thin flakes ; to weave ; to pare turf, &c. ; to strip off the skin or hide ; to mix, mingle ; to pilfer straw, hay, &c. in handfuls.

Flaught, Flaucht, *n.* a spreading or a flapping of wings ; hurry, bustle, flutter ; sudden fright ; a number of birds on the wing.— *v.* to flutter ; to palpitate ; to tremble. —*adv.* with wings outspread ; at full length ; with great eagerness.

Flaught-bred, *adv.* at full length ; with great eagerness.

Flaughter, *n.* a skinner ; a carder of wool.

Flaughter, *n.* a man who cuts peats with a ' flaughter-spade ' ; a thin turf pared from the ground.—*v.* to pare off turf from the ground.

Flaughter, *v.* to flutter as a bird ; to flicker, waver, move hither and thither aimlessly ; to flurry, alarm, frighten. — *n.* a flutter, fluttering motion.

Flaughter, *v.* to fell, prostrate.—*n.* a heavy fall ; a knock-down blow.

Flaughterer, *n.* one who cuts peats with a ' flaughter-spade.'

Flaughter-fail, -feal, *n.* a long turf or peat.

Flaughterin', *n.* a light shining fitfully, a flickering ; a fluttering, quivering, palpitation.

Flaughter-spade, *n.* a two-handed spade, for cutting turfs, sods, and peats ; a boys' game, called also the ' Salmon-loup.'

Flaughts, Flauchts, *n.* instruments used in carding wool.

†**Flaune,** *n.* a pancake.

Flaunter, *v.* to waver ; to flinch. Cf. Flanter.

Flaunty, *adj.* eccentric; flighty. Cf. Flanty.

Flaur, *n.* a strong smell or flavour.

Flaurie, *n.* a drizzle.

Flaver, *n.* the grey-bearded oat.

Flaw, *n.* a storm of snow; rage, passion; in *pl.* snow-flakes.

Flaw, *n.* in *phr.* 'fire-flaw,' the sting-ray. Cf. Fiery-flaw.

Flaw, *n.* an extent of land under grass; a broad ridge.

Flaw, *n.* a lie, a fib.—*v.* to lie; with *awa,* to exaggerate in narration; to cheat, defraud.

Flaw, *n.* the point of a horse-nail, broken off by the smith, after it has passed through the hoof.

Flaw, *v. pret.* fled; flew.

Flaw, *n.* a thin layer of turf or peat cut for fuel; the place in a moss where peats are spread to dry.—*v.* to cut or pare peat-moss.

Flaw, *n.* a failure, blunder; an injury, accident.

Flawkit, *ppl. adj.* used of cattle: white in the flanks.

Flawmont, *n.* a narrative, story.

Flaw-moss, *n.* a moss on which peats are spread to dry.

†Flawn, *n.* a pancake. Cf. Flaune.

Flaw-peat, *n.* soft, light, spongy peat.

Flay, *v.* to pare the turf off grass or moss-land.—*n.* a skin.

Flay, *n.* a flea.

Flay-a-louse, *n.* a skinflint; a very mean person.

Flaze, *v.* used of cloth: to fray out, ravel out; of a sharp instrument: to turn its edge.

Flea, *v.* to flay.

Flea, *v.* to free from fleas.

Flea, *n.* a fly. Cf. Flee.

Fleach, *n.* a flea.—*v.* to free from fleas. Cf. Flech.

Flea'd, *ppl. adj.* frightened. Cf. Fley.

Fleaks, *n.* fissures between the strata of a rock.

Flea-luggit, *adj.* hare-brained, unsettled.

Fleasocks, *n.* wood-shavings.

Flea-sticker, *n.* a tailor.

Fleat, *n.* a thick mat under a saddle to prevent chafing.

Fleat, *v. pret.* scolded. Cf. Flite.

Flech, *n.* a flea; a little, frivolous, light-headed person.—*v.* to free from fleas.

Flech, *v.* to beat soundly; to fall upon; to scold.

Flechan, Flechin, *n.* a small quantity or sprinkling of anything; a particle; a flake of snow.

Flechter, *n.* a thin turf.—*v.* to pare off turf from the ground. Cf. Flaughter.

Flechts, *n.* the forked parts of a spinning-wheel in which the teeth are set; the part of the fanners of a winnowing-machine that raises the wind.

Flechy, *adj.* swarming with fleas.

Fleck, *n.* a flea. Cf. Flech.

Fleck, *n.* a flake of snow; a flake, a variety of carnation.—*v.* to spot, bespatter.

Fleckert, *ppl. adj.* flecked, dappled; torn, mangled.

Fleckie, *n.* a speckled cow; a pet name for such a cow.

Fleckit, *n.* a spirit-flask. Cf. Flacket.

Fleckit, *ppl. adj.* used of the sky: dappled with clouds.

Fleckit-fever, *n.* spotted fever.

Fled, *ppl. adj.* fugitive.

Flee, *v.* to frighten. Cf. Fley.

Flee, *n.* a fly; a whit, jot; a fit of passion or temper.—*v.* to fly as a bird; to fall into a passion.

Flee-about, *n.* a gadabout; a flighty person.

Flee-cap, *n.* a head-dress formerly worn by elderly ladies, formed by two conjoined crescents standing out by means of wire from a cushion on which the hair was dressed.

Fleech, *v.* to flatter, fawn; to coax, cajole; to beseech, importune; to beguile.—*n.* flattery.

Fleech, *v.* used of a carpenter: to shave off spills in planing wood.

Fleecher, *v.* to flutter.

Fleeching, *n.* flattery, cajolery.—*ppl. adj.* used of the weather: falsely assuming a favourable appearance; flattering, deceitful.

Fleechingly, *adv.* flatteringly.

Fleed, *n.* a head-ridge, on which the plough is turned.

Flee'd, *ppl.* frightened.

Fleefu', *adj.* fearful. Cf. Fley.

Fleeg, *v.* to frighten. Cf. Fleg.

Fleegarie, Fleegerie, *n.* a vagary, whim; finery, frippery; a gewgaw; a fastidious person, one fond of trifles, &c.

Fleegarying, *ppl. adj.* busying one's self about trifling articles of dress.

Fleegest, *n.* a paper fly-catcher.

Fleegirt, *n.* a small quantity of anything.

Flee-haunted, *adj.* haunted by flies.

Fleeing, *ppl. adj.* flying.

Fleeing, *n.* fly-fishing.

Fleeing-adder, *n.* the dragon-fly.

Fleeing-buss, *n.* a whin-bush on fire.

Fleeing-dragon, *n.* the dragon-fly; a paper kite.

Fleeing-merchant, *n.* a pedlar; travelling merchant.

Fleeing-passion, *n.* a towering passion.

Fleeing-pinner, *n.* a head-dress with the ends of the lappets flying loose. Cf. Pinner.

Fleeing-tailor, *n.* a travelling tailor.
Fleeing-washerwoman, *n.* a travelling washer-woman.
Fleeing-yett, *n.* an unlatched gate.
Fleem, *n.* a veterinary lancet, a fleam.
Fleem, *v.* to scare; to banish. Cf. Flem.
Fleeock, *n.* a small fly.
Fleep, *n.* a stupid fellow; a cowardly, hulking fellow.
Fleer, *v.* to ogle; to make a wry face; to whimper.—*n.* a scornful laugh, a mock.
Fleer, *v.* to floor.—*n.* a floor.
Fleerach, *n.* a giddy talker in a shrill voice. Cf. Flairach.
Fleeringly, *adv.* mockingly.
Fleerish, *n.* a piece of steel for lighting tinder or match-paper on a flint. Cf. Flourish.
Fleerish, *v.* to embroider with floral designs, &c.
Fleesh, *n.* a fleece.
Fleesh, *n.* attack, assault, onset.
Fleesome, Fleesum, *adj.* frightful.
Fleesomelie, *adv.* frightfully.
Fleesomeness, *n.* frightfulness.
Flee's-wing, *n.* a particle, atom, the least.
Fleet, *v.* to remove, shift. Cf. Flit.
Fleet, *v.* to flow; to float.—*n.* a number of fishing-lines or nets; the overflow of water; a flat bog or swamp, out of which water flows from the hills.
Fleetch, *v.* to flatter. Cf. Fleech.
Fleet-dyke, *n.* a 'dyke' for preventing inundation.
Fleeter, *n.* a utensil for skimming broth, &c., in cooking.
Fleeter, *n.* a bumper.
Fleetfu', *adj.* fleeting.
Fleet-water, *n.* water which overflows ground.
Flee-up, *n.* a flighty, irascible person.
Flee-up-i'-the-air, *phr.* a contemptuous phrase for a person of light build or no weight.
Fleg, *n.* a stroke, a random blow; a kick; a fit of temper; an exaggeration; a lie.—*v.* to kick.
Fleg, Flegg, *v.* to frighten, frighten away; to take fright.—*n.* a fright, scare.
Fleg, *v.* to flutter, fly from place to place; to walk with a swinging step.
Flegarie, *n.* a vagary, whim. Cf. Fleegarie.
Fleggar, *n.* an exaggerator; a liar.—*v.* to kick.
Fleggin, *n.* a lazy, lying fellow, who goes from door to door.
Flegging, *ppl. adj.* timid.
Flegh, *n.* a flea. Cf. Flech.
Fleghings, *n.* the dust caused by flax-dressing.
Flegmagearie, *n.* a whim, fancy.
Flegmaleeries, *n.* needless finery, frippery.
Fleia, *n.* a landing-net used by fowlers in Skye.
Fleighter, *v.* to flutter; to palpitate. Cf. Flaughter.

Fleighterin, *n.* a fluttering; palpitation.
Fleip, *v.* to strip, peel. Cf. Flipe.
Fleir, *v.* to jeer; to whimper. Cf. Fleer.
Fleit, Fleid, *ppl. adj.* frightened. Cf. Fley.
Fleit, *v.* to float.—*n.* the overflowing of water. Cf. Fleet.
Fleitch, *v.* to coax, wheedle, &c.—*n.* cajolery Cf. Fleech.
Fleitness, *n.* fear, fright.
Flem, Fleme, *v.* to scare; to banish.
Flemens-firth, *n.* an asylum for outlaws.
Flench, *v.* to flinch, yield.
Flench, *v.* to slice the blubber from a whale's body; to flense.
Flench-gut, *n.* blubber laid out in long slices; the part of the hold into which it is thrown before being barrelled up.
Flenders, *n.* splinters, shivers. Cf. Flinders.
Flenis, *n.* fragments.
Fleock, *n.* a small fly. Cf. Fleeock.
Flep, *n.* a fall. Cf. Flap.
Flesh, *v.* to shave off the flesh on the under-side of a hide in the process of tanning.—*n.* butcher's meat.
Flesh-and-blood, *n.* the blood-root, or tormentil.
Flesh-and-fell, *phr.* the whole carcass and skin.
Flesh-boat, *n.* a meat-tub.
Fleshing, *n.* the business of a butcher.
Flet, Flett, *n.* a house; the inner part of a house; a flat, a story of a house.
Flet, *n.* a straw mat under a horse's saddle. Cf. Fleat.
Flet, Flett, *n.* a saucer; the saucer of a flower-pot. Cf. Flat.
Flet, *v. pret.* did scold. Cf. Flyte.
Flether, *v.* to flatter, fawn, wheedle.—*n.* in *pl.* fair words. Cf. Flaither.
Fleuchan, Flewchan, *n.* a snow-flake, a sprinkling of anything. Cf. Flechan.
Fleuk, *n.* a flounder. Cf. Fluke.
Fleuk, *n.* a parasite in the liver of sheep. Cf. Fluke.
Fleume, *n.* phlegm. Cf. Floam.
Fleunkie, *n.* a flunkey.
Fleup, *v.* to dance without lifting the feet.—*n.* in *pl.* broad feet.
Fleurie, *n.* the ace of spades. Cf. Flowerie.
Fleuwn, *ppl.* fled, flown.
Flew, *n.* a horn, a trumpet.
Flewat, Flewet, *n.* smart blow; a blow with the back of the hand.
Flews, *n.* a sluice, used in irrigation.
Fley, *v.* to frighten, scare; to put to flight; to be afraid; to warm slightly, take the chill off.—*n.* a fright; fear. Cf. Flee, Fleg.
Fleyit, Fleyt, *ppl. adj.* timorous; shy; abashed.
Fleyr, *v.* to jeer. Cf. Fleer.
Fleysome, *adj.* fearful; terrifying. Cf. Fleesome.

Flich, *v.* to fly.

Flichan, *n.* a sudden glow of heat; a sudden surprise, a fright.

Flichan, *n.* anything very small; a snow-flake; a flake of soot. Cf. Flechan.

Flicher, *v.* to flutter; to hover, flap the wings; to flirt, giggle, titter; to coax.—*n.* a rustle, flutter; a giggle; a giggler.

Flicher, *n.* a sprinkling.

Flicht, *n.* a small spot of dirt among food; a snow-flake.

Flicht, *v.* to fluctuate, flutter; to make a great show.—*n.* flight; the part of a spinning-wheel which twists the thread, and, by means of a 'tooth,' guides it to the pirn; the part of a winnowing-machine that raises the wind. Cf. Flechts, Flichter.

Flichtened, *ppl. adj.* flecked, sprinkled with.

Flichter, *v.* to flutter; to flap the wings; to move quiveringly in the air; to run with outspread arms; to startle, alarm; to throb, palpitate; to pinion, bind.—*n.* a flutter; a flicker; a throb; a great number of small objects flying in the air; a snow-flake; the 'flicht' of a winnowing-machine.

Flichteriff, *n.* unsteadiness.—*adj.* unsteady, fickle, flighty.

Flichtering, *ppl. adj.* fluttering, throbbing; unsteady, changing.—*n.* a fluttering, flickering, palpitation.

Flichtering-fain, *adj.* throbbing with happiness.

Flichter-lichtie, *n.* a light-headed, unsteady person.

Flichtersome, *adj.* unsteady, whimsical.

Flichtery, *adj.* flighty, fickle.

Flichtfu', *adj.* fluttering, flickering.

Flichtmafleathers, *n.* articles of adornment, finery, frippery, trifles.

Flichtrife, *adj.* changeable, unsteady. Cf. Flichteriff.

Flichtriveness, *n.* fickleness, flightiness.

Flichty, *adj.* flighty.

Flick, *n.* a small quantity, a modicum, a 'touch.'

Flicker, *v.* to whirl; to hover; to titter; with *at*, to make light of.—*n.* a rustle; a giggle. Cf. Flicher.

Flick-pie, *n.* a suet-pudding.

Flied, *ppl. adj.* frightened. Cf. Fley.

Fliep, *n.* a fool.

Fliet, *n.* a flute.

Flighan, *n.* a flake; a sprinkling. Cf. Flechan.

Flight, *v.* to scold. Cf. Flite.

Flighter, *v.* to pinion, bind.

Flighter, *v.* to flutter.—*n.* a flighty woman. Cf. Flichter.

Flighty, *adj.* hasty, quick.

Fligmagary, *n.* a whim.

Flim, *n.* an illusion; a whim.

Flim-flae, *n.* flattering speech; a compliment.

Flim-flam, *n.* nonsense.

Flimrikin, *n.* a flimsy article. Cf. Flinderkin.

Flinch, *v.* to flense a whale for blubber. Cf. Flench.

Flinch, *v.* to coax, flatter.

Flinder, *n.* a splinter; a fragment.—*v.* to break in pieces.

Flinder, *v.* used of cattle: to break loose and scamper about.

Flinderkin, *n.* a weak person; a flimsy article; a thin garment.

Flindrikin, *adj.* flirting.

Flin'er, *n.* a splinter.

Fling, *v.* used of a horse: to kick, strike with the hind-feet, to throw its rider; to throw in wrestling; to jilt, disappoint, cheat; to reject, throw over; to dance vigorously, caper; to beat, thresh grain; to go off at a tangent in a fit of ill-humour; to go at hastily and forcibly.—*n.* a dance, the 'Highland Fling'; the act of flinging; a sudden and hasty movement; a rebuff, rejection; a stroke, blow; a disappointment, a disappointment in love; a fit of ill-humour; the knack of using a tool or working properly; gait, style of walking; the act of kicking, dancing, &c.

Fling-bag, *n.* a bag for the shoulder.

Flinger, *n.* a dancer; a kicking horse.

Flinging-tree, *n.* a flail, the lower part of a flail; a piece of timber hung as a partition between two horses in a stable; the pole of a carriage; a swingle-tree.

Fling-stick, *n.* a 'rowly-powly' man who frequents fairs.

Fling-strings, *n.* in *phr.* 'to tak' the fling-strings,' to lose one's temper, become restive.

Flinner, *n.* a splinter. Cf. Flinder.

Flinrickin, Flinriken, *n.* very thin cloth; a mere rag. Cf. Flinderkin.

Flint-specks, *n.* flint-glass spectacles.

Flip, *n.* the flap of a saddle.

Flipe, *v.* to strip, tear off; to fleece; to turn up or down, fold back; used of a stocking: to turn it partially inside out.—*n.* the folded-back edge of a knitted woollen 'cowl' or night-cap; a fold, flap; a thin piece of skin; a contemptuous name for a person, a 'fellow.'

Flipe, *v.* to fall suddenly, to flop. Cf. Flap.

Flipin, *ppl.* looking absurd.

Flipper, *v.* to move the hands in walking.

Flird, *n.* a thin piece of anything; anything thin, insufficient, or threadbare; vain finery.

Flird, *n.* a sneer, a gibe.

Flird, *v.* to flaunt, flutter, flounce; to move about from place to place restlessly.—*n.* a foolish, trifling, fickle person.

Flirdie, *adj.* giddy, unsettled.

Flirdin'-aboot, *ppl. adj.* unsettled, restless; skittish.

Flirdoch, *n.* a flirt; a foolish trifler.—*v.* to flirt.

Flirdome, *n.* affectation, ostentation, pretence.

Flirn, *v.* to twist, distort.

Flirr, *v.* to gnash.

Flirr, *v.* to fly out in a passion upon one; to interrupt rudely.

Flirry, *n.* a blossom.

Flirt, *v.* to take short, swift flights.

Flisk, *v.* to whisk; to move quickly hither and thither; to frisk, to be restive under the yoke; to make restless, uneasy; to displease, fret; to switch.—*n.* a swift movement; a whim; a caper; a trifling, skipping person; a moment.

Fliskie, *n.* a frolicsome girl, a 'romp.'—*adj.* skittish, lively, frisky, restive.

Fliskmahaigo, *n.* a 'fliskmahoy.'

Fliskmahoy, *n.* a giddy, ostentatious person; a giddy, gawky girl.

Flist, *n.* a flash, a slight explosion, as of gunpowder, or of air confined in a bottle when the cork is drawn; an explosion of temper; a flash of wit, &c.; a keen, smart stroke, a fillip; a flying shower of snow, a squall; a small quantity of gunpowder exploded.—*v.* to make a slight explosion; to 'flare up,' explode in passion; to snap the fingers; to rain and blow at the same time.

Flist, *n.* a boast; a fib; one who boasts or fibs.—*v.* to boast, to fib.

Flisterin', *ppl. adj.* flustering, flighty.

Flistert, *ppl. adj.* flustered, flushed.

Flistin, *n.* a slight shower.

Flisty, *adj.* irascible, passionate; stormy, squally.

Flit, *v.* to remove, transport, shift, change; to remove from one house to another; to assist one in moving; to cause one to remove; to shift a tethered animal from one place in a field to another; to pass away, depart, die; to leave, quit.—*n.* a change of residence.

Flitch, *v.* to move or flit.

Flitcher, *v.* to flutter like young nestlings when their dam approaches.—*n.* in *pl.* light flying flakes.

Flitchers, *n.* the 'men' used in playing the game of 'corsiecrown.'

Flite, *v.* to scold, chide; to flout, jeer; to quarrel, wrangle; to reprimand.—*n.* a scolding; a gibe; a scolding match, wrangle; a bully.

Flitepock, *n.* a double chin.

Fliter, *n.* a scold, one given to scolding.

Flitfold, *n.* a movable sheepfold.

Flither, *v.* to flutter.—*n.* a stir, bustle, fluster. Cf. Flitter.

Fliting, *n.* a scolding; the act of scolding.

Fliting-bridle, *n.* the 'branks,' a bridle put on scolding women as a punishment.

Fliting-free, *adj.* at liberty to scold without retort or being scolded.

Fliting-hot, *adj.* hot with scolding.

Fliting-match, *n.* a scolding match.

Flitten, *ppl.* removed. Cf. Flit.

Flitter, *v.* to flutter, bustle, shake.—*n.* a flutter, stir, fluster.

Flittering, *n.* a shaking.

Flitters, *n.* splinters, 'flinders'; rags, tatters.

Flitting, *n.* a removal to another house; the furniture removed thither; the decay of seed that does not come to maturity.

Flitting-chack, -shack, *n.* a vibrating sound. Cf. Chack.

Flitting-day, *n.* the removal term-day.

Flitting-feast, *n.* an entertainment when the mother, after child-bearing, came to the fire, and resumed her household duties.

Flix, *n.* a flux.

Floam, *n.* phlegm. Cf. Flume.

Floame, Floamie, *n.* a large or broad piece of anything.

Floan, *v.* used of women: to show attachment or court regard indiscreetly; to go about idly; to hang over the fire.—*n.* a lazy, untidy person, specially a woman.

Float, *n.* the act of floating; the scum of a boiling broth-pot; a fleet; a timber-raft for conveyance down a river.—*v.* to pilot a timber-raft down a river.

Float, *n.* the strip of a ploughed field between two open furrows, three poles or so in breadth.

Floater, *n.* one who pilots or 'floats' a timber-raft.

Floathing, *n.* a thin layer or stratum.

Floating, *ppl. adj.* vacillating, undecided.

Float o' feet, *n.* the fat of boiled legs of oxen.

Float-whey, *n.* the curdled scum of boiled whey.

Flobby, *adj.* used of clouds: large and heavy, indicating rain.

Flocht, *v.* to flutter; to flirt.—*n.* a bustling or gaudy person; a flirt; a sudden gust of passion; a sudden change of opinion. Cf. Flaught, Flucht.

Flochter, *v.* to flutter; to flicker; to give free vent to joy.—*n.* a flutter. Cf. Flaughter.

Flochterin, *n.* a fluttering; palpitation.

Flochtersome, *adj.* easily elated or fluttered under impulse of joy.

Flochtrous, *adj.* flurried; terrified.

Flochtry, *adj.* flurried, confused; terrified; alarming.

Flochty, *adj.* unsteady, whimsical, volatile.

Flockmele, *adv.* in flocks.

Flock-raik, *n.* a range of pasture for a flock of sheep.

Flodden, *ppl.* flooded.

Flodge, *n.* a big, fat, awkward person.—*v.* to hobble, walk clumsily.

Floe, *n.* a bog, morass. Cf. Flow.

Flog, *n.* a flogging.

Floggan, *ppl.* walking fast.

Floichen, *n.* a large flake of snow or soot. Cf. Flechan.

Floisterin', *n.* hurry, bustle, confusion.

Floit, *n.* a petted person.

Flonkie, *n.* a flunkey.

Flood, *n.* the sea.

Floody, *adj.* flooding, flooded.

Flooency, *n.* influenza.

Flooer, *v.* to flower.—*n.* a flower. Cf. Flower.

Flook, *n.* diarrhœa.

Flook, *n.* a flounder. Cf. Fluke.

Flook, *n.* a parasite in the liver of a sheep. Cf. Fluke.

Flook-mou'd, *adj.* having a crooked mouth.

Floonge, *v.* to fawn as a dog ; to flatter.

Floop, *adj.* awkward. Cf. Flup, Fleep.

Floor, *n.* a portable threshing-floor ; the sea-bottom ; a house.—*v.* to bring forward an argument ; to table a motion.

Floor-bands, *n.* the bands which secure the bottom boards of a boat to the keel.

Floor-head, *n.* the surface of a floor.

Floor-stane, *n.* the hearth-stone.

Flor, Flore, *v.* to strut about as if vain of one's clothes ; to cut a dash ; to live extravagantly ; to flourish about.

Florence, *n.* Florence wine.

Florentine, *n.* a kind of pie.

Florie, *adj.* vain, volatile ; conceited ; dashing, flashy.—*v.* to cut a dash.

Florier, *n.* a dashing, extravagant person.

Floring, *ppl. adj.* lavish of time, money, dress, foppery.

Flory, Florrie, *v.* to cut a dash, flourish about. —*n.* a dressy, showy person ; a vain, empty fellow.

Flory-heckles, *n.* an empty-headed fop.

Flosh, *n.* a swamp ; a body of standing water overgrown with reeds, weeds, &c.

Floshan, *n.* a shallow puddle of water.

Flosk, *n.* the cuttle-fish, sea-sleeve, or anker-fish.

Floss, *n.* the common rush ; the leaves of the red canary grass ; material made from the common rush by shaking out the pith.

Flossie-cap, *n.* a cap made of rushes.

Flossy, *adj.* reedy ; covered with reeds or rushes.

Flot, *n.* part of land ploughed at one turn, usually four rigs. Cf. Float.

Flot, *n.* the scum of broth when boiling. Cf. Float.

Flotch, *n.* a big, fat, dirty, tawdry woman. —*v.* to move with ungraceful action and awkward dress. Cf. Flodge.

Flotch, *v.* to weep, sob.

Flotter, *v.* to float ; to wet, to splash.

Flottins, *n.* the curdled scum of whey when boiled.

Flot-whey, *n.* 'flottins.' Cf. Float-whey.

Flought, *v.* to flutter. Cf. Flocht, Flaught.

Floughter, *v.* to flutter. Cf. Flaughter, Flochter.

Floughterty, *adj.* flighty.

Floughtrous, *adj.* alarmed. Cf. Flochtrous.

Flounge, *n.* the act of plunging or floundering in water ; the act of flouncing.

Flour-bread, *n.* wheaten bread.

Flour'd, *adj.* used of sheep : scabby and losing their wool.

Flourish, Flourice, *n.* a steel for striking fire from flint to kindle match-paper. Cf. Fleerish.

Flourish, *n.* blossom.—*v.* to cut a dash, make a fine display.

Flourished, *ppl. adj.* covered with blossom.

Flouse, *v.* to turn or blunt the edge of a tool or the point of a nail. Cf. Flaze.

Flouster, *v.* to fluster.—*n.* a fluster.

Floustering, *n.* flurry.

Flow, *n.* a bog, morass ; quicksand ; the sea, a sea-basin.

Flow, *n.* a chimney-cowl, open at one side and turning with the wind, to prevent smoke.

Flow, Flowe, *n.* a jot, a particle ; a small quantity of meal, &c.

Flow, *v.* to exaggerate a story.—*n.* an exaggerated story.

Flowan, *n.* a small portion of meal, flour, flax, &c.

Flow-dyke, *n.* a drain along the banks of a river ; a wall or bank to prevent a river from overflowing.

Flower, *n.* a nosegay ; an edge-tool used in cleaning laths.—*v.* to embroider floral and other designs on muslin, &c.

Flower-basket, *n.* an arrangement for growing flowers in beds on a lawn.

Flowered, *adj.* used of sheep : scabby and losing their wool.

Flowerer, *n.* one who 'flowers' muslin, &c.

Flowerie, *n.* the ace of spades.

Flowering, *n.* floral embroidery ; the act of flowering muslin.

Flowff, *v.* to flutter. Cf. Flaff.

Flowin'-ee, *n.* a hole in a drinking-vessel, beyond which it could not be filled.

Flow-moss, *n.* a very wet, spongy moss.

Flown, *ppl.* muddled, overcome with drink.

Flownie, *n.* a small portion of any light or dusty substance, as of meal, thrown on a draught of water.—*adj.* downy; trifling, without substance; frivolous.

Flowther, *v.* to confuse; to flood.—*n.* a hurry. Cf. Fluther.

Flowy, *adj.* used of peat: light, spongy.

Flozen, *v.* to cause to swell; to become swollen.

Flozent-up, *ppl. adj.* fat and flabby.

Fluchan, *n.* a flake; a sprinkling. Cf. Flechan.

Flucht, *v.* to agitate, flutter, frighten: to make a great show; to flirt.—*n.* a bustling, bouncing, flashy person. Cf. Flocht.

Fluchter, *v.* to make a great fuss or talking; to 'flucht.' Cf. Flaughter.

Fludder, *v.* to confuse, agitate; to flood. Cf. Fluther.

Fludder, *v.* to fawn, cajole, pretend regard.

Flude, *n.* flood.—*v.* to flood.

Fluet, *n.* a slap, a blow. Cf. Flewat.

Fluff, *n.* a flap of the wings; a slight puff or gust; a slight explosion.—*v.* to puff, blow out; to flap.—*adv.* with a puff.

Fluff, *n.* a sea anemone.

Fluff, *v.* to disappoint.

Fluffer, *v.* to disconcert; to agitate; to flutter; to palpitate; to move excitedly.—*n.* palpitation; mental agitation; a quick vibration and its sound; in *pl.* loose leaves, fragments.

Fluff-gib, *n.* an explosion of gunpowder.

Flught, *v.* to agitate. Cf. Flucht.

Flughter, *v.* to fuss in talking.

Fluir, *n.* the floor.

Fluish, *n.* a flood. Cf. Flush.

Fluk, *n.* a flux.

Fluke, *n.* a parasitic insect in the liver of sheep. Cf. Flook.

Fluke, *n.* diarrhœa. Cf. Flook.

Fluke, *n.* a flounder. Cf. Fleuk, Flook.

Fluke, *n.* a duck's bill.

Fluke-mow'd, *adj.* having a crooked mouth like a flounder's.

Flum, *n.* flattery.

Flume, *n.* phlegm.

Flumgummery, *n.* fussy ceremony; senseless display in trifles.

Flummery, *n.* needless show; useless ornaments; flattery.

Flunge, *v.* to skip; to caper.

Flunkey-chap, *n.* a waiter, servant.

Flunkey-craft, *n.* the trade of a man-servant.

Flunkey-lord, *n.* a lord in waiting.

Flup, *n.* an awkward and foolish person.—*adj.* awkward. Cf. Floop.

Flup, *n.* sleet.

Flure, *n.* the floor.

Fluris fever, *n.* scarlet fever.

Flurish, *n.* blossom. Cf. Flourish.

Flurr, *v.* used of spray: to be scattered.

Flurrikin, *ppl. adj.* speaking in a flurry.

Flurrish, *v.* to blossom.—*n.* a blossom.

Flush, *v.* used of water: to run fast and full; to bud, blossom.—*n.* a sudden rise in a stream; a run of water; a farm watering-place; a marshy place, a surface-drained place after peats have been cut; snow thawing, 'slush'; a superabundance, a surfeit; a rich and rapid growth of grass; blossoms, &c.; a large flow of milk from cows.

Fluster, *v.* to be in a bustle.

Flutch, *n.* an inactive person.

Flutchy, *adj.* inactive.

Fluther, *v.* to pretend great regard. Cf. Fludder.

Fluther, *v.* to flutter; to confuse, agitate; to overflow.—*n.* a hurry, bustle; an abundance creating confusion; a rising of a river: used of snow: a thick driving.

Fluthers, *n.* loose flakes of a stone; laminæ of a stone.

Fluthery, *adj.* flabby, soft; boggy, marshy.

Flutteration, *n.* frivolity, unsettlement.

Flutter-baw, *n.* a puff-ball.

Fluze, *v.* to turn the edge or point of an instrument. Cf. Flouse.

Fly, *v.* to frighten. Cf. Fley.

Fly, *adj.* sly; smart.

Fly, *v.* with *out* or *up*, to take offence quickly. Cf. Flee.

Flyam, *n.* a large seaweed tangle, growing round the shore.

Flyave, *n.* a flake; a thin stratum of rock.—*v.* to take or come off in flakes.

Fly-cap, *n.* an elderly lady's head-dress, formed like two crescents conjoined and wired so as to stand out from the cushion on which the hair was dressed. Cf. Flee-cap.

Fly-cup, *n.* a secret or surreptitious cup of tea, one taken on the sly.

Flye, *v.* to frighten.

Flyer, *v.* to jeer. Cf. Fleer.

Flyfe, *n.* a fit, a turn.

Flyker, *v.* to flutter; to flirt. Cf. Flicher.

Flyndrig, *n.* an impudent woman; a deceiver. —*v.* to deceive, beguile.

Flype, *v.* to ruffle the skin; to turn inside out.—*n.* a piece of skin; a shred; a fold, lap, flap. Cf. Flipe.

Flype, *n.* a lout, stupid fellow.

Flypeshard, *v.* to castrate.

Flypin', *ppl.* looking abashed, shamefaced.

Flyrd, *v.* to flaunt, flutter. Cf. Flird.

Flyre, *v.* to gibe; to ogle; to look surly; to go about complaining; to whine, whimper. Cf. Fleer.

Flyre-up, *v.* to flare up; to break into passion. —*n.* a great display.

Flyte, *v.* to scold.—*n.* a scold. Cf. Flite.

Flyte-poke, *n.* a double chin.

Foal, *n.* a cake or bannock ; any soft, thick bread.

Foal, *v.* used jocularly of a horse : to throw its rider.

Foal's-fit, *n.* the mucus hanging from a child's nose.

Foam, *n.* a state of great heat and perspiration ; a great rage.—*v.* to stream out, bubble up ; to be very heated ; to rage. Cf. Faem.

Foaming-drunk, *adj.* excessively or raging drunk.

Foarrie, *adj.* used of a cow : not in calf, but giving no milk.

Fob, *v.* to breathe hard, pant ; to sigh ; to catch the breath.

Fochel, *n.* a girl from sixteen to twenty. Cf. Foichal.

Fochen, Fochten, *ppl.* fought ; exhausted, distressed. Cf. Fecht.

Focht, *v. pret.* and *ppl.* fought.

Fochtin-milk, *n.* buttermilk.

Fock, *n.* people. Cf. Fowk.

Fodder-door, *n.* a barn- or straw-house door.

Foddering, *n.* fodder ; provisions.

Fode, *v. pret.* fed.

Fodge, *n.* a fat, squat person ; one with chubby cheeks. Cf. Fodge.

Fodgel, *adj.* fat ; squat, plump.—*n.* a fat, good-humoured person ; a fat, thriving person or animal.—*v.* to prosper, thrive ; to waddle, as a fat, clumsy person.

Fodgie, *adj.* fat and squat.

Fodmell, *n.* a weight of lead, 70 lb.

Fodyell, *adj.* fat, squat. Cf. Fodgel.

Fodyellin, *adj.* waddling.

Fog, *n.* moss.—*v.* to become moss-covered ; to acquire wealth ; to furnish, supply.

Fog, *v.* to eat heartily.

Fog-clad, *adj.* moss-covered.

Fogel, *adj.* fat, squat. Cf. Fodgel.

Fogget, *ppl.* moss-covered ; furnished, supplied.

Foggie, Fogie, *n.* an invalid or garrison soldier ; an old fellow.

Foggie, Foggie-bee, *n.* a small, yellow humble-bee.

Foggie-bummer, -toddler, *n.* a 'foggie-bee.'

Fogging-ewes, *n.* old ewes past bearing.

Foggy, *adj.* mossy, spongy ; sapless.

Foggy, *adj.* dull ; lumpish ; mentally in a fog.

Foggy-peat, *n.* a fibrous, soft surface-peat.

Foggy-rose, *n.* a moss-rose.

Fog-house, *n.* a summer-house lined with moss.

Fog-moss, *n.* tall grass used as fodder.

Fog-theekit, *adj.* moss-covered.

Fog-turf, *n.* mossy turf.

Foichal, *n.* a cant term for a girl from sixteen to twenty years of age ; a little, thickset child ; a small, weak person trying to grapple with his work, but unable to do it.—*v.* to do anything with difficulty or unskilfully through weakness.

Foichel, *n.* a young foal. Cf. Fychell.

Foichlin', *n.* unskilful working through weakness.

Foigil, *n.* a bundle of yarn, straw, &c.; a tangle, confused mass.

Foigilled, *adj.* tangled, in a lump, ravelled.

†**Foilzie**, *n.* foil, gold-leaf. Cf. Foolzie.

†**Foison**, *n.* pith, ability ; nourishing power, nourishment, nutritive substance ; inherent vigour, power ; power of feeling. Cf. Fizzen, Fushion.

Foisonach, *n.* waste straw, dried grass, and like refuse.

Foisonless, *adj.* dry, innutritious ; insipid ; without 'body' or substance ; withered, not succulent ; without strength or 'backbone' ; weak, useless. Cf. Fushionless, Fizzenless.

Foisonlessness, *n.* the condition of being 'fushionless.'

Foistering, Foishtering, Foistring, *n.* hurry, disorder ; slovenly, scamped work.

Foistest, *adj.* next of age.

Foiter, *v.* to puzzle.—*n.* a puzzle ; a difficulty ; a muddle.

Fold, *v.* to bend double. Cf. Fauld.

Foldings, *n.* wrappers, used in that part of the dress which involves the posteriors.

Fole, *n.* a thick bannock. Cf. Foal.

Folk, *n.* men-servants, work-people. Cf. Fowk.

Folla, *v.* a fellow. Cf. Follow.

Follieshat, *n.* the jelly-fish.

Follifil, *adj.* very foolish. Cf. Folly-foo.

Follo, *v.* to follow. Cf. Follow.

Follow, *n.* a fellow.

Follow, Folloo, *v.* to court.

Follow-Dick, *n.* a servile follower.

Follower, *n.* a young animal following its mother.

Following, *n.* a doctor's regular patients.

Folly, *n.* a useless, or foolish, or too costly building.

Folly-foo, *adj.* very foolish.

Folm, *n.* used of the weather : a long spell ; of mist, &c. : a volume of rolling cloud.

Folm, *v.* to turn upside-down, overturn.—*n.* anything that upsets the stomach.

Folp, *n.* a whelp ; a term of contempt.—*v.* to whelp ; to give birth to.

Fond, *adj.* glad, happy ; anxious, eager.

Fondament, *n.* a foundation ; fundamental fact or truth.

Fond-like, *adj.* doting.—*adv.* affectionately.

Fondness, *n.* gladness.

Fone, *n.* foes.

Fonned, *adj.* prepared.

Foo, *adv.* why.

Foo, *adv.* how.

Foo, *adj.* full; tipsy. Cf. Fou.

Fooanever, *adv.* however. Cf. Howanever.

Foochtir, *n.* confusion; a fussy, muddling style of working; an unmethodical worker. —*v.* to work awkwardly, fussily, or unmethodically.

Foodge, *v.* in marble-playing: to take unfair advantage by thrusting the hand forward. Cf. Fouge.

Foodjie, *n.* a fugitive; a coward. Cf. Fugie.

Fooever, *conj.* and *adv.* however.

Foof, *n.* a stench.

Foof, *int.* an excl. of impatience, disgust, &c.

Foogee, Foojie, *n.* a coward. Cf. Fugie.

Fool, *adj.* foolish, silly.—*v.* to play truant.

Fool, *adj.* foul.

Fool, *n.* a fowl.

Foolage, *adj.* foolish.

Fool-body, *n.* an idiot; a 'natural'; a foolish person.

Fool-folk, *n.* fools, foolish persons.

†Foolie, *n.* a leaf.

Foolie, *n.* in *phr.* 'foolie, foolie,' a children's game.

Foolies, *n.* a mountebank's tricks.

Fool-like, *adj.* foolish.

Fool's-parsley, *n.* the lesser hemlock.

Fool's-stones, *n.* the male and female orchis, *Orchis morio.*

Fool-thing, *n.* a silly, foolish girl or woman.

Fool-tongit, *adj.* foolish-speaking.

†Foolyie, *n.* gold-leaf, foil. Cf. Foilzie, Fulye.

Foomart, Foomert, *n.* the polecat. Cf. Foumart.

Foon, *ppl.* found.

Foon, Foond, *v.* to found.—*n.* a foundation.

Foondit, *n.* with a negative, nothing at all. Cf. Foundit.

Fooner, *v.* to founder.

Foongan, Foonyiean, *n.* the fawning of a dog; flattery.

Foonge, Foonyie, *v.* to fawn as a dog; to flatter.

Foor, *v. pret.* fared, travelled.

Foord, *v.* to ford.

Foor-days, *adv.* late in the afternoon. Cf. Fure-days.

Foorich, Foorigh, Fooroch, *n.* bustle; a state of agitation; a rage, a person of bustling manners; ability, energy. —*v.* to hurry, bustle; to work in a flurried manner.

Foorichan, *n.* a state of bustle or confusion.

Fooriochie, Foorioghie, *adj.* hasty, passionate.

Foorochie, *adj.* bustling.

Foorsday, *n.* Thursday.

Foose, *n.* the house-leek.

Foosht, Foost, *n.* anything useless or needless, lying by or stored up; a dirty fellow, one who breaks wind.—*v.* to be mouldy, to decay; to smell foul; to break wind behind; to store up, hoard.

Fooshtie, *adj.* mouldy, musty; of corn: damp, mouldy.

Fooshtit, *ppl. adj.* fusty, musty.

Foost, Foostin, *n.* a sickness, nausea.

Foosty, *adj.* mouldy; fusty. Cf. Fooshtie.

Foosum, *adj.* dirty.

Foosumness, *n.* dirtiness.

Foot, *v.* to travel or go on foot; to dance; to knit a new foot to an old stocking; used of a horse: to kick; to set peats on end to dry on the moss.—*n.* speed, rate of going; the lower part of a street, town, &c.; in *pl.* the acceleration of a curling-stone by sweeping in front of it; progress; ability to walk or run. Cf. Fit.

Foot-ale, *n.* a feast given to her 'gossips' by a woman recovered from child-bearing; drink given by the seller to the buyer at a cattle-fair.

Foot-an'-a-half, *phr.* a boys' game like leap-frog.

Footch, *int.* hush!

†Footer, Footre, *n.* a term of greatest contempt.—*v.* to ridicule; to disapprove; to hinder.

†Footer, *v.* to bungle; to work hastily, unskilfully, and in a manner that calls for contempt; to fuss about, fiddle with.—*n.* bungle; confusion; a bungler, a silly, useless person.

Footer, *n.* activity, successful exertion. Cf. Foutre.

Footer-footer, *v.* to strut like a peacock; to walk affectedly.

Footerin, *n.* awkward, hasty working.—*ppl. adj.* clumsy, unskilful.

Footh, *n.* abundance. Cf. Fouth.

Footilie, *adv.* meanly; obscenely.

Footiness, *n.* meanness; obscenity.

Footing, *n.* entrance money, or something paid by way of it as a fine; putting new feet to old stockings; in *pl.* small heaps of peat set on end to dry.

Footing-ale, *n.* an entertainment given by parents when a child begins to walk.

Footith, *n.* a bustle; a riot; an awkward predicament. Cf. Futith.

Footlad, *n.* a foot-boy.

Footman, *n.* a pedestrian; a foot-passenger; a metal stand for holding a kettle before the fire.

Foot-pad, *n.* a footpath.

Foot-peat, *n.* a peat cut vertically by the cutter pressing the spade down with his foot.

Foot-soam, *n.* an iron chain eight or ten feet long, extending from the muzzle of the plough and fixed to the yoke of the oxen next the plough.

Footy, *adj.* base, mean; paltry; obscene, indecorous.

Fooze, *n.* the common house-leek. Cf. Foose.

Foozle, *v.* to fuss; to palaver.

Fopperies, *n.* delusions, false miracles, &c.

For, *prep.* with *vb.* 'to be,' to desire, incline to, purpose; with *vb.* 'to go' understood, expresses motion to a place; with *vbs.* of asking and fearing, as to, regarding; in the direction of; for want of; on account of; as to, so far as regards; by; of.—*conj.* because; lest; until.—*n.* a 'wherefore.'

For a, *phr.* what a !; as a.

For-a-be, *conj.* notwithstanding.

Forage, *v.* to procure, get hold.

Foraivert, *adj.* much fatigued.

Foraneen, *n.* the time between breakfast and midday, forenoon.

Foranent, *prep.* over against. Cf. Forenent.

For-as-meikle-as, *conj.* forasmuch as.

Forat, *v.* to forward.

For a that, *conj.* notwithstanding.

Forbear, Forbeir, Forbeer, *n.* a forefather, ancestor. Cf. Forebear.

Forbearer, *n.* an ancestor; progenitor.

Forbes' hour, *phr.* eleven o'clock, p.m., when public-houses, &c., must close under the Forbes Mackenzie Act.

Forbodin, *ppl. adj.* unlawful; unhappy.

Forby, Forbye, Forbyse, *prep.* besides, in addition to; with the exception of.—*adv.* besides, in addition, over and above; on one side, out of the way; near by.—*adj.* uncommon, superior.—*n.* an addition, appendix.

Forcasten, *ppl. adj.* cast off; neglected.

Force, *n.* a great number; the greater part; consequence, importance.

Forced-fire, *n.* fire from the friction of two pieces of dry wood together.

Forcely, *adv.* forcibly.

Forcing, *ppl. adj.* used of the weather: likely to bring crops to maturity.

Forcy, *adj.* used of the weather: 'forcing'; forward with work; pushing on work.

Fordal, *n.* progress, advancement; in *pl.* stock not exhausted.—*adj.* in advance, ready for future use.—*v.* to store up for future use.

Fordal-rent, *n.* rent paid in advance on entry.

Forddeddus, *n.* the violence of a blow.

Fordel, *n.* progress.—*v.* to store up for future use.

Forder, *v.* to further, promote; to succeed, advance.—*adj.* further; progressive.—*adv.* moreover, further.

Forderance, *n.* advancement.

Forder-'im-hither, *n.* a piece of showy dress worn by a woman to draw young men to court her.

Fordersome, *adj.* expeditious.

Fordling, *n.* stock or provision for the future. Cf. Fordal.

For-done, *ppl. adj.* quite worn out.

For-drunken, *ppl. adj.* quite worn out with drinking; quite drunk.

Fordwart, *adv.* forward.—*v.* to forward.

For-dweblit, *ppl.* quite feeble. Cf. Dwable.

Fore, *adv.* before.—*prep.* before.—*n.* priority; the front; help; advantage; anything cast ashore; a finish.—*phr.* 'to the fore,' remaining.

Fore-and-after, *n.* a hat turned up in front and behind.

Fore and back, *phr.* in front and behind.

Fore-bait, *n.* crushed limpets scattered near the hooks as bait.

Fore-bargain, *v.* to bargain beforehand.

Forebear, *n.* an ancestor. Cf. Forbear.

Forebreast, *n.* the front of a cart; the front seat in a church-gallery.

Fore-breathing, *n.* premonitory symptoms.

Fore-breed, -breadth, *n.* the front breadth of a dress, petticoat, &c.

Fore-brees, -broos, *n.* the forehead.

Forebroads, *n.* the milk which is first drawn from a cow.

Foreby, *prep.* besides.—*adv.* besides. Cf. Forby.

Fore-byar, *n.* a forestaller.

Fore-cappy, *n.* the stone used to sink nets at the bow of a boat.

Fore-cast, *n.* forethought; an omen, forewarning; a premonition of death, &c.

Fore-crag, -craig, *n.* the front of the throat.

Fore-day, *n.* the day between breakfast and noon.

Fore-days, *adv.* towards noon; towards evening.

Fore-day's-dinner-time, *n.* a late hour for dinner.

Fore-done, *ppl. adj.* exhausted. Cf. For-done.

Fore-door, *n.* the front-door; the front of a common cart.

Fore-é-fire, *n.* the kitchen and living-room of an old Caithness house; the part of the kitchen where the family sat.

Fore-end, *n.* the anterior part; the beginning; a first instalment.

Forefalted, *ppl.* subjected to forfeiture. Cf. Forfaulted.

Fore-fowk, *n.* ancestors.

Fore-front, *n.* the forehead.

Foregain, Foregainst, *prep.* opposite to.

Fore-gang, *n.* a 'wraith,' apparition of a person about to die, a light foreboding death or disaster.

Fore-go, *n.* a foreboding, an omen.

Fore-hammer, *n.* a sledge-hammer.

Forehand, *n.* the start as to time or advantage ; the fore-quarters of a horse, cow, &c. ; the first player in a curling-rink.—*adj.* first in order.—*adv.* beforehand.

Forehandit, *adj.* rash ; foreseeing, far-seeing.

Forehand-payment, *n.* payment in advance.

Forehand-rent, *n.* a year's rent paid on entry, or six months after entry.

Forehand-stone, *n.* the stone first played in a curling-rink.

Forehead, *n.* the bow of a boat ; effrontery, boldness.

Forehorn, *n.* a projection at the bow of a boat.

Foreign, *adv.* abroad.

Foreigneering, *adj.* foreign, not local.

Forelan, *n.* boxes in a fish-curing yard, in which herrings, &c., are placed, preparatory to being cured.

Foreland, *n.* a house facing the street.

Forelang, *adv.* erelong.

Foreleet, *v.* to outstrip, surpass.

Foreleit, *v.* to forsake, abandon ; to forget. Cf. Forleet.

Fore-loofe, *n.* a furlough.

Foremaist, *adj.* most excellent, 'first class' ; foremost.

Fore-mak, *n.* bustling preparation for an event.

Foreman, *n.* the ninth person in a deep-sea fishing-boat, who cleans the boat, and does odd jobs in it.

Foremither, *n.* an ancestress.

Forenail, *v.* to spend on credit before the money is gained ; to anticipate one's wages extravagantly.

Forename, *n.* the Christian name.

Foreneen, *n.* the time between breakfast and midday ; the forenoon.

Forenent, *prep.* opposite, facing, over against, in opposition to ; in exchange for ; towards.

Forenicht, *n.* the early part of the night ; the interval between twilight and bedtime.

Forenichter, *n.* one who spends the evening in a neighbour's house.

Fore-nickit, *ppl. adj.* prevented by a trick.

Forenoon, Forenoon bread, *n.* a luncheon or spirits taken between breakfast and dinner.

Forentres, *n.* a porch ; a front entrance to a house.

Fore-paid, *adj.* paid in advance.

Fore-pairt, *n.* the front of a person.

Fore-pocket, *n.* a front pocket.

Fore-rent, *n.* 'forehand-rent.'

Fore-rider, *n.* a leader, forerunner.

Fore-room, *n.* the compartment of a fishing-boat next the bow.

Fore-run, *v.* to outrun, outstrip.

Fores, *n.* perquisites given by bargain to a servant in addition to his wages.

Fore-seat, *n.* a front seat.

Foreseen, *ppl. adj.* provided, supplied ; acquainted, thoroughly understood or instructed.

Fore-sey, *n.* that side of the backbone of beeves which is not the sirloin ; the short ribs. Cf. Sey.

Foreshot, *n.* the whisky that first comes off in distillation ; in *pl.* the milk first drawn from a cow.

Foreshot, *n.* the projection of the front of a house over part of the street on which it is built.

Foresichted, Foresichtie, *adj.* foreseeing, provident.

Foreside, *n.* the front.

Foresinger, *n.* a precentor.

Foreskip, *n.* precedence of another in a journey ; advantage given in a contest, &c.

Fore-spaul, *n.* a foreleg.

Forespeak, *v.* to injure by immoderate praise, according to popular superstition ; to bewitch ; to consecrate by charms ; to speak of evil beings so as to make them appear.

Forespeaker, *n.* an advocate ; one who bewitches another, or injures him by immoderate praise.

Forespeaking, *n.* immoderate praise supposed to injure the person spoken of.

Forespoken, *ppl. adj.* bewitched.

Forespyke, *v.* to 'forespeak.'

Foret, *adv.* forward. Cf. Forrat.

Fore-thinking, *ppl.* prudent.

Forethouchtie, *adj.* provident.

Fore-tram, *n.* the front part of the shaft of a cart.

Forfairn, *ppl. adj.* worn out ; forlorn ; abused.

Forfaughlit, *ppl. adj.* worn out ; jaded.

Forfaughten, *ppl. adj.* worn out.

Forfaulted, *ppl.* subjected to forfeiture, attainted.

Forfaulture, *n.* forfeiture.

Forfecht, *v.* to overtask one's self, to be over come with fatigue.

Forfeit, *n.* an offence.—*v.* to subject to forfeiture.

Forfeitry, *n.* forfeiture.

Forfend, *v.* to prevent, forbid ; to defend.

Forfeuchen, *ppl. adj.* exhausted.

Forfight, *v.* to be overcome with fatigue ; to wear one's self out. Cf. Forfecht.

Forfleeit, *ppl. adj.* terrified, stupefied with terror. Cf. Fley.

Forflitten, *ppl.* severely scolded.—*n.* a severe scolding. Cf. Flite.

Forfluther, Forflutter, *v.* to discompose, disorder.—*n.* confusion, discomposure. Cf. Fluther.

Forfochen, Forfocht, Forfochten, Forfoochen, *ppl. adj.* worn out. Cf. Forfecht.

Forforn, *ppl. adj.* worn out ; forlorn. Cf. Forfairn.

Forfouchen, Forfouchten, Forfought, Forfoughten, Forfowden, Forfuchan, *ppl. adj.* exhausted, worn out ; out of breath. Cf. Forfochen.

Forgadder, Forgader, *v.* to meet together. Cf. Forgather.

Forgain, Forgainst, *prep.* against, opposite to.

Forgather, Forgaither, *v.* to assemble, to meet for a special purpose ; to encounter, meet with, meet by chance ; to consort with ; to come together in marriage ; with *up*, to become attached to.

Forgathering, *n.* an assembly ; a social gathering ; an accidental meeting.

Forge, *v.* used of children : to copy another's work and pass it off as one's own.

Forgedder, Forgethar, *v.* to meet together. Cf. Forgather.

Forgeit, *v. pret.* let fly.

Forger, *n.* a child who habitually copies another's work.

Forget, *n.* a neglect ; an omission ; an oversight.

Forgettil, Forgettle, *adj.* forgetful.

Forgettilness, *n.* forgetfulness.

Forgie, *v.* to forgive.

Forgrutten, *ppl. adj.* tear-stained.

Forhow, Forhoo, Forhooie, Forhui, *v.* to forsake, abandon.

Forit, *phr.* if it be not so.

Forjaskit, Forjeskit, *ppl. adj.* jaded, fatigued.

Forjidged, *ppl. adj.* jaded with fatigue.

Fork, *n.* diligent search.—*v.* to 'pitch-fork' into ; to pitch hay or corn ; to search for ; to look after one's own interest.

Forker, *n.* one who 'forks' at a stack.

Forker, *n.* an earwig.

Forking, *n.* the division of a river into one or more streams ; a branch of a river at its parting from the main body ; the parting between the thighs ; looking out or searching for anything.

Forknokit, *ppl. adj.* quite knocked up.

Forky-, Forkit-tail, *n.* an earwig.

Forlaithie, *v.* to loathe ; to disgust.—*n.* disgust ; a surfeit.

Forlane, *adj.* quite alone, forlorn.

Forlat, *v.* to deal a blow.

Forlatten, *ppl.* used of a blow : dealt.

Forlay, *v.* to lie in ambush.

Forle, *v.* to whirl, turn, twist.—*n.* a turning, a twist ; a small wheel ; a whorle ; a stone ring on the end of a spindle, making it revolve.

Forleet, *v. pret.* dealt a blow. Cf. Forlat.

Forleet, Forleit, *v.* to abandon ; to forget.

Forleith, *v.* to loathe. Cf. Forlaithie.

Forlet, Forlete, *v.* to abandon ; to forget. Cf. Forleet.

Forlethie, *v.* to loathe. Cf. Forlaithie.

Forloff, *n.* a furlough.

Forlore, *adj.* forlorn.

Forlorn, *adj.* used of time : miserable, wretched.

Forlut, *v. pret.* dealt a blow.—*ppl. adj.* used of a blow : dealt. Cf. Forlat.

Form, *v.* to point, direct.

Formalist, *n.* an expert in legal forms, writs, styles, &c.

Former, *n.* a kind of chisel. Cf. Furmer.

Fornackit, *n.* a fillip ; a sharp blow.

Fornail, *v.* to spend money before receiving it. Cf. Forenail.

Fornens, Fornenst, *prep.* opposite to. Cf. Forenent.

Forniaw, Fornyauw, *v.* to fatigue, tire.

Fornyawd, *ppl. adj.* fatigued.

Forpit, *n.* the fourth part of a peck.

Forra, *adj.* used of a cow : not giving milk ; not in calf.

Forra, *adv.* a fishing term : forward ; in *phr.* 'in the same forra,' said of two fishing-boats which, when casting lines, lie in the same stretch east and west.

Forragate, *n.* the rowing while fishing-nets are being hauled.

Forrage, *n.* gun or pistol wadding.

Forrage-clout, *n.* wadding for gun or pistol.

Forrat, Forret, Forrit, *adv.* forward.

Forretsome, *adj.* of a forward disposition.

Forridden, *ppl.* worn out with hard riding.

Forrow, *n.* as much as is carted or carried at one time or turn.

Forrow-cow, *n.* a cow not in calf. Cf. Farrow.

Forsay, *v.* to deny, gainsay.

Forscomfisht, *ppl. adj.* overcome by heat ; nearly overcome by bad smells.

Forsee, *v.* to overlook ; to neglect ; to oversee, superintend.

Forsel, *n.* a straw or 'bent' mat to protect the back of a horse carrying a burden.—*v.* to harness.

Forsens, *n.* the refuse of wool.

Forset, *v.* to overpower with work ; to surfeit ; to overload.—*n.* surfeit.

Forsey, *n.* the short ribs of beeves. Cf. Foresey.

Forslitting, *n.* castigation ; a satirical reprimand.

Forsman, *n.* a foreman.

Forspeak, *v.* to bewitch, charm. Cf. Forespeak.

Forst, *adj.* embanked.

Forsta', *v.* to understand.

Forstand, *v.* to withstand ; to understand.

Fortaivert, *ppl.* much fatigued. Cf. Foraivert.

Fortak, Fortack, *v.* to aim or deal a blow.

Forth, *adv.* out of doors, abroad.—*prep.* forth from, outside of.—*n.* the open air.

Forth-coming, *n.* accounting for money, production of accounts.

Forther, *adv.* formerly.

Forthersum, *adj.* rash; of forward manner; of an active disposition. Cf. Fordersome.

Forthert, *adv.* forward.

Forthgeng, *n.* the entertainment given at the departure of a bride from her own or her father's house.

Forthiness, *n.* frankness, affability. Cf. Forthy.

Forthink, *v.* to repent, regret.

Forth-right, *adv.* forthwith.—*adj.* straight-forward.

Forth-setter, *n.* a publisher; an author; a setter forth.

Forthshaw, *v.* to show forth.

Forthy, *adj.* early in production; productive; frank, cheerful.

Fortifee, *v.* to pet, indulge; to encourage, abet.

Fortifier, *n.* an aider and abettor.

Fortravail, *v.* to fatigue greatly.

Fortune-maker, *n.* one prosperous in business.

Forwakit, *ppl. adj.* worn out with watching.

Forwandered, *ppl. adj.* lost, strayed.

Forward, *adv.* of a clock, &c.: in advance of the correct time.—*adj.* eager, energetic, zealous; present, arrived; intoxicated. Cf. Forret.

Forwardness, *n.* eagerness.

Forweery't, *ppl. adj.* worn out with fatigue.

Forworn, *ppl. adj.* exhausted with fatigue.

Foryawd, *ppl. adj.* fatigued. Cf. Fornyawd.

Foryet, *v.* to forget.

Foryettil, *adj.* forgetful.

Foryoudent, *ppl. adj.* overcome with weariness; breathless.

Forzmin, *n.* a foreman. Cf. Forsman.

Fosie, Fosy, *adj.* spongy, soft.

Fossa, *n.* grass growing among stubble.

Fossee, *n.* a fosse.

Fosset, Fossetin, *n.* a rush-mat for keeping a horse's back unchafed.

Foster, *n.* a foster-child; an adopted child; progeny.—*v.* to suckle.

Fostern, *n.* Shrove-Tuesday. Cf. Fastern.

Fotch, *v.* to change horses in a plough; to change situations; to exchange.—*n.* an exchange of one thing for another.

Fotch, *v.* to flinch.

Fotch-plough, *n.* a plough that is worked with two yokings a day; a plough used in killing weeds; a plough in which horses and oxen are yoked together. Cf. Fatch-pleugh.

Fother, *n.* fodder.—*v.* to give fodder.

Fothering, *n.* fodder; provisions.

Fothersome, *adj.* rash. Cf. Forthersome.

Fots, *n.* footless stockings.

Fottie, *n.* one whose stockings, trousers, boots, &c. are too wide; a plump, short-legged person or animal; a female wool-gatherer, who went from place to place for the purpose of gathering wool.

Fottit-thief, *n.* a thief of the lowest description.

Fou, *adv.* how.

Fou, *adv.* why.

Fou, *adj.* full; well-fed, filled to repletion; intoxicated, drunk; well-to-do, rich; puffed up, conceited.—*adv.* very, much; fully.—*n.* a fill; tipple; contents, what fills; a firlot, a bushel of grain.—*v.* to make full, to fill.

Fou, *n.* a pitchfork; a kicking, tossing; a heap of corn in the sheaves, or of bottles of threshed straw.—*v.* to kick, toss; to throw up sheaves with a pitchfork. Cf. Fow.

Fouat, *n.* a cake baked with butter and currants.

Fouat, *n.* the house-leek.

Fouchen, *ppl. adj.* wearied in struggling.

Foucht, Fouchten, *ppl.* fought.—*ppl. adj.* troubled.

Foud, *n.* the thatch and sods of a house when taken from the roof; foggage, long coarse grass not eaten down in summer.

Fouet, *n.* the house-leek.

Fou-ever, *adv.* however.

Fouge, *v.* to 'fudge,' or cheat at marbles by unfairly advancing the hand before playing a marble.—*n.* the act of playing thus.

Fouger, *n.* one who 'fouges' at marbles.

Fou-handit, -han't, *adj.* well-to-do; losing nothing in a bargain.

Fou-hoose, *n.* open house; a hospitable house.

Fouish, *adj.* slightly drunk.

Fouk, *n.* folk. Cf. Fowk.

Foul, *adj.* used of the weather: bad, gloomy.—*adv.* foully.—*n.* a storm, bad weather; devil; evil.—*v.* to soil legally or find guilty.

Foul a-ane, -bit, -drap, *phr.* devil a-one, -bit, -drop.

Foul and fair, *phr.* with *come,* whatever may happen.

Foulbeard, *n.* a blacksmith's mop for his trough.

Foul-befa', -fa', *phr.* devil take! evil befall!

Foul-farren, *adj.* of foul appearance.

Foulmart, *n.* a polecat. Cf. Foumart.

Foul-may-care, *n. phr.* devil may care. Cf. Deil-ma-care.

Foul-tak-ye, *phr.* devil take you! evil take you.

Foul thief, *phr.* the devil.

Foul water, *n.* part of a Halloween rite, the choice of which by a person blindfolded portended marriage to a widow or to a widower.

Foulzie, *v.* to foil, defeat; to defile.—*n.* filth, street-sweepings, dung. Cf. Fulyie.

Foulzie-can, *n.* a pail for holding house refuse, ordure, &c.

Foulzie-man, *n.* a scavenger.

Foumart, *n.* the polecat; an offensive person; a sharp, quick-witted person.

Foumart-faced, *adj.* having a face like a polecat.

Foumartish, *adj.* having a strong or offensive smell.

Fou-moo't, *adj.* having all one's teeth sound.

Found, *n.* the foundation of a building; the area on which the foundation is laid; foundation, truth, substance.—*v.* to warrant; to have good grounds for an action at law.

Founder, *v.* to collapse, break down; used of a horse: to stumble violently; to cause to stumble; to fell; to dismay; to perish or be benumbed with cold; to astonish.

Founding, *n.* laying the foundation-stone.

Founding-pint, *n.* drink, &c., given to workmen at the laying of the foundation of a house.

Foundit, *n.* with a negative: nothing at all, not the least particle.

Foundit-hait, *phr.* absolutely nothing.

Found-stane, *n.* a foundation-stone; origin, beginning.

Foundy, *v.* to founder.

Founer, *v.* to collapse. Cf. Founder.

Four-hours, *n.* a refreshment taken about four o'clock.

Four-hours-at-een, *n.* four o'clock in the afternoon.

Fourioghie, *adj.* hasty, passionate. Cf. Fooriochie.

Four-lozened, *adj.* having four panes of glass in a window-frame.

Four-luggit, *adj.* having four handles.

Four-nookit, *adj.* four-cornered.

Four-part-dish, *n.* an old measure holding the fourth of a peck. Cf. Forpit.

Fours, *n.* all fours.

Foursome, Foursum, *n.* a company of four.—*adj.* performed by four together.

Four-stoopit-bed, *n.* a four-post bed.

Fourthnight, *n.* a fortnight.

Four-ways, *n.* four cross-roads.

Fouscanhaud, *n.* a Celtic keeper of a low public-house.

Fouse, *n.* the house-leek. Cf. Foose.

†Fousion, *n.* pith, substance. Cf. Foison.

Fousome, *adj.* copious; somewhat too large; satiating; luscious. Cf. Full.

Fousome, *adj.* nauseous; disgusting; dirty. Cf. Foul.

Fousomeness, *n.* dirtiness.

Fousticat, *n.* 'what-d'ye-call it?' How is it that you call it?

Fousty, *adj.* fusty; mouldy, musty; used of corn: mouldy or damp, having a musty smell. Cf. Fooshtie.

†Fousun, *n.* pith, substance. Cf. Foison.

Fout, *n.* a spoiled child.

Fout, *n.* a fool, a simpleton.

Fout, *n.* a sudden movement.

Foutch, *v.* to exchange.—*n.* an exchange. Cf. Fotch.

†Fouter, *v.* to bungle.—*n.* a bungle; a bungler. Cf. Footer.

†Fouter, *n.* a term of deepest contempt.—*v.* to ridicule. Cf. Footer.

Fouth, *n.* abundance, fill.

Fouthily, *adv.* prosperously, plentifully.

Fouthless, *adj.* useless.

Fouthlie, *adv.* plentifully.

Fouthy, *adj.* prosperous, well-to-do; hospitable, liberal.

Fouthy-like, *adj.* having the appearance of prosperity or abundance.

Foutie, *adj.* mean; obscene, smutty; paltry. Cf. Footy.

Foutilie, *adv.* meanly, basely; obscenely.

Foutiness, *n.* meanness; obscenity.

Foutrack, *int.* an excl. of surprise.

Foutre, *n.* successful exertion.

Foutsome, *adj.* forward; officious, meddling.

Fouty, *adj.* obscene. Cf. Foutie.

Fow, *v.* to kick, toss; to throw up sheaves with a pitchfork.—*n.* a corn-fork, a pitchfork; a kicking, tossing; a heap of sheaves or of bottles of straw.

Fow, *n.* the house-leek.

Fow, *adj.* full; drunk.—*n.* a firlot; a bushel. Cf. Fou.

Fow, *adj.* foul.

Fower, *adj.* four.

Fowie, *adj.* well-to-do; a term of disrespect; *phr.* 'a fowie body,' an old hunks.

Fowl, *n.* a bird of any kind.

Fowlie, *n.* a chicken.

Fowlie-bree, *n.* chicken broth.

Fowmart, *n.* a polecat.

Fowner, *v.* to founder. Cf Fooner.

Fows, *n.* the house-leek.

Fowsie, *n.* a fosse. Cf. Fossee.

Fowsum, *adj.* somewhat too large; luscious; too sweet. Cf. Fousome.

Fowsum, *adj.* nauseous. Cf. Fousome.

Fowt, *n.* a fool. Cf. Fout.

Fowth, *n.* plenty. Cf. Fouth.

Fowty, *adj.* mean; paltry. Cf. Footy.

Fox, *v.* to dissemble.

Foxter-leaves, *n.* the foxglove.

Foy, *n.* a farewell feast to or by one leaving a place, ending an apprenticeship, or finishing a job.—*v.* to be present at such a feast.

Foy, *adj.* foolish, silly.

†Foyard, *n.* a fugitive.

Foyll, *n.* a defeat, foil.

Foze, *v.* to wheeze; to breathe with difficulty; to emit saliva.—*n.* difficulty in breathing.

Foze, *v.* to lose flavour, become fusty.

Foziness, *n.* sponginess; obtuseness of mind, stupidity.

Fozle, *n.* a weasel.

Fozle, Fozzle, *v.* to wheeze.—*n.* a wheeze.

Fozlin, *n.* great exertion with want of strength. —*ppl. adj.* weak; breathing with difficulty.

Fozy, *adj.* wet, moist with saliva, dribbling.

Fozy, Fozzy, *adj.* light, spongy, soft, porous; fat, bloated; stupid, dull-witted; hazy, foggy; obscured by haze or fog.

Fra, *prep.* from.

Fraat, *adv.* nevertheless; 'for all that.' Cf. Frithat.

†Fracaw, *n.* a hubbub; a brawl.

Fracht, *n.* what can be carried or carted at one time.

Frack, *adj.* ready, eager; bold, forward; stout, firm, hale, vigorous in old age. Cf. Freck.

Frae, *prep.* from.—*adv.* from the time that.

Fraesta, *adv.* pray thee; notwithstanding.

Fragalent, *adj.* advantageous, profitable; undermining.

Fraik, Fraick, *v.* to cajole, wheedle; to coax. —*n.* flattering, coaxing; a flatterer; a wheedling person.

Fraikas, *n.* much ado in a flattering sort of way.

Fraiky, *adj.* coaxing, wheedling.

Frail, *n.* a flail.

Fraim, *adj.* strange, foreign, not of kin; cold, reserved, unfriendly; distant, far off.—*n.* a stranger, one unrelated by blood. Cf. Frem.

Frain, *v.* to ask.—*n.* an inquiry. Cf. Frayn.

Fraise, *n.* a disturbance, fuss; bustle, excitement; flattery, cajolery, vain talk.—*v.* to flatter, wheedle.

Fraise, *n.* a calf's pluck.

Fraiser, *n.* a flatterer, wheedler.

Fraisie, *adj.* given to flattery or vain talk.

Fraisilie, *adv.* in a flattering, 'fraising' way.

Fraisiness, *n.* addiction to flattery, &c.

Fraising, *n.* flattery, cajolery.—*ppl. adj.* flattering.

Fraisle, *v.* to flatter, pay court to.

Fraist, Fraiz'd, *ppl. adj.* greatly astonished; having a wild, staring look.

Frait, *n.* trouble, fret.

Fraith, *v.* to froth, foam.—*n.* froth, foam.

Fraize, *v.* to wheedle, flatter. Cf. Fraise.

Frake, *n.* a freak; a whim. Cf. Freak.

Frake, *v.* to wheedle. Cf. Fraik.

Fraky, *adj.* coaxing, wheedling.

Frame, *v.* to succeed.—*n.* a skeleton.

Framed, Framet, Frammit, *adj.* strange; cold, distant. Cf. Frem.

Frample, Frammle, *v.* to gobble up; to put in disorder.—*n.* a confused mass; disordered clothes or yarn.

Frampler, *n.* a disorderly person.

Frandie, *n.* a hay-cock; a small rick of sheaves.

Frane, *v.* to ask; to insist, urge warmly.— *n.* an inquiry. Cf. Frayn.

Frank, *n.* the heron.

Frank, *adj.* used of a horse: willing, eager, not needing whip or spur.

Frank-tenement, *n.* a freehold.

Frap, *v.* to blight; to destroy.

Frappe, *adj.* insane, sullenly, melancholy.

Fra't, *adv.* notwithstanding, 'for all that.'

Frath, *adj.* reserved in manner.

Fraucht, Fraught, *n.* a freight, load, what carts can bring at a time; two bucketfuls of water; passage money, boat-hire.—*v.* to freight; to load.

Frauchtless, *adj.* insipid; without weight or importance.

Frauchty, *adj.* liberal; hospitable.

Fraud, *v.* to defraud.

Fraudling, *n.* the act of defrauding, committing of fraud.

Frawart, *adj.* froward.

Frawfu', *adj.* bold, impertinent; sulky, scornful.

Fray, *n.* terror, panic.—*v.* to frighten, daunt; to be afraid.

Frayn, *v.* to ask; to insist; to urge strongly. —*n.* inquiry.

Freak, *n.* a strong man; a fellow; a fool; a foolish fancy. Cf. Freik.

Freak, *v.* to fret.

Freak, *v.* to cajole. Cf. Fraik.

Freat, *n.* a superstitious fancy. Cf. Freit.

Freath, *v.* to froth, foam; to make soap-suds; to lather; to wash clothes slightly before smoothing them with the iron.—*n.* soap-suds, froth; a slight washing up of clothes before ironing them.

Freazock, *v.* to coax, wheedle, cajole. Cf. Fraise.

Frecht, *v.* to frighten. Cf. Fricht.

Freck, *adj.* ready; stout, hale. Cf. Frack.

Freck, *v.* to cajole. Cf. Fraik.

Freckle, *adj.* active, hot-spirited.

Frecky, *adj.* coaxing. Cf. Fraiky.

Free, *adj.* frank, outspoken; genial, familiar; liberal, ready, willing, under no restraint of conscience; unmarried; made free of burghal privileges; divested of; friable, easily crumbled; used of cakes: short.

brittle; of corn: so ripe as to be easily shaken.—*n.* soft sandstone, freestone; in *pl.* Free Church members.

Free-coup, *n.* a place for emptying rubbish.

Freedom, *n.* the right of pasturing on a common; permission, leave.

Free-gaun, *adj.* frank, affable.

Freelage, *n.* an heritable property as distinguished from a farm tenanted.—*adj.* heritable.

Freely, *adv.* quite, very; thoroughly.

Freeman, *n.* a neutral party.

Free-martin, *n.* a female twin-calf where the other is a bull, supposed naturally incapable of ever having offspring.

Freen, Freend, *n.* a friend; a relation.

Freesk, *v.* to scratch; to curry; to rub roughly or hastily; to walk or work briskly; with *up*, to beat soundly.—*n.* a hasty rub, work done hastily.

Freet, *n.* butter, cheese, &c. Cf. Fret.

Freet, *n.* a superstitious fancy or saying; an omen, a charm; a superstitious ceremony or rite; a fancy, whim, trick; a trifle.

Freet, *n.* anything fried; oatcake, &c., fried with dripping, butter, &c.

Freethe, *v.* to foam, froth. Cf. Freath.

Free-trade, *n.* smuggling.

Free-trader, *n.* a smuggler.

Freevolous, *adj.* trifling; small, simple.

Free-ward, *n.* freedom.

Free-willers, *n.* Arminians, believers in free-will alone.

Freff, *adj.* shy; intimate.

Freicht, *v.* to frighten. Cf. Fricht.

Freight, *n.* two bucketfuls of water. Cf. Fraucht.

Freik, *n.* a strong man; a fellow; a fool; a foolish fancy. Cf. Freak.

Frein, *v.* to whine. Cf. Frine.

Freisk, *v.* to rub briskly; to scratch; to work hastily. Cf. Freesk.

Freit, *n.* a superstitious fancy or practice; a charm. Cf. Freet.

Freit, *v.* to eat; to eat into. Cf. Fret.

Freith, *n.* liberal wages.

Freith, *v.* to froth, foam. Cf. Freath.

Freitten, *ppl. adj.* pitted, seamed, as with smallpox.

Freity, *adj.* superstitious; credulous as to omens, &c.

Freize, *v.* to freeze.

Frem, Fremd, Freme, Fremit, Fremmit, *adj.* strange, foreign; unrelated by blood; distant, reserved; unfriendly, estranged; far off.— *n.* a stranger; one not a blood relation.

Fremd-folk, *n.* strangers in contrast with relations.

Fremd-sted, *adj.* forsaken by friends and cast upon strangers.

Fren, *adj.* strange, foreign; 'fremd'; acting like a stranger.

Frenauch, *n.* a crowd.

French-butterfly, *n.* the common white butterfly.

French-jackie, *n.* the boys' game of 'gap.'

French-puppy, *n.* the eastern poppy.

French-saugh, *n.* the Persian willow-herb.

French-wallflower, *n.* the purple-coloured wallflower.

Frenchy, *n.* a boys' marble, of greenish-yellow colour.

Frend, *n.* a relation by blood or marriage. Cf. Friend.

Frenn, *v.* to rage, to be in a frenzy.

Frennishin, Frenisin, *n.* rage, frenzy; a half-asleep, dazed, or mentally-confused state.

Frenyie, Frenzie, *n.* a fringe.—*v.* to fringe.

Frenzy, *v.* with *up*, to madden, inflame.

Frequent, *adj.* numerous, great in concourse. —*v.* to acquaint, give information; with *with*, to associate with.

Frequently, *adv.* numerously.

†Frere, *n.* a brother.

Fresch, *int.* an excl. of contempt.

Fresh, *adj.* used of land: free from stock; unsalted; novel, new; sober, not drunk; excited with drink; used of the weather: thawing, wet, cold, open.—*n.* a flood in a river; a thaw.—*v.* to thaw.

Fresh-water-muscle, *n.* the pearl mussel.

Fret, *v.* to eat, devour; to eat into.—*n.* a quarrel, revolt.

Fret, Frett, *n.* a superstitious fancy. Cf. Freet.

Fret, *n.* the product of milk; butter, cheese, &c.

Fretch, *n.* a flaw.

Fret-taker, *n.* a woman supposed to have the power of lessening the 'profit' of her neighbours' cows, and of increasing that of her own.

Fretty, *adj.* fretful, peevish.

Freuch, Freugh, *adj.* used of wood: brittle; of corn: dry.

Frey, *n.* stir, hurry; cause of anxiety, &c.

Frezell, *n.* a steel for striking fire. Cf. Frizzel.

Friars'-chicken, *n.* chicken broth with eggs dropped into it.

Friar-skate, *n.* the sharp-nosed ray.

Fribble, *v.* to curl; to frizzle.—*n.* a trifler, a good-for-nothing fellow.

Fricht, *v.* to frighten, scare away.—*n.* fright.

Frichtedly, *adv.* in a fright.

Frichten, *v.* to frighten.

Frichtfu', *adj.* frightful, terrible; bad, annoying.

Frichtsome, *adj.* frightful; causing fear.

Frichtsomely, *adv.* fearfully.

Fricht-the-craw, *n.* a scarecrow.

Fricksome, *adj.* vain ; vaunting.

Friday's-bairn, *n.* a child born on Friday.

Friday's-bawbee, -penny, *phr.* a weekly half-penny or penny given to a child on Friday as pocket-money.

Frie, *adj.* friable.—*n.* freestone. Cf. Free.

Fried-chicken, *n.* 'friars'-chicken.'

Friend, Frien', *n.* a relation by blood or marriage.—*v.* to befriend.

Friended, *ppl. adj.* having friends or relations.

Friend-stead, *adj.* befriended, having friends.

Friesk, *v.* to rub briskly. Cf. Freesk.

Friet, *v.* to eat into. Cf. Fret.

Frig, *v.* to potter about.

†Frigassee, *n.* a fricassee.

Friggle-fraggles, *n.* trifles ; useless orna-ments of dress.

Frim-fram, *n.* a trifle ; a whim.

Frimple-frample, *adv.* promiscuously ; in a tangled fashion. Cf. Frample.

Frine, *v.* to whine ; to fret peevishly.

Frisk, *n.* a dance ; a caper ; a jig.—*v.* to cause to dance.

Frisksome, *adj.* sportive, frisky.

Frisky, *adj.* staggering from drink.

Frist, *v.* to delay ; to give a debtor time to pay ; to give credit, sell on trust.—*n.* delay, respite ; credit, trust.

Fristing, *n.* delay, suspension.

Frith, *n.* a wood ; a clearing in a wood.

Frithat, Frithit, *adv.* nevertheless, 'for a' that.' Cf. Fraat.

Fritter, *v.* to scatter ; to reduce to fragments. —*n.* a fragment.

Frizz, *n.* a curl.

Frizzel, *n.* the hammer of a gun or pistol ; a piece of steel for striking fire from a flint.

Frizzel-spring, *n.* the spring of a gun or pistol.

Frizzle, *n.* a hissing, sputtering sound, as of frying.

Frizzle, *v.* to flatter, coax ; to make a great fuss.

Froad, *v.* to froth, foam.—*n.* froth, foam.

Froath-stick, *n.* a stick for whipping up cream, &c.

Froch, *adj.* brittle ; dry. Cf. Freuch.

Frock, *n.* a sailor's or fisherman's knitted woollen jersey.

Frock, *n.* the term used in distinguishing the different pairs in a team of oxen, as hind-, mid-, fore-frock. Cf. Throck.

Frock-soam, *n.* a chain fixed to the yoke of the hindmost oxen in a plough, and stretched to that of the pair before them.

Frocky, *adj.* brittle. Cf. Freuch.

Froe, *n.* froth.

Frog, *v.* to snow or sleet at intervals.—*n.* a flying shower of snow or sleet.

Frog, Frogue, *n.* a young horse between one and two years old ; a colt about three years old.

Froichfu', *adj.* perspiring.

Froie, *n.* froth. Cf. Froe.

From, *prep.* in reckoning time by the clock : before a certain hour.

†Frone, *n.* a sling.

Front, *n.* in *phr.* 'in front of,' before in point of time.

Front, *v.* to swell, distend, used of meat in boiling.

Front-briest, *n.* the front-pew in a church gallery.

Fronter, *n.* a ewe four years old.

Frontispiece, *n.* the front, or front view of a house.

Fronty, *adj.* passionate ; high-spirited, free in manner ; healthy-looking.

Frooch, *adj.* brittle ; dry. Cf. Freuch.

Frost, *n.* ice ; a poor hand at ; an ignoramus. —*v.* to become frozen or frost-bitten ; to spoil through frost ; to prepare horses' shoes for frost ; used of the hair : to turn gray or white.

Frost-rind, *n.* hoar-frost.

Frost-, Frosty-win', *n.* a freezing wind.

Frost-, Frosty-wise, *adj.* tending to frost.

Frosty-bearded, *adj.* having a gray or white beard.

Frosty-pow, *n.* a gray head.

Frothe, *v.* to wash slightly.—*n.* a slight washing.

Frothing-stick, *n.* a stick or horse-hair whisk for whipping cream or milk. Cf. Froath-stick.

Frothy, *adj.* good at early rising ; early at work ; energetic. Cf. Forthy.

Frou, *n.* froth. Cf. Froe.

†Frow, *n.* a big, fat woman.

Frowdie, *n.* a big, lusty woman.—*adj.* used of a woman : big, lusty.

Frowdie, *n.* a woman's cap ; a 'sowback mutch,' with a seam at the back, worn by old women.

Frowngy, *adj.* frowning, gloomy, lowering.

Frozening, *n.* a freezing ; the act of being frozen.

Fruesome, *adj.* coarse-looking ; frowsy.

Frugal, *adj.* frank, kindly, affable.

Fruize, *v. pret.* froze.

Frump, *n.* a badly dressed woman.

Frump, *n.* an unseemly fold or gathering in any part of one's clothes.

Frumple, *v.* to wrinkle ; to crease ; to crumple.

Frumpses, *n.* ill-humour, sulks.

Frumpy, *adj.* peevish.

Frunce, *n.* a plait.

Frunsh, *v.* to fret, whine ; to frown, gloom ; to pucker the face.

Frunter, *n.* a ewe in her fourth year. Cf. Fronter.

Frunty, *adj.* free in manner; healthy-looking; keen, eager, forward. Cf. Fronty.

Fruozen, *ppl. adj.* frozen.

Frush, *n.* a collection of fragments.—*adj.* brittle, crumbling; frail, fragile; tender-hearted; frank; forward.

Frushness, *n.* brittleness.

Fry, *n.* a number of children; a clique, set, crew.

Fry, *n.* a disturbance, tumult; stir, bustle.—*v.* to be in a passion; to be pestered or in a state of agitation.

Frythe, *v.* to fry; to feel great indignation.

Frything-pan, *n.* a frying-pan.

Fu, *adv.* how. Cf. Fou.

Fu, *adv.* why. Cf. Foo.

Fu', *adj.* full; tipsy. Cf. Fou.

Fu', *adj.* dirty. Cf. Foul.

Fud, *n.* the buttocks; the female pudendum; the brush of a hare or rabbit; a queue, or the hair tied behind.

Fud, *v.* to whisk, scud, like a rabbit or hare; to frisk; to walk with short, quick steps.—*n.* a quick, nimble walk; a small man who walks with short, quick steps. Cf. Whid.

†**Fudder,** *n.* a gust of wind; a flurry; the shock occasioned by a gust of wind; a sudden noise; a stroke, a blow; a hurry, hasty motion.—*v.* to move hurriedly; to patter with the feet; to run to and fro in an excited and aimless manner.

Fudder, *n.* a large quantity; a cartload; a certain weight of lead; a great number; a confederacy.

Fudder, *conj.* whether.

Fudder-flash, *n.* a flash of lightning.

Fuddie, *n.* the 'fud' of a rabbit or hare; a hare.

Fuddie-hen, *n.* a hen without a tail.

Fuddie-skirt, *n.* a short coat or vest.

Fuddik, *n.* a very short person who walks with a quick, nimble step.

Fuddle, *v.* with *in,* to sow seed in wet weather, or when the soil is in a 'puddle.'

Fuddle, *n.* a drinking-bout; intoxication.

Fuddum, *n.* snow drifting at intervals.

Fuddy, *n.* a name given to the wind personified.

Fuddy, *n.* the bottom of a corn-kiln.

Fudgel, *adj.* plump, fat, and squat. Cf. Fodgel.

Fudgie, *adj.* short and fat.

Fudgie, *n.* a fugitive; a coward. Cf. Fugie.

Fudie-skirt, *n.* a short coat or vest.

Fuding, *ppl. adj.* gamesome; sportive; frisky.

Fudle, *v.* to fuddle.

Fueling, *n.* the cutting of peats for fuel.

Fuff, *v.* to puff, blow; to breathe heavily; used of a cat: to spit, make a hissing sound; to sniff; with *away,* to go off in a 'huff' or fuming; with *off, out, up,* to blaze up suddenly, to explode.—*n.* an explosive sound; a splutter; the hissing sound made by a cat; a puff of wind; a short smoke of tobacco; a whiff of any odour; a sudden outburst of anger.—*int.* an excl. of displeasure or contempt; pooh!

Fuffers, *n.* a pair of bellows.

Fuffily, *adv.* hastily; scornfully.

Fuffin, *n.* puffing.

Fuffit, *n.* the British long-tailed titmouse.

Fuffle, Fuffel, *v.* to ruffle, rumple; to dishevel.—*n.* fuss; violent exertion.

Fuffle-daddie, *n.* a foster-father.

Fuffy, *adj.* light, soft, spongy; short-tempered.

Fug, *n.* moss. Cf. Fog.

Fuggie, *n.* a coward. Cf. Fugie.

Fuggie, *n.* a small yellow bee. Cf. Foggie.

Fuggie-bell, *n.* a truant.

Fuggie-the-skweel, *n.* a truant from school.

Fuggy, *adj.* mossy. Cf. Foggie.

Fugie, Fugè, Fugee, *n.* a fugitive from law; a cock that will not fight; a coward; a blow given as a challenge to fight.—*adj.* fugitive, running away, retreating.—*v.* to run away, play truant from.

Fugie-blow, *n.* a blow challenging to fight; the 'cowardly-lick.'

Fugie-cock, *n.* a cock that will not fight.

Fugie-warrant, *n.* a warrant to arrest a debtor intending to flee.

Fugle, *v.* to signal; to give an example of.

Fuhre, *v.* to go.

Fuilteachs, *n.* half of January and half of February O.S.

†**Fuilyie,** *v.* to foil, get the better of; to soil.

Fuir-days, *phr.* late in the afternoon.

Fuirsday, *n.* Thursday.

Fuish, *v. pret.* fetched.

Fuishen, *ppl.* fetched.

Fuist, *n.* a fusty smell.—*v.* to acquire a fusty smell. Cf. Foosht.

Fuit, *n.* the house-leek. Cf. Fouat.

Fule, *n.* fool.—*adj.* foolish.

Fule, *n.* a fowl.

Fule-bodie, *n.* a foolish person.

Fule-thing, *n.* a foolish creature; a silly, giddy coquette.

Fulfil, *v.* to fill up or to the full.

Full, *adj.* puffed up, conceited; used of herrings: in good condition; fully.—*n.* contents; a firlot, a bushel of grain; a herring before it spawns.—*v.* to fill. Cf. Fou.

Full-begotten, *adj.* lawfully begotten.

Fulmar, *n.* a species of petrel.

Fulp, *n.* a whelp.—*v.* to whelp; to give birth to. Cf. Fup.

†**Fulsie,** *v.* to soil, defile; to foil, defeat.—

n. filth, dung, street-sweepings. Cf. Foulzie, Fuilyie.

Fulsome, *adj.* copious, giving abundance; used of a garment: somewhat too large; of food: satiating, 'filling,' surfeiting, luscious, rich. Cf. Fousome.

Fulsomeness, *n.* lusciousness.

Fultacks, *n.* half of January and half of February O.S. Cf. Fuilteachs.

Fulthy, *adj.* mean, niggardly.

†Fulye, Fulzie, *n.* a leaf; leaf-gold.

†Fulyie, Fulzie, *v.* to soil; to defeat, foil. Cf. Foulzie, Fuilyie.

Fum, *n.* a useless, slovenly woman.

Fumart, *n.* a polecat. Cf. Foumart.

Fume, *n.* scent, fragrance.

Fummert, *ppl. adj.* benumbed; torpid.

Fummils, *n.* a whip for a top.

Fummle, Fummel, *v.* to upset. Cf. Whummle.

Fummle, *v.* to fumble; to disturb by handling or poking; with *out*, to extract slowly and unwillingly.—*n.* weakly doing of work; needless, foolish, or awkward handling.

Fummlin', *ppl. adj.* unhandy at work; weak.

Fumper, *v.* to whimper; to sob; to hint, mention.—*n.* a whimper; a whisper. Cf. Whimper.

Fun, *ppl. adj.* found.

Fun, *n.* gorse. Cf. Whin.

Fun, *v.* to joke; to indulge in fun.—*n.* a hoax; a practical joke.

Funabeis, *adv.* however.

Fund, *ppl. adj.* found.

Fund, *n.* a foundation. Cf. Found.

Fundament, Fundment, *n.* a foundation; a founding.

Fundamental, *n.* the seat of the breeches; in *pl.* the fundamental doctrines of religion.—*adj.* adhering to the 'fundamentals,' orthodox.

Funder, *v.* to founder; to collapse. Cf. Fooner.

Fundy, *v.* to founder; to become stiff with cold. Cf. Funnie.

Funeral-letter, *n.* an invitation to attend a funeral.

Funeralls, *n.* funeral expenses, escutcheon, ceremonies, &c.

Funeuch, *adj.* glad, pleased, merry.

Fung, *v.* to strike, beat; to kick; to throw with force; to anger; to annoy, offend; to work briskly; to work in a temper; to lose one's temper; to give forth a sharp, whizzing sound.—*n.* a blow, thrust, kick; a 'bang' out, the pet, a fit of bad temper.—*adv.* violently, with a 'whiz.'

Fung, *n.* beer.

Fung about, *v.* to drive hither and thither at high speed.

Fungel, *n.* an uncouth, suspicious-looking person or beast.

Funger, *n.* a whinger, hanger.

Fungibles, *n.* movable goods which may be valued by weight or measure, as grain or money.

Fungie, *adj.* apt to take offence.

Funk, *v.* used of a horse: to shy, kick up the heels; with *off*, to throw the rider; with *up*, to lift up smartly; to die.—*n.* a kick, a smart blow; a rage; opposition; in *pl.* humours.

Funk, *v.* to faint; to become afraid; to shirk, fail; to fight shy of; to wince; to cheat in marbles by playing without keeping the hand on the ground, or by jerking or stretching the arm, and so obtaining an unfair advantage.—*n.* a jerk of the arm unfairly accelerating a marble; a fright, alarm, perturbation.

Funker, *n.* a horse or cow that kicks; a kicker.

Funkie, *n.* one who is afraid to fight.

Fun-mill, *n.* a mill for bruising 'whins' or furze for food for horses, &c.

Funnie, Funie, *v.* to become stiff with cold; to be benumbed; to founder. Cf. Fundy.

Funniet, *ppl. adj.* easily affected by cold.

Funny, *adj.* strange, curious, unwonted; eccentric; merry, producing mirth or ridicule.

Funny, *n.* a game of marbles, where the marbles are set on a line, and the ones that are hit are restored to their owners.

Funny-bone, *n.* the elbow-joint.

Funs, *n.* furze, 'whins.'

Funsar, *n.* an unshapely bundle of clothes.

Funschoch, Funschick, *n.* a sudden grasp; energy and activity at work.

Funseless, *adj.* without strength; dry, withered; sapless. Cf. Fusionless.

Fup, *n.* a whelp, a pup.—*v.* to whelp, to pup. Cf. Fulp.

Fup, *n.* a whip; a cut from a whip; a blow; a moment.—*v.* to whip, beat. Cf. Whip.

Fuppertie-geig, *n.* a base trick.

Fur, *n.* a furrow; a furrowing, ploughing. —*v.* to furrow; to rib stockings.

Furage, *n.* wadding for gun or pistol.

Fur-ahin, *n.* the hindmost right-hand horse in a plough.

Fur-beast, *n.* the horse that walks in the furrow in ploughing.

Furc, *n.* the gallows.

Furder, *adj.* more remote.—*adv.* further.—*v.* to aid; to provoke; to speed; to succeed. —*n.* luck, success; progress.

Furdersome, *adj.* active; expeditious; rash, venturesome; forward; favourable, forwarding.

Fur-drain, *n.* a small trench ploughed periodically in the land for drainage.

Fure, *adj.* firm, fresh; sound.

Fure, *n.* a furrow. Cf. Fur.

Fure, *v.* to go.—*v. pret.* went.

Fure-days, *phr.* late in the afternoon.

Fur-felles, *n.* furred skins.

Furfluthered, *ppl. adj.* disordered; agitated. Cf. Forfluther.

Fur-horse, *n.* the horse that treads the furrow in ploughing.

Furhow, *v.* to forsake, abandon. Cf. Forhow.

Furich, *n.* bustle. Cf. Foorich.

Furiositie, *n.* madness, insanity.

Furious, *adj.* insane, mad; extraordinary; excessive.—*adv.* uncommonly; excessively. Cf. Feerious.

Furl, *v.* to whirl, wheel, encircle; to spin a teetotum, &c.—*n.* a short spell of stormy weather; a sharp attack of illness.

Furlad, Furlet, *n.* a firlot.

Furlie, *n.* a turner.

Furlie-fa', *n.* a trifling excuse; a showy, use-less ornament.—*v.* to make trifling excuses before doing anything.

Furligig, Furligiggum, *n.* a 'whirligig'; a light-headed girl; a child's toy of four cross-arms with paper sails attached, which spin round in the wind on the end of a stick. Cf. Whirligig.

Furloff, *n.* a furlough. Cf. Fore-loofe.

Furlpool, *n.* a whirlpool.

Furly birs, *n.* the knave of trumps.

Furm, *n.* a form, a bench.

†**Furmage,** *n.* cheese.

Furmer, *n.* a flat chisel.

Furnishings, *n.* furniture; belongings.

Furniture, *v.* to furnish; to have furniture.

Furoch, *n.* bustle. Cf. Foorich.

Furr, *n.* a furrow. Cf. Fur.

Furr, *v.* to choke up, clog with any substance; to be incrusted, as a kettle.—*n.* the incrustation in a kettle.

Furrage, *n.* wadding for gun or pistol. Cf. Forrage.

Furret, *adv.* forward.

Furrochie, *adj.* feeble, infirm from rheumatism or old age.

Furrow, *v.* to forage.

Furrow cow, *n.* a cow not with calf. Cf. Farrow.

Fur-scam, *n.* the second horse from the right hand in a four-abreast team in an old Orkney plough.

Fursday, *n.* Thursday.

Fur-side, *n.* the iron plate in a plough for turning over the furrow.

Fur-sin, *n.* the cord to which the hook of a plough is attached.

Furth, *adv.* forth.—*prep.* out of.—*n.* the open air.

Furthie, *adj.* thrifty, managing; frank, affable; hospitable. Cf. Forthy.

Furthilie, *adv.* frankly; without reserve.

Furthiness, *n.* frankness, affability.

Furthsetter, *n.* a setter forth; a publisher; an author. Cf. Forthsetter.

Furth-the-gait, *adv.* in *phr.* 'fair furth-the-gait,' honestly.—*adj.* holding a straightfor-ward course.

Furthy, *adj.* frank, affable; unabashed; forward, impudent; early in production. Cf. Forthy.

Furtigue, *n.* fatigue.

Fury, *n.* madness.

Fuschach, Fushach, *n.* a fluffy mass; a rough bundle or truss carelessly made up. Cf. Fusschach.

Fush, *n.* fish.—*v.* to fish.

Fush, Fushen, *v. pret.* and *ppl.* fetched.

†**Fushen, Fushon,** *n.* 'foison'; pith, vigour, &c. Cf. Fissen, Foison.

Fushica'd, *n.* what-do-you-call-it? Cf. Fous-ticat.

Fushica'im, *n.* what-do-you-call-him?

†**Fushion,** *n.* pith; substance. Cf. Foison.

Fushionless, *adj.* pithless; tasteless, feeble. Cf. Fissenless.

Fushloch, *n.* waste straw about a barn-yard; a rough bundle, an untidy mass.

†**Fushon,** *n.* pith; substance. Cf. Foison.

Fusht, *int.* whisht! hush!

†**Fusion,** *n.* 'foison'; pith, substance, vigour.

Fusionless, *adj.* pithless; tasteless.

Fusker, *n.* a whisker; beard and whiskers.

Fusky, *n.* whisky.

Fusky-pig, *n.* a whisky-jar.

Fusle, *v.* to whistle; to rustle.—*n.* a bustle. Cf. Fissle.

Fuslin, *ppl. adj.* trifling.

Fu'some, *adj.* nauseous, loathsome, disgust-ing. Cf. Fousome.

Fusschach, *v.* to work hastily and awkwardly. —*n.* an untidy bundle.

Fusschle, Fusschal, *n.* a small, untidy bundle of hay, straw, rags, &c.

Fussle, *n.* a sharp blow.—*v.* to beat sharply.

Fussle, *n.* a whistle.—*v.* to whistle.

Fussle, *n.* fusel-oil.

Fussock, *n.* an untidy bundle. Cf. Fusschach.

Fustit, *ppl. adj.* musty. Cf. Foosht.

Fustle, *v.* to whistle.

Fustle fair oot, *phr.* to be straightforward.

Fute, Fut, *n.* a foot. Cf. Foot.

Fute, *n.* a fool. Cf. Fout.

†**Futer, Futor,** *n.* a term of deepest contempt. —*v.* to ridicule. Cf. Footer.

Futher, *pron.* and *conj.* whether.

Futher, *n.* the future.

Futher, *n.* a large quantity; a number; a gathering.

Futher, *n.* the whizzing sound of quick motion. Cf. Whither.

†**Futher, Futhir,** v. to bungle. Cf. Footer.

Futherer, n. in *phr.* 'peat-futherer,' one who supplies peats.

Futhil, v. to work or walk clumsily.—n. hasty, clumsy working or walking; a fussy, clumsy person; a short and stout person.

Futith, Futoch, n. bustle; a riot; a dilemma. Cf. Footith.

Futrat, n. a weasel. Cf. Futteret.

†**Futter,** v. to bungle. — n. a bungle; a bungler. Cf. Footer.

†**Futter,** n. a term of the greatest contempt. Cf. Footer.

Futteret, Futterad, n. a weasel; a term of contempt. Cf. Whitteret.

Futtle, n. a knife, a whittle.—v. to whittle.

Futtle, v. to work or walk clumsily. Cf. Futhil.

Futtle-the-pin, n. an idler.—v. to be idle; to be too long in doing anything.

Futtlie-bealin, n. a whitlow.

Futty, adj. neat, trim; expeditious. Cf. Fittie.

Futty, Futy, adj. mean, paltry, worthless; meaningless. Cf. Footy.

Fuze, n. strength, pith.

†**Fuzen, Fuzhon, Fuzzen,** n. pith; substance, vigour. Cf. Foison.

Fuzzle, n. beverage, 'tipple.'

Fuzzlet, n. a smart blow. Cf. Fussle.

Fuzzy, adj. buzzing, fizzing, hissing.

Fuzzy, adj. fluffy, feathery.

Fy, int. an excl. calling to notice, hurry, or a summons.

Fy, n. whey.

Fyaach, v. to fidget; to 'fike' here and there.

Fyachle, v. to loaf about; to work at anything softly; to move about in a silly, 'feckless' way; with *down*, to fall softly down.

Fyak, n. a woollen plaid. Cf. Faik.

Fyantich, adj. in fair health; hilarious.

Fyantish, adj. plausible; fulsome in compliments or welcome; used of lovers: showing or expressing great fondness.

Fyarter, n. an expression of contempt for any bad quality that is not immoral or dishonest.

Fy-blots, n. the scum formed on boiling whey.

Fy-brose, n. 'brose' made with whey.

Fychel, n. a young foal; a fondling name for a young foal. Cf. Foichal.

Fye, adj. doomed; acting as if doomed. Cf. Fey.

Fye-haste, n. a great hurry.

Fyeuch, v. to smoke a pipe.—n. a short smoke. Cf. Feuch.

Fyeuch, int. an excl. of disgust. Cf. Feuch.

Fyfteen, adj. fifteen.

Fy-gae-by, n. a jocular name for diarrhœa.

Fy-gae-to, n. a fuss, disturbance, bustle.

Fy-gruns, n. the finely-divided sediment formed after whey cools.

Fyke, n. the fish, Medusa's head.

Fyke, v. to fidget. Cf. Fike.

Fyke-fack, n. a troublesome job; a small household job. Cf. Fike-fack.

Fykesome, adj. fidgety.

Fyle, v. to bring in guilty, condemn; to soil, defile. Cf. File.

Fyooack, n. a very small quantity of anything.

Fyoonach, n. used of snow: a sprinkling, as much as just whitens the ground.

Fyow, adj. few.

Fysigunkus, n. a man devoid of curiosity.

Fyte, v. to cut wood with a knife.—n. a cut. —*phr.* 'to fyte the pin,' to be too long in doing anything. Cf. White.

Fyte, adj. white. Cf. White.

Ga', n. the gall of an animal; a gall-nut; a disease of the gall affecting cattle and sheep; spite; a grudge. Cf. Gall.

Ga', n. an abrasion or sore on the skin; a trick or bad habit; a crease in cloth; a layer of different soil from the rest, intersecting a field; a furrow, a drain; a hollow with water springing in it.—v. to rub, excoriate; to irritate; to chafe, fret, become pettish.

Ga', v. *pret.* gave.

Ga, v. to go. Cf. Gae.

Gaabril, n. a big, uncomely, ill-natured person.

Gaa-bursen, adj. short-winded.

Gaad, n. a goad. Cf. Gad.

Gaadie, adj. showy; tricky. Cf. Gaudy.

Gaa-grass, n. a plant growing in streams, used for disease of the gall.

Gaan, adj. straight, near.—adv. tolerably. Cf. Gain.

Gaan, *ppl.* going.

Gaap, v. to stare. Cf. Gaup, Goup.

Gaar, n. oozy vegetable stuff in the bed of streams and ponds; hardened rheum from the eyes; a thin poultice of oatmeal and cold water. Cf. Garr.

Gaar, v. to scratch; to gore.—n. a scratch; a seam. Cf. Gaur.

Gaa-sickness, n. gall-disease in cattle and sheep.

Gaat, n. a gelded pig.

Gaave, v. to laugh loudly. Cf. Gaff.

Gab, *n.* impertinent talk ; prating ; entertaining conversation ; the mouth, the tongue ; one who talks incessantly ; the palate, taste ; appetite. —*v.* to speak impertinently ; to reply impertinently ; to chatter ; to play the tell-tale.

Gab, *n.* the hook on which pots are hung at the end of the 'crook.'

Gab, *n.* in *phr.* 'the gab o' May,' the last days of April ; weather anticipating that of May.

†Gabbart, Gabbard, *n.* a lighter ; an inland sailing-vessel.

Gabbart, *n.* a mouthful, morsel ; a fragment, bit of anything.

Gabber, *n.* a talkative person ; jargon. —*v.* to gabble, jabber.

Gabber, *n.* a broken piece ; what has come to grief. Cf. Gaber.

Gabber-stroke, *n.* the garboard-strake of a boat.

Gabbet, *n.* a gobbet ; a mouthful ; the palate, taste.

Gabbie-labbie, *n.* confused talking.

Gabbing, *n.* talk, chatter, gabble.

Gabbing-chat, *n.* a chatterer ; a tell-tale ; a talkative child who tells of all he hears.

Gabbit, *adj.* having a mouth or tongue ; gossipy ; talkative ; used of milk : passed through the mouth.—*n.* a mouthful ; a bit of anything.

Gabble, *v.* to scold ; to wrangle.

Gabbock, Gabbot, *n.* a mouthful ; a fragment.

Gabbock, *n.* a talkative person.

Gabby, *n.* the mouth ; the palate ; the crop of a fowl.

Gabby, *adj.* talkative ; fluent. —*n.* a pert chatterer.

Gaber, *n.* a lean horse.

Gaber, *n.* a fragment ; anything broken. Cf. Gabber.

Gaberlunzie, *n.* a wallet that hangs on the loins.

Gaberlunzie, Gaberlunyie, Gaberloonie, *n.* a licensed beggar ; a mendicant ; the calling of a beggar.

Gaberlunzie-man, *n.* a beggar who carries a wallet.

Gaberosie, *n.* a kiss.

†Gabert, *n.* a lighter. Cf. Gabbart.

Gaberts, *n.* a kind of gallows for supporting the wheel of a draw-well ; three poles of wood, like a 'shears,' forming an angle at the top, for weighing hay.

Gab-gash, *n.* petulant chatter ; vituperation.

Gabiator, *n.* a gormandizer.

Gable-end, *n.* the end wall of a building. Cf. Gavel.

Gable-room, *n.* a room at the gable of a house.

Gab-nash, *n.* petulant chatter ; a prattling, forward girl. Cf. Snash-gab.

Gab-shot, *n.* having the under jaw projecting beyond the upper. Cf. Gebshot.

Gab-stick, *n.* a spoon ; a large wooden spoon.

Gack, *n.* a gap.

Gad, *n.* an iron bar ; a goad for driving horses or cattle ; a fishing-rod ; the gad-fly.

Gad, *n.* in *phr.* 'a gad of ice,' a large mass of ice.

†Gad, *n.* a troop or band.

Gad-boy, *n.* the boy who went with the ploughman and 'goaded' his team.

Gadder, *v.* to gather ; to assemble ; to amass money. Cf. Gaither.

Gadderin, *n.* an assembly, meeting ; a festering lump.

Gaddery, *n.* a collection.

Gaddie, *adj.* gaudy ; showy ; tricky.

Gadding-pole, *n.* a goad or pointed stick for driving horses or cattle.

Gade, *n.* a 'gad,' goad.

Gade, *v. pret.* went.

Gade, *v. pret.* gave.

Gadge, *v.* to dictate impertinently ; to talk idly with stupid gravity.

Gadge, *n.* a standard, a measure ; a search, scrutiny, look-out ; a hunt or watch for one's own interests.—*v.* to measure.

Gadger, *n.* an exciseman ; a gauger ; one who is on the watch for gifts, &c.

Gadie, *adj.* showy ; tricky.

Gadje, *n.* a person, used contemptuously.

Gadman, Gadsman, *n.* the man or boy in charge of a plough-team, for driving the team with a 'gad' ; a ploughman.

Gadwand, *n.* a 'gadding-pole.'

Gae, *n.* the jay.

Gae, *n.* a sudden break in a stratum of coal.

Gae, *v.* to go ; used of animals : to graze ; to die.

Gae, *v.* to give.—*v. pret.* gave.

Gae aboot, *v.* used of a disease : to prevail in a locality.

Gae awa, *int.* an excl. of contempt, ridicule, surprise, &c.—*v.* to swoon ; to die.

Gae back, *v.* used of cows : to stop or lessen the milk they give.

Gae-between, *n.* a servant who does part of the housemaid's work and part of the cook's.

Gaebie, *n.* the mouth ; palate ; the crop of a fowl. Cf. Gabby.

Gae-by, *v.* to befall.

Gae-bye, *n.* a cheat, an evasion.

Gae by oneself, *phr.* to go off one's head.

Gaed, *v. pret.* went.

Gaed, *v. pret.* gave.

Gae-doon, *n.* the act of swallowing ; appetite ; a guzzling or drinking match.—*v.* to be hanged, executed.

Gae-lattan, *n.* an accouchement; verge of bankruptcy.

Gaen, *ppl.* gone.

Gaen, *ppl.* given.

Gaen, *prep.* used of time : before, within.—*conj.* before, until ; if. Cf. Gin.

Gae-owre, *v.* to swarm; to excel, transcend ; to cross, as a bridge.

Gaeppie, *n.* a large horn spoon, requiring a widely-opened mouth.

Gaet, *n.* a child ; a brat ; a bastard. Cf. Gett.

Gaet, *n.* rags, bits.

Gaet, *n.* a way. Cf. Gate.

Gae the country, *phr.* to tramp as a beggar or itinerant hawker.

Gae thegither, *v.* to be married.

Gae through, *n.* a great tumult ; much ado about nothing.—*v.* to bungle ; to waste ; to come to grief.

Gae-to, *n.* a brawl, squabble ; a drubbing.

Gae to the bent, *phr.* to abscond from creditors or other pursuers.

Gae wi', *v.* to court; to go to wreck; to coincide.

Gaff, *v.* to interchange merry talk, to 'daff'; to laugh loudly.—*n.* a loud laugh ; rude, loud talk ; impertinence.

Gaffa, Gaffaw, *v.* to laugh loudly ; to guffaw.—*n.* a loud laugh, a guffaw.

Gaffäer, *n.* a loud laugher.

Gaffer, *n.* a loquacious person.

Gaffer, *n.* a grandfather ; an elderly man ; a term of respect ; an overseer.

Gaffin, *ppl. adj.* light-headed, thoughtless, giddy.

Gaffnet, *n.* a large fishing-net, used in rivers.

Ga-fur, *n.* a furrow in a field for letting water run off.

Gag, *n.* a joke, hoax.—*v.* to ridicule ; to hoax, deceive, play on one's credulity.

Gag, *n.* a filthy mass of any liquid or semi-liquid substance.

Gag, *n.* a chap in the hands, a deep cut or wound ; a rent or crack in wood, a chink arising from dryness.—*v.* used of the hands : to chap, crack ; to break into chinks or cracks through dryness.

Gage, *n.* wage, salary.

Gage, *n.* a standard, measure ; a search. Cf. Gadge.

Gager, *n.* an exciseman. Cf. Gauger.

Gaggee, *n.* one who is hoaxed.

Gagger, *n.* one who hoaxes or deceives.

Gagger, *n.* a large, ugly mass of any liquid or semi-liquid substance ; the under-lip ; a large, ragged cloud ; a deep, ragged cut or wound ; a large, festering sore.—*v.* to cut or wound so as to cause a ragged edge.

Gagger-lip, *n.* a large, protruding lip.

Gaggery, *n.* a deception, hoax.

Gagging, *n.* a hoax ; a hoaxing.

Gaggle, *v.* to laugh affectedly or immoderately ; to giggle ; to chirp mournfully ; used of geese : to sound an alarm.

Gaibloch, *n.* a morsel ; a fragment.

Gaiby, *n.* a gaby ; a stupid person.

Gaid, *v. pret.* went.

Gaig, *n.* a rent or crack in the hand caused by dry weather; a crack in wood.—*v.* to crack from dryness. Cf. Gag.

Gail, *n.* a gable. Cf. Gavel.

Gail, *v.* to tingle, smart with cold or pain; to crack, split open with heat or frost ; to break into chinks ; used of the skin : to chap.—*n.* a crack, fissure ; a chink, split in wood. Cf. Gell.

Gail, *v.* to pierce, as with a loud, shrill noise.

Gailies, *adv.* tolerably, fairly well. Cf. Gayly.

Gailins, *adv.* 'gailies.'

Gaily, *adj.* in good health and spirits, very well.—*adv.* tolerably, moderately.

Gain, *adj.* used of a road or direction : near, straight, direct.—*adv.* nearly, almost; tolerably, pretty.

Gain, *v.* to fit ; to suffice ; to suit, correspond to shape or size.

Gäin, *ppl.* going.

Gain, *prep.* used of time : before.—*conj.* until . if. Cf. Gaen, Gin.

Gainage, *n.* the implements of husbandry : land held by base tenure by sockmen or *villani.*

Gain-coming, *n.* return.

Gainder, *v.* to look foolish ; to stretch the neck like a gander.—*n.* a gander. Cf. Gainter.

Gainer, *n.* a gander.

Gainer, *n.* a winner at marbles.

Gainful, *adj.* profitable, lucrative.

Gäin-gear, *n.* the 'going' or moving machinery of a mill, &c. ; persons going to wreck.

Gaingo, *n.* human ordure.

Gainly, *adj.* proper, becoming, decent. Cf. Ganelie.

Gainstand, *v.* to withstand, resist, oppose.

Gainter, *v.* to use conceited airs and postures. Cf. Gainder.

Gainterer, *n.* one who puts on conceited airs.

Gair, *n.* a strip or patch of green on a hillside ; a triangular strip of cloth, used as a 'gore' or gusset ; a strip of cloth ; anything like a strip or streak ; a crease.—*v.* to dirty ; to become streaked ; to crease ; to become creased. Cf. Gore.

Gair, *adj.* greedy, rapacious, intent on gain ; thrifty, provident ; niggard, parsimonious.—*adv.* niggardly ; greedily.—*n.* covetousness, greed.

Gair-carlin, *n.* the mother-witch ; a witch ; a hobgoblin ; a scarecrow. Cf. Gyre-carlin.

Gair'd, *ppl. adj.* used of a cow : brindled, streaked ; 'flecked.'

Gairdy, *n.* the arm. Cf. Gardie.

Gairfish, *n.* the porpoise.

Gair-gathered, *adj.* ill-got.

Gair-gaun, *adj.* rapacious, greedy.

Gairie, *n.* a striped or streaked cow ; the black and yellow striped wild bee ; the name of a streaked cow. Cf. Kaery.

Gairies, *n.* vagaries, whims.

Gairly, *adv.* greedily.—*adj.* rapacious.

Gairn, *n.* a garden.

Gairner, *n.* a gardener.

Gairner's-gertans, *n.* the ribbon-grass.

Gairock, *n.* the black and yellow striped wild bee.

Gairsy, *adj.* plump, 'gaucy.' Cf. Gawsy.

Gairten, *n.* a garter. Cf. Garten.

Gairun, *n.* a sea-trout. Cf. Gerron.

Gairy, *adj.* variegated ; streaked with different colours.

Gairy, *n.* a steep hill or precipice ; moorland ; a piece of waste land.

Gairy-bee, *n.* a 'gairock' or 'gairie.'

Gairy-face, *n.* a piece of waste land, a 'gairy.'

Gaishen, Gaishon, *n.* a skeleton, an emaciated person ; a hobgoblin ; anything regarded as an obstacle in one's way.

Gaislin, *n.* a gosling ; a fool ; a term of disparagement to a child.

Gaist, *n.* a ghost ; a term of contempt.

Gaist coal, *n.* a coal which, when it is burned, becomes white.

Gait, *n.* pace, motion ; rate of walking.

Gait, *n.* a goat.

Gait, *v.* to set up sheaves on end or singly to dry.

Gait, Gaite, *n.* a way ; a fashion ; a distance. —*v.* to make one's way. Cf. Gate.

Gait-berry, *n.* a blackberry.

Gaited, *ppl. adj.* paced, walking.

Gaiten, Gaitin', *n.* the setting up of sheaves to dry ; a single sheaf set up to dry.

Gaiter-berry, *n.* a blackberry.

Gaitet, *ppl. adj.* used of a horse : broken in, accustomed to the road.

Gaither, *v.* to gather ; to meet together ; to grow rich ; to save money ; in butter-making : to collect or form during churning ; to collect corn enough in the harvest-field to make a sheaf ; to collect money ; to pick up anything ; to raise from the ground ; of a 'rig' : to plough a ridge so as to throw the soil towards the middle.

Gaithered, Gaithert, *ppl. adj.* rich, well-to-do, said of one who has saved money.

Gaithered gear, *n.* savings, hoard of money amassed.

Gaitherer, *n.* one who collects corn for binding into sheaves ; a gleaner.

Gaithering, *n.* a crowd ; a company ; saving, frugality ; in *pl.* amassed wealth, money saved.

Gaithering-bell, *n.* a tocsin ; a bell summoning citizens to a town meeting.

Gaithering-coal, -peat, -turf, *n.* a large piece of coal, peat, or turf put on a fire at night to keep it alive till morning.

Gaithering-peat, *n.* a fiery peat sent by Borderers to alarm a district in time of threatening danger.

Gaitlin, *n.* a little child, brat ; the young of animals ; in *pl.* boys of the first year at Edinburgh High School and Edinburgh Academy.

Gaitlins, *adv.* towards, in the direction of.

Gaitsman, *n.* one employed in making passages in a coal-mine.

Gaitwards, *adv.* in the direction of, towards.

Gaivel, *v.* to stare wildly ; used of a horse : to toss the head up and down.

Gaivle, *n.* the hind parts, posteriors ; a gable. Cf. Gavel.

Gaivle-end, *n.* the posteriors.

Gaizen, *adj.* used of a wooden tub, barrel, &c.: warped, leaking from drought ; thirsty. —*v.* to warp, leak from drought ; to parch, shrivel ; to dry up, fade. Cf. Gizzen.

Gakie, *n.* the shell, *Venus mercenaria.*

Galant, *v.* to play the gallant. Cf. Gallant.

†Galash, *v.* to mend a shoe by a band round the upper leather.

Galashoes, *n.* overshoes.

Galasses, *n.* braces. Cf. Gallowses.

Galatians, *n.* a boys' Christmas mumming play. Cf. Goloshin.

Galavant, *v.* to gad about ; to philander. Cf. Gallivant.

Galavanting, *n.* love-making.

Galdragon, *n.* a sorceress, sibyl.

Galdroch, *n.* a greedy, long-necked, unshapely person.

Gale, *n.* an afflatus, an uplifting of the spirit.

Gale, *n.* a gable. Cf. Gavel.

Gale, *n.* used of geese : a flock.

Gale, *v.* to tingle ; to ache. Cf. Gell.

Gall, *n.* a disease of the gall among sheep and cattle ; spite ; a grudge.

Gall, *n.* a crease, a wrinkle in cloth ; a layer of a different kind of soil from the rest in a field ; a wet, spongy, unfertile spot in a field.

Gall, Gall-bush, *n.* the bog-myrtle.

Gall, Gall-flower, *n.* a beautiful growth on roses, briars, &c., resembling crimson moss.

Gallacher, *n.* an earwig. Cf. Golach.

Galla-glass, *n.* an armour-bearer.

Galland, *n.* a young fellow. Cf. Callant.

Gallan-nail, *n.* one of the bolts which attach a cart to the axle.

Gallant, *v.* to play the gallant or cavalier by escorting a woman in public; to flirt; to go about idly and lightly in the company of men, to 'gallivant.'—*n.* a woman who goes about in the company of men.—*adj.* large; improperly familiar; jolly.

Gallanter, *n.* a man or woman who goes much in the company of the other sex.

Gallanting, *ppl. adj.* gay, roving with men or women.

Gallantish, *adj.* fond of going about with men.

Gallan-whale, *n.* a sort of large whale frequenting the Lewis.

Gallasches, *n.* overshoes. Cf. Galashoes.

Gallayniel, *n.* a big, gluttonous, ruthless man.

Gallehooing, *n.* a stupefying, senseless noise.

Gallet, *n.* a term of endearment, 'darling.'

Galley, *n.* a leech.

†Galliard, *adj.* gay, gallant; brisk, cheerful, lively.—*n.* a gay, lively youth; a dissipated character; a quick, lively dance.

Galliardness, *n.* gaiety.

Gallion, *n.* a lean horse.

Gallivant, *v.* to jaunt, go about idly or for pleasure, show, &c.; to philander, act the gallant to; to make love to; to 'keep company' with.

Gallivanter, *n.* an incurable flirt; a gasconader.

Gallivaster, *n.* a tall, gasconading fellow.

Galloglach, *n.* an armour-bearer.

Gallon, *n.* a Scots gallon, equalling nearly three imperial gallons.

Gallon-tree, *n.* a cask holding liquor.

Galloper, *n.* field-piece used for rapid motion against an enemy in the field.

Galloway-dyke, *n.* a wall built firmly at the bottom, but no thicker at the top than the length of the single stones, loosely piled the one above the other.

Galloway-whin, *n.* the moor or moss whin, *Genista anglica.*

Gallowglass, *n.* an armour-bearer.

Gallow-ley, *n.* a field on which the gallows was erected.

Gallows, *n.* an elevated station for a view; three beams erected in triangular form, for weighing; braces.—*adj.* depraved, rascally.

Gallowses, *n.* braces, suspenders for trousers; leather belts formerly used as springs for carriages.

Gallows-face, *n.* a rascal.

Gallows-faced, *adj.* having the look of a blackguard, 'hang-dog.'

Gallows-foot, *n.* the space immediately in front of the gallows.

Gallows-tree, *n.* the gallows.

Gall-wood, *n.* wormwood.

Gally-fish, *n.* the char. Cf. Gallytrough.

Gally-gander, *n.* a fight with knives. Cf. Gully-gander.

Gallyie, *v.* to roar, brawl, scold.—*n.* a roar, a cry of displeasure.

Gallytrough, *n.* the char.

Galnes, *n.* compensation for accident at death, paid by the person who occasioned it.

†Galope, *v.* to belch.

†Galopin, *n.* an inferior servant in a great house.

Galore, *n.* abundance.—*adv.* abundantly.

Galpin, *n.* a lad, a *gamin,* 'city-arab.'

Galravitch, -vidge, -vich, -vish, *v.* to raise an uproar; to gad about; to romp; to live or feast riotously; to lead a wild life.—*n.* up roar, noise, a romp, riot; a drinking-bout. Cf. Gilravage.

Galravitching, *n.* riotous feasting; noisy, romping merry-making.

Galrevitch, *v.* to 'galravitch.'

Galshochs, *n.* indigestible articles, unsuitable foods; kickshaws.

Galsoch, *adj.* fond of good eating.

Galt, *n.* a sow when castrated or spayed.

Galy, *n.* a quick dance, a 'galliard.'

†Galyard, Galyeard, *adj.* gay, brisk. Cf. Galliard.

Galyie, *v.* to roar, bellow. Cf. Gallyie.

Gam, *n.* a tooth; a gum, lip, mouth.—*adj.* used of teeth: irregular, overlapping, twisted. —*v.* used of teeth: to grow in crooked and overlapping.

Gamaleerie, Gamareerie, *adj.* foolish; big. boned, lean, long-necked and awkward; grisly in appearance.—*n.* a foolish, clumsy person.

†Gamashes, Gamashins, Gamashons, *n.* leggings, gaiters.

Gamawow, *n.* a fool.

Gamb, *n.* a tooth; anything overlapping. Cf. Gam.

†Gambade, *v.* to prance, strut, march jauntily.

Gambadoes, *n.* leather leggings for use on horseback.

Game, *n.* a trick, knack, dodge; courage, pluck.—*adj.* plucky.

Game, *adj.* lame, deformed.

Game-fee, *n.* a fine formerly imposed by church courts for immorality. Cf. Buttock-mail.

Game-hawk, *n.* the peregrine falcon.

Game-leg, *n.* a deformed leg, a leg with a club-foot.

Gameral, *n.* a fool, a stupid fellow. Cf. Gomeril.

Gamf, *v.* to gape; to gulp, devour, eat greedily; to snatch like a dog.—*n.* the act of 'gamfing.'

Gamf, *v.* to be foolishly merry; to mock, mimic.—*n.* a buffoon. Cf. Gamp.

Gamfle, *v.* to trifle, idle, neglect work ; to spend time in idle talk or dalliance.

Gamfrell, Gamfrel, *n.* a fool ; a forward, presumptuous person.

Gamie, *n.* a familiar term for a gamekeeper.

†**Gammawshins,** *n.* leggings. Cf. Gamashes.

Gammel, *v.* to gamble.

Gammereerie, *adj.* foolish. Cf. Gamaleerie.

Gammerstel, *n.* a foolish, gawky girl.

†**Gammon, Gammond, Gammont,** *n.* the leg or the thigh of a person ; in *pl.* the feet of an animal ; pettitoes.

Gammul, *v.* to gobble up.

Gamon, *n.* a leg, a thigh. Cf. Gammon.

Gamp, *v.* to be foolishly merry ; to laugh loudly ; to mimic, mock.—*n.* an idle, meddling person ; a buffoon ; an empty-headed, noisy fellow.—*adj.* sportive, playful.

Gamp, Gamph, *v.* to gape ; to devour greedily ; to snatch like a dog. Cf. Gamf.

Gamphered, *ppl. adj.* used of embroidery : flowery, bespangled.

Gamphil, *v.* to sport ; to flirt ; to run after girls. Cf. Gamfle.

Gamphrell, *n.* a fool ; a forward fellow. Cf. Gamfrell.

Gamrel, *n.* a fool. Cf. Gomeril.

Gam-teetht, *adj.* having twisted or overlapping teeth.

Gam-tooth, *n.* an overlapping tooth.

Gan, *n.* the mouth, throat ; in *pl.* the gums, toothless jaws. Cf. Ganne.

Gan, *n.* the gannet.

Gan, *v. pret.* began.

Ganch, *v.* to snap with the teeth ; to snarl, bite ; to gnash the teeth ; to stammer ; to be very ugly.—*n.* a wide gape ; the snapping of a dog.

Gandays, *n.* the last fortnight of winter and the first fortnight of spring. Cf. Gaundays.

Gander, *n.* a stupid person, a ' goose.' Cf. Gainder, Gainter.

Gandiegow, *n.* a stroke, punishment ; a nonsensical trick, a prank.

Gandier, *n.* a braggart.

Gandy, *v.* to talk foolishly ; to brag ; to chatter pertly.—*n.* a brag, a vain boast ; pert, foolish talk ; a pert talker.

Gandying, *n.* foolish, boasting talk ; pertness.

Gane, *ppl.* gone.

Gane, *v.* to suffice ; to suit, fit. Cf. Gain.

Gane, *conj.* if ; before. Cf. Gin, Gaen.

Gane, *adj.* near, short ; convenient ; active, expert. Cf. Gain.

Ganelie, *adj.* proper ; seemly ; decent.

Gang, *n.* gait, style of walking ; pace ; a journey ; a road, path ; a drill, furrow ; the channel of a stream ; a cattle-walk for grazing ; the right of pasture ; a freight of water from a well ; as much as can be carried or carted at a time ; a family, band, retinue ; a company ; a flock ; a row of stitches in knitting ; a set of horse-shoes.

Gang, *v.* to go ; to walk ; to die. Cf. Gae.

Gangable, *adj.* passable, fit for travelling ; tolerable ; used of money : current.

Gang aboot, *n.* a travelling hawker.

Gang aff, *v.* to waste.

Gang agley, *v.* to go astray.

Gang-atween, *n.* a go-between ; an intercessor.

Gang awa', *v.* to faint.

Gang-by, *n.* a go-by ; escape, evasion.

Gange, *v.* to prate tediously ; with *up,* to chat pertly.

Ganger, *n.* a walker, pedestrian ; a shop-walker ; a fast-going horse.

Ganger, *n.* an overseer or foreman of a gang of workers.

Ganger, *v.* to become gangrenous.

Gangeral, Gangerel, Gangeril, *n.* and *adj.* vagrant. Cf. Gangrel.

Gangery, *n.* finery.

Ganging, *n.* the furniture of a mill which the tenant must uphold.

Ganging, *ppl. adj.* going ; active ; stirring.

Ganging-body, *n.* a tramp, beggar.

Ganging-gate, *n.* a field-path ; a footpath in contrast to a roadway for carts, &c.

Ganging-graith, *n.* the ' ganging ' of a mill.

Ganging-gudes, *n.* movable goods.

Ganging-man, *n.* a male tramp or beggar.

Ganging-plea, *n.* a hereditary or permanent lawsuit.

Gangings-on, *n.* ongoings, behaviour.

Ganging-water, *n.* something laid past for future needs, a ' nest-egg.'

Ganglin, *adj.* straggling ; of awkward tallness.

Gang on, *v.* to behave.

Gang ower, *v.* to transcend.

Gangrel, Gangril, *n.* a vagrant, tramp ; a child beginning to walk, an unsteady walker ; in *pl.* furniture, movables.—*adj.* creeping ; walking with short steps ; vagabond, itinerant, vagrant, strolling ; applied to creeping vermin.

Gangrill-gype, *n.* a spoiled child.

Gangs, *n.* spring-shears for clipping sheep or grass borders in gardens.

Gang-there-out, *adj.* wandering, vagrant.

Gang throw, *v.* to waste ; to bungle.

Gang together, *v.* to be married.

Gangway, *n.* a field-path, a footpath in contrast to a roadway.

Gang wi', *v.* to go to ruin, break down ; to waste.

Gangyls, *n.* in *phr.* to ' be a' guts and gangyls,' to be fit for nothing but eating and walking.

Ganien, *n.* foolish boasting. Cf. Gandying.

Gank, *n.* an unlooked-for trouble.

Ganna, *ppl.* going to.

Ganne, *n.* the mouth, throat ; in *pl.* the jaws without the teeth. Cf. Gan.

Gannyie, *v.* to talk foolishly. Cf. Gandy.

†Gansald, *n.* a severe rebuke. Cf. Gansel.

Gansch, *v.* to snatch with open jaws ; to snarl.—*n.* a gape, a dog's snatch. Cf. Ganch.

†Gansel, Gansell, *n.* a garlic sauce for goose ; an insolent retort, something spicy, snappish, or disagreeable in speech.—*v.* to scold, upbraid ; to bandy testy language ; to gabble.

Gansey, Ganzy, *n.* a seaman's jersey.

Gansh, *v.* to snap at anything, to ' gansch.'—*n.* a snap with the teeth. Cf. Ganch.

†Ganshel, *v.* to scold ; to bandy words. Cf. Gansel.

Gant, *v.* to yawn, gape ; to stutter.—*n.* a yawn ; a stutter.

Gant-at-the-door, *n.* an indolent lout.

Gantress, *n.* a wooden stand for barrels.—*v.* to set barrels on a ' gantress.'

Gap, *v.* to gape; to stare with open mouth. Cf. Gaup, Gowp.

Gape, *n.* a gap.—*v.* in *phr.* to ' gape one's gab,' to open wide one's mouth.

Gape-shot, *adj.* open-mouthed.

Gappock, *n.* a gobbet ; a morsel ; a bit of anything. Cf. Gabbock.

Gapus, *n.* a fool ; one noisily foolish.—*adj.* noisily foolish ; stupid. Cf. Gaupus.

Gar, *v.* to make, cause ; to induce, compel.—*adj.* compulsory, forced.

Garavitch, *v.* to live riotously. Cf. Galravitch.

Garb, *n.* a young bird ; a young child. Cf. Gorb.

Garbals, *n.* in *phr.* 'guts and garbals,' entrails.

Garbel, *n.* a young unfledged bird. Cf. Gorbal.

†Garbel, Garboil, Garbulle, *n.* a broil, uproar, brawl. — *v.* to make a brawling, scolding noise.

†Gardeloo, *n.* a warning cry when household slops were thrown from a window to the street. Cf. Gardyloo.

Garden, *v.* to plant in a garden.

Gardener's-gartens, -garters, *n.* the ribbon-grass.

†Garderobe, Gardrop, *n.* a wardrobe.

†Gardevin, *n.* a big-bellied bottle ; a square bottle ; a bottle holding two quarts ; a whisky-jar ; a case or closet for holding wine-bottles, decanters, &c. ; a cellaret.

Gardie, Gardy, *n.* the arm.

Gardin, *n.* a large chamber-pot. Cf. Jordan.

Gardy-bane, *n.* the bone of the arm.

Gardy-chair, *n.* an arm-chair.

†Gardyloo, *n.* a warning cry about dirty water thrown from windows on to the streets.

Gardy-moggans, *n.* long sleeves or 'moggans' for covering the arms.

Gardy-pick, *n.* an expression of great disgust.

Gare, *adj.* keen, eager, ready ; rapacious ; parsimonious ; intent on making money ; active in managing a household. Cf. Gair.

Gare, *n.* a triangular strip of cloth used as a gusset ; a strip or streak ; a crease.—*v.* to become streaked ; to dirty ; to crease. Cf. Gair.

Gare, Gare-fowl, *n.* the great auk.

Gare-gaun, *adj.* rapacious, greedy.

Garg, *v.* to creak.—*n.* a creaking sound. Cf. Jirg.

Gargrugous, *adj.* austere in person and in manners.

Garlands, *n.* straw ropes put round the head of a stack.

Gar-ma-true, *n.* a hypocrite ; a make-believe.

Garmunshoch, *adj.* ill-humoured, crabbed.

Garnel, *n.* a granary, corn-chest. Cf. Girnel.

Garnet, *n.* the gurnard. Cf. Girnot.

Garr, *n.* mud ; rheum. Cf. Gaar.

Garraivery, *n.* folly, frolicsome rioting, revelling ; loud uproar.

Garrard, *n.* a hoop, a 'gird'; in *phr.* 'ca the garrard,' keep the talk going.

Garravadge, *v.* to make an uproar, &c. Cf Galravitch.

Garret, *n.* the head ; the skull.

Garrochan, *n.* a kind of oval shellfish, three inches long, found in the Firth of Clyde.

Garron, Garran, *n.* an inferior kind of horse, small, and used for rough work ; an old, stiff horse ; a thickset animal ; a stout, thickset person.

Garron, *n.* a large nail, a spike-nail.

Garry-bag, *n.* the abdomen of unfledged birds.

Garse, *n.* grass.

Garsummer, *n.* gossamer.

Gart, *v. pret.* and *ppl.* made, compelled. Cf. Gar.

Garten, Gartan, Gartane, Garton, *n.* a garter.—*v.* to bind with a garter.

Garten-berries, *n.* blackberries, brambleberries.

Garten-leem, *n.* a portable loom for weaving garters.

Garten-man, *n.* one who does the swindling trick of 'prick-the-garter.'

Garten-pricker, *n.* a 'garten-man.'

Garter, *n.* the game of 'prick-the-garter,' a form of 'fast-and-loose.'

Garth, *n.* a house and the land attached to it : an enclosure for catching salmon ; a shallow part or stretch of shingle on a river, which may be used as a ford.

Garvie, Garvock, *n.* the sprat.

Garwhoungle, *n.* the noise of the bittern in rising from the bog ; the clash of tongues.

Gascromh, *n.* a trenching spade of semicircular form, with a crooked handle fixed in the middle.

Gash, *n.* a chin ; a projection of the under-jaw.—*adj.* used of the chin : projecting.—*v.* to project the under-jaw ; to distort the mouth in contempt.

Gash, *n.* talk, prattle ; loquacity ; pert language ; insolence.—*adj.* talkative ; affable, lively ; wise, sagacious ; shrewd ; witty, sharp ; trim, neatly dressed ; well-prepared ; used of the weather : bright, pleasant. — *v.* to talk freely ; to converse, chatter.

Gash, *adj.* grim, dismal, ghastly.—*adv.* dismally.

Gash-beard, *n.* a person with a long, protruding chin ; one with a long, peaked beard.

Gash-gabbit, *adj.* having a long, protruding chin ; having a distorted mouth ; loquacious ; shrewd in talk.

Gashin, *ppl. adj.* having a projecting chin.

Gashin, *ppl. adj.* chattering ; insolent in speech ; talking.

Gashle, *v.* to distort, writhe ; to argue fiercely or sharply.

Gashlin, *n.* a noisy, bitter argument.—*ppl. adj.* wry.

Gashly, *adv.* shrewdly, wittily, smartly.

Gash-moo't, *adj.* having a distorted mouth.

Gashy, *adj.* wide, gaping, deeply gashed.

Grashy, *adj.* talkative, lively ; stately, handsome, well-furnished.

†Gaskin, *n.* a rough, green gooseberry, originally from Gascony.

Gasoliery, *n.* a chandelier.

Gasping, *ppl. adj.* feeble, fainting, expiring.

Gast, *n.* a fright, a scare. – *adj.* frightened, terrible.

Gast, *n.* a gust of wind.

Gaste, *n.* a term of contempt.

Gastly-thoughted, *adj.* frightened at, or thinking of, ghosts.

Gastrel, *n.* the kestrel.

Gastrous, *adj.* monstrous.

Gastrously, *adv.* monstrously.

Gat, *v. pret.* got.

Gate, *n.* a way ; route ; distance ; a street, thoroughfare ; a journey.

Gate, *n.* a method ; fashion ; knack ; habit, trick. Cf. Gait.

Gate, *n.* a goat. Cf. Gait.

Gate, *n.* a sheaf set on end singly to dry. Cf. Gait.

Gate-end, *n.* a road-end ; quarters, place of abode ; a neighbourhood.

Gate-farren, *adj.* comely ; of respectable appearance.

Gateless, *adj.* pathless.

Gatelins, *adv.* directly, in the way towards.

Gate-slap, *n.* an opening in a wall, hedge, &c., for a gateway.

Gateward, Gatewards, *adv.* straight, directly.

Gather, *v.* used of butter : to form or collect in the churn. Cf. Gaither.

Gatheraway, *n.* a travelling rag-and-bone-man.

Gathering, *n.* a collection of pus under the skin.

Gatten, *ppl.* 'gotten,' got.

Gatty, *adj.* enervated ; gouty.

Gaubertie-shells, *n.* a hobgoblin supposed to combine loud roaring with barking like little dogs, and the sound of shells striking against each other.

Gauciness, *n.* stateliness.

Gaucy, *adj.* plump, jolly ; large ; portly, stately ; well-prepared ; comfortable, pleasant.,

Gaucy-gay, *adj.* fine, handsome, gay.

Gaud, Gaude, *n.* a prank ; a habit, custom ; a toy, plaything ; an ornament ; in *pl.* pomps.—*v.* to make a showy or gaudy appearance.

Gaud, *n.* a rod ; a goad ; a rind of board, about nine feet long, used on a calm day to lay the corn slightly before the man who cuts it. Cf. Gad.

Gaudé-day, *n.* a festive day.

Gaudering, *n.* finery, tawdriness.

Gaudery, *n.* 'gaudering.'

Gaud-flook, *n.* the saury pike.

Gaudnie, *n.* a semi-aquatic bird, ? the water-ouzel.

Gaudsman, *n.* a ploughman, as using the 'gaud' or goad. Cf. Gadman.

Gaudy, *adj.* tricky ; mischievous.

Gauff, *v.* to laugh loudly. Cf. Gaff.

Gauffin, *adj.* light-headed ; foolish, giddy ; thoughtless. Cf. Gaff.

Gaufnook, *n.* the saury pike. Cf. Gaud-flook.

Gauge, *n.* a search, scrutiny. Cf. Gadge.

Gauger, *n.* one who is ever looking after his own interests.

Gaugnet, *n.* the sea-needle or needle-fish.

Gauk, *v.* used of young women : to behave foolishly or lightly with men.

Gaukie, *n.* a foolish, forward, vain woman ; a foolish person.—*v.* to play the fool. to 'gauk' with men.—*adj.* giddy, foolish.

Gaukit, *adj.* foolish, giddy, awkward.

Gaul, *n.* bog-myrtle ; Dutch myrtle.

Gaulf, *n.* a horse-laugh.—*v.* to laugh loudly. Cf. Gaff.

Gaulp, *v.* to gape, yawn; to stare. Cf. Gaup.

Gaum, *v.* to acknowledge by curtsy. Cf. Goam.

Gaumeril, Gaumeral, *n.* a stupid fellow; a dunce. Cf. Gomeril.

Gaump, *v.* to be foolishly merry. Cf. Gamp.

Gaump, *v.* to sup greedily, as if likely to swallow the spoon. Cf. Gamf.

Gaun, *v.* to go.—*ppl. adj.* going.—*n.* lapse.

Gaun, Gaund, *n.* the butter-bur.

Gaun-a-du, *n.* a resolution never acted on.

Gaunch, *v.* to snap as a dog, snarl. Cf. Ganch.

Gaun-days, *n.* the last fortnight of January and the first of February.

Gauner, *v.* to bark; to scold loudly.—*n.* a barking; a fit of scolding.

Gaunge, *v.* to boast, exaggerate; to fib; to talk pertly, chatter.—*n.* boasting, brag; pert, silly talk. Cf. Gange.

Gaunna, Gauna, *ppl.* going to.

Gaunt, *v.* to gape, yawn.—*n.* a yawn. Cf. Gant.

Gaun-to-dee, *n.* a state near death.

Gauntrees, *n.* a wooden stand for barrels.—*v.* to set on a wooden frame. Cf. Gantress.

Gaup, *v.* to gape, yawn; to open the mouth widely; to gaze vacantly or with open mouth; to swallow greedily, gulp.—*n.* a vacant, staring person; a stupid, vacant stare; a wide, open mouth; a large mouthful; chatter. Cf. Goup.

Gaup-a-liftie, *n.* one who carries his head high.

Gaupish, *adj.* inclined to yawn.

Gaupus, *n.* a vacant, staring person; a booby, blockhead. Cf. Gapus.

Gaupy, *n.* a 'gaupus.'—*adj.* gaping.

Gaur, *v.* to make; to compel. Cf. Gar.

Gaur, *v.* to scratch; to seam or cut into; to 'gore.'—*n.* a seam, scratch, a cut made by a sharp point drawn over a smooth surface.

Gausy, *adj.* big, jolly. Cf. Gaucie.

Gaut, *n.* a boar-pig; a gelded boar; a sow.

Gautseam, Gautsame, *n.* hog's-lard.

Gavall, Gavawll, *v.* to revel, live riotously.

Gavalling, *n.* revelling, riotousness; a feast, a merry-making.

Gavel, *n.* a gable; the gable-end of a building.

Gavelag, Gavelock, *n.* an earwig; an insect like an earwig but longer.

Gavelock, *n.* an iron crowbar, a lever.

Gavel-winnock, *n.* a gable-window.

Gavil, Gavel, *n.* a railing, a hand-rail.

Gaw, *n.* a channel or furrow for drawing off water; a hollow with water-springs in it.

Gaw, *n.* in *phr.* 'gaw o' the pot,' the first runnings of a still.

Gaw, *n.* a gall-nut.

Gaw, *n.* a habit, a trick.

Gaw, *v.* to gall; to rub; to irritate; to chafe; to become pettish.—*n.* a sore place or abrasion of the skin; a crease or wrinkle in cloth; a layer of different soil from the rest in a field.

Gaw, *n.* the gall; a disease of the gall among sheep and cattle; bitterness, malice, spite.

Gawan, *n.* a daisy, a 'gowan.'

Gawd, *n.* a goad. Cf. Gad.

Gawd, *n.* a toy, plaything; a trick, habit. Cf. Gaud.

Gawdnie, *n.* the yellow gurnard. Cf. Gaudnie.

Gawe, *v.* to go about staring. Cf. Goave.

Gawf, *v.* to laugh boisterously. Cf. Gaff.

Gaw-fur, *n.* a furrow for draining off water.

Gaw-haw, *v.* to talk loudly.

Gawk, Gawkie, *v.* used of young women : to behave forwardly.—*n.* a foolish, forward woman. Cf. Gauk.

Gawk, *n.* a fool; a lout.

Gawkie, *v.* to stroll about.

Gawkie, *n.* the horse-cockle shell.

Gawkiness, *n.* clownishness.

Gawkit, *adj.* stupid; awkward.

Gawkitness, *n.* stupidity, lack of sense.

Gawky, *adj.* clownish; stupid.—*n.* a lout, bumpkin; a fool, simpleton.

Gawless, *adj.* without gall or bitterness; harmless; innocent.

Gawlin, *n.* a fowl less than a duck, regarded as a prognosticator of fair weather.

Gawmfert, *ppl. adj.* flowery; bespangled. Cf. Gampher'd.

Gawmp, *v.* to mock. Cf. Gamp.

Gawn, *ppl.* going.

Gawntress, *n.* a stand for barrels. Cf. Gauntrees.

Gawp, *v.* to gape, to yawn; to swallow up greedily.—*n.* a large mouthful. Cf. Gaup.

Gawrie, *n.* the red gurnard.

Gawries, *n.* vagaries, whims. Cf. Gairies.

Gawsie, Gawsy, *adj.* plump; portly; jolly; large. Cf. Gaucy.

Gay, Gayan, *adv.* pretty much, middling.

Gay-carlin, *n.* the mother-witch. Cf. Gyre-carlin.

Gaye, *adj.* considerable; tolerable.—*adv.* very; rather. Cf. Gey, Gay.

Gaylies, Gayly, *adj.* in fair health.—*adv.* pretty well.

Gaynoch, *adj.* gluttonous; avaricious. Cf. Geenyoch.

Gayt, *n.* a child; a brat. Cf. Gett.

Gaze, *n.* a sight, spectacle.

Gazen, *adj.* leaky from shrinkage in drought; thirsty; dry.—*v.* to warp; to leak from drought. Cf. Gizzen.

Gazzard, *n.* talk, gossip.

†**Geal,** *v.* to freeze ; to congeal, as jelly.—*n.* extreme cold, ice ; jelly.

Geal-caul, *adj.* cold as ice.

†**Gean,** *n.* the wild cherry ; its fruit.

Gear, *n.* dress, garb ; accoutrements ; a sword, weapon, &c. ; harness ; apparatus of all kinds ; household goods ; property, money, wealth, cattle ; stuff, material ; fare, food ; spirits ; trash, rubbish, doggerel ; an affair, matter of business ; 'goings on' ; the smallest quantity, atom ; in *pl.* the twisted threads through which the warp runs in the loom ; a set of 'shear-legs.'— *v.* to harness a horse.

Gear-carlin, *n.* a witch, hobgoblin ; an evil spirit. Cf. Gyre-carlin.

Gear-gatherer, *n.* a money-making man ; one prosperous in business.

Gear-grasping, *adj.* money-grabbing, avaricious.

Gearing, *n.* dress ; fishing-tackle.

Gearless, *adj.* moneyless ; without property.

Gear nor gweed, *phr.* neither one thing nor another.

Gear-pock, *n.* purse ; money-bag.

Geat, *n.* a way, street. Cf. Gate.

Geat, *n.* a child, a brat. Cf. Gett.

Geave, *v.* to stare, gape ; to look in an unsteady manner. Cf. Goave.

Gebbie, *n.* the crop of a fowl ; the stomach. Cf. Gabby, Kaebie.

Geb-shot, *adj.* having the lower jaw projecting beyond the upper. Cf. Gab-shot.

Geck, *v.* to mock, deride, scoff at ; to trifle with, deceive ; to toss the head in scorn or pertness ; to look derisively ; to look shyly ; to exult ; to look fondly ; to be playful, sportive.—*n.* scorn, contempt, derision ; a passing sarcasm, scoff ; a toss of the head, a scornful air ; an act of deception, a cheat.—*phr.* ' to geck one's heels,' to dog one's heels, pursue.

Geckin', *ppl. adj.* pert ; light-headed ; lively, sportive.

Geck-neck, *n.* a wry neck.

Geck-neckit, *adj.* having a wry neck.

Ged, Gedd, *n.* the pike ; a greedy or avaricious person ; anything under water fastening a hook so that it cannot be pulled out.

Gedder, *v.* to gather. Cf. Gaither.

Gedderer, *n.* a female gatherer in the harvest-field.

Geddery, *n.* a miscellaneous collection, a heterogeneous mass.

Geddock, *n.* a small staff or goad.

Ged-staff, *n.* a pointed staff.

Gedwing, *n.* an ancient-looking person ; an antiquary.

Gee, *int.* a call to horses to start or move faster ; a call to horses to turn to the left ;

an excl. of surprise.—*v.* to stir, move, change place ; to move aside ; to turn, tilt ; to swerve from, shirk.—*n.* a move, motion to one side ; a turn. Cf. Jee.

Gee, *n.* a fit of ill-temper, sullenness, stubbornness ; a sudden pique, offence ; a whim, fit of doing anything ; a knack, facility for anything. Cf. Jee.

Geeble, *n.* a small quantity of any liquid, used contemptuously.—*v.* to shake a liquid, spill, splash over ; to lose, destroy ; to cook badly ; with *on*, to use constantly, as an article of food.

Geeblick, *n.* a very small quantity of liquid.

Geebloch, *n.* a quantity of worthless liquid.

Geed, *adj.* good.

Geeg, *n.* a joke ; a hoax. Cf. Gag.

Geeg, *v.* to laugh in a suppressed way, giggle ; to quiz, laugh at.—*n.* fun, frolic ; a gibe. Cf. Gig.

Geegaw, *n.* a gewgaw, a trifle.

Geegs, *n.* the sounding-boards, pegs, and wheels in a mill. Cf. Gig.

†**Geel,** *v.* to freeze ; to congeal.—*n.* jelly ; ice. Cf. Geal.

Geelim, *n.* a rabbet-plane.

†**Geen,** *n.* the wild cherry. Cf. Gean.

Geen, *ppl.* gone.

Geen, *ppl.* given. Cf. Gien.

Geenyoch, Geenoch, *adj.* gluttonous, voracious ; avaricious.—*n.* a covetous, insatiable person.

Geenyochly, *adv.* gluttonously ; greedily.

Geenyochness, *n.* gluttony, covetousness.

Geer, *n.* tools, apparatus ; goods ; wealth ; stuff. Cf. Gear.

Geese, *n.* a goose ; a large curling-stone.

Geet, *n.* a child. Cf. Gett.

Geetle, *v.* to spill over.—*n.* a small quantity.

Geetsher, *n.* a grandfather. Cf. Gutcher.

Geevelor, *n.* a gaoler.

Gee-ways, *adv.* aslant ; obliquely.

Geezen, *v.* to shrink from drought ; to become leaky. Cf. Gizzen.

Geg, *n.* an implement for spearing fish.—*v.* to poach fish by a 'geg.'

Geg, *n.* a joke ; a hoax. Cf. Gag.

Geg, *n.* a crack in wood ; a chink caused by dryness ; a chap in the hands.—*v.* to chap ; break into clefts and chinks through dryness. Cf. Gaig.

Geg, *n.* the article used in the game of 'smuggle the geg' ; the holder of the article.

Gegger, *n.* the under-lip. Cf. Gagger.

Geggery, *n.* a deception.

Gehl-rope, *n.* the rope that runs along the end of a herring-net.

Gehr, *v.* to become streaked ; to crease. Cf. Gair.

Geig, *n.* a net for catching the razor-fish.

Geik, *v.* to toss the head. Cf. Geck.

†Geill, *v.* to congeal.—*n.* jelly. Cf. Geal.

Geing, *n.* human ordure, dung. Cf. Gaingo.

Geing, *n.* any intoxicating liquor.

Geir, *n.* accoutrements, dress; money. Cf. Gear.

Geisan, Geisen, *v.* to become leaky through drought; to warp. Cf. Gizzen.

Geit, *r.* a child. Cf. Gett.

Geit, *adj.* mad; out of one's senses.—*n.* a madman, a stupid fellow; an idiot. Cf. Gyte.

Geitter, *v.* to talk much and foolishly; to work awkwardly and triflingly.—*n.* nonsense; foolish chatter; a stupid person; ruin.

Geitteral, *n.* a very stupid person.

Geizen, *v.* to leak; to warp. Cf. Gizzen.

Geiz'ning, *ppl.* growing parched.

Gekgo, *n.* a jackdaw; a magpie. Cf. Jacko.

Gelaver, *v.* to talk foolishly; to gossip. Cf. Glaiver.

Gell, *adj.* used of animals: barren; of cows: not giving milk. Cf. Yell.

Gell, *n.* a gable. Cf. Gavel.

Gell, *v.* to sing loudly; to bawl in singing; to quarrel noisily.—*n.* a shout, yell; a brawl, wrangle; sport, a frolic; glee; a 'spree'; a drinking-bout; briskness of sale.

Gell, *adj.* used of the weather: sharp, keen; of persons: sharp, keen in business; of a market: brisk in the sale of goods.

Gell, *v.* to thrill with pain, throb, ache; to tingle; to crack from heat or frost, to chap.—*n.* a crack in wood, a chap. Cf. Gail.

Gell, *n.* a leech; a tadpole. Cf. Gill.

Gell, *v.* to cheat, fleece, 'gull.' Cf. Gill.

Gelleck, *n.* a crowbar. Cf. Gavelock.

Gelleck, *n.* an earwig; a small beetle like an earwig. Cf. Golach.

Gellie, *v.* to roar, brawl, scold.—*n.* a roar. Gallyie.

Gellie, *n.* a leech; a tadpole. Cf. Gill.

Gelloch, *n.* a shrill cry; a yell.

Gelloch, *n.* a crowbar. Cf. Gavelock.

Gelloch, Gellock, *n.* an earwig. Cf. Gelleck.

Gelly, *adj.* merry, pleasant; upright; worthy; jolly. Cf. Jelly.

Gelly-flower, *n.* the gillyflower. Cf. Gilly-flower.

Gelore, *n.* plenty. Cf. Galore.

Gelt, *n.* money.

Gelt, *adj.* barren. Cf. Gell.

Gemlick, Gemblet, *n.* a gimlet.

Gemm, *n.* a game.

Gemmle, *n.* a long-legged man.

Gen, *int.* a word used as a cry of pain.

Gen, *prep.* against.—*conj.* if. Cf. Gin.

Gend, *adj.* playful.—*adv.* playfully.

Gener, *n.* a gender in grammar.

Geng, *v.* to go. Cf. Gang.

Genie, Geni, *n.* genius.

Genious, *adj.* ingenious: having genius or intelligence.

Genivin, *adj.* genuine.

Gennick, *adj.* genuine, not spurious.

Gent, *n.* a very tall, thin person; anything very tall.

Gent, *v.* to spend time idly.

Gentilities, *n.* gentlefolk; gentry.

Gentiness, *n.* gentility; genteel manners: daintiness, elegance.

Gentle, *adj.* well-born; gentlemanly.—*n.* one of gentle birth; in *pl.* gentry.—*phr.* 'gentle and simple,' high and low.

Gentle-beggars, *n.* poor relations.

Gentlemanie, Gentlemanny, *adj.* belonging to a gentleman; like a gentleman.

Gentle-persuasion, *n.* the Episcopal form of religion.

Gentle-woman, *n.* the name formerly given to the housekeeper in a family of distinction.

Gentrice, *n.* good birth; people of gentle birth; honourable disposition, generosity; gentleness.

†Genty, Gentie, *adj.* noble; courteous; high-born; having good manners; neat, dainty, trim; tasteful, elegant; used of dress: well-fitting, becoming, 'genteel.'

Genyough, *adj.* ravenous. Cf. Geenyoch.

Geordie, *n.* a guinea in gold; a designation of a rustic; ? a coarse, cheap roll or 'bap.' —*phr.* 'by the Geordie,' by St George.

George, *n.* in *phr.* 'George's daughter,' a musket; a 'yellow George,' a guinea in gold.

Ger, *v.* to compel. Cf. Gar.

Ger, *n.* an iron hoop; a top. Cf. Gird.

Geravich, *v.* to make an uproar. Cf. Gal ravitch.

Gerg, *v.* to make a creaking noise. Cf. Girg, Jirg.

Gerletroch, *n.* the char. Cf. Gallytrough.

Gern, *n.* a boil, tumour.

Gernis, *n.* the state of being soaked. Cf. Jerniss.

Gerr, *adj.* awkward, clumsy.

Gerrack, *n.* a coal-fish of the first year.

Gerran, *n.* a sea-trout.

Gerran, Gerron, *n.* an inferior kind of horse, &c. Cf. Garron.

Gerrit, Gerrat, *n.* a little salmon.

Gerrock, *n.* a layer in a pile that is gradually built up.

Gerse, Gerss, *n.* grass.—*v.* to pasture, graze; to eject, cast out of office.

Gerse-cauld, *n.* a slight cold affecting horses.

Gersie, *adj.* grassy ; interspersed with grass.

Gerslouper, *n.* a grasshopper.

Gersome, *n.* a 'grassum.' Cf. Grassum.

Gerss-fouk, *n.* cottars.

Gerss-gawed, *adj.* cut or galled by grass.

Gerss-house, *n.* a house possessed by a tenant, with no land attached to it.

Gerss-ill, *n.* a disease among sheep.

Gerss-man, *n.* the tenant of a house without land attached to it.

Gerss-meal, *n.* the grass that will keep a cow for a season.

Gerss-nail, *n.* a long piece of hooked iron, with one end attached to the scythe-blade and the other to its handle.

Gerss-park, *n.* a field in grass.

Gerss-puckle, *n.* a blade of grass.

Gerss-strae, *n.* hay.

Gerss-tack, *n.* the lease which a 'gerss-man' has of his house.

Gert, *v. pret.* made.—*ppl.* compelled. Cf. Gar.

Gertan, Gertin, *n.* a garter. Cf. Garten.

Geshon, *n.* a skeleton. Cf. Gaishen.

Gesning, *n.* the reception of a guest. Cf. Guestning.

Gess, *v.* to go away clandestinely.

Gest, *n.* a joist.—*v.* to place joists.

Gester, *v.* to walk proudly, to make conceited gestures.

Get, *v.* to beget ; to earn ; to learn by heart ; to take ; to find ; to marry ; to be called ; to manage ; to manage to reach a place or thing ; to cause cream to turn to butter by churning ; to receive a blow ; to be deceived.—*n.* the food brought by birds to their young ; a catch of fish ; begetting, procreation ; offspring ; a contemptuous name for a child ; a bastard ; a 'gett,' 'brat.'

Get a' by, *phr.* to finish off.

Get ahin, *v.* to fall into arrears.

Get awa', *v.* to die.

Get hands on, *phr.* to strike, assault.

Gether, *v.* to gather. Cf. Gaither.

Get in ahin, *phr.* to prove the wiser, or cleverer ; to get the better of.

Get it, *v.* to be scolded, chastised ; to suffer ; to pay for it.

Get one's bed, *phr.* used of a woman : to be confined.

Get owre, *v.* to get the better in a bargain.

Get roon, *v.* to master ; to accomplish.

Gett, *n.* a child ; a bastard ; in *pl.* boys attending the lowest class, or junior classes, of an academy. Cf. Get.

Gett, *n.* a way ; a street ; a habit ; a knack. Cf. Gate.

Gettable, *adj.* attainable.

Gett-farrant, *adj.* comely. Cf. Gate-farren.

Get the cauld, *phr.* to catch cold.

Get the length of, *phr.* to go as far as.

Gettlin, *n.* a little child ; a brat ; the young of animals.

Gettward, *adv.* on the way towards.

Get upon, *v.* to be struck on.

Get with, *v.* to be struck with a missile, &c.

Geudam, *n.* a grandmother. Cf. Gudame.

Gevil, *n.* a gable. Cf. Gavel.

Gevil, *n.* a railing ; a hand-rail. Cf. Gavil.

Gewgaw, *n.* a Jew's-harp.

Gewlick, *n.* an earwig. Cf. Gelloch, Golach.

Gewlick, Gewlock, *n.* an iron lever. Cf. Gavelock.

Gey, *adj.* 'fast,' wild, 'pretty'; tolerable : large, great, 'good,' considerable.—*adv.* very, considerably, 'pretty'; indifferently.

Gey an, Gey and, *adv.* somewhat, tolerably ; considerably, rather.

Geyl, *n.* the gable of a house. Cf. Gavel.

Geylies, Geyly, *adv.* rather, much.—*adj.* in fair health.

Geysan, Geysen, Geyze, Geyzen, *v.* to warp from drought ; to parch, wither ; to leak. Cf. Gizzen.

Gezling, *n.* a gosling ; a fool.

Ghaist, *n.* a ghost ; a piece of coal that burns white, retaining its shape.

Ghaist-coal, *n.* a piece of coal that burns white, retaining its shape.

Ghaist-craft, *n.* a place haunted by ghosts.

Ghaist-cramp, *n.* an injury supposed to be owing to a ghostly visitation.

Ghaistlin, *n.* a ghost, used contemptuously.

Ghaist-rid, *adj.* ghost-ridden.

Ghast, *adj.* frightened.—*n.* a fright. Cf. Gast.

Ghoul, *n.* a ghastly spectacle, terrible object ; an envious, grudging, gloomy person.

Ghoulie, *adj.* haunted by horrid spectres.

Giann, *n.* a giant.

Gib, *n.* a tom-cat ; a castrated cat.

Gib, *n.* the beak or hooked upper-lip of a male salmon.

Gib, *n.* toffy, candy ; a sweetmeat made of treacle and spices.

Gibain, *n.* an oily substance procured from the solan goose, used as a sauce for porridge.

Gibb, *n.* in *phr.* 'Rob Gibb's contract,' a toast expressive of mere friendship.

Gibbag, *n.* a roll of flax prepared for spinning on the distaff.

Gibber, *n.* nonsense, foolish talk.

Gibber-gabber, *v.* to talk idly and confusedly.

Gibberish, *n.* a confused mixture ; idle talk.

Gibbery, *n.* gingerbread.

Gibbery-man, -wife, *n.* a man or woman who sells gingerbread.

Gibbet, *n.* a chimney crane for suspending a pot over a fire.

Gibbet-gab, *n.* a strong double hook for suspending pots.

Gibbet-pan, *n.* the largest pan used in cooking.

Gibbie-gabble, *n.*. nonsense.—*adj.* foolish.— *v.* to babble.

Gibble, *n.* a small quantity of liquid, &c. Cf. Geeble.

Gibble, *n.* a tool of any kind ; in *pl.* articles, wares ; odds and ends.

Gibble-gabble, *n.* idle, confused talk, babble. —*v.* to talk loudly or rapidly.

Gibblet, Giblet, *n.* any small iron tool.

Gibby, *n.* the bent end of a walking-stick.

Gibby-gabble, *n.* nonsense.—*adj.* foolish. Cf. Gibbie-Gabble.

Gibby-stick, *n.* a stick with a turned handle ; a walking-stick.

Gib-gash, *n.* a fluent talker about nothing.

Giblet-check, *n.* a check in a wall to let a door fold back close to it.

Giblich, *n.* an unfledged crow.

Gibloan, *n.* a muddy ' loan ' or miry path, so soft as not to admit of walking on it.

Gibrie, Gibbrie, *n.* gingerbread. Cf. Gibbery.

Gidd, *n.* a pike, a ' ged.' Cf. Ged.

Giddack, *n.* the sand-eel.

Gidder, *v.* to gather ; to lift and put on one's hat or cap.

Gie, *adv.* tolerably ; rather. Cf. Gey.

Gie, *v.* to pry.

Gie, *v.* to give ; to relax, give way ; to thaw ; to give a blow.

Giean, *ppl. adj.* given to prying.

Giean, *adv.* rather. Cf. Geyan.

Giean-carlins, *n.* old women of a prying nature, supposed to be troublesome at Hallowe'en to any one they found alone. Cf. Gyre-carlin.

Gied, *v. pret.* gave.

Gied, *v. pret.* went.

Gielainger, Gielanger, *n.* a bad debtor ; a cheat, swindler. Cf. Gileynour.

Gi'en, *ppl. adj.* gratuitous, given as a gift ; plighted, pledged ; with *to*, inclined to, having a propensity to.

Gi'en-horse, *n.* a gift-horse.

Gi'en-rig, *n.* a piece of land set apart for the devil, the ' gudeman's croft.'

Gie 's, *v.* give us.

Gies 't, *v.* give us it.

Giezie, *adj.* given to prying into matters which do not concern one's self.

Gif, *conj.* if ; whether.

Giff-gaff, *n.* reciprocity, mutual services, giving and taking ; mutual conversation.— *v.* to exchange in a friendly way ; to bandy words ; to converse promiscuously.

Giff-gaffy, *adj.* friendly, talkative.

Gift, *n.* a contemptuous term for a person.— *v.* to give as a present.

Gig, *n.* a giddy girl ; a prostitute ; a silly, flighty fellow ; a trifler.

Gig, *v.* to make a creaking noise.—*n.* a creaking noise. Cf. Jeeg.

Gig, *n.* anything that whirls ; an ingenious artifice ; a curiosity ; a charm ; a winnowing-fan ; a jig ; a state of flurry.

Gig, *v.* to laugh in a suppressed manner, giggle. —*n.* fun, frolic ; a gibe ; a prank, trick ; a whim.

Gig, *n.* the article held in the game of ' smuggle-the-gig.' Cf. Geg.

Gig, *v.* to trot, to walk briskly ; to jerk.

Giggery, *n.* odds and ends, things of little value.

Giggie, *adj.* brisk, lively, hearty ; full of tricks.

Giggle, *v.* to jog, shake about.—*n.* a slight jerk, shake.

Giggleby, *n.* a silly, giggling girl.

Giggle-trot, *n.* in *phr.* ' to tak' the giggle-trot,' said of a woman who marries when she is far advanced in life.

Giggum, *n.* a trick.

Giglet, *n.* a girl.

†**Gigot**, *n.* the hind-haunch of a sheep, a leg of mutton.

Gig-trot, *n.* habit ; jog-trot.

Gihoe, *n.* a kind of conveyance.

Gike, *n.* the stalk of lovage, hemlock, &c., of which children make squirts ; keksy.

Gil, *n.* a ravine. Cf. Gill.

Gilainger, *n.* a swindler. Cf. Gileynour.

Gilaver, *v.* to chatter, talk foolishly.—*n.* idle or gossiping talk. Cf. Glaiver.

Gilbert, *n.* an ill-shapen piece of dress.

Gilbow, *n.* a legacy. Cf. Jillbow.

Gild, *adj.* clever, capable ; full-grown, great ; loud, light-hearted.—*n.* clamour, uproar, noise, an outburst.—*v.* to make a clamour about ; to pay court to.

Gildee, *n.* the whiting pout.

Gileynour, *n.* a cheat, swindler, a bad debtor.

Gilgal, *n.* a hubbub, confused noise.

Gilkie, *n.* a lively young girl, a ' gilpy.'

Gill, *n.* the lower-jaw, the flesh under the chin or ears ; the mouth, throat.

Gill, *n.* a ravine ; a narrow glen with precipitous or rocky sides, or wooded and with a stream running at the bottom ; a dingle, ' den ' ; a mountain stream.

Gill, *n.* a leech ; a tadpole.

Gill, *v.* to cheat, ' gull.'

Gill, *v.* to tipple, drink, tope.

Gillé-gapous, *n.* a booby. Cf. Gilly-gaupus.

Gillem, *n.* a rabbet-plane. Cf. Geelim.

Gillet, *n.* a giddy young woman, a flirt ; a young woman approaching puberty.

Gill-flirt, *n.* a thoughtless, giddy girl.

Gill-gatherer, *n.* a leech-gatherer.

Gill-ha', *n.* a house that cannot protect dwellers from the weather; a house where workmen live in common during a job, or where each prepares his own food; a lonely house in a glen.

Gillhoo, *n.* a woman who is not counted economical.

Gillie, *n.* a gill of whisky, &c.

Gillie, *n.* a giddy young woman.

Gillie, *n.* a man-servant; a male attendant.

Gillie-birse, *n.* an ornament or head-dress consisting of a hair-cushion or pad, worn on a woman's forehead, over which her hair was combed.

Gillie-callum, *n.* the Highland sword dance, and its tune. Cf. Killum-callum.

Gillie-casfliuch, -casflue, *n.* the one of a chief's attendants who had to carry him over fords.

Gillie-comstrian, *n.* one who led his chief's horse in difficult places.

Gillie-gascon, *n.* an empty, talkative vapourer.

Gillie-more, *n.* a chief's armour-bearer.

Gillie-trusharnish, *n.* a chief's baggage-man, or knapsack-bearer.

Gillie-wetfoot, *n.* a chief's attendant for beating the bushes; a worthless fellow, swindler, a debtor who runs off; a running footman; a bum-bailiff.

Gillie-wheesels, -wheesh, *n.* gipsies, robbers.

Gillie-whitefoot, *n.* a beater of the bushes.

Gilligachus, *n.* a fool.

Gilliver, *n.* the gillyflower.

Gill-kickerty, *n.* in *phr.* 'gang to gill-kickerty,' 'go to Jericho.'

Gill-maw, *n.* a glutton, a voracious eater.

Gillock, *n.* a gill; a small measure of drink.

Gillore, Gillour, *n.* plenty; wealth. Cf. Galore.

Gill-ronie, *n.* a ravine abounding with brushwood.

Gill-rung, *n.* a long stick used by leech-gatherers to rouse leeches from deep holes.

Gill-sipper, *n.* a tippler.

Gill-stoup, *n.* a drinking-vessel holding a gill, a pitcher; the common periwinkle, from its resemblance to a pitcher.

Gill-towal, *n.* the horse-leech.

Gill-wheep, *n.* a cheat; a jilting.

Gill-wife, *n.* an ale-wife, one who sells liquors.

Gilly-cacus, *n.* a booby. Cf. Gilligachus.

Gillyflower, *n.* the clove-pink or carnation; wallflower; the hoary, shrubby stock; a thoughtless, giddy girl.

Gilly-gaukie, *v.* to spend time idly and foolishly.

Gilly-gaupus, -gaupie, *n.* a fool, booby, giglet, half-witted person.—*adj.* giddy and foolish.

Gilly-vine, *n.* a black-lead pencil. Cf. Keeli-vine.

Gilp, *n.* a big, fat person or animal; a person of disagreeable temper.

Gilp, *n.* a small quantity of water, &c.; a dash or splash of water; thin, insipid liquid.
—*v.* to jerk, spurt; to spill, splash, dash liquids; to be jerked.

Gilpin, *n.* a very big, fat person; a child or young animal when large and fat.

Gilpin, *n.* a smart young fellow; a 'gilpy.'

Gilpy, *adj.* used of eggs: not fresh, stale.

Gilpy, Gilpey, *n.* a lively young person; a roguish or mischievous boy; a soft, stupid person; a brisk, light-hearted girl; a young, growing girl.

Gilravage, Gilravachy, *v.* to behave tumultuously; to live riotously; to romp; to ravage.—*n.* a tumult, noisy mirth; a disorderly company; a depredation. Cf. Galravitch.

Gilravager, *n.* a riotous, forward fellow; a depredator; a wanton fellow.

Gilravaging, *n.* riotous behaviour at a merry meeting; depredation.

Gilreverie, *n.* revelry; riotousness and wastefulness.

Gilse, *n.* a young salmon, a grilse.

Gilt, *n.* a young sow when castrated. Cf. Gylte.

Gilt, *n.* money.

Gilt, *n.* a haystack with rectangular base; a construction made of cleaned straw.

Gilter, *adj.* lively, light-hearted.

Giltit, *adj.* gilded.

Gim, *adj.* neat, spruce. Cf. Jim.

Gimblet, *n.* a gimlet. Cf. Gemlick.

Gimcrack, *adj.* tawdry, fantastic.

Gimlet-tool, *n.* a gimlet.

Gimmels, *n.* tools, implements of various kinds.

Gimmer, *n.* a ewe from one to two years old, or that has not yet borne young; a contemptuous name for a woman.

Gimmer, *v.* to court and enjoy.

Gimmer-hill, -hillock, *n.* in *phr.* 'on the gimmer-hill' or 'gimmer-hillock,' unmarried; childless.

Gimmer-pet, *n.* a two-year-old ewe.

Gimp, *adj.* slender; neat; scanty, tight; narrow; deficient in quantity. — *adv.* scarcely.—*v.* to contract, curtail; to make too narrow; to give short measure, room, or weight, &c. Cf. Jimp.

Gin, *prep.* used of time: against; by; in time for; within.—*conj.* by the time that; until; if, whether.

Gin, *n.* the bolt or lock of a window or a door.

Gin, *adj.* greedy of meat.

Ginch, *n.* ginger. Cf. **Ginge.**

Ginch, *n.* a small piece.

Ginchick, *n.* a very small piece.

Ginchock, *n.* a rather small piece.

Gin-cough, *n.* the whooping-cough.

Gindle, *v.* to tickle trout. Cf. **Ginnle.**

Gineough, *adj.* gluttonous. Cf. **Geenyoch.**

Ging, *v.* to go. Cf. **Gang.**

Ging, *n.* gait. Cf. **Gang.**

Ging-bang, *n.* a party; an affair. Cf. **Jing-bang.**

Ginge, *n.* ginger.—*adj.* made with ginger.

Ginge-brace, -bras, *n.* gingerbread, spice-cake.

Ginge-bread, *n.* gingerbread.—*adj.* flimsy, soft, delicate; affecting dignity; gaudy; made of gingerbread.

Gingebread-man, -wife, *n.* a man or woman who sells gingerbread; the figure of a man or woman in gingerbread; a flighty, delicate, affected man or woman.

Ginger, *n.* a child's posteriors.

Ging-go, *n.* nonsense; a confused mass.

Gingich, *n.* the chief climber or leader in rock-climbing for sea-fowl in the Western Isles.

Gingle, *v.* to jingle.—*n.* an instant; noisy mirth. Cf. **Jingle.**

Gingling, *ppl. adj.* noisy, chattering.

Gin-goon, *adv.* ding-dong.

Gink, *v.* to titter; to laugh in a suppressed fashion.—*n.* a trick; a tittering.

Ginker, *n.* a dancer.

Ginkie, *adj.* light-headed, giddy, tricky, frolicsome.—*n.* a giddy, light-headed girl; a giglet.

Ginkum, *n.* a trick; an inkling; a hint.

Ginnaguid, *adj.* 'ne'er-do-well,' good-for-nothing.

Ginnel, *n.* a street-gutter.

Ginnel, *v.* to tickle trout. Cf. **Ginnle.**

Ginners, *n.* the gills of a fish.

Ginnle, *v.* to tickle trout, catch fish by groping under banks and stones with the hands; to 'guddle.'

Ginnle, *v.* to tremble, shake; to cause to tremble.—*n.* tremulous motion; the sound caused by vibration.

Ginnles, *n.* the gills of a fish.

Ginnling, *n.* tickling trout.

Ginnling, *n.* the noise caused by vibration.

Gin'st, *phr.* than it has.

Gip, *n.* the point of a fish's jaw.

Gip, *v.* to 'gut' fish for curing.

Gipe, *n.* one who is greedy, voracious, or avaricious.—*adj.* keen, ardent, very hungry. Cf. **Gype.**

Gipe, *n.* a stupid, awkward, foolish person; a foolish stare.—*v.* to stare foolishly; to act foolishly. Cf. **Gype.**

Gipper, *n.* a woman who 'guts' or cleans fish; a 'gippie.'

Gippie, *n.* a small knife used in 'gutting fish.

Gipping, *n.* gutting fish in the herring season.

Gipsy, *n.* a term of contempt for a woman or girl, and sometimes of endearment; a woman's cap plaited on the back.

Gipsy-herring, *n.* the pilchard.

Gird, *n.* a girth; a hoop for a barrel or tub; a child's hoop.—*v.* to put on a hoop; to 'ring' a wheel; to encircle with a belt or girth; to keep fast to a thing.

Gird, *v.* to strike, push; to drive smartly; to erect one's self with energy or violence; to drink hard; to scoff at.—*n.* a push, thrust; a blow, knock; a gust of wind; a very short space of time; a reproach, rebuke.

Girden, Girdin, *n.* a ligament which binds a thing round; a saddle-girth.

Girder, *n.* a cooper.

Girderings, *n.* suckers from an ash-tree, used as hoops.

Girding, *adj.* belonging to the trade of coopers.—*n.* girthing.

Girdit, *ppl. adj.* hooped with wood or iron.

Girdle, *n.* a circular iron plate with bow handle, for baking oatcake, scones, &c.

Girdle-braid, *adj.* of the breadth of a 'girdle.'

Girdle-cake, *n.* a cake baked on a 'girdle.'

Girdle-farl, *n.* a quarter of the circular oatcake which is cut into four while baked on the 'girdle.'

Girdle-scone, *n.* a flour or barley-meal scone baked on a 'girdle.'

Girdlesmith, *n.* a maker of 'girdles.'

Girdless, *adj.* without hoops.

Gird-the-cogie, *n.* the name of an old Scots tune.

Girg, *v.* to creak; to gurgle, as water-logged shoes in walking.—*n.* a creaking sound; the sound of wet boots in walking, or of creaking shoes. Cf. **Jirg.**

Girkienet, *n.* a woman's outer jacket. Cf. **Jirkinet.**

Girl, *n.* a girdle.

Girl, Girle, *v.* to tingle, thrill, dirl; to shudder, shiver; to set the teeth on edge.

Girl, *v.* to feel a sudden sensation of cold. Cf. **Grill.**

Girn, *v.* to grin; to snarl; to show or gnash the teeth in rage or scorn; to twist the features, grimace; to gape, like a dress so tightly fastened as to show the under-garment.—*n.* a snarl, grin; a whimper; fretful fault-finding; a smile; distortion of the face; a gape in a too tight dress.

Girn, *n.* a snare, trap, gin, noose of wire or cord to catch birds, rabbits, trout, and other small animals; a seton to keep up an issue, an issue.—*v.* to catch birds, rabbits, &c., by means of a 'girn.' Cf. **Grin.**

Girn, *n.* the last handful of grain shorn in the harvest-field. Cf. Kirn.

Girn-again, *n.* a peevish, cross-grained person; an habitually fretting child.

Girnel, Girnal, *n.* a granary; a meal-chest.— *v.* to store up in granaries.

Girnel-house, *n.* a large granary; a miller's granary.

Girnel-kist, *n.* a meal-chest.

Girnel-man, *n.* a land-steward in charge of the grain and meal paid as part of the rent.

Girner, *n.* a garner, a 'girnel.'

Girnie, *n.* a peevish person; a fretting child. —*adj.* peevish, fretful.

Girnie-gib, -gibbie, *n.* a peevish person.

Girnigo, Girnigae, *n.* a peevish person.—*adj.* peevish, fretful.

Girnigo-gash, -gibbie, *n.* a peevish person.

Girningly, *adv.* with a grin; fretfully.

Girnot, *n.* the grey gurnard. Cf. Garnot.

Girr, *n.* a hoop. Cf. Gird.

Girran, Girron, *n.* a small boil. Cf. Guran.

Girran, *n.* an inferior kind of horse. Cf. Garron.

Girrebbage, *n.* an uproar. Cf. Gilravage.

Girrel, *v.* to thrill. Cf. Girl.

Girs, Girse, Girss, *n.* grass. Cf. Gerse.

Girsie, *adj.* interspersed with grass. Cf. Gersy.

Girskaivie, *adj.* hare-brained.

Girsle, *n.* a gristle; a quill-pen; the throat. Cf. Grisle.

Girslie, *adj.* gristly, full of gristles. Cf. Grisly.

Girslin, *n.* a slight frost, a thin scurf of frost.

Girst, *ppl.* pastured on grass.

Girst, *n.* grist; the quantity of corn sent to a mill to be ground; the fee paid in kind for grinding.—*v.* to grind and dress grain. Cf. Grist.

Girst, *n.* size, measurement, texture, thickness; the form of the surface of linen, wood, &c., as to smoothness. Cf. Grist.

Girster, *n.* one who brings grain to be ground at a mill.

Girt, *adj.* great, large.

Girt, *n.* the girth; a girth.

Girth, *n.* a neckcloth; a hoop of iron or wood.

Girth, *n.* a sanctuary, place of refuge; a circle of stones environing the ancient places of judgment, popularly supposed to be sanctuaries.

Girthgate, *n.* a safe road, the way to a sanctuary.

Girthing, *n.* a saddle-girth, harness. Cf. Girding.

Girtholl, *n.* a sanctuary.

Girtle, *n.* a small quantity of any fluid.—*v.* to pour in small quantities; to work with liquids; with *up,* to throw up, splash; with

out, over, to spill in small quantities; with *at, with,* to use constantly, as an article of food.

Girt o' the leg, *phr.* the calf of the leg.

Girzy, Girzie, *n.* a maid-servant.

Gisn, *v.* to leak from drought. Cf. Gizzen.

Gite, *adj.* mad; enraged.—*n.* a madman, an idiot.

Gite, *n.* a child, a brat. Cf. Gett.

Gitters, *n.* mud, mire, 'gutters.'

Gitty, *n.* a term of endearment to a child, or 'geit.'

Give, *conj.* if. Cf. Gif.

Give, *v.* to give way; used of ice, frost: to thaw; to give a blow; with *down,* to reduce or lower a fine, &c. Cf. Gie.

Gizen, *adj.* dry; thirsty. Cf. Gizzen.

Gizen, *n.* the gizzard of a fowl; a person's throat. Cf. Gizzen.

Gizy, *n.* a wig.

Gizy-maker, *n.* a wig-maker.

Gizz, *n.* a wig; the face, countenance.

†Gizzen, *n.* childbed. Cf. Jizzen.

†Gizzen, *n.* the gizzard of a fowl; a person's throat.

Gizzen, *adj.* used of wooden vessels: leaking owing to drought; dry; thirsty; parched. — *v.* used of wooden vessels: to warp, twist, or crack, and become leaky from drought; to dry up from heat; to be parched; to wither, fade, shrivel; to parch from thirst.

Gizzen-bed, *n.* childbed.

Gizzen-clout, *n.* an infant's binder.

Gizzy-maker, *n.* a wig-maker.

Glaamer, *v.* to grope. Cf. Gloomer.

Glaar, *n.* mud, ooze, filth; slippery ice, slipperiness.—*v.* to make muddy, slippery. Cf. Glaur.

Glabber, *v.* to chatter, gabble; to speak indistinctly.—*n.* foolish, idle talk.

Glack, *v.* in *phr.* to 'glack one's mitten,' to bribe, 'tip.'

Glack, *n.* a trick; deception.—*v.* to trifle; to flirt; to deceive. Cf. Glaik.

Glack, *n.* a ravine, a defile; the fork of a tree, road, &c.; the angle between the thumb and the forefinger; an opening in a wood where the wind blows briskly; a handful or small portion; as much grain as a reaper holds in his left hand; a 'snack,' slight repast.

Glad, Glade, *adj.* smooth, easy in motion; slippery; not to be trusted.

Glad content, *phr.* specially content.

Glaff, *n.* a glimpse, a 'gliff.'

Glaff, *n.* a sudden blast or puff of wind.— *v.* to waft, blow gently.

Glag, *v.* to make a choking noise in the throat.—*n.* a choking sound in the throat. Cf. Glog, Glock.

Glagger, *v.* to 'glag.'—*n.* a 'glag.'

Glagger, *v.* to search, pursue, or desire eagerly. —*n.* a keen pursuit; avaricious greed.

Glaggy, *adj.* soft, sticky, 'claggy.'

Glaiber, *v.* to chatter, gabble.—*n.* idle talk. Cf. Glabber.

Glaid, *adj.* glad. Cf. Gled.

Glaid, *adj.* smooth. Cf. Glad.

Glaid, *n.* the kite. Cf. Gled.

Glaiger, *n.* a hard, whitish marble, made of earthenware.

Glaik, *n.* a trick; a deception; an illusion of the eye; a gleam, reflection of light; a glance of the eye; the bat; in *pl.* scoffs, gibes; a jilting; an idle, good-for-nothing person; a puzzle-game; a child's puzzle.— *v.* to trifle; to flirt; to fool; to wanton; to wander idly; to spend time playfully; to jeer, make 'game' of; to shine, dazzle; to deceive, beguile.

Glaikery, *n.* coquetry, trifling, light-headedness.

Glaikie, *adj.* pleasant. Cf. Glaiky.

Glaikit, Glaigit, *ppl. adj.* senseless, silly; giddy, thoughtless; affected; petted.

Glaikitly, *adv.* lightly, foolishly, affectedly, pettishly.

Glaikitness, *n.* levity, giddiness; affectation; pettedness.

Glaiky, *adj.* giddy, thoughtless; pleasant, charming.—*n.* a giddy girl.

Glaim, *v.* to burn with a bright flame.—*n.* a flame.

Glaip, *v.* to gulp food or drink.

Glair, *n.* mud, mire. Cf. Glaur.

Glair-hole, *n.* a mire.

Glairie, *n.* mud.

Glairie-flairies, *n.* gaudy trappings. Cf. Glare.

Glairy, *adv.* showy.

Glairy-flairy, *adj.* gaudy, showy.

Glaise, *n.* in *phr.* 'a glaise o' the fire,' warming one's self hurriedly at a strong fire. Cf. Glaize.

Glaister, *n.* a thin covering of snow or ice.

Glaister, *v.* to babble, talk indistinctly; to howl, to bark; to speak foolishly.

Glaisterie, *adj.* sleety; miry.

Glaiver, *n.* chatter, gossip. — *v.* to talk foolishly, babble. Cf. Glaver.

Glaize, *v.* to smooth over; to graze in passing; to glaze.

Glaize, *n.* a warming at a fire.

Glaizie, *adj.* glittering; glossy; smooth, sleek, shining like glass.

Glak, *n.* a trick; an illusion. Cf. Glaik.

Glakit, *ppl. adj.* senseless; giddy; thoughtless. Cf. Glaikit.

Glam, *n.* a loud, prolonged cry; noise, clamour.

Glam, *v.* to clutch at; to eat greedily.—*n.* the hand. Cf. Glaum.

Glamack, *n.* a snatch; an eager grasp; a handful; a mouthful.—*v.* to snatch at, clutch; to eat greedily.

Glamer, *n.* glamour.—*v.* to bewitch, fascinate; to dazzle.

Glamer, *n.* noise, clamour.

Glamer bead, *n.* an amber bead used in enchantment.

Glamerie, *n.* witchcraft, magic, fascination Cf. Glamourie.

Glamerify, *v.* to bewitch, cast a spell.

Glamer-micht, *n.* power of enchantment.

Glammach, *v.* to snatch at, clutch; to grope for, search one's pocket; to eat greedily.— *n.* a clutch, grasp; a handful; a morsel.

Glammer, *n.* a spell, fascination; witchery. —*v.* to bewitch, beguile; to dazzle; to bind with a spell.

Glammie, *n.* a mouthful. Cf. Glaum.

Glamorous, *adj.* magical, supernatural.

Glamour-gift, *n.* the gift of fascinating or enchanting.

Glamourie, *n.* witchcraft; fascination; a spell.

Glamp, *v.* to grasp, clutch at; to grope; to gulp, eat greedily; to sprain.—*n.* a snatch, gulp, grasp; a groping search in the dark; a sprain.

Glance, *v.* to cause to glance; to brighten the eye.

Glancing-glass, *n.* a glass used by children to reflect sun-rays on any object; applied to a minister of the gospel who has more show or flashiness than solidity.

Glant, *v. pret.* shone.

Glar, Glare, *n.* mud. Cf. Glaur.

Glare, *n.* a fine show, a gaudy appearance. Cf. Glairy.

Glarry, *adj.* muddy; smooth and shining, like wet mud. Cf. Glaurie.

Glasgow-magistrate, *n.* a red herring.

Glash, *n.* a hollow on the slope of a hill. Cf. Clash.

Glashan, *n.* the coal-fish.

Glashtroch, *n.* continuous rain causing dirty roads.

Glasin-wricht, *n.* a glazier.

Glasp, *n.* a clasp, grasp.

Glass, *n.* in *pl.* glasses filled with water, and having the white of an egg dropped into them, used at Fastern's-e'en and Hallowe'en as predictions of the future. — *v.* to glaze, furnish windows with glass.

Glassack, *n.* a 'glassey.'

Glass-breaker, *n.* a tippler, a hard drinker.

Glass-chack, *v.* to plane down the outer part of a sash, to fit it for receiving the glass.

Glassen, *adj.* made of glass.

Glasser, Glassier, *n.* a glazier.

Glasser, *n.* a marble or ‘taw’ made of glass.

Glassey, *n.* a sweatmeat made of treacle; a glass marble.

Glassin, *n.* glass-work, panes of glass.

Glassing, *n.* a planing, smoothing.

Glassin-wright, *n.* a glazier.

Glassites, *n.* followers of the Rev. John Glas (1695-1773), otherwise called Sandemanians.

Glassock, *n.* the coal-fish.

Glaster, *v.* to babble; to bawl. Cf. **Glaister.**

Glasterer, *n.* a boaster.

Glastrious, *adj.* contentious; boastful.

Glatton, *n.* a handful.

Glaum, *v.* to clutch; to grope.—*n.* a clutch; a mouthful. Cf. **Glam.**

Glaum, *v.* to stare, ‘glower.’

Glaumer, Glaumour, *n.* glamour. Cf. **Glamer.**

Glaump, *v.* to grasp ineffectually; to grope; to sprain. Cf. **Glamp.**

Glaums, *n.* a horse-gelder’s instruments.

Glaund, Glaun, *n.* a clamp of iron or wood.

Glaur, Glawr, *n.* mud, dirt, ooze; slippery ice, slipperiness. - *v.* to make muddy, dirty, or slippery; to wade or stick in mud.

Glaurie, *adj.* muddy, filthy; smooth and shining like wet mud; used of the weather: wet, causing mud.—*n.* mire, soft mud.

Glauroch, *n.* a soft, muddy hole.

Glaver, *v.* to chatter, babble.—*n.* foolish talk, chatter. Cf. **Claver.**

Glawnicy, *n.* an ocular deception caused by witchcraft.

Glazie, *adj.* glazed; glassy; smooth. Cf. **Glaizie.**

Glead, *n.* a spark; a flame.—*v.* to burn. Cf. **Gleed.**

Gleakit, *adj.* senseless; giddy; petted. Cf. **Glaikit.**

Gleam, *n.* in *phr.* ‘gang gleam,’ to take fire.

Glebber, Glebor, *v.* to gabble, chatter. Cf. **Glabber.**

Gled, *adj.* glad.

Gled, Glede, *n.* the kite; the buzzard; a greedy person.

Glede’s whissle, *n.* an expression of triumph.

Glede-wylie, *n.* a children’s game.

Gledge, *v.* to glance at, take a side view; to look askance, leer; to look slyly or archly; to spy.—*n.* a glance, glimpse; an oblique look; a sly or arch glance.

Gled-like, *adj.* like a kite.

Glee, *v.* to squint; to look sideways.—*n.* a squint; a mark, track, straight course.—*adv.* awry, ‘agley.’

Glee, *adj.* merry, gleeful.

Gleed, *n.* a spark, a red ember; a cinder; a fire, flame, a glare, glow.—*v.* to burn; to smoulder. Cf. **Glead.**

Gleed, *ppl. adj.* squinting; blind of an eye; crooked, awry, oblique.—*adv.* crookedly; astray.

Gleed-eyed, *adj.* squinting.

Gleed-looking, *adj.* appearing to have a squint.

Gleed-necked, *adj.* wry-necked, crooked.

Gleeitness, *n.* obliqueness; the state of being squint-eyed.

Gleek, *v.* to gibe; to trifle; to flirt.—*n.* a trick; an illusion. Cf. **Glaik.**

Gleemock, *n.* a faint or deadened gleam, like that of the sun through fog.

Glee-mou’d, *adj.* having the mouth awry.

Gleen, *v.* to shine, glitter, gleam.—*n.* a bright light, gleam.

Gleesh, *v.* to burn with a strong, clear fire.—*n.* a strong, clear fire.

Gleeshach, *n.* a strong, clear fire. Cf. **Grieshach.**

Gleet, *v.* to shine, glance, glitter.—*n.* a glance, a glitter, the act of shining.

Gleet, *ppl. adj.* squinting; blind of an eye awry, crooked.—*adv.* crookedly.

Gleeyed, *ppl. adj.* squinting.

Gleg, *n.* a gadfly, ‘cleg.’

Gleg, *v.* in *phr.* ‘to be aff the gleg,’ to be off the track, to miss the mark. Cf. **Glee.**

Gleg, *adj.* clear-sighted, of quick perception; keen, sharp, eager; brisk, nimble; quick in movement; bright, smart, gay, vivid sparkling; keen of appetite, hungry; sharp edged; of ice: keen, slippery; clever; pert in manner; attentive; avaricious.—*adv.* cleverly.

Gleg-e’ed, *adj.* sharp-eyed.

Gleg-glancing, *adj.* quick-sighted.

Gleg-hawk, *n.* the sparrow-hawk.

Gleg-lug’d, *adj.* quick of hearing.

Glegly, *adv.* cleverly, keenly, attentively; briskly; quickly; brightly, flashingly.

Glegness, *n.* keenness; quick perception.

Gleg-set, *adj.* sharp, keen.

Gleg-sichted, *adj.* quick-sighted.

Gleg-sure, *adj.* certain, ‘cocksure.’

Gleg-tongued, *adj.* sharp-tongued.

Gleg-witted, *adj.* sharp-witted.

Gleib, *n.* a piece, part of anything. Cf. **Glibe.**

Gleid, *n.* a spark, flame.—*v.* to illuminate. Cf. **Gleed.**

Gleid, *ppl. adj.* squint-eyed; oblique. Cf. **Glee.**

Glen, *n.* a daffodil.

Glender-gane, *adj.* in a bad condition, physical, moral, or financial.

Glender-gear, *n.* ill-gotten substance.

Glendrie-gaits, *n.* far-away errands.

Glendronach, *n.* a particular brand of whisky.

Glengarry, *n.* a man’s or boy’s oblong woollen cap.

Glengore, *n.* venereal disease.

Glenlivat, *n.* whisky distilled at Glenlivet.

Glent, *v.* to shine, sparkle; to flash, twinkle; of flowers: to blossom; to glance, peep; to squint; to pass suddenly.—*n.* a gleam, sparkle; an instant; a sudden blow; a glance, glimpse; a sly look.

Glentin-stanes, *n.* small white stones, used by children to strike fire.

Gleshan, *n.* the coal-fish. Cf. Glashan.

Gless, *n.* a glass.—*v.* to drink a glass of spirits, &c.

Glesser, *n.* a variegated glass marble. Cf. Glasser.

Glessy, *n.* a sweetmeat made with treacle. Cf. Glassey.

Glet, *n.* ooze, slime, viscid matter; phlegm.—*v.* to discharge watery serum. Cf. Glitt.

Gletty, *adj.* slimy; green with slime or ooze.

Gley, *v.* to squint; to overlook.—*n.* a squint. Cf. Glee.

Gleyd, *n.* an old horse; an old fellow. Cf. Glyde.

Gley'd, Gleyed, Gleyt, *ppl. adj.* squinting.

Gley-eyed, -e'et, *adj.* cross-eyed.

Gley-mou'd, *adj.* having a crooked mouth.

Gleytness, *n.* obliqueness; obliqueness of vision.

Glib, *adj.* cunning, sharp or slippery in one's dealings; easily swallowed.

Glib, Glibbe, *n.* a twisted lock of hair.

Glibbans, *n.* a sharp person.

Glibber-glabber, *v.* to talk idly and confusedly.—*n.* frivolous and confused talk.

Glibby, *adj.* talkative, glib.

Glibe, *n.* a piece of anything. Cf. Gleib.

Glib-gabbit, -mou'd, -tongued, *adj.* fluent, voluble, talkative.

Glibly, *adv.* smoothly.—*adj.* easily swallowed.

Glibs, *n.* a sharper.

Glid, *adj.* slippery, smooth, polished. Cf. Glad.

Glide, *ppl. adj.* squinting. Cf. Glee, Gley'd.

Glide-aver, *n.* an old horse.

Glie, *v.* to squint. Cf. Glee.

Glieb, *n.* a field; a glebe.

Gliff, *n.* a glimpse, glance, a brief view; a flash, gleam, anything appearing for a moment; an instant, a moment; a sudden fright or shock; a glow, an uneasy feeling of heat; a short sleep.—*v.* to look quickly, glance; to flash, gleam; to frighten, startle, surprise.

Gliffie, *n.* a moment, a small moment.

Gliffin, *n.* a gleam; a sudden glow or heat; a sudden sensation; an instant; a surprise, fright; something very small.

Glifring, *n.* a feeble attempt to grasp anything.

Glim, *n.* a candle, lantern, a light.

Glim, *adj.* blind.—*n.* an ineffectual attempt to lay hold of an object; a slip, tumble; a disappointment.

Glim, *n.* venereal disease.

Glime, *v.* to look askance or asquint; to glance slyly; to gaze impertinently with a side-look.—*n.* a sly glance, a sidelong look.

Glim-glam, -glaum, *n.* 'blind-man's buff.'

Glimmer, *v.* to blink, as from defective vision; to wink; with *owre,* to overlook.—*n.* mica, or 'sheep's siller.'

Glimmie, *n.* the person blindfolded in 'blind-man's buff.'

Glimp, *n.* a glimpse, glance, cursory look; the least degree. –*v.* to blink.

Glinder, *v.* to peep through half-closed eyes.

Glink, *v.* to sparkle, gleam; to cast a side-glance, catch a glimpse of; to give a fleeting glance; to jilt.—*n.* a gleam, flash; a light affection; a side-look.

Glinkit, *ppl. adj.* light-headed; giddy.

Glint, *v.* to twinkle; used of flowers: to blossom; to catch a glimpse of; to peer, peep, look furtively; to glance off at an angle.—*n.* a glitter; an instant; anything sudden; a glimpse, peep, squint. Cf. Glent.

Glintin, *n.* a gleam; early dawn.

Glintle, *v.* to sparkle, gleam, flash.

Glisk, *n.* a flash, sparkle, gleam of light; a passing glance, a transient view; an instant, moment; anything transitory or slight, a short, brisk movement; a glance at or over.

Gliskie, *n.* a rapid glance.

Gliss, *v.* to shine, gleam, glisten; to glance.

Glist, *v.* to glisten.

Glister, *n.* a clyster.

Glister, *n.* a thin covering of snow or ice. Cf. Glaister.

Glitt, *n.* slime, ooze; phlegm. Cf. Glet.

Glittilie, *adv.* slimily. Cf. Gletty.

Glittiness, *n.* ooziness.

Glitty, *adj.* oozy, slimy; having a surface so smooth as not to sharpen edge-tools.

Glive, *n.* a glove.

Gloam, *n.* the gloaming, dusk, evening.—*v.* to become dusk, to grow dark.

Gloamd, *n.* the twilight at evening.

Gloamin', *adj.* belonging to evening twilight. —*v.* to darken, become dusk. –*n.* twilight.

Gloamin'-fa', *n.* dusk; fall of evening.

Gloamin'-grey, -hour, *n.* twilight.

Gloamin'-hushed, *adj.* still as in twilight.

Gloamin'-light, *n.* twilight.

Gloamin'-shot, *n.* an interval at twilight which workmen within doors take before using lights; a twilight interview; nightfall.

Gloamin'-star, -starn, *n.* the evening star.

Gloamin'-tide, -time, *n.* twilight.

Gloamin'-tryst, *n.* an evening tryst or appointment to meet.

Gloam't, *ppl. adj.* dusk, in the state of twilight.

Gloan, *n.* substance, strength.

Gloan, Gloanin, *n.* feverish excitement.

Glock, *v.* to gulp ; to gurgle, flow through too narrow an opening.—*n.* a gulp ; a gurgle ; the noise of water, &c., flowing through too narrow an opening.

Glocken, *v.* to astound, to start from fright.—*n.* a frightened start ; a sudden shock ; an unlooked-for disaster.

Glockenin', *n.* a sudden shock from fright, a 'glocken.'

Gloff, *n.* a sudden fright ; a sudden change of atmosphere, or of temperature ; a twinge. —*v.* to take fright ; to feel a sudden shock ; to shiver or shudder from shock, as of plunging into cold water. Cf. Gliff.

Gloff, *v.* to have unsound sleep.—*n.* disturbed sleep.

Gloffel, *n.* a short sleep.

Gloffin, *n.* a short, unquiet sleep.

Glog, *v.* to gulp down ; to shake a liquid, cause it to gurgle.—*n.* a hasty draught ; a gurgling sound. Cf. Glag, Glock.

Glog, *adj.* black, dark ; appearing deep ; slow.

Gloggie, *adj.* insipid, artificial, unnatural.

Gloggie, *adj.* used of the atmosphere : dark, hazy, muggy.

Glog-rinnin, *adj.* used of a river : running slowly, dark and deep.

Gloidin, *ppl. adj.* awkward. Cf. Gloit.

Gloit, *v.* to work with the hands in any liquid, miry, or viscous substance ; to do anything dirtily or awkwardly.

Gloit, *n.* a blockhead, 'lubber,' lout ; a soft, delicate person.

Gloitry, *adj.* dirty, miry, sloppy, wet and slippery.

Gloken, *v.* to astound. Cf. Glocken.

Glomin, *n.* the gloaming.

Glonders, *n.* the sulks, a bad temper, frowns.

Gloom, *n.* in *pl.* the sulks, depression.

Gloomer, *n.* one who frowns.

Gloomer, *v.* to grope. Cf. Glaamer.

Glooming, *ppl. adj.* frowning.

Gloot, *v.* to look sullen ; to pout, sulk.—*n.* a pout, a sullen look. Cf. Gloat.

Gloove, *n.* a glove.

Glore, *n.* glory.—*v.* to glory.

Glore, *v.* to glow, shine.

Glorg, *v.* to do dirty work.—*n.* a nasty compound of any kind.

Glorgie, *adj.* bedaubed, miry, dirty ; used of the weather : sultry, warm, suffocating.

Glorious, *adj.* excited or hilarious from drink.

Glory, *int.* in *phr.* 'my glory!' an excl. of surprise.—*n.* fun, merriment, hilarity.

Glose, *n.* a specious show, a delusion. Cf. Gloze.

Glose, *n.* a blaze ; the act of warming one's self at a quick fire.—*v.* to blaze.

Gloss, *n.* a low, clear fire, without smoke or flame ; the act of warming one's self at such a fire.

Gloss, *v.* to adorn, give a bright hue.

Glossator, *n.* a glosser ; a commentator.

Glossins, *n.* flushings in the face.

Glotten, *v.* to thaw gently.—*n.* a partial thaw.

Glottenin, *n.* a partial thaw ; a slight rise in a river, with change of colour, and froth on the surface.

Glouf, *n.* a sudden blast ; a fright.—*v.* to scare. Cf. Gluff.

Glouk, *n.* the sound made by crows or ravens over carrion.

Gloum, *v.* to gloom, frown.—*n.* a frown ; the gloaming.

Glouminly, *adv.* in a frowning manner.

Glour, *v.* to stare.—*n.* a stare. Cf. Glower.

Glourer, *n.* an eye ; a starer, a merely curious onlooker at a deathbed.

Glourie, *n.* one who stares.

Glouriks, *n.* the eyes.

Gloushteroich, *n.* the dregs of soup.

Gloushteroich, *adj.* used of the weather : boisterous, gusty.

Glousterie, Glousteroich, Glousterin, *adj.* used of the weather : gusty, blustering.—*n.* boisterous, changeable weather. Cf. Glysterin.

Glout, *v.* to pout, sulk.—*n.* a pout, sullenness.

Glouten, *v.* to thaw gently.—*n.* a partial thaw. Cf. Glotten.

Glow, Glowe, *n.* a blaze.

Glower, Glowr, Glowre, *v.* to stare, gaze ; to look threateningly, scowl.—*n.* an intent or angry look ; a stare ; a frown ; a leer ; vision.

Gloweret-like, *adj.* stormy-looking.

Glowering, *ppl. adj.* vacant-looking ; overcast ; scowling ; gleaming, clear.

Glowm, *v.* to frown ; to gloom.—*n.* a frown ; the gloaming.

Gloy, *n.* straw ; cleaned straw, straw used for thatching, &c.; a superficial threshing.—*v.* to give grain a hasty threshing.

Gloyd, *n.* an old horse ; an old fellow ; a disagreeable person. Cf. Glyde.

Gloy-stane, *n.* the stone or floor on which grain is threshed.

Gloze, *n.* a specious show, delusion, mistaken idea.

Gloze, *v.* to blaze.—*n.* the clear flame of a fire. Cf. Gloss, Glose.

Glozing, *ppl. adj.* blazing.

Glozing, *ppl. adj.* flattering, fawning, deceitful. —*n.* romancing.

Gluck, *n.* a gurgling sound. Cf. Glock.

Gludder, *n.* the sound of a body falling into mud, slush, &c.—*v.* to do dirty work, or work in a dirty manner; to swallow food in a slovenly or disgusting way.

Gluddery, *adj.* wet, unctuous, slippery to the touch.

Glue, *n.* in *phr.* 'candy-glue,' candy of a sticky kind, in stalks or lumps.

Gluff, *n.* a sudden blast, gust; a whiff; a twinge; a sudden scare.—*v.* to scare, startle; to surprise. Cf. Gliff, Gloff.

Gluff, *adj.* sullen, gloomy.

Gluffin, *n.* a boisterous brawler; a frightful appearance.

Gluffus, *n.* an ugly person.

Glugger, *v.* to swallow liquids with a noise in the throat.

Gluggery, *adj.* flaccid, like young and soft animal food.

Gluive, *n.* a glove.

Glum, *adj.* sour, sulky, moody.

Glumch, *v.* to look sad or moody. Cf. Glumsh.

Glumf, *v.* to look sulky. Cf. Glump.

Glumfie, *adj.* moody; 'grumpy.' Cf. Glumpy.

Glumly, *adv.* sullenly, moodily.

Glump, Glumph, *v.* to look sulky, gloomy, discontented.—*n.* a morose or sulky person; in *pl.* the 'dumps.'

Glumpish, *adj.* sulky, surly; mopish; morose.

Glumpy, *adj.* sour-looking; 'grumpy;' low-spirited.

Glumsh, *v.* to look sulky, frown; to whine, grumble, be querulous; to be dogged.—*n.* a frown, pout, sulky look or fit; in *pl.* the 'dumps.'—*adj.* gloomy, sour-looking.

Glumsh, *v.* to swallow food with haste and noise. Cf. Glunsh.

Glumshous, *adj.* sulky.

Glunch, *v.* to frown; to grumble.—*n.* a sullen look; a dogged fit.—*adj.* sour-looking.

Glunchingly, *adv.* moodily, fretfully.

Glunchy, *adj.* morose, bad-tempered; dogged.

Glunder, *v.* to look sulky.

Glundering, *ppl. adj.* gaudy, glaring, calculated to please a vulgar taste.

Glundie, *n.* an inert, awkward lout; a fool; a sullen look; a plough-'redder,' one who clears the plough-coulter of earth, &c.—*adj.* sullen, inactive.

Glune-amie, Glunimie, *n.* a Highlander; a rough, unpolished, boorish man; a fondling term used of a cow.

Glunner, *n.* an ignorant, sour-tempered fellow; in *pl.* the sulks. Cf. Glunter.

Glunny, *n.* an inert, awkward lout. Cf. Glundie.

Glunsch, Glunsh, *v.* to look sulky. Cf. Glunch.

Glunsh, *v.* to swallow food hastily and noisily.

Glunshoch, *n.* one who has a morose look; a sulky person.

Glunt, *v.* to emit sparks. Cf. Glent.

Glunt, *v.* to look sullen; to pout, scowl.—*n.* a sour look, a suspicious look over the shoulder or sideways; in *pl.* the sulks.

Gluntch, *v.* to look sullen. Cf. Glunch.

Glunter, *n.* one who has a morose look, a sour-tempered person; in *pl.* the sulks. Cf. Glunt.

Gluntie, *n.* a sour look.

Gluntie, *adj.* tall, meagre, and haggard.—*n.* an emaciated woman.

Gluntoch, *n.* a surly, sullen, stupid person.

Glunyieman, *n.* a Highlander. Cf. Gluneamie.

Glup, *v.* to beguile, wheedle; to make a conquest of.

Glush, *n.* anything pulpy; sleet, slush; mud.

Glushie, *adj.* slushy; abounding in half-melted snow.

Glut, *n.* a drink, gulp.—*v.* to swallow with effort at one gulp.

Gluther, *v.* to swallow greedily; to splutter; to make a gurgling sound in the throat.—*n.* a rising or filling of the throat; a gurgling sound in it caused by emotion and preventing distinct articulation; an ungraceful noise made in swallowing. Cf. Gludder.

Gluthery, *adj.* used of roads: muddy. Cf. Gludder.

Gluts, *n.* two wedges used as leverage in tempering a plough; wedges used in tightening the hooding of a flail.

Glutter, *v.* to swallow quickly. Cf. Gluther.

Glutters, *n.* wet mud, soft earth, 'gutters.' Cf. Gludder.

Gly, *v.* to squint. Cf. Glee.

Glyack, *n.* the last sheaf cut in harvest, the 'clyack' sheaf.

Glybe, *n.* glebe land.

Glyde, *n.* an old horse; an old fellow; a person of disagreeable temper. Cf. Gleyd.

Glyde, *n.* an opening; a road; a glade.

Glysterie, Glysterin, *adj.* boisterous, gusty, stormy. Cf. Glousterie.

Gnaff, *n.* any small or stunted creature; a poor-looking creature.

Gnap, Gnape, *v.* to gnaw, bite, nibble; to snap at; to attempt to mince one's words affectedly; to taunt, censure snappishly.—*n.* a bite, mouthful, morsel of anything eatable; mincing, affected speech.—*adj.* hungry.

Gnapping, Gnaping, *ppl. adj.* eager, earnest; given to fault-finding and taunting.

Gnap-the-ween, *n.* very thin oatcake; any kind of very light bread.

Gnarl, *n.* biting, rough treatment.

Gnarlish, *adj.* used of temper: crusty, crabbed.

Gnarly, *adj.* twisted ; cross-grained.

Gnarr, *n.* a hard knot in wood.

Gnarr, *v.* to find fault in a snarling manner ; to quarrel.—*n.* the growl of an angry dog ; peevishness. Cf. Nyirr.

Gnash, *n.* pert, insolent talk, bluster.—*v.* to prate, give impudence. Cf. Nash.

Gnashicks, *n.* the red bear-berry.

Gnat, *v.* to gnaw ; to grind the teeth.—*n.* a bite ; a snap.

Gnatter, *v.* to grumble, worry ; to wrangle. Cf. Nyatter.

Gnattery, *adj.* ill-tempered, peevish, querulous.

Gnaw, *n.* a slight, partial thaw.

Gneck, *n.* a notch.—*v.* to cut notches.

Gneep, Gneip, *n.* a booby, ninny ; a foolish fellow.

Gnegum, *n.* a tricky disposition ; a fiery, pungent flavour in edibles.

Gneigie, *adj.* sharp-witted, ' knacky.'

Gneisle, *v.* to gnaw.

Gneut, Gneutie, *n.* a stupid person.

Gneutick, Gneutickie, *n.* a stupid person.

Gnew, *v. pret.* gnawed.

Gnib, *adj.* ready, quick, clever in action ; light-fingered ; stingy, mean ; sharp-tempered, curt ; sharp in demanding one's own ; keen of appetite.

Gnibbich, *n.* a little person of thin, sharp features and curt manners.—*adj.* mean, stingy ; curt in manners.

Gnidge, *v.* to press, squeeze ; with *off,* to rub off, to peel off by rubbing.—*n.* a squeeze. Cf. Knidge.

Gnip, *v.* to eat, crop ; to taunt, complain constantly about.—*n.* a morsel, mouthful. Cf. Nip.

Gnipick, Gnipickie, *n.* a morsel of anything edible. Cf. Nippock.

Gnipper, *n.* the smallest piece of anything edible.

Gnipper for gnapper, or **gnopper,** *phr.* the sound made by a mill in grinding ; the very smallest particle.

Gnippin, *n.* continual petty taunting.

Gnissle, *v.* to gnaw. Cf. Gneisle.

Gnorly, *adj.* twisted, knotty. Cf. Gnarly.

Go, *v.* used of animals : to graze ; to die.—*n.* distress, excitement, fuss ; a drunken frolic, ' spree.' Cf. Gae.

Goab, *n.* the worked-out part of a mine.

Goab-fire, *n.* the spontaneous ignition of small coal in a worked-out part of a mine, producing white ' damp.'

Goad, *n.* a fishing-rod. Cf. Gad.

Goadloup, *n.* the military punishment of running the gauntlet.

Goadsman, *n.* the driver of a team of oxen. Cf. Gadsman.

Goaf, *n.* a foolish person, a simpleton. Cf. Goff.

Goafish, *adj.* stupid, foolish.

Goak, *int.* an excl. of surprise, and of imprecation.

Goal, *n.* a gaol.

Goam, *v.* to pay attention to, heed, care for, take notice of ; to acknowledge by curtsy.

Goam, *v.* to gaze about wildly or idly.

Goan, *v.* to lounge.

Goan, *n.* a wooden dish for meat.

Goare, *n.* a hurt, wound.

Goarling, *n.* an unfledged bird ; anything very young. Cf. Gorlin.

Goarling-baird, *n.* the first downy hairs appearing on the chin.

Goarling-hair, *n.* the down of unfledged birds.

Go-ashores, Go-shores, *n.* better clothes than working or sea-going clothes.

Goat, *n.* a drain, ditch, gutter ; a narrow cavern or inlet into which the sea enters ; a slough, deep, miry place. Cf. Gote.

Goat-chaffer, *n.* the nightjar.

Goat's beard, *n.* vapour in the sky foreboding storm.

Goat-whey-quarters, *n.* a place of resort for the drinking of goat's-milk.

Goave, *v.* to stare idly or vacantly ; to look with a roving eye ; to look steadily with uplifted face ; to throw up and toss the head from side to side ; to gaze with fear ; to flaunt ; to play the flirt.—*n.* a broad, vacant stare.

Goave-i-th'-wind, *phr.* a vain, foolish, light-headed person.

Goavie, *int.* an excl. of surprise. Cf. Govie.

Goaving, *ppl. adj.* stupid ; staring ; coquetting ; startled ; tossing the head.

Goaving-wild, *adj.* staring stupidly ; foolishly eager.

Gob, *n.* a lump of meat, &c. ; a mouthful.

Gob, *n.* the mouth ; a beak ; a grimace.

Gobich, *n.* the goby.

Goblet, Gobblet, *n.* a cast-iron kettle.

Goch, *int.* an excl. of pain.

Gock, *n.* a deep wooden dish, a ' cogue.'

Gock, *n.* the cuckoo ; a simpleton. Cf. Gowk.

Gockie, *n.* a stupid person, a ' gawky.'

Gockie, Gockie-cog, *n.* a deep wooden dish.

Gockmin, *n.* a sentinel, watchman.

Godderlitch, *adj.* sluttish ; sanctimonious. Cf. Gotherlisch.

Godin, *n.* the smallest amount or atom, a trace.

God-left, *adj.* God-forsaken.

Godrate, *adj.* cool, deliberate.

Godrately, *adv.* coolly.

Godsend, *n.* used in Orkney and Shetland : a shipwreck ; flotsam and jetsam coming ashore ; a drove of ' ca'in whales ; ' a boat-fare.

God's-penny, *n.* earnest-money, ' arles.'

God's truth, *n.* the very truth.

Goer-bye, *n.* a passer-by.

Goff, *n.* a fool, simpleton.

Goffish, *adj.* foolish. Cf. Goafish.

Gog, *n.* the mark aimed at in playing quoits, &c.

Gogar, *n.* whey boiled with a little oatmeal, as food.

Gogar-worm, *n.* a worm of serrated form used as bait in fishing.

Gogge, *v.* to blindfold.

Goggie, *adj.* elegantly dressed.

Goggle, *n.* in *pl.* the eyes, especially when protruding ; spectacles ; blinds applied to horses that are apt to be scared.

Goggle-eyes, *n.* spectacles ; goggles worn by stone-breakers.

Goglet, Goglet-pot, *n.* a small pot with a long handle.

Gohams, *n.* bent pieces of wood on each side of a horse to support panniers, ' hames.'

Go-harvest, Goe-hairst, -harst, *n.* the latter end of summer ; the time from the end of harvest till the beginning of winter.

Goit, *n.* a young unfledged bird.

Goitling, *n.* a ' goit.'

Goke-a-day, *int.* excl. of wonder and satis-faction.

Gokman, *n.* a sentinel. Cf. Gockmin.

Golach, *n.* a beetle ; an earwig ; a centipede.

Golaichie, Golaigh, *n.* a low, short-legged hen ; a low, short-legged woman.

Golden-crest, -cuttie, *n.* the gold-crest.

Golden-grass, *n.* the seed of the crested dog's-tail grass.

Golden-maw, *n.* the glaucous gull.

Golden-wren, *n.* the gold-crest.

Golder, *n.* a shout.—*v.* to shout. Cf. Gollar, Guller.

Gold-foolyie, *n.* leaf-gold.

Goldie, *n.* the goldfinch ; the ladybird ; a cow of a light-yellow colour ; the yellow gurnard.

Goldie-duck, *n.* the golden-eye.

Gold-spink, *n.* the goldfinch. Cf. Gowd-spink.

Goles, *n.* the corn-marigold. Cf. Gool.

Goles, *n.* disguised form of ' God,' used in petty oaths. Cf. Golly.

Golinger, *n.* a contemptuous term ; a cheat. Cf. Gileynour.

Golk, *n.* the cuckoo ; a fool. Cf. Gowk.

Gollan, *n.* the marsh-marigold ; the common daisy. Cf. Gowan.

Gollar, Goller, *v.* to emit a gurgling sound ; to speak indistinctly and loudly ; to bark violently ; to growl.—*n.* a gurgling sound ; a shout ; a fierce bark. Cf. Gulder.

Gollering, *n.* a gurgling sound, as of an animal being strangled.

Gollersome, *adj.* passionate ; boisterous.

Golley, *v.* to bawl. Cf. Golly.

Gollie, *n.* bawling. Cf. Golly.

Gollies, *v.* to scold.

Gollimer, *n.* one who eats greedily.

Golling, *n.* a method of trenching moss to produce new soil.

Gollop, *v.* to gulp ; to swallow hastily.

Golly, *n.* a disguised form of ' God,' used in petty oaths. Cf. Goles.

Golly, *v.* to bawl at the top of the voice, make a loud noise ; to burst into loud weeping.—*n.* a barking or bawling noise. Cf. Gollie, Gollies.

Goloch, *n.* an earwig.

Golore, *n.* plenty. Cf. Galore.

Goloshin, Goloshan, *n.* a stupid fellow ; a ninny ; the name of a character in a ' Hogmanay' masque. Cf. Galatians.

Gomach, *n.* a fool. Cf. Gommoch.

Gome, Gom, *v.* to pay attention to. Cf. Goam.

Gomer, *n.* coursing term, used of a greyhound or a hare.

Gomeril, *n.* a gambrel.

Gomeril, Gomeral, Gommeral, *n.* a fool, blockhead.—*adj.* half-witted, stupid.

Gomf, *n.* a fool, or one who wishes to seem so. Cf. Gump, Gumphie.

Gommoch, *n.* a fool, idiot, simpleton.

Gomrell, *n.* a stupid fellow. Cf. Gomeril.

Gone, *ppl. adj.* of a woman : pregnant ; thin, wasted.—*adv.* ago, since.—*conj.* since.

Gone-away-land, *phr.* Hades.

Gone a week, month, &c., *phr.* a week, month, &c., ago.

Gone corbie, *n.* a dead man.

Gone man, *n.* a man who is ' done for.'

Goner, Gonner, *n.* a mouth disease in cattle ; a pig's snout.

Goner, *n.* a person in bad health and not likely to recover.

Gonial, *n.* a large, ill-shaped person ; a stupid fellow ; flesh of a sheep fit for food, though not killed by the knife of a butcher.

Gonial-blast, *n.* a great storm in January 1794, in the south of Scotland, destroying many sheep.

Gonk, *v.* to disappoint ; to jilt.—*n.* a dis-appointment, jilt. Cf. Gunk, Begunk.

Gonsir, *n.* a big, stupid, clumsy person. Cf. Gunsar.

Gonterniblicks, *n.* gladness.

Gonternichs, *int.* an excl.

Gonterns, Gontrans, Gontrins, Gontrum, *int.* an excl. of joyous admiration.

Gontrum-niddles, *int.* an exclamation of joy, &c.

Gonyell, *n.* a large, ill-shaped person; a stupid fellow. Cf. Gonial.

Goo, *n.* the gull; a fool.—*v.* to seduce, allure. Cf. Gow.

†Goo, *n.* taste, relish, liking, gusto; odour, smell.

Goo, *v.* used of infants: to coo.

Good, *adj.* large; long; of good birth.—*n.* wealth, substance; in *pl.* cattle, sheep; smuggled articles.—*v.* to manure. Cf. Gude.

Good cheap, *adj.* cheap.—*adv.* cheaply, gratis.

Good dame, *n.* a grandmother.

Good deed, *n.* a benefaction, a gift.

Goodin, *n.* manure; manuring.

Goodly, *adj.* godly, religious.—*adv.* well, conveniently.

Goodly-neighbour, *n.* a fairy.

Goodman, *n.* the head of a house or family; a husband; a manager, chief, overseer, head-gaoler; a tenant-farmer; a small proprietor farming his own land; a name for the devil; with *the*, a child's name for God. Cf. Gudeman.

Good neighbour, *n.* a fairy, a brownie.

Good-place, *n.* a child's name for heaven.

Goodsir, *n.* a grandfather.

Goodwife, *n.* the mistress of a house, a wife; a landlady of an inn; a female farmer, a farmer's wife. Cf. Gudewife.

Good-willer, *n.* a well-wisher.

Good-willie, *adj.* wishing well.

Goody, *n.* an old woman; a child's name for a sweet.

Goog, *n.* an unfledged bird; the young of animals; soft young meat.

Googg, *n.* a large, open, festering sore; a heavy cloud.

Gook, *n.* the cuckoo; a simpleton.

Gool, *v.* to howl.—*n.* a howl. Cf. Gowl.

Gool, Goold, *n.* the corn-marigold.

Goold, *n.* gold.—*adj.* golden.

Gooldie, *n.* the goldfinch. Cf. Goldie.

Gool-fittit, *adj.* used of fowls: having yellow legs and feet.

Goolie, *n.* a large knife.—*v.* to cut. Cf. Gully.

Gool-riding, *n.* an old custom of riding through a parish to watch against the growth of 'gools.'

Goon, *n.* a gown.

Goonie, *n.* a child's night-dress.

Goor, *n.* broken ice and half-melted snow in a thaw.—*v.* used of streams: to become choked with masses of ice and snow in a thaw.

Goose, *v.* to iron linen clothes; to use a tailor's goose; to smooth.—*n.* a large stone used in curling.

Goose-cleavers, *n.* the catch-weed or cleavers.

Goose-corn, *n.* wild oat or field brome-grass.

Goose-dub, *n.* a goose-pond.

Goose-ee, *n.* a blind, stupid eye.

Goose-girse, *n.* the soft brome-grass; the rough brome-grass.

Goose-pan, *n.* a pan for stewing a goose; the largest pot or pan used in cooking.

Goose-pear, *n.* a kind of pear.

Goose-seam, -same, *n.* goose-grease.

Goose-wings, *n.* the peculiar appearance which the foresail and mainsail of a schooner-rigged vessel assume when it is running before the wind, these sails being then spread to opposite sides.

Goosey-weasen, *n.* a goose's neck; a person's long neck.

Goosing-iron, *n.* a tailor's 'goose,' a flat-iron.

Goosy, *n.* a call to swine; a young sow. Cf. Gussie.

Gootar, *n.* a trench, drain. Cf. Gutter.

Gope, *v.* to palpitate; to pulse. Cf. Goup.

Gopin, *n.* a hand with the fingers touching the root of the thumb; a handful. Cf. Gowpen.

Gor, *int.* an excl. or oath. Cf. Gore.

Gorachen, *n.* hard work.

Goravich, *n.* uproar. Cf. Galravitch.

Gorb, *n.* an unfledged bird.

Gorb, *adj.* greedy, voracious.

Gorbal, Gorbel, *n.* an unfledged bird.

Gorbie, *n.* a raven. Cf. Corbie.

Gorbit, Gorbet, *n.* a newly-hatched bird; a child.

Gorble, *v.* to eat greedily; to swallow voraciously. Cf. Gorb.

Gorblet, *n.* an unfledged bird; a child.

Gorblet-hair, *n.* the down of unfledged birds.

Gorblin, *n.* an unfledged bird; anything very young and bare.

Gor-, Gore-crow, *n.* the carrion crow.

Gord, *v.* used of running water, &c.: to stop, be pent up. Cf. Gourd.

†Gorded, *ppl. adj.* frosted over; covered with crystallizations; benumbed. Cf. Gourd.

Gordlin, *n.* a nestling, an unfledged bird. Cf. Gorblin.

Gore, *n.* hardened rheum from the eyes; the eye. Cf. Gaar.

Gore, *int.* a disguised form of 'God,' used in exclamations and oaths.

Gore, *n.* a strip of land at the side of a field; a strip of cloth.—*v.* to plough the 'gores' of a field. Cf. Gair.

Gore-pate, *int.* an excl. Cf. Gore, Gorr.

Gorfy, *adj.* coarse in appearance.

Gorge, *v.* to squeak; to make a squelching sound, as when one walks with shoes full of water. Cf. Girg.

Gorgetches, *n.* a calf's pluck; the heart, liver, and lights.

Gorie, *int.* a disguised form of 'God,' used in expletives.

Gorkie, *adj.* nauseous, disgusting.

Gorl, *v.* to surround the thatch of a stack with straw ropes. Cf. Girl.

Gorlin, *n.* a neckcloth.

Gorlin, Gorlan, *adj.* bare, unfledged.—*n.* a nestling, unfledged bird. Cf. Goarling.

Gorlin-hair, *n.* the down of an unfledged bird. Cf. Goarling-hair.

Gorlins, *n.* a ram's testicles.

Gormaw, *n.* the cormorant ; a greedy person, a glutton.

Gorr, *int.* an excl. or oath. Cf. Gore.

Gorroch, Gorrach, *v.* to mix and spoil porridge ; to imbed in mire ; to spoil, bungle.—*n.* anything dirty and sticky ; a sloppy mess, mud ; a bungle, 'hash'; a bungler ; an untidy, slovenly worker.

Gorsh, *int.* an excl. or oath. Cf. Gosh.

Gorsk, *n.* strong, rank grass.—*v.* used of grass : to grow in luxuriant patches through cattle-droppings. Cf. Gosk.

Gorsy, *adj.* furze-clad.

Gort, *n.* a gout of blood, &c.

Gos, *n.* the goshawk. Cf. Goss.

Gosh, Goshie, *int.* a disguised form of 'God,' used in expletives. Cf. Gweeshie.

Goshen, Goshins, *int.* 'gosh !'

Gosk, *n.* chickweed.

Gosk, *n.* strong, rank grass.—*v.* used of grass : to grow in luxuriant tufts.

Gosky, *adj.* rank, coarse ; luxuriant ; used of animals : large in size, but feeble.

Goslin, *n.* an unfledged bird ; a fool.

Gospel-greedy, *adj.* fond of attending church.

Gospel-hearer, *n.* a church attender.

Gospel-hearted, *adj.* truly pious.

Gospel-kail, *n.* evangelical preaching.

Gospel-lad, *n.* a Covenanter.

Gospel-minister, *n.* an evangelical minister.

Goss, *n.* a silly, good-natured man ; a mean, griping person.

Goss, *n.* a 'gossip,' an intimate.

Goss, *n.* the goshawk.

Gossie, *n.* a 'gossip,' an intimate ; a fellow, person. Cf. Goss, Gossip.

Gossie-fain, *adj.* fond of a gossip.

Gossip, *n.* a god-parent, sponsor at baptism ; an intimate friend invited to a baptism ; a boon companion, crony.

Gossiprie, *n.* intimacy.

Gossips' wake, *n.* a gathering of friends and neighbours after the mother's recovery, to congratulate the parents, and drink to the child's prosperity.

Gossok, *n.* a term applied in derision to an old type of an inhabitant of Wigtownshire.

Go-summer, Go o' summer, *n.* the latter end of summer.

Got, Gote, *n.* a drain, a ditch ; a narrow inlet of the sea ; a slough, &c.

Gotch, *v.* to botch, mar.—*n.* a bungle, muddle.

Goth, *int.* a disguised form of 'God,' used in oaths, &c.

Gotherligh, *adj.* used of persons : confused, in disorder.

Gotherlisch, Gotherlitch, *adj.* sanctimonious, of unreal but pretentious piety; foolish, godless ; sluttish.—*n.* want of delicacy of feeling and manner.

Gothill, *int.* in *phr.* 'an' or 'in gothill,' if God will.

Gott, *n.* a drain ; a slough. Cf. Got.

†**Gou,** *n.* taste, relish ; a smell. Cf. Goo.

Gouch, *n.* a bad smell. Cf. Guff.

Goucher, *n.* a grandfather. Cf. Gutcher.

Gouck, *v.* to stare vacantly. Cf. Gouk.

Gouck, *n.* the cuckoo ; a fool, &c. Cf. Gowk.

Goud, *v. pret.* began. Cf. Begoud.

Goud, *n.* gold.—*adj.* golden.

†**Gouda,** *n.* a Dutch cheese of spherical shape.

Gouden, *adj.* golden.

Gouden-bobbed, *adj.* with golden blossoms.

Gouden-knap, *n.* a variety of pear.

Goudie, *n.* the keeper of a key of the box of a Glasgow trade incorporation, the box-master.

Goudie, *n.* a gouda-cheese. Cf. Gouda.

Goudie, *n.* a blow, stroke.

Goudie, *n.* the goldfinch. Cf. Goldie.

Goudie, *n.* in *phr.* 'heels o'er-' or 'heelster-goudie,' head over heels, topsyturvy.

Goudie, *n.* a jewel ; a fondling term of address.

Goudie, *n.* the dragonet ; the gurnard.

Goudie, *n.* the name given to a light-yellow-coloured cow.

Goudie-duck, *n.* the golden-eye duck.

Goud-links, *n.* golden locks.

Goudnie, *n.* the golden-eye.

Goudnie, *n.* the yellow gurnard.

Goudriff, *adv.* ? reverently, respectfully.

Goudspink, *n.* the goldfinch.

Goudspring, *n.* the goldfinch.

Goudy aumous, *n.* a 'gaudeamus,' a feast, a merry-making.

Gouf, *n.* a foolish person. Cf. Goff, Guff.

Gouff, *n.* a blow, stroke, 'bang'; ruin, wreck.—*v.* to strike, hit, cuff.

Gouff, *n.* a puff of wind ; a slight wind ; a whiff, smell, savour ; a bad smell. Cf. Guff.

Gouff, *v.* to laugh immoderately ; to let wind from the mouth.—*n.* a guffaw ; a loud, sudden noise ; a suppressed bark or snort. Cf. Guff.

Goufmalogie, *n.* a woollen petticoat formerly worn by women, having on its border large horizontal stripes of different colours.

Goug, *n.* a young solan goose.

Gouk, *v.* to gaze about idly or foolishly.

Gouk, *n.* the cuckoo ; a fool. Cf. Gowk.

Gouken, *n.* a handful, a 'gowpen.'

Goukmey, *n.* the gray gurnard. Cf. Goudnie.

Goul, *n.* the soul.

Goul, *v.* to howl, yell, whine ; to scold, growl, threaten ; used of wind : to blow boisterously.—*n.* a yell, howl ; a cry of indignation ; the growl or howl of a dog. Cf. Gowl.

Gould, *n.* gold.—*adj.* golden.

Gouldie, *n.* the goldfinch.

Gouldspink, *n.* the goldfinch.

†Goule, *n.* the throat, neck, gullet.

Goulie, *adj.* sulky ; scowling.

Gouling, *ppl. adj.* used of weather : stormy.

Goulkgalister, Goulkgaliter, *n.* a pedantic, conceited fellow; a simpleton ; a wanton rustic.

Goull-bane, *n.* the top of the thigh-bone as it enters the cavity in which it moves.

Goulmaw, *n.* the cormorant. Cf. Gormaw.

Goulock, *n.* a beetle ; an earwig. Cf. Golach.

Goup, *v.* to palpitate, throb, beat ; to ache.—*n.* a single beat or throb of pain.

Goup, *v.* to scoop, lave with the two hands ; to hollow out.

Goup, *v.* to gape, yawn ; to stare with open mouth, vacantly ; to gulp.—*n.* a vacant, staring person ; a fool, simpleton ; a stupid stare ; a wide-open mouth ; chatter, 'jaw'; a gulp. Cf. Gaup.

Goupen, Goupan, Goupin, *n.* the hollow of the hand in semi-globular shape to receive anything ; a handful ; a perquisite of a miller's servant in the shape of a handful of meal. Cf. Gowpen.

Gouph, *v.* to laugh boisterously. Cf. Gouff.

Goupin, *n.* the throbbing of a wound or sore.

†Gourd, *adj.* stiff, unwieldy, difficult to open or move, stiffened by exposure to the air ; used of ice : not slippery.

Gourd, *v.* used of running water : to be pent up, stop. Cf. Gord.

Gourdness, *n.* stiffness ; want of slipperiness.

Gouries, *n.* the garbage of salmon.

Gourlins, Gourlock, *n.* the root of the earth-chestnut.

Gouster, *v.* to bully ; to storm with wind and rain.—*n.* a passionate outburst of scolding ; a violent, unmanageable fellow ; a swaggerer.

Gousterous, Goustrous, *adj.* boisterous, rude, violent ; of the weather : dark, wet, blustering, stormy ; frightful.

Gousterous-looking, *adj.* stormy-looking.

Gousty, *adj.* tempestuous, stormy, gusty.

Gousty, *adj.* waste, desolate, dreary, gloomy ; ghastly, ghostly, unearthly ; haggard by age or disease ; emaciated ; pale, sickly.

†Gout, *n.* taste.

Goutcher, *n.* a grandfather. Cf. Gutcher.

Gouthart, *ppl. adj.* affrighted, scared.

Goutherfow, *adj.* amazed, terrified.

†Goutte, *n.* a drop ; a large drop of rain. Cf. Gut.

Govan, *ppl. adj.* flaunting, coquetting. Cf. Goave.

Govance, *n.* good-breeding.—*adj.* well-bred.

Govanendy, *int.* an excl. of surprise.

Gove, *v.* to move awkwardly ; to stare idly.—*n.* a vacant stare. Cf. Goave.

Govellin, *ppl. adj.* staggering, as if drunk ; hanging loosely and ungracefully ; used of the appearance of the eyes in intoxication.

Govie, *int.* an excl. of surprise.

Govie-dick, *int.* excl. of surprise.

Goving, *ppl. adj.* used of startled cattle : staring, tossing the head. Cf. Goave.

Govit, *ppl. adj.* hollowed out.

Govus, *n.* a simple, stupid person.

Gow, *n.* the gull ; a fool.—*v.* to entice, seduce ; to sway ; to bend, lead.

Gow, *n.* a halo, circle round the sun or moon, a 'brough,' portending bad weather.

Gow, *n.* in *phr.* to 'tak the gow,' to run off without paying one's rent, debts, &c.

Gow, *adj.* petted, spoiled, applied to a pampered dog.

Gowan, *n.* the buttercup.

Gowan, *n.* the generic name for the daisy ; the common or mountain daisy.—*phrs.* 'not to care a gowan,' not to care in the least ; to 'cow the gowan,' an expression of surprise, to beat everything.

Gowaned, *adj.* daisied.

Gowan-gabbit, *adj.* used of the sky : bright, fine, deceptively clear ; of the face : having much red and white, marking a delicate constitution.

Gowan-head, *n.* the head or flower of a daisy.

Gowan-shank, *n.* the stalk of a daisy.

Gowan-sparkled, *adj.* sprinkled with daisies.

Gowan-speckled, *adj.* speckled with daisies.

Gowan-tap, *n.* the flower of a daisy.

Gowany, *adj.* daisied ; bright, fair in appearance ; deceptively fine.

Gowd, *n.* gold.—*adj.* golden. Cf. Goud.

Gowdanook, *n.* the saury pike. Cf. Gowdnook.

Gowden, *adj.* golden. Cf. Gouden.

Gowdie, *n.* a jewel ; gold-cloth, gold-lace ; a term of endearment. Cf. Goudie.

Gowdie, *n.* the dragonet ; the gurnard. Cf. Goudie.

Gowdie, *n.* the goldfinch ; the ladybird. Cf. Goudie, Goldie.

Gowdie, *n.* a Dutch cheese. Cf. Gouda.

Gowdie, *n.* in *phr.* 'heels o'er gowdie,' topsy-turvy. Cf. Goudie.

Gowdie, *n.* a yellow-coloured cow. Cf. Goudie.

Gowdnie, *n.* the yellow gurnard. Cf. Gawdnie.

Gowdnie, *n.* the golden-eye duck.

Gowdnook, *n.* the saury pike.

Gowds, *n.* a term of familiarity used by old women in conversing.

Gowdspink, *n.* the goldfinch.

Gower, *v.* to induce; to tempt; to draw over.

Gowet, *ppl.* induced, persuaded. Cf. Gow.

Gowf, *n.* a bad savour affecting the throat. Cf. Gouff.

Gowfer, *n.* a golfer.

Gowff, *n.* a stroke; golf.—*v.* to strike. Cf. Gouff.

Gowff, *n.* a fool, simpleton. Cf. Goff, Guff.

Gowfin, *n.* a noisy, silly fellow, a fool.

Gowgair, *n.* a mean, greedy, selfish person.

Gow-glentie, *n.* a sharp, interesting child.

Gowishness, *n.* folly.

Gowk, *v.* to stare idly, gaze vacantly. Cf. Gouk.

Gowk, *v.* to wander up and down, knock about.

Gowk, *n.* the cuckoo; a fool, blockhead; a clumsy person, a clown.

Gowk and titling, *n. phr.* the cuckoo and any bird of the 'tit' species; the young cuckoo and its foster-mother; an incongruous pair; a pair of inseparable friends.

Gowk-bear, *n.* the golden maiden-hair.

Gowken, *n.* a handful. Cf. Gowpen.

Gowkit, *adj.* foolish, stupid, awkward; used of a woman: light-headed, giddy.

Gowkitly, *adv.* stupidly, foolishly.

Gowk-like, *adj.* like a fool.

Gowkoo, *n.* the cuckoo.

Gowkoo-clock, *n.* a cuckoo-clock.

Gowk's errand, *n.* a fool's errand.

Gowkship, *n.* a fool.

Gowk's hose, *n.* the Canterbury bell.

Gowk's meat, *n.* the wood-sorrel.

Gowk's shillins, *n.* the yellow rattle.

Gowk's spit, spittle, *n.* the froth on plants discharged by the insect Cicada.

Gowk's-thimmles, -thummles, *n.* the harebell.

Gowkston, *n.* in *phr.* to 'make John Gowkston of,' to make a cuckold of.

Gowk-storm, *n.* a storm of several days at the end of April or the beginning of May; an evil or obstruction of short duration.

Gowky, *n.* a fool.

Gowl, *n.* a hollow between hills, a defile; a gap, opening.

Gowl, *n.* anything large and empty.

Gowl, *v.* to howl, yell, growl; used of wind: to blow fitfully with a hollow sound.—*n.* a howl, yell, growl. Cf. Goul.

Gowling, *ppl. adj.* howling, growling; boisterous, stormy; sulky, scolding. — *n.* loud and angry scolding.

Gowlock, Gowlick, *n.* an earwig; a beetle. Cf. Golach.

Gowls, *n.* the private parts.

Gowlsome, *adj.* large.

Gowly, *adj.* howling, growling; boisterous; scolding.—*n.* a fretful, crying child.

Gowmeril, *n.* a stupid person. Cf. Gomeril.

Gown-alane, *adj.* without a cloak or upper covering for a gown; dowerless.

Gownie, *n.* a child's night-dress. Cf. Goonie.

Gown-men, *n. togati.*

Gow'ny, *adj.* daisy-clad.

Gowp, *v.* to gulp; to gape, yawn; to gaze vacantly.—*n.* a mouthful; a vacant stare; a staring person, fool, simpleton. Cf. Gaup.

Gowp, *v.* to throb, palpitate; to ache.—*n.* a throb of pain. Cf. Goup.

Gowp, *n.* in *phr.* a 'gowp in the lift,' a squint.

Gowpen, Gowpan, Gowpin, *n.* the hollow of the hand; the two hands held together so as to form a bowl; a handful; specially a double handful; a great quantity, an indefinite amount.—*v.* to lift or ladle out with the two hands extended and united; to deal out in handfuls. Cf. Goupen.

Gowpin, *n.* the throbbing of a wound or sore. Cf. Gowp.

Gowpinfu', *n.* as much as the two hands can hold when in a concave form.

Goupinfu' o' a' thing, *phr.* a contemptuous term to designate one who is a medley of every absurdity.

Gowrie, *n.* in *phr.* 'heels o'er gowrie,' topsy-turvy. Cf. Goudie.

Gowries, *n.* the garbage of salmon. Cf. Gouries.

Gowst, *v.* to speak loudly or angrily; to threaten. Cf. Gouster.

Gowstly, *adj.* ghastly.

Gowsty, *adj.* waste, desolate; used of persons: pale, sickly. Cf. Gousty.

Gowsty, *adj.* tempestuous, gusty. Cf. Gousty.

Goy, *v.* to allure, seduce, decoy. Cf. Gow.

Goyit, *ppl. adj.* foolish, silly.

Goyler, *n.* the Arctic gull.

Gozen, *v.* to dry in the sun. Cf. Gizzen.

Grab, *v.* to seize with violence or unfair means; to cheat; to filch.—*n.* a grasp, clutch; the number of things seized; an advantageous bargain; a grasping, miserly person.

Grab, *n.* food, provisions.

Grabbin', *ppl. adj.* inclined to cheat.

Grabble, *v.* to grope with the hands for stones on the ground.

Grabbles, *n.* a disease of cows affecting their limbs and rendering them unable to walk.

Grabby, *adj.* greedy, avaricious, grasping.

Grace, *n.* good qualities, virtue.

Grace an' growin', *phr.* a good wish for a new-born child, spiritual and temporal prosperity.

Grace-drink, *n.* a drink taken after grace at the close of a meal.

Gracie, *adj.* well-behaved; devout, religious.

Gracie, *n.* a pig, 'grice'; a fat, ungraceful woman of loose character.

Gracious, *adj.* pleasant, friendly; agreeable.

Graddan, *n.* a coarse kind of oatmeal, prepared by scorching grain in a pot over the fire, and then grinding it in a hand-mill; coarse snuff in large grains, made from toasted tobacco-leaves.—*v.* to parch grain by scorching the ear.

Grade, *v.* to make ready. Cf. Graid.

Graduality, *n.* in *phr.* 'by a graduality,' gradually.

Graduwa, Gradawa, *n.* a graduate; a doctor with a medical degree.

Grafel, *v.* to grovel.

Graff, *n.* a grave; a ditch, trench, hole; the sea-bottom.

Graff, *adj.* coarse, vulgar; gross, obscene. Cf. Groff.

Graff, *n.* a graft.

Graffstane, *n.* a gravestone.

Graft, *v.* to grapple, wrestle.

Graft, *n.* a grave.

Grafter, *n.* an engrafter.

Graicie, *n.* a pig; a fat, ungraceful woman of loose character. Cf. Gracie.

Graid, *v.* to prepare, make ready, 'graith.'

Graidly, *adj.* orderly; proper, fit.—*adv.* decently; thoroughly.

Graig, *v.* to belch; to make a noise in the throat; to hesitate in speech, grumble about; to utter an inarticulate sound of contempt or scorn; to find fault.

Graigin, *n.* hesitation.

Grain, *n.* a branch of a tree; a branch of a river, of a valley or ravine; the prong of a fork.

Grain, *n.* a particle; a little bit; in *pl.* the refuse of malt, used for feeding cattle, 'draff.'

Grain, *v.* to groan.—*n.* a groan.

Grainer, *n.* a tanner's or skinner's knife for taking hair off skins.

Graintal-man, *n.* the keeper of a granary, a 'girnel-man.' Cf. Grintal-man.

Grainter, *n.* a 'girnel-man.' Cf. Grinter.

Graip, *n.* a three- or four-pronged fork, used in farming and gardening operations.

Graip, *v.* to gripe; to grope; to cross-examine.

Graiper, *n.* a blind man, one who gropes.

Grait, *n.* a grating.

Graith, *v.* to make ready for use, equip; to steep in a ley of stale urine for bleaching.—*n.* accoutrements; clothes, furniture; equipment; harness for horses; apparatus, tools, machinery, &c.; substance, wealth; stuff, material; company, companions; a lather for washing clothes; stale urine, used for washing.

Graithing, *n.* any kind of equipment, furnishing, provision, or preparation; vestments.

Gralloch, *v.* to disembowel the carcass of a deer, &c. Cf. Groilach.

Gram, *n.* anger, passion.

†Gramacie, *int.* 'gramercie,' 'many thanks.'

†Gramarie, *n.* magic.

†Gramashes, Gramashons, *n.* gaiters reaching to the knees; riding-hose.

Gramloch, *adj.* avaricious, grasping.

Gramlochlie, *adv.* graspingly.

Gramlochness, *n.* a very worldly disposition.

Grammar, Grammarian, *n.* a grammar-school boy.

Grammar-folk, *n.* educated people.

Grammaticals, *n.* grammar.

Grammaw, *n.* a voracious eater, a greedy person.

Grammle, *v.* to scramble.

†Gramoches, *n.* riding-hose. Cf. Gramashes.

†Gramowrie, *n.* magic. Cf. Gramarie.

Grampus, *n.* an ignoramus; a greedy fellow.

Gramshoch, *adj.* used of grain, &c.: coarse, rank; of the sky: heavy, lowering, portending heavy snow or rain.—*n.* an appearance in the sky portending snow, &c.

Gramultion, *n.* common-sense, 'gumption.'

Gran, *n.* a grandmother.

Gran, *v. pret.* ground.

Grand, Gran', *adj.* capital, first-rate, excellent; eloquent; used of the weather: fine; showily dressed.—*adv.* grandly, finely.

Grandam, *n.* a grandmother.

Grand-bairn, *n.* a grandchild.

Grand-dad, -daddy, *n.* a grandfather.

Grandery, *n.* grandeur, display.

Grandey, Grandie, *n.* a grandfather.

Grandgore, *n.* venereal disease.

Grand-gutcher, *n.* great-grandfather; ancestor.

Grandsher, *n.* a great-grandfather.

Grane, *n.* a branch; the fork of a river, the branch of a valley. Cf. Grain.

Grane, *v.* to groan.—*n.* a groan.

Grange, *n.* a barn or granary; the granary of a religious house.

Graniean, *n.* crying or screaming; a prolonged scream.

Grannam, Grannum, *n.* a grandmother.

Granny, *n.* a grandmother; an old woman; an old, tough hen; a grandfather.

Granny moil, *n.* a very old, false, flattering woman.

Granny's mutches, *n.* the columbine.

Grant, *v.* to consent.

Grant, *v.* to grunt, moan.

Grap, Grape, *v.* to grope; to examine; to search.

Grape, *n.* a three- or four-pronged fork used in farming and gardening.

Graper, *n.* a blind man, one who gropes his way.

Grapple, *v.* to drag for dead bodies in water. —*n.* a grip in wrestling.

Grapple-airn, *n.* a grappling-iron.

Grappling, *n.* a method of catching salmon.

Grapploch, *v.* to grasp, seize.

Grapus, *n.* a hobgoblin; the devil.

Grashloch, Grashlagh, *adj.* stormy, boisterous, blustering.

Grass, *v.* to pasture; to graze; to turn out of office. Cf. Gerse.

Grassum, *n.* a payment to a landlord by a tenant on entering a farm.

Grat, *v. pret.* wept.

Grat, Grate, *n.* a grating.

Grate, *adj.* grateful; friendly; on terms of intimacy.

Grate, *v.* to annoy, irritate; to hurt, grieve; to grate upon.

Grathe, *v.* to make ready. Cf. Graith.

Gratification, *n.* a reward, a 'tip,' a douceur.

Gratify, *v.* to recompense, to 'tip,' give a gratuity, requite; in *pass.* to receive a gratuity.

Gratis, Gratus, *adj.* gratuitous.

Graulse, *n.* a young salmon. Cf. Grawl.

Grauvat, *n.* a cravat. Cf. Gravat.

Gravaminous, *adj.* serious, of grave import; grievous, burdensome, irritating.

Gravat, *n.* a cravat; a knitted woollen comforter for the neck.

Grave, *n.* a pit or hollow.—*v.* to dig ground with a spade; to dig for shellfish in the sand; to bury, inter persons.

Gravel, *v.* to embarrass, confuse, bring to a standstill.

Gravestane-gentry, *n.* the dead and buried.

Graveyaird-chorus, *n.* a cough symptomatic of approaching death.

Graveyaird-deserter, *n.* a sickly person who lingers long.

Gravitch, *v.* to gad about in a dissipated way; to 'gilravage.'

Grawl, *n.* a young salmon, a grilse. Cf. Graulse.

Grawl, *v.* to grope, search for.

Gray, *n.* a slight breath of wind; a taste, 'nip,' whiff of spirits; a drubbing, thrashing.

Gray, *n.* an arithmetic-book in use about the middle of the 19th century, so named from its author.

Gray, *adj.* sombre, sad, disastrous.—*n.* morning twilight; evening twilight; a badger; in *pl.* a dish of 'kale' and cabbage beaten together.—*v.* to dawn.

Gray-beard, *n.* a large earthenware jar for holding liquor, &c.

Gray bread, *n.* coarse bread made of rye or oats.

Gray-corn, *n.* light corn.

Gray-crow, *n.* the hooded crow.

Gray-dark, *n.* dusk.

Gray daylight, *n.* dawn.

Gray diver, *n.* the red-breasted merganser.

Gray duck, *n.* the wild duck.

Gray fish, *n.* the fry of the coal-fish; the coal-fish.

Gray folk, *n.* the fairies.

Gray gate, *n.* an evil course, a bad end.

Gray geese, *n.* large boulders on the surface of the ground.

Gray groat, *n.* a silver groat, a fourpenny-piece.

Gray heads, *n.* heads of gray-coloured oats, growing among others of another colour.

Gray heads, *n.* coal-fish of the size and firmness of haddocks.

Gray hen, *n.* the female blackcock.

Gray-jar, -jug, *n.* a 'gray-beard,' whisky-jar.

Gray-lennart, -linnet, -lintie, *n.* the linnet.

Gray ling, *n.* the coal-fish.

Gray lord, *n.* a fully-grown coal-fish.

Gray mare, *n.* a wife who rules her husband.

Gray meal, *n.* oatmeal.

Gray oats, *n.* a kind of oats yielding a good crop on thin, gravelly soil.

Gray paper, *n.* brown packing-paper.

Gray-pig, *n.* a 'gray-beard,' whisky-jar.

Gray plover, *n.* the knot.

Gray podley, *n.* the coal-fish.

Gray scool, *n.* a particular shoal or 'school' of salmon.

Gray thrush, *n.* the fieldfare.

Gray yogle, *n.* the short-eared owl.

Greaf, *n.* a grave; a trench. Cf. Graff.

Grean, *n.* the muzzle or upper-lip of cattle, pigs, &c.

Greasehood, *n.* a long, shallow, iron vessel for melting tallow.

Greaser, *n.* a thrashing, beating. Cf. Greezer.

Greasy, *adj.* used of roads: slippery from mud or wet; of the sky: dim, misty, portending rain.

Great, *adj.* of large dimension, of large build; pregnant; full, overflowing with emotion, ready to weep; used of a river: flooded, swollen; boastful, vain.—*n.* piece-work; sum total, gross amount. Cf. Grit.

Great, *adj.* familiar, friendly. Cf. Grate.

Greatably, *adv.* greatly, much.

Great-bred, *adj.* high-bred.

Great-ewe, *n.* a ewe big with young.

Great-hearted, *adj.* having a full heart, ready to cry.

Great-line, *n.* a line used in catching fish of large size.

Greatness, *n.* width, girth, circumference of a body.

Great-printed, *adj.* having large type.

Great whaup, *n.* the French curlew.

Greave, *n.* a farm overseer. Cf. Grieve.

Grecie, *n.* a little pig. Cf. Gracie.

Gredden, *n.* a coarse kind of oatmeal.—*v.* to scorch corn. Cf. Graddan.

Greddon, *n.* the sweepings of a peat-stack or peat-box; the remains of fuel.

†Gree, *n.* the first place, palm, prize, highest honours; vogue, celebrity; a gradation.

Gree, *n.* tinge, dye; ichor from an animal's sore; the fat exuding from boiling fish.

†Gree, *n.* favour, loving-kindness.

Gree, *v.* to agree, come to an agreement; to reconcile, arrange.

Greeable, *adj.* harmonious; living in peace and goodwill; kind, obliging.

Greeance, *n.* concord, agreement; the first of the festivities incident to a fisher's bridal, when the betrothal took place formally in presence of parents and friends.

Gree'd, *ppl. adj.* boiled so as to exude fat.

Gree'd, *ppl. adj.* agreed, reconciled.

Greed, *v.* to covet.—*n.* covetousness.

Greedy gled, *n.* the kite; a term of disparagement for a grasping person; a children's game. Cf. Gled, Gledwylie.

Greek, *n.* in *phr.* to 'become short of the Greek,' to become speechless.

Greek, *n.* daybreak.

Greek, *n.* the grain or peculiar distinguishing texture or quality of a stone.

Greement, *n.* agreement, concord.

Green, *v.* to long for, yearn after.

Green, *adj.* young, vigorous; fresh, not dry; simple, inexperienced; immature; unseasoned; fresh, unsalted; raw, mild, rainy, without frost or snow; used of a grave: recently opened.—*n.* a bleaching-ground, lawn; grass-land; the sods that cover a grave.—*v.* to grow green.

Green-back, *n.* the viviparous blenny.

Green-bone, *n.* the gar-pike or sea-needle; the viviparous blenny.

Green-brees, *n.* a cesspool; a stagnant pool beside a dunghill.

Green coaties, *n.* fairies.

Green corn, *n.* corn sown with vetches for green fodder in summer.

Green cow, *n.* a cow recently calved.

Green crop, *n.* a turnip-crop.

Greeney, *n.* the greenfinch.

Green gaisling, *n.* a foolish person, a 'goose.'

Green-goose, *n.* a young goose.

Green gown, *n.* the loss of virginity in the open air; sod, turf on a grave.

Green grass, *n.* a children's singing game.

Green horn, *n.* a horn-spoon of greenish colour.

Green-horned, *adj.* simple, silly, foolish.

Greenichy, *adj.* greenish.

Greening, *ppl. adj.* becoming green.

Green kail, *n.* plain green colewort.

Green-kail-worm, *n.* a green caterpillar; a person of puny appearance or girlish look.

Greenland dove, *n.* the black guillemot.

Green-lennart, -linnet, -lintie, -lintwhite, *n.* the greenfinch.

Green milk, *n.* the milk of a newly-calved cow.

Green-milk-woman, *n.* a cow recently calved.

Green sloke, *n.* the oyster-green or sea-lettuce.

Green Tables, *n.* the Court of Session.

Green-wife, *n.* a female greengrocer.

Green yair, *n.* a species of pear.

Greep, *n.* a small trench for draining a field; an open drain in a cowhouse for carrying off dung and water, lying between two rows of stalls. Cf. Gruip, Grip, Groop.

†Greese, *n.* a step.

Greeshoch, Greeshough, *n.* a red, glowing, flameless fire; red-hot embers; a glowing affection.

Greesome, *adj.* gruesome.

Greet, *v.* to cry, weep, lament.—*n.* a fit of weeping; a tear, sob, whine.

Greet, *adj.* great. Cf. Great.

Greet, *n.* the peculiar distinguishing texture of a stone. Cf. Greek.

Greetie, *n.* a child's short cry or whimper.

Greetin', *n.* crying, tears.

Greetin'-cheese, *n.* a cheese from which oily matter oozes.

Greetin'-faced, *adj.* looking as if ready to cry, puling.

Greetin' fu, *adj.* maudlin drunk, at the tearful stage of drunkenness.

Greetin'-meetin', *n.* the last meeting of a town-council, &c., before new members are elected; a farewell meeting.

Greetin-washin, *n.* the last washing a servant does before leaving her 'place.'

Greety, *n.* in *phr.* 'to be on the greety,' to be always crying.

Greezer, *n.* a thrashing, a beating. Cf. Greaser, Creesh.

Gregory, *n.* Gregory's powder.

Greice, *n.* a pig. Cf. Grice.

Greik, *n.* daybreak.

Greim, Greme, *n.* soot, grime.—*v.* to begrime.

Grein, *v.* to long for. Cf. Green.

Greit, *v.* to cry, weep. Cf. Greet.

Greking, *n.* daybreak.

Gress, *n.* grass.

Gressum, *n.* a 'grassum' paid by a tenant to a landlord.

Greth, *n.* harness; soapsuds. **Cf.** Graith.

Grett, *adj.* great.

Grettin, *ppl.* wept.

Grettlin, *n.* a fishing-line. Cf. Great-line.

Grew, *n.* a greyhound.

Grew, *adj.* gray.

Grew, *v.* to shiver.—*n.* a shiver.—*adj.* horrible. Cf. Grue.

Grewan, Grewhund, Grew'n, *n.* a greyhound.

Grewing, *n.* a shivering; an aguish feeling of cold.

Grewse, *v.* to shiver with cold, ague. Cf. Groose.

Grewsome, *adj.* gruesome.

Grey, Grey dog, *n.* a greyhound. Cf. Grew.

Grey-grooning, *ppl. adj.* hunting with greyhounds.

Gribble, *v.* to feel with the fingers, make a manual examination.

Grice, *n.* a young pig.

Grice-mites, *n.* small potatoes for feeding pigs.

Grice-pan, *n.* a pan or pot for boiling pigs' meat.

Grice-sty, *n.* a pig-sty.

Griddled, *ppl. adj.* completely entangled; nonplussed.

†Grie, *n.* a gradation; a prize. Cf. Gree.

Grien, *v.* to long for. Cf. Green.

Grieshoch, Grieshach, *n.* a red, flameless fire. Cf. Greeshoch.

Grieve, *n.* a farm-overseer, or foreman.—*v.* to act as 'grieve.'

Grieveship, *n.* the situation occupied by a 'grieve.'

Grill, *v.* to shiver, thrill. Cf. Girl.

Grime, *n.* coal-dust, soot, smoke.—*v.* to sprinkle, to cover thinly.

Grimes-dike, *n.* a ditch made by magic.

Grimie, *adj.* swarthy in complexion; blackened with soot.

Griming, *n.* a sprinkling.

Grimly, *adj.* grim, terrible.

Grin, *n.* a snare; a noose of wire or hair for catching trout, &c. Cf. Girn.

Grind, *ppl. adj.* ground.

Grind, *v.* to study hard; to prepare a student for examination; used of a cat: to purr.

Grindable, *adj.* used of grain: fit for grinding. Cf. Grundable.

Grinder, *n.* a hard student; a student's 'coach.'

Grinstane, *n.* a grindstone.

Grinstane-ways, *adv.* like a grindstone.

Grintal-man, *n.* the keeper of a granary. Cf. Graintal-man.

Grinter, Grinter-man, *n.* one who had charge of a laird's granary.

Grinwan, *n.* a rod or stick with a hair-noose for catching trout. Cf. Girn, Grin.

Grip, *n.* the trench behind cattle in a cowshed, for dung; a furrow or drain for draining a field. Cf. Groop.

Grip, *v.* to grasp with the arms, embrace, seize; to apprehend, arrest; to catch after pursuit or in a trap; to search, feel with the hands.—*n.* a seizure; an embrace; a struggle; intelligent comprehension; in *pl.* a sharp pain; colic; a wrestling; blows.

Gripe, *v.* to grip.

Gripper, *n.* a midwife; in *pl.* antennæ; nippers, a shoemaker's tool.

Grippie, *n.* a grasp of the hand.

Gripping, *n.* a disease of sheep disabling them from moving the neck but in one way. —*ppl. adj.* avaricious, grasping.

Grippit, *ppl. adj.* greedy, grasping; sprained.

Gripple, *adj.* griping, grasping, miserly.

Grippy, *adj.* disposed to defraud; greedy, close-fisted; griping.

Grisk, *adj.* greedy, avaricious.

Griskin, *n.* a young pig. Cf. Grice.

Grisle, *n.* gristle; a quill-pen; the throat. Cf. Girsle.

Grisly, *adj.* gristly, full of gristles.

Grisset, *n.* a long, shallow, iron vessel for melting tallow. Cf. Greasehood.

Grist, *n.* size, measurement, texture, thickness of anything, grain of wood, &c. Cf. Girst.

Grist, *n.* the multure or fee paid in kind at a mill for grinding.—*v.* to grind and dress grain. Cf. Girst.

Grister, *n.* one who brings grist to a mill.

Grit, Grite, *adj.* great; overflowing with emotion; ready to cry; swelled with rain; pregnant. Cf. Great.

Grit, *adj.* intimate. Cf. Grate.

Grit, *n.* a grinding sound; a gnashing of teeth; the grain of stones.

Grithe, *n.* girth.

Grit-hearted, *adj.* ready to cry, having a full heart.

Gritness, *n.* width, girth, circumference. Cf. Greatness.

Grit-yowe, *n.* a gravid ewe.

Grizzie, *n.* Grizzel, Griselda, the name often given to a cow.

†Grizzle, *n.* a gooseberry. Cf. Grozer, Groset.

Groak, *v.* to look at one watchfully and suspiciously; to whimper, cry for anything.

Groaning-malt, -maut, *n.* ale brewed on occasion of a confinement.

Groatie, *adj.* made of groats.

Groatie, Groatie-buckie, *n.* a species of cowrie-shell found about John o' Groat's.

Grobble, *v.* to swallow hastily and greedily. Cf. Grouble.

Groff, *adj.* large, coarse, rough, thick; coarse-featured; used of language: coarse, vulgar, obscene, gross.

Grofflins, *adv.* prone, on one's face. Cf. Groufflins.

Groff-meal, *n.* coarse, large-grained meal.

Groff-write, *n.* large text in handwriting.

Groilach, *n.* the intestines of a deer. Cf. Gralloch.

Grole, *n.* porridge, gruel. Cf. Growl.

Gromish, *v.* to crush severely parts of the body.

Groncie, *n.* anything large or fine of its kind.

Grone, *n.* a pig's snout.

Groo, *v.* to shudder, shiver.—*adj.* ugly; horrid. Cf. Grue.

Groo, *n.* water partly congealed.—*v.* to choke up water by half-congealed ice. Cf. Grue.

Groof, *n.* the belly. Cf. Grouf.

Groogle, *v.* to disorder, disfigure by much handling. Cf. Gruggle.

Grool, *n.* a stone bruised to dust; refuse; a kind of moss beaten into peat.—*v.* to bruise to dust; to crush in battle.

Groop, *n.* an open drain in a cowhouse floor for dung and urine. Cf. Grip.

Grooschin, **Grooshan**, *n.* any disgusting liquid or viscous stuff. Cf. Groushan.

Groose, *v.* to shudder, shiver; to be chill or aguish. Cf. Growze.

Groosh, *adj.* excellent.

Groosie, *adj.* used of the face: coarse of skin, greasy.—*n.* a big, fat, awkward person.

Groot, *n.* the refuse of fish-livers after the oil is extracted; any evil-smelling thing. Cf. Grute.

Grooze, *v.* to shudder. Cf. Growze.

Groozle, *v.* to breathe with difficulty; to speak huskily. Cf. Gruzzle.

Groozlins, *n.* intestines.

Gropsey, *n.* a glutton.

Gropus, *n.* a stupid person.

Grose, *v.* to graze, rub off the skin; to rub off the sharp edge of a tool.

†**Grose**, **Groser**, **Groset**, *n.* a gooseberry.

Grosie, *adj.* of coarse, greasy face.—*n.* a big, fat, clumsy woman. Cf. Groosie.

Gross, *v.* to total, to amount to.

†**Grosser**, **Grossart**, **Grosset**, *n.* a gooseberry.

Grosset-buss, *n.* a gooseberry-bush.

Grotty, *adj.* made or consisting of groats. Cf. Groatie.

Grou, **Groue**, *adj.* ugly, misgrown; horrid.— *n.* a shivering, horror. Cf. Grue.

Grouble, *v.* to swallow hastily. Cf. Grobble.

Grouf, **Grouff**, *n.* the front of the body, especially of the stomach.—*v.* to lie flat on the face or prone.

Grouf, *adj.* large, thick, coarse; vulgar, obscene. Cf. Groff.

Grouff, *v.* to sleep in a restless manner; to

breathe heavily; to snore, grunt.—*n.* a short, restless sleep; a sleep with a short, noisy snore.

Groufflins, *adv.* prone.

Grougrou, *n.* the corn-grub.

Grouk, *n.* to become enlivened after sleep.

Grouk, *v.* to overlook watchfully and sus- piciously. Cf. Groak.

Grounch, *v.* to grunt like a pig; to growl, grumble; to give a droning sound.—*n.* a grunt, growl; the droning sound of a bag- pipe; a grumble.

Ground, *n.* a grave, a 'lair,' belonging to a person or family; a farm; the bottom of anything.—*v.* to bring to the ground; to strengthen. Cf. Grun.

Ground ebb, *n.* extreme low water; the lower part of the foreshore.

Groundie-swallow, *n.* groundsel.

Ground-lair, *n.* the burial-ground pertaining to a family or person.

Ground-maill, *n.* the duty or fee paid for the right of interment in a churchyard.

Ground-master, *n.* a landlord.

Ground-rotten, *n.* the brown rat.

Grounds, *n.* refuse of flax.

Ground-sill, **-sel**, *n.* the threshold of a house; a door-sill of wood or stone.

Ground-stane, *n.* a foundation-stone; a basis, foundation.

Ground-wa-stane, *n.* the foundation-stone of a wall.

Ground-wren, *n.* the willow-warbler.

Grounge, *v.* to look sullen; to grumble, &c. Cf. Grounch.

Grouse, *v.* to shiver; to be chill. Cf. Growze.

Groushan, *n.* any disgusting liquid or semi- liquid substance. Cf. Grooschin.

Grousome, *adj.* gruesome; very uncomely.

Grousy, *adj.* shivering with cold. Cf. Growze.

Grousy, *adj.* having a coarse and greasy skin. Cf. Groosie.

Grout, *n.* the refuse of fish-livers after the oil has been melted out; any dirty, ill-smelling, oily substance. Cf. Grute.

Grouty, *adj.* full of sediment, muddy; some- what rough; rough in manners, rustic, un- polished.

Grovel, *v.* to grope in a stooping posture.

Grow, *n.* growth; a crop.—*adj.* favourable to growth.

Grow, **Growe**, *v.* to shiver, shudder. Cf. Grue.

Growble, *v.* to swallow hastily. Cf. Grobble.

Grow-grey, *adj.* becoming gray.—*n.* clothes made of wool of the natural colour.

Grow-grey wool, *n.* wool of the natural colour.

Growing, *n.* growth; produce.

Growk, *v.* to overlook watchfully; to grudge; to grumble. Cf. Groak.

Growl, *n.* a grumbler.

Growl, *n.* oatmeal porridge. Cf. Gruel.

Growp, *n.* a greedy person.

Growse, *v.* to shiver.—*n.* a chill. Cf. Growze.

Growshie, *adj.* favourable for vegetation.

Growsin, *n.* a shivering fit; the feeling of the skin when chilled.

Growsome, *adj.* gruesome.

Growth, *n.* an excrescence on the body; full growth, maturity.

Growthilie, *adv.* luxuriantly.

Growthiness, *n.* luxuriance, fertility.

Growthy, *adj.* well-grown, tall; luxuriant, fertile; growing fast and large; favourable for vegetation.

Grow-weather, *n.* weather good for vegetation.

Growy, *adj.* promoting growth and vegetation.

Growze, *v.* to shiver, tremble; to have a chill before an ague-fit.—*n.* a chill, a shivering-fit, a cold, aguish feeling.

†Grozart, Grozel, Grozer, Grozet, Grozzle, *n.* a gooseberry. Cf. Grose.

Grozen, *v.* to crush, bruise.

Grozle, *v.* to breathe with difficulty. Cf. Gruzzle.

Gru, *n.* half-frozen water. Cf. Grue.

Gru, *n.* a particle, an atom.

Gruan, Gruant, *n.* a greyhound. Cf. Grewan.

Grub, *n.* food.

Grub, *v.* to toil for; to grasp at parsimoniously.—*n.* a greedy or stingy person.

Grubbing, *ppl. adj.* grasping. greedy.

Grubby, *adj.* dirty, grimy.

Grudge, *v.* to murmur at, bear a grudge against.

Grudge, *v.* to squeeze, press down; with *up*, to press up; used of water checked in its course, or ice with water swelling underneath: to rise, to bulge up.

Grudgeful, *adj.* unforgiving, bearing malice.

Grue, *v.* to shudder with fear or repulsion; used of the flesh: to creep; to feel chilled; to sigh or groan like wind before a storm. —*n.* a shiver, tremor; a feeling of horror. —*adj.* afraid, suspicious of danger; horrible, frightful.

Grue, *n.* half-frozen water; floating snow or ice.—*v.* with *up*, used of water: to be choked up with floating snow or melting ice.

Grue, *n.* a greyhound.

Grueing, *n.* a shuddering repulsion or fear; an aguish sensation of cold.

Gruel, *n.* oatmeal porridge.

Gruel-tree, *n.* a porridge-stick, 'spurtle.'

Grufe, *n.* the front of the body. Cf. Grouf.

Grufe, *v.* to sleep restlessly. Cf. Gruff.

Grufeling, *ppl. adj.* closely wrapped up and comfortable in a lying posture; used in ridicule.

Grufelins, *adv.* prone, on one's face. Cf. Groufflins.

Gruff, *v.* to sleep restlessly; to snore.—*n.* a short, restless sleep. Cf. Grouf.

Gruff, *n.* a short, thick, well-dressed man.

Gruff, *adj.* used of the voice: hoarse, rough.

Gruff, *n.* the front of the body. Cf. Grouf.

Gruffer, *n.* a grandfather.

Grufflins, *adv.* prone. Cf. Groufflins.

Gruggle, *v.* to put out of order by much handling. Cf. Groogle.

Grugous, *adj.* grim, grizzly.

Gruilch, *n.* a thick, squat, fat person or animal. Cf. Grulsh.

Gruilchin, Gruilchinie, *n.* a very thick, squat, fat person or animal.

Gruinnich, *n.* disgust, repulsion.—*v.* to disgust.

Gruip, *n.* a cow-house drain. Cf. Groop.

Gruishack, *n.* a red-hot, flameless fire. Cf. Greeshoch.

Gruize, *v.* to shiver; to be chill. Cf. Growze.

Grule, *n.* a mixture of fluid and solid parts in an effusion from an old wound.

Grull, *v.* to bruise to dust.—*n.* a stone bruised to dust. Cf. Grool.

Grullion, *n.* a hotch-pòtch; a mixture of various foods.

Grulsh, Grulch, *n.* a thick, squat, fat person or animal. Cf. Gruilch.

Grulshy. *adj.* clumsy, awkward, coarsely grown.

Grumly, *adj.* fault-finding, irritable, given to grumbling; surly; grim.

Grumly, *adj.* thick, muddy, full of dregs; gravelly; unpleasant; unsociable; not affable.

Grumly-like, *adj.* forbidding in manner and look.

Grummle, *v.* to grumble; to grudge, have a spite against.—*n.* a grudge, spite; a quarrel, misunderstanding; a grumble.

Grummle, Grummel, *n.* crumbs, fragments; dregs, mud.—*v.* to make muddy or turbid.

Grummlie, Grummely. *adj.* thick, muddy, 'grumly.'

Grumous, *n.* a bloody effusion from an old wound.

Grump, *v.* to crunch a hard or brittle substance with the teeth.

Grumph, *v.* to grunt, grumble.—*n.* a grunt; a pig.

Grumphie, *n.* a pig.

Grumple, *v.* to feel with the fingers; to 'grabble.'

Grumply, *adj.* surly, out of humour, grumpy.

Grun, *n.* an inclination to evil.

Grun, Grund, *v.* to grind.—*ppl. adj.* ground; whetted on a stone.

Grun, Grund, *n.* ground; land; a grave. Cf. Ground.

Grunch, *v.* to grunt, growl, drone. Cf. Grounch.

Grundable, *adj.* used of grain : that may be ground. Cf. Grindable.

Grundavie, *n.* ground ivy.

Grunded, *ppl. adj.* ground ; whetted on a stone.

Grunded-spice, *n.* ground pepper.

Grundie-swallie, Grun-i-swallow, *n.* groundsel.

Grund-rotten, *n.* the brown rat.

Grunge, *v.* to grunt. Cf. Grounch.

Grungy, *n.* a grudge ; a deep, revengeful feeling.

Grunie, *n.* a small farm.

Grunistule, Grunnishule, *n.* groundsel.

Grunkle, *n.* a grunt ; an animal's snout. Cf. Gruntle.

Gruns, *n.* grounds, sediment.

Grunsie, *n.* a sour fellow.

Grunsie, *adj.* having much grounds ; dreggy.

Grunstane, *n.* a foundation-stone ; a foundation.

Grunstane, *n.* a grindstone.

Grun-swall, -swallow, *n.* groundsel.

Grunt, *v.* to grumble, complain. — *n.* a grumble, complaint.

Gruntch, *v.* to grunt. Cf. Grounch.

Grunter, *n.* a pig.

Gruntie, Grunty, *n.* a pig.

Gruntle, *n.* a grain, fragment.

Gruntle, *v.* to grunt in a low key ; to groan slightly ; used of infants : to make a low, cooing sound. — *n.* a grunting noise ; the moan of a sick cow ; an infant's cooing.

Gruntle, Gruntill, *n.* the snout ; the face in general. Cf. Grunkle.

Gruntle-thrawn, *adj.* wry-faced.

Gruntling, *n.* a groaning noise.

Grun-wark, *n.* the preparatory work in laying the foundation of a building ; groundwork.

Grunyie, *v.* with *at*, to grumble, find fault with ; with *at* or *with*, to disgust. — *n.* disgust.

Grunyie, Grunzie, *n.* the snout, mouth ; the face, visage.

Grunzie, *adj.* having sediment, dreggy. Cf. Grunsie.

Gruous, *adj.* grim, grizzly ; awe-inspiring.

Grup, *v.* to grip, grasp. — *n.* a grip. Cf. Grip.

Grupe, *n.* the channel of a cow-house for receiving dung, &c. Cf. Groop.

Gruppit, *ppl. adj.* sprained, strained ; greedy, grasping. Cf. Grippit.

Gruppy, *adj.* greedy ; parsimonious. Cf. Grippy.

Gruse, Gruss, *v.* to crush, press, squeeze.

Gruse, *n.* half-frozen water. Cf. Grue.

Grush, *v.* to crumble. — *n.* what has crumbled down.

Grush, Grushie, *adj.* of thriving growth ; thick ; flabby ; frowsy.

Grushach, Grushaw, *n.* a red, flameles fire. Cf. Greeshoch.

Grusle, *v.* to speak huskily. Cf. Gruzzle.

Grut, Grute, *n.* the refuse of fish-livers after oil has been extracted. Cf. Grout.

Grut, *adj.* great ; swollen. Cf. Grit.

Gruttin, Grutten, *ppl.* cried. Cf. Greet.

Gruze, *v.* to shiver. Cf. Growze.

Gruzin, *n.* a creeping of the flesh ; a shivering.

Gruzlins, *n.* intestines. Cf. Groozlins.

Gruzzle, *v.* to bruise, press together.

Gruzzle, Gruzle, *v.* to speak huskily, breathe heavily ; to eat voraciously ; to grunt. — *n.* a grunt ; a loud breathing. Cf. Groozle.

Gryce, Gryse, *n.* a pig. Cf. Grice.

Gryfe, *n.* a claw, talon.

Gryking, *n.* dawn. Cf. Greek, Greking.

Grymie, *adj.* swarthy in complexion. Cf. Grimie.

Gryming, *n.* a sprinkling.

Grype, *v.* to grip. Cf. Grip.

Gu, *n.* a fool. Cf. Gow.

Guad, *v.* used of a horse : to be restive or troublesome in harness.

Guard, *n.* the old name for an Edinburgh night-watchman ; a guard-house, prison, ward ; one curling-stone preventing another from being dislodged. — *v.* to protect a curling-stone from being dislodged, by putting another in front of it.

Guard-fish, *n.* the sea-pike.

Guardsman, *n.* a warder, sentinel, watcher.

Guck, *n.* a duck.

Guck, *n.* the cuckoo ; a fool. Cf. Gowk.

Guckrie, *n.* folly.

Gud, *n.* God.

Gudame, *n.* a grandmother.

Gud day, *n.* a salutation. Cf. Gude-day.

Guddle, *v.* to catch trout by groping with the hands under the stones or banks of a stream ; to dabble as a duck ; used of children : to play in the gutters, mud, or puddles ; to do work of a dirty or greasy nature. — *n.* toil, turmoil ; dirty work ; a mess, muddle.

Guddle, *v.* to mangle ; to haggle ; to cut awkwardly.

Guddler, *n.* one who catches fish with his hands.

Gude, *n.* God.

Gude, *adj.* good ; considerable, large ; used of time or distance : long, lengthy ; well-born. — *n.* wealth, substance ; in *pl.* livestock. — *adv.* well. — *v.* to manure, enrich with manure.

Gude anes, *n.* one's best clothes.

Gude-billie, *n.* a brother-in-law.

Gude-bit, *n.* a good berth ; a long time ; a long space.

Gude-bluid, *n.* a brave fellow.

Gude-breid, *n.* bread baked for special domestic events, as marriages, &c.

Gude-brither, *n.* a brother-in-law.

Gude-cheap, *n.* a good bargain.—*adj.* costing little or nothing.

Gude-day, *n.* a salutation, bidding 'good-day.'

Gude-deed, *n.* a bribe, a favour, a benefaction.

Gude-deed, *int.* a mild expletive.

Gude-dochter, -dother, *n.* a daughter-in-law.

Gude-e'en, *n.* a salutation, bidding 'good-evening.'

Gude-father, -faither, -fader, *n.* a father-in-law.

Gude few, *phr.* a good many.

Gude-folk, -fowk, *n.* fairies, elves, 'brownies.'

Gude fores, *n.* good qualities.

Gude-for-nocht, *n.* a good-for-nothing person. —*adj.* worthless.

Gude-gaun, *adj.* proceeding steadily.

Gudeless, *adj.* wicked, hurtful; terrible, frightful.—*adv.* exceedingly, very.

Gudelie, *adj.* godly.

Gudelie, *adj.* goodly.—*adv.* easily, conveniently, well, properly, with a good grace.

Gudelie-neighbour, *n.* a fairy, 'brownie.'

Gudeliheid, *n.* glory, goodliness.

Gude livin', *adj.* pious.—*n.* good or luxurious food.

Gude lock, *n.* a good quantity.

Gude-man, *n.* the master of a house; a husband; a master, chief; the head of a prison; a farmer who is not a proprietor; a yeoman, a small farmer who farms his own land; the devil; with *the*, a child's designation of God.

Gudemanlike, *adj.* becoming a husband.

Gudeman's acre, *n.* the spot of ground reserved by a farmer for himself when he resigns his farm to his son.

Gudeman's-craft, -field, -taft, *n.* a portion of land dedicated to the devil and left untilled.

Gudeman's milk, *n.* the milk first skimmed from the pan after the cream has been taken off.

Gude-mither, *n.* a mother-in-law.

Gude neighbours, *n.* fairies, 'brownies.'

Gude-nicht, *n.* a salutation, bidding 'good-night'; a farewell.

Gude rest, *n.* an evening salutation, 'good-night.'

Gude-sister, *n.* a sister-in-law.

Gude-son, *n.* a son-in-law.

Gude troth, *int.* a mild expletive.

Gude-wife, *n.* the mistress of a house, a wife; the landlady of an inn, &c.; a woman-farmer.

Gudewill, *n.* love, affection; a gratuity, 'tip'; perquisite of an under-miller; parents' consent to a daughter's marriage.

Gude-willie, -willied, -willit, *adj.* hospitable, hearty, kindly, generous, liberal.

Gude words, *n.* a child's name for its prayers.

Gudge, *n.* anything short and thick; a short, thick-set person.

Gudge, *v.* to probe, poke; to press out or make to bulge by wedges or by a lever or 'pinch'; to poke or probe for trout under the stones or banks of a stream, 'guddle'; to stuff, cram with food, play the glutton.

Gudgeon, *n.* a 'noodle,' fool, one easily deceived.

†Gudget, Gudgeat, *n.* a camp-servant.

Gudget, *n.* a glutton.—*v.* to be gluttonous.— *adj.* short and thick, fat from over-eating.

Gudgick, *n.* a short, thick-set person.

Gudgie, *adj.* short and thick, stout.

Gudin, *n.* manure. Cf. Goodin.

Gueed, *n.* God.

Gueed, *adj.* good. Cf. Gude.

Gueedly, *adj.* religious, godly.

Gueedly, *adv.* easily, with a good grace.—*adj.* goodly.

Gueel, *n.* the corn-marigold. Cf. Gool.

†Guerdon, *n.* protection, safeguard.

†Guergous, *adj.* martial; warlike in appearance.

Guess, *n.* a riddle, conundrum; an opinion.

Guessie, *n.* a principal actor in the child's game of 'Namie and Guessie.'

Guest, *n.* anything which the superstitious think portends the arrival of a stranger.

Guest, *n.* a ghost, spectre.

Guesten, *v.* to lodge as a guest.

Guest-house, *n.* a house of entertainment.

Guestning, *n.* reception as a guest. Cf. Gesning.

Guff, *n.* a puff of wind; a whiff, savour; an inhalation; a bad smell.

Guff, *v.* to laugh boisterously; to babble; to let wind from the mouth.—*n.* a guffaw; a loud, sudden noise; a suppressed bark or snort.

Guff, *n.* a fool, simpleton. Cf. Goff.

Guffa, *n.* a boisterous laugh.

Guffer, *n.* the viviparous blenny.

Guffie, *adj.* foolish, stupid.—*n.* a fool; a rustic, clown; a noisy person.

Guffie, *adj.* chubby, 'chuffy'; fat about the cheeks or temples.

Guffiness, *n.* fatness about the cheeks or temples.

Guffish, *adj.* foolish.

Guffishlie, *adv.* foolishly.

Guffishness, *n.* foolishness.

Guffle, *v.* to puzzle, nonplus.

Guff nor sty, *phr.* nothing at all.

Guggle, *v.* to gurgle hysterically.

Guid, *n.* God.

Guid, *adj.* good. Cf. Gude, Gweed.

Guidal, *n.* guidance, control, management.

Guide, *v.* to treat; to try, handle, use; to manage, control, look after; to manage economically; to save; to keep, in excls. of surprise.—*n.* a manager in control of money or property.

Guider, *n.* the leader of a party or faction; a guardian, adviser; with *good,* a managing, economical housewife.

Guideship, *n.* guidance; usage, treatment; management.

Guidet, *ppl. adj.* harassed, troubled.

Guide ye, *int.* an excl. of contempt.

Guid-fit, *n.* a lucky foot.

Guid-fitter, *n.* one who has a lucky foot.

Guidsake, *int.* for God's sake !

Guid-the-fire, *n.* a poker.

Guid-the-gate, *n.* a halter for a horse.

Guik, *n.* the cuckoo; a fool. Cf. Gowk.

Guild, *n.* the society of the burgesses of a royal burgh.

Guild, Guild-tree, *n.* the barberry.

Guild, *n.* the corn-marigold. Cf. Gool.

Guild, *adj.* clever, capable; loud.—*n.* clamour, noise; an outburst. Cf. Gild.

Guildee, *n.* the young of the coal-fish.

Guilder-faugh, *n.* old lea land, once ploughed and then left to lie fallow.

Guildry, *n.* the society of the burgesses of a royal burgh.

Guile, *v.* to beguile.

Guile, *n.* the corn-marigold. Cf. Gool.

Guiltfou, *adj.* full of guilt.

†Guind, *n.* a wild cherry, a 'gean.'

Guinea-gowd, *n.* a fine quality of gold of which guineas were coined.

Guinea-note, *n.* a bank-note for a guinea.

Guisard, *n.* a mummer.

Guise, *v.* to go mumming, to masquerade; to decorate.—*n.* a merry-making, frolic; a mumming, masquerade; the parts in a play.

Guiser, *n.* a mummer; a masquerader.

Guissern, *n.* a coarse, lusty woman. Cf. Gusehorn.

Guissern, *n.* the gizzard. Cf. Gusehorn.

Guissie, *int.* a call to a pig.—*n.* a young pig. Cf. Gussie.

Guissock, *n.* a superstitious observance.

Guiz, *n.* a wig. Cf. Gizz.

Guizard, *n.* a mummer.—*v.* to act as a mummer.

Guize, *v.* to go mumming.

Gukkow, *n.* the cuckoo; a simpleton. Cf. Gowk.

Gulch, *v.* to eructate.—*n.* a glutton; a thick, ill-shaped person; an eructation.

Gulchin, *n.* a big, fat, short person.

Gulchy, *adj.* of gross, thick habit of body.

Gulder, *v.* to shout, speak boisterously; to bark threateningly; to growl loudly and with menace; to make a gurgling sound; to speak indistinctly.—*n.* a loud, sudden shout of surprise or anger; the angry growl of a dog; a gurgling sound; the sound of water escaping through a narrow orifice or channel; the sound of choking or strangulation; half-articulate speech; the sound of a turkey-cock.

Guldersome, *adj.* passionate, boisterous; given to snarling.

Guldie, *n.* a tall, black-faced, gloomy-looking man.

Gule, *n.* the corn-marigold. Cf. Gool.

Gule, *adj.* yellow.

Gulefittit, *adj.* yellow-footed or -legged.

Guleravitch, *v.* to live riotously. Cf. Galravitch.

Gulf, *n.* a big hole or rut caused by a 'rooting' sow.

Gulghy, *n.* a beetle, a cockchafer. Cf. Golach.

Gull, *v.* to flout, sneer at, make fun of.

Gull, *n.* a large trout.

Gull, *n.* a thin, cold mist, accompanied with a slight wind; a chill; a rather low estimate of a person or thing.—*adj.* chill, marked by a cold wind.—*v.* to be covered with a thin mist, to grow misty.

Gull, *v.* to thrust the finger forcibly under the ear, to 'catlill'; to shout; to growl loudly. —*n.* a loud shout; a growl.

Guller, *v.* to gurgle.—*n.* a gurgling sound. Cf. Gulder.

Guller's spree, *phr.* a heavy drinking-bout.

†Gullet, Gullot, *n.* a water-channel.

Gulliegaup, *v.* to injure severely; to take by the throat, strangle.

Gulliegaupus, *n.* a big, stupid person.

Gulliegaw, *v.* to wound with a sharp weapon. —*n.* a deep cut or gash with sword or knife; a broil.

Gulliewillie, *n.* a blustering, quarrelsome fellow; a swamp covered with grass or herbs; a quagmire.

Gullimont, *n.* a glutton.

Gullion, *n.* a mean wretch.

Gullion, *n.* a quagmire; mud.

Gull-maw, *n.* the greater black-backed gull.

Gulloot, *n.* a big, ugly fellow.

Gully, *n.* a large knife; a butcher's knife; a carving-knife; a sword.—*v.* to cut, gash.

Gully, *v.* to swallow; to gulp.

Gully, *n.* a sink.

Gully-gander, *n.* a fight with knives.

Gully-hole, *n.* the orifice of a sink; a gutter-hole, mouth of a drain or sewer.

Gully-knife, *n.* a large knife.

Gullymudge, *v.* to stick or stab with a large knife.

Gullyvant, *v.* to gad about. Cf. Gallivant.

Guloch, *n.* an iron lever, a 'pinch,' 'gavelock.' Cf. Gewlick.

Gulp, *n.* a big, unwieldy child.

Gulpin, *n.* a young child ; a simpleton, greenhorn ; a raw, unwieldy fellow.

Gulsach, Gulsoch, *n.* a surfeit ; a voracious appetite.

Gulsach, Gulschoch, *n.* the jaundice.—*adj.* jaundiced.

Gulsch, Gulsh, *v.* to belch.—*n.* a glutton. Cf. Gulch.

Gulschy, *adj.* gross in body. Cf. Gulchy.

Gulset, *n.* the jaundice. Cf. Gulsach.

Gulshock, *adj.* in *phr.* a 'gulshock scoot,' a boy's pop-gun made from a hollow-stemmed plant.

Gulzie, *n.* a knife ; a large knife. Cf. Gully.

Gum, *n.* the condensed moisture on the windows and walls of a crowded church, hall, &c. ; a thin film on anything ; coal or peat dust, 'coom.'—*v.* to become covered with condensed vapour, or with a thin film.

Gum, *n.* the palate.

Gum, *n.* disturbance, variance, a 'dust'; a misunderstanding.

Gum, *n.* a disguised form of 'God,' used as an expletive.

Gumflate, *v.* to swell, inflate ; to perplex, bamboozle.

Gumflerman, *n.* the bearer of a funeral banner. Cf. Gumphion.

Gumflower, *n.* an artificial flower.

Gumly, *adj.* muddy, 'grumly'; gloomy. Cf. Gummle.

Gummel, Gummul, *v.* to gobble up. Cf. Gammal.

Gummeril, *n.* a fool, simpleton. Cf. Gomeril.

Gummle, *v.* to make muddy ; to confuse, perplex.

Gump, *v.* to grope ; to grope for trout, to 'guddle.'

Gump, *n.* the whole of anything ; a large piece or portion.

Gump, Gumph, *n.* a fool, blockhead, 'sumph'; a silly woman ; a plump child, rather overgrown ; in *pl.* the sulks.—*v* to go about in a stupid way ; to sulk.

Gumph, *v.* to beat, defeat, get the better of.

Gumph, *n.* a bad smell ; the entrails of a skate.

Gumphie, *n.* a fool, a simpleton.

Gumphieleerie, *adj.* stupid, silly.

Gumphion, *n.* a funeral banner.

Gumping, *n.* a piece cut out of the whole of anything ; the part of a 'rigg' on a harvest-field, separated from the rest, that is left uncut.

Gumple, *v.* to become sulky ; to show bad humour.—*n.* a surfeit ; in *pl.* the sulks.

Gumple-face, *n.* a downcast face.

Gumple-faced, *adj.* chop-fallen, sulky.

Gumple-feast, *n.* a surfeit.

Gumple-foisted, *adj.* sulky, ill-humoured.

Gumplin, *n.* a long, sulky fit.

Gumpshion, *n.* 'gumption.'

Gumption, *n.* common-sense ; shrewdness ; quickness of understanding.

Gumptionless, *adj.* foolish ; without 'gumption.'

Gumptious, *adj.* self-important ; bumptious ; fault-finding, quarrelsome ; having 'gumption.'

Gumpus, *n.* a fool.

Gumral, *adj.* foolish ; frivolous. Cf. Gomeril.

Gumsheon, Gumshion, Gumtion, *n.* 'gumption'.

Gumstick, *n.* a stick used by teething children.

Gun, *v.* to interchange talk, to gossip.

Gun, *n.* a tobacco-pipe.—*v.* used of blasting-charges : to explode without effect.

Gunch, *n.* a large piece, a 'hunch.'

Gundie, *n.* the fatherlasher.

Gundie, *adj.* greedy, voracious.

Gundie-guts, *n.* a voracious person ; a fat, pursy fellow.

Gundy, *n.* a sweetmeat made of treacle and spices ; candy, toffy.

Gundy, *n.* a push, shove.

Gundy-balls, *n.* globular 'gundies.'

Gundyman, *n.* a seller of 'gundies.'

Gundyman, *n.* a ploughman's assistant, who, with a long pole fastened to the plough-beam, had to help the ploughman by pushing the plough off or to him, as occasion required.

Gundymonger, *n.* a seller of sweetmeats or 'gundy.'

Gundywife, *n.* a female 'gundymonger.'

Gunk, *v.* to jilt, disappoint ; to take or set aback.—*n.* a disappointment, a jilt. Cf. Begunk.

Gunkerie, *n.* the act of duping, jilting, tricking.

Gunkie, *n.* a dupe.

Gunnack, *n.* a species of skate.

Gunnald, *ppl. adj.* with great jowls.

Gunnals, *n.* gills ; jowls, great hanging cheeks. Cf. Gunnles.

Gunner, *n.* a sportsman, one who takes a shooting.

Gunner, *n.* the yellow-ammer.

Gunner, *v.* to gossip ; to talk loud and long. —*n.* gossip, noisy talk ; a blustering talker.

Gunnerflook, *n.* the turbot.

Gunner-room, *n.* a sort of committee-room, a 'parlour' or meeting-room, in which matters are discussed. Cf. Gunner, Gun.

Gunning, *n.* a familiar talk.

Gunning, *n.* the sport of shooting.

Gunnled, *ppl. adj.* having large jowls.

Gunnles, *n.* gills; jowls. Cf. Ginnles.

Gun-plucker, *n.* a kind of fish with a wide mouth.

Gunpowder, *n.* tea.

Gunsar, Gunsir, *n.* a big, clumsy, ungainly, stupid person.

Gunsh, *n.* a short, thick-set fellow.

Gunshy, *adj.* thick-set.

Gun-sleeves, *n.* sleeves wider at the shoulder than at the wrist.

Gun-stane, *n.* a gun-flint.

Guran, *n.* a pustule, a small boil.

Guranie, *adj.* full of small boils.

Gurbit, *n.* an unfledged bird, a raw youth. Cf. Gorbit.

Gurg, *v.* to make a creaking noise. Cf. Girg.

Gurgrugous, *adj.* ugly; austere. Cf. Gargrugous.

Gurgy, *adj.* fat; short-necked; with protuberant belly.

Gurk, *n.* a fat, short person; a fine, well-conditioned fellow; the thriving young, large for their age, of any live-stock; a term of address.

Gurkas, *n.* a 'gurk.'

Gurkin, *n.* a very fat, short person.

Gurl, Gurle, *v.* to growl as a dog; to snarl, mutter; of the wind: to rush, roar, howl as in a storm; of water: to issue or escape with a gurgling noise; of an infant: to crow, coo, 'gurgle.'—*n.* a growl; a narrow spot where a confined stream pours with force and gurgling sound.—*adj.* surly, quarrelsome; rough, stormy, bitter.

Gurl, *v.* to flatter.—*n.* flattery, deceit.

Gurliewhirkie, *n.* unforeseen evil: premeditated revenge.

Gurlin', *n.* flattery.

Gurling, *ppl. adj.* growling, snarling; surly.

Gurly, *adj.* used of a dog: given to growling, growling loudly; of the weather: boisterous, threatening to be stormy, bitter, bleak; of fluids: gurgling; of infants: 'crowing,' 'gurgling'; of persons: surly, rough, cross; of a tree: gnarled.

Gurly, *adj.* deceitful, fair-spoken.

Gurn, *n.* a snare.—*v.* to trap. Cf. Girn.

Gurnel, Gurnle, *n.* a strange-shaped, thick man; a fisherman's tool for fixing stakes in the sand to spread nets on.

Gurnet, *n.* the gurnard.

Gurr, *v.* to growl as a dog, snarl; to rumble; to purr as a cat.—*n.* the growl, or snarl, of a dog.

Gurr, *n.* mud; hardened rheum of the eyes. —*v.* to soil, defile. Cf. Garr.

Gurr, *n.* a strong, thick-set person; a knotty stick or tree.

Gurrag, *n.* a pimple, pustule. Cf. Guran.

Gurran, *n.* a very strong, thick-set person; one with a stubborn temper.

Gurr-gurr, *v.* to growl continuously, or for a time.

Gurr-gurring, *n.* a long, low growl or snarl; a rumbling, snarling sound.

Gurrie, *v.* to growl; to 'gurr.'

Gurring, *n.* a low growl.

Gurron, *n.* anything large or fine of its kind; a sturdy lad. Cf. Garron.

Gurry, *n.* a dog-fight; a loud, angry wrangle; a brawl; a hurry, bustle, confusion.

Gurry-wurry, *n.* a dog-fight, 'collieshangie,' wrangle.—*adj.* snarling, growling.

Gurth, *n.* crushed curd.

Gurthie, *adj.* heavy, oppressive; weighty, solid; corpulent, fat; nauseating, burdensome to the stomach.

Guschach, *n.* the fireside. Cf. Coutchack.

Guschet, *n.* a gusset; a pocket at or near the arm-pit; the clock of a stocking; a triangular piece of land, interposed between two other properties.

Guschet, Gusset-house, *n.* a house at a corner, forming a division between two streets.

Guschetie, *n.* a small 'guschet.'

Guse, *n.* a goose. Cf. Goose.

Guse, *n.* the long gut or 'rectum.'

Gusehorn, *n.* a coarse, lusty woman.

Gusehorn, *n.* the gizzard.

Gush, *n.* in *phr.* to 'play gush,' to bleed profusely.

Gushat, Gushet, *n.* a gusset. Cf. Guschet.

Gushel, *n.* a small dam made in a gutter or streamlet to intercept water.

Gushel, *n.* an awkward lout; a clumsy, untidy worker.—*v.* to work untidily.

Gush-hole, *n.* an outlet in a wall for the escape of water.

Gushing, *n.* the grunting of a pig.

Gussie, *n.* a young sow; a call to a sow. Cf. Goosy.

Gussie, *n.* a coarse, lusty woman. Cf. Gusehorn.

Gussie, *n.* a division of an orange.

Gust, *n.* a taste, relish, liking, gusto.—*v.* to taste, smell; to give relish or appetite; to please the palate; to flavour.

Gust, *n.* a contemptuous term for an officious, flighty, talkative woman, who means nothing in her talk.

Gustard, *n.* the great bustard.

Gustfu', *adj.* full of relish; palatable, savoury; enjoying a relish.

Gustily, *adv.* luxuriously, daintily.

Gustless, *adj.* without taste or appetite, with no power to relish.

Gusty, *adj.* pleasing the palate, savoury, appetizing; fond of good living; with an appetite.

Gut, *n.* the gout.

Gut, Gutt, *n.* a drop. Cf. Goutte.

Gut, *n.* in *pl.* the belly, stomach; the contents of anything; the inside of anything.

Gut an' ga', *phr.* the whole contents of the stomach violently ejected.

Gutcher, *n.* a grandfather; grandsire.

Gut-haniel, *n.* a colic.

Gut-pock, *n.* the stomach, belly; the crop of a fowl.

Gut-pot, *n.* a receptacle for the entrails of herrings.

Gutrake, *n.* provisions got with difficulty or improperly.

Gut-scraper, *n.* a fiddler.

Gutser, *n.* a grandfather. Cf. Gutcher.

Gutsily, *adv.* gluttonously.

Gutsiness, *n.* gluttony, voracity; greediness.

Gutsy, *adj.* greedy, gluttonous, voracious; used of a house: capacious, roomy, commodious.

Guttag, *n.* a knife for gutting herrings.

Gutter, *n.* the mark or trace of tears on the cheeks; mud, mire, puddles, 'dubs'; the act of doing work untidily or dirtily; a dirty, untidy worker.—*v.* to bemire, bedaub with mud; to work dirtily, slovenly, and unskilfully; to eat into the flesh, fester; to lay a gutter.

Gutter, *n.* a person who guts herrings; a person who unpacks herring-boxes.

Gutter, *v.* used of running water: to gurgle, make a noise.

Gutter-blood, -bleed, -bluid, *n.* a street-arab, a low-born person; one born within the same town or city as another; one whose ancestors have been in the same town or city for some generations.—*adj.* brought up in the same locality and in the same rank of life.

Gutterel, *adj.* rather gluttonous.—*n.* a fat, young pig.

Gutterer, *n.* an unskilful, dirty worker.

Gutter-gaw, *n.* a sore caused by mud, &c., in one who walks with bare feet.

Gutter-hole, *n.* a sink or kennel; a receptacle for kitchen refuse or filth.

Gutterin', *ppl. adj.* untidy and unskilful in work.

Gutter-teetan, *n.* the rock pipit.

Guttery, *adj.* muddy, full of puddles, miry; mud-stained.

Guttie, *n.* a minnow. Cf. Gutty.

Guttiness, *n.* capaciousness of belly; thickness; grossness.

Guttle, *v.* to gorge, guzzle; to reach to the guts.

Guttrell, *adj.* rather gluttonous. Cf. Gutterel.

Gutty, *adj.* pot-bellied, corpulent; thick, gross; greedy, gluttonous.—*n.* a fat, corpulent person; a minnow.

Gutty bottle, *n.* a big-bellied bottle.

Guy, *adv.* rather, very. Cf. Gey.

Guy, *v.* to guide; to have charge of a bill in parliament.

Guylte, *n.* a full-grown pig. Cf. Gilt.

Guynoch, *adj.* gluttonous, voracious; greedy of money.—*n.* an insatiable, covetous person. Cf. Geenyoch.

Guyser, *n.* a mummer. Cf. Guiser.

Guzle, *v.* to guzzle.

Guzzhorn, *n.* the gizzard.

Guzzle, *v.* to take by the throat, throttle, choke.—*n.* the throat.

G'wa, *int.* an excl. of surprise, incredulity.

Gweed, *n.* God. Cf. Gude.

Gweed, *adj.* good. Cf. Good, Gude.

Gweed-frauchty and gweed-willie, *phr.* generous and ready to give to the poor.

Gweedin, *n.* manure. Cf. Goodin.

Gweel, *n.* the corn-marigold. Cf. Gule.

Gweeshie, Gweeshtins, *int.* a disguised form of 'God,' used in excls. of great surprise and mild oaths. Cf. Gosh.

Gwick, *n.* the movement of the mouth and the sound made in swallowing.—*v.* to move the mouth in swallowing; to make the sound as of swallowing.

Gwite, *n.* a child, brat, 'geat.' Cf. Gett.

Gy, *n.* a scene, show, performance; a gathering; estimation, respect; a strange, hob goblin-looking fellow, a 'guy.'

Gy, *adj.* prodigal; wild; considerable.—*adv.* rather; very. Cf. Gey.

Gya, *v. pret.* gave.

Gyaan, Gyaen, Gyan, *ppl.* going.

Gyaggers, *int.* an excl. of disgust.

Gyang, *v.* to go. Cf. Gang.

Gyang, *n.* a gang; gait. Cf. Gang.

Gyangals, *n.* in *phr.* 'to be a' guts and gyangals,' to be fit for nothing but eating and drinking. Cf. Gangyls.

Gyangrel, *n.* a tramp, vagrant. Cf. Gangrel.

Gyang-water, *n.* something laid past for the future; a 'nest-egg.' Cf. Ganging-water.

Gyaun, *ppl.* going.

Gy-carlin, *n.* a mother-witch. Cf. Gyrecarlin.

Gye, *adj.* wild; considerable.—*adv.* rather. Cf. Gey.

Gyem, *n.* a game.

Gyld, *adj.* clever; light-hearted.—*n.* clamour. Cf. Gild.

Gyle, *n.* wort; the vat in which wort is fermented; a tun-dish.

Gyle, *n.* a gaol.

Gyle, *n.* a gable. Cf. Gavel.

Gyle-fat, *n.* the vat used for fermenting wort.

Gyle-house, *n.* a brew-house.

Gylie, Gylies, *adv.* considerably; rather. Cf. Geylie.

Gymp, *v.* to talk freely; to taunt, gibe.—*n.* a quirk; a gibe.

Gynk, *v.* to titter; to laugh in a suppressed manner.—*n.* a trick. Cf. Gink.

Gynkie, *adj.* giddy, tricky, frolicsome.—*n.* a reproachful designation of a woman; a light-hearted girl.

Gyp, *n.* a woman's skirt or short petticoat. Cf. Jupe.

Gype, *v.* to stare foolishly; to act like a fool.—*n.* a foolish stare; a fool, lout; an awkward, stupid fellow. Cf. Gipe.

Gype, *adj.* hungry; voracious; keen; ardent; eager.

Gypelie, *adv.* keenly; quickly; nimbly.

Gyper, *n.* nonsense, fun; joking.

Gyperie, *n.* foolishness.

Gypit, *adj.* foolish.

Gypitness, *n.* foolishness.

Gyre, *n.* a powerful, malignant spirit.

Gyre, *adj.* gaudy; glaring.

Gyre-carle, *n.* a water-sprite, 'kelpie'; a giant; an ogre.

Gyre-carlin, *n.* a mother-witch, a witch; a hobgoblin; a scarecrow. Cf. Giean-carlins.

Gyre-fu', *adj.* fretful, ill-tempered; discontented.

Gyre-leukin, *adj.* impish-looking; odd-looking.

Gyrie, *n.* a stratagem; circumvention.

Gyrin', *adj.* gaudy, of a bright or glaring colour.

Gyrn, *n.* a snare, trap. Cf. Girn.

Gyrn, *v.* to grin; to show the teeth like a dog; to fret, whine.—*n.* a grin. Cf. Girn.

Gysan, Gysen, *adj.* leaky from shrinking, dry.—*v.* to leak from shrinking; to parch. Cf. Gizzen.

Gysard, Gysart, *n.* a mummer. Cf. Guizard.

Gyse, *v.* to masquerade; to disguise.—*n.* a merry-making; a disguise. Cf. Guise.

Gyse, *n.* mode, fashion; guise.

Gyser, *n.* a mummer.

Gyte, *adj.* mad; out of one's senses.—*n.* a madman; a foolish, idiotic person; ruin; pieces.

Gyte, *n.* a child, a brat. Cf. Gett.

Gyte, *n.* a goat.

Gyte, Gytt, *n.* a small sheaf of corn set by itself to dry in a field.—*v.* to set up such sheaves. Cf. Gait.

Gytlin, *adj.* rural, belonging to the fields.

Gytlin, *n.* a contemptuous or angry designation for a child. Cf. Gettlin.

Gytting, *n.* the act of setting up single sheaves to dry. Cf. Gaiten.

Gyve-airns, *n.* gyves, fetters for the legs.

Gyzen, *adj.* leaking from drought warping staves. Cf. Gizzen.

†**Gyzen**, *n.* childbed. Cf. Gizzen, Jizzen.

Gyzen-clout, *n.* an infant's binder.

Ha', *n.* a hall; a house, home; a farmhouse; a cottage; the chief manor-house; a house in a township; a room of a house; the kitchen of a farmhouse.

Ha', *n.* low-lying land beside a stream. Cf. Haugh.

Haadie, *n.* a haddock. Cf. Haddie.

Haaf, *n.* the deep or open sea; deep-sea fishing ground.

Haaf, *adv.* half.

Haaf-boat, *n.* a boat adapted for deep-sea fishing.

Haaf-eel, *n.* the conger-eel. Cf. Heaweeel.

Haaf-fish, *n.* the great seal.

Haaf-fishing, *n.* deep-sea fishing.

Haafing, *n.* deep-sea fishing.

Haaflin, *n.* a half-grown boy.—*adj.* half-grown. Cf. Halflin.

Haaf-lines, *n.* deep-sea fishing-lines.

Haaf-man, *n.* a deep-sea fisherman.

Haaf-seat, *n.* a deep-sea fishing ground.

Haal, *n.* a hold; the support given to a child learning to walk; walk.—*v.* to offer sufficient resistance. Cf. Had haal.

Haaliget, *adj.* light-headed; disreputable; violent. Cf. Hallockit.

Haalyan, *n.* a clumsy fellow; a clown; a scamp. Cf. Hallion.

Haanyal, *n.* a greedy dog. Cf. Haniel.

Haap, *v.* to hop.—*n.* a hop. Cf. Hap.

Haap, *v.* used of horses: to turn to the right from the driver.—*int.* a call to a horse to turn to the right.

Haar, *n.* a raw, foggy, easterly wind; a mist; drizzling rain; hoar-frost.

Haar, *n.* a huskiness in the throat; an impediment of speech.—*v.* to speak hoarsely and thickly.

Haary, *adj.* used of wind: cold, keen, biting.

Haas, *n.* the neck; gullet. Cf. Halse.

Haave, *n.* a large pock-net used in fishing.—*v.* to fish with a pock-net. Cf. Halve, Hauling.

†**Haave**, *adj.* pale, wan.

Haaver, *n.* a half-share; a sharer who holds a half; in *pl.* 'haavers!' children's claim to have half of any treasure-trove; in *phr.* 'haavers and shaivers!' a children's excl. when they find anything of the nature of treasure.—*adj.* used of cattle, &c.: held in partnership.—*v.* to halve; to share in partnership; to divide into two.

Hab, *n.* the hob of a fireplace. Cf. Hob.

Habber, *n.* a stammerer, one who speaks 'hickly; a clumsy person; the act of snarling or growling like a dog.—*v.* to stutter, stammer; to snarl.

†**Habberdyn-fish,** *n.* dried cod; barrelled cod.

Habbergaw, *n.* hesitation; suspense; an objection.

Habberjock, *n.* a turkey-cock; a big, stupid person who speaks thickly.

Habbernab, *v.* to touch glasses in drinking, hobnob.

Habbers, *n.* 'halvers,' a copartnery of equal shares between two.

Habbie, *adj.* stiff in motion, as a hobby-horse.

Habbie, *n.* a hobby.

Habbie-gabbie, *v.* to throw money to be scrambled for.

Habble, *n.* the act of snapping; a dog's growling noise; perplexity, a fix; tumult, disorder; a squabble.—*v.* to snap like a dog; to confuse; to stammer; to speak confusedly; to gabble, talk fast; to wrangle. Cf. Hobble.

Habble, *v.* to hobble, walk with difficulty; to limp; to shake, jolt; to dandle, toss; to move unsteadily with a quivering motion; to swarm with insects or vermin; to embarrass.—*n.* a shake, toss. Cf. Hobble.

Habble-hobble, *n.* a 'rumpus,' hubbub.

Habble-jock, *n.* a turkey-cock.

Habbler, *n.* a squabbler, one who provokes or likes squabbles.

Habble-sheuf, *n.* an uproar, tumult, confusion.

Habbleshow, *n.* a disorderly crowd, rabble; a hubbub. Cf. Hobbleshow.

Habblie, *adj.* used of cattle: having big bones, ill-set; used of ground: soft, quaking.

Habbling, *n.* confusion, wrangling; confused talk.—*ppl. adj.* given to petty quarrelling.

Habbocraws, *int.* a shout to scare crows from corn-fields, &c.

Habby, *adj.* stiff in motion.

Habeek-a-ha, *int.* a cry that marbles, &c., forfeited in school-hours are to be scrambled for out of doors.

Haberdash, *n.* small wares, miscellaneous articles.

Haberschon, *n.* an habergeon, a jacket of mail or scale armour.

Ha'-Bible, *n.* a large family Bible.

†**Habil, Habile,** *adj.* competent; able, qualified; passable; liable.

Habiliments, *n.* outfit. Cf. Abuliement.

Hability, *n.* legal competence.

Ha'-bink, *n.* the bank of a 'haugh' overhanging a stream.

Habit and repute, *phr.* notorious; held and reputed to be.

Habit-sark, -shirt, *n.* a woman's riding-shirt.

†**Hable,** *adj.* passable; liable. Cf. Habil.

Hachle, *n.* a sloven, slut; a dirtily-dressed person.

Hack, *v.* used of the stomach: to turn against.

Hack, *n.* a pronged implement for drawing dung from a cart; a mark; a fissure; a chap in the skin; an indentation, or piece of indented sheet-iron, for steadying a curler's feet when playing.—*v.* to chop; to chap; to be cracked.

Hack, *v.* to hawk, to peddle.

Hack, *n.* a wild, moorish place, a 'hag.' Cf. Hagg.

Hack and manger, *phr.* free quarters.

Hack and sweep, *phr.* a clean sweep.

Hack-a-thraw, *n.* a determined fellow. Cf. Hawk-a-thraw.

Hack-berry, *n.* the bird-cherry. Cf. Hagberry.

Hack-door, *n.* a door between a farm-kitchen and the farmyard.

Hacker, *v.* to hack in cutting; to cut small, hash.

Hackery-lookit, *adj.* rough, gruff; marked by smallpox.

Hacking, *n.* the chapping of hands or feet from cold.

Hacking-stock, *n.* a butcher's block.

Hackit, *ppl. adj.* used of the tongue: biting, caustic; of hands or feet: chapped.

Hackit, *adj.* used of animals: white-faced. Cf. Hawkit.

Hackit-flesh, *n.* a charm of carrion for injuring a neighbour's live-stock.

Hackit-kail, *n.* 'hackum-kail.'

Hackster, *n.* a butcher; a cut-throat.

Hackstock, *n.* a butcher's block.

Hackum-kail, *n.* chopped colewort, &c.

Hackum-plackum, *adv.* in equal shares of payment.

Ha'clay, *n.* potter's earth; a tough, clammy, blue clay, used for colouring the walls of farm-cottages.

Had, *n.* a hold, grip; a holding; a house; a den, an animal's hole; a place of retreat or concealment; a support; a leading-string; restraint; power of retention.

Had, *v.* to hold, grip; to keep, maintain; to look after, preserve; to uphold, to occupy; to keep busy; to burden, harass; to restrain, hinder, detain; to withhold; to be held as true or generally accepted; to bet, wager; to accept as a bargain; to regard an engagement binding; to preserve for stock; of seeds: to keep to the ground, come up short; to go on one's way; of things: to go on; of health: to progress; of the weather: to continue; to stay, remain; to restrain one's self, refrain from; to cease, stop; used of fish: to lurk for shelter.

Had, *v. pret.* took.—*ppl.* taken.

Had a care, *phr.* to take care; to beware.

Had aff, *v.* to keep off.—*int.* a ploughman's call to his horses, in some districts to turn to the right, in others to the left.

Had affen, *v.* to defend, protect.

Had aff ye, *phr.* go ahead !

Had again, *v.* to resist ; to arrest, stop.—*n.* a check, opposition.

Had a hough, *phr.* to assist at a confinement.

Had at, *v.* to persist in ; not to spare or let alone.

Had awa, *v.* to hold off, keep away ; to wend one's way.

Had awa frae, *phr.* except.

Had back, *int.* a ploughman's call to his horses to turn to the left.

Had by, *v.* to go past ; to refrain from.

Haddag, *n.* a haddock.

Hadden, *ppl. adj.* held.

Hadden and dung, *phr.* sorely worried and troubled.

Hadder, *n.* a holder ; the part of a flail held by the thresher ; a needle-cushion ; a niggard.

Hadder and pelter, *n.* a flail.

Haddie, *n.* a haddock.

Haddies, *n.* a measure of dry grain.

Haddies cog, *n.* a measure of dry grain, one-third or one-fourth of a peck. Cf. Haddish.

Haddin, *ppl. adj.* holding ; certain, sure.

Haddin, *n.* the act of embracing ; a holding of house or land on lease; property, living; furniture, equipment ; farm-stock ; an entertainment, feast, merry-making.

Haddin-caaf, *n.* a calf preserved for stock.

Haddish, *n.* one-third of a peck, or, according to some, one-fourth.

Haddo-breeks, *n.* the haddock's roe.

Haddock-sand, *n.* sea-ground frequented by haddocks.

Had dog, *n.* a sheep-dog.

Hadds ye, *phr.* expressing the acceptance of an offer or bargain.

Hade, *v. pret.* hid.

Had fit wi', *phr.* to keep pace with, equal.

Had forrit, *v.* to go forward.

Had haal, *n.* a hold, grip.—*v.* to keep hold ; to offer sufficient resistance.

Had in, *v.* to confine ; to contain without leaking ; to save or limit expenses ; to keep up supply.

Had in wi', *phr.* to curry favour ; to keep in one's good graces.

Had o' health, *n.* a sign of health.

Had on, *v.* to stop ; to continue.

Had out, *v.* to pretend ; to affirm strenuously; to dwell, lodge ; to present a gun ; to be of full measure or weight ; to suffice to the last ; to frequent regularly.

Had-poke, *n.* a beggar ; a churl.

Had sae, *v.* to cease, give over.—*n.* a sufficiency.

Had the crack, *phr.* to keep conversation going.

Had till'd, *v.* to be in health.

Had to, *v.* to maintain ; to go one's way ; to shut, keep shut ; to keep going or at work.

Had up, *v.* used of weather : to keep fair.

Had up to, *phr.* to make up to, court, woo.

Had up with, *phr.* to keep pace with.

Had with, *v.* to agree with ; to consume, indulge in.

Hae, *v.* to have ; to take ; to receive ; to carry to burial ; to understand.—*n.* property.

Hae and cry, *n.* a fuss ; a 'hue and cry.'

Hae-been, *n.* an ancient rite, custom, institution, or person.

Haed, *v. pret.* had.—*ppl.* taken for burial. Cf. Hae.

Haed, *n.* an atom, particle. Cf. Haet.

Hael, *v.* to hide. Cf. Heal.

Haellens, *adv.* certainly ; completely. Cf. Haillins.

Haem, *n.* in *pl.* the two curved pieces of wood or iron resting on a horse's collar, and supporting the traces. Cf. Hame.

Haem-blade, *n.* the half of a horse's collar.

Haem-houghed, *adj.* having houghs shaped like 'hames.'

Haemilt, *adj.* homely ; home-made ; tame.—*v.* to domesticate. Cf. Hamald.

Ha'en, *ppl.* had ; had to.

Haen, *v.* to preserve land for hay, &c.; to spare, lay by. Cf. Hain.

Haerst, *n.* harvest. Cf. Hairst.

Haet, *n.* an atom, whit, particle, used generally with negatives.

Haev, *n.* a fisherman's hand-basket for carrying bait.

Haf, Haff, *n.* the deep sea. Cf. Haaf.

Haf, Haff, *adj.* half. Cf. Half.

Hafer, Haffer, *n.* a half-share. Cf. Haaver.

Haffet, Haffat, Haffit, *n.* the side of the face ; the temple ; in *pl.* locks of hair, especially on the temples.

Haffet-clawing, *n.* face-scratching.

Haffet-close, *adv.* very close together, cheek to cheek.

Haffet-links, *n.* locks of hair on the temples.

Haffins, *n.* manners. Cf. Haivins.

Haffins, *adj.* half-grown.—*adv.* half, partially. Cf. Halflins.

Hafflin, *n.* a trying-plane, used by carpenters.

Hafflin, Haflin, *n.* a half-grown boy ; a boy employed at a stable or farm ; a hobble-dehoy. Cf. Halflin.

Haft, *n.* the right-hand side of a band of reapers. Cf. Heft.

Haft, *n.* usual pasture ; a domicile ; a haunt.—*v.* to accustom sheep or cattle to a new pasture ; to dwell ; to accustom to live in a place ; to become domiciled. Cf. Heft.

Haft and point, *n.* the outermost party on each side in a field of reapers.

Hag, *n.* an ill-tempered, violent woman; a scold; a dirty, slovenly woman.

Hag, *v.* to hew, chop; to hack; to cut or carve clumsily; to bungle.—*n.* a hack, notch; a stroke with an axe, &c.; a selection of timber for felling; brushwood.

Hag, *n.* wild, moorish, broken ground. Cf. Hagg.

Hag-a-bag, *n.* huckaback; refuse of any kind.

Hag-airn, *n.* a blacksmith's chisel.

Hag-berry, *n.* the bird-cherry.

Hag-block, -clog, *n.* a chopping-block.

Hages, *int.* a disguised form of 'Jesus,' used in petty oaths and excls.

Hagg, *n.* wild, broken ground; a piece of soft bog in a moor; a hole in a 'moss' from which peats have been cut; a water-hollow, wet in winter and dry in summer; an islet of grass in the midst of a bog.

Hagg, *n.* a stall-fed ox; one who tends fat cattle.

Hagg, *v.* to harass, fatigue.

Hagg, *v.* used of cattle: to butt with the head, to fight.

Hagg, *v.* to hew. Cf. Hag.

Haggart, *n.* a stackyard.

Haggart, *n.* an old, useless horse.

Hagger, *n.* one who uses a hatchet, one employed to cut down trees.

Hagger, *v.* to cut roughly and unevenly, hack, mangle.—*n.* a large cut with a jagged edge.

Hagger, *v.* to rain gently.—*n.* fine, small rain.

Haggeral, *n.* a very large cut; an open, festering sore.

Hagger'd, *ppl. adj.* mangled, full of notches.

Haggerdash, *n.* disorder; a broil.—*adv.* in confusion.

Haggerdecash, *adv.* topsyturvy.

Haggerin', *n.* the act of cutting unevenly.

Haggerin', *ppl. adj.* in *phr.* 'haggerin' and swaggerin',' in an indifferent state of health, not prospering in business, &c.

Haggersnash, *n.* offals; a spiteful person; tart language.—*adj.* spiteful, tart.

Haggerty-tag, -tag-like, *adv.* in an untidy, ragged manner.—*adj.* ragged.

Haggerty-taggerty, *adj.* tattered, ragamuffin.

Haggies, *n.* a haggis.

Haggils, *n.* trammels.

Haggin, *ppl. adj.* given to butting with the head.

Haggis, Haggise, *n.* a sheep's maw containing the minced lungs, heart, and liver of the sheep, mixed and cooked with oatmeal, suet, onions, pepper, and salt.

Haggis-bag, *n.* the sheep's maw containing the ingredients of a haggis; a wind-bag; a contemptuous term for anything; the paunch; a lumpish, soft-headed person: a 'pudding-head.'

Haggis-fed, *adj.* fed on haggis.

Haggis-fitted, *adj.* used of a horse: having the pasterns swelled like a haggis.

Haggish, *n.* a haggis.

Haggis-headed, *adj.* soft-headed, stupid.

Haggis-heart, *n.* a soft, cowardly heart.

Haggis-kail, *n.* the water in which a haggis is boiled.

Haggis-supper, *n.* a supper mainly of haggis.

Haggit, *ppl. adj.* tired; careworn.

Haggle, *v.* to mar a piece of work; to work clumsily or improperly; to struggle; to advance with difficulty.

Haggle-bargle, *n.* one with whom it is difficult to come to terms in bargaining; a stickler.

Hagglie, *adj.* rough, uneven; unevenly cut.

Hagglin, *adj.* rash, incautious.

Haggling, *ppl. adj.* used of the weather: vexatious, trying.

Haggrie, *n.* an unseemly mass, a mess.

Haggy, *adj.* full of 'haggs,' rough, broken, boggy.

Haghle, *v.* to walk slowly and clumsily; to drag the legs, shuffle along. Cf. Hauchle, Hechle.

Hagil, *v.* to haggle.

Hagil-bargain, -bargin, *n.* a stickler in bargaining; a keen wrangle in cheapening a thing.

Hagmahush, *n.* a sloven.—*adj.* slovenly and awkward.

Hagman, *n.* a wood-cutter; one who fells and sells wood.

Hagmana, *n.* New-year's Eve, Dec. 31. Cf. Hogmanay.

Hagmark, *n.* a boundary-mark.

Hag-rid, *ppl. adj.* suffering from nightmare.

Hag-ride, *v.* to bewitch; to give nightmare.

Hag-stane, *n.* a boundary-stone.

Hag-wife, *n.* a midwife.

Hag-wood, *n.* a copse-wood fitted for a regular felling of trees in it.

Hag-yard, *n.* a stackyard. Cf. Haggart.

Ha' hoose, *n.* the manor-house.

Hah-yaud, *int.* a shepherd's call to his dog to make a wide sweep round the flock he is driving.

Haiches, Haichus, *n.* force, impetus; a heavy fall, and its noise.

Haid, *n.* a whit, atom. Cf. Haet.

Haid, *v. pret.* hid.

Haid nor maid, *phr.* extreme poverty.

Haig, *n.* a violent, ill-tempered woman. Cf. Hag.

Haig, *v.* used of cattle: to butt with the head. Cf. Hagg.

Haig, *v.* to loiter; to lounge; to beat; to kidnap.—*n.* a gossiping, gadabout, tattling woman. Cf. Haik. .

Haigel, Haigle, *v.* to haggle. Cf. Hagil, Haggle.

Haigh, *n.* a steep bank, a precipice, a 'heuch.'

Haigle, *v.* to walk or carry with difficulty. Cf. Hauchle.

Haigs, *int.* an excl.; a petty oath, 'fegs!' 'heth!' Cf. Hegs.

Haik, *n.* a rack or manger for fodder; a sparred box for holding turnips, &c., for sheep feeding in a field; a triangular wooden frame with small nails for drying fish; a rack on which cheeses are hung to dry; an open cupboard hanging on a wall; the part of a spinning-wheel, armed with teeth, which guides the spun thread to the 'pirn.'

Haik, *v.* to wander aimlessly, loiter, lounge; to drag about to little purpose; to tramp, trudge; to beat, batter; to kidnap, abduct.—*n.* an idle, lounging fellow; an animal that wanders restlessly in a field, or strays from it; a forward, tattling woman, a gossiping gadabout.

Haiked, Haikit, *adj.* used of animals: white-faced; stupid, foolish. Cf. Hawkit.

Haiker, *n.* an animal that 'haiks' in a field or from it.

Hail, *n.* small shot, pellets.

Hail, *v.* to shout, roar.

Hail, *v.* to drive a ball to the goal.—*n.* the cry raised when the ball is so driven; the act of driving the ball so; the goal at 'shinty,' football, &c.; in *pl.* a game resembling hockey played at the Edinburgh Academy; the place for playing off the ball.

Hail, *n.* a small quantity of a liquid; a drop.—*v.* to flow, run down in large and rapid drops; to pour down.

Hail, *v.* in *phr.* 'to hail a hundred,' a weaver's term.

Hail, Haill, *v.* to haul, pull, drag along.—*n.* a haul of fish.

Hail, Haill, *adj.* hale; free from injury; safe and sound; healthy, vigorous, robust; whole, complete, entire.—*n.* health, vigour, soundness; welfare, well-being; the whole, sum-total.—*adv.* wholly.

Hail an' a-hame, *phr.* quite at home; in good spirits.

Hail an' fere, *phr.* in perfect health.

Hail-an-hadden, *phr.* complete, entire.

Hail-ba', *n.* a boys' game at ball, known also as 'han-an-hail.'

Hail-head, *adv.* in *phr.* to 'go hail-head,' to go on express errand or sole purpose.

Hail-headit, *adj.* unhurt; whole and entire.

Hail-heartit, *adj.* of unbroken spirit; with the whole heart.

Hail-hide, *adj.* unhurt; safe and sound; with a whole skin.

Hailick, *n.* a romping, giddy girl. Cf. Hallock.

Hailing-muff, *n.* a mitten used by fishermen to protect their hands when hauling their lines.

Haillick, *n.* the last blow or kick of the ball that sends it beyond the line and gains the game.

Haillins, *adv.* certainly, completely.

Hailly, *adv.* wholly, utterly.

Hail-oot drinks, *n.* a toast calling to leave no heel-taps.

Hail-ruck, *n.* the sum-total of a person's property; the whole of a collection of things.

Hail-scart, *adj.* without a scratch, quite safe or unhurt.

Hail-skinn't, *adj.* having a whole, unbroken, or healthy skin.

Hailsum, *adj.* wholesome, health-giving, sound.

Hailumly, *adv.* certainly, completely.

Hail-water, *n.* a heavy fall of rain; a rush of rain like a waterspout.

Hail-wheel, *adv.* in wholesale fashion; in quick succession.

Hailwort, Hailwur, *n.* the whole number of things or persons. Cf. Hale-ware.

Hailzin, *n.* a vigorous setting-down.

Haim, *n.* home. Cf. Hame.

Haim, *n.* in *pl.* the curved pieces of wood or iron attached to a horse-collar and supporting the traces. Cf. Hame.

Haimald, *adj.* homely, domestic; home-grown, home-made, home-bred; tame, domestic, not wild.—*v.* to domesticate. Cf. Hamald.

Haimart, Haimert, *adj.* belonging to home; home-grown, home-keeping, homely, simple; condescending in manner, not haughty.—*adv.* homeward. Cf. Hamert.

Haimartness, *n.* a childish attachment to home.

Haimhald, *v.* to prove anything to be one's own property; to domesticate. Cf. Hamhald.

Haimo'er, *adv.* homewards.—*adj.* homely, rustic, unpolished; home-keeping. Cf. Hame-owre.

Hain, *n.* a haven; a shelter, place of refuge.

Hain, *v.* to enclose, defend by a hedge; to preserve grass for hay; to preserve from harm; to shield; to economize; to hoard, be penurious; to save exertion, spare trouble, &c.; with *off* or *from*, to abstain from; to cease raining; to keep one's self chaste.

Hainberries, *n.* raspberries; wild raspberries.

Hainch, *n.* the haunch.—*v.* to throw under the leg or thigh, by striking the hand against the thigh ; to jerk.

Hainch, *v.* to halt, limp. Cf. Hinch.

Hainch-bane, *n.* the haunch-bone.

Hainch-deep, *adv.* up to the haunches.

Hainch-hoops, *n.* hoops over which the skirts were draped.

Hainchil, *v.* to roll from side to side in walking. Cf. Henchil.

Hainch-knots, *n.* bunches of ribbons worn on the hips.

Hainch-vent, *n.* a triangular bit of linen or gore between the front and back tails of a shirt.

Hainer, *n.* a thrifty, saving person who takes care of his or her ' things,' &c.

Haing, *v.* to hang.

Haingle, *v.* to go about feebly; to loaf about; to dangle.—*n.* a lout, booby, a clumsy fellow; in *pl.* influenza; a state of ennui.

Haining, *ppl. adj.* thrifty, penurious.—*n.* a field in which a crop or grass is protected ; thrift, parsimony ; in *pl.* earnings, savings.

Haining-broom, *n.* broom reserved for use.

Haining-time, *n.* the time of cropping, when fields or crops were enclosed for protection from cattle.

Haip, *n.* a sloven. Cf. Heap.

Hair, *n.* a filament of flax or hemp ; the sixth of a hank of yarn ; a very small portion of anything.—*v.* to free from hairs.

Hair, *n.* the last pickle corn to be cut on a farm. Cf. Hare.

Hair-and-wair, *n.* contention, disagreement. Cf. Here and were.

Hair-breed, *n.* a hairbreadth.

Haired, *ppl. adj.* used of a cow : having a mixture of white and red, or of white and black, on the skin.

Hairen, *adj.* made of hair.

Hairey, *n.* the devil. Cf. Harry.

Hair-frost, *n.* hoar-frost.

Hair-hanged, -hung, *adj.* hanging by the hair, like Absalom.

Hairiken, *n.* a hurricane.

Hair-kaimer, *n.* a hairdresser.

Hair-knife, *n.* a knife used to free butter from hairs.

Hair-lug, *n.* a particular fishing-fly. Cf. Hare's lug.

Hairm, *n.* harm.—*v.* to harm.

Hairm, *v.* to grumble, fret ; to be ill-tempered ; to 'harp' on a trifling fault, &c., and upbraid the offender.

Hairmer, *n.* one who 'harps' on trifles.

Hairmin', *n.* fretfulness, grumbling ; the continuous 'harping' on faults or trifles.

Hairmless, *adj.* unharmed, safe and sound.

Hair-mould, *n.* mouldiness caused by dampness.

Hairn, *n.* in *pl.* brains. Cf. Harn.

Hairn-pan, *n.* the skull, brain-pan.

Hairp, *v.* to harp ; to grumble ; to reflect on one with repeated upbraiding.—*n.* a harp ; a wire instrument for sifting. Cf. Harp.

Hairriel, *n.* what impoverishes land. Cf. Herrial.

Hairry, *v.* to harry, plunder ; to rob nests. Cf. Herry.

Hairse, *adj.* hoarse.

Hairse, *n.* a lustre ; a triangular frame for holding lights in a church.

Hairselie, *adv.* hoarsely.

Hairseness, *n.* hoarseness.

Hair-shagh, -shard, -shaw, *n.* a hare-lip, a cleft lip.

Hairshill, *v.* to injure ; to waste.

Hairship, *n.* a foray ; booty, prey ; plundering by force. Cf. Herschip.

Hairst, *n.* harvest ; an engagement for harvest any kind of autumn crop.—*v.* to harvest, to work in the harvest-field.

Hair-stane, *n.* boundary-stone.

Hairst-day, *n.* a day during harvest.

Hairst-folks, *n.* harvesters.

Hairst-hog, *n.* a sheep smeared at the end of harvest, when it ceases to be a lamb.

Hairst-home, *n.* winter.

Hairst-maiden, *n.* a figure formed of a sheaf, surmounting the last load of corn brought home. Cf. Maiden.

Hairst-Monday, *n.* a fair on the Monday occurring four weeks before the anticipated beginning of the local harvest.

Hairst-mune, -meen, *n.* the harvest-moon.

Hairst-play, *n.* the school holidays during harvest.

Hairst-queen, *n.* the belle of the harvest-home dance.

Hairst-rig, *n.* the harvest-field, or a section of it ; the man and woman who reap together on a 'rig' of the field.

Hairst-roup, *n.* a sale by auction at a harvest-fair.

Hairst-shearer, *n.* a reaper at harvest with the 'hook.'

Hairst-vacance, *n.* school vacation in harvest.

Hairt, *n.* heart. Cf Heart.

Hair-tether, *n.* a tether made of hair, supposed to be used in witchcraft.

Hairturk, *n.* a cloth used for ladies' riding-skirts.

Hairy, *v.* to harry. Cf. Herry.

Hairy-brotag, *n.* any large, hairy caterpillar.

Hairy-bummler, *n.* a name given to certain kinds of crabs.

Hairy-hutcheon, *n.* the sea-urchin.

Hairy-moggans, *n.* hose without feet.

Hairy-oobit, -oubit, *n.* any large, hairy cater-pillar.

Haiser, Haisre, *v.* to dry clothes in the open air and sun.

Haisert, *ppl. adj.* half-dried, surface-dried.

Haisk, *v.* to make a noise like a dog when anything sticks in his throat. Cf. Hask.

Haisle, *v.* to dry, mellow in the sun ; to dry on the surface.—*n.* the first process in drying linen. Cf. Haiser, Aisle.

Haiss, *adj.* hoarse.

Haist, *v.* to make haste.

Haist, *n.* the harvest. Cf. Hairst.

Haister, *v.* to speak or act without considera-tion ; to do anything in a slovenly manner ; to toast bread badly ; to serve a great dinner confusedly.—*n.* a person who does things confusedly ; a slovenly woman ; a confusion, hodge - podge, mess ; a great dinner confusedly set down.

Haisters, *n.* one who speaks or acts confusedly.

Haistert, *ppl. adj.* hurried.

Haistines, *n.* early peas, 'hastings.'

Haistow, *n.* a call to make haste.

Hait, *n.* an atom, particle. Cf. Haet.

Haith, *int.* an excl. of surprise, &c., faith !

Haitsum, *adj.* unkind ; hateful.

Haiveless, *adj.* wasteful ; slovenly ; incom-petent.

Haiver, *n.* a gelded he-goat. Cf. Aver.

Haiver, *v.* to talk nonsense.—*n.* in *pl.* non-sense. Cf. Haver.

Haiverel, *n.* a foolish talker.—*v.* to talk nonsense. Cf. Haverel.

Haives, *n.* hoofs.

Haivins, Haivens, *n.* manners, good be-haviour.

Haiviour, *n.* behaviour.

Haivrel, *n.* a foolish talker.

Haivrelly, *adj.* talking like a fool.

Haizart, *v.* to venture to do or to conjecture ; to hazard.

Haizer, Haizre, *v.* to dry clothes in the open air. Cf. Haiser.

Haizert, *ppl. adj.* half-dried.

Haizie, *adj.* dim ; not seeing distinctly ; muddled ; crazy. Cf. Hazie.

Hake, *v.* to wander aimlessly. Cf. Haik.

Hake, *n.* a frame for drying cheeses ; a frame for drying fish. Cf. Haik.

Hal', *n.* an abode. Cf. Ha'.

Halakit, *ppl. adj.* light, giddy. Cf. Hall lockit.

Halan-, Halin-shaker, *n.* a ragged fellow. Cf. Hallanshaker.

Halbert, *n.* a halberd ; a very tall, thin person.

Hald, *v.* to hold ; to cease. *–pret.* held. *n.* a hold ; the bank of a stream under which trouts lie ; a dwelling. Cf. Had.

Halden, *ppl.* held. Cf. Hadden, Holden.

Halder, *n.* a holder. Cf. Hadder.

Hale, *n.* health.

Hale-head, *adv.* in *phr.* 'to go hale-head,' to go on express errand.

Halelie, *adv.* wholly. Cf. Hailly.

Halescart, *adj.* safe and sound.

Halesome, *adj.* wholesome. Cf. Hailsum.

Haleumlie, *adv.* certainly ; completely. Cf. Hailumly.

Haleware, Halewar, Halewur, *n.* the whole ; the whole number of things or persons ; the 'whole hypothec.'

Hale-water, *n.* a heavy fall of rain, as if from a waterspout.

Hale-wheel, *adv.* all at once, wholesale.

Halewort, *n.* the whole. Cf. Hailwort.

Half, *n.* in *pl.* equal shares claimed by children who find anything.—*adj.* preced-ing numerals indicating an hour : half-past the preceding hour.—*v.* to halve.

Half-acre, *n.* a small field or allotment.

Half-auld, *adj.* middle-aged.

Half-bend, *adv.* used of a gun, pistol : half-cock.

Half-cousin, *n.* a first cousin once removed.

Half-dealsman, *n.* a fisherman who shares in the profits.

Halfer, *n.* one who has a moiety of a thing ; a half-share. Cf. Haaver.

Half-fou, *n.* two pecks, or half a bushel.

Half-fou, *adj.* half-drunk.

Half-gable, *n.* a gable common to two houses.

Half-gane, *adj.* about the middle of preg-nancy.

Half-gates, *adv.* half-way.

Half-jack, *adj.* half-witted.

Half-lade, *n.* a large straw basket, two of which, when filled and slung on a pony's back, form a load.

Halflin, *n.* a carpenter's plane. Cf. Hafflin.

Halflin, *adj.* half-grown, youthful.—*n.* a half-grown boy, a stripling ; a farm- or stable-boy ; a hobbledehoy ; a half-witted person, a fool.

Halflins, *adv.* half, partially, nearly ; half-way, in equal shares.—*adj.* half, partial ; half-grown, young.

Halflinswise, *adv.* partly, in a slight measure ; half-heartedly.

Half-loaf, *n.* half of a loaf which happens to exceed the number allotted to the reapers, which loaf, divided into two, is given, one half to the men, and the other half to the women, to be scrambled for.

Half-mark-, -merk-bridal, *n.* a clandestine marriage.

Half-mark-kirk, *n.* a church in which clan-destine marriages were formerly celebrated.

Half - mark - marriage, *n.* a clandestine marriage.

Half-mark-marriage-kirk, *n.* a 'half-mark-kirk.'

Half-marrow, *n.* a spouse; yokefellow; mate.

Half-moon-flask, *n.* a large flask formerly used in smuggling, and almost encircling the body of the smuggler.

Half-mutchkin, *n.* half a pint.

Half-net, *n.* the right to half of the fishing by one net.

Half-nothing, *n.* little or nothing, next to nothing, a very small sum.

Half-on, *adj.* well on the way to become drunk.

Half-one, *n.* used in golfing: the handicap of a stroke deducted every second hole.

Half-penny deevil, *n.* a kind of cheap sweet-cake.

Half-roads, *adv.* half-way.

Half-sarkit, *adj.* half-clothed.

Half-sea, *adj.* tipsy.

Half-water, *adv.* half-way between the boat and the sea-bottom.

Half-ways, *adv.* half, partly.

Half-web, *n.* the red-necked phalarope; the gray phalarope.

Half-whaup, *n.* the bar-tailed godwit.

Halicat, Halicut, *ppl. adj.* giddy, romping, crazy. Cf. Hallockit.

Halick, *n.* a giddy girl. Cf. Hallock.

Halidome, *n.* lands holding of a religious foundation.

Halison, *n.* a comfortable saying.

Halk-, Hawk-hen, *n.* a hen formerly demanded from each house in Orkney, to feed the king's hawks, when his falconer went thither to collect hawks.

Halkit, *adj.* used of animals: white-faced. Cf. Hawkit.

Hall, *n.* a house, cottage, farmhouse, farm-kitchen. Cf. Ha'.

Hallach, Hallach'd, *adj.* crazy. Cf. Hallock.

Hallachin, *n.* noisy, foolish conduct.—*ppl. adj.* noisy, foolish.

Hallack, *n.* a hillock.

Halla'-day, *n.* All-hallows-day.

Hallan, Hallen, *n.* a partition - wall in a cottage between the door and the fire-place; the space within the partition, a porch, lobby; a screen; a dwelling, cottage; a buttress built against a weak wall to keep it from falling; the space above the cross-beams of the couples of a house; a turf seat outside a cottage.

Hallan-door, *n.* an outer door.

Hallanshaker, *n.* a ragged fellow, tramp, beggar; a knave, rascal of shabby appearance.

Hallanshaker-looking, *adj.* unkempt, ragged in appearance.

Hallan-stane, *n.* a doorstep, threshold.

Hallarackit, *adj.* wildly excited, giddy. Cf. Hallirackit.

Hallens, Hallins, *adv.* partially, half. Cf. Halflins.

Hallens, *n.* in *phr.* 'to gae by the hallens,' of a child : to go by holds. Cf. Halls.

Hallick, Hallik, *n.* a wild, giddy girl.

Hallickit, *ppl. adj.* wild, giddy. Cf. Hallockit.

Hallie, *n.* romping.

Hallie-balloo, *n.* a hubbub, uproar.

Hallier, *n.* a half-year.

Halligit, *ppl. adj.* wild, giddy. Cf. Hallockit.

Hallion, *n.* a clumsy fellow, a clown; an idle, lazy scamp; a servant out of livery; an inferior servant doing odd jobs; a domineering, quarrelsome, vulgar woman.

Hallior, *n.* the last quarter of the moon when much on the wane.

Hallirackit, Hallyrackit, *adj.* giddy, romping; hare-brained.

Hallirakus, *n.* a giddy, hare-brained person.

Hallock, *v.* to behave foolishly and noisily.—*adj.* crazy.—*n.* a hoyden.

Hallockit, *ppl. adj.* wild, giddy, romping; half-witted.—*n.* a romp, a hoyden : a noisy, restless person.

Halloo-balloo, *n.* an uproar.

Hallop, *v.* to frisk about precipitately.—*n.* a hasty, precipitate person.

Halloper, *n.* a giddy and precipitate person.

Hallopin, *ppl. adj.* unsteady, unsettled, foolish.

Hallow, *adj.* hollow, sunken.—*n.* a hollow, valley.—*v.* to hollow, make hollow.

Hallow-baloo, *n.* an uproar.

Hallow-day, *n.* All-hallows-day.

Hallowe'en, *n.* the eve of 'Hallow-day.'

Hallowe'en-bleeze, *n.* a bonfire kindled cn Hallowe'en.

Hallow-fair, *n.* a fair held in the beginning of November.

Hallow-fire, *n.* a Hallowe'en bonfire.

Hallow-market, *n.* a market held on 'Hallow-day.'

Hallowmas, *n.* the season of All hallows; the first week of November.

Hallowmas-rade, *n.* the general assembly of 'warlocks' and witches, supposed to have been held about 'Hallowmas.'

Halls, *n.* in *phr.* 'to walk by the halls,' used of a child : to support itself while learning to walk. Cf. Hallens.

Hallum, *n.* the woody part of flax.

Hally, *adj.* holy.

Hally-balloo, -baloo, *n.* an uproar.

Hally-bally, *n.* a great noise or uproar.

Hallyie, *n.* romping.

Hallyoch, *n.* a gabbling noise as heard in listening to a strange tongue.

Haloc, Halok, *adj.* light, giddy.—*n.* a light, giddy girl. Cf. Hallock.

Haloo-balloo, *n.* an uproar.

Halowhou, *n.* a child's caul; a membrane. Cf. Helie-how.

Halse, Hals, *n.* the neck; the throat, gullet; a defile; a shallow in a river; a hug.—*v.* to hug, embrace.

Halser, *n.* a hawser.

Halshe, *n.* a noose, loop.

Halsome, *adj.* wholesome, health - giving. Cf. Hailsum.

Halt, *n.* a defect; a defect of speech.

Halter, *v.* to bridle; to secure a husband.

Haluck, *n.* a giddy girl. Cf. Hallock.

Haluckit, *ppl. adj.* giddy, light-headed. Cf. Hallockit.

Halve-net, *n.* a fixed net, within water-mark, to prevent fish returning with the tide. Cf. Haave.

Halver, *n.* a sharer; an equal share.—*adj.* held in partnership.—*v.* to halve; to hold in partnership. Cf. Haaver.

Haly, Halie, *adj.* holy.

Haly, *adj.* cautious, in no hurry. Cf. Hooly.

Halyear, *n.* a half-year. Cf. Hallier.

Ha'-maiden, *n.* the bride's-maid at a wedding; the 'maiden kimmer' who lays the infant in the father's arms at a baptism. Cf. Maiden-kimmer.

Hamald, *v.* to prove anything to be one's own property. Cf. Hamhald.

Hamald, *adj.* homely, domestic, household; home-grown; home-made, not foreign; tame, not wild.—*v.* to domesticate.

Hamart, *adj.* home-grown; home-keeping; homely; courteous. Cf. Hameart.

Hame, *n.* a ham.

Hame, *n.* in *pl.* two curved pieces of wood or iron resting on the collar of a horse, and supporting the traces.

Hame, *n.* home.—*adj.* to the point, direct.

Hame-airted, *adj.* directed homewards.

Hameald, *adj.* home - grown; vernacular; vulgar. Cf. Hamald.

Hameart, *adv.* homewards.—*adj.* homeward; homely; home-grown; belonging to home; home-keeping; condescending, courteous.

Hameartness, *n.* attachment to home.

Hame-at, *adj.* belonging to home; home-made. Cf. Hameart.

Hame-blade, *n.* a ham-bone.

Hame-blade, *n.* the half of a horse-collar.

Hame-body, *n.* one not a stranger.

Hame-bred, *adj.* unpolished.

Hame-bringing, *n.* bringing home; importation, importing.

Hame-coming, *n.* arrival home; festivities, &c., on an arrival home.

Hame-dealing, *n.* plain speaking.

Hame-drauchtit, *adj.* selfish, looking after one's own interests.

Hame-drawn, *adj.* 'hame-drauchtit.'

Hame-fair, -fare, *n.* the removal of a bride from her own or her father's house to that of her husband; the home-coming of a newly-married couple.

Hame-gäin, -gaun, *n.* a return-journey.—*adj.* going homeward.

Hame-girse, *n.* private pasture, in contrast to common.

Hame-houghed, *adj.* used of a horse: straiter above than below the hough; having houghs shaped like 'hames.'

Hameil, *adj.* homely; home-grown. Cf. Hamald.

Hameit, *adj.* home-grown; home-keeping. Cf. Hameart.

Hamel, *adj.* homely. Cf. Hamald.

Hame-lan', *adj.* used of farm-servants: living in the farmhouse.

Hameld, Hamelt, *adj.* homely. Cf. Hamald.

Hameliness, *n.* homeliness; familiarity.

Hamely, *adj.* friendly, familiar, 'at home.'

Hamely-spoken, *adj.* plain-spoken, unaffected.

Hame-made, *n.* a home-made article.

Hame-o'er, -owre, *adj.* homely, humble; rude, rustic; coarse, unpolished; home-keeping.—*adv.* homewards.

Hamert, *adj.* homely; home-grown. Cf. Hameart.

Hame-sang, *n.* a song of home, country, &c.

Hamesome, *adj.* homely.

Hamespun, *adj.* spun at home; mean, contemptible, vulgar; rustic, homely, humble.

Hamesucken, *n.* the crime of violently assaulting a man in his own house.—*adj.* fond of one's home; selfish.

Hamet, *adj.* homely. Cf. Hameart.

Hameward, Hamewart, *adj.* homely, courteous.—*adv.* homewards. Cf. Hameart.

Hamewith, -wuth, *adj.* homeward.—*adv.* homewards.—*n.* self-interest.

Hamhald, *adj.* homely; home-grown.—*v.* to prove a thing to be one's own property and not another's; to domesticate. Cf. Hamald.

Hamie, *adj.* homely, domestic, suggestive of home.

Hamil, Hamilt, *adj.* homely. Cf. Hamald.

Hamit, *adj.* home-grown; home-made. Cf. Hameart.

Hamlan, Hamlin, *n.* a trick, wile.

Hamly, *adj.* homely.

Hammal, Hammel, *adj.* homely, domestic. Cf. Hamald.

Hammel, *n.* an open shed for sheltering cattle; a stage on posts to support hay, corn, &c.

Hammer, *v.* to thrash; to work or walk noisily and clumsily; to stumble.—*n.* a blow with a hammer; clumsy, noisy walking; a noisy, clumsy person; the sledge-hammer in athletic games.

Hammer, *v.* to stammer; to hesitate in speaking, ' hum and haw.'

Hammer-and-block, -study, *n.* a boys' bumping game.

Hammer and tongs, *phr.* high words; in curling: a stone played with sweeping force.

Hammerer, *n.* a big, clumsy person with unwieldy feet; a noisy, clumsy worker.

Hammerflush, *n.* sparks from an anvil.

Hammergaw, *v.* to argue pertinaciously.

Hammerin', *n.* a severe thrashing.

Hammerman, *n.* a worker in iron, tin, &c.; a member of a blacksmiths' incorporation.

Hammer-thrower, *n.* one who throws a large hammer in athletic games.

Hammil, Hammle, *adj.* hornless.—*v.* to remove the beards of barley after threshing. Cf. Hummel.

Hammirt, *adj.* homely, vernacular. Cf. Hamert.

Hammit, Hammot, *adj.* used of corn: growing close, but short in the straw; plentiful, with many grains on one stalk.

Hammle, *v.* to walk in an ungainly, stumbling way.

Hamp, *v.* to halt in walking; to stutter; to read with difficulty and much mispronunciation.—*n.* a halt in walking; a stutter.

Hamper, *n.* one who cannot read fluently.

Hamphis, *v.* to surround; to confine.

Hamrel, *n.* a heedless walker; a frequent stumbler.

Hamsh, *v.* to eat noisily and voraciously.

Hamshackle, *v.* to prevent an animal from straying by fastening its head to one of its forelegs.

Hamshoch, Hamsheugh, *n.* a sprain or contusion on the leg; a severe bruise accompanied by a wound; a severe laceration of the body; a misfortune, an untoward accident; a disturbance; a harsh and unmannerly intermeddling in any business.— *adj.* much bruised and lacerated; used of critics: severe, censorious. Cf. A:nshach.

Hamstram, *n.* difficulty.

Han, *n.* hand.—*v.* to hand.

Han-an-hail, *n.* a game at hand-ball, played at Dumfries.

Hanbeast, *n.* the horse a ploughman guides with the left hand.

†Hanch, *v.* to snap like a dog when anything is thrown to it; to devour greedily.—*n.* a voracious snatch.

Hanchman, *n.* a personal attendant, henchman.

Hand, *n.* an adept, clever performer; handwriting; a business or job, good or bad; help; the horse that walks on the left-hand side in ploughing; direction; a fuss; in *pl.* the use of her hands for a servant's own benefit in her spare hours.

Hand-afore, *n.* the fore-horse on the left hand in a plough.

Hand-ahin, *n.* the last horse on the left hand in a plough.

Hand-bellows, *n.* a small pair of bellows.

Hand-bind, *n.* a grip in wrestling.

Hand-bound, *adj.* fully occupied.

Hand-braid, -breed, -brode, *n.* a handbreadth.

Hand-canter, *n.* a quick canter.

Hand-clap, *n.* a moment, instant.

Hand-darg, *n.* handiwork, toil; wages of manual labour.

Handed, *ppl. adj.* hand in hand.

Handel, *n.* a slight refreshment before breakfast, a ' morning-piece'; a ' snack.'

Hand-fast, *v.* to betroth by joining hands for cohabitation before marriage; to contract in order to marriage.

Hand-fasting, *n.* cohabitation for a year with a view to ultimate marriage.

Hand-frandie, *n.* a small stack of corn that can be reached by the hand.

Handful, *n.* a heavy charge, task, or responsibility.

Handgun, *n.* a pistol; a pop-gun.

Hand-habble, *adv.* summarily and quickly, off-hand.

Hand-haill, *adj.* hand-whole; fit for one's work.

Hand-hap, *n.* a chance, hazard.

Handiconeive, *adv.* in company; conjunctly.

Handicuff, *n.* a blow with the hand.

Hand-idle, *adj.* idle, with unoccupied hands.

Hand-ladder, *n.* a light ladder, easily carried by the hand.

Handlawwhile, *n.* a little while.

Handle, Han'le, *n.* fishing-tackle.—*v.* to secure; to get money from; to treat, deal with; to drag up a curling-stone by the handle.

Hand-lecks, *n.* mittens.

Handler, *n.* one who handles a cock in a cock-fight.

Handless, *adj.* awkward in the use of the hands; clumsy in working; apt to let things fall.

Handling, *n.* business; stewardship, charge; interference; an entertainment; a merry-making.

Hand-making, *n.* manufacturing by hand and not by machinery.

Hand-money, *n.* ready money.

Hand-payment, *n.* a beating.

Hand-plane, *n.* a smoothing-plane.

Hand-prap, *n.* a walking-stick.

Hand-rackle, *adj.* rash in striking; careless, inconsiderate; active, ready.

Hand-reel, *n.* an old reel used for winding and numbering the hanks of yarn.

Hand-rick, *n.* a small stack, not too high to be reached by the hand.

Handsel, *n.* an inaugurative gift for luck; an auspicious beginning; a good omen; the first money received for sale of goods; the first purchaser; a morning-lunch, given before breakfast; guerdon, reward; a punishment, a smack of the hand; the earnest given on completing a bargain.—*v.* to give money, &c., to celebrate a new undertaking, possession, &c.; to inaugurate; to drink success; to pay earnest money on a bargain; to try or use a thing for the first time.

Handsel-e'en, *n.* the eve of the first Monday of the New Year.

Handselling, *n.* the inauguration, first use, payment, purchase, &c.

Handsel-Monday, *n.* the first Monday of the New Year.

Handsel-smell, *n.* a smell instead of a taste in 'handselling' liquor.

Hansdel-Tuesday, *n.* the first Tuesday of the New Year.

Handsel-wife, *n.* the woman, usually the bride's mother, who distributes the 'handsel' or gifts at a marriage.

Handshaking, *n.* close engagement, grappling; an intermeddling; a correction, punishment.

Hand-shoes, *n.* gloves.

Hand-skair, *n.* the lowest part of a fishing-rod.

Handsome, *adj.* used of the weather: fine, bright.

Hand-spaik, -spake, *n.* a handspike, used for carrying the dead to the grave.

Hand-staff, *n.* the handle of a flail; a walking-stick.

Hand-stone, *n.* a pebble, a stone that can be lifted by the hand.

Hand-streik, -straik, *n.* a blow with the hand; in *pl.* hand-to-hand fighting.

Hand's-turn, *n.* a single act of doing a piece of work.

Hand's-while, *n.* a little while.

Hand-thief, *n.* one who thieves with the hands.

Hand-wailed, -waled, *adj.* carefully selected; picked by hand; remarkable.

Hand-wailling, *n.* particular or accurate selection.

Hand-wave, *v.* to strike a measure of grain with the hand; to give good measure.

Hand-waving, *n.* a mode of measuring grain by striking it with the hand.

Hand-write, *n.* handwriting; penmanship.

Handy, *adj.* dexterous, clever; useful, good; suitable, seemly; near by, close at hand.—*adv.* easily, without trouble.—*n.* a child's hand, a small hand.

Handy, *n.* a small tub or pail with upright handle, for carrying milk, water, &c.; a milk-pail; a wooden dish for food.

Handy-fu', *n.* the fill of a milk-pail, &c.

Handy-grips, *n.* close quarters in grappling.

Handy-micht, *n.* main force, strength of hand.

Handy-stane, *n.* a stone that can be thrown with the hand.

Hane, *v.* to save; to spare. Cf. Hain.

Ha'net, *n.* the right to half of the fishing of one net. Cf. Half-net.

Han'-for-nieve, *phr.* 'cheek by jowl'; abreast; walking in familiar, friendly fashion.

Hangall, *v.* to entangle. Cf. Hankle.

Hangarel, *n.* a stick, post, or peg on which halters, bridles, &c., or anything may be hung.

Hang-choice, *n.* the necessary choice of one of two evils.

Hangers, *n.* braces for trousers.

Hangie, *n.* a hangman; the devil; a drift-net.

Hanging gate, *n.* a bar hung across a small stream to prevent any one passing it.

Hanging-lock, *n.* a padlock.

Hanging-side, *n.* the side of a door to which the hinges are usually attached.

Hanging-tow, *n.* a hangman's rope.

Hangit, *ppl. adj.* cursed, damned.

Hangit-faced, *adj.* having a look that seems to point to the gallows.

Hangit-like, *adj.* shamefaced, hang-dog like.

Hangle, *v.* to delay a decision; to hang in suspense.

Hang-net, *n.* a net with a very large mesh.

Hangrell, *n.* a peg or post for hanging anything on. Cf. Hangarell.

Haniel, *n.* a greedy dog; an idle, slovenly person; a term of abuse.—*v.* to have a jaded appearance from extreme fatigue or from slovenliness.

Haniel slyp, *n.* an uncouthly-dressed person, an ugly fellow, a vulgar dependant.

Haning, *n.* a field where the grass or crop is preserved; in *pl.* savings through thrift or parsimony. Cf. Haining.

Hank, *n.* a rope, coil; a knot, loop; a lock of hair; a skein of cotton, thread, &c.; hold, influence.—*v.* to make up into coils, &c.; to fasten, tie up; to put together; to gall with a rope or cord by tying it too tightly; to catch or hang on a hook; to muzzle.

Hank, *n.* the lee-side of a boat.

Hanker, *v.* to loiter, linger, loaf about; to hesitate, ponder, hesitate in speaking.—*n.* hesitation, doubt, regret.

Hankering, *n.* hesitation.

Hankie, *n.* a bucket narrower at the top than the bottom, with an iron handle, used for carrying water.

Hankle, *v.* to fasten by tight tying; to entangle, involve; to wind up into a coil.

Hankle, *n.* the ankle.

Hankle, *n.* a quantity, a considerable number, a 'hantle.'

Hank-oarsman, *n.* the rower who sits near the helmsman.

Hanky, *n.* a handkerchief.

Hannie, *n.* a child's hand.—*adj.* handy, suitable. Cf. Handy.

Hannie, *n.* a milk-pail, &c. Cf. Handy.

Hanniel, *n.* a greedy dog. Cf. Haniel.

Hannies, *n.* oatcakes.

Hanniwing, *n.* a term of contempt.

Hanny, *adj.* light-fingered. Cf. Handy.

Hans, *n.* in *phr.* 'Hans in kelder,' an unborn child, a toast formerly drunk to the health of an expected infant.

Hansel, *v.* to handsel.

Hansh, *v.* to snap at like a dog. Cf. Hanch.

Hant, *v.* to practise; to frequent, resort to; to provide a haunt for.—*n.* a custom, practice, habit. Cf. Haunt.

Hanterin, Hantrin, *n.* a moment, a short space of time.—*adj.* occasional. Cf. Anterin.

Hantle, *n.* a large quantity or number; much.

Hanty, *adj.* convenient, handy; manageable with ease; handsome.

Hanyel, Hanziel, *n.* a greedy dog; a lout. Cf. Haniel.

Hap, *v.* to cover, envelop, surround; to cover for warmth, tuck up in bed; to clothe, dress; to cover over, bury; to protect with a covering of earth, straw, litter, &c.; to thatch; to conceal, hush up, cover out of sight; to shield, shelter; to make up a fire so as to keep it alive through the night.—*n.* a covering, wrap; a coverlet, rug; a thick outer garment; dress; with *up*, a heavy fall or cover of snow.

Hap, *v.* used of horses or yoke-oxen: to turn to the right.—*int.* a call to a horse to turn to the right.

Hap, *v.* to hop; to dance; to caper; to limp; to revolve; to cause to hop; used of tears: to drop fast.—*n.* a hop; a rustic dance, a light leap.

Hap, *n.* the fruit of the briar.

Hap, *v.* in *phr.* 'hap weel, rap weel,' hit or miss.

Hap, *n.* an implement for scraping up sea-ooze to make salt with.

Hap-border, *n.* the border of a shawl or wrap.

Hape, *v.* used of horses and yoke-oxen: to turn to the right. Cf. Hap.

Hape, *n.* a halfpenny.

Happen, *n.* the path trodden by cattle, especially on high grounds.

Happen, *v.* to befall, happen to; with *on*, to light upon, meet in with, come upon by chance.

Happening, *n.* an event, a casual occurrence. —*ppl. adj.* casual, chance, occasional.

Happer, *n.* the hopper of a mill.

Happer, *n.* a vessel made of straw for carrying grain to the sower.

Happer-arsed, *adj.* shrunken about the hips.

Happer-bauk, *n.* the beam on which the hopper rests.

Happered, *adj.* shrunken.

Happer-gaw, -gall, *v.* to sow grain unevenly. —*n.* a blank in growing corn, caused by unequal sowing.

Happer-hippit, *adj.* shrunken about the hips; lank.

Happie, *n.* a rustic dance; a short hop.—*v.* to hop.

Happins, *n.* clothes.

Happit, *ppl. adj.* covered, wrapped up; buried.

Happit, *v.* to hop.

Happity, *n.* a man with a club foot.—*adj.* lame.

Happity-kick, *n.* used of an ill-assorted couple: inability to walk together in step, incompatibility.

Happle, *v.* used of tears: to trickle, roll down the cheeks.

Happorth, *n.* halfpennyworth.

Happy, *adj.* lucky, fortunate, boding good luck.

Happy-go-lucky, *adv.* at all hazards, by chance.

Haps, *adv.* perhaps, perchance.—*n.* happenings; strange occurrences.

Hapshackle, *v.* to bind the feet of cattle together, to keep them from straying.—*n.* a shackle, fetter; a ligament for confining a horse or cow.

Hap-stap-and-loup, *n.* hop, skip, and jump.

Hap-stumble, *n.* a chance stumble.

Hap-the-beds, *n.* the game of hop-scotch or 'pallall.'

Hap-warm, *n.* a warm wrap or covering.— *adj.* covering to create or maintain warmth.

Har, Harr, *adj.* cold and raw.—*n.* a cold, easterly haze or fog. Cf. Haar.

Har, *n.* the post of a door or gate to which the hinges are fastened.

†Harberie, *n.* a port, harbour; harbourage; shelter.

Harborous, *adj.* furnishing shelter.

Harbour, *n.* lodging; hospitable entertainment.—*v.* to give house-room, hospitality, &c.

Hard, *v. pret.* heard.

Hard, *adj.* close-fisted; used of spirits : strong, undiluted ; of ale : sour ; having unequal surfaces so as to prevent close contact of parts.—*adv.* used of the wind : strongly, boisterously ; tightly, quickly.—*n.* whisky ; difficulty ; hardship; the place where two pieces of wood join too closely together.

Harden, *n.* coarse cloth made of the 'hards' of flax or hemp ; sackcloth.—*adj.* made of sackcloth or 'harden.'

Harden, *v.* to roast on embers; to toast bread ; used of prices : to advance.

Harden-gown, *n.* a coarse linen or sackcloth gown, worn by offenders against the Seventh Commandment when under church-discipline.

Harden-poke, *n.* a bag or sack made of sackcloth.

Hardens, *n.* the thin, hard cakes that come off the sides of a pot in which porridge has been boiled.

Harden-sark, *n.* a coarse linen or hempen shirt.

Harden-wab, *n.* a web of coarse linen cloth.

Hard-fish, *n.* dried and salted cod, ling, &c.

Hard-food, *n.* dry food and corn as opposed to grass ; dry victuals as opposed to fluid or semi-fluid.

Hard-handed, *adj.* stingy, niggardly, close-fisted.

Hard-head, *n.* the gray gurnard ; the father-lasher ; a kind of sea-scorpion.

Hard-head, *n.* a small coin of mixed metal formerly current.

Hard-head, *n.* the sneezewort.

Hard-headit, *adj.* unyielding, stubborn.

Hard-heartit, *adj.* heart-breaking, distressing.

Hard-horn, *adv.* tightly.

Hardiness, *n.* bravery.

Hardlies, *adv.* hardly, scarcely.

Hard-meat, *n.* hay and oats as opposed to grass or to boiled bran, &c.

Hard-nickle-down, *n.* a game of marbles.

Hard-pushed, *adj.* hard-pressed ; hard put to it.

Hards, *n.* what of boiled food, as porridge, &c., adheres to the pot.

Hards, *n.* torches of rags dipped in tar.

Hard-set, *adj.* scarcely able.—*adv.* hardly.

Hardship, *n.* a difficulty, a strait, a 'tight place.'

Hard-tree, *n.* hardwood, close-grained timber.

Hard-words, *n.* abusive language, vituperation.

Hard-wrocht, *ppl. adj.* hard-earned.

Hardy, *adj.* strong, robust ; of good constitution ; used of the weather : frosty.

Hare-bouk, *n.* the body of a hare.

Hare-shard, -shaw, -shie, -skart, *n.* a hare-lip.

Hare's-lug, *n.* a particular kind of fishing-fly.

Haricles, *n.* the pluck of an animal. Cf. Harigalds.

Harie-hurcheon, hutcheon, *n.* a children's game in which the players hop round in a ring, with their bodies resting on their hams, and arms akimbo.

Ha'-rig, *n.* the right-hand 'rig' of a company of reapers ; the first ridge in a harvest-field, so called because reaped by the farm-domestics or members of the farmer's family.

Harigald, *n.* in *phr.* 'head and harigald money,' a sum payable to colliers and salters in bondage when a female of their number, by bearing a child, added to their owner's property or 'live-stock.'

Harigalds, Harigals, Harigells, *n.* the pluck of an animal ; locks of hair.

Hark, *v.* to whisper.—*n.* a whisper ; a secret wish or desire.

Harken, *v.* to hearken ; to hear one repeat a lesson.

Harker, *n.* a listener.

Harkie, Harky, *n.* a pig or sow ; a boar-pig.

Harking, *n.* a whispering.

Harl, Harle, *n.* the reed or brittle stem of flax separated from the filament ; the side fibre of a peacock's tail-feather, used for dubbing flies in fishing.

Harl, Harle, *v.* to drag, tug, trail along the ground, pull ; to drag one's way with difficulty ; to draw one's self along feebly ; to scrape or rake together ; to grapple with. —*n.* the act of dragging or trailing ; a haul, collection, gathering of things ; money or property wrongly acquired ; a small quantity of anything ; what is obtained with difficulty or rarely ; a mud-rake or scraper for roads ; a slattern ; a big, untidy, coarse, cross-grained person.

Harl, Harle, *v.* to rough-cast a wall with a mixture of mortar and small gravel.—*n.* the mixture used for rough-cast.

Harle, Harle-duck, *n.* the goosander; the red-breasted merganser.

Harle-a'-hame, *adj.* selfish, grasping.

Harle-net, *n.* a haul-net.

Harley, *n.* the swift.

Harlin, *n.* rough-casting ; the mixture used for rough-casting.

Harlin, Harlin-favour, *n.* some degree of affection ; an inclination or liking.

Harmless, *adj.* unharmed, safe and sound.

Harn, *n.* coarse cloth of flax or hemp. Cf. Harden.

Harn, *n.* in *pl.* the brain ; brains.

Harness-cask, *n.* a receptacle on board ship,

in which meat, after being taken from the pickle-cask, is kept ready for use.

Harness-lid, *n.* the lid or covering of a 'harness-cask,' with a rim coming a small way down the outside of the cask.

Harness-plaid, *n.* a plaid of fine manufacture, formerly an indispensable part of a respectably married bride's outfit.

Harnless, *adj.* brainless.

Harn-pan, *n.* the skull, brain-pan.

Harn-wab, *n.* a web of coarse linen cloth. Cf. Harden-wab.

Harp, *n.* a mason's oblong riddle for riddling sand, &c.; a kind of 'search' for cleansing grain; the part of a mill which separates the 'dust' of grain from the 'shilling.'—*v.* to riddle or sift with a 'harp.'

Harper crab, *n.* the crab, *Cancer araneus*, the Tammy Harper.

Harr, *n.* an east wind. Cf. Haar.

Harr, *n.* the upright part of a door or gate to which the hinges are fastened. Cf. Har.

Harrage, Harriage, *n.* service due by tenants, in men and horses, to their landlords. Cf. Average.

Harragles, Harrigals, *n.* an animal's viscera. Cf. Harigalds.

Harragraf, *n.* a designation of men not usually taken out to curling matches by the Kippen Club.

Harran, Harren, *n.* coarse linen cloth. Cf. Harden.

Harren, *n.* in *pl.* the brain. Cf. Harn.

Harrie, *adj.* stubborn.

Harriment, *n.* spoliation.

Harrist, *n.* harvest. Cf. Hairst.

Harro, *int.* hurrah! an excl. of surprise; an outcry for help.—*v.* to hurrah, halloo.

Harrow, *v.* to arouse, stir.

Harrow-fair, *n.* an annual fair held in Edinburgh.

Harrow-plough, *n.* a plough for killing weeds in turnip-fields.

Harrow-slaying, *n.* the destruction of grass seeds by rain, before they have struck root, when the mould has been too much pulverized.

Harrowster, *n.* a spawned naddock.

Harrow-teeth, *n.* oppression, exaction, extortion.

Harry, *n.* a harrow.

Harry, *adj.* stubborn. Cf. Harrie.

Harry, *n.* the devil; an opprobrious epithet applied to a woman.

Harry, *v.* to rob birds' nests. Cf. Herry.

Harry-hurcheon, -hurtchon, *n.* a children's game. Cf. Harie-hurcheon.

Harry-purcan, *n.* blind-man's buff.

Harship, *n.* ruin. Cf. Herschip.

Hart, *n.* the heart.—*v.* to stun by a blow given over the heart. Cf. Heart.

Hary, *int.* hurrah! Cf. Harro.

Has-been, *n.* a custom of long standing; one of the old school; a thing past service.

Hase-bane, *n.* the neck-bone.

Hash, *n.* a mess, muddle; a confused mas; a great crash; careless, wasteful use; noisy tumult, riotous strife; nonsense; ribaldry; a heavy fall of rain; a wasteful, slovenly person; a foolish, nonsensical person; a blockhead; a scamp; a vulgar term of endearment for a boy.—*v.* to slash; to damage, destroy; to bruise, ill-treat, abuse; to make a mess of; in harvesting with the scythe: to cut so fast that the man behind the scytheman falls to the rear, or the man in front is pushed forward by the man behind.

Hash-a-pie, *n.* a lazy, slovenly fellow, fonder of eating than of working.

Hasher, *n.* a long knife with a handle, fixed on a board, and worked with the hand, for slicing turnips, &c.

Hashie, *adj.* coarse, rough.

Hashiness, *n.* slovenliness in dress.

Hash-loch, *n.* waste, refuse.

Hashlock, *n.* the fine wool on a sheep's throat; the 'halse-lock.' Cf. Haslock.

Hashly, *adv.* in a slovenly manner.

Hash-mash, *adv.* slap-dash.

Hash-methram, *adv.* topsyturvy; in a state of disorder.

Hashrie, *n.* careless destruction, reckless waste.

Hashter, *n.* ill-planned or slovenly executed work.—*v.* to work in a hurried, slovenly, wasteful manner. Cf. Hushter.

Hashter't, *ppl. adj.* hurried, flustered, flurried.

Hashy, *n.* a mess, muddle, noise, riot; an old sermon preached over again.—*adj.* wet, sleety, slushy; slovenly, careless, wasteful, destructive.

Hashy-holey, *n.* a boys' game.

Hask, *adj.* hard and dry to the touch; harsh and dry to the taste; rigorous, harsh.—*v.* to give a short, dry cough; to clear the throat, hawk.

Hask, *n.* the throat, soft palate. Cf. Hass, Halse.

Hasky, *adj.* dry, parched; husky; rank in growth; coarse to the taste; dirty, slovenly; of coarse workmanship.

Haslet, *n.* the liver, lights, &c., of a pig, &c.

Haslie, *adj.* covered with hazels. Cf. Hazley.

Haslig, *n.* the wool on the neck of a sheep. Cf. Haslock.

Hasloch, *n.* waste, refuse.

Haslock, *n.* the fine wool on the throat of a sheep.

Hasp, *n.* a latch, clasp.—*v.* to fasten with a latch.

Hasp, *n.* a hank of yarn, worsted, &c.; the fourth part of a spindle; with *ravelled,* a difficulty; confusion, disorder.

Haspal, Hasple, *n.* a sloven, with his shirt-neck open; a clownish fellow.

Haspan, Haspin, *n.* a stripling.

Hass, *n.* the neck, throat; a gap, opening.— *v.* to clasp round the neck, kiss. Cf. Halse.

Hassie, *n.* a confused mass, a heterogeneous mixture. Cf. Hashy.

Hasslin-tooth, *n.* a back-tooth. Cf. Aslin-tooth.

Hassock, Hassick, *n.* a tuft of coarse grass; anything bushy; a 'shock' of hair; a large, round turf used as a seat.

Hastard, *adj.* irascible.

Haster, Hasther, *v.* to hurry, drive to work; to fluster.

Hastern, Hastered, *ppl. adj.* used of oats, &c.: early, soon ripe.

Hastings, *n.* a kind of early pea. Cf. Haistines.

Hastow, *v.* with *pron.* hast thou?

Hastrel, *n.* a confused person; one who is always in haste.

Hasty, *n.* murrain in cattle.

Hasty-brose, *n.* 'brose' hastily made with oatmeal and boiling water or milk.

Hat, *v. pret.* did hit.

Hat, *n.* a heap.

Hat, *n.* a salutation with the uplifted hat.— *v.* to salute by raising the hat.

Hat, *v.* to hop.—*n.* a hop.

Hatch, *n.* a jolt.—*v.* to move by jerks, to 'hotch.' Cf. Hotch.

Hatch-door, *n.* a wicket or half-door.

Hatchel, *v.* to shake in carrying.

Hatch-hole, *n.* a trap-door.

Hatch-way, *n.* the sliding panel of a box-bed.

Hate, *n.* a whit, an atom. Cf. Haet.

Hateral, *n.* a large quantity; a dirty, confused mass. Cf. Hatterel.

Haterent, *n.* hatred.

Hatery, *adj.* matted; dishevelled. Cf. Hatry.

Hatesum, *adj.* unkind; hateful.

Hather, *n.* heather.

Hathish, *n.* a dry measure, the fourth of a peck. Cf. Haddish.

Hatrel, Hatrell, *n.* a large quantity; a jumble. Cf. Hatterel.

Hatry, *adj.* matted; disordered, dishevelled. —*n.* a jumble.

Hatter, *n.* an irregular and numerous gathering of any kind; a great number of small insects crawling together; a jumble; an eruption on the face; a collection of sores, a rush of pimples.—*v.* to harass, vex, hurt; to exhaust; to move in confusion and a mixed state; to gather in crowds; to speak thickly and confusedly.

Hatterel, *n.* a large quantity; a jumble; a collection of sores.

Hatting owre the bonnets, *n.* a boys' game.

Hattit kit, *n.* a dish of sour or coagulated cream; a preparation of new milk and fresh butter-milk.

Hattock, *n.* a small hat.

Hattrel, *n.* the core or flint of a horn.

Hatty, *n.* a form of the game of leap-frog, each boy leaving his cap on the back as he leaps over; a game played with pins on the top of a hat.

Hauber, *n.* oats. Cf. Haver.

Hauch, *n.* low-lying, level ground by the side of a river or stream.

Hauch, *v.* to hawk, clear the throat of phlegm; to expel anything from the throat by force of the breath; to hesitate, 'hum and haw'; to make a fuss before doing anything.—*n.* an effort to clear the throat.

Hauchal, *n.* a deformed or crippled person. Cf. Hauchle.

Hauchan, *n.* mucus expelled from the throat.

Hauch-grund, -land, *n.* low-lying land by the side of a river or stream.

Hauchle, *v.* to walk lamely or with difficulty; to hobble, drag the feet in walking; to shamble.

Hauchlin', *ppl. adj.* slovenly. Cf. Hachle.

Hauchs, *n.* the three points into which the upper part of a ploughshare is divided and by which it clasps the wood.

Hauchty, *adj.* haughty.

Haud, *n.* a hold.—*v.* to hold; to preserve a calf for stock.

Haud, *n.* a squall.

Hauden, *ppl.* held.

Haudin, *n.* a holding.

Haudin-calf, *n.* a calf kept to grow to maturity.

Haud-richt, *n.* a safe, right, and wise counsellor.

Hauf, *adj.* half.

Hauf, *n.* a resort, place of resort; a haunt. Cf. Howff.

Hauf-an-snake, *v.* to divide equally.

Hauf-cock, *adj.* half-tipsy.

Hauflin, *adj.* half-grown.—*n.* a half-grown lad. Cf. Halflin.

Hauf-on, *adj.* half-drunk.

Haugaw, *n.* a rag-gatherer, a midden-raker. Cf. Hawgaw.

Haugh, *n.* a hough, hock.—*v.* to throw a stone under the hough.

Haugh, *n.* low, level ground beside a stream.

Haugh, Haught, *v.* to clear the throat.

Haugh-grun', *n.* a 'haugh.'

Haugull, *n.* a cold, damp, easterly wind blowing from the sea in summer.

Haugullin, *adj.* drizzling, damp and cold.

Hauk, *n.* an implement for hauling dung from a cart. Cf. Hack.

Hauka, *n.* a rag-gatherer. Cf. Hawgaw.

Haukie, Hawky, *n.* a white-faced cow; a clumsy fellow; a prostitute. Cf. Hawkie.

Haukit, *adj.* used of animals: white-faced; stupid.

Haukum-plaukum, *adj.* every way equal.

Haul, *n.* a large quantity or amount, as of money.

Haul, Hauld, *v.* to hold; used of trout: to flee under a stone or bank for safety.—*n.* a habitation. Cf. Hold.

Hauling, *n.* fishing with a pock-net. Cf. Haave, Halve.

Haulket, *adj.* used of animals: having a white face. Cf. Hawkit.

Haully, *n.* a hauling, rough handling in dragging a prisoner, &c.

Haumer, *n.* a hammer. Cf. Hammer.

Haumshoch, *n.* a sprain, bruise.—*adj.* lacerated. Cf. Hamshoch.

Haun, *n.* a hand.

Haunch, *v.* to snap, bite. Cf. Hanch.

Haunch-buttons, *n.* the buttons on the back of a coat.

Haunch-knots, *n.* bunches of ribbon worn on ladies' gowns at the haunches.

Haunchman, *n.* a henchman.

Haunie, *n.* a child's hand.—*adj.* handy. Cf. Hannie.

Haunle, *v.* to handle.—*n.* a handle.

Haunlins, *n.* festive parties. Cf. Handling.

Haunsh, *v.* to snap. Cf. Hanch.

Haunt, *v.* to practise; to resort to; to consort with; to provide a haunt for.—*n.* a custom, habit; a notion, a queer fancy.

Hauntskip, *n.* a place of resort.

Haunty, *adj.* convenient; not troublesome; handsome.

Haup, *v.* used of yoked animals: to turn to the right. Cf. Hap.

Haup, *v.* to limp; to hop.—*n.* a hop. Cf. Hap.

Haup, *n.* the hip of a rose.

Haupie-stap-and-jump, *n.* hop, step, and jump.

Haur, *v.* to speak with a 'burr.'—*n.* the act of so speaking. Cf. Haar.

Haur, *n.* a cold, easterly wind, bringing fog. Cf. Haar.

Haurk, *int.* a huntsman's encouraging call to foxhounds.

Haurl, *v.* to drag.—*n.* a slatternly woman. Cf. Harle.

Haurn, *v.* to roast; to toast on the embers; to 'fire' a bannock. Cf. Harden.

Haurrage, *n.* a blackguard crew of people.

Haury, *adj.* foggy, misty.

Hause, *n.* the neck, throat; a hug, embrace.—*v.* to embrace. Cf. Halse.

Hause-bane, *n.* the neck-bone.

Hauselet, *n.* a pig's pluck. Cf. Haslet.

Hauselock, Hausslock, *n.* the wool on a sheep's neck. Cf. Haslock.

Haut, *v.* to limp; to hop.—*n.* limping; a hop.

Haut, *n.* a grove, holt.

Haut, *v.* to gather or rake with the fingers.

Hauter, *n.* one who can hop.

Haut-stap, -stride, -and-loup, *n.* hop, step, and jump.

Hauve, *n.* a pock-net.—*v.* to fish with a pock-net. Cf. Haave.

Hauve-net, *n.* a fixed net within water-mark, to prevent fish returning with the tide. Cf. Halve-net.

Hauver, *n.* oats.

Hauver-meal, *n.* oatmeal.

Have, *v.* to carry; to have enough; to understand; to take, receive.- *n.* property. Cf. Hae.

Haveless, *adj.* wasteful, incompetent; slovenly; of bad manners, unrefined.

Havence, Havens, *n.* manners, behaviour. Cf. Haivins.

Haver, *n.* oats.

Haver, *v.* to talk at random, incoherently, nonsensically; to hesitate; to fuss about little or nothing; to work lazily.—*n.* nonsense, foolish talk; a piece of folly or nonsense; a silly whim; a stupid chatterer; a lazy, idle fellow; fussy hesitation; one who hesitates.

Haver, *n.* a possessor; one who has information or deeds bearing on a case in court; a legal term.

Haver, *n.* a sharer, partner; an equal share. —*v.* to halve, to hold in partnership. Cf. Haaver, Halver.

Haver, *v.* to toast before the fire. Cf. Haurn.

Haveral, *n.* a half-witted person; a talkative, garrulous person; a fool.—*adj.* foolish, silly, nonsensical; talking foolishly.—*v.* to talk nonsense, 'blether.'

Haveral-hash, *n.* a silly, nonsensical person.

Haver-bannock, *n.* an oatmeal-bannock.

Haverel, *n.* a gelded he-goat. Cf. Aiver, Haiver.

Haverelism, *n.* a habit of foolish, nonsensical talking.

Haveren, *n.* a sloven.

Haverer, *n.* a foolish talker.

Haver-jannock, *n.* an oatmeal-cake or bannock.

Haver-meal, *n.* oatmeal.—*adj.* made of oatmeal.

Haveron, *n.* a gelded he-goat. Cf. Haverel.

Havers, *n.* nonsense; foolish talk.—*int.* nonsense!

Haver-sack, *n.* a bag hung at a horse's head, containing his oats, &c.

Haver-straw, *n.* oat-straw.

Haves, *n.* goods; effects. Cf. Have.

Havings, *n.* possessions.

Havings, *n.* manners, behaviour. Cf. Haivins.

Haviour, *n.* behaviour.

Havoc-burds, *n.* the large flocks of small birds which fly about the fields after harvest.

Haw, *adj.* bluish-gray, or pale-green ; livid, pale, wan.

Haw, *n.* a hall, house. Cf. Ha'.

Haw-berry, *n.* the fruit of the hawthorn.

Haw-buss, *n.* the hawthorn-tree.

Hawflin, *n.* a stripling. Cf. Halflin.

Hawgaw, *n.* a rag-gatherer, a midden-raker.

Hawgh, *v.* to hawk, to clear the throat of phlegm.—*n.* an effort to clear the throat of phlegm. Cf. Hauch.

Hawick-gill, *n.* a liquid measure of half an English pint.

Hawing, *ppl. adj.* huzzaing, resounding.

Hawk, *n.* a dung-fork. Cf. Hack.

Hawk, *v.* to hesitate ; to hum and haw.

Hawkathraw, *n.* a country carpenter.

Hawk-hen, *n.* a hen formerly levied from each house to feed the king's hawks. Cf. Halkhen.

Hawkie, *n.* a white-faced cow ; a name for a cow ; the bald coot ; a stupid, clumsy fellow ; a whore.—*phr.* 'brown hawkie,' a barrel of ale.

Hawkin' and swaukin', or swappin', *phr.* irresolute, wavering in mind ; in indifferent health ; struggling with difficulties in worldly circumstances, borrowing from one to pay another.

Hawking, *ppl. adj.* sharp, hawk-like.

Hawkit, *adj.* of animals : bearing a white face ; foolish, stupid.

Hawk-studyin', *n.* the steady hovering of a hawk over its prey before pouncing upon it.

Hawk-teuchin, *ppl.* clearing the throat of phlegm.

Hawm, *v.* to waste time ; to loiter ; to work in a slovenly way.

Hawmer, *v.* to hammer.

Hawmerer, *n.* a big, clumsy person with ungainly feet.

Hawmering, *ppl. adj.* big and clumsy.

Hawnet, *n.* the right to half of the fishing of one net. Cf. Half-net.

Hawnie, *n.* a wooden milk-pail with an upright handle. Cf. Handy.

Hawse, *n.* the throat. Cf. Halse.

Haw-stones, *n.* the seeds contained in the haw.

†Hawtane, *adj.* haughty.

Hawthorndean, *n.* a species of apple.

Haw-tree, *n.* the hawthorn-tree.

Hawy, *adv.* heavily.

Haw-year, *n.* a year in which haws abound.

Hay, *v.* to hie, hasten.

Hay, *n.* hay-harvest.

Hay-bird, *n.* the willow-warbler.

Hay-bog, *n.* a damp hay-meadow.

Hay-broo, *n.* a decoction of hay.

Hay-dash, *n.* the turning and tossing of hay in drying it.

Ha' year olds, *n.* cattle eighteen months old.

Hay-fog, *n.* aftermath ; foggage after hay.

Hay-folk, *n.* haymakers.

Hay-fow, *n.* a hay-fork.

Hay-knife, *n.* a large knife for cutting hay in the stack.

Haymakers, *n.* a country-dance.

Hay-mow, *n.* a large hay-stack.

Hay-neuk, *n.* the stall where hay is stored for immediate consumption when brought in from the stack.

Hays, Hayes, *n.* the steps of a round country-dance.

Hay-soo, *n.* a large, oblong stack of hay, shaped like a sow.

Hay-spade, *n.* a sharp, heart-shaped spade for cutting the hay in stack.

Hay-worker, *n.* a haymaker.

Hazardful, *adj.* hazardous.

Haze, *v.* to half-dry, dry on the surface, in the open air.

Haze, *n.* the glazing of the eyes of the dying.

Hazel-oil, *n.* a drubbing.

Hazel-raw, *n.* the lungwort.

Hazel-shaw, *n.* an abrupt flat piece of ground, at the bottom of a hill, covered with hazels.

Hazely, Hazelly, *adj.* used of soil : poor, light, loose.

Hazie, Hazzie, Hazy, *adj.* weak in understanding, crazy ; muddled ; dim, not seeing distinctly.—*n.* a stupid, thick-headed person, a numskull.

Hazley, Hazelly, *adj.* covered with hazels.

He, *n.* the goodman of the house ; a male ; a man ; anybody. — *adj.* having masculine manners or appearance.

Head, *n.* an atom, whit. Cf. Haet.

Head, *n.* the hair of the head ; the ears of grain on a single stem of corn ; the froth of ale, &c. ; the hood of raw hide on the upper end of the 'soople' of a flail ; a measure of wool or twine ; the higher part of a street ; a hill, an eminence ; the source of a river ; the volume of water in a stream ; in curling : one single contest between two rinks, the majority of twenty-one 'heads' winning the game.—*adj.* chief ; best.—*v.* to behead ; to have as a head or top ; to put in the head of a cask.

Head and hide, Head and tail, *advs.* completely.

Head-back, *n.* the rope that runs along the side of a herring-net and carries the corks.

Head-band, *n.* the band or rope fastening a cow to the stall; the band at the top of a pair of trousers; a 'head-back' of a herring-net.

Head-billie-dawkus, *n.* the person in chief charge, the 'presiding genius.'

Head-buil, *n.* the best family residence on an estate, the manor-house; the chief estate.

Head-bummer, *n.* the head of the house; the principal person.

Head-busk, *n.* a head-dress, an ornament for the head.

Headcadab, *n.* a clever, sharp person; an adept; one quick of understanding.

Head-court, *n.* formerly a court of justice for a county, a sheriffdom, and a regality; a special meeting of citizens called by the magistrates of a burgh for counsel and decision on matters affecting the community.

Head-cut, *n.* the cut of a fish which includes the head.

Head-dyke, *n.* a wall dividing the green pasture of a farm from the heather.

Header, *n.* a stone or brick in a wall having the end outwards.

Head-hing, *n.* a droop of the head.

Head-hurry, *n.* the thick or the midst of any pressing business.

Head-ice, *n.* the ice at the tee of a curling-rink.

Head-ill, *n.* jaundice in sheep.

Heading, *n.* scorn.

Heading, *n.* an execution by beheading.

Heading-hill, *n.* the hill where criminals were beheaded.

Heading-man, *n.* a headsman, executioner.

Heading-sheaf, *n.* the sheaf placed on the top of a stack; the crowning act.

Head-lace, *n.* a narrow ribbon for binding the head.

Headless, *adj.* thoughtless, heedless; fatherless, orphaned.

Head-light, *adj.* giddy, dizzy, light-headed.

Head-lightness, *n.* dizziness.

Headlins, *adv.* headlong, precipitately.

Head-man, Headsman, *n.* the master or chief; an overseer; a stalk of rib-grass.

Head-maud, *n.* a plaid covering head and shoulders.

Headmost, *adj.* topmost.

Headocks, *n.* a children's game of chance, with pins as stakes.

Head-rig, *n.* the strip of land in a field on which the plough turns.

Head-room, *n.* sufficient height of ceilings, &c., room to move the head; freedom; opportunity to take liberty to do one's will; the ground lying between a 'haugh' and the top of a hill.

Head-rowm, *n.* the outer boundaries of a feu or toft.

Headset, *n.* a Highland reel or dance.

Head-shave, -sheaf, *n.* the last sheaf placed upon the top of a stack; the climax, finishing touch.

Head-skair, *n.* the highest part of a fishing-rod.

Head-speed, *n.* a state of great excitement. Cf. Speed.

Head-stall, *n.* the head of a house.

Head-stock, *n.* a leader for the yearly cock fight, formerly common in schools.

Head-stone, *n.* in *pl.* stones resembling various members of the body, and lying round 'healing wells'; used to rub the affected parts of the body corresponding to them.

Head-stoop, *adv.* in headlong haste.

Head-suit, *n.* a head-dress, a covering for the head.

Head-swell, *n.* jaundice in sheep.

Head-theekit, *adj.* having the head covered.

Head-town, *n.* a county town.

Head-washing, *n.* an entertainment given to his comrades and friends by one who has newly entered a profession, received promotion, or made an expedition he never made before.

Head-win, *n.* the leading band of reapers on the harvest-field.

Heady, *adj.* clever, giving proof of brains.

Heady-craw, *n.* the 'hoodie' crow; a somersault.—*adv.* head-foremost.

Heady-maud, *n.* a plaid covering head and shoulders. Cf. Head-maud.

Heady-peer, Head-y-peer, -a-peer, *adj.* equal in height.—*n.* in *pl.* equals, compeers.

Heague, *v.* used of cattle: to push with the head in trying their strength.

Heal, *adj.* healthy; whole.—*n.* health; welfare; nourishment. Cf. Hail.

Heal, *v.* to conceal.

Heald-twine, *n.* the thread of which the healds are made.

Healey, *adj.* haughty. Cf. Heally.

Healfull, *adj.* healthy, healthful.

Heal-hadin', -makin', *n.* salvation.

Healing-blade, -leaf, *n.* the leaf of the plantain.

Heally, *adj.* haughty; disdainful; high and mighty; ill-tempered.—*v.* to esteem slightly; to disdain; to take an affront in silence; to abandon, to forsake in contempt.—*n.* dudgeon; consciousness of insult.

Heally-fu', *adj.* full of disdain.

Health, *v.* to drink healths.

Healthsome, *adj.* wholesome; health-giving.

Healy, *int.* softly!—*adv.* fairly, gently.—*v.* to wait, be patient. Cf. Hooly

Heam-houghed, *adj.* used of a horse : having its hind-legs shaped like the 'hames' of a horse's collar.

Heap, *n.* one fill of the firlot, heaped till it can hold no more ; a great deal ; a slovenly woman.—*adv.* very much ; higgledy-piggledy.

Heap-mete, *n.* liberal measure.

Hear, *v.* to treat ; to reprove.—*phr.* 'to be heard for,' to be heard of, or on account of, to be known for.

Hearing, *n.* information, news ; a scolding ; an opportunity of preaching to a congregation as a candidate for the pastorate.

Hearken, *v.* to listen by stealth ; to hear a lesson repeated ; to listen to ; to whisper ; with *in*, to prompt secretly ; to pay a visit.

Hearkenin', *n.* encouragement.

Hearkenin'-win', *n.* a comparative lull in a storm, followed by a destructive blast.

Hearse, *n.* a lustre, a sconce with lights ; a frame for holding candles in a church.

Hearse, *adj.* hoarse.

Hearst, *n.* harvest.

Hearsto, *v.* with *pron.* hearest thou?

Heart, *n.* the stomach ; spirits, cheer ; the middle of anything ; used of land : good, fertile condition.—*v.* to strike or fall on the region of the heart ; to stun, to deprive of the power of breathing, sensation, &c., by a blow near the region of the heart ; to sicken, nauseate ; with *up*, to hearten.

Heart-anguished, *adj.* heart-sore.

Heart-axes, *n.* the heartburn. Cf. Axes.

Heart-brunt, *adj.* very fond, greatly enamoured.

Heart-eident, *adj.* with a firm or steadfast heart.

Heartening, *n.* encouragement.

Heartful, *adj.* sad-hearted.

Heart-gashed, *adj.* cut or stricken to the heart.

Heart-hale, *adj.* heart-whole ; inwardly sound and healthy.

Heart-hankering, *n.* heart-longing.

Heart-hanking, *adj.* used of a maiden : attractive and entangling the affections.

Heart-heezer, *n.* a comfort, what cheers the heart or raises the spirits.

Heart-heezing, *adj.* exhilarating, heart-cheering, encouraging.

Hearth-money, *n.* a tax levied on each hearth in a house.

Heart-hole, *n.* the centre of a fire.

Heart-hove, *adj.* heaved from the heart, deep.

Heart-hunger, *n.* a ravenous desire for food.

Heart-hunger'd, *adj.* starved, very hungry.

Heartie, *n.* a little heart ; a child's heart.

Heart-kittlin', *adj.* heart-affecting.

Heart-loup, *n.* a heart-beat.

Heart-o'-the-earth. *n.* the self-heal.

Heart o' the nut, *n.* the main point.

Heart-richt, *n.* the right or due of the heart or affections.

Heart-sabbit, *adj.* sad, mournful.

Heart-sair, *adj.* heart-sore ; annoyed.—*n.* a great vexation.

Heart-scad, -scald, -scaud, *n.* heartburn ; bitter grief.

Heart's-gree, *n.* delight.

Heart-shot, *n.* a hearty burst of laughter.—*int.* an excl. after sneezing.

Heartsome, *adj.* hearty.

Heartsomely, *adv.* merrily, cheerfully.

Heartsomeness, *n.* cheerfulness.

Heart-thirled, *adj.* bound by the affections.

Heart-wear, *n.* an illness of the heart.

Heart-worm, *n.* the heartburn.

Hearty, *adj.* cheerful ; liberal ; exhilarated by drink ; having a good appetite ; plump, inclining to corpulence ; used of land : in good condition.—*n.* a term of address, a good fellow.

Heary, *n.* a conjugal endearing term of address. Cf. Herie.

Hease, *v.* to hoist. Cf. Heeze.

Heasie, *n.* a hoist. Cf. Heezy.

Heastie, *n.* the murrain. Cf. Hasty.

Heasty, *adj.* hasty.

Heat, *n.* a heating, warming ; a thrashing ; a round, bout.—*v.* used of hay or corn : to become hot in the stack through premature stacking ; to thrash so as to heat the skin affected.—*adj.* hot. Cf. Het.

Heathens, *n.* gneiss. Cf. Heath-stones.

Heather and dab, *n.* an obsolete style of roofing houses, &c.

Heather-and-dub, *adj.* rough, poor, tawdry.

Heather-bell, *n.* the flower of the heath.

Heather-bill, *n.* the dragon-fly. Cf. Atherbill.

Heather-birn, *n.* the stalks and roots of burnt heather.

Heather-bleat, -bleet, *n.* the common snipe.

Heather-bleater, -bluiter, -blutter, *n.* the common snipe.

Heather-brae, *n.* a heather-clad slope.

Heather-cat, *n.* a cat becoming wild and roving among the heather : a wild, roving person.

Heather-clu, *n.* the ankle.

Heather-cock, *n.* the ring-ousel.

Heather-cowe, *n.* a tuft of heather ; a broom made of heather.

Heather-lintie, *n.* the linnet ; the mountain linnet or twite.

Heather-peep, -peeper, *n.* the common sandpiper.

Heather-range, -reenge, *n.* the hydrangea.

Heather-tap, *n.* a tuft of heather ; a broom made of heather.

Heather-theekit, *adj.* thatched with heather.

Heathery, *adj.* abounding in heather; living among heather; rough, dishevelled, hairy.

Heathery-heidit, *adj.* used of a mountain: having the summit clad with heather; of the human head: rough, dishevelled, 'touzy.'

Heath-shield-fern, *n.* the shield-fern.

Heath-stones, *n.* gneiss. Cf. Heathens.

Heauveless, *adj.* colourless, meaningless, insincere. Cf. Haveless.

Heave, *v.* to rise up, come into view; to become swollen; to puff up; used of cattle: to become distended by overeating fresh clover, &c.; to exalt, puff up with conceit.—*n.* a push, shove; a throb, a heaving motion.

Heaven's-hen, *n.* the lark.

Heaviers, *n.* large-sized cattle, taken in to be kept during winter.

Heavy, *adj.* used of the uterus: gravid; advanced in pregnancy; large, copious.

Heavy charge, *n.* a heavy trial or burden, such as the care of a number of young children.

Heavy end, *n.* the worst or heaviest part.

Heavy-fitted, *adj.* advanced in pregnancy.

Heavy handful, *n.* a 'heavy charge.'

Heavy-headit, *adj.* dull, slow of apprehension.

Heavy-heartit, *adj.* used of the atmosphere: lowering, threatening rain.

Heavysome, *adj.* heavy, weighty; dull, drowsy.

Heawe-eel, *n.* the conger. Cf. Haaf-eel, Heevil.

Heben, *n.* ebony.—*adj.* made of ebony.

Heben-wood, *n.* ebony.

He-broom, *n.* the laburnum.

Hebrun, Heburn, *n.* a goat of three years old that has been castrated.

Hech, *int.* an excl. of surprise, contempt, sorrow, weariness, pain.—*v.* to cry 'hech!' to pant, 'pegh.'—*n.* the act of panting, hard breathing.

Hechen, *n.* the fireside.

Hech-hey, *int.* heigh-ho!

Hech-how, *n.* the hemlock.

Hech-how, *int.* heigh-ho!—*adj.* wearisome, causing one to say 'hech-how!'—*n.* bad circumstances or health.

Hech-how-aye, *int.* heigh-ho! aye!

Hech-how-hum, *int.* an excl. of despondency.

Hechle, *v.* to breathe short and quick after exertion; to exert one's self in climbing a steep incline or surmounting a difficulty; with *on*, to advance with difficulty as to bodily health or temporal circumstances.

Hecht, *n.* height; a hill, elevation; a help, a lift up; the greatest degree of increase.—*v.* to lift up, raise.

Hecht, *v.* to promise; to offer; to offer; to threaten; to call or name; to be called or named.—*n.* a promise, offer, engagement.

Hecht, *ppl.* promised.

Hech-wow, *int.* an excl. of regret, depression.

Heck, *n.* a whore.

Heck, *int.* a call to horses to come to the left or near side.

Heck, *n.* a rack for cattle; a wooden grating placed across a stream. Cf. Hack.

Heckabirnie, *n.* any lean, feeble creature.

Heckam-peckam, Heckam-peckam-lass, *n.* the name of an angler's fly.

Heck-door, *n.* the door between a farm kitchen and the byre or stable.

Hecked, *adj.* used of cows: white-faced.

Heckery-peckery, *n.* a boys' game.

Hecket, *n.* a hay-rack in a stable.

Heck-hens, *n.* an additional rent charge paid in fowls and eggs. Cf. Halk-hens.

Heckie-, Heckle-birnie, *n.* a substitute for the word 'hell'; a children's game, of the nature of running the gauntlet.

Heckle, *n.* a sharp pin; a hackle, a comb with steel teeth for dressing flax and hemp; a thorn in one's side.—*v.* to dress flax with a 'heckle'; to cross-question a candidate for parliamentary or municipal honours at a public meeting; to examine searchingly; to scold severely; to tease, provoke.

Heckle, *n.* the neck-feathers of a cock.

Heckle-back, *n.* the fifteen-spined stickleback.

Heckle-biscuit, *n.* a kind of biscuit, punctured in baking by a wooden disc full of spikes or 'heckles.'

Heckle-pins, *n.* the teeth of a 'heckle.'

Heckler, *n.* a flax-dresser; a severe examiner; a chastiser.

Heckling. *n.* flax-dressing; questioning; scolding; a dispute.

Hecklin-kame, *n.* a 'heckle.'

Hector, *v.* to oppose with vehemence.

Hedder, *n.* heather.

Hedder-hillock, *n.* a heather-clad hill.

Hedder-reenge, *n.* the hydrangea.

Heddery, *adj.* heathery; of the head: rough, shaggy; ruffled.

Heddle-twine, *n.* the thread of which heddles are made. Cf. Heald-twine.

Hedge, *v.* to protect; to equivocate; to shuffle in narration.

Hedgehog-holly, *n.* the holly.

Hedge-root, *n.* the foot of a hedge as a shelter.

Hedge-spurgy, *n.* the hedge-sparrow.

Hedry, *adj.* heathery; dishevelled; of the head: rough, 'tousled.' Cf. Heddery.

Hedy-pere, *adj.* of equal stature. Cf. Heady-peer.

Hee, *adj.* high.

Hee-balou, *n.* a lullaby.

Heed, *n.* the head.

Heed, *v. pret.* held. Cf. Had.

Heef, *n.* a hoof.

Heel, *n.* health. Cf. Heal.

Heel, *v.* to conceal. Cf. Heal.

Heel, *n.* the part of an adze into which the handle is fixed; the part of a golf-club nearest the handle; the stern of a boat; the bottom crust of a loaf; the last remaining part of a cheese; the end, finish, wind up, close; in *pl.* increased speed to a curling-stone by sweeping before it.—*v.* to take to one's heels; to strike with the heel of a golf-club; to haul by the heels; to send one heels over head on to one's back.

Heelan', *adj.* Highland. Cf. Hielan.

Heel-and-fling-board, *n.* a spring-board.

Heel-cap, *v.* to patch stocking-heels with cloth.

Heel-cutter, *n.* a shoemaker's shaping-knife; a shoemaker.

Heeld, *v.* to hold.—*v. pret.* held.

Heeld, *v.* to bend downwards or to one side.

Heel-hole, *n.* the hole in the handle of a spade.

Heelie, *adj.* haughty; crabbed; ill-tempered. Cf. Heally.

Heelie, *adj.* slow.—*adv.* slowly. Cf. Hooly.

Heeliegoleerie, *adv.* topsyturvy.—*n.* in *pl.* frolicsome tricks.

Heelifow, *adj.* scornful, full of pride. Cf. Heally-fu'.

Heel-pins, *n.* two pieces of wood driven into the ground, forming a frame for the treddles of a loom.

Heel-ring, *n.* a shoe heel-piece.

Heel-seat, *n.* ? a board over the bottom of a boat; a seat at the stern.

Heel-shakin', *n.* dancing.

Heel-shod, *adj.* having iron heel-pieces.—*n.* an iron heel-piece.

Heels ower-body, -craig, -gowdie, -gowrie, *advs.* topsyturvy, in great disorder.

Heels-ower-head, *adv.* topsyturvy; without particular enumeration or distinction.

Heelster-gowdie, *adv.* head over heels.

Heelster-head, *adv.* heels over head.

Heel-strop, *n.* the parting kick; the finishing touch.

Heely, *adj.* haughty, disdainful; ill-tempered. —*v.* to regard disdainfully or with slight esteem.—*n.* a state of offence, consciousness of insult. Cf. Heally.

Heely, *adv.* softly, cautiously, slowly.—*adj.* slow.—*int.* softly!—*v.* to go slowly, gently, or cautiously. Cf. Hooly.

Heemlin, *adj.* humbling, humiliating.

Heemlin, *ppl. adj.* used of a continuous rumbling sound.

Heep, *n.* a heap; a slovenly woman.—*v.* to heap. Cf. Heap.

Heepie-creep, *adv.* in a creeping, sneaking manner.

Heepocreet, *n.* a hypocrite.

Heepy, *n.* a fool; a stupid person; a melancholy person.

Heer, Heere, *n.* a filament of flax or hemp; the sixth part of a hank, or the twenty-fourth part of a spindle. Cf. Hier.

Heeroad, *n.* the highway.

Heery, *n.* a term of conjugal endearment. Cf. Herie.

Heeryestreen, *n.* the night before last.

Heese, *v.* to hoist.—*n.* a hoist, a heave. Cf. Heeze.

Heest, *n.* haste.—*v.* to hasten, make haste.

Heesty, *adj.* hasty.

Heet, *n.* a whit, a 'haet.' Cf. Haet.

Heetie-kneetie, *n.* with a *negative:* absolutely nothing, neither one thing nor another.

Heevil, *n.* the conger. Cf. Heawe-eel, Haaf-eel.

Heeze, *v.* to hoist, heave; to exalt; to dance vigorously; to carry hurriedly; to travel fast.—*n.* a hoist; help, furtherance; a toss or lift of the head; a swing; swinging. Cf. Hoise.

Heezy, *n.* a hoist, heave; a lift or help upwards; a tossing; one who tosses another; anything discomposing.

Heezy, *adj.* creaking.

Heff, *n.* a place of rest; an accustomed pasture. —*v.* to accustom to a place. Cf. Heft.

Heffing, *n.* keep, maintenance.

Heft, *n.* an accustomed pasture; a resting-place; a domicile.—*v.* to accustom sheep or cattle to new pasture; to dwell; to domicile; to become familiarized to a station or work.

Heft, *v.* to confine or restrain nature; to let a cow's udder get hard and large by not withdrawing her milk.

Heft, *v.* to lift up; to carry aloft.

Heft, *v.* to pose, nonplus.

Heft, *n.* a haft, a handle.—*v.* to fix, as a knife in its haft.

Heft and blade, *n.* the whole disposal of a thing; the whole.

Hefted, *ppl. adj.* used of cattle: swollen.

Hefted-milk, *n.* milk not drawn off from a cow for some time.

Hefter, *v.* one who watches sheep in new pasture to keep them from straying.

Heftet, *adj.* accustomed to live in a place.

Hefty, *adj.* weighty, not easy to lift.

Heg-beg, *n.* the nettle.

Hegh, *v.* to pant, breathe with difficulty, 'pech.' Cf. Hech.

Heghen, *n.* the fireside. Cf. Hechen.

Hegh-hey, -how, *int.* heigh-ho!

Heghle, *v.* to breathe short and quick after exertion. Cf. Hechle.

Heght, *n.* a heavy fall.

Heght, *v.* to promise, offer; to threaten. Cf. Hecht.

Hegs, *int.* an excl.; a petty oath, 'fegs!' Cf. Haigs.

Heh, *int.* an excl. of surprise. Cf. Heich.

Heich, *int.* a call to attract attention; an excl. of surprise, sorrow, &c.—*v.* to cry 'heich!' or 'hey!' Cf. Hech.

Heich, *adj.* high; tall; used of an animal's ears: pricked, erect; protuberant, big; used of the wind: north; proud, haughty; in high spirits, excited, 'raised.'—*n.* a height, hill; a slight eminence, a knoll. Cf. High.

Heichness, *n.* height; highness.

Heicht, *n.* height.—*v.* to raise.

Heid, *n.* head.—*v.* to behead; to cut off the tops of turnips. Cf. Head.

Heid, *n.* state or quality; 'hood.'

Heid-speed, *n.* a landlord, as contrasted with his factor.

Heid-turning, *adj.* used of liquor: intoxicating.

Heidy, *adj.* clever. Cf. Heady.

Heifer, *v.* to earmark castrated cows.

Heiffle, *n.* a 'toolyie' or tussle with a young wench.

Heigh, *int.* an excl. of surprise. Cf. Heich, Hech.

Heigh, *adj.* high.—*n.* a height.

Heigh-hey, -how, *int.* an excl. of weariness or sorrow. Cf. Hech-how.

Heigh-jing-go-ring, *n.* a girls' game.

Heigh-ma-nannie, *n.* in *phr.* 'like heigh-ma-nannie,' at full speed.

Height, *n.* a help, lift up; the greatest degree of increase.—*v.* to lift up; to raise in price. Cf. Hecht.

Height, *v. pret.* promised. Cf. Hecht.

Heik, *int.* a call to horses to go to the left.

Heild, *v.* to hide. Cf. Heal.

Heild, *v.* to bend over or to the side. Cf. Heeld.

Heildit, Heilit, *v. pret.* held.

Heilie, *adj.* ill-tempered. Cf. Heally.

Hein-shinned, *adj.* with large, prominent shin-bones; in-shinned.

Heir-oye, *n.* a great-grandchild. Cf. Ier-oe.

Heirscap, Heirskip, *n.* heirship, inheritance.

Heirship, *n.* a foray; booty; ruin; mischief.

Heirs-portioners, *n.* co-heirs or co-heiresses.

Heis, Heise, Heize, *v.* to hoist. Cf. Heeze.

Heisie, *n.* a lift; a furtherance. Cf. Heezy.

Heiyearald, *n.* a heifer eighteen months old.

Held, *v. pret.* ran off; took to heels. Cf. Heel.

Helden, *ppl.* held.

Heldigoleerie, *adv.* topsyturvy. Cf. Heelie-goleerie.

Hele, *v.* to hide. Cf. Heal.

Helie, *adj.* holy. Cf. Haly.

Helie, *adj.* proud. Cf. Heally.

Heliefu', *adj.* proud, arrogant. Cf. Heally-fu'.

Helie-how, *n.* a caul or membrane.

Helimly, *adv.* actually; wholly. Cf. Hailumly.

Helit, *ppl. adj.* concealed. Cf. Heal.

Helkite, *n.* a dishonest or 'shady' person. Cf. Hellicat.

Hell, *adj.* whole. Cf. Hail.

Helldom, *n.* misery, utter wretchedness.

Hellenshaker, *n.* a tramp, vagrant. Cf. Hallanshaker.

Hell-, Hell's-holes, *n.* dark nooks supposed to be haunted by 'bogles.'

Hell-hot, *adj.* as hot as can be.

Hellicat, Hellicate, *adj.* wild, unmanageable; giddy, light-headed; extravagant.—*n.* a wicked creature; a villain. Cf. Hallockit.

Hellie-lamb, *n.* a ludicrous designation of a hump on the back.

Hellie-man, *n.* the devil.

Hellie-man's-rig, *n.* a piece of land dedicated to the devil.

Hellier, Hellzier, *n.* half a year. Cf. Hallier.

Hellim, *n.* a helm.

Hell-jay, *n.* the razor-bill.

Hellocat, *adj.* wild, unruly. Cf. Hallockit.

Hellock, *n.* a romp. Cf. Halok.

Hell-weed, *n.* the lesser dodder.

Hell-words, *n.* words or spells of evil omen.

Helly, *adj.* holy. Cf. Haly.

Helm, *n.* in *phr.* 'a helm of weet,' a great fall of rain.

Helm, *v.* to turn, guide, govern.

Helmy, *adj.* rainy.

Help, *v.* to mend, repair; to lift, to relieve of a burden; with *to,* to refrain from.

Helpener, Helpender, *n.* an assistant.

Helper, *n.* an assistant teacher; an assistant to a minister.

Helply, *adj.* helpful.

Helter, *n.* a halter.—*v.* to put on a halter.

Helter-cheeks, *n.* a halter or bridle encompassing the head of a horse or cow, the 'branks'; a cow wearing such a halter.

Helter-shank, *n.* a rope attached to a horse's head-stall.

Helter-skelter, *adj.* confused; careless.

Helter-skeltering, *n.* and *adj.* hurrying.

Hely, *adj.* holy. Cf. Haly.

Hem, *n.* the edge of a stone.

Hem, *n.* a horse-collar. Cf. Haim.

Hemlock, *n.* any hollow-stemmed umbelliferous plant.

Hemlock-skite, *n.* a squirt made of the stem of a hemlock. Cf. Humlock.

Hemmel, *n.* a covered shed for cattle; a stage on posts to support fodder, &c., for cattle. Cf. Hammel.

Hemmil, *n.* a heap; a crowd, multitude.—*v.* to surround a beast in order to capture it; to surround with a multitude.

Hemp, *n*. a rope; a halter; a hangman's halter; in *phr*. 'to haud the hemp on the hair,' to push on with arrears of work.

Hempie, *n*. the hedge-sparrow.

Hemp-looking, *adj*. fit for the gallows.

Hemp-riggs, *n*. 'riggs' of fertile land on which hemp was formerly grown.

Hempshire-gentleman, *n*. one who is qualifying for the gallows.

Hemp-string, *n*. a hangman's halter.—*v*. to hang by the neck.

Hempy, *adj*. wild, riotous; giddy, reckless, romping.—*n*. a rogue, one who deserves to be hung; a giddy, wild, romping, mischievous girl.

Hen, *n*. an opprobrious epithet applied to a woman; a term of endearment for a wife, &c.—*v*. to break a bargain, withdraw from an engagement.

Hen-a-haddie, *n*. a 'to-do,' an outcry.

Hen-bauk, *n*. a rafter on which hens roost.

Hen-bird, *n*. a chicken following its mother; a hen.

Hen-broth, *n*. chicken-broth.

Hench, *n*. the haunch.—*v*. to throw missiles under the leg or thigh by striking the hand against the thigh. Cf. Hainch.

Hench, *v*. to halt, limp.—*n*. a halt, limp; lameness. Cf. Hinch.

Hench-hoop, *n*. the hoop worn by ladies in the eighteenth century.

Henchil, *v*. to roll from side to side in walking. Cf. Hainchil.

Hench-vent, *n*. a gore, a piece of linen put into the lower part of a shirt to widen it so as to give vent for the haunch.

Hend, Hende, *adj*. used in ballad poetry: clever; courteous.—*n*. a young fellow. Cf. Hind-chiel.

Hender, *v*. to hinder.—*n*. hindrance.

Hendersum, *adj*. causing hindrance.

Hen-hearted, *adj*. timid, cowardly, chicken-hearted.

Hen-laft, *n*. the joists of a country cottage, on which the poultry roosted.

Henmaist, *adj*. last, hindmost.

Hen-man, *n*. a poultry-tender.

Hen-mou'd, *adj*. toothless.

Henners, *n*. a boys' swing-game.

Hennie, *n*. a term of endearment for a woman.

Henny, *n*. honey.

Henny, *adj*. apt to draw back from a bargain.

Henny-byke, -beik, *n*. a honey-hive.

Henou, *int*. an order to a number of persons to pull or lift all at once. Cf. Eenow.

Hen-party, *n*. a tea-party of wives exclusively.

Hen-pen, *n*. a hen-coop; the dung of hens.

Hen's care, *n*. care exercised without judgment.

Henscarts, *n*. fleecy clouds thought to betoken wind or rain.

Hen's cavey, *n*. a hen-house.

Hen's croft, *n*. a portion of a corn-field frequented and damaged by fowls.

Hen's flesh, *n*. the state of the skin when the pores stand up through cold, making it rough like a plucked fowl; 'goose-flesh.'

Hen's gerse, -girss, *n*. a hen's keep.

Hen's taes, *n*. bad writing; 'pot-hooks.'

Hensure, *n*. a giddy young fellow.

Hen's ware, *n*. the edible fucus.

Hent, *v*. *pret*. and *ppl*. caught, laid hold of.

Hent, *n*. a moment of time. Cf. Hint.

Hent, *adj*. posterior, hind. Cf. Hind.

Hen-wife, *n*. a woman in charge of poultry, or who sells poultry; a man who meddles with his wife's department of domestic affairs.

Hen-wifely, *adj*. like a 'hen-wife.'

Hen-wile, *n*. a stratagem.

Herald, *n*. the diving-goose; the heron.

Herald-duck, *n*. the diving-goose; the dun-diver.

Herb, *n*. any wild plant used medicinally.

Herbery, *n*. a haven or harbour; a shelter; a small loch, a stream. Cf. Harberie.

Herbour, *n*. a shelter.—*v*. to give shelter. Cf. Harbour.

Herd, *n*. a shepherd; a farm-servant or boy who tends cattle; a pastor; a 'guard' placed on the ice in curling, to prevent the winning stone being displaced.—*v*. to tend cattle, &c.; to drive away, scare; to gather in a crop; to keep in trust or charge.

Herd, *n*. the coarse refuse of flax. Cf. Hards.

Herd-club, *n*. the stick, partly notched in a peculiar way, and generally made of ash, formerly used by herd-boys in the north-east of Scotland.

Herding, *n*. the place and work of a 'herd.'

Herding-tree, *n*. a herd-boy's stick.

Herdship, *n*. the driving away of cattle wrongfully. Cf. Heirship.

Herd's-man, *n*. the common skua, thought to protect young lambs from the eagle.

Herd-widdiefows, *n*. cattle-stealers.

Hereabout, *adj*. belonging to the immediate neighbourhood.

Here and were, *n*. contention, disagreement.

Hereanent, *adv*. concerning this.

Hereawa', *adv*. in or to this quarter.—*adj*. belonging to this quarter.

Herefore, *adv*. on this account, hence.

Hereschip, *n*. the plundering of cattle. Cf. Heirship.

Hereward, *adv*. hither, hitherward.

Hereyesterday, *n*. the day before yesterday. Cf. Eve-yesterday.

Hereyestreen, *n*. the night before yesternight. Cf. Eve-yestreen.

Herezeld, *n*. the best beast on the land, given to the landlord on the death of the tenant.

Herie, *n.* a conjugal term of endearment ; a term addressed to a female inferior. Cf. Heary.

Heritor, *n.* a landed proprietor in a parish, liable to pay public burdens.

Heritrix, *n.* a female 'heritor.'

Herle, *n.* a heron ; a mischievous dwarf ; an ill-conditioned child or little animal.

Herling, *n.* the salmon-trout.

Herling-house, *n.* a net in which 'herlings' are caught.

Hern, *n.* the heron.

Hern, *n.* in *pl.* brains. Cf. Harn.

Hern-bluter, **-bliter**, *n.* the snipe.

Hern-fern, *n.* a plant taken from ditches for protection against witches, &c.

Heron-bluter, *n.* the snipe.

Heronious, *adj.* careless, bold, daring.

Heronsew, **Heronshew**, *n.* the heron.

Herral, *n.* a heron. Cf. Herle.

Herral-necked, *adj.* long-necked.

Herrial, **Herrieal**, *n.* what causes loss, ruin ; a great, costly expenditure.

Herrier, *n.* a plunderer. Cf. Herryer.

Herrinband, *n.* a string warped through the different skeins of yarn to keep them separate when boiled.

Herring-drave, *n.* a drove or shoal of herring.

Herring-drewe, *n.* a 'herring-drave,' as an attraction to idle fellows and bankrupts, so that a bankrupt who fled from his creditors was said to have gone to the 'herring-drewe.'

Herring-soam, *n.* the fat of herrings.

Herring-tack, *n.* a shoal of herrings.

Herrin-head, *n.* a retreating forehead ; a person with a retreating forehead, used contemptuously.

Herry, *v.* to plunder ; to rob nests, &c. Cf. Harry.

Herryer, *n.* a robber ; a plunderer of birds' nests.

Herryment, *n.* plunder ; the cause of plunder.

Herry-water, *n.* a net that catches small fish ; a person who takes all he can get.

Hersche, **Herse**, *adj.* hoarse. Cf. Hairse.

Hersel', *pron.* used by a Highlander as the same as 'himself'; a nickname of a Highlander.

Hersel, *n.* a flock of sheep, &c. Cf. Hirsel.

Herseness, *n.* hoarseness.

Hership, **Herschip**, *n.* the act of plundering. Cf. Heirship.

Herskit, *n.* heartburn. Cf. Heart-scad.

Hersum, *adj.* strong, rank, harsh.

Hervy, *adj.* mean ; having the appearance of great poverty.

Heshie-ba, *n.* a lullaby.—*int.* a call to a baby to sleep. Cf. Hush-a-ba.

He-slip, *n.* a lad, young boy.

Hesp, *n.* a clasp, a hook.—*v.* to fasten. Cf. Hasp.

Hesp, *n.* a hank of yarn. Cf. Hasp.

Hespy, *n.* a boys' game. Cf. Hie-spy.

Hess, *adj.* hoarse. Cf. Haiss.

Hester, *v.* to hesitate ; to pester, trouble.

Het, *v.* to strike, hit.

Het, *adj.* hot, warm, comfortable.—*n.* heat.

Het a hame, *adj.* comfortable at home.

Het beans and butter, *n.* a children's game, like 'hunt the thimble.'

Het bitch, *n.* a bitch in the rutting season.

Het drinks, *n.* warm, cordial drinks.

Het-fit, *adv.* at full speed, immediately.

Heth, *int.* an expletive : 'faith !' Cf. Haith.

Het hands, *n.* a children's game of piling hands one on another and withdrawing them in rotation.

Hether, *n.* heath ; ling. Cf. Hadder.

Hetherig, *n.* the end of a field on which the horses and plough turn. Cf. Head-rig.

Hethery, *adj.* used of the hair : shaggy ; ruffled. Cf. Heathery.

Hetly, *adv.* hotly.

Het pint, *n.* a drink composed of ale, spirits, &c., drunk on New Year's Eve, on the night preceding a marriage, and at child-bearing.

Het rows and butter-bakes, *n.* a boys' game.

Het seed, *n.* early grain ; early peas.

Het skin, *n.* a drubbing, thrashing.

Het skinned, *adj.* irascible, hot-tempered.

Het spurred, *adv.* at full speed, at once.

Het stoup, *n.* a 'het pint.'

Hettle, *adj.* fiery ; irritable ; hasty, eager.

Hettle, *n.* the name given by fishermen on the Firth of Forth to a range of rocky bottom lying between the roadstead and the shore.

Hettle-codling, *n.* a species of codling caught on the 'hettle.'

Het tuik, *n.* a bad taste, as of meal made from corn heated in the stack.

Het waters, *n.* ardent spirits.

Het weeds, *n.* annual weeds, like field-mustard, &c.

Heuch, **Heugh**, *n.* a crag, cliff, rugged steep ; a hollow, a deep glen ; a deep cleft in rocks ; a coal-pit ; the shaft of a coal-mine ; a hollow made in a quarry.

Heuch, *int.* an exclamation, generally used in dancing Scotch reels.—*v.* to cry 'heuch !' Cf. Hooch.

Heuch, **Heugh**, *n.* a disease of cows, supposed to arise from want of water, or from bad water, attacking the stomach and eventually inflaming the eyes.

Heuch-head, *n.* the top of a cliff or precipice.

Heuchle-bane, *n.* the hip-bone or -joint, the huckle-bone.

Heuch-, Heugh-man, *n.* a pitman.

Heuchster, Heughster, *n.* a pitman.

Heuck, *n.* a reaping-hook; a reaper in harvest. —*v.* to hook.

Heuck, *n.* a disease of cows affecting the eyes. Cf. Heuch.

Heuck-bane, *n.* the hip-bone, huckle-bone.

Heuck-stane, *n.* blue vitriol, used for removing the 'heuck' disease among cattle.

Heuk, *v.* to itch. Cf. Yeuk.

Heuk, *v.* to hook.—*n.* a hook; a reaping-hook.

Heul, *n.* a mischievous boy; one that acts in a headstrong, regardless, or extreme fashion; a cross-grained person.

Hevicairies, *int.* an excl. of surprise, a contraction of 'have a care of us!'

Hew, *n.* a crag, precipice. Cf. Heuch.

Hew, *n.* look, appearance; a slight quantity, a 'dash.'—*v.* to colour. Cf. Hue.

Hewl, *n.* a mischievous boy. Cf. Heul.

Hewmist, *adj.* last, hindmost.

†Hexe, *n.* a witch.

Hey, *int.* a call to attract attention.—*v.* to cry 'hey!' Cf. Heich.

Hey-ma-nannie, *n.* full speed.

Heynd, *adj.* clever; courteous. Cf. Hend.

Heypal, *v.* to limp, go lame.—*n.* sciatica; rheumatic pains in the upper part of the thigh; a good-for-nothing fellow; a term of contempt. Cf. Hypal.

Heypalt, *n.* a cripple; an animal whose legs are tied; a sorry-looking fellow or horse; a sheep which 'casts' its fleece as the result of some disease. Cf. Hypalt.

Heyrd, Heyrt, *adj.* furious, raging.

Heytie, *n.* the game of 'shinty' or hockey.

Hey Wullie wine and How Wullie wine, *n.* an old fireside play of the peasantry, the aim of which was, by rhyming question and answer, to find out the sweethearts of the players.

Hezard, *v.* to dry clothes by bleaching. Cf. Haiser, Haisle.

Hezekiah, *n.* in *phr.* 'proud as Hezekiah,' excessively proud.

Hibble, *v.* to confine.

Hic, *v.* to hesitate. Cf. Hick.

Hiccory, *adj.* cross-grained, ill-tempered.

Hich, *v.* to hoist; to hitch; to lift with an upward heave.—*adj.* high. Cf. Heich.

Hich, *int.* an excl. of surprise, sorrow, contempt, &c. Cf. Hech.

Hicht, *v.* to promise; to call by name. Cf. Hecht.

Hicht, *n.* height.—*v.* to raise, to lift up. Cf. Heicht.

Hichtit, *ppl. adj.* in great anger, 'raised.'

Hick, *v.* to hesitate in bargaining or speaking. —*n.* an expression of hesitation; a stammer. —*int.* a call to horses to turn to the right.

Hick, *v.* to make a clicking sound in the throat like a sob; to hiccup; to cry at short intervals; to whimper.—*n.* a clicking sound in the throat; the hiccup.

Hickertie-pickertie, *adv.* higgledy-piggledy, one upon another.

Hickery-pickery, *n.* 'hiera picra,' a drug compounded of Barbadoes aloes and canella bark.

Hickety-bickety, *n.* a boys' outdoor game.

Hid, *pron.* it.

Hidance, *n.* shelter, a hiding-place.

Hidder, *adv.* hither.

Hidder and tidder, *adv.* hither and thither.

Hiddie, *n.* the hooded crow, the carrion crow. Cf. Hoodie.

Hiddie-giddie, *n.* a disorderly noise, a disturbance.—*adv.* topsyturvy, in confusion; hither and thither.—*adj.* confused, giddy, wanton.

Hiddie-giddie, *n.* a short piece of wood with a sharp point at each end, fixed on the trace for keeping horses or oxen apart in ploughing.

Hiddie-pyke, *n.* a miser, niggard.

Hiddils, Hiddles, *n.* shelters, hiding-places; concealment.

Hiddle, *v.* to hide.—*adv.* secretly, mysteriously.

Hiddle, *n.* a heald, a heddle.

Hiddlin, *adj.* hidden, secret.

Hiddlins, *adj.* secret, clandestine.—*adv.* secretly, stealthily.—*n.* a place or state of concealment.

Hiddlinsly, *adv.* secretly.

Hiddlinways, Hiddlinwise, *adv.* secretly, by stealth.

Hiddly, *adj.* hidden; sheltered from view, concealing.

Hiddrick, *n.* the head-ridge on which a plough turns.

Hide, *n.* the skin of a human being; a term of contempt applied to the females of domestic animals, also to human beings, especially women; the nap of a hat.—*v.* to beat, thrash; to curry; to skin an animal.

Hide, *v.* to put carefully by; to treasure.—*n.* a hiding-place.—*int.* the cry given by the concealed player in 'hide-and-seek.'

Hide-a-bo-seek, *n.* the game of 'hide-and-seek.'

Hide and hair, *n.* the whole of a thing.

Hide-and-seek, *n.* 'blind-man's buff.'

Hide-bind, *n.* a disease of horses and cattle causing the hide to stick closely to the bones.

Hidee, *n.* the player who hides himself in 'hide-and-seek.'

Hide-i'-the-heather, *n.* a tramp, vagrant.

Hidet, *v. pret.* hid.—*ppl.* hidden.

Hide-the-mare, *n.* a child's game of searching for a hidden article. Cf. Kittly-cowt.

Hiding, *n.* a severe thrashing.

Hidlance, *n.* secrecy; concealment. Cf. Hiddlins.

Hidle, *v.* to hide. Cf. Hiddle.

Hidlin, *adj.* hidden. Cf. Hiddlin.

Hidlins, *adv.* secretly. Cf. Hiddlins.

Hidmaist, *adj.* hindmost.

Hidy, *adj.* hidden; secret; hiding.

Hidy-corner, *n.* a secret corner in which to hide things.

Hidy-hole, *n.* a place in which a person or thing is hidden; a subterfuge.

Hie, *adj.* high.

Hie, Hie-here, *int.* a call to horses to turn to the left.

Hielan', Hieland, Hielant, *adj.* Highland; silly; clumsy.

Hielan' blue, *n.* Highland whisky.

Hielan' Donald, *n.* a pony or 'sheltie' formerly reared in the Highlands by the crofters and brought to the Lowlands.

Hielan'-fling, *n.* a Highland step-dance.—*v.* to dance the 'Hielan'-fling.'

Hielan'-man's funeral, *n.* a funeral lasting more than a day, and occasioning much whisky-drinking.

Hielan'-man's ling, *n.* walking quickly with a jerk.

Hielan' passion, *n.* a violent but temporary outburst of anger.

Hield, *v.* to shield, protect.

Hier, *n.* the sixth part of a 'hesp' of yarn. Cf. Hair.

Hiersome, *adj.* coarse-looking.

Hiertieing, *n.* a mocking or jeering salutation.

Hiese, *v.* to hoist. Cf. Heeze.

Hie-spy, *n.* a form of the game of 'hide-and-seek.'—*int.* the call given by the players when ready in their hiding-places.

Hie-wo, *int.* a call to horses to turn to the left; also to turn to the right.

Higgle, *v.* to argue.

High, *adj.* tall; used of a dog's ears: erect; of the belly: protuberant; of the wind: north; proud; in high spirits. Cf. Heich.

High-bendit, *adj.* dignified in appearance; aspiring, ambitious.

High-cocked-hat, *n.* a hat with the brim thrice cocked.

High-flies, *n.* swings at fairs.

High gate, *n.* the high-road, highway.

High-henched, *adj.* having high or projecting thigh-bones.

High jinks, *n.* an obsolete drinking game. Cf. Hy jinks.

High-jumper, *n.* a parasite found in wool.

High-kilted, *adj.* with short or tucked-up petticoats; verging on indecency.

Highland gill, *n.* two gills.

Highle, *v.* to carry with difficulty. Cf. Hechle.

High sniffingness, *n.* airs of importance.

High street, *n.* the highway.

High-style, *adj.* bombastic, grandiose.

Hight, *v.* to promise. Cf Hecht.

Hight, *v.* to trust, resort to.

Hight, *v.* to raise, heighten, enhance.

High-twal', *n.* midday.

High-year-old, *adj.* used of cattle: a year and a half old. Cf. Heiyearald.

Hig-rig-ma-reel, *adv.* higgledy-piggledy.

Hig-tig-bizz, *int.* a form of words used by boys to startle cattle.

Hike, *v.* to move the body suddenly by the back joint; used of a boat: to toss up and down, swing.

Hike, *int.* a call to horses to come to the near side. Cf. Heck.

Hilch, *v.* to halt, hobble.—*n.* a halt, a limp.

Hilch, *n.* a shelter from wind or rain.

Hilch, *n.* in *phr.* the 'hilch of a hill,' the brow or higher part of the face of a hill, whence one can get a full view on both hands, of that side of the hill.

Hildegaleerie, Hildegulair, Hiligulier, *adv.* topsyturvy. Cf. Heeliegoleerie.

Hildie-gildie, *n.* an uproar. Cf. Hiddy-giddy.

Hill, *n.* a heap of rubbish or things in disorder; a common moor.

Hill, *n.* a hull, a husk.

Hillan, *n.* a hillock; a small artificial hill; a heap.

Hill-ane, *n.* a fairy.

Hillan-piet, *n.* the missel-thrush.

Hill-bird, *n.* the fieldfare.

Hill-burn, *n.* a mountain-stream.

Hill-chack, *n.* the ring-ousel.

Hill-dyke, *n.* a wall dividing pasture from arable land.

Hiller, *n.* a small heap, a mound of rubbish.

Hiller, *n.* a stout, untidy person.

Hill-folk, *n.* dwellers in hilly regions; Covenanters, Cameronians, or Reformed Presbyterians; fairies.

Hill-gait, *n.* a hilly road; a hill-road.

Hill-head, *n.* the top of a hill or of an acclivity.

Hilliebalow, -baloo, -belew, -bullow, -buloo, *n.* a 'hullaballoo,' an uproar.

Hilliegeleerie, *n.* a frolic.—*adv.* topsyturvy. Cf. Heeliegoleerie.

Hilling, *n.* grazing on hill-pasture.

Hill-linty, *n.* the twite.

Hill-man, *n.* a dweller among hills; a Covenanter, a Cameronian.

Hilloa, *n.* a call to attract attention.—*int.* 'hullo!'

Hillocket, *ppl. adj.* giddy, light-headed, wild Cf. Hallockit.

Hill-plover, *n.* the golden plover.

Hill-slack, *n.* a pass between two hills.

Hill-sparrow, *n.* the meadow-pipit.

Hill-worn, *adj.* wearied with hill-walking.

Hilly, *adj.* used of the sea : rough, heaving, having huge waves.

Hilly-baloo, *n.* an uproar.

Hilly-ho, *int.* a hunting cry, 'tally-ho!'

Hilsh, *v.* to walk lamely.—*n.* a halt, a hobble. Cf. Hilch.

Hilt, *n.* in *phr.* 'hilt and hair,' every particle ; with *nor*, nothing at all.

Hilted-rung, -staff, *n.* a crutch.

Hilter-skilter, *adv.* in rapid succession, helter-skelter.

Hiltie, *n.* a crutch.

Hiltie - skiltie, Hilty - skilty, *adv.* helter-skelter.

Him lane, *phr.* himself alone.

Himsel', Himsell, *pron.* the head of the house ; the husband as spoken of to or by his wife ; the master as spoken of to or by his servant ; one in full possession of his faculties.

Hin, *adj.* belonging to the back or rear. Cf. Hind.

Hinch, *v.* to halt, limp.—*n.* a limp, halt ; lameness.

Hinch, *v.* to throw missiles under the leg or thigh by striking the hand against the thigh ; to jerk.—*n.* the haunch. Cf. Hainch.

Hincher, *n.* a lame person.

Hincum, *n.* what is put up into balls. Cf. Hinkum.

Hind, *n.* a farm-servant, hired yearly and occupying a farm-cottage.

Hind, *n.* a thin layer.

Hind, *adj.* rearward ; belonging to the back ; spare, extra.—*n.* the rear, back ; the very last.—*adv.* behind.—*prep.* behind.

Hindberry, *n.* the wild raspberry.

Hind-chiel, *n.* a youth ; a young fellow.

Hind-door, *n.* the movable back-board of a box-cart.

Hinderin, *n.* the close, latter end, hind end.

Hinderlets, *n.* the back parts, posteriors.

Hinding-work, *n.* a farm-servant's work.

Hindish, *adj.* rustic, clownish, clumsy.

Hindling, *n.* one who falls behind, a loser in a game.

Hindmaist, *adj.* hindmost.

Hind-squire, *n.* a young fellow ; a young squire.

Hine, *adv.* away, afar, to a distance.—*v.* to take one's self off.—*n.* a departure.

Hine-awa, *adj.* far-away.—*adv.* to a distance.

Hin'-en', *n.* the last part, the latter end.

Hiner, *v.* to withhold, keep back from ; to hinder. Cf. Hinner.

Hine-till, *adv.* as far as ; to the distance of.

Hing, *v.* to hang, be suspended ; to hang, suspend ; to be in suspense.—*n.* the trick,

fashion of a thing ; the knack of putting a thing.

Hing an' hangie, *v.* to delay, dawdle.

Hingar, Hinger, *n.* a curtain, hanging ; a pendant ; a necklace.

Hingar-at-lug, *n.* an ear-ring.

Hing-dringing, *adj.* lingering, dwelling tediously on a topic.

Hinged-brig, *n.* a drawbridge.

Hinging, *n.* a courting, wooing.

Hinging, *ppl. adj.* used of a market or sale : dull, not brisk.

Hinging-chafted, *adj.* having pendulous cheeks.

Hinging-lug, *n.* a grudge or enmity toward one ; in *pl.* despondency.

Hinging-luggit, *adj.* having drooping ears ; disappointed ; dull, despondent ; sulky, out of temper ; having a grudge at one.

Hinging-mou'd, *adj.* in low spirits.

Hingings, *n.* bed-curtains.

Hinging-shouthered, *adj.* having sloping shoulders.

Hingle, *v.* to loiter. Cf. Haingle.

Hing-thegither, *adj.* clannish.

Hingum-tringum, *adj.* in weak health ; in low spirits ; disreputable, worthless.

Hin-hairst, *n.* the end of harvest ; the time between harvest and winter.

Hin-han', *adj.* last.—*n.* the last of a series ; the last player in a curling-rink.

Hin-heid, *n.* the back of the head.

Hink, *v.* to hesitate.—*n.* hesitation, a misgiving.

Hinklin, *n.* an inkling.

Hink-skink, *n.* very small beer.

Hinkum, *n.* what is tied up into balls ; a young and mischievous boy or girl.

Hinkum-booby, *n.* a children's singing-game.

Hinkum-sneevie, -snivie, *n.* a silly, stupid person.—*adj.* stupid, lounging, slothful.

Hinmaist, *adj.* the last, latest, final.—*n.* the end, the last remains.

Hin-man, *n.* the man behind ; the man who is last.

Hinner, *v.* to hinder ; to withhold or keep back from.—*n.* hindrance.

Hinner, *adj.* hind, hinder, back, posterior ; last, latter, as regards time.—*n.* in *pl.* the posteriors ; the hind-quarters of an animal.

Hinner-en, *n.* the back of anything ; the end ; the end of life ; the last remnant of anything ; refuse ; the worst of anything.

Hinner-lans, -lats, -lets, -lins, -liths, *ns.* back parts, buttocks ; hind-quarters.

Hinnerly, *adv.* at the last ; finally.

Hinnermaist, *adj.* last.—*n.* the latest.

Hinner nicht, *n.* the last or latest night.

Hinnersum, *adj.* tedious ; wearisome ; causing hindrance or delay.

Hinny, *n.* honey; a term of endearment. Cf. Honey.

Hinny-crock, *n.* a honey-jar.

Hinny-mark, **Honey-mark**, *n.* ? a mole on the body. Cf. Honey-drap.

Hinny-pig, *n.* a honey-jar.

Hinny-pigs, -**pots**, *n.* a children's game.

Hin-shelving, *n.* an extra board put on the back-board of a box-cart.

Hin-side, *n.* the back, the rear.

Hint, *v.* with *about* or *after*, to watch quietly; to go about quietly or slyly; to teach quietly, to indicate slightly.—*n.* an opportunity, occasion; a moment of time.

Hint, *v.* to disappear quickly, vanish; with *back*, to start back.

Hint, *v.* to throw a stone by striking the hand sharply against the thigh, to 'hinch.'

Hint, *v.* to hunt.

Hint, *v.* to lay hold of. Cf. Hent.

Hint, *v.* to plough up the bottom furrow between 'rigs.'

Hint, *adv.* and *prep.* behind. Cf. Hind.

Hint-a-gowk, *n.* the derisive name given to an April-fool.

Hintins, *n.* the furrows with which ploughmen finish their 'rigs.'

Hint o' hairst, *n.* the end of harvest; the time between harvest and winter.

Hip, *v.* to skip over, omit, miss; to hop.—*n.* an omission, the passing over.

Hip, *n.* the border or edge of a district; the shoulder of a hill; a round eminence towards the extremity, or on the lower part, of a hill; a protection, shelter.

Hip, *int.* a call to a horse to go to the right or off side, or to go on.—*v.* to cry 'hip!' Cf. Hup.

Hip and hollion, *adv.* entirely.

Hip-hop, *adv.* with repeated hops.

Hiplocks, *n.* the coarse wool about the hips of sheep.

Hippal, *n.* sciatica; rheumatic pains in the upper part of the thigh.

Hippen, Hippin, *n.* a baby's hip-napkin.

Hippertie-skippertie, *adv.* in a skipping fashion. Cf. Hippity-skippertie.

Hippertie-tipperty, *adj.* childishly exact; affectedly neat. Cf. Hippity-tippertie.

Hippet, Hippit, *ppl. adj.* hurt in the thigh; having the muscles of the back, loins, and thighs overstrained by stooping at work; wearied.

Hip-piece, *n.* a piece of beef cut from the thigh of an ox.

Hippie-dippie, *n.* a castigation; a 'skelping' on the hips or buttocks.

Hippit, *ppl. adj.* passed over; exempted; excused.

Hippity-haincher, -**hincher**, *n.* a lame person.

Hippity-skippertie, *adv.* in a frisking, skipping fashion.

Hippity-tippertie, *adj.* unstable; flighty, frivolous; childishly exact; affectedly neat

Hip-shot, -**shotten**, *adj.* lamed in the hip; with a sprained or dislocated thigh.

Hip-the-beds, *n.* the game of hop-scotch.

Hirch, *v.* to shiver; to thrill with cold; to shrug the shoulders.—*n.* a shrug.

Hirch and kick, *n.* a kicking-game in which the player had no other impetus than a shrug of the shoulders when toeing the line.

Hird, *v.* to tend cattle.—*n.* a flock, a herd; a cattle-tender, shepherd. Cf. Herd.

Hirdie-club, *n.* a herd's stick or club.

Hirdie-girdie, *adv.* topsyturvy. — *adj.* disorderly. — *n.* a tumult, disorder. Cf. Hiddie-giddie.

Hirdsale, Hirdsel, *n.* a flock of sheep. Cf. Hirsel.

Hirdum-dirdum, *n.* confusion, noisy mirth, uproar.—*adj.* uproarious, confused.—*adv.* topsyturvy.

Hire, *v.* to enrich land with various manures; to make food palatable or appetizing.

Hire, *v.* to let on hire; to engage as a servant; to accept, welcome.—*n.* a dealing, trading transaction.

Hired, *ppl. adj.* used of food: seasoned with various condiments.

Hire-house, *n.* service; the place or house to which a servant is engaged to go.

Hire-man, *n.* a hired servant, farm-labourer.

Hire-quean, *n.* a servant-girl.

Hirer, *n.* a person engaged for farm-work by the day or for a short time; one who lets on hire; a horse-jobber.

Hireship, *n.* service; the place of a servant.

Hirewoman, *n.* a maid-servant.

Hirie-harie, *n.* the hue and cry after a thief. Cf. Hirrie-harrie.

Hiring-pint, *n.* drink consumed at the hiring of a horse, &c.

Hirling, *n.* the salmon-trout, 'herling.' Cf. Herling.

Hirm, *v.* to fret, grumble. Cf. Hairm.

Hirne, *n.* a corner, recess.

Hirp, *n.* a mason's riddle; a wire-cloth frame for sifting grain or meal in milling.—*v.* to harp on one topic; to riddle or sift with a 'harp.' Cf. Harp.

Hirple, Hirpil, *v.* to limp, walk as a cripple; to move unevenly, hobble.—*n.* a limp, halt; a cripple.

Hirploch, Hirplock, *n.* a cripple, a lame creature.

Hirr, *v.* to hound on a dog.—*int.* an expression used in hounding on a dog; a herd's call to his dog to drive up cattle.

Hirrie, *v.* to rob; to plunder nests. Cf. Harry.

Hirrie - harrie, *n.* the hue and cry after a thief; a broil, tumult.—*adv.* tumultuously.

Hirro, *int.* hurrah! an outcry for help.—*v.* to hurrah, halloo. Cf. Harro.

Hirsel, Hirsle, *n.* a flock of sheep; the stock of sheep on a farm; a spiritual flock; the feeding-place of a flock of sheep; a gathering, company; a large collection of people or of things.—*v.* to arrange different kinds of sheep in separate flocks; to arrange or dispose persons in order.

Hirsel, Hirsle, Hirschle, *v.* to move or glide resting on the hams; to slide with grazing or friction; 'o move in a creeping or trailing manner with a slight grating noise; to move a body with much friction or effort; to cause to slide; to work in a hurried, careless, or slovenly fashion; to be slovenly in dress.—*n.* a sliding, grazing movement; the noise made by a heavy body being drawn over another; an auger used for boring when red - hot. Cf. Hurschle, Hushel.

Hirsel aff, *v.* to die easily or gently.

Hirsel yont, *v.* to move farther off.

Hirsil-rinning, *adj.* gathering sheep at a distance.

Hirsp, *v.* to jar; to rasp.

Hirst, *n.* a resting-place; a small eminence on a rising ground; a small wood; a ridge; a bank; the bare, hard summit of a hill; a sandbank on the brink of a river; a shallow in a river; a sloping bank or wall of stonework, formerly used in mills as a substitute for a stair.

Hirst, *n.* a great number; a large quantity of anything.

Hirst, *v.* to slide with grazing or friction.

Hirstin, *n.* a dwelling-place.

Hirstle, *v.* to breathe roughly, wheeze.—*n.* a wheeze. Cf. Hurstle.

Hirstlin, *n.* the sound of rough breathing.—*ppl. adj.* wheezing.

Hirsty, *adj.* dry, bare, barren.

Hirtch, *v.* to move gradually or with jerks; to approach slyly or in wheedling fashion.—*n.* a slight motion or jerk, a slight push.

Hirtchin-harie, *n.* a children's game. Cf. Harie-hurcheon.

His, *poss. pron.* God's.

His, *pron.* us.

Hise, *v.* to hoist.—*n.* a hoist; help. Cf. Heeze.

Hish, *v.* to hiss; to make a hissing sound to hound on a dog or to drive away an animal. Cf. Husch, Hiss

Hish, *int.* hush!

Hishie, *v.* to lull to sleep, to sing a lullaby. Cf. Hush.

Hishie, *n.* in *phr.* 'neither hishie nor wishie,' not the slightest sound.

Hishie-ba, -baw, *int.* an expression used in lulling a child to sleep.—*n.* a lullaby.—*v.* to lull to sleep. Cf. Hush-a-ba.

Hisht, *int.* hush!

Hisk, Hiskie, *int.* a call to a dog.—*n.* a dog; a hissing sound. Cf. Isk.

His lane, *phr.* himself alone.

Hiss, *v.* to drive off an animal, or hound on a dog, by making a hissing sound.—*int.* a sound used in so doing. Cf. Hish.

Hissel, *n.* a flock of sheep. Cf. Hirsel.

Hissel', His sel', *pron.* himself, used emphatically. Cf. Himsel'.

Hissie, *n.* a housewife; a hussy, used contemptuously; a young girl, a 'lass,' wench; a mare, a jade; a needle-case, a case for needles, thread, &c.

Hissieskip, *n.* housewifery.

Hist, *n.* a great number. Cf. Hirst.

Hist, *v.* to haste; to hasten.

Hist away by, *int.* a shepherd's call to his dog to be off.

Hist-hast, *h.* a confusion, disorder.

Histie, *adj.* dry, barren. Cf. Hirsty.

Historicals, *n.* historical statements, history.

Hit, *v.* to throw forcibly; with *it,* to manage, succeed; to agree.

Hit, *pron.* it, used emphatically; the 'he' or 'she' in certain games.

Hitch, *v.* to move about with jerks; to 'hotch'; to hop on one leg; to creep; to linger.—*n.* a sudden movement; a push, a slight temporary assistance; a difficulty; an obstruction in mining, when the coalseam is interrupted by a different stratum or sudden rise or inequality; a row of knitting.

Hite, *adj.* furious, mad; excessively keen. Cf. Hyte.

Hither-and-yont, *adv.* hither and thither; backwards and forwards; topsyturvy, in confusion.

Hitherawa, *adv.* hither.

Hither-come, *n.* advent, descent, pedigree.

Hither-thither, *adv.* hither and thither.

Hithin, *n.* the eye of the 'souple' of a flail, the 'hooding.'

Hithom-tithom, *n.* a dish of sweet and sour 'sowens.'

Hitten, *ppl.* hit, struck.

Hiv, *n.* a hoof.

Hiv, *v.* to have.

Hive, *n.* a crowd, a swarm of people.—*v.* to go in crowds.

Hive, *v.* to swell; to cause to swell. Cf. Heave, Hove.

Hive, *n.* a haven.

Hives, *n.* any eruption on the skin from an internal cause; the red and the yellow gum; a feverish complaint among children.

Hivie, *adj.* in easy circumstances; well-to-do; affluent.

Hiving-sough, *n.* the peculiar buzzing sound made by bees before they hive.

His, *pron.* us.

Hizard, *v.* to dry clothes by bleaching. Cf. Hezard.

Hize, *v.* to ramble; to romp about.

Hizzie, *n.* a housewife; a hussy. Cf. Hissie.

Hizzie-fallow, *n.* a man who interferes in a housewife's department.

Hniusle, *v.* to nuzzle.

Ho, *n.* a stop, delay, cessation.

Ho, *n.* a stocking.

Ho, *n.* a cover; a coif, head-dress; a child's caul. Cf. Hoo, How.

Hoak, *v.* to dig, excavate. Cf. Howk.

Hoakie, *n.* a fire that has been covered up with cinders, when all the fuel has become red.

Hoakie, *int.* used as a petty oatn.

Hoam, *n.* level, low ground beside a stream, a holm; an islet, an inland in a lake; a depression, hollow. Cf. Howm.

Hoam, *n.* the dried grease of a cod.

Hoam, *v.* to give a disagreeable taste to food by confining the steam in the pot when boiling; to spoil provisions by keeping them in a confined place. Cf. Oam.

Hoam'd, *ppl. adj.* used of animal food: having a fusty taste from being kept too long.

Hoars, *n.* white hairs; old age.

Hoarse, *n.* a hoarse note of a fowl.

Hoars-gowk, *n.* the common snipe; the green sandpiper. Cf. Horse-gowk.

Hoast, *n.* a cough; a hem, a vulgar mode of calling on one to stop; a matter attended with no difficulty.—*v.* to cough; to belch up, bring forth; to hem, to call on one to stop.

Hoatie, Hoats, *n.* a term used in the game of 'pearie' or peg-top, of a 'pearie' that bounces out of the ring without spinning.

Hob-and-nob, *v.* to hobnob.

Hobble, Hoble, *v.* to shake, jolt; to dandle; to shake with a quivering motion; to swarm with vermin or any kind of living creatures, insects especially; to embarrass, hamper; to tie an animal's legs so as to prevent it from straying.—*n.* a swarm of any kind; a shake, toss; a predicament; a confused fight; any apparatus for 'hobbling' an animal. Cf. Habble.

Hobble, *n.* a fool; a blockhead.

Hobble-bog, *n.* a quagmire; soft, wet, quaking ground.

Hobbled, *ppl. adj.* perplexed; put about; confined.

Hobble-quo, *n.* a quagmire; a scrape, dilemma.

Hobbler, *n.* a stout ferry-boat.

Hobbleshow, Hobbleshaw, Hobbleshew, Hobbleshue, *n.* a hubbub, tumult; commotion; a rabble; a tumultuous gathering.

Hobblie, *adj.* used of ground: soft, quaking under foot.

Hobby, *n.* the merlin.

Hobby-horse, *n.* a hobby, favourite avocation.

Hobby-tobby, *n.* the appearance, dress, &c. of an awkward, tawdry woman.

Hob Collinwood, *n.* the four of hearts in the game of whist.

Hobois, *int.* a hunting cry to the dogs.

Hoboy, *n.* a hautboy or oboe; a player on the hautboy.

Hobshanks, *n.* knees.

Hoburn saugh, *n.* the laburnum.

Hoch, *n.* the leg of an animal; the leg or lower part of a man's thigh; the ham, thigh, hip.—*v.* to hamstring; to throw a missile under the thigh; to throw the leg over a person in contempt of his small stature; to tramp, trudge along.

Hoch, *int.* an excl. of grief, weariness, joy, &c.

Hoch-anee, *int.* an excl. of grief.

Hoch-ban, *n.* a band passing round the neck and one of the legs of a restless animal.— *v.* to tie a 'hoch-ban' to a cow, &c.

Hoch-bane, *n.* the thigh-bone.

Hoch-deep, *adv.* up to the thighs; as deep as the thighs.

Hochen, *n.* the fireside. Cf. Hechen.

Hocher, *n.* one who houghs cattle.

Hoch-hey, *int.* an excl. of weariness.

Hoch-hicht, *v.* to stand on one leg and put the other over any object.

Hoch-hiech, *adj.* as tall as a full-grown man's leg.

Hoch-hone, *int.* an excl. of grief, 'ochone!'

Hochie, *n.* a keg, cask, small barrel.

Hochimes, *n.* bent pieces of wood, slung on each side of a horse, as supports for panniers. Cf. Houghams.

Hochle, *v.* to walk with short steps; to sprawl, shamble, shuffle in walking; to walk clumsily; to do anything clumsily or awkwardly; to tumble lewdly with women in open day.—*n.* a sloven; a person regardless of dress or appearance.

Hochmagandy, *n.* fornication.

Hoch-wow, *int.* an excl. of grief, weariness, &c.

Hock, *v.* to scoop out, dig. Cf. Howk.

Hocker, *v.* to bend, stoop; to crouch over the fire. Cf. Hoker.

Hockerie-topner, *n.* the house-leek.

Hockerty-cockerty, *adv.* riding on a person's shoulders, with a leg over each.

Hockery-packery, -pokery, *n.* sharp practice, anything mysterious or underhand; hocus-pocus.

Hocking, *n.* scraping out a hole with the hands or with a hoe.

Hocus, *n.* a stupid fellow, fool, simpleton.

Hocus, *n.* juggling, artful management, hocus-pocus.

Hod, *v.* to jog along; to ride badly.

Hod, *v.* to hide; to put carefully by; to treasure. Cf. Hide.

Hod, *v. pret.* hid.—*ppl.* hidden.

Hod, *n.* a hood; the hob of a fireplace; the back of a fireplace, the 'cat-hud'; a small enclosure or shelf built at the side of a fireplace; a portion of a wall built with single stones, or with stones which go from side to side at short intervals. Cf. Hood.

Hodded, *v. pret.* did hide.

Hodden, *ppl.* hid, hidden.

Hodden, Hoddin, *n.* homespun cloth of wool of the natural colour, a coarse, thick cloth worn by the peasantry and smaller farmers; a covering made of hodden.—*adj.* clad in homespun; made of hodden; homely, coarse.

Hodden-breeks, *n.* homespun breeches.

Hodden-clad, *adj.* clad in homespun.

Hodden-gray, *n.* gray homespun.—*adj.* clad in hodden-gray.

Hoddie, *n.* the hooded crow; the carrion-crow; a hired mourner. Cf. Hoodie.

Hoddin, *ppl.* riding heavily.

Hoddins, *n.* small stockings, such as are worn by children.

Hoddit, *v. pret.* hid.

Hoddle, *v.* to waddle; to walk awkwardly; to dance clumsily.—*n.* a waddle, jog-trot; a step, a pace.

Hoddle, *n.* a clumsy rick of hay or corn.

Hoddler, *n.* one who waddles.

Hoddle-trossie, *n.* bread twice steeped in hot water, and pressed twice.

Hoddy, *adj.* in good condition.

Hoddy, *adj.* hidden, concealed; suitable for concealment.

Hoddy-corner, *n.* a cunning place for hiding things.

Hoddy-table, *n.* a small table which goes under a larger one when not in use.

Hode, *v.* to hide.—*pret.* hid.

Hoden, *n.* homespun. Cf. Hodden.

Hodge, *v.* to move with an awkward, heaving motion; to stagger; to shake with laughter; to hitch up; to push roughly.—*n.* a shove; a jolt; a big, awkward person, a fool.

Hodgil, *n.* a dumpling.

Hodgil, *v.* to move by jerks and with difficulty; with *about*, to carry about constantly; to hobble, to move slowly and clumsily.—*n.* a push; a stout, clumsy person.

Hodin, *n.* 'hodden.'

Hodlack, *n.* a rick of hay.

Hodle, *n.* a small roadside inn.

Hodle, *v.* to walk or move more quickly than a child. Cf. Hoddle.

Hodle-makenster, *adj.* rustling.

Hodler, *n.* one who waddles.

Hodlins, *adv.* secretly. Cf. Hiddlins.

Hoe, *n.* a single stocking. Cf. Ho.

Hoe, *n.* a stop, delay. Cf. Ho.

Hoeshin, *n.* a stocking without a foot; a term of abuse. Cf. Hoshen.

Hog, *n.* a cant name for a shilling.

Hog, Hogg, *n.* a young sheep before it has lost its first fleece; a curling-stone which does not pass over the distance-score; the distance-score or line in curling.—*v.* to clip or make pollards of trees.

Hog, Hogg, *v.* to jog, shog.

Hog and score, *n.* one sheep added to every twenty, a 'cledscore.'

Hog and tatie, *n.* 'braxy' mutton stewed with potatoes, onions, pepper, and salt.

Hog-backed, *adj.* round-backed.

Hoger, *n.* a footless stocking. Cf. Hogger.

Hog-fence, *n.* a feeding-ground for sheep; a fence for enclosing sheep.

Hoggart, *ppl. adj.* of stockings: footless. Cf. Hogger.

Hogged, *ppl. adj.* fallen behind in means or business.

Hogger, *n.* a footless stocking worn as a gaiter; an old stocking used as a purse.

Hogget, *n.* a hogshead, a large cask or barrel.

Hoggie, *n.* a young sheep.

Hogging, *n.* a place where sheep, after becoming 'hogs,' are pastured.

Hogging-score, *n.* the distance-line in curling. Cf. Hog-score.

Hoggling, *ppl.* in *phr.* 'hoggling and boggling,' unsteady, moving backwards and forwards.

Hogg-reek, *n.* a blizzard of snow.

Hog-ham, *n.* hung mutton of a sheep that has died of disease or been smothered in the snow.

Hoghle, *v.* to hobble, to limp. Cf. Hochle.

Hoghmanay, *n.* the 31st of December. Cf. Hogmanay.

Hog-house, *n.* a pig-sty, a piggery.

Hog in hairst, *n.* a young sheep smeared at the end of harvest, and ceasing then to be a lamb.

Hog-lamb, *n.* a sheep of about a year old.

Hogling, *n.* a pig.

Hogmanay, -ae, -ee, *n.* the last day of the year; a gift given to children who ask it on New Year's Eve; an entertainment given to visitors on Hogmanay.

Hogmena, -ay, *n.* Hogmanay.

Hogmina, -ay, *n.* Hogmanay.

Hogmonay, Hogmynae, *n.* Hogmanay.

Hogrel, Hoggrel, *n.* a sheep of about a year old.

Hogry, *adj.* awkward and confused in manner or dress. Cf. Huggrie.

Hogry-mogry, *adj.* in a confused state, disorderly, untidy, slovenly. Cf. Huggry-muggry.

Hog-score, *n.* the distance-line in curling.

Hog-shouther, *n.* a game in which the players push each other with the shoulders.—*v.* to jostle or push with the shoulders.

Hoguemennay, *n.* Hogmanay.

Hogyet, *n.* a hogshead. Cf. Hogget.

Hoichle, Hoighle, *v.* to walk with short steps.—*n.* a person who pays no attention to dress. Cf. Hochle.

Hoighlin, *ppl. adj.* doing anything clumsily.

Hoilie, *adv.* slowly.—*v.* to go softly. Cf. Hooly.

Hoise, *v.* to hoist, elevate, raise; to brag, vaunt; to bluster, rant; to talk, gossip.—*n.* a hoist, a lift upward.

Hoispehoy, *n.* a game like 'hide-and-seek,' 'hie-spy.'

Hoist, *v.* to cough.—*n.* a cough. Cf. Hoast.

Hoisting, *n.* the assembling of a host or army. Cf. Hosting.

Hoit, *n.* a foolish, awkward, clumsy person; a hobbling or awkward motion; a shrug, a motion of the shoulders.—*v.* to move awkwardly; to run or walk clumsily.

Hoited, *ppl. adj.* clumsy, awkward; clumsily shaped or made.

Hoitering, *ppl.* moving in a stiff, clumsy manner.

Hoity-toity, *n.* an awkward, tawdry appearance.

Hoke, *v.* to dig.—*n.* the act of digging. Cf. Howk.

Hoker, *v.* to crouch over the fire; to bend over.

Hokery-packery, -pokery, *n.* sharp practice; anything underhand or mysterious, cantrips.

Hoky, *int.* an expletive. Cf. Hoakie.

Holden, *ppl. adj.* held.

Holder, *n.* a needle-cushion.

Holding, *adj.* sure, certain.

Hole, *n.* cover, shelter; a sheep-mark; in *pl.* a game of marbles, the 'kypes.'—*v.* to bore a hole, perforate; to wear into holes; to have holes; to dig, dig out; to hide; to disappear; to take to earth.

Hole-ahin, *n.* a term of reproach for one who falls behind.

Holen, *n.* the holly.

Holie, *n.* a game of marbles, the 'kypes.'

Holie-pie-thingies, *n.* patterns of sewing and knitting; small holes cut out of linen and stitched round.

Holing, *n.* the depth of coal displaced at a blasting.

Holk, *v.* to search; to burrow. Cf. Howk.

Holl, *v.* to excavate, to hollow out; to pierce, penetrate.

Holl, *v.* to stay in a place without occupation; to haunt a place in a lazy, idle fashion; to loaf; to be content with mean work; to work hard and accomplish little; to work sluggishly and dirtily.—*n.* a lazy, idle meeting or gossiping.

Hollan, *n.* a partition wall in a cottage between the door and the fire. Cf. Hallan.

Hollan, Holland, *n.* the holly.

Holland, Hollan, *adj.* Dutch.

Holland-bools, *n.* Dutch marbles, striped and variegated.

Holland-bush, *n.* a holly-bush.

Holland-duck, *n.* the scaup.

Holland-hawk, *n.* the great northern diver. Cf. Allan hawk.

Hollen, *n.* the holly.

Holleu, Holo, *n.* a halloo, loud shout.

Hollie, *adj.* having holes, holed.

Hollin, *n.* a 'hallan.'

Hollin, *n.* the holly.

Hollin, Hollin-aboot, *ppl. adj.* lazy; unskilful, awkward.

Hollion, *n.* in *phr.* 'o'er hip and hollion,' completely, entirely.

Hollis-bollis, Hollos-bollos, *adv.* completely. Cf. Holus-bolus.

Hollow, *n.* a carpenter's tool, plane; in *phr.* 'hollows and rounds,' casements used in making any kind of moulding, whether large or small, in wood.

Hollow, *adj.* moaning, having a dismal sound; speaking in hollow tones.

Hollow meat, *n.* poultry.

Holsie-jolsie, *n.* a confused mass of food; swine's meat.

Holt, *v.* to halt; to stop.

Holt, *n.* a wooded hill; a small haycock; a small quantity of manure before it is spread.

Holus-bolus, *adv.* completely, all at once.

Holy-band, *n.* the kirk-session.

Holy-dabbies, *n.* 'petticoat-tails'; cakes of shortbread, formerly used as communion-bread.

Holy-doupies, *n.* 'holy-dabbies.'

Holy-fair, *n.* a name formerly given to the days set apart in connection with the Lord's Supper in a district.

Holy-how, *n.* a membrane on the head, with which some children are born, the loss of which was regarded as a bad omen.

Home, *n.* a holm.

Home-bringer, *n.* an importer from abroad.

Home-dealing, *n.* close dealing with a man's conscience.

Homester, *n.* a stay-at-home.

Homie-omrie, *n.* a hotch-potch; a miscellany.

Homing, *n.* level and fertile ground, properly on the bank of a stream or river. Cf. Howm.

Hommel, *adj.* hornless. Cf. Hummel.

Hommel-corn, *n.* beardless grain.

Hommelin, *n.* the fish, rough ray.

Hone, *v.* to whine, complain, murmur.

Honest, *adj.* honourable; respectable; chaste. —*adv.* honestly.

Honest-come, *adj.* honestly obtained; well-earned.

Honest hour, *n.* the hour of death.

Honest-like, *adj.* good-looking; of respectable appearance; goodly, substantial; liberal; used of a child: plump, lusty.

Honestly, *adv.* decently, respectably, honourably.

Honest man, *n.* a kindly designation of an inferior.

Honesty, *n.* honour; respectability; what becomes one's station in life, kindness, liberality; a handsome, valuable gift; a thoroughly good article worthy of the giver.

Honey, *n.* a pet; a sweetheart; a term of endearment for a woman or a child.—*adj.* honeyed, sweet as honey. Cf. Hinny.

Honey-bee, *n.* a working bee.

Honey-blab, -blob, *n.* the contents of a bee's honey-bag; a term of endearment; a variety of gooseberry.

Honey-byke, *n.* a hive of honey.

Honey-cherrie, *n.* a sweet variety of cherry.

Honey-doo, *n.* a pet, sweetheart.

Honey-drap, *n.* a mole on the skin.

Honey-flower, *n.* any flower yielding honey.

Honey-month, *n.* the honeymoon.

Honey-mug, *n.* a vessel containing honey.

Honey-oil, *v.* to flatter, 'butter up.'

Honey-pear, *n.* a variety of the pear.

Honey-spot, *n.* a mole on the skin.

Honey-ware, *n.* a species of edible seaweed.

Honner, *v.* to honour.

Honneril, *n.* a foolish, talkative person.

Honnie, *n.* a term of endearment. Cf. Honey.

Hoo, *int.* a cry intended to scare; a call to draw attention.—*v.* to frighten away birds; to drive away; to holloa, shout; used of an owl: to hoot; of the wind: to sigh, moan, howl drearily. Cf. Hou.

Hoo, *adv.* how; why. Cf. How.

Hoo, *n.* a head-dress, cap, nightcap; a child's caul. Cf. How.

Hoo, *n.* a piece of wood used in building the couples of a roof.

Hooch, *int.* an excl. of disgust.

Hooch, *int.* an excl. of joy, &c.; a shout during the dancing of a reel.—*v.* to cry 'hooch!'—*n.* a shout, hollo, the 'hooch'

used in reels; the sound made by forcing the breath through the narrowed lips; a smell, savour.

Hood, *n.* a sheaf of corn placed on the top of a 'stook' to protect it from rain; the hob at the side of a fireplace for pots, &c.; the back of a fireplace, built like a seat; a small enclosure or shelf built at the side of a fireplace; a space of a stone wall built at short intervals, and marked by stones which go from side to side.—*v.* to cover corn 'stooks' by putting on 'hood-sheaves.'

Hooded, *ppl. adj.* of a hen: tufted, having a tuft on the head.

Hooded crow, *n.* the pewit gull or black-headed gull; the carrion-crow.

Hooded mew, *n.* the pewit gull.

Hoodie, *n.* the hooded crow or the carrion-crow; a hired mourner.

Hoodie-craw, *n.* the 'hoodie.'

Hooding, *n.* the leather strap or thong connecting the hand-staff and the 'souple' of a flail.

Hoodling-how, *n.* a kind of cap.

Hood-neuk, *n.* the corner beside the fireplace.

Hoodock, *adj.* foul and greedy, like a 'hoodie' or carrion-crow, miserly.

Hood-sheaf, *n.* a sheaf of corn laid on the top of a 'stook' to protect it from rain.

Hood-stane, *n.* a flagstone set on edge as a back to a fire on a cottage hearth; a stone used in building a 'hudd,' 'hood,' or portion of a wall.

Hooferie, *n.* folly.

Hooger, *n.* a footless stocking. Cf. Hogger.

Hooh, *int.* a cry. Cf. Hoo.

Hoo-hooing, *ppl.* crying out, calling out.

Hooick, *n.* a small stack in a field, built in a wet harvest.

Hooie, *v.* to barter, exchange.—*n.* an exchange, barter; a boys' word in exchanging knives under cover.

Hooing, *n.* loud shouting.

Hook, *n.* the bend of a river, the land enclosed by such a bend; a reaping-hook; a reaper, a shearer. Cf. Heuck.

Hook, *v.* to run off.

Hook, *v.* to dig. Cf. Howk.

Hook-bane, *n.* the hip-bone.

Hook-busser, *n.* one who 'busks' or dresses fly-hooks.

Hooker, *n.* a reaper, one who wields a sickle.

Hooker, *n.* whisky; a 'dram.'

Hookers, *n.* the bended knees, 'hunkers.'

Hookie, *n.* a meaningless excl. or mild expletive. Cf. Hoky.

Hook-penny, *n.* a penny given weekly to reapers in addition to their wages.

Hool, *v.* to remove the outer husk of any vegetable or fruit; to geld.—*n.* a husk, pod, outer skin of fruit; a case; a shell; a cheese rind.

Hool, v. to conceal; to cover, wrap up.—n. an outer covering; the pericardium; the body.

Hool, adj. beneficial; friendly, kind.

Hoolachan, n. a Highland reel.

†Hoolet, n. an owl; an owlet. Cf. Howlet.

Hoolie, adv. softly.

Hoolie-gool-oo-oo, n. the hoot of an owl.

Hooliness, n. slowness, tardiness.

Hooloch, n. a falling or rolling mass; an avalanche of stones, &c.

Hooly, Hoolyie, adv. slowly, cautiously, gently. —v. to go softly or slowly; to pause.—int. 'take time!'

Hooly and fairly, adv. fair and softly, slowly and gently.

Hoom, n. a herd, a flock.

Hoom, v. to give an unpleasant taste to food by confining the steam in the pot when boiling; to spoil provisions by keeping them in a confined place. Cf. Hoam.

Hoomet, n. a large flannel nightcap; a child's under-cap; a man's Kilmarnock bonnet.

Hoometet, ppl. adj. covered with a 'hoomet.'

Hoon, v. with off, to delay, postpone.

Hoon, v. to whine, complain, murmur. Cf. Hone.

Hoop, n. the circular wooden frame surrounding the millstones, and keeping the meal from being lost.—v. to speed, hurry.

Hoop, v. to hope.

Hoord, v. to hoard.

Hoose, n. a house. Cf. House.

Hoosht, int. hush!—v. to order silence. Cf. Husht.

Hoosie, n. a small house.

Hoot, Hoots, int. an excl. of doubt, contempt, irritation, dissatisfaction.—v. to pooh-pooh, discredit, doubt.

Hoot awa, int. tuts! nonsense!

Hoot ay, int. to be sure!

Hoot fie, int. O fie!

Hoot-toot, -toots, int. excl. of strong dissatisfaction or jocular contradiction.

Hoot-toot-toot, int. an excl. of annoyance.

Hoove, v. to stay, tarry.

Hoozle, n. the housel, sacrament of the Lord's Supper.

Hoozle, n. a socket for a handle in tools; the head of a hatchet, &c.; a paper band round a bundle of papers, keeping them together.

Hoozle, v. to wheeze; to breathe with a wheezing sound, as if out of breath.—n. heavy breathing; an inhalation; a big pinch of snuff.

Hoozle, v. to perplex, puzzle, pose; to drub smartly.

Hoozling, ppl. adj. breathing hard.—n. a wheezing.

Hoozling, n. a severe drubbing.

Hop, v. to dance; to caper; to revolve; to drop fast. Cf. Hap.

Hop-clover, n. yellow clover.

Hope, Hop, n. a hollow among the hills; a hill.

Hope, n. a small bay; a haven.

Hoped, ppl. in phr. 'better hoped,' more hopeful.

Hope-fit, n. the lowest part of a 'hope,' or valley among hills.

Hope-head, n. the highest part of a 'hope,' or valley among hills.

Hop-my-fool, n. a game of chance.

Hopple, v. to fasten two legs of an animal to prevent it from straying.—n. the rope or strap so used. Cf. Hobble.

Hoprick, n. a wooden pin driven into the heels of shoes.

Horl, Horal, n. a small iron or wooden ring used as a pulley; a castor; a small wheel.

Horn, n. a drinking-vessel; a draught of liquor; a comb; a spoon made of horn; a snuff-box made from the sharp end of a horn; a horn formerly used as a cupping-glass; a hard excrescence on the foot; a hair-comb; the continuation of the stern of a boat; the nose; the spout of a teapot; part of a large bell; a cloud resembling a boat in shape, a 'Noah's Ark.'—v. to make hard and horny; to bleed by cupping; to cuckold; to draw up a curling-stone by the handle and so put it out of play.

Horn-bouet, -bowet, n. a hand-lantern, in which thin horn was used for glass.

Horn-cutty, n. a short spoon made of horn.

Horn-daft, adj. quite mad, outrageous; very foolish.

Horn-dry, adj. very dry; thirsty; craving for drink.

Horneck, n. the root of the earth-nut.

Horned, ppl. adj. cuckolded.

Hornel, n. the sand-lance, when of large size.

Horn-end, n. the parlour or better end of a house.

Horner, n. a maker of horn-spoons; one who is sent to Coventry; one who was 'put to the horn.'

Horn-golach, n. an earwig.

Horn-haft, n. a haft made of horn.

Horn-hard, adj. very hard.—adv. soundly, profoundly.

Horn-head, adv. with full force, without pause.

Horn-idle, adj. quite idle, thoroughly at leisure.

Hornie, n. the 'horneck.'

Hornie, n. the devil.

Hornie, n. a children's game, played with clasped hands and thumbs extended.

Hornie, *n.* a horned cow; the name of such a cow.

Hornie, *n.* in *phr.* 'fair hornie,' fair-play.

Hornie-goloch, *n.* an earwig.

Hornies, *n.* horned cattle.

Horning, *n.* a supply of drink; a cuckolding; the legal process of 'putting to the horn'; in *phrs.* 'letters of horning,' 'horning and caption,' an order requiring a debtor to pay his debt on pain of being declared a rebel; a letter of amercement.

Horn-mad, *adj.* raving mad; outrageously irritated.

Horn-mark, *n.* a mark branded on the horn of a sheep, ox, &c.

Hornock, *n.* the devil. Cf. Hornie.

Horns, *n.* in the game, 'a' horns to the lift,' where the horn represents the forefinger.

Hornshottle, *adj.* used of the limbs: dislocated; of the teeth: loose; shaken to pieces.

Horn-spune, -speen, *n.* a spoon made of horn.

Horn-tammie, *n.* a laughing-stock, a butt.

Horny, *adj.* having horns; strong, fortified; noisy as a horn; amorous, lecherous; having 'horns' or corns on the feet.

Horny-goloch, *n.* an earwig.

Horny-holes, *n.* a game of four persons, played with a bat like a walking-stick, and frequently a sheep's horn for a 'cat.'

Horny-hoolet, *n.* the long-eared owl.

Horny-luck, *n.* a variety of the game of 'tig.'

Horny-rebels, *n.* a children's game.

Horny-worm, *n.* a short, thick worm with a tough skin, enclosing a sort of chrysalis, which becomes the long-legged fly called by children 'spin-Mary.'

Horrals, *n.* very small wheels, castors. Cf. Horl.

Horrid, *adj.* great, extraordinary.—*adv.* exceedingly, extraordinarily.

Horse, *n.* horses; a mason's large trestle; a mason's hod; a frame or rack for drying wood; a screen or frame for airing linen, a clothes-horse; a wooden implement for drawing off liquors, a faucet.—*v.* to mount; to ride on horseback; to punish or hurt by striking or bumping the buttocks of a person on a stone, &c.

Horse and hattock, *int.* a call to get ready to ride off; the witches' and fairies' call to be off.

Horse-beast, *n.* a horse.

Horse-buckie, *n.* the white whelk.

Horse-cock, *n.* a small kind of snipe.

Horse-corn, *n.* the small corn separated by riddling.

Horse-couper, -cowper, *n.* a horse-dealer.

Horse-coupin', *adj.* horse-dealing.—*n.* the trade of a 'horse-couper.'

Horse-feast, *n.* food without liquid of any kind. Cf. Horse-meal.

Horse-foal, *n.* a colt.

Horse-gang, *n.* a fourth of land that is ploughed by four horses, belonging to as many tenants.

Horse-gear, *n.* harness, saddlery.

Horse-gell, *n.* the horse-leech.

Horse-gowan, *n.* the ox-eye daisy.

Horse-gowk, *n.* the green sandpiper; the snipe.

Horse-grace, *n.* a rhyme describing how a horse should be treated by its driver on a journey.

Horse-hirer, *n.* one who lets out horses for riding, &c.

Horse-hoe, *n.* a hoe, or hoeing implement, drawn by a horse.—*v.* to use a 'horse-hoe.'

Horse-kirn, *n.* a churn driven by a horse.

Horse-knot, *n.* the black knapweed.

Horse-load, *n.* the load which a horse can carry.

Horse-mackerel, *n.* the scad.

Horse-magog, *n.* a boisterous, frolicsome clown.

Horse-malison, *n.* one who is very cruel to horses.

Horseman, *n.* a farm-servant in charge of a pair of horses.

Horseman's word, *n.* the secret password which a farm-servant gets from his fellows in order to become a member of the Horseman's Society, and receive help in the training of a refractory horse.

Horse-meal, *n.* food without any liquid. Cf. Horse-feast.

Horse-muscle, -mussel, *n.* a large mussel; the pearl-mussel.

Horse-nail, *n.* in *phr.* 'to make a horse-nail of a thing,' to do it clumsily and imperfectly.

Horse-setter, *n.* one who lets out horses for riding, &c.

Horse-sheet, *n.* a horse-cloth.

Horse-stang, *n.* the dragon-fly.

Horse-supperin', *n.* the horse's evening meal.

Horse-tailor, *n.* a saddler.

Horse-thristle, *n.* the bur.

Horse-tree, *n.* the swingle-tree, to which the horse is harnessed when drawing a pair of harrows.

Horse-troch, *n.* a drinking-trough for horses, &c.

Horse-well-grass, *n.* the brooklime.

Horsing wadge, *n.* a large wedge used in quarrying.

Hort, *v.* to maim; to hurt.—*n.* a hurt.

Hose, Hosen, *n.* a single stocking; a footless stocking; the sheath of corn; the seed-leaves of grain; a socket for the handle of a tool.

Hose-doup, *n.* the medlar.

Hose-fish, *n.* the cuttle-fish. Cf. O-fish.

Hose-gerse, *n.* meadow soft grass.

Hose-net, *n.* a small net, resembling a stocking, affixed to a pole ; an entanglement, a difficulty.

Hoshen, *n.* a footless stocking ; a wide, loose house slipper ; a term of abuse ; a bad, pithless worker.

Hosie, *n.* the cuttle-fish.

Ho-spy, *n.* the game of 'hie-spy.' Cf. Hiespy.

Host, *v.* to cough ; to hem.—*n.* a cough. Cf. Hoast.

Hosta, *int.* an excl. of surprise or hesitation. Cf. Husta.

Host-bell, *n.* the bell rung at the celebration of mass ; used in one place in Perthshire formerly to call children into school.

Hostilar, *n.* an innkeeper. Cf. Hostler.

Hostillar, Hostellar, *n.* a hostelry.

Hostilogies, *n.* retainers, henchmen.

Hosting, *n.* the raising or gathering of an army or host.

Hostler, Hostlier, *n.* an innkeeper.

Hostler-house, *n.* a hostel ; a house of public entertainment.

Hostler-wife, *n.* a landlady ; an innkeeper's wife.

Hot, Hott, *n.* a small heap of anything carelessly put up ; a pannier used for carrying dung ; a 'hot'-load, a small heap of manure or lime drawn from a cart in a field for spreading. Cf. Hut.

Hot, *adj.* comfortable. Cf. Het.

Hotch, Hotchen, *v.* to jerk, move clumsily, lurch ; to fidget ; to hitch ; to shake with laughter ; to shrug the shoulders ; to move along in a sitting posture ; to sit closer ; to limp ; to swarm ; to cause to jerk ; to heave.—*n.* a jerk, jolt, shove, shrug ; a big, unwieldy person.

Hotchie, *n.* a general name for puddings.

Hotchle, *v.* to walk clumsily ; to hobble ; to limp.—*n.* a jerk, a hitch.

†Hotch-potch, *n.* a vegetable soup with pieces of mutton boiled in it ; a medley, a confused jumble.

Hot-load, *n.* a heap of manure or lime in a field for spreading.

Hots, *n.* a term used in the game of 'pearie' or peg-top. Cf. Hoatie.

Hott, *v.* to move by sudden jerks ; to shake with laughter. Cf. Hotch.

Hotter, *v.* to move unsteadily or awkwardly ; to hesitate ; to shake with laughter ; to totter, hobble ; to shudder, shiver ; to shake, jolt, vibrate ; to boil slowly, simmer ; to make a bubbling noise in boiling ; to crowd together ; to move like a toad ; to rattle, clatter, make a loud noise ; to 'blatter.'— *n.* a swarm, a crowd of small animals in motion, the motion made by such a crowd ; the agitation of boiling water ; a jolting, shaking-up ; a shaking, heaving mass. Cf. Hatter.

Hotter-bonnet, *n.* a person overrun with vermin, lice, &c.

Hottie, *n.* a name given to one who has something pinned to his back of which he is unconscious.

Hottish, *adj.* rather hot.

Hottle, Hottel, *n.* an hotel.

Hottle, *n.* the bubbling sound of boiling.

Hottle, *n.* anything tottering or not firmly based.

Hot-trod, -tred, *n.* the pursuit of Border 'rievers' with bloodhounds and bugle-horn.

Hou, *v.* used of an owl : to hoot ; of the wind : to howl, moan ; to shout.—*int.* a cry to scare birds ; a cry to call attention. Cf. Hoo.

Hou, *n.* a piece of wood used in the couples of a roof ; a 'roof-tree.' Cf. Hoo.

Hou, *adv.* how ; why. Cf. Hoo.

Hou, *n.* a nightcap. Cf. How.

Houan, *ppl. adj.* howling.

Houch, *v.* to hoot as an owl.—*n.* the moaning of the wind. Cf. Hooch.

Houchty-pouchty, *adj.* 'high and mighty.'

Houck, *n.* a haunt ; a continued stay in one place in idleness.—*v.* to haunt, frequent ; to loaf, lounge.

Houd, *n.* a swing ; a wriggling ; a swaying. —*v.* to swing ; to wriggle ; to sway, rock ; to float heavily. Cf. Howd.

Houdee, *n.* a flatterer, a fawning person. Cf. Howdoye.

Houdin-tow, *n.* a swing-rope.

Houdle, *n.* the simultaneous movement of a large number of insects, as ants.—*v.* to move so. Cf. Howdle.

Houdy, *n.* a midwife. Cf. Howdie.

Houff, *n.* a haunt.—*v.* to haunt. Cf. Howff.

Houffie, *adj.* used of a place : snug, comfortable.

Houg, *n.* a grip, grasp, hug.

Hough, *v.* to cry 'hooch !' Cf. Hooch.

Hough, *n.* a man's leg or thigh.—*v.* to throw a stone under the uplifted thigh. Cf. Hoch.

Hough, *adj.* giving a hollow sound ; empty, hollow ; low, mean ; in poor health ; in low spirits. Cf. Howe.

Houghams, *n.* bent pieces of wood, slung on each side of a horse, to support dung-panniers.

Houghle, *v.* to limp ; to hobble. Cf. Hochle.

Houghlin, *n.* lewd tumbling, sexual intercourse.

Houghmagandie, *n.* fornication. Cf. Hoch magandie.

Hought, *ppl. adj.* undone, overthrown.

Hough up, *adv.* as high as the 'hough.'

Houh, *adj.* hollow. Cf. Howe.

Houin, *n.* the dreary whistling of the wind. Cf. Hou.

Houk, *v.* to heap.

Houk, *v.* to dig. Cf. Howk.

Houlat, *v.* to reduce to a henpecked state ; to go about downcast and peevish ; to look miserable.

†Houlat, Houlet, Houlit, *n.* an owl. Cf. Howlet.

Houlat-like, *adj.* having a meagre, feeble appearance ; puny.

Hound, *n.* a large, ill-favoured dog ; a low, mean fellow ; a greedy, avaricious, grasping person.—*v.* to hunt with dogs ; with *out*, to instigate, incite to mischief.

Hounder-out, *n.* an inciter to mischief ; an instigator. Cf. Out-hounder.

Hound-hunger, *n.* the ravenous appetite of a dog.

Hound-thirsty, *adj.* thirsty as a hound.

Houp, *n.* hope.

Houp, *n.* hops.

Houp, *n.* a mouthful of any drink ; a mouthful of food ; a taste of any liquid.—*v.* to drink by mouthfuls.

Houpin, *n.* the drinking by mouthfuls.

Hour, *n.* in *pl.* o'clock, time of day.

Housal, *adj.* domestic, household.

House, *n.* the workhouse, poorhouse ; a portion of a house occupied by one tenant ; in curling : the circle round the tee within which stones must lie to count.—*v.* to shelter ; used of hay or corn : to get under cover in rick or in barn.

House an' ha', *phr.* house and hall, completely, a clean sweep.

House-ba', *n.* a girls' game of ball.

House-carle, *n.* a household servant.

House-devil, *n.* 'a devil at home, a saint abroad.'

House-dirt, *n.* the dust of a house.

House-end, *n.* the gable of a house.

House-fast, *adj.* confined to the house by illness, duty, &c.

House-gear, *n.* household goods.

House-haddin', *n.* housekeeping.

House-head, -heid, *n.* the head of the house ; the ridge of the house-roof.

House-heat, -heating, *n.* a house-warming on entering a new house.

House-hicht, *n.* a person of small stature.— *adj.* in an excited or angry state.

Householdry, *n.* charge of a household ; household utensils.

Housel, *adj.* belonging to the house, household.

Housel, *n.* the socket of the handle of a dungfork.

House-maill, *n.* house-rent.

Housen, *n.* houses.

House-riggin', *n.* the ridge at the top of a house.

House-side, *n.* a big, clumsy person.

House-things, *n.* articles of furniture ; household goods.

Housewifeskep, *n.* housekeeping.

Housie, *n.* a small house.

Houster, *v.* to gather together confusedly.—*n.* one whose clothes are ill put on. Cf. Haister.

Houstrie, *n.* soft, bad, nasty food ; trash, trumpery.

Houstring, *ppl. adj.* bustling but confused.

Hoat, *int.* tuts ! Cf. Hoot.

Hout fy, *int.* for shame !

Houther, *v.* to push ; to blow fitfully.—*n.* a push ; a rocking motion ; the act of fornication ; a violent tossing ; confusion, havoc ; a blast of wind.

Houthering, *n.* rough, clumsy romping.

Houtie croutie, *n.* the haunches, hams.

Houttie, *adj.* testy, irritable.

Houxie, *int.* a call to a cow.

Houzle, *v.* to wheeze.—*n.* heavy breathing. Cf. Hoozle.

Hove, *v.* to rise up, come into view ; to heave ; to swell ; to puff up ; used of cattle : to become distended by overeating fresh clover, &c. ; to exalt, puff up with conceit.

Hove, Hove lady, *int.* a call to a cow to come and be milked.

Hoved, *ppl. adj.* used of light, loose soil : puffed up.

Hoven, Hoving, *n.* used of cattle : flatulence, distention from overeating ; of cheese : swelling or undue rising.

Hover, *v.* to stay, pause ; to take time, wait. —*n.* suspense, hesitation, uncertainty ; of the weather : a state of uncertainty.

How, *n.* a coif, head-dress ; nightcap ; a hood ; a child's caul.

How, *n.* a piece of wood, wh'n joins the couple-wings together at the top, on which rests the roof-tree of a thatched house. Cf. Hoo.

How, *v.* to reduce ; to drain ; to thin.—*n.* reduction, diminution. Cf. Howe.

How, Howe, *int.* an excl. to draw attention ; one of joy or grief.—*v.* to cry 'how !' with grief. Cf. Hoo.

Howanabee, Howanawbee, *adv.* however.

Howanever, *adv.* however.

How-backit, *adj.* sunk in the back. Cf. Howe-backit.

Howch, *adj.* hollow. Cf. Howe.

Howd, *v.* to sway, rock ; to wriggle ; to bump up and down, move by jerks.—*n.* a motion from side to side ; swaying, jerking ; wriggling ; a sudden gust of wind. Cf. Houd.

Howd, *v.* to hide.

Howd, *v.* to act as a midwife; to deliver a woman in labour.

Howd, *n.* a great quantity.

Howder, *v.* to heap together confusedly; to crowd, swarm, huddle; with *on*, to put on one's clothes hurriedly and carelessly.

Howder, *v.* to push.—*n.* a pushing; a strong blast of wind. Cf. Houther.

Howder, *v.* to hide.

†**Howdie**, *n.* a young hen; a young unmarried woman. Cf. How-towdie.

Howdie, *n.* a midwife.

Howdie-fee, *n.* a midwife's fee.

Howdiefication, *n.* a confinement, accouchement.

Howdieing, Houdying, *n.* a confinement, childbed.

Howdieing-fee, *n.* a midwife's fee.

Howdle, *v.* to move up and down; to sway; to rock to sleep; to crowd together, swarm, move hither and thither; to limp; to walk in a heaving, clumsy way; with *about*, to carry clumsily.—*n.* a swarm, a wriggling mass; the motion of such a mass of small creatures; a crowd in motion.

Howdler, *n.* one who walks in a limping, heaving manner.

Howdlins, *adv.* secretly, clandestinely. Cf. Hiddlins.

Howdoye, *n.* a sycophant. Cf. Houdee.

†**Howdy-towdy**, *n.* a young hen. Cf. How-towdie.

Howe, *adj.* hollow, deep, concave; empty; hungry, famished; used of sounds: hollow, deep, low, guttural; poor, humble, mean; in low spirits; in bad health.—*n.* a hollow; a hollow space; a valley, glen; a flat tract of land; the track of a curling-stone towards the tee; the depth or middle of a period of time; reduction, diminution.—*v.* to reduce; to thin; to drain, diminish in quantity or number.

Howe, *n.* a hoe.—*v.* to hoe.

Howe-backit, *adj.* hollow-backed, sunk in the back.

Howe-doup, *n.* the medlar. Cf. Hose-doup.

Howe-dumb-dead, *n.* used of night: the middle, when silence reigns.

Howe-hole, *n.* a hollow; a valley; a depression; a hole.

Howe-hoose, *n.* an area-dwelling; a house below the street-level.

Howe-howm, *n.* a vale, a low-lying plain.

Howen, *ppl. adj.* hewn.

Howen, *ppl. adj.* hoed.

Howe o' the year, *n.* the winter solstice.

Hower, *n.* a hoer.

Howe-speaking, *n.* speaking in a low, deep voice; speaking like a ventriloquist.

Howe-wecht, *n.* a circular implement of sheepskin stretched on a broad hoop, for lifting grain, chaff, &c. in barns.

Howf, *n.* a severe blow on the ear, given with a circular motion of the arm.

Howf, *n.* liking, desire for.

Howff, Howf, *n.* a place of resort or concourse; haunt; a much-frequented tavern; an abode, residence; a stay at a place; a shelter; a cemetery, burial-place, mausoleum.—*v.* to haunt, frequent; to lodge, abide, reside, take shelter; to lodge, house, cause to live, shelter; with *up*, to bury.

Howffie, *adj.* comfortable, cosy.

Howffin, Howfin, *n.* a clumsy, foolish person.

How-hum, *int.* alas!

Howick, *n.* a small rick in a field in a wet harvest. Cf. Hooick.

Howie, *n.* a small plain.

Howk, *n.* an internal disease of common occurrence among cattle, of the nature of acute indigestion.

Howk, *v.* to dig out; to excavate; to burrow; to grub; to pull out, draw out, 'rype'; to rummage, to search out, hunt out; to sound or 'pump' a person.—*n.* the act of digging, excavation.

Howk-back, *n.* a sunk back.

Howk-backit, *adj.* having a sunk back.

Howk-chowk, *v.* to make a noise as if poking in deep mud.

Howker, *n.* a digger.

Howking, *n.* an excavation; the act of sounding or 'pumping' any one.

Howl, *n.* a hollow, a depression.

†**Howlet**, *n.* an owl; an owlet; a term of reproach.

Howlet-blind, *adj.* blind as an owl.

Howlet-een, *n.* eyes like an owl's, large and staring.

Howlet-faced, *adj.* having a face like an owl's.

Howlet-haunted, *adj.* frequented by owls.

Howlety, *adj.* like an owl.

Howlety-hoo, *n.* the cry of an owl.

Howm, *n.* low-lying, level ground near a stream; a field; a walled field; an islet; a 'holm.' Cf. Hoam.

Howmet, *n.* a little cap. Cf. Hoomet.

Hownabe, *adv.* however. Cf. Howanabee.

Hownicht, *n.* midnight.

Howp, *n.* hope.—*v.* to hope.

Howp, *n.* a mouthful; a taste of any liquid. Cf. Houp.

How-sheep, *int.* a shepherd's call to his dog to pursue sheep.

Howsoever, *adv.* indeed, in fact.

Howsomever, *adv.* however; nevertheless; in any case.

How soon, *adv.* as soon as.

Howster, *v.* to gather together confusedly.—*n.* one whose clothes are badly put on. Cf. Houster.

Howstrie, *n.* soft, bad food; a mixture of different sorts of meat. Cf. Houstrie.

Howther, *v.* to push.—*n.* a push; a 'touzling.' Cf. Houther.

Howthering, *n.* rough romping, 'touzling.'

Howthir, *v.* to hobble in walking; to work hastily and untidily.—*n.* an awkward, hasty walker; a sloven, slattern; unseemly haste. Cf. Huther.

Howtie, *adj.* irritable, ready to sulk. Cf. Houttie.

Howtilie, *adv.* in an angry and sulky manner.

Howtiness, *n.* anger and sulkiness.

†**How-towdy,** *n.* a hen that has never laid; a young unmarried woman.

Howts, *int.* tuts! Cf. Hoot.

Hoxter-poxter, *adv.* in great confusion.

Hoy, *int.* an excl. to draw attention.—*n.* a shout, cry.—*v.* to call to, hail, summon; to incite, provoke; to set on dogs.

Hoyden, *adj.* inelegant, homely, commonplace.

Hoyse, *v.* to hoist.—*n.* a lift by a rope, or by an upward thrust. Cf. Hoise.

Hoys net, *n.* a 'hose-net.' Cf. Hose-net.

Hoyster, *v.* to hoist.

Hoyte, *v.* to hoist, raise on the shoulders.

Hoyte, *v.* to walk or run clumsily; to amble. —*n.* a foolish, clumsy person; a hobbling or awkward motion; a shrug. Cf. Hoit.

Hu, *int.* an excl. of anger, rage, &c.

Huam, *n.* the moan of an owl in the warm days of summer.

Hubbie, *n.* a dull, stupid, slovenly fellow.

Hubble, *n.* an uproar, tumult; a stir, bustle.

Hubble, *v.* to shake, dandle, quiver; to limp. —*n.* a shake. Cf. Hobble.

Hubblebub, *n.* the riff-raff, the rabble.

Hubble-show, -shew, -shoo, *n.* a hubbub; tumult. Cf. Hobbleshow.

Huch, *v.* to warm the hands by breathing on them.

Huck, *v.* to haggle, play the huckster.

Huckie, *n.* the pit in which ashes are held under the fire.

Huckie-buckie, *n.* a game in which children slide down a hill sitting on their 'hunkers.'

Hud, *v.* to hide. Cf. Hod.

Hud, *v.* to hold. Cf. Had.

Hud, *n.* a mason's hod.

Hud, Hudd, *n.* the back of a fireplace in the houses of the peasantry, built of stone and clay, not unlike a seat; a small enclosure or shelf at the side of the fire, formed of two stones set erect, with one laid across the top as a cover; the flat plate which covers the side of a grate; the seat opposite

the fire on a blacksmith's hearth; a portion of a wall built with single stones going through from side to side. Cf. Hood.

Hudden, Huddem, *n.* homespun.—*adj.* homely. Cf. Hodden.

Hudden, *ppl. adj.* held.

Hudder, *v.* to heap together in disorder; to crowd, swarm; to huddle; to work confusedly. Cf. Howder.

Hudderin, *n.* meat condemned as unwholesome.

Hudderon, Hudderen, *n.* a dirty, ragged person; a big, fat, flabby woman.—*adj.* dirty and ragged; ugly, hideous. Cf. Huddroun.

Hudderone, *n.* a young heifer.

Huddery, *adj.* rough, shaggy; dishevelled; tawdry; slovenly.

Huddin, *n.* homespun.

Huddin, *n.* a child's cap or hood.

Huddle, *v.* to gather together greedily; to crowd together in a little room or space; to lie down in the grave.

Huddle-muddle, *adv.* secretly.

Huddroun, *adj.* hideous, ugly; flabby and slovenly in person; empty, ill-filled.—*n.* a dirty, ragged person; a big, fat, flabby woman.

Huddry, *adj.* rough, shaggy; slovenly; tawdry. Cf. Huddery.

Hudds, *n.* hardened clay, used as a back to a grate.

Huddy, Huddy-craw, *n.* a hooded or carrion crow. Cf. Hoodie.

Huddy-droch, *n.* a squat, waddling person.

Hude, *n.* the back of a fireplace in a peasant's cottage. Cf. Hud.

Huderon, *n.* a dirty, ragged person. Cf. Hudderon.

Hudge, *v.* to amass.—*n.* a great quantity.

Hudge, *v.* to speak in a suppressed manner; to spread evil reports. — *n.* suppressed talking.

Hudge-mudge, *n.* secrecy, 'hugger-mugger'; a suppressed talking; a talk aside in a low voice. —*adv.* secretly, underhand. —*v.* to whisper, talk in a suppressed voice.

Hudgie-drudgie, *n.* a drudge; an incessant talker.—*v.* to toil, drudge.—*adj.* toiling, slaving.

†**Hudibrass,** *v.* to hold up to ridicule.

Hud-nook, *n.* the corner beside the fireplace.

Hudron, Hudroun, *n.* veal fed on pasture and not on milk. Cf. Hudderin.

Hudroun veal, *n.* veal of the worst quality.

Hud-stane, *n.* a flag-stone set on edge as a back to a fire on a cottage hearth; a stone used in building a 'hud.' Cf. Hud.

Hue, *n.* look, appearance; a slight quantity, a 'soupçon.'—*v.* to colour.

Huerunt, *n.* the heron.

Hueta, *int.* an excl. of surprise and hesitancy; 'see here.'

Huferie, *n.* folly. Cf. Hooferie.

Huff, *v.* used of a bruise : to swell; in baking : to rise; to become angry, take offence; to offend; to scorn; to bully; to get rid of by bullying; to get on smartly with work.—*n.* a fit of temper, a 'tiff'; offence; haste, hurry.

Huff, *v.* to humbug; to disappoint; to illude.—*n.* a humbug; a disappointment.

Huff, *int.* an excl. of surprise or suddenness.

Huff, *v.* in draughts : to remove a piece from the board, which an opponent should have played to take another piece.

Huffle-buffs, *n.* old clothes.

Hufflit, *n.* a blow with the hand on the side of the head.

Huffy, *adj.* proud; choleric.

Hufud, *n.* a stroke on the head. Cf. Hufflit.

Hug, *v.* to cling close to.

Hugeous, *adj.* huge, large.

Hugert, *ppl. adj.* wearing footless stockings.

Hugger, *n.* a coarse, footless stocking. Cf. Hogger.

Hugger, *v.* to shudder, shiver; to crouch with cold or disease; to crowd together from cold.—*n.* a state of shivering or crouching from cold or disease.

Huggerfu', *n.* a stockingful.

Huggerie, *adj.* awkward and confused in dress or manner. Cf. Hogry.

Huggorin, *ppl. adj.* bent down from cold or disease.

Hugger-mugger, *n.* secrecy.—*adv.* secretly.—*v.* to act or speak secretly; to conceal.

Huggert, *ppl. adj.* wearing footless stockings; used of stockings : footless.

Huggert, *ppl. adj.* bent with cold or disease; shrunken.

Hugget, *n.* a hogshead; a large cask. Cf. Hogget.

Huggrie, *adj.* awkward in manner. Cf. Huggerie.

Huggry-muggry, *adj.* secret; slovenly, untidy, disorderly.—*n.* clandestine conduct.—*adv.* secretly.

Hughyal, *v.* to hobble. Cf. Hochle.

Hugrie, *adj.* awkward in dress or manner. Cf. Huggerie.

Hugy, *adj.* huge.

Hui, *int.* begone! Cf. Hoy.

Huick, Huickie, *n.* a small rick of corn. Cf. Hooick.

Huie, *v.* to frighten away birds.—*int.* a cry to scare birds. Cf. Hoo.

Hui-hoi, *int.* a cry used by fishermen when heaving all together in launching their boats.

Huik, *n.* a hook.

Hull, *adj.* cautious. Cf. Hooly.

Huild, *v. pret.* did hold.

Huird, *n.* a hoard.

Huisht, *int.* hush!

Huisk, *n.* an untidy, dirty, unwieldy woman.

Huist, *n.* a heap; an overgrown, clumsy person.

Huister, *n.* an uncomplimentary term for a woman, implying lasciviousness. Cf. Huster.

Huister, *v.* to gather together confusedly. Cf. Houster.

Huit, *n.* a heap.

Huive, *v. pret.* did heave; did swell. Cf. Hove.

Huke, *v.* to hook.—*n.* a hook; a reaping hook. Cf. Heuck.

Huke-bane, *n.* the haunch-bone.

Hulbie, *n.* any object that is large and unwieldy.

Huldie, *n.* a nightcap.

Hule, *n.* a mischievous fellow; a rake. Cf. Heul.

Hule, *n.* a pod; a husk; a child's caul; a covering. Cf. Hool.

Hulgy, *adj.* having a hump.

Hulgy-back, *n.* a hunchbacked person.

Hulgy-backed, *adj.* hunchbacked.

Halie, *adj.* cautious, tardy. Cf. Hooly.

Huliness, *n.* tardiness. Cf. Hooly.

Hulk, *v.* to skulk lazily about; to hang about a place.—*n.* a lazy, clumsy person; an idle, good-for-nothing lout.

Hulking, *ppl. adj.* skulking, idle.

Hull, *n.* a hill; the elevated site of a peat-stack.

Hullachan, *n.* a Highland reel. Cf. Hool-achan.

Hull-cock, *n.* the fish smooth-hound.

Huller, *n.* a stout, untidy person. Cf. Hiller.

Hullerie, *adj.* erect, bristling; used of a hen : with feathers standing up; of the head confused after hard drinking; slovenly; of walls : ill-built, crumbling, friable.

Hullerie, *adj.* used of the weather : raw, damp, and cold.

Hullie-bullie, -bulloo, *n.* a noisy tumult, hurly-burly. Cf. Whillie-billow.

Hullion, *n.* wealth; goods; property; a burden, heap.

Hullion, *n.* a clumsy fellow; a sloven. Cf. Hallion.

Hullockit, *ppl. adj.* giddy, romping, crazy.—*n.* a romp. Cf. Hallockit.

Hully, *adj.* having a husk or shell or rind; husky, hoarse.

Hully-belloo, *n.* a noisy tumult.

Hulster, *n.* a holster.

Hulster, *v.* to carry a burden with difficulty and awkwardly; to walk with heavy, ungraceful step.—*n.* the pushing up of a burden ; a big, awkward person.

Hulter-corn, *n.* hulled grain ; husked corn.

Huly, *adj.* slow ; patient.—*int.* slowly! Cf. Hooly.

Hum, *n.* the milt of a cod-fish.

Hum, *v.* to stammer ; to speak hesitatingly ; to whip a top ; to strike.—*n.* hesitation, indecision ; an evasive answer ; an expression of scorn.

Hum, *v.* to cheat, impose upon, humbug.—*n.* a cheat, trick, sham.

Hum, *v.* to feed, as birds do their young by billing ; to transfer food from one's mouth to an infant's ; to chew food for infants.—*n.* a morsel of chewed food given to infants ; in *pl.* mouthfuls of chewed food.

Hum, *adj.* out of humour ; sullen.

Humanity, *n.* the classics, especially Latin ; a classical education.—*phr.* 'the Humanities,' the study of the classics.

Humble, *adj.* hornless. Cf. Hummel.

Humble-bummel, *n.* a deep ravine with a stream flowing through it over numerous cataracts.

Humch, *v.* to be in a sulky mood.—*n.* a fit of sulking.

Humdrum, *n.* a dull, stupid person, without interest in anything ; in *pl.* dejection.—*v.* to talk in a humdrum, prosy way.

Humdrumming, *n.* hesitation, insincerity.

Humdudgeon, -durgon, *n.* needless complaint, fuss, or noise ; a big, stupid person of an evil disposition.

Humet, *n.* a flannel nightcap. Cf. Hoomet.

Humil, *adj.* hornless. Cf. Hummel.

Humist, *adj.* hindmost.

Humlag, *n.* a hornless cow.

Humle, *adj.* hornless.

Humlie, *n.* a hornless ox, cow, &c.

Humlock, Humloch, *n.* hemlock, the cowparsley ; any hollow-stemmed, umbelliferous plant. Cf. Hemlock.

Humlock, *n.* a hornless cow ; a person with a shaved head, or whose hair has been cut off.

Humlock-skite, *n.* a squirt made from the hollow stalk of hemlock.

Humma, *n.* a grip with the thumb and four fingers placed together. Cf. Hummie.

Hummel, Hummle, *v.* to humble ; to cast down, overthrow.—*adj.* downcast ; lowlying.

Hummel, Hummil, Hummle, *adj.* hornless ; wanting, lacking ; used of handwriting : plain, without flourishes.—*v.* to remove the beards of barley after threshing ; to chew carelessly.

Hummelcorn, *n.* beardless grain ; the lighter kind of grain.—*adj.* poor, mean, shabby.

Hummel-doddy, *adj.* hornless.—*n.* a woman's

flat and mean head-dress ; a hornless ox, polled Angus, Aberdeen, or Galloway. Cf. Doddy.

Hummel-drummel, *adj.* morose and taciturn.

Hummel-mittens, *n.* woollen gloves with only the thumb separated.

Hummer, *v.* to murmur, grumble.

Hummer, *n.* a small top.

Hummie, *n.* a hump.

Hummie, *n.* a grasp taken with the thumb and four fingers pressed together ; the space thus included, excluding the palm ; a pinch of anything, as much as can be taken up between the thumb and the four fingers.—*v.* to lift up the thumb and fingers.

Hummie, *n.* the game of 'shinty' or hockey ; the hooked stick used in the game.—*int.* a cry used in the game to a player to keep on his own side.

Hummie-fou, *n.* a pinch of anything.—*v.* to lift up the 'hummies.'

Hummilt, *ppl. adj.* having no horns.

Humming, *ppl. adj.* used of ale or liquor : strong, heady, foaming.

Humming-bumming, *n.* a humming sound.

Hummlie, *n.* a hornless ox, cow, &c.

Hummock, *n.* a grasp with the thumb and fingers together. Cf. Hummie.

Humorous, *adj.* whimsical, inconstant, capricious, pettish.

Humour, *n.* pus or matter from a sore ; bad temper ; advice, opinion.

Humourousness, *n.* caprice, pettishness, bad temper.

Humoursome, *adj.* capricious, fanciful ; droll, witty, humorous.

Hump, *n.* an arched back ; a hillock, knob ; ill-humour, the 'sulks.'—*v.* to be dissatisfied, sulk ; to carry on the back or shoulders.

Hump-glutteral, *n.* the flesh of a sheep that has died a natural death, and not of disease.

Humph, *n.* coal when it approaches the surface of the ground and becomes useless.

Humph, *n.* a 'hum' in hesitating speech.

Humph, *n.* a bad smell or taste as indicating some degree of putridity.—*v.* to sniff as if detecting a bad smell ; to smell or taste of putridity ; to begin to putrefy.

Humph, *n.* a hump.—*v.* to carry on one's back.

Humph-backit, *adj.* hunchbacked.

Humphed, *ppl. adj.* having a tainted smell.

Humpher, *n.* a hurried movement in rising, a bolt upright.

Humphy, *adj.* tainted, having a bad taste or smell.

Humphy, *n.* a hunchback.—*adj.* hunchbacked.

Humphy-back, *n.* a hunched back.

Humple, *n.* a hillock.—*v.* to exhibit a hump ; to walk with a stoop ; to hump the shoulders ; to assume a semicircular form.

Humple, *v.* to walk lame, limp; to stumble; to walk feebly and awkwardly. Cf. Hammle.

Humple, *v.* to ride at the crupper behind another.

Humpling, *ppl. adj.* shambling.

Humpling, *ppl. adj.* exhibiting a hump.

Humplock, *n.* a small heap; a knoll; a lump; a protuberance.

Hump-shouldered, -shouthered, *adj.* hunchbacked, high-shouldered.

Humpy-back, *n.* a hunched back.

Humpy-backit, *adj.* hunchbacked.

Hums, *n.* expressions of love, endearing names.

Humsh, *v.* to eat noisily and greedily. Cf. Hamsh.

Humstrum, *n.* a slight peevish fit, the pet.

Humstrum, *n.* inferior music.

Hunch, *v.* to hoist up, shove; to push; to shrug the shoulders up.—*n.* an awkward bending movement of the body.

Hund, *n.* a hound; an avaricious person.—*v.* to incite. Cf. Hound.

Hunder, *n.* a hundred; a measure of garden ground, 15 ft. by 18 ft. in extent.—*phr.* 'a lang hunder,' six score.

Hune, *v.* to loiter; to stop.—*n.* delay; a loiterer; a lazy, silly person.

Hune, *v.* to stammer from shyness, or from conscious guilt.—*n.* one who stammers.

Hune, *v.* to whine, murmur, fret. Cf. Hone.

Hung, *ppl. adj.* used of milk: coagulated by the heat of the weather, placed in a linen bag, and hung up until the whey, &c., has dripped from it, and only a thick, creamy substance is left.

Hunger, *v.* to starve, withhold necessary food; used of land: to manure insufficiently.—*n.* a period of privation.

Hunger-rot, *n.* rot in sheep arising from a deficiency of every kind of food.

Hungersome, *adj.* hungry; causing hunger; with rather keen an appetite.

Hungrisum, *adj.* voracious, eager.

Hungrisumlike, *adv.* somewhat voraciously.

Hungrisumness, *n.* a state of hunger.

Hungry-ground, *n.* ground credited to be so much enchanted that a person passing over it would faint if he did not use something to support nature.

Hungry-haunch, *adj.* starved, poorly fed.

Hungry-hillock, *n.* 'hungry-ground.'

Hungry hour, *n.* the dinner-hour from noon to one o'clock.

Hungry welcome, *n.* a cold reception.

Hungry-worm, *n.* a worm supposed to cause hunger, especially in children.

Hunker, *v.* to squat on the haunches with the hams near the heels; to make one squat down so; to watch in a crouching position;

to stoop, yield, submit.—*n.* in *pl.* the hams resting on the legs near the heels.

Hunkerings, *n.* genuflections, prostrations.

Hunker-slide, *v.* to slide sitting on one's 'hunkers'; to act in a mean, unmanly, underhand way.

Hunkerticur, *v.* to slide sitting on one's 'hunkers.'

Hunker-tottie, *adv.* in a 'hunkering' position.

Hunkert-wise, *adv.* in a squatting position.

Hunkertys, *adv.* 'hunkert-wise.'

Hunks, *n.* a lazy slut; a drab.

Hunner, *n.* a hundred.

Hunt, *v.* to drive by force; to search for; to frequent, haunt.—*n.* in *phr.* 'neither hunt nor hare,' absolutely nothing.

Hunter, *n.* used of a cat: a good mouser, one which preys on birds, rats, young rabbits, &c.

Hunter's beer, *n.* a weaver's treat.

Huntiegouke, *n.* a fool's errand. Cf. Hunt-the-gowk.

Hunting-hawk, *n.* the peregrine falcon.

Huntsman's moon, *n.* the October moon.

Hunt-the-glaiks, *v.* to go on a fool's errand.

Hunt-the-gowk, *v.* to go on a fool's errand. —*n.* a fool's errand, an April errand; an April fool, a person sent on a fool's errand. —*adj.* of the character of a fool's errand.

Hunt-the-hare, *n.* the game of 'hare and hounds.'

Hunt-the-slipper, *n.* a young people's sport.

Hunt-the-staigie, *n.* a boys' game in which one player tries to catch the others with his hands clasped; if he catch one, the two join hands and try to catch another, and so on.

Hunt-the-unity-staigie, *n.* the game of 'hunt-the-staigie.'

Hunty, *n.* the game of 'hare and hounds.'

Huoven, *ppl. adj.* heaved; swelled, 'hoven.'

Hup, *int.* a call to a horse to go to the right; a call to a horse, cow, &c. to go on.—*v.* to cry 'hup' to a horse, &c.; to go forward.

Hupe, *n.* the wooden circular frame surrounding millstones. Cf. Hoop.

Hur, *v.* to snarl, growl. Cf. Hurr.

Hurb, *n.* a term of endearment applied to a mischievous child; a term of contempt for a short, thick-set person; an awkward fellow; a puny, dwarfish person.

Hurble, *n.* a lean, meagre object.

†**Hurcheon, Hurchent, Hurchin,** *n.* a hedgehog. Cf. Urchin.

Hurd, *n.* a hoard.—*v.* to hoard. Cf. Huird.

Hurdle, *v.* to crouch, squat like a hare; to contract the body like a hedgehog, cat, &c.; to curtsy, bow.

Hurdon, *n.* a woman with large hips.

Hurdy, *n.* in *pl.* the buttocks; the hips and adjoining parts.

Hurdy-bane, *n.* the thigh-bone.

Hurdy-caikle, *n.* pain in the loins of reapers from stooping.

Hurdy-gurdy, *n.* a contemptuous name for a harp.

Hure, *n.* a whore.

Huredom, *n.* whoredom.

Hure-quean, -quine, *n.* a whore.

Huril, *n.* the heron; a mischievous dwarf. Cf. Herle.

Hurk, *v.* to stay idly in a place; to do little; with *about*, to go about in a lazy, underhand fashion.

Hurkel, *v.* to crouch. Cf. Hurkle.

Hurker, *n.* a semicircular piece of iron put on an axle-tree, inside of the wheel, to prevent friction on the cart-body.

Hurkie, *n.* the fish, bib.

Hurkle, *n.* a 'horse-hoe' for cleaning turnips.

Hurkle, *adj.* lazy, careless, slovenly; troublesome, unmanageable; unpleasant. Cf. Hurk.

Hurkle, *v.* to crouch, cower, squat down; to draw one's self together; to submit; to shrug the shoulders; to walk with difficulty owing to rickety legs; to advance in a crouching position, or on hands and feet.

Hurkle-backit, *adj.* hunchbacked; having stooping shoulders.

Hurkle-bane, *n.* the hip-bone.

Hurkled, *ppl. adj.* wrinkled.

Hurkle-durkle, *n.* laziness, sluggishness.—*v.* to lie long in bed; to lounge.

Hurklin, *ppl. adj.* misshapen, drawn together.

Hurl, *n.* a kind of Dutch tobacco.

Hurl, *n.* a drive; a lift on the road; a train-journey; an airing in a carriage, &c.; a confused mass of material thrown or falling down with violence; the noise caused by the violent fall of material, or of carts on a hard road; a scolding.—*v.* to wheel, trundle; to whirl; to rush; to roll; to drive in a conveyance.

Hurl, *v.* to toy; to dally amorously.

Hurl-barrow, *n.* a wheel-barrow; a hand-cart.

Hurl-come-gush, *n.* a great and sudden rush or onset.

Hurler, *n.* one who wheels a barrow; a peat-wheeler.

Hurley, *n.* a wheel; a two-wheeled barrow used by hawkers, porters, &c.; a hand-cart for light goods; a truckle-bed.

Hurley, *adj.* last. Cf. Hurly.

Hurley-barrow, *n.* a two-wheeled barrow or hand-cart.

Hurley-bed, *n.* a truckle-bed.

Hurley-cart, *n.* a hand-cart; a toy-cart.

Hurley-hacket, *n.* a small trough or sledge for sliding down an inclined plane or a hillside, a toboggan; an ill-hung carriage, a sliding game down a smooth bank.

Hurley-house, *n.* a large house fallen into disrepair, or nearly in ruins.

Hurlie, *n.* a tumult.

Hurling, *ppl. adj.* quickly passing, rushing.

Hurling, *n.* rough dalliance, as on the harvest-field.

Hurloch, *n.* a falling or rolling mass; an avalanche of sand, stones, &c. Cf. Hooloch.

Hurloch, *adj.* cloudy. Cf. Urluch.

Hurly, *n.* a noise, tumult.

Hurly, *adv.* and *adj.* last.

Hurly, *n.* a wheel; a hand-cart. Cf. Hurley.

Hurly, *int.* in *phr.* 'hurly hawkie!' a milkmaid's call to her cows.

Hurly-buck-out, *n.* the last, the hindmost person.

Hurly-burley, *n.* the last, the hindmost person.

Hurly-burly, *n.* a storm of wind.—*adj.* tempestuous, tumultuous.

Hurly-go-thorow, *n.* a racket, disturbance.

Hurly-gush, *n.* the gushing forth of water.

Hurly-hacket, *n.* a racket, disturbance.

Hurly-hindmost, *n.* the last, the hindmost person.

Huron, *n.* the heron. Cf. Huerunt, Huril.

Huroosh, *n.* a disturbance.

Hurr, *v.* to whir round.

Hurr, *v.* to snarl like a dog.—*n.* rough breathing; hoarseness.

Hurried, *ppl. adj.* in *phr.* 'hurried enough,' having enough to do, having one's work cut out before one, an expression of difficulty; busy; having much to do in little time; in a hurry.—*adv.* quickly.

Hurrok, *n.* the brent-goose.

Hurroo, Hurroe, Hurro, *int.* hallo! hurrah!—*n.* a hallo; a murmuring noise as of the sea on a pebbly shore; a hurly-burly; a noisy commotion.

Hurry, *n.* a press of work; a riot, commotion; a quarrel, scolding.

Hurry-burry, *n.* confusion, noise.—*adv.* with extra hurry; in confusion.

Hurry-scurry, *n.* an uproar, tumult.

Hurschle, Hurstle, *v.* to move or slide with grazing or friction. Cf. Hirsel.

Hurstle, *v.* to breathe roughly from phlegm in the windpipe.—*n.* a rattling sound in the windpipe.

Hurstling, *n.* the sound of rough breathing; wheezing.

Hurst-rigg, *n.* the harvest-field.

Hurtit, *ppl.* hurt.

Hurtsome, *adj.* hurtful.

Husband-land, *n.* a division of land such as might be ploughed, or mown with a scythe.

Husband-toon, *n.* a farmstead.

Husband-work, *n.* household work.

Husch, v. to scare birds by a slight noise. Cf. Hush.

Husch, v. to lull to sleep. Cf. Hush.

Huschle, v. to move with friction. Cf. Hirsel.

Huschle-muschle, n. great confusion.—v. to put into great confusion.

Huschoue, v. to frighten birds.—int. a cry to scare birds away.

Hush, v. to lull asleep, sing a lullaby ; to go to sleep.—n. a whisper, the slightest noise. —adj. hushed, quiet.

Hush, n. a sudden gush or rush ; a swell or rolling motion of the sea ; abundance.—v. to rush, gush forth ; to force forward, cause to rush.

Hush, int. a cry in order to scare birds.—v. to scare birds by a slight noise.

Hush, n. the lump-fish.

Hush-a-baa, n. a lullaby.—v. to lull a child to sleep.

Hushel, v. to move or slide with friction. Cf. Hirsel.

Hushel, n. a worn-out implement ; a person out of order, or useless for work ; a sloven ; a confused mass of things.

Hushel-bushel, n. an uproar.

Hushel-mushel, n. a state of great confusion. —v. to put into great confusion.

Hushie, v. to lull a child. Cf. Whushie.

Hushie, n. in phr. 'hushie or whishie,' the slightest intimation given most cautiously.

Hushie-ba, n. a lullaby.—v. to lull asleep.— int. an expression used to lull a child to sleep.

Hushion, n. a footless stocking. Cf. Hoshen.

Hushle, v. to move with friction. Cf. Hirsel.

Hushloch, n. a confused heap ; a tangled mass ; hasty, slovenly work ; a hasty or slovenly worker. Cf. Hushoch.

Hushlochy, adv. all of a heap.—adj. hurried ; careless ; slovenly.

Hushly, adj. disordered, untidy.

Hush-mush, -musch, n. secret talking, rumour ; bustling disorder.—v. to speak much secretly. —adv. in bustling disorder.

Hush nor mush, phr. not a single whisper.

Hushoch, v. to work carelessly or hurriedly ; to dress in a slovenly style ; to heap up loosely.—n. a confused heap ; a loose quantity of anything ; slovenly work.

Hushochy, adj. hurried ; careless ; slovenly.

Husht, int. hush !—v. to order silence.

Hushter, n. ill-arranged work ; work done in a slovenly way.—v. to work in a slovenly or wasteful way. Cf. Hashter.

Hushy-baa, -baw, n. a lullaby.—v. to lull to sleep.

Huskit, ppl. adj. husky, hoarse.

Hussey-skep, n. housewifery.

Hussil, Hussle, v. to move the clothes about the shoulders ; to shrug the shoulders. Cf. Hustle.

Hussle-bussle, n. a confusion.

Hussock, n. a tuft of coarse grass ; a shock of hair ; the earth adhering to the root of a cabbage-stock when pulled. Cf. Hassock.

Hussyfe, n. a housewife ; a wench, hussy. Cf. Hissie.

Hussyfe-skep, n. housewifery.

Husta, Husto, int. an excl. of surprise and hesitance.

Huster, n. a contemptuous designation of a woman.

Hustle, v. to work hard ; to shrug the shoulders.

Hustle, v. used of a child : to coo ; of a cat : to purr.

Hustle-farrant, n. one who wears tattered clothes.

Hut, n. an overgrown, indolent person ; a slattern.

Hut, n. a small heap ; a heap of dung laid down in a field ; a small stack built in the field.—v. to put up grain in the field in a small stack. Cf. Hot.

Hut, int. a call to a careless horse.

Hut, n. a square basket formerly used for carrying out dung to the fields, the bottom of which opened.

Hutch, n. a cottage ; an embankment to hinder water from washing away the soil ; a deep pool in a river underneath an over-hanging bank.

Hutch, n. a small heap of dung ; a small rick or temporary stack of corn. Cf. Hut.

Huther, n. a slight shower ; a wetting mist.— v. to fall in slight showers ; to rain inter-mittently.

Huther, v. to work confusedly. Cf. Howder.

Hutherin, n. a young heifer ; a stupid fellow ; a mongrel sort of greens, raised from the seed of common greens and cabbages grown too near each other.

Huthering, Hutheron, ppl. adj. confused ; awkward ; hurried in walking or working ; of a stout woman : slovenly.—n. a lazy, slovenly girl or woman, a slattern.

Huther-my-duds, n. a tatterdemalion ; a ragged person.

Huthery, adj. untidy.

Huthir, v. to walk clumsily, hobble ; to work hurriedly and slovenly.—n. a slattern ; a slovenly worker ; a hasty walker ; unbe-coming haste. Cf. Howthir.

Huthran, ppl. adj. 'huthering,' acting with confused haste.

Hutie-cuittie, n. a copious draught of in-toxicating liquor.

Hutock, n. a small stack. Cf. Hut, Hutch.

Huts, *int.* tuts ! Cf. Hoot.
Hutten, *ppl.* hit.
Huuy, *int.* begone ! Cf. Hui.
Huz, *pron.* us.
Huzle, Huzzle, *v.* to wheeze.—*n.* a wheeze. Cf. Hoozle.
Huzzh, *v.* to lull a child to sleep. Cf. Hush.
Huzzh-baw, *n.* a lullaby.
Huzzie, Huzzy, *n.* a hussy; a lass, a wench; a jade. Cf. Hissie.
Huzzie, *n.* a case for needles, thread, &c.
Huzzie-baw, *n.* a lullaby. Cf. Hushie-ba.
Hwill, *n.* a small skiff. Cf. Whill.
Hwrinket, *n.* improper language.—*adj.* perverse, stubborn.
Hy, *int.* a call to horses to turn towards the left. Cf. Hie.
Hyaave, *adj.* gray; sallow; livid. Cf. Haw.
Hyank, *v.* to cut in lumps.—*n.* a lump; a big slice.
Hyauve, *adj.* gray; black and white. Cf. Hyaave.
Hychle, *v.* to walk with difficulty while carrying a burden. Cf. Hechle.
Hyde, *n.* a hide; a disagreeable fellow.
Hyeave, *adj.* sallow; livid. Cf. Haw.
Hy jinks, *n.* drinking by lot.
Hyke, *v.* to hoist; to toss up and down. Cf. Hike.
Hykerie-pykerie, *n.* a mixture of Barbadoes aloes and canella bark. Cf. Hickery-pickery.
Hymnler, *n.* a hymn-singer.
Hynail, *n.* a greedy dog; a greedy person. Cf. Hanniel.
Hynd, Hynde, *n.* a farm-servant. Cf. Hind.
Hynd-wynd, *adv.* straight; by the nearest road.
Hyne, *n.* a farm-servant. Cf. Hind.
Hyne, *adv.* far away.—*n.* a departure.
Hyne, *v.* to hoist.
Hyne-awa, *adj.* distant.—*adv.* to a great distance.
Hynt, *v. pret.* caught up; laid hold of.—*ppl.* gathered up. Cf. Hent.
Hypal, *v.* to limp.—*n.* sciatica.
Hypal, *n.* a good-for-nothing person; a person with loose, tattered clothes; one who is hungry or voracious.
Hypalt, Hypald, *adj.* crippled.—*n.* a cripple; a strange-looking fellow; a sheep that casts its fleece from disease; a lean, old, starved horse; an animal whose legs are tied.

Hype, Hyp, *n.* the fruit of the dog-rose.
Hype, *n.* a big, unruly person; a term sometimes of respect, sometimes of disrespect.
Hyple, *v.* to limp.—*n.* sciatica. Cf. Hypal.
Hyple, *n.* a dishonest old woman; a 'hypal'
Hypocreeties, *n.* shams, hypocrisies.
Hypocrip, *n.* a hypocrite.
Hypothec, *n.* a legal security for rent or money due; the former right of a landlord to claim rent of his tenant, in preference to other creditors; in *phr.* 'the whole hypothec,' the whole concern or collection.
Hyppal, *v.* to limp. Cf. Hypal, Hyple.
Hysch, *v.* to lull a child to sleep. Cf. Hush.
Hyse, *v.* to romp; to banter; to brag; to bluster, rant.—*n.* an uproar, rant; a wild frolic; a brag; banter; a practical joke; a 'cock-and-bull' story.
Hy-spy, *n.* the game of 'hie-spy' or 'hespy.'
Hyste, *v.* to hoist.
Hyster, *v.* to hoist.
Hyte, *int.* a call to horses to go on.—*v.* to urge a horse.
Hyte, Hyt, *adj.* mad, raging, 'gyte.'
Hyter, *v.* to walk with tottering gait; to work weakly and clumsily.—*n.* weak and clumsy working; walking with tottering steps; confusion; ruin; nonsense; a weak, stupid person.—*adv.* with weak, tottering steps; in a state of ruin.
Hytering, *ppl. adj.* weak; stupid; unskilful.
Hyter-skyter, *n.* walking with tottering steps; a lot of arrant nonsense.—*v.* to walk with tottering steps.—*adv.* with weak steps; in ruin.
Hyter-styte, *n.* stupidity; nonsense; utter ruin.—*adj.* stupid, silly, mad-like.—*adv.* madly, stupidly; in ruin.—*v.* to walk with tottering steps.
Hyte-styte, *adj.* mad-like; in a state of madness.—*n.* nonsense; utter ruin.
Hyuck, Hyuk, *n.* a hook.
Hyule, *n.* an out-of-the-way person; a mischievous person; a rake. Cf. Heul, Hule.
Hyven, *n.* heaven.
Hyves, *n.* an eruption on the skin. Cf. Hives.
Hyvie, Hyvy, *adj.* in easy circumstances. Cf. Hivie.
Hyze, *v.* to hoist.—*n.* fun, a frolic; a practical joke, a 'rise.' Cf. Hyse.
Hyzzie, *n.* a hussy; a quean. Cf. Hissie.

I, *prep.* in.
Ice-ground, *n.* a curling-rink.
Icelet, *n.* an icicle.
Iceshoggle, Iceshockle, *n.* an icicle.
Ice-stane, *n.* a curling-stone.

Ice-tangle, *n.* an icicle.
Ichie nor ochie, *adj.* irresolute, wavering.—*n.* not a sound, nothing. Cf. Eechie.
Icker, *n.* an ear of corn.
Icksy-picksy, *adj.* alike.

Idder, *conj.* and *adv.* either.

Idder, Ider, *adj.* other ; each other.

Idderwise, *adv.* otherwise.

Ident, *adj.* diligent, industrious. Cf. Eident.

†Idiot, *n.* an unlearned person.

Idioticals, *n.* foolish things, nonsense ; things of no moment.

Idiotry, *n.* idiocy ; folly.

Idiwut, *n.* an idiot, a simpleton. Cf. Ediwut.

Idledom, *n.* idleness.

Idleset, Idleseat, *n.* idleness ; a useless or frivolous amusement.—*adj.* disposed to idleness.

Idleteth, Idelty, *n.* idleness ; in *pl.* idle frolics.

I dree, I dree I dropped it, *n.* a girls' singing game.

Ie, *n.* an island. Cf. Ea.

Ield, *adj.* used of a cow : not giving milk. Cf. Yeld.

Ier-oe, *n.* a great-grandchild. Cf. Air-oe.

Ieskdruimin, *n.* a species of salmon at the Isle of Harris.

Ignorant, *n.* an ignorant person.

Ile, *n.* the fishing-ground inside the main tidal current, in the space between two points where there is a counter-current.

Ile, *n.* a wing of a church ; a half-transept ; an 'aisle.'

Ile, *n.* oil. Cf. Oil.

Ilk, *n.* the same name, place, nature, or family.—*phr.* 'of that ilk,' indicating that the person so designated has the same surname as his property or title.

Ilk, *adj.* each ; every.—*n.* each one.

Ilka, *adj.* each ; every ; common, ordinary.

Ilka body's body, *n.* a universal favourite ; a time-server.

Ilka day, *n.* a lawful day, a week-day.—*adv.* daily.—*adj.* pertaining to the week-days ; ordinary.

Ilka-day's claise, *n.* week-day garments in contrast to Sunday's.

Ilka-deal, *adv.* every whit ; altogether.

Ilk ane, *n.* each one.

Ilka-where, *adv.* everywhere.

Ill, *adj.* vicious, immoral ; used of money : forged ; noxious ; grieved, sorrowful ; stormy ; hard, difficult ; unkind, cruel, harsh ; severe ; angry ; with *about*, eager after, very fond of ; with *for*, having a vicious propensity to ; with *to*, hard to bargain with or to deal with in settling an account.—*adv.* badly.—*n.* misfortune, harm ; illness, pain ; disease ; difficulty.

Ill able, *adj.* hardly able ; unable.

Ill-aff, *adj.* poor, miserable, ill-used ; perplexed.

Ill-ane, *n.* a bad character ; the devil.

Ill-best, *n.* the best of a bad job ; the best of the bad.

Ill-bind, *n.* a bad shape or form of an article of dress.

Ill-bit, *n.* hell.

Ill-boden, *adj.* poorly furnished or stocked.

Ill-brew, -broo, *n.* an unfavourable opinion ; no great liking.

Ill-brocht-up, *adj.* badly trained.

Ill-canker't, *adj.* not well-disposed.

Ill-chance, *n.* bad luck.

Ill-cleckit, *adj.* misbegotten, base-born.

Ill-coloured, *adj.* discoloured.

Ill-contrickit, *adj.* knavish, mischievous.

Ill-contrived, *adj.* tricky, mischievous ; badly behaved, ill-tempered ; awkward ; badly constructed.

Ill-convenient, *adj.* inconvenient.

Ill-cuisten, *adj.* badly sown with the hand.

Ill-curponed, *adj.* ill - conditioned, surly, churlish ; cross.

Ill-deedy, *adj.* mischievous, evilly disposed.

Ill-dereyt, *adj.* untidy, disorderly.

Ill-designed, *adj.* evilly disposed.

Ill-doer, *n.* an evil-doer.

Ill-doin', -deein', *adj.* badly behaved ; leading an evil life.

Ill-done, -deen, -dune, *adj.* wrong, mischievous, cruel, ill-advised.

Ill-dread, *n.* an apprehension of evil, of something bad.

Ill-dreaded, *adj.* fearing or expecting evil.

Ill-dreader, *n.* one anticipating or suspicious of evil.

Ill-eased, *adj.* reduced to a state of inconvenience ; inconvenient.

Ill-e'e, *n.* the 'evil eye' ; dislike.

Illegal, *n.* an illegality.

Ill-end, *n.* a bad end, a miserable death.

Illest, *adj.* worst.

Ill-fashed, *adj.* greatly troubled ; much worried.

Ill-fashioned, *adj.* vulgar in habits, ill-mannered ; quarrelsome.

Ill-faur'd, -far'd, *adj.* unbecoming, unmannerly ; out of place ; unpleasant, unsavoury ; not looking well or healthy ; ill-tempered ; mean ; scurvy ; clumsy ; ugly, not good-looking.

Ill-fauredly, *adv.* clumsily ; meanly, shabbily.

Ill-fit, *n.* a 'foot' or person supposed to bring bad luck.

Ill-fitter, *n.* one who has the 'ill-fit.'

Ill-gab, *n.* bad language, abusive talk, insolence of speech.—*v.* to use such language.

Ill-gabbit, *ppl. adj.* foul-tongued ; vituperative.

Ill-gainshoned, -gaishoned, *adj.* mischievous ; mischievously disposed.

Ill-gait, -gate, *n.* an evil way, a bad habit.

Ill-gaited, -gaetit, -gettit, *adj.* having bad habits.

Ill-gi'en, *adj.* evilly disposed, given to evil; niggardly.

Ill-gotten, *adj.* base-born; illegitimate.

Ill-greein', *adj.* quarrelsome.

Ill-grun, -grunyie, *n.* a bad, knavish disposition.

Ill-gruntet, *adj.* 'grumpy,' ill-natured.

Ill-grunyiet, *adj.* evilly disposed.

Ill-guide, *v.* to mismanage; to ill-treat; to train or bring up badly; to advise wrongly.

Ill-hadden, *adj.* unmannerly, ill-mannered.

Ill-hain't, *adj.* saved with no good result.

Ill-hair't, *adj.* ill-conditioned; surly, churlish.

Ill-hairtit, -heartit, *adj.* malevolent, illiberal.

Ill-hairtitness, *n.* malevolence.

Ill-happit, *adj.* ill-clad; with poor or scanty clothes.

Ill-hauden-in, *adj.* saved to no good purpose.

Ill-hear, *v.* to chide, scold.

Ill-hearing, *n.* a scolding.

Ill-hivard, *adj.* ill-natured. Cf. Ill-hyvered.

Ill-hued, *adj.* ill-favoured.

Ill-hung, *adj.* used of the tongue: impudent, insolent; vituperative.

Ill-hyver, *n.* awkward behaviour; ill-humour.

Ill-hyvered, *adj.* awkward; abusive; ill-looking, ill-skinned; ill-tempered.

Illighten, *v.* to enlighten.

Illiquid, *adj.* not legally ascertained.

Ill-jaw, *n.* bad language; an abusive tongue. —*v.* to use abusive language.

Ill-jaw't, *adj.* foul-tongued, abusive.

Ill-kennin', *adj.* hardly knowing.

Ill-kessen, *adj.* badly sown with the hand.

Ill-learned, *adj.* badly taught; inexperienced.

Ill-leggit, *adj.* having unshapely legs.

Ill-less, *adj.* harmless, innocent; with no evil disposition.

Ill-less guidless, *adj.* having neither good nor bad habits, character, &c.

Ill-like, *adj.* not looking well; ugly.

Ill-likit, *adj.* unpopular.

Ill-liver, *n.* an immoral person.

Ill-living, *adj.* immoral. *n.* immoral conduct.

Ill-luckit, *adj.* unlucky; bringing bad luck.

Ill-making, *adj.* mischief-making.

Ill-man, *n.* a child's name for the devil.

Ill-minded, -min't, *adj.* evil-minded.

Ill-min'in, *n.* forgetfulness; unmindfulness.

Ill-minted, *adj.* ill-meant; with evil intentions.

Ill-mou, *n.* abusive, insolent language.—*v.* to use such language.

Ill-mou'd, *adj.* insolent; vituperative.

Ill-muggent, *adj.* abusive, insolent; evilly disposed.

Ill-name, *n.* a bad name; a bad reputation.

Ill-off, *adj.* poor. Cf. Ill-aff.

Ill-one, *n.* a bad character. Cf. Ill-ane.

Ill-paid, -pay't, *adj.* very sorry.

Ill-paired, *adj.* badly matched, ill-assorted.

Ill-part, *n.* hell.

Ill-payment, *n.* a bad debt.

Ill-place, *n.* hell.

Ill-prat, -prot, *n.* a mischievous trick.

Ill-prattie, -pretit, -prottit, *adj.* mischievous, roguish.

Ill-put-on, *adj.* badly or carelessly dressed.

Ill-red-up, *adj.* untidy; in a state of disorder.

Ill-saired, -ser'd, *adj.* badly served; not having enough to eat at a meal.

Ill-santafied, *adj.* not spiritually edifying.

Ill-sar'd, *adj.* unsavoury.

Ill-scrapit, *adj.* used of the tongue: abusive, rude.

Ill-set, *v.* to become badly. — *adj.* evilly disposed; spiteful.

Ill-setness, *n.* opposition; spite; churlishness.

Ill-shaken-up, *adj.* used of dress: disordered, untidy, uncomely.

Ill-shapit, *adj.* badly behaved.

Ill-side, *n.* a defect, blemish.

Ill-sitten, *adj.* ungainly in gait from long sitting at work.

Ill-sorted, *adj.* displeased, dissatisfied; ill-assorted.

Ill-speaker, *n.* an evil speaker, a slanderer.

Ill-spent, *adj.* misspent.

Ill-ta'en, *adj.* taken amiss.

Ill-tasted, *adj.* unpleasant.

Ill-teth'd, *adj.* malevolent; ill-conditioned.

Ill-thief, -thing, *n.* the devil.

Ill-thochted, *adj.* suspicious; evilly disposed.

Ill-thriven, *adj.* lean, not thriving.

Ill-tochered, *ppl. adj.* poorly dowered. Cf. Tocher.

Ill-tongue, *n.* evil speaking; bad language.

Ill-tongued, *adj.* foul-tongued; difficult to pronounce.

Ill-trick, *n.* a mischievous trick.

Ill-trickit, -tricky, *adj.* mischievous, roguish.

Ill-turn, *n.* a turn for the worse.

Ill-upon't, *adj.* in bad health; much fatigued; spiritless, woe-begone.

Ill-used, *adj.* put to a wrong use.

Ill-waled, *adj.* badly chosen.

Ill-wared, *adj.* ill laid out; misspent.

Ill-washen, *adj.* badly washed; expressive of contempt.

Ill-ween, *n.* bad language; bad news.—*v.* to use abusive language.

Ill-will, *v.* to wish evil.

Ill-willed, -willied, *adj.* sulky; ill-tempered; grudging; unwilling.

Ill-willer, *n.* an adversary; one who wishes evil to another.

Ill-willie, -willy, *adj.* ill-tempered, spiteful; disobliging; grudging, niggardly; reluctant. —*adv.* reluctantly.

Ill-win, *adj.* ill-won.

Ill-win', *n.* an evil report, slander.

Ill-wish, *n.* an imprecation; a malicious wish.

Ill-wull, *n.* ill-will.

I-lore, *int.* woe is me! Cf. Elore.

Image, *n.* a wooden figure carved by the fairies in the likeness of a person intended to be stolen; a figure of clay or wax used in witchcraft; a pitiful object; an oddity; a 'sight.'

Imaky-amaky, *n.* the ant.

†Imbase, *v.* to debase coin.

†Imbecill, *v.* to damage. Cf. Embezill.

Imber, *n.* the great northern diver. Cf. Ember.

†Imbezilling, *ppl.* exposing to loss, damage.

Imbog, *v.* to engulf, as in a bog.

Ime, *n.* soot; a thin coat or scum deposited on a surface.

Imey, *adj.* sooty.

Imhim, *int.* an excl. of assent. Cf. Imphim.

Immedant, *adj.* immediate.

Immedantly, *adv.* immediately.

Immer, *n.* the great northern diver. Cf. Ember.

Immick, Imok, *n.* the ant. Cf. Eemock.

Immis, *adj.* variable. Cf. Emmis.

Imp, *n.* a shoot, a sucker; a length of hair twisted, forming part of a fishing-line.

†Impasch, Impeach, *v.* to hinder. Cf. Empesch.

Imper, *v.* to be overbold, to presume.

Imperence, *n.* impudence.

Impertinence, *n.* petulance; an insolent person.

Impertinent, *adj.* uncivil, petulant.

Imphim, Imph, Imphm, *int.* an excl. of assent.

Impiddent, *adj.* impudent.

Implement, *n.* fulfilment.

Importance, *n.* means of support; source of gain.

Imposition, *n.* the right or permission to levy a tax.

Imprestable, *adj.* impracticable.

Imprieve, *v.* to disprove; to impeach. Cf. Improve.

Imprieve, *v.* to improve.

Improbation, *n.* a legal term: the act of 'improving.'

†Improve, *v.* a legal term: to prove a statement untrue, or that a thing has not taken place.

Improver, *n.* a legal term: one who proves a writ to have been forged, or that an allegation is false.

†Impune, *n.* impunity.

Impunge, *v.* to impugn.

Imrie, *n.* the scent of roasted meat.

Imrigh, *n.* a kind of strong soup made from the best parts of beef.

In, *prep.* in the midst of, occupied with; near, close; into; on, upon; with.—*adv.* inside,

within the house, at home; used of a gathering: met, going on; used of the harvest; gathered, stacked; shrunken, fallen in; of the sea: at high tide; of a railway train, &c.: arrived at a station; on good terms; friendly; approving of, agreeing to.—*v.* to go or come in; to put, push, or get in.—*n.* an entrance.

In, *conj.* if, 'an,' 'gin.'

In about, *adv.* in or to the immediate neighbourhood, near.

Inairt, *adj.* inward; quite genuine, sincere.

In and in, *adj.* used of cattle, sheep, horses, &c.: bred wholly from the same stock.

In at, *prep.* to, at.

In atween, *prep.* between.

Inawe, Inawn, *v.* to owe.

Inbearing, *ppl. adj.* officious, meddlesome; eager to ingratiate one's self; persuasive, impressive in speech.

Inbiggit, *ppl. adj.* selfish, morose, reserved.

Inbreak, *n.* a portion of 'in-field' pasture-land broken up or tilled; a breach in or into.

Inbred fever, *n.* a disease similar to influenza.

Inbring, *v.* to import; to bring in; to pay in; to collect forces or taxes.

Inbringer, *n.* an importer; an introducer, one who brings in.

Inbrocht, *ppl. adj.* imported; introduced; paid in.

In-by, -bye, *adj.* low-lying.—*adv.* nearer towards the speaker; in the inner part of a room, house, &c.—*v.* to come near.—*prep.* beside.

Incall, *v.* to invoke; to pray; to call in or on.

Incaller, *n.* a petitioner.

Incalling, *n.* invocation, prayer.

Incast, *n.* what is given over and above the legal measure or exact sum.

Inch, *n.* an island; low-lying land near a river or stream.

Inch, *n.* in *phr.* 'an inch of time,' the least moment of time.—*v.* to live sparingly, to grudge spending.

Inch-muckle, *n.* a piece as small as an inch.

Incident, *adj.* incidental; occurring as a possible consequence.

Incidently, *adv.* not of set purpose.

Income, *n.* advent, entrance; a new-comer, an arrival; an internal disease, not due to accident or contagion, an ailment without apparent external cause; an abscess, running sore; deficiency from a stated or expected quantity of things weighed or measured; what is thrown ashore by the sea.—*ppl. adj.* introduced; come in.

Income ware, *n.* weeds or wrack cast ashore by the sea.

Incoming, *n.* conversion and accession to the church.—*ppl. adj.* ensuing, succeeding.

†**Incontinent,** *adv.* forthwith, immediately, at once.

Inconvene, Inconveen, *adj.* inconvenient.—*n.* inconvenience.

Inconveniency, *n.* hardship, inconvenience.

Inconvenient, *n.* inconvenience.

Incormant, *n.* a share, portion.

In-country, *n.* the interior of a country; an inland district.

Ind, *v.* to bring in; to house or stack grain.

Indecent, *adj.* disreputable.

Indecent-like, *adj.* disreputable-looking; apparently unseemly.

Indeed no, *phr.* no, indeed.

Indemnify, *v.* to compound a felony by relieving the criminal from penalties; to free from the consequences of rebellion, &c.

Indent, *v.* to carve, engrave; to engage; to warrant; to make a compact.—*n.* an indenture.

Indew, *adj.* indebted.

India, *n.* india-rubber.

Indian fuel, *n.* tobacco.

Indian rubber, *n.* india-rubber.

Indict, *v.* to appoint a meeting authoritatively; to summon.

Indicted, *ppl. adj.* addicted, inclined.

Indignance, *n.* indignation.

Indignify, *v.* to disgrace.

†**Inding,** *adj.* unworthy, shameful.

Indiscreet, *adj.* rude, uncivil.

Indiscreetly, *adv.* rudely, uncivilly.

Indiscretion, *n.* incivility, rudeness, discourtesy.

Indite, *v.* to 'indict,' summon a meeting.

Indoor-face, *n.* a face not affected by exposure to the weather.

Indorsate, *ppl.* endorsed.

Indraught, *n.* suction of air; a strong current, vortex; toll or duty collected at a port.

Indrink, *n.* shrinkage, diminution of quantity or number.—*v.* to shrink in, turn out less.

Indumious, *adj.* very bad; of the weather: extraordinarily stormy. **Cf.** Ondeemas.

Induring, *prep.* during.

Indwall, *v.* to inhabit.

Indwelling, *n.* a habitation, residence.

Inease, *v.* to allay, set at rest.

Infall, *n.* an invasion; a hostile attack, onslaught.

Infamous, *adj.* branding with infamy.

Infang, *v.* to cheat, gull; to get into one's clutches.

Infang thief, *n.* a thief caught by a baron within his own territory; the privilege conferred on a landlord of trying such a thief. **Cf.** Fang.

Infar, Infare, *n.* the home-coming of a bride; the feast given at her reception in her new nome.

Infar-cake, *n.* a cake broken over the bride's head as she crossed the threshold of her new home.

Infatuate, *ppl. adj.* infatuated; mad, foolish.

Infauld, *v.* to enfold.

Infeft, *v.* to invest formally with property, enfeoff.—*ppl.* invested with, possessed of.

Infeftment, *n.* investiture, legal possession.

†**Infestuous,** *adj.* extraordinary.

Infield, *n.* arable land continually cropped and manured. - *adj.* pertaining to 'infield.'

Infit, *n.* an introduction; influence, footing.

Infittin, *n.* influence, footing.

Inflame, *n.* inflammation.

Infleenzy, *n.* influenza.

Inforce, *v.* to aid, to second, to abet; to compel by inward impulse.

Infore, *n.* an 'infar.'

Ingaan, Ingäin, *n.* an entrance.—*adj.* entering, assembling, ingoing.

Ingaan-mouth, *n.* the mouth of a coal-pit with a horizontal direction.

Ingadder, Ingaither, *v.* to collect, ingather.

Ingae, *v.* to enter.

Ingäin' tenant, *n.* a tenant who succeeds another on a farm, &c., which has been let. Cf. Ingo.

Ingan, *n.* an onion.

Ingang, *n.* lack, deficiency, shrinkage; entrance, beginning.

Ingangs, *n.* intestines.

Ingate, *n.* an entrance.

Ingate and outgate, *adv.* within and without, completely.

Ingeniously, *adv.* ingenuously, frankly.

Ingenuity, *n.* ingenuousness.

Inger, *n.* a gleaner.

Inger's pot, *n.* a quantity of all kinds of grain dried in a pot and ground into meal.

Ingetting, *n.* a gathering in; a receiving; collection.

Ingine, *n.* an engine; a weapon used with gunpowder.

†**Ingine,** *n.* ingenuity; quickness of intellect, ability; knowledge, invention; disposition; a person of ability; a genius; an ingenious person. Cf. Engine.

Ingiver, *n.* one who delivers a thing, either for himself or for another.

Ingle, *n.* fire, flame; a fire in a room; the furnace of a kiln; a hearth, fireplace, fireside; a chimney-corner; a faggot or bundle of fuel; a burning peat, coal, or log.

Ingle-berry, *n.* a fleshy growth on the bodies of oxen. Cf. Angleberry.

Ingle-biel, *n.* fireside shelter.

Ingle-bole, *n.* a chimney-recess for holding small articles.

Ingle-bred, *adj.* home-bred.

Ingle-cheek, *n.* the fireside.

Ingle-end, *n.* the end of a room where the fire is, the 'fire-end.'

Ingle-gleed, *n.* the blaze of a fire; a blazing fireside; hearth-coal.

Ingle-lichtit, *adj.* lighted by the fire.

Ingle-lowe, *n.* the flame or blaze of a fire, firelight.

Ingle-lug, *n.* the fireside, the hearth.

Ingle-mids, *n.* the centre of a fire.

Ingle-neuk, -nook, *n.* a chimney-corner, a corner by the fireside.

Ingle-ring, *n.* the fireside-circle.

Ingle-save, *n.* a device for saving fuel.

Ingle-side, *n.* the fireside.

Ingle-stane, *n.* the hearthstone.

Inglin, *n.* fuel.

Inglisher, *n.* an Englishman.

Ingo, *v.* to enter.

Ingothill, *phr.* 'if God will,' 'God willing.'

†Ingrat, *n.* an ungrateful person.—*adj.* ungrateful.

Ingrate, *adj.* ungrateful.

Ingrowth, *n.* increase.

Ingy, *v.* to bring forth lambs.

Ingyang, *n.* entrance; shrinkage. Cf. Ingang.

Ingyre, *v.* to push one's self forward artfully; to 'worm' one's way into.

†Inhabile, *adj.* incompetent, disqualified; inadmissible as a witness.

†Inhabilitie, *n.* disability, unfitness, inability.

Inhable, *v.* to disable, disqualify, prevent.

Inhadden, Inhaudin, *ppl. adj.* continuously supplied; selfish; fawning, cringing; frugal, penurious.—*n.* frugality, parsimoniousness.

Inhaddin eldin, *n.* fuel which needs constant renewal.

Iniquity, *n.* inequity.

Iniquous, *adj.* iniquitous, unfair.

†Injury, *n.* contumely, reproach, abuse.

Injustified, *ppl. adj.* not put to death.

Inker, *n.* an ink-bottle.

Inker-pinker, *n.* small beer.

Ink-holder, *n.* a vessel containing ink.

Inkle-weaver, *n.* a weaver of coarse tape.

Inkling, *n.* a faint or half-concealed desire or inclination; a small measure or degree.

In-kneed, *adj.* knock-kneed.

Ink-pud, *n.* a vessel for holding ink.

Inks, *n.* low-lying lands on the banks of a river, overflowed by the sea at high-tide, and covered by short, coarse grass; shore pasture.

Ink-standish, *n.* an inkstand.

Inlaik, Inlack, Inleak, *n.* a deficiency, lack. —*v.* to be deficient, to lack; to die.

Inlair, *n.* a 'mill-lade.'

Inler, *n.* one who is in office; one of the government party.

In-life, *adj.* alive.

In-liftin', *adj.* used of animals: too weak to rise without help.

Inlying, *n.* child-bearing; a confinement.

In-meat, *n.* the edible viscera of any animal; food given to animals within doors.

Inmix, *v.* to interfere.

Inn, *v.* to bring in grain from the field. Cf. Ind.

Inn, *n.* a house; in *pl.* an inn; in games: the goal.

Inner, *adj.* in *phr.* 'inner water,' water entering a house through the foundation.— *n.* in *pl.* under-garments.

Innerly, *adj.* situated in the interior of a country; low-lying, snug, not exposed; used of land: fertile; towards the shore, keeping near the land; in a state of near neighbourhood; neighbourly, sociable; affectionate, compassionate.

Innerly-hearted, *adj.* of a feeling disposition.

Innes, *n.* an inn.

Inning, *n.* the bringing of corn from the field. Cf. Inn, Ind.

Inno, *prep.* in; into; within; close beside.

Innocent, *n.* an imbecile, idiot; a half-witted person.

Inorderlie, *adv.* irregularly.

In-ower, -o'er, -owre, *adv.* near, close to the speaker; over; beside, close to; close at hand; within, to within, on the premises; in and over.

In-owre and out-owre, *phr.* backwards and forwards, thoroughly; violently, with complete mastery.

Inpervenient, *adj.* unforeseen, unprovided for.

Input, Inpit, *v.* to put in.—*n.* a contribution to a collection; help, assistance; entrance, beginning; the feeding of children; balance in change of money; what one is instructed or inspired by another to do in a bad cause; a setting up or settlement in business with financial help.

Inputtin, Inpitten, *n.* the feeding of children.

Inputter, *n.* one who instructs, or suggests to, another; one who places another in a certain situation.

Inquest, *ppl. adj.* inquired at.

Inquietation, *n.* disturbance.

Inring, *n.* a movement of a curling-stone, either to displace the winner or to lie within the ring around the tee; the segment of the surface of a curling-stone which is nearest the tee. Cf. Outring.

Inscales, *n.* the racks at the lower end of a 'cruive' in a river.

Inseam, *n.* the seam attaching the welt to the insole and upper of a shoe or boot.

Inseam-elshin, *n.* a shoemaker's awl for making the 'inseam.'

Inseat, Inset, *n.* the kitchen of a farm-house;

the 'mid-room,' between the kitchen and the parlour.

Insense, *v.* to make to understand ; to explain ; to instil ; to enlighten as to, to 'put sense into.'

Insett, *ppl. adj.* substituted temporarily for another.

Insh, *n.* low-lying land near a river. Cf. Inch.

Inside, *n.* the inner parts of the body.—*adv.* in a room, house, &c., within.

Insight, Insicht, *n.* the furniture of a house, household goods ; implements of husbandry kept within doors.—*adj.* relating to 'insight.'

Insightit, *ppl. adj.* having insight into.

Insight-kennage, *n.* knowledge, information.

Insignificate, *v.* to make void ; to reduce to nothing ; to deprive of authority.

Insist, *v.* to prolong a discourse ; to persevere ; with *for,* to incist upon having.

In sma', *adv.* briefly.

Insnorl, *v.* to entangle, inveigle.

Insook, *n.* used of frost : a touch, a slight amount ; of the tide : an inrush.

Insook, *n.* a bad bargain ; a fraud, 'suck in.'

Inspraich, Inspraith, Inspreght, *n.* furniture, household goods.

Inspreight, *adj.* domestic ; pertaining to what is within a house.

†**Instance,** *n.* insistence, effort.

Instancy, *n.* eagerness, urgency.

Instore, *v.* to store up.

Instriking, *n.* the throwing back into the body of an eruption through cold, &c.

Instruct, *v.* to prove or show clearly ; to equip, furnish.

Instrument, *n.* a formal document in proof of any deed of a civil or an ecclesiastical court, or of a member of that court.

Insucken-multure, *n.* the duty payable at a mill by tenants whose land is astricted to it. Cf. Sucken.

In 't, *conj.* with *pron.* if it.

Intae, *prep.* into ; in.

In-taed, *adj.* having the toes turned inward.

Intak, *n.* an inhalation ; the bringing home of the crop ; a contraction ; the narrowing of a stocking in knitting ; the place in a seam where the dimensions are narrowed ; a piece of land enclosed from moor, common, &c. for cultivation ; the part of the body of flowing water taken from the main stream ; the place where this water is taken off ; a dam across a stream to turn off water ; a cheat, swindle, fraud ; a swindler.—*v.* to take a fortified place.

Intaker, *n.* a receiver of stolen goods.

Intakin', *n.* the part of a farm newly reclaimed from moor.—*ppl. adj.* deceptive, fraudulent, swindling.

Inteer, *adj.* entire, unbroken.

Intellects, *n.* wits, senses.

Intellectuals, *n.* intellect, mental capacity.

Intelligence, *n.* a friendly understanding, agreement.

Intend, *v.* a legal term : to prosecute ; to raise an action.

Intenet, *ppl.* intended.

Intent, *v.* to intend ; to raise an action.—*n.* a litigation, lawsuit ; superintendence, onlooking.

Intercommon, -commune, *v.* to hold intercourse with proscribed persons ; to forbid such intercourse.

Intercommuner, *n.* one who holds intercourse with proscribed persons ; one who treats between persons at variance.

Intercommuning, *n.* holding intercourse with proscribed persons.

Interdick, *v.* to interdict.

†**Interesse,** *v.* to interest ; to have an interest.

Interlocutor, *n.* a legal term : a judgment exhausting the points immediately under discussion in a cause, which becomes final if not appealed against in due time.

†**Intermell,** *v.* to intermingle, intermeddle.

†**Interpell,** *v.* to importune ; to interdict ; to warn against.

Interpone, *v.* to interpose.

Interrogator, *n.* judicial examination.

†**Interteen, Intertenie,** *v.* to entertain ; to support ; to maintain ; to pay for the support of.

Interteniement, *n.* support, maintenance.

Interval, *n.* the time between the hours of public worship.

Intervald, *v.* to interrupt, cause an interval.

Intervert, *v.* to intercept ; to appropriate to another than the original purpose.

In-through, -throw, *adv.* towards the fireplace, or the speaker, in a room.—*prep.* by means of, through from the outside to the centre.

Inthrow and outthrow, *phr.* in every direction.

Intill, *prep.* into ; in, within.

Intimmers, *n.* the intestines, 'inside.'

Intire, *adj.* intimate, very familiar.

Into, *prep.* in, within.

Intown, Intoon, *n.* land or pasture adjacent to the farm-house.—*adj.* adjacent to the farm-house.

In-town, -toon-weed, *n.* an annual weed.

Intrals, *n.* the entrails, the interior of the body.

Intromission, *n.* interference with another's money or effects ; in *pl.* goings on with a person.

Intromit, *v.* to meddle with another's effects, &c. ; to interfere ; to associate with.

Invade, *v.* to assail, assault a person.

Invaird, *v.* to put within, place inside.

Invasion, *n.* an assault on a person.

Inveet, *v.* to invite.—*n.* an invitation.

Inveetors, *n.* articles taken over by inventory at a valuation in taking a farm.

Inventor, *n.* an inventory.

Invert, *v.* used of money: to pervert to wrong ends; to practise malversation.

Invest, *v.* to take possession of one's own property.

Invigor, *v.* to invigorate.

†**Invitor,** *n.* an inventory.

Invock, *v.* to invoke.

Invyfull, *adj.* envious.

Inward, Inwaird, *adj.* living within.—*v.* to put within, place inside.

Inwick, *v.* a curling term : to send a stone through a 'port' or 'wick,' to strike the 'inring' of a stone seen through that 'wick.'—*n.* a station in which a stone is placed very near the tee, after passing through a narrow 'port.'

Inwith, *adv.* to within; towards the low country; secretly; inclining downwards; inclining inwards.—*prep.* within.

Inwork, *n.* indoor or domestic work.

Ion, *n.* a horse; a cow a year old.

Ire, *n.* a passion.—*phr.* 'an ire o' wraeth,' a fit of wrath.

Irie, Irey, *adj.* melancholy, gloomy; causing fear. Cf. Eerie.

Irish, *n.* an Irishman.

Irish blackgauds, *n.* a variety of potato.

Irish blackguard, *n.* a variety of snuff.

Irisher, *n.* an Irishman.

Irk, *n.* weariness, pain.—*v.* to grow weary.

Irm, *v.* to whine; to question fretfully and persistently. Cf. Yirm.

Iron, Irne, *n.* a sword; a horse-shoe; a 'girdle' for baking; in *pl.* the coulter, sock, &c. of a plough; thin plates on the edges of the soles of clogs.

Iron-eer, -ever, Iron-near, *n.* iron ore, chalybeate matter.

Iron-eer spot, *n.* a spot on linen caused by oxide of iron.

Iron-eer-well, *n.* a mineral well.

Iron-eery, *adj.* chalybeate; impregnated with iron.

Iron-heater, *n.* a toaster, made of strong iron wire or slender rods.

Iron-house, *n.* a room in a prison where prisoners were put or kept in irons.

Iron-soupled, *adj.* having links or hinges of iron.

Iron-tings, *n.* fire-tongs.

Irony, *adj.* hard or strong as iron.

Irr, *int.* a shepherd's call to his dog to pursue cattle.

Irremediless, *adj.* irremediable.

Irrepairable, *adj.* irreparable.

Irresponsal, *adj.* insolvent.

Irresponsality, *n.* irresponsibility; insufficiency.

Irritancy, *n.* the rendering void of a contract, lease, or deed, the terms of which are no longer observed; a legal term.

Irritate, *v.* to render a deed, &c., null and void, the terms of which are no longer observed by the party in whose favour it was granted.

Irrnowt, *int.* a shepherd's call to his dog to pursue cattle. Cf. Irr.

Irrogat, *ppl. adj.* of a sentence or doom: judicially pronounced.

Is, *conj.* as.

I's, I'se, *pron.* with *v.* I shall; I am.

Isca, *int.* a call to a dog. Cf. Isk.

Isel, *n.* a hot cinder. Cf. Aizle.

Ish, *n.* issue, exodus; the act of passing out; termination.

Isher, *n.* an usher.

Isherie, *n.* an usher's office.

Ish-wish, *int.* a call to a cat to come for its food.

Ising, *n.* the silvering of a looking-glass.

Isk, Iskie, Iskey, Iskiss, *int.* a call to a dog. Cf. Isca.

Iskie-bae, *n.* 'usquebaugh,' whisky. Cf. Usquebaugh.

Isle, *n.* anger.—*v.* to be angry.

Isle, *n.* a hot cinder. Aizle.

Is na, Is nae, *neg. v.* is not.

I-spy, *n.* the game of 'hie-spy.' Cf. Hie-spy.

Iss, *int.* a call to a dog to attack. Cf. Hiss.

It, *pron.* that.—*adv.* there.—*n.* in games : the 'he' or chief player; used possessively, its.

Item, *n.* a small creature; an 'object'; a puny creature. Cf. Eetim.

Ither, *n.* the udder of a cow, mare, or goat.

Ither, *adj.* other; each other.

Ithin, *prep.* and *adv.* within.

Itinerarly, *adv.* in an itinerant way, in one not stationary.

Its, *poss. pron.* in *phr.* 'its lane,' by itself, alone.

Itsel', *pron.* itself.

Iver, *adv.* ever.

Ivver-yestreen, *n.* the day before yesterday. Cf. Eve-yestreen.

Ivy-tod, *n.* an ivy-bush.

Iwis, *adv.* certainly. Cf. Awis.

Iwyte, *adv.* assuredly. Cf. Awat.

Ixey-pixey, *adj.* equally matched. Cf. Icksy-picksy.

Izel, Izle, *n.* a smut or flake of soot from a chimney; a hot cinder. Cf. Aizle.

Izzat, Izzit, Izzard, *n.* the letter Z.—*adj.* zigzag.

Jaabard, *n.* an animal out of condition; a fish out of season. Cf. Jabart.

Jaager, *n.* a pedlar; a boat for taking the first catch of herrings from the deep-sea fishing to land. Cf. Jagger.

Jaap, *v.* used of water: to dash and rebound in waves; to splash, bespatter; to throw water, &c.—*n.* a dash of water. Cf. Jaup.

Jab, *v.* to prick sharply; to shut up, embarrass.—*n.* a prick, a sharp thrust. Cf. Job.

Jabart, *n.* a lean, useless horse; an animal in poor condition; a fish out of season.

Jabb, *n.* a large, open creel lined with a net for catching the fry of coal-fish.

Jabb, *v.* to fatigue, exhaust.—*n.* a big, lean, uncomely person; a big-boned, lean, weakly animal.

Jabber, *n.* chatter; idle talk.

Jabble, *v.* used of water: to ripple, break in irregular wavelets; to shake the liquid in a vessel; to spill; to cook badly; to use constantly an article of food.—*n.* a ripple on the surface of water, small broken waves of the sea; a confusion of a liquid and its sediment; weak soup, tea, &c.; a quantity of any liquid, or of wishy-washy drink; turmoil, confusion.

Jabble, *n.* a large, blunt needle; a knife; a 'shable.'

Jabbled, *ppl. adj.* agitated; stormy.

Jabblick, *n.* a quantity of worthless liquid or half-liquid food.

Jabblin, *ppl. adj.* weak, washy, insipid.

Jabbloch, *n.* a mess of liquid or half-liquid food; weak, watery liquor.

Jacey, *n.* a jersey made of coarse wool; any coarse woollen fabric.

Jachlet, *ppl. adj.* blown or bent to one side.

Jack, *n.* a half-contemptuous name for a single person, a fellow; a leathern drinking-vessel; a jackdaw; a roller for a towel; in *pl.* small bones, pebbles, &c., used in a children's game; a privy, 'jakes.'

Jack, *n.* a jacket.

Jack-and-the-lantern, *n.* Will-o'-the-Wisp; *ignis fatuus.*

Jacket, *n.* the skin of a potato.

Jack-in-the-bush, *n.* the navel-wort.

Jack-jag-the-flae, *n.* a tailor.

Jacko, *n.* the jackdaw; the magpie.

Jack's alive, *n.* a game played with a lighted piece of paper or match.

Jacksnipe, *n.* the snipe; the dunlin.

Jacky-forty-feet, *n.* a centipede.

Jacky-tar, *n.* a sailor; the sailor's hornpipe.

Jacob's-ladder, *n.* the belladonna.

Jacobus, *n.* a gold coin, in value £18, 16s. Scots.

Jacolet, *n.* chocolate.

Jad, *n.* a jade; a worthless woman; a lass, girl; a mare, a horse; an old, worn-out horse.—*v.* to jade.

Jadder, *n.* the stomach.

Jadin, *n.* the stomach of a cow.

Jadstane, *n.* the common white pebble, found on the sand or beds of rivers.

Jae, *v.* used of water: to dash, surge.—*n.* a wave. Cf. Jaw.

Jaffled, *ppl. adj.* jaded.

Jag, *n.* calf-leather; a hunter-fashion of boots, jack-boot.

Jag, *n.* a leather bag or wallet; a pocket; a saddle-bag; a cloak-bag.

Jag, *n.* fatigue.

Jag, *v.* to 'jog,' jerk roughly.—*n.* a sharp jerk, a jolt; a rut.

Jag, *v.* to pierce, prick with a sharp instrument, thorn, &c.; to vex, irritate; to rankle; to pain.—*n.* a prick or tear made by nail, thorn, &c.; a thorn, prickle.

Jag-armed, *adj.* armed with a sharp point or sting.

Jager, *n.* a pedlar. Cf. Jagger.

Jagg, *n.* an iron collar formerly used as an instrument of punishment. Cf. Jougs.

Jagger, *n.* a prickle.

Jagger, *n.* a pedlar, a hawker, a fish-hawker; a boat, or 'jogger,' which is used to land the first-caught herrings in the deep-sea fishing.

Jagger-steamer, *n.* a steamer for the transport of herrings.

Jagget, *n.* a full sack or pocket dangling at every motion from an awkward position.

Jagget, *ppl. adj.* prickly.

Jaggie, *adj.* prickly; sharp-pointed; piercing.

Jaggie, *adj.* full of ruts; having a jerking or jolting motion.

Jag-the-flea, *n.* a contemptuous name for a tailor.

Jaip, *v.* to jape, jest.—*n.* a jest.

Jaiper, *n.* a jester, a buffoon.

Jairble, *v.* to spill here and there on a table in taking food.—*n.* in *pl.* a small portion of liquor left by one who has often been drinking from the same glass. Cf. Jirble.

Jairblins, *n.* dregs of tea, &c.; drops of liquid spilt here and there.

Jaisy, *n.* a wig. Cf. Gizz.

Jake, Jak, *v.* to trifle, dally; to waste time. Cf. Jauk.

Jake-easy, *adj.* quite willing.

Jaker, *n.* an idler, trifler.

Jakmen, *n.* a landlord's fighting retainers.

Jallup, *n.* a brisk purgative, jalap; something to stir one up.

†Jalouse, Jaloose, &c., *v.* to suspect; to guess, imagine.

Jalousings, *n.* suspicions.

Jalp, *v.* used of water: to dash and rebound in waves; to splash. Cf. Jaup.

Jam, *v.* to put to inconvenience; to press or 'corner' in an argument.

Jam, Jamb, *n.* a projection, buttress, or wing of a building; the projecting side of a fireplace; the upright support of a fireplace; a corner made by a projection; anything large and clumsy; a big, ugly animal.

Jamb-friends, *n.* intimate or fireside friends.

Jamb-, Jam-stane, *n.* the side stone of a fireplace.

Jamf, *v.* to mock; to trifle. Cf. Jamph.

Jamfle, *v.* to shuffle in walking. Cf. Jamphle.

Jamie, *n.* a rustic, clown.

Jammer, *v.* to cry fretfully. Cf. Yammer.

Jammerer, *n.* an incessant, foolish talker. Cf. Yammerer.

Jamp, *v. pret.* jumped.

Jamper, *n.* a tool for boring rocks, stones, &c., a jumper.

Jamph, *v.* to make game of; to mock, jeer, sneer; to shuffle, make false pretences; to act the part of a male jilt; to trifle, spend time idly; to walk slowly and idly, lounge. —*n.* a mock, jeer, sneer; an habitual trifler; trifling over work.

Jamph, *v.* to tire, fatigue; to destroy by jogging or friction; to chafe; to drive to difficulties, straits, or extremities; to travel with extreme difficulty, as through mire; to trudge, plod.

Jampher, *n.* a male jilt; an idler; a scoffer.

Jamphing, *n.* the act of a male jilt.

Jamphit, *ppl. adj.* reduced to extremities.

Jamphle, *v.* to shuffle in walking owing to too wide shoes.

Jampt, *v. pret.* jumped.

Jander, *v.* to talk foolishly. Cf. Jaunder.

Jandies, *n.* jaundice.

Janet-jo, *n.* a children's game; a dramatic entertainment among young rustics.

†Jangle, *v.* to prattle, chatter.

Jangler, *n.* a prater; a quarreller, wrangler.

Janiveer, *n.* January.

Jank, *v.* to trifle. —*n.* a shuffling trick, giving one the slip.

Janker, *n.* a long pole attached to two wheels, for carrying logs fastened to it by chains.

Jankit, *ppl. adj.* fatigued.

Jank off, *v.* to run off.

Jank-the-labour, *v.* to trifle at work. —*n.* a trifler at work.

Janner, *v.* to talk foolishly. Cf. Jaunder.

Jannerer, *n.* an idle, foolish talker.

Jannock, *n.* a thick oatmeal bannock.

Jaut, *v.* to go on a pleasure-trip; to trip along. —*n.* an excursion, jaunt.

Janty, *adj.* cheerful.

Januar, Janwar, *n.* January.

Jap, *v.* used of water: to dash in waves. Cf. Jaup.

Japin, *n.* a jerk, smart stroke. Cf. Jaupin.

Japper, *n.* a hollow, broken wave.

Japple, *v.* to stamp on clothes when washing them; to get the feet wet. —*n.* a liquid mess. Cf. Jabble.

Jarble, *n.* an old, tattered garment.

Jarg, *v.* to make a harsh, grating or creaking sound; to creak. —*n.* a harsh, grating or shrill sound as of a rusty or creaking hinge. Cf. Girg.

Jarg, *n.* a trick played on one.

Jargative, *adj.* disputatious.

Jargle, *v.* to produce a shrill sound repeatedly.

†Jargon, *n.* chatter; banter.

Jargoning, *n.* idle talk, chattering.

Jar-hole, *n.* a sink, 'jaw-hole.'

Jarie, *n.* a boy's marble.

Jarness, *n.* a marshy place. Cf. Jerniss.

Jarr, *v.* to wrangle, quarrel; to disturb, ruffle.

Jaskin, *n.* a person occasionally employed in work to which he has not been regularly bred. Cf. Joskin.

Jaskit, *ppl. adj.* jaded, worn out, 'disjaskit.'

Jasp, *n.* a spot, blemish; a particle. Cf. Jesp.

Jass, *n.* a violent throw, dash; a heavy blow; the noise of a heavy blow. —*v.* to dash, throw with violence.

Jassich, *n.* a dull, heavy blow or fall. —*v.* to shake violently. Cf. Jossich.

Jatter, *v.* of the teeth: to chatter.

Jaub, *v.* to prick sharply. Cf. Jab.

Jaubber, *v.* to chatter, talk idly; to speak rapidly and indistinctly. —*n.* chatter, idle talk, jabber. Cf. Gabber.

Jauchle, *v.* to walk as with feeble joints; to make shift, do with difficulty. —*n.* a shift.

Jaud, *n.* a jade; an old, done horse. Cf. Jad.

Jaudie, *n.* the stomach of a pig; a 'pudding'; a pudding of oatmeal and lard, with onions and pepper, enclosed in a sow's stomach.

Jaudie, *n.* a little jade, a little girl running wild on the streets, ragged, dirty, and unkempt.

Jaug, *n.* a leather bag or wallet; in *pl.* saddlebags. Cf. Jag.

Jauk, *v.* used of shoes: to be too large and loose upon the feet in walking.

Jauk, *v.* to trifle, spend time idly; to walk slowly, waste time in walking. —*n.* an idler, a trifler over his work, trifling over work.

Jauk, *v.* to dodge ; to stoop, duck. Cf. Jouk.

Jauker, *n.* a trifler, idler.

Jaukery, *n.* joking, trifling.

Jaukin, *n.* delay ; idling, trifling, dallying ; flirting.—*ppl. adj.* habitually trifling over work.

Jaumle, *v.* to jumble ; to shake.

Jaumph, *v.* to travel with exertion. Cf. Jamph.

Jaumph, *n.* fun, a joke. Cf. Jamph.

Jaumpt, *v. pret.* jumped.

Jaunder, Jauner, *v.* to talk idly and foolishly ; to maunder.—*n.* idle talk ; rambling conversation ; a foolish talker.

Jaunder about, *v.* to go idly about from place to place with no proper object.

Jaunt, *v.* to trip along ; to go jauntily.

Jaunt, *v.* to taunt, gibe, jeer.—*n.* a taunt, a gibe.

Jaunt-coal, *n.* a kind of coal.

Jaunting-bottle, *n.* a pocket-flask.

Jauntingly, *adv.* jauntily.

Jaunty, *adj.* cheerful. Cf. Janty.

Jaup, *v.* used of water : to dash and rebound in waves ; of the liquid contents of a vessel : to dash against its side ; to splash ; to bespatter with mud or water ; to spill ; to throw water, &c., over anything or any person.—*n.* a dash of water ; a broken wave ; a short, cross sea ; a spot or splash of mud, dirty water, &c.; a quantity of liquid ; dregs ; the sound made by shoes full of water ; a slap, a slight blow ; ruin, destruction.

Jaup, *v.* to fatigue, weary.

Jaupie, Jauppie, *v.* to spill, scatter, separate into small portions of liquid.

Jaupin, *n.* a jerk, a smart stroke.—*ppl. adj.* breaking in waves.

Jaur, *v.* to quarrel ; to jar. Cf. Jarr.

Jaur-hole, *n.* a sink, 'jaw-hole.'

Jaurnoch, *n.* filth ; washings of dishes, &c.

Jave, *v.* to push hither and thither. Cf. Jeve.

Jave, *n.* the upper crust of a loaf of bread.

Javel, *n.* a blow, an injury.

Jaw, *n.* talk, chatter ; abusive or insolent talk ; coarse raillery.—*v.* to talk, chatter ; to vituperate, give insolence or abusive language.

Jaw, *v.* used of water : to dash, splash, surge ; to dash or pour a quantity of water.—*n.* a dash or spurt of water ; a quantity of water thrown out with a jerk or dash ; a wave, billow, breaker ; a large quantity of any liquid.

Jaw-blade, *n.* the jaw.

Jaw-box, *n.* a sink under a tap ; an indoor sink for dirty water.

Jawcked, *ppl. adj.* baffled in an attempt ; deceived with hope.

Jawd, *n.* a jade ; an old, worn-out horse, &c. Cf. Jad.

Jawdie, *n.* the stomach of a pig ; a 'pudding.' Cf. Jaudie.

Jaw-hole, *n.* a place into which dirty water, &c., are thrown ; a cesspool, midden ; a sink leading to a sewer.

Jaw-lock, *n.* lock-jaw.

Jawner, *v.* to talk foolishly.—*n.* in *pl.* foolish prattle. Cf. Jaunder.

Jawp, *v.* used of water : to dash and rebound in waves.—*n.* in *pl.* spots of mire, &c., thrown on a person. Cf. Jaup.

Jawp, *n.* a jape ; a nasty, mean trick.

Jawther, *v.* to engage in idle or frivolous talk.—*n.* in *pl.* idle, frivolous talk.

Jay-piet, -pyet, *n.* the jay.

Jay-teal, *n.* the common teal.

†**Jeal,** *v.* to freeze ; to be benumbed with cold ; to congeal as jelly.—*n.* extreme cold ; jelly Cf. Geal.

Jealous, *adj.* suspicious, apprehensive. Cf. Jalouse.

†**Jealouse,** *v.* to suspect. Cf. Jalouse.

Jealousy, *n.* suspicion.

Jeanie, *n.* a generic name for a country damsel.

Jeast, *n.* a joist.

Jebber, *v.* to chatter, to jabber.—*n.* in *pl.* idle talk ; absurd chattering. Cf Jibber.

Jeck, *v.* to neglect a piece of work. Cf. Jauk.

Jecko, *n.* the jackdaw ; the magpie.

Jeddart, *adj.* connected with Jedburgh.

Jeddart-cast, *n.* a legal trial after the infliction of punishment.

Jeddart-jug, *n.* a brass jug containing about eight gills, used as a standard of dry and liquid measure.

Jeddart-jury, *n.* a jury that tries a case after the infliction of punishment.

Jeddart-justice, *n.* punishment before trial ; a general condemnation or acquittal.

Jeddart-law, *n.* punishment before trial.

Jeddart-staff, *n.* a kind of battle-axe ; a halbert.

Jedge, *n.* the order or warrant of a Dean of Guild.

Jedgry, *n.* the act of gauging.

Jee, *v.* to stir, move ; to cause to move ; to move aside ; to swerve.—*n.* a turn, a swerve ; a side-motion.—*int.* a call to horses. Cf. Gee.

Jee, *n.* a fit of ill-temper ; a knack. Cf. Gee.

Jeeack, Jceak, *v.* to squeak, to creak.—*n.* a creaking noise.

Jeeble-jabble, *n.* any weak fluid, any mixture spoilt by being tossed about. Cf. Jabble.

Jeedge, *v.* to judge ; to adjudge.

Jeeg, *v.* to creak.—*n.* a creaking noise.—*adv.* with a creaking noise.

Jeeg, *n.* a silly fellow; a giddy girl; a prostitute.

Jeeg, *v.* to dance briskly; to trot, walk briskly. Cf. Jig.

Jeeg, *v.* to taunt; to scoff.—*n.* a taunt; a gibe; an oddity.

Jeeg, *v.* to laugh in a suppressed fashion; to quiz.—*n.* fun, frolic.

Jeegets, *n.* little sounding-boards, pegs, and wheels in a piece of machinery.

Jeeggit, *v.* to move from side to side; to jog, to ride or walk at a jog-trot.

Jeegin, *n.* a creaking sound.

Jeegle, *v.* to jog; to shake about.—*n.* a slight jerk. Cf. Giggle.

Jeegle, *v.* to make a jingling or creaking noise.—*n.* the creaking of a door on its hinges.

Jeegler, *n.* an unfledged bird.

†Jeel, *v.* to freeze; to congeal as jelly.—*n.* extreme cold; jelly. Cf. Geal.

Jeelie, *n.* jelly.

Jeelie-piece, *n.* a piece of bread spread with jelly.

Jeelie-pig, *n.* a jelly-jar.

Jeelt, *ppl. adj.* chilled, frozen; jellied.

Jeer, *v.* to scorn, mock.

Jeery, *adj.* jesting.

Jeest, *n.* a joist.

Jeestie, *n.* a joke; a jesting matter or manner. —*adj.* jesting.

Jeet, *n.* a worthless person; a term of contempt.

Jeetle, *v.* to delay; to be idle. Cf. Juitle.

Jeetle, *n.* a small quantity.—*v.* to spill, shake over. Cf. Geetle.

Jeety, *adj.* bright; neat.—*adv.* neatly.

Jeezy, *n.* a wig. Cf. Gizz, Gizzy.

Jeggin, *ppl. adj.* creaking. Cf. Gig.

Jeggle-jaggle, *v.* to waver to and fro in order to save one's self from a fall.

Jehoy, *v.* to cease, give over.

Jeissle, *n.* a multitude of things thrown together without order.

Jeist, *n.* a joist.

†Jeistiecor, *n.* a jacket; a waistcoat with sleeves. Cf. Justiecoat.

Jellily, *adv.* merrily, gaily.

†Jelly, *adj.* upright; worthy; excellent in its kind; pleasant, agreeable; jolly. Cf. Gellie.

Jellyflower, *n.* the clove-pink; the wallflower. Cf. Gilly-flower.

Jellyteen, *n.* gelatine.

†Jelouse, *v.* to suspect. Cf. Jalouse.

Jemmies, *n.* a species of woollen cloth.

Jen, *n.* a generic name for a country damsel.

Jenk, *v.* to elude. Cf. Jink.

Jenkin's-hen, *n.* a hen that never knew a cock; an old maid.

Jennock, *adj.* fair, honest.—*phr.* 'to do the jennock,' to behave fairly. Cf. Gennick.

Jenny, *n.* a spinning-wheel.

Jenny, *n.* a generic name for a country damsel.

Jenny, *n.* a centipede.

Jenny-a'-thing shop, *n.* a general dealer's shop.

Jenny-cut-throat, *n.* the whitethroat.

Jenny-guid-spinner, *n.* the daddy-long-legs.

Jenny-heron, *n.* the heron.

Jenny-langlegs, *n.* the daddy-long-legs.

Jenny Mac, *n.* a girls' game.

Jenny-mony-feet, *n.* a species of centipede.

Jenny-nettle, *n.* the daddy-long-legs.

Jenny-spinner, *n.* the daddy-long-legs; a toy, a teetotum.

Jenny-wren, *n.* the wren.

Jenny Wullock, *n.* a woman who gives no trouble in child-bearing.

†Jentie, *adj.* courteous; genteel; dainty, neat; tasteful. Cf. Genty.

Jeoparty-trot, *n.* a quick motion between walking and running; a contemptuous designation for one who walks in this fashion; a coward.

Jeoperd, *n.* a risky undertaking; a bold venture.

Jerg, *v.* to creak.—*n.* a creaking sound. Cf. Girg.

Jerk, *v.* to eject a person; to walk smartly; to make a splashing sound as of water in one's shoes; to move, to rise briskly or suddenly.—*n.* a smart blow; a stroke of good fortune; a trick; an instant.

Jerkin, *n.* a beating, thrashing.

Jerkin, *n.* a gathering, or kind of low picnic.

Jerkined, *adj.* wearing a jerkin.

Jerniss, *n.* the state of being soaked with water. Cf. Jarness.

Jeroboam, *n.* a large bottle, bowl, or goblet; its contents.

Jesmie, *n.* jasmine.

Jesp, *n.* a gap in the woof; a seam in one's clothes.

Jessie, *n.* a wig. Cf. Gizz.

Jet, Jett, *n.* to strut; to flaunt about.

Jethart, *adj.* relating to Jedburgh. Cf. Jeddart.

Jether, *v.* to talk idly. Cf. Jawther.

Jet-tribe, *n.* crows.

Jeuk, *v.* to stoop, duck. Cf. Jouk.

Jeuk, *n.* a duck.

Jeve, *v.* to push hither and thither.—*n.* a push with the elbow.

Jevel, *n.* a rascal, ne'er-do-weel; a 'gaol-bird.'

Jevel, Jevvel, *v.* to joggle; to shake; to spill a large quantity of any liquid at once; to move obliquely.—*n.* the dashing of water.

Jevelor, *n.* a gaoler. Cf. Geevelor, Jivvle.

Jew, *v.* to cheat, defraud.

Jewel, *n.* a term of endearment.

Jew's-ears, *n.* a species of lichen.

Jew's-roll, *n.* a penny loaf, round on the top, and with a reddish-brown glaze.

Jib, Jibb, *v.* to milk a cow closely ; to fleece.

Jibber, *v.* to chatter, talk nonsense.—*n.* in *pl.* silly talk.

Jibberage, *n.* gibberish.

Jibber-jabber, *v.* to talk foolishly.—*n.* noisy, foolish talk.

Jibbings, *n.* the last milk, or 'strippings,' taken from a cow.

Jibble, *v.* to spill ; to lose, to destroy ; to cook badly.—*n.* a quantity of any liquid. Cf. Geeble.

Jick, *v.* to avoid by a sudden jerk of the body ; to elude ; with *school,* to play truant. — *n.* a sudden jerk ; the act of eluding.

Jicker, *v.* to ride smartly ; to trot ; to go quickly about anything.

Jickering, *ppl. adj.* gaudy but tawdry in dress.

Jicky, *adj.* used of a horse : apt to shy and swerve suddenly.

Jie, *v.* to turn aside quickly. Cf. Gee, Jee.

Jie, *int.* a call to a horse to go on. Cf. Gee.

Jiffing, *n.* an instant.

Jiff-jaffs, *n.* a fit of the 'blues.'

Jiffle, *v.* to shuffle restlessly ; to fidget.—*n.* a shuffling movement ; a fidget.

Jiffy, Jiffey, *n.* an instant ; a hurry.—*v.* to hurry.—*adv.* with haste.

Jig, *n.* a jerk, shake, swing ; a sudden pull ; an illegal fishing instrument.—*v.* to dance vigorously or boisterously ; to play the fiddle ; to walk briskly ; to jerk, tilt ; to rock or sway, as a ladder under a person's movement ; to give a sudden pull ; to catch fish illegally with a 'jig.' Cf. Gig.

Jig, *n.* a certain measure of yarn ; a method of measuring yarn.

Jig, *n.* a spinning-top ; anything that whirls ; a winnowing-fan. Cf. Gig.

Jig, *v.* to creak. Cf. Jeeg.

Jiggate, *n.* a sail shaped like a leg of mutton.

Jigger, *n.* one who 'jigs' for herrings.

Jigger, *n.* a contemptuous designation applied to a person ; an oddity.

Jigger, *n.* a vehicle for carrying trees from a wood ; a 'janker.'

†Jigget, Jiggot, *n.* a leg of mutton, a 'gigot.'

Jigget, *v.* to jog ; to move from side to side. Cf. Jeeggit.

Jiggle, *v.* to make a jingling noise ; to creak. —*n.* a creaking noise. Cf. Jeegle.

Jiggle, *v.* to shake, jog.—*n.* a slight jerk or shake. Cf. Giggle.

Jiggle-jaggle, *adj.* irregular, uneven, zigzag.

Jile, *n.* gaol.—*v.* to put in gaol.

Jiling, *n.* imprisonment.

Jill-bow, *n.* a legacy. Cf. Gilbow.

Jillet, Jilly, *n.* a giddy girl ; a flirt, a jilt ; a young woman entering puberty.

Jill-flirt, *n.* a giddy, flirting girl.

Jilp, *v.* to dash water upon one.—*n.* a spurt of water. Cf. Gilp.

Jilp, *n.* a big, fat person or animal ; a person of disagreeable temper. Cf. Gilp.

Jilt, *v.* to throw water upon one.—*n.* a dash of water.

Jim, *adj.* neat, spruce. Cf. Jimp.

Jimmer, *v.* to make a disagreeable noise on a violin.—*n.* the sound made by a badly played violin.

Jimmy, *adj.* neat, spruce, smart ; handy, dexterous ; neatly made.

Jimp, *n.* a thin piece of leather, put between the outer and inner soles of a shoe.

Jimp, *adj.* slender, small, neat ; scanty ; tight ; narrow ; short in quantity.—*adv.* scarcely ; straitly.—*v.* to curtail, contract ; to make too narrow ; to give too little measure, weight, room, &c.

Jimp, *n.* a coat, a loose jacket ; in *pl.* easy stays, open in front. Cf. Jump.

Jimp, *v.* to leap.

Jimper, *n.* a fisherman's jersey. Cf. Jumper.

Jimpey, *n.* a short gown without skirts, reaching only to the middle, worn by cottage women ; a kind of easy stays.

Jimply, *adv.* scarcely ; narrowly.

Jimp-middled, -waisted, *adj.* slender-waisted.

Jimpy, *adj.* slender.—*adv.* slenderly ; tightly.

Jimrie-cosie, *n.* a comfortable supply of drink.

Jimy, *n.* a white pudding.

Jin, *n.* the bolt or lock of a door.

Jinch, *adj.* neat, spruce, smart.

Jing, *n.* jingo, used in common oaths.

Jing-bang, *n.* in *phr.* the 'hale jing-bang,' the whole party or affair.

Jingle, *n.* gravel, shingle.

Jingle, *n.* the smooth water at the back of a stone in a river.

Jingle, *n.* noisy mirth ; an instant.

Jingle-the-bonnet, *n.* a game in which the players put a coin each into a cap, and, after shaking them together, throw them on the ground. He who has most heads, when it is his turn to jingle, gains the coins put into the cap.

Jingle-the-key, *n.* the cry of the yellow-ammer.

Jingling, *ppl. adj.* noisy, chattering ; wordy and unmeaning.

Jingo-ring, -ringle, *n.* a girls' game in which, hand in hand, they dance in a circle singing.

Jinipperous, *adj.* spruce ; trim ; stiff.

Jink, *n.* a chink ; a long, narrow aperture, as when a window is slightly open.

Jink, *v.* to elude; to dodge, swerve quickly aside; to slouch behind a wall; to play tricks; to frolic; to cheat, trick; to move nimbly, turn quickly; to escape, avoid; to spend time idly; to move the arm, as in fiddling; with *in*, to enter a place suddenly and secretly; to dance briskly.—*n.* a sudden turn; a slip; a trick; a frolic; an escape; a game; a particular point or turn in a dispute.

Jinkam's-, Jinking's-hen, *n.* an old maid. Cf. Jenkin's-hen.

Jinker, *n.* a fast horse; a lively, giddy girl; an immoral woman; a wag.

Jinket, *v.* to junket, to make merry; to gad about.

Jinkie, *n.* a small chink.

Jinkie, *n.* a children's game of sudden turns to avoid being caught.

Jinking, *n.* a frolic, trick; a quick movement. —*ppl. adj.* wriggling; dexterous; evasive; crafty; gay, sportive.

Jinniprous, *adj.* trim; spruce. Cf. Jinipperous.

Jinny, *n.* a generic name for a country girl. Cf. Jenny.

Jipper, *v.* to peril; to jeopard.

Jipperty, Jippordy, *n.* jeopardy.

Jirble, *v.* to shake the liquid contents of a vessel so as to spill them; to pour out unsteadily; to empty a small quantity of liquid backwards and forwards from one vessel to another.—*n.* in *pl.* the dregs left by one often drinking from the same glass, cup, &c.

Jirbling, *n.* the spilling of liquids; the changing of liquids from vessel to vessel; in *pl.* dregs of tea, &c.; spots of liquid spilt here and there.

Jird, *v.* to gird; to strike, push.—*n.* a push. Cf. Gird.

Jirg, *v.* to creak, gurgle, jar.—*n.* a creaking sound. Cf. Girg.

Jirger, *n.* anything that causes a creaking sound.

Jirgle, *v.* to empty a small quantity of liquor from one vessel to another.—*n.* a small quantity of liquor; dregs left in a glass.

Jirgum, *v.* to jerk, as if using a fiddle-bow.

Jirk, *v.* to gnash one's teeth, to 'chirk.' Cf. Chirk.

Jirk, *v.* to unload, disburden; to unload a vessel so as to defraud the revenue.

Jirk, *v.* to jerk; to fidget. Cf. Jerk.

Jirkin, *n.* a sort of bodice worn by women.

Jirkinet, *n.* a woman's outer jacket or 'jirkin.'

Jirt, *v.* to squirt. Cf. Chirt.

Jirt, *n.* a jerk.

Jisk, *v.* to caper.

Jisp, *n.* a flaw, fracture, or small orifice. Cf. Jesp.

Jist, *adv.* just.

Jit, *n.* sour or dead liquor. Cf. Joot.

Jivvle, *n.* a gaol; a house sparsely furnished like a gaol. Cf. Jevelor.

Jize, *n.* in *phr.* 'jize be here,' an expletive, 'joys be here.'

†**Jizzen, Jizzen-bed**, *n.* child-bed. Cf. Gizzen.

Jizzy, *n.* a wig. Cf. Gizz, Gizzy.

Jo, *n.* a sweetheart; a term of endearment, 'my dear.' Cf. Joe.

Joan Thomson's man, *n.* a man who yields to the influence of his wife.

Joater, *v.* to wade in mire.

Joatrel, *n.* one who wades in mire.

Job, *n.* a prickle.—*v.* to prick, prod.

Job, *n.* a difficult or unfortunate affair; an affair; in *pl.* excrement.—*v.* to trade in; to act improperly.

Jobber, *n.* one who does odd jobs of work.

Jobbernowl, *n.* the head.

Jobbet, *ppl. adj.* fatigued. Cf. Jabb.

Jobbie, *adj.* prickly.

Jobbie, *n.* a little job, a small piece of business.

Job-troot, *n.* a jog-trot.

Jock, *n.* a country fellow; a bull.

Jockey, *n.* a gipsy; a strolling minstrel.

Jockey-coat, *n.* a greatcoat.

Jockey's-grun, -ground, *n.* a boys' game.

Jock-hack, *n.* a rough-rider; a horse-breaker.

Jock-hasty, *n.* a coarse riddle for rough-dressing grain.

Jock Hector, *n.* an excl. equivalent to 'Jack Robinson.'

Jockie, Jocky, *n.* a country fellow, rustic; a pig.

Jockie-blindman, *n.* blind-man's buff.

Jock-landy, *n.* a foolish, destructive person.

Jock-leg, *n.* a large clasp-knife. Cf. Jockteleg.

Jock-neb, *n.* a turkey-cock's nose; the bloodless appearance of a half-starved bard's nose.

Jock-needle-Jock-preen, *n.* in *phr.* to 'play Jock-needle-Jock-preen,' to play tricks on one, to play fast and loose.

Jock-startle-a-stobie, *n.* exhalations from the ground on a warm summer day.

Jock Tamson, *n.* whisky.

Jock-te-leear, *n.* a small almanac, the weather predictions of which seldom came true.

†**Jockteleg, Jock-tae-leg, Jocktaleg**, *n.* a clasp-knife; a large pocket-knife; a large knife for kitchen use.

Jocktie, *n.* the wheat-ear; the whin-chat; the stone-chat.

Jocky-haggis, *n.* part of the intestines; the stomach.

Jocky-Ketch, *n.* a hangman, 'Jack Ketch.'

Jocky-landy, *n.* anything blazing foolishly given as a child's plaything.

Joctibeet, *n.* the wheat-ear; the whin-chat; the stone-chat. Cf. Jocktie.

Joe, *n.* a sweetheart; a term of affection, 'my darling.'

Jog, *n.* a slow, steady pace.

Jog, *v.* to prick or pierce.—*n.* a prick, a thorn. Cf. Jag.

Jogg, *v.* to confine in the 'jougs' or pillory. —*n.* in *pl.* the 'jougs.' Cf. Jougs.

Jogger, *n.* a state of tremulousness.

Joggle, *v.* to lurch; to jog on.—*n.* a push; a lurch; the reeling of a carriage.

Jogglie, *adj.* shaky; tottering.

John, *n.* a country fellow; a rustic. Cf. Jock.

John, *n.* a demijohn.

John Barley, *n.* 'John Barleycorn.'

John Barleycorn, *n.* malt liquor; whisky.

Johndal, *n.* a contemptuous name for a young ploughman or 'bothy' lad.

John Dominie, *n.* a schoolmaster.

John Heezlum Peezlum, *n.* the man in the moon.

Johnie Barley, *n.* 'John Barleycorn.'

John Jillets, *n.* a term of contempt for a man.

Johnny, *n.* a countryman; a greenhorn, a simpleton; a half-glass of whisky; whisky.

Johnny-cheats, *n.* a cheating pedlar.

Johnny Ged's hole, *n.* a grave-digger.

Johnny Lindsay, *n.* a young people's game.

Johnny Maut, *n.* 'John Barleycorn.'

Johnny Napier, *n.* a note of the Galloway Bank, of which the late John Napier of Mollance was manager.

Johnny Pyot's term-day, *n.* the day after the Day of Judgment; never and for ever.

Johnny-raw, *n.* a country clown, a greenhorn.

Johnny Rover, *n.* a boys' game.

Johnny-stand-still, *n.* a scarecrow.

John o' Groat's buckie, *n.* the *Cyprœa Europœa.*

Johnsmas, *n.* St John's Day, Midsummer Day.

John's (St) nut, *n.* two nuts growing together in one husk, supposed to secure one against witchcraft.

Johnstone's (St) ribband, -tippet, *n.* a halter for hanging a criminal.

John Thomson's man, *n.* a husband who yields to his wife's influence.

Joice, *n.* juice.

Joined, *ppl. adj.* in *phr.* 'a joined member,' a church member.

Joinering, *n.* carpentry, joinery.

Joiner-word, *n.* the password of a carpenters' guild.

Joiner-work, *n.* carpentry.

Joint, *n.* in *phr.* 'a word out of joint,' a word improper in any respect, as approaching profanity or indecency.

Joint-harl, *v.* to point a wall or fill its joints with mortar.

Jointure, *n.* a juncture.

†**Joise,** *v.* to enjoy, to possess. Cf. Joyse.

Joiter, *n.* an idler, loiterer, ne'er-do-weel.

Joke-, Jack-, Jock-fellow, *n.* an intimate, one treated as an equal, a yoke-fellow.

Joke-fellow-like, *adj.* apparently intimate; friendly.

Jokie, *adj.* jocular; fond of a joke.

†**Jolliment,** *n.* mirth, jollity.

Jollock, *adj.* jolly; hearty; fat, healthy.

Jolly-cheekit, *adj.* bright, comely.

Jolster, *n.* a mixture; a hodge-podge; a quantity of ill-prepared victuals.

Joog-jooging, *ppl.* going pit-a-pat.

Jook, *v.* to duck or stoop so as to evade a blow. Cf. Jouk.

Jookerie, *n.* juggling. Cf. Joukerie.

Jookery-cookery, *n.* artful management.

Jookery-pawkrie, -paikerie, *n.* artful management; juggling; roguery.

Jookie, *n.* a slight swerve.

†**Joop, Joopan,** *n.* a woman's skirt or short-gown. Cf. Jupe.

Joot, *n.* sour or dead liquor; used contemptuously of tea; a tippler.—*v.* to tipple.

Jordan, *n.* a chamber-pot; a urinal; an open cesspool.

†**Jordeloo,** *n.* a warning cry formerly given by servants in the higher stories of Edinburgh houses when about to throw dirty water, &c., into the streets; the contents of the vessel used. Cf. Gardyloo.

Jore, *n.* a mixture of semi-liquid substances; a mire, slough.

Jorg, *n.* the noise of shoes when full of water. Cf. Girg.

Jorgle, *n.* the noise of broken bones grating.

Jorinker, *n.* a bird of the titmouse species.

Jork, *v.* to make a grating noise. Cf. Chirk.

Jorram, *n.* a slow and melancholy boat-song; a song in chorus.

Jorum, *n.* a loud thunder-crash.

Jorum, *n.* in *phr.* 'push about the jorum,' the name of an old Scottish reel, or the tune adapted to it.

Jorum-jingler, *n.* ? a fiddler.

Joskin, *n.* a raw country youth; a farm-servant; a yokel.—*adj.* of the nature of a 'joskin.'

Joss, *v.* to jostle.—*n.* a jostle.

Jossich, *n.* a dull, heavy blow or fall; the dull sound of such.—*v.* to shake or dash violently; to shake to pieces; to jerk heavily backwards and forwards. Cf. Jass, Yachis.

Jossle, *v.* to push through a crowd; to hustle; to shake.—*n.* a push, shake; a big, clumsy cart or gig.—*adv.* roughly, by pushing.

Jossler, *n.* a big person of rude manners; an ugly, clumsy conveyance.

Jossling, *ppl. adj.* wobbling, having an unsteady motion.

Jot, *n.* a light job; an occasional piece of work; in *pl.* petty domestic work.—*v.* with *about*, to engage in light kinds of work.

Jotter, *v.* to engage idly in light and petty kinds of work; to do odd jobs.

Jotteral, *n.* odd, mean, or dirty work; anything about to fall in pieces.

Jotterie, *n.* odd or dirty work.

Jotterie-horse, *n.* a horse of all work.

Jotterie-man, *n.* a man of all work.

Jotterie-wark, *n.* work of all kinds, such as does not belong to a regular servant.

Jottle, *v.* to busy one's self with trifles, to accomplish little.

Jottler, *n.* a man of all work, an 'orra' man.

Jottling-man, *n.* a 'jottler.'

Jottrell, *n.* odd, mean, or dirty work. Cf. Jotteral.

Joucat, *n.* a liquid measure, a gill.

Jouf, *n.* a sort of 'bed-gown.' Cf. **Jupe.**

Joug, *v.* to shake, jog, jolt.

Jougging, *n.* jolting, 'joggling.'

Jougs, *n.* bad liquors.

†**Jougs**, *n.* an instrument of punishment, of the nature of the pillory, placed on the offender's neck.

Jouk, Jouck, *v.* to duck so as to avoid a blow; to evade, dodge; to swerve suddenly; used of a stream: to wind, meander; of a light: to flicker, appear and disappear; to bow, make obeisance, curtsy; to cheat, swindle; to jilt; to play truant.—*n.* a swerve, stoop, or duck to avoid a blow; a bow, curtsy; a shelter from a storm or a blow; a dodge, trick.

Jouker, *n.* a truant.

Joukerie, *n.* trickery, double-dealing, jugglery. Cf. Jookerie.

Jouking, *ppl. adj.* cunning, deceitful.—*n.* artful conduct.

Joukit, *ppl. adj.* cunning.

Jouk-the-squeel, *n.* a truant from school.

Jouky-daidles, *n.* a term of affection given to a child.

Joundie, *v.* to jog with the elbow; to jostle; to gush.—*n.* a shake; a push, blow; a sudden impulse to one side. Cf. Jundy.

†**Joup**, *n.* a woman's skirt or short petticoat. Cf. Jupe.

Jourdan, *n.* a chamber-pot. Cf. Jordan.

Journey-wark, *n.* journeyman's work.

†**Jouse**, *adj.* proud, joyous.

Joust, *n.* a joist.

Joustle, *v.* to push through a crowd. Cf. Jossle.

Jow, *v.* to ring or toll a bell; to knell, ring, toll; to ring a bell by moving its tongue; to move, to attract attention; to rock, roll; to surge, come in waves or floods; to spill the liquid contents of a vessel by moving it from side to side; used of a river: to roll forcibly in flood; with *in*, to ring a bell quickly, so as to indicate that the ringing will soon stop; with *on*, to jog on.—*n.* a knock, push; a single pull or toll of a bell; the ringing of a bell; the sound of a bell; the dashing of water in waves, wavelets, or ripples; water thus dashed.

Jow, Jowie, *n.* a fir-cone. Cf. Ewe.

Jowgs, *n.* the 'jougs.' Cf. Jougs.

Jowing-in-bell, *n.* the curfew-bell.

Jowl, *n.* in *phrs.* 'jowl to jowl,' close together, cheek to cheek; 'cheek for jowl,' side by side.

Jowl, *v.* to jolt or shake rudely.—*n.* the knell or clang of a bell.

Jowler, *n.* a heavy-jawed dog; a foxhound.

Jowp, *n.* a skull, head; a term of contempt, denoting stupidity.

Joy, *n.* a term of endearment or friendly address.

†**Joyeusity**, *n.* jollity, joyousness.

Joy-glad, *adj.* glad and joyous.

†**Joyse**, *v.* to enjoy; to possess.

Jubilee, *n.* any merry-making, as at the New Year.

Jubious, *adj.* dubious; suspicious; jealous.

Jubish, *v.* to suspect.—*adj.* dubious.

Jucat, *n.* a gill measure. Cf. Joucat.

Juck, *n.* a duck.

Juck, Juckie, *n.* a large, white, earthenware marble.

Judge, *v.* to curse.

†**Judgeable**, *adj.* that may be judged.

Judgment, *n.* one's senses, wits.

Judgment-like, *adj.* threatening some token of divine judgment; mysterious; awful.

Judgment-timed, *adj.* indicative of judgment by coincidence of time.

Judicate, *v.* to think, imagine.

Judicious, *adj.* intelligent.

Juffle, *v.* to walk hastily; to shuffle.—*n.* in *pl.* old shoes down at the heels.

Juffler, *n.* a shuffler in walking.

Jug, *n.* an old measure of capacity kept at Stirling.

Juggie, *n.* a jug or small vessel for drinking punch.

Juggins, Juggons, *n.* rags.

Juggle, *v.* to cheat, swindle.

Juggle, *v.* to shake, 'joggle.'

Juggs, *n.* an iron collar on the neck of a criminal, which was fastened to a wall or post. Cf. Jougs.

Jugle, *v.* to cheat. Cf. Juggle.

Juice, *n.* gravy; sauce.

Juik, *v.* to duck, dodge.—*n.* a trick. Cf. Jouk.

†**Juip,** *n.* a woman's skirt; a flannel shirt. Cf. Jupe.

Juist, *adv.* very; quite; only. Cf. Just.

Juit, *n.* tasteless drink; dead liquor. Cf. Joot.

Juitle, *v.* to delay; to be idle, dilatory.

Juitlin', *ppl. adj.* dilatory; tricky, impudent.

Juke, *v.* to duck; to dodge; to evade. Cf. Jouk.

Juliflower, *n.* the gillyflower.

Jum, *n.* a clumsily-built, awkward-looking house.

Jum, *adj.* reserved; not affable.

Jumle, *v.* to jolt; to confuse; to muddle; to jumble. Cf. Jummel.

Jumly, *adj.* muddy, turbid.—*n.* the sediment of ale.

Jumm, *n.* the hollow moaning of the sea in a storm.

Jummel, Jummle, *v.* to jolt; to jumble.—*n.* a splash, dash; a shock.

Jummlie, *adj.* muddy. Cf. Jumly.

Jump, *n.* a coat, a loose jacket; in *pl.* easy stays, open in front.

Jump, *v.* used of a garment made too tight: to burst asunder; to tally, coincide; with *at,* to accept eagerly; used of a gun: to recoil at one's shoulder; of crops: to start growing.

Jump, *adj.* neat, slender, 'jimp.'

Jumpables, *n.* a bodice; stays.

Jumper, *n.* a maggot found in cheese, cooked meat, ham, &c.

Jumper, *n.* a fisherman's jersey.

Jumper-yarn, *n.* coarse worsted for knitting a 'jumper.'

Jumpie, *n.* a short-tailed spencer worn by women. Cf. Jump.

Jumping-cattle, *n.* fleas.

Jumping-jack, *n.* a child's toy made with a merry-thought, thread, and shoemaker's wax; a figure of a man made of pasteboard or thin wood, the limbs of which are pulled by a string; a fickle, unstable person.

Jumping-on-lid, *n.* the lid of a ship's cask in which pickled meat is kept ready for use. Cf. Harness-lid.

Jumping-rope, -tow, *n.* a skipping-rope.

Jump-strap, *n.* a strap for a pair of stays.

Jump-the-cuddy, *n.* a boys' game.

Jumze, *n.* anything larger than needful. Cf. Jum.

Junction, *n.* a juncture.

Juncturer, *n.* an old name for a greatcoat.

Jund, *n.* a large piece of anything. Cf. Junt.

Jund, *n.* a jolt. Cf. Junt.

Jundie, *n.* anything larger than strictly needful.

Jundie, Jundy, *v.* to jog with the elbow; to jostle; to move or rock from side to side; to gush.—*n.* a shake, push; a wrench causing pain; a blow, a dash, a blow from being knocked about; a sudden impulse to one side.

Jundy, *n.* the trot; the ordinary course.

Juniper, *n.* in *phr.* 'Janet Juniper's stinking butter,' a nickname for a wife's daughter whom no man will marry because of her laziness, conceit, and pride, and who, if married, would lie like stinking butter on her husband's stomach while she lived.

Juniper-nebbed, *adj.* self-conceited.

Junketin, *n.* a country festival; a merry-making.

Junkit, *adj.* stout, sturdy.

Junky, *adj.* stout, sturdy.

Junnice, *n.* a jostle; a blow; a jog.

Junnie, Junny, *v.* to jog; to shake a vessel containing liquor so as to produce the sound of dashing.—*n.* a severe blow, a painful sprain or wrench. Cf. Jundie.

Junrell, *n.* a large, irregular mass of stone or other hard matter.

Junt, *n.* a large piece of anything; a large quantity of any liquid; a squat, clumsy person.

Junt, *n.* a jolt; a heavy fall or blow.

†**Jupe, Jup,** *n.* a woman's skirt; a woman's short-gown, upper garment, or 'bed-gown'; a man's loose coat, a greatcoat; a flannel shirt or jacket; in *pl.* loose stays, a piece of flannel used instead of stays, 'jumps'; a kind of pelisse for children.

Jurble, *v.* to shake the liquid contents of a vessel so as to spill them. Cf. Jirble.

Jurg, Jurge, *v.* to make a creaking noise. Cf. Girg.

Jurnummle, *v.* to crush; to disfigure; to bamboozle.—*n.* the act of crushing or disfiguring.

Jurnal, *v.* to coagulate.

Jurr, *n.* the noise of a small waterfall descending among stones and gravel.

Jurr, *n.* a servant girl.

Jurram, *n.* a slow and melancholy boat-song. Cf. Jorram.

Jurrie-worrieing, *n.* a growling noise like that of a dog about to worry.

Juskal, *n.* a tale, traditional tale.

Just, *v.* to adjust.—*adj.* accurate, exact.

Just, *adv.* very, extremely; quite, only, none other than.

Justiciary-power, *n.* the power of judging in matters of life and death.

†**Justicoat, Justiecor,** *n.* a sleeved waistcoat. Cf. Jeistiecor.

Justify, *v.* to inflict capital punishment or other penalty; to punish arbitrarily; to judge; to acquit legally.

Just na, *int.* just so!

Just now, *adv.* immediately, by-and-by.

Jute, *n.* a jade, a term of reproach applied to a woman.

Jute, *n.* sour or dead liquor; a tasteless drink; a tippler.—*v.* to tipple. Cf. Joot.

Jute, *n.* whisky.

Jutter, *n.* a tippler.

Juttie, *n.* a tippler.

Juttle, *v.* to shake liquids; to tipple.

Juttler, *n.* a tippler.

Juttling, *ppl. adj.* weak, wishy-washy.

Juxter, *n.* a juggler.

Jybe, *v.* to taunt.—*n.* taunt, a gibe.

Jyple, *n.* a person with badly-made clothes.

Ka, *n.* the jackdaw. Cf. Kae.

†**Kabbelow,** *n.* salted codfish hung for a few days.

Kabbelow, *n.* potatoes and cabbage mashed together.

Kabbie-labbie, -llaby, -lyabbie, *n.* a wrangle, gabble.—*v.* to wrangle, dispute.

Kabbie-llabiein, *ppl. adj.* fretful.

Kach, *n.* excrement.—*v.* to void excrement. —*int.* an excl. warning children not to touch anything dirty.

Kacky, *v.* to void excrement; to befoul with excrement.

Kade, *n.* the sheep-louse. Cf. Kaid.

Kadgie, *adj.* in high spirits. Cf. Cadgie.

Kae, *n.* the jackdaw; a thievish or mischievous person; the jay; a neat, little person; the jackdaw's cry; a caw.—*v.* to caw.

Kae, *v.* to invite; in *phr.* 'kae me and I'll kae you,' invite me and I'll invite you. Cf. Call, Claw.

Kae, *int.* an excl. of disbelief, contempt, disgust.

Kaebie, *n.* the crop of a fowl. Cf. Gebbie.

Kae-hole, *n.* a jackdaw's hole or nest in a tower.

Kaery, *adj.* of many colours, applied to sheep. Cf. Gairie.

Kae-wattie, *n.* the jackdaw.

Kae-witted, *adj.* scatter-brained.

†**Kahute,** *n.* a little house; a ship's cabin. Cf. Cahute.

Kaiber, *n.* a pole, rafter. Cf. Caber.

Kaible, *n.* the crop of a fowl.

Kaid, *n.* the sheep-louse; in *pl.* a disease of sheep.

Kaid, *v.* used of cats: to desire the male. Cf. Kate.

Kaiding, *n.* the state of a cat desiring the male.

Kaiding-time, *n.* the time when a cat desires the male.

Kaif, *adj.* familiar.

Kaigh, *int.* an excl. of contempt, disgust. Cf. Kach.

Kail, *n.* a race at a wedding, the prize being a kiss from the bride.

Kail, *n.* colewort; broth made of colewort and other greens; food, dinner.

Kail-bell, *n.* the dinner-bell.

Kail-blade, *n.* a leaf of colewort.

Kail-broo, *n.* water in which colewort has been boiled.

Kail-brose, *n.* the scum of 'kail-broth' mixed with oatmeal.

Kail-broth, *n.* vegetable soup boiled with meat.

Kail-castock, -custock, *n.* the stem of the colewort.

Kail-cog, *n.* a wooden 'bicker' for holding broth, mashed colewort, &c.

Kail-gully, *n.* a large knife for cutting down and slicing colewort.

Kailie, *adj.* of colewort. Cf. Kailly.

Kail-kennin, *n.* cabbages and potatoes mashed together.

Kail-kirk, *n.* a Glassite church, where the members dined together after service.

Kailly, *adj.* used of colewort, cabbage, &c.: producing leaves fit for the pot; smeared with broth, greasy.

Kailly-brose, *n.* 'kail-brose.'

Kailly-worm, *n.* the cabbage caterpillar.

Kail-pat, *n.* a large broth-pot; the extreme division at either end of the space divided into eight parts, in the game of 'beds' or hop-scotch.

Kail-pat-whig, *n.* one who stops at home from church on Sundays.

Kail-root, -reet, *n.* the stump of a colewort-stem that has been cut.

Kail-runt, *n.* a colewort-stem stripped of its leaves; a full-grown plant of colewort; a term of contempt.

Kail-runtle, *n.* a 'kail-runt,' used contemptuously.

Kail-seed, *n.* colewort-seed; 'wild oats.'

Kail-seller, *n.* a greengrocer.

Kail-stick, *n.* a rod for stirring boiling broth.

Kail-stock, *n.* a plant of colewort, a 'castock.'

Kail-straik, *n.* straw laid on beams, anciently used instead of iron, for drying corn

Kail-supper, *n.* one who is fond of broth, a name given to Fifeshire people.

Kail-time, *n.* dinner-time.

Kailwife, *n.* a woman who sells colewort; a scold.

Kailworm, *n.* a caterpillar which feeds on 'kail' and cabbage; a tall, slender person dressed in green.

Kailyard, *n.* a kitchen-garden; a small cottage garden.

Kaim, *n.* a comb; a honeycomb.—*v.* to comb. Cf. Kem.

Kaim, *v.* with *down,* used of a horse: to strike with the forefeet; to rear.

Kaim, *n.* a low ridge; the crest of a hill; a pinnacle resembling a cock's comb; a camp or fortress; a mound.

Kaim-cleaner, *n.* horse-hair used for cleaning combs.

Kaiming-stock, *n.* the stock on which the combs were fixed for dressing wool, 'rippling' lint, and breaking flax.

Kain, *n.* rent in kind. Cf. Cane.

Kainer, *n.* a water-bailiff. Cf. Kenner.

Kaip, *v.* to keep.—*n.* possession. Cf. Keep.

Kaip, *v.* to catch. Cf. Kep.

Kair, *n.* mire; a puddle.

Kair, *v.* to take the broken straws and grass out of corn after threshing.

Kair, *v.* to toss to and fro; to mix up; to handle too much.—*n.* much handling.

Kaird, *n.* a gipsy, tinker. Cf. Caird.

Kaird-turners, *n.* small bad money forged by tinkers.

Kairins, *n.* pieces of straw, grass, &c., removed from newly-threshed grain by turning it over with outspread fingers.

Kairn, *n.* a heap of stones. Cf. Cairn.

Kairney, *n.* a small heap of stones.

Kairs, *n.* rocks through which there is an opening.

Kairy, *adj.* having different coloured stripes. —*n.* wool of different colours; a small breed of sheep. Cf. Kaery.

Kaisart, *n.* a cheese-press; a frame on which cheeses are placed to ripen.

Kaivan, *n.* the act of rearing; the act of climbing.

Kaive, *v.* to topple over; used of a horse: to toss the head, to paw the ground, rear, plunge; to climb; to push backwards and forwards; to walk awkwardly.—*n.* the act of climbing.

Kaiver, *v.* to waver in mind. Cf. Caiver.

Kaiving, *ppl. adj.* rearing and plunging, as a habit.

Kaivy, *n.* a great number of living creatures, especially human beings.

Kaizar, *n.* a 'kaisart.'

Kale, *n.* colewort. Cf. Kail.

Kalwart, *adj.* used of the weather: keen, very cold.

Kamb, Kame, *v.* to comb.—*n.* a comb; a honeycomb.

Kame, *n.* a low ridge; the crest of a hill. Cf. Kaim.

Kamshacle, *adj.* difficult to repeat. Cf. Camshauchle.

Kamster, *n.* a wool-comber.

Kane, *n.* rent in kind. Cf. Cane.

Kaner, *n.* a water-bailiff. Cf. Kainer, Kenner.

Kannie, *adj.* careful; prudent. Cf. Cannie.

Kaper, *n.* a piece of buttered oatcake bearing a piece of cheese. Cf. Caper.

Kaping, *n.* a coping.

Kar, *adj.* left-handed. Cf. Car.

Karrach, *n.* the game of 'shinty.'

Karriewhitchet, *n.* a fondling term for a child.

Karshab, *int.* a cry used in the game of 'shinty.'

Kartie, *n.* a kind of louse resembling a crab, a crab-louse.

Katabella, *n.* the hen-harrier.

Kate, *v.* used of cats: to desire the male. Cf. Kaid.

Katherane, *n.* a 'cateran' riever.

Kathil, *v.* to beat very severely; to pulp.— *n.* pulp; an egg beaten up.

Katie-, Katty-clean-doors, *n.* a child's name for the snow.

Katie-hunkers, *n.* sliding on the ice in a crouching position.

Katie-wren, *n.* the common wren.

Katty, *n.* the 'jack' in the game of bowls.

Katy-handed, *adj.* left-handed.

Kauch, *n.* a bustle, fluster, uneasiness of mind, anxiety.—*v.* to bustle, fluster. Cf. Caigh.

Kaur, *n.* calves.

Kaur-, Kaury-handit, *adj.* left-handed. Cf. Car.

Kave, *n.* a bottle; a spirit-flask.

Kave, *n.* a hencoop, a 'cavie.'

Kave, *v.* to clean grain from broken straws, chaff, &c.

Kavel, *n.* a lot.—*v.* to divide by lot. Cf. Cavel.

Kavel, *n.* a low, mean fellow. Cf. Cavel.

Kavel-mell, *n.* a sledge-hammer; a large hammer for breaking stones.

Kaver, *n.* a gentle breeze. Cf. Caver.

Kay, *n.* the jackdaw. Cf. Kae.

Kay, *int.* an excl. of contempt. Cf. Kae.

Kazzie, *n.* a sack or net of plaited straw. Cf. Cazzie.

Keach, Keagh, *n.* bustle, fluster.—*v.* to bustle. Cf. Kauch.

Keady, *adj.* wanton.

Keal, *n.* colewort. Cf. Kail.

Keal *n.* a wedding-race, the prize being a kiss from the bride. Cf. Kail.

Keallach, *n.* a small cart; a conical, wicker manure basket. Cf. Kellach.

Keam, *n.* a honeycomb; a young girl's bosom, as beautiful and sweet. Cf. Kaim.

Keam-drappit, *adj.* used of honey: dropped from the comb.

Keaming-stock, *n.* the stock on which the combs were fixed for dressing wool, &c. Cf. Kaiming-stock.

Keap-stone, *n.* a copestone.

Keasen, *v.* to dry up, shrink. Cf. Kizen.

Keave, *v.* used of horned cattle: to toss the horns threateningly; to threaten. Cf. Kaive.

†Keave, *n.* a large tub for fermenting beer; a large vessel for holding vitriol. Cf. Keeve.

Keavie, *n.* a species of crab.

Keavie-cleek, *n.* a hooked iron implement for catching crabs.

Keavle, *n.* that part of a field that falls to one when divided by lot. Cf. Cavel.

Keaw, *n.* a jackdaw. Cf. Kae.

Keb, *n.* the sheep-louse; any small creature; an infant.

Keb, *v.* to beat severely.—*n.* a blow; a thrust.

Keb, *v.* used of ewes: to bring forth a still-born lamb; to abandon a lamb; with *at*, to refuse to suckle.—*n.* a ewe that has brought forth immaturely, or been accidentally prevented from suckling; a sow-pig that has been littered dead.

Kebar, Kebbre, *n.* a rafter; a strong person of stubborn disposition; a companion, neighbour. Cf. Caber.

Kebback, *n.* a cheese. Cf. Kebbuck.

Kebbie, *v.* to chide, quarrel.

Kebbie, Kebbie-stick, *n.* a walking-stick with a curved handle; a shepherd's crook.

Kebbie-lebbie, *n.* an altercation when a number of people talk at once.—*v.* to carry on an altercation. Cf. Kabbie-labbie.

Kebbuck, Kebbock, *n.* a whole cheese.

Kebbuck-creel, *n.* a cheese-basket.

Kebbuck-end, *n.* the remains of a cheese.

Kebbuck-heel, -stump, *n.* a 'kebbuck-end.'

Kebec, *n.* a cheese.

Keb-ewe, *n.* a ewe that has lost her lambs.

Keb-house, *n.* a shelter for young lambs in the lambing-time.

Kebrach, Kebritch, *n.* very lean meat. Cf. Cabroch.

Kebrock, *n.* anything big and clumsy. Cf. Cabroch.

Kebruch, *n.* meat unfit for use.—*adj.* lean; rapacious. Cf. Kebrach.

Kebs, *n.* the game of 'knuckle-bones.'

Kebuck, *n.* a cheese.

Kech, *n.* a girl's shoe.

Kecher, *v.* to cough continuously.

Kecht, *n.* a consumptive cough.

Keck, *v.* to draw back from a bargain; to flinch. Cf. Cock.

Keck, *v.* to faint or swoon suddenly.

Keck, *n.* a linen covering for the head and neck. Cf. Keek.

Keckle, *v.* to cackle; to laugh heartily; to chuckle; to giggle; to show signs of eagerness, joy, temper.—*n.* a chuckle; noisy laughter; giddy behaviour; loud chatter; foolish, idle talk.

Keckle-, Keckling-pins, *n.* knitting-pins, knitting-wires.

Kecklor, *n.* a hen.

Ked, *n.* a sheep-louse. Cf. Kaid.

Kedge, *v.* to stuff; to fill with food.

Kedge, *adj.* active, brisk.

Kedge, *v.* to toss about; to move a thing quickly from one place to another. Cf. Cadge.

Kedge-kyte, *n.* a large, protuberant belly; a glutton.

Kedgie, *adj.* brisk, lively. Cf. Cadgie, Kidgie.

Kee, *n.* humour. Cf. Key.

Keech, *v.* used of children: to void excrement.—*n.* dirt.

Keechan, *n.* a small rivulet.

Keechie, *adj.* dirty.

Keechin, *n.* in distillation, the liquor after it has been drawn from the grains and fermented, before going through the still.

Keechle, *v.* to cough.—*n.* a cough, coughing. Cf. Keuchle.

Keed, *n.* the cud.

Kee-how, *n.* the game of 'hie-spy.'—*int.* a cry made in the game.

Kee-hoy, *n.* a variety of 'hie-spy.'

Keek, *n.* a linen covering for the head and neck.

Keek, *v.* to look, peep; to pry.—*n.* a peep, a stolen glance.

Keek-a-bo, Keek-bo, *n.* the game of 'peep-bo.'—*int.* a cry during the game.

Keek-bogle, *n.* the game of 'hide-and-seek.'

Keeker, *n.* a gazer, spectator; a 'black-eye'; in *pl.* the eyes.

Keek-hole, *n.* a peep-hole.

Keeking-glass, *n.* a looking-glass; a telescope.

Keek-keek, *int.* a cry in the game of 'hide-and-seek.'

Keek-roon-corners, *n.* a spy.

Keeky-bo, *n.* the game of 'bo-peep.' Cf. Keek-a-bo.

Keel, *n.* a small vessel, a lighter; the spine; the lower part of the body, the breech.—*v.* used of a ship: to plough the seas; to overturn, knock down.

Keel, *adj.* cool.—*v.* to cool.

Keel, *n.* ruddle; any marking substance, black or red.—*v.* to mark with ruddle; to mark a person or thing as an expression of dissatisfaction, contempt, jealousy, &c.

Keel, *n.* a large, clumsy person, animal, or thing.

Keel, *v.* to cease; with *in*, to give over, come to an end.

Keel, *n.* a mark on the warp showing the weaver where to cut his cloth.

Keelack, *n.* a pannier for carrying dung to the fields. Cf. Kellach.

Keelan, *n.* a big, awkward person.

Keelavine, *n.* a pencil of black-lead. Cf. Keelyvine.

Keelavine-pen, *n.* a 'keelavine.'

Keel-draught, *n.* the part of the keel below the garboard-strake; a false keel.

Keel-hauled, *ppl.* intoxicated.

Keel-hauling, *n.* a severe questioning, scolding, rating.

Keelick, *n.* anger, trouble, vexation; a stroke, a blow. Cf. Keelup.

Keelie, *adj.* reddish; coloured by ruddle.

Keelie, *n.* a street-arab; a pickpocket.

Keelie, *n.* a long plank or beam for amusing children; the game played, a kind of seesaw.—*v.* to play the game on a 'keelie.' Cf. Killie.

Keelie, *n.* the kestrel.

Keelie-craig, *n.* a crag on which the kestrel nests.

Keelie-hawk, *n.* the kestrel.

Keeling, *n.* a large cod.

Keel-row, *n.* a Galloway country-dance; a popular bridal tune.

Keelup, *n.* a blow, a stroke. Cf. Keelick.

Keelyvine, Keelivine, *n.* a lead-pencil.

Keen, *v.* to wail over a corpse.

Keen, *adj.* used of a horse, dog, &c.: eager; of the weather: severe, cold; avaricious, devoted to self-interest; with *for*, desirous of; with *to*, eager, anxious to.

Keen-bitten, *adj.* eager, sharp; hungry.

Keenk, *v.* to cough; to labour for breath. Cf. Kink.

Keen-killer, *n.* an eager shooter of game.

Keep, *v.* to watch over; to fare in health; to attend regularly.—*n.* possession; charge, keeping; in *pl.* marbles kept by a winner; food kept up from previous meals.

Keep, *v.* to catch what is thrown to one. Cf. Kep.

Keeper, *n.* the catch of a clasp; the guardring of a wedding-ring; in *pl.* store-cattle.

Keepet, Keeped, Keepit, *v. pret.* and *ppl.* kept.

Keeping, *n.* board and lodging; guard.

Keeping off, *prep.* except.

Keep 's, *int.* an excl. of surprise.

Keer, *n.* a cure.—*v.* to cure.

Keerie, *n.* a call to a lamb or sheep.

Keerie-oam, *n.* a game similar to 'hie-spy.'

Keerikin, *n.* a sharp and sudden blow that knocks one down; a fall.

Keeriosity, *n.* curiosity; in *pl.* curious habits.

Keerious, *adj.* curious.

Keeroch, *n.* a contemptuous name for any strange mixture, particularly a medicinal compound; a 'soss.'—*v.* to mess about, make a 'soss.'

Keers, *n.* a thin gruel given in the spring to feeble sheep.

Keesich, *int.* a word used by one entering a room where a person is already seated, and requesting a seat.

Keeslip, *n.* the dried stomach of a calf used for curdling milk; rennet; a plant resembling southernwood, used as a substitute for rennet.

Keessar, *n.* a big, ugly person or animal, particularly a woman.

Keest, *n.* sap; substance. Cf. Kyst.

Keest, *v. pret.* and *ppl.* cast; vomited. Cf. Cast.

Keestless, *adj.* tasteless, insipid; giving no nourishment; without substance; spiritless.

Keet, *n.* the ankle. Cf. Cuit, Queet.

Keeth, *v.* to make known; to become known. —*n.* an appearance. Cf. Kythe.

Keething-sight, *n.* the view of the motion of a salmon, by marks in the water.

Keetikins, *n.* gaiters. Cf. Cuitikins, Queetikins.

†**Keeve,** *n.* a tub; a mashing-vat. Cf. Keave.

Keezlie, *adj.* used of soil: unproductive, barren.

Keff, *n.* in *phr.* to be 'in a gay keff,' to have one's spirits elevated.

Keffel, *n.* an old or inferior horse.

Keh, *int.* an excl. of contempt, &c. Cf. Kae.

Keig, Keik, *n.* a wooden trumpet, formerly blown in the country districts of Aberdeenshire at 5 P.M.

Keik, *v.* to pry. Cf. Keek.

Keil, *n.* a hay-cock.—*v.* to put hay into cocks. Cf. Coil.

Keil, *n.* ruddle. Cf. Keel.

Keill, *n.* a lighter. Cf. Keel.

Keilling, *n.* large cod. Cf. Keeling.

Keiltch, *v.* to heave a burden farther up on one's back; to jog with the elbow.—*n.* an upward heave; one who heaves upwards.

Keilup, Keilop, *n.* a blow, a stroke. Cf. Kellup.

Keis, *n.* a large straw basket for carrying on the back. Cf. Keyse.

Keisen, Keizen, *v.* to dry up, parch, shrink. Cf. Gizzen, Keasen.

Keist, *v. pret.* and *ppl.* cast. Cf. Keest.

Keisty, *adj.* lecherous.

Keisyl-staue, *n.* a flint-stone.

Keith, *n.* a bar laid across a river to prevent salmon going farther up.

†Keit you, *int.* an excl. of impatience; get away! Cf. Kit.

Keize, Keizie, *n.* a sort of basket made of straw. Cf. Cazzie.

Kekle, *v.* to cackle. Cf. Keckle.

Kelch, *n.* a thump; a push.—*v.* to push. Cf. Kilch.

†Kelder, *n.* the womb.—*phr.* 'Hans in kelder,' a child in the womb.

Kelk, *n.* the roe of cod, ling, &c.

Kell, *n.* a child's caul; an incrustation of grime, &c.; the scurf, &c., on a child's head; dandriff; a network cap for a woman's hair; the hinder part or crown-piece of a woman's cap.

Kellach, Kellachy, *n.* a small cart of wicker fixed to a square frame and tumbling shafts; a conical basket of coarse wicker for carrying manure to the fields; anything built high or narrow, or in a slovenly way.

Kellop, *n.* a stroke, blow. Cf. Keilup.

Kelp, *n.* a raw-boned youth.

Kelpie, *n.* a water-sprite, a river-horse; a rawboned youth.

Kelshie, *adj.* crabbed, rude. Cf. Calshie.

Kelso boots, *n.* heavy shackles put on prisoners' legs.

Kelso convoy, *n.* escorting a friend a short distance.

Kelso-rung, *n.* a Kelso cudgel, classed along with 'Jeddart staves.'

Kelt, *n.* a salmon spent after spawning, a foul fish.

Kelt, *n.* frieze cloth, generally of native black wool.

Kelt-coat, *n.* a coat of coarse homespun made of black and white wool.

Kelter, *n.* money.

Kelter, *v.* to move at full speed; to move in an undulating manner; to move uneasily, 'wamble'; used of the stomach and of the conscience : to be uneasy with qualms; to tilt; to upset; to fall headlong; to struggle violently, as a hooked fish.—*n.* a somersault, a fall heels over head. Cf. Kilt.

Kelt-hooks, *n.* hooks for catching 'kelts.'

Keltie, *n.* the kittiwake.

Keltie's mends, *n.* a bumper to be drunk by a reluctant or unfair drinker in a company. Cf. Kelty.

Kelty, *n.* a child.

Kelty, Keltie, *n.* plenty; a bumper to be drunk by those who do not drink fair; a reluctant or unfair drinker.

Kem, Keme, Kembe, *v.* to comb.—*n.* a comb. Cf. Kaim, Keam.

Kembit, *n.* the pith of hemp.

Kembo, *adv.* akimbo.

Kemester, *n.* a wool-comber.

Keming-stock, *n.* the stock on which combs are placed in dressing wool. Cf. Kaiming-stock.

Kemmin, *n.* an active and agile child or small animal.

Kemp, *n.* a stalk and seed-head of rib-grass or lancet-leaved plantain; a game played with these; crested dog's-tail grass.

Kemp, *v.* to fight, struggle; to contend for mastery; to compete, especially in the harvest-field.—*n.* a competition; strife; a champion; an impetuous person.

Kempel, *v.* to cut in separate parts for a purpose; to cut wood into billets.—*n.* a piece, fragment; a piece cut off.

Kemper, *n.* a reaper 'kemping' in harvest; one who strives; a competitor.

Kempin, *n.* striving on the harvest-field; a struggle for superiority in any form.

Kemple, *n.* a measure of straw or hay, containing forty 'bottles.'

Kemps, *n.* a variety of potatoes.

Kemp-seed, *n.* a name given to the seed of the rib-grass; in *pl.* the 'seeds' or husks of oats, when meal is made; the 'reeings' or riddlings of the sieve.

Kemp-stane, *n.* a stone placed to mark where the first player reaches with the 'putting-stone,' the player who throws farthest beyond being the winner.

Kempy, *n.* a bold, impetuous person. Cf. Kemp.

Kemster, *n.* a wool-comber.

Kemstock, *n.* a capstan.

Ken, *n.* a headland. Cf. Kenn.

Ken, *v.* to know; to be acquainted with; to recognize; to destroy.—*n.* knowledge; one's own mind; recognition; sight, view.

Ken, *n.* 300 stone weight of cheese; the quantity of cheese made by a farmer in one season. Cf. Cain.

Kenable, *adj.* easily known or recognizable.

Kendal-ben, *n.* very thick shoe-leather for soles.

Kendle, *v.* to kindle, to bring forth.

Kendle, *v.* to kindle a fire, &c.

Kendlin', *n.* what is used to kindle a fire.

Kendlin-brand, *n.* a brand or live-coal for kindling a fire.

Kendlin-peat, *n.* a live-peat for kindling a fire.

Kendlin-stuff, *n.* materials for lighting fires.

Kendlin-wood, *n.* matchwood, splinters or chips of wood for lighting fires.

Ken-gude, *n.* a caveat; a lesson or example to teach, warn, or profit by.

Kenilt, *ppl. adj.* kindled.

Kenk, *v.* to choke. Cf. Kink.

Ken-kind, *n.* kind, species, genus. Cf. Kin-kind.

Kenle, *v.* to kindle a fire.

Kenless, *adj.* unknown.

Kenlin, *n.* what is used to light a fire.

Ken-mark, *n.* a distinguishing mark.

Kenn, *n.* a headland, point; in *pl.* the district along the banks of the Ken in Galloway, the Glenkens.

Kennan, *n.* knowledge. Cf. Kenning.

Kenna-what, *n.* a nondescript.

Kenned, *v. pret.* knew; *ppl.* known.

Kennelling, *n.* firewood.

Kenner, *n.* a water-bailiff; the overseer of the crew of a salmon-coble. Cf. Kainer.

Kennet, Kenet, *n.* a small hound, a beagle.

Kenning, Kening, *n.* knowledge, experience; recognition, acquaintance; a small portion of anything; a very little; the distance a person can see.

Ken-no, *n.* a cheese made to be eaten at a birth by the 'gossips.'

Kens, *n.* rent paid in kind. Cf. Cane.

Kensie, *n.* a rustic. Cf. Kenyie.

Kenspeckle, *adj.* easily recognised from some peculiarity; conspicuous, notable.—*n.* a distinguishing mark or feature.

Kent, *n.* a long pole used by shepherds for leaping ditches, &c.; a long, lank person.— *v.* to pole a boat or punt.

Kent, *v. pret.* knew.—*ppl. adj.* known, familiar.

Kent-face, *n.* an intimate, an acquaintance.

Kent-fit, *n.* a familiar footstep.

Kent-fowk, *n.* people familiarly known.

Kent-grun', *n.* a familiar district.

Kenyie, Kenzie, *n.* a rustic; in *pl.* fighting fellows.

Keoch, *n.* a wooded glen.

Kep, *n.* a cap.—*phr.* 'to hing up one's kep to,' to pay one's addresses to, to court.

Kep, Kepp, *v.* to catch anything thrown or falling; to catch with the hand; to fasten up the hair; to intercept; to hinder progress, turn or head back an animal; to encounter, meet accidentally; to prepare for; to gather up on the way.—*n.* reach, range; a catch.

Kep, *v.* to keep. Cf. Keep.

Kep o' steill, *n.* a steel head-piece.

Keppie, *adj.* quick at turning back an animal.

Kepping-kaim, *n.* a large comb for keeping up a woman's hair on the back of her head.

Keppit, *ppl.* kept.

Kep-stone, *n.* the copestone. Cf. Capestone.

Ker, *n.* the soft kernel of suet.

Ker, *adj.* left-handed; awkward; morally wrong. Cf. Car.

Kerbit, *adj.* peevish, 'crabbit.'

Ker-cake, *n.* a cake baked specially for Fastern's E'en. Cf. Car-cake.

Kerd, *v.* to card wool. Cf. Caird.

Ker-handit, *adj.* left-handed.

Kerk, *v.* to scold; to nag.

Kerl, *n.* a tall candlestick.

Kerlin, *n.* an old woman. Cf. Carline.

Kern, Kerne, *n.* a foot-soldier armed with a dart or a 'skean'; a vagabond, a sturdy beggar.

Kernel, *n.* a hard gathering or gland in the neck. Cf. Wax-kernel.

Kerrag, *n.* a contemptuous term applied to a woman.

Kerse, *n.* a water-cress; a cress. Cf. Carse.

Kerse, *n.* an alluvial plain near a river. Cf. Carse.

†**Kerse**, *n.* a cherry.

Kersen, *v.* to baptize, to christen.

Kertch, *n.* a woman's head-dress. Cf. Curch.

Kertie, *n.* a kind of louse. Cf. Kartie.

Kerve, *v.* to carve.—*n.* a cut, an incision.

Kerwallop, *adv.* pit-a-pat.

Kest, *n.* a chest. Cf. Kist.

Kest, *v. pret.* cast. Cf. Keist.

Ket, Kett, *n.* carrion; the flesh of animals that have died of disease, 'braxy'; a worthless fellow; a term of contempt.

Ket, Kett, *n.* couch-grass, 'quicken'; a spongy peat composed of tough fibres of moss, &c.; exhausted land; a fleece.

Ket, *adj.* irascible.

Ketch, *v.* to catch hold of and throw down.

Ketle, *v.* to kitten.

Ketlin, *n.* a kitten.

Ketrail, *n.* a term of great contempt and abhorrence.

Kett, *v.* to shield, protect.

Kettach, *n.* the fishing-frog or sea-devil.

Kettie-neetie, *n.* the dipper.

Kettle, *n.* a church bell, used in contempt; a Tweedside feast or social party, in which salmon is the main dish.

Kettle of fish, *n.* a salmon feast.

Kettle-pan, *n.* a cooking utensil.

Kettlin, *n.* a kitten.

Kettrin, *n.* a 'cateran.'

Ketty, *adj.* used of grass: matted with couch-grass; of peats: spongy, fibrous.

Keuchle, *v.* to cough.—*n.* a cough; the act of coughing.

Keude, *adj.* hare-brained, wild. Cf. Cude.

Keuill, *v.* to have intercourse.

Keuk, *v.* to cook.—*n.* a cook.

Keul, *n.* a lot. Cf. Kevel, Cavel.

Keulins, *n.* young people in general.

Keuter, *v.* to coax, wheedle. Cf. Cuiter, Cuter.

Keuve, *v. pret.* kneaded; chewed much. Cf. Kiauve.

Keve, v. to push, toss. Cf. Kaive.

†Kevee, n. in phr. 'on the kevee,' with a flow of spirits bordering on derangement, with a 'bee in the bonnet.'

Kevel, n. a staff, cudgel.

Kevel, Kevil, v. to walk or climb clumsily; to hold or wield awkwardly.

Kevel, n. a low, mean fellow. Cf. Cavel.

Kevel, v. to quarrel, wrangle; to scold.—n. a quarrel. Cf. Cavil.

Kevel, n. a lot.—v. to cast lots. Cf. Cavel.

Kever, n. a gentle breeze, causing a slight motion of the water. Cf. Caver.

Kevie, n. a hencoop. Cf. Cavie, Kave.

Kevins, n. the refuse separated from grain. Cf. Cavings.

Kew, v. pret. struggled; wrought hard.—n. an overset from great fatigue. Cf. Keuve, Kiauve.

Kew, v. to clew up.—n. a clew; a queue.

Kewl, n. a halter put under the jaws and through the mouth of a horse not easily managed.

Kex, n. human excrement.

Key, n. the seed of the ash; a spanner, screw-wrench; mood, frame of mind.—v. to fasten with a key, lock.

Key-cold, adj. cold as a key, quite cold; thoroughly indifferent or unconcerned.

Keysart, n. a cheese-press. Cf. Kaisart.

Keyse, n. a large straw basket, with a rope of hay or straw, for carrying on the back.

Keytch, v. to toss; to drive backwards and forwards.—n. a toss.

Kiaugh, n. a bustle, anxiety.—v. to fluster. Cf. Kauch.

Kiauve, v. to knead; to chew hard; to struggle, sprawl; to pull to and fro; to work hard.—n. a kneading; hard chewing; a struggle, tumbling; hard toil. Cf. Keuve, Kew.

Kibble, adj. strong, active; compactly framed.

Kibbling, n. a cudgel; a roughly-cut stick.

Kibbock, n. a cheese. Cf. Kebbuck.

Kich, n. human excrement. Cf. Kach.

Kichen, Kichin, adj. disgusting; disagreeable; used of children especially: having a disagreeable temper.

Kick, n. a novelty.

Kick, v. to walk with a silly, haughty air; to show off; to beg successfully for money; to play tricks; to tease; with up, to make or raise disturbance, &c., to die.—n. a trick, practical joke; a puzzle; the knack, trick; contemptuous and summary dismissal; in pl. fine airs.

Kick-at-the-benweed, adj. headstrong, unruly.

Kick-ba, n. a football; the game of football.

Kick-bonnety, n. a boys' game, in which one boy's cap is used as a football until the owner can seize another's cap, which then becomes the football.

Kicken-hearted, adj. faint-hearted.

Kicker, v. to titter; to laugh in a suppressed manner.—n. a titter; a suppressed laugh.

†Kickshaw, n. a novelty; a curio. Cf. Kick.

Kick-up, n. a tumult, uproar; a great stir or row.

Kicky, adj. smartly dressed, showy; aspiring beyond one's station; pert, clever, lively; saucy; repulsive.

Kid, v. to toy; to render pregnant.

Kid, n. the sheep-louse. Cf. Kaid.

Kiddet, ppl. adj. pregnant, with child.

Kiddy, adj. wanton. Cf. Keady.

Kidgie, adj. friendly; familiar; lovingly attached. Cf. Cadgie.

Kie, v. to detect; to show, to 'kythe.'

Kiel, n. ruddle. Cf. Keel.

Kies, n. keys.

Kiest, v. pret. cast.

Kiff, n. a fool. Cf. Coof.

Kiffle, v. to cough from a tickling sensation in the throat.—n. a tickling or troublesome cough.

Kiffling-cough, n. a slight cough, caused by a tickling.

Kift, n. a talk, a chat, a gossip over liquor.

Kigger, v. to mess about with soft or semi-liquid foods.

Kiggle-kaggle, v. in curling: to make a succession of 'inwicks' up a 'port' to a certain object.

Kigh, v. to cough from a tickling in the throat. —n. a short, tickling cough.

Kighen-hearted, adj. faint-hearted. Cf. Kicken-hearted.

Kigher, v. to cough from a tickling in the throat.—n. a short, tickling cough. Cf. Kecher.

Kigher, v. to titter.—n. a titter. Cf. Kicker.

Kighle, v. to have a short, tickling cough.— n. a short, tickling cough.

Kilbaigie, n. whisky formerly distilled at Kilbaigie in Clackmannan county.

Kilch, v. used of horses: to throw up the hind-legs, specially when tickled on the croup; with up, to raise one end of a plank by sitting on the other.

Kilch, v. to push.—n. a thump, blow; a heavy fall; a catch.

Kilches, n. wide-mouthed trousers, worn by male children. Cf. Calshes.

Kildoch, n. the herling.

Kile, n. chance, opportunity. Cf. Kyle.

†Kiles, n. ninepins.

Kilfud-yoking, n. a fireside disputation.

Kilk, n. the roe of cod, ling, &c. Cf. Kelk.

Kill, *v.* to overcome; to exhaust; to hurt severely.

Kill, *n.* the opening in a stack for ventilation.

Kill, *n.* a kiln.—*v.* to dry in a kiln.

Killach, *n.* a small cart. Cf. Kellach.

Kill-barn, *n.* a barn attached to a kiln.

Kill-beddin, *n.* the straw in a kiln on which grain was spread to dry.

Kill-briest, *n.* the part of a kiln built above the arch of the open space in front of the fireplace.

Kill-cow, *n.* a matter of consequence, a serious affair.

Kill-door, *n.* the raised steps at the entrance to a kiln.

Kill-dry, *v.* to dry in a kiln.

Kill-ee, *n.* the fireplace of a drying-kiln.

Killer, *n.* a finishing blow, a 'settler.'

Kill-fuddie, *n.* the aperture by which fuel is put into the kiln, the inner part of the 'killogie.'

Killfudyoch, *n.* a fireside disputation. Cf. Kilfud-yoking.

Kill-head, *n.* in curling: a large number of stones all lying near the 'tee.'

Kill-huggie, -hogie, *n.* an open space in front of the fireplace in a kiln. Cf. Killogie.

Killick, *n.* the fluke of an anchor; the 'mouth' of a pick-axe.

Killicoup, *n.* a somersault, a tumble head over heels.

Killie, *n.* an amusement for children with a long plank, see-saw; the plank by which a child is raised.—*v.* to raise a child on the long end of a 'killie.' Cf. Keelie.

Killieleepsie, Killileepie, *n.* the common sandpiper.

Killiemahou, *n.* an uproar; a confusion.

Killimanky, *n.* a petticoat made of calamanco; a petticoat.

Killin, *n.* cod. Cf. Keeling.

Killing-clothes, *n.* clothes worn by a butcher in the slaughter-house.

Killing-times, *n.* the times immediately preceding the Revolution of 1688, during which the Covenanters suffered.

Killin-kites, *n.* a designation of the inhabitants of Colvend in Galloway, from codfish being their chief sustenance.

Kill-kebber, *n.* a kiln-rafter; a support for a kiln. Cf. Caber.

Kill-man, *n.* the man in charge of a kiln.

Kill-meat, *n.* a perquisite of the 'shillings' of a mill, falling to the under-miller.

Kill-moulis, *n.* a hobgoblin, represented as having no mouth.

Killogie, *n.* the open space in front of the fireplace in a kiln.

Killogue, *v.* to confer secretly; to plot, conspire. Cf. Collogue.

Kill-pot, *n.* the pot in which grain was dried in a kiln at a farmstead.

Kill-ravage, *n.* a disorderly mob, engaged or engaging in some outrage. Cf. Gilravage.

Kill-rib, *n.* a support for a kiln; a kiln-rafter.

Kill-ring, *n.* the open space in front of the fireplace in a kiln.

Kill-spendin, *n.* an old name for the kiln-fire.

Kill-stickles, *n.* pieces of drawn straw on which grain was laid to dry in 'strae-kilns.'

Kill-strae, *n.* straw used in kilns, on which grain was laid.

Kill-trees, *n.* thin laths on which straw was laid, to bear the corn spread on it for kiln-drying.

Killum-callum, *n.* the Highland sword-dance, 'Gillie-callum.'

†**Killyvie,** *n.* a state of alertness, '*qui là vive?*'

Killy-wimple, *n.* a gewgaw; an ornament; a grace note in singing.

Kilmarnock, *n.* a Kilmarnock 'cowl'; a man's woven cap in shape of a 'Tam o' Shanter.'

Kilmarnock whittle, *n.* a betrothed person of either sex.

Kiln, *n.* a frame of wood on a corn-staddle, for ventilating a stack. Cf. Kill, Boss.

Kilsh, *v.* to push. Cf. Kilch.

Kilshes, *n.* wide trousers worn by children. Cf. Calshes.

Kilt, *n.* the proper way or 'knack' of doing a thing; 'the trick.'—*v.* to do a thing neatly and skilfully.

Kilt, *n.* the slope of a stone, especially in a staircase; an unnatural or ungraceful elevation of the voice.

Kilt, *v.* to tuck up the skirts, &c.; to roll up the sleeves; to elevate; to lift up quickly; to run quickly; to pack off with.—*n.* a tuck.

Kilt, *v.* to overturn.—*n.* an upset. Cf. Kelter.

Kilt, *n.* a Hebridean name for home-made cloth of any or no colour. Cf. Kelt.

Kilter, *n.* cheer, entertainment.

Kiltie, *n.* one who wears a kilt or a very short dress; a soldier in a Highland regiment.—*adj.* wearing a kilt.

Kiltie, *n.* a salmon that has been spawning. Cf. Kelt.

Kilting, *n.* the portion of a dress, &c., that is tucked up; the lap of a woman's petticoat that is tucked up.

Kiltit, *ppl. adj.* tucked up.—*phr.* 'high-kiltit,' used of language verging on indecency or coarseness.

Kilt-rack, *n.* the machinery for raising the rack of a mill.

Kilty, *n.* fornication.

Kim, *n.* a cistern, a tub; a large baling-ladle.

Kim, *adj.* keen; spirited; spruce.

Kimmen, Kimmin, *n.* a milk-pail; a small tub; a large, shallow tub used in brewhouses.

†Kimmer, *n.* a 'gossip'; a godmother; a midwife; a young woman; a contemptuous name for a woman; a reputed witch; a male companion.—*v.* to bring forth a child. Cf. Cummer.

Kimmerin, *n.* an entertainment at the birth of a child.

Kimpal, *n.* a truss of drawn straw for thatch.

Kimplack, *n.* a very large piece.

Kimple, *n.* a piece of any solid substance.

Kimplet, *n.* a piece of moderate size.

Kin', *adj.* kind.

Kin, *v.* to kindle, light.

Kin', *n.* kind; nature; custom, wont; sort.—*adv.* somewhat, in some degree.

Kin-awa, *n.* kindred abroad.

Kin-a-wise, *adv.* in a way, in a sort.

Kin-bot, -boot, *n.* a fine paid to the kindred of a slaughtered person as compensation.

Kinch, *n.* the arm-pit.

Kinch, *n.* a loop; a twist or doubling given to a rope, &c.; a sudden twist in wrestling; an unfair or unexpected advantage; a favour; a hold.—*v.* to twist, loop; to tighten by twisting.

Kinch-pin, *n.* a pin or stick used in twisting ropes, &c., to tighten them. Cf. Kinkinpin.

Kin cogish, *n.* the law by which a chief was answerable for every member of his clan.

Kind-gallows, *n.* a name given to the gallows of Crieff.

Kindle, *v.* used of small animals: to litter. Cf. Kendle.

Kindlie, *n.* the tenure of a 'kindlie-tenant.'

Kindlie-possession, *n.* the land held by a 'kindlie-tenant.'

Kindlie-rowm, -room, *n.* a 'kindlie-possession.'

Kindlie-tenant, *n.* a tenant whose ancestors have long resided on a farm, and who claims a right to retain a farm through long possession by his ancestors.

Kindlike, *adv.* in a kindly manner.

Kindling, *n.* fire or light applied to combustibles.—*ppl. adj.* blushing, ruddy.

Kindly, *adj.* natural, according to nature; thriving, in good condition; favourable for growth, &c.—*adv.* heartily, cordially.

Kindness, *n.* friendship, affection, liking; the right on which a man claimed to retain a farm in consequence of long possession by his ancestors.

Kine, *adj.* kind.

King, *n.* an adept; the ladybird.

King and Queen of Cantelon, *n.* a boys' game, in which the boy who is king tries to catch the other players when running between two goals.

King-coll-awa', -gollowa, *n.* the ladybird.

King-collie, *n.* the ladybird.

King-come-a-long, *n.* a boys' game, in which the two sides strive which can secure most captives for the king.

King-cup, *n.* the marsh-marigold.

King Dr Ellison, *n.* the ladybird.

Kingervie, *n.* a species of wrasse.

King Henry, *n.* a boys' game.

Kingle-kangle, *n.* loud, confused, and ill-natured talk.

King of Bane, King of the Bean, *n.* a character in Christmas revels. Cf. Bane.

King of Cantland, *n.* a boys' game. Cf. King and Queen of Cantelon.

King of the herrings, *n.* the fish *Chimaera monstrosa.*

King's chair, *n.* the hands crossed to form a seat; a game played with the hands so crossed.

King's claver, *n.* melilot, a species of trefoil.

King's covenanter, *n.* a children's game. Cf. King and Queen of Cantelon.

King's cushion, *n.* a seat formed by crossing the arms; the game played with such a seat.

King's ellwand, *n.* Orion's belt.

King's hat, *n.* the second stomach of a ruminant.

King's head, *n.* the 'king's hat.'

King's hood, *n.* the 'king's hat'; the great gut, part of a sheep's 'tripe.'

King's horn *n.* the hue and cry. Cf. Horn.

King's keys, *n.* in *phr.* to 'mak king's keys,' to force open the door of a house, room, chest, &c., by virtue of a legal warrant in the king's name.

King's land, *n.* land formerly in possession of the Crown.

King's man, *n.* an exciseman.

King's weather, *n.* the exhalations rising from the earth on a warm day.

King's will, *n.* the king's good pleasure as to a sentence.

Kink, *n.* a bend; a crease; a fold.—*v.* to curl.

Kink, *v.* to laugh restrainedly; to choke with laughter; to choke, catch the breath convulsively, cough, as in whooping-cough; to vomit.—*n.* a convulsive fit of laughter, a catch of the breath; the sound of whooping-cough; a faint; a whiff; in *pl.* the whooping-cough.

Kinken, *n.* a small barrel, a keg.

Kinkens, *n.* an evasive answer to an inquisitive child. Cf. Kinshens.

Kink-host, -hoast, *n.* the whooping-cough; a severe loss; an utter disgust.

Kinkin, *ppl. adj.* used of a cough : choking, convulsive.

Kinkind, Kinkine, Kinkin, *n.* kind, variety, sort.

Kinkin-pin, *n.* a lever or pin for tightening ropes, &c., by twisting. Cf. Kinch-pin.

Kinkit, *ppl.* used of twisted ropes when untwisted : knotted, curled.

Kinkoch, *n.* the whooping-cough.

Kinnen, Kinning, *n.* a rabbit, a coney.

Kinrent, Kinred, *n.* a kindred ; a clan.

Kinrick, *n.* a kingdom.

Kinsh, *n.* a lever used in quarrying, &c., a ' pinch.'

Kinsh, Kinsch, *n.* a twist.—*v.* to twist. Cf. Kinch.

Kinshens, *n.* an evasive answer. Cf. Kinkens.

Kintra, *n.* a country, region, district.—*adj.* belonging to the country ; rustic ; rural. Cf. Country.

Kintra clash, *n.* country or district gossip or news.

Kintra-clatter, *n.* talk or reports current in a district.

Kintra cleadin, *n.* rustic apparel, homespun.

Kintra-crack, *n.* country talk.

Kintra-cuisser, -cousser, *n.* an itinerating stallion serving mares.

Kintra-dance, *n.* a country-dance.

Kintra fowks, *n.* country people, rustics.

Kintra-side, *n.* a country district.

Kintye, *n.* the roof-tree.

Kinvaig, *n.* a tippet ; a small plaid.

Kiow-ow, *n.* in *pl.* tittle-tattle : foolish talk ; trifles, things of a trivial nature.—*v.* to trifle in discourse or conduct.

Kiowowy, *adj.* particular ; fastidious.

Kip, *v.* to take another's property by fraud or force.

Kip, *v.* to play truant.—*n.* a truant.

Kip, *n.* a house of ill-fame.

Kip, *n.* haste, hurry.

Kip, Kipp, *n.* a hook ; a tilt or upward turn of the nose ; anything that is beaked ; a sharp-pointed hill ; a jutting point or knob on a hill.—*v.* to turn up at the point of a horn, nose, &c. ; to turn up at the side of a hat or bonnet.

Kipe, *n.* a hole in a game of marbles. Cf. Kype.

Kiple, *v.* to couple.

Kip-nebbit, -nosed, *adj.* used of the nose : tip-tilted, turned up at the tip ; having a ' pug-nose.'

†Kippage, *n.* a ship's crew or company.

Kippage, *n.* disorder, confusion ; a dilemma, ' fix ' ; a paroxysm of rage, a passion.

Kippen, *n.* a rabbit.

Kipper, *n.* a salmon after spawning ; a salmon or herring salted and cured.—*v.* to cure fish by salting and hanging them up, or drying them in smoke.

Kipper, *n.* a large bowl ; a large quantity of food.—*v.* to eat heartily.

Kipper, *v.* to trifle.

Kipperdy smash, *n.* a children's game.

Kipper-kaper, *adj.* easy-going, as of a tired or lazy horse.

Kipper-nose, *n.* a hooked or beaked nose.

Kippie, *adj.* left-handed.—*n.* a left-handed person ; the left hand.

Kippie, *n.* a small hill.—*adj.* having the points of horns turned up.

Kipping, *n.* truancy.

Kipple, *n.* a couple, pair ; a rafter-beam.— *v.* to couple, fasten together ; to marry, match. Cf. Couple.

Kipple-bawk, *n.* a roof-beam, rafter.

Kipple-fit, *n.* the foot of a rafter.

Kipple-hoe, *n.* a straight piece of wood laid across the top of the couple or rafter.

Kippling, *n.* a rafter ; a coupling.

Kippling-kaim, *n.* a comb for fastening up the hair.

Kir, *adj.* cheerful ; fond, amorous, wanton ; consequential.

Kire, *n.* a choir.

Kirk, *n.* a church ; the Church ; a congregation ; the building set apart for public worship ; ecclesiastical courts.—*v.* to attend church ; to church a woman after child-birth ; to escort a newly-married couple to the church on the first Sunday after marriage ; to lodge the ball into the hole in the game of ' kirk-the-gussie.'

Kirk-attender, *n.* a church-goer.

Kirk-beadle, *n.* the church-officer ; the ' minister's man.'

Kirk-bell, *n.* the church-going bell, summoning to church.

Kirk-book, *n.* the kirk-session's record or minute-book.

Kirk-box, *n.* the name formerly given to the fund for the church-poor, derived from fines, gifts, collections, legacies, &c.

Kirk-brae, *n.* the hill on which a church stands.

Kirk-brod, *n.* the plate at the church-door, or the ' ladle,' for receiving collections.

Kirk-clachan, *n.* a village or hamlet containing a church.

Kirk-claes, *n.* Sunday clothes.

Kirk-court, *n.* a church court or judicature.

Kirk-door, *n.* a church-door.—*phr.* to ' do anything at the kirk-door,' to do it openly and unblushingly.

Kirk-door-plate, *n.* the offertory-plate at the main entrance of a church.

Kirk-dyke, *n.* a churchyard wall.

Kirk dues, *n.* fines formerly exacted for breaches of the seventh commandment, &c.; church dues, contributions regularly paid for church purposes.

Kirker, *n.* a member or adherent of a church.

Kirk-fever, *n.* excitement over church affairs.

Kirk-fouk, *n.* the members of a congregation; church-goers; those going to or returning from church; church officials; ecclesiastical office-bearers.

Kirkfu', *n.* a churchful, a congregation.

Kirk-gate, *n.* the churchyard gate.

Kirk-gate, *n.* the way leading to a church.

Kirk-gaun', *adj.* church-going; frequenting church.—*n.* attendance at church.

Kirk-greedy, *adj.* eager and regular in church attendance.

Kirk-green, *n.* a church green; a churchyard.

Kirk-hammer, *n.* the tongue of a church bell.

Kirk-herd, *n.* a minister, a pastor; a ruling elder.

Kirk-hill, *n.* a hill on which a church stands.

Kirk-hole, *n.* a grave in a churchyard.

Kirking, *n.* church-going; the first attendance of a newly-married couple at church, generally on the first Sunday after marriage.

Kirking party, *n.* the newly-married couple and their friends met to attend church for the first time after the marriage.

Kirk-keeper, *n.* a regular church attender.

Kirk knock, *n.* the church clock.

Kirk knowe, *n.* the knoll on which a church stands.

Kirk-ladle, *n.* a box with long wooden handle for taking collections inside a church.

Kirklands, *n.* lands formerly belonging to a church; glebe-lands.

Kirkle, *n.* a 'kirtle.' Cf. Kirtle.

Kirkless, *adj.* used of a minister or preacher: without a church or charge; of people: not attending church.

Kirk liggate, *n.* a churchyard gate.

Kirk-loaning, *n.* a lane leading to a church.

Kirk-loom, *n.* a pulpit.

Kirk-lover, *n.* a lover of church.

Kirkman, *n.* an ecclesiastic.

Kirk-master, *n.* a deacon of an incorporated trade; a member of a town-council, whose office is to take charge of the fabric, &c., of the churches which are under the care of the council.

Kirk member, *n.* a communicant of a church.

Kirk-mouse, *n.* a church mouse.

Kirk-occasion, *n.* church service; the dispensation of the Communion. Cf. Occasion.

Kirk-officer, *n.* the 'kirk-beadle.'

Kirk-park, *n.* a park adjoining a church.

Kirk-pad, -path, *n.* a path leading to a church.

Kirk-plate, *n.* the 'plate' at the church-door for the offertory.

Kirk-reekit, *adj.* bigoted.

Kirk-road, *n.* a church road; a right-of-way leading to a church.

Kirk-scandalisin', *n.* a causing of scandal to a church.

Kirk-seat, *n.* a church-pew.

Kirk-session, *n.* the lowest Presbyterian Church court, having spiritual oversight of the congregation.

Kirk-shoon, *n.* Sunday shoes reserved for church-going.

Kirk-shot, *n.* fishings on a river, near or belonging to a church.

Kirk-skailing, *n.* dismission of congregation after service.

Kirk-steeple, *n.* a church steeple, formerly used often as a prison.

Kirk-stool, *n.* a stool taken to church before the introduction of pews.

Kirk-style, -stile, *n.* the gate of a churchyard or of a wall round the church; steps in a churchyard wall by which persons pass over; the houses adjoining a churchyard.

Kirk-supper, *n.* the festivity after the 'kirking' of a newly-married pair.

Kirk-tables, *n.* communion tables at which communicants sit.

Kirk-the-gussie, *n.* a game with a large ball which one set of players strive to beat with clubs into a hole, while the other set strive to drive it away.

Kirk-time, *n.* the hour for beginning public worship; the time during which it lasts.

Kirk-town, *n.* a village or hamlet where there is a parish church.

Kirk-wa', *n.* a church wall.

Kirk-waddin, *n.* a marriage in church.

Kirkward, *adv.* towards church.

Kirk-wark, *n.* the church fabric and what concerns it.—*phr.* 'maister of the kirk-wark,' a 'kirk-master.'

Kirk-weather, *n.* weather admitting of church-going.

Kirk-wipe, *n.* a club-foot.

Kirk-wiped, *adj.* having a club-foot.

Kirk wynd, *n.* a church lane.

Kirkyard, *n.* a churchyard.

Kirkyard-deserter, *n.* a very aged or infirm person.

Kirkyard gate, *n.* the way to the churchyard.

Kirkyard-like, *adj.* apparently likely to die soon.

Kirk-yett, *n.* the churchyard gate, church-gate.

Kirn, *n.* a churn; the act of handling or nursing too much; the act of working in a lazy, slovenly manner; a disgusting mixture, mire; the last handful of grain cut on the harvest-field; the harvest-home.—*v.* to churn; to mix, stir up; to handle constantly and messily; to over-nurse or take too much care of a child; to work in a disgusting way; to be improperly familiar.

Kirn, *n.* a kernel; a grain of corn.

Kirnan-rung, *n.* the upright rod used in old churns to stir the milk.

Kirn-bannock, *n.* a bannock specially baked for the harvest-home.

Kirn-cut, *n.* the last cut handful of corn on the harvest-field.

Kirn-dancing, *n.* dancing at the 'kirn-supper.'

Kirn-dollie, *n.* a female figure or image made of the last cut of grain. Cf. Maiden.

Kirnel, *n.* a kidney.

Kirnen, *n.* familiarity; improper familiarity.

Kirn-feast, *n.* the harvest-home festival.

Kirnie, *n.* a pert, impudent boy who apes a man and would be thought one.

Kirning, *n.* a churning; what has been churned at a time.

Kirning-stone, *n.* a stone heated red-hot to heat the churn before use.

Kirning-water, *n.* hot water to mix with butter-milk in a churn.

Kirn-milk, *n.* butter-milk; the precipitate of curd which occurs when hot water is poured into a churn containing butter-milk.

Kirn-rung, *n.* the rod used for stirring milk in a churn. Cf. Kirnan-rung.

Kirn-staff, *n.* the 'kirn-rung,' 'churn-staff.'

Kirn-staff, *n.* the sun-spurge.

Kirn-stick, *n.* a stupid person.

Kirn-supper, *n.* the harvest-home feast.

Kirn-swee, *n.* an implement for lightening the manual labour of churning.

Kirny, *adj.* used of corn: full of grains.

Kirr, *adj.* cheerful. Cf. Kir.

†**Kirry-wirry,** *n.* a burlesque serenade given to old people marrying again, or marrying young people; a 'charivari.' Cf. Carry-warry.

Kirsen, *v.* to baptize, christen.—*adj.* Christian; proper, suitable, decent.

Kirsenmas, Kirsmas, *n.* Christmas. Cf. Christenmas.

Kirsnin, *n.* baptism.

Kirssan-crab, *n.* a blackish variety of crab.

Kirstal, *n.* and *adj.* crystal.

Kirsty, *n.* a whisky-jar.

Kirtle, *n.* a woman's outer petticoat, or short skirt; a gown; dress.—*v.* to clothe, dress.

Kiryauw, *v.* to caterwaul.—*n.* a noise, great outcry; an ado.

Kish, *n.* shining powdery matter that separates from pig-iron too long kept molten.

Kisle-stane, *n.* a flint stone.

Kislop, *n.* the fourth stomach of a calf. Cf. Keslop.

Kissie, *n.* a kiss.

Kissing-signal, *n.* at rustic balls, the signal given by the fiddler making a squeaking sound like a kiss, at which the men kiss their partners and then begin dancing.

Kissing-strings, *n.* strings tied under the chin.

Kissing-time, *n.* the time for kissing at a rustic ball.

Kiss-my-loof, *n.* a fawner; a useless person.

Kiss-the-caup, *v.* to drink, take refreshment. —*n.* a tippler.

Kist, *n.* a chest, box; a chest of drawers; a coffin, a 'cruive'; a shop-counter; the chest of the body.—*v.* to lay up in a chest; to place in a coffin.

Kist, *n.* sap, substance; spirit; taste. Cf. Kyst.

Kistfu', *n.* a boxful.

Kistfu' o' whistles, *n.* an organ.

Kisting, *n.* the act of placing a dead body in a coffin; the religious service often accompanying that act.

Kist o' whistles, *n.* an organ.

Kistit, *adj.* dried up, sapless; without substance.

Kistit, *ppl. adj.* put in a chest; put in a coffin.

Kistless, *adj.* tasteless. Cf. Keestless.

Kist-lid, *n.* the lid of a chest.

Kist-locker, *n.* a box-like locker in a chest, for holding valuables, &c.

Kist-neuk, *n.* the corner of a chest, where money was often concealed.

Kist-shaped, *adj.* shaped like a chest.

Kist-weed, *n.* the woodruff.

Kit, *n.* any wooden vessel used for milk, butter salted, sugar, &c., or for washing dishes; a small fiddle; a set of tools.—*v.* to pack in a kit.

Kit, *n.* the whole collection of persons or things.

Kit, *n.* the ankle. Cf. Keet, Coot.

†**Kit,** *v.* to pack off; in *phr.* 'kit ye,' get out of the way! Cf. Keit you.

Kitchen, *n.* a relish or condiment with food; something to make plain fare more palatable; an allowance for milk, butter, beer, to servants; a tea-urn.—*v.* to season; to give a relish to food; to save; to be sparing of.

Kitchener, *n.* a cook.

Kitchen-fee, *n.* dripping.

Kitchen-fowk, *n.* servants.

Kitchen-lass, *n.* a maid-servant, kitchen-maid.

Kitchenless, *adj.* without relish, seasoning, or condiment.

Kitchen-lum, *n.* the kitchen chimney.

Kitchie, *n.* a kitchen ; an addition or relish to plain fare.—*v.* to season, give a relish to.

Kitchie-boy, *n.* a boy who serves in a kitchen.

Kitchie-umman, *n.* a kitchen-maid.

Kite, *n.* the stomach. Cf. Kyte.

Kite-clung, *adj.* having the belly shrunk from hunger ; herring-gutted.

Kited, *adj.* intestinal.

Kitefu', *n.* a bellyful.

Kith, *n.* acquaintance, friends not related by blood, or not 'kin.'

Kith, *v.* to show, appear. Cf. Kythe.

Kithag, *n.* an unmanageable woman.

Kithan, *n.* an unmanageable rogue.

Kithless, *adj.* friendless.

Kit-kae, *adv.* pit-a-pat.

Kitlin, *n.* a kitten.

Kitt, *n.* a brothel ; a privy ; a urinal.

Kitt, *v.* to lose all one's money at the gaming-table or otherwise.

Kitt, *n.* the whole number or quantity.

Kitter, *v.* to fester.

†**Kittie**, *int.* get out of the way ! Cf. Keit you.

Kittie, *n.* a name given to any kind of cow. Cf. Kitty.

Kittie, *n.* a loose woman, a 'cutty'; a term of disrespect for a woman who may not, however, be light-headed ; a romping, merry girl. Cf. Kitty.

Kittie-cat, *n.* a bit of wood, or any substitute for it, hit in the game of 'shinty' or other games.

Kitting, *n.* the act of packing in a kit.

Kittit, *ppl.* stripped of all one's possessions, by misfortune or otherwise. Cf. Kitt.

Kittle, *v.* to tickle ; to please, flatter ; to caress, fondle, 'cuddle'; to itch ; to stir up, enliven, stimulate what is jaded ; to rouse, interest ; to prick, stab ; to puzzle, perplex ; to get or put into a bad humour ; to sweep before a curling-stone in motion ; to strike up a tune on an instrument ; to warm up and show life in speaking ; used of a horse : to become restive or excited ; of the wind : to rise ; to compose, work at, make up.—*n.* a tickling sensation ; cunning, cleverness, skill.

Kittle, *adj.* easily tickled, tickly, ticklish ; itching ; difficult, not easily managed or done, 'ticklish'; unsteady, nicely balanced ; uncertain, fickle ; variable ; dangerous, critical ; obscure, intricate, not easy to understand or to pronounce ; excitable, nervous, fidgety ; skittish ; touchy, easily angry, keen-tempered ; clever, apt ; cunning, smart ; humorous, entertaining ; used of an angle, sharp ; scrupulous, squeamish.

Kittle, *v.* used of cats, &c.: to bring forth young ; to be generated in the imagination or affections.

Kittle-breeks, *n.* a nickname for a person of irascible temper.

Kittle-leggit, *adj.* nimble, quick at dancing.

Kittlen, *n.* a kitten.

Kittlesome. *adj.* sensitive to tickling ; itchy.

Kittle-strips, *n.* a rope with a noose at each end, into which a person's feet are put, he being placed across a joist or beam, in which position he has to balance himself so nicely as to be able to lift something laid before him with his teeth, without being overturned.

Kittlet, *ppl. adj.* interested ; aroused ; excited.

Kittle thairm, *v.* to play the fiddle.

Kittley, *adj.* ticklish ; obscure. Cf. Kittly.

Kittlie-cowt, **-kow**, *n.* a children's game of searching for a hidden handkerchief or other article.

Kittling, *n.* a tickling sensation ; the act of being tickled ; anything that tickles the fancy.—*ppl. adj.* stirring, affecting.

Kittling, *n.* a kitten ; the bringing forth of kittens.

Kittly, *adj.* itchy ; ticklish ; difficult ; intricate.

Kitt-neddy, *n.* the sandpiper.

Kittock, *n.* a romping girl ; a loose woman. Cf. Kittie.

Kitty, *n.* a disrespectful name for a young woman ; a common name for a cow ; the kittiwake ; any of the smaller gulls.

Kitty, *n.* a small bowl.

Kitty-langlegs, *n.* the daddy-longlegs.

Kitty-needy, **-neddy**, *n.* the sandpiper.

Kitty-stick, *n.* a small stick on which the 'pirns' are put in order that the thread may be wound off them.

Kitty-wren, *n.* the common wren.

Kiutle, *v.* to fondle ; to embrace. Cf. Cuitle.

Kivan, *n.* a gathering of people ; a covey. Cf. Kivin.

†**Kive**, *n.* a mashing-vat used in brewing. Cf. Keeve.

Kiver, *v.* to cover.—*n.* a cover.

Kivering, *n.* a covering ; woollen cloth for bed-coverings and saddle-cloths.

Kivilaivie, *n.* a crowd of low persons.

Kivin, Kivvan, *n.* a gathering of people ; a promiscuous crowd ; a bevy ; a covey.

Kivvy, *n.* a covey.

Kizen, Kizzen, *v.* to dry up ; to parch ; to shrink ; to wither. Cf. Gizzen.

Kizzen, *n.* a cousin.

Klamoos, Klamoz, *n.* an outcry, a loud noise.

Kleg, *n.* a gadfly. Cf. Cleg.

Klem, *adj.* imperfectly done, badly done, of little value ; unprincipled.

Klint, *n.* a rough stone ; an outlying stone. Cf. Clint.

Klippert, *n.* a shorn sheep. Cf. Clippart.

Klipsheers, *n.* the earwig. Cf. Clipshears.

Kllauch, *v.* to work in a filthy, disgusting manner.—*n.* the act of working so.

Klot, *v.* to scrape up mud, dung, ashes, &c.—*n.* a hoe for scraping, a 'claut.'

Klyock, *n.* the last sheaf in harvest, 'claaick.'

Klyte, *n.* a heavy fall.—*v.* to fall heavily. Cf. Cloit, Clite.

Knab, *v.* to strike, to beat.—*n.* a blow. Cf. Nab.

Knab, *n.* the apex of a rock or hill; a rocky headland. Cf. Nab.

Knab, *n.* a sturdy boy; a stout, thick-set animal.

Knabb, Knab, *n.* a person of consequence, rank, wealth, &c.; a pretentious, conceited person; a chief, leader. Cf. Nab.

Knabbish, *adj.* well off pecuniarily or socially; pretentious, dressing above one's means or station; genteel.

Knabbry, *n.* the lower class of gentry.

Knabby, *adj.* well-to-do; pretentious; wealthy.

Knablich, *n.* a strong, thick-set person or animal.—*adj.* sour, cantankerous.

Knablick, *adj.* irregularly shaped.—*n.* a stone or pebble with several angles that moves under the foot when trod on. Cf. Knibb-lach.

Knabrie, *n.* the lower gentry. Cf. Knabbry.

Knabsie, *n.* a short, stout, strong person or animal.

Knack, *v.* to crack, snap with a clicking sound, as with finger and thumb; to strike together; to make a harsh sound with the throat; to talk amusingly, chatter; to tell, narrate; to indulge in repartee; to poke fun at.—*n.* a snap, crack; a click, a clicking noise in the throat; a habit; a scheme, a tricky pretence, trick; a knick-knack; a joke, a witty saying, a smart answer.

Knack, *v.* to knock.—*n.* a knock. Cf. Knock.

Knackers, *n.* two flat pieces of wood or bone used as castanets; the testicles.

Knacket, *n.* one smart in reply or retort.

Knackety, *adj.* handy, expert at nice work; finical; self-conceited.

Knacks, *n.* a disease in the throat of fowls fed on too hot food. Cf. Nacks.

Knacksy, *adj.* quick at repartee; pleasant, amusing; clever.

Knackum, *n.* a sharp blow.

Knack up, *v.* to compliment, flatter.

Knackuz, *n.* a chatterer; a quick, snappish speaker.

Knacky, *adj.* handy, ingenious, expert; acute and facetious; entertaining, vivacious; cunning, crafty.

Knag, *n.* a knob or peg on which to hang articles; the projection of a knot in a tree.

Knag, *n.* a keg, small barrel; a small wooden vessel with a handle. Cf. Knog.

Knag, *n.* the green woodpecker.

Knaggie, *n.* a small barrel.

Knaggie, *adj.* having protuberances like rock, &c.; bony; tart, ill-humoured; of wood: full of knots.

Knaggim, *n.* a disagreeable after-taste.

Knaglie, *adj.* having many protuberances.

Knaivatick, *adj.* mean, knavish.

Knak, *v.* to snap the fingers.—*n.* a trick. Cf. Knack.

Knap, *n.* a knob, protuberance, bump; a knot in wood; a hillock, knoll; a bunch of heather; the ascent of a rising ground; the knee-cap; the point of the elbow; a stout, thick-set person; a wooden vessel, a milk-vat.

Knap, *n.* an eccentric person.

Knap, *v.* to knock; to strike sharply; to pat; to break stones, chip, hammer; to snap in two; to cleave; to snap with the teeth; to eat greedily; of a clock: to tick; to speak affectedly, to try to speak fine English, to clip one's words.—*n.* a blow; a tap, slight stroke; a bump; a snap, bite; a morsel.

Knap-dodgil, -dogik, *n.* any person, animal, or thing that is short and stout.

Knap-dorlak, -dorle, *n.* a large piece of any-thing solid.

Knaper, *n.* in *phr.* 'ilka knipper and knaper,' every particle.

Knap-for-naught, *n.* any morsel that just serves for a mouthful.

Knap-knap, *v.* to tap; to knock against.

Knap-knapping, *n.* a tapping; the sound of tapping.

Knap of the knee, *n.* the knee-pan.

Knappal, *n.* a boy between ten and sixteen years of age.

Knapparts, Knapperts, *n.* the bitter vetch.

Knappel, Knappild, *n.* a thick stick or staff; in *pl.* oak-staves from Memel, Danzig, &c.

Knapper, *n.* a hammer for stone-breaking.—*v.* to rattle, jolt.

Knappery, *adj.* used of roads: having loose road-metal, causing jolting.

Knappik, *n.* a stout, thick-set person or animal.

Knappin', *n.* the noise of tapping or smart strokes.

Knappin'-hammer, *n.* a hammer used in stone-breaking.

Knappin'-hole, *n.* the hole out of which two 'shinty'-players try to drive the ball in opposite directions.

Knappish, *adj.* tart, snappish.

Knappit, *ppl. adj.* affected, spoken mincingly.

Knapplach, Knapplack, *n.* a large lump or protuberance; a stout, thick-set person or animal.

Knapply, *adj.* short and stout, dumpy, thick-set.

Knappy, *adj.* abounding in lumps, in small, roundish lumps.

Knappy, *adj.* brittle. Cf. Nappie.

Knappy, *adj.* used of ale, &c.: strong.—*n.* strong liquor. Cf. Nappy.

Knapsack, *n.* a boys' game.

Knapscap, *n.* a steel bonnet, a head-piece.

Knapseck-drill, *n.* a severe scolding.

Knapskull, *n.* a 'knapscap.'

Knark, *v.* to crunch with the teeth; to crack, creak.—*n.* a snap with the teeth, a bite.

Knarly, *adj.* gnarly, knotty.

Knarrie, *n.* a bruise; a hurt; an abrasion.

Knash, *v.* to strike; to gnaw.

Knauperts, *n.* the crowberry. Cf. Krauperts.

Knaur, *n.* a knot of wood. Cf. Knirr.

Knave, *n.* a man-servant, a lad; an under-miller.

Knave-bairn, *n.* a man-child.

Knave-servant, *n.* a dishonest servant.

Knaveship, *n.* a customary due of meal paid to the under-miller.

Knaw, *v.* to know.

Knawlege, *n.* knowledge; trial, examination; an inquest.

Kned, *v.* generally used of animals: to pant, breathe heavily; to exhaust.—*n.* short, laboured breathing.—*ppl. adj.* exhausted; hard pushed or driven.

Knedeuch, *n.* a musty taste or smell.

Knee, *v.* to bend in the middle; to be broken down; to mend or patch clothes at the knees; to press down with the knees.—*n.* a bow, curtsy; a crank; a small hill.

Knee-bairn, *n.* a child too young to walk.

Knee-breekit, *adj.* wearing knee-breeches.

Knee-breeks, *n.* knee-breeches.

Knee-breekums, *n.* knee-breeches.

Kneef, *adj.* alert, active; intimate; fairly healthy, in good spirits after illness; quick-tempered; difficult.

Kneef-like, *adj.* hale-looking; of strong appearance.

Kneefly, *adv.* briskly.

Kneefy, *adj.* stout and active; agile.

Knee-heigh, *adj.* as high as one's knee.

Knee-height, *n.* the height of one's knee.

Knee-ill, *n.* a cattle disease affecting the knees.

Kneep, *n.* a lump; a promontory; a big, stupid person.

Kneeplach, *n.* a big lump; a large clot.—*v.* to strike and cause a lump.

Kneeple, *n.* a big lump.—*v.* to cause a big lump.

Knee-pock, *n.* a baggy trouser-knee.

Knee-shell, -shall, *n.* the knee-pan.

Kneetle, *v.* to strike with the knuckles; to hit, knock, tap.

Kneetling, *n.* a thrashing.

Kneeve, *n.* the fist. Cf. Neive.

Kneevick, *adj.* grasping, covetous.

Kneevle, *n.* a lump; a clot; a knot.

Kneevle, *v.* to beat severely. Cf. Knevell.

Kneevlick, Kneevlack, *v.* to press down with force; to strike so as to cause a lump.—*n.* a stroke producing a lump; a severe beating; a large lump; a large protuberance.

Kneggum, *n.* a disagreeble after-taste. Cf. Knaggim.

Kneggum, *n.* a trick, prank; a bad practice.

Kneif, *adj.* alert; intimate; quick-tempered. Cf. Kneef.

Kneip, *v.* to knock, strike lightly or smartly. Cf. Knap.

Kneister, *v.* to creak; to smother a laugh.

Knell, *v.* to talk loudly. Cf. Nell.

Knelling, *ppl. adj.* sounding an alarm; uneasy, alarmed, troublesome.

Knell-kneed, *adj.* knock-kneed.

Knet, *v. pret.* knitted; knotted.

Knevell, *v.* to beat severely; to thump with fists; to knock about.—*n.* a severe thrashing. Cf. Kneevle, Nevell.

Knewel, *n.* a wooden pin in the end of a halter for holding by; the cross-bar of an albert watch-chain.

Knib, *n.* a small piece of wood fixed in the end of a rope, fixed also in the loop in the end of another rope, so as to act like a swivel.

Knibblach, Knibbloch, *n.* a lump, a knob, a small piece; a small, round stone or clod; the swelling caused by a fall or blow. Cf. Knablick.

Knibblochie, Knibblockie, *adj.* rough, uneven; used of a road in which many small stones rise up and make walking hurtful.

Knible, *adj.* nimble, clever.

Knicht, *n.* a knight.

Knick, *v.* to crack, click; to cause to click, crack. Cf. Knack.

Knickity-knock, *adv.* in *phr.* 'to fa' knickity-knock,' to fall so as to strike the head first on one side and then on the other.

Knick-knack, Knick-nack, *n.* a whim, caprice; a precise person; one who is neat and skilful in delicate work.

Knick-knacket, *n.* a knick-knack, a trifle; in *pl.* odds and ends, curios.

Knickle, *n.* a knuckle. Cf. Knuckle.

Knickum, *n.* a tricky boy. Cf. Nickum.

Knidder, *v.* to keep under. Cf. Nidder.

Knidge, *n.* a strong squeeze, heavy pressure; a nudge; a short, strong person or animal. —*v.* to press down forcibly, squeeze; to nudge. Cf. Gnidge.

Knidgel, *n.* a short, strong person.

Knidget, *n.* a mischievous, saucy boy or girl.

Knidgie, *adj.* short, strong, and thick.
Knief, *adj.* alert. Cf. Kneef.
Kniefly, *adv.* vivaciously.
Kniel, *n.* a wooden pin in the end of a halter. Cf. Knewel.
Knievel, *n.* a lump. Cf. Kneevle.
Knife, *n.* in *phr.* 'a black knife,' a small dirk.
Kniff, *adj.* alert. Cf. Kneef.
Kniffy, *adj.* agile. Cf. Kneefy.
Kniggum, *n.* a disagreeable after-taste. Cf. Knaggim.
Knight, *n.* a close-stool.
Knip, *v.* to bite, nibble.
Knip, *n.* a blow.
Knip, *n.* a small bundle of things strung together at one end of a string.
Kniper, *n.* in *phr.* 'ilka kniper and knaper,' every particle.
Knippach, *n.* two or three small fish tied together.
Knipper-knatlich, *adj.* stingy; particular and slightly eccentric.
Knipperty-knaps, *n.* odds and ends, knick-knacks.
Knipsie, *n.* a malapert, mischievous boy or girl.
Knirls, *n.* a kind of measles; chicken-pox. Cf. Nirls.
Knirr, *n.* a knot of wood; a wooden ball or knot of wool used in the game of shinty; anything small or stunted in growth, used contemptuously of a decrepit old woman who outlives the usual span of life. Cf. Knurr.
Knit, *v.* to tie; to overfill, burst.
Knitch, *n.* a bundle tied round.—*v.* to truss, tie, bundle, tie round.
Knitchell, *n.* a bundle, a number of things tied together.
Knite, *v.* to strike, beat; to gnaw. Cf. Knoit.
Knittal, *n.* braces; a trouser-belt.
Knittan, *n.* a surfeit.
Knitten, *ppl. adj.* knitted.
Knitting, Knitten, *n.* tape.
Knitting-pins, *n.* knitting-needles.
Knitting-sheath, *n.* a small sheath, generally of a hen's quills, into which knitters thrust their wires.
Knivel, *n.* the short horn of a young beast; a snuff-box made from such a horn.
Knivel, Knivvle, *v.* to beat, thrash. Cf. Knevell.
Knivelach, *n.* a blow that causes a swelling.
Knivvelin, *n.* a thumping.
Knob, *n.* a lump; the head.
Knobbet, *adj.* having knobs.
Knobby, *adj.* having knobs; short and plump.
—*n.* a walking-stick with a hooked head.

Knock, *n.* a little sheaf of cleaned straw of four or five inches in diameter.
Knock, *n.* a hill, a knoll.
Knock, *n.* a clock; in *phr.* 'Jock-strike-the-knock,' the hammer of a clock, which jerks back before striking.
Knock, *v.* to strike with a sharp blow; to pound; to hull barley.—*n.* a sharp blow; a door-knocker; a sort of beetle for beating yarn-webs, &c., in bleaching.
Knock-beetle, *n.* one who is severely beaten.
Knock-dodgel, *adj.* short and thick.
Knock-him-doon, *adj.* downright; turbulent.
Knock-house, *n.* a clock-house.
Knockie, *adj.* clever, smart, 'knacky.'
Knockin'-knees, *n.* knock-knees.
Knockin'-mell, *n.* a mallet for beating the hulls off barley, or linen after bleaching.
Knockin'-stane, *n.* a stone-mortar in which barley was hulled by the 'knockin'-mell'; a large, flat stone on which linen was beaten after bleaching.
Knockit, *n.* a lunch between breakfast or dinner; a midday meal; a small cake or loaf baked for children.
Knockit-barley, -bear, *n.* barley hulled in the 'knockin'-stane' with the 'knockin'-mell.'
Knock-maker, *n.* a clockmaker.
Knock-me-down, *adj.* knock-down.
Knock-strings, *n.* the cords supporting the weights of a clock.
Knog, Knogie, *n.* anything short, thick, and stout; a small cask, a firkin. Cf. Knag.
Knoist, *n.* a large lump. Cf. Knoost.
Knoit, *n.* a large piece of anything; a knob.
Knoit, *v.* to strike, knock, beat; used of the knees: to knock together, tremble; to plod on; to gnaw.—*n.* a sharp blow, the sound of a heavy stroke.
Knoiter, *v.* to knock, strike sharply; used of the knees; to tremble.
Knoity, *adj.* knobbed, knobby.
Knoll, *n.* a large piece of anything, a lump.—*v.* to knead.
Knoll, *n.* a knell; the sound of a bell tolling.
Knooff, *v.* to converse familiarly. Cf. Knuff.
Knool, *v.* to beat with the knuckles or clenched fist; to beat on the knuckles in a game of marbles; to knuckle down.
Knool, *n.* a wooden pin fixed in the end of a halter. Cf. Knewel.
Knoop, *n.* a knob; a lump; a peg to hang anything on; that part of a hill which towers or projects above the rest.
Knoose, *v.* to bruise. Cf. Knuse.
Knoost, *n.* a large lump, a piece. Cf. Knoist.
Knoozing, *n.* a beating. Cf. Knuse.
Knop, *n.* a knob, a protuberance; a peg. Cf. Knoop.
Knop, *v.* to strike sharply. Cf. Knap.

Knorel, Knorle, *n.* a lump, knob; a clot, &c. Cf. Knurl.

Knorelick, *n.* a 'knorlack.'

Knorlack, *n.* a large lump, a protuberance; a large clot; a swelling.

Knorlag, *n.* a small lump or knob.

Knorlie, *adj.* having small lumps or knobs Cf. Knurly.

Knorrie, *n.* a wheal raised by a blow; a 'knorlack.'

Knot, *n.* a lump; a pretty large piece of anything round or square; a lump of sugar; used of a little dry oatmeal in porridge; a clod of earth; a short, strong, thick-set person or animal; the mark, where a branch has budded in the wood, at the bottom of a boat, supposed in Shetland and Orkney to betoken the fortune of the boat; a 'cut' or 'lot' to be cast; a joint in straw, grass, &c.; a cluster, group; in *phr.* 'aff at the knot,' crazy, insane.—*v.* to gather together, to form groups; to knot thread in a particular way; to do tatting; to knit.—*ppl.* and *ppl. adj.* knotted.

Knot-grass, *n.* the oat-grass.

Knotless, *adj.* used of thread: without knots. —*phr.* 'like a knotless thread,' quietly, easily, without check.

Knottik, *n.* a small, strong, thick-set person.

Knotty, *n.* a game like 'shinty'; the ball used in the game.

Knotty-porridge, *n.* porridge with lumps of dry or uncooked oatmeal in it.

Knotty-sowans, *n.* 'sowans' badly boiled so as to have lumps.

Knotty-tams, -tammies, -tommies, *n.* lumps of meal in porridge.

Knoul, *n.* a knob; an excrescence, a swelling. Cf. Knule.

Knoul, *n.* a wooden pin fixed at the end of a halter. Cf. Knewel.

Knout, *n.* the ball or piece of wood used in 'shinty.' Cf. Noot.

Knout, Knowt, *n.* cattle. Cf. Nowt.

Knout-berry, *n.* the cloudberry.

Know, *v.* to press down with the fists or knees.

Knowe, Know, *n.* a knoll; a protuberance; the head.

Knowel, *n.* a wooden pin fixed at the end of a halter. Cf. Knewel.

Knowie, *adj.* full of knolls.

Knowing, *ppl. adj.* intelligent, well-instructed.—*n.* a very small quantity.

Knowledge, *n.* a trial or inquest by a jury.

Knowledgeable, *adj.* intelligent, well-informed.

Knowledge-box, *n.* the head; any one full of information.

Knowsh, *n.* a lump, a large protuberance.

Knowt, *v.* to plod on. Cf. Knoit.

Knub, *n.* a smart blow; a short club.—*v.* to thump.

Knublack, Knublock, *n.* a lump, knob; a small, round object; a swelling caused by a blow or fall. Cf. Nubblock.

Knuckle, *n.* the length of the second finger from the tip to the knuckle.—*v.* to measure a 'knuckle'; with *in*, a term in playing marbles; with *down*, to shoot a marble with the knuckles on the ground, to expose the knuckles to the 'nags' as a punishment; to bend, submit; to knead.

Knuckled-cake, *n.* oat-cake or bannocks kneaded with the knuckles instead of being rolled out with a rolling-pin.

Knuckler, *n.* a marble.

Knuckles, *n.* a punishment at the game of marbles.

Knudge, *n.* a short, thick-set, strong person or animal.

Knudgie, *adj.* short, thick-set, and strong.

Knuff, Knuiff, *v.* to converse familiarly. Cf. Knooff.

Knuist, *n.* a large lump. Cf. Knoost.

Knule, *n.* a wooden pin fixed in the end of a halter. Cf. Knewel.

Knule, *v.* to beat with the knuckles or clenched fist. Cf. Knool.

Knule, *n.* a knob, knot; a swelling, excrescence.

Knuled, *ppl. adj.* henpecked.

Knule-kneed, *adj.* having swelled or enlarged knee-joints; knock-kneed.

Knule-knees, *n.* swollen knee-joints.

Knule-taed, *adj.* having toes with swollen joints.

Knule-taes, *n.* toes swollen at the joints.

Knurl, Knurle, *n.* a lump, protuberance, knob; a clot; a game resembling cricket, in which a wooden ball or 'knurl' is struck with a bat; a knot in twine, thread, &c.; a dwarf, hunchback; a term of contempt.—*v.* to strike so as to raise a lump.

Knurley, *adj.* having small lumps or knobs.

Knurlin, *n.* a dwarf.—*adj.* dwarfish.

Knurly, *adj.* used of wood: knotty, hard; ill-shapen, rough; stunted in growth.

Knurr, *n.* a knot of wood, a round, knotty projection on a tree; the wooden ball used in 'shinty'; anything small or stunted in growth. Cf. Knirr.

Knuse, *v.* to press down with the hands or knees, to bruise; to beat with the fists; to knead. Cf. Knoose.

Knushy, *adj.* thick, gross.—*n.* a strong, firm boy.

Knusly, *adv.* snugly, comfortably.

Knut, *v.* to halt slightly; used of a horse: to jerk on its pasterns when setting a foot on a round stone.—*n.* a slight halt.

Knutle, *v.* to strike with the knuckles ; to repeat feeble blows frequently.

Knuzle, *v.* to press with the knees, to squeeze. Cf. Knuse.

Knyaff, *n.* a dwarf, a very small person or animal.

Knyp, Knype, *n.* a sharp blow, the sound of a blow.—*v.* to inflict a smart blow ; to knock with violence. Cf. Knip.

Knyte, *n.* a lump of anything. Cf. Knoit.

Knyte, *v.* to strike. Cf. Knoit.

Kob, *n.* a gold coin, a Jacobus. Cf. Jacobus.

Kok, *v.* to faint.

Koks, *n.* a child's name for excrement.

Koky, *v.* to evacuate excrement.

Kook, *v.* to appear and disappear by fits.

Kool, *n.* a sailor's 'sou'-wester.'

Koom, *n.* coal- or peat-dust ; crumbs. Cf. Coom.

Koopie, *v.* to chide.

Koost, *v. pret.* did cast.

Koot, *n.* the ankle. Cf. Cuit.

Korkalit, Korkie-lit, *n.* a red dye. Cf. Corkie-lit.

Korkir, *n.* the lichen which furnishes 'korka-lit.' Cf. Corkir.

Korter, *n.* a quarter or 'farle' of oatcake.

Kouk, *v.* to retch. Cf. Cook.

Koum, *n.* soot, dust. Cf. Coom.

Kounger, *v.* to snub. Cf. Coonjer.

Kow, *n.* a goblin.

Koyt, *v.* to beat, flog.

Kracht, *n.* craft, wickedness.

Krang, *n.* the body of a whale divested of blubber.

Krauperts, *n.* the crowberry. Cf. Knau-perts.

Krechle, *v.* to make a hoarse, croaking sound. Cf. Craickle.

Kreish, *n.* grease. Cf. Creish.

Krocket, *n.* the oyster-catcher.

Krunkled, *ppl. adj.* wrinkled, crinkled.

Kued, *adj.* hare-brained. Cf. Cude.

Kuit, Kute, *n.* an ankle. Cf. Coot, Cuit.

Kurchie, *n.* a kerchief for neck or head.

Kurt, *adj.* sparing.

Kustril, *n.* a foolish fellow. Cf. Custril.

Kuter, *v.* to coax, wheedle ; to nurse delicately, 'cocker'; to converse clandestinely and intimately. Cf. Cuiter.

Kuttikins, *n.* gaiters. Cf. Cuitikins.

Kweed, *n.* the cud.

Kweel, *v.* to cool.—*adj.* cool.

Kwile, Kwyle, *n.* a piece of burning peat or coal.

Kwintra, *n.* the country.

Kwyte, *n.* a coat.

Kyaard, *n.* a tinker. Cf. Caird.

Kyan, *n.* cayenne-pepper.

Kyardin, *n.* a scolding. Cf. Kyaard.

Kyarlin, *n.* an old man. Cf. Carlin.

Kyarn, *n.* a heap, cairn.

Kyauve, *v.* to knead. Cf. Kiauve.

Kye, Ky, *n.* cows, kine.

Kye-herd, *n.* a cow-herd.

Kye-time, *n.* the time of milking cows.

Kyeuk, *v.* to cook.

Kyle, *n.* a sound, a strait.

†**Kyle**, *n.* a ninepin ; in *pl.* the game. Cf. Kile.

Kyle, *n.* a chance, opportunity. Cf Kile.

Kyle, *n.* a haycock.—*v.* to put hay into cocks.

Kyle-alley, *n.* a ninepin-alley.

Kylevine, *n.* a lead-pencil. Cf. Keelavine.

Kyloe, Kylie, Kylock, *n.* a breed of small Highland cattle.

Kymond, *n.* a milk-pail. Cf. Kimmen.

Kyow-ow, *v.* to trifle. Cf. Kiow-ow.

Kyowowy, *adj.* fastidious. Cf. Kiowowy.

Kype, *n.* a cup-shaped hole in the ground, used in playing marbles ; in *pl.* the game played with such holes.

Kypie, *n.* a game played with a bat and a soft ball.

Kypie, *adj.* left-handed. Cf. Kippie.

Kypie-hole, *n.* a hole in the game of 'kypes.'

Kyrtle, *n.* a short skirt. Cf. Kirtle.

Kysle-stane, *n.* a flint-stone.

Kyst, *n.* sap, substance. Cf. Keest.

Kystless, *adj.* without substance ; tasteless. Cf. Keestless.

Kytch, *v.* to hitch up on the back ; to toss over the head. Cf. Keytch.

Kyte, *n.* the belly, stomach. Cf. Kite.

Kyte-clung, *adj.* with a shrunken belly.

Kyted, *ppl. adj.* intestinal.

Kyte-fu', *n.* a bellyful.

Kyth, *n.* kith.

Kythe, *v.* to show ; to make known ; to become known ; to appear, show one's self ; to look, seem ; to become friendly.—*n.* an appearance, show.

Kythesome, *adj.* of prepossessing appearance.

Kything, *n.* an appearance, manifestation.—*ppl. adj.* revealing itself ; used of the sky : brightening.

Kything-sight, *n.* a salmon-fisher's sight of a fish by marks in the water.

Kytie, *adj.* corpulent from good living.

Kytock, *n.* the belly.

Laaboard, *n.* a tailor's lap-board. Cf. Labord.

Laager, *v.* to besmear with dirt. Cf. Lagger.

Laan, *n.* land, ground. Cf. Land.

Lab, *n.* a blow ; a throw with a swing.—*v.* to beat severely; to pitch or toss with a swing ; to walk with a swinging gait ; to fall flatly.

Lab, Labb, *n.* a piece, lump ; a portion.—*v.* to devour in lumps.

Lab, *adj.* drunk.

Labach, *n.* a long story about nothing.

Labb, *n.* the sound of lapping waves.

Labber, *v.* to slobber in eating or drinking ; to let fall food in eating ; to soil, bespatter. —*n.* the act of slobbering, and the noise it causes.

Labe, *v.* to lay on a burden.

Labey, Labie, Labbie, *n.* the flap or skirt of a coat or shirt.

Labichrie, *n.* a long story about nothing. Cf. Labach.

Labie, *n.* a large, irregular piece. Cf. Lab.

†Labile, *adj.* liable or apt to err.

Labord, Labroad, *n.* a tailor's lap-board.

Labour, *v.* to till land ; to plough.—*n.* tillage.

Labouring, *n.* a farm.

Labourous, *adj.* labouring.

Labster, *n.* a lobster.

Labster-tae, *n.* a lobster's claw.

Lace, *v.* to mix spirits with tea, &c.

Lacer, *n.* a shoe tied with a lace.

Lacer, *n.* spirits for 'lacing' tea, &c.

Lacerate, *v.* to destroy a deed by tearing it up.

Lacht, *n.* a loft ; an upper floor or room. Cf. Laft.

Lachter, *n.* a sitting of eggs ; all the eggs laid by a hen before ' clocking '; a brood of young chickens, &c. ; as much cut grain as a reaper carries in one hand ; a lock of hair or wool ; a flake or layer of hay, &c. ; the site of a house.—*v.* to gather up cut grain. Cf. Lauchter.

Lachter-stead, *n.* the site of a house.

Lack, *v.* to slight, depreciate ; to vilify.—*n.* vilification ; scandal, disgrace, slight.

Lackanee, *int.* alas ! Cf. Alakanee.

Lacken, *n.* coarse German cloth.

Lad, *n.* a kindly term of address to a man ; a bachelor ; a male sweetheart ; a young man-servant ; a term of commendation or the reverse.

Lad-bairn, *n.* a male child.

Ladder, *n.* the framework of a cart for carrying straw, &c. ; a gallows.—*v.* to apply a ladder for ascending.

Ladder-to-Heaven, *n.* the Jacob's ladder plant.

Laddie, *n.* a boy ; a term of affection for a boy or youth ; a male sweetheart. Cf. Lad.

Laddie-bairn, *n.* a male child.

Laddie-band, *n.* a band of boys.

Laddie-days, *n.* boyhood.

Laddie-herd, *n.* a herd-boy.

Laddie-hood, *n.* boyhood.

Laddie-in-jacket, *n.* a novice.

Laddie-wean, *n.* a male child.

Laddikie, *n.* a little lad ; a term of endearment for a lad or boy.

Laddock, *n.* a 'laddikie.'

Lade, *n.* a watercourse leading to a mill.

Lade, *v.* to lead.

Lade, *v.* to load.—*n.* a load.

Lade, *ppl.* laden.

Lade-man, *n.* a miller's carter.

Laden, *v.* to load, to burden.—*n.* a load, a burden.

Ladenin-time, *n.* the time of laying in winter provisions.

Lading, *n.* a burden.

Ladle, *n.* a small wooden box with long handle, formerly in general use in collecting offerings in churches ; a tadpole. Cf. Laid lick.

Lad's love, *n.* southernwood.

Lad-wean, *n.* a male child.

Lady, *n.* a 'laird's' wife.—*adj.* fit for a lady. —*v.* to be the mistress ; to be the wife of a ' laird.'

Lady-bracken, *n.* the female fern.

Lady-hen, *n.* a lark.

Lady Landers, *n.* the ladybird.

Ladyness, *n.* ladylikeness.

Lady of the meadows, *n.* meadow-sweet.

Lady-preen, *n.* a small kind of pin.

Lady's-, Ladies'-bedstraw, *n.* the yellow bedstraw.

Lady's-, Ladies'-fingers, *n.* the kidney vetch ; the honeysuckle.

Lady's-, Ladies'-garten-berries, *n.* brambleberries.

Lady's-o'-heaven's-hen, *n.* the wren.

Lady's-, Ladies'-smock, *n.* the cuckoo-flower.

Lady-toed, *adj.* used of a horse : turning out the hoofs of the fore-feet in running.

Lae, *v.* to leave.—*n.* the rest, remainder.

Laenarly, *adj.* lonely ; exceptional.

Laep, *v.* to lap as a dog.

Laesion, *n.* lesion ; injury.

Laesir, *n.* leisure.

†Laethran, *n.* a light-headed, loose woman ; a lazy, idle person. Cf. Latheron.

Lafe, *n.* the remainder. Cf. Lave.

Laffin, *n.* a ceiling ; a joisted, boarded ceiling. Cf. Lafting.

Laffy, *adj.* soft, flaccid; not pressed together.

Laft, *n.* an upper floor; a church-gallery; a loft.

Laft, *n.* fitness of soil for seed. Cf. Lauch.

Lafting, *n.* a boarded ceiling; a ceiling, flooring; a story.

Laftit, *ppl. adj.* used of grain: kept on the floor of a 'laft' or granary.

Lag, *n.* in *phr.* 'lag at the bools,' a challenge to play at marbles.

Lag, *adj.* slow, sluggish; laggard; late, last of all.

Lagabag, *n.* the hindmost, a loiterer.

Lagen, Laggan, *n.* the projection of the staves of a barrel beyond its bottom. Cf. Laggen.

Laggan, *ppl. adj.* fatiguing.

Laggen, *n.* the projection of the staves of a barrel, &c., beyond its bottom; the angle formed by the side and bottom of a barrel, &c.—*v.* to repair the 'laggen' of a hooped vessel.—*phr.* to 'ungirth the laggen,' to give birth to a child.

Laggen-, Lagen-gird, *n.* the bottom hoop of a tub, barrel, &c.—*phr.* to 'cast a laggen-gird,' to give birth to an illegitimate child.

Lagger, *v.* to bemire; to sink in a mire; to overburden, to stagger under a load; to walk with difficulty; to walk loiteringly.—*n.* a miry place, mud; in *pl.* spots of mud.

Laggert, *ppl. adj.* miry; overburdened.

Laggery, *adj.* miry, dirty.

Laggie, *n.* a goose.—*int.* a call to geese.

Laggie, *adj.* slow, inactive.

Laggie-bag, *n.* the hindmost. Cf. Lagabag.

Lagging, *ppl. adj.* toilsome; exhausting; slow-moving.

Laggit oot, *ppl. adj.* worn out.

Laich, *adj.* low; short of stature; below the level of a street, &c., underground; prostrate, sick; in low spirits; lowly, of low birth, humble; used of the wind: southerly.—*n.* a hollow, low-lying land; a plain; the lower part or side of anything, years of age, &c.—*v.* to lower; to cease, stand still; to higgle about a price. Cf. Low.

Laich-browed, *adj.* used of a close: with a low entry.

Laich country, *n.* the Low Country; the Lowlands.

Laich croft, *n.* a low-lying croft.

Laichen, *v.* to lower.

Laichen, *n.* a large quantity of anything. Cf. Laigan.

Laich kirk, *n.* the area of a church, in contrast to the galleries; the low church of a town, in contrast to the high or principal church.

Laich-lifeo, *adj.* pertaining to 'low life,' mean, despicable.

Laichness, *n.* lowness.

Laich-shop, *n.* a shop below the level of a street.

Laich-sprung, *adj.* of lowly birth.

Laid, *n.* the pollack.

Laid, *ppl. adj.* used of crops: flattened by a storm; lain; compelled.—*v. pret.* lay.

Laid, *n.* a load.

Laid-drain, *n.* a drain in which stones were so laid as to give free passage to the water.

Laidlick, *n.* a tadpole.

†Laidly, *adj.* loathly; lascivious; clumsy.

Laidner, *n.* a larder; provisions for winter.

†Laidron, *n.* a lazy slattern; a loose woman. Cf. Latheron.

Laif, *n.* a loaf.

Laig, *n.* silly talk, gossip; a gossiper.—*v.* to talk idly, loudly, foolishly; to gossip.

Laig, *v.* to wade.

Laigan, *n.* a large quantity of anything.

Laigen, Laiggen, *n.* the angle between the staves of a barrel and the bottom. Cf. Laggen.

Laiger, Laigger, *v.* to bemire. Cf. Lagger.

Laigh, *adj.* low. Cf. Laich.

Laighen, *v.* to lower. Cf. Laichen.

Laighie-braid, *n.* a thick-set person or animal.

Laighland, *adj.* lowland.

Laiglen, *n.* a milk-pail. Cf. Leglen.

Laik, *n.* a toy; in *pl.* marbles staked in playing. Cf. Lake.

Laikin, *ppl. adj.* used of rain: intermittent. Cf. Leak.

Laik-wake, *n.* a watch by the dead.

Laiky, *adj.* moist; used of showers: intermittent.

†Lailly, *adj.* loathly.

Laim, *n.* earthenware. Cf. Lame.

Laimiter, *n.* a lame person. Cf. Lamiter.

Lain, *adj.* lonely. Cf. Lane.

Lainch, Lainsh, *v.* to throw; to launch; to pay out; to set about vigorously; to spring.—*n.* a launch.

Laing, *v.* to take long strides.

Laip, *v.* to lap like a dog.

Lair, *n.* a bed; a resting-place; a family grave.—*v.* to lie, rest; to sink to rest; to bury.

Lair, *n.* a quagmire, bog, quicksand; mud.—*v.* to sink in mud, snow, &c.; to stick fast in mud, snow, &c.; to struggle in a 'lair.'

Lair, *n.* lore; learning; education; schooling.—*v.* to learn; to teach.

Lair, *n.* a layer; a slice of beef, &c.; a patch of moss for drying peats.—*adj.* thick in layers.

Lairach, *n.* the site of a building; the traces of a foundation or ruin; the foundation on which a stack rests; a peat-moss; a heap of materials; a cairn of stones. Cf. Larach.

Lairach-cairn, *n.* a heap of stones.

Lairag, *n.* the lark. Cf. Laverock.

Laird, *n.* a lord; a landlord of a house; a landed proprietor.

Lair'd, *ppl. adj.* stuck in mud, snow, &c.

Lairdie, *n.* a small 'laird.'

Lairdlin, *n.* a lordling; a petty 'laird.'

Lairdliness, *n.* lordliness.

Lairdly, *adj.* lordly.

Lairdship, *n.* lordship; landed or house property; ownership of land or houses; the rank or dignity of a 'laird.'

Lairer, *n.* a herd-boy's staff for driving cattle, &c., to their resting-place.

Lairick, *n.* the larch. Cf. Larick.

Lair-igigh, *n.* the green woodpecker.

Lairing-staff, *n.* a herd-boy's 'lairer.'

Lairoch, *n.* a site. Cf. Larach.

Lairock, *n.* the lark. Cf. Laverock.

Lair-stane, *n.* a tombstone.

Lairt, *adj.* used of hair: streaked with gray. Cf. Lyart.

Lairy, *adj.* wet, slushy; boggy, swampy.

Laish, *n.* a heavy fall of rain. Cf. Lash.

Lait, *n.* the pollack. Cf. Lythe.

Lait, *n.* manner, bearing; a habit, custom; a trick, prank, bad habit.

Lait, *v.* to search for; to induce; to entice.

Lait, *v.* to reduce the temper of iron when too hard; to plate with tin, &c. Cf. Late.

†Laiteran, *n.* the elders' pew near the pulpit. Cf. Lateran.

Laith, *n.* the pollack. Cf. Lythe.

Laith, *adj.* loath.—*n.* a loathing.—*v.* to loathe.

Laithfu', *adj.* bashful; shy of invitations; loathsome; wilful.

Laithless, *adj.* unregretful; quite willing; not shy.

Laith-lounkie, *adj.* in low spirits.

†Laithly, *adj.* foul; repulsive; loathly; lascivious.

†Laithron, *n.* a term of contempt; a lazy, idle person; a sloven; a loose woman.

Laitin, *n.* thin sheet-metal; tin-plate. Cf. Latten.

Laive, *n.* the rest, remainder.

.Laive, *v.* to bale water; to throw water with the hand or with a vessel.—*n.* a quantity of water thrown; the drawing or throwing of water.

Lake, *v.* to undervalue.—*n.* a disgrace; want. Cf. Lack.

Lake, *n.* a small, stagnant pool.

Lake, *n.* play; a plaything; in *pl.* marbles staked in various games.—*v.* to play, sport.

Laldie, *n.* punishment, beating.

Lall, *n.* a lazy, inactive person.

Lallan, *adj.* belonging to the Lowlands of Scotland.—*n.* the Lowland dialect; in *pl.* the Lowlands of Scotland.

†Lamar, Lamer, *n.* amber. Cf. Lammer.

Lamb, *n.* a term of endearment.

Lamb-gimmer, *n.* a ewe lamb of a year old.

Lambie, *n.* a young lamb; a term of endearment.

Lamb's lettuce, *n.* corn-salad.

Lamb's tongue, *n.* corn-mint.

Lamb-tiend, *n.* the tithe of wool.

Lamb-time killing, *n.* the time when lambs are killed for food.

Lame, *adj.* slow-footed; clumsy.

Lame, *n.* crockery, earthenware; a broken piece of earthenware.—*adj.* made of earthenware or porcelain.

Lamely, *adj.* slow; halting.

Lame pig, *n.* an earthenware jar or other vessel.

Lamer, *n.* a thong; the lash of a whip.

Lamgammachy, *n.* a long, rambling speech; much foolish talk; rhymes repeated in girls' games.

Lamiter, Lameter, *adj.* lame.—*n.* a cripple; one deformed.

Lammas, *n.* the beginning of August; a Scottish term.

Lammas-fair, *n.* a fair held at 'Lammas.'

Lammas-flood, -rain, -spate, *n.* heavy rain and floods about 'Lammas.'

Lammas-nicht, *n.* the night of August 1.

Lammas-stream, *n.* a strong and high spring-tide in August.

Lammas-tide, *n.* the 'Lammas' season.

Lammas-whiting, *n.* the young of the salmon-trout.

†Lammer, *n.* amber.—*adj.* made of amber.

Lammer-bead, *n.* an amber bead.

Lammermoor-lion, *n.* a sheep.

Lammer-wine, *n.* amber wine, an imaginary liquor esteemed a sort of elixir of immortality.

Lammie, Lammikie, Lammikin, *n.* a young lamb, a term of endearment; a kid.

Lammie-loo, *n.* a darling child.

Lammie-sourocks, *n.* the sorrel-dock.

Lamoo, *n.* in *phr.* 'to gang down like lamoo,' to be easily swallowed.

Lamp, *n.* in *phr.* 'lamp o' the watter,' phosphorescence on the sea.—*v.* to shine as a lamp.

Lamp, *v.* to stride; to walk quickly and with long steps; to beat, thrash; to hammer on a sole, heel, &c.; to vanquish, conquer.—*n.* a long, heavy step, a great stride.

Lamp, *v.* used of the ground: to be covered with gossamer from dew or slight frost.

Lamper, *n.* one who takes long, heavy strides.

Lamper, Lamper-eel, *n.* a lamprey.

Lamper, *v.* used of milk: to coagulate, to 'lapper,' without artificial means.

Lampin', *n.* a beating; a defeat.

Lampit, *n.* a limpet.

Lampy, *adj.* having a striding gait.

Lamy, *n.* the common guillemot.

Lan', *n.* land; ground. Cf. **Land.**

Lance, *n.* a lancet.—*adj.* lancet-shaped.

Lance, *v.* to leap, bound forward.

Lancers, *n.* teeth.

Land, *n.* that portion of a field, or 'rig,' which a band of reapers could cut together at one bout; arable land; a house of different stories, let out in tenements; a story, a tenement in such a house.—*v.* to end, to finish a business.

Land, *n.* a hook like the letter S.

Landart, *adj.* rustic.

Land-biding, *adj.* 'stay-at-home.'

Land-burst, *n.* a series of a few breakers at a tidal change, or occasionally during a storm.

Land-fall, *n.* the flood-tide.

Land-folk, *n.* country people, rustics.

Landgates, *adv.* towards inland.

Land-horse, *n.* the horse that treads on the unploughed land.

Landimere, Landemeer, *n.* the march of a property; the ceremony of 'beating the bounds.'

Landimere's-day, *n.* the day on which the bounds are beaten or the marches are examined.

Landin, Landen, *n.* the end of a furrow in a ploughed field; the name given by a band of reapers to the 'rig' on which they worked; the reaping of their 'rig.'

Landlash, *n.* a great fall of rain with high wind.

Landlord, *n.* the head of the family.

Land-louper, *n.* a vagabond; an adventurer; an unsettled person; one who flees the country to escape his creditors or arrest.

Land-loupin', *adj.* rambling from place to place as a vagrant.

Land-lubbing, *adj.* pertaining to a 'land-lubber' or rustic.

Landmail, *n.* rent of land in money or kind.

Landman, *n.* a landowner; a landsman; an inhabitant of the country.

Land-march, -merch, *n.* a boundary. Cf. **Landimere.**

Land-, Land's-mark-day, *n.* the day on which a burgh's boundaries are beaten or marches ridden.

Land-master, *n.* landowner.

Land-metster, *n.* a measurer of land, a land-surveyor.

Landrien, *adv.* in a straight course and quickly.

Land-sea, *n.* heavy breakers on a beach.

Land-setting, *n.* land-letting.

Land-setting cop, *n.* a fee paid by the tenant at the letting of a farm.

Land-side, *n.* the side of a plough next the unturned soil.

Land's lord, *n.* a landowner.

Landstail, *n.* the parapet of a bridge; the part of a dam-head which connects it with the adjoining land.

Land-stane, *n.* a stone found in the soil of a field.

Land-tide, *n.* the undulating motion of the air, seen on a hot day.

Land-tow, *n.* a cable for fastening a boat to the shore.

Land-tripper, -trippit, *n.* the common sand-piper.

Landwart, *n.* the country; inland districts.—*adj.* rural, rustic; boorish.—*adv.* towards the country.

Landwart-bred, *adj.* brought up in the country.

Landwart-men, *n.* rustics in contrast with citizens.

Landwart-town, *n.* a country farm-house; a country-house.

Land-waster, *n.* a spendthrift.

Landways, *adv.* by land.

Land-whaup, *n.* the curlew.

Lane, *n.* a brook of which the motion is scarcely perceptible; the hollow course of a large rivulet; meadow-land; the smooth, imperceptible flow in a river.

Lane, *v.* to hide, keep secret. Cf. **Layne.**

Lane, *adv.* alone.—*adj.* lonely; solitary; dreary.—*n.* with *pers. pron.* and *poss. adj.,* self, selves; *phrs.* 'him lane,' 'his lane,' by himself; 'her lane,' by herself; 'them lane,' 'their lane,' by themselves.

Laneful, *adj.* forlorn.

Lanely, *adj.* lonely; alone; single.

Lan'en, *n.* the end of a furrow. Cf. **Landin.**

Lanerly, *adj.* alone; single; exceptional, singular.

Lanesome, *adj.* lonely.

Lang, *v.* to long for.—*n.* homesickness; desire.

Lang, *prep.* along.—*adv.* for a long time.

Lang, *adj.* long; tall; great; slow; tedious, wearisome; lasting.—*n.* length, extent; a long time; tedium.

Langainsyne, *adv.* long ago.

Langal, *n.* a tether for sheep. Cf. **Langel.**

Lang-back-seen, *adv.* long ago.

Lang board, *n.* a long table in a farm-house, at which master and servants sat at meals.

Lang bowls, *n.* a game in which heavy leaden bullets were thrown from the hand, and in which he who threw the farthest, or reached a fixed point with fewest throws, was victor.

Lang bullet, *n.* an iron bullet or a round stone, round which a broad garter was wound, the end of which was held in the hand, while the bullet was forcibly thrown forward on the highway, and acquired a rotary motion, making it move forward with extreme rapidity. Cf. **Lang bowls.**

Lang-chafted, *adj.* having long jaws.

Lang-craig, *n.* a long neck; a purse; an onion that goes to a stalk.

Lang-craigit, *adj.* long-necked.

Lang-craigit heron, *n.* the heron.

Lang-day, *n.* the Day of Judgment.

Lang-draughtit, *adj.* very foreseeing or politic.

Langel, *n.* a tether fastening an animal's fore- and hind-legs together on one side; a hindrance.—*v.* to hobble an animal; to fetter.

Langelt, *n.* a shackle.—*v.* to shackle an animal.

Langemark-day, *n.* the day for riding the marches. Cf. Landmark-day.

Lang-endwise, *adv.* lengthwise.

Langer, *n.* weariness; tedium; ennui; longing; homesickness.

Langersome, *adj.* tedious; slow; causing ennui.

Langet, *n.* a shackle for an animal.—*v.* to shackle an animal.

Lang-eyed, -e'ed, *adj.* long-sighted, sharp-sighted.

Lang-fingert, *adj.* thievish.

Lang frae syne, *adv.* long ago.

Lang-gabbit, *adj.* talkative.

Lang gae, *n.* a long time.

Lang-gaithered, *adj.* used of money, &c.: taking long to accumulate.

Lang-gate, *n.* the path skirting the old Nor' Loch, now Princes Street, Edinburgh.

Lang halter time, *n.* the season of the year when, the fields being cleared, travellers and others claimed a common right of occasional passage.

Lang hame, *n.* the grave, heaven.

Lang-heidit, *adj.* shrewd; far-seeing; intelligent.

Langie-spangie, *n.* a game of marbles, played with large marbles out along a road.

Langije, *n.* abusive language.

Lang-kail, *n.* a colewort or cabbage unmashed or unchopped.

Lang-kail-gullie, -knife, *n.* a knife for cutting 'lang-kail.'

Langle, *n.* a hobble for an animal. Cf. Langel.

Lang-least-buik, *n.* a ledger.

Lang-leggit-tailor, *n.* the daddy-longlegs.

Lang length, *n.* full length, full extent; a long time.

Langletit, *ppl. adj.* having a fore- and a hind-leg shackled, to prevent straying or running. Cf. Langel.

Langlins, *prep.* along.—*adv.* slowly, long drawn out.

Lang-lip, *n.* a fit of sulking; a sulky, morose person.

Lang-lippit, *adj.* sulky; morose; melancholy.

Langlit, Langlet, *n.* a shackle for an animal. Cf. Langelt, Langel.

Lang-lonen, *n.* long-continued loneliness.

Lang-Lowrie, *n.* a large bell tolled at 10 P.M. in many towns.

Lang-lug, *n.* a large portion; in *pl.* a donkey; an eavesdropper.

Lang-luggit, *adj.* long-eared; quick of hearing; given to eavesdropping.

Lang megs, *n.* a kind of apple.

Lang-neb, *n.* a long beak or nose; a forward intrusion.

Lang-nebbit, *adj.* long-nosed; quick of understanding; prying, intrusive; having a long point or prong; preternatural; used of words: difficult to pronounce or to understand, polysyllabic, pedantic.

Langour, *n.* ennui. Cf. Langer.

Langrin, *n.* the 'long run.'

Langs, *prep.* along.

Lang saddle, *n.* a long wooden seat with a high back and ends; a folding bed.

Lang sands, *n.* in *phr.* 'to leave one to the Lang sands,' to throw one out of a share of property to which he has a just claim.

Lang sang, *n.* a noise made by the waves on the bar of a harbour.

Lang seat, *n.* a 'lang saddle.'

Lang seen, *adv.* long ago.

Lang settle, *n.* a 'lang saddle.'

Lang-shankit, *ppl.* long-legged; having a long handle.

Lang sheep, *n.* sheep of the Cheviot breed.

Lang sicht, *n.* a great deal.

Langside, *adv.* alongside.

Lang siller, *n.* a large price.

Lang since syne, Langsinsyne, *n.* and *adv.* long ago.

Langsome, Langsum, *adj.* slow; tedious, weary; rather long; rather tall; lengthy, 'dreich;' late, behind time.

Langsomelie, *adv.* tediously.

Langsomeness, *n.* tediousness; delay.

Langspiel, *n.* a small harp.

Lang-spool, *adj.* long-limbed.

Langsyne, *adv.* long ago.—*adj.* ancient, old-time.—*n.* ancient days, days of old.

Lang-taed, *adj.* used of a 'tawse': having long strips at its end.

Lang-tailed, *adj.* tedious, prolix; longing, covetous.

Lang-taw, *n.* a game of marbles.

Lang tholance, *n.* long-suffering.

Lang-tochered, *adj.* well-dowered.

Lang-tongued, *adj.* voluble, garrulous; talebearing; unable to keep secrets; given to exaggeration.

Languish, *adj.* longish; used of a forehead: high.

Lang-war-day, *n.* the month of March.

Langways, -wise, *adv.* lengthways.
Lang Whang, *n.* the bleakest part of Carnwath Moor.
Langwidge, *n.* languor, languishing.
Lang-wund, *adj.* tedious, long-winded, involved.
Lanland, *n.* all the stories of a house.
Lannimor, *n.* an adjuster of marches between conterminous landowners.
Lanstell, *n.* the parapet of a bridge. Cf. Landstail.
Lant, *n.* three-card loo; a cheat; a dilemma. —*v.* to play the game of 'lant;' to cheat; to bring to a stand, to reduce to a dilemma; to jeer at.
Lant, *n.* confusion; commotion.
Lant, *n.* land, ground.
Lante, *v. pret.* did lend.
Lanter-loo, *n.* five-card loo.
Lantern-chafts, *n.* lantern-jaws.
Lantron, *n.* a lantern.
Lantron, *n.* Lent. Cf. Lentrin.
Lap, Lapp, *n.* a drink; what can be licked by the tongue; the noise of water among stones; a plash; a pool.
Lap, Lapp, *v.* to mend, patch; to wrap round. —*n.* a wrap; a patch; a flap; the lobe of the ear; the lapel of a coat, &c.; a saddle-flap.
Lap, *v. pret.* did leap.
Lap, *n.* a small quantity. Cf. Leap.
Lap-love, *n.* the climbing buckweed; the corn convolvulus.
Lapper, *v.* used of water: to ripple, lap, dash gently.
Lapper, *v.* to clot, curdle, coagulate; to besmear; to cover so as to clot; used of damp soil: to harden by drought; to become lumpy, claggy; to make soil muddy by working it in wet weather. —*n.* a clot of blood; a coagulated mass; curdled or sour milk; snow in a slushy state.
Lappert milk, *n.* milk coagulated without artificial means.
Lappie, *n.* a plash; a pool.
Lappings, *n.* slobberings from an animal's mouth.
Lapron, *n.* a leveret.
Lapster, *n.* a lobster.
Lapster-clap, *n.* a stick with iron hook for catching lobsters on the shore at extreme low tide.
Lapstone, *n.* the stone on which a shoemaker hammers his leather.
Larach, *n.* the site of a building; a heap; ruins; a peat-moss. Cf. Lairach.
Larbal, *adj.* lazy, sluggish.
Larboard, *adv.* beneath board.
Larcenry, *n.* larceny.
Lare, *n.* a resting-place. Cf. Lais,

Lare, *v.* to learn; to teach.—*n.* learning. Cf. Lair.
Lare, *n.* a layer. Cf. Lair.
Lare-maister, *n.* a schoolmaster, teacher.
Large, *adj.* liberal; self-important; plentiful.
Larick, *n.* the larch. Cf. Lairick.
Larick, *n.* the lark, 'laverock.'
Larick's lint, *n.* the great golden maidenhair. Cf. Laverock's-lint.
Larie, *int.* an excl. of surprise. Cf. Lorie.
Larie, *n.* laurel.
Lark, *v.* to play, frolic, make mischievous fun.—*n.* a frolic, 'spree'; mischievous fun.
Larrie, *n.* jesting, gibing; a practical joke; hoax.
Larrup, *v.* to thrash, beat soundly.—*n.* a blow.
Larry, Lary, *n.* a servant.
Larum, *n.* an alarm, noise, stir, bustle.
Las-a-day, *int.* an excl. of fear, surprise, &c.
Lash, *n.* a heavy fall of rain; a dash of water; a quantity, great abundance.—*v.* with *out,* to kick from behind; to lavish money, live extravagantly; to dash water, &c.; to throw forcibly, act violently; used of water: to fall with violence, dash, splash, rush; of rain: to fall in torrents; to work vigorously.
Lash, *adj.* relaxed from weakness or fatigue; feeble; lazy.
Lashings, *n.* abundance; great quantities.
Lashness, *n.* relaxation through great exertion; looseness of conduct.
Lask, *n.* diarrhœa or 'scour' in cattle. Cf. Lax.
Laskar, *n.* a large armful of hay or straw.
Laskit, *n.* elastic.
Lass, *n.* a girl; a young woman; a female sweetheart; a daughter; a maid-servant; a woman; a term of address.
Lass-bairn, *n.* a female child.
Lassie, *n.* a young 'lass'; a term of endearment. Cf. Lass.
Lassie-bairn, *n.* a female child.
Lassie-boy, *n.* a tomboy.
Lassie-days, *n.* girlhood.
Lassie-hood, *n.* girlhood.
Lassie-lad, *n.* an effeminate boy.
Lassie-like, *adj.* girlish; used of a boy: effeminate.
Lassie-wean, *n.* a female child, a daughter.
Lassikie, Lassockie, *n.* a young or little 'lassie.'
Lassock, *n.* a young 'lass.'
Lassock-love, *n.* a girl-sweetheart.
Lass-quean, *n.* a female servant.
Lass-wife, *n.* a girl-wife.
Last, *n.* a measure of herrings; a measure of arable land; a measure of tonnage; a dry measure of varying amount.
Last, *n.* durability, continuance; stay, power of lasting.—*v.* to hold out, live, survive.

Last-day, *n.* yesterday ; the other day, a day or two ago.

Lasten, *adj.* last.

Laster, *adj.* later.—*adv.* later.

Lastest, *adj.* latest.—*adv.* last, lastly.

Lasty, *adj.* lasting, durable, serviceable.

Lat, *v.* to let, hinder.—*n.* a hindrance.

Lat, *v.* to let, allow.

Lata, *n.* loyalty. Cf. Lawtie.

Lat a be, *phr.* not to mention ; to omit.

Latace, *n.* lettuce.

Lat be, *v.* to let alone.—*adv.* much less.

Latch, *n.* a mire, swamp ; a rut, the track of a cart-wheel.

Latch, *n.* a loop of thread on the edge of a garment for fastening on a hook or button ; the cord connecting the foot-board and the wheel of a spinning-wheel.

Latch, *v.* to catch.

Latch, *n.* part of a moss where peats are spread to dry.

Latch, *v.* to idle, loiter.—*adj.* indolent.—*n.* an idler or indolent person.

Latchard, *n.* a loop of thread on the edge of a dress for fixing on a button or hook ; a loop of thread fixing a footless stocking by passing over the second toe.

Latchet, *n.* a smart blow.

Latchy, *adj.* full of ruts.

Late, *v.* to reduce the temper of hard iron or steel by heating it ; to plate tin. Cf. Lait.

Late, *n.* a late hour ; a recent time.

†Lateran, Latern, *n.* the precentor's desk below the pulpit ; the raised pew round the foot of the pulpit, where the elders sat, and parents brought their children for baptism.

Lateth, *n.* loyalty. Cf. Lawtie.

Late-wake, *n.* a watch beside the dead. Cf. Lyke-wake.

Lat-gae, *v.* to let off, fire ; to break wind ; to ' raise ' a psalm-tune.

Lather, *v.* to work vigorously.

Lather, *n.* a ladder. Cf. Ladder.

Lather, *n.* leather. Cf. Leather.

†Latheron, Latherin, Lathron, *n.* a lazy, idle person ; a sloven, slut ; a loose woman ; a term of contempt.—*adj.* lazy, vulgar ; slovenly, sluttish. Cf. Laidron.

Lathie, *n.* a ' laddie.'

Latiner, *n.* one who is learning Latin.

Latna, *neg. v.* let not.

Lat o'er, *v.* to swallow.

Lat oot, *v.* to pay out straw gradually in twisting straw-ropes.

Latron, *n.* a latrine.

Latt, *n.* a shelf formed of laths.

Latten, *ppl.* let, allowed.

Latter-meat, *n.* meat sent from the master's to the servant's table.

†Latteron, *n.* a precentor's desk. Cf. Lateran.

Latter-oot, *n.* the person who pays out straw in twisting straw-ropes.

Lat wi', *v.* to yield to, indulge.

Lauch, *n.* law ; custom ; condition ; fitness of soil ; a tavern-bill.

Lauch, *v.* to laugh ; used of the eye : to light upon with pleasure.—*n.* a laugh.

Lauchablest, *adj.* most laughable.

Lauchen, *ppl.* laughed.

Laucher, *n.* a laugher.

Lauchfull, *adj.* lawful.

Lauchter, *n.* a setting of eggs ; what grain a reaper can carry in one hand ; a layer ; a lock of hair, wool, &c.—*v.* to gather up cut grain. Cf. Lachter.

Lauchterins, *n.* what remains after a mass of anything has been removed.

Lauchty, *adj.* used of teeth : projecting, long, tusk-like.

†Laudron, *n.* a lazy, idle fellow ; a sloven. Cf. Latheron.

†Laudry, *n.* a heated discussion or questioning.

Laugh, *n.* a loch, lake.

Laughen, *ppl.* laughed.

Laughify, *v.* to laugh at.

Laughing-rain, *n.* rain from the south-west, with a clear sky-line.

†Laumer, *n.* amber. Cf. Lammer.

Laun, *n.* land, estate. Cf. Land.

Launder, *n.* a laundry-maid.—*v.* to wash and dress clothes.

Laup, *v. pret.* leaped.

Lave, *n.* the remainder.

Lave, *v.* to lavish.

Lave, *v.* to draw water, to bale ; to throw water.—*n.* a quantity of water thrown.

Lave, *n.* the guillemot. Cf. Lavy.

Lavellan, *n.* a kind of weasel ; a mythical creature, living in lakes, &c., and squirting poison to a great distance.

Lave-luggit, *adj.* having long, drooping ears.

Laverock, Laveruck, *n.* the lark.

Laverock-heich, *adv.* as high as the lark soars.

Laverock-heicht, *n.* the height to which a lark soars.

Laverock's-lint, *n.* the golden maidenhair ; the dwarf-flax.

Lavrick, Lavrock, *n.* the lark.

Lavrie, *adj.* used of broth : well-cooked ; having good and plentiful ingredients.

Lavy, *adj.* lavish, profuse, liberal.

Lavy, *n.* the common guillemot.

Law, *n.* litigation, lawsuits ; disputatious talk ; so much time or space granted in a race, and pursuit of game.—*v.* to go to law ; to take every advantage of law against the defender ; to lay down the law ; to determine.

Law, *n.* a roundish or conical hill.

Lawage, *n.* acting lawfully.

Law-biding, *adj.* able to answer a charge; waiting the regular course of law instead of fleeing; observing the laws.

Lawbor, *n.* labour.—*v.* to labour; to cultivate the soil.

Lawborable, *adj.* that may be ploughed.

Law-brod, -buird, *n.* a tailor's lap-board.

Law burrows, *n.* legal security given by a person that he will not injure another in person or property.

Lawe, *v.* to lower. Cf. Low.

Law-folk, *n.* lawyers.

Law-free, *adj.* not legally convicted or condemned.

Lawful-day, *n.* an ordinary weekday.

Lawin, *n.* a tavern-bill, the reckoning.

Lawin-clink, -coin, *n.* money for payment of the 'lawin.'

Lawin-free, *adj.* scot-free, exempt from paying a share of the 'lawin.'

Lawland, *adj.* belonging to the Lowlands of Scotland. Cf. Lallan.

Lawly, *adv.* in legal form.

Lawn, Lawning, *n.* grass land.

Law-paper, *n.* a will, a testamentary deed.

Law-plea, *n.* a lawsuit.

Law-pleaing, *n.* litigation.

Lawrence-fair, *n.* a fair held on St Lawrence's Day.

Lawrencemas, *n.* August 23.

Lawrie, *n.* a fox. Cf. Lowrie.

Law-sovertie, *n.* legal security.

Law Sunday, *n.* the name given to a particular Sunday between the end of March and Whitsuntide.

Lawtie, Lawtith, *n.* loyalty, fidelity, honesty. Cf. Lata.

Lawtifull, *adj.* most loyal, full of loyalty.

Law-work, *n.* the experience of conviction of sin or repentance under the Law.

Lax, *n.* relief, release.—*v.* to relax, grow feeble.

Lax, *n.* a salmon.

Laxat, *adj.* laxative, aperient.

Lax-fisher, *n.* a salmon-fisher.

Lay, *n.* a slip of wood coated with sand or emery, for sharpening a scythe.

Lay, *n.* the slay of a loom; that part to which the thread is fixed, and which, as it moves, lays the threads of the web parallel, shot by shot, in weaving.

Lay, *n.* grass-land, pasture, lea.

Lay, *n.* a turning-lathe.

Lay, *v.* used of crops: to flatten by wind or rain; to wager; to alleviate; to allay; to repair the worn edge of a plough-coulter by adding fresh iron; to 'smear' sheep with ointment; to thresh; to lie, rest.—*n.* the parting of the wool when the sheep is smeared; the lie of the land, the direction in which a thing lies or moves; a foundation; a temporary lull of waves; a chance.

Lay about, *v.* to turn, put about; to fight vigorously.

Lay aff, *v.* to talk volubly; to hurt, injure.

Layan, *n.* the curing of a rickety child in a smithy, by bathing it in a tub of water heated by plunging hot irons into it.

Lay at, *v.* to beat severely; to work vigorously.

Lay away, *v.* used of hens, &c.: to lay eggs in out-of-the-way places.

Lay-buird, *n.* a lap-board.

Lay by, *v.* to stop, cease; to injure one's self by overwork; to be laid aside from illness.

Lay down, *v.* to knock or trample down; to sow out in grass; to bury; to seduce a woman.

†**Laydron,** *n.* a lazy knave; a sloven.

Layer, *n.* a resting-place. Cf. Lair.

Layer, *n.* the Manx shearwater.

Lay-fitted, *adj.* used of the foot: flat-soled, springless, and much turned out.

Lay from, *v.* used of a horse: to kick violently, to 'fling' out.

Lay in, *v.* used of a woman: to be confined; to work vigorously.

Laying money, *n.* money in hand.

Laying time, *n.* the season, about November, for smearing sheep.

Lay into, *v.* to beat severely; to work vigorously; to eat greedily.

Lay money, *n.* false coin.

Layne, *v.* to conceal. Cf. Lane, Lean.

Lay on, *v.* to beat severely; to work hard; used of rain, &c.: to fall heavily; to 'fall to' on food, to eat much.—*n.* a good meal.

Lay on to, *v.* to thrash, beat severely.

Lay out, *v.* to explain clearly.

Lay out for, *v.* to get ready for; to abuse, scold.

Lay past, *v.* to put by.

Lay pock, *n.* the ovary of a fowl.

Layt, *v.* to seek for. Cf. Lait.

Lay-to, -tae, *n.* a contest, fight; a holdfast at the head of a cow's stall, to which the cow is tied.

Lay-to, -till, *v.* to shut a door, &c.; to lay hold of; to apply, put on; to lay to the charge of; to work vigorously, to set to work; to eat greedily.

Lay up, *v.* to serve a meal; to cast on stitches in knitting.

Lay upon, *v.* to strike, beat severely.

Lazy, *v.* to render lazy.

Lazy-bed, *n.* a method of planting potatoes, which secures the trenching of the plot in two or three years.

Lea, *adj.* unploughed.—*adv.* in grass. Cf. Ley.

Lea, *v.* to leave.

Lead, *v.* to play first in a curling-rink ; to carry, cart, hay, straw, peats, &c.—*n.* a mill-race, an artificial water - course ; as much hay, &c., as a horse and cart can take in one journey ; the course over which curling-stones are driven ; the first player in a curling-rink ; in *pl.* a game of curling.

Lead, *n.* a dialect ; a rhyme, song ; a screed. Cf. Leed.

Lead, *n.* the weight at the end of the pendulum of a clock ; a weaving term.

Lead-brash, *n.* a disease affecting animals at Leadhills.

Lead-bullaxe, *n.* a roughly-pointed piece of lead used as a pencil or as a ruler.

Lead-draps, *n.* small shot.

Leaden-heart, *n.* a charm hung round the neck to promote recovery from unaccountable ailments.

Leader, *n.* the person who plays the first stone in a curling-rink ; a carrier, carter ; a tendon, sinew ; a pipe for conveying water.

Leading, *n.* carting hay, straw, peats, &c. ; provisions.

Lead master, *n.* a leader, general.

Lead-pike, *n.* a 'lead-bullaxe.'

Lead-stane, *n.* the weight that sinks a fishing-line.

Leaf, *n.* a loaf. Cf. Laif.

Leaf-alane, *adj.* quite alone.

Leaful, *adj.* lawful. Cf. Leiful.

Leaful, *adj.* sad, lonely ; wistful. Cf. Leeful.

Leafu'-lane, *adj.* quite alone.

Leag, *n.* talk, gossip. Cf. Laig.

Leager, *v.* to encamp.

Leager-lady, *n.* a soldier's wife ; a female camp-follower ; used contemptuously.

League, *v.* to hurry off.

Leaky, *n.* an irregularity in the tides in the Firth of Forth.

Leaky-tide, *n.* the 'leaky' in the Firth of Forth.

†**Leal,** *adj.* loyal, faithful ; sincere, true ; genuine ; true to the mark ; of a blow : severe, smart, well-directed.—*n.* truth.—*adv.* truly.

Lea-laik, *n.* natural shelter for cattle, such as is furnished by glens or overhanging rocks.

Lea-laik-gair, *n.* well - sheltered grazing ground ; the place where two hills join together and form a kind of bosom.

Lea-lane, *adj.* quite alone. Cf. Lee-lane.

Lea-lang, *adj.* livelong. Cf. Lee-lang.

Leal-come, *adj.* honestly gained.

Leal-gude, *adj.* truly good.

Leal-heartit, *adj.* true-hearted, faithful, loyal.

Leal-loved, *adj.* dearly and truly loved.

Leally, *adv.* loyally, honestly.

Lealty, *n.* loyalty, fidelity.

Leam, *n.* a gleam, flash ; flame, blaze.—*v.* to gleam, shine, flash.

Leam, *v.* to take nuts out of the husk.

Leam, *n.* a dog-leash.

Leam, *n.* earthenware, crockery. Cf. Lame.

Leamer, *n.* a ripe nut ready to fall from the husk. Cf. Brown-leamer.

Leaming, *ppl. adj.* used of nuts : ripe and separating easily from the husk.

Lean, *v.* with *down*, to be seated, to lie down, recline.—*n.* means of leaning ; a resting-place.

Lean, *v.* to conceal, connive at. Cf. Layne.

Lean, *adv.* scantily.

Leanet, *adj.* well-inclined, affable, frank.

Leaning-stock, *n.* a post or block of wood for resting on. Cf. Stock.

Leap, *n.* a small quantity, a measure. Cf. Lap.

Leap, *v.* with *on*, to mount a horse ; to dance, frisk about ; to flee in haste ; with *into*, to change suddenly from one party to another ; to burst open, break out ; with *out*, to break out in an illegal or disorderly way ; used of frost : to give way ; of wood : to spring ; to become red with blushing.—*n.* a small cataract. Cf. Loup.

Leaping ague, *n.* St Vitus's dance.

Leaping-block, *n.* a horse-block.

Leaping-ill, *n.* a disease of sheep. Cf. Louping-ill.

Leaping-on-stone, *n.* a stone horse-block.

Lear, *v.* to teach ; to accustom, train ; to learn.—*n.* learning, education, knowledge ; a habit, custom. Cf. Lair.

Lear, *v.* with *up*, to brighten up, lighten. Cf. Leure.

Lear, *adv.* rather. Cf. Leefer.

Lea-rig, *n.* a grass field, an unploughed 'rig.'

Learless, *adj.* unlearned.

Learn, *v.* to teach ; to threaten punishment ; to accustom.

Learning, *n.* education, schooling.

Learock, *n.* the lark, 'laverock.'

Leary, *n.* the light of a candle, lamp, &c. : a lamp-lighter. Cf. Leerie.

Leary-licht-the-lamps, *n.* a lamp-lighter ; a teasing name given to a lamp-lighter by children.

Lease, *v.* to hold, possess.

†**Lease,** *v.* to injure. Cf. Lese.

Lease-haud, *n.* possession, holding by a lease.

Lease-me-on, *phr.* an expression of preference. Cf. Leese-me-on.

Leash, *n.* a long piece of rope, cord, &c., rope enough, freedom, liberty ; anything very long.—*v.* to tie together ; to marry ; to tie up with twine ; to walk or move quickly ; with *off*, to unroll, to speak from memory ; to speak much ; with *at*, to work vigorously and with speed ; with *away*, to go cleverly off.

Leash, *adj.* supple. Cf. **Lish**.

Leasing-maker, *n.* a liar; a spreader of lies.

Leasing-making, *n.* lying; the uttering of falsehood against the king or his counsellors to the people, or to the king or government against the people.

Leasome, *adj.* lonely. Cf. **Leesome**.

Least, *adv.* at least.

Least, *conj.* lest.

Least-ways, **-wise**, *adv.* at least, at any rate.

Leasum, *adj.* lawful.

Leasumlie, *adv.* lawfully.

Leath, *n.* the 'lay' of a weaver's loom. Cf. **Lay**.

Leath, *v.* to loiter; to delay.

Leath, *adj.* unwilling, loath. Cf. **Laith**.

Leather, *n.* the skin; untanned hide; a cow's udder; a heavy blow.—*v.* to beat, thrash; to do anything vigorously and speedily; to hurry; to plod on or pound away at anything; to scold; to tie tightly; to cover with leather.

Leather, *n.* a ladder.

Leathering, *n.* a thrashing; a scolding.

Leather-shod, *adj.* supplied with boots and shoes.

Leatherty-patch, *n.* a country-dance.

Leathfow, *adj.* loathsome. Cf. **Laithfu'**.

Leaugh, *adj.* low. Cf. **Laich**.

Leauw, Leaw, *n.* a place for drawing nets on at a river-side.

Leave, *v.* to allow, permit, let; to have leave.

Leave, *n.* the remainder.

Leave, *adj.* dear, beloved. Cf. **Lief**.

Leave aside, *v.* to put aside, not to count, to except.

Leave be, *v.* to let alone, let be.

Leaven, *n.* dough set for fermentation.

Leave out, *n.* permission to leave school for a few minutes.

Leaves, *n.* leavings, scraps.

Lebb, Leb, *n.* as much liquid, meat, &c. as can be taken into the mouth or thrown by the hand at one time.—*v.* to lick up food; to swallow hastily; to throw small quantities of liquid or of meal by hand or a small vessel into the mouth; to get through work quickly.

Lebber, Leber, *v.* to bedaub; to beslobber.— *n.* in *pl.* droppings of food or drink from the mouth. Cf. **Labber**.

Lebber-beards, *n.* broth made of greens, thickened with oatmeal.

Lebbie, *n.* the fore-skirt of a man's coat. Cf. **Labey**.

Leck, *n.* a flagstone; any stone that stands a strong fire; a hard subsoil of clay and gravel.

Leck, *v.* to moisten; to sprinkle; to pour water over a substance to get a decoction; to drip, ooze; to leak; to drain off.—*n.* a leak; a drip; a pit for soaking bark in tanning.

Leck-ee, *n.* the pit which holds the tan-liquor and supplies the tan-pits.

Lectern, *n.* the precentor's desk. Cf. **Lateran**.

Ledder, *n.* a ladder.

Ledder, *n.* leather.

Leddy, *n.* a lady.

Leddy-launners, *n.* the ladybird.

Led-farm, *n.* a farm on which the tenant does not reside.

Ledge, *v.* to allege; with *upon*, to accuse.

Ledge, *v.* to jut out; to overhang.

Ledge, *v.* with *on*, to travel at a good pace; to work quickly; with *out*, to go fast at the start; to begin work with a dash.

Ledgin', *n.* a parapet, especially of a bridge.

Ledgit, *n.* the top of the inner half of a window.

Ledington, *n.* a kind of apple.

Lee, *n.* shelter from wind or rain.—*adj.* sheltered.

Lee, *n.* the ashes of green weeds.

Lee, *adj.* lonely, used as an intensive.

Lee, *n.* in *phr.* 'little lee,' slender means of escape.

Lee, *n.* lea, grass land.—*adj.* untilled.

Lee, *v.* to leave.

Lee, *v.* to tell lies.—*n.* a lie.

Lee, *v.* to love.

Lee-a-lawly, *n.* a children's game. Cf. **King** of Cantland.

Leear, Leearie, *n.* a liar.

Leech, *n.* a doctor, surgeon.—*v.* to bleed, doctor.

Leech, *v.* to pin or splice two pieces of wood together.— *n.* a piece of wood used to splice a broken shaft, &c.

Leechence, *n.* license.

Leed, *n.* the metal, lead.

Leed, *n.* a dialect, language; a song, rhyme; a long, rambling speech; a yarn; a particular line of argument or talk.—*v.* to speak much with little meaning.

Leef, *adj.* unwilling. Cf. **Laith**.

Leef, *n.* the hand. Cf. **Loof**.

Leefer, *adv.* rather. Cf. **Liefer**.

Leefow, Leefu', *adj.* kindly, compassionate.

Leefow, *adj.* wilful, obstinate.

Leefow, Leeful, *adj.* lonely, sad, wistful.

Leefow-heartit, *adj.* kindly, sympathizing.

Leeft, *v. pret.* left.

Leefu-lane, -leen, *adj.* all alone, quite by one's self.

Leein'-like, *adj.* unlike the truth.

Leek, *n.* in *phr.* 'as clean as a leek,' completely, perfectly.

Leekrife kail, *n.* broth with abundance of leeks.

Leeky, *adj.* used of the hair : much in need of the curling-tongs.

†**Leel**, *adj.* loyal. Cf. **Leal**.

Lee-lane, -lone, *phr.* with a *poss. pron.*, quite alone ; single.

Lee-lang, *adj.* livelong ; whole.

Lee-like, *adj.* having the appearance of falsehood.

Leem, *n.* a tool, an implement.

Leem, *n.* a loom.

Leem, *n.* a light.—*v.* to shine. Cf **Leam**.

Leem, *n.* earthenware ; a wide-mouthed vessel for holding anything. Cf. **Lame**.

Leem, *v.* to separate nuts from the husk. Cf. **Leam**.

Leemer, *n.* a ripe nut ready to fall from the husk. Cf. **Leamer**.

Leen, *n.* a wet, grassy place in a moor ; a lowlying piece of grass in a farm.

Leen, *int.* cease !—*v.* to cease. Cf. **Lin**.

Leen, *adj.* alone. Cf. **Lane**.

Leenge, *v.* to slouch, lounge.

Leenger, *n.* a slouching, lazy fellow.

Leengyie, *adj.* used of a weaver's web : of a raw or thin texture.

Leeno, Leenon, *n.* thread gauze, leno.

Leenzie, *n.* the loin. Cf. **Leingie**.

Leep, *v.* to parboil, scorch, scald ; to warm hastily ; to boil for a short time ; to perspire freely ; to sit over a fire.—*n.* a great heat ; a hasty warming ; a lounge over a fire.

Leep, *v.* to cheat, cozen, deceive. Cf. **Loopy**.

Leepan day, *n.* a hot, moist day.

Lee-penny, *n.* a charm, consisting of a stone set in gold, in the possession of the Lockharts of Lee.

Leeper, *adv.* very, superlatively. Cf. **Lepper**.

Leeping, *ppl. adj.* used of the weather : hot, moist.

Leepit, *ppl. adj.* chilly, loving a fire ; meagre, thin.

Leer, *n.* a look, glimpse.—*v.* to scowl, frown.

Leer, *adv.* rather. Cf. **Liefer**.

Leeret-gray, *adj.* 'lyart-gray.' Cf. **Lyart**.

Leerie, *adj.* blinking, casting sidelong glances.

Leerie, *n.* a light ; a lamp-lighter. Cf. **Leary**.

Leerie, *n.* a cock, chanticleer.

Leerie-la, -law, *n.* the crow of a cock ; cockcrow.

Leerielarach, *n.* a wrangle, a brisk quarrel.

Leeroch, Leerrach, *n.* the site of an old building ; a peat-moss ; local position. Cf. **Larach**.

Leerrach, *v.* to talk much foolishly ; to deliver a long, uninteresting speech, &c. ; with *aboot* and *at*, to repeat from memory ; to speak in an unknown tongue.—*n.* rambling talk ; a foolish book or writing.

Leese, Lees, *v.* to unravel, disentangle ; to arrange ravelled bits of pack-thread by collecting them into one hand ; to gather anything into the hand ; to pass a coil of rope through the hand ; to arrange, trim, sort ; to loosen the fibres of a rope ; with *out*, to spin out, be prolix, to prolong.—*n.* the thread in winding yarn ; *phr.* to 'get the lees of a thing,' to get a right understanding of it.

Leese, *v.* to be pleased to.

Leese, *v.* to lose ; to cause to lose.

Leese-me-on, *phr.* an expression of extreme pleasure in, or affection for, a person or thing.

Leesh, *n.* a heavy fall of rain ; a quantity.—*v.* to lash ; to work vigorously. Cf. **Lash**.

Leesh, *n.* a long piece of rope ; silk twine, part of the mounting of a silk-weaver's loom.—*v.* to hurry forward. Cf. **Leash**.

Leeshach, *n.* a long piece of rope, twine, &c.—*v.* with *off*, to unroll ; to speak from memory ; to tell news at length. Cf. **Leash**.

Leeshince, Leeshins, *n.* license ; leisure.

Leesing, *n.* falsehood ; a lie.

Leesk, *n.* the groin. Cf. **Lisk**.

Leesome, Leesim, *adj.* pleasant ; loving ; lovable. Cf. **Lovesome**.

Leesome, *adj.* lonely.

Leesome, *adj.* lawful ; permissible. Cf. **Leisome**.

Leesome, *adj.* easily moved to pity.

Leesome-lane, *adj.* quite alone.

Leesome-like, *adj.* 'eerie,' ghostly.

Leester, *n.* a salmon-spear. Cf. **Leister**.

Leesum, *adj.* speaking in a lying or hyperbolical manner.

Leesumlie, *adv.* lawfully.

Leesum-like, *adj.* like lying.

Leet, *n.* a lot, portion ; a separate division ; a selected list of candidates or nominees ; a nomination to office by election.—*v.* to nominate, to make a select list of candidates ; to enrol, establish.

Leet, *n.* an unseemly mass of liquid or semiliquid stuff ; ichor distilling through the pores of the body.—*v.* to ooze slowly.

Leet, *v.* to pretend, feign, make a thing appear so or so ; to 'let on,' notice, mention ; to attend to, listen to.

Leet, *n.* dialect.—*v.* to ramble in speech. Cf. **Leed**.

Leet, *v.* to reduce the temper of metal. Cf. **Lait**.

Leetach, *n.* an unseemly mass of any liquid or semi-liquid substance ; a 'leet' or watery sore.

Leetach, *v.* to talk a great deal foolishly ; to deliver a speech or sermon ; to repeat from memory.—*n.* incoherent talk, rambling speech ; a poor, lengthy piece of literature. Cf. **Leed**.

Leetch, v. to pin or splice two pieces of wood together. Cf. Leech.

Leeth, adj. reluctant, loath. Cf. Laith.

Leethfu', adj. loathsome; slow, reluctant; bashful, modest, discreet. Cf. Laithfu'.

Leethfu', **Leethfow**, adj. compassionate. Cf. Leefow.

Leet-lyte, v. to fall flat violently.—n. a heavy fall.—adj. flat.

Leeve, v. to live.

Leeve, adv. willingly, gladly. Cf. Lief.

Leevin, n. a living being. Cf. Living.

Leevin-lane, adj. quite alone. Cf. Leefu'-lane.

Leeze, v. to unravel. Cf. Leese.

Leeze-me-on, phr. an expression of great pleasure. Cf. Leese-me-on.

Left, ppl. adj. destitute, abandoned, God-forsaken; widowed.

Left-about, n. an abrupt dismissal.

Left ane, n. the largest bannock of a batch.

Lefter, n. a shallow wooden vessel, larger than a 'cog.'

Left-hand, adj. wrong.

Left-handed, adj. sinister, malicious; dubious, doubtful; used of a child: illegitimate.

Left-loof, adj. sinister, malicious.

Leg, v. to lie, to sleep with.

Leg, n. a flat, wooden, leg-shaped board, for stretching stockings after washing; an upright post resting on the ground, giving support to a house; a 'leg-dollar'; in pl. increased speed to a curling-stone.—v. to walk, to run away, to take to one's heels.

Legacie, n. the state or office of a papal legate.

Legacy, v. to bequeath.

Legal, n. time allowed before the foreclosure of a mortgage.

Legality, n. legal proof; legal knowledge; legal action; a lawsuit.

Legate, v. to bequeath.

Legation, n. a legal formality.

Legator, n. a legatee.

Leg-bail, n. a kick on the legs; escape; flight from justice instead of seeking bail.

Leg-bane, n. the shin.

Leg-brod, n. a leg-shaped frame for stretching stockings.

Leg-, **Legged-dollar**, n. a Manx dollar; a dollar worth £2, 16s. Scots, bearing the impression of a man in arms with one leg visible and a shield covering the other.

Lege, v. to allege.

Legen-girth, n. the bottom hoop of a tub or cask. Cf. Laggen-gird.

Leg-foot, n. the foot or bottom of a thing.

Leggat, n. a stroke at golf or ball which for some reason or other is not counted.

Leggate, n. a small, self-closing gate. Cf. Liggate.

Leggen, **Leggin**, n. the angle at the bottom of a cask or tub. Cf. Laggen.

Leggen-gird, n. the bottom hoop of a cask or tub.

Leggie, v. to run, to use one's legs.—n. a child's leg.

Leggin, n. loose bits of wool from near the sheep's feet.

Leggums, n. leggings, gaiters.

Legible, adj. fair, equitable.

Leg-ill, n. a disease in sheep causing lameness.

Legitim, n. the lawful share of movables falling to a child on the father's death.

†Legitime, adj. legitimate.

Leg-length, n. the length of a stocking.

Leglin, n. a milk-pail with an upright handle.

Leglin-girth, n. the lowest hoop of a milk-pail; phr. 'to cast a leglin-girth,' to bear an illegitimate child.

Leg-o'er-im, adv. with one leg over the other.

Leg-o'-mutton, adj. huge, brawny.

Leg-on, n. brisk walking or working.

Leg-out, n. a quick walk.

Legs, n. legends.

Legs and arms, n. used of a story: currency given to it.

Leid, n. the metal, lead.

Leid, n. a load.

Leid, n. a mill-race. Cf. Lade.

Leid, n. a language, dialect. Cf. Leed.

Leid, n. an inkling, a partial idea.

Leif, adj. unwilling, loath. Cf. Laith.

Leif, adj. dear.—adv. gladly. Cf. Lief.

Leifer, adv. rather.

Leifsum, adj. pleasant. Cf. Leesome.

Leifsum, adj. compassionate. Cf. Leesum.

Leifu', adj. lawful.

Leifu', adj. discreet, modest. Cf. Laithfu'.

Leifu', adj. sad, lonely. Cf. Leeful.

Leifu'-lane, adj. quite alone.

†Leil, adj. loyal, honest, upright; used of a blow: smart.—adv. smartly, severely.

Leill, n. a single stitch in marking on a sampler.

Leillie, n. in the lullaby, 'Leillie-baw-loo-loo.'

Lein, v. to conceal. Cf. Lane, Layne.

Lein, v. to cease. Cf. Lin.

Leinfou, adj. kindly; feeling; sympathetic.

Leinfou-heartit, adj. 'leinfou.'

Leingie, n. the loin. Cf. Lunyie.

Leingie-shot, adj. used of a horse: having the loins dislocated.

Leip, v. to parboil; to scald. Cf. Leep.

Leippie, n. the fourth of a peck. Cf. Lippie.

Leir, v. to teach.

Leirichie-larachie, v. to whisper together.—n. mutual whispering.

Leis, *v.* to arrange.

Leisch, *n.* a long piece of rope. **Cf. Leash.**

Leish, *adj.* active, nimble; supple; tall; lithe. **Cf. Lish.**

Leish, Leisch, *n.* a heavy fall of rain.—*v.* to dash, to lash. **Cf. Lash.**

Leish, *n.* a long piece of rope; liberty.—*v.* to couple; to marry. **Cf. Leash.**

Leisher, *n.* a tall, active fellow; an extensive tract; a long journey.

Leishin', *ppl. adj.* tall and active; used of a field, farm, parish, &c.: extensive; of a journey: long.

Leisin, *n.* lying, lies. **Cf. Leasing.**

Leis-me-o', *phr.* an expression of great pleasure.

Leisome, *adj.* lawful. **Cf. Leasum.**

Leisome, Leisum, *adj.* pleasant, lovable. **Cf. Leesome.**

Leisome, *adj.* warm, sultry.

Leissure, *n.* pasture between two corn-fields; any grazing ground.

Leister, *n.* a barbed fish-spear with prongs.—*v.* to spear fish.

Leit, *n.* a piece of horse-hair used as a fishing-line.

Leit, *n.* a watery discharge from a sore, &c. —*v.* to ooze. **Cf. Leet.**

Leit, *v.* to pretend; to think; to give a hint of. **Cf. Leet.**

Leit, *v.* to nominate.—*n.* a select list of candidates. **Cf. Leet.**

Leitch, *v.* to loiter.

Leiugh, *adj.* low. **Cf. Laich.**

Leive, *adj.* dear. **Cf. Lief.**

Lek, *v.* to moisten; to leak.—*n.* a leak. **Cf. Leck.**

Le-lane, *int.* be quiet! let alone!

†**Lele,** *adj.* loyal; true. **Cf. Leal.**

Leil, *v.* to mark, take aim.

Leloc, *adj.* lilac-coloured.

Lemanry, *n.* an illicit amour; harlotry.

Leme, *n.* a gleam.—*v.* to gleam. **Cf. Leam.**

Leme, *n.* earthenware. **Cf. Lame.**

Lemp, *v.* to stride, walk with long strides. **Cf. Lamp.**

Lempit, *n.* a limpet.

Lempit-cuddie, *n.* a small creel for gathering limpets.

Lempit-ebb, *n.* the shore between high and low tide, where limpets are gathered.

Lempit-pick, *n.* an iron chisel for detaching limpets from rocks.

Len, *v.* to conceal. **Cf. Layne, Lean.**

Len, *v.* to sit down; to sit in a sloping position; to lean.—*n.* a resting-place; a sloping position. **Cf. Lean.**

Len', *v.* to lend.—*n.* a loan. **Cf. Lend.**

Lench, *v.* to launch; to throw. **Cf. Lainch.**

Lend, *v.* to give a blow.—*n.* a loan.

Lend, *n.* the loin.

Lendit, *adj.* used of black cows: having a white stripe over the loins.

Length, *n.* stature, tallness; a point of distance or time; with *poss. adj.* one's house.

Lenk, *n.* a link of horse-hair connecting hooks and fishing-line.

Lenner, *n.* a lender.

Lenno, *n.* a child.

Lennochmore, *n.* a big child.

†**Lent,** *adj.* slow.

Lent, *n.* the game of three-card loo. **Cf. Lant.**

Lented, *ppl. adj.* beaten in the game of 'lent.'

Lenten, *n.* the spring.

Lenten, *ppl.* allowed, let.

†**Lent fever,** *n.* a slow fever.

†**Lent-fire,** *n.* a slow fire.

Lenth, *n.* length. **Cf. Length.**

Lenthie, *adj.* prolix, long.

†**Lently,** *adv.* slowly.

Lentrin, Lentren, Lentron, *n.* Lent; the spring.

Lentrin-kail, *n.* broth made without beef; poor fare.

Lentrins, *n.* lambs that die in spring soon after birth.

Leomen, *n.* a leg; the bough of a tree.

Lep, *v.* to sup or lick with the tongue; to lap. **Cf. Lap.**

Lepe, *n.* a slight boiling. **Cf. Leep.**

Leper-dew, *n.* a cold, frosty dew.

Lepit peats, *n.* peats dug out of the solid moss, without being baked.

Leppie, *n.* the quarter of a peck. **Cf. Lippie.**

Lerk, *v.* to contract; to shrivel.

Lerrick, Lerrock, *n.* the larch. **Cf. Larick.**

Lerroch, *n.* the site of a building; the artificial bottom of a stack. **Cf. Lairach.**

†**Lese,** *v.* to injure, wrong; to offend.

Lesed, *ppl. adj.* legal term: injured, wronged.

Lesion, *n.* legal term: injury, wrong.

Lesk, *n.* the groin. **Cf. Lisk.**

Less, *conj.* unless.—*prep.* except, with the exception of.

Less, *conj.* lest.

Lesser, *n.* a smaller quantity or amount.

Lesum, *adj.* lawful, permissible. **Cf. Leasum, Leesome.**

Let, *v.* to let go; to emit, give out; to lance. **Cf. Lat.**

Let at, *v.* to assail.

Let bug, *v.* to give a hint, 'let on.' **Cf. Bug.**

Let gae, *v.* to 'raise' a tune.

Leth, *n.* disgust. **Cf. Laith.**

Lethargy, *n.* coma; a trance.

Lether, *v.* to leather, beat.

Lether, *n.* a ladder.

Letherin, *n.* a beating; a scolding.

Lethfu', *adj.* shy, modest, bashful. Cf. Laithfu'.

Lethie, *n.* a surfeit : a disgust.

Let intil, *v.* to strike.

Let licht, *v.* to admit, allow.

Let off, *v.* to fire a gun ; to break wind ; to make a great display.

Let on, *v.* to make known, mention ; to indicate by signs ; to take notice of ; to pretend, feign ; to give one's self concern about ; to explain.

Let on the mill, *v.* to scold.

Let out, *v.* to go on : used of a school, church, &c. : to be dismissed.

Let out on, *v.* to break out into scolding.

Lett, *n.* a lesson ; a piece of instruction ; a ticket on a house showing it is to be let.

Letten, *ppl.* permitted, suffered.

Lettengo-wort, *n.* a laxative.

Letter, *n.* a spark on the wick of a candle, supposed to indicate the arrival of a letter : in *pl.* legal writs.—*v.* to write, paint, or carve letters on signboards, gravestones, &c. ; to teach letters, instruct.

†**Letteran, Letterin**, *n.* the precentor's desk. Cf. Lateran.

Lettered, *ppl. adj.* bearing an inscription ; used of invitations : sent by letter.

Lettered-cakes, *n.* cakes with words inscribed on them, generally with sugar.

Lettered-sweeties, *n.* large, flat lozenges, with mottoes, &c., printed on them, 'conversation-lozenges.'

†**Letterene**, *n.* a desk for writing. Cf. Lateran.

Letter-gae, *n.* the precentor in a church. Cf. Let gae.

Lettering, *n.* letter-cutting on a tombstone.

†**Lettern, Letteron, Lettrin**, *n.* the precentor's desk. Cf. Lateran.

Let wit, Let to wit, *v.* to inform, give to know.

Let with it, *v.* to admit ; to mention, inform.

Leuch, Leugh, *v. pret.* laughed.

Leuch, Leugh, *adj.* low in situation : squat, not tall.—*n.* the low part ; a dale. Cf. Laich.

Leuchen, Leughen, *ppl.* laughed.

Leuchly, *adv.* in a low situation.

Leuchness, *n.* lowness of stature ; lowness of situation.

Leug, *n.* a tall, ill-looking man.

Leuk, *v.* to look.—*n.* a look.

Leur, *adv.* rather. Cf. Liefer.

Leure, *n.* a gleam, a faint ray.

Leusking, *ppl. adj.* absconding. Cf. Lusking.

Leut, *n.* a sluggard. Cf. Lute.

Levellers, *n.* a name given to the Galloway peasantry who objected to landlords fencing-in fields, on the ground that herding cattle by their children would no longer be necessary.

Leven, *n.* lightning.

Leven, *n.* a lawn ; an open space between woods.

†**Lever**, *v.* to unload from a ship.

Lever, *adv.* rather. Cf. Liefer, Lure.

Levin-bolt, *n.* a thunder-bolt.

Levrick, *n.* the lark. Cf. Laverock.

Lew, *v.* to warm, make tepid.—*n.* a heat.—*adj.* lukewarm. Cf. Loo.

Lewands, *n.* butter-milk and meal boiled together.

Lewder, *v.* to move heavily.—*n.* a blow with a cudgel : a hand-spike for lifting a mill-stone. Cf. Lowder.

Lewer, Lewre, *n.* a hand-spike ; a long pole ; a lever.

Lewgh, *adj.* low. Cf. Laich.

Lew-warm, *adj.* lukewarm.

Ley, *n.* grass-land.

Ley-cow, *n.* a cow not giving milk and not in calf.

Ley-crap, *n.* a lea-crop.

Ley-metal, *n.* an alloy of tin and lead.

Leytch, *v.* to loiter.

Lezzure, *n.* pasture. Cf. Leissure.

Liam, *n.* a hair-rope.

Liart, *adj.* used of the hair : streaked with gray. Cf. Lyart.

Lib, Libb, *v.* to geld.

Libbag, *n.* a short-handled horn-spoon.

Libber, *n.* a castrator ; a sow-gelder.

Libber, *n.* a lubberly fellow.

Libby, *n.* the quarter of a peck. Cf. Lippie.

†**Libel**, *n.* a legal indictment.—*v.* to indict ; to draw up a 'libel.'

Libelt, *n.* a long discourse ; a long treatise.

Liberality, *n.* a gift, present.

Libet, *n.* a eunuch ; a gelded animal.

Lice, *n.* the seeds of the wild rose.

Licent, *ppl. adj.* licensed.

Lich-bird, *n.* the night-jar.

Liche-fowl, *n.* the night-jar.

Licht, *v.* to light, kindle.—*n.* a light ; light ; a will-o'-the-wisp ; a 'corpse-candle' ; in *pl.* with *auld*, conservatives in theology and ritual ; with *new*, progressives in theology and ritual.

Licht, *adj.* not heavy ; dizzy ; giddy ; thoughtless, foolish.—*v.* to lighten ; to make light of ; to undervalue.

Licht, *v.* to alight ; to reach one's destination ; to happen.

Lichtavised, *adj.* of light, fair complexion.

Licht-coal, *n.* a piece of splint coal put on a fire to give a light.

Lichten, *v.* to give light, enlighten.—*n.* a flash of lightning.

Lichten, *v.* to lighten, alleviate.

Lichtening, *n.* dawn ; daybreak ; lightning.

Lichtenly, *adv.* disparagingly, scornfully.

Lichter, *adj.* used of a woman : delivered of a child.—*v.* to unload ; to deliver a woman of a child.

Lichters, *n.* a horse's blinkers.

Licht-farran, *adj.* light in conduct, giddy.

Licht-fit, *adj.* nimble ; giddy, flighty ; of loose character.

Licht-heeled, *adj.* active, nimble.

Lichtie, *adj.* light-headed, foolish.—*n.* a giddy woman.

Lichtin'-in-eldin, *n.* small brushy fuel, as furze, thorns, &c.

Lichtless, *adj.* despondent.

Lichtlie, *adj.* light of foot.—*adv.* expeditiously.

Lichtlie, *v.* to make light of, disparage ; to undervalue, think little of ; of a bird : to forsake its nest.—*n.* scorn, slight, jilting.

Lichtliefow, *adj.* scornful, haughty.

Lichtlifie, *v.* to make light of, slight ; to undervalue.

Lichtlifiean, *n.* disparagement ; the act of disparaging.

Lichtly-shod, *adj.* bare-footed.

Licht-o'-day, *n.* the white phlox.

Licht-o'-spald, *adj.* light of foot.

Lichts, *n.* the lungs.

Lichtsome, *adj.* well-lighted ; light in colour.

Lichtsome, *adj.* light in weight ; nimble ; cheerful, lively ; pleasant, delightful ; used of a sick person : easier, better, brighter ; light, trifling, fickle.

Lichtsomely, *adv.* pleasantly ; joyously ; brightly.

Lichtsomeness, *n.* cheerfulness, gaiety ; pleasant variety.

Lichty, *adj.* near daylight.

Lick, *v.* to strike ; to fight ; to carry on a prosecution.—*n.* a taste, a small quantity ; a pinch of snuff ; a daub of paint, &c.; a blow ; speed ; a wag, a fellow ; a cheat ; in *pl.* a thrashing, punishment, deserts.

Licken, *v.* to lay to one's charge.

Licker, *n.* liquor.

Lickie, *n.* a small hooked wire for drawing the thread through the hack of a spinning-wheel.

Licklie, *v.* to lay to one's charge.

Lick-lip, *adj.* fawning.

Lick-ma-dowp, *n.* a servile flatterer.

Lick-my-loof, *adj.* fawning, cringing.

Lick-penny, *n.* a scamp, rascal.

Lick-spit, *n.* a servile flatterer.

Lick-up, *n.* a lock of hair that will not lie flat ; a horse's martingale ; a 'lock-up,' prison ; a bar of iron hindering the chains from slipping off the swingle-tree of a plough ; a scrape, plight, difficulty.

Licquory-stick, *n.* a stick of liquorice or liquorice-root.

Lid, *v.* to shut, close.

Lidded, *ppl. adj.* furnished with flaps.

Lidder, *adj.* idle, lazy ; loathsome.—*n.* laziness. Cf. Lither.

Lidderie, *adj.* feeble and lazy.

Lidderlie, *adv.* lazily.

†**Lidderon, Lidrone**, *n.* a lazy, idle fellow. Cf. Latheron.

Liddisdale-drow, *n.* a shower that wets an Englishman to the skin.

Lide, *v.* to glide through.

Lide, *v.* to thicken ; to become mellow. Cf. Lithe.

Lie, *n.* a sheltered, warm place ; a calm.—*adj.* warm, sheltered. Cf. Lithe.

Lie, *n.* a black speck on a tooth.—*v.* to make an erroneous statement without intending to lie. Cf. Lee.

Lie, *v.* to be ill in bed ; to lie idle ; to sleep ; used of a ewe : to bring forth lambs ; to lay.—*n.* used of a place : exposure, natural situation ; the direction in which a thing moves or is placed ; the situation of a golf-ball ; rest.

Lie-a-bed, *n.* a late riser, a sluggard.

Lie-by, *v.* to lie idle ; to lie unused ; to keep off.—*n.* a mistress ; a neutral.

Lied, *n.* a dialect. Cf. Leed.

Lie-day, *n.* an idle day.

Lief, *n.* the palm of the hand, the 'loof.'

Lief, *adj.* dear, beloved.—*adv.* gladly, willingly.

Lief-alane, -on-lone, *adj.* quite alone.

Liefer, *adv.* rather.

†**Liefhebber**, *n.* a lover.

Liefsum, *adj.* pleasant. Cf. Leesome.

Liefu' lane, *adj.* quite alone.

Lie in, *v.* to be in childbed.

Lie out, *v.* used of cattle : to lie in the fields at night ; to be delayed in receiving money due, or in entrance on inherited property.

Lierachie, *n.* a hubbub.

Liesh, *adj.* tall ; active. Cf. Lish.

Lies-making, *n.* treasonable falsehood.

Liesome, *adj.* warm, sultry.

Liesome, *adj.* lawful.

Liesome, *adj.* pleasant, lovable.

Liesome-like, -looking, *adj.* having the appearance of lies.

Lie throut, *v.* to lie out of doors.

Liethry, *n.* a crowd. Cf. Lithry.

Lie-time, *n.* days on which harvesters are not engaged on harvest work proper.

Lie to, *v.* to incline to love.

Lieugh, *adj.* low. Cf. Laich.

Lieutenantry, *n.* the lieutenancy of a county or district.

Lieve, *adj.* dear.—*adv.* willingly, gladly. Cf. Lief.

Liever, *adv.* rather. Cf. Liefer.

Lievetenant, *n.* lieutenant.

Life, *n.* a living person or animal.

Life-knife, *n.* a pocket-knife.

Life-like, *adj.* in *phrs.* 'life-like and death-like,' used of the uncertainty of life ; 'living and life-like,' in vigorous health.

Life-safe, *n.* a warrant to spare an offender's life.

Life-sick, *adj.* sick of life.

Life-stoup, *n.* a mainstay, chief support of life.

Life-thinking, *adj.* in *phr.* 'living and life-thinking,' in vigorous health.

Life-tie, *n.* a hold on life ; one for whose sake alone another lives.

Liffy, *n.* a blow on the hand. Cf. Loofie.

Lifie, Lifey, *adj.* lively; spirited ; merry; active ; life - giving, exhilarating. — *adv.* quickly, alertly.

Lifieness, *n.* vigour, vitality.

Lifily, *adv.* vigorously, briskly ; heartily ; merrily.

Lift, *n.* the firmament, sky.

Lift, *v.* to gather root - crops ; to cut corn, hay, &c. ; to collect money, rates, taxes, subscriptions, &c. ; to steal, pilfer ; to steal cattle, &c. ; to exhume a dead body ; to 'flit,' remove, transport, shift cattle ; to break up ground ; to take out of pawn ; to strike up a tune, 'raise' the psalm, &c. ; to rise and depart ; to disperse ; to ascend ; to carry out the dead to burial ; of the chest : to heave.—*n.* a burden, a weight to be lifted, the lifting of a burden ; a large quantity ; a theft ; a drove of cattle ; a trick in a game of cards ; the first break or ploughing ; help, encouragement, promotion ; a helpful drive given on a road to one on foot ; a heave of the chest in difficult breathing or oppressive sickness ; the rise of a wave, the swell of the sea ; an ill-turn ; a large sum of money ; the matter.—*int.* a call to a horse to lift its foot.

Lift and lay, *n.* a number of men wielding the scythe.—*adv.* stroke for stroke ; on an equality.

Lifted, *ppl. adj.* elated ; conceited ; joyously grateful.

Liften, *ppl.* lifted.

Lifter, *n.* one who gathers corn in harvest-fields, or gathers root-crops ; a cattle-stealer ; a shallow wooden bowl in which milk is set for cream ; a flat, rectangular, perforated door-key which lifted the latch ; the valve of a pair of bellows ; in *pl.* the name formerly given to those who held that the minister, at the Communion, should lift the bread before the thanksgiving. Cf. Anti-lifters.

Lift-fire, *n.* lightning.

Lift-hanse, *n.* the left hand.

Liftie, *n.* dirt on the streets adhering to the feet.

Lifting, *n.* removal ; the carrying forth of a coffin from the house to burial ; used of the mouth : something to eat.

Liftward, *adj.* and *adv.* heavenward.

Lig, *v.* to talk much, gossip.—*n.* much talk, gossip ; the noise of talking. Cf. Liglag.

Lig, *v.* to lag, fall behind.

Lig, *v.* used of ewes : to bring forth.

Lig, Ligg, *v.* to lie, recline ; to lodge ; to know carnally ; to lay, let lie.

Liggate, Ligget, *n.* a self-closing gate.

Ligger, Liggar, *n.* a foul salmon.

Ligger-lady, *n.* a female camp-follower. Cf. Leager-lady.

Light, *v.* to undervalue. Cf. Licht.

Lighter, *n.* in *pl.* the blinkers of a horse.

Lighter, *adj.* of a woman : delivered of a child. Cf. Lichter.

Lightfeet, *n.* a greyhound.

Liglag, *n.* a confused noise of tongues ; a great deal of idle talk ; a strange language ; an unintelligible discourse.—*v.* to prate. Cf. Lig.

†**Lignate,** *n.* an ingot or mass of metal which has been melted.

Likamy-docks, *n.* the pillory, 'jougs,' gyves, &c.

Like, *adj.* in golf: equal, even ; likely, probable.—*adv.* probably ; about, nearly.—*conj.* as, just as ; as if.—*n.* a match, equal ; the even stroke in golf.—*v.* to be on the point of, to be likely.

Like, *v.* to please, be agreeable to ; used impersonally.

Like, *n.* an unburied corpse ; the watch kept over it. Cf. Lyke.

Like as, *conj.* as if ; as also.

Likeliness, *n.* comeliness, good looks.

Likely, *adj.* promising ; likely to do well ; good-looking.—*adv.* probably.—*n.* likelihood, probability.

Likelys, *adv.* likely.

Liken, Liking, *ppl. adj.* on the point of, likely to do, bear, &c.

Liker, *adj.* better fitted for ; more suitable to. —*adv.* more likely.

Likery-stick, *n.* a stick of liquorice or liquor-ice-root. Cf. Liquor-stick.

Likesome, *adj.* like.

Likewake, *n.* the watch by the dead. Cf. Lykewake.

Liking, Likein, *n.* appearance ; condition.

Liking, *n.* favour ; good graces ; a darling.

Likmy-docks, *n.* the pillory. Cf. Likamy docks.

Lill, *n.* the hole of a wind instrument.

Lillilu, Lillyloo, *n.* a lullaby ; a refrain.

Lilly, *adj.* charming, lovely.

Lilly-lowe, *n.* a bright flame, blaze.

Lilt, *v.* to sing softly; to hum: to sing briskly; with *out* or *off*, to finish off one's drink merrily or quickly; with *up*, to begin a song or music; to dance to music; to leap lightly over a fence.—*n.* a song; a cheerful tune; a mournful tune; the hole of a wind instrument; a long and frequent 'pull' in drinking.

Lilti-cock, *n.* one who walks limping or jerking himself.—*adj.* walking in a limping or jerking way.

Lilting, *ppl.* limping.

Liltit, *ppl. adj.* paired for a dance.

Lily, *adj.* charming, lovely.

Lily, *n.* aphthæ or thrush in children.

Lily, *n.* the white lily or poet's narcissus; the daffodil.

Lily-can, *n.* the yellow water-lily.

Lily-oak, *n.* the lilac.

Limb, Lim, *n.* the butt of a fishing-rod; a creature, a tool, agent, used contemptuously; a mischievous child or person.

Limb-free, *adj.* with relaxed limbs, as in sleep.

Lime, *n.* glue.

Lime-man, *n.* a lime-burner; a dealer in lime.

Lime-quarrel, *n.* a lime-quarry.

Lime-red, *n.* the rubbish of lime-walls.

Lime-shells, *n.* burnt lime unslaked.

Limestone-beads, *n.* St Cuthbert's beads, fossil *entrochi.*

Lime-wark, *n.* a place where limestone is dug and burnt.

Limm, *n.* a mischievous child or woman; a 'limmer.' Cf. Limb.

Limmer, *n.* a rascal, rogue; a prostitute; a loose woman or girl; a playful or contemptuous term applied to a woman, without any charge of immorality; a familiar term of address to a man or a woman.

Limmer, *n.* a limber, a wagon- or cart-shaft.

Limp, *v.* to cause to limp.

Limpus, *n.* a worthless woman.

Lin, *n.* flax.

Lin, *n.* a waterfall.—*v.* to hollow out the ground by force of water.

Lin, *n.* a shrubby ravine.

Lin, *v.* to cease; to rest. Cf. Lint.

Linarich, *n.* a green sea-plant, used as an astringent.

Linch, *v.* to halt; to limp; to hop.—*n.* a hop.

Lincum-green, *n.* a green-coloured cloth manufactured at Lincoln.

Lincum-twyne, *n.* packthread; a very fine thread; a Lincoln texture.

Lind, *n.* the loin. Cf. Lend.

Linder, *n.* a woollen or flannel undershirt.

Lindsay, *n.* linsey-woolsey. Cf. Linsey.

Line, *n.* the boundary of the Highlands; any written or printed authority: a doctor's prescription; a certificate of proclamation of banns, or of marriage, or of Church membership, or of character; a short letter of introduction.—*v.* to measure with a line; to thrash.

Line, *v.* used of dogs: to impregnate.

Line, *n.* flax.

Line, *v.* to bestow gifts; with *one's loof,* to bribe one.

Lineboard, *n.* the starboard.

Line-grip, *n.* strength and skill to handle a fishing-line.

Line-him-out, *n.* a boys' game in which the players beat one of their number with their caps.

Line-man, *n.* a line- or white-fisher.

Linen, Linnen, *n.* the white sheet worn by immoral offenders in doing public penance; in *pl.* underclothing, shirts, a shroud, winding-sheet.

Linen-winsey, *n.* linsey-woolsey.

Liner, *n.* one who measures by line.

Liner-out, *n.* one who prefers the reading of a psalm line by line before singing.

Line-scoll, *n.* a box to hold fishing-lines.

Ling, *n.* a long, thin grass or species of rush.

Ling, *n.* a line; a quick career in a straight line.—*v.* to walk quickly with long step; to gallop.

Lingal, Lingel, *n.* shoemakers' thread. Cf. Lingle.

Lingan, Lingin, *n.* shoemakers' thread; the taw or lash to a whip.

Lingcan, *n.* the body.

Linge, *v.* to flog, beat.

Lingen-ends, *n.* shoemakers' thread-ends.

Linget, *n.* a rope binding a fore-foot of a horse to a hind one.

Linget, *n.* the seed of flax, linseed; flax-thread.

Linget-oil, *n.* linseed-oil.

Linget-seed, *n.* the seed of flax, linseed.

Lingit, *ppl. adj.* narrow; thin; small; used of an animal: very lank in the belly.

Lingit, *ppl. adj.* flexible, supple; pliant, agile.

Lingit-claith, *n.* cloth of a soft texture.

Lingity, *adj.* slender.

†**Lingle**, *n.* shoemakers' thread; a leather thong; a fetter; anything to tie with; anything of considerable length; a tall, lanky person.—*v.* to fasten with shoemakers' thread; to fasten, fetter; to hobble an animal; with *off,* to unwind, unroll; to reel off a speech, &c.

Lingle-back, *n.* a person with a long, weak back.

Lingle-end, *n.* the point of a shoemaker's waxed thread.

Lingle-tailed, *adj.* draggle-tailed.

Ling-tow, *n.* a rope used by smugglers.

Ling-tow-man, *n.* a smuggler; one who carried inland smuggled goods.

Lingy, *adj.* trashy; limp; helpless.

Lining, *n.* a measurement; permission to build from the Dean of Guild's Court of a burgh according to plans given in to, and passed by, the Court.

Lining, *n.* food and drink.

Lining-out, *n.* the old practice of reading the psalms to be sung line by line.

Linjet, *n.* flax-seed. Cf. Linget.

Link, *n.* a length of hair or fine gut, attaching a hook to a line; a joint; the division of a peat-stack; a straw-rope fastening the thatch of a stack, &c.; a lock of hair; in *pl.* the chain by which a pot, &c., hangs over a fire from the 'crook'; a string of sausages resembling links in a chain.—*v.* to walk arm in arm; to join; to twine arms; to marry; to cease moving about; to lift a pot from the links of a 'crook'; with *down*, to lower on the links of a chain, to unhook; with *on*, to hang upon a chain or 'crook'; with *away*, to carry off by the arm.—*phr.* the 'links of misery,' the extreme of starvation.

Link, *v.* to walk briskly; to trip along; used of money: to flow in rapidly and in plenty.

Link, *n.* in *pl.* the windings of a river; the rich ground lying among these windings; sandy knolls, a stretch of sandy, grass-covered ground near the seashore.

Lin-, Linn-keeper, *n.* a large fresh-water trout, supposed to keep possession of a particular pool or linn.

Linket, *ppl. adj.* swift.

Linkie, *adj.* sly, roguish, waggish.—*n.* a wag, rogue; a person on whom no reliance can be placed.

Linkingly, *adv.* swiftly, lightly.

Linkome-green, *n.* a green cloth of Lincoln manufacture.

Linkome-twyne, *n.* packthread. Cf. Lincum-twyne.

Links-goose, *n.* the common sheldrake.

Link-stane, *n.* a stone attached to a rope to keep a 'link' of a peat-stack upright.

Linky, *adj.* flat and grassy.

Linn, *n.* the precipice over which water falls; the cascade of water; the pool at the base of the fall.—*v.* to hollow out the ground by the force of water.

Linn, *n.* a piece of wood placed under a boat's keel to facilitate drawing it up on the beach.

Linnen, *n.* a lining.

Linn-lier, *n.* a 'lin-keeper.' Cf. Lin-keeper.

Lin-pin, *n.* a linch-pin.

Lins, *n.* rollers by which a boat is drawn over the beach, and by which it is propped up. Cf. Linn.

Linset, *n.* linseed.

Linset-bows, *n.* the pods containing the flax-seed.

Linsey, *n.* linsey-woolsey.

Linsh, *v.* to hop.—*n.* a hop. Cf. Linch.

Lint, *v.* to relax; to unbend; to cease from work.—*phr.* to 'lint one's hough,' to sit down for a little. Cf. Lin.

Lint, *n.* flax.

Lint-bells, *n.* the flowers of the flax.

Lint-bennels, *n.* the seed of the flax.

Lint-bow, *n.* the pod containing flax-seed.

Lint-brake, *n.* an implement for breaking and softening flax.

Lint-coble, *n.* a pond or pit for steeping flax.

Lintel-ale, *n.* ale given at the completion of building-work.

Lint-haired, *adj.* having flaxen locks.

Lint-hole, *n.* a 'lint-coble.'

Lintie, *n.* the linnet; the twite.

Lintie-whytie, Lintiwhite, *n.* the linnet.

Lint-locks, *n.* flaxen hair.

Lint-pot, *n.* a 'lint-coble.'

Lint-ripple, *n.* a toothed implement for separating the seeds of flax from the stalk.

Lintseed, *n.* linseed.

Lint-straik, *n.* a handful of newly-dressed flax.

Lint-tap, *n.* as much flax as is put on the distaff at a time.

Lint-wheel, *n.* a spinning-wheel.

Lintwhite, *adj.* flaxen-coloured.

Lint-white, *n.* the linnet.

Linty, *adj.* flaxen.

Lion, *n.* a coin of the value of £2, 8s. Scots.

Lip, *n.* edge, boundary.—*v.* to taste; to be full to the brim; to rise to the edge of a bank; to break pieces from the face of edge tools.

Lip-deep, *adj.* superficial, only from the lips; very deep, up to the brim; up to the lips.

Lip-fou, *adj.* quite full; tipsy.

Lip-licker, *n.* one who licks his lips at the sight of some dainty.

Lippen, *v.* to trust, depend upon; to have confidence in; to entrust to; to expect.

Lippen, *ppl.* leaped. Cf. Luppen.

Lippen, *v.* to taste, sip, put one's lips to.

Lippening, *ppl. adj.* occasional; thoughtless; accidental.

Lipper, *n.* a slight swell or ruffle on the surface of the sea; a ripple, wavelet.—*v.* to ripple, break in small waves; to rise and fall gently on the waves.

Lipper, *n.* a large festering surface on the skin.—*adj.* covered with smallpox or any cutaneous eruption.

Lipper, *n.* a leper; a contemptuous term applied to a dog.

Lipper, *v.* to lap up.

Lipper, *adv.* very, exceedingly, superlatively.

Lippering, *ppl. adj.* full, overflowing.

Lipperjay, *n.* a jay or jackdaw.

Lipper owre, *v.* to be so full as to run over.

Lippet, *ppl. adj.* edged, having a border.

Lippie, *n.* the fourth part of a peck; a liquid measure; a bumper.

Lippie, *n.* a child's lip.

Lipping, Lipping-fou, *adj.* full to the brim.

Lip-rapping, *adj.* lip-knocking; used of a kiss: resounding.

Liquefy, *v.* to spend money in drink.

Liquidly, *adv.* clearly beyond dispute.

Liquor-, Liqurry-stick, *n.* a stick of liquorice. Cf. Likery-stick.

Liquory, *adj.* sweet-toothed, fond of sweets.

Liquory-knots, *n.* the bitter vetch.

Lirb, *v.* to sip.

Lire, *n.* the flesh or muscles of any animal, as distinguished from the bones; lean beef.

Lire, *n.* the complexion; that part of the skin which is colourless; the air.

Lire, *n.* the udder of a cow or other animal. Cf. Lure.

Lirk, *n.* a crease, wrinkle; a fold in the skin or flesh; a double; a subterfuge; a crevice or hollow in a hill.—*v.* to fold, crease, rumple; to contract, shrivel.

Lirky, *adj.* full of creases, wrinkled.

Lirt, *v.* to deceive, jilt, beguile.—*n.* deception, fooling; cheating.

Liry, *n.* the pogge. Cf. Lyrie.

Lish, *adj.* lithe; supple; agile.

Lisk, *n.* the groin, flank.

Liss, *v.* to cease, stop.—*n.* cessation, release, respite from pain.

Lissens, *n.* release; an interval free from pain, &c.

Lissim, *adj.* lawful.

List, *adj.* agile; lively; eager.—*n.* appetite. —*v.* to choose.

List, *v.* to write down on a list; to enlist as a soldier.

List, *v.* to listen to.

Listen, *v.* to listen to.

Listener, *n.* the ear.

Lister, *n.* a dyer. Cf. Litster.

Lister, *n.* a fish-spear. Cf. Leister.

Listing, *n.* list for stockings.

Lit, *n.* a dye. Cf. Litt.

Lit, *v.* to edge. Cf. Litt.

Litany, *n.* a long, unmeaning effusion.

Litch, *n.* a smart blow.—*v.* to strike over.

Litch, *v.* to loiter. Cf. Latch.

Lite, *n.* dung. Cf. Loit.

Lit-fat, *n.* a dyer's vat. Cf. Litt-fat.

Lith, *n.* a gate; a gap in a fence.

Lith, *adj.* soft, gentle. Cf. Lithe.

Lith, *n.* a joint of the body; a division of an orange or onion, &c.; a ring round the base of a cow's horn.—*v.* to disjoint, dislocate.

Lithe, *v.* to listen, hearken.

Lithe, *n.* a shelter.—*adj.* sheltered.—*v.* to shelter.

Lithe, *v.* to thicken broth, &c., by adding oatmeal; to thicken water with mud, &c.

Lithe, *adj.* soft, gentle; mild, pleasant; agile, active.—*n.* encouragement, favour.

Litheless, *adj.* comfortless, cold.

Lithely, *adv.* warmly, genially.

Litheness, *n.* genial warmth.

Lither, *adj.* idle, lazy.—*n.* sloth, laziness.—*v.* to idle, loaf.

Lither, *adj.* yielding, undulating.

Litherlie, *adv.* lazily.

Litheside, *n.* a liking, kindly regard.

Lithesome, *adj.* active, brisk, agile.

Lithesome, Lithsome, *adj.* sheltered, shady; warm, cosy.

Lithet, *ppl. adj.* thickened, spiced.

Lithics, *n.* meal and cold water boiled to be a poultice. Cf. Lythocks.

Lithie, *adj.* warm, comfortable.

Lithing, *n.* a paste of flour or oatmeal for thickening broth, gravy, &c.

Lithry, *n.* a crowd.

Lithy, *adj.* thickened; thick and smooth, as porridge.

Litigious, *adj.* prolix, tedious; vindictive.

Litster, *n.* a dyer.

Litt, *n.* a dye; a tinge, hue, stain, any colouring liquid.—*v.* to dye; to colour; to stain; to blush.

Litt, *v.* to edge.

Litterstane, *n.* a brick-shaped stone, about two feet long and one foot in breadth and depth, formerly borne to builders in litters.

Litt-fat, -vat, *n.* a vat for dye-stuff.

Litt-house, *n.* a dye-house.

Littin', *ppl. adj.* blushing.

Litt-kettle, *n.* a dyer's kettle.

Little ane, *n.* a baby; a small child.

Little boukit, *adj.* of small size; of small authority or influence.

Little-coatie, *n.* a petticoat.

Little-dinner, *n.* a morsel taken in the morning before going to work.

Little-doucker, *n.* the little grebe.

Little-ease, *n.* a lock-up.

Little-felty-fare, *n.* the redwing.

Little-good, -goodie, *n.* the sun-spurge.

Little-gude, *n.* the devil.

Littleman, *n.* a young ploughman: a learner at the plough.

Littlenie, *n.* a very small or young child.

Little-pickle, *n.* the little tern.

Littler, *adj.* less.

Little-room, *n.* a room smaller than the best room in a farmhouse, and used by the farmer and his family for common meals, talk, &c.

Littlest, *adj.* least.

Little-whaup, *n.* the whimbrel.

Little-wit, *adj.* of little intelligence.

Littleworth, *adj.* worthless.—*n.* a worthless person.

Littlie, *adj.* rather little.

Littlin, *n.* a baby, young child.

Litt-pat, *n.* a pot used in dyers' work.

Liung, *n.* an atom, whit.

Liv, *n.* the palm of the hand. Cf. Loof.

Live-day-long, *n.* the livelong day.

Livefu-, Livin-lane, *adj.* quite alone. Cf. Leafu'-lane.

Livellan, *n.* a mythical creature haunting swamps, and squirting poison to a great distance. Cf. Lavellan.

Liven, *v.* to enliven, brighten.

†**Liver,** *v.* to unload a vessel.

Liver, *adj.* active, sprightly, lively.

Liver-bannocks, *n.* bannocks baked with fish-livers between them.

Liver-crook, -cruke, *n.* intestinal inflammation in calves.

Liver-cup, *n.* a cup-shaped dumpling filled with fish-livers.

Liver-grass, *n.* the liverwort.

Liver-head, *n.* the head of a fish stuffed with livers.

Liverock, *n.* the lark. Cf. Laverock.

Livery-downie, *n.* a haddock stuffed with livers, meal, &c.

Liveryman, *n.* a livery-servant.

Livery-meal, *n.* meal given to servants as part of their wages.

Livfu', *n.* as much liquid as will lie on the palm of the hand. Cf. Liv.

Living, *ppl. adj.* alive, in life; used of fire: blazing, glowing.—*n.* a living being, a person; food, fare; a farm.

Living-body, *n.* a live person too weak to do anything.

Living-like, *adj.* likely to live long; healthy, healthy-looking.

Livrie, *adj.* well-cooked; used of liquid food: well-thickened. Cf. Lavrie.

Lixie. *n.* a woman who collected knives, forks, and spoons, on loan, for a 'penny-bridal,' and got her dinner for her trouble.

Lizures, *n.* selvages of cloth or of a weaver's web.

Lizzure, *n.* a pasture; grass-land. Cf. Leissure.

Llabbach, *v.* to speak in an unknown tongue; to speak much with little meaning; to talk incoherently; to repeat from memory; to unroll. - *n.* incoherent talk or writing; a long piece of worthless cloth; an uncomely article of dress; a long piece of twine, &c.; a quantity of strong drink.

Llarg, *v.* to lodge in wet masses, as grass, corn.—*n.* a wet mass in the midst of a dry sheaf.

Llauve-cairn, *n.* a beacon-cairn. Cf. Lowe.

Lo, *v.* to allow, grant.

Lo, *n.* a corpulent person.

Load, *n.* a large number or quantity; used of illness: a very severe cold.—*v.* to lay to one's charge.

Loaden, *ppl.* laden, loaded.

Loaden, *v.* to load, burden; to load a gun.

Loadning, *n.* lading.

Load-stone, *n.* a curling-stone.

Loadstone-watch, *n.* a compass.

Loaf-bread, *n.* a wheaten loaf.

Loags, *n.* footless stockings.

Loake, *n.* one of the multures of a mill. Cf. Lock.

Loal, *v.* to mew, to caterwaul. Cf. Loll.

Loamy, *adj.* slothful.

Loan, *n.* provisions; rations; pay, wages.—*v.* to lend.

Loan, *n.* a lane; a narrow street; the space between the middle of a street and the houses on either side; an opening between fields of corn for driving cattle home; a small piece of ground near a farm or village where cows are milked, a milking-park; a paddock; a small common.

Loan-end, *n.* the end of a 'loan.'

Loan-head, *n.* the upper end of a 'loan.'

Loaning, *n.* a lane, a bypath; a milking-park; a paddock.

Loaning-dyke, *n.* a wall dividing arable from pasture land.

Loaning-green, *n.* a milking-green.

Loan-money, -silver, *n.* pay, wages; bounty.

Loan-soup, *n.* milk given to passengers through the 'loan' at milking-time; milk fresh from the cow.

Loatch, *n.* a corpulent, lazy person. Cf. Lotch.

Loave, *v.* to offer for sale; to offer at lower price for anything in purchasing.

Loavenenty, *int.* an excl. of surprise. Cf. Lovanenty.

Lob, *n.* a lump.

Lobbach, *n.* a lump.

Lobster-clap, *n.* a hooked staff for picking out lobsters from crevices in the rocks.

Lobster-kist, *n.* a floating box in which lobsters are kept alive until sold.

Lobster-toad, *n.* the deep-sea crab, *Cancer araneus.*

Local, *v.* to assign among different land-holders their respective portions of an increase of the parish minister's stipend.

Locality, *n.* the apportioning of the increase of a parish minister's stipend; the lands held by a widow in liferent, in terms of her marriage contract.

Lochaber-axe, *n.* a halberd hooked at the back.

Lochaber-trump, *n.* a Jews'-harp.

Lochan, Lochen, *n.* a small loch or lake.

Locherin', *adj.* drenched with moisture. Cf. Loggerin'.

Loch-head, *n.* the head of a loch.—*phr.* in curling: 'to loch-head of desolation,' driving a stone with extreme vigour, so as to scatter all before it.

Loch-learoch, *n.* a small, gray water-bird, seen on Lochleven.

Loch-leech, *n.* the medicinal leech.

Loch-liver, *n.* a jelly-fish.

Loch-lubbertie, *n.* the jelly tremella, a gelatinous plant found in pastures after rain.

Loch-reed, *n.* the common reed-grass.

Lochter, *n.* a layer; the eggs laid in one season. Cf. Lachter.

Lock, *n.* a difficulty, deadlock, dilemma, a knotty point.—*v.* to enclose; to clutch; to embrace.

Lock, *n.* a small quantity of anything; one of the multures of a mill.

Lockanties, *int.* an excl. of surprise.

Locken-gowlan, *n.* the globe-flower.

Locker, *n.* the globe-flower.

Locker, *v.* to curl.

Lockerby-lick, *n.* a wound in the face.

Locker-gowlan, *n.* the globe-flower.

Lockerie, *adj.* used of a stream: rippling.

Locker-strae, *n.* a school-pointer.

Lockfast, *n.* a locked cupboard, &c.

Lockhole, *n.* a keyhole.

Lockhole execution, *n.* serving a writ by leaving it in the defendant's keyhole.

Lockin-gowan, *n.* the globe-flower.

Lockintee, *int.* oh strange! Cf. Lockanties.

Lockin'-tree, *n.* the 'rung' that served to bar the door.

Lockman, Locksman, *n.* the public executioner.

Locus, *n.* ashes so light as to be easily blown about.

Lodamy, *n.* laudanum. Cf. Lowdamer.

Loddan, Lodden, *n.* a small pool.

Lodden, Loden, *v.* to load. Cf. Loaden.

Lodge, *n.* a fishing-hut.—*v.* used of grain: to lie flat through wind or rain.

Lodge-fish, *n.* fish caught by lodge-men.

Lodge-man, *n.* the occupant of a fishing-hut.

Lodging, *n.* a dwelling-house.

Lodging-maill, *n.* the rent of lodgings, house-rent.

Lodomy, *n.* laudanum.

Loe, *v.* to love.—*n.* love.

Loesome, *adj.* lovable; lovely; winsome, beloved; affectionate.

Loft, *v.* to lift the feet high in walking. Cf. Laft.

Lofted-house, *n.* a house of two or more stories.

Loft-house, *n.* the upper part of a house used as a warehouse; the whole building of which the loft is so used.

Lofting, *n.* a joisted, boarded ceiling; a ceiling or flooring; a story. Cf. Lafting.

Loftit, *ppl. adj.* used of grain: stored on a loft- or a granary-floor.

Log, *n.* the substance which bees gather to make their wax.

Log, *n.* a stocking without a foot. Cf. Loags.

Logamochy, *n.* a long, rambling, dull story or speech.

Logan, *n.* a handful of money, marbles, &c. thrown to be scrambled for by a crowd of boys; a scramble for such things.—*v.* to throw any articles to be scrambled for.

Logerhead, *n.* a blockhead.

Logg, *adj.* lukewarm.

Loggar, Logger, *v.* to hang loosely and largely.—*n.* a stocking without a foot; a gaiter.—*adj.* loose-hanging, drooping.

Loggerin', *adj.* drenched with moisture. Cf. Locherin'.

Loggie, *n.* a wooden pail with upright handle. Cf. Luggie.

Logie, Loggie, *n.* the open space before a kiln-fire; a fire in a snug place; a snug place for a fire; a ventilating hole at the foundation of a stack.

Logies, *int.* an excl. of surprise.

Logive, *adj.* extravagant; careless.

Log-water, *n.* lukewarm water. Cf. Logg.

Loichen, *n.* a quantity of anything soft, like porridge.

Loin, *n.* an allowance. Cf. Loan.

Loit, *n.* a turd; a horse's dropping.—*v.* to excrete. Cf. Lite.

Loit, *n.* a spirt of boiling water ejected from a pot; any liquid suddenly ejected from the mouth.—*v.* to spirt; to bubble forth; to eject from the stomach.

Loit, *n.* a lazy person. Cf. Loyt.

Lokadaisy, *int.* an excl. of surprise.

Loke, Loks, *int.* an excl. of surprise and mirth.

Lokker, *v.* to curl.—*adj.* curled. Cf. Locker.

Lolaby, *n.* a screaming child.

Loll, *v.* to embrace, fondle.—*n.* a lazy fellow. Cf. Lall.

Loll, *v.* to excrete.—*n.* human excrement.

Loll, *v.* to caterwaul, to mew. Cf. Loal.

Lolling, *ppl. adj.* lazy, indolent.

Loltidoll, *n.* the largest species of potato.

Lome, *n.* a tool, utensil ; a tub. Cf. Loom.

Lomon, Lomin', *n.* a leg.

Lon, *v.* to lend.

Lonachies, *n.* couch - grass ; couch - grass gathered in heaps for burning.

Londer, *v.* to tramp heavily and wearily.

London-pride, *n.* the common rose-campion.

Lone, *n.* a lane, avenue ; a byroad ; a milking-paddock. Cf. Loan.

Lone, *adj.* dreary.—*phr.* 'one's lone,' one's self. Cf. Lane.

Lone, *n.* a place of shelter.

Lone, *n.* provisions, rations. Cf. Loan.

Loneful, *adj.* forlorn.—*adv.* forlornly.

Lonely, *adj.* alone, single ; exceptional.—*adv.* singly, only.

Lonesum-like, *adj.* lonely.

Long, *v.* to become weary.

Long, *adj.* tall ; numerous ; tedious. — *n.* length. Cf. Lang.

Long, *adv.* and *prep.* along.

†Longavil, Longueville, *n.* a species of pear.

Longe, *v.* to tell a fair story ; to flatter.

Longie, *n.* the guillemot.

Longish, *adj.* used of the forehead : high.

Longsome, *adj.* tedious ; rather tall. Cf. Langsome.

Loning, *n.* a lane. Cf. Loaning.

Lonkor, *n.* a hole in a 'dyke' through which sheep may pass. Cf. Lunkie.

Lonnach, *n.* a long piece of twine or thread ; a ragged article of dress ; a long rigmarole. —*v.* to talk a great deal ; to unroll ; to deliver a speech, &c.

Lonnachs, *n.* couch-grass. Cf. Lonachies.

Loo, *v.* to love.

Loo, *adj.* lukewarm. Cf. Lew.

Lood, *adj.* loud ; famous.—*adv.* aloud.

Lood-spoken, *adj.* outspoken.

Loof, *n.* the palm of the hand ; help ; a hoof.

Loof, *v. pret.* luffed.

Loof-bane, *n.* the centre of the palm of the hand.

Loof-bread, *n.* a hand's-breadth.

Loof-fu', *n.* a handful.

Loofie, *n.* a stroke on the palm of the hand, a 'palmie' o1 'pandie' ; a fingerless mitten for the hand ; a flat stone resembling the palm, and formerly used in curling.

Loofie channel-stane, *n.* a 'loofie' formerly used in curling.

Loofie-lair, *n.* proficiency in fisticuffs, &c.

Loof-licker, *n.* a fawning, cringing person.

Loogan, *n.* a rogue.

Loogard, *n.* a slap on the ear. Cf. Lugard.

Look, *v.* with *in* on, to call on ; with *on*, to watch beside a dying person ; to inspect, examine.—*n.* the face, the appearance.

Looker, *n.* the eye.

Lookin'-to, *n.* a prospect, a future.

Lool, *v.* to sing in a dull and heavy manner. Cf. Loll.

Loom, *n.* an implement ; utensil ; a vessel of any kind.—*v.* to weave.

Loom, *n.* mist, fog ; the hazy appearance of land as seen from the sea or on the horizon.

Loombagus, *n.* lumbago.

Loom-bred, *adj.* bred to weaving.

Loom-post, *n.* a post forming part of a loom.

Loom-shop, *n.* a weaving-shop.

Loom-stance, -stead, *n.* the place where a loom stands.

Loomy, *adj.* misty, hazy.

†Loon, *n.* a limb ; a loin. Cf. Lunyie.

Loon, *n.* a rascal ; a ragamuffin ; an idle, stupid fellow ; a fellow ; the native of a place ; the follower of a trade ; a servant ; a person of low rank ; a peasant, rustic ; a boy, a lad ; a loose woman, paramour.

Loonder, *v.* to beat severely. Cf. Lounder.

Loonfow, *adj.* rascally.

Loonie, *n.* a boy, a little lad.

Loonie, *adj.* imbecile ; crazy ; lunatic. — *s.* an idiot, a 'natural,' a lunatic.

Loon-ill, *n.* malingering to shirk work.

Loon-like, *adj.* rascally ; shabby, tattered ; like a lad or boy.

Loon-looking, *adj.* rascally.

Loon-quean, *n.* a loose woman.

Loon's-piece, *n.* the uppermost slice of a loaf.

Loop, *n.* a stitch in knitting ; a piece of knitting ; the winding of a river, lake, or glen ; the channel of a stream left dry by the water changing its course.— *v.* to join in marriage ; to hang in a noose.

Loop, *n.* a trick, a tricky scheme ; a wile.

Loopy, *adj.* crafty, deceitful.

Loor, *adv.* rather.—*v.* to prefer. Cf. Liefer.

Loor, *v.* to lurk ; to crouch ; to skulk.—*n.* a lurking-place.

Loosable, *adj.* that may be loosed.

Loose, *adj.* open, unlocked ; ripe.—*v.* to unyoke horses or cattle ; to unload ; to cease working ; to be dismissed. Cf. Lowse.

Loose, *n.* a louse.

Loose-behind, *adj.* not costive.

Loose-footed, *adj.* disengaged ; free from entanglements.

Loose-tongued, *adj.* voluble, gossiping.

Loosey, *adj.* lousy. Cf. Lousy.

Loosht, *n.* a lazy lounger.

Looshtre, *n.* a heavy, soft blow.—*v.* to strike with a heavy, soft blow.

Looshtrin, *n.* a heavy beating.

Loosing, *ppl. adj.* laxative, purgative.

Loosome, *adj.* lovable. Cf. Loesome.

Loossie, *adj.* used of the skin : covered with dandriff.

Looster, *v.* to lounge, idle.—*n.* indolence; a lazy, slothful person.

Loostrie, *adj.* lazy, idle.

Loot, *v.* to stoop. Cf. Lout.

Loot, *v. pret.* permitted, let.

Looten, *ppl.* allowed, let.

Loothrick, *n.* a wooden lever. Cf. Lowder.

Lootin o', *adj.* esteemed, held in estimation.

Loot on, *v. pret.* with *neg.* did not give any sign. Cf. Let on.

Loove, *n.* love; a lover.

Looves, *n.* the palms of the hands. Cf. Loof.

Loozy, *adj.* lousy. Cf. Lousy.

Lope, *v.* to lop off.

Lope, *v. pret.* leapt.

Lopper, *v.* to coagulate. Cf. Lapper.

Lopper, *v.* to ripple. Cf. Lipper.

Lopper-gowan, *n.* the yellow ranunculus.

Lord, *n.* a judge of the Court of Session; a 'laird.'—*int.* an excl. of surprise.

Lord Harry, *int.* an expletive.

Lordlifu', *adj.* rich, sumptuous; extravagantly liberal.

Lordly, *adj.* proud; difficult to please; very liberal.

Lordsake, *int.* an excl. of surprise.

Lord's fool, *n.* a born fool, a 'natural.'

Lore *n.* talk, conversation.

Lorle, Lorie-me, *int.* an excl. of surprise.

Lorimer, *n.* a clockmaker.

Lorrach, *n.* a disgusting mess; ill-cooked food; a long piece of wet, dirty cloth, twine, &c.

Lorum, *n.* lore, learning.

Lose, *adj.* loose.

Losel, Lossel, *n.* a lazy rascal.

Lose-leather, *n.* loose skin from falling away of flesh.

Losh, *n.* a corrupt form of 'Lord.'—*int.* an excl. of surprise or wonder; used alone and in various combinations.

Loshie, Loshie-goshie, *int.* 'losh!'

Loshins, Loshtie, *int.* 'losh!'

Losin, *n.* a pane of glass. Cf. Lozen.

Loss, *v.* to lose.

Lossie, *adj.* used of a crop: causing loss, waste by vacancies.

Lossiness, *n.* the state of being 'lossie' or unprofitable.

Lost, *ppl.* at a loss.

Lot, *n.* a building 'feu'; a quantity of grain, generally the twenty-fifth part, given to the thresher as his wages; a great number, the whole of several articles.

Lotch, *n.* a handful or considerable quantity of something semi-liquid.

Lotch, *n.* a corpulent, lazy person.—*adj.* lazy.

Lotch, *v.* to limp; to jog.

Loth, *adj.* unwilling. Cf. Laith.

Lotman, *n.* a thresher, at so much per boll.

Lotten, *ppl.* allowed, let.

Lottie, *n.* a small collection or number.

†Louable, *adj.* praiseworthy.

Louch, *v.* to slouch; to bend the back in walking. Cf. Loutch.

Louchter, *n.* a setting of eggs. Cf. Lachter.

Loud, *adv.* aloud. Cf. Lood.

Lougs, *n.* stockings without feet. Cf. Loags.

Loun, *n.* a rascal; a strumpet. Cf. Loon.

Loun, Lound, *adj.* quiet, calm; sheltered. Cf. Lown.

Lounder, Louner, *v.* to beat severely; to do anything with vehemence; to scold.—*n.* a heavy blow; energy at work.

Loundering, *n.* a severe beating.—*ppl. adj.* used of a blow: resounding.

Lounfow, *adj.* rascally. Cf. Loonfow.

Lounge, *v.* to thrust forward violently.—*n.* a lunge.

Lounlie, *adv.* in a sheltered position; under protection morally; softly, with a low voice. Cf. Lownly.

Loun's-piece, *n.* the uppermost slice of a loaf.

Loup, *v.* to leap, jump, spring; to jump over; to throb, pulsate; to dance, frisk; to run, run off, escape; to move quickly; to run like a hare or rabbit; used of horses and bulls: to engender; of frost: to give way at sunrise; to burst, break out of an enclosure; to swell with anger, heat, &c.; to pass from one owner to another; with *aff,* to ramble in a speech or story; with *back,* to refuse suddenly to keep a bargain; with *down,* to lower one's first offer in bargaining; to dismount; with *on,* to mount on horseback, to equip a company of horse; with *up,* to raise one's price in bargaining. —*n.* a leap, spring, bound; the distance jumped; a place where a river becomes so contracted by rocks that it can be easily leapt; a small cataract; a disease of sheep affecting their limbs.

Loup, *n.* a loop.

Loup-counter-lad, *n.* a shopkeeper, salesman.

Loupen, *ppl.* leapt.

Loupen-steek, *n.* a broken stitch in a stocking; anything amiss.

Louper, *n.* a vagabond, a fugitive from the law. Cf. Land-louper.

Louper-dog, *n.* the porpoise.

Loup-garthe, *n.* a gauntlet to be run.

Loup-hunt, *n.* an idle errand; the search for adventure.—*v.* to go abroad early in the morning; to go in search of adventures.

Loupie, *adj.* crafty, tricky. Cf. Loopy.

Loupin'-ague, *n.* St Vitus's dance.

Loupin and leevin, *adj.* used of fish: freshly caught; of persons: in health and spirits.

Loupin'-ill, *n.* the disease of sheep affecting their movements.

Loupin'-on-stane, *n.* a horse-block.

Loup-the-bullocks, *n.* the game of leap-frog.

Loup-the-cat, *n.* a term of contempt.

Loup-the-dyke, *adj.* unsettled, runaway, not keeping in bounds.

Loup-the-tether, *v.* to break bounds; to throw off restraint.—*adj.* wild, that cannot be restrained.

Loupy, *n.* a short leap.

Loupy for loup, *adv.* with short leaps.

Loupy for spang, *phr.* with short leaps.

Lour, *v.* to lurk, crouch; to skulk.—*n.* a lurking-place.

Lour, *v.* to prefer.

Lourd, *ppl.* rather; in *phr.* 'I had lourd,' I had much rather.

†Lourd, *adj.* dull; lumpish; stupid; sottish, gross.

†Lourdand, *n.* a lazy, stupid person. Cf. Lurdane.

Lourdly, *adv.* stupidly.

Lourdy, *adj.* lazy, sluggish.

Lourie, *n.* the name of a bell rung at ten o'clock P.M. in some towns.

Lour-shouthered, *adj.* round-shouldered. Cf. Lout-shouthered.

Loury, *adj.* used of the weather: gloomy, threatening.

Lousance, *n.* freedom from bondage.

Louse, *adj.* loose, free. Cf. Lowse.

Louse, *v.* to look for lice; to take lice from the person or clothes.

Lousen, *v.* to loosen. Cf. Lowsen.

Louss, *v.* to loosen. Cf. Lowse.

Louster, *v.* to lounge; to idle. Cf. Looster.

Lousy, *adj.* dirty, shabby, mean; used contemptuously.

Lousy-arnut, *n.* the earth-nut.

Lout, *v.* to stoop; to bend low; to bow; to curtsy.

Loutch, *v.* to slouch; to bow down the head and raise the shoulders; to have the appearance of a blackguard; to loiter. Cf. Louch.

Louthe, *n.* abundance.

Louther, *v.* to loiter, idle; to walk or move with difficulty; to carry anything with difficulty; to be entangled in mire, snow, &c.; to beat severely.—*n.* an idler, trifler, a good-for-nothing person; a tall, uncomely person; a sharp blow. Cf. Lowder.

Louther, *n.* a lever or handspike for lifting millstones. Cf. Lowder.

Louthering, *ppl. adj.* lazy, awkward, lumbering.

Louthertree, *n.* a lever for lifting millstones.

Lout-shouthered, *adj.* round-shouldered; off the perpendicular. Cf. Lour-shouthered.

Louty, *adj.* slow, lazy.

Louze, *v.* to loosen. Cf. Lowse.

Lovanenty, Loveanendie, Lovenanty, *int.* an excl. of surprise, alarm, &c.

Love-bairn, *n.* an illegitimate child.

Love-begot, *n.* an illegitimate child.—*adj.* illegitimate.

Love-begotten, *adj.* illegitimate.

Love-blink, *n.* a glance of love.

Love-clap, *v.* to embrace fondly.

Love-daft, *adj.* madly in love.

Love-darg, *n.* a friendly day's ploughing given to a neighbour.

Love-dotterel, *n.* the doting love felt by old unmarried people.

Love-fraucht, *adj.* full of love.

Love-glint, *n.* a glance of love.

Love-in-idleness, *n.* the *Viola tricolor*.

Loveit, Lovite, *n.* a term expressing the royal regard for a person mentioned or addressed, as in a Royal Commission.

Love-links, *n.* the creeping Jenny.

Love-lowe, *n.* the flame of love.

Lovenenty, *int.* an excl. of surprise. Cf. Lovanenty.

Lovens, Loving, *int.* an excl. of surprise.

Loverin-iddles, *int.* an excl. of surprise.

Lovers' links, *n.* stonecrop.

Lovers' loaning, *n.* a lane frequented by lovers.

Lover's loup, *n.* the leap of a despairing lover over a precipice; the place where such a leap has occurred.

Love-stoond, -stound, *n.* the pang of love.

Lovetenant, *n.* lieutenant.

Love-tryste, *n.* a lovers' meeting by appointment.

Lovich, Lovitch, *adj.* lavish.

Lovy-ding, *int.* an excl. of surprise.

Low, *v.* to degrade; to lower; to abate, cease; to higgle as to a price.

Low, *v.* to allow. Cf. Lo.

Low, *adj.* weak, extremely weak; of small stature; lower, downstairs; used of the wind: blowing from the south. Cf. Laich.

Low, *n.* a flame. Cf. Lowe.

Lowan, *adj.* calm, still. Cf. Lown.

Lowance, *n.* allowance; share; permission.

Lowdamer, Lowdamy, *n.* laudanum. Cf. Lodomy.

Lowden, *v.* to lull, abate; to reduce to calmness, to quiet; to silence; to bring down; to speak a little; to stand in awe of another.

Lowder, *n.* a wooden lever; a handspoke for lifting a millstone; any long, stout, rough stick; a stroke or blow.—*v.* to beat; to move heavily. Cf. Louther, Lewder.

Lowdomary, *n.* laudanum. Cf. Lodomy.

Lowe, *n.* a flame, blaze, light; a glow; a rage.—*v.* to flame, blaze, glow; to parch with thirst from great heat.

Lowed, *ppl.* lowered.

Lowen, adj. calm, quiet, serene. Cf. Lown.
Lowering, ppl. adj. stooping. Cf. Lour.
Lowie, n. a big, lazy person.
Lowie-lebbie, n. a hanger-on about kitchens.
Lowins, n. liquor after it has once passed through the still.
Lowins, n. an allowance, a share. Cf. Lowance.
Lowland, adj. low-lying. Cf. Lallan.
Low-lifed, adj. mean, despicable; of low habits.
Lowly-legged, adj. short-legged.
Lowmin, n. a limb. Cf. Loymin.
Lowmost, adj. lowest.
Lown, n. a rascal; a lad. Cf. Loon.
Lown, adj. calm, serene, sheltered; tranquil, unagitated; silent, quiet; soft, gentle, low; secret.—adv. softly, in a low voice.—n. stillness, shelter; a sheltered place.—v. used of the wind: to abate, fall.
Lownder, v. to beat severely. Cf. Lounder.
Lowner-like, adj. more like a 'lown' or beggar.
Lowness, n. shortness of stature; extreme weakness.
Lown-hill, n. the sheltered side of a hill.
Lownly, adv. in shelter; quietly; softly; in a low tone; in stillness; languidly.
Lownness, n. stillness, quietness.
Lown-side, n. the sheltered side of a wall, hill, &c.
Lown-warm, adj. soft and warm.
Lowp, v. to leap. Cf. Loup.
Lowp, v. to lop.
Lowrie, n. the fox.
Lowrie-like, adj. having the crafty look of a fox.
Lowrie-tod, n. the fox. Cf. Tod-lowrie.
Lowsance, n. liberty; deliverance.
Lowse, adj. loose, free, unrestrained; lax in morals; thoughtless; used of the weather: mild, genial.
Lowse, v. to lose.
Lowse, v. to loosen; to set free; to stop working; to unharness, unyoke; to unload, discharge a cargo; used of perspiration: to break out; to set to work energetically, to begin; to say grace before a meal; to redeem an article pawned; used of a cow: to show signs of milk in the udder; to thaw. —n. a rush, a race.—phr. 'lowse us,' say grace for us.
Lowse leather, n. pendulous skin on one that has lost flesh.
Lowsely, adv. loosely.
Lowsen, v. to loosen; to unyoke horses, cows.
Lowseness, n. diarrhœa; dysentery.
Lowse siller, n. small change.
Lowsing, n. the end of working.
Lowsing-time, n. the end of a day's work; the time for unyoking horses and stopping farm-work.

Lowsy naturæ, n. a *lusus naturæ*.
Lowt, v. to stoop. Cf. Lout.
Lowter, v. to walk heavily. Cf. Lowder.
Lowttie, adj. loutish; heavy and inactive.
Lowying, ppl. adj. idling; lounging.
Loy, adj. sluggish, inactive.
Loyester, n. a stroke, a blow.
Loymin, Loym, n. a limb.
Loyness, n. inactivity.
Loyt, n. a lazy person. Cf. Loit.
†Lozen, Lozin, Lozzen, n. a pane of glass.
Lozenge-lion, n. an ancient coin.
Lozenger, n. a lozenge.
Luac-, Luag-Friday, n. a fair held in Tarland, in Aberdeenshire, on a Friday in July.
Lub, n. anything heavy and unwieldy.
Lubbard, Lubbert, n. a lout; a coward; a lubber.
Lubber-fiend, n. a benevolent sprite; a 'brownie.'
Lubbertie, adj. lazy; sluggish, lubberly.
Lubin, n. a children's singing game.
†Lubrick, adj. vacillating; slippery.
Luce, n. brightness.
Luce, n. scurf, dandriff; the slimy matter scraped off in shaving.
Lucht, n. a lock of hair.
Luchter, n. a handful of corn in the straw; a setting of eggs. Cf. Lachter.
Luck, v. to prosper; to have good-luck; to happen by good-fortune.
Luck, n. a lock.—v. to shut up, fasten, enclose.
Lucked, ppl. adj. fated; having good or ill luck or fate.
Lucken, n. a bog.
Lucken, v. to prosper; to cause to thrive.
Lucken, n. the globe-flower. Cf. Luckengowan.
Lucken, v. to knit the brows; used of cloth, &c.: to pucker, gather into folds; of a cabbage: to grow firm in the heart.
Lucken, ppl. adj. close; shut up; contracted; locked, bolted; webbed.
Lucken, n. an unsplit haddock, half-dried.
Lucken-booth, n. the old 'Tolbooth' of Edinburgh; in pl. booths made to be locked up by day or night.
Lucken-browed, adj. heavy-browed; having the eyebrows close to each other.
Lucken-footed, adj. web-footed; having the toes joined by a film.
Lucken-gowan, -gowlan, n. the globe-flower. Cf. Lockin-gowan.
Lucken-haddock, n. an unsplit haddock, half-dried.
Lucken-handed, adj. having the fist contracted, with the fingers drawn down to the palm; close-fisted.
Lucken-toed, adj. web-footed, 'lucken-footed.'

Lucken-toes, *n.* toes joined by a film or web.

Lucker, *n.* an eye.

Luck-penny, *n.* money given back by the seller to the buyer for luck.

Luckrass, *n.* a cross-grained, cantankerous old woman.

Lucky, Luckie, *n.* a familiar term of address to an elderly woman; a midwife; a grandmother; a grandfather; a wife, mistress; a helpmate; a landlady, mistress of an ale-house; a witch.

Lucky, *adj.* of good omen; over and above the standard measure or stipulated quantity; abundant, full; larger; bulky; more than enough. —*adv.* perhaps.

Lucky-dad, -daddy, -deddy, *n.* a grandfather.

Lucky-foot, *n.* a person whom it is lucky to meet on a road.

Lucky-like, *adj.* looking like good-fortune.

Lucky-measure, *n.* that which exceeds what can legally be claimed; overflowing measure.

Lucky-minnie, *n.* a grandmother; a term of reproach to a woman.

Lucky-minnie's 'oo', *n.* a fleecy substance growing on a plant in wet ground.

Lucky-plack, *n.* the fee for the proclamation of marriage-banns.

Lucky-pock, *n.* a lucky-bag.

Lucky-roach, *n.* the father-lasher or hard-head.

Lucky's-lines, *n.* a plant growing in deep water near the shore.

Lucky's-mutch, *n.* the monk's-hood.

Lucky's 'oo', *n.* 'lucky-minnie's 'oo'.'

Lucky-words, *n.* words which Shetland fishermen use only at the deep-sea fishing.

Lucre, *n.* in tautological *phr.* 'lucre of gain,' profit of gain.

Lucriss, *n.* a cantankerous old woman. Cf. Luckrass.

Lucy-arnut, *n.* the earth-nut. Cf. Lousy-arnut.

Ludging, *n.* a lodging, a house. Cf. Lodging.

†**Ludibrie,** *n.* derision; an object of derision.

Lue, *adj.* lukewarm. Cf. Loo, Lew.

Lue, *v.* to love. Cf. Loe.

Luely, *adv.* softly.

Luesome, *adj.* lovely; lovable. Cf. Loesome.

Lufe, Luff, *n.* the palm of the hand. Cf. Loof.

Lug, *adj.* used of crops: growing too little to ear or root, and too much to stem.

Lug, Lugg, *n.* the ear; the handle of a jar, cup, jug, &c.; the projection on a bucket, &c., to which the handle is attached; a tuft or tassel at the side of a bonnet or cap; a knot; one of the two tufts at the top of a full sack by which it is lifted and carried

on the back; a corner, recess; the side of a chimney; a corner of a herring-net, the loop on the end of a fishing-line; the 'tongue' of a boot or shoe.—*v.* to cut off the ears.

Lug, *n.* the sand-worm, the lug-worm.—*v.* to dig for lug-worms.

Lugard, *n.* a blow on the ear.

Lug-bab, *n.* an ear-ring; a tuft or knot of ribbons or tassel on the side of the cap over the ear.

Lug-bane, -been, *n.* part of the head of a fish.

Lug-drum, *n.* the ear-drum.

Lug-fin, *n.* the fin of a fish nearest the ear.

Luggie, *n.* the horned owl; a crop-eared person.

Luggie, *adj.* heavy, sluggish.

Luggie, *n.* a wooden pail or dish with a handle formed by the projection of one of the staves above the others; a boys' game.

Luggie, *n.* a hut or lodge in a park; a very small cottage.

Luggit, *ppl. adj.* having ears, having handles, eared.—*n.* a blow on the ear.

Luggy, *adj.* used of crops: growing more to stem than to grain or root.

Lug-haul, *v.* to pull by the ears.

Lug-horn, *n.* a stethoscope; an ear-trumpet.

Lught, *n.* a lock of hair. Cf. Lucht.

Lughter, *n.* a setting of eggs. Cf. Lachter.

Lug-knot, *n.* a knot of ribbons at the side of the bonnet over the ear.

Lug-lachet, *n.* a box on the ear.

Lug-length, *n.* the distance at which one can hear another speak.

Lug-locks, *n.* curls hanging behind the ear.

Lug-mark, *n.* a distinguishing mark cut on the ear of a sheep.—*v.* to cut such marks, to earmark; to punish by cropping the ears.

Lug of, *adv. phr.* near to.

Lug-stanes, *n.* stones attached as sinkers to the lower side of a herring-net.

Lug-yerkit, *adj.* struck on the ear; pulled by the ears.

Luig, *n.* a hovel. Cf. Luggie.

Luik, *v.* to look.

Luive, Luif, *n.* the palm of the hand. Cf. Loof.

Luke, *adj.* lukewarm, tepid.

Luke, *v.* to look.

Luke's-mass, *n.* the festival of St Luke, Oct. 18.

Lull, *v.* to sleep gently.

Lulls, *n.* bagpipes.

Lum, Lumb, *n.* a chimney; a chimney-corner; a chimney-stalk; the chimney-top; a 'chimney-pot' hat.

Lum, v. to rain heavily.—n. in phr. 'a lum of a day,' a very wet day.

Lumberload, n. a heavy, useless load; a corpulent, overfed body.

Lumbersome, adj. cumbrous.

Lumbery, adj. useless, rubbishy.

Lum-cheek, n. the fireside, the side of the chimney.

Lum-cleek, n. the hook on which a pot is hung in cooking.

Lume, n. a utensil, a loom. Cf. Loom.

Lum-hat, n. a 'chimney-pot' hat, a dress-hat.

Lum-heid, n. the chimney-top.

Lummle, n. the filings of metal.

Lump, n. a fat pig; a dull, heavy person; a mass, quantity; a great wave, a large mass of water.—v. to beat, thump; to raise a lump by a fall or blow.

Lumper, n. one who furnishes ballast for ships.

Lum-pig, n. a chimney-can or -cowl.

Lumping pennyworth, n. good measure or weight.

Lumpit, ppl. adj. collective.

Lump o' butter, n. a soft, easy-going, useless person.

Lum-reek, n. smoke from a chimney.

Lum-root, n. the base of a chimney where it rises from the roof.

Lum-sooper, n. a chimney-sweep.

Lum-tap, n. the top of a chimney or of the funnel of a steamer.

Lum-tile, n. a chimney-can made of clay.

Luncart, n. a temporary fireplace out of doors for the use of washerwomen.

Lunch, Luncheon, n. a large piece of anything, of food.

Lunchick, n. a bulky package carried on the haunch under the coat.

Lunchock, n. the angle made by the thighs and belly.

Lunder, Lundre, v. to beat heavily. Cf. Lounder.

†**Lunets,** n. spectacles.

Lungie, n. the guillemot. Cf. Longie.

Lunie, Luny, n. a lunatic; an imbecile.—adj. mad, crazy; silly. Cf. Loonie.

†**Lunie,** n. the loin.

Lunie-bane, n. the hip-bone.

Lunie-joint, n. the hip-joint.

Lunie-shot, adj. having the hip-joint dislocated or sprung.

Lunk, adj. lukewarm.

Lunkie, Lunky, n. a small hole left for the admission of animals; a hole for sheep in a stone 'dyke.'

Lunkie, adj. used of the weather: close and sultry.

Lunkie-hole, n. a hole in a stone 'dyke' for sheep.

Lunkieness, n. oppressiveness of atmosphere, sultriness.

Lunkit, ppl. adj. lukewarm; half-boiled.

Lunner, n. a smart stroke. Cf. Lounder.

Lunnon, n. London.

Lunsh, v. to loll.

Lunshing, ppl. adj. idle, lounging.

Lunt, n. a light; a match; a lighted match; smoke, the smoke of a pipe; smoke with flame; anything used to light a fire; a column of flame; hot vapour of any kind. —v. to emit smoke in puffs or columns; to blaze; to smoke a pipe.

Lunt, v. to walk quickly; to walk with a great spring.—n. a great rise and fall in walking.

Lunt, v. to sulk.—n. a fit of sulking.

Luntus, n. a contemptuous name for an old woman.

†**Lunyie, Lunzie,** n. the loin. Cf. Lunie.

Luppen, ppl. leapt. Cf. Loup.

Luppen-steek, n. a dropped stitch.

Luppin, n. looping for a hat.

Lurch, n. a tricky way.

Lurd, n. a blow with the fist.

†**Lurdane, Lurden, Lurdoun,** n. a lazy, stupid person; an idle fellow; a worthless man or woman.—adj. lazy, stupid, worthless; heavy; severe.

Lurdenly, adv. stupidly; lazily; clownishly.

Lurder, n. a lazy, worthless person.

Lurdy, adj. lazy.

Lure, adv. rather. Cf. Liefer.

Lure, n. the udder of a cow, as used for food. Cf. Lire.

Lure, n. the fleshy or muscular parts of an animal. Cf. Lire.

Lurk, v. to live quietly in seclusion; to idle, loaf about; to lower so as to hide.

Lurk, n. a crease; a fold. Cf. Lirk.

Lusbirdan, n. a low-statured people once living in the Hebrides; pigmies.

Luscan, n. a sturdy, thieving beggar.

Lush, n. strong drink.

Lusking, ppl. adj. absconding.

Lusome, adj. not smooth; rough, unpolished.

Lusome, adj. lovable.

Luss, n. dandriff. Cf. Luce.

Lust, n. an appetite for food. Cf. List.

Lustheid, n. amiableness.

Lusty, adj. pleasant; sturdy; healthy-looking; fat; powerful.

Lute, n. a sluggard; a lout.

Lute, v. pret. and ppl. allowed, let.

Luthir, adj. idle, lazy. Cf. Lither.

Luther, Luthir, n. a heavy blow. Cf. Leather.

Lutten, ppl. let, allowed.

Luve, v. to love.

Luves, n. hands. Cf. Loof.

Ly, *n.* the pollack.

Lyaach, *adj.* low. Cf. Laich.

Lyaach-fire, *n.* a fire on a hearthstone, and not in a grate.

Lyaag, *n.* gossip, talk. Cf. Laig.

Lyaagen, *n.* the extreme edge. Cf. Laggen.

Lyaagens o' the air, *n.* the extreme edge of the visible sky, the horizon.

Lyaager, *v.* to bemire; to overload. Cf. Lagger.

Lyaat, *n.* **a** very small quantity, especially of liquid.

Lyabach, *n.* a long story about little or nothing. Cf. Llabach.

Lyabber, *v.* to slobber; to bespatter. Cf. Labber.

Lyam, *n.* a rope made of hair. Cf. Liam.

Lyardly, *adv.* sparingly.

Lyart, *adj.* used of hair : streaked with gray, hoary; streaked with red and white; of fallen leaves : variegated, changed in colour.

Lyaug, *n.* silly talk, gossip. Cf. Lyaag.

Lychtle, Lychtlie, *v.* to despise, make light of. Cf. Lichtlie.

Lydder, *adj.* lazy. Cf. Lither.

Lye, *n.* pasture-land. Cf. Lea.

Lying-in-wife, *n.* a midwife.

Lying-money, *n.* money not used.

Lying-side, *n.* the side of a carcass of beef which has all the spinous processes of the vertebræ left on it.

Lying-storm, *n.* a prolonged storm.

Lying-time, *n.* the time worked by a miner between the date of making up the pay-bill and the date of the pay-day.

Lyke, *n.* an unburied corpse; the watch kept over a dead body until the funeral.

Lyke-wake, *n.* the watch kept over a body between death and burial.

Lyke-waker, *n.* a watcher by the dead.

Lymphad, Lymfad, *n.* a galley.

Lyowder, *n.* a long, stout, rough stick. Cf. Lowder.

Lyre, Lyrie, *n.* the Manx shearwater.

Lyre, *n.* the flesh and muscular parts of an animal. Cf. Lire.

Lyred, *adj.* having locks of hair of iron-gray. Cf. Lyart.

Lyrie, *n.* the pogge; the whiting pollack.

Lyse-hay, *n.* hay from pasture-land, not from meadow.

Lyst, *v.* to listen.

Lyt, *n.* a few; a small quantity or number.

Lytach, *n.* a large mass of wet substance; speech in an unknown tongue; a long, rambling piece of news; a long, disconnected piece of literature.—*v.* to work with liquid or semi-liquid substances, to perform domestic work; to work unskilfully and awkwardly; to speak in an unknown tongue; to speak much in a rambling, confused manner.

Lyte, *n.* an untidy mass of any wet substance; a heavy fall; the sound of a heavy fall.—*v.* to throw any wet substance in a mass to the ground; to fall flat; to work unskilfully.—*adv.* flat and heavily.

Lyter, *n.* a large mass of any wet substance. Cf. Lytach.

Lythe, *n.* the immature pollack. Cf. Lait.

Lythe, *v.* to thicken broth, &c., with oatmeal or flour, or by boiling; to thicken water with mud, &c. Cf. Lithe.

Lythe, Lyth, *adj.* soft, gentle, pleasant; flexible; agile.—*n.* favour; countenance. Cf. Lithe.

Lythe, Lyth, *n.* shelter.—*adj.* sheltered from the weather.—*v.* to shelter. Cf. Lithe.

Lythesome, *adj.* sheltered, shaded; warm, genial.

Lythesome, *adj.* engaging, of genial disposition.

Lythet, *ppl. adj.* thickened; spiced.

Lythie, *adj.* warm, comfortable. Cf. Lithie.

Lything, *n.* softening; soothing; a smooth paste of flour or oatmeal and water or milk, for thickening soup, gravy, &c.

Lythocks, *n.* a mixture of oatmeal and cold water stirred over a fire until it boils and thickens; used as a poultice. Cf. Lithics.

Lythy, *adj.* thickened; thick and smooth like porridge.

Lytrie, *n.* a mass of anything in disorder; a crowd of small creatures in disorder.—*adj.* used of a mass of semi-liquid substance : dirty and disordered.

Lytt, *v.* to nominate.—*n.* a list of nominations, or of candidates, for election. Cf. Leet.

Ma, *adj.* more, in quantity or number. Cf. Mae.

Ma, *v.* to mow. Cf. Maw.

Ma, *pron. adj.* my.

Maa, *n.* the common sea-gull; the herring-gull. Cf. Maw.

Maa, *v.* to mow.

Maa, *n.* a whit; a jot.

Maa, *n.* the bleat of a lamb.

Maa-craig, *n.* a rock frequented by gulls.

Maad, *n.* a shepherd's plaid. Cf. Maud.

Maader, *int.* a call to a horse to come to the near side. Cf. Maether.

Maain, *ppl.* mowing.—*n.* what a man can mow in a day.

Maak, *n.* the milt of a fish.

Maak, *n.* a match, equal. Cf. **Maik.**

Maan, *ppl. adj.* mown.

Maavie, *n.* the maw of a fish; any small animal's stomach; a rennet-bag. Cf. **Mauvie.**

Mabbie, *n.* a woman's cap.

Macabaa, Macabaw, *n.* a kind of snuff.

Macalive-cattle, *n.* cattle appropriated, in the Hebrides, to a child sent out to be fostered.

†**Macaroni, Maccaroni**, *n.* a fop, dandy.

Macdonald's disease, *n.* an affection of the lungs.

Macer, *n.* a mace-bearer, an officer who keeps order in law-courts.

Macfarlane's bouat, *n.* the moon.

Mach, *n.* might. Cf. **Maught.**

Mach, *n.* a maggot. Cf. **Mawk.**

Machars, *n.* the part of Wigtownshire washed by the Solway Firth and the Bay of Luce.

Machers, *n.* bent-grown, sandy tracts by the sea.

Machie, *n.* a conveyance, a gig, a cart. Cf. **Machine.**

Machine, *n.* a vehicle, carriage, cart.

Machle, *v.* to busy one's self in vain.

Machless, *adj.* feeble; powerless. Cf. **Maught-less.**

Macht, *n.* strength, might. Cf. **Maught.**

Mack, *v.* to make.

Mack, *n.* fashion; shape.—*adj.* neat, tidy. Cf. **Make.**

Mackaingie, *n.* in *phr.* 'fair mackaingie,' full scope.

Mackdom, *n.* figure, shape. Cf. **Makedom.**

Mackerel-sture, *n.* the tunny.

Macker-like, *adj.* more becoming; more suitable.

Mack-like, *adj.* tidy, neat; seemly; suitable; well-proportioned.

Mackly, *adj.* 'mack-like.'

Macmillan-folk, Macmillanites, *n.* the followers of Macmillan, one of the founders of the Reformed Presbyterian Church.

Macon, *n.* a hare. Cf. **Mawkin.**

Macrel, *n.* a mackerel.

Mad, *adj.* keen, eager; angry, vexed.—*v.* to madden.

Mad, *n.* a sort of net, fixed on four stakes, for catching salmon and trout.

Mad, *n.* a maggot; the larva of a maggot.

Mad, *n.* a shepherd's plaid. Cf. **Maud.**

Madam, *n.* a fine lady; a mistress; a hussy.

Madded, *ppl. adj.* mad, foolish.

Madden, *v.* to anger, vex.

Madder, *n.* a vessel used in mills for holding meal. Cf. **Mather.**

Madder drim, Madden drim, *n.* madness; folly; mad pranks.

Maddie, *n.* a large species of mussel.

Maddis, *n.* a lunatic.

Made, *ppl. adj.* fatigued.

Made, *n.* a maggot. Cf. **Mad.**

Made with, *ppl.* affected by.

Madge, *n.* a playful or contemptuous term for a woman.

Mad-leed, *n.* a mad strain.

Madlins, *adv.* madly.

Madlocks, *n.* milk-brose.

Mae, *adj.* more. Cf. **Ma, Moe.**

Mae, *n.* the bleat of a sheep or lamb; a child's name for a sheep; a sheep-call.—*v.* to bleat softly.

Maeg, *n.* a hand; a big, clumsy hand; in *pl.* the flippers of a seal.—*v.* to handle; to handle injuriously. Cf. **Maig.**

Maegsie, *n.* the possessor of big, clumsy hands.

Mael, *n.* a spot; an iron stain.—*v.* to spot, stain. Cf. **Mail.**

Maelyer, *n.* the quantity of corn ground at a time. Cf. **Melder.**

Maen, *n.* a moan; lamentation; complaint. —*v.* to moan; to pity; to show signs of pain; to mourn; to condole with.

Maese, *v.* to allay; to soothe; to settle; to mellow fruit. Cf. **Mease.**

Maeslie, *adj.* speckled, spotted; poor, inferior. Cf. **Mizzle.**

Maeslie-shankit, *adj.* having the legs spotted from being too near a fire.

Maet, *n.* meat; food.—*v.* to feed. Cf. **Meat.**

Maet-haill, *adj.* able to take one's food with an appetite.

Maether, *int.* a carter's call to his horse to come to the near side. Cf. **Comether.**

Maffling, *n.* blundering, bungling.

Mag, *n.* a large, clumsy hand. Cf. **Maeg.**

Magerful, *adj.* masterful, exercising undue influence.

Magg, Mag, *n.* a halfpenny; a small gratuity, 'tip.' Cf. **Maik.**

Magg, *v.* to carry off clandestinely.

Maggative, Maggativous, *adj.* full of whims; crotchety.

†**Magger**, *prep.* in spite of, 'maugre.'

Maggie, *n.* a young woman or girl; a jade; a collier's term for a kind of till or clay.

Maggie, *n.* the common guillemot; a magpie.

Maggie Findy, *n.* a woman capable of shifting for herself.

Maggie-mony-feet, *n.* a centipede.

Maggie-Rab, -Robb, *n.* a bad halfpenny; a bad wife.

Maggit, *n.* a maggot; a whim, fancy; a fad.

Maggle, *v.* to mangle; to bungle.

Maggoty-heidit, *adj.* whimsical, capricious.

Maggoty-pow, *n.* a whimsical, crotchety person.

Magin, *ppl.* wondering; speculating; talking as if at a loss.

Magistrand, *n.* a student about to become M.A. at Aberdeen University.

Magistrate, *n.* a red herring.

Magot, *n.* a maggot; a whim.

Magowk, *v.* to make an April fool of one.

Magpie, *n.* a chatterer.

†Magre, *prep.* in spite of.

Mags, *n.* a tip, a small fee for service. Cf. Magg.

†Magyers, *v.* to spite.

Mahers, *n.* a tract of low land, of a marshy and moory nature. Cf. Machers.

Mahoun, *n.* a name given to the devil.

Maich, *n.* marrow; might; strength; an effort. Cf. Maught.

Maicherand, *ppl. adj.* weak, feeble; incapable of exertion.

Maichless, *adj.* wanting bodily strength. Cf. Maughtless.

Maick, *n.* a halfpenny; a small gratuity. Cf. Magg.

Maid, *n.* a maggot; the larva of a maggot. Cf. Mad, Maith.

Maid, *ppl.* fatigued. Cf. Made.

Maid, *n.* the last handful of corn cut in harvest.

Maiden, *v.* to lay a child in the arms of its parent when it is presented for baptism.—*n.* an old maid; a designation formerly given to the eldest daughter of a farmer; the bride's-maid at a wedding; she who laid the child in the arms of its parent when it was presented for baptism; the last handful of corn cut in harvest, dressed with ribbons to resemble a young woman; the feast of harvest-home; a wisp of straw put into a hoop of iron, used by a smith for watering his fire; an ancient instrument for holding the broaches of pirns until the pirns are wound off; an instrument for beheading, like the guillotine; the skate, thornback.

Maiden-chance, *n.* a first chance.

Maiden-day, *n.* the day when the last sheaf of the harvest is cut.

Maiden-feast, *n.* the feast given on the last day of harvest.

Maiden-hair, *n.* the muscles of oxen when boiled.

Maiden-kimmer, *n.* the maid who attends the 'kimmer,' or matron who has the charge of the infant at 'kimmerings' and baptisms; the maid who lays the infant in the father's arms at a baptism.

Maiden-night, *n.* the night of the harvest-feast.

Maiden-play, *n.* the harvest-home amusement.

Maiden-skate, *n.* the skate, thornback.

Maiden Trace, *n.* the name of an old popular tune, often played when a bride and her maidens walked thrice round the church before the celebration of the marriage.

Maid-in-the-mist, *n.* navelwort.

Maidship, *n.* a maiden condition; an unmarried state.

Maie, *n.* the bleat of a lamb. Cf. Mae.

Maig, *v.* to handle a thing so as to render it disgusting.—*n.* a clumsy hand. Cf. Maeg.

†Maigers, *prep.* in spite of, 'maugre.'

Maighrie, *n.* money; valuable effects.

Maigintie, Maiginties, *int.* excl. of surprise.

Maik, *n.* a halfpenny; a small gratuity. Cf. Magg.

Maik, *n.* fashion; design; figure, shape; kind, species; variety; quantity of what is made. Cf. Mack.

Maik, *n.* an equal, match, 'marrow'; an image, model; resemblance.

Maikint, *adj.* confident. Cf. Makint.

Maikless, *adj.* matchless.

Mail, Maill, *n.* rent; a contribution levied.

Mail, *n.* a spot in cloth; a mark, an iron stain.—*v.* to spot, stain.

Mail, *n.* food; a meal; the milk given by a cow or a herd at one milking.—*v.* to feed; to have meals. Cf. Meal.

Mail, *n.* a travelling-bag.

Mail-duty, *n.* rent.

Mailer, *n.* the quantity of corn ground at a time. Cf. Melder.

Mail-free, *adj.* rent-free.

Mail-garden, *n.* a garden, the produce of which is grown for sale.

Mailie, Maillie, *n.* a pet-ewe; the name for a pet cow or ewe.

Mailin, *n.* a purse.

Mailin, Mailen, *n.* a farm, holding; its rent.

Mailinder, *n.* the holder of a farm.

†Maille, *n.* a gold coin.

Mailler, Mailer, *n.* a cottager who gets waste land rent-free for a number of years to improve it; a rent-paying farmer.

Maillyer, Mailyer, *n.* the quantity of corn ground at a time. Cf. Melder.

Mail-man, *n.* a farmer.

Mail-payer, *n.* a rent-paying farmer.

Mail-rooms, *n.* hired lodgings.

Mails, *n.* various species of goose-foot.

Mails, *n.* small perforated scales of metal attached to the heddle through which the warp passes, used in weaving.

Mailt-house, *n.* a house for which rent is paid.

Main, *n.* patience.—*adj.* thorough; staunch. —*adv.* very much; quite.

Main, *v.* to moan; to express pain; to pity. —*n.* a moan, complaint. Cf. Maen.

Main-braces, *n.* part of the equipment of a carriage of the old fashion for supporting its body.

Main-comb, *n.* a comb for a horse's mane, &c

Maine-bread, *n.* fine white bread, manchet.

†**Maingie,** *n.* a family household ; a retinue ; a crowd. Cf. Menyie.

Mainly, *adv.* very, exceedingly.

Mainners, *n.* manners.

Main-rig, *n.* land of which the ridges were possessed alternately by different persons.

Mains, *n.* the home-farm on an estate.

Mainsmore, *n.* good-will or free grace.

Mainswear, *v.* to swear falsely. Cf. Manswear.

Main-sweat, *n.* the death-sweat.

Mainto, *n.* obligation to one ; debt. Cf. Mento.

Mair, *adj.* more.

Mairattour, *adv.* moreover.

Mairch, *n.* a boundary. Cf. March.

Mairdil, *v.* to be overcome with fatigue.—*adj.* moving heavily from fatigue, size, or bodily weakness.

†**Mairdle,** *n.* a large lot; an unpleasant quantity. Cf. Mardle.

Mairower, *adv.* moreover.

Mairritch lickness, *n.* a likelihood of marriage.

Mairt, *n.* winter provision of beef, made at Martinmas.

Mairtimas, *n.* Martinmas.

Maischloch, *n.* mixed grain. Cf. Mashloch.

Maise, Mais, *n.* a measure of herrings. Cf. Maze.

†**Maise,** *v.* to soothe ; to soften ; to mellow fruit. Cf. Mease.

Maise, *v.* to mix ; to blend or incorporate in one mass. Cf. Meise.

Maised, *ppl. adj.* used of fruit : mellow, spoiled from too long keeping. Cf. Mease.

Maiser, *n.* a macer.

Maiser, *n.* a drinking-cup of maple, a mazer.

Maishie, *n.* a basket for odds and ends. Cf. Maizie.

†**Maison-dieu, -dew,** *n.* a hospital.

Maissery, *n.* macership.

Maist, Maista, *adj.* most.—*adv.* almost.—*n.* the greatest number, degree, &c.

Maister, *n.* master ; an overmatch ; a schoolmaster.—*v.* to master. Cf. Master.

Maister, *n.* stale urine ; chamber-lye. Cf. Master.

Maister-can, *n.* an earthen vessel for preserving stale urine.

Maisterfu', *adj.* masterful.

Maister-laiglen, -tub, *n.* a wooden vessel for holding stale urine.

Maister-wud, *n.* the timber of agricultural buildings originally paid for by the landlord.

Maistlins, *adv.* mostly ; almost.

Maistly, *adv.* mostly ; almost.

Maistry, *n.* mastery ; skill, power.

Mait, *n.* meat, food.

Maith, *n.* a maggot.—*v.* to become infested with maggots. Cf. Mad, Maid.

Maitter, *n.* matter.

†**Maivie,** *n.* the song-thrush. Cf. Mavis.

Maizick, *n.* music. Cf. Music.

Maizie, *n.* a basket for odds and ends.

Maizie, *n.* a 'binder'; a flannel undershirt.

Majirk, *n.* a queer, old-fashioned article or machine.

Major, *v.* to walk to and fro with a military air, swagger.

Major-mindit, *adj.* haughty in demeanour.

Mak, *v.* to make ; to compose poetry ; to make up accounts ; of dung : to become fit for use ; to do, to have business ; to meddle ; to pretend ; to matter, be of consequence : to reach ; of the tide : to rise, flow.

Mak, *n.* fashion ; style ; figure, form ; sort, kind. Cf. Maik, Mack.

Mak, *n.* a match, equal, 'marrow'; an image, model, likeness. Cf. Maik, Mack.

Mak aff, *v.* to run away, scamper off.

Make, *n.* figure, form. Cf. Maik.

Make, *n.* a halfpenny ; a small gratuity. Cf. Maik.

Make-bate, *n.* a mischief-maker.

Makedom, *n.* figure, shape. Cf. Maikdom.

Make-down, *v.* used of spirits : to dilute ; of a bed : to make it ready.

Maker, *n.* a poet.

Mak for, *v.* to prepare for.

Mak fore, *v.* to be of advantage.

Making, *n.* used of tea, &c.: the quantity made at a time ; in *pl.* the materials of which a thing is made ; germs.

Makint, *adj.* assured ; confident.

Makintly, *adv.* assuredly ; confidently.

Mak into, *v.* to make one's way into, sail into.

Mak in wi', *v.* to get into one's good graces.

Makly, *adv.* equally.

Makly, *adj.* seemly ; well-proportioned. Cf. Mackly.

Mak of, *v.* to make much of ; to profit by ; to do with ; to pat.

Mak-on, *n.* a pretence.

Mak one's self away, *v.* to commit suicide.

Mak oot, *v.* to extricate one's self ; to prove ; to find out truth or fact.

Mak sleepy, *adj.* soporific.

Maksna, *v. neg.* matters not.

Mak stead, *v.* to be of use.

Mak throw, *v.* to struggle through.

Mak to, *v.* to make towards ; to approximate so far towards.

Mak up, *v.* to intend, decide ; to get out of bed ; to arrange, prepare ; to raise, collect ; to invent ; to make a fortune ; to break. — *n.* a fabrication ; anything made up of odds and ends.

Mak up for, v. used of rain : to threaten.

Mak upon, v. to prepare.

Mak up one's self, v. to recoup one's self for expenditure, labour, &c.

Mak up to, till, v. to overtake ; to accost; to make matrimonial overtures.

Mak up with, v. to be pleased with, satisfied with, profited by.

†Mal-accord, n. disagreement ; disapproval.

Malagruized, ppl. adj. disordered, rumpled.

Malagruze, v. to bruise ; to rumple.

Malapavis, n. a mischance ; a misfortune.

Malavogue, v. to beat, chastise.

Malchance, n. mischance.

Male, n. rent. Cf. Mail.

Male, n. a meal.

Male, n. five hundred herrings.

Male, n. a spot ; a stain.—v. to spot, to stain. Cf. Mail.

Male-a-forren, n. a meal over and above what is consumed ; a meal beforehand.

†Malefice, n. a bad action ; injury by witches.

Maleficiat, ppl. adj. injured by witchcraft.

Male-free, adj. rent-free. Cf. Mail-free.

Malegrugrous, adj. grim, ghastly ; looking discontented.

Maliceful. adj. sickly ; in bad health.

Malicin, Mallasin, n. a curse.

Maligrumph, n. the spleen.

Malishy, n. the militia.

Malison, n. the Evil One.

Malkin, n. a half-grown girl ; a hare. Cf. Mawkin.

Mall, n. in phr. 'mall in shaft,' all right, fit for work.

Mallachie, adj. of a milk-and-water colour.

Mallagrugous, adj. grim ; ghastly ; looking discontented.

Mallat, v. to feed.

Malleables, n. ironwork.

Mallow, n. the sea-wrack Zostera marina.

Malm, v. to soften and swell by means of water ; to steep ; to become mellow.

Malmieness, n. mellowness.

Malmy, adj. used of fruit : mellow, juiceless ; of food : vapid, tasteless ; soft, yielding, gentle.

†Malorous, adj. evil, unfortunate; malicious.

Malt, n. any liquor made from malt. Cf. Maut.

Malt and meal, n. food and drink.

Malvader, v. to stun by a blow ; to injure.

Malvadering, n. a beating, a defeat.

Malverish, adj. ill-behaved ; good for nothing.

†Malverse, n. a crime ; a misdemeanour.— adj. criminal.—v. to do wrong ; to give an erroneous judgment ; to misemploy or pervert an office, trust, &c.

†Malvesy, n. malmsey wine.

Mam, n. a child's name for 'mother.'

Mament, n. a moment.

Mamie, n. a wet-nurse ; a foster-mother. Cf. Mammy.

Mamikeekie, n. a smart, sound blow.

Mammock, n. a fragment ; a bit.

Mammy, n. a child's name for 'mother'; a midwife ; a nurse ; a foster-mother.

Mamore, n. a big field.

Mamp, v. to nibble ; to mop ; to eat as one does who has no teeth ; to speak querulously. Cf. Mump.

Mam's-fout, -pet, n. a spoiled child.

Man, n. a husband ; a familiar term of address.

Man, v. must ; to order haughtily or masterfully. Cf. Maun.

Man, v. to accomplish by means of strength ; to 'manage,' succeed ; to effect by any means. Cf. Maun.

†Manadge, Manawdge, n. a kind of club or benefit society of near neighbours.

Manadge-circle, n. the whole number of contributors to the 'manadge.'

Manadge-wife, n. the woman-treasurer of the 'manadge.'

Manage, v. to get through with ; to reach with some difficulty.

Man-body, n. a full-grown man.

Man-bote, n. compensation fixed by law for manslaughter.

Man-browed, adj. having hair growing between the eyebrows.

Manco, n. calamanco, a kind of cloth.

Mand, n. a bread-basket, shaped like a corn-sieve, and made of plaited willows and straw. Cf. Maund.

Mandate, v. to commit a sermon to memory before preaching it.

Mandel-buttons, n. mantle-buttons, buttons for a loose upper garment.

Mander, v. to handle ; to deal.

Mane, n. a moan ; a complaint.—v. to complain. Cf. Maen.

Mane, n. the wool on a sheep's neck ; the top of a sheaf of oats.

Manelet, n. the corn-marigold.

Man-faced, adj. having masculine features.

Manfu'-like, adj. manly, man-like.

Mang, Mangs, prep. among.

Mang, v. to maim, bruise ; to overpower.—n. a mixture. Cf. Ming.

Mang, v. to become frantic; to render frantic; to feel great but suppressed anxiety ; to long for eagerly ; to gall ; with at, to be angry with.—n. strong, suppressed feeling or anger.

Manglumtew, n. a heterogeneous mixture.

Manheid, n. bravery ; fortitude.

Man-hive, n. a populous town.

Manish, v. to manage ; to pull through. Cf. Manage.

Manitoodlie, *n.* a term of endearment for a male child.

†**Mank,** *v.* to fail; to be deficient; to impair, spoil. —*n.* a want; a deficiency, short-coming; the shying of an animal, causing it to stop. —*adj.* defective; at a loss.

Man-keeper, *n.* the water-newt or 'esk'; a small lizard.

Mankey, *n.* calamanco. Cf. Manco.

†**Mankie,** *v.* to miss; to fail. —*n.* a 'pear' which misses its aim and remains in the ring, in the game of pegtop.

Mankie, *n.* calamanco. Cf. Manco.

Manling, *n.* a mannikin.

Man-muckle, *adj.* come to the height of a full-grown man.

Mann, *v.* to 'manage.' Cf. Maun.

Mannagie, *n.* a mannikin. Cf. Mannie.

Manner, *v.* to mock; to mimic; to sound indistinctly or mockingly as an echo. Cf. Maunder.

Mannerin', *n.* mockery; mimicry.

Mannie, Manikie, Mannikie, *n.* a little man; a term of endearment for a small boy.

Mannin', *ppl. adj.* imperious. Cf. Man, Maun.

Manno, *n.* a big man.

Mannor, Manor, *v.* and *n.* manure.

Man o' mean, *n.* a beggar.

Man o' sin, *n.* the Pope.

Manritch, *adj.* used of a woman: masculine.

Manse, *n.* a Scottish minister's official residence.

Mansemas Day, *n.* Dec. 31 N.S.; Dec. 20 O.S.

Mansie, *n.* a mannikin.

Manswear, *v.* to commit perjury. Cf. Mainswear.

Mansworn, *ppl. adj.* perjured.

Mant, *v.* to stammer, stutter. —*n.* a stutter.

†**Mantay,** *n.* a mantle, gown. Cf. Manty.

Manteel, *n.* a mantle.

Manter, *n.* a stammerer.

Manting, *n.* stuttering; stumbling. —*ppl. adj.* stammering.

†**Manto,** *n.* a mantle, gown.

†**Manty,** *n.* a gown; the stuff of which the gown is made.

Manty-coat, *n.* a lady's loose coat.

Manty-maker, *n.* a dressmaker.

†**Manumission,** *n.* graduation, as making 'free' of a university.

†**Manumit,** *v.* to confer an academical degree; to laureate.

Many, *adj.* much. —*n.* with *a*, a great number; with *the*, the majority, the departed. Cf. Mony.

†**Manzy,** *n.* a household; retainers. Cf. Menyie.

Maoll, *n.* a promontory. Cf. Mull.

Map, *n.* a portrait, likeness.

Map, *v.* to nibble as a sheep, rabbit, &c. —*n.* a rabbit. —*int.* a call to a rabbit.

Map and mell, *v.* to live at board and bed, as a wife with a husband.

Mappy, *n.* a rabbit. —*int.* a call to a rabbit.

Mapsie, *n.* a pet sheep; a young hare.

Mar, *n.* an impediment in speech; a defect. —*v.* to irritate, annoy.

Marb, *n.* the marrow.

Marbel, *adj.* feeble, inactive, slow, lazy; reluctant. Cf. Mervil.

Marble, *n.* an alley made of fine white clay and streaked with red and blue lines.

Marble-bools, *n.* marbles used in playing.

Marbled, *ppl. adj.* used of meat: composed of fat and lean in layers.

Marchandye, *n.* merchandise.

Marchant, *n.* a merchant. Cf. Merchant.

March-balk, *n.* a narrow ridge, serving as a march between the contiguous lands of different proprietors.

March-dyke, *n.* a boundary wall or fence.

Marches, *n.* part of a weaver's loom.

March-man, *n.* a Borderer.

March-stane, *n.* a boundary-stone.

Mardel, *n.* a fat, clumsy woman. —*adj.* big, fat; clumsy. Cf. Merdal.

†**Mardle,** *n.* a crowd; a great number of vermin. Cf. Meirdel.

Mardle, Mardel, *n.* a gossiper; an idle, lounging woman.

Mare, *n.* the wooden figure of a horse, used as a military punishment; a trestle supporting scaffolding; a mason's or bricklayer's hod or trough.

Marefu', *n.* a hodful.

Mareillen, *n.* the frog-fish.

Mare's-tails, *n.* long, streaky clouds portending rain.

Marestane, *n.* a rough, hatchet-shaped stone, hung up in a stable to protect the horses from being hag-ridden.

Margent, *n.* a margin, bank, beach.

†**Margullie, Margulie,** *v.* to disfigure, mangle; to bungle; to abuse.

Marican, *n.* a kind of pear.

†**Mariken,** *n.* a dressed goatskin, morocco.

Mariken shoon, *n.* morocco-leather shoes.

Marinel, *n.* a mariner.

Marish, *adj.* marshy.

Maritage, *n.* money paid to the superior by the heir of his dead vassal, if unmarried before the death, or at puberty, as the value of his 'tocher.'

Mark, *n.* a silver coin, worth 13s. 4d. Scots, or 13⅓d. stg.; a division of land; a nominal weight. Cf. Merk.

Mark, *adj.* dark. —*n.* darkness. Cf. Mirk.

Mark, *n.* a conspicuous figure, a 'spectacle'; the supposed mark of the devil on a witch's body; the aim in shooting.—*v.* to aim in shooting.

Market, *n.* sale; traffic; a matrimonial engagement or match.

Market-fare, *n.* a 'fairing' bought for a sweetheart at a market.

Market-ripe, *adj.* used of a woman : marriageable.

Market-stance, *n.* the field, &c., on which a market is held.

Market-stead, *n.* the site of a market.

Mark-land, *n.* a division of land, varying in extent.

Mark nor burn, Mark nor horn, *n.* not the least vestige or trace of anything lost.

Mark o' mouth, *n.* indication of age by the teeth.

Mark-stane, *n.* a boundary-stone; in *pl.* stones defining the extent of a 'mark' of land.

Marl, Marle, *v.* to become mottled, variegated; to streak, spot.—*n.* a mottle, an indistinct mark on the skin caused by cold; in *pl.* the measles.

Marl, Marle, *v.* to marvel.

Marled, *adj.* mottled; chequered.

Marled-salmon, *n.* the gray trout, a species of salmon.

Marley, *n.* a red clay marble.

†**Marlion, Marlin,** *n.* the merlin; the sparrow-hawk; the kestrel.

Marl-midden, *n.* a compost of marl and earth.

Marmaid, *n.* a mermaid; the frog-fish; a species of limpet.

†**Marmite,** *n.* a large cooking-pot.

Maroonjus, Marounjous, *adj.* harsh; outrageous; obstreperous; in bad humour.

Marr, *v.* used of a cat : to purr; of an infant : to coo; with *up*, to make a noise like two cats provoking each other to fight; to urge or keep one to work.

Marr, *n.* an obstruction; an injury. Cf. Mar.

Marriage, *n.* the duty payable on the marriage of a ward whose lands were held of a superior.

Marriage-bone, *n.* a fowl's merrythought.

Marriage-chack, *n.* a sound like the ticking of a watch, portending marriage.

Marriage-lines, *n.* a marriage certificate given to the bride.

Marriage-sark, *n.* a shirt made by the bride, to be worn by the bridegroom on their marriage-day.

Marrott, *n.* the common guillemot; the razor-bill.

Marrow, *n.* a name given to *The Marrow of Modern Divinity,* a work published in 1718 by Edward Fisher, the doctrines of which influenced the Evangelicals of the Scottish Kirk in the 18th century.

Marrow, *n.* a match, equal; a facsimile; one of a pair; a partner, mate, companion; a spouse, lover; an atom.—*v.* to match; to wed, mate; to pair; to unite; to keep company with.

Marrow-kirk, *n.* a Church which favoured the 'Marrow' doctrine.

Marrowless, *adj.* without a peer or equal; odd, not of a pair, not matching; companionless; without a husband or wife; widowed, unmarried.

Marrow-men, *n.* ministers who preached the 'Marrow' doctrine.

Marry, *v.* with *on* or *upon,* to be married to.

Marsh-bent, Marsh-bent-grass, *n.* the fine-top grass.

Marsh-woundwort, *n.* the marsh-betony.

Mar's year, *n.* the year 1715.

Mart, *n.* a cow or ox fattened, killed, and salted about Martinmas, for winter use; meat pickled and stored for winter; one who lives in ease and prosperity.

†**Marter,** *n.* a mess.—*v.* to mutilate. Cf. Martyr.

Marth, *n.* marrow, pith.

Martin-a-bullimus, -of-bullion's Day, *n.* July 4, the feast of the Translation of St Martin.

Martinmas, *n.* St Martin's Day; the 11th of November; the November term-day.

Martinmas-foy, *n.* a ploughman's farewell feast at Martinmas.

Martin-swallow, *n.* the martin.

Martlet, *n.* the marten.

†**Martyr,** *n.* a dirty or spoilt condition; a mess; anything causing a mess.—*v.* to mutilate, bruise severely; to torture; to subject to great pain; to bungle, confuse; to work in a dirty, clumsy fashion; to be-daub, bespatter with dirt.

†**Martyreese,** *v.* to victimize, 'martyr.'

Martyring, *n.* ill-treatment.

Marval, *n.* marble.

Marvel, *v.* to marvel at.

Mary, Marie, *n.* a maid of honour; a female attendant.

Mary-knot (St), *n.* a triple knot.

Marymas, *n.* Sept. 8, the festival of St Mary.

Mary's-knot (St), *n.* in *phr.* 'to tie with St Mary's knot,' to hamstring.

Mary-sole, *n.* the smear or dab.

Maschle, Mashle, *n.* a mixture; a mess; a state of confusion.—*v.* to reduce to a confused mass; with *up,* to be closely related by marriage and blood.

Mash, *n.* a mess; a soft, pulpy mass.

Mash, *n.* a mason's large hammer.—*v.* to crush stones.

Mash-fat, *n.* a large tub for mashing malt in brewing.

Mash-hammer, *n.* a mason's large hammer.

Mashie, *n.* a particular kind of golf-club.

Mashlach, Mashlich, *n.* mixed grain. Cf. Mashloch.

Mashlam, *n.* mixed grain. Cf. Mashlum.

Mashlie, *n.* mixed grain, peas and oats; the broken parts of a moss.

Mashlie-moss, *n.* a moss that is much broken up.

Mashlin, *ppl. adj.* mixed; blended carelessly or coarsely.—*n.* mixed grain.

Mashloch, Mashlock, *n.* a coarse kind of bread; mixed peas and oats.—*adj.* mingled, blended; promiscuous.

Mashlum, *n.* mixed grain; the flour or meal of different kinds of grain; a mixture of edibles.—*adj.* mixed; made from different kinds of grain.

Mash-man, *n.* one who has charge of the mashing of malt at a brewery.

Mash-pot, *n.* a teapot.

Mash-rubber, *n.* a 'mash-fat.'

Mask, *n.* a mesh of a net; a crib for catching fish.—*v.* to catch fish in a net.

Mask, *n.* a quantity; a mass.

Mask, *v.* to infuse tea, malt, &c.; used of a storm : to be brewing; to be in a state of infusion or preparation.—*n.* a mash for a horse.

Maskert, *n.* the marsh-betony.

Masking, *n.* a sufficient quantity of tea, &c., for an infusion.

Masking-fat, *n.* a large tub for mashing malt in brewing.

Masking-loom, *n.* a brewing utensil.

Masking-pat, *n.* a teapot.

Masking-rung, *n.* a rod for stirring mash in the mash-tub.

Maskis, *n.* a mastiff.

Mask-rudder, *n.* an instrument for stirring the mash in the vat.

Masle, *n.* mixed grain.

Maslin, *n.* mixed grain. Cf. Mashlum.

†Mason-due, *n.* a hospital. Cf. Maison-dieu.

Mason-word, *n.* a Masonic password.

Mass, *n.* a title prefixed to the Christian name of a minister of religion.—*int.* used in excls. and in oaths.

Mass, *n.* pride, haughtiness; self-conceit.

Mass and meat, *n.* prayers and food.

Masser, *n.* a mace-bearer. Cf. Macer.

Mass-John, *n.* a minister of religion.

Massy, *adj.* self-important; conceited; boastful.

Master, *n.* a landlord, 'laird'; a schoolmaster; a baron's or viscount's eldest son.

Master, *n.* stale urine. Cf. Maister.

Masterdom, *n.* mastery.

Masterful, *adj.* great in size; powerful; violent, forcible.

Master-graith, *n.* the chain fastening the harrow to the swingle-tree.

Masterman, *n.* an employer; an overlooker.

Master of mortifications, *n.* the member of a town council who has charge of funds 'mortified' or bequeathed to the town.

Master-pen, *n.* a bird's chief feather.

Master-tree, *n.* the swingle-tree nearest the plough, &c.

Master-wood, *n.* the principal beams in the roof of a house. Cf. Maister-wud.

Master-work, *n.* work on the home-farm exacted from the neighbouring tenants of small holdings.

Mast-head, *n.* the extreme, the utmost limit, the very end.

†Mastin, *n.* a mastiff.

Mat, *n.* a woollen bed-coverlet.

Mat, *v.* may. Cf. Mote.

Ma't, *n.* malt.

Matash, *n.* a moustache.

Match, *v.* to marry, mate.

Match-paper, *n.* brown paper soaked in a solution of saltpetre, and used with flint and steel for lighting pipes, &c.

Match-stick, *n.* a splint of wood tipped with sulphur, for kindling.

Mated-out, *ppl. adj.* exhausted with fatigue.

Mat-grass, *n.* the wire-bent.

Mather, *n.* a dish for holding meal. Cf. Madder.

Matie, Mattie, *n.* an immature herring; a fat herring.

Matrimonial, *n.* an affair of marriage.

Matter, *n.* a quantity or variety of food.

Mattle, *v.* to nibble.

Matty, *adj.* matted.

Mauch, *n.* a maggot. Cf. Mawk.

Mauch, *n.* marrow; power. Cf. Maught.

Mauch, *adj.* moist, damp. Cf. Moch.

Mauchless, *adj.* without power to move. Cf. Maughtless.

Maucht, *adj.* tired, worn-out; puzzled, baffled; out of heart.

Maucht, *n.* marrow; power. Cf. Maught.

Mauchy, *adj.* dirty, filthy. Cf. Mochy.

Maud, *n.* a shepherd's plaid.

Maud, *n.* a net for catching salmon, &c. Cf. Mad.

Maudin-plaid, *n.* a shepherd's plaid.

Maudlin-hood, *n.* a woollen hood.

Maughsome, *adj.* loathsome.

Maught, *n.* strength, ability; an effort; marrow.

Maughtless, *adj.* feeble, impotent.

Maughtlessly, *adv.* feebly.

Maughtly, *adv.* mightily, strongly.

Maughty, *adj.* mighty; powerful.

†Maugre, *n.* ill-will; spite; vexation; blame; injury. Cf. Maigers.

Mauk, *n.* a maggot. Cf. **Mawk.**
Maukie, *adj.* full of maggots.
Maukin, *n.* a hare. Cf. **Mawkin.**
Maukiness, *n.* the state of being 'maukie.'
Maukin-mad, *adj.* mad as a hare.
Maukrel, *n.* a mackerel.
Maul, *n.* a female paramour, a 'doxy.'
Maulifuff, *n.* a young woman without energy; one who fusses to little effect.
Mauly, *n.* a 'maulifuff.'
Maum, *v.* to soften and swell by means of water; to mellow. Cf. **Malm.**
Maument, *n.* a moment.
Maumie, *adj.* mellow. Cf. **Malmy.**
Maumieness, *n.* mellowness.
Maun, *v.* must; to order imperiously. Cf. **Man.**
Maun, *v.* to manage; to accomplish by energy or by any means.
Maun, *adv.* used as a superlative: very.
†**Maun,** *n.* a basket. Cf. **Maund.**
Mauna, *v. neg.* must not.
Maun-be, *n.* a necessary act or result.
†**Maund,** *v.* to beg.
†**Maund,** *n.* a hamper.
†**Maunder,** *n.* a beggar.
Maunder, *n.* a gossip; a babbler.—*v.* to talk idly, incoherently, foolishly; to sound indistinctly as an echo.
Maundrel, *n.* a gossip, a babbler; in *pl.* idle tales; foolish, fevered fancies.—*v.* to babble.
Maund-wecht, *n.* a winnowing-sieve of untanned sheep- or calf-skin stretched on a wooden hoop.
Mauner, *v.* to 'maunder.'
Mauning, *ppl. adj.* imperious.
Maunna, *v. neg.* must not.
Maunnering, *n.* incoherent talk.
Maunt, *v.* to stutter. Cf. **Mant.**
Mausie, *adj.* used of persons: stout; of cloth: strong.—*n.* a stout person; a slovenly woman; strong, thick, warm cloth. Cf. **Mawsie.**
Maussie, *adj.* quiet; cautious, wary. Cf. **Mawse.**
Maut, *n.* malt. Cf. **Malt.**
Maut-bree, *n.* malt liquor.
Mauten, *v.* used of bread: to become tough and heavy; of grain: to sprout when being steeped.
Mauten, Mautent, *ppl. adj.* used of grain: having a peculiar taste because not properly dried; of bread: not properly baked, moist; dull, sluggish.
Mauten'd-loll, -lump, *n.* a heavy, sluggish person.
Mautit, *ppl. adj.* malted.
Maut-kiln, *n.* a malt-kiln.
Mautman, *n.* a maltster.
Maut-siller, *n.* money for malt.

Mauvering, *n.* threatening language or demeanour.
Mauvie, *n.* the maw of a fish; the stomach of any small animal; a rennet-bag.
Maverish, *adj.* ill-behaved. Cf. **Malverish.**
Mavie, *n.* the slightest noise. Cf. **Meevie.**
†**Mavis, Mavie, Mavish,** *n.* the song-thrush.
Mavis-skate, *n.* the sharp-nosed ray. Cf. **May-skate.**
Maw, *v.* used of a cat: to mew.
Maw, *n.* the human mouth.
Maw, *v.* to mow —*n.* a single sweep of the scythe.
Maw, *n.* the common gull.
Maw, *n.* an atom, whit.
Maw-bag, *n.* an animal's stomach.
Mawch, *n.* a maggot. Cf. **Mawk.**
Mawch, *n.* strength, power. Cf. **Maught.**
Mawd, *n.* a shepherd's plaid. Cf. **Maud.**
Mawer, *n.* a mower.
Mawin, *n.* the quantity mowed in a day.
Mawk, *n.* a maggot; the larva of the blue-bottle fly.—*v.* to be infested with maggots.
Mawkin, *n.* a half-grown girl; a girl engaged to do light housework; a hare.
Mawkiness, *n.* the state of being infested with maggots.
Mawkin-fly, *n.* the blue-bottle fly.
Mawkin-hippit, *adj.* having thin hips like a hare.
Mawkin-mad, *adj.* mad as a March hare.
Mawkit, *ppl. adj.* infested with maggots.
Mawk-worm, *n.* a maggot.
Mawky, *adj.* full of maggots.
Mawm, *v.* to steep; to mellow. Cf. **Malm.**
Mawment, *n.* an image, effigy.
Mawn, *n.* a basket. Cf. **Maund.**
Mawner, *v.* to mimic. Cf. **Manner.**
Mawp, *v.* to mope; to wander about thoughtfully or listlessly.
Maws, *n.* the mallow.
Mawse, *n.* a joke, jest. Cf. **Mows.**
Mawse, *adj.* quiet; wary. Cf. **Maussie.**
Mawsie, *adj.* stout, strapping, 'sonsie'; thick, strong. — *n.* a stout woman; a stupid, slovenly woman; a drab, a trollop; a poorsounding fiddle; a piece of thick, strong, warm dress material; a knitted semmit worn over the shirt by old men, a 'surcoat.'
Mawster, *n.* a mower.
Mawten, *v.* to sprout. Cf. **Mauten.**
Maxie, *n.* a *maximus*, or the gravest error in a Latin version.
May, *n.* a maid, maiden.
May, *n.* the bleat of a sheep. Cf. **Mae.**
Maybe, Maybes, *adv.* perhaps, possibly.—*n.* a possibility.
May-bird, *n.* the whimbrel; a person born in May.

May-gobs, *n.* cold weather about the second week of May.

May-gosling, *n.* a 'fool' made on May Day as on the 1st of April.

Mayock-fluke, *n.* the flounder.

May-puddock, *n.* a young frog.

May-shell, *n.* the bone of a cuttle-fish.

May-skate, *n.* the sharp-nosed ray. Cf. Mavis-skate.

May-spink, *n.* the primrose.

Maze, *n.* five hundred herrings. Cf. Maise.

Maze, *v.* to wonder; to be amazed.

Mazerment, *n.* bewilderment; confusion.

Mazie, *n.* a straw net; a basket made of straw-rope. Cf. Maizie.

Mazing, *adv.* amazingly.

Meace, *n.* a meal, dinner, mess.

Mead, *n.* mood. Cf. Meid.

Meadow, *n.* boggy land producing coarse grass.

Meadow-hay, *n.* the hay produced on boggy land.

Meadow-kerses, *n.* the cuckoo-flower.

Meadow-queen, *n.* the meadow-sweet, spiræa.

Meadow-rocket, *n.* the marsh-orchis.

†Meagries, *n.* miseries; ills.

†Meagrim, *n.* a whim, fancy; an absurd notion; a caprice.

Meal, *n.* soil, mould. Cf. Meel.

Meal, *n.* oatmeal.—*v.* used of grain: to produce meal.

Meal, *n.* the quantity of milk given by a cow or herd at one milking.—*v.* to feed. Cf. Mail.

Meal, *n.* rent; payment of dues on land let. Cf. Mail.

Meal-a-forren, *n.* a meal of meat over and above what is consumed.

Meal-and-ale, *n.* a mixture of oatmeal, ale, sugar, and whisky, prepared when all the grain crop is cut.

Meal-and-bree, *n.* 'brose.'

Meal-and-bree-nicht, *n.* Hallowe'en.

Meal-and-kail, *n.* oatmeal and mashed 'kail.'

Meal-and-thrammel, *n.* a little meal in the mouth of a sack at a mill, having some water or ale poured in and stirred about.

Meal-ark, *n.* a large meal-chest.

Meal-bowie, *n.* a meal-barrel.

Meal-cog, *n.* a small wooden vessel for holding meal.

Mealer, *n.* the quantity of oats ground at one time. Cf. Melder.

Meal-girnel, *n.* a 'meal-ark.'

Meal-hogyett, *n.* a barrel for holding oatmeal.

Mealin, *n.* a 'meal-ark'; oatcake or barley scones soaked in milk; in *pl.* meal for dusting over bannocks before baking them. —*v.* to dust or sprinkle with meal.

Mealing, *n.* a farm; a holding; rent of a farm. Cf. Mailin.

Me-alive, *int.* an excl. of surprise; a mild oath.

Meal-kail, *n.* oatmeal and mashed 'kail.'

Meal-kist, *n.* a meal-chest.

Meal-kit, *n.* a kit for holding meal.

Mealler, *n.* a cottager who, rent-free for so many years, improves waste land; a farmer paying rent. Cf. Mailler.

Meal-maker, *n.* a miller.

Meal-monger, *n.* a meal-seller.

Meal-mou'd, *adj.* soft-spoken; plausible; afraid to speak out.

Mealock, Meallock, *n.* a crumb of oatcake, &c.

Mealom, *n.* a very mealy potato.

Meal-o'-meat, *n.* a meal; victuals.

Meal-pock, *n.* a meal-bag; a beggar's wallet for holding meal.

Meal's corn, *n.* any species of grain; any food made of corn.

Meal-seeds, -sids, *n.* the husks of oats sifted out of the meal.

Meal-shells, -shillings, *n.* mill-seeds.

Meal's meat, *n.* food for one meal.

Meal-stand, *n.* a ploughman's barrel for holding his oatmeal.

Meal-stane, *n.* a rough stone weighing generally about 17 lb., formerly used in weighing oatmeal.

Mealtith, *n.* a meal; the quantity of milk given by a cow or herd at one milking. Cf. Meltith.

Meal-wind, *v.* to rub a cake or bannock over with meal before putting it on the 'girdle,' and again after it is first turned.

Mealy, *adj.* dusty with meal; stained with meal.

Mealy-bag, *n.* a beggar's wallet for holding meal.

Mealy-mou'd, *adj.* afraid to speak out; plausible; soft-spoken.

Mean, *n.* a means, instrumentality; means, property.

Mean, *adj.* held in common or equal shares; in bad health or condition.

Mean, *v.* to complain, lament; to complain against; to seek sympathy, redress, justice; to moan; to indicate pain; to pity; to resent, blame.—*n.* a moan, complaint. Cf. Maen.

Mean-born, *adj.* of lowly birth.

Meaner, *n.* an arbiter who adjusts in equal portions land held in common by various tenants; in *pl.* common lands.

Meantime, *n.* in *phr.* 'in the middle of mean-time,' meanwhile.

Mear, *n.* a mare. Cf. Mare.

Mearen, *n.* a strip of uncultivated ground of various breadth between two corn-ridges.

†Mease, *v.* to soothe, assuage, calm; to settle; to soften, mellow fruit.

Measie, *n.* a basket made of straw-rope. Cf. Mazie.

Measle, *v.* to have the legs spotted by sitting too near a fire; to speckle, blotch, mottle. Cf. Mizzle.

Measly, *adj.* contemptible; spotted, speckled. Cf. Maeslie.

Measly-shankit, *adj.* having the legs spotted by heat, &c. Cf. Maeslie-shankit.

Measure, *n.* moderation.

Measurely, *adv.* in moderation, moderately.

Meat, *n.* victuals; board; food for animals; flesh.—*v.* to feed; to board; to fill out the corn for a horse.

Meat-hale, -haill, *adj.* having a good, healthy appetite.

Meathie, *n.* a measure; a landmark. Cf. Meethe.

Meaths, *n.* maggots. Cf. Maith.

Meaties, *n.* food for infants.

Meat-like, *adj.* like one well-fed.

Meat-loom, *n.* a vessel in which food is cooked or served.

Meat-mither, *n.* the mistress of a house; one who serves out food.

Meat-rife, *adj.* abounding in meat.

Meat-wedder, *n.* a wedder ready for the butcher.

Meat-year, *n.* the season for crops, &c.

Meazie, *n.* a basket made of straw-rope. Cf. Mazie.

Meazle, *v.* to speckle. Cf. Measle.

†Meble, *adj.* movable.

†Meckant, *adj.* romping, frolicsome.

Med, *v.* must.

Meddem, *n.* a tickling in the nose, portending the arrival of a visitor.

Medding, *n.* a dung-heap.

Meddle, *v.* to meddle with; to hurt; to assault; to annoy; to have to do with.

Medicamenting, *n.* medical attendance.

Medicine, *n.* anything nauseous, bitter, or disagreeable.

Mediciner, *n.* a doctor, physician.

Meduart, *n.* meadow-sweet.

Meed, *n.* a mood. Cf. Meid.

Meed, *n.* a landmark. Cf. Meethe.

Meedge, *n.* a landmark. Cf. Meethe.

Meef, *adj.* hot, sultry. Cf. Meeth.

Meek-tasted, *adj.* sweet or mild of taste.

Meel, *n.* oatmeal.

Meel, *n.* soil, mould; in *pl.* dry earth; pulverized mould, the grave.—*v.* to crumble; to bury. Cf. Mool.

Meelack, *n.* a crumb. Cf. Mealock.

Meelick, *n.* the same spot where the 'pitcher' spins in striking a marble.

Meen, *n.* the moon.

Meen, *v.* to indicate pain; to pity, condole. Cf. Mean.

Meen, *adj.* held in common. Cf. Mean.

Meener, *n.* an adjuster. Cf. Meaner.

Meenint, Meenont, *n.* a minute.

Meenlicht, *n.* moonlight.

Meenlichty flitting, *n.* a moonlight 'flitting' by a tenant unable to pay his rent.

Meer, *n.* a mare.

Meeran, *n.* a carrot.

Meer-browed, *adj.* having the eyebrows meeting so as to cover the bridge of the nose.

Meerie, *n.* a young or little mare.

Meer-swine, *n.* the dolphin, the porpoise. Cf. Mere-swine.

Mees, *v.* to soothe; to mellow. Cf. Mease.

Meeschle, *n.* a mixture; a state of confusion. —*v.* to mix; to throw into confusion. Cf. Maschle.

Meeschle-maschle, *n.* great confusion; a confused mass.—*adj.* confused; much intermarried.

Meese, *n.* locating a spot at sea by observing certain landmarks.

Meesery, *n.* misery.

Meesh-mash, *n.* a muddle. Cf. Mish-mash.

Meet, *adj.* exact, exactly corresponding to; close-fitting.

Meet, *v.* with *in with*, to meet with.

Meet-bodied-coat, *n.* a 'meet-coat.'

Meet-coat, *n.* a coat exactly fitting the body, as distinguished from a greatcoat.

Meeten, *ppl.* measured, meted.

Meeth, *adj.* hot, sultry, close; exhausted with heat. Cf. Mooth.

Meeth, *adj.* modest; mild; gentle.

Meethe, Meeth, *n.* a measure; a mark; a landmark for vessels at sea; a mark by which observations are made or an object is detected; a hint, innuendo.—*v.* to mark a place at sea by the bearings of landmarks.

Meethness, *n.* sultriness; extreme heat.

Meeths, *n.* bodily activity, alertness.

Meet-marrow, *n.* a facsimile; a fellow, companion.

Meeve, *v.* to move.

Meevie, *n.* the slightest noise.—*phr.* 'naither meevie nor mavy,' not the slightest sound.

Meexter-maxter, *adv.* 'mixty-maxty,' in confusion.

Meezle, *v.* to cause the legs to be speckled by sitting close to a fire. Cf. Measle.

Meg, *n.* a woman; a country girl.

Meg-cut-throat, *n.* the whitethroat.

Meg Dorts, *n.* a sulky, pettish woman or girl.

Meggification, *n.* an exaggeration; an untruth.

Meggy-mony-feet, *n.* the centipede.

Megh, *n.* the big toe.

Megirkie, *n.* the woollen cloth worn by old men in winter to protect head and throat.

Megirtie, *n.* a kind. of cravat, held by two clasps.

Megisty, *int.* an excl. of surprise. Cf. Megsty.

Meg-mony-feet, *n.* the centipede.

Meg-o'-mony-feet, *n.* the centipede.

Megrim, Megram, *n.* a whim ; a foolish fancy.

Megsty, Megsty me, *int.* an excl. of surprise.

Meg-wi'-the-mony-feet, *n.* the centipede ; the crab ; the lobster.

Meid, *n.* appearance ; bearing, courage ; mood, disposition.

Meid, *n.* a measure ; a landmark ; a sign ; a hint.—*v.* to define by certain marks. Cf. Meethe.

Meid, *n.* a reward, recompense.

Meigh, *adj.* still, oppressive, close. Cf. Meeth.

Meikle, *adj.* much ; great. Cf. Muckle, Mickle.

Meikledom, *n.* size.

Mein, *adj.* common. Cf. Mean.

Mein, *n.* an attempt.

Mein, *v.* to show signs of pain ; to complain. Cf. Mean.

Meing, *v.* to mingle, blend ; of corn : to become mixed in colour.

Meinging, *n.* the act of mixing.

Meingyie, *v.* used of grain : to begin to change colour.

Meingyie, *v.* to hurt ; to lame.

†Meingyie, Meinzie, *n.* a household ; retainers. Cf. Menyie.

Meir, *n.* a mare.

†Meirdel, *n.* a confused crowd of persons or animals ; a large family of little children ; a huddled mass of small insects. Cf. Mairdle.

Meirie, *n.* a young mare.

Meise, Meis, *v.* to assuage, soothe ; to become calm ; to ripen or mellow fruit. Cf. Mease.

Meise, *v.* to mix ; to incorporate. Cf. Maise.

Meishachan, *n.* a subscription dance.

Meisle, Meissle, *v.* to waste imperceptibly ; to crumble down in eating ; to expend on trifles ; to eat little and slowly.—*n.* a small piece.

Meislen, Meisslen, *v.* to waste away by degrees ; to eat little and slowly.—*n.* a very small piece.

Meit, *n.* meat.

Meith, *adj.* sultry. Cf. Meeth.

Meith, *n.* a mark ; a sign.—*v.* to define by certain marks. Cf. Meethe.

Meith, *v.* might. Cf. Mith.

Mekil, Mekle, *adj.* much ; great. Cf. Mickle.

Mekildom, *n.* largeness of size.

Mekilwort, *n.* the deadly nightshade.

Mel, *n.* meal, ground grain. Cf. Meal.

Melancholious, *adj.* melancholy ; sombre ; bilious.

Melancholy, *n.* love-sickness ; mischief.

Melder, *n.* the quantity of oats ground at one time ; with *dusty,* the last milling of the crop of oats ; the last child born in a family.

Meldren, *n.* a 'melder.'

Meldrop, *n.* the foam that falls from a horse's mouth, or the drop at the bit ; the drop at the end of an icicle ; any drop in a pendent state, as a drop at the nose.

Meldweed, *n.* the white goosefoot.

Melg, *n.* the milt of fish.

Melgraf, Mellgrave, *n.* a quagmire, quicksand ; a break in a highway.

†Meliorat, *v.* to improve.

Mell, *n.* a mallet ; a 'beetle' ; a large wooden hammer ; a big, heavy fist ; the prize given to the last in a race or contest ; a blow with a mallet ; a heavy blow with any weapon ; a big, strong, stupid person.—*phr.* 'mell for mell,' blow for blow.—*v.* to hammer ; to beat with a 'mell.'

Mell, *v.* to feed ; to have meals. Cf. Meal, Mail.

†Mell, *v.* to mix ; to be intimate ; to meddle, interfere ; to join battle ; to match, equal. —*n.* a company.

Mell, *adj.* mellow.

Mell, *v.* used of corn in the straw : to become damp.

Meller, *n.* a 'melder.'

Mellering, *n.* waste meal ; the refuse meal gathered after grinding the sweepings of a meal-mill.

Mellin, *n.* a meal-chest.—*v.* to dust with meal. Cf. Mealin.

Melling, *n.* a mixture.

Mellison, *n.* a curse, malison.

Mellow, *adj.* genial by drink ; ripe, ready.

Mellowish, *adj.* slightly intoxicated.

Mells, *n.* in *phr.* to 'gree like butter and mells,' not to agree well.

Mellsman, *n.* a stonemason ; one who can wield a 'mell.'

Melly, *adj.* mellow ; pleasant, tender.

Melmont-berry, *n.* the juniper berry.

Melodious, *adj.* used as an intensive *adj.*

Melt, *v.* to be almost overcome with heat ; used of money : to spend in drink.

Melt, *n.* the milt of a fish.

Melt, *v.* to knock down by a stroke on the side ; to bruise, knock.

Melt, *n.* the male fish.

Melt, *n.* the spleen.

Melt-hole, *n.* the space between the ribs and the pelvis in man and in animals.

Meltie-bow, *n.* a mystic figure on a herd-boy's club, which was supposed to protect the cows from hurt if th- · ' ' · them on the side.

Meltin-blow, *n.* the finishing-stroke.

Meltith, Melteth, Meltaith, Meltit, *n.* a meal; the quantity of milk yielded by a cow at a milking. Cf. Mealtith.

Meltith-buird, *n.* a table on which meals are served.

Meltith-hale, *adj.* having a good appetite; 'meat-hale.'

Melvie, *v.* to cover or soil with meal.—*adj.* soiled with meal.

Melvyin, *n.* a dusting with meal.

Melwand, *v.* to rub bannocks with meal in baking. Cf. Meal-wind.

Melyie, *n.* a coin of small value.

Mem, *n.* madam, ma'am.—*v.* to call one madam or ma'am.

Memorandum, *n.* a memorial inscription.

Memt, *ppl. adj.* connected by, or attached from, blood, alliance, or friendship.

Men', *v.* to mend.

Men, *n.* laymen who occupy a prominent place in the religious life of the Highlands.

†**Menage,** *n.* a local benefit-club among neighbours. Cf. Manadge.

Mend, *v.* to make better; to mend for one; to become convalescent; to reform, improve in character.—*n.* a patch, repair; improvement or recovery of health.

Mendable, *adj.* reparable; capable of amendment.

Mendiment, *n.* amendment.

Mends, *n.* amends, compensation; revenge; amendment; improvement.—*phr.* 'to the mends,' over and above.

Mene, *v.* to bemoan; to indicate pain. Cf. Mean.

Mene, *n.* an attempt.

Mene, *adj.* common. Cf. Mean.

Men-folk, -fowk, *n.* males, men.

Meng, *v.* to mix, blend; used of corn: to become mixed in colour. Cf. Meing.

Menge, *v.* to soothe.

†**Mengyie, Menji,** *n.* a household; retainers. Cf. Menyie.

Mennent, Mennon, Menon, *n.* a minnow.

Mens, Mense, *n.* amends. Cf. Mends.

Mensal-kirk, *n.* a church appropriated by the patron to the bishop, and made thenceforth a part of his own benefice.

Mense, *n.* honour, respect, reverence; a great deal; recompense; thanks; decency, propriety; discretion; good manners; a credit; an ornament.—*v.* to adorn; to do credit or honour to; to make up for; to become.—*phr.* 'to mense a board,' to preside at table.

Menseful, *adj.* becoming, seemly, discreet; creditable, respectable; courteous, respectful, mannerly; hospitable, liberal; clean, neat.

Mensefullie, *adv.* with propriety; becomingly.

Menseless, *adj.* unmannerly, ill-bred; uncultured; greedy; selfish; immoderate in price; incalculable.

Men's house, *n.* a farm 'bothie,' where menservants cook their own food.

Mensworn, *ppl. adj.* perjured. Cf. Mansworn.

Ment, *v.* to pretend or threaten to strike; to attempt ineffectually.—*n.* such a movement or threat. Cf. Mint.

Ment, *v. pret.* and *ppl.* mended.

Ment, *n.* mental capacity.

Mentals, *n.* wits.

Mention, *n.* a trifle; a little bit of anything.

Mentith, *n.* a dish; a meal. Cf. Meltith.

Mento, *n.* obligation; debt. Cf. Mainto.

Meny, *v.* to indicate pain; to complain. Cf. Mean.

†**Menyie, Menze, Menzie,** *n.* a household, family; a train of followers, a company of retainers; a crowd of persons; a multitude of things.—*v.* to crowd; to mix confusedly.

Meow, *v.* to mew.—*n.* a cat's mew.

Mercat, *n.* a market. Cf. Market.

Mercatable, *adj.* marketable.

†**Mercatorian,** *adj.* commercial.

Merch, *n.* a march; a boundary.

Merch, *n.* marrow; pith, strength.

Merchandise, *v.* to trade as a merchant.

Merchandising, *n.* shopping; retailing; shopkeeping.

Merchant, Merchan', *n.* a shopkeeper, a retailer; a buyer, customer; shopping.

Merchiness, *n.* the state of being marrowy.

Merchless, *adj.* without marrow; pithless.

Merchy, *adj.* marrowy; full of marrow.

Merciful, *adj.* used of the weather: favourable, seasonable, mild; lucky, fortunate.

†**Merciment,** *n.* mercy; discretion; disposal.

Mercury-docken, *n.* the 'smear-docken,' the good King Henry.

Mercury-leaf, *n.* the plant, dog's mercury.

Mercy, *int.* used in excl. of surprise.—*n.* in *pl.* whisky, &c.

Merdal, *n.* a fat, clumsy woman.—*adj.* big, fat, stout. Cf. Mardel.

†**Merdle,** *n.* a confused crowd of persons or animals. Cf. Meirdel.

Mere, *n.* a small pool caused by moisture of the soil; a pool easily dried by the heat.

Mere-swine, *n.* the dolphin; the porpoise.

Mergh, *n.* marrow. Cf. Merch.

Merghless, *adj.* without marrow, pithless.

Mergie me, *int.* an excl. of surprise.

Mergin, *adj.* largest; most numerous.

Mergle, *v.* to wonder; to express surprise.

Meridian, *n.* a midday drink of liquor.

Merk, *n.* a silver coin, worth 13⅓d. stg.; a measure of land. Cf. Mark.

Merk, *adj.* dark. Cf. Mirk.

Merkerin, *n.* the spinal marrow.

Merl, *v.* to candy; to become sweet and gritty.

Mer-lady, *n.* a mermaid.

†**Merle,** *n.* the blackbird.

Merled, *ppl. adj.* variegated; mottled. Cf. Marl.

Merlie, *adj.* candied.

Merligo, *n.* dizziness, vertigo. Cf. Mirligo.

Merlin, *n.* a mermaid.

Merlins, *int.* an excl. of surprise.

Mermaid, *n.* the frog-fish.

Mermaid's-glove, *n.* a kind of sponge.

Mermaid's purse, *n.* the egg-case of fishes whose skeleton is cartilaginous.

Merridge, *n.* a marriage.

Merrigle, *n.* a miracle; a ridiculous spectacle; a mischievous boy.—*adj.* mischievous.

Merrily-go, *n.* vertigo. Cf. Mirligo.

Merriment, *n.* a source of merriment.

Merry, *v.* to marry.

Merry - begotten, *adj.* illegitimate. — *n.* an illegitimate child.

Merry-dance, *n.* the aurora borealis.

Merry - dancers, *n.* the aurora borealis; vapours rising from the earth on a warm day, and seen flickering in the atmosphere.

Merry-hyne, *n.* a disgraceful dismissal; a good riddance.

Merry-man, *n.* a merry-andrew, a clown; a chieftain's retainer.

Merry-matanzie, *n.* an expression in the girls' singing game of 'jingo-ring'; a children's singing game.

Merry-meat, *n.* a feast at the birth of the first child.

Merry-meetings, *n.* New-Year's Day merry-makings.

Merry-night, *n.* a festive entertainment.

Merry-pin, *n.* an excited or merry mood.

Merse, *n.* a fertile spot of ground between hills; alluvial land beside a river; ground gained from the sea, converted into moss.

Mert, *n.* an ox, &c., killed and salted at Martinmas. Cf. Mart.

†**Merter,** *n.* a mess.—*v.* to mutilate. Cf. Martyr.

Mertimes, *n.* Martinmas.

Mert-maill, *n.* rent due at Martinmas.

†**Mertyreese,** *v.* to torment. Cf. Martyreese.

Mervadie, *adj.* used of cake: sweet and brittle.

Merve, *adj.* sweet; mellow. Cf. Mervy.

Mervel, *v.* to marvel.

Mervil, *adj.* nervous, trembling; inactive in mind or body.

Mervy, *adj.* used of fruit: rich, mellow; savoury.

Mes, Mess, *n.* a title prefixed to the Christian name of a minister of religion. Cf. Mass, Mass-John.

†**Meschant,** *adj.* wicked; mischievous; a worthless person. Cf. Mischant.

Mese, *v.* to soothe. Cf. Mease.

Mese, *n.* five hundred herrings. Cf. Maise.

Mesh, *n.* a net for carrying fish.

Meshie, *n.* a basket made of straw-rope. Cf. Maizie.

Meslin, *n.* mixed corn. Cf. Mashlum.

Mess, *n.* a meal.—*v.* in *phr.* 'to mess and mell,' to have familiar intercourse; to mingle at one 'mess.'

Mess, *n.* a muddle; a scrape, plight.

Messan, Messin, Messen, Messon, *n.* a small dog; a small, insignificant person.

†**Messan-dew,** *n.* a hospital. Cf. Maison-dieu.

†**Messanter,** *n.* a mishap. Cf. Mishanter.

Messenger, Messenger-at-arms, *n.* a sheriff's officer.

Mess-John, *n.* a minister.

Mess-priest, *n.* a Roman Catholic priest.

Mester, *n.* stale urine. Cf. Maister.

Met, *v.* may. Cf. Mot, Mat.

Met, *n.* a measure. Cf. Mett.

Metal, *v.* to make or repair a road with broken stones.

Meter, *n.* a person legally authorized to measure.

Meth, *n.* a landmark. Cf. Meethe.

Methe, *n.* a maggot. Cf. Maith.

Methody, *n.* a Methodist.

Metster, *n.* a person legally authorized to measure.

Met-stick, *n.* a piece of wood for measuring the foot.

Mett, *n.* a measure of herring, of coals, &c.; a boundary, a boundary-stone.—*v.* to measure.

Mettage, *n.* measurement.

Mettle, *adj.* capable of enduring great fatigue; spirited.

Met-wand, *n.* a measuring-rod.

Meugle, *v.* to dabble in mud.

Meul, *v.* to mew like a cat. Cf. Mewl, Miol.

†**Mevies,** *n.* the song-thrush. Cf. Mavis.

Mew, *n.* a son-in-law.

Mew, *n.* an enclosure.

Mewl, *v.* to cry, whine; to mew like a cat.

Mewt, *v.* to mew as a cat.

Mey, *n.* the bleat of lambs. Cf. Mae.

Meycock, *n.* the may-cock, the gray plover.

Meyse, *v.* to soothe. Cf. Mease.

Meysel, Meyzle, *v.* to waste or disappear gradually. Cf. Meisle.

Meyseln, *v.* to eat little and slowly, to consume by degrees. Cf. Meislen.

Miauve, *v.* to mew as a cat.—*n.* a cat's mew

Micel, *v.* to waste imperceptibly.—*n.* a small piece. Cf. Meisle.

Michael, *n.* a term applied to a girl.

Michaelmas-moon, *n.* the harvest-moon ; the produce of a raid at this season, as constituting the portion of a daughter.

Michen, *n.* the common spignel. Cf. Muilcioun.

Micht, *n.* might.—*v.* might.

Micht-be-better, *adj.* showing some signs of improvement.

Michty, *adj.* mighty; stately, haughty; strange, surprising ; used of liquor : strong.—*adv.* very, exceedingly.

Michty me, *int.* an excl. of surprise.

Mickle, *adj.* great, big ; much, abundant ; grown-up ; eminent, important ; proud, haughty.—*adv.* much, greatly ; very.—*n.* a large amount, a great deal. Cf. Muckle.

Mickle-bag, *n.* the stomach.

Mickle-bookit, *adj.* full-bodied ; great with child ; bulky.

Mickle-chair, *n.* a large arm-chair.

Mickle-cheild, *n.* the devil.

Mickle-coat, *n.* a greatcoat.

Mickle-deil, *n.* the devil.

Mickledom, *n.* size, bulk.

Mickle-Friday, *n.* the Friday on which a large fair is held.

Mickle-hell, *n.* hell itself.

Mickle-horned, *adj.* having large horns.

Mickle-man, *n.* a head farm-servant ; a man of means.

Mickle-maun, *adj.* very big, very fine.

Mickle-mou'd, *adj.* having a large mouth.

Mickle-neived, *adj.* large-fisted.

Mickleness, *n.* size, bulk.

Mickle-preen, *n.* a large pin for fastening shawls.

Mickle-rin-wheel, *n.* the large wheel of a spinning-wheel.

Mickle-Sunday, *n.* a Communion Sunday.

Mickle-tochered, *adj.* largely dowered.

Mickle-toe, -tae, *n.* the big toe.

Mickle-wame, *n.* a big belly ; the stomach of a cow.

Mickle-wheel, *n.* the large wheel of a spinning-wheel.

Mickle-worth, *n.* great value ; great reputation.

Mickly, *adv.* greatly, much.

Mid-aged, *adj.* middle-aged.

Mid-couple, *n.* the swipple of a flail.

Midden, *n.* a dunghill ; a dirty, slovenly woman.

Midden-cock, *n.* a dunghill-cock ; the principal cock in the poultry-yard.

Midden-creel, *n.* a basket for manure, &c.

Midden-croon, *n.* the top of a dunghill.

Midden-dub, *n.* a dunghill-pool.

Midden-dung, *n.* dung from a dunghill.

Midden-dyke, *n.* the wall of a dunghill.

Midden-feil, *n.* turf mixed with manure to form a dung-heap.

Midden-head, *n.* the top of a dunghill.— *phr.* to 'be heard on the midden-head,' to quarrel openly.

Midden-heap, *n.* a dunghill.

Midden-hen, *n.* a common barn-door hen.

Midden-hole, *n.* a dunghill ; a dunghill-puddle.

Midden-lairach, *n.* the site of a dunghill.

Midden-makin', *n.* the making of a dunghill.

Midden-mavis, *n.* a raker of dust-bins, dung-heaps, &c.

Midden-monarch, *n.* a cock.

Midden-mount, *n.* a rampart or mound made of dung, rubbish, &c.

Midden-mylies, *n.* the goosefoot ; the wild spinach.

Midden-peel, *n.* a dunghill-pool.

Midden-scarter, *n.* a hen.

Midden-stead, *n.* the site of a dunghill.

Midden-tap, *n.* the top of a dunghill.

Midder, *n.* a mother.

Middle, *n.* the waist.

Middle, *v.* to meddle.

Middled, Midled, *ppl. adj.* used of sheep : earmarked by a bit cut out of the middle of the ear.—*n.* a sheep-mark so made.

Middle-erd, *n.* the earth, the world ; the nether regions.

Middlemaist, *adj.* nearest the middle.

Middlin, *adj.* tolerable ; mediocre ; fairly well, indifferent, not very well.—*adv.* moderately, tolerably.

Middlinly, *adv.* not perfectly ; moderately.

Middlins, *adv.* moderately.

Middrit, *n.* the midriff ; in *pl.* the heart and 'skirts' of a bullock.

Midge, *n.* a mosquito ; a very diminutive person.—*v.* to move slightly.

Midge-merchant, *n.* a petty trader or shopkeeper.

Mid-grund, *n.* a fishing-ground in a middle position.

Midgy, *n.* a midge.

Mid-house, *adv.* half-way.

Midlen, *adv.* moderately. Cf. Middlin.

Midlert, *n.* this world. Cf. Middle-erd.

Mid-man, *n.* a mediator.

Mid-noon, *n.* noon.

Mid-person, *n.* a middleman between two others.

Mid-place, *n.* a middle room between a 'but' and a 'ben' in a three-roomed house ; a bedcloset.

Mid-room, *n.* a 'mid-place'; the middle compartment in a boat.

Mids, Midse, *n.* the midst, middle ; a medium ;

a middle course; the open furrow between two ridges; in *pl.* means, ways, methods. —*v.* to strike a medium; to come to an agreement.

Mids-day, *n.* midday.

Mids-man, *n.* a mediator. Cf. Mid-man.

Mid-stick, *n.* the middle-stick of a kite, &c.

Midtime o' day, *n.* midday.

Midwart, *adv.* towards the middle.

Mid-water, *n.* the middle of a stream, lake, or sea.

Midwife-gallop, *n.* full gallop; a great speed.

Mields, *n.* the dust of the grave, the 'mools.'

Miff, *n.* a slight quarrel; a 'tiff,' a 'huff.'—*v.* to offend, 'huff.'

Mights, *n.* means, help.

Mighty, *adj.* large in quantity or size. Cf. Michty.

Milcie, *n.* a milk-strainer. Cf. Milk-sye.

Milcie-wall, *n.* a wall in a dairy with a window of perforated tin or zinc.

Mildrop, *n.* any pendent drop. Cf. Meldrop.

Milds, *n.* the goosefoot. Cf. Mails, Miles.

Mile, *n.* the wild celery.

Mile, *n.* millet.

Milens, *n.* crumbs. Cf. Moolin.

Miles, *n.* wild spinach; the goosefoot.

Miles, *n.* 'flooks,' or small insects in the diseased entrails of sheep.

Militate, *v.* to take effect, operate without opposition.

Milk, *n.* an annual school-holiday, on which the scholars presented their teacher with a small offering, of which milk originally formed the chief part; the semi-liquid of the ear of corn before it hardens.—*v.* used of a cow: to yield milk; to steal, pilfer; to rook.—*adj.* milch.

Milk and meal, *n.* milk-porridge; 'milk-brose.'

Milk-ass, *n.* an ass giving milk.

Milk-bowie, *n.* a milk-pail.

Milk-boyne, *n.* a milk-tub.

Milk-brose, *n.* a dish of milk and raw oatmeal.

Milk-broth, *n.* broth made of milk and barley.

Milk-cattle, *n.* milch-cows.

Milk-cow, *n.* a milch-cow.

Milker, *n.* a cow that gives milk.

Milk-gowan, *n.* a yellow flower, the dandelion.

Milk-herrie, *n.* the loss of milk, or of 'profit' of milk, through witchcraft.

Milk-house, *n.* the dairy; the house or room where milk is stored.

Milking-kye, *n.* milch-cows.

Milking-loan, *n.* the milking-park.

Milking-shiel, *n.* a milking-shed.

Milking-slap, *n.* the entrance to the milking-field.

Milk-keg, *n.* a milk-tub.

Milk-kye, *n.* milch-cows.

Milk-lue, *n.* lukewarm, of the temperature of milk warm from the cow.

Milk-madlocks, *n.* milk-porridge.

Milkmaid's-path, *n.* the Milky-way.

Milk-may. *n.* a milkmaid.

Milk-meat, *n.* milk-porridge; any food of which milk is an ingredient.

Milkness, *n.* dairy produce; milk; a dairy; dairy work.

Milk-ort, -wort, *n.* the root of the harebell.

Milk-potage, *n.* milk-porridge.

Milk-saps, *n.* bread steeped in boiled milk and sweetened.

Milk-sieve, *n.* a milk-strainer.

Milk-sile, *n.* a milk-strainer.

Milk-span, *n.* a milk-pail.

Milk-stoup, *n.* a milk-pail.

Milk-sye, -syth, *n.* a milk-strainer.

Milk-woman, *n.* a wet-nurse.

Milky, *adj.* used of grain: when the ear is soft and fills, but does not grow white.

Mill, *n.* a snuff-box.—*v.* to manufacture; to steal.

†**Mill,** *n.* a boys' fight; a scrimmage.—*v.* to beat, drub.

Mill-bannock, *n.* a large circular cake of oatmeal, a foot in diameter, and one inch thick.

Mill-bitch, *n.* a small bag clandestinely hung up by the miller to receive meal for his own profit. Cf. Black-bitch.

Mill-burn, *n.* a stream driving a mill.

Mill-capon, *n.* a person begging of those who had corn grinding at a mill.

Mill-claise, *n.* a miller's working clothes.

Mill-clap, *n.* a piece of wood, or clapper, that strikes and shakes the hopper of a mill.

Mill-cloose, *n.* the boxed woodwork which conducts the water into the mill-wheels; the sluice of a mill-race.

Milldew, *n.* cold, raw weather; wet, foggy weather.

Mill-dozen, *n.* every thirteenth peck of grain milled, payable to the owner or laird of the mill.

Milled, *ppl. adj.* intoxicated.

Mill-e'e, *n.* the 'eye' or opening in the cases of a mill, through which the meal falls into the bin.

Miller, *n.* the quantity of corn ground at a time. Cf. Meller.

Miller, *v.* to crumble.—*n.* in *pl.* small crumbs.

Millering, *n.* the waste meal gathered after grinding the sweepings of a mill. Cf. Mellering.

Miller's-thumb, *n.* the young of the bib; the river bullhead; the goldcrest.

Millert, *n.* a miller.

Millert's lift, *n.* an upward thrust with a lever.

Mill-fish, *n.* the turbot.

Mill-fud, *n.* a girl who works in a mill or factory.

Mill-gruel, *n.* milk-porridge.

Mill-haave, *n.* a vessel for measuring 'corn-shillings.'

Millie, *n.* a small mill.

Millin, *n.* a crumb of bread ; the least bit of solid food ; a particle.

Mill-knave, *n.* the miller's man who received the 'knaveship' as his perquisite.

Mill-lade, *n.* a mill-race, or its channel.

Mill-lichens, *n.* the entry into the place where the inner mill-wheel goes.

Mill-reek, *n.* the lead distemper to which workers in lead are subject.

Mill-ring, *n.* the open space in a mill between the runner and the wooden frame surrounding it ; the meal remaining in the 'ring' or on the millstones, which becomes the miller's perquisite ; the dust of a mill.

Mill-shilling, *n.* husked grain running from the 'mill-e'e.'

Mill-steep, *n.* a lever fixed to the machinery of corn-mills, by which the millstones can be adjusted closer or otherwise.

Mill-stew, *n.* the dust of a mill.

Mill-swine, *n.* a miller's swine.

Millthromie, *n.* the fish, hardhead.

Mill-timmer, *n.* a thick, round piece of timber, used as a prop in a mill.

Mill-trows, *n.* the sluice of a mill-race.

Millvader, *v.* to confuse, bamboozle.

Mill-wand, *n.* a beam or pole used for transporting a millstone from a quarry to the mill.

Milne-clap, *n.* the clapper of a mill.

Milne-knave, *n.* the miller's man who received the 'knaveship' as his perquisite.

Milnhirst, *n.* the place on which lie the crubs, within which the millstone rubs.

Miln't, *ppl. adj.* milled.

Milord, *n.* a haggis, as 'chieftain of the pudding race.'

Milryn, *n.* a coin worth £2, 17s. Scots.

Milsie, *n.* a milk-strainer. Cf. Milk-sye.

Milsie-wall, *n.* a wall with crenated battlements ; the wall of a dairy with a sort of window of perforated tin. Cf. Milcie-wall.

Milt, *v.* to melt.

Milt-hole, *n.* the space between the ribs and the pelvis.

Milt-token, *n.* prognosticating weather from cuts in the spleen of an ox killed about Martinnas.

Mim, *adj.* prudish ; prim ; demure ; affecting great moderation in eating or drinking ; affecting squeamishness in admitting what cannot be denied ; quiet, mute.—*v.* to act in a prim, affected manner ; to protest affectedly.

Mimicate, *v.* to mimic ; to pretend, sham.

Mimin, *n.* affected protesting.

Mimlie, *adv.* primly, affectedly.

Mim-mou'd, *adj.* affectedly proper in speech or action ; shy at speaking out ; reticent ; soft-spoken.

Mim-mou'dness, *n.* affected modesty in speech.

Mimness, *n.* prudishness.

Mimp, *v.* to speak or act affectedly.—*adj.* prim, demure.

Mim-spoken, *adj.* shy at speaking out.

Min, *n.* man ; a familiar term of address.

Min, *v.* must. Cf. Man, Maun.

Min', *v.* to mind.—*n.* mind. Cf. Mind.

Minace, *v.* to threaten, menace.

†**Minawa**, *n.* a minuet.

Mince, *v.* to dance with short steps ; to tone down, lessen, extenuate ; to derogate from ; to disown.

Minch, *v.* to cut into very small pieces ; to mince.—*n.* a crumb.

Minch-house, *n.* a small alehouse or inn.

Minchick, *n.* a very small piece.—*v.* to cut or break into small pieces.

Minchickie, *n.* a very small piece indeed.

Minch-meat, *n.* mince-meat.

Mincing, *ppl. adj.* trivial, trifling ; disparaging.

Mind, *v.* to mine ; to dig in a mine.—*n.* a mine.

Mind, *n.* memory ; a reminder ; affection.—*v.* to remember ; to remember in a will ; to remind ; to notice ; to take care of ; to have a mind to ; to wish.

Minding, *n.* recollection ; a very small quantity, a 'thocht.'

Mindless, *adj.* heedless ; forgetful.

Mine, *n.* mien, figure, carriage.

Mineerum, *n.* a stir, fuss, a great ado ; an awkward plight, a scrape. Cf. Minneer.

Minent, *n.* a minute.

Mines, *pron.* mine.

Ming, *v.* to mix.—*n.* a mixture.

Ming a mang, *v.* to mix up together. Cf. Mang.

Mingle-mangle, *adj.* confused, irregular.

Ming-mang, *n.* confusion.

Mingse, Minkse, *v.* to mingle.

Minikin, *n.* anything very small.—*adj.* of the smallest size.

Minikin preen, *n.* the smallest size of pin.

Minister, *n.* in *pl.* small spiral shells found on the seashore.

Ministerial, *adj.* becoming a minister.

Minister's-mark, *n.* a mark on sheep ; having both ears cut off.

Mink, *n.* a noose ; a ring of straw or rushes,

used in adjusting the yoke on an ox.—*v.* to tie fast ; to halter ; with *up*, to coil a rope in the hand.

Minkie, *n.* a noose, 'mink.'

Minkster, Minxter, *n.* a mixture.

Minna, *v. neg.* may not ; must not.

Minneer, *n.* a great noise.—*v.* to make a great noise.

Minnie, *adj.* many.

Minnie, *n.* a mother ; a pet name for 'mother'; a dam.—*v.* to join a lamb to its own mother in a flock ; used of a lamb : to run to its own mother.

Minnie, *n.* 'the cup of remembrance,' a toast on Yule Eve formerly in the North.

Minnie's-bairn, *n.* mother's pet.

Minnie's-daut, -dawtie, *n.* mother's pet.

Minnie's-man, *n.* a henpecked husband.

Minnie's-mouthes, *n.* those who must be wheedled into any measure by kindness, coaxing, &c.

Minnin, Minnon, *n.* the minnow. Cf. Mennent.

Minnock, *n.* the minnow.

Minnoyt, *ppl. ?* annoyed.

†**Minowaye**, *n.* a minuet. Cf. Minawa.

Minsh, *v.* to mince. Cf. Minch.

Minsbach, *adj.* mean, niggardly ; inhospitable.

Minshoch, *n.* a two-year-old she-goat.

Minstrell, *n.* a minster.

Minswear, *v.* to swear falsely. Cf. Manswear.

Mint, *n.* peppermint.

Mint, *n.* a very large quantity or sum of money.

Mint, *v.* to insinuate, hint, use innuendo ; to feign ; to aim at ; to attempt ; to intend, purpose ; to venture, dare.—*n.* an aim ; an attempt, effort ; a threat ; a blow, stroke ; an insinuation, hint ; a feint.

Minteen, *v.* to maintain.

†**Minua**, *n.* a minuet. Cf. Minawa.

Minum, *n.* a minim ; a musical note, a song.

Minute, *n.* a first draught of a written agreement ; in *pl.* a short interval for play during school-hours.—*v.* to make short notes or a first draught of a written agreement.

Minute-time, *n.* the short interval for play during school-hours.

Minyar, *n.* anything untoward.

Miogs, *n.* clumsy hands. Cf. Maig.

Miol, *v.* to cry or mew like a cat.

Miracle, Miraikle, *n.* an object of amazement ; a 'spectacle'; a mockery ; a mischievous boy ; a very large quantity, a wonderful lot.—*v.* to wonder ; to tease.

Mirac'lous, *adj.* very drunk ; clumsy, helpless. —*adv.* excessively.

Mird, *v.* to meddle ; to venture, attempt ; to make amorous advances ; to toy amorously ; to fawn upon, coax.—*n.* flattery, coaxing.

Mire, *n.* a bog, swamp.—*v.* to 'bog'; ta 'lair'; to entangle in a dispute.

Mire-bumper, *n.* the bittern.

Mire-duck, *n.* the wild duck.

Mireena, *n.* merino.

Mire-side, *n.* the edge of a bog.

Mire-snipe, *n.* the snipe ; an accident, misfortune, plight ; a person with hard features.

Mirk, *adj.* dark, obscure, murky, dusky.—*n.* darkness, gloom ; night.—*v.* to darken, overcast.

Mirk-dim, *adj.* dark, gloomy.

Mirk-eyed, *adj.* dark-eyed.

Mirkin, *n.* darkness, nightfall.

Mirkins, *adv.* in the dark.

Mirklins, *adv.* in the dark.

Mirk-Monanday, *n.* Monday, Mar. 24, 1652, when the sun was totally eclipsed.

Mirkness, *n.* darkness.

Mirk-night, *n.* midnight ; the darkest hour of night.

Mirknin, *ppl. adj.* darkening, growing dark. —*n.* the dusk, twilight.

Mirksome, *adj.* rather dark ; somewhat gloomy ; dusky.

Mirky, *adj.* dark, gloomy, murky.

Mirky, *adj.* merry, smiling ; light-hearted.

Mirl, *v.* to crumble.—*n.* a crumb. Cf. Murl.

Mirl, Mirle, *v.* to speckle ; to become variegated.—*n.* in *pl.* the measles. Cf. Marl.

Mirligo, Mirlego, Mirlygo, *n.* a small, upright, fast-revolving spinning-wheel ; dizziness, vertigo, causing disordered vision ; in *pl.* ridiculous fancies ; mad frolicsomeness, the effect of drinking.

Mirly, *adj.* speckled, spotted, variegated.

Mirly-breasted, *adj.* having a speckled breast.

Mirran, *n.* a carrot. Cf. Meeran.

Mirrot, *n.* a carrot.

Mirsgim, *n.* the angler-fish.

Mirthsome, *adj.* mirthful, merry.

Misacker, *v.* to injure severely. Cf. Missaucher.

†**Misanter**, *n.* a misfortune. Cf. Mishanter

Misbeet, *v.* to disarrange ; to mismatch.

Misbegot, Misbegotten, *adj.* illegitimate.—*n.* an illegitimate child.

Misbegowk, *n.* a deception ; a disappointment.

Misbehadden, *ppl. adj.* used of language : unbecoming ; ill-natured ; ill-trained ; indiscreet ; incautious.

Misbelief, *n.* unbelief.

Misbeseem, *v.* to misbecome ; not to suit.

Miscall, Misca', *v.* to speak evil of ; to scold, vituperate ; to call names.

Miscaller, Misca'er, *n.* one who mispronounces in reading.

Miscarriage, *n.* a misfortune ; misconduct.

Miscarry, *v.* to misbehave ; to behave indecently.

Mischancy, *adj.* unlucky ; risky, dangerous.

†**Mischant,** *adj.* wicked ; mischievous ; worthless.

Mischanter, *n.* a misfortune ; in *phr.* 'Auld Mischanter,' the devil. Cf. Mishanter.

Mischant-fow, *adj.* cruel.

Mischantlie, *adv.* wickedly.

Mischantness, *n.* wickedness.

Mischant-, Mischan-pratt, *n.* a mischievous trick.

Mischief, *n.* a severe hurt ; injury, harm ; a mischievous, vexatious person ; the devil.

Mischieve, *v.* to injure, hurt, damage.

Mischievin, *n.* a severe injury ; a cruel beating.

Mischievous, Mischeevous, *adj.* hurtful, painful ; cheating, tricky.

Miscomfist, *ppl. adj.* nearly stifled by a bad smell.

Misconstruct, *v.* to misconstrue.

Miscontent, *adj.* discontented.

Miscontented, *ppl. adj.* discontented.

Miscontentment, *n.* discontent ; a grievance.

Misconvenient, *adj.* inconvenient.

Miscook, *v.* to cook badly ; to bungle, mismanage.

Miscounselled, *ppl. adj.* ill-advised.

Misdeedy, *adj.* mischievous, 'ill-deedie.'

Misdiet, *v.* to have food irregularly.

Misdoot, *v.* to doubt, disbelieve ; to suspect ; to mistake. — *n.* a doubt, mistrust.

Misdootins, *n.* doubts, suspicions.

Misemployment, *n.* malversation of money, &c.

Miser, *n.* a wretch ; a miserable being.

Misert, *adj.* miserly, avaricious ; parsimonious. — *n.* a miser.

Misertish, *adj.* miserly, very parsimonious.

Misert-pig, *n.* a child's money-box made of earthenware.

Misfarin, *ppl. adj.* ill-grown.

Misfet, *v.* to offend one.

Misfortunate, Misfortinit, *adj.* unfortunate.

Misfortune, *n.* the giving birth to an illegitimate child.

Misfuir, *v.* to fare badly.

Misgae, *v.* to go wrong ; to miscarry ; of a cow : to abort.

Misgate, *n.* a going astray, transgression, misdeed.

Misgie, Misgive, *v.* to fall through, miscarry ; used of a pistol, &c. : to miss fire.

Misgieins, *n.* misgivings.

Misgoggle, Misgoogle, *v.* to spoil, mar ; to rumple ; to mismanage, bungle. Cf. Misguggle.

Misgrow, *v.* to grow stunted, crooked, ill-shaped.

Misgrugle, *v.* to rumple, handle roughly ; te disfigure ; to deform.

Misguggle, *v.* to disfigure, mar ; to handle roughly ; to 'misgrugle.'

Misguide, *v.* to mismanage, waste, misspend ; to ill-use, injure.

Misguided, *ppl. adj.* used of a woman : seduced.

Misgully, *v.* to handle a 'gully' clumsily ; to mangle in cutting or carving.

Mishandle, *v.* to mismanage, bungle ; to handle awkwardly.

†**Mishanter,** *n.* a misfortune, accident ; ill-luck ; a name for the devil. — *v.* to meet with an accident, hurt, or bruise.

Mishappens, *n.* unfortunateness.

†**Mishent,** *adj.* wicked.

Mishently, *adv.* wickedly.

Mishguggle, *v.* to 'misguggle.'

Mish-mash, *n.* a hodge-podge ; a muddle. — *v.* to mingle ; to throw into confusion. — *adv.* in confusion. — *adj.* put in confusion.

Mish-masherie, *n.* things in a confused state.

Misinclined, *adj.* disinclined.

Misinformer, *n.* a false informer.

Misk, *n.* a piece of land, partly earth, partly moss ; land covered with coarse, rough, moorish grasses.

Misken, *v.* not to recognize ; to ignore, disown ; not to know of ; to misunderstand ; to leave unnoticed, not to meddle with ; to assume airs of superiority ; with *one's self,* to forget one's proper station.

Misk-grass, *n.* the grass growing on a 'misk.'

Misknow, *v.* to 'misken.'

Mislair, *v.* to misinform. Cf. Mislear.

Misle, *n.* the mistletoe.

Misle, *v.* to speckle. Cf. Mizzle.

Mislear, *v.* to misinform ; to lead astray, seduce.

Misleard, Misleart, Misleer'd, *ppl. adj.* unmannerly, ill-bred ; mischievous ; greedy.

Mislearin, *n.* an error, mistake.

Misle-shinned, *adj.* having speckled legs. Cf. Mizzle.

Mislike, *v.* to displease.

Misliken, *v.* to disparage, depreciate ; to do discredit to.

Mislippen, *v.* to disappoint ; to deceive ; to distrust, suspect ; to mismanage ; to neglect.

Mislooin, *n.* derision.

Misluck, *n.* misfortune ; ill-luck. — *v.* to miscarry ; not to prosper.

Mislushious, *adj.* rough ; malicious ; ill-natured.

Mismacht, Mismaight, *ppl. adj.* mismatched, disordered.

Mismae, *v.* to disturb.

Mismaggle, *v.* to disarrange, rumple ; to mar, spoil.

Mismake, Mismack, v. to shape clothes improperly; to trouble, disturb, unsettle; to blush.

Mis-mannered, adj. unmannerly, uncivil; unbecoming.

Mis-manners, n. ill-breeding; incivility.

Mismar, v. to disarrange, mar.

Mismarrow, Mismorrow, v. to mismatch.—n. anything that is wrongly matched.

Mismaucher, v. to render useless.

Misminnie, v. used of a lamb: to lose its mother, to be put to suck a strange ewe; of a child: to miss its mother.

Mismove, Mismuve, Mismuive, v. to disturb; to disconcert, flurry.

Misnurtured, adj. ill-bred.

Misorder, n. irregularity; disorderly proceeding.

Mis-portion, v. with one's self, to eat to excess.

Misprood, adj. unduly proud.

Misreckon, v. to miscalculate.

Mis-red, -rid, ppl. adj. entangled, complicated, ravelled.

Mis-remember, v. to forget.

Miss, n. a paramour, mistress.

Miss, v. to avoid; to fail to happen; to fail to germinate or grow; to dispense with, do without.—n. absence, loss; one whose death or removal is regretted; a fault.

Missaucher, Missaucre, v. to destroy, ruin; to hurt severely; to bruise, mangle.—n. ruin; severe injury; pain caused by bruises, &c.

Miss but, v. to fail to; to avoid.

Mis-seem, v. to ill-become.

Mis-set, v. to put out of temper; to displease; to disorder.

Misshieff, n. mischief. Cf. Mischief.

Missing, ppl. adj. used of the tide: not full.

Mission, v. to send on a mission.

Missionar, n. an itinerant preacher.

Missive, n. a provisional lease; an informal contract preceding the formal one.

Miss-John, n. a minister. Cf. Mess-John.

Missle, v. to decamp. Cf. Mizzle.

Misslie, adj. lonely; much missed, regretted. Cf. Mistlie.

Misslieness, n. loneliness; regret for one absent.

Missour, n. measure.

Misspeak, v. to speak favourably of one whose conduct does not justify such praise.

Mis-swear, v. to swear falsely.

Mis-sworn, ppl. adj. perjured.

Mistaen, Misteen, ppl. mistaken.

Mistak, v. to mistake; to do wrong.—n. in phr. 'nae mistak but,' without doubt.

Mistell, v. to misinform.

Mistemper, v. to put out of gear.

Mistent, v. to neglect; not to take heed to.—n. a slip, mistake.

Mister, n. a master; a term of address, 'sir.'

Mister, n. stale urine. Cf. Master.

†**Mister,** v. to lack; to be necessary; to need.—n. want, need, necessity.

Misterfu', adj. needy, in straits.

Misteuk, v. pret. mistook.

Mist fawn, n. mist like a white spot of ground.

Misthrive, v. to thrive badly.

Mistime, v. to play out of tune or time; to put out of one's usual routine.

Mistimeous, adj. unpunctual; not to be trusted for punctuality; untidy, clumsy; not to be depended on.

Mistiming, n. irregularity or unpunctuality as to times.

Mistlie, adj. dull, solitary, from the absence of some one; bewildered on a road; dreary, 'eerie.' Cf. Misslie.

Mistraucht, adj. distraught.

Mistress, n. a title formerly given to the wife of a principal tenant, and to a minister's wife; a familiar term for a wife.

Mistryst, v. to miss an appointed meeting; to fail to keep a promise; to visit with trouble, &c.; to frighten, perplex without cause or against expectation.

Misuser, n. one who injures another.

Mitch, n. the support near the stern of a large boat, on which the lowered mast rests.

Mite, v. to pick out mites.—n. anything small and inferior.

Mitel, v. used of mites: to eat away; of money when changed: to be spent gradually. Cf. Mitle.

Mith, v. might.

Mith, n. a mark. Cf. Meethe.

Mither, n. mother; the origin, source; an old potato.

Mither-in-law, n. a step-mother.

Mitherland, n. native land.

Mither-nakit, adj. quite naked.

Mither-o'-the-mawkins, n. the little grebe; a witch; an uncanny person.

Mither-o'-thousands, n. the ivy-leaved toad-flax.

Mither's heart, n. the shepherd's purse.

Mither-wife, n. a wife and mother.

Mithrate, Mithret, n. the diaphragm. Cf. Middrit.

Mitle, v. used of mites: to eat away; to waste slowly. Cf. Mitel.

†**Mitten,** n. a glove, specially a worsted glove; a gauntlet.

Mittilat, v. to mutilate, to maim.—n. a person with disabled limbs.

Mittle, v. to mutilate, to hurt.

Mix, v. used of grain: to change colour; to

grow pale from illness; to disorder the body; to join with a company.

Mixed, *ppl. adj.* muddled with drink.

Mixen-varlet, *n.* a contemptuous designation.

Mixie-maxy, *n.* a miscellaneous mixture; a state of confusion.—*adj.* confused, jumbled.

Mixter-maxter, *n.* and *adj.* 'mixie-maxy.'

Mixty-maxty, -maxie, *n.* and *adj.* 'mixie-maxy.'

Mizzle, *v.* to decamp.

Mizzle, Mizle, *v.* to speckle.—*n.* in *pl.* measles.

Mizzle-shinned, *adj.* with the shins speckled by the heat of a fire.

Mizzlie, Mizly, *adj.* speckled; variegated. Cf. Maeslie.

Mo, *adj.* more. Cf. Mae, Moe.

Moach, *adj.* moist; close; misty; putrescent. —*v.* to grow mouldy, putrid. Cf. Moch.

Moagre, *n.* a muddle, a clumsy mess, disorder. Cf. Mogre.

Moakie, *n.* a pet name for a calf.

Moan, *v.* to indicate pain. Cf. Maen.

Moary, *adj.* heathy. Cf. Moory.

Moat, *n.* a mote; an atom; a minute creature.

Moat, *n.* an earthen mound.

Moat-hill, *n.* an earthen mound of considerable size.

Moatie, *adj.* tiny; full of motes.

Mob, *n.* a school of whales.

†Mobile, *n.* the mob, rabble.

Moch, *n.* a moth.

Moch, *n.* a maggot. Cf. Mawk.

Moch, *adj.* moist, damp; close, foggy; mouldy, putrescent.—*v.* to grow mouldy; to approach putrescence; to be putrid.

Moch, *n.* a heap.

Moch-eaten, *adj.* moth-eaten.

Mocher, Mochre, *v.* to coddle; used of cows: to soothe before milking; to busy one's self with trifles or paltry work; to work in the dark.

Moch-flee, *n.* a moth.

Mochie, *adj.* full of moths.

Mochie, Mochy, *adj.* moist, misty, 'muggy'; dirty; becoming mouldy or putrid.

Mochness, *n.* moistness causing mouldiness or putrescence.

Mochrum-elder, -laird, *n.* the cormorant.

Mocht, *ppl. adj.* becoming putrid.

Mock, *n.* fun; a jest; a flout; a sham; a swindle.

Mockage, *n.* mockery.

Mockrife, Mockriff, *adj.* scornful.

Modder, *v.* to mutter.

Model, *n.* the very image.—*v.* to organize.

Moderate, *v.* to preside in a Presbyterian Church court; to preside at the election, calling, or ordination of a pastor.

Moderate, *adj.* composed, calm, cool; used of the weather: calm.—*n.* a name given to

a party in the Church of Scotland in the 18th and 19th centuries, in contrast to the Evangelical party.

Moderation, *n.* presiding in a Church court at the election, calling, or ordination of a pastor; calmness; settled weather.

†Moderator, *n.* the minister who presides in a Presbyterian Church court.

Modgel, *n.* a noggin; the usual quantity of drink.

Modie-brod, *n.* the mould-board of a plough. Cf. Mowdie-brod.

Modification, *n.* arrangement, adjustment.

Modify, *v.* to arrange proportionally; to arrange the contributions of heritors to a parish minister's stipend.

Modish, *adj.* polite, courteous.

Modyware, *n.* a mole. Cf. Moudiewarp.

Moe, *v.* to cry as a calf. Cf. Mae.

Moe, *adj.* more. Cf. Mae.

Moem, *n.* a scrap.

Mogen, *adj.* ? common, public; watched.

Moggan, Moggen, Moggin, *n.* a stocking; a footless stocking; a stocking used as a purse; a long stocking-like sleeve for a woman's arm; in *pl.* the legs.

Mogh, *adj.* moist, mouldy; putrescent. Cf. Moch.

Mogh, *n.* a moth. Cf. Moch.

Moghie, *adj.* full of moths. Cf. Mochie.

Mogran, *adj.* clumsy.

Mogre, *n.* a bungle; a clumsy mess.—*v.* to work in a dirty way; to handle clumsily.

Moich, *adj.* moist and putrescent. Cf. Moch.

Moichness, *n.* mouldiness; damp causing putrescence.

Moider, *v.* to stupefy; to dull the brain by drinking.

Moiken, *n.* the spignel. Cf. Michen.

Moil, *n.* drudgery, hard labour; bustle, din; turmoil.

Moilie, Moiley, *n.* a hornless bullock or cow; a mild, good-natured person, who is tame even to silliness.

Moist, *v.* to moisten.

Moisterless, *adj.* lacking moisture.

Moistify, *v.* to moisten.

Moisty, *adj.* moist.

Mokie, *n.* a stupid, silly fellow.

Mokre, *v.* to coddle. Cf. Mocher.

Mokriff, *adj.* scornful. Cf. Mockrife.

Molashed, *adj.* drunk.

Molass, Molash, *n.* whisky made from molasses.

Moldewort, *n.* the mole.

Mole-blind, *adj.* blind as a mole.

Moleery-tea, *n.* the common milfoil; the goose-tongue.

Moley, Molie, *n.* a familiar name for a mole-catcher.

Mollachon, *n.* a small cheese.

Mollan, *n.* a long, straight pole, such as is used in fish-yards.

Mollat, *n.* the bit of a bridle.

Mollets, *n.* sly winks; fantastic tricks.

Mollify, *v.* to tone down a charge, statement, &c.

Molligrant, Molliegrunt, Moligrant, Mollygrant, *n.* whining, complaining. — *v.* to whine.

Molligrubs, Molligrumphs, *n.* a stomach-ache; a fit of temper.

Mollion, *n.* the mass of the people, 'the million.'

Moll-on-the-coals, *n.* a gloomy-minded, melancholy woman.

Mollop, Mollup, *v.* to toss the head haughtily.

Molloping, *ppl. adj.* haughty, disdainful.

Molluka, *n.* the Molucca-bean or -nut, once used as a charm in the Western Islands.

Moloss, *adj.* loose; dissolute in conduct. Cf. Molashed.

Molten, *v.* to melt; to melt into laughter, tears, &c.

Moment-hand, *n.* the second-hand of a clock or watch.

Mon, *v.* must. Cf. Maun.

Mon, *n.* man, a term of address.

Monanday, Mononday, *n.* Monday. Cf. Mirk.

Monday's haddie, *n.* a stale fish.

Mone, *v.* to moan; to complain. Cf. Maen.

Money-nifferer, *n.* a money-changer.

Monger, *n.* a trader, dealer.

Mongs, *prep.* among. Cf. Mang.

Monie, Mony, *adj.* many. Cf. Many.

Monie lang, *adv.* for a long time past.

Moniest, Monniest, *adj.* most in number.

Moniment, *n.* a monument; a 'spectacle'; a ridiculous or insignificant person; a fool.

Moniplies, Monieplies, Monnyplies, Monyplies, *n.* the third stomach of a ruminant, with its many parallel folds; the human intestines.

Monk, *n.* a head-stall. Cf. Munks.

Monk-fish, *n.* the angler-fish.

Monk's-rhubarb, *n.* the patient dock.

Month, *n.* the Grampian range towards its eastern extremity.

Monthly-bird, *n.* the fieldfare.

Monyest, *adj.* most.

Monyfaulds, *n.* the third stomach of a ruminant. Cf. Moniplies.

Moo, *n.* the mouth.

Moo, *v.* to low as a cow.—*n.* the low of a cow.

Moo, *n.* a large rick of hay or corn; a mow.

Moo-band, *n.* a halter; speech; a hint; a word.—*v.* to articulate; to mention as a great secret; to hint cautiously; to understand. Cf. Mow-band.

Moo-bit, *n.* a morsel; food.

Mooch, *v.* to sneak about, play the spy. Cf. Mouch.

Moocher, *n.* a loafer on the lookout for what he can pick up on the sly; a sharper.

Moo-cue, *n.* a twisted halter for curbing a young horse.

Moodie, *n.* a mole.

Moodie-hill, *n.* a molehill.

Moodge, *v.* to 'mudge,' move, stir.

Moody-warp, *n.* the mole.

Moo-frachty, *adj.* palatable; pleasant to the taste.

Moofu', *n.* a mouthful; a meal; a scanty livelihood.

Moofu' o' a prayer, *n.* a short prayer.

Moogan, *n.* a long, footless stocking. Cf. Moggan.

Moogard, *n.* the mugwort.

Moogard, *n.* a worthless person or thing; a mess, a muddle. Cf. Mogre.

Moo-hause, *n.* a trap-door opening.

Moo-heich, *adv.* as high as one's mouth.

Mool, *n.* a bluff headland.

†Mool, *n.* a slipper. Cf. Muils.

Mool, *n.* in *pl.* broken chilblains; a disease of the heels.

Mool, *n.* a mould; the small piece of bone, &c., round which cloth is wrapped to form a button. Cf. Mule.

Mool, *n.* mould; soil good for working; pulverized dry earth; the soil for a grave, the grave; in *pl.* a grave, the earth of a grave, dust.—*v.* to bury; to crumble; to have carnal intercourse with.

Mool-board, *n.* the mould-board of a plough.

Mool-button, *n.* a button of cloth wrapped round a piece of bone.

Moold, *n.* the ground, earth. Cf. Mould.

Mooler, *v.* to crumble, moulder.

Moolet, Moolat, *v.* to whine; to murmur; to sob.

Moolicks, *n.* crumbs. Cf. Meelack.

Moolie, *n.* a soft, ill-baked marble.—*adj.* full of crumbs or small pieces of soil, friable, crumbling; soft, flabby.

Moolie-pudding, *n.* a boys' game, in which one boy with clasped hands tries to touch the others.

Mooligrubs, *n.* a colic; a fit of bad temper. Cf. Molligrubs.

Moolin, *n.* a crumb.

Mooliness, *n.* the state of being full of crumbs.

Mooly, *adj.* mouldy.

Mooly, *adj.* earthy; earth-stained; savouring of the grave.

Mooly-heel, *n.* a heel affected by chilblains; in *pl.* chilblains.

Moo-maein, *n.* the lowing of cattle.

Moo-mawin, *ppl.* hinting, mooting.

Moon, Moonie, *n.* the goldcrest. Cf. Moony.

Moon-broch, *n.* a halo round the moon.
Moonlicht-flittin', *n.* a decamping by night with one's goods to escape from one's creditors or landlord.
Moonog, *n.* the cranberry or crawberry.
Moony, *n.* the goldcrest.
Moop, *v.* to nibble; to mump; to keep company with; used of nose and chin: to approach each other through loss of teeth in old age. Cf. Moup.
Moop, *v.* to impair by degrees; to fall off, fail. Cf. Moup.
Moop, *v.* to have sexual intercourse; to consort with.
Mooping, *n.* fantastic conduct; grimacing.
Moo-pock, *n.* a horse's nosebag.
Moor, *n.* peaty land; peat-mud.
Moor-band, *n.* a surface of peat-moss wasted to a kind of light black earth, often mixed with sand.
Moor-bird, *n.* any bird nesting on a moor.
Moor-burn, *n.* the annual burning of part of a moor; an outbreak of temper; a dispute, conflict.
Moor-duck, *n.* the wild duck.
Moor-fail, *n.* turf cut from the surface of a moor.
Moor-, **Muir-fowl-egg**, *n.* a species of pear.
Moor-grass, *n.* the silver-weed.
Moor-hags, *n.* holes made in moor or moss by peat-cutting. Cf. Moss-hag.
Moor-ill, *n.* the red-water in cattle.
Moor-poot, **-pout**, *n.* the young of a moor-bird; a young grouse.
Moor-sickness, *n.* a wasting sickness affecting sheep in autumn.
Moor-spade, *n.* a spade for cutting the turf of moor or peat.
Moory, *adj.* heathy; of a brown or heather colour.
Moose, **Moosie**, *n.* a mouse.
Moose-web, *n.* a cobweb; gossamer; phlegm in the throat.
Moosie, *adj.* downy, covered with soft hair.
Moost, *n.* a nasty smell.—*v.* to grow mouldy.
Moost, *n.* hair-powder.—*v.* to powder the hair.
Moosty, *adj.* covered with hair-powder.
Moot, *v.* to hint, suggest.
Moot, *v.* to moult. Cf. Mout.
Mooten'd, *ppl. adj.* moulted.
†**Mooter**, *n.* a multure.—*v.* to take multure for grinding corn.
Mooter, *v.* to mutter.
Mooter, *v.* to fret; to fall off through friction; to take away piecemeal. Cf. Mouter.
Mooter-the-melder, *n.* a miller.
Mooth, *adj.* foggy, misty; damp and warm; soft, calm, comfortable; cheerful, jolly.
Mooth, *n.* the mouth.

Moothfu', *n.* a mouthful. Cf. Moofu'.
Moothlie, *adj.* softly.
Moothu, *n.* a mouthful.
Mootie, *adj.* tiny. Cf. Moatie.
Mootie, *adj.* parsimonious, niggardly.
Mootit-like, *adj.* puny; looking like shrinking in size.
Mootle, *v.* to nibble; to fritter away. Cf. Moutle.
†**Mootre**, *n.* the miller's payment in meal.
Moozlie, *v.* used of hay, &c.: to become mouldy or rot through damp.—*n.* dry-rot.
Mop, *n.* a grimace.
Moral, *n.* the exact likeness.
Moral-legger, *n.* a boys' marble, hard, ring-streaked, or piebald.
Moray coach, *n.* a cart.
Morbid, *adj.* morbific, causing disease.
†**Mord-de-chien**, *n.* a disease of horses, glanders. Cf. Mortersheen.
More, *adj.* greater; longer. Cf. Mair.
Morgoz'd, *ppl. adj.* confused.
Morie-morning, *n.* to-morrow morning.
Morken, **Morkin**, *n.* a dead sheep, 'braxy'; the skin of a dead sheep.
Morn, *n.* with *the*, to-morrow.
Morn-come-never, *adv.* never.
Mornie-, **Morn-i'-'e-morning**, *n.* the early morning.
Morning, *n.* a glass of liquor taken before breakfast; a slight repast taken some hours before breakfast.
Morning-blink, *n.* early morning light.
Morning-bout, *n.* a morning walk.
Morning-drink, *n.* alcoholic refreshment before breakfast.
Morning-gift, *n.* a husband's gift to his wife on the morning after marriage.
Morning-mun, *n.* the dawn; increasing daylight.
Morn-wind, *n.* morning wind.
Morrice-dance, *n.* a morris-dance.
Morroch, *v.* to trample in mud; to soil.
Morrot, *n.* the guillemot; the razor-bill. Cf. Marrott.
Morrough, *n.* a merman.
Morrow, *n.* a companion, match. Cf. Marrow.
Morsel, *n.* a slight meal; food spoilt in cooking.
Morsing-horn, *n.* a powder-flask.
Mort, *n.* the skin of a sheep that dies.—*adj.* in *phr.* 'a mort cauld,' a very severe cold.
Mortal, *adj.* great, extreme; single, individual; complete, whole; dead-drunk.—*adv.* very, exceedingly.—*n.* the mortal remains.
Mortal-drunk, **-fou**, *adj.* dead-drunk.
Mortally, *adv.* excessively, very.
Mortar, *n.* coarse reddish clay.
Mortar-stone, *n.* a hollow stone formerly used as a mortar for husking grain.
Mort-cloth, **-claith**, *n.* a funeral pall.

†**Mortersheen**, *n.* the most fatal species of glanders.

†**Mortfundit**, *ppl. adj.* chilled to death, cold as death ; foundered with cold.

Morth, *n.* murder. Cf. Murth.

Morth, *n.* in *phr.* 'a morth o' cauld,' a very severe cold.

Mort-heid, *n.* a death's-head ; a turnip hollowed out and cut in the form of a face, and lighted with a candle ; the death's-head moth.

Morthling, *n.* the skin of a shorn lamb or sheep. Cf. Murling.

†**Mortichien**, *n.* a disease of horses, glanders. Cf. Mortersheen.

Mortification, *n.* giving in mortmain ; lands or funds so given.

Mortifier, *n.* one who bequeaths lands or funds in mortmain.

Mortify, *v.* to give in mortmain for religious, &c., purposes.

Mort-safe, *n.* a cast-iron frame, formerly used to prevent a grave being violated by 're-surrectionists.'

Mort-woo', *n.* the wool from the skin of a sheep that has died a natural death.

Morungeous, *adj.* in a very bad humour. Cf. Maroonjus.

Moses' table, *n.* a kind of granite.

Moshin-hole, *n.* the touch-hole of a piece of ordnance.

Mosker, *v.* to decay, crumble away.

Moss, *n.* a place where peats may be dug ; peat ; various kinds of cotton-grass. — *v.* to cut and prepare peats.

Moss-bailie, *n.* one who has charge of a peat-moss.

Moss-bluter, *n.* the common snipe ; the bittern.

Moss-boil, *n.* a fountain which boils up in a moss.

Moss-bummer, *n.* the bittern.

Moss-cheeper, *n.* the meadow-pipit, titlark.

Moss-corn, *n.* the silver-weed.

Moss-crop, *n.* various species of cotton-grass ; the silver-weed.

Moss-duck, *n.* the wild duck. Cf. Moor-duck.

Moss-earth, *n.* peaty soil.

Mosser, *n.* one who cuts and prepares peats.

Moss-fa', *n.* a ruinous building.

Moss-fa'en, *adj.* used of trees : fallen into a bog, and gradually covered with moss.

Moss-farmer, *n.* a moorland farmer.

Moss-flow, *n.* a watery moss. Cf. Flow-moss.

Moss-fog, *n.* mosses growing in a bog or swamp.

Moss-grieve, *n.* a 'moss-bailie,' one in charge of a peat-moss.

Moss-hag, *n.* a place out of which peats have been cut.

Mossin', *n.* peat-cutting.

Mossin'-time, *n.* the peat-cutting season.

Moss-laird, *n.* the owner of a moorland farm.

Moss-leerie, *n.* a will-of-the-wisp.

Moss-maill, *n.* rent for right of cutting peats.

Moss-mingin, *n.* the cranberry.

Moss-oak, *n.* bog-oak ; a seat made of bog-oak.

Moss-owl, *n.* the short-eared owl.

Moss-seat, *n.* a mossy seat.

Moss-stock, *n.* trunks and stumps of bog-oak.

Moss-thief, *n.* a Border riever.

Moss-thristle, *n.* the marsh-thistle.

Moss-trooper, *n.* a Border freebooter.

Moss-willow, *n.* the *Salix fusca*.

Most, *adj.* chief, principal. — *adv.* almost ; mostly. — *n.* the majority. Cf. Maist.

Most, *n.* a mast.

Mosted, *ppl. adj.* crop-eared.

Mot, Mote, *v.* may ; might.

Mot, *n.* a small hill. Cf. Mote.

Mot, *n.* a speck of dust ; a mote, a dot, a mark aimed at.

Motch, *v.* to eat little slowly and secretly ; to waste imperceptibly. — *n.* slow, quiet eating ; fondness for dainties ; imperceptible use ; thriftlessness.

Mote, *n.* a very small particle ; a crumb ; a tiny creature ; a single stalk of straw or hay ; a flaw, drawback from. — *v.* to pick motes out of anything ; to search for and catch lice. — *phr.* to 'mote the blankets,' to pick at the bedclothes, a sign of the approaching death of a patient.

Mote, *ppl.* used of money : gradually spent.

Mote, *n.* a rising ground, a knoll. Cf. Moat.

Mote-hill, *n.* a little hill on which conventions were held.

Motey, *adj.* full of motes or minute creatures ; tiny.

Moth, *adj.* warm, sultry. Cf. Mooth.

Motheat, *v.* to injure one's reputation secretly and slowly.

Mother, *n.* in *phr.* 'the mother on beer,' the lees working up, and forming a thick mould on the top.

Moth-hawk, *n.* the nightjar.

Motie, *adj.* used of the cheeks : ornamented with black patches.

Motion-hole, *n.* the touch-hole of a cannon. Cf. Moshin-hole.

Mott, *n.* an earthen mound. Cf. Moat.

Mottie, *adj.* profane.

Mottie, *n.* a mark to be aimed at ; a dot.

Motty, *adj.* spotted ; full of minute creatures ; full of motes ; tiny.

Mottyoched, *ppl. adj.* matted. Cf. Muttyoched.

Motty-sun, *n.* the appearance when a sunbeam shines through an aperture and shows floating atoms of dust.

Mou, *n.* the mouth. Cf. Moo.

Mou, *n.* a mow.

Mou-ban, *n.* a halter; speech; a word.—*v.* to articulate. Cf. Moo-band.

Moubit, *n.* a mouthful; food.

Mouch, *n.* a moth; the larva of a clothes-moth. Cf. Moch.

Mouch, *v.* to idle or sneak about.

Moucher, *v.* to sneak about, to spy.

Moud, *n.* a moth.

Moud, *n.* mould, earth; the grave.

Moudie, *n.* a mole; a mole-catcher.

Moudie-hillan, -hill, *n.* a molehill.

Moudie-hoop, *n.* a molehill.

Moudie-man, *n.* a mole-catcher.

Moudie-poke, *n.* a bag to put moles in.

Moudie-skin, *n.* a moleskin.

Moudiewarp, Moudiewart, Moudiewort, *n.* a mole; a short, dark person with a profusion of hair; a term applied to children.

Moudiewarp-burd, *n.* the mould-board of a plough.

Moudiewarp-hill, *n.* a molehill.

Moug, *n.* a mug.

Mought, *n.* might; marrow. Cf. Maught.

Mougre, *v.* to creep, crawl over.

Moul, *v.* to become mouldy.

Moul, *n.* mould, soil; the grave. Cf. Mool.

Moul, *n.* a broken chilblain. Cf. Mool.

Mould, *n.* the grave; soil. Cf. Mool.

Mould, *adj.* mouldy.

Mould, *n.* a candle made in a mould.

Moulder away, *v.* used of laws, customs, &c.: to become obsolete.

Mouldie, *adj.* savouring of the grave.

Mouldywarp-burd, *n.* the mould-board of a plough.

Moulie-draps, *n.* drops left in the bottom of a glass.

Mouligh, *v.* to whine, whimper.

Mouligrant, *n.* a grumbling, whining. Cf. Molligrant.

Mouligrubs, *n.* an ill-humour. Cf. Molligrubs.

Moull, *n.* refuse of meal at a mill, generally used to feed swine.

Moulter, *n.* a multure; payment for grinding corn.

Mouly, Moully, *adj.* mouldy.

Mouly-heels, *n.* chilblains on the heels.

Mouly-penny, *n.* a miser.

Mounge, *v.* to munch; to whine, grumble; to go about listlessly, gloomily. Cf. Munge.

Mount, *v.* to make ready; to equip; to get ready for setting off.—*n.* a weaving term.

Mountain-blackbird, *n.* the ring-ousel.

Mountain-dew, *n.* whisky.

Mountain-dul e, *n.* the mountain laver.

Mountain-folks, -men, *n.* the Covenanters; the sect of the Cameronians.

Mountain-spate, *n.* a mountain-torrent.

Mountain-thrush, *n.* the ring-ousel.

Mount-caper, *n.* the marsh orchis.

Mounting, *n.* furnishing; a trousseau; a 'mount' in weaving, a weaver's apparatus.

Moup, *v.* to nibble; to mump; to keep company with.

Moup, *v.* to fail off, fail; to cast off, drop.

Mouper, *v.* to nibble continuously.

Moupit-like, *adj.* in apparent ill-health, drooping.

Mourie, *n.* a gravelly sea-beach; a stratum of mixed sand and gravel.

Mourn, *v.* used of cattle: to moan.—*n.* a murmuring sound.

Mournings, *n.* mourning garb.

Mourning-string, *n.* a streamer worn on the hat in token of mourning, 'dule-string.'

Moury, *adj.* mellow.

†**Mous**, *n.* a joke; a matter of jesting. Cf. Mows.

Mouse, *n.* the bulb of flesh at the end of a shank of mutton.

Mouse-ear, *n.* the mouse-ear chickweed.

Mouse-end, *n.* the end of a leg of mutton where the 'mouse' is situated.

Mouse-fa', *n.* a mouse-trap.

Mouse-web, -wab, -wob, *n.* a cobweb; phlegm in the throat.

Mouse-webbed, *ppl. adj.* covered with cobwebs.

Moust, *n.* a nasty smell.

Moust, *n.* hair-powder.—*v.* to powder the hair.

Mou'-strings, *n.* the strings that tie the open end of a pillow-slip, &c.

Mout, *v.* to moult; with *away*, to lessen gradually, take away piecemeal.

Moutch, *v.* to idle, loaf about. Cf. Mouch.

Moutchit, *n.* a contemptuous term applied to children; a 'smatchet.'

Mouten, *v.* to melt.

Mouter, *v.* to fret; to fall off through friction. Cf. Mooter.

†**Mouter**, *n.* multure; a miller.—*v.* to take multure for grinding corn.

Mouth, *n.* a mouthful; a trap-door opening; the bowl of a spoon.—*v.* to speak; to proclaim; to feel hungry; to crow. Cf. Moo.

Moutin', *ppl. adj.* moulting.

Moutle, *v.* to nibble; to fritter away, to take away piecemeal. Cf. Mootle.

†**Mouze**, *n.* a joke. Cf. Mows.

Mow, *n.* a large rectangular stack of hay, &c.; a heap, pile.—*v.* to pile up hay, &c.

†**Mow**, *n.* a grimace.

Mow, *n.* the mouth.

Mow-band, *n.* a halter; speech.—*v.* to articulate; to mention; to understand. Cf. Moo-band.

Mowbit, *n.* a morsel; food.

Mowch, *v.* to loaf about, sneak. Cf. Mouch.

Mowdie, *n.* a mole. Cf. Moudie.

Mowdie-brod, *n.* the mould-board of a plough.

Mowdie-hoop, *n.* a molehill.

Mowdiewark, -wart, -wort, *n.* a mole. Cf. Moudiewarp.

Mowe, *n.* dust.

Mowe, *v.* to copulate.

†Mowes, *n.* a joke. Cf. Mows.

Mowr, *n.* a mock, jeer, flout.

†Mows, Mowse, Mowze, *n.* a joke, jest.

Moy, *adj.* affecting great moderation in eating or drinking; modest; demure.

†Moyen, Moyan, *n.* means; ability; influence; management.—*v.* to accomplish by means; to manage; to succeed through influence.

Moyener, *n.* one who uses his influence for another.

Moyenless, *adj.* powerless, inactive; without influence.

Moylie, *n.* a hornless bullock; a soft, good-natured, silly person. Cf. Moilie.

Mozie, *adj.* swarthy, dark in complexion; acrimonious; ill-natured; sour-looking.

Mozie, *n.* a person of weak intellect, an idiot. —*adj.* rotten, mouldy, decayed; over-ripe.

Mucht, *n.* might, power. Cf. Maught.

Muck, *n.* dung in a wet state; mud, mire; any kind of filth; a worthless person.—*v.* to clean a 'byre' or stable; to manure with dung; to soil one's self; to use dirty practices in any way.

Muckafy, *v.* to defile, soil.

Muck-creel, *n.* a large 'creel' or hamper, formerly used for carrying dung to the fields.

Muck-fail, *n.* a mixture of sward and dung used as a manure.

Muck-hawk, *n.* a dung-fork.

Muck-heap, *n.* a dunghill.

Muck-hole, *n.* an opening in a cow-house wall for throwing out dung.

Muck-kishie, *n.* a 'muck-creel.'

Muckle, *adj.* large. Cf. Mickle.

Muckle-chair, *n.* an arm-chair.

Muckle-coat, *n.* a greatcoat.

Muckle Friday, *n.* the Friday on which a large fair is held.

Muckle man, *n.* a full-grown and qualified farm-servant; a man of means.

Muckle-mou'd, *adj.* having a large or wide mouth.

Muckleness, *n.* largeness of size.

Muckle-worth, *adj.* of great value.

Muckly, *n.* the fair on 'Muckle Friday.'

Muck-man, *n.* a scavenger.

Muck-midden, *n.* a dungheap.

Muck-rotten, *adj.* quite rotten.

Mucky, *adj.* dirty; slatternly; messy; untidy. —*n.* a privy.

Mucky-fit, *n.* a ploughman; a farm-labourer.

Mucky-heap, *n.* a dirty, slatternly woman or girl.

Mucky-house, *n.* a privy.

Mud, *n.* a small nail used in the heels of shoes, having a small head.

Mud, *v.* must.

Mud-bedraiglet, *adj.* mud-bedraggled.

Muddle, *v.* to work fussily and do little; to be busy clandestinely; to lie upon and tickle a person; to have carnal knowledge of a woman.

Muddock, *n.* a child's name for 'mother.'

Muddy, *adj.* used of style: not lucid, obscure, confused; muddled with drink.—*v.* to make muddy.

Mud-fever, *n.* an affection of the legs of horses that are clipped in winter, occasioned by muddy roads.

Mud-fish, *n.* fish salted in barrels.

Mudge, *v.* to move, stir; to budge; to talk of secretly, to hint at.—*n.* a movement; a stir; a rumour.

Mudgeon, Mudyeon, *n.* a movement of the face, indicating displeasure, contempt, mockery, &c. Cf. Murgeon.

Mudwart, *n.* a mole. Cf. Moudiewart.

Mue, *v.* to low as a cow.

Muff, *v.* to mow; to trim the beard, &c.

Muffatees, Muffitees, *n.* wristlets of knitted wool, &c., worn in cold weather.

Muffed, *ppl. adj.* used of a hen: tufted.

Muffie-wren, *n.* the willow-warbler.

Muffit, *n.* the whitethroat.

Muffe, *n.* a mitten with only two divisions.

Mufty, *n.* a tufted fowl. Cf. Muffed.

Mug, *v.* to drizzle.—*n.* a drizzling rain.

Mug, *n.* the mouth; the face.

Mug, *v.* to soil, defile; to use dirty practices. —*n.* dung. Cf. Muck.

Mug, *n.* the hole into which a ball or marble is thrown or rolled.—*v.* to play a marble as in 'kypes,' or throw a ball into a hole; to strike a ball out from a wall.

Mug, Mugg, *n.* a kind of sheep with a good coat of wool.

Muggan, *n.* a footless stocking. Cf. Moggan.

Muggart, Mugger, *n.* the mugwort. Cf. Moogard.

Muggart-kail, *n.* a dish composed of mug wort; mugwort-broth.

Mugger, *n.* a hawker of crockery.

Mugg-ewe, *n.* a sheep with a good coat of wool.

Muggie, *n.* a small mug; a game of marbles, the 'kypes'; the hole into which a marble or ball is played.—*v.* to put the marble or ball into the hole ; to strike a ball out from a wall. Cf. Mug.

Muggin, *n.* a long, footless stocking. Cf. Moggan.

Muggle, *v.* to drizzle.—*n.* a drizzle.

Muggly, *adj.* drizzling ; damp, foggy.

Muggons, Muggins, *n.* mugwort.

Muggy, *adj.* drizzling ; foggy ; tipsy.

Mugg-yarn, *n.* wool from a 'mug' sheep.

Muil, *n.* mould, soil. Cf. Mool.

Muilcioun, *n.* the spignel. Cf. Michen.

Muilen, *n.* a crumb of bread.

Muilie, *adj.* full of crumbs. Cf. Moolie.

†**Muils**, *n.* slippers, cloth or list shoes. Cf. Mool.

Muin, *n.* the goldcrest. Cf. Moony.

Muir, *n.* a moor. Cf. Moor.

Muir-burn, *n.* a contest, dispute. Cf. Moerburn.

Muist, *n.* an unpleasant smell ; mouldiness.— *v.* to become mouldy. Cf. Moost.

Muist, *n.* hair-powder.—*v.* to powder the hair. Cf. Moost.

Muist, *n.* musk. Cf. Must.

Muist-box, *n.* a musk-box ; a box for smelling at.

Muisty, *adj.* mouldy ; musty.

Muisty, *adj.* covered with hair-powder.

Muith, *adj.* foggy ; damp and warm. Cf. Mooth, Meeth.

Mulberry, *n.* the white beam-tree.

Mulder, *v.* to crumble ; to moulder.—*n.* in *pl.* small crumbs.

Mule, *n.* a mould. Cf. Mool.

Mule, *n.* mould, soil.—*v.* to crumble. Cf. Mool.

Mule, *n.* a promontory. Cf. Mull.

Mule, *n.* a chilblain. Cf. Mool.

†**Mules**, *n.* slippers.

Mulie, *adj.* full of crumbs ; pulverized. Cf. Moolie.

Mulin, Mullen, *n.* a crumb. Cf. Moolin.

Muliness, *n.* the state of being full of crumbs.

Mulk, *n.* milk.

Mull, *n.* a promontory.

Mull, *n.* a mill.

Mull, *n.* a mule.

Mull, *n.* a snuff-box.

Mull, *n.* the mouth.

Mullach, *n.* a term of endearment among women.

Muller, *v.* to crumble.—*n.* in *pl.* small crumbs ; mould, soil.

Muller, Mullert, *n.* a miller.

Mulligrumphs, *n.* a colic ; a sulky fit. Cf. Mullygrubs.

Mullion, *n.* a shoe made of untanned leather.

Mulliwark, *n.* a mole. Cf. Moudiewarp.

Mulloch, *n.* the crumbled dust of a peat-stack.

Mullock, *n.* a hornless cow.

Mully, *n.* a small tin snuff-box.

Mullygrubs, *n.* a colic ; a fit of sulks, low spirits.

Mulock, *n.* a crumb. Cf. Meelack.

Mulrein, *n.* the frog-fish. Cf. Mareillen.

Multer, *n.* multure.

Multiples, *n.* the folds of a dress.

Multure, *n.* the toll of meal taken by a miller for grinding corn ; a miller.—*v.* to take toll of meal for grinding corn ; to defraud.

Multure-free, *adj.* exempt from multure-dues.

Multure-man, *n.* a miller's man. Cf. Knaveship.

Multurer, *n.* the tacksman of a mill, a miller.

Mum, *v.* to talk or sing in a low, inarticulate voice ; to mutter.—*n.* a mutter ; a low, inarticulate sound.—*adj.* silent.—*int.* hush !

Mumbudjit, *n.* silence.

Mumge, *v.* to grumble, fret. Cf. Munge.

Mummed, *ppl. adj.* benumbed ; tingling from heat after cold.

Mummer, *n.* one who speaks or sings in a low, inarticulate voice.

Mummle, *v.* to mumble ; to chew without teeth.

Mummy, *n.* bits, fragments. Cf. Mammock.

Mumness, *n.* numbness.

Mump, *v.* to hint ; to aim at ; to whisper.— *n.* a whisper, surmise.

Mump, *v.* to nibble ; to chew without teeth ; to gnaw ; to grimace, screw up the mouth ; to mimic ; to speak affectedly or mincingly ; to complain, murmur ; to mope.—*n.* used contemptuously of a toothless old woman.

Mump, *v.* to hitch ; to move by jerks.

Mumpit-like, *adj.* dull, stupid-like.

Mumple, *v.* to seem as if going to vomit ; to chuckle.

Mump-the-cuddie, *n.* a children's game, in which they sit on their hams, with a hand on each hough, and thus hitch forward to reach the goal.

Mumt-like, *adj.* having the appearance of stupor. Cf. Mummed.

Mun, *v.* must. Cf. Maun.

Mun, *n.* a small, trifling article ; a short-handled spoon.

Mun, *n.* man.

Mun, *n.* an old person with a very little face ; in *pl.* the mouth, the face, the hollow behind the jaw-bone ; the jaws.

Munanday, Munnonday, Munonday, Mununday, *n.* Monday.

Munch, *v.* to chew without teeth ; to eat voraciously ; to mumble ; to grumble.

Mund, *n.* in *pl.* the face ; the jaws. Cf. Mun.

Munder, *v.* to maunder ; to babble, gossip.— *n.* a babbler, a gossip. Cf. Maunder.

Mune, *n.* the moon.

Munelichty, *adj.* moonlight.

Munge, *v.* to mumble ; to grumble ; to moan ; to bellow ; to betray a secret ; to mention.

Munge, *v.* to munch, chew ; to chew with difficulty. Cf. Munch.

Munk, *v.* to diminish ; to bring below the proper size ; to cut the hair of the head very close.

Munkie, *n.* a short rope with a loop at one end for receiving a ' knool ' or peg at the other, used for fastening up cattle in a ' byre.'

Munks, *n.* a halter for a horse. Cf. Monk.

Munn, *n.* a short-handled spoon. Cf. Mun.

Munn, *n.* in *pl.* the face, jaws. Cf. Mun.

Munshock, *n.* the red-bilberry. Cf. Moonog.

Munsie, *n.* a short-handled spoon. Cf. Mun.

Munsie, *n.* a designation of contempt or ridicule ; a contemptible figure ; a ' spectacle ' through ill-treatment ; the knave in a pack of cards.

Munt, *v.* to go off, take one's self off.

Munt, *v.* to mount.

Munt, *v.* to aim at ; to hint. Cf. Mint.

Muntin, *n.* a bride's trousseau ; mounting ; the whole of a weaver's apparatus.

Mupetigage, *n.* a term of endearment addressed to a child.

Mur, *v.* to purr as a cat. Cf. Murr.

Murbled, *ppl. adj.* lamed, halting. Cf. Murmled.

Murchen, *n.* ? a hare.

Murder, *v.* to kill by accident ; to harass, trouble.

Murdiegrups, *n.* a colic. Cf. Mullygrubs.

Mure, *n.* a moor. Cf. Moor.

†**Mure,** *v.* to immure.

Mure-burn, *n.* strife. Cf. Moor-burn.

Mureland, *adj.* pertaining to a moor.—*n.* an upper and less cultivated region.

Murelander, *n.* a dweller in a ' mureland.'

Mureman, *n.* a ' murelander.'

Murgeon, *v.* to mock ; to grumble ; to make faces ; to mimic.—*n.* a murmur ; muttering, mumbling ; in *pl.* grimaces ; violent gesture ; taunts ; grumblings. Cf. Mudgeon.

Murgeon-maker, *n.* one who makes ' murgeons.'

†**Murgully,** *v.* to bungle ; to spoil ; to abuse. Cf. Margullie.

Murjin, *n.* a grimace. Cf. Murgeon.

Murk, *adj.* dark, gloomy. Cf. Mirk.

Murkie, *adj.* merry, gay ; light-hearted. Cf. Mirky.

Murkle, *n.* a term of reproach or contempt.

Murlain, *n.* a round, narrow-mouthed basket ; a wooden half-peck measure.

Murle, *v.* to crumble, pulverize ; to moulder away ; to eat slowly and in small portions. —*n.* a fragment, crumb ; the act of eating in a slow, quiet manner.

†**Murle,** *v.* used of an infant : to coo, murmur, ' croodle '; to talk to one's self in a low voice ; to reduce to a murmur ; to hum a tune.

Murlick, *n.* a crumb. Cf. Murlock.

Murlin, *n.* a round, narrow-mouthed basket. Cf. Murlain.

Murling, *n.* a crumb, fragment.—*ppl. adj.* crumbling ; eating slowly and quietly ; dainty in eating.

Murling, *n.* a gentle noise, a soft murmur ; a very froward, whining, ill-natured child.

Murling, *n.* the skin of a young lamb or sheep after it has been shorn.

Murloch, *n.* the young dogfish ; the smooth-hound.

Murlock, *n.* a crumb, fragment.

Murly, *adj.* friable, crumbly.—*n.* any small object ; a crumb ; a fondling term for an infant.

Murly-fikes, *n.* an infant.

Murmell, *v.* to murmur ; to ' croodle ' like an infant.

Murmled, *ppl. adj.* halting, lamed.

Murmur, *v.* to murmur at, complain or grumble against.

Murmuration, *n.* murmuring ; mumbling.

Murn, *v.* to mourn. Cf. Mourn.

Murneful, *adj.* mournful.

Murphy, *n.* a potato.

Murphy, *n.* morphia.

Murr, *v.* to purr as a cat ; used of infants : to make a low, murmuring sound. Cf. Marr.

Murrain, *n.* a nuisance ; used as an execration.

Murre, *n.* the razor-bill.

Murreungeous, *adj.* harsh ; outrageous. Cf. Maroonjus.

Murrie, *adj.* merry.

Murrlin, *n.* a froward child ; a gentle noise, whining. Cf. Murling.

Murroch, *n.* shellfish.

Murrs, *n.* the edible roots of *Potentilla anserina*.

Murt, *n.* the skin of a young lamb or of a sheep soon after it has been shorn, or before castration.

Murth, *n.* murder.

Murther, *v.* to murmur softly as a child.

Murther, *v.* to kill by accident ; to harass, trouble.

Murther, *n.* a great number. Cf. Muther.

Musch, *n.* a small person with a shock of dark hair.

†**Muschin,** *adj.* bad ; mischievous. Cf. Mischant.

Muschin-pratt, *n.* a mischievous trick ; used ironically : ' a great deed.'

Muschle, *v.* to mix clumsily. Cf. Mushle.

Muscle, *n.* a mussel.

Mush, *n.* a mash ; a pulp ; a mass of things

tossed together in confusion; the slow, constant consumption of anything. — *v.* to consume or use slowly and wastefully. Cf. Mushle.

Mush, *n.* a muttering; whisper, hint.

Mush, *v.* to cut out with a stamp; to nick, notch, scallop; to make into flounces; to plait. — *n.* a nick, notch, as is made by scissors.

Mush, *n.* one who goes between a lover and his sweetheart, a 'black-foot.'

Mushed-out, *ppl. adj.* scalloped; flounced.

Mushie, *n.* a mushroom.

Mushik, *n.* a little person with much dark hair. Cf. Musch.

Mushin, *n.* scalloped or crimped work; plaiting; cloth so ornamented.

†Mushin, *adj.* bad, mischievous. Cf. Mischant.

Mushinfow, *adj.* cruel.

Mushle, *v.* to throw into confusion; to mix clumsily; to be connected by blood and affinity; to consume slowly; to eat slowly. — *n.* confusion; slow and constant consumption of anything; the act of eating slowly. Cf. Mush.

Mushlin, *n.* one who is fond of dainty food eaten secretly.

Mushoch, *n.* a heap of grain laid aside in a corner for seed.

Mushoch-rapes, *n.* ropes for surrounding a 'mushoch.'

Music, *n.* instrumental music in churches, in contrast to vocal music alone.

Musicianer, Musitioner, *n.* a musician.

Musicker, *n.* a musician; a player on any musical instrument.

Music-tunes, *n.* church music; psalm-tunes.

Musk, *n.* pulp; a confused heap. Cf. Mush.

Musk-almond, *n.* a sweetmeat; an almond coated with sugar.

Musken, *n.* a measure equal to an English pint, 'mutchkin.'

Muslin-kail, *n.* broth made simply of water, barley, and greens.

Muslin-mouth, *n.* a prim mouth.

Mussel-, Mussle-brose, *n.* 'brose' made from mussels boiled in their own sap, which is mingled with oatmeal.

Mussel-draig, *n.* an implement for gathering mussels.

Mussel-ebb, *n.* the mussel-ground as exposed at low-tide.

Mussel-mou', *n.* a mouth shaped like a mussel, and closing tightly.

Mussel-mou'd, *adj.* having a 'mussel-mou'.'

Mussel-pecker, -picker, *n.* the oyster-catcher.

Mussel-scaup, *n.* a bed of mussels.

Mussle, *v.* to throw into confusion. Cf. Mushle.

Mussy, *adj.* messy; slippery.

Must, *n.* musk. Cf. Muist.

Must, *n.* hair-powder. Cf. Muist.

Must, *n.* a disagreeable smell.—*v.* to mildew. Cf. Muist.

Mustard-bullet, *n.* a bullet used for bruising mustard-seed.

Mustard-stone, *n.* a stone used for bruising mustard-seed in a stone or wooden vessel.

Musted, *ppl. adj.* mouldy, musty.

Musted, *ppl. adj.* powdered; covered with hair-powder.

Muster, *v.* to talk with great volubility.—*n.* extreme loquacity.

Musterer, *n.* an incessant talker.

Musty, *adj.* powdered; covered with hair-powder. Cf. Moosty.

Mutch, *n.* a woman's cap; an infant's cap; a man's night-cap.

Mutch-cap, *n.* a night-cap.

Mutched, *ppl. adj.* wearing a 'mutch.'

Mutchit, *n.* a contemptuous name for a child.

Mutchkin, *n.* a liquid measure equal to an English pint.

Mutchkin-bottle, -bowl, -cup, -stoup, *n.* a vessel large enough to hold a 'mutchkin.'

Mutch-string, *n.* the string of a woman's cap.

Mute, *v.* to complain; to reveal a secret.—*n.* a quarrel; a whisper; a grievance. Cf. Moot.

Mute, *n.* a small utensil fixed on the bridge of a violin to deaden or soften the tone.

†Muter, Mutter, *n.* multure.

Muth, *adj.* used of persons: exhausted with heat or fatigue; of the weather: hot, sultry; cheerful; soft, comfortable. Cf. Meeth, Mooth.

Muther, *n.* a great number.

Mutineer, *v.* to mutiny.

Muttie, Mutty, Muttie-measure, *n.* a measure like a bushel, though smaller, with a division or bottom at a particular point within the circular walls, one end of the measure holding half a peck of oatmeal, and the other holding the same; used in taking multure.

Mutton-ham, *n.* a leg of mutton cured like ham.

Mutton-kail, *n.* mutton-broth.

Mutton-tee, *n.* a 'mutton-ham.'

Muttyoched, *ppl. adj.* matted together. Cf. Mottyoched.

†Mutur, Muture, *n.* multure.

Muxter-maxter, *n.* a confused heap; a miscellaneous collection. Cf. Mixty-maxty.

Muzzel-thrush, *n.* the missel-thrush.

Muzzle, *n.* the face; the lower part of the face.

Muzzy, *adj.* muddled with drink; dazed from injury to the head.

My, *int.* an excl. of astonishment or surprise.
Myaakin, *n.* a hare. Cf. Mawkin.
Myaat, *n.* the short, faint mew of a cat.
Myach, *n.* might; ability. Cf. Maught.
Myak, *n.* a match, equal; an image, model. Cf. Make.
Myarl, *v.* to become mottled; to variegate. Cf. Marl.
†Myarter, *v.* to disfigure; to bedaub. Cf. Martyr.
Myaut, *n.* the slightest sound. Cf. Myaat.
Myauve, *v.* to mew like a cat. Cf. Miauve.
Myckie, *adj.* dirty. Cf. Mucky.
Myginich, *n.* a coward, a beaten one, a 'fugie.'
Myid, Myed, *n.* a measure. Cf. Meethe.
Myles, *n.* various species of goosefoot. Cf. Mails.

Mylies, *n.* the small rings on a fishing-rod through which the line runs.
Mylk, *n.* milk.
Mynd, *n.* a mine in which metals or minerals are dug.—*v.* to dig in a mine.
Myogre, *v.* to bungle; to spoil work by doing it dirtily or clumsily. Cf. Mogre.
Mype, *v.* to speak a great deal; to be very diligent.
†Mysel, *n.* a leper.—*adj.* leprous.
Mysel, Mysell, *pron.* myself; by myself.
†Myster, *n.* a need. Cf. Mister.
Mystification, *n.* mystery.
Myter, *n.* a large number. Cf. Muther.
Myth, *v.* to measure; to mark. Cf. Meethe
Myth, *n.* marrow.
Mythie, *adj.* marrowy, full of marrow.
Myting, *n.* a fondling name for a child.

Na, *int.* an excl. of surprise.
Na, *adv.* not.
Na, *conj.* than, 'nor.'
Na, *adj.* no, none.
Naag, *v.* to tease; to nag.
Naak, *n.* the great northern diver.
Naar, *adv., prep.,* and *adj.* near. Cf. Near.
Nab, *n.* a smart stroke; a blow on the head. —*v.* to strike; to peck.
Nab, *n.* an important person; a conceited person; in *phr.* 'his nabs,' his lordship. Cf. Knab.
Nab, *n.* the head.
Nab, *v.* to catch, seize suddenly; to steal; to take into custody. — *n.* a snatch; a theft.
Nab, *v.* to speak affectedly; to attempt to speak fine English. Cf. Knap.
Nab, *n.* the summit of a rock or hill; a rocky headland.
†Nabal, *n.* a narrow-minded, greedy person; a churlish person.—*adj.* churlish; stingy; narrow-minded.
Nabalish, *adj.* covetous, griping, grasping.
Nabb, *n.* a peg or nail on which anything is hung.
Nabber, *n.* a pilferer, thief.
Nabbery, *n.* theft, pilfering.
Nabbery, *n.* the lesser gentry. Cf. Knabbry.
†Nabble, *n.* a churlish person. Cf. Nabal.
Nabby, *adj.* well-to-do; of rank; trim, well-dressed; pretentious, dressed above one's station. Cf. Knabby.
Nabity, *n.* a well-dressed person.—*adj.* neat, trim, 'nabby.'
†Nable, *n.* a churl. Cf. Nabal.
Nabrie, *n.* the lesser gentry. Cf. Nabbery.
Nace, *adj.* destitute.
Nack, *n.* a trick, knack.

†Nacket, *n.* an impertinent, mischievous child; a precocious child; a person of small size.
Nacket, *n.* the bit of wood, stone, or bone used in the game of 'shinty'; a small roll of tobacco; a quantity of snuff made up.
Nacket, *n.* a small cake or loaf; a piece of bread eaten at noon. Cf. Nocket.
Nacketie, *adj.* expert in doing any piece of nice work; self-conceited.—*n.* one neat in person and work. Cf. Knackety.
Nackie, *n.* a loaf of bread; a small cake.
Nackie, *adj.* clever, ingenious, expert. Cf. Knacky.
Nackit, *n.* a lunch. Cf. Nocket.
Nackit, *n.* a person of small size. Cf. Nacket.
Nacks, *n.* a disease in the throat of fowls fed on too hot food; pip.
Nackuz, *n.* one who tells a tale pretty sharply. Cf. Knackuz.
Nadder, *n.* an adder.
Nadkin, *n.* the taint of meat too long kept; any disagreeable taste or odour.
Nae, *adj.* no, none.—*adv.* not.
Naegait, *adv.* in no wise; nowhere.
Nael, *n.* the navel.
Naelins, *adv.* used as a *neg.* interrogative.
Nael-string, *n.* the umbilical cord.
Nae mows, *phr.* no joke; dangerous.
Nae rizzon, *n.* an insufficient reason.
Nae-say, *n.* a refusal; the option of refusing, what is undeniable.—*v.* to refuse; to contradict. Cf. Nay-say.
Naeslin, *ppl.* used of horses: nuzzling; pulling well in double harness; well-matched.
Naet, *adj.* neat.—*adv.* neatly. Cf. Nate.
Naet, *n.* nought.
Naether, *pron., adj.,* and *conj.* neither.
Naething, *n.* nothing.
Naetie, *adj.* natty; tidy; handy, deft.

Naetly, *adv.* neatly ; completely ; exactly.
Naff, *v.* to bark, yelp ; to talk pertly or snappishly ; to walk with short steps. Cf. Nyaff.
Naffin, *n.* idle talk, chatter.
Naffle, *v.* to trifle ; to walk with short steps. Cf. Nyaffle.
Naffle, *v.* to rumple.
Naffy, *adj.* affable ; on good terms ; gossipy, 'newsy.'
Nag, *v.* to strike smartly ; to snap, bite ; to nick, notch ; to find fault with continually and peevishly ; to jeer ; to labour persistently and painfully.—*n.* a snap, bite ; a nick, notch, a hack ; an indentation with a sharp instrument ; a snappish retort ; a stroke in the game of ' nags ' ; in *pl.* a game at marbles in which the loser is struck on the knuckles by other players with their marbles.
Nag, *n.* the ball used in ' shinty,' &c.
Nag, Nagg, *n.* a peg or nail on which to hang hats, clothes, &c.; the short stump of a broken-off branch. Cf. Knag.
Nag, *n.* a saddle-horse.
Naggie, *n.* a cup ; a noggin. Cf. Noggie.
Naggle, *v.* to fret continuously.
Naggly, *adj.* touchy, fretful ; peevish, ill-natured ; sarcastic.
Naggy, *adj.* snappish, cross.
Nag-nail, *n.* an ingrowing nail ; a bunion.
Nagy, *n.* a pony.
Naig, *n.* a riding-horse ; a nag ; a stallion.—*v.* with *awa'*, to move like a horse that has a long, quick, and steady pace.
Naig-graith, *n.* harness.
Naigie, *n.* a horse, a pony.
Nail, *n.* a trigger ; in *pl.* loose tufts of wool ; refuse of wool.—*v.* to catch unawares ; to arrest ; to steal ; to settle a bargain ; to clench an argument ; to aim at successfully ; to kill ; to strike ; with *off*, to say or repeat rapidly.
Nail, *n.* a particular pain in the forehead.
Nailer, *n.* a ' clincher.'
Nail-horn, *n.* a nail.
Nailing, *n.* a beating.
Nain, *adj.* own.—*phr.* 'by one's nain,' by one's self.
Nain-folk, *n.* one's particular friends or supporters ; one's kinsfolk.
Nainsel', *pron.* one's own self ; a nickname for a Highlander.
Naip, *n.* the ridge of a roof.
Naipkin, *n.* a napkin ; a handkerchief.
Naipry, *n.* napery.
Nairrow, *adj.* narrow ; stingy.
Naise, *n.* the nose. Cf. Neeze.
Naish, *adj.* delicate in health. Cf. Nesch.
Naisty, *adj.* nasty. Cf. Nasty.
Nait, *adj.* neat.

Naither, *conj., pron.,* and *adj.* neither.
Naitherans, *adv.* and *conj.* neither.
Naithers, *adv.* and *conj.* neither.
Naithing, *n.* nothing.
Naithless, *adv.* nevertheless.
Naitie, *adj.* stingy. Cf. Nittie.
Naitie, *adj.* natty ; neat, clever in mechanical operations. Cf. Naetie.
Naitir, *n.* nature.—*adj.* natural ; growing naturally.
Naitir-woo', *n.* fine wool. Cf. Nature-wool.
Naitral, *adj.* natural, native.—*n.* one's nature ; an imbecile. Cf. Natural.
Naivel, *v.* to pommel, buffet. Cf. Nevell.
Nake, *v.* to bare ; to make naked.
Naked, Nakit, *adj.* scanty, insufficient ; unarmed, defenceless ; destitute ; sole ; simple.
Naked-corn, *n.* thin-eared corn.
Naked-truth, *n.* spirits neat.
Nale, *n.* an alehouse.
Nam, *v.* to seize quickly and rather violently.
Name, *n.* a clan ; a group of persons bearing the same name ; a reputation for ; a report. —*v.* to report that two persons are courting or engaged to each other ; to baptize.
Name-daughter, *n.* a girl who bears one's name.
Name-father, *n.* a person whose Christian name one bears.
Nameliheid, *n.* fame, glory.
Namely, *adj.* famous, celebrated.
Namers-and-guessers, *n.* 'namie-and-guessie.'
Name-son, *n.* a boy who bears one's name.
Namie-and-guessie, *n.* a children's guessing-game.
Nam-nam, *adj.* pleasant to the taste ; sweet. Cf. Nyum.
Namshach, *v.* to hurt severely.—*n.* an accident, misfortune. Cf. Amshach.
Nancy-pretty, *n.* London pride, 'none-so-pretty.'
Nane, *adj.* none.
Nane, *adj.* own. Cf. Nain.
Nanes, *n.* the nonce.
Nanny, *n.* a she-goat.
Nap, *n.* a soporific, a soothing.
Nap, *n.* a wooden vessel or dish, made with staves ; a milk-vat. Cf. Knap.
Nap, *n.* ale, strong beer ; the head on ale ; the head.
Nap, *n.* a bit, a morsel, a ' snack.'—*v.* to bite. Cf. Gnap.
Nap, *n.* a joke, jest, fun ; a trick.
Nap, *n.* a shin of beef.
Nap, *v.* used of a fishing-line : to be released when a hook is caught on the bottom, by means of the recoil of a strong pull suddenly stopped.
Nap, *adj.* expert, clever ; ready, eager.
Nap, *n.* an eccentric person. Cf. Knap.

Nap, *v.* to knock; to hammer.—*n.* a blow, tap. Cf. Knap.

Naper, *n.* the head.

†Napery, *n.* bed and table linen, sometimes including blankets; a closet for household linen.

Napkin, *n.* a pocket-handkerchief; a kerchief for the head or neck.

Napper, *n.* a mallet, beetle. Cf. Knapper.

Nappie, *n.* a short sleep.

Nappit, *ppl. adj.* crabbed; ill-humoured.

Napple, Napple-root, *n.* the heath-pea.

Nappy, *n.* strong ale; any alcoholic drink.— *adj.* used of ale or beer: foaming; of any liquor: strong, 'heady'; excited by liquor, tipsy; strong, vigorous.

Nappy, Nappie, *adj.* brittle; used of the tongue: snappish, tart.

Nappy, *n.* a wooden dish. Cf. Nap.

Nappy-boin, *n.* a small tub. Cf. Boyne.

†Napron, Naperon, *n.* an apron.

Napsie, *n.* a little, fat animal, such as a sheep. Cf. Knabsie.

Napskap, *n.* a headpiece, a steel bonnet. Cf. Knapscap.

Nar, *conj.* nor; than, if, that.

Nar, *adv., prep.,* and *adj.* near. Cf. Near.

Narder, *adv.* and *adj.* nearer.

Nardest, *adv.* and *adj.* nearest.

Narg, *v.* to nag; to fret; to jeer.—*n.* continual quarrelling. Cf. Nag.

Nargle, *adj.* jeering.

Nar-hand, *adv.* 'near-hand'; hard-by; nearly. —*prep.* near to.—*adj.* neighbouring; niggardly.

Narly, *adv.* narrowly.

Narr, *v.* to snarl, as dogs.

Narration, *n.* a great noise or clamour.

Narrow, *adj.* stingy; close, searching.

Narrow-nebbit, *adj.* narrow-minded, bigoted.

Nar-side, *n.* the left side of a horse, &c.

Na-say, *n.* a refusal. Cf. Nay-say.

Nase, *n.* the nose.

Nash, *v.* to prate; to talk pertly.—*n.* pert, insolent talk.

Nash, *adj.* delicate in health. Cf. Naish.

Nashag, *n.* the bearberry.

Nash-gab, *n.* a forward, prattling girl; insolent talk. Cf. Snash-gab.

Nash-gabbit, *adj.* pert, talkative, gossiping.

Nashie, *adj.* talkative, chattering.

Nask, *n.* a withe for binding cattle.

Nastified, *adj.* nasty, disgusting.

Nasty, *adj.* ill-tempered.—*v.* to commit a nuisance.

Nat, *n.* a person of short stature and short temper.

Natch, *v.* to lay hold of violently; to notch; to loop or sling.—*n.* a notch, an incision made in cutting cloth.

Nate, *v.* to need; to use.—*n.* use, employment.

Nate, *adj.* neat; pretty; exact; precise; identical; mere.—*adv.* exactly. Cf. Neat.

Nateral, *adj.* natural. Cf. Natural.

Natheless, Nathless, *adv.* nevertheless.

Nather, *conj., pron.,* and *adj.* neither.

Nathing, *n.* nothing.

Nation, *n.* a division of students according to birthplace in the Universities of Glasgow, St Andrews, and Aberdeen.

Native, *n.* one's birthplace.

Natkin, *n.* a disagreeable taste or smell. Cf. Nadkin.

Natrie, Nattrie, *adj.* ill-tempered; grumbling; querulous.

Natter, *v.* to grumble, fret; to tease, worry, nag; to talk in an unfriendly way; to debate; to wrangle.—*n.* peevish chattering, grumbling.

Natterin, *ppl. adj.* chattering fretfully.

Nattle, *v.* to nibble; to gnaw.

Natty, *adj.* handy, deft. Cf. Naetie.

Natural, *adj.* due to birth alone; affable; simple, kind; of the weather: genial.—*n.* an idiot, imbecile; a half-witted person; one's nature or constitution.

Naturality, Naturalty, *n.* natural affection; natural disposition.

Nature, *adj.* spontaneously producing rich herbage, &c.; rich, nourishing.

Nature-clover, *n.* rich natural clover.

Nature-grass, *n.* rich natural grass.

Nature-ground, *n.* land producing rich natural grass.

Nature-hay, *n.* hay produced by the ground spontaneously.

Natureness, *n.* spontaneous fertility in rich herbage; richness and exuberance of natural grass.

Nature-wid, *n.* natural wood.

Nature-wool, *n.* fine wool; wool pulled off from the sheep's back instead of being shorn.

Nauchle, *n.* a dwarf.

Nauchlie, *adj.* dwarfish.

Naughtafee, *v.* to make naught of; to disparage.

Naukie, *adj.* asthmatical; short-winded.

Nauks, *n.* a disease affecting the throat of fowls fed on hot food. Cf. Nacks.

Naum, *n.* a heavy blow with a bludgeon.

Naur, *adj., prep.,* and *adv.* near.

Naval, *v.* to pommel. Cf. Nevell.

Nave, *n.* a fist. Cf. Neive.

Navel, *n.* the very centre; the very front.

Navus-bore, *n.* a hole in wood where a knot has dropped out.

Nawn, *adj.* own. Cf. Nain.

Nawus-, Nawvus-bore, *n.* a 'navus-bore.'

Naxie, *n.* one who tells a tale pretty sharply. Cf. Nackuz.

Nay-say, *n.* a refusal; the option of refusing; what cannot be denied or contradicted.—*v.* to deny; to refuse; to contradict.

Nay-sayer, *n.* one who denies.

Nay-saying, *n.* a refusal.

Naze, *n.* a promontory.

Neal, *v.* to soften.

Neap, *n.* a turnip.

Neaphle, *n.* a thing of no value.

Neapit, *ppl. adj.* used of tides: low.

Near, *n.* a kidney.

Near, *adv.* nearly; exactly; narrowly; sparingly.—*adj.* close; short; left: narrow; stingy, niggardly.

Near-about, *adv.* almost.

Near-begaun, *adj.* stingy, parsimonious.

Near-behadden, *adj.* stingy, miserly.

Near-bludit, *adj.* closely connected by blood.

Near-by, *adv.* close to, near at hand; almost.

Near-cut, *n.* a short-cut, the nearest way.

Nearer-hand, *adv.* nearer.

Near-friend, *adj.* closely related.

Near-gaun, *adj.* stingy, miserly.

Near-geddert, *adj.* used of money: gathered by parsimony.

Near-hand, *adv.* hard by. Cf. Nar-hand.

Near-hand-gate, *n.* the nearest way.

Near-handness, *n.* nearness; a short distance; niggardliness.

Near-hand-road, *n.* a short-cut.

Nearlins, *adv.* nearly, almost.

Nearmaist, *adj.* nearest.—*adv.* almost.

Near miss, *n.* almost a miss; almost a hit.

Nearness, *n.* niggardliness.

Near-o'-ane, *n.* not one.

Near one's self, *adj.* niggardly; tenacious of one's own property; very careful as to one's self-interest.

Near-strings, *n.* the strings connected with the kidneys.

Near-the-bane, *adj.* niggardly.

Nease, *n.* the nose.

Neast, *adj.* nearest, next. Cf. Neist.

Neat, *adj.* pretty, pleasing to the eye; exact; mere; identical.—*adv.* exactly, nett.

Neath, *prep.* beneath.—*adv.* under, lower than.

Neath-maist, -mest, *adj.* lowest, undermost.

Neat land, *n.* land for grazing neat cattle.

Neat's-fire, *n.* fire from the friction of two pieces of wood. Cf. Need-fire.

Neaty, *adj.* mere; identical. Cf. Netty.

Neave, *n.* the fist. Cf. Neive.

Neavil, *v.* to pommel. Cf. Nevell.

Neb, Nebb, *n.* the tip or point of anything; the snout; the nib of a pen; oatmeal and water mixed up together in a wooden dish, rolled like cucumbers, and boiled; the time between dawn and sunrise; pungency; pungency in liquor.—*v.* to peck, to scold; to bill and coo, kiss, caress; to make a pen of a goose-quill.

Neb and feather, *phr.* completely.

Nebbily, *adv.* sharply, smartly.

Nebbit, *ppl. adj.* having a beak or nose; pointed, edged; having a hooked head on a staff. Cf. Lang-nebbit.

Nebbock, *n.* the nose.

Nebby, *adj.* sharp, ill-natured, smart.

Neb-cap, *n.* an iron toe-plate on shoe or clog.

Nebed, *ppl. adj.* pointed. Cf. Nebbit.

Nebfu', *n.* a beakful; a very small quantity of whisky, &c.

Neb-o'-the-mire-snipe, *n.* the utmost extremity.

Neb-o'-the-morning, *n.* the time between dawn and sunrise.

Nebsy, *n.* an impudent old woman.

Necessar, *adj.* necessary.—*n.* in *pl.* necessary things.

Necessitat, *ppl. adj.* necessitated, compelled.

Necessitous, *adj.* necessary.

Nechram, *n.* horse-leather.

Neck, *n.* the neck-piece or cape of a coat, covering the neck and shoulders; a weaving term.—*v.* to kill, behead; to put the arm round the neck; to court.

Neck-break, *n.* ruin, destruction; what brings to an unlooked-for end.

Neck-cutter, *n.* a headsman, executioner.

Neck-deep, *adv.* up to the neck.

Neck-herring, *n.* a smart stroke.

Necking, *n.* courting.

Neckit, *n.* a tippet for a child.

Neckle, *v.* to entangle.

Neckless, *adj.* of a button: without a shank.

Neck-napkin, *n.* a neckerchief.

Neck-verse, *n.* Psalm li. 1, sung at executions.

Ned, Neddy, *n.* a donkey, a simpleton.

Neddar, Neddir, *n.* an adder. Cf. Nether.

Nedder, *conj., pron.,* and *adj.* neither.

Neddercap, *n.* a cross-grained person.

Nedderin, *conj.* and *adv.* neither.

Nedeum, *n.* a gnawing pain.—*v.* of pain: to gnaw; to mutter curses to one's self.

Neebour, *n.* a neighbour. Cf. Neighbour.

Need, *v.* to do of necessity; to use.

Need-be, *n.* a necessity; expediency.

Needcessitate, *v.* to necessitate.

Needcessity, *n.* necessity, a state of need; in *pl.* things needful for life.

Need-fire, *n.* fire caused by friction of two pieces of wood, used as a charm for murrain, &c.; a beacon fire; spontaneous ignition.

Needfu', *adj.* needy, necessitous.—*n.* in *pl.* necessaries.

Needlach, *n.* a small, young eel.

Needle, *n.* a fallen leaf of the larch or Scotch fir; a 'spark' of fire or boiling matter that pricks the spot of skin on which it falls; a cheat, swindle; anything of the smallest.— *v.* to sew with a needle; to work backwards and forwards; to thread one's way through.

Needle-cases, *n.* a children's singing-game.

Needle-dumper, *n.* a seamstress.

Needle-e'e, *n.* in *phr.* 'through the needle-e'e,' the children's game of 'thread-the-needle,' the game of 'oranges and lemons.'

Needle-fish, *n.* the shorter pipe-fish, the sea-needle.

Needles-e'e, *n.* a 'nutshell.'

Needle-speed, *n.* the utmost speed.

Needle-steik, *n.* a needle-stitch.

Need-made-up, *adj.* hastily prepared, as immediately necessary.—*n.* anything so prepared.

Needment, *n.* a requirement, anything necessary.

Neednail, *v.* to clinch a nail.

Neef, *n.* need, difficulty. Cf. **Kneef.**

Neeger, Neegre, *n.* a negro; a hard worker; an adept. Cf. **Nigger.**

Neeger, Neigre, *n.* a niggard; a mean, low fellow; a lout; an iron 'cheek' for a grate, used as a coal-saver. Cf. **Niggar.**

Neek-nack, *adv.* rapidly moving in and out, or to and fro, as in play.

Neemit, *n.* dinner.

Neen, *adj.* none.

Neen, *n.* noon.

Neep, *n.* a turnip; a bulky, old-fashioned watch in hinged case; a disagreeable person; anything ugly of its kind; in *pl.* the time between the final hoeing of turnips and the harvest.—*v.* to serve cattle with turnips.

Neep, *n.* a promontory.

Neep-brose, *n.* a dish of oatmeal mixed with mashed turnips.

Neep-cutter, *n.* a turnip-cutter.

Neep-grun', *n.* ground in which turnips are sown.

Neep-hack, -hawk, *n.* a pronged mattock for raising turnips from the frozen ground; a turnip-rack for feeding cattle or sheep out of doors with turnips in winter.

Neep-heid, *n.* a turnip-head; a stupid person.

Neep-heidit, *adj.* dull, stupid.

Neepkin, *n.* a napkin; a pocket-handkerchief.

Neep-like, *adj.* like a turnip; stupid.

Neepour, *n.* a neighbour.

Neep-reet, *n.* growing turnips.

Neep-seed, *n.* turnip-seed; the time for sowing turnip-seed.

Neep-shaw, *n.* a turnip-top.

Neepyun, *n.* a napkin.

Neer, *n.* a kidney. Cf. **Near.**

Ne'er-be-licket, *phr.* not a whit.

Ne'er-day, *n.* New Year's Day; a New-Year's Day present.

Ne'er-do-gude, *adj.* past mending; irreclaimable.

Ne'er-do-weel, *n.* an incorrigible in wickedness, folly, or indolence.

Ne'erless, *adv.* nevertheless.

Neese, *n.* a sneeze.

Neeshin, *v.* used of an animal: to desire the male.

Neeshin, *n.* sneezing; snuff, 'sneeshin.'

Neeshin-mill, *n.* a snuff-box.

Neest, *adj.* nearest, next.

Neet, *n.* a parsimonious person, a niggard.

Neet, *n.* a 'nit,' the egg of a louse; a louse.

Neety, *adj.* miserly, stingy.

Neety-cud, *n.* a low fellow who does mean things.

Neeve, *n.* a fist. Cf. **Neive.**

Neever-day, *n.* New Year's Day. Cf. **Ne'er-day.**

Neever-e'en, *n.* New Year's Eve.

Neevie-neevie-nick-nack, *n.* a guessing-game, played with a small article hidden in one closed hand moved over the other.

Neeze, *v.* to sneeze.—*n.* a sneeze. Cf. **Neese.**

Neeze, Neez, *n.* the nose. Cf. **Niz.**

Neffit, *n.* a pigmy; a chit.

Neffle, *v.* to pommel.—*n.* a blow with the fist. Cf. **Nevell.**

Neffow, Neffu', *n.* a handful.—*v.* to take in handfuls; to handle an animal. Cf. **Neive-fu'.**

Neg, *v.* to bite, snap; to nag. Cf. **Nag.**

Negleck, *v.* to neglect.—*n.* neglect.

Negleckfu', *adj.* negligent, apt to neglect.

Neibour, *n.* a neighbour.

Neicher, Neigher, *v.* to neigh; to whinny. Cf. **Nicker.**

Neidfire, *n.* fire produced from the friction of two pieces of wood; a beacon-fire. Cf. **Need-fire.**

Neidnail, *v.* to fasten by clinched nails. Cf. **Neednail.**

Neif, *n.* difficulty. Cf. **Neef.**

Neif, *n.* the fist. Cf. **Neive.**

Neiffer, *v.* to barter. Cf. **Niffer.**

Neighbour, *n.* a companion, comrade, good friend; a partner; a fellow-servant; a bedfellow; a husband or wife; a match, a 'marrow,' one of a similar pair.—*adj.* neighbouring, fellow.—*v.* to consort with; to work along with, or in partnership; with *ill*, to disagree. Cf. **Neiper.**

Neighbourhood, *n.* friendly, social relations.

Neighbourless, *adj.* not matching, not of a pair.

Neighbourlike, *adj.* like one's neighbours; friendly, sociable.

Neighbourliness, *n.* friendship, companionship.

Neigher, v. to whinny. Cf. Nicker.

Neigre, n. a term of reproach. Cf. Niggar.

Neil, n. in phr. 'Auld Neil,' the devil.

Neilship, n. in phr. 'his Neilship,' the devil.

Neip, n. a turnip. Cf. Neep.

Neiper, n. a neighbour.

Neiperheed, n. friendship, social relations.

Neiperty, n. partnership; the embrace of copulation; companionship.

Neir, n. a kidney. Cf. Near.

Neis, n. the nose; a ness. Cf. Nose.

Neisht, adj. next.

Neist, adj. nearest.—adv. next.—prep. next to, on this side of.

Neistmost, adj. next.

Neistways, adv. in a short time after.

Neis-wise, adj. having an acute sense of smell; quick of perception, or pretending to be so.

Neith, prep. under. Cf. Neath.

Neithers, adv. notwithstanding, either.

Neive, n. the fist; the hand; the closed hand; a handful; cheating at marbles by stretching the hand over the score; a measure of length; in pl. fisticuffs, boxing.—v. to catch with the hands, 'guddle'; to turf the ridge of a house so as to hold and cover the ends of the thatch; to cheat at marbles by extending the hand unduly.

Neivefu', n. a handful. Cf. Nievefu'.

Neive-shaking, n. a women's quarrel, scolding-match; a windfall.

Neivie-nick-nack, n. a guessing-game played with the 'neives.' Cf. Neevie-neevie-nick-nack.

Nek, n. the neck.—v. to embrace. Cf. Neck.

Nell, v. to talk loudly or fluently.

Nellin, ppl. adj. loquacious, frivolous.

Nell-kneed, adj. knock-kneed. Cf. Knell-kneed.

Nens, Nenst, Nent, prep. opposite to; regarding. Cf. Anent.

Nepos, Nepus-gable, n. a gable in the middle of the front of a house.

Neppit, ppl. adj. short in size, quantity, or number. Cf. Nippit.

Ner, conj. than. Cf. Nor.

Nerby, prep. near to.—adv. nearly; almost.

Nerlins, adv. nearly, almost.

Nerr, v. to snarl or growl as a dog; to purr as a cat; to fret.—n. a growl; a purr. Cf. Nurr.

Nerve, n. capacity, ability; in pl. an attack of nervousness; strong excitement.

Nervish, adj. nervous.

Nervously, adv. forcibly.

Nesch, adj. of delicate health.

Ness, adj. destitute, necessitous. Cf. Nace.

Nesscock, Nesscockle, n. a small boil, a hot pimple. Cf. Arse-cockle.

Nesslin, n. the smallest and weakest bird in the nest.

Net, adv. neatly.

Net, n. the omentum or caul covering the intestines.—v. to enclose sheep by nets.

Neth, prep. beneath.—adv. under.

Nether, adj. lower; nearer, next.

Nether, n. an adder. Cf. Nadder.

Nether, pron. and conj. neither.

Netherans, adv. and conj. neither. Cf. Naitherans.

Nether-end, n. the posteriors.

Nethermaist, adj. lowest.—n. the lowest part.

Nether-stane, n. an 'adder-bead,' used as a charm against 'elf-shots.'

Nethmist, adj. undermost.

Net-silk, n. knitted silk, used for stockings.

Nett, adv. exactly. Cf. Neat.

Nettercap, n. a spider. Cf. Ettercap.

Netterie, adj. ill-natured; sarcastic. Cf. Attery.

Nettery, n. a spider.

Nettle, v. to puzzle.

Nettle-broth, n. broth made of young nettles, as a substitute for greens.

Nettle-earnest, adj. in deadly earnest.

Nettle-kail, n. 'nettle-broth.'

Nettlesome, adj. peevish, quarrelsome, irritating.

Nettlie, adj. ill-humoured, fretful, exasperating.

Nettly, adv. exactly.

Netty, adj. mere, sheer.

Netty, n. a woman who traverses the country in search of wool.

Neucheld, ppl. adj. used of a cow: newly-calved, with calf. Cf. New-cal'.

Neuck, Neuk, n. a nook, recess, interior angle; a niche, crevice; a corner-seat by the fire; an out-of-the-way place; childbed; a corner, the corner of a garment or any piece of cloth; a fair share of work, of a treat, &c.—v. to check, humble, 'corner'; to outwit, take in, trick.

Neukatyke, n. a shepherd's collie.

Neukie, adj. having corners.

Neukit, ppl. adj. having corners; crooked; short-tempered, sharp.

Neuk-stane, n. a corner-stone.

Neuk-time, n. twilight, as the season for pasture or gossiping among work-people.

Neull, n. a small horn. Cf. Nool.

Neulled, adj. having very short horns.

Nev, Neve, n. the fist. Cf. Neive.

Neval, adv. in phr. to 'fa' a-neval,' used of an animal lying helpless on its back. Cf. Aval.

Nevell, Nevel, v. to strike with the fist, pommel; to grasp, pluck out; to knead; to pinch with the fingers.—n. a blow with the fist or elbow.

Nevermas, *n*. a time that never comes.

Nevilling, *n*. a pommelling.

Nevil-stone, *n*. the keystone of an arch.

†**Nevo, Nevoy, Nevey**, *n*. nephew.

New, *v*. to curb, master, humble; to beat severely.

New, *adj*. recently happened.—*adv*. newly.—*n*. in *phr*. 'in the new,' anew.

Newance, *n*. something new or unusual; the first kiss given to a person by a child on getting a new garment.

New-bread, *n*. a novelty.

New-brent, *adj*. quite new.

New-cal', -ca'd, *adj*. used of a cow: lately calved; with calf, pregnant. Cf. Neucheld.

New-cheese, *n*. a cheese made of the milk of a newly-calved cow.

New-come, *adj*. newly come, fresh.

Newfangle, *n*. a novelty.—*adj*. fond of novelty; pleasant to strangers; new-fashioned.

Newfangled, *adj*. vain of a new thing; in a new and strange position; innovating.

Newfangledness, *n*. love of novelty; an innovation, novelty.

Newhaven-gill, *n*. a measure of two gills.

Newing, *n*. barm; yeast.

Newings, *n*. novelties; news. Cf. Newance.

Newis, *adj*. earnestly desirous; parsimonious, greedy, keeping in.

New Light, *adj*. liberal and progressive in doctrine.

Newlins, Newlans, *adv*. very lately; newly, recently.

Newmost, *adj*. nethermost, lowest.—*n*. the nethermost.

Newous, *adj*. very eager; parsimonious. Cf. Newis.

Newous, *adj*. fond or full of what is new, newfangled.

Newouslie, *adv*. in a novel or new-fashioned way.

Newousness, *n*. 'newfangledness'; an innovation, love of novelty.

New-pan, *n*. a widow's second husband.

Newrgift, *n*. a New Year's Day gift.

News, Newse, *n*. gossip; talk; the subject of talk; a newspaper.—*v*. to tell as news; to talk over the news; to gossip, talk.

New's day, *n*. New Year's Day.

Newser, *n*. a retailer of news; a gossip.

Newsfu', *adj*. full of gossip.

News-gizzened, *adj*. empty of, or hungering for, news.

Newsie, *adj*. talkative; gossiping.

Newsing, *n*. gossip.—*ppl. adj*. gossiping.

News-lassie, *n*. a newspaper-girl.

Newspaper-billy, *n*. a press reporter.

Newspaper-woman, -man, *n*. a great reader of newspapers.

New-Year-day, *n*. New Year's Day; a present given on New Year's Day.

Next, *adj*. next but one.

Nextan, Nexten, *adj*. next.

Neypsie, *adj*. prim; precise in manners.

Niaff, *v*. to yelp, bark.—*n*. a pert, saucy person. Cf. Nyaff.

Nib, *n*. the human nose; a narrow strip of land; a long, projecting headland; a point, tip; a nibble, a snapping bite.

Nibbawa, Nibawa, *adj*. snappish, crusty.

Nibbie, *n*. a walking-stick with a crooked head; a shepherd's crook.

Nibbits, *n*. two pieces of oatcake buttered and placed face to face.

Nibble, *n*. the stump of a pen.

Nibble, *v*. to fidget with the fingers; to snatch stealthily.

Nibbock, *n*. a beak, bill.

Niber, *n*. a neighbour.

Nibwise, *adj*. ready to take offence or take up a wrong meaning.

Niccar, *v*. to neigh. Cf. Nicker.

Nice, *adj*. difficult, critical; fine.

Nice-gabbit, *adj*. difficult to please with food; prim, particular of speech.

Nicelies, *adv*. nicely.

Niceness, *n*. a difficulty; a ticklish business.

Nicety, *n*. a dainty, a luxury; a nice thing.

Nicher, *n*. a neigh, whinny; a snigger.—*v*. to whinny; to snigger. Cf. Nicker.

Nicherin, *n*. a neighing, whinnying. Cf. Nickerin.

Nichil, *n*. nothing. Cf. Nickle.

Nicht, *n*. night; the evening; a curtain-lecture.—*v*. to darken; to benight; to spend the night, lodge for the night; to spend the evening with; to visit after dark; to stop work for the day; to cease working at the close of daylight.

Nicht-at-eenie, *n*. the time of night when children play, &c., before bed-time.

Nicht-bour, *n*. a bedchamber.

Nicht-bussing, *n*. a woman's night-cap.

Nicht-cap, *n*. some liquor taken before going to bed.

Nicht-come, *n*. nightfall.

Nicht-cowl, *n*. a night-cap.

Nicht-cowled, *adj*. wearing a night-cap.

Nicht-hawk, *n*. a large white moth which flies about hedges on summer evenings; a person who ranges about at night.

Nicht-hawking, *adj*. given to roam at night.

Nichting-time, *n*. the time when daylight closes and outdoor labour ceases.

Nichtit, *ppl*. benighted; darkened by night.

Nicht-kep, *n*. a night-cap.

Nichtless, *adj*. with no night.

Nicht-mirk, *n*. the darkness of night.

Nicht-mutch, *n*. a woman's night-cap.

Nicht-rail, *n.* a covering for the head worn at night ; a night-dress.

Nichtside, *n.* the course of the evening.

Nicht-things, *n.* coal, peats, water, &c. brought in at night for use next morning.

Nick, *n.* a name for the devil.

Nick, *n.* a score, mark ; a cleft, crevice, groove ; the angle between the beam and handle of a plough ; a hollow or pass through hills ; in *pl.* the knuckles.—*v.* to cut ; to reap ; to stab ; to wrinkle ; to bite ; to snap off ; to thwart ; to cut one short ; to refuse curtly ; to deprive.

Nick, *n.* a wink ; a gibe, jeer ; a retort.—*v.* to answer in a mocking or insulting way.

Nick, *v.* to click ; to play a marble smartly with thumb and first finger ; to aim at marbles.—*n.* a creaking sound ; a click ; a smart blow.—*phr.* 'to play nick,' to sound like something suddenly giving way. Cf. Knick.

Nick, *v.* to steal ; to cheat ; to seize ; to catch away.—*n.* an act of trickery or deceit ; a policeman.

Nick, *v.* to drink heartily.

Nickelty, *n.* the letter N on a tee-totum, signifying 'nothing.'

Nickem, Nickim, *n.* a mischievous, tricky boy ; a wag.

Nicker, *n.* a water-sprite.

Nicker, *n.* the marble with which a boy aims, a 'pitcher.'

Nicker, *v.* to neigh, whinny ; to give a suppressed laugh, snigger.—*n.* the neighing of a horse ; light laughter ; a snigger.

Nickerers, *n.* creaking shoes, new shoes which creak.

Nickerie, *n.* a term of endearment for a child.

Nickerin', *n.* a neighing, whinnying.

Nickery, *adj.* knavish.

Nickey, Nickie, Nickie-ben, *n.* the devil.

Nickie-frog, *n.* a contemptuous name for a Frenchman.

Nickit, Nicket, *n.* a small notch.

Nickle, *v.* to aim with a marble briskly ; to handle ; to set up type.—*n.* a sharp stroke such as impels a 'pitcher' at marbles ; a player at marbles. Cf. Nick.

Nickle, *n.* a knuckle. Cf. Knickle.

Nickle, *n.* in *phr.* 'N-nichil, nickle-naething,' said when the tee-totum displays N uppermost ; nothing at all.

Nick-nack, *adv.* with steady motion or clicking sound.

Nick-nack, *n.* a gimcrack ; in *pl.* smallwares. Cf. Knick-knack.

Nick-nacket, *n.* a trinket. Cf. Knick-knacket.

Nick-nackity, *adj.* precise, punctilious.

Nick-nacky, *adj.* dexterous in doing nice work.

Nick on the horn, *n.* another year of life.

Nicks, *v.* to aim at anything near.

Nickstick, *n.* a tally.

Nickstick bodie, *n.* one who proceeds exactly by rule ; one who does nothing without a return in kind.

Nickum, *n.* a mischievous boy. Cf. Nickem.

Nicky-nacky, *adj.* gimcrack ; useless, trifling ; speaking mincingly.

Nid, *v.* to nod slightly.

Nidder, *conj.* neither.

Nidder, *adj.* lower. Cf. Nether.

Nidder, *n.* the second shoot made by growing grain.

Nidder, *v.* to depress ; to straighten ; to undervalue, depreciate ; to put out of shape by frequent handling.

Nidder, *v.* to shiver ; to shiver with cold ; to subject to hunger ; to pinch with cold ; to shrivel ; to pine, fret, wither ; to blast and bite with frost or wind ; to plague.

Niddle, *v.* to work quickly with the fingers without doing much ; to trifle with the fingers.

Niddle, *v.* to overcome and rob.

Niddle, *v.* used of birds : to bill and coo, to frisk about each other at pairing-time.

Niddling, Nidling, *ppl. adj.* trifling.

Niddy-noddy, *n.* a palsied movement of the head ; in *pl.* assumed airs, showy manners, as shown by the movement of the head.

Nidge, *n.* a heavy squeeze, pressure ; a nudge. —*v.* to squeeze, press down ; to nudge. Cf. Knidge.

Nidgell, *n.* a fat, forward young man ; a lover no one can displace.

Nidity-nod, *adv.* bobbing up and down.

Nid-noddy, *adj.* falling asleep.

Nidy-noy, *adv.* with affected gait ; with mincing or bobbing step.

Nief, *n.* a female bond-servant.

Niegre, *n.* a niggard ; a lout. Cf. Niggar.

Niest, *adj.* next.

Nieve, Niev, *n.* the fist. Cf. Neive.

Nievefu', *n.* a handful ; a small quantity of anything dry ; any person or thing very small and puny ; anything comparatively of little or no value ; a death's-hold of what is viewed as worthy of grasping.

Nieveshaking, *n.* something dropped from the hand of another ; a windfall.

Nievle, *v.* to strike with the fist.—*n.* a blow. Cf. Nevell.

Nievling, *n.* milking a cow by grasping the teat with the whole hand.

Niffer, *v.* to exchange, barter ; to haggle in bargaining.—*n.* an exchange, barter.

Nifferer, *n.* a barterer.

Niffle, *v.* to trifle ; to be in any respect insignificant.

Niffle-naffle, v. to trifle away time.

Niff-naff, n. a trifle; anything very small; a small person; a silly peculiarity of temper; fussiness.—v. to trifle; to talk in a silly way; to toy; to take finicking trouble.

Niff-naffy, adj. fussy; over-particular about trifles.

Nif-niff, Niffy-naff, v. to trifle. Cf. Niff-naff.

Nig, n. in phr. 'nigs and naws,' knick-knacks, oddments. Cf. Nig-nag.

Nigg, v. to complain, fret; to nag.

Niggar, n. a niggard; a mean fellow; a lout; an iron cheek to a grate, used for economy of fuel.

Nigger, n. a hard worker; an adept. Cf. Neeger.

Niggerality, n. meanness, niggardliness.

Nigger'd, adj. in reduced circumstances.

Niggerhead, n. a white cowrie.

Niggerhead, n. negrohead tobacco.

Niggle, v. to hack; to cut with a blunt implement.

Nigher, v. to neigh. Cf. Nicker.

Nigh-hand, adv. nearly.

Night, v. to lodge during the night. Cf. Nicht.

Nightingale, n. a moth.

Nig-ma-nies, n. sundry trifles; needless ornaments; gewgaws; a bride's 'things.'

Nig-nag, -nac, n. a knick-knack; a worthless trifle.

Nig-nay, -nae, -naw, -nye, n. a trifle; a knick-knack; a plaything; a gewgaw.—v. to do what is useless or is without good result; to show reluctance; to work in a trifling way.

Nig-nayin, ppl. adj. whimsical; full of crotchets.

Nigre, n. a niggard; a lout. Cf. Niggar.

Nikkienow, n. a term of reproach.

Nile, n. a plug for the water-hole in the bottom of a boat.

Nile-hole, n. the hole for the 'nile.'

Nill, Nil, v. to be unwilling; in phr. 'nill ye, will ye,' whether you will or no.

Nim, n. steam, vapour, warm air. Cf. Oam.

Nim, v. to catch up quickly; to walk with brisk, short steps, or mincingly.

Nimble, adj. clever, astute.

Nimble-gawn, adj. nimble; loquacious.

†Nimious, adj. oppressive, exceeding due bounds, excessive.

Nimmit, n. dinner.

Nimp, n. a very small piece. Cf. Nip.

Nine-eyed-eel, n. the lamprey.

Nineholes, n. the game of nine-men's morris; the piece of beef that is cut out immediately below the breast.

Nine O's, n. a game in which nine O's in three parallel columns are to be joined by lines which must not cross each other.

Ninepence, n. in phr. 'to a ninepence,' to a T.

Ninesome, adj. consisting of nine.

Nineteen, n. a nineteen years' lease of a farm.

Ninny-niawing, n. whinnying.

Ninycumpook, n. a nincompoop.

Nip, v. to graze; to eat daintily; to taste sharp; to smart; to tingle with cold; to be niggardly, to stint; to cheat; to snatch; to steal; to run off quickly.—n. a squeeze; a bite; a bite in fishing; the pain of a pinch or bite; a sharp, pungent flavour; a burning, biting taste; a keen feeling in the air; a small bit of anything; a share of a burden, &c.; an advantage in bargaining; speed, rate.

Nip-caik, n. an eater of delicacies in secret.

Nipick, n. a very small piece. Cf. Nippock.

Nipkin, n. a napkin; a pocket-handkerchief.

Nip-lug, n. a schoolmaster; quarrelling to the point of blows.

Nip-necks, v. used of horses: to bite each other's neck.

Nipour, n. a neighbour. Cf. Neiper.

Nipper, n. a small quantity of strong liquor.

Nipper, n. a sharp retort; a 'settler.'

Nipper, n. a niggard; a tooth; in pl. tongs; forceps.

Nipperkin, n. a small measure of liquor. Cf. Niprikin.

Nipper-nebbit, adj. having a sharp beak.

Nipperren, n. a small quantity.

Nipperty, adj. mincing, affected.

Nipperty-tipperty, adj. childishly exact, affectedly neat; quick, rattling in rhythm.

Nippily, adv. smartly, sharply.

Nipping, n. a smarting pain; a tingling.—ppl. adj. sharp; pungent; tingling, aching; cold, freezing; short in size or weight; niggardly; tricky.

Nippit, ppl. adj. niggardly; short in size or weight; scanty; used of clothes: tight-fitting, pinched-in; starved-looking; apt to give short weight or measure; narrow-minded, bigoted; snappish, short-tempered.

Nippitness, n. stinginess.

Nippock, n. a very small piece.

Nippy, adj. sharp; pungent, biting, causing to tingle; bitter of speech; scanty; tight in fit; too little; stingy; keen to take advantage; tricky.—n. a very small bit.

Niprikin, n. a small morsel. Cf. Nipperkin.

Nipscart, n. a niggard; a cross, ill-tempered person.

Nipshot, adv. aslant, backwards.

Nipsicker, adj. cross, captious; severely exact.

Nir, n. anything small or stunted; a term of contempt.

Nirb, *n.* a dwarf; anything of stunted growth.

Nirl, *n.* a knot; an induration on the skin; a fragment; a small piece; a dwarfish person.—*v.* to pinch with cold; to cause to shrink or shrivel; to break into small pieces.

Nirled, *ppl. adj.* shrunken, shrivelled; stunted.

Nirlie, *adj.* stunted in growth; puny; niggardly.

Nirlie-headed, *adj.* used of wheat: having a small head.

Nirling, *ppl. adj.* keen, nipping, frosty, drying.

Nirlock, *n.* a small, hard lump or swelling on the feet or hands.

Nirls, Nirles, *n.* an eruption on the skin, like measles or chicken-pox.

Nirr, *v.* to snarl or growl like a dog. Cf. Nurr.

Nirrange, *n.* an orange.

Nirt, *n.* a very small piece.

Nirty, *adj.* small.

Nis, Nise, *n.* the nose. Cf. Naise, Neeze.

Nis-bit, *n.* the iron or bit that passes across the nose part of a horse's bridle or 'branks.'

Nisser, *v.* to contract; to dry up; to become stunted. Cf. Nizzer.

Nissle, *v.* to beat with the fists; to thrash.

Nissling, *n.* a thrashing.

Nistie-cock, *n.* a small boil or pimple. Cf. Nesscock.

Nis-wise, *adj.* far-seeing; having an acute sense of smell. Cf. Neis-wise.

Nit, Nite, *n.* the egg of a louse; a louse.

Nit, *v.* to knit, fasten.

Nit, *n.* a nut; a hazel-nut.

Nit, *n.* a female wanton.

Nitch, *n.* a bundle or truss.

Nitch, *n.* a notch, incision.

Nite, *v.* to strike a sharp blow. Cf. Nyte.

Nit-grit, *adj.* as large as a nut.

Nither, *v.* to depress; to depreciate. Cf. Nidder.

Nither, *v.* to shiver; to shrivel; to pine away; to pinch with cold. Cf. Nidder.

Nither, *adj.* lower, nether.

Nither, *conj., adj.,* and *pron.* neither.

Nithered, *ppl. adj.* trembling with cold; withered, wasted.

Nitherie, *adj.* withered, blasted, feeble.

Nitmyug, *n.* a nutmeg.

Nit-saw, *n.* a salve for clearing the head from lice.

Nitter, *v.* to grumble constantly.

Nitter, *v.* to shiver with cold. Cf. Nither.

Nitteret, *ppl. adj.* sulky; ill-natured.—*n.* a sulky-looking face.

Nitterie, *adj.* ill-natured.

Nitters, *n.* a greedy, grubbing, impudent, withered woman.

Nittie, *n.* a female wanton. Cf. Nit.

Nittie, *adj.* niggardly; covetous. Cf. Neetie.

Nitting, *n.* tape. Cf. Knitting.

Nittle, *v.* to irritate. Cf. Nettle.

Nittled, *adj.* having small, stunted horns.

Nittles, *n.* horns peeping through the skin; the small, stunted horns of sheep.

Nittles, *n.* the pieces of string used for tying full sacks. Cf. Knittle.

Nitty, *adj.* lousy.

Nitty, *n.* a knave, a rascal; a term of abuse.

Nitty, *adj.* clever, agile; neat; small. Cf. Naetie.

Nit-wud, *n.* a wood of hazel-nut trees.

Niv, Nivv, *n.* the fist. Cf. Neive.

Nivel, *v.* to pommel. Cf. Nevell.

Nivie-nick-nack, *n.* a game of choice, played with an article in one of the closed fists.

Nivlock, *n.* a handle of wood, round which the end of a hair-tether is fastened. Cf. Knewel.

Nivvi-nivvi-nak-kak, *n.* 'nivie-nick-nack.'

Nivvil, *n.* a handful.

Nix, *v.* to aim at anything near. Cf. Nicks.

Nixie, *n.* a water-nymph.

Nixin, *n.* a game resembling 'rowly-powly.'

Niz, Nizz, *n.* the nose.

Niz-bit, *n.* the iron that passes over a horse's nose and joins the 'branks' together.

Nizzart, *n.* a lean person with a hard, sharp face.—*ppl. adj.* contracted.

Nizzelin', *ppl. adj.* niggardly; from greed, spending time on trifles.

Nizzer, *v.* to contract; to become dried up or stunted in growth.

Nizzertit, *adj.* stunted in growth.

Nizzey, *n.* the nose.

Nizzin, Nizin, *n.* a drubbing; exposure to the weather.

Nizzle, *v.* to pommel. Cf. Nissle.

Nizzlin, *n.* direct exposure to a severe storm.

No, *adv.* not; used as an interrogative after a positive statement.

Noah's ark, *n.* clouds assuming the shape of a boat, regarded as a sign of the weather.

Nob, *n.* a knob; a rounded hill; the nose; the toe of a boot.

Nob, *n.* an interloper in a trade, a 'black-leg.'—*v.* to act as a 'blackleg.'

Nob-berry, Nobe-berry, *n.* the cloudberry.

Nobbut, Nobut, *adv.* only; nothing but.

Nobby, *n.* a rich man; a 'swell.'

†Nobilitat, *v.* to confer a peerage, ennoble.

Noble, *n.* the armed bullhead.

†Nocent, *adj.* guilty.

Nocht, *n.* nought.

Nochtie, *adj.* puny in size; contemptible in appearance; bad; unfit for any purpose; valueless; trifling.

Nock, *n.* a notch; the notch on a spindle or an arrow.

Nock, *n.* a clock. Cf. Knock.

Nock, *n.* a hill. Cf. Knock.

Nock, *n.* the corner of a sailyard.

Nock, *v.* to tire out, exhaust.

Nocket, *n.* a luncheon; a slight repast between breakfast and dinner; a small cake.

Nocket-time, *n.* the time for taking a 'nocket.'

Nod, *v.* to fall asleep in one's chair; to go on one's way briskly and carelessly. — *n.* a nap.—*phr.* 'the land of Nod,' sleep.

Nodder, *conj.* neither. Cf. Nowther.

Noddle, *n.* the temper; the head, used contemptuously.

Noddle-araid, *adv.* head-foremost.

Noddy, *n.* a sleepy person.

Noddy, *n.* a kind of tea-cake baked with currants.

Noddy, *n.* a simpleton. Cf. Audie.

Noddy, *n.* a one-horse coach, moving on two wheels, and opening behind; a one-horse coach of the ordinary kind, with four-wheels.—*phr.* 'on Shanks' noddy,' on foot.

Nodge, *v.* to strike with the knuckles.—*n.* a stroke with the knuckles.

Nodge, *v.* to sit or go about in a dull, stupid state; with *along*, to travel leisurely.

Nodie, *n.* the head.

Nog, *n.* a small wooden vessel; a mug.

Nog, *n.* a wooden peg used in thatching with sods; a knob; a hooked stake driven into the wall; a projecting small handle of a scythe.

Nogg, *v.* to stroll leisurely nodding the head.

Noggan, *n.* a noggin.

Noggie, *n.* a small wooden vessel, a mug. Cf. Naggie.

Noggit, *n.* a small cake; a luncheon. Cf. Nocket.

Noint, *v.* to anoint.

Nointment, *n.* ointment.

Noisome, *adj.* noisy.

Noit, *n.* a small rocky height; a projecting knob on the foot.

Noit, *v.* to strike smartly.—*n.* a smart stroke. Cf. Knoit.

Noiting, *n.* a beating.

Noitled, *ppl. adj.* drunk with spirits.

Noityon, *n.* a 'noit' on the foot. Cf. Nutyon.

Nokkit, *n.* a midday meal. Cf. Nocket.

Noll, *v.* to press, beat, or strike with the knuckles.—*n.* a strong push or blow with the knuckles.

Noll, *n.* a knoll; a large piece of anything. Cf. Knoll.

Noll, *n.* a noodle.

Nolt, *n.* cattle; black cattle; a stupid fellow. Cf. Nowt.

Noltish, *adj.* stupid.

Nolt-tath, *n.* luxuriant grass, manured by cattle.

Nombles, *n.* the entrails of a deer, sheep, &c.

No mere man, *n.* a supernatural being, a goblin.

Non, *n.* a name given towards the middle of the 19th century to the 'Non-intrusion' section of the Church of Scotland.

Non-compear, *v.* not to appear in answer to a citation.

Non-conform, *adj.* not conforming.

None, *adv.* not; in no wise.

Nonentity, *n.* a sinecure; a nonplus; a deadlock.

None-so-pretty, *n.* London pride.

None-such, Nonsuch, *adj.* unparalleled.—*n.* a quite exceptional person or thing.

Non-fiance, *n.* want of confidence.

Non-plush, *v.* to nonplus.

Non-residentin, *adj.* non-resident.

Noo-a-days, *adv.* now, in these days.

Noof, *adj.* sheltered from the weather; snug; neat, trim.—*v.* to enjoy one's self leisurely; to be snug and comfortable.

Noof, *v.* to chat familiarly. Cf. Knooff.

Noofly, *adv.* neatly; handsomely.

Noofy, *adj.* silly; 'feckless.'

Nooh, *v.* of the wind: to blow gently. Cf. Nough.

Nook, *v.* to check; to humble; to trick, outwit, take in.—*n.* a corner seat; a crevice; a trick. Cf. Neuck.

Nookit, *ppl. adj.* crooked; sharp; short-tempered.

Nool, *n.* a small horn; one not part of the skull, but attached to the skin. Cf. Knule.

Nool, *v.* to beat with the knuckles. Cf. Knool.

Nooled, *ppl. adj.* having mere stumps of horns.

Nool-kneed, *adj.* knock-kneed. Cf. Knule-kneed.

Nooning-piece, *n.* a piece of bread as luncheon.

Noony, *n.* a luncheon.

Noop, *n.* the fruit of the cloudberry. Cf. Nup.

Noop, *n.* a round projection.

Noop, *v.* to walk with downcast eyes and nodding head.

Noor, *adv.* not.

†Noorish, *n.* a nurse. Cf. Nourice.

Noos, *n.* news; gossip.

Noosle, *v.* to nuzzle; to nestle close for warmth; to root with the snout like a pig; to seize by the nose.

Noost, *v.* to cudgel, belabour.

Noost, *n.* the action of the grinders of a horse in chewing.

Noot, *n.* the ball struck in playing at 'shinty.' Cf. Knout.

Noozle, *v.* to nuzzle. Cf. Noosle.

Noozle, *v.* to squeeze; to press down with the knees. Cf. Knuzle.

Nor, *conj.* than; although; if; that; in *phr.* 'deil nor,' little would one care although.

Norawa', *n.* Norway.

Norawa'-wifie, *n.* the little auk.

Nordereys, *n.* the Northern Hebrides.

Norie, *n.* a whim, fancy.

Norie, *n.* the puffin.

†Norish, *n.* a nurse. Cf. Nourice.

Norit, *adv.* northward. Cf. Norward.

Norl, *n.* a lump; a protuberance.—*v.* to rise in lumps. Cf. Knurl.

Norland, *n.* the north country; a north country man.—*adj.* northern.

Norland-blue, *n.* Highland whisky.

Norlander, *n.* one who lives in the north.

Norland-Nettie, *n.* a Highland woman who bartered small articles of dress for wool.

Norlick, *n.* a tumour caused by a blow. Cf. Knorlack.

Norlin, *adj.* northern. Cf. Norland.

Norlins, *adv.* northwards.

Norloc, *n.* a large cyst or growth on a person's head. Cf. Knorlack.

Nor'loch trout, *n.* a jocular term formerly applied to a joint or leg of mutton.

Norrat, Norrart, *adv.* northward. Cf. Norward.

Norrie, *n.* a name for a sow.

Norrie, *n.* a whim. Cf. Norie.

North, *v.* used of the wind: to blow from the north.—*n.* in *phr.* 'Cock o' the North,' a name for the Dukes of Gordon.

Northart, *adj.* northward. Cf. Norward.

North-bye, *adv.* towards the north.

North-cock, *n.* the snow-bunting.

North-dancers, *n.* the aurora borealis.

Northern-hareld, *n.* the long-tailed duck.

Northlins, *adv.* northwards. Cf. Norlins.

Norward, *adv.* northward.—*adj.* northern.— *n.* the north, the direction of the north.

Nor-wastert, *n.* a bitter blast; anything of a cold, rude nature.

Norwegian teal, *n.* the scaup.

Nose, *n.* the projecting part of anything; a promontory; an immediate approach.—*v.* to rub with the nose; to suck. Cf. Neeze, Niz.

Nose-band, *n.* a loop of stout cord to which one end of a lead-stone or sinker is attached, the other being fastened to the fishing-line.

Nose-feast, *n.* a storm.

Nosel, *n.* a small socket or aperture.

Nose-nippin', *adj.* used of the weather: cold, freezing, 'snell.'

Nose-o'-wax, Nosy-wax, *n.* a pliable fellow; an easily imposed on simpleton.

Noseskip, *adj.* nasal.

Nose-specks, *n.* spectacles.

Nosetirl, Nostirle, *n.* a nostril.

Nose-wise, *adj.* having an acute sense of smell. Cf. Neis-wise.

Noshin, *n.* a notion.

Nosie-nappie, *n.* a nursery term for the nose.

Nossock, *n.* a good drink of liquor, a 'dram.'

Nost, *n.* noise; talking; speculation about any subject.

Not, *n.* a knob; a ball; a point, conclusion; a head. Cf. Note.

Not, *v. pret.* and *ppl.* needed.

Notable, *adj.* used of a woman: clever, industrious, capable.

Notandums, *n.* notes, memoranda.

†Notar, Nottar, *n.* a notary.

Not-a-will, *adv.* not voluntarily.

†Notch up, *v.* to reckon, count.

Note, *n.* a spoken remark; a saying; notice; a bank-note for £1.

Note, *n.* a knob, ball; a head; a point, conclusion. Cf. Knoit.

Note, *n.* necessity, need; occasion for.—*v.* to use, have occasion for; to enjoy; to need.

Noteless, *adj.* unknown; unnoted.

Noth, *n.* nothing; the cipher o.

Notice, *v.* to attend to, to take care of.

Notion, *n.* a fancy which may lead to love-making; a liking for; a whim; a pretence of being, doing, &c.

Notionate, *adj.* self-opinionated; fanciful.

Notour, *adj.* notorious; determinedly persistent.

Notourly, *adv.* notoriously.

Not-payment, *n.* non-payment.

Nott, *v. pret.* and *ppl.* needed.

Nott, *n.* a knob. Cf. Note.

Nott-and-loopwark, *n.* a process in weaving.

Notten, *ppl.* needed.

Nouchtie, *adj.* puny; trifling. Cf. Nochtie.

Noud, *n.* the gray gurnard. Cf. Knowd.

Nough, *v.* used of the wind: to blow gently.

Nought, *adj.* worthless.—*adv.* in no wise. Cf. Nocht.

Nought, *n.* cattle. Cf. Nowt.

Noup, *n.* a nob. Cf. Knop.

†Nourice, *n.* a nurse.

Nourice-fee, *n.* a wet-nurse's wages.

Nouricerie, *n.* a nursery.

Nourice-skap, -ship, *n.* the place of a nurse; nurse's wages.

†Nouse, *n.* sense; intelligence.

Nouse, *n.* nothing.

Nout, *n.* cattle. Cf. Nowt.

Novation, *n.* an innovation.

Novelles, *n.* novels, works of fiction; news.

Novels, *n.* tidings, news.

Novity, *n.* a novelty.

Now, *int.* an excl. of discontent.—*n.* the present time.

Now, *v.* used of the wind : to blow gently ; to talk foolishly.

Nowan, *ppl. adj.* silly, loquacious.

Now and talk, *v.* to talk loudly and in a silly manner. Cf. Nough.

Nowd, *n.* the gray gurnard. Cf. Knowd.

No weel, *adj.* unwell.

Nown, *adj.* own. Cf. Nain.

Nowt, *n.* cattle ; black cattle ; a stupid fellow, a lout.

Nowt, *v.* to injure ; to beat. Cf. Knoit.

Nowt-beast, *n.* an animal of the ox tribe.

Nowt-doctor, *n.* a veterinary surgeon.

Nowt-feet, *n.* calves' feet ; cow-heel.

Nowt-feet-jeel, *n.* calf-foot jelly.

Nowt-head, *n.* a blockhead ; a coward.

Nowther, *conj.* neither.

Nowt-herd, *n.* a cattle-herd ; a keeper of black cattle.

Nowt-hide, *n.* ox-leather.

Nowt-horn, *n.* an ox-horn, used as a trumpet.

Nowtit, *ppl. adj.* used of a potato : hollow in the heart.

Nowt-leather, *n.* ox-leather.

Nowt-market, *n.* a cattle-market.

Nowt-tath, *n.* grass growing luxuriantly from dung. Cf. Nolt-tath.

No-wyss, *adj.* foolish ; thoughtless ; deranged.

Noy, *n.* annoyance ; harm ; mischief.

Noyit, *ppl. adj.* vexed ; wrathful.

Nozle, *n.* a small socket or aperture. Cf. Nosel.

Nozzle, *v.* to nuzzle ; to nestle closely. Cf. Noosle.

Nub, *n.* a club-foot.

Nub-berry, *n.* the knout-berry. Cf. Nob-berry.

Nubbie, *n.* a staff with a hook or knob.—*adj.* short and plump ; dumpy ; having knobs. Cf. Knobby.

Nubbie, *n.* an unsocial person, worldly, yet lazy.

Nubblock, *n.* a knob ; an induration ; the swelling made by a blow or fall. Cf. Knublack.

Nuce, *adj.* destitute. Cf. Nace.

Nuck, *n.* a corner. Cf. Neuck.

Nuck, *v.* to notch ; to make nooks or angles ; to make verses the lines of which are not of equal length.

Nuckle, Nuckelt, *adj.* of a cow : newly calved. Cf. New-cal'.

Nucky, *n.* a small corner ; the tassel of a cap, the knob of a night-cap ; a fish-hook.

Nud, *n.* the pull of a fish on a fishing-line. Cf. Nug.

Nudge, *n.* a stroke or push with the knuckles ; a slight movement ; exertion ; grief, annoyance, pain.—*v.* to stir one's self ; to molest.

Nudge, *n.* a short, thick-set person. Cf. Knudge.

Nudie, *n.* a simpleton. Cf. Noddy.

Nufe, *adj.* neat, spruce. Cf. Noof.

Nug, Nugg, *v.* to nudge, jog with the elbow ; to nod.—*n.* the pull of a fish on a fishing-line. Cf. Nud.

Nuget, Nugget, *n.* a lump of anything ; a short, thick-set person. Cf. Knudge.

Nuif, *adj.* intimate.

Nuif, *adj.* neat, trim. Cf. Noof.

Nuik, *n.* a corner. Cf. Neuck.

Nuikey, *adj.* having corners.

Nuil, *n.* the navel. Cf. Nael.

†**Nuisant**, *adj.* hurtful.

Nuist, *n.* a large piece of anything.

Nuist, *v.* to eat continually, to be ever munching ; to beat, bruise.—*n.* a greedy, ill-disposed, ignorant person ; a blow. Cf. Noost.

Nule, *v.* to beat with the knuckles. Cf. Knool.

Nule, *n.* a knob. Cf. Knule.

Nule-kneed, *adj.* knock-kneed. Cf. Knule-kneed.

Null, *v.* to finish off ; to reduce to nothing.

Null, *n.* a small horn. Cf. Nool.

Null, *v.* to beat with the knuckles. Cf. Knool.

Nully, *v.* to nullify.

Numb, *adj.* of a boat : slow in sailing, almost motionless.

Number, Nummer, *n.* a statement of quantity.

Number-sorrow, *adj.* hardy ; rough, weakly. Cf. Umber-sorrow.

Numeration, *n.* the counting of money in paying it over.

Nump, *v.* to nibble.

Nun, *n.* the blue titmouse.

Nunce, *n.* a nuncio.

Nup, Nupe, *n.* the fruit of the cloudberry. Cf. Noop.

Nupe, *n.* a protuberance. Cf. Noop.

Nurday, *n.* New Year's Day.—*adj.* appropriate to New Year's Day.

Nure-gift, *n.* a New Year's gift or treat.

Nurg, Nurgle, *n.* a short, squat, savage man.

Nurgling, *n.* a person of cat-like disposition.

†**Nurice, Nurish**, *n.* a nurse. Cf. Nourice.

Nurl, Nurle, *n.* a knot ; a lump ; a tumour. —*v.* to strike so as to raise lumps ; to become knotty ; to rise in lumps. Cf. Knurl.

Nurling, *n.* a person of a 'nurring' or ill-tempered disposition.

Nurlock, *n.* a small, hard swelling, an induration on the skin.

Nurly, *adj.* lumpy, knotty, hard. Cf. Knurly.

Nurr, *v.* to snarl or growl like a dog ; to purr as a cat ; to fret, be discontented.—*n.* the sound made by a cat. Cf. Nirr.

Nurr, *n.* a hard knot of wood ; the ball used in the game of 'knur and spell.'

Nurr, *n.* a decrepit person.

Nurrilled, *ppl. adj.* shrunken, stunted in growth. Cf. Nirled.

Nurring, *ppl. adj.* feline, cat-like.

Nurris-braid, *adv.* working too eagerly to last long.

†Nurrish, *n.* a nurse. Cf. Nourice.

Nurrit, *n.* an insignificant or dwarfish person.

Nurse, *n.* a hardy tree planted to shelter a more tender one.

Nuse, *v.* to knead. Cf. Knuse.

Nut, *n.* the head. Cf. Nit.

Nut-brae, *n.* a 'brae' abounding in hazel-nut trees.

Nutting-tyne, *n.* a nut-hook.

Nutyon, *n.* a projecting knob on the foot. Cf. Noit.

Nuzzle, *v.* to root like a pig; to seize by the nose; used of an approaching storm : to assail. Cf. Noosle.

Nyaakit, *adj.* naked.

Nyaakit-like, *adj.* scantily clad.

Nyabok, *n.* a small, talkative person. Cf. Yabbock.

Nyaff, *n.* a trifle, a thing of no value; anything small of its kind; a dwarf. Cf. Knyaff.

Nyaff, *v.* to bark, yelp; to talk forwardly and frivolously; to argue snappishly; to trifle and be weakly in working; to take short steps.—*n.* a little dog's yelp; frivolous chatter; a wrangle over a trifle; a pert chatterer.

Nyaffet, *n.* a conceited little creature.

Nyaffing, *ppl. adj.* chattering; peevish; haggling; idle, insignificant; contemptible.— *n.* idle talk, prattle.

Nyaffle, *v.* to trifle away time; to potter about; to loiter; to take short steps.—*n.* a trifle; a thing of no value; anything very small.

Nyam, *v.* to chew.—*int.* a child's excl. over anything good to eat. Cf. Nam.

Nyamff, *adj.* hungry.

Nyap, *v.* to snap or bite at. Cf. Gnap.

Nyaph, *n.* the female nymphæ, &c.

Nyarb, *v.* to fret; to be discontented.—*n.* a peevish complaint, a fretful quarrel.

Nyarg, *v.* to jeer; to nag. Cf. Narg.

Nyargie, *adj.* jeering.

Nyargle, *v.* to wrangle.—*n.* one who loves to wrangle or dispute.

Nyarr, *v.* to snarl as a dog; to cry as an angry cat; to find fault peevishly.—*n.* a dog's growl; peevishness; peevish fault-finding.

Nyat, *v.* to strike sharply with the knuckles. —*n.* a smart stroke with the knuckles.

Nyatrie, *adj.* peevish, petulant. Cf. Gnattery, Natrie.

Nyatt, *n.* a person of short temper, a gnat. Cf. Nat.

Nyatter, *v.* to chatter; to speak fretfully; to scold; to tease; to gossip in an unfriendly fashion; to gnash the teeth like a trapped rat; to quarrel, wrangle. — *n.* peevish chatter. Cf. Gnatter.

Nyatter, *v.* to rain slightly with a high wind.

Nyatterie, *adj.* cross-tempered.

Nyauchle, *n.* a dwarf. Cf. Nauchle.

Nyaukit, *adj.* naked.

Nyawn, *adj.* own. Cf. Nain.

Nyber, *n.* a neighbour. Cf. Neighbour.

Nyim, Nyimmie, *n.* a very small piece. Cf. Nimp.

Nyirb, *n.* great peevishness. Cf. Nyarb.

Nyirr, *v.* to snarl as a dog. Cf. Nyarr.

Nyit, *v.* to strike sharply with the knuckles. Cf. Nyat.

Nyle, *n.* the navel.

Nyod, *int.* a modified form of 'God,' used as an excl. or oath.

Nyow, *v.* to curb; to maul. Cf. New.

Nyow, *adj.* new.

Nyowan, *n.* a beating.

Nyowmost, *adj.* nethermost, lowest. Cf. Newmost.

Nyse, *v.* to pommel. Cf. Knuse.

Nyte, *v.* to strike smartly; to rap. Cf. Knyte.

Nyuckfit, *n.* the snipe.

Nyuk, *n.* a corner, nook. Cf. Neuck.

Nyum, *v.* to chew. Cf. Nyam.

Nyum-nyum, *int.* a child's excl. of pleasure in anything good to eat. Cf. Nam-nam.

Nyurr, *v.* to snarl as a dog. Cf. Nurr, Nyarr.

O, *n.* a grandson, grandchild. Cf. Oye.

O', *prep.* of. Cf. Of.

O', *prep.* on. Cf. On.

O, *int.* oh!

Oachening, *n.* early dawn; the night just before daybreak.

Oaf, *n.* an elf; an animal whose face is so covered with hair that it can scarcely see.— *v.* to walk stupidly. Cf. Ouph.

Oaff, *adj.* decrepit; worn down with disease.

Oak, *n.* an oaken cudgel. Cf. Aik.

Oak-eggar, *n.* a moth.

Oakie, *n.* the common guillemot.

Oak-nut, *n.* an acorn.

Oam, *n.* steam, vapour; a blast of warm air; a close, warm air.—*v.* to blow with a warm, close air. Cf. Aem.

Oar, *v.* to row; to ferry.

Oast, *n.* a dug-out place above high-water into which a boat is drawn when it is to be some time on shore.

Oat-fowl, *n.* the snow-bunting.

Oath, *n.* in *phr.* to 'gie one's oath,' to take an oath.—*v.* to swear to anything.

Oat-land, *n.* land for growing oats.

Oat-leave, *n.* in old husbandry: the crop after bear or barley. Cf. Aitliff.

Oats and beans and barley, *n.* a singing-game.

Oatseed, *n.* oats for seed; the time of sowing oats. Cf. Aitseed.

Oat-skiter, *n.* the wild angelica, through the hollow stems of which children shoot oats.

O ay, *int.* O yes!

Obedience, *n.* obeisance; a bow; a curtsy.

Obeisance, *n.* subjection.

Obering, *n.* a hint; an inkling of something important.

†Obfusque, *v.* to darken.

Obit, *n.* a particular length of slate.

Objeck, *n.* a miserable creature; one diseased or deformed; an objection.—*v.* to object.

Obleegement, *n.* a favour, service.

Obleish, *v.* to oblige.

Obleisment, Obleistment, *n.* an obligation, bond.

Obleist, Oblist, *ppl.* come under obligation.

Oblish, *v.* to oblige.

Oblishment, *n.* an obligation.

Obscure, *adj.* secret; concealed; clandestine.—*v.* to conceal, hide.

Observe, *n.* an observation, remark.—*v.* to guard.

Obstic, *n.* an obstacle; an objection.

Obstrapulosity, *n.* obstreperousness, restiveness.

Obstrapulous, Obstropalous, *adj.* obstreperous; unmanageable, refractory.

Obtemper, *v.* to obey; to fulfil an injunction, &c.

Occasion, *n.* cause, reason; necessity; the dispensation of the Sacrament of the Lord's Supper.

Occupier, *n.* one engaged in business, work, &c.

Occupy, *v.* to labour, work.

Occur, *n.* interest, usury. Cf. Ocker.

Och, *int.* an excl. of sorrow, &c.

Ochaine, Ochanee, Och-hey, Och-hey-hum, Och-hone, Och-hon-a-rie, Och-hon-o-chrie, Och-how, *ints.* excls. of sorrow, &c.

Ochening, *n.* the night just before dawn. Cf. Oachening.

Ochie, *n.* in *phr.* 'neither eechie nor ochie,' absolutely nothing.

Ocht, *n.* aught; anything; a whit; a person of consequence.—*adj.* any. Cf. Aucht.

Ocht, *v.* ought. Cf. Aucht.

Ocht, *ppl.* possessed of. Cf. Aucht.

Ochtlins, *adv.* in the least degree; in any degree.—*n.* anything at all.

Ocker, Ockar, *n.* interest, usury.—*v.* to increase, add to.

Ockerer, *n.* a usurer; a money-changer.

Ock-name, *n.* a distinguishing name or 'to-name.' Cf. Eke-name.

Od, *n.* a disguised form of 'God,' a minced oath, an expletive, used in various combinations.

Odd, *adj.* occasional; sequestered, solitary. —*adv.* singularly, out of the usual course, fashion, &c.—*n.* a point of land; a handicap to a weaker player.

Odd-come-shortlies, *n.* an occasion close at hand.

Odd-like, *adj.* strange-looking.

Odd or even, *n.* a guessing-game played with small articles in a closed hand.

Odds, *n.* consequence; change.

Oddses, *n.* differences.

Odd time, *n.* leisure; a chance time.

Odious, *adj.* exceeding. — *adv.* exceedingly, used as an intensive.

Odiously, *adv.* exceedingly, terribly.

Od-zookers, *int.* an excl. of surprise, &c.

Oe, *n.* a small island.

Oe, *n.* a grandchild. Cf. Oye.

Oen, *n.* an oven.

O'er, *prep.* over; upon; on account of; concerning; across, on the other side of; past, beyond.—*adv.* across; off; asleep; too, too much; very. — *adj.* upper, higher; superior in power, &c.—*v.* to cross; to go, jump, run, swim, &c., across; to endure, surmount, survive; to recover from; with *refl. pron.* to manage for one's self, control one's self.

O'er-abürd, *adv.* overboard.

O'er-anent, *prep.* over against.

O'erback, *n.* a cow that has failed to have a calf when three years old.

O'er-bladed, *ppl. adj.* hard-driven in pursuit.

O'erblaw, *v.* used of a storm: to blow over; to cover with driven snow.

O'er-Bogie, -Boggie, *n.* a marriage not celebrated by a minister.—*v.* to contract such a marriage.

O'er-brim, *v.* to overflow.

O'er-by, *adj.* neighbouring; past and gone. —*adv.* at no great distance.—*n.* a place not far off.

O'ercast, *v.* to overturn; to cloud over; to overlay; to recover from, as an illness or wound.—*n.* an outcast, castaway.

O'erclad, *ppl adj.* overspread, thickly covered.

O'ercome, *v.* to come or cross over; to surpass; to prove too much for, baffle; to

revive from a swoon; to recover from.—*n.*
overplus; the refrain of a song, the burden
of a discourse or speech; a hackneyed
phrase, or one frequently used by a person;
a voyage, a journey, passage across the sea;
outcome, issue.

O'er-coup, *v.* to upset, capsize; to retch.

O'er-crow, *v.* to overcome; to exult over; to
overlook a view, house, &c.

O'er-crown, *n.* a particular kind of woman's
cap or 'mutch,' so cut as not to require a
crown, and rendering a bonnet unnecessary.

O'er-driven, *ppl. adj.* used of persons: overworked, oppressed with work.

O'er-end, *v.* to set on end; to turn over end-
wise; to be turned topsy-turvy.—*adj.* erect,
upright, on end.

O'er-fa'in, *n.* the time of childbirth, a
woman's confinement.

O'er-foughten, -fochen, *adj.* over-exhausted;
quite prostrate.

O'er-fret, *adj.* decorated all over.

O'er-gae, *v.* to go over; used of time: to
elapse; to become overdue; to overrun;
to overburden, exhaust; to domineer over,
oppress; to superintend. Cf. O'er-gang.

O'er-gaff, *v.* to cloud over; to overcast.

O'er-gane, *ppl. adj.* past and gone.

O'er-gang, *v.* to overrun, overspread, to outrun; to elapse; to exceed; to surpass;
to master, overpower; to superintend.—
n. a right of way; oppression; superintendence; an overseer; the director of a
gang of workmen; a coat of paint, plaster,
&c.; a scraping, raking, harrowing.

O'er-ganger, *n.* an overseer, superintendent,
&c.

O'er-gangin, *ppl. adj.* unmanageable; domineering.

O'er-gaun, *n.* a passage, crossing; a going or
falling over; a falling asleep; a coat of
paint, &c.; a washing, scouring, &c.; a
raking, harrowing, &c.—*ppl. adj.* unmanageable.

O'ergaun-rapes, *n.* the vertical ropes keeping
down the thatch of a stack.

O'er-get, *v.* to overtake, come up with; to
overreach.

O'er-gilt, *adj.* gilded over.

O'er-grip, *v.* to strain, overstrain.

O'er-gyaun, *n.* a fault-finding.

O'er-hand, *n.* the upper hand, mastery.

O'er-harl, *v.* to oppress; to treat with
severity, to 'haul over the coals'; to turn
over; to examine roughly.

O'er-heeze, *v.* to elate unduly.

O'er-heid, *adv.* overhead; wholly; on an
average; taken in the gross.

O'erhie, O'erhigh, O'er-hye, *v.* to overtake.

O'erhing, *v.* to overhang.

O'er-hip, *n.* a way of fetching a blow with the
sledge-hammer over the arm.

O'erlay, *n.* a cravat, neckcloth; a kind of
hem, in which one part of the cloth is laid
over the other.—*v.* to belabour, drub; to
hem in such a way that one part of the
cloth is laid over the other.

O'er-leat, -leet, *n.* something that is folded
over another.

O'er-ling, *adj.* covering over.

O'er-loup, -lop, *n.* a trespass; excess, occasional self-indulgence; the stream-tide at
the change of the moon; an occasional
trespass of cattle; the act of leaping over a
fence.—*v.* to overleap.

O'er-lyin, *n.* in *phr.* 'at the o'erlyin,' ready to
lie or fall down from fatigue.

O'er-mills, *n.* remnants; the remains of
anything.

O'ermist, *adj.* uppermost; farthest off.

O'er mony, *phr.* too many; too strong; more
than a match.

O'er nice, *adj.* too fastidious.

O'er ocht, *phr.* beyond comparison.

O'er-peer, *n.* one who excels; a superior.

O'erplush, *n.* surplus, overplus.

O'er-put, *v.* to recover from; to survive.

O'er-qualled, *ppl. adj.* overrun, overspread.

O'er-rack, -rax, *v.* to overreach; to overstrain.

O'er-rin, *v.* to run over; used of animals: to
multiply too greatly.

O'ers, *n.* excess.

O'er-sea, *adj.* foreign.

O'ersee, *v.* to manage, superintend; to overlook, pass over, forget.

O'erseen, *ppl. adj.* watched over when dying.

O'erset, *v.* to upset, overturn, disorder; to
upset mentally.—*ppl. adj.* deranged.

O'ershot, *n.* the surplus, remainder.

O'er-side, *adv.* overboard, over the side.

O'erslide, *v.* to slide or glide past.

O'erspade, *v.* to cut land into narrow trenches.
—*n.* heaping the earth upon an equal quantity of land not raised.

O'er-spang, *v.* to pursue; to overleap; to
bound over.

O'er-stent, -stented, *ppl. adj.* exorbitant,
overcharged.

O'erswak, *n.* the rush or noise of a wave
breaking on the beach.

O'er-syle, *v.* to cover, conceal; to beguile.

O'ertack, *v.* to overtake.

O'ertake, *v.* to take aback, put to confusion;
to overcome; to succeed in a task though
pressed for time; to fetch one a blow; in
pass. to become drunk.

O'ertap, *v.* to overtop.

O'er-tirvie, *v.* to overcome; to upset.

O'er-tramp, *v.* to oppress: to trample on.

O'er-tree, *n.* the single handle or stilt of an Orcadian plough.

O'erturn, *n.* the refrain or chorus of a song ; an upheaval, revolution, change of circumstances, &c. ; used of money : turning over for profit in business.

O'er-wales, *n.* the refuse of anything from which the best is taken.

O'erway, *n.* the upper or higher way.

O'er-week, *v.* to overstay one's welcome by not departing in the week of arrival.

O'er-weekit, *ppl. adj.* used of meat : kept too long.

O'erweill, *v.* to exceed.

O'er wi', *adj.* done with, finished with.

O'er-woman, *n.* a woman chosen to give a casting vote in a cause in which the arbiters are equally divided.

O'er-word, *n.* a word or phrase frequently repeated ; the chorus or burden of a song.

O'eryeed, *v. pret.* overwent, overpassed.

Oey, *n.* a grandchild. Cf. Oye.

Of, *prep.* from, out of ; on ; during ; on account of ; as regards ; at ; used of time : to, before.

Off, *prep.* beyond, past ; without ; from.—*adv.* out of.—*adj.* committed to memory.—*v.* to go off ; with *with*, to doff. Cf. Aff.

Off-cap, *n.* a salutation by lifting the cap.

Off-come, *n.* an apology ; a subterfuge, pretext.

Offend, *v.* to injure.

Offer, *v.* to attempt ; to show promise or intention.—*n.* choice, disposal ; an attempt ; a projecting or overhanging bank that has been undermined by the action of a stream.

Offering, *n.* a small quantity ; an imperfect performance.

Off-faller, *n.* an apostate ; one who falls away.

Off-falling, *n.* defection ; a declension in health or appearance ; moral declension.

Offgang, *n.* the firing of a cannon, &c.

Off-going, *n.* death ; departure from life ; the firing of a cannon.

Offhand, *adv.* and *adj.* extempore. Cf. Aff-hand.

Officiar, *n.* an officer ; an official.

Offish, *n.* an office.

Offishness, *n.* reserve.

Offnin, *adv.* often.

Off-put, *n.* an excuse ; postponement.

Off-set, *n.* a recommendation. Cf. Aff-set.

Offskep, *n.* the utmost boundary of a landscape.

Ofi, *n.* an outhouse ; a privy.

O-fish, *n.* the cuttle-fish. Cf. Hose-fish.

Oft, *adj.* frequent. Cf. Aft.

Ogertful, *adj.* nice, squeamish ; affecting delicacy of taste.

Oggit, *ppl. adj.* surfeited. Cf. Ug.

Oghie, *n.* in *phr.* 'neither eechie nor oghie,' absolutely nothing. Cf. Ochie.

Ogie, Oggie, *n.* the open space before the fireplace of a kiln ; a 'killogie.' Cf. Logie.

Oglet, *n.* a theodolite, as something to spy with.

Ogress, *n.* a giantess with large, fiery eyes, supposed to feed on children.

Ogrie, *n.* a giant with the same character and propensities as the 'ogress.'

Ohn, *neg. pref.* equivalent to un-.

Ohon, *int.* alas ! Cf. Ochanee.

Oie, Oi, *n.* a grandchild. Cf. Oye.

Oil, *v.* to soothe, comfort ; with *lug*, to flatter in speech.

Oilan-auk, *n.* the great northern diver. Cf. Allan-hawk.

Oilcoat, *n.* an oilskin coat.

Oil-muggie, *n.* a vessel for holding oil.

Oil of aik, *n.* a beating with an oaken cudgel.

Oil of hazel, *n.* a beating.

Oil of malt, *n.* whisky ; malt liquor.

Oily-gaun, *adj.* plausible, flattering.

Oily pig, *n.* an oil-jar.

Oindroch, *n.* a weak, puny creature ; a coward. Cf. Undoch.

Oisie, *int.* an excl. of wonder, or as a call to attention. Cf. Oyse.

†**Oist,** *n.* a host, an army.

Old, *adj.* eldest. Cf. Auld.

Old-mouthed, *adj.* toothless from age.

Oleit, Olied, Olicht, Olit, Ollath, *adj.* prompt, willing ; active, nimble ; sprightly ; handsome. Cf. Evleit.

Ome, *n.* steam, vapour. Cf. Oam.

Omne-gatherum, -gaddrum, *n.* a miscellaneous collection ; a medley ; the unincorporated craftsmen of a burgh.

On, *neg. pref.* generally used with *ppls.*

On, *prep.* on to, upon ; in ; about ; regarding ; of ; for ; to ; at ; against ; by means of.—*adv.* continually ; agoing ; on the fire, cooking, boiling ; with speed, force of forward movement ; in drink, tipsy ; with *with*, courting, keeping company.—*v.* with *with*, to put on.

Onbeast, *n.* a monster ; a ravenous beast ; a noxious member of human society ; a raging toothache.

Onbethankit, *ppl. adj.* unthanked.

Onbraw, *adj.* ugly ; unbecoming ; unhandsome. Cf. Braw.

Onbrawness, *n.* ugliness.

Oncarry, Oncairy, *n.* a stir, bustle ; frolic, merriment ; flighty conduct.

Oncarryings, *n.* behaviour, 'ongoings,' 'oncarries.'

Oncast, *n.* a misfortune, burden ; the first row of loops in knitting ; the casting of a row of loops.—*v.* to begin knitting with an 'oncast.'

Once-, One's-errand, *n.* a special errand.—*adv.* purposely, expressly.

Oncome, *n.* a fall of rain or snow; the beginning of any business or movement, as an assault; an attack of disease the cause of which is unknown.

Oncost, *n.* expense before profit; extra expense.—*adj.* causing extra expense.

Ondeemas, *adj.* incalculable; extraordinary; incredible; what cannot be reckoned. Cf. Undemis.

Ondeemously, *adv.* excessively.

Onding, *n.* a heavy fall of rain or snow; an attack; oppression; turmoil.—*v.* to rain heavily. Cf. Ding.

Ondingin', *n.* an 'onding' of rain or snow; a torrent of words.

Ondo, *v.* to undo.

Ondocht, *n.* a weak, puny creature. Cf. Undoch.

Ondraw, *n.* a wrapper or garment for occasional use.

One, *adj.* only.—*n.* a degree, step; a blow, rebuff; some one. Cf. Ae, Ane.

One-erie, *n.* a child's word in counting out rhymes for regulating games. Cf. Anery.

Oner, *prep.* under.

Onerosity, *n.* the payment of an 'onerous' price.

Onerous, *adj.* not gratuitous; sufficiently advantageous; implying the payment of a sufficient price.

Onfa', Onfall, *n.* a heavy fall of snow or rain; a misfortune; an onslaught, attack; a mysterious disease.

Onfa'en, *adj.* unfallen.

Onfarrant, *adj.* senseless; rude. Cf. Unfarrant.

Onfeel, Onfeelin, *adj.* unpleasant; disagreeable; uncomfortable; rough, not smooth. Cf. Unfeel.

Onfeirie, *adj.* infirm; unwieldy. Cf. Unfeiroch, Unfiery.

Onfrack, *adj.* inactive, not alert.

Ongae, *n.* stir; fuss; 'to-do.'

Ongäines, Ongauns, Ongyauns, *n.* 'ongoings'; procedure; conduct, behaviour; fuss.

Ongang, *n.* the starting of machinery; proceedings; conduct.

Ongangings, *n.* 'ongoings'; conduct, behaviour.

Ongetting, *n.* welfare, manner of getting on.

Ongoings, *n.* proceedings, conduct, behaviour.

Ongraithe, *v.* to unharness.

Onhing, *n.* patient waiting; a mean and lazy staying in a place.

Onie, Ony, *adj.* any.

Onie-gate, *adv.* any way; in any place or direction.

Onie-gates, *n.* used in the game of marbles:

the claim of a player to play at any part of the ring.

Oniehow, *adv.* anyhow; at any rate.

Oniewhaur, *adv.* anywhere.

Onken, *v.* not to know or recognize. Cf. Unken.

Onkennable, *adj.* unknowable; immemorial.

Onkent, *adj.* unknown. Cf. Unkenned.

Onker, *n.* a small portion of land.

Onlat, *n.* the setting of machinery in motion; the allowing water to flow to move machinery.

Onlauchful, *adj.* unlawful.

Onlay, *n.* a fall of snow or rain; a surfeit.

Onlayin', *n.* castigation, the act of beating severely.

Onless, *prep.* except.

Onlife, *adj.* alive.

Onlouping, *n.* the act of mounting a horse.

Onmarrow, *n.* a partner in business, a sharer in a concern.

Onnawars, *adv.* unawares, unexpectedly.

Onnerstan', *v.* to understand.

Onnersteed, *ppl.* understood.

On o', On on, *prep.* on upon.

Onpricket, *adj.* used of cattle: without 'pricking' or 'startling' in hot weather.

Onputting, *n.* dress, clothes.

Onricht, *adj.* dishonest; unjust. Cf. Unricht.

Onset, *n.* an outhouse; a farmstead.

Onset, *v.* to attack.

Onsettin', *adj.* not handsome, ugly.

Onsleepit, *adj.* not having slept.

Onstanding, *adj.* determined.

Onstead, *n.* a farmstead; a homestead.

Ontack, Ontak, *n.* a bustle, fuss; airs; assumption.

Ontakin', *n.* approach; beginning.—*ppl. adj.* taking on airs; taking or buying on credit; reckless in expenditure, dishonest.

Onter, *v.* used of horses: to rear.

Onter, *v.* to venture. Cf. Aunter.

Ontill, *prep.* on to, upon; unto.

Onto, *prep.* 'ontill.'

Ontron, *n.* evening. Cf. Orntren.

On-uptaken, *ppl. adj.* not taken up.

Onwaiter, *n.* a patient waiter for a future good.

Onwaiting, *adj.* patiently waiting.—*n.* patient waiting.

Onwal, *n.* interest on money, profit on capital. Cf. Annual.

Onweetin, *adj.* unknowing; involuntary; unknown.

Onwittins, *adv.* without being privy to; without the knowledge of.

Onwyne, *n.* the left hand.

Onwyner, *n.* the foremost ox on the left hand in ploughing.

Onwyte, *n.* an expectant wait; waiting on a sick person or on one dying.

Onwytin, *adj.* and *n.* 'onwaiting.'

Oo', *n.* wool.

Oo, *pron.* we.

Oo', *int.* O ! oh !

Oo, *n.* a grandson. Cf. **Oye**.

Oo ay, *int.* O yes !

Oobit, *n.* a woolly worm, or long-haired caterpillar ; a hairy, unkempt person.

Ooder, *n.* an exhalation. Cf. **Ouder**.

Oof, **Ooff**, *n.* an elf ; a lout ; a weak, harmless person.—*v.* to walk stupidly.

Ooff, *v.* used of peaty soil : to cause oats to die out before ripening.—*adj.* decrepit ; worn down by disease. Cf. **Oaff**.

Oof-looking, *adj.* wearing a stupid look.

Ooin', *n.* and *ppl. adj.* wooing.

Ooin', *n.* woollen material.—*adj.* woollen.

Ook, *n.* a week.

Ook-day, *n.* a week-day.

Ookly, *adj.* weekly.

Ool, *v.* to treat harshly ; to treat as an oddity.

Oolat, **Oolert**, *n.* an owl ; an owlet. Cf. **Hoolet**.

Ooly, *n.* oil. Cf. **Ulzie**.

Oom, *n.* steam, vapour. Cf. **Oam**.

Ooman, *n.* a woman.

Oon, *n.* a wound.

Oon, *neg. pref.* un-. Cf. **Ohn**, **On**.

Oon, *n.* an oven. Cf. **Oen**.

Oon, *adj.* addled ; applied to an egg without a shell.

Oondisjeested, *ppl. adj.* undigested.

Oondomious, **Oondeemis**, *adj.* incalculable. Cf. **Undemis**.

Oon egg, *n.* a wind egg, a soft egg without a shell.

Oonerstan', *v.* to understand.

Oonfashed, *adj.* untroubled.

Oonfersell, *adj.* inactive, inert ; not lively.

Oonleedful, *adj.* lacking in diligence or industry.

Oonlicklie, *adj.* unlikely.

Oonpatientfu', *adj.* impatient.

Oonslocken, **Oonslockened**, *adj.* unslaked, unquenched.

Oontimeous, *adj.* untimely, unseasonable.

Oonweelness, *n.* an illness.

Oonwutty, *adj.* wanting wits. Cf. **Unwitty**.

Oop, *v.* to splice, to bind with thread or cord ; to unite.

Oor, *poss. adj.* our.

Oor, *pron.* and *v.* we are.

Oor, *n.* hour.

Oor, **Ool**, *v.* to creep, cower, crouch ; to move slowly and feebly.

Oora, *adj.* odd ; occasional. Cf. **Orra**.

Oorat, **Oorit**, *ppl. adj.* cold, miserable, shivering ; weak, drooping.

Oorat, *n.* a wart. Cf. **Rat**, **Wrat**.

Oore, *adv.*, *prep.*, and *conj.* ere. Cf. **Or**.

Oorie, *adj.* 'eerie'; apprehensive ; superstitious, afraid, melancholy, depressing, dismal ; languid, sickly-looking, drooping ; bleak ; chilly.

Oorie-like, *adj.* looking much fatigued.

Oorieness, *n.* chilliness.

Ooriesum, *adj.* timorous.

Oorlich, *adj.* cold, chilly, 'oorie.' Cf. **Urluch**.

Oose, *n.* a house.

Ooss, *n.* fibrous stuff put into an inkstand to prevent spilling. Cf. **Ooze**.

Oot, *adv.* out. Cf. **Out**.

Ootaltie, *n.* anything that sets off the person.

Ootbrack, *n.* an eruption ; a quarrel.

Oot-cast, *n.* a quarrel.

Ooten, *prep.* out of.

Ooterin, **Ootrin**, *adj.* outward, from without.

Ooth, *n.* value, worth.

Ootlie, *n.* outlay.

Ootlin, *n.* a stranger; an outcast ; the despised or neglected member of a family. Cf. **Outlin**.

Ootmaist, *adj.* outermost.

Oot-turn, *n.* the yield of grain in threshing.

Ootwyle, *n.* refuse.—*v.* to select. Cf. **Outwale**.

Oowen, *adj.* woollen.

Ooy, *adj.* woolly.

Ooze, *n.* the nap or 'caddis' that falls from yarn, cloth, &c. ; cotton or silk ; fibrous stuff put into an inkstand to prevent the ink from spilling.

Oozlie, *adj.* slovenly, unkempt ; broken-down ; miserable ; dark - featured.—*adv.* in a slovenly way.

Oozlie-looking, *adj.* slovenly in appearance.

Oozlieness, *n.* slovenliness.

Ope, *v.* to open.—*adj.* open.

Open, *adj.* used of the weather : mild, without frost or snow ; of a sow or heifer : unspayed.—*n.* an opening, a hole ; the front suture of the skull. Cf. **Apen**.

Open-steek, *n.* a peculiar kind of stitch in sewing.—*adj.* having like ornaments in architecture.

Open the mouth, *v.* to begin to preach as a licentiate of the Church.

Opentie, *n.* an opening.

Operate, *v.* a legal term ; in *phr.* to 'operate payment,' to procure or enforce payment.

Opery, *n.* belongings, tackle, miscellaneous property.

Opignorate, *v.* a legal term ; to pledge.

Opine, *n.* opinion.

Opingyon, *n.* opinion.

Oppone, *v.* to oppose; to bring forward evidence against a prisoner at the bar.

†**Opprobry**, *n.* reproach ; opprobrious language ; scornings.

Optics, *n.* eyes.

Or, *prep.* before; until.—*conj.* than; before; till.

Ora, *adj.* odd; occasional. Cf. Orra.

Orange-fin, *n.* sea-trout fry in the Tweed.

Oranger, *n.* an orange.

Orchin, *n.* a hedgehog. Cf. Urchin.

Orchle, *n.* a porch.

Ord, *n.* a steep hill or mountain.

Ordeen, *v.* to ordain; to design for a special purpose.

Order, *v.* to put in order.—*n.* in *phr.* 'to take order,' to adopt measures for bringing under proper regulations, or to secure a certain result.

Orderly, *adv.* regularly.

Ordinances, *n.* the administration of the Lord's Supper and the services connected with it.

Ordinar, Ordnar, *adj.* ordinary; usual.—*adv.* ordinarily, fairly, rather.—*n.* custom, habit; usual condition or health.

Ordinarie, *n.* one's usual course, health, &c.

Ordinary, *n.* a 'Lord Ordinary' in the Court of Session.

Ore, *conj.* before. Cf. Or.

Orf, *n.* a puny, contemptible creature. Cf. Urf.

Orhie, *v.* to overtake. Cf. O'erhie.

Orie, *adj.* apprehensive; dismal; chilly. Cf. Oorie.

Origin, *n.* an orange. Cf. Oranger.

Original sin, *n.* debt on an estate to which one succeeds; the living proofs of youthful incontinence; a cant term.

†**Orishen,** *n.* a reproachful term for a savagely behaved person, an 'Orson.' Cf. Oshen.

†**Orlache, Orlage, Orloge,** *n.* a clock; the dial-plate of a clock.

Orlang, *n.* a complete year.

Orlie, *adj.* relating to Orleans.

Orling, *n.* a dwarfish person or child. Cf. Urling.

Or'nar, *n.* one's usual course of health. Cf. Ordinar.

Orntren, *n.* evening; the repast between dinner and supper.

Orp, *v.* to weep convulsively; to fret, repine; to chide habitually.

Orphant, *n.* an orphan.

†**Orphelin,** *n.* an orphan.

Orpie-leaf, *n.* orpine.

Orpiet, Orpit, *ppl. adj.* fretful, querulous.

†**Orpy, Orpey, Orpie,** *n.* orpine, a species of house-leek.

Orra, Orrie, Orro, Orrow, *adj.* unmatched, odd, without a fellow; occasional, doing odd jobs; having no settled occupation; spare, superfluous; unoccupied, not engaged; sundry; idle, low, worthless, vagabond, disreputable; out of the common,

strange.—*adv.* oddly; unusually.—*n.* what is left over; a fragment, scrap; in *pl.* odds and ends; superfluous things.

Orra-beast, *n.* an odd horse used in doing odd jobs.

Orraest, *adj.* most 'orra.'

Orra-fowk, *n.* beggars, tramps.

Orra-lad, -loun, *n.* a boy employed on odd jobs.

Orrals, Orrels, *n.* anything left over; refuse; odds and ends.

Orra-man, *n.* a farm-labourer who does odd jobs and not stated work.

Orraster, *n.* a low, vagabond fellow; a term of contempt.

Ort, *v.* to pick out the best part of food and leave the rest; to throw away provender; to crumble or waste food; to reject anything; to give away a daughter in marriage without regarding the order of seniority of the others.—*n.* in *pl.* refuse.

Orzelon, *n.* a kind of apple. Cf. Oslin.

Oshen, *n.* a person of mean disposition.

Osler, *n.* an ostler.

Oslin, *n.* a species of apple.

Osnaburgh, Osenbrug, *n.* coarse linen cloth or ticking.

Ostensible, *adj.* used of persons: prominent, conspicuous in public life.

Ostentation, *n.* too much of any article.

†**Ostler,** *n.* an innkeeper. Cf. Hostler.

Osy, *n.* an easy-going, good-tempered person. Cf. Easy-osy.

O' them, *phr.* some of them.

O'-them-upo'-them, *n.* cold flummery, used instead of milk, with boiled flummery; the same substance used at once both as meat and drink, or in a solid and fluid state.

Other, *adj.* additional, successive, another; next, succeeding.—*pron.* each other, one another.—*adv.* otherwise, else.—*n.* other way or thing. Cf. Ither.

Other gaits, *adv.* in another direction.

Othersome, *pron.* some others.

Otherwheres, *adv.* elsewhere.

Otherwhiles, *adv.* at other times.

Otter, *n.* the barb of a fish-hook; an illegal fishing implement used by poachers.

Otter-grains, *n.* the dung of the otter.

Otterline, *n.* a cow in calf in her second year. Cf. Etterlin.

Ou, *n.* wool.

Ou, *int.* oh!—*v.* to ejaculate; to say 'ou!'

Ou ay, *int.* oh yes!

Oubit, *n.* a hairy caterpillar. Cf. Oobit.

Ouch, *int.* an excl. of pain, disgust, &c.—*n.* the sound of a forcible expulsion of the breath. Cf. Ough.

Ouchin', *ppl. adj.* used of the wind: sighing, blowing gently.

Oucht, *n.* anything. Cf. Ocht.

Ouchtlans, *adv.* in any respect. Cf. Oughtlins.

Ouder, *n.* a haze, light mist; flickering exhalations from the ground on a warm day.

Ouer, *prep.* over. Cf. O'er.

Ouf, *n.* an elf; a lout. Cf. Ouph.

Ouf-dog, *n.* a wolf-dog.

Ouff, *v.* to bark.—*n.* the sound of a dog barking.

Oufish, *adj.* elvish.

Oufish-like, *adj.* elf-like.

Gug, *v.* to surfeit; to loathe; to disgust. Cf. Ug.

Ough, *int.* ugh! an excl. of pain or disgust. —*n.* the sound of forcible expulsion of breath.

Ough, *v.* used of the wind: to blow gently.

Ought, *v.* to own. Cf. Aucht.

Oughtlins, *adv.* at all; in any degree.—*n.* anything at all. Cf. Ochtlins.

Oughtlins, *n.* anything that ought to be done, duty.

Ougsum, *adj.* horrible. Cf. Ugsome.

Ouk, *n.* a week.

Oukly, *adj.* weekly.

Oulie, *n.* oil. Cf. Ulzie.

Ouncle-weights, *n.* weights formerly used about farmhouses, generally of sea-stones of various sizes, regulated to some standard.

Oup, *v.* to splice; to warp round a joint or break. Cf. Oop.

Ouph, Ouphe, *n.* an elf; a lout. Cf. Ouf.

Ouphish, *adj.* elfin; loutish.

Ouphish-like, *adj.* elf-like.

Our, Oure, *v.* to overawe.—*prep.* over, beyond. Cf. O'er.

Ourback, *n.* a cow which has not a calf when three years old. Cf. O'erback.

Ourheid, *adj.* untidy.

Ourie, Oury, *adj.* chill; sad. Cf. Oorie.

Ouriness, *n.* sadness, melancholy.

Ourlay, *n.* a cravat.

Ourman, *n.* an arbiter, overman.

Oursel's, *refl. pron.* ourselves.

Ourthort, *prep.* athwart.

Ourword, *n.* a refrain. Cf. O'erword.

Ouse, *n.* an ox.

Ouse-, Oussen-bow, *n.* a wooden collar used for draught oxen.

Ouse-John, *n.* a cowherd.

Ousel, *n.* the blackbird.

Ousel, *n.* the sacrament of the Lord's Supper.

Ousen-milk, *n.* flummery unboiled, used as milk.

Ousen-staw, *n.* an ox-stall.

Ouster, *n.* the armpit. Cf. Oxter.

Out, *adv.* used of a meeting, &c.: dispersed; over; projecting, curving outwards; current, published, circulating; aloud; fully; throughout; finished.—*adj.* gone, empty;

worn-out, torn; mistaken, in error; extinguished, gone out; not in friendship.— *prep.* beyond; along; without, free from.— *n.* in *pl.* those out of office, &c.—*phr.* ' outs and ins,' the whole details, particulars.

Out, *v.* to eject, oust; with *with,* to pull or draw out, to tell out, divulge; to betray, speak aloud; to vent, expend.

Out, *int.* an excl. of surprise, reproach, &c. Cf. Hoot.

Out-about, *adj.* and *adv.* out of doors.

Out alas, *int.* alas!

Out-amo', *adv.* away from.

Outance, *n.* an outing; a going out.—*adv.* out of doors.

Out-an'-out, *adv.* wholly, entirely.

Out ay, *int.* a strong affirmative.

Out-back, *adv.* back foremost.

Outbaits, *n.* common for pasture.

Out-bearing, *n.* endurance to the end.—*ppl. adj.* blustering, bullying.

Outbock, *v.* to vomit forth; to pour out.

Outbrade, *v.* to draw out; to start out.

Outbreak, *n.* an eruption on the skin; a quarrel, a strife; a fit of drinking; transgression; an 'outcrop'; land recently improved.

Outbreaker, *n.* an open transgressor of the law.

Outbreaking, *n.* transgression, sin.

Outburst, *v.* to burst out, break forth.

Outburthen, *v.* to overburden.

Outby, *adv.* outside, out of doors; near by; at a distance; in the direction of.—*adj.* out of doors, open-air; out-of-the-way, more remote.

Outca', *n.* a pasture to which cattle are 'ca'd' or driven; a wedding feast given by a master to a favourite servant.

Outcast, *n.* a quarrel, disagreement.—*v.* to quarrel, fall out.

Outcasten, *n.* a dispute, contention.

Outcome, *n.* appearance; increase, product; termination; upshot; surplus, excess beyond a measured quantity.

Outcoming, *n.* development of youthful promise.

Out-dichtins, *n.* the refuse of grain.

Outdo, *v.* to overcome.

Outdoor, *n.* work out of doors on a farm.

Out-dyke, Out-o'-dykes, *adv.* in unfenced pasture.

Outen, *adv.* out of doors.—*prep.* out of.

Outen-under, *prep.* out from under.

Outer, *n.* one who frequents balls and entertainments.

Outerlin', *n.* an alien; an outcast; the member of a family who is treated as an outsider; the weakling of a brood, &c.

Outerly, *adv.* outwards.—*adj.* used of the wind: blowing from the shore.

Outfall, *n.* the water that escapes from, or runs over, a weir or dam ; a fall of rain, &c.; an incident, accident ; a quarrel, contention ; the ebb-tide.

Outfalling, *n.* a quarrel.

Outfang-thief, *n.* the right of a feudal lord to try a thief who is his own vassal, although taken with the 'fang' or booty within the jurisdiction of another ; the thief so taken.

Outfarm, *n.* an outlying farm on which the tenant does not reside.

Outfeedle, *n.* an outlying field ; the land farthest from the farmstead.

Outfield, *n.* arable land, not manured, but constantly cropped, lying some distance from the farmstead.—*adj.* used of land : outlying and of inferior quality.

Outfight, *v.* to confront ; to fight to the last.

Outfit, *n.* the expense of fitting out.

Outflow, *n.* the ebb-tide.

Out-foul, *n.* wild-fowl.

Out-fy, *int.* an excl. of reproach.

Outgae, *n.* outlay, expenditure.—*v.* to expend.

Outgaein, *n.* a going out of doors ; a removal, departure ; the feast given to a bride before she leaves her father's or master's house for that of her husband.—*ppl. adj.* expiring ; removing, 'flittin'.'

Outgane, *ppl. adj.* past, beyond, older than ; exceeding a limit.

Outgang, *n.* a departure ; the giving up of a tenancy ; exit, egress ; excess over a certain weight or measure.

Outganging, *n.* an outgoing ; a going out of doors.

Outgate, Outgaet, *n.* a way out, exit, outlet, an issue ; gadding about, visiting ; ostentatious display ; a market, a demand, sale.

Outget, *n.* a way out, deliverance ; an opening, opportunity, demand.

Outgie, *n.* expenditure, outgiving, outlay.

Outgoer, *n.* a removing tenant.

Outgoing, *ppl. adj.* removing from a house, farm, &c. Cf. Outgaein.

Outheidie, *adj.* rash, hot-headed.

Outher, *adv.* and *conj.* either.

Outherans, *adv.* either. Cf. Eitherens.

Outhery, *adj.* used of cattle : not in a thriving state, as shown by their leanness, rough skin, and long hair.

Outhounder, *n.* an instigator, an inciter to mischief. Cf. Hounder-out.

Out-hoy, *n.* an outcry.

Outing, *n.* a vent for commodities ; the act of going out or abroad ; a gathering of men and women for amusement ; the open sea.

Outish, *adj.* roguish ; showy ; fond of public amusements.

Outkeek, *n.* an outlook, a peep out.—*v.* to peep out.

Outlabour, *v.* to exhaust by too much labour.

Out-lack, -laik, *n.* overweight ; overmeasure

Out-laid, -layed, *ppl. adj.* expended.

Outlair, *n.* an egg laid by a hen out of her proper nest. Cf. Outlayer.

Outlan, *n.* an alien, stranger ; an incomer from the country to the town, or from one parish to another.—*ppl. adj.* outlying, distant ; far from neighbours ; strange, alien ; wandering. Cf. Ootlin.

Outlander, *n.* a stranger, foreigner, 'outlan.'

Outlandish, *adj.* out-of-the-way, remote.

Outlans, Outlens, *n.* freedom to go in and out ; holidaying.

Outlayer, *n.* a hen that lays out of the regular nest ; an egg laid by such a hen ; a stone lying detached in a field.

Outlay gear, *n.* a stock of furniture, implements, 'plenishin'.'

Outlaying, *ppl. adj.* used of a hen : laying eggs away from the regular nest.

Outleap, *n.* an outbreak, outburst. Cf. Outloup.

Outler, *adj.* not housed - *n.* a beast that lies outside in winter ; one who is out of office.

Outletting, *n.* an emanation ; the operation of divine grace.

Outlie, *n.* outlay, expenditure.

Outlier, *n.* an 'outler'; a stone lying out detached in a field.

Outlin, *n.* an alien ; an outcast. Cf. Ootlin.

Outlins, *n.* freedom ; liberty to go in and out at will ; recreation. Cf. Outlans.

Outloup, *v.* to leap out.

Outly, *n.* money which lies out of the hands of the owner either in trade or at interest.

Outly, *adv.* fully, completely.

Outlyer, *n.* a person who sleeps in the open air at night.

Outlying, *ppl. adj.* used of cattle : lying out at night in winter ; distantly related ; used of money : spent on, laid out, put out.

Outmarrow, *v.* to outmatch ; to out-manœuvre.

Out of, *prep.* in excess of, going beyond ; destitute of.

Out on, *adv.* hereafter, by-and-by.—*prep.* out of. Cf. Outen.

Out oner, *prep.* from under.

Outouth, *adv.* outwards. Cf. Outwith.

Outowre, *adv.* out from any place ; quite over ; across, beyond ; outside.

Out-owre-by, *adv.* at a good distance.

Outplay, *v.* to beat at play.

Outpittin, *n.* the excrement of infants ; attending thereto. Cf. Outputting.

Outpour, *n.* a downpour of rain or snow.

Output, *n.* appearance, style of dress, 'get up.'—*v.* to dismiss, eject ; to furnish, equip soldiers ; to issue coin ; to publish.

Outputter, *n.* one who furnishes and equips soldiers; an employer, instigator; one who passes counterfeit coin; one who circulates false or calumnious reports.

Outputting, *n.* passing coin; equipment; the publishing of libels, &c.

Outrake, *n.* an extensive walk for sheep or cattle; an expedition.

Outrate, *v.* to outnumber; to outdo, outrun.

Out-red, *n.* a military expedition.

Outred, *v.* to extricate; to finish out a business; to clear off debt; to fit out; to 'redd' out, put in complete order. —*n.* rubbish, what is cleared off or swept out; clearance, finishing.

Outreike, *n.* outfit, rigging out.—*v.* to fit out, equip levies.

Outreiker, *n.* one who equips others for service.

Outrigg, *n.* equipment; appearance, preparation.—*v.* to equip.

Out-ring, *n.* a curling term: the outward bias given to a stone by touching the outside of another.

Outrook, Outrug, *n.* the backward wash of a wave after breaking.

Outrun, *v.* to run out, come to an end.—*n.* pasture land attached to a farm.

Outrunning, *n.* expiration, termination.

Outs, *int.* an excl. of impatience. Cf. Hoot.

Outscold, *v.* to scold excessively or loudly.

Outseam-awl, *n.* a peculiar kind of shoemaker's awl.

Outset, *v.* to set out, start, set about; to set off ostentatiously, to make a tawdry display of finery.—*n.* an outfit; a start in life; the provision for a child leaving home, or a daughter at her marriage; the publication of a book; an ornament, offset, what sets off the appearance; an ostentatious display of finery, &c.; an outhouse, an addition enlarging a room or building; waste land brought under cultivation; patches of newly-cultivated land.

Out-shinned, *adj.* having the shins turned outwards.

Outshot, *n.* the projection of a building or wall; an out-building or lean-to of a house; pasture, untilled ground on a farm; ebb-tide; a visible attack of illness.—*adj.* projecting outside.

Outshot-window, *n.* a bay window.

Outside, *n.* the farther side of anything; the heart of the matter; the utmost extent.— *prep.* beyond the usual course of.

Outsider, *n.* one who is not a relative.

Outside worker, *n.* a field-worker.

Outsiftins, *n.* the refuse of grain.

Outsight, *n.* goods or implements for use out of doors. Cf. Insight.

Outsight, *n.* prospect of egress.

Outsight-plenishing, *n.* implements for use out of doors.

Outsole, *n.* the outer sole of a boot.

Outspeckle, *n.* a laughing-stock.

Outspew, *v.* to pour forth.

Outspout, *v.* to spout forth; to dart out.

Outstaffs, *n.* the poles of a poke- or pout-net.

Outstand, *v.* to stand out against, withstand.

Outstander, *n.* an opponent; a firm opposer.

Outstanding, *n.* resistance, opposition.—*ppl. adj.* great, enormous.

Out-steek, *n.* a kind of shoe.

Outstrapolous, Outstropolous, *adj.* obstreperous.

Outstriking, *n.* an eruption on the skin.

Outstrucken, *adj.* having an eruption on the skin.

Outsucken, *n.* the freedom of a tenant from 'thirlage' to a mill; duties payable by those who have such freedom.—*adj.* free from 'thirlage' to a mill.

Outsuckener, *n.* one not 'thirled' to a mill.

Outsucken-multure, *n.* the duties payable by those who come voluntarily to a mill.

Out-tak, *n.* goods bought on credit; outlay; yield, return.

Out-taken, *ppl.* as *prep.* except, excepting.

Outter, *n.* a frequenter of balls and merry-makings. Cf. Outer.

Out-the-gait, *adj.* honest.

Out-things, *n.* objects outside.

Out-through, -throw, *prep.* through to the opposite; completely through.—*adv.* thoroughly.

Outtie, *adj.* addicted to company; much disposed to go out.

Out-tope, *v.* to overtop.

Out-town, *n.* an outlying field on a farm.

Out-town multures, *n.* duties payable by those who come voluntarily to a mill.

Out-trick, *v.* to outdo by trickery.

Out-turn, *n.* a finish, result in the end; increase, productiveness.

Out upon, *prep.* advanced in.

Out upon, *int.* an excl. of reproach or anger.

Outwag, *v.* to wave; to hold out and wave.

Outwair, *v.* to expend.

Outwairin, *adj.* wearisome.

Outwale, *n.* refuse; the pick or choice.—*v.* to choose out, select.

Outwalins, *n.* refuse; leavings.

Outward, *adj.* cold, distant, reserved; not kind.

Outwardness, *n.* distance; coldness; unkindness.

Outwatch, *n.* an outpost, picket, watch.

Outwick, *n.* a curling term: the bias given to a stone by touching the outside of another.

Out-winterers, *n.* cattle not housed in winter.

Outwith, Outwuth, *prep.* outside of.—*adv.* separate from ; beyond.—*adj.* abroad ; more distant, not near.—*n.* the outlying parts.

Out with, *phr.* at variance with ; fallen out with.

Outwittins, *adv.* unwittingly ; without the knowledge of.

Out-woman, *n.* a woman who does outdoor work.

Outwork, *n.* outdoor work ; field-work.

Outworker, *n.* a field-worker.

Outworthy, *v.* to excel.

Outwyle, *v.* to select. Cf. Outwale.

Ouze, *n.* the nap that falls from yarn, cloth, &c. Cf. Ooze.

Ouzel, *n.* the sacrament of the Lord's Supper. Cf. Ousel.

Ouzily, *adj.* unkempt. Cf. Oozlie.

Oven, *n.* a shallow pan or metal pot with lid, in which loaves are baked, burning peats being piled on the top of the lid ; the closeness felt on opening a room long shut up.—*v.* to bake in an oven.

Oven-builder, *n.* the willow-warbler.

Oven-cake, *n.* a cake made of oatmeal and yeast, and baked in an oven.

Over, *v.* to cross. Cf. O'er.

Overbalance, *v.* to outnumber ; to get the better of.

Overbid, *v.* to outbid.

Overcap, *v.* to overhang, project over.

Overcoming, *n.* crossing over.

Overenyie, *n.* southernwood.

Overgive, *v.* to give up, surrender.

Overing, *n.* superiority ; control ; a by-job ; in *pl.* odds and ends.

Overish, *adj.* in *phr.* 'all overish,' qualmish, feeling 'creepy.'

Overitious, *adj.* excessive, intolerable ; boisterous, violent, headstrong.

Overlap, *v.* to be folded over ; to lay one slate or stone so as partially to cover another.—*n.* the place where one thin object partially covers another ; a surplus ; the hatches of a ship.

Overlarded, *ppl. adj.* covered with fat or lard.

Overleather, *n.* the upper leather of a shoe.

Overlook, *v.* to bewitch ; to look on one with the 'evil eye.'—*n.* an omission, oversight.

Overlouping, *ppl. adj.* exultant.

Overly, *adj.* excessive ; superficial ; careless ; remiss ; incidental.—*adv.* excessively, very ; too, too much ; superficially, briefly, hastily ; incidentally, by chance.

Overreach, *v.* to overtake ; to overrate, assess too highly ; to extend over.

Oversailyie, *v.* to build over a close, leaving a passage below ; to arch over.

Oversman, *n.* a foreman, overseer ; an umpire when two arbiters disagree.

Overspaded, *ppl. adj.* half-trenched.

Over-the-matter, *adj.* excessive.

Overthink, *v.* to think over.

Overthwart, *prep.* across.

†**Overture,** *n.* in Presbyterian Churches : the opening-up or introduction of a subject to the notice of a superior court.—*v.* to bring up an 'overture.'

Over-ward, *n.* the upper 'ward' or district of a county.

Ow, *int.* an excl. of surprise.

Ow ay, *int.* oh yes !

Owder, *n.* an exhalation ; a haze. Cf. Ouder.

Owdiscence, *n.* a hearing, audience. Cf. Audiscence.

Owe, *v.* to own, possess.

Owe, *adj.* owing, indebted to. Cf. Awe.

Ower, *v.*, *prep.*, and *adv.* over. Cf. O'er, Over.

Owerling, *adj.* covering over.

Ower-lippin, *ppl.* overflowing.

Ower-thrang, *adj.* too busy ; too crowded.

Owff, *v.* to bark. Cf. Ouff.

Owg, *v.* to shudder. Cf. Ug.

Owght, *n.* a cipher, nought.

Owing, *n.* in *phr.* 'eghin and owing,' humming and hawing.

Owk, Owke, *n.* a week. Cf. Ouk.

Owme, *n.* steam, vapour ; hot air. Cf. Oam.

Own, *v.* to claim as owner ; to recognize ; to identify ; to acknowledge relationship ; to support, favour ; not to let a curling-stone alone, but help it up by sweeping before it. Cf. Awn.

Owrance, *n.* ability ; superiority ; mastery.

Owre, *prep.* over. Cf. O'er.

Owrhye, *v.* to overtake. Cf. O'erhie.

Owrie, *adj.* superstitious ; sad ; chilly. Cf. Oorie.

Owrim and owrim, *n.* the shearing by a band of reapers of grain not portioned out to them by 'rigs.'

Owrter, *adv.* farther over.

Owsal, *n.* the blackbird.

Owse, *n.* an ox. Cf. Ouse.

Owssen-staw, *n.* an ox-stall.

Owther, *adv.*, *conj.*, and *pron.* either. Cf. Outher.

Owtherins, *adv.* either. Cf. Outherans.

Owthor, *n.* an author.

Ox, *n.* a steer of the third year.

Ox-e'e, *n.* the blue tit ; the ox-eye daisy.

Oxengate, Oxgang, Oxgate, *n.* a measure of land varying according to the nature of the soil.

Ox-money, -penny, *n.* a tax on oxen paid to a landlord by tenants.

Oxter, *n.* the armpit ; the armhole of a coat, &c. ; the breast, bosom.—*v.* to go arm in arm ; to lead by the arm ; to embrace ; to take by the arms ; to carry under the arm ; to elbow.

Oxter-deep, *adv.* up to the armpits.

Oxterfu', *n.* an armful.

Oxterfu'-ket, *n.* a worthless fellow.

Oxter-lift, *n.* as much as can be carried between the arm and the side, or in a semi-circle formed by the arms and the breast.

Oxter-pocket, -pouch, *n.* a breast-pocket.

Oxter-staff, *n.* a crutch.

Oy, Oye, *n.* a grandchild; a grandson; a nephew.

Oyess, *n.* Oyez, as used by heralds and public criers three times in succession, to give legal effect.

Oyess, *n.* a niece.

Oyse, *n.* oysters.

Oyse, *n.* Oyez.

Ozelly, *adj.* slovenly; unkempt; swarthy. Cf. Oozlie.

Ozle, *n.* the line attaching cork buoys to a herring-net.

Pa', *n.* a rich or fine cloth. Cf. Pall.

Pa', *n.* a hand. Cf. Paw.

†**Pa'**, *n.* a trick; a quick movement. Cf. Paw, Pavie.

Paak, *v.* to beat, chastise. Cf. Paik.

Paal, *n.* a mooring-post. Cf. Pall.

Paalie-maalie, *adj.* in bad health, sickly.

Paamie, *n.* a stroke on the palm of the hand from a 'tawse.' Cf. Palmy.

Paat, *v.* to poke with the hand or a stick. Cf. Paut.

Pab, *n.* the refuse of flax, 'pob.' Cf. Pob.

Pabble, *v.* to bubble like boiling water.

†**Pace**, *n.* the weight of a clock.—*v.* to weigh with the hand. Cf. Paise.

Pace, *n.* Easter.

Pace-day, *n.* Easter Day.

Pace-egg, *n.* an Easter-egg, hard-boiled and coloured, given as a toy to a child.

Pace-even, *n.* Easter Saturday.

Pace-market, *n.* a market held at Easter.

Pace-ree, *n.* a time about Easter when storms were expected.

Pace-Saturday, *n.* Easter Saturday.

Pace-Sunday, *n.* Easter Day.

Pack, *n.* a pact, compact.

Pack, *n.* the shepherd's part of a flock which is allowed free grazing in return for his services in looking after the whole herd.

Pack, *n.* property, belongings; a measure of wool, 18 stones Scots, or 240 lb.; a heavy mass of clouds, a thunder-cloud.—*v.* to play as partner at cards; with *upon*, used of a retort: to come home.—*adj.* intimate, familiar, friendly.

Packad, *n.* a shallow wooden box, or 'backet,' for carrying ashes.

Packald, *n.* a pack-load.

Pack and peil, *v.* to load and unload; to trade unfairly.

Packet, *n.* a pannier.

Pack-ewes, *n.* the ewes allowed to a shepherd instead of wages.

Pack-house, *n.* a warehouse for goods imported or to be exported.

Packie, *n.* a packman, pedlar.

Packies, *n.* heavy masses of clouds.

Packlie, *adv.* familiarly.

Packman-rich, *n.* a species of bear having six rows of grains to the ear.

Packmantie, *n.* a portmanteau.

Pack-merchant, *n.* a packman; in *pl.* heavy masses of clouds, 'packies.'

Packness, *n.* familiarity, intimacy.

Paction, *v.* to bargain; to make an agreement.

Pad, *n.* a nag.

Pad, *n.* a path; a beaten track.—*v.* to make a path on a new track; to go on foot; to send away on foot.

Padda, Paddan, *n.* a frog.

Padder, *v.* to tread; to beat down by frequent treading. Cf. Patter.

Paddie-stule, *n.* a toadstool.

Paddit, *ppl. adj.* used of a track: beaten hard by treading.

Paddle, *n.* a long-handled spud for cutting thistles, weeds, &c.; a stake-net.—*v.* to cut off with a spud; to hoe.

Paddle, *n.* the lump-fish.

Paddle, *v.* to walk slowly or with short steps; to toddle; to tramp about in wet and mud.—*n.* the act of walking with short, quick steps, or tramping in mud or water.

Paddle, *v.* to finger, handle, feel lovingly.

Paddle-doo, *n.* a frog formerly kept in a cream-jar for luck.

Paddled-rounall, *n.* a circular spot in a field worn bare by oxen following one another round and round.

Paddler, *n.* a child just beginning to walk; a small person walking with short, uncertain steps.

Paddling, *ppl. adj.* walking, wandering aimlessly; trifling, petty; useless.

Paddock, *n.* a frog; a toad; a term of reproach or contempt; a low, frog-shaped sledge for carrying large stones.

Paddock, *n.* a small farm.

Paddock-cheeks, *n.* yellow, inflated cheeks, like those of a frog.

Paddock-cruds, *n.* frogs' spawn. Cf. Paddock-rud.

Paddock-dabber, *n.* one that dabs at or kills frogs.

Paddock-flower, *n.* the marsh-marigold.

Paddock-hair, *n.* the down on unfledged birds and on the heads of babies born without hair.

Paddock-loup, *n.* as far as a frog can leap; the game of leap-frog.

Paddock-pipe, *n.* various species of the horse-tail.

Paddock-rud, -ride, -reed, *n.* the spawn of frogs or toads.

Paddock-spit, -spittles, *n.* the 'cuckoo-spit,' the white froth secreted on plants by cicadas.

Paddock-spue, *n.* frogs' spawn.

Paddock-stone, *n.* the toadstone.

Paddock-stool, *n.* a toadstool; a term of contempt.

Paddock-stool bonnet, *n.* a cap shaped like a toadstool.

Paddow, *n.* a frog; a toad.

Paddy, *n.* a frog.

Paddy, *n.* a packman, pedlar.—*phr.* 'to come Paddy,' to befool.

Paddy-fair, *n.* a fair held at Brechin in memory of St Palladius. Cf. Paldy-fair.

Paddy-ladle, *n.* a tadpole.

Padell, *n.* a spud. Cf. Paddle.

Padjell, *n.* an old pedestrian; one who has often won foot-races.

Padle, *n.* a spud. Cf. Paddle.

Padle, *n.* the lump-fish. Cf. Paddle.

Padroll, *v.* to patrol.

Pady, *n.* a frog.

Paece, *n.* Easter. Cf. Pace.

†Paedaneous judge, *n.* a petty judge who tried only trifling cases, and sat only on a low seat. Cf. Pedaneous.

Paedle, *n.* the lump-fish.

Paedle, *v.* to totter. Cf. Paddle.

Paelag, *n.* a porpoise. Cf. Pellock.

Paet, *n.* a peat.

Paffle, *n.* a small portion of land; a 'pendicle.'

Paffler, *n.* one who occupies a small farm.

Paght, *n.* the custom on goods.

Paick, *v.* to beat. Cf. Paik.

Paid, *n.* a path; a steep ascent. Cf. Pad.

Paid, *ppl. adj.* in *phr.* 'ill-paid,' very sorry.

Paidle, *v.* to hoe.—*n.* a hoe; a short spud.

Paidle, *v.* to walk with short steps; to wander aimlessly. Cf. Paddle.

Paidle, *n.* a nail-bag.

Paiferal, *n.* a stupid fellow.

Paighled, *ppl. adj.* overcome with fatigue; panting with exertion. Cf. Peghle.

Paigle, *n.* the dirty work of a house. Cf. Pegil.

Paik, *n.* a low character; a term of reproach for a woman.

Paik, Paike, *v.* to beat, strike; to chastise; to walk steadily and continually.—*n.* a

stroke, blow; in *pl.* a deserved punishment, 'licks.'

Paiker, *n.* a street-walker.

Paiket, *ppl. adj.* in *phr.* 'paiket wi' poverty,' pinched by poverty.

Paikie, *n.* a female street-walker; a prostitute.

Paikie, *n.* a piece of skin doubled, for defending the thighs from the peat-spade in cutting peats.

Paikie, *n.* an occasional day-labourer.

Paikie-dog, *n.* a dog-fish.

Paiking, *n.* a beating, chastisement.

Paikit-like, *adj.* like a prostitute; looking shabby and worn-out.

Paikment, *n.* a beating, 'paiking.'

Pail, *n.* a hearse.

Pail, *v.* to test the quality of a cheese by a boring instrument. Cf. Pale.

Pailie, *adj.* impotent, feeble; poor in size.— *n.* a feeble, inanimate being; a sickly or deformed lamb. Cf. Paulie.

Pailin, *n.* a stake-fence.—*v.* to surround with a paling.

Paill, *n.* in *phr.* to 'haud paill wi',' to match a thing with another.

Pain, *n.* pains, trouble; a penalty; in *pl.* rheumatism.

Painch, *n.* a paunch; in *pl.* tripe.

Painch-lippit, *adj.* used of a horse: having lips like a 'painch.'

Painful, *adj.* painstaking; laborious.

Pain-piss, *n.* a disease of horses, the 'batts.'

Painsfu', *adj.* painful.

Paint, *n.* the painted woodwork in a room or house.

Paip, *n.* the Pope.

Paip, *v.* to strike. Cf. Pop.

Paip, *n.* a cherry-stone used in a children's game; the game played with cherry-stones.

Paipie, *n.* the game played with cherry-stones.

Paipoch, *n.* the store of cherry-stones from which the 'castles' or 'caddles' are supplied. Cf. Caddle, Castle.

Pair, *n.* a set or number of anything; a single article; in *pl.* a card-game.—*v.* to marry; with *with,* to match with, agree with.—*phr.* 'a pair o' carritches,' a catechism.

Pair, *v.* to grow worse; to diminish.

Pairing, *ppl. adj.* matrimonial.

Pairk, *n.* a park; a field.

Pairle, *n.* two rounds of a stocking in knitting.

Pairless, *adj.* companionless, without a fellow or match.

Pairnmeal, Pairns, *n.* the coarsest kind of meal made of bran and wheat-siftings.

Pairt, *n.* a part.—*v.* to part, divide. Cf. Part.

Pairtisay, *n.* anything done by, or belonging to, more persons than one. Cf. Partisie.

Pairtisay wa', *n.* a party-wall.

Pairtisay wark, *n.* work done by a number of persons.

Pairtisay web, *n.* a web wrought for several owners, of whom each contributes a share of the materials.

Pairtrick, *n.* a partridge.

Pairt-tak', *v.* to side with ; to defend.

†**Paise, Pais,** *v.* to weigh in the hand ; to poise.—*n.* the weight of a clock ; a weight used by a weaver to keep his web extended.

Paise, Paiss, *n.* Easter. Cf. Pace.

Pait, *n.* a pet ; an advocate related to a judge, and favoured by him. Cf. Peat.

Paiter, *v.* to beat with light, rapid blows ; to walk with short, quick steps ; to patter.

Paiter, Paitter, *v.* to chatter ; to mutter.—*n.* loquacity, chatter ; a word ; a loquacious person. Cf. Patter.

Paith, *n.* a steep, narrow, rugged pathway. Cf. Path.

Paitlich, *adj.* favourite, favoured.

Paitlich-gown, *n.* ? a kind of neckerchief.

Paitric, Paitrick, *n.* a partridge.

Pake, *n.* a term of contempt for a woman. Cf. Paik.

Pake, *v.* to beat. Cf. Paik.

Pakey, *adj.* shrewd ; cunning. Cf. Pawky.

Pakkald, *n.* a packet. Cf. Packald.

Palach, *n.* the porpoise. Cf. Pellock.

Palall, *n.* hop-scotch. Cf. Pall-all.

Palaulays, *n.* hop-scotch, 'beds.' Cf. Pall-all.

Palaver, Palaiver, *n.* idle talk, nonsense ; a wearisome talker ; a silly, ostentatious person ; fussy show.—*v.* to talk over ; to gossip ; to behave ostentatiously ; to jest.

Paldy fair, *n.* a fair held at Brechin in memory of St Palladius.

Pale, *v.* to test a cheese by an incision ; to tap for the dropsy.—*n.* an instrument for testing a cheese.

Pale, *n.* in *pl.* a paling.

Pale, *n.* a faucet.

Pale, *n.* any kind of fine cloth. Cf. Pall.

Pale, *v.* to call, summon ; in *phr.* to 'pale a candle,' on seeing a dead-candle, to demand a view of the person's face whose death it portends. Cf. Pell.

†**Palerine,** *n.* a woman's cloak or tippet, a pelerine.

Paley, *adj.* feeble, impotent. Cf. Paulie.

Paley, *adj.* pale, pale-faced.

Paley-footed, *adj.* flat-footed, splay-footed, having the feet turned in.

Paley-lamb, *n.* a very small or feeble lamb.

Paling, *v.* to surround with a paling.

Paling-wall, *n.* a paling.

Palinode, *n.* a legal term ; a recantation demanded of a libel, in addition to damages.

†**Palissade,** *n.* a row of trees planted close.

Pall, *n.* a large pole ; a mooring-post ; a stay for the feet in pulling horizontally.—*v.* to get a purchase for the feet against a post, in pulling ; used of a horse : to strike with the forefeet.

Pall, Palle, *n.* any rich or fine cloth.

Pall, *v.* to puzzle, baffle ; to beat, surpass.—*n.* a puzzle. Cf. Paul.

Pallach, Pallack, *n.* the porpoise. Cf. Pellock.

Pallach, *v.* to puzzle ; to beat.

Palladies, *n.* hop-scotch.

Pall-all, Pallalls, Pallally, *n.* hop-scotch, 'beds'; the piece of slate, stone, &c. with which the game is played.

Pallawa, *n.* a species of sea-crab, a 'keavie' or 'pillan'; a dastardly fellow.

Pallet, *n.* the head ; a ball.

Pallet, *n.* a pelt ; an undressed sheepskin.

Pallie, *adj.* weak. Cf. Paulie.

Pallo, *n.* a porpoise. Cf. Pellock.

Pally, *adj.* palsied.—*n.* a palsied hand.

Pally-wat, *n.* a term of contempt. Cf. Pallawa.

Palm, *n.* the common willow ; in *pl.* its catkins.

Palm, *v.* to lay hands on ; to squeeze the hand.

†**Palmer,** *v.* to wander about ; to saunter ; to walk clumsily, feebly, or with a shuffling gait.—*n.* clumsy walking ; one who goes about in shabby clothes, either from poverty or from slovenliness. Cf. Pawmer.

Palmerer, *n.* a clumsy, noisy walker.

Palmering, *ppl. adj.* rude, clumsy ; walking feebly ; wandering.

Palm-fair, *n.* a fair beginning on the fifth Monday in Lent, and lasting two days.

Palmy, *adj.* abounding in catkins.

Palmy, *n.* a blow on the palm of the hand from a schoolmaster's 'tawse' or cane.—*v.* to inflict 'palmies.' Cf. Pandy.

Palsified, *ppl. adj.* palsied.

Paly, *adj.* pale, whitish.

Pamisample, *n.* the shell *Bulla lignaria.*

Pammy, *n.* a stroke on the hand with a 'tawse.' Cf. Palmy.

†**Pamphie,** *n.* the knave of clubs ; the knave of any suit of cards ; the pam.

Pamphil, *n.* a square enclosure made with stakes for cattle ; a small house ; a square pew. Cf. Pumphel.

Pamphlete, Pamphelet, *n.* a plump young woman.

Pan, *n.* the skull, head ; a piece of timber laid lengthwise on the top or posts of a house, to which the roof is attached.

Pan, *v.* to correspond ; to tally ; to unite.

Pan, *n.* the curtain or drapery hanging from the frame of a bed. Cf. Pawn.

Pan, *n.* a hard, impenetrable crust below the soil.

Pan and kaiber, *n.* a peculiarly constructed roof. Cf. Pan.

†**Panash,** *n.* a plume worn in the hat.

†**Pance,** *v.* to dress a wound. Cf. Panse.

Pand, *n.* the valance of a bed.

Pander, *v.* to wander about, in a silly, aimless way, from place to place ; to trifle at work.

Pandore, Pandoor, *n.* a large oyster.

Pan-drop, *n.* a kind of sweetmeat.

Pandy, *n.* a stroke on the palm of the hand with a 'tawse' or cane.—*v.* to inflict 'pandies.' Cf. Palmy.

Panel, Pannel, *n.* the bar or dock in a court of justice ; a prisoner at the bar.—*v.* to bring to the bar for trial.—*phr.* to 'enter upon pannel,' to appear at the bar.

Pang, *v.* to pain ; to ache.

Pang, *v.* to pack to the utmost ; to cram, stuff full.—*adj.* close-packed, choke-full, crammed.

Pang, *n.* strength, force. Cf. Bang.

Pang fu'. *adj.* crammed to the full.

Panicat, *ppl. adj.* panic-stricken.

Pan-jotrals, *n.* a dish made of various kinds of meat ; a sort of fricassee ; a 'gallimaufrie'; the 'slabbery' offals of the shambles.

Pan-kail, *n.* broth made of coleworts cut small, seasoned with 'kitchen-fee,' butter, or lard, and thickened with oatmeal.

Pan-loaf, *n.* a baker's loaf baked in a pan, and hard and smooth on the sides and bottom.

†**Pannel,** *n.* a sack filled with straw.

Pannelling, *n.* part of a saddle.

Pans, *n.* a description of Church lands.

†**Panse,** *v.* to think ; to dress a wound.

Pan-soled, *adj.* used of 'baps' : flat and hard on the underside, from being fired there.

Pant, *n.* the mouth of a town-well or fountain.

Pant, *n.* a back-stroke.

Pantin, Pantoun, *n.* a slipper.

†**Pantouffles,** *n.* slippers.

Pantry, *n.* a larder ; a 'press.'—*v.* to lay up in store.

Pant-well, *n.* a covered well.

Pan-velvet, *n.* rough velvet ; plush.

Pan-wood, *n.* fuel used at salt-pans for purposes of evaporation ; small coals, coal-dust.

Pany, *adj.* used of a field : difficult to plough, owing to stones, &c., on it.

Pap, *n.* the projection of the mouth ; a teat.

Pap, *n.* weavers' paste for dressing their webs.

Pap, *v.* to pop ; to fire off a gun ; to rouse suddenly ; to thrust quickly ; to run, come, go quickly or suddenly ; with *about*, to move from place to place ; to fall quickly or lightly, drop.—*n.* a spot or speck.

Pap, *v.* to knock, beat ; to aim at ; to throw, pelt.—*n.* a blow ; a pat, tap.

Paparap, *n.* a pronged implement.

Pap-bairn, *n.* a sucking child.

Pape, *v.* to pop. Cf. Pap.

Pape, *n.* a cherry-stone. Cf. Paip.

Pape, *n.* the Pope.

†**Papejay,** *n.* a parrot ; a popinjay. Cf. Papingoe.

Paper, *n.* the MS. of a sermon not preached extempore ; accommodation bills ; bills instead of cash ; bank-notes ; a begging petition written for a person begging.—*v.* to advertise in the newspapers ; to report to the newspapers.

Paper-dragon, *n.* a boy's paper-kite.

Paper-glory, *n.* glory or fame by writings.

Paperie, *n.* a small paper ; a short paper.

Paper-lead, *n.* sheet-lead ; tinfoil-paper.

Paper-lord, *n.* a lord by courtesy alone.

Paper-minister, *n.* a minister who reads his sermons.

Paper-news, *n.* newspapers.

Paper-note, *n.* a bank-note.

Paper-pound, *n.* a bank-note of £1.

Paper-sermon, *n.* a sermon read, and not preached extempore.

Papery, *n.* Popery, Romanism.

Papin, *n.* a beverage of whisky, small-beer, and oatmeal.

†**Papingoe, Papinjay,** *n.* a parrot ; a wooden bird formerly shot at in a yearly trial of skill, a popinjay.

Papingoe-ball, *n.* the yearly ball held at the shooting of the 'papingoe.'

Papish, *n.* a Papist, a Roman Catholic.

Papism, *n.* Popery.

Papist-stroke, *n.* a cross ; a ludicrous term used by young people.

Papistry, *n.* Romanism, Popery.

Paple, *v.* to bubble. Cf. Papple.

Pap-milk, *n.* breast-milk.

Pap-o'-the-hass, *n.* the uvula.

Pappan, *v.* to cocker, pamper ; to bring up young people or animals too indulgently or delicately. Cf. Peppin

Pappant, *adj.* rich, rising in the world ; rendered pettish by over-indulgence ; very careful of one's health.

Pappin, *n.* weavers' paste.

Pappin, *n.* a thrashing ; the sound made by hail, &c., beating against anything.

Papple, *n.* the corn-cockle, and its seed.

Papple, *v.* to bubble, boil up like water ; to tumble about or swirl with a quick, bubbling motion ; to purl ; to boil with indignation ; to perspire violently. Cf. Popple.

Papple-roots, *n.* the roots of the corn-cockle.

Pappy, *adj.* conceited ; puffed up with pride ; presumptuous.

Par, *n.* a young salmon, the samlet.

Parade, *n.* a procession.—*v.* to cut a dash, strut about.

Para-dog, *n.* a dog constantly at his master's heels ; a constant companion ; a parasite. Cf. Pirrie-dog, Penny-dog.

†**Paraffe, Paraffle,** *n.* ostentatious display ; embroidery.

Paraffling, *n.* a trifling evasion.

Paragon, *n.* a rich cloth imported from Turkey. Cf. Barragon.

Paraleeses, *n.* paralysis.

Paralytic, *n.* a stroke of paralysis.

Paramuddle, *n.* the red-tripe of cattle.

Paraphernally, *n.* a matter, an affair ,occurrence ; a story ; a rigmarole.

†**Paraphernals, Parapharnauls,** *n.* a wife's personal dress and ornaments.

Paraphrases, *n.* the Scottish metrical version of other portions of Scripture than the Psalms.

†**Paratitle,** *n.* an explanatory sub-title.

Paraud, Parawd, *n.* a procession. Cf. Parade.

†**Pardi,** *int.* a French oath : 'by God !'

Pardoos, *n.* violence ; a 'bang.'—*adj.* violently.

Pare, *v.* to cut off the surface of a moss or moor ; to run a plough lightly among thinned turnips to check weeds.

†**Paregally,** *adv.* particularly.

†**Parfait,** *v.* to perfect.

Parich, *n.* a small, neatly-dressed person. Cf. Parrich.

Parish, *n.* the ring with the tee in the centre at the end of a curling-rink.

Parishen, *n.* a parish. Cf. Parochine.

Paritch, Parritch, *n.* oatmeal porridge.

Park, *n.* a grass-field ; a paddock.

Park-breed, *n.* the breadth of a 'park.'

Park-dyke, *n.* a field-'dyke,' or wall of stone or turf enclosing a field.

Parl, *v.* to puzzle ; to baffle. Cf. Pall.

Parlamentar, *n.* a member of Parliament.

†**Parle,** *n.* speech ; a talk, conversation ; an argument, a war of words.—*v.* to talk, converse.

Parled, *ppl.* paralyzed.

Parley, Parlie, *n.* a small, thin gingerbread cake sprinkled with small 'sweeties'; a 'parliament.' Cf. Parliament-cake.

†**Parley, Parlie, Parly,** *v.* to converse.—*n.* a long conversation ; a truce, especially in certain games. Cf. Barley.

†**Parleyvoo,** *v.* to speak French, or in a foreign tongue.—*n.* speech, talk, used in ridicule of the French ; a lover's talk.—*adj.* foreign, French.

Parliament, Parliament-cake, *n.* a 'parley'-cake, supposed to have been used by members of the Scottish Parliament during their sittings.

Parliamenter, Parlimenter, *n.* a member of Parliament.

Parliamentin chield, *n.* a member of Parlia ment.

Parliament-man, *n.* a 'Parliamenter.'

†**Parlicus,** *n.* a résumé of various speeches, sermons, or addresses, given at their close ; a flourish at the end of a word in writing ; the space between the thumb and the fore-finger when they are extended ; in *pl.* peculiarities of conduct, whims, oddities.— *v.* to give a résumé of speeches, and especi ally of sermons preached at a communion-season. Cf. Pirlicue.

Parlously, *adv.* in an extraordinary manner.

Parochial, *n.* in *phr.* 'to gang on the paro chial,' to accept parish relief.

Parochine, *n.* a parish. Cf. Parishen.

Parochiner, *n.* a parishioner.

†**Parpane,** *n.* the parapet of a bridge ; a partition-wall ; a wall.

Parpane-wall, *n.* a partition-wall.

Parpell-wall, *n.* a partition-wall.

Parpin, *adj.* perpendicular.

†**Parqueer, Parquier,** *adj.* accurate ; skilful ; thoroughly instructed.—*adv.* by heart. Cf. Perqueer.

Parr, *n.* a young salmon. Cf. Par.

Parrach, *n.* oatmeal porridge.

Parrach, Parrich, Parrick, *n.* a small field, a paddock ; a small enclosure in which a ewe is confined to suckle a strange lamb ; a crowd, a collection of things huddled to-gether ; a group.—*v.* to shut up a ewe with a strange lamb to induce her to suckle it ; to crowd together confusedly.

Parrich, *n.* a person of small stature, very neatly and finely dressed ; a term of endear-ment to an infant or young child.

Parritch, Parridge, *n.* oatmeal porridge ; used as a *pl.*

Parritch-bicker, *n.* a porringer.

Parritch-broo, *n.* water for boiling porridge.

Parritch-cap, -coggie, *n.* a porringer.

Parritch-hale, *adj.* quite able to take one's ordinary food.

Parritch-hertit, *adj.* soft-hearted.

Parritch-hours, *n.* meal-times, breakfast.

Parritch-kettle, *n.* a porridge-pot.

Parritch-luggie, *n.* a porringer.

Parritch-meal, *n.* oatmeal for porridge.

Parritch-pan, *n.* a porridge-pot.

Parritch-pat, -pingle, *n.* a porridge-pot.

Parritch-spurkle, -spurtle, *n.* a rod for stirring porridge.

Parritch-time, *n.* meal-time.

Parritch-tree, *n.* a rod for stirring porridge.

Parrlie, *n.* a small barrel.

Parrock, Parrok, *n.* a paddock, a small stall for lambs. Cf. Parrach.

Parrot, Parrot-coal, *n.* a species of coal that burns very clearly, a 'cannel' coal, giving a loud, cracking noise on being placed on the fire.

Parry, *v.* to put off, delay, tarry, loiter.

Parry, *n.* in *phr.* 'whan ane says Parry a' says Parry,' when anything is said by a person of consequence it is echoed by every one.

Parrymyak, *n.* a match, equal.

†**Parsel,** *n.* parsley.

Parsley-breakstone, *n.* the lady's mantle.

Parson-gray, *adj.* dark gray.

Part, *n.* a place, a district; that which is incumbent on, or becomes, one; interest, share, concern.—*v.* to part with, abandon; to divide; to share; to distribute; to side with, favour; to depart.—*phrs.* 'to part with bairn' or 'with patrick,' to abort, to give birth prematurely.

Par-tail, *n.* bait taken from the tail of a young salmon or 'parr.'

Partal-door, *n.* the door leading from the dwelling-house to the 'byre.'

Partal-wall, *n.* the wall separating the dwelling-house from the 'byre.'

Partan, Parten, Partin, Parton, *n.* the common crab; a term of contempt.

Partan-cage, *n.* a crab-trap, a sparred-cage for keeping crabs alive when caught.

Partan-cartie, *n.* an empty crab-shell used as a toy-cart.

Partan-crab, *n.* a crab.

Partan-face, *n.* a term of contempt.

Partanfu', *adj.* as full as a crab.

Partan-haar, *n.* a seasonable time for catching crabs.

Partan-handit, *adj.* close-fisted; gripping like a crab; greedy.

Partan-, Partan's-tae, *n.* a crab's claw.

Partawta, *n.* a potato.

Parteeclar, *adj.* particular.

Partic, *adj.* particular.

Particate, *n.* a rood of land.

Particle, *n.* a small piece of land.

Particular, *adj.* precise; careful; very attentive.

Particularities, Partickilarities, *n.* the particulars, details; whims, particular fancies.

Particularness, *n.* caution; precision.

Partiere-wall, *n.* a boundary-wall common to two proprietors.

Partisie, *adj.* proper to, or done by, more than one person. Cf. Pairtisay.

Partle, *v.* to trifle at work.—*n.* a trifle; a small part.

Partlet, *n.* a woman's ruff.

Partner, *n.* a spouse.—*v.* to be a partner of or to.

Partrick, *n.* a partridge.

Part-take, *v.* to side with.

Party, *v.* to side with.

Party-match, *n.* a party contest.

Party-pot, *n.* a pot with several owners.

Pas, *v.* to pace, measure.

Pasch, Pase, *n.* Easter.

Paseyad, *n.* a woman who has nothing new to wear at Easter.

Pash, *v.* to bruise to powder.

Pash, *n.* the head.

Pashy, *adj.* having a good head, brainy.

†**Pasment,** *n.* livery.

†**Pasper, Paspie,** *n.* samphire.

Paspey, *n.* a kind of dance.

Pass, *v.* with *off*, to spend; to let a thing go or slip; to remit; to have or finish a meal; to pass by, avoid; to surprise, puzzle.—*n.* an aisle, a passage in a church, or between rows of seats.—*phr.* to 'draw one's pass,' to withdraw one's self or one's offer.

Passage, *v.* to progress.

Passe, *n.* a hint to resign an office.

Passeneip, *n.* parsnip.

Passors, *n.* a pair of compasses.

Pass-gilt, *n.* current money.

Passingly, *adv.* occasionally.

Passivere, *v.* to exceed.

Pastorauling, *ppl.* playing at shepherds and shepherdesses; used of lovers walking in the fields together.

Pastoraulity, *n.* the act of 'pastorauling.'

Past-ordinar, *adj.* extraordinary, 'by-ordinar.'

Pasty, *adj.* pale, sallow.

Pasty, *n.* a nickname for a bill-sticker.

Pat, *n.* a pot.

Pat, *v.* *pret.* put.

Pat, *n.* the head, the top of the head, pate.

Pat, *v.* used of the heart: to beat fast.

Pat, *adj.* appropriate; ready, fluent; pleasant.

Pat, Pate, *n.* a judge's favourite advocate through whom interest was made for clients. Cf. Peat.

Patawtie, *n.* a potato.

Patelet, *n.* a woman's ruff. Cf. Partlet.

Patent, *adj.* ready, willing; disposed to listen; open; available.

Pater, *v.* to chatter, be tiresomely loquacious.—*n.* a loquacious person. Cf. Paiter.

Pates, *n.* steps at the corners of the roofs of houses to facilitate reaching the top.

Path, *n.* a steep, narrow way; the world, the way through life.

Pathed, *ppl. adj.* used of a subject: often treated of or discussed.

Pathlins, *adv.* by a steep and narrow way.

Patience, *n.* used as an expletive.

Patient, *n.* in *phr.* 'patient of death,' a death-agony; one who waits; one who delays his decision.

Patientfu', *adj.* very patient.

Patlet, *n.* a woman's ruff. Cf. Partlet.

Pat-luck, *n.* pot-luck.

Paton, *n.* a patten.

Patrick, Patridge, *n.* a partridge.

†**Patron,** *n.* a pattern.

Patronate, *n.* the right of presenting to a benefice.

Patron-call, *n.* the patronage of a church.

Patship, *n.* the being a judge's 'peat.' Cf. Pat, Peat.

Patter, *v.* to move with quick, sounding steps; to tread down, trample underfoot.—*n.* the act of walking with quick, short steps.—*adv.* with a quick succession of sharp strokes; with quick, sharp - sounding steps. Cf. Paiter.

Patter, *v.* to be loquacious; to mutter, mumble; to engage in a low or whispering conversation. Cf. Paiter.

Patterar, *n.* one who repeats prayers.

Patter-patter, *v.* to fidget about; to move restlessly in and out.

Pattie, Patty, *n.* a small pot.

Pattie, *adv.* pit-a-pat.

Pattle, *n.* a plough - staff, a small, long-handled spade, used for cleaning a plough.

Pattle, *v.* to move the hands backwards and forwards in any yielding substance.

Pauce, *v.* to prance with rage; to stride in irritation.

Pauchel, *v.* to tout for 'tips' by slight services.

Pauchle, *v.* to struggle, make way with difficulty.

Pauchty, *adj.* haughty. Cf. Paughty.

Paucky, *adj.* shrewd. Cf. Pauky.

Pauge, *v.* to prance; to 'pauce'; to pace about artfully till an opportunity occurs for fulfilling any plan; to tamper with; to venture on what is hazardous in a foolhardy manner.

Paughtily, *adv.* haughtily.

Paughty, *adj.* haughty, proud; ambitious; consequential, impertinent, forward; saucy, insolent; discreet.

Pauk, *n.* a trick, wile; a sly, clever way.

Paukery, *n.* slyness, craftiness.

Paukily, *adv.* shrewdly, craftily, cleverly.

Paukiness, *n.* shrewdness; cunning; craftiness.

Pauky, *adj.* shrewd; cunning; knowing, artful; insinuating; used of the eye: wanton, arch; lively.

Paul, *n.* a hold; a detent; a leaning-place, a mooring-post.—*v.* to strike with the forefeet. Cf. Pall.

Paul, *v.* to puzzle, baffle; to surpass.—*n.* a puzzle. Cf. Pall.

Paulie, *adj.* used of a bodily member: impotent, feeble; of lambs: small in size; of the mind: insipid, inanimate; lame, dislocated, distorted.—*n.* an inferior or sickly lamb; the smallest lamb in a flock; a feeble, inanimate being.

Paulie-footed, *adj.* flat-footed; splay-footed. Cf. Paley-footed.

Paulie-merchant, *n.* one who traverses the country buying inferior lambs.

Paum, *n.* the palm of the hand.—*v.* to lay hands on, finger; to squeeze the hands. Cf. Palm.

Paum, *n.* the common willow. Cf. Palm.

Paumy, *n.* a stroke on the hand with a 'tawse,' &c. Cf. Palmy.

Paunch, *n.* in *pl.* tripe; the entrails, the sides of the belly.—*v.* to swallow greedily. Cf. Painch.

Paunchings, *n.* tripe.

Paut, *v.* to paw; to push out the feet alternately when one is lying down; to stamp with the foot in anger; to strike with the foot, kick; to move the hand, as if groping in the dark; to search with a rod or stick in water or in the dark; to make a noise when so searching; to make short, convulsive movements with the hands; to pat; to set to work slowly or aimlessly; to move about gently or leisurely.—*n.* a kick, a stamp on the ground; a pat; a heavy, weary walk; a poker.

†**Pauw,** *n.* a trick; a quick movement. Cf. Paw.

Pavean, Paveen, *ppl. adj.* pretentious.

†**Pavee,** *n.* a trick. Cf. Pavie.

Pavement, *v.* to pave; to furnish with a flooring.

Paver, *n.* a paving-stone.

†**Pavie,** *n.* a trick; a part in a play or business; exertion; a bustle; quick muscular movement.—*v.* to make fantastic gestures, to act as a clown. Cf. Paw.

Paw, *n.* a hand.

Paw, *n.* a step; gait; 'the pas.'

†**Faw,** *n.* a trick; the slightest motion; one who cannot make the slightest exertion; a quick, ridiculous, or fantastic movement; a ceremonious fluster; a stir, bustle; a conceited, dressed-up person.—*v.* to make fantastic movements.

Pawchle, Pawchlie, *n.* a frail, old body; one low in stature and weak in intellect.

Pawk, *n.* a trick. Cf. Pauk.

Pawkery, Pawkrie, *n.* -lyness. Cf. Paukerie.

Pawkie, *n.* a woollen mitten having a thumb, and without fingers.

Pawky, *adj.* shrewd; sly. Cf. Pauky.

Pawl, *v.* to claw the air, to make an ineffectual effort to clutch.

Pawlie, *n.* the stone, &c., used in hop-scotch. Cf. Pall-all.

Pawlie, *adj.* weak; impotent. Cf. Paulie.

Pawm, *n.* the uppermost grain in a stalk of corn.

Pawm, *n.* the palm of the hand. Cf. Palm.

Pawm, *n.* the common willow. Cf. Palm.

†**Pawmer,** *n.* one who goes from place to place shabbily dressed.—*v.* to go about idly from place to place. Cf. Palmer.

†**Pawmie,** *n.* the knave of clubs; the knave of any suit of cards. Cf. Pamphie.

Pawmie, *n.* a stroke on the palm with a 'tawse,' &c.—*v.* to inflict such a stroke. Cf. Palmy.

Pawn, *n.* a narrow curtain fixed to the top or the bottom of a bed. Cf. Pan.

Pawn, *n.* a pawnshop.—*v.* to palm off a worthless thing as one of great value.

Pawn, *n.* the timbers in a thatched roof placed under the 'cabers,' and stretching from gable to gable. Cf. Pan.

Pawnd, *n.* a pledge, security.—*v.* to pledge, pawn.

Pawrlie, *n.* a small, thin gingerbread-cake. Cf. Parley.

Pawt, *v.* to poke with the hand or a stick. Cf. Paut.

Pawvis, *v.* to dally with a girl.

Pay, *v.* to beat, drub; to punish; to defeat, conquer; to smart, pay the penalty, suffer; to run, walk smartly; with *up*, to work energetically.—*n.* a drunken bout following the payment of wages; in *pl.* punishment.

Payment, *n.* a thrashing.

Pays, *n.* Easter.

Paysyad, *n.* a woman with nothing new to wear at Easter. Cf. Paseyad.

Pay-way, *adj.* valedictory.—*n.* a farewell; a 'foy.'

Pay-wedding, *n.* a wedding at which guests contribute to the cost of the feast.

Pea, *a.j.* tiny; as small as a pea.—*n.* in *pl.* peasemeal.

Pea-and-thummils, *n.* a thimble-rigging game.

Peace, *n.* Easter. Cf. Pace.

Peace-warn, *v.* to serve a notice of ejectment.

Peace-warning, *n.* a notice of ejectment.

Peaceyaud, *n.* a woman with nothing new to wear at Easter. Cf. Paseyad.

Pea-gun, *n.* a pea-shooter.

Peak, *n.* the sharp point of a sea-cliff or rock; a triangular piece of linen, binding the hair below a cap; a very small quantity; a ray.—*v.* used of a spire, mast, &c.: to end in a sharp point; to show a peak or sharp point.

Peak, *v.* to chirp; to squeak; to speak in a whisper or thin, weak voice; to complain of poverty—*n.* the chirp of a bird; the squeak of a mouse; an insignificant voice; a small person with a thin, weak voice.

Peakie, *adj.* small; petty, trifling. Cf. Pickie.

Peaky, *adj.* sharply pointed.—*n.* a steel knitting-pin; a knitter; in *pl.* knitting.

Peaky-worker, *n.* a knitter.

Peal, *v.* to call, summon. Cf. Pale, Pell.

Peal, *v.* to peel.—*n.* a particle. Cf. Peel.

Peal, *v.* to equal, match.—*n.* a peer; an equal. Cf. Peil.

Peaner, *n.* a small, cold-looking, ill-clad person.

Peanerflee, *n.* one with the appearance of lightness and activity.

†**Peanie,** *n.* a turkey-hen.

Peanie, *n.* a pinafore.

Pea-pluffer, *n.* a tin pea-shooter.

Pear, *n.* a peg-top. Cf. Peerie.

Pear, *v.* to appear.

Pearl, *v.* to stud with pearls.—*n.* a cataract in the eye.

Fearl, *n.* a kind of ornamental lace used for edging.—*v.* to edge with lace; to border; to ornament with a knitted border.

Pearl, *n.* in *phr.* to 'cast up a pearl,' to purl a stitch instead of making it plain; the seam-stitch in a knitting stocking.

Pearled, *ppl. adj.* bordered with lace.

Pearlin, *n.* lace; a kind of thread lace.

Pearling, *n.* a string of pearls; in *pl.* tears.

Pearlin-keek, *n.* a cap with a lace border.

Pearl-lace, *n.* an ornamental lace, used as an edging.

Pearl-shell, *n.* the pearl-mussel.

Peart, *adv.* scarcely, hardly; smartly.

Peary, *n.* a peg-top. Cf. Peerie.

Peary, *adj.* small. Cf. Peerie.

Peas, *n.* glassy marbles used as 'pitchers.'

Pease, *int.* a call to calves, pigeons, &c. Cf. Pees.

Pease-bannock, *n.* a bannock made of pease-meal.

Pease-bogle, *n.* a scarecrow set up in a field of peas.

Pease-bread year, *n.* a year towards the close of the 18th century, when peasemeal was used as a substitute for oatmeal and barley-meal.

Pease-brose, *n.* 'brose' made of peasemeal.

Pease-bruizle, *n.* field-peas boiled in their pods.

Pease-clod, *n.* a coarse roll or 'bap' made of peasemeal.

Pease-cod-tree, *n.* the laburnum.

Pease-kill, *n.* 'pease-bruizle'; a confused scramble.

Pease-lilts, *n.* 'pease-brose.'

Pease-meal, *adj.* soft, flabby; doughy.

Pease-mum, *n.* in *phr.* to 'play pease-mum, to mutter.

Pease-pudding-faced, *adj.* mealy-faced.

Peaser, *n.* a strong bumper of liquor.

Peaseweep, *n.* the lapwing. Cf. Peesweep.

Peasie-whin, *n.* greenstone. Cf. Peysie-whin.

Pea-splitting, *adj.* hair - splitting ; driving hard bargains.

Peas-scone, *n.* a 'scone' made of peasemeal.

Peat, *n.* a pet ; a term of endearment ; used also contemptuously ; a name formerly given to advocates who were related to judges and favoured by them.

Peat, *n.* a magpie. Cf. Pyat.

Peat-bank, *n.* the place whence peats are cut.

Peat-bree, -brew, *n.* peaty-water.

Peat-breest, *n.* the 'peat-bank.'

Peat-broo, *n.* 'peat-bree.'

Peat-broo, *n.* the 'peat-bank.'

Peat-cashie, *n.* a large basket or 'creel' for holding or carrying peats.

Peat-caster, *n.* one who cuts peats.

Peat-castin', *n.* peat-cutting.

Peat-claig, *n.* a place built for holding peats.

Peat-clod, *n.* a single peat ; a piece of peat.

Peat-coom, *n.* peat-dust.

Peat-corn, *n.* peat-dust, peat-dross.

Peat-creel, *n.* a peat-basket.

Peat-crue, *n.* the place where peat is stored.

Peat-days, *n.* days on which peats are cut, or are 'led' home.

Peat-digger, *n.* a peat-cutter.

Peat-fitter, *n.* one who sets peats on end to dry.

Peat-futherer, *n.* a retailer or carter of peats.

Peat-grieshoch, *n.* red-hot peat.

Peat-hagg, *n.* a hole from which peat has been cut ; a 'peat-hole' containing water ; the rough, projecting margin of a 'peat-hole' when the hole has grown up again : a hump of peat on the surface of a moss.

Peat-hole, *n.* a hole from which peats have been dug.

Peat-house, *n.* a house where peats are stored.

Peat-lair, *n.* the place where peats are spread and 'fitted' to dry.

Peat-lowe, *n.* the blaze of a peat-fire.

Peatman, *n.* a retailer of peats.

Peat-meal, *n.* peat-dust.

Peat-mould, *n.* peat-dust ; peaty soil.

Peat-mow, *n.* a large stack of peats ; a heap of peat-dust.

Peat-neuk, *n.* the corner at the kitchen fire-side, where peats were stored for immediate use ; a place facing the entrance door, between two doors, one of which opened into the kitchen, and the other led to the other rooms of the house.

Peat o' sape, *n.* a bar of soap, so called from its resemblance to a peat.

Peat-pot, -pat, *n.* a hole from which peat has been dug.

Pea-tree, *n.* the laburnum.

Peat-reek, *n.* peat-smoke ; the flavour imparted to whisky distilled by means of peat ; Highland whisky.

Peat-reekit, *adj.* filled, discoloured, or flavoured by peat-smoke.

Peat-reek-whisky, *n.* Highland whisky, distilled over peat-fires.

Peat-shieling, *n.* a hut built of peat.

Peat-spade, *n.* a 'flaughter-spade,' used for cutting peats.

Peat-stane, *n.* the corner-stone at the top of a house-wall.

Peaty, *n.* a judge's 'peat.' Cf. Peat.

Peavor, *n.* hop-scotch. Cf. Peever.

Pech, *n.* a Pict. Cf. Pecht.

Pech, *v.* to pant, puff ; to breathe hard ; to sigh heavily ; to cough shortly and faintly. —*n.* a heavy sigh, deep breath ; laboured breathing ; an exclamatory, forcible expiration after exertion.

Pechan, *n.* the gullet, the crop ; the stomach.

Pechie, *adj.* short of breath, given to panting.

Pechin, *n.* a fit of short, faint coughing.

Pechle, *n.* a parcel or packet carried secretly.

Pechle, *v.* to pant.

Pech-pech, *n.* the sound of forcible expiration during violent exertion.

Pecht, *n.* a Pict ; a term of contempt.

Pecht-, Pech-stane, *n.* a prehistoric monumental stone.

Peck, *n.* a large quantity or number.

Peck, *v.* to beat, strike. Cf. Paik.

Peck-bit, *n.* that part of a 'muttie-measure' which holds a peck.

Peckin, *n.* a small quantity.

Peckish, *adj.* hungry.

Peckle, *v.* to peck.

Peckman, *n.* one who carried smuggled spirits through the country in a vessel like a peck-measure.

Peculiar, *n.* a particular line of business, work ; a peculiarity.

Ped, *n.* a professional runner ; the tramp, walking.

†**Pedaneous,** *adj.* used of inferior judges who had not a bench, but sat on a low seat.

Pedder, *n.* a pedlar.

Pedee, *n.* a kind of footboy.

Pedlar's drouth, *n.* hunger.

Pedrall, *adj.* toddling.—*n.* a child beginning to walk.

Pee, *v.* used of children : to urinate ; to wet with urine.

Peeack, Peeak, *v.* to chirp. Cf. Peak.

Peeackin, *ppl. adj.* speaking or singing in a thin or querulous voice.

Peeak, *v.* to look sickly.

Peeble, *n.* a pebble ; an agate.—*v.* to throw pebbles at.

Peebruch, *n.* a pibroch.

Peece, *n.* a piece. Cf. Piece.

Peechack, *n.* a small-sized marble.

Peefer, *v.* to whine ; to be petulant ; to trifle and be feeble in working.—*n.* a very useless person ; a 'cypher.' Cf. Piffer.

Peefering, *ppl. adj.* insignificant ; useless ; trifling.

Peeggirin-blast, *n.* a heavy shower ; a stormy blast.

Peek, *v.* to look sickly ; to peak.

Peek, *v.* to chirp.

Peek, *n.* the sharp point of a sea-cliff ; a triangular piece of linen, binding the hair beneath the cap ; a very small quantity ; a ray. Cf. Peak.

Peekie, *n.* a small ray or point of light.

Peekie, *adj.* small ; insignificant. Cf. Pickie.

Peeking, *ppl. adj.* ill-tempered ; complaining.

Peeky, *adj.* sharp-pointed.—*n.* a steel knitting-pin ; a knitter. Cf. Peaky.

Peel, *v.* to rub or take off the skin ; to take off one's clothes.—*n.* a particle ; a blade of grass.

Peel, *n.* a pool.

Peel, *n.* a pill ; anything disagreeable, unpleasant, nauseous.—*v.* to prescribe or administer pills.

Peel, *v.* to equal, match. Cf. Peil.

Peel-a-bane, *n.* very freezing weather.

Peel-a-flee, *n.* a person insufficiently clad ; a creature out of its element.

Peel-an'-eat, *adj.* sickly-looking, delicate.

Peel-an'-eat, *n.* potatoes presented at table unpeeled ; the eating of such potatoes.

Peeled egg, *n.* a windfall.

†**Peelemel,** *adv.* pell-mell.

Peeler, *n.* a crab that has cast its shell.

Peeler, *n.* a policeman.

Peel-garlick, *n.* a simpleton ; a weak, wasted, miserable-looking person.

Peelie, *adj.* thin, meagre.—*n.* a scarecrow.

Peelie-wally, *n.* a tall, slender, sickly-looking young person ; a tall, slender plant or shoot.

Peeling, *ppl.* travelling lightly clad on a windy day.—*n.* a paring ; peel ; skin.

Peeling, *n.* a thrashing.

Peelock, *n.* a potato boiled in its skin ; ' peel-an'-eat.'

Peel-reestie, *n.* a stirring, mischievous child or youth.

Peel-ringe, -range, *adj.* thin ; not able to endure the cold.—*n.* a skinflint ; a tall, thin person ; a cold person.

Peelrushich, *n.* anything that comes with a rush or in a torrent ; a rush, a torrent.

Peel-shot, *n.* the dysentery of cattle.

Peel-wersh, *adj.* wan, sickly-looking.

Peem-pom, *n.* a pom-pom, the ball of coloured worsted once worn by infantry in front of the shako.

Peen, *n.* a pin.

Peen, *n.* a pane of glass.

Peen, *n.* the sharp point of a mason's hammer. —*v.* to strike with a hammer.

Peenge, *v.* to whine, fret ; to complain of cold or hunger ; to pretend poverty.

Peenged, *ppl. adj.* delicate ; shrunken.

Peenging, *ppl. adj.* starved-looking ; sickly ; fretful.

Peengy, *adj.* fretful, ill-tempered ; pinched with cold ; unable to bear cold.

Peenie, *n.* a pinafore. Cf. Pinny.

Peenie, Peenie-rose, *n.* a peony.

Peenish, *v.* to stint, limit.

Peenjure, *v.* to hamper ; to confine.

Peeoye, Peeoe, *n.* a small cone of moistened gunpowder, made by boys as a firework.

Peep, *n.* the dawn ; a peep-hole.

Peep, *v.* to whine, complain ; to pule.—*n.* the meadow-pipit ; a feeble sound ; a whisper.

Peepag, *n.* a reed or pipe made of green straw, used by boys to make a sound.

Peeper, *n.* a looking-glass ; in *pl.* spectacles ; the eyes.

Peeper, *n.* a complaining person.

Peep-glass, *n.* a telescope.

Peepie, *adj.* fretful, whining.—*n.* a fretful and tearful child.

Peepie-weepie, *adj.* used of a whining disposition.

Peep-sma', *n.* one who is weak in body and mind ; one who keeps in the background. —*v.* to keep in the background ; to take a humble place ; to 'sing small.' Cf. Pipe-small.

Peer, *n.* a match, equal.—*v.* to equal ; to match.

Peer, *adj.* poor.

Peer, *n.* a pear ; a peg-top.

Peerer, *n.* one who stares.

Peerie, *n.* a peg-top ; the game of top-spinning.

Peerie, *adj.* small.

†**Peerie,** *adj.* timid, fearful.

Peerie, *adj.* peeping, peering ; sharp-looking ; disposed to examine narrowly.

Peerie, *v.* to flow in a small stream, as through a quill ; to purl.—*n.* a small quantity of fluid.

Peerie-breeks, *n.* short trousers ; a person with short legs.

Peerie-foal, *n.* a small bannock.

Peerie-man, *n.* an iron or wooden frame for holding bog wood or 'fir-candles' for lighting purposes. Cf. Peer-man.

Peerie-pinkie, *n.* the little finger.

Peerie-wee, *adj.* very small.

Peerie-weerie, *n.* a slow-running stream. Cf. Peerie.

Peerie-weerie, *adj.* blinking; small-eyed; sore-eyed.—*n.* a mysterious, hidden person.

Peerie-weerie, -wirrie, *adj.* very small.—*n.* anything very small; the little finger or toe.

Peerie-weerie-winkie, *adj.* excessively small.

Peerie-winkie, *n.* anything very small; the small finger or toe.

Peerie-write, *n.* small-text handwriting.

Peer-man, *n.* a beggar; a frame of iron or wood on a rod three or four feet long, set in a stone socket, and holding 'fir-candles' or bog-wood, for lighting a room; a pile of four upright sheaves, with one laid on the top, in a wet harvest; the blade-bone, or broiled remains of a shoulder of mutton.

Peer-mate, *adj.* of equal rank.

Peer-page, *n.* a 'peer-man' for lighting purposes.

Peer's-house, *n.* the workhouse.

Pees, *int.* a call to pigeons, calves, &c.

Peeser, *n.* an unfledged pigeon.

Peesie, *n.* the lapwing. Cf. Peesweep.

Peeskie, *n.* short wool; stunted grass.—*adj.* dry, withered, shrivelled; short, stunted. Cf. Piskie.

Peesweep, Peesweep, *n.* the lapwing.

Peesweep-like, *adj.* sharp-featured, with a feeble appearance and a shrill voice.

Peesweepy, *adj.* poor, pitiful, silly, whining.

Peesweet, *n.* the lapwing; the cry of the lapwing.

Peetly-pailwur, *n.* an endearing term for a child.

Peety, *n.* pity.

Peeuk, *v.* to chirp; to peep.

†**Peevee,** *n.* a trick; a fantastic bodily movement; bustle; a conceited, dressed-up person.—*v.* to make fantastic gestures. Cf. Pavie, Paw.

Peever, Peevor, *n.* the game of hop-scotch; the stone or slate used in the game.

Peever, *v.* used of children: to urinate.

Peever, *v.* to tremble, quiver. Cf. Piver.

Peeveralls, Peeveral-al, *n.* the game of hop-scotch.

Peewit, *n.* the cry of the lapwing.

Peff, *n.* a dull, heavy blow or fall; the sound made by such; a dull, heavy step in walking; the sound of such; a big, stupid person.—*v.* to beat with dull, heavy blows; to beat severely; to walk with heavy step; with *in* or *down*, to drive.—*adv.* with heavy step; with a dull, heavy fall. Cf. Beff.

Peffin, *n.* a very big, stout person.

Peg, Pegg, *n.* a leg, foot; a step; the ball used in 'shinty'; a blow with the fist.—*v.* to hammer, beat; to hurry on; to work

hard; to eat greedily; with *out*, to pay or give out.

Peg, *n.* a policeman.

Peggin'-awl, *n.* a shoemaker's awl for entering pegs driven into the heels of shoes.

Pegh, *v.* to breathe heavily. Cf. Pech.

Peghin, *n.* the stomach. Cf. Pechan.

Peghle, *v.* to pant from exertion. Cf. Pechle.

Peght, *n.* a Pict. Cf. Pecht.

Pegil, *n.* the rough or dirty work of a house. —*v.* to do such work.

Peg-pie, *n.* a magpie.

Peg-puff, *n.* an 'old' young woman; a young woman with the manners of an old one.

Pegral, *adj.* paltry.

Pehoy, *n.* a sneeze.

Pehts, *n.* in *phr.* to 'make pehts and kail of,' to beat very severely; to destroy.

Peifer, *v.* to shake, quiver. Cf. Piver.

Peifer, *v.* to whimper.—*n.* a 'cypher.' Cf. Piffer.

Peik, *n.* a long piece of lead, used for ruling paper.

Peikthank, *adj.* ungrateful.

Peil, *v.* to equal, match.—*n.* a peer, an equal.

Peil, *v.* in *phr.* to 'pack and peil,' to conduct business in an unfair way.

Peild, *ppl.* made bald.

Peinge, *v.* to whine. Cf. Peenge.

Peinor-pig, *n.* an earthenware money-box.

Peir, *n.* an equal. Cf. Peer.

Peisled, *ppl. adj.* in easy circumstances; smug.

Peist, *v.* to work feebly.—*n.* a little, weak person.

†**Pejorate,** *v.* a legal term: to prejudice; to make worse.

Pele, *v.* to puncture. Cf. Pale.

Peley-wersh, *adj.* sickly. Cf. Peel-wersh.

Pell, *n.* a useless, worn-out thing; a thick, dirty piece of cloth; a term of abuse; a lazy, dirty, worthless person; a tuft of clotted wool; dried dirt adhering to an animal's hind-quarters; in *pl.* rags, tatters.

Pell, *n.* very sour butter-milk.

†**Pell,** *n.* a heavy dash, blow, or fall; the sound of such a blow or fall.—*v.* to dash, drive, strike violently; to walk with a heavy, dashing step.—*adv.* with great force or violence.

Pell, *v.* to summon. Cf. Pale.

Pellack-whale, *n.* a porpoise. Cf. Pellock.

Pellad, *n.* a tadpole.

Pell and mell, *v.* to rush pell-mell.

Pell-clay, *n.* pure, tough clay, 'ball-clay.'

Pellet, Pellot, *n.* a skin.

Pellets, *n.* two leaden compresses, applied to prevent undue bleeding.

Pellile, *n.* the redshank.

Pell-mell, *n.* a scrimmage; a headlong rush; confusion.—*adj.* confused, hap-hazard.

Pellock, Pelloch, Pelluck, *n.* the porpoise.

Pelonie, *n.* a dress for young boys : an old-fashioned, long, tight-fitting overcoat. Cf. Polonaise.

Pelt, *n.* rags, rubbish ; a piece of thick, dirty dress.

Pelt, *v.* to beat, strike, thrash ; to work with energy ; to hurry.—*n.* a stroke or blow ; a downpour ; a heavy fall ; the noise made by a falling body.—*adv.* violently.

Pelt, *n.* a sheepskin without the wool ; used as a term of reproach in *phr.* ' foul pelt.'

Peltag, *n.* a coal-fish in its second year.

Pelter, *n.* a passion, temper ; a state of excitement.

Peltin-pock, *n.* a bag for guarding the thighs from the ' flaughter-spade ' in peat-cutting ; a worthless dress or bag.

Peltry, *n.* a skin.

Peltry, *n.* trash, rubbish ; ill-cooked food ; wet and stormy weather.—*adj.* worthless ; wet and stormy.

Pemmint, *n.* a thrashing ; payment. Cf. Payment.

Pen, *n.* a feather, quill ; part of a kail-stem or ' castock'; a snuff-spoon, a piece of quill used for taking snuff ; a spoon.—*v.* to take snuff with a ' pen.'

Pen, *n.* a hill ; a high, pointed, pyramidal hill. Cf. Pin.

Pen, *n.* the dung of fowls. Cf. Hen-pen.

Pen, *n.* an old, saucy man with a sharp nose.

Pen, *n.* condition ; humour ; ' pin.' Cf. Pin.

Pen, *n.* an arch, archway ; a small conduit ; a sewer. Cf. Pend.

Pence, *n.* money ; a fortune.

Pencefu', *adj.* proud. Cf. Pensefu'.

Penceless, *adj.* penniless.

Pence-pig, *n.* an earthenware money-box. Cf. Penny-pig.

Pencey, *adj.* quiet. Cf. Pensy.

Pench, *n.* the paunch. Cf. Painch.

Pend, *n.* an archway ; a covered way ; a covered sewer, a conduit.—*v.* to arch.

Pendenter-knock, *n.* a clock hanging on a wall, a ' wag-at-the-wa'.'

Pendice of a buckle, *n.* that which receives the one latchet, before the shoe is straightened by means of the other.

Pendicle, *n.* an appendage ; a pendant ; a small piece of land attached to a larger ; a small farm, a croft ; a church or parish depending on another.

Pendicler, *n.* one who farms a ' pendicle'; an inferior tenant.

Pending, *n.* an archway, a ' pend'; making a ' pend.'

Pendit, *ppl. adj.* arched.

†**Pendle, Pendule,** *n.* a pendant ; an ear-ring.

Pen-driver, *n.* a clerk ; an author.

Pend-stane, *n.* a stone for building an arch.

Pen-fauld, *n.* the close in a farmstead, for holding cattle.

Penfu', *n.* a spoonful ; a mouthful ; a good meal.

Pen-gun, *n.* a child's pop-gun made of a quill ; a loquacious person of small stature.

Pen-head, *n.* the upper part of a ' mill-lead,' where the water is carried off from the pond to the mill.

Penkle, *n.* a rag, a fragment.

Pen-mouth, *n.* the entrance to a ' pend' or covered gateway.

Penn, *n.* a ' pend.'

Pennander, *n.* a standard-bearer, one who carries a pennant.

Pennar, Pennart, *n.* a pen-case ; a tin cylinder for holding pens, &c.; a penman ; a composer ; a scribbler.

Pennarts, *n.* revenge ; retribution. Cf. Pennyworth.

Penned, *ppl. adj.* arched, ' pendit.'

Penneth, *n.* a pen-case.

Pennirth, *n.* a tin pen-case. Cf. Pennar.

Penny, Pennie, *n.* money ; cash ; earnings ; a fortune ; a sum of money.

Penny, *n.* the act of eating ; daintier fare than ordinary.—*v.* to eat much with gusto ; to feed, fare.

Penny-bake, *n.* a penny biscuit or roll.

Penny-boo, *n.* a large top.

Penny-brag, *n.* a game.

Penny-breid, *n.* a penny loaf ; penny loaves.

Penny-bridal, *n.* a wedding the guests at which contribute to the cost of the feast.

Penny-cookie, *n.* a penny bun.

Penny-cress, *n.* the wild cress.

Penny-dog, *n.* a person that dogs another's footsteps, as a dog follows his master ; a mean, sneaking fellow.

Penny-fee, *n.* wages in money.

Penny-friend, *n.* a deceitful, interested friend.

Penny-Herioters, *n.* balls formerly made by the boys of George Heriot's Hospital.

Penny-maill, *n.* rent paid in money.

Penny-maister, *n.* an old term for the treasurer of a town-guild, or incorporated trade, &c.; a ' box-master.'

Penny-note, *n.* a forged £1 note.

Penny-pap, *n.* a penny roll.

Penny-pig, *n.* an earthenware money-box, used by children. Cf. Peinor-pig, Pine-pig.

Penny-reels, *n.* dances at which admission was paid for.

Penny-rent, *n.* rent paid in money.

Penny-siller, *n.* money ; hard cash ; a dowry.

Penny-stane, *n.* a flat, circular stone, used as a quoit ; a quoit ; in *pl.* the game played with these stones.

Penny-stane-cast, *n.* the distance to which a man can throw a quoit.

Penny-stipend, *n.* a minister's salary in money.

Penny-wabble, *n.* very weak beer sold at a penny a bottle.

Penny-wedding, -waddin', *n.* a 'penny-bridal.'

Penny-whaup, -wheep, -whip, *n.* very weak beer sold at a penny a bottle.

Penny-widdie, *n.* a haddock dried without being split. Cf. Pin-the-widdie.

Penny-winner, *n.* a scanty wage-earner.

Pennyworth, *n.* a purchase; a bargain; revenge, retribution; value for money paid; also a term of contempt. Cf. Pennarts.

Pen-point, *n.* a pen-nib.

†**Pense,** *v.* to walk conceitedly, with measured step.

Pensefu', *adj.* thoughtful, meditative; proud, conceited.

Pensefu'ness, *n.* conceit, affectation.

†**Pensel,** *n.* a banneret, a small pennon. Cf. Pinsel.

Penshens, *n.* tripe. Cf. Painch.

Pensieness, *n.* self-conceit, affectation.

Pensilie, *adv.* in a self-important manner.

Pension, *n.* pay; salary.

†**Pensioner,** *n.* a boarder *en pension.*

Penstraker, *n.* the whin-lintie; the yellow-ammer.

†**Pensy,** *adj.* quiet, thoughtful; pensive; sedate; proud, affected; smart, foppish; tidy in dress and appearance.

Pent, *n.* paint.

Penty, *v.* to fillip.—*n.* a fillip.

Penure, *adj.* penurious.

Penure-pig, *n.* a miser, niggard.

Penury, *n.* scarcity; lack, deficiency.

Pen-work, *n.* copying; writing.

Pep, *n.* a cherry-stone. Cf. Paip.

Peppen, Peppin, Pepin, *v.* to cocker; to rear delicately. Cf. Pappan.

Pepper, *v.* to dust or sprinkle with powder, &c.; to tickle.—*n.* irritation, passion.

Pepper-curn, -curns, *n.* a hand-mill for grinding pepper.

Pepper-dulse, -dilse, *n.* the edible jagged fucus.

Peppin, *n.* a baby.

Peppoch, *n.* the store of cherry-stones from which the 'castles,' or 'caddles,' of 'paips' are supplied.

Perambulation, *n.* the itinerating of a judge going on circuit.

Perconnon, Percunnance, *n.* condition, term, understanding.

†**Perdé,** *int.* an oath. Cf. Pardi.

†**Perdews,** *n.* the forlorn hope.

†**Perdue,** *adj.* driven to extremities, so as to use violent means.

Pere, *v.* to pour; to stream. Cf. Pirr.

Perelt, *adj.* paralytic. Cf. Perils.

Perempt, *adj.* peremptory.

Peremptor, Peremper, *adj.* peremptory; exact; precise.—*n.* a peremptory demand; an allegation for the purpose of defence.—*phrs.* 'at one's peremptors,' at one's wits' end; 'upon one's perempers,' being so very exact and precise.

Peremptourly, *adv.* precisely; unalterably.

Perfeck, *adj.* perfect; thorough, utter.—*adv.* thoroughly, utterly.

Perfeckshous, *adj.* perfect.

Perfite, Perfit, Perfyt, *adj.* perfect, exact, neat; finished, complete, utter.—*v.* to finish, bring to completion or perfection.

Perfite age, *n.* the age of twenty-one; majority.

Perfitely, *adv.* thoroughly, in finished style.

Perfiteness, *n.* exactness; neatness; perfection.

Perfumed, *ppl. adj.* thorough, 'out-and-out'; used intensively.

Perfurnish, *v.* to furnish thoroughly.

Pergaddus, *n.* a heavy fall or blow.

Perie, *n.* a peg-top. Cf. Peerie.

Perils, Perls, *n.* a shaking of head or limbs, resulting from a paralytic affection.

Perish, *v.* to kill or starve with cold or hunger; to be benumbed with cold; to destroy, injure, murder; to devour, eat up; to squander, waste.

Perishment, *n.* severe cold; a severe chill.

Perjim, *adj.* neat.

Perjink, Perjinct, *adj.* precise, particular, nice; neat; finical.—*n.* a precise, particular, finical person; in *pl.* 'p's and q's.'

Perjinkety, *adj.* extreme as to neatness, &c., finical.—*n.* in *pl.* preciseness, niceties, particulars, details; peculiarities; odd ways; naughty tricks.

Perk, *n.* a bird's perch; a clothes-line; a peg; a small wooden skewer for plugging a hole; an affected little girl; a pole, a perch.—*v.* to perch; to brighten up.

Perkin, *n.* a thin, round gingerbread biscuit, with a piece of almond in the centre.

Perk-tree, *n.* a pole to support a clothes-line.

Perky, *adj.* saucy, pert.

Perlie, *n.* a money-box. Cf. Pirlie.

Perlie, *n.* anything small; the little finger.—*adj.* difficult to please. Cf. Pirlie.

Perlin, *n.* lace. Cf. Pearlin.

Perlyaag, *n.* rubbish, bits of all kinds; a mixture of odds and ends; something nauseous or unpalatable.

Permusted, *ppl. adj.* scented.

Pernickety, Pernackety, Pernicketty, Perneekity, Pernickity, Pernicked, Pernicky,

adj. particular, fastidious, finical; difficult to please, fidgety; dainty, nice.—*adv.* particularly, fastidiously, daintily.—*n.* in *pl.* niceties, 'p's and q's.'

Perpen, *n.* a partition. Cf. Parpane.

Perple, *n.* a wooden partition.

Perplin, *n.* a 'cat and clay' wall between the kitchen and the 'spence' of a cottage.

†**Perqueer, Perquire, Perqueir, Perquer,** *adj.* accurate, exact; elaborate, skilled.—*adv.* accurately, exactly, by heart; distinctly, separately.

Perqueerly, *adv.* accurately, by heart.

Perr, *n.* a breeze; energy. Cf. Pirr.

Perrackit, *n.* a little, smart child; a sagacious, talkative child.

Perrie, *adj.* small. Cf. Peerie.

Perris, Perrishin, *n.* a parish. Cf. Parochine, Parishen.

Pershittie, *adj.* precise; prim.

†**Persil,** *n.* parsley. Cf. Parsel.

Personality, *n.* personal peculiarity; personal appearance.

Persowdy, *n.* a medley, an incongruous mixture. Cf. Powsowdy.

Perteen, *v.* to pertain, belong to.

Pertrick, *n.* a partridge.

Pertrubill, *v.* to perturb, trouble greatly.

Pery, *n.* a peg-top. Cf. Peerie.

Pesky, *adj.* 'plaguy'; tiresome.

Pesse-pie, *n.* a pie baked for Easter.

Pessments, *n.* livery. Cf. Pasment.

Pess-Sunday, *n.* Easter Sunday.

Pest, *v.* to pester, plague.

†**Pestillette,** *n.* a small pistol, a pistolet.

Pestration, *n.* annoyance, worry, plague.

Pesty, *adj.* troublesome, 'plaguy.'

Pet, *n.* a very fine day in the midst of bad weather.—*v.* to feed delicately, pamper; to sulk, take offence.

Petal, *n.* a plough-staff. Cf. Pattle.

Pet day, *n.* a fine day in bad weather.

Peter, *n.* in *phrs.* to 'make a Peter of,' to befool, ill-use; to 'put the Peter on,' to snub, annoy.

Peter-Dick, *n.* a dancing step in which the movements of the feet correspond to these words when said at the same time.

Peter's pleugh, *n.* the constellation *Ursa major.*

Peter's staff, *n.* the constellation Orion's sword or belt.

Peth, *n.* a steep, narrow path. Cf. Path.

Pether, Pethir, Pethirt, *n.* a pedlar.

Pethlins, *adv.* by a steep declivity.

Petitour, *n.* one entitled to raise an action by which something is sought to be decreed by the judge in consequence of a right of property in the pursuer.

Pet-loll, *n.* a favourite, darling.

Petrie-ball, *n.* a black-ball used by shoemakers.

Pett, Pettit, *n.* the skin of a sheep without wool.

†**Petticoat-tails,** *n.* a kind of tea-bread, baked with butter; small cakes.

Pettie, *n.* a sea-bird.

Pettie, *adj.* small.—*n.* a man's short woollen under-vest.

Pettie-pan, *n.* a white-iron pastry-mould.

Pettie-point, *n.* a particular kind of sewing-stitch.

Pettle, *n.* a foot.

Pettle, *v.* to pet, 'cocker'; to make much of; to indulge; to take care of one's self.

Pettle, *n.* a plough-staff. Cf. Pattle.

Petty-whin, *n.* the needle-furze.

Peuchling, *n.* a slight fall of snow. Cf. Peughle.

Peugh, *int.* an excl. of disgust, contempt, &c.

Peughle, *v.* to attempt anything feebly; to do anything inefficiently; to cough in a stifled manner; used of rain: to drizzle continuously; of snow: to fall in fine particles; to eat little and slowly, nibble without appetite; to sneak off; to whine.—*n.* a stifled cough; a nibble, a small bit such as a sick ox takes at a time. Cf. Peul, Pyoul.

Peught, *adj.* asthmatic.

Peuk, *v.* to whine, whimper, wail.

Peul, *v.* to pule, whine, fret; to eat without appetite; to sneak away.—*n.* a small bite, such as a sick ox takes. Cf. Peughle.

Peust, *adj.* in comfortable circumstances; smug and self-satisfied every way.—*n.* one who is thick and heavy. Cf. Puist.

Peuter, *v.* to whine, whimper.

Peuter, Peuther, *v.* to canvass; to bustle about seeking votes; to go about aimlessly; to potter; to appear working yet accomplishing nothing. Cf. Pouter.

Peuter-fac't, *adj.* having a complexion of the colour of pewter.

Peutherer, *n.* a worker in pewter.

Peutring, *n.* the act of canvassing.

Peveral, *n.* the flat stone, &c., with which 'hop-scotch' is played. Cf. Peeveralls.

Pew, *n.* the least breath of wind or smoke; the least ripple on the sea; a small quantity.—*v.* used of smoke: to rise, be wafted.

Peweep, *n.* the lapwing.

Pewil, Pewl, *v.* to 'peughle' or 'peul.' Cf. Peughle, Peul.

Pewit, *n.* the lapwing.

Pewter, *v.* to canvass. Cf. Peuter.

Pewtring, *ppl. adj.* bungling.

Pey, *v.* to pay; to punish.

Peyay, *int.* a milkmaid's call to calves to come to their mothers.

Peychle, *n.* a fat person.

Peysie-whin, *n.* the greenstone. Cf. Peasie-whin.

Peysle, Peyzle, *n.* any small tool used by a rustic.

Peyster, *n.* a miser who feeds voraciously.

Peyvee, *n.* a trick; a contortion. Cf. Paw, Pavie.

Peyzart, Peysert, *n.* a miser.—*adj.* miserly.

Phairg, *v.* to work vigorously; to rub or beat severely.—*n.* the act of rubbing.

Phaple, *n.* the under-lip; the countenance. Cf. Faiple.

Pheare, *n.* a companion, a 'fere.'

Pheer, *v.* in ploughing : to mark off the ridges by one or two furrows. Cf. Feer.

Pheerin, *n.* the act of turning a plough; the furrow or furrows that mark off the breadth of the ridges.

Pheerin-pole, *n.* a pole used by ploughmen in opening up the furrows.

Pheugh, Pheuch, *int.* an excl. of contempt, disgust, &c.

Phieton, *n.* a phaeton.

Philabeg, *n.* the leather pouch worn in front of a Highlander's kilt; a kilt; a fillibeg.

Philander, *v.* to prance, caper, as a horse.

Phingrim, *n.* a coarse woollen cloth. Cf. Fingerin, Fingrom.

Phink, *n.* a species of the finch.

Phinnick, Phinoc, *n.* a species of gray trout. Cf. Finnac.

Phizz, *n.* a beard.

Phleme, *n.* a farrier's lancet, a 'fleam.'

Phraise, Phrase, *v.* to talk insincerely; to use coaxing, flattering, fussy speech glibly; to brag.—*n.* smooth, insincere, glib speech; voluble, unmeaning talk; fuss, ado.

Phraiser, *n.* a braggart; a wheedling person.

Phraising, *ppl. adj.* given to flattery, &c.—*n.* fair speech, flattery; the act of cajoling.

†Phrenesie, *n.* frenzy.

Physical, *adj.* relating to physic, drugs, &c.; medical; medicinal, healing.

Pibrach, Pibrugh, *n.* Highland bagpipe music; a pibroch.

Pibroch-reed, *n.* a bagpipe.

Picher, *n.* a flurry, bustle; work done with bustle and uselessly; a bother, perplexity; a weak, bustling person; one who works in a flurry without plan or method.—*v.* to work in a hurry and bustle; to be bothered or perplexed in one's work.

Picherty, *n.* a difficulty; embarrassment. Cf. Pickelty.

Picht, *v.* to work weakly.—*n.* a very diminutive and deformed person.

Pick, *n.* a pickaxe; a soldier's pike; an instrument for detaching limpets from a rock. —*v.* to indent; to hew stone; to detach limpets.

Pick, *n.* pitch.—*v.* to bedaub with pitch.

Pick, *v.* to throw stones at; used of animals; to abort.

Pick, *v.* to pilfer; to peck, eat in small quantities or with poor appetite; to choose; to find fault with.—*n.* choice; a selected article; a peck; a very small quantity; a little food; a meal; a pique, grudge, quarrel.

Pick, *n.* a spade in playing-cards; in *pl.* the suit of spades.

Pick, *v.* to dress, beautify.—*n.* a thread of gold, silk, &c.; an implement used in embroidering. Cf. Pyke.

Pick, *n.* a marble used as a mark to aim at.

Pickal, *n.* a miller.

Pick and dab, *n.* potatoes and salt.

Pick and wale, *n.* the best choice; a selection to choose from.

Pickaternie, *n.* the common tern; the Arctic tern. Cf. Pictarnie.

Pick-black, *adj.* black as pitch.

Pick-dark, *adj.* pitch-dark.

Pickelty, *n.* a difficulty; a plight; embarrassment; suspense, eagerness.

Picken, *n.* a picking, a scrap of food.

Picken, Pickenie, *adj.* used of cheese : pungent from the action of mites.

Picker, *n.* a young fish, a codling.

Picker, *v.* to bustle.—*n.* a bustle. Cf. Picher.

Picker, *n.* a petty thief.

Picker, *n.* the implement for pushing the shuttle across the loom.

Picker, *n.* an implement of embroidery.

Pickerel, *n.* the dunlin.

Pickery, *n.* petty theft.

Picket, *v.* to dash a marble against the knuckles of losers in a game.—*n.* such a blow on the knuckles; in *pl.* the penalty of losing at tennis paid by holding up the hand against the wall while others strike it with the tennis-ball.

Picketarnie, *n.* the tern. Cf. Pictarnie.

Pickie, *n.* 'hop-scotch.'

Pickie, *adj.* insignificant; petty.

Pickie, *n.* a wooden pole with iron hook, used for striking fish into a boat.

Pickie-burnet, *n.* a young black-headed gull.

Pickie-fingered, *adj.* given to pilfering.

Pickie-laird, *n.* a small proprietor.

Pickie-man, *n.* a miller's servant ; a miller.

Pickietar, Pickietarnie, *n.* the tern. Cf. Pictarnie.

Pickin, *adj.* used of cheese : tart, pungent. Cf. Picken.

†Pickindail, *n.* a ruff or collar with star-shaped points, a piccadill.

Pickit, *ppl. adj.* meagre ; bare ; niggardly.

Pickle, *n.* a grain of corn ; any small seed ; a small particle ; a small quantity ; a few.

Pickle, *v.* to pilfer; to pick up as a blrd; to pick up a tune note by note; to dawdle.

Pickle, *n.* the brain.

Pickled primineary, *n.* a quandary.

Pickman, *n.* a pikeman.

Pickmaw, Pickmire, *n.* the black-headed gull.

Pick-mirk, *adj.* pitch-dark.—*n.* total darkness.

Picktelie, *n.* a plight, difficulty. Cf. Pickelty.

Pickthank, *adj.* ungrateful.—*n.* a mischief-maker; a fault-finder.

Picktooth, *n.* a toothpick.

Pi-cow, *n.* 'hide-and-seek,' a game of assaulting and defending a 'castle' or 'fort.'

Pictarnie, Pictarn, *n.* the common tern; the Arctic tern.

Pictarnitie, *n.* the black-headed gull.

Picts' houses, *n.* underground erections.

Pictur', Pickter, *n.* a 'sight,' 'spectacle'; used contemptuously.

Piddie, *v.* to urinate; a child's term.

Piddle, *v.* to 'piddie'; a child's term.

Piddle, *v.* to trifle with one's foot; to take short steps.

Pidge, *v.* to confine in small space.

Pie, *n.* a mess, scrape; a conical potato-pit.

Pie, *n.* a magpie.—*v.* to peer like a magpie; to squint.

Pie, *n.* an eyelet for a lace; a hole made in patterns of knitting, embroidery, &c.

Piece, *conj.* although.

Piece, *n.* with *of* omitted, a part of anything; an abusive term for a woman; a recitation; an indefinite space or distance; a slice of bread, &c., given to children as lunch; a place, room; a hogshead of wine; with *the,* apiece.

Piece-time, *n.* lunch-time.

Piefer, *v.* to whimper; to fret for little; to be petulant; to work feebly.—*n.* a 'cypher.' Cf. Piffer.

†Piege, *n.* a snare, trap for rats or mice.

Pie-hole, *n.* an eyelet for a lace; a hole in patterns of knitting or embroidery. Cf. Pie.

Piel, *n.* an iron wedge for boring stones.

Piepher, *v.* to whimper.—*n.* a very useless creature. Cf. Piffer.

Pier, *n.* a quay or wharf.

Piercel, *n.* a gimlet.

Pierie, *n.* a peg-top. Cf. Peerie.

Pierie, *adj.* little. Cf. Peerie.

Piet, *n.* a magpie.

Piew, *n.* a very faint breath of wind or ripple on water.—*v.* used of smoke: to ascend. Cf. Pew.

Piffer, *v.* to whimper; to complain peevishly; to do anything feebly in a trifling way.—*n.* an utterly useless person, a 'cypher.'

Pifferin', *ppl. adj.* trifling, insignificant; complaining.

Pig, Pigg, *n.* an earthenware jar or pitcher; a stone bottle; a hot-water bottle; a chamber-pot; an ornamental or common flower-pot; a chimney-can; any article of crockery; a potsherd.

Pig and ragger, *n.* a pedlar who exchanges crockery for rags and bones.

Pig-ass, *n.* an ass for drawing a cart with crockery for sale.

Pigful, *n.* what fills an earthenware 'pig.'

Pigger, *n.* an earthenware marble.

Piggery, *n.* a collective name for pigs.

Piggery, *n.* a pottery; a crockery-shop; earthenware.

Piggie, *n.* a small earthenware jar or bottle.

Piggin, *n.* an earthenware swine-trough.

Pigman, *n.* a male seller of crockery.

Pigs and whistles, *n.* wreck and ruin; useless knick-knacks.

Pigshop, *n.* a crockery-shop.

Pigwife, *n.* a female seller of crockery.

Pik, *v.* to strike lightly with anything sharp-pointed. Cf. Pick.

Pik, *n.* pitch. Cf. Pick.

Pike, *n.* applied to a tall, thin, sharp-featured person; the rib of an umbrella; a cairn of stones on the highest point of a hill.

Pike, *v.* to pick; to gather; to pick bare; to scratch with the finger-nail; to pilfer, practise petty thieving; to trim and clean flower-beds; to nibble, to eat sparingly or with little appetite; to eat pasture bare; to emaciate.—*n.* a small quantity of food; anything to pick up and eat. Cf. Pick.

Pike, *n.* the spade in playing-cards. Cf. Pick.

Pike, *n.* a pique. Cf. Pick.

Pike, *v.* to dress, adorn.—*n.* a stitch or thread of gold, &c.; an instrument used in embroidery. Cf. Pyke.

Pike-a-plea-body, *n.* a litigious person.

Pikeman, *n.* a miller; a miller's servant. Cf. Pickie-man.

Pike out, *v.* to delineate; to prick out.

Piker, *n.* a wire for cleaning the vent of a gun.

Pikes, *n.* short, withered heath.

Pikes, *n.* a drubbing. Cf. Paik.

Pikethank, *n.* a meddlesome, officious person; a slanderous mischief-maker.—*adj.* ungrateful.—*phr.* 'for pikethank,' for mere thanks. Cf. Pickthank.

Pikie, *adj.* given to pilfering.

Piking, *n.* nourishment, food; livelihood.

Pikit, *ppl. adj.* emaciated, lean, pinched.

Pikit, *ppl. adj.* spiked, pointed.

Pikle, *n.* a pitchfork.

Pik-mirk, *adj.* pitch-dark.

Pi-ku, *n.* 'hide-and-seek.' Cf. Pi-cow.

Pilch, *n.* anything hung before the thighs to preserve them from injury in the 'casting' of peats with a 'flaughter-spade.'

Pilch, *n.* a tough, skinny piece of meat; anything short and gross; a short, fat person. —*adj.* thick, gross. Cf. Bilch.

Pilcheck, *n.* a worthless fellow, a rake. Cf. Pilshach.

Pilcher, *n.* the marble which a player uses in his hand to pitch with; a 'pitcher.'

Pile, *n.* a small quantity.

Pile, *n.* fat or grease as a scum on soup, &c.; grease skimmed off the liquor in which fat meat has been boiled.

Pile, *n.* a blade or stalk of straw, grass, &c.; a single grain.

Pile, *n.* the motion of the water made by a fish rising to the surface.

†Pile, *n.* the reverse of a coin; money; in *phr.* 'with neither cross nor pile,' without a single coin.

Pilget, *n.* a quarrel, broil; a conflict; a difficulty, plight. —*v.* to quarrel; to get into difficulty.

Pilgeting, Pilgatting, *n.* the act of quarrelling.

Pilgie, *n.* a quarrel. —*v.* to quarrel; to toil, struggle.

Pilgrim, *v.* to go on pilgrimage.

Pilgrimer, *n.* a pilgrim.

Pilk, *v.* to pick, pluck; to take out of a husk or shell; to pilfer.

Pilkings, *n.* the last-drawn milk, 'strippings.'

Pill, *n.* anything unpleasant; anything very small.

Pillan, *n.* a small, greenish sea-crab, used for bait, the shear crab.

Pillarachie, *n.* hubbub, confusion. Cf. Pitleurachie.

Pillenrichie, *n.* a 'pillarachie.'

Pillgarlic, *n.* a person or thing of no value; a weakling; a simpleton. Cf. Peelgarlick.

Pillie, *n.* a pulley.

Pilliewinkes, *n.* the thumbscrew; thumbkins. Cf. Pilniewinks.

Pillie-winkie, *n.* a barbarous sport against young birds among children. Cf. Pinkie-winkie.

Pillions, *n.* rags, tatters.

Pillonian, *n.* a kind of coarse blue cloth. Cf. Pollonian.

Pillow, *n.* a tumultuous noise.

Pillowbere, *n.* a pillow-slip.

Pilly, *n.* a boys' game, the cry used in the game.

Pillyshee, *n.* a pulley. Cf. Pullisee.

Pilniewinks, *n.* an instrument of torture formerly used, of the nature of 'thumbkins' or thumbscrews.

Pilshach, Pilshock, *n.* a piece of thick, dirty cloth; a dirty, ugly piece of dress; a low, coarse, dirty fellow. Cf. Pilcheck.

Piltack, Piltock, Piltick, *n.* a coal-fish in its second year.

Piltin-pyock, *n.* a bag for guarding the thighs from the 'flaughter-spade' in peat-cutting.

Pimginet, *n.* a small red pimple; one resulting from over-indulgence in spirits.

Pimpin, *adj.* mean, scurvy.

Pimrose, *n.* the primrose.

Pin, *n.* a small, neat person or animal; a person of small stature; the latch of a door; a fiddle-peg; humour, temper; a point, peak, summit; the hip-bone; a leg; anything used for closing or filling up, a small stone for filling up a crevice in a wall.— *v.* to attach; to fasten; to stop a hole or crevice in masonry by driving something in; to fill; to seize, grasp; to steal, pilfer.

Pin, *v.* to strike by throwing or shooting; to make a small hole by throwing a stone, &c.; to drub.—*n.* a sharp stroke or blow, a blow from an object thrown; a severe beating; speed, haste in running.

Pinch, *v.* to economize; to stint; to puzzle, put to the pinch.—*n.* hunger; the smallest possible portion; a difficulty.

Pinch, *n.* an iron crowbar.

Pincher, *n.* in *pl.* pincers, tweezers.

Pincing, *ppl. adj.* pinching; chilling.

Pind, *v.* to impound; to 'poind'; to distrain.

Pinding, *n.* costiveness in lambs.

Pine, *v.* to suffer pain; to inflict pain; to take pains, toil; to fret, complain; to dry or cure fish by exposure to the weather.—*n.* grief, pain, misery; pains, trouble; used of sheep: a wasting disease. Cf. Pining.

Pine, *v.* used of wind: to blow strongly.

Pine-, Piner-pig, *n.* an earthenware money-box.

Piner, *n.* a strong breeze from N. or N.E.

Piner, *n.* an animal that does not thrive.

Piner, *n.* one who prepares mortar for the mason; a labourer; a carter; a scavenger; a porter. Cf. Pynour.

Ping, *v.* to strike, dash against.—*n.* the noise of a hard substance striking against metal, &c.

Pinge, *v.* to whine. Cf. Peenge.

Pingil, *v.* to strive. Cf. Pingle.

Pinging, *ppl. adj.* thumping, resounding.

Pinging, *ppl. adj.* sordid, miserly, mean, 'pinching.'

Pingle, Pingle-pan, *n.* a small saucepan; a small tin pan with a long handle.

Pingle, *v.* to strive, compete; to quarrel; to struggle, toil, contend with difficulties.—*n.* a struggle for a livelihood; a combat; a turmoil; a difficulty; labour, toil without much result.

Pingles, *n.* a pedlar's varied stock-in-trade made up in bundles.

Pingling, *n.* striving for subsistence with not much success; constant, irksome application; difficult or tiresome work.

Ping-pong, *n.* a jewel fixed to a wire with a long pin at the end, and worn in front of the cap.

Pinie, *n.* a game.

Pining, Pining and vanquishing, *n.* a wasting disease of young sheep; tubercular consumption.

Pinion, *n.* a pivot.

Pinit, *ppl. adj.* starved, hungry-looking.

Pink, *v.* to deck, to dress up.—*n.* an example or type of utmost perfection; a term of endearment used by a young man to his sweetheart; the prettiest, the best.

Pink, *v.* to contract the eye; to glimmer.—*n.* a small gleam of light.

Pink, *v.* to trickle, drop, drip; to bespot.—*n.* a drop; the sound of a drop; a very small hole; a very small spot.—*adv.* drop by drop, in drops.

Pink, *v.* to strike smartly with any small object, as a marble; to poke, push; to beat, punish.

Pinkerton, *n.* a person of small intelligence. Cf. Pinkie.

Pinkie, *n.* the clove-pink.

Pinkie, *adj.* small; glimmering; used of the eyes: narrow, drooping.—*n.* a blindfolded person; a person of small intelligence; anything very small; the little finger; the smallest size of candle; the weakest small-beer.

Pinkie-finger, *n.* the little finger.

Pinkie-nail, *n.* the nail of the little finger.

Pinkie-small, *n.* anything very small.

Pinkie-winkie, *n.* a barbarous pastime against birds among young children. Cf. Pilliewinkie.

Pinkle-pankle, *n.* the tinkling sound of a little liquid in a bottle, jar, &c.—*v.* to make a tinkling sound, as of a little liquid in a jar, &c.

Pinkling, *n.* a thrilling, tinkling motion.

Pink-pank, *v.* to make a tinkling sound, as by twitching the strings of a musical instrument.

Pin-leg, *n.* a wooden leg.

Pinler, *n.* a forester; a field-watcher. Cf. Pundler.

Pin-mittens, *n.* woollen gloves knitted by men on wooden pins.

Pinn, *v.* to suffer pain. Cf. Pine.

Pinn, *n.* a leg. Cf. Pin.

Pinn, *v.* to drub. Cf. Pin.

Pinnance, *n.* a pinnace.

Pinner, *v.* to dash, roll; to move quickly and noisily. Cf. Binner.

Pinner, *n.* a woman's head-dress, with lappets pinned to the temples, reaching down to the breast, and fastened there.

Pinner-pig, *n.* a child's earthenware money-box. Cf. Pine-pig.

Pinnet, *n.* a streamer; a pennant.

Pinning, *n.* diarrhœa in sheep.

Pinning, *n.* a surfeit.

Pinning, *n.* a small stone for fitting into a crevice in a wall.

Pinning, *ppl.* running quickly.

Pinning-awl, *n.* a shoemaker's awl for pegging shoes.

Pinnit, *ppl. adj.* used of lambs: seized with diarrhœa.

Pinny, *n.* a pinafore.

Pinnywinkles, *n.* the thumbkins. Cf. Pilniewinks.

†Pinsel, *n.* a streamer; a banneret.

Pint, *n.* a measure equal to two English quarts.

Pint, *v.* to point.

Pint, *n.* a point; a shoe-tie.

Pintacks, *n.* a children's game in which the stakes are pins.

Pin-the-widdie, *n.* a small dried haddock, unsplit; a very thin person.

Pintill-fish, *n.* the pipe-fish.

Pinto, Pintoe, *n.* a wooden lever for turning a weaver's beam.

Pin-tooth, *n.* a pin-cushion.

Pint-pig, *n.* a child's money-box. Cf. Pine-pig.

Pint-stoup, *n.* a pint-measure; a drinking-vessel; a spiral shell of the genus *Turba*, resembling a 'pint-stoup.'

Piona, *n.* the peony.

Piot, *n.* the magpie.

Pioted, *ppl. adj.* variegated; piebald.

Pi-ox, *n.* 'hide-and-seek'; a game of siege and defence. Cf. Pi-cow.

Pioy, Pioye, *n.* a conical firework of moistened gunpowder. Cf. Peeoye.

Pipe, *n.* the throat; in *pl.* the bagpipe.—*v.* used of the wind: to whistle loud, howl; to cry, weep; to frill with an Italian iron.

Pipe-bent, *n.* a stalk of the dog's-tail grass.

Pipe-gun, *n.* a pop-gun.

Piper, *n.* a singer, vocalist; a half-dried haddock; the sea-urchin; the daddy-long-legs or crane-fly.

Piper, *n.* a marble made of pipeclay.

Pipe-reek, *n.* tobacco-smoke.

Piper-faced, *adj.* pale, delicate-looking.

Piper-fu', *adj.* very drunk.

Piper's invite, *n.* the last asked to a convivial meeting or party.

Piper's news, *n.* stale news.

Pipe-shank, *n.* a pipe-stem.

Pipe-shankit, *adj.* used of the legs: long and thin.

Pipe-skill, *n.* skill in playing the bagpipe.

Pipe-small, *n.* a silly, useless person; one feeble in body and mind. Cf. Peep-sma'.

Pipe-stapple, *n.* the stem of a clay pipe; anything very brittle; a blade of dog's-tail grass; in *pl.* broken pieces of a pipe-stem; a children's plaything, consisting of a green pea pierced by two pins at right angles, and placed at the upper end of a pipe-stem, which is held vertically and blown gently through.

Pipin'-fou, *adj.* very drunk, 'fou as a piper.'

Piping, *n.* a frill.

Piping-hot, *adj.* used of lessons : said by a pupil fresh from learning them, and not likely to remember them long.

Piping-iron, *n.* an Italian iron.

Pipple, *v.* to cry; to whimper.

Pipple-papple, *v.* to patter; to pop, do anything with a sudden noise or motion.—*adv.* with a popping sound or motion.

Pir, *n.* a breeze, a flaw of wind. Cf. Pirr.

Pirie, *n.* a peg-top. Cf. Peerie.

Pirie's chair, *n.* a punishment in a boys' game, when a wrong answer to a question was given.

Pirjinct, Pirjink, *adj.* exact, precise. Cf. Perjink.

Pirk, *n.* a clothes-line. Cf. Perk.

Pirkas, Pirkus, *n.* a perquisite; a thing not worth having.

Pirkle, *v.* to prick.—*n.* a thorn. Cf. Prickle.

Pirl, *v.* to spin round as a top; to push or roll gently along; used of a brook : to purl; to whirl; to twist, twine, curl; to twist horsehair into a fishing-line; to poke, stir; to fumble, grope; to handle overmuch; to work needlessly, in a trifling way, or easily; to shoot.—*n.* a whirl, a twist, curl; a ripple on the surface of water; a gentle stirring; undue handling; work done easily, with little accomplished.

Pirlag, *n.* a small, round lump of dung. Cf. Purl.

Pirlet, *n.* a puny, contemptible figure.

Pirlewoot, *n.* marmalade.

Pirley pease-weep, *n.* a boys' game.

Pirl-grass, *n.* creeping wheat-grass.

†Pirlicue, Pirliecue, *n.* a brief recital at the close of a series of sermons, addresses, &c. of the chief points treated; a flourish at the end of a word in writing; the space between the forefinger and thumb extended; in *pl.* whims, oddities.—*v.* to give a *résumé* of previous sermons, &c., specially at the close of a Communion season.

Pirlie, *n.* a money-box.

Pirlie, *n.* anything small; the little finger.— *adj.* difficult to please.

Pirlie, *adj.* crisp; tending to curl up.

Pirlie-pig, *n.* an earthenware money-box.

Pirlie-skinned, *adj.* having a crisp, curly coat.

Pirlie-wee, *adj.* small.

Pirlie-weeack, *n.* anything small of its kind

Pirlie-wheel, *n.* the small spinning-wheel.

Pirlie-winkie, *n.* the little finger.

Pirlie-wirlie, *n.* a term of contempt.

Pirlin, *ppl. adj.* crisp, curly.

Pirlin, *n.* the selecting of potatoes by feeling for them with the hand.

Pirlin-stick, -wand, *n.* a rod for stirring 'shilling seeds' to make them burn when they are used as fuel.

Pirlit, *n.* a puny figure. Cf. Pirlet.

Pirn, *n.* a reel or bobbin on which yarn or thread is wound; the bobbin of a shuttle; yarn wound on 'pirns'; a reel of cotton; the reel of a fishing-rod; a wheel; an ill-turn.—*v.* to reel; to run to and fro.

Pirn-cap, *n.* a wooden dish used by weavers for holding their quills or reeds round which the yarn was wound.

Pirned, *ppl. adj.* having unequal threads or colours; striped.

Pirn-girnel, *n.* a box for holding 'pirns' while being filled.

Pirn-house, *n.* a weaver's shed.

Pirnickerie, *adj.* troublesome; precise. Cf. Pernickety.

Pirnie, *adj.* used of cloth or a web : of unequal threads or unlike colours; striped, variegated.—*n.* a night-cap.

Pirnie-cap, *n.* a striped woollen night-cap.

Pirnie-castle, *n.* a contemptuous designation for the harvester on the 'rig' that is generally behind the rest.

Pirn of ale, *n.* three gallons of ale.

Pirn-stick, *n.* the wooden 'broach' on which the quill or 'pirn.' is placed while the yarn is reeled off; in *pl.* thin legs, spindle-shanks.

Pirn-wheel, *n.* a wheel for winding bobbins.

Pirnwife, *n.* a woman who fills the 'pirns' with yarn.

Pirn-winding, *n.* the act of winding 'pirns.' —*adj.* engaged in winding 'pirns.'

Pirr, *n.* a gentle breath of wind; a breeze; a stirring up; vigour, energy; a flurry, 'birr'; a pettish fit.—*v.* to blow gently, to freshen; to spring up or forth, as blood from a lancet-wound. Cf. Pere.

Pirr, *adj.* neat, trim; gaily dressed; precise in manner; having a tripping mode of walking; walking with a spring.

Pirr, *n.* the common tern; the tern's cry.

Pirr-egg, *n.* the tern's egg.

Pirrie, *adj.* neat; precise. Cf. Pirr.

Pirrie, *v.* to follow a person from place to place like a dependant.

Pirrie-dog, *n.* a dog that follows his master

closely; one who is constant companion to another; a parasite. Cf. Para-dog, Penny-dog.

Pirrihouden, *adj.* fond, doating.

Pirwee, *n.* a flighty or excited mood.

Pirweeans, *n.* a conceited, flighty person.

Pirzie, *adj.* conceited.

Pish, *v.* to make water.—*n.* a jot.

Pishminnie, *n.* an ant.

Pishminnie-hillan, -tammock, *n.* an ant-hill.

Pishmother, *n.* an ant.

Pisk, *n.* a dry, scornful-looking girl.

Pisket, *adj.* dried, shrivelled; dry, reserved in manner.

Piskie, *adj.* dry, withered, shrivelled; short, stunted. Cf. Peeskie.

Piskie, *adj.* marshy.

Pisminnie, *n.* an ant.

Piss, *int.* a call to a cat; an excl. to drive away a cat.—*v.* to hiss in order to drive off; to incite a dog to attack.

Piss-a-bed, *n.* the dandelion.

†**Pistolet, Pistolette,** *n.* a small pistol. Cf. Pestilette.

Pisweip, *n.* the lapwing. Cf. Peesweep.

Pit, *v.* to put.—*phrs.* to 'pit one down,' to execute one; to 'pit one's self down,' to commit suicide.

Pit, *n.* a colliery; a dungeon; a pit for drowning women; a conical heap of potatoes, turnips, &c. partially sunk in the ground and covered with straw and earth.—*v.* to cover a heap of potatoes, &c., with straw and earth; to mark as with smallpox.

Pitata, Pitawta, Pitatay, Pitattie, *n.* a potato.

Pit-bank, *n.* the mound around a coal-mine.

Pitcake, *n.* the plover.

Pitch, *v.* to affix; to start a tune; with *into*, to attack, assail vigorously.

Pitcher, *n.* the marble with which a boy aims; the piece of slate or stone used in hop-scotch.

Pitchie, *n.* the game of hop-scotch.

Pitching-ring, *n.* the ring in playing marbles.

Pitch-pea, *n.* the wild vetch.

Pit-dark, *adj.* dark as a pit.

Pit-for-pat, *adv.* pit-a-pat.

Pith, *n.* substance; marrow.—*phrs.* 'pith of hemp,' the hangman's rope; 'pith of malt,' whisky.

Pithfu', *adj.* used of words: powerful, pithy.

Pithy, *adj.* used of ale: strong.

Pitiful, *adj.* to be regretted.

Pitifu'-market, *n.* the marriage-market for widows.

Pitleurachie, *n.* hubbub, confusion. Cf. Pillarachie.

Pit-life, *n.* a collier's life.

Pit-mirk, *adj.* dark as a pit.—*n.* intense darkness.

Pit-mirkness, *n.* intense darkness.

Pit-stones, *n.* boundary-stones that mark different parts of a peat-moss.

Pitten, *ppl.* put, placed.

Pitter-patter, *v.* to beat continuously with light, rapid strokes; to fall in hasty, repeated drops, like hail; to walk to and fro, in and out of doors; to move up and down with a clattering noise with the feet; to repeat prayers hastily and mechanically.—*n.* the act of making light, rapid strokes; the sound of such strokes; the act of walking with a quick, short step; the sound of such step.—*adv.* all in a flutter.

Pitterty-pat, *adv.* pit-a-pat.

†**Pittivout,** *n.* a small arch or vault.

Pitty, *adj.* small; petty.

Pitty-patty, -pat, *adv.* pit-a-pat.—*adj.* unsteady, tottering, pattering.—*n.* the fluttering movement of a perturbed heart.

Pity, *n.* in *phrs.* 'it's a pity of one,' expressive of compassion for one; to 'think pity of one,' to feel sorry for one.—*int.* pity *me!* an excl. of surprise or self-commiseration.—*v.* to be sorry; used *impersonally*, it fills one with pity.

Piver, *v.* to shake, tremble, quiver.

Piwipe, *n.* the lapwing. Cf. Peesweep.

Piz, Pizz, *n.* peas; a single pea.

Piz, *n.* a very small person; a dwarf. Cf. Pizie.

Pizan, *n.* in *phr.* to 'play the pizan with one,' to get the better of one.

Pize, *n.* a mild form of execration.

Pizen, *n.* poison.

Pizie, Pizzie, *n.* a very small marble; a dwarf; a mischievous child. Cf. Piz.

Pizzant-like, *adj.* poisoned-like; shrivelled, wasted, withered.

Placad, *n.* a placard. Cf. Placket.

Place, *n.* a passage of Scripture, the text of a sermon; a landed proprietor's mansion-house; a small holding.—*v.* to ordain or settle a minister in a charge.

Placing, *n.* a minister's settlement in a charge.

Plack, *n.* a copper coin, worth one-third of a penny stg., or four pennies Scots; the smallest coin; the least amount of money.

Plack, *n.* a plaything. Cf. Playock.

Placket, *n.* a placard; a public proclamation.

Plackless, *adj.* penniless, poor.

Plack-pie, *n.* a pie costing a 'plack.'

Plack's-worth, *n.* what is of very little value.

Pladd, *n.* a plaid.

Plaff, *adv.* suddenly; with the sound of a slight explosion.

†**Plagiary,** *n.* an abductor; a legal term.

Plague, *n.* used in various expletives; trouble.

Plagued, Plagit, *ppl. adj.* used as a term of abuse, or as an intensive.

Plaguely, *adv.* very, excessively; greatly.

Plaguesome, *adj.* annoying, troublesome.

Plaguey, *adv.* very, excessively.

Plaid, *n.* a plaid used as a blanket.—*v.* to clothe.

Plaiden, *n.* coarse woollen twilled cloth.— *adj.* made of 'plaiden.'

Plaiden-ell, *n.* an ell of 38·416 inches, used in measuring 'plaiden.'

Plaiden-merchant, *n.* a dealer in 'plaiden.'

Plaid-neuk, *n.* the sewed-up corner of a plaid, used for carrying a lamb, &c.

Plaig, Plaik, *n.* a plaything. Cf. Playock.

Plaik, *n.* a plaid; a loose covering for the body.

†**Plain**, *adj.* used of a court, meeting, &c.: full.

Plain, *v.* to complain. Cf. Plainyie.

Plainen, *n.* coarse linen.

Plain-soled, *adj.* flat-footed.

Plain-, Plane-stanes, *n.* the pavement; a flagged roadway; the exchange of a town, as paved with flat stones.

Plaint, *v.* to complain.

Plaintless, *adj.* uncomplaining.

Plainyie, *v.* to complain.—*n.* a complaint; a dissent.

†**Plait**, *v.* to cross the legs; to throw one leg over the other in walking or running; to mark with folds or wrinkles.—*n.* a fold, a 'pleat.'

Plait-backie, *n.* a 'bedgown' reaching to the knees, with three plaits on the back.

Plaithie, *n.* a plaid.

Plaitings, *n.* the two pieces of iron below the sock of a plough.

Plane, *n.* the sycamore.

Plane-footed, *adj.* flat-footed.

Plane-soled, *adj.* flat-footed.

Plane-tree, *n.* the maple.

Plank, *n.* a regular division of land, in contrast to the irregular divisions of 'run-rig'; a piece of land in cultivation, longer than broad; a strip of land between two open furrows.—*v.* to place, settle; to divide or exchange pieces of land possessed by different people, and lying intermingled with one another, so that each person's property may be thrown into one field.

Planker, *n.* a land-measurer.

Planky, *n.* candy; a sweetmeat. Cf. Plunkie.

Planky, *n.* a large marble.

Plant, *v.* to supply a district with a minister.

Plant-cot, *n.* a small enclosure for rearing cabbage-plants.

Planting, *n.* a plantation.

Plantry, *n.* garden grounds; plantations.

Plant-toft, *n.* a bed for rearing young cabbages, &c.

Plap, *adv.* plop; with a sudden splash.

Plapper, *v.* to make a noise with the lips or by striking a flat-surfaced body in water.—*n.* the act of doing so; the noise so made.— *adv.* with a splashing noise.

Plash, *v.* to dash through water; to rain heavily; to wash or scour perfunctorily; to work with the hands in a liquid; to work ineffectually.—*n.* a splash of rain, mud; a heavy downfall of rain, snow, &c.; a quantity of liquid or semi-liquid dashed violently; a 'mess' of ill-cooked liquid food.—*adv.* with a splash.

Plash-fluke, *n.* the plaice.

Plashie, *n.* the plaice.

Plashie, *adj.* wet; wetting; miry; apt to daub; full of dirty water.

Plashing-wet, *adj.* used of clothes: soaked with water so as to make a splashing sound.

Plash-mill, *n.* a fulling-mill, a 'waulkmill.'

Plash-miller, *n.* a fuller.

Plasket, *n.* an evil trick. Cf. Plisky.

Plat, *n.* a plot of ground.

Plat, *adj.* flat; clear, plain, distinct.—*adv.* very, quite; due, direct.—*n.* a cake of cow's dung.

Plat, *v.* *pret.* did intertwine; with *up*, erected. —*n.* a plait of hair. Cf. Plait.

Plat, Platt, *n.* a plot; a plan; those who form a plan.

Platch, *n.* a flat foot.—*v.* to make a heavy noise in walking with short, quick steps.

Platch, *v.* to splash; to bespatter, besmear. —*n.* a splash; a clot; a large piece of anything; a big spot.

Platch, *v.* to patch; to mend clumsily.—*n.* a patch; a piece of cloth used as a patch.

Platchack, *n.* a large patch.

Platchen, Platchin, *v.* to cover with spots; to besmear.—*n.* a very big spot or clot.

Platchen, *v.* to patch, mend clumsily.—*n.* a big or clumsy patch.

Platchie, *adj.* splashy, bespattering, besmearing.

Plate, *v.* to clinch a nail.

Plate-jack, *n.* ancient coat-armour, platemail.

Plate-man, *n.* the man in charge of the offertory plate at a church door.

†**Platoon**, *n.* a volley; the report of a shot; a sudden scare or shock.

Platten, *v.* to rivet; to clinch a nail.

Platten-stone, *n.* a large flat stone used by blacksmiths in riveting horse-shoe nails to prevent their coming out.

Platter, *v.* to dabble among a liquid or semi-liquid; to walk smartly in water or mud.— *n.* dabbling in water, mud, &c.; the noise so caused.—*adv.* with such a sharp, continuous noise.

Play, *v.* to boil with force.

Play, *n.* any game; a holiday; a school vacation.

Play-act, -ack, *v.* to act plays; to recite.

Play-acting, *n.* acting.—*ppl. adj.* theatrical.

Play-actoring, *adj.* dramatic; theatrical.

Play at, *v.* to nibble at; to begin to enjoy.

Play brown, *v.* used of strong broths; to take on a brown colour in boiling.

Play by, *v.* to play against; to play false.

Play-carl-again, *v.* to give as good as one gets.

Play-day, *n.* the day when school holidays are given out; a day which is a half-holiday at school.

Playding, *n.* coarse woollen cloth. Cf. Plaiden.

Play-fair, *n.* a toy, plaything.

Playing-at-the-pitcher, *n.* the game of hop-scotch.

Playing-bairn, *n.* a playmate.

Play-marrow, *n.* a playmate.

Playock, Playick, Playke, *n.* a plaything, toy; a trifle.

Playrife, *adj.* playful.

Playrifety, *n.* playfulness; fondness of sport; abundance of play, sport, fun.

Playsome, *adj.* playful, sportive.

Plea, *n.* a lawsuit; the subject of a lawsuit; a quarrel, debate; wrangling, strife.—*v.* to go to law; to plead, sue; to quarrel, wrangle.

Plead, *v.* to argue, debate, quarrel.—*n.* a quarrel, strife.

Plea-house, *n.* a law-court, court-house.

Plean, *v.* to complain. Cf. Plain.

Pleasance, *n.* pleasure, delight.

Please, *v.* to relish, like.—*n.* pleasure; a pleasant word; a choice, a say.

Pleat, *v.* to plait.—*n.* a plait.

Pleck-pleck, *n.* the cry of the oyster-catcher.

Pledge, *v.* to be sure; to provide, furnish.

Pledge-house, *n.* a house in which debtors were confined.

Plee, *n.* a lawsuit; a quarrel. Cf. Plea.

Pleen, *v.* to complain. Cf. Plain.

Pleengie, *n.* the young of the herring-gull.

Pleep, *v.* to chirp; to speak in a fretful tone of voice.—*n.* the plaintive chirping of sea-fowl.

Pleepin, *n.* the chirping of a bird.—*ppl. adj.* complaining, pleading poverty or sickness.

Pleesh-plash, *v.* to splash. Cf. Plish-plash.

Pleesk, *v.* to dash and wade through water. Cf. Plesk.

Pleesure, *v.* to please, gratify.—*n.* pleasure.

Pleet, *v.* to complain in a low, peevish tone.

Pleeter, *n.* a complaint; a peevish tone.

Plencher-nails, *n.* large nails used in planking.

†Plene, *adj.* full, abundant. Cf. Plain.

Plenish, *v.* to furnish a house; to stock a farm.—*n.* furniture.

Plenisher, *n.* one who 'plenishes.'

Plenishing, *n.* furniture, furnishing; goods; stock.

Plenishment, *n.* furnishing.

Plenshing-nail, *n.* a flooring-nail.

Plenshir, *n.* a large nail for floors.

Plenstanes, *n.* a pavement. Cf. Plainstanes.

Plent, Plente, *v.* to complain.—*n.* complaint. Cf. Plaint.

Plenty, *adv.* sufficiently.

Plenyie, Plenzie, *v.* to complain. Cf. Plainyie.

Pleoch, Pleochan, *n.* a plough.

Plep, *n.* anything weak or feeble.

Pleppit, *adj.* feeble; creased; not stiff; flaccid.

Plesk, *v.* to dash through water.

†Plet, Plett, *v.* to plait.—*v. pret.* plaited. Cf. Plait.

Plet, *v.* to rivet; to clinch. Cf. Plate.

Plet, *adv.* due, direct. Cf. Plat.

Plettin, *v.* to rivet. Cf. Platten.

Plettin-stone, *n.* a large flat stone used by a smith for clinching horse-shoe nails. Cf. Platten-stone.

Pleuat, *n.* a green turf or sod, used for covering houses. Cf. Plood.

Pleuch, Pleugh, *n.* a plough; as much land as a plough can till; a plane for making a 'groove and feather'; a match-plane.—*v.* to plough; to 'groove and feather'; to use a match-plane.

Pleuch-airns, -irnes, *n.* the coulter and ploughshare of a plough.

Pleuch-bred, *adj.* bred to the plough.

Pleuch-bridle, *n.* what is attached to the head of a plough-beam, to regulate the breadth or depth of the furrow.

Pleuch-fittit, *adj.* having heavy, dragging feet.

Pleuch-gang, -gate, *n.* as much land as can be properly tilled by a plough, about forty Scotch acres.

Pleuch-gear, -graith, *n.* the harness and equipment of a plough.

Pleuch-gudes, -goods, *n.* plough-oxen.

Pleuch-lad, *n.* a ploughboy; a ploughman.

Pleuch-land, *n.* arable land.

Pleuch-man, *n.* a ploughman.

Pleuch-pettle, *n.* a small paddle for clearing earth from the plough.

Pleuch-shears, *n.* a bolt with a crooked head for regulating the 'bridle,' and keeping it steady, when the plough requires to be raised or depressed on the furrow.

Pleuch-sheath, *n.* the head of a plough, on which the 'sock' or ploughshare is put.

Pleuch-staff, *n.* the 'pleuch-pettle.'

Pleuch-stilts, *n.* the handles of a plough.

Pleuch-tail, *n.* the 'pleuch-stilts,' the rear of a plough.

Pleuk, *n.* a pimple. Cf. Plook.

Pleuter, *v.* to wade through water or mud. Cf. Plouter.

Pleutery, *n.* anything wet, dirty, or disagreeable. Cf. Ploutery.

Plew, *n.* a match-plane; a plough. Cf. Pleuch.

Plewman, *n.* a ploughman.

†Pley, *n.* a lawsuit; a quarrel.—*v.* to go to law; to quarrel. Cf. Plea.

Plichen, *n.* a plight, condition.

Plichen, *n.* a peasant.

Plicht, *v. pret.* plighted.

Plicht, *n.* a plight.

Plie, *v.* to ply; to fold, plait.—*n.* a fold, plait. Cf. Ply.

Plies, *n.* thin strata of freestone.

Plingie, *n.* the young of the herring-gull. Cf. Pleengie.

Plirrie, *n.* the young of the herring-gull.

Plish, *v.* to splash.

Plish-plash, *v.* to splash.—*adv.* in a splashing manner.—*n.* a splashing in a liquid; the noise so made.

Plisky, *n.* a trick, prank; a mischievous trick; a practical joke; a plight; a fray, 'scrimmage.'—*adj.* tricky, mischievous; frolicsome.

Plit, *n.* the slice of earth turned over by a plough; a furrow.

Plitch-platch, *n.* a splashing. Cf. Plish-plash.

Pliver, *n.* the plover.

Plleuter, *v.* to wade through mud. Cf. Plouter.

Plloud, Pllout, *v.* to waddle; to splash; to wade through mud, &c.; to put down suddenly and heavily; to fall with a short, heavy fall; to exert one's self.—*n.* a short, heavy fall; a splash into liquid; the noise of such a splash; a waddle; a fat, thickset person or animal; a plump child. Cf. Ploud, Plout.

Ploat, *v.* to plunge into hot water. Cf. Plot.

Plock, *n.* a 'plack,' worth one-third of an English penny.

Plodder, *v.* to toil continuously.

Ploiter, *v.* to wade through mud or water. Cf. Plouter.

Ploiterie, *n.* anything wet, dirty; refuse. Cf. Ploutery.

Plonk, *n.* a tree buried in a moss.

Ploo, *v.* to plough. Cf. Pleuch.

Plood, *n.* a green sod.

Ploog, *n.* a pimple. Cf. Plook.

Plook, *n.* a pimple; a spot on the skin; a small knob near the top of a metal measure for liquid.—*v.* to set the 'plook' on a vessel for measuring liquids.

Plook-besprent, *adj.* pimply, covered with pimples.

Plook-faced, *adj.* having pimples on the face.

Plookie, *adj.* full of little knobs: pimply.

Plookie-faced, *adj.* 'plook-faced.'

Plookiness, *n.* the being covered with pimples.

Plook-measure, *n.* measure up to the 'plook' of a vessel.

Plooky, *n.* a slight stroke or blow.

Ploom, *n.* a plum.

Plooman, *n.* a ploughman.

Plooster, *v.* to toil in mud or filth; to splash among water.—*n.* a mess, muddle, bungle.

Plop, Plope, *v.* to plunge, plump, flop; to fall or drop suddenly and noisily into water. —*n.* the sound made by a small object falling into water from a height.—*adv.* suddenly, with a 'plop.'

Plore, *v.* to work among mire, as children amusing themselves.

Plorie, *adj.* a piece of ground converted into mud by treading, &c.

Plot, Plote, *v.* to plunge into boiling water; to scald; to make boiling hot; to burn, scorch, make hot.—*n.* a scald or burn with boiling water; a hot, stewing, or perspiring condition.

Plot, Plott, *v.* to pluck off feathers; to make bare, flecce, rob.

Plotch, *v.* to dabble; to work slowly.

Plotcock, *n.* the devil.

Plot-het, *adj.* so hot as to scald.

Plotter, *v.* to wade through water or mud. Cf. Plouter.

Plotter-plate, *n.* a wooden platter with a place in the middle for salt.

Plottin, *n.* a plan, scheme.

Plotting, *ppl. adj.* sweating profusely.

Plottin-het, *adj.* scalding hot.

Plottit, *ppl. adj.* fleeced, plucked.

Plottit, *ppl. adj.* fond of heat; unable to bear cold.

Plotty, *n.* a rich and pleasant hot drink, made with spices, wine, and sugar, mulled; any hot drink, as tea.

Plouckie, *adj.* pimpled.

Ploud, *n.* a green sod. Cf. Plood.

Ploud, *v.* to waddle in walking; to fall with a short, heavy fall; to endeavour.—*n.* a waddling pace; a short, heavy fall; a thickset, fat person or animal; a plump child. Cf. Plout.

Plouder, *v.* to wade or walk with difficulty through water, mud, &c. Cf. Plouter.

Plouk, *n.* a pimple. Cf. Plook.

Ploumdamis, *n.* a damson.

Plounge, *v.* to plunge.—*n.* a plunge.

Ploup, *v.* to plunge. Cf. Plop.

Ploussie, *adj.* plump, well-grown.

Plout, *v.* to splash; to fall with a splash suddenly; to put down suddenly and heavily; to wade through water or mud.— *n.* a fall into liquid; a splash; the noise of a fall or splash; a heavy shower of rain:

the act of walking in water, mud, or wet soil.—*adv.* suddenly, plump.

Plout, *v.* to scald. Cf. Plot.

Plout, *v.* to poke.—*n.* a poker. Cf. Pout.

Plouter, *v.* to wade through water or mud; to flounder, splash; to dabble in liquid; to do wet or dirty work; to work awkwardly or slovenly; to dawdle; to potter about at trifling tasks.—*n.* a splash, plunge; a splashing sound; walking through water or mud; wet, disagreeable work; ill-cooked food.—*adv.* with a noisy splash.

Plouterin', *ppl. adj.* weak, unskilful at work, laborious with little result.

Ploutery, *n.* anything wet, dirty, or disagreeable; wet weather; refuse; ill-cooked food.—*adj.* wet and dirty, disagreeable.

Ploutie, *n.* a sudden fall.

Ploutin', *ppl. adj.* weak and clumsy at work.

Plout-kirn, *n.* the common churn, worked by an upright 'staff.'

Plout-net, *n.* a small, stocking-shaped net, affixed to two poles.

Ploutter, *n.* a clumsy, untidy person; a great and noisy talker. Cf. Plouter.

Plover, *n.* the golden plover. Cf. Pliver.

Plover's page, *n.* the dunlin; the jack-snipe.

Plow, *n.* a plough. Cf. Pleuch.

Plowable, *adj.* arable.

Plowp, *v.* to plunge. Cf. Plop.

Plowster, *v.* to toil in mud or filth.—*n.* a bungle, muddle. Cf. Plouter.

Plowt, *v.* to scald. Cf. Plot.

Plowter, *v.* to wade through mud, &c. Cf. Plouter.

Ploy, *n.* amusement, sport; a frolic, escapade; a practical joke; employment, business; a serious matter; a procession; a quarrel.

Pluchie, *n.* a ploughman.

Pluck, *n.* courage, spirit; what can be plucked; a small quantity of grass, &c.; a two-pronged implement, with teeth at right angles to the shaft, for taking dung out of a cart, or for uprooting turnips in hard frost; the armed bullhead; a reverse of fortune, a loss, a calamity; in *pl.* herrings damaged by the net.

Pluck, *n.* a pimple. Cf. Plook.

Plucked, *ppl. adj.* high-spirited, brave.

Plucker, *n.* the great fishing-frog; the father-lasher.

Plucking pin, *n.* a weaving implement used in hand-looms for pushing or pulling the shuttle across the loom.

Pluckless, *adj.* spiritless.

Pluck-measure, *n.* measure up to the 'plook' of a drinking-vessel. Cf. Plook.

Pluck-up, *n.* an eager struggle or demand for an article on sale or for gift; a rise in price of an article owing to its scarcity.

Plucky-face't, *adj.* having a pimpled face.

Pluff, *v.* to emit a short, sharp breath; to puff, pant, blow; to blow peas, pellets, &c. through a tube; to set fire to suddenly; to explode gunpowder; to throw out hair-powder in dressing the hair; to throw out smoke in quick, successive whiffs.—*n.* a puff, blast, shot; a slight explosion; a pinch, a small quantity of snuff, powder, &c.; a powder-puff; a piece of bored 'bourtree,' used as a bellows; a rotten and dried mushroom (the 'devil's snuff-mill'), which falls to dust when touched; a pear with a fair outside, but rotten inside; the act of throwing on hair-powder.

Pluffer, *n.* a pea-shooter; a shooter, marksman.

Pluff-grass, *n.* the creeping, and the meadow, soft-grass.

Pluff-gun, *n.* a pop-gun, a pea-shooter.

Pluffins, *n.* anything easily blown away, as the refuse of a corn-mill.

Pluffy, *adj.* fat, swollen, chubby.

Plug, *v.* to strike with the fist.

Pluke, Pluik, *n.* a pimple. Cf. Plook.

Plum, *n.* a deep pool in a river or stream; the noise made by a stone when plunged into a deep pool; the straight, the right direction.

+Plumache, Plumashe, *n.* a plume of feathers.

Plumb, *n.* a plum.

Plumb, *n.* a plunge. Cf. Plump.

Plum-damas, -dames, -damis, -damy, *n.* a damson; a Damascene plum.

Plum-duff, *n.* a suet dumpling, usually eaten with beef.

Plume, *n.* a plummet, plumb-weight.

Plume, *n.* a plum.

Plummet, *n.* the pommel of a sword.

Plump, *n.* a plunge; a heavy shower falling straight down; a ducking.—*v.* to rain heavily, like a thunder-shower.—*adv.* falling heavily and perpendicularly.

Plump, *n.* a clump of trees.

Plumpit, *ppl. adj.* plump, protuberant.

Plump-kirn, *n.* a common upright churn. Cf. Plunge-churn.

Plumpy, *adj.* plump; chubby.

Plumrock, *n.* the primrose.

Plunge-churn, *n.* a churn driven with an upright 'staff.'

Plunk, Plung, *n.* the sound made by a heavy body falling from a height into water; the sound of a cork being drawn; the sound of emitting tobacco-smoke; a sound imitating the cry of the raven; a sudden blow or stab; the 'pitching' of a marble by thumb and forefinger; a short, stout, thickset person, animal, or thing.—*v.* to drop or throw anything so as to produce a hollow sound or a crackling noise; to plump, plunge; to draw a cork; to croak like a raven; used in the game of marbles: to give a fair and full hit, to 'pitch' a marble. —*adv.* suddenly, smartly; at once.

Plunk, *v.* to desert, shirk; to play truant; to stand still, balk, like a vicious horse, 'reist.'

Plunkart, *n.* a person or thing, short, stout, and thickset.

Plunker, *n.* a large marble.

Plunker, *n.* a truant; a horse given to balking.

Plunkie, *n.* a trick; a practical joke.—*adj.* tricky, not to be trusted.

Plunkie, *n.* a sweetmeat made of molasses.

Plunkin, *n.* a game at marbles.

Pluskie, *n.* a trick. Cf. Plisky.

Plut, *v.* to splash; to put down heavily and suddenly. Cf. Plout.

Ply, *v.* with *on*, to push on; to fold, plait. —*n.* a plight, condition.

Ply, *n.* a lawsuit. Cf. Plea, Pley.

†Ply, *n.* a frolic. Cf. Ploy.

Plyaak, Plyaack, *n.* a toy, plaything. Cf. Playock.

Plyde, *n.* a plaid.

Plype, *v.* to walk or dabble in water, mud, &c.; to fall 'plump' into water; to work in slovenly fashion among any liquid.—*n.* dabbling or walking in water, mud, heavy ground, &c.; working in a slovenly way in liquids; a fall into water; the noise made by a fall into water or mud; a heavy fall of rain.—*adv.* with a 'plype.' Cf. Plap, Flop.

Plypper, *v.* to make a noise with the lips or by striking a flat-surfaced body in water. Cf. Plapper.

Plyvens, *n.* the flowers of the red clover.

Po, *n.* a chamber-pot.

Po, *int.* pooh!

Poach, *v.* to poke; used of cattle: to trample soft ground into mud and holes; to poke in a wet substance; to work in a wet or semi-liquid substance in a dirty, slovenly way; to drive backwards and forwards; to play about with food, mess.—*n.* a puddle; wet soil trampled by cattle; a muddle, mess, confusion.

Poacher-court, *n.* a nickname for a kirk-session.

Poachie, *n.* a child's game.

Poachie, *n.* a nursery name for porridge.

Poaching, *n.* the trampling of sward into holes.—*ppl. adj.* clumsy and dirty at work.

Poachy, *adj.* used of land: soft, wet, full of puddles, trampled into holes.

Poan, *n.* the fresh-water herring, guiniad; the vendace. Cf. Powan.

Poatch, *v.* to poke. Cf. Poach.

Pob, *n.* the refuse of flax, often used for pop guns.

Pob-bob, *n.* a hubbub.

Pob-tow, *n.* 'pob.'

Pock, *n.* a bag, wallet, poke, sack; a bag-shaped fishing-net; the stomach of a fish; a bag growing under the jaws of a sheep, an indication of the rot; the rot.—*v.* to catch fish in a net; to be seized with the rot.

Pock, *n.* the pustule caused by vaccination; in *pl.* smallpox.

Pock-arr, *n.* a mark left by smallpox.

Pock-arred, Pockard, *adj.* marked with smallpox.

Pock-arrie, *adj.* full of the marks of smallpox.

Pock-broken, *adj.* marked with smallpox.

Pocked, *ppl. adj.* marked with smallpox; used of sheep: having a disease resembling scrofula.

Pocket-hankie, *n.* a pocket-handkerchief.

Pocket-napkin, -naipkin, *n.* a pocket-handkerchief.

Pocket-pick, *v.* to pick one's pocket.

Pockey-ort, Pockiawrd, *adj.* marked with smallpox. Cf. Pock-arred.

Pock-faced, *adj.* having the face marked with smallpox.

Pock-freitten, *adj.* pitted by smallpox. Cf. Freitten.

Pockmanteau, Pockmanky, Pockmanty, *n.* a portmanteau.

Pock-markit, *adj.* marked with smallpox.

Pock-net, *n.* a bag-shaped fishing-net, a ring-net.

Pock-neuk, *n.* the bottom corner of a sack; one's own resources or means.

Pock-pit, *n.* a scar left by smallpox.—*v.* to mark with smallpox.

Pock-pud, -pudding, *n.* a bag-pudding; a term of contempt for an Englishman; a glutton.

Pock-shakings, *n.* the youngest and last child of a family; the small, weak pigs of a litter.

Pock-staff, *n.* the pole to the end of which a 'pock'- or ring-net is suspended.

Pocky, *adj.* subject to smallpox.

Pockyawr'd, *adj.* marked with smallpox. Cf. Pock-arred.

Pod, *n.* a little person; a small and neat animal.

Pod, *v.* to walk with short steps.

Pod, *n.* a louse.

Pod, *int.* a call to pigeons.

Podder, *v.* to potter; to dawdle; to walk slowly to and fro; to produce slowly and with difficulty.

Poddle, *v.* to walk with short, unsteady steps. Cf. Pod.

Poddlie, *n.* an immature coal-fish. **Cf.** Podley.

Poddlit, *ppl. adj.* used of poultry : plump, in good condition.

Poddock, Podduck, *n.* a frog ; a rude sledge for drawing stones. **Cf.** Paddock.

Poddock-cruds, *n.* frog-spawn. **Cf.** Paddock-rud.

Podge, *n.* a short, fat person.

Podge, *n.* hurry, bustle, confusion ; a jumble, mixture.

Podgel, Podgal, *n.* a strong, thickset person.

Podle, *n.* a tadpole.

Podle, *n.* a fondling name for a thriving child.

Podle, *v.* to 'toddle.' **Cf.** Poddle.

Podley, Podlie, Podle, *n.* an immature coal-fish ; the pollack.

Podsy, *adj.* pudgy. **Cf.** Bodsie.

Poem-book, *n.* a book of poems.

Poeteeze, *v.* to write poetry.

Poeter, *n.* a poet ; a poetaster.

Poffle, *n.* a small farm ; a 'pendicle.' **Cf.** Paffle.

Poik, *n.* a poke, bag.

Poind, *n.* a silly, inactive person, easily imposed on.

Poind, Poin, *v.* to distrain ; to impound.—*n.* a distraint. **Cf.** Pind.

Poindable, *adj.* capable of being distrained.

Poinder, *n.* a distrainer. **Cf.** Pundler.

Poind-fauld, *n.* a pound ; an enclosure for strays.

Poinding, *n.* a distraint ; a warrant for distraint.

Poinding-plea, *n.* an action or suit to distrain.

Poiner, *n.* a mason's labourer ; a scavenger ; one who digs and sells peat, sods, clay, &c. **Cf.** Piner, Pynour.

Point, *n.* a bodkin ; a boot- or shoe-lace ; a stay-lace ; the left-hand side of a 'bandwin'; the portion of a harvest-field reaped by the left half of a 'bandwin'; the leader of a 'bandwin'; state of body.—*phr.* to 'be first in the point,' to lead as scythesman in harvest.

Point-bitch, *n.* a bitch-pointer.

Pointed, *ppl. adj.* used of a person : particular, precise, exact, punctual, tidy.

Point-game, *n.* in curling : a game played by each player for himself, at the various shots, to win the 'single-handed' medal.

Poinyel, *n.* a burden carried by a traveller.

Poison, *n.* anything offensive ; a term of contempt.—*v.* to spoil food; to mar.—*adj.* used of persons : bad, disgusting.

Poisonable, *adj.* poisonous.

Poist, *v.* to urge, push ; to cram the stomach with food.

Poist, *n.* a post.

Poister, *v.* to pamper, pet, spoil.

Pok, *n.* a bag ; the bag of a bagpipe ; the rot in sheep. **Cf.** Pock.

Poke, *n.* the smallpox.

Poke, *v.* to do digging-work lazily ; to dawdle ; to grope about in the dark; to walk with a dull, heavy footfall ; to carry the head and shoulders thrust forward ; with *at,* to meddle with ; to make fun of.— *n.* a blow ; the hollow sound of a blow ; the act of groping in the dark or in a hole.—*adv.* suddenly and with a hollow sound ; awkwardly and with heavy footfall.

Pokeful, *n.* a sufficiency ; surplus.

Pokemantie, *n.* a portmanteau. **Cf.** Pockmanteau.

Poke-up, *adj.* turned up, 'tip-tilted.'

Pokey, *adj.* shrewd. **Cf.** Pawky.

Pol, Pole, *v.* to cut the hair.—*n.* the head. **Cf.** Pow.

†**Poldach,** *n.* marshy ground beside a body of water.

Pole, *n.* a walking-stick.

Pole-tree, *n.* the pole of a carriage.

Police, *n.* a policeman.

Police-dung, *n.* town manure applied to fields.

Policy, *n.* in *pl.* the pleasure-grounds of a country mansion.

Polisher, *n.* a policeman.

Polist, Polisht, *ppl. adj.* polished ; accomplished educationally ; finished, complete, in an opprobrious sense ; fawning, designing.

Polist lair, *n.* a 'finishing' education.

†**Politique,** *n.* policy, plan.

Polka, *n.* a woman's jacket.

Poll, *n.* the top or crown of anything ; the head or striking-part of a hammer ; a poll-tax.—*v.* to win a battle ; with *up,* to raise the head, to show the head. **Cf.** Pow.

Pollac, *n.* the guiniad-powan.

Pollachie, *n.* the crab-fish.

Pollan, *n.* a fresh-water herring ; a vendace. **Cf.** Poan, Powan.

Pollicate, *n.* a kind of web or cloth.

†**Pollie, Polly,** *n.* a turkey. **Cf.** Poullie.

Pollie-cock, *n.* a turkey-cock.

Pollock, *n.* the young of the coal-fish.

Pollonian, Polonian, *n.* a surtout ; a person clad in old-fashioned garments ; a dress for young boys. **Cf.** Polonaise.

Polly-shee, *n.* a pulley attached to a pole, from which a rope runs to a window, for hanging clothes to dry ; peculiar to Dundee.

Polly-wag, -woug, *n.* a tadpole.

Polonaise, Polonie, *n.* a dress for young boys, including a sort of waistcoat with loose, sloping skirts ; a greatcoat for boys ; a dress formerly worn by men in the Hebrides; a surtout; a person clad in old-fashioned garments. Cf. Pelonie.

Polsterer, *n.* an upholsterer.

†**Pomate, Pomet,** *n.* pomatum.—*v.* to grease with pomatum.

Pome, *n.* a poem.

†**Pompidoo,** *n.* an article of feminine apparel; a kind of chemise; a dress cut low and square in the neck.

Ponage, *n.* pontage; the place of a ferry.

Pones, *n.* long meadow-grass; the duffel-grass. Cf. Pounce.

Poney-cock, *n.* a turkey; a peacock.

Pong, *n.* a kind of embroidery.

†**Pong-pong,** *n.* a trinket.

Poo, *n.* a crab. Cf. Pow.

Poo, *v.* to pull.—*n.* a pull.

Pooch, *v.* to pouch.—*n.* a pocket.

Poochle, *adj.* shy, reserved; proud.

Poodle, *n.* a 'pattle,' a plough-staff.

Poodge, Pooge, *n.* a thickset, short, fat person; anything short and fat of its kind; one who feeds well; a small hut, a hovel. Cf. Pudge.

Pooer, *n.* power. Cf. Power.

Poof, *v.* to puff.—*n.* breath.—*adv.* in a breath.—*int.* an excl. of contempt, disgust, &c. Cf. Puff.

Pooin, *n.* a pulling.

Pook, *v.* to pull with nimbleness or force; to pull gently; to pluck a fowl; to pull the hair; to moult; to take or eat in small quantities, peck.—*n.* the disease to which moulting fowls are subject; a very small quantity; a 'pick'; in *pl.* the feathers on a fowl, when they begin to grow after moulting; down, or any like stuff, adhering to one's clothes; the ends of threads; unconsidered trifles.

Pook and rook, *v.* to pillage.

Pookie, *adj.* starved-looking, thin and bony; shabby in appearance.

Pookit, *ppl. adj.* plucked; pinched; starved-looking, 'pookie.'

Pookit-like, *adj.* looking like a plucked chicken; puny, meagre, diminutive.

†**Poolie,** *n.* a louse.

†**Poollie,** *n.* a turkey. Cf. Pollie.

Poolly-woolly, *n.* the cry of the curlew.

Poon, *v.* to distrain. Cf. Poind.

Poon, *n.* a pound.

Poop, *v.* to break wind backwards. Cf. Proop.

Poopit, *n.* a pulpit.

Poopit-fit, *n.* a pulpit-foot.

Poopit-man, *n.* a minister, preacher.

Poor, *adj.* out of condition: used endearingly.—*n.* a poor, or unfortunate, or contemptible creature.—*v.* to impoverish.

Poor, *v.* to pour.

Poor-bodie, *n.* a poor creature; a delicate person; a beggar.

Poorie, *n.* a small, meagre person.

Poorie, *n.* a small vessel, with a spout, for holding liquids; a small quantity of liquid, &c.—*adj.* used of a stream: pouring, rushing along. Cf. Pourie.

Poorin', *n.* a very small quantity of any liquid; in *pl.* the dregs or leavings of a liquid, 'heel-taps.' Cf. Pourin'.

Poorish, *adj.* not very well.

Poorit, *ppl. adj.* impoverished; meagre.

Poor John, *n.* a cod in poor condition.

Poorly, *adv.* in poverty; softly, gently.

Poor-man, *n.* a beggar; a frame of iron or wood on a rod three or four feet long, set in a stone socket, and holding 'fir-candles' for lighting a room; a heap of four upright sheaves of corn with one laid on the top in wet weather; the blade-bone or broiled remains of a shoulder of mutton. Cf. Peer-man.

Poor-man of mutton, *n.* the remains of a shoulder of mutton broiled for supper or for next day. Cf. Peer-man.

Poor man's weather-glass, *n.* the common pimpernel; the knotted figwort.

Poor-page, *n.* an iron or wooden frame for holding 'fir-candles.' Cf. Peer-page.

Poor's-house, *n.* the workhouse. Cf. Peer's-house.

Poortith, Poortha, Poortoth, *n.* poverty; leanness, weakness from lack of food.

Poortith-struck, *adj.* poverty-stricken.

Poor widow, *n.* a children's game.

Poor Willie, *n.* the bar-tailed godwit.

Poos, *n.* a sort of sour cake, the dough of which was moistened with water poured off 'sowens.'

Poosion, Pooshan, *n.* poison.

Poosioning, *ppl. adj.* noisome, poisonous, disagreeable.

Poossie, *n.* a kitten; a cat; a hare.

Poost, *v.* to push; to overload the stomach. Cf. Poist.

Poot, *n.* a small haddock; anything small; a young trout; a pullet; young game, &c. Cf. Pout.

Pootch, *n.* a pocket.

Pootie, *adj.* niggardly, mean, stingy.

Poot-poot-poot, *int.* a call to young pigs at feeding-time.

Pop, *v.* to fire a gun; to shoot; to put, place; with *up,* to startle, rouse up suddenly; with *about,* to go about; to drop; to fall quickly or lightly.—*n.* a spot, speck. Cf. Pap.

Pop, *v.* to strike, knock; to shoot at; to pelt, throw.—*n.* a knock, blow; a pat, tap. Cf. Pap.

Pope, *n.* a name given by seamen to the puffin.

Poper, *n.* the boy who swept out a school-room instead of paying fees.

†**Popingoe**, *n.* a parrot. Cf. Papingoe.

Popist, *n.* a papist.—*adj.* popish.

Pople, Popple, *v.* to bubble, boil up like water; to boil with indignation. Cf. Papple.

Poppin, Popin, *n.* weavers' paste. Cf. Pappin.

Poppin'-job, *n.* an odd job; a small piece of work.

Popple, *n.* the corn-cockle. Cf. Papple.

Poppy-show, *n.* a peep-show. Cf. Puppy-show.

Pop-the-bonnet, *n.* a game played with two pins on the crown of a hat.

Popular, *adj.* populous.

Pore, *v.* to purge or soften leather, so that the stool or bottom of the hair may come easily off.

Poring-iron, *n.* a poker. Cf. Purring-iron.

Pork, *v.* to grub, poke about, rout about; to poke, thrust.

Pork-bree, *n.* soup made of fresh pork.

Pork-ham, *n.* a ham in contrast to a mutton-ham.

Porkling, *n.* a young pig.

Porkmanky, Porkmanty, *n.* a portmanteau. Cf. Pockmanteau.

Porky, *n.* a pig.

Porpus, *n.* a porpoise; a stupid or self-important person.

Porpy, *n.* a porpoise.

Porr, *v.* to prick, stab; to poke a fire.—*n.* a thrust with a sword; a kick; the sound of a sharp instrument piercing flesh. Cf. Purr.

Porrage, Porritch, *n.* porridge. Cf. Parritch.

Porridge-tree, *n.* a rod for stirring porridge.

Porring-iron, *n.* a poker. Cf. Purring-iron.

†**Port**, *n.* the carriage of an article.

Port, *n.* a gate, gateway; in curling or bowling: a passage left between two stones or bowls.

Port, Porte, *n.* a lively tune on the bagpipe; a catch, glee.

Port, *v.* in *phr.* 'port the helm,' a boys' game, suggested by contact with seafarers.

Portage, *n.* the goods allowed to be put on board a vessel as a passenger's private store or luggage.

Port-day, *n.* the day (in old times) for hiring harvesters near the West Port of Edinburgh.

Porteous-roll, *n.* a list of persons indicted to appear before the Justice-aire, given by the Justice-Clerk to the Coroner, that he might attach them in order to their appearance; the list of criminal causes to be tried at the circuit-courts.

Porter, *n.* a weaving term, denoting a certain number of threads forming a section of a warp; a ferryman.

†**Porterage, Porteretch, Portridge**, *n.* a portrait.

Porterer, *n.* a portrait.

Portie, *n.* air, mien, bearing.

Portioner, *n.* the occupier of part of a property originally divided among co-heirs; the possessor of a small portion of land.

Portmantle, Portmankle, Portmanty, *n.* a portmanteau.

Portule, *n.* a cry, howl.—*phr.* 'to sing portule,' to cry out. Cf. Port-youl.

Portus, *n.* a skeleton.

Port-vent, *n.* part of the bagpipe.

Port-youl, -yeul, *n.* a cry, howl.

Pory, *adj.* used of bread: light, spongy, 'porous.'

Pose, *n.* a hoard; a secret store; savings.—*v.* to hoard up, amass.

Pose, *v.* to examine, question.

Posel, *n.* a small heap.

Posellie, *n.* a very small heap.

Posh, Poshie, *n.* a nursery name for porridge.

Positeevest, *adj.* most positive.

Posnett, *n.* a bag for holding money; a net-purse.

†**Poss**, *v.* to push; to pound; to dash violently backwards and forwards in water for the purpose of cleaning or rinsing clothes, &c. Cf. Post.

Poss, *n.* a hoard. Cf. Pose.

Posse, Possey, *n.* a large muster of men.

Possess, *v.* to give legal possession or investiture.

Posset-masking, *n.* the making and drinking of possets.

Possibles, *n.* means, wherewithal.

Possile, *n.* a small heap. Cf. Posel.

Possing-tub, *n.* a tub for washing clothes or 'tramping' blankets.

Possit, *adj.* possible.

Possody, *n.* a ludicrous term of endearment. Cf. Powsowdy.

Post, *n.* a stratum in a quarry.

Post, *n.* a postman; postage.—*v.* to convey, accompany.

Post, *v.* to knead clothes with hands, or 'tramp' them with feet, in order to wash them. Cf. Poss.

Post and pan, *n.* a method of building walls with upright posts tied with 'pans' or cross-pieces of timber, making a framework to be filled up with stones and clay or mud.

Postie, *n.* a familiar name for a postman.

†**Postit**, *ppl. adj.* in *phr.* 'postit wi' sickness,' overpowered by sickness.

Post-letter, *n.* a letter posted.

Post-sick, *adj.* bedridden, confined to bed with illness.

Posture, *n.* site, local position.

Posy. *n.* a cluster; a small collection; an un savoury smell.

Pot, *n.* a small-still; the last division in the game of hop-scotch; ruin.—*v.* to stew; to boil in water to reduce to a jelly when cold; to boil in order to preserve. Cf. Pat.

Pot, Pott, *n.* a pit; a deep hole or cavity; a deep pool or hole in water; a hole from which peats have been dug.—*v.* to plant or set in a pit; to dig peats out of a hole.

Pot, *v.* to trample soft or wet soil, as cattle do. Cf. Poach.

Potards, *n.* dotards.

Potato-beetle, *n.* a potato-masher.

Potato-bing, *n.* a covered potato-heap.

Potato-bogle, *n.* a scarecrow.

Potato-box, *n.* the mouth.

Potato-bread, *n.* bread made of flour and mashed potatoes.

Potato-doolie, *n.* a scarecrow.

Potatoes and point, *n.* only potatoes to eat.

Potato-mould, *n.* a field on which potatoes have been grown, and which is considered rich enough to give a crop of oats without further manure.

Potato-scones, *n.* scones made of flour and potatoes.

Pot-brod, *n.* a pot-lid.

Pot-brose, *n.* oatmeal stirred quickly into hot milk.

Potch, *v.* to drive backwards and forwards; to thrust. Cf. Poach.

Potch, *n.* a jumble, a hodge-podge.

Potching, *ppl. adj.* clumsy and dirty at work.

Potchy, *n.* a name for a poacher.

Pot-cleps, *n.* pot-hooks.

Pot-dyed, *adj.* dyed in a pot.

Pote, *n.* a poker. Cf. Paut, Pout.

†**Potecary,** *n.* an apothecary.

Potent, *n.* a crutch.

Pot-head, *n.* the 'caain'' whale.

Potie, *v.* to stew in a pot. Cf. Pottie.

Potie, *n.* a boy's marble. Cf. Pottie.

Potingarie, Potinger, *n.* an apothecary; a cook.

Potle-bell, *n.* in *phr.* to 'ring the potle-bell,' a children's way of confirming a bargain, by hooking together the little fingers of the right hand and shaking the hands up and down, and repeating, 'Ring the potle-bell, Gin ye brack the bargain ye 'll gang to hell.'

Pot-lid, *n.* a curling-stone played so as to rest on the tee.

Pot-metal, *n.* cast-iron.

Pot-piece, *n.* an old name for the piece of ordnance called a mortar.

Potridge, *n.* a portrait. Cf. Porterage.

Pot-shkirt, *n.* a piece of a broken kettle for holding oil; a potsherd.

Pot-stick, *n.* a 'spurtle,' stirring-rod.

Pot-still, *n.* a small whisky-still.

Pot-stuff, *n.* vegetables for cooking; plants grown in pots.

Pottage, Pottish, *n.* porridge.

Pottage-meal, *n.* oatmeal.

Pottage-pan, *n.* porridge-pot.

Potterlow, *n.* fragments, small pieces; utter ruin.

Potter-skink, *n.* wreck and ruin; bits.

Potterton-hen, *n.* the black-headed gull.

Pottie, *n.* a little pot.

Pottie, *n.* a red clay marble.

Pottie, Potty, *adj.* stewed or preserved in a pot.—*v.* to stew in a pot.

Pottie-head, *n.* a dish made from the flesh of an ox-head or pig's head boiled to a jelly.

Pottingar, *n.* a cook; a druggist.

Pottinger, *n.* a jar, a small earthen vessel; a porringer.

Pottit-heid, *n.* 'pottie-head.'

Potty, *n.* putty.—*v.* to putty; to suit, work, do.

Pou, *n.* a pool; a slow-running stream.

Pou, *v.* to pull, pluck.—*n.* a pull.

†**Pouce,** *n.* a flea.

Pouch, *n.* a pocket; a purse.—*v.* to pocket; to steal; to pocket food, &c.; to swallow; to eat greedily.

Pouch-clout, *n.* a pocket-handkerchief.

Pouch-companion, *n.* a pocket-companion.

Poucher, *n.* one who pockets food, &c., on the sly.

Pouch-flap, *n.* a pocket-flap.

Pouchfu', *n.* a pocketful.

Pouching, *ppl. adj.* greedy; fond of good living.

Pouchless, *adj.* pocketless; poor; impecunious.

Pouch-lid, *n.* a pocket-flap.

Pouch-pistol, *n.* a pocket-pistol.

Pouch-room, *n.* pocket-space.

Pouch-strings, *n.* purse-strings.

Pouder, *n.* dust; gunpowder; hair-powder. —*v.* to powder; to wear hair-powder; to 'corn' beef, salt it slightly.

Pouff, *n.* a dull, heavy blow or fall; the sound of such; the act of walking heavily or wearily; a big, stupid person.—*v.* to give dull, heavy blows; to dash down violently; to drive, hammer; to fall heavily; to walk with dull, heavy step.—*adv.* with a dull, heavy blow; with heavy or weary steps.

Pouffin, *n.* a big, stupid person.

Pouk, *v.* to poke; to grope in the dark. Cf. Poke.

Pouk, *n.* a mischievous sprite; 'Puck.'

Pouk, *n.* a small pit or hole containing water or mud; a deep hole.

Pouk, *n.* a poke, bag.

Pouk, *v.* to pull, pluck. —*n.* a disease to which moulting fowls are subject; a very small quantity. Cf. Pook.

Pouken-pin, *n.* weaving term: a 'plucking-pin,' used in handloom weaving.

Poukery, *n.* slyness. Cf. Pawkery.

Poukit, *ppl. adj.* plucked; lean, bony; shabby in appearance; puny, meagre; stingy. Cf. Pookie, Pookit.

†**Poulie,** *n.* a louse. Cf. Powlie.

†**Poullie,** *n.* a turkey. Cf. Pollie.

Poullie, *v.* to look plucked-like.

Poullie-hen, *n.* a turkey-hen.

Poullie hens, *n.* plucked-looking hens.

Pounce, *v.* to spring or pounce upon.

Pound, Poun, *n.* a weight varying in locality and as to articles weighed.

Pound, *n.* a small enclosure; a sheepfold.

Poundlaw, *n.* money paid for delivery of goods 'poinded' or impounded.

Pound-piece, *n.* a sovereign.

Pound Scots, *n.* the twelfth of a pound sterling.

Pounie, *n.* a pony.

†**Pounie,** *n.* a peacock; a turkey-hen. Cf. Pownie.

Pount, *n.* a point.

Pouny, *adj.* puny, little.

Poupit, *n.* a pulpit. Cf. Poopit.

Pour, *adj.* poor.

Pour, *n.* power. Cf. Power.

Pour, *v.* to drain off water in which potatoes have been boiled; to dish a meal by emptying the vessel in which it has been cooked; to rain heavily and fast. —*n.* a steady flow; a heavy shower; a small portion of liquid.

Pourie, *n.* a vessel with a spout; a decanter; a cream-jug; a very small quantity of any liquid or dry substance. —*adj.* used of a stream: rushing, rapid. Cf. Poorie.

Pourin', *n.* a small quantity of liquid or spirits; in *pl.* the thin liquid poured off from 'sowens' after fermentation; the dregs or leavings of a liquid.

Pourit, *ppl. adj.* impoverished; meagre. Cf. Poorit.

Pourtith, *n.* poverty. Cf. Poortith.

†**Pouse,** *v.* to push; to thrust. —*n.* a push; a blow. Cf. Pouss.

Pousion, Pousin, Poushon, Pushion, *n.* poison; used as a term of contempt for a disagreeable person; an eyesore; anything offensive. —*v.* to spoil; to spoil food in cooking. —*adj.* used of persons: bad, contemptible, disgusting.

Pousioning, *ppl. adj.* poisonous, noisome.

Pousle, *v.* to puzzle; to search uncertainly for anything; to trifle. —*n.* an airy and finical person; one who boasts of wealth with little reason for doing so.

Pousowdy, *n.* sheep's-head broth; a mixture of meal and milk; any mixture of incongruous foods. Cf. Powsowdy.

†**Pouss, Pousse,** *v.* to push, thrust; to wash clothes by frequent lifting and kneading in the tub. —*n.* a push; a blow. Cf. Poss.

Pouss, Poust, *v.* to snuff a candle.

Poussie, *n.* a cat; a hare.

†**Poust,** *n.* strength, vigour; bodily power.

Poust, *n.* the person who plays second of three players in the game of marbles or 'buttons.' —*v.* to put a person in such a position.

†**Pouster, Pousture,** *n.* bodily ability, the power of using a limb, &c.

†**Poustie,** *n.* power, ability, bodily strength; in *phr.* 'lege poustie,' full strength; legitimate power.

Pout, *n.* in *phr.* 'to play pout,' to make the least noise or exertion.

Pout, Pout-worm, *n.* a grub destructive of springing grain, the 'tory,' the larva of the 'daddy-long-legs.'

Pout, *v.* to cause to pout, render sullen.

Pout, *n.* a poker. —*v.* to poke; to push with the foot. Cf. Paut.

Pout, *v.* to start up suddenly, as from under water; to make a noise when doing so.

Pout, *n.* a pullet; a young turkey; a young partridge or moorfowl; an unfledged bird; the sound made by a chicken; a term of endearment for a young child, young girl, a sweetheart; anything small; a small haddock; a small trout. —*v.* to shoot at young partridges.

Pout, *v.* to stumble or stagger from drink. Cf. Pouter.

Pouter, *n.* a sportsman who shoots young partridges or moorfowl.

Pouter, *v.* to poke; to stir with finger or instrument; to rake as among ashes; to work carelessly and unskilfully; to go about aimlessly or to the annoyance of others; to walk backwards and forwards; to trifle; to make a noise or splash in liquid. —*n.* a careless worker; an aimless walker; a poking, stirring. Cf. Peuter, Peuther.

Pouther, *n.* pewter.

Pouther, *v.* to canvass; to bustle about seeking votes. Cf. Peuther.

Pouther, *n.* powder, dust; hair-powder; gun-powder. —*v.* to powder; to wear hair-powder; to 'corn' beef.

Poutie, *adj.* niggardly, mean. Cf. Pootie

Pouting, *n.* spearing salmon.

Pouting-season, *n.* the shooting season.

Pout-net, *n.* a round net fastened to two poles, thrust under the banks of a river to force out fish.

Poutry, *n.* poultry.

Pousle, *v.* to puzzle. Cf. Pousle.

Povereeze, *v.* to exhaust ; to impoverish.

Poverty-pink, *n.* the clover *Trifolium.*

Povie, *adj.* snug, comfortable, well-off ; spruce ; self-conceited.

Pow, *n.* a crab.

Pow, *n.* a slow-running stream in flat lands ; a marshy place ; a small creek with landing-place for boats ; the wharf itself.

Pow, *v.* to strike.

Pow, *n.* the head, the poll ; a head of hair ; the head of a hammer.—*v.* to cut the hair ; with *up,* to raise up the head ; to win, secure.

Powan, *n.* the fresh-water herring, the guiniad ; the vendace.

Powan, Powin, *n.* a pound.

Powart, *n.* a seal.

Powart, *n.* a tadpole. Cf. Pow-head.

Powder, *n.* dust ; used in curling : strength in driving a stone.—*v.* to sprinkle butter or beef slightly with salt ; with *up,* to powder the hair. Cf. Pouther.

Powder-brand, *n.* a disease in grain.

Powder-deil, *n.* a small cone of moistened gunpowder, used as a firework.

Powder-pan, *n.* the priming-pan of a firelock.

Powder-pouch, *n.* a powder-flask.

Powder-room, *n.* a powder-magazine.

Pow-ee, *n.* a small fresh haddock.

Poweed, Powet, *n.* a tadpole. Cf. Pow-head.

Power, *n.* a large number or quantity, a great deal ; a military force ; power to dispose of ; possession.

Powerful, *adj.* used of liquor : strong, potent ; plentiful.

Pow-head, *n.* a tadpole ; a vesuvian match ; the minute-hand of a clock.

Pow-high, *adv.* as high as the head.

†**Powie,** *n.* a young turkey. Cf. Poullie.

Powie, Powit, *n.* a tadpole. Cf. Pow-head.

†**Powin,** *n.* a peacock. Cf. Pownie.

Powk, *n.* a poke, bag. Cf. Pock.

Powk, *v.* to pluck. Cf. Pook.

Powk, *v.* to poke ; to grope.—*n.* a thrust, blow. Cf. Poke.

Powk-powking, *n.* repeated poking ; digging ; groping ; walking heavily.

Powl, *v.* to walk or move rapidly.

Powl, *n.* a pole.

Powlick, *n.* a tadpole. Cf. Pow-head.

†**Powlie,** *n.* a louse. Cf. Poulie.

Pownie, *n.* a pony ; a trestle for support of temporary tables, &c.

†**Pownie, Powney,** *n.* a peacock ; a turkey-hen.

Pownie-cock, *n.* a peacock.

Powowit, *n.* a tadpole. Cf. Pow-head.

Powrit, *n.* a tadpole. Cf. Pow-head.

Powsowdy, Pow's-sowdy, Pow-sodie, *n.* sheep's-head broth ; milk and meal boiled together ; a mixture of incongruous foods.

Powster, *n.* posture ; local position.

Powt, *v.* to poke with hand or stick ; to make short and, as it were, convulsive movements with the hands or feet ; to spear salmon ; used of a horse : to paw the ground, to stamp.—*n.* a kick, stamp ; a short, convulsive movement ; a slight blow. Cf. Paut.

Powt, *n.* a pullet ; a young game-bird. Cf. Pout.

Pow-tae, *n.* a crab's claw.

Powter, *v.* to do little, easy jobs ; to rummage in the dark ; to poke ; to stir with the finger or any instrument ; to potter about.—*n.* a poking, stirring ; a careless worker. Cf. Pouter.

Powtle, *v.* to creep out like a mole.

Pow-wow, *n.* a child's head.

Pox, *n.* a plague ; an imprecation.—*v.* to plague ; to break so as to render useless.

Poy, *v.* to work diligently and anxiously ; with *upon,* to use persuasion so as to exercise undue influence.

Poyn, Poynd, *v.* to distrain. Cf. Poind.

†**Practicate,** *ppl. adj.* practised.

†**Practician,** *n.* one who treats of legal procedure.

†**Practick, Practique,** *n.* legal precedent ; uniform practice in law ; form of procedure. Cf. Pratick.

†**Practise,** *v.* to suborn, bribe a witness ; to tamper with.

†**Practiser,** *n.* one who ' practises.'

†**Practitioner,** *n.* a writer on ' practicks.'

Prad, *n.* a steed.

Praise, *n.* a name for God.

Praise-be-thankit, *int.* an excl. of thanks to God.

Praiss, *n.* a strong but ineffectual inclination to go to stool. Cf. Priest.

Pran, Prann, *v.* to wound, bruise ; to squeeze ; to scold, reprimand.—*n.* a bruise, squeeze ; anything crushed to fragments ; coarsely ground oatmeal ; the bran of oatmeal.

Prance, *v.* to dance, caper ; to dance vigorously.

Prancer, *n.* a vigorous dancer.

Prang, *n.* a prong ; a prop, support.

Prank, *v.* to play tricks on ; to play fast and loose with ; to prance.

Pranket, *n.* a childish prank.

Pranksome, *adj.* full of pranks, lively.

Pranning, *n.* a squeeze, bruise. Cf. Pran.

Prap, *n.* a prop ; a molehill ; a tall chimney-stalk ; a mark.—*v.* to prop ; to set up as a mark ; to aim at, throw at a mark ; to assist ; to pelt.

Prapper, *n.* a prop, support.

Prappin, *n.* a game in which stones are thrown at a mark.

Prap-prap, *v.* used of tears : to trickle, to roll quickly down in drops.

Prat, Prate, Pratt, *n.* a trick ; a roguish or wicked act.—*v.* to become restive, as a horse, &c.

Pratfu', *adj.* tricky ; used of children : mischievous.

†**Pratick, Prattick, Prattik,** *n.* practice ; legal procedure ; a precedent ; a piece of policy ; an experiment ; a project ; a mischievous trick ; a trick of legerdemain ; a warlike exploit ; an achievement of stratagem or policy ; any wicked act.

Prattle, *v.* used of a stream : to flow noisily.

Pratty, *adj.* tricky, mischievous.

Prawn, *v.* to injure on the head ; to 'brain.' Cf. Pran.

Prawta, *n.* a potato.

Preace, Preas, *v.* to press ; to importune ; to endeavour, make an effort.—*n.* pressure, trouble ; a difficulty.

Preaching, *n.* a sermon ; a religious service, especially at a Communion season.

Preaching-tent, *n.* a covered erection for an open-air pulpit at a Communion season.

Preceese, *adj.* precise, particular.—*adv.* precisely, exactly.

Precent, *v.* to lead the singing as a precentor.

Precept, *n.* a legal injunction ; a written order from a superior ; an order to pay money.

Precognition, *n.* a preliminary judicial examination of witnesses ; a legal term.

Precognosce, *v.* to make preliminary judicial investigation of a case by examination of witnesses ; a legal term.

Precunnance, *n.* an understanding, condition. Cf. Perconnon.

Predick, *v.* to predict.

Predominant, *n.* a dominant passion or sin.

Pree, *v.* to prove, experience, venture upon ; to attain ; to taste, partake of ; to give relish to ; to kiss ; to stop at a place to try for fish.—*n.* a taste, a small portion. Cf. Preeve, Prieve.

Preeay, *int.* a call to calves.

Preef, Prief, *n.* proof.

Preein', *n.* proof, experience ; a testing, tasting ; a taste, bite, sup ; a tippling.

Preek, *v.* to be spruce ; to dress up ; to be conceited ; to stimulate.—*n.* impatient eagerness to accomplish anything. Cf. Prick.

Preekin, *n.* the killing of oxen, &c., with a sharp chisel driven into the neck behind the head. Cf. Prickin.

Preen, *n.* a pin ; a fish-hook ; in *pl.* a game played with pins lifted from the ground by wetted thumbs.—*v.* to pin.

Preen, *v.* to deck one's self out ; to dress the hair.

Preen-cod, -cushion, *n.* a pin-cushion.

Preen-heid, *n.* a pin-head.

Preen-heidit, *adj.* small-brained.

Preen-hook, *n.* a fish-hook.

Preening, *ppl. adj.* used of water : just at the boiling-point, when small bubbles like pin-points shoot to the surface.

Preen-point, *n.* a pin-point.

Preen's-worth, *n.* a pin's worth.

Prees, *n.* a crowd, a press. Cf. Preace.

Preest, *n.* a minister.

Preest-cat, *n.* a fireside-game with a stick reddened in the fire. Cf. Priest-cat.

Preeve, *v.* to prove ; to try, test ; to taste ; to experience, enjoy ; to meddle with.—*n.* a taste. Cf. Pree.

Preface, *n.* profession, pretence ; a short explanation of the verses of a psalm given by the minister before they were sung at the beginning of the service.—*v.* to give such a 'preface.'

Preferment, *n.* preference.

Pregnancy, *n.* fullness, ripeness, richness of promise.

Pregnant, *adj.* full, complete ; rich in promise, clever ; solid, weighty.

Prein, *n.* a pin. Cf. Preen.

Preise, *v.* to press. Cf. Preace.

Prejinctly, *adv.* with minute nicety.

Prejink, Prejinct, *adj.* precise, prim ; finical ; neat, smart ; hypercritical. Cf. Perjink.

Prejinkitie, *n.* minute nicety or accuracy.

Prejinkness, Prejinctness, *n.* niceness ; insistence on trifles.

Prejudge, *v.* to prejudice ; to be to the prejudice of.

Prejudice, *n.* injury, damage.

Premit, *v.* to premise.

Premunitories, *n.* premonitory symptoms of illness.

Prent, *n.* print ; a pat of butter marked with a die ; in *pl.* newspapers.—*adj.* printed.

Prent-buik, *n.* a printed book.

Prentice-foy, *n.* a feast at the end of an apprenticeship.

Prentice-haun', *n.* a novice ; a novice's effort.

†**Prequeer,** *adv.* by heart ; thoroughly. Cf. Perqueer.

Presairve, *v.* to preserve.

Prescript, *n.* a doctor's prescription.

Prescrive, Prescryve, *v.* to prescribe.

Present, *n.* a white speck on a finger-nail, as an augury of a gift.—*v.* to bring before a judge.—*phr.* 'present to,' used of a pistol : to present at.

Presently, *adv.* just now.

Preserve, *v.* used in excl. of surprise.—*n.* in *pl.* spectacles used to preserve the sight, but magnifying little or nothing.

Preses, *n.* a president or chairman.

Press, *v.* to crowd a room, &c. ; to urge a guest

to eat or drink.—*n.* a squeeze, pressure; a wall-cupboard with shelves, &c.

Press-bed, *n.* a box-bed with doors.

Press-door, *n.* the door of a wall-cupboard.

Pressfu', *n.* what fills a 'press.'

Press-gang, *n.* a group of romping children.

†**Prestable**, *adj.* payable.

Prestoune-ale, *n.* Prestonpans beer.

Pret, *n.* a trick. Cf. Prat.

Pretfu', *adj.* full of tricks.

†**Prettick**, *n.* practice; a piece of policy; a trick. Cf. Pratick.

Prettikin, *n.* a feat, trick. Cf. Pratick.

Pretty, *adj.* small; small and neat; handsome, well-made; bold, stalwart, warlike; polite, cultured; fine, excellent, fragrant; considerable; insignificant, petty.—*adv.* prettily; tolerably.—*phr.* 'pretty little girl of mine,' a children's singing-game.

Pretty dancers, *n.* the aurora borealis.

Pretty-Nancy, *n.* the London pride.

Prevade, *v.* to neglect.

Preveen, *v.* to prevent, hinder; to anticipate; to interpose in another judge's jurisdiction.

Prevention, *n.* a legal term: the interposition of one judge in another's jurisdiction.

Preventive-man, *n.* a coastguard.

Preztry, *n.* a presbytery.

Price, *v.* to ask in marriage.—*n.* in *phr.* to 'speer a woman's price,' to ask her in marriage.

Pricie, *n.* a small or low price.

Prick, *n.* a wooden bodkin or pin for fastening one's clothes; a pike; an iron spike.—*v.* to pin; to fasten; to discover a witch by searching for and pricking the supposed 'devil's marks' on her person; used of cattle: to run fast, 'startle,' in hot weather, from the torment of flies, &c.; to dress gaudily, adorn; to stimulate; to copy music in manuscript; to stick; to set forward prominently. Cf. Preek.

Pricker, *n.* the basking shark; a contemptuous name for a tailor; one who discovered witches by 'pricking.'

Prick-haste, *n.* hot haste.

Prickie-and-jockie, *n.* a child's game played with pins, like 'odds or evens.'

Prickie-sockey, *n.* the game of 'prickie-and-jockie.'

Prickin, *n.* a method of killing oxen, &c., with a sharp chisel driven home on the neck behind the animal's head.—*ppl. adj.* sharp-pointed, piercing; fond of dress; conceited; forward.

Prickle, *v.* used of the hair: to stand up; to have a pricking sensation.—*n.* a pricking sensation; a muzzle set with projecting nails; a tool used by bakers for pricking holes in bread; the 'crampit' or perforated

sheet-iron on which a curler stands to play.

Prickly-tang, *n.* the *Fucus serratus.*

Prickmaleerie, *adj.* stiff, precise.

Prickmedainty, **Prickmadenty**, **Prickmydainty**, *adj.* finical in language and manners, conceited.—*n.* one who is finical in dress and carriage.

Prick's-worth, *n.* anything of the lowest imaginable value.

Prick-the-clout-loon, *n.* a nickname for a tailor.

Prick-the-garter, *n.* a cheating game played at fairs.

Prick-the-loops, *n.* the same cheating game played at fairs.

Prick-the-louse, *n.* a contemptuous designation of a tailor.

Pride, *v.* to be proud of, take pride in.

Prided, *ppl.* proud.

Priding, *n.* the pride, one of whom others are proud.

Prie, *v.* to taste. Cf. Pree.

Prief, *n.* proof. Cf. Preeve.

Priest, *n.* used of a Presbyterian minister; in *phr.* to 'be one's priest,' to kill one.

Priest, *n.* a strong but ineffectual inclination to go to stool.

Priest-cat, *n.* a children's or fireside game, played with a stick made red in the fire and handed round.

Priest-dridder, *n.* the dread of priests.

Priest's pintle, *n.* the rose-root.

Prieve, *v.* to prove; to taste. Cf. Preeve, Pree.

Prig, **Prigg**, *v.* to importune, plead; to haggle: to beat down the price.—*n.* entreaty, pleading.

Prigger, *n.* one who beats down the price of an article; an importunate person.

Prigging, *n.* haggling; entreaty.

Prigmedainty, *adj.* finical in dress or manners. Cf. Prickmedainty.

Prignickitie, *adj.* precise in trifles; trim. Cf. Pernickety.

Priler, *n.* a marble which, on striking another, spins round in the place of contact.

Prim, *v.* to close firmly; to press closely or primly.

Primadainty, *n.* a finical person. Cf. Prickmedainty.

†**Primanaire**, *n.* trouble, confusion.

†**Primar**, *n.* the *primarius* or principal of a college or university.

†**Primariat**, *n.* the principalship of a college or university.

Prime, *adj.* ready, eager; primed with liquor.—*adv.* capitally.—*n.* the best.

Prime, *v.* to fill, load; to intoxicate, excite with drink; to excite to the point of an outburst of temper.

Primely, *adv.* capitally, very well.

Primp, *v.* to dress smartly or affectedly; to deck; to behave prudishly or affectedly.— *n.* a person of stiff, affected manner.

Primpie, *adj.* affected in dress or manner.— *n.* an affected person.

Primpit, *ppl. adj.* 'primpie'; pursed - up, primly set; ridiculously stiff in demeanour.

Primpsie, Primsie, *adj.* demure, precise; affected.

Prin, Prine, *n.* a pin. Cf. Preen.

Principal, *adj.* used of the weather: excellent, prime.

Pringle, *n.* a small silver coin about the value of a penny.

Prinkin', *n.* the act of twinkling or shining brightly.

Prinkle, *v.* to tingle, prickle; to touch; to cause to tingle; used of a boiling pot: to send up small bubbles.

Prinkle, *n.* a young coal-fish.

Prinkling, *n.* a tingling sensation arising from stoppage of the circulation of the blood.

Print, *n.* a pat of butter impressed with a die; in *pl.* newspapers.—*adj.* printed.

Priperty miss, *n.* a children's singing and dancing game.

†Prise, *v.* to wrench, force open.—*n.* a lever; a push with a lever.

Prison, *v.* to imprison.

Prisoners, Prisoners'-relief, *n.* the game of 'prisoners' base.'

Prisoning, *n.* imprisonment.

Prisonment, *n.* imprisonment.

Privado, *n.* a confidential private supporter.

Privates, Privities, *n.* the privy parts.

Priving, *n.* a tasting. Cf. Preeve.

Privy, Privy-saugh, *n.* the privet.

Prization, *n.* valuation.

†Prize, *v.* to set a value on, appraise.

†Prize, *v.* to capture, to seize as a prize.

Prizer, *n.* an appraiser.

Proadge, *v.* to push with a stick. Cf. Prodge.

Prob, *v.* to probe, pierce, stab, prod.—*n.* a prod; a jog.

Probable, *adj.* provable.

Probationer, *n.* a licensed preacher eligible for a settled charge and ordination.

Process, *v.* to bring to trial; to raise an action in a court; to try judicially.

Prochy, *int.* a call to cows. Cf. Proochy.

Prockie, *int.* a call to horses.

Proctrie, *n.* procuration.

Procurator-fiscal, *n.* an official who institutes and carries on criminal proceedings in the inferior courts in Scotland.

Procutor, *n.* a procurator; a solicitor.

Prod, *n.* a prodigal.

Prod, *v.* to stir about, shuffle; to jog.—*n.* a wooden skewer; a prick with a pointed instrument; a stake; a thorn, prickle; a sting; a 'craw-prod,' or pin fixed on the top of a gable, to which the ropes fastening the thatch of a cottage were attached; a house-thatcher; a poke, a stir. Cf. Brod.

Prod, *v.* to move with short steps like a child.

Proddle, *v.* to prick, goad, stab.

Prodie, *n.* a toy.

Prodigious, *adj.* prodigal, very wasteful.

Prodin, *n.* a child's foot; a small foot.

†Proditor, *n.* a legal term: a traitor, a betrayer.

Prodle, *v.* to move quickly with short steps. —*n.* a small horse which takes short steps.

Prodler, *n.* a small horse, one that 'prodles.'

Profane, *v.* to swear.

Profession, *n.* a religious denomination; a yearly examination formerly held in some of the universities as to the progress of the students during the preceding year.

Professionist, *n.* a professing Christian whose profession is an empty one.

Professor, *n.* a professing Christian; one who claims an unusual amount of religious faith and fervour.

Proffer, *n.* an offer of marriage; a tender of services.

Profit, *n.* the expected yield of milk or butter, &c.

Profite, *adj.* exact; clever. Cf. Perfite.

Prog, Progg, *v.* to probe; to prod, prick; to stir up, poke.—*n.* a goad; a prick; a probe; a spike; a thorn, prickle; an arrow; a sting; a poke, thrust; a pointed sarcasm, retort; food. Cf. Brog.

Proggles, *n.* the spines of a hedgehog.

†Progne, *n.* the swallow.

Prognostic, Prognostication, *n.* an almanac.

Prog-staff, *n.* an iron-pointed staff.

Progue, *v.* to probe. Cf. Prog.

Proitle, *v.* to stir; to poke out trout from under banks.

Projeck, *n.* a project; resource.

Proke, *v.* to poke; to poke the fire. Cf. Prog.

Proker, *n.* a poker.

Prokitor, *n.* a procurator, solicitor.

Proll, *v.* in *phr.* to 'proll thumbs,' to lick and strike thumbs in confirmation of a bargain.

Promiscuously, *adv.* by chance, casually.

Promish, *v.* to promise.

Promoval, *n.* promotion, furtherance.

Promove, Promuve, *v.* to promote, further; to prompt.

Pron, *v.* to bruise; to squeeze, crush; to hurt; to scold.—*n.* a bruise, squeeze; anything crushed to fragments or coarsely ground; flummery and the substance from which it is made; the bran of oatmeal. Cf. Pran.

Pronack, *n.* a fragment, splinter; a crumb; a crumb of dough in kneading oatmeal.

Prone, *v.* to squeeze. Cf. Pran.

Pronn, *n.* provisions.

Pronning, *n.* a bruise, a squeeze.

Prontag, *n.* a splinter. Cf. Pronack.

Proo, *int.* a call to oxen to come near; a gentle call to a horse.

†**Proochy**, *int.* a call to a cow or oxen.

Proochy-lady, -madame, *int.* a call to a cow.

Prood, *adj.* proud.

Proof, *n.* a Scripture text proving a doctrine, specially in the Shorter Catechism; a proof-text; a mode of ascertaining the amount of grain in a corn-stack, when it is to be sold.

Proof a-shot, *adj.* shot-proof.

Proof-barley, -corn, *n.* barley or corn from selected sheaves.

Proof-man, *n.* a person appointed to determine the amount of grain in a stack.

Proof of lead, or shot, *n.* a fancied protection from leaden bullets by witchcraft.

Proonach, *n.* a fragment; a crumb. Cf. Pronack.

Proop, *v.* to break wind backward.—*n.* the act of doing so. Cf. Poop.

Prop, *n.* a leg; a landmark; a molehill.—*v.* to aid, encourage; to set up a landmark; to designate by landmarks; to aim or throw at a mark. Cf. Prap.

†**Propale**, *v.* to publish, proclaim abroad.

Proper, *adj.* thorough, complete; excellent; fine; well made or grown.

Property, *n.* a good quality, as opposed to a failing.

Prophet's chamber, *n.* a room occupied by a probationer or minister going from home on duty.

†**Propine, Propyne**, *v.* to present, give; to propitiate; to pledge in drinking; to touch glasses.—*n.* a gift, a gift in recognition of services; drink-money; the power of giving; disposal.

Propone, *v.* to bring forward a legal defence; to propose; to lay down.

Proppit, *ppl. adj.* marked out, appointed.

†**Proqueer**, *adv.* by heart. Cf. Perqueer.

†**Prorogat**, *ppl. adj.* used of a jurisdiction to which a defendant submits willingly, though it be not altogether otherwise competent.

Prose, *v.* to put into prose.

Prose-folk, *n.* people who talk in prose.

Prose-hash, *n.* a prosy fool or blockhead.

Proselyte, *v.* to proselytize, bring over to one's views or ways.

Prospect, Prospect-glass, *n.* a telescope.

Pross, *v.* to give one's self airs; to behave overbearingly.

Prossie, *adj.* annoyingly nice and particular in dress or work.

Prostrate, *v.* to prostitute.

Prot, *n.* a trick. Cf. Prat.

†**Protick, Prottik**, *n.* legal procedure; a trick. Cf. Pratick.

Protty, *adj.* tricky, mischievous. Cf. Pratty.

Protty, *adj.* handsome, elegant; possessing mettle. Cf. Pretty.

Prou, *int.* a call to cattle. Cf. Proo.

Proud, *adj.* glad, pleased; protuberant; used of the projection in a haystack during building, whence it needs dressing; of a roof: highly pitched.

Proud, *v.* to prod. Cf. Prod.

Proudful, *adj.* full of pride; used of skins: swollen by the operation of lime.

Proudish, *adj.* rather proud.

Proudness, *n.* used of skins: the state of being swollen out.

Prove, *v.* to enjoy. Cf. Pree, Preeve.

Proven, *ppl.* proved; attested: a legal term.

†**Provend, Provand**, *n.* provender; provisions.

Proverb, *v.* to quote proverbs.

Proves', Provo', Provost, *n.* the chief magistrate of a burgh.

Provide, *v.* to furnish a bride's outfit of dress, household linen, &c., and also the bridegroom's contribution; to promote.

Providing, *n.* a bride's outfit, trousseau.

Provokesome, *adj.* provoking.

Provoking, *ppl. adj.* tempting the appetite.

Provokshon, *n.* provocation.

Provostry, *n.* a provost's tenure of office. Cf. Proves'.

Prow, *int.* a call to cattle. Cf. Proo.

†**Prowan**, *n.* provender. Cf. Provend.

Prowie, *n.* a cow.

Prowse, *v.* to give one's self airs. Cf. Pross.

Prowsie, *adj.* finical in dress and manner used contemptuously. Cf. Prossie.

Pru, Prui, Prroo, *int.* a call to cattle. Cf. Proo.

†**Prutchee**, *int.* a call to a cow. Cf. Proochy.

Prute no, *int.* an excl. of contempt.

Pruve, *v.* to prove.

Pry, *n.* the carex-grass.

Pry, *n.* refuse, small trash; inferior vegetables.

Prym, *v.* to fill. Cf. Prime.

†**Pryze**, *v.* to appraise, value. Cf. Prize.

Psalm, *n.* in *phr.* 'to take up the psalm, to act as precentor.

Ptru, Ptroo, Ptrui, *int.* a call to cattle or horses. Cf. Proo.

Ptruch, Ptruchie, *int.* a call to a cow. Cf. Proochy.

Ptrueai, Ptrumai, *int.* a call to cattle.

Pu', *v.* to pull.—*n.* a pull.

Puady, *n.* a kind of cloth. Cf. Puddy.

Public, *n.* a public-house, inn.—*adj.* adapted to the times.

Public-room, *n.* a reception-room.

Publisht, *adj.* plump.

Puchal, Puchil, *adj.* well-off, thriving ; of small stature ; neat ; conceited ; consequential.

Pucker, *n.* a state of perplexity, agitation, &c. ; a difficulty, confusion.

Puck-hary, *n.* a certain sprite or hobgoblin.

Puckle, *n.* a small quantity. Cf. Fickle.

Pud, *n.* a pudding.

Pud, *n.* the belly ; a plump, healthy child ; an endearing name for a child.

Pud, *n.* an ink-holder.

Pud, *n.* an innkeeper.

Pudden-band, *n.* catgut.

Pudder, *n.* bustle ; to-do ; pother.

Puddie, *n.* a fondling term for a child. Cf. Pud.

Puddill, *n.* a pedlar's pack ; a pedlar's wallet.

Pudding, Puddin, *n.* in *pl.* the intestines ; the intestines of a pig, &c., filled with various ingredients.

Pudding-bree, -broo, *n.* the water or broth in which puddings have been boiled.

Pudding-heidit, *adj.* stupid, thick-headed.

Pudding-leather, *n.* the stomach.

Pudding-leggie, *n.* a fat, chubby leg.

Pudding-pin, *n.* a skewer or pin for pricking puddings when boiling.

Pudding-prick, *n.* a 'pudding-pin.'

Puddle, *n.* a state of disorder or perplexity ; the act of working in such a state ; a slow, dirty, untidy worker.—*v.* to walk through puddles, or on muddy roads, or on marshy ground ; to play with hands and feet in water ; to work dirtily and untidily ; to engage laboriously and frivolously in the Popish ceremonies ; to tipple.

Puddling, *ppl. adj.* weak, trifling ; untidy, dirty.

Puddock, *n.* a frog. Cf. Paddock.

Puddock-pony, *n.* a tadpole.

Pud-dow, *n.* a pigeon.

Puddy, *n.* a frog. Cf. Padda.

Puddy, *n.* a kind of cloth ; paduasoy.

Pudge, *n.* a small house, a hut ; anything small and confined ; a short, thickset, fat person or animal ; anything short and fat.

Pudgel, *adj.* fond of good living.

Pudget, *n.* a short, fat person.—*adj.* short, fat, corpulent ; inclined to feed well.

Pudgettie, *adj.* short and fat ; having a large belly.

Pudgick, *n.* a short, fat person or animal.— *adj.* short and fat, corpulent.

Pudgy, *adj.* podgy, short and fat.

Pudill, *n.* a state of disorder. Cf. Puddle.

Pudjel, *n.* a fat, round person.

Pue, *n.* a faint breath of wind or ripple on water.—*v.* used of smoke : to rise. Cf. Pew.

Pueshen, *n.* poison.

Puff, *n.* breath, one's wind ; panting ; flattery. —*v.* to pant ; to boast, brag.—*adv.* in a breath, all at once. Cf. Poof.

Puffer, *n.* one who bids at a sale, not to purchase, but only to raise the price, one who 'sweetens.'

Puffery, *n.* puffing advertisements.

Puffing, *n.* pastry puffs.

Puffle, *v.* to puff up, swell.

Puff-the-wind, *n.* bellows.

Puft, *n.* a puff of wind.

Pug, *n.* a monkey ; a small locomotive engine.

Pug, *v.* to pull.

Puggy, *n.* a monkey ; a drunken man.—*v.* to play tricks, befool.

Puggy, *v.* with *up,* to show temper.

Puggy-like, Pug-like, *adj.* like a monkey.

Pugh, *int.* pooh !

Puh, *v.* used of smoke : to rise. Cf. Pew.

Pui, *int.* in *phr.* 'pui ho, pui hup !' calls to calves.

Puik, *v.* to pluck, pull. Cf. Pook.

Puin, *v.* to distrain. Cf. Poind.

Puint, *n.* a point.

Puir, *adj.* poor.—*v.* to impoverish. Cf. Peer, Poor.

Puirtith, *n.* poverty. Cf. Poortith.

Puist, *adj.* in comfortable circumstances ; snug and self-satisfied.—*n.* one who is thick and heavy.

Puist, *v.* to urge, push ; to cram the stomach. Cf. Poist.

Puist-body, *n.* a person in easy circumstances.

Puistie, *adj.* in easy circumstances.

Puk, *v.* to pluck. Cf. Pook.

Puke, *n.* an evil spirit. Cf. Pouk.

†**Pulchrie,** *adj.* beautiful.

Pule, *n.* a puff of smoke.—*v.* to puff out smoke.

Pule, *v.* to eat without appetite ; to sneak off. Cf. Peughle, Peul.

Pulicate, *n.* a kind of weaver's web. Cf. Pollicate.

Pull, *v.* to trim the sides of a rick by pulling out the projecting straw. Cf. Pu, Poo.

Pullion, *n.* a saddle.

Pullisee, Pullishee, *n.* a pulley on a pole with a rope stretching to a window, for drying clothes. Cf. Polly-shee.

Pull-ling, *n.* the mosscrop, cotton-grass.

Pulloch, *n.* a young crab.

†**Pully,** *n.* a turkey. Cf. Poullie.

Puloch, *n.* a patch, a clout.

Pult, *n.* a dirty, lazy woman.—*v.* to go about in a lazy, dirty manner.

Pultie, *n.* a short-bladed knife ; one that has been broken and has had a new point ground on it.

Pultring, *ppl.* rutting ; lascivious.

Pultron, *n.* a poltroon.

Pultrous, *adj.* lustful, lascivious.

Pumfil, Pumfle, *n.* an enclosure for cattle ; a square pew. Cf. Pumphel.

Pump, *n.* a beer-shop.

Pump, *v.* to break wind backwards.—*n.* wind broken backwards.

Pumphel, Pumppil, *n.* a railed-in enclosure for cattle ; a square church-pew.—*v.* to enclose cattle in a 'pumphel.'—*adj.* enclosed, boxed-in.

Pumpit, *adj.* hollow ; used of trees : rotten at the core.

Pumrose, *n.* the primrose. Cf. Pimrose.

Pun, *n.* a sham.

Pun, *n.* a pound in weight or money.

Punce, *v.* to beat ; to push by striking ; to push with the head or a stick.—*n.* a blow with the fist ; a thrust.

Punce, *v.* to pierce or punch with a bradawl.

Punch, *v.* to strike with the foot ; to jog with the elbow.—*n.* a slight push, a jog.

Punch, *n.* an iron crowbar. Cf. Pinch.

Punch, *adj.* thick and short.

Punch and Polly, *n.* a Punch and Judy show.

Punch-bowl, *n.* in *phr.* 'the bottom of the punch-bowl,' a figure in an old dance ; a girls' dancing and singing game.

Punchik, *n.* any person, animal, or thing that is short, stout, and strong.

Punckin, *n.* the footsteps of horses or cattle in soft ground. Cf. Punkin.

Punctual, *adv.* precisely, especially.

Punctuality, *n.* a detail, point, nicety, technicality.

Pund, *n.* an enclosure ; a sheepfold. Cf. Pound.

Pund, *n.* a pound in money or weight.

Pundar, *n.* a person who has charge of hedges, woods, &c., and who 'pounds' straying cattle.

Pundie, *n.* a small tin mug for heating liquids ; a drinking-jug ; drink, liquor.

Pundler, Punler, *n.* a stalk of peas bearing two pods ; one who watches fields or woods to prevent thefts and impound straying cattle.

Punger, *n.* the large edible crab.

Punish, *v.* to reduce much in cutting or dressing, a workman's term ; to devour ; to eat or drink heavily of.

Punk-hole, *n.* a 'peat-pot' or hole in a moss.

Punkin, *n.* footsteps of horses or cattle in soft ground.

Punky, *n.* the game of 'kypes' at marbles.

Puns, *n.* the duffel-grass.

Punse, *v.* to emboss. Cf. Punce.

Punsh, *v.* to punch. Cf. Punch.

Punyie, Punzie, *v.* to prick, spur.—*n.* a prick.

Puock, *n.* a bag. Cf. Pock.

Pup-gallanter, *n.* a 'swell' or coxcomb that plays the gallant.

Puppie-show, *n.* a puppet-show.

Puppish, *adj.* puppyish.

Pur, *v.* to prick ; to poke. Cf. Purr.

†Purchase, *n.* an amour ; an intrigue ; one's wits.—*v.* to obtain, procure, secure.

Purcill, Pursill, *n.* the edible fucus, *Fucus esculentus.* Cf. Pursill.

Pure, *adj.* poor.—*v.* to impoverish. Cf. Peer, Poor.

Pure pride, *n.* ostentatious grandeur without means of supporting it.

Purfeit, Purfittie, *adj.* short-necked, corpulent, of asthmatical make.

†Purfile, Purfloe, *n.* an edging ; the border of a woman's dress.—*v.* to purfle.

Purfillit, Purfled, *ppl. adj.* short-winded.

Purge, *v.* to acquit ; to clear a court of those who are not members.

Purie, *n.* a small, meagre person. Cf. Poorie.

Purify, *v.* to fulfil the conditions of a bond.

Purl, *n.* a portion of the dung of sheep or horses ; dried cow-dung, used for fuel.

Purl, *v.* to spin round ; to twine, curl ; to grope for potatoes ; to fumble ; to form the stitch that produces the 'fur' in a stocking.—*n.* the seam-stitch in a knitted stocking. Cf. Pirl.

Purled-steek, Purlin-steek, *n.* the stitch that produces the 'fur' in a stocking.

Purled stocking, *n.* a ribbed or 'furred' stocking.

†Purlicue, *n.* a flourish at the end of a word in writing ; a recapitulation ; a peroration. —*v.* to recapitulate. Cf. Pirlicue.

Purlie, Purlie-pig, *n.* a money-box. Cf. Pirlie.

Purlusion, *n.* anything noxious or disgusting. —*v.* to render noxious.

Purn, *n.* a quill or 'pirn' of yarn. Cf. Pirn.

Purpie, *n.* purslane.

Purpie, *adj.* of purple colour.—*n.* the colour purple.

Purpie-fever, *n.* typhus.

Purple, *n.* blood.—*v.* to appear as purple.

Purply, *adj.* purple.

Purpose, *n.* neatness, tidiness ; exactness, taste.—*adj.* exact, methodical ; neat, neatly dressed ; well-adjusted.

Purpose-like, *adj.* suitable to its purpose ; used of a woman : capable, managing.— *adv.* suitably to an end.

Purposeness, *n.* neatness, exactness ; method ; capacity.

Purr, *v.* to prick, stab ; to poke ; to kick.— *n.* a kick ; a stab ; the sound of a sharp instrument piercing the flesh. Cf. Porr.

Purr, *n.* a buzzing sound.

Purring-iron, *n.* a poker.

Purry, *n.* a kind of porridge or pudding made of 'kail' and oatmeal, 'tartan-purrie.'

Purse-browed, *adj.* having a pursed-up forehead.

Purse-hingers, *n.* purse-strings; purse-strings attaching a purse to the person.

Purselin, *n.* purslane.

Purselled, *ppl. adj.* used of the mouth: pursed.

Purse-moo, *n.* the purse-mouth; a boat-shaped cloud.

Purse-penny, *n.* any coin kept in the purse and neither exchanged nor given away.

Purse-pest, *n.* a highwayman; a pickpocket.

Purser, *n.* a town-treasurer.

Pursikie, *n.* a small purse; a small fortune.

Pursill, *n.* as much money as fills a purse.

Pursuable, *adj.* that may be prosecuted at law.

Pursual, *n.* most earnest urging; a prosecution; a trial, attempt.

Pursue, *v.* to walk or run with great energy; to assault; to urge earnestly; to prosecute at law.

Pursuer, *n.* a plaintiff, prosecutor.

Pursuit, *n.* an assault; a prosecution.

Pursy, *adj.* purse-proud.

Push, *n.* pressure of work, &c.

Pushen, Pushion, Pushon, Pusion, *n.* poison. Cf. Pousion, Poison.

Pushlock, Puslick, *n.* cows' dung dropped in the fields; dung of cattle, horses, and sheep.

Push-pin, *n.* a child's game, played with three pins.

Pussickie, *n.* a kitten; a fondling term for a child.

Pussy-bawdrons, *n.* a cat.

Put, *v.* to send; to compel.

Put, *n.* a dimple; a hollow in the cheek or chin.

Put about, *v.* to put on clothes; to annoy, inconvenience; to vex, harass; to disconcert; to report, circulate; to publish.

Put afore, *v.* to put in front of.

Put against, *v.* to oppose.

Put at, *v.* to set to, apply one's self; to dun; to appeal for help; to push against.

Put away, *v.* to lay by, save.

Put-back, *n.* a disadvantage, drawback.

Put-by, *n.* a makeshift, a substitute; a hoard, a 'nest-egg.'—*v.* to lay carefully aside; to hoard, save; to bury; to support, satisfy, entertain; to defray cost; to delay, postpone; to divert from a purpose, &c.; to hold out beyond; to serve one's turn, do for an occasion or as a makeshift.

Put by on, *v.* to serve one's turn; to be satisfied with.

Put by one's self, *adj.* greatly excited.

Put down, *v.* to kill, execute, hang; to bury; in *phr.* to 'put one's self down,' to commit suicide.

Put-hand-, -hands-, -in, -to, -on, *v.* to lay violent hands on, assault; to kill, to kill one's self.

Puther, *v.* to canvass. Cf. Peuther.

Puther, *n.* pewter.

Put in, *v.* to unharness, put in the stable; to advance, deposit, or invest money; to pass, endure; to fulfil; to suffer as punishment; to cart corn, &c., from the field to the farmyard.

Put in a foot, *v.* to hurry.

Put in for, *v.* to tender, give in an offer.

Put in the cries, *v.* to give in for publication the banns of marriage.

Put in the pin, *v.* to give up drinking.

Put-off, *n.* an excuse, evasion, pretext; unnecessary delay.—*v.* to squander, waste.

Put on, *n.* a style of dress, clothes.—*v.* to clothe, dress; to put or keep on one's hat, cap, &c.; to dun; to press, embarrass; to push forward, to hasten with increasing speed; to pretend; to acquire a language; to impute to.

Put out, *v.* to discover; to publish; to make a person known who wishes to be concealed; to exert, put forth; to expend, lay out money; to bake.

Put owre, *v.* to survive, last until; to tide over, suffice for; to swallow.

Put past, *v.* to lay aside, save; to dissuade; to give a distaste to; to exempt one from an imputation or charge.

Putt, *v.* to push, thrust; to butt; to pat; to push gently as a hint; to throw a heavy stone from the shoulder in athletic games; to throb.—*n.* a push; a thrust; the recoil of a gun; the act of 'putting' the stone; used in golf: a slight push of the ball into a hole; position, ground; attempt, effort; a buttress of a wall; a jetty, a mass of stones placed in a river to divert the current; one's ground or point.

Putt and row, *n.* great exertion.

Putten, *ppl.* put.

Putter, *n.* one who 'putts' the stone; an animal that butts.

Putter, *n.* a small petard or piece of ordnance.

Putterling, *n.* a small petard.

Put through, *v.* to publish, spread abroad.

Putting, *ppl.* pouting.

Putting-stane, *n.* a heavy stone used in 'putting.'

Put to, or till, *v.* to interrogate straitly; to

straiten; to be put out of countenance; to shut, close; to harness, yoke; to put together in order to propagate; to apprentice to a trade or profession; to set to work, begin; to subject to, make to endure or suffer.

Puttock, *n.* the buzzard.

Put up, *v.* to be lodged; to raise, erect; to settle, have a home of one's own; to endure; to vomit; to incite.

Put upon, *v.* to put on one's clothes; to oppress; to impose upon; to put pressure on.—*ppl. adj.* oppressed, hardly treated.

Put up to, *v.* to incite; to teach, instruct.

Puzhun, *n.* poison.

Puzzle, *v.* to cause intricacy; to get bewildered on a strange road or in a fog. Cf. Pousle.

Py, *n.* a loose riding-coat or frock.

Py, *n.* a magpie. Cf. Pie.

Pyaavan, *adj.* peevish, sickly.

Pyaavie, *n.* a short turn of illness.

Pyardie, *n.* the magpie.

Pyat, *n.* the boy or man who, when a stack begins to taper, is perched on its eaves to catch the sheaves from the fork and toss them to the builder.

Pyat, Pyet, *n.* a magpie; a forward child; a chatterer.—*adj.* piebald; having large white spots; used of words: meaningless, chattering, ornate.

Pyated, *ppl. adj.* freckled, piebald.

Pyat-horse, *n.* a piebald horse.

Pyatie, *adj.* parti-coloured; freckled; cloudy in appearance.

Pyck, *n.* a pike.

Pydle, *n.* a cone made of rushes, for catching fish.

Pye, *n.* a magpie.—*v.* to pry; to peer; to squint. Cf. Pie.

Pyetty, *adj.* 'pyatie.'

Pyfer, *v.* to whimper; to work feebly.—*n.* a useless creature. Cf. Peefer, Piffer.

Pygral, *adj.* paltry. Cf. Pegral.

Pyke, *v.* to dress, beautify, deck.—*n.* a stitch or thread of gold, silk, &c.; an implement used in embroidering. Cf. Pick.

Pyke, *v.* to steal, pilfer. Cf. Pike.

Pyke, *v.* to pick.

Pyker, Pycker, *n.* one charged with petty theft.

Pykering, *n.* petty theft, pilfering.

Pyket, Pykeit, *ppl. adj.* used of wire: barbed.

Pykie, *adj.* given to stealing.

Pykie-pock, *n.* chicken-pox.

Pykin-awl, *n.* a shoemaker's awl for picking out pegs, &c.

Pykis, *n.* short, withered heath.

Pykit, Pykeit, *ppl. adj.* meagre-looking; shrunken.

Pykle, *n.* a hay-fork.

Pyle, *n.* a Border peel or fortress.

Pyle, *n.* fat on the surface of soups, &c. Cf. Pile.

Pyle, *n.* a small quantity.

Pyle, *n.* a blade or stalk of grass; a single grain of corn.

Pyne, *n.* pain, lingering pain; grief.—*v.* to suffer pain; to cause pain. Cf. Pine.

Pyne-doublet, *n.* a hidden coat of mail.

Pyne-, Pynt-pig, *n.* a child's earthenware money-box. Cf. Pine-pig.

Pyocher, *n.* a troublesome cough.

Pyochter, *v.* to cough vigorously to get rid of phlegm.

Pyock, *n.* a bag, a sack. Cf. Pock.

Pyotie, *adj.* having large white spots; piebald. Cf. Pyatie.

Pyoul, *v.* to fret, whine; to eat without appetite, little and slowly; to sneak off; used of snow: to fall in a continuous drizzle.—*n.* a small bite; a stifled cough. Cf. Peughle, Peul.

Pyowe, *n.* a cone of damp gunpowder, made by boys as a firework. Cf. Peeoye.

Pyowter, *v.* to poke or potter about; to work without care or skill. Cf. Pouter.

Pyrl, *v.* to twist, twirl, whirl. Cf. Pirl.

Pyrn, *n.* a bobbin. Cf. Pirn.

Pyrr, *n.* the par or samlet; the salmon.

Pysent, *adj.* of light behaviour.

Pysert, *n.* a miser. Cf. Peyzart.

Pyslit, *ppl. adj.* in easy circumstances. Cf. Peisled.

Pyssle, *n.* a thing of no value; a trifle.

Pyster, *v.* to hoard up.

Pystery, *n.* a hoard, anything hoarded up.

Pytane, *n.* a term of endearment; a young child.

Qua, *v.* to come away; only imperatively used. Cf. Quay.

Qua, Quaa, *n.* a bog, quagmire. Cf. Quaw.

Quaakin, *ppl. adj.* quaking.

Quack, *n.* an instant.

Quacking, *ppl. adj.* quaking.

Quad, *adj.* base, bad, vile.—*n.* a bad state.

†**Quadre,** *v.* to square, quadrate.

Quadruply, *n.* a fourth reply; a defender's rejoinder to a pursuer's 'triply.'—*v.* to make such reply or rejoinder: a legal term. Cf. Duply, Triply.

Quaff, *n.* a draught.

Quag, *n.* a quagmire; the soft part of a bog.

Quaich, *v.* to scream wildly.—*n.* a wild scream.

Quaich, *n.* a two-eared drinking-cup. Cf. Quaigh.

Quaick, *n.* a heifer. Cf. Quey.

Quaigh, *n.* a small, shallow drinking-cup, with two 'ears' for handles.

Quaik, *n.* a heifer. Cf. Quey.

Quaikin-ash, *n.* the aspen.

Quail, *v.* to quell; used of the wind : to lull; to quiet down.

Quaintance, *n.* acquaintance.

Quair, Quaire, *n.* a quire of paper.

Quairn, *n.* a small stone hand-mill for grinding corn, a quern.

Quairn, *n.* a grain, seed, a small particle.

Quairny, *adj.* granulated ; in small particles.

Quaist, *n.* a rogue ; a wag.

Quaisten, *n.* a question.—*v.* to question.

Quaisten-buik, *n.* the Shorter Catechism.

Quait, *adj.* quiet ; secret, private.—*v.* to silence.

Quaiten, *v.* to quiet ; to assuage pain.

Quait-tongued, *adj.* not talkative ; of sober and gentle speech.

Quake, *n.* a heifer. Cf. Quey.

Quakers' meeting, *n.* a silent gathering or assembly.

Quaking, Quakkin, *ppl. adj.* used of a bog: moving, trembling.

Quaking-ash, *n.* the aspen.

Quaking-bog, *n.* a moving quagmire.

Quaking-qua, *n.* a moving quagmire. Cf. Bobbin-quaw.

Qualify, *v.* to prove ; to authenticate, make good ; to testify to.

Quality, *n.* the gentry ; the upper classes ; reservation, condition.

Quality-binding, *n.* a sort of worsted tape used for binding the borders of carpets.

Quall, *v.* to quell ; to be subdued ; to quail. Cf. Quell.

Quantance, *n.* acquaintance.

Quar, *n.* a quire of paper. Cf. Quair.

Quarnelt, *ppl. adj.* having angles.

Quarrant, *n.* a kind of shoe made of untanned leather.

Quarrel, *n.* a stone-quarry ; materials from a quarry.—*v.* to quarry ; to raise stones from a quarry.

Quarrel, *v.* to challenge, reprove, check ; to object to, question.

Quarrel-head, *n.* the head of a dart for a cross-bow.

Quarrellable, *adj.* open to challenge, challengeable.

Quarrelsome, *adj.* fault-finding ; litigious ; fond of contradicting.

Quarry-hole, *n.* a disused quarry.

Quartan, *n.* a quart ; a quarter.

Quarter, *n.* the quarter of a circular oatcake ; a quarter of a pound.

Quarter-cake, *n.* a 'farl' or fourth part of a circular oatcake.

Quarterer, *n.* a respectable beggar who was furnished with lodgings in a parish ; a lodger.

Quarter-ill, *n.* a disease affecting one of the quarters of sheep or young cattle.

Quartering-house, *n.* a lodging, quarters.

Quarterly, *adv.* through each quarter of a town.

Quartor-wife, *n.* a poor woman quartered in a house by the parish.

Quartril, *n.* the 'quarter-ill.'

Quat, *v.* to quit, give over ; to abandon : to resign ; to exonerate ; to stop working.

Quat, *v. pret.* omitted.—*ppl. adj.* rid, free.

Quate, *adj.* quiet.

Quaten, *v.* to quiet.

Quattit, *v. pret.* quitted.

Quauk, *v.* to quake.

Quaukin-aish, *n.* the aspen.

Quave, *v.* used of a 'brae': to go up or down zigzag.

Quaver, *n.* a tremulous cry or voice.

Quaw, *n.* a quagmire ; a hole out of which peats have been cut ; an old pit overgrown with grass, &c.

Quay, *v. imperat.* come away ! get along ! Cf. Qua.

Quay, *n.* a heifer. Cf. Quey.

Quay-neb, *n.* the point of a pier, the projecting part of a quay.

Quazie, *adj.* queasy.

Que, *n.* a heifer. Cf. Quey.

Queach, *n.* a small two-handled drinking-cup. Cf. Quaigh.

Queak, *v.* to squeak or cry like the young of rats, mice, &c.—*n.* a gentle squeak ; the cry of the young of small animals.

Quean-bairn, -lassie, *n.* a female child ; a young girl.

Quease, *v.* to wheeze.

Quech, *n.* a two-handled drinking-cup. Cf. Quaigh.

Qued, *adj.* bad, vile. Cf. Quad.

Quee-beck, *n.* the cry of a startled grouse.

Queecher, *v.* to work lazily and unsatisfactorily.

Queed, *n.* a tub ; a vessel for holding fish ; a wooden chamber-pot.

Queed, *n.* the cud.

Queedie, *n.* a small tub ; a small wooden chamber-pot, used in a nursery. Cf. Cootie.

Queedie, *n.* the cud.

Queek, *n.* a gentle squeak. Cf. Queak.

Queel, *v.* to cool.—*n.* a cooling ; what cools one.

Queem, *adj.* pleasant ; calm, smooth ; neat ; filled up to the general level ; close and tight, fitting exactly ; deep.—*v.* to fit exactly.

Queemer, *n.* one skilled in fitting joints ; a wheedler.

Queemly, *adj.* exactly adapted.—*adv.* calmly, smoothly.

Queemness, *n.* exact adaptation.

Queen, *n.* a quean ; a damsel ; a loose woman ; a term of endearment or of contempt.

Queen, *n.* a quern.

Queen Anne, *n.* a girls' rhyming-game in which a ball is used ; a gun such as was used in Queen Anne's reign.

Queen Anne's thrissel, *n.* the musk-thistle.

Queen-cake, *n.* a small sweet cake, made without pastry.

Queen's chair, *n.* a method of carrying a person. Cf. King's chair.

Queen's cushion, *n.* a 'queen's chair.'

Queen's cushion, *n.* the cropstone.

Queen's head, *n.* a postage-stamp.

Queentra, *n.* the country. Cf. Quintry, Kwintra.

Queeple, *v.* to quack like a duckling.—*n.* a duckling's quack. Cf. Wheeple.

Queer, *n.* the choir or chancel of a church ; a vault in a church ; the persons composing a choir.

Queer, *adj.* entertaining, amusing, humorous. —*adv.* queerly.—*n.* in *pl.* news, any things odd or strange. —*v.* to puzzle ; to treat curiously.

Queerach, *v.* to work weakly and triflingly ; to nurse too daintily.—*n.* working in a weak and trifling way ; overnursing daintily.

Queer-gotten, *adj.* used of uncertain parentage.

Queerikens, *n.* the hips. Cf. Wheerikins.

Queerish, *adj.* feeling rather unwell ; rather queer.

Queerishness, *n.* an uneasy sensation.

Queersome, *adj.* rather queer.

Queerways, *adj.* strange, nervous, squeamish.

Queery, *n.* a queer thing ; a curious circumstance.

Queery, *n.* a query.

Queese, *v.* to wheeze.

Queesitive, *adj.* inquisitive.

Queesitiveness, *n.* inquisitiveness, curiosity.

Queest, *v. pret.* did cast.

Queest, *n.* the wood-pigeon.

Queet, *n.* the ankle ; a gaiter. Cf. Coot.

Queeter, *v.* to work in a weak, trifling manner. —*n.* working in a weak, trifling manner.

Queeth, *n.* the coal-fish in the second year.

Queetie, *adj.* low, mean. Cf. Wheetie.

Queetikins, *n.* gaiters ; short leggings.

Queezie, *adj.* queasy.

†**Queez-maddam,** *n.* the French jargonelle pear. Cf. Cuisse-madame.

Queff, Quegh, Queich, *n.* a two-handled drinking-cup. Cf. Quaigh.

Queine, *n.* a quean. Cf. Queen.

Queir, *n.* the choir or quire of a church.

Quell, *v.* to quench, extinguish ; to quail ; to cease ; to grow quiet. Cf. Quall.

Quelt, *n.* a kilt.

Queme, *v.* to fit exactly. Cf. Queem.

Quene, *n.* a quean. Cf. Queen.

Quentry, *n.* country. Cf. Quintry.

Quenyie, *n.* a corner. Cf. Quinzie.

Querd, *n.* a vessel formerly used for holding fish. Cf. Queed.

Querious, *adj.* curious.

Quern, *n.* the gizzard of a fowl.

Quern, *n.* a grain, granule. Cf. Quairn.

Querney, *n.* a species of rot in sheep.

Quernie, *adj.* used of honey : abounding in granules. Cf. Quairny.

Quernie, *n.* a grain of corn ; an indefinite number or quantity. Cf. Curnie.

Quernie, Quernock, *n.* a small quern or stone hand-mill for grinding corn.

Querty, *adj.* lively, possessing a flow of animal spirits ; active.

Query, *n.* a queer thing. Cf. Queery.

†**Quest,** *v.* to search for game ; used of a dog : to give tongue on a scent, to hunt.—*n.* a request, petition.

Question, *n.* in *pl.* the Shorter Catechism.

Questionary, *adj.* used of examinations : oral, *vivâ voce.*

Question-book, *n.* the Shorter Catechism.

Quet, *n.* the guillemot.

Quey, Queyag, *n.* a heifer until she has had a calf.

Queyit, *adj.* quiet.—*n.* rest, quietude.

Queyl, *n.* a haycock. Cf. Coil, Cole.

Queyn, Queynie, *n.* a damsel, wench, quean. Cf. Queen.

Queyoch, *n.* a heifer. Cf. Quey.

Queyt, *n.* a coat. Cf. Quite, Kwite.

Quhaip, Quhawp, *n.* an evil spirit, a goblin, supposed to haunt the eaves of houses at night on the lookout for evil-doers. Cf. Whaup.

Quhey, *n.* a heifer, 'quey.'

Quhult, *n.* anything big of its kind. Cf. Welt.

Qui, *n.* a heifer.

Quib, *n.* a quip ; a gibe.

Quibow, *n.* the branch of a tree.

Quich, *n.* a small round-eared cap, worn by women under another, and showing only the border.

Quick, *adj.* piercing, sharp.

Quick-and-quidder, *adv.* quickly, swiftly.

Quicken, *n.* the mountain-ash, 'rowan'; the couch-grass.

Quickenin, *n.* fermenting ale or beer thrown into ale, porter, &c. that has become dead or stale.

Quick-horn, *n.* a horn taken from a living animal.

Quid, *n.* the cud.

Quiddie, *n.* the cud. Cf. Queedie.

Quiddie, *n.* a small tub; a small wooden chamber-pot. Cf. Queedie.

Quide, *n.* a 'quiddie'; a small tub.

Quie, *n.* a heifer. Cf. Quey.

Quierty, *adj.* lively. Cf. Querty.

Quiet, *adj.* used of persons: concealed, skulking. Cf. Quait.

Quieten, *v.* to quiet, pacify; to allay. Cf. Quaten.

Quietlin-wise, *adv.* quietly.

Quiff, *n.* a whiff of a pipe, a short smoke.

Quile, *n.* a coal; a burning coal.

Quile, *n.* a haycock.—*v.* to pile haycocks. Cf. Coil, Cole.

Quill, *v.* to write.—*n.* the throat.

Quill, *n.* a weaver's reed; a bobbin.

Quill, *n.* a bung.

Quill-fatt, *n.* a vat having a bung.

Quilt, *v.* to thrash.

Quim, *adj.* familiar. Cf. Queem.

Quim and cosh, *adj.* familiarly intimate.

Quin, *v.* in *phr.* 'to quin thanks,' to give thanks. Cf. Con.

Quine, *n.* a quean; a girl. Cf. Queen.

Quinie, *n.* a young girl.

Quinkins, *n.* the scum or refuse of any liquor; nothing at all.

Quinter, *n.* a ewe in her third year, a 'twinter.'

Quintry, Quintra, *n.* country. Cf. Kwintra, Queentra.

Quinzie, *n.* a corner.

Quirk, *n.* an advantage, not positively illegal, but inconsistent with honour and strict honesty.—*v.* to cheat; to elude by stratagem.

Quirkle, *n.* a puzzle, the answer to which depends on a catch or quibble.

Quirklum, *n.* a little arithmetical puzzle, the answer to which depends on a quibble.

Quirksome, *adj.* subtle.

Quirky, *adj.* intricate; playful.

Quirn, *n.* a quern, a small stone hand-mill.

Quirty, *adj.* lively. Cf. Querty.

Quisquous, *adj.* nice, perplexing, subtle; difficult to discuss.

Quistical, *adj.* whimsical, fantastic, queer; odd-looking.

Quit, *n.* an ankle. Cf. Queet.

Quitchie, *adj.* very or scalding hot.

Quit-claim, *v.* to renounce a claim.

Quits, *adj.* quiet.

Quite, *n.* a coat; a petticoat.

Quite, *v.* to play quoits; to skate; to play at curling.—*n.* a quoit; the act of skating. Cf. Quoit.

Quiting, *n.* the game of curling.

Quiting-stone, *n.* a curling-stone.

Quittance, *n.* riddance.

Quiyte, *n.* an ankle. Cf. Queet.

Quiz, *v.* to question closely.

Quizzing-glass, *n.* an eyeglass.

Quo', *v. pret.* quoth.

Quoif, *n.* a cap, 'mutch,' coif.

Quoit, *v.* to skate; to curl. Cf. Quite.

Quoiting-stane, *n.* a curling-stone.

Quoits, *n.* in *phr.* 'a' oot o' the quoits,' quite astray, all wrong.

Quorum, *n.* a company, assemblage, 'core.'

Quote, *v.* in *phr.* to 'quote a paper,' to endorse the title of a paper: a law term.

Quott, Quote, *n.* the portion of goods of one deceased, appointed by law to be paid for the confirmation of his testament, or for the right of intromitting with his property.

Quoy, Quoyach, *n.* a heifer. Cf. Quey.

Qurd, *n.* a clot of excrement; a term of reproach for a person.

Quy, Quyach, *n.* a heifer. Cf. Quey.

Quyle, *n.* a coal. Cf. Quile.

Quyle, *n.* a haycock.—*v.* to put hay into cocks. Cf. Coil.

Quyne, *n.* a damsel. Cf. Queen.

Quynyie, Quynyie, *n.* a corner. Cf. Quinzie.

Quyte, *n.* a coat; a petticoat. Cf. Quite.

Quyte, Qwyte, *v.* to skate; to play at curling. —*n.* the act of skating. Cf. Quite, Quoit.

Ra, *n.* a roe-deer.

Ra, *adj.* raw.

Raal, *adj.* real.—*adv.* very. Cf. Real.

Ra'an, *ppl.* riven, torn.

Raan, *n.* the roe of a fish. Cf. Ran, Raun.

Raand, *n.* a stripe; a streak of dirt; a mark, stain. Cf. Rand.

Raan-fleuk, *n.* the turbot.

Raaze, *v.* to raise; to excite. Cf. Raise.

†**Rabate,** *v.* to abate.

Rabbie-rinnie-hedge, *n.* the goose-grass.

Rabbit's-kiss, *n.* a penalty in the game of forfeits, in which a man and a woman have each to nibble an end of the same piece of straw until their lips meet.

Rabblach, *n.* nonsense; incoherent speech or nonsense; a confused mass; an ill-built wall, &c.; a stunted tree.—*v.* to rattle off nonsense; to repeat a lesson, &c., carelessly or hastily; with *up*, to build carelessly and in a hurry.

Rabble, Rablo, *v.* to speak indistinctly and quickly; to gabble; to work hastily or carelessly; to mob riotously.—*n.* confused, careless speech; incoherent reading or talking; a gabble; hasty, careless work; a ruinous mass, a building falling to decay; a careless, hurried worker; a foolish story.

Rabblement, *n.* confused talk; chatter.

Rabbler, Rabler, *n.* a quick reader; one who speaks or reads indistinctly; a careless, hasty worker; a rioter, mobber.

Rabbling, *n.* the act of mobbing; a violent ejectment.

†Rabiator, Rabiawtor, *n.* a violent bully; a robber, plunderer.

Rabscallion, *n.* a low, worthless fellow; a tatterdemalion.

Race, *n.* a freight of water from a well; a quick errand; the train of historical narration.

Racer, *n.* a common trull; an attendant at races.

Racer-horse, *n.* a racehorse.

Rach, *n.* a hound; a thievish animal; a poacher; a night-wanderer.—*adj.* loose in morals, unsteady. Cf. Ratch.

Rachan, *n.* a plaid worn by men; rough cloth from which sailors' 'dreadnoughts' are made; a scarf, cravat. Cf. Rauchan.

Rachle, *n.* a loose heap.—*v.* to heap up loosely. Cf. Ruckle.

Rachled, *ppl. adj.* used of faces: wrinkled, worn.

Rachlie, *adj.* dirty and disorderly.

Rachlin, *adj.* unsettled; harebrained; noisy, clamorous.

Rack, *n.* a blow; a shock; ruin.

Rack, *n.* used of mutton: the neck or scrag.

Rack, *n.* a racking pain; a wooden shelved frame attached to a wall, for holding plates, &c.; in *pl.* an apparatus for roasting meat; a piece of wood used in feeding a mill; reach, extent; a shallow ford of considerable breadth.—*v.* to suspend; to strain; to wrench.

Rack, *n.* the course in curling over which the stones are driven.

Rack, *v.* used of the clouds: to clear.—*n.* the foam of the sea; driving clouds, mist, smoke, &c.

Rack, *v.* to heed, care.—*n.* care.

Rack, *n.* couch-grass.

Rackabimus, *n.* a sudden or unexpected stroke or fall.

Rackad, Rackart, *n.* a racket, noise; uproar; hurly-burly; reproof; a crashing blow.

Rack-bone, *n.* that part of the harness of a twelve-ox plough by which the first pair was connected with the bridle.

Rackel, *adj.* rash; stout. Cf. Rackle.

Racket, *n.* a spasm of pain; a smart and violent blow.

†Racket, *n.* a dress-frock. Cf. Rockat.

Racking-pin, *n.* a piece of wood used to tighten ropes. Cf. Rack-pin.

Racking-wage, *n.* a too liberal wage.

Rackle, *n.* a loose heap.—*v.* to pile up loosely.

Rackle, *adj.* rash; fearless; sturdy, stout; strong in old age; strong and clumsy. Cf. Raucle.

Rackle, *n.* a chain; the chain of a tin pipe-lid; the clank of a chain.—*v.* to clank, rattle; to shake forcibly; to chain; to take the kinks out of a rope for one winding it into a ball.

Rackle-handit, *adj.* careless; headstrong; ready to strike.

Rackleness, *n.* vigorous health and briskness in old age.

Rackler, *n.* a land-surveyor.

Rackless, *adj.* reckless.

Rackless-handit, *adj.* reckless, headstrong.

Racklessly, *adv.* recklessly.

Rackle-tongued, *adj.* rough-tongued, harsh of speech.

Rackligence, *n.* accident, chance.

Rackmereesle, *adv.* higgledy-piggledy.

Rackon, *v.* to reckon; to fancy; to suppose.

Rack-pin, *n.* a stick for twisting or tightening ropes.

Racks, *v.* to stretch. Cf. Rax.

Rack-staff, -stick, *n.* a 'rack-pin.'

Rack-stock, *n.* a rack; the rack for torture.—*phrs.* to 'tak' rack-stock,' to claim everything that belongs to one; to 'tak' one owre the rack-stock,' to call one to account severely for some mistake.

Racky, *adj.* used of the weather: gusty, stormy.

Rad, Rade, *adj.* afraid, timorous.—*v.* to fear.

Rad, *adj.* quick.

Raddle, *v.* to beat soundly with a stick.

Rade, *n.* a ridiculous enterprise or expedition. Cf. Raid.

Rade, *v. pret.* rode.

Rade-goose, *n.* the barnacle-goose. Cf. Rood-goose.

Radgie, *adj.* used of a horse, &c.: becoming excited and plunging wildly.

Radicle, *n.* a reticule.

Radly, *adv.* quickly.

Rae, *n.* an enclosure for cattle. Cf. Ree.

Rae, *n.* a roe-deer.

Rael, *n.* a rail; a line or row.—*v.* to set in a row. Cf. Rail.

Rael, *adj.* real; true.—*adv.* very, thoroughly. Cf. Real.

Rael, *v.* to entangle.—*n.* a tangle. Cf. Ravel.

Raeling, *n.* a tangled thread. Cf. Ravelin.

Raem, *n.* cream.—*v.* to cream; to foam. Cf. Ream.

Raen, *n.* a raven.

Raen, v. to whimper; to repeat monotonously. Cf. Rane.

Raep, v. to reap.

Raeper, n. a reaper.

Raff, n. a flying shower.

Raff, n. a rank, rapid growth; worthless stuff, refuse; the 'riff-raff'; plenty, abundance.— v. to abound, overflow; to rant, roar, carouse.—adj. cheerful; contented.

Raffan, Raffing, ppl. adj. merry, ranting, carousing; roving; hearty.

Raffel, n. doeskin.

Raffish, adj. sportive; rough.

Raffy, adj. used of corn: rank, coarse, rapidly growing; of a crop: thick and thriving; drunken, dissipated; liberal, generous; plentiful.—n. a large quantity of forced growth, exhausting the soil.

Raft, n. a large number or quantity; a crowd.

Rag, Ragg, n. a low, worthless person; a contemptuous designation of anything very lean and thin; used of corn: a partial winnowing.—v. to pierce a fish with the hook in fishing; used of corn: for the ear to show out of the shot blade; to put corn for the first time through the winnowing-machine. Cf. Raggle.

Rag, v. to tease; to reproach, scold violently, abuse.—n. rough chaffing; a debate, quarrel; the act of severe reproaching.

Ragabanes, n. the skeleton of a fish, &c.

Rag-a-bash, Rag-a-brash, Rag-a-buss, -bush, n. a tatterdemalion; a low rascal; a vagabond.—adj. very poor; mean, paltry, contemptible; good for nothing.

Rag-fallow, -fauch, n. grass-land broken up in the summer after the hay is cut, ploughed three times, and then dunged.

Ragger, n. a ragman, one who exchanges crockery, &c., for rags.

Raggety, adj. ragged, untidy.

Raggle, v. to ruffle the skin; used in architecture: to jag, to groove one stone to receive another; to winnow corn partially.—n. a reglet in architecture; a partial winnowing of corn.

Raggle, v. to wrangle, dispute.—n. a wrangle, a bicker.

Raggling, Ragling, n. the vacant space between the top of the walls and the slates of a house.

Ragglish, Raglish, adj. used of the weather: rough, boisterous; harsh, severe, coarse, worthless.

Raggy, n. a ragman.—adj. ragged.

Raggy-folks, n. rag-gatherers.

Raglat-plane, n. a plane used by carpenters in making a groove for shelves of drawers, &c.

Ragnails, n. broken bits of skin round the finger-nails.

Rag-pock, n. a bag for holding rags, &c.

Rag-tag, adj. reduced to rags by drink.

Ragweed, n. ragwort, Senecio.

Raible, v. to speak confusedly; to gabble. —n. a foolish story. Cf. Rabble.

Raichie, v. to scold.—n. the act of scolding.

Raid, n. a ridiculous enterprise or expedition. Cf. Rade.

Raid, n. a road for ships.

Raid, v. pret. rode.

Raid-goose, n. the barnacle-goose. Cf Rood goose.

Raik, v. to rake; to collect. Cf. Rake.

Raik, v. to heed, matter. Cf. Reck.

Raik, n. an idle person, a stroller by night; a dog that does not stay at home.—v. used of cattle, dogs, persons: to stray, to roam about. Cf. Rake.

Raik, n. the extent of a pasturage for sheep or cattle; a swift pace; what a person can cart or carry at a time from one place to another; the extent of a fishing-ground; the direction of clouds driven by the wind. —v. to run, fly. Cf. Rake.

Raik, n. attainment; width, reach.—v. to reach; to hand; to stretch; to strike a blow. Cf. Reach.

Raik, n. a weed which grows around a water-spring or in a well.

Raiker, n. a hard worker. Cf. Raker.

Raikin, adv. readily. Cf. Raking.

Rail, n. a woman's jacket; an upper garment worn by women; the upper portion of an infant's nightdress.

Rail, n. a line or row.—adj. railed.—v. to fit with a band, bar, or border; to enclose; to set in a row.

Rail, v. to rail at, abuse.

Rail, v. to ravel; to entangle. Cf. Ravel.

Railed, ppl. entangled, ravelled.

Rail-ee'd, adj. wall-eyed, 'ringle-ee'd.'

Railie, Railly, n. a woman's jacket. Cf. Rail.

Raillich, n. a thin, worthless piece of cloth.

Rail-stick, -tree, n. a large beam in a 'byre,' fixed about two feet above the heads of the cows, into which the upper ends of stakes are fixed.

Rail-train, n. a railway train.

Rail-wand, n. the railing of a stair.

Raim, n. cream.—v. to froth. Cf. Ream.

Raim, n. idle, unmeaning talk.—v. to repeat the same thing over and over. Cf. Rane.

Rain-bird, n. the green woodpecker.

Raing, n. a circle; a circular streak.—v. to encircle, to streak in a circular manner.

Raing, n. a row, a rank.—v. to rank up; to follow in a line.

Rain-goose, n. the red-throated diver.

Rainie, *n*. idle, unmeaning talk. Cf. Rane.

Rainiebus, *n*. a boys' game, to recover caps scattered at a distance from a line drawn across the playground.

Rain-tree, *n*. an umbrella.

Rain-tree, *n*. the beam in a chimney or over a fire, on which pots, kettles, &c. are hung. Cf. Ran-tree.

Rainy day, *n*. a day of adversity.

Raip, *n*. a rope. Cf. Rape.

Raipie, Raipy, *adj*. viscous, ropy; used of thread, &c.: coarse, rough.

Rair, *n*. a roar. Cf. Roar.

Raird, *v*. to brag; to bandy ill-language; to roar; to break wind backwards; to make a noise by eructation; to make a loud noise; to scold; to make a crackling sound; used of sheep and cattle: to bleat, to low.—*n*. a loud noise, clamour; a riot; confusion; a sudden report; the noise of eructation; the backward breaking of wind; lowing; bleating; a scold.

Rairdie, *n*. a wild frolic; a riot; a quarrel.

Rairuck, *n*. a small rick of corn.

Raise, *v*. to cause bread to rise; to leaven; to cause to ferment; to start a tune; to sing; to excite, infuriate, madden; used in curling: to move a stone out of the way.—*n*. a jest, wild fun, a 'rise.'

Raise, *v. pret*. arose, rose.

Raise-an'-wand, Raise-an'-dwang, *n*. an apparatus for bringing a millstone home from the quarry. Cf. Raising-dwang.

Raised-like, *adj*. apparently under great excitement; mad-like.

Raise-net, *n*. a net that rises and falls with the tide.

Raise-net-fishing, *n*. allowing the lower part of the net to rise and float with the flowing tide and to fall with the ebbing.

Raiser, *n*. one who helps another to rise in life.

Raising, *n*. an alarm, rousing.

Raising-dwang, *n*. the apparatus formerly used for bringing a millstone home from the quarry.

Raisin-wine, *n*. a name given to French brandy.

Rait, *n*. a file of soldiers. Cf. Ratt.

Raith, *n*. a quarter of a year.

Raith, *n*. a circular earthwork or mound, a 'rath.'

Raither, *adv*. rather.

Raitherly, *adv*. rather.

Raivel, *v*. to entangle; to wander in speech; to unravel.—*n*. a tangle; confusion; ravelled thread. Cf. Ravel.

Raivel, *n*. a rail, railing; a weavers' instrument for spreading yarn; the cross-beam in a 'byre' to which the stakes of the cows are fastened; in *pl*. the tops of a cart; the rowels of spurs.—*v*. to rail in. Cf. Ravel.

Raivelin, Raivlin, *n*. a tangled thread; a loose, unravelled thread; used of rhyme: loose odds and ends. Cf. Ravelling.

Raivel-stick, *n*. the 'raivel' of a 'byre.' Cf. Rail-stick, -tree.

Raivery, *n*. delirium. Cf. Ravery.

Raize, *v*. to anger. Cf. Raise.

Rajie, *adj*. used of an animal: becoming excited and plunging about wildly. Cf. Radgie.

Rak, *n*. flying clouds.—*v*. used of the clouds: to clear. Cf. Rack.

Rak, *v*. to heed, care, reck. Cf. Raik.

Rak, *n*. the rheum or scum which gathers in the eyes during sleep; the scum on stagnant water. Cf. Rawk.

Rake, *v*. to clear a grate or fire of ashes; to turn and smooth burning seaweed in kelp-making; to accumulate, gather; to search thoroughly; to recall old scandals, &c.; to bank up a fire; to bury; to clear the eyes; to rub any part of the body with the hands; used of food: to disagree with.—*n*. an implement like a rough golf-iron, with a handle like a spade's, used in kelp-making.

Rake, *n*. a track, path; a walk for cattle, &c.; the direction of clouds driven by the wind; a journey; a journey to and fro to fetch anything, the thing so fetched, a load; a large quantity; a swift pace; a rapid growth of crops, &c.; great energy: work done speedily; work to be done within a given time; one who works with fuss, but carelessly; in *pl*. the duty exacted at a mill of three 'gowpens.'—*v*. to do anything with speed or energy; to run; to fly; used of cattle, &c., ploughing: to turn to the left.

Rake, *v*. to range, stray; to roam, wander; to stroll idly; to walk about late at night. —*n*. a lounger; one who roams at night; an aimless wanderer.

Rake, *v*. to fit out. Cf. Reek.

Rake, *v*. to reach; to hand, pass; to stretch; to extend; to arrive. Cf. Reach.

Rakel, *adj*. rash, fearless; strong, stout. Cf. Rackle.

Raker, *n*. a hard worker.

Raker, *n*. a vagabond.

Raking, *n*. a flight, clearance.—*ppl. adj*. energetic; quick; used of clouds: gathering, scouring.—*adv*. readily.

Raking-coal, -piece, *n*. a large lump of coal used to keep a fire alight through the night.

Rakless, *adj*. rash; careless.

Rale, *adj*. real; true. Cf. Real.

Ralliach, *adj*. slightly stormy.

Rallion, *n*. a ragged fellow. Cf. Rullion.

Rallion, *n.* clattering noise. Cf. **Rullion.**

Rallion-shout, *n.* a loud, noisy shout.

Rally, *v.* to crowd; to sport in a disorderly fashion; to go to and fro in disorder.—*n.* a rush, quick pace; a crowd.

Rally, *v.* to scold.

Rally, *adj.* mean, not handsome or genteel.

Rally, *n.* a woman's upper garment. Cf. **Rail.**

Ralyie, *v.* to crowd. Cf. **Rally.**

Ram, *n.* a headstrong fellow.

Ram, *v.* to push violently; to stuff with food; to use a person as a battering-ram, by way of punishing him; with *about*, to knock about; with *in*, to crush or burst in.

Ramack, *n.* a stick; a large, rugged piece of stick; a scrap; a worthless article. Cf. **Rammack.**

Ramack, *n.* a large, raw-boned person who speaks and acts heedlessly; a backbiter; a double-dealer; a false-hearted fellow. Cf. **Ramagiechan.**

Ramack-a-dodgil, *n.* anything large.

Ramagiechan, *n.* a large, raw-boned person who speaks and acts heedlessly; a backbiter; a double-dealer; a false-hearted fellow. Cf. **Ramack.**

†Ramasht, *ppl. adj.* summed-up, totalled.

Rambaleugh, *adj.* tempestuous, stormy; used of the temper: stormy.

†Rambarre, *v.* to repulse; to stop, restrain.

Rambask, *adj.* robust. Cf. **Rambusk.**

Rambaskious, Rambaskish, *adj.* rough, rude, unpolished.

Ramble, *v.* to dance; to wander or talk in sleep or delirium.—*n.* a digression in writing or speaking; a drinking-bout; a spree.

Ramble, *n.* mixed grain. Cf. **Rammel.**

Ramblegarie, *n.* a forward person.—*adj.* disorderly. Cf. **Rumblegarie.**

Ramblin', *ppl. adj.* loose, talkative, untrustworthy.

Ramblin-, Ramlin-lad, *n.* a tall, fast-growing boy. Cf. **Rumbling.**

Ramblin-syver, *n.* a drain filled up to the surface with loose stones. Cf. **Ramle.**

Rambooze, *adv.* suddenly and with headlong speed.

Rambounge, *n.* a severe bout of labour.

Rambusk, Rambust, *adj.* robust. Cf. **Rambask.**

Rambusteous, *adj.* rude, of boisterous manners. Cf. **Rambaskious.**

Rame, *v.* to shout, roar; to talk nonsense; to ask for anything repeatedly and fretfully; to whimper; to ply with questions; to keep reiterating the same words.—*n.* a cry; a reiterated cry; repetition of the same sound.

Ramfeezled, *ppl. adj.* fatigued, exhausted; overworked; worn-out; confused.

Ramfeezlement, *n.* disorder, caused by fatigue or otherwise; confused discourse; a violent quarrel.

Ramfoozle, *v.* to disorder; to turn topsy-turvy.

Ramgeed, Ramjeed, *adj.* furious, crazy; confused with drink.

Ramgunshoch, *adj.* rugged; morose; rough, rude.

Ramiegeister, *n.* a sharp stroke; an injury. Cf. **Remigester.**

Ramished, Rammist, *ppl. adj.* furious, crazy; confused with drink; ill-rested; sleepy from broken sleep. Cf. **Rammish.**

Ram-lamb, *n.* a male lamb.

Ramle, *n.* a big-boned, scraggy animal. Cf. **Rammel.**

Ramle, *n.* rubbish; fragments of stones; a wall, &c., unsubstantially built; a heap of ruins; brushwood.—*adj.* used of drains: filled with broken stones.

Ramlin, *ppl. adj.* rambling; loose, talkative. Cf. **Rambling.**

Rammack, *n.* a stick; a scrap; anything worthless. Cf. **Ramack.**

Rammack, *n.* a large, raw-boned, clumsy, heedless person. Cf. **Ramack.**

Rammage, *adj.* used of a road: rough-set.

†Rammage, *n.* the sound emitted by hawks.

Rammage, *adj.* rash, thoughtless; furious; of strong sexual instinct; violent; strong.—*v.* to be driven about under the impulse of any powerful passion; to go about in an almost frenzied state. Cf. **Rammish.**

Rammaged, *ppl. adj.* delirious from drink. Cf. **Ramished.**

Rammekins, *n.* a dish of eggs, cheese, and bread-crumbs mixed like a pudding.

Rammel, *n.* a heap of ruins; brushwood; small branches.—*adj.* branchy. Cf. **Ramle.**

Rammel, *n.* mixed grain.

Rammel, *n.* a big-boned, scraggy animal.—*adj.* used of straw: rank and strong. Cf. **Ramle.**

Rammelin, *ppl. adj.* rambling; talkative, loose. Cf. **Ramlin.**

Rammelsome, *adj.* rough, troublesome.

Rammely, *adj.* used of persons and animals: tall, loosely made.

Rammer, *n.* a knock, rap.

Rammish, Rammis, *v.* to go about under the influence of strong passion. Cf. **Rammage.**

Rammle, *v.* to ramble. Cf. **Ramble.**

Rammleguishon, *n.* a sturdy, rattling fellow.

Rammy, *n.* a horn-spoon.

Ramp, *v.* to romp; to prance; to stamp about in fury; to use violent language; to boil vigorously; to trample.—*n.* a romp; a tomboy; passion.—*adj.* riotous; vehement, violent, disorderly; headstrong.

Ramp, *v.* used of milk : to become ropy.

Ramp, *adj.* rank ; rancid ; strong-smelling.

Ramp, *n.* a shirt.

Rampage, Rampauge, *v.* to prance about with fury ; to rage, storm ; to romp about noisily.—*n.* disorderly conduct ; a rage, fury.

Rampageous, Rampaginous, *adj.* boisterous, noisy ; furiously angry.

Rampager, Rampauger, *n.* one who 'rampages,' a restless, romping person.

Rampan, *adj.* used of bread, of bannocks : kept too long, and showing small white filaments like gossamer.

†Rampar, Ramper, *n.* the lamprey.

Rampar-eel, *n.* the lamprey.

Ramper, *n.* a noisy, stamping fellow.

†Rampier, Rampire, *n.* a rampart.

Ramping-mad, -wud, *adj.* raving mad.

Rample, *v.* to romp, scramble.

†Ramplon, *n.* the lamprey.

Ramplor, Rampler, *n.* a gay, roving fellow. —*adj.* roving, unsettled.

Ramplosity, *n.* a roving disposition ; boisterousness.

†Rampron-eel, *n.* the lamprey.

Ramps, *n.* a kind of garlic, the wild garlic.

Rampse, *adj.* harsh to the taste ; rank ; used of spirits : fiery, strong. Cf. Ramsh.

Ram-race, -rais, *n.* the race taken by two rams before each shock in fighting ; a short race to give impetus in leaping ; running with the head down, as if to butt with it ; a headlong rush ; a boys' rough game, sometimes given as a punishment. —*adj.* headstrong, impetuous, precipitate. Cf. Sheep-race.

Ram-reel, *n.* a reel danced by men alone, a 'bull-reel.'

Ramscooter, *v.* to send flying in a panic.

Ramscullion, -callion, *n.* an offensively dirty person ; a low vagrant.

Ramse, *adj.* harsh to the taste. Cf. Ramsh.

Ramsh, Ramsch, *v.* to eat greedily and noisily. —*n.* a single act of masticating noisily coarse or rank food, as raw vegetables. Cf. Ransh.

Ramsh, *adj.* strong, robust ; harsh to the taste ; rash, arrogant ; acting too soon or too forcibly ; lascivious, lustful ; rank, foul ; used of spirits : strong, fiery. Cf. Rampse, Rammage, Rammish.

Ramsh, *n.* wild garlic. Cf. Ramps.

Ramshackle, *adj.* rickety ; unmethodical ; disorderly, wild ; dissipated, unsteady.—*n.* a wild, idle fellow ; a thoughtless fellow.

Ramshackle, *v.* to ransack ; to search for closely.

Ramshackled, Ramshachled, *ppl. adj.* loose, disjointed ; rickety ; in a crazy state.

Ramskeerie, *n.* a wild, restless romp ; a madcap, tomboy.

Ramskerie, *adj.* restive and lustful as a ram.

Ram-skulled, *adj.* sheepish.

Ramstacker, Ramstalker, *n.* a clumsy, awkward, blundering fellow.—*v.* to act in a blundering, awkward manner.

Ramstageous, *adj.* coarse ; rough ; strong ; austere ; boisterous. Cf. Ramstougar.

Ramstam, Ram-stram, *adj.* headlong, precipitate ; headstrong, heedless, impetuous ; forward ; thoughtless.—*adv.* precipitately ; at random ; rudely ; regardlessly of obstacles ; at headlong speed. —*n.* a giddy, forward person ; an impetuous, reckless person ; the strongest home-brewed beer.—*v.* to walk, push, or run forward in a headlong, rude, reckless manner.

Ramstam-like, *adv.* as with headlong speed.

Ramstamphish, *adj.* rough, blunt, unceremonious ; forward and noisy.

Ramstamran, *ppl. adj.* rushing headlong.

Ramstougar, Ramstougerous, *adj.* rough and strong ; used of cloth : rough ; of a woman : big, vulgar, masculine ; boisterous in manner ; disposed to be riotous ; quarrelsome ; austere ; heedless, harebrained.

Ramstugious, *adj.* coarse. Cf. Ramstageous.

Ram-tam, *adv.* precipitately. Cf. Ramstam.

Ramtanglement, *n.* confusion, disorder.

Ran, *n.* the roe of a fish.

Ran, *n.* the 'rowan' or mountain-ash.

Ran, *n.* a border ; a selvage, list. Cf. Rand.

Rance, *v.* to prop with stakes ; to barricade ; to fill completely ; to choke up.—*n.* a wooden prop ; the cross-bar which joins the lower part of the frame of a chair together ; the cornice of a wooden bed.

Rancie, *adj.* used of the complexion : red, sanguine.

Rancil, Ransel, *v.* to search for missing goods ; to rummage, ransack ; to grope for.

Rancor, *v.* to cause or enhance rancour.

†Rancountor, *v.* to encounter.—*n.* a rencontre.

Rand, *n.* a border ; a strip or selvage of cloth, list ; a stripe ; a strip of leather securing the heel of a shoe to the sole.

Rand, *n.* what can be melted at a time.

Rand, *v.* to thicken, strengthen by thickening or doubling ; to strengthen a stocking-heel by darning or doubling.

†Ran-dan, *n.* a carouse ; violence.

Rander, *v.* to ramble in talk ; to talk idly.—*n.* a great talker ; in *pl.* idle talk ; idle rumours.

Rander, *n.* order.

Rander, *v.* to render ; to surrender ; to melt down fat, &c.

†Rander, *v.* to darn ; to seam up with wide

stitches.—*n.* a careless worker; work badly done. Cf. Ranter.

Randified, *ppl. adj.* scolding.

Randit, *ppl. adj.* streaked.

†**Randivoo**, *n.* rendezvous.

Random-splore, *n.* a chance frolic.

†**Randon**, *n.* a drunken carouse; force, violence.

Randy, *n.* a frolic; a wild practice; a wild, reckless person; a beggar; a ruffian; a scolding virago; a loose, disorderly woman; an indelicate, romping hoyden, a tomboy; a thief; occasionally a term of affection for a young, lively female child.—*adj.* wild, unmanageable; disorderly, disreputable; vagrant; quarrelsome; scolding; abusive. —*v.* to scold, vituperate; to frolic.

Randy-beggar, *n.* a 'sturdy beggar,' one who extorts alms by menaces; a tinker.

Randy-like, -looking, *adj.* looking like a 'randy.'

Rane, *n.* idle talk frequently repeated; a frequent repetition of one sound; a metrical rigmarole; a fable.—*v.* to repeat the same thing over and over; to murmur monotonously; to rhyme; with *down*, to speak evil of, to disparage.

Rane, *n.* a border. Cf. Rand.

Ranegill, *n.* a masterful, turbulent person or criminal. Cf. Rannygill.

Rang, *n.* a row, rank. Cf. Raing.

Rang, *v. pret.* reigned.

Range, *v.* to search for thoroughly; to rush about noisily and roughly; to give a clattering, ringing motion, as when crockery or a piece of iron falls; to crash; to poke a fire; to clear out the bars of a grate; to agitate water by plunging, for the purpose of driving fish from their holds.—*n.* a thorough search; a clearing out; a stroll; a clattering or clanging noise; a strip of land; a shelf; a settle; the seat round the pulpit that was reserved for the elders, or for parents bringing their children for baptism; a row, a rank. Cf. Reenge.

Range, *v.* to clear out; to rinse.—*n.* a handful of heather tied together to clean out pots and pans, &c., a 'heather-ranger,' '-range.' Cf. Ringe.

Rangel, Rangle, *n.* a crowd; used of stones: a heap.

Ranger, *n.* one who goes about noisily.

Ranger, *n.* a scrubber made of heather for pots, pans, &c.

Rangiebus, Range-the-bus, *n.* a boys' game. Cf. Rainiebus.

Rangle-tree, *n.* a cross-beam in a chimney, or a 'swee' for hanging pots. Cf. Rannel-tree.

Rangunshock, *v.* to roar incessantly.

Rank, *adj.* strong, sturdy, formidable;

thorough; wild, rugged; used of a boat: top-heavy.

Rank, *v.* to arrange one's costume; to get one's self ready in regard to clothes; with *out*, to bring forward and arrange; to rummage; to bring out, prepare.

Rankreenging, Rankringing, *adj.* wild, coarse; lawless.

Rannel-, Rannle-, -bauk, -tree, *n.* a cross-beam in a chimney on which the 'crook' hung. Cf. Rantle-tree.

Rannie, *n.* the wren.

Rannoch, *n.* bracken.

Rannock, *n.* lake-weed; ooze.

Rannygill, *n.* a bold, impudent, unruly person. Cf. Ranegill.

Ranse, *v.* to prop with sticks. Cf. Rance.

Ransh, *v.* to take large mouthfuls, eat voraciously; to crunch with the teeth. Cf. Ramsh.

Ranshackle, Ransheckle, *v.* to ransack. Cf. Ramshackle.

Ransie, *adj.* used of the complexion: red, sanguine. Cf. Rancie.

†**Ransivall**, *n.* a garden pea, a large, pasty pea.

Ransom, *n.* an extravagant price or rent.

Rant, *v.* to frolic, romp; to revel; to live a fast life; to roister; used of a fire: to roar, blaze.—*n.* a merrymaking; a rough, noisy frolic; a jollification; a lively story or song.

Ranter, *n.* a roving, jovial fellow; a reveller; a scold.—*v.* to roam, to rove about, as an animal broken loose.

†**Ranter**, *v.* to sew a seam across roughly; to darn coarsely; to join; to attempt to reconcile statements that do not tally; to work hurriedly and carelessly.—*n.* one who does anything carelessly; anything badly done.

Ranting, *ppl. adj.* roistering; blazing; in high spirits; exhilarating.—*n.* noisy mirth in drinking.

Rantingly, *adv.* with great glee; in a jovial, riotous fashion.

Ranting-place, *n.* a place for revelling.

Rantle-tree, *n.* the cross-beam in a chimney; the end of a rafter or beam; a tall, rawboned person. Cf. Rannel-tree.

Rantle-tree, *n.* the mountain-ash.

Ran-tree, *n.* the beam over the fire on which pots, &c., are hung.

Ran-tree, *n.* the 'rowan-tree' or mountain-ash.

Rantry, Rantry-tree, *n.* the mountain-ash.

Rant up, *v.* to mend, repair clothes. Cf. Ranter.

Ranty, *adj.* lively, cheerful, gay; tipsy, riotous.

Ranty-tanty, *n.* a weed with reddish leaf, growing among corn; the broad-leaved dock; a kind of beverage distilled from heath and other vegetable substances, formerly used by the peasantry.

†**Ranverse,** *v.* to reverse; to overturn a decision on appeal; to refute.

Rap, *n.* a counterfeit copper coin of the nominal value of a halfpenny, used in Ireland in the reign of George I.; a counterfeit coin of any kind; a cheat; an impostor.

Rap, *n.* a rope; in *phr.* 'rap and stow,' root and branch.

Rap, *v.* to rap at; to knock heavily; to tap; to arouse by knocking; used of tears: to fall in quick succession, in pattering drops; to sound as if knocked on; with *off*, to go off hastily and with a noise; to act expeditiously; with *to*, to fasten a door, &c.; with *up*, to knock up, awaken by knocking; with *upon*, to come upon, knock up against.—*n.* a moment; a knock at a door; a stroke.

Rap, *v.* to seize, snatch; to carry off.

Rap, *n.* the vegetable, rape.

Rape, *n.* a rope; a line of rope carried across a room or the front of the fireplace; a band for a sheaf or stack; any worthless piece of dress or cloth of considerable length; a measure, a rood.—*v.* to wind up in a ball; to coil; to bind sheaves or stacks; to tie clumsily; to unroll, wind out; to fray out.

Raperie, *n.* a ropery, a rope-walk.

Rape-thackit, -theekit, *adj.* with thatch secured by ropes.

Raping-band, *n.* a rope-band for carrying a basket on the shoulder, or for tying it so as to keep in its contents.

Raploch, Raplock, Raplach, Raplack, *n.* coarse woollen cloth, homespun and undyed; a plaid of such cloth; the skin of a hare littered in March, and killed at the end of the year.—*adj.* coarse; homely; rough; homespun.

Rapper, *n.* wrapper-leather.

Rapperdandy, *n.* the bear-bilberry.

†**Rapple,** *n.* the beat of a drum.

Rapple, *v.* to grow quickly and rankly, used of vegetation and of young persons; to do work hurriedly and imperfectly; to intertwist threads in sewing.

Rapple, *v.* to put on clothes in haste; to 'warple,' wrap clothes around.

Rapple-rat-tat, *n.* the beat of a drum.

Rapt, *n.* robbery; rapine; abduction.

Rapture, *n.* a fit of temper; a state of violent anger or strong excitement.

Rapturous, *adj.* outrageous.

Rare, *v.* to roar; to give out a continuous loud report like the cracking of a large field of ice.—*n.* a roar. Cf. Raird.

Rare, *adj.* grand, fine.—*adv.* very.

Raree, *n.* a raree-show, a 'spectacle.'

Rarely, *adv.* excellently, capitally.

Rarish, *adj.* rather rare.

†**Rase,** *v.* to abrade the skin; to shave. Cf. Raze.

Rase, *v. pret.* rose.

Rash, Rasch, *adj.* brisk, agile; hale, hearty in old age.—*v.* with *out*, to blab, to publish imprudently.

Rash, Rasch, *v.* to pour down; to descend heavily; to dash down; to dash, rush about; to thrust; to make any forcible exertion; to twinge with pain.—*n.* a sudden fall; a sudden twinge or twitch; a rush of rain, &c.

Rash, Rasch, *n.* a crowd, a number of anything; a row of any article, as needles used in weaving.

Rash, *n.* the rush.

Rash-bonnet, *n.* a cap made of rushes.

Rash-buss, *n.* a clump of rushes.

Rashen, *adj.* made of rushes.

Rash-hat, *n.* a hat made of rushes.

Rashie, *adj.* covered with rushes.

Rashie-wick, *n.* a rush-wick.

Rash-, Rashie-mill, *n.* a toy-mill made of rushes.

Rash-pyddle, *n.* a bag-net of rushes, for catching fish.

Rash-rape, -tow, *n.* a rope made of rushes.

Rash-whish, *n.* a whizzing sound.

Raskill, *n.* a young deer.

Rasp, *v.* to rub a ring up or down over a twisted rod attached to a door, the sound serving as a bell or knocker, to 'tirl at the pin'; used of the heart: to make it sore, to cut it to the quick.

Rasp, *n.* a raspberry; a raspberry-plant.

Rasper, *n.* one who speaks in an exasperating manner.

†**Rasp-house,** *n.* a house of correction, 'bridewell.'

Rat, *n.* rote. Cf. Rat-rhyme.

Rat, *n.* a scratch; a rut, a wheel-track on a road.—*v.* to scratch, score; to make deep ruts.

Rat, *n.* a wart. Cf. Oorat, Wrat.

Ratch, *n.* the little auk.

Ratch, *n.* a white mark or streak, generally on the face of a horse.—*v.* to mark with lines, stripes, &c.

Ratch, *n.* a hound; a poacher; a night-wanderer.—*adj.* unsteady, loose in morals. Cf. Rach.

Ratch, *n.* the lock of a musket.

Ratch, *v.* to tear away so roughly or clumsily as to cause a fracture.

Ratchal, Ratchell, *n.* a hard, rocky crust below the soil; the stone called wacken-porphyry.

Ratch't, *ppl. adj.* ragged; in a ruinous condition.

Rate, *v.* to be priced.

Rate, *n.* a file of soldiers. Cf. Ratt.

Rate, *v.* to beat, flog.

Rath, Rathe, *adj.* early, quick.—*adv.* soon.

Rathely, *adv.* quickly.

Ratherest, Ratherly, *adv.* much rather. Cf. Raitherly.

Rathest, *adv.* sooner, much rather.

Rathy, Rathie, *n.* a good, quick-growing crop of hay, weeds, &c.

Ratify, *v.* to clear up, settle.

Ratihabit, *v.* to confirm, approve.

Ratihabition, *n.* a legal term : confirmation, approval.

Ration, *n.* reason.

Rationality, *n.* reason, sense.

Rat-rhyme, *n.* anything repeated by rote ; a long rigmarole ; nonsense.—*v.* to repeat from memory without attaching any meaning to the words.

Rat's-tail, *n.* the greater plantain.

Ratt, *n.* a file of soldiers.

Rattan, Ratten, Ratton, *n.* a rat ; a small person or animal ; a sly person ; a term of endearment.

Rattan-fa', *n.* a rat-trap.

Rattan-flitting, *n.* the removal of rats in a body from one haunt to another.

Rattan-houkit, *adj.* dug or holed by rats.

Rattan's-rest, *n.* a state of perpetual turmoil or bustle.

Rattan-stamp, *n.* a rat-trap.

Rattle, *v.* to pronounce the letter R with a 'burr' ; to do anything with energy and speed ; to talk much loosely and foolishly ; with *down*, to undo work carelessly ; to strike, beat.—*n.* a sudden smash ; impetus ; a chatterer ; a stupid fellow ; a smart, quick blow.

Rattle-bag, *n.* anything that makes a rattling noise ; a loud clatter ; a noisy, fussy person who excites alarm.

Rattler, *n.* a loud, noisy, talkative fellow ; a child's rattle.

Rattle-shot, *n.* a shot fired as a salute.

Rattle-skull, *n.* one who talks much without thinking ; a stupid, silly fellow.

Rattle-trap, *adj.* rickety, worn-out.—*n.* in *pl.* odds and ends ; 'traps.'

Rattley, Rattlie, *n.* a child's rattle.

Rattling, *ppl. adj.* rollicking ; lively ; wild, noisy.

Rattling-fou, *adj.* boisterously drunk.

Rattrum, *n.* anything repeated by rote. Cf. Rat-rhyme.

Rauch, *adj.* foggy ; hoarse. Cf. Rawk.

Rauchan, *n.* a plaid ; a mantle.—*adj.* plaiden.

Rauchel, *adj.* fearless ; strong. Cf. Raucle.

Rauchle, *n.* a loose heap of stones, &c. ; a 'rickle.' Cf. Rackle.

Rauchly, *adj.* rough, boisterous.

Raucht, *ppl. adj.* frosted.

Raucht, *v. pret.* and *ppl.* reached. Cf. Raugh.

Raucht, *n.* the act of reaching ; a blow, stroke. Cf. Raught.

Raucie, *adj.* coarse.

Rauck, *v.* to snatch with anything pointed ; to mark with a nail ; to rummage.—*n.* a mark, scratch. Cf. Rauk.

Raucking, *n.* the noise of a nail scratching a slate.

Raucle, Rauckle, *adj.* fearless ; boisterous ; headstrong ; strong and sturdy in old age. —*n.* any rough person or thing. Cf. Rackle.

Raucle-haundit, *adj.* ready to strike.

Raucleness, *n.* vigour in old age.

Raucle-tongue, *n.* a rough, vigorous, plain-speaking tongue.

Raucle-tongued, *adj.* plain - speaking, out-spoken.

Raugh, *v.* to reach ; to hand, fetch ; to stretch, hold out ; to give a blow.

Raughan, Raughen, *n.* a plaid. Cf. Rauchan.

Raughel, *n.* a term of contempt. Cf. Raucle.

Raught, *v. pret.* reached for.—*n.* the act of reaching ; a blow, dash.

Rauhhel, *n.* a small three-pronged fork, used to break potatoes boiling in a pot.

Rauk, *adj.* hoarse, misty.—*n.* a mist. Cf. Rawk.

Rauk, *v.* to stretch ; to reach.

Rauk, *v.* to scratch ; to search, rummage ; with *out*, to search out ; with *up*, to put in order.

Rauky, *adj.* misty, foggy. Cf. Rawky.

Raul, *n.* a rail ; a line or row.—*v.* to set in a row. Cf. Rail.

Raullion, *n.* a shoe made of untanned leather ; a rough dress ; a big, coarse-looking person or animal. Cf. Rullion.

Raul-tree, *n.* a long piece of strong wood, placed across 'byres,' to put the end of cow-stakes in. Cf. Rail-tree.

Raun, *n.* the roe or spawn of a fish ; a female fish, as a salmon or herring ; the turbot.

Raun, *n.* the mountain-ash. Cf. Rowan.

Raun'd, *ppl. adj.* having roe.

Raunel-, Raunle-tree, *n.* the cross-beam in a chimney. Cf. Rantle-tree.

Rauner, *n.* the female salmon, having roe.

Raun-fleuk, *n.* the turbot.

Rauns, *n.* the awns of barley.

Raun-tree, *n.* the mountain-ash. Cf. Rowan-tree.

Raup, *n.* a three-pronged instrument for bruising potatoes for supper.—*v.* to prepare potatoes thus.

Raut, *n.* a scratch ; a rut.—*v.* to scratch. Cf. Rat.

Raut, *n.* a wart. Cf. Wrat.

Raux, *v.* to extend, stretch ; to stretch the limbs. Cf. Rax.

Rave, *v.* to bawl ; to make a loud noise ; used of the wind : to make a wild, roaring sound.—*n.* a vague report ; an almost incredible story.

Rave, *v.* to roam, stray ; to rove.

Rave, *v. pret.* tore, did tear.

Rave, *v.* to reave, take by violence.

Ravel, *n.* a rail, railing ; the cross-beam in a 'byre' to which the tops of the cow-stakes are fastened ; an instrument with pins in it, for spreading out yarn on the beam before it is wrought ; the rowel of a spur ; in *pl.* the 'tops' of a cart.—*v.* to fit or enclose with a railing. Cf. Raivel.

Ravel, *v.* to wander in speech ; to unravel the loops in knitting ; to tangle or curl up like a hard-twisted thread.—*n.* a ramble ; a tangle ; confusion ; incoherent speech ; in *pl.* ravelled thread.

Ravelled-hesp, *n.* an intricate business.

Ravelling, Ravelin', *n.* a tangled thread ; a loose, unravelled thread ; frayed textile fabric ; odds and ends of rhyme.

Ravel-lock, *n.* a kind of river-lock.

Ravel-stick, -tree, *n.* the cross-beam in a 'byre' to which the tops of the cow-stakes are fastened. Cf. Rail-tree.

Ravery, *n.* delirium ; a violent fit of temper and loud vociferation.

Ravin, *adv.* exceedingly.

Raving, *ppl. adj.* riving.

Ravlin', *n.* 'ravelling.'

Raw, *n.* undiluted whisky.—*v.* used of corn : to grow soft.—*adj.* of the weather : cold and damp.

Raw, *n.* a row, a rank ; a row, a street ; in *pl.* parallel ridges. Cf. Row.

Rawchan, *n.* a man's plaid. Cf. Rachan.

Rawel, *n.* a rail. Cf. Ravel.

Raw-footed, *adj.* barefooted.

Raw-gabbit, *adj.* speaking confidently on a subject of which one is ignorant.

Rawk, *n.* a mist, fog. Cf. Rauk.

Rawk, *v.* to scratch ; to search, rummage.—*n.* a scratch. Cf. Rauck.

Rawk, *n.* the rheum that gathers about the eyes in sleep ; the scum on stagnant water. Cf. Rak.

Rawky, *adj.* foggy, damp, raw and cold.

Rawlie, Rawly, *adj.* unripe ; not fully grown ; moist, damp, raw.

Rawn, *n.* the fragment of a rainbow.

Rawn, *n.* a scratch ; a furrow ; a discoloured stripe.

Rawn, *adj.* afraid.

Rawn, *n.* a fish-roe. Cf. Raan.

Rawned, *ppl. adj.* furrowed ; striped so as to be disfigured ; streaked.

Rawn-fleuk, *n.* the turbot.

Rawn-tree, *n.* the mountain-ash. Cf. Rowan-tree.

Rawsie, *adj.* coarse. Cf. Raucie.

Rawt, *n.* a wart. Cf. Rat.

Rawt, *v.* to scratch.—*n.* scratch. Cf. Rat.

Rax, *n.* an andiron ; in *pl.* an iron instrument consisting of links or hooks on which the spit was turned at the fire.

Rax, *n.* a boys' game, also called 'cock.' Cf. Rax-king-of-Scotland, Rex.

Rax, *v.* to extend, stretch ; to hand, pass, reach ; to stretch out the body or limbs on waking ; to strain, overstrain ; to wrench ; to rack ; to grow.—*n.* a stretch, reach ; the act of stretching or reaching ; a strain ; a sprain ; a wrench of limb or muscle.

Raxed-craig, -neck, *n.* the neck of a person who has been hanged.

Raxing, *ppl. adj.* elastic, easily stretched ; used of pain : racking ; increasing, growing.—*n.* a hanging.

Rax-king-of-Scotland, Raxie-boxie, *n.* a boys' game, in which one player tries to catch others as they rush across a line.

Rax-me-doon, *n.* a better kind of coat, that can readily be put on in place of one's working-coat.

Raxter, *n.* a long walk.

Ray, *v.* to array ; to make ready.

Ray, *n.* rye.

Ray, *adj.* mad, wild. Cf. Ree.

Ray, *n.* a song, poem.

†**Raze**, *v.* to abrade the skin ; to shave.—*n.* an erasure.

Razer, *n.* a measure of grain.

Razon-berry, *n.* the red currant.

Razor-ride, *v.* to shave.

Re, *int.* a call to a horse to turn to the right.

Rea, *n.* an evil spirit.

Reach, *v.* to strike.—*n.* ability, capacity ; attainment. Cf. Reak.

Reach, *v.* to retch.

Read, *v.* to advise ; to warn.—*n.* warning, advice ; a reading. Cf. Red.

Read, *adj.* red. Cf. Red.

Read, *n.* spawn. Cf. Redd.

Reade, *n.* a kind of sceptre.

Reader, *n.* a preacher who reads his sermons ; one who read the lessons and prayers when ministers of the Scottish Church were few ; used of cups : a fortune-teller examining grounds of tea in a cup.

Readily, Readilys, Read'ly, *adv.* probably ; naturally ; easily.

Reading, *n.* family worship.

Reading-priest, *n.* a minister who reads his sermon.

Ready, *adj.* on the point of.—*v.* to prepare

food; to put on one's 'things.'—*n.* ready-money.

Ready-handit, *adj.* clever with the hands; quick and handy.

Reak, *n.* a trick; a 'rig'; an artifice.

Reak, *v.* to reach; to hand; to fetch; to extend; to thrust; to arrive; to fetch a blow.—*n.* ability, capacity; attainment.

Reak, *v.* to fit out, equip. Cf. Reek.

Real, *adj.* eminently good; true, staunch; used of money, rent, &c.: paid in cash.—*adv.* very; thoroughly.—*n.* reality.

Real, *n.* a rail; a line, row. Cf. Rail.

†**Real,** *n.* a gold coin.

Real-tree, *n.* the beam in a 'byre' to which the cow-stakes were fixed. Cf. Rail-tree.

Ream, *n.* cream, thick cream; froth, foam; water lying near the surface of a well, &c. —*v.* to skim off cream; to rise as cream; to froth, foam, mantle; to overflow; to buzz; used of thoughts: to keep hold of the mind.—*adj.* smooth as cream; used as cream; made of cream.

Ream, *v.* to prose on; to talk at length; to cry fretfully and repeatedly; to repeat the same sound. Cf. Rame.

Ream-bowie, *n.* a small barrel in which cream is kept.

Ream-breid, *n.* oatcake or bannocks baked with cream.

Ream-cheese, *n.* a cheese made from cream.

Ream-crowdy, *n.* oatmeal mixed with cream.

Ream-dish, *n.* a dish for holding cream.

Reamed-milk, *n.* skim-milk.

Reamer, *n.* a milk-skimmer.

Ream-fu', *adj.* full to overflowing.

Reaming-calm, *n.* a calm with the sea smooth as cream.

Reaming-cap, -dish, *n.* a milk-skimmer.

Reaming-fu', *adj.* full to overflowing.

Reamish, *n.* a disturbance. Cf. Reemish.

Reamishing, *adj.* noisy, disturbing.

Ream-jug, *n.* a cream-jug.

Ream-kirn, *n.* a churn.

Ream-milk, *n.* unskimmed milk.

Ream-pig, *n.* a jar for holding cream.

Reamy, *adj.* creamy.

Reard, *n.* noise, report.—*v.* to make a loud noise. Cf. Raird.

Reardie, *n.* a wild frolic; a riot, a quarrel.

Rearie, Rearum, *n.* a wild frolic; a riot, a quarrel.

Reason, *n.* a reasonable price; justice, right.

Reasonable, *adj.* used of distance: fairly near, not very far.

Reast, *n.* a hen-roost.

Reast, *v.* to smoke; to dry by heat of sun or fire. Cf. Reest.

Reath, *n.* the quarter of a year. Cf. Raith.

Reathy, *adj.* ready.

Reave, *v.* to rave, roam; stray. Cf. **Rave.**

Reave, *v. pret.* tore. Cf. Rive.

Reave, *n.* a robber; a Border thief.

Reavel, *v.* to ravel. Cf. Ravel.

Reavel, *n.* a rail. Cf. Ravel.

Reaver, *n.* a freebooter, a plunderer.

Reaverie, *n.* robbery, spoliation.

Reaving, *ppl. adj.* used of a fire: brisk, strong. Cf. Reeving.

Reaving-wind, *n.* a high wind.

Rebaghle, *n.* reproach.

Rebat, *n.* the cape of a mantle.

†**Rebat,** *v.* to retort.

Rebbit, *n.* a polished stone for a window, door, or corner.

Rebig, *v.* to rebuild.

Rebleat, *v.* used of a ewe: to bleat in response to her lamb.

Rebook, *v.* to rebuke.

Reboon, Rebound, *v.* to vomit; to be squeamish; to be like to vomit; to repent.—*n.* the sound of a shot fired.

Rebunctious, *adj.* refractory.

†**Rebute,** *n.* a rebuff.

Recant, *v.* to revive from debility or sickness.

Receipt, Receit, Recept, *n.* accommodation, capacity; shelter; the harbouring of criminals; the receiving of stolen goods; a receiver of stolen goods.—*v.* to receive, welcome; to entertain; to shelter a criminal or outlaw; to receive stolen goods.

Receipter, *n.* one who entertains; one who shelters criminals; a receiver of stolen goods.

Receive, *n.* a power of receiving; an appetite, a good stomach.

Recently, *adv.* early.

Reck, *n.* a track, a course; used in curling: the 'rink.' Cf. Rack.

Reck, *v.* to take heed of; to matter. Cf. Rack, Raik.

Reck, *v.* to reckon, deem, think.

Reck, *v.* to reach, hand. Cf. Reak, Raugh.

Reckle, *n.* a chain. Cf. Rackle.

Reckon, *v.* to conjecture; to pretend.

†**Reclaim,** *v.* a legal term: to object, oppose; to appeal against a decision.

Reclaiming Note, *n.* a formal notice of appeal.

Reclamation, *n.* an appeal to a higher court.

Recognosce, *v.* a legal term, used of a superior: to reclaim heritable property from a vassal who has failed to observe the terms of his tenure.

Recognose, *v.* to reconnoitre.

Recollection, *n.* the memory of the dead.

Reconvalesce, *v.* to recover health after a relapse.

Reconvene, *v.* to cite again a person for the same crime of which he was proved innocent.

Reconvention, *n.* a counter-charge; a renewed citation; a legal process raised by a person prosecuted for a crime, in which he calls for the defence all such witnesses as he thinks might be brought to testify against him.

Recounter, *v.* a tradesman's technical term: to invert; to reverse.

Recour, *v.* to recover; to regain health; to obtain.

†**Recrue,** *v.* to recruit.—*n.* a party of recruits.

†**Recule,** *v.* to recoil, retreat, revert.

Recuperate, *v.* a legal term: to recover, regain.

Recur, *v.* to have legal recourse for recovering damages or the relief of expenses.

†**Recusance,** *n.* refusal.

Red, *adj.* bloody.—*v.* to redden, to become red.

Red, *n.* the green ooze found in the bottom of pools.

Red, *adj.* afraid. Cf. Rad.

Red, Redd, *v.* to advise, counsel; to warn; to explain, solve; to foretell, predict; to guess; to imagine, suppose; to beware, be cautious.—*n.* advice, counsel, warning.

Red, *v. pret.* rode.

Red, *n.* the Rood; Rood Day. Cf. Rood.

Redact, *v.* to reduce.

Red-aitin, *n.* a savage sort of fellow. Cf. Red-etin.

†**Redargue,** *v.* a legal term: to contradict; to accuse, blame.

Red-belly, *n.* the char.

Red-cap, Red-capie-dossie, *n.* a spectre or elf with very long teeth, supposed to haunt old castles.

Red-close, *n.* the throat, the gullet.

Red-coat, *n.* a name specially given during the Rebellion to those who served under King George; a lady-bird.

Red-cock, *n.* an incendiary fire.

Red-cock crawing, *n.* fire-raising.

Red-cole, -coal, *n.* red cabbage.

Red-comb, *n.* a large-toothed comb.

Red-cowl, *n.* a 'red-capie-dossie.'

Red-cross, *n.* the fiery cross.

Redd, Red, *v.* to set in order; to prepare; to tidy, clean up; to dress or comb the hair; to disentangle, unravel; to clear up, sort; to clear, clean out, open up; to adjust, mark out; to arbitrate, judge; to quell a fray; to compose a quarrel; to separate combatants; to correct, set right; to criticize, sum up faults; to scold, rebuke.—*n.* tidying, cleaning; a clearance; the removal of an obstruction; litter, rubbish, remains; a cleaner, an instrument for cleaning or clearing out anything; energy, speed, ability to work; progress, despatch; a will, a testamentary settlement of affairs.

Redd, Red, *adj.* ready, willing, prepared; active, able; clear, not closed up, free from crowd, obstacles, encumbrances; clear, fluent, distinct; done with one's work or business.—*adv.* readily.

Redd, *n.* spawn; a spawning-ground.—*v.* to spawn.—*adj.* used of fish: in the spawning state.

Redd, Red, *v.* to rid, to free.—*ppl. adj.* rid, free.

Redd, *v. pret.* rode.

Redd, *adj.* afraid.

Reddance, *n.* riddance, clearance.

Reddand, *n.* the bend of the beam of a plough at the insertion of the coulter.

Reddans, *n.* combings; odds and ends left over.

Red-day, Rood-day, *n.* May 3; Sept. 14.

Redden, *v.* to cause to blush.

Reddendo, *n.* the clause in a feu-charter defining the duty which the vassal has to pay to the superior.

Redder, *adv.* rather.

Redder, *n.* a large-toothed comb; one who tries to settle a dispute or part combatants.

Redder's-blow, -lick, *n.* the blow that falls on one who tries to part combatants.

Redder's-part, *n.* the 'redder's-blow.'

Redd-hand, *n.* a clearance.

Redd-handit, *adj.* active, capable, neat; having little in possession.

Reddin, *n.* a clearance, a riddance.

Reddin'-blow, -straik, *n.* the 'redder's-blow.'

Reddins, *n.* spawn.

Red-doup, *n.* a kind of bumble-bee.

Redd thrums, *v.* to quarrel about trifles.

Redd-up, *ppl. adj.* neat, tidy; put in order. —*n.* the making things neat, clean, and orderly.

Reddy, *adj.* ready.—*v.* to prepare food. Cf. Ready.

Rede, *n.* a fairy of some kind.

Rede, *n.* a wraith; the apparition of a person, seen when he is alive.

Rede, *n.* the fourth stomach of a ruminant. Cf. Reed.

Rede, *v.* to counsel.—*n.* advice. Cf. Read, Redd.

Rede, *adj.* fierce, impetuous, wild; excited; drunk.

Rede, *n.* a reed; part of a weaver's loom.

Rede, *adj.* timorous. Cf. Rad.

Rede, *ppl. adj.* aware.

Rede, *n.* spawn. Cf. Redd.

Red-early, *n.* grain that has begun to sprout in the stack.

Rede-goose, *n.* the rood-goose, barnacle-goose. Cf. Rade-goose.

Red-etin, -eitin, *n.* the name of a giant or monster; a savage, barbarous person.

Red-even, -e'en, *n.* the eve of May 3; the evening of May 3; the eve of September 14; the eve of Beltane. Cf. Rood.

Red-fish, *n.* fish in a spawning state.

Red-fisher, *n.* a salmon-fisher.

Red-glove grozer, *n.* a kind of red gooseberry.

Red-gown, *n.* an arts student of the Universities of St Andrews, Glasgow, and Aberdeen.

Red-hand, *n.* a bloody hand.—*adv.* in the very act.

Red-hawk, *n.* the kestrel.

Red-headit, *adj.* hot-tempered.

Red-heckle, *n.* a kind of fishing-fly.

Red-hunger, Reid-hunger, *n.* the rage of hunger.

Red-hungered, *adj.* ravenous from hunger.

Redie, *n.* a red clay marble.

Red-kail, *n.* red cabbage. Cf. Red-cole.

Red-kaim, *n.* a large-toothed comb. Cf. Red-comb.

Red-land, *n.* ploughed land.

Red-lane, *n.* the throat, gullet.

Redlins, *adv.* readily; perhaps, probably.

Red-mad, *adj.* raging mad; furious; intensely eager.

Redment, *n.* a putting in order; a settlement of affairs, &c.

Red-nakit, *adj.* quite naked.

Red-neb, *n.* the kidney-bean potato.

Redound, *v.* of money: to fall to be paid.

Red-rot, *n.* the sundew.

Red-sauch, *n.* a species of red willow.

Red-shank, *n.* the dock, after it has begun to ripen; a contemptuous name for a Highlander, from his bare legs.

Red-sheuch, -seuch, *n.* the stomach.

Redsman, *n.* one who clears away rubbish; one who tries to settle a dispute or part combatants.

Red-tail, *n.* the redstart.

Red the rook, *v.* to detect a fraud.

Red-wame, *n.* the char.

Redware, *n.* sea-girdles, seaweeds growing in shallow waters.

Redware-cod, -codlin, *n.* a species of cod.

Redware-fishick, *n.* the whistle-fish.

Red-wat, *adj.* wet with blood; blood-stained.

Red-water, *n.* a disease of cattle and sheep.

Redwing-mavis, *n.* the redwing.

Red-wode, -wood, -wud, *adj.* raging mad; insane; furious; eager.

Redwood, *n.* the reddish wood found in the heart of trees.

Red-waur, *n.* a name given by Newhaven fishermen to a species of fucus used by children for painting their faces. Cf. Yaur.

Ree, *n.* an enclosure from a river or the sea, open towards the water, to receive small vessels; a harbour; the hinder-part of a mill-dam; a sheepfold, an enclosure for cattle; an enclosure for coal on sale; a 'wreath' of snow.—*v.* to enclose with a wall of stone or turf; used of snow: to drift into 'wreaths.'

Ree, *n.* a period of stormy weather occurring about Whitsuntide.—*adj.* used of weather: windy, clear, and frosty; bleak.

Ree, *v.* to riddle corn, beans, &c. by an eddying movement.—*n.* a riddle smaller than a sieve.

Ree, *adj.* crazy, delirious; rude, wild; unmanageable; used of a horse: high-spirited, restive; excited with drink; tipsy.—*n.* a state of temporary delirium, excitement.—*v.* to become excited.

Reeans, *n.* the coarser damaged beans which do not pass through the sieve.

Reeble, *v.* to read or recite quickly, gabble; to work hastily or confusedly.—*n.* careless or indistinct speech or reading; careless, hurried work; a ruinous mass; one who works carelessly or in a hurry. Cf. Ribble, Rabble.

Reeble, *n.* a greedy person or animal.

Reebler, *n.* a careless worker or speaker.

Reeble-rabble, *n.* a rabble; great confusion. —*adv.* in great confusion.—*v.* to crowd in great confusion.—*adj.* confused, disorderly.

Reechnie, *adj.* rough in appearance or manner. —*n.* a person of ungainly, rough appearance or manners.

Reed, *n.* part of a weaver's loom.

Reed, *n.* the fourth stomach of a ruminant.

Reed, *n.* a cattle-yard; a bay, roadstead. Cf. Ree.

Reed, *conj.* lest, for fear that.—*v.* to fear, apprehend. Cf. Rad.

Reed, *v.* to advise, counsel. Cf. Read, Redd.

Reed, *n.* the Rood. Cf. Rood.

Reed, *v.* to spawn.—*n.* spawn. Cf. Redd.

Reed, *adj.* red. Cf. Red.

Reed, *adj.* fierce, wild; drunk. Cf. Rede.

Reediemadeasy, Reedy-ma-deezy, *n.* a child's first reading-book.

Reeding-plane, *n.* a carpenter's plane which forms three rows at once; a 'centre-bead' plane, making two or more beads.

Reed-mad, *adj.* distracted. Cf. Red-mad.

Reeds, *n.* a method of catching the young coalfish with a hand-line from a boat anchored near the shore.

Reef, *n.* a rumour.—*v.* to talk vivaciously. Cf. Reeve.

Reef, *n.* a skin-eruption; mange; the itch.

Reef, *n.* a roof.

†Reefart, Reefort, *n.* the radish.

Reefart-nosed, *adj.* having a nose coloured or shaped like a radish.

Reef'd, *ppl.* rumoured.

Reef-saw, *n.* an ointment for the itch.

Reefu', *adj.* roaring loud; rueful. Cf. Rierful.

Reefy, *adj.* scabby; having the itch.

Reegh, *n.* a harbour. Cf. Ree.

Reeing-riddle, *n.* the sieve for 'reeing' beans. Cf. Ree.

Reek, *n.* smoke; a smoke, a whiff of a pipe; mist, fog; scent, smell; a house with a chimney; a quarrel among people in the same house; a family misunderstanding.—*v.* to smoke; to soil with smoke; to perspire.

Reek, *n.* a blow.

Reek, *v.* to equip; to rig out; to dress, accoutre; to make ready.

Reek, *v.* to reach; to extend; to stretch; to arrive.—*n.* attainment. Cf. Reach.

Reek, *n.* a trick; a wile. Cf. Reak.

Reeker, *n.* anything out of the common.

Reek-fowl. -hen, *n.* a hen paid as a tax; the tax itself.

Reekie, Auld Reekie, *n.* Edinburgh.

Reekim, Reekum, *n.* a smart blow; a riot, quarrel.—*v.* to strike a smart blow; to box.

Reekin', *n.* an outfit, 'plenishin'.'

Reekiness, *n.* smokiness.

Reekin'-house, *n.* an inhabited house; a household.

Reekit, *ppl. adj.* rigged out; well-dressed; furnished with an outfit.

Reek-money, -penny, *n.* a tax on every chimney.

Reek-ridden, *adj.* smoke-ridden.

Reek-shot, *adj.* used of the eyes: sore and watery without apparent cause.

Reek-stained, *adj.* smoke-begrimed.

Reeky, *adj.* smoky, smoking.

Reeky Peter, *n.* a candlestick for 'fir-candles.' Cf. Peer-man.

Reel, *n.* a lively dance peculiar to Scotland.—*v.* to dance a 'reel.'

Reel, *n.* the spool of a spinning-wheel; the spinning-wheel; a bobbin.—*v.* to wind or unwind a bobbin; with *on*, to rattle on; to push on rapidly.

Reel, *v.* to romp; to travel; to roam; to roll; to knock violently; used of thunder: to peal; to wrestle, contend.—*n.* a confused or whirling motion; turmoil; mental confusion; a loud, rattling noise; a peal, a thunder-clap.

Reel, *n.* in *phr.* 'oot o' reel,' not in a healthy condition.

Reel, *n.* a rail; a line or row. Cf. Rail.

Reel-about, *v.* to go to and fro in a rambling and noisy way; to romp; to whirl round in a dance.—*n.* a lively, romping person.

Reel-fittit, *adj.* club-footed; having the feet turned inwards so that the legs are crossed in walking and the feet make a curve.

Reeling, *ppl. adj.* in confusion; intoxicated; disordered in thought and speech.—*n.* a whirling motion made by bees; confusion of ideas; intoxication; bustle; a loud, clattering noise.

Reel-rall, -rawl, *n.* a state of confusion; turmoil.—*v.* to move or work confusedly; to walk in aimless, disorderly fashion.— *adv.* in confusion; topsy-turvy, helter-skelter.

Reel-rally, *adj.* staggering under the influence of liquor.

Reel-tree, *n.* the beam in a 'byre' to which cow-stakes are fixed. Cf. Rail-tree.

Reel-yeukin, *adj.* itching to dance a 'reel.'

Reem, *n.* a rumour.

Reem, *n.* cream; froth; foam.—*v.* to skim off cream; to froth; to buzz in the head. Cf. Ream.

Reemage, *v.* to rummage noisily. Cf. Reemmage.

Reemish, Reemis, *n.* a loud, rumbling noise; the sound of a heavy fall or blow; a disturbance, 'row'; stir, bustle; a thorough and noisy search; a weighty blow.—*v.* to make a loud, rumbling noise; to search thoroughly and noisily.

Reemle, *v.* to emit or cause a sharp, tremulous noise; to roll or push forward.—*n.* a continuous sharp, tremulous sound or motion; a confused, falling sound, a rumble.—*adv.* with a sharp, tremulous sound.

Reemle-rammle, *v.* to make a great deal of noise; to behave noisily and rompingly.— *n.* a great noise; noisy, rollicking behaviour; rambling speech or talk.—*adv.* in a rude, noisy manner; with a low, heavy sound; with a jingling and confused sound.

Reemmage, *v.* to search thoroughly; to rummage noisily. Cf. Reemish.

Reemous, *n.* a falsehood; a false report; a clamour. Cf. Reem, Reemish.

Reenge, *v.* to range; to search for thoroughly; to romp; to give out a clattering, ringing sound; to clear the bars of a grate.—*n.* a thorough search; a stroll; a border; a row, rank; a shelf; a settle; a semicircular seat round a pulpit reserved for the elders and baptismal purposes. Cf. Range.

Reenge, *v.* to clean out; to rinse. —*n.* a handful of heather used as a scrubber. Cf. Range.

Reenger, *n.* one who goes about noisily.

Reep, *v.* to rip; to cleave; to utter impetuously.—*n.* rubbish; a rascal; a person, good or bad. Cf. Rip.

Reepal, *n.* a person, irrespective of character.

Reepan, Reepin, *n.* a lean person or animal; a low character; a tell-tale.

Reerd, *n.* a loud noise. Cf. Raird.

Reerie, *n.* a wild frolic; a free fight: a wordy battle. Cf. Rearie.

Ree-ruck, *n.* a small rick of corn put up to be easily dried.

Reese, *v.* to blow briskly.—*n.* a puff, blast.

Reese, *v.* to praise. Cf. Roose.

Reeshle, Reeshil, *v.* to rustle; to clatter, crackle; to beat soundly; to hustle; to drive with blows; to shake up; to knock up against.—*n.* a rustle; a loud clattering or rattling sound; the ringing of a bell; a sounding blow; a sharp shaking; a tottering ruin; a loose heap.—*adv.* with a crackling sound.

Reeshler, *n.* a noisy or flurried worker.

Reeshlin', *ppl. adj.* forward, bustling, prompt.

Reeshlin-bland, *n.* a scourge.

Reeshlin-dry, *adj.* so dry as to make a rustling sound.

Reeshly, *adj.* rude, rowdy; troublesome; given to rows; stirring; rattling; noisy.

Reesie, *adj.* blowing briskly; used of a horse: frisky. Cf. Reezie.

Reesil, *v.* to rustle. Cf. Reeshle.

Reesin, *ppl. adj.* vehement, forcible, strong.

Reesk, *n.* coarse grass growing on downs; waste land yielding only benty grasses; a marshy place. Cf. Risk.

Reeskie, *adj.* abounding in 'reesk,' coarse grass, &c.

Reesle, *v.* to rustle. Cf. Reeshle.

Reest, *v.* to be restive; to refuse to proceed; used of a horse: to 'balk,' to turn.—*n.* a fit of stubbornness or refusal to move on; one who becomes stubborn.

Reest, *v.* to smoke; to dry in the sun or by fire; used of a well: to dry up.—*n.* the place where fish, hams, &c. are smoked.

Reest, *v.* to make up a fire for the night; to owe; to arrest; to distrain for debt. Cf. Rest.

Reest, *n.* a roost.—*v.* to roost. Cf. Roost.

Reested, *ppl. adj.* restive; stiff, tired; unwilling.

Reested, *ppl. adj.* smoke-dried; shrivelled up.

Reester, *n.* a restive, 'balking' horse; a resister; an obstinate, wayward person.

Reester, *n.* a salted and dried salmon; a kipper.

Reestle, *n.* a resounding blow. Cf. Reeshle.

†Reestle, *v.* to warm at the fire. Cf. Rizzle.

Reestlin'-rustlin, *adj.* used of corn: so dry as to rustle. Cf. Reeshle.

Reesty, *adj.* restive, unwilling to move, 'balking'; obstinate, mulish.

Reet, *n.* root.—*v.* to uproot.

Reet, *v.* to turn up the ground with the snout; to turn things clumsily; to rummage: to struggle for a living. Cf. Root.

Reeve, *n.* a cattle-pen: a sheepfold.—*v.* to shut up in a 'reeve.'

Reeve, *v.* to burn with a strong, bright flame.

Reeve, *v.* to talk vivaciously and incoherently; to rumour.—*n.* a rumour.

Reeve, *v.* to rivet, clinch. Cf. Roove.

Reeve, *v.* to split asunder; to tug; to tear. —*v. pret.* did burst, tore. Cf. Rive.

Reeve, *v.* to rob, plunder. Cf. Reave.

Reeve, *v.* to twist cotton or yarn into rope-form for spinning; to twist; to fasten.—*n.* a twist of rope. Cf. Rove.

Reever, *n.* anything large or quickly moving; a roaring fire; a high wind; a swift boat; a stout, active person.

Reever, *n.* a robber, freebooter.

Reeving, *ppl. adj.* high, strong: burning brightly.

Reeving-wind, *n.* a high wind.

Reeze, *v.* with *behind,* to break wind.

Reeze, *v.* to praise.—*n.* high praise. Cf. Roose.

Reeze, *v.* to pull one about roughly.

Reeze, *v.* to blow briskly. Cf. Reese.

Reezie, *adj.* wild, frolicsome, partially tipsy; used of a horse: frisky. Cf. Reesie.

Reezing-horse, *n.* a healthy horse.

Reezlie, *adj.* used of ground: having a cold bottom, producing coarse grass.

Refe, *n.* the itch. Cf. Reef.

Refeese, *v.* to refuse.

Refeir, *n.* in *phr.* to 'the refeir,' in proportion.

Refell, *v.* to refute, repel.

Refer, *n.* a reference; a thing referred.—*v.* to delay, defer.

Reff, *v.* to rob, spoil.

Refind, *v.* to refund.

Refleck, *v.* to reflect.

Reform, *v.* to repair.—*n.* repair.

Refound, *v.* to charge to the account of; to refund.

Refresher, *n.* liquid refreshment.

Reft, *v. pret.* stole.—*ppl.* stolen. Cf. Reave.

Reft, *v. pret.* tore. Cf. Rive.

Refted, *ppl.* stolen. Cf. Reave.

Refuse, *n.* a refusal, rejection.

Refusion, *n.* the act of refunding.

Refusticat, *v.* to recover consciousness, revive.

Regalia, *n.* privileges pertaining to the Crown.

Regalis, Regalles, *n.* districts having the privileges of a regality.

Regality, *n.* a territorial jurisdiction granted by the king, with lands given 'in free regality,' and conferring on the person receiving it the title of 'lord of regality.'

Regard, Regaird, *v.* to fall to the lot of; to concern.

Regardless, Regairdless, *adj.* reckless, careless; regardless of God and man.

†**Regent**, *n.* the old title of a university professor. — *v.* to discharge the office of a university professor.

Regentry, Regency, *n.* a university professor's office.

Regibus, *n.* a boys' game. Cf. Rangiebus.

Regiment, *v.* to form into a regiment. — *n.* government.

Registrate, *v.* to register. — *ppl.* registered.

Reglar, *adj.* regular; thorough, complete. — *adv.* regularly, always.

†**Regorge,** *v.* to regurgitate.

Regret, *n.* a complaint; a grievance.

Rehable, *v.* to rehabilitate; to reinstate.

Reib, *n.* colewort growing tall with little or no leaf; a cabbage that does not stock properly; a lean, thin person or animal; an animal that does not thrive. Cf. Ribe.

Reibie, *adj.* tall and thin; lean, lank, slender.

Reick, *v.* to equip. Cf. Reek.

Reid, *n.* the fourth stomach of a ruminant. Cf. Reed.

Reid, *adj.* red. Cf. Red.

Reid, *v.* to prepare; to tidy. Cf. Redd.

Reid, *adj.* fierce, wild. Cf. Rede.

Reid, *n.* the Rood. Cf. Rood.

Reid-hunger, *n.* a ravenous appetite.

Reif, Reife, *n.* robbery; plunder. — *adj.* plundering. Cf. Reave.

Reif, *n.* the itch. Cf. Reef.

†**Reifart,** *n.* a radish. Cf. Reefart.

Reiffar, *n.* a robber.

Reif randy, *n.* a sturdy beggar.

Reif-saw, *n.* itch-ointment.

Reify, *adj.* having the itch.

Reigh, *n.* a harbour. Cf. Ree.

Reik, *n.* smoke. Cf. Reek.

Reik, *n.* a blow. Cf. Reek.

Reik, *v.* to equip. Cf. Reek.

Reik, *v.* to reach; to stretch out. — *n.* a reach; a 'rink,' the course of a stone in curling. Cf. Reach.

Reik, *n.* a trick; a stratagem; a prank. Cf. Reak.

Reikim, Reikum, *n.* a smart blow; a riot. — *v.* to strike a smart blow. Cf. Reekim.

Reiking, *n.* an outfit, personal garments, 'rig.'

Reikit, *ppl. adj.* furnished with all needful clothes.

Reil, *v.* to whirl; to romp; to roam. — *n.* a turmoil. Cf. Reel.

Reilibogie, *n.* confusion; tumult, disorder. Cf. Reel.

Reiling, *n.* a loud, clattering noise.

Reimis, *n.* a loud, clattering noise. Cf. Reemish.

Reinge, *v.* to rinse. Cf. Range, Ringe.

Reinge, *v.* to rap hard; to rush about roughly. Cf. Range.

Reingin', *n.* a hard rapping.

Reinzies, *n.* reins.

Reip, *v.* to search; to search one's pockets; to rifle a pocket; to clean out a pipe. — *n.* a clearing out. Cf. Ripe.

Reird, *v.* to make a loud noise. Cf. Raird.

Reise, *v.* to praise. Cf. Roose.

Reise, *n.* a branch; brushwood. Cf. Rise.

Reishle, Reishil, *v.* to rustle; to beat soundly. Cf. Reeshle.

Reishlin, Reishillin', *ppl. adj.* noisy; forward; prompt. — *n.* a sound beating.

Reisk, *v.* to scratch so as to make a noise. — *n.* such a scratching noise. Cf. Risk.

Reisk, Reisque, *n.* coarse grass growing on downs; a morass. Cf. Reesk.

Reiskie, *n.* a big, boorish person, especially such a woman.

Reisle, Reissil, Reissle, *v.* to rustle. Cf. Reeshle.

Reist, *n.* the instep of the foot.

Reist, *v.* to sprain or strain the wrist. Cf. Wrest.

Reist, *v.* to be restive. Cf. Reest.

Reist, *v.* to dry by the heat of the sun or fire. Cf. Reest.

Reist, *v.* to make up a fire for the night; to arrest, distrain. Cf. Rest.

Reister, *n.* a kippered salmon. Cf. Reester.

Reisum, *n.* a stalk or ear of corn; an atom, particle; the smallest possible quantity. Cf. Rissom.

Reit, *n.* a root.

Reithe, *adj.* keen, ardent.

Reive, *n.* a name given to circular mounds with regular fosses, which are considered to be ancient Caledonian forts.

Reive, *v.* to plunder. Cf. Reave.

Reive, *v.* to tear. Cf. Rive.

Reiver, *n.* a robber, freebooter.

Rejag, *v.* to give a smart answer, or one reflecting on the person to whom it is addressed. — *n.* a repartee, retort.

Rejeck, *v.* to reject.

Relapser, *n.* one who relapses into scandalous sin.

Release, *v.* to relax; to remove a duty on goods.

Releich, *v.* to enlarge, release.

Relevancy, *n.* the legal sufficiency of facts stated, in a 'libel' or in a defence, to infer punishment or exculpation.

Relevant, *adj.* a legal term: valid; sufficient to warrant the conclusion in a 'libel' or in a defence.

Relict, *n.* a relic; ruins.

Relief, *adj.* an ecclesiastical term, applied to congregations that withdrew from the Church of Scotland in order to be free from the evils of patronage in presentation to livings, and free to choose their own ministers.

Relish, *v.* to give relish to.

Relisher, *n.* one that relishes.

Remain, *n.* a posthumous publication; literary 'remains.'

Remaining, *ppt. adj.* future.

Remaining state, *n.* a future state.

†Remanent, *adj.* remaining, other.—*n.* a remainder.

Remark, *n.* in *phr.* 'in remark,' notable, remarkable, exceptional.

Remarkable, *n.* any thing or event remarkable or noteworthy.

Remarking, *n.* a remark; criticism.

Remb, *v.* to rave; to tell lies. Cf. Rame.

Rember, *n.* one who tells improbable stories.

Reme, *v.* to foam. Cf. Ream.

†Remede, Remeed, *n.* remedy. Cf. Remeid.

Remedie, *n.* a certain latitude of degrees of fineness in silver on either side of the standard in coining formerly, to save the labour of precision.

Remeeve, *v.* to remove.

†Remeid, Remead, Remied, *n.* a remedy, cure; redress, relief.—*v.* to remedy, redress.

Remeid of law, *n.* a legal term, applicable to the obtaining of justice by appeal to a superior court.

Remember, *v.* to remind.

Rememberful, *adj.* full of old memories.

Remembering-prayer, *n.* the intercessory prayer in public worship.

Remigester, *n.* a sharp blow; an injury. Cf. Ramiegeister.

Remind, *v.* to keep in mind, remember.

Remish, *n.* a loud, rumbling noise; a disturbance. Cf. Reemish.

Remit, *v.* used of a person: to pardon him.

Remnant, *n.* a small piece, a 'flinder'; a feeble old creature, a physical wreck.

Remove, *v.* to die.—*n.* an intervening degree of relationship; an old horseshoe removed and replaced; the act of re-shoeing a horse with the old shoes.

Removedly, *adv.* remotely.

Ren, *v.* to run. Cf. Rin.

Renaige, *v.* to revoke at cards.—*n.* a revoke.

Renchel, *v.* to beat with a stick.

Renchel, *n.* a tall, thin person.

Rendal, *n.* land held by a tenant in discontiguous plots; land held by several tenants in one field. Cf. Run-rig.

Render, *v.* to melt fat, butter; to discharge pus.—*n.* melted fat, dripping.

Render, *n.* a rate; a degree.

Rendered fat, *n.* melted fat.

Renderment, *n.* melted fat, dripping.

Renk, *n.* a curling-rink. Cf. Rink.

Rennal, *n.* land held by a tenant in discontiguous plots. Cf. Rendal.

Rennet, *n.* in *phr.* 'rig and rennet,' land held by tenants in places here and there, or land held by several tenants in one field.

Rensh, *v.* to rinse.

Renshel, *v.* to beat or drive with a stick. Cf. Renchel.

Rent, *v.* to rend, tear, crack.

Rental, *n.* a favourable lease; the annual rent.

Rentaller, *n.* one who possesses a farm or land by 'rental.'

Rent-dues, *n.* arrears of rent.

Rent-racker, *n.* a rack-renter; a harsh collector of rents.

Rep, Repp, *v.* to rip; with *out*, to unwind anything knitted. Cf. Rip.

Repair, *n.* a gathering of people, concourse.

†Reparty, *v.* to reply, retort.

Repeal, *v.* to recall a sentence; to set aside a verdict on appeal.

Repeat, *v.* to demand money back; to recover; to call back.—*n.* the repetition of lines in psalm-singing.

Repeater, *n.* a repeating psalm-tune.

Repentance, *n.* in *phr.* 'stool of repentance,' the stool or seat in church formerly occupied by offenders against the Seventh Commandment, for public rebuke.

Repentance-gown, *n.* a white sheet of coarse linen worn by those who occupied the 'stool of repentance,' or had otherwise to undergo public penance.

Repentance-, Repenting-stool, *n.* the 'stool of repentance.'

Repetition, *n.* repayment; recovery or restoration of money.

†Replegiation, *n.* the handing of a prisoner over to the jurisdiction to which he was subject.

Replenish, *v.* to refurbish, clean up anew.

Reploch, *n.* coarse woollen cloth. Cf. Raploch.

Repone, *v.* to replace; to restore to office or status, &c.; to reply.—*n.* a legal reply.

Report, *v.* to obtain; to carry off.

†Repose, *v.* to replace, reinstate, 'repone.'

Reposition, *n.* reinstatement; restoration to ecclesiastical status.

†Repouss, *v.* to repulse, repel.

Reppet, *n.* a disturbance; a wrangle. Cf. Rippet.

Reppoch, *n.* a ragged garment; in *pl.* tatters.

Repree, *v.* to reprove.

Reprivell, *n.* a reprieve.

Reproach, *v.* to bring or be a cause of reproach.

Reprobate, *v.* to contradict the evidence of a witness; to challenge a verdict as against evidence: a legal term.

Reprobation, *n.* contradictory evidence of one witness against another.

Reprobator, *n.* one who 'reprobates' evidence or a verdict.

Reprobature, *n.* the act of 'reprobating.'

Repute, *adj.* reputed ; habitually reported.

Requeesht, *v.* to request.

Requittance, *n.* requital.

Resaitt, *v.* to harbour ; to receive stolen goods. Cf. Receipt, Reset.

Reschell, Reshill, *v.* to beat soundly ; to rustle. Cf. Reeshle.

Reseeduary, *n.* a minister who did not leave the Established Church of Scotland at the Disruption in 1843. Cf. Residuary.

Resent, *v.* to appreciate ; to applaud.

Resentments, *n.* feelings of gratitude, appreciation.

Reserve, *n.* a reservation ; a tree reserved in a 'hag' or cutting of an allotted portion of wood.

Reset, *v.* to receive stolen goods. Cf. Receipt.

Reset, *n.* resin. Cf. Roset.

Resetter, *n.* a receiver of stolen goods.

Reshill, *n.* a rumbling or clattering noise. Cf. Reeshle.

Resident, *v.* to reside.

Residenter, *n.* a resident.

Residenting, *ppl. adj.* residing, resident.

Residuary, *n.* a name formerly given to ministers who remained in the Established Church of Scotland at the Disruption in 1843.

†**Resile,** *v.* to flinch, recoil ; to withdraw ; to beguile, deceive ; to resist in argument ; to respite.

Reskal, *n.* a rascal.

Resolve, *v.* to terminate ; to clear up or settle doubts ; to convince.

Resp, *v.* to grate, rub with a file.—*n.* a file ; a grating sound. Cf. Risp.

Resp, *n.* long, coarse grass ; a stalk of straw ; a bulrush. Cf. Risp.

Respeck, *v.* to respect ; to be solicitous for ; to drink one's health.—*n.* respect ; in *pl.* interest, emolument, advantage.

Respect, *n.* a respite.

Respective, *adj.* respectful, full of regard to.

Respond, *n.* the return made by a precept from Chancery on an application for sasine.

Responsal, *adj.* responsible ; substantial as to means, &c.

Responsible, *adj.* of good standing ; respectable ; substantial. Cf. Sponsible.

Resputt, *n.* respite. Cf. Respect.

Ress, *n.* a freight of water from a well. Cf. Race.

Ressum, *n.* an atom, particle. Cf. Rissom.

Rest, *n.* the place where a curling-stone should stop ; the part of a spade on which the foot rests.

Rest, *v.* to make up a fire for the night ; to be indebted to one, owe ; to arrest, distrain for debt.—*n.* a remnant ; a relic ; in *pl.* arrears of money due, rent, &c.

Rest, *v.* to twist, sprain ; to wrest.—*n.* a sprain. Cf. Wrest.

†**Restaur,** *v.* to make restitution.

†**Restauration,** *n.* restitution, reparation for injury, &c.

Resting-chair, *n.* a long chair, shaped like a settle.

Resting-clod, -peat, *n.* a peat-sod for 'resting' a fire.

Resting-owing, *adj.* remaining indebted to one.

Restrick, *v.* to restrict.

Restringent, *n.* an astringent.

†**Resume,** *v.* to repeat ; to recapitulate, summarize.

Resurrectioner, Resurrector, *n.* a resurrectionist, body-snatcher.

Ret, *v.* to steep flax in order to separate the woody core from the fibre.

Ret, *v.* to score ; to slit ; to furrow. Cf. Rit.

Reteir, *v.* to retreat, retire.

Reth, *n.* a quarter of a year. Cf. Raith.

Retical, *n.* a reticule.

†**Retour,** *v.* to return ; to make a return in writing as to the service of an heir, or the value of lands.—*n.* the legal return made to a brief issued from Chancery, or as to the value of lands ; a great amount.

Retreat, *v.* to retract.

Retrench, *v.* to reduce the amount of a fine.

Retrinch, *v.* to compel the return of anything unjustly obtained.

Retroact, *v.* to make an Act retrospective.

Retrocess, *v.* to give a back-place.

Rett, *n.* a quarter of a year. Cf. Raith.

Retting, *n.* the steeping of flax or hemp in order to separate the woody core from the fibre.

Reunde, *v.* to cough loudly and hoarsely ; to grind ; to make an unpleasant grinding sound. Cf. Roond.

Reuth, *n.* wild mustard-seed.

Reuth, *n.* ruth, pity.

†**Revally,** *n.* the signal given about daybreak to awaken soldiers.

Reve, *v.* to rob. Cf. Reave.

Revel, *n.* a severe blow ; a back-stroke.

Revel, *n.* a rail. Cf. Ravel.

Revel, *v.* to ravel ; to unravel. Cf. Ravel.

Rever, *n.* a robber. Cf. Reaver.

Reverence, *n.* a respectful greeting ; power ; one's mercy ; a title of respect given to a minister or priest ; in *phr.* to 'be in one's reverence,' to be under obligation to one.

Reverie, *n.* a rumour; a vague report.—*v.* to report.

Revers, *n.* in *phr.* 'at the revers,' at random.

Reverser, *n.* a proprietor who has the right of redemption over lands he has mortgaged, by paying the mortgage.

Reversion, *n.* the right of redemption of a mortgaged property.

Revert, *v.* to recover from a swoon or from sickness.

†**Revestrie**, *n.* the vestry of a church.

Revil, *n.* the point of a spur, a rowel.

Revisie, *v.* to inspect again; to revise.

Revure, Revoore, *adj.* dark and gloomy; thoughtful; having a look of calm scorn or contempt.

Rew, *v.* to roll.

Rew, Rewe, *v.* to repent; to change one's mind regarding something done or intended; to pity.—*n.* regret, repentance. Cf. Rue.

Rewayle, Rewayl'd, *adj.* untidy, slovenly; ravelled, disordered.

Rewl, *v.* to be entangled. Cf. Ravel.

Rewth, *n.* a cause for repentance.

Rex, *n.* a boys' game. Cf. Rax.

Rexa-boxa-king, *n.* the game of 'rex.' Cf. Rax-king-of-Scotland.

Rex-dollar, *n.* a coin worth £2, 18s. Scots.

Reyk, *n.* a blow. Cf. Reek.

Reyle, *v.* to entangle. Cf. Ravel.

Reyl-tree, *n.* a cross-beam in a 'byre' to which the cow-stakes are attached. Cf. Rail-tree.

Reyve, *v.* to tear asunder. Cf. Rive.

Rhaem, Rhaim, *n.* a commonplace speech; a rhapsody; a monotonous repetition.—*v.* to reiterate; to repeat by rote; to lay off a long rigmarole. Cf. Rame.

Rhane, *n.* idle, unmeaning repetition; a metrical jargon; a reiteration of the same thing.—*v.* to rhyme; to repeat the same thing constantly; to murmur monotonously. Cf. Rane.

Rheemous, *n.* clamour. Cf. Reemous.

Rheum, *n.* in *pl.* rheumatism.

Rheumateese, Rheumatiz, *n.* rheumatism.

Rheumatics, *n.* rheumatism.

Rheumatis't, *adj.* afflicted with rheumatism.

Rhind, *n.* a rind; a piece cut off a board; list or selvage. Cf. Rind.

Rhind, *n.* a footpath, roadway.

Rhind-mart, *n.* a whole carcass of cow or ox; a 'mart.'

Rhone, *n.* a spout for carrying off rain-water; a small patch of ice formed on a road. Cf. Rone.

Rhume, *v.* to shout; to talk nonsense. Cf. Rame.

Rhyme, *v.* to reiterate. Cf. Rame.

Rhymeless, *adj.* unreasonable; regardless.

Rhyming-ware, *n.* compositions in rhyme; minor poetry.

Rhynd, Rhyne, *n.* hoar-frost. Cf. Rind.

Rhynde, *v.* to melt, liquefy fat; to distil whisky. Cf. Rind.

Rhyne, *v.* to grumble, growl; to mutter in discontent. Cf. Rhane.

Riach, *adj.* dun; ill-coloured.

†**Rial**, *n.* a gold coin; a silver coin bearing the name of the reigning sovereign. Cf. Royal.

Riauve, *n.* a row, a file.

Rib, *n.* a wife; the bar of a grate; a strip of anything; the slight ridge in stockings.—*v.* to half-plough land, by leaving an alternate furrow unploughed.

Ribbing, *n.* a half-ploughing.

Ribbit, *n.* a hewn stone at the side of a door, &c. Cf. Rebbit.

Ribble, *v.* to read quickly; to gabble; to work carelessly, hastily, and confusedly.—*n.* careless speech, reading, or working; a ruinous mass; a careless worker. Cf. Rabble.

Ribble-rabble, *n.* a rabble; great confusion. —*v.* to crowd in great confusion.—*adv.* in great confusion.

Ribblie, *n.* a disorderly gathering.

Ribblie-rabblie, *adj.* disorderly.

Ribbon, *n.* in *phr.* 'St Johnston's ribbon,' a halter.

Ribe, *n.* a colewort tall and with little or no leaf; a cabbage that does not stock properly; a lean person or animal.

Rib-grass, *n.* the ribwort plantain.

Ribie, *adj.* tall, with little foliage; lank, tall and thin.

Rib-ploughing, *n.* 'ribbing,' a particular kind of ploughing. Cf. Rib.

Rice, *n.* a twig, branch; brushwood; branches used for hedging.—*v.* to throw branches into a river to frighten the salmon. Cf. Rise.

Rich, *adj.* full.—*v.* to become rich.

Richnie, *n.* a name given in anger to a woman.

Richt, *adj.* right in health; in sound mind; exercising reason.—*v.* to put to rights; to mend. Cf. Right.

Richteous, *adj.* righteous.

Richtfu', *adj.* rightful.

Richt-like, *adj.* according to justice; in good health.

Richtly, *adv.* certainly, positively.

Rick, *n.* smoke. Cf. Reek.

Rick, *v.* to pierce with a hook by a sudden pull or jerk.—*n.* a tug or pull; a sharp movement.

Rickam, *n.* a smart blow. Cf. Reekim.

Ricket, *n.* a racket, disturbance; a policeman's rattle.

Ricket, *adj.* unsteady, rickety.

Rickety-dickety, *n.* a wooden toy made for children.

Rickle, *n.* a loose heap, pile, or stack; a low stone fence built before a drain; a very lean person or animal; a living skeleton.—*v.* to put into a heap; to stack; to pile up loosely.

Rickle-dyke, *n.* a wall firmly built at the bottom, but having the top only the thickness of the single stones loosely piled the one above the other.

Rickler, *n.* one who builds up loosely; a bad stone-builder.

Rickling, *n.* a method of preserving corn in small stacks.

Rickling, *n.* the youngest or smallest of a brood, litter, or family; a weakling.

Rickly, *adj.* loosely built; rickety, unsteady; dilapidated.

Rickmaster, *n.* a 'rittmaster'; a captain of horse.

Rickmatick, *n.* concern, affair; collection, 'hypothec.'

Rick-thacking, *n.* the thatching of ricks.

Rick-yard, *n.* a stackyard.

Rictum-tictum, *adj.* conjuring.

Rid, *v.* to despatch, discharge, accomplish, get through with; to comb the hair; to disentangle; to part combatants. Cf. Redd.

Rid, *adj.* ready.—*adv.* readily, fluently.

Rid, *adj.* red. Cf. Red.

Rid, *n.* spawn. Cf. Redd, Rude.

Rid, *v. pret.* rode.

Ridable, *adj.* fordable on horseback.

Rid-comb, *n.* a comb for the hair.

Ridden-meal, *n.* money paid by an incoming tenant for getting the liberty of the farm before the term expires.

Ridder, *n.* one who parts combatants. Cf. Redder.

Ridding-comb, *n.* a 'rid-comb.'

Riddins, *n.* spawn.

Riddle, *v.* to pierce; to mangle.

Riddle, *v.* to puzzle; to solve.

Riddle-turning, *n.* a method of divination by means of a riddle fixed on the extended points of a pair of scissors.

Riddlin-heids, *n.* what has been sifted out; refuse.

Riddlin' in the reek, *n.* a rough and ready method of getting rid of a fairy changeling.

Riddlum, Riddleum, *n.* a riddle, conundrum.

Ride, *n.* spawn. Cf. Redd.

Ride, *v.* to ford on horseback; to be fordable on horseback; to ride in procession to the Parliament House; to ride on a plundering raid; to drive a curling-stone with such force as to knock a rival one out of the way; to bowl strongly.—*n.* a hard throw in bowls; a passage by water; the current or swell of the sea.

Ride, *adj.* rough. Cf. Royd, Royet.

Rider, *n.* a Scottish gold coin worth £8, 2s. Scots.

Rider, *n.* a curling-stone that forcibly dislodges one blocking its way; used in bowling: a forcibly-thrown bowl.

Ride-tail-tint, *v.* to back one horse against another in a race, so that the losing horse is lost by the owner.

Rid-handit, *adj.* clever with the hands. Cf. Redd-handit.

Ridicule, *n.* a practical joke.

Ridiculous, *adj.* used of the weather: unseasonable.

Ridie-roosie, *n.* a ride pick-a-back.

Riding, *n.* marauding, freebooting; a Border raid.

Riding-graith, *n.* riding equipment.

Riding-money, *n.* a tax paid in connection with the quartering of dragoons on the Covenanters.

Riding-pie, -py, *n.* a loose riding-coat or frock.

Riding-time, *n.* the breeding season of sheep.

Rief, Rieft, *v.* to plunder.—*n.* plunder. Cf. Reif, Reave.

Riefer, *n.* a robber. Cf. Reiffar.

Rien, *ppl.* riven.

Riep, *n.* a slovenly-dressed girl; a rascal.—*v.* to rip. Cf. Rip.

Rier, *v.* to roar. Cf. Rair.

Rierfu', *adj.* roaring. Cf. Reefu', Reird.

Riesle, *v.* to rustle; to thwack. Cf. Reeshle.

Riest, *v.* to make up a fire for the night. Cf. Rest.

†Rifart, *n.* a radish. Cf. Reefart.

Rife, Riff, *n.* the itch. Cf. Reef.

Rife, *adj.* ready; quick.

Riffraff, Rifraff, *n.* a low, mean person.—*adj.* disreputable; shabby; scurvy.

Rifle, *v.* in *phr.* 'rifle the ladies' pouches,' the shepherd's purse.

Rift, *v.* to belch, eructate; to come back unpleasantly to the memory; to boast, exaggerate.—*n.* an eructation; unbridled talk; exaggeration; frank conversation.

Rift, *n.* a look; appearance; a slit made in a sheep's ear.—*v.* to mark sheep with a 'rift.'

Rifted, *ppl. adj.* riven, split.

Rifting-full, *adj.* full to repletion.

Rifty, *adj.* belching forth abuse.

Rig, *n.* a half-castrated animal; a male animal with imperfectly developed organs.

Rig, Rigg, *v.* to cheat, trick.—*n.* a frolic; a trick; a spree.—*phr.* 'on the rig,' wandering about at night.

Rig, Rigg, *v.* to deck out; to set up; to prepare, trim.—*n.* equipment; good condition; working order.

Rig, Rigg, *n.* a ridge; a long, narrow hill; the spine of a person or animal; the space between the furrows of a field; a section of a ploughed field; a section of a field; a field; the first furrow turned in ploughing; a drill for potatoes, &c.—*v.* to plough; to make ridges in a field by ploughing.

†Rigadoon, Rigadown-daisy, *n.* a lively dance on the grass at a wedding.

Rig and bauk, *n.* a field with alternate strips of corn and pasture.

Rig and fur, *n.* the ridge and furrow of a ploughed field; the whole field; the ribbing of stockings, &c.

Rig-and-rendal, *n.* the old land system of 'runrig,' where the small farms are parcelled out in discontiguous plots. Cf. Rendal.

Rig-back, -bane, *n.* the spine, backbone.

Rig-end, *n.* the buttocks; the lower end of the spine; the end of a 'rig' in ploughing, or of a section of a field in reaping.

Rig-fidge, *n.* a gentle blow on the back.

Rig-fish, *n.* the backbone of a fish.

Rigget-cow, *n.* a cow with white stripe along the backbone.

Riggin, *n.* a term of reproach to a woman; a tall, ungainly woman.

Rigging, *n.* clothing; outfit.

Rigging, *n.* the backbone; the head, skull; the ridge of a roof; the rafters forming the roof; the roof itself; shelter under a roof. —*v.* to roof in, cover with a roof.

Rigging-stone, *n.* a stone forming part of the ridge of the roof.

Rigging-tree, *n.* the ridge-beam of the house; the 'roof-tree.'

Riggit, *ppl. adj.* used of cattle: having a white streak or white and brown streaks along the back.

Rigglin, *n.* an animal with one testicle.

Riggly, *adj.* unsteady, rickety, wriggling.

Riggs and shaws, *n.* the entire estate.

Riggy, Rigga, *n.* a name given to a cow having a stripe along the back.

Rig-head, *n.* the strip of land at the sides of a field where the plough turns.

Right, *adj.* large; good; thorough; sane, 'canny'; in good health; sober.—*adv.* thoroughly.—*v.* to put in order, repair.

Rightlins, *adv.* by rights; of a certainty; rightly.

Right now, *adv.* just now, immediately.

Right-recht, *v.* to judge justly, aright.

Rights, *n.* title-deeds.

Right-side, *n.* the side of a cake that was uppermost when first placed on the 'girdle.'

Right-so, -sua, *adv.* in like manner, just so.

Right way, *n.* the true story, the real facts of a case.

Rigibus, *n.* a boys' game. Cf. Rangiebus, Regibus.

Riglan, Riglen, *n.* a half-castrated animal. Cf. Rigglin.

Rigmalorum, *n.* a rigmarole.

Rigmarie, Rig-ma-ree, *n.* a base coin; a mischievous frolic; a tumult, uproar; any frail, thin membrane.

Rigmarole, *adj.* long-winded and incoherent.

Rigs, *n.* a boys' game; 'rangiebus.'

Rigwiddie, Rigwoodie, Rigwuddie, *adj.* stubborn in disposition; deserving the 'widdie' or halter; ill-shaped; lean, bony.—*n.* the rope or chain crossing the back of a yoked horse; one who can bear much fatigue or hard usage; a wild trick or prank.

Rigwiddie-nag, *n.* a half-castrated horse.

Rike, *v.* to reach, stretch. Cf. Reach.

Rik-ma-tik, *n.* affair, concern. Cf. Rickmatick.

Rile, *v.* to entangle, ravel.

Rile, *v.* to irritate, annoy.

Rilling, *n.* a shoe made of rough, untanned leather, a 'rivelin.'

Rim, *n.* a circular haze, a halo; in *phr.* 'rim of the belly,' the peritoneum.

Rim, *n.* a ream of paper.

Rim-bursin, *n.* a rupture of the abdominal muscles to which horses and cows are subject.

Rim-burst, *n.* hernia.

Rim-burstenness, *n.* the condition of having hernia.

Rime, *n.* a fog, mist; the death-sweat.

Rim-fou, *adj.* brim-full.

Rimil, *v.* to rumble.

Rimless, *adj.* reckless, regardless. Cf. Rhymeless.

Rimmed, *ppl. adj.* brimmed.

Rimmer, *n.* the iron hoop round the upper millstone, to keep it unbroken.

Rimpin, *n.* a lean cow; an old, ugly woman.

Rim-ram, *adv.* in disorder.

Rim-raxin, *n.* a good feed; a surfeit; what food one can retain, having eaten until the stomach is distended.

Rin, *v.* to run; used of liquid: to flow; to suppurate; used of the eyes: to water; of a road: to be covered with liquid mud; to curdle.—*n.* a run; a small stream; a ford where the water is shallow and ripples. Cf. Run.

Rin, *v.* to darn stockings. Cf. Rund.

Rin, *v.* to melt; to liquefy fat by heat; to distil whisky. Cf. Rind.

Rin-aboot, *v.* to go about, wander from place to place.—*n.* a gadabout; a vagabond;

one who 'tramps' the country.—*adj.* running about, scampering to and fro.

Rin ahin, *v.* to run at one's heels or behind; to follow closely; to fall into arrears, run into debt.

Rin at, *v.* to assault; to fall upon a person.

Rin-awa', *n.* a runaway; the bolting of horses; the ring-finger.—*adj.* runaway.

Rind, *v.* to liquefy fat by heat; to melt; to distil whisky.

Rind, *n.* a piece cut off a board; list, selvage; the wrapping of list on the handle of a golf-club, under the leather.

Rind, *n.* hoar-frost. Cf. Rhynd.

Rindle, *v.* to trickle, flow gently.—*n.* a brook, rivulet.

Rin doon wi', *v.* to pour down the throat of a hand-fed animal.

Rind-shoon, *n.* shoes with the uppers of cloth woven or plaited out of list.

Rine, *n.* list or selvage; a piece cut off a board. Cf. Rind.

Rine, *n.* hoar-frost. Cf. Rind.

Rinegate, Rinagate, *n.* a runagate, vagabond. —*adj.* worthless.

Rin-'em-owre, *n.* a children's game, played in the open street, in the middle of which one tries to catch those who try to cross within bounds. Cf. Burrie.

Ring, *n.* a prehistoric circular fort or entrenchment; a game of marbles placed in a circle; a mark on a cow's horn by which her age may be known; the meal which falls round the millstone, between it and the surrounding case.—*v.* to form a ring; to encircle or surround with a wall; to put a ring in a bull's nose or in a pig's snout; to put a ring round a wheel; used of a mill: to fill the crevices round the millstone with the first grain ground after the stones are picked.

Ring, *v.* to tingle, vibrate.—*n.* the striking of a public clock; a solitary coin to ring or jingle on a counter; a slap, blow.

Ring, *v.* to reign; to behave noisily or imperiously; to urge on; to overpower.

Ring, *n.* a race. Cf. Rink.

Ring, *v.* to wring.

Ring aboot at, *v.* to make a great noise; to behave imperiously.

Ringan, *ppl. adj.* used intensively, as in *phr.* 'a ringan deevil,' a very devil.

Ring-corn, *n.* the meal which in grinding falls round the millstone, between it and its case.

Ring-outter, *n.* an implement used by curlers for marking the rings at the ends of the rinks.

Ring down, *v.* to overpower; to overbear.

Ringe, *v.* to rinse.—*n.* a rinse, a cleansing; a small scrubber for cleaning pots, &c. Cf. Range.

Ringe, *v.* to go about noisily; to beat a drum —*n.* a clattering or rumbling noise. Cf. Range.

Ringe-heather, *n.* the cross-leaved heather. Cf. Rinse-heather.

Ringer, *n.* a scrubber or whisk for cleaning pots, &c.

Ringer, *n.* one who ranges about noisily.

Ringer, *n.* a stone which lies within the ring immediately surrounding the tee in curling; a 'pot-lid.'

Ring-fowl, *n.* the reed-bunting.

Ringie red belt, *n.* a children's game, played with a burning splint of wood rapidly turned in a circle, while doggerel lines are repeated.

Ring in, *v.* used of a church bell: to ring with increased speed, indicating that service is about to begin; to be near death.

Ring in, *v.* to yield; to cease; to acknowledge defeat.

Ringing, *ppl. adj.* very energetic; domineering.—*adv.* intensely.

Ringit, *ppl. adj.* used of a sow: having a ring through the snout; having a great quantity of white visible round the iris of the eye.

Ringle, *n.* a ringing sound, as of a loose horse-shoe.

Ringle, *n.* a cluster, group.

Ringled, *ppl. adj.* ringed; marked in rings.

Ringle-e'e, *n.* a wall-eye; a wall-eyed animal.

Ringle-e'ed, *adj.* wall-eyed; having too much white in the eye.

Ring-malt, *n.* 'ring-corn.' Cf. Ring corn.

Ring-necked loon, *n.* the great northern diver.

Ring owre, *v.* to hold in subjection.

Ring-straik, *n.* an instrument used for stroking down grain in a bushel measure.

Ring-tail, *n.* the hen-harrier (female).

Ring-tails, *n.* small remnants; miscellaneous odds and ends; arrears of rent; 'heel-taps.'

Ringum-craggum, *adv.* right through and through.

Ringy, *n.* a game with marbles placed in a ring.

Rink, *n.* a race; a course; the course over which curling-stones are driven; a set of players in a 'rink' at curling or quoits; a number of articles set in order; the act of setting in order; a line of division.—*v.* to range up and down; to roam hither and thither; to climb about; to clamber on to an elevated position; to mount some forbidden place; to arrange, set in order.

Rink, *v.* to surround, encircle.

Rink, *v.* to rattle; to move with a sharp sound; to search or rummage noisily and thoroughly.—*n.* a rattling sound; noisy movement or conduct.

Rink, *n.* a strong man.

Rinker, *n.* a tall, thin, long-legged horse ; a tall, raw boned woman ; a harridan.

Rinketer, *n.* a 'rinker,' a harridan.

Rink-fair, *n.* a yearly public market held a few miles south of Jedburgh.

Rink-medal, *n.* the medal played for by 'rinks,' and held by the winning 'rink,' in curling.

Rink-room, *n.* the arena for jousting.

Rink's-end, *n.* the goal.

Rinlet, *n.* a small stream.

Rinn, *v.* to melt. Cf. Rind.

Rinn, *v.* to run. Cf. Rin.

Rinnagate, *n.* a runagate ; a worthless person. —*adj.* vagabond.

Rinnal, *n.* a small stream ; a rivulet.—*v.* to trickle. Cf. Rindle.

Rinner, *n.* the upper millstone.

Rinner, *n.* a clue of yarn ; a stream, brooklet.

Rinner, *n.* butter melted with tar for sheep-smearing.

Rinnin', *n.* a running sore, an ulcer, abscess ; the flowing of matter from a sore ; in *pl.* scrofula ; in *pl.* the drift of a remark ; the main lines of anything ; the run of an argument.

Rinning-bill, *n.* a furious or mad bull.

Rinning-darn, *n.* a disease in cows causing a severe flux.

Rinning-knot, -noose, *n.* a slip-knot.

Rinning-mink, *n.* a slip-knot.

Rino, *n.* ready-money.

Rin on, *v.* to push ; to butt as a furious bull, &c.

Rin out, *v.* to leak ; not to contain.

Rin owre, *v.* to continue without pause ; to boil over ; to overflow ; to overrun.

Rinrig, *n.* a wile ; a prank, trick ; a deep-laid scheme.

Rinse, Rinze, *v.* with *down*, to wash down. —*n.* a scrubber of heather-stems.

Rinse-, Rinze-heather, *n.* the cross-leaved heather. Cf. Ringe-heather.

Rin-shackel, *n.* a shackle which runs on a chain, with which a cow is bound in the 'byre.'

Rin-the-country, *n.* a fugitive ; one who flees the country for his misdeeds.

Rintherout, Rin-there-out, *n.* a gadabout ; a needy, homeless vagrant ; a tramp.—*adj.* given to roaming or gadding about.

Rin up, *v.* to pour into, fill up.

Rin-wa', *n.* a partition ; a wall dividing a house from one side to the other.

Rin-watter, *n.* just enough money, laid past or in hand, to pay one's way ; a struggle to make ends meet.

Riot, *n.* in *phr.* 'in full riot,' in full swing.

Rip, *v.* to cleave ; to saw wood with the grain ; to undo insufficient or badly done work ; used of cloth : to shrink so as to tear ; with *up*, to disclose, open up ; to recall old stories, grievances, &c ; to scold ; to speak impetuously ; to curse.—*n.* a rush, great speed ; anything worthless ; a reckless person ; a rascal ; a slovenly-dressed girl ; a cheat.

Rip, *v.* to search. Cf. Ripe.

Rip, Ripp, *n.* a handful of unthreshed corn or hay ; an unbound sheaf, or part of one.

Rip, *n.* an osier basket, for holding eggs, spoons, &c.

Ripe, *adj.* prevalent, abundant, rife.—*v.* to ripen.

Ripe, *v.* to search thoroughly ; to investigate narrowly ; to rob or pick one's pocket ; to clear from an obstruction ; to clean or clear out a pipe ; to break up pasture ; in *phr.* to 'ripe the ribs,' to clear the bars of a grate of ashes, cinders, &c.—*n.* a clearing-out.

Ripe-pouch, *n.* a pickpocket.

Riper, *n.* anything used for clearing a small hole or a tobacco-pipe.

Ripet, *ppl. adj.* ripened.

†Riphet, *n.* a radish. Cf. Reefart.

Riple, *v.* to take the seed off flax. Cf. Ripple.

†Riposte, *n.* a reply, retort ; a short, sharp answer.—*v.* to retort, reply.

Rippet, Rippart, Rippit, *n.* a noisy disturbance ; a romp ; an uproar ; a brisk, short quarrel ; mental disturbance or care ; a bitter-tempered, chattering creature.—*v.* to make a disturbance ; to quarrel ; to scold ; to wrangle.

Rippie, *n.* a poke-net fixed to a hoop, for catching crabs.

Ripping, *ppl. adj.* given to cleaning-out. Cf. Ripe.

Rippish, *adj.* cleanly, fastidious. Cf. Ripe.

Ripple, Rippill, *v.* to separate the seed of flax from the stalk ; with *out*, to undo badly-done work ; to separate ; to tear in pieces ; used of birds : to eat grains of standing corn ; to drizzle ; used of clouds : to open up, disperse, clear off.—*n.* an instrument with teeth like a comb for 'rippling' flax.

Ripple, *n.* a painful illness ; a fatal disease ; in *pl.* kidney trouble ; backache.

Ripple-, Rippling-grass, *n.* the ribwort plantain.

Rippler, *n.* one who 'ripples' flax.

Rippling, *n.* the operation of separating the seed of flax from the stalks.

Rippling-kaim, *n.* a toothed instrument for 'rippling' flax.

Rippon, *n.* an old, broken-down horse.

Rip-rap, *v.* used in curling : to drive on with great force, knocking the stones out of the way.—*adv.* with great violence.

Ris, *v. pret.* rose.

Risart, *n.* a red currant. Cf. Rizzard.

Rise, *v.* used of soap : to lather well in washing clothes ; to ascend, climb ; used of food : to be vomited, to have the taste repeated in the mouth ; to raise.—*n.* a steep ascent ; a practical joke.

Rise, *n.* a twig ; in *pl.* brushwood ; the branches of trees when lopped off.

Rise-up-Jack, *n.* magic, conjuring.

Rishle, *n.* a rod, wand. Cf. Rissle.

Rising, *ppl. adj.* approaching, nearing a certain age.

Risk, *v.* to make a harsh, grating sound, like the tearing of roots ; to cut grass with a reaping-hook ; to rasp ; to thrust, plunge. —*n.* a tug, pull ; a rasping, grating sound.

Risk, *n.* wet, boggy land. Cf. Reesk.

Riskish, *adj.* wet, boggy.

Risle, *n.* a rod, wand. Cf. Rissle.

Risp, *v.* to grate ; to rub with a file ; to rub hard bodies together ; to grind the teeth ; to rasp ; to whet a knife ; to make a harsh, grating sound ; to use the 'tirling-pin' ; to knock, rattle.—*n.* a harsh, grating sound ; the friction of two rough bodies ; a whetting ; a carpenter's file ; a 'tirling-pin,' used as a knocker or a door-bell.

Risp, Risple, *n.* long, coarse grass ; a stalk of hay or straw ; a bulrush.

Risp-grass, *n.* long, coarse grass.

Rispings, *n.* filings ; grated bread.

†Rissar, *v.* to dry in the sun ; to bleach in the open air. Cf. Rizzar.

Rissle, *n.* a rod, wand. Cf. Rishle.

Rissle, *n.* a red currant. Cf. Rizzle.

Rissom, *n.* a stalk or ear of corn ; an atom, particle ; the smallest possible quantity.

Rist, *v.* to make up a fire for the night.—*n.* rest. Cf. Rest.

Ristle, *n.* a kind of small plough, used to draw a deep line in the ground in order that a big plough might more easily follow.

Rit, Ritt, *v.* to incise, furrow ; to score, scratch, mark ; to cut open, slit ; to plunge ; to cut a slit in a sheep's ear.—*n.* a scratch, a slight incision ; a sheep's earmark ; a rent, opening ; a chasm ; a groove.

Rit, *n.* root. Cf. Root.

Rit-fure, *n.* the first furrow opened in ploughing ; a furrow to run off surface water in a ploughed field.

Ritnacrap, *n.* 'root nor crap,' or 'top' ; a mystery. Cf. Root.

†Ritt-master, *n.* a captain or master of horse. Cf. Rickmaster.

Rittocks, *n.* the refuse of tallow, when it is first melted and strained.

Riv, *v.* to sew roughly or slightly.

Riv, *v.* to rivet, clinch. Cf. Reeve, Roove.

Riv, *n.* a cattle- or sheep-pen. Cf. Reeve.

Riv, *v.* to rive. Cf. Rive.

Riva chair, *n.* a cleft in a rock, forming a seat.

Rive, *v.* to tear one's food ; to eat ravenously ; to pull with force ; to burst asunder ; to 'burst' from overeating ; to plough fallow, to break in new land ; used of clouds : to break ; used of a storm : to rage ; to fight, struggle together, romp roughly ; to work energetically ; to struggle on ; to toil on ; to plunge forward.—*n.* a rent, a tear ; a tug, wrench ; a piece torn off ; used of food : a piece torn off and hastily eaten ; the break of day ; a worthless lot ; energy in work, much work accomplished ; a meal to repletion, a surfeit.

Rive, *v.* to rob. Cf. Reave.

Rivel-ravel, *n.* a rigmarole, rhapsody ; nonsense.

Riven, *ppl. adj.* stolen, plundered. Cf. Reave.

Riven'd, *ppl. adj.* riven, torn.

River, *n.* a robber.

River, *n.* an energetic worker.

Rivin' fu', *adj.* full to bursting.

Riving, *ppl. adj.* energetic ; used of a storm : raging.

Riz, *v. pret.* rose.

†Rizar, Rizer, Rizar, *v.* to dry in the sun. Cf. Rizzar.

Rizer, *n.* a red currant. Cf. Rizzard.

Rizle, *v.* to beat violently. Cf. Rishle.

†Rizzar, Rizzer, Rizzor, *v.* to dry in the sun ; to cook by drying in the sun ; to bleach or dry clothes in the open air.—*n.* drying by heat, by sun-heat ; a haddock dried in the sun. Cf. Rissar.

Rizzard, Rizzart, Rizzer, *n.* a red currant. Cf. Risart.

Rizzard-haddie, *n.* a dried haddock.

Rizzen, *n.* reason.

Rizzer-berry, *n.* a red currant.

Rizzim, *n.* a stalk of corn, &c. ; an atom. Cf. Rissom.

Rizzle, *n.* a red currant.

†Rizzle, *v.* to dry by the heat of the sun or fire. Cf. Reestle.

Rizzle-buss, *n.* a red-currant bush.

Road, *n.* a direction.—*v.* to make a beaten track by repeated walking ; used of small birds : to run along the ground before the sportsman, instead of flying ; of a sporting dog : to follow game closely, to track by scent.

Road-collup, *n.* a portion of the booty paid by the robber to the laird or chief through whose lands he drove his prey.

Roadman, *n.* a carter, one who drives stones for repair of public roads ; a man in charge of the roads in a district; one in charge of the ways of a mine.

Road-money, *n.* a tax for the maintenance of the public roads.

Road-reddens, -ribbins, *n.* mud raked to the side in cleaning roads.

Road-scrapings, *n.* 'road-reddens.'

Road-side room, *n.* room to pass.

Road-stamper, *n.* a wooden leg.

Road-stoor, *n.* dust on the roads.

Roak, *n.* mist, vapour, fog. Cf. Rawk, Rouk.

Roaky, *adj.* damp; foggy, misty. Cf. Rawky, Rouky.

Roan, *n.* a roan-coloured cow.

Roan, *n.* the roe of a fish. Cf. Rawn.

Roan, *n.* a spout for carrying off water. Cf. Rone.

Roan, *n.* a tangle of brushwood, thorns, &c.; a coarse substance adhering to flax. Cf. Rone.

Roan, Roan-tree, *n.* the mountain-ash. Cf. Rowan.

Roap, *v.* to cry aloud; to sell by auction. Cf. Roup.

Roar, *v.* to cry, weep; used of a bird : to emit a loud cry; to emit a loud continuous report, as the cracking of a field of ice; used in curling : to rush with great speed; with *in*, to salute loudly.—*n.* a loud report, as a noisy eructation. Cf. Rair.

Roarer, *n.* a broken-winded horse; the barn-owl; a curling-stone driven too forcibly.

Roarer, *n.* anything large of its kind. Cf. Rorie.

Roaring-buckie, *n.* a kind of sea-shell.

Roaring-fou, *adj.* noisily drunk.

Roaring-game, -play, *n.* the game of curling.

Roary, *adj.* drunk; noisily drunk; gaudy, glaring, flashy.

Roasen, *ppl. adj.* roasted.

Roasen-like, *adj.* looking as if roasted.

Roast, *v.* to scald; to burn severely; to 'chaff,' jest.—*n.* a rough jest.

Roasted cheese, *n.* toasted cheese.

Rob, *n.* black-currant jam or jelly.

Robbie-boy, Rob-boy, *n.* a hoyden, a tomboy.

Robin-a-ree, *n.* a game played with a lighted stick.

Robin-breestie, *n.* the robin.

Robin-redbreast, *n.* the wren.

Robin-rin-the-hedge, -roun'-the-hedge, *n.* the goose-grass.

Roborate, *v.* to corroborate; to confirm legally.

Robrie, *n.* robbery.

Robustious, *adj.* robust, healthy, vigorous.

Roch, *adj.* rough; plentiful. Cf. Rouch.

Rock, *v.* to reel under the influence of drink.

Rock, *n.* a distaff.

†Rockat, Rocket, *n.* a rochet; a loose upper cloak.

Rock-banes, *n.* fossil bones.

Rock-blackbird, *n.* the ring-ouzel.

Rock-cod, *n.* the cod-fish.

Rock-doo, *n.* the wild pigeon.

Rockel, *n.* a porch, vestibule.

Rocker, *n.* one who frequents or attends a 'rocking.'

Rockety-row, *n.* a game in which two persons stand back to back, and, with arms intertwined, lift each other alternately.

Rock-heartit, *adj.* stony-hearted.

Rocking, *n.* a visit to a neighbour's house for the evening with 'rock' and spindle; a friendly gathering of neighbours with their 'rocks' and spindles; a spinning-'bee'; a lovers' assignation.

†Rocklay, Rockley, *n.* a short cloak. Cf. Rokeley.

Rockle, *n.* a pebble.

Rocklie, *adj.* abounding in pebbles.

Rock-lintie, *n.* the rock-pipit.

Rockly, *n.* a distaff. Cf. Rock.

Rockman, *n.* a cragsman who catches sea-fowl.

Rock-starling, *n.* the ring-ouzel.

Rocky, *n.* the twite.

Rodd, *n.* spawn. Cf. Redd.

Rodden, Roddin, *n.* the mountain-ash; the fruit of the mountain-ash; the red berry of the hawthorn, wild rose, and sweet briar. Cf. Rowan.

Rodden-fleuk, *n.* the turbot.

Roddie, *n.* a narrow road; a short footpath. Cf. Roddin.

Roddikin, *n.* the fourth stomach of a ruminant animal.

Roddin, *n.* a sheep-track; making tracks or narrow paths.

Rodding-time, *n.* spawning-time.

Rode, *n.* a raid, foray.

Rode, *ppl.* ridden.

Roden, Rodin, Roden-tree, *n.* the mountain-ash. Cf. Rodden.

Rodger, *n.* anything large and ugly; a big ugly animal; a big person of rude manners. —*v.* to beat with violence.

Rodikin, *n.* the fourth stomach of a ruminant. Cf. Roddikin.

Roebuck-berry, *n.* the stone-bramble berry.

Roen, *n.* a border, selvage, list; a shred. Cf. Rand, Rund.

Rogerowse, *adj.* free of speech, outspoken.

Rogie, *n.* a little rogue; a term of endearment for a child.

Rogue, *v.* to swindle, cheat.

Rogue-money, *n.* a tax for the apprehension and punishment of offenders.

Roid, *adj.* used of children: frolicsome; romping; riotous; tomboyish. Cf. Royd.

Roik, *n.* a thick mist. Cf. Rawk, Rouk.

Roil, *n.* a disturbance, storm.

Roil-fittit, *adj.* having the feet turned outwards.

Roin, *n.* a strip of cloth, selvage. Cf. Royne.

Roister, *n.* a bully; a noisy, blustering fellow; a romp.—*adj.* noisy, dissolute, riotous. Cf. Royster.

Roisting, *ppl. adj.* noisy. Cf. Roysting.

Roit, *v.* to go about aimlessly and idly; to be troublesome; to cause confusion and noise; to stir up strife.—*n.* a forward, disorderly person; an unruly animal; a babbler; a term of contempt for a woman. Cf. Royte.

Roke, *n.* fog, mist. Cf. Rouk.

Roke, *n.* a distaff. Cf. Rock.

†Rokelay, *n.* a short cloak; a ' roquelaure.'

Roll, *v.* to wrap up; to wind up; to wheel; to tie up in sheaves.—*n.* a roll of wool; a distaff; a roller. Cf. Row.

Roller, *n.* a rolling-pin; a roll of carded wool ready for spinning; a strickle for a bushel measure.

Rolloching, Rollying, *adj.* frank, free, speaking one's mind freely.

Rolment, *n.* a register, record.

Roly-poly, Rolli-poly, *n.* a name given to various games of chance played at fairs.

Romage, *v.* to rummage; to ransack; to rampage.—*n.* a disturbance. Cf. Rummage.

Roman Catholic, *n.* the red admiral butterfly.

Romantics, *n.* romancings; exaggerations.

Romble, *v.* to rumble; to stir violently; to beat. Cf. Rummle.

Rome-believer, *n.* a Roman Catholic.

Rome-blinkit, *adj.* become somewhat sour.

Romie, *n.* a small brown marble.

Rommle, *v.* to rumble; to beat, to stir violently. Cf. Rummle.

Rond, *n.* a border; a stripe; a selvage. Cf. Rand.

Rond, *v.* to thicken the heels of stockings by darning. Cf. Rand.

Rone, Ron, *n.* a tangle of brushwood, thorns, &c.; a thick growth of weeds; a coarse substance adhering to flax, which has to be scraped off in 'heckling.'

Rone, *n.* a spout for carrying off rain water; ice formed on a road by the freezing of running water or melted snow.

Rone, *n.* sheepskin dressed to imitate goatskin; roan leather.

Roneless, *adj.* lacking rain-spouts.

Rong, *v.* used of a bell: to toll like a funeral or passing-bell.

Rong, *n.* an edge, list, selvage. Cf. Rung.

Ronie, *adj.* covered with rime or sheets of ice.

Ronkly, *adj.* wrinkled. Cf. Runkly.

Ronn, *n.* a spout for rain-water; an erection of wood or metal to carry water from one place to another. Cf. Rone.

Ronnachs, *n.* couch-grass.

Ronnal, Ronnel, *n.* the female of salmon, trout, or any other fish.

Ronnet, *n.* rennet.

Ronnet-bags, *n.* the rennets for coagulating milk.

Roo, *n.* a pile of peats set on end to dry.—*v.* to pile up.

Roo, *n.* an enclosure in a grass field, in which cattle are penned up during the night.

Rood-day, *n.* the day of the Invention of the Cross, May 3 in the Romish calendar, or the Elevation of the Cross, Sept. 14 O.S. or Sept. 25 N.S.

Rood-day in barlan, *n.* May 3.

Rood-day in hairst, *n.* Sept. 25.

Rooden, *n.* the mountain-ash. Cf. Roddin.

Rood-eve, *n.* the eve of May 3; the eve of Sept. 25; the eve of 'Beltane,' June 21.

Rood-fair, *n.* a fair held on 'Rood-day.'

Rood-goose, *n.* the barnacle-goose. Cf. Radegoose.

Roodoch, Roodyoch, *n.* a hag, beldame; a deluded wretch; a savage; a villain. Cf. Ruddoch.

Rood's mass, *n.* Sept. 25.

Roof, *n.* the ceiling of a room.

Roof-rotten, *n.* the black rat.

Roof-timbers, *n.* the rafters.

Roof-tree, *n.* the beam forming the angle of a roof; one's house, home; a toast to the prosperity of one's family.

Roog, *v.* to pull hastily or roughly; to tear; to pull to pieces.—*n.* a rough or hasty pull; an article got much under its value.

Rook, *n.* a disturbance, uproar; a noisy company; a set of boisterous companions; a house swarming with inmates.—*v.* to cry like a raven or crow.

Rook, *n.* a heap, pile.—*v.* to pile up in heaps.

Rook, *n.* in *phr.* 'one's hindmost rook,' one's last farthing.

Rook, *v.* to moult.—*n.* moulting; a thin, lean animal; a term of contempt.

Rook, *v.* to clear, bare; to plunder; to cheat and despoil; to devour; to cut close.

Rook, *n.* thick mist. Cf. Rouk.

Rookery, *n.* a disturbance; a noisy quarrel.

Rookery, *n.* robbery, pillage.

Rooketty-coo, *v.* to bill and coo; to fondle.

Rooketty-doo, *n.* a tame pigeon.

Rookit, *ppl. adj.* hoarse.

Rookit, *ppl. adj.* used of a bird: moulting; of an article of dress: bare and scrimpy.

Rookit, *n.* a rissole.

†Rookly, *n.* a short coat. Cf. Rokelay.

Rooky, *adj.* misty.

Rooky, *adj.* hoarse.

†Roolye, Roolyie, *v.* to rumble; to stir about things noisily.

Roolying-tree, -stick, *n.* a stick for stirring potatoes in washing them.

Room, *n.* the best sitting-room in a small house; a compartment in a boat; a farm; a portion of land; a possession; an official situation: place in logical sequence; place in a literary work.—*adj.* roomy; unoccupied.

Room-and-kitchen, *adj.* two-roomed.

Roomatics, *n.* rheumatism.

Room-end, *n.* the end of a cottage in which the best room is situated.

Roomily, *adj.* with abundance of room.

Roon, *n.* a fish roe or spawn; a female fish; the turbot. Cf. Raun.

Roon, *v.* to whisper; to speak much and often about one thing. Cf. Roun.

Roon, Roond, *adj.* round. Cf. Round.

Roon, Roond, *n.* a shred, list, selvage. Cf. Rand, Rund.

Roond, *v.* to make a loud, hoarse noise in coughing; to grind; to make a disagreeable noise, as by grinding.

Roond-shoon, *n.* shoes made of lists plaited across each other; carpet-shoes. Cf. Rund-shoon.

Roonses, *n.* used in marbles: the claim of a player to shift to a better position at the same distance from the ring.

Roop, *n.* in *phrs.* 'roop and stoup,' 'stoup and roop,' entirely, wholly.

Roop, *v.* to shout; to cry hoarsely; to croak; to sell by auction. — *n.* a hoarse cold; hoarseness; a sale by auction. Cf. Roup.

Roop, *v.* to plunder; to devour; to ransack. Cf. Roop.

Roopit, *ppl. adj.* hoarse.

Roos, *n.* fine rain accompanied by high wind.

Roose, Roos, *v.* to praise, extol; to boast; to exaggerate or flatter in praising; to rouse.—*n.* praise, commendation; a laudatory toast; a boast.

†Roose, *v.* to water; to sprinkle with water; to use a watering-pot. Cf. Rouse.

Roose, *v.* to salt a large quantity of fish together, preparatory to curing them. Cf. Rouse.

Rooser, *n.* a boaster; one given to self-commendation.

Rooser, *n.* a watering-pot.—*v.* to water with a 'rooser.' Cf. Rouser.

Rooser, *n.* anything very large; a big lie. Cf. Rouser.

Roosh, *n.* a broil; a flux in sheep put on new pasture. Cf. Rush.

Rooshie-doucie, *n.* a tumultuous rush; a scrimmage.

Rooshoch, *adj.* coarse; robust; half-mad.

Rooshter, *n.* a severe blow.

Roosil, *v.* to cudgel. Cf. Reeshle.

Roosing, *ppl. adj.* flattering; praising.—*n.* boasting.

Roosing, *ppl. adj.* resounding; used of a fire: blazing, roaring; strong; large; of a lie: big.—*n.* a noise; noisy mirth. Cf. Rousing.

Roost, *n.* the inner roof of a cottage, composed of spars reaching from the one wall to the other; a garret.—*v.* to rest, sleep.

Roost, *n.* rust; a brownish blight on wheat.

Roost, *v.* used of a horse: to become restive. Cf. Reest, Rust.

Rooster, *n.* a cock.

Roostit, *ppl. adj.* rusted; parched, dry.

Roosty, *adj.* used of the throat: rough, hoarse.

Roosty, *adj.* stubborn, restive, irritable. Cf. Rusty.

Root, *n.* the base of a hedge; in *phr.* 'root and crap,' wholly, root and branch.—*v.* to uproot.

Root, *v.* to burrow; to rummage; to turn things over in search of anything; to 'rub along,' make shift.

Root, *v.* to roar, bellow.—*n.* a bustle, confusion. Cf. Rout.

Rooter, *v.* to work in a rough, hurried manner. —*n.* rude, unskilful work; a boorish person. Cf. Router.

Rootering, *ppl. adj.* unskilful; boorish.

Rooth, *n.* a rowlock. Cf. Rowth.

Root-hewn, *adj.* perverse, froward.

Roove, *v.* to rivet, clinch; to settle a point beyond possible alteration.—*n.* an iron rivet; a washer of iron on which a nail is clinched. Cf. Reeve, Riv.

Rooze, *v.* to praise; to flatter. Cf. Roose.

Roozer, *n.* a watering-pot.

Rope, *n.* a band for the thatch of a stack.—*v.* to band sheaves or stacks. Cf. Rape.

Roped-e'en, *n.* sore eyes, with rheumy matter hardened on the eyelashes.

Rope-ravel, *n.* a hand-rail made of rope.

Roper's-ree, *n.* a rope-walk.

Roplaw, *n.* a young fox.

Roploch, *n.* coarse cloth. Cf. Raploch.

Roppin, *v.* to wrap; to rope, tie.

Ropple, *v.* to draw the edges of a hole coarsely together; to work in a hurry and imperfectly. Cf. Rapple.

Ropple, *v.* to grow up quickly and rankly. Cf. Rapple.

Ropy, *adj.* used of twine or thread: very coarse and rough.

Ropy-e'en, *adj.* having rheumy matter hardened on the eyelashes.

Rorie, *n.* a cabbage-plant run to stalk without having formed a heart.

Rorie, Rorie-boulder, *n.* anything large of its kind. Cf. Roarer.

Rory, *adj.* drunk, 'roarin' fu"; gaudy, glaring, 'loud.'

†Rosa solis, *n.* the sundew.

Rose, *n.* erysipelas; used of potatoes: the crown end of the tubers; the part of a watering-pan that scatters the water.—*v.* used of a wound: to inflame.

Rose fever, *n.* erysipelas.

†Roseir, *n.* a rose-bush; an arbour of roses.

Rose-kaim, *n.* a fowl with a red or rose-coloured comb.

Rose-kaimed, *adj.* used of fowls: having a tightly-curled comb.

Rose-lenart, -lintie, *n.* the red-breasted linnet.

Rose-noble, *n.* the knotted figwort.

Rosert, *n.* resin.

Roset, Rosit, *n.* resin; cobblers' wax.—*v.* to rub with resin or with cobblers' wax.—*adj.* used of wood: resinous.

Roset-end, Roset-end-thread, *n.* the end of a shoemaker's waxed thread.

Rosetty, *adj.* covered with resin or cobblers' wax.

Rosetty-end, *n.* a shoemaker's waxed thread-end.

Rosie, *n.* a red clay marble.

Rosieways, *adv.* like roses.

Rosin, *n.* a bramble-thicket. Cf. Rossen.

Rosin, *n.* boasting. Cf. Roose.

Rosit, *n.* a quarrel; a disturbance.

Rossen, *n.* a bramble-thicket; a clump of thorns or briars.

Rosseny, *adj.* abounding in brushwood.

Rosy, *adj.* red.

Rot, Rott, *v.* used in oaths and imprecations; to steep flax.

Rot, *n.* six soldiers of a company.

Rot, *v.* to scratch. Cf. Rote.

Rotch, Rotchie, *n.* the little auk. Cf. Ratch.

Rotcoll, *n.* the horse-radish.

Rote, *n.* a line cut or drawn along a surface; a scratch or mark made by a point; a row. —*v.* to draw lines along a surface; to scratch with a sharp point; to make rows for cabbage, &c.

Rot-grass, *n.* the midge-grass.

Rothos, *n.* an uproar, tumult.

Rot-master, *n.* a non-commissioned officer, inferior to a corporal.

Rot-, Rott-rime, *n.* repetition by rote. Cf. Rat-rhyme.

Rot-stone, *n.* a soft stone used for scrubbing.

Rottack, Rottick, Rottich, *n.* old, musty corn; anything stored up until it becomes musty; in *pl.* grubs in a beehive; old rubbishy odds and ends stored up for possible use, but never used; lumber.

Rotten, *adj.* rainy; damp.

Rotten, Rottan, Rotton, Rottin, *n.* a rat. Cf. Ratten.

Rotten-fa', *n.* a rat-trap.

Rotten-whin, *n.* whin or trap rock of a brittle or inadhesive variety.

Rotten yow, *n.* an unwholesome person given to much expectoration.

Rouch, *adj.* rough; used of the face: long-bearded and moustached; hoarse; plentiful; well-off; luxuriant, sappy; used of a bone: having plenty of meat left on it; of the weather: stormy.—*adv.* roughly.—*n.* the coarser part of anything; the greater part of anything.—*v.* to roughen or 'frost' the shoes of a horse.

Rouch, *n.* a rowlock; the part of the gunwale between the thowls. Cf. Rowth.

Rouch and ready, *adj.* used of a meal: plentiful, but roughly served.

Rouch and richt, *adv.* entirely.—*adj.* indifferently well; rough in manners.

Rouch and round, *n.* rude plenty.—*adj.* used of a meal: plentiful, but roughly served.

Rouch girs, *n.* rough benty grass; the rough cocksfoot-grass.

Rouch-handit, *adj.* violent, daring.

Rouchle, *v.* to toss about.

Rouchness, *n.* roughness; rude plenty; abundance.

Rouch-red, *n.* a variety of potato.

Rouch-rider, *n.* a circus equestrian.

Rouch-rullion, *n.* a rude, rough fellow.

Rouchsome, *adj.* somewhat rough; rather rude in manners; rustic, unpolished.

Rouchsome-like, *adj.* rough-looking.

Rouch-spun, *adj.* rude, blunt; rough in manner or speech.

Rouchton, *n.* a strong, rough fellow.

†Roudas, Roudes, *adj.* rude, unmannerly; rough; old, haggard, grim.—*n.* a virago; an ill-natured, ugly old woman; a strong, masculine woman. Cf. Rudas.

Roudoch, *n.* a hag, beldame; a deluded wretch.—*adj.* sulky. Cf. Ruddoch.

Rouen, *ppl.* torn, riven; used especially of old pieces of dress and wooden dishes split.

Roufu', *adj.* rueful, sorrowful-looking.

Roug-a-rug, *int.* a fishwife's cry.

Rough, *n.* a rush.

Rough, *adj.* raw.

Rough, *adj.* plentiful. Cf. Rouch.

Rough bear, *n.* a coarse kind of barley.

Roughie, *n.* a withered bough, brushwood; dried heather; a torch; the torch used in leistering salmon; a wick clogged with tallow instead of being dipped.

Roughish meadow-grass, *n.* the bird-grass.

Rough tea, *n.* a 'high tea'; a 'knife-and-fork tea.'

Roughy, *n.* in *phr.* 'Auld Roughy,' a name given to the devil.

Rouk, *n.* a rook ; a rapacious person.—*v.* to deprive of everything, plunder. Cf. Rook.

Rouk, Rouke, *n.* fog, mist. Cf. Rawk.

Rouk, *n.* a riot, disturbance.

Roukery, *n.* pillage. Cf. Rookery.

Rouky, *adj.* foggy, misty. Cf. Rawky.

Roul, *n.* a colt ; a pony a year old. Cf. Rowl.

Roulie-poulie, *n.* a name given to various games of chance played at fairs. Cf. Roly-poly.

Roum, *n.* a room ; a farm ; an office or situation.—*v.* in *phr.* to 'soum and roum,' to pasture in summer and fodder in winter. Cf. Room.

Roun, *n.* the roe of a fish. Cf. Raun.

Roun, Round, *v.* to whisper ; to speak much and often about one thing.

Rounall, *n.* anything circular, as the moon.

Round, Roun, *adj.* used of coals : consisting of lumps or large pieces free from dross ; full, abundant.—*n.* the immediate neighbourhood ; a round of beef ; an accustomed way ; the way a thing should go round ; a semicircular wall of stone and 'feal,' for sheltering sheep.—*v.* to turn round.

Round, Roun, *adv.* in *phr.* 'round by,' nearer, closer in.—*v.* in *phr.* to 'get round,' to recover health.

Round-aboot-fire, *n.* the circle of persons sitting round the fire.

Round-about, *n.* a circular fort or encampment ; a fireplace with the grate so detached from the wall that persons may sit round it ; an oatcake or gingerbread cake of circular form, pinched all round with the finger and thumb ; circumlocution.

Round-about fireside, *n.* a fireplace with detached grate round which all may sit on every side.

Round-eared, *adj.* used of a woman's cap : shaped like a beehive and surrounding the ears.

Rounder, *n.* a whisperer.

Rounders, *n.* the game of prisoners' base.

Round-sound, *n.* the seed-vessels of the honesty.

Roung, *n.* a cudgel. Cf. Rung.

Rounge, *v.* to devour greedily.

Rounstow, *v.* to cut off the ears of sheep, and so obliterate distinctive marks of ownership.

Roun-tree, *n.* the mountain-ash. Cf. Rowan-tree.

Roup, *n.* the ore-weed.

Roup, *v.* to plunder ; to devour ; to explore.

Roup, *v.* to vomit.

Roup, *v.* to shout ; to cry hoarsely ; to croak ;

to sell by auction ; to sell up.—*n.* hoarseness ; the croup ; a disease affecting the throat or mouth of fowls ; a sale by auction.

Roup, *n.* a close mist.

Roup, *n.* in *phr.* 'stoup and roup,' entirely. Cf. Roop.

Roup-bill, *n.* a bill announcing an auction.

Roup-day, *n.* the day of sale by auction.

Rouped-price, *n.* the price realized at an auction.

Rouper, *n.* one who sells his goods by auction ; an auctioneer.

Roup-folk, *n.* people attending an auction.

Roup-green, *n.* the grass plot on which an auction is held.

Roupie, *adj.* overgrown with ore-weed.

Roupie, *adj.* hoarse.

Rouping, *n.* an auction.

Rouping-wife, *n.* a woman who buys at auctions to sell again.

Roupit, *ppl. adj.* hoarse ; spent with shouting.

Roup-roll, *n.* the list of articles to be sold at auction.

Roup-wife, *n.* a female auctioneer.

Roupy, *adj.* viscous, ropy.

Roupy-weather, *n.* foggy weather that makes one hoarse.

Rouse, *v.* to stir up a fire.—*n.* a reveille ; a state of excitement, a hurry.

†**Rouse,** *v.* to sprinkle with water.

Rouse, *v.* to salt herrings slightly.

Rouse, *v.* to praise ; to flatter.—*n.* commendation ; a boast. Cf. Roose.

Rouse away, *int.* haul away ! the call of a fresh-water boatswain.

Rouser, *n.* a watering-pot.

Rouser, *n.* anything very large ; a big lie.

Rousing, *ppl. adj.* resounding ; used of a fire : brisk, blazing, roaring ; strong, large ; used of a lie : big, 'thumping.'—*n.* noisy, unruly mirth.

Rousing-bell, *n.* a bell rung at 8 A.M. to arouse the 'upland' people to get ready for church.

Rousling, *ppl. adj.* rousing ; bustling. Cf. Roussillin.

Roussil, *v.* to rouse.

Roussillin, *ppl. adj.* bustling and cheerful.

Roust, *v.* to rust.—*n.* rust.

Roust, *v.* to rouse ; to rout out.

Roust, *v.* to roar ; to bellow ; to make a loud noise as on a trumpet.—*n.* a roar, a bellow ; the act of roaring or bellowing.

Rouster, *n.* a stroke, a blow.

Roustit, *ppl. adj.* rusted ; parched, dry. Cf. Roostit.

Roustree, *n.* the crossbar on which a crook is hung.

Rousty, *adj.* rusty ; hoarse.

Rout, *v.* to go to parties.

Rout, *n.* the brent-goose.

Rout, *v.* in *phrs.* to 'rout about, to poke about, to go from place to place rummaging ; to 'rout out,' to clear out.—*n.* in *phrs.* to 'rin the rout,' to gad or run about ; to 'tak' the rout,' to take to flight.

Rout, *v.* to low loudly, as cattle ; to bellow, roar ; to bray ; to make any loud noise ; to snore ; to break wind backwards.—*n.* the prolonged or angry low of a cow ; a donkey's bray ; a loud noise ; a bustle, commotion, disturbance.

Rout, *v.* to strike, beat.—*n.* a heavy blow.

Router, *n.* a cow.

Router, *v.* to do work roughly and in a hurry. —*n.* rude, unskilful work ; a person of boorish manners.

Routh, *n.* plenty, abundance.—*adj.* abundant, well-supplied. Cf. Rowth.

Routh, *n.* a rowlock ; the act of rowing.

Routhily, Routhlie, *adv.* abundantly, plentifully.

Routhless, *adj.* profane ; regardless of God and man.

Routhrie, *n.* plenty, abundance.

Routhy, *adj.* abundant ; well-furnished.

Routing, *ppl. adj.* noisy, blustering ; loud-sounding.

Routing-well, *n.* a well that makes a rumbling noise, predicting a storm.

Rove, *ppl.* riven.

Rove, *v.* to be delirious ; to rave ; to talk in one's sleep ; to have high animal spirits.— *n.* a stroll, ramble ; a wandering.

Rove, *v.* to twist yarn into rolls preparatory to spinning ; to twist ; to fasten.—*n.* a twist of rope ; a roll of cotton or yarn, to be drawn into thread by the spindle.

Rovers, *n.* in *phr.* 'at rovers,' at random.

Roving, *ppl. adj.* of unsettled character ; merry, excitable ; full of animal spirits ; used of the weather : unsettled.—*adv.* quite, excessively.—*n.* delirium, raving.

Roving-fu', *adj.* full to overflowing.

Row, Rowe, *v.* to roll ; to wrap up ; to wind, turn, move round ; with *up*, to wind up a clock ; to tie a sheaf of corn ; to make carded wool into a roll for spinning ; to nod through drowsiness ; with *about*, to be advanced in pregnancy ; used of tears : to flow.—*n.* a roll of wool ; a roll for a woman's hair ; a roll of tobacco ; a roller ; a fat, plump person.

Row, *n.* a street in a coal-mining village ; a ridge of ground ; genus, class, set.—*v.* to set out, sow, plant, place, or stand in rows ; to come up in rows.

Rowan, *n.* the mountain-ash ; its fruit.

Rowan, *n.* a flake of wool ; in *phr.* to 'cast a rowan,' to bear an illegitimate child.

Rowan, *n.* the roe of a fish ; a turbot. Cf. Raun.

Rowans, Rowins, *n.* wool made up in long rolls ready for spinning.

Rowan-tree, *n.* the mountain-ash.

Rowar, *n.* a row of carded wool ready to be spun. Cf. Roller.

Row-chow-tobacco, Rowity-chow-o'-tobacco, *n.* a game of boys in a line, holding each other's hands, and gradually coiling themselves round one at the extremity (who is called the pin), in imitation of a tobacconist winding up his roll round a pin.

Row-de-dow, Rowdy-dow, *n.* a disturbance, uproar ; a bitter quarrel.

Rowdy-dowdy, *adv.* with great confusion and noise ; in noisy disorder.

Rower, *n.* a roller ; one who wheels peats for drying.

Row-footed, *adj.* rough-footed, rough-shod.

Rowin-pin, *n.* a roller for flattening dough.

Rowk, *n.* fog, mist. Cf. Rouk.

Rowl, *v.* to roll.

Rowl, *n.* a colt, a year-old pony. Cf. Roul.

Rowle, *v.* to rule.

Rowley-powley, Rowly-powly, *n.* various games of chance played at fairs. Cf. Roly-poly.

Rowm, *n.* a situation ; a possession in land ; a place in a literary work, or in logical sequence. Cf. Room.

Rowme, *adj.* clear, empty.

Rowmmill, *v.* to clear, as a tobacco-pipe when choked, or as a fire by poking. Cf. Rummle.

Rown, Rownd, *n.* the roe of a fish ; a turbot. Cf. Raun.

Rown, *v.* to whisper. Cf. Roun.

Rowns, *n.* the berries of the mountain-ash.

Rown-tree, *n.* the mountain-ash.

Rowp, *n.* a sale by auction. Cf. Roup.

Rowsan, *ppl. adj.* vehement ; used of a fire : blazing briskly. Cf. Rousing.

Rowt, *n.* a rabble ; a party. Cf. Rout.

Rowt, *v.* to rout ; to poke. Cf. Rout.

Rowt, *v.* to bellow, roar. Cf. Rout.

Rowt, *n.* a heavy blow. Cf. Rout.

Rowth, *n.* plenty. Cf. Routh.

Roxle, *v.* to grunt ; to speak hoarsely.

†Roy, *n.* a king.

Royal, *n.* royalty ; a gold coin ; applied to certain silver coins in conjunction with the name of the reigning sovereign.

Royal, *adj.* at an advanced stage of drunkenness, 'glorious.'

Royal blue, *n.* whisky.

Royal bracken, *n.* the flowering or royal fern.

Royaleese, *v.* to play the king.

Royality, *n.* royalty.

Royalty, *n.* territory under the immediate jurisdiction of the king.

†**Royd, Royet, Royat. Royit,** *adj.* frolicsome, romping, tomboyish ; riotous, mischievous ; wild ; stormy ; unruly ; dissipated.—*v.* to romp ; to feast well.

Royetness, *n.* romping, wildness.

Royetous, *adj.* wild, unruly.

Royl-fittit, *adj.* having the feet turned outward. Cf. Roil-fittit.

Royne, *n.* a selvage. Cf. Roin.

Royne, *v.* to growl ; to grumble. Cf. Rhyne.

Royst, *adj.* wild ; dissolute.

Royster, *n.* a bully.—*adj.* noisy, riotous.

Roystering, *ppl. adj.* swaggering, blustering.

Roysting, *ppl. adj.* noisy.

Royston-crow, *n.* the hooded crow.

Roy't, *adj.* frolicsome ; unruly. Cf. Royd.

Royt, Royte, *v.* to go aimlessly or idly from place to place ; to be troublesome ; to cause confusion and noise ; to stir up strife.—*n.* a forward, disorderly person ; an unruly animal.

Rozered, *ppl. adj.* rosy ; resembling a rose.

Rozet, *n.* cobblers' wax, resin. Cf. Roset.

Rub, *v.* to rob ; to practise robbery.

Rub, *n.* an indirect reproof ; an insinuation ; a hard, grasping person.—*v.* with *on* or *upon*, to impute, impose.

Rubbage, *n.* rubbish.

Rubber, *n.* a robber.

Rubber, *n.* a scrubber.

Rubbers and reengers, *n.* a children's game, 'through the needle-e'e.'

Rubbery, *n.* robbery.

Rubbidge, *n.* rubbish.

Rubbing-bottle, *n.* a liniment.

Rubbings, *n.* a liniment.

Rubbing-stick, *n.* a stick used by shoemakers to rub leather into smoothness.

Rubbing-stock, *n.* a post set up for cattle to rub themselves against.

Ruber, *n.* a cask ; a wine-cask.

†**Rubiator,** *n.* a bully ; a swearing, worthless fellow. Cf. Rabiator.

Ruch, *adj.* rough ; plentiful.—*adv.* roughly. Cf. Rough.

Ruck, *n.* the majority, the bulk ; a mass.

Ruck, *n.* a rick, stack.—*v.* to build in a stack.

Rucker, *n.* one who builds in a stack.

Ruckle, *n.* a loose heap, a pile ; in *pl.* old, useless articles ; ruins. Cf. Rickle.

Ruckle, *n.* a crease ; a wrinkle.—*v.* to rumple, wrinkle.—*adj.* rough, uneven.

Ruckle, *v.* to breathe with difficulty ; to make a harsh, rattling sound in the throat.—*n.* a hoarse, gurgling sound made in hard breathing ; the death-rattle.

Ruckly, *adj.* rickety ; unsteady, dilapidated.

Ruction, Ruckshun, *n.* a quarrel ; a disturbance.

†**Rudas,** *adj.* bold, masculine ; stubborn, rude ; rough, unmannerly ; haggard, old.—*n.* a virago ; an ill-natured, ugly old woman.

Rudd, *n.* spawn. Cf. Redd.

Rudder, *n.* wreck, ruin, smash.

Rudder, *n.* an implement for stirring the mash in brewing.

Ruddikin, *n.* the fourth stomach of a ruminant. Cf. Roddikin.

Ruddin, *n.* the berry of the mountain-ash ; anything very sour. Cf. Rodden.

Rudding-time, *n.* spawning-time.

Ruddoch, *n.* a beldame, hag ; a deluded wretch ; a monster, villain.—*adj.* sour-looking, sulky. Cf. Roodoch, Rudas.

Ruddoch, Ruddock, *n.* the robin.

Ruddy, *n.* ruddiness, ruddy complexion.

Ruddy, *v.* to make a loud, reiterated noise ; to rumble.—*n.* a thud ; a loud, reiterated noise.

Ruddying, *n.* a loud knocking.

Rude, *n.* the complexion ; the red colour of the complexion.

Rude, *n.* spawn.

Rude, *n.* the Cross, Rood. Cf. Rood.

Rude, *n.* a rood of ground.

Rude-goose, *n.* the barnacle-goose.

†**Rudes,** *n.* an old, wrinkled, ill-natured woman. Cf. Rudas.

Rudjen, *v.* to beat.

†**Rudous,** *adj.* rude, haggard, old ; used of a woman : strongly masculine. Cf. Rudas.

Rue, *n.* regret, repentance ; in *phr.* to 'take the rue,' to change one's mind, draw back from a promise or engagement.

Rue-bargain, *n.* smart-money for breaking a bargain.

Ruech, *n.* a hill-pasture, cattle-run, summer shieling. Cf. Ruith.

Rueless, *adj.* unregretful.

Ruend, *n.* a selvage, list. Cf. Rund.

Ruff, *v.* to beat a drum ; to applaud by stamping with the feet.—*n.* the noise made by the beating of a drum ; applause made by stamping with the feet.

Ruff, *n.* an eruption on the skin.

Ruff, *v.* to ruffle ; to put in disorder.

Ruffe, *n.* fame, celebrity.

Ruffle, *v.* to insult ; to threaten.—*n.* an insurrection ; a skirmish.

Rufflet-sark, *n.* a frilled shirt.

Ruffy, *adj.* unkempt ; used of cabbages : not properly hearted.

Ruffy, *n.* a withered bough ; brushwood ; a torch used in leistering salmon ; a wick clogged with tallow. Cf. Roughie.

Ruffy-headed, *adj.* having rough, unkempt hair.

Ruft, *v.* to eructate. Cf. Rift.

Rug, Rugg, *n.* a kind of cloth for clothes.

Rug, Rugg, *v.* to pull forcibly, tug, tear.—

n. a pull, tug, bite ; dragging power ; a severe throb of pain ; an unfair advantage ; a good bargain or investment.

Rug and rive, *v.* to drag forcibly, to contend violently for possession ; to pull or haul in a quarrel.

Ruggin', *n.* used of a fowl : one tough, not easy to carve or eat.

Ruggly, *adj.* unsteady, rickety ; causing unsteady pulling or tugging. Cf. Rugl.

Ruggy-duggy, *n.* a rough, boisterous person.

Rugh, *adj.* rough. Cf. Rough.

Rugl, *v.* to shake, tug backwards and forwards.—*n.* a shake, tug, a pull backwards and forwards.

Rug-saw, *n.* a wide-toothed saw.

Ruh-heds, *n.* turfs for fuel, cut with grass adhering ; rough heads.

Ruik, *n.* a rick. Cf. Ruck.

Ruil, *n.* an unruly person or animal ; an awkward female romp.

Ruin, *v.* to soil ; to spoil.

Ruind, *n.* a border, selvage : a shred. Cf. Rand, Rund.

Ruint, *v.* to make a harsh, grating sound. Cf. Roond.

Ruise, Ruiss, *v.* to extol, praise ; to flatter. Cf. Roose.

Ruit, *n.* a root.

Ruith, *n.* hill-pasture, cattle-run ; a summershieling.

Rule, *n.* an unruly person or animal ; an awkward female romp. Cf. Ruil.

Rule o' contrary, *n.* a girls' game.

Rule-o'er-thoum, *adv.* slap-dash ; off-hand ; without consideration or accuracy.

Rulie, *adj.* unruly, talkative. Cf. Ruil.

Rullion, *n.* a shoe made of untanned leather ; a piece of thick, rough cloth ; a rough dress ; a big, coarse-looking person or animal ; a term of contempt or pity ; a noise, clatter.—*adj.* coarse ; loud, noisy.

Rullion-hand, *n.* a rude, coarse hand.

Rullion-shout, *n.* a loud, noisy shout.

Rullye, *v.* to crowd ; to sport in disorderly fashion ; to go backwards and forwards in disorder.— *n.* a rush ; a crowd. Cf. Rally.

Rum, *n.* in *phr.* 'christened rum,' rum and water.

Rum, *adj.* ingenious, especially in mischief or wickedness ; excellent of its kind.

Rumatics, *n.* rheumatism.

Rumballiach, *adj.* used of the weather : stormy ; of a person : quarrelsome.

Rumble, *v.* to shake, stir violently, push about ; to knock about ; to rummage ; to clear a tube, pipe, &c. by rod or wire.—*n.* a stir, anything causing a rumbling sound, a thunder-peal ; a cumbersome house, room, or piece of furniture. Cf. Rummle.

Rumblegarie, *adj.* disorderly ; confused in manner ; forward.—*n.* a forward person ; a romp ; a rambling, roving person.

Rumble-gumption, *n.* common-sense. Cf. Rummle-gumption.

Rumble-tumble, *n.* the rumbling sound of rushing water.—*adj.* hurried ; confused ; noisy.

Rumbling, *ppl. adj.* hungry, having a growing appetite. Cf. Ramblin-lad.

Rumel-, Rumle-gumption, -gumshion, -gumtion, *n.* common-sense ; smartness of mind.

Rumgumption, *n.* common-sense ; shrewdness.

Rumgunshoch, Rumgunshach, *adj.* used of soil : rocky, stony ; of persons : coarse, rude, unkind.—*n.* a coarse, rude person.

Ruminage, *v.* to rummage.

Rumish, *v.* to make a clattering noise in falling.—*n.* a loud, clattering noise. Cf. Reemish.

Rumlieguff, *n.* a rattling, foolish fellow.

Rummage, *v.* to rampage, storm, rage.—*n.* a great noise or disturbance.

Rummer, *n.* the mat on which the 'toddytumbler' was placed.

Rummiss, *n.* a loud, clattering noise. Cf. Rumish.

Rummle, Rummell, *n.* rubbish ; broken stones ; an unsubstantial, hurriedly built wall ; a heap of ruins.—*adj.* used of drains : formed of loose or broken stones. Cf. Ramle.

Rummle, Rummil, *v.* to rumble ; to stir violently ; to push or poke about ; to beat, knock about ; to rummage ; to clear a tube or pipe with rod or wire.—*n.* a rumble ; a thunder-peal ; anything causing a rumbling sound ; a large, inconvenient house or room ; a cumbrous piece of furniture. Cf. Rumble.

Rummle-de-thump, *n.* mashed potatoes ; a mess of potatoes and cabbage.

Rummled tatties, *n.* mashed potatoes.

Rummle-, Rummil-gairie, *n.* a rambling person ; a forward person ; a romp.— *adj.* disorderly, confused ; forward. Cf. Rumblegarie.

Rummle-, Rummel-, Rummil-gumption, -gumshon, *n.* common-sense ; shrewdness.

Rummle-hobble, *n.* confusion, disorder.

Rummle-kirn, *n.* a gully on a wild, rocky shore.

Rummle-, Rummel-shackin, *adj.* raw-boned ; loose-jointed.

Rummle-skeerie, -skerie, *n.* a madcap ; a wild, reckless romp.

Rummle-thump, *n.* potatoes and cabbage.

Rummlety-thump, *n.* mashed potatoes; 'rummle-thump.' Cf. Rummle-de-thump.

Rummlin-kirn, *n.* a gully on a wild, rocky shore.

Rummlin-sive, -syver, *n.* a drain filled up to the surface with loose stones for percolation.

Rump, *n.* an ugly, raw-boned animal, especially a cow; a contemptuous name for a person.

†Rump, *v.* to break; to cut off close; to smash, beat; to deprive a person of all his property or money, as by gambling.

Rump and dozen, *n.* the wager of a rump of beef and a dozen of wine, as a dinner.

Rump and stump, *adv.* wholly, root and branch.

Rumping, *ppl. adj.* reduced in size; growing less and less.

Rumping-shaft, *n.* a rod used by the weaver when he went to the warehouse for money for payment in advance.

Rumple, *n.* the rump; the rump-bone; the tail.

Rumple-bane, *n.* the rump-bone.

Rumpled, *ppl. adj.* used of the brain: confused.

Rumple-fyke, *n.* the itch when it has got a firm hold.

Rumple-knot, *n.* a bunch of ribbons worn at the back of the waist.

Rumple-routie, *n.* the haunch.

Rumple-tumple, *v.* to roll in play down a declivity.

Rumption, *n.* a noisy bustle within doors, driving everything into confusion.

Rumpus, *v.* to quarrel; to behave boisterously.

Rumpy-bum coat, *n.* a short, tailless coat.

Run, *n.* a border; a selvage. Cf. Rund.

Run, *v.* to compete with in running; to land smuggled goods; to fix with melted lead; to leak, let in water; to curdle.—*n.* a smuggling voyage; the track of an animal; a stretch of pasturage; a small water-channel; a pipe for carrying water from a roof, a 'rone'; a squall, blast; heavy surge on a shore caused by a past or approaching gale; business, line of goods, &c. Cf. Rin.

Run, *v.* to thicken the heels of stockings by darning. Cf. Rund.

Runagate, *adj.* vagabond; roving, unsettled. —*n.* a worthless person.

Runch, *n.* wild mustard; the wild radish.

Runch, *n.* a large, raw-boned person or animal. Cf. Runshick.

Runch, *n.* an iron instrument for twisting nuts on screw-bolts; a wrench or screw-key.

Runch, *adj.* used of whisky-punch: strong.

Runch, *v.* to crunch; to grind the teeth; to wrench, rive.—*n.* the act of crunching any harsh edible substance, or of grinding the teeth; a bite, a piece of anything taken out with the teeth; the noise of a sharp instrument piercing the flesh.

Runchie-week, *n.* the first week in May.

Runchy, Runchie, *adj.* large, raw-boned.

Runckle, Runcle, *n.* a crease, wrinkle. Cf. Runkle.

Runcy, *n.* a woman of coarse manners and doubtful character.

Rund, *n.* a border; a selvage, a list; a shred. Cf. Rand.

Rund, *v.* to thicken or protect the heels of stockings by darning or sewing. Cf. Rand.

Rund, *v.* to make a harsh, grating sound; to grind. Cf. Roond.

Rundale, *n.* the division of a farm between two persons; the working of a farm in partnership. Cf. Rendal, Run-rig.

Run-deil, *n.* a thorough devil; an incorrigible villain.

Rundge, *v.* to gnaw.

Rund-shoon, *n.* shoes made of list or selvages of cloth. Cf. Roond-shoon.

Rune, *n.* a selvage; a border. Cf. Rund.

Rung, *n.* a cudgel, staff; a stout piece of wood; a bough; a rail on the side of a cart; a bar in a chair; the spoke of a wheel; an ugly, big-boned person or animal; a contemptuous term for an old person, particularly an old woman; the stroke of poverty.—*v.* to cudgel. Cf. Runk.

Rung, *v. pret.* reigned.

Rung, *ppl. adj.* exhausted by running.

Rung, *n.* an edge, selvage, list.

Rung-cart, *n.* a cart the sides of which are made of round pieces of wood.

Runge, *v.* to rummage, to search eagerly.

Runged-stool, *n.* a stool or chair with the seat and back formed of 'rungs.'

Rung-gin, *n.* a gin worked by a 'rung-wheel.'

Rung-in, *ppl.* worn-out by fatigue. Cf. Ring in.

Rungle, Rungil-tree, *n.* a beam across a chimney for hanging pots on; a 'rantle-tree.'

Rung-wheel, *n.* a wheel with spokes which are driven by the cogs of a wheel geared into it. Cf. Rung-gin.

Runigate, *adj.* vagabond. Cf. Runagate.

Run in, *v.* to pour in.

Runjoist, *n.* a strong spar laid alongside of a roof which is to be thatched.

Runk, *n.* a fold, plait, crease; a term of anger or contempt applied to a woman; an old woman, a hag; a scandal-monger, gossip; an old, outworn, lean animal; a broken or twisted and useless branch of a tree.—*adj.* wrinkled.

Runk, *v.* to deprive one of one's possessions by any means; to attack or undermine one's character; to ruin; to satirize.

Runkar, *n.* the lump-fish.

Runkle, *v.* to wrinkle, crease, crumple.—*n.* a wrinkle, crease, crumple.

Runkly, *adj.* wrinkled, creased, crumpled.

Run-knot, *n.* a slip-knot, a knot that cannot be untied.

Run-metal, *n.* cast-iron.

Run-milk, *n.* curdled milk.

Runnagate, *adj.* vagabond; worthless.

Runner, *n.* a small channel for water; a kennel, gutter; the slice which extends across the forepart of a carcass of beef under the breast.

Running-dog, *n.* a dog given to roaming.

Running-trade, *n.* smuggling.

Run off, *v.* to pour out.

Run out, *v.* to leak; to pour into, fill up.

Run-rig, Run-ridge, *n.* land where the alternate ridges of a field belong to different owners, or are worked by different tenants.

Runse, *n.* the noise of a sharp instrument piercing the flesh. Cf. Runch.

Runse, *n.* the wild mustard; the wild radish. Cf. Runch.

Runsh, *v.* to crunch. Cf. Runch.

Runshag, Runshick, *n.* the wild mustard; the wild radish.

Runsheoch, *n.* a large, raw-boned person. Cf. Runch.

Runt, *n.* an ox or cow of small breed; an old ox or cow; a short, thickset person; an old person; a withered old man or woman, a hag; a cabbage- or 'kail'-stem, the dry, hard stalk of a plant; a short, thick stick, a 'rung,' cudgel; the tail or rump of an animal; a shaft or handle.—*v.* to grow old.

Runt, *v.* to rush out; to bounce, prance.

Runt, *v.* to rend, tear; used of cloth: to make a loud ripping sound when cut or torn.

Runt, *v.* to take all a person's money.

Runted, *ppl. adj.* stunted in growth.

Runted, *ppl. adj.* used in the game of marbles: having lost all one's marbles.

Run-the-road, -the-rout, *adj.* vagrant, gadabout.—*n.* one who has no fixed residence; a tramp, a gadabout.

Run to, *v.* to have recourse to, resort to.

Run upon, *v.* to shame, disgust, grieve.

Run-wull, *adj.* run wild; out of reach of the law.

Ruppit, *n.* an uproar, quarrel, disturbance. Cf. Rippet.

Ruralach, *n.* a rustic, native of a rural district.

†Ruse, *v.* to sprinkle with water. Cf. Rouse.

Ruse, *v.* to extol; to boast.—*n.* praise, flattery. Cf. Roose.

Ruse, *v. pret.* did rise.

Ruser, *n.* a boaster; a flatterer.

Ruser, *n.* a watering-pan.

Rush, *n.* diarrhœa in sheep, when first put on new or rank pasture; a broil.—*v.* to throw down with violence.

Rush, *n.* a rash, skin eruption.

Rush-fever, *n.* scarlet-fever.

Rushie, *n.* a broil, quarrel; a tumult.

Rushie-doucie, *n.* a tumultuous rush; a scrimmage.

Rushy, *adj.* thatched with rushes.

Rushy-wick, *n.* a rush-wick.

Rusie, *v.* to praise. Cf. Roose.

Rusk, *v.* to claw, scratch vigorously; to pluck roughly.

Rusk, *v.* to risk.—*n.* risk.

Ruskie, Rusky, *adj.* healthy, vigorous, stout; strong, of force.—*n.* a strong person of rough manners; a very stout woman.

Ruskie, Ruskey, Rusky, *n.* a seed-basket used in sowing; a basket of straw for holding oatmeal; a straw beehive; a coarse straw hat worn by peasant girls and others.

Russel, Russle, Rustle, *n.* a red currant. Cf. Rizzle.

Russel-buss, *n.* a red-currant bush.

Rusty, *adj.* used of the throat: rough, hoarse.

Rute, *n.* a blow. Cf. Rout.

Ruth, *n.* plenty. Cf. Routh.

Ruth, *adj.* kind.

Ruth, *n.* a rowlock. Cf. Rowth.

Ruthag, *n.* a young edible sea-crab.

Ruthe, *n.* the seeds of the spurrey.

Ruther, *n.* a rudder.

Ruther, *n.* an uproar; a noise; outcry.—*v.* to storm, bluster; to roar.

Rutherair, *n.* an uproar.

Ruthie, *n.* the noise in the throat or chest caused by oppressed breathing.

Rutle, *v.* to rattle; to breathe with a rattling sound, as in dying persons.—*n.* a rattling sound in the throat, the death-rattle.

Ruve, *v.* to rivet. Cf. Roove.

Ruz, Ruzie, *v.* to extol. Cf. Roose.

†Ryal, *n.* a gold coin. Cf. Royal.

Rybat, *n.* a hewn stone at the side of a window or door. Cf. Rebbit.

Rybe, *n.* a cabbage that does not heart properly; a thin, lean person or animal. Cf. Reib.

Ryce, *n.* a branch, twig; brushwood. Cf. Rise.

Rye-craik, *n.* the landrail.

Rye-kail, *n.* rye broth.

†Ryefart, *n.* a radish. Cf. Reefart.

Ryfe out, *v.* to break up land; to reclaim waste land. Cf. Rive.

Ryke, _v._ to reach.

Ryle, _v._ to entangle. Cf. Raivel.

Rymeless, _adj._ unreasonable; reckless. Cf. Rhymeless.

Rynd, _v._ to get one's affairs in order.

Rynd, _n._ a long strip of cloth. Cf. Rind.

Rynes, _n._ reins.

Rynk, _n._ a course; the course in curling, quoiting, &c. Cf. Rink.

Rynmart, _n._ a whole carcass of beef; a 'mart.' Cf. Rhind-mart.

Ryot, _n._ an assault; an illegal interference a breach of the peace.

Rype, _adj._ ripe; ready.—_v._ to ripen. Cf. Ripe.

Rype, _v._ to ransack; to rifle, to search one's pockets, &c.; to clean out a pipe; to clear the bars of a grate.—_n._ a clearing-out.

Ryss, _n._ a twig; brushwood. Cf. Rise.

Ryve, _v._ to burst asunder; to eat voraciously; to struggle on.—_n._ a rent; what is torn off; a worthless lot. Cf. Rive.

S, _n._ an iron hook shaped like the letter s.

'S, _v._ is.

Saan, _n._ sand. Cf. Sand.

Saan-blin', _adj._ purblind.

Saat, _n._ salt. Cf. Saut.

Sab, _n._ a sob; a gust, a gale of wind; a land-storm; the noise of the sea.—_v._ to sob; to make a hissing noise, as green wood, &c., in a fire; used of flowers : to fade.

Sab, _v._ to soak, saturate.

Sab, _v._ used of flooring, &c.: to subside, settle down; of a wooden floor : to make an elastic movement on the fall of a heavy body or the starting of a joist.—_n._ such an elastic motion of a floor.

Sabbathly, _adv._ on every Sabbath.

†Sabelline, _n._ sable.

Sacban, Sackbaun, _n._ an apparition, preceding a person, and portending sudden death in the house at which it stops.

†Sachet, _n._ a small sack. Cf. Sacket.

Sachless, _adj._ useless; feeble; guiltless.

Sack, _n._ a sackcloth or coarse linen garment worn by offenders in public penitence; a bottle; a term of contempt for a man.—_v._ to put into a sack or pocket. Cf. Seck.

Sacken, _n._ sacking.

Sacken-goun, -sark, -weed, _n._ a 'sack-goun.'

Sacket, _n._ a bag, a small sack; a short, dumpy person; a determined little fellow.

Sackety, _adj._ short and thick.

Sack-goun, _n._ the garb of an offender doing public penance.

Sackie, _adj._ short and thick.—_n._ a short, dumpy person.

Sackit, _n._ a small bag. Cf. Sacket.

Sackless, _adj._ blameless; guiltless, innocent; simple, inoffensive, harmless; useless, silly, feeble.

Sacklessly, _adv._ innocently.

Sacrament-time, _n._ a communion season.

†Sacrify, _v._ to consecrate.

Sacrist, _n._ a university mace-bearer, who has also charge of the cleaning of class-rooms, &c.

Sad, _adj._ solid, firm, compact, beaten hard;

used of bread, &c.: heavy; singular, remarkable, uncommon; great; flat, close to the ground.—_v._ to consolidate by tramping or otherwise; to sink, settle down; to grow solid; to sadden.—_n._ a heavy, downward, consolidating movement.

Sadden, _v._ to consolidate, beat down.

Saddle, Sadle, _n._ the part of a stall between the manger and the 'grip' or drain; a settle, a wooden seat. Cf. Sattle.

Saddle-gear, _n._ saddlery.

Saddle-irons, _n._ stirrups.

Saddle-my-nag, _n._ a boys' game.

Saddle-seat, _n._ a saddle-horse.

Saddle-sick, _adj._ sore from long riding.

Saddle-tae-side, -tae-sidlins, _adv._ side-saddle, not astride.

Saddle-tore, _n._ a saddle-bow.

Saddle-turside, _n._ a settle.

Sade, _n._ a thick sod or turf for burning; sward.

Sadjell, _n._ a lazy, unwieldy animal.

Sadlies, _adv._ sadly; to a great degree, greatly.

Sae, _adv._ so; as.

Sae, _n._ a bucket; a milk-pail; a tub. Cf. Say.

Sae-be, Saebeins, Saebins, _conj._ if so be, provided that; since.

Saed, _n._ a full-grown coal-fish. Cf. Saithe.

Saeg, _v._ to set the teeth on edge by eating anything sour. Cf. Seg.

Saeg, Saege, _n._ a name given to various species of rushes, reeds, and sedges; the water-flag. Cf. Sag, Segg.

Sael, _v._ to bind cattle in their stalls.—_n._ a rope or chain for binding cattle in their stalls. Cf. Seal.

Sae-like, _adj._ similar.

Saelkie, _n._ a seal, sea-calf; a big, stout person. Cf. Sealch.

†Saem, _n._ lard; hog- or goose-lard; fat; grease; train-oil. Cf. Saim.

Saer, _adj._ sore. Cf. Sair.

Saet, _n._ a full-grown coal-fish. Cf. Saithe.

Sae-tree, _n._ a pole for carrying pails.

Saewyse, _adv._ in such wise.

Saf, Saff, Safe, v. to save.

Safer, n. a safe.

Saft, adj. muddy; used of the weather: damp, drizzling, rainy; used of a horse: out of condition, tender; pleasant, easy; gentle; weak, simple, effeminate; easily imposed on; half-witted, foolish; amorous, 'spoony.'—adv. gently, lightly, easily.—n. cut tobacco in contrast to cake or twist; ale in contrast to whisky.

Saft-cake, n. oatcake before it is dried.

Saft-e'ened, adj. disposed to weep; soft-hearted.

Saften, v. to soften; to thaw.

Saft-fisted, adj. effeminate.

Saft-fittit, adv. quietly.

Saft-hand, n. a foolish, inexpert person.

Saft-heid, n. a simpleton, a fool.

Saft-heidit, adj. silly, foolish.

Saftick, n. the shore-crab after it has cast its shell. Cf. Safty.

Saftness, n. weakness of character.

Saft-side, n. in phr. 'one's saft-side,' one's weakness, one's good graces.

Saft-skinned, adj. sensitive; 'thin-skinned.'

Saft-soles, n. a simpleton, fool.

Saft-tobacco, n. cut tobacco.

Saft-veal, n. a simpleton.

Saft-win', n. flattery.

Safty, n. a crab that has cast its shell; a simpleton; a person easily duped; a weak, effeminate person.

Sag, n. a name given to various species of rushes, reeds, and sedges; the water-flag. Cf. Saeg, Segg.

Sagan, n. a devil; Satan.

Sag-backit, adj. used of a horse: having a sunk back.

Saggon, n. the water-flag; various species of rushes, reeds, and sedges. Cf. Sag.

Saght, v. pret. sought.

Saick, n. a sack. Cf. Seck.

Saickless, adj. guiltless; feeble. Cf. Sackless.

Saicretfu', adj. secretive.

Said, n. a thick sod for burning. Cf. Sade.

Said, n. a mature coal-fish. Cf. Saithe.

Saidle, n. a saddle. Cf. Saddle.

Saidle-turside, n. a settle.

Said-sae, n. a report.

Saig, v. to sag; to press down; to cause to bend.

Saig, n. a rush; a reed; a sedge. Cf. Sag, Segg.

Saig, n. a bull castrated when fully grown. Cf. Segg.

Saigh, v. to sigh.

Saikless, adj. innocent; feeble. Cf. Sackless.

Sail, v. to ride in a vehicle.—n. a ride in a vehicle; in phr. 'to keep a low sail,' to live quietly.

Sail-fish, n. the basking shark.

Sailing-Jack, n. the 'Blue Peter,' the flag used as a signal for sailing.

Saille, n. happiness. Cf. Seel.

Sailor-lad, n. a girls' dancing and singing game.

†Sailzie, Sailyie, n. an assault.—v. to assail.

†Saim, n. lard; goose-grease; fat; fish-oil.

†Sain, v. to make the sign of the Cross; to bless; to consecrate; to shield from evil influences of fairies, witches, &c.; to absolve of.—n. a blessing. Cf. Shane.

Sainins, n. a scolding; what one thinks of another's bad conduct.

Sainless, adj. unblessed, graceless, profane.

Saint, v. to bless. Cf. Sain.

Saint Causlan's flaw, n. a shower of snow in March.

Saint John's nut, n. a double nut.

Saint Mary knot, n. a triple knot.

Saint Mary's knot, n. in phr. to 'tie with St Mary's knot,' to hamstring.

Saint Monday, n. the day on which workmen spend Saturday's wages on drink.

Saint Peter's wort, n. the hypericum or hardhay.

Saint Sair, n. St Serf.

Saint Sair's fair, n. a fair held on St Serf's Day.

Saint's bell, n. the small church-bell rung just before service begins.

Saip, n. soap.—v. to soap. Cf. Soap.

Saip-blotts, n. soap-suds.

Saipman, n. a soap-boiler.

Saip-sapples, n. soap-suds.

Saipy, adj. soapy.

Sair, adj. sore; aching; sad, sorrowful; costly; heavy, great; 'sorry,' puny, scanty; niggardly; used of the weather: tempestuous.—adv. sorely, grievously; very, greatly; very well.—n. a wound, bruise; a crack, fracture; sorrow.

Sair, v. to serve, serve out; to treat; to serve along with an article of food; to supply with alms; used of clothes: to fit, be large enough for; to satisfy; to suffice for; with of, to satisfy with, to tire of; with out, to deal out, divide.—n. a small quantity of food, a morsel, a 'grain.'

Sair, v. to taste, smell, savour; to be appetizing; with out, to scent out, smell out.—n. a taste, smell; a stench; wit, spirit, courage; a gentle breeze; unction.

Sair aff, adj. straitened in means; greatly to be pitied.

Sairch, v. to search.—n. a search.

Sair-dowed, adj. sorely worn by grief.

Sair-dung, adj. hard put to.

Sair-fit, n. a time of need.

Sair-han', n. a mess, muddle.

Sair-heel, *n.* a time of need ; a tender spot.

Sair-heid, *n.* a headache.

Sair-hertit, *adj.* sad of heart.

Sairie, *adj.* poor ; silly ; feeble ; sorry ; sorrowful ; contemptible ; innocent ; needy ; empty.

Sairie-man, *n.* an expression of affection, often used to a dog.

Sairing, *n.* a serving, a helping ; a sufficiency of food ; a sufficient punishment ; an alms.

Sairing, *n.* a taste ; the smallest quantity or portion of anything.

Sairious, *adj.* serious.

Sairless, *adj.* savourless, tasteless, insipid. Cf. Saurless.

Sair-lump, *n.* a boil.

Sairly, *adv.* severely ; greatly ; sorely ; used intensively.

Sair miss't, *adj.* greatly missed ; deeply regretted.

Sairness, *n.* soreness.

Sair pechin', *adj.* sorely panting.

Sair-six, *n.* a rotation of crops, two each of grass and cereals, one of turnips, and one of cereals.

Sair-sought, -socht, *adj.* much exhausted ; nearly worn-out by age or weakness ; eagerly desired, anxiously sought.

Sair-sunk, *adj.* deeply sunk.

Sair-vroucht, -wroucht, -wrocht, *adj.* hard-worked.

Sair wame, *n.* colic.

Sair-won, *adj.* hardly earned.

Sairy, *adj.* sufficiently large.

Sairy, *adj.* sorry ; sorrowful. Cf. Sairie.

Sairy man, *n.* a poor fellow. Cf. Sairie-man.

Sait, *n.* a seat, chair.

Saithe, *n.* the mature coal-fish.

Saitisfee, *n.* what satisfies one, enough ; satisfaction.

Sakeless, *adj.* innocent ; feeble. Cf. Sackless.

Sakes, *int.* an excl. of anger or surprise.

Sal, Sall, *v.* shall.

Sal, Sall, *int.* a strong expletive.

Salamander, *n.* a large poker with a flat heated end for lighting fires.

Salariat, *ppl. adj.* salaried, receiving pay.

Sald, *ppl. adj.* sold.

Salder, *v.* to solder.

Sale, *n.* used of a doctor : practice.

†Salebrosity, *n.* a rough or uneven place.

Salerife, *adj.* saleable.

Sal-fat, *n.* a salt-cellar. Cf. Salt-fat.

Salie, Sallie, *n.* a hired mourner, a funeral mute. Cf. Saulie.

Sallet, *n.* salad.

Sally Walker, *n.* a children's singing-game.

Salmon-e'en, *n.* eyes like a salmon's.

Salmon-fishers, *n.* a children's singing-game.

Salmon-flounder, *n.* the flounder.

Salt, *n.* a salt-cellar ; the sea ; cost, penalty ; sarcasm ; in *pl.* Epsom salts.—*adj.* costly, expensive.—*v.* to snub. Cf. Saut.

Salt-bed, *n.* the place where ooze fit for making salt is found.

Salter, *n.* one who salts fish ; a shrewd, sharp-tongued person.

Salt-fat, *n.* a salt cellar.

Saltie, *n.* the dab.

Saltless, *adj.* senseless ; disappointing.

Saltly, *adv.* smartly ; at a heavy price.

Salt-master, *n.* an owner of 'salt-pans.'

Salt-pan, *n.* a shallow pond for making salt by evaporation.

Salt-upon-salt, *n.* refined salt.

Salty, *adj.* salt, tasting of salt.

†Salvage, *n.* a savage, barbarian.—*adj.* savage.

Salve, *v.* to save ; to prevent ; to obviate.

Saly, *n.* a funeral mute. Cf. Saulie.

†Same, *n.* lard. Cf. Saim.

Same-like, *adj.* similar.

Samen, Samine, *adj.* same ; used as a noun with *the.*

Sammer, *v.* to adjust ; to assort, match ; to agree.

Sample-swatch, *n.* a sample as pattern.

Samson, *n.* an adept, proficient.

San', Sand, *n.* a sandy-bottomed fishing-ground. —*v.* to run ashore on sand ; to nonplus.

San'-blin', *adj.* purblind.

Sanchich, *adj.* imperious and impertinent. Cf. Sanshach.

Sand, *v.* to disappear. Cf. Sant.

Sand-back, *n.* the sand-martin.

Sand-bed, *n.* an inveterate drunkard.

Sand-bunker, *n.* a small well-fenced sand-pit.

Sand-chappin', *n.* the pounding of sandstone finely for sprinkling on floors.

Sandel, Sandle, Sandile, *n.* the sand-eel ; the smelt or sperling.

Sand-fleuk, *n.* the smear-dab.

Sand-jumper, *n.* a sand-hopper, beach-flea.

Sand-kep, *n.* a wall of sand built on the beach by children to withstand the rising tide.

Sand-lairag, *n.* the common sandpiper.

Sand-lark, *n.* the common sandpiper ; the ringed plover.

Sandling, *n.* the sand-eel. Cf. Sandel.

Sand-loo, *n.* the ringed plover.

Sand-louper, *n.* a sand-hopper ; a small species of crab.

†Sandrach, *n.* bee-bread, the food provided for young bees.

Sand-tripper, *n.* the common sandpiper ; the ringed plover.

Sandy, *n.* the common sandpiper ; the sand-eel.

Sandy, *n.* a nickname for a Scotsman ; in *phr.* 'Auld Sandy,' the devil.

Sandy Campbell, *n.* a pig.

Sandy Fry, *n.* the devil.

Sandy-giddack, *n.* the sand-eel.

Sandy-laverock, *n.* the ringed plover. Cf. Sand-lairag.

Sandy-loo, *n.* the ringed plover. Cf. Sand-loo.

Sandy-mill, *n.* in *phr.* to 'big a sandy-mill,' to be in a state of intimacy.

Sandy-swallow, *n.* the sand-martin.

†Sane, *v.* to cross; to bless; to heal. Cf. Sain.

Sane, *n.* a message; a prayer. Cf. Send.

Sang, *v. pret.* singed.

†Sang, *int.* an oath, expletive; 'blood!'

Sang, *n.* song; a note, strain; a fuss, outcry, a saying.

Sang-buke, *n.* a book of songs.

Sang-note, *n.* a voice for singing; a singing note.

Sang-schule, *n.* a music-school; a class for learning to sing.

Sangster, *v.* to sing.—*n.* a songster.

Sanguine, *adj.* bloody, blood-stained.

Sanna, *v. neg.* shall not.

Sannal, *n.* the sand-eel. Cf. Sandel.

Sanneg, *n.* a kind of pear, ? the 'swan-egg.'

Sannie, *adj.* sandy.

Sannie, *n.* a Scotsman. Cf. Sandy.

Sannock-garner, *n.* the devil.

Sanshach, Sanshagh, Sanshauch, Sansheuch, Sanshuch, *adj.* wily, crafty; sarcastically clever; proud, distant; disdainful; petulant, saucy; nice, precise, peevish.

Sansie, *adj.* lucky; thriving; stout. Cf. Sonsy.

Sant, *v.* to disappear, be lost; to vanish noiselessly downward.

Sant, *n.* a saint.

Santliness, *n.* saintliness.

Sap, *n.* liquid of any kind; milk, beer, &c. taken with solid food; juice, gravy; sorrow; tears provoked by vexation or affliction.—*v.* to saturate; to moisten; to flow forth.

Sap, *n.* a simpleton, ninny, fool, 'softy.'

Sap, *n.* a sup; a gulp; a mess of food.

Sape, *n.* soap. Cf. Saip.

Sapless, *adj.* used of the weather: rainless, dry.

Sap-money, *n.* an allowance to servants for milk, liquor, &c.

Sapp, *n.* a bunch; a cluster of worms strung on worsted, for eel-fishing.—*v.* to catch or 'bob' for eels.

Sapple, *n.* a soap- or foam-bubble; in *pl.* soap-suds.—*v.* to steep or soak in soapy water, &c.

Sappy, *adj.* saturated with moisture; sodden; wet, rainy, muddy; savoury; given to drink; lively in liquor; used of kisses: sweet, pleasing; fat, plump; used of a sermon: given with unction; used of a bargain: very profitable.

Sappy-headed, *adj.* silly; stupid.

Saps, *n.* sops.

Sap-spale, *n.* sapwood, the soft layer of wood next the bark of a tree.

Saps-skull, *n.* a simpleton; a blockhead.

Sar, Sare, *v.* to savour. Cf. Sair.

Sarbit, *int.* an excl. of sorrow.

Sare, *adj.* sore.—*n.* a sore. Cf. Sair.

Sareless, *adj.* unsavoury. Cf. Sairless.

Sargeat, *n.* a kind of cloth; ? serge.

Sark, *n.* a shirt; a chemise; a nightdress.

Sark-alane, *adj.* wearing only a 'sark.'

Sarken, Sarking, *adj.* belonging to a shirt or to cloth for shirts.

Sarkfu', *n.* a shirtful; in *phr.* 'a sarkfu' o' sair banes,' the result of great fatigue, of violent exertion, or of a sound beating.

Sarking, *n.* coarse linen shirting; the wood above the rafters and immediately under the slates.

Sarkit, *n.* a short shirt or blouse.—*ppl. adj.* dressed in or possessing a shirt; used of a roof: covered with 'sarking.'

Sarkless, *adj.* without a shirt; poverty-stricken.

Sark-neck, *n.* the collar or neckband of a shirt.

Sark o' God, *n.* a surplice.

Sark-tail, *n.* the bottom of a shirt; the skirt or lower part of a dress.

Sarless, *adj.* used of a soft, limp, useless person, or of one who does not care to do too much work.

Sarrie, *adj.* sorry; feeble. Cf. Sairie.

†Sasine, *n.* investiture, 'seizin.'

Sasser-meat, *n.* sausages.

Saster, *n.* a pudding of meal and minced meat, or of minced hearts and kidneys salted, put into a 'bag' or 'tripe.'

Sat, *n.* salt. Cf. Saut.

Satchell-baggie, *n.* a wallet.

Satericals, *n.* satire.

Satisfee, *n.* enough.

Satisfice, *v.* to satisfy.

Satteral, *adj.* tart, quick-tempered. Cf. Sittrel.

Satterday, *n.* Saturday.

Satterday's slop, *n.* the time from Saturday afternoon till sunrise on Monday, during which it is unlawful to catch salmon.

Sattle, *v.* to determine a quarrel; to reduce to silence; to settle, decide; to induct a minister into a charge.

Sattle, *v.* to settle; to settle down.—*n.* a wooden seat like a sofa; a passage-way behind cows in a 'byre,' and between the urine-channels.

Sattle-chair, *n.* a long, sofa-shaped chair, frequently found in farm-kitchens and farm-cottages, and used as a bed for children.

Sattler, *n.* what determines a quarrel or reduces a person to silence.

Sattle-stane, *n.* a stone at the fireside, used as a seat.

Sattril, *adj.* sarcastic.

Saturday kebbuck, *n.* a cheese made of the overnight and morning's milk, poured cream and all into the 'yearning-tub.'

Saturday's-bairn, *n.* a child born on Saturday, who is supposed to have to work for a living.

Saturday's bawbee, *n.* a halfpenny given every Saturday to a child as pocket-money.

Sauce, *n.* impertinence; vanity, pride, display.

Saucer-meat, *n.* sausages.

Sauch, *n.* a willow.

Sauch, *n.* a hollow, murmuring sound. Cf. Sough.

Sauch-buss, *n.* a willow, a willow-bush.

Sauch-creel, *n.* a basket made of willow.

Sauchen, Sauchin, Saughen, *adj.* belonging to or made of willow; soft, weak, not energetic; of a sour, stubborn disposition; unsociable.—*n.* a willow.—*v.* to make supple or pliant.

Sauchen-toup, *n.* a simpleton, one easily duped.

Sauchen-tree, *n.* a willow-tree.

Sauchen-wand, *n.* a willow-wand, osier.

Sauchie, *adj.* abounding in willows; made of willow.

Saucht, *v. pret.* and *ppl.* sought.

Saucht, *n.* rest, quiet, peace.

Sauch-tree, *n.* a willow-tree.

Sauch-wand, *n.* a willow-wand.

Saucy, *adj.* scornful; proud, vain, conceited.

Saud, *n.* a sod. Cf. Sod.

†Sauf, Sauff, *v.* to save.—*prep.* except. —*adj.* safe.

Saugh, *n.* a willow. Cf. Sauch.

Saughe, *n.* the sum given in name of salvage.

Saugher, *v.* to walk or act in a lifeless, inactive manner.

Saughran, Saughrin, *adj.* listless, inactive; sauntering; taking good care of one's self.

Saught, *n.* ease, quiet. Cf. Saucht.

Saul, *n.* soul; spirit, mettle.—*int.* used as an expletive.

Saul, Sauld, *v. pret.* and *ppl.* sold.

Saulfu', *n.* enough to daunt the soul.

Saulie, Saullie, *n.* a funeral mute, a hired mourner; a black plume.

Saulless, *adj.* spiritless, dastardly.

Saully, *v.* to move or run from side to side; to rock or swing like a small boat at anchor. —*n.* a run from side to side; a continuous rising and falling; a swaying, swinging motion.

Saul-sleper, -sleeper, *n.* a minister who neglects the care of souls.

†Sault, *n.* a start; a leap; the start of a plough when it meets a stone. Cf. Soutt.

†Saumont, Saumon, *n.* a salmon.

Saumont-loup, *n.* a boys' game.

Saumont-raun, *n.* the roe of salmon.

Saun, *n.* sand.

Saun-blin', *adj.* purblind, near-sighted.

Saunt, *n.* a saint.

Saunt, *v.* to disappear, vanish like a spectre. Cf. Sant.

Saunter away, *v.* to waste time.

Saup, *n.* a sup; a moderate quantity of liquid. Cf. Sap.

Saur, *v.* to savour; to smell.—*n.* a savour; a smell. Cf. Sair.

Saur, Saurin, *n.* the smallest portion of anything. Cf. Sairing.

Saurless, *adj.* tasteless. Cf. Sairless.

Saut, *n.* salt; the sea; cost, penalty, smart. —*v.* to salt, pickle; to snub; to have revenge upon; to check; to heighten in price.—*adj.* costly; severe, painful.

Saut-backet, *n.* a salt-box of wood.

Saut-bree, *n.* salt-water.

Saut-cadger, *n.* an itinerant seller of salt.

Saut-cuddie, *n.* a salt-box.

Sauter, *n.* a cadger of salt; a salt-maker. Cf. Salter.

Saut-fat, -fit, *n.* a salt-cellar; a salt-box.

Saut-girnel, *n.* a salt-box.

Sautie, *n.* the dab, a species of flounder.

Sautie, Sauty, *adj.* tasting of salt.

Sautie-, Sauty-bannock, *n.* an oatmeal pancake, baked for Fastern's Eve.

Saut-kist, *n.* a salt-box.

Sautless, *adj.* insipid, saltless; senseless, without wit; disappointing.

Sautly, *adv.* dearly, highly in price.

Sautman, *n.* an itinerant seller of salt.

Saut-water, *n.* the sea; the seaside.

Saut-water-fleuk, *n.* the dab.

Saut-water-fowk, *n.* visitors to the seaside.

Savage, *n.* a young animal difficult to rear.

†Savendie, Sauvendie, *n.* sagacity, knowledge.

Savendle, *adj.* strong, secure; trustworthy; to be depended on. Cf. Sevendle.

†Savie, *n.* common-sense, perception.—*adj.* wise, sagacious, experienced.

Saving, *n.* the savings bank.—*prep.* except.

Savour, *n.* a bad smell; a disgust; unction in preaching.—*v.* to taste; to scent out. Cf. Sair, Saur.

Savoury, *adj.* possessing unction.

Saw, *n.* a salve, an ointment.

Saw, *v.* to sow. Cf. Sow.

Saw-bill, *n.* the goosander; the red-breasted merganser.

Sawcer, *n.* a maker or seller of sauces.

Sawer, *n.* a sower.

Sawf, *n.* a prognostication.

Sawins, *n.* sawdust.

Sawin'-sheet, *n.* a sheet used in sowing grain.

Sawlie, *n.* a funeral mute. Cf. Saulie.

Sawmer, *v.* to agree ; to adjust. Cf. Sammer.

†**Sawmon,** *n.* a salmon. Cf. Saumont.

Sawney, Sawnie, *n.* a Scotsman. Cf. Sandy.

Sawnie, *adj.* sandy.

Sawr, *n.* a gentle breeze ; a disgust. Cf. Sair.

Sawstick, Sawstock, *n.* a log of rough-hewn timber.

Sawt, *n.* salt. Cf. Saut.

Sax, *adj.* six.

Sax, *v.* to scarify with a sharp instrument.

Saxon shilling, *n.* a shilling of English money.

Saxpence, *n.* sixpence. Cf. Sixpence.

Saxt, *adj.* sixth.

Say, *n.* a speech ; a thing to say ; a saying ; a proverb ; an opinion, and the right to express it ; authority, influence, voice.

Say, *v.* to assay ; to test ; to try, prove ; to taste.—*n.* an assay ; an attempt ; a trial-piece of work. Cf. Sey.

Say, Saye, *n.* a bucket, milk-pail, tub. Cf. Sae.

Say, *n.* a kind of woollen cloth formerly made by families for their own use. Cf. Sey.

Say again, *v.* to disapprove of, find fault with.

Say-awa', *v.* to go on with what one is saying ; to say grace ; to begin to eat ; to 'fall to.' —*n.* loquacity ; a discourse, narrative ; confused talking.

Sayer, *n.* a poet.

Say for, *v.* to vouch for.

Say-hand, *n.* an assay, trial.

Saylch, *n.* a seal, a sea-calf. Cf. Sealch.

Say-piece, *n.* a trial-piece of work ; a first attempt at anything.

Say-shot, *n.* a trial-shot ; an opportunity in a game to regain by one stroke all that one had previously lost ; an attempt.

Scaad, *v.* to scold. Cf. Scaul.

Scaam, *v.* to singe, scorch. Cf. Scam.

Scaap, *n.* a scalp ; thin soil. Cf. Scalp.

Scab, *n.* the itch, as it appears in the human body.

Scabbit, *ppl. adj.* used of land : thin, bare, gravelly, rocky ; used of vegetation : thin, patchy ; mean, paltry ; worthless ; shabby, ill-looking.

Scabble, *v.* to scold, squabble.

Scubely, *adj.* untidy ; naked.

Scabert, *n.* a scabbard, sheath.

Scab-full, *adj.* chock-full.

Scad, Scadd, *n.* a colour obliquely or slightly seen as by reflection ; the reflection itself ; a faint gleam ; the variegated scum of mineral water.

Scad, *n.* the ray.

Scad, *v.* to soil by frequent use ; used of dress : to fade, soil.

Scad, *v.* to scald ; to heat a liquid to the boiling-point or slightly under ; to burn, scorch ; to be inflamed ; to trouble, vex ; to disgust.—*n.* anything that scalds ; any hot drink, as tea ; a scorch, burn ; an inflamed part of the body ; trouble, pain, injury ; disgust.

Sca'd, *ppl. adj.* scalled ; scabbed, scurfy ; affected with skin-disease, as eczema or ringworm.

Scaddaw, Scaddow, *n.* a shadow.

Scaddem, *n.* an incompetent smith.

Scadden, *adj.* thin, not obese.—*n.* a person of spare figure.

Scadderized, *ppl. adj.* used of persons : dry, withered.

Scaddin, *n.* the quantity scalded or to be scalded.

Scaddit-ale, -beer, *n.* a drink made of hot ale or beer and a little meal, of the consistency of gruel.

Scaddit-whey, *n.* whey boiled on a slow fire so as to become curdy.

Scaddit-wine, *n.* mulled wine.

Scade, *n.* a colour seen by reflection. Cf. Scad.

Scad-head, *n.* a scrofulous disease of the head, causing the hair to fall off.

Scadie, *adj.* burning, causing a tingling sensation.

Scadlips, *n.* thin broth apt to scald the lips.

Sca'd-man's-head, *n.* the sea-urchin's shell.

Scaff, *n.* food ; provisions ; anything got by dishonourable or importunate begging ; the act of going about in an idle or frolicsome manner ; merriment, diversion.—*v.* to provide food ; to devise means for obtaining food ; to 'sponge,' 'sorn'; to collect by dishonourable means ; to eat greedily ; to wander about idly.

Scaff, *n.* a heavy, but brief, shower of rain.

Scaff-and-raff, *n.* abundant provisions ; the dregs of the populace.

Scafferie, *n.* the contents of a larder.

Scaffie, *n.* a scavenger.

Scaffing, *n.* food of any kind ; abundance of provisions ; aimless wandering.

Scaff-raff, *n.* the dregs of the populace, the 'riff-raff.'

Scaffy, *adj.* used of a shower of rain : heavy, but soon over.

Scag, *n.* putrid fish.—*v.* to render putrid by exposure to sun and air ; to spoil a dress by carelessness or untidiness in wearing it ; to spoil the appearance of a thing. Cf. Skag.

Scaich, *v.* to obtain a thing by any means ; to obtain by craft ; to filch, steal ; to roam about for food; to go about in a silly, idle, vain manner.—*n.* a disappointment; an outlook, search. Cf. Skaigh.

Scaicher, *n.* one who 'sponges,' or who obtains anything by artful means. Cf. Skaigher.

Scail, *v.* to disperse; to scatter.—*n.* a scattering. Cf. Skail.

Scailie, *v.* to squint. Cf. Skelly.

Scaill, *v.* to disperse. Cf. Skail.

Scair, *v.* to splice.—*n.* a splice; a joint in carpentry. Cf. Skair.

Scairt, *v.* to scratch. Cf. Scart.

Scairt, *v.* to run quickly. Cf. Skirt.

Scairt, *ppl. adj.* scared, frightened. Cf. Scar.

Scairy, *n.* a shadow, reflection; a metaphor.

Scaith, *n.* injury; loss; scathe. Cf. Skaith.

Scaithless, *adj.* unharmed; harmless.

Scalbert, *n.* a low-minded, evil-living person. —*adj.* low-minded; evil-living. Cf. Scawbert.

Scalch, *n.* a morning dram or drink.

Scald, *v.* to heat; to scorch; to vex.—*n.* a hot drink; vexation. Cf. Scad.

Scald, *v.* to scold.—*n.* a scolding; one who scolds. Cf. Scaul.

Scal'd, *ppl. adj.* scabbed. Cf. Sca'd.

Scaldachan, *n.* an unfeathered nestling.

Scald-berry, *n.* the fruit of the blackberry.

Scalder, *n.* a jelly-fish.

Scalder, *n.* a sore or inflamed place.

Scaldricks, *n.* wild mustard; the wild radish. Cf. Skeldick.

Scale, *v.* to disperse; to spread about; to spill. Cf. Skail.

†**Scale-stairs**, *n.* a straight staircase in contrast to a spiral.

Scalie, *v.* to squint. Cf. Skelly.

Scall, *v.* to scold; to abuse. Cf. Scald.

Scall, *v.* to scald.—*n.* a scald. Cf. Scad.

Scallag, *n.* a bond-servant who worked five days for his master and one for himself.

Scallion, *n.* the leek.

Scallyart, *n.* a blow, stroke.

Scalp, *n.* the head, skull, as a term of contempt; a small bare knoll; thin soil barely covering rock beneath; a bank of sand or mud exposed at low tide; an oyster- or mussel-bed.—*v.* to pare off the surface of soil; to cut turf; to scrape. Cf. Scaup.

Scalpy, *adj.* bare, barren; thinly covered with soil. Cf. Scaupy.

Scalve, *n.* a shelf. Cf. Skelf.

Scam, **Scame**, *n.* a spot.—*v.* to singe, scorch; to scald slightly with steam or boiling water. Cf. Scaum.

Scamble, *v.* to shamble; to dodge about.

Scambler, *n.* a 'sponger' for food, a meal-time visitor.

Scamells, *n.* shambles Cf. Skemmel.

Scamp, *v.* to roam about idly; with *off*, to hurry off; to play mischievous tricks.—*n.* idle wandering; work badly or lazily done; a swindler.

Scan, *n.* what one can see or know; a view.

Scance, *v.* to reflect on, ponder; to glance at, scan; to look with contempt; to give a slight account of; to put to the proof; to reproach; to reflect censoriously; to form a hasty judgment.—*n.* a glance; a quick look; a hasty survey in the mind; a cursory inspection; a brief calculation; blame, reproach, scandal.

Scance, *v.* to glitter; to shine; to make a great display; to exaggerate in conversation. —*n.* a glance; a gleam.

Scancer, *n.* a showy person; an exaggerator; a gleam; a light.

Scancing, *ppl. adj.* good-looking; bouncing.

Scanclashin ?, *n.* scanty increase; a small remainder. Cf. Scantlishin.

Scandal, *v.* to scandalize ecclesiastically.

Scandal-crack, *n.* talk involving scandal.

Scandaleese, *v.* to talk or spread scandal.

Scandal-jobber, *n.* a scandal-monger.

Scandal-potion, *n.* a sarcastic name for tea.

Scannach, *v.* to gleam, shine.

Scanse, *v.* to climb.

Scanse, *v.* to glitter. Cf. Scance.

Scanse, *v.* to scan; to test. Cf. Scance.

Scansed, *ppl. adj.* seeming, having the appearance of.

Scant, *adj.* scarce, rare; few; deficient, needy; poor, badly off; parsimonious, sparing.— *adv.* scarcely.—*n.* scarcity, lack; poverty.

Scantack, *n.* a fishing-line with hooks for night-fishing in rivers, &c. Cf. Seantack.

Scantily, *adv.* scarcely.

Scantling, *n.* the juncture of a wall with the roof of a house.

Scantling, *n.* a rude sketch; a rough draft of a deed; a scanty measure or portion.—*adj.* small, very scanty.

Scantling-line, *n.* a fishing-line fixed on the bank of a stream for night-fishing; a 'scantack.'

Scantlins, *adv.* scarcely, hardly.

Scantlishin, *n.* scanty increase; a small remainder.

Scantly, *adv.* scarcely.

Scant o' grace, *n.* a graceless fellow.

Scap, *n.* the head; a bed of mussels; poor soil. Cf. Scalp, Scaup.

Scap, **Scape**, *n.* a beehive. Cf. Skep.

Scape, *n.* a landscape.

Scape-the-gallows, *n.* a thoroughly bad fellow.

Scapethrift, *n.* a spendthrift; a worthless fellow.

Scar, *n.* a bare place on the side of a steep hill, from which the sward has been washed

down by rains; a cliff, precipice; a spit
of sand or gravel running into a lake or
loch; in *pl.* rocks through which there is
an opening. Cf. Scaur.

Scar, *v.* to scare, frighten; to take fright;
used of a horse: to shy.—*n.* a fright; a
panic; an object of alarm.—*adj.* scared,
timid, shy; wild, untamed.

Scarce, *adj.* with *of*, short of.

Scarcement, *n.* the row of stones which
separates the slates of two adjoining roofs;
the edge of a ditch where thorns are to be
planted; a projection among rocks; a shelf
among rocks; the part which projects when
a 'dyke' is suddenly contracted.-

Scarce Thursday, *n.* a fair held at Melrose
on Maunday-Thursday. Cf. Skirisfurisday.

Scarcht, *n.* a hermaphrodite.

Scarcraw, *n.* a scarecrow.

Scare, *v.* to take fright.—*n.* an ugly person.—
adj. easily frightened, shy; wild; affectedly
modest; given to shying. Cf. Scar.

Scare, *v.* to splice.—*n.* a splice. Cf. Skair.

Scare, *n.* a share, a portion; pot-luck. Cf.
Skair.

Scarey, *adj.* terrifying.

Scarf, *v.* to wrap, envelop.

Scarf, *n.* the cormorant. Cf. Scart.

Scar-gait, *adj.* used of a horse: easily frightened.

Scargivenet, *n.* a girl from twelve to fourteen
years of age; a half-grown woman.

Scarnoch, *n.* a number, multitude; a noisy
tumult.

Scarnoghin, *n.* a great noise.

Scarred, *ppl. adj.* bare; precipitous.

Scarrie, *adj.* bare, rocky; full of precipices.

Scarrow, *n.* faint light; reflected light; a
shadow.—*v.* to emit a faint light; to shine
through clouds.

Scarsement, *n.* the row of stones separating
the slates of two adjoining roofs. Cf.
Scarcement.

Scart, *v.* to scratch; to strike a match; to
scrape; to clean any vessel with a spoon;
to scrape together money, &c.; to oppress
by extortion; to make a scraping, rasping
sound; to write; to write indistinctly; to
draw; to sculpture; to scatter.—*n.* a
scratch; a scratching; a stroke of the pen;
a scrap of writing; the smallest quantity of
anything; a puny or meagre-looking person;
a saving, industrious person; a niggard; a
rasping sound. Cf. Scrat.

Scart, *n.* the cormorant.

Scart, *ppl. adj.* scared.

Scartel, *n.* a scraper. Cf. Scartle.

Scart-free, *adj.* safe and sound; unharmed;
· free of expense.

Scartins, *n.* what is scraped out of any vessel.

Scartle, *v.* to scrape together by many little
strokes; to collect money by long and continuous small savings; to scatter.—*n.* an
iron tool for raking out a stable or 'byre.'

Scart-the-bowl, *n.* a niggard, skinflint.

†**Scash**, *v.* to beat, batter; to crush or press
roughly or carelessly; to squabble; to twist,
turn awry; to tread on the side of one's foot;
to turn the toes inward; to walk affectedly;
to be careless as to dress.—*n.* a blow; a
thump; a twist, wrench; a turning to one
side.—*adj.* twisted, turned to one side.—
adv. in a twisted manner; with a waddling,
shuffling gait.

Scash-foot, *n.* a foot with the toes turned
inward.

Scash-footed, *adj.* having the toes turned
inward.

Scashie, *v.* to squabble. — *n.* a wrangle.
squabble. Cf. Scash.

Scashle, *v.* to squabble, wrangle; to twist,
turn away; to tread on one side of the
foot; to turn the toes inward; to waddle
or shuffle in walking; to be careless about
one's dress.—*n.* a squabble, wrangle; a
scuffle; a twist, wrench; a turning to one
side; a waddling, shuffling walk; the noise
of shuffling feet along the ground.—*adv.* in
a waddling, shuffling manner.

Scash-mouthed, *adj.* having the mouth awry.

†**Scass**, *v.* to beat; to twist. Cf. Scash.

Scat, *n.* the sharp sound of a bullet striking a
hard substance.

Scate, *n.* a skate. Cf. Skate.

Scath, *n.* injury; loss; damage. Cf. Skaith.

Scatted, *ppl.* with *up*, littered-up.

Scatter, *v.* to stud, dot over.—*n.* a dispersion.

Scatter-cash, -good, *n.* a spendthrift.

Scatterment, *n.* a scattering, as of shot.

Scattermouch, *n.* an ill-conditioned rascal.

Scatter-witted, *adj.* senseless, hare-brained.

Scatyun, *n.* a small potato.

Scau, *v.* to lose colour. Cf. Scaw.

Scaubert, *n.* a scabbard.

Scaud, *n.* the appearance of light; a faint
gleam. Cf. Scad.

Scaud, *v.* to scald; to scorch.—*n.* a burn;
vexation; a contemptuous name for tea.
Cf. Scad.

Scaud, *ppl. adj.* scabbed; scurfy. Cf. Sca'd.

Scaudie, *adj.* burning; causing a tingling
sensation. Cf. Scadie.

Scauding, *n.* the quantity to be scalded at a
time. Cf. Scaddin.

Scaudit, *ppl. adj.* scalded.

Scaud-man's-head, *n.* the sea-urchin's shell.
Cf. Sca'd-man's-head.

Scaud o' day, *n.* the daybreak.

Scauff, *n.* provisions; a loafer.—*v.* to provide
food; to 'sponge.' Cf. Scaff.

Scaul', *v.* to scald. Cf. Scad.

Scaul, Scauld, *v.* to scold.—*n.* a scold; a scolding. Cf. Scald.

Scaum, *v.* to burn, scorch, singe; to envelop in a mist or haze, to shade.—*n.* a burn, scorch; the mark of a burn or singeing; a thin haze, a light vapour. Cf. Scam.

Scaumer, *n.* a pirate; a plunderer; a cattle-stealer.

Scaum o' the sky, *n.* the thin vapour of the atmosphere.

Scaumy, *adj.* misty, hazy.

Scaup, Scaulp, *n.* the head, skull; thin rocky soil; a bank of mud or sand exposed at low tide; an oyster- or mussel-bed; in *phr.* 'a peer scaup,' poor soil.—*v.* to scrape. Cf. Scalp.

Scaur, *n.* a bare place on the side of a hill; a cliff. Cf. Scar.

Scaur, *v.* to frighten.—*n.* a scare.—*adj.* timid; wild; prudish. Cf. Scar.

†**Scaurabee**, *n.* a term of contempt.

Scaured, *ppl. adj.* bared; precipitous.

Scaurie, *adj.* bare, rocky; full of precipices. Cf. Scarrie.

Scaurt, *n.* the cormorant. Cf. Scart.

Scaut, *ppl. adj.* scabbed. Cf. Sca'd.

Scavie, *n.* a trick, prank. Cf. Shavie.

Scaw, *n.* a barnacle.

Scaw, *v.* to become faded; to change or fade in colour, as a dress; to spoil, destroy; to destroy a colour.—*n.* a faded or spoilt mark.

Scaw, *v.* to scab.—*n.* a scab; a scall; the itch.

Scawbert, *n.* a pretentious person, one who wishes to appear above his rank; a strongly-made person of a stubborn, disagreeable temper. Cf. Scalbert.

Scawd, *n.* a faint gleam of light. Cf. Scad.

Scaw'd, Scaw't, *ppl. adj.* used of a dress: faded in colour; used of land: having bare brown patches; worthless.

Scaw'd, Scaw't, *ppl. adj.* scalled, scabbed; used of the face: having many carbuncles. Cf. Sca'd.

Scaw'd-like, *adj.* faded in colour.

Scawip, Scawp, *n.* a scalp; a bare knoll. Cf. Scalp.

Scelet, Scellet, *n.* a skeleton; a form, appearance. Cf. Skelet.

Scent, *n.* a bad smell; a sniff; the least particle.

Scentage, *n.* aroma, flavour.

Scent-bean, *n.* a fragrant bean, carried in snuff-boxes to perfume the snuff.

Scent-dog, *n.* a pointer.

Sch (*for many* **Sch** *words see* **Sh** *words*).

Schachel, *v.* to distort. Cf. Shachle.

Schafe, *n.* a slice. Cf. Shave.

Schafts, *n.* the jaws, cheeks. Cf. Chafts, Shafts.

Schald, *adj.* shallow.—*n.* a shallow place. Cf. Shald.

Schamlich, *v.* to shamble.—*adj.* shambling, weak in the legs, puny.—*n.* a weak, puny person or animal.

Scharge, *n.* a puny child. Cf. Sharger.

Schavel, *n.* a rogue.

Schaw, *n.* a wood of small size; a glade; a grove.

Schech, *v.* to search; to obtain by craft; to filch. Cf. Skaigh.

Schell-fowl, *n.* the sheldrake.

†**Schelm, Schellum**, *n.* a rascal, rogue. Cf. Skellum.

Schenachy, *n.* a bard; a story-teller; a chronicler of heroic deeds. Cf. Seannachie.

Scheu, *v.* to scare away, to 'shoo.'

Schew, *v.* to swing. Cf. Shew.

Schiff, *n.* a sieve.

Schlaffert, *n.* a blow, buffet. Cf. Sclaffert.

Schluchten, *n.* a hollow between two hills. Cf. Scluchten.

Scholard, *n.* a scholar; one who can read and write.

School, *v.* to train an animal. Cf. Schule.

School, *n.* a swarm, a great number; a shoal.

Schooling-frock, *n.* a dress worn at school.

School-penny, *n.* a school-tax.

Schowd, *v.* to waddle in walking; to swing. Cf. Showd.

Schowdin-rope, *n.* a swing.

Schowy, *adj.* containing fragments of broken flax, &c. Cf. Shows.

Schroynock, *n.* noise.

Schugh, *n.* a drain, a furrow.—*v.* to furrow; to plant temporarily. Cf. Sheugh.

Schule, *n.* a shovel.—*v.* to shovel. Cf. Shool.

Schule, *n.* a school.—*v.* to educate; to correct, rebuke; to train an animal.

Schule-brod, *n.* a school-board.

Schule-callant, *n.* a schoolboy.

Schule-craft, *n.* a school-education.

Schule-gaen, *adj.* attending school.

Schule-lear, -lare, *n.* education.

Schule-wean, *n.* a school-child.

Schute-stock, *n.* a bevel.

Sciatics, *n.* sciatica.

Scibe, *n.* a low, worthless fellow. Cf. Skibe.

Scig, *n.* a shelter; a ruse.—*v.* to shade; to hide. Cf. Scug.

Sciver, *n.* a skewer. Cf. Skiver.

Sclaff, *v.* to strike with the open hand, or with anything having a flat surface; to throw down flat; to walk clumsily without lifting the feet properly; to shuffle along.—*n.* a blow with the open hand; a slight blow; the noise made by a slight blow, or a flat, soft fall, or in shuffling the feet; a thin, light shoe; an old, worn shoe used as a slipper; anything thin and solid.—*adv.* flat, plump; with light, flat step.

Sclaffard, *n.* a slight blow; a 'sclaffert.' Cf. Sclaffert.

Sclaffer, *v.* to 'sclaff.'—*n.* a 'sclaff'; in *pl.* worn-out shoes.—*adv.* with a 'sclaff.'

Sclaffert, Sclafferd, *n.* a 'sclaff'; a rock lying horizontally in thin beds.—*v.* to 'sclaff.'

Sclaffert, *n.* the mumps.

Sclaff-fitted, *adj.* flat-footed.

Sclaip, *v.* to drag the feet in walking. Cf. Sclaup, Sclype.

Sclait, *n.* slate.

Sclaitey, *n.* a marble made of slate.

Sclamb, *v. pret.* climbed. Cf. Sclimb.

†Sclander, *n.* slander, scandal.—*v.* to slander.

Sclanderer, *n.* a slanderer; one who creates scandal.

Sclarried, *ppl. adj.* bedaubed, besmeared. Cf. Sclaurie, Clarried.

Sclasp, *v.* to clasp.—*n.* a clasp; the act of clasping.

Sclatch, *n.* an unseemly, semi-liquid mess; a large clot of mud or filth; a large spot or mark on the skin; an uncomely patch; a big, lubberly fellow; a heavy fall into water or mud, a splash; the noise of a splash; a stroke or slap with the palm of the hand; a bespattering with mud.—*v.* to bespatter, bedaub; to perform work inefficiently and clumsily; to dash violently; to fall heavily; to walk with a heavy, lumbering step.—*adv.* heavily, violently; with clumsy, lumbering gait.

Sclate, Sclat, *n.* a slate.—*v.* to cover with slate.—*adj.* of slate.

Sclate-band, *n.* a stratum of slate among bands of rock.

Sclate-pen, *n.* a slate-pencil.

Sclater, *n.* a slater.

Sclater, *n.* the wood-louse.

Sclater's eggs, *n.* little white eggs like beads found in ploughed land.

Sclate-stane, *n.* a small bit of slate; a stone resembling slate.

Sclattie, *n.* a slate.

Sclaty, *adj.* slaty, like slates; abounding in slates.

Sclaup, *v.* to shuffle in walking; to walk in loose slippers.

Sclaurie, *v.* to splash with mud; to soil one's clothes; to calumniate, vilify; to scold; to call names; to pour forth abusive language. —*n.* soft mud; any semi-viscous substance, as jelly. Cf. Slaurie.

Sclave, Sclaive, *v.* to slander, calumniate.

Scleeberie, Sclibbrie, *n.* a large piece of land of little value.

Scleet, Scleit, *v.* to slide or slip smoothly or rapidly; to walk so as to wear down shoes

at one side, or as if splay-footed.—*adj.* smooth, sleek.

Sclectin-fittit, Scleetan-feeted, *adj.* having plain soles; splay-footed; given to treading one's shoes on one side.

Sclender, *adj.* slender.

Sclender, Sclenter, *n.* a loose, thin stone lying on the face of a 'scaur'; the face of a hill covered with small, loose stones.

Scienderie, *adj.* covered with small, loose stones.

Sclent, *v.* to slope; to look obliquely; to look askance; to hit or throw obliquely; to be guilty of immoral conduct; to diverge from truth, fib; to give a slanting direction; to dart askance; in relation to the eyes: to squint; to pass obliquely; to cut so as to produce a slanting side.—*n.* obliquity; acclivity, ascent; a glance; a squint.

Sclentin-ways, *adv.* obliquely.

Scleurach, *n.* a person untidy in dress and gait.

Sclibberie, *n.* a large area, generally of poor land. Cf. Scleeberie.

Sclidder, *v.* to slide, slip; to slide on ice.—*n.* in *pl.* loose stones on a slope. Cf. Slidder, Sclithers.

Scliff, *v.* to drag the feet in walking; to walk with a dull, heavy step; to stride sideways in passing with anything having a flat surface; to rub against.—*n.* dragging of the feet, a dull, heavy step; a side stroke or rub in passing; the noise made by 'scliffing'; an old broken shoe or slipper; an untidy slattern.—*adv.* with a trailing, shuffling motion.

Scliffan, *n.* a thin, useless shoe.

Scliff-sclaff, *adv.* with a dragging, shuffling step, as with loose shoes or slippers.

Sclimb, Sclim, *v.* to climb.

Sclimpet, *n.* a small, thin piece of rock or anything else.

Sclinner, *adj.* slender.

Sclither, *v.* to slide. Cf. Sclidder, Slither.

Sclitherie, *adj.* slippery.

Sclithers, *n.* loose stones lying on a hillside; places where numerous small stones lie.

Scloit, *n.* a worn-out shoe; a large, clumsy foot; an untidy, clumsy fellow.—*v.* to fall heavily. Cf. Sclyte.

Sclon, Sclone, *n.* a large piece of anything flat like a pancake.

Sclowff, *v.* to walk with a heavy tread like a flat-footed person.

Scloy, *v.* to slide.—*n.* a slide. Cf. Scly.

Scluchten, *n.* a flat-lying ridge. Cf. Schluchten.

Sclute, *v.* to throw down or pour out in a mass; to fall flat; to fall flat in mud or loose soil; to walk clumsily and with dragging feet; to walk with the toes much turned out.—*n.* a thin, semi-liquid mass; the fall of such a mass, and its sound; a large, clumsy foot; a lout, an awkward, clumsy fellow; a person of untidy habits.—*adv.* flat, plump; with heavy, awkward step.

Sclutt, *n.* soft and coarse till.

Sclutter, *v.* to dawdle.—*n.* a sloven. Cf. Slutter.

Scly, *v.* to slide.—*n.* a slide; a sliding motion; the place on which one slides.

Sclypach, *v.* to 'sclype.'—*n.* a 'sclype.'—*adv.* with force. Cf. Sclype.

Sclype, *v.* to dash down violently; to fall flat and heavily; to walk with a heavy, splashing step; to tear, rend; to strip off in flakes or thin shreds.—*n.* a heavy blow with the palm of the hand or anything having a flat surface; a heavy fall; the noise made by such a blow or fall; a large clot or spot; a large, thin piece of anything; a clumsy hand or foot; a misshapen shoe or bonnet; a term of contempt for a person of dirty habits; a man not much respected.—*adv.* with force. Cf. Sklype.

Sclyre, *v.* to slide.—*n.* a slide. Cf. Sklyre.

Sclytach, *v.* to 'sclyte'; used intensively.

Sclyte, *v.* to throw down or pour out so as to cause a sharp sound; to fall heavily.—*n.* a thin, semi-liquid mass; a heavy fall; the sharp sound made by such a fall; a worn-out shoe; a large, clumsy foot; a clumsy, untidy fellow.—*adv.* flatly; suddenly, as with a fall. Cf. Cloit.

Sclyter, *v.* to 'sclyte'; used intensively.—*n.* a quantity, mass.

Sclyterach, *v.* to 'sclyter'; used intensively.

Scoan, *n.* a round, flat cake. Cf. Scon.

Scob, Scobb, *n.* a splint; a wooden gag; a limber rod of willow, hazel, &c. used for fastening down thatch; the rib of a basket. —*v.* to put in splints; to gag; to keep the mouth open by cross-pieces of wood; to peg down thatch; to take long stitches in sewing; to sew clumsily; to dip the shuttle in weaving, so that the woof appears above the warp.

Scob, Scobe, *v.* to scoop out roughly; to test a cheese by a scoop.—*n.* an instrument for scooping.

Scob, Scobe, *n.* an onion planted after vegetation has begun.

Scoberie, Scobrie, *n.* the act of careless sewing, or sewing with long stitches.

Scobie, *n.* a birchen trout-rod.

Scob-seibow, *n.* an onion allowed to remain in the ground during winter; the young shoot from an onion of the second year's growth.

Scodge, *v.* to look sly; to pilfer; to sneak about idly; to do housework; to drudge.

Scodger, *n.* a lazy lounger.

Scodgie, *n.* one who does the dirty work of a kitchen; a drudge; a mean, underhand fellow; a suspicious-looking person.—*v.* to act as a drudge; to clean, scrub.

Scodgie-lass, *n.* a female drudge.

Scog, *v.* to shelter; to secrete; to take shelter; to hide.—*n.* shelter; a sheltered place. Cf. Scug.

Scoggy, *adj.* shady.

Scogie, *n.* a kitchen-drudge, a scullion. Cf. Scodgie.

Scoil, *v.* to squeal.—*n.* a squeal.

Scok, *v.* to shelter; to shade. Cf. Scug.

Scokky, *adj.* shady.

Scold, *n.* a scolding. Ct. Scaul.

Scold, *v.* to drink healths. Cf. Scoll.

Scolder, *n.* a drinker of healths.

Scold's bridle, *n.* the 'branks,' an instrument for punishing scolding women.

Scoll, Scol, *v.* to drink to one's health, to toast; to drink hard.—*n.* the drinking of healths, a toast.

Scolle, Scole, *n.* the skull, head; the brain; brains, ability.

Scolp, *v.* to scallop.

Scomfish, *v.* to suffocate, stifle, choke, from heat, smoke, or bad smells; to spoil by heat, &c.; to disgust.—*n.* a state of suffocation; a dislike.

Scon, *v.* to crush flat; to beat with the open hand or a flat surface; to inflict corporal punishment, generally on the buttocks.—*n.* a stroke with the palm of the hand, &c.

Scon, *v.* to make flat stones skip along the surface of water; used of flat bodies: to skip along, as in 'ducks and drakes.' Cf. Scun.

Scon, *n.* a flat, round cake of flour, &c., baked on a 'girdle'; anything flat or round like a 'scon'; a piece of dried dung used as fuel; a sample or specimen of anything; the old broad Lowland 'bonnet.'

Scon-, Scone-cap, *n.* a man's flat, broad 'bonnet.'

Scounce, *n.* a slight erection as a shelter from the wind; a stone-hewer's shed; a screen; a seat fixed in the wall or near the fireplace.—*v.* to guard, protect; to take up a position of security; to keep off, turn aside; to extort, cheat; to trick out of; to jilt or slight a woman.

Scone, *v.* to beat with the open hand, generally on the breech. Cf. Scon.

Scone, *n.* a flat, round cake of flour, &c., baked on a 'girdle.' Cf. Scon.

Sconfice, Sconfis, *v.* to suffocate; to disgust. Cf. Scomfish.

Sconner, v. to disgust; to loathe. Cf. Scunner.

Scoo, n. a flat basket into which herrings are put when gutted. Cf. Scull.

Scoo, adj. awry.—n. anything badly made. Cf. Scoy.

Scooder, v. to scorch. Cf. Scowder.

Scooed, ppl. adj. twisted; badly made. Cf. Scoy'd.

Scoof, v. to shuffle the feet; to graze.—n. a kind of battledoor. Cf. Scuff.

Scoog, v. to shade; to shelter.—n. a shelter; a pretext. Cf. Scug, Scog.

Scook, v. to skulk, to hide; not to look one straight in the face.—n. a skulking, cowardly fellow. Cf. Scouk.

Scool, n. a swelling in the roof of a horse's mouth.

Scool, n. a shoal of fish. Cf. School.

Scool, v. to scowl.

Scooneral, n. a scoundrel.—adj. scoundrelly.

Scoonge, v. to go about like a dog; to 'cadge' for invitations to meals; to pilfer. Cf. Scounge.

Scoop, n. an offertory ladle, generally a small box with a long handle; a baler; a spoonful; a wooden drinking-cup, a 'caup'; a draught of liquor; the peak of a cap; a poke-bonnet.—v. to core an apple, &c.; to dig out the contents and leave the shell, crust, or rind of anything; to sup; to drink off, quaff; to bale a boat.

Scoop, n. range; scope; room; liberty; length of rope. Cf. Scoup.

Scoopie, n. an old-style poke-bonnet.

Scoor, n. the rattle of a hail-shower; a shower, a squall with rain. Cf. Scour.

Scoor, v. to scour; to clear out a ditch, drain, &c.; to clear, rid, free; to purge; with out, to drink off; to flog; to whip a top; to scoop.—n. a cleansing; a laxative, a purgative; diarrhœa; a big draught or dose of liquor; severe rebuke. Cf. Scour.

Scoor, v. to scamper; to plunge, drive; to discover, lay hands on, find.—n. pace; a quick walk; a run of water; a channel. Cf. Scour.

Scoorie, n. a squall with rain; a severe scolding.—adj. squally. Cf. Scoury.

Scoorie, adj. shabby, threadbare, ragged; mean in conduct; idle; disreputable; dried, parched in appearance; wasted.—n. a blackguard, a mean, disreputable person. Cf. Scourie.

Scoorin, n. a severe scolding; a drubbing; diarrhœa.

Scooriness, n. shabbiness of dress.

Scoorins, n. a kind of coarse flannel; serge. Cf. Scourins.

Scoorin' things, n. gaudy ornaments.

Scoor-the-buggie, n. the youngest child of a family.

Scoor-the-gate, n. a kind of ale causing diarrhœa.

Scoor-the-huddie, n. a chimney-sweep.

Scoor-the-kintry, adj. vagrant.—n. a vagabond.

Scoosh, v. to run for shelter: to plunge.

Scoot, n. the common guillemot; the razorbill. Cf. Skutie.

Scoot, n. a term of contempt applied to man or woman; a camp-trull; a braggadocio.

Scoot, n. a wooden drinking-vessel.

Scoot, v. to squirt; to spout; to eject water forcibly; to throw off liquid excrement; to hurry off; to dart away.—n. a squirt, syringe; a pop-gun, 'pluffer'; a gush or flow of water from a roof, and the pipe from which it flows; liquid excrement; diarrhœa.

Scoot, v. to loaf about.

Scooter, n. a squirt, syringe.

Scooter, n. the scattering of money among children at a marriage.—v. to scatter money to children at a marriage.

Scoot-gun, n. a squirt, syringe.

Scooth, n. scope; freedom of action. Cf. Scouth.

Scooti-allan, n. the Arctic gull.

Scootie, adj. low, mean, beggar-like.

Scootie, n. a wooden drinking-vessel.

Scootiefu', n. the full of a drinking-cup.

Scootiekin, n. a dram of whisky.

Scootle, v. to spill anything when carrying it. Cf. Scutle.

Scoove, v. to fly equably and smoothly. Cf. Scove.

Scop, n. range; length of rope. Cf. Scoup.

Scope, n. a gag. Cf. Scob.

Score, v. to mark a supposed witch with a cross cut on the brow, or 'above the breath,' as a protection from her cantrips.—n. a line drawn in games; a circle drawn to keep off ghosts, witches, &c.; the line in marble-playing; a deep, narrow, ragged indentation on a hillside; a narrow street on a slope; absolution from scandal; matter, affair.

Scorie, n. a game of marbles.

Scorlins, n. slimy, cord-like seaweed.

Scorn, n. jest, ridicule; a slight in love; the rejection of an offer of marriage; insult, reproach, blame.—v. to mock; to rally a woman about her lover; to allege an existing courtship between a young man and a maiden; to jilt.

Scornsum, adj. scornful; troublesome, bothering; slippery.

Scory, adj. used of a hedgehog's cheeks: wrinkled, lined. Cf. Scoury.

Scoscie, n. a starfish.

Scot, *v.* to pay taxes.

Scot, *n.* a Scotsman as distinguished from a Shetlander; in *phr.* 'Scots and English,' a boys' game.

Scotch, *n.* in *phr.* 'Scotch and English,' a boys' game.

Scotch, *n.* an ant.

Scotch-collops, *n.* beef scotched, or sliced, and stewed with onions, pepper, and salt; beef minced and stewed.

Scotch-, Scots-convoy, *n.* the accompanying of a visitor the whole way home.

Scotch cuddy, *n.* a pedlar; a travelling draper.

Scotch ell, *n.* 37·0958 inches.

Scotch European, *n.* a Scotsman living on the Continent.

Scotch fiddle, *n.* the itch.

Scotch gale, *n.* the bog-myrtle.

Scotch mark, *n.* a moral or physical defect distinguishing a particular individual.

Scotch mile, *n.* 1984 yards.

Scotch mist, *n.* a small but wetting rain.

Scotch nightingale, *n.* the sedge-warbler.

Scotify, *v.* to translate into Scotch.

Scots, *adj.* Scottish.—*n.* the Scotch language. Cf. Scotch, Scot.

Scots-rider, *n.* a gold coin worth £8, 2s. Scots.

Scots-room, *n.* room to swing the arms.

Scots Willie, *n.* a small codlin.

Scouder, *v.* to scorch, singe. Cf. Scowder.

Scouderin', *ppl. adj.* threatening; chastising, rebuking.

Scoudrum, *n.* chastisement.

Scouff, *v.* to sweep; to swoop.

Scouff, *n.* a low blackguard; a male jilt; a blusterer.—*adj.* empty; blustering.

Scoug, *v.* to shelter; to hide.—*n.* a shade; a ruse. Cf. Scug.

Scougie, *n.* a kitchen drudge.—*v.* to drudge. Cf. Scodgie.

Scouk, *v.* to skulk; to scowl; to look angry, sulky, or furtive; to go about stealthily, as if guilty; to conceal, hide; to seek shelter or hiding; to dash or flow under.—*n.* a frown, scowl; a sour, forbidding look; an evil look; a skulking, cowardly fellow; one with a downcast or dogged look; shade, shelter, protection.—*adv.* sulkily, sullenly; secretly, clandestinely.

Scouking, *ppl. adj.* ill-looking; ashamed to look up; furtive.

Scoul, *v.* to scold.

Scoulie-horned, *adj.* having the horns pointing downwards.

Scoulin, *v.* a scolding.

Scoult, *v.* to beat with the open hand; to thrash.—*n.* a blow on the palm of the hand. Cf. Scult.

Scounge, *v.* to go to and fro like a dog; to fish for invitations; to pilfer.

Scoup, *v.* to run, scamper, move briskly; to skip, leap; to spring from a place; to go off.—*n.* a blow; a sudden fall.

Scoup, *n.* a ladle; a scoop.—*v.* to hollow out; to quaff. Cf. Scoop.

Scoup, *n.* scope; range; liberty, license; length of rope; plenty of room.

Scouper, *n.* a dancer; a light, unsettled person.

Scoup-hole, *n.* a subterfuge.

Scour, *v.* to clear out; to purge; to flog.—*n.* a purgative; a cleansing; a cleanser; diarrhœa; a big draught; a severe scolding. Cf. Scoor.

Scour, *v.* to scamper; to discover.—*n.* a quick pace; a run. Cf. Scoor.

Scour, *n.* a shower; a squall. Cf. Scoor.

Scourge, *v.* to act very severely; to be a hard taskmaster; used of land: to exhaust the strength of the soil.

Scourger, *n.* one whose duty it was to rid a parish of sturdy beggars.

Scourging-hyre, *n.* an executioner.

Scourin', *n.* diarrhœa; a beating; a severe scolding. Cf. Scoorin.

Scouriness, *n.* shabbiness of dress.

Scourins, *n.* a coarse flannel. Cf. Scoorins.

Scourse, *n.* a subject of conversation.

Scoury, *adj.* shabby; mean; idle; parched in appearance.—*n.* a blackguard. Cf. Scoorie.

Scoury, *adj.* showery; squally. Cf. Scoorie.

Scoury-looking, *adj.* disreputable in appearance.

Scout, *n.* a small boat; a handy, open sailing-boat, used by smugglers.

Scout, *n.* a cobbler.

Scout, *v.* to eject liquid forcibly; to spout; to hurry off.—*n.* a squirt. Cf. Scoot.

Scout, *n.* a term of contempt for man or woman. Cf. Scoot.

Scout, *n.* the guillemot; the razor-bill. Cf. Scoot.

Scouth, *n.* room, freedom, scope, liberty to range; abundance.

Scouth and routh, *n.* freedom to range and plenty to eat.

Scouther, *n.* a slight, flying shower; a storm of wind and rain; a slight fall of snow.—*v.* to rain or snow slightly; to drizzle.

Scouther, *v.* to scorch.—*n.* a burn. Cf. Scowder.

Scouther, *v.* to make a stone skim the surface of the water.

Scouther, *n.* sea-blubber. Cf. Scowder.

Scouthered, *ppl. adj.* spoiled by rain.

Scoutherie, *adj.* abounding in flying showers; threatening rain.

Scoutherie-like, *adj.* like flying showers, threatening such.

Scoutherin, *n.* a slight quantity of fallen snow.

Scoutherin', *ppl. adj.* threatening, rebuking, chastising. Cf. Scouder.

Scoutherum *n.* a very slight shower.

Scouthie, *adj.* roomy, capacious, of large size.

Scouthry, *adj.* threatening rain. Cf. Scoutherie.

Scouti-aulin, *n.* the Arctic gull.

Scoutie, *n.* a term of contempt. Cf. Scootie.

Scout-mouth, *n.* a pursed-up mouth.

Scout-mouthed, *adj.* having a 'scout-mouth.'

Scove, *v.* to fly equably and smoothly; used of a bird : to poise on the wing.

Scovie, *n.* a fop.—*adj.* foppish.

Scovie-like, *adj.* having a foppish look.

†Scow, *n.* a small boat made of willows, &c., covered with skins.

Scow, *n.* a barrel-stave; a thin plank, from which barrel-staves are made; the outside board of a tree; a stick; a twig; in *pl.* brushwood, firewood; a bit, fragment; the fragments cut from planks; anything broken in small and useless pieces; anything tall, thin, and bony.—*v.* to knock in staves; to smash in pieces; to trim; to cut off rags or tatters.

Scowb, *n.* a splint; a sapling; a gag.—*v.* to splice; to gag; to sew clumsily; to put in splints. Cf. Scob.

Scowb and scraw, *n.* a wattle used in thatching with straw or thin pieces of turf, 'scraws.'—*adj.* all snug.

Scowder, *v.* to scorch, singe, burn; to brown in toasting.—*n.* a burn, scorch, singe; a hasty toasting; sea-blubber, owing to its power of scorching the skin; severity; painful experience.

Scowder-doup, *n.* a ludicrous designation for a smith.

Scowf, *n.* a blusterer; empty blustering; a low scoundrel. Cf. Scouff.

Scowff, *v.* to swallow at one draught.

Scowk, *v.* to skulk; to look sulky. Cf. Scouk.

Scowman, *n.* the man in charge of a 'scow' or a lighter.

Scowner, *v.* to disgust. Cf. Scunner.

Scowp, *n.* scope; range; liberty; length of rope. Cf. Scoup.

Scowp, *v.* to run, scamper; to skip.—*n.* a blow. Cf. Scoup.

Scowr, *n.* a slight shower; a squall. Cf. Scoor.

Scowrie, *n.* a scurry, bustle.

Scowrie, *n.* a scurvy fellow.—*adj.* shabby; mean. Cf. Scoorie, Scoury.

Scowry, *adj.* showery. Cf. Scoorie, Scoury.

Scowry, *adj.* scouring.

Scowth, *n.* room. Cf. Scouth.

Scowther, *n.* a slight shower; a squall. Cf. Scouther.

Scowther, *v.* to scorch. Cf. Scowder.

Scoy, *adj.* askew, awry.—*n.* anything badly made. Cf. Scoo.

Scoy'd, *ppl. adj.* twisted; badly made or done.

Scoyloch, *n.* an animal that plaits its legs in walking.

Scra', *n.* a thin slice of turf, a 'divot.' Cf. Scraw.

Scrab, *n.* a stunted or withered tree or shrub; a root; a stump of heather; a puny, shrivelled person; a thin, shrivelled limb; an undergrown, scraggy animal.

Scrab, *v.* to scratch, scrape, claw.

Scrabbie, *adj.* stunted; shrivelled.

Scrabble, *n.* a stunted tree or shrub; a thin, shrivelled limb; a puny, shrivelled person; a small, scraggy animal.

Scrabble, *v.* to tease wool.

Scrabblich, *n.* a stunted tree or shrub; a 'scrabble.' Cf. Scrabble.

†Scrabe, *n.* the Manx shearwater.

Scraber, Scrabber, *n.* the black guillemot.

Scra'-built, *adj.* built with thin turfs. Cf. Scra'.

Scrach, *v.* to scream.—*n.* a scream. Cf. Scraich.

Scrachle, *v.* to scramble, crawl, creep; to move with difficulty.—*n.* a crawl, clamber. Cf. Scrauchle.

Scrae, *n.* a shoe; an old, shrivelled shoe; a thin, skinny person or animal; anything thin or shrivelled; a skeleton; fish dried in the sun, unsalted; an ill-natured, fault-finding person; an excitable person.—*adj.* spare, meagre, lean.

Scrae-fish, *n.* unsalted fish dried in the sun.

Scrae-shankit, *adj.* having long, thin legs; spindle-legged.

Scraffle, *v.* to scramble for loose coins.—*n.* a scramble, struggle.

Scraggy, *adj.* small; spare.

Scraich, Scraigh, *v.* to shriek, scream; to cry like an alarmed hen; to neigh; to make a harsh, grating sound.—*n.* a shriek; a bird's scream or shrill cry; an urgent cry; a harsh, discordant sound; a lean, short person with a shrill voice; used of day : the dawn. Cf. Screigh.

Scraicher, *n.* one who 'scraichs.'

Scraighton, *n.* a person fond of screaming.

Scraik, *v.* to scream, screech.—*n.* a screech; used of day : the break, the dawn. Cf. Scraich.

Scraip, *v.* to scrape. Cf. Scrape.

Scrall, *v.* to crawl.

Scrammle, *v.* to scramble.

Scramp, *v.* to cramp, pinch; to stint of anything.

Scran, *n.* food; a collection of miscellaneous provisions; victuals; ability; means for effecting a purpose.—*v.* to gather together; to scrape a livelihood; to save by frugality; to collect; to gain, catch; to spend money on sweets, &c.

Scranch, *v.* to grind between the teeth, crunch.

Scranel, *n.* a morsel.

Scrank, *adj.* lank, lean, ill-shaped, slender; used of writing: thin, sprawling, ill-formed. —*n.* a lean, slender person; ill-formed, sprawling writing.—*v.* to make ill-formed letters; to write in a sprawling hand.

Scrankit, *ppl. adj.* shrunken, puny.

Scranky, *adj.* lean, meagre; lank, scraggy; wrinkled; empty, shrunken; used of letters: ill-formed.—*n.* a coarse-featured person.

Scranky-looking, *adj.* thin, scraggy in appearance.

Scranky-shankit, *adj.* thin-legged.

Scranny, *adj.* thin, meagre, scraggy; of inferior quality, scanty.—*n.* an ill-natured old woman.

Scran-pock, *n.* a beggar's wallet for scraps; a bag carried by camp-followers to hold the spoil taken from the dead or wounded in battle.

Scran-wallet, *n.* a beggar's wallet for scraps.

Scrap, *n.* scrap-iron.

Scrap, *n.* a wallet, scrip.

Scrap, *v.* to fight; to box; to gather up; to bow, make obeisance.

Scrape, *v.* to make a scraping noise; to grub in the earth; to bow moving the foot; to shave; to gather or save money with difficulty, toil, and pinching; with *along,* to manage to live; to express scorn or derision.—*n.* a mark or scratch made by a pen; a short letter, writing; a shave; an obeisance; a pinch, difficulty in earning or saving money; a miser.

Scrape-hard, *n.* a miser; one who has difficulty in 'making ends meet.'

Scraper, *n.* a barber; a fiddler; an instrument for cleaning a 'byre'; a hat.

Scrapie, *n.* a miser.

Scrapit, *ppl. adj.* in *phrs.* 'ill-scrapit,' ill-speaking, foul-mouthed; 'weel-scrapit,' well-speaking, civil of speech.

Scrapit-face, *n.* a person of thin, haggard face.

Scraple, *n.* an instrument for cleaning a baking-board; one for cleaning a 'byre' or stable.

Scrapon, *v.* to hamper, scrimp.—*n.* a hinderer. Cf. **Scrupon.**

Scrapper, *n.* a contemptuous name for a fiddler. Cf. Scraper.

Scrat, *v.* to scratch; to make a scratching noise; to dig; to rake together; to toil for a living; to scratch with a pen; to write; to scatter.—*n.* a scratch; a meagre, scraggy, mean-looking person; a small fish; a puny, tiny child. Cf. Scart.

Scratch, *n.* in *phr.* 'up to the scratch,' thoroughly competent.

Scratch, *n.* a hermaphrodite.

Scrath, *n.* the cormorant. Cf. **Scart.**

Scratter, *n.* a coarse heather-scrubber for cleaning pots, &c.

Scratty, *adj.* small, insignificant, puny, thin.

Scrauch, Scraugh, *v.* to scream; to shriek; to utter a loud and discordant sound. Cf. Scraich.

Scrauchle, *v.* to crawl; to scramble.—*n.* a clamber.

Scraunky, *adj.* lean; lank; used of letters: ill-formed. Cf. Scranky.

Scraut, *v.* to scratch, scrape; to make a scratching noise.—*n.* a scratch or scrape. Cf. Scrat.

Scraw, *n.* a thin strip of turf; a sod for thatching a roof, used also for hens confined to peck at; in *phr.* 'scob and scraw,' giving the idea of snugness, like the roof of a house when the turfs are well secured. Cf. Scob.

Scraw-built, *adj.* built of sods.

Scrawdyin, *n.* a sickly, puny child.

Scray, *n.* an old shoe; a thin, skinny person. —*adj.* spare, lean. Cf. Scrae.

Screa, *n.* an old shoe. Cf. Scrae.

Screak, *v.* to screech, scream. Cf. Scraich, Skreek.

Scree, *n.* the débris collected on a steep mountain-side.

Screeby, *n.* the scurvy; the scurvy-grass. Cf. Scrooby.

Screech, *v.* to scream as a hen, &c. Cf. Scraich.

Screech-bird, -thrush, *n.* the fieldfare.

Screed, *n.* a long, thin strip of paper, cloth, land, &c.; a piece, bit; a rent, tear; a gap; the sound of tearing; the sound of scraping, used of a fiddle-bow on the strings; used of a pistol: shot; a large portion; a long discourse or statement; a piece of poetry; a long list; a drinking-bout, a revel; a quick movement; a snatch; anything torn off; a lie.—*v.* to tear, rend; to scream, to produce a sharp, shrill sound; to play on the fiddle; to talk tediously; to recite rapidly; to reel off; to repeat a lie, to lie; to write down at length; to do anything smartly and with spirit.

Screedge, *v.* to tear; to 'screed.'

Screef, *n.* scurf, dandriff; a thin film or

crust; a slight covering; lichen; the hard
'skin' or surface of arable land.—*v.* to
become covered with scurf, a thin film, or
hard crust; to pare a surface; to come off
in flakes of scurf. Cf. Scruff.

Screege, *v.* to scourge.

Screegh, *v.* to screech. Cf. Screigh.

Screek, *v.* to shriek.—*n.* a shriek; used of
day: daybreak, cockcrow.

Screel, *v.* to scream.

Screemage, *v.* to skirmish.—*n.* a skirmish.
Cf. Scrimmage.

Screen, *v.* to hide; to protect; to cover with
a plaid or cloak.—*n.* a large scarf worn over
the head; a plaid, cloak.

Screenge, *v.* to scrub or rub vigorously; to
pry searchingly.—*n.* a blow with a flexible
weapon. Cf. Scringe.

Screeny, *adj.* shady, screening.

Screeve, *v.* to glide along swiftly; to career;
to reel off a story; to talk, read, or sing
fast and continuously.—*n.* a lengthy, familiar
talk or chat: a learned dissertation. Cf.
Scrieve.

Screeve, *v.* to write; to scratch, scrape; to
peel.—*n.* a letter; a writing; handwriting;
a large scratch. Cf. Scrive.

Screever, *n.* a clever fellow; an expeditious
worker.

Screever, *n.* an inferior writer; a mean scribe.

Screg, *n.* a shoe. Cf. Scrae.

Scregh, *v.* to screech. Cf. Screigh.

Screigh, Screich, *v.* to shriek, scream.—*adj.*
shrill, screeching.—*n.* a shrill cry; a lean
person with a shrill voice; used of day:
the dawn. Cf. Scraich.

Screigh, *n.* whisky.

Screigh o' day, *n.* daybreak. Cf. Scraich.

Screik, *v.* to scream. Cf. Scraik.

Screive, *v.* to glide swiftly along. Cf. Screeve,
Scrieve.

Screive, *v.* to drag aside. Cf. Scrive.

Scremerston-crow, *n.* the hooded crow.

Scremit, *adj.* stingy.

Screnoch, *n.* a shrill cry; a yell; a tumult;
a noisy person.—*v.* to shout, yell; to make
a disturbance. Cf. Scroinoch.

Screw, *v.* to bore or move like a screw; used
in golf: to drive widely to the left hand.
—*n.* in *phr.* 'a screw higher,' a higher level.

Screw, *n.* the shrew-mouse.

Screw, *n.* a great number; a state of disorder.
—*v.* to swarm. Cf. Scrow.

Screw-driver, *n.* a carpenter's turnscrew.

†**Screwtore,** *n.* an escritoire. Cf. Scritor.

Screyb, *n.* a crab-apple. Cf. Scribe.

Scribble, *v.* to tease wool. Cf. Scrabble.

Scribe, *n.* a crab-apple.

Scribe, *v.* to write; to inscribe.—*n.* a mark
with a pen; a letter; a scrap of writing.

Scriddan, Scridan, *n.* a mountain-torrent.

Scrie, *n.* a great number; a crowd. Cf.
Screw.

Scrie, *v.* to cry; proclaim.—*n.* a noise; a
proclamation. Cf. Scry.

Scriech, Scriegh, *v.* to shriek. Cf. Scraich.

Scried, *n.* a drinking-bout. Cf. Screed.

Scrieve, *v.* to move quickly and gently along;
to troll a song.—*n.* a long, familiar talk.
Cf. Screeve.

Scrieve, *v.* to write; to scrape.—*n.* anything
written; a large scratch. Cf. Scrive.

Scrieve, *v.* to drag aside. Cf. Scrive.

Scrieving, *n.* the sound of a player putting
very much wind into his bagpipe.

Scriff, *n.* the scruff of the neck.

Scriff, *n.* scurf; a thin crust; a film. Cf.
Screef.

Scriffin, Scriffan, *n.* a small quantity; a
membrane; a film.

Scrift, *n.* a recitation from memory; a long-
winded story; a written composition; a
fabrication; a falsehood.—*v.* to rehearse
from memory fluently; to magnify in narration; to fib.

Scrim, *v.* to strike; to beat vigorously; to
bustle about; to work with energy and
success; to search vigorously; to move
swiftly; to rinse; to rub vigorously.

Scrim, *n.* thin, coarse cloth, used for window-
blinds; buckram.

Scrimge, *v.* to rub vigorously, to scrub; to
beat severely; to ransack, go searching from
place to place.—*n.* a hard rub; a severe
beating; a thorough search. Cf. Scringe.

Scrimger, *n.* a greedy, covetous person; a
person of disagreeable disposition and
manners.

Scrimmage, *n.* a hard rubbing; a severe
beating; a thorough, noisy, fussy search.
—*v.* to skirmish; to scramble; to rub
violently; to beat severely; to search
thoroughly and noisily. Cf. Scrummage.

Scrimmish, *n.* a skirmish.

Scrimp, *v.* to straiten; to straiten as to food
or money; to stint, pinch; to oppress by
extortion; to give short weight or measure;
to dole out scantily.—*adj.* narrow; parsimonious, niggardly; short in weight or
measure; deficient mentally.—*adv.* barely.

Scrimp, *v.* to kick violently; to act energetically. Cf. Scrim.

Scrimpiness, *n.* cutting, measuring, or weighing
out articles on sale with very great exactness.

Scrimpit, *ppl. adj.* niggardly.

Scrimpitly, *adv.* scarcely, barely, hardly.

Scrimpitness, *n.* scrimpness, scantiness.

Scrimply, *adv.* scantily; scarcely, barely;
sparingly.

Scrimps, *n.* narrow means; a short allowance.

Scrimpy, *adj.* niggardly, mean ; scanty.

Scringe, *v.* to scrub or rub vigorously ; to purge ; to scourge, flog ; to search carefully, pry about ; to run forcibly ; to wander about, turning over everything ; to glean.— *n.* a thorough cleansing ; a rub, a rubbing ; the sound of rubbing ; energetic working ; a lash, stroke ; a severe beating ; a prying, eager search ; a thorough rummage ; a gleaning ; a mean, miserly person ; a searcher ; a loose woman.—*adv.* with a sharp blow. Cf. Scrimge.

Scringe, *v.* to shrink ; to wince ; to shrivel.

Scringer, *n.* a person of energetic character, ill-disposed ; a gleaner ; one who pries about looking out for trifles ; anything large of its kind.

Scringing, *n.* fishing at night with small nets and no torches ; in *pl.* gleanings.

Scrip, *n.* a bill, reckoning.

Scripturalist, *n.* a firm believer in Holy Scripture.

†**Scritor,** *n.* an escritoire.

Scrive, *v.* to write ; to scrape, peel ; to make a harsh sound by scratching metal.—*n.* a piece of writing, a letter ; a written statement ; handwriting ; a large scratch. Cf. Screeve.

Scrive, *v.* to tear, drag asunder.

Scrive, *v.* to glide swiftly along ; to move in furious career. Cf. Screeve.

Scrivening-paper, *n.* writing-paper.

Scriver, *n.* a writer ; a paymaster ; a secretary.

Scrobe, *v.* to scratch.

Scrobie, *n.* the scurvy. Cf. Scrubie.

Scroch, *v.* to scorch, used of a sultry, oppressive day, or of a withering wind.

Scrochen't, *ppl. adj.* used of peats : sufficiently dried on the surface to allow them to be 'footed' ; twisted or gnarled by excessive heat.

Scrog, *n.* the tilt given to a cap or 'bonnet' on the head.

Scrog, Scrogg, *n.* a stunted shrub, tree, or branch ; a thorn-bush ; rough land covered with stunted bushes and underwood, the crab-apple ; a long, crooked, scraggy limb. —*adj.* stunted.

Scrog-apple, *n.* the crab-apple.

Scrogg-buss, *n.* a stunted bush.

Scrogged, *ppl. adj.* used of vegetation : thorny ; stunted ; twisted.

Scroggy, Scrogie, *adj.* stunted ; thorny ; abounding in stunted bushes or underwood.

Scroinoch, Scroinach, *n.* a shrill cry ; a yell ; a tumult ; a noisy fuss ; a noisy person.—*v.* to shout, yell ; to make a noisy disturbance.

Scroit, *n.* used of children or grown persons : a worthless, contemptible number.

Scroll, Scrol, *v.* to write.

Scronach, Scronnoch, *v.* to shout, yell.—*n.* tumult. Cf. Scroinoch.

Scrooby, *n.* the scurvy.

Scrooby-grass, *n.* the scurvy-grass.

Scrooch, Scrouch, *v.* to scorch. Cf. Scroch.

Scroof, *n.* the back of the neck ; the back of a coat-collar. Cf. Scruff.

Scroof, Scroofe, Scrooff, *n.* scurf ; a thin crust ; a film. Cf. Scruff.

Scroofin, *n.* a thin covering or scurf. Cf. Scruffin.

Scrout, *n.* a worthless set of persons. Cf. Scroit.

†**Scrow,** *n.* a scrap ; a damaged skin, fit only for making glue ; an odd bit or scrap taken from a skin ; in *pl.* various kinds of small insects found in pools and springs.—*v.* to cut off scraps, ears, and torn pieces from skins.

Scrow, *n.* a slight shower of rain.

Scrow, *n.* a number ; a crowd ; a swarm ; riot ; hurly-burly.—*v.* to swarm ; to gather in numbers. Cf. Screw, Scrie.

Scrub, *n.* a joiner's fore-plane or jack-plane ; a niggard, a mean, grasping person ; in *pl.* the husks of oats, &c.—*v.* to scrape, scratch ; to scrape together money, to live parsimoniously.

Scrubber, *n.* a small bundle of heather for cleaning pots, &c.

Scrubbieness, *n.* sordid parsimony.

Scrubble, *v.* to struggle ; to raise an uproar. —*n.* a struggle ; a difficulty to be overcome in accomplishing any work ; a squabble, uproar.

Scrubby, *adj.* lean.

Scrubie, *n.* the scurvy. Cf. Scrooby.

Scrubie-grass, *n.* the scurvy-grass.

Scrubily, *adv.* scurvily.

Scrudge, *v.* to scourge.—*n.* a scourge.

Scrufan, Scrufin, *n.* a thin covering. Cf. Scruffin.

Scruff, *n.* the back of the neck, the nape : the back of a coat-collar.

Scruff, Scruf, Scrufe, *n.* scurf, dandriff ; a thin crust or covering ; a film ; the surface of land or water.—*v.* to take off the surface of anything ; to graze, touch slightly ; to handle any subject superficially ; to plough carelessly and slightly ; to be covered with a film.

Scruffin, *n.* a thin covering or scurf ; the surface of earth.

Scruffin-time, *n.* the time for preparing land for one crop in succession to another, and covering the seed.

Scrug, *v.* in *phr.* to 'scrug one's bonnet,' to cock one's cap in order to look smart or bold. Cf. Scrog.

Scrug, *n.* a stunted bush. Cf. Scrog.

Scruinnich, *v.* to shout, yell. Cf. Scroinoch.

Scruity, *n.* the scurvy. Cf. Scrubie.

Scrummage, *n.* a scrimmage; a skirmish; a quarrel; a scramble; a hard rubbing; a severe beating; a thorough search.—*v.* to skirmish, quarrel, riot; to rub briskly; to beat severely; to search noisily. Cf. Scrimmage.

Scrump, *v.* to make a crackling noise in eating crisp bread; to make crisp; to bake hard; to crunch hard bread; used of bread: to become crisp.—*n.* crisp and hard bread. Cf. Scrumple.

Scrumpie, *adj.* crisp.

Scrumpit, *ppl. adj.* crisp, baked hard.

Scrumple, Scrumpill, *v.* to make crisp; to bake hard or roast too much by the fire; to shrivel by means of the fire; to become crisp.—*n.* anything crisp; crisp bread.

Scrumple, *v.* to crease, wrinkle, ruffle.

Scrumplie, *adj.* crisp.

Scrunch, *v.* to eat noisily.—*n.* a crunching, grating sound.

Scrunge, *v.* to rub with force; to scrub; to loaf about idly.—*n.* a rub, the act of rubbing; a severe beating; energetic working; a thorough search. Cf. Scringe.

Scrunt, *n.* anything stunted or worn down; the stump of a quill-pen; a cabbage-stalk; a stunted, insignificant person; a mean, miserly person; a walking skeleton.

Scrunt, *v.* to grate; to produce a harsh sound by grating or scraping; to scratch, scrape, scrub; to oppress or grind down.—*n.* a harsh, grating sound.

Scruntin', *ppl. adj.* stunted, dwarfed.

Scruntiness, *n.* stuntedness; scrubbiness; stubbiness.

Scruntit, *ppl. adj.* stunted, dwarfed; meagre, thin, undergrown; raw-boned.

Scruntit-like, *adj.* 'scruntit' in appearance.

Scrunty, *adj.* stunted in growth; thin, meagre; raw-boned, scraggy; stubbed, short and thick; mean, niggardly, stingy.

Scrupon, *v.* to hamper.—*n.* one who hampers.

Scrupulous, *adj.* doubtful, suspicious; curious, inquisitive.

†Scrutoire, *n.* the writing-desk or escritoire, forming the upper part of a chest of drawers. Cf. Scritor.

Scry, *n.* a great number; a crowd. Cf. Screw, Scrow.

Scry, *v.* to cry, proclaim; to announce publicly.—*n.* noise, clamour; a public proclamation of sales, fairs, banns of marriage, &c.

Scrymge, *v.* to rub vigorously; to beat severely. Cf. Scrimge.

Scrymger, *n.* a greedy, covetous person; a disagreeable person. Cf. Scrimger.

Scrynge, *v.* to rub vigorously; to search carefully. Cf. Scringe.

Scrynoch, *n.* noise, tumult.—*v.* to shout, yell. Cf. Scroinoch.

Scubble, *v.* to soil, as a schoolboy does his book.

Scud, *v.* to cause a thin stone to skim along the surface of still water; to rain slightly or in drifting showers; to quaff; to raise froth or foam upon; to slap with the open hand, with a 'tawse,' or with a ferule; to dust with a rod; to beat or whip.—*n.* a sudden movement; the rush of a stream; a sudden shower with wind, a squall; foam, froth; a blow, a slap; in *pl.* a whipping, 'licks'; foaming beer or ale.

Scud, *n.* the skin; nudity, nakedness.

Scudder, *v.* to burn slightly; to harden by heat; to brown with the fire. Cf. Scowder.

Scudder, *v.* to shudder.

Scudderin, *n.* shuddering.

Scuddie, *n.* a game like 'shinty'; the club used in such a game.

Scuddievaig, *n.* a 'scullion,' rogue. Cf Scurryvaig.

Scudding-seat, *n.* the seat in a school on which punishment was inflicted.

Scudding-stane, *n.* a thin stone used in 'ducks and drakes.'

Scuddle, *v.* to cleanse, wash; to act as a kitchen drudge; to do housework in a slatternly way; to soil, sully; to put an article of dress out of shape or colour by careless usage; to walk in a slovenly way.—*n.* a cleansing, scrubbing; kitchen drudgery; a kitchen drudge, scullion; a dress much worn or soiled; a slovenly, untidy style of working or walking.—*adv.* in a slatternly way.

Scuddle, *v.* to scurry, hurry; to wander from home in order to shirk work or duty.

Scuddler, *n.* a youngster.

Scuddler, *n.* a child who wanders from home to shirk work.

Scuddlin-boy, *n.* a young scullion or kitchen boy.

Scuddrie, *adj.* showery.

Scuddy, *adj.* naked; unfledged; scant; too small; penurious.—*n.* an undressed infant; an unfledged bird.

Scuddy-naked, *adj.* stark-naked.

Scudgie, *n.* a kitchen-drudge; a mean fellow. Cf. Scodgie.

Scudle, *v.* to wash; to act as kitchen drudge. Cf. Scuddle.

Scue, *adj.* askew. Cf. Skew.

Scuff, Scufe, *v.* to shuffle the feet, scrape with the shoes in walking; to graze; to touch lightly in passing; to brush aside; to injure slightly; to cuff, slap; to treat a subject superficially; to tarnish dress by wearing or doing rough work; to work in a light, careless manner.—*n.* a shove with the foot in walking; a slight touch or graze in passing; a puff of wind; the slight performance of work; a hasty brushing; a bat for playing at hand-ball; a battledoor.—*adv.* with a whizzing sound.

Scuff, *n.* the nape or 'scruff' of the neck.

Scuff, *n.* a sudden and passing shower of rain. —*v.* to rain slightly.

Scuff, *n.* a mean, sordid fellow.—*v.* to pilfer from the poor, or in any mean way.

Scuff, *v.* to drink off.

Scuffet, *n.* a smith's fire-shovel.

Scuffle, *v.* to work roughly and superficially; to shuffle with the feet; to whiz, to grate slightly; to graze; to rub lightly; to tarnish.—*n.* a shuffle; a graze; a slight rub; a slight grating sound; doing work superficially.—*adv.* with a whizzing sound.

Scuffle, *n.* a Dutch hoe.—*v.* to use a Dutch hoe.

Scuffle, *n.* a mop for cleaning out ovens.

Scuffy, *adj.* shabby, flimsy; worthless.

Scufter, *n.* a policeman.

Scug, *n.* a twig; a small branch.

Scug, *n.* a shade; a sheltered place; the declivity of a hill; shelter, protection; a pretext, ruse; a frown, a gloomy countenance.—*v.* to shade; to shelter, protect; to hide; to take shelter, refuge; to go in a stooping posture; to flow under; to frown, have a gloomy countenance; to crouch in order to avoid a blow; to move stealthily.

Scuggers, *n.* footless stockings worn over the shoes as gaiters, or over the arms.

Scugging-faced, -looking, *adj.* of a gloomy countenance.

Scugways, Scugwise, *adv.* stealthily.

Scuit, *n.* a wooden drinking-vessel. Cf. Scoot.

Scuit, *v.* to walk awkwardly with the feet turned much out owing to flat soles. Cf. Skute.

Sculder, *n.* ruin.

Sculder, *n.* an under-cook.

Sculduddery, Sculdudry, Sculduldry, *n.* fornication; grossness; obscenity; filthy talk; vulgar, low people; rubbish, tatters. —*adj.* adulterous; immoral; obscene, indecent, foul-mouthed.

Scule, *n.* a great collection of animals; a great number of persons. Cf. School.

Scule-time, *n.* the time one is at school.

Scule-wean, *n.* a school-child. Cf. Schule.

Scull, *n.* a fisherman's shallow wicker basket; a wickerwork cradle.

Scull, *v.* to walk in zigzag fashion; to wander.

Scull, *n.* a close-fitting cap or hat. Cf. Skull.

Scull-bonnet, *n.* a tightly-fitting cap formerly worn by judges and lawyers.

Scull-gab, *n.* a cloud shaped like a boat.

Scull-hat, *n.* a skull-cap.

Scullion, Scullian, *n.* a rogue, knave. Cf. Cullion.

Scull-row, *n.* the notch in the stern of a boat for the oar when only one is used to propel the boat.

Scult, *n.* a stroke with the open hand; a blow on the palm of the hand, a 'pandy' or 'pawmie.'—*v.* to beat with the open hand, thrash; to punish by striking the palm.

†Scum, *n.* anything skimmed; skimmed milk; a thin coating of ice; a greedy fellow, a hunks; a scamp, rascal; a worthless person. —*v.* to shave; to scrape clean; to catch the herrings that fall from the nets as they are hauled; to glance; to look at hurriedly.

Scum, *v.* to strike on the mouth.

Scumfish, *v.* to suffocate, stifle, choke with heat, smoke, or bad smell; to spoil by heat or bad smell; to disgust; to overpower. —*n.* a state of suffocation; a dislike, disgust.

Scummer, *n.* the boy who in a herring-boat catches the fish that drop from the nets when being hauled; the poke-net on the end of a pole by which he catches the falling fish.

Scummerins, *n.* the scrapings of a pot.

Scum-milk, *n.* skimmed milk.

Scummings, *n.* anything skimmed; skimmed milk.

Scun, *n.* plan; craft; intention.

Scuncheon, *n.* the corner-stone of a building; a stone forming a projecting angle; a square dole or piece of bread, cheese, &c.

Scunder, *v.* to loathe, dislike, disgust. Cf. Scunner.

Scunfis, Scunfish, *v.* to suffocate; to choke. Cf. Scumfish.

Scunge, *v.* to slink about; to fawn like a dog for food; to drive out like a dog; to gallop, run quickly.—*n.* a sly fellow; a vicious man.

Scunner, *v.* to loathe; to feel disgust; to shudder with repugnance; to scare; to flinch from; to cause to surfeit; to be sick; to disgust, sicken, cause loathing; to hesitate. —*n.* dislike, disgust; a surfeit; the object of loathing; what excites disgust.

Scunnerashen, *n.* anything disgusting, an abomination.

Scunnerfu', *adj.* disgusting, loathsome, abominable.

Scunnersome, *adj.* loathsome, 'scunnerfu'.'

Scuntion, *n.* a stone forming a projecting angle. Cf. Scuncheon.

Scuppit-beaver, *n.* a shovel-shaped hat.

Scur, *n.* a small fresh-water shrimp; the May-fly, fresh from the larva.

Scur, *n.* a scab. Cf. Scurr.

Scurdy, *n.* moorstone; a resting-place; a favourite seat.

Scurfuffle, *v.* to tarnish.—*n.* the act of tarnishing; a tarnished article of dress.

Scurl, *n.* the scab formed over a wound or sore.

Scurly, *adj.* covered with a scab.

Scurly, *adj.* scurrile; opprobrious.

Scurr, *n.* the scab formed over a wound or sore; the rough surface of a stone; a small horn of ox or cow, not fastened to the skull but hanging by the skin alone; a low rascal; a sheriff-officer's assistant; anything low.— *v.* used of a sore: to become covered with a scab.

Scurrie, *n.* the shag.

Scurrie, *adj.* low, dwarfish; not thriving.

Scurrie, *n.* a cow with 'scurrs' or short horns.

Scurrie-man, *n.* a wandering fellow.

Scurrie-whurrie, *n.* a hurly-burly, tumult.

Scurroch, Scurrock, *n.* the least particle.

Scurry, *v.* to scour; to go about from place to place; to wander about aimlessly.

Scurryvaig, Scurrivaig, *v.* to run about in an unsettled manner; to live idly and in dissipation.—*n.* a scamp; a vagabond; a clumsy person; an idle, unsettled person, a 'scullion'; a course of dissipation; a spree.

Scurvy, *n.* a mean, contemptible person.

Scushel, Scushle, *v.* to slide; to shuffle in walking; to make a noise in walking in shoes too big or down at the heels; to work carelessly and in slovenly fashion; to spoil an article of dress by bad usage.—*n.* a shuffle; a shuffling noise from walking in old or ill-fitting shoes; an old, worn-out shoe; slovenly unmethodical working; work so done; a clumsy person in gait or work; a clumsy, ill-made thing.—*adj.* clumsy, ill-made.

Scushy, *n.* money, cash.

Scutch, *v.* to beat; to switch, cane; to shear or trim with a hook; to walk pushing the feet lightly forward; to move quickly; to touch lightly with a duster, &c.; to push or carry forward.—*n.* a cut at the top of a twig or thistle; the trimming of a hedge; the cutting down of thistles; a shuffle or scraping movement of the feet; a slight whizzing or grating sound; a light, quick manner of working; a beating, dusting; a bill-hook.—*adv.* with a grating sound.

Scutcher, *n.* a dirty, slovenly, clumsy worker; a scutch used in flax-dressing.

Scutching, *n.* in *pl.* waste tow, refuse flax; twigs, thistles, &c. lopped off.

Scutching-knife, *n.* a bill-hook.

Scutching-spurkle, *n.* a stick for beating flax.

Scutching-tow, *n.* the refuse of flax after scutching.

Scute, *n.* a wooden drinking-vessel. Ct. Scoot.

Scuter-hole, *n.* a dirty puddle. Cf. Scutterhole.

Scutle, *v.* to pour from vessel to vessel; to spill liquid in doing so; to cook.—*n.* in *pl.* liquid tossed from vessel to vessel.

Scuttal, *n.* a pool of filthy water, a 'jaw-hole.'

Scutter, *v.* to run off hastily, as if in panic, to scuttle; to bungle, make a mess; to work ignorantly, awkwardly, and in a 'messy' manner.—*n.* a mess, muddle; dirty, confused work; dirty, messy working; a slovenly, untidy worker.

Scutter-hole, *n.* a filthy puddle.

Scutterie job, *n.* work of an indefinite character.

Scuttle-dish, *n.* a large, flat dish set below the spigot of an ale-barrel to catch the drops.

Scuttlin-flour, *n.* flour made of refuse wheat.

Scuttlins, *n.* light or refuse wheat, ground apart into inferior flour.

Scybel, *n.* a low, worthless fellow; a lazy, worn-out horse. Cf. Skybal.

Scypal, *adj.* lacking, deficient, short. Cf. Skypal.

Scyre, *adj.* sheer, utter, complete. —*adv.* utterly. Cf. Skeer.

Scythe, *v.* to eject quickly, 'skite,' squirt from the mouth through the teeth. Cf. Seethe.

Scytheman, *n.* a mower.

Scythe-shank, *n.* the long handle of a scythe.

Scythe-sned, *n.* the handle of a scythe.

Scythe-straik, *n.* a piece of hardwood covered with sand, for sharpening scythes.

Se, *v.* shall.

Sea-box, *n.* a box for holding fishermen's provisions at the deep-sea fishing.

Sea-breach, -break, *n.* a breaker.

Sea-bree, *n.* the waves of the sea.

Sea-breed, *n.* the food of fishes.

Sea-breeks, *n.* breeches worn by fishermen at sea.

Sea-broken, *adj.* shipwrecked.

Sea-candle, *n.* the phosphorescence of the sea.

Sea-carr, *v.* to embank.—*n.* a sea-wall, an embankment.

Sea-cashie, *n.* a wicker fish-basket.

Sea-cock, *n.* the puffin; the foolish guillemot.

Sea-coulter, *n.* the puffin.

Sea-crow, *n.* the razor-bill.

Sea-daisy, *n.* the thrift.

Sea-dog, *n.* a meteor seen on the horizon before sunrise, or after sunset, viewed by sailors as a sure portent of bad weather.

Sea-dovie, *n.* the black guillemot.

Sea-edge, *n.* the margin of the sea.

Seafarin', *n.* sea-voyaging.

Sea-fike, *n.* a marine plant which, when rubbed on the skin, causes irritation.

Sea-fire, *n.* the phosphorescence of the sea.

Seag, *n.* a name given to various species of plants having sword-shaped leaves. Cf. Segg.

Sea-goo, *n.* a sea-gull.

Sea-growth, *n.* the names given by fishermen to various species of *sertularia, flustra,* &c. adhering to small stones, shells, &c.

Sea-haar, *n.* a sea-fog.

Sea-hack, *n.* a temporary thaw occasioned by the salt vapour during the rising tide; a short thaw between frosts.

Sea-hen, *n.* the common guillemot; the piper or *Trigla lyra.*

Seal, *n.* a rope or chain for binding cattle in the stall.—*v.* to bind or fasten cattle in the stalls. Cf. Seill.

Seal, *n.* a favourable occasion; happiness.—*v.* to wish health and happiness to the wearer of an article of new clothing. Cf. Seel.

Sea-lark, *n.* the dunlin.

Sealch, *n.* a pustule, a large blackhead; a bunion.

Sealch, Sealgh, *n.* a seal, sea-calf.

Sealch's-bubble, *n.* a jelly-fish.

Sealch-skin, *n.* a sealskin.

Sea-light, *n.* the phosphorescence of the sea.

Seal of cause, *n.* a writing granted to a body of craftsmen or guild by a royal burgh, and sealed with the burgh seal, conveying or confirming privileges.

Seam, *n.* a crack in crockery; a piece of sewing or weaving; used of teeth: a row.

†**Seam,** *n.* hog's-lard; goose-grease; fat; fish-oil. Cf. Saim.

Sea-maiden, *n.* a mermaid.

Seaman-body, *n.* a sailor.

Sea-maw, *n.* the common gull; the black-headed gull.

Sea-meath, -meeth, *n.* a landmark to those out at sea.

Sea-milkwort, *n.* the black saltwort.

Sea-mouse, *n.* the dunlin.

Seannachie, *n.* a Highland bard; a story-teller; a chronicler of heroic achievements.

Seantack, *n.* a baited fishing-line, one end of which is fastened to the bank of the river, and the other kept across the stream by a weight. Cf. Scantack.

Seap, *v.* to percolate slowly; to ooze, leak. Cf. Seip.

Sea-peek, *n.* the dunlin.

Sea-pellock, *n.* the porpoise.

Sea-pheasant, *n.* the turbot.

Sea-pie, -pyet, *n.* the oyster-catcher.

Sea-poacher, *n.* the armed bullhead.

Sea-qubaup, -whaup, *n.* a species of gull of a dark colour.

Search, *n.* a fine sieve; a strainer.—*v.* to sift or strain through a fine sieve.

Searcher, *n.* a civil officer formerly employed in Glasgow to apprehend idlers on the streets on Sunday during public worship. Cf. Seizer.

Sear-claith, *n.* a cerecloth.

Sea-snipe, *n.* the dunlin.

Season-side, *n.* the duration of the season.

Sea-spire, *n.* sea-spray.

Sea-swine, *n.* the ballan-wrasse.

Seat, *n.* one of the boards over the bottom of a boat; a fishing-ground; a sitting in a church.

Seat-board, *n.* the seat of a handloom.

Seat-breast, -breist, *n.* the book-board of a pew.

Seath, *n.* the coal-fish. Cf. Saithe.

Seath, *n.* part of a plough.

Seat-house, *n.* the manor-house on an estate.

Seatie, *n.* a small or low seat.

Seat-maill, *n.* pew-rent.

Sea-tod, *n.* the ballan-wrasse.

Sea-tow, *n.* a rope for fastening or anchoring a fishing-boat.

Sea-tree, *n.* a pail-pole. Cf. Sae-tree.

Seat-tree, *n.* a weaver's seat while at the loom.

Seawa, *v.* to say grace; to fall to.—*n.* loquacity. Cf. Say-awa'.

Sea-waur, *n.* algæ thrown up by the sea, used as manure.

Sea-woman, *n.* a mermaid.

Sea-worm, *n.* a crab.

Sea-wynd, *n.* an alley leading to the sea.

†**Sebow,** *n.* a small onion. Cf. Sybo.

Seceder, *n.* a seceder from the Established Church of Scotland; one who differs from another.

Seceder-body, *n.* a 'seceder,' a member of the Secession Church.

Seceder-face, *n.* a sanctimonious face.

Seceder-plan, *n.* the plan of supporting a Church by voluntary contributions without State aid.

Secession, *n.* the Church of 'Seceders.'

Sech, *v.* to sigh. Cf. Sich.

Seck, *n.* a sack.

Seck, *n.* the wine, sack.

Seckcloth, *n.* sackcloth.

Seck-gown, *n.* the garment worn by an offender while doing public penance.

Seckless, *adj.* innocent; feeble. Cf. Sackless.

Secky-ban, *n.* an apparition. Cf. Sacbaun.

Second-handed, *adj.* second-hand.

Second-sichtit, *adj.* having the power of foreseeing the future.

Secret, *n.* a coat of mail worn under the outer dress.

†Secretar, Secreter, *n.* a secretary; a keeper of secrets.

Secret Council, *n.* the Privy Council.

Secretful, *adv.* secretly.

Sect, *n.* set, class; sex.

Secured, *ppl. adj.* provided for, secured from want.

Sedan-bread, *n.* a soda-scone.

Sedgeband, *n.* an apparition. Cf. Sacbaun.

Sedge-singer, *n.* the sedge-warbler.

Sedging, *n.* a disease in the roots of oaks caused by insects.

Sedimateese, *v.* to choke or stop up with sediment.

See, *v.* to give, hand, lend, let one have.

See-about, *v.* to acquire an accurate knowledge of one's surroundings.

See-after, *v.* to look after, attend to; to try to find, inquire about.

See and, *v.* to see if.

See-awa', *v.* to outlive, survive.

See'd, *v. pret.* saw.

Seed, *n.* the husk of oats; the inner covering of grain, recovered in grinding; a very small quantity; a fragment; seed-time; spring; a hot-tempered person.—*v.* to sow; used of mares and cows: to have the udder begin to swell before giving birth.

Seed-bird, *n.* the gray wagtail; the common gull.

Seed-fire, *n.* a fire made with 'seeds' or husks of oats.

Seed-foullie, *n.* the pied wagtail.

Seed-fur, *n.* the furrow into which the seed is to be cast.

Seedge, *n.* rate, speed.

Seed-lady, -laverock, *n.* the pied wagtail.

Seed-like, *adj.* used of land: apparently fit to receive seed.

Seedlins, *n.* youngsters; learners.

Seedsman, *n.* a sower.

Seedy, *adj.* full of 'seeds' or husks; made of, or containing, the husks of oats. Cf. Siddie.

Seedy-broo, *n.* 'sowens' in the first stage of steeping, before the 'seeds' have fallen to the bottom of the tub; the second brewing of ale or home-made beer; weak ale.

Seefer, *n.* a worthless, lazy, or drunken loafer; an impudent, empty-headed rascal; a 'cipher.'—*adj.* diminutive. Cf. Sieffer.

Seeing-glass, *n.* a looking-glass.

Seek, *v.* to fetch, bring; to court, ask in marriage; to invite; to ask as a price; to make a bid, offer a price; to overtask, use-up; to attack; to beg; to live by begging; to ask for.

Seek, *v.* to soak.

Seek, *v.* to ooze; to leak.

Seek-and-hod, *n.* the game of 'hide-and-seek.'

Seek awa', *v.* to seek to go away.

Seek in, *v.* to seek to enter in.

Seek out, *v.* to fetch out; to ask leave to go out of school.

Seel, *n.* a favourable occasion; happiness.

Seelfu', *adj.* pleasant, happy, blessed, foreboding good.

Seelfu'ness, *n.* complacency; sweetness of disposition; happiness of temper.

Seelible, *adj.* pleasant, happy, delightful.

Seelie-hoo, -how, *n.* a child's caul, thought to bring luck to its possessor; any quaint head-dress.

Seely, *adj.* happy, blessed.

Seely-court, *n.* the fairy court.

Seely-wight, *n.* a fairy.

Seem, *n.* resemblance, appearance.

†Seem, *n.* lard; fat. Cf. Saim.

Seemilar, *adj.* similar. Cf. Similar.

Seemless, *adj.* unseen.

Seemly, *adj.* comely, winsome.

Seen, *v. pret.* saw.

Seen, *ppl. adj.* looking, showing; familiar; versed, practised, expert.

Seen, *adv.* ago, since; then; afterwards.— *prep.* since.—*conj.* seeing that; therefore. Cf. Syne.

Seen, *adv.* soon.

Seenil, *adv.* seldom, rarely.—*adj.* rare, infrequent; single; singular.

Seenillie, *adv.* remarkably, singularly.

Seenil-times, *adv.* rarely, seldom.

Seenlins, *adv.* rarely, seldom.

Se'ennicht, *n.* a week; the seventh night.

Seep, *v.* to percolate slowly; to soak; to ooze.—*n.* a small quantity of liquor imbibed; a small spring; moisture. Cf. Seip.

Seep-sabbin', *n.* the sound of dripping, trickling water, or of a brook.

Seer, *n.* one who has the 'second-sight.'

Seer, *adj.* sure.

Seerie, *adj.* weak, feeble. Cf. Sairie.

Seerly, *adv.* surely.

Seerup, *n.* syrup.

Seestou, Seestow, Seestoo, *int.* an excl. used as emphasis, to attract attention. Cf. Sestuna.

Seet, *n.* soot.

Seet, *n.* a seat; the cover of the narrow place over the keel of a boat. Cf. Seat.

Seeth, Seethe, *n.* the coal-fish. Cf. Saithe.

Seeth, *v.* to boil; to be nearly boiling.

Seethe, *v.* to draw in or squirt out water through the teeth. Cf. Scythe.

Seg, *v.* to bend down from superincumbent weight; to sink, subside; to press or shake down; used of liquids: to sink down; of drink: to influence the drinker.

Seg, *v.* to set the teeth on edge by eating anything sour.

Seg, *n.* a grip.

Seg-backit, *adj.* used of a horse : having the back hollow or sunk.

Segg, Seg, *n.* a name given to various plants with sword-shaped leaves ; the yellow iris.

Segg, *n.* a bull castrated when of full age.

Seggan, *n.* a name given to various plants with sword-shaped leaves ; the yellow iris.

Seggit, *ppl. adj.* walking heavily and stumbling from weariness.

Seggit-cow, *n.* a cow with calf.

Seggit-teeth, *n.* teeth set on edge.

Segg-root, *n.* the root of a 'segg.'

Seggy, *adj.* sedgy, overgrown with reeds, &c.

Seggy-boat, *n.* a toy boat made of sedges, rushes, &c.

†**Seibow,** *n.* a young onion. Cf. Sybo.

Seich, *v.* to sigh. Cf. Sich.

Seiger, *n.* a besieger.

Seik, *v.* to seek.

Seil, *v.* to strain ; to filter ; to rinse clothes. —*n.* a sieve, strainer for milk, &c.

Seil, Seile, *n.* a favourable occasion ; happiness. Cf. Seel.

Seiler, *n.* a strainer.

Seilfu', *adj.* pleasant, happy. Cf. Seelfu'.

Seill, *v.* to bind cattle in their stalls.—*n.* a rope or chain for doing this. Cf. Seal.

Seily, *adj.* happy. Cf. Seely.

†**Seim,** *n.* lard, grease, &c. Cf. Saim.

Seim, *n.* resemblance ; appearance. Cf. Seem.

Seimly, *adj.* winsome. Cf. Seemly.

Seindle, Seinle, *adv.* seldom.—*adj.* rare ; singular. Cf. Seenil.

Seip, *v.* to ooze ; to leak ; to percolate slowly ; to cause to drop or trickle ; to drain to the dregs in drinking ; to drain of moisture ; to soak through ; to sink slowly and disappear.—*n.* a leakage ; a puddle ; a state of wetness ; a mouthful of liquid ; a sip, drop ; what remains in a bottle ; a small spring or stream of water ; the dregs of a liquid. Cf. Sipe.

Seipage, *n.* leakage.

Seiped, *ppl. adj.* dried up, drained of moisture.

Seipin', *ppl. adj.* very wet, dripping.

Seirie, *adj.* distant, reserved, haughty ; cynical in manner.

Seise, *v.* to give formal possession.

Seissle, *v.* to confuse, disorder ; to trifle ; to spend time needlessly ; to be inactive or unhandy.

Seissler, *n.* a trifler.

Seizer, *n.* an officer whose duty was to apprehend persons idling in the streets during public worship on Sunday. Cf. Searcher.

†**Sejoin,** *v.* to disjoin, separate.

Sek, *n.* a sack.

Seker, *adj.* firm, sure. Cf. Sicker.

Sekerly, *adv.* surely, firmly. Cf. Sickerly.

Sel', Sell, *pron.* and *adj.* self. Cf. Sell.

Selch, Selchie, Selcht, *n.* a seal, sea-calf. Cf. Sealch.

Selcouth, *adj.* strange, rare, uncommon.

Sele, *n.* a favourable occasion ; happiness. Cf. Seel.

Sele, *n.* a rope or chain to bind cattle in their stalls.—*v.* to bind cattle. Cf. Seal.

Self, *adj.* original, pristine ; natural ; undyed.

Self and same, *adj.* the very same.

Self-tenderness, *n.* care for one's own health.

Selkhorn, *n.* a small, hard pimple ; a blackhead. Cf. Shillcorn.

Selkie, *n.* a seal, sea-calf. Cf. Sealch.

Selkirk-bannock, *n.* a sweet cake of flour baked with currants.

Selkit, Selkith, *adv.* seldom. Cf. Selcouth.

†**Sell, Selle,** *n.* a seat, stool ; a saddle, pillion.

Sell, *v.* to throw away an advantage.

Sell, *n.* a favourable occasion ; happiness. Cf. Seel.

Sell, *v.* to bind cattle in their stalls.—*n.* a chain to bind cattle. Cf. Seal.

Sellag, *n.* the fry of the coal-fish.

Sellat, Sellat-pan, *n.* a small pan or pot with a lid.

Sellet, *n.* a salad.

Sellible, *adj.* pleasant, happy. Cf. Seel.

Sellie, *n.* self.—*adj.* selfish. Cf. Sel'.

Sell't, Selt, *v. pret.* and *ppl.* sold.

Sel'-sappit, *adj.* self-satisfied ; self-conceited.

Selvage, *n.* a border, edge ; the bank of a stream.—*v.* to form a border, line, or margin.

Selver, *n.* a salver.

Sely, *adj.* happy, blessed. Cf. Seely.

Sely-how, *n.* a child's caul. Cf. Seelie-hoo.

†**Sem,** *n.* hog's-lard. Cf. Saim.

Semble, *n.* the parapet of a bridge.

Semi, Semie, *n.* a second year's student at a Scottish university, especially Aberdeen University.

Semi-bachelor, *n.* an old designation of a second year's student at Edinburgh University.

Semi-bajan, *n.* a 'semi-bachelor.'

Semi-class, *n.* second-year students at Aberdeen University.

Semi-year, *n.* the second year of a student's curriculum.

Semmit, *n.* a flannel or knitted woollen undershirt, a 'binder.'

Semmle, *v.* to arrange, put in order.

†**Sempeternum,** *n.* a species of woollen cloth.

Semple, *adj.* of lowly birth ; in common life. —*n.* the commonalty.

Sempleness, *n.* a low condition of life.

Sempster, *n.* a sempstress.

†**Sen,** *v.* to cross ; to bless. Cf. Sain.

Sen, *adv.* ago.—*prep.* since.—*conj.* seeing that. Cf. Sin.

Sen', *v.* to send.

Senachie, Sennachie, *n.* a bard ; a story-teller. Cf. Seannachie.

Send, *n.* a message ; a prayer ; a messenger ; one sent in advance of the bridegroom to summon the bride.—*v.* to require by message something to be done.

Send-down, *n.* a message sent down.

Send-up, *n.* a message sent up.

Sengreen, *n.* in *phr.* 'small marsh-sengreen,' the hairy stonecrop.

Senil, Sennil, *adv.* seldom. Cf. Seenil.

Senlins, *adv.* seldom.

Sen's, *int.* save us ! bless us ! Cf. Sain.

Sense, *n.* essence, pith.—*v.* to put a sense upon ; to put meaning into ; to scent out.

Senselessest, *adj.* most senseless.

Sense-thrawin, *adj.* used of drink : confusing the senses.

Senshach, *adj.* used of children : wise, sensible ; well-behaved.

Sensible, *adj.* conscious in an illness ; evident, beyond doubt.

Sensible drunk, *adj.* drunk, but conscious.

Sensuals, *n.* passions.

Sen syne, *adv.* since then ; ago. Cf. Sin syne.

Sent, *n.* a small quantity, a 'scent.' Cf. Sint.

Sen't, *v.* with *pron.* send it.

Sentence-silver, *n.* money paid by the person losing his case towards the salary of the judges, and by the prosecutor also.

Sequels, *n.* small parcels of corn or meal given as a fee to the mill-servants, in addition to what is paid to the multurer, 'knaveship,' 'bannock and lock'; children of serfs ; the young of animals.

†**Sequestrate,** *v.* to set apart a day for a special purpose : a legal term.

Ser', Sere, *v.* to serve, be a servant ; to treat ; to give an animal food, or alms to a beggar ; with *out,* to deal, to satisfy, suffice ; to suit, become, be appropriate to.—*n.* enough to eat, sufficiency of food. Cf. Sair.

Sere, *v.* to sear ; to wither up, blast.

Sereachan-, (?) Screachan-aittin, *n.* a bird with a larger body than a large mall, of bluish colour, with a bill of carnation colour, and given to shrieking hideously.

Serf, *n.* 'sowens' before fermentation has fully begun.

Serin', *n.* a helping of food ; a sufficiency of food ; in *pl.* deserts ; punishment. Cf. Sairin.

Serk, *n.* a shirt. Cf. Sark.

†**Serplath,** *n.* eighty stones of wool.

Serplins, *n.* the soapy water in which clothes have been boiled.

Serse, *int.* an excl. of surprise. Cf. Sirce.

Ser't, *ppl.* said of one who has had quite enough.

†**Servad, Servat,** *n.* a serviette, table-napkin ; a towel ; a small tray.

Servant, *n.* a clerk, secretary. Cf. Servitor.

Servant-lass, *n.* a maid-servant.

Serve, *v.* to supply food to animals or to beggars ; to suffice. Cf. Sair, Ser.

Serve, *v.* to deserve.

Serve, *v.* to preserve.

†**Servet,** *n.* a serviette ; a salver. Cf. Servad.

Service, *n.* an assurance of respect ; a place of service ; assistance given by unskilled labourers to masons and carpenters while building or repairing a house ; a round of wine, spirits, &c. formerly given to the persons attending a funeral ; any serving of whisky, &c.

Servin', *n.* a helping of food ; a sufficiency ; punishment. Cf. Sairin.

Servin'-chiel, *n.* a man-servant.

Servin'-lass, -woman, *n.* a maid-servant.

†**Servitor,** *n.* an apprentice or clerk of a judge, advocate, &c. ; a secretary, man of business ; a servant, attendant.

Servitrix, *n.* a female servant ; a lady's-maid.

Servitude, *n.* service, employment.

Sesquaster, *v.* to sequester ; to sequestrate.

Sess, *v.* to assess.—*n.* an assessment.

Session, *n.* the elders of a Presbyterian congregation in session, the kirk-session.—*v.* to give in names to the clerk of the kirk-session for proclamation of banns ; to summon before the session.

Session-book, *n.* the kirk-session record of its proceedings.

Sessioner, *n.* a member of the kirk-session.

Session-saints, *n.* elders of the kirk.

Session-siller, *n.* a parish dole distributed by the kirk-session.

Sestuna, *int.* an excl. of admiration. Cf. Seestou.

Set, Sett, *n.* a potato, or part of one, used for planting ; a shape, figure ; a pattern, the pattern of a tartan ; kind, manner ; the knack of doing a thing ; the nature or requirement of the material worked ; the fixed quantity of an article regularly supplied ; a check in growth ; an attack, onset ; impulse, force ; a shock ; a difficult task, problem ; a disgust ; a lease ; a billet on a house showing that it is to be let ; the chartered constitution of a burgh ; a sta-

tionary net, the place in a river where it is
fixed ; a warp, twist ; a paving-stone ; a
whetstone for a razor ; the pointing of a
sporting dog ; a band of reapers, and the
number of ridges they cut at one time ;
the socket in which a precious stone is set ;
in *pl.* corn put up in small stacks.

Set, *v.* to seat ; to place a hen on eggs in
order to hatch them ; to assign work ; to
settle, get in order ; to put milk into a pan
for the cream to rise ; to set a fishing-line
or net ; to work according to a pattern ; to
plant potatoes, 'kail,' &c. ; to make, impel, induce ; to beset ; to bring to a halt ;
to puzzle ; to nauseate, disgust ; used of
a dog : to mark game ; to let, lease ; to
escort for part or the whole of a short
journey ; to send, despatch ; to become,
suit, beseem ; to sit ; to cease to grow,
become mature ; to stiffen, congeal, become hard or solid ; to start, begin ; to set
off.

Set, *ppl. adj.* stunted in growth, squat,
no longer growing ; bent, warped ; firm,
resolute ; obstinate, self-willed, settled in
opinion or purpose ; disposed, affected, or
inclined, either ill or well ; distressed,
afflicted, cast down.

Set-aff, *v.* to dismiss, turn off ; to fob off,
shift off ; to put away ; to take one's self
off ; to slip off ; to loiter, linger, delay,
waste time ; to set in motion ; to fire off,
explode ; to deliver a speech glibly, tell
a fluent story ; to make a great display ; to
plant ; to quit ; to keep off.—*n.* a dismissal ; a shift, evasion ; an offset ; anything that counterbalances another ; delay ;
a dilatory person ; a pretence ; a start ;
anything that becomes a person.   Cf.
Aff-set.

Set after, *v.* to hurry after, pursue, set out
after.

Set at, *v.* to attack ; to incite.—*n.* a battle,
contest.

Set awa', *v.* to go, set off.

Set-back, *n.* a rebuff ; a check ; the rejection
of an offer of marriage.

Set by, *v.* to lay or put by ; to save ; not to
take into account ; to substitute for something better ; to make to suffice ; to satisfy ;
to esteem greatly ; to value highly.—*n.* a
substitute ; a makeshift.

Set caution, *v.* to give security.

Set-down, -doon, *v.* to place food on the
table ; to write down ; to rebuff, snub ;
to settle in marriage.—*n.* a snub, rebuff ;
a settlement in marriage, a 'doon-set,'
'-sitting.'—*ppl. adj.* used of a meal : sit-
down, formal, regularly prepared or provided.

Set fire, *v.* with *in* or *till,* used of a pipe or
cigar : to light it.

Set-gear, *n.* money bearing interest.   Cf.
Settle-gear.

Seth, *n.* the coal-fish.   Cf. Saithe.

Set hame, *v.* to start for home ; to escort
homeward.

Seth-ill, *n.* a disease of sheep in their side,
causing them to walk leaning to one side.
Cf. Side-ill.

Set house, *v.* to begin housekeeping, set up
house.

Set in, *v.* to bring in a meal, to arrange or
spread it on a table ; used of the weather :
to last.—*ppl. adj.* likely to continue long,
permanent.

Set on, *v.* to fall upon, attack ; to set to a
task ; to accommodate ; to be well off ; to
make a start ; used of a fire : to prepare and
light it ; used in curling : to aim or direct a
stone ; to do well by.—*n.* a violent scolding ; a strong effort to persuade.—*ppl. adj.*
provided ; treated ; resolved upon, bent
upon ; engrossed with, devoted ; used of
food : burned in cooking ; ill-thriven, short.

Set out, *v.* to eject, put out forcibly ; to
publish ; to array one's self in order to
conquest in courting ; to embellish ; to set
off by ornament or contrast.—*n.* a feast ; a
display ; an important event ; a joke, fun.

Set owre, *v.* to overset, capsize.—*n.* a capsize,
overturn.

Set rent, *n.* a certain portion allotted to a
servant or cottager when working for his
master.   Cf. Settrin.

Set-stane, *n.* a whetstone for a razor, &c.

Sett, *n.* a decree.

Setten, Settin, *ppl. adj.* set.

Setter, *n.* one who lets anything out for hire ;
a baker's tool.

Setterel, *adj.* thickset ; dwarfish.—*n.* a squat
person.

Setter out, *n.* a publisher ; one who circulates
anything.

Setting, Settin', *n.* the number of eggs a hen
sits on to hatch ; the letting or leasing of
a house, farm, &c. ; a portion of land ; a
measure of bulk ; a sufficiency of anything.
—*ppl. adj.* growing mature ; becoming,
suitable ; comely, graceful.

Setting-dog, *n.* a spaniel, a setter.

Setting-down, *n.* a settlement in marriage ; a
provision made with a view to marriage.

Setting of the sculls, *n.* the carrying or
'creeling' of bride and bridegroom in
baskets or 'sculls.'

Setting-step, *n.* a step in the sword-dance.

Settle, *v.* to compose a quarrel ; to silence ;
to kill.

Settle, *v.* with *up,* to attend to, make comfortable; to induct or place a minister to a particular charge.—*n.* shape, build, form of body; a settling-down; the fall of night; calmness, ease.

Settle-bed, *n.* a settle that forms a bed by night.

Settle-gear, *n.* money yielding interest. Cf. Set-gear.

Settler, *n.* what reduces one to silence; a conclusive argument or blow.

Settlin, *n.* what reduces one to silence or submission.

Settlins, *n.* the dregs of beer; sediment.

Set to, *v.* to begin; to fight; to turn to; to settle down to; in *phr.* 'set to the gate,' to set off, go off.—*n.* a fight; a quarrel; a scolding-match; a state of things, pass, crisis.

Set together, *v.* to marry.

Settral, *adj.* unconvinced by argument.

Settrel, Settril, *adj.* thickset. Cf. Setterel.

Settrell, *n.* young sprouts that shoot forth in spring from coleworts planted in the beginning of winter.

Settrin, *n.* the portion of a servant or cottager, consisting of different kinds of food, when working for his master. Cf. Set rent.

Set tryst, *v.* to make an appointment to meet.

Set up, *v.* to cause, occasion; to restore to health or prosperity; to cure, make good; to elate; to ornament, set off; to disgust, nauseate; used of razors: to sharpen.—*ppl. adj.* conceited, proud, vain, affected; elated.

Seuch, Seugh, *n.* a ditch, drain, open gutter; a trench; a furrow.—*v.* to plant temporarily in a furrow. Cf. Sheuch.

Seugh, *n.* a hollow, murmuring sound, a rushing sound like that of the wind; a deep sigh. Cf. Sough.

Sevendle, Sevennil, *adj.* strong, secure, sufficient; trustworthy; to be relied on. Cf. Savendle.

Seven senses, *n.* all one's wits.

Seven-shift, *n.* a seven years' course of cropping.

Seventeen-hunner linen, *n.* a very fine linen, produced by a reed with 1700 divisions.

Severals, *n.* several persons or things.

Severely, *adv.* thoroughly.

Sewawra, *n.* a kind of cravat, ? a 'suwarrow.'

Sewster, *n.* a sempstress.

Sey, *n.* the opening of a gown or shift through which the sleeve passes; the part of a dress between the armpit and the breast; a part of the back of an ox cut up for beef. Cf. Back-sey, Fore-sey.

Sey, *n.* the coal-fish. Cf. Saithe.

Sey, *v.* to try, test; to assay, prove; to essay; to taste.—*n.* an assay; an attempt; a trial-piece of work. Cf. Say.

Sey, *n.* a bucket; a milk-pail. Cf. Sae, Say.

Sey, *n.* a woollen cloth formerly made by families for their own use; a kind of serge.

†**Sey,** *n.* a stuff which contained silk.

Sey, *v.* to strain through a sieve; to strain milk.—*n.* a sieve; a strainer for milk, &c. Cf. Sie.

Sey, *v.* to see.

Seyal, *n.* a trial.

†**Seybie, Seybo, Seybow,** *n.* a young onion. Cf. Sybo.

Sey-clout, *n.* a cloth through which any liquid is strained.

Seyd, *n.* a sewer, a passage for water.

Sey-dish, *n.* a milk-strainer.

Seyer, *n.* a fine sieve for straining milk.

Seyg, *v.* to sink. Cf. Seg.

Seyl, *v.* to strain, filter. Cf. Seil.

Seyle, *n.* happiness; a favourable occasion. Cf. Seel, Seal.

†**Seymar,** *n.* a loose upper garment; a scarf.

Sey-milk, *adj.* a milk-strainer.

Seyndle, *adv.* seldom. Cf. Seenil.

Sey-piece, *n.* a trial-piece. Cf. Say-piece.

Sey-sones, -sowens, *n.* a sieve for straining 'sowens.'

Seyster, *v.* to mix incongruously.—*n.* an incongruous mixture or medley of edibles.

Sgian-dhu, *n.* a dirk; a dagger. Cf. Skean-dhu.

Sha, *int.* an inciting call to a dog to chase another animal.

Shaak, *n.* chalk.

Shaal, *n.* a shell.

Shaal, *adj.* shallow. Cf. Shall.

Shaard, *n.* a shard, sherd. Cf. Shaird.

Shaave, *n.* a saw.—*v.* to saw. Cf. Shauve.

Shaave, *v.* to sow.

Shaavin-basket, *n.* a basket for sowing seed.

Sha-awa', *int.* a call to a dog to chase another animal.

Shab, Shabb, *v.* to smuggle; to send anything away privately; used of the sun: to sink slowly, to set.

Shabble, Shable, *n.* a crooked sword or hanger; an old, rusty sword; a small, insignificant person or thing.

Shach, *v.* to distort; to shape anything obliquely; to jilt or desert a woman.

Shach-end, *n.* the fag-end of a web where the cloth becomes inferior in quality.

Shachle, Schachel, *v.* to distort; to wear out of shape; to cripple; to walk in a shambling or knock-kneed fashion; to waddle; to wriggle.—*n.* a feeble, puny, misshapen person or animal; anything worn-out or badly put together; a shanty; a contemptuous term for a leg.

Shachle, *n.* a shackle; the wrist. Cf. Shackle.

Shachled-shoes, -shoon, *n.* a person of no

further use; a woman discarded by her lover.

Shachlieness, *n.* knock-kneedness.

Shachlin', *ppl. adj.* mean, paltry, unsatisfactory; unsteady, infirm.—*n.* a puny weakling.

Shachl't, *adj.* shuffling.

Shachly, *adj.* shambling, shuffling; jolting; shaking.

Shack, *v.* to shake.—*int.* a word of incitement to a dog to worry another animal. Cf. Shake.

Shack-a-fa', **Shackiefa**, *v.* to wrestle.

Shackelt, *ppl.* hindered, kept down.

Shackle, *n.* a hobble for a horse; the wrist; the ankle.—*v.* to hobble horses, to tie their forelegs together.

Shackle, *v.* to shamble; to distort. Cf. Shachle.

Shackle, *v.* to joggle, to 'shoggle.' Cf. Shockel.

Shackle-bane, *n.* the wrist-bone; the knuckle-bone.

Shacky, *adj.* shaky.

Shade, *n.* a cultivated field.

Shade, *n.* a sheath; a sheath for knitting-pins.

Shade, *v.* to part asunder; to part the hair with a comb.—*n.* a parting in the hair; used of land : a division; a narrow dividing-way. Cf. Shed.

Shade-knife, *n.* a knife carried in a sheath.

Shadow-half, *n.* the northern exposure of land; the shady side.

Shae, *n.* a shoe.

Shaep, *v.* to shape. Cf. Shape.

Shaetery, *n.* cheating; 'cheatery.'

Shaffie, *n.* a frivolous excuse. Cf. Sheeffie-shaffie.

Shaft, *v.* to put a handle to any implement.

Shaftmon, **Schaftmon**, *n.* the measure of the fist with the thumb extended, taken as six inches.

Shafts, *n.* the cheeks, jaws. Cf. Chaft.

Shafts, *n.* a kind of woollen cloth.

Shag, *n.* the cormorant.

Shag, *n.* a bull castrated at full age. Cf. Segg.

Shag, **Shagg**, *n.* tail-corn; the refuse of barley or oats.

Shag-coat, *n.* a coat of rough cloth.

Shagged, *ppl. adj.* shaggy.

Shaghle, *v.* to distort; to wear out of shape. Cf. Shachle.

Shagmahoch, *n.* a small, misshapen person.

Shags, *n.* in *phr.* 'to go shags,' to go shares.

Shaimit-reel, *n.* the first dance after a marriage ceremony, the 'shame-reel.'

Shair, *v.* to rub one substance against another; to grate, grind.

Shair, *adj.* sure.

Shaird, *n.* a shard, sherd; a fragment, shred; a small portion; an old, unseaworthy boat; a piece of furniture badly put together; a little, despicable creature; an unhealthy dwarf; a puny or deformed child; a petulant, mischievous child.

Shairn, **Shairin**, *n.* cows' dung. Cf. Sharn.

Shairny, *adj.* bedaubed with 'sharn.'—*n.* the person who cleans out the cow-house.

Shaivle, *v.* to distort; to become distorted. Cf. Shevel.

Shak, **Shake**, *v.* to wrestle.—*n.* a shock; a wrestling-bout; emaciation by disease or long confinement; refuse corn; corn shorn when green.

Shak a fa', *v.* to wrestle; to exert one's self to the utmost.—*n.* a wrestling-match.

Shak a fit, or leg, *v.* to dance.

Shak-and-tremble, *n.* the quaking-grass.

Shak-im-troose, *n.* an old Scotch reel. Cf. Shantrews, Shawintrewse.

Shaking, *n.* the smallest quantity; the last remains.

Shakin's o' the pock, or pot, *n.* the youngest child of a family.

Shakit, *v. pret.* shook.

Shakker, **Shaker**, *n.* part of a threshing-mill; a fit of ague; nervous tremor.

Shakky trimmles, *n.* nervous tremors.

Shaklock, *n.* a lazy 'ne'er-do-weel'; an idle loafer.

Shak o' a fit, *n.* a dance.

Shak o' a hand, *n.* a very short time.

Shak one's crop, *v.* to vent one's ill-humour; to speak loudly and vehemently.

Shak-, **Shake-rag**, *n.* a beggar; a tatterdemalion.

Shak-rag-like, *adj.* like a tatterdemalion.

Shak the feet, *v.* to shake dust, mud, &c. off one's feet; to dance.

Shak-wind, *n.* a wind that shakes the ripened grain; a blustering wind.

Shaky, *adj.* used of a road : causing jolting.

Shaky-mill, *n.* the death-watch. Cf. Chacky-mill.

Shald, *adj.* shallow.—*n.* a shallow place, a shoal. Cf. Shall.

Shale, *n.* alum ore.

Shale, *adj.* shallow. Cf. Shall.

Shalk, *n.* a servant; a workman; a farm-servant.

Shall, *n.* a shell; part of the old 'crusie'-lamp, for holding the oil and wick and for catching the drip; a portion, fragment; the scale suspended from a balance for weighing; in *pl.* burnt limestone before it is slaked.

Shall, *adj.* shallow.—*v.* to spear or 'leister' salmon in shallow water.

Shall, *n.* a shawl.

Shallmillens, *n.* fragments.

Shalloch, *adj.* plentiful, abundant; used of corn: short in the stalk, but growing very close, with many grains on one stalk.

Shalloch, *n.* a small, shallow tin vessel.

Shallochy, *adj.* shallow.

Shalt, Shaltie, *n.* a pony; a small horse. Cf. Sheltie.

Sham, *v.* to cheat, trick, deceive; to shirk; to treat lightly.

Sham, *v.* to strike.

Sham, *v.* to make faces.

†**Sham,** *n.* a leg. Cf. Shaum.

Sham, *n.* shame. Cf. Shame.

Shamble, *v.* to rack the limbs by striding too far; to distort, writhe; to make a wry face or mouth.

Shamble-chafts, *n.* a wry, distorted mouth.

Shamble-shankit, *adj.* having crooked legs.

Shamble-shanks, *n.* crooked legs; a person with crooked legs.

Shambling, *ppl. adj.* unevenly set.

Shambo, Shambo-leather, *n.* chamois leather, shammy.

Shame, *n.* in imprecations: the devil, 'sorrow.' —*v.* to be ashamed; in *phr.* to 'think shame,' to be ashamed.

Shamed-, Shame-reel, *n.* the first dance after a marriage ceremony, danced by bride and best man and bridegroom and bride's-maid. Cf. Shaimit-reel.

Shame-fa', *int.* an imprecation.

Shameful, *adj.* modest; shy, bashful.

Shameful-reel, *n.* the 'shame-reel.'

Shame-spring, *n.* the dance-music for the 'shame-reel.'

Sham-gabbit, *adj.* having the upper jaw protruding, or an underhung mouth.

Shamlichin, *n.* shambling, irregular gait in walking. Cf. Schamlich.

Shamloch, *n.* a cow that has not calved for two years.

Shammel, Shammil, *v.* to shamble; to distort, to rack the limbs by striding too far. Cf. Shamble.

†**Shammy,** *n.* hockey, 'shinty.'

Shamp, *v.* to take one's self off.

Shan, *adj.* backward, averse; reluctant. Cf. Shandy.

Shan, *adj.* pitiful, silly; poor, shabby; paltry. Cf. Shand.

Shanachy, *n.* a bard; a story-teller. Cf. Seannachie.

Shand, *adj.* worthless.—*n.* base coin.

Shan-dre-dan, *n.* any old, rickety, quaint-looking conveyance; a jocular name for a vehicle.

Shandy, *adj.* shy, reluctant. Cf. Shan, Shanny.

†**Shane,** *v.* to heal, cure; to break the spell of witchcraft; to wish good-luck by super-stitious practices.—*n.* that which breaks the spell of witchcraft. Cf. Sain.

Shang, *n.* a sort of luncheon, a 'bite' between meals; a 'piece.'

Shan-gabbit, *adj.* having a sunken cheek and prominent jaw. Cf. Sham-gabbit.

Shangan, Shangin, Shanjan, *n.* a stick cleft at one end for putting on a dog's tail.

Shangie, *adj.* thin, meagre, lean.

Shangie, Shanjie, Shangy, *v.* to enclose in a cleft piece of wood.—*n.* a cleft stick for a dog's tail, a 'shangan'; an ornament for a horse's tail; a shackle running on the stake to which a cow is bound in the 'byre'; a chain; a leash or chain for coupling dogs; a loop of gut or hide round the mast of a boat into which the lower end of the sprit is slipped; a trouble, pest, 'plague'; a quarrel, 'scrummage,' a 'collyshangy.'

Shanginess, *n.* leanness, meagreness.

Shangy-mou'd, *adj.* hare-lipped; having a cleft mouth; having the mouth much to one side.

Shank, *n.* the leg of a stocking; a stocking in process of being knitted; a handle, shaft; a stem; the stem of a tobacco-pipe; the stalk of a plant; the trunk of a tree; the projecting point of a hill joining it to the plain; the shaft or pit of a coal- or lead-mine.—*v.* to travel on foot; to walk; to run; to hurry off; to send off without ceremony; to depart; to knit stockings; to fit with a handle; to sink a shaft; to shrivel up, shrink, wither.

Shank, *n.* a salmon after spawning; the smallest of the kelt tribe.

Shank-bane, *n.* a leg; the shin-bone.

Shanker, *n.* a knitter of stockings; a sinker of shafts; one present at the throwing of the bride's stocking.

Shankie, *n.* the leg.

Shankit, *ppl.* set or started on the way.

Shanks, *n.* with 'Auld,' a name for Death. Cf. Shanky.

Shank's mare, *n.* one's own legs.—*adv.* afoot.

Shank's naig, naigie, or naggie, *n.* 'shank's mare.'

Shank's noddy, or pair, *n.* 'shank's mare.'

Shank-steels, *n.* the legs.

Shankum, *n.* a man or beast with long, slender legs.

Shanky, *n.* in *phr.* 'Auld Shanky,' Death.

Shanna, *v. neg.* shall not.

Shannach, *n.* a bonfire lighted on Hallowe'en. Cf. Shinich.

Shannag, *n.* an ant.

Shannagh, Shannach, *n.* in *phr.* 'it is ill shannagh in you to do so and so,' it is ill on your part, or unwise of you, or un-grateful of you to do so and so.

Shannel, *n.* subsoil; hard, unyielding subsoil as the foundation of a building. Cf. Channel.

Shanny, *adj.* shy, bashful; lacking in energy and push. Cf. Shan, Shandy.

Shantrews, *n.* a Highland tune and dance. Cf. Shak-im-troose.

Shantrum, *n.* a Highland dance.

Shanty, *n.* a chamber-pot. Cf. Chanty.

Shap, *n.* a shop. Cf. Chap.

Shap, *n.* the soil at the foot of a wall, hedge, &c.

Shap, *v.* to mash. Cf. Chap.

Shap, *n.* the pod of peas or beans; an empty pod. Cf. Shaup.

Shape, Shap, *v.* to devise; to cut out; to succeed; to show promise; to go, depart; to drive off; to intend, contrive, manage; to set about.—*n.* an attitude; an article; conduct, manner, mood.

Shapings, *n.* the shreds or clippings of cloth.

Shapper, *n.* a beetle for mashing potatoes.

Shappin-stick, -tree, *n.* a 'shapper.' Cf. Chappin-stick.

Shard, *n.* an old, unseaworthy boat; a piece of furniture badly put together; a little, despicable creature; an unhealthy dwarf. Cf. Shaird.

Shard, *n.* cow-dung.

Share, *adj.* sure.

Share, *v.* in *phr.* 'to share a staff,' to distribute blows.

Share, *v.* to pour off the lighter parts of a liquid; to separate a liquid from the dregs; used of liquids: to separate in a vessel into two or more parts.

Sharg, *adj.* tiny, lean, shrivelled; mean.—*n.* a starveling; a tiny, mischievous creature.

Shargan, *n.* a lean, scraggy person; a weakly child.

Shargar, Sharger, *n.* a thin, stunted person; a weakly child; a starveling; an ill-thriven person or animal.—*v.* to stunt in growth; to become stunted.

Shargar-like, *adj.* lean and stunted, or ill-thriven in appearance.

Shargar-stone, *n.* a stone which was supposed to stop the growth of any one who crept underneath it.

Sharge, *v.* to sharpen, grind.

Shargie, *adj.* thin, shrivelled.

Sharginess, *n.* thinness.

Sharings, *n.* the useless or less valuable part of a liquid, whether poured off or remaining in the vessel.

Shark, *n.* a shirt. Cf. Sark.

Sharle-pin, *n.* a pin of wood or an iron bolt used instead of hinges.

Sharlins, *n.* the whole arrangement of pivots for hinges.

Sharn, *n.* cow-dung.—*v.* to soil with 'sharn.'

Sharn-hole, *n.* the hole that receives the 'sharn' from 'byres.'

Sharny, *adj.* bedaubed with 'sharn.'—*n.* one who cleans out a 'byre.'—*v.* to bedaub with 'sharn.'

Sharny-faced, *adj.* having a very dirty face.

Sharny-peat, *n.* 'sharn' mixed with coaldust, dried in the sun and used for fuel.

Sharon, *n.* 'sharn.'

Sharp, *adj.* used of land: sandy, gravelly; used of weather: cold, frosty, keen, brisk. —*adv.* quickly.—*v.* to sharpen; to 'rough' a horse in frosty weather.—*n.* a sharpening.

Sharpen, *v.* to 'rough' a horse in frosty weather.

Sharping-stone, *n.* a whetstone; a severe lesson learned by experience.

Sharps, *n.* coarse flour containing much bran; turnip-tops; pods of beans.

Sharp-set, *adj.* keen; sharp-witted.

Sharrachie, *adj.* used of the weather: cold, chill, piercing.

Sharrow, *adj.* sharp, sour, bitter in taste; keen. Cf. Shirragh.

Sharrow-craver, *n.* one who acts the part of a dun.

Sharry, *n.* a quarrel; a dispute.—*v.* to quarrel. Cf. Sherra-moor.

Shathmont, *n.* the measure of the fist with the thumb extended; six inches. Cf. Shaftmon.

Shatter, *v.* used of the teeth: to chatter; to rattle, as the windows of a carriage.

Shatter, *v.* to chirp; to chatter.

Shauchle, Schaughle, *v.* to shuffle in walking; to distort.—*n.* an ill-shaped person. Cf. Shachle.

Shaughle-bane, *n.* the wrist-bone. Cf. Shackle-bane.

Shauk, *v.* to shake.

Shaul, Shauld, *adj.* shallow. Cf. Shall, Shald.

Shault, Shaultie, *n.* a pony. Cf. Shelt, Sheltie.

+**Shaum,** *n.* a leg; a limb. Cf. Sham.

Shaum, *v.* to warm one's self by thrusting the lower part of the body close to the fire.—*n.* a warming, a sitting very near the fire to get warm.

Shaup, *n.* the shell or pod of peas or beans; an empty pod; anything empty, worthless, or shrivelled; a fragment, a broken piece. —*v.* to shell peas or beans.

Shaupie, *adj.* lank, thin; not well filled-up.

Shaupit, *ppl. adj.* furnished with pods.

Shauve, *v.* to saw.—*n.* a saw.

Shauvens, *n.* sawdust.

Shav, *v.* to saw. Cf. Shauve.

Shave, *n.* a slice; the wheel of a pulley.—*v.* to gall.

Shave, *v.* to sow.

Shave, *n.* a trick. Cf. Shavie.

Shavel. *v.* to distort. Cf. Shevel.

Shavelin, *n.* a tool for smoothing hollow or circular wood or plaster.

Shaver, *n.* a wag, a queer fellow; a youngster.

Shavie, *n.* a trick; a practical joke; an uproar; a disappointment. Cf. Scavie.

Shaving, *n.* the candle-grease that gutters down the side of a candle; a nicety.

Shaving-whittle, *n.* a weaver's tool.

Shaviter, *n.* a term of contempt; a blackguard.

Shaviter-like, *adj.* having the appearance of a blackguard.

Shavling, *n.* a shaveling; a contemptuous name for a priest.

Shaw, *n.* a grove, a flat piece of ground at the foot of a hill or steep bank; in *pl.* the leaves or stalks of turnips, potatoes, and other esculent roots.—*v.* to cut off the tops of turnips, potatoes, &c.

Shaw, *v.* to sow. Cf. Shave.

Shaw, *n.* in *pl.* refuse flax or hemp. Cf. Shows.

Shaw, *v.* to show.—*n.* a show; a sight, view.

Shaw, *int.* a call to a dog to chase another animal. Cf. Sha.

Shawd, *adj.* shallow. Cf. Shald.

Shawintrews, *n.* a hornpipe-dance. Cf. Shantrews.

Shawl, *adj.* shallow. Cf. Shall.

Shawlie, *n.* a small shawl for the shoulders or head.

Shawlness, *n.* shallowness.

Shawlt, Shawltie, *n.* a pony. Cf. Shelt.

Shawn, *ppl.* shown.

Shawp, *n.* a pod. Cf. Shaup.

Shawpy, *adj.* lanky, thin. Cf. Shaupie.

Shay, *n.* a chaise.

She, *n.* the mistress of a house; 'the wife'; a woman.

Sheaf, *n.* a slice; the wheel of a pulley.—*v.* to slice. Cf. Sheave.

Sheal, *n.* a hut or cottage for temporary use by shepherds, fishermen, sportsmen, &c.; a night-shed for sheltering sheep; a shelter; a summer dwelling.—*v.* to shelter; to put sheep under cover. Cf. Shiel.

Sheal, *v.* to shell; to husk. Cf. Sheel.

Shealin, *n.* the husk of seeds.—*ppl. adj.* fitted for husking grain. Cf. Sheelin.

Shealin, *n.* a hut, 'bothie,' for temporary use of shepherds, &c., during summer. Cf. Shielin.

Shealocks, *n.* the lighter part of grain. Cf. Shillacks.

Shear, *v.* to cut through; to reap with a sickle; to part.—*n.* a knife; the blade of the 'maiden' or guillotine; a shorn sheep;

a reaping; a cut, slice; a particular sheep-mark; the ridge of a hill; the fork of the legs.

Shear-bane, *n.* the pubic-bone.

Shear-blade, *n.* a blade of a pair of scissors; a knife for cutting 'kail.'

Shear-feather, *n.* the part of a plough that cuts out the furrow.

Shear-grass, *n.* long, coarse grass; couch-grass.

Shear-keavie, *n.* a kind of crab.

Shearman, *n.* a cloth-worker.

Shearn, *n.* cow-dung. Cf. Sharn.

Shears, *n.* scissors.

Shear-smith, *n.* a maker of 'shears.'

Shear-tail, *n.* the tern.

Sheath, *n.* a metal plough-head; a holder of needles during knitting, often made of a tied bunch of hens' quills.

Sheath-whittle, *n.* a sheath-knife.

Sheave, *n.* a slice.—*v.* to slice.

Sheavick, *n.* a paring, a small slice.

Sheavle, *v.* to distort; to walk unsteadily. Cf. Shevel.

Shed, *n.* a shade, shady place; a shelter.—*v.* to shade.

Shed, Shede, *v.* to part, separate, divide; to part lambs and calves from their mothers; to rake out a fire; to make a parting in the hair of the head or the wool of a sheep; to cut into slices; to cut off a part; to cease, leave off.—*n.* a parting in the hair or in a sheep's wool; a slice; a piece cut off; used of land: a particular piece set apart; an interstice; the space between the different parts of the warp in a loom.

Shed, *n.* an abode.—*v.* to place in sheds.

Shedder-salmon, *n.* a female salmon just after spawning.

Shedding, *n.* a parting of the hair; the intersection of cross-roads; the separation of lambs from sheep; the sheep drafted out from the flock.

Sheddo, *n.* a shadow.

Shed of corn, *n.* a field set apart for corn.

Shed of land, *n.* a portion of land.

Shed of teeth, *n.* the interstices between the teeth.

Shee, *n.* a slice; a pulley-wheel. Cf. Sheave.

Shee, *n.* a shoe.—*v.* to shoe.

Shee-bree, *n.* water in the shoes.

Sheed, *v.* to part; to slice.—*n.* a portion of land. Cf. Shed.

Sheeffie, *v.* to hesitate; to make frivolous excuses.

Sheeffie-shaffie, *v.* to shilly-shally.—*n.* a frivolous excuse.

Sheeg, *v.* to shake. Cf. Shieg.

Sheegle, *v.* to shake, joggle; to be rickety. Cf. Shiegle, Shoggle.

Sheel, *n.* a shovel.—*v.* to shovel. Cf. Shool.

Sheel, Sheeld, *n.* a temporary residence for shepherds, &c., in summer; a shelter.—*v.* to put sheep under cover. Cf. Sheal.

Sheel, *v.* to shell; to husk. Cf. Sheal.

Sheeld-peat, *n.* peat cut horizontally.

Sheelfa, *n.* the chaffinch. Cf. Shilfa.

Sheelin, *n.* a hut; a cottage; a temporary summer residence. Cf. Shealin.

Sheelin, *n.* the husk of seeds, chaff.—*ppl. adj.* pertaining to husking. Cf. Shealin.

Sheelin-coug, *n.* a dish for holding mussel-bait, &c., when shelled.

Sheeling-hill, *n.* an eminence where grain can be winnowed.

Sheeling-seeds, *n.* the husks of grain.

Sheelock, *n.* an unfilled ear of corn. Cf. Shillacks.

Sheemach, Sheemich, *n.* a mass of matted hair or fibre; thick matted cloth; a pad of a straw rope used as a pack-saddle; a thing of no value; anything much damaged.

Sheen, *n.* shoes. Cf. Shee.

Sheen, *adj.* shining.—*n.* a gleam, sparkle; used of the eye: the pupil.—*v.* to shine; to glitter.

Sheenies, *n.* children's shoes.

Sheep-bucht, -bught, *n.* a small sheepfold.

Sheep-dead, *n.* a disease of sheep from 'flukes' in the liver.

Sheep-drains, *n.* surface drains on moorland.

Sheep-faws, *n.* retreats beneath the moors for sheep in winter.

Sheep-gang, *n.* pasturage for sheep.

Sheep-head, Sheep's-head, *n.* a dish of boiled sheep's head.

Sheep-head-broth, -kail, *n.* broth made from a sheep's head.

Sheep-head-sword, *n.* a basket-hilted sword.

Sheep-herd, *n.* a shepherd.

Sheep-hog, *n.* a sheep before its first shearing.

Sheep-lifter, *n.* a sheep-stealer.

Sheep-lifting, *n.* sheep-stealing; the removal of sheep by their buyer.

Sheep-muckle, *adj.* as big as a sheep, full-grown.

Sheep-net, *n.* a net hung on stakes for enclosing sheep when feeding in a turnip-field.

Sheep-race, *n.* a boys' game; a 'ram-race.' Cf. Ram-race.

Sheep-ree, *n.* an enclosure for sheep built with stone or turf.

Sheep-rent, *n.* the rent of a sheep-farm.

Sheep-rive, *n.* pasturage for sheep.

Sheep-rodding, *n.* a sheep-track.

Sheep-rot, -root, *n.* the butterwort; the pennywort.

Sheep's-cheese, *n.* the root of the couch-grass or 'quicken.'

Sheep-shank, *n.* a person or thing of no value or consequence.

Sheepshank-bane, *n.* a nobody, a 'sheep-shank.'

Sheep-silver, -siller, *n.* mica; an allowance to ploughmen, instead of permission to keep a sheep or two.

Sheep-smearing, *n.* an application of tar and melted butter to sheep in winter for warmth.

Sheep's-suorag, -sorrel, -sourock, *n.* a kind of sorrel.

Sheep-stell, *n.* an enclosure for sheep.

Sheep's tothins, *n.* sheep's droppings.

Sheep-taid, -tade, *n.* a tick or sheep-louse.

Sheep-tathing, *n.* the confinement of sheep to a particular portion of ground until their droppings manure it.

Sheep-tiend, *n.* a tithe on lambs or sheep.

Sheep-troddles, *n.* the droppings of sheep.

Sheep-walk, *n.* a sheep-track.

Sheer, *v.* to shear; to part. Cf. Shear.

Sheer, *n.* a lurch, swerve.

Sheer, *n.* the sweeping stroke of a sword.

Sheer, *adj.* odd, singular. Cf. Skire.

Sheer, *adj.* sure.

Sheer-blade, *n.* a blade of a pair of scissors; a 'lang-kail' knife.

Sheer-cloth, *n.* a cerecloth.

Sheerless, *adj.* without scissors.

Sheerly, *adv.* thoroughly, entirely.

Sheerly, *adv.* surely.

Sheerman, *n.* a cloth-worker. Cf. Shearman.

Sheermouse, *n.* the shrew, field-mouse.

Sheers, *n.* scissors.

Sheet, *v.* to shoot; used of rain: to fall at brief intervals of sunshine.—*ppl.* shot. Cf. Shoot.

Sheet, *n.* a winding-sheet.

Sheets, *n.* the sweetbread. Cf. Cheats.

Sheet-styth, *adj.* shot dead.

Sheeve, *n.* a slice.—*v.* to slice. Cf. Sheave.

Sheevick, *n.* a small slice, a paring, shaving.

Sheevil, *v.* to distort. Cf. Shevel.

Shee-wisp, *n.* a little straw in the shoes to keep the feet warm.

Sheggan, *n.* a reed. Cf. Seggan.

Sheil, *v.* to shell. Cf. Sheal.

Sheil, Sheild, *n.* a hut for shepherds, &c. Cf. Sheal.

Sheilin, *n.* a temporary residence for shepherds, &c. Cf. Shealin.

Sheilin, *n.* the husk of seeds.

Sheiling-hill, *n.* a winnowing hill.

Sheilin-mill, *n.* a mill for husking grain.

Sheimach, *n.* a matted mass of fibrous stuff; a kind of pack-saddle; anything damaged. Cf. Sheemach.

Sheive, *n.* a slice; a slice of bread, &c. Cf. Shive.

Sheld-fowl, *n.* the common sheldrake.

Shelf, *v.* to lay on a shelf; to put past.

Shelf, *n.* a rock or reef under water; a shoal, shallow.

Shelf, *n.* a splinter; a splint for a broken limb. Cf. Skelf.

Shelfa, Shelfy, *n.* the chaffinch. Cf. Shilfa.

Shelf-press, *n.* a walled cupboard with shelves.

Shelister, *n.* the water-flag.

Shelky, *n.* the seal, sea-calf. Cf. Sealch.

Shell, *n.* the husk of oats, peas, &c.; in *pl.* burnt limestone before it is slaked.—*v.* to husk grain; to pay out or down; used of sheep: to have snow frozen in their wool. Cf. Sheal.

Shell, *n.* a cell.

Shellach, *n.* a young boy.

Shellachie, *adj.* used of the weather: cold, piercing. Cf. Sharrachie.

Shellaggy, *n.* the tussilago or colt's-foot.

Shell-gold, *n.* gold leaf.

Shelling, *n.* grain freed from husks.

Shelling-, Shellen-seeds, *n.* the fine husks of grain enclosing the meal; the husks of grain, chaff, generally. Cf. Shealin.

Shell-lime, *n.* unslaked lime.

Shellocks, *n.* ears of corn without kernels. Cf. Shillacks.

Shell-sickness, *n.* a disease of sheep, affecting the omentum and larger intestines.

Shell-wherry, *n.* a small boat used along the coast for bringing up cockles and mussels.

Shell-wife, *n.* a woman who procures and sells shell-fish.

Shell-wing, *n.* the 'shelving' of a cart. Cf. Shelving.

Shelly-coat, Shellicoat, *n.* a water-sprite; a coat made of shells worn by the water-sprite; a bum-bailiff, sheriff's messenger; the tortoise-shell moth.

†**Shelm**, *n.* a rascal, a 'skellum.' Cf. Schelm.

Shelm, *n.* the pieces of wood forming the upper frame of a cart, into which the starts or posts in the sides are mortised.

Shelments, *n.* the frame or rail, extending over the wheels, which is laid on a corn-cart for carrying a load of corn or hay; the longitudinal bars of the sides of a close cart.

Shelpit, *adj.* pale, sickly; pinched. Cf. Shilpit.

Shelter-stell, *n.* an enclosure or shelter for sheep, of stone or a clump of trees. Cf. Stell.

Sheltie, Shelt, *n.* a pony; a Shetland pony. Cf. Shalt.

Shelve, *n.* a shoal, shallow. Cf. Shelf.

Shelving, *n.* additional boards fixed to the sides of a cart to increase its capacity. Cf. Shilbin.

Shelvy, *adj.* shelving, shoaling.

Shend, *v.* to abash, confound; to disgrace; to chide; to mar, destroy, ruin.

Shendship, *n.* ruin, confusion.

Shent, *ppl.* destroyed. Cf. Shend.

Shenty, *n.* hockey; 'shinty.' Cf. Shinty.

Shepherd-check, *n.* shepherd-tartan, a small black-and-white check pattern in cloth.

Shepherd-land, *n.* pastoral districts.

Shepherd's-club, -gourd, *n.* the great mullein.

Shepherd's-needle, *n.* the wild chervil.

†**Shephroas**, *n.* kid-gloves.

Sherarim, *n.* a squabble. Cf. Sharry.

Shere, *v.* to shear.

Sheriff-gloves, *n.* an old perquisite of the sheriff of Edinburgh after each of the two great local fairs.

Shern, *n.* cow-dung. Cf. Sharn.

Sheroo, *n.* the shrew-mouse. Cf. Shirrow.

Sherp, *adj.* sharp.—*v.* to sharpen.

Sherra, Sherry, *n.* a sheriff.

Sherra-moor, *n.* the battle of Sheriffmuir in 1715; a row, confusion; a scrimmage; a loud scolding.

Sherra-, Sherry-officer, *n.* a sheriff-officer.

She-slip, *n.* a young girl.

Sheth, Shethe, *n.* the stick with which a mower whets his scythe; any object coarse and ugly; an ugly person.

Sheth, *n.* the 'sheath' of a plough. Cf. Sheath.

Sheuch, *v.* to distort. Cf. Shach.

Sheuch, Sheugh, *int.* an excl. used for driving off intruding poultry, &c.—*v.* to frighten away by word or gesture; to hasten away. Cf. Shoo.

Sheuch, Sheugh, *n.* a ditch, drain; a furrow, trench; a small stream; a ravine; the hollow of the neck; in *phr.* 'to be in a sheuch,' to be in a difficulty.—*v.* to make ditches, furrows, &c.; to dig for peats or coals; to plant temporarily in a furrow with a view to transplanting; to cover over.

Sheughly, *adj.* rickety, shaky, unsteady, 'shoggly.'

Sheuk, *v. pret.* shook.

Sheuken, *ppl.* shaken.

Sheul, *n.* a shovel. Cf. Shool.

Shevel, *v.* to distort; to become distorted; to walk unsteadily and obliquely.—*n.* a distortion. Cf. Sheyle.

Shevel-, Sheveling-gabbit, *adj.* having a distorted mouth.

Sheveling-heeled, *adj.* used of a shoe: twisted or down at the heel.

Shevel-mouthed, *adj.* having a distorted mouth.

Shevel-shot, *adj.* twisted, deformed; having the joints distorted.

Shew, *v.* to swing; to move up and down; to shove.—*n.* a swing; a see-saw; a shove.

Shew, *int.* an excl. in scaring away poultry,

dogs, &c.—*v.* to scare away poultry, crows, &c.; to cry 'shoo!' Cf. Shoo.

Shew, *v. pret.* showed.

Shew, *v.* to sew. Cf. Shoo.

Shewe, *v. pret.* sowed. Cf. Shaw.

Sheyld, Sheylt, *ppl. adj.* distorted in any way.

Sheyle, *v.* to distort the face; to make faces; to look askance.—*n.* a wry face, a distortion of the features. Cf. Shevel.

Shiacks, *n.* light black oats, variegated with gray stripes, and bearded like barley.

Shiauve, Shiave, *v.* to sow. Cf. Shave.

Shick, *n.* the cheek.—*v.* to set the head, as a bull intending to toss.

Shick-blade, *n.* the cheek-bone.

Shicked, *ppl. adj.* wry-necked.

Shie, *n.* a shoe.

Shieg, *v.* to joggle; to be rickety. Cf. Sheeg.

Shiegle, *v.* to joggle; to be loose and rickety. Cf. Sheegle.

Shiek, *n.* the cheek; the side of anything; insincere or boastful talk. Cf. Cheek.

Shiel, Shield, *n.* a hut, cottage; a shepherd's summer shelter.—*v.* to enclose or shelter in a 'shiel.' Cf. Sheal.

Shiel, *v.* to husk grain; to shell. Cf. Sheal.

Shielin, *n.* the husk of seeds; grain freed from the husk. Cf. Shealin.

Shieling, *n.* a hut, cottage. Cf. Shealin.

Shiemach, *adj.* malignant; reproachful.

Shiffle-shaffle, *v.* to shuffle in walking.

Shift, *v.* to escape; to evade, elude; to hesitate; to try shifts; to swallow.—*n.* a rotation of crops; management.

Shiftin'-claes, *n.* a change of clothes after working hours.

Shifty, *adj.* ingenious; resourceful.

Shig, *v.* to make temporary small stacks in the harvest field.—*n.* a small, temporary stack in the harvest field.

Shilbins, Shilbands, *n.* a frame or boards for adding to the carrying capacity of an ordinary cart. Cf. Shilmonts.

Shile, *v.* to make wry faces; to squint at. Cf. Sheyle.

Shilfa, Shilfaw, Shilfey, Shilfy, *n.* the chaffinch.

Shilfa-cock, *n.* a male chaffinch.

Shilf-corn, *n.* a blackhead; a small, hard pimple. Cf. Shillcorn.

Shill, *n.* a shovel; an arrangement on the front of the plough-beam to regulate the width and depth of the furrow. Cf. Sheal.

Shill, *v.* to shell; to remove the husks from corn; to fall or remove from the shell. Cf. Sheal.

Shill, Schill, *adj.* shrill, loud, noisy.

Shill, *adj.* chill.

Shillacks, Shillicks, Shillocks, *n.* the lighter part of grain; light grain blown aside in winnowing.

Shillcorn, Shilcorn, *n.* a blackhead. Cf. Chilcorn.

Shilling, *n.* in *phr.* to 'spit shillings,' to have the mouth so dry from hard drinking that the saliva spit on the ground lies like a shilling.

Shilling, Shillen, *n.* grain freed from the husk.

Shilling-hill, *n.* a rising ground where grain can be winnowed by the wind. Cf. Sheilin-hill.

Shilling-, Shillen-seeds, *n.* the husks of oats.

Shilly, *adj.* used of the wind: shrill, howling, loud.

Shilly, *v.* to distort. Cf. Sheyle.

Shilly-shally, *adj.* weak, delicate; poor, inferior; undecided.

Shilmine, *n.* a 'shilmont.'

Shilmonts, *n.* the frame laid on a common cart, for carrying a load of hay or straw; the longitudinal bars for the sides of a close cart, to increase its capacity. Cf. Shelments.

Shilp, *n.* a pale, sickly girl.—*adj.* acid to the taste.

Shilpit, *adj.* pale, sickly; weak; pinched, shrunken, and starved-looking; puny, small, insignificant, timid; insipid, tasteless, 'wersh'; thin, inferior, worthless; used of corn-ears: ill-filled.

Shilpitness, *n.* weakness, feebleness; tremor.

Shilpy, Shilpie, *adj.* 'shilpit'; cold and wet.—*n.* a weak, sickly, timid person; a sycophant.

Shil-shal, *n.* a dainty, delicacy.

Shilt, Shilty, *n.* a pony. Cf. Shalt, Sheltie.

Shilvin, *n.* additional boards to the side of a cart. Cf. Shelving.

Shim, *v.* to weed with a hoe.—*n.* a hoe.

Shimee, *n.* a chemise.

Shimmer, *n.* one of the cross-bars in a kiln for supporting the ribs on which the grain is laid to dry.

Shin, *n.* shoes. Cf. Sheen.

Shin, *n.* the slope of a hill; the ridgy part of a declivity, with a hollow on each side.—*v.* to climb with hands and legs, to swarm up.

Shincough, *n.* the whooping-cough.

Shine, *v.* to fling; to throw violently.—*n.* a display; a treat; a merrymaking.

Shiner, *n.* a candlestick; a light on a branched candlestick.

Shinicle, *n.* a bonfire lighted on Hallowe'en.

Shinnen, Shinan, Shinnon, *n.* a sinew. Cf. Sinen.

Shinners, *n.* cinders; the refuse of a blacksmith's stithy.

Shinnock, *n.* the game of 'shinny' or 'shinty.'

Shinny, *n.* the game resembling hockey.

Shinny-ball, *n.* the ball used in 'shinny.'

Shinny-club, *n.* the curved stick used in 'shinny.'

Shin-side, *n.* the front part of the leg, the shin.

Shinty, *n.* the game 'shinny'; the ball and the club used in the game.

Shiolag, *n.* the wild mustard. Cf. Skellock.

Shipper, *n.* a shipmaster, skipper.

Shire, *n.* Wigtownshire, as distinguished from Kirkcudbright, or the Stewartry, in Galloway.

Shire, *adj.* used of liquids : clear, not muddy, thin, watery ; used of cloth : thin ; scrimp, strait, exact in measure ; mere, utter, complete.—*v.* to pour off liquor from dregs. Cf. Share.

Shire-lick, *n.* a smart fellow.

Shirie, *adj.* used of liquids : thin, watery ; used of cloth : thin, loosely woven ; proud, conceited.

Shirins, Schirins, *n.* liquid poured off.

Shirl, *adj.* shrill.

Shirle, *n.* a piece of turf for fuel. Cf. Shirrel.

Shirp, *v.* to shrink, shrivel ; to waste or pine away.

Shirpit, *ppl. adj.* thin and tapering to a point.

Shirpit-looking, *adj.* of thin, shrunken appearance.

Shirra, *n.* a sheriff. Cf. Sherra.

Shirragh, Shirroch, *adj.* sour, acrid.

Shirraghie, Shirrochy, *adj.* looking sour, haughty, or passionate.

Shirragle, Shirraglie, *n.* a contention, squabble.

Shirra-muir, -meer, *n.* the battle of Sheriffmuir in 1715 ; a tumult. Cf. Sherra-moor.

Shirrang, *n.* a wrangle, squabble.—*v.* to wrangle noisily.

Shirrel, *n.* a piece of turf for fuel.

Shirret, Shirrot, *n.* a turf ; a 'divot.'

Shirrow, *n.* the shrew-mouse. Cf. Sheroo.

Shirt, *n.* a woman's shift.

Shirt, *n.* the winter rape ; wild mustard.

Shirt-gown, *n.* a bodice.

Shirt-washings, *n.* the water in which clothes have been washed.

Shit, *n.* a chit ; a child ; a puny, insignificant person or animal ; a term of contempt.

Shit, *v.* to shoot.

Shite, *v.* to void excrement.—*n.* excrement.

Shite-house, *n.* a privy.

Shit-faced, *adj.* having a small face.

Shither, *v.* to shiver.

Shither, *n.* people, folk ; a fellow.

Shitten, *ppl. adj.* dirty ; mean, despicable ; insignificant in appearance.

Shitten-like, *adj.* dirty looking ; mean, despicable ; insignificant in appearance.

Shittle, *n.* anything good for nothing.

Shittle, *n.* a shuttle.

Shiv, Shive, *v.* to push, shove ; with *by*, to succeed.—*n.* a shove.

Shive, *n.* a slice of bread.—*v.* with *aff*, to live upon another, to save or help one's self at another's cost. Cf. Sheave.

Shive, *n.* a 'sive,' chive, one of the leek-tribe.

Shivel, *n.* a shovel.—*v.* to shovel.

Shivelavat's-hen, *n.* a hen that has ceased to lay ; a woman past child-bearing.

Shivereens, *n.* fragments, atoms, shivers.

Shivering-bite, *n.* a piece of bread eaten immediately after bathing.

†**Shiverons, Shivrons,** *n.* chevrons.

Shivers, *n.* torn clothes, rags, tatters.

Shluist, *n.* a large, heavy person ; an ungainly or ungraceful person ; a sluggard. Cf. Slust.

Shluster, *v.* to swallow ungracefully.

Sho, *n.* a shoe.

Sho, *v.* to scare away. Cf. Shoo.

Shoad, *n.* a portion of land. Cf. Shed.

Shoak, *n.* a shock ; a moment.

Shoar, *v.* to threaten ; to scold. Cf. Shore.

Shoas, *n.* the refuse of flax or hemp. Cf. Shows.

Shochad, *n.* the lapwing.

Shochle, *v.* to distort ; to waddle. Cf. Shachle.

Shochle, *n.* an icicle. Cf. Shoggle.

Shochles, *n.* legs, a term of contempt.

Shochling, *ppl. adj.* waddling ; wriggling ; mean ; paltry.—*n.* irregularity of gait.

Shock, *n.* a paralytic stroke ; a moment.

Shock, *v.* to choke.

Shock, *ppl.* shaken.

Shockel, *v.* to shake about ; to joggle. Cf. Shoggle.

Shocking, *adv.* exceedingly.

Shocks, *n.* the jaws ; the 'chafts.' Cf. Chouks.

Shod, *v.* to furnish with shoes ; to shoe a horse ; to fit with a metal tip, band, or ring ; to put a tire on a wheel ; to fit iron toe- and heel-pieces on shoes ; to cover the soles with hobnails.—*n.* a shoe ; an iron tip or point ; the tire of a wheel ; an iron toe- or heel-piece on a shoe.

Shoddie, *n.* a child's shoe ; the iron point of a pikestaff, or pivot of a top.

Shodless, *adj.* shoeless.

Shod-shool, -shule, *n.* a wooden shovel fitted with iron.

Shoe, *v.* to put a tire on a wheel.—*n.* the hopper of a mill.

Shoe-bree, *n.* water in the shoes.

Shoe-clouter, *n.* a cobbler, a mender of shoes.

Shoel, *v.* to distort ; to grimace.—*n.* a grimace. Cf. Showl.

Shoelin, *ppl. adj.* distorted.

Shoe-mou', *n.* the open part of a shoe.

Shoes, *n.* the refuse of flax or hemp; the refuse of hay. Cf. Shows.

Shoe-the-auld-mare, *v.* to play a dangerous game of balancing one's self on a wooden beam slung between two ropes, and going through a number of 'antics' without falling.

Shoe-the-naig, *n.* a blacksmith.

Shoe-wisp, *n.* a little straw in the shoes or boots in order to keep the feet warm.

Shog, Shogg, *v.* to shake; to jog, jolt; to jog along; to swing to and fro, rock a cradle; with *about*, to keep about, remain alive.— *n.* a push, nudge; a blow; a swing-rope.

Shog-bog, *n.* a quaking bog; one on which a light person can walk without sinking.

Shoggie, *v.* to swing to and fro as a pendant; to swing.—*n.* a push; a slight blow; a swing.—*adj.* unstable.

Shoggie-shew, -shoo, -shue, *n.* a swing; a see-saw; the gallows.—*adv.* with a swaying, swinging motion.

Shoggie-shooin', *adj.* used of a long ladder: unsteady under a person moving on it.

Shogging, Shogging-tow, *n.* a swing-rope.

Shoggle, *n.* an icicle; a large piece of ice floating down a river when a thaw comes.

Shoggle, *n.* a clot of blood.

Shoggle, Shogle, *v.* to shake, jolt, rock; to totter; to trot slowly, jog along; to shake or settle down.—*n.* a jolt, jog; a shake.

Shoggly, *adj.* shaky, insecure, tottering.

Shog-shog, *v.* to jolt or shake frequently or continuously.

Shogue, *v.* to 'shog.'—*n.* a 'shog.'

Shol, *n.* a shovel; a shovel-shaped slit in a sheep's ear.

Shol-markit, *adj.* marked with a 'shol,' or born with one. Cf. Shool.

Shon, *n.* a bog, quagmire.

Shone, *n.* shoes.

Shony, *n.* a sea-god to whom sacrifice was formerly offered in the island of Lewis at Hallowe'en.

Shoo, *int.* an excl. to scare away poultry and other intrusive birds and animals; an excl. of surprise, disdain, &c.—*v.* to cry 'shoo!' to scare away; to hasten away.

Shoo, *v.* to swing; to rock to and fro; to see-saw; to back water in rowing; to back a cart.—*n.* a swing; a rocking motion; a rope on which to swing; a see-saw. Cf. Shoggie-shoo.

Shoo, *pron.* she.

Shoo, *v.* to sew.

Shoo, *v.* to sue.

Shooch, *n.* a ditch; a furrow.—*v.* to dig. Cf. Sheuch.

Shood, *n.* the distant noise of animals passing. Cf. Shud.

Shooder, *n.* the shoulder.

Shooder-heid, *n.* the shoulder-blade.

Shooer, *n.* a shower.

Shoog, *v.* to shake; to jolt. Cf. Shog.

Shoogie, *v.* to sway as a pendant; to swing. Cf. Shoggie.

Shoogle, *v.* to shake; to tremble; to dangle. Cf. Shoggle.

Shoo-gled's-wylie, *n.* a children's or boys' game.

Shook, Shooken, *ppl.* shaken.

Shooken, *n.* dues of 'thirlage' paid at a mill; the tenants of an estate bound to send their grain to the mill belonging to the landlord. Cf. Sucken.

Shookie, *int.* a word used in calling horses.

Shool, *n.* a shovel; a spade; a shovel-shaped distinguishing mark in a sheep's ear.—*v.* to shovel; to clean with a shovel; to drag the feet; to shuffle; to mark a sheep's ear with a shovel-shaped mark.

Shool, *v.* to husk grain. Cf. Shill.

Shool, *v.* to twist; to grimace.—*n.* a grimace. Cf. Showl.

Shool-bane, *n.* the shoulder-blade.

Shoolfu', *n.* a shovelful.—*adv.* in shovelfuls.

Shool-staff, *n.* a shovel-handle; a crutch.

Shool-the-board, *n.* the game of 'shovel-board.'

Shoomach, Shoomich, *n.* a diminutive person. Cf. Sheemach.

Shoon, *n.* shoes.

Shoon, *adv.* soon.

Shoonies, *n.* a child's shoes.

Shoonless, *adj.* shoeless.

Shoop, *v. pret.* shaped.

Shoor, *v. pret.* shore. Cf. Shear.

Shoory, *adj.* showery.

Shoost, *v.* to drive off; with *on*, to urge on. Cf. Shoo.

Shooster, Shooster-body, *n.* a sempstress.

Shoot, *n.* a throw of a fishing-net or lines; a push; a puny or imperfect young animal. —*v.* to empty a cart by tipping; to cast fishing-lines or -nets into the sea; to push, thrust; to push off from the shore in a boat and cast a net in a river; to bulge out and give way; to run to seed; to avoid, escape; to separate the worst animals from a drove or flock; to select in purchasing cattle or sheep.

Shoot, *v.* to suit; to please.

Shoot-about, *v.* to get through a time of special difficulty; to be in ordinary health; to satisfy with food.

Shoot aff, *v.* to run off, hurry off.

Shoot by, *v.* to put off, delay; to palm off, substitute; to get through a crisis; to satisfy with a slight or homely meal.—*n.* a makeshift.

Shooter, *n.* a sportsman; a member of a shooting-party.

Shoother, *n.* the shoulder. Cf. Shouther.

Shooting-blade, *n.* the upper leaf of a corn-plant.

Shooting-brod, *n.* a target.

Shoot o'er, *v.* to overpass, get through a period of time; to satisfy; to palm off upon.

Shoot-stick, *n.* an arrow.

Shoot-stock, *n.* a mason's or joiner's tool; a 'bevel.'

Shoow, *v.* to sew. Cf. Shoo.

Shop, *v.* to rap, 'chap'; to hammer.

Shop, *adj.* used of certain plants, as comfrey, eyebright, lungwort, speedwell, and valerian: common, officinal.

Shop-hauder, *n.* a shopman, shopkeeper.

Shop-keeper, *n.* an article in a shop remaining long unsold.

Shoppie, *n.* a small shop.

Shoppie, *n.* a teetotum.

Shore, *n.* a steep rock; a rocky coast; a quay, wharf; a game of marbles.

Shore, *n.* a sewer, drain.

Shore, Schore, *n.* a chieftain.

Shore, *v.* to threaten; to scold; to threaten rain; to be cloudy; to call off; to urge; to hound; to offer; to promise; to favour; to bestow upon.

Shore, *v.* to count, reckon.

Shore, *v.* to cut.—*ppl.* shorn.

Shoreside, *n.* the shore.—*adj.* pertaining to the shore.

Shore-snipe, *n.* the common-snipe.

Shore-teetan, *n.* the rock-pipit.

Shorling, *n.* the skin of a newly-shorn sheep.

Short, *adj.* laconic; tart; quick, urgent; early. —*adv.* soon; recently.—*v.* to amuse, divert, make time seem short; to become angry or short-tempered.—*n.* a short time.

Shortcome, *n.* a shortcoming.

Short-coupled, *adj.* thickset, compact in body.

Short-cuts, *n.* a method of drawing 'cuts' or lots.

Shorten, *v.* to put a baby into short clothes for the first time.

Short-ended, -ainded, *adj.* short-winded. Cf. Aynd.

Shortener, *n.* what shortens or lessens.

Shortgown, *n.* a gown without skirts, reaching only to the middle, worn by female cottagers and servants.

Short-heeled field-lark, *n.* the tree-pipit.

Short-heeled-lark, *n.* the skylark.

Short hours, *n.* the early morning; the small hours.

Shortie, *n.* shortbread, shortcake.

Short kail, *n.* vegetable broth.

Shortlies, Shortlins, *adv.* shortly, quickly, soon.

Shortly, *adv.* tartly.

Shorts, *n.* the refuse of flax; the refuse of hay, straw, &c.

Short-set, *adj.* short and stout, thickset.

Short shed, *n.* in *phr.* 'salving from short shed to short shed,' 'smearing' sheep slightly on the back, neck, and upper parts of the sides.

Short sheep, *n.* a blackfaced forest breed of sheep.

Short-shift, *n.* a day's work of fewer hours than usual; short-time.

Short side, *n.* in *phr.* 'the short side of day,' dawn, early morn.

Short sinsyne, *adv.* lately, not long ago.

Shortsome, *adj.* amusing, diverting, not tedious or 'dreich'; pleasantly situated.— *v.* to divert; to while away time; to keep from ennui.

Shortsyne, *adv.* recently, not long ago.

Short-trot, *n.* a fit of temper; snappishness.

Short while, *adv.* recently.

Short-writing, *n.* shorthand.

Shot, *n.* a division of land.

Shot, Shott, *n.* speed, progress; a blasting in quarrying; a blasting charge of gunpowder, dynamite, &c.; used in curling: a stone lying nearest the tee; a thread shot home when the shuttle passes across the web; a sudden attack of illness; a shooting-pain; the spout that carries water to a mill-wheel; one of the boxes of a mill-wheel receiving the water carried to it; a compartment in the stern of a fishing-boat; a fishing-station on a salmon-river; a projecting window; a hinged window opening outwards; an ill-grown ewe; a refuse animal left after the best of a flock or herd have been chosen; a young weaned pig; a gelded pig; a set of heavy breakers followed by the lull caused by the backwash; the end or aim of action; an outburst; one's turn to play in any game, the stroke or move made; very strong whisky.

Shot, *ppl. adj.* cast at by fairies; used of herring: recently spawned.—*n.* a danger-signal of street-children on the appearance of a policeman.

Shot, Shote, *v.* to shoot.

Shot, *ppl.* shut.

Shot-about, *n.* an alternate move or play in a game.—*adj.* striped, of various colours.

Shot-a-dead, *n.* death from a fairy dart.

Shot blade, *n.* the upper leaf of a corn-plant, the part of a corn-stalk enclosing the ear.

Shot brae, *n.* an avalanche causing a 'scar' on a hillside or bank.

Shot heuch, *n.* a steep bank from which the surface has fallen through the action of rain or flood undermining.

Shot-hole, *n.* a loophole in a wall of an old castle or 'keep.'

Shot-pig, *n.* a young pig taken out of the litter; a gelded pig.

Shot star, *n.* a meteor; the jelly tremella, a gelatinous substance found in pastures, &c., after rain.

Shot stern, *n.* the jelly tremella.

Shotten, *ppl. adj.* shot.

Shottle, *adj.* short and thick, squat.

Shottle, Shottel, *n.* a shuttle; a small drawer; a small, hinged box in a trunk. Cf. Shuttle.

Shot-whaup, *n.* a species of curlew.

Shot-window, *n.* a projecting window.

Shou, *v.* to see-saw.—*n.* a see-saw. Cf. Shoo.

Shoud, *v.* to swing; to waddle. Cf. Showd.

Shoudder-bane, *n.* the shoulder-blade.

Shough, *n.* a drain; a furrow. Cf. Sheuch.

Shoughie, *adj.* short and bandy-legged.

Shoulfall, *n.* the chaffinch. Cf. Shilfa.

Shout, *v.* to shout at, assail with shouts; used of a woman: to be in labour.

Shouther, *n.* the shoulder.—*v.* to lift and carry on the shoulder; to push with the shoulder.

Shouther-bane, *n.* the shoulder-blade.

Shouther-cup, *n.* the socket of the shoulder-blade.

Shouther-heich, *adj.* as high as the shoulder.

Shouther-heicht, *n.* the height of the shoulder.

Shouther-lyar, *n.* a joint of beef, coarse, and fit only for broth or beef-tea.

Shouther-pick, *n.* a pickaxe.

Shouther-shawl, *n.* a small shawl thrown over the shoulders or head.

Shouting, *n.* parturition, childbed-labour.

Shovel-groat, *n.* a game of draughts. Cf. Shool-the-board.

Show, *n.* a see-saw. Cf. Shou, Shoo.

Show, *n.* indication, sign; a sight. Cf. Shaw.

Show, *n.* a coppice; a glade; a 'shaw.'

Showd, Showdie, *v.* to waddle; to swing on a rope or on a see-saw; to rock like a ship tossed by waves; to dandle a child; to rock to sleep.—*n.* a swing, a see-saw; the act of swinging; a swing-rope; a rocking motion; a jaunt, a short journey, a 'lift' on a road. —*adv.* with a rocking motion, or a swaying, waddling gait.

Showdin-tow, *n.* a swing-rope.

Showdy-towdy, *n.* a see-saw.

Shower, Showre, *n.* a sharp attack of pain; a throe, a paroxysm; in *pl.* the pangs of childbirth; a strong push, a sudden turn. —*v.* to give a helping hand; to push or turn forcibly.

Showerickie, Showerockie, *n.* a slight or gentle shower.

Show-fair, *n.* anything more showy than likely to be useful.

Showing-horne, *n.* a 'shoeing-horn,' any article of food that makes men drink more liquor.

Showl, *v.* to twist, distort the face; to grimace.—*n.* a grimace, a distortion of the face. Cf. Schowl.

Showlie, *adj.* deformed by being slender and crooked.

Shows, *n.* the refuse of flax, hemp, hay, straw, &c.

Show-shop, *n.* a place of great display or show.

Show-wife, *n.* a show-woman.

Shrauky, *adj.* scraggy, shrunken.

Shreud, *v.* to shroud.

Shrew, *v.* to curse.

Shriegh, *v.* to shriek.

Shriek o' day, *n.* daybreak.

Shrift, *n.* one who shrives a penitent.

Shrive-days, *n.* days for shriving penitents.

Shroud, *n.* a piece of charred wick, or melted wax or tallow running down the side of a candle, regarded as an omen of death or disaster.—*v.* to clothe, cover.

Shrugg, *n.* a quiver, a convulsion.

Shu, *int.* an excl. to scare poultry, &c.—*v.* to frighten away by word or gesture. Cf. Shoo.

Shuch, Shugh, *n.* a trench, a furrow. Cf. Sheuch.

Shuck, *v. pret.* shook.

Shuck, *v.* to throw out of the hand, to chuck.

Shucken, *n.* mill-dues; tenants bound to grind at a mill. Cf. Sucken.

Shuckenwort, *n.* chickweed.

Shud, Shude, *n.* the coagulation of any liquid body; a large piece of floating ice.

Shud, *v. pret.* should.

Shue, *v.* to swing.—*n.* a swing; a see-saw. Cf. Shoo, Shou.

Shue, *v.* to sew.

Shue, *v.* to scare poultry. Cf. Shoo.

Shuest, *v.* to drive off; to urge. Cf. Shoost.

Shuffle, *v.* with *out*, to hand out, pay.

Shuffle-cap, *n.* the game of 'jingle-the-bonnet.'

Shuffle-the-brogue, *n.* the game of 'hunt the slipper.'

Shug, *int.* a call to a horse to come to the hand.

Shug, *v.* to jog; to jolt.—*n.* a nudge, shove. Cf. Shog.

Shug-bog, *n.* a bog that shakes under one's feet. Cf. Shog-bog.

Shuggie, *v.* to move from side to side; to swing. Cf. Shoggie.

Shuggie-shou, -shue, *n.* a swing; a see-saw.

Shuggle, *v.* to sway; to rock; to become rickety. Cf. Shoggle.

Shug-shug, *v.* to jog continuously. Cf. Shog-shog.

Shuil, Shule, *n.* a shovel. Cf. Shool.

Shuir, *v. pret.* shore.

Shuit, *v.* to shoot.

Shuit, *v.* to suit.

Shuk, *v. pret.* shook.

Shul, Shull, *n.* a mark cut in a sheep's ears, shaped like a shovel. Cf. Shool, Shol-markit.

Shull, *n.* a shoal.

Shullie, *n.* a small shoal.

Shulock, *v.* to sweep the stakes in a game.

Shulocker, *n.* one who sweeps the stakes.

Shun, *v.* to move aside ; to make room for.

Shune, *n.* shoes.

Shunner, Shuner, *n.* a cinder.

Shunner-stick, *n.* charcoal.

Shure, *v. pret.* did shear.

Shurf, *n.* a puny, insignificant person ; a dwarf.

Shurl, *v.* to cut with shears.

Shurl, *n.* snow slipping from a roof ; the noise it makes.

Shurlin, *n.* a sheep newly shorn. Cf. Shorling.

Shurlin-skin, *n.* the skin of a sheep taken off after the wool has been shorn.

Shurral, *n.* a piece of turf for fuel. Cf. Shirrel.

Shushlach, *n.* an untidy, slovenly woman.

Shusy, *n.* a dead body taken from the grave. Cf. Susy.

Shusy-lifter, *n.* a resurrectionist.

Shut, *n.* a shutter ; riddance ; a close, an end ; in *phr.* 'shut of day,' the twilight.—*ppl.* with *of* or *on*, rid of.

Shut, Shute, *v.* to shoot.

Shute, *n.* soot.

Shuten, *ppl.* shot.

Shuther, *n.* the shoulder. Cf. Shouther.

Shuther, *v.* used of loose earth, &c. : to fall down in a heap, to slip.

Shutted, Shutten, *ppl. adj.* shut.

Shuttle, *n.* a hollow in the stock of a spinning-wheel, in which the first filled bobbin is kept till the other is ready to be reeled with it ; a small drawer or box in a press, chest, or escritoire ; a shop-till.—*v.* to weave ; to dart backwards and forwards ; to thrust, push ; to eject forcibly.

Shuttle-airm, *n.* the arm with which the weaver throws the shuttle.

Shuttle-cock, *v.* to play at battledoor and shuttle-cock.

Shuttle-gabbit, *adj.* having a misshapen mouth.

Shuttle of ice, *n.* a miniature glacier ; a sloping slide on which children can toboggan.

Shuttle-ploy, *n.* weaving.

Shuttler, *n.* a weaver.

Shy, *adj.* averse, unwilling.—*v.* to shun.

Shyauve, Shyaave, *v.* to sow. Cf. Shave.

Shyle, *v.* to make faces.—*n.* a grimace. Cf. Sheyle.

Shyre, *adj.* used of liquids : clear, not muddy, thin, watery ; used of cloth, &c. : thin ; used of crops : scanty ; complete, utter.—*v.* to pour off a liquid from its dregs. Cf. Shire.

Shyrie, *adj.* used of liquids : watery ; used of cloth : thin, loosely woven ; proud, conceited. Cf. Shirie.

Sib, *adj.* closely related ; akin ; of the same blood ; friendly, intimate ; bound by ties of affection ; like, having similar qualities ; being in like circumstances ; having right or title to ; improperly intimate.—*n.* kindred, relations.

†Sibba, Sibow, *n.* a young onion. Cf. Sybo.

Sibbens, *n.* the itch ; a venereal disease. Cf. Sivven.

Sib-like, *adj.* friendly.

Sibly, *adv.* closely ; affectionately.

Sibman, *n.* a relation, kinsman.

Sibness, *n.* nearness of blood, relationship ; friendliness.

Sic, *v.* to sigh ; to sob.

Sic, *adj.* such.—*n.* a similar person or thing. —*adv.* so.

Sicca, Siccan, *adj.* such a, such an.

Siccar, *adj.* secure, sure. Cf. Sicker.

Siccart, *ppl.* secured, firmly settled.

Sicen, Sicin, *adj.* such an.

Sich, *v.* to sigh.—*n.* a sigh.

Sicher, *v.* to sigh and sob.

Sichin-like, *adj.* like one in trouble.

Sicht, *n.* sight ; a great number or quantity ; used of the eye : the pupil.—*v.* to inspect.

Sichter, *n.* a great quantity of small objects seen at once.

Sichtly, *adj.* personable.

Sicht-seeing, *ppl. adj.* seeing ghosts.

Sichty, *adj.* striking-looking.

Sick, Sicken, *adj.* such, such an.

Sick, *n.* sickness.

Sicken-like, *adj.* such-like.

Sicker, *adj.* secure, safe ; firm ; sure, certain ; steady, unyielding, to be relied on ; prudent, cautious in money matters, grasping ; severe, harsh ; used of a bargain : hard, stiff.—*adv.* securely, firmly, safely ; certainly, assuredly.—*v.* to make sure ; to fasten firmly ; to make certain.

Sickerly, *adv.* securely, safely, firmly ; surely, certainly ; assuredly ; severely.

Sickerness, *n.* security ; firmness ; assurance ; severity ; custody ; prison.

Sick-fu', *adj.* full to bursting.

Sick-house, *n.* a hospital.

Sickie, *int.* a sheep-call.

Sick-laith, *adj.* very unwilling.

Sickle, *v.* to reap with a sickle.

Sickle-sweep, *n.* a curve like that of a sickle.

Sicklike, *adj.* of the same kind. —*adv.* in the same manner.

Sickly-looking, *adj.* used of the moon : hazy, watery.

Sickness, *n.* 'blackwater' or 'braxy' in sheep.

Sickrife, *adj.* sickly ; slightly sick.

Sick-saired, *adj.* satiated to loathing, thoroughly sated.

Sick-sorry, *adj.* very sorry ; extremely unwilling.

Sick-tired, *adj.* very weary of ; weary to nausea ; utterly disgusted.

Sickwise, *adv.* in such a manner.

Siclike, *adj.* like such a person or thing ; such-like.

Sicsae, *adv.* just so.

Sicsame, *adj.* just the same, self-same.

Sid, *v.* should.

Sid, *n.* the inner covering of grain ; a fragment. Cf. Seed, Side.

Sidderwood, *n.* southernwood.

Siddie, *adj.* full of husks of oats, full of 'sids.' Cf. Seedy.

Siddle-siddle, *adv.* with sidelong movement.

Side, *n.* a district, region ; the side of. Cf. Athis'd.

Side, *n.* time. —*adj.* used of a traveller : too late ; overtaken by night.

Side, *adj.* wide, long ; hanging low down ; trailing.

Side, *adj.* hard, severe ; strong ; rough.

Side, *prep.* beside.

Side, *n.* a husk of oats ; the inner covering of grain removed by grinding ; a fragment. Cf. Seed, Sid.

Side and wide, *adj.* large in every way.

Side-board, *n.* a movable board for heightening the side of a cart.

Side-coat, *n.* a long coat, a greatcoat ; a long waistcoat.

Side-dish, *n.* a person invited to an entertainment in order to make game of one or more of the guests.

Side-dykes, *n.* in *phr.* to 'rin side-dykes with one,' to keep company or be on friendly terms with one.

Side-for-side, *adv.* alongside, in the same line, at the same place. Cf. Sidy-for-Sidy.

Side-ill, *n.* a disease affecting cows and sheep in the side. Cf. Seth-ill.

Side-langel, *v.* to tie the fore- and hind-leg of an animal on the same side to prevent straying.

Side-legs, *adv.* side-saddle ; with legs on one side, as ladies ride.

Side-lichts, *n.* side-whiskers.

Sideling, *adj.* having a declivity ; sidelong ; oblique. —*adv.* sideways, obliquely.

Sidelins, Sidelans, *adv.* sideways ; with legs on one side ; alongside ; aside ; furtively. —*adj.* slanting, sidelong. —*n.* a declivity.

Side-sark, *n.* a long shirt.

Side-school, *n.* a school auxiliary to the principal one in a parish.

Side's-man, *n.* an umpire, referee.

Side-springs, *n.* elastic-sided boots.

Side-stap, *n.* a false step causing a wrench to a limb.

Side-tailed, *adj.* long-tailed.

Side-wipe, *n.* an indirect censure or sarcasm ; a blow on the side ; a covert blow.

Sid-fast, *n.* rest-harrow. Cf. Sit-fast.

Sidle, *v.* with *off*, to slip off.

Sidlin, *adj.* sidelong. Cf. Sideling.

Sids, *n.* in *phr.* 'never to say sids,' never to mention the subject, never to say anything, though expected to say something.

Sidy-for-sidy, Sidie-for-sidie, *adv.* on a footing with ; in a line of equality. Cf. Side-for-side.

Sidyways, *adv.* to one side.

Sie, *v.* to strain milk through a sieve. —*n.* a strainer. Cf. Sey, Sye.

Sie, *n.* the opening of a gown for the insertion of the sleeve ; part of the back of an ox cut up for beef. Cf. Sey.

Siecan, *adj.* such an.

Sieffer, *n.* an impudent, empty-headed rascal ; a worthless, lazy, or drunken loafer, a 'cipher'; a playful term of endearment applied to children. —*adj.* diminutive.

Siege, *n.* a chase with a view to chastisement.

Sieging, *n.* a scolding.

Siep, *v.* to percolate. Cf. Seep.

Siepher, *n.* a lazy, worthless fellow. Cf. Sieffer.

Sier, *v.* to salve ; to apply a salve, balm, &c.

Sieve, *v.* to pass through a sieve ; to become full of holes like a sieve.

Sieve and sheers, *n.* a method of divination with a riddle and scissors.

Siever, *n.* a miller's man ; any one who sifts grain.

Sievewricht, *n.* a maker of sieves.

Sievins, *n.* fine particles that have passed through a sieve.

Sifflication, *n.* a supplication, petition.

Sift, *v.* used of snow : to fall in fine flakes as through a sieve ; to bandy words ; with *out*, to find out a secret.

Sifting, *n.* a sprinkling.

Sigg, *n.* a callus on the skin.

Sigh, *n.* a seer, one who pretends to predict the future.

Sight, *n.* a station on a river for observing the movements of salmon. —*v.* to spy from a station the movements of salmon in order to direct the casting of the net ; to inspect, examine. Cf. Sicht.

Sightman, *n.* the fisherman who observes the movements of salmon.

Signbrod, *n.* a sign-board.

Sik, Sike, *v.* to sigh ; to sob.—*n.* a sigh. Cf. Sic.

Sik, *v.* to seek.

Sike, *n.* a small rill ; a marshy bottom or hollow with one or more small streams.

Sike, *adj.* such.

Sike, *n.* in *phr.* to ' flay the sikes from one,' to give one a good beating.

Siken, Sikken, *adj.* such an.

Siker, Sikker, *adj.* firm ; sure ; fast. Cf. Sicker.

Sikie, *adj.* full of rills.

Sikkle, *n.* a bicycle.

Silder, *n.* and *adj.* silver.

Sile, *n.* a beam, a rafter, a ' couple' ; the lower part of a rafter ; an iron bar inserted across the centre of the ' eye' of a hand-mill.

Sile, *n.* soil.

Sile, *n.* the young of herring ; milt. Cf. Sill.

Sile, *v.* to strain, filter ; to rinse clothes.—*n.* a strainer, milk-sieve. Cf. Seil.

Sile-blade, *n.* one of the upright beams of a ' sile' ; the side of a ' sile.'

Siler, *n.* a strainer for milk. Cf. Seiler.

Silit, *ppl. adj.* fallen behind, at a distance.

Silkey, Silkie, *n.* a seal, sea-calf. Cf. Sealch.

Sill, *n.* a beam, rafter ; a beam lying on the ground-floor, a ' sleeper.'

Sill, *n.* milt ; herring-fry.

Sillabe, *n.* a syllable.

Siller, *n.* silver ; money ; payment ; price.—*adj.* of silver.—*v.* to pay ; to bribe with money.

Siller-bag, *n.* a money-bag.

Siller-blind, *adj.* blinded by wealth.

Siller-buckie, *n.* the gray, purple-streaked pyramid shell.

Siller-day, *n.* pay-day.

Siller-dodge, *v.* to cheat out of money, to embezzle.

Siller-duty, *n.* rent or dues paid in money alone.

Siller-gatherer, *n.* a money-gatherer, a miser.

Siller-ginglers, *n.* the quaking-grass.

Siller-grip, *n.* a miser, a ' money-grubber.'

Siller-hair-grass, *n.* the mouse-grass.

Siller-holes, *n.* excavations made in working minerals, &c.

Sillerie, *adj.* rich in money.

Sillerieness, *n.* richness in money.

Sillerless, *n.* poor, impecunious.

Siller-maill, *n.* rent paid in money alone.

Siller-marriage, *n.* a marriage to which the guests contributed money.

Siller-owl, *n.* the barn-owl.

Siller-plover, *n.* the knot.

Siller-pock, *n.* a money-bag.

Siller-poun', *n.* a pound in silver.

Siller-rent, *n.* rent paid in money alone.

Siller-Saturday, *n.* pay-day.

Siller-sawnie, *n.* the pearly-top ; the periwinkle.

Siller-shakers, -shakle, *n.* the quaking-grass.

Sill-fish, *n.* a male fish, a milter. Cf. Sill.

Sillist, *adj.* laying aside work in the meantime.

Sillup, *n.* a syllable. Cf. Sillabe.

Silly, *adj.* good, worthy : pure, innocent, young ; a term of endearment or compassion ; weak, feeble, frail ; sickly, delicate ; lean, meagre ; timid, spiritless ; fatuous, imbecile.—*v.* to show weakness, act foolishly.

Silly-how, -hoo, *n.* a child's caul ; any curious head-dress. Cf. Seelie-hoo.

Silly man, *n.* a term of compassion, ' poor fellow.'

Silly-willy, *n.* a foolish person.

Sillywise, *adj.* somewhat weakened in mind or body.

†Silvendy, *adj.* solvent ; trustworthy ; safe. Cf. Sevendle, Solvendo.

Silver-work, *n.* silver plate.

Sim, *n.* a hint ; a slight notice or warning.

Simie, Symie, *n.* a name of the devil ; in *phr.* ' like simie or symie,' used of two things that are quite like each other.

Similar, *adj.* in *phr.* ' similar the same,' exactly, or nearly, the same.

Simmer, *v.* to cool, subside.

Simmer, *n.* the principal beam in the roof of a building ; one of the supports laid across a kiln.

Simmer, *n.* summer.—*v.* to bask ; to enjoy the warmth and brightness of summer ; to pasture cattle in the open in summer.

Simmer and winter, *v.* to harp on the same string ; to be minute and prolix in narration ; to ponder, ruminate ; to adhere to permanently. Cf. Summer.

Simmer-lift, *n.* the summer sky.

Simmerscale, *v.* used of beer, &c. : to cast up scales in summer, when it begins to sour.—*n.* in *pl.* the scales thus cast up.

Simper-faced, *adj.* having a simpering face.

Simple, *adj.* of humble birth.—*n.* used in weaving : that part of a weaver's harness to which the figure intended to be wrought is committed.—*v.* to feed on herbs or ' simples.'

Simulate, *ppl. adj.* dissembling ; insincere ; pretended ; unreal.

Simulatlie, *adv.* under false pretences ; hypocritically.

Sin, *n.* the sun.

Sin, *n.* a son.

Sin, *adv.* since; ago; since then.—*prep.* since; from the time that.—*conj.* since; seeing that. Cf. Syne.

Sin, *n.* blame.—*v.* to make to sin; to injure by sin.

†Sinacle, *n.* a sign; the slightest trace; a particle, grain.

Sinal, *adv.* seldom. Cf. Seenil.

Since, *adv.* afterwards; then.

Sinceder, *n.* a seceder from the Established Church. Cf. Seceder.

Sincere, *adj.* grave; apparently serious.

Since syne, *adv.* since then.

Sind, Sinde, *v.* to rinse; to wash down food with drink; to quench.—*n.* a slight washing; a drink with or after food. Cf. Synd.

Sinder, *v.* to sunder, part.

Sindering-day, *n.* the day of parting after a merrymaking.

Sindill, Sindle, *adv.* seldom.

Sindle-times, *adv.* seldom. Cf. Seenil.

Sindoon, *n.* sundown.

Sindry, *adj.* sundry, several.—*adv.* asunder; in pieces.

Sine, *v.* to rinse. Cf. Sind.

Sine, *adv.* ago; then; in that case; late.—*prep.* since.—*conj.* since; because; therefore. Cf. Sin, Syne.

Sin-eater, *n.* a person called in, when any one died, to eat the sins of the deceased, which would have kept him haunting his relatives.

Sin-eating, *n.* the custom of placing a bit of bread upon the plate of salt laid upon the breast of a corpse, by a person known as the 'sin-eater,' who, for money, at the same time partook of it, thereby, as it was believed, absorbing all the sins of the deceased.

Sinen, *n.* a sinew. Cf. Shinnen.

Sing, *v.* used of animals: to hum, buzz, to purr; to wheeze; with *out*, to call aloud, shout.

Sing, *v.* to singe.—*n.* used of food: the point of burning.

Singeing-dust, *n.* the dust from stuff-goods quickly passed over a flame.

Singing-cake, *n.* a cake given to carol-singers at 'Hogmanay.'

Singing-e'en, *n.* the last night of the year, 'Hogmanay.'

Singing-glasses, *n.* musical glasses.

Singing-lines, *n.* popular secular lines used for teaching psalm-tunes.

Singing-schule, *n.* a singing-class for the practice of psalmody.

Singit, *ppl. adj.* singed; evil-smelling; puny, shrivelled; in *phr.* a 'singit hair,' next to nothing.

Single, *adj.* few, slight; small; used of letters of the alphabet: not capital; of liquor: weak, under-proof, without addition or accompaniment; of a waistcoat: one without a lining; of a man: one without means of defence; of the Shorter Catechism: a copy without Scripture-proofs; singular, not plural.—*adv.* alone; singly.—*n.* in *pl.* a handful or a few ears of gleaned corn; the talons of a hawk.—*v.* used of turnips, &c.: to thin out with the hand; of flax: to prepare it for making thread.

Single-Book, *n.* the Shorter Catechism without proof-texts.

Single-en', *n.* a house of one apartment.

Single-flooring, *n.* a kind of nail.

Single-horse-tree, *n.* the 'swingle-tree' or stretcher of a plough, by which one horse draws.

Single-note, *n.* a £1 bank-note.

Singler, *n.* one who 'singles' turnips, &c.

Single sailor, *n.* a man before the mast.

Single-sided, *adj.* widowed.

Single soldier, *n.* a private soldier.

Singles questions, *n.* the Shorter Catechism without proof-texts.

Single-straw, *n.* straw gleaned as 'singles.'

Single-tongued, *adj.* truthful.

Singular combat, *n.* single combat.

Sinile, *adv.* seldom. Cf. Seenil.

Sink, *v.* to lose sight of a landmark on the horizon; to overpower with liquor; to excavate a pit-shaft; to cut the die used for coining money; to curse, swear, used in imprecations.—*n.* a place where superabundant moisture stagnates in the ground; the shaft of a mine; a waste, a throwing away of money; a weight, the weight of a clock.

Sinkation, *n.* cursing.

Sinker, *n.* a miner; a stone attached to each lower corner of a drift-net; a weight attached to the rope of a horse's stall-collar.

Sinking rope, *n.* a drift-line to which smuggled kegs of spirits were attached and weighted.

Sinkler, *adj.* used of codfish: thin, with large head and thin body.

Sinky, *adj.* yielding, given to sinking.

Sinle, Sinnle, *adv.* seldom. Cf. Seenil.

Sinn, *v.* to wash down; to rinse. Cf. Sind.

Sinna, *v. neg.* shall not.

Sinna, Sinnan, *n.* a sinew.

Sinnacle, *n.* a viciously-disposed person.

Sinnen, Sinnin, *n.* a sinew.

Sinnery, Sinnry, *adj.* sundry, several. Cf. Sindry.

Sinnet, *n.* merry-plait.

Sinnie, *n.* senna.

Sinnie-fynnie, *n.* the black guillemot.

Sinno, Sinnon, Sinon, *n.* a sinew.

Sinry, *adj.* sundry.

Sinsheen, *n.* sunshine.

Sinsyne, *adv.* ago, since then. **Cf. Sin, Syne.**

Sint, Sinter, *n.* a small quantity; a morsel, a 'scent.'

Sinwart, *adv.* towards the sun.

Sip, *v.* to sup fluid food with a spoon; to drink, not necessarily in small mouthfuls.

Sipage, *n.* a leakage.

Sipe, Sip, *v.* to distil; to shed; to ooze, trickle, leak; to percolate slowly; to soak; to cause to drop or trickle; to drain to the dregs; to soak through; to sink slowly and disappear.—*n.* a leakage; a sip, a drop; a state of wetness; a puddle; a slight spring of water; the remainder of the contents of a bottle, &c.; the dregs of a liquid. **Cf. Seip.**

Siping, *ppl. adj.* soaking.—*n.* in *pl.* oozings, leakings from an insufficient cask, &c.

Sipit, *ppl. adj.* drained of moisture, dried up.

Siplin, *n.* a sapling.

Sipper, *n.* supper. **Cf. Supper.**

Sipple, *v.* to sip continuously, to tipple.—*n.* a tipple. **Cf. Sirple.**

Sir, *n.* a term of address used by Highlanders to a lady; in *pl.* applied to a number of persons of both sexes.—*int.* an excl. of astonishment, without regard to the number or sex of the persons addressed.

Sirce, Sircy, *int.* an excl. of surprise, as above; 'sirs!'

†Sirdon, Sirdoun, *n.* a low, plaintive, bird-like cry.—*v.* to emit such a cry.

Sirdoning, *n.* the singing of birds.

Sire, *n.* a sewer, gutter. **Cf. Siver.**

Siree, *n.* sir.

Sir-John, *n.* a close-stool.

Sirken, *adj.* tender of one's body; tender of one's credit.

Sirkenton, *n.* one afraid of pain or cold; one who keeps near the fire.

Sirple, *v.* to sip often.—*n.* a sip; a small quantity of liquid.

Sirree, *n.* a soiree, a social gathering, a 'swarry.'

Sirse, *int.* an excl. of surprise. **Cf. Sirce.**

Siskie, *int.* seest thou!

Sist, *v.* a legal term: to stop procedure; to cite, summon; to stay.—*n.* a delay of legal procedure; a summons, citation.

Sistance, *n.* the smallest possible quantity of food, &c.

Sister-bairn, *n.* a sister's child; a cousin on the mother's side.

Sister-part, *n.* a daughter's portion; less than one's right; nothing at all.

Sistren, *n.* sisters.

Sit, Sitt, *v.* to lie; to remain in the same position; to continue in a house or farm during a lease; to cease to grow; to become stunted; used of a wall, &c.: to sink, settle;

to seat; to set; to ignore, disregard, refuse, disobey; to suit, fit, become.—*n.* the state of sinking; continuance in a place.

Sit, *ppl.* sat.

Sit doun, *v.* to become settled, established; to continue; to settle on the lungs; to become bankrupt.—*n.* a settlement in marriage, 'down-sitting.'

Site, *n.* anxious care; suffering; punishment.

Site o' claise, *n.* a suit of clothes.

Sitfast, *n.* a large stone fast in the earth; the creeping crowfoot; the rest-harrow.

Sith, *conj.* seeing that; because; although.

Sith, *adj.* true.—*n.* truth.—*v.* to make one believe; to impose on one by flattery. **Cf. Sooth.**

Sith, *n.* in *phr.* 'oh sith!' an excl. of sorrow.

Sithe, *v.* to strain through a sieve; to strain milk.—*n.* a sieve; a milk-strainer.

Sithe, *n.* a scythe.

Sithe, *n.* satisfaction for injury.—*v.* to give legal compensation.

Sithement, *n.* legal compensation; satisfaction for injury.

Sithence, *adv.* since that time.—*conj.* seeing that.

Sitherwood, *n.* southernwood. **Cf. Sidderwood.**

Sithes, *n.* chives.

Sithe-sned, *n.* the handle of a scythe.

Sithe-straick, *n.* a piece of hardwood greased and sprinkled with flinty sand, for sharpening a scythe.

Sit-house, *n.* a dwelling-house, as distinguished from a house used for any other purpose.

Sit in, *v.* to sit to the table, draw in or near.

Sit on, *v.* to remain in a place or house; used of food: to stick to the pan, burn in cooking.

Sit-on-ma-thoom, *n.* a contemptuous term for a diminutive person.

Sit-sicker, *n.* the upright crowfoot; the cornfield crowfoot.

Sit still, *v.* to continue in a tenancy of house, farm, &c.

Sitten, *ppl. adj.* used of eggs: being hatched; stunted in growth; not thriving.

Sitten-doun, *adj.* used of weather: settled; of a cold, &c.: having taken hold of one, difficult to get rid of

Sitten-like, *adj.* ill-thriven in appearance.

Sitten-on, *adj.* stunted, small; burnt and stuck to the pan in cooking.

Sitten-up, *adj.* careless, neglectful, specially as to religious duties.

Sitter, *n.* a rebuff, 'settler.'

Sittet, *v. pret.* sat.

Sittie-fittie, *n.* the ladybird.

Sittin', *n.* a situation, berth.

Sittin'-board, *n.* the seat of a pew.

Sittin'-down, *n.* a resting-place; a settlement

in marriage; bankruptcy.—*adj.* settled, chronic, continued; used of a meal: partaken of by the company seated at table.

Sitting-drink, *n.* a drink of long duration taken in company.

Sit to, *v.* to settle down to, set in for; used of food: to stick to the pan in cooking.

Sittrel, *adj.* peevish; discontented. Cf. Satteral.

Sit under, *v.* to attend regularly the ministry of any particular preacher.

Sit up, *v.* to watch over a dead body at night; to become careless as to one's religious profession or duties.

Sit upon, *v.* to draw near to, sit near to; to fit, become, suit.

Sit with, *v.* to disregard, endure, put up with.

Siv, *n.* a sieve.

Sive, *v.* to drain.

Siver, *n.* an open drain, a gutter.

Sives, *n.* chives, small onions.

Sivven, *n.* the raspberry; in *pl.* a venereal disease resembling a raspberry. Cf. Sibbens.

Sixpence, *adj.* sixpenny.—*n.* in *phr.* to 'spit sixpence,' to be very thirsty from hard drinking. Cf. Shilling.

Six-quarter cattle, *n.* cattle from eighteen months to two years old.

Sixteen-hundred, *n.* very fine linen. Cf. Seventeen-hundred.

Size, *v.* to estimate the value of a thing or the character of a person.—*n.* importance; estimation.

Size, *n.* an assize.

Size, *n.* chives.

Sizer, *n.* a juryman.

Sizzen, Sizzon, *n.* a season.

Sizzle, *v.* to make a hissing sound like water on hot iron; to fizz.—*n.* a hissing sound as in frying.

Sk (*for* Sk *words see also* Sc).

Skaal, *v.* to scold.

Skad, *v.* to scald. Cf. Scad.

Skadderized, *ppl. adj.* used of persons: withered. Cf. Scadderized.

Skaddin, Skadden, *adj.* dry, shrivelled.—*n.* anything dry and shrivelled; a thin, shrivelled person; a very lean animal.

Skaddow, *n.* a shadow. Cf. Scaddaw.

Skae, *v.* to aim with; to direct to.

Skae, *n.* excrement, solid or liquid. Cf. Skee.

Skaeny, *n.* packthread, twine. Cf. Skeengie.

Skaetch, *v.* to skate.—*n.* a skate.

Skaetcher, *n.* a skater; a skate.

Skafe, *n.* a merry, frolicsome person; a wag.

Skaff, *n.* food; an idle wanderer; a sponger; fun.—*v.* to sponge for food; to find a livelihood. Cf. Scaff.

Skaffing, *n.* any kind of food.

Skafrie, *n.* the contents of a larder.

Skaicher, *n.* a sponger. Cf. Skaigher.

Skaicher, *n.* a gentle scolding term applied to a child.

Skaif, *n.* a shabby person; a worthless fellow. Cf. Scaff.

Skaig, *v.* to stride along clumsily; to walk briskly, scud along.—*n.* a quick motion; a scudding along; an unpleasant person; a woman of uncertain temper.—*adv.* with force; flat.

Skaigh, *v.* to obtain by craft or wiles; to obtain by any means; to pilfer, steal; to sponge for food; to roam idly and foolishly. —*n.* a disappointment; a search; an outlook.

Skaigher, *n.* one who goes about seeking food; a sponger; one who obtains by artful means.

Skaik, *v.* to bedaub; to separate awkwardly or dirtily one thing from another, or part of a thing from the rest; to spread.

Skail, Skaill, *v.* to unrip; to tear asunder; to dismiss or disperse a meeting; to scatter, spread about; to spill; to upset; to fire a gun; used of a meeting: to break up, disperse; to depart from a place; used of a wall: to jut outwards; used of a house: to dismantle it, give up housekeeping; to pass over; to retreat.—*n.* a dispersion, dismission; the noise of waves breaking on the shore; a hurricane, a scattering wind or storm; anything scattered or separated from its fellows; a thin, shallow vessel for skimming milk.

Skailach, *n.* a sharp cry; a scream, yell. Cf. Skelloch.

Skail-dish, *n.* a thin, shallow dish for skimming.

Skail-drake, *n.* the sheldrake.

Skailer, *n.* a scatterer, disperser.

Skailin', *n.* dispersion, dismission.

Skailin'-time, *n.* the time of dismission; the hour when a congregation, school, or meeting breaks up.

†Skailit, *n.* a small bell. Cf. Skellat.

Skaillie, *n.* blue slate; slate-pencil.

Skaillie-burd, *n.* a writing-slate.

Skaillie-pen, *n.* a slate-pencil.

Skailment, *n.* a scattering, dispersion.

Skailset, *v.* to separate, scatter, disperse.

Skail-water, *n.* the superfluous water let off by a sluice before it reaches the mill.

Skail-wind, *n.* a hurricane.

Skailyie, *n.* slate-pencil.

Skaim, *v.* to scheme.

Skainya, *n.* packthread. Cf. Skeengie.

Skaip, *n.* a beehive. Cf. Skep.

Skair, *n.* the bare part of a hillside; a bare, steep bank. Cf. Scaur.

Skair, *v.* to splice.—*n.* a splice; the joining of a fishing-rod's parts; a joint in carpentry.

Skair, *v.* to share.—*n.* a share, portion.

Skair, *v.* to scare; to frighten off; to be scared. —*n.* a scare, a fright.—*adj.* timid, shy, affectedly modest.

Skair-Furisday, *n.* Maundy-Thursday.

Skairgifnock, *n.* a girl half-grown or entering on puberty. Cf. Scargivenet.

Skairin, *n.* a share.

Skair-like, -looking, *adj.* of wild or frightened looks.

Skair-scon, *n.* a pancake baked and eaten on Shrove Tuesday.

Skairt, *ppl. adj.* scared.

Skait, *n.* a paper-kite. Cf. Skate.

Skait-bird, *n.* Richardson's skua.

Skaitch, *v.* to skate.

Skaith, *v.* to injure, damage; to defame.—*n.* injury, damage, loss; danger, expense.

Skaithfu', *adj.* hurtful, injurious.

Skaithie, *n.* a fence of stakes or bunches of straw placed before the outer door, or a wall of stone, turf, or boards at the outside of a door, as a shelter from wind.

Skaithless, *adj.* unhurt; harmless.

Skaithly, *adj.* hurtful.—*n.* a young romp.

Skaith-seeker, *n.* one who seeks to harm others.

Skaitie-purse, *n.* the ovarium of the skate.

Skaive, *v.* to calumniate; to spread abroad a matter.

Skaivie, Skaivy, *n.* a trick, prank; the result of a mad prank; a disappointment; a mishap; an affront.—*adj.* hare-brained; delirious, on the verge of insanity.—*v.* to play pranks; to wander idly, aimlessly, or foolishly.

Skaivle, *v.* to put out of shape, wear to one side; to twist; to totter in walking; to walk affectedly.—*adj.* twisted, out of shape.

Skaldocks, *n.* wild mustard. Cf. Scaldricks.

Skale, *v.* to disperse; to scatter.—*n.* a dispersion; a skimming-dish. Cf. Skail.

Skale-stairs, *n.* a straight or square staircase.

Skaley, *v.* to squint. Cf. Skelly.

Skalk, *n.* a morning drink. Cf. Scalch.

Skall, *n.* the right to the next turn of the mill in grinding.

Skallag, *n.* a bond-servant who carried kelp and did the hard work.

Skalrag, *adj.* shabby in appearance.—*n.* a tatterdemalion.

Skam, *n.* a mark; a spot, stain.—*v.* to singe, scorch. Cf. Scaum.

Skambler, Skamler, *n.* a visitor at meal-times; a sponger.

Skammit, *ppl. adj.* scorched, singed.

Skance, *v.* to reflect on, ponder; to scan; to glance at contemptuously; to give a slight narration; to test, try; to reproach, censure; to conjecture.—*n.* a glance; blame; scandal. Cf. Scance.

Skance, Skanse, *v.* to glitter; to make a great display, especially in talk; to exaggerate. —*n.* a gleam. Cf. Scance.

Skanes, *n.* dandriff showing in the hair of the head.

Skantack, *n.* a fishing-line set with hooks for night-fishing. Cf. Scantack.

Skap, *n.* the scalp; the head.

Skar, Skare, *n.* a steep, bare bank; a rocky or sandy spit running into the sea; in *pl.* rocks through which there is an opening. Cf. Scaur.

Skar, *v.* to frighten.—*n.* a fright.—*adj.* timid, shy.

Skar, *adj.* left.

Skare, *v.* to scare.—*n.* a scare.—*adj.* scared.

Skare, *v.* to splice. Cf. Scare.

Skare, *v.* to share.

Skar-gait, *adj.* used of a horse; easily scared.

Skar-handit, *adj.* left-handed. Cf. Skerhandit.

Skarin, *n.* a share.

Skarnoch, *n.* a crowd; a tumult. Cf. Scarnoch.

Skarrach, *n.* a flying shower; a squall with rain; a large quantity of drink.

Skarrow, *n.* reflected light; faint light; a shadow. Cf. Scarrow.

Skart, *v.* to scratch; to scrape; to write.— *n.* a scratch; a scrap of writing; a puny person; a niggard; a rasping sound. Cf. Scart.

Skart, *n.* the cormorant. Cf. Scart.

Skart, *ppl. adj.* scared.

Skart-free, *adj.* safe and sound.

Skartle, *v.* to scrape money together by many continuous small economies; to scrape together by many little strokes; to scatter.— *n.* an iron dung-scraper.

Skashie, *n.* a wrangle.—*v.* to wrangle.

Skashle, *v.* to quarrel; to twist; to tread on the side of the foot; to shuffle in walking.—*n.* a squabble; a twist, wrench; a shuffling walk, and the noise of it.—*adv.* with a waddling or shuffling gait.

Skatch, *v.* to skate. Cf. Sketch.

Skatcher, *n.* a skater; a skate.

Skate, *n.* a paper-kite.

Skate, *n.* the ovarium of the skate; a term of contempt; a boy or girl of little worth.

Skate-bree, *n.* the water in which a skate has been boiled.

Skate-rings, *n.* jelly-fish.

Skate-rumple, *n.* the hinder part of a skate; a thin, awkward-looking person.

Skate-sheers, *n.* appendages on the lower part of the male skate's body, resembling a pair of scissors.

Skath, *v.* to injure. Cf. Skaith.

Skathie, *n.* a fence. Cf. Skaithie.

Skatie-goo, *n.* Richardson's skua.

Skau, *n.* a state of ruin, destruction. Cf. Skew.

Skaud, *v.* to scald. Cf. Scad.

Skaud, *ppl. adj.* scabbed. Cf. Sca'd.

Skaul, *v.* to scold.

Skaum, *v.* to scorch, singe.—*n.* the mark of burning. Cf. Scaum.

Skaur-wrang, *adj.* quite wrong; totally out of the way morally.

Skavie, *n.* a laughable trick. Cf. Skaivie.

Skavie, *v.* to put out of shape. Cf. Skaivie.

Skean, Skean-dhu, *n.* a dirk; a short sword; a knife; a dirk stuck in the stocking when the Highland costume is worn. Cf. Sgian-dhu.

Skear, *v.* to scare, frighten.—*n.* a fright.—*adj.* timid; wildly excited; rousing.

Skearie, *adj.* frightened, nervous, restive.—*n.* a madcap.

Skebel, Skebal, *n.* a mean, worthless fellow. Cf. Skybal.

Skeblous, *adj.* rascally, evil-disposed.

Skech, *v.* to obtain by craft; to sponge; to steal, pilfer. Cf. Scaich.

Skedaddle, *v.* to spill.

Skee, *v.* to void excrement.—*n.* liquid excrement. Cf. Skae.

Skeeb, *v.* to go about carelessly in a vain manner, flourishing a knife or other sharp instrument; to carry anything about carelessly.—*n.* a large knife, a cutting instrument; a staff or stick.—*adv.* with vain parade.

Skeebrie, *n.* thin, light soil.—*adj.* worthless. Cf. Skibbrie.

Skeebroch, *n.* very lean meat.

Skeech, Skeegh, *adj.* timid; coy; shy; proud. Cf. Skeigh.

Skeechan, *n.* treacle-beer.

Skeeg, *n.* the smallest portion of anything; a drop.

Skeeg, *v.* to lash; to strike with the open palm.—*n.* a blow, a 'skelp'; a blow with the open palm on the breech; in *phr.* 'to play skeeg,' to become suddenly bankrupt.

Skeegat, Skeegit, *n.* a stroke on the naked breech.

Skeegers, *n.* a whip made of sedges for whipping tops; a whip.

Skeel, *n.* a tub; a bucket; a wooden drinking-vessel with a handle. Cf. Skeil.

Skeel, *n.* a mouth-disease of horses. Cf. Scool.

Skeel, *v.* to shelter, screen.—*n.* a screen, shelter.

Skeel, *v.* to prove, test; to matter, avail.—*n.* skill; knowledge, experience; medical advice; approbation, liking for; confidence in; a proof, trial. Cf. Skill.

Skeel-duck, -goose, *n.* the common sheldrake.

Skeelie, Skeelie-pen, *n.* a slate-pencil. Cf. Skaillie.

Skeeliegolee, *n.* weak gruel; thin broth.

Skeeling-goose, *n.* the common sheldrake.

Skeel-like, *adj.* like a tub or water-barrel.

Skeelly, *n.* weak gruel; thin broth; skilly.

Skeely, *adj.* skilful, clever; wise, knowing; skilled in the healing-art. Cf. Skilly.

Skeelygallee, *n.* weak tea. Cf. Skeeliegolee.

Skeely-wife, *n.* a midwife; a woman expert in nursing, healing, &c.

Skeen, Skeen-dhu, *n.* a dirk, dagger. Cf. Skean.

Skeengie, Skeenzie, Skeeny, *n.* packthread, twine.

Skeenk, *v.* to scatter; to split; to pour from vessel to vessel. Cf. Skink.

Skeenkle, *v.* to sparkle, glitter. Cf. Skinkle.

Skeep, *n.* a scoop; a baling-scoop.

Skeer, *v.* to scare. Cf. Skear.

Skeer, *adj.* sheer, utter.—*adv.* quite, utterly.

Skeer-eyed, *adj.* squinting.

Skeer-wittit, *adj.* quite silly, foolish.

Skeer-wud, *adj.* sheer mad.

Skeet, *v.* to squirt; to eject fluid; to slide, skate; to hasten, move quickly.—*n.* diarrhœa; a squirt, syringe. Cf. Scoot, Skite.

Skeetack, Skeetick, *n.* the cuttle-fish.

Skeeter, *n.* the cuttle-fish.

Skeetle, *v.* to drop.

Skaetlich, Skeetlichie, *n.* a drop; a small shower.

Skeetlie, *n.* a drop; a small shower.

Skeevers, *n.* the leather used for binding school-books, which is sliced into two. Cf. Skiver.

Skeg, *v.* to strike with the open hand.—*n.* a blow with the palm of the hand. Cf. Skeeg.

Skegh, *v.* to void excrement. Cf. Skee.

Skegh, *v.* to filch. Cf. Scaich.

Skeibalt, *n.* a scoundrel. Cf. Skybal.

Skeigh, *n.* a round, movable piece of wood put upon the spindle of the large wheel of a spinning-wheel to prevent the worsted from slipping off.

Skeigh, Skeich, *adj.* timid, given to starting; spirited, mettlesome, skittish; coy, shy; prudish; disdainful, proud; fierce-looking; used of drugs: unpleasant to taste; reserved, keeping aloof.—*adv.* timidly; briskly; skittishly; coyly, shyly; proudly, loftily.—*n.* haughtiness.

Skeigh-bill, *n.* a wild, skittish, 'raised' bull.

Skeighish, *adj.* rather skittish.

Skeighness, *n.* timidity; skittishness; coyness; pride, disdain.

Skeil, *n.* a tub; a wooden drinking-vessel with handle.

Skeil, *n.* skill; experience. Cf. Skill.

Skeill, *v.* to scatter, disperse. Cf. Skail.

Skeillie, *n.* a scattering.—*v.* to scatter. Cf. Skail.

Skeilly, Skeily, *n.* slate-pencil. Cf. Skaillie.

Skeily, *adj.* wise, expert ; skilful. Cf. Skilly.

Skein, Skein-durk, *n.* a dirk. Cf. Skean.

Skein-ochil, *n.* a small dirk, a concealed one.

Skeir, *v.* to scare. Cf. Skear.

Skeitch, *v.* to skate. Cf. Sketch.

Skelb, *n.* a splinter of wood ; a thin slice of anything.—*v.* to cut off in thin slices, to separate in laminæ. Cf. Skelf.

Skelbin, *n.* a splinter ; a thin piece ; a small, thin person.

Skelby, *adj.* full of splinters ; tending to splinters.

Skeldick, Skeldock, *n.* the wild mustard ; the wild radish. Cf. Skellock.

Skeldrake, Skelldrake, Skelduck, *n.* the common sheldrake ; the oyster-catcher.

Skeldroch, *n.* hoar-frost.

Skelet, *n.* a skeleton ; form, appearance.

Skelf, *n.* a shelf ; a frame containing shelves ; a ledge on a cliff ; a splinter.—*v.* to splinter ; to peel off in flakes.

Skelfy, *adj.* laminated ; tending to splinters ; full of splinters ; shelving.

Skell, Skel, *v.* to scatter. Cf. Skail.

Skell, *n.* the right of the earlier comer to the next turn of the mill in grinding. Cf. Skall.

Skellach, *n.* a hubbub.

Skellachin, *n.* a shrill laughter.

Skellad, Skellat, *n.* a pan, saucepan ; a skillet. Cf. Skellet.

Skellag, Skellach, *n.* wild mustard. Cf. Skellock.

†**Skellat, Skellit,** *n.* a bell ; a hand-bell.

Skellat, *n.* an imaginary spirit.

Skellet, *n.* a skillet ; cast-metal.—*adj.* made of tinned iron.

Skell-faced, *adj.* having a wry, distorted face ; squinting.

Skellie, *n.* wild mustard. Cf. Skellock.

†**Skellie,** *n.* a bell ; a hand-bell. Cf. Skellat.

Skellied, *ppl. adj.* squinting.

Skellie-man, *n.* a bellman ; a public crier.

Skellihewit, *n.* a rumpus.

Skelloch, *n.* a scream, shriek, yell ; a blow, what provokes a scream.—*v.* to scream, shriek, yell.

†**Skelloch-bell,** *n.* a small bell ; a hand-bell.

Skellock, Skellack, *n.* the wild mustard ; the wild radish. Cf. Skellag.

Skellop, *v.* to beat ; to run fast. Cf. Skelp.

†**Skellum,** *n.* a rascal, scamp, scoundrel. Cf. Schelm.

Skelly, *n.* the chub.

Skelly, *n.* slate ; slate-pencil. Cf. Skaillie.

Skelly, *n.* a rock ; a skerry.

Skelly, *v.* to squint ; to look sideways ; to do anything crookedly ; to throw or shoot beside the mark ; to digress ; to exaggerate, narrate incorrectly.—*n.* a squint ; a cast in the eye.—*adj.* squinting ; having a squint.

Skelly-coat, *n.* a goblin ; a water-sprite. Cf. Shelly-coat.

Skelly-ee, *n.* a squint eye.

Skelly-ee'd, *adj.* cross-eyed, having a squint.

Skelp, *v.* to strike with the open hand or a flat surface ; to whip, beat, drub ; to hammer iron, leather, &c. ; to throb, pulsate ; used of a clock : to tick ; to drive with blows ; to drive hard ; to cause a rapid movement ; to write hastily ; to move quickly, run, dash ; to act with energy, spirit, suddenness, or violence.—*n.* a stroke with the open hand ; a smack, blow ; a dash, splash ; a dash of liquid ; a stride, leap.—*adv.* with violence, energy, or spirit.

Skelp, *n.* a splinter of wood ; a splint ; any large superficial area.—*v.* to run or break into splinters ; to apply splints to a broken limb ; to dig, plough, or cut turf. Cf. Skelb, Skelf.

Skelp-doup, *n.* a contemptuous designation of a schoolmaster.

Skelper, *n.* one who 'skelps' with the open hand ; a quick walker.

Skelpie, Skelpy, *adj.* deserving to be whipped. —*n.* a worthless person ; a mischief-maker ; a mischievous girl.

Skelpie-limmer, *n.* an opprobrious term applied to a girl.

Skelpin', *ppl. adj.* making a noise ; used of a kiss : 'smacking' ; vigorous ; clever, agile. —*n.* a beating with the open hand.

Skelp-the-dub, *n.* a contemptuous name for one accustomed to do dirty work.—*v.* to act like a foot-boy.

Skelt, *v. pret.* spilt. Cf. Skail.

Skelter, *v.* to hurry off.—*adv.* rapidly ; at headlong speed.

Skelve, *n.* a thin slice.—*v.* to separate in laminæ. Cf. Skelf.

Skelvy, *adj.* having various laminæ ; shelving.

Skemmel, Skemmil, *v.* to kill and skin animals in the shambles.—*n.* in *pl.* the shambles ; a butchers' market.

Skemmel, Skemmil, Skemmle, *v.* to throw the legs out in an awkward manner, as if one had not proper command of them in walking ; to walk or climb over slight obstructions ; to scramble over rocks, walls, &c. ; to wander ; to go astray ; to scramble ; to romp ; to throw things about in a careless and slovenly way.—*adj.* having the feet thrown outwards.—*n.* a tall, thin, ungainly person.

Skemmling, *n.* a foolish way of throwing the legs.

Skemp, *n.* a scamp; a worthless fellow.

Skene-occle, *n.* a concealed dirk. Cf. Skein-ochil.

Skenk, *n.* a shin of beef; soup made from the shin. Cf. Skink.

Skenkle, *v.* to sparkle, twinkle. Cf. Skinkle.

Skeoch, *n.* a very small cave; a large chink in a cliff.

Skep, Skepp, *n.* a large basket; a bowl-shaped vessel with handle for ladling; a straw beehive; the contents of a beehive. —*v.* to knock one's hat over his eyes; to enclose in a hive; to go to rest for the night; with *in*, to make acquaintance with.

Skep, *v.* to escape. Cf. Scape.

Skeplet, *adj.* mean, tattered, ragged.—*n.* a hat out of shape.

Skep-moo, *n.* the mouth of a beehive.

Skeppack, *n.* the game of 'tig.' Cf. Skibbie.

Skeppit, *ppl. adj.* having the hat tilted over the eyes and nose from behind.

Sker, *adj.* left.

Sker, *v.* to frighten. Cf. Skear.

Sker-handit, *adj.* left-handed.

Skerie, *adj.* somewhat restive; easily startled.

Skerr, *n.* a ridge or rock; a bare precipice. Cf. Scaur.

Skerriegifnot, *n.* a girl from twelve to fourteen years. Cf. Scargivenet.

Skerry, Skerry-blue, *n.* a variety of potato.

Skerry, *n.* a shadow. Cf. Scairy.

Sketch, *v.* to skate.—*n.* a skate.

Sketcher, *n.* a skater; a skate.

Sketchers, *n.* two wooden legs with a cross-bar, for supporting a tree during the opera-tion of sawing.

Skeu, *adv.* awry.

Skeuch, Skeugh, *v.* to distort.—*n.* a distor-tion. Cf. Skew.

Skeut, *v.* to twist, distort; to walk awkwardly, putting down the feet with force; to throw or fall flat.—*n.* a twist; anything clumsy and misshapen; a broad, flat hand or foot; an ill-fitting, clumsy shoe; an untidy, cross-tempered woman; a skate.—*adv.* with awk-ward, heavy step; flatly, heavily.

Skeut-fittit, *adj.* having flat, turned-out feet.

Skevl, *v.* to twist, distort. Cf. Skaivle.

Skevrel, *v.* to move unsteadily in a circular way.

Skew, *adv.* in a distorted manner; with a waddling, affected gait. —*n.* anything crooked; a twist, turn; the oblique part of a gable on which the roof rests; a shade, shadow; a wooden chimney-cowl; a state of ruin.—*v.* to slant; to twist about; to walk in an affected manner; to distort; to build obliquely; to cover the gables of a thatched roof with sods.

Skew, *n.* a skewer.

Skew, *v.* to eschew; to seek shelter from.

Skewed, *ppl. adj.* demented; bemused with drink; distorted.

Skew-fittit, *adj.* splay-footed.

Skewl, *v.* to twist, distort; to deflect from the plumb-line; to waddle, walk affectedly.—*n.* a twist.—*adv.* in a twisted manner; with a waddling gait.

Skew-mouth, *n.* a crooked mouth.

Skew-mouth plane, *n.* a kind of joiner's plane.

Skey, *adj.* skittish. Cf. Skeigh.

Skeyb-horn't, *adj.* having the horns far asunder.

Skeybil, *n.* a rascal. Cf. Skybald.

Skeyf, *n.* a shrivelled dwarf.

Skeyg, *v.* to move nimbly in walking.—*n.* a quick motion. Cf. Skaig.

Skeyg for skeyg, *adv.* at full speed.

Skeys, *v.* to run off quickly.

Skeytch, *v.* to skate. Cf. Sketch.

Ski, *v.* to slide.

Skiach, *n.* the hawthorn fruit.

Skian, *n.* a dirk. Cf. Skean.

Skib, *n.* a stroke, blow.

Skibbie, *n.* the game of 'tig.' Cf. Skeppack.

Skibbrie, Skibrie, *n.* thin, light soil; any worthless stuff.—*adj.* worthless.

Skibby, *n.* a left-handed person.

Skibe, *n.* a low, worthless, niggardly fellow. Cf. Skype.

Skibel, *n.* a scamp; a low, worthless fellow. Cf. Skybal.

Skice, *v.* to run off quickly. Cf. Skeys.

Skichen, *n.* a disgust at food from over-nicety in taste.—*v.* to disgust; to become dis-gusted.—*adj.* haughty; showing contempt and disgust.

Skick, Skich, *v.* used of cattle: to frisk about.—*adj.* frisky.

Skid, *v.* to slide, slip; to look squint at an object.

Skiddaw, *n.* the common guillemot.

Skiddie, *adj.* oblique; squint.

Skiddie-look, *n.* a squint look.

Skiddle, *n.* a contemptuous name for tea or any insipid liquid.

Skiech, *adj.* skittish; coy. Cf. Skeigh.

Skiel, *n.* a tub. Cf. Skeil.

Skieldrake, *n.* the sheldrake.

Skien, *n.* a dirk. Cf. Skean.

Skier, *adj.* sheer, utter.—*adv.* quite, utterly. Cf. Skeer.

Skiff, *v.* to skim lightly along the ground; to move or dance lightly and easily; to fly lightly and airily; to blow over; to brush, or graze, or wipe off gently; to cause a thin, flat stone to skim along the surface of water; to rain or snow slightly; to work carelessly and superficially.—*n.* a skip; a slight whizzing sound by a body 'skiffing'; a slight movement; a slight graze; a light touch; a sketchy description; art or facility in operation; a slight or flying shower. Cf. Skift.

Skiffer, *v.* to rain, snow, or hail gently.—*n.* a slight shower. Cf. Skifter.

Skiffie, *n.* the tub used for bringing up coals from the pit.

Skiffle, *v.* to scuffle.

Skift, Skifft, *v.* to shift; to glide over; to move lightly and easily; to graze slightly; to wipe gently; to cause a flat stone to skim along the surface of water; to rain or snow slightly; to work carelessly and superficially.—*n.* a skip; a slight whizzing sound; a light movement; a slight graze or hurt; a light touch; a slight shower; art or facility in operation; a shaving of wood. Cf. Skiff.

Skifter, *v.* to rain, snow, or hail very gently. —*n.* a slight shower.

Skifting, *n.* a skimming; a thin shaving from a larger piece.

Skig, *v.* to flog.—*n.* a stroke on the breech. Cf. Skeeg.

Skig, *n.* the least quantity of anything. Cf. Skeeg.

Skiggle, *v.* to sprinkle, scatter; to spill in small quantities.

Skight, *v.* to fly off hastily; to slide suddenly. Cf. Skite.

Skiken, *n.* disgust at food. Cf. Skichen.

Skile, *v.* to scatter, disperse. Cf. Skail.

Skill, *n.* medical aid or advice; favour, liking; proof.—*v.* to prove; to avail. Cf. Skeel.

†**Skillat, Skillet**, *n.* a small bell. Cf. Skellat.

Skiller, *v.* to warp.

Skillock, *n.* wild mustard. Cf. Skellock.

Skilly, *adj.* clever, skilful. Cf. Skeely.

Skilly, *n.* slate-pencil. Cf. Skaillie.

Skilly-wife, *n.* a midwife.

Skilp, *v.* to strike smartly; to run swiftly. Cf. Skelp.

Skilt, *v.* to drink copiously, to swill.—*n.* a draught, drink.

Skilt, *v.* to move quickly and lightly; to skip. —*n.* a contemptuous name for a girl; a 'hizzie.'

Skim, *v.* to evade; to shirk the truth.

Skime, *v.* to gleam with reflected light; to give a side-glance. — *n.* the glance of reflected light; a glance of the eye.

Skimmer, Skimmar, *v.* used of light: to flicker; to shimmer, glitter; to have a flaunting appearance, as when women are lightly and showily dressed; to dust lightly or quickly over the surface of anything; to fall in a light, drizzling shower; to glide rapidly; to act or move quickly; to flutter

lightly; to frisk; used of swallows: to skim the surface of smooth water.—*n.* the flickering rays of light; a slight sprinkling of any powdery substance; a low flight of birds.

Skimmerin, *n.* a low flight; a sprinkling.

Skimmering look, *n.* the characteristic look of an idiot or lunatic.

Skimp, *v.* to stint, curtail, 'scrimp.'—*adj.* small, scanty; used of weight or measure: short, scant.

Skin, Skine, *n.* a parchment deed; a particle, grain.—*v.* to exact to the full; to hide, represent under a false appearance; with *up*: to put the best face on a story or a bare-faced lie.—*adj.* skin-deep, superficial.

Skin, *n.* a term of extreme contempt.

Skin-bane, *adj.* naked; very poor.

Skincheon, *n.* used of drink: a hearty pull.

Skin-claes, *n.* oilskins; waterproof overalls.

Skin-flype, *v.* to flay, take off the skin in 'flypes.'

Skinfu', *n.* a bellyful of drink or food.

Skinie, Skiny, *n.* packthread. Cf. Skeengie.

Skink, *n.* a shin or knuckle of beef; a bad piece of flesh; soup made from the shin of beef; soup in general.

Skink, *v.* to pour out for drinking; to decant; to serve with drink; to drink, tipple; to charge glasses and drink healths; with *over*: to drink together in ratifying a bargain, &c. —*n.* liquor, drink; a draught; a drinking-bout.

Skink, *v.* to scatter, disperse, separate, split; to pour from vessel to vessel in order to mix thoroughly; to crush to pieces; to break by crushing the sides of anything together.—*n.* a small portion; a chip, shred; a crush, smash; the sudden pressure or blow that causes a smash.

Skink-broth, *n.* soup made from the 'skink.'

Skinker, *n.* a server of drink; a butler; a drinker, tippler.

Skink-hoch, *n.* the shin of beef.

Skinking, *ppl. adj.* thin, liquid, 'wersh.'

Skinkle, *v.* to sparkle, twinkle, shine; to make a showy appearance. —*n.* lustre, glitter, sparkle.—*adj.* glittering, sparkling.

Skinkle, *v.* to sprinkle; to spill in small quantities; to sow thinly.—*n.* a sprinkling, scattering; a very small quantity.

Skinklin, *n.* the sparkling of a bright irradiation.

Skinklin, *n.* a sprinkling; a small portion or quantity.

Skinkling, *n.* meat that is nearly cold.—*adj.* used of meat: out of season; tainted; unpleasant to the taste.

Skinny, *n.* a roll of bread.

Skint, *n.* a drop of liquid thrown; a very small quantity of liquid.—*v.* to splash with mud, &c. ; to throw drops of liquid on anything.

Skin-the-louse, *n.* a contemptuous name for a niggard.

Skin-whole, *adj.* unharmed, sound of body.

Skiollag, *n.* the wild mustard. Cf. Skellock.

Skip, *v.* to make a stone skim along the surface of water ; to leap lightly across.

Skip, *v.* used in curling : to act as captain of a rink. —*n.* the captain of a rink.

Skip, *v.* to slide on ice.

Skip, *n.* the peak of a cap.

Skip, *n.* a beehive. Cf. Skep.

Skipjack, *adj.* nimble, sportive.

Skipped, *ppl. adj.* used of a cap: peaked.

Skipper, *n.* the 'skip' or captain of a curling-rink ; the head man on board a fishing-boat. —*v.* to act as captain of a boat.

Skip-rape, *n.* a skipping-rope.

Skip-rig, *n.* ? an article of ladies' dress.

Skir, *n.* a rock in the sea ; a small rocky islet ; a cluster of rocks.

Skirdoch, *adj.* flirting ; easily scared.

Skire, *adj.* mad. Cf. Sheer.

Skire, *adj.* sheer, utter.—*adv.* quite, utterly. Cf. Skeer.

Skire, *n.* cloth, &c., of a loud colour. Cf. Skyre.

Skirg, *v.* to romp about.

Skirge, *n.* a termagant ; a brawling woman ; a 'scourge.'

Skirge, *v.* to pour liquor backwards and forwards from one vessel to another to mellow it.—*n.* a dash of hot water.

Skirgiffin, *n.* a half-grown woman. Cf. Scargivenet.

Skirin, *ppl. adj.* of a loud colour. Cf. Skyrin'.

Skirisfurisday, *n.* Maundy-Thursday.

Skirl, *v.* to scream ; to sing shrilly ; to give forth any discordant, shrill sound ; to fry ; to frizzle, as in frying.—*n.* a shriek, scream, shrill sound ; a squall of wind with rain or snow ; a blow producing a scream.

Skirlag, *n.* a long, thin leaf, as of corn, held stretched between the thumbs held parallel, which, when blown upon, emits a musical sound.

Skirl-crake, *n.* the turnstone.

Skirlie, *n.* used of snow : a slight shower.

Skirlie, *n.* a hasty-pudding of meal, suet or dripping, pepper, salt, and chopped onions, cooked, and eaten generally with mashed potatoes.

Skirling-pan, *n.* a frying-pan.

Skirl-in-the-pan, *n.* the frizzling sound made by butter frying in a pan ; anything fried in butter in a pan ; a drink composed of oatmeal, whisky, and ale, mixed and heated in a pan, and given to gossips at 'in-lyings.'

Skirllie-weeack, *v.* to cry with a shrill voice —*n.* a shrill cry ; a little person with a shrill voice.

Skirl-naked, *adj.* stark-naked.

Skirl o' wind, *n.* a stiff breeze.

Skirl up, *v.* to sing high notes forcibly.

Skirly, *n.* a stew made of oatmeal, fat, pepper, salt, and onions. Cf. Skirlie.

Skirp, *v.* to splash, bespatter ; to rain slightly ; to besprinkle.—*n.* a splash ; a drop of rain ; a small clot ; a sprinkling ; a slight shower.

Skirpin, *n.* the gore, or strip of thin cloth, on the hinder part of breeches.

Skirr, *v.* to scurry ; to rush ; to scour, hunt.

Skirrivaig, *v.* to run about in an unsettled way. Cf. Scurryvaig.

Skirry-whirry, *n.* a hurly-burly, tumult. Cf. Scurrie-whurrie.

Skirt, *n.* a large overall petticoat used in riding by women ; a 'short-gown'; the slope of a hill ; the close, end.

Skirt, *v.* to run rapidly ; to hurry off ; to elude, run away stealthily.

Skirvin', *n.* a thin coating of snow, earth, &c.

Skist, *n.* a chest, box. Cf. Kist.

Skit, *n.* a taunt, sneer ; a practical joke ; a trick ; a humorous story or picture ; a foolish action ; a piece of silly ostentation. —*v.* to asperse by oblique taunts ; to make game of.

Skit, *v.* to caper like a skittish horse ; to flounce.—*n.* a capering, restive horse ; one who skips about ; a vain, empty creature ; a woman of frivolous or immoral character ; a disagreeable woman; a sharp, passing shower.

Skit, *v.* to glide or pass quickly. Cf. Skite.

Skit, *v.* to steal.

Skitch, *v.* to skate. Cf. Sketch.

Skite, *n.* a trick ; an ill-turn ; a spree, jollification ; a nasty person ; a meagre, starved-looking person ; a strange-looking, ugly person.

Skite, *n.* the yellow-ammer.

Skite, *v.* to move in leaps and bounds ; to fly off quickly ; to run swiftly and lightly ; to slip or slide suddenly on a smooth or frozen surface ; to rebound, as hail ; to fly off at a tangent ; to fly off in a slanting direction ; to make a flat, thin stone skim the surface of water ; to squirt ; to spit ; to eject liquid forcibly ; to project with force ; to have diarrhœa ; to splash ; to rain slightly.—*n.* the act of sliding or slipping ; a turn in skating, curling, &c. ; a skate ; the act of squirting, or spitting forcibly or through the teeth ; a squirt, syringe ; a sharp, passing shower ; a small quantity of any liquid ; a 'mouthful' of spirits ; diarrhœa in animals ; the dung of a fowl ; a dash ; a sudden fall ; a sudden blow delivered sideways and causing a slanting rebound ; an accident, a misadventure; with *ill*, an unfortunate event. —*adj.* fleet, active.—*adv.* with sharp force.

Skiter, *n.* skater ; a squirt ; a sea-bather.

Skiter, *v.* to go quickly from place to place ; to travel hither and thither.

Skites, *n.* hemlock, from being used to make 'skiters' or squirts as toys.

Skitten, *adj.* pampered ; over-nice as to food. Cf. Skichen.

Skitter, *n.* a thief.

Skitter, *v.* to have diarrhœa.—*n.* liquid excrement ; diarrhœa ; anything impure or incongruous, which, when mixed with what is valuable, renders the whole useless.

Skitterfu', *adj.* afflicted with diarrhœa.

Skittery-deacon, *n.* the common sandpiper.

Skittle, *n.* a contemptuous name for tea or any insipid liquid. Cf. Skiddle.

Skiuldr, *n.* the jelly-fish, Medusa.

Skive, *v.* to cut longitudinally into equal slices ; to slit leather.

Skive, *v.* to move quickly.

Skiver, *n.* a skewer.—*v.* to fasten with a skewer ; to disperse.

Skivers, *n.* the leather used for binding school-books, which is sliced into two.

Skivet, Skivat, *n.* a sharp blow.

Skivet, *n.* a blacksmith's fire-shovel.

Skivie, *adj.* silly. Cf. Skaivie.

Sklaeve, Sklaive, *v.* to slander, reproach. Cf. Sclave.

Sklaff, *v.* to strike with the open hand or anything flat ; to shuffle along.—*n.* a slight slap with anything flat, &c. ; the noise of such a slap ; a thin shoe ; an old slipper.—*adv.* with a light, flat gait. Cf. Sclaff.

Sklaffard, Sklaffirt, *n.* a blow with the flat hand on the side of the head ; anything thin and tough ; a thin, light shoe ; a horizontal rock lying in thin beds.—*v.* to shuffle along, as with loose slippers. Cf. Sclaffert.

Sklaffer, *v.* to 'sklaff.'—*n.* a 'sklaff.'—*adv.* with a 'sklaff.' Cf. Sclaffer.

Sklafford-hole, *n.* a ventilating-hole in a barn wall.

Sklaik, *v.* to bedaub.—*n.* smeary stuff. Cf. Slaik.

Sklaikie, *adj.* smeary.

Sklait, *n.* slate. Cf. Sclate.

Sklammer, *v.* to clamber ; to scramble ; to wander idly.

Sklap, *v.* to slap ; to go slap. --*n.* a slap.

Sklàp-dunt, *n.* a slap-dash blow.

Sklash, *v.* to dash ; to strike with anything wet ; to splash ; to lick ; to give a slobbering kiss.—*n.* a heavy shower ; a dash of anything wet ; a violent dash ; a loud crash ; a wet kiss ; a lick ; a sloven.—*adv.* forcibly.

Sklatch, *n.* an unseemly mass ; a large clot

of mud, &c. ; a big stain ; a big, lubberly fellow ; a heavy fall into mud, &c. ; a stroke with the palm of the hand.—*v.* to bedaub ; to dash violently. --*adv.* violently. Cf. Sclatch.

Sklatching, *n.* an unseemly mass ; a large clot of mud, &c.

Sklate, *n.* slate. Cf. Sclate.

Sklater, *n.* a slater ; a wood-louse.

Sklave, *v.* to calumniate ; to reproach. Cf. Sclave.

Skleeny, *adj.* thin, slender. Cf. Sklenie.

Skleet, *v.* to glide rapidly ; to slide ; to wear down shoes on one side, or as one splay-footed.—*adj.* sleek, smooth. Cf. Scleet.

Skleet, *v.* to throw forcibly ; to empty out in a mass ; to walk with a stumping step.--*n.* a heavy fall or dash ; a heavy, stumping gait.—*adv.* forcibly.

Skleeting-fittit, *adj.* splay-footed ; wearing down one side of the shoes.

Skleff, *adj.* thin and flat ; shallow ; flat-footed.—*n.* a thin slice.

Sklefferie, *adj.* separated into laminæ.

Skleff-fittit, *adj.* flat-footed.

Sklender, *adj.* thin, slender.

Sklenderie, Sklendry, *adj.* thin, slender, lank ; faint, slight.

Sklenie, *adj.* thin, slender.

Sklent, *v.* to slope ; to slant ; to look obliquely or askance ; to fall into moral obliquity ; to fib ; to err doctrinally ; to give a slanting direction ; to squint ; to cut so as to diverge from the straight.—*n.* obliquity ; a glance ; a squint ; a slope. Cf. Sclent.

Sklent, *v.* to tear, rend ; to split ; to splinter. —*n.* a tear, a rent.

Skleush, *v.* to dash or fall softly ; to drag one's steps.—*n.* a soft dash or fall ; the act of dragging one's steps ; the sound of such a fall or dragging ; a misshapen, worn shoe ; a slatternly woman.

Skleushing, *ppl. adj.* slatternly.

Skleut, *v.* to fall flat ; to walk clumsily or with turned-out toes.—*n.* the fall of a semi-liquid mass ; a lout. Cf. Sclute.

Skleutch, *v.* to slouch ; to walk in a dirty, slovenly manner.—*n.* a sloven ; an untidy woman.

Skleuter, *v.* to flow through a narrow orifice with a spluttering sound ; to walk in a careless, awkward way ; to work in slovenly fashion. —*n.* an untidy mass of liquid or semi-liquid matter ; the noise of the projection of liquids or semi-liquids through a narrow orifice ; messing among liquids or semi-liquids in a slatternly way ; a woman of filthy habits. Cf. Slutter.

Skleuterie, *adj.* wet and dirty.

Skley, *v.* to slide.—*n.* a slide. Cf. Scly.

Sklice, *v.* to slice.—*n.* a slice.

Sklidder, *v.* to slide, slip; to make slippery; to slouch in walking; to slur one's words; to delay.—*n.* the slide of a scale; loose stones on a hillside.—*adj.* slippery. Cf. Slidder.

Skliff, *v.* to drag the feet in walking; to graze, rub against.—*n.* a dull, dragging gait; a side-stroke with a flat article; an old, worn shoe, &c.; an untidy person.—*adv.* with a dragging, shuffling motion. Cf. Scliff.

Skliffer, *v.* to 'skliff.'—*n.* a 'skliff.'—*adv.* with a shuffling motion.

Sklifferie, *adj.* separated into laminæ. Cf. Sklefferie.

Sklim, *v.* to climb. Cf. Sclimb.

Sklinner, *n.* a splinter.—*adj.* slender. Cf. Sklinter.

Sklint, *v.* to slope. Cf. Sclent.

Sklint, *v.* to tear; to rend; to splinter. Cf. Sklent.

Sklinter, *v.* to splinter; to break off in laminæ.—*n.* a splinter.—*adj.* slender.—*adv.* in splinters; with speed.

Sklire, *v.* to slide on ice. Cf. Sklyre.

Sklite, *v.* to throw forcibly. Cf. Sclyte.

Sklitter, *v.* to throw down with sharp force and noise; to fall heavily.—*n.* a heavy fall and its sound; a worn-out shoe; a heavy, clumsy foot; a clumsy, untidy fellow. Cf. Sklyter.

Sklone, *v.* to squeeze a plastic substance flat.—*n.* a mass of plastic substance; a mass of snow or sleet; a big snowflake; an easy-going person.

Sklouff, Skloof, *v.* to strike a dull, heavy blow; to strike sideways or in passing with a flat surface; to rub against; to walk with dull, heavy step; to drag the feet.—*n.* a blow with the open hand or with a flat surface; the noise of a rub or blow; the act of walking with dull, heavy step, or with dragging feet; the sound so produced; an old, worn shoe or slipper; a big, clumsy shoe or boot; an easy-going, untidy person.—*adv.* with a dull, heavy sound; with a shuffling, trailing motion; flat, 'plump.'

Sklouffer, *v.* to 'sklouff.'—*n.* a 'sklouff.'—*adv.* with a 'sklouff.'

Sklout, Sklouter, *n.* cow-dung in a thin state.

Skloy, *v.* to slide on ice.—*n.* a slide. Cf. Scly.

Sklufe, *v.* to strike a dull, heavy blow; to graze. Cf. Sklouff.

Skluff, *n.* anything large.

Sklush, Sklussh, *n.* slush; liquid mud. Cf. Slush.

Sklute, *n.* a semi-liquid mass; a lout; a big, clumsy foot; an untidy woman.—*v.* to empty out in a mass; to fall flat or plump; to drag the feet. Cf. Sclute.

Skly, *v.* to slide.—*n.* the place where one slides; a slide. Cf. Scly.

Sklyde, *v.* to slide.—*n.* a slide.

Sklypach, *v.* to dash down violently; to 'sklype.'—*n.* a 'sklype.'—*adv.* with a 'sklype.'

Sklype, *v.* to dash down violently; to fall flat and heavily; to walk with heavy, splashing step; to tear, rend; to strip off in thin shreds or flakes; to 'flype' a stocking.—*n.* a heavy blow with the open hand on a flat surface; a slap; a box on the ears; a heavy fall; the noise of such blow or fall; a large clot or spot; a large, thin piece of anything; a clumsy hand or foot; a mis-shapen shoe, glove, or bonnet; a person of lazy or dirty habits.—*adv.* with force. Cf. Clype.

Sklyre, *v.* to slide.—*n.* a slide; the act of sliding.

Sklytach, *v.* to 'sklyter.'—*n.* a 'sklyter.'—*adv.* with a 'sklyter.' Cf. Clytach.

Sklyte, *v.* to fall heavily.—*n.* a heavy fall; a clumsy foot; an old shoe. Cf. Sclyte.

Sklyter, *v.* to throw down or pour out with force and a sharp sound; to fall heavily.—*n.* a thin, semi-liquid mass; a heavy fall; the sharp sound of such a fall; a worn-out shoe; a large, clumsy foot; a clumsy, untidy fellow; a term of reproach.—*adv.* flatly; suddenly, as with a fall.

Sklyterach, *v.* to 'sklyter.'—*n.* a 'sklyter.'—*adv.* with a 'sklyter.'

Skoddy, *adj.* shady, verging on dishonesty.

Skodge, Skodgie, *n.* a drudge.—*v.* to act as a drudge. Cf. Scodgy.

Skoffrie, *n.* scoffing, mockery.

Skole, Skolt, *v.* to drink hard; to drink healths. Cf. Scoll.

Skon, *v.* to beat with the flat of the hand or with a flat surface; to crush flat.—*n.* a blow with a flat surface. Cf. Scon.

Skon, Skone, *n.* a flat, round cake of flour or barley-meal; anything round and flat; a specimen. Cf. Scon.

Skonce, *n.* a thin partition; a wall to defend from the wind; a shed for hewing stones; a 'hallan.'—*v.* to guard; to keep off. Cf. Sconce.

Skonke, *n.* part of a fishing-net.

Skonner, *v.* to disgust. Cf. Scunner.

Skooder, *v.* to scorch, singe. Cf. Scowder.

Skoog, *v.* to shade, shelter, hide.—*n.* a shade, &c. Cf. Scug.

Skook, *v.* to conceal; to hide one's self. Cf. Scouk.

Skookin-like, *adj.* ill-looking; furtive; sullen.

Skool, *n.* a shoal of fish.

Skoom, *n.* scum. Cf. Scum.

Skoor, *v.* to clean out a drain, &c.; to purge. Cf. Scour.

Skoot, *v.* to squirt; to eject liquid excrement. —*n.* a squirt. Cf. Scoot.

Skoot, *n.* a term of contempt; a braggadocio. Cf. Scoot.

Skoot, *n.* sour or dead liquor. Cf. Skute.

Skord, *v.* to scratch. Cf. Score.

Skore, *v.* to score; to scratch.—*n.* a line marking a goal. Cf. Score.

Skouder, *n.* a flying shower.—*v.* to drizzle. Cf. Skouther.

Skough, *v.* to shade.—*n.* a shade. Cf. Scug.

Skoup, *n.* a scoop. Cf. Scoop.

Skouper, *n.* a dancer; a flighty person. Cf. Scouper.

Skour, *n.* a slight shower; a gust. Cf. Scour.

Skourick, *n.* a thing of no value; a particle.

Skout, *n.* the guillemot. Cf. Scoot.

Skouth, *n.* abundance, scope. Cf. Scouth.

Skouther, *n.* a flying shower. Cf. Scouther.

Skouther, *v.* to burn, singe. Cf. Scowder.

Skoutt, *n.* a small boat. Cf. Scout.

Skow, *n.* barrel-staves after the barrel has been broken up.

Skow, *n.* a small boat made of willows, &c., and covered with skins; a flat-bottomed boat used as a lighter.

Skowder-doup, *n.* a blacksmith. Cf. Scowder-doup.

Skowel, Skowl, *v.* to twist, distort. Cf. Skewl.

Skowff, *v.* to quaff, drink off. Cf. Scuff.

Skowrie, *adj.* shabby, ragged. Cf. Scoury.

Skowther, *n.* a slight shower. Cf. Scouther.

Skowther, *v.* to scorch. Cf. Scowder.

Skoyl, *v.* to squeal.—*n.* a squeal.

Skrach, *v.* used of birds: to scream; to shriek.—*n.* a shrill cry. Cf. Scraich.

Skrae, *n.* an old, worn shoe; a thin person; a skeleton; a fault-finder.—*adj.* thin, meagre. Cf. Scrae.

Skrae, *n.* a wire sieve for sifting grain.

Skrae-fish, *n.* sun-dried, unsalted fish.

Skrae-shankit, *adj.* having long, thin legs.

Skraich, Skraigh, *v.* used of birds: to scream. Cf. Scraich.

Skraik, Skrake, *v.* to cry as a startled fowl; to scream, screech; to cry importunately and discontentedly. —*n.* the cry of a startled fowl; a scream, shriek.

Skran, *n.* a miscellaneous gathering of edibles; scraps of human food thrown to dogs; daily bread; power or means to accomplish. —*v.* to collect miscellaneous things by fair means or foul. Cf. Scran.

Skrank, *adj.* lank; used of writing: sprawling.—*n.* a lean person; sprawling, bad writing.—*v.* to write in a scrawling hand. Cf. Scrank.

Skranky, *adj.* lank; slender; scraggy; used of a purse: lean, empty; used of writing: ill-formed.—*n.* a coarse-featured person. Cf. Scranky.

Skran-pock, *n.* a beggar's wallet.

Skrat, Skratt, *v.* to scratch; to struggle for a living; to save frugally; to write with a pen; to scatter. Cf. Scrat.

Skrauch, Skraugh, *v.* used of birds: to scream; to bawl. Cf. Scraich.

Skrauchle, *v.* to scramble; to move with difficulty.—*n.* a scramble. Cf. Scrauchle.

Skrea, *n.* a post or prop for a clay or wattled wall.

Skreagh, *v.* used of birds: to scream. Cf. Scraich.

Skree, *n.* a wire sieve for sifting corn. Cf. Skrae.

Skreech, Skreegh, *v.* to scream. Cf. Scraich.

Skreed, *v.* to cry, scream; to speak rapidly; to do anything quickly; to talk or write at length; to tear, rend.—*n.* a shred; a long strip of anything; a rent, tear; the sound of a tear; a shrill sound; a long harangue; a long list, document, &c.; a revel. Cf. Screed.

Skreef, *n.* scurf; a thin covering; lichen. Cf. Screef.

Skreek, *v.* to shriek. Cf. Skraik.

Skreek o' day, *n.* cock-crow; daybreak.

Skreemage, *n.* a hard rubbing; a severe beating; a noisy, bustling search. Cf. Scrimmage.

Skreen, *v.* to protect; to ward off; to hide. Cf. Screen.

Skreenge, *v.* to scour vigorously; to search carefully; to glean.—*n.* a thorough cleansing; a lash; a sound drubbing; a loose woman; a searcher. Cf. Scringe.

Skreenger, *n.* a vigorous, energetic person; anything large of its kind; one who pokes about for trifles.

Skreenings, *n.* gleanings.

Skregh, Skrech, *v.* to scream. Cf. Scraich.

Skreich, Screigh, *v.* to scream. Cf. Scraich.

Skreigh, *n.* whisky.

Skreigh o' day, *n.* daybreak; cock-crow.

Skreik, *v.* to scream. Cf. Skraik.

Skrew, *n.* the shrew-mouse.

Skriech, Skriegh, *v.* to scream. Cf. Scraich.

Skriek, *v.* to scream, shriek. Cf. Skraik.

Skriet, *v.* to shriek; to cry; to proclaim.

Skrieve, *v.* to glide swiftly along; to talk, read, or write fast and continuously.—*n.* a lengthy talk. Cf. Screeve.

Skrieve, *v.* to write; to peel; to scrape.—*n.* handwriting; a letter, writing. Cf. Scrive.

Skriever, *n.* a smart worker; a clever fellow.

Skriever, *n.* an inferior writer; a poor scribe.

Skriff, *n.* scurf, dandriff. Cf. Screef.

Skriff, *n.* a scrap of writing.

Skriffin, *n.* a film; a thin skin. Cf. Striffan, Scriffin.

Skrift, *v.* to recite or rehearse from memory; to fib; to exaggerate; to fabricate.—*n.* a recitation; a fabrication, falsehood. Cf. Scrift.

Skrille, *n.* a shrill cry. Cf. Skirl.

Skrim, *v.* to strike vigorously; to crush; to bustle. Cf. Scrim.

Skrimmage, *n.* a severe beating; a thorough, noisy search. Cf. Scrimmage.

Skrimp, *v.* to stint, pinch.—*adj.* scanty. Cf. Scrimp.

Skrine, *n.* unboiled 'sowens.'

Skringe, *v.* to rub violently. Cf. Scringe.

Skrinkie, Skrinkit, *adj.* lank; slender; wrinkled; shrivelled.

Skrinkie-faced, *adj.* having wrinkles on the face.

Skrow, *n.* the shrew-mouse. Cf. Screw.

Skrow, *n.* a scroll.

Skrow, *n.* a great number; a great uproar.

Skrow, *n.* a slight shower of rain.

Skrow, *n.* a scrap; in *pl.* damaged skins; scraps taken from skins; small insects in fresh-water pools.—*v.* to cut off scraps or torn pieces from skins. Cf. Scrow.

Skrucken, *v.* to shrivel; to cause to shrivel. —*n.* anything dry or shrivelled.—*ppl. adj.* shrivelled, shrunken.

Skruf, *n.* scurf; a thin crust.—*v.* to graze; to be covered with a film. Cf. Scruff.

Skruff, *n.* the back of the neck; the back of a coat-collar. Cf. Scruff.

Skrummage, *n.* a severe beating; a thorough, noisy search. Cf. Scrimmage.

Skrumple, *v.* to make crisp; to over-roast; to bake hard; to become crisp.—*n.* anything crispy; crisp bread. Cf. Scrumple.

Skrumplie, *adj.* crisp.

Skrumplit, *ppl. adj.* shrunk; shrivelled by means of fire.

Skrunge, *v.* to rub with force; to wander about idly. Cf. Scrunge.

Skrunk, *v.* to shrink; to crumple; to become withered or dry.

Skrunkilt, *ppl. adj.* pinched, scanty.

Skrunkit, *ppl. adj.* pinched, scanty.

Skrunkle, *v.* to shrink; to crumple; to 'skrunk.'

Skrunt, *v.* to produce a harsh or rough noise by rubbing or scratching on a board with a blunted point.—*n.* the sound so produced. Cf. Scrunt.

Skrunt, *v.* to start for; to walk off. Cf. Strunt.

Skrunt, *n.* anything stunted or worn down;

a stump; a stunted, insignificant person; a miserly person. Cf. Scrunt.

Skruntin, *n.* a continuous, harsh, grating sound.

Skruntiness, *n.* scrubbiness.

Skruntit, *ppl. adj.* stunted, dwarfed; meagre, thin.

Skrunty, *adj.* meagre; raw-boned; niggardly, stingy. Cf. Scrunty.

Skry, *v.* to cry; to proclaim.—*n.* a proclamation, public intimation by a crier. Cf. Scry.

Skube, *n.* a hearty drink.

Skube, *n.* anything hollowed out.

Skud, *v.* to run quickly; to rain slightly; to drink copiously.—*n.* a blow; in *pl.* ale. porter.

Skuddievaig, *n.* a rogue. Cf. Scuddievaig.

Skuddler, *n.* a youngster.

Skudge, *v.* to buffet, box the ears.

Skudge, Skudgy, *n.* a kitchen drudge. Cf. Scodgie.

Skue, *adj.* off the straight. Cf. Skew.

Skuff, *n.* the nape of the neck.

Skuff, *v.* to shuffle the feet; to graze; to cuff. Cf. Scuff.

Skug, *v.* to flog.

Skug, *n.* a shade; a shelter.—*v.* to shade; to take shelter. Cf. Scug.

Skugging-faced, -looking, *adj.* of gloomy face.

Skuggy, *adj.* shady.

Skug-ways, -wise, *adv.* clandestinely.

Skuik, *v.* to hide one's self; to skulk; to scowl. Cf. Scouk.

Skuil, *n.* a school.

Skuil, *n.* a great collection of animals. Cf. School.

Skuill, *n.* a mouth-disease of horses. Cf. Scool.

Skuir-Fuirsday, *n.* Maundy-Thursday. Cf. Skirisfuirsday.

Skul, *n.* a scullion.

Skulduddery, *n.* fornication. Cf. Sculduddery.

Skule, *n.* school.

Skule, *n.* a great swarm or school of animals. Cf. School.

Skule, *n.* a mouth-disease of horses. Cf. Scool.

Skuler, *n.* a story-teller, narrator.

Skules, *n.* feeding-stalls for cattle.

Skull, *n.* a tightly-fitting cap or hat.

Skull, *n.* a swarm, shoal. Cf. School.

Skull, *n.* a shallow, wicker basket; a wicker-work cradle.

Skull, *v.* to wander; to zigzag.

Skulldavie, *n.* a kind of woman's hat; any large-sized hat.

Skult, *v.* to beat.—*n.* a blow with the open hand. Cf. Scult.

Skultie, *adj.* naked, nude.

Skumfish, Skunfis, *v.* to disgust. Cf. Scumfish.

Skunge, *v.* to fawn like a dog for food; to slink about. Cf. Scunge.

Skunkle, *v.* to glitter. Cf. Skinkle.

Skunner, *v.* to disgust.—*n.* a disgust. Cf. Scunner.

Skup, *n.* a scoop-shaped bonnet.

Skur, Skurr, *n.* the rough, projecting part of a stone; a small horn hanging to the skull of an animal by the skin alone; the scab formed over a wound or sore; a low rascal; a sheriff-officer's underling. Cf. Scurr.

Skurl, *n.* the scab formed over a wound or sore. Cf. Scurl.

Skurr, *v.* to scurry; to whiz. Cf. Skirr.

Skurrie, *n.* a cow with 'skurs' or short horns.

Skurrie, *v.* to go about from place to place idly and lazily. Cf. Scurry.

Skurrieman, *n.* a wandering fellow; a vagrant.

Skurroch, Skurrock, *n.* a cant term for cash; a particle. Cf. Skourick.

Skurryvaig, Skurivaig, Skurrievarg, *n.* a scamp; a vagrant; a 'spree.'—*v.* to lead a vagrant life, or one of idleness and dissipation. Cf. Scurryvaig.

Skushle, *v.* to shuffle in walking.—*n.* an old, worn-out shoe. Cf. Scushel.

Skute, *n.* sour or dead liquor.

Skute, *v.* to walk awkwardly, from being flat-soled.

Skute, *v.* to squirt.—*n.* a squirt. Cf. Scoot, Skite.

Skutie, *n.* a wooden drinking-vessel. Cf. Scootie.

Skutie, Skutock, Skuttock, *n.* the common guillemot. Cf. Scoot.

Skutter, *v.* to work unmethodically. Cf. Scutter.

Skweel, *n.* a school.

Skweelin'-days, *n.* school-days.

Skwype, *v.* to tear, rend.—*n.* a tear, rent.

Sky, *n.* twilight, dawn; the red light in the sky before or after sunset; the ridge or summit of a hill.—*v.* to skim along the horizon; to hurry along; used of the weather: to clear up.

Skyb, *n.* a low, worthless, mean fellow. Cf. Skibe.

Skybal, Skybald, Skybil, Skyble, *n.* a low, worthless fellow; a scoundrel; a lazy, useless ne'er-do-well; a tatterdemalion; a ragged urchin; a lean person or animal; a worn-out horse; a lazy horse; a gelded goat; thin, poor land.—*adj.* mean, low; ragged; used of the legs: poor, long, bare, and thin. Cf. Skypal.

Skybaleer, *v.* to rail against, abuse.

Skybrie, *n.* thin, light soil. Cf. Skibbrie.

Skyeman's puzzle, *n.* a most difficult question.

Skyeow, *adj.* askew. Cf. Skew.

Sky-goat, *n.* the bittern.

Sky-high, *v.* to throw up into the air.

Skyir-Thuirsday, *n.* Maundy-Thursday.

Sky-laverock, *n.* the skylark.

Skyle, *v.* to scatter.—*n.* dispersion. Cf. Skail.

Skylights, *n.* a half-filled wine-glass; the space between the wine and the rim.

Skyllie, Skylie, *n.* slate-pencil. Cf. Skaillie.

Skyme, *v.* to glance or gleam with reflected light.—*n.* the glance of reflected light. Cf. Skime.

Skynk, *v.* to pour out liquor.—*n.* liquor. Cf. Skink.

Skyow, *v.* to go askew; to differ in opinion; to wrangle slightly. Cf. Skew.

Skyowl, *v.* to distort. Cf. Skewl.

Skyowt, *ppl. adj.* distorted; half-drunk. Cf. Skewed.

Skypal, Skypel, *adj.* ugly, worthless.—*n.* a mean, worthless fellow; a person of unpleasant temper and manners. Cf. Skybal.

Skypal, *adj.* short, lacking, deficient.

Skype, *n.* a mean, worthless fellow; a lean person of disagreeable manner and temper. Cf. Skibe.

Skype, *v.* to wander idly from place to place.

Skyr, *n.* a rock in the sea. Cf. Skir.

Sky-racket, *n.* an uproar; a great noise.

Skyre, *v.* to shine, glitter; to make a foolish display of gaudy dress; to look in a silly, amazed manner.—*n.* anything brightly coloured or gaudy; a brightly-coloured, tawdry piece of dress; a person with a foolish, amazed look.

Skyre, *adj.* sheer, utter. Cf. Skeer.

Skyre, *v.* to scare; to startle; to be shy. Cf. Skear.

Skyre-leukin, *adj.* shining; brilliant, showy, of bright, gaudy colour; having a vacant, foolish look.

Skyrie, *adj.* bright; glaring; glowing.

Skyrin, *ppl. adj.* shining; making a great show; gaudy.

Skyt, *v.* to slide; to squirt. Cf. Skite.

Skytch, *v.* to skate.—*n.* a skate. Cf. Sketch.

Skytchers, *n.* skates; skaters.

Skyte, *v.* to eject liquid; to squirt; to slide; used of scones: to bake them expeditiously.—*n.* a slap. Cf. Skite.

Skyte, *n.* a skit; a trick; a spree; an unpleasant fellow. Cf. Skite.

Skyter, *n.* a squirt; a sea-bather; a skater.

Skytes, *n.* hemlock, from being used as toy 'skyters.'

Skytie, *n.* a slight, passing shower.

Skytle, *v.* to move from side to side, applied to the movement of liquid when carried in a vessel and shaken.

Sla, *n.* a sloe. Cf. Slae.

Slab, *n.* a thick slice; a large piece; a tall, thin person; a lubberly fellow.

Slab, *n.* to sup eagerly and greedily.

Slabber, *v.* to swallow one's words in speaking.—*n.* mud, slush; a slovenly, dirty fellow.

Slabbergash, *n.* a slovenly, drivelling fellow.

Slabbergaucie, *n.* a 'slabbergash.'

Slabbery, *adj.* rainy; sloppy; muddy.

Slab-step, *n.* a flat door-step.

Slachter, *v.* to slaughter.

Slack, *adj.* slow; short of work; thinly occupied, not filled; not trustworthy; loose in conduct; reluctant to pay a debt; used of money: slowly paid.—*n.* a loose, baggy part of anything, as of trousers; a ewe that has missed a lamb; in *pl.* trousers.—*v.* to become flaccid, cease to be distended; to cease, pause; to slacken; to grow remiss, become neglectful; used of business: to become less busy.

Slack, *v.* to cover up a fire with dross or slack to lessen consumption.

Slack, *n.* an opening between hills; a pass; a hollow; a dip in the ground; a glade; a hollow, boggy place; a morass; the narrowest part of an animal's ribs; used of the throat: the narrowest part.

Slack, *v.* to slake, quench the thirst.

Slacken, *v.* to slake; to quench thirst. Cf. Slocken.

Slacken, *v.* to enfeeble.

Slack-ewe, -yowe, *n.* a ewe past bearing.

Slackie, *n.* a kind of sling, made of an elastic rod split at the end.

Slack-jaw, *n.* impudent speech; loose, frivolous talk; rude, uncivil, coarse language.

Slade, *n.* a hollow between rising grounds, one with a streamlet flowing in it.

Slade, *adj.* slovenly; dirty; disagreeable. Cf. Slaid.

Slade, *v. pret.* slid, did slide.

Sladge, *n.* a sloven; one who muddies his clothes in walking; a dirty, coarse woman. —*v.* to walk through mire and dirt in a lounging, slovenly way; to work in a slovenly way so as to soil one's clothes. Cf. Slodge, Sludge.

Slae, *n.* the sloe; the fruit of the whitethorn.

Slae, *n.* a weaver's reed. Cf. Slay.

Slae-berry bloom, *n.* the flower of the blackthorn.

Slae-black, *adj.* black as a sloe.

Slae-board, *n.* the board to which the 'slae' of a weaver is affixed.

Slaeie, *adj.* abounding in sloes or sloe-bushes.

Slae-stick, *n.* a blackthorn staff.

Slae-thorn, *n.* the blackthorn; a blackthorn staff.—*adj.* bent, twisted, crooked.

Slag, Slagg, *adj.* moist, wet, soft; thawing.

—*n.* a lump of any soft substance; a portion, mess; a quagmire, slough. —*v.* to soften; to moisten; to besmear; with *up*, to lift in large spoonfuls; to gobble up greedily.

Slag-day, *n.* a curlers' designation of a day of thaw.

Slagger, *v.* to besmear with mud; to eat carelessly. Cf. Slaiger.

Slaggie, *n.* an unseemly mess of anything wet or soft; food dirtily mixed; slatternly work; the act of working in a slatternly manner.— *adj.* thawing; soft; miry; wet, drizzling.

Slaich, *v.* to bedaub, besmear; to paint carelessly; to spit mucus; to eat liquid food in a dirty, disgusting manner; to wash or scour in a slatternly fashion.—*n.* slime; anything wet and muddy, or soft and disgusting; the act of eating in a dirty, disgusting manner.

Slaichie, *adj.* slimy, wet, moist; disgusting.

Slaid, *v.* to walk with long steps and a lounging gait.—*n.* an indolent sloven; a procrastination; a heavy, inactive, unwieldy person; a rather disagreeable person.—*adj.* slovenly, dirty, disagreeable.

Slaid, *n.* a valley between two hills. Cf. Slade.

Slaid, *v. pret.* did slide.

Slaig, *adj.* moist. Cf. Slag.

Slaiger, *v.* to besmear with mud, bedaub; to beslobber; to waddle in mud; to eat slowly and carelessly; to make a gurgling noise in the throat; to walk slowly and carelessly.—*n.* the act of bedaubing; slatternly work; a quantity of some soft substance; a nasty mess of anything wet or soft; the act of taking food in a slovenly manner; food dirtily mixed; the act of making a gurgling sound in the throat; the growl of a dog.

Slaigerer, *n.* one who bedaubs; a dirty walker.

Slaigerin, *n.* a bedaubing.

Slaigersom, *adj.* dirty or slovenly in taking food, walking, or working.

Slaigh, *v.* to bedaub. Cf. Slaich.

Slaik, *v.* to lick with the tongue; to lick up or eat greedily and noisily; to kiss in a slabbering manner; to bedaub, smirch; to lounge, hang about; to carry off and eat sweetmeats, &c., clandestinely.—*n.* a lick with the tongue; a slabbering or wet kiss; anything laid hold of clandestinely in small portions; a small quantity of anything soft, semi-liquid, or viscous that smears; such a quantity of such a substance applied to anything; a daub, smear, dirty mark; a slight wipe, or brush-over, or bedaubing; a careless wash; the act of bedaubing or smearing; a slight stroke; a pat, slap; a low, mean sneak. Cf. Slake.

Slaik, *n.* vegetable, oozy stuff in river-beds. Cf. Slake.

Slaiker, *n.* a dauber; a sneak.

Slaiky, *adj.* streaked with dirt; used of thick mucus in the mouth, as in great thirst.

Slain, *n.* a wooded 'cleugh' or precipice.

Slaines, *n.* in *phr.* 'letter of slaines,' letters subscribed, in the case of slaughter, by the wife or executors of the one slain, acknowledging that satisfaction has been given, or otherwise soliciting the pardon of the offender.

Slainge, *n.* one who clandestinely carries off anything that seems palatable.

Slaipie, *n.* a mean fellow; a plate-licker.— *adj.* indolent, slovenly.

Slair, *v.* to lick up in a slatternly manner; to eat greedily and noisily; to gobble one's food; to outstrip in eating.

Slairg, *n.* a quantity of any semi-fluid substance.—*adj.* slimy, viscous, adhesive.—*v.* to bedaub; to plaster; to besmear with mud; to beslobber; to take food in a slovenly or careless manner; to walk slowly and carelessly.

Slairgie, *adj.* unctuous; slimy, adhesive.

Slairk, *v.* to lick with the tongue; to lick up greedily; to wet; to smear.—*n.* a lick with the tongue; a pat; a slap; a daub; a 'slaik.' Cf. Slaik.

Slairp, *v.* to lick up in a slatternly manner; to eat greedily and noisily; to 'slairg.'—*n.* a slovenly woman.—*adj.* slovenly; 'handless.'

Slairt, *v.* to lick up in a slatternly manner; to gobble; to outdo in eating; to outdo; to go about sluggishly.—*n.* a silly, dastardly fellow.—*adj.* slovenly, 'handless.'

Slairy, *v.* to bedaub through carelessness; food, &c., taken so as to bedaub one's clothes.

Slaister, *v.* to be engaged in wet, dirty work; to bedaub, bespatter; to make a wet, sloppy, or dirty mess; to move clumsily through a muddy road; to do anything in a dirty, slovenly, careless, or awkward way.—*n.* a dirty, disgusting mess; working in a mess; the act of bedaubing; a miscellaneous mixture; slovenly work; a lazy, untidy worker; a sloven.

Slaistering, *n.* liquid spilt by carelessness.

Slaister-kyte, *n.* a foul feeder; a gormandizer; a 'belly-god.'

Slaisters, *n.* a slovenly, dirty person; one who bedaubs himself.

Slaistry, Slaistery, *adj.* wet, dirty, messy; apt to spill; slovenly, careless, untidy.—*n.* dirty work; drudgery; kitchen-refuse.

Slait, *n.* the track of cattle through standing corn.

Slait, *v.* to level; to depreciate; to abuse grossly, maltreat; to wipe.

Slait, *v. pret.* did slit.

Slait, *n.* a dirty, slovenly person.—*adj.* dirty, slovenly; careless in dress. Cf. Slate.

Slaither, *v.* to flatter.

Slaiver, *n.* saliva; spittle; slobber.—*v.* to dribble; to eject saliva; to cajole. Cf. Slaver.

Slake, *v.* to lick with the tongue; to wet, daub. Cf. Slaik.

Slake, *n.* a morass; a narrow pass between two hills. Cf. Slack.

Slake, *n.* the oozy, vegetable stuff in riverbeds; naval laver. Cf. Slaik.

Slake, *n.* a rocky hill; waste land near the shore, covered at high tide.

Slake, *n.* a blow on the chops. Cf. Slaik.

Slakken, *n.* in *phr.* 'slakkens o' night,' night watches.

Slaky, *adj.* streaked with dirt. Cf. Slaiky.

Slam, *v.* to beat, bang; to do anything violently.—*n.* the sound of a bang.

Slam, *n.* a portion of anything acquired by force or craft.

Slamach, Slammach, *v.* to slobber; to eat hastily and in a slovenly manner; to eat stolen food; to seize unfairly.—*n.* a large quantity of soft food swallowed hastily and in slovenly fashion; food gained by force or craft.

Slammachs, *n.* gossamer.

Slammikin, *n.* a drab; a slut; an untidy person.

Slamp, *adj.* pliant, supple, flexible; plump, taut.

Slander, *n.* scandal.

Slane, *n.* a wooded precipice. Cf. Slain.

Slang, *n.* talk, chat.

Slang, *v. pret.* slung.

Slanger, *v.* to linger, go slowly.

Slank, *adj.* thin, lanky.

Slank, *v. pret.* did slink.

Slanlas, Slanlus, *n.* the greater plantain.

Slant, *n.* opportunity.

Slap, *v.* to slam a gate, &c.; to excel, beat.— *n.* a large quantity.—*adv.* with sudden force.

Slap, *v.* to separate threshed grain from broken straw by means of a riddle.—*n.* a riddle for separating grain from broken straw before winnowing.

Slap, *n.* a narrow pass between two hills; a gap or temporary opening in a hedge, fence, &c.; a notch in the edge of a sword.—*v.* to break into gaps.

Slap-bang, *adj.* loud; forcible.

Slapie, *n.* a mean fellow. Cf. Slaipie.

Slaping, *n.* the making of a gap.

Slapper, *n.* anything large of its kind.

Slapping, *adj.* tall and strong; stalwart; strapping.

Slap-riddle, *n.* a riddle for separating threshed grain from straw, chaff, &c.

Slaps, *n.* slops; liquor or liquid food of poor quality.

Slarg, *v.* to bedaub. Cf. Slairg.

Slargie, *adj.* unctuous; viscous. Cf. Slairgie.

Slary, Slarie, *v.* to bedaub. Cf. Slairy.

Slash, *v.* to dash liquid, splash, bespatter; to rush, dash; to walk violently on a wet and muddy road; to lick; to give a slabbering kiss; to work in what is wet and flaccid.— *n.* a quantity of anything wet or semi-liquid thrown with violence; a heavy shower; a great quantity of broth or other food that may be supped; a violent dash; the act of walking violently through mud or water; a loud, crashing noise; a lick; a slabbering kiss; a light brushing-over; a sloven.—*adv.* with violence.

Slashy, *adj.* wet, sloppy, dirty.—*n.* a slatternly woman.

Slatch, *v.* to dabble among mire; to move heavily, as in a miry road.—*n.* a heavy fall or crash; a sloven, slattern. Cf. Sclatch.

Slate, *v. pret.* did slit.

Slate, *n.* a flat rock; a thin piece of wood nailed to the shank of an oar to prevent it from chafing. Cf. Sclate.

Slate, *adj.* slovenly, dirty, careless as to dress. —*n.* a dirty sloven.

Slate, *v.* to depreciate, disparage. Cf. Slait.

Slate-ban', *n.* a stratum of slate among bands of rock; schist.

Slater, *n.* a wood-louse.

Slating, *n.* a roof; a covering, not necessarily of slates.

Slauch, Slaugh, *n.* slime; expectoration; the act of expectorating; a wet covering; a thin film; a haze; mire; the eating of slimy food; the working in a viscous substance.—*v.* to bedaub; to do slimy work; to eat slimy food; to expectorate. Cf. Slauke.

Slauchie, *adj.* slimy. Cf. Slaukie.

Slauchter, *n.* the destruction of springing grain by grubs.

Slauchter-bucht, *n.* a 'bucht' or pen in which sheep were killed.

Slauke, *n.* the oozy, slimy vegetation of river-beds. Cf. Slake.

Slaukie, *adj.* slimy; flaccid; unctuous; slow in speech or motion.—*adv.* slowly.

Slaukie-spoken, *adj.* drawling in speech.

Slaum, *v.* to slobber; to blubber; to smear.

Slaunt, *n.* opportunity. Cf. Slant.

Slaupie, *adj.* indolent and slovenly. Cf. Slaipie.

Slaurie, *v.* to splash with mud; to slander;

to scold.—*n.* mud; anything gelatinous or viscous, like jelly. Cf. Sclaurie.

Slaver, *v.* to slobber; to talk fast; to flatter. —*n.* slobber; fulsome flattery; plausible speech.

Slaver-brewing, *adj.* causing the saliva to flow.

Slavermagullion, *n.* a foolish, lubberly person.

Slavery, *adj.* slobbering; used of the weather: damp, wet.

Slaw, *adj.* slow.

Slaw-fittit, *adj.* slow-footed.

Slaw-gaun, *adj.* slow-going.

Slawk, *n.* slimy vegetation in streams. Cf. Slake.

Slawlie, *adj.* slowly.

Slawm, *v.* to slobber.

Slawmach, *v.* to slobber; to eat stolen food, sweets, &c. Cf. Slamach.

Slawmin, *n.* blubbering.

Slawness, *n.* slowness.

Slawpie, *adj.* indolent and slovenly. Cf. Slaipie.

Slay, *n.* the hand-board of a loom.

Slay, *v.* to pulverize soil too much by harrowing.

Slayworm, *n.* the slow-worm.

Slead, *n.* a sledge.

Sleak, Sleake, *v.* to lick with the tongue. Cf. Slaik.

Sleath, *n.* sloth. Cf. Sleeth.

Sleck, *v.* to groan when overcharged with food.

Sled, *v. pret.* did slide.

Sled, *n.* a low cart or framework without wheels for carrying heavy loads.—*v.* to slip, miss one's footing.

Sled, *adv.* aslant.

Sledder, *n.* one who drives goods on a 'sled.'

Slederie, *adj.* slippery. Cf. Sliddery.

Sled-full, *n.* a cartload.

Sledge, *n.* a sledge-hammer.

Sledging-mill, *n.* a sledge-hammer.

Sled-saddle, *n.* a saddle for a horse yoked in a cart.

Slee, *adj.* sly; clever; skilful.—*v.* to slip; to escape from a task; with *at*, to look at slyly; to place or carry off anything craftily or on the sly.

Sleeband, *n.* an iron band going round the beam of a plough to strengthen it where the coulter is inserted.

Sleech, *n.* silt; sea-wrack; the oozy, vegetable substance found in river-beds; slime; designing flattery; in *pl.* foreshores on which silt is deposited by the tide, 'slob-lands.'— *v.* to coax, cajole.

Sleechy, *adj.* slimy.

Sleegh, *n.* the oozy, vegetable substance found in river-beds. Cf. Sleech.

Sleek, *adj.* used of the ground: smooth,

slippery; sly, cunning; plausible.—*adv.*
slyly, stealthily.—*v.* to smooth the hair;
to fill a measure level at the top; to fill
to overflowing; to lay out carefully; to
slip neatly under cover; to flatter, soothe,
propitiate; to work or walk in a sly
manner.

Sleek, *n.* a measure of fruit, &c., containing
40 lb.

Sleek, *n.* sleet; snow and rain mixed.

Sleek, *n.* mire, slime; miry clay in the bed of
a river on the sea-shore. Cf. Sleech.

Sleeked-ful, *n.* a level measureful.

Sleeken, *v.* to make sleek.

Sleeker, *n.* an instrument for smoothing and
stretching leather.

Sleek-gabbit, *adj.* smooth-tongued; flattering.

Sleekie, Sleeky, *adj.* sly, crafty, insinuating;
deceitful.—*n.* a person of sly, fawning disposition; a term of endearment for a child.

Sleekie, *adj.* sleety.

Sleekit, *ppl.* *adj.* smooth and glossy; un-
ruffled; smooth-tongued; plausible; sly;
hypocritical.

Sleekit-gabbit, *adj.* smooth-tongued.

Sleekit-like, *adj.* sly; cunning.

Sleekitly, *adv.* artfully; cajolingly; slyly.

Sleekitness, *n.* fair show; wheedling.

Sleekly, *adv.* smoothly, easily; slyly.

Sleek-warm, *adj.* sleek and warm.

Sleeky-tongued, *adj.* of plausible speech.

Sleely, *adv.* cleverly, skilfully; slyly.

Sleeness, *n.* slyness.

Slee-nested, *adj.* used of birds' eggs: laid or
hatched in a cunningly hidden nest.

Sleenge, *v.* to slink off or about; to lounge
about idly; to hang the ears. Cf. Slounge.

Sleenger, *n.* an idle lounger.

Sleenie, *n.* a guinea.

Sleep, *v.* used of a limb: to be benumbed
through cold or want of circulation; of a
top: to spin so fast and smoothly that no
movement is visible; in law: to be dormant
or in abeyance; with *in,* to oversleep one's
self.

Sleep-drink, *n.* a sleeping-draught.

Sleeper, *n.* the dunlin.

Sleep-hungry, *adj.* sleepy, craving for sleep.

Sleepies, *n.* field brome-grass; wild-oats.

Sleepin'-fou, *adj.* dead-drunk.

Sleepin'-Maggie, *n.* a top; a kind of humming-top.

Sleepin'-room, *n.* a bedroom.

Sleepit, *v. pret.* slept.

Sleepry, *adj.* sleepy.

Sleep-sang, *n.* a lullaby.

Sleepy-dose, *n.* the ragwort.

Sleepy-fivvers, *n.* a disease affecting the
patient with a strong tendency to sleep;
laziness at work.

Sleepy-heid, -heidit, *adj.* sleepy; stupid.

Sleepy-Maggy, *n.* a rude humming-top.

Sleesh, *n.* a slice.

Sleet, *n.* a load.

Sleetch, *n.* fat mud from shores, used as
manure. Cf. Sleech.

Sleeth, *adj.* sly, cunning.

Sleeth, *adj.* slothful.—*n.* a sloven; a sluggard.

Sleeth-like, *adj.* idiotic; sottish.

Sleethy, *adj.* slovenly.

Sleeve-button, *v.* to put on sleeve-buttons.

Slegger, *n.* a janker; a pole fixed to the axle
of two high wheels, used for carrying trees.

Slegie, *adj.* smooth.

Sleicht, *v.* to dismantle; to jilt; to pass time.
—*n.* the act of jilting. Cf. Slight.

Sleik, *n.* mire, slime. Cf. Sleek.

Sleik, *adj.* sleek; soft. Cf. Slick.

Sleik-worm, *n.* a worm bred in the ooze of
river-beds.

Sleip-eyed, *adj.* with the inside turned out;
disdainfully rejected.

Sleipit, *v. pret. ppl.* slept.

Sleitchock, *n.* a flattering woman. Cf. Sleech.

Slekit, *adj.* deceitful. Cf. Sleekit.

Slenk, *v. pret.* slunk.

Slerg, *v.* to debaub; to gobble. Cf. Slairg.

Slerk, *v.* to lick up greedily. Cf. Slairk.

Slerp, *v.* to eat greedily and noisily.—*n.* a
slovenly woman. Cf. Slairp.

Slester, *v.* to bespatter; to make a wet, dirty
mess. Cf. Slaister.

Slesterin', *ppl. adj.* untidy; besmeared with
food.

Sletch, *n.* oozy mud in river-beds or on the
sea shore. Cf. Sleech.

Sleug, *n.* a queer-looking person; an ill-
behaved fellow.

Sleugh-hound, *n.* a sleuth-hound.

Sleumin, *ppl. adj.* backbiting; gossipy; given
to raising or spreading reports.—*n.* a faint
rumour; hearsay. Cf. Slooming.

Sleutch, *v.* to slouch; to lounge about; to
shirk work or danger.

Sleuth, *adj.* hungry; voracious; keen.

Sleuth, *v.* to act slothfully; to work carelessly;
to neglect. Cf. Sloth.

Sleuthan, Sleuthun, *n.* a lazy, good-for-
nothing person. Cf. Slughan.

Slever, *n.* slaver.—*v.* to eject saliva. Cf.
Slaiver.

Slevery, *adj.* used of the weather: damp, wet.
Cf. Slavery.

Slew, *v.* to edge round, avoid.

Slew, *n.* a moor.

Slewie, *v.* to walk with a heavy, swinging gait.
—*n.* the act of walking with such a gait.

Slib, Slibbie, *adj.* slippery.

Slibber, *n.* slipperiness; a cause of slipperiness.

Slibberkin, Slibrikin, *adj.* sleek, glossy.—*n.* a term of endearment.

Slicht, *v.* to forsake, neglect; to jilt; to spend time.—*n.* a jilting, slight by a lover. Cf. Slight.

Slicht, *n.* sleight; a trick; the knack of doing anything.

Slicht, *adj.* slight; worthless. Cf. Slight.

Slicht-me-not, *adj.* not to be slighted.

Slick, *adj.* sleek, smooth; glossy; soft; sharp, quick; sly, cunning.—*v.* to sleek.—*adv.* exactly; quickly. Cf. Sleek.

Slick, *n.* river-bed ooze. Cf. Sleech, Sleek.

Slick, *n.* a measure of fruit, &c., containing 40 lb. Cf. Sleek.

Slickit, *ppl. adj.* smooth; shining; smooth-tongued; flattering; deceitful; insinuating. Cf. Sleekit.

Slick-tongued, *adj.* smooth-tongued; plausible.

Slick-worm, *n.* a worm bred in the ooze of rivers.

Slid, *adj.* slippery; sly, cunning; smooth-tongued; wheedling.

Slidder, Slider, *v.* to slide, slip; to make slippery; to slip away quietly; to walk with a lazy, slouching gait; to pronounce indistinctly from rapid speaking, to slur one's words; to delay without reason.—*n.* ice; the slide of a scale; loose stones in large numbers lying on a hillside; the place where such stones lie.—*adj.* slippery; unstable.

Slidderin', *ppl. adj.* slippery; unstable.

Sliddery, Sliddry, *adj.* used of food: loose and flaccid, easily eaten; slippery, smooth; sly, deceitful, not trustworthy; squandering, spendthrift; mutable, fleeting, uncertain.

Slide, *v.* to go quickly or unobserved; to steal away, slip off; to pass quietly; to sneak; to carry stealthily; to fib.—*n.* passage, passing away unnoticed; a fib, a deviation from truth.

Slider, *n.* a skate; a round case or stand for a decanter, which can be passed along an uncovered table.

Slide-thrift, *n.* the game of 'first off the board' at draughts.

Slidin', *ppl. adj.* given to fibbing.

Slidness, *n.* slipperiness; smoothness of metre.

Slieck, *n.* a measure of fruits, &c., weighing 40 lb.

Sliek, *n.* river-bed ooze. Cf. Sleek.

Sliep, *v.* to slip.

Slieth, *n.* a sloven; a sluggard.—*adj.* slothful. Cf. Sleeth.

Slieth-like, *adj.* idiotic; sottish.

Slieve-fish, *n.* the cuttle-fish.

Sliggy, *adj.* deceitful, sly; loquacious.

Slight, *v.* to dismantle, demolish; to forsake, neglect, jilt; used of time: to while away. —*n.* the act of one who jilts a woman.

Slight, *adj.* smooth, slippery; worthless in character, unscrupulous.

Slightly, *adv.* slightingly.

Slike, *n.* river-bed ooze. Cf. Sleek.

Slim, *adj.* insufficient; naughty, worthless; sly.—*n.* a careless workman.—*v.* to 'scamp' work; to slur over; to trifle.

Slime, *v.* to idle when not watched; to render eye-service.

Slimer, *n.* an eye-servant; one who cannot be trusted to work unwatched.

Slimly, *adv.* slightly, thinly; superficially; hastily.

Slimmer, *adj.* delicate; easily hurt; slender.

Slim-o'er, *n.* work carelessly done.

Sling, *v.* to strike; to walk with a long stride. —*n.* a throw, cast; a blow; a long, striding step.—*adv.* with a long, quick step; like a stone from a sling.

Slinge, *v.* to sneak; to slink away. Cf. Sleenge.

Slinger, *v.* to move unevenly; to reel; to be in danger of upsetting.

Slink, *v.* to cheat, gull, deceive.—*n.* a cheat; a greedy starveling, one that would slyly purloin and devour everything; a sneak.—*adj.* used of coin: false, forged.

Slink, *n.* the flesh of an animal prematurely born; ill-fed veal; inferior meat.

Slink, *adj.* lank, slender; not fed; poor, insolvent; of no account.—*n.* a tall, limber person; a weak, starved creature; anything poor and weak of its kind.

Slink, *n.* greasy mud; sludge.

Slink-beast, *n.* a weak or worthless animal.

Slinken, *v.* to grow long and thin.

Slinkin, *n.* deceit.—*ppl. adj.* deceitful.

Slink-kid, *n.* an aborted kid.

Slink o' veal, *n.* veal from an aborted calf; a term of reproach for a person.

Slinky, *adj.* tall and slender; lank. Cf. Slunkie.

Slinky-veal, *n.* the flesh of a very young calf.

Slint, *n.* a slovenly, untidy, awkward man.

Slinter, *n.* a 'slint.'

Slip, *v.* to let slip; to convey by stealth; to slit; to open with a sharp point.—*n.* a trick; an upper petticoat; a loose frock; a stripling; a growing girl; a delicate, slender person; a slit, incision; a wooden frame on the top of a cart to enlarge its capacity; a certain quantity of yarn as it comes from the reel, containing twelve 'cuts.'

Slip, *adj.* glib.

Slip-airn, *n.* an oval ring connecting the plough with the swingle-trees.

Slip awa', *v.* to die.

Slip-body, *n.* a loose bodice.

Slip-by, *n.* a careless performance; a pretence at anything; a makeshift.

Slip-coffin, *n.* a coffin with a hinged bottom, allowing the corpse to fall out when lowered into the grave.

Slip-ma-labour, -lawber, *n.* a careless worker; an unreliable servant.—*adj.* careless in working, perfunctory.

Slipper, *n.* slippery ice.

Slippery, *adj.* overpowered by sleep. Cf. Sleepry.

Slippit, *ppl. adj.* slipped; escaped from restraint; aborted.

Slippy, *adj.* slippery; sly; untrustworthy; quick, sharp, prompt.

Slipshod, *adj.* wearing shoes but not stockings.

Slip-slaps, *n.* thin liquid food, ' slops.'

Slister, *v.* to make a mess. Cf. Slaister.

Slit, *n.* a splinter; a splinter of rotten timber.

Slit, *n.* a particular sheep-mark.

Slite, *v.* to rip up anything sewed.—*n.* the act of ripping up. Cf. Slyte.

Slither, *v.* to slip, slide; to glide or drag one's self along; to drag the feet in walking, shuffle.—*n.* a bed of loose stones on a hillside. Cf. Sklidder, Slidder.

Slithery, *adj.* slippery, unstable; sly; untrustworthy. Cf. Sliddery.

Slithy, *adj.* slippery.

Slitter, *n.* a sloven, slattern.

Slitter, *n.* a break in cloth where the woof has given way and only the warp is left.

Slittery, *adj.* sluttish.

Slittie, *n.* a small slit.

Slive, *n.* a slice.

Sliver, *n.* a large, thin slice of beef, &c., cut off.

Sliver, Slivver, *n.* slaver, saliva dribbling from the mouth.—*v.* to slobber; to give wet kisses; to eat untidily.

Slivery, *adj.* slavering.

Slo, *n.* the porous bone inside the horns of cattle.

Sloak, *n.* a bog; a slough. Cf. Slock.

Sloak, *v.* to quench, drench; to slake. Cf. Slock.

Sloaking, *n.* a drenching.

Sloan, *n.* a greedy, covetous person.

Sloan, *n.* a scolding-match.

Sloap, *n.* a lazy, tawdry woman. Cf. Slaupie.

Sloat, *v.* to drink plentifully.—*n.* a voracious fellow.

Sloatch, *n.* an idle, lazy, sloven.—*v.* to go about in a lazy, slovenly manner. Cf. Slotch.

Slobber, *v.* to work untidily; to muddle; to fit loosely.

Slobber, *n.* imperfectly twisted woollen thread. Cf. Slubber.

Slobbery, *adj.* viscous, sticky.

Slob-lands, *n.* flat, muddy foreshores.

Sloch, *v.* to expectorate; to take food in a slovenly, disgusting manner; to work in a viscid substance. — *n.* mucus, phlegm, slime; the act of expectorating; the working carelessly in any sticky stuff.

Sloch, *v.* to do anything carelessly.

Sloch, *n.* the core of a horn; the sheath of a straw, pea, bean, &c.

Sloch, *v.* to slake, drench. Cf. Slock.

Slochan, *n.* a lubberly fellow.

Slocher, *v.* to suffer from cold, asthma, bronchitis, &c.; to take liquid food in a slobbering manner; to be slovenly in dress and gait; used of a pig: to wallow in mud. —*n.* difficult breathing from asthma; the noise of breathing through mucus; the taking food in a slobbering manner; one who breathes with difficulty; a slovenly eater; an untidy, slovenly person.

Slochie, *adj.* slimy, dirty, disgusting.

Slock, *v.* to slake, drench; to extinguish a fire; to go out, as a fire.—*n.* a drink, draught; intoxicating drink.

Slock, *n.* slime; mucus. Cf. Sloch.

Slock, *n.* a hollow between hills; a bog. Cf. Sloak, Slack.

Slocken, *v.* to slake; to drench; to quench thirst; to quench a fire.

Slockener, Slockening, *n.* a thirst-quencher.

Slocker, *v.* to suffer from asthma, &c. Cf. Slocher.

Slocking, *n.* a drenching; a quenching of thirst.

Slodge, *n.* a slattern, sloven. Cf. Sladge, Sludge.

Sloe, *n.* the bony core of a horn. Cf. Slo.

Slogan, *n.* a to-name used to distinguish a person from others of the same name; an ' eke-name.' Cf. Slughorne.

Slogg, *n.* a quagmire, slough; a quantity of any soft substance.—*v.* to soften, moisten, besmear. Cf. Slag.

Slogger, *v.* to go about in a slovenly way, or with stockings hanging down about the ankles; to eat in a greedy or slovenly manner.—*n.* a dirty sloven.

Sloggerin, *ppl. adj.* slovenly.

Sloggorne, *n.* a hereditary peculiarity in a family or race. Cf. Slughorne.

Slogie, *n.* a loose ' bed-gown' hanging down to the knees.

Slogy, Slogy-riddle, *n.* a wide-meshed riddle, used for potatoes, onions, &c.

Sloit, *n.* a lazy, stupid, dirty fellow; a sloven. —*v.* with *awa'*, to pass on carelessly.

Sloiter, *v.* to engage in any wet and dirty

work ; to eat in a slovenly, dirty way ; to
breathe through nasal mucus ; to work or
walk in a slovenly, loitering manner ; to
overnurse. — *n.* a wet, dirty mess ; nasal
mucus ; a sloven, one dirty in person or at
food ; the taking of food in a slovenly
manner ; the noise made in eating thus ;
the doing of anything, or walking, in a
slovenly fashion ; overnursing.

Slok, Sloke, *v.* to slake. Cf. Slock.

Sloke, *n.* the oozy vegetable substance in
river-beds ; a name given to various edible
sea-weeds. Cf. Sleek.

Sloken, Slokin, *v.* to slake ; to spend money
on drink. Cf. Slocken.

Slomie, *adj.* flaccid, blown up ; relaxed, enfeebled. Cf. Sloomy.

Slong, *n.* a sling. Cf. Slung.

Slonk, *n.* a mire ; a ditch ; the noise made by
wading or sinking in a miry bog, and when
walking with shoes full of water.—*v.* to
wade through a mire ; to sink in mud.

Slooch, *n.* a term of contempt.—*v.* to slouch.

Slooie, *v.* to fleece one by a trick or fraud ;
to take advantage of one in a bargain.

Sloom, *n.* a report. Cf. Slooming.

Sloom, *n.* a slumber ; a light doze ; an unsettled sleep. — *v.* to slumber ; to doze
lightly ; to become powerless through fear,
&c. ; to move slowly and silently ; to
wander aimlessly or sneakingly ; used of
plants : to become flaccid and droop
through frost ; to waste, decay.

Sloomin', *ppl. adj.* slinking ; sneaking.

Slooming, *ppl. adj.* backbiting ; gossipy ;
given to raising reports.—*n.* a faint rumour ;
a report, hearsay.

Sloomit, *ppl. adj.* sullen, evil-looking ; with
a hang-dog air ; wily, sly.

Sloomy, *adj.* sleepy, sluggish ; used of animals : relaxed, enfeebled ; of vegetables :
damp, beginning to putrefy.

Sloomy corn, *n.* grain not well filled.

Sloon, *n.* a suppressed rumour. Cf. Sloom,
Slooming.

Sloonge, *v.* to lounge.—*n.* an idler. Cf.
Slounge.

Sloop, *v.* with *doun*, to descend obliquely.

Sloos, *n.* a sluice ; a dash of water.—*v.* to
dash water from a vessel.

Sloot, *n.* a sloven ; a low fellow. Cf. Sloit,
Slute.

Slooter, *n.* a lumpish, inactive person. Cf.
Skleuter, Slutter.

Sloottery, *adj.* slovenly.

Slop, *n.* a gap. Cf. Slap.

Slop, *v.* to slap.—*n.* a slap, blow.

Slope, Slop, *v.* to cheat, defraud ; to evade
payment of debts, rent, &c.

Slope, Slop, *n.* a smart, tight-fitting article of

dress, made of white or striped unbleached
linen, in shape a cross between a sleeved
waistcoat and a common jacket ; a cotton
smock-frock.

Sloped gaw, *n.* an open drain.

Slopping, *ppl. adj.* sloping.

Slorach, *v.* to work in a semi-liquid substance in an untidy way ; to eat in a dirty,
slovenly way ; to expectorate. — *n.* work
dirtily done ; the eating of food in a disgusting way ; a dirty, disgusting mess.

Slorg, *v.* to ' slork.'

Slork, *v.* to make a disagreeable noise in eating ; to eat up in large mouthfuls ; to walk
through slush with wet shoes which regorge the water in them.

Slorp, *v.* to swallow ungracefully and noisily ;
to draw in the breath convulsively ; to
bungle ; to do anything in a noisy, slatternly way.—*n.* a sop ; a mess of food ; a
spoonful of food ; a spoonful of food taken
ungracefully ; a sloven ; an uncouth person.

Slorpie, *adj.* slovenly, tawdry.

Slorping, *ppl. adj.* slovenly, tawdry.

Slorrich, *n.* an unsavoury mess of food. Cf.
Slorach.

Slort, *n.* a lazy, stupid, slovenly fellow. Cf.
Sloit.

Slot, *n.* a sum of money ; a windfall of money
unlooked for.

Slot, *n.* a hollow in a hill or in the human
body.

Slot, *n.* the track or trail of a traveller.

Slot, Slott, *n.* a cross-bar ; a wooden bar or
support in a cart.—*v.* to bolt, bar, fasten
securely.

Slotch, *n.* an idle, lounging, slovenly fellow ;
a glutton, a greedy, slovenly eater.—*v.* to
lounge about in a lazy, slovenly fashion.

Slote, *n.* the bolt or bar of a door.

Sloth, *v.* to neglect slothfully. Cf. Sleuth.

Slott, *n.* a lazy, stupid, dirty sloven.—*v.*
with *awa'*, to pass on in a careless manner.
Cf. Sloit.

Slotter, *v.* to act in a slovenly manner ; to
gobble one's food noisily, like a duck ; to
slobber ; to breathe through nasal mucus ;
to engage in wet, dirty work ; to overnurse ;
to pass time sluggishly or idly ; to idle,
loiter. — *n.* a filthy mess ; a sloven in
person or at food ; eating or drinking
in a slobbering manner ; the noise thus
made ; overnursing ; working or walking
in a slovenly manner. Cf. Sloiter.

Slotter-hodge, *n.* a dirty, slovenly fellow in
person and at food.

Slottry, *adj.* slumbering, drowsy ; inactive.

Slouan, *n.* a sleuth-hound. Cf. Sleugh-
hound.

Slouch, *v.* with *away*, to slip away from a

place where there is anything to do or to fear. Cf. Sleutch.

Slouch, *v.* to wet, drench. Cf. Slock.

Slouch, *n.* a deep ravine or gully. Cf. Slough.

Slouching, *n.* a wetting, drenching.

Sloug, Slough, *n.* a slow, idle, lounging person ; a lazy, awkward fellow.

Slough, *n.* a husk, the skin of a berry ; a coat ; a petticoat ; a warm wrapper.

Slough, *n.* a voracious eater and drinker ; a lean, hungry person or animal ; a mean, selfish person.

Slough, *n.* a deep ravine.

Slough-dog, -hound, *n.* a sleuth-hound.

Slouk, *n.* various species of algæ ; the oozy vegetable substance in river-beds. Cf. Sloke.

Sloum, *n.* a slumber.—*v.* to slumber ; to become powerless through fear. Cf. Sloom.

Sloum, *n.* the green scum that gathers on stagnant pools.

Sloun, *n.* an indolent, good-for-nothing person.—*v.* to idle away one's time. Cf. Slowan.

Sloung, *n.* a sling. Cf. Slung.

Slounge, *v.* to lounge, idle about, walk with a slovenly gait ; to go from place to place catering for a meal ; to hang the ears, look sour.—*n.* an idler ; a skulking, sneaking, vagabond fellow ; a glutton ; a stupid, dull-looking fellow ; a dog that goes about with hanging ears, prying for food.

Slounge, *v.* to plunge ; to splash, dash water ; to make a plunging noise.—*n.* a plunge, splash ; its sound ; a great fall of rain ; a complete drenching. Cf. Slunge.

Slounge o' weet, *n.* a heavy fall of rain.

Slounger, *n.* a loafer ; an idle sneak ; one who goes about sponging for food.

Sloungin'-like, *adj.* having a downcast, tired appearance or gait.

Sloupe, *n.* a stupid, silly person.

Slouper, *n.* a sloven ; a knave who tries to slip off stealthily. Cf. Slyper.

Slouster, *v.* with *awa'*, to work in a slovenly way ; to work among liquid or semi-liquid stuff.—*n.* a sloven ; food ill-prepared. Cf. Slaister.

Slouter, *v.* to eat up greedily and untidily.

Slouth, *v.* to neglect.—*n.* sloth. Cf. Sloth.

Slouthfu', *adj.* inactive, idle.

Slouth-hound, *n.* a sleuth-hound.

Slowan, *n.* a sloven ; a sleuth-hound.—*v.* to idle one's time. Cf. Slouan, Sloun.

Slow-belly, *n.* a louse.

Slow-hound, *n.* a sleuth-hound.

Slow-thumbs, *n.* one who dawdles at work.

Sloy, *n.* a slide. Cf. Skloy.

Sloyt, *n.* a lazy, stupid, dirty fellow. Cf. Sloit.

Sluan, *n.* a sleuth-hound ; a man of disreputable character ; a lazy lounger. Cf. Slowan, Slouan.

Slub, *n.* slime.

Slubber, *v.* to swallow with a gurgling noise ; to work carelessly ; to idle.—*n.* mire, mud, slush ; the act of swallowing with a gurgling noise ; food overboiled or of a flaccid nature.

Slubber, *n.* half-twined or ill-twined woollen thread.

Slubber-de-gullion, *n.* a mean, dirty fellow.

Slubbery, *adj.* slimy ; used of food : loose, flaccid, overboiled.

Slubby, *adj.* slimy.

Sluch, *n.* a sloppy mess ; mud. Cf. Slutch.

Slucken, *ppl. adj.* looking lean and empty, like a tired, ill-fed horse. Cf. Slunken.

Sludder, *n.* a liquid or semi-liquid mess.—*v.* to eat in a slovenly way ; to eat noisily ; to articulate indistinctly ; to slur over. Cf. Sluther.

Sluddery, *adj.* soft, flaccid.

Sludge, *n.* a wet, muddy place ; ground-ice ; a sloven ; one who muddies himself walking or working ; a coarse, dirty woman.— *v.* to bemire one's self walking or working. Cf. Sladge.

Slue, *v.* to twist ; to slew.

Slug, *n.* a loose wrapper or upper covering worn for dirty work.

Slug, Slug road, *n.* a road through a narrow defile between two hills.

Slug, *n.* a sluggard ; a short sleep.—*v.* to move slowly.

Slug, *n.* in *phr.* 'a slug for the drink,' one who drinks continually but never becomes drunk.

Sluggy, *v.* to swallow greedily.

Slugh, *n.* a mean fellow. Cf. Sloug.

Slughan, *n.* a lazy, good-for-nothing person.

Slughorne, Sloggorne, *n.* a hereditary feature or characteristic of a family or race. Cf. Slogan.

Sluice, Sluich, *n.* the flow of water from a sluice ; a dash of water ; an outburst.—*v.* to dash water out of a vessel or over a person or thing.

Sluich-board, *n.* a sluice-gate.

Sluip, *n.* a lazy, clumsy fellow. Cf. Slype.

Sluist, *n.* a large, heavy person ; a sluggish person ; an ungraceful person. Cf. Slust.

Sluit, *n.* a lazy, clumsy person ; a glutton ; a sloven. Cf. Slute.

Sluiter, *v.* to dawdle over work ; to snore.— *n.* a clumsy sloven ; a glutton ; a noisy splash. Cf. Slutter.

Slum, *n.* a slight doze.—*v.* to slumber. Cf. Sloom.

Slummish, *v.* to trifle away one's time.

Slump, *n.* a marsh; a swamp; a dull noise of something falling into a hole.—*v.* to sink or stick in a wet, miry place; to fall suddenly into anything wet or miry; to plump in.—*adv.* plump.

Slump, *n.* a large quantity; a lump sum.

Slump, *n.* a remnant.

Slumpert, *n.* a large quantity; what is not measured.

Slumpie, *adj.* marshy, swampy.

Slump number, *n.* the whole number.

Slump-wise, *adv.* in the lump or mass; without measure.

Slump-work, *n.* work taken in the lump.

Sluneoch, Sluneuch, *n.* a brutal, mischievous person.—*v.* to lounge idly about.

Slung, *n.* a sling.—*v.* to sling; to walk with long steps and a swinging gait.

Slung, *n.* a tall, lank fellow; a sneaking, low fellow. Cf. Slounge.

Slunge, *v.* to plunge; to dash water; to splash.—*n.* a fall of rain; a complete drenching. Cf. Slounge.

Slunge, *v.* to lounge.—*n.* an idler, a sneak; a glutton. Cf. Slounge.

Slunk, *n.* mire; a quagmire; a slough.—*v.* to wade through a mire or a moor. Cf. Slonk.

Slunk, *n.* a lazy shirker of work or duty; a sneak.

Slunk, *n.* veal from a calf cut out of the mother. Cf. Slink.

Slunk, *n.* a tall, thin, awkward person.

Slunken, *ppl. adj.* lank, lean, empty in appearance, like a tired horse not fed fully on its journey. Cf. Slucken.

Slunker, *v.* to slink, go off stealthily.

Slunkie, *n.* a tall, thin person. Cf. Slinky.

Slunyoch, *v.* to lounge about idly. Cf. Sluneoch.

Slupe, *n.* a sloven. Cf. Slype, Sluip.

Slur, *v.* to sneer, make fun of.—*n.* scorn.

Slure, *v.* to swallow ungracefully; to pour; to pour dirty water on one.

Slurich, *n.* flaccid food, in swallowing which a noise is made. Cf. Slorach.

Slush, *n.* a wet, muddy place, plashy ground; a pool; dirty water; slops; sloppy food; weak liquor; a flow of water; a large body of water; any liquid or semi-liquid stuff dashed or thrown; an indefinite quantity of anything; a dirty sloven, a drudge; the act of walking with slatternly, trailing steps, or through soft mud or water; the noise of such walking; the doing of drudgery or dirty work; misshapen, worn shoes.—*v.* to dash water; to splash; to fall in a soft, wet mass; to walk through mud or water; to walk with a slovenly gait; to do rough, dirty work; to drudge; to 'toil and moil.' —*adv.* with violence. Cf. Skleush.

Slushie, *adj.* abounding in melting snow; weak, sloppy, 'wishy-washy.'

Slushit, *ppl. adj.* slovenly; untidy in dress.

Slushitness, *n.* slovenliness; untidiness.

Slust, *n.* a sluggish person; an unwieldy, ungraceful person.

Slutch, *n.* a sloppy mess; a hanger-on; a parasite.—*v.* to move heavily, as in a deep, soft road.

Slute, *n.* a very contemptuous term; a slow, lazy animal; a lazy, clumsy person; a sloven; a glutton; a drunkard; a low, greedy fellow.

Sluther, *n.* a quagmire; dirty, slatternly work. —*v.* to work carelessly and hurriedly; to go carelessly; to eat in a slovenly way. Cf. Sludder.

Sluthery, *adj.* muddy, wet; slimy.

Slutter, *v.* to spill or slobber in cooking or eating food; to work in a slovenly manner; to loiter, dawdle at work; to snore; to make a noise through the nostrils when half-asleep.—*n.* a big, clumsy sloven; a glutton; a noisy splash. Cf. Skleuter.

Sluttery, Sluttrie, *adj.* slovenly.

Sly, *v.* to go or come silently or stealthily; to look in a sly manner; to place or remove slyly; to escape from a task. Cf. Slee.

Slyaag, *v.* to besmear. Cf. Slagg.

Slyaager, *v.* to besmear. Cf. Slagger.

Slycht, *v.* to dismantle. Cf. Slight.

Sly-goose, *n.* the common sheldrake.

Slylins, *adv.* slyly.

Slype, *v.* to strip off, peel; to press gently downwards; to move freely, as a weighty body drawn through mud; to fall over, as a wet furrow from the plough; used of a plough: to turn over a furrow.—*n.* a sledge used in agriculture; a coarse, worthless fellow; a term of contempt.

Slype, *adv.* aslant, aslope.

Slype-eyed, *adj.* cross-eyed.

Slyper, *n.* one who seemingly wishes to sneak away, from fear of detection; one who is tawdry and slovenly in dre...

Slyple, *n.* a lazy person, a 'sl

Slyppies, *n.* roasted peas, ea

Slyre-lawn, *n.* a species of '

Slyster, *v.* to do dirty, messy work; to be-daub. Cf. Slaister.

Slyte, *v.* to move easily or smoothly; to sharpen an edged tool.

Sma', *adj.* small; young.—*n.* a small thing; a small sum of money; a small quantity.

Sma'-bouket, *adj.* of small bulk; shrunken.

Smacher, *n.* a large number; a confused crowd; a mess, a mixture; confusion; trash; a fondling term for a child.—*v.* to collect in a crowd; to crowd; to eat stealthily or in small pieces what is pleasant to the taste.

Smachrie, Smachirie, *n.* a great number; a confused gathering; a miscellaneous collection; a jumble; trash; a hodge-podge of eatables; confectionery.—*adj.* trashy, worthless.

Smack, *n.* style, fashion.—*v.* to drink with enjoyment.

Smack, *n.* a loud kiss; an instant.—*v.* used of guns : to give a loud report; to speed.—*adv.* with force.

Smackie, *n.* a little kiss.

Smacle, *n.* as much, 'as mickle.'

Smad, *v.* to stain; to discolour.—*n.* a stain; a spot of mud or grease on clothes. Cf. Smud.

Sma' drink, *n.* very weak beer.

Sma' evens, *n.* a very small quantity.

Sma'-fairns, *n.* the intestines, the guts.

Sma'-folk, *n.* people of low rank.

Smag, *n.* a small piece; a tit-bit; anything small and nice.

Smagrie, Smaggrie, *n.* a large crowd of small objects in confusion; a dainty; a dainty mixture. Cf. Smachrie.

Smaicher, *n.* a large number. Cf. Smacher.

Smaichery, *n.* a great number; confectionery. Cf. Smachrie.

Smaik, *n.* a mean, scurvy fellow; a sneak; a rascal.

Smair, Smairie, *v.* to 'smear'; to besmear. Cf. Smear.

Smair-caryin, *n.* the spinal marrow. Cf. Smergh-kerien.

Smair-docken, *n.* the common dock; the good King Henry. Cf. Smear-docken.

Smairg, *v.* to bedaub; used of sheep : to 'smear' or salve.

Smalie, *adj.* small, little. Cf. Smally.

Small, *adj.* young; inferior in station.—*n.* anything small. Cf. Sma'.

Small blue-hawk, *n.* the merlin.

Small doucker, *n.* the little grebe.

Small waters, *n.* two or three small lochs lying near each other.

Small-write, *n.* small-text in handwriting.

Smally, *adj.* small; puny; undersized.

Sma'-maw, *n.* the common gull.

Smarrich, *v.* to crowd in a confused, secret, or underhand way; to work weakly and unskilfully; to eat, talk, or work clandestinely; to eat dainties secretly.—*n.* a confused crowd; a group of persons engaged in secret work or talk; an untidy heap. Cf. Smacher.

Smart, *v.* to smarten, urge on; to punish.

Smash, *v.* to shiver; to beat down in battle; to beat severely; to hurl with a crash; to push forward vigorously or recklessly.—*n.* a heavy, dashing blow; the shreds of anything broken; the sound of breaking.

Smashables, *n.* things liable to be broken breakages.

Sma' sheen, *n.* fine shoes, dress-shoes.

Smasherie, *n.* the act of smashing; a smash; used of an epidemic : great loss of life.

Smashing, *ppl. adj.* big; burly, strapping.

Sma' still, Sma' still whisky, *n.* whisky distilled in small stills, and thought superior to the product of a large still.

Smatchard, Smatchart, Smatcher, Smatchert, *n.* a pert, impudent child; a scurvy fellow; a small, contemptible person.

Smatchet, Smatched, Smatchit, *n.* a 'smatchard'; used as a term of contempt or dislike.

Smatter, Smathir, *v.* to break in bits, to smash; used of children and small objects : to swarm, crowd, or move confusedly; to be busily engaged with trifles; to pretend to work; to work or speak in a slow, hesitating, confused way; to deal in smallwares; with *awa'*, to spend in a trifling way; to consume food by eating often and little at a time.—*n.* a heap of small objects in confusion or motion; confusion; the doing of anything awkwardly or confusedly; a little person weak and unskilful at work; a trifle, scrap, a thing of small value; a small sum of money.

Smatterie, *n.* a quantity of small objects; a family of young children; a flock.

Smawly, *adj.* small; puny. Cf. Smally.

Smeadum, *n.* force of character; spirit. Cf. Smeddum.

Smeak, *v.* to smoke.—*n.* smoke. Cf. Smeek.

Smear, *v.* to rub sheep with a compound of tar and train-oil or butter.—*n.* an ointment for 'smearing' sheep.

Smear, *n.* marrow; pith; vigour of mind or body. Cf. Smergh.

Smear-docken, *n.* the dock; the good King Henry; both of which were used in making a salve for stings, sores, &c.

Smearing-house, *n.* a hut for 'smearing' sheep.

Smearing-stool, *n.* a stool with a spoked bottom, so as to admit the legs of a sheep and keep it steady during the 'smearing.'

Smearless, *adj.* pithless; unhandy; languid, senseless. Cf. Smerghless.

Smeary, *n.* a sheep that has been 'smeared'; a person all besmeared.—*adj.* greasy, viscid.

Smechle, *v.* to fumble.

Smeddum, *n.* the powder of ground malt; dust; powder; force of character; mettle, spirit; liveliness; sagacity, good sense, intelligence.

Smeddumfu', *adj.* intelligent; full of spirit or sagacity.

Smeddumless, *adj.* lacking intelligence, spirit, or sagacity.

Smeeg, *n.* a kiss.

Smeek, *v.* to smoke; to dry in smoke; to fumigate; to kill with smoke.—*n.* smoke; tobacco-smoke; fumes; a pungent, foul smell; a stuffy, close atmosphere; a quarrel, high words between husband and wife.

Smeek, *v.* to infect; to smite.

Smeeky, *adj.* smoky; giving forth a foul, pungent smell.

Smeer, *v.* to 'smear.' Cf. Smear.

Smeer, *n.* marrow; pith; vigour of body or mind. Cf. Smergh.

Smeerikin, *n.* a hearty kiss; a stolen kiss.

Smeerless, *adj.* pithless, untidy, 'handless.' Cf. Smerghless.

Smeeth, *adj.* smooth.—*adv.* smoothly.

Smeethly, *adv.* smoothly.

Smeethness, *n.* smoothness.

Smeik, *v.* to smoke; to dry in smoke.—*n.* smoke. Cf. Smeek.

Smell, *v.* to feel; to impart a smell.—*n.* a small quantity; a 'taste' of liquor.

Smeller, *n.* a small quantity of drink.

Smelt, *n.* salmon-fry; a term of contempt, applied generally to a child.

Smelt, *n.* a smooth spot on the sea.

Smeltering, *ppl. adj.* applied to the roaring sound of devouring flames.

Smerg, *v.* to besmear. Cf. Smairg.

Smergh, Smer, *n.* marrow; pith; vigour of mind or body; sense.

Smergh-kerien, *n.* the spinal marrow.

Smerghless, *adj.* pithless; unhandy; insipid; languid; senseless.

Smert, *v.* to smarten. Cf. Smart.

Smertish, *adj.* rather smart.

Smertry, *adj.* savoury; fat, marrowy.

Smeth, *adj.* smooth. Cf. Smeeth.

Smeu, *n.* the willow-warbler. Cf. Smeuth.

Smeuch, *v.* to smoke fiercely; to emit fumes; to drizzle thickly. — *n.* smoke; fumes; smell; thick, drizzling rain.

Smeuchie, *adj.* smoky; drizzly.

Smeuchter, *v.* to burn slowly with much smoke; to drizzle; to work slowly and unskilfully; to eat slowly and sparingly; to consume or waste slowly.—*n.* a fire burning slowly with much smoke; a drizzling shower or wetting mist; the doing of work slowly and unskilfully; slow and sparing eating; a slow wasting.

Smeuth, *n.* the willow-warbler.

Smewlikin, *adj.* sly.

Smewy, *adj.* savoury; marrowy; fat.

Smiach, *n.* sagacity, 'smeddum.'

Smiaggered, *ppl. adj.* besmeared.

Smick, *n.* a dainty; anything somewhat old and worthless.

Smiek, *n.* a spot; a tincture.

Smicker, *v.* to smirk; to smile fawningly; to grin.

Smiddle, *v.* to smuggle; to hide; to work stealthily.

Smiddy, *n.* a blacksmith's workshop; a brisk conversational gathering such as takes place in a 'smiddy.'

Smiddy-boll, *n.* a payment in grain made to a blacksmith.

Smiddy-coom, -gum, *n.* small coal used in a smithy.

Smiddy-seat, *n.* a croft attached to a smithy.

Smiddy-sparks, *n.* sparks from a smith's anvil.

Smid-meal, *n.* a coarse meal. Cf. Smeddum.

Smikker, *v.* to grin; to smirk. Cf. Smicker.

Smill, *n.* fragments; leavings.—*v.* to fall in pieces. Cf. Smuil.

Smiok, *n.* a dish of good food.—*v.* to feed on the best.

Smir, *n.* fine rain. Cf. Smurr.

Smircle, *v.* to smile; to giggle. Cf. Smirkle.

Smird, *v.* to gibe, jeer.

Smird, *n.* a smart tap on the knuckles, or on any other part of the body, with the finger-tips, or with the tip of a 'tawse.'

Smirikin, *n.* a stolen kiss. Cf. Smeerikin.

Smirk, *v.* to smile pleasantly.—*n.* a pleasant smile.—*adj.* pleasant; smiling.

Smirkingly, *adv.* smilingly.

Smirkle, *v.* to smile; to giggle; to laugh in a suppressed manner.—*n.* a smile; a suppressed laugh.

Smirky, *adj.* smiling; good-natured-looking; cheerful; in good health.

Smirky-faced, *adj.* good-natured-looking.

Smirl, *n.* a roguish trick; a mocking smile; a sneering laugh.—*v.* to smirk; to smile or laugh in a mischievous, mocking mood.

Smirn, *v.* to drizzle.—*n.* a drizzle; a slight shower of rain.

Smirr, *n.* a drizzle; fine rain.—*v.* to drizzle. Cf. Smurr.

Smirtle, *v.* to smile; to giggle; to laugh in a suppressed manner; to smile bashfully.—*n.* a smile; a suppressed laugh.

Smit, *n.* a clashing noise.

Smit, *n.* a spot; a stain; infection, contagion; potato disease or blight; a moral stain.—*v.* to infect by contagion; to stain, pollute, contaminate; to attack, smite.

Smitch, *n.* a stain, a speck; a spot on the skin, blemish; a moral stain; a slur.

Smitch, *n.* an impudent boy; a chit. Cf. Smytch.

Smitchcock, *n.* a grilled or broiled chicken.

Smite, *n.* a blow; a hit.

Smite, *n.* a mite; an atom; a small portion; a puny, insignificant person.

Smith-body, *n.* a contemptuous term for a blacksmith.

Smithereens, *n.* bits; splinters; shivers.

Smithers, *n.* 'smithereens.'

Smithy-chat, *n.* gossip among frequenters of a smithy.

Smitsome, *adj.* infectious.

Smittable, *adj.* infectious.

Smittal, *adj.* contagious. Cf. Smittle.

Smit-thumbs, *n.* a pledge for the fulfilment of a bargain, by licking and pressing the thumbs.

Smittin, *ppl. adj.* infectious.

Smittin'-sickness, *n.* any infectious disease; infection.

Smittle, *v.* to infect by contagion.—*adj.* infectious; contagious.

Smittleness, *n.* infection; contagion.

Smittlish, *adj.* infectious; contagious.

Smittral, *adj.* infectious; contagious.

Smitty, *adj.* dirty, smutty; impure.

Smoar, *v.* to smother. Cf. Smoor.

Smoch, *n.* the smoke of burning wet, rotten wood.—*v.* to burn and smoke like rotten wood.

Smocher, *v.* to breathe with difficulty from cold.

Smock-faced, *adj.* smooth-faced; pale-faced.

Smod, *n.* a stain; a speck. Cf. Smud.

Smoghie, *adj.* close, stuffy, smoky; sultry.

Smoik, *n.* a dish of good food. Cf. Smiok.

Smoir, *v.* to smother. Cf. Smoor.

Smoit, *n.* a foolish or obscene chatterer.

Smoke, Smok, *n.* a smoked fish; hot ashes; an inhabited house with one chimney at least. Cf. Smeek.

Smoky, *n.* a chemise.

Smoky, *n.* a smoked haddock; one unsplit and smoked.

Smolder, *v.* to smother.

Smollicher, *n.* in *phr.* 'a black smollicher,' a person with very dark features.

Smolt, *adj.* used of the weather: fair; clear; mild.

Smolt, *n.* a contemptuous name for a child.

Smoo, *v.* to smile placidly or benignantly; to smile, smirk; to laugh in one's sleeve; to suppress a laugh.—*n.* a placid or benignant smile.

Smoochter, *v.* to burn slowly with much smoke. Cf. Smeuchter.

Smoodge, Smoog, *v.* to laugh quietly; to laugh in one's sleeve. Cf. Smudge.

Smoogle, *v.* to smuggle; to hush up. Cf. Smuggle.

Smooin', *adj.* sly; sneaking. Cf. Smuin.

Smook, *v.* to put away, hide; to draw on or off, as a stocking; with *about*, to go about clandestinely; to pilfer.

Smook, *n.* a drizzling rain, driving before the wind.

Smook, *v.* to suffocate bees by burning sulphur.

Smook, *adj.* thievish, pilfering.

Smookit, *ppl. adj.* smoked.

Smookit, *ppl. adj.* cunning, artful.

Smool, *v.* to secure by underhand means; to filch; to wheedle; to slip away.

Smool, *v.* to look sulky.

Smool, *n.* small bits.—*v.* to crumble. Cf. Smuil.

Smoolachan, *n.* a kiss.

Smoolet-like, *adj.* sulky-looking.

Smoor, *v.* to smother, suffocate, stifle; to oppress by heat; to drown; to suppress; to conceal; to obscure; to extinguish a light.—*n.* a stifling smoke; a stuffy atmosphere; a smothering.

Smoor, *n.* a drizzling mist or rain. Cf. Smurr.

Smoorich, *v.* to hide, conceal; to kiss.—*n.* a stolen kiss; a hearty kiss.

Smoorich, *n.* a cloud of dust, smoke, or driving snow, like to choke one.

Smoorikin, *n.* a stolen kiss. Cf. Smeerikin.

Smoor-thow, *n.* heavy snow with strong wind, threatening to suffocate one.

Smoory, *adj.* close, stifling; hot.

Smooshter, *v.* used of a fire: to give more smoke than flame, to 'smoost.'

Smoost, *v.* to smoulder; to emit smoke; to burn gradually away without blazing. Cf. Smuist.

Smoot, *v.* to shuffle off; to hide stealthily.

Smoot, *v.* to smother.

Smoot, *n.* salmon-fry; a small speckled trout. Cf. Smout.

Smooth, *v.* to render useless. Cf. Smeeth.

Smooth, *n.* the willow-warbler. Cf. Smeuth.

Smootrikin, *adj.* tiny and active.—*n.* a puny person or animal; a fondling term.

Smore, *v.* to smother, suffocate. Cf. Smoor.

Smore of rain, *n.* close, small rain without wind. Cf. Smurr.

Smorie, *adj.* drizzly, rainy. Cf. Smurr.

Smot, Smott, Smote, *n.* a stain; a sheep-mark; a number of sheep bearing the same mark; mouldiness gathering on what is kept in a damp place; moral pollution; a slur or stain on character.—*v.* to stain; to mark sheep with tar, ruddle, &c.

Smote, *ppl.* smitten.

Smotter, *v.* to besmear; to bespatter.

Smoukie, *n.* a little, cunning, fawning child; a playful epithet applied to a child.

Smoukie, *n.* a species of bird of prey.

Smoupsie, *n.* a stripling.

Smourock, *n.* a hearty kiss. Cf. Smoorich.

Smouster, *v.* to eat clandestinely.

Smout, *n.* salmon-fry; a smolt; a small speckled trout; a small person or animal; a fondling term for a child; a trifling little boy or girl.

Smout, *adj.* used of the weather: clear, fair, mild. Cf. Smolt.

Smoutter, *v.* to eat often and little at a time.

Smouty, *adj.* obscene, smutty.

Smow, *v.* to smile, smirk.—*n.* a placid or benignant smile. Cf. Smoo.

Smowe, *v.* to stink.

Smucht, *n.* a smouldering.

Smuchty, *adj.* smoky.

Smud, *n.* a dirty speck; any stain.—*v.* to stain, blacken.

Smud, *n.* a stench.

Smuddoch, *n.* a smouldering fire with much smoke.

Smudge, *v.* to laugh quietly or in a suppressed manner; to laugh in one's sleeve.—*n.* a suppressed laugh or smile.

Smue, *v.* to laugh in one's sleeve. Cf. Smoo.

Smue, *v.* to smoke; to drizzle thickly.—*n.* thick, stifling smoke; thick, drizzling rain.

Smueie, *adj.* drizzling thickly.

Smug, *v.* to hide, conceal; to go about stealthily; to toy amorously in secret.

Smug, *v.* to dress well.

Smug, *v.* to laugh in one's sleeve. Cf. Smudge.

Smuggart, *n.* a puny and disagreeable person.

Smuggle, *v.* with *up*, to conceal, hide.

Smuggle-boots, *n.* a boys' game.

Smuggle-the-gig, -gag, -keg, *n.* a boys' game.

Smugglins, *adv.* by means of smuggling.

Smuggy, *adj.* muggy, foggy, drizzling.

Smugly, *adj.* amorous; sly and well-dressed.

Smuik, *v.* to smoke bees. Cf. Smook.

Smuil, *v.* to sneak; to slip through one's fingers; with *in*, to wheedle, curry favour; to crumble; to fall in pieces; to cajole; to slip away.—*n.* small pieces; fragments; leavings.

Smuin, *adj.* sly; sneaking.

Smuir, *v.* to smother. Cf. Smoor.

Smuirach, *n.* very small coal.

Smuist, *v.* to smoulder; to emit smoke.—*n.* the act of burning in a smouldering, smoky way; disagreeable smoke; a smouldering, suffocating smell, as of burning sulphur, &c.

Smuister, *v.* used of the air: to smother.

Smuister, *v.* to work lazily and feebly; to idle over the fire. Cf. Smyster.

Smuisty, *adj.* smoky.

Smulachin, *adj.* puny, looking poorly.

Smule, *v.* to cajole. Cf. Smuil.

Smult, *v.* to crop very short.

Smurach, **Smuroch**, *n.* a hearty kiss; a stealthy kiss. Cf. Smoorich.

Smurachin, *n.* a hearty kiss.

Smurack, **Smuragh**, *n.* a slight drizzle; a summer shower; peat-dust; a slight smoke.

Smure, *v.* to suffocate. Cf. Smoor.

Smurl, *v.* to smirk.—*n.* a mocking smile. Cf. Smirl.

Smurl, *v.* to eat little and slowly; to eat secretly; to waste imperceptibly.

Smurlin', *ppl. adj.* fond of dainties and of eating them secretly.

Smurr, *n.* a drizzle; fine rain; snow falling thickly.—*v.* to drizzle.

Smurtle, *v.* to smile. Cf. Smirtle.

Smusch, *n.* a short, dark person with abundant hair.

Smuschle, *v.* to eat slowly. Cf. Smushle.

Smush, *n.* smoke; dirt; a disagreeable, sulphurous smell from smoke and dust.— *adj.* dirty; stinking.

Smush, *v.* to bruise; to grind to powder; to eat secretly anything got improperly; to waste or decay slowly.—*n.* a bruised, crushed mass; anything reduced to pulp or powder; refuse, scraps; refuse hay or straw; a slight, drizzling rain.—*adj.* broken, fragmentary.

Smushach, **Smuschach**, *v.* to eat slowly; to decay slowly.—*n.* what is small or in fragments; a dainty person, small in stature and dark in complexion.—*adj.* small; dark.

Smushagh, *n.* a suffocating smell caused by a smothered fire.

Smushlach, *n.* a bruised, broken, crumbled state; fragments, scraps, leavings.

Smushle, *v.* to eat slowly; to eat in secret; to use slowly; to waste slowly; to drizzle. —*n.* eating slowly or secretly; a lot of tit-bits; a dainty meal or tit-bit; a person fond of dainties and of secret eating; a small person of dark complexion; a slow wasting; fragments, leavings; a slight, drizzling rain.

Smushlin, *adj.* fond of dainty fare.

Smushy, *adj.* foul, dirty; stinking.

Smuster, *n.* a large cluster of things.

Smutchack, *n.* a contemptuous name for a child, a 'smatchet.'

Smutchless, *adj.* stainless, spotless.

Smyaager, *v.* to besmear. Cf. Smiaggered.

Smyach, *n.* sagacity, capability. Cf. Smiach.

Smyle, *v.* to crumble; to fall in pieces.—*n.* fragments. Cf. Smuil.

Smysle, *v.* to sear.

Smyster, *v.* to work lazily and feebly; to idle sitting over a fire; to talk or laugh to one's self, as in a day-dream.— *n.* working lazily and feebly; an idle, dreamy state; a weak and unskilful worker; an idler; a listless person.

Smytch, *n.* a puny, pert fellow; an impudent boy; a term of contempt, anger, &c.

Smytcher, *n.* a 'smytch'; an impudent child. Cf. Smatchard.

Smyte, *n.* a small bit; a particle. Cf. Smite.

Smyteral, *n.* a collection of small objects.

Smytrie, Smytterie, *n.* a collection of small individuals, children, &c.

Sna, Snaa, *n.* snow.

Snab, *n.* the projecting part of a hill or rock; the bank, rock, or hill itself which projects; a steep ascent.

Snab, *n.* a shoemaker; a cobbler; a shoe-making or cobbling apprentice or boy.

Snabbie, *n.* the chaffinch.

Snachel, *n.* a puny, contemptible bantling. Cf. Snackel.

Snack, *n.* a snap. — *v.* to snap, bite; to snatch; to break with a snap.

Snack, *adj.* quick, sharp, alert; smart, clever, or cute. — *adv.* quickly, cleverly; exactly, to the moment. — *n.* a keen, active person; a good bargainer; a person of short stature.

Snackel, *n.* a puny bantling. Cf. Snachel.

Snackit, *n.* a small person of keen, active disposition.

Snackly, *adv.* cleverly, adroitly; intelligently.

Snackus, *n.* a fillip.

Snacky, *adj.* clever, acute, 'knacky'; tricky, quirky.

Snaff, *v.* to sniff in a surly, jeering manner; to find fault in a surly manner.

Snag, *n.* a protuberance; the bolt of a door. — *v.* to cut off branches with an axe, &c.

Snag, *v.* to snap, bite; to chide and taunt; to scold severely; to snarl; to banter; to 'nag.' — *n.* a snap, bite; a quarrel; a snarl; a violent scolding; a slight repast, snack; a dainty; any kind of confectionery; in *pl.* shares, very small things.

Snagger, *v.* to snore loudly and gruntingly; to snarl. — *n.* a snore; a snoring; a growl with an attempt to bite; a bite.

Snaggerel, *n.* a puny, contemptible bantling. Cf. Snachel.

Snagger-snee, *n.* a large knife, originally from Germany.

Snaggery, *n.* trashy, indigestible food; trashy sweet-stuff.

Snaggin, *n.* raillery.

Snaggy, *adj.* sarcastic; morose; cross, ill-tempered; snappish.

Snaid, *n.* a band of ribbon for confining the hair. Cf. Snood.

Snaig, *n.* a worthless fellow; the obtaining of money by fair or foul means.

Snaik, *n.* a black or gray slug.

Snaik, *v.* to sneak; to walk or move furtively and secretly; to walk or work slowly and indolently. — *n.* an indolent person; the working or walking indolently. Cf. Snake.

Snaikach, *adj.* creeping, crawling.

Snalker, *n.* an indolent person.

Snail, *v.* to go slowly, loiter.

Snail-caup-e'en, *n.* eyes like a snail's.

Snail-slaw, *adj.* very slow.

Snak, *adj.* quick, sharp. Cf. Snack.

Snake, *v.* to sneak; to do anything in a low, underhand fashion; to work slowly. Cf. Snaik.

Snakin', *ppl. adj.* exulting and sneering.

Snam, *v.* to snap at anything greedily.

Snang, *v.* to twang. Cf. Besnang.

Snap, *v.* to seize an opportunity; to take advantage of; to overcharge; to get the advantage in argument; to toy; to eat hastily or greedily; to make a sharp, cracking noise with the fingers; used of a gun: to go off accidentally; to stumble, trip suddenly; to snub, cut any one short. — *n.* a quick movement; a small portion of food, a snack, a morsel; a bit; a fragment; a small, crisp gingerbread cake, a 'brandy-snap'; a brief, sudden interval; a moment; an angry dispute; a sharp blow; a sudden stumble. — *adj.* brittle, crisp; quick, active; smart, acute; short-tempered, snappish; eager to find fault.

Snap-dyke, *n.* a stone fence from four to six feet high, suitable for enclosing sheep.

Snap-gun, *n.* a firelock as contrasted with a matchlock.

Snap-haunce, *n.* the spring of the lock of a gun or pistol; the whole gun or pistol.

Snaply, *adv.* hastily, quickly.

Snap-maker, *n.* a maker of pistols and guns with triggers.

Snapper, *v.* to stumble, trip; to fall suddenly; to fall into a scrape. — *n.* a false step, a stumble; a failure in morals; a perplexity, entanglement; a misfortune; an unforeseen accident.

Snapper, Snappert, *adj.* tart; hasty; curt.

Snappering-stone, *n.* a stumbling-stone.

Snappous, Snappus, *adj.* testy; hasty in temper.

Snappy, *adj.* keen in business; disposed to take advantage of another; cross, ill-tempered.

Snapsy, *adj.* tart, surly, snappish.

Snap-the-louse, *n.* a cant name for a tailor.

Snapur, *n.* a foolish and impudent person; one reckless in his speaking.

Snap-wark, *n.* a firelock.

Snap-wife, *n.* a woman who sells ginger-bread-snaps.

Snar, Snare, *adj.* severe; ill-tempered, surly; prudent, diligent, managing; keen in bargaining, disposed to overreach; rigid; firm to the grasp. Cf. Snarre.

Snarbled, *adj.* pinched, shrivelled.

Snar-gab, *n.* abusive language; 'jaw.'

Snark, v. to snore ; to grumble, fret, find fault. Cf. Snork.

Snarl, n. a broil, quarrel, wrangle.

Snarlinger, adj. more quarrelsome.

Snarly, adj. snappish, surly.

Snarre, adj. ill-tempered ; surly ; diligent ; managing ; keen at a bargain ; firm to the grasp.

Snash, v. to snap, bite ; to vituperate ; to sneer ; to gibe.—n. abusive language ; impudence ; sneers ; gibes.—adv. snappishly ; pertly.—adj. pert, saucy.

Snash-gab, n. prating ; petulant talking ; a prattling, forward boy or girl. Cf. Gabnash, Nash-gab.

Snashter, n. trifles.

Snashtrie, n. trash ; trifles ; low chat.

Snath, v. to prune timber-trees. Cf. Sned.

Snauchle, v. to walk slowly with lingering steps ; to saunter. — n. a weakling ; a dwarf.

Snaur, adj. tart ; severe ; prudent ; managing ; firm to the grasp. Cf. Snarre.

Snaw, n. snow.—v. to be snowed up.

Snaw-ba', n. a snowball ; a joke, sarcasm.

Snaw-bird, n. the snow-bunting ; any winter bird.

Snaw-brack, n. a quick thaw.

Snaw-breakers, n. sheep scraping the hardened surface of the snow to find food.

Snaw-bree, -broo, -broth, n. melted snow.

Snaw-drift, n. fine, driving snow.

Snaw-flaigh, -flake, -fleck, n. the snowbunting.

Snaw-flight, -fowl, n. the snow-bunting.

Snaw-hoord, n. an accumulation of snow.

Snawie, adj. snowy.

Snawie-ba', n. a snowball.

Snawie-fowl, n. the snow-bunting.

Snawie-heads, n. large masses of white clouds.

Snaw-o'-the-rink, n. snow on the sides of a curling-rink.

Snaw-powther, n. fine, driving snow.

Snaw-rink, n. a snow-covered track.

Snaw-shurl, n. snow slipping from the roof of a house ; the noise it makes.

Snaw-tooried, adj. snow-capped.

Snaw-wreath, n. a snow-drift.

Snaw-wreathed, adj. blocked by snowdrifts.

Snaw-wride, n. a snow-drift.

Snayaavie, adj. snowy. Cf. Snyaavie.

Sneaker, n. a small bowl of punch.

Snear, v. to snort ; to emit a hissing sound. —n. a snort ; the hiss of an adder. Cf. Sneer.

Sneb, v. to snub ; to correct, punish. Cf. Snib.

Sneck, n. a door-latch ; a small bolt.—v. to fasten the latch of a door ; to secure by a latch or catch.—adv. with a sudden snap or catch.

Sneck, v. to snap, bite.—n. a snatch of food, a 'bite.' Cf. Snack.

Sneck, v. to cut sharply, incise ; to strike smartly ; to close, fill up ; to stop an incision or gap ; to drink off ; to finish up.— n. the act or power of cutting ; a slight cut or incision ; a cut suddenly given ; a portion of a wall built with single stones, or stones which go from side to side. Cf. Snick.

Sneck, v. to sneak ; to pilfer ; to grab at. Cf. Snick.

Sneck-draw, n. an intruder ; a crafty, artful person ; a sly person ; a covetous person ; one who from long practice has acquired facility.

Sneck-drawer, n. a 'sneck-draw.'

Sneck-drawin', adj. crafty, sly.—n. craft, cunning.

Snecker, n. a sharper.

Sneck-harl, v. to 'harl' or rough-cast a wall with mortar.

Sneck-pin, v. to put in small stones between the larger ones in a wall, and daub the seams with mortar.

Sneck-trap, n. a spring rat-trap.

Sned, n. a branch pruned off.—v. to prune ; to lop off ; to hew or polish stones with a chisel ; to remove excrescences ; to emasculate.

Sned, n. the shaft or pole of a scythe.

Sned, n. the thin link of hair to which a hook is tied, and by which it is attached to the fishing-line. Cf. Snood.

Snedder, n. one who lops off branches or turnip-tops.

Sneddins, n. the prunings of trees.

Sned-kail, n. colewort or cabbages, of which the old stalks, after they have begun to sprout, are divided by a knife, and set in the earth for future produce.

Sneed, n. a band or ribbon used to confine the hair ; a coil or twist ; a twisted line or rope ; a link of hair with hook attached. Cf. Snood.

Sneeg, v. to neigh ; to snort. Cf. Sneg.

Sneel, v. to be lazy ; to lack energy ; to remain idle ; to go about stealthily.—n. the doing of anything lazily ; an indolent person ; an inactive person. Cf. Snool.

Sneel, v. to snivel ; to speak through the nose.

Sneep, n. the glitter of a white colour.—adj. glittering, white. Cf. Snip.

Sneer, v. to snort ; to snore ; to inhale by the nostrils ; to hiss ; to give forth a hissing sound.—n. a snort, inhalation by the nostrils ; an adder's hiss ; the act of a horse with cold in throwing mucus from its nostrils.

Sneerag, *n.* a child's toy, made of the larger bone of a pig's foot and two worsted strings, and worked so as to give a snoring sound. Cf. Snorick.

Sneesh, *n.* snuff; a pinch of snuff.—*v.* to take snuff.

Sneesher, *n.* one who takes snuff.

Sneeshin, Sneeshen, Sneeshan, *n.* snuff; a pinch of snuff; anything of little value; anything that gives comfort or pleasure.

Sneeshin-box, *n.* a snuff-box.

Sneeshin-horn, *n.* a small horn used as a snuff-box.

Sneeshinie, *adj.* snuffy.

Sneeshin-mill, -mull, *n.* a snuff-box.

Sneeshin-pen, *n.* a small bone-spoon or quill used in taking snuff.

Sneest, *n.* an air of disdain; impertinence; a snarl; a taunt.—*v.* to treat with scorn or contempt; to sneer, sniff; to snarl; to taunt. Cf. Snuist.

Sneesty, *adj.* scornful; sneering; contemptuous.

Sneet, *v.* to loiter; to walk slowly and stupidly; to work lazily or unskilfully; to remain idly.—*n.* the walking or working lazily; a stupid, indolent person. Cf. Sneut.

Sneet, *n.* sleet.

Sneeter, *v.* to 'sneet'; to sleep a light, short sleep; to weep, 'blubber.'—*n.* a 'sneet'; a short sleep.

Sneety, *adj.* sleety.

Sneevel, Sneevle, Sneevil, *v.* to snivel; to breathe or speak through the nose.—*n.* a snuffle; a heavy breathing through the nose; a whimper. Cf. Snivel.

Sneevlin', *ppl. adj.* whining; cringing; snivelling; used in contempt.

Sneeze, *v.* to take snuff; with *upon,* to sneer at, despise.

Sneezing, *n.* snuff. Cf. Sneeshin.

Sneezing-mill, *n.* a snuff-box.

Sneezing-tobacco, *n.* snuff.

Sneg, *n.* a low term for gain.

Sneg, *v.* to neigh; to snort.—*n.* the neigh of a horse.

Sneg, *v.* to cut with a sharp instrument; to cut off or short; to interrupt; to check; to invite a broil.—*n.* a sudden cut; an incision. Cf. Snag, Sneck.

Snegger, *n.* a horse; the neigh of a horse.

Sneill, *v.* to be lazy.—*n.* a lazy person. Cf. Sneel.

Sneish, Sneishin, *n.* snuff. Cf. Sneesh, Sneeshin.

Sneishter, *v.* to scorch. Cf. Sneyster.

Sneist, *n.* a taunt. Cf. Sneest.

Sneisty, *adj.* sneering; taunting. Cf. Sneesty.

Sneith, *adj.* smooth; polished; refined.

Snell, *adj.* quick, sharp; keen, eager; fierce; severe; painful; cold, piercing, bracing; pungent; acrimonious, tart; sarcastic; austere; clear-sounding; firm, resolute.—*adv.* quickly; pungently; very, exceedingly.

Snell-gabbit, -tongued, *adj.* sharp-tongued; caustic in speech.

Snelly, *adj.* 'snell'; keen, chilly.—*adv.* coldly, bitterly, keenly; tartly; severely.

Sneut, *n.* a silly, stupid person. Cf. Sneet.

Sneuter, *n.* a 'sneut.'

Snew, *v. pret.* did snow.

Snewn, *ppl.* snowed.

Sneyster, *v.* to sear, scorch. Cf. Sniester.

Sneyster, *n.* a severe blast in the face. Cf. Snister.

Sniauve, *v.* to snow.—*n.* snow.

Snib, *v.* to check; to snub; to bolt, bar, fasten; to trap; to cut, cut short; to shape, point; to cut short as to money; to castrate; to snuff a candle.—*n.* a check, a snub; a cut; a smart stroke; a small bolt for fastening a door; a fastening, catch; a button.

Snibb, *adj.* chastised; frightened.

Snibbelt, *n.* a small piece of wood at the end of a tether, which is slipped through an eye at the other end to fasten it.

Snibbert, *v.* to loiter; to work stupidly.—*n.* a person of sharp, hard features and little force of character.

Snibbert, *n.* the nose. Cf. Snubbert.

Snibbertick, Snibbertickie, *n.* a 'snibbert.'

Snibbit, *n.* a 'snibbelt'; anything curtailed of its proper proportions.—*ppl. adj.* curtailed of its proper proportions.

Snibble, Sniblet, *n.* a 'snibbelt.'

Sniblich, *n.* a collar of plaited straw or rushes, formerly used to bind a cow to the stake.

Snichen, *n.* snuff. Cf. Sneeshin.

Snicher, *v.* to snigger; to titter; to laugh in one's sleeve. Cf. Snicker.

Snichter, *v.* to sniff, snuffle. Cf. Snicker.

Snick, *v.* to cut sharply; to notch; to strike smartly; to fill up.—*n.* a notch. Cf. Sneck.

Snick, *v.* to pilfer; to grab at; to sneak; in *phr.* 'to draw a snick,' to cheat. Cf. Sneck.

Snick, *n.* a latch. Cf. Sneck.

Snick-drawing, *adj.* latch-lifting; stealthy. Cf. Sneck-drawing.

Snicker, *v.* to snigger.—*n.* a derisive, sneering laugh; a snigger.

Snid, *n.* a ribbon used to confine the hair; a short hair-line.—*v.* to confine the hair with a 'snood.' Cf. Snood.

Sniest, *n.* a taunt. Cf. Sneest.

Sniester, *v.* to cauterize.

Sniesty, *adj.* taunting.

Sniff, *n.* a trifle; a very small piece.

Sniffle, *v.* to sniff, snuffle; to be slow in motion or action; to trifle.—*n.* a sniff; slowness of motion or action; trifling delay; a slow person; a trifler; a driveller; in *pl.* difficulty of breathing through the nostrils caused by cold.

Sniffle-bit, *n.* a snaffle.

Sniffler, *n.* a trifler; a driveller.

Snifflttie-foot, *n.* the green crab.

Snifle, *n.* a snaffle.

Snift, *v.* used of hail: to whiz, rattle briskly in falling.

Snifter, *v.* to sniff, snuffle; to inhale sharply through the nose; to scent a smell; to sob. —*n.* a sniff, snuffle; a quick inhalation by the nose; a suppressed laugh or sob; a sneering laugh; a cutting repartee; the effect of a strong purgative; a severe blast, storm; a reverse; a defeat; in *pl.* a severe cold in the head; a disease of animals and fowls causing stoppage of the nostrils.

Snifterin', *n.* a severe exposure to stormy weather.

Snig, *v.* to cut, chop off; to pull suddenly; to jerk.—*n.* a sudden, sharp pull.

Sniggert, *n.* one chargeable with wilful malversation.

Sniggle, *v.* to snigger; to laugh sneeringly; to giggle.

Sniggle, *v.* to poach fish by snaring them in a mean way.

Snip, *n.* a scrap; a fragment; a share; a narrow stripe down the face of a horse; a spell, snap; a tailor.—*v.* to run with short steps; to slip off quickly or suddenly; to stumble slightly.

Snip, *adj.* glittering; of a bright colour; white.—*n.* the dazzling of something white.

Snipe, *n.* a thin, hard-featured person with a prominent nose.

Snipe, *n.* a snub; a sarcasm; a muzzle on a pig's snout; a smart blow; a fillip; a loss, a reverse of fortune; a cheat, fraud; one who cheats, defrauds; a contemptuous designation for any one; a mean, insignificant person; a scolding; a sharp-tongued woman; a tailor, 'snip.'—*v.* to snub; to give a smart blow; to scold; to muzzle a pig; to cheat; to bring loss to one.

Snipie-nebbit, *adj.* having a long, sharp nose.

Snipper, *n.* a small, insignificant person.

Snippert, Snippart, *n.* a crumb, a very small bit of anything; a small person of sharp disposition.—*adj.* quick, tart in speech; addicted to giving short weight or measure.

Snippiltin', *ppl. adj.* roaming; hunting after: 'raking.'

Snippin, *ppl. adj.* dazzling.

Snippit, *ppl. adj.* used of a horse: having a white stripe down the face.

Snippit, *ppl. adj.* used of the nose: snub; scanty; niggardly, pinching.

Snippy, *adj.* tart in speech, sharp-tongued; speaking with a sharp accent; used of one who gives scant measure in cutting cloth.— *n.* a sharp-tongued person; a scold.

Snippy, *n.* a horse with a white-striped face.

Snip-white, *adj.* dazzling white.

Snirk, *v.* to draw up the nose in contempt or displeasure.

Snirl, *v.* to sneeze; to laugh involuntarily and in a suppressed manner.

Snirl, *v.* to tangle; to contract like hand-twisted yarn; to ruffle or wrinkle.—*n.* a knot, tangle. Cf. Snurl.

Snirt, *n.* an insignificant, diminutive person.

Snirt, *v.* to laugh in a suppressed manner; to breathe sharply and in a jerking way through the nostrils; to sneer.—*n.* a suppressed laugh; nasal mucus; a snort.

Snirtle, *v.* to laugh in a suppressed manner; to sneer.—*n.* a suppressed laugh; a sneer.

Snish, Snishin, *n.* snuff. Cf. Sneesh, Sneeshin.

Snisle, *v.* to singe; to burn partially; to harden by heat.

Snister, *n.* a severe blast in the face.

Snisty, *adj.* saucy, pert. Cf. Sneesty.

Snitan, Snitern, *adj.* loitering; putting off time.

Snitch, *n.* a noose, a loop.

Snitchers, *n.* handcuffs.

Snite, *n.* a small, insignificant person or thing.

Snite, *v.* to blow the nose with finger and thumb; to wring the nose; to snuff a candle; to taunt, gibe.—*n.* a smart blow.

Snitian, *n.* snuff. Cf. Sneeshin.

Snitter, *n.* a biting blast.

Snivel, *v.* to breathe hard through the nose; to speak through the nose.—*n.* a snuffle; a heavy breathing through the nose; speaking through the nose, a nasal twang; in *pl.* a disease affecting animals.

Snivelling, *ppl. adj.* mean-spirited; whining.

Snoak, *v.* to smell about like a dog; to scent. Cf. Snook.

Snob, *n.* a cobbler. Cf. Snab.

Snocher, Snocker, *v.* to breathe heavily and noisily through the nose; to slobber with the nose like a pig in a trough; to snort, snore.—*n.* a snort; a loud snore; difficult breathing through the nose owing to mucus; in *pl.* stoppage of the nostrils from cold.

Snock, *v.* to snort contemptuously; to turn over with the nose, as a dog or pig; to poke into.

Snod, *adj.* smooth, level; neat, trim, tidy;

snug, comfortable.—*v.* to trim, prune, lop; to put in order; to make neat and tidy; to castrate; with *off*, to finish off.

Snod, *v. pret.* did prune. Cf. Sned.

Snoddie, *n.* a neatly-dressed person.

Snoddie, *n.* a ninny, a stupid fellow.

Snoddy, *adj.* neat, trim.—*adv.* deftly, neatly.

Snodge, *v.* to walk deliberately.

Snodit, *ppl. adj.* dressed; tidied.

Snodless, *adj.* untidy.

Snodly, *adv.* evenly, smoothly; neatly, tidily; snugly.

Snog, *adj.* neat, handsome, trim, tidy; snug.

Snog, *v.* to jeer, flout.

Snoick, *adj.* virgin, chaste; used of ships, &c.: watertight.

Snoid, *n.* a ribbon to confine the hair. Cf. Snood.

Snolt, *n.* a young, conceited person who speaks little; an upstart, a swaggerer; an intruder.

Snoit, *n.* nasal mucus.—*v.* to blow the nose with finger and thumb. Cf. Snite, Snot.

Snoiter, *v.* to breathe strongly through the nose. Cf. Snotter.

Snoity, *adj.* having the nose dirty with mucus, 'bubbly.' Cf. Snotty.

Snoke, *v.* to smell about like a dog. Cf. Snook.

Snoker, *v.* to breathe heavily through the nose. Cf. Snocher.

Snoker, *n.* one who smells at objects like a dog; in a bad sense: a rake. Cf. Snooker.

Snoo, *v. pret.* snowed.

Snood, *n.* a ribbon or band for confining the hair; a short hair-line; the thin line by which hooks are attached to a fishing-line; a coil, a twist; a twisted line or rope; a twist of temper; a threatening twist of the head.—*v.* to confine the hair with a 'snood'; to tie a hair-line on a fishing-hook; to coil, twist; to tangle; used of cattle: to threaten with the head.

Snooded folks, *n.* virgins, unmarried maidens.

Snoodless, *adj.* without a 'snood'; used of a maid who has lost her virginity.

Snoofmadrune, *n.* a lazy, inactive person.

Snook, *v.* to smell with a loud inhalation; to sniff; to scent as a dog; to scent; to pry about; to sneak.—*n.* a smell; a sniff. Cf. Snowk.

Snooker, *n.* one who smells at objects like a dog; a rake, a profligate fellow.

Snool, *n.* an abject; a cringing person; one easily overborne; a weak fool; anything mean or paltry; a tyrant; one who frightens or overbears.—*v.* to submit tamely and weakly; to act meanly and without spirit; to give in, cringe, sneak; to overbear, frighten, subdue; to dispirit; to snub; to walk warily or stealthily.

Snool-, Snool'd-like, *adj.* craven; weak; subdued; dispirited.

Snoot, *n.* the snout; the nose; the face; the mind, head; a point, a projection; the point of an anvil; the peak of a cap; the muzzle of a gun.

Snootit, *ppl. adj.* used of a cap or 'bonnet': peaked.

Snoove, *v.* to move smoothly and steadily; to glide; to walk with a steady step; to sneak; to move looking to the earth; to walk carelessly; to move like a top.

Snoovle, *v.* to move slowly; to walk in a slow, lazy way.

Snoov-snoove, *v.* to glide; to move steadily along.

Snooze, *v.* to sleep, doze.—*n.* a nap.

Snoozle, *v.* to sleep, doze; used of a dog: to sniff and poke with the nose.

Snore, *v.* to snort; to roar; to make a loud noise; to rush with a roaring sound; used of an engine: to puff.—*n.* a snort, roar; a loud, roaring noise; a disease affecting animals.

Snorick, *n.* a child's toy made from a pig's leg-bone. Cf. Sneerag.

Snork, *v.* to snort; to clear the throat noisily. —*n.* the snort of a frightened horse.

Snorl, *n.* a ravel in twine or thread; a kink in a rope; a scrape, plight, difficulty, dilemma.—*v.* to tangle, ravel; to confuse; to place in a difficulty. Cf. Snirl.

Snort, *n.* a twist, kink; a tangle.

Snory-bane, *n.* a child's toy made from a pig's leg-bone. Cf. Snorick.

Snosh, *adj.* fat and contented; comfortable.

Snoshie, *n.* a fat, comfortable man.

Snot, *n.* the snuff of a candle or lamp; used of soot: a small lump; a mean, dirty person; a despicable person; a dolt, dunce; a fool.—*v.* to blow the nose with finger and thumb; to snivel.

Snotter, *n.* nasal mucus, snot; the red membraneous portion of a turkey-cock's beak; a sniggering laugh; anything of little weight or value.—*v.* to let mucus run from the nose; to snuffle, snore, snort; to cry, weep, 'blubber'; to snivel.

Snotter-box, *n.* the nose; a term of contempt.

Snotter-cap, *n.* a dull, stupid, boorish fellow.

Snottery, *adj.* running with nasal mucus; speaking through mucus.

Snotties, *n.* the nostrils.

Snottit, *ppl. adj.* smeared with nasal mucus.

Snotty, *adj.* having the nose dirty with mucus; peevish, snappish; rude, impudent; 'high and mighty.'—*n.* a dolt.

Snouff, *n.* the snuffing sound made by a dog.

Snouk, Snowk, *v.* to smell as a dog. Cf. Snowk.

Snout, n. impudence ; a point ; the face. Cf. Snoot.

Snouter, n. a peaked cap.

Snouthie, adj. drizzly, rainy ; dark.

Snow, v. to be snowed up. Cf. Snaw.

Snow-flake, n. the snow-bunting.

Snowk, v. to smell like a dog ; to poke with the nose ; to sniff, snuffle ; to pry curiously ; to seek out.—n. a smell, used ludicrously. Cf. Snook.

Snow-tappit, adj. covered with snow.

Snubbert, n. a loose knot or lump ; a contemptuous name for the nose ; the snout.

Snude, n. a ribbon for confining the hair. Cf. Snood.

Snuff, v. to breathe ; to inhale sharply ; to sniff in contempt or displeasure.—n. a short, quick, contemptuous inhalation ; a breath of fresh air ; anger ; scorn ; a very small quantity ; anything of very little value ; in pl. an excl. of contempt.

Snuff-bean, n. a bean kept in a snuff-box to scent the snuff.

Snuff-girnel, n. a snuff-jar.

Snuff-hauder, n. the nose.

Snuff-horn, n. the tip of a horn used as a snuff-box.

Snuffie, adj. snuff-coloured ; sulky ; displeased.

Snuffilie, adv. sulkily.

Snuffiness, n. sulkiness.

Snuff-man, n. a tobacconist.

Snuff-mill, -mull, n. a snuff-box.

Snuff-pen, n. a small bone-spoon or quill for taking snuff.

Snuff-tankard, n. a snuff-jar.

Snuffy-like, adj. snappish, 'huffy.'

Snug, adj. secret, quiet ; convenient ; neat.— v. to put in order ; to make tight, trim.— n. the snuggery in a tavern. Cf. Snog.

Snug, v. to strike, push, butt ; to scold ; to reprimand severely.—n. a stroke ; a thrust or push with the head. Cf. Snog.

Snug, n. a small branch lopped off a tree.

Snuggit, ppl. adj. used of houses : built snugly and compactly together.

Snuie, v. used of horned cattle : to toss the head, as if angry.

Snuifie, adj. awkward, sheepish.

Snuift, v. pret. went stealthily. Cf. Snoove.

Snuist, v. to sniff. Cf. Sneest.

Snuister, v. to laugh in a suppressed manner through the nose.—n. a suppressed laugh.

Snuister, n. a sweet.

Snuit, v. to move carelessly, inactively, and in a stupefied manner.

Snuitter, v. to laugh in a suppressed manner through the nose.—n. a suppressed laugh.

Snuittit, ppl. adj. having the foolish, dazed look of one half-drunk.

Snuive, v. to glide gently and equably ; to sneak. Cf. Snoove.

Snule, n. an abject ; a craven. Cf. Snool.

Snurkle, v. to run into knots, as a hard-twisted thread.

Snurl, Snurrl, v. to twist, tangle ; to 'snurkle'; to ruffle ; to wrinkle.—n. a tangle. Cf. Snirl.

Snurley, Snurlie, adj. twisted ; knotty.

Snurt, v. to laugh in a suppressed manner. Cf. Snirt.

Snurtle, v. to 'snurt'; to sneer. Cf. Snirtle.

Snush, n. snuff. Cf. Sneesh.

Snush, adj. fat and contented. Cf. Snosh.

Snut, v. to curl the nose disdainfully.

Snuve, v. to glide gently. Cf. Snoove.

Snyaave, Snyauve, v. to snow. Cf. Sniauve.

Snyaavie, adj. snowy.

Snyb, v. to snub. Cf. Snib.

Snype, n. a snub ; a smart blow ; a fraud on one ; a term of contempt. Cf. Snipe.

Snyte, n. a smart blow ; nasal mucus.—v. to blow the nose with finger and thumb ; to snuff a candle. Cf. Snite.

Snyte, v. to walk feebly, or slowly and stupidly ; to loiter ; to work stupidly and lazily.—n. a stupid, lazy person.

Snyter, v. to loiter.—n. a stupid, lazy person.

So, conj. as. Cf. Sae.

Soak, v. to drink hard.

Soaken, v. to soak.

Soakie, adj. plump ; of full habit.—n. a fat woman.

Soal, n. a sole ; the under-surface of a curling-stone ; a window-sill. Cf. Sole.

Soal-tree, n. a beam on the ground supporting other upright beams. Cf. Sole-tree.

†Soam, n. fat ; lard. Cf. Saem.

Soam, n. the air-bladder of a fish.

Soam, n. the rope or chain by which horses or oxen are yoked to the plough.—v. to drive the plough.

Soap-bell, n. a soap-bubble.

Soap-blotts, n. soapsuds.

Soaper, n. a soap-boiler.

Soaperie, n. a soapwork.

Soap-man, n. a soap-boiler.

Soap-sapples, n. soapsuds.

Soapy-blots, -sapples, -suds, n. soapsuds.

Sob, v. to make a hissing sound, as of green wood, &c., in a fire ; used of flowers : to fade.—n. a gust of wind ; a land storm ; the noise of the sea. Cf. Sab.

Sober, adj. steady ; poor, mean, indifferent ; diminutive, slender, weakly ; fairly well.

Soberly, adv. sparingly, frugally.

Sobersides, n. a creature of 'sober' habits.

Soch, v. to swill.—n. a copious draught. Cf. Sooch.

Socher, v. to make much of one's self ; to

live delicately ; to be overcareful as to one's food and drink.—*adj.* lazy, effeminate ; inactive from delicate living.

Socherer, *n.* a lazy, effeminate person.

Socht, *v. pret.* and *ppl.* sought.

Society-people, *n.* the sect of the Cameronians.

Sock, *n.* a schoolboys' term for sweetmeats or dainties.

Sock, *n.* a ploughshare.

Sock, *v.* to sink into. Cf. Sog.

Sock, *n.* a frame, rest, support.

Sock, *n.* a socket.

Sock, *n.* the right of a baron to hold a court within his own domains.

Sockie, *n.* a person who walks with a manly air.—*v.* to walk with a manly air.

Sockin-hour, *n.* the time between daylight and candlelight ; time for ceasing to work ; a rest-time.

Sockin of the tide, *n.* the last of a tide, either of the ebb or of the flood.

Sockman, *n.* a tenant bound by certain restrictions and to certain services by his lease.

Sock-mandrill, *n.* a facsimile of a plough-head cast in metal.

Sock-neb, *n.* the point of the ploughshare.

Socy, *v.* to walk with a manly air. Cf. Sockie.

Sod, *adj.* sad.

Sod, Sodd, *n.* a rough saddle of coarse cloth or skin stuffed with straw ; a heavy person ; a dead-weight.—*adj.* firm, steady ; sedate, respectable ; careful. —*v.* to cover with sods ; to make solid.—*adv.* securely.

Sod, *n.* a roll or 'bap' made of coarse flour.

Sod, *n.* the rock-dove.

Sod, *n.* a sudden and singular sound made in a pot or pan while used in cooking, regarded as a portent of death.—*adj.* singular, unaccountable.

Soda, *n.* bicarbonate of soda or baking-soda ; carbonate of soda or washing-soda.

Soda-drink, *n.* aerated water.

Soda-scone, *n.* a 'scone' made with bicarbonate of soda.

Soddie, *n.* a seat made of sods.

Sodger, Sodjer, *n.* a soldier ; the ribwort plantain ; in *pl.* a game played with the stems of the plantain ; the small fiery sparks on the bottom of a pot just taken from the fire.—*v.* to be a soldier ; used of turnips : to have the leaves turn red and stop growing.

Sodger-blade, -body, *n.* a soldier.

Sodger-folk, *n.* soldiers.

Sodgerize, *v.* to act as a soldier ; to be drilled.

Sodgerly, *adj.* soldierly.

Sodger's bite, *n.* a large bite.

Sodger's buttons, *n.* the white burnet-rose.

Sodger's feather, *n.* the plant honesty.

Sodger-thee'd, *adj.* 'soldier-thighed,' or having little or no money in one's pocket.

Sodlies, *adv.* sadly ; to a great degree.

Sod-like, -looking, *adj.* having a singular appearance.

Sod-seat, *n.* a seat of sods or turfs.

Sod track, *n.* a sad state.

Sody, *n.* soda. Cf. Soda.

Soft, *adj.* muddy ; wet, rainy ; silly ; amorous. Cf. Saft.

Soft-dud, *n.* a weakling ; one without bodily stamina.

Soften, *v.* to thaw.

Softness, *n.* weakness of character ; amorousness.

Softy, *n.* a simpleton.

Sog, *v.* to sink, press down.

Soger, Sojer, *n.* a soldier. Cf. Sodger.

So'h, *v.* to hum over a tune. Cf. Souf, Souch.

Sok, *n.* surety.—*v.* to guarantee.

Soil, Soilyie, *n.* dirt, ashes, house refuse ; the manure collected from the streets of a town. —*adj.* soiled, dirtied.

Sol, *n.* a window-sill. Cf. Sole.

Solate, *adj.* sedate, staid ; trustworthy. Cf. Solid.

†Solatious, Solacious, *adj.* cheerful ; comforting.

Soldier, *n.* the ribwort plantain ; a spark of fire on the bottom of a pot just taken from the fire.—*v.* used of turnip-leaves : to turn red. Cf. Sodger.

Sole, *n.* the under-surface of a curling-stone ; a window-sill ; a bottom shelf ; subsoil.— *v.* in *phr.* to 'sole one's boots,' to make a profit.

Sole, *n.* a potato-basket.

Sole, *n.* a swivel. Cf. Sowle, Sule.

Sole-ale, *n.* ale given at the finishing of the window-sills.

Sole-clout, -shoe, *n.* an iron plate fastened to the part of the plough which runs on the ground, to save the wooden heel from being worn.

Sole-fleuk, *n.* the sole.

Solemncholy, *adj.* solemn ; sober.

Solemn-leaguing, *adj.* covenanting ; adhering to the Solemn League and Covenant.

Sole-tree, *n.* a beam reaching from one wall of a cow-house to the opposite, into which the under-end of each stake or post is mortised, forming the crib or manger.

Solicit, Sollisit, *adj.* solicitous ; anxious. Cf. Solist.

Solid, *adj.* sedate, staid ; capable ; sane, sober, *compos mentis ;* thorough, utter, whole.—*n.* in *pl.* solidity of character, moral worth, gravity.

Solidness, *n.* solidity of character, steadiness, gravity.

Solist, *v.* to solicit.—*adj.* solicitous, careful, anxious.

Solistar, *n.* one who solicits anything.

Solistation, *n.* solicitation, interest, influence.

Solistnes, *n.* anxiety.

Solute, *adj.* general, not close; declamatory, diffuse.

Solutive, *adj.* laxative.

†Solvé, *n.* that member of a college who exacts the lines.

†Solvendie, Solvendo, *adj.* solvent, sufficient to pay one's debts; trustworthy; safe; to be depended on; firm, strong; sufficient for the purpose. Cf. Savendle.

Solvendiness, *n.* a state of trustworthiness.

Somat, *adv.* somewhat.

Some, *adv.* in some degree; somewhat; rather; in *phr.* 'and some,' much more so, used to denote pre-eminence in what has been mentioned before.

Somebody, *n.* a lover; a sweetheart.

Somedeal, *adv.* in some measure.—*n.* a fairly large amount.

Somegate, *adv.* somehow; in some way; somewhere.

Somepairt, *adv.* somehow; somewhere.

Something, *adv.* somewhat.

Son, *n.* a familiar term of kindly address without implying sonship.

Son-afore-the-father, *n.* the common colt's-foot; the cudweed.

Sonce, *n.* prosperity. Cf. Sonse.

Soncy, *adj.* lucky. Cf. Sonsy.

Sones, *n.* 'sowens.' Cf. Sowen.

Song, *n.* a fuss, outcry. Cf. Sang.

Sonk, *n.* a seat; a couch; a bag of straw; a pad of straw used as a saddle or cushion.

Sonk, *v.* to drivel; to loiter; to be in a dejected state.

Sonk-dyke, *n.* a wall or 'dyke' built with stone or sods on one side and filled with earth on the other.

Sonkie, *n.* a low stool; a man like a sackful of straw.

Sonk-pocks, *n.* the bags tied to the 'sonks' on the back of a tinker's ass, in which children, baggage, goods, &c. were carried.

Sonnet, *n.* a song; a verse; nonsensical talk or writing.

Sons, *n.* 'sowens.' Cf. Sowen.

Sonse, *n.* luck; prosperity; used in good wishes.

Sonsy, Sonsie, *adj.* lucky, fortunate, happy; thriving; plump, buxom, stout; jolly; comely, good-looking; cheerful, pleasant; sensible; placid; tractable, good-tempered; comfortable; plentiful; cordial.

Sonsy-faced, -looking, *adj.* of buxom, pleasant, jolly appearance.

Sonsy-folk, *n.* lucky 'first-foots' on New Year's Day.

†Sonyie, *n.* excuse. Cf. Essonyie.

Soo, *v.* to smart; to tingle; to throb.—*n.* an ache, a throb. Cf. Sou.

Soo, *n.* a sow, pig. Cf. Sow.

Soo, *n.* a large rectangular stack of hay or straw.—*v.* to stack. Cf. Sow.

Sooans, Sooins, *n.* 'sowens.' Cf. Sowen.

Sooback, *n.* a woman's cap of a peculiar kind. Cf. Sowback.

Sooch, *v.* to swill; to swig off.—*n.* a copious draught.—*adj.* drunken, swigging.

Sooch, Soogh, *n.* a hollow, murmuring sound; the sighing of the wind. Cf. Souch.

Sood, *v. pret.* should.

Soodie, *n.* a hodge-podge; a miscellaneous mixture; broth; a gross, heavy person; one who is big and clumsy; a dirty woman. Cf. Soudie.

Sooh, *v.* to swill. Cf. Sooch.

Sook, *v.* to suck; to pull at a pipe; to drink leisurely; to dry up by the action of the wind; to drain, exhaust by overcropping; with *in*, to flow in slowly and quietly; to ingratiate one's self.—*n.* a sip, drink, a 'suck'; a whirlpool; wet, boggy ground; loose straw rubbish; a rapid drying of the ground or atmosphere; drought; a stupid fellow, a 'duffer'; in *pl.* the flowers of the red clover, sucked by children.

Sookag, *n.* a head of clover.

Sooker, *n.* the sucker of a tree.

Sooker, *n.* a horse-leech; the young of the cod and other fish; a boy's toy, consisting of a disc of wet leather with a string through the centre, used for suction.

Sookie, *n.* the flower of the red clover; a call-word for a calf, a pet name for a calf.—*adj.* spongy; oozy; untidy.

Sookie-soo, *n.* the flower of red clover.

Sookie-soorach, *n.* the common wood-sorrel and other acid plants.

Sookin'-bairn, *n.* a sucking-child.

Sookin'-bottle, *n.* a baby's feeding-bottle.

Sookin'-stirk, *n.* an unweaned steer; one who depends on others longer than is necessary.

Sookin' turkey, *n.* a fool, ninny; a childish, peevish person.

Sookit, *ppl. adj.* used of fish: partially dried, semi-putrescent; fatigued, exhausted.

Sool, *n.* a swivel. Cf. Sole, Sule.

Soolyie, *n.* used as a most disrespectful term for tribe, race, lot, crew.

Soom, *v.* to hum, buzz.

Soom, *v.* to swim; to float; to cause to float.—*n.* a state of great wetness; a flooding; a pool; a swim.

Soom, *n.* a state of swoon, giddiness, faintness.—*v.* to turn giddy ; to swoon ; to spin as a top ; to cause to spin.

Soom, *n.* the number of sheep or cattle proportioned to a pasture ; the pasture proportioned to sheep or cattle ; twenty sheep. Cf. Soum.

Soomer, *n.* a swimmer.

†**Soommence,** *n.* a legal summons.

Soon, *adj.* used of distance : quick, near, direct.

Soon, Soond, *v.* to swoon, faint ; to spin a top. Cf. Sound.

Soon, Soond, *v.* to sound ; to test the acoustics of a building ; to pronounce, utter ; to scold.—*n.* a sound, a rumour.

Soon, Soond, *adj.* sound ; orthodox ; sound asleep ; used of a period of time : whole, uninterrupted ; smooth, unwrinkled.

Soonie, *adj.* made of the husks and siftings of oatmeal ; used of butter : containing, or adulterated with, 'sowens.'

Soons, *n.* 'sowens.' Cf. Sowen.

Soony, *v.* to swoon. Cf. Sound.

Soop, *v.* to sweep ; to quicken the speed of a curling-stone by sweeping the path clear in front of it ; to work or walk energetically. —*n.* a sweep ; the acceleration of a curling-stone by sweeping. Cf. Sweep.

Sooper, *n.* a whisk or bunch of feathers for dusting, &c.

Sooping, *n.* the act of sweeping ; what is swept up.

Soopit, *v. pret.* and *ppl.* swept.

Soople, *v.* to wash, soak.—*n.* a soaking, washing ; the act of soaking, washing. Cf. Sapple, Soup.

†**Soople,** *adj.* supple ; limp, soft ; quick, nimble ; glib ; swaying from side to side, as with drink ; tractable, agreeable, affable ; clever, cunning, 'slippery,' quirky.—*v.* to make supple ; to soften dry ground with rain.

Soople, *n.* the striking-part of a flail ; a cudgel.—*v.* to cudgel, beat severely.

Soopled, *ppl. adj.* used of a flail : furnished with a 'soople.'

Soople-neckit, *adj.* having a supple neck ; cringing.

Soopleness, *n.* nimbleness ; craftiness, cunning.

Soople Tam, *n.* a top ; a child's toy pulled by a string so as to cause it to shake and seem to dance.

Soor, *adj.* sour ; bitter, pungent ; surly, cross ; sullen, forbidding ; used of the weather : cold, wet, inclement ; of land : cold, wet, unfertile.—*n.* anything unpleasant or bitter.

Soorag, Soorak, *n.* the common sorrel. Cf. Sourock.

Soor-bread, *n.* oat-cake baked at Christmas with sour leaven.

Soor-cake, *n.* 'soor-bread'; a kind of oat-cake baked for St Luke's Fair at Rutherglen.

Soor-cogue, *n.* a preparation of milk eaten with sugar and cream.

Soord, *n.* a sword.

Soor-dook, *n.* buttermilk.

Soor-draps, *n.* acid drops.

Soor-faced, -faced-like, *adj.* surly-looking.

Soor-fish, *n.* fish kept till it is 'high.'

Soor-grass, *n.* sedge-grass.

Soorick, *n.* the sorrel. Cf. Sourock.

Soorin, *n.* a disappointment.

Soorish, *adj.* rather sour ; somewhat surly or sullen.

Soor-leek, -lick, *n.* the common sorrel.

Soor-like, *adj.* ill-tempered, cross.

Soor-like-faced, *adj.* surly-looking.

Soor-like-moo'd, *adj.* surly-looking.

Soor-lookit, *adj.* surly-looking.

Soor milk, *n.* buttermilk.

Soor-moo'd, *adj.* surly-looking.

Soorness, *n.* sullenness, ill-temper, surliness.

Soorock, *n.* the common sorrel. Cf. Sourock.

Soorock-faced, *adj.* sour-faced.

Soose, *v.* to souse ; to soak. Cf. Souce.

Soose, *v.* to box the ears ; to cuff ; to let fall or drop heavily.—*n.* a heavy, swinging blow. Cf. Souse.

Soosh, *v.* to beat severely ; to flog ; to taunt, upbraid teasingly ; to sue at law ; to punish ; to fine.—*n.* a heavy blow.

Sooshin, *n.* a beating ; abusive language.

Soosler, *n.* a thin fish of any of the larger sorts ; a debilitated animal.

Sooslin, *n.* a 'soosler.'

Sootar, Sooter, *n.* a shoemaker. Cf. Souter.

Sooth, *adj.* true, faithful, loyal.—*int.* truth ! —*v.* to make one believe ; to flatter.

Sooth, *v.* to swoon.

Sooth, *adj.* south. Cf. South.

Sooth-aboot, *adj.* southern ; belonging to the south.

Soother, *v.* to coax, flatter ; to soothe.

Soothfast, *adj.* trustworthy ; honest ; true.

Soothfow, *adj.* 'soothfast.'

Soothlan', *adj.* southern ; from the south ; belonging to the south.—*n.* the south ; one who comes from the south.

Soothlin, *adj.* southern.

Soothlins, *adv.* toward the south.

Soothly, *adv.* truly ; softly, gently.

Sooth-ower, *adv.* southwards.

Sooth side, *n.* the bright, the sunny side.

Sooth thro', *adj.* southern.

Sootiman, *n.* a sweep.

Sootipillies, Sootpillies, *n.* the bulrush.

Soot-stour, *n.* soot, sooty dust.

Soot-water, *n.* sooty water.

Sooty, Sootie, *n.* a sweep ; a name for the devil.

Sooty-scon, *n.* a cake baked with soot to be used on Fastern's-eve in superstitious ceremonies.

Sop, *n.* juice, gravy; a sup. Cf. Sap.

Sord, *n.* a sword.

Sord, *n.* the oblique cross-bar in a reclining gate.

†Sordes, Sords, *n.* filth; washings; off-scourings; refuse.

Sore, *adj.* sorry; aching; poor; harsh; tempestuous. Cf. Sair.

Sore head, *n.* a headache; a time of possible future need, a 'rainy day.'

Sore-heady, *n.* a small cylindrical cake wrapped in buttered paper, resembling a person with a headache, who seeks relief by wearing a bandage round the head.

Sorie, *v.* to sorrow.

Soret, *adj.* of a sorrel colour.

Sorn, Sorne, *v.* to take food or lodging by force or threats; to sponge; to live at free quarters; to idle, loaf about.

Sorner, *n.* one who sponges upon another; an idle fellow; a sturdy or threatening beggar.

Sornie, *n.* the fireplace of a kiln, and the opening beyond by which the heat enters.

Sorning, *n.* the exacting of free board and lodgings.

Sorple, *v.* to scrub with soap and water.

Sorplins, *n.* soapsuds.

Sorrow, Sorra, *n.* a euphemism for the devil, &c., in imprecations; with a *noun* or *pronoun*, an expression of the utter absence of the thing or person mentioned; a troublesome child; a plague, pest; a fellow.

Sorrowful, *adj.* troublesome.

Sorrow-rape, *n.* a rope or strap slung across the shoulders of persons carrying a handbarrow, and attached to the 'steels' or 'trams' of it, to relieve the arms of the bearers.

Sorry, *n.* sorrow; a troublesome child.—*adj.* poor, pitiable. Cf. Sairie.

Sorry man, *n.* a kindly designation of a dog.

Sort, *n.* a moderate number or quantity; in *pl.* payment.—*v.* to tidy one's self; to dress; with *by*, to put away; to mend; to put to rights; to feed and litter cows, horses, &c.; to supply one's requirements satisfactorily; to agree, harmonize; to come to an understanding; used of animals: to serve the female with the male; to punish, scold, put to rights morally; with *with*, to consort with.

Sorting, *n.* a scolding; a punishment.

Sorting-stell, *n.* an enclosure into which sheep are driven in order to be separated from each other.

Sortless, *adj.* useless, good-for-nothing.

Sorts, *n.* in *phr.* 'that's your sorts,' an expression of high satisfaction with an action or thing.

Sosh, *n.* a co-operative store.

Sosh, *adj.* addicted to company and the bottle; frank, free, affable; quiet, contented; cheerful; snug, comfortable; lazy, indolent; plump, broad-faced.

Sosherie, *n.* social intercourse; boon companionship; a convivial club.

Soshie, *n.* the manager of a co-operative store.

Soshul, *n.* a social meeting, a soiree.

Soss, *v.* to boil or cook slowly, to 'sotter.'

Soss, *n.* an incongruous or badly-cooked mixture of foods; liquid food; liquor; a mess, slop; a wet, dirty substance; a state of dirt and mess; a muddle; muddled work; a dirty, lazy woman; a slattern; over-tender nursing.—*v.* to mix anything incongruously; to work in dirt and disorder; to nurse over-tenderly; to remain idly in a place.

Soss, Sosse, *v.* to sit or fall down heavily, or as a dead weight; to swill like a hog.—*n.* a heavy fall; the sound of a heavy, soft body falling or squatting down.

Sosserie, *n.* a bad mess, a 'soss.'

Sossing, *n.* an incongruous mixing of foods or medicines.

Soss-poke, *n.* the stomach.

Sot, *n.* an idiot; a stupid person.—*v.* to drink sottishly.

Sot, *adv.* used in assertion, contradicting a previous negation.

†Sott, *n.* the start of a plough when it meets a large stone. Cf. Sault.

Sotten, *ppl.* set.

Sotter, *v.* to boil or cook slowly; to simmer; to bubble, sputter, crackle in boiling or frying; to scorch any part of the body; to burn with hot iron in a foundry.—*n.* a slow boiling; a scorch or burn; the noise made in boiling or frying.

Sotter, *n.* an indefinite number of insects or other small animals collected together; things mixed up in a heterogeneous mass.—*v.* to cluster closely in cutaneous eruptions.

Sotter, *v.* to saturate; to work dirtily or unskilfully; to nurse disgustingly; to 'potter' about; to remain idly in a place.—*n.* a state of utter wetness; a filthy, disgusting mass; a large festering sore; a dirty, clumsy person.

Sotter, *n.* in shinty, the first thwack at the ball.

Sottle, *v.* to sound as porridge, broth, &c. in boiling.

Sou, *n.* a sow. Cf. Sow.

Sou, *n.* a large rectangular stack. Cf. Sow.

Sou, *v.* to smart, tingle. — *n.* an ache, a throb. Cf. Soo.

Soucan, *n.* a single-ply straw rope.

Souce, *v.* to souse; to wash, soak.—*n.* a plunge in water.—*adv.* with a sudden splash.

Souce, *v.* to strike; to cuff.—*n.* a box on the ears. Cf. Souse.

Souch, *n.* a hollow, murmuring sound; the moaning of the wind; a gentle hum; a deep sigh; the sound of heavy breathing; a slumber, restless sleep; a whining style of preaching or praying; a strain, way of speaking; feeling, opinion; a rumour; a story; a scandal; talk; the sound of a blow or a missile in the air; a stroke, blow.—*phr.* 'a calm souch,' silence, a quiet tongue.—*adj.* silent, quiet, tranquil.—*v.* to make a hollow, murmuring sound; used of the wind: to sigh; to make a rushing sound, whir, whiz; to breathe heavily, especially in sleep; with *awa'*, to breathe one's last; to slumber, sleep restlessly; to sing softly; to hum over a tune; to whine; to speak in a whining voice; to swoop; to whisk; to strike; to beat severely; to work or walk with great briskness.

Soucht, *v. pret.* and *ppl.* sought.

Soucye, *n.* the heliotrope.

†**Soud**, *n.* a sum; a hoard; a quantity; a large sum or quantity; a small quantity of liquor.

Soud, *v. pret.* should.

†**Souder**, *v.* to solder; to melt with heat; to burn; to fasten together; to repair, put to rights; to unite; to agree, suit; to compose a quarrel; to reconcile.—*n.* solder.

Soudie, *n.* a heterogeneous mixture; hodge-podge; broth; sheep's-head broth; milk and meal boiled together; a gross, heavy person; a big, clumsy person; a dirty woman.

Soudlan, *adj.* southern. Cf. Soothlan.

Soue, *v.* used of the wind: to sigh, moan.

Souf, Souff, *v.* to sleep in a disturbed manner: to breathe heavily in sleep; to whistle in a low tone; to hum over a tune; to sing; used of the wind: to blow gently.—*n.* a disturbed sleep; heavy breathing in sleep; a low whistle or singing; strain; humour. Cf. Sooch, Souch.

Souff, *v.* to strike.—*n.* a stroke. Cf. Souch.

Souff, Souffe, *v.* to drink, quaff.—*n.* a draught; a lazy, drunken fellow; a fool, simpleton; a stupid person.

†**Souffle**, *n.* a blow; a box on the ear.

Souffle, *n.* a stupid, lazy, drunken fellow.—*v.* to drink. Cf. Souff.

†**Souflet**, *n.* a stroke, a blow.

Souft, *ppl. adj.* exhausted.

Sough, *n.* a sigh; the sound of wind; a rumour.—*v.* to make a whizzing sound. Cf. Souch

Sough, *n.* a ditch; a trench. Cf. Sheugh.

Soughless, *adj.* noiseless.

Souk, *v.* to suck; to have the trick of flattering. Cf. Sook.

Soukie-clover, *n.* the flower of the red clover. Cf. Sookie.

Soul, *n.* spirit, mettle. Cf. Saul.

Soul-couper, *n.* one who sells his soul.

†**Souldart**, *n.* a soldier.

Soul-heezin', *adj.* uplifting the soul.

†**Soult**, *n.* the start of a plough on its striking a large stone. Cf. Sault.

Soum, Soume, *n.* twenty sheep; the number of sheep or cattle proportioned to a pasture. —*v.* to fix the number of animals to be kept on land which is occupied by more than one proprietor or tenant.

Soum, *v.* to surmise.

Soum, *v.* to swim. Cf. Soom.

Soum, *n.* the rope or chain attaching oxen or horses to the plough. Cf. Soam.

Soum, *n.* the air-bladder of a fish.

Soum and roum, *n.* pasture in summer and fodder in winter.

Soun', *adj.* sound; orthodox; sound asleep; used of a period of time: whole, unbroken; level, smooth.

Soun', *v.* to sound; to test the acoustics of a building; to utter, pronounce; to scold.

Sound, *v.* to swoon; to stun; to spin a top; to spin as a top.—*n.* a swoon, faint.

Soundly, *adv.* properly; regularly.

Soup, *v.* to soak, drench; to drink copiously. —*n.* a soaking, washing; a state of wetness; a big draught; a piece of ground always wet or muddy.

Soup, *v.* to sweep; to clear the path before a curling-stone; to walk briskly; to work energetically.—*n.* a sweeping movement; sweepings. Cf. Sweep.

Soup, *v.* to sup; to drink, tipple; to eat liquid food from a spoon.—*n.* a sip, mouthful; a small quantity of liquid; an indefinite quantity of liquid; a small portion of sustenance, such as is taken with a spoon. Cf. Sup.

Soupet, *ppl. adj.* water-logged.

Soupet, *ppl. adj.* wearied, spent; emaciated.

Soupie,, *n.* a sling.

Souping-wet, *adj.* soaking.

Soupit, *v. pret.* and *ppl.* swept.

†**Souple**, *adj.* supple; flexible; cunning; limp, yielding. Cf. Soople.

Souple, *n.* the striking-part of a flail.—*v.* to cudgel. Cf. Soople.

†**Soup-meagre**, *n.* a thin soup.

Soup-tatties, *n.* potato soup.

Soup-the-causey, *n.* a scrub, niggard; one who would do the meanest thing for money

Sour, *v.* used of lime: to slake. Cf. Soor.

Sourock, Sourack, Sourick, *n.* the sorrel.
Sourock-faced, *adj.* sour-faced.
†**Sous, Souse,** *n.* a 'sou,' a halfpenny.
Souse, *n.* a plunge into water.—*adv.* with a sudden splash. Cf. Souce.
Souse, *v.* to thump, cuff; to box the ears; to fall of a heap; to sit down suddenly with a bump; to let fall heavily, drop.—*n.* a blow on the head; a box on the ear; a heavy fall or its sound; a load; a dirty, mixed mass of food, &c., a 'soss.'—*adv.* with sudden violence.
Soust feet, *n.* pickled cow-heel.
Souter, Soutar, Soutor, *n.* a shoemaker, cobbler.—*v.* to botch, spoil utterly; to give up, yield; to get the better of, worst.
Souter's brandy, *n.* buttermilk.
Souter's clod, *n.* a kind of coarse wheaten bread, sold for a halfpenny a roll.
Souter's deevil, *n.* a shoemaker's awl.
Souter's ends, *n.* a kind of twine, 'rosetty-ends.'
Souter's grace, *n.* a mock appeal to St Crispin, the patron saint of shoemakers.
Souter's howlet, *n.* an opprobrious term of address.
Southen, *adj.* southern.
†**Souther,** *v.* to solder. Cf. Souder.
Southland, Southlin, *adj.* southern. Cf. Soothlan', Soothlin.
Southlins, *adv.* southwards.
Southron, *adj.* southern; English as distinguished from Scottish.—*n.* a southerner; an Englishman.
Soutrie, *n.* a miscooked liquid dish. Cf. Souter.
†**Soutt, Sout,** *n.* a leap, bounce; the start or bounce of a plough when it meets a stone. Cf. Sault.
Soutt, Sout, *v.* to sob.
Soutter, *n.* a shoemaker. Cf. Souter.
Sove, *v.* in *phr.* to 'sove awa' hame,' to go home quickly.
†**Soverty,** *n.* surety.
Sow, *n.* a dirty, swinish person; a game played by a number of persons with 'shinties'; the small piece of wood or bone used in the game of 'sow'; a small heap of cherry-stones in a children's game. Cf. Soo.
Sow, Sowe, *n.* a large rectangular stack; a cluster of objects; anything in a state of disorder; a bride's outfit.—*v.* to stack hay or straw in a 'sow.'
Sow, *v.* with *out*, to sow for grass. Cf. Saw.
Sow-back, *n.* a woman's cap with a raised fold running lengthways from the brow to the back of the head.
Sow-back-, -backit-mutch, *n.* a 'sow-back.'
Sow-, Soo-brock, *n.* a badger.

Sowce, *n.* flummery; 'brose,' 'sowens'; porridge, &c.
Sowce, *v.* to box one's ears. Cf. Souse.
Sow-crae, *n.* a pig-sty, piggery.
†**Sowd,** *n.* a quantity. Cf. Soud.
†**Sowder,** *v.* to solder; to combine. Cf. Souder.
Sowdie, *n.* a hodge-podge; anything boiled to 'smush.' Cf. Soudie.
Sow-driver, *n.* the player who tries to drive the 'sow' into the holes in the game of 'sow.'
Sowe, *n.* a winding-sheet.
Sowen, Sowan, Sowin, *v.* to smear with 'sowens.'—*n.* weavers' paste; in *pl.* a dish made by steeping and fermenting the husks, 'seeds,' or siftings of oats in water, and then boiling.—*adj.* made of 'sowens'; containing 'sowens.'
Sowen-boat, -bowie, *n.* a small barrel used in preparing 'sowens.'
Sowen-brod, *n.* the board used by weavers for laying their paste on the web.
Sowen-cog, *n.* a wooden vessel for holding weavers' paste.
Sowen-crock, *n.* a jar for holding weavers' paste.
Sowenie-mug, *n.* a contemptuous name for a weaver.
Sowening, *n.* the custom of smearing neighbours' doors with 'sowens.'
Sowen-kit, *n.* a vessel in which 'sowens' are made.
Sowen-mug, *n.* a dish for holding 'sowens' when made.
Sowen-pot, *n.* a 'sowen-kit.'
Sowens-breakfast, *n.* a breakfast of 'sowens.'
Sowen-seeds, -sids, *n.* the husks of oats used for making 'sowens.'
Sowen-sieve, *n.* a sieve for straining 'sowens,' and freeing them from the husks used in making them.
Sowens-nicht, *n.* Christmas Eve, o.s., when parties were held for sharing 'sowens,' bread, cheese, and ale, and when it was the practice to besmear the doors of neighbours with 'sowens.'
Sowens-pan, *n.* a 'sowen-kit.'
Sowen-splatter, *n.* weavers' paste.
Sowens-porridge, *n.* porridge made of cold 'sowens' by mixing them with oatmeal while on the fire.
Sowens-say, -sey, *n.* a 'sowens-sieve,' a strainer affixed to the 'sowen-tub.
Sowen-suds, *n.* weavers' paste.
Sowen-tub, *n.* a 'sowen-kit.'
†**Sower,** *v.* to solder. Cf. Souder.
Sower-bread, *n.* a flitch of bacon.
Sowf, *n.* a draught; a sot. Cf. Souff.
Sowf, *v.* to hum over a tune. Cf. Souf.

Sowff, *n.* a stroke, a blow; a 'souch.' Cf. Souch.

Sowgh, *v.* to make a whizzing sound. Cf. Souch.

Sowie, *n.* a small heap of cherry-stones, used in a children's game. Cf. Sow.

Sowings, *n.* 'sowens.' Cf. Sowen.

Sow-in-the-kirk, *n.* the game of 'sow.'

Sowk, *v.* to drench.—*n.* a sot, tippler.

Sow-kill, *n.* a lime-kiln dug out of the earth.

Sowl, *v.* to pull by the ears.

Sowle, *n.* a swivel.

Sow-libber, *n.* a castrator or spayer of swine.

Sowloch, *v.* to wallow like a sow.

Sow-luggit, *adj.* with hanging ears, with ears like a sow.

Sowm, Sowmp, *n.* the chain that passes between the oxen by which the plough was drawn; traces for dragging ordnance; the ropes by which hay is fastened on a cart. Cf. Soam.

Sowm, *v.* to swim. Cf. Soom.

Sowm, Sowme, *n.* the number of sheep or cattle proportioned to a pasture; as much grass as will pasture one cow or five sheep. Cf. Soom.

Sownack, *n.* a Hallowe'en bonfire.

Sowns, *n.* 'sowens.' Cf. Sowen.

Sowp, *v.* to soak, drench.—*n.* a soaking, washing. Cf. Soup.

Sowp, *n.* a sip; a drink; a drop; liquid food. Cf. Soup.

Sowr, *adj.* sour. Cf. Soor.

Sowroo, *n.* sorrow, used in imprecations.

Sow's coach, *n.* the game of 'hot-cockles.'

Sowse, *v.* to thump. Cf. Souse.

Sow-siller, *n.* hush-money; a bribe to pervert justice.

Sow's-mou, *n.* a piece of paper rolled on the hand, and twisted at one end, to hold small quantities of groceries.

Sow's-tail, *n.* a spoiled knot in binding sheaves.

Sowster, *n.* a sempstress.

Sowter, *n.* a shoemaker. Cf. Souter.

Sowth, *n.* a stroke; a 'souch.' Cf. Souch.

Sowth, *adj.* true. Cf. Sooth.

Sowth, *v.* to whistle in a low tone. Cf. Souch.

†Sowther, *v.* to solder. Cf. Souder.

†Soy, *n.* silk, silken material.

Spa, *n.* drink, liquor.

Spaad, *n.* a spade.

Space, *n.* a pace.—*v.* to measure by paces; to pace.

Spacier, *v.* to walk; to march.

Spack, *v. pret.* spoke, spake.

Spade'l, *n.* a spadeful.

Spade-peat, *n.* a large surface turf for placing at the back of the hearth on which a peat-fire burns.

Spading, *n.* a trench of a spade in depth; the depth of soil raised at one time by a spade.

Spae, *v.* to foretell; to tell fortunes; to prophesy; to forebode.

Spae, *n.* the opening or slit in a gown, petticoat, &c.

Spae-book, *n.* a book of necromancy or witch-spells.

Spae-craft, *n.* the art of fortune-telling.

Spaedom, *n.* witchcraft; prognostication.

Spaeg, *n.* a skeleton. Cf. Spaig.

Spae-man, *n.* a diviner, soothsayer; a male fortune-teller.

Spaer, *n.* a fortune-teller, soothsayer.

Spae-trade, *n.* the art of fortune-telling.

Spae-wife, -woman, *n.* a female fortune-teller.

Spae-work, *n.* 'spae-craft.'

Spaig, *n.* a hand; a paw; a limb. Cf. Spyogg.

Spaig, *n.* a skeleton; a tall, lanky person; a person with long, ill-shaped legs.

Spaigin, *n.* a tall, lanky person.

Spaik, *n.* a spoke; the spoke of a wheel; a bar of wood; a branch or slip of a tree planted to grow; in *pl.* the spokes on which a coffin is borne to the grave.

Spaik, *v.* to speak.

Spail, Spaill, *v.* to work or walk with energy. —*n.* the act of working so; a quantity; an amount of work; anything long.

Spail, *n.* a splinter, chip, or shaving of wood; a lath of wood; a lath or thin plank used in wooden houses for filling up the interstices of the beams; the guttering of a candle. Cf. Spale, Spell.

Spain, *v.* to wean.

Spaining-brash, *n.* milk-fever; the illness of infants resulting from their being weaned.

Spaining-time, *n.* the season for weaning lambs; weaning-time.

Spainyie, *adj.* Spanish.—*n.* a West Indian cane sometimes smoked by boys; used also for weavers' reeds and the reeds of bagpipes.

Spainyie-flee, *n.* cantharides or Spanish-fly.

Spainyie-flee-blister, *n.* a fly-blister.

Spair, *adj.* spare, thin.

Spair, *n.* an opening or slit in gown, petticoat, trousers, &c. Cf. Spare.

†Spairge, *v.* to sprinkle, bespatter, scatter; to slander; to rough-cast a wall; to whitewash. — *n.* a dash, a sprinkling; what is sprinkled; a dram of spirits; a dash of contumely.

Spairk, *v.* to bespatter with spots; to fly off in sparks.—*n.* a spark; a speck. Cf. Spark.

Spait, *n.* a flood; a sudden rush of water. Cf. Spate.

Spaive, *v.* to spay; to bear spaying. Cf. Spave.

Spaiver, *n.* one who spays or castrates.

Spaiver, *n.* the flap in front of small-clothes ; the slit at the fork of the trousers.

Spaivie, *n.* the spavin in horses.—*v.* to walk as if spavined.

Spaiviet, *ppl. adj.* spavined.

Spak, *v. pret.* spoke.—*ppl.* spoken.

Spake, *n.* a spoke.

†**Spald,** *n.* the shoulder ; a limb. Cf. Spaul.

Spald, *v.* to split open. Cf. Speld.

Spalder, *v.* to split open. Cf. Spelder, Spaller.

Spalding, *n.* a small fish split open, gutted, and dried. Cf. Spelding.

Spale, *n.* a chip of wood ; a lath ; a wood-shaving ; a lath or thin plank for filling the interstices between the beams of a wooden house ; the guttering of a candle.

Spale, *n.* energetic and speedy working. Cf. Spail.

Spale-board, *n.* a thin plank.

Spale-box, *n.* a box made of very thin wood for holding ointments, &c.

Spale-horned, *adj.* used of cattle : having the horns thin and broad.

†**Spallard,** *n.* an espalier ; a trained fruit-tree.

Spaller, *v.* to split open ; to injure the body in striding ; to sprawl.

Spalliel, *n.* a cattle disease.

Spalsh, *n.* a splash of colour, dirt, &c. Cf. Spelch.

Spalter, *v.* to sprawl.—*n.* a sprawl. Cf. Spaller.

Spalyin, *adj.* flat-footed.

Span, *v.* to yoke horses to any sort of carriage.

Span, *v.* to grasp with both hands together ; used of life : to spend, pass.—*n.* the span of life, threescore and ten ; a grasp ; the act of grasping ; a definite portion.

Spane, *v.* to wean. Cf. Spain, Spean.

Spang, *v.* to grasp ; to span.—*n.* the act of grasping.

Spang, *v.* to leap with elastic force ; to spring ; to cause to leap ; to stride along, walk quickly.—*n.* a leap, bound, spring ; a long stride ; a bang, a smart blow ; a fillip.

Spang-cockle, *n.* a game, played with marbles, nuts, &c. placed on the second joint of the forefinger and smartly spun off by the application of the thumb.

Spang-fire-new, *adj.* quite new.

Spanghew, Spanghue, *v.* to jerk anything violently into the air by placing it on one end of a board, the middle of which rests on a wall, &c., and striking the other end smartly ; to torture frogs, yellow-ammers, &c. thus ; to bend back one end of a bough, and suddenly release it so as to strike a person.

Spangie, *n.* an animal fond of leaping.

Spangie, *n.* a boys' game, the game of 'boss and span.' Cf. Spawnie.

Spangiehewit, *n.* a barbarous sport of boys with young yellow-ammers, frogs, &c.

Spanging, *ppl. adj.* nimble, active.

Spang-new, *adj.* quite new, span-new.

Spang-tade, -taid, *n.* a barbarous sport of children with frogs and toads. Cf. Spanghew.

Spanhew, *v.* to 'spanghew.'

Spank, *v.* to stride, run.—*n.* a leap, bound, speed.

Spank, *v.* to sparkle ; to shine.

Spank, *n.* a spark ; spirit. Cf. Spunk.

Spanker, *n.* an active, tall, well-made person ; in *pl.* long, thin legs.

Spankering, *adj.* nimble, agile and tall.

Spanker-new, *adj.* quite new, span-new.

Spanking, *ppl. adj.* smart ; active ; showy ; sprightly.

Spankingly, *adv.* smartly ; rapidly ; in dashing style.

Spanky, *adj.* sprightly, frisky ; smart, well-dressed. — *n.* one who moves rapidly, a 'spanker.'

Spar, *v.* to shut ; to bar a door with a wooden bolt.

Spar, *adv.* in a state of opposition ; wide apart. Cf. Aspar, Sparr.

Spare, *n.* the slit in a gown, petticoat, or front of a pair of trousers.

Spare, *adj.* deficient, lacking ; meagre.

Spare, *v.* to save, retrench ; to save from ; to do without.

Sparely, *adv.* scantily, poorly.

Spareness, *n.* scantiness, poverty.

†**Sparge,** *v.* to dash ; to bespatter. Cf. Spairge.

Sparginer, Spargiter, *n.* a plasterer.

Spar-hawk, *n.* the sparrow-hawk.

Spark, *n.* a speck, spot ; an atom ; a spirt, jet of boiling water, mud, &c.; a spot of dirt, &c.; a small quantity of liquor, a 'nip' of whisky.—*v.* to strike a light or match ; to fall or strike in drops ; to fly off in bits ; to scatter seeds thinly ; to bespatter with spots ; to rain slightly ; to sparkle.

Spark in the hawse, or throat, *n.* a craving for liquor.

Spark in the wick, or candle, *n.* an omen indicating the arrival of a letter.

Sparkle, *n.* a spark ; a gleam of light ; in *pl.* large flying sparks of fire or burning wood, straw, &c.

Sparklit, *ppl. adj.* speckled. Cf. Spreckle.

Sparling, *n.* the smelt. Cf. Sperling.

†**Sparple, Sparpel,** *v.* to scatter ; to sprinkle ; to spread abroad.

Sparr, *v.* to place the legs and arms so as to resist a strain.—*adv.* in a state of opposition.

Sparrible, *n.* a sparable.

Sparrow, *n.* the corn-bunting. Cf. Spurgie.

Sparrow-blastit, *adj.* dumfounded.

Sparrow-drift, -hail, *n.* very small shot, for small birds.

Sparrow-hawk, *n.* the merlin.

Sparry, *adj.* sharp-pointed, like a sparable.

Sparrygrass, *n.* asparagus.

Sparse, *adj.* used of writing : widely spread, far apart.

Spart, *n.* the dwarf-rush. Cf. Sprat.

Spart, *v.* to scatter dung with a 'muck-hack.'

Spartle, *v.* to leap, spring ; to paw ; used of a child . to sprawl, kick about.

Sparty, *adj.* abounding in rushes.

Spash, *n.* the foot.

Spat, *n.* a spot, a place. Cf. Spot.

Spat, *n.* a quarrel, 'tiff.'

Spat, *n.* a gaiter, legging.

Spatch, *n.* a large spot ; a patch ; a plaster.

Spate, *n.* a flood ; a sudden flood in a river ; a sudden, heavy downfall of rain.—*v.* to flood ; to rain heavily ; to overwhelm ; to punish severely.

Spate-ridden, *adj.* carried along by a flood.

Spathie, *n.* a spotted river-trout.

Spatril, *n.* a kind of shoe ; a gaiter ; in *pl.* the notes in music.

Spatterdashes, *n.* gaiters, leggings.

Spattle, *n.* a spatula ; a 'pattle' or plough-spade.

Spattle, *n.* a slight inundation, a little 'spate.'

Spaud, *n.* a spade.

Spaud, *v.* to hasten, go quickly.

†Spaul, *n.* the shoulder or forequarter of an animal ; a leg, limb ; a feeble stretching of the limbs.—*v.* to push out the limbs feebly. Cf. Spule.

Spauld, *v.* to split. Cf. Spald.

†Spauld, *n.* the shoulder ; a limb, leg. Cf. Spaul.

Spauldrochie, *adj.* long-legged.—*n.* a long-legged fellow.

Spauly, *adj.* leggy ; having too much leg for beauty.

Spave, *v.* to spay.

Spaver, *n.* one who spays cattle.

Spaver, *n.* a slit in front of the trousers. Cf. Spaiver, Spare.

Spavie, *n.* the spavin in horses.—*v.* to walk as if having the spavin. Cf. Spaivie.

Spavy-fittit, *adj.* having feet that make one walk as if spavined.

Spawer, *n.* a slit in the front of the trousers. Cf. Spare.

†Spawl, *n.* a limb. Cf. Spaul.

Spawly, *adj.* leggy. Cf. Spauly.

Spawn, *n.* a span in the game of 'spawnie.'

Spawnie, *n.* a boys' game with buttons, in which one player throws his button to a distance, and another throws his as near as possible, winning the button if he reaches within a 'spawn' of it. Cf. Spangie.

Spay, *v.* to tell fortunes. Cf. Spae.

Speak, *v.* to bespeak ; to be on friendly terms ; to attend, hearken to ; to come and hear what one has to say.—*n.* a speech ; talk, gossip ; a conversation ; a subject of talk or of gossip.

Speakable, *adj.* affable.

Speak-a-word-room, *n.* a small waiting-room or parlour in a large house.

Speak for, *v.* to bespeak, engage.

Speak hame, *v.* to answer.

Speak ill, *v.* to scold.

Speak in, *v.* to make a short call on one in passing.

Speak to, *v.* to rebuke ; to threaten ; to chastise ; to ask in marriage ; to bear witness to.

Speal, *v.* to climb. Cf. Speel.

Speal, *n.* a play, game. Cf. Spiel.

†Speal, *n.* a limb ; the shoulder-blade. Cf. Spaul.

Speal, Speall, *n.* a thin shaving. Cf. Spell, Spail.

Speal-bone, *n.* the shoulder-bone of mutton.

Spean, *v.* to wean. Cf. Spain.

Speaning-brash, *n.* illness affecting infants on being weaned.

Spear, *v.* to taper, rise to a point.

Spear, *v.* to ask, inquire. Cf. Speer.

Spearmen, *n.* the ancient city-guard, or city-officers, attending the authorities.

Spearwind, *n.* a gust of rage ; a violent passion. Cf. Spirewind.

Speat, *n.* a flood. Cf. Spate.

Speated, *ppl. adj.* used of a river : in flood.

Speave, *v.* to spay animals. Cf. Spave.

Speavie, *n.* spavin. Cf. Spavie.

Specialies, *adv.* especially.

Speck-glass, *n.* a spectacle-glass.

Speckilation, *n.* a spectacle. Cf. Speculation.

Speckits, *n.* spectacles.

Speckle, *n.* kind, quality.

Specks, Spects, *n.* spectacles.

Spectacle, *v.* to examine through a pair of spectacles.—*n.* in *pl.* the merrythought of a fowl.

Speculation, *n.* the power of vision ; a spectacle ; a subject of remark or gossip ; an object of contempt ; a fanciful rumour ; a romance.

Speddart, *n.* a spider ; a tough old creature, tight as a wire.

Spedlin, *n.* a child just beginning to walk. Cf. Spodlin.

Speech-crier, *n.* a street seller of speeches, &c.

Speechman, *n.* a 'speech-crier.'

Speed, *n.* a state of excitement, a quarrel.—*v.* to give success.

Speedard, Speeder, *n.* a spider. Cf. Speddart.

Speedy, Speedy-fit, *n.* a child that can run alone.

Speeho, *n.* a rumpus; outburst; uproar.

Speel, *v.* to climb, to ascend; to climb vertically upwards by hands and feet.—*n.* a climb, an ascent.

Speel, *v.* to play, sport, amuse one's self; to slide on ice.—*n.* a game, play, match. Cf. Spiel.

Speelick, *n.* a smart blow or tap; a hard blow.

Speeliewally, *n.* a tall, thin, delicate-looking person; a tall, thin, young shoot or plant.

Speen, *n.* a spoon.

Speen, *v.* to wean. Cf. Spean.

Speendrift, *n.* snow driven by the wind from the ground; spindrift; spray.

Speengie-rose, *n.* the peony.

Speeock, *n.* a stake or log of wood.

Speer, *v.* to ask, inquire, question; to ask in marriage, pop the question.—*n.* a search, investigation; an inquisitive person.

Speer, *v.* to spirt; to squirt.

Speere, *n.* an opening in a house-wall, through which inquiries were made and answered in the case of strange visitors.

Speerings, *n.* inquiry, investigation, interrogation; news, tidings; prying inspection.

Speerin' word, *n.* the right to ask in marriage.

Speerit, *n.* spirit.

Speerity, *adj.* spirited.

Speer-wundit, *adj.* out of breath with exertion.

Speet, *n.* a spit; a skewer. Cf. Spit.

Speet, *n.* spite; a cause of grief; a disappointment.

Speg, *n.* a pin or peg of wood.

Speikintare, *n.* the common tern.

Speil, *v.* to climb. Cf. Speel.

Speil, *v.* to play.—*n.* a match between two curling-clubs. Cf. Spiel.

Speinty, *n.* a spawned fish, a 'spent' herring.

Speir, *n.* an opening in a house-wall for asking and answering questions. Cf. Speere.

Speir, *v.* to ask. Cf. Speer.

Spek, *v.* to speak.

Spel, *v.* to play. Cf. Spiel.

Spelch, *v.* to splash. Cf. Spelsh.

Speld, *v.* to split open; to spread open; to expand.

Spelder, *v.* to split, cut up; to tear open; to draw asunder; to toss the limbs in walking; to stretch out the legs; to sprawl; to rack the limbs in striding. Cf. Spalder, Spaller.

Spelder, *n.* one who splits fish for curing.

Speldin, Speldane, *n.* a small fish, split open, salted, and dried in the sun.

Spelding, *ppl. adj.* broken; awkward; halting.

Speldrin, *n.* a 'speldin.'

Speldron, *n.* an awkward, sprawling, loose-limbed person; a term of contempt.

Spele, *v.* to climb. Cf. Speel.

Spelk, *n.* a splinter; a thin piece of wood; a sharp splinter of iron flying from the mass to which it belongs; a splint for a broken limb; a very thin person or thing; a young, slender boy or girl.—*v.* to splinter; to put in splints; to set a broken limb.

Spelked, *ppl. adj.* used of wood: ragged.

Spell, *n.* a splinter of wood, &c.; a thin shaving; a lath or thin plank for filling up interstices between the beams in wooden houses. Cf. Spale.

Spell, *n.* spelling; a spelling-lesson.—*v.* to tell, narrate; to discourse; to asseverate falsely; to exaggerate; to decipher.

Spell, *v.* to spoil, destroy. Cf. Spill.

Spellan, *n.* a fish split, salted, and dried in the sun. Cf. Speldin.

Spell-book, *n.* a spelling-book.

Spell-wind, *n.* a gust of rage; a violent outburst of passion. Cf. Spirewind.

Spell-woman, *n.* a female fortune-teller, a 'spaewife.'

Spelsh, *v.* to dash a liquid or semi-liquid substance; to splash, bespatter; to dash or fall heavily into a liquid or semi-liquid substance; to splash through mud or water.—*n.* any liquid or semi-liquid thrown violently; the act of throwing it so; a fall into mud, water, &c.; the sound of such fall.

Spen, *v.* to spend. Cf. Spend.

Spen, *v.* to wean. Cf. Spean.

†**Spence,** *n.* a spare room on the same flat as the kitchen; a country parlour; a larder; a room containing a loom.—*v.* to put into the inner or spare room of a house.

Spence-door, *n.* a door between the kitchen and the pantry or the inner room.

Spend, *v.* used of time: to pass; to waste.—*n.* wasting, expense.

Spend, *v.* to spring; to gallop.—*n.* a spring, bound; an elastic motion.

Spend, *v.* to wean. Cf. Spean.

Spendrife, *adj.* prodigal; extravagant. - *n.* a spendthrift.

Spengyie, Spengie, *adj.* Spanish.—*n.* a West Indian cane. Cf. Spainyie.

Spenn, *v.* to button or lace one's clothes.

†**Spens, Spense,** *n.* a larder; a parlour. Cf. Spence.

Spentacles, Spenticles, *n.* spectacles.

Speochan, *n.* a tobacco-pouch. Cf. Speuchan.

Sper, *v.* to bolt or bar a door. Cf. Spar.

Sper, Spere, *v.* to ask, inquire. Cf. Speer.

Spere, *n.* an opening in a house-wall for asking and answering questions. Cf. Speere.

†Sperfle, *v.* to scatter; to sprinkle. Cf. Sparple.

Sperk, *n.* a spark. Cf. Spark.

Sperling, *n.* the smelt. Cf. Sparling.

†Sperple, *v.* to scatter; to sprinkle. Cf. Sparple.

Spert, *n.* the dwarf-rush. Cf. Spart.

Sperthe, *n.* a battle-axe.

Speshie, *n.* species.

Speuchan, *n.* a tobacco-pouch, a ' spleuchan.'

Speug, *n.* the house-sparrow; a tall, thin person. Cf. Spug.

Speugle, *n.* anything extremely slender.

†Speul, *n.* the shoulder-blade. Cf. Spaul, Spule.

Spew, *v.* to pour forth contents; to pour forth smoke, &c. ; used of corn: to have the ear firm ; of snow: to drive strongly in a blizzard.—*n.* an outpouring of smoke, &c.

Spewing, *ppl. adj.* giving out smoke ; used of sores: exuding, running.

Spewing-fou, *adj.* disgustingly drunk, drunk to sickness.

Spey, *v.* to tell fortunes. Cf. Spae.

Spey-codlin, *n.* a salmon.

Speyk, *v.* to speak ; to talk, gossip.—*n.* talk, gossip. Cf. Speak.

Spice, *n.* a small quantity ; a sample ; a specimen ; pepper ; pride ; a blow, thwack. —*v.* to pepper, as with shot ; to beat, thwack.

Spice-box, -buist, *n.* a pepper-box.

†Spicerie, *n.* a specimen, 'a touch'; in *pl.* groceries.

Spicket, *n.* a spigot ; a wooden tap.

Spicy, *adj.* smart, showy, neat; peppered; peppery, testy, proud.

Spidarroch, *n.* a day's work with a spade ; the ground that can be dug with a spade in a day.

Spider-legs, *n.* long, thin legs ; a person with long, thin legs.

Spidert, *n.* a spider. Cf. Speddart.

Spider-webster, *n.* a spider.

Spiel, *v.* to play, sport.—*n.* a play, game.

Spier, *v.* to ask, inquire. Cf. Speer.

Spiffer, *n.* anything very fine or showy; a smartly-dressed person.

Spiffin, *adj.* fine, capital.

Spig, *n.* a spigot.

Spike-nail, *n.* a long nail.

Spilder, *v.* to cut or split open. Cf. Spelder.

Spile-tree, *n.* a long pole supported horizontally, on which fishermen hang their lines in order to clean the hooks.

Spilgie, *adj.* long and slender.—*n.* a tall, meagre person ; a long limb.

Spilk, *n.* a splinter ; a splint.—*v.* to splinter ; to put in splints. Cf. Spelk.

Spilk, *v.* to shell peas ; to beat smartly.—*n.* a smart blow.

Spilkins, *n.* split-peas.

Spill, *v.* to spoil, ruin, destroy ; to pour forth, overflow.—*n.* a ruin, wreck ; a sum of money.

Spilth, *n.* what is spilled ; overflow ; waste.

Spin, *n.* a spoon.

Spin, *v.* used of the heart: to beat quickly ; of the blood : to course rapidly ; to prosper quickly, succeed.—*n.* a drinking-bout.

Spindle, *n.* four hanks of yarn ; a tall, thin person.—*adj.* tall and slender.—*v.* used of plants : to grow tall and lanky with great rapidity ; of grain : to shoot out.

Spindle-shanks, *n.* long, thin legs ; a person having such legs.

Spindle-wood, *n.* splinters.

Spindly, *adj.* tall and thin ; overgrown.

Spink, *n.* the goldfinch.

Spink, *n.* a diminutive person.

Spink, *n.* the pink, in general ; the primrose ; the polyanthus.

Spink, *adj.* used of ale : brisk, strong, good.

Spinkie, *n.* a dram or glass of spirits.

Spinkie, *adj.* slender and active.

Spin'le, *n.* a spindle. Cf. Spindle.

Spin'le-neb, -nib, *n.* in *phr.* 'at the spin'le-neb wi',' at the end of one's resources or exertions.

Spinly, *adj.* tall and slender. Cf. Spindly.

Spin-Maggie, -Mary, *n.* a daddy-longlegs.

Spinnel, *n.* a spindle. Cf. Spindle.

Spinner, *n.* a daddy-longlegs.

Spinner, *v.* to run or fly swiftly ; to move in a spiral form.—*n.* a smart rate of speed ; a smart, swift rush or dash.

Spinnie, *n.* a wheel.

Spinning-boy, *n.* a weaver.

Spinning-day, *n.* a day formerly given by tenants' daughters to spinning for the laird's wife.

Spinning-jenny, *n.* a spinning-wheel; a daddy-longlegs.

Spinning-Maggie, -Meg, *n.* a daddy-longlegs.

Spinnie, *v.* used of grain: to shoot out. Cf. Spindle.

Spintie, *adj.* lean ; thin.

Spiog, *n.* a paw, hand, foot. Cf. Spoig.

Spire, *n.* a small, tapering tree, generally a fir-tree, of a size fit for paling.—*v.* to soar upwards ; to aspire.

Spire, *n.* the stem of an earthfast 'couple,' reaching from the floor to the top of a cottage wall, partly inserted in and partly standing out of the wall ; a wall between the fire and the door, with a seat in it ; the lower part of a 'couple.'

Spire, *n.* spray.

Spire, *v.* to wither ; to cause to fade.

Spires, *n.* small particles of spittle projected from the mouth.

Spirewind, *n.* a gust of rage. Cf. Spearwind, Spellwind.

Spirg, *n.* as much liquid as will moisten the lips.

Spirie, *adj.* tall, slender ; used of growing plants : tall and weak.

Spirie, *adj.* warm, parching with drought.

Spiring, *ppl. adj.* aspiring, soaring.

Spirit, *v.* to inspire, inspirit.

Spirity, *adj.* spirited ; lively ; full of life.

Spirk, *v.* to emit sparks ; to spirt.—*n.* a small blot or mark. Cf. Spark.

Spirl, *v.* to run about in a light, lively way.

Spirl, *adj.* slender. Cf. Spirlie.

Spirlicket, *n.* a particle ; an atom.

Spirlie, *adj.* slender, thin, spindly.—*n.* a slender spiral column of smoke, vapour, &c. ; a slender person.

Spirlie-legget, *adj.* having thin legs.

Spirling, *n.* a commotion, broil.

Spirling, *n.* a smelt. Cf. Sperling.

Spirnling, *n.* a small 'burn'-trout ; a 'spir-ling.'

Spirran, *n.* a spider ; a horrid old woman ; a hag.

Spirt, *n.* the dwarf-rush. Cf. Spart.

Spirtle, *n.* a wooden stirring-rod, a 'spurtle.' Cf. Spurtle.

Spiry, *adj.* tall, slender. Cf. Spirie.

Spiry, *adj.* parching with drought. Cf. Spirie.

Spit, *v.* to rain slightly ; to be very angry with one.—*n.* the spitting of a consumptive patient ; an outburst ; a slight disputation ; a small, hot-tempered person, a 'spitfire'; a slight shower.

Spit, *n.* a stick or skewer on which fish are hung to dry.—*v.* to put fish on a skewer to dry.

Spit, *n.* the depth of a spade in digging.

Spital, Spittal, *n.* a hospital ; the site of an old, demolished hospital.

Spit-deep, *adj.* of the depth of a spade in digging.

Spite, *n.* provocation ; a disappointment.—*v.* to provoke, vex ; to exasperate ; to scorn, despise.

Spither, *n.* foam, spume, froth.

Spit in one's face, *v.* to reproach ; to take revenge on one.

Spit-stick, *n.* a pointed piece of wood or iron prong on which meat is roasted ; used contemptuously of a small sword or rapier.

Spitten, *n.* spittle. Cf. Spittin.

Spitten, *n.* a puny, mischievous creature ; a little person of hot temper ; a mettlesome, little animal ; a person of low rank.—*adj.* of lowly birth.

Spitter, *n.* a very slight shower ; in *pl.* small drops of snow or rain wind-driven.—*v.* to rain or snow slightly.

Spitterie, *adj.* spurting or flying out irregularly without connection of parts.

Spittin, *n.* a spit, spittle.

Spittle, *n.* the act of spitting ; a thing of no account or value.

Spitty, Spittie, *n.* ? horse.

Splacher, *v.* to splash ; to fall with a splash.

Splae, *n.* a stroke ; a great display. Cf. Splay.

Splae, *v.* to fasten down the edges of a seam. —*n.* the hem so made. Cf. Splay.

Splae-seam, *n.* a hem-seam, one side of which only is sewn down.

Splairge, Splarge, *v.* to splash, sprinkle with liquid mud, &c. ; to bespatter, besmear ; to fall in fragments or scattered splinters.—*n.* a splash of mud, &c. ; anything spattered or splashed.

Splart, *v.* to chatter ; to quarrel.

Splash, *n.* a patch of colour.

Splash, *adj.* splay.

Splash-feet, *n.* splay-feet.

Splash-fluke, *n.* the plaice.

Splat, *v. pret.* did split.

Splatch, *n.* a splash ; a bespattering of mud, &c. ; anything so broad or full as to exhibit an awkward appearance, as a clumsy seal on a letter.—*v.* to splash, bedaub.

Splatchin, *v.* to bedaub.—*n.* a splash or patch of dirt.

Splatter, *v.* to splash with water, mud, &c. ; to besprinkle, bespatter ; to dash or splash hastily through water, mud, &c. ; to splutter ; to come out in spirts or in a rush ; to scatter ; to walk or run with a rattling noise.—*n.* a splash, splutter ; a sharp, rattling noise, the causing of such a noise ; a rush, dash ; a sudden stir or bustle ; an outcry, hubbub ; a wrangle ; in *pl.* uproarious mirth.—*adv.* with a splashing noise.

Splatter-dash, *n.* an uproar ; a splutter ; the sound as of racing among mud, &c.

Splay, *n.* a great display or show ; a quarrel ; a stroke.

Splay, *v.* to fasten down the edges of a seam ; to mend a tear in cloth by sewing the edges together without adding a patch.—*n.* the hem made in fastening down the edges of a seam. Cf. Splae-seam.

Splay, *v.* to skin ; to flay.

Splechrie, *n.* furniture ; an unmarried woman's clothes and furniture ; what a bride brings with her to her husband's house ; the executory of a defunct person or his movable goods left to his heirs.

Splee-fitted, *adj.* splay-footed.

Spleet, *v.* to split.—*ppl.* split.—*n.* a chip.

Spleeted on, *phr.* departed from.

Spleet-new, *adj.* quite new. Cf. Split-new.

Spleetrin, *ppl.* spilling.

Spleit, *v.* to split.

Splender, *n.* a splinter. Cf. Splinder.

Splender-new, *adj.* quite new.

Splenner, *v.* to stride. Cf. Splinner.

Splent, *n.* armour for the legs and arms, worn like splints. Cf. Splint.

Splerg, *v.* to splash in walking in mud. Cf. Splairge.

Splerrie, *v.* to splash in or with mud; to 'splatter.'

Splet, *ppl.* split.

Spleuchan, *n.* a tobacco-pouch; a large purse or pouch. Cf. Speuchan.

Spleut, *v.* to burst forth with a spluttering noise; to fall flat into mud, &c.; to walk in an ungainly and splashing manner.—*n.* a sudden spluttering gush or rush; the noise of such a rush; any weak or watery drink; a quantity of liquid or semi-liquid substance spilled in an unseemly mass.—*adv.* with a spluttering gush; with an unbecoming, splashing step.

Spleutter, *v.* to 'spleut'; to spill awkwardly.—*n.* a 'spleut,' splutter; ruin.—*adv.* with a 'spleut.'

Spleutterie, *adj.* weak and watery; used of the weather: very rainy.—*n.* weak, watery, dirty food; an unseemly, dirty mess.

Splew, *v.* to spit out, spew.

Spley, *v.* to fasten down the edges of a seam. Cf. Splay.

Splinder, *n.* a splinter; a fragment.—*v.* to splinter; to be shivered into fragments.

Splinder-new, *adj.* quite new.

Splinkey, *adj.* tall and lank; spindly.

Splinner, *n.* speed, force.—*adv.* with speed. Cf. Splenner.

Splinner, *n.* a splinter. Cf. Splinder.

Splint, *n.* a hard, laminated variety of bituminous coal.

Splint, *n.* armour worn on the legs and arms.

Splinter-new, *adj.* quite new.

Splirt, *v.* to eject liquid forcibly; to spit out.

Splish-splash, *adv.* in a splashing manner.

Split, *n.* a weaving term: a single thread in plain linen work, a 'dent'; in *pl.* the divisions of a weaver's reed.

Split, *v.* used in curling: to separate two stones lying closely together; in ploughing: to lay the furrows on each side off from the line at which the ploughing of the part is to be finished.

Split an oath, *v.* to swear.

Split-new, *adj.* quite new.

Split-nut, *n.* a beech-nut.

Splitten, *ppl. adj.* split.

Splitter, *v.* to splutter; to make a spluttering noise.

Splitter, *n.* one who splits fish in order to take out the backbone.

Splittie, *n.* a split, disagreement, division.

Splitting-full, *adj.* full to bursting.

Spliung, *n.* a mean, disagreeable person. Cf. Splung.

Sploit, *v.* to spout, squirt; to splash.—*n.* a squirt; an expectoration; a little liquid filth.

Sploit, *n.* an exploit; a trick, joke.

Sploiter, *v.* to spout, 'sploit.'

Splore, *n.* a frolic, a 'spree'; a 'revel; an outing; a game, romp, play; an escapade; a drinking-bout; a debauch; a quarrel; a scrimmage; an outbreak; a disturbance, 'rumpus,' fuss; a sudden movement.—*v.* to frolic; to riot; to show off; to let a thing be known with startling results; to boast, brag.

Splore, *v.* to explore.

Splore, *adj.* in *phr.* 'little splore pearls,' spittle, drops of saliva ejected in speaking.

Splorroch, *n.* the sound made by walking in wet or mud.

Sploy, *n.* a frolic; a frolicsome or funny story; a 'ploy.'

Spluchan, *n.* a tobacco-pouch. Cf. Spleuchan.

Splung, *v.* to carry off by stealth; to filch; to walk with striding, swinging, stealthy gait.—*n.* a mean, disagreeable person.

Splunt, *v.* to court under cloud of night.—*n.* such courting. Cf. Sprunt.

Splunting, *ppl. adj.* amorous.—*n.* the running after girls at night.

Splurt, *n.* a spurt; a splutter; a sudden movement.

Splute, *v.* to exaggerate in narration.—*n.* an exaggerator.

Splutter, *v.* to splash, besprinkle; to gush out noisily; to spill awkwardly and dirtily; to ramble about noisily; to walk with a dirty, splashing step.—*n.* weak, watery liquid; an unseemly mess of spilt liquid or semi-liquid stuff; a fuss, disturbance; rain.—*adv.* with a sharp, spluttering noise; with a dirty, splashing step.

Spluttery, *adj.* weak and watery; rainy.—*n.* a nasty, dirty mess.

Splytten, *ppl.* split.

Splyuchan, *n.* a large purse; a tobacco-pouch. Cf. Spleuchan.

Spoach, Spoatch, *v.* to poach, to pick up trifles; to search for anything; to lounge about for meat or drink.—*n.* a poacher; a picker-up of trifles.

Spoacher, *n.* a poacher: one who lounges about in search of a meal, &c.

Spodlin, *n.* a child learning to walk. Cf. Spedlin.

Spog, *n.* the spoke of a wheel.

Spogshave, *n.* a spokeshave.

Spoig, *n.* a paw, hand, foot; a limb. Cf. Spyogg.

Spoilzie, Spoilyie, *v.* to plunder; to spoil. —*n.* depredation; plunder. Cf. Spulyie.

Spoke, *ppl.* spoken.

Spoke, *n.* a wooden bar used for carrying a coffin to the grave. Cf. Spaik.

Sponga, *n.* a flecked cow. Cf. Spunga.

Sponge, *n.* a baker's mop; putrid moisture issuing from the mouth, eyes, &c. after death; a low, sneaking person on the look-out for food; a wandering dog; a person inclined to steal.—*v.* to ooze; used of a dead body: to exude putrid moisture; to prowl about in search of food.

Sponk, *n.* a spark. Cf. Spunk.

Sponsefu', *adj.* responsible, respectable, 'sponsible.'

Sponsibility, *n.* responsibility.

Sponsible, *adj.* respectable, trustworthy, honourable; of good standing and repute; substantial, well-to-do.

Sponsible-looking, *adj.* of respectable appearance.

Spool, *n.* a weaver's shuttle.

Spool-fittit, *adj.* splay-footed; having the feet twisted outwards like a weaver's shuttle.

Spoolie, *v.* to plunder. Cf. Spulyie.

Spoom, *v.* to swoop; used of a hawk: to dart after its prey.

Spoon, *n.* part of the breast.—*v.* to attempt to feed with a spoon.

Spoon-bill-duck, *n.* the scaup.

Spoonge, *v.* to sponge for food. Cf. Sponge.

Spoon-hale, *adj.* able to enjoy one's food; in capital health.

Spoon-mouth, *n.* the hollow part of a spoon.

Spoon-shaft, -shank, *n.* the handle of a spoon.

Spoot, *v.* to spout; to spew; to run in a frisky way.—*n.* a spout; a spurt; a frisky run. Cf. Spout.

Spoot, *n.* the razor-fish. Cf. Spout.

Spootcher, *n.* a bucket with long handle for baling. Cf. Spoucher.

Spooter, *n.* a squirt, syringe; a tin tube for shooting peas.

Spootragh, *n.* drink of any kind. Cf. Spoutroch.

Sporge, *v.* to sprinkle. Cf. Spairge.

Sporne, *ppl.* spared.

Spot, *n.* any person or thing remarkable, or that attracts attention. Cf. Spat.

Spotch, *v.* to poach; to go seeking trifles. Cf. Spoach.

Spot-preen, *n.* a kind of pin used in playing with the teetotum.

Spottie, *v.* to run with great speed.—*n.* a 'will-o'-the-wisp.'

Spotty, *n.* a designation of a fox.

Spoucher, *n.* a long-handled wooden ladle, used to bale a boat or lift fish out. Cf. Spootcher.

Spounge, *v.* to sponge for food. Cf. Sponge.

Spousal, *adj.* betrothed.

Spouse, Spouss, *v.* to put one's fortune out to nurse.

Spout, *v.* to spurt; to come with a rush; to dart forth; to run forth briskly; to run in a frisky way; to press rapidly through a narrow gap; to spue; to recite, give a recitation, to 'orate.'—*n.* a spurt; a sudden rush; a frisky run; a boggy part of a road; a boggy spring; a runnel of water; a waterfall; a large coal-shoot; a horn, trumpet; a squirt, syringe; a shot-gun.

Spout, Spout-fish, *n.* the razor-fish.

Spouter, *n.* a squirt. Cf. Spooter.

Spout-gun, *n.* a pop-gun.

Spoutie, *adj.* vain; foppish.

Spoutiness, *n.* the state of having many boggy springs.

Spoutroch, *n.* any kind of drink; weak, washy drink.

Spout-well, *n.* a well with a pump or spout.

Spout-whale, *n.* a porpoise.

Spouty, *adj.* marshy; abounding in springs.

Sprach, *v.* to scream, shriek.—*n.* a shriek. Cf. Spraich.

Sprachle, Sprachel, *v.* to scramble; to clamber; to sprawl. Cf. Sprauchle.

Sprack, *adj.* lively, animated; brisk, smart, nimble.

Sprack, *n.* a spark.—*v.* to throw off sparks.

Sprackle, *v.* to sprawl. Cf. Sprauchle.

Sprag, *n.* a piece of wood or iron inserted in the spokes of a wheel to arrest progress.—*v.* to insert a 'sprag' in the spokes of a wheel; to check one's progress.

Spraghle, *v.* to sprawl. Cf. Sprauchle.

Spraich, *v.* to cry shrilly or peevishly; to scream; to wail.—*n.* a cry; a shriek; a wail; a child's scream; a crowd, swarm; cock-crow.

Spraichle, *v.* to sprawl. Cf. Sprauchle.

Spraich o' day, *n.* daybreak.

Spraichrie, *n.* cattle-'lifting'; stolen goods. Cf. Spreagherie.

Spraickle, *v.* to sprawl. Cf. Sprauchle.

Spraigherie, *n.* stolen goods. Cf. Spreagherie.

Spraikle, *v.* to speckle. Cf. Spreckle.

Spraing, Sprain, *n.* a long stripe or streak; a variegated streak; a streamer; a shade of colour.—*v.* to streak ; to stripe ; to variegate ; to tint ; to embroider with sprays on silk.

Spraint, *v.* to run or spring forward ; to 'sprint.'

Spraith, *n.* a crowd ; a quantity, large number.

Sprallich, *v.* to sprawl.

Sprallich, *v.* to shriek.—*n.* a loud, shrill cry.

Sprangle, *v.* to struggle ; to spring in order to get free ; to sprawl.

Sprangled, *ppl. adj.* used of hens : speckled.

Sprat, **Spratt**, *n.* long rough grass growing on marshy places ; the jointed-leaved rush. Cf. Spret, Sprot.

Spratoon, *n.* the red-throated diver.

Sprattle, **Spratle**, *v.* to scramble ; to struggle ; to sprawl.—*n.* a scramble ; a struggle ; a sprawl.

Sprauch, *n.* a sparrow ; the house-sparrow. Cf. Sprug.

Sprauch, *v.* to sprawl.

Sprauchle, **Spraughle**, **Sprawchle**, *v.* to climb, clamber ; to scramble ; to struggle towards ; to sprawl.—*n.* a struggle ; a scramble ; a sprawl.

Sprauge, *n.* a long, lean, clumsy finger, toe, hand, or foot. Cf. Sprog.

Sprawls, *n.* limbs ; pieces, shreds ; tatters.

Spread, *v.* in *phr.* to ' spread a piece,' to butter bread.

Spreading-drink, *n.* an old trade drinking-custom.

Spreagh, *n.* cattle-' lifting ' ; plunder, spoil.

Spreagherie, *n.* cattle-' lifting ' ; small booty, movables of an inferior kind ; stolen goods.

Spreat, *n.* the jointed-leaved rush. Cf. Sprat, Spret, Sprot.

Spreath, *n.* cattle-' lifting.' Cf. Spreagh.

Sprech, *v.* to scream. Cf. Spraich.

Sprecherie, *n.* stolen goods ; movables of no great value. Cf. Spreagherie.

Spreckle, *v.* to speckle ; to become speckled. —*n.* a speckle ; a freckle.

Spreckly, *adj.* speckled, spotted.

Spree, *n.* a frolic ; merrymaking ; a jollification ; a quarrel, fight, hubbub, disturbance. —*v.* to frolic ; to make merry ; to spend money in a 'spree' ; to indulge in drunken, noisy, or riotous mirth.

Spree, *adj.* brisk, lively, 'spry' ; neat, trim, gaudy, spruce.—*v.* to smarten up ; to make spruce.

Spreet, *n.* a mischievous young person.

Spreeth, *n.* in *phr.* 'a great spreeth o' fowk,' a crowd of people much scattered.

Spreich, *v.* to scream. Cf. Spraich.

Spreich, *n.* cattle-' lifting.' Cf. Spreagh.

Spreicherie, *n.* movables of little value ; cattle-' lifting.' Cf. Spreagherie.

Spreid, **Spreed**, *v.* to spread.

Spreiden, *ppl.* spread.

Spreidit, *v. pret.* did spread.

Spreit, *n.* the jointed-leaved rush. Cf. Spret.

Sproith-hunting, *n.* the search for, and salving of, the wreckage and cargo of timber-laden ships.

Sprend, *v.* to spring suddenly forward. Cf. Sprent.

Sprent, *n.* an opening ; a hole.

Sprent, *v.* to sprinkle.—*ppl.* sprinkled.

Sprent, *v.* to spring suddenly forward ; to sprint.—*n.* the spring at the back of a pocket-knife ; the spring or elastic force of any-thing ; any elastic body ; the spine ; the iron clasp that fastens down the lid of a chest or trunk. Cf. Sprint.

Sprentacles, **Sprenticles**, *n.* spectacles.

Spret, **Sprett**, *n.* the jointed-leaved rush. Cf. Sprit.

Spretty, *adj.* full of rushes.

Sprety, *adj.* sprightly. Cf. Spirity, Spritty.

Sprewl, **Spreul**, *v.* to sprawl, scramble, struggle.—*n.* a struggle ; one who struggles hard against difficulties, implying a diminutive person.

Spried, *v. pret.* did spread.

Sprig, *n.* the house-sparrow. Cf. Sprug.

Sprig, *n.* a tune, piece of music. Cf. Spring.

Sprig, *adj.* brisk, active.

Sprightful, *adj.* sprightly.

Sprightfulness, *n.* sprightliness ; sparkle.

Sprighty, *adj.* sprightly.

Spring, *n.* a quick, lively tune.

Spring, *v.* to work briskly and rapidly.

Springald, **Springal**, *n.* a stripling.

Springer, *n.* a trout, so called from its leaping.

Spring-head, *n.* a fountain-head ; a source, origin.

Spring-juices, *n.* the name of a nauseous medicinal potion compounded of brooklime, scurvy-grass, and other ingredients.

Springle, *n.* a stripling. Cf. Springald.

Springlin, *n.* a young fellow. Cf. Springald.

Sprint, *v.* to spring, leap forward.—*n.* the spring or clasp of a knife, &c. Cf. Sprent.

Sprit, *n.* the jointed-leaved rush. Cf. Spret.

Sprit, *adv.* quite.

Sprithy, *adj.* full of rushes. Cf. Spritty.

Sprit-new, *adj.* quite new.

Spritt, *v.* to run off suddenly.

Sprittl't, *ppl. adj.* speckled, spotted. Cf. Spruttled.

Spritty, *adj.* full of spirit ; inspiriting ; inspired. Cf. Spirity.

Spritty, *adj.* full of rushes ; full of tough roots.

Sproag, *v.* to court under cloud of night. Cf. Sprog.

Sproaging, *n.* courting under cloud of night.

Sprog, *n.* a long, lean, clumsy finger, toe, hand, or foot. Cf. Sprauge.

Sprog, *n.* a house-sparrow. Cf. Sprug.

Sprog, *v.* to court under cloud of night.

Sprone, *n.* sea-birds' liquid dung.—*v.* used of birds: to eject liquid dung.

Sproo, *n.* a disease, other than the thrush, affecting the mouths of infants.

Sprool, *n.* a hand-line for deep-sea fishing; a wire or piece of whalebone fixed crosswise at the end of a line, carrying a 'snood' and a hook at each end.

Sproot, *v.* to sprout.—*n.* a child.

Sproot, *v.* to spirt from the mouth.

Sprootens, *n.* the sproutings of potato 'eyes.'

Sproot-sail, *n.* a sprit-sail.

Sproozle, Sproosle, *v.* to struggle.—*n.* an anxious bustle; a hurried exertion.

Sprose, *v.* to boast, brag; to swagger, make a great show; to commend one's self ostentatiously; to magnify in narration.—*n.* brag, bravado; ostentatious appearance, swagger; a by-word.

Sproser, *n.* a braggart, boaster.

Sprosie, *adj.* ostentatious in language; much given to self-praise.

Sprot, Sprote, *n.* a coarse kind of grass; the jointed-leaved rush; the withered stem of any plant, broken and lying on the ground; refuse of plants gathered for fuel; a chip of wood flying from a carpenter's tool; the end of a stalk of grain, or branch of a tree, blown off by a high wind. Cf. Sprat, Spret, Sprit.

Sprotten, *adj.* made of 'sprots.'

Sproug, *n.* the house-sparrow. Cf. Sprug.

Sproulzie, *n.* a fierce conflict; a sharp skirmish.

Sprouse, *v.* to brag, boast. Cf. Sprose.

Sprouser, *n.* a braggart. Cf. Sproser.

Sprout, *v.* to rub off the sprouts of potatoes. —*n.* a child; offspring.

Sprout, *v.* to spirt from the mouth.

Sprowse, *v.* to brag. Cf. Sprose.

Spruch, *v.* to smarten up. Cf. Sprush.

Sprud, *n.* a spud for removing limpets from a rock.

Sprug, *n.* the house-sparrow.

Sprung, *ppl. adj.* tipsy.

Sprunt, *v.* to run quickly; to run among the stacks after the girls at night. Cf. Splunt.

Sprunting, *n.* running among the stacks after the girls at night.

Sprush, *adj.* spruce, neat, smart.—*v.* to deck, smarten up; used of birds: to raise up the feathers; to dress up finely; to set in order. —*n.* a decking out; a setting in order.

Sprushle, *v.* to struggle. Cf. Sproozle.

Spruttings, *n.* sproutings.

Spruttled, *ppl. adj.* speckled, spotted. Cf. Sprittl't, Spurtlit.

Spry, *adj.* brisk, nimble; sprightly, lively; spruce; smartly dressed.

Spryauch, *v.* to scream harshly.—*n.* a shrill scream; a little, active, noisy person. Cf. Spraich.

Spryly, *adv.* quickly, briskly.

Spryness, *n.* sprightliness, liveliness.

Spud, *n.* a potato; a potato-set; a fondling-name for a small boy.

Spuddy, *n.* a fondling-name for a small boy.

Spudyoch, *n.* any sputtering produced by ignition; a small cone of moistened gunpowder set fire to at the apex, a 'peeoy'; a diminutive person who speaks or acts rapidly.

Spue, *v.* used of smoke: to pour forth. Cf. Spew.

Spug, *n.* the house-sparrow; a tall, thin person. Cf. Speug.

Spuilzie, Spuilie, Spuilyie, Spuilly, *v.* to plunder. Cf. Spulyie.

Spule, *n.* a thin, flat piece of wood.

Spule, *n.* a weaver's shuttle. Cf. Spool.

†**Spule,** *n.* the shoulder; a limb. Cf. Spaul.

Spule-bane, -blade, *n.* the shoulder-bone or -blade.

Spule-fittit, *adj.* splay-footed; with the feet turned outwards.

Spulie, *n.* a spool.

Spulp, *v.* to collect and retail scandal; to be a busybody or eavesdropper.

Spulper, *n.* a busybody, an eavesdropper; a collector of scandal.

Spulyie, Spulzie, *v.* to plunder, sack; to spoil, lay waste; to romp.—*n.* depredation; a plundering raid; the act of spoiling; spoil, booty, plunder; illegal meddling with movable goods.

Spulyiement, *n.* spoil, booty.

Spulyie-play, *n.* a plundering raid; a popular outbreak of destructiveness.

Spulyier, *n.* a plunderer.

Spun, *n.* tobacco-twist.

Spune, *n.* a spoon. Cf. Spoon.

Spune-drift, *n.* snow drifted from the ground by a whirling wind.

Spune-hale, *adj.* able to take one's usual food. Cf. Meat-hale.

Spung, *n.* a heavy blow.

Spung, *v.* to stride. Cf. Spong.

Spung, *v.* to broach a cask of wine, &c.

Spung, Spunge, *n.* a purse that closes with a spring; a fob.—*v.* to rob; to pick one's pocket.

Spung, *n.* the leg of a fowl, 'drumstick.'

Spunga, *n.* a flecked cow.

Spung and rung, *n.* the stick or board on which boys 'spang-hewed' a toad.

Spunge, *n.* putrid moisture oozing from a dead body. Cf. Sponge.

Spungit, *ppl. adj.* flecked, mottled.

Spunk, *n.* a spark of fire; a very small fire; the spark of life; an old-fashioned match tipped with sulphur, used for kindling purposes; a lucifer-match; spirit, pluck, vivacity: a person of quick temper; a person who has more spirit than bodily strength; a small portion of any principle of intelligence or action. —*v.* to sparkle, twinkle; with *out*, to come to light, become known; with *up*, to fire up, flash forth.

Spunk-backet, *adj.* having a slender back.

Spunk-basket, *n.* a basket for holding 'spunks.'

Spunk-box, *n.* a match-box; a tinder box.

Spunk-flask, *n.* a powder-flask.

Spunkie, *n.* a small fire; a will-o'-the-wisp; a lively young fellow; a false teacher; an irritable person; phosphorescence of the sea; liquor, whisky.—*adj.* haunted by will-o'-the-wisps; irritable, fiery; lively, spirited; plucky, mettlesome.

Spunkie-clootie, *n.* the devil.

Spunkie-haunted, *adj.* haunted by will-o'-the-wisps.

Spunkie-howe, *n.* a hollow haunted by will-o'-the-wisps.

Spunkie-piece, *n.* a fowling-piece.

Spunk-maker, -man, *n.* a maker of matches.

Spunk-seller, *n.* one who sells matches.

Spunk-wood, *n.* matchwood; small splinters.

Spur, *n.* a spirituous stimulant.—*v.* to run fast; to kick about, sprawl; to scrape, as a cock or hen on a dunghill.

Spur, Spurr, *n.* the sparrow; a little person of lively disposition; a tall, thin person.

Spur, Spure, *v.* to ask. Cf. Speer.

Spur, *n.* a disease in rye.

Spur-bauk, *n.* a cross-beam in the roof of a house.

Spurd, *n.* the house-sparrow; a little person of lively disposition.

Spurdie, *n.* the house-sparrow; any thin object nearly worn out.

Spure, *v. pret.* did ask. Cf. Speer.

Spur-faang, *n.* a person of a sour, dogged disposition; an atom; a very small piece.

Spurg, *n.* the house-sparrow.

Spurgaw, *v.* to apply spurs; to gall with spurs; to irritate.

Spurgie, *n.* the house-sparrow; a nickname for one whose step is like the hop of a sparrow.

Spur-hawk, *n.* the sparrow-hawk; a little person of lively disposition.

Spurkle, *n.* a wooden stirring-rod; a broad 'spattle' for thatching with, or for beating flax. Cf. Spurtle.

Spurl, *v.* to sprawl, kick about. Cf. Spur.

Spur-leathers, *n.* understrappers, people of no importance.

Spurmuick, *n.* an atom; a particle.

Spurrie-how, *n.* the sparrow-hawk.—*v.* to run as fast as a sparrow-hawk flies.

Spurtle, *v.* to move the feet restlessly; to kick with the feet.

Spurtle, Spurtil, *n.* a wooden rod for stirring porridge, &c., when boiling; a wooden or iron 'spattle' for turning bread in firing; a ludicrous name for a sword.

Spurtle-blade, *n.* a sword.

Spurtle-braid, *n.* a wooden 'spattle' for turning bread in firing; a wooden stirring-rod.

Spurtle-leggit, *adj.* having 'spurtle-legs.'

Spurtle-legs, *n.* thin, spindly legs.

Spurtle-stick, *n.* a 'spurtle-braid.'

Spurtlit, *ppl. adj.* speckled, spotted. Cf. Spruttled.

Spur-whang, *n.* a leather strap or thong of a spur; a thing of little or no worth.

Sputter, *v.* to splutter.—*n.* a splutter, outcry, fuss.

Spyaller, *v.* to sprawl. Cf. Spaller.

Spy-ann, *n.* a variety of 'hide-and-seek.'

Spyauck, *n.* an example, guide.

Spy-glass, *n.* an eye-glass.

Spyke, *v.* to speak.

Spy-knowe, *n.* a hill on which a watch is set.

Spyle, *v.* to sample cheese with a scoop.

Spyler, *n.* a cheese-scoop.

Spyle-tree, *n.* a long pole, supported horizontally, on which fishing-lines, after use, are gathered for the cleaning of the hooks. Cf. Spile-tree.

Spyndle, *n.* four hanks of yarn. Cf. Spindle.

Spyniel, *n.* a 'spyndle.'

Spynner, *v.* to run swiftly, to move with a spinning motion. Cf. Spinner.

Spyo, *n.* the game of 'hide-and-seek.'

Spyogg, *n.* a paw, hand, foot, a limb. Cf. Spiog, Spoig.

Spyug, *n.* the house-sparrow. Cf. Spug.

Spyung, *v.* to carry off clandestinely; to filch; to walk with long, quick steps; to stride along stealthily.—*n.* a person of disagreeable temper and manners; a worthless fellow. Cf. Spung.

Spy-wife, *n.* an inquisitive woman.

Squaach, *v.* to scream; to squawk.—*n.* the noise a hare makes when a-killing. Cf. Squaich.

Squaar, *adj.* square.

Squabash, *n.* a splutter.

Squach, *v.* to cry out; to squawk. Cf. Squaich.

Squack, *v.* to cry out; to cry as a child.

Squad, *n.* a number of people; a 'crew'; a 'core'; a squadron.

Squade, *n.* a squadron.

Squagh, *v.* to scream. Cf. Squaich.

Squaich, Squaigh, *n.* a loud scream; the cry of a bird or beast when being caught.—*v.* used of a fowl: to scream; to squall.

Squaint, *adj.* squinting. Cf. Squint.

Squair, *n.* a gentle depression between two hills.

Squall, Squal, *n.* a row; a disturbance; a wrangle; a burst of temper.

Squalloch, Squallach, Squalach, *v.* to scream, squeal, squall.—*n.* a loud cry. Cf. Skelloch.

Squalloching, *ppl. adj.* noisy in manners and shrill in voice.

Squander, *v.* to disperse, scatter.

Square, *v.* to assume a fighting or pugilistic, forward attitude.—*n.* an equal game in golf.—*adv.* exactly, properly.

Square-man, *n.* a carpenter.

Squares, *n.* the game of hop-scotch.

Square-wricht, *n.* a joiner who works in the finer kinds of furniture.

Squash, *v.* to splash; to dash water; to fall heavily into water.—*n.* the act of splashing; a dash of water; the sound of a heavy fall into water.—*adv.* slap-dash; with a sudden fall.

Squat, *n.* a contemptuous movement of the nose.

Squat, *v.* to strike with the open hand.—*n.* a blow thus given.

Squatter, Squater, *v.* to crouch, squat; to flap or flutter in the water, as a duck; to move quickly; to scatter; to squander.

Squatter, *n.* a large collection of small objects; a swarm.

Squattle, *v.* to squat, settle down; to sprawl.

Squattle, *v.* to swill, drink deeply.

Squaw-hole, *n.* a broad, shallow, muddy pool.

Squeal, *v.* to grumble, scold; with *on,* to inform against.—*n.* an outcry; a broil; a debauch, 'spree.'

Squech, *v.* to squall. Cf. Squaich.

Squeeb, *n.* a name given to an obnoxious person. Cf. Squib.

Squeef, *n.* a mean, disreputable person; one shabby in appearance and conduct.

Squeefy, *adj.* disreputable, mean-looking.

Squeek-squaakin, *adj.* used of shoes or boots: creaking.

Squeeky, *adj.* squeaking.

Squeel, *n.* a school.—*v.* to educate.

Squeel, *n.* too great sourness of buttermilk for use.

Squeel, *n.* a great number of people.

Squeel, *v.* to grumble. Cf. Squeal.

Squeem, *n.* the motion of a fish as observed by its effect on the surface of the water, including the idea of the shadow made by the fish.

Squeengy, Squeergy, *v.* to wander, as a dog, from place to place.

Squeery, *v.* to 'squeengy.'

Squeesh, *v.* to squeeze; to squash; used of water, &c.: to squirt, gush out.—*n.* the sound of water suddenly poured out.

Squeeter, *v.* to scatter; to work weakly and unskilfully.—*n.* weak, unskilful work; a confused mess; a 'scutter'; a weak, careless, or unskilful worker.

Squeeterer, *n.* a 'squeeter.'

Squeetering, Squeetrin, *ppl. adj.* weak and unskilful; scattering.

Squeever, *n.* a squall of wind.

Squelch, *v.* to make a noise, as when walking in wet boots.

Squelching, *n.* a drenching.

Squent, *adv.* diagonally.

Squib, *n.* used of lightning: a flash; a name given to an obnoxious person.

Squibe, *v.* used of a top: to run off to the side when it ceases to spin.

Squigged, *adj.* crooked.

Squile, *v.* to squeal.—*n.* a squeal.

†**Squinacy,** *n.* a quinsy.

Squint, *v.* to look slyly; to go in a slanting direction; to slant.—*n.* a passing glance.—*adj.* squinting.

Squinty, Squiny, *n.* a woman's cap.

Squinty-mutch, *n.* a 'squinty.'

Squirbile, *adj.* ingenious; versatile.

Squirl, *n.* an ornamental twist, tail, or flourish in writing.

Squirr, *v.* to throw with a whirling motion; to make a thin stone skim along the water or the surface of the land; to go off quickly; to whirl.

Squirrly-wirly, *n.* an ornamental appendage to clothes, &c.

Squirt, *adv.* with a bang.

Squish, *v.* to squash; used of water: to gush suddenly out. Cf. Squeesh.

Squiss, *v.* to beat up an egg.

Squodgie-wark, *n.* hard drudgery; a scullion's work. Cf. Scodgy.

Squoil, *v.* to squeal.—*n.* a squeal.

Squrbuile, *adj.* ingenious. Cf. Squirbile.

Sramullion, *n.* a fit of ill-humour; a fit of pettishness; a 'huff.' Cf. Stramullion.

Sruffle, *v.* to scrape the surface of anything; to 'scuffle' the surface of ground and kill weeds.

St, *int.* a call to a dog, by way of inciting it.

Sta, *n.* a stall; a surfeit; a feeling of dislike; a nuisance, annoyance.—*v.* to surfeit; to cloy; to disgust; to weary. Cf. Staw.

Sta, *v. pret.* stole.

Stab, *n.* a prickle, thorn. Cf. Stob.

Stab, *n.* a stake; a wooden post; a stool, seat.—*v.* to fix stakes into the ground; to stake off, enclose with stakes.

Stab and stow, *adv.* completely.

Stab-callant, *n.* a short, thick fellow.

Stab-gaud, *n.* a set-line for fishing, fixed to a small stake thrust into the bank to preserve the line from being carried off.

Stable, *n.* a marsh or bog in which a horse has foundered.

Stabled, *ppl. adj.* used of a horse: foundered in a marsh or bog.

Stable-meal, *n.* the liquor drunk in an inn by farmers in return for stabling for their horses.

Stabler, *n.* a stable-keeper.

Stab-munted, *adj.* used of a gap in a hedge: repaired with stakes.

Stacher, *v.* to stagger, totter.—*n.* a stagger, reel.

Stachie, *adj.* stiff, lazy, not energetic.

Stachie, *n.* an uproar, disturbance; a frolic. Cf. Stashie.

Stack, *v. pret.* stuck.

Stack, *v. pret.* and *ppl.* stabbed, butchered.

Stack, *n.* in *pl.* a game of 'hide-and-seek' among stacks in a stackyard; 'barley-bracks.'

Stacker, *v.* to stagger, reel.—*n.* a stagger. Cf. Stacher.

Stacket, *n.* a palisade, stockade.—*v.* to palisade.

Stack-meels, **-mools**, *n.* peat-dust and broken peat found at peat-stacks.

Stack-mou', *n.* the end of a peat-stack at which peats are taken away.

Stacky, *n.* a stack; a stackyard.

Staddle, *n.* the lower part of a corn-stack as far as the sides are upright; a small temporary stack.

Staddle, *n.* a mark made by one thing lying on another.

Staddling, *n.* a surface-blemish.

Staddling, *n.* the foundation of a stack; the materials of it.

Stadge, *n.* a fit of ill-humour; a pet, huff.

Staffage, *adj.* dry in the mouth; not easily swallowed.

Staff and baton, *n.* a symbol of the resignation of property or feudal right into the hands of another.

Staff and burdon with one, *n.* an open rupture with one.

Staff-end, *n.* a proper distance, arm's-length.

Staff-man, *n.* a baton-man.

Staff-swerd, *n.* a sword-stick.

Staffy-nevel, *n.* a staff in hand; a cudgelling.—*adj.* in *phr.* a 'staffy-nevel job,' a fight with cudgels.

Stag, *n.* a young horse; a stallion. Cf. Staig.

Stag, *n.* a stake, pile.—*v.* to stake; to drive stakes into the ground.

Stag, *adj.* used of skins: dried simply in the open air.

Stage, *n.* an informal trial; the bar.—*v.* to accuse without formal trial; to put on trial.

Stage, *v.* to walk about in a stately or prancing manner; to saunter. Cf. Stairge, Staig.

Staggering-bob, *n.* a very young calf, or its veal.

Staggie, *adj.* used of grain: thin.

Staggrel, *n.* one who staggers in walking.

Stagher, *v.* to stagger. Cf. Stacher.

Staidle, *n.* a staddle; the lower part of a stack. Cf. Staddle.

Staig, *v.* to stalk with a slow, stately step; to walk where one should not be found.—*n.* a slow, stately step. Cf. Staik, Stairge.

Staig, *n.* a stallion; a young courtier. Cf. Stag.

Staigh, *v.* to stuff, cram; to gorge. Cf. Stech.

Staik, *n.* butcher's meat.

Staik, *v.* to walk with a slow, stately step; to stalk where one should not be found.—*n.* a slow, stately step; the act of walking so. Cf. Staig.

Staik, *v.* to accommodate, supply; to suit, satisfy. Cf. Stake.

Stail, *n.* the foundation or under-part of a stack; the mother-hive of bees.—*v.* to lay properly the bottom sheaves of a stack.

Stail, *n.* a gathering of urine.—*v.* used of horses and cattle: to urinate.

Staill, **Staille**, *n.* a foundation. Cf. Stail.

Stail-sheaf, *n.* a bottom sheaf of a stack.

Stainch, *adj.* staunch.—*v.* to stanch; to stay hunger. Cf. Stanch.

Staincher, *n.* a stanchion.

Staincher-fittit, *adj.* ? with feet like stanchions, owing to stiff fetlock-joints.

Staing, *n.* the mast of a boat; a pole. Cf. Stang.

Stainzie, *v.* to stain; to fade in colour.

Stair, *n.* a flight of stairs.

Stair-fit, *n.* the bottom of a flight of stairs.

Stairge, *v.* to walk very magisterially; to prance. Cf. Staig.

Stair-heid, *n.* the top of a flight of stairs.

Stair-heid manawge, *n.* a sort of fireside accommodation-bank for the housewives in a tenement, with weekly contributions and 'draws.' Cf. Manadge.

Stair-pit, *n.* a coal-pit in which the miners could descend or ascend by a ladder erected from top to bottom in short lengths.

Staithle, *n.* the under-part of a stack. Cf. Staidle.

Staive, *v.* to sprain; to push against: to go about aimlessly.—*n.* a sprain; a heavy blow. Cf. Stave.

Staivelt, *n.* a stupid person.

Staiver, *n.* an easy-going person; a saunter; in *pl.* bits, fragments.—*v.* to saunter; to wander; to tumble. Cf. Staver.

Stake, *v.* to supply. Cf. Staik.

Stake, *v.* to stalk. Cf. Staik.

Stake and rice, **rise**, or **ryse**, *n.* a fence of upright stakes interlaced with boughs, wattles, &c.; a partition or wall of brush-wood or lath; anything incomplete, sketchy, or in outline or skeleton.

Stakey, *n.* a game at marbles in which stakes are played for.

Stakker, *v.* to stagger. Cf. Stacher.

Stale, *n.* the mother-hive of bees; the under-part of a stack. Cf. Stail.

Stale, *adj.* barren.—*v.* to disgust.

Stale, *v. pret.* stole.

Stale-fishing, *n.* fishing with a 'stell-net.'

Stale-sheaf, *n.* a sheaf laid at the bottom of a stack.

Stalk, *n.* a handle; a pipe-stem.

Stalk, *n.* a quantity.

Stall, *n.* a manger; a surfeit.—*v.* to surfeit. Cf. Staw.

Stall, *v.* used of horses and cattle: to urinate. Cf. Stail.

Stallange, Stallinge, *n.* rent paid for a market-stall.

Stallanger, Stallinger, *n.* one who pays rent for a market-stall; a person, not a freeman, who, for a consideration to his corporation, is allowed to carry on business for a year.

Stalliard, *adj.* stout, vigorous, valiant; stately, gallant. Cf. Stalward.

Stallworthe, *adj.* brave and strong; stalwart.

Stallyoch, *n.* a thick stalk of grain standing by itself.

Stalward, *adj.* used of persons: valiant, 'stalliard'; of things: stout, strong; hard, severe; stormy, tempestuous.

Stalyard, *n.* a steelyard.

Stam, *v.* to strike down the feet with violence in walking.

Stamach, Stamack, Stamick, *n.* the stomach. Cf. Stomach.

Stamachet, *ppl. adj.* stomached.

Stamachless, *adj.* without appetite.

Stamfish, *adj.* strong, robust; coarse, rank; unruly.

Stammacker, Stammager, *n.* a stomacher; a busk; a slip of stay-wood used by women.

Stammackie, *n.* a child's stomach.

Stammagust, Stammagast, *n.* a disgust at food; a disagreeable surprise.

Stammel, *n.* a coarse kind of red.

Stammel, Stammle, *v.* to stumble. Cf. Stample.

Stammer, *v.* to stagger, stumble; to blunder; to hesitate, falter.—*n.* a stumble, stagger.

Stammeral, *n.* an awkward blunderer; a blockhead; a stammerer; one who falters in speech.—*adj.* half-witted.

Stammerel, *n.* friable stone.

Stammerers, *n.* detached pieces of limestone.

Stammering, *ppl. adj.* rude, noisy; awkward, blundering.

Stamp, *n.* a trap; a snare.

Stamp, *n.* the cramp; a qualm of conscience; remorse.

Stamp-cole, *n.* a small rick of corn or hay erected in the field.

Stamphish, *adj.* robust. Cf. Stamfish.

Stampin-irons, *n.* branding-irons.

Stample, *v.* to stumble, stagger, totter; to stumble in upon.

Stam-ram, *v.* to go into a thing recklessly; to walk roughly and noisily.—*adj.* noisy, rough walking.—*n.* a noisy, rude person.—*adv.* rudely, noisily, recklessly. Cf. Ram-stam.

Stan, *v.* to stand. Cf. Stand.

Stan, *n.* a stone. Cf. Stane.

Stanart, *n.* a standard. Cf. Standart.

Stan-blin, *adj.* quite blind.

Stance, *n.* a standing-place, station; the line from which marbles are played; a stand-still; a site; a building-area; a stall; a separate place for each animal in a stable or 'byre'; the field, &c., in which a fair or cattle-market is held.—*v.* to station.

Stanch, *adj.* staunch; in good health; reso-lute.—*n.* satisfaction, surfeit.—*v.* to satisfy with food or drink; to stanch blood; to desist, stay; to recall a dog from pursuit.

Stanchel, *n.* a stanchion; a wooden or iron window-bar.—*v.* to supply with stanchions.

Stanchel, *n.* the kestrel.

Stancher, *n.* a stanchion; an iron window-bar.

Stanch-girss, *n.* the yarrow or milfoil.

Stancie, *n.* a 'stance.'

Stancle, *n.* the wheatear; the stonechat. Cf. Steinkle.

Stand, *v.* to place, set, make to stand; used of a clock, &c.: to stop; to rise up; to continue, last; to hesitate, scruple, refrain; to object; to cost; to continue solvent; to play in a game of cards; to treat to.—*n.* a stall at fair or market; the goods exposed thereon for sale; a barrel set on end; a water-bucket; a standstill; a place to make a halt at; a complete suit of clothes, or of single articles forming a set; cost, outlay. —*int.* a call to horses to halt or stand still.

Standart, *n.* stature; an old inhabitant; one with a long residence.

Stand at, *v.* to feel great disgust at food, so as to be unable to swallow or to retain it.

Stander, *n.* a pillar; an animal's leg; a barrel set on end.

Stand for, *v.* to be surety for; to sail towards.

Stand good, *v.* to be surety for; to hold good, be settled.

Standie, *n.* a small or shabby stall at a fair.

Stand in, *v.* to cost.

Stand in for, *v.* to be surety for.

Standing, *ppl. adj.* able to stand; healthy; used of colour : fast.

Standing-bands, *n.* tethers for cows standing in a ' byre.'

Standing-bed, *n.* a bed with posts, one that cannot be folded up.

Standing-drink, *n.* a hasty drink, one taken standing.

Standing-graith, **-gear**, *n.* the fixtures in the machinery of a mill.

Standing-stone, *n.* an upright gravestone.

Stand one hard, *v.* to vex, grieve one.

Stand owre, *v.* to remain unpaid or undetermined.

Stand the session, *v.* to appear before the kirk-session for discipline.

Stand up, *v.* to hesitate, stickle, be irresolute ; to spend time idly.

Stand upon, *v.* to insist on.

Stand-yont, **-yon**, *v.* to stand aside ; to get out of the way.

Stane, *n.* a stone ; a curling-stone ; the rocky sea-shore.—*v.* to set with stones ; to place a heavy stone on a cheese.—*adv.* as used intensively : utterly, completely.

Stane-bark, *n.* liverwort, a lichen yielding a purple dye.

Stane-crib, *n.* a gaol.

Stane-blin, *adj.* stone-blind, quite blind.

Stane-cast, *n.* a stone's-throw.

Stane-chack, **-chacker**, *n.* the stonechat; the whinchat ; the wheatear.

Stane-chapper, *n.* a stone-breaker ; a contemptuous name for a geologist.

Stanecher, *n.* a stanchion. Cf. Stancher.

Stane-clod, *n.* a stone's-throw.

Stane-couples, *n.* stone arches instead of timber, across which rough spars were laid for supporting thatch.

Stane-dead, *adj.* quite dead.

Stane-dumb, *adj.* quite dumb ; totally silent.

Stane-dunder, *n.* an explosion of firearms ; the sound of a heap of stones falling.

Stane-dyke, *n.* a stone wall.

Stane-falcon, *n.* the merlin.

Stane-fish, *n.* the spotted blenny.

Stane-gall, *n.* the kestrel. Cf. Stanel.

Stane-graze, *n.* a bruise from a stone.

Stane-hertit, *adj.* stony-hearted.

Stane-horse, *n.* a stallion.

Stane-knot, *n.* a very tight knot.

Stanel, *n.* the kestrel or wind-hover. Cf. Stane-gall.

Stane-loppen, **-loupin**, *adj.* bruised ; crushed, as by a stone.

Stane-naig, *n.* a stallion.

Stane-pecker, *n.* the purple sandpiper ; the turnstone ; the stonechat.

Staneraw, *n.* the rock-liverwort, a lichen producing a purple dye.

Staners, *n.* small stones and gravel on the margin of a river or lake. Cf. Stanner.

Stane-still, *adj.* still as a stone ; utterly without motion.

Stane-wark, *n.* masonry ; building of stone.

Stane-wod, **-wud**, *adj.* stark mad.

Stang, *v.* to sting ; to pierce, prick ; to shoot with pain.—*n.* a sting ; the act of piercing or stinging ; a sudden, sharp pain ; a dart ; the beard of barley ; the needle-fish ; in *pl.* a fit of passion.

Stang, *n.* a pole, post ; a long wooden bar ; an iron-shod pole used in floating rafts of wood down a river, like a large punting-pole ; the mast of a boat ; a boat-pole.—*v.* to cause to ride the 'stang,' to subject a wife-beater or an unfaithful husband to punishment by carrying him from place to place astride a pole borne on the shoulders of others, accompanied by a noisy and contemptuous crowd.

Stangie, *n.* a tailor.

Stang o' the trump, *n.* the chief actor ; the best of the lot ; the most attractive of a company.

Stangrill, *n.* an instrument for pushing in the straw in thatching.

Stanie, *n.* a small stone marble.

Stanieraw, *n.* rock-liverwort. Cf. Staneraw.

†Stank, *n.* a pool, a pond ; a stagnant or slow-flowing ditch ; a moat ; a very wet, marshy piece of ground ; an open drain ; a surfeit.—*v.* to drain land by open ditches ; to protect by a ditch, moat, &c. ; to entrench ; to bank up, strengthen the bank of a stream ; to fill up ; to satisfy, sate, surfeit; to stagnate.

Stank, *v.* to prick, sting ; to thrill with pain. —*n.* a sting ; a sharp, shooting pain. Cf. Stang.

Stank, *v.* to gasp for breath ; to breathe deeply.

Stank-bree, **-broo**, *n.* the edge of a pool ; the brow of a ditch.

Stank-hen, *n.* the moor-hen.

Stankie, *n.* the moor-hen.

Stankit, *ppl. adj.* moated ; surrounded by a ditch.

Stank-lochen, *n.* a stagnant pool or lakelet.

Stank-up, *v.* to render stagnant.

Stanlock, *n.* the gray lord or coal-fish in its first year ; an overgrown coal-fish.

Stannel, *n.* the kestrel. Cf. Stanel.

Stanner, *n.* small stones and gravel in the bed or by the margin of a stream.

Stanner, *n.* a stander ; a pillar ; an animal's leg. Cf. Stander.

Stanner-bed, *n.* a bed of gravel.

Stannerie, *n.* a lichen used for dyeing purple. Cf. Staneraw.

Stanner-steps, *n.* stepping-stones placed across the bed of a stream.

Stannery, *adj.* gravelly.

Stannin, *ppl. adj.* standing. Cf. Standing.

Stannyel, *n.* a stallion. Cf. Stanyel.

Stanse, *n.* a site. Cf. Stance.

Stant, *v.* to stint; to restrict.—*n.* a fixed task. Cf. Stent.

Stant, *v.* to assess, rate, tax; to confiscate.—*n.* assessment. Cf. Stent.

Stany, *adj.* stony.—*n.* a boy's marble made of stone. Cf. Stony.

Stanyel, *n.* a stallion.

Stanyel, *n.* the kestrel. Cf. Stannel.

Stap, *n.* the stave of a cask, tub, wooden bicker, &c.—*phr.* to 'fa' a' staps,' to become extremely debilitated; to fall to pieces.

Stap, *v.* to step; with *awa'*, to die. Cf. Step.

Stap, *v.* to stop; to stuff. Cf. Stop.

Stap-mither, *n.* a stepmother.

Stap-mither year, *n.* a year of great scarcity and of high prices for food, &c.

Stappack, *n.* a mixture of oatmeal and cold water, 'drammock.'

Stappie, *n.* a game of marbles, in which the player takes a step forward before firing at a number of marbles placed within a fixed area.

Stappil, *n.* a stopper. Cf. Stapple.

Stappin, *n.* stuffing for filling fishes' heads.

Stappin-stane, *n.* a stepping-stone.

Stappit-heads, *n.* haddocks' heads stuffed with a mixture of oatmeal, suet, onions, and pepper. Cf. Crappit-heads.

Stapple, *n.* a staple for fixing wire to posts; an 'eye' in a gate-post for holding a hook to fasten the gate.

Stapple, *n.* a stopple, stopper, plug; a pipe-stem; a handful of straw tied at one end, used for thatching.

Stapplick, *n.* a stopper; a catch or fastening for a bar or bolt.

Stapplick, *n.* a pipe-stem; a handful of straw tied at one end, used for thatching.

Star, *n.* the pupil of the eye; a speck in the eye; cataract.

Stare, *v.* to face; used of a horse's or cow's coat: to stand out when roughened by cold, &c.

Stare, *adj.* austere, stern; used of the voice: strong; harsh and rough. Cf. Stour.

Starglint, *n.* a shooting-star.

Staring-mad, *adj.* very mad.

Stark, *adj.* used of liquor: potent, intoxicating; stiff, unbending; rigid in death; quite naked; sheer, arrant, utter.—*adv.* utterly, altogether; strenuously.

Starn, *adj.* stern.

Starn, *n.* the stern of a ship, &c.

Starn, *n.* a star; the eye; the pupil of the eye. Cf. Stern.

Starn, Starne, *n.* a grain, a particle; a very small quantity; the outermost point of a needle.

Starn, *n.* the starling.

Starned, *ppl. adj.* starred.

Starn-fall, *n.* the fungus, *Nostoc commune.*

Starnie, *n.* a very small quantity.

Starn-keeper, *n.* an astronomer; a star-gazer.

Starnless, *adj.* starless.

Starn-licht, *n.* starlight; the flash of light seen when the eye receives a slight blow.

Starny, *adj.* starry.

Starr, Star, *n.* various species of sedges; the lesser tufted sedge; the moss-rush.

Starrach, *adj.* used of the weather: cold; disagreeable; boisterous.

Star-sheen, *n.* starlight.

Starshie, *n.* a frolic; banter; an uproar, disturbance. Cf. Stashie.

Start, *v.* to shrink asunder, spring asunder.—*n.* a short space of time.

Start, *n.* an upright post mortised into the shafts of a cart, into which the boards of the side are nailed; one of the pieces of wood which support the 'awes' of a mill-wheel.

Startle, *v.* to take fright; used of cattle: to run about wildly in hot weather; to bustle about.—*n.* a scare.

Startle-o'-stovie, *n.* undulating exhalations seen rising from the ground in very hot weather.

Startling, Startling-fit, *n.* used of a woman: a desire for matrimony.

Start-up, *n.* an upstart; an interloper.

Starty, *adj.* apt to start; used of a horse: skittish, nervous.

Starve, *n.* a fit of abstinence.

Starwart, Starwort, *n.* stitchwort.

Stash, *n.* an uproar; a frolic.

Stashie, Stashy, *n.* an uproar; a disturbance, 'row'; a frolic; banter.—*v.* to frolic; to banter.

Stassel, *n.* a support for a stack to raise it above the ground; the corn which is undermost in a stack.—*v.* to build small, temporary stacks. Cf. Stathel.

State, *n.* a state of excitement, fuss, temper, &c.—*v.* to set up, establish; to endure; to instate, invest.

Stated, *ppl. adj.* situated.

Stathel, Stathle, *n.* a support for a stack; the sheaves at the foundation of a stack; a small, temporary rick.—*v.* to build in small, temporary ricks. Cf. Staddle, Stassel.

Sta'-tree, *n.* the stake in a cow-house to which a cow is bound.

Statute, *v.* to ordain; to decree by statute.

Staucher, *v.* to stagger. Cf. Stacher.

Stauchie, *adj.* close, stuffy. Cf. Stoich.

Stauf, *n.* a staff.

Staug, *v.* to stalk where one ought not to be. Cf. Staig.

Stauk, *n.* a stalk.

Stauk, *v.* to stalk.

Staul, *v.* to squint.—*n.* a squint.

Staul, *v. pret.* stole.

Staumer, *v.* to stagger; to falter. Cf. Stammer.

Staumrel, *n.* a blockhead; an awkward blunderer.—*adj.* half-witted.

Staun, Staund, *v.* to stand.—*n.* a barrel set on end, to contain water, beef, &c.; a stall. Cf. Stand.

Staunder, *n.* a pillar. Cf. Stander.

Staup, *n.* a stave of a cask. Cf. Stap.

Staup, *v.* to stride, stalk; to take long, awkward steps; to walk uncertainly, as in darkness.—*n.* a long, clumsy stride; an awkward step; a tall, awkward person.

Staup, *v. pret.* stepped.

Staupen, *ppl. adj.* awkwardly tall; stalking awkwardly.

Stav, *n.* disgust at food. Cf. Staw.

Stave, *v.* to push, drive; to beat against; to thump vigorously; to consolidate iron instruments by striking them perpendicularly on the anvil when they are half-cooled; to sprain; to walk quickly; to walk awkwardly; to walk aimlessly, or as in a reverie; to totter.—*n.* a heavy blow; a push, dash; a sprain.

Stave, *n.* a short song.

Stave-aff, *n.* an excuse, evasion; a delay.

Stavel, *v.* to stumble; to wander aimlessly.— *n.* a stumble. Cf. Stevel.

Staver, *v.* to saunter, walk listlessly; to totter; to stagger; to stumble; to wander.—*n.* a saunter; an easy-going, pleasant person; in *pl.* pieces, ruin.

Staverall, *n.* a blundering, awkward, foolish person.

Stavie, *v.* to saunter; to dawdle.

Staw, *v.* to surfeit, satiate; to disgust; to cloy; to weary, tire.—*n.* a surfeit, disrelish; a dislike, aversion; a nuisance, annoyance; a stall, a stall in a stable.

Staw, *v. pret.* stole.

Stawmer, *v.* to stagger; to hesitate. Cf. Stammer.

Stawn, *ppl.* stolen.

Stawn, *n.* a stall or stand in a market.—*v.* to stand. Cf. Stand.

Stawp, *n.* a stave of a barrel, &c. Cf. Stap.

Stawp, *v.* to take long, awkward strides. Cf. Staup.

Stawsome, *adj.* disgusting, nauseous, surfeiting.

Stay, *adj.* steep, ascending; stiff to climb. Cf. Stey.

Stay, *v.* used of a servant: to remain to the end of his or her term; to renew an engagement for a new term of service; to put to the bar.—*n.* a fixed abode.

Stayband, *n.* a horizontal plank in a door; a narrow linen band brought through the tie of an infant's cap, and fastened to its frock, to keep the head from being thrown too far back; a band for keeping the brim of a hat fast to the top.

Stayedly, *adv.* deliberately.

Stay in, *v.* to adhere to a party, church, &c.; not to separate or go forth from it.

Stay-measure, *n.* the size of corsets.

Stead, *n.* a site; a place, situation; the bottom or foundation of anything; a track, mark, impress, print; a farmhouse and buildings; a mass; a large number or quantity; a stone used to sink deep-sea fishing-lines.—*v.* to bestead; to lay a foundation; to gather, collect.—*adv.* instead.

Steadable, *adj.* necessary; serviceable; standing in good stead.

Stead-hook, *n.* the hook next to the stone used to sink the deep-sea fishing-lines. Cf. Steethe.

Steading, *n.* a site; building-land; a farmhouse and buildings; the buildings as distinguished from the farmhouse.

Stead-sheaf, *n.* a sheaf at the bottom of a stack.

Steak, *v.* to shut, close. Cf. Steek.

Steak-raid, *n.* that portion of the live-stock taken in a predatory raid which was supposed to belong to any proprietor through whose lands the prey was driven.

Steal, *n.* a theft; anything stolen.—*v.* used in golfing: to hole an unlikely 'put' from a distance.

Steal, *n.* the shaft of a barrow or plough.

Steal-bonnets, *n.* a romping game played with hats or 'bonnets' laid down at opposite ends of a field, like 'Scotch and English.'

Steal-corn, *n.* a nursery name for the forefinger.

Steal't, *v. pret.* stole.—*ppl.* stolen.

Steal-the-pigs, *n.* a game representing the stealing and recovery of a woman's children.

Steal-wads, *n.* the game of 'steal-bonnets.'

Steam-mill, *n.* a travelling steam threshing-mill.

Stear, *n.* a starling.

Steave, *adj.* stiff; sturdy; obstinate. Cf. Steeve.

Stech, *v.* to stuff, cram; to fill to repletion; to gorge, gormandize; to stuff one's self; to smell unpleasantly, stink; to groan, pant, 'pech'; to have a great many clothes on the body; to loiter; to confine one's self to a very warm room.—*n.* a greedy manner of eating, guzzling; cramming in food; a groan; a heap, crowd; a confused mass; a great number crowded in little space; heat.

Stechie, *n.* an over-feeder, gormandizer, glutton.—*adj.* heavy, stiff in the joints, lazy.

Stechle, *v.* to rustle; to emit a whistling, snoring sound through the nose. Cf. Stichle.

Sted, Stedd, *n.* a site.—*v.* to bestead. Cf. Stead.

Stedding, *n.* a farmhouse and buildings. Cf. Steading.

Steddy, *v.* to make or keep steady.

Stede, Stedt, *n.* a site. Cf. Stead.

Stee, *adj.* steep; difficult to climb. Cf. Stay.

Steech, *n.* something obnoxious.

Steed, *v. pret.* stood.

Steed, *n.* a site; an impress. Cf. Stead.

Steedge, *v.* to walk with slow, heavy step.—*n.* a slow, heavy walk; a big person of slow, quiet disposition.

Steeding, *n.* a farmstead. Cf. Steading.

Steek, *v.* to push; to butt with the horns; to shut, fasten; to clench; to stitch, sew.—*n.* a stitch; a loop in knitting; an article of clothing; a fragment, the least bit; a stitch in the side; a sharp, painful blow; a quick pace.

Steek-and-hide, *n.* a game like 'hide-and-seek.'

Steeker, *n.* a boot-lace, shoe-tie.

Steekie-nevvle, *n.* a clenched fist.

Steekin-slap, *n.* a gap with a gate opening and shutting.

Steekit, *ppl. adj.* used of a fog: thick, enveloping.

Steel, *n.* a needle: a steelyard.—*v.* to rough horse-shoes.

Steel, *n.* a wooded precipice; the lower part of a ridge projecting from a hill where the ground declines on each side.

Steel, *n.* a handle; the shaft of a hand-barrow. Cf. Steal.

Steel, *n.* a covering for a sore finger. Cf. Steil.

Steel, *n.* a stool.

Steel-bow, *n.* goods on a farm which are the property of the landlord, and may not be removed by an outgoing tenant.

Steel-bowed, *adj.* set apart for a special purpose; guaranteed, inviolate.

Steel-rife, *adj.* overbearing.

Steel-wamit, *adj.* ? having a 'wizened' podex.

Steely, *adj.* covered with steel.

Steen, *n.* a stone.

†Steen, *v.* to spring.—*n.* a spring. Cf. Stend.

Steenie, *adj.* stony.—*n.* a boy's stone marble; a boys' game. Cf. Stany, Stony.

Steenie, *n.* a gold coin; a guinea. Cf. Steinie.

Steenie-pouter, *n.* the sandpiper.

Steep, *v.* to drench with rain or wet; to curdle milk for cheese; in *phr.* 'to steep the withies,' to get ready.—*n.* a tub; the small spearmint; the quantity of malt steeped at a time.

Steep-grass, *n.* butterwort.

Steepin, *n.* a stipend, minister's salary; in *pl.* contributions to a stipend.

Steepin', *n.* a drenching with rain.

Steeple, *n.* a very tall, thin person; a small, square heap of partially-dried fish; a large stack of such fish.

Steeple, Steepil, *n.* a staple for fixing wire on posts.

Steeple, *n.* a stopper, plug. Cf. Stopple.

Steeple-root, *n.* the base of anything.

Steepy, *adj.* steep.

Steer, *v.* to stir; to bestir one's self; to go, depart; to bustle about, be in a stir; to work confusedly; to stir, poke, mix; to cause to move; to disturb; to injure; to plough slightly; to plough the ground a second time when it has to be ploughed thrice. —*n.* a stir; a poke; a disturbance, commotion, fuss; with *cauld*, a mixture of oatmeal and cold water.

Steer, *adj.* austere, stern; used of the voice: harsh, rough. Cf. Stare, Stour.

Steerabout, *n.* a restless, stirring person; stirabout.

Steerach, *v.* to crowd in disorder; to fill to excess in a disorderly manner; to work dirtily and confusedly. — *n.* a disorderly crowd; domestic disorder; dirty, disorderly working; a quantity of ill-cooked food.

Steerin', *ppl. adj.* used of children: restless, lively, troublesome.

Steerin-fur, *n.* a slight ploughing.

Steerless, *adj.* lifeless, lacking energy.

Steerman, *n.* a steersman.

Steer-pin, *n.* a pin in the stilt of the old Orkney plough.

Steer-tree, *n.* the stilt in the beam of a plough, regulating its motion.

Steerum, *n.* a stir; excitement.

Steer-water, *n.* the wake of a boat.

Steery, *n.* a stir, disturbance, commotion; a tumultuous assembly; a mixture.—*adj.* stirring; in commotion.

Steery-fyke, *n.* bustle, commotion with confusion.

Steet, *n.* a prop; a shore for a boat.—*v.* to prop, support with pillars. Cf. Stut.

Steeth, *n.* the bottom, foundation; a stone attached to a buoy-rope serving as an anchor to deep-sea fishing-lines. Cf. Stead.

Steethe-stone, *n.* the first of the stones let down as an anchor to deep-sea fishing-lines.

Steeval, *adj.* used of food : firm, substantial, made with little water.

Steeve, *adj.* stiff, firm ; strong, sturdy ; used of food : thick, substantial, stiff in substance ; steep, inaccessible ; staunch to principle, true, trusty ; obstinate, stubborn. —*v.* to stuff, cram.

Steevely, *adv.* firmly.

Steevie, *n.* a quantity of thick, stodgy food. Cf. Stivey.

Steevin', *ppl. adj.* strong, stiff.

Steg, Stegg, *n.* a gander.—*v.* to stalk about.

Steg, *v.* to bring to a standstill.

Stegh, *v.* to stuff with food ; to pant. Cf. Stech.

Steichle, Steichel, *v.* to stifle, suffocate ; to be in a state of suffocation ; to crowd to suffocation.—*n.* a close, stifling air ; a state of suffocation ; a crowd of people or animals packed together to suffocation.

Steichly, *adj.* used of air : close, foul, suffocating.

Steick, *v.* to push ; to stitch. Cf. Steik.

Steid, *n.* a place ; a mass.—*v.* to found. Cf. Stead.

Steigh, Steich, *v.* to groan or pant from over-eating or over-exertion.—*n.* a stifled groan. Cf. Stech.

Steigh, *adj.* steep ; stiff to climb. Cf. Stay.

Steigh, *v.* to look big.

Steighle, *v.* to stifle. Cf. Steichle.

Steik, *v.* to close ; to stitch. Cf. Steek.

Steil, *n.* a covering for a sore finger.

Steil, *n.* a shaft, handle.

Steil, *n.* a stand or framework for support ; a stack-prop. Cf. Stell.

Steilbow, *n.* goods on a farm belonging to the landlord. Cf. Steel-bow.

Steill'd, *v. pret.* stole.

Stein, *n.* a stone.

Steing, *n.* a pole. Cf. Sting.

Steinie, *adj.* stony.—*n.* a little stone. Cf. Stane.

Steinie, *n.* a gold coin. Cf. Steenie.

Steinie gate, *n.* the place where stones, gathered from a field, are collected.

Steinkle, *n.* the stonechat ; the wheatear.

Steir, *v.* to stir ; to bustle. Cf. Steer.

Steit, *v.* to stumble ; to stagger. Cf. Stite, Stoit.

Steit, *n.* nonsense, 'buff.' Cf. Stite.

Steiter, *v.* to stumble ; to stagger. Cf. Styter, Stoiter.

Steith, *n.* a place ; a mass, large number. Cf. Stead.

Steive, *adj.* firm, stiff ; true, good.—*v.* to stuff. Cf. Steeve, Stive.

Stell, *v.* used of horses and cattle : to urinate. Cf. Stail.

Stell, *n.* a still.

Stell, *n.* a prop, support ; a stack-prop ; a supporting framework ; an enclosure for sheep ; a plantation or clump of trees for shelter ; a deep pool in a river where net-fishing for salmon can be carried on ; in *pl.* indentations in ice to steady the feet in curling.—*v.* to place, set, fix ; to plant firmly ; to point ; to prop ; to stop ; to bring to a stand ; to stand ; in *phr.* to 'stell a gun,' to take aim with it.

Stell, *adj.* steep ; precipitous.

Stellage, *n.* the ground on which a market is held.

Stell-dyke, *n.* the wall of an enclosure for sheep.

Stell-fishing, -fishery, *n.* fishing with a 'stell-net' ; the place of such fishing.

Stellfitch, *adj.* used of rank flax or grain : dry, coarse.

Stell-net, *n.* a net, fixed by stakes in or across a river, for catching salmon.

Stell-pat, *n.* a pot-still ; a small, illegal still.

Stell-shot, *n.* a shot fired from a gun resting on some object to secure accuracy of aim.

Stellvitch, *adj.* used of flax : coarse, dry. Cf. Stellfitch.

Stelt, *n.* a crutch ; a stilt. Cf. Stilt.

Stem, *n.* the peak of a cap.

Stem, *v.* to stanch ; in quarrying : to ram a blasting-charge home.—*n.* a check ; the utmost extent of anything ; a dam in a stream or ditch.

Stem, *n.* a particle, atom ; a glimpse ; a glance. Cf. Stime.

Stembod, *n.* a symbol of citation, as a staff, arrow, axe, or cross.

Stem-bonnet, *n.* a peaked cap.

Stemple, *n.* a plug used by lead-miners.

†Sten', *v.* to extend ; to spring. Cf. Stend.

Stench, *adj.* staunch, firm, strong ; diligent. —*v.* to satisfy with food, &c. Cf. Stanch.

Stenchel, *n.* an iron or wooden window-bar. Cf. Stanchel.

Stencher, *n.* a stanchion ; an iron window-bar. Cf. Stancher.

†Stend, *v.* to stretch ; to bound, spring up, rear ; to walk with long strides, hasten ; to turn, twist, bend.—*n.* a bound, leap ; a long stride ; a sudden movement in the wrong direction.

Steng, Stengy, *n.* a pole, rail ; the mast of a boat. Cf. Stang, Sting.

Stenloch, Stenlock, *n.* an overgrown coal-fish or sillock. Cf. Stanlock.

Stenloch-hooks, *n.* hooks for catching coal-fish.

†Stenn, *v.* to spring. Cf. Stend.

Stenners, *n.* gravel or small stones on a river's bank. Cf. Stanners.

Stennis, *n.* a sprain.—*v.* to sprain slightly.

Stensil, *n.* a stanchion. Cf. Stanchel.

Stent, *v.* to stint; to leave off, cease, stop; to straiten, restrict; to allot; to prescribe a fixed task; to measure out.—*n.* a fixed task; an allotted portion of work; a limited allowance of pasturage.

†Stent, *v.* to extend, stretch out.—*n.* an utmost stretch, extent; a bound, limit.—*adj.* outstretched; tight; stretched to the utmost; taut.

†Stent, *v.* to assess, rate, tax; to confiscate.—*n.* an assessment, rate, tax.

Stent, *v.* to place.

Stented, *ppl.* limited.

Stented, *ppl. adj.* hired, engaged.

Stenter, Stentor, *n.* an assessor, an imposer of a tax.

Stentless, *adj.* unlimited.

Stent-master, *n.* an assessor of a town or parish.

Stent-net, *n.* a net stretched across a river and fixed by stakes.

Stent-roll, *n.* an assessment-roll.

Stenye, *v.* to sting.

†Stenyie, Stenzie, *v.* to stretch, extend.

Stenzie, *v.* to stain. Cf. Stainzie.

Step, *v.* to go away, depart; to pass over, omit, neglect.—*n.* a distance; a way; a walk, stroll; in *pl.* stepping-stones.

Step, *n.* the stave of a cask, &c. Cf. Stap.

Step-aside, *v.* to act in an underhand manner; to go wrong.

Step-awa', *v.* to depart, die.

Step-bairn, *n.* a stepchild.

Step-ben, -in, -in-by, *v.* to come or go into a room or house.

Step-dame, *n.* a stepmother.

Step-minnie, *n.* a stepmother.

Stepmother-year, *n.* a cold, unfavourable year.

Step on, *v.* to advance, grow old.

Step-over, *n.* a foot-bridge; a short distance across.

Steppe, *n.* the stave of a tub, &c. Cf. Stap.

Stepping, *n.* a way, path.

Steppit, *v. pret.* stepped.

Step-stanes, *n.* stepping-stones.

Stere, *adj.* austere, stern; used of the voice: strong; harsh, rough. Cf. Stare.

Sterk, *adj.* stark; potent; strenuous.—*adv.* utterly, strenuously. Cf. Stark.

Sterk, *n.* a young ox or heifer; a steer; a stupid, lumpish fellow. Cf. Stirk.

Sterling, *n.* a smelt.

Stern, Sterne, *n.* a star. Cf. Starn.

Stern-licht, *n.* starlight.

Sterny, *adj.* starry.

Stert, *v.* to start.—*n.* a short space of time. Cf. Start.

Stertle, *v.* to startle. Cf. Startle.

Stertlin'-fit, *n.* used of a woman: a desire for marriage. Cf. Startling.

Sterve, *v.* to starve. Cf. Starve.

Stethel, *n.* a small, temporary stack; a support for a stack; the bottom corn of a stack.—*v.* to build small, temporary stacks. Cf. Stathel, Staddle.

Steuch, *n.* dust; stew; a bad smell.—*v.* to drizzle. Cf. Stew.

Steug, *n.* a thorn, prickle; a spike; anything sharp-pointed; an arrow; a rusty dart; a stab, prick; a hasty stitch with a needle; light, coarse stitching.—*v.* to stab; to prick; to stitch; to sew lightly and coarsely.

Steur, *adj.* austere. Cf. Stare.

Steut, *n.* anything long and pointed, or large and sharp-edged; a big, stupid person.—*v.* to go about in a silly, stupid way.

Steutal, *n.* a 'steut.'—*v.* to 'steut.'

Steve, *adj.* stiff; firm; obstinate. Cf. Steeve.

Stevel, *v.* to stagger into a place into which one ought not to go; to stumble.—*n.* a stumble.

Stevel, *adj.* used of food: firm, substantial. Cf. Steeval.

Steven, Stevin, *n.* a loud voice; a ranting; an uproar.

Stew, *n.* dust, a cloud of dust; vapour; smoke; spray; an offensive smell.—*v.* to smell unpleasantly; to rain slightly.

Stew, *n.* a commotion; a state of fright, perplexity, excitement.

Stew, *v.* to burn.—*n.* a state of heat or great perspiration.

Steward, Stewart, *n.* the sheriff of a 'stewartry.'

Stewartry, *n.* the jurisdiction over an extent of territory nearly equivalent to that of a 'Regality'; the territory over which such jurisdiction extends; now the county of Kirkcudbright.

Stewg, *n.* a rusty nail. Cf. Steug.

Stewle, *n.* the foundation of a rick or haystack.

Stewrn, *v.* to besprinkle lightly with a powder.—*n.* a small quantity of anything powdered.

Stewrnin, *n.* a very small quantity of anything powdered.

Stey, *adj.* steep; hard to climb. Cf. Stay.

Stey, *v.* to stay; to dwell; to check. Cf. Stay.

Steyme, *n.* a particle; a glimpse. Cf. Stime.

Stibble, *n.* stubble.

Stibble, v. to stumble. Cf. Stevel.

Stibble-butter, n. butter from the milk of cows fed on the stubble after harvest, considered the best for salting.

Stibbled-lea, n. a stubble-field.

Stibble-field, -land, n. a stubble-field.

Stibbler, n. a horse turned loose after harvest into the stubble; a labourer in harvest who goes from ridge to ridge, cutting and gathering the handfuls left by those who in their reaping go regularly forward; a probationer of the Church without a settled charge.

Stibble-rig, n. a stubble-field; the leading reaper on a ridge.

Stibblert, Stibblart, n. a young fellow; a stripling.—adj. well-grown, plump.

Stibble-win, v. to cut down a ridge of corn before another, the one cut down being between that other and the standing corn.

Stibbly, adj. covered with stubble; used of hair: short and stiff, stubbly.

Stich, n. something obnoxious. Cf. Steech.

Stichle, v. to snore; to breathe with difficulty through the nostrils; to rustle.

Stichles, n. the hot embers of the fuel of a kiln.

Stichlie, adj. filled with fibres.

Stick, n. in pl. furniture; lumber in a house; in phr. 'nae great sticks,' no great 'shakes.'

Stick, v. to butcher; to gore, butt with horns; to stake peas, &c.; to stitch.—n. a pedestal; a stitch; a loop in knitting; the least article of clothing; a term of disparagement for a person.

Stick, v. to hesitate; to break down; to fail in one's profession or examinations; to bungle; to spoil in the execution.—n. a stoppage, halt, standstill; a breakdown; a bungle; a state of hesitation.

Stickamstam, Stickamstan, n. a thing of no value; supposed to signify a halfpenny Scots, the twenty-fourth of an English penny.

Stick and stow, adv. completely.—n. the whole of a thing.

Stick-armed, adj. armed with drumsticks.

Stick by, v. to adhere to.

Sticker, n. a fish-spear.

Sticker, n. a difficulty; a poser.

Stick fast, v. to take firm hold.

Stick in, v. to persevere.

Sticking, ppl. adj. stiff; disobliging; obstinate; unwilling.

Sticking-bull, n. a horned bull in the habit of attacking people.

Sticking-piece, n. that part of an animal's neck where the knife is inserted to kill it.

Stick into, v. to devote one's self to; to attack.

Stick in with, v. to devote one's self to.

Stick it, v. with pron. to remain; to halt.

Stickit, v. pret. and ppl. adj. stabbed, gored.

Stickit, v. pret. stuck.—ppl. adj. unsuccessful or failing in one's profession or business from want of ability or means; dwarfed; stunted in growth; unfinished.

Stickit coat, n. a coat which is a misfit.

Stickit job, n. a bungled or unfinished job.

Stickit minister, n. a probationer who fails to obtain a settled charge.

Stickit stibbler, n. a 'stickit minister.' Cf. Stibbler.

Stickle, n. bustle, haste; confusion.

Stickle, n. stubble; a spar of a kiln for supporting the hair-cloth, or straw, on which the grain is laid; the trigger of a gun or pistol.

Sticklie, n. the stickleback.

Stickly, adj. rough; bristly, prickly; stubbly; used of soil: intermixed with the stems of trees.

Stickly, adj. stickling.

Stick out, v. to hold out.

Sticks and staves, n. wreck and ruin.

Stickumstam, n. a thing of no value. Cf. Stickamstam.

Stick up to, v. to begin to court, to pay one's addresses to; to ingratiate one's self with; to prepare to fight.

Stick with, v. to displease; to be objectionable to.

Sticky-fingered, adj. thievish, 'tarry-fingered.'

Stid, n. an impression. Cf. Stead.

Stiddie, n. an anvil; a blacksmith's forge; a smithy.

Stiddle, v. to straddle.

Stied, n. a place; a large number. Cf. Stead.

Stiek, v. to prick; to stitch; to close. Cf. Steek.

Stieve, adj. stiff; obstinate; substantial.—v. to stuff, cram. Cf. Steeve.

Stieve-hertit, adj. stout of heart.

Stife, n. a sulphureous smell; a close, stifling atmosphere; the bad smell from a chimney; a smoky smell.

Stiff, adj. sturdy, strong; obstinate; self-willed; unyielding; supercilious, 'starchy'; burdensome; difficult; rich, wealthy.—v. to stiffen.

Stiff-back, n. a game resembling 'sweer-tree,' in a trial of strength.

Stiffen, Stiffin, v. to starch clothes. — n. starch.

Stiffener, Stiffner, n. a starched cravat; an article used to stiffen a neckcloth.

Stiffening, n. starch, for clear-starching.

Stiffing, n. starch.

Stiffle, *v.* to stifle.

Stiffle, *v.* to stumble, stagger ; to walk as if stupefied. Cf. Stevel.

Stifler, *n.* the gallows.

Stiggy, *n.* a stile or passage over a wall or fence by means of steps.

Stigil, *n.* a clownish fellow.

†Stigmatize, *v.* to brand with red-hot irons.

Stike criech, *n.* a 'stike-raid.'

Stike-raid, *n.* a ' raid collop.' Cf. Steak-raid.

Stilch, *n.* a fat, unwieldy young man.

Stile, *n.* a gate ; a sparred gate ; a passage over a wall.

Stile, *v.* to place, set. Cf. Stell, Still.

Still, *adj.* taciturn, reserved, somewhat morose. —*n.* the interval between ebb- and flood-tide. —*v.* to be at rest, cease ; to be quiet.—*int.* a command to horses to stand still.

Still, *adv.* always.

Still, *n.* a prop, support.—*v.* to place. Cf. Stell, Stile.

Still and on, *adv.* nevertheless, yet.

Still as a stap, *adj.* quite still.

Still-stand, *n.* a stand-still ; a cessation of hostilities.

Stilp, *v.* to step, stalk ; to walk with long strides ; to go on crutches or on stilts.

Stilper, *n.* a stalker ; one who has long legs ; in *pl.* crutches, stilts.

Stilper, *v.* to walk with long, awkward strides, lifting the feet high.—*n.* awkward walking with high steps by a long-legged person.

Stilpert, Stilpart, *n.* a long-legged, lanky person or animal ; a stilt ; the act of walking with long legs, lifting the feet high ; in *pl.* stilts.—*v.* to walk in this awkward fashion.

Stilp-stilpin, *ppl.* sauntering, stumping.

Stilt, *n.* a crutch ; in *pl.* poles with rests for the feet, about 2½ inches from the ground, used for crossing a river at a ford ; a shaft ; the handle of a plough.—*v.* to halt, limp ; to go on crutches ; to walk stiffly and awkwardly ; to hop ; to cross a river on stilts or poles.

Stiltit, *ppl. adj.* used of heels : high.

Stime, *v.* to look as one whose vision is indistinct ; to move awkwardly from defective vision ; to open the eyes partially ; to peer. —*n.* the faintest form of any object ; a glimpse, gleam of light ; the least particle, atom ; a look ; a glance ; a disease of the eye.

Stimel, *n.* a reproachful term for one who does not see what another wishes him to see.

Stimey, *n.* one who is clumsy through defective vision ; one who sees indistinctly.

Stimmer, *v.* to go about in a confused manner.

Stimpart, Stimpert, *n.* quarter of a peck ; used of ground : as much as will produce a quarter of a peck of flax-seed ; a young person who can barely 'shear' out the fourth part of a ridge ; an unskilful 'shearer.'

Stimy, *n.* the predicament of a golf-player whose opponent's ball lies in the line of his 'put.'

Sting, *n.* a forked instrument used in thatching ; the pipe-fish.—*v.* to feel a tingling, smarting sensation ; to thatch, or repair thatch, with a 'sting.'

Sting, *n.* a pole, post, shaft, &c. ; the mast of a vessel.—*v.* to push ; to push with a pole. Cf. Stang.

Sting and ling, *phrs.* 'to carry sting and ling,' to carry with a long pole resting on the shoulders of two people ; 'sting and ling,' entirely, bodily ; by force ; the use of both pole and rope in managing unruly animals.

Stinge, *adj.* stiff, austere, forbidding ; hard, difficult.

Stinger, *n.* a mender of thatched roofs ; an insect's mandible.

Stingin' spurtle, *n.* an instrument used in thatching for pushing in the straw. Cf. Sting.

Stingy, *adj.* bad-tempered, irritable ; of poor appetite.

Stink, *v.* to disgust by smell ; to capture a prisoner in the game of 'Scots and English.'—*n.* a prisoner in such a game.

Stinkard, *n.* a dirty, disagreeable person ; a prisoner in the game of 'Scots and English.'

Stinker, *n.* a prisoner in the game of 'Scots and English.'

Stinkin', *adj.* saucy, haughty.

Stinking Davies, *n.* the common ragwort.

Stinking Elshander, *n.* the common tansy.

Stinking-ill, *n.* a disease of sheep, causing a strong, sulphureous smell when the dead body is opened.

Stinking Roger, *n.* figwort.

Stinking-weed, *n.* the common ragwort.

Stinking Willie, *n.* the common ragwort ; the water ragwort ; the common tansy.

Stinkle, *n.* the stonechat ; the wheatear. Cf. Steinkle.

Stint, *v.* to leave off ; to stop in growth ; to stunt ; to restrict one's food. — *n.* an allotted task, a 'stent'; trouble, sorrow, vexation.

Stipend, Stipen, *n.* a minister's salary ; a benefice. Cf. Steepin.

Stippety-stap, *n.* a short, mincing gait.

Stir, *v.* to plough slightly ; to disturb so as to injure. Cf. Steer.

Stir, *n.* sir.

Stirabout, *n.* a porridge-stick; meal and water without salt. Cf. Steerabout.

Stirdy, *n.* in *phr.* 'to steer one's stirdy,' to trouble one's head. Cf. Sturdy.

Stirk, *n.* a steer; a stupid fellow; a stout man.—*v.* to be with calf.

Stirkie, *n.* a little 'stirk.'

Stirk-like, *adj.* stolid.

Stirk's-, Stirkie's-sta', *n.* the place in a cow-house appropriated to a 'stirk'; the place, generally the father's bosom, assigned to a child when the mother has a younger baby.

Stirra, Stirrah, *n.* 'sirrah'; a sturdy boy; a stripling; a man.

Stirring, *ppl. adj.* in good health; active after an illness.—*n.* a slight or second ploughing.

Stirring-furrow, *n.* the second ploughing across the first; the seed-furrow.

Stirrow, *n.* a fellow; a stripling. Cf. Stirrah.

Stirrup-dram, *n.* a parting glass of spirits, or of ale, from a host to his departing guest after he has mounted.

Stirrup-stockings, *n.* woollen riding-gaiters.

Stirve, *v.* to starve.

Stishie, *n.* an uproar; a banter; a frolic.—*v.* to banter; to frolic. Cf. Stashie.

Stitch, *n.* an article of clothing; a nickname for a tailor; a furrow or drill of turnips, potatoes, &c.

Stitch-through, *adv.* straight through; without delay.

Stitchum, *n.* a nickname for a tailor.

Stite, *n.* nonsense, 'buff'; one who talks nonsense.

Stite, *v.* to stumble so as to go aside; to move about stiffly and unsteadily; to walk with short, sharp step; to totter, stagger; to rebound; to cause to rebound.—*n.* a stagger; a rebound; a spring; a sharp, short step in walking.—*adv.* with a sharp rebound; with a sharp, short step.

Stith, *adj.* used of a rope: taut; strong, lusty; dead, stiff in death.

Stithe, *n.* place, station. Cf. Stead.

Stivage, Stivvage, *adj.* stout; fit for work.

Stive, *adj.* firm, stiff, strong, rigid; true, good.—*v.* to stuff, cram. Cf. Steeve, Steave.

Stivel, *v.* to stagger. Cf. Stevel.

Stively, *adv.* firmly; stoutly.

Stiveron, *n.* any very fat food, as a 'haggis.'

Stivet, *n.* a short, stout man; a stubborn, wilful person.

Stivey, *n.* a large quantity of stodgy food. Cf. Steevie.

Stivven, Stiven, *v.* to stiffen with cold; to freeze to death.—*n.* freezing weather.

Stoan, *v.* used of trees, &c.: to send out suckers from the roots.—*n.* a quantity of suckers from the roots.

Stoar, *adj.* large; tall; stout; stern; ill-tempered. Cf. Stour.

Stob, *n.* a stake, post; a spike; the stump of a tree; a thorn, prickle; a small, sharp-pointed splinter; the puncture made by a prickle, &c.; a small boring instrument, a brad-awl; a coarse nail; that part of a rainbow which seems to rest on the horizon when no more of it is seen.—*v.* to stab; to prick, pierce; to dress a corn-stack by driving in the ends of the sheaves with a pitchfork; to uncover a peat-bank by cutting off the rough surface; to push or hurt the foot accidentally against a stone, &c., projecting from the ground. Cf. Stab.

Stob-bairn, *n.* an unprovided-for child.

Stobbans, *n.* broken pieces of straw after threshing.

Stobbed, *ppl. adj.* used of a bird: unfledged.

Stobby, *adj.* rough, stubbly; bristly, unshaven; beset with posts.

Stob-feather, *n.* a short, unfledged feather on a plucked fowl; such a feather as appears first on a young fowl.—*v.* to feather one's nest; to provide furniture, &c., for a young couple.

Stob-feathered, *ppl. adj.* unfledged; used of a young couple: having provision or furniture.

Stob-spade, *n.* an instrument for pushing in straw in thatching.

Stob-thack, *v.* to thatch with 'stobs' or stakes to keep down the thatch.—*adj.* thatched with 'stobs.'

Stob-thacker, *n.* one who 'stob-thacks.'

Stock, *n.* the stem of a cabbage-plant or 'kail'-plant; the front part of a bed; the part of a spinning-wheel to which the wheel is attached; a strong, thickset, well-built person; a term of pity or contempt for an old, feeble, or useless person, or for a child; one whose joints are stiffened by age or disease; a pack of cards.—*v.* to amass money; used of plants: to branch out into various shoots immediately above ground; to become stiff; to be benumbed.

Stock and brock, *n.* the whole of one's property.

Stock-and-horn, *n.* a toast given by farmers, referring to sheep-stock and cattle.

Stock-and-horn, *n.* a musical instrument composed (1) of the stock, which is the hinder thigh-bone of a sheep, or a piece of elder, with stops in the middle; (2) of the horn, or smaller end of a cow's horn, cut so as to admit the stock; and (3) of an oaten reed held by the lips, and playing loose in the smaller end of the stock.

Stock-annet, *n.* the common sheldrake. Cf. Strok-annet.

Stock-duck, *n.* the wild-duck.

Stocket, *ppl. adj.* trimmed ; stiffened.

Stock-hawk, *n.* the peregrine falcon.

Stockie, *n.* a piece of cheese, or of fish, between two pieces of bread.

Stocking, *n.* farm stock and implements, in contradistinction from the crop.

Stocking, *n.* the sending forth of various stems.

Stocking, Stocken, *n.* an old stocking used as a purse ; savings ; a hoard or ' pose ' of money.

Stocking-feet, *n.* the feet clothed in stockings without shoes.

Stocking-foot, -leg, *n.* an old stocking used as a purse ; savings ; a banking-account.

Stocking-needle, *n.* a darning-needle.

Stocking-seamer, *n.* a woman who sews the seams of stockings.

Stockit, *ppl. adj.* hard, stubborn of disposition.

Stockit-siller, *n.* amassed money.

Stock-owl, *n.* the eagle owl.

Stock-purse, *n.* a purse held in common.

Stock-saint, *n.* a graven image of a saint.

Stock-storm, *n.* snow continuing to lie on the ground.

Stock-whaup, *n.* the curlew.

Stocky, *adv.* plainly, respectably.—*n.* a person of respectable, simple habits ; an ordinary, stay-at-home person.

Stoddart, Stoddert, *n.* a grassy hollow among hills.

Stoddy, *v.* to study; to guard against; to keep firm.

Stodge, *n.* thick, satisfying food ; repletion ; a fat, thickset person ; one deformed.—*v.* to eat to repletion ; to walk with short, heavy steps.

Stodge, *n.* a fit of ill-humour ; a pet.

Stodger, *n.* one who walks with short, heavy steps.

Stodgie, *adj.* ill-humoured ; pettish ; sulky.

Stodgy, *adj.* used of food : stiff and substantial ; fat ; short and stout.

Stoer-mackrel, *n.* the tunny.

†**Stog,** *v.* to stab, pierce ; to drive in a tool too deeply in working with wood ; to probe with a stick, or pole ; to cut or reap unevenly ; to jag.—*n.* a stab, thrust ; a sharp-pointed instrument ; a thorn, prickle ; a small, sharp splinter in the flesh : a piece of decayed tree standing out of the ground ; stubble too high or uneven ; a short, irregular horn, or one bent backwards.

Stog, *v.* to walk heavily or awkwardly ; to plod on.—*n.* a stamp ; a heavy pressure of the foot ; a person with awkward gait.

Stoggie, *adj.* rough ; used of cloth : coarse and rough ; of stubble : uneven in height ; of a comb : having some of the teeth broken.

Stoich, *n.* foul, bad, suffocating air ; a close,

sulphureous smell.—*v.* to fill with bad or suffocating air.

Stoichert, *ppl. adj.* overloaded with clothes ; overpowered with fatigue ; suffocated, overpowered by fumes, &c.

Stoif, *n.* a suffocating smell ; a sulphureous smell arising from the burning of bad coal ; a smoky smell. Cf. Stife.

Stoif, *n.* a stove.

Stoit, *v.* to stagger, stumble ; to walk carelessly ; to rebound, bounce ; to skip about. —*n.* a stagger, stumble ; a springy gait ; the proper method of handling a tool, or manner of working. Cf. Stite, Stot.

Stoit, *n.* nonsense. Cf. Stite.

Stoit, *n.* an awkward, blundering, or foolish person.

Stoiter, *v.* to stagger, stumble, totter.—*n.* a stagger ; a tottering gait. Cf. Styter.

Stoitle, *v.* to stagger ; to fall gently from weakness.—*n.* the act of staggering.

Stoitlin', *ppl. adj.* of unsteady gait.

Stoke, *n.* a foolish person ; a blockhead. Cf. Stookie.

Stole, *ppl.* stolen.

Stole, *n.* a stool ; the ' stool of repentance.' Cf. Stool.

Stole, *n.* a single stalk of corn.

Stoll, *n.* a place of safety ; a covert, shelter.

Stolum, Stolm, Stoltum, *n.* a large piece of anything broken off another piece ; a large quantity of anything ; a good slice, as of bread or cheese ; a supply or store ; as much ink as a pen takes up at a time.

Stomach, *n.* desire ; power to brook.—*v.* to retain on the stomach ; to tolerate, put up with. Cf. Stamach.

Stomatick, *n.* a medicine good for the stomach ; a stomachic.

Ston, *v.* to stun ; to clang. Cf. Stound.

Stonach, *n.* a stone marble. Cf. Stony.

Stondy, *n.* a stone marble. Cf. Stony.

Stone, *n.* a curling-stone.—*v.* to set a ring with stones. Cf. Stane.

Stoned-horse, *n.* a stallion.

Stone-lands, *n.* tenement-houses built of stone.

Stoner, *n.* a stone marble.

Stonern, *adj.* made or built of stone.

Stone-thrust, *n.* a small pier or projecting quay.

Stong, *n.* a pole ; the mast of a boat. Cf. Stang.

Stonk, *v.* to be sullen. Cf. Stunk.

Stonkerd, *adj.* silent and sullen. Cf. Stunkard.

Stony, *n.* a stone marble ; a boys' game, with a large stone set up in an open place, and a smaller stone set on its top.

Stoo, *v.* to crop ; to nip off ; to mark a sheep by a slit in the ear or piece cut off it.—*n.* a cut ; a slice ; a ' whang.' Cf. Stow.

Stoo, *v.* to stun; to astound. Cf. Stound.

Stoo, *v.* to tingle, throb, smart.—*n.* an ache, twinge. Cf. Stound.

Stood, *n.* a mark on a sheep's ear; half the ear cut across.

Stoog, *n.* the central matter in a boil.

Stooin, *n.* the tender sprout of a cabbage, &c.

Stook, *v.* used of corn; to bulk in the stook.

Stook, *n.* a kind of wedge formerly used in sinking coal and lead mines.

Stook, *n.* a small horn; a horn pointing backwards.

Stook and stour, *adv.* wholly, altogether.

Stooker, *n.* one who arranges the sheaves in a stook.

Stookie, *n.* a small stook of corn.

Stookie, *n.* a bullock with horns turned backwards.

Stookie, Stookey, *n.* a foolish person; a blockhead.—*adj.* bashful; awkward.

Stookie, *n.* a boy's red clay marble.

Stookit, *ppl. adj.* having irregular horns, or horns turning backwards.

Stook o' rags, *n.* one whose clothing is ragged.

Stook-ways, *adv.* after the manner in which stooks of corn are set up.

Stooky, *adj.* having stooks of corn.

Stooky-Sunday, *n.* the Sunday in harvest on which the greatest number of stooks is seen in the fields.

Stool, *n.* a small trestle used to support a coffin, &c.; a seat in church on which offenders formerly did public penance.

Stool, *n.* a place where wood springs up spontaneously after having been cut down; a single stalk.—*v.* used of a tree: to shoot out after being cut down; of corn: to ramify, shoot out stems from the same root.

Stool-bent, *n.* moss or heath-rush.

Stool of a beard, *n.* a bushy beard.

Stool of repentance, *n.* the seat in a church on which offenders had to do public penance.

Stoom, *v.* to frown; to look sulky.

Stoon, Stoond, *v.* to ache; to tingle.—*n.* an ache, throb; a whim. Cf. Stound.

Stoon, Stoond, *n.* a portion of time; a moment. Cf. Stound.

Stoon, Stoond, *v.* to stun; to resound.—*n.* a heavy blow. Cf. Stound.

Stoonie, *adj.* moody and capricious.

Stoop, *n.* a pillar; a post; an animal's limb; a supporter; a staunch adherent; used in coal-mining: a massive pillar of coal, left to support the roof; a piece of the shaft of a cart projecting behind; a wooden bench beside a cottage door.—*v.* to leave pillars of coal to support the roof in a mine.

Stoop-and-room, *n.* the old method of working out coal, leaving pillars to support the roof.

Stoop and roop, *n.* the whole.—*adv.* wholly, 'stump and rump.'

Stoop-bed, *n.* a bed with posts; one with very short posts and no tester.

Stoopie, *n.* a wooden water-pitcher. Cf. Stoup.

Stooping, *n.* a place where the coal has been worked out except for the pillars left to support the roof.

Stoopit, *ppl. adj.* furnished with posts.

Stoopit, *ppl. adj.* bent, stooping.

Stoopit-bed, *n.* a bed with posts.

Stoop-shouldered, -shouthered, *adj.* round-shouldered.

†Stoor, *v.* to stir, move quickly; to gush; to pour out leisurely; to rise in a cloud of dust, smoke, &c.—*n.* a bustle, stir; a fight; flying dust; liquid pouring from a vessel. Cf. Stour.

Stoor, Stoore, *adj.* tall, stout; hardy, sturdy; stiff, unyielding; stern; austere; rough, hoarse; deep-sounding. Cf. Stour, Stare.

Stoor, *n.* a stiff breeze. Cf. Stour.

Stoor, *int.* avast! get away!

Stoordie, *int.* a call to a dog.—*n.* a dog.

Stoorie-woorie, *adj.* restless, excitable, bustling. Cf. Stour.

Stoorum, Stooram, *n.* thin porridge; gruel. Cf. Stourum.

Stoosie, *adj.* squat; strong and healthy.—*n.* a stout and healthy child. Cf. Stoushie.

Stoot, *adj.* stout; healthy, strong; well-grown; used of liquor: strong; plucky; stubborn.—*adv.* sturdily; strenuously.

Stoot, *n.* a prop, support.—*v.* to prop; to support with stakes or pillars. Cf. Steet, Stut.

Stoot, *v.* to stutter. Cf. Stutt.

Stooter, *v.* to stumble.

Stooter, *n.* nonsense.

Stooth, *v.* to lath and plaster a wall.

Stoot-hertit, *adj.* stout of heart.

Stoothin, Stoothing, *n.* lathing and plastering; the surface 'stoothed.'

Stoove, *v.* to stumble.

Stop, *v.* to stuff. Cf. Stap.

Stopple, *n.* a pipe-stem; a tube of small bore. Cf. Stapple.

Store, *v.* to win all a boy's marbles in a game.

Store, *v.* to enable, equip.—*n.* sheep or cattle; lean stock bought for fattening.

Store-farm, *n.* a farm consisting chiefly of a walk for sheep.

Store-farmer, *n.* one who works a 'store-farm' as tenant or owner.

Store-man, *n.* the store-keeper at a colliery village.

Store-master, *n.* the tenant of a sheep-farm.

Storey, *n.* the grub of the daddy-long-legs. Cf. Story.

Storg, *n.* a large pin.

Storging, *n.* the noise a large pin makes in going through flesh.

Storm, *n.* a fall of snow.—*v.* used of the weather : to be stormy.

Storm *n.* as much ink as a pen takes up at a dip. Cf. Stolum.

Storm-cock, *n.* the field-fare.

Storm-finch, *n.* the stormy petrel.

Storming, *n.* stormy weather.

Storm-steddit, -sted, *adj.* storm-stayed.

Storm-water, *n.* surface water.

Storm-window, *n.* a window raised from the roof, and slated above and on each side.

Story, *n.* in *phr.* a ‘bonny story,’ a fine state of matters.

Story, *n.* the grub of the daddy-long-legs. Cf. Torie.

Story-tell, *v.* to tell lies, fib.

Story-worm, *n.* a grub; a slug. Cf. Story, Torie.

Stot, Stott, *v.* to stagger, totter; to walk with uneven, unsteady step; to rebound, bounce ; to cause to rebound; to bounce or spring in walking; to walk ungracefully; to stutter, stammer.—*n.* a stagger ; a stumble ; the gait of a cripple ; the act of rebounding; a rebound ; a rebounding blow ; sudden motion ; a bouncing gait ; a leap or step in dancing ; the swing of a tune ; the ‘go’ or ‘trick’ of a thing ; a stutter, stammer ; jerky speech ; a standstill ; a hindrance.— *adv.* bouncingly ; with a rebound.

Stot, Stott, *n.* a young bull or ox ; a bull of any age ; one that has been castrated ; a stupid, clumsy fellow.—*v.* to take the bull.

Stot-ba', *n.* a game of ball.

Stot-calf, *n.* a castrated bull-calf.

Stot's-milk, *n.* unboiled flummery, used as a substitute for milk when that is scarce.

Stot-sticker, *n.* a butcher.

Stotter, *n.* a ball that ‘stots.’

Stotter, *v.* to stagger, stumble ; to totter ; to walk clumsily ; to rebound.—*n.* a stumble, stagger ; the act of stumbling or tottering. Cf. Stoiter.

Stou, *v.* to crop; to lop off; to mark a sheep by cutting off a bit of the ear.—*n.* a cut, slice. Cf. Stow.

Stou, *v.* to ache; to tingle.—*n.* a throb; an ache ; a thrill. Cf. Stound.

Stou, *v.* to stun with a blow or with noise ; to benumb ; to astound.—*n.* a heavy blow. Cf. Stound.

Stouchy, *adj.* squat ; strong and healthy. Cf. Stoushie.

Stouff, *n.* dust. Cf. Stuff.

Stouff, *v.* to walk lazily and heavily.—*n.* the act of walking with such a step ; the sound of such a step ; a slow, stupid person.—*adv.* with a lazy, heavy step.

Stouin, *ppl. adj.* stolen.

Stouins, *n.* croppings of cabbage or colewort. Cf. Stowan.

Stouk, *n.* a stook, a shock of corn.

Stound, Stoun, *v.* to ache ; to throb; to tingle, smart ; to thrill with glee.—*n.* an intermittent, throbbing pain ; a sharp, sudden pang; a twinge ; an ache ; a thrilling sensation; a throb, wave ; a whim.

Stound, Stoun, *n.* a moment; a portion of time.

Stound, Stoun, *v.* to stun with a blow or loud noise ; to sound, resound ; to clang; to astonish ; to astound ; to baffle, perplex.— *n.* a heavy blow ; a resounding noise.

Stoup, *n.* a deep, narrow vessel for holding liquids ; a flagon of wood ; a jug with a handle ; a liquid measure ; a measure of liquor ; a wooden water-pail.

Stoup, Stoupe, *n.* a post, pillar ; a support. Cf. Stoop.

Stoup, *n.* a stupid person.—*adj.* stupid. Cf. Stupe.

Stoup and roup, *adv.* completely.

Stoupfu', *n.* as much liquor as fills a ‘stoup’; a bucketful.

Stoupie, *n.* a small liquid measure.

†**Stour, Stoure**, *v.* to stir ; to move or run quickly ; to pour or gush out; to pour leisurely from a vessel held on high; to sprinkle ; to rise in a cloud, as of dust, spray, smoke, &c. ; to raise a dust ; to drive, as snow.—*n.* a quarrel, strife ; a bustle ; a state of perturbation ; vexation ; excitement ; severe reproof ; a stiff breeze ; a storm ; dust, dust in motion ; fine-driven snow ; chaff; any powdered substance; flour ; a cloud of spray ; a smoke-like fog. —*adv.* in a gush.

Stour, Stoure, *adj.* tall, large, stout ; robust, sturdy, strong : stiff, stubborn, unyielding ; rough in manner ; austere, stern ; ill-tempered ; used of the voice : rough, hoarse, harsh.—*adv.* severely, strongly. Cf. Stare.

Stour, Stoure, *n.* a stake ; a long pole.

Stourage, *n.* direction, management.

Stourfu', *adj.* stirring, exciting.

Stourie, Stoury, *n.* bustle, stir.—*adj.* restless, bustling, excitable ; dusty ; used of the weather : marked by driving dust or snow. Cf. Stocrie-woorie.

Stourie, *adj.* long and slender, gaunt.

Stourin, *n.* a slight sprinkling of any powdery substance.

Stour-looking, *adj.* stern-looking, of austere looks.

Stourly, *adv.* strongly, sturdily ; sternly, austerely.

Stour-mackerel, *n.* the scad.

Stourness, *n.* largeness, bigness.

Stour-o'-words, *n.* a wordy discourse.

Stourum, Stourreen, *n.* thin porridge or gruel; a warm drink containing oatmeal and milk, with boiling water poured over the mixture.

Stoushie, Stousie, Stoussie, *adj.* squat; strong and healthy.—*n.* a stout and healthy child.

Stout, *adj.* strong; healthy; proud; stubborn.—*adv.* sturdily. Cf. Stoot.

Stouter, *v.* to stumble; to trip in walking.

Stouth, *n.* theft, robbery; stealth.

Stouth and rief, *n.* robbery with violence. Cf. Stouthrief.

Stouth and routh, *n.* plenty, abundance.

Stouthrie, *n.* provision, furniture.

Stouthrie, Stoutherie, *n.* theft; stolen or smuggled goods.

Stouthrief, Stouthreef, Stouthreif, Stouthrife, *n.* robbery with violence.

Stove, *n.* a feverish illness; a ground-mist; food that has been stewed.—*v.* to stew in a pot; to bleach blankets with sulphur.

Stove, *v.* to stave; to knock in; to push; to wrench, sprain. Cf. Staive.

Stovies, *n.* mashed potatoes; stewed potatoes; Irish stew.

Stovins, *n.* the first or tender shoots of green. Cf. Stooin.

Stow, *v.* to store, furnish; to stuff.

Stow, *v.* to crop, lop off; to mark sheep by cutting out a piece of the ear.—*n.* an incision; a cut; a piece.

Stow, *v.* to steal.

Stowan, Stowen, *ppl.* and *ppl. adj.* stolen.

Stowan, Stowin, *n.* the tender sprout of cabbage or other greens. Cf. Stooin.

Stowed, *ppl. adj.* stolen.

Stowen, *ppl. adj.* stowed.

Stowen, *n.* a greedy fellow.

Stowenlins, *adv.* stealthily.

†**Stower,** *v.* to run quickly; to pour out; to raise a dust.—*n.* a stir; spray, dust; strife. Cf. Stour.

Stowf, *v.* to steam; to rise up as steam.

Stowff, Stowffin, *n.* a slow and measured gait in walking. Cf. Stouff.

Stowfie, *adj.* short and thick.—*n.* a short, thickset person or child.

Stowin, *n.* silence.

Stowk, *n.* a stook, a shock of corn.

Stowl, *v.* to ramify, as corn. Cf. Stool.

Stowlins, *adv.* stealthily.

Stown, *ppl. adj.* stolen.

Stownlins, *adv.* stealthily.

Stown-wyes, *adv.* by stealth.

Stowp, *n.* a post, pillar; support. Cf. Stoop.

Stowp, *n.* a liquid measure. Cf. Stoup.

†**Stowre,** *v.* to run quickly. Cf. Stour.

Stowsie, *adj.* squat. Cf. Stoushie.

Stow-struntin, *n.* a kind of coarse garter made at Stow.

Stowth, *n.* stealth. Cf. Stouth.

Stoy, *v.* to saunter; to loiter.—*n.* a saunter.

Stoyte, *v.* to stagger. Cf. Stoit.

Stoyter, *v.* to stagger. Cf. Stoiter.

Stra, *n.* straw.

Straa, in *phr.* 'to say "straa" to one,' to find fault with one, to lay anything to one's charge.

Strab, *n.* anything hanging or lying loosely, or adhering to a person's clothes; a shred, a tatter; a loose straw sticking out from a sheaf or stack; an end of thread; a withered leaf.

Strabble, *n.* anything hanging loosely; a shred, tatter; a long, withered stalk of grass; a piece of straw, thread, &c.—*v.* to hang in long tatters.

Strabblie, *adj.* full of 'strabbles,' or long fibres or strips.

Strabush, Strabash, *n.* tumult, uproar.

Strachle, *v.* to struggle. Cf. Strauchle.

Stracht, *adj.* straight.

Strack, *adj.* strict.

Strack, *v. pret.* struck.

Stracummage, *n.* uproar, tumult.

Straddle, *v.* to stroll; to wander about aimlessly.—*n.* the small saddle on the back of a cart or carriage horse for supporting the 'back-band' and the shafts.

Strade, *v. pret.* strode.

Strae, *n.* straw; a thing of nought.

Strae-boots, *n.* wisps of straw tied round the feet and legs.

Strae-breadth, *n.* the breadth of a straw.

Strae-dead, *adj.* quite dead.

Strae-death, *n.* a death in bed in contrast to a violent one; a natural death.

Strae-drawn, *n.* a sheep-mark; a thin slice cut from the top to the bottom of an animal's ear.

Strae-headit, *adj.* yellow- or flaxen-haired.

Strae-hoose, *n.* a house or shed for holding straw.

Straein, *adj.* made of straw. Cf. Sträen.

Strae-kiln, *n.* a kiln dug in the face of a hillock, and roofed with pieces of trees covered with drawn straw, on which corn was put, a fire being lighted in front, with openings at the back to draw the heat.

†**Straemash,** *n.* uproar. Cf. Stramash.

Sträen, *adj.* made of straw; of wattled straw.

Strae-sonks, *n.* a wreath of straw used as a cushion or load-saddle.

Strae-wisp, *n.* one easily swayed or influenced.

Strag, Stragg, *n.* an irregular person of ill-defined purpose; a tramp; a thin-growing, 'straggly' crop.

Straggelt, *ppl. adj.* used of a child: stray, forsaken.

Stragger, *n.* a straggler.

Straggly, *adj.* sparse, straggling.

Straicht, *adj.* straight. Cf. Straight.

Straid, *v. pret.* strode.

Straidle, *v.* to straddle; to saunter. Cf. Straddle.

Straiffin, *n.* a thin, membranous film. Cf. Striffin.

Straight, *adv.* frankly; seriously.—*v.* to put to rights; to tidy; to lay out a dead body. —*n.* a straight line.

Straight-tongued, *adj.* plain-speaking, outspoken, honest.

Straik, *n.* a scythe-sharpener.

Straik, *n.* whisky; in *phr.* 'cauld straik,' raw whisky.

Straik, *n.* a tract of country; ground traversed; the strip of ground passed over at one turn in harrowing; the act of travelling over a tract of ground; an excursion.—*v.* to traverse a tract of land; to take an excursion.

Straik, *v.* to stroke; to smooth; to comb; smooth with a comb; to render even or smooth what tends to overflow; to level down grain in measuring it; to tune a fiddle, to draw the bow over the fiddle-strings; to anoint or spread with any unctuous or viscous substance; used of birds: to preen the feathers.—*n.* a stroke, buffet; a pat, caress; a stroking or smoothing; the act of anointing or spreading with an unctuous or viscous substance; a flat piece of wood, or a small rolling-pin, used for levelling grain, &c., heaped up in the measure; the grain so rubbed off the top of the measure; a very small quantity; a mere handful.

Straik, *n.* a stroke, a blow.

Straik, Straike, *n.* a bushel; a measure of corn, &c.

Straik, *n.* a streak; a stripe; a ray of the sun; in *pl.* the narrow boards or planking forming the sides and bottom of a boat.— *v.* to streak; to stripe. Cf. Strake.

Straik, *v.* to stretch; to extend; to lay out a dead body. Cf. Streek.

Straik, *n.* a small roll or bundle of flax when dressed.—*v.* to tie up flax in 'straiks,' ready for 'scutching.' Cf. Strick.

Straiked, *v. pret.* struck.

Straiked, *ppl. adj.* levelled to the brim of the measure.

Straiker, *n.* that with which corn, &c., is levelled to the brim of the measure.

Straikin, *n.* in *phr.* 'straikin o' daylicht,' daybreak.

Straikin, *n.* coarse linen used for shirts; in *pl.* the refuse of flax.

Straikin-stick, *n.* a stick for marking sheep with tar.

Straikit-measure, *n.* exact measure.

Straik o' day, *n.* daybreak.

Strain, *n.* temperament. Cf. Strynd, Streind.

Strain, *v.* to sprain; to extort; to squeeze.— *n.* a sprain.

Strait, *adj.* straight.—*v.* to straighten. Cf. Straight.

Strait, *adj.* used of an article of clothing: too small, tight; of a bargain: hard, close; hard at driving a bargain; straitened, in want of; steep.—*v.* to tighten, to stretch tight; to take a good, hearty meal.

Strait bields, *n.* a shelter formed by a steep hill.

Straith, *n.* a strath.

Straitie, *n.* the shank of the leg.

Straitnedness, *n.* straitness; the being straitened.

Strak, *v.* to stretch. Cf. Streek.

Strak, *v. pret.* struck.

Strake, *n.* a streak. Cf. Straik.

Strake, *n.* a scythe-sharpener. Cf. Straik.

Strake, *v.* to stroke. Cf. Straik.

Strake, *n.* a small roll of flax, ready for 'scutching.' Cf. Strick.

Strake, *v. pret.* struck.—*n.* a blow, stroke.

Stram, *n.* a big person.—*v.* to walk in a rude, noisy manner.

Stram, *adj.* stupid.—*n.* a stupid person.

†Stramash, *n.* an uproar; a tumult; a disturbance; fuss; a smash, crash; wreck and ruin.—*v.* to break in pieces, wreck.

Strammel, *n.* straw.

Stramp, *v.* to tread or stamp on; to trample; to tread under foot; to tramp, walk.—*n.* a stamp, tread; a walk, step, tramp.

Stramper, *n.* one who tramples.

Stramulleugh, *adj.* cross, sour, ill-natured.

Stramullion, *n.* a strong, masculine woman, a virago; a row, broil; a fit of bad temper; a display of pettishness.

Stramullyoch, *adj.* cross, ill-natured. Cf. Stramulleugh.

Stramulyert, *adj.* aghast; panic-stricken.

Stramyulloch, *n.* a broil, battle; a disturbance, tumult.

Strand, Stran', *n.* a stream, rivulet; a gutter; a channel or drain for water.

Strand-scouring, *n.* clearing out the gutters.

Strang, *n.* urine; human urine formerly preserved as a lye.

Strang, *adj.* strong.—*n.* strong ale.

Strang, *v. pret.* and *ppl.* strung.

Strange, *adj.* aloof.—*v.* to think strange; to wonder.—*n.* in *phr.* 'strange be here!' an excl. of surprise.

Stranger, *n.* a small bit of tea-leaf in a cup of tea, supposed to indicate the arrival of a stranger; a moth fluttering toward one, supposed to indicate the arrival of a stranger or a letter.

Strang-pig, -tub, *n.* a vessel for preserving urine as a lye.

Strang-thewed, *adj.* having strong thews.

Strap, *n.* a band for a sheaf of corn; a bunch. —*v.* to be hanged.

Strap, *n.* treacle.

Strap, *n.* a fellow, a 'chap.'

Strap, *n.* an end of thread. Cf. Strab.

Strap-oil, *n.* a castigation.

Strapper, *n.* the man on a farm who has charge of the farmer's horse and gig.

Strapping, *adj.* tall and handsome.

Strath, *n.* a valley or plain through which a river runs.

Strathspey, *n.* a Highland dance, like a reel, but slower; the music for this dance.

Stratlin, *n.* a step; a straddling, striding step.

Strauchen, *v.* to straighten. Cf. Strauchten.

Strauchle, *v.* to struggle; to toil, strive.

Straucht, Straught, *adj.* straight.—*v.* to make straight; to stretch; to smooth out; to lay out a dead body.—*n.* a straight line.—*adv.* straightway.

Strauchten, Straughten, *v.* to straighten; to lay out the dead.

Straucht-forrit, -for'at, *adj.* straightforward. —*adv.* forthwith.

Straucht-gaun, *adj.* straightforward.

Strauchting-brod, *n.* a board on which the dead are laid out.

Strauchtly, *adv.* straightforward; forthwith.

Straucht-oot-the-gate, *adj.* straightforward, upright.

Strauchtway, *adv.* straightway.

Strauchty-squinty, *adj.* winding, zigzag; not straight.

Straun, *n.* a rivulet; a gutter. Cf. Strand.

†**Stravaig, Stravag, Stravague, Stravaug,** *v.* to saunter, stroll; to go about aimlessly and idly.—*n.* a stroll, saunter; aimless walking.

Stravaiger, *n.* a saunterer; a wanderer; a vagabond; a seceder from a religious community.

Strave, *v. pret.* strove.

Straw, *n.* childbed. Cf. Strae.

Straw, *v.* to strew, spread.

Strawage, *n.* what is strewn.

Strawn, *n.* a string, as of beads.

Strawn, *n.* a stream; a gutter. Cf. Strand.

Straw-theekit, -thackit, *adj.* thatched with straw.

Stray, *adj.* lost, not at home, strange.—*n.* a lost child or animal.

Stray, *n.* straw. Cf. Strae.

Streach, *n.* a straining of the law, &c.; a quibble. Cf. Stretch.

Streah, *n.* a 'round,' a term used to denote a mode of drinking practised by the chief men

of the Western Islands, who sat in a circle until they became drunk.

Streak, *v.* to stretch. Cf. Streek.

Streamer, *n.* in *pl.* the Aurora Borealis or Northern Lights.—*v.* to streak; to cover with straggling flashes of light, like the Aurora Borealis.

Streamie, *n.* a streamlet.

Streamoury, *adj.* having streams of light from the Aurora Borealis.

Stream-tide, *n.* a flowing tide.

Streap, *n.* a rivulet. Cf. Stripe.

Streauw, *n.* straw.

Streaw, *n.* the shrew-mouse.

Strechen, *v.* to straighten.

Strecht, *adj.* straight.

Streck, *v.* to stretch. Cf. Streek.

Streck, *adj.* strict. Cf. Strick.

Streck, *v.* to strike. Cf. Strike.

Streek, *v.* to stretch; to stretch one's self; to bear stretching without breaking; to lie down at full length; to lay out a dead body; to draw the first furrow in autumn or spring; to plough; to exert one's self; to set to work; to engage in work; to go quickly, or at full speed; to hasten; to walk along; to saunter; to smooth out.— *n.* a stretch; full length; the longitudinal direction of a stratum of coal in a mine; one's course, way, opinion; speed, rapid progress; any kind of exertion; bustle, tumultuous noise, disturbance; dawn, daybreak.

Streek, *v.* to stroke. Cf. Straik.

Streek, Streek o' lint, *n.* a handful of flax being dressed. Cf. Strick.

Streeker, *n.* a very tall person.

Streeking, *n.* used of ploughing: the drawing of the first furrow at the beginning of spring.

Streeking-buird, *n.* the board on which a dead body is laid out.

Streeking o' day, *n.* dawn.

Streekit claith, *n.* an umbrella.

Streek o' day, *n.* dawn.

Streel, *v.* to urinate forcibly; to pour from vessel to vessel. Cf. Strule.

Streen, *n.* last night, yesterday evening, in *phr.* 'the streen.' Cf. Yestreen.

Streend, *v.* to strain, sprain.—*n.* a sprain. Cf. Streind.

Streenge, *v.* to beat, scourge.—*n.* a stroke.

Streenzie, *v.* to sprain; to extort; to distrain; to squeeze.—*n.* a sprain.

Streetch, *v.* to stretch.

Streeve, *v. pret.* strove.

Streffin, *n.* a membranous film. Cf. Striffin.

Streik, *v.* to stretch; to lay out a dead body. Cf. Streek.

Streik, *n.* a handful of flax; a bundle of dressed flax. Cf. Strick.

Streikin, *ppl. adj.* tall and active.

Streiking-burd, -buird, *n.* a board for laying out a dead body.

Strein, *n.* last night. Cf. Streen.

Streind, *n.* a peculiar cast or disposition of a person; strain; temperament. Cf. Strain.

Streind, *v.* to sprain, strain.—*n.* a sprain, strain.

Streive, *v. pret.* strove.

Strek, *v.* to stretch. Cf. Streek.

Strek, *n.* a handful of flax which is being dressed. Cf. Strick.

Strekin, *n.* used of ploughing: drawing the first furrows at the beginning of spring.

Strength, Stren'th, *n.* a stronghold; an ample supply.

Strenie, *adj.* lazy, sluggish.

Strenkel, Strenkle, *v.* to sprinkle. Cf. Strinkle.

Strenthie, *adj.* strong, powerful.

†**Stress,** *v.* to incommode; to overtax; to strain at the swingle-tree.—*n.* an effort; a pressing demand; distraint; a forced duty, fine, &c.

Stret, Strett, *adj.* strait; tight; straitened; steep.—*v.* to tighten; to take a hearty meal. Cf. Strait.

Stretan, *n.* a good, hearty meal.

Stretch, *v.* to lay out a dead body; to walk with dignity; to walk a long distance; to take a walk.—*n.* a quibble; a straining of law, equity, evidence, &c.; a walk; a distance.

Stretcher, *n.* an implement for stretching Shetland shawls, drying washed flannels, &c.

Streten, *v.* to tighten; to straiten; to eat heartily. Cf. Stret.

Streyck, Streyk, *v.* to strike.

Strib, *v.* to milk neatly; to drain the last drops from a cow's udder. Cf. Strip.

Stribbings, *n.* the last drops of milk drawn from a cow's udder. Cf. Strippings.

Strick, *n.* a handful of flax which is being dressed.—*v.* to tie up flax in handfuls or small rolls for milling.

Strick, *v.* to dress barley.

Strick, *adj.* rapid, swift.—*n.* used of a river: the most rapid part.

Strick, *v.* to strike.

Strick, *adj.* strict, rigid, in principles and in practice.—*adv.* strictly.

Stricken, *ppl. adj.* fought.

Stricken hour, *n.* a whole hour.

Stricklie, *adv.* strictly.

Strickness, *n.* austereness; strictness.

Strict, *v.* to stroke.

Strict, *n.* a strict way; in *pl.* formalities, ceremonies; strict terms.

Strict, *adj.* used of a stream: rapid. Cf. Strick.

Striddle, *v.* to straddle; to sit astride; to stride.—*n.* a stride; the gait of a man with bent legs.

Striddle-legs, *adv.* astride.

Stride, *n.* walking power; the legs; the fork of the legs.

Strided, *v. pret.* strode.

Stride-legs, *adv.* astride, with legs apart.

Stridelins, Stridlins, *adv.* astride, with legs apart.

Striek, *v.* to stretch. Cf. Streek.

Strieking, *ppl. adj.* tall and active. Cf. Streikin.

Strif, *n.* a struggle for a livelihood.

Striferiggs, *n.* patches of common land; debatable land.

Striffen, *n.* starch. Cf. Stiffen.

Striffin, Striffen, *n.* a thin, membranous film; a thin skin; the thin, filmy substance made of the after-birth of a cow and used for covering the mouths of bottles, &c.

Striffle, *v.* to move in a fiddling or shuffling way; to assume an air of importance.—*n.* a shuffling motion.

Strik, *v.* to tie up what is reaped.

Strike, *v.* used in curling: to dislodge a stone by striking it forcibly with another; of a horse: to kick out behind, 'fling'; to start a tune; to smooth, level.

Strike, *v.* to stretch; to hurry. Cf. Streek.

Strike, *n.* a handful of flax in process of dressing. Cf. Strick.

Striken, *ppl. adj.* struck.

Striking-teck, *n.* the cutting of heather with a short scythe.

Strin, Strinn, *n.* a thin, narrow stream of water, &c.; the channel of a river; used of a pipe: a short smoke.—*v.* to flow in a thin, narrow stream.

Strin, *n.* the milk drawn from a cow's teat by one motion.

String, *n.* meaning, drift; the thread of an argument, &c.; a lineal measure of twenty-four ells; a cord for making watches and clocks act as 'repeaters' by pulling; in *pl.* the root-fibres of a plant.

String, *v.* to feel a passion for; to feel the stirrings of animal desire.

String, *n.* a tide, current.

String, *v.* to move or fly in a long line; to walk, run, or fly in single file; to hang by the neck; to be hanged; used of turnips: to spring regularly in the drills.

Stringie, *adj.* stiff, affected; narrow; 'dour'; discontented.

Stringin', *n.* tape; a kind of narrow web used for trouser-braces; strings for knee-breeches.

String-of-tide, *n.* a rapid tideway.

Strings, *n.* inflammation of the intestines of calves.

Strink, *v.* to dole out in small quantities; with *it*, to pine away.

Strinkle, *v.* to sprinkle; to strew. Cf. Strenkel.

Strinkling, *n.* a sprinkling.

Strinnent, *ppl.* measuring out very carefully into a scale anything that is to be weighed, such as dangerous drugs. Cf. Strink.

Strintle, Strinnle, *v.* to trickle; to flow in a small stream.—*n.* a very small stream; a narrow channel or groove.

Strip, Stripe, *v.* to draw the last milk from a cow; to cleanse or wipe by drawing between the finger and thumb compressed, or drawing the fingers or hand along the surface; to walk, stride; to draw the feet along the ground; to walk or send one off.—*n.* a stripe; a stripling.

Strip, *n.* a stirrup.

Stripe, *n.* a narrow piece of ground.—*v.* to thrust; to whip.

Stripe, Strip, *n.* a rill; a small stream; a small, open drain; a long, narrow plantation.

Stripey, *n.* a red-and-yellow worm, used for bait.

Striphin, *n.* a film. Cf. Striffin.

Strip-irons, *n.* stirrup-irons.

Strip-leathers, *n.* stirrup-leathers.

Stripped, Strippit, *ppl. adj.* striped.

Strippings, *n.* the last and richest milk drawn from a cow.

Strippit, *ppl. adj.* clean milked.

Stritchie, *adj.* lazy, sluggish.

Strive, *v.* to be restive; to find fault with, object to.—*n.* an effort, struggle.

Strived, *v. pret.* strove.

Striven, *ppl. adj.* at variance; on bad terms; not friendly.

Stroak, *v.* to lay out a dead body; to draw the last milk from a cow's udder. Cf. Stroke.

Stroakings, *n.* the last milk taken from a cow, 'strippings.'

Stroan, *v.* to urinate; to stream. Cf. Strone.

Stroap, *n.* treacle. Cf. Strap.

Strobble, *v.* to slouch, shamble in walking; to walk awkwardly.

Strodd, Strod, *v.* to stride along; to strut; to walk fast without speaking. Cf. Strodge.

Stroddle, *n.* anything very small or worthless, a 'straw.'

Strodge, *v.* to stride along; to walk fast without speaking. Cf. Strodd.

Strods, *n.* a pet; a sulky fit; one of ill-humour.

Strok-annet, *n.* the common sheldrake. Cf. Stock-annet.

Stroke, Strok, *n.* a streak or line; the least possible; the point of striking in a clock.

Stroke, *v.* to lay out a dead body; to draw the last milk from a cow.

Stroke, *v. pret.* did strike.

Strokings, *n.* the last milk drawn from a cow. Cf. Stroakings.

Strokit, *ppl. adj.* striped, in lines or streaks.

Stroller, *n.* a strolling player or showman.

Strommel, *v.* to stumble.

Stronachie, *n.* the fifteen-spined stickleback.

Strone, Stron, *n.* a hill terminating a range; the end of a ridge of hills.

Strone, *v.* to walk about in a sulky mood.

Strone, Stron, *v.* to urinate; to stream; to pour; to milk into; to spout forth as from a water-pipe.—*n.* the act of urinating copiously; a streamlet.

Strong, *adj.* harsh to the taste.—*n.* strong ale. Cf. Strang.

Stronge, *adj.* bitter to the taste; forbidding, stern. Cf. Strounge.

Strong waters, *n.* ardent spirits.

Strood, *n.* a suit of clothes; a complete set of anything; a worn-out shoe.

Strood, *n.* a foolish song. Cf. Strowd.

Stroods, *n.* the sails of a boat.

Strool, *v.* to urinate forcibly. Cf. Streel, Strule.

Strool, *n.* a certain length of lace, &c. Cf. Stroul.

Stroonge, *adj.* harsh, bitter. Cf. Strounge.

Stroop, *n.* the spout of a pump, kettle, tea-pot, &c.

Stroopit, *ppl. adj.* having a spout.

Stroopless, *adj.* without a spout.

Stroosh, *n.* a heavy blow on anything soft or yielding.

Strooshie, *n.* a squabble, a 'hurly-burly.' Cf. Strush.

Stroot, *adj.* stuffed full; drunk; vainglorious. Cf. Strute.

Stroozle, *v.* to struggle. Cf. Struissle.

Strop, *n.* treacle. Cf. Strap.

Strops, *n.* braces. Cf. Strap.

Stroud, *n.* a senseless, silly song. Cf. Strowd.

Stroud, *n.* a disturbance. Cf. Strowd.

Stroud, *n.* a worn-out shoe; a suit or set of anything. Cf. Strood.

Stroul, *n.* any stringy substance found among food; a long piece of anything.

Strounge, *adj.* harsh to the taste; morose; of forbidding aspect or manner.—*v.* to take the pet; to sulk.

Stroungely, *adv.* harshly, forbiddingly.

Stroungey, *adj.* quarrelsome; sulky.

Stroup, *n.* the spout of a pump, kettle, tea-pot, &c. Cf. Stroop.

Stroupie, *n.* a teapot.

Stroussie, *n.* a squabble. Cf. Strooshie.

Strouth, *n.* force, violence.—*v.* to compel; to use violence.

Strouthy, *adj.* strong.

Strow, *n.* a turmoil; a quarrel; variance; strife; a pet, sulky fit; a short illness.—*adj.* hard to deal with.

Strow, *n.* the shrew-mouse. Cf. Streaw.

Strowd, *n.* a senseless, silly song.—*v.* to sing in a stupid, bad style.

Strowd, *v.* to stride along; to strut; to walk fast without speaking. Cf. Strodd.

Strowd, *n.* a disturbance; a quarrel. Cf. Strow.

Strowl, *n.* any stringy substance found in food. Cf. Stroul.

Strow-mouse, *n.* the shrew-mouse.

Strown, *v.* to urinate; to stream. Cf. Strone.

Stroy, *v.* to destroy.

Struble, *v.* to trouble, vex.

Strublens, *n.* disturbance.

Struchle, *adj.* untidy. Cf. Strushel.

Strucken, *ppl. adj.* struck; stricken.

Strucken hour, *n.* a whole hour.

Strucken up, *ppl. adj.* metamorphosed into stone by the agency of evil spirits.

Struckle, *n.* a pet, sulky fit.

Struie, *v.* in threshing with the flail: to strike so that the straw is moved to the end of the threshing-floor; to squander; to scatter things about.

Struissle, Struisle, Struishle, *v.* to struggle. —*n.* a struggle, tussle; a brawl, squabble. Cf. Stroozle, Strush.

Struit, *n.* stubbornness. Cf. Strute.

Strule, *v.* to urinate forcibly; to pour from vessel to vessel; to emit liquid in a stream. —*n.* a stream. Cf. Streel.

Strum, *n.* a pet, sullenness.—*adj.* pettish, sullen.—*v.* to be pettish, sullen; to gloom, take offence.

Strum, *n.* the first draught of the bow over the fiddle-strings; the sound of a bagpipe.

†**Strumash**, *n.* an uproar, tumult. Cf. Stramash.

Strummel, *n.* the remainder of tobacco, left with the ashes, in a tobacco-pipe.

Strumming, *n.* a loud, murmuring noise; a thrilling sensation, sometimes implying giddiness; confusion.

Strummy, *adj.* pettish, sullen.

Strump, *n.* a broken bit of straw.

Strune, *v.* to urinate. Cf. Strone.

Strung, *v.* to sulk.—*n.* a sulky fit; in *pl.* the sulks. Cf. Strounge.

Strunge, *adj.* harsh, bitter; forbidding, surly, sullen. Cf. Strounge.

Strungely, *adv.* harshly, forbiddingly. Cf. Stroungely.

Strungie, *adj.* quarrelsome; sulky. Cf. Stroungey.

Strunk, *v.* to sulk. Cf. Strung.

Strunt, *n.* a pet, pique; a sulky fit; a person of sulky disposition.—*v.* to affront, offend, insult.

Strunt, *n.* anything long and narrow.

Strunt, *v.* to walk sturdily; to strut; to walk with dignity; to walk about in a sullen mood.

Strunt, *n.* any kind of spirituous liquor.

Strunt, *v.* to cut short.

Struntain, Struntin, *n.* coarse worsted tape less than an inch broad. Cf. Stow-struntin.

Struntum, *n.* the name of a fiddler's tune.

Strunty, *adj.* short, contracted; stumpy; stunted; short-tempered; easily offended; out of humour.

Strush, *n.* a disturbance, quarrel; tumult; a state of disorder.—*v.* to go about in a lazy, careless, slovenly manner.

Strushan, *n.* a disturbance, tumult.

Strushel, Strushal, *adj.* untidy, disorderly; slovenly.—*v.* to go about in a lazy, careless, slovenly manner.

Strushelness, *n.* untidiness in dress; slovenliness.

Strushil, *v.* to struggle.—*n.* a struggle, a brawl. Cf. Struissle.

Strushlach, *n.* an untidy, slovenly woman.

Strussel, Strussle, *v.* to struggle.—*n.* a struggle. Cf. Struissle.

Strute, *n.* stubbornness, obstinacy.

Strute, *adj.* stuffed full; drunk, 'glorious' in drink; vainglorious.

Struve, *v. pret.* strove.

Struy, *v.* to scatter things about. Cf. Struie.

Stryke, *v.* to stretch. Cf. Streek.

Strynd, Stryne, *n.* strain, disposition; used of persons of the same kindred. Cf. Streind.

Stryne, *v.* to strain, sprain. Cf. Strain.

Strypal, *v.* to hang in loose, unwieldy folds or tatters; to walk with long, unsteady steps, or with wavering gait, like tall persons. — *n.* anything long and rather flexible; a tall, slender person; a good-looking, tall person.

Strype, *n.* a small stream, a rill. Cf. Stripe.

Strypie, *n.* a very small rill.

Stryth, *n.* the labouring animals on a farm.

Stuan, *n.* the tender sprout of a cabbage, &c. Cf. Stooin.

Stub, Stubb, *n.* a bristle; a short, stumpy hair.

Stubble-butter, *n.* butter from the milk of cows grazing in stubble-land.

Stubble-end, *n.* the posteriors.

Stubble-goose, *n.* the graying or gray lag goose.

Stubble-rig, *n.* a stubble-field.

Stubblin, *adj.* short and thickset.

Stubbly, *adj.* stubble-clad.

Stubbly, *adj.* strong, sturdy; healthy.

Stubie, *n.* a large bucket or pitcher, narrower at the top than at the bottom, with an iron handle, for carrying water ; a 'water-stoup.'

Stucken, Stuchin, Stuckin, *n.* a stake driven into the ground to support a paling or sheep-net. Cf. Stuggen.

Stucken, *ppl.* stuck. Cf. Stick.

Studderts, *n.* grassy patches on hillsides, or between hills where there is a fresh spring of water. Cf. Stoddart.

Studdie, Study, Studdy, *n.* an anvil, a stithy. Cf. Stiddie.

Stude, *v. pret.* stood.

Studgel, *adj.* stout, sturdy.

Stue, *n.* dust. Cf. Stew.

Stue, *v.* to crop, lop off. Cf. Stoo, Stow.

Stuff, *n.* dust.

Stuff, *v.* to garrison.

Stuff, *n.* luggage, baggage, belongings ; corn, grain ; produce ; liquor, whisky ; physic ; vigour ; in *pl.* provisions.

Stuffen, *n.* starch. Cf. Stiffen.

Stuffily, *adv.* toughly, perseveringly.

Stuffiness, *n.* ability to endure fatigue.

Stuffing, *n.* croup ; difficult breathing from accumulated phlegm.

Stuffrie, *n.* stuff ; material ; an article of any kind.

Stuffy, Stuffie, *adj.* stout and firm ; sturdy ; mettlesome ; able to endure.—*n.* a sturdy, persevering fellow.

Stug, *n.* a masculine woman, one who is stout and raw-boned.

†Stug, *v.* to stab ; to prick with a sword ; to jag ; to cut corn unevenly.—*n.* a prickle, thorn ; a stab, thrust ; any clumsy, sharp-pointed thing, as a large needle ; a short, irregular horn bent backwards ; a piece of a decayed tree standing out from the ground ; in *pl.* stubble of uneven length. Cf. Stog.

Stuggen, *n.* a post, stake ; an obstinate person.

Stugger, *n.* a big, ungainly woman. Cf. Stug.

Stuggy, *adj.* rough ; used of stubble : uneven in height ; of a comb : having some of the teeth broken. Cf. Stoggie.

Stughie, *n.* anything that fills to repletion ; satisfying food.

Stughrie, *n.* great repletion.

Stuir, *adj.* tall, stout ; sturdy ; inflexible ; stern ; harsh. Cf. Stour, Stare.

Stule, *n.* a stool. Cf. Stool.

Stult, *n.* a crutch. Cf. Stilt.

Stultie, *n.* one who uses a crutch.

Stumfish, *adj.* robust ; coarse ; rank ; unruly. Cf. Stamfish.

Stummle, *v.* to stumble.

Stump, *n.* an old person ; a fragment of a rainbow appearing on the horizon ; a man with a wooden leg ; a blockhead, a stupid

person ; in *pl.* legs.—*v.* to walk with a wooden leg ; to hobble ; to walk briskly ; to walk heavily ; to halt.

Stumpart, *n.* a person of awkward, stupid, or stumbling gait ; such a gait.—*v.* to walk with such a gait.

Stumper, *v.* to 'stumpart.'—*n.* a 'stumpart.' —*adv.* with an awkward gait.

Stumpers, *n.* legs.

Stumpie, *n.* a nickname for a person with a wooden leg ; a short, squat bottle.

Stumpish, *adj.* stupid, blockish.

Stumpit, *ppl. adj.* stumpy, short.

Stumple, *v.* to walk with a stiff, hobbling motion ; to stump off.

Stumpy, *adj.* thickset, short and stout ; used of a leg : amputated, mutilated ; of a pen, pencil, &c. : worn to a stump, blunted.—*n.* a short, thickset person ; a small, good-natured person ; an endearing name for a child ; anything mutilated ; an amputated leg ; a short, much-worn quill-pen ; the stump of a tooth showing above the gum ; a bottle ; a man with a wooden leg.

Stumral, *adj.* used of a horse : given to stumbling.

Stun, *v.* to astonish, startle.—*n.* a start, surprise.

Stunch, *n.* a lump of food, as of bread and beef.

Stund, *v.* to ache, throb. Cf. Stound.

Stungle, *v.* to sprain a joint or limb ; to sprain slightly.

Stunk, *v.* to be silent or sullen ; to sulk.—*n.* in *pl.* a sulky fit.

Stunk, *n.* a stake in a game.

Stunkard, *adj.* sullen, silent ; obstinate.

Stunkardy, *adj.* 'stunkard.'

Stunkle, Stunkel, *n.* a sullen or pettish fit : the sulks.

Stunkus, *n.* a stubborn girl.

Stunner, *n.* a big, foolish man.

Stunt, *v.* to cut off from ; to curtail.—*n.* a stunted tree, &c.

Stunt, *v.* to stamp ; to walk smartly.

Stuog, *n.* a masculine woman. Cf. Stug.

Stup, *n.* a post, pillar, support. Cf. Stoop.

Stupe, *n.* a stupid person ; a dullard ; a fool.

Stupid-fou, *adj.* stupid with drink.

Stuppie, *n.* a small wooden vessel for carrying water. Cf. Stoupie.

Stur, *adj.* harsh ; austere. Cf. Stour, Stare.

Stur, *v.* to stir.—*n.* a stir.

Sturdied, *adj.* afflicted with the 'sturdy.'

†Sturdy, *adj.* stupid ; giddy-headed.—*n.* vertigo, a disease affecting the brain of sheep and other animals ; a sheep affected with 'sturdy' ; the darnel, and its seed ; giddiness caused by eating or drinking anything with which darnel-seed has been mixed; the head; a fit of obstinacy or giddiness.

Sturdy, *n.* a sturdy leg.

Sture, *adj.* robust; rough in manner; hoarse. Cf. Stour, Stare.

Sturken, *v.* to become stout after an illness, or after childbirth; to coagulate, congeal. —*adj.* of sour disposition and cold manners. Cf. Sturten.

Sturnill, *n.* an ill turn, a ' back-set,' a relapse.

Sturoch, Sturroch, *n.* oatmeal stirred into milk or water.

†Sturt, *v.* to startle; to stir; to vex, trouble. —*n.* strife, discussion; trouble, vexation; wrath.—*adj.* turbulent, contentious.

Sturten, *adj.* of a sour disposition and cold manners. Cf. Sturken.

Sturtin, *adj.* frightened.

Sturtin-straigin, *n.* coarse thread, formed of blue and red worsted.

Sturtle, *v.* to startle; used of cattle : to run about wildly in hot weather. Cf. Startle.

Sturty, *adj.* causing trouble.

Stushagh, Stushach, *n.* a suffocating smell arising from a smothered fire.

Stushie, Stushy, *n.* an uproar; commotion. Cf. Stashie.

Stut, *v.* to prop, support with stakes or pillars. —*n.* a prop, support.

Stute, Stutt, *v.* to stammer, stutter.

Stuter, *n.* a stammerer.

Stutherie, *n.* a confused mass.

Stuthy, *n.* an anvil. Cf. Stiddie.

Stutter, *v.* to stagger, stumble; to totter; to rebound. Cf. Stotter.

Sty, *v.* to put a pig into a sty.

Stychie, *n.* an unseemly mass; great confusion; a confused crowd.

Stychle, *v.* to suffocate. Cf. Steichle.

Stychly, *adj.* foul, suffocating.

Styen, *n.* a sty on the eyelid.

Style, *v.* to give a person his proper name in speaking or writing.

Style, *n.* a gate. Cf. Stile.

Styme, Stym, *n.* a glimpse; a particle; the faintest form of an object. Cf. Stime.

Stymel, *n.* one who does not see what another wishes him to see. Cf. Stimel.

Stymie, *n.* one who sees indistinctly, or is clumsy through defective vision. Cf. Stimey.

Styoo, *n.* dust.

Styte, *n.* nonsense, ' buff.' Cf. Stite.

Styte, *v.* to totter; to stumble so as to go to one side. Cf. Stite.

Styter, *v.* to totter; to stagger.—*n.* a totter; a staggering gait. —*adv.* with tottering steps. Cf. Stoiter.

Styter, *n.* the smallest bit.

Styth, Stythe. *adj.* firm, steady; strong; lusty; stiff; stiff in death, rigid; dead. Cf. Stith.

Stythe, *n.* a place; a station. Cf. Stead.

Styther, *v.* to toddle; to totter; to saunter. Cf. Styter.

Sualter, *v.* to flounder in water. Cf. Swatter, Squatter.

Sub, *adj.* of near kin. Cf. Sib.

Sub-customer, *n.* an under custom-house officer.

Sub-feu, *n.* a ' feu ' granted by one who himself holds his property as subject to a superior.—*v.* to grant a right to heritable property, on condition of the payment of a certain duty to one who is himself subject to a superior.

†Subite, *adj.* sudden.

Subject, Subjeck, *n.* in *pl.* property, effects. —*v.* to submit, become subject to.

†Submisse, *adj.* submissive; moderate; gentle.

Subscrive, Subscryve, Subscrieve, *v.* to subscribe, sign one's name.

Subscriver, *n.* one who subscribes his name.

Subservant, *n.* an under-servant.

Subsist, *v.* to stop, cease, desist; to support, maintain—*n.* a subsistence.

†Substancious, Substantious, *adj.* powerful; possessing ability; substantial; effectual.

Substrack, Substract, *v.* to subtract; to withdraw from.

Subtack, *n.* a sub-lease.

Succar, Succour, Succre, *n.* sugar. Cf. Sucker.

Succar-saps, *n.* pap abundantly sweetened with sugar.

Succeed, *v.* to cause to prosper.

Succles, *n.* stone-crop.

Succre-ale, *n.* liquorice. Cf. Sugarallie.

†Succumb, *v.* to lose one's cause; to fail in an action at law.

Such, *adv.* so. Cf. Sic.

Suck, *v.* to pull at a pipe; to drink leisurely. —*n.* a whirlpool. Cf. Sook.

Sucken, *ppl. adj.* sunk.

Sucken, *n.* a territory subjected to a certain jurisdiction; the privilege or obligation of tenants to grind at a certain mill; the jurisdiction attached to a mill; the miller's dues. —*adj.* legally astricted to grind at a certain mill; under obligation to employ any tradesman, shopkeeper, &c.—*v.* to astrict the grinding of corn.

Suckener, *n.* one who is bound to grind at a certain mill.

Suckens, *n.* a grapple used by fishermen to recover lost lines.

Sucker, *n.* a horse-leech; a boy's toy. Cf. Sooker.

Sucker, *n.* sugar; a term of endearment.— *v.* to sugar. Cf. Sugar.

Suckered, Suckert, *ppl. adj.* used of a child : pampered, spoilt, fondled.

Suckler, *n.* a lamb nursed by hand.

Sucky, *n.* clover ; a pet name.—*int.* used as a call-name for a calf. Cf. Sooky.

Sud, *v.* should.

Sud, *n.* the south.

Sud, *n.* seed.

†Sudart, Suddart, *n.* a soldier. Cf. Souldart.

Suddard, Suddart, *adv.* southward.

Suddent, *adj.* sudden.—*adv.* suddenly.—*n.* in *phr.* 'on a suddent,' on the spur of the moment.

Suddent-like, *adv.* suddenly.

†Suddenty, *n.* suddenness ; a mishap, harm, mischief.

Suddle, Suddil, *v.* to soil, sully, defile.—*n.* a stain ; a much-worn article of dress.

Sudereys, *n.* the southern Hebrides.

†Sudge, Sudgess, *adj.* subject to.

Sudroun, *adj.* southern ; English. — *n.* an Englishman ; the English language.

Suffer, *v.* to suffer capital punishment.

†Sufflet, *n.* a blow. Cf. Souflet.

Sug, *v.* to saturate.

Sug, *n.* a stout woman. Cf. Sugg.

Sugarallie, Sugarelly, Sugar-ally, *n.* liquorice ; a policeman.

Sugarallie-button, *n.* a sweetmeat made of liquorice, a Pomfret cake.

Sugarallie-water, *n.* a solution of liquorice and water, made by children.

Sugar-bools, *n.* round sugar-plums.

Sugar-peas, *n.* sweet-peas.

Sugar-piece, *n.* a slice of bread buttered and sprinkled with sugar.

Sugar-tap, *n.* a kind of sweetmeat.

Sugg, *v.* to sink ; to press down ; to move heavily or in a rocking manner.—*n.* a sow ; a stout person ; an easy-going woman or child.

Suggan, *n.* a thick coverlet ; a saddle of straw or rushes.

Suggie, *n.* a young sow ; a young cow ; a fat person.

Suggy, *adj.* wet, marshy, boggy.

Sugh, *n.* a gentle murmur or hum ; the moaning of the wind ; a rumour ; a stroke. Cf. Souch.

Sugh, *n.* a ditch, drain ; a trench, furrow. Cf. Seuch.

Suh, *int.* a call to dogs to seek.

Suill, *n.* a swivel. Cf. Sool.

Suit, *v.* used of clothes : to fit close ; to provide one's self.

Suit, *v.* to sue for.

Suld, *v.* should.

†Sule, *v.* to soil, sully.

Sule, *n.* a ring with a swivel. Cf. Sole, Sool.

Sulfitch, *adj.* used of a smell : suffocating.

Sulk down, *v.* used of the brows : to droop sulkily.

Sullige, *n.* 'soil,' dung ; sediment, refuse conveyed by water.

Sum, *adj.* some.—*adv.* somewhat.

Sumf, Sumff, *n.* a simpleton. Cf. Sumph.

Summar, *adj.* summary.

Summer, *v.* to pasture cattle in summer. Cf. Simmer.

Summer-blink, *n.* a passing gleam of sunshine.

Summer-cloks, *n.* sunbeams dancing in the atmosphere on a fine summer day.

Summer-cout, *n.* the quivering appearance of the atmosphere on a warm day ; a swarm of gnats dancing in the air ; a lively young fellow.

Summer-flaws, *n.* the quivering appearance of the atmosphere on a warm day ; a swarm of gnats dancing in the air.

Summer-growth, *n.* various species of *Sertulariæ, Flustræ,* &c., attached to small stones or shells ; 'sea-growth.'

Summer-haar, *n.* a slight breeze from the east which often rises after the sun has passed the meridian.

Summering, *n.* in *pl.* cattle a year old.

Summering-ground, *n.* pasture kept for summer-feeding.

Summer-lift, *n.* the summer sky.

Summer-preachings, *n.* preparatory services for the Communion, when it was formerly held once a year in country parishes during summer.

Summer-scale, *n.* in *pl.* the scales which rise on the top of beer beginning to sour.—*v.* to cast up such scales.

Summer-snipe, *n.* the common sandpiper.

Summer-sob, *n.* a summer storm ; frequent slight rains in summer.

†Summons, *v.* to summon ; to summon to a superior law-court.

Summonser, *n.* a server of a summons.

Sump, *n.* the pit of a mine ; the well of a mine below the working level, where water collects before being pumped to the surface ; drainage ; a drain ; mud ; a sudden, heavy fall of rain.—*v.* to be wet ; to soak, drench.

Sumped, *ppl. adj.* drenched.

Sumph, *n.* a soft, blunt fellow ; a simpleton, stupid blockhead, fool ; a surly, sulky person.—*v.* to be stupid and 'dottish' ; to remain in a state of stupor ; to be of a sullen, sulky temper ; to look sullen.

Sumphie, *adj.* stupid, foolish ; sulky, sullen.

†Sumphion, *n.* a musical instrument, a kind of drum.

Sumphish, *adj.* stupid, foolish ; sulky, sullen.

Sumple, *adj.* pliable, easily imposed on.—*n.* a simpleton, fool.

Sun, *n.* a son.

Sun-birsled, *adj.* sunburnt.

Sunblink, *n.* a sunbeam; a gleam of sunlight.

Sun-broch, *n.* a halo round the sun.

Sunday-blacks, *n.* black clothes worn by men at church.

Sunday-claise, *n.* dress for going to church.

Sunday-name, *n.* a full baptismal name.

Sunday-sark, *n.* a clean or finer shirt worn on Sunday.

Sunday's face, *n.* a solemn face, a serious look.

Sunday's morning, *n.* Sunday morning.

Sunday-squeel, -schule, *n.* a Sunday-school.

Sunder with, *v.* to part from; to part with. Cf. Sinder.

Sun-dew-web, *n.* the gossamer.

Sundry, *adj.* separate, distinct.—*adv.* apart, asunder. Cf. Sindry.

Sune, *adv.* soon. Cf. Soon.

Sun-fish, *n.* the basking shark.

Sun-flaucht, *n.* a gleam of sunshine; a sunbeam.

Sung, *ppl. adj.* singed.

Sun-gates, *adv.* with the sun, from east to west.

Sun-glaff, *n.* a passing sunbeam.

Sungle, *adj.* single.—*v.* used of lint: to separate flax from the core.

Sun-glint, *n.* a sunbeam; a gleam of light.

Sun-go-down, *n.* sundown, sunset.

Sunk, *n.* the back of the fire.

Sunk, *n.* a seat, couch; a straw pad as cushion or saddle. Cf. Sonk.

Sunk, *v.* to drivel, loiter; to be in a low or dejected state. Cf. Sonk.

Sunkan, Sunken, *ppl. adj.* sullen, sour; ill-natured; splenetic.

Sun-kep, *n.* a sun-bonnet.

Sunket, *n.* a lazy person.

Sunket, Sunkit, *n.* in *pl.* provisions of any kind.—*adv.* somewhat, slightly.

Sunkie, *n.* a low stool; a man like a sackful of straw. Cf. Sonkie.

Sunkit-, Sunket-time, *n.* meal-time.

Sunkots, *n.* something. Cf. Sunket.

Sunk-pocks, *n.* the bags tied to the 'sunks' on the back of a tinker's ass, in which goods, baggage, children, &c. were carried.

Sunny-half, -side, *n.* the south side of anything; land with a southern exposure.

Sun-saut, *n.* salt made from sea-water.

Sunsheen, *n.* sunshine.

Sunsheeny, *adj.* bright with sunshine.

Sunshines, *n.* a children's singing game.

Sunside, *n.* the sunny side of anything; used of the heart: the good side.

Sun-singit, *adj.* sunburnt.

Sun-sittin, *adj.* used of eggs: injured by the heat of the sun.

Sunways, *adv.* with the sun, from east to west.

†Sunyie, Sunzie, *n.* an excuse, an objection.

Sup, *v.* to drink; to feed and give bedding to horses, cattle, &c. for the night.—*n.* a mouthful; a small quantity of liquid, porridge, &c.; an indefinite quantity of liquid; used of whisky: a drink; of spoon-meat: a spoonful; in *phr.* 'bit and sup,' food and drink.

Supe, *v.* to sweep. Cf. Soop.

Super, *n.* a superintendent.

Superior, *n.* the landlord to whom feu-duties are payable.

Superiority, *n.* ownership of land by a 'superior'; the ground-rents payable to him.

†Supernumerary, *adj.* used of votes: constituting the difference in number between majority and minority.

†Superplus, *n.* the surplus.

†Supersault, *n.* a somersault.

Superscription, *n.* a subscription.

Superscryve, *v.* to subscribe.

Suppable, *adj.* that may be supped.

Supper, *v.* to provide a person with supper; to feed horses, cattle, &c. with food for the night.

Suppie-mae, *n.* a pet sheep.

Supping-sowens, *n.* 'sowens' supped with a spoon, in contrast to 'drinking-sowens.'

Supple, *adj.* limp; nimble; 'slippery.'—*v.* to soften. Cf. Soople.

Supple, *n.* the striking part of a flail; a leg. Cf. Soople.

Supplicant, *n.* one in deep distress, an object of pity.

Supplication-well, *n.* a holy well.

Supply, *n.* a 'locum tenens,' especially for a minister's pulpit.

Suppone, *v.* to suppose; to hope, expect.

Suppose, *v.* to substitute in a supposititious way.—*conj.* although.

†Suppost, *n.* a supporter; a scholar in a college.—*v.* to put one in the room of another.

Surce, *n.* a common mode of addressing a number of people of both sexes.—*int.* an excl. of surprise, &c. Cf. Sirs.

†Surcoat, *n.* an under-waistcoat; a knitted semmit worn over the shirt by old men.

Sure, *adj.* sour.

Sure, *adv.* surely.

Surely, *adj.* certain, true.—*n.* certainty; truth.

Surface-man, *n.* a labourer in charge of roads.

Surf-duck, *n.* the common scoter.

†Surfeit, Surfeid, Surfet, *adj.* excessively painful or cruel; arrogant.

Surfle, Surfel, *v.* to overcast; to gather or spread a wider edge over a narrower; to ornament with edging, embroidery, &c.—

n. an overcast; a trimming; an edging, embroidery; a border of fur; the hem of a gown.

Surfy, *v.* to satisfy; to avail.

Surly, *adv.* surely.—*n.* a certainty.

Surly, *adj.* rough, boisterous; stormy.

Surprise, *v.* to be surprised; to wonder.

Surree, *n.* a social gathering, with tea, music, speeches, &c.

Surrender, *n.* speed, haste, a great rate.

Surrock, *n.* the sorrel. Cf. Sourock.

Survivance, *n.* survival.

Sush, *v.* to beat, to flog; to punish, fine; to upbraid.—*n.* a heavy blow. Cf. Soosh.

Sush, Sushing, *n.* used of the wind: a rushing sound.

Sushie, *v.* to shrink.

Susket, *n.* a shot; the report of a shot.

Suskit, *ppl. adj.* used of clothes: threadbare, much worn.

Suspeck, *v.* to suspect.

Suspection, *n.* suspicion.

Suspender, *n.* a law term: one who brings in a suit of 'suspension.'

Suspense, *v.* to suspend.

Suspension, *n.* a suit seeking a stay of execution of a judgment or a charge.

†**Sussie, Sussy,** *n.* care; hesitation.—*v.* to hesitate; to be careful; to care; to trouble.—*adj.* careful, attentive to.

Sussnin, *n.* a very small quantity.

Sustain, *v.* a legal and ecclesiastical term: to admit as valid; to approve of; to confirm.

Sustainer, *n.* one who entertains another at bed and board.

Sustainment, *n.* sustenance, nourishment.

Susy, *n.* a dead body taken from the grave. Cf. Shusy.

Susy-lifter, *n.* a resurrectionist.

Sut, *adv.* an expression of strong affirmation in reply to a negative. Cf. Sot.

Sute, *v.* to shoot.

Suth, *n.* truth. Cf. Sooth.

Suthart, *adj.* southward, southern.

Sutieman, *n.* a sweep.

Sutor, Sutter, *n.* a shoemaker. Cf. Souter.

Sutten, *ppl. adj.* sat; in *phr.* 'sutten on,' stunted in growth.

Suwaawra-wursit, *n.* a particular kind of yarn used in knitting petticoats.

Swaadge, *v.* used of the stomach: to grow empty; in *phr.* to 'swaadge a fill of the stomach,' to digest its contents. Cf. Swage.

Swaagin, *ppl.* wagging; fluttering, as a bird's wing. Cf. Swagging.

Swaat, *n.* the thin part of 'sowens.' Cf. Swat.

Swab, *v.* to wipe, mop; to go about in a loose, idle fashion.—*n.* a term of contempt for a drunkard; a loose, idle fellow.

Swab, *n.* the pod of a pea.

Swabbish, *adj.* mean, despicable.

Swabble, *v.* to beat with a long, supple stick. —*n.* a supple, pliant rod; a tall, thin, overgrown person.

Swabblin', *n.* a drubbing.

Swabblin'-stick, *n.* a cudgel.

Swabing, *n.* a beating, drubbing.

Swable, *v.* to beat with a long, pliant stick. Cf. Swabble.

Swack, *n.* a hard blow; a violent fall; a sudden gust; a severe blast of wind.—*v.* to throw with force; to strike violently sword against sword; used of wind: to blow suddenly and violently.

Swack, *n.* a large quantity, a collection; a share; a deep draught of liquor.—*v.* to drink deeply and in haste; to drink greedily, swill.—*adj.* abundant and good. Cf. Swag.

Swack, *adj.* limber, supple, pliant; nimble, agile; active, clever; elastic; used of a slight bar of iron, or piece of wood, &c.: slender, weak, fragile.

Swacken, *v.* to make supple or pliant; to become supple; to grease an axle.

Swacken, *v.* to beat very severely.

Swacking, Swackan, *ppl. adj.* clever; tall; active; of a large size.

Swad, *n.* a soldier.

Swad, Swaddie, *n.* the Swedish turnip.

Swaddle, *v.* to twist about, as for ease on a saddle.

Swaddlins, *n.* long-clothes; baby-linen.

Swadge, *v.* to assuage. Cf. Swage.

Swaf, *n.* a gust, blast, swirl of wind.

Swag, *v.* to move backwards and forwards; to swing to and fro.—*n.* motion; inclination from the perpendicular; a leaning to; a swinging motion; a swaying gait; a depression in the ground caused by mining; a bag, a wallet, a schoolboy's pocket; a festoon used as an ornament to beds, &c.

Swag, *n.* a large draught of any liquid. Cf. Swack.

Swage, *v.* to assuage; used of the full stomach: to grow empty by digestion; to digest food; to quiet; to still. Cf. Swaadge, Swauge.

Swagger, *v.* to stagger, reel; to feel as if intoxicated.—*n.* an inclination to one side; a stagger.

Swaggie, *n.* the act of swinging.

Swagging, Swaging, *ppl. adj.* bulging; pendulous; fluttering as a bird's wing; wavering; wagging.

Swaif, *n.* a gust, a blast. Cf. Swaf.

Swaif, *v.* to swoon. Cf. Swarf.

Swail, *n.* a gentle rising in the ground with a corresponding declivity.

Swailsh, *n.* a part of a mountain or hill which slopes more than the rest.

Swaip, *v.* to sweep.

Swaip, *adj.* slanting. Cf. Aswaip.

Swaipelt, *n.* a piece of wood, like the head of a crosier, put loosely round the fore-fetlock of a horse to impede its progress.

Swaird, *n.* sward.

Swairf, *v.* to swoon. Cf. Swarf.

Swaish, *adj.* used of the face: full, suave, and benign. Cf. Swesh.

Swaith, *n.* a wreath of mist; a lock of hair. Cf. Swathe.

Swaits, *n.* new ale or wort. Cf. Swat.

Swak, *adj.* supple; limber. Cf. Swack.

Swak, *v.* to throw with force; to wield a sword vigorously. Cf. Swack.

Swakken, *v.* to render supple. Cf. Swacken.

Swal, Swall, *v.* to swell.

Swald, Swalled, Swalt, *v. pret.* did swell.

Swald, Swalled, Swallen, *ppl.* swelled.

Swall, *v.* to devour; to swallow; used in imprecations.

Swallin, *n.* a swelling.

Swallow, *n.* the martin; the stormy petrel.

Swally, *v.* to swallow.—*n.* the throat.

Swam, *n.* a large quantity.

Swamp, *adj.* thin, not gross; not swelled.—*v.* to become thin.

Swamped, *ppl. adj.* a slang word for 'imprisoned.'

Swampie, *n.* a tall, thin fellow.

Swander, *v.* to be seized with giddiness; to fall into a wavering or insensible state; to want resolution or determination.—*n.* a fit of giddiness which comes on at a sudden emergency or surprise, and may induce apoplexy.

Swane, *n.* a young man, a swain.

Swank, *adj.* slender, thin, not corpulent.—*n.* a tall, thin man.

Swank, *adj.* supple, pliant; active; stately; jolly.—*n.* a clever young fellow.—*v.* to be supple.

Swankie, Swanky, *n.* a smart, active, strapping young fellow or girl; anything large of its kind.—*adj.* supple, active, agile.

Swanking, *ppl. adj.* supple, agile, active; moving quickly; stout and healthy-looking; used of a blow: heavy.

Swankit, *v. pret.* toiled, worked hard. Cf. Swink.

Swanky, *adj.* tall and thin; loosely put together.

Swanky-like, *adj.* active-looking.

Swap, *n.* the cast of countenance; the general appearance.—*v.* to resemble in appearance or temperament; used of a young, growing animal: to form or shape.

Swap, *n.* an immature and a partially formed pod.—*v.* used of peas, &c.: to form into pods.

Swap, *v.* to exchange; to lose; to excel, outvalue; to vouch.—*n.* the thing exchanged; an exchange.

Swap, *v.* to strike violently; to wield a sword vigorously; to thrash; to set down with a bang; to throw with a sudden, swinging motion; to cast a fishing-line; with *off*, to knock off, dispose of.—*n.* a heavy blow; a sudden stroke; a slap.—*adv.* with sudden force; quickly, smartly.

Swap, *v.* to roll tightly round; to gird; to twist over; to put straw ropes over the thatch of a rick or house by throwing a large ball of rope.—*n.* a twist, turn.

Swapper, *n.* the person with whom one exchanges.

Swappert, *adj.* nimble, agile. Cf. Swipper.

Swappet-beast, *n.* an animal exchanged for another.

Swarch, *n.* a rabble, crowd; a tumultuous gathering. Cf. Swarrach.

Sward, *n.* a sod for burning.—*v.* to cover with grass.

Sware, *n.* the most level spot between two hills; a steep pass; the declivity of a hill. Cf. Swire.

Swarf, Swarff, *v.* to swoon, faint; used of the breath: to stop, as in a swoon; to cause to swoon; to exhaust; to stupefy.—*n.* a swoon, fainting fit; stupor.

Swarfish, *n.* the spotted blenny.

Swargh, *n.* a crowd, rabble. Cf. Swarrach.

Swarl, *v.* to swirl. Cf. Swirl.

Swarrach, Swarrack, Swarrich, *n.* a large, untidy heap; a confused mass; a quantity of liquid; a closely-packed crowd.—*v.* to crowd together in confusion.

Swarricking, *n.* a confused crowd.

Swarth, *n.* sward; the surface of the ground.

Swarth, *n.* exchange, excambion.

Swarth, *n.* a swoon. Cf. Swarf.

Swarth, *v.* to darken.

Swarth-broo'd, *adj.* black-browed.

Swart-head, *n.* the edible part of the head of the large tangle.

Swart-tangle, *n.* the large *red* tangle.

Swarve, *v.* to swoon. Cf. Swarf.

Swarve, *v.* to swerve; to incline to one side.

Swash, *v.* to beat; to dash violently; to slash; used of a tail: to swish; to walk haughtily; to swagger, bounce.—*n.* a splash, a dash of water; a rush, dash; a heavy blow; a fall; the sound of a blow, fall, &c.; a large quantity; a corpulent person; ostentation, a swaggering gait; a swaggerer, a fop.—*adj.* of a broad make, corpulent; fuddled; showy, gaudy, ostentatious; haughty.

Swasher, *n.* a tall person of ostentatious manners, a swaggerer; anything large and showy.

Swashing, *ppl. adj.* striking, startling.

Swashy, *adj.* showy, gaudy; swaggering; soft-spoken; of a broad make; fuddled; soft, squashy; damp.

Swat, *v.* to sweat.—*v. pret.* did sweat.—*ppl.* sweated.

Swat, *n.* in *pl.* drink; new ale; small-beer; the thin part of 'sowens' fermented into a weak beer.—*v.* to tipple.

Swat-a-day, *int.* an excl. of surprise, &c.

Swatch, *n.* a sample, pattern; a piece cut off as a pattern.—*v.* to match; to make or supply according to pattern.

Swate, *v. pret.* did sweat.—*ppl.* sweated.

Swathe, *n.* a wreath of mist; a lock of hair.

Swathel, *n.* a strong man; a hero.

Swatle, *v.* to swallow noisily. Cf. Swattle.

Swatroch, *n.* substantial food. Cf. Swattroch.

Swatt, *n.* weak beer. Cf. Swat.

Swatter, Swather, *v.* to flutter and splash in water, as a duck; to move quickly and awkwardly; to 'squatter.'

Swatter, *n.* a large collection especially of small objects in quick motion; a confused mass; an untidy heap.

Swattle, *v.* to swallow greedily and noisily; to swill.—*n.* the act of swallowing greedily; thin soup or other liquid.

Swattle, *v.* to beat soundly with a stick or wand.

Swattlin, *n.* a drubbing.

Swattroch, *n.* substantial food; strong liquor.

Swauge, Swauje, *v.* used of an overloaded stomach: to subside gradually by digestion. Cf. Swaadge.

Swauger, *n.* a large draught.

Swauger, *v.* to stagger. Cf. Swagger.

Swauk, *n.* a hard blow; a sudden gust.—*v.* to strike heavily; used of wind: to blow hard. Cf. Swack.

Swaukin, *ppl. adj.* hesitating.

Swaul, *v.* to swell; to increase in bulk.—*n.* a swelling. Cf. Swell.

Swauled, *ppl. adj.* swelled.

Swaultie, *n.* a fat animal.

Swaunder, *v.* to become giddy suddenly.—*n.* a sudden giddy fit. Cf. Swander.

Swaup, *v.* to cool a spoonful of food by putting it into one's own mouth before giving it to a child.

Swaup, *adj.* strapping.

Swaup, *n.* the cast of a countenance. Cf. Swap.

Swaup, *n.* an immature and partially-filled pod. Cf. Swap.

Swaup, *v.* to swop, exchange. Cf. Swap.

Swauve, Swave, *v.* to swoon. Cf. Swarf.

Swaver, *v.* to stagger, totter, walk feebly; to hesitate; to be undecided.—*n.* a stagger; an inclination to one side.

Swaw, *v.* to produce waves; to ruffle the surface of the water, as by the movements of a fish; to swing.—*n.* a wave; an undulation of the water or slight movement of the surface by a fish swimming near the surface, or by any body thrown into the water.

Swawin, *n.* used of water: the rolling of a body of water under the impression of the wind.

Sway, *n.* the line of grass as it falls from the scythe or mowing-machine.

Sway, *v.* to weigh or press down; to be irresolute; with *off*, to turn aside.—*n.* a swing; a side-movement; an inclination to one side; a lever; a crane; a flat iron rod, pivoted and suspended in a chimney, for the hanging of pots and kettles. Cf. Swee.

Sway-boat, *n.* a swing-boat.

Sway-chain, *n.* a chain hanging from the 'sway' in a chimney.

Sway-crook, *n.* the hook and chain suspended from the 'sway' in a chimney.

Swayed, *ppl. adj.* used of growing grass, &c.: waved by the wind.

Swayl, *v.* to swaddle. Cf. Sweel.

Sway-swaw, -sway, *n.* a state of suspense, indecision. Cf. Swee-sway.

Sweal, *v.* used of a candle: to flare and gutter; to melt away; to carry a candle so as to make it blaze away.

Sweal, *v.* to swaddle; to swathe. Cf. Sweel.

Sweal, *v.* to whirl round; used of water: to eddy. Cf. Sweel.

Sweal, *v.* to rinse; to souse. Cf. Swill.

Sweap, *v.* to scourge.—*n.* a stroke, blow. Cf. Sweep.

Swear, *v.* to put on oath.—*n.* an oath.

Swear, *adj.* lazy, reluctant; niggardly. Cf. Sweer.

Swearer, *n.* one who administers an oath.

Sweart, *adj.* slow; lazy; unwilling. Cf. Sweert.

Sweat, *v.* used of cheese: to exude oily matter in ripening.—*n.* a state of great anxiety or exciting effort.

Swebar, *n.* the iron bar or 'sway' in a chimney, for hanging pots, &c. Cf. Sway.

Swech, *v.* used of rushing water: to sound.

Sweching, Swechan, *n.* a rushing sound, as of a waterfall; a hollow, whistling sound, as of the wind.

Swecht, *n.* the force of a moving body;

violence; a burden; weight; force; a
multitude; a great quantity.

Sweckery, *n.* trickery. Cf. Swick.

Swedge, *n.* an iron chisel with bevelled edge,
for making a groove round the edge of a
horse-shoe.—*v.* to groove a horse-shoe for
receiving nails.

Swee, *v.* to swing; to weigh down; to be
undecided; to turn aside.—*n.* a swing; a
movement or inclination to one side; a
lever; a pivoted iron rod, suspended in
a chimney, from which pots, &c., are hung
above the fire by a chain. Cf. Sway.

Swee, *n.* the line of grass cut down by the
mower.

Swee-bauk, *n.* a balance-beam.

Swee-chain, *n.* the chain hanging from the
'swee.'

Swee-crook, *n.* the 'swee-chain' and its hook.

Sweeg, *n.* a poor home-made candle. Cf. Sweig.

Sweege, *v.* to ooze between the staves of a tub.

Sweek, *v.* to cheat, trick.—*n.* the knack of
doing a thing properly. Cf. Swick.

Sweel, *v.* to swaddle; to wrap round; to
wrap in a winding-sheet.—*n.* the act of
swathing; as much cloth as goes round
a person's body.

Sweel, *v.* to whirl round; to swing anything
round with the hands; to make water in
a vessel eddy.—*n.* a circular motion, an
eddy; the act of turning rapidly round;
anything with a circular motion; the rippling sound of a streamlet.

Sweel, *v.* to cleanse by throwing water; to
rinse; to swallow; to drink copiously.—*n.*
a copious draught. Cf. Swill.

Sweel, *n.* a swivel. Cf. Sule.

Sweeler, *n.* a bandage; a swaddling-band.

Sweem, *v.* to swim; to float. Cf. Swim.

Sweeng, *v.* to swing.

Sweens, *n.* 'sowens.' Cf. Sowen.

Sweep, *v.* to quicken the speed of a curling-
stone by sweeping the path before it; to do
anything briskly.—*n.* the rope by which
stones are tied to the corners of a herring-
net; a stretch of land; sweepings; a scamp,
rascal.

Sweep, *v.* to whip; to scourge; to strike
with a club.

Sweeped, *v. pret.* and *ppl.* swept.

Sweeper, *n.* a bunch of feathers for dusting;
one who sweeps before a curling-stone.

Sweepie, *n.* a sweep.

Sweepit, *v. pret.* and *ppl.* swept.

Sweep-stone, *n.* the stone tied to the corner
of a herring-net to sink it.

Sweep-the-causey, *n.* one who would do the
meanest thing for money.

Sweer, *v.* to swear; to put on oath.—*n.* an oath.

Sweer, *v. pret.* swore.

Sweer, Sweere, *adj.* slow, lazy, reluctant;
not liberal or ready to spend or give.—*n.*
a lazy time; a short rest during working
hours in field labour; darkness.—*v.* to be
lazy; to rest for a short time during working hours.

Sweer-arse, *n.* a children's game, played by
two seated on the ground, feet to feet,
holding a stick by their hands, and trying
which shall raise the other up by main
strength.

Sweerd, *adj.* lazy; reluctant. Cf. Sweert.

Sweer-drauchts, *n.* the game of 'sweer-arse.'

Sweer-draun, *adj.* reluctant.

Sweered, *v. pret.* swore.

Sweer-Jenny, Kitty, *n.* an instrument for
winding yarn.

Sweerman's-lift. load, *n.* an undue burden
borne by a lazy person to save a double
journey; more than one can accomplish.

Sweerness, *n.* laziness.

Sweerock, *n.* a lazy girl.

Sweer-out, *adj.* unwilling to turn out; hard
to draw.

Sweert, *adj.* reluctant; slow; lazy.

Sweerta, Sweerty, *n.* laziness, sloth; a fit of
laziness.

Sweer-tree, *n.* an instrument for winding
yarn; a youths' game resembling 'sweer-
arse'; the stick used in the game.

Sweer-up, *adj.* unwilling to get up in the
morning.

Sweer will, *n.* reluctance.

Sweery, *adj.* lazy; slow; unwilling.

Sweesh, *v.* to swish; to move with a swishing
motion.

Swee-sway, *adj.* in suspense; hesitating. Cf.
Sway-swaw.

Swee-swee, *v.* to make a chirping noise.

Sweet, *adj.* used of butter: not salted, fresh.

Sweet, *v.* to sweat.

Sweet-breeds, *n.* the diaphragm of an animal.

Sweet-cicely, *n.* the great chervil.

Sweeten, *v.* to bribe; to bid at a sale without
intending to buy.

Sweet-gale, *n.* the bog-myrtle.

Sweet-heap, *n.* a home-brewing term: the
heap into which the malt was gathered
after it had been spread long enough evenly
on the barn-floor.

Sweet-heart, *v.* to court, to act as a lover.

Sweet-hearting day, *n.* courting-time.

Sweet-heat, *n.* a home-brewing term: the
proper point of heat at which malt was removed from the 'sweet-heap' to be kiln-
dried at once.

Sweetie, *n.* a sweetmeat, goody; a sweetheart; a considerable sum of money.

Sweetie-bench, *n.* a sweet-stall.

Sweetie-bun, *n.* a large cake, made about

Christmas, of flour, raisins, currants, orange-peel, almonds, and spices.

Sweetiecook, *n.* a sweetmeat ; a sugar-coated bun.

Sweetie-laif, *n.* a 'sweetie-bun.'

Sweetie-man, *n.* a retailer of sweets.

Sweetie scon, *n.* a 'sweetie-bun.'

Sweetie-shop, *n.* a confectioner's or sweet-shop.

Sweetie-stand, *n.* a sweet-stall.

Sweetie-wife, *n.* a woman who sells sweets.

Sweetie-wiggy, *n.* a sweet cake or roll, baked with butter and currants. Cf. Wig.

Sweet-lippit, *adj.* fond of sweet things.

Sweet Mary, *n.* the rosemary.

Sweet-milk cheese, *n.* cheese made of un-skimmed milk.

Sweet-milker, *n.* the day on which sweet-milk cheese is made.

Sweet-William, *n.* the common tope.

Sweevil, *n.* a swirl ; an eddying movement.

Sweg, *n.* a copious draught ; a quantity ; a large number. Cf. Swig.

Sweig, *n.* a very bad home-made candle.

Sweigh, *v.* to swing ; to sway. Cf. Sway, Swee.

Sweil, *n.* a swivel ; a ring containing a swivel ; Cf. Sweel, Sule.

Sweil, Sweill, *v.* to whirl round.—*n.* anything with a circular motion ; an eddy. Cf. Sweel.

Sweir, *v.* to swear.

Sweir, *adj.* lazy. Cf. Sweer.

Sweired, Sweirt, *adj.* lazy ; reluctant. Cf. Sweert.

Sweirta, Sweirtie, *n.* laziness. Cf. Sweerta.

Sweit, *v.* to sweat.

Sweited, *v. pret.* did sweat.—*ppl.* sweated.

Swelchie, *n.* a seal. Cf. Sealch.

Swelchie, Swelchee, *n.* a whirlpool.

Swell, *v.* to swagger ; to play the swell.—*n.* a sensation, excitement, figure.

Swell, *n.* a bog, a mire. Cf. Swile.

Swelled-kye, *n.* cattle swelled by flatulence.

Swelt, *v.* to melt, broil with heat.

Swelt, *ppl.* melted, suffocated with heat.

Swelting-cod, *n.* a cod in poor condition.

Sweltry, *adj.* sultry.

Swerd, *n.* a sword.

Swerd-slipper, *n.* a sword-cutler.

Swere, *adj.* lazy. Cf. Sweer.

Swerf, Swerve, *v.* to swoon. Cf. Swarf.

Swesh, *adj.* used of the face : full, suave, be-nignant.

Swey, *v.* to sway ; to swing.—*n.* a pivoted rod in a chimney from which pots, &c., hang by a chain. Cf. Sway, Swee.

Swick, *v.* to cheat ; to win by cheating ; to deceive ; to blame.—*n.* fraud, deceit ; any kind of trick ; a cheat ; a swindler ; the knack of doing a thing properly ; ability,

knowledge ; approbation, good opinion ; blame ; responsibility in the sense of blame-worthiness.—*adj.* clear of anything.

Swick an' trick, *adj.* unscrupulous and tricky.

Swicker, *n.* a deceiver.

Swickful, *adj.* deceitful.

Swicky, *adj.* deceitful ; sportively tricky ; roguish.

Swidder, *v.* to hesitate.—*adj.* hesitating, in two minds. Cf. Swither.

Swidderin, Swiddern, *ppl.* trying to make up one's mind.

Swiel, *v.* to whirl round ; used of water : to eddy. Cf. Sweel.

Swieth, *adv.* quickly. Cf. Swith.

Swiff, *n.* a rapid motion and the whirring or whizzing sound it produces ; a 'soughing' sound ; a whiff, a puff, breath ; a short interval, a snatch of sleep, &c.—*v.* to move with a rushing sound ; to whiz.

Swiff a sleep, *v.* to have a short, disturbed sleep.

Swiff awa', *v.* to swoon, faint.

Swift, *n.* a reeling-machine used by weavers.

Swig, *n.* a quantity ; a considerable number.

Swig, *n.* art ; skill ; knowledge ; manner. Cf. Swick.

Swig, *v.* to sway ; to move from side to side ; to walk with a rocking motion ; to turn suddenly ; to walk quickly ; to work ener-getically.—*n.* the act of turning suddenly.

Swil, *n.* a swivel. Cf. Sweel, Sule.

Swile, *n.* a bog in a meadow. Cf. Sweel.

Swilie, *adj.* full of bogs.

Swilkie, *n.* a large whirlpool in the sea. Cf. Swelchie.

Swill, *v.* to rinse, wash out ; to souse ; with *away* or *down*, to wash down ; with *up*, to wash up.—*n.* a washing, rinse. Cf. Sweel.

Swill, *v.* to swaddle ; to wrap round. Cf. Sweel.

Swill, *v.* to whirl round anything with the hands. Cf. Sweel.

Swilter, *v.* to agitate water, or any liquid ; to undulate in a pail, &c.

Swim, *n.* a state of great wetness ; a flooding. Cf. Soom.

Swim, *n.* a swoon ; a giddiness, faintness.—*v.* to swoon, turn giddy ; to spin, as a top ; to cause to spin. Cf. Soom.

Swimmed, *v. pret.* swam.

Swine-arnot, *n.* the marsh betony or clown's allheal.

Swine-bread, *n.* the pig-nut.

Swine-fish, *n.* the wolf-fish.

Swine-gotten, *adj.* used as an opprobrious epithet.

Swine-meat, *n.* pigs'-wash.

Swine-pig, *n.* a pig.

Swine-pot, *n.* a large pot or caldron for boil-ing pigs' food.

Swine-ree, *n.* an enclosure where pigs are reared, the pig-sty within it.

Swine's arnuts, *n.* the tall oat-grass with tuberous roots.

Swine's cresses, *n.* the fool's cress.

Swine-shott, *n.* a young pig.

Swine's-maskert, -mosscroft, *n.* the marsh betony.

Swine's-murricks, *n.* the tuberous roots of the tall oat-grass.

Swine's-saim, -saem, *n.* hog's-lard.

Swine-sty, *n.* a pig-sty.

Swine-thistle, *n.* the sow-thistle.

Swing, *n.* the hawser of a fishing-boat.

Swinge, *v.* to walk with a heavy, swinging gait.—*n.* a blow; a heavy, swinging gait.—*adv.* with such a gait.

Swingeing, Swinging, *ppl. adj.* large, excellent; 'thumping.'—*n.* a whipping, a beating.

Swingeour, Swinger, *n.* a sluggard, drone; a rogue, rascal; a bankrupt.

Swinging-tree, *n.* a flail.

Swingle, *v.* to separate flax or hemp from the stalk or pith by beating it.—*n.* the striking part of a flail.

Swingler, *n.* an instrument used for beating flax.

Swingler, *n.* a swindler.

Swingle-tree, *n.* the stock over which flax is scutched; the movable part of a flail which strikes the grain.

Swingle-wand, *n.* an instrument for beating flax.

Swingling-hand, *n.* a wooden lath or 'sword' for dressing flax.

Swingling-post, *n.* a sloping post firmly fixed in the barn-floor, over which flax was held to be dressed.

Swingling-stock, *n.* an upright board, three feet long, mortised into a foot or 'stock,' over which the flax was held in order to be beaten.

Swing-lint, -lind, *n.* an instrument for breaking flax.

Swing-tree, *n.* the swingle-tree of a plough.

Swink, *v.* to work hard.—*n.* labour, toil.

Swipe, *n.* a heavy driving stroke; a circular motion.—*v.* to move circularly, as in using a scythe.

Swipe, *v.* to drink hastily and greedily, to gulp.—*n.* a copious draught.

Swipe, *v.* to sweep. Cf. Sweep.

Swipper, Swippert, *adj.* quick, nimble; sudden; hasty, tart.—*adv.* suddenly, quickly.

Swipper-like, *adv.* hastily, with ill-temper.

Swippertly, *adv.* swiftly, suddenly.

Swippit, *ppl.* swept.

Swipple, *n.* the striking part of a flail; a cudgel.—*v.* to cudgel. Cf. Soople.

Swire, *n.* a level spot, or steep pass, between mountains; the descent of a hill; a declivity near the top of a hill. Cf. Sware.

Swirl, Swirel, *v.* to turn or wheel round; to unroll; to turn out verses or rhymes; to brandish; to be seized with giddiness; to carry off, as by a whirlwind.—*n.* a facial contortion; a twist in the grain of wood; a twist; a curl; a sweep, curve; a tuft of hair on the head that refuses to lie flat, a 'cowlick'; a state of confusion; the vestiges left by a whirling motion of any kind.

Swirlin', Swirlon, *ppl. adj.* used of the human body: distorted.

Swirling, *n.* giddiness, vertigo.

Swirly, *adj.* curly; used of wood: full of twists or knots, contorted, gnarled; of grass: twisted, entangled, and difficult to cut; inconstant, fluctuating, ever in rotation.

Swish, *v.* used of water: to rush noisily; of the wind: to blow loudly and fiercely.—*n.* a rush of water, and its sound; a slight fall or sprinkling of water.—*int.* an excl. indicating the sound of a swift, sudden stroke.

Switch, *n.* a slight blow, as with a switch; a fillip.—*v.* to thresh with a thin stick.

Swite, *v.* to sweat. Cf. Sweat.

Swith, Swithe, *adv.* quickly, suddenly.—*adj.* swift, instant; eager.—*v.* to hasten, to get away.—*int.* begone! quick!

Swither, *v.* to dry up, wither; to parch with heat.

Swither, *v.* to doubt, hesitate; to be undecided or in perplexity; to cause doubt or apprehension; to shake one's resolution.—*n.* doubt, hesitation; a dilemma; a flurry; a panic, 'funk.' Cf. Switter.

Swither, *v.* to overpower forcibly; to rush; to whiz; to put forth all one's strength; to assert one's self, assume a superior dignity or merit; to swagger; to hector.—*n.* a severe blow, such as makes one stagger or become giddy; a trial of strength in exerting mind or tongue.

Swithly, *adv.* swiftly, eagerly.

Switter, *v.* to work confusedly.—*n.* entanglement, confusion; confused working; excitement, fluster, panic. Cf. Swither.

Swoaping, *ppl. adj.* used of the tail of a horse: swishing, sweeping.

Swoich, *v.* to give forth a hollow, whistling sound. Cf. Souch.

Swole, *ppl.* swollen, swelled.

Swoof, *v.* to swoop; to move with a whizzing sound. Cf. Swuff.

Swoom, *v.* to swim. Cf. Soom.

Swoon, *n.* in *phr.* 'in the swoon,' said of corn, the seed of which has lost strength ere the plant is fairly rooted.

Swoop, *v.* to sweep. Cf. Soop.

Swooper, *n.* a bunch of feathers for dusting. Cf. Sweeper.

Swoople, *n.* the striking part of a flail. Cf. Soople.

Swoor, *v. pret.* swore.—*ppl.* sworn. Cf. Swear.

Swoorn, *ppl.* sworn.

Sword, *n.* the leaf of the common yellow iris; a cross-bar in a door or gate.

Sword-claught, *n.* a sword-thrust.

Sword-slipper, -sliper, *n.* a sword-cutler.

Sword-straik, *n.* a sword-stroke.

Swound, *v.* to swoon, faint.—*n.* a swoon; a fainting fit.

Swow, *n.* a dull, murmuring sound.—*v.* to emit such a sound.

Swown, *ppl. adj.* swollen.

Swuff, *v.* to swoop; to move with a whizzing sound; to breathe loudly in sleep; to whistle or hum a tune in a low key or under the breath, to 'sowf'; to faint, swoon. —*n.* the act of whizzing.

Swunged, *ppl.* beaten. Cf. Swinge.

Swuppert, *adj.* nimble, agile; quickly gliding. Cf. Swipper.

Swure, Swuir, *v. pret.* swore.

Swurl, *v.* to swirl. Cf. Swirl.

Swurn, *ppl.* sworn.

Swuther, *v.* to doubt. Cf. Swither.

Swutten, *ppl.* sweated.

Swye, *v.* to sway, to swing. Cf. Sway, Swee.

Swyke, *v.* to deceive, trick.—*n.* a fraud, trick. Cf. Swick.

Swyl, *v.* to swaddle. Cf. Sweel.

Swyle, *n.* a bog. Cf. Swile.

Swylie, *adj.* full of bogs.

Swype, *n.* knowledge, art, skill.

Swype, *v.* to sweep. Cf. Sweep.

Swype, *n.* the exact image or likeness. Cf. Swap.

Swype, *n.* a heavy blow with a stick, &c. Cf. Swipe.

Swype, *v.* to drink hastily and greedily.—*n.* a copious draught.

Swyppirt, *adj.* nimble; sudden; hasty, tart. Cf. Swipper.

Swyre, *n.* the descent of a hill; a pass between two hills. Cf. Swire.

Swyte, *v.* to sweat. Cf. Sweat.

Swyth, Swythe, *adv.* swiftly. Cf. Swith.

Sy, *v.* to strain a liquid. Cf. Sie, Sey.

Sy, *n.* a scythe.

Sy, *n.* the opening of a gown. Cf. Sey.

†**Sybo, Sybie, Syboe, Sybow,** *n.* a young onion; a shallot.

Sybor, *n.* an open drain; a sewer. Cf. Siver.

Sybo-short, *adj.* of short temper.

Sybow-tail, *n.* the tail of an onion.

Syde, *v.* to side with, support.

Syde, *adj.* wide and long; hanging low down. Cf. Side.

Sye, *n.* a scythe.

Sye, *n.* the small wild onion. Cf. Sives.

Sye, *n.* the coal-fish. Cf. Sey.

Sye, *v.* to strain a liquid.

Sye-dish, *n.* a milk-strainer. Cf. Sey-dish.

Sye-milk, *n.* a 'sye-dish.'

Syer, *n.* a strainer.

Sye-sones, -sowens, *n.* a sieve for straining 'sowens.'

Syke, *n.* a small rill. Cf. Sike.

Syle, *v.* to betray; to circumvent.

Syle, *v.* to filter; to strain a liquid. Cf. Sile.

Syle, *n.* a beam; a rafter. Cf. Sile.

Syllab, Syllap, Sylib, *n.* a syllable.—*v.* to divide into syllables.

Sylling, *n.* ceiling.

†**Symar,** *n.* a loose upper garment; a scarf. Cf. Seymar.

Symie, *n.* the devil.

Symion-brodie, *n.* a cross-stick; a children's toy.

Syn, *adv.* since, ago.—*prep.* since.—*conj.* since. Cf. Sin, Syne.

Synd, Synde, *v.* to rinse; to wash down with drink; to draw through water.—*n.* a rinsing; a drink; a drink taken with or just after food; a deluge. Cf. Sind.

Syndins, *n.* water for washing out a dish.

Syndry, *adj.* sundry.—*adv.* asunder.

Syne, *v.* to 'synd.'

Syne, *n.* a small quantity of anything.

Syne, *adv.* ago, since; from that time; then, at that time; afterwards; next in time; in that case; late.—*prep.* since.—*conj.* since; then, thereupon, therefore.

Syneteen, *adj.* seventeen.

Syning-glass, *n.* a looking-glass.

Synle, *adv.* seldom. Cf. Seenil.

Synn, *v.* to wash down. Cf. Synd.

Synner, *v.* to sunder. Cf. Sinder.

Syp, *v.* to sup; to drink, not necessarily in small mouthfuls. Cf. Sip.

Sype, *v.* to percolate slowly; to ooze; to cause to trickle; to soak through. Cf. Sipe.

Syple, *n.* a saucy, big-bellied person.

Syre, *n.* a sewer; a gutter; an open drain; a ditch. Cf. Siver.

Syse, *n.* an assize; a jury. Cf. Size.

Syser, *n.* a juryman.

Syte, *n.* compensation. Cf. Syth.

Syte, *n.* anxious care. Cf. Site.

Syth, *n.* compensation, satisfaction; atonement.

Syth, Sythe, *v.* to strain through a sieve.—*n.* a sieve; a milk-strainer.

Sythe, *n.* a scythe.

Sythment, *n.* compensation, damages.

Syver, Syvor, *n.* a sewer, an open drain. Cf. Siver.

Syzzle, *v.* to shake.

Ta, Taa, *n.* a sucker or stolon of sedge, couch-grass, &c.

Taa, *n.* a marble, a taw.

Taaie, *adj.* fibrous.

Taanle, *n.* a bonfire. Cf. Tawnle.

Taapie, *n.* a stupid, slovenly girl. Cf. Tawpie.

Taat, *n.* a matted tuft of wool or hair. Cf. Taut.

Taatie, *n.* a potato. Cf. Tatie.

Taave, *v.* to struggle; to toil; to distress.— *n.* difficulty, toil; stress. Cf. Tyaave.

Taave, *v.* to toughen by working with the hands. Cf. Tyaave.

Taave, *v.* to tease out; to entangle; to caulk; to close up a hole, &c., by stuffing. Cf. Tyaave.

Taave-taes, *n.* pit-fir split into fibres and twisted for ropes.

Taavin-skate, *n.* skate separated into filaments.

Tab, *adj.* used of a cat: brindled, striped.— *n.* a male cat; a pet name for a cat.

Tab, *n.* a loop for hanging a coat, &c.

Tabacca, *n.* tobacco.

Tabbet, Tabbit, *n.* opportunity of advantage occurring.

Tabbit, *ppl. adj.* used of a cap: having the corners folded up.

Tab-cat, *n.* a pet cat.

Tabernacle, *n.* the bodily frame; a full habit of body.

Taberin, *n.* a beating. Cf. Tabour.

Tabet, *n.* bodily sensation, feeling; strength.

Tabetless, *adj.* numb, without sensation; heedless, foolish.

Table, *n.* the Communion Table; a water-course at the side of a road to carry off water; a map, chart.—*v.* to board.

Table-cloot, *n.* a table-cloth.

Table-seat, *n.* a square church-pew containing a table; in *pl.* seats set apart for communicants.

Table-tombstane, *n.* a flat gravestone.

Tabling, *n.* the stone coping of a wall or gable; a ledge on a slope in which a hedge may be planted.

Tabour, *v.* to drub, thrash.—*n.* in *pl.* a drubbing. Cf. Toober.

Tabrach, Tabragh, *n.* animal food nearly in a state of carrion.

Ta-brig, *n.* a drawbridge. Cf. To-brig.

Taby, *n.* watered silk or other stuff, tabby.

Tach, *v.* to drive a nail so as to give it a slight hold; to fasten on slightly.—*n.* a fringe; a shoulder-knot.

†**Tach, Tache,** *v.* to soil; to slander; to fatigue.—*n.* a stain, blot. Cf. Tash.

Tacht, *adj.* tight, tense; strict, severe.

Tack, *v.* to fasten; to keep together; to nail. —*n.* a stitch; a slight fastening; the membrane attaching the tongue to the lower part of the mouth; a time, spell; a manœuvre, expedient.

Tack, *n.* a hobnail. Cf. Tacket.

Tack, *v.* to take; to marry; to charge, as a price; to cost time or trouble; used of fish: to rise readily to bait; to deliver a blow; to strike against; to be seized with pain, &c.; to affect, happen to; to burn brightly; to betake one's self to; to take a contract for work; to understand; to acknowledge; to take for granted; to induce, cause to come.— *n.* a catch or haul of fish, &c.; a lease, holding, farm; a state of excitement, grief, fuss, &c.; a bargain, one's word or promise.

Tackad, *n.* a hobnail. Cf. Tacket.

Tack-duty, *n.* rent.

Tacket, Tackit, *n.* a hobnail; used of whisky: a pimple caused by drink.—*v.* to drive 'tackets' into boots, &c.

Tacket, *n.* a restless, unruly boy.

Tacket-boot, *n.* a hobnailed boot.

Tacket-soled, *adj.* hobnailed.

Tackety, *adj.* hobnailed.

Tackety-shoed, *adj.* wearing hobnailed shoes.

Tackie, *n.* a game in which one chases his playmates; the one who chases.

Tackit, *ppl. adj.* tongue-tied.

Tackle, Tackel, *n.* an arrow.

Tackle, *v.* to catch with fishing-tackle; to punish; to take to task; to accost; with *to*, to set vigorously to work.

Tack on, *v.* to buy on credit.

Tacksman, *n.* a leaseholder; a tenant-farmer; a toll-keeper.

Tack the gate, *v.* to set off, depart.

Tack wi', *v.* to acknowledge.

Tacle, *n.* an arrow.

Taddy, *n.* a snuff bearing the name of its maker.

Taddy-powder, -snuff, *n.* 'taddy.'

Tade, *n.* a toad; a term of contempt, disgust, &c.; a term of endearment for a child; a child.

Tade, *n.* the tick, sheep-louse.

Tae, *prep.* to.

Tae, *n.* a toe; the branch of a drain; the prong of a fork.

Tae, *num. adj.* the one, contrasted with the other.

Tae-bit, *n.* a toe-plate for a shoe.

Taebit, *n.* strength. Cf. Tabet.

Tae-breeth, *n.* the smallest possible distance.

Tae'd, *ppl. adj.* pronged.

Taed, *n.* a toad. Cf. Tade.

Taedie, *n.* a fondling name for a child.

Tae-ee, *n.* a pet, fondling.

Tael-duck, *n.* the teal.

Taen, *num. adj.* the one, contrasted with the other.

Taen, *v. pret.* took.—*ppl.* taken.

Taen, *v.* to lay hands on the head of one caught in games.

Taen-awa, *n.* a changeling.

Taening, *n.* the act by which one 'taens' another in games.

Tae-shod, *n.* an iron toe-piece on boot or shoe.

Tae's length, *n.* the shortest distance possible.

Tae-stane, *n.* the stone at the foot of a grave.

Taesty, *adj.* palatable, tasteful. Cf. Tasty.

Taet, *n.* a lock of hair, wool, or fibrous substance; a small quantity of anything.—*v.* to pluck wool, &c., in small quantities. Cf. Tait.

Taff, *n.* turf.

Taff-dyke, *n.* a turf fence.

Taffel, Taffil, *n.* a small table.

Tafferel, *adj.* giddy, thoughtless; ill-dressed.

Taffie, *n.* a sweetmeat of boiled treacle and flour, eaten only at Hallowe'en.

Taffle, *v.* to tire; to wear out with fatigue; to ravel, ruffle.

Taft, *n.* the thwart of a boat.

Taft, *n.* a toft, messuage, homestead; a bed for plants. Cf. Toft.

Taftan, *n.* a toft, homestead. Cf. Toftin.

Taft-hoose, *n.* the house attached to a toft.

Tag, *adj.* tag-rag.

Tag, *n.* any small, nasty thing adhering to a. larger; the white hair at the tip of the tail of an ox or cow; a disease of sheep, scab on the tail.—*v.* to have the tip of the tail white; with *after*, to follow closely at the heels.

Tag, *n.* anything used for tying, binding, &c.; a strap; a shoe-tie; a thong; a long, thin slice; a piece; a schoolmaster's 'tawse.'—*v.* to bind, fasten; to punish with the 'tawse.'

Tag, *v.* used of the moon: to wane.

Tag, Tagg, *n.* fatigue; a burden; in *phr.* 'in the tag,' always kept hard at work.—*v.* to exhaust; to tire; to oppress with toil.

Tag and rag, *n.* every bit, the whole.

Taggie, *n.* a cow whose tail is white at the tip.

Taggit, *ppl. adj.* used of a woman: wearing a frock shorter than the petticoat underneath. Cf. Tag-tailed.

Taggit, *ppl. adj.* used of cattle: having the tip of the tail white.

Taggle, Taggil, *v.* to delay, hinder; to harass.

Tagh, *n.* tallow. Cf. Tauch.

Taghairm, *n.* a mode of divination formerly used in the Highlands.

Taght, *adj.* stretched out; tightened. Cf. Tacht.

Tag-tailed, *adj.* used of a woman: wearing a frock shorter than the petticoat underneath.

Tah, *n.* tallow. Cf. Tauch.

Tahie, *adj.* greasy; used of the weather: warm and moist.

Taid, *n.* the droppings of cattle or sheep.—*v.* to dung land with 'taid' in pasturing or folding cattle, &c. Cf. Tathe.

Taid, *n.* a toad; a term of contempt or disgust; a fondling name for a child.

Taidie, *n.* a pet designation for a little child.

Taid-stule, *n.* a mushroom.

Taifle, *n.* a small table. Cf. Taffel.

Taigle, *v.* to entangle; to 'tackle' with, to harass; to weary; to detain, delay, hinder; to occupy one's time; to tarry, loiter, dawdle.—*n.* a hindrance, cause of delay. Cf. Taggle.

Taiglesum, *adj.* causing hindrance.

Taigsum, *adj.* 'taiglesum.'

Taigy, *n.* a cow with white at the tip of the tail. Cf. Taggie.

Taik, *n.* a stroll, saunter.

Taiken, *n.* a token; evidence; a small quantity, pinch. Cf. Taken.

Taikin, *n.* a kind of cloth, ticking.

Taikle, *n.* tackle.

Tail, *n.* the posteriors, the train of a robe, the bottom of a skirt at the back; a retinue or following; the pendulum of a clock; the hind-part of a cart or plough; the stern of a boat or ship; a fish; a horse-leech; the end of a portion of time; the lower end of a field; used in weaving: a number of cords stretching over pulleys in the harness-box, and connecting the 'simple' with the yarn; the tap-root of a turnip; in *pl.* inferior sheep drafted out of the fat or young stock; onion-leaves; the lighter grains or refuse grains from threshing.

Tail-board, *n.* the door of a close cart.

Tailer, *n.* a tool for cutting off the tap-roots of turnips.

†**Tailie,** *n.* a slice. Cf. Tailyie.

Tail-ill, *n.* an inflammatory disease of a cow's tail.

Taillyer, *n.* a tailor.

Tail-meal, *n.* meal made from the lighter part of grain.

Tail-net, *n.* the herring-net first shot and farthest from the boat.

Tailor-body, *n.* a tailor, used contemptuously.

Tailor-man, *n.* a 'tailor-body.'

Tailor's-gartens, *n.* the ribbon-grass.

Tailor's-nip, *n.* a pinch given to a boy wearing new clothes for the first time.

Tail-pressed, *adj.* closely pressed.

Tail-rot, -slip, *n.* 'tail-ill.'

Tail-toddle, *n.* conjugal rights.

Tail-tynt, *n.* in *phrs.* to 'ride tail-tynt,' to stake one horse against another in a race, so that the losing horse is lost to its owner; to 'play tail-tynt,' to make a fair exchange.

Tail-win, *n.* the last band of reapers.

Tail-wind, *n.* in *phr.* to 'shear wi' a tailwind,' to cut grain, not straight across the ridge, but diagonally.

Tail-worm, *n.* 'tail-ill.'

Tail-wyrin, *n.* the finish of anything to be gathered up, as the end of a 'bout' in a corn-field.

†Tailyie, Tailzie, *n.* a cut or slice of meat; a large piece of meat; an entail.—*v.* to entail.

Tailyour, *n.* a tailor.

Taing, *n.* a tang, prong; anything ending in a point; the tongue of a Jews' harp; a flat tongue of land projecting into the sea. Cf. Tang.

Taings, *n.* tongs.

Tainty, *adj.* attentive; watchful. Cf. Tenty.

Taipet, *n.* bodily sensation. Cf. Tabet.

Taipetless, *adj.* benumbed; heedless, foolish. Cf. Tabetless.

Taird, *n.* a term of gross contempt, used of men and animals; a gibe, taunt, sarcasm.

Tairdie, *adj.* satirical; peevish, sulky. Cf. Tardie.

Tairge, *v.* to beat, thrash; to keep under discipline; to scold vigorously; to cross-examine, question closely.—*n.* a scold.

Tairger, *n.* a scold, virago; a quarrelsome woman.

Tairgin, *n.* a severe scolding or cross-examination.

Tairin, *ppl. adj.* excessive; boisterous; strenuous; violent. Cf. Taring.

†Tais, *n.* a cup, glass. Cf. Tass.

Taisch, *n.* the voice of a person about to die; 'second sight.' Cf. Task.

Taise, *v.* to tease. Cf. Tease.

†Taisie, *n.* a cup, a glass. Cf. Tass.

Taissle, Taisle, *v.* to entangle, twist; to toss; to disorder, jumble; to handle too much; to puzzle a person in an examination; to confuse, perplex; to tease, irritate.—*n.* the act of mixing or jumbling; disorder caused by wind; too much handling; a puzzle, a puzzling; a vexing, a teasing; a severe tussle. Cf. Teasle.

Taiste, *n.* the black guillemot. Cf. Teistie.

Taistril, Taistrill, *n.* a dirty, gawkish, 'feckless' woman; a careless girl regardless of her dress.

Tait, *n.* a lock of hair, wool, &c.; anything like hair, wool, hay, straw, &c., plucked; a small sheaf; a small quantity of anything.

—*v.* to pluck any fibrous stuff in small quantities.

Taith, *n.* the dung of pastured sheep or cattle; a tuft of grass growing where dung has been dropped in a field.—*v.* to manure land by pasturing or feeding sheep or cattle on it. Cf. Tathe.

Tait-lock, *n.* a small matted lock of hair, wool, &c.

Taiver, *v.* to wander; to delay; to rave or talk wildly or foolishly.—*n.* in *pl.* wild, raving words; tatters, rags.

Taiversum, *adj.* tiresome, tedious.

Taivert, *ppl. adj.* wandering; foolish, senseless, raving; stupid with drink; boiled to rags; fatigued.

†Taizie, *n.* a cup, goblet. Cf. Tass.

Tak, *v.* to sew, stitch.

Tak, Take, *v.* to marry; to cost time and trouble; used of fish: to take the bait readily; to strike, deliver a blow; to catch in, strike against; to seize, as with pain, sickness, panic, &c.; to happen to, affect; to take fire, burn brightly; to betake one's self to; to haunt; to contract for work; to acknowledge; to understand, to take for granted; to cause to come, bring.—*n.* a catch of fish; a lease, 'tack'; a situation; a state of excitement, &c. Cf. Tack.

Tak aff, *n.* a mimic; a jester.—*v.* to go off, betake one's self.

Tak-bannets, *n.* a game in which 'bonnets' are generally the pledges, and in which the side that carries off most of these one by one is the winner.

Taken, *n.* a token.

Take in, *n.* a cheat.

Take on, *v.* to undertake; to engage for.

Take-up, *n.* a tuck.—*v.* to register.

Take with, *v.* to acknowledge, admit.

Takie, *adj.* used of victuals: lasting.

Taking, *n.* a state of excitement; a capture; a pinch of snuff.

Tal, *int.* an expletive.

Tale, *n.* one's own account or story.

Tale-pyet, -piet, -py't, *n.* a tale-bearer; a tell-tale.

Taler, Talor, *n.* state, condition.

Tale's man, *n.* one who gives or originates a piece of news; the authority for a statement.

†Taliation, *n.* adjustment of one thing to another.

Talking, *n.* a scolding.—*ppl. adj.* talkative, 'blethering.'

Tallan, Tallin, *n.* tallow. Cf. Tallon.

Talliwap, *n.* a blow, a stroke.

Tallon, Tallown, *n.* tallow.—*v.* to grease with tallow.

Tallow-leaf, *n.* the fat covering the entrails of animals.

Tallowny-faced, *adj*. sallow.

Tallow-powk, *n*. a bag through which melted tallow is strained in refining.

Tally-ho-the-hounds, *n*. a boys' game.

Taltie, *n*. a wig.

†Talyee, *n*. a joint of beef; an entail. Cf. Tailyie.

†Tambourer, *n*. an embroiderer of silk, &c., stretched on a circular frame.

†Tambour-major, *n*. a drum-major.

Tamer, *n*. the sharp-nosed eel; the broad-nosed eel.

Tammachless, *adj*. used of a child : not eating with appetite; tasteless, insipid.

Tammas, *n*. the puffin.

Tammasmas, *n*. the feast of St Thomas, Dec. 21.

Tammie, *n*. a loaf of bread.

Tammie-cheekie, *n*. the puffin.

Tammie-Harper, *n*. the crab, *Cancer araneus*.

Tammie-herl, *n*. the heron.

Tammie-louper, *n*. a child's toy made of black tangle.

Tammie-noddie-heid, *n*. the butterfly chrysalis.

Tammie-Noddy, *n*. the puffin.

Tammie-Norie, -Norrie, *n*. the puffin; the razor-bill; a simpleton.

Tammie-reekie, *n*. a cabbage-stalk hollowed out and filled with lighted tow.

Tammie-toddy, *n*. a kind of spindle.

Tammie-wake, *n*. the cock-sparrow.

Tammil, *v*. to scatter from carelessness, or from design, as money in a crowd by candidates at an election.

Tammock, *n*. a hillock; a little knoll.

Tam o' cheeks, *n*. the puffin.

Tam o' tae end, *n*. a ludicrous designation for the larger end of a pudding.

Tamper away, *v*. to find or take one's way.

Tamson's bairns, or man, *n*. in *phr*. 'to be John Tamson's bairns,' or 'man,' to be of one stock, on an equality. Cf. John Thomson's man.

Tamson's mear, *n*. walking, 'Shank's naigie.'

Tam-taigle, *n*. a rope fastening a hind-leg to a fore-leg of a horse or cow to prevent straying.

Tam-tary, Tamtarrie, *n*. detention under frivolous pretences; the state of being hindered.

Tamteen, *n*. a tontine.

Tam-tram, *v*. to play; to play fast and loose.

Tam-trot, *n*. a kind of toffee.

Tan, *v*. to rebuke; to keep one steadily at work. Cf. Taun.

Tan, *n*. a temporary hut.

Tandle, *n*. a bonfire. Cf. Tawnle.

Tane, *ppl*. taken; taken aback.

Tane, *num. adj*. the one.

Tane-awa, *n*. a decayed, unhealthy, puny

child; a suspected changeling substituted by the fairies.

Tane doon, *adj*. enfeebled by illness; reduced in circumstances; diluted.

Tang, *n*. a species of seaweed, a tangle.

Tang, *n*. a prong; a pike; a sting; a piece of iron used for fencing anything else; a low tongue of land projecting into the sea; the tongue of a Jews' harp. Cf. Taing.

Tang, *n*. a twang, timbre of the voice. Cf. Tong.

Tang, *n*. a strong or unpleasant flavour.

Tang, *adj*. straight, tight.

Tanghal, *n*. a bag, satchel. Cf. Toighal.

Tangie, *n*. a sea-sprite appearing sometimes as a small horse, sometimes as an old man; a young seal.

Tangle, *v*. to entangle.—*adj*. tall and feeble; loose in the joints; relaxed through fatigue, too tired to stand up.—*n*. a tall, lank person; an icicle; a species of seaweed; a state of perplexity; in *pl*. the knots of scroll-work cut on Celtic crosses.

Tangle-backit, *adj*. long and lean in the back, lanky.

Tangleness, *n*. indecision, fluctuation; pliability of opinion.

Tangle-wise, *adj*. long and slender, lanky.

Tangly, *adj*. long and slender.

Tang o' the trump, *n*. the tongue of a Jews' harp; the chief personage or actor in a company.

Tangs, *n*. tongs.

Tang-sparrow, *n*. the shore pipit.

Tang-whaup, *n*. the whimbrel.

Tanker, Tankor, *n*. a tankard.

Tanker, *n*. a large, ugly person, or lean animal.

Tanker-backit, *adj*. hunch-backed, round-shouldered, having an ungainly back.

Tanker-mouthed, *adj*. used of dogs : having large, forbidding mouths.

Tankle, *n*. an icicle. Cf. Tangle.

Tannage, *n*. a tannery.

Tanner, *n*. the small root of a tree; the root of a tooth, corn, or boil; the part that is fitted into a mortise.

Tanneree, *n*. a tannery.

Tanny, *adj*. tawny, dark-complexioned.—*n*. a mulatto; a dark-complexioned person.

Tansy, *n*. in *phr*. 'my delight's in tansies,' a children's singing-game.

Tant, *v*. to argue captiously, wrangle; to rage.

Tant, *v*. to upset one's digestion. Cf. Taunt.

Tantaleeze, *v*. to tantalize; to aggravate; to taunt.

Tantallon, Tantallan, *n*. in *phr*. 'to ding doun Tantallon,' to exceed all bounds, to attempt the impossible.

Tanter, *v.* to quarrel; to dispute captiously; to rage.

Tanterlick, *n.* a severe blow.

Tantin', *ppl. adj.* raging; squally, stormy.

Tantivy, *adv.* quickly.

Tantrum, *n.* a whimsy, whim, vagary; a fluster; ill-temper; in *pl.* high airs, affected airs.

Tantrum-fit, *n.* a fit of ill-temper.

Tanty-ranty, *n.* fornication.

Tan-yaird, *n.* the poorhouse, as if old people were sent thither to be got rid of, like old horses to the tannery.

Tap, *n.* a boys' top.

Tap, *n.* the top; the head; the tip; a tuft on the head of a bird; a tuft of hair; the woollen knob on the top of a 'bonnet'; a fir-cone; a hill; a heap; the quantity of flax put on the distaff; cream, the surface of milk; in *pl.* the best sheep or lambs in a flock.—*v.* to snuff a candle; to lead off in a dance, &c.; to parade, walk in stately fashion.—*adj.* excellent.

Tap-an-teerie, *adv.* upside-down. Cf. Tap-salteerie.

Tap-bird, *n.* in *phr.* 'the tap-bird of the nest,' the best of a family.

Tap-castle, *n.* the upper part of a weaver's loom.

Tap-dressed, *adj.* smartly beaten; manured on the surface.

Tape, *v.* to use sparingly; to stint.

†**Tapee,** *n.* the fore-part of the hair when put up with pins; a small cushion worn by old women at the 'opening' of the head, to keep up the hair.

Tapered, *ppl. adj.* used of a building: high and frail.

Taper-tail, *adv.* topsy-turvy.

Tapet, *n.* bodily sensation. Cf. Tabet.

Tapetless, *adj.* heedless.

Tap-flude, *n.* high flood.

Tapie, *n.* a giddy, foolish, or slovenly girl. Cf. Tawpie.

Tapis, *n.* a top-coat.

Tapisht, *ppl.* lurking.

Tapi-toorie, *n.* anything raised to a point. Cf. Tappie-toorie.

Tap-knot, *n.* the human head; a knot of ribbons on a woman's cap.

Taplash, *n.* bad small-beer; the dregs of liquor.

Taploch, *n.* a giddy, hare-brained girl. Cf. Tawpie.

Tapmaist, *adj.* uppermost.

Tapman, *n.* a ship with tops.

Tap o' lint, *n.* the quantity of flax put on a distaff.

Tapone staff, *n.* the stave in which the bung-hole of a cask is.

Tap o' tow, *n.* 'tap o' lint'; an irascible person; a shaggy-headed child.

Tapoun, *n.* a tap-root; a long fibre at a root. Cf. Tappin.

Tappenie, *int.* a term used in calling a hen.

Tapper, *n.* one who taps a cask, a 'drawer.'

Tappie, *n.* a crested hen.

Tap-piece, *n.* a hat, a cap.

Tap-pickle, *n.* the uppermost grain in a stalk of oats.

Tappie-toorie, -tourie, *n.* anything raised very high to a point; the knob of pastry on the top of a covered pie; a 'tappiloorie.'

Tappie-tourock, *n.* a 'tappie-tourie.'

Tappie-tousie, *n.* a children's game, in which one holds another by the hair of the head and asks questions; a shaggy head of hair.

Tappiloorie, *n.* anything raised high on a slight or tottering foundation.

Tappin, *n.* the root of a tree; the tap-root of a turnip, &c.; a long, thin person.

Tappin, *n.* a crest; the tuft of feathers on the head of a cock or hen; the woollen knob on the top of a 'bonnet'; the top of the head; the head; the noddle. Cf. Toppen.

Tappin'd, Tappent, *ppl. adj.* crested, tufted.

Tappinless, *adj.* without a tassel or knob.

Tappit, *ppl. adj.* crested, having a top.

Tappit-hen, *n.* a crested hen; a Scottish quart-measure of ale or claret, having a knob on its lid; a measure containing three English quarts; a large bottle of claret, holding three magnums or Scots pints.

Tappity, *adj.* tufted, crested.

Tapple, *v.* to topple.

Tappy, *n.* a hare-brained or slovenly girl. Cf. Tawpie.

Tappy, *n.* the crown of a child's head.

Tap-rooted, *adj.* deeply rooted.

Tap-rung, *n.* the highest point, summit.

Tapsalteerie, Tapselterrie, *adv.* topsy-turvy, upside-down.—*n.* a state of disorder; a topsy-turvy manner.

Tapsie-teerie, Tapsill-teerie, *adv.* topsy-turvy.

Tapsman, *n.* the principal servant in charge; the man in charge of a drove.

Tap-swarm, *n.* the first swarm from a hive of bees; a body of people who are the first to leave their former connection.

Tap-sweat, *n.* a profuse perspiration.

Tap, tail, and mane, *n.* neither head nor tail of a matter.

Taptee, *n.* a state of eager desire. Cf. Taptoo.

Tap-thrawn, *adj.* perverse; headstrong; disputatious.

Taptoo, *n.* a gaudy ornament on the head; a violent passion. Cf. Tiptoo.

Tap-tree, *n.* a solid and rounded piece of wood used as a bung in a brewing vat or cask.

Tap-wark, *n.* part of a weaver's 'mounting.'

Tarans, *n.* the souls of unbaptized children.

Tar-buist, *n.* the box holding tar for sheep-marking.

Tard, *n.* a dirty person. Cf. Taird.

Tardie, *adj.* peevish, sulky, sarcastic. Cf. Tairdie.

Tards, *n.* a schoolmaster's 'tawse.'

Tare, *v.* to tear.

Taretathers, *n.* what is torn in shreds.

Targat, Target, *n.* a tassel; an ornament for the hat; a shred, a tatter; a long, thin slice of dried fish.

Targe, *v.* to beat, thrash; to keep in order; to discipline; to scold loudly or severely; to cross-question; to examine rigorously.— *n.* a scold, a virago.

Targed, *ppl. adj.* tattered; shabby in appearance.

Targer, *n.* a scold, a virago, a 'vixen.'

Targing, *n.* a severe cross-questioning.

Taring, *n.* the common tern.

Tarj, *n.* a dirty person.

Tarle, Tarl, *v.* to work lazily; to be lazily disposed; to labour under disease.—*n.* a weak, puny person or animal; a dirty person.

Tar-leather, *n.* a strong slip of leather, salted and hung, used for coupling the staves of a flail.

Tarloch, Tarlack, Tarlich, Tarlogh, *n.* a mean fellow; a sturdy, brawling woman; a dirty female tatterdemalion; a silly, inactive girl; any creature or thing puny, weak, and worthless; a horse restive at the plough, &c.—*v.* to go about lazily; to labour under disease. — *adj.* weak, peevish; stormy; squeamish, not caring for food; restive; 'fashious,' 'pernicketty.'

Tar-mop, *n.* a mop for tarring with.

Tarnation, *n.* damnation.—*adj.*, *adv.*, and *int.* used as expletive and as intensive.

Tarnish, *n.* anything that tarnishes.

Tarnty, *n.* trinity.

Tar-pig, *n.* a jar of tar for marking sheep.

Tarpit, *v.* to interpret.

Tarragat, *v.* to interrogate.

Tarragatin, *n.* a strict examination; the act of examining strictly.

Tarran, *n.* a peevish, ill-tempered person. Cf. Tirran.

Tarras, *n.* a terrace.

Tarret, *n.* the common tern. Cf. Tarrock.

Tarrie, *n.* trouble.

Tarrie, *n.* a terrier dog.

Tarrock, *n.* the common tern; the Arctic tern; the kittiwake. Cf. Tirracke.

Tarrow, *v.* to tarry, linger; to loathe; to find fault with food, to refuse food peevishly; to complain; to be sick and weakly; used of springing corn: not to thrive.—*n.* a slight illness; used of grain springing: exhaustion of strength, inability to draw nourishment from the soil; a loathing.

Tarrower, *n.* one who 'tarrows' as to food.

Tarry, *adj.* used of the hands: adhesive, light-fingered.

Tarry-breeks, *n.* a sailor.

Tarry-fingered, *adj.* light-fingered, pilfering.

Tarry-fingers, *n.* dishonest fingers; a dishonest person.

Tarry-handit, -haun'd, *adj.* dishonest, pilfering.

Tarrymichie-clay, *n.* a fine kind of clay.

Tarry-neives, *n.* 'tarry-fingers.'

Tarry-trick, *n.* cheating, pilfering.

Tarsie-versie, *adv.* walking backwards; in confusion. Cf. Tersy-versy.

Tart, *adj.* used of gossip: stinging, painful.

Tartan, *n.* the Scottish Lowland dialect; the Highland dialect; Highland manners or customs; 'tartan-purry.'

Tartan-purry, *n.* a pudding of red cabbage and oatmeal.

Tarter, *n.* noise made by scrambling about.

Tartle, *v.* to hesitate; to hesitate in recognizing a person; to boggle, scruple; used of a horse: to shy, jib; to recognize.—*n.* hesitation in recognizing.

Tartle, *v.* to rend, tatter.

†**Tartuffish,** *adj.* sour, sulky, stubborn.

†**Tarveal,** *v.* to fatigue; to vex; to travail.— *n.* fatigue.—*adj.* fretful, ill-tempered.

Tascal-money, *n.* money formerly given in the Highlands for information as to 'raided' cattle.

†**Tash,** *v.* to soil, tarnish; to bespatter; to cast a stain on a person, injure by calumny; to upbraid; to weary out; with *about*, to throw things carelessly about so as to damage them.—*n.* a stain, spot, flaw; an affront, reproach; disgrace. Cf. Tach.

Tashellie, *adj.* used of animals: having the hair or wool matted with dirt, dung, &c.

Tasht, *ppl. adj.* well-worn; frayed.

Task, *v.* to impose a task or lesson.

Task, *n.* the angel or spirit of any person. Cf. Taisch.

Tasker, *n.* a labourer at piece-work.

Taskit, *ppl. adj.* over-fatigued with work.

Taskit-like, *adj.* appearing to be greatly fatigued.

Tass, Tas, *n.* a small heap of earth; a large bunch; a cluster of flowers.

†**Tass, Tasse,** *n.* a cup, glass; a goblet, bowl.

Tassel-stane, *n.* the projecting stone above the door of a castle or 'keep,' from which evil-doers, &c., were hung.

†**Tassie,** *n.* a 'tass'; a small glass, &c.

Tassle, Tassell, *v.* to entangle; to toss; to tease. Cf. Taissle.

Taste, v. to partake of refreshments; to take a dram; to give relish or appetite to; to please the palate; to quench hunger or thirst; to appreciate mentally.—n. used of drink: a dram, a sip; of any liquid: a small quantity.

Taster, n. a dram; a mouthful of spirits.

Taster, n. a sea-fowl. Cf. Taiste.

Tasting, n. a small quantity of anything; a mouthful of food or drink.

Tasty, adj. savoury; appetizing; neat, dainty; attractive.

Tat, n. a tuft of hair, wool, &c.—v. to mat, to lie in tufts.

Ta-ta, int. good-bye!

Tatch, v. to drive a nail so as to give it a slight hold; to fix slightly by a nail.—n. a fringe; a shoulder-knot. Cf. Tach.

Tate, n. a tuft of wool, &c.; a little sheaf of straw for making baskets, ropes, &c. Cf. Tait, Taut.

Tatelock n. a small lock of hair.

Tathe, Tath, v. to dung; to make grass grow in tufts by droppings of horses, cattle, sheep, &c.—n. droppings of cattle, sheep, &c. on land; the luxuriant grass grown on droppings, or manure applied otherwise. Cf. Taith, Toath.

Tathe-faud, n. a field on which cattle, &c., are shut up at night to manure the ground with their droppings.

Tathil, n. a small table.

Tathing, n. the raising of rank grass by manure.

Tatie, Tattie, n. a potato; the head; a term of contempt.

Tatie-beetle, n. a potato-masher.

Tatie-bing, n. a potato-heap.

Tatie-blots, n. water in which potatoes have been boiled.

Tatie-bogie, -bogle, n. a scarecrow among growing potatoes.

Tatie-boodie, n. a 'tatie-bogie.'

Tatie-broo, n. potato-soup.

Tatie-chapper, n. a potato-masher.

Tatie-doolie, n. a scarecrow in a potato-field.

Tatie-dreel, n. a potato-drill.

Tatie-grab, n. a way of grabbing and eating potatoes from the dish.

Tatie-graip, n. a flat-pronged fork for digging potatoes.

Tatie-grun', n. a potato-field or patch.

Tatie-head, n. a stupid head.

Tatie-howker, n. a potato-digger.

Tatie-kro, n. a corner in a house boarded to keep potatoes from frost.

Tatie-liftin, n. potato-digging.

Tatie-like, -laek, adj. used of ground: looking fit to grow potatoes.

Tatie-müld, n. a potato-field or -patch.

Tatie-pairer, n. a potato-peeler.

Tatie-peck, n. a peck measure for potatoes.

Tatie-peels, n. potato-skins.

Tatie-pat, n. a potato-pot.

Tatie-pit, n. a potato-heap protected to preserve potatoes from frost.

Tatie-pourins, n. water in which potatoes have been boiled.

Taties and dab, n. potatoes boiled in skins, dipped in salt, and eaten.

Taties and point, n. potatoes eaten, with a small bit of beef or fish, which is not, however, eaten, but is pointed to with the potato.

Tatie-scon, n. a scone made of flour and mashed potatoes.

Tatie-settin', n. potato-planting.

Tatie-shaws, n. potato-stems.

Tatie-soup, n. potato-soup; in phr. 'the ticket for tatie-soup,' an expression of the highest praise.

Tatie-trap, n. the human mouth.

Tatie-walin', n. sorting out potatoes.

Tatie-warks, n. farina or starch mills dealing with potatoes.

Tatie-washins, n. water in which potatoes have been washed.

Tatshie, adj. dressed in slovenly manner.

Tatter, v. to tear, rend in pieces; to rave, talk in delirium.

Tatter, v. to hurry, go at great speed.

Tatter-wallop, n. a woman who does not mend her clothes; in pl. fluttering rags; hanging rags.—v. to hang in rags.

Tattery, adj. tattered, ragged.

Tattle, n. a clot of dirt adhering to the tail of a cow or sheep. Cf. Tittle.

Tattrel, n. a rag.

Tatty, adj. matted; rough and shaggy.

Tauch, Taugh, n. tallow; grease.—v. to grease.

Tauch, Taugh, n. the threads of large ropes.

Tauchey, Taughie, adj. greasy, clammy; used of the weather: warm, moist, or misty.

Tauchey-faced, adj. greasy-faced.

Taucht, v. pret. did teach.—ppl. adj. taught.

Taucht, n. tallow that has been melted.

Taud, n. a toad.

Taudy, n. a child.

Taudy, n. the breech, buttocks.

Taudy-fee, n. a fine for having an illegitimate child, 'buttock-mail.'

Tauk, n. talk.—v. to talk.

Taul', Tauld, v. pret. and ppl. told.

Taum, n. a rope; a line; a fishing-line, one made of horse-hair; a long thread of any viscous or glutinous substance; gossamer. —v. to draw out any viscous substance into a line. Cf. Toum.

Taum, v. to fall gently asleep; to swoon.—

n. a fit of drowsiness; a fit of faintness or sickness; an ungovernable fit of ill-humour. Cf. Tawm.

Taums, *adj.* ropy, glutinous. Cf. Toums.

Taun, *v.* to urge one on with taunts.

Taundle, Taunel, *n.* a bonfire. Cf. Tawnle.

Taunt, *v.* with *at,* to mock at.

Taunt, *v.* to upset the digestion.

Taupie, *n.* a foolish woman. Cf. Tawpie.

Taupiet, *adj.* foolish; inactive and slovenly.

Taupin, *n.* the root of a tree; a lanky person. Cf. Tappin.

Tauploch, *n.* a giddy, flighty girl.

Taupsaleery, *adj.* topsy-turvy. Cf. Tapsalteerie.

Taur, *n.* tar.

Taurd, *n.* a large piece.

Taurie, *n.* a terrier. Cf. Tarrie.

Taury, Taurrie, *adj.* tarry. Cf. Tarry.

Taut, *v.* to mat; to entangle; to run into tufts; to make rugs of thick worsted yarn. —*n.* a mat; matting; a tuft of hair, wool, &c.; in *pl.* thick worsted yarn for making rugs. Cf. Tawt.

Taut, *v.* to drag or dash to the ground; to drag to and fro.—*n.* a heavy dash; abuse by dragging or dashing about. Cf Tawt.

Tauther, *v.* to abuse by dragging to and fro. —*n.* such abuse.

Tauthereeze, *v.* to 'tauther.'

Tautie, *n.* a potato. Cf. Tatie.

Tautie-bogle, *n.* a scarecrow.

Tautit, *ppl. adj.* used of the hair: matted; shaggy, ragged.

Tautit-rug, *n.* a thick bed-coverlet.

Tauty, *adj.* used of the hair: matted, shaggy.

Tauty-headit, *adj.* shaggy-headed.

Tauven, *ppl. adj.* tired.

Tavar, Taver, *v.* to wander; to talk foolishly. —*n.* in *pl.* rags; raving talk. Cf. Taiver.

Tavernry, *n.* tavern expenses.

Tavert, *ppl. adj.* stupid; doted.

Taw, *v.* to knead; to work in mortar; to tumble about; to spoil by too much handling; to pull, lay hold of; to whip.—*n.* a whip; the point of a whip; a difficulty; a great to-do; hesitation, reluctance.

Taw, *v.* to suck greedily and continuously like a hungry child.

Taw, *n.* a streak of light.

Tawdy, *n.* a child. Cf. Taudy.

Tawdy, *n.* the buttocks, the breech. Cf. Towdy.

†Taweal, *n.* fatigue. Cf. Tarveal.

Tawen, Tawan, *v.* to disfigure by overhandling; to pull, lay hold of; to tumble about; to knead.—*n.* a difficulty, a great ado; hesitation; reluctance.

Tawie, *adj.* tame; tractable; allowing to be handled; quiet; gentle.

Tawm, *v.* to fall asleep gently; to swoon.—*n.* a drowsy fit; a fit of sickness or fainting; an ungovernable temper.

Tawm, *n.* a fishing-line; a long thread of viscous matter; gossamer.—*v.* to draw out a viscous substance into a line. Cf. Taum.

Tawnle, Tawnel, *n.* a bonfire, a large fire.

Tawny, *n.* a dark-complexioned person; a mulatto. Cf. Tanny.

Tawnymichie-clay, *n.* a fine kind of clay. Cf. Tarrymichie-clay.

Tawpie, Tawpa, *n.* a foolish, awkward, giddy, idle, or slovenly girl; a foolish fellow; a blockhead.—*adj.* foolish, awkward, slovenly, ill-conditioned; tawdry.

Tawpie-headit, *adj.* having a silly, stupid head.

Tawploch, *n.* a giddy-brained girl. Cf. Taploch.

Tawrds, *n.* a schoolmaster's 'tawse.' Cf. Tards.

Tawse, Taws, *n.* a leather strap cut into thongs at one end, for the use of schoolmasters to punish with. —*v.* to whip, scourge, belabour. Cf. Taw.

Tawse-swasher, *n.* one who uses the 'tawse.'

Tawse-taes, *n.* the thongs at the end of a 'tawse.'

Tawt, *v.* to drag or push to the ground; to abuse by dragging to and fro.—*n.* abuse by such dragging.

Tawt, *v.* to mat; to run into tufts. Cf. Taut.

Tawthrie, *adj.* disordered; confused; slovenly. Cf. Toutherie.

Tawtie, *n.* a potato; a stupid person.

Tawtie, *adj.* matted; shaggy.

Tax, *v.* to find fault with; to scold.

Taxative, *adj.* a forensic term: having the power of reduction from the force of an argument or plea, as enfeebling it.

Taxed-ward, *n.* a forensic term: the wardship of a minor, in which a limited sum is accepted in lieu of the whole 'casualties.'

Tax-man, *n.* a tax-collector.

Tax-master, *n.* a task-master.

Tay, *n.* tea.

Taythe, *n.* the droppings of cattle, &c., on an enclosed part of a field. Cf. Tathe.

Taz, *n.* a 'tawse' of a schoolmaster.—*v.* to whip, scourge.

Tazie, *n.* a romping, foolish girl; a mischievous child.

T'chach, *int.* an excl. of wonder, disgust, &c.

Tcheuch, *int.* tush!

T'chuchet, *n.* the peewit or lapwing. Cf. Teuchit.

Tea, *v.* to take tea with one.

Tea and eating, *n.* a 'rough' or 'high' tea.

Teach, *v.* to preach.

Teached, *v. pret.* taught.—*ppl.* taught.

Tea-chit-chat, *n.* cakes, &c., eaten at tea.

Tead, *v.* to ted hay, &c.

Tead, *n.* a toad; a child. Cf. Tade.

Tea-doins, *n.* a tea-party.

Teae, *num. adj.* the one.

Tea-fight, *n.* a tea-party.

Teagie, *n.* a cow with tail tipped with white. Cf. Tag.

Teagle, *v.* to hinder; to detain; to loiter. Cf. Taigle.

Tea-haun, *n.* a tea-drinker.

Tea-kitchen, *n.* a tea-urn.

Teal, *n.* a busybody; a mean fellow.

Teal, *v.* to wheedle; to inveigle by flattery, entice.

Teal, *n.* a tail; the posteriors. Cf. Tail.

Teal-duck, *n.* the common teal.

Tealer, *n.* one who wheedles or entices.

Tealie, *adj.* encouraging; offering inducements.

Tea-man, *n.* a tea-drinker.

Tean, Teane, *num. adj.* the one.

Tean, *n.* sorrow, grief; anger; temper; vexation.—*v.* to vex; to tease. Cf. Teen.

Tear, *v.* to stir the colours for block calico-printing.

Tear, *v.* to tease; to hurry along; to bustle about; to work hard and with speed; to rage.—*n.* a great hurry; a raging storm; in *pl.* cracks, rents, tatters.

Tear, *v.* to shed tears.

Tearancy, *n.* a rage, violence; outrageous haste.

Tear-blob, *n.* a tear-drop.

Tear-boy, *n.* a boy employed to stir the colours in block calico-printing.

Tearer, *n.* a virago, vixen, shrew.

Tearer, *n.* a 'tear-boy.'

Tearing, *ppl. adj.* excessive, very great; used intensively; boisterous, blustering; energetic, strenuous; passionate, violent.

Tear-in-twa, *adj.* savage, violent.

Teartathers, *n.* torn shreds. Cf. Taretathers.

Teary, *adj.* tearful.

Tease, Teaze, *v.* to disentangle; to open up matted wool for carding; to tear in pieces; to toss about in gossip; to drive; to stir up meal so as to make it look bulkier in the measure. Cf. Tize.

Tea-shine, *n.* a tea-party.

Tea-skittle, *n.* a tea-party.

Teasle, Teazle, *v.* to entangle, twist; to tease, vex.—*n.* disorder; a severe tussle; a puzzle. Cf. Taissle.

Teat, *n.* a tuft; a small quantity of anything. Cf. Tait.

Teathe, *n.* cattle-droppings. Cf. Tathe.

Teather, *n.* a tether. Cf. Tedder, Tether.

Tea-twine, *n.* twine with which a parcel of tea is tied up.

Teauve, *v.* to struggle; to toil; to wade heavily. Cf. Tyaave.

Tea-water, *n.* water for making tea.

Teaz, *v.* to prop a golf-ball.—*n.* the prop of earth on which the golf-ball is placed when first struck off.

Tebbit, *n.* energy; bodily sensation. Cf. Tabet.

Tebbitless, *adj.* pithless.

Teck, *n.* a tack, change of direction.

Teckle, *v.* to tackle.—*n.* tackle.

Teckle, *n.* an arrow. Cf. Tackle.

Ted, *v.* to scatter; to spill; to spread out; to arrange in order; to tidy.—*n.* the act of tidying.

Ted, *n.* a toad; a term of contempt or disgust; a child; a diminutive person. Cf. Taid.

Tedd, *ppl. adj.* ravelled, entangled.

Tedder, *n.* a tether.—*v.* to tether. Cf. Tether.

Teddie, *n.* a little child. Cf. Taidie.

Teddy, *adj.* used of corn: winnowed, ready for carting to the stackyard.

Tedisum, Tediousome, *adj.* tedious, wearisome.

Tedy, *adj.* peevish, fretful, cross.

Tee, *adv.* too, also.

Tee, *n.* a buckle attached to the collar or saddle of a horse.

Tee, *prep.* to. Cf. To.

Tee, *num. adj.* the one. Cf. Tane.

Tee, *n.* a tittle, a T.

Tee, *n.* the mark set up to aim at in certain games; a small cone of earth, &c., from which a golf-ball is driven.—*v.* to place a golf-ball on such a cone.

Teed, *ppl. adj.* used of a cow: in full milk.

Teedle, *v.* to sing a song without words.

Teedy, *adj.* peevish, cross.

Tee-fa', *n.* a building leaning on another. Cf. To-fall.

Teeger, *n.* a tiger; a virago.—*v.* to look fierce.

Tee-head, *n.* the circle round the tee at the end of each rink, within which curling-stones must lie to count in the game.

Tee-hee, Te-he, *n.* loud, derisive laughter; silly laughter; giggling.—*v.* to laugh in a silly way; to giggle; to laugh loudly.—*int.* an excl. of derisive laughter.

Teel, *n.* a tool.

Teel, *v.* to till; to toil, work at.

Teel, *v.* to entice; to wheedle. Cf. Teal.

Tee-leuk, *n.* a look to, attention to; a prospect.

Teelie, *adj.* encouraging. Cf. Teal.

Teelie, *n.* a small job or piece of farm-work.

Teelie, *n.* any agricultural implement.

Teely, *v.* with *back*, to recover, restore; to coax back.

Teem, *v.* to pour, pour out; to rain heavily, pour in torrents; to empty; to unload a

cart; to grant liberally; to bale out water.
—*n.* a downpour or torrent of rain.—*adj.*
empty. Cf. Toom.

Teem, *v.* to overflow.

Teem on, *v.* to beat severely; to work energetically and with speed. — *n.* a severe
beating.

Teems, *n.* a piece of fine crape or muslin
tightened on a circular rim of wood, for
dressing flour for pastry, &c.; a fine hair
sieve.—*v.* to sift.

Teen, *n.* sorrow, grief; wrath, rage; revenge;
vexation.—*v.* to trouble; to tease, vex.

Teen, *n.* a tithe. Cf. Teind.

Teen, *ppl.* taken. Cf. Tane.

Teen, *n.* a tune; the twang of a dialect. Cf.
Tune.

'Teen, *adv.* at even.

Teen, *num. adj.* the one. Cf. Tane.

Tee-name, *n.* a nickname; an additional
name to distinguish persons of the same
name, a 'to-name.'

Teenfu', *adj.* wrathful.

Teenge, *n.* colic in horses.

Teeock, *n.* the lapwing.

Teep, *n.* a type.

Teep, *n.* a tup, ram.

Teep, *v.* to stint. Cf. Tape.

Teepical, *adj.* typical.

Teeple, *n.* a slight stroke or touch.—*v.* to
touch or strike lightly.

Teer, *v.* to stir colours for block calico-printing.

Teer, *v.* to tear. Cf. Tear.

Teeribus and Teri odin, *n.* the war-cry of
Hawick. Cf. Teribus.

Teers, *n.* tares, vetches.

Tee-shot, *n.* a curling-stone played so as to
rest on the 'tee.'

Teesick, *n.* a spell of illness.

Teesie, *n.* a gust of passion.

Teessit, *n.* the line first shot from a fishing-
boat; the man whose line is first shot.

Teet, *v.* to peep; to peep or pry clandestinely.
—*n.* a peep; a stolen glance; a chirp; the
slightest sound; the least word.

Teet-bo, Teetie-bo, *int.* peep-bo!—*n.* the
game of 'peep-bo.'

Tee-tee, T.T., *n.* a teetotaler.

Teeth, *n.* a tooth.

Teeth, *n.* temper; spirit, mettle. Cf. Teth.

Teeth, *n.* the fragment of a rainbow appearing
on the horizon.

Teethache, *n.* toothache.

Teethe, Teeth, *v.* to fix teeth in a spiked
instrument; to impress, indent; to indent
a wall with mortar on the outside.

Teethed, *ppl. adj.* having or furnished with
teeth.

Teethfu', *n.* a toothful; a small quantity of
liquid.

Teething-bannock, -plaster, *n.* an oatmeal
cake given to a child when first teething.

Teethless, *adj.* toothless.

Teethrife, *adj.* toothsome, palatable.

Teethy, *adj.* testy; crabbed; tart; used of
dogs: showing the teeth.

Teetle, *n.* title.

Teetlin, *n.* the meadow pipit; the rock pipit.

Tee-tot, *n.* a teetotaler.

Teetotal, *n.* teetotalism; a teetotal society.

Teetotally, *adv.* totally, quite.

Teeuck, *n.* the lapwing. Cf. Teeock.

Teevoo, *n.* a male flirt.

Teewheep, Teewhoap, *n.* the lapwing.

Tee-wheet, Tee-wit, *n.* the lapwing or peewit.
Cf. Teuchit.

Teicher, *v.* to ooze from the skin; to distil
almost imperceptibly.—*n.* the appearance
of a fretted sore.

Teidsome, *adj.* tedious. Cf. Tedisum.

Teight, *ppl. adj.* fatigued.

Teil, *n.* a busybody; a mean fellow. Cf. Teal.

Teil, Teill, *v.* to till the soil; to toil. Cf.
Teel.

Tein, *n.* sorrow; rage.—*v.* to provoke; to
vex. Cf. Teen.

Teind, Tein, *v.* to tithe; to draw tithes.—*n.*
a tithe; a church-tithe.

Teind, *v.* to light.—*n.* a spark of fire; a spark
on a candle-wick. Cf. Tine.

Teind, *n.* the prong of a fork; a tine; the act
of harrowing.

Teind-Court, *n.* the court of law dealing with
the tithes of the Established Church of
Scotland.

Teind-free, *adj.* exempt from tithe-paying.

Teind-lamb, *n.* a tithe-lamb.

Teind-sheaves, *n.* sheaves payable as tithes.

Teind-siller, *n.* tithe-money.

Teind-skate, *n.* a skate or fish payable as tithe.

Teist, *n.* a handful.

Teistie, *n.* the black guillemot.

Tek, *n.* a dog; an otter. Cf. Tike.

Telegraft, *n.* a telegram.

Tell, *v.* to recognize; to distinguish; to pay;
to count.

Tellable, *adj.* fit to be told.

Tell'd, Telt, *v. pret.* and *ppl.* told.

Telling, *ppl.* to the advantage of; having
effect.—*n.* a story; talk; what is worth
telling; advice, warning; a scolding, reprimand.

†**Telyie**, *n.* a slice cut off; an entail. Cf.
Tailyie.

†**Temerare**, *adj.* rash.

†**Temming**, *n.* a very coarse, thin, woollen
cloth. Cf. Timming.

Temp, *v.* to tempt.

Temper, *v.* to regulate or adjust machinery
or the rate of its movement.

Temperament, *n.* a legal term : the qualifying of a confession.

Temper-pin, *n.* a wooden screw for tightening the band of a spinning-wheel ; a fiddle-peg ; temper, disposition.

Temper-thrawing, *adj.* souring the temper.

Temples, *n.* long thin rods which stretch the web on the loom.

Temptashious, *adj.* tempting, inviting.

Temptsome, *adj.* tempting, inviting.

Tenandry, *n.* tenure ; tenancy ; the collective tenants on an estate, tenantry.

Tenant-sted, *adj.* occupied by a tenant.

Tend, *v.* to attend to ; to attend at regularly. Cf. Tent.

Tend, *v.* to intend.

Tender, *adj.* delicate, ailing ; circumspect, scrupulous ; pathetic ; akin, closely related. —*v.* to make tender, delicate, soft ; to have regard for, care for.

Tenderly, *adj.* poorly, unwell.

Tenderness, *n.* delicacy of health ; regard, consideration ; scrupulousness.

Tendle, *n.* firewood ; brushwood used for fuel.

Tendle-knife, *n.* a knife or bill-hook for cutting firewood.

Tene, *n.* sorrow ; rage ; vexation.—*v.* to provoke. Cf. Teen.

Tenendrie, *n.* tenure ; tenancy ; the tenantry.

Tenfauld, *adj.* tenfold.

Tengs, *n.* tongs. Cf. Taings.

Ten-hours, *n.* ten o'clock ; a slight feed to horses in the yoke in the forenoon.

Ten-hours'-bite, *n.* the slight feed given to horses in the yoke in the forenoon.

Tennel, Tennle, *n.* firewood. Cf. Tendle.

Tennendrie, *n.* tenantry ; tenancy ; tenure. Cf. Tenandry.

Tennrills, *n.* dry twigs ; tendrils.

Tenon, *n.* a tendon.

Tenony-hough, *n.* the joint of a beast's hind-leg.

Tenor, *n.* the cross-bar between the legs of a chair.

Tenor-saw, *n.* a tenon-saw ; a thin back-saw.

Tenpenny-nail, *n.* a large, strong nail.

Tensome, Tensum, *n.* a company of ten.

Tent, *n.* an open-air pulpit of wood with a projecting roof.

Tent, *v.* to attend to, look after ; to herd animals ; to notice ; to heed ; to listen to ; to beware, take care ; to incline.—*n.* care, heed ; a look ; notice, attention ; time, patience.—*adj.* watchful ; keen, intent, observant.

Tentie, Tenty, *adj.* careful, heedful, cautious, watchful.—*adv.* carefully, attentively, cautiously.

Tentily, *adv.* carefully, cautiously, heedfully.

Tentive, *adj.* attentive, careful.

Tentless, *adj.* careless, heedless, inattentive ; uncared for, unattended.

Tentlessly, *adv.* incautiously, carelessly.

Tently, *adv.* carefully.

Tent-preaching, *n.* preaching from a 'tent.'

Tent-reader, *n.* one who read the lessons from a 'tent.'

Teppit, *n.* bodily sensation. Cf. Tabet.

Teppitless, *adj.* benumbed ; without sensation or sense.

†Terbuck, *v.* to make a false move in play ; to check an opponent's false move in play. —*n.* a false-move in play, a slip ; a check in a game of skill. Cf. Trebuck.

†Terce, *n.* a widow's right to a life-rent of one-third of her deceased husband's heritage.

Terced, *ppl. adj.* divided into three parts.

Tercer, *n.* a widow who enjoys a 'terce.'

Terd, *n.* a term of contempt ; a taunt ; sarcasm. Cf. Taird.

Tergat, *n.* a tassel, an ornament for the hat ; a shred. Cf. Targat.

†Tergiverse, *v.* to use subterfuge.

Teri, *n.* a native of Hawick.

Teribus ye Teri odin, *n.* the war-cry of Hawick.

Terlis, *n.* a lattice ; a wicket. Cf. Tirless.

Termagant, *n.* a ptarmigan.

Termin life, *adv.* forever, finally.

Term-time, *n.* Whitsunday ; Martinmas.

Terr, *v.* to strip thatch, &c., from a roof. Cf. Tirr.

Terrible, *adj.* great ; tremendous ; extraordinary.—*adv.* extremely.

Terrie, *n.* a terrier. Cf. Tarrie.

Terrier, *n.* a man of bad temper and character ; a pugnacious fellow.

Terrification, *n.* terror ; any thing or person causing terror.

Terrifick, *adj.* terrified.

Terry, *int.* used as an expletive or oath.

Terse, *v.* to dispute, debate.—*n.* a dispute, contention.

Tersy-versy, *adv.* topsy-turvy. Cf. Tarsie-versie.

Tert, *adj.* tart.

Tertian, *n.* a third year's student in Arts at Aberdeen University.

Tertle, *v.* to recognize, take notice of. Cf. Tartle.

Teryvee, *n.* a rage, fit of temper ; stir, bustle. Cf. Tirrivee.

Tesment, Tesmont, Testment, *n.* a last will ; a legacy.

Test, *n.* a will, testament.—*v.* to bequeath by will.

Test, *n.* a small cylindrical piece of wood, formerly kept in a school, in an aperture near the door, and in the master's sight,

without which being in its place no boy
was allowed to get outside.

Testament, *n.* a legacy; the New Testament
as distinguished from the Old.—*v.* to leave
by will.

Testamentar, *adj.* testamentary.

Testament-man, *n.* a Protestant.

Testie, *n.* the black guillemot. Cf. **Teistie.**

Testificate, Testificat, *n.* a passport; a certificate, testimonial.

Testification, *n.* a certificate, testimonial.

†**Testoon, Testan, Teston,** *n.* silver coin
varying in value, generally 5s. Scots.

Tet, *n.* a lock of hair, wool, &c. Cf. **Tait.**

Teth, *n.* temper, disposition; spirit, mettle.

Teth, *int.* an expletive; a euphemism for
'faith!' Cf. **Heth.**

Tether, *n.* a hangman's halter or rope; a tow-
rope.—*v.* to moor a vessel; to confine; to
bind; to restrain; to marry, get married.
Cf. **Tedder.**

Tether-chack, *n.* a spike of iron or wood for
fixing a tether in the ground.

Tether-en', *n.* a rope's end; the end of one's
fortune.

Tether-faced, *adj.* ill-natured in looks.

Tether-length, *n.* the length of a tether; a
long distance; calamity at the end of a
reckless career.

Tether-safe, *n.* a tether that holds fast.

Tether's-end, *n.* extremity; the farthest possible length.

Tether-stake, *n.* a 'tether-chack'; the upright
post in a stall to which a cow is tethered.

Tether-stick, *n.* a 'tether-chack.'

Tether-string, *n.* a rope, halter.

Tether-tow, *n.* a cable, hawser.

Tets, *int.* an excl. of impatience. Cf. **Tits.**

Tett, *n.* a lock of hair, wool, &c. Cf. **Tait.**

Tetter, *v.* to hinder, 'tether.'

Tetty, *adj.* having a bad temper; gusty. Cf.
Titty.

Tetuz, *n.* anything tender; a delicate person.

Teu, *v. pret.* strove hard.—*ppl.* striven hard.
Cf. **Tew.**

†**Teu,** *n.* the nozzle of a blacksmith's bellows;
a blacksmith's long pincers. Cf. **Tew.**

Teuch, *n.* a draught of any kind of liquor. Cf.
Deuch.

Teuch, *adj.* tough; used of the heart: hard,
not easily broken; of a contest: keen,
pertinacious; tedious, protracted.—*adv.*
stoutly, sturdily.

Teuchatie, *n.* a young or little lapwing.

Teuchin', *ppl.* used of tough phlegm: clearing
the throat of it, hawking.

Teuchit, Teuchat, *n.* the lapwing or peewit.

Teuchit-storm, *n.* the gale popularly asso-
ciated with the arrival of the green plover
or lapwing.

Teuchly, *adv.* toughly; tenaciously.

Teuckie, *n.* a hen; a chicken; used as a
nickname. -*int.* 'chucky!' a call to fowls.

Teud, *n.* a tooth.

Teudle, *n.* the tooth of a rake or harrow, a
tine.—*v.* to insert teeth; to renovate the
teeth of a reaping-hook, &c.

Teudless, *adj.* toothless.

Teug, *n.* a rope, a halter. Cf. **Tug.**

Teugh, *int.* an excl. of disgust, impatience,
contempt.

Teugh, *adj.* tough. Cf. **Teuch.**

Teugs, *n.* trousers; the thighs of a pair of
breeches; clothes, 'togs.'

Teuk, *v. pret.* took.

Teuk, *n.* a disagreeable taste, a by-taste.

Teukin, *ppl. adj.* quarrelsome, troublesome;
used of the wind: shifting, variable.

Teum, *adj.* empty. Cf. **Toom.**

Teurd, *n.* a nasty mess; excrement. Cf.
Turd.

†**Teut-meut,** *n.* a dispute.—*v.* to whisper; to
mutter. Cf. **Toot-moot.**

Tevel, Tevvel, *v.* to confuse; to put into
disorder.

†**Tew,** *n.* the nozzle of the bellows of a forge,
&c.; a blacksmith's long pincers; iron hardened with a piece of cast-iron; in *pl.* the
leather catches of a drum, by which the
cords are tightened; the cords of a drum.

Tew, *v.* to knead; to exhaust, fatigue;
to overpower; to fidget; to toil, labour;
to work constantly; to work hard; to
be eagerly employed about anything; to
struggle, strive.—*v. pret.* toiled.—*n.* a
struggle, difficulty; hard work, toil.—*adj.*
fatigued.

Tew, *v.* used of grain: to become damp and
acquire a bad taste.—*n.* a bad taste occasioned by dampness. Cf. **Tewk.**

Tew, *v.* to make tough; to make meat tough
by roasting it with too slow a fire. Cf.
Teuch.

Tew, *int.* an excl. of disgust, &c. Cf.
Teugh.

Tew, *v. pret.* did amble. Cf. **Tiawe.**

Tewel, Tewl, *n.* a tool; a ship.

Tewhit, Tewit, *n.* the lapwing. Cf. **Tee-
wheet, Tee-wit.**

Tew-iron, *n.* the nozzle of the bellows of a
forge; the long pincers of a blacksmith.

Tew-iron, -arne bore, *n.* iron hardened with
cast-iron to make it stand the fire in a
forge.

Tewkie, *n.* a hen.—*int.* a call to fowls. Cf.
Teuckie.

Teynd, *n.* a tithe.—*v.* to tithe. Cf. **Teind.**

Teypard, *adj.* used of a building: high and
frail.

Thaar, *v.* to need. Cf. **Thar.**

T'hach, *int.* an excl. of disgust, contempt.

Thack, *v.* to thwack.

Thack, *v.* to thatch, cover, roof.—*n.* thatch; a thatching; a roof or covering of straw; materials for thatching; the hair of the head.—*adj.* thatched; used for thatching.

Thack and rape, *n.* cover for stacks against wind and rain; home comforts.

Thack-bunch, *n.* a bunch of straw drawn for thatching.

Thack-covered, *adj.* thatched.

Thacker, *n.* a thatcher.

Thack-gate, *n.* the sloping edge of the gable-tops of a h use, when the thatch covers them.

Thackit-stick, *n.* an umbrella.

Thack-lead, *n.* leaden roofing.

Thackless, *adj.* not roofed; without thatch; uncovered, hatless.

Thack-nail, -pin, *n.* a peg for fastening down thatch.

Thack-rape, -raip, *n.* a rope of straw or coir for securing thatch.

Thack-spurkle, -spurtle, *n.* a tool used in thatching.

Thack-stones, *n.* square slabs of sandstone used for slates.

Thack-strae, *n.* straw prepared for thatch.

Thack-threid, *n.* a coarse, strong thread for tying down thatch.

Thae, *dem. pron.* and *adj.* those, these.

Thaft, *n.* a rower's bench in a boat.

Thaimsels, *refl. pron.* themselves.

Thain, *adj.* insufficiently cooked. Cf. Thane.

Thair, *adv.* there.

Thair, *pron.* their.

Thair, *v.* to need. Cf. Thar.

Thairf, *adj.* sad.

Thairfish, *adj.* of heavy countenance; lumpish.

Thairm, *n.* the belly of man or beast; the gut of a beast; the intestines twisted; catgut; a fiddle-string; in *pl.* bonds.—*v.* to play on a stringed instrument.

Thairm-band, *n.* a catgut cord for turning a spinning-wheel.

Thairsels, *refl. pron.* themselves.

Thait, *n.* a plough-trace; an inclination, liking. Cf. Theat.

Thaivil, *n.* a stirring-rod; a 'spurtle.' Cf. Thivel.

Thak, *n.* thatch. Cf. Thack.

Than, *adv.* then.

Than, *conj.* used to express a wish: would that.—*adv.* else; elsewhere.

Than a days, *adv.* in those days.

Thane, *n.* a vane.

Thane, *adj.* used of meat: underdone, raw; of meal: moist, or made of oats not thoroughly kiln-dried.

Thank, *v.* to suffice. —*n.* obligation to a person; something to be thankful for.

Thankful, *adj.* used of payment: sufficient, satisfactory.

Thanse, *adv.* else, otherwise.

Thar, *v.* to need. Cf. Ther, Thurst.

That, *pron.* this; used to avoid repeating a previous word or statement; also in emphatic reiteration of an assertion; who.—*adj.* this; those; such.—*adv.* so, to such a degree; very.—*conj.* because, seeing that; alas! that, in apology for an oath, &c.

Thatch-gate, *n.* the sloping edge of the gable-tops of a house, when the thatch covers them. Cf. Thack-gate.

Thaten, *adj.* that.

Thaur, *v.* to need. Cf. Thar.

Thaut, *n.* a sob.—*v.* to sob. Cf. Thout.

Thawart, *adj.* froward; obstinate. Cf. Thrawart.

Thaw-wind, *n.* a wind bringing a thaw. Cf. Thow-wind.

The, *adj.* used as a *poss. pron.;* indefinitely with some words, as 'church,' 'school,' 'wife'; before certain diseases, as 'cold,' 'measles,' 'fever'; before certain languages or sciences; used for 'a' or 'an' before weights and measures distributively; for 'to' or 'this' with 'day,' 'morn,' 'night,' &c.

Theak, *v.* to thatch; to cover, clothe, protect. — *n.* thatch; thatching material; heather used as litter for cattle. Cf. Thack.

Theaker, *n.* a thatcher.

Theaking, *n.* thatch; thatching; a roof; clothing.

Theat, *n.* a leather band fastened round a horse, to which long chains are attached and then fixed to plough or harrow; a rope, trace, chain for drawing; a liking, inclination for; in *phr.* 'oot o' theat,' unreasonable, extortionate as to price; out of practice; out of order.

Theck, *n.* thatch.—*v.* to thatch. Cf. Theak.

Thee, *n.* the thigh.

Thee, *v.* to thrive, prosper.

Theedle, *n.* a porridge-'spurtle.'

Theef, *n.* an escape of flatulence; a bad smell.

Theegh, *n.* the thigh.

Theek, *n.* thatch.—*v.* to thatch. Cf. Theak, Thack.

Theel, *n.* a porridge-'spurtle.' Cf. Theedle, Thivel.

Theet, *n.* a rope, chain, trace; a liking for. Cf. Theat.

Theeveless, *adj.* listless. Cf. Thieveless.

Theevil, *n.* a porridge-'spurtle.' Cf. Thivel.

Theft-boot, *n.* the securing of a thief against the punishment due by law.

Theftdom, *n.* thieving.

Theftuous, Theftous, *adj.* thievish.

Theftuously, *adv.* thievishly.

The furth, *adv.* out-of-doors ; abroad.

Theg, *v.* to beg ; to solicit gifts on special occasions. Cf. Thig.

Thegidder, Thegither, *adv.* together.

Theigh, *n.* the thigh. Cf. Thee.

Theik, Theick, *n.* thatch.—*v.* to thatch. Cf. Theak.

Theil, *n.* a porridge-'spurtle.' Cf. Theel.

Theim, *n.* the belly or intestines ; catgut ; a fiddle-string. Cf. Thairm.

Theirsels, *refl. pron.* themselves.

Theivil, *n.* a porridge-'spurtle.' Cf. Thivel.

Theivil-ill, -shot, *n.* a pain in the side.

Them, *n.* Providence, the Powers above.— *pron.* those.—*adj.* those.

Them-lane, *adv.* by themselves alone.

Themsel', *refl. pron.* himself, herself ; themselves.

Then, *conj.* than.

Then-a-days, *adv.* in former days ; some time ago.

The now, the noo, *adv.* just now.

†**Theort,** *n.* a large, double-necked lute, with two sets of tuning-pegs, a theorbo.

Thepes, *n.* the fruit of the gooseberry ; of the gorse ; of the thorn.

The piece, *adv.* apiece.

Ther, *v.* to need. Cf. Thar.

Thereanent, *adv.* concerning that.

Thereawa', *adv.* thereabouts ; in that quarter ; about that time ; that way, to that purpose.

There-ben, *adv.* there in a 'ben-room.'

There-but, *adv.* there in a 'but-room.'

Thereby, *adv.* thereabouts as to time, quantity, quality.

There-bye, *adv.* past there or that way.

There-east, *adv.* in the east ; eastward.

Thereckly, *adv.* directly.

There-fra, *adv.* from that place, thence.

Therein, *adv.* within doors, at home.

Thereout, Thereoot, *adv.* outside, out-of-doors ; out. Cf. Throut.

Theretill, Theretull, *adv.* thither ; thereto ; in addition to.

There-up, *adv.* upwards.

Therm, *n.* the belly of man or beast ; catgut ; a fiddle-string. Cf. Thairm.

†**Thesaurer,** *n.* a treasurer.

†**Thesaury,** *n.* the treasury.

These, *pron.* and *adj.* those.

Theself, *refl. pron.* itself.

Thestreen, *n.* last night, 'yester-even.'

Thet, Thete, *n.* a trace. Cf. Theat.

Thewless, *adj.* feeble, inactive. Cf. Thowless.

They'se, *pron.* and *v.* they shall.

Thick, *adj.* thickset ; stupid ; numerous ;

frequent ; friendly, intimate ; criminally familiar.—*n.* a crowd.

Thick, *n.* thatch. Cf. Theak.

Thickness, *n.* fog, mist ; intimacy, familiar friendship.

Thickset, *n.* strong, thick cloth ; in *pl.* clothes made of 'thickset.'

Thick-thrang, *adj.* thickly crowded.

Thie, *n.* a thigh.

Thief, *n.* a term of vituperation not implying dishonesty, a rascal.

Thief, *n.* a bad smell. Cf. Theef.

Thief-animal, *n.* a thievish person.

Thief-bute, -bote, *n.* the crime of taking money or goods from a thief to shelter him from justice.

Thiefer-like, *adj.* more thief-like.

Thief-like, *adj.* having the appearance of a blackguard ; giving grounds for an unfavourable impression as to conduct or design ; plain, ugly, hard-looking ; used of dress : unbecoming, not handsome.

Thief-loon, *n.* a thief, thievish rascal.

Thief-riever, *n.* a thief ; a cattle-stealer.

Thiefy, *adj.* thievish.

Thieval, *n.* a porridge-'spurtle.' Cf. Thivel.

Thieveless, *adj.* listless, spiritless ; lacking energy ; cold, bleak ; shy, reserved ; frigid, forbidding. Cf. Thowless.

Thieveless-like, *adj.* indifferent, unconcerned.

Thievelessly, *adv.* feebly ; aimlessly ; without energy or force.

Thiever, *n.* a thief.

Thieves'-hole, *n.* gaol ; a bad dungeon reserved for thieves.

Thieve-thrum'd, *adj.* made of stolen 'thrums.'

Thig, *v.* to beg, to borrow ; to solicit gifts on certain occasions ; to be a genteel beggar ; to entice ; to entreat ; to tease.—*n.* begging, borrowing.

Thigger, *n.* a mendicant ; a genteel beggar.

Thigging, *n.* the grain, &c., collected by begging ; the act or practice of begging.

Thigging-bit, *n.* an article got by 'thigging.'

Thigster, *n.* a beggar.

Thill, *n.* a coarse subsoil of gravel and clay. Cf. Till.

Thilse, *adv.* else, otherwise.

Thimba-fu', *n.* a thimbleful.

Thimber, *adj.* gross ; heavy ; massive.

Thimble, Thimmel, *n.* the harebell.

Thimble-ha', *n.* a tailor's workshop.

Thin, *adj.* thin-skinned, touchy ; easily jealous ; scantily provided with ; few, scarce.— *n.* a thin or slender part.—*v.* to lessen in numbers ; to pick out the bones of a fish's head, and collect the fleshy parts.

Thine's, *pron.* thine.

Thing, *n.* a state of affairs ; a depreciatory

designation of a person ; a term of endearment for a child, a girl, or a sweetheart : with the *def. art.* and a preceding negative, a term of disapprobation ; without the negative, a term of great approbation ; before the *rel. pron.* that ; those ; with an intensive *adj.*, an amount, quantity, number.

Thingiment, *n.* a thing the name of which is unknown or forgotten.

Thingum, *n.* a person or thing whose name is unknown or forgotten.

Thingumbob, *n.* a thing the name of which is unknown or forgotten ; a useless article.

Thingum-dairie, *n.* a 'thingumbob.'

Think, *v.* to feel ; to experience ; to expect ; to wonder ; with *on*, to recollect. — *n.* thought, opinion.

Think long, *v.* to become weary for ; to be long expecting.

Think shame, *v.* to feel ashamed.

Think sorry, *v.* to feel sorry.

Thinter, *n.* a three-year-old sheep. Cf. Thrinter.

Thir, Thirs, *pron.* and *adj.* these ; those.

Thir-ben, *adv.* there in the 'ben-room.'

Thirds, *n.* brewers' grains.

Thirdsman, *n.* an arbiter between two.

Thirdy, *n.* a penny loaf of inferior flour.

Thirl, Thirle, *v.* to perforate, drill ; to pierce, penetrate ; to thrill, cause to vibrate ; to tingle.—*n.* a hole ; a thrill.

Thirl, *v.* to come under legal obligation ; to bind a tenant by lease to grind his grain at a certain mill ; to subject to ; to be dependent on.—*n.* the obligation to grind at a certain mill ; the land held under this obligation ; the tenant so bound.

Thirlage, *n.* thraldom ; servitude to a particular mill ; the miller's multure ; a mortgage.

Thirlage-man, *n.* a man bound to grind at a certain mill.

Thirl-hole, *n.* the hole into which the coulter of a plough is fixed.

Thirlin', *ppl. adj.* piercingly cold.

Thirling-mill, *n.* the mill at which tenants are bound to grind.

Thirl-pin, *n.* a pivot on which doors without hinges turned.

Thirsels, *refl. pron.* themselves.

Thirssle, *n.* the song-thrush.

Thirssle-cock-lairag, *n.* the song-thrush.

Thirsty, *adj.* causing thirst.

This, *n.* this time.—*adj.* these.

Thissle, *n.* a thistle.

Thistle-cock, *n.* the corn-bunting.

Thistle-finch, *n.* the goldfinch.

Thistle-tap, *n.* thistledown.

Thivel, *n.* a porridge-'spurtle' ; a cudgel. Cf. Theevil.

Thiveless, *adj.* inactive ; remiss ; spiritless. Cf. Thieveless.

Thoch-been, *n.* the collar-bone of a fowl, the merrythought.

Thocht, *n.* thought ; a very little of anything ; a moment. — *v. pret.* did think. — *ppl.* thought.

Thochted, *ppl. adj.* anxious, concerned.

Thochtie, *n.* a very little.

Thochtiness, Thoghtiness, *n.* thought, anxiety.

Thochty, *adj.* thoughtful ; reflective ; attentive.

Thof, *conj.* though.

Thoft, *n.* the rower's seat in a boat. Cf. Thaft.

Thoft, *n.* a toft, homestead, messuage. Cf. Toft.

Thoftin, *n.* a 'thoft,' the house built upon a toft ; the using and right of such house.

Thole, *v.* to bear, suffer, tolerate ; to allow, grant, permit ; to require ; to advantage ; to admit of ; to wait, hold out.

Tholeable, *adj.* tolerable, bearable.

Thole an assize, *v.* to stand one's trial.

Tholemoody, *adj.* patient.

Thole-pin, *n.* a peg fastening a double door.

Tholesum, *adj.* bearable.

Thole-weel, *n.* patient endurance.

Thon, *pron.* that, 'yon.'—*adj.* yonder.

Thonder, Thonner, *adj.* and *adv.* yonder.

Thong, *n.* a shoe-tie.

Thongs, *n.* tongs.

Thoom, *n.* the thumb.—*v.* to handle, spread, or clean with the thumb ; to compress with the thumb.

Thoomack, *n.* a violin-peg.

Thoom-licking, *n.* a mode of confirming a bargain.

Thoom-raip, *n.* a rope of hay or straw twisted round the thumb.

Thoom-simmon, *n.* a 'thoom-raip.'

Thoom-syme, *n.* an instrument for twisting ropes of straw, &c.

Thoo's, *poss. adj.* thy.

Thoosan, *adj.* thousand.

Thoosan-leaved-clover, *n.* yarrow.

Thoosan-taes, *n.* the centipede.

Thor, *n.* durance, confinement.

Thorle, Thorl, *n.* the fly of a spindle or spinning-wheel, the pivot on which a wheel revolves ; the whorl of a wooden clock ; the loop or tag by which a button is sewn on.

Thorle-pippin, *n.* a species of apple in form like the fly of a spindle.

Thorn, *n.* the hawthorn ; a sharp, prickly spine on certain fish.

Thorn, *v.* to eat heartily.

Thorny-back, *n.* the thorn-back.

Thorough, Thorow, *adj.* wise, sane.

Thorough, *prep.* and *adv.* through.

Thorough-go-nimble, *n.* small-beer ; diarrhœa.

Thorow, Thorrow, *prep.* and *adv.* through. Cf. Through.

Thorter, *adj.* used of wood : cross-grained.— *prep.* across, athwart.—*v.* to thwart, oppose ; to plough or harrow crosswise ; to go backwards and forwards on anything, as in sewing ; used of an argument : to sift or try it thoroughly.

Thorter-ill, *n.* a paralysis affecting sheep. Cf. Thwarter-ill.

Thorter-knot, *n.* a knot in wood.

Thorter-ower, *prep.* across, athwart.

Thorter-ploughing, *n.* cross-ploughing.

Thorter-throw, *v.* to pass an object backwards and forwards.

Though, *conj.* nevertheless.

Thought, *n.* a source of grief or trouble ; a small quantity of anything ; a short time ; a short distance, a nicety. Cf. Thocht.

Thought-bane, *n.* the merrythought of a fowl.

Thoughty, *adj.* thoughtful.

Thouless, *adj.* inactive, feeble. Cf. Thowless.

Thoum, *n.* the thumb. Cf. Thoom.

Thoumart, *n.* the polecat ; a contemptuous term for a curious or eccentric person. Cf. Foumart.

Thou's, *pron.* and *v.* thou art.

Thout, *v.* to sob.—*n.* a sob. Cf. Thaut.

Thow, Thowe, *v.* to thaw ; used of hardened blood : to wash off.—*n.* a thaw ; a profuse sweat.

Thow-hole, *n.* the south.

Thowless, *adj.* lacking energy, spirit, mettle ; useless ; tasteless.

Thowlessness, *n.* lack of energy ; laziness ; listlessness.

Thowlie, *adj.* lazy ; listless.

Thow-lousin, *n.* a thaw.

Thow-wind, *n.* a wind bringing a thaw.

Thraa, Thra, *v.* to throw ; to twist ; to be perverse. Cf. Thraw.

Thrae, *prep.* from.

Thrae, *adj.* backward ; reluctant ; stiff, stubborn. Cf. Thraw.

Thraep, *v.* to persist in arguing. Cf. Threap.

Thraif, *n.* twenty-four sheaves. Cf. Thrave.

Thraim, *v.* to dwell or harp on.

Thrain, *v.* to harp constantly on one subject. —*n.* a constant repetition ; a refrain. Cf. Threne.

Thraip, *v.* to insist ; to argue. Cf. Threap.

Thraldom, *n.* servitude, as to property ; trouble.

Thrall, *v.* to oppress.—*n.* oppression ; restraint ; worry. Cf. Thraw.

Thram, *n.* a twisted thread ; a loose end. Cf. Thrum.

Thram, *v.* to prosper, thrive ; used also in malediction.

Thramle, Thrammle, *v.* to wind ; to reel.

Thrammel, Thrammle, *n.* a rope to fasten cattle in a stall.

Thrammel, *n.* a little oatmeal put into the mouth of a sack at a mill, with a little water or ale, and stirred about.

Thrang, *v.* to throng ; to crowd towards a place ; to become crowded.—*adj.* pressed for space ; crowded ; numerous, thick ; intimate, familiar ; busy, absorbed in work ; used of work : pressing.—*adv.* in plenty ; busily.—*n.* a large quantity ; intimacy ; business ; pressure of work ; a busy time ; bustle ; confusion ; a throng, crowd ; constant employment. Cf. Throng.

Thrangerie, *n.* a bustle, stir ; a busy time.

Thrangetty, Thrangatie, Thrangity, *n.* a press of work ; the state of being busy ; great intimacy.

Thrape, *v.* to insist on, argue pertinaciously ; to browbeat ; to wrangle.—*n.* an assertion ; an argument ; a tradition. Cf. Threap.

Thrapple, *n.* the windpipe, neck.—*v.* to throttle ; to entangle with cords ; with *up*, to gobble up, devour in eating.

Thrapple-deep, *adj.* up to the throat.

Thrapple-girth, *n.* a collar or cravat.

Thrapple-hearse, *adj.* hoarse.

Thrapple-plough, *n.* the old wooden plough with one ' stilt.'

Thrash, *n.* a rush. Cf. Thresh.

Thrash, *v.* to thresh.—*n.* a beating ; a threshing ; threshed grain ; a dashing noise as of rain.—*phr.* ' wi' a thrash,' immediately.

Thrashel, *n.* a threshold. Cf. Threshel.

Thrashen, *ppl.* threshed.

Thrasher, *n.* the striking part of a flail.

Thrashin'-mull, *n.* a threshing-mill.

Thrashin-tree, *n.* a flail.

Thratch, *v.* to gasp convulsively, as in the death-throes.—*n.* the oppressed and violent respiration of one in the death-throes.

Thrave, *n.* twenty-four sheaves of grain ; a large number or quantity ; a crowd.—*v.* to work by ' thraves ' in harvest, and be paid accordingly.

Thrave, *v. pret.* throve.

Thraver, *n.* a reaper paid according to the ' thraves ' he cuts down.

Thraving, *n.* paying according to the ' thraves ' cut.

Thraw, *n.* a throe.—*v.* to suffer pain, writhe.

Thraw, *v.* used of young people : to grow rapidly.

Thraw, *adj.* awry ; stubborn ; unyielding ; cross ; adverse.

Thraw, *v.* to oppress.—*n.* oppression.

Thraw, *v.* to throw, cast ; to twist ; to wreathe ; to wrench, sprain ; to wring the neck ; to torture by twisting ; to turn a key ; to distort, pervert ; to oppose, thwart ; to warp ;

to provoke to anger; to contend, argue, contradict; to carry a measure with a strong hand.—*n.* a twist, wrench; a sprain; wriggling; one turn of the hand in twisting; anger, ill-humour; perversity; a fit of stubbornness; a quarrel; a wrangle; a reverse of fortune; trouble; pressure; a crowd; a rush.

Thrawart, Thrawort, *adj.* twisted, crooked; perverse, stubborn; ill-tempered, cross; adverse, unfavourable.—*adv.* in confusion, pell-mell.

Thrawart-like, *adj.* seemingly cross or reluctant.

Thrawartness, *n.* frowardness, perverseness.

Thraw-cock, *n.* an instrument for twisting straw-ropes.

Thraw-cruik, -crook, *n.* an instrument for twisting straw-ropes.

Thraw-gabbit, *adj.* peevish.

Thraw-mouse, *n.* the shrew-mouse.

Thrawn, Thrawin, *ppl. adj.* thrown; twisted, distorted, misshapen; uneven, crooked; cross-grained, ill-tempered; perverse, stubborn; disobedient; used of the weather: disagreeable, bitter.—*adv.* crossly.

Thrawn-body, *n.* a cross, perverse person.

Thrawn-days, *n.* a petted child.

Thraw-neckit, *adj.* having the neck twisted by hanging.

Thrawn-faced, *adj.* with distorted features, surly-faced.

Thrawn-gabbit, *adj.* with a twisted mouth; peevish, quarrelsome, contradictory.

Thrawn-headed, *adj.* perverse.

Thrawnly, *adv.* crossly.

Thrawn-mou'd, *adj.* twisted in the mouth.

Thrawn-muggent, -natured, *adj.* perverse.

Thrawnness, *n.* perverseness, stubbornness.

Thrawn-rumplet, *adj.* with twisted rump.

Thrawn-stick. *n.* a queer, obstinate, ill-tempered fellow.

Thraw-rape, *n.* an instrument for twisting ropes of straw.

Thraw-sitten, *adj.* lazy, stupefied.

Thraws-spang, *n.* an iron rod so fastened to a plough as to prevent it being straightened by the draught.

Thraw-wark, *n.* work for twisting ropes.

Thread, *n.* the thread of life.—*v.* to draw in, as upon a thread; to pay out a rope slowly.

Thread-dry, *adj.* quite dry.

Thread-lapper, *n.* a spinner of thread.

Thread of blue, *n.* anything smutty in talk or writing.

Thread-pirn, *n.* a reel for thread.

Thread the needle-e'e, *n.* a young people's game.

Threap, *v.* to assert firmly, insist on; to reiterate pertinaciously; to urge, press, heap;

to haggle over a bargain; to argue; to wrangle; to complain.—*n.* a pertinacious assertion; an indictment; a statement of facts; an argument; a wrangle; a quarrel; a tradition; a saying often repeated.

Threaper, *n.* a pertinacious asserter.

Threap-knot, *n.* a groundless assertion made in order to find out truth, or to prevent what is dreaded.

Threat, *v.* to threaten.

Threatful, *adj.* threatening; threatening-looking.

Threave, *n.* twenty-four sheaves. Cf. Thrave.

Threave, *v.* throve.

Threaver, *n.* a reaper who is paid by the number of 'threaves' he cuts down.

Threaving, *n.* payment by the 'threaves' cut.

Three-cockit, *n.* a three-cornered hat.

Three-cord, *adj.* three-ply.

Threed, *n.* thread.

Three faces in a hood, *n.* the pansy.

Threefauld, *adj.* threefold.

Three-fold, *n.* the bog-bean.

Three-four, *adj.* three or four.

Three-girr'd, *adj.* girded with three hoops.

Threen, *n.* a refrain. Cf. Threne.

Three-neukit, *adj.* three-cornered.

Threep, *v.* to assert pertinaciously. Cf. Threap.

Threepenny, *n.* a first reading book.

Threeple, *adj.* treble.

Three-plet, *adj.* three-ply; threefold.

Threep-tree, *n.* the beam of a plough.

Threesh, *v. pret.* thrashed.

Threesht, *v. pret.* threshed.

Threesome, *n.* three together; a reel which is danced by three alone.

Three-stand, *adv.* in three portions.

Three sweeps, *n.* a girls' singing game.

Three-taed, *adj.* three-pronged.

Three threads and thrums, *n.* a cat's purring.

Three thrums, *n.* a cat's purring.

Threeve, *v. pret.* throve.

Threeve, *n.* twenty-four sheaves. Cf. Thrave.

Three-yirl'd, *adj.* three years old.—*n.* an animal three years old.

Threft, *adj.* reluctant; perverse. Cf. Thairf.

Threin, *ppl. adj.* thriven.

Threip, *v.* to argue; to insist. Cf. Threap.

Threish, *v.* to entreat one in a kind way; to flatter. Cf. Treesh.

Threishin, *n.* courting.

Thremmel, *v.* to squeeze, wring; to extort.

Threne, Thren, *n.* a song, a refrain; a ghost-story, a superstitious tradition; a vulgar adage.—*v.* to tell ghost-stories, &c. Cf. Thrain.

Thresh, *n.* a rush. Cf. Thrash.

Thresh, *n.* a beating. Cf. Thrash.

Threshen, *ppl.* threshed.

Threshie, *n.* a rush.

Threshie-coat, *n.* an old working-coat.

Threshing-tree, *n.* a flail.

Threshwart, Threshwort, *n.* a threshold.

Threshy mill, *n.* a threshing-mill.

Threshy-wick, *n.* a rush-wick.

Thresum, *n.* three together. Cf. Threesome.

Thresury, *n.* the treasury.

Thretten, *adj.* thirteen.

Thretty, *adj.* thirty.

Threuch, Threuch-stane, *n.* a flat tombstone. Cf. Through-stone.

Threush, *v. pret.* thrashed, beat.

Thrid, *adj.* third.

Thrid, *n.* thread.

Thriep, *v.* to insist on. Cf. Threap.

Thriest, *n.* constraint.

Thrieve, *n.* twenty-four sheaves. Cf. Thrave.

Thrieveless, *adj.* thriftless; not promising success.

Thrift, *n.* prosperity; luck; success; work, employment, business; industry.

Thriftin, *n.* luck; success.

Thriftless, *adj.* unprofitable; unsuccessful; 'thrieveless.'

Thrifty, *adj.* thoughtful, considerate; saving time or trouble.

Thrim, *n.* a twisted thread; a loose end. Cf. Thrum.

Thrimble, Thrimle, Thrimmle, Thrimal, *v.* to finger anything as if unwilling to part with it; to crowd, press; to wrestle; to fumble; to press, squeeze through. Cf. Thrumble.

Thrime, *n.* a triplet in verse.

Thrimp, *v.* to press, squeeze; to press or push in a crowd; to push; used of schoolboys on a bench: to push all before them from end to end.—*n.* schoolboys' pushing.

Thrim-thram, *n.* a term of ridicule or contempt; used in evasive answers. Cf. Trim-tram.

Thring, *v.* to press, squeeze; to push one's way in.

Thrinter, *n.* a sheep of three winters.

Thrip, *v.* to insist. Cf. Threap.

Thriplin'-kame, *n.* a comb for separating the seed of flax from the stalks.

Thrissel, Thrissle, Thrisle, *n.* a thistle.

Thrissly, *adj.* abounding in thistles; testy.

Thrist, *n.* thirst.—*v.* to cause thirst.

Thrist, *v.* to thrust; to squeeze, hug; to wring.—*n.* a thrust, push; a squeeze, hug; the action of the jaws in squeezing the juice of a quid of tobacco.

Thrist, *v.* to spin.

Thristle, *n.* a thistle.

Thristle-, Thrissel-cock, *n.* the song-thrush.

Thristle-cock-lairag, *n.* the common bunting.

Thristled, *ppl. adj.* used of banners: bearing the emblem of the thistle.

Thristly, *adj.* abounding in thistles; bristly; testy, snappish.

Thriv, *n.* twenty-four sheaves. Cf. Thrave.

Thriv, *v. pret.* throve.

Thrivance, *n.* prosperity, success; prosperous industry.

Thrive, *n.* the way to prosperity.

Thriven, *ppl. adj.* thriving; prosperous; well-nourished. Cf. Threin.

Thriver, *n.* a thriving animal.

Thriver, *n.* a reaper paid by the 'threaves' he cuts. Cf. Threaver.

Throat, *n.* a narrow entrance.

Throat-cutter, *n.* a cut-throat.

Throch, *prep.* through.—*v.* to carry through, accomplish.

Throch, *n.* a sheet of paper; a small literary work.

Throch-and-through, -throw, *adv.* completely through, through and through.

Throch-stane, *n.* a flat tombstone.

Throck, *n.* the lower part of a plough to which the share is attached; a term given to certain pairs of oxen in a twelve-oxen plough. Cf. Frock.

Throck, *v.* to crowd, throng.—*n.* a throng, a crowd.

Throng, *n.* a large quantity; intimacy; pressure of work; a busy time; a bustle.—*v.* to become crowded.—*adj.* crowded, pressed for room; very busy; numerous; intimate; improperly familiar; used of work: pressing.—*adv.* busily. Cf. Thrang.

Throngness, *n.* a crowded state.

Throoch, Throoch-stane, *n.* a flat tombstone. Cf. Through.

Throok, *n.* an instrument for twisting ropes of straw, &c.

Throosh, *v. pret.* threshed.

Throosh, *v.* to play truant.

Throosh-the-schule, *n.* a truant.

Throost, *v. pret.* did thrust.—*ppl.* thrust.

Throother, *adj.* unmethodical. Cf. Through-ither.

Thropit, *v.* to go.

Thropple, Throple, *n.* the windpipe, throat, neck.—*v.* to throttle; to seize by the throat; to entangle with cords. Cf. Thrapple.

Thropple-deep, *adj.* up to the throat.

Thropple-girth, *n.* a collar; a neckcloth.

Thropple-hearse, *adj.* hoarse.

Throssil, *n.* the song-thrush.

Throstle, *v.* to warble.

Throther, *adj.* unmethodical. Cf. Through-ither.

Throuch, *prep.* through.—*v.* to carry through; to penetrate.—*adj.* active, expeditious; capable. Cf. Through.

Throu'-come, *n.* a trying experience through which one passes.

Throu'-'dder, *adj.* unmethodical.

Througal, *adj.* frugal, thrifty.

Througallity, *n.* frugality.

Througang, *n.* a passage through.

Througawn, *adj.* persevering.

Through, Throwe, *prep.* across; on the other side of; during.—*adv.* up and down; thoroughly.—*adj.* finished; going through, penetrating; active, expeditious.—*n.* a grazing-range.—*v.* to advance, to go through with; to perfect, make thorough; to prove.

Through, *n.* a flat tombstone.

Through-art, *n.* a narrow passage or close between the barn and the 'byre' of a farmstead.

Through-band, *n.* a long binding stone which goes the whole breadth of a wall.

Through-bear, *v.* to sustain, support, provide; to bear through to the end of a work or difficulty.

Through-bearin', *n.* a livelihood; means of sustenance; support through work, difficulty, danger unto the end.

Through-coming, *n.* a livelihood; a coming through.

Through-gäin, -gäen, -going, *adj.* active, pushing; prodigal, wasteful; passing through. —*n.* a severe examination; a thorough reprimand; a thorough overhaul; a passage through; a thoroughfare; transit; a livelihood; support under difficulties to their end.

Through-gäin close, *n.* an open narrow passage from one street to another.

Through-gäin entry, *n.* a passage from the front to the back of a house.

Through-gang, *n.* a thoroughfare; a passage; a close scrutiny; labour; perseverance; energy.

Through-gang close, *n.* an open passage from one street to another.

Through-ganging, *ppl. adj.* active; having a great deal of action.

Through-gaun, *n.* a livelihood.—*adj.* active. Cf. Through-gäin.

Through-hands, *adv.* under consideration; under reprimand.—*adj.* used of work, &c.: undertaken or finished.

Throughither, *adv.* in confusion; pell-mell; among each other; unmethodically.—*adj.* confused, disorderly, unmethodical; harum-scarum; careless in working; mentally confused; intimate; living in close proximity. —*n.* a confusion, disturbance; in *pl.* mixed sweets.

Throughitherness, *n.* want of method, confusion.

Throughither-witted, *adj.* weak or confused mentally.

Through-pit, -put, *n.* activity, expedition.

Through-pittin, *adj.* active, expeditious.—*n.* a bare subsistence; a rough handling; a severe examination.

Through-stane, *n.* a flat tombstone.

Through-stane, *n.* a stone going through a wall; a 'through-band.'

Through-the-bows, *n.* a severe scolding; a thorough dealing; a strict examination.

Through-the-muir, -meer, *n.* a quarrel, wrangle; a fault-finding.

Through-the-needle-e'e, *n.* a young people's game.

Through-the-wad-laddie, *n.* a wrangle; a fault-finding.

Through time, *adv.* gradually; in the course of time.

Throut, *adv.* out-of-doors. Cf. Thereout.

Throu'ther, *adj.* unmethodical. Cf. Throughither.

Throw, *v.* to vomit; to throw off; to twist; to twist the neck; to turn a key; to distort, pervert; to thwart.—*n.* a twist, sprain; a turn of the hand; a quarrel; perversity; a reverse of fortune; a press. Cf. Thraw.

Throw, Throwe, *prep.* and *adv.* through. Cf. Through.

Throwder, *adj.* muddled; unmethodical. Cf. Throughither.

Throw-gang, *adj.* affording a thoroughfare.

Throwlie, *adv.* thoroughly.

Throwther, *adj.* confused. Cf. Throughither.

Thruch, Thrugh, *n.* a flat tombstone. Cf. Through.

Thruish, *v. pret.* threshed.

Thrum, *n.* a loose end of any kind; a particle; a tangle, mess; the debts a man, leaving a place, leaves unpaid; close and loving intercourse; an engagement to marry; courting with a view to marriage; a fit of ill-humour; a foolish whim; in *pl.* threads needed from the yarn in beginning to weave.—*v.* to raise a tufted pile on knitted or woollen stuffs; to enwrap in a careless fashion; to entangle; to act on a foolish whim, to sulk; to twirl the fingers in a shy, awkward manner.

Thrum, *v.* to strum; to hum, 'croon'; to repeat over again; used of a cat: to purr. —*n.* a drumming noise; a strain, a hum; the purring of a cat; a theme; a narrow passage for water between rocks.

Thrumble, *v.* to fumble. Cf. Thrummil.

Thrum-cutter, *n.* a weaver.

Thrum in the graith, *n.* a hitch in an undertaking.

Thrummer, *n.* an itinerant minstrel; a contemptible musician.

Thrummil, Thrummle, *v.* to fumble, grope; to handle awkwardly or overmuch; with *out* or *up*, to deal out cash in small quantities; to bring forth after a confused search ; to throng ; to press into or through a crowd with effort.—*n.* the act of fumbling, groping, or handling overmuch.

Thrummle, *v.* to tremble.—*n.* a tremor.

Thrummy, *n.* a very coarse woollen cloth with rough, tufted surface.—*adj.* shabbily dressed ; wearing old, worn-out clothes.

Thrummy-cap, *n.* a cap made of 'thrums' or weavers' ends.

Thrummy-mittens, *n.* mittens woven from 'thrums.'

Thrummy-tailed, *adj.* used of a woman : wearing fringed gowns or petticoats.

Thrummy-wheelin, *n.* coarse worsted spun on the large wheel.

Thrump, *v.* to press ; to press, as in a crowd ; to push.—*n.* the act of pushing. Cf. Thrimp.

Thrunter, *n.* a three-year-old ewe. Cf. Thrinter.

Thrush, *n.* a rush. Cf. Thresh.

Thrush-buss, *n.* a clump of rushes.

Thrushe, *v. pret.* threshed.

Thrushe, *v. pret.* thrashed.

Thrusle, Thrustle, *n.* a thistle. Cf. Thristle.

Thrust, *v.* to thirst ; to cause to thirst.—*n.* thirst.

Thrustle-cock, *n.* the song-thrush.

Thrusty, *adj.* thirsty.

Thry, *adj.* cross, contrary.

Thryne, *ppl. adj.* thriving, prosperous ; well-nourished.

Thryst, *n.* an engagement. Cf. Tryste.

Thud, *v.* to fall heavily ; to make a noise in falling ; to move or drive quickly ; used of wind : to blow in gusts, to rush with a hollow sound ; to beat, thump ; to beat hard and with a noise.—*n.* a buffet, thump ; a blow with the fist ; a gust of wind.

Thud, *v.* to wheedle ; to flatter.—*n.* the act of wheedling or flattering.

Thuddering, *ppl. adj.* used of the wind : blowing in gusts.

Thulmart, *n.* a polecat. ·Cf. Thoumart, Thummart.

Thumb, *v.* to compress with the thumb. Cf. Thoom.

Thumbikins, *n.* thumbkins, an instrument of torture applied us a screw to the thumbs.

Thumble, Thummle, *n.* a whip for driving a top.

Thumble, Thummle, *n.* a thimble ; in *pl.* round-leaved bell flowers, harebells. Cf. Thimble.

Thummart, Thummert, *n.* a polecat ; a person of singular and awkward appearance.

Thump, *v.* to walk or dance with energy ; to work vigorously.—*n.* a lump ; anything big of its kind.

Thumper, *n.* a gross lie.

Thumpers, *n.* the hammers of a fulling-mill.

Thumping, *ppl. adj.* large, big, stout.

Thum-steil, -stule, *n.* a covering for a sore thumb, as the finger of a glove.

Thunder, *n.* a hailstorm ; a thundering noise ; a heavy blow ; a thunderbolt.

Thunder-and-lightning, *n.* the common lungwort.

Thunder-bolt, *n.* a stone hatchet or 'celt'; a fossil belemnite.

Thunder-flower, *n.* the common red poppy.

Thundering-drouth, *n.* a strong drought.

Thunder-plump, *n.* a heavy thunder-shower.

Thunder-slain, *adj.* struck by lightning.

Thunder-speal, -spale, *n.* a thin piece of wood, two or three inches wide and six inches long, with notched sides, tied to some yards of twine, and whirled round the head by boys to make mimic thunder.

Thunder-speat, -spate, *n.* a heavy thundershower, -storm.

Thunner, *n.* thunder. Cf. Thunder.

Thur, *pron.* and *adj.* these. Cf. Thir.

Thurst, *v.* to thrust.—*n.* a thrust, stab.

Thurst, Thurt, *v. pret.* needed. Cf. Thar.

Thus-gates, *adv.* in this way or manner.

Thwang, *n.* a leathern thong ; a shoe-tie.

Thwankin, *ppl. adj.* used of clouds : mingling in thick and gloomy succession.

Thwart, *adv.* crosswise.

Thwart-bawk, *n.* a cross-beam in a roof.

Thwarter, *adj.* cross-grained. Cf. Thorter.

Thwarter-ill, *n.* a paralysis affecting sheep. Cf. Quarter-ill.

Thwartlins, *adv.* crosswise.

Thwartour, *adv.* athwart.

Thwricken, *v.* to choke with thick, smouldering smoke.

Thysel', *refl. pron.* thyself.

Tiachersum, *adj.* ill-disposed.

Tial, *n.* a latchet ; anything used for tying ; a tying.

Tiawe, *v.* to amble.

Tib, *n.* a tub.

Tibbet, *n.* one length of hair in a fishing-line ; a link. Cf. Tippet.

Tibbie-thiefie, *n.* the cry of the sandpiper.

Tibbit, Tibet, *n.* bodily sensation. Cf. Tabet.

Tibb's eve, *n.* a time that never comes.

Tibeethe, *n.* the 'tolbooth,' gaol. Cf. Tolbooth.

Tic, *n.* credit. Cf. Tick.

Tice, *v.* to entice ; to coax ; to move slowly and cautiously ; to attract, allure ; to treat kindly. — *n.* kind treatment ; a coaxing manner of treating.

Tich, *v.* to touch.

Tichel, Tichil, Tichle, *n.* a number, band, troop ; anything attached to another ; any article kept secretly.—*v.* to join hands in children's games.

Tich'en, Tichten, v. to tighten.

Ticher, v. to laugh in a suppressed manner; to titter.—n. a titter.

Ticher, n. a small fiery pimple; an eruption on the face; a dot of any kind. Cf. Ticker.

Ticher, v. to ooze from the skin.—n. the appearance of a fretted sore. Cf. Teicher.

Ticht, v. to tighten.—adj. tight.

Tichtly, adv. tightly; firmly; assuredly. Cf. Tightly.

Ticht-trag, n. a low, mean person.

Ticht wecht, n. barely the exact weight.

Tick, v. to buy on credit; to give credit.

Tick, n. a children's game of 'tig'; a state of activity; a small speck or spot on the skin.

Ticker, n. a dot of any kind; a small eruption on the skin.

Ticket, n. a bill given for money lent on promise to pay; a pat, a slight stroke; a smart blow; a drubbing.

Ticket, n. the correct thing; an oddity, a queer 'figure.'

Tickle, v. to puzzle.

Tickle, adj. difficult; nice; delicate.

Tickler, n. anything very puzzling or difficult; a person difficult to deal with.

Tickles, n. spectacles.

Tickle-tails, adv. applied to any children's game in which they hold each other by the hand. Cf. Tichel.

Tickly, adj. easily tickled, touchy; puzzling, difficult.

Ticksie, n. a quarrel, wrangle; a scolding. Cf. Dixie.

Tick-tack, n. the ticking sound of a clock; an instant.

Tick-tack-toe, Tic-tac-toe, n. a children's game played on a slate, like 'noughts and crosses.'

Ticky-molie, n. a boy's prank.

Ticquet, n. a bill; a written promise to pay. Cf. Ticket.

Tid, n. the proper time or season for agricultural operations; season, tide; the suitable condition of soil for cultivation; mood, humour, temper; a fit of ill-humour.—v. to choose the proper time.

Tid, n. a term of endearment. Cf. Taid.

Tid and quid, n. a term used by old farmers to denote a farm in a state of thriving rotation.

Tidder, adj. 'tother,' the other; successive; additional.

Tiddie, adj. cross in temper; used of land: difficult to catch the proper season for ploughing, owing to its quality; uncertain; eccentric.

Tiddler, n. a small trout.

Tiddy, n. tidy; smart, expeditious.

Tide, n. the sea, ocean; the water in a dock;

the seashore; the quantity of fish taken ashore at one time.

Tide-race, n. a strong tidal current.

Tidy, adj. plump and thriving; lucky, favourable; pregnant.

Tie, v. to marry; to bind by moral obligation. —n. a tie-wig; obligation; a trick, deception.

Tie-hie, n. loud laughter; silly laughter. Cf. Tee-hee.

Tiend, n. a tithe. Cf. Teind.

†Tiercer, n. a widow claiming her third of her husband's property.

Tiff, n. a fit of anger or bad temper; a wanton or dallying struggle.—v. to scold; to show strong feelings of offence; to delay; to struggle against.

Tiff, v. to quaff.—n a small draught.

Tiff, n. order; condition, plight; mood, humour; mood of the moment; a period of time, with the notion of tediousness. Cf. Tift.

†Tiff, v. to put in order; to adjust. Cf. Tift.

Tiff, v. to eject anything from the mouth.— n. a sudden gust of wind; afflatus, inspiration; a whiff, sniff; a sudden flight; a great haste. Cf. Tift.

Tiffle, n. a slight breeze or ripple of wind.

Tiffy, adj. of uncertain temper.

Tiffy, adj. in good condition; healthy, well; smart.

Tift, n. order, condition; mood, humour; a 'dreich' period of time.

†Tift, v. to put in good order; to adjust; to deck.

Tift, n. a sudden breeze; a whiff; a sudden flight.—v. to eject from the mouth.

Tift, v. to quaff. Cf. Tiff.

Tift, n. a 'tiff'; a fit of anger.—v. to scold. Cf. Tiff.

Tift, v. to throb, tingle with pain.

Tiftan, n. the act of decking.

Tifter, n. a quandary; a stiff breeze with a stormy sea.

Tifter, n. a quarrel.

Tiftie, adj. uplifted, inspired.

Tiftin, n. a scolding; a quarrelling bout.

Tift o' tow, n. a sudden blaze of kindled flax.

Tifty, adj. petulant; touchy; quarrelsome.

Tifty, adj. in good condition; healthy.

Tig, v. to tap; to touch lightly; to play the game of 'touch'; to dally; to caress; to treat scornfully; to trifle with; to work carelessly; used of cattle: to run hither and thither, irritated by flies or boys; to go off in a pet; to take a sudden whim.—n. a twitch, tap, pat; a light touch in the game of 'touch'; the game of 'touch'; the player in the game who tries to touch the others, the one who is touched; a sharp blow; a

stroke causing a wound ; a hard bargain ;
a pet, fit of ill-humour.

Tig-an'-tie, *phr.* 'touch and go.'

Tig-biz, *n.* the cry of boys to incite cattle to
run to and fro.

Tig'd, *ppl. adj.* tired, wearied.

Tiger, *n.* a virago.—*v.* to look fierce. Cf.
Teeger.

Tiger-tarran, *n.* a waspish child.

Tiggel, *v.* to undermine ; to tamper with.

Tigger, *n.* the 'toucher' in the games of 'tig'
and 'hie-spy.'

Tigger, *n.* a tiger ; a virago.

Tiggle-taggle, *v.* to haggle in bargaining.

Tiggy, *adj.* pettish.

Tigher, *v.* to ooze from the skin. Cf. Teicher.

Tigher, *v.* to titter ; to laugh in a suppressed
manner. Cf. Ticher.

Tight, *adj.* neat, trim ; well-shaped ; good-
looking ; tidy, in good order ; sound, whole,
healthy ; dexterous, skilful ; ready for action ;
used of ale, &c.: good, strong, pleasing ;
stingy ; hard up ; used of money : scarce ;
tipsy.—*adv.* tightly ; strenuously.—*v.* to
tighten ; to stretch ; with *up*, to tidy, put
in order.—*n.* a setting in order.

Tight-bound, *adj.* strong, well-made, strapping.

Tight-locked, *adj.* used of comrades : close
bound.

Tightly, *adv.* cleverly ; deftly ; promptly ;
actively ; thoroughly ; minutely ; severely,
sharply.

Tigmateeze, *v.* to pull one about.

Tig-me-if-you-can, *n.* the game of 'tig' or
'touch.'

Tigsam, Tigsum, *adj.* hindersome ; tedious.
Cf. Taigsum.

Tig-tag, *v.* to trifle ; to be busy while doing
nothing ; to shilly-shally ; to be tedious in
bargaining, to haggle. Cf. Tiggle-taggle.

Tig-tailed, *adj.* used of a woman : wearing a
frock shorter than the petticoat underneath.
Cf. Tag-tailed.

Tig-tire, *v.* to keep in ; to annoy ; to make
sport by teasing.—*n.* a practical joke.

Tig-tow, *n.* the game of 'tig'; dallying.—*v.*
to play at 'tig'; to play fast and loose ; to
act capriciously ; to dally with ; to be off
and on ; to pat mutually ; to stroke gently
backwards and forwards.

Ti-hi, *n.* silly laughter. Cf. Tee-hee.

Tike, *n.* a dog, hound, cur ; a churl, a currish
fellow, a boor ; a mischievous, tiresome
child ; a playful term of reproach for a
child ; a Yorkshireman ; an overgrown man
or beast ; the common otter.

Tike, *n.* ticking for covering a bed or bolster,
&c.; the bed or bolster itself.

Tike-and-tryke, *adv.* higgledy-piggledy.

Tike-auld, *adj.* very old.

Tiked, *adj.* currish.

Tike-hungry, *adj.* ravenous as a dog.

Tiken, *n.* ticking. Cf. Tike.

Tike's-testament, *n.* nothing left as a legacy.

Tike-tire, -tyrit, *adj.* dog-tired.

Tike-tulyie, *n.* a dogs' quarrel, 'collieshangie';
a coarse scolding match.

Tilavie, *n.* a sudden fit of temper. Cf.
Tirrivie.

Tile, *n.* a drain-pipe ; a hat.

Tiled, *ppl. adj.* used of fish : dried.

Tile-stone, *n.* a brick.

Till, *n.* hard, unproductive, gravelly clay ;
hard or soft shale.

Till, *n.* stuff ; drink.

Till, *v.* to entice, allure, tempt. Cf. Teal.

Till, Til, *conj.* before, until ; to such a degree
that.—*prep.* to ; at ; by ; for ; of ; after ; about.

Tillage, *v.* to till, cultivate.

Till-band, *n.* pudding-stone.

Tiller, *n.* a till ; a money-box.

Tillie-lick, -licket, *n.* an unexpected blow ;
an unexpected calamity or reverse of fortune ; in *pl.* taunts and sneers

†**Tillie-soul,** *n.* a place to which a gentleman
sent the horses and servants of his guests,
when he did not choose to entertain the
former at his own cost.

Tilliwhillie, *n.* the curlew.

Tillowie, *int.* tally-ho ! a cry to encourage
hounds on to the chase.—*n.* used of drink :
as much as urges the drinker on.

Tilly, *adj.* of the nature of 'till,' or unproductive clay soil.

Tilly-clay, *n.* cold clay, unproductive soil ;
coldness of heart.

Tilly-pan, *n.* a skillet ; a pan for lifting water.

Tilt, *n.* a high-minded state ; trouble, annoyance.

Tilt, *n.* filth ; plight, condition.

Tilter, *n.* the man that delivers the sheaves
from a reaping-machine with a rake.

Tilting-machine, *n.* a reaping-machine requiring a man to knock off the sheaves
with a rake.

Tilyer, *n.* a tailor.

Tim, *v.* to pour ; to empty out. Cf. Teem.

Timber, *adj.* unmusical. Cf. Timmer.

Timber-man, *n.* a timber-merchant.

Timber-mare, -horse, *n.* the 'wooden horse'
formerly used as a military punishment.

Time, *n.* thyme.

Time, *n.* life ; lifetime ; the time of parturition ; the death-hour ; the duration of
apprenticeship or contract of service ; the
act of once harrowing a field.

Time-mark, *n.* an epoch.

Timeous, Timous, *adj.* opportune ; keeping
time ; keeping proper hours.—*adv.* betimes.

Timeously, *adv.* opportunely; in good or proper time.

Timersome, *adj.* timorous.

Time-taker, *n.* one who lies in wait for an opportunity of effecting his purpose; used in a bad sense.

Timmer, *v.* to act strenuously, continuously, and successfully in any work requiring exertion.

Timmer, *n.* timber, wood; a wooden dish or cup; a stick, cudgel; a leg, limb; a piece of furniture.—*v.* to beat, cudgel.—*adj.* wooden, made of wood; unmusical, without an ear for music.

†**Timmer,** *n.* a legal quantity of forty or fifty skins packed within boards.

Timmer-breeks, *n.* a coffin.

Timmer-goods, *n.* wooden articles.

Timmerin, *n.* a cudgelling, thrashing.

Timmer-man, *n.* a timber-merchant.

Timmer-market, *n.* an ancient fair held in Aberdeen on the last Wednesday of August for the sale of small fruits, timber articles, toys, &c.

Timmer-tune, *n.* a poor, unmusical voice.

Timmer-tuned, *adj.* having no ear or voice for music.

†**Timming,** *n.* a coarse, thin, woollen cloth.

Timothy, *n* the cat's-tail grass.

Timothy, *n.* haste, bustle; an agitated state; a jorum of drink.

Timoursome, *adj.* timorous.

Timpany, Timpan, *n.* the middle part of the front of a house raised above the level of the rest, so as to resemble a gable and give an attic in the roof.

Timpany-gable, *n.* a 'timpany.'

Timpany-window, *n.* a window in the 'timpany'-gable.

Tim'pin,' *ppl. adj.* tempting.

Timse, *n.* a sieve, riddle. Cf. Teems.

Timty, *n.* a method of digging the ground and covering it with sea-ware in the Isle of Lewis.

Tin, *n.* any article made of tin, a tin mug, &c.

Tin, *n.* the prong of a fork; the tooth of a harrow; a tine; the branch of a stag's horn. Cf. Teind.

Tinchel, Tinchill, Tinckell, *n.* a circle formed by sportsmen to encircle deer; a gin, trap, snare.

Tinclarian, *adj.* tinker-like; composed of tinkers. Cf. Tinkler.

Tindel, *n.* tinder. Cf. Tundle.

Tine, *v.* to kindle.—*n.* a spark of fire; a spark on the side of the wick of a candle. Cf. Teind.

Tine, *v.* to lose; to forfeit; to lose a cause in a court of justice; to be lost, perish.

Tin-egin, *n.* forced fire, as an antidote to murrain.

Tineless, *adj.* used of a harrow: without tines.

Tineman, *n.* an appellation given to one of the lords of Douglas, who lost almost all his sons in battle.

Tinesel, *n.* loss. Cf. Tinsel.

Tining, *n.* in *phr.* 'at the tining and the winning,' at a critical point between loss or gain, ruin or safety.

Ting, *n* a tongue of land jutting into the sea. —*v.* used of cattle: to swell up through eating clover, &c.

Ting, *v.* to ring, jingle; to resound.—*n.* a ringing sound, a tinkle; the sound of a clock striking, or of a small bell.

Ting-a-ling, *n.* the sound of a small bell; the imitation of such; a ringing sound; a clock that strikes.

Tingle, *v.* to tinkle; to jingle; to ring a bell.

Ting-tang, *n.* the sound of a bell; a monotonous repetition; an oft-told tale.

Tink, *n.* a tinker.—*v.* to rivet with a tinkling sound.

Tink, *v.* to tinkle.—*n.* a tinkle, ring; the sound of a small bell.

Tinker, *n.* a gipsy, a 'randy' beggar. Cf. Tinkler.

Tinker-bairn, *n* a tinker's child.

Tinker-tongue, *n.* an abusive tongue.

Tinkle, *v.* to trifle; to work carelessly and lazily.

Tinkle, *v.* with *on*, to ring chimes about one, or to praise one unduly.

Tinkler, *n.* a tinker; a gipsy, vagabond; an opprobrious term; a virago.—*adj.* like a 'tinkler.'

Tinkler-bairn, *n.* a tinker's child.

Tinkler gipsy, *n.* a wandering gipsy.

Tinkler-jaw, *n* a loud, scolding tongue; coarse, abusive language.

Tinkler-lass, *n.* a gipsy-girl; a tinker's daughter.

Tinkler's-curse, -tippence, -whussel, *n.* anything utterly worthless; a jot, atom.

Tinkler-tongue, *n.* a 'tinkler-jaw.'

Tinkler-trumpet-tongue, *n.* a loud, abusive tongue.

Tinkler-wife, *n.* a term of contempt for a woman; a woman of low character and companions; a virago.

Tinkle-sweetie, *n.* a bell formerly rung in Edinburgh at eight o'clock P.M., when shops were closed for the night.

Tinkling-tool, *n.* a tinker's tool.

Tinner, *n.* a tinsmith.

Tinnie, *n.* any small tin vessel; a tin canister; a tinsmith.

Tinnikin, *n.* a small tin vessel.

Tinnykit, *n.* a 'tinnikin.'

Tinsel, Tinsall, *n.* loss; forfeiture. Cf. Tine.

Tinsey, Tinsy, *n.* tinsel.

Tinsey-tailed, *adj.* having a bright, shining tail.

Tint, *v.* to lose.

Tint, *v. pret.* and *ppl.* lost. Cf. Tine.

Tint, *n.* a taste; a foretaste; evidence, indication; tidings, information.

Tint, *adj.* used of a child: spoilt, petted.

Tinte, *n.* loss. Cf. Tine.

Tintoe, *n.* the pin used in turning the cloth-beam of a loom.

Tip, *n.* a tup, ram.—*v.* to take the ram; to serve with the ram.

Tip, *n.* a term marking great excellence in a person or thing; the belle of a ball or party; the best of anything; an overdressed person, a 'swell'; a match, an equal.—*v.* to go on tiptoe; to equal, match; to excel, exceed; to overcome.

Tip, *v.* to tap; to kick in football; to empty by tipping; to drink off; to milk a cow with a small yield; to pull down the teats preparatory to milking a cow; to put to silence; to disappoint, nettle, mortify.—*n.* a tap; a notch; a place where rubbish is thrown down, a rubbish-heap; a small quantity of liquid; anything that silences a person, a 'settler.'

Tip, *n.* ale sold for twopence a pint. Cf. Tippenny.

Tipie, *adj.* trim, tidy; neatly dressed.

Tipney, *n.* small-beer at twopence a pint. Cf. Tippenny.

Tippanize, Tippenize, *v.* to tipple small-beer.

Tippen, *n.* the hair that binds a hook to a fishing-line. Cf. Tippet.

Tippence, *n.* twopence.

Tippenny, *n.* small-beer sold for twopence a pint; a child's first reading-book, costing twopence.

Tippenny-hoose, *n.* an ale-house.

Tipper, *n.* a horse used for the tipping of wagons in making a railway, &c.

Tipper, *n.* a well-dressed person of either sex; a 'swell.'

Tipper, *v.* to walk on tiptoe, or unsteadily; to totter; to place in an unsteady position.

Tipper-taiper, *v.* to totter.

Tippertin, *n.* a bit of card with a pin passed through it, resembling a teetotum.

Tipperty, *adj.* unstable; walking stiffly, with mincing gait, or in a flighty, ridiculous manner.

Tipperty-like, *adv.* mincingly, in a flighty, ridiculous gait.

Tippet, *n.* one length of twisted hair or gut in a fishing-line; a handful of straw bound together at one end, used in thatching. Cf. Tibbet.

Tippet, *n.* in *phr.* 'St Johnstone's Tippet,' a hangman's halter.

Tippet-stane, *n.* a round stone with a hook in its centre for twisting 'tippets.'

Tippet up, *ppl. adj.* nicely dressed.

Tippy, *n.* the height of fashion.—*adj.* dressed in the highest fashion.

Tipsie, *n.* drink, liquor.

Tiptoo, *n.* a violent passion.—*v.* to be in a violent passion. Cf. Taptoo.

Tir, *v.* to strip off one's clothes. Cf. Tirr.

Tiravie, *n.* a fit of tempter; a commotion, an outbreak. Cf. Tirrivee.

Tirbad, *n.* the turbot; the halibut.

Tird, *v.* to strip, denude; to scatter; to work vigorously. Cf. Tirr.

Tire, *n.* a 'snood' or narrow band for the hair of women; an ornamental edging used by cabinet-makers and upholsterers; the metal edging or ornaments of coffins.

Tire, *n.* fatigue, stiffness; tiredness, the feeling of tiredness.

Tirivee, Tiryvee, *n.* a passion. Cf. Tirrivee.

Tirl, Tirle, *v.* to vibrate, quiver; to thrill; to make a thrilling sound; to make a rattling or scraping sound so as to attract attention at a door; to whirl; to rotate rapidly; to twist; used of the wind: to veer; to cause to vibrate; of the sun: to drive its course; to touch the strings of an instrument and produce vibrations of sound; to cause to twirl, roll, or whirl; to turn over; to strip, denude; to unroof; to strip off thatch or slates; to uncover a house; to pare the surface of a peat-moss.—*n.* a thrill; a vibration; a tremor; a twirl, whirl; a fall over and over; the act of rotating; a bout, a short spell at anything, as of drinking, dancing; a gentle breeze; a substitute for the trundle of an old Shetland mill. Cf. Dirl.

Tirlass, Tirless, Tirlies, *n.* a trellis; the lattice of a window; a latticed grating or rail; a wicket, a small gate; a woven wire frame.—*v.* to lattice.

Tirless-yett, *n.* a turnstile.

Tirlest, *ppl. adj.* trellised.

Tirl-grind, *n.* a turnstile, a revolving gate.

Tirling-pin, *n.* a bar of iron, notched or twisted like a rope, placed vertically on a door, with a ring of iron slung to it, formerly used as a knocker.

Tirling-ring, *n.* the ring which was 'tirled' round the 'tirling-pin,' to make a rattling noise at the door.

Tirl-mill, *n.* a primitive grinding-mill of Shetland.

Tirl-o'-win, *n.* a good winnowing wind.

Tirly, *n.* an ornamental waving line in scroll-work or carving; the ornament itself; a winding in a footpath.

Tirly-toy, *n.* a trifle, a toy; a 'tirly.'

Tirly-wirly, Tirly-wirl, Tirly-whirly, *n.* a

flourish; a fanciful ornament; any figure or decoration; the clock of a stocking; a whirligig; an ingenious contrivance.—*adj.* intricate, winding, intertwisted.—*adv.* round and round like a whirligig.

Tirma, *n.* the sea-pie or oyster-catcher.

Tirr, *v.* to strip, denude; to uncover with force; to unroof; to tear off a covering, thatch, slates, &c.; to remove the surface or subsoil in quarrying; to pare the surface of a peat-moss before cutting peats; to despoil one of property; to undress, pull off one's clothes.—*n.* what is removed from the bed of a quarry.

Tirr, *v.* to snarl; to speak in ill-temper.—*n.* a cross, peevish child; an angry or excited condition.—*adj.* crabbed, quarrelsome, in ill-temper.

Tirracke, Tirrik, Tirrock, *n.* the common tern; the Arctic tern; the kittiwake when young. Cf. Tarrock.

†**Tirran, Tirrane**, *n.* a tyrant; a perverse, ill-tempered person.

Tirrivee, Tirreveoch, Tirravie, Tirrievie, *n.* a passion, rage; a fit of temper; a commotion, bustle; excitement.

Tirrle, *v.* to vibrate. Cf. Tirl.

Tirr-wirr, *n.* a quarrel, wrangle; a contest; a complaint; a scolding.—*v.* to wrangle.—*adj.* growling, quarrelsome.

Tirr-wirrin', *ppl. adj.* growling, quarrelsome; fault-finding.

Tirry, *adj.* angry; cross, ill-tempered.

Tirry-mirry, *n.* a fit of passion; wild, excited mirth.

Tirryvie, *n.* a fit of temper. Cf. Tirrivee.

Tirry-wirry, *n.* a wrangle; a fit of passion; a contest; a scolding-fit.

Tirse, *v.* to pull with a jerk; to tear.—*n.* a tug, a jerk; a sudden gale.

Tirve, *n.* a turf.

Tirvin, *n.* sod taken from the top of peat.

Tir-wir, *adj.* growling.

Tiryvee, *n.* a fit of temper. Cf. Tirrivee.

Tise, *v.* to entice.

Tisha, *n.* a sneeze; the sound of sneezing.

Tissle, *n.* a tussle, a struggle, a 'dissle.' Cf. Taissle.

Tissle, *n.* a gew-gaw, a trifle, tinsel.

Tit, *n.* a teat, the nipple of the breast.

Tit, *n.* a mood, humour; a fit of temper. Cf. Tid.

Tit, *v.* to jerk; to snatch; to twitch; to tap; to pull.—*n.* a sudden jerk or pull; a tug; a snatch; a twitch; a tap; in *pl.* a disease of horses causing their legs to be spasmodically contracted.

Tita, *adv.* rather, sooner. Cf. Titter.

Tit-an'-taum, *n.* a fit of ill-humour.

Titbo-tatbo, *n.* the game of 'peep-bo.' Cf. Teet-bo.

Tite, *v.* to totter; to fall over; to walk with short, unsteady, or jerking steps.—*n.* such walking; a little person.—*adv.* with short, or jerking steps. Cf. Toit.

Tite, *adj.* straight, direct.—*adv.* directly. Cf. Tyte.

Tithand, *n.* tidings, news.

Tither, *adj.* the other, 'tother.'

Tithy, *adj.* plump, thriving. Cf. Tidy.

Titing, *n.* the titlark or meadow-pipit.

Title, *v.* to tattle; to talk idly; to whisper.—*n.* gossip, small talk; an idle talker; a whisper. Cf. Tittle.

Title, *v.* to tug repeatedly at one's coat-tails.

Titlene, Titlin, *n.* the meadow-pipit or titlark; the hedge-sparrow.

Tits, *int.* tuts! 'toots!'

Titsam, *adj.* short-tempered; touchy.

Titt, *v.* to jerk. Cf. Tit.

Tit-ta, *n.* a child's name for 'daddy' or father.

Titter, *adv.* rather, sooner.

Titter, *v.* to totter; to walk with weak or faltering steps; to shiver; to tremble; to quiver; to twitter; to work in a weak, trifling manner; to gossip.—*n.* a sorry plight; a weak, unsteady gait; work done in a weak, trifling manner; silly gossip; one who gossips.

Tittersome, *adj.* used of the weather: fickle, unsettled; backward; of a horse: restless, nervous.

Titter-totter, *n.* a see-saw.

Tittish, *adj.* captious, testy.

Tittivate, *v.* to dress up, make one's self smart; to flatter, tickle.

Tittivation, *n.* a smartening, making spruce.

Tittle, *v.* to tickle.

Tittle, *v.* to tattle; to prate idly; to whisper.—*n.* gossip, idle talk; a whisper. Cf. Title.

Tittle, *n.* a clot of dirt hanging at the tail of a cow or sheep. Cf. Tattle.

Tittle, *n.* anything small.

Tittlin, *n.* the meadow-pipit; the hedge-sparrow. Cf. Titlene.

Tittlins, *adv.* in the way of whispering, tattling, &c.

Titty, *n.* a child's word for 'sister'; a young girl.

Titty, *adj.* captious, testy; ill-tempered, 'teethy'; used of the wind: gusty, boisterous.

Titty-billy, *n.* an equal; a match; the strongest marks of resemblance, as of sister and brother.

Titular, *n.* a layman who after the Reformation had a donation of church-lands; a person having a legal title to the parsonage teinds of such parishes as had been 'mortified' to the monasteries.

Titup, *v.* to canter, gallop.

Tiv, *prep.* to.

Tivee, *n.* a fit of passion. Cf. **Tirrivee**.

Tize, *v.* to entice.

Tize, *v.* to add to the apparent bulk of meal by stirring it up or 'teasing' it. Cf. **Tease**.

Tizzle, *v.* to stir up or turn over; to ted hay. Cf. **Tousle**.

T'nead, *v.* to exhaust, fatigue; to dislike, annoy.

To, *prep.* at; by; for; on, upon; towards, with; in comparison with; in response to; belonging to.—*adv.* with a verb of motion understood; shut, close, in place; down.

Toachie, *int.* a call to a cow.

Toad, *n.* a term of contempt, dislike, or disgust; a term of endearment for a child; a child. Cf. **Taid**.

Toad, *n* a fox. Cf. **Tod**.

Toad-red, -rid, -rud, *n.* the spawn of toad or frog.

Toad's-e'e, *n.* jealousy.

Toad-spue, *n.* 'toad-red.'

Toad-stane, *n.* a stone formerly thought to be formed within a toad, and used with a certain formula for stanching the flow of blood.

Toad-stool, *n.* a mushroom.

To-airn, *n.* a piece of iron with a perforation wide enough to admit the pipe of the smith's bellows, built into the wall of his forge, to preserve the pipe from being consumed by the fire.

Toalie, *n.* a small, round cake of any kind of bread.

Toam, *v.* to rope. Cf. **Tome**.

To-an'-fro, *n.* indecision, wavering.

Toast, *v.* to tease; to vex; to toss. Cf. **Tost**.

Toaster, *n.* an iron frame for toasting oatcake before a fire.

Toath, *n.* sheep's dung. Cf. **Tathe**.

Tobacco-flour, -meal, *n.* snuff.

Tobacco-night, *n.* an irreverent name for a lyke-wake.

Tobacco-snipe, *n.* a boy-worker under a tobacco-spinner.

To'booth, *n.* a town-hall; a prison. Cf. **Tolbooth**.

To-bread, *n.* a biscuit given by a baker in addition to a shilling's worth or so purchased from him.

To-brig, *n.* a drawbridge.

Tocher, *n.* the dowry brought by a woman at marriage.—*v.* to dower.

Tocher-band, *n.* the deed signed regarding a bride's dowry.

Tocher-fee, -gear, -guid, *n.* a marriage dowry.

Tocherless, *adj.* without a dowry.

Tocherodarach, *n.* a sergeant of court; a thief-taker. Cf. **Tosheoderoch**.

Tocher-purse, *n.* a woman's dowry.

Tod, *int.* a corruption of the word 'God,' used as excl. of surprise, &c. Cf. **Dod**.

Tod, *n.* a disparaging term applied to a child. Cf. **Toad**.

Tod, *n.* a small species of crab.

Tod, *n.* a small, round cake of any kind of bread, given to pacify or please children.

Tod, *n.* a fit of the sulks.

Tod, *n.* a fox.

Tod, *n.* a glass of toddy.

Tod-and-lambs, *n.* a game played with wooden pins on a perforated board.

Tod-brod, *n.* the board on which the game 'tod-and-lambs' is played.

Toddie, *n.* the 'tod,' or small, round cake, given to children.

Toddle, *n.* a small cake or 'scone.'

Toddle, *v.* to walk with feeble, uncertain steps; to waddle; to stagger under the influence of drink; to saunter; used of a stream: to purl, to move with gentle sound; to make a murmuring sound in boiling.—*n.* a child just beginning to walk; a neat little person.

Toddler, *n.* one who walks with short steps; a child learning to walk.

Toddy, *n.* a glass of toddy.

Todgie, *n.* a small, round, flat cake.

Tod-hunting, *n.* fox-hunting.

Todie, *n.* a small, round cake given to children. Cf. **Toddie**.

Todie, *n.* a child. Cf. **Taudy**.

Tod-i'-the-fauld, *n.* a boys' game.

Todle, *v.* to waddle; to saunter. Cf. **Toddle**.

Todlen, *n.* a rolling, short step.

Todler-tyke, *n.* a kind of bumble-bee.

Todlich, *n.* a child beginning to walk.

Tod-like, *adj.* fox-like, crafty.

Tod-lowrie, *n.* the fox; a children's game.

To-draw, *n.* a resource, refuge; something to which one can draw in danger or threatening circumstances.

Tod's-bairns, -birds, *n.* an evil brood; a froward young generation.

Tod's-hole, *n.* a fox's hole; a secret hiding-place; the grave.

Tod's-tail, Tod-tail, *n.* a children's game in which they chase each other in single file; Alpine club-moss.

Tod's-turn, *n.* a sly trick; a base, crafty trick.

Tod-touzing, *n.* a method of fox-hunting by shooting, 'bustling,' 'guarding,' &c.

Tod-track, *n.* the traces of a fox's feet in snow.

Tod-tyke, *n.* a mongrel between a fox and a dog.

Toe, *n.* the prong of a fork; the branch of a drain. Cf. **Tae**.

To-fall, To-fa, *n.* used of day or night: the

close ; a building annexed to a larger, against which the roof rests ; a 'lean-to'; a porch ; a support ; a burden.

Toft, *n.* a bed for plants of cabbage, &c.; land once tilled but now abandoned. Cf. Taft.

Toft-field, *n.* a field belonging to a toft or messuage.

Toft-house, *n.* the house attached to a toft or messuage.

Toftin, *n.* a toft ; a messuage, the house built on a toft ; the holding of this house ; the right to hold it. Cf. Taftan.

To-gang, *n.* encounter ; meeting ; access.

To-gaun, *n.* a drubbing.

Togersum, *adj.* tedious ; tiresome.

To-hooch, *int.* an excl. of disgust. Cf. T'chach.

Toighal, *n.* a parcel ; a budget ; luggage ; any troublesome appendage. Cf. Tanghal.

Toiled, *ppl. adj.* hard-wrought.

Toil-sprent, *adj.* toil-worn.

Toist, *n.* the black guillemot. Cf. Taiste.

Toit, *v.* to totter from age ; to walk feebly ; to saunter ; to dawdle ; to tease.—*n.* a sudden attack of illness ; a fit of bad temper. Cf. Tite, Tout.

Toited, *ppj. adj.* feeble ; tottering.

Toiter, *v.* to walk about feebly ; to totter.

Toity, *adj.* testy, snappish ; easily offended.

Token, *n.* a metal ticket given as a mark of admission to the Communion. Cf. Taiken.

†Tokie, *n.* an old woman's head-dress, resembling a monk's cowl.

Tokie, *n.* a child's pet-name.

Tolbooth, Tolbuith, *n.* the town-gaol ; the town-hall.

Tolerance, *n.* leave, permission.

Tolie, *n.* a small, round cake of any kind of bread. Cf. Toalie.

Toll, *n.* a turnpike ; a taker of tolls ; a turn-pike-keeper. — *v.* to take 'multure' for grinding corn.

Toll-bar, *n.* a turnpike.

Toll-free, *adj.* without payment.

Tollie, *n.* a turnpike-keeper.

Tollie, *n.* excrement ; in *pl.* horse-dung.

Tolling, *n.* the sound made by bees before they swarm.

Toll-road, *n.* a turnpike-road.

Toll-roup, *n.* the sale by auction of the right to take tolls at a turnpike.

Toll-tax, *n.* the toll paid at a turnpike.

Toll-ticket, *n.* a square scrap of printed paper, available for the day of issue, stating that it cleared certain neighbouring turn-pikes.

To-look, *n.* a look to ; an outlook ; matter of expectation ; a prospect ; something laid up for the future ; a marriage portion.

Tolor, *n.* state, condition. Cf. Taler.

Tolsey, *n.* a place where toll was paid.

Tolter, *v.* to totter, hobble ; to move un-equally ; to be unstable. — *n.* an insecure erection.— *adj.* unstable, out of the per-pendicular.

Toltery, *adj.* insecure, unstable, shaky ; not perpendicular.

To-luck, *n.* a 'luck-penny,' something given in above a bargain for 'luck' to the buyer.

Tom, *n.* a rope ; a horse-hair fishing-line. Cf. Tome.

Tomack, *n.* a hillock. Cf. Tammock.

Toman, *n.* a twelvemonth. Cf. Towmond.

Toman, *n.* a hillock ; a mound ; a thicket.

Tome, *adj.* empty. Cf. Toom.

Tome, Tombe, *n.* a line for a fishing-line ; a long thread of any glutinous, viscous sub-stance ; a rope.—*v.* to draw out any viscous substance into a line ; to hang in long glutin-ous threads.

Tōmekins, *n.* an implement for twisting three strands into a rope.

Tomerall, *n.* a horse two years old.

Tomes, *adj.* ropy ; drawing out like toasted cheese. Cf. Toums.

Tome-spinner, *n.* a whorl used for twisting hair-lines.

Tommack, *n.* a hillock. Cf. Tammack.

Tommie-wake, *n.* the cock-sparrow.

Tomminaul, *n.* an ox or heifer a year old.

Tommy, *n.* a loaf of bread. Cf. Tammie.

Tommy-book, *n.* a book for entering goods bought on credit.

Tom-noddy, -norry, *n.* the puffin.

Tomon, *n.* a twelvemonth, a year. Cf. Towmond.

Tomontal, *n.* a yearling cow or colt.

To-morrow, *adv.* used of past time : the next day.

To-morrow morning, *adv.* used of past time : next morning.

Tom o' tae end, *n.* a haggis.

Tomshee, *n.* a fairy hillock.

Tom-taigle, *n.* a hobble for a horse or cow.

Tom-thumb, *n.* the willow-warbler.

Tom-trot, *n.* a kind of toffee.

To-name, *n.* a name added to one's surname to distinguish him from another with the same Christian name and surname. Cf. Tee-name, Eke-name.

Tong, *v.* to ring, toll a bell ; used of a bell : to sound loudly or harshly.—*n.* a twang in speaking.

Tongablaa, *n.* a continuous gabble.

Tongue, *n.* dialect ; manner of speaking ; abuse, violent language.—*v.* to talk im-moderately ; to scold, abuse.

Tongue-betroosht, -betrusht, *adj.* outspoken, too ready with the tongue.

Tongue-deavin', *adj.* voluble ; deafening with a loud tongue.

Tongue-, Tongue's-end, *n.* the tip of the tongue.

Tongue-ferdy, *adj.* loquacious, glib-tongued.

Tongue o' butter, *n.* a flattering, smooth tongue.

Tongue of the trump, *n.* the person of most importance ; the chief or best performer.

Tongue-raik, *n.* elocution ; fluency.

Tongue-roots, *n.* the tip of one's tongue.

Tongue-strabush, *n.* strife of tongues.

Tongue-tack, *v.* to silence; to hinder freedom of speech.

Tongue-tackit, *ppl. adj.* tongue-tied, having an impediment in speech owing to the tongue being fastened to a film or membrane ; slow of speech ; suddenly or unusually silent ; mealy-mouthed, not outspoken ; mumbling from the influence of drink.

Tongue-thief, *n.* a slanderer.

Tonguey, *adj.* able to speak up for one's self ; loquacious, in a bad sense.

Tonnoch'd, *ppl. adj.* covered with a plaid. Cf. Tunag.

Too, *prep.* to. Cf. To.

Toober, *v.* to beat, strike.—*n.* a quarrel. Cf. Tabour.

Tooberin, *n.* a drubbing. Cf. Taberin.

Toofall, *n.* a lean-to building ; the fall of evening, the gloaming. Cf. To-fall.

Toog, *n.* a small hillock.

Too-hoo, *n.* a hullabaloo ; an outcry of pleasure or of pain ; a spiritless person, a 'softy.' Cf. Tu-hu.

Took, *n.* a nasty taste or smell. Cf. Teuk.

Took, *n.* the beat of a drum ; the sound of a trumpet.—*v.* used of drums or trumpets : to beat or sound.

Took, *v.* to pull, jerk.—*n.* a pull, jerk ; a blow, slap.

Toolie, Toolzie, Tooly, *n.* a broil.—*v.* to fight. Cf. Tuilyie.

Tool-skep, *n.* a tool-basket.

Toolter, *adj.* unstable, shaky. Cf. Tolter.

Toom, *adj.* empty ; thin, lean ; lacking understanding ; shallow, empty-sounding, vain. —*v.* to empty, pour out ; used of rain : to pour down ; to discharge.—*n.* a place into which rubbish is emptied. Cf. Teem.

Toom, *n.* a fishing-line ; a long thread of viscous substance.—*v.* to draw such substance into a line. Cf. Taum, Tome.

Toom-brained, *adj.* empty-headed.

Toom-clung, *adj.* empty from want of food.

Toomed, *ppl. adj.* used of a woman : delivered of a child.

Toom-halter, *n.* the end of one's resources.

Toom-handed, *adj.* empty-handed.

Toom-heid, *n.* an empty-headed person.

Toom-heidit, *adj.* empty-headed.

Toom-like, *adj.* empty ; used of clothes hanging loosely on one : empty-looking.

Toom-looking, *adj.* empty-looking.

Toomly, *adv.* emptily.

Toom of rain, *n.* a heavy torrent of rain.

Toom-skinned, *adj.* hungry, hungry-looking.

Toom-spoon, *n.* an empty spoon ; applied to an unedifying preacher.

Toom-tail, *adv.* used of a plough : coming back without making a furrow ; of a cart : going with a load and returning empty.

Toom-the-stoup, *n.* a 'toss-pot'; a drunken fellow.

Toom-the-timmer, *v.* to empty the wooden 'cog' or drinking-vessel.

Toon, *n.* a town ; a village ; a hamlet ; a farmstead ; a country-seat ; the farm-people ; the household.

Toon-bodies, *n.* townspeople, townsfolk.

Toon-born, *adj.* born in a town.

Toon-dyke, *n.* the 'dyke' or wall enclosing a township.

Toon-end, *n.* the end of a road leading to a farm ; the end of the main street of a village or town.

Toon-foot, -fit, *n.* the lower end of a village or village street.

Toon-gate, *n.* the chief thoroughfare of a town or village.

Toon-guard, *n.* a civic watchman ; the men composing a guard-company.

Toon-heid, *n.* the upper part of a town or village, or of its main street.

Toon-hoose, *n.* the town-hall ; the court-house of a town.

Toon-keeper, *n.* the person in charge of a farmstead on Sunday.

Toon-land, *n.* cleared land near a township.

Toon-loan, *n.* an open, uncultivated piece of land near a village or farmstead ; the wider area beyond the narrow strip in front of a farmhouse.

Toon-loon, *n.* a boy of the town.

Toon-neighbours, *n.* tenants of adjacent farms.

Toon-rot, *n.* a soldier of the city-guard.

Toon-row, *n.* the privileges enjoyed by a village or community.

Toon's-bairn, *n.* a native of the same town.

Toon's-bodies, *n.* townspeople.

Toon's-lad, *n.* a townsboy, a 'toon's-bairn.'

Toon's-piper, *n.* the piper employed to make civic proclamations.

Toon's-talk, *n.* common report, the talk of the town.

Toon-wife, *n.* a woman born and bred in a town.

Toop, *n.* a tup, ram. Cf. Tup.

Toopick, Toopichan, Toopichen, *n.* a pinnacle; a summit; a cupola; a turret; a steeple; a narrow pile raised so high as to be in danger of falling; the top that finishes off the thatch of a stack.

Toopikin, *n.* a 'toopick.'—*v.* to build high without stability; to place high. Cf. Toupican.

Toop-lamb, *n.* a young ram.

Toor, *n.* a turf or peat. Cf. Turr.

Toor, *n.* a tower; a small heap; a knot of hair; a short worsted knob on the top of a man's woollen cap.—*v.* used of hay: to rise on the rake in raking; of a fire: to blaze freely.

Toor, *n.* a weed.

Toor, *adj.* wearisome, difficult.

Toor-battle, *n.* a boys' fight with bits of peat.

Toor-, Tour-dyke, *n.* a fence of turf or peat.

Toore, *v. pret.* tore.

Toorie, *n.* a small peat or turf.

Toorie, *n.* a very small heap; a knot of hair; a worsted knob on a man's 'bonnet.'

Toorie-top, *n.* a worsted knob for a 'bonnet' or cap.

Toorish, *int.* a dairymaid's call to a cow to stand still, or to come to be milked.

Toorock, *n.* a small tower; a small heap.

Toosh, *n.* a nasty person.

Toosh, *n.* a woman's 'short-gown' or 'curtoush.' Cf. Toush.

Tooshlach, *n.* a small bunch of straw. Cf. Tushloch.

Toosht, *v.* to dash about; to toss about; to roll or heap up carelessly.—*n.* a heavy toss or dash; an untidy heap of straw, litter, &c.; a dirty, slovenly woman; a person whose conduct is under reproach.

Tooshtie, *n.* a small quantity.

Tooskie, *n.* a tuft of hair on each cheek below the ear.

Toosle, *v.* to ruffle; to dishevel; to embrace roughly. Cf. Touzle.

Toosy, Toosey, *adj.* dishevelled; shaggy, frowzy. Cf. Tousy.

Toosying, *ppl. adj.* dishevelling.

Toot, *v.* used of a bird: to whistle, sing; to trumpet abroad, spread a report; to whine; to express dissatisfaction or contempt.—*n.* a boast, brag; a puff.—*int.* an excl. of contempt, tut!

Toot, *v.* to jut out; to project.—*n.* a projection; a jutting out.

Toot, *v.* to tipple; to drink copiously.—*n.* a drinking-bout; a copious draught.

Toot, *v.* to toss about; to disturb. Cf. Tout.

Tooter, *v.* to babble, gossip.—*n.* a horn, trumpet, a tin or wooden whistle; silly gossip; a humbug; a gossip, babbler.

Tooteroo, *n.* a bungle; a bad job.

Tooteroo, *n.* a warning signal, as of a motorcar.

Toothfu', *n.* a moderate quantity of strong liquor.—*v.* to tipple; to drink in small quantities.

Toothrife, *adj.* palatable.

Toothsome, *adj.* easily chewed; having a sweet tooth.

Toothy, *adj.* having many or large teeth; given to biting; belonging to a tooth; crabbed; sarcastic; hungry. Cf. Teethy.

Tootie, Tooty, *n.* a drunkard; a dram.

Tootin, *n.* a reproachful term for a woman.

Tootin', *ppl.* tippling from a bottle at short intervals.

Tooting-horn, *n.* an ox-horn for blowing.

Tooting-trumpet, *n.* a pitch-pipe.

Tootle, *v.* to chirp; to play on a horn or other wind-instrument; to mutter; to talk foolishly; to gossip.—*n.* silly gossip; a silly, gossiping person.

Tootle, *v.* to drink; to tipple.

Tootlie, *adj.* unsteady.

†**Toot-moot,** *n.* a low, muttered conversation; the muttering at the beginning of a quarrel; a dispute.—*v.* to whisper; to converse in low, muttering tones.—*adv.* in a whisper. Cf. Teut-meut.

Toot-mootre, *n.* talk of the nature of hints, insinuations, &c.

Toot-net, *n.* a large fishing-net anchored.

Tootoroo, *n.* a warning signal. Cf. Tooteroo.

Toots, *int.* tuts! tush!

Toot's-man, *n.* one who warns by a cry to haul the 'toot-net.'

Tootter, *v.* to babble, gossip. Cf. Tooter.

Tootter, *v.* to work in a weak, trifling way.—*n.* ruin; a weak and trifling worker.

Toot-too'in', *n.* the blowing of a horn.

Toozle, *v.* to ruffle the hair, &c.; to ruffle the temper. Cf. Touzle.

Toozy, *adj.* dishevelled; shaggy. Cf. Tousy.

Toozy-looking, *adj.* shaggy-looking.

Top, *v.* to set aside by a superior authority, real or pretended. Cf. Tap.

Tope, Top, *v.* to oppose, contend.—*n.* opposition.

Topp, *adj.* excellent. Cf. Tap.

Toppin, *n.* a crest of feathers; the top of the head. Cf. Tappin.

Topping, *ppl. adj.* leading, being at the head of affairs; managing; prominent.

To-put, *v.* to affix; to set or put one to work.—*n.* anything needlessly or incongruously added; a fictitious addition.

To-putter, *n.* one who holds another to work; a taskmaster.

†**Toque,** *n.* a cushion worn on the forepart of the head, over which a woman's hair was combed.

Tor, Tore, *n.* a high hill; a high rock. Cf. Torr.

Torchel, *v.* to pine away; to die; to relapse into disease; to draw back from a design or purpose. Cf. Torfel.

Tore, Tor, *n.* the pommel of a saddle; the knob at the corner of a cradle.

Torfel, Torfle, *v.* to pine away; to decline in health; to relapse into disease; to toss about; to draw back from a design or undertaking. —*n.* the state of being unwell; declining health.

Torie, *n.* the grub of the daddy-long-legs, an insect that consumes germinating grain.— *v.* to be eaten by the 'torie.'

Torie-eat, *v.* used of the 'torie': to eat the springing grain.

Torie-eaten, *ppl. adj.* used of land: poor, moorish soil, exhausted by cropping, very bare, and bearing only scattered tufts of sheep's fescue; eaten by the 'torie.'

Torie-worm, *n.* the hairy caterpillar; the grub-worm, the 'torie.'

†Tork, *v.* to torture or pain by continuous puncturing, pinching, nipping, or scratching.

Torment, *n.* a severe pain.

Tormentatious, *adj.* troublesome.

Tormentors, *n.* an instrument for toasting bannocks, oat-cakes, &c.

Tornbelly, *n.* a herring having its belly torn open.

Torn-doun, *adj.* reduced in circumstances.

Torne, *n.* a tower.

Torpit, *n.* turpentine.

†Torque, *v.* to torture by pinching, nipping, &c. Cf. Tork.

Torr, *n.* a high rock; a hill; wet, rocky land.

Torran, Torrie, *int.* a call to a bull.

Torrie, *n.* peas roasted in the sheaf.

Torrie, *n.* the 'torie-worm,' the 'torie.' Cf. Torie.

Torry, *n.* a lug-sail boat.

Torwooddie, *n.* an iron draught-chain for a harrow.

Tory, *n.* the grub of the daddy-long-legs. Cf. Torie.

Tory, *n.* a term of contempt and dislike, applied to a child or grown person; a disreputable or deceitful person; a tyrannical person; a term of endearment for a child.

†Tosh, Tosch, *adj.* neat, trim, tidy; tight; comfortable; happy; familiar, friendly.— *n.* a small, neat, tidy person or thing.—*v.* to tidy; to touch up, smarten.—*adv.* neatly; tightly; smoothly.

Tosh, *n.* a woman's 'short-gown.' Cf. Toush.

Tosheoderoch, *n.* a thief-catcher; a sergeant of court.

Toshings, *n.* additions to a person's means and comfort.

Toshly, *adv.* neatly, snugly.

Toshoch, *n.* a comfortable-looking young person; a neat, tidy-looking girl.

Toshod, Toschod, *n.* a small, trim person or thing.

Tosht up, *ppl. adj.* very tidily or finely dressed.

Toshy, *adj.* neat, tidy.

Tosie, *adj.* tipsy; slightly intoxicated; intoxicating; cosy, snug; cheerful, pleasant.— *n.* a cheerful glow on the face.

Tosie, *n.* the mark at which curling-stones are aimed. Cf. Tozee.

Tosie-mosie, *adj.* slightly intoxicated.

Tosily, *adv.* cosily, snugly.

Tosiness, *n.* cosiness, snugness, warmth.

Tosk, *n.* the torsk.

Toss, *v.* to toss off; to discuss, debate.

Toss, *v.* to toast, drink to the health of.—*n.* a toast; a beauty; a belle frequently toasted.

Tossie, *adj.* tipsy; snug. Cf. Tosie.

Tossil, *n.* a tassel.

Tossle, *v.* to ruffle, dishevel. Cf. Touzle.

Tost, *v.* to tease; to vex; to toss.

Tostit, *ppl. adj.* severely afflicted; troubled with difficulties and opposition; tossed.

Tot, *n.* anything very small; a small child; a dram; a term of endearment for a child.

Tot, *v.* to move with short or feeble steps, like a child or infirm person; to toddle; to totter.

Tot, *n.* the total, the sum.

Total, *adj.* teetotal.

Totaller, *n.* a teetotaler.

Totch, *v.* to toss about; to rock a cradle with the foot; to move with short, quick steps. —*n.* a sudden jerk.

Tote, *n.* the whole. Cf. Tot.

Tote, *v.* to walk feebly; to totter; to move about leisurely; to take things easily. Cf. Tot.

Tothe, Toth, *n.* sheep's dung; droppings of cattle, &c., enclosed in a 'toth-fold.'—*v.* to manure land by means of a 'toth-fold.' Cf. Tathe.

To the fore, *adj.* still remaining; coming to the front.

Toth-, Tothed-fold, *n.* an enclosure in a field for cattle, &c., to manure land. Cf. Tathe.

Tother, *adj.* that other; next.—*pron.* the other in conjunction with the one. Cf. Tidder, Tither.

Tother, Tothir, *n.* rough handling; putting into disorder.—*v.* to throw into disorder; to handle roughly; to dash.

Tott, *n.* anything very small; a child. Cf. Tot.

Tottery, *adj.* changeable, fickle.

Tottie, *v.* to move with short steps; to cause to move, drive.

Tottie, *n.* a term of endearment for a little child.

Tottie, *adj.* snug; warm.

Tottin, *ppl. adj.* walking with short steps, tottering.

Tottle, *v.* to walk feebly or with short steps; to toddle; to totter; used of a stream: to purl; to boil, simmer; to make a noise in boiling.—*n.* a little, toddling child; the noise made by boiling liquid.

Tottle, *adj.* warm, snug.

Tot-totterin, *ppl.* tottering for a while.

Tottum, *n.* a small child beginning to walk. Cf. Totum.

Tottum, *n.* a teetotum. Cf. Totum.

Totty, *adj.* small, 'wee.'

Totty, *adj.* shaky; dizzy.

Totum, *n.* a term of endearment for a little child, or one beginning to walk; a neat, little, or undersized person or animal.

Totum, *n.* a teetotum; the game of teetotum.

Toty, *adj.* small, puny, tiny.

Toubooth, *n.* a town-hall. Cf. Tolbooth.

Touch, *v.* to hurt; to punish; to equal; to come up to; to play upon the fiddle; to preach with vigour; with *up*, to animadvert on one; with *with*, to meddle with. —*n.* an attack of illness; touchwood, tinder; a very small portion of time; a sensible impression; a feeling of interest.

Touch-bell, *n.* the earwig.

Touched, *ppl. adj.* slightly intoxicated.

Touchet, Touchit, *n.* the lapwing, peewit. Cf. Teuchit.

Touchie, *n.* a very short space of time.

Touch-spale, *n.* the earwig.

Touck, *n.* the tuck of a drum. Cf. Took.

†**Toudie,** *n.* a hen that has never laid. Cf. How-towdie.

Tough, *adj.* hard.—*adv.* stoutly. Cf. Teuch.

Touk, *n.* an embankment to hinder water from washing away the soil.—*v.* to shorten; to eat greedily. Cf. Tuck.

Touk, *n.* a tug; a hasty pull; a blow.—*v.* to pull, jerk.

Touk, *v.* to beat a drum; used of a drum: to sound. Cf. Took.

†**Toulzie,** *n.* a broil, disturbance. Cf. Tuilyie.

Toum, *n.* a fishing-line; the gossamer. Cf. Tome, Taum.

Toum, *adj.* empty. Cf. Toom.

Touman, Toumon, *n.* a year. Cf. Towmond.

Toums, *adj.* ropy; glutinous. Cf. Tomes.

Toun, *n.* a town; a farm. Cf. Toon.

Tounit, *n.* knitting; manufacturing of wool. Cf. Townit.

Toup, *n.* a foolish fellow. Cf. Tawpie.

†**Toupee,** *n.* a top-knot.

Toupican, *n.* a tuft of straw neatly finishing the top of a rick of straw or hay when thatched. Cf. Toopikin.

Tour, *n.* one's way, one's steps; an expedition.—*v.* to speed.

†**Tour,** *n.* a turn; alternation.

Tour, *n.* a tower; a small heap. Cf. Toor.

Tour, Toure, *n.* a turf, sod, peat. Cf. Turr.

Toure-battle, *n.* a boys' fight with bits of peat.

Tourin, *ppl.* towering.

Tourkin-calf, -lamb, *n.* a calf or lamb covered with the skin of another for suckling purposes. Cf. Tulchan.

Tourock, *n.* a small tower; a little heap. Cf. Toorock.

Touse, *v.* to dishevel, ruffle up; to pull about roughly; to thrash.—*n.* an untidy or shaggy head of hair.

Tousel, Tousle, *v.* to ruffle. Cf. Touzle.

Touselled-looking, *adj.* dishevelled.

Toush, *n.* a woman's 'short-gown.'

Tousily, *adv.* roughly.

Touss, Tousse, *v.* to ruffle. Cf. Touse.

Toussie, *adj.* dishevelled. Cf. Tousy.

Toustie, *adj.* testy, irritable.

Tousy, *adj.* disordered, dishevelled; rough, shaggy; unkempt; rollicking; used of the weather: rough; of a fight: rough, stubborn; of food: roughly abundant.—*adv.* rudely, roughly.

Tousy-faced, *adj.* hairy-faced.

Tousy-headed, *adj.* having a shaggy head.

Tousy-like, *adj.* ruffled, shaggy; rough-looking.

Tousy-pousie, *adj.* rough, shaggy.

Tousy-tailed, *adj.* having a shaggy tail.

Tousy-tea, *n.* a tea with rough plenty, a 'knife and fork tea.'

Tout, *n.* a slight and passing attack of illness; a pet, fit of temper.—*v.* to attack suddenly; to have a sudden illness; to have a fit of temper; to irritate; to twit.

Tout, *v.* to toss about; to disorder; to disorder by quibbling or litigation; to disturb, harm.

Tout, *v.* to toot; to sing as a bird; to trumpet abroad; to express dissatisfaction or contempt.—*n.* a brag. Cf. Toot.

Tout, *v.* to drink copiously.—*n.* a large draught. Cf. Toot.

Touter, *n.* a friendly glass.

Touter, *n.* one who banters, teases, and annoys.

Touther, *v.* to put into disorder.—*n.* a state of disorder. Cf. Towther.

Toutherie, *adj.* disordered; confused, slovenly.

Toutie, *adj.* irritable.—*n.* a person easily vexed; an irritable person; one subject to frequent ailments.

Toutie, Touttie, *adj.* throwing into disorder.

Toutie, *n.* a humorous term for a child.
Toutit, *ppl. adj.* disordered ; blown about by the wind.
Toutle, *v.* to put clothes in disorder.
Toutle, *v.* to tipple.
†Tout-mout, *n.* a muttered conversation. Cf. Toot-moot.
Toutom, *n.* a teetotum. Cf. Totum.
Touts, *int.* tuts !
Touttie-wind, *n.* a boisterous wind.
Touze, *v.* to disorder ; to ruffle. Cf. Touse.
Touzle, Touzzle, *v.* to ruffle, dishevel, disarrange ; to toss hay, &c. ; to embrace roughly ; to grapple indecorously with a woman ; to romp rudely ; to wrestle. —*n.* a struggle, tussle ; a shake ; rough dalliance ; a troublesome effort.
Touzlie, *adj.* used of the hair : in confusion, ruffled.
Touzy, *adj.* dishevelled. Cf. Tousy.
Tove, *v.* to talk familiarly, cheerfully, and at length ; to chat ; to sound cheerfully ; to flaunt about with girls ; to keep company, as lovers ; to flatter ; to praise.—*n.* a chat, a friendly gossip.
Tove, *v.* to cause to swell ; to rise in a mass ; to make a dense smoke ; to smell strongly in burning ; to fly back ; to return.
Tovie, *adj.* babbling ; talking incoherently ; garrulous in liquor ; fuddled ; pleasant, warm, comfortable.
Tovize, *v.* to flatter ; to cajole.
Tow, *n.* flax or hemp in a prepared state ; what specially occupies one's attention.
Tow, *v.* with *down*, to let one down with a rope.—*n.* a clock-chain ; a rope ; a bell-rope ; a ship's cable ; a coil of hair ; a hangman's halter ; a line for deep-sea fishing.
Tow, *v.* to give way ; to fail ; to perish, die.
Towairds, *prep.* towards.
Towal, *n.* a horse-leech.
Tow-band-tether, *n.* a hempen tether.
Towbeeth, Towbuith, *n.* the town-gaol. Cf. Tolbooth.
Tow-card, *n.* a card for carding flax.
Towdent, *ppl. adj.* tidied, tidy ; in *phr.* 'ill-towdent hair,' unkempt locks.
Towder, *v.* to disorder. Cf. Towther.
†Towdie, *n.* a hen that never laid ; a young unmarried woman. Cf. How-towdie.
Towdy, *n.* the buttocks. Cf. Taudy.
Towdy, *n.* a child. Cf. Taudy.
Towen, Towin, *v.* to maul ; to subdue by severity ; to tame ; to tire.
Tower, *n.* a small heap. Cf. Toor.
Towerick, *n.* a summit ; anything elevated. Cf. Towrickie.
Towey-headit, *adj.* flaxen-haired.
Towfud, *n.* an opprobrious term.
Tow-gravat, *n.* a hangman's halter.

Tow-gun, *n.* a popgun, for which pellets of 'pob' or refuse flax are used.
Towie, *n.* a small coil or twist of hair.
Towk, *n.* a bustle ; a set-to.
Towk, *n.* the beat of a drum. Cf. Touk.
Towk, *v.* to tuck ; to shorten.—*n.* a tuck. Cf. Touk.
Towl, *n.* a toll ; a turnpike ; a tollman.—*v.* to collect tolls.
Towlie, *n.* a turnpike-keeper ; a levier of tolls. Cf. Tollie.
Towling, *n.* the sound of bees before swarming. Cf. Tolling.
Towm, *n.* a hair fishing-line. Cf. Taum, Tome.
Tow-man, *n.* the man who holds the halyards and controls the sail of a boat.
Towmond, Towmont, Towmonth, *n.* a twelve-month, year.
Towmondall, Towmontill, Towmontell, *n.* a yearling cow or colt ; a yearling.
Town, *n.* a farmstead.
Town, *v.* to beat ; to tame. Cf. Towen.
Townin', *n.* a drubbing.
Township, *n.* a farm occupied by two or more farmers of the same hamlet, in common, or separately.
Tow-plucker, *n.* a heckler of flax.
Tow-raip, *n.* a hempen rope or halter.
†Towre, *n.* a turn in rotation.
Towrickie, *n.* a summit ; anything raised on a height. Cf. Towerick.
Tow-rock, *n.* the flax-distaff.
Tow-row, *n.* a hubbub ; a romp.
Towse, *v.* to ruffle. Cf. Touse.
Towsing, *n.* a ruffling.
Towsle, *v.* to ruffle. Cf. Touzle.
Towsy, *adj.* shaggy ; dishevelled. Cf. **Tousy.**
Towt, *n.* a fit of illness. Cf. Tout.
Towt, *v.* to toss about. Cf. Tout.
Tow-tap, *n.* the portion of flax in the distaff.
Towther, *n.* a state of disorder ; a tussle ; an untidy, slovenly person ; a 'tousling.'—*v.* to put in disorder. Cf. Touther.
Towzie, Towzy, *adj.* shaggy ; dishevelled. Cf. Tousy.
Towzle, *v.* to ruffle. Cf. Touzle.
Toxie, Toxy, *adj.* tipsy.
Toxified, *ppl. adj.* tipsy.
Toy, *n.* a fancy, a conceit.
Toy, Toy-mutch, *n.* a woman's linen or woollen cap, with a deep fall hanging down on the shoulders.
Toyt, *n.* a fresh-water mussel found in the Tay.
Toyt, Toyte, *v.* to totter. Cf. Toit.
Tozee, *n.* the mark at which stones are aimed in curling. Cf. Tosie.
Tozie, Tozy, *adj.* muddled ; tipsy ; snug, warm.—*n.* a fire. Cf. Tosie.
Tozy-mozy, *adj.* slightly tipsy.
Traap, *n.* a slut.

Traapach, *adj.* slattern.

Traboond, *n.* a rebound; a blow removing out of its place the thing struck.

†**Trabuck,** *v.* to make a false move in play.— *n.* such a move. Cf. Trebuck.

Trace, *v.* to follow up; to obey; to search by travel.

Trace, *n.* a trestle for scaffolding.

Trace, *n.* a trice; a short, sudden movement.

Traced, *ppl. adj.* laced; bound with gold lace.

Tracer, *n.* an extra horse placed before one in the shafts.

Trachle, Trachel, *v.* to draggle; to trail; to drag one's feet, trudge; to spoil through carelessness or slovenliness; to drudge; to overtoil; to burden; to fatigue; to trouble; to hinder; to injure corn or grass by treading on it.—*n.* a long, tiring exertion; drudgery; struggle, toil; trouble; a trudge, tramp; a drag, burden, hindrance; a sloven; an incompetent person.

Trachler, *n.* one who grows weary in walking; one who drags himself or 'trails' along.

Trachlie, *adj.* dirty, slovenly, wet; apt to entangle; fatiguing, exhausting; drudging; burdensome.

Track, *v.* used of tea: to draw, to infuse; to train an animal to go in traces or harness. —*n.* a feature, lineament; an ugly or unusual spectacle, oddity; any person or thing presenting a remarkable appearance; used of an untidy person: a 'figure,' a 'sight'; an earthenware teapot.

Track, *n.* a tract; a tractate.

†**Track,** *v.* to barter. Cf. Troke.

Track, *v.* to search.

Track, *n.* a period, 'spell'; course of time; a tract.

Track-boat, *n.* a canal-boat drawn by horses.

Tracker, *n.* a funnel. Cf. Tracter.

Trackie, *n.* an earthenware teapot.

Trackie-pottie, *n.* a 'trackie.'

Trackle, *v.* to draggle. Cf. Trachle.

Track pot, *n.* a 'trackie.'

Track pot-ware, *n.* earthenware teapots, cups, saucers, &c.

Tract, *n.* a track; a path.

Tractable, *adj.* used of land: cultivable, in good order; properly treated.

Tracter, *n.* a funnel for pouring liquids into bottles, casks, &c.

Trade, *n.* fuss, ado; material, stuff; in *pl.* bodies of craftsmen in burghs.

Trades-lad, *n.* a journeyman, or an apprentice to a tradesman.

Tradesman, *n.* an artisan, handicraftsman.

Trading-body, *n.* a trader, merchant.

Tradition, *n.* the delivery of goods to a customer.

Trad-wuddie, *n.* the iron hook and swivel or chain connecting the swingle-tree with the plough or harrow. Cf. Tread-widdie.

Trae, *adj.* stubborn, stiff Cf. Thraw.

Traeddit, *v. pret.* trod.

Traesh, *v.* to entreat one in a kindly or flattering manner; to court; to call cattle. —*n.* cajolery, flattery.—*int.* a call to cattle. Cf. Treesh.

Traess, *n.* a trestle. Cf. Trace.

Traeve, *n.* twenty-four sheaves. Cf. Thrave.

Trafeck, Trafeque, *n.* intercourse; dealing; stir.—*v.* used of bees: to be busy searching flowers. Cf. Traffick.

Traffical, *adj.* with much traffic.

Traffick, Traffeck, Traffike, Traffique, *n.* discussion; intercourse, familiarity; small things, light, useless articles.—*v.* to have dealing with; to hold familiar intercourse; to conspire secretly with a person.

Trafficker, Traffiquer, *n.* one who has dealings or intercourse; a trader; a secret agent.

Trafike, *n.* small affairs. Cf. Traffick.

Trag, *n.* trash, rubbish; dregs; anything useless or worthless; a low, mean person; something unpleasant to handle.

Tragle, *v.* to bemire, wet.

Tragullion, *n.* an assortment, a collection; a company of not very respectable persons. Cf. Tregallion.

Traich, *v.* to wander; to trace; to waste away. Cf. Traik.

Traichie, *adj.* slimy, ropy.

Traichin, *ppl. adj.* of sickly constitution; lazy, dirty, disgusting.

Traicle, *n.* an idler, gadabout.

Traicle, *n.* treacle.

Traik, *v.* to wander idly to and fro; to stroll, saunter; to gad about; to wander; to use circumlocution; to lose one's self; used of poultry: to stray; to follow lazily; to dangle after; to court; to walk with difficulty; to trudge; to track, trace; to waste away; to decline in health; to draw out any sticky, ropy substance; to nurse over-daintily.—*n.* idle lounging; a stroll; wandering to and fro aimlessly; a long, tiring tramp; difficult walking; weakness, declining health; weariness; loss, disaster, bad fortune; the drawing out of any viscous substance; dirty, slovenly working; the working in liquid or semi-liquid material; too dainty nursing; a dirty, slovenly person; an illness; a weakly person; the loss of sheep by death from whatever cause; the flesh of sheep that have died from disease or accident; the worst portion of a flock of sheep.— *adj.* weak; in a declining state; languid.

Traikie, *adj.* slimy, ropy; in poor health; delicate-looking; drooping.

Traikieness, *n.* leanness.

Traikin, *ppl. adj.* straggling, having a sickly constitution; lazy, dirty, disgusting.

Traikit, *ppl. adj.* weary, fatigued; consumptive-looking; in poor circumstances; used of birds: wet, drooping, having dirty, disordered feathers; draggled, disordered in dress.

Traikit-like, *adj.* draggled and tired from trudging or ranging about; used of birds: having wet, dirty, disordered feathers.

Traikit-tyke, *n.* a tired or lounging dog.

Traikle, *n.* treacle.

Traikle, *n.* an idler, lounger; a gadabout.

Trail, *n.* a trudge; a long, tedious walk; a lazy, dirty person; a sloven; a well-worn or shabby article of clothing; a rag.—*v.* to drag forcibly, to haul along; to walk slowly, lazily, in a slovenly fashion; to loiter, saunter idly; to gad about; to drag one's feet from weariness.

Trail, *n.* a part, portion; a quantity.

Trailach, Trailoch, *v.* to draw; to go about in a lazy, slovenly fashion; to work in a slovenly fashion; to over-nurse in a slovenly or disgusting fashion. — *n.* a long, dirty piece of rope, dress, &c.; idle wandering to and fro; dirty, lazy working; one of slovenly habits; a wearer of dirty or shabby clothes; a person given to idle wandering; a gossip.—*adj.* lazy, slovenly.

Trailachin', *ppl. adj.* slovenly; always drudging.

Trail-cart, *n.* a box with shafts like a carriage, but without wheels, mounted on a mass of brushwood.

Trailer, *n.* used in fly-fishing: the hook at the end of the line.

Trail-hunt, *n.* a dog-race in which dogs follow a 'trail' dragged over the ground by hand.

Trailing, *ppl. adj.* slovenly, slatternly, untidy.

Traily, Traillie, *n.* a person who 'trails' about in shabby clothes; one who wanders idly gossiping here and there.

Train, *n.* a rope used for drawing harrows, &c.; a small cone of moistened gunpowder, serving to prime a toy-gun.—*v.* to tamper with, work upon, draw on.

Traishur, *v.* to go about in a lazy, slovenly manner.—*n.* a dull, stupid person; a big, ugly, or old and lean animal.

Traissle, Traissel, *v.* to tread or trample down.

Traist, *n.* trust.

Traivel, *v.* to travel. Cf. Travel.

Traivellin' man, *n.* a tramp, a vagrant.

†Traiviss, *n.* a stall in a stable; a smith's frame for shoeing horses. Cf. Traverse.

Trake, *v.* to wander from place to place; to fatigue. Cf. Traik.

Trallop, *n.* a trollop.—*v.* to hang loosely. Cf. Trollop.

Tram, *n.* a beam; a bar; a shaft of a barrow, cart, carriage, &c.; a prop, pillar; a supporter; a limb; a leg; a tall, ungainly person, one with long limbs.

†Tramble-net, *n.* a trammel-net.

Tramless, *adj.* without shafts.

Trammals, *n.* luggage used in travelling.

Tramp, *v.* to wash blankets in soapsuds by tramping on them in a tub; to trudge; to dance clumsily, or heavily, or vigorously; to catch flounders by stamping with bare feet on the sand until they rise.—*n.* a stamp with the feet; a trudge; a mechanic travelling in search of work; the part of the spade on which the foot rests in digging; a plate of iron worn in the centre of a ditcher's boot in digging; a perforated and slightly spiked piece of sheet-iron on which a curler stands when playing a stone; a piece of spiked iron fastened to a curler' boot by a leather strap to prevent his slipping during play.

Tramp-coll, *n.* a hayrick compressed by tramping.

Tramped-pike, *n.* a 'tramp-coll.'

Tramper, *n.* a travelling hawker; a tinker; one who travels in search of work.

Trampers, *n.* feet; heavy boots.

Trampet, *n.* a 'tramp' or 'crampet' on a curler's boot.

Trampilfeyst, *adj.* unmanageable. Cf. Amplefeyst.

Tramping, *ppl. adj.* vagrant.

Tramp-pick, *n.* a narrow kind of spade or 'pick' used for turning up very hard soils, with a projection for the foot to rest on.— *v.* to use a 'tramp-pick.'

Tramsach, *n.* a tall, ungainly person; a large, lean, ugly horse or other animal.

†Trance, Transe, *n.* a passage within a house; a lobby; an entrance-hall; an alley, a 'close'; a passage, a crossing over; a narrow space.

Trance-door, *n.* a passage-door; the door leading to the kitchen.

Trance-window, *n.* a passage-window.

Trancing, Transing, *ppl. adj.* used of a middle wall: passing across a house from wall to wall.

Trangam, *n.* a trinket; a toy.

Trankle, *n.* a small hayrick.

Tranklum, *n.* a useless trifle; a trinket; a tool. Cf. Trantlum.

Transack, Transeck, *v.* to transact; to dispose of, finish; not to decide, but pass from a decision. —*n.* a transaction; dealing; trade.

Transcrive, *v.* to transcribe.

Transires, *n.* goods sent for exportation.

Transirie, *n.* a custom-house permit; a transiré.

Translate, *v.* an ecclesiastical term: to transfer a minister from one charge to another.

†**Transmew, Transmue,** *v.* to transmute, transform, change.

Transmugrify, *v.* to metamorphose; to transform.

Transpire, *v.* used of smoke: to issue from a chimney.

Transport, *v.* to transfer a minister from one charge to another.—*n.* a minister so transferred; excitement, indignation.

Transportable, *adj.* used of a minister: entitled to, or capable of, transference from one charge to another.

Transportation, *n.* transference from one ministerial charge to another; the carrying of a corpse from house to grave.

Transum, *n.* a transom.

Transume, *v.* to copy, transcribe.

Transum-plait, *n.* an iron plate or bar for a transom.

Transumpt, *n.* a copy.

Trantalum, *n.* a trinket; a useless article. Cf. Trantlum.

Trantle, Trantel, *n.* a trundle; the sound made by trundling; a deep rut made by a wheel.—*v.* to trundle; to roll along; to make a noise by rolling along.

Trantle-bole, -hole, *n.* a hole for the reception of odds and ends. Cf. Bole.

Trantles, *n.* trifling or superstitious ceremonies; movables of little use or value; odds and ends; children's toys; a workman's various tools.

Trantlins, *n.* articles of little value.

Trantlum, Trantloom, *n.* a useless or worthless article; a trifle; a trinket; a toy; in *pl.* odds and ends; gear; old tools.

Trap, *n.* a movable flight of stairs leading up to a loft.

Trap, *n.* a trap-door; a hatch; any vehicle on springs.—*v.* used in games: to catch; in finding things: to seize and claim; in school-life: to take another's place in a class by answering a question when he failed.

Trap, *v.* to deck.—*n.* in *pl.* personal belongings, baggage.

†**Trapane,** *n.* craft, cunning. Cf. Trepan.

Trap-creel, *n.* a wicker lobster-trap; a creel for keeping crabs alive.

Trapes, Trapez, *v.* to trudge; to walk untidily, as with a trailing dress; to wander aimlessly; to gad about.

Traping, Trappan, *n.* tape. Cf. Trapping.

Trapper, *n.* one who answers where another fails in school, and takes his place.

Trapping, *n.* tape; small wares; trimmings; frippery.

Trapping-lesson, *n.* a school-lesson, in which children gain or lose places in the class according to their answers.

Trap-pit, *n.* a pit in which animals are caught.

Trapse, *v.* to seize and claim an article found.

Trash, *n.* low, disreputable people; riff-raff; a worthless person; a mischievous girl.

Trash, *v.* to trudge wearily through wet and dirt; to jade, to overheat or override a horse; to maltreat.

Trash, *v.* to thrash; used of rain: to dash, pour.—*n.* a heavy fall.

Trashery, *n.* trash, rubbish.

Trash-like, *adj.* good-for-nothing.

Trashtrie, *n.* trashy food or drink; pap, sops.

Trashy, *adj.* rainy; very wet; stormy.

Trattle, *n.* a pellet of sheep-dung. Cf. Trottle.

Trattle, Trattil, *v.* to prattle, chatter.—*n.* in *pl.* tattle; idle talk.

Trattler, Tratler, *n.* a prattler; a chatterer.

Trauchle, Traughle, *v.* to draggle; to drudge. Cf. Trachle.

Trave, *n.* twenty-four sheaves of grain.

†**Travel, Travail,** *n.* exertion, work; trouble. —*v.* to labour; to work soil; to fatigue.

Travel, *v.* to walk, journey on foot; to go about begging or peddling small wares; to lead about a stallion.—*n.* a journey on foot.

Travelled, *ppl. adj.* used of soil: worked; fatigued.

Traveller, *n.* a pedestrian; a tramp; a travelling beggar; a travelling pedlar, a packman.

Travellyie, *n.* a disturbance. Cf. Trevally.

†**Traverse, Travesse,** *n.* a journey across; a reverse of fortune; a partition between two stalls in a stable; a stall in a stable; a smith's shoeing-shed or framework for shoeing horses; a retired seat in a church or chapel, with a screen across; a shop-counter or desk.—*v.* to fit up into stalls.

Travish, *v.* to sail backwards and forwards; to carry in procession; to trail.

Trawlie, *n.* a ring through which the chain or rope passes between the two horses or oxen in a plough to prevent it from trailing on the ground. Cf. Troly.

Tray, *adj.* stiff, stubborn. Cf. Thraw, Trae.

Treacle-ale, -beer, *n.* a thin, light beer made with treacle.

Treacle-peerie, *n.* 'treacle-ale.'

Treacle-piece, *n.* a piece of bread or oat-cake spread with treacle.

Treacle-scone, *n.* a scone baked with treacle.

Treacley, *adj.* pleasing; flattering.

Treader. *n.* a cock; a male bird.

Treadle, *v.* to go frequently and with difficulty.

Tread-widdie, -wuddy, *n.* the iron hook and swivel connecting a swingle-tree with a plough or harrow.

Treasonrie, *n.* treachery.

Treat, *v.* to entreat, urge.—*ppl.* urged.

Treave, *n.* twenty-four sheaves of grain.

Treb, *n* a long earthen rampart.

Treble, *n.* a particular dance tune.

†**Trebuchet,** *n.* a military engine for throwing stones.

†**Trebuck,** *v.* to make a false move in play; to catch one doing so; to check him for doing so.—*n.* a slip or false move in play; a check or trip in a game of skill.

Treck, *n.* fatigue. — *adj.* diseased, dying, lingering. Cf. Traik.

Treck, *int.* an expletive, as 'troth!' Cf. Treggs.

Treck, *v.* to infuse tea. Cf. Track.

Treck, *v.* to wander, stray. Cf. Traik.

Treckle, *n.* treacle.

Treck-pot, *n.* a teapot. Cf. Track-pot.

Tred, *v.* to tread.

Tredden, *ppl.* trodden.

Tredder, *n.* a male bird; a cock. Cf. Treader.

Tred-widdie, *n.* the iron hook or swivel connecting the swingle-tree with a plough or harrow. Cf. Tread-widdie.

Tree, *n.* wood; a staff, cudgel; a stirring-rod for porridge, &c.; a pole or bar of wood; an axle-tree; a swingle-tree; a barrel; an archery bow.

Tree and trantel, *n.* a piece of wood going behind a horse's tail, used as a crupper to keep the horse from being tickled under the tail.

Tree-clout, *n.* a piece of wood formerly put on the heels of shoes.—*adj.* having wooden heels.

Tree-clout shoon, *n.* shoes with wooden heels.

Tree-creeper, *n.* the common *Certhia* or creeper.

Tree-goose, *n.* the barnacle-goose.

Treein, *adj.* wooden.

Tree-ladle, *n.* a wooden ladle.

Tree-leg, *n.* a wooden leg.

Tree-leggit, *adj.* having a wooden leg.

Treen, *n.* trees.

Treen, *adj.* wooden, made of wood.

Treen-mare, *n.* a 'wooden horse' used as an instrument of military punishment.

Treeple, *adj.* triple.

Treeple, *v.* to dance, trip; to beat time with the feet. Cf. Tripple.

Treeplet, *n.* a triplet.

Treesh, Treesch, *v.* to entreat in a kindly and flattering way; to cajole; to court; to call to cattle.—*n.* enticement; cajolery; flattery.—*int.* a call to cattle.

Treeshin, *n.* courting.

Tree-speeler, *n.* the common *Certhia* or creeper.

Treetle, *v.* to trickle in drops or very small quantities; to work at anything weakly and unskilfully.—*n.* a trickle; a very small quantity of liquid.—*adv.* in drops.

Treevolie, *n.* a scolding. Cf. Trevally.

Trefold, *n.* the trefoil; the water trefoil.

Tregallion, Tregullion, *n.* a collection; a miscellaneous assortment; a company not thought respectable.

Treggs, *int.* 'troth!' used as an oath. Cf. Trogs.

Trein, *adj.* wooden. Cf. Treein.

Treissle, *v.* to abuse by treading. Cf. Traissle.

Treit, *v.* to entreat. Cf. Treat.

Trek, *adj.* diseased, dying, lingering.—*v.* to wander; to walk about. Cf. Traik.

Tremble, *n.* a fit of trembling; a tremor, shiver; in *pl.* ague; palsy or ague in sheep. Cf. Trimle.

Trembling-axies, -exies, -fevers, *n.* the ague.

Trembling-ill, *n.* a disease of sheep, the 'leaping-ill.'

Tremendious, *adv.* exceedingly.

Tremmle, Tremel, *v.* to tremble.

Trencher, *n.* one who trenches ground, or drains land by making open drains; a drainer.

Trencher-bread, *n.* bread not of the first quality.

Trenching, *adj.* trenchant.

Trenchman, *n.* a support for the head of one learning to swim.

Trendle, *n.* a wheel; a whirlwind.—*v.* to trundle. Cf. Trindle.

Trene, *adj.* wooden. Cf. Treein.

Trenk, *n.* a narrow, open drain; a rut.—*v.* to be full of ruts. Cf. Trink.

Trenket, *n.* an iron heel-piece.

Trenle, *n.* a wheel.—*v.* to trundle. Cf. Trindle.

†**Trepan,** *v.* to seduce; to cheat, trick.—*n.* a trick; a plot; a scheme.

Treple, *n.* a particular dance tune. Cf. Treble.

Tres-ace, *n.* a catching game, played by six players generally.

Tress, Trest, *n.* a frame of wood; a trestle; a beam; the support of a table.

Trestarig, *n.* a very strong spirit, thrice distilled from grain.

Tret, *v. pret.* and *ppl.* treated; entreated.

Treuless, *adj.* faithless; truthless; false. Cf. Trew.

Trevally, Trevaillie *n.* a disturbance; a catastrophe; a scolding; a quarrelling.

Trevallyie, *n* a mean retinue or train.

†**Trevis, Trevesse, Trevise,** *n.* anything laid across, as a bar; a stall of a stable; a partition between two stalls; a smith's shoeing frame or shed; a desk or counter of a shop; a screened-off pew in a church. —*v.* to fit up into stalls. Cf. Traverse.

Trew, *v.* to trust, believe. Cf. Trow.

Trewan, *n.* a trowel. Cf. Trooen.

Trewan, *n.* a truant. Cf. Troo.

Trews, *n.* trousers; the short trousers worn under a kilt; stockings and breeches all of a piece.

Trewsers, *n.* trousers.

Trewsman, *n.* a Highlander, a wearer of the kilt, &c.

Treykle, Triacle, *n.* treacle.

Trial, *n.* a difficulty; a trouble; drudgery; affliction; effort; proof, evidence; in *pl.* examinations and discourses prescribed by presbyteries for licensing preachers and ordaining ministers.

Tribble, *n.* trouble. Cf. Trouble.

Tribe, *n.* a contemptuous designation for a set or crowd of people.

Tricker, *n.* a trigger; a latch, spring; a wooden leg; a piece of spiked iron to fix on the ice for steadying a curler in playing his shot.

Trickit, Tricked, *ppl. adj.* tricky, wicked.

Tricky, *adj.* mischievous, playful, waggish.

Triddle, *v.* to trudge, tramp, go on. Cf. Treadle.

Triffle, *n.* a trifle; a small sum.

Trig, *adj.* smart, active; quick, clever; brisk, nimble; neat, tidy, trim; spruce; tight.— *v.* to tidy up; to make neat; to settle; to dress smartly and finely; to bedeck.

Trigger, *n.* the place from which a curler plays his shot; the spiked iron plate on which he steadies himself. Cf. Tricker.

Triggin, *n.* finery; decking out.

Triggs, *n.* plough-traces made of twisted strips of horse-hide and dried.

Triggy, *adj.* neat, orderly.

Trigly, *adv.* quickly, briskly; neatly, smartly, sprucely.

Trig-made, *adj.* neatly made.

Trigness, *n.* neatness; orderliness.

Trig up, *n.* a tidying up.—*v.* to set in order, tidy up.

Trikle, *n.* treacle.

†**Trilapser,** *n.* one who falls into the same sin thrice.

Trill, *n.* treble.

Trillichan, *n.* the oyster-catcher.

Trim, *v.* to beat, thrash, castigate; to scold, chide.—*n.* temper, disposition, mood; haste, speed.

Trim, *n.* a poor kind of ale.

Trimle, *v.* to tremble.

Trimmer, *n.* anything of superior quality, fine, or pleasing to the eye; a scold, a virago.

Trimmie, *n.* a disrespectful term applied to a young girl; a name for the devil.

Trimming, *n.* a beating; a scolding.

Trimmle, *v.* to tremble; to shiver.—*n.* a tremor. C.. Tremble.

Trim-tram, *n.* a term expressing ridicule or contempt.

†**Trincat,** *v.* to lie indirectly. Cf. Trinquet.

Trinch, *v.* to trench.

Trindle, *n.* a wheel; the felloe of a wheel, a trundle; the cradle of a mill-wheel; a small wheel for a trundle-bed; a whirlwind.—*v.* to trundle, roll; to move with a rolling gait; to bowl along. Cf. Trintle.

Tring, *n.* a series, a succession of things; a 'string.'

Tringal, *n.* anything long and ugly; a tall, uncomely person.—*v.* to walk in a loose, slovenly fashion.—*adv.* with loose, slovenly gait.

Tringum, *n.* anything ugly and worthless; a person of loose character.—*adj.* worthless, loose.

Trink, Trinck, *n.* a trench; a narrow, open drain for the passage of water; a narrow channel between rocks on a sea-coast; the bed of a river or stream; the water flowing in a 'trink'; a rut; used in flag quarries: a long, narrow stone.—*v.* to become filled with ruts.

Trink-about, *n.* a trinket, gewgaw, ornament.

Trinker, *n.* one who does not pay his share of a tavern-bill.

Trinket, *n.* a trifle; a small article of any kind.

†**Trinket,** *v.* to lie indirectly; to correspond clandestinely with an opposite party; to tamper with; to have dealings with. Cf. Trinquet.

Trinketing, *n.* clandestine correspondence with an opposite party.

Trinkie, *n.* a narrow channel between rocks on the sea-coast.—*adj.* filled with ruts.

Trinkit, *ppl. adj.* having trenches, ditches, or drains.

Trinkle, *v.* to trickle; to fall slowly in drops or in a tiny stream; to sprinkle.—*n.* a trickle; a succession of drops, a drip; the sound of trickling water.—*adv.* drop by drop. Cf. Trinkle, Trintle.

Trinkle, *v.* to tingle; to thrill.

Trinklems, *n.* trinkets, gewgaws; knick-knacks; odds and ends.

Trinkum, *n.* a trinket; a knick-knack.

Trinkum-trankums, *n.* trinkets, gewgaws; fallals.

Trinle, *n.* a wheel. — *v.* to trundle. Cf. Trindle.

Trinnel, *n.* the entrails of a calf.

Trinnle, *n.* the cradle of a mill-wheel. Cf. Trindle.

Trinnle, Trinnel, *v.* to trickle; to fall in a tiny, gentle flow; to drip; to give forth a slight sound in trickling or dropping. — *n.* a trickle; a gentle stream of liquid, or of falling grain; the sound thereof. Cf. Trintle.

†**Trinquet,** *v.* to lie indirectly; to tamper with; to correspond clandestinely.

Trintle, *v.* to trickle; to fall in drops or in a small, steady flow; to walk or move slowly; to sprinkle; to spread a small quantity of anything over a surface. — *n.* a drop; a drip; a tiny flow of drops; the sound thereof; a man's following. Cf. Trinkle, Trinnel.

Trintle, *v.* to roll, trundle. — *n.* a roll, a wheel round; a turn or gentle movement in dancing. Cf. Trindle.

Trintle aff, *v.* to drop off or away.

Trip, *v.* to hurry; to go off quickly. — *n.* a short dance.

Tripe, *n.* a term of contempt, generally used of a tall, lanky person. Cf. Trype.

Tripes, *n.* the entrails; the stomach; the 'inner man.'

Triping, *n.* coal brought to the 'bank' of a mine before it is screened.

Triple, *v.* to dance. Cf. Tripple.

Triply, *v.* to make a rejoinder to a 'duply.' — *n.* a reply to a 'duply' or rejoinder.

Tripple, *v.* to dance, trip; to beat time with the feet in dancing.

Trip-trout, *n.* a game of shuttlecock in which a ball is used instead of a cork and feathers.

Trist, *v.* to squeeze; to thrust.

Trist, Triste, *v.* to afflict; to appoint to meet; to betroth. Cf. Tryst.

Trittle-trattles, Tritle-trantles, *n.* children's toys; trifles. Cf. Trantle.

Triv, *v.* to push; to drive.

†**Trivage,** *n.* a partition between two stalls. Cf. Traverse.

Trixie, *n.* the tune 'Hey trix, trim go trix, under the greenwood tree,' an old popular melody.

†**Troak,** *v.* to deal; to barter. Cf. Troke.

Troaker, *n.* a secret agent; a pedlar. Cf. Troker.

Troap, *n.* a boys' game like that of 'trap.'

Troch, *n.* an extraordinary fellow; a 'rough customer'; anything of little value.

Troch, *n.* a flat tombstone. Cf. Through.

Troch, *n.* a trough. Cf. Trough.

†**Trock,** *v.* to bargain, deal; to exchange. — *n.* odds and ends. Cf. Troke.

Trocker, *n.* a low trader; an exchanger of goods.

Trockery, *n.* odds and ends.

Trockie, *n.* a teapot. Cf. Trackie.

Trod, *n.* a tread; a footstep; a track, pursuit. — *v.* to trace, track by the footsteps.

Trod, *v.* to trot; to half-run and half-walk.

Troddle, Trodle, *v.* to toddle; to walk with short steps like a little child; to go; to slip; to tumble; used of a stream: to purl; to glide gently.

Trodge, *v.* to trudge; to saunter.

Trod-widdie, *n.* the chain fastening a harrow to the swingle-tree. Cf. Tread-widdie.

†**Trogg, Trog,** *v.* to barter; to exchange; to truck; to have underhand dealings; to use trickery. — *n.* in *pl.* old clothes. Cf. Troke.

Trogger, *n.* a pedlar; one who barters or exchanges; a collector of old clothes; an Irish vagrant; a vagrant.

Troggin, *n.* pedlars' wares.

Trogs, *int.* 'troth!' as an oath.

Trogue, *n.* a young horse.

Troistry, *n.* the entrails of a beast; offal.

Troitle, *v.* to gossip.

Trojan, *n.* a big, overgrown person, a giant; an active, sturdy person.

†**Troke, Trok,** *v.* to barter, exchange; to deal, bargain, in a small way; to have dealings with; used of an underhand or improper character: to associate, be on friendly terms with; with *in*, to tamper with; to work for money; to potter; to be busy about trifles; to spread abroad news. — *n.* barter; a bargain; goods; small articles or wares; lumber; trash; dealings, business; negotiation; intercourse; illicit intercourse; fondling, dalliance, toying; a matter of business; an odd job; an errand.

Troker, *n.* one who exchanges goods; a dealer, pedlar; a low trader; a secret agent.

Trokery, *n.* articles of small value; a miscellaneous collection of odds and ends.

Trokings, *n.* dealings; friendly terms.

Trolie, *n.* any long, unshapely thing that trails on the ground; a slovenly girl or woman. Cf. Troll.

Trolie, *n.* any object that has length disproportionate to its breadth; the dung of cows, horses, or persons; in *pl.* entrails.

Troll, *n.* a slovenly person; a trull; a long, unshapely thing trailing on the ground. — *v.* to walk, work, or dress in a slovenly fashion; to trail; to carry about in a slovenly fashion.

Troll, *n.* any object with length disproportionate to its breadth; the dung of animals and persons. Cf. Trolly.

Trollibags, Trolliebags, *n.* the paunch of a slaughtered animal; tripe.

Trollop, Trollope, v. to hang in a wet or loose state; to work in a dirty, slovenly fashion; to walk in a slovenly way; to slouch; to lead a loose life.—n. a large, loose, hanging rag; a tatter; a large, straggling mass of anything; a dirty, idle sloven; a woman of loose life.

Trolloping, ppl. adj. slatternly, untidy.

Trollops, n. a slattern; a dirty, idle, slovenly woman.

Trollopy, adj. slovenly.

Trolly, n. a slovenly girl; any long, unshapely thing trailing on the ground. Cf. Trolie.

Trolly, n. anything having length disproportionate to its breadth; human or animal excrement; in pl. entrails. Cf. Trolie.

Trolollay, int. a term occurring in a rhyme used by children at 'Hogmanay.'

Troly, n. a ring through which the chain or rope passes between the two horses or oxen in a plough, preventing it from trailing on the ground.

†**Tron,** n. a weighing-machine; a market. Cf. Trone.

Tronach, n. the crupper used with a pack-saddle, formed of a piece of wood, and connected with the saddle by a cord at each end.

†**Trone,** n. a steelyard; a weighing-machine; a market; a market-place; a pillory; the standard of weight used at the public steel-yard.

Trone, n. a truant.—v. to play truant.

Trone, n. a trowel.

Troner, n. the person in charge of the 'trone,' the weighman.

Tronie, Tronnie, n. a truant.

Tronie, n. a traditionary, rhyming saw; anything often repeated; a long story; trifling conversation; a darling.

Tron-kirk, n. a church near the 'trone.'

Tron-, Trone-lord, n. a sweep who was stationed at the 'trone.'

Tron-, Trone-man, n. a sweep; a 'trone-lord.'

Tron-, Trone-weight, n. the standard weight used at the 'trone.'

Troo, v. to play truant. Cf. Trow.

Troo, v. to trust, believe; to make one believe. Cf. Trow.

Trooen, n. a trowel. Cf. Trone.

Trooie, n. a truant.

†**Trooker,** n. a contemptuous term applied to a woman. Cf. Trucker.

Troolian, n. the common cuttle-fish.

Troon, n. a trowel. Cf. Trone.

Troop, n. a loose woman.

†**Troos,** v. to tuck up; to truss.—n. a tuck. Cf. Trouss, Tross.

Troosh, int. a call to cattle. Cf. Treesh.

Trooshlach, Trooshloch, n. rubbish; anything worthless.

Trooshter, n. a thing; anything worthless.

Troost, n. used in playing marbles: a sort of 'lien' that the winner has on the loser for his favourite marble or 'pitcher' when it is the last to be lost.

Troot, n. a trout. Cf. Trout.

Trootie, n. a small trout; a fondling term for a child.

Trootle, v. to walk with quick, short steps; to move slowly; used by nurses of children beginning to walk.

Trooy, int. a call to cattle.

†**Troque,** v. to barter. Cf. Troke.

Trosk, n. a stupid fellow.

†**Tross,** v. to pack up; to truss; to pack off; to set out. Cf. Trouss.

Trot, v. used of a stream: to flow briskly, to run with noise; to play truant; to tease jestingly; to make sport of, or ridiculous.—n. a raid or expedition by horsemen.

Trot-cosie, -cozy, n. a woollen hap, covering the back of the neck, the shoulders, and the breast, for keeping the throat warm.

Troth, int. in truth! verily!—n. truth.—v. to betroth.

Troth-plight, -plighted, adj. affianced, betrothed.

Trottee, n. a person who is made sport of.

Trotter, n. one who makes sport of another; a truant; in pl. a sheep's feet.

Trotter-board, n. the treadle of a spinning-wheel.

Trotter-speed, n. great celerity.

Trottie, n. a bad humour.

Trottie, n. a child that has learned to walk or run about the floor.

Trottle, Trottel, v. to babble; to make a babbling noise; to chatter. Cf. Trattle.

Trottle, n. a small, round pellet of sheep-dung. Cf. Trattle.

Trottlick, n. a hard pellet of dung.

Trou, v. to credit a person or thing. Cf. Trow.

†**Trou,** n. a wretched hole of a lodging.

Troublance, n. pain, trouble.

Trouble, v. to go to, attend; to clutch, finger, like a dying person.—n. an ailment, complaint; a fault or hitch in coal-strata.

Trouch, n. a trough.

Trouff-gate, n. a right of way for carrying peats from a common or moss.

Trough, n. the wooden conduit conveying water to a mill-wheel; a long wooden dish used in common by a family; a vale, valley, the lower ground through which a river runs.

Trough-stane, n. a stone-trough.

Trouk, n. a slight but teasing complaint.

Troulins, Troulis, adv. truly.

†**Trounce**, *v.* to hustle about ; to drive off.

Trounce, *v.* to trudge ; to travel fast.

Trouse, *n.* the short trousers worn under a kilt. Cf. Trews.

Troush, *int.* a call to cattle.

Trousing, *n.* a combination of trousers and stockings in one.

†**Trouss**, *v.* to tuck up ; to shorten.—*n.* a tuck or fold sewed in a garment to shorten it.

Trouster, *n.* a tuck to shorten a garment.

Trout, *v.* to fish for trout.

Trouter, *n.* a trout-fisher.

Trouth, Troutha, *n.* truth.—*int.* 'troth !' Cf. Trowth.

Troutie-burn, *n.* a trout-streamlet.

Troutsho, *n.* a term of contempt ; a ludicrous term for a Highlander.—*int.* an excl. of contempt.

Trove *n.* a turf.

Trow, *n.* a double-boat, used in salmon-spearing.

Trow, *n.* a short fit of sickness.—*v.* to have a short fit of sickness. Cf. Drow.

Trow, *n.* a trough ; a conduit carrying water to a mill-wheel ; the lower ground through which a river runs. Cf. Trough.

Trow, *v.* to play truant. Cf. Troo.

Trow, *n.* a fairy ; a goblin ; the devil.

Trow, *v.* to troll ; to roll over ; to roll over and down ; to put in rotatory motion ; to cause to roll or spin ; to toss up a liquid with a spoon, &c.; to season a cask by rinsing it with wort before it is used ; to nurse carefully.—*n.* a continued tossing up of a liquid by a spoon, &c.; careful nursing.

Trow, *int.* a call to cattle.

Trow, *v.* to feel sure ; to make one believe.

Trowen, Trowan, *n.* a trowel.

Trower, *n.* a truant.

Trowie, *adj.* sickly.

Trowl, *v.* to draw gently upwards a line with hooks stretched across a stream and fastened to a rod on each side.

†**Trowse**, *v.* to tuck up.—*n.* the tuck of a petticoat or dress. Cf. Trouss.

Trowse, Trows, *n.* the conduit carrying water to a mill. Cf. Trow, Trough.

Trowth, *n.* truth.—*int.* truly ! verily ! Cf. Troth.

Troyt, *n.* an inactive person.

Tru, *v.* to trust. Cf. Trew.

†**Trua**, *v.* to play truant. Cf. True.

Trual, *n.* a trowel.

Truan, *n.* a trowel. Cf. Trone.

†**Truant**, *v.* to play truant.

Truce, *v.* to keep quiet ; to hush up.

†**Truce**, to tuck up. Cf. Trouss.

†**Truck**, *n.* odds and ends ; trash.—*v.* to barter ; to traffic.

Truck, *v.* used of tea : to draw, to infuse. Cf. Track.

†**Trucker**, *n.* a term of contempt for one who has offended or is deceitful ; a waggish or tricky person. Cf. Trooker.

Truckery, *n.* odds and ends ; miscellaneous articles ; crockery.

Truckle, *n.* a truckle-bed.

Truckler, *n.* an underhand person ⋅ one who scamps his work.

Truck-pot, *n.* a teapot. Cf. Track-pot.

Trudder, *n.* lumber ; trumpery ; confusion.

Trudge-back, *n.* a humpback.

Trudget, *n.* a trick ; a mischievous prank.

Trudget, *n.* a paste of barley-meal and water, used by tinkers to prevent a newly-soldered vessel from leaking.

True, *v.* to play truant. Cf. Trow, Troo.

True, *v.* to trust, believe. Cf. Trow.

True, *adj.* used of ice : perfectly smooth and level.

True-blue, *n.* a rigid Presbyterian ; a person of integrity and steadiness.

Truelins, Trulines, *adv.* truly ; indeed.—*n.* truth.

True-love, *n.* one whose love is pledged to another ; the herb Paris.

Truey, *int.* a call to cattle. Cf. Trooy.

Truff, *n.* a turf ; a sod ; a peat.

Truff, *v.* to pilfer, steal.

Truggs, *n.* a lazy worker ; used as a nickname.

Trugs, *int.* 'troth !' used as an oath. Cf. Trogs.

Trui, *int.* a call to cattle. Cf. Trooy.

†**Truiker**, *n.* a rascal, scoundrel. Cf. Trucker.

Truint, *n.* a trowel. Cf. Trone.

Truish, *int.* a call to cattle. Cf. Treesh.

Truish, *n.* breeches and stockings made of a piece. Cf. Trews.

†**Trukier**, *n.* an offender, a deceiver ; a wag. Cf. Trucker.

Trull, *n.* a foolish or silly person ; a slattern.

Trullion, *n.* a low, dirty fellow ; a foolish or silly person.

Trullion, *n.* a sort of crupper.

Truly, Trulie, *adj.* not false or fictitious.—*n.* one's word or honour, used in mild oaths. —*int.* an excl. of surprise.

Trum, *n.* a thread, a weaver's thrum.

Trummle, Trumle, *v.* to tremble.—*n.* a tremor.

Trump, *n.* a Jews' harp.—*v.* to play on the Jews' harp.

†**Trump**, *v.* to deceive, cheat.

Trump, *v.* to go off in consequence of disgrace or necessity.

Trump-about, *n.* a game at cards. Cf. Trumph-about.

†**Trumper**, *n.* a deceiver ; a term of contempt.

Trumph, *n.* a trifle.

Trumph, Trumf, Trumph-card, *n.* a trump, trump-card.

Trumph-about, *n.* in *phr.* to 'play trumph-about,' to be on an equality or footing with ; to retaliate ; to do equal deeds of valour.

Trumphery, Trumphy, *adj.* trumpery.—*n.* rubbish ; a disreputable woman ; odds and ends.

Trumphy, *n.* a stupid woman or girl. Cf. Tumfie.

Trumpie, *n.* Richardson's skua.

Trumpket, *n.* a spiral or 'turnpike' stair.

Trumplefeyst, *n.* a qualm or fit of sickness.

Trumposie, *adj.* guileful ; cross-tempered, perverse.

Truncher, *n.* a wooden platter, a trencher.

Truncher-spear, *n.* a pointless spear.

Trundle, Trunle, *v.* used of a stream : to flow along briskly. Cf. Trindle.

Trundle, *n.* an animal's entrails. Cf. Trinnel.

Trunkie, *n.* a small trunk.

Truntle, *v.* to trundle ; to roll along. Cf. Trintle.

Truse, *v.* to hush up. Cf. Truce.

Trushel, *n.* a sloven ; a person untidy in dress ; a confused mass of things lying carelessly together.

Trushter, *adj.* worthless. Cf. Trooshter.

†**Truss,** *n.* a large bundle.—*v.* with *up*, to pack up.

Trust, *v.* to buy on credit or trust.—*n.* credit ; the charge or care of a turnpike ; the body formerly in charge of the district-roads, or turnpikes.

Trustful, *adj.* trustworthy.

Trustman, *n.* a creditor.

Trustre, *n.* butter.

Trust-road, *n.* a turnpike-road ; one under the charge of the road-trustees of a district.

Trutchie, *n.* a fondling term for a cow.—*int.* a call to a cow. Cf. Truish.

Truthful, *adj.* honest ; upright.

Trutle, *v.* to be slow in motion. Cf. Trootle.

Truyll, *n.* a trull ; a sloven.

Try, *v.* to taste.—*n.* a trace of anything lost.

Trying trotty, *n.* a trot to test the paces of a horse.

Trykle, *n.* treacle.

Trypal, *n.* a tall, lanky, ill-shaped person.— *v.* to walk or work in a slovenly fashion. —*adj.* tall, ill-made ; slovenly.—*adv.* in a slovenly manner.

Trype, *n.* a long, lanky person ; a term of contempt.—*v.* to walk in a slovenly manner. —*adv.* in a slovenly manner.

Trysht, *v.* to coax ; to wheedle ; to entice.— *n.* coaxing ; wheedling.

Tryst, Tryste, *n.* an appointment to meet ; an appointed meeting ; a rendezvous ; a fixed cattle-market or fair ; a meeting or concourse ; a merry-making ; a betrothal, engagement to marry ; a journey taken by a company pledged to travel together ; trouble, annoyance ; difficulty ; affliction.— *v.* to engage to meet ; to agree to bargain · to appoint a meeting ; to fix a time for, to appoint, arrange ; to bespeak, order in advance ; to betroth ; to engage to marry ; to fit in with, agree ; to deal with, come to terms ; to visit ; to afflict, try ; to invite, induce, entice ; to decoy.

Tryst-breaker, *n.* one who breaks an appointment or engagement.

Trysted-hour, *n.* an hour appointed for meeting.

Tryster, *n.* one who convenes others, fixing the time and place of meeting.

Tryster-time, *n.* the courting-time.

Trysting, *n.* a meeting by appointment ; an engagement to meet.

Trysting-place, -spot, *n.* the appointed place for meeting.

Trysting-style, *n.* a stile at which lovers meet.

Trysting-time, *n.* the time appointed for meeting.

Trysting-tree, *n.* a tree at which lovers meet by agreement.

Tryst-nicht, *n.* the night on which it is agreed to meet.

Tryst-stane, *n.* a stone anciently erected, marking a rendezvous.

Tryst-word, *n.* a password.

Trytle, *v.* to lag ; to act perfunctorily.

Tuachim, *n.* ? a token ; in *phr.* 'their ain tuachim be't,' an expression of a wish to escape evils that have befallen others.

Tuag, *n.* a small hillock ; a hillock on the top of a height. Cf. Toog.

Tuam, *n.* the nozzle of a smithy forge. Cf. Tew-iron.

Tub, *n.* a smuggler's keg containing four gallons.—*v.* to line a fault in a pit with wood or iron casing so that it will hold or keep back water.

Tucht, *n.* vigour.

Tuchtless, *adj.* pithless, feeble ; inactive.

Tuck, *v.* used of drums : to beat or sound. Cf. Took.

Tuck, *v.* to shorten, cut short.—*n.* a jetty on the side of a river ; an embankment. Cf. Touk.

Tuck, *v.* to pull, jerk.—*n.* a pull, jerk. Cf. Took.

Tuck, *int.* a call to poultry.

Tuckie, *int.* a call to poultry, 'chuckie!'

Tucky, *adj.* mean, shabby ; contemptible.

†**Tue,** *n.* the nozzle or tube of the bellows of a forge. Cf. Tew.

Tue, *v.* to toil hard.—*pret.* did struggle or toil.—*ppl. adj.* fatigued. Cf. Tew.

Tued, *ppl. adj.* fatigued; killed; destroyed.

Tufa, *n.* an appendage. Cf. To-fall.

Tuff, *n.* a tuft of feathers or ribbons.

Tuffie, *v.* to ruffle; to disorder by frequent handling.

Tuffie-pack, *n.* a nickname for a pedlar.

Tug, *v.* used of a door: to prevent it from being opened from the inside by placing a stout sapling across the outside and fastening it to the latch.—*n.* raw hide, of which plough-traces were formerly made; a plough-trace.

Tug and rug, *v.* to haggle over a bargain.

Tuggin, *n.* the beech or stone marten.

Tuggle, *v.* to pull by repeated jerks; to contend about by pulling; to handle roughly; to toss backwards and forwards; to fatigue with travelling or toil; to overwork; to keep under.—*n.* a contention by pulling.

Tught, *n.* vigour. Cf. Tucht.

Tug-the-tow, *n.* a church-bellman.

Tug-whiting, *n.* a species of whiting, a whiting caught by hand-line.

Tu-hu, *n.* a spiritless person. Cf. Too-hoo.

Tuick, *n.* the sound of a drum or trumpet. Cf. Took.

Tuik, *n.* a spell; a turn.

Tuik, *n.* a cook.

Tuik, *n.* a by-taste; a disagreeable taste. Cf. Teuk.

Tuik, *v. pret.* took, did take.

†Tuilyie, Tuilzie, *n.* a quarrel, broil, fight; a scrimmage, battle; toil, labour, trouble; a wrangle; a wordy dispute.—*v.* to quarrel, scuffle, fight; to wrangle, dispute; to toil, work hard; used of lovers: to struggle or play together, 'touzle.'

Tuilyiement, *n.* toil, exertion, great struggle.

Tuilyie-muilyie, -mulie, *n.* a 'tuilyie.'

Tuilyiesum, *adj.* quarrelsome.

Tuilyie-wap, *n.* a boys' game, in which they clasp one another's hands, press together, and end in falling all together in a mass.

Tuim, *adj.* empty. Cf. Toom.

Tuin, *n.* tune; temper, mood; the twang of a dialect. Cf. Teen, Tune.

Tuish, *n.* a flabby infant.

Tuive, *v.* to swell or rise, as the effect of leaven; to operate as yeast; to fly back.

Tuke, *v.* to jerk; to chuck under the chin. Cf. Tuck.

Tukie, *n.* a hen.—*int.* a call to fowls. Cf. Teuckie.

Tukie-hen, *n.* a hen.

Tulcan, *n.* a calf-skin stuffed with straw. Cf. Tulchan.

Tulch, *n.* a stout person of sulky, stubborn temper.

Tulchan, Tulchain, Tulchin, *n.* a calf-skin stuffed with straw, used to induce a cow to give her milk; a bag generally made of the skin of a calf; a chubby, dwarfish child.

Tulchan-bishop, *n.* the name given in the beginning of the 17th century to a bishop who accepted a bishopric with the condition of assigning the temporalities to a secular person.

Tulchan-calf, *n.* a 'tulchan.'

Tulie-mulie, *n.* a squabble. Cf. Tuilyie-muilyie.

Tull, *prep.* till, until.

Tullihoo, *n.* a disturbance.

†Tullisaul, *n.* a place to which a gentleman sent the horses and servants of his guests when he would not entertain them himself. Cf. Tillie-soul.

Tulloch, *n.* a hillock; a fortune, legacy; a 'heap' of money.

Tulloch, *n.* a well-known Scotch reel; its tune; a noisy tune.

Tullochgorum, *n.* the reel of Tulloch, or 'Tulloch's' rant.

†Tully, *v.* to wrangle; to fight. Cf. Tuilyie.

Tullyat, *n.* a contemptuous term for a bundle.

Tulshie, *n.* a sour-looking person. Cf. Tulch.

Tulshoch, *n.* a carelessly-arranged bundle; a heap; applied contemptuously to a person.

†Tulyie, Tulzie, *n.* a broil. Cf. Tuilyie.

Tum, *n.* a cant name for a tumbler or glass.

Tumble, *v.* to toss; to wander about.

Tumble-cart, *n.* a box or sledge set on wooden wheels fixed on a wooden axle, which tumbled or turned together; a tumbrel.

Tumbler, *n.* the porpoise; a small, lightly-made cart.

Tumbler-cart, *n.* a 'tumble-cart.'

Tumble yell, *v.* used of cows: suddenly to cease to give milk.

Tumbling-car, *n.* a 'tumble-cart.'

Tumbling-Tam, *n.* a large, thick penny-piece of copper.

Tumbling-Tam, *n.* a sieve for riddling coals.

Tumbling-trees, *n.* wheels in which wheel and axle formed one piece and revolved together.

Tumbous, Tumbus, *n.* anything large; a big, lazy person.—*adj.* large and slovenly.

Tume, *adj.* empty. Cf. Toom.

Tumfie, *n.* a dull, stupid, slow, awkward person.—*adj.* dull and stupid.

Tumick, Tummock, *n.* a hillock, a small mound; a small spot of elevated ground; a grassy knoll.—*v.* to build up to a high point dangerous to stability.

Tummle, Tumle, *v.* to tumble. Cf. Tumble.

Tummlers, *n.* part of a weaver's loom.

Tummle the wullcat, *v.* to tumble heels over head.

Tump, *n.* a small mound or hillock.

Tumph, Tumphy, *n.* a dull, slow, awkward person. Cf. Tumfie.

Tumple, v. to tumble; to roll over.—n. a tumble; a roll.

Tumult, n. the land attached to a cottar's house.

Tunag, n. a sort of shawl or short mantle worn by Highland women. Cf. Tonnoch'd.

Tunch, v. to push or jog with the elbow.—n. a jog with the elbow. Cf. Dunch.

Tundle, n. tinder. Cf. Tindel.

Tundle-box, n. a tinder-box.

Tune, n. the tone of a dialect; mood, temper; trim, order.—v. to hum or sing a tune; with *up*, to induce one to do something silly or wrong.

Tune-lines, n. popular rhymes sung to Psalm-tunes instead of verses of the Psalms, in teaching children psalmody.

Tun'er, n. tinder.

Tunie, adj. of uncertain temper or changeable moods.

Tunnel, n. the throat.

Tup, Tupe, n. a ram; a foolish fellow; an unpolished person.

Tup-head, adj. used of a sword: having the handle ending in a miniature figure of a ram's head.

Tup-headed, adj. stupid, foolish.

Tup-hog, n. a male ram, after weaning, until the first shearing.

Tup-horn, n. a ram's horn, often used as a drinking-cup, or as a snuff-box.

Tup-i'-the-wind, n. in *phr.* ' to rin like a blind tup-i-the-wind,' said of a woman who haunts the company of men in her eagerness to be married.

Tup-lamb, n. a male lamb.

Tuppens, n. twopence. Cf. Tippence.

Tup-yeld, -eild, n. a ewe that proves barren.

Tuquheit, n. the lapwing. Cf. Teuchit.

Turbot, Turbet, n. the halibut.

Turbot-reeklins, n. strips of halibut dried in peat-smoke.

Turchie, adj. squat, short and thick.

Turd, n. excrement; a lump of excrement; a very contemptuous term for a person. Cf. Taird.

Ture, v. *prat.* tore.

Ture, n. a turf. Cf. Turr.

Turf-farm, n. a farm of which the tenant pays so much to the proprietor for the peats he cuts.

Turk, adj. angry, annoyed. — n. a savage, violent man; a tiresome, mischievous child.

†Turkas, Turkesse, Turkis, n. a pair of pincers; a griping, oppressive man.

Turken, v. used of a young foal: to harden; to wax stout.

Turkey, n. a term of contempt; a pouch, purse, or pocket-book made of Turkey leather.

Turkey-hide, n. a wallet, or a pocket-book, of Turkey leather.

Turkey-Jock, n. a turkey-cock.

Turkie, n. a small bottle of straw.

Turlie-whurlie, n. a fanciful ornament; a flourish; a whirligig. Cf. Tirly-wirly.

Turmet, Turmut, n. a turnip.

Turmoil, v. to work hard; to toil.

Turmour, n. turmeric.

Turn, n. an attack of illness or faintness; a surprise, a fright; a piece of work, a job; a service, help; a trick; an escapade, a whim; an appearance before a court of law; a check, rebuff; disposition, manner; style; bent, liking; time, season; used of milk, &c.: the beginning to sour; the change in the shortening or lengthening of the day; a short stroll.

Turn, v. to turn a corner; to drive animals into a field, stable, or other place; to turn from one's purpose; to change; to grow, become; used of milk: to curdle.

Turner, n. an old copper coin worth two pennies Scots.

Turner, n. the man who holds and turns the instrument that twists straw-ropes.

Turner-aside, n. one who deviates from a particular course.

Turnie, n. a slight turn; a short walk.

Turnie-box, n. a box turning on a pivot in a door, used for passing food into a cell or room.

Turning, n. a qualm; nausea; the calf of the leg; the space between the ankle and the calf.

Turning-lay, -loom, n. a turning-lathe.

Turning-tree, n. a wooden stirring-rod, a 'spurtle.'

Turnip, n. a thick, clumsy, old-fashioned watch with cases.

Turnip-heid, n. a blockhead.

Turnip-lantern, n. a hollowed turnip used to hold a candle in boys' play.

Turnip-oats, n. oats sown after turnips.

Turnip-shaw, n. a turnip-top.

Turnip-shawer, n. one who cuts off turnip-tops, or 'sneds' turnips.

Turnip-singler, n. one who thins out young turnips by the hand.

Turn-out, n. a stroll; a gathering of people; an outfit.

Turnpike, Turnpike-stair, n. a narrow, spiral staircase.

Turn-screw, n. a screw-driver.

Turn-tail, n. a fugitive.

Turr, n. a turf, sod, peat.—v. to remove the turf from waste land; to pare the surface of a moss before cutting peats. Cf. Toor.

Turriefax-day, n. never.

Turris, n. turfs. Cf. Turr.

Turrish, v. used of a cow : to stand still ; to be quiet.—*int.* a call to a cow to stand still.

Turry, v. to pare off turf before cutting peats. Cf. Turr.

Turrying-spade, n. the spade with which the surface of a moss is pared off to get at the peat below.

Turryvee, n. a passion ; a commotion. Cf. Tirrivee.

Turry-wurry, n. a quarrel, wrangle. Cf. Tirr-wirr.

Tursable, adj. portable ; capable of being packed up.

†Turse, Turs, v. to truss ; to bundle or pack up ; to adjust one's clothes ; to take an infant from the cradle and dress it ; to send away ; to take one's self off ; to walk ; to set to work ; to carry partly and drag partly a burden with difficulty.—*n.* a truss, bundle ; a load ; the dressing of an infant ; labour or difficulty in carrying ; an amount, a quantity.

Tursin, n. a bundle ; baggage.

Tursk, n. the torsk. Cf. Tusk.

Turskil, n. a spade for cutting peats. Cf. Tuskar.

†Turss, v. to truss. Cf. Turse.

Turven, n. peats ; sods.

†Turze, v. to truss. Cf. Turse.

Tuse, n. potato-soup.

Tuse, int. an excl. used to incite a bull.

Tush, n. a tusk ; an animal's tooth.

Tush, v. to express displeasure.

Tushalagy, n. the tussilago or coltsfoot. Cf. Dishilago.

Tushkar, n. a spade for cutting peats. Cf. Tuskar.

Tushloch, Tuschlich, n. a small bundle or truss ; a small cock of hay, straw, &c.

Tushloch, Tuschlach, n. a cake of cow-dung, so dry that it may be burned.

Tushy-lucky-gowan, n. the coltsfoot.

Tusk, n. the torsk.

Tusk, v. to cut peat from above.

Tusk, v. to change the contents of one bag into another ; to pluck or pull roughly, as a horse tears hay from a stack.

Tuskar, Tuskar-spade, n. a peat-spade.

Tuskin, n. the act of turning a man upside-down, so that his money, &c., drop from his pockets.

Tusk-spade, n. a peat-spade.

Tusky, adj. having tusks.

Tussle, v. to embrace roughly ; to ruffle. Cf. Touzle.

Tussock, n. a tuft of hair ; a tuft of heather, or coarse grass.

Tute, v. to jut out ; to project.—*n.* a jutting out ; a projection. Cf. Toot.

Tutie, n. a woman-tippler ; a child who drinks a great deal.

Tutie-ta, Tutie-tatie, n. the sound of a trumpet ; a child's name for a trumpet. Cf. Tutti-taiti.

†Tut-mute, n. a low, muttered conversation.—*v.* to whisper. Cf. Toot-moot.

Tutor, n. the legal guardian of a boy under fourteen or a girl under twelve.

Tutory, n. tutorship, teaching ; guardianship ; tutelage ; the period of life under tutorship.

Tuts, int. an excl. of impatience.

Tutti-taiti, -tatti, n. the sound of a trumpet ; a child's name for a trumpet.—*int.* an excl. of impatience ; in *phr.* ' Hey tutti-tatti,' or ' taiti,' the name of an old Scottish tune.

Twa, Twae, adj. two ; a few.—*n.* a pair ; a couple.

Twa-beast-tree, n. the swingle-tree of a two-horse plough.

Twa-cord, adj. two-ply, having two strands.

'Twad, *pron.* with v. it would.

Twae'rie, adj. two or three ; a few. Cf. Two-three.

Twa-faced, adj. hypocritical, insincere.

Twa-facedness, n. duplicity ; insincerity.

Twa-fald, -fauld, adj. twofold ; double ; bent double from age or infirmity.

Twa-hand barrow, n. a barrow propelled by two persons.

Twa-handit, adj. double.

Twa-handit-, Twa-hand, -crack, n. a familiar conversation between two persons ; a *tête-à-tête.*

Twa-handit wark, n. work so badly done as to require to be done over again.

Twa-horse farm, n. a farm requiring two horses to work it.

Twa-horse tree, n. a swingle-tree stretcher of a plough which two horses draw.

Twa-horse wark, n. a ' twa-horse farm.'

Twal, Twall, adj. twelve.

Twal-at-e'en, n. midnight.

Twal-cup, n. a midday cup of tea.

Twal-hoors, n. twelve o'clock ; noon ; lunch or liquor taken at noon.

Twal-hoors' bell, n. midnight ; a public clock striking at midnight.

Twal-hundred, adj. used of linen : fine, good.

Twalmonth, n. a year. Cf. Towmond.

Twa-lofted, adj. two-storeyed.

Twal-o'-nicht, n. midnight.

Twal-oxen plough, n. a heavy wooden plough that was drawn by twelve oxen.

Twal-pence, n. one shilling sterling.

Twal-pennies, n. one shilling Scots ; one penny sterling.

Twal-penny, adj. costing a shilling.

Twal-pennyworth, n. the value of a penny sterling.

Twal-pint hawkie, n. a cow yielding twelve pints at a milking.

Twalsome, *adj.* consisting of twelve.—*n.* a company of twelve.

Twalt, *adj.* twelfth.

Twang, *n.* a dialect accent, a brogue; the vernacular speech of a district betraying the natives.

Twang, *n.* a tinge, a spice, a little, a 'touch.'

Twang, *n.* a twinge; a sudden, acute pain.

Twa-part, *n.* two-thirds.

Twa-pennies, *n.* a copper coin of the value of an English halfpenny.

Twa-penny, *adj.* cheap, insignificant. Cf. Tippenny.

Twa-shear, *n.* a sheep that has been twice shorn.

Twa-skippit, *adj.* used of a man's cap: having two peaks.

Twasome, Twaesum, *n.* a company or family of two, a couple, pair.—*adv.* doubly.—*adj.* double, twofold; performed by two persons.

Twa-storeyed, *adj.* used of a chin: double.

Twa-three, Twar-three, *adj.* two or three; a few.

Twaum, *n.* a pet, a temper.

Tway, *adj.* two.

Twa-year-auld, *n.* an animal two years old.

Tweddle, *v.* to work cloth so that the woof seems to cross the warp vertically.

Tweedle, *v.* to play the bagpipes; to play the fiddle carelessly or clumsily; to sing.

Tweedle, *v.* to twiddle; to twirl; to twist; to be busy about trifles. Cf. Twiddle.

Tweedle-dee, *n.* a sorry fiddler; careless or indifferent singing.

Tweedle-dee and tweedle-dum, *v.* to strum, play at random.

Tweedle-dum-tweedle-dee, *n.* clumsy fiddling.

Tweedlin' oot an' in, *n.* the swerving to right and left of a learner on a bicycle.

Tweel, *adv.* and *int.* truly, indeed. Cf. Atweel.

Tweel, *v.* to twill; to weave cloth diagonally.—*n.* twill; the texture of literary composition. Cf. Tweddle.

Twee-licht, *n.* twilight.

†**Tweelie, Tweelzie**, *n.* a broil, quarrel.—*v.* to contend. Cf. Tuilyie.

Tweelin, *adj.* pertaining to cloth that is 'tweeled.'

Tweemay, *int.* a call to calves to come for their portion of milk.

Tween, *prep.* between.

Tweesh, Tweesht, Tweest, *prep.* betwixt, between. Cf. Atweesh, Betweesh.

Tweet, *v.* to whittle.

Tweetins, *n.* chips cut from wood with a knife.

Tweetle, *n.* a public assembly attended by young people, who each paid a halfpenny for each dance they indulged in.

Tweeze, *v.* to pinch.

Tweezelick, Tweezelock, *n.* an implement for twisting ropes.

†**Tweillie, Tweillie**, *n.* a quarrel. Cf. Tuilyie.

Twenty, *adj.* numerous, plentiful.

Twet, *n.* a fatiguing spell of work.

Tweyt, *v.* to whittle.

Tweytins, *n.* whittlins. Cf. Tweetins.

Twice't, *adv.* twice.

Twiddle, *v.* to be busy about trifles; to circumvent, cozen.—*n.* used of the sea: a succession of small waves caused by a light breeze.

Twiddle, *v.* to play the bagpipes; to play the fiddle carelessly. Cf. Tweedle.

Twiddle-deo, *n.* useless ornaments on a woman's dress, frippery.

Twiddle-twaddle, *adj.* trifling, idle.

Twig, *v.* to glance at; to see through a dodge, &c.—*n.* a glance.

Twig, *v.* to pull with a jerk or quickly; to twitch; to turn; to wound the skin of a sheep in shearing.—*n.* a quick pull.

Twig, *v.* to contain, hold in.

Twig, *v.* to put cross-ropes on the thatch of a house.

Twig-rape, *n.* a cross-rope for the thatch of a house.

Twilt, *n.* a quilt.—*v.* to quilt.

Twime, *n.* a couplet.

Twin, *v.* to be a twin; to resemble closely.

Twin, *v.* to separate from one another; to part, sever; to divide; to part with; to deprive; to extract by stratagem or importunity.

Twin-bairns, *n.* twins.

Twine, *v.* to chastise.

Twine, *n.* a tie, bond; a contortion; a twist, turn; an intricate vicissitude.—*v.* to turn; to wriggle; to wind, meander; to deviate; to fasten, bind; used of cheese: to become leathery, tough; to join; to join in marriage; to spin, weave; to stretch out, prolong; to represent, state, or put a case.

Twine, *n.* a short attack of illness; a twinge of pain; weakness resulting from disease.

Twine, *v.* to put one to the utmost stretch of his power in working; to labour to the utmost of one's powers; to toil; to walk with great difficulty.—*n.* hard labour; a difficult task.—*adv.* with great difficulty.

Twine, *v.* to sever, part from. Cf. Twin.

Twiner, *n.* one who separates or 'teds' hay by tossing.

Twine-spinner, *n.* a rope-maker.

Twingle, *v.* to twine round; to turn, twist.

Twingle-twangle, *v.* to twang.

Twink, *v.* to twitch, jerk.

Twink, *n.* a twinkling; an instant.

Twinkling, *n.* a tingling.

Twinkling-of a bed-post, -of a cat's tail, *n.* an instant.

Twinter, *n.* a beast two years old, specially a sheep; a sheep from fifteen months up to four years old.

Twinter-ewe, *n.* a ewe three times shorn.

Twinty, *adj.* twenty; numerous. Cf. **Twenty**.

Twirk, *n.* a twitch.

Twirl, *n.* a grace note in singing; a flourish of words; a twinge.

Twish, *prep.* between. Cf. **Tweesh**.

Twisle, Twissle, Twistle, *v.* to twist; to fold; to wrench.—*n.* a shaking, tossing; a grip; a wrestling; a twist.

Twist, *v.* to twist yarn for weaving.—*n.* the peculiar screwing of the arms known as the 'frog's march'; a bond, a tie.

Twister, *n.* one who twists yarn for weaving; an implement for twisting straw-ropes.

Twisting, *n.* thread.

Twisty-thraws, *n.* colic.

Twit, *n.* used in weaving: anything that entangles, or gives resisting power to, the thread.

Twit, *v.* to chirp, twitter.—*n.* a bird's short, occasional chirp.

Twitch, *v.* to draw tightly together; to twinge.—*n.* an instrument made of a stick and loop of cord for the nose of a restive horse.

Twitch, *v.* to touch.—*n.* an instant of time, a touch.

Twitching, *n.* a twinge.

Twite, *v.* to whittle wood.

Twitter, *v.* to tremble; to quiver; to flicker; to sparkle; used of lightning: to gleam fitfully.—*n.* a fluster, flurry.

Twitter, *n.* the thin part of unevenly-spun thread; anything very thin or feeble.

Twittery, *adj.* spun very small; slender; without strength or substance.

Twit-twitter, *v.* to twitter.

Two, *n.* a few; a couple, pair. Cf. **Twa**.

Twolt, *n.* a quilt. Cf. **Twilt**.

Two-part, *n.* two-thirds.

Two-penny, *n.* a child's first reading-book; very small beer. Cf. **Tippenny**.

Twosome, *n.* two together.

Two-three, *adj.* two or three. Cf. **Twa-three**.

Twull, *adj.* twelve. Cf. **Twall**.

Twullsome, *n.* a company of twelve; twelve together. Cf. **Twalsome**.

Twunty, *adj.* twenty.

Twussle, *v.* to twist. Cf. **Twisle**.

Twyne, *v.* to sever, part. Cf. **Twin**.

Tyaave, *v.* to struggle, wrestle; to strive, toil; to struggle on; to wade; to labour under disease.—*n.* difficulty, struggle, pinch; toil, toiling; a hurry, stir.

Tyaave, *v.* to tease out; to ravel; to caulk. Cf. **Taave**.

Tyaave, *v.* to knead dough; to work up any-

thing sticky; to roughen a thing by work it with the hands; to meddle. Cf. **Tew**.

Tyach, *v.* to besmear. Cf. **Tyauch**.

Tyakin, *n.* a token; in *phr.* 'their ain tyakin be 't,' an expression of a desire to escape evils that have befallen others. Cf. **Tuachim**.

Tyal, *n.* a latchet; anything used for tying. Cf. **Tyal**.

Tyang, *n.* the prong of a fork. Cf. **Tang**.

Tyangs, *n.* tongs. Cf. **Tangs**.

Tyaou, *v.* to knead; to fidget. Cf. **Tew**.

Tyaou, *v.* to work hard; to toil.—*n.* a struggle, a laborious effort. Cf. **Tyaave**.

Tyauch, *v.* to besmear with grease or viscous stuff; to chew much; to swallow reluctantly from disgust; to be weak in health.—*n.* a short fit of illness.—*int.* an excl. of disgust, impatience, &c.

Tyauchie, *adj.* greasy; viscous; of weak health.

Tyauve, Tyave, *v.* to tease out; to caulk. Cf. **Taave**.

Tyauve, *v.* to struggle. Cf. **Taave**.

Tyauve, *v.* to knead. Cf. **Tew**.

Tyawen-skate, *n.* skate wrought with the hands into filaments. Cf. **Taavin-skate**.

Tyburn top, *n.* a close crop, a 'prison-cut,' used of the hair.

Tyce, *v.* to move slowly and carefully.

Tyce, *v.* to entice. Cf. **Tice**.

Tydie, *adj.* lucky; pregnant. Cf. **Tidy**.

Tye, *v.* to marry. Cf. **Tie**.

Tye, *n.* a pigtail.

Tyesday, *n.* Tuesday.

Tyeuve, *v. pret.* struggled. Cf. **Tyaave**.

Tygie, *n.* a cow with a white-tipped tail. Cf. **Taigie**.

Tyke, *n.* a dog; a rough, clownish fellow. Cf. **Tike**.

Tyke, *n.* tick, ticking; the case of a pillow or bed. Cf. **Tike**.

Tyke and tryke, *adv.* higgledy-piggledy.

Tyken, Tykan, *n.* ticking.

Tyken-weaver, *n.* a weaver of ticking.

Tyle, *v.* to cover.

Tyle, *v.* to close the door of a mason lodge.

Tyler, *n.* the door-keeper of a mason lodge.

†**Tylie**, *n.* a slice; a joint. Cf. **Taillie**.

Tymmer, *n.* timber. Cf. **Timmer**.

Tympany, Tympany-gavel, *n.* a gable in the middle of a house-front. Cf. **Timpany**.

Tynd, *n.* the prong of a fork; the tooth of a harrow; a harrowing. Cf. **Teind**.

Tynd, *n.* anger, sorrow. Cf. **Teen**.

Tynde, *v.* to kindle. Cf. **Teind**.

Tyne, *n.* the prong of a fork.

Tyne, *v.* to lose; to forfeit. Cf. **Tine**.

Tynin', *n.* a grubbing, harrowing.

Tynin', *n.* the losing.

Tynsell, *n.* loss; forfeiture. Cf. **Tinsel**.

Type, *n.* a sign, picture.

Type, *v.* to trail about in weakness or weariness; to struggle, labour hard.—*n.* hard labour accompanied by much walking; a weak, hard-working woman.

Typin' job, *n.* any employment that makes serious inroads on the constitution or physical strength.

Typit, *ppl. adj.* exhausted by toil.

Tyraneese, *v.* to overwork.

Tyre, *n.* a 'snood' or ribbon as a band for the hair. Cf. Tire.

Tysse, *v.* to entice. Cf. Tice.

Tyst, *v.* to entice; to stir up.

Tyste, Tystie, *n.* the black guillemot. Cf. Teistie.

Tystril, *n.* a light wanton; a dirty, slovenly woman. Cf. Taistril.

Tyte, *v.* to pull, jerk; to tap.—*n.* a tap. Cf. Tit.

Tyte, *adv.* straight, directly. Cf. Tite.

Tyte, *v.* to totter, tumble; to walk with short, unsteady steps.—*n.* continuous walking with short steps; a little person.—*adv.* with short steps. Cf. Tite.

Tytle, *v.* to walk with short steps.—*n.* the act of walking so.

Tytle, *v.* to tattle; to gossip.—*n.* idle talk; an idle talker. Cf. Tittle.

Tytter, *v.* to totter; to quiver. Cf. Titter.

Tyty, *n.* a grandfather.

Tyu, *v. pret.* kneaded. Cf. Tew, Tyaou.

Tyuchle, *n.* a tough morsel.—*v.* to chew something tough.

Tyuts, *int.* an excl. of impatience. Cf. Tuts, Toots.

Ubit, *adj.* dwarfish. Cf. Wobart.

Ubit, *n.* a hairy caterpillar. Cf. Oobit.

Ubitous, *adj.* very small, useless.

Uccle, *n.* the image of any one.

Udder-clap, *n.* a tumour on the udder of ewes, caused by the return of milk after being 'yeld.'

Udderlock, *v.* to pluck the wool from a ewe's udder for cleanliness, or free access of the lambs to the teats.—*n.* a lock of wool from the udder of a ewe.

Ug, Ugg, *v.* to feel disgust or abhorrence; to loathe; to cause disgust, nauseate; to vomit. —*n.* a feeling of repulsion, disgust, nausea; an object of disgust; a person of disagreeable, disgusting manners.

Ugertfow, *adj.* nice; squeamish. Cf. Ogertful.

Ugfou, *adj.* disgusting; scornful.

Uggin, *ppl. adj.* disgusting, loathsome; frightful.—*n.* a loathing.

Ugly, *adj.* ill-tempered; nasty.—*n.* a collapsible shade worn formerly in front of a woman's bonnet.

Ugsome, Ugsum, Uggsum, *adj.* disgusting; frightful; ghastly; horrible.

Ugsomelike, *adj.* ghostly-looking.

Ugsumness, *n.* loathsomeness, repulsiveness; frightfulness; horror.

Uhu, Uh-uh, *int.* an excl. of affirmation or approbation, used specially by children.

Ui, *n.* an isthmus or neck of land.

Uikname, *n.* a nickname. Cf. Eke-name.

†**Uily,** *n.* oil.—*adj.* oily; greasy.

Uily-pig, *n.* an oil-jar.

Uim, *n.* steam, vapour. Cf. Oam.

Uke, *n.* a week. Cf. Ouk.

†**Ulie,** *n.* oil. Cf. Uily.

Ulky, *adj.* every. Cf. Ilka.

Ull, *adj.* ill. Cf. Ill.

Ull-eesin', *n.* ill-usage.

Ull-wull, *n.* ill-will.

†**Ulzie, Ulyie, Uly,** *n.* oil. Cf. Uily.

Umbersorrow, *adj.* hardy; resisting disease or the effects of bad weather; rugged; of a surly disposition; rude, uncultivated; delicate, weakly.

Umbrell, *n.* an umbrella; in *pl.* honour paid to a person by drinking his health, and then inverting the glasses.

Umcast, *v.* to bind or splice by wrapping round.

Umist, Umast, *adj.* uppermost, highest. Cf. Eemost.

Umman, Uman, *n.* woman. Cf. Woman.

Umph, Umph'm, Umphum, *int.* an excl. of doubt, disapproval, or contempt; a murmur of assent, used by children especially.

Umquhile, Umquhill, Umwhile, *adj.* former, whilom; of old; late, deceased.—*adv.* formerly, some time ago.

Umrage, *n.* spite, ill-feeling; umbrage.

Umshy, *n.* a lump from a blow on the head.

Un, negative particle in composition. Cf. On, Ohn.

Unable, *adj.* infirm.

Unacquaint, Unacquant, *adj.* ignorant; not familiar; having no acquaintance.

Unacquaintedness, *n.* ignorance.

Unacquantit, *adj.* ignorant, unwitting.—*adv.* unwittingly.

Unafeard, *adj.* unafraid.

Unamendable, *adj.* irremediable, irreparable.

Unapproven, *adj.* not approved.

Unassoilzied, *adj.* unpurged from sin.

Unbauld, *adj.* humble, self-abased.

Unbeast, *n.* the toothache. Cf. Onbeast.

Unbeen, *adj.* not thoroughly closed in or made tight.

Unbekent, *adj.* unknown.

Unbeknown, *adj.* unknown, unperceived.

Unbeknownst, *adj.* unknown.

Unbethought, *v. pret.* not bethought.

Unbiddable, *adj.* perverse ; intractable ; not to be counselled.

Unbiggit, *adj.* unbuilt. Cf. Big.

Unboding, *adj.* unpropitious ; unpromising.

Unbonnet, *v.* used of a man : to take off his cap.

Unbonny, *adj.* ugly, not 'bonny'; unhealthy. Cf. Bonny.

Unbowsome, Unbousome, *adj.* unbending, unyielding ; unable to bend ; stiff, obstinate.

Unbristle, *v.* to shave a bristly beard.

Unbrizzed, *adj.* unbruised.

Unbrunt, *adj.* unburnt.

Unbusket, *adj.* unadorned. Cf. Busk.

Unca, *adj.* strange, unknown ; weird. Cf. Unco.

Unca'd, *adj.* uninvited.

Uncannily, *adv.* carelessly ; weirdly ; dangerously.

Uncanny, *adj.* awkward, inexpert ; imprudent ; unearthly, ghostly ; dangerous from supernatural causes ; ominous, weird, unlucky ; possessing supernatural powers ; dangerous ; mischievous ; open to suspicion of evil ; severe ; rude ; very hurtful.

Uncapable, *adj.* incapable.

Uncaring, *adj.* free from care ; heedless, careless.

Uncassable, *adj.* unbreakable ; that cannot be annulled.

Uncawket, *adj.* unchalked ; without an account being sent.

Unce, *n.* an ounce.

Uncessant, *adj.* incessant.

Unchance, *n.* a misfortune, calamity ; a mischance.

Unchancy, *adj.* unlucky ; ill-omened, ill-fated ; unfortunate ; mischievous ; risky ; not safe to meddle with.

Unclear, *adj.* undecided.

Uncle Tom is very sick, *n.* a singing game.

Uncloured, Unclowred, *adj.* unbeaten ; unwounded. Cf. Clour.

Unco, *adj.* unknown, strange ; foreign ; hardly recognizable ; 'uncouth'; weird, 'uncanny'; terrible ; reserved in manner ; uncommon ; extraordinary, very great.—*adv.* extremely, unusually, very.—*n.* a novelty ; a curiosity ; anything strange ; wonder, stir ; a stranger ; in *pl.* news ; strange tidings.

Unco body, *n.* a stranger ; a simple, unpretending, unimportant person.

Unco fork, *n.* strangers.

Uncoft, *adj.* unbought.

Unco-guid, *n.* an ironical designation of such persons as make a great profession of piety and are strait-laced in their religion.

Uncolie, Uncolies, Uncoly, *adv.* strangely ; very much ; extremely.

Uncolike, *adj.* strange ; strange-looking.

Uncolins, *adv.* in a strange or odd fashion or manner.

Unco-looking, *adj.* having a strange, wild look.

Unco man, *n.* a stranger.

Uncome, *adj.* not come, not arrived.

Uncommon, *adv.* uncommonly.

Uncompulsed, *adj.* unforced.

Unconess, *n.* strangeness, reserve.

Unconstancy, *n.* a lack of constancy.

Unconstant, *adj.* not constant.

Uncorn, *n.* wild oats.

Uncounselfow, *adj.* unadvisable.

Uncouth, *adj.* peculiar in dress, appearance, looks ; strange, unfamiliar.

Uncouthness, *n.* want of acquaintance.

Uncouthy, *adj.* 'eerie,' under the influence of superstitious fears ; dreary ; causing fear ; unseemly ; unfriendly.

Uncover, *v.* to drive a fox out of cover.

Uncraized, *adj.* unshattered ; unshaken.

Unction, *n.* an auction.

Unctioneer, Uncshoneer, *n.* an auctioneer.

Uncustomed, *adj.* smuggled, not having paid duty.

Undainty, *adj.* unbecoming, improper.

Undecent, *adj.* indecent ; unbecoming.

Undeemint, *adj.* countless, incalculable.

Undeemis, Undeemas, Undumous, *adj.* extraordinary, incredible ; immense, incalculable ; that cannot be reckoned.

Undeemously, *adv.* excessively.

Undegrate, *adj.* ungrateful.

Undemus, Undeimis, *adj.* extraordinary. Cf. Undeemis.

Undeniable, *adj.* unexceptionable.

Under, Un'er, *prep.* elliptically for 'under pretence of.'

Underbod, *n.* the swelling of the sea under a floating object.

Undercoat, -cote, -cot, *v.* used of a sore : to fester under a superficial scurf brought over it by improper treatment.

Under-cotie, *n.* a petticoat.

Underfit, *adj.* used of peat : dug beneath the feet instead of laterally.

Under-fur-sowing, *n.* sowing in a shallow furrow.

Undergang, *v.* to undergo, endure.

Undergore, *adj.* in a state of leprous eruption.

Underly, *v.* to endure, undergo ; to be subjected to.

Undermind, *v.* to undermine.

Undermine, *v.* to work secretly upon one ; to threaten, alarm.

Undermoor, *n.* in a deep peat-moss where two persons cut peats : the part cut by the second below the first cutter.

Undernight, *adv.* under cloud of night, by night.

Underside, *n.* the under surface.

Undersook, *n.* an undercurrent flowing, against that on the surface.

Understane, *n.* the nether millstone; a foundation, beginning.

Under-subscriber, *n.* one who subscribes a written statement.

Underthoom, *adv.* secretly; in an underhand manner.

Under water, *n.* water about the foundations of a house.

Undicht, Undight, *adj.* undressed; undecked; unwiped.

Undichtit, *adj.* unwiped.

Undoch, Undocht, *n.* a weak, puny creature; a coward; a silly, incapable, worthless person.—*adj.* sickly, puny, weak, contemptible. Cf. Dought.

Undoomis, *adj.* extraordinary; incalculable. Cf. Undeemis.

Undought, *n.* a weak, puny creature. Cf. Undoch.

Undraikit, *adj.* not drenched. Cf. Draik.

Une, *n.* an oven; the oppressive air of a room long shut up. Cf. Oen.

Unease, *n.* an uneasy state.

Uneasy, *adj.* troublesome, causing uneasiness.

Unedicat, *adj.* uneducated.

Uneirdly, *adj.* unearthly.

Uneith, *adj* not easy.—*adv.* hardly.

Unequal, *adj.* unfair, unjust.

Uneven, *adj.* out of sorts.

Unever, *adv.* never.

Unevitable, *adj.* inevitable.

Unfaceable, *adj.* ugly, not fit to be seen.

Unfain, *adj.* unwilling; not fond.

Unfandrum, *adj.* bulky; unmanageable.

Unfankle, *v.* to unwind, disentangle. Cf. Fankle.

Unfarrant, *adj.* ill-informed, senseless; slow of apprehension; rude, unmannerly. Cf. Farrand.

Unfashion, *n.* unfashionableness.

Unfauld, *v.* to unfold.

Unfavourable, *adj.* used of persons: unfavourably placed.

Unfeil, *adj.* uncomfortable, unpleasant; rough, coarse; not smooth. Cf. Onfeel.

Unfeiroch, *adj.* feeble, frail; unwieldy. Cf. Feerie.

Unfeued, *adj.* not disposed of in 'feu.' Cf. Feu.

Unfierdy, *adj.* feeble, infirm; unfit for action; overgrown, unwieldy. Cf. Feerdy.

Unfiery, *adj.* feeble, weak; unwieldy. Cf. Feery, Onfeirie.

Unfleggit, *adj.* not frightened, unalarmed. Cf. Fleg.

Unfond, *adj.* not fond.

Unforbidden, *adj.* unruly, disobedient.

Unforlattit, *adj.* unforsaken; used of wine: new, fresh. Cf. Forleit.

Unformal, *adj.* irregular; not according to form.

Unforsained, *adj.* undeserved.

Unfothersum, *adj.* used of the weather: not favourable to vegetation. Cf. Unfurthersome.

Unfree, *adj.* not enjoying the liberties of a burgess; liable to custom-duty.

Unfreelie, *adv.* very.—*adj.* heavy, unwieldy; frail, feeble.

Unfriend, Unfreen, *n.* an opponent; an enemy.

Unfriendship, *n.* unfriendly terms, enmity, ill-will.

Unfrugal, *adj.* lavish, given to expense.

Unfurthersome, *adj.* used of the weather: unfavourable to vegetation; unpropitious; difficult.

Unfylt, *adj.* undefiled, unsoiled. Cf. File.

Unganed, *adj.* inappropriate.

Ungang, *v.* to deceive, to lead to mistake.

Ungear, Ungeir, *v.* to unclothe; to unharness; to castrate. Cf. Gear.

Ungentilely, *adv.* rudely, impolitely. Cf. Genty.

Ungifted, *adj.* not given.

Ungirth, *v.* to take off a hoop. Cf. Girth.

Unglaured, *adj.* unsoiled. Cf. Glaur.

Ungraithe, *v.* to unharness.

Ungrate, *adj.* ungrateful.

Unguiled, *adj.* not beguiled or caught by guile.

Unhabile, *adj.* used of witnesses: legally incompetent.

Unhalesome, *adj.* unwholesome.

Unhalsed, *adj.* unsaluted.

Unhandsome, *adj.* shabby; knavish.

Unhanty, Unhaunty, *adj.* inconvenient; over-large; very fat; unwieldy, clumsy.

Unhappit, *adj.* without warm clothes; uncovered.

Unheartsome, *adj.* melancholy, cheerless; used of the weather: bad, uncomfortable; slightly ailing.

Unhearty, *adj.* disheartened; cheerless; wretched, sad; slightly ailing; feeling cold; used of the weather: cold and damp, uncomfortable.

Unhine, Unhyne, *adj.* extraordinary, unparalleled in a bad sense; immense, excessive in a bad sense.

Unhive, *v.* to deprive of cover or shelter.

Unhonest, *adj.* dishonest.

Unhonesty, *n.* dishonesty.

Unhousened, *adj.* unburied.

Unicorn-fish, *n.* the narwhal.

Unintenet, *adj.* unintended, unintentional.

†University, *n.* an entire community; as incorporation.

Unkaimed, Unkamed, *adj.* unkempt; uncombed.

Unken, *v.* to fail to recognize; to be ignorant or unwitting.

Unkennable, *adj.* innumerable; unknowable.

Unkenned, Unkent, *adj.* unknown, strange, unfamiliar.

Unkensome, *adj.* unknowable, unknown.

Unkilt, *v.* to let down a tuck or what was 'kilted' up.

Unkin', *adj.* unkind.

Unkipple, *v.* to uncouple.

Unkirs'en, *adj.* unchristian; unfit for human food.

Unkirsen'd, Unkirstened, *adj.* unbaptized.

Unko, Unka, *adj.* strange; foreign. Cf. Unco.

Unlaw, *n.* a breach of law; an unjust act; an injury; a fine fixed by law; a law without real authority.—*v.* to fine; to pay a fine.

Unleared, *adj.* uneducated, untaught.

Unleeze, *v.* to disentangle.

Unleisum, *adj.* unlawful.

Unless, *prep.* except.

Unlibbet, *adj.* not gelded.

Unlife-like, *adj.* likely to die; not having the appearance of living or recovering from disease.

Unlife-rented, *adj.* not life-rented.

Unlink, *v.* to rise up from a stooping position.

Unlo'esome, Unloosome, Unluesome, Unlusum, *adj.* unlovely; disgusting, repulsive.

Unloesom-, Unluesom-like, *adj.* unattractive, unpleasant-looking.

Unmackly, *adj.* deformed, unshapely.

Unmelled, Unmeled, *adj.* not meddled with.

Unmensefu', Unmencefu', *adj.* disorderly; unmannerly; unbecoming; indiscreet; ungenerous; used of the weather: rough, unseasonable.

Unnaturality, *n.* imbecility.

Unnest, *v.* to dislodge.

Unorderlie, *adv.* irregularly.

Unpaid, *ppl.* without having paid.

Unpalliable, *adj.* that cannot be palliated.

Unpassible, *adj.* impassable.

Unpatient, *adj.* impatient.

Unpaunded, *adj.* unpledged.

Unperfeit, *adj.* imperfect.

†Unpignorate, *v.* to pledge.

Unpossible, *adj.* impossible.

Unproper, *adj.* improper.

Unpurpose, *adj.* awkward; untidy; inexact.

Unpurpose-like, *adj.* seemingly awkward, or not adapted to the purpose to which a thing is applied.

Unpurposeness, *n.* slovenliness.

Unquarrelable, *adj.* unchallengeable.

Unquit, *adj.* unrequited.

Unream, *v.* used of milk: not to skim the cream off.

Unreason, *n.* disorder.

Unreave, *v.* to unravel, unwind.

Unreddable, *adj.* that cannot be disentangled, or 'redd' up.

Unregular, *adj.* irregular.

Unremeadfu', *adj.* irremediable. Cf. Remeid.

Unrest, *n.* a troublesome person; one who causes disquietude.

Unreverentlie, *adv.* irreverently.

Unricht, *adj.* dishonourable, unjust; wrong.

Unrid, *adj.* entangled.

Unrig, *v.* to unroof.

Unringed, *adj.* used of pigs: without a ring in the nose.

Unriped, *adj.* unexplored, unsearched, not investigated.

Unrude, *adj.* rude; hideous; diabolical, vile; base.

Unruleful, *adj.* unruly; ungovernable; lawless.

Unsaucht, *n.* trouble, disquietude. Cf. Saucht.

Unscabbit, *adj.* used of potatoes: not scabbed.

Unscaured, *adj.* unscared, undaunted.

Unseal, Unsell, Unseel, *n.* a wicked, worthless person; a self-willed, naughty child.

Unseally, Unseely, *adj.* worthless, wretched; unlucky.

Unsensible, *adj.* insensible; imperceptible; destitute of sense or reasoning power.

Unseyed, *adj.* untried, unproved.

Unshappen, *adj.* misshapen.

Unsicker, *adj.* insecure; not to be depended upon.

Unskaithed, *adj.* uninjured.

Unslockenable, *adj.* unquenchable; inextinguishable.

Unslot, *v.* to unfasten a door, &c., by drawing back the bolt or 'slot.'

Unsnarre, *adj.* blunt, not sharp. Cf. Snar.

Unsneck, *v.* to lift a latch. Cf. Sneck.

Unsned, *adj.* not pruned or cut. Cf. Sned.

Unsnib, *v.* to unbolt, unfasten. Cf. Snib.

Unsnick, *v.* to unlatch. Cf. Unsneck.

Unsnod, *adj.* untidy, in disorder. Cf. Snod.

Unsocht, *adj.* not sought.

Unsonsy, *adj.* unlucky; ominous; causing ill-luck; mischievous; disagreeable; plain, ill-looking, thin; slovenly, untidy. Cf. Sonsy.

Unspairket, *adj.* not bespattered.

Unspeaned, *adj.* unweaned.

Unspoilyied, *adj.* not despoiled.

Unspoken water, *n.* water from under a bridge, over which the living pass and the dead are carried, brought in the dawn or twilight to the house of a sick person, without the bearer's speaking either in going or returning; used in various ways as a most powerful charm by the superstitious for healing the sick.

Unstint, *adj.* unstinted ; unchecked ; without limit.

Unstout, *adj.* not stubborn.

Unstraighted, Unstrauchted, Unstreekit, *adj.* used of a dead body : not laid out for burial.

Unsure, *adj.* insecure, unsafe ; uncertain, unreliable.

Unsuspect, *adj.* not open to suspicion.

Unswack, *adj.* stiff ; not nimble or agile. Cf. Swack.

Unswackened, *adj.* used of an axle : ungreased, without oil.

Unsweel, *v.* to unwind ; to unwrap.

Untasty, *adj.* without good taste.

Untauld, *adj.* untold.

Untellable, *adj.* unfit to be told ; impossible to tell.

Untelling, *adj.* impossible to tell ; past words or reckoning.

Untender, *adj.* inconsiderate ; not circumspect.

Untented, *adj.* uncared for ; careless ; unconsidered.

Untentie, *adj.* careless.—*adv.* heedlessly ; incautiously ; noisily.

Untested, *adj.* used of a deed, will, &c. : without the testing clause.

Unthack, Untheek, *v.* to take off thatch ; to uncover.

Unthinkingness, *n.* thoughtlessness.

Unthocht, *adj.* unthought.

Unthochtfu', *adj.* thoughtless, inconsiderate.

Unthocht-lang, *adj.* without feeling ennui.

Unthocht o', *adj.* carelessly done.

Untholeable, *adj.* unbearable ; intolerable. Cf. Thole.

Unthraw, *v.* to untwist ; to unlock. Cf. Thraw.

Unthreshen, *adj.* not threshed.

Unticht, *adj.* used of the mind : wandering, weak.

Untochered, *adj.* without a dowry. Cf. Tocher.

Untolerable, *adj.* intolerable.

Untrig, *adj.* untidy ; slovenly. Cf. Trig.

Untrim, *adj.* not trim ; dishevelled.

Untrusty, *adj.* not trustworthy.

Unwarly, *adj.* unworldly ; supernatural ; uncouth ; clumsy ; unwieldy.

Unwaukit, *adj.* unwatched.

Unweel, *adj.* unwell ; of an ailing constitution.

Unweelness, *n.* ill-health ; an ailment.

Unwillie, *adj.* illiberal.

Unwinnable, *adj.* invincible, impregnable.

Unwitten, Unweetin, *adj.* unknowing, involuntarily ; unknown.

Unwittins, *adv.* unconsciously ; with no knowledge.

Unwitty, *adj.* lacking wit.

Unwordily, *adv.* unworthily.

Unwordy, *adj.* unworthy.

Unyerthly, *adj.* unearthly.

Unyokit, *adj.* unyoked ; finished.

Up, *adv.* above.—*adj.* open ; grown up ; excited, irritated.—*v.* to stand, rise, or jump up.

Up-again, *adv.* over again.

Up-a-land, *adj.* at a distance from the sea.

Upbang, *v.* to force to rise by beating ; to rise up with a ' bang.'

Upbear, *v.* to confirm, bear out.

Upbig, *v.* to build up.

Upbig, *adj.* conceited ; having a high opinion of one's self.

Upbirl, *v.* to rise quickly.

Upbow, *n.* a fiddler's action in striking an opening chord.

Up-brak, *n.* the breaking up.

Upbring, *v.* to bring up ; to educate, train ; to maintain during youth.—*n.* education, training : maintenance in youth.

Upbuckle, *v.* to buckle or fasten up.

Upbuller, *v.* to boil, bubble, or throw up.

Upbye, *adv.* up yonder ; up the way ; upstairs.

Up by yonder, *adv.* up yonder ; a little farther up.

Upcast, *v.* to raise up, elevate ; to turn over ; to reckon, calculate ; used of clouds : to gather ; to reproach, cast in the teeth, upbraid.—*n.* an upset ; a reproach ; a taunt ; an occasion of reproach.

Up-casting, *n.* the rising of clouds above the horizon, threatening rain.

Up-chokit, *ppl. adj.* choked up.

Up-coil, *n.* a kind of game with balls.

Upcome, *n.* promising appearance ; upshot ; bodily growth ; ascent.

Upcoming, *n.* ascent ; adolescence.

Updraw, *v.* to overtake, come up with ; to pick and draw a sheep from a flock ; to understand.

Up-drinking, *n.* an entertainment given to her ' gossips ' by a woman on her recovery from child-bearing.

Up-end, *v.* to set upright on end.

Up-fan'd, *adj.* used of a turkey's tail : spread out like a fan.

Up-feshin, -fess, -fessin, *n.* training, education, upbringing.

Up-fuirdays, *adv.* up before sunrise.

Up-gabble, *v.* to gobble up.

Upgae, *n.* an upward break in a mineral stratum.

Upgäen, *adj.* used of a market : rising ; wild, reckless.

Upgang, *n.* the act of ascending, ascent ; a sudden rise of wind and sea.

Upget, *v.* to rise up.

Upgive, *v.* to give up, surrender; to avow, 'own up.'

Upgiver, *n.* a legal term: one who delivers up to another.

Upgiving, *n.* the act of delivering up.

Upgrowing, *adj.* growing, adolescent.

Upgrown, *adj.* grown up.

Uphadd, Uphald, Uphaud, *v.* to uphold; to support, maintain; to defend; to provide for, furnish; to keep in repair or good condition; to raise, hold aloft; to affirm, maintain in argument; to warrant, vouch for; to believe in, accept as true; used of the weather: to clear.—*n.* support, maintenance; a prop; one who maintains another; the act or obligation of keeping in good repair; chief delight; ruling desire. Cf. Uppal.

Uphand, *adv.* with uplifted hand.

Uphauder, *n.* an upholder.

Upheese, *v.* to lift or hoist up.

Uphunt, *v.* to hunt up.

Up-ings, *n.* new or mended clothes, &c.

Up-i'-the-buckle, *adj.* ambitious, intent on rising in the social scale.

Up-jumlet, *adj.* jumbled up.

Upland, *adj.* on high or hilly ground; inland; rustic.

Uplayer, *n.* the person who loads ponies with peats at a peat-hill.

Uplift, *v.* to cheer; to collect rates, dues, &c.—*ppl.* uplifted.

Upliftable, *adj.* leviable.

Uplifted, *ppl. adj.* elated; excited; rendered proud.

Uplifter, *n.* a collector; a tax-gatherer.

Uplifting, *ppl. adj.* elevating; inspiring.—*n.* elation; pride; collection; exaction.

Uplight, Uplicht, *n.* brightening after a shower.

Uplins, *adv.* upwards.

Uploppin, *ppl. adj.* easily excited; jumping hurriedly at conclusions.

Uplös, Uppleuse, *v.* to disclose, discover.

Upmak, *v.* to make up; to compensate; to enrich; to supply a deficiency; to elate.—*n.* style, making; a fabrication, invention; a contrivance.

Upmaker, *n.* one who makes up an untrue story or false rumour.

Upo, Upon, *prep.* on; to; with; at; in.

Uppal, *n.* support; chief delight or pursuit, hobby; what gives one a good start in life and leads to prosperity.—*v.* used of the weather: to clear; to build up in health. —*adj.* fine, clearing up. Cf. Uphadd.

Upper, *n.* the uppermost.

Upper end, *n.* the head.

Upper mes, *n.* those who sat at table 'above the salt.'

Upper-moor, *n.* the one who cuts on the top where a moss is deep, and two persons cut, the one below the other.

Uppil, *adj.* used of the weather: clear, clearing up. Cf. Uppal.

Uppil aboon, *adj.* clear overhead.

Uppins, *adv.* a little way upwards.

Uppish, *adj.* aspiring, ambitious; bold, audacious.

Up-pit, -put, *v.* to erect.—*n.* lodging, entertainment; the power of secreting to prevent discovery.

Upple, *v.* used of the weather: to clear.

Up-putter, *n.* an erector, a builder; an instigator.

Up-putting, -pitting, *n.* accommodation; lodging; entertainment for man and beast; erection, building.

Upred, *adj.* tidied, put in order.

Upride, *v.* to cause to ride-a-cock-horse.

Upright, Upricht, *n.* a golf-club of which the head is at nearly right angles to the shaft. —*adj.* pure, genuine, as opposed to what is false or adulterated.

Upright bur, *n.* the fir-moss, *Lycopodium selago.*

Uprin, *v.* to come up to running.

Uprising, *n.* a removal from a house, farm, &c.

Upseed-time, *n.* seed-time.

Upset, *v.* to recover from an illness, wound, calamity, &c.—*ppl. adj.* pointing upwards; tip-tilted.

Upsetting, *ppl. adj.* forward, ambitious; stuck-up, proud; vehement.—*n.* assumption of right or superiority; aspiring or ambitious behaviour; a fitting up.

Upsetting-like, *adj.* appearing to have a spirit of assumption and self-elevation.

Upsides, *adv.* quits; on an equal footing.

Upsides wi', *adj.* revenged on.

Upsitten, *ppl. adj.* callous, listless, indifferent.

Upsitting, *n.* an entertainment given after the recovery of a woman from childbirth; indifference, callousness, listlessness.

Upsitting-time, *n.* the time when a woman gets up after childbirth.

Upskail, *v.* to scatter upwards.

Upspeak, *v.* to speak up.

Upspiel, *v.* to climb up.

Upstack, *v.* to put up in stacks.

Upstanding, *ppl. adj.* tall, erect, well made; upright, honourable; determined.—*n.* used of crops: pith, substance.

Upstart, *n.* a stick set upon the top of a wall, but not reaching the summit, in forming the woodwork of a thatch-roof.

Upstikket, *adj.* stuck-up; too particular.

Upstirrer, *n.* an inciter; a raiser of strife or rebellion.

Upstirring, *n.* quickening of the mind or spirit.

Up-strut, *v.* to strut proudly.

Uptail, *v.* to turn tail, run off.

Uptak, Uptack, Uptake, *v.* used of one's self: to reform; of a psalm, &c.: to start the tune; to levy fines, collect money, dues, &c.; to make out an inventory or list; to understand.—*n.* comprehension, understanding, intelligence; used of weather: a gale of wind; a storm.

Uptaker, *n.* a collector.

Uptaking, *n.* understanding, comprehension; the act of collecting.

Up-through, *adv.* in the upper part of the country; upwards through to the other side.—*adj.* living or situated in, or belonging to, the upper part of the country.

Up-throwing, *n.* puking; vomiting.

Up to, *adj.* skilled in; equal to.

Up-ty, *v.* to put in bonds.

Upwart, *adj.* upward; elevated.

Upwauken, *v.* to wake up.

Up-with, *n.* an ascent, a rising ground.—*adj.* taking a direction upwards; uphill; on an equal or superior footing; equal to.—*adv.* upwards.

Upwreil, *v.* to wriggle up.

Urchin, *n.* a hedgehog. Cf. Hurcheon.

Ure, *n.* soil; barren, ferruginous soil; mud, clay.

Ure, *n.* colour, tinge; a stain on linen caused by iron; the 'fur' adhering to iron vessels in which water is kept. Cf. Eer.

Ure, *n.* a haze in the air; a coloured haze which sunbeams cause in summer, in passing through the air; sweat, perspiration; a slow heat from embers; a suffocating heat.

Ure, *n.* the udder of a sheep or cow. Cf. Ewer.

Ureie, *adj.* coloured, stained.

Ure-lock, *n.* a lock of wool pulled from a ewe's udder. Cf. Ewerlock, Udderlock.

Ure-red, *n.* small reddish stones in muddy clay.

Urey, *adj.* hazy; filled with moisture or haze; clammy, covered with perspiration.

Urf, *n.* a stunted, ill-grown person or child, a crabbed or peevish little person; a dirty, insignificant person; a dwarf; a fairy. Cf. Orf.

Urf-like, *adj.* stunted, puny in appearance.

Urie, *adj.* furred, encrusted with metallic scum.

Urisk, *n.* a Highland name for a satyr.

Urisum, *adj.* frightful; terrifying. Cf. Ooriesum.

Urling, *n.* a dwarfish person or child.

Urluch, Urlich, *adj.* cloudy, dull; stupid, silly-looking, dazed. Cf. Oorlich.

Urn, *n.* a grave, tomb.

Urn, *v.* to pain, torture.

Urp, *v.* to become pettish.

Ury, *adj.* hazy. Cf. Urey.

Ury, *adj.* furred with metallic scum. Cf. Urie.

Us, *pron.* me.

Use, *n.* interest of money.

Use, *v.* to frequent; to familiarize; to grow accustomed to a place.

Used, *ppl. adj.* accustomed; tried; expert.

Useless, *n.* the crab's claw or lady's thumb.

Ush, *v.* to usher; to escort; to lead, guide.

Ush, Usch, ¼. to issue; to flow out copiously; to empty; to cleanse.—*n.* the entrails of a slaughtered animal.

Usque, *n.* whisky.

Usqueba, Usquebae, Usquebagh, Usquebah, Usquabae, Usquebey, Usquibae, *n.* whisky.

Usual, *n.* usual health or circumstances.

Utgie, Utgien, *n.* outlay, expenditure.

Uther, *n.* an udder.

Utherlock, *v.* to pull the wool from a ewe's udder in order to facilitate suckling. Cf. Udderlock, Urelock.

Utole, *n.* a symbol for the 'infeftment,' or the resignation of an annual rent.

Utterance, *n.* outrance; extremity of distress, &c.

Utter House, *n.* the Outer House in the Court of Session.

Utteridge, *n.* utterance, power of speech.

Utwith, *adv.* beyond. Cf. Outwith.

---

†**Vacance, Vacans,** *n.* a vacation; holidays; a vacancy.

†**Vacillancy,** *n.* vacillation.

†**Vacillant,** *adj.* vacillating.

Vady, *adj.* great, strong; gay; vain. Cf. Vaudy.

†**Vaedge, Vaege,** *v.* to journey. Cf. Vage.

Vagabond-money, *n.* a tax levied in one-half from landlords and one-half from tenants, according to their means and substance, to meet the weekly charges that might arise sufficient to sustain the poor.

Vagabone, *n.* a vagabond.

†**Vage,** *n.* a voyage; a journey by land; a short journey to fetch or carry; an expedition.—*v.* to go on an expedition.

†**Vage,** *v.* to wander. Cf. Vaig.

Vaging, *n.* loafing about.

Vagral, *adj.* vagrant.

†**Vague,** *v.* to wander. Cf. Vaig.

†**Vaicance,** *n.* a vacation. Cf. Vacance.

†**Vaig, Vaige,** *v.* to roam, stroll, wander; to loaf about; to be discursive.—*n.* a wanderer; a vagabond, an idler.—*adj.* wandering; easily swept away.

Vaiger, *n.* a wanderer; a vagrant.

Vaigie, *n.* a romp.

Vaiging, *n.* idle strolling, loafing about.

Vaigrie, *n.* a whim; a freak; a piece of folly; a vagary.

†**Vaik,** *v.* to be vacant; to vacate; to scatter so as to empty; to be dismissed; to be unoccupied; to be at leisure.

Vailye, *v.* to value.—*n.* value, worth.

Vaiper, *v.* to vapour. Cf. Vapour.

Vairie, *v.* to begin to show symptoms of delirium. Cf. Vary.

Vairtie, *adj.* early up; wide-awake; cautious; industrious. Cf. Vertie.

Vaishle, *n.* a vassal; a maid-servant.

†**Vake,** *v.* to be vacant; to vacate. Cf. Vaik.

†**Valawish,** *adj.* profuse; lavish. Cf. Volage.

Valentine's deal, -dealing, *n.* a method by billets with names written on them in a company, by which a person whose name was written became the drawer's valentine from one 14th Feb. to the next.

Valetudinariness, *n.* weak health.

Validate, *ppl. adj.* validated.

†**Valises,** *n.* saddle-bags.

†**Valour,** *n.* worth, value.

Valuedom, *n.* value.

Vamp, *v.* to improve, set off; to mend.

Vamper, *v.* to present an ostentatious appearance; to pose.

Vandie, *adj.* vain, ostentatious.—*n.* a vain, vaunting fellow; a braggart; a self-conceited person. Cf. Vaunty.

Vane, *int.* a call to a horse to come near.

Vankish, *v.* to entwine, twist. Cf. Wankish.

Vanquish, *n.* a wasting disease of sheep, caused by the pernicious quality of a certain grass.

Vantie, *adj.* ostentatious. Cf. Vaunty.

Vapour, *v.* to bully; to threaten violence; to frisk about, caper; to stroll, saunter.

Vare, *n.* the spring. Cf. Voar.

Variorum, *n.* a constant change; a medley; variation; diversion; a long rigmarole; a repeating Psalm-tune; in *pl.* odds and ends.

Varlet, *n.* a wizard, 'warlock.'

Varsal, *adj.* universal.

Vary, *v.* to show symptoms of delirium in illness.—*n.* a quandary, uncertainty, loss.

Vassal, *n.* a tenant paying for land to the superior an annual feu-duty.

†**Vassalage,** *n.* an exploit; a brave deed.

Vast, *n.* a great number or quantity.

Vastage, *n.* waste ground.

Vaudy, Vaudie, *adj.* great, strong; uncommon; showy, gay; proud, vain; conceited; elated; forward; merry.

Vaunty, *adj.* boastful, proud; vain; exultant; ostentatious; merry; wanton; showy.—*n.* a vain, boastful person; a braggadocio.

Vaw, *int.* a call to a horse to come to one.

†**Veadge, Veage,** *n.* a voyage. Cf. Vage.

†**Veak,** *v.* to become vacant. Cf. Vaik.

†**Veal,** *n.* a calf; the carcass of a calf.

Veand, *adj.* superannuated.

†**Veef,** *adj.* brisk, lively. Cf. Vive.

Veem, *n.* a close heat over the body, with redness of face and some perspiration; a state of elation, exaltation, or excitement of spirit.

Veeper, *n.* a viper.

Veeperate, Veeperit, *adj.* venomous, vicious; sharp-tempered; bitterly abusive.

Veesion, *n.* a vision; a thin, meagre person or animal.

Veesit, *v.* to visit; to punish; to inspect.

†**Veesy, Veesie,** *n.* a look, view.—*v.* to aim at. Cf. Vizy.

†**Veev, Veeve,** *adj.* brisk, lively.—*adv.* briskly; vividly.

†**Veevers,** *n.* provisions. Cf. Vivers.

†**Veill,** *n.* a calf.

†**Venall,** *n.* an alley. Cf. Vennel.

†**Vendue,** *n.* an auction.

Vendue-warehouse, *n.* an auction-room.

†**Venge,** *v.* to avenge.

Vengeable, *adj.* cruel, destructive.—*adv.* excessively.

Vengeance, *n.* used as an oath.

Venim, *n.* venom; malice; a spiteful person.

Venison, *n.* goat's flesh.

†**Vennel,** *n.* an alley, a narrow lane.

Vent, *n.* a hole; the anus of a fowl; a chimney.—*v.* used of a chimney: to draw: to smoke; to issue false coin.

†**Vent,** *n.* progress, speed; a sale.—*v.* to sell.

Venter, *v.* to venture.—*n.* anything driven ashore by tide or wind.

Venterer, *n.* one who looks for articles driven ashore by tide or wind.

Ventoner, *n.* a vintner.

Venus, *adj.* impure, immoral.

Vera, *adv.* very.

Verge, *n.* a belt or strip of planting.

Vergus, *n.* verjuice.

Verilies, *adv.* verily.

Vermin, *n.* a term applied playfully to a child.

Versant, *adj.* versed in, conversant.

Version, *n.* an exercise in translating a piece of English into Latin.

Verter, *n.* virtue; a charm for curing certain diseases.

Verter-water, *n.* water found in the hollows of tombstones and rocks, a charm for warts.

Verter-well, *n.* a well possessing medicinal virtue.

Vertie, *adj.* cautious, prudent; industrious: eager; wide-awake; early up, early at business.

'Verties, 'Vertise, *v.* to advertise; to warn.

Vertue, *n.* thrift, industry.

Vertuous, *adj.* thrifty, industrious.

Verylies, *adv.* verily.

Veshell, *n.* a vessel.

†Vesie, *v.* to visit; to inspect; to take aim. Cf. Vizy.

Vessel, *n.* a cow's udder.

Vetcher, *n.* a man of a very suspicious appearance.

†Veve, *adj.* alive.

Vex, *v.* to fret, grieve, be sorry.—*n.* a trouble; vexation; a cause of vexation or worry.

Vexsome, *adj.* grievous, sad.

†Veyage, Viage, *n.* a journey; voyage. Cf. Vage.

Vicinity, *n.* close resemblance.

Vicious, *adj.* used of the weather: severe. Cf. Vitious.

Victual, *n.* grain of any kind; standing corn.

Victualler, *n.* a grain-dealer; a corn-factor.

†Vievers, *n.* provisions. Cf. Vivers.

Vile, *adj.* dirty. Cf. Vyld.

Villanious, *adj.* villainous.

†Vincus, *v.* to conquer.

Vindicat, *v.* to relieve, deliver.

†Vinel, *n.* an alley.

Vintiner, *n.* a vintner.

Violent, *v.* to act violently; to bring very strong pressure to bear. — *adj.* extremely strong.

†Violer, *n.* a fiddler.

Violing, *n.* fiddling.

Viparously, *adv.* malignantly.

Viperean, *adj.* viperous, venomous.

Viporous, *adj.* venomous.

Vir, Virr, *n.* force, vigour, 'go'; activity, impetus.—*v.* to move or walk with energy. —*adv.* by force. Cf. Birr.

Virgin-honey, *n.* honey from the hive of the second swarm from the parent stock.

Virgus, *n.* verjuice. Cf. Vergus.

†Virl, Virle, Virrel, *n.* a ferrule; an encircling band or ring put round any body to keep it firm.—*v.* to ring round.

Virtue, *n.* thrift. Cf. Vertue.

Virtuous, *adj.* thrifty.

Vise, *n.* the indication of the direction that a mineral stratum has taken when interrupted in its course.

†Visie, *n.* a scrutinizing view. Cf. Vizy.

Vision, *n.* a thin, meagre person or animal.

Visit, *v.* to punish; to inspect ecclesiastical records, &c.

Visitation, *n.* the public yearly visit of magistrates, &c., to a burgh grammar-school to distribute prizes, &c.

Visitation - acquaintance, *n.* a visiting acquaintance.

Visnomy, *n.* physiognomy.

÷Vissy, *n.* a gaze. Cf. Vizy.

Vital, *adj.* having vitality.

Vitcher, *n.* a visitor.

Vitiate, Vitiat, *ppl. adj.* vitiated.

Vitiosity, *n.* what vitiates an animal or article.

Vitious, *adj.* unauthorized; legally informal, irregular; fierce, fiery.

Vitiousness, *n.* fierceness; unmanageableness.

Vittle, *n.* grain; standing corn; in *pl.* victuals. — *v.* to support or supply with victuals. Cf. Victual.

Vittler, *n.* a corn-merchant.

Vivacity, *n.* the degree of life in a new-born child.

†Vive, *adj.* vivid; life-like; clear; living; lively; brisk, vigorous; fresh.

Vively, *adv.* clearly, vividly; to the life.

Vive-prent, *n.* print easily read.

†Vivers, Vivres, *n.* provisions, food.

Vivual, *adj.* alive; identical, self-same.

Vivuallie, *adv.* in life; identically.

†Vizy, Vizzy, *n.* a look; a scrutinizing gaze; the sight of a gun. —*v.* to look; to scrutinize; to visit for inspection; to aim at.

Vizzie-drap, *n.* the sight of a gun.

Vizzy-hole, *n.* a peep-hole or small wicket in the door or gate of a castle or fort for spying.

Vizzying-port, *n.* the door or gate of a castle or fort having a 'vizzy-hole.'

Vizzyless, Vizyless, *adj.* used of a gun: not sighted.

Voar, Vor, *n.* the spring; seed-time.

Voar-fee, *n.* wages for work done in seed-time.

Voar-time, *n.* spring-time.

Vocable, *n.* in *pl.* a vocabulary.

Voce, *n.* voice.

Vogerous, *adj.* boastful, vaunting.

Vogie, Voggie, *adj.* vain; merry, cheerful; vaunting; fondly, kindly; caressing.

Vogue, *n.* reputation; humour, mood; a strong inclination.

Voice, *n.* a vote. —*v.* to vote.

Voicer, *n.* a voter.

Vokie, *adj.* vain. Cf. Vogie.

†Volage, *adj.* giddy; inconsiderate; profuse, lavish, prodigal.—*v.* to talk ostentatiously.

†Volageous, *adj.* very giddy and light; very boastful.

†Volanting, *adj.* paying a flying visit; flying from one's creditors.

Vole-mouse, *n.* the short-tailed or field-mouse.

†Voler, *n.* a thief.

†Volish, *v.* to talk ostentatiously. Cf. Volage.

Volisher, *n.* an ostentatious talker.

†Voluntar, *adj.* voluntary.

Voluptuous, *adj.* used of repairs on a house: unnecessarily luxurious or convenient.

Vomiter, *n.* an emetic.

Vougie, *adj.* vaunting. Cf. Vogie.

Vour, *n.* the spring. Cf. Voar.

Vouss, *n.* the liquor of hay and chaff boiled.

Voust, Voost, *v.* to boast, brag.—*n.* a boast; vaunting.

Vouster, *n.* a braggart; a boaster.

Voustin, *n.* boasting.

Vousty, *adj.* given to vain boasting.

†**Vout,** *n.* a vault ; a deep hole.

Vow, *int.* an excl. of surprise, admiration, sorrow, &c. Cf. Wow.

Vowbit, *n.* a hairy worm ; the caterpillar of the tiger-moth ; a puny creature. Cf. Oobit, Woubit.

Vowgie, *adj.* vain. Cf. Vogie.

Vowky, *adj.* vain. Cf. Vogie.

Vowl, *v.* used in card-playing : to draw all the tricks.—*n.* a deal that draws all the tricks, a vole.

Vowst, *v.* to boast.—*n.* a boast.

Vowster, *n.* a boaster.

†**Vowt,** *n.* a vault.

Vrack, *n.* wreck, ruin. Cf. Wrack.

Vrack, *n.* wrack, sea-ware. Cf. Wrack.

Vracket, *ppl. adj.* shattered, dismembered.

Vraith, *n.* an apparition. Cf. Wraith.

Vran, *n.* the wren. Cf. Wran.

Vrang, *adj.* wrong. Cf. Wrang.

Vrap, *v.* to wrap.

Vrapper, *n.* a wrapper ; a woman's loose jacket or blouse.

Vrat, *v. pret.* wrote.

Vratch, *n.* a wretch. Cf. Wratch.

Vrath, *n.* wrath.

Vreath, *n.* a snow-'wreath.'

Vreet, *v.* to write. Cf. Write.

Vreetin', *n.* writing.

Vricht, *n.* a wright. Cf. Wricht.

Vrite, *v.* to write.

Vriter, *n.* an attorney. Cf. Writer.

Vrocht, *ppl.* wrought. Cf. Wrocht.

Vrutten, *ppl.* written.

Vung, *v.* to move swiftly with a buzzing sound.—*n.* a buzzing or humming sound.

Vyaachle, *n.* a vehicle.

Vyaag, Vyaug, *n.* a woman of rude manners. —*adj.* incorrigible.

Vyld, *adj.* dirty, filthy ; worthless.

Vyldness, *n.* dirt, filth.

Vyokie, *adj.* vain ; cheerful. Cf. Vogie.

Wa', *n.* a wall.

Wa', *n.* a way.

Wa', *int.* an excl. of contempt.

Wa', *v.* to choose.—*ppl. adj.* chosen ; strongest ; best. Cf. Wale.

Wa, Waah, *int.* well ! why ! Cf. Waw.

Waajer, *v.* to wager.

Waak, *v.* to wake ; to watch.

Waal, *v.* to weld ; to comply with. Cf. Wall.

Waalaquyte, *n.* an under-vest. Cf. Wylie-coat.

Waalin-heat, *n.* the heat at which iron will weld.

†**Waalipend, Waalipenn,** *v.* to slight, under-value ; to vilipend.

Waan, *n.* hope ; prospect of success. Cf. Wan.

Waanly, *adj.* hopeful.

Waap, *v.* to beat. Cf. Wap.

Waapon, *n.* a weapon.

Waar, *v.* to spend ; to wager. Cf. Ware.

Waar, *n.* sea-wrack.—*v.* to manure with sea-wrack. Cf. Ware.

Waar-blade, *n.* a blade of sea-wrack.

Waarcaist, *n.* a heap of sea-wrack.

Waariebowg, *n.* a bladder of the yellow tangle.

Waariebug, *n.* a tumour on cattle caused by the larva of the gadfly ; a warble.

Waarsche, *adj.* tasteless ; weak and watery. Cf. Wairsh.

Waar-strand, *n.* a beach on which seaweed is cast up.

Waat, *n.* a welt ; a fissure ; a weal or mark made by a blow. Cf. Welt.

Waav, *v.* to signal by a wave of the hand.

Waavle, *v.* to stagger. Cf. Wavel.

Wab, *n.* a web ; the omentum.—*v.* to weave.

Wa'baw, *n.* a hand-ball for playing against a wall.

Wabble, Wable, *v.* to wobble, hobble.—*n.* hobbling. Cf. Wauble.

Waberan-, Wabert-leaf, *n.* the great plantain.

Wab-fittit, *adj.* web-footed.

Wabran-, Wabron-leaf, *n.* the great plantain.

Wabster, *n.* a weaver ;-a spider. Cf. Webster.

Wa-cast, *n.* a castaway ; anything worthless or to be despised ; a piece of extravagance.

Wace, *n.* wax.

Wach, *adj.* moist, clammy. Cf. Wack.

Wachie, *adj.* wet ; foggy ; swampy.

Wachle, Wachel, *v.* to waggle ; to fatigue greatly ; to puzzle. Cf. Wauchle.

Wacht, *n.* a guard, a watch.

Wacht, *v.* to quaff.—*n.* a big drink. Cf. Waught.

Wack, *adj.* damp ; clammy ; swampy ; foggy ; rainy.

Wackness, *n.* moisture, humidity.

Wad, *v.* would.

Wa'd, *ppl. adj.* chosen, choice.

Wad, *n.* a pawn ; a pledge ; a forfeit ; a wager.—*v.* to pledge ; to engage one's self ; to wager.

Wad, *v.* to marry, wed.

Wad, *v. pret.* and *ppl.* married.

Wad-be-at, *n.* one who aspires above his station.

Wadd, *n.* a pledge. Cf. Wad.

Wadd, *n.* black-lead ; a lead-pencil.

Wadder, *n.* weather.

Wadder, *n.* a wether.

Waddie, *n.* a twig with smaller shoots branching from it, which being plaited together, it becomes a kind of whip. Cf. Widdie.

Waddin, *ppl. adj.* strong, like two pieces of iron welded into one.

Waddin', *n.* a wedding.

Waddin'-ba's, -baws, *n.* money scattered at a wedding.

Waddin'-braws, *n.* wedding-clothes, a trousseau.

Waddin'-coat, *n.* the coat a bridegroom wears at his marriage.

Waddin'-day, *n.* the wedding-day.

Waddin' o' craws, *n.* a large flock of crows.

Waddin'-sark, *n.* a shirt made by the bride for the bridegroom before the wedding.

Waddin'-store, *n.* the wedding-feast.

Waddin'-treat, *n.* a feast given on the fourth day of the marriage festivities by the young men at their own expense, as a compliment to the newly-married, and as a return for the liberality of their entertainment.

Waddler, *n.* one who would keep house, or act, properly, but does not. Cf. Walder.

Wadds, *n.* various games of forfeits, played within doors and in the open air ; the game of 'Scots and English.'

Wadds and wears, *n.* a rhyming game of forfeits, formerly common in Galloway farm-kitchens.

Waddy, *adj.* great, strong ; uncommon ; gay, showy ; proud, vain ; forward ; merry. Cf. Vaudy.

Wade, *v.* to wager.

Wade, *v.* used of the sun or moon : to gleam at intervals through clouds or mists ; to ford a river.

Wadeable, *adj.* fordable.

Waden, *adj.* young and supple.

Wader, *n.* the heron.

Wadge, *n.* a wedge.

Wadge, *v.* to brandish threateningly.—*n.* the act of so brandishing.

Wadie, Wady, *adj.* strong ; showy ; plucky ; gay. Cf. Vaudy.

Wad-keeper, *n.* one who takes charge of forfeits or pledges.

Wadna, *v. neg.* would not.

Wa'-drap, *n.* water dropping from the eaves of a house, 'wall-drop.'

Wadset, *n.* a mortgage ; a deed from a debtor to a creditor assigning the rents of land until the debt is paid ; a pledge.—*v.* to mortgage ; to pawn ; to alienate land, &c., under reversion.

Wadset o' an aith, *n.* a bet.

Wadsetter, *n.* one who holds another's property in 'wadset.'

Wad-shootin, *n.* shooting at a mark for a prize or 'wad.'

Wae, *n.* woe.—*adj.* woeful, sorrowful ; vexed.

Waeak, *v.* to whine.—*n.* a whine. Cf. Wëak.

Wae-begane, *adj.* woe-begone.

Wae-days, *n.* days of adversity.

Waefleed, *n.* the water of a mill-stream after passing the mill, the 'away-flood.'

Waefu', *adj.* woeful ; sad ; miserable.

Waefu'some, *adj.* sad ; sorry ; wretched.

Waeg, *n.* the kittiwake.

Wae-hearted, *adj.* sad-hearted ; sad.

Waelike, *adj.* sorrowful, sad-looking.

Waely, *adv.* sadly.

Waen, *n.* a child. Cf. Wean.

Waeness, *n.* sadness, sorrow ; vexation.

Waeock, *v.* to squeak ; to whine. Cf. Wëak.

Waese, *n.* a small bundle of hay or straw, larger than a wisp ; a bundle of wheat-straw 'drawn' for thatching ; a bundle of sticks or brushwood placed on the wind side of a cottage-door to ward off the blast ; a circular pad of straw placed on the head for carrying a tub, basket, &c.; a straw collar for oxen ; a bulky neck-tie.

Wae's-heart, *int.* alas for you ! Cf. Waste-heart.

Wae's me, *int.* woe is me !

Waes my fell, *int.* an excl. of mingled sadness and astonishment.

Waesome, *adj.* sorrowful, sad.

Waesomelike, *adj.* sad.

Waesomely, *adv.* sadly.

Waesuck, Waesucks, *int.* alas !

Wae wags ye, *int.* an excl. of imprecation.

Wae-wan, *adj.* pale with grief.

Wae-weirdit, *adj.* doomed to woe.

Wae-worn, *adj.* grief-stricken.

Wae worth, *int.* woe betide ! woe worth !

Waey, *n.* way. Cf. Way.

Waff, *v.* to wave ; to flap ; to fan ; to flutter ; to excel in vigorous dancing.—*n.* a flapping ; a wave of the hand ; a flag, signal ; a puff of wind ; a current or gust of wind caused by the swift passage of a moving body ; a whiff ; an odour assailing the nostrils ; a slight touch from a soft body in passing ; a slight, sudden ailment ; a touch of cold ; a passing glimpse ; a good or bad influence ; a wraith.—*adj.* brief, fleeting.

Waff, *adj.* strayed, wandering alone ; solitary ; woe-begone ; vagabond-like ; unprincipled ; wild ; immoral ; shabby ; of poor quality ; feeble, paltry ; worn-out, weak in mind ; low-born ; hard, difficult.—*n.* a waif, vagrant ; a rascal ; a low, idle fellow ; one who keeps bad company.—*v.* to wander idly.

Waffel, *adj.* limp. Cf. Waffle.

Waffer, *n.* used in mining : a break or dip ; a fault.

Waffer, *adj.* strayed, wandering.

Waffie, *n.* a worthless fellow ; one given to idleness or low company.

Waffil, *v.* to wave about. Cf. Waffle.

Waffinger, *n.* a vagabond ; a good-for-nothing fellow.

Waffish, *adj.* used of persons : disreputable, immoral ; of things : worthless.

Waffle, *v.* to turn over anything lightly. Cf. Wuffle.

Waffle, *v.* to wave about ; to flap in the wind. —*adj.* flexible, pliant.

Waffleness, *n.* pliability, limberness.

Waffler, *n.* a weak, undecided person.

Waff-like, *adj.* of disreputable appearance ; shabby-looking ; weak.

Wafflin, *ppl. adj.* hesitating, unsteadied, vacillatory.

Waff-looking, *adj.* of disreputable, suspicious appearance.

Waffly, *adj.* hesitating, undecided.

Waffness, *n.* a shabby appearance.

Waft, *n.* a puff of wind ; a whiff ; a passing smell or taste ; a passing glimpse ; a benevolent or favourable influence ; one who, under the appearance of friendship, holds a person up to ridicule.

Waft, *n.* weft, woof.

Waft and warp, *v.* to weave.

Wafters, *n.* pinions.

Wag, Wagg, *v.* to move about ; to keep going ; to shake ; to wave ; to beckon with hand or head ; used of the tongue : to chatter. — *n.* a waving motion ; a signal with the hand ; a flag ; a contemptuous designation of a fellow ; in *pl.* tricks, conduct.

Wa-gâen, Wa-gang, *n.* a departure ; a disagreeable taste after swallowing a thing ; the channel in which water runs from a mill.—*adj.* going away ; leaving a farm, &c.

Wa-gâen-, Wa-gang-crap, *n.* the last crop of a tenant leaving his farm. Cf. Way-gang-crop.

Wag along, *int.* a driver's call to his oxen.

Waganging, *n.* going or passing along.

Wa'gate, *n.* speed, progress. Cf. Waygate.

Wag-at-the-wa, *n.* a cheap clock, hanging on a wall, with pendulum and weights exposed ; a spectre supposed to haunt the kitchen, and to wag backwards and forwards on the crook before a death in the house.

Wage, *n.* wages.

Wage, *v.* to wager.

Waggie, *n.* a 'waggity.'

Waggity, Waggity-wa, *n.* a 'wag-at-the-wa.'

Waggle, *v.* to waddle ; to walk along unsteadily.—*n.* a bog, quagmire, marsh.—*adv.* swaying from side to side. Cf. Wiggle.

Waggle-Waggle, *adv.* swaying from side to side.

Waggly, *adj.* waggling, unsteady.

Waggy, *n.* the pied wagtail.

Wagh, *adj.* smelling of damp ; musty. Cf. Waugh.

Waghorn, *n.* a fabulous personage, supposed to be a far greater liar than the devil, and therefore the king of liars ; a name for the devil.

Wag-o'-the-pen, *n.* a scrap of writing ; the least bit of a letter.

Wag-string, *n.* one who is hanged.

Wag-tawse, *n.* a schoolmaster.

Wag-wits, *n.* a waggish person.

Wa'-head, *n.* the empty space at the head of a cottage-wall, that is not beam-filled, where articles are deposited ; the 'crap o' the wa'; 'wall-head.'

Waible, *v.* to walk unsteadily from feebleness. Cf. Wauble.

Waichle, *v.* to stagger ; to waddle ; to fatigue. Cf. Wauchle.

Waicht, *n.* a hoop with a skin stretched over it, used for winnowing or carrying corn.—*v.* to winnow. Cf. Weight.

Waiden, *adj.* young and active, supple. Cf. Waden.

Waidge, *v.* to brandish. Cf. Wadge.

Waif, *n.* a stray animal.—*adj.* solitary ; in a strange place ; paltry, weak, inferior ; worn-out.

Waif, *v.* to wave ; to flap ; to fluctuate. Cf. Waff.

Waif-beast, *n.* a stray animal whose owner is unknown.

Waif-woman, *n.* a woman without property or connections.

Waigle, *v.* to waddle ; to waggle. Cf. Waggle, Wiggle.

Waik, *v.* to watch.—*n.* a watch ; a company of musicians who serenade on the street early in the morning.

Waik, *adj.* weak.

Waik-leggit, *adj.* weak in the legs.

Waikly, *adj.* weakly.

Waikness, *n.* weakness.

Wail, Waile, *v.* to choose, select. Cf. Wale.

Wail-a-wins, *int.* an excl. of surprise, pity, or sorrow. Cf. Weel-a-wins.

Wailed, *ppl. adj.* mourned, lamented.

Wailow, *v.* to fade ; to wither ; to dwindle. Cf. Wallow.

Waim, *n.* the womb ; the belly. Cf. Wame.

Wain, *v.* to remove, convey.

Wain, *n.* a child. Cf. Wean.

Waingle, *v.* to flutter ; to wag ; to dangle ; to flap. Cf. Wingle.

Wainisht, *adj.* 'vanished'; pinched, thin.

Wainness, *n.* childishness ; feebleness.

Wainscot, *n.* oak.—*adj.* oaken.

Waint, *n.* a glimpse, a passing view ; a moment. Cf. Went.

Waint, *n.* an alley; the bend of a fishing-line not cast at a stretch.—*v.* used of liquids: to turn sour; to become flavourless.

Waip, *v.* to strut, to swagger. Cf. Wap.

Waipon, *n.* a weapon.

Waipon-shaw, *n.* a kind of ancient military parade. Cf. Wapenshaw.

Wair, *n.* a pillow-slip.

Wair, *n.* the spring. Cf. Voar.

Wair, *v.* to spend.—*n.* goods. Cf. Ware.

Wair, *n.* sea-wrack.—*v.* to manure with sea-wrack. Cf. Ware.

Wair, *n.* wire.

Wairawons, *int.* well-a-day!

Waird, *v.* to award. Cf. Ward.

Waird, *v.* to guard; to preserve; to watch for; to fasten a mortised joint by driving a pin through it.—*n.* the pin so used; a division of a county; a guard; confinement. Cf. Ward.

Waird, *n.* fate.—*v.* to predict one's fate.—*adj.* ghostly; ill-fated. Cf. Weird.

Wairder, *n.* one who mortises joints with pins.

Waird-house, *n.* the guard-house.

Wairdless, *adj.* ill-fated; unprosperous; purposeless; 'regardless.' Cf. Weirdless.

Wairin, *n.* the strip of wood forming the top of the gunwale of a boat.

Wairin', *n.* leisure. Cf. Waring.

Wairn, *v.* to warn. Cf. Warn.

Wairsh, *adj.* rather saltless; tasteless; squeamish; insipid to the mind; delicate; faint; easily affected; raw; having no fixed principles.

Wairsh-crap, *n.* the third crop from the 'outfield.'

Wairshless, *adj.* insipid.

Wairsh-like, *adj.* sickly-looking, sorry-looking.

Wairsh-looking, *adj.* 'wairsh-like.'

Wairshly, *adj.* sickly, feebly.

Wairshness, *n.* insipidity.

Wairsh-stamack'd, *adj.* squeamish.

Waister, *n.* a spendthrift.

Waistin, *n.* wasting; consumption.

Waist-leather, *n.* a leather belt for the waist.

Waistrel, *n.* a spendthrift. Cf. Wastrel.

Waistry, *n.* prodigality, waste, extravagance.

Wait, *n.* the water-course from a mill.

Wait, *v.* to happen, befall.

Wait, *v.* with *on,* to watch beside those near death.—*n.* arrangement to lie in wait.

Wait, *v.* to know; to inform; to assure. Cf. Wat.

Waite, *v.* to blame; to reproach with. Cf. Wite.

Waiter, *n.* a person charged with guarding the gates of Edinburgh; a tray.

Waiter, *adj.* water.

Waiter, *n.* a token.

Waiter-wench, *n.* a maid-servant.

Waith, *n.* cloth made into clothes; a woman's plaid.

Waith, *adj.* strong-spirited.

Waith, *v.* to stray.—*n.* what strays and is unclaimed; flotsam and jetsam; a straying.—*adj.* wandering, roaming, straying.

Waithman, *n.* a hunter.

Waive, *v.* to wield; with *up,* to raise up.

Wak, *adj.* moist; rainy. Cf. Wack.

Wa'k, *v.* to walk.

Wake, *v.* to wander.

Wake, *v.* to watch; to keep watch; to keep watch over a corpse.—*n.* the watch held over the dead between death and burial; an annual fair. Cf. Wauk.

Wake, *adj.* weak. Cf. Waik.

Wake, *v.* to full cloth. Cf. Walk.

Waken, *ppl. adj.* awake.

Waken, *v.* to become excited; to grow violent in language; to revive a dormant legal action; to watch over.

Wakening, *n.* the revival of a dormant legal action; a severe scolding.

Wakerife, Wakrife, *adj.* wakeful, sleepless; easily wakened; watchful.

Wakerifely, *adv.* wakefully.

Wakerifeness, *n.* wakefulness; sleeplessness.

Wakness, *n.* humidity.

Wal, *n.* a well.

Wal, *v.* to choose. Cf. Wale.

Wal, *v.* to weld. Cf. Wall.

Wal-a-day, *int.* alas! well-a-day!

Walaquyte, *n.* an under vest or coat. Cf. Wyliecoat.

Walaway, Walaways, *int.* an excl. of sorrow.—*n.* a lamentation; an object of pity or contempt; a name for the devil.

Walawaying, *n.* a lamentation.

Walcome, *adj.* welcome.

Wald, *v.* to weld. Cf. Wall.

Wald, *v.* to wield; to manage; to govern; to possess.

Wald, *v.* would.

Walder, *n.* one who would act, but fails to do so.

Walding-heat, *n.* the right degree of heat for welding iron; fitness for a particular object or design being carried out.

Waldritch, *adj.* unearthly. Cf. Eldritch.

Wale, *v.* to weld. Cf. Wall.

Wale, *v.* to thrash.—*n.* a weal; the verge of a mountain.

Wale, *v.* to choose, select, pick out; to woo; to look out for.—*n.* choice; choosing; the choicest; the pick; the equal, match.—*adj.* choice, select, picked.

Waled, *ppl. adj.* the best and bravest, the strongest.

Wale-wight, *adj.* chosen, strongest, best and bravest.

Walgan, Walgon, *n.* a wallet; a pouch; something large and roomy; an ill-made or dirty article of dress.—*v.* to go about ill-dressed in an idle and slovenly fashion.

Walgie, *n.* a woolsack made of leather; a calf-skin bag; a 'walgan.'

†**Walise,** *n.* a portmanteau.

Walk, *v.* to leave or be dismissed from a situation; used of a shoe: to be loose at the heel.—*n.* a procession.

Walk, *v.* to full cloth; to render hard and callous, as by hard work; used of flannel, &c.: to shrink after wetting; to beat, thrash.

Walk, *v.* to wake; to watch. Cf. Wauk.

Walken, *v.* to awake; to awaken. Cf. Waken, Wauken.

Walker, *n.* a fuller.

Walking-rod, *n.* a walking-stick.

Walkit, *ppl. adj.* used of the hand: rendered hard by toil.

Walkitness, *n.* callousness.

Walk-mill, *n.* a mill for fulling cloth.

Walk-miller, *n.* a fuller.

Walkrife, *adj.* wakeful. Cf. Wakerife.

Walkster, *n.* a fuller.

Wall, *v.* to choose. Cf. Wale.

Wall, *n.* the crust of cheese round the width.

Wall, *n.* a well; a spring of water; a whirlpool in the sea.—*v.* to well up, as water.

Wall, *v.* to weld.

Wallach, Walloch, *v.* to cry, as a peevish child; to scream; to wail; to use many circumlocutions.—*n.* a wail; a howl; a scream; a noisy blusterer; the lapwing.

Wallach, *v.* to wallow; to walk with difficulty.—*n.* the act of wallowing, and of walking with difficulty; a noisy step, thump, or fall.—*adv.* with heavy, labouring step.

Wallachie-weit, *n.* the lapwing.

Wallachin', *ppl. adj.* noisy, demonstrative in manner.

Wall-a-day, *int.* alas! well-a-day!

Wallagoo, *n.* a silly person.

Wallan, *v.* to wither, fade.—*adj.* withered, faded. Cf. Wallow.

Wallap, *n.* the lapwing. Cf. Wallop.

Wallawae, Wallyway, *int.* alas!— *n.* a lamentation. Cf. Walaway.

Wall-carses, *n.* water-cress. Cf. Wall-girse.

Walle, *n.* a choice. Cf. Wale.

Wallee, *n.* a spring in a quagmire; a spring or pool of water; the orifice of a well; a source.

†**Wallees,** *n.* saddle-bags; pockets to an under-waistcoat.

Waller, *n.* a confused crowd in quick motion.

Waller, *v.* to wallow; to roll on the ground; to toss about, as a fish on dry land. Cf. Wallow.

Wallet, *n.* a small, neatly-made person; a fondling term; a valet.

Wallflower, *n.* a children's singing and dancing game.

Wall-girse, *n.* the water-cress. Cf. Wall-carses.

Wall-girse kail, *n.* the water-cress.

Walli-drag, Walli-dreg, *n.* a feeble, ill-grown person or animal; the youngest bird in the nest; the youngest daughter of a family; a 'wastrel.' Cf. Wally-draigle, Wari-drag.

Wallies, *n.* the intestines.

†**Wallies,** *n.* saddle-bags.

Wallies, *n.* finery; toys. Cf. Wally.

Wallie-tragle, *n.* a 'walli-drag.' Cf. Wally-draigle.

Wallifou fa', *int.* 'bad luck to!' an imprecation.

Walling, *n.* a cementing, a close alliance with.

Wallink, *n.* the brooklime. Cf. Wellink.

†**Wallipend,** *v.* to undervalue; to vilipend.

Walloch, *v.* to walk with difficulty; to wallow. Cf. Wallach.

Walloch, Wallock, *n.* a Highland dance, the 'Highland Fling.'

Walloch-goul, *n.* a noisy, blustering, demonstrative person. Cf. Wallach.

Walloch-goul, *n.* a woman of slovenly appearance. Cf. Wallach.

Wallop, *n.* the lapwing.

Wallop, *v.* to dance; to gallop; to move fast, shaking the body or clothes; to flounder; to tumble over; to kick about; to move heavily; to waddle; used of the heart: to go pit-a-pat; to flutter; to dangle loosely; to chatter; to scold; to talk volubly; to dash with a swinging force.—*n.* a gallop; a dance; a quick movement agitating one's clothes; a sudden, heavy plunge; a leap; the act of dangling loose; a fluttering; a fluttering rag, a dangling tatter; a beat of the heart.—*adv.* with a lurch, plunge, or jump.

Wallop, *v.* to boil violently with a bubbling sound.

Wallop, *v.* to beat, thrash; to knock.—*n.* a blow; a thrashing.

Wallopy-week, -weep, -weet, *n.* the lapwing.

Wallow, *v.* to walk or run in a helpless, lumbering fashion.

Wallow, *v.* to fade, wither; to dwindle.

Wallowwa, Wallowae, *int.* an excl. of sorrow.—*n.* a lamentation; the devil. Cf. Walaway.

Wall-pepper, *n.* ginger.

Wall-rae, *n.* the green growth on damp walls; fresh-water algæ.

Walls of Troy, *n.* a labyrinth.

Wall-tea, *n.* a tea at which the guests sit round the walls and not at the table.

Wall-water, *n.* water that penetrates a wall, or runs down its surface.

Wall-water, *n.* water from a well.

Wall-wight, *adj.* strongest and best; stalwart. Cf. Wale-wight.

Wallwood, *adj.* wild-wood.

Wallwort, *n.* the dwarf elder.

Wally, *adj.* beautiful, excellent; fine, thriving; jolly, pleasant; ample, large.—*n.* a toy; a gewgaw; a choice ornament; good luck.

Wally, *v.* to fade. Cf. Wallow.

Wally, *n.* a small flower. Cf. Waly.

Wally, *int.* an excl. of lamentation.—*n.* a lamentation. Cf. Waly.

Wally-draig, *n.* a 'wally-draigle.'

Wally-draigle, *n.* a feeble, ill-grown person or animal; the youngest bird in a nest; the youngest daughter; a sloven; a worthless woman; a 'wastrel'; a vagrant; three sheaves set up without the 'hood-sheaf' to dry speedily. Cf. Wary-draggle.

Wally-draiglin, *adj.* weak and worthless; dirty.

Wally-dye, *n.* a toy. Cf. Wally.

Wally-dye, *int.* well-a-day! alas!

Wally-fa' ye, *int.* 'good luck to you!'

Wally-flower, *n.* wallflower.

Wally-gowdie, *n.* a term of endearment.

Wally-kwite, *n.* an under-coat. Cf. Wylie-coat.

Wally-stane, *n.* a nodule of quartz, used as a plaything by children. Cf. Wally.

Wally-waeing, *n.* a lamentation. Cf. Walawaying.

Wally-wallying, *n.* lamentation.

Wa-look, *n.* a suspicious, downcast look away from the person one addresses.

Walsh, *adj.* insipid.

Walshness, *n.* insipidity.

Walshoch, *adj.* insipid.

Walt, *n.* a welt; a crust of cheese; a weal caused by a blow; a blow; anything large of its kind.—*v.* to beat.

Waltams, *n.* straps to keep trousers from mud.

Walter, *v.* to welter; to wallow; to roll and twist about; to swell, surge; to overturn. —*n.* an upset; confusion; a change causing confusion.

Walth, *n.* wealth; plenty, abundance.

Walthy, *adj.* wealthy; plentiful, abundant.

Walt-sheep, *n.* a fallen sheep.

Waly, *n.* a small flower.

Waly, *adj.* goodly; beautiful; jolly. Cf. Wally.

Waly, *int.* an excl. of woe.—*n.* a lamentation.

Waly-coat, *n.* an under-coat. Cf. Wylie-coat.

Waly-draigle, *n.* the youngest bird in a nest. Cf. Wally-draigle.

Waly-draiglin, *adj.* dirty.

Waly sprig, *n.* a small flower, a daisy.

Wamb, *n.* the womb; the belly. Cf. Wame.

Wamble, *v.* used of the intestines: to rumble, roll, or stir uneasily; to quiver, shake, undulate; to turn over and over; to revolve; to wriggle, writhe; to twist about the body; to stagger; to walk clumsily or unsteadily; to wallow.—*n.* an undulating motion; a wriggle; the movement of the stomach in digesting food.—*adv.* with an undulating or writhing motion.

Wamblin, *n.* a puny child with a big belly; a weak, restless child. Cf. Wamelin.

Wambly, *adj.* insecure, shaky, unsteady.

Wame, *n.* the belly; the stomach; the womb; a hollow; room, capacity of holding.—*v.* to fill the belly.

Wamefu', *n.* a bellyful.

Wame-gird, *n.* a horse's belly-band.

Wame-ill, *n.* stomach-ache.

Wamel, Wamle, *v.* to 'wamble.'

Wamelin, Wamlin, *n.* a big-bellied, puny child. Cf. Wamflin.

Wame-tow, *n.* a horse's belly-band.

Wamfil, *adj.* weak; useless; helpless; limp.

Wamfle, *v.* to flap; to flutter; to sully.

Wamflet, *n.* the water of a mill-stream after passing the mill. Cf. Waefleed.

Wamflin, *n.* a big-bellied, puny child; a weak, restless child.

Wamie, *adj.* big-bellied; corpulent.

Wamil, *v.* to 'wamble.'

Waminess, *n.* corpulence.

Wammle, *v.* to roll; to undulate. Cf. Wamble.

Wammlin, *n.* a restless child.

Wampasin, *n.* a winding street or lane.

Wampish, Wampes, *v.* to fluctuate; to move backwards and forwards; to move like an eel or adder; to brandish, flourish; to make curvilinear dashes, like a large fish in the water.—*n.* the motion of an adder.

Wample, Wamphle, *v.* to wriggle; to writhe; to intertwine; to twist; to wind, as a stream.—*n.* an undulating motion; a wriggling motion, like that of an eel.—*adj.* slender, easily bent. Cf. Wimple.

Wampler, *n.* a rake, a wencher.

Wampuz, *v.* to toss about in a threatening, boasting manner; to fluctuate; to go backwards and forwards. Cf. Wampish.

Wan, *adj.* used of water: black, gloomy.

Wan, *v. pret.* dwelt. Cf. Won.

Wan, *adj.* not fully round or plump.

Wan, *n.* hope; a prospect of success; a liking for anything.

Wan, *n.* a direction.—*adv.* in the direction of.

Wan', *n.* a wand; a fishing-rod. Cf. Wand.

Wan, *v. pret.* and *ppl.* won.

Wan, *v. pret.* wound.

Wan, *pref.* a negative prefix corresponding to 'un.'

Wancanny, *adj.* 'uncanny'; unlucky. Cf. Canny.

Wanchance, *n.* a mishap; misfortune.

Wanchancy, *adj.* unlucky; boding evil; wicked; dangerous.

Wan-cheekit, *adj.* having thin cheeks.

Wancheerie, *adj.* cheerless; sad.

Wancouth, *adj.* uncouth; strange.

Wand, *n.* a switch; a stick; a willow wand; wicker; a fishing-rod; a sheriff-officer's rod, the symbol of his authority.—*adj.* made of willow; wicker.

Wand, *v. pret.* wound.

Wand-bed, *n.* a wicker-bed.

Wand-birn, *n.* a straight burn on the face of a sheep.

Wand-chair, *n.* a wicker-chair.

Wandeedy, *adj.* mischievous, 'ill-deedy.'

Wander, *v.* to travel begging, hawking, &c.; to lose one's self, or one's way; to confuse, perplex.—*n.* confusion.

Wandered, *ppl. adj.* strayed; lost; confused.

Wanderer, *n.* a fugitive Covenanter.

Wandering-folks, *n.* beggars; hawkers; vagrants.

Wandering-sailor, *n.* the ivy-leaved toad-flax.

Wandocht, Wandough, Wandout, *adj.* weak; puny; silly; contemptible.—*n.* a weak, puny creature; a silly and inactive person; a worthless person.

Wand of peace, *n.* the wand of an officer of justice, with which he touched a rebel to make him prisoner.

Wane, *n.* a dwelling; a habitation.

Wane, *n.* a child. Cf. Wean.

Wanearthly, Wanerthly, *adj.* unearthly; supernatural; ghostly.

Wanease, Waneis, *n.* uneasiness; vexation. —*v.* to put one's self about.

Wan'er, *v.* to wander. Cf. Wander.

Wanfortune, *n.* misfortune.

Wanfortunate, *adj.* unfortunate.

Wangle, *v.* to wag; to dangle.

Wangrace, Wangrease, *n.* oatmeal gruel, with a little butter and honey.

Wangrace, *n.* wickedness; lack of grace; a blackguard, scamp.

Wangracefu', *adj.* wicked; graceless; ungraceful.

Wangracie, *adj.* blackguardly; ill-behaved.

Wanhap, *n.* misfortune; a mishap.

Wanhappie, *adj.* unlucky, unfortunate.

Wanhelt, *n.* ill-health, sickness.

Wanhope, *n.* despair.

Wanion, *n.* bad luck, mischief; used as an imprecation.

Wanjoy, *n.* misery, sorrow.

Wankill, *adj.* unstable.

Wankish, *v.* to twist, entwine.

Wanlas, *n.* a surprise.

Wanle, *adj.* agile, lithe, nimble; strong, healthy.

Wanless, *adj.* hopeless. Cf. Wan.

Wanlie, *adj.* auspicious, hopeful; agreeable; comfortable.

Wanliesum, *adj.* unlovely.

Wanlit, *adj.* unlit, darkened.

Wanluck, *n.* misfortune; bad luck.

Wannel, Wannle, *adj.* agile; robust. Cf. Wanle.

Wannel, *v.* to stagger, be unsteady.

Wanner, *v.* to wander.

Wanny, *adj.* pale, ill-looking.

Wanown't, *adj.* unclaimed; not acknowledged.

Wanreck, *n.* mischance; ruin.

Wanrest, *n.* unrest, inquietude; the cause of inquietude; the pendulum of a clock.

Wanrestfu', *adj.* restless.

Wanrestie, *adj.* restless.

Wanruly, *adj.* unruly.

Wansday, *n.* Wednesday.

Wanshaiken, *adj.* deformed.

Wansonsy, *adj.* mischievous; unlucky,

Want, *n.* a mental defect, a weakness of intellect; a search for anything missing.—*v.* with *for,* to need; to do without; to search, seek; to ask; to seek a wife; to be unmarried; to deserve.

Wanter, *n.* a bachelor; a widower; one seeking a wife.

Wanthrift, *n.* unthrift.

Wanthriven, *adj.* not thriving; stunted; in a state of decline.

Wantin', *ppl. adj.* deficient in intellect.—*prep.* without.

Wanton, *n.* a girth; a horse's belly-band.

Wanton-meat, *n.* an entertainment of spirits, sweetmeats, &c., given to those in a house at the birth of a child. Cf. Blithemeat.

Wanton-yeuk, *n.* a disease of horses of the nature of the itch.

Wanty, *n.* a horse's belly-band.

Wanuse, *n.* a misuse, abuse, waste.

Wanut, *n.* a walnut.

Wanweird, *n.* misfortune, ill-luck, ill-fate.

Wanwordy, *adj.* unworthy, worthless.

Wanworth, Wanwuth, *adj.* unworthy; useless, valueless.—*n.* an undervalue; a very low price; a cheap bargain; anything worthless or of little value, a mere nothing; a worthless person.

Wanwuth, *n.* a surprise.

Wanyoch, *adj.* pale, wan.

Wap, *v.* to wrap, fold up; to make a loose bundle; to bind with thread, twine, &c.; to splice with cord; to swaddle.—*n.* a wrappage; a roll or tie; a thread for tying; cord for splicing; turns of string twisted round a rope or other string; a bundle of straw.

Wap, *v.* to strut; to walk haughtily, or with a bustling air.—*n.* a vain, bustling style of walking; vain, showy, vulgar conduct; a vain person, one with showy manners, with a vain, silly manner.

Wap, *v.* to strike smartly; to strike with a swing; to flog, thrash; to thresh with a flail; to flap; to seize quickly; to thrust; to 'whip'; to throw; to cast; to dash violently; to pitch; to excel, surpass; to riot; to quarrel; to wrestle.—*n.* a sweeping or swinging movement; a stroke of an oar; a knock; a smart stroke; the sound of a smart blow; a disturbance; a riot; a round, fall, or throw in wrestling; in *pl.* a large amount, plenty,—*adv.* with a flop; violently. Cf. Whap.

Wapenshaw, Wapinschaw, *n.* an exhibition of arms formerly made at certain times in every district; a competition in rifle-shooting on a large scale.

Wapin, *n.* a loose dress worn by a fisherman at work.

Wa-pit, *v.* to put away. Cf. Wayput.

Wappan, Wapping, *ppl. adj.* exceptionally large or fine; strapping, huge, stout; used of persons: vain, showy, vulgar.

Wapper, *n.* anything exceptionally large or fine; a great falsehood; a big, fat, or strapping person.

Wapper, *n.* a showy, vain, vulgar person; a beau; a belle.

Wappin', *n.* a flapping of wings.

Wapping, *n.* a fisherman's loose working-dress. Cf. Wapin.

Wappon, *n.* a weapon.

Wappy, *adj.* neat, natty; dressing fashionably; careful as to dress and appearance.

War, *v.* were.

War, *n.* goods, stuff. Cf. Ware.

War, *v.* to defend; to lead, herd. Cf. Wear.

War, *adj.* cautious, wary; aware, conscious.

War, *adj.* worse.—*adv.* the worse.—*n.* a defeat; something rather bad.—*v.* to put to the worse; to overcome; to excel; to get the better of; to requite for an injury; to injure.

Warba-blade, *n.* the greater plantain.

Warbie, Warback, *n.* a maggot bred in the backs of cattle; a warble.

Warble, *n.* a bump, a swelling; a lean, scraggy person.

Warble, *v.* to play the quicker measures of a piece of bagpipe-music in which there are many grace-notes.

Warble, *v.* to swing; to reel; to wriggle; to worm one's way.

Warbler, *n.* a combination of five or more grace-notes in a piece of bagpipe-music.

War-brook, *n.* a large heap of seaweed cast ashore.

Ward, *v.* to award, assign.—*n.* an award; what one thoroughly deserves.

Ward, *v.* to watch for; to keep off, guard against; to confine; to go to prison; to fasten a mortised joint by driving a pin through it.—*n.* a division of a county; a piece of pasture; land enclosed on all sides for young animals; a beacon-hill, a signal-hill; confinement.

Ward, *n.* the world.

Ward and warsel, *n.* security; a pledge.

Warden, *n.* a particular kind of pear. Cf. Wash-warden.

Ward-fire, *n.* a beacon-fire.

Ward-hill, *n.* a beacon-hill.

Wardle, *n.* the world; in *pl.* times.

Wardle's-make, *n.* an earthly mate or spouse.

Wardle's winner, *n.* a world's wonder, in a bad sense.

Wardly, *adj.* worldly.

Wardly-wary, *adj.* worldly-wise.

†**Wardroper,** *n.* a wardrobe-woman.

Ware, *ppl.* worn.

Ware, *n.* stuff; rhymes; money for spending. —*v.* to spend; to bestow upon; to squander; to wager.

Ware, *v.* to manure with seaweed.

Ware, *n.* the spring. Cf. Voar.

Ware, *adj.* worse. Cf. War.

Ware, *adj.* wary. Cf. War.

Ware, *n.* wire.

Ware-bear, *n.* barley manured with seaweed.

Wareblade, *n.* the blade of seaweed.

Ware-caist, *n.* a heap of seaweed.

Ware-cock, *n.* the blackcock.

Ware-strand, *n.* the part of the beach on to which the seaweed is washed.

Ware-time, *n.* spring; the early time of youth.

Warf, *n.* a puny, contemptible creature; a dwarfish person; a fairy. Cf. Urf.

War-far'd, -faured, *adj.* worse-looking.

War-gang, *n.* a pennon.

War-hawk, *int.* beware! take care!

Waridrag, *n.* the youngest of a brood; a very young child. Cf. Wary-draggle.

Waring, *n.* leisure. Cf. Wairin.

†**Warison,** *n.* the note of assault.

Wark, *v.* to ache; to throb.

Wark, *n.* work; a fuss; a show of affection; a structure, 'works'; a religious revival.— *v.* to knit; to net; used of material, &c.: to lend itself easily to work; of a pipe: to draw; to manage, control; to struggle convulsively; to purge; to ferment; to cause pain; to retaliate; to sprain.

Wark-a-day, *adj.* working, everyday.

Wark-claes, *n.* working-clothes.

Wark-day, *n.* a work-day; a week-day.

Wark-fit, *adj.* fit for work.

Wark-folk, *n.* working-people, labourers.

Wark-leem, -loom, -lume, *n.* a tool, implement.

Warkless, *adj.* unable to work.

Wark-like, *adj.* industrious.

Wark-little, *adj.* lazy.

Warkly, *adj.* given to work; industrious.

Wark-machine, *n.* any machine or contrivance.

Warkman, *n.* a jobber; a porter; an Aberdeen 'shore-porter.'

Warkrife, *adj.* industrious; fond of work; hard-working.

Wark-stot, *n.* a work-ox, an ox used for ploughing.

Wark-worn, *adj.* toil-worn.

Warl, *v.* to whirl.

Warl, Warld, *n.* the world; worldly goods; a large number.

Warldlie, *adj.* worldly; parsimonious.

Warld-like, *adj.* like the rest of the world; not unnatural.

Warld's gear, *n.* worldly substance; with a negative, nothing at all.

Warld's-make, *n.* an earthly mate or spouse.

Warld's waster, *n.* a spendthrift.

Warld's worm, *n.* a miser, niggard.

Warld's wunner, *n.* a spectacle for all beholders; a person of notorious or surprising conduct.

Warl-gear, *n.* worldly substance.

Warlin, *n.* a worldling.

Warlock, Warlick, *n.* a wizard.

Warlock-breef, *n.* enchantment; a wizard's spell.

Warlock-craigie, *n.* a wizards' rock. Cf. Warlock-knowe.

Warlock-fecket, *n.* a magic jacket woven from the skins of water-snakes at a certain period of a March moon.

Warlockin, *n.* a mischievous imp; an imp of darkness.

Warlock-knowe, *n.* a hill where wizards were thought to meet.

Warlockry, *n.* wizardry; magical skill.

Warly, *adj.* worldly; parsimonious. Cf. Warldlie.

Warm, *n.* the act of warming.—*v.* to thrash.

Warm-wise, *adj.* rather warm, sultry.

Warn, *v.* to cite, summon; to invite verbally to a meeting, funeral, &c.; to give verbal intimation; used of a clock: to click before striking.

Warn, *v.* to warrant. Cf. Warran.

Warna, *v. neg.* were not.

Warney, *n.* a boys' game.

Warniement, *n.* warning, notice.

Warning, *n.* the clicking sound of a clock before striking; a death-omen, a portent; a notice; a citation; a verbal invitation to attend a funeral, &c.

Warnish, Warnice, Warnis, *v.* to warn.

Warnishment, *n.* warning.

Warnisin, *n.* warning.

Warp, *v.* to make an embankment with piles and brushwood; used of bees: to take flight; to make a bleating sound.—*n.* the number four, used by fishwives in counting oysters; a smart blow; a stroke of the oar in rowing.

Warp and waft, *n.* every bit.—*adv.* completely.

Warping-dinner, *n.* a dinner or food given to a weaver by those who brought their own yarn to his handloom.

Warping-pins, *n.* the machine in which threads are arranged into warps.

Warping-wheel, *n.* a machine for arranging threads into warps.

Warple, Warpel, *v.* to entangle; to intertwine; to twist or wind round; to wriggle; to twist the limbs about in the tumbling and tossing of children; to confuse or be confused in any business; to struggle.

Warr, *adj.* worse. Cf. Waur.

Warrach, Warrack, *n.* a knotted stick; a stubborn, ill-tempered person; a stunted, ill-grown person; a puny child; a worthless fellow.—*v.* to scold; to vituperate; to blackguard.

Warrachie, *adj.* rough and knotty, gnarled, like the trunk of a tree.

Warran, Warrand, *v.* to warrant; to assure; to 'be bound' or 'go bail.'—*n.* a security; a surety.

†Warrandice, Warrandiss, *n.* a surety; security for the fulfilment of a bargain, or that goods are as they are represented; a warranty; a legal warrant.

Warrer, *adj.* more wary.

Warricoe, *n.* a bugbear. Cf. Worricow.

Warroch, *v.* to wallow; to struggle in mud.

Warroch, *n.* a knotted stick. Cf. Warrach.

Warry, *int.* take heed! look out!—*adj.* wary, heedful.

Warry, *adj.* pertaining to seaweed.

Warse, *adj.* worse. Cf. Waur.

Warsh, Warsche, *adj.* tasteless. Cf. Wairsh.

Warsle, Warstle, Warsal, Warsel, Warsell, *v.* to wrestle; to strive; to struggle; to grapple with difficulties; used of time: to pass bringing toil and sorrow; with *through*, to come out successful, overcome difficulties, &c.—*n.* a wrestle; a struggle; a tussle; a grapple with a difficulty.

Warsler, *n.* a wrestler.

Warst, *adj.* worst.

Warstan, *adj.* worst.

Warstling-herrings, *n.* 'herrings all alive!' an Edinburgh fishwife's cry.

Wart, *v.* with *pron.* were it.

Wart, *n.* a beacon-hill; an elevated signalling-station; the beacon kindled on a 'wart.' Cf. Ward.

Warth, *n.* the apparition of a living person, a 'wraith.' Cf. Wraith.

Warthill, *n.* a beacon-hill. Cf. Wardhill.

Wart nor, *v.* with *pron.* and *neg.* had it not been for; were it not for.

Wartweil, *n.* the skin at the base of the finger-nail when loose or fretted.

Warwoof, Warwooph, *n.* a puny child; an undergrown person; a 'were-wolf.'

Wary, *int.* look out! Cf. Warry.

Wary-draggle, *n.* a puny hog or young sheep; a feeble, worn-out person or animal; the youngest of a brood; a young child. Cf. Wally-draigle.

Wa's, *n.* ways; in *phr.* 'come your wa's,' come away.

Wash, *n.* liquid mud; weak, washy drink; stale urine formerly used for washing clothes.

Wash-bine, -boyne, *n.* a wash-tub.

Washen, *ppl. adj.* washed.

Washer, *n.* a washerwoman.

Washer-wife, *n.* a washerwoman, laundress.

Washing-boyne, -boin, *n.* a wash-tub.

Washing-say, *n.* a wash-tub.

Wash-mug, *n.* a chamber-pot.

Wash-tub, *n.* a large tub or cask for storing urine for washing clothes. Cf. Maister-can.

Wash up, *n.* a ducking.

Wash-warden, *n.* a coarse, sour winter pear. Cf. Worry-carl.

Wash words, *v.* to converse.

Washy-waulker, *n.* a cloth-fuller.

Wasie, *adj.* sagacious; of quick apprehension; gay, playful, lively.

Wasp-bike, -bink. *n.* a wasps' nest.

Wasper, *n.* a fish-spear; a 'leister.' Cf. Wawsper.

Waspet, *ppl. adj.* thin about the loins.

Wassel, *n.* oat-cake baked with yeast. Cf. Westel.

Wassel, *adv.* westwards. Cf. Wessel.

Wassie, *n.* a horse-collar. Cf. Waese.

Wassock, *n.* a pad worn by milkmaids to relieve the pressure of their pails on their heads; a kind of bunch put on a boring 'jumper' to prevent the water used in boring from leaping up into the quarrier's eyes. Cf. Waese.

Wast, *adj.* west.

Wastage, *n.* a waste; a place of desolation.

Wast-bye, *adv.* westward.

Wastcoat, *n.* a waistcoat.

Waste, *adj.* wasted.—*n.* disused workings in a coal-mine; coal-mining refuse; remnants of weft, broken threads, &c., in weaving; consumption, phthisis.

Waste-heart, *int* alas for you! Cf. Wae's-heart.

Wastel, Wastel-bread, *n.* thin oat-cake baked with yeast.

Wastell, *n.* in *phr.* 'Willy Wastell,' a children's rhyming game.

Wasteness, *n.* waste.

Waster, *n.* an extravagant person; an idler; an imperfection in the wick of a candle causing guttering.—*v.* to waste; to spend needlessly.

Waster, *n.* a fish-spear; a 'leister.' Cf. Wawsper.

Waster, *adj.* western. — *v.* to go or drift westwards.

Wasterfu', *adj.* wasteful; extravagant; lavish.

Wasterfully, *adv.* extravagantly; wastefully.

Wasterfulness, *n.* extravagance; lavishness.

Wasterie, *n.* waste; wastefulness.

Wasterous, *adj.* wasteful.

Wasting, *n.* consumption, a decline.

Wastland, *adj.* western.—*n.* the west country. Cf. Westland.

Wastle, *adv.* westward. Cf. Wessel.

Wastlin, *adj.* western.—*n.* the west country.

Wastlins, *adv.* westward.

Wast-ower, *adv.* westward.

Wastrel, Wastril, *n.* a spendthrift; a 'ne'er-do-weel'; a vagrant; a thin, unhealthy-looking person.—*adj.* vagabond; wasteful; thin, wasted.

Wastroy, Wastrie, *n.* a waste; extravagance; wastefulness.

Wastrife, *adj.* extravagant; wasteful. — *n.* extravagance; wastefulness.

Wat, *n.* an outer garment.

Wat, *v.* to know; to inform; to assure; to be sensible of.

Wat, *v.* to pledge, promise. Cf. Wad.

Wat, *n.* a welt. Cf. Waat.

Wat, *adj.* wet; given to intemperance in drink.—*n.* moisture. Cf. Wet.

Wa'taking, *n.* carrying off by theft or violence.

Watch, *n.* a watch-dog; an outpost; a hill of a certain height.

Watch-glass, *n.* an hour-glass.

Watch-house, *n.* a police-station.

Watchie, *n.* a watchmaker.

Watch-light, *n.* a rush-light.

Watch-mail, *n.* a duty imposed for maintaining a garrison.

Watchman, *n.* the uppermost grain in a stalk of corn.

Watch-money, *n.* blackmail.

Watchword, *n.* a note of warning; a hint to be on one's guard.

Wate, *n.* a mill-race. Cf. Wait.

Wate, *v.* to know. Cf. Wat.

Water, Watter, *n.* a river, a good-sized stream; a lake; a pool in a river; a wave;

a heavy sea ; a disease of sheep, 'shell-sickness'; the banks of a river ; the district bordering a river.—*v.* to wash down any food ; used of the mouth : to make it water.

Water-berry, *n.* water-gruel.

Water-betony, *n.* the water-figwort.

Water-blackbird, *n.* the dipper.

Water-blinks, *n.* the water-chickweed.

Water-brash, *n.* watery acid eructations.

Water-brod, *n.* a bench or board on which water-pails rest.

Water-broo, *n.* water-gruel.

Water-brose, *n.* oatmeal stirred into boiling water until the mixture is thick and rather stiff.

Water-burn, *n.* the phosphorescence of the sea.

Water-calf, *n.* the placenta of a cow.

Water-corn, *n.* the grain paid by farmers for the maintenance of the 'dams' and races of the mills to which they are astricted.

Water-cow, *n.* a water-sprite inhabiting a lake.

Water-cow, *n.* a water-beetle.

Water-craw, *n.* the water-ousel or dipper ; the coot ; the great northern diver.

Water-custom, *n.* the custom of going to a well near midnight of 31st Dec. to draw the first water of the new year, a custom supposed to bring good luck for the year.

Water-deevil, *n.* a water-sprite, a 'kelpie.'

Water-dog, *n.* the water-rat.

Water-draucht, *n.* the outlet of water from a loch.

Water-droger, *n.* the last-born of a litter.

Water-dyke, *n.* a wall or embankment to keep a river or stream in flood from over-flowing the adjoining lands.

Water-eagle, *n.* the osprey.

Water-elder, *n.* the guelder-rose.

Waterfall, *n.* a watershed.

Waterfast, *adj.* water-tight ; capable of re-sisting the force of rain.

Water-fishings, *n.* river-fishings.

Water-fit, *n.* the mouth of a river ; a village or hamlet at the mouth of a river or stream.

Water-fur, *n.* a furrow made to drain off surface-water.—*v.* to form furrows in ploughed land for draining off the water.

Water-gang, *n.* a mill-race ; a water-course ; a right to draw water along a neighbour's ground to water one's own.

Water-gate, *n.* a road leading to a watering-place ; the act of voiding urine ; an advan-tage over a man.

Water-gaw, *n.* the fragment of a rainbow appearing in the horizon ; seen in the north or east, a sign of bad weather.

Water-gled, *n.* a revenue-officer, a preventive-officer.

Water-hole, *n.* a pond.

Water-horse, *n.* a water-goblin, a 'kelpie.'

Water-ill, *n.* a disease of cows affecting their water.

Watering, *n.* drink for a horse.

Watering-pan, *n.* a watering-pot.

Water-kail, *n.* broth made without meat, and only with vegetables.

Water-kelpie, *n.* a mischievous water-sprite, a river-horse.

Water-kit, *n.* a wooden bucket for holding water, narrower at top than at bottom, and having a wooden handle fixed across the top.

Water-kyle, *n.* meadow-land possessed by the tenants of an estate in common, or by rotation.

Water-lamp, *n.* marine phosphorescence.

Water-laverock, *n.* the common sandpiper.

Waterloo, *v.* to overcome ; to overcome by strong drink.

Water-mouse, *n.* a water-rat.

Water-mouth, -mow, *n.* the mouth of a river.

Water-neb, *n.* the mouth of a river.

Water-of-Ayr stone, *n.* a stone highly valued for hones and boys' marbles.

Water-peggie, *n.* the water-ousel or dipper.

Water-purpie, -purple, *n.* the common brook-lime.

Water-pyet, *n.* the water-ousel or dipper.

Water-run, *n.* a water-spout or gutter under the eaves of a house.

Water-saps, *n.* invalids' food.

Water-sapwort, *n.* the hemlock dropwort.

Waterside, *n.* a river-bank.

Water-skater, *n.* an insect that glides, or skates, or darts along the surface of stag-nant pools.

Water-slain-moss, *n.* peat-earth carried off by water and then deposited.

Water-stane, *n.* a pebble from a brook.

Water-stoup, *n.* a 'water-kit'; the common periwinkle, from its resemblance to a pitcher.

Water-table, *n.* the ditch or gutter on each side of a road for carrying off water.

Water-tabling, *n.* the work of making or cleaning 'water-tables.'

Water-tath, *n.* luxuriant grass owing to excess of moisture.

Water-thraw, *n.* 'water-brash.'

Water-tiger, *n.* a swimming water-beetle.

Water-twist, *n.* a particular kind of yarn.

Water-wader, *n.* a home-made candle of the worst kind.

Water-wag, -waggie, *n.* the wagtail.

Water-wan, *n.* part of a water-mill, the axle.

Water-water, *n.* water from a stream, as con-trasted with water from a well.

Water-weak, -weik, *n.* a frail, delicate person.

Water-weikit, *adj.* frail, delicate.

Water-wraith, -waith, *n.* a water-sprite.

Watery, *n.* the pied wagtail.

Watery-braxy, *n.* inflammation of a sheep's bladder through over-distention.

Watery-nebbit, -nibbit, *adj.* of a pale and sickly countenance ; having a watery nose.

Watery-pleeps, *n.* the common sandpiper ; the redshank.

Watery-pox, *n.* the chicken-pox.

Watery-wagtail, *n.* the yellow wagtail.

Wat-finger, *n.* little effort.

Wath, *n.* a ford.

Wather, *n.* weather.

Wat-lookin', *adj.* threatening rain.

Watreck, *int.* an excl. of surprise or pity.

Watshod, *adj.* used of the eyes : brimful of tears.

Watsunday, *n.* Whitsunday term.

Watten, *v.* to wet.

Watter-vraith, *n.* a water-sprite.

Wattie, *n.* a blow.

Wattin, *n.* a wetting.

Wattle, *n.* a twig ; a switch ; a billet of wood ; an entanglement of a line, thread, or twine ; in *pl.* the rods laid on the framework of a roof to lay the thatch on.—*v.* to strike with a switch, cane, &c. repeatedly.

Watty, *n.* an eel ; the pied wagtail ; the white-throat.

Wauble, *v.* to wobble ; to swing ; to reel ; to undulate ; to walk unsteadily from weakness.—*n.* the act of so walking ; weak, watery food or drink.—*adj.* slender, easily shaken ; of a weak, watery flavour.—*adv.* tremulously ; with weak, faltering steps.

Wauch, *adj.* moist, clammy. Cf. Wack.

Wauch, *adj.* musty, stale ; faint ; wan ; worthless.—*n.* the taste or smell of anything stale or decomposing. Cf. Waugh.

Wauch, *v.* to drink deeply.—*n.* a big drink. Cf. Waught.

Wauch, Wauck, *v.* to full cloth. Cf. Walk.

Wauchie, *adj.* clammy.

Wauchie, *adj.* of a sallow and greasy face ; feeble, weak.

Wauchle, Wauchile, *v.* to move backwards and forwards ; to waggle ; to waddle ; to stagger ; to walk as fatigued ; to fatigue greatly ; to struggle, strive with difficulties ; to puzzle.—*n.* an unsteady movement ; a struggle ; a difficulty ; weary work.

Waucht, *v.* to quaff.—*n.* a copious draught. Cf. Waught.

Waucht, *n.* weight.

Wauchty, *adj.* weighty ; corpulent ; valiant. Cf. Wechty.

Waud, *n.* black-lead ; a black-lead pencil. Cf. Wadd.

Waud, *v.* to wade.

Wauf, *v.* to wave ; to flap ; to scare or drive away birds or beasts. Cf. Waff.

Wauf, *adj.* strayed ; solitary ; vagabond. Cf. Waff.

Waufish, *adj.* hardly respectable. Cf. Waffish.

Waufle, *v.* to waver in the air, as snow, chaff, or any light substance.—*n.* a slight fall of snow.

Wauge, Wauje, *v.* used with *nieve :* to shake one's fist at a person.

Waugh, *v.* to drink deeply. Cf. Waught.

Waugh, *adj.* insipid ; nauseous to taste or smell ; musty ; smelling of damp ; wan and pale ; sallow and greasy ; debased, worthless.

Waugh, Waughie, *adj.* moist, damp ; clammy. Cf. Wack, Wauchie.

Waughle, *v.* to waggle ; to puzzle. Cf. Wauchle.

Waughorn, *n.* the king of liars ; the devil. Cf. Waghorn.

Waught, *v.* to drink deeply ; to quaff.—*n.* a copious draught ; a big drink.

Waught, *n.* weight.

Waughy, *adj.* feeling faint or sick ; wan, sallow. Cf. Wauchie.

Wauk, *v.* to wake ; to watch ; to watch over. Cf. Wake.

Wauk, *v.* to walk. Cf. Walk.

Wauk, *adj.* moist, damp. Cf. Waugh.

Wauk, Wauck, *v.* to full cloth ; to render hard or callous ; to beat, to thrash ; used of cloth, &c. : to shrink after wetting. Cf. Walk.

Wauken, *v.* to awake ; to become animated ; to use violent language ; to awaken ; to revive a dormant legal process ; to watch over. Cf. Waken.

Wauken, *ppl. adj.* awake ; disinclined for sleep.

Wauken, *v.* to chastise.

Waukening, *n.* the act of awaking, or of awakening ; outrageous scolding.

Wauker, *n.* a watcher ; one who watches clothes during the night.

Wauker, *n.* a fuller.

Waukerife, *adj.* wakeful. Cf. Wakerife.

Waukfere, *adj.* able to go about. Cf. Fere.

Wauking, Waukan, *n.* the act of watching ; the night-watch kept over a corpse unburied, or of one buried in resurrectionist times, or over clothes, or over the 'fauld' or sheepfold.

Waukit, *ppl. adj.* used of the hands : hardened, rendered callous by hard work.

Waukitness, *n.* callousness of skin.

Waukmill, *n.* a fulling-mill.

Waukmiller, *n.* a fuller.

Waukrife, *adj.* wakeful.

Waukster, *n.* a fuller.

Waul, *v.* to roll the eyes ; to gaze wildly ; to gaze drowsily.

Waul, *adj.* nimble, agile.

Waul, *int.* an excl. of sorrow.

Waul, *n.* a well.

Waul, *v.* to weld; to comply; to consent. Cf. **Wall.**

Waul, Waule, *v.* to choose, to pick out.—*n.* choice; 'the pick.' Cf. **Wale.**

Wauld, *v.* to wield; to possess; to manage. Cf. **Wield.**

Wauld, *n.* the plain open country, without wood.

Waulie, *adj.* agile. Cf. **Waul.**

Waulie, *adj.* jolly. Cf. **Waly.**

Wauliesum, *adj.* causing sorrow.

Wauling-heat, *n.* the proper temperature for welding iron. Cf. **Walling-heat.**

Waulk, *v.* to full cloth. Cf. **Wauk.**

Waulking-wicker, *n.* a basket used in fulling cloth.

Waumish, *adj.* uneasy, 'all-overish,' squeamish.

Waumle, *v.* to rumble; to roll; to move awkwardly. Cf. **Wamble.**

Waund, *n.* a fishing-rod. Cf. **Wand.**

Wauner, *v.* to wander.

Waup, *v.* to strike sharply; to flog. Cf. **Wap.**

Waup, *n.* an outcry.

Waur, *v.* to defeat; to beat off; to ward off.

Waur, *n.* the spring. Cf. **Voar.**

Waur, Waure, *adj.* wary, cautious; aware. Cf. **War.**

Waur, *adj.* worse.—*n.* in *phr.* 'ten waurs,' a great misfortune, a great pity. Cf. **War.**

Waur, *n.* goods.—*v.* to spend money. Cf. **Ware.**

Waurn, *v.* to warrant. Cf. **Warran.**

Waurst, *adj.* worst.

Wausie, *adj.* weary, tired and sore; bored.

Wausper, *n.* a fish-spear, a 'leister.' Cf. **Wawsper.**

Waut, *n.* a border, a selvedge; a welt. Cf. **Walt.**

Wauw, *v.* to caterwaul. Cf. **Waw.**

Wave, *v.* to signal by a wave of the hand.

Wavel, *v.* to move backwards and forwards; to stagger; to wave.

Wavel, *n.* a weevil.

Wavelock, *n.* an implement for twisting ropes of hay, straw, &c.

Waver, *v.* to be slightly delirious.

Wavy, *adj.* voyaging by sea.

Waw, *n.* a wall.

Waw, *int.* an excl. of sorrow; of pleasure, admiration. Cf. **Wow.**

Waw, *int.* well! why! pshaw! an excl. of expostulation, contempt, or encouragement.

Waw, *v.* to mew as a cat, caterwaul; to wail.—*n.* the mew of a cat; the wail of an infant.

Wawf, *adj.* stray; solitary; disreputable. Cf. **Waff.**

Wawl, *v.* to look wildly; to roll the eyes. Cf. **Waul.**

Wawl, *v.* to howl; to whine; to mew as a cat.

Waws, *n.* used of cheese: the crust round the width. Cf. **Wall.**

Wawsper, *n.* a fish-spear; a 'leister.'

Waxen-, Wax-kernel, *n.* a glandular swelling in the neck.

Way, *n.* a state of anxiety, anger, perturbation, &c.; the direction of; a tradition, saw; cause, reason; in *phr.* 'to make way of one's self,' to commit suicide.—*adv.* away. Cf. **Wa'.**

Way, *int.* a call to a horse to stop.

Way-bread, *n.* the greater plantain.

Way-burn-leaf, *n.* the greater plantain.

Way-gang, *n.* departure; death; a leave-taking, or farewell social meeting; a flavour; a disagreeable taste; a whiff; a whisper; a faint sound; the channel of water running from a mill. Cf. **Wa-gäen.**

Way-gang-crop, *n.* the last crop belonging to a tenant before he leaves his farm.

Way-ganging, Way-going, *n.* a 'way-gang.' —*adj.* departing, outgoing.

Way-ganging-crop, *n.* 'way-gang-crop.'

Waygate, Wayget, *n.* room, space; the tail-race of a mill; progress, speed.

Waygaun, *adj.* outgoing.—*n.* a departure; death.

Waygoe, *n.* a place where a body of water breaks out.

Way-kenning, *n.* the knowledge of one's way from a place.

Waylay, *v.* to hide; to lay aside.

Wayleave, *n.* right of way, privilege of passage.

Waylook, *n.* the look of one who does not look at the person to whom he is speaking. Cf. **Wa-look.**

Wayput, *v.* to put away; to make away with.

Wayputting, *n.* execution; murder; burial.

Waywart, *adj.* preparatory, preliminary; warning.

Waz, *n.* a small bundle of straw, &c.; a bulky necktie; a straw collar for oxen. Cf. **Waese.**

Wazban, *n.* a waistband.

Wazie, *adj.* sagacious; sensible; of quick apprehension. Cf. **Wasie.**

Wazzan, *n.* the windpipe, the weasand.

We, *adj.* small. Cf. **Wee.**

Weagh, *v.* to waggle.

Weak, *v.* to weaken. Cf. **Waik.**

Wĕak, *v.* to squeak; to whine, whimper; to scream; to utter loud cries, as an animal; to whistle at intervals.—*n.* a squeak; a chirp; a little, thin person with a squeaky voice. Cf. **Queak.**

Weal, *v.* to choose.—*n.* 'the pick.' Cf. Wale.

Wealth, *n.* abundance ; enough. Cf. Walth.

Wealth and worle, *n.* abundance to choose from.

Weam, *n.* the belly. Cf. Wame.

Weam-ill, *n.* belly-ache.

Wean, *n.* a child ; an infant.

Weanie, *n.* a little child.

Weanly, *adj.* childish ; feeble ; slender ; ill-grown.

Weanock, *n.* a little child.

Weapon-shaw, *n.* a muster of arms ; a scrimmage. Cf. Wapenshaw.

Wear, *v.* to last ; to retain vigour ; to serve for wearing ; to use ; to grow, become ; to cause to become ; to make gradually ; to waste away ; to live in wedlock with a person ; to walk quietly, go slowly ; to pass on.—*n.* clothing ; fashion in dress.

Wear, *v.* to long for, desire earnestly. Cf. Weary.

Wear, *v. pret.* wore.

Wear, *n.* ware, goods. Cf. Ware.

Wear, *v.* to watch, guard ; to stop ; to turn aside ; to cause to veer ; to lead cattle, sheep, &c. gently to an enclosure ; to guide, help on ; to incite.—*n.* a defence ; a hedge ; a guard ; a guard in fencing ; force, restraint.

Wearables, *n.* clothes.

Wear awa, *v.* to pass away slowly ; to fade away ; to draw near to death ; to make time pass.

Wear-a-wins, *int.* an excl. of sorrow.

Wear by, *v.* to pass by.

Weard, *adj.* weird.—*n.* a fateful being. Cf. Weird.

Weardie, *n.* the youngest or feeblest bird in a nest.

Wear down, *v.* to descend slowly and surely ; to grow old.

Weared, *v. pret.* wore.—*ppl.* worn.

Wearifu', *adj.* tedious ; dismal, dreary ; tiresome, vexatious.

Wear in, *v.* used of time : to pass slowly ; to while away ; to bring to a close ; to move slowly and cautiously to a place ; to lead carefully, or drive slowly, cattle, sheep, &c.

Wear in by, *v.* to move cautiously towards a place.

Wearing, *ppl. adj.* tedious, tiresome, trying.

Wear in o', or **in til,** *v.* to acquire by degrees.

Wear off, *v.* to ward off.

Wear off, *v.* to pay off gradually.

Wear on, *v.* to near slowly ; to introduce gradually.

Wear out, *v.* to decline ; to apostatize ; to exhaust.

Wear round, *v.* to recover health ; to prevail in ; to gain one's favour.

Wear through, *v.* to waste ; to get through ; to endure ; to while away time.

Wear up, *v.* to grow up ; to grow old ; to waste away.

Weary, Wearie, *adj.* wearisome ; monotonous ; tedious ; sad, sorrowful ; disastrous ; vexatious ; troublesome ; bad ; feeble, puny, sickly.—*n.* a feeling of weariness ; a girls' singing game.—*v.* to long for, desire earnestly.—*adv.* sadly.

Weary, Wearie, *n.* the deuce ; a nuisance, trouble.

Weary-fa', *int.* as an imprecation, a curse.

Weary-wae, *adj.* weary with woe.

Weasan, Weason, *n.* the gullet, windpipe.

Wease, *n.* a small bundle of hay or straw ; a bundle of sticks or brushwood placed at the side of a cottage-door to keep off wind. Cf. Waese.

Weased, *ppl. adj.* uneasy, anxious. Cf. Weezet.

Weasel-body, *n.* an inquisitive, prying person.

Weasses, *n.* a species of breeching for the necks of horses. Cf. Waese.

Weather, *n.* a wether.

Weather, *n.* a storm ; rough weather ; the weather-side ; a season, a condition of things ; means, method.—*v.* to keep clear of ; to make way with difficulty.

Weather-brack, *n.* a break or change in the weather.

Weather-cock, *n.* in *phr.* 'aneth the weather-cock,' imprisoned in the church steeple, in which offenders formerly were confined.

Weather-dame, *n.* a weather-prophetess.

Weather-days, *n.* the time for sheep-shearing.

Weather-fender, *n.* protection from the weather.

Weather-fu', *adj.* boisterous, stormy.

Weather-gaw, *n.* the lower part of a rainbow left visible above the horizon ; a fine day during much bad weather ; brightness before a storm ; a gleam of sunshine between storms ; anything so favourable as to seem to indicate the reverse.

Weather-gleam, *n.* a clear sky near a dark horizon ; used of objects seen in the twilight or dusk : near the horizon ; a place exposed to the wind.

Weather-gloom, *n.* a 'weather-gleam.'

Weather-wear, *n.* the severity or wearing influence of the weather.

Weather-wiseacre, *n.* a weather-prophet ; one who is weather-wise.

Weathery, *adj.* stormy, unsettled.

Weave, *v.* to knit ; to wind in pursuit.

Weaven, Weavin, *n.* a moment.

Weaver, *n.* a knitter of stockings ; a spider.

Weaver-kneed, *adj.* knock-kneed.

Weaverty-waverty, *n.* a contemptuous name for a weaver.

Weazle-blawing, *n.* a disease of the roots of the fingers.

Weazon, Weazen, *n.* the windpipe. Cf. Weasan.

Weaz't, *ppl. adj.* excited. Cf. Weezet.

Web, *n.* the omentum or caul; the epidermis, —*v.* to weave, fabricate. Cf. Wab.

Web-glass, *n.* a magnifying-glass for examining a web of cloth.

Webis, *n.* the common ragwort; the tansy. Cf. Weebo.

Web-o'-the-body, *n.* the omentum.

Web's end, *n.* the last moment.

Webster, *n.* a weaver; a knitter of stockings; a spider.

Webster-craft, *n.* the art of weaving.

Wecht, *n.* a weight; the standard by which a thing is weighed; a great amount; a bundle of fishing-lines; in *pl.* a pair of scales.—*v.* to weigh; to feel the weight of; to depress, dispirit.

Wecht, *n.* an unperforated sheepskin or calf-skin stretched over a hoop, for winnowing or carrying corn; a sort of tambourine.—*v.* to winnow, fan.

Wechtfu', *n.* as much as a 'wecht' will contain.

Wechtsman, *n.* a winnower who uses a 'wecht.'

Wechty, *adj.* weighty.

Wechty-fittit, *adj.* advanced in pregnancy.

Wechty-tochered, *adj.* well-dowered.

Wed, *n.* a pledge; a forfeit.—*v.* to pledge; to wager. Cf. Wad.

Wed, *v. pret., ppl.,* and *ppl. adj.* married. Cf. Wad.

Wed, *ppl.* and *ppl. adj.* weeded.

Wed, *ppl.* faded, vanished. Cf. Wede.

Wedder, *n.* a wether.

Wedder, *n.* weather. Cf. Weather.

Weddinger, *n.* a wedding-guest; in *pl.* the whole marriage party.

Weddin-sou, *n.* a trousseau.

Wede, Wede-away, *v.* to die out; to cause to vanish; to destroy.—*ppl.* and *ppl. adj.* faded, vanished, removed by death.

Wedless, *adj.* unmarried.

Wedset, *n.* a mortgage. Cf. Wadset.

Wee, *adj.* little; young; of low station, humble; on a small scale; close-fisted; mean, despicable.—*n.* a short time; a while.

Wee, *v.* to weigh.—*n.* in *pl.* a balance beam and scales.

Weeack, Weeak, *v.* to squeak; to chirp; to whine. Cf. Wëak.

Wee-ane, *n.* a child. Cf. Wean.

Wee-bauk, *n.* a small cross-beam nearest the angle of a roof.

Weebis, Weebie, *n.* ragwort. Cf. Weebo.

Wee bit, *adj.* little, puny.—*n.* a small bit of anything; used often contemptuously of persons of small stature.

Weebo, *n.* the common ragwort; the tansy.

Wee-boukit, *adj.* small-bodied; in small compass.

Wee cheese, wee butter, *n.* a children's play in which two children, back to back with linked arms, lift each other alternately, the one crying 'Wee [weigh] cheese,' the other 'Wee butter,' when their turns come to lift.

Weed, *n.* a worthless person.—*v.* to thin out plants; to single turnips.

Weed, *n.* a garment; dress; a winding-sheet; grave-clothes.

Weed, *n.* a chill causing inflammation of milk-ducts in a woman's breasts after confinement; a disease of horses and cattle; pains of labour.

Weed, *ppl.* faded. Cf. Wede.

Weeder, *n.* one who thins out plants.

Weeder-clips, *n.* an instrument for pulling up weeds growing among grain.

Weedins, *n.* plants weeded out, or cut out, in thinning trees, turnips, &c.

Weedit, *ppl. adj.* used of the hair: thin, sparse.

Weedock, *n.* a weed-hook for grubbing up weeds.

Weedock, *n.* a little weed.

Weedow, Weeda, Weedy, *n.* a widow; a widower.

Wee-drap, *n.* whisky; a little whisky.

Weefil, *n.* a contemptuous designation of an extravagant person.

Weegilty-waggiltie, *adj.* unstable, wavering.

Weegle, *v.* to waggle. Cf. Wiggle.

Weegler, *n.* one who waddles.

Weeglie, *adj.* having a wriggling motion in walking.

Wee-hauf, *n.* a half-glass of whisky.

Wëek, *v.* to squeak; to chirp. Cf. Wëak.

Week, *n.* a corner, angle; a corner of the eye or of the mouth. Cf. Wick.

Week-teeth, *n.* a canine tooth.

Weel, *n.* an eddy; a pool; a deep, still part in a river.

Weel, *v.* to choose, pick out. Cf. Wale.

Weel, *n.* happiness, prosperity, weal.

Weel, *adj.* well; healthy; used of food: well-cooked.—*adv.* well, very, quite.—*int.* an excl. of contentment, resignation, impatience, surprise, &c.

Weel-a-day, *int.* alas! well-a-day!

Weel-aff, *adj.* well off.

Weel-a-wat, *int.* assuredly!

Weel-a-weel, *int.* an excl. of resignation, well, well!

Weel-a-wins, Weel-a-wons, *int.* an excl. of pity, sorrow, &c.

Weel-awyte, *int.* assuredly !

Weel-bred, *adj.* polite, civil.

Weel-comed, *adj.* come of good family, or stock ; legitimate.

Weel-countit, *adj.* counted correctly or to the full amount.

Weel-creeshed, *adj.* used of a pig : well-fattened.

Weeld, *v.* to gain over; to subdue. Cf. Wield.

Weel-doin', *adj.* prosperous, well-to-do ; well-behaved ; of good character.

Weel done to, *adj.* well cared for.

Weel-ees't, *adj.* well-treated.

Weel-faced, *adj.* of comely face.

Weel-faird, *adj.* ' weel-faured.'

Weel-fardy, *adj.* well-favoured.

Weelfare, *n.* welfare.

Weel-farrand, *adj.* good-looking, comely.

Weel-faured, -faurt, *adj.* good-looking.

Weel-faurtly, *adv.* handsomely ; with good grace ; distinctly ; openly.

Weel-faurtness, *n.* comeliness.

Weel-favoured, *adj.* good-looking.

Weel-fished, *adj.* with a good supply of fish ; a whale-fishing term.

Weel-flittin, *adj.* a sarcastic word applied to one who scolds another, and himself deserves a scolding. Cf. Flite.

Weel-foggit, *adj.* used of one who has earned or saved plenty of money.

Weel-gäin, -gaun, *adj.* used of a horse : spirited ; of machinery, &c.: going or working smoothly.

Weel-gaited, *adj.* used of a horse : thoroughly broken in.

Weel-geizened, -gizzened, *adj.* very thirsty.

Weel-girst, *adj.* well-fed on good grass.

Weel-hain't, *adj.* well-kept ; saved to good purpose ; not wasted ; saved by frugality.

Weel-handit, *adj.* clever with the hands ; expert.

Weel-hauden in, *adj.* ' weel-hain't.'

Weel-head, *n.* an eddy ; the centre of an eddy.

Weel-heartit, *adj.* kind-hearted ; hopeful, not cast down.

Weel-hung, *adj.* used of the tongue : ready, fluent, glib.

Weelins, *n.* power over one's self to keep one's feet after a paralytic shock, &c.

Weel-kent, -kenned, *adj.* well-known ; conspicuous ; familiar.

Weel-leared, -learnit *adj.* well-informed ; well-educated.

Weel-leggit, *adj.* having good, strong, shapely legs.

Weel-lickit, *adj.* used of speech : careful, plausible ; well-whipped.

Weel-like, *adj.* good-looking; looking in good health.

Weel-likit, *adj.* much liked.

Weel-lo'ed, *adj.* dearly loved.

Weel-lookin', -lookit, *adj.* good-looking, looking well.

Weel man, *int.* a common form of address.

Weel-meatit, *adj.* used of grain : full in the ear ; well-fed.

Weel-mindit, -min't, *adj.* well brought to recollection.

Weel-natured, *adj.* good-natured.

Weelness, *n.* good health.

Weel on, *adj.* far gone in drink.

Weel-paid, *adj.* well-satisfied ; well-punished.

Weel-pang't, *adj.* well-stuffed or crammed.

Weel-pitten on, -putten on, *adj.* well-dressed.

Weel-raxed, *adj.* widely stretched.

Weel-redd-up, *adj.* tidy ; made thoroughly tidy. Cf. Redd.

Weel sae, *adv.* very ; too.

Weel-saired, *adj.* well-served ; feasted ; deservedly punished.

Weel-set, *adj.* well-disposed ; partial ; sharp set ; very hungry.

Weel-set-on, *adj.* used of a stack, &c : well-built ; well-provided.

Weel-settin', *adj.* good-looking ; well set up.

Weel-sleekit, *adj.* well-beaten.

Weel's-me-on, *int.* blessings on ! happy am I with ! an excl. expressive of very great pleasure.

Weel-socht, *adj.* greatly exhausted.

Weel-sookit, *adj.* almost exhausted.

Weel-standing, *adj.* used of a house : well-furnished.

Weel-thrashen, *adj.* well-whipped.

Weel-tochered, *adj.* well-dowered.

Weel-to-do, *adj.* nearly drunk ; tipsy.

Weel-to-leeve, -to-live, *adj.* in easy circumstances ; half-drunk.

Weel-to-pass, *adj.* prosperous, well-to-do.

Weel-to-see, *adj.* good-looking.

Weel-wal'd, *adj.* well-chosen. Cf. Wale.

Weel-war, *adj.* much the worse.

Weel-wared, -waurt, *adj.* well-spent ; well laid out ; well-earned, well-deserved ; well done, properly awarded.

Weel-warst, *adj.* the very worst.

Weel-willed, *adj.* kindly disposed ; generous ; very willing.

Weel-willer, *n.* a friend ; a well-wisher.

Weel-willie, -willied, *adj.* well-disposed towards one ; liberal ; very willing.

Weel-willin, *adj.* kindly disposed ; favourable ; complacent ; well-meaning.

Weel-wintered, *adj.* used of cattle : well-fed in winter.

Weel-wish, *n.* a good wish.—*v.* to wish well.

Weel-wished, *ppl. adj.* given with good-will.

Weel-won, *adj.* well-earned.

Weem, *n.* a natural cave ; an artificial cave ;

an underground passage; an underground building.

Weemen, Weemen-bodies, *n.* women.

Ween, *v.* to boast.—*n.* a boast; a boaster.

Ween, *n.* a child. Cf. **Wean.**

Weeness, *n.* smallness; meanness of spirit.

Weeoch, *n.* a little while.

Weeock, Weeok, *v.* to squeak; to chirp. Cf. **Wëak.**

Wee oor, *n.* one o'clock A.M.

Weep, *v.* used of cheese: to exude; to ooze.

Weepers, *n.* strips of muslin or cambric stitched on the cuffs of a coat or gown, as a sign of mourning, often covered with crape; mourners for the dead.

Weer, *v.* to turn away, or back, an animal.

Weer, *n.* doubt; fear.

Weer, *n.* wire.

Weer, *v.* to wear.

Weerd, *n.* destiny; a fateful being. Cf. **Weird.**

Weerdie, *n.* a queer, uncanny, weird person.

Weerigills, *n.* quarrels; the act of quarrelling.

Weerit, *n.* the young of the guillemot; a peevish child.

Weerock, *n.* a corn; a bunion; a callosity. Cf. **Wyrock.**

Weers, *n.* in *phr.* 'on the weers o',' on the point of.

Weer-stanes, *adv.* in a state of hesitation. Cf. **Weer.**

Wees, *n.* a balance beam and scales.

Wee-saul't, *adj.* having a little soul.

Wee-schule, *n.* an infant school.

Weese, *n.* a wisp or small bundle of hay or straw. Cf. **Waese.**

Weese, *v.* to ooze. Cf. **Weeze, Wooze.**

Weesh, *int.* a call to a horse to go to the right. Cf. **Weest.**

Weesh, *v. pret.* washed.

Weeshen, *ptl.* washed.

Weeshie, *adj.* delicate; watery.—*v.* to hesitate. Cf. **Wishy.**

Weesht, *int.* hush! Cf. **Whisht.**

Weesp, *n.* a measure of fish; a small quantity.

Weest, *adj.* depressed with dullness.

Weest, *int.* a call to a horse to go to the right. Cf. **Weesh.**

Weet, *adj.* wet.—*v.* to wet.—*n.* rain; a small quantity of liquor. Cf. **Wat, Wet.**

Weet, *n.* the cry of the chaffinch.

Weet, *v.* to wit, know.

Wee-taws, *n.* a small 'taws' used for slight offences.

Wee thing, *n.* a child; a darling; a trifle.

Wee-thocht, *n.* a very little thing; a trifle; a particle.

Weetie, *adj.* rainy; wet.

Weetit, *ppl.* wetted.

Weet-my-fit, *n.* the quail.

Weetness, *n.* wet; rainy weather; anything drinkable.

Weeuk, *v.* to chirp. Cf. **Wëak.**

Wee way, *n..* a small trade or business; a retail trade.

Weeze, *v.* to ooze.

Weeze, *n.* a wisp of straw. Cf. **Waese.**

Weezen, *v.* to wither; to shrivel. Cf. **Wizzen.**

Weezet, *ppl. adj.* excited over some new possession, or over the prospect of it.

Weff, *adj.* of a musty smell. Cf. **Waugh.**

Weffil, Weffle, *adj.* limber, flexible, pliant. Cf. **Waffle.**

Weffilness, *n.* limberness, pliancy.

Wefflin, Wefflum, *n.* the water-course at the back of a mill-wheel. Cf. **Waefleed.**

Weght, *n.* weight.—*v.* to burden. Cf. **Weight.**

Weght, *n.* a skin stretched over a hoop, used for winnowing. Cf. **Weight.**

Wehaw, *int.* a cry that displeases or alarms horses.

Weibis, *n.* the common ragwort. Cf. **Weebo.**

Weicht, *n.* weight.

Weicht, *n.* a skin stretched over a hoop. Cf. **Weight.**

Weid, *n.* a garment.

Weid, *n.* a chill causing inflammation of the milk-ducts after a woman's confinement. Cf. **Weed.**

Weidinonfa, *n.* a chill, fever, the onfall of a 'weid.' Cf. **Wytenonfa.**

Weigh, *n.* a weight or measure of dry goods.

Weigh-bauk, *n.* a balance; in *pl.* scales; a state of indecision.

Weigh-beam, *n.* a balance.

Weigh-brods, *n.* the boards used as scales in a large balance.

Weigh-scale, *n.* a pair of scales; a steelyard.

Weight, *n.* a skin stretched over a hoop, for winnowing.—*v.* to winnow grain. Cf. **Wecht.**

Weight, *n.* the standard by which anything is weighed; a great amount or sum; a bundle of fishing-lines; a pair of scales; one's own place, or influence; the weight of a blow, &c.—*v.* to feel the weight of; to burden, oppress; to dispirit.

Weightsman, *n.* one who winnows with a 'weight.' Cf. **Wechtsman.**

Weighty, *adj.* heavy, corpulent; valiant, doughty.

Weighty-fitted, *adj.* advanced in pregnancy.

Weik, *n.* a corner or angle. Cf. **Wick.**

Weik, *n.* a rush-wick.

Weil, *v.* to choose. Cf. **Wale.**

Weil, Weill, *n.* prosperity, happiness. Cf. **Weel.**

Weil, *n.* a whirlpool; an eddy. Cf. **Weel.**

Weil, Weill, *adj.* well.—*adv.* very, quite. Cf. **Weel.**

Weild, *v.* to manage, govern. Cf. Wield.

Weil'd, *ppl. adj.* chosen, choice. Cf. Wale.

Weil'd-wight, *adj.* strongest and best. Cf. Wall-wight.

Weilycoat, *n.* an under-coat. Cf. Wylie-coat.

Weind, *n.* thought.—*v.* to ween.

Weint, *n.* a moment; a transient sight. Cf. Went.

Weint, *n.* a narrow passage, an alley; the bend of a fishing-line when not cast in one stretch.—*v.* used of milk: to turn sour. Cf. Waint.

Weir, *n.* war.

Weir, *v.* to watch; to stop, turn aside; to collect and drive cattle, &c., gently; to herd; to help on.—*n.* a hedge, a fence; an enclosure. Cf. Wear.

Weir, *n.* cows and ewes giving milk.

Weir, *n.* doubt, fear. Cf. Weer.

Weir-buist, -buse, *n.* a partition between cows in a byre.

Weird, *n.* a fateful being; a dealer in the supernatural; disaster; a fateful story; a prediction, prophecy.—*v.* to doom to; to adjure by the knowledge of impending fate; to predict; to waft kind wishes; to make liable to; to expose to evil.

Weird, *n.* the world. Cf. Ward.

Weird, *adj.* troublesome. Cf. Wierd.

Weird, Weirded, *ppl. adj.* fated; destined; predicted; determined.

Weird-fixed, *adj.* fateful; destined.

Weird-fu', *adj.* fateful.

Weirdin, *ppl. adj.* employed for the purpose of divination.

Weirdless, *adj.* ill-fated; unprosperous; improvident; purposeless; worthless.

Weirdlessness, *n.* wastefulness; mismanagement; improvidence.

Weird-light, *n.* the light of one's destiny.

Weird-like, *adj.* ominous.

Weirdly, *adj.* ghastly; fate-bringing; 'eerie'; happy, prosperous.

Weirdly-cake, *n.* a cake broken at Christmas so as to portend the future.

Weirdman, *n.* a seer.

Weird-set, *adj.* fateful; destined.

Weirdy, *adj.* fateful.

Weirfu', *adj.* warlike.

Weir-glove, *n.* a war-glove or gauntlet.

Weir-harness, *n.* armour.

Weir-horse, *n.* a stallion.

Weiriegills, *n.* quarrels. Cf. Weerigills.

Weir-men, *n.* armed men, warriors.

Weirs, *n.* in *phr.* 'on weirs,' in danger of; on the point of. Cf. Aweers.

Weir-saddle, *n.* a war-saddle.

Weise, Weisse, *v.* to direct; to lead; to use policy for attaining an object; to turn by art rather than strength; to manoeuvre; to advise; to lure; to persuade; to beguile; to wheedle; to draw or let out anything cautiously, so as to prevent it from breaking; to spend; to use; to withdraw; to incline, slip away. Cf. Wise.

Weish, *v. pret.* washed.

Weit, *adj.* wet.—*v.* to wet; to rain. Cf. Weet.

Weize, *v.* to incline; to direct. Cf. Weise, Wise.

Weke, *n.* a narrow 'port' in a curling-rink. Cf. Wick.

Welcome-hame, *n.* the repast presented to a bride as she enters the bridegroom's house; a festivity on the day after a newly-married pair have made their first appearance at church; a welcome given to a newly-engaged ploughman.

Wel'd, *ppl.* welded.

Weld, *v.* to manage successfully; to exercise. Cf. Wield.

Wele, *n.* happiness, prosperity. Cf. Weil.

Wele, *v.* to choose. Cf. Wale.

Wele, *n.* an eddy. Cf. Weil.

Welk, *v.* to wither.

Well, *n.* a whirlpool; an eddy. Cf. Weel.

Well, *n.* the hollow centre of an Irish car, used as a receptacle for luggage. Cf. Wall.

Well, *n.* happiness, weal. Cf. Weel.

Well, *v.* to weld. Cf. Wall.

Well, *adj.* used of meat: well-cooked.—*adv.* quite, very. Cf. Weel.

Well-a, Well-a-day, *int.* alas!

Well-a-wins, *int.* an excl. of sorrow.

Well-ee, -ey, *n.* a spring in a quagmire; a spring of water; the orifice of a well.

Weller, *v.* to crave; to call for.

Well-head, *n.* the spring from which a marsh is supplied.

Wellicot, *n.* an under-vest. Cf. Wylie-coat.

Well-shanker, *n.* a well-digger.

Well-sitting, *ppl. adj.* favourably disposed.

Well's-me, *int.* an excl. of pleasure.

Well-strand, *n.* a stream flowing from a well.

Well-stripe, *n.* a 'well-strand.'

Well-warst, *adj.* the very worst.

Well-wight, *adj.* stalwart; strongest and best. Cf. Wall-wight.

Welt, *n.* a seam; the crust of cheese; a weal made by a blow; a blow; anything large of its kind.

Welter, *v.* to overturn, upset; to reel, stagger, stumble.—*n.* a confused noise.

Welth, *n.* wealth; abundance; a sufficiency. Cf. Walth.

Wench, *n.* a female servant.

Wene, *n.* a habitation, a lodging. Cf. Wane.

Weng, *n.* a penny.

Went, *n.* a narrow lane or passage; the bend

of a fishing-line when not cast at one stretch; a short time.—*v.* to turn sour. Cf. Waint.

Went, *n.* a transient glimpse; a moment. Cf. Waint.

Wer, *poss. adj.* our.

Wer, *adj.* wary. Cf. Waur.

Werd, *v.* to award. Cf. Ward.

Werd, *n.* weird; fate. Cf. Weird.

Werdie, *n.* the youngest bird in a nest.

Werk, *v.* to ache. Cf. Wark.

Werk, *v.* to work. Cf. Wark.

Wer-nain, *poss. adj.* our own.

Wer nainsels, *refl. pron.* our ownselves.

Wersels, *refl. pron.* ourselves.

Wersh, *adj.* tasteless; weak and watery. Cf. Wairsh.

Wery, *adj.* wearisome. Cf. Weary.

Wery, *n.* the deuce, used in expletives.

We'se, *pron.* with *v.* we shall.

Weslin, *adj.* western.

Wesp, *n.* a wasp. Cf. Wasp.

West-bye, *adv.* westward. Cf. Wast-bye.

Wester, *n.* a fish-spear. Cf. Waster.

Westlin, *n.* the west country.—*adj.* western.

Westlins, *adv.* westward.

Wet, *v. pret.* waited.

Wet, *adj.* given to drink.—*n.* moisture; a drizzling rain; wet weather; a small quantity of liquid; water; a wetting; wet clothes.—*v.* to rain; to drizzle; used of a river: to water, irrigate. Cf. Wat, Weet.

Wet-bird, *n.* the chaffinch.

Wete, *n.* hope.

Wet finger, *n.* an effort.

Wet fish, *n.* fresh fish.

Wether-bell, *n.* the bell worn by the bell-wether.

Wether-bleat, *n.* the snipe.

Wether-gammon, *n.* a leg of mutton.

Wether-haggis, *n.* a haggis boiled in a sheep's stomach.

Wether-hog, *n.* a male sheep of the second season.

Wether-lamb, *n.* a male lamb.

Wet-looking, *adj.* threatening rain.

Wetness, *n.* rainy weather; anything drinkable.

Wet-shod, *adj.* wet-footed; brimful of tears.

Wet-shoe ford, *n.* a ford that just wets the feet of the forders.

Wetting, *n.* a small quantity of liquor; a convivial feast.

Wetty, *adj.* wet.

Wevil, *v.* to wriggle. Cf. Waffle.

Wew, *v.* to mew as a kitten.

Wewleck, Wewlock, *n.* an instrument for twisting ropes of straw.

Wey, *n.* a way. Cf. Way.

Wey, *pron.* we.

Wey, *v.* to weigh.

Wey, *adj.* little.—*n.* a little. Cf. Wee.

Weyke, *adj.* weak. Cf. Waik.

Weykness, *n.* weakness.

Weynt, *n.* a narrow passage. Cf. Waint.

Weynt, *n.* a moment; a transient sight. Cf. Went.

Weyso, *n.* a small bundle of hay or straw. Cf. Wease.

Weyse, *v.* to lead; to turn by art; to use policy. Cf. Weise, Wise.

Weysh, *int.* a call to a horse to turn to the right. Cf. Weesh.

Weyve, *v.* to weave.

Weyver, *n.* a weaver; a knitter.

Wez, *pron.* us; we.

Wha, *pron.* who.

Whaal, *n.* a whale; a long, unbroken wave. Cf. Whale.

Whaap, *n.* the curlew. Cf. Whaup.

Whaap, *n.* the sheltered part of a hill.

Whaap-neb, *n.* the beak of a curlew. Cf. Whaup-neb.

Whaarl, *v.* to whirl.

Whack, *v.* to cut in large slices; to pull out smartly; to surpass.—*n.* a cut; a slice; a large portion of food or drink; a great number.

Whack, *v.* to quack; to drink copiously or with gulping noise.

Whacker, *n.* anything large of its kind; a great lie.

Whacking, *ppl. adj.* big, 'thumping.'

Whackle, *v.* to fish with fly.

Whae, *pron.* who.

Whaff, *v.* to wave; to flap.—*n.* a whiff. Cf. Waff.

Whaile, *v.* to flog, thrash. Cf. Wale.

Whaingle, *v.* to whine.

Whaish, *v.* to wheeze as one that has taken cold.

Whaishle, *v.* to 'whaish,' wheeze.

Whaisk, *v.* to speak huskily, or with difficulty, owing to a throat affection; to hawk; to clear one's throat; to gasp violently for breath. Cf. Whesk.

Whaisle, Whaizle, *v.* to wheeze in breathing. —*n.* the wheezing sound of the lungs when one is under a severe cold. Cf. Wheezle.

Whaky, *n.* whisky. Cf. Whawkie.

Whale, *v.* to flog. Cf. Wale.

Whale, *adj.* whole. Cf. Whole, Hail.

Whale, *n.* a large species of cuttle-fish, the 'whale-skate'; in *pl.* long, unbroken waves.

Whale-blubs, *n.* the sea-jelly.

Whale-money, *n.* money paid to whalers for blubber, &c.

Whale-ruck, *n.* the whole collection of things. Cf. Hail-ruck.

Whale-skate, *n.* a large species of cuttle-fish.

Whalm, *v.* to whelm ; to turn a vessel upside-down ; to come in large numbers ; used of a crowd : to surge.

Whalp, *v.* to bring forth whelps. — *n.* a whelp ; a term of contempt.

Whalpin, *n.* a whipping.

Wham, *n.* a swamp ; a hollow in a field ; a wide, flat glen through which a brook runs ; a corrie.

Wham, *pron.* whom.

Wham, *n.* a blow ; a bend.

Whamble, Whamal, Whamel, Whammel, Whammle, *v.* to upset ; to turn upside-down ; to capsize ; to invert a vessel ; to cover over with a vessel ; to toss to and fro ; to tumble about ; to move quickly ; to overcome ; to throw off ; to pour over, swallow liquor ; to turn round. — *n.* a violent overturn ; a capsize ; a tumble ; a toss ; a turn ; a rocking ; a state of confusion, or of being overturned.

Whame, *n.* the belly. Cf. Wame.

Whample, *n.* a stroke, blow ; a cut ; a chip.

Whan, *adv.* when.

Whan-a-be, *adv.* notwithstanding ; however.

Whand, *n.* a wand. Cf. Wand.

Whand-cage, *n.* a wicker-cage.

Whang, *n.* a thong ; a long strip of leather ; a leather lace for boot or shoe ; a whip-lash ; a rope ; a band ; anything long and supple.

Whang, *v.* to beat, thrash ; to lash ; to cut in large lumps ; to slice. — *n.* a blow or lash with a whip ; a lump ; a large piece or slice.

Whang-bit, *n.* a leathern bridle.

Whangkin, *n.* a lump ; a portion.

Whank, *v.* to beat, flog ; to cut off large portions. — *n.* a stroke, a violent blow with the fist ; the act of striking.

Whanker, *n.* anything larger than common of its kind.

Whankin, *n.* a lump ; a portion. Cf. Whang-kin.

Whap, *v.* to strike smartly ; to beat ; to cast down ; to wrestle ; to excel. — *n.* a blow ; a disturbance ; a sweeping movement. — *adv.* violently ; flop. Cf. Wap.

Whap, *n.* the curlew. Cf. Whaup.

Whapie, *n.* a little whelp, a young puppy.

Whapper, *n.* anything excessive in its kind or beyond expectation ; a great lie, a 'whopper.'

Whapping, *ppl. adj.* stout, lusty, exceptionally big, fine, good.

Whar, *adv.* where ; whither.

Wharle, *v.* to roll the letter *r*. Cf. Whirl.

Wha's, *pron.* with *v.* who is.

Wha's, Whase, *pron.* whose.

Whasle, *v.* to wheeze. Cf. Wheezle, Whaisle.

Whassl-whiesl, *v.* to wheeze in breathing.

Whate, *v. pret.* did whittle. Cf. White.

Whaten, Whatten, Whatena, *adj.* what kind of.

Whatever, *adv.* in any circumstances ; at all, on any account.

What-for, *n.* punishment, retribution.

What-like, *adj.* resembling what.

Whatna, *adj.* what kind of. Cf. Whaten.

Wha-to-be-married-first, *n.* the name of a card-game.

Whatrack, Whatreck, Whatrecks, *int.* an excl. of surprise, indifference, contempt ; what matters it ? no matter !

Whatreck, *conj.* nevertheless.

Whatrick, *n.* a weasel. Cf. Whitteret.

What's-comin'-next ? *adj.* uncertain what is to happen next.

Whatsomever, Whatsomer, *adj.* whatsoever. — *adv.* whenever. — *n.* anything of importance.

Whatt, *v. pret.* cut, whittled. Cf. White.

Whattie, *n.* the white-throat. Cf. Watty.

Whaubert, *n.* a lean, tall, ungainly person. Cf. Wheebert.

Whaugh, *int.* an excl. of surprise or disapproval.

Whauk, *v.* to thwack. — *n.* a heavy blow. Cf. Whack.

Whauk, Whauky, *n.* whisky. Cf. Whawkie.

Whaum, *n.* a blow ; a bend. Cf. Wham.

Whaum, *n.* a hollow on a hill. Cf. Wham.

Whaumle, Whaumil, *v.* to upset. Cf. Whamble.

Whaund, *n.* a wand. Cf. Wand.

Whaup, *n.* a curlew — *v.* to make an unpleasant noise ; to 'tootle' clumsily on a flute.

Whaup, *n.* a pod in its earliest stage ; a capsule ; an empty pod ; a term of contempt for a disagreeable person ; a lout ; a lazy person ; a scamp. — *v.* to form into pods.

Whaup, *v.* to wheeze.

Whaup, *n.* an outcry ; a fuss.

Whaup, *n.* in *phr.* 'a whaup in the raip,' something wrong, a hitch somewhere ; a fraudulent trick ; a 'spoke in one's wheel.'

Whaupie-mou'd, *adj.* having a mouth like the curlew.

Whaupin, *ppl. adj.* very big ; stout ; 'whopping.' Cf. Whapping.

Whaup-neb, *n.* a curlew's beak ; with *Auld,* a name for the devil.

Whaup-nebbit, *adj.* having a long, sharp nose.

Whaup-neckit, *adj.* used of a bottle : long-necked.

Whaur, *adv.* where ; whither.

Whaurie, *n.* a misgrown or a mischievous child ; a fondling term, or a jocular, reproachful term, addressed to a child

Whaurtee, *adv.* whereto ; whither.

Whauzle, *v.* to wheeze. Cf. Wheezle, Whaisle.

Whawbert, *n.* a tall, lean, clumsy, ungainly person. Cf. Wheebert.

Whawk, *v.* to thwack. Cf. Whack.

Whawkie, *n.* whisky.

Whawmle, *v.* to upset. Cf. Whamble.

Whawp, *n.* a curlew. Cf. Whaup.

Whawp, *n.* a pod. Cf. Whaup.

Whazle, *v.* to wheeze. Cf. Wheezle.

Whëak, *v.* to squeak; to whine; to whistle at intervals.—*n.* a squeak. Cf. Wëak.

Wheasle, *v.* to wheeze. Cf. Wheezle.

Wheat, *v.* to whittle. Cf. White.

Wheck, *v.* to thwack. Cf. Whack.

Wheeber, *v.* to whistle a tune.

Wheeber, Wheebre, *v.* to beat severely; to dash; to walk hurriedly and clumsily.—*n.* a tall, ungainly person.

Wheebert, *n.* a tall, ungainly person.

Wheebert, *v.* to whistle.

Wheebring, *ppl. adj.* hurried and clumsy in manner.

Wheech, *n.* a stench.—*int.* an excl. of disgust with a stench. Cf. Feegh.

Wheef, *n.* a passing glimpse. Cf. Whiff.

Wheef, *n.* a fife, a flute.—*v.* to play the fife or the flute.

Wheefer, *n.* a fifer; a flute-player.

Wheefle, *v.* to play on the flute or the fife.—*n.* a shrill, intermittent note, with little variation of tone. Cf. Wheeple.

Wheefle, *v.* to puff; to blow away; used of the wind: to blow in puffs, to drive before it; to veer.

Wheefler, *n.* a fifer or a flute-player.

Wheegee, Wheejee, *n.* a whim, fancy; a 'maggot'; in *pl.* superfluous ornaments in dress.—*v.* to beat about the bush, to be long-winded in speech.

Wheegil, *n.* a piece of wood for pushing in the end of the straw-rope with which a sheaf is bound.

Wheegle, *v.* to wheedle, coax, flatter.—*n.* a wheedling.

Wheel, *n.* an eddy; a pool. Cf. Weel.

Wheel, *v.* to drive in a wheeled vehicle; to whirl in dancing; to hurry; to bid at an auction simply to raise the price.—*n.* a wheel round; a spinning-wheel.

Wheel-abouts, *n.* used of horses: paces.

Wheel-band, *n.* a band passing round a wheel and causing it to revolve; what keeps any business going.

Wheel-bird, *n.* the nightjar.

Wheel-chargeman, *n.* one who wheels pig-iron to the smelting-furnace.

Wheeler, *n.* one who bids at an auction simply to raise the price; one who wheels peats in a moss.

Wheelin, *n.* coarse worsted spun on the large wheel from wool that has been only carded.

Wheelmagig, *n.* anything whirling rapidly along.

Wheel-treck, *n.* the part of a spinning-wheel armed with teeth.

Wheel-wricht, *n.* in *phr.* to 'make a wheel-wricht of a woman,' to seduce her.

Wheem, *n.* a whim.

Wheem, *adj.* gentle; smooth; calm; neat, tidy; close, tight. Cf. Queem.

Wheemer, *v.* to whimper; to go about muttering complaints. Cf. Whimper.

Wheen, *n.* a number; a quantity; a party, group; a division; somewhat; a few.

Wheenge, *v.* to whine. Cf. Whinge.

Wheep, *v.* to give a sharp, intermittent, whistling sound; to squeak; to whistle.—*n.* a sharp, shrill sound, cry, or whistle.

Wheep, *v.* to whip; to fly nimbly.—*n.* an instant. Cf. Whip.

Wheep, *n.* used with *penny:* small-beer at a penny a bottle; whisky at a penny a quartern.

Wheeper, *n.* a jocular name for a tuning-fork.

Wheeple, *v.* to utter short, sharp, melancholy cries, like a curlew or plover; to whistle; to try to whistle; to whistle in an almost inaudible tone.—*n.* a shrill, intermittent cry of certain birds; a whistle; an unsuccessful attempt to whistle. Cf. Queeple.

Wheepler, *n.* a whistler.

Wheeps, *n.* an instrument for raising the 'bridgeheads' of a mill.

Wheeriemigo, *n.* a gimcrack; an insignificant person.—*v.* to work in a trifling, insignificant manner; to play fast and loose. Cf. Wheerim.

Wheerikins, *n.* the hips.

Wheerim, Wheeram, Wheerum, *n.* anything insignificant; a toy; a plaything; a trifling excuse; a trifling peculiarity; an insignificant, trifling person; the act of working in a trifling, imperfect way.—*v.* to turn; to work in a trifling way; to play fast and loose.

Wheerip, *v.* to whimper, whine; to torment by mourning. Cf. Whyripe.

Wheesh, *int.* a call to a horse to go to the right. Cf. Weesh.

Wheesh, *adv.* with a whiz or swish.

Wheesht, *int.* hush!—*n.* silence; a hush. Cf. Whisht.

Wheesk, *v.* to creak gently.—*n.* a creaking sound.

Wheest, *int.* hush!—*n.* silence. Cf. Whisht.

Wheet, *n.* a whit.

Wheet, Wheetie, *int.* a call to poultry, especially ducks.—*v.* used of young birds: to twitter, chirp or 'cheep.'—*n.* a very young bird; a duck.

Wheet-ah, *n.* the cry of the tern.

Wheetie, *n.* the white-throat.

Wheetie, *adj.* low, mean, shabby.

Wheetie-like, *adj.* having the appearance of meanness.

Wheetie-wheet, *n.* a very young bird. Cf. Wheet.

Wheetie-whitebeard, *n.* the white-throat.

Wheetle, *v.* to wheedle.

Wheetle, *int.* a call to ducks.—*v.* used of birds: to 'cheep.'—*n.* a young duck.

Wheetle-wheetie, *n.* a very young bird.

Wheetle-wheetle, *n.* the 'cheep' of a young bird.

Wheetlie, *int.* a call to ducks.—*v.* to 'cheep' as a young bird.

Wheety, *int.* a call to poultry. Cf. Wheet.

Wheety-what, *v.* to shilly-shally.—*n.* an idle pretence; vague language; a person unscrupulous as to means used to gain his end. Cf. Whittie-whattie.

Wheezan, *n.* the noise carriage-wheels make when moving fast.

Wheeze, *v.* to coax; to flatter; to urge.—*n.* flattery; a deception.

Wheeze, *v.* to whiz; to move briskly.—*n.* the whizzing sound of a flame or gas-jet; the hissing sound of water and hot iron in contact. Cf. Whiz.

Wheezie, *v.* to blaze with a hissing sound.—*n.* a blaze making such a sound.

Wheezie, *v.* to steal fruit, peas, and vegetables.—*n.* such theft.

Wheezle, *v.* to breathe with difficulty; to wheeze; used of the wind: to whistle.—*n.* a wheeze; the act of wheezing; the difficult breathing of asthma.

Wheezle-rung, *n.* a strong stick used by country-people for lifting a large boiling-pot off the fire.

Wheezloch, *n.* the state of being short-winded; a disease of horses affecting their wind.

Whegle, *v.* to wheedle. Cf. Wheegle.

Wheich, *n.* fine wheaten bread.

Wheich, *n.* whisky.

Whelm, *v.* to turn a vessel upside-down so as to be a cover; to come in overwhelming numbers.

Whelp, *n.* a silly, stupid fellow; a foolish braggart.

Wheme, *adj.* gentle; calm. Cf. Wheem.

When-a-be, **When-a-by**, *adv.* however; nevertheless.

Whenever, *conj.* as soon as.

Where, *n.* a place. Cf. Whaur.

Whereas, *n.* a warrant of apprehension, of which it is the opening word.

Whereawa', *adv.* where; whereabouts.

Wherefrae, *adv.* whence.

Where-out, *adv.* whence, out of which.

Whereto, *adv.* whither; why, wherefore.

Whesk, *v.* to speak huskily; to gasp violently. Cf. Whaisk.

Whet, *n.* a small dram of spirits.

Whether or no, *adv.* in any case; willingly or unwillingly. Cf. Fither.

Whew, **Whe-ew**, *n.* the shrill cry of a bird, as the plover; a whistle.—*v.* to whistle; used of a plover: to cry.

Whey-beard, *n.* the white-throat.

Whey-bird, *n.* the woodlark.

Whey-blots, *n.* the scum of boiling whey.

Whey-brose, *n.* 'brose' made with whey.

Whey-cream, *n.* the cream left in the whey after the removal of the curd.

Whey-drap, *n.* a hole from which whey has not been pressed out of the cheese, and in which it putrefies.

Whey-ee, *n.* a 'whey-drap.'

Whey-faced, *adj.* pale-faced; beardless.

Whey-parritch, *n.* porridge made with whey.

Whey-sey, *n.* a tub in which milk is curdled.

Whey-spring, *n.* a 'whey-drap' or 'whey-ee.'

Whey-white, *adj.* white as whey; very pale.

Whey-wullions, *n.* a dish for dinner, formerly common among peasants, consisting of the porridge left at breakfast beaten down with fresh whey, with an addition of oatmeal.

Whezle, *n.* a weasel.

Whick, *v.* to dash or rush with a soft, whizzing sound.—*n.* a soft, whizzing sound; a blow accompanied by such a noise; the hiss of an adder when angered.—*adv.* with a soft, whizzing sound.

Whicker, *v.* to giggle.—*n.* a giggle. Cf. Whihher.

Whickie, *adj.* crafty; knavish.

Whid, *n.* a light, nimble, noiseless movement; a start, a spring; a whisk; a quick run; a hare's hasty flight; an instant.—*v.* to move nimbly and noiselessly; to run or fly quickly; to frisk; to whisk or scamper as a hare.—*adv.* nimbly.

Whid, *v.* to fib; to exaggerate; to equivocate; to deceive.—*n.* an exaggerated statement; a fib, lie.

Whidder, *pron., adj., adv.,* and *conj.* whether.

Whidder, *adv.* whither.

Whidder, *v.* to flutter; used of the wind: to bluster; of a bullet, arrow, &c.: to pass with a whizzing sound. Cf. Whither.

Whiddle, *v.* to flutter about, as birds at pairing-time; to move with quick, short flight; to go lightly and quickly.

Whiddy, *n.* a hare.—*adj.* unsettled, unsteady.

Whiff, *n.* a glimpse; a transient view; a short time, a 'jiffy'; a slight or passing touch.—*v.* to smoke a pipe.

Whiff, *n.* a fife; a flute.—*v.* to play on a fife or a flute. Cf. Wheef.

Whiffinger, *n.* a vagabond. Cf. Waffinger.

Whiffle, *v.* to drive before the wind. Cf. Wheefle.

Whiffle, *v.* to play the fife or flute. Cf. Wheefle.

Whiffler, *n.* a fifer; a flute-player.

Whig, *n.* an old name for a Covenanter, a Presbyterian, or a dissenter from the Established Church of Scotland, used contemptuously.

Whig, Whigg, *n.* the sour part of cream, spontaneously separated from the rest; the thin part of a liquid mixture.—*v.* used of stale churned milk : to throw off a sediment.

Whig, *v.* to go quickly; to move at a steady, easy pace; to jog along; to work nimbly and heartily; to drink copiously.—*n.* a copious draught.

Whig, *n.* fine wheaten bread; a small, oblong roll, baked with butter and currants. Cf. Wig.

Whigamore, *n.* a 'Whig,' a Presbyterian Covenanter.

Whiggery, *n.* the practices and tenets of the Presbyterian Covenanters.

Whiggle, *v.* to waddle; to move loosely; to wriggle; to trifle; to idle; to work listlessly.—*n.* the act of waddling; a swing in the gait; a trifle; a gimcrack, toy; anything more ornamental than useful. Cf. Wiggle.

Whiggonite, *n.* a 'Whig.'

Whigling, *n.* a contemptuous name for a modern Whig.

Whigmaleerie, Whigmeleerie, *n.* a game played with pins for drink at a drinking club; a gimcrack; a fantastic, useless ornament; a whim, crotchet; a foolish fancy.—*adj.* whimsical, odd.

Whig-mig-morum, *n.* the name of a tune; party politics. Cf. Whip-meg-morum.

Whihher, *v.* to move through the air with a whizzing noise; to flutter quickly, as a bird; to titter; to laugh in a suppressed manner.

Whike, *n.* the hiss of an angry adder. Cf. Whick.

Whil, Whill, *conj.* until. · Cf. While.

While, *conj.* until.—*prep.* since; from.

Whileag, *n.* a little while. Cf. Whilock.

While as, *adv.* as long as.

Whileoms, *adv.* at times.

Whiles, *adv.* sometimes; at other times; now and then.

While-sin, -syne, *adv.* a while ago; some time back.

Whilesome, *adj.* former, whilom.

Whilie, *n.* a short time.

Whilk, *pron.* which.

Whilkever, *pron.* whichever.

Whilking, *ppl. adj.* complaining.

Whill, *n.* a small skiff.

Whillie-billow, Whillabaloo, *n.* an uproar; an outcry. Cf. Hullie-bullie.

Whilliegoleerie, *n.* a hypocritical fellow; a wheedler; a selfish flatterer.

Whillie-lu, Whilli-lu, Whilly-lou, *n.* an air in music; a prolonged strain of melancholy music; an outcry; a hubbub.

Whillie-whallie, *v.* to coax; to wheedle; to dally; to loiter.

Whilly, *v.* to cheat; to wheedle; to gull.

Whillybaloo, *n.* an uproar.

Whillywha, Whillywhae, Whillywhaw, *adj.* not to be depended on; wheedling; flattering.—*n.* a flatterer; one not to be depended on; a deceitful, wheedling person; a cheat; cajolery, flattery.—*v.* to flatter; to cajole; to wheedle; to delay; to be undecided.

Whilock, Whileock, *n.* a short space of time; a little while.

Whilockie, *n.* a very little while.

Whilom, *conj.* while, whilst.

Whiloms, *adv.* sometimes.

Whilper, *n.* anything large of its kind.

Whilt, *n.* a blow; perturbation; a pit-a-pat condition. Cf. Whult.

Whiltie-whaltie, *n.* a state of palpitation.—*v.* to palpitate; to dally; to loiter.—*adj.* in a state of palpitation, pit-a-pat.

Whim-ma-gary, *adj.* whimsical, fanciful.

Whimmer, *v.* to cry feebly, like a child; to whimper.

Whimper, *v.* to grumble; to make complaints; to sound as running water.—*n.* the cry of a dog at the sight of game; a whisper.

Whimple, *v.* to cover; to meander. Cf. Wimple.

Whimsey, Whimsy, *n.* a capricious liking; a fanciful device.

Whim-wham, *n.* a whim, fancy, fad; a kickshaw.

Whin, *n.* whinstone, ragstone.

Whin, *n.* a number; a few. Cf. Wheen.

Whin, *n.* furze.

Whin-bloom, *n.* furze-blossom.

Whin-buss, *n.* a furze-bush.

Whin-chacker, *n.* the whinchat.

Whin-clad, *adj.* furze-covered.

Whin-clocharet, *n.* the whinchat.

Whin-cowe, -kow, *n.* a furze-bush; a branch of furze.

Whinge, *v.* to whine; to cry fretfully and peevishly; to 'whimper' as a dog.—*n.* a whine, moan; a low, complaining cry.

Whinger, *n.* one who whinges.

Whinger, *n.* a short dagger, used as a knife at meals, and also as a weapon; a sword.

Whin-hoe, *n.* an adze-shaped hoe for stubbing up furze.

Whinil, *n.* a bottle of straw. Cf. Winnel.

Whinilstrae, *n.* a stalk of withered grass. Cf. Windlestrae.

Whink, *v.* to bark, as an untrained collie-dog in pursuit of game, when, breathless and impatient, he loses sight of a hare.—*n.* the suppressed bark of a sheep-dog; a whine.

Whinkens, *n.* flummery, 'sowens.'

Whinlet, *n.* young furze.

Whin-linnet, *n.* the linnet.

Whin-lintie, *n.* the whinchat.

Whin-mull, *n.* a rude kind of mill for crushing young furze for fodder.

Whinner, *v.* to neigh.

Whinner, *v.* to pass swiftly with a humming sound; to thunder or whiz along; to strike with force and loud noise; used of corn, &c.: to rustle to the touch through severe drought.—*n.* the whizzing sound of rapid flight or motion; a thundering sound; a thundering or resounding blow.

Whinnering-drouth, *n.* a severe drought, followed by a sifting wind.

Whinny, *adj.* producing 'whins' or furze; furze-clad.

Whinny, *v.* to cry as a snipe or a lapwing.

Whinny-buss, -cowe, *n.* a furze-bush.

Whinny-knowe, *n.* a furze-clad knoll.

Whin-pod, *n.* the seed-vessel of the furze.

Whinsie, *adj.* whimsical.

Whin-sparrow, *n.* the hedge-sparrow.

Whinstane, *n.* a name given to a curling-stone.

Whip, *v.* to warp, splice.

Whip, *v.* to run quickly, rush; to jerk; to drink off.—*n.* a sudden movement; a single swift blow; a moment; an attack or touch of illness; a sip; a hurried drink of liquor; in *pl.* punishment.—*adv.* smartly, suddenly.

Whip-col, *n.* a drink composed of rum, whipped eggs, and cream.

Whip-licker, *n.* one who has a horse and cart to hire.

Whip-ma-denty, *n.* a fop; a conceited dandy.

Whipman, *n.* a carter.

Whip-meg-morum, *n.* the name of a tune; 'Whiggery.'

Whipper-snapper, *n.* a cheat; a trick.

Whippert, *adj.* hasty, tart, irritable.

Whippert-like, *adj.* showing irritation in speech or manner.

Whipper-tooties, *n.* silly scruples; frivolous difficulties.

Whipple, *v.* to utter short, sharp cries, as a curlew or plover. Cf. Wheeple.

Whippy, *n.* a term of contempt applied to a young girl; a 'cutty.'—*adj.* clever; agile.

Whipshard, *v.* to whip, scourge.

Whip-the-cat, *n.* an itinerant tailor.—*v.* to itinerate as a tailor from house to house plying his trade.

Whip-together, *n* food, the ingredients of which are coarse, hastily mixed and badly cooked.

Whir, *v.* to whiz. Cf. Whirr.

Whirken, *v.* to strangle; to choke.

Whirkins, *n.* the posteriors. Cf. Wheerikins.

Whirky, *v.* to fly with a whizzing sound, like a startled partridge.

Whirl, *v.* used of the eyes: to roll; to wheel, 'hurl'; to drive; to speak with the uvular utterance of the *r.*—*n.* an eddy, whirlpool; a drive; a very small wheel or whorl; the fly-wheel of a spindle; a kind of apple shaped like the fly-wheel of a spindle; a fanciful ornament.

Whirl-barrow, *n.* a wheelbarrow.

Whirlbone, *n.* the knee-pan.

Whirligig, *n.* any rapidly revolving object; a turning of fortune; a trifle; a fanciful ornament; a child's toy, consisting of four cross-arms with paper sails attached, which spin round in the wind; a whimsical notion; an untrustworthy person; a light-headed girl. Cf. Furligig.

Whirligigum, Whirliegigin, *n.* a 'whirligig,' fanciful ornament.

Whirlimagig, *n.* a strange fancy; a sudden whim.

Whirliwhaw, Whirliwha, Whirly-wha, *n.* a useless ornament; a gimcrack; a trifle: a high and difficult trill in singing.—*v.* to gull, cheat; to mystify.

Whirlmagee, *n.* an unnecessary ornament.

Whirly, *adj.* like an 'adder-bead.'—*n.* an eddy; a whirlpool; a small wheel; a castor; a wheelbarrow; a two-wheeled barrow with two legs; a truckle-bed; a colliery-hutch.

Whirly, *adj.* weak, delicate.

Whirly-bed, *n.* a truckle-bed.

Whirly-birlie, *n.* a rapid, circular motion; anything that whirls round; a child's toy.

Whirly-mill, *n.* a toy water-wheel or mill.

Whirly-stane, *n.* an 'adder-bead.'

Whirmel, *v.* to upset. Cf. Whamble.

Whirr, *v.* to purr as a cat; to speak with the uvular utterance of the *r*; to whirl a thing round so fast as to make a whizzing sound; to move or drive along with great speed.—*n.* a smart blow; haste, hurry.

Whirret, *n.* a blow.

Whirrock, *n.* a knot in wood caused by the growth of a branch from the place; a corn or bunion on the foot; a pimple on the sole of the foot; a boil. Cf. Weerock.

Whirry, *v.* to hurry off; to whirl away.

Whiscar, *n.* a bunch of feathers for dusting with. Cf. Whisker.

Whish, *n.* a rushing or whizzing sound; a

swish; a slight sound, as of falling water;
the least whisper; a rumour, noise.—*v.* to
whiz; to rush with a whizzing noise; to
whistle, as the wind.

Whish, *int.* hush !—*v.* to hush; to be or remain silent; to soothe.—*n.* the sound made
by saying 'whish'; the slightest sound; a
whisper.—*adj.* quiet, silent.

Whish, *int.* a cry to scare away fowls, &c.—
v. to scare away fowls by saying 'whish !'
Cf. Wheesh.

Whishie, *n.* the slightest sound; a whisper.

Whishie, *n.* the white-throat.

Whisht, *int.* hush !—*v.* to hush, quiet, silence;
to be silent.—*n.* one's tongue as 'held' or
kept silent; the slightest sound; a whisper;
a faint rumour.—*adj.* hushed, silent, quiet.

Whisk, *n.* a one-horse conveyance; a blow;
a slight cleaning; in *pl.* a machine for
winding yarn on a 'quill' or 'clue.'—*v.* to
curry a horse; to lash, switch.

Whisk, *n.* whisky.

Whisker, *n.* a bunch of feathers for dusting
with; a beard, moustache, and whiskers;
a knitting-sheath; a blustering wind. Cf.
Fusker.

Whiskie, *n.* a kind of gig or one-horse chaise.
Cf. Whisk.

Whiskied, *ppl. adj.* tipsy, drunk with whisky.

Whisking, *ppl. adj.* great, sweeping.—*n.* palpitation of the heart.

Whiskit, *ppl. adj.* used of a horse: curried;
having a switched tail.

Whiskybae, *n.* 'usquebaugh,' whisky.

Whisky-bukky, *n.* a compound of oatmeal
and whisky rolled together into a ball of
two or three pounds weight.

Whisky-can, *n.* any vessel from which whisky
can be drunk; drinking, the intemperate
use of whisky.

Whisky-fair, *n.* a gathering to drink whisky;
a drunken revel.

Whisky-house, *n.* a public-house with no bar.

Whisky-maker, *n.* a distiller.

Whisky-pig, *n.* a whisky-jar, a 'graybeard.'

Whisky-pistol, *n.* a spirit-flask.

Whisky-plash, *n.* a liberal supply of whisky,
a drinking-bout.

Whisky-splore, *n.* a drunken revel, a drinking-bout.

Whisky-tacket, *n.* a pimple supposed to be
caused by intemperance.

Whisky-wife, *n.* a woman who sells whisky.

Whissel, Whissle, *v.* to whistle. Cf. Whistle.

Whissle, Whissel, *v.* to change money. Cf.
Wissel.

Whissle, *n.* a blow. Cf. Whistle.

Whissuntide, *n.* Whitsunday.

Whist, *int.* hush ! Cf. Whisht.

Whistle, *v.* to play on a reed, pipe, fife, or

flute.—*n.* a pipe, fife, or flute; a smart
blow; in *pl.* organ-pipes.

Whistle, *v.* to change money. Cf. Wissel.

Whistle-band, *n.* a fife-band.

Whistle-binkie, *n.* one who attends a penny-
wedding without paying anything, and has
no right to share in the festivities, and who
may sit on a 'bink' or bench by himself,
and whistle for his own amusement or that
of the company.

Whistle-kirk, *n.* a church with an organ in it;
an Episcopal church.

Whistle-kirk-minister, *n.* an Episcopal
clergyman.

Whistle-kist, *n.* an organ, a 'kist o' whistles.'

Whistle over, *v.* to swill liquor.

Whistler, *n.* a small, gray water-bird haunting
Lochleven, called also a 'Loch-learock';
anything exceptionally large; in *pl.* the
farmers on a large estate, who inform the
landlord as to rent and value of their
neighbours' farms, when he is about to
raise his rents.

Whistle-the-whaup, *n.* one who is supposed
to be making fun of another.

Whistle-whistle, *v.* to go on whistling.

Whistle-wood, *n.* a smooth wood used by
boys for making whistles; the willow; the
plane-tree.

Whistling-duck, *n.* the coot.

Whistling-plover, *n.* the golden plover.

Whit, *n.* a bit; an action; a deed.

Whit, *v.* to milk closely; to draw off the
dregs.

Whit, *adj.* what.

Whit, *v.* to cut; to whittle.

White, *n.* wheat.

White, *v.* to whittle; to shave off portions of
wood, &c., with a knife.—*n.* a cut; a
whittling.

White, *adj.* used of coin: silver.—*n.* silver
coin; the ling, a fish; a good action; in
pl. white clothes.—*v.* to flatter.

White aboon-gled, *n.* the hen-harrier.

White-airn, *n.* sheet-iron coated with tin,
white-iron.

White-bonnet, *n.* one who bids at a sale only
to raise the price.

White-bread, -breid, *n.* wheaten bread from a
baker's shop.

White-chaff't, *adj.* white-cheeked.

White-corn, *n.* wheat, barley, and oats alone.

White-crap, *n.* 'white corn.'

White-drap, *n.* snow.

White-fish, *n.* sea-fish, as haddocks, cod,
ling, tusk, &c.

White-fisher, *n.* one who fishes for white-fish
in the sea.

White-fish-in-the-net, *n.* a sport in which
two persons hold a plaid pretty high, over

which the rest of the company leap, and he who is entangled loses the game.

White folk, *n.* flatterers, wheedlers.

White Geordie, *n.* a shilling. Cf. Geordie.

White hare, *n.* an alpine hare.

White-hass, -hawse, *n.* a sheep's gullet; a favourite meat-pudding.

White-horned owl, *n.* the long-eared owl.

White-horse, *n.* the fish, fuller ray.

White-iron smith, *n.* a tinsmith.

White-land, *n.* land which is not moss or peat.

White-legs, *n.* the smaller wood, branches, &c. of a cutting.

White-lintie, *n.* the white-throat.

White-lip, *n.* a flatterer, a wheedler.

White-liver, *n.* a flatterer.

Whitely, *adj.* white, pallid; delicate-looking. —*adv.* pallidly; with a white appearance.

Whitely-faced, *adj.* white-faced.

White-maw, *n.* the herring-gull.

White-meal, *n.* oatmeal, as distinguished from barley-meal.

White-money, *n.* silver coin.

Whiten, *n.* small fish, the young of the salmon-trout. Cf. Whiting.

Whitening, *n.* pulverized chalk, freed from impurities, used for whitewashing, cleaning plate, making putty, &c.

White-pow'd, *adj.* white-headed.

White-pudding, *n.* a pudding of oatmeal, suet, and onions, stuffed in one of the intestines of a sheep, and tied tightly into sections.

Whiter, *n.* one that whittles; a knife for whittling.

Whiteret, *n.* a weasel. Cf. Whitrack.

White-sark, *n.* a surplice.

White-sarkit, *adj.* surpliced.

White-seam, *n.* plain needlework.—*v.* to do plain needlework.

White-shilling, *n.* a shilling in silver.

White-shower, *n.* a snow-shower.

White-siller, *n.* silver coin; small change in silver.

White-siller shilling, *n.* a shilling in silver.

White-skin blankets, *n.* blankets to be used without sheets.

White-spate, *n.* a flood in which the water is not muddy.

White-victual, *n.* wheat, barley, and oats alone.

White-washen, *ppl. adj.* used of the complexion: pale, pallid.

White wind, *n.* flattery; wheedling.

White wood, *n.* the outermost circles of oak-trees found in peat-bogs.

White-wren, *n.* the willow-warbler.

Whitey-brown thread, *n.* strong, unbleached thread.

Whither, *v.* to flutter; used of the wind: to bluster, rage; of an arrow, bullet, or other missile: to whiz by in its flight; to rush along; to whirl along with a booming sound; to beat, belabour.—*n.* a shaking; a slight attack of illness; a gust of wind; the sound of a rushing, violent movement; a stroke; a smart blow; the noise of a hare starting from its den.

Whither, *n.* a direction.

Whither, *conj.* whether.

Whither and beyont, *adv.* where and how far.

Whither-spale, *n.* a child's toy of a piece of notched lath to which a cord is attached to swing it round and cause mimic thunder; a thin, lathy person; a versatile person who is easily turned from his opinion or purpose.

Whitie, *n.* a species of sea-trout, probably the salmon-trout.

Whitie, *n.* a flatterer.

Whitie-whatie, *v.* to shilly-shally.—*n.* an idle pretence. Cf. Whittie-whattie.

Whiting, *n.* the young of the salmon-trout.

Whiting, *n.* the language of flattery.

Whitings, *n.* wood-shavings; thin slices cut off with a knife.

Whitlie, *adj.* pallid. Cf. Whitely.

Whitling, *n.* a species of sea-trout; the bull-trout in its first year.

Whitling-stone, *n.* a whetstone. Cf. Whittle.

Whitna, *adj.* what kind of. Cf. Whaten, Whatna.

Whitrack, Whitreck, Whitruck, *n.* a weasel.

Whitrack-skin, *n.* a purse made of a weasel's skin.

Whitred, Whitrat, Whitrit, *n.* a weasel.

Whitter, *n.* a hearty draught of liquor, whisky, &c.; a social glass.

Whitter, *n.* any weak stuff; anything weak in growth.

Whitter, *v.* to chirp, warble, twitter; to speak low and rapidly; to chatter, prattle. —*n.* loquacity, chatter. Cf. Twitter.

Whitter, *v.* to lessen by taking away small portions; to fritter.

Whitter, *n.* a token; a sign; a tree reserved in cutting timber. Cf. Witter.

Whitter, *v.* to move with lightness and speed; to scamper; to patter along; to shuffle about.

Whitteret, Whitterit, Whittrit, *n.* a weasel. Cf. Whitrack.

Whitterick, Whitterock, Whittrick, *n.* a weasel. Cf. Whitrack.

Whitterick, *n.* the curlew.

Whitter-whatter, *v.* to converse in a low tone of voice.—*n.* trifling conversation; chattering; tittle-tattle; a garrulous woman.

Whittery, *n.* weak stuff. Cf. Whitter.

Whittie, *adj.* low, mean. Cf. Wheety.

Whittie-whattie, *v.* to shilly-shally; to make frivolous excuses; to talk frivolously; to whisper.—*n.* an idle pretence; a vague, shuffling, or coaxing speech; a frivolous excuse; one who employs every means to gain his end.

Whittins, *n.* the last milk drawn from a cow, and the richest.

Whittle, *n.* a butcher's knife; a carving-knife, a 'gully'; a reaping-hook; a steel for sharpening knives; a state of uneasiness, or of being on the edge or fidgety.—*v.* to trim wood by paring it; to sharpen.

Whittle, *n.* a whitlow.

Whittle-case, *n.* a sheath for a knife.

Whitty, Whittie, *n.* the white-throat.

Whitty-whaws, *n.* silly pretences.

Whiver, *v.* to quiver.

Whiz, *v.* to move rapidly; used of water, &c.: to hiss on hot iron, stones, &c.—*n.* the hissing sound of hot iron in water.

Whizz, *v.* to inquire, cross-question, 'quiz.'

Whizzle, *v.* to make a hissing sound.

Whoa, *int.* an interjectional sound, used by a speaker in a hurry, to introduce a sentence.

Whoick, *int.* a call to dogs.

Whole, *adj.* healthy; well in health; with a *pl. n.,* all. Cf. Hail.

Whole-bodied cart, *n.* a cart with fixed shafts.

Whole hypotheo, *n.* the whole collection, number, &c.

Whole-ruck, *n.* the whole collection, number, &c. Cf. Hail-ruck.

Whole water, *n.* very heavy rain. Cf. Hail-water.

Whollup, *v.* to fawn, wheedle. Cf. Whullup.

Whomble, Whomel, Whomil, Whoml, Whomle, *v.* to upset. Cf. Whamble.

Whommel, Whommil, Whommle, *v.* to upset. Cf. Whamble.

Whon, *n.* a worthless person.

Whoogh, *int.* an excl. of surprise, delight, &c.; used by dancers, for mutual excitation.

Whoorle, *n.* a very small wheel; the fly-wheel of a spindle. Cf. Whirl.

Whoosh, *int.* an excl. expressive of a swift, sudden, rushing motion.

Whop, *v.* to strike; to throw. Cf. Whap.

Whopin, *ppl. adj.* big.

Whopper, *n.* any person or thing exceptionally large. Cf. Whapper.

Whopper-snapper, *n.* a little, presumptuous person; a cheat, a fraudulent trick. Cf. Whipper-snapper.

Whorl-bane, *n.* the 'whirlbone' or the knee-pan.

Whorlie, *adj.* like an 'adder-bead.' Cf. Whirly.

Whosle, *v.* to wheeze; to breathe heavily.

Whow, *int.* an excl. of admiration or pleasure Cf. Wow.

Who-yauds, *int.* a call to dogs to pursue horses.

Whozle, Whozzle, *v.* to breathe hard.—*n.* a difficulty in breathing. Cf. Whosle.

Whripe, *v.* to whimper. Cf. Whyripe.

Whud, *v.* to frisk; to whisk, as a hare.—*n.* a whisk, a hasty flight. Cf. Whid.

Whud, *n.* a fib, a lie.—*v.* to fib.

Whudder, *v.* to make a whizzing or rushing sound.—*n.* such a sound. Cf. Whither.

Whuff, *n.* a transient view; a whiff; a taste; an instant.—*v.* to puff; to smoke a pipe. Cf. Whiff.

Whuffle, *v.* to turn anything over lightly; to rumple. Cf. Wuffle.

Whuffy, *n.* an instant, a 'jiffy.' Cf. Whiff.

Whulk, *pron.* which. Cf. Whilk.

Whulli-goleerie, *n.* a wheedling fellow. Cf. Whillie-goleerie.

Whullilow, *n.* an outcry; a hubbub. Cf. Whillie-lu.

Whullup, *v.* to fawn, wheedle; to curry favour.

Whully, *v.* to cheat; to gull; to wheedle. Cf. Whilly.

Whully-wha, *v.* to flatter; to say soft things as a lover. Cf. Whilly-wha.

Whulper, *n.* anything large of its kind. Cf. Whilper.

Whult, *n.* a blow from a fall; a blow with a stick; the noise of such a fall; anything very large of its kind; a large piece. Cf. Whilt.

Whulter, *n.* anything large of its kind; a large potato; a large trout.

Whulting, *ppl. adj.* thumping, sounding; large.

Whumble, Whumel, Whumil, Whumle, *v.* to upset. Cf. Whamble.

Whumgee, *n.* a vexatious whispering; a trivial trick.

Whummils, *n.* a whip for a top.

Whummle, Whummel, Whummil, *v.* to upset. Cf. Whamble.

Whummle, *n.* a wimble.

Whummle-bore, *n.* a hole bored by a wimble. Cf. Wimble-bore.

Whumpie, *n.* a wooden dish containing liquid food enough for two persons.

Whumple, *v.* to wrap; to wind; to squirm. Cf. Whimple, Wimple.

Whun, *n.* the common furze. Cf. Whin.

Whun, Whunn, *n.* whinstone. Cf. Whin.

Whun, *n.* a worthless person. Cf. Whon.

Whunce, *n.* a heavy blow; the sound of such a blow.

Whunge, *v.* to whine; to 'whimper' as a dog. Cf. Whinge.

Whun-lintie, *n.* the red-linnet.

Whunner, *v.* to thunder or whiz along. Cf. Whinner.

Whup, *v.* to whip. Cf. Whip.

Whupers, Whuppers, *n.* a family of itinerant drivers.

Whupper, *n.* anything unusually large or fine; a great lie. Cf. Whapper.

Whuppie, *n.* a contemptuous term applied to a woman. Cf. Whippy.

Whuppin, *ppl. adj.* exceptionally large or fine. Cf. Whapping.

Whuppity-stourie, *n.* the name of a certain 'brownie.'

Whuppy, *adj.* quick, smart. Cf. Whippy.

Whuram, *n.* grace-notes or slurs in singing; any ornamental piece of dress.

Whur-cocks, *int.* a call given when game-birds rise.

Whurken, *v.* to choke, strangle. Cf. Whirken.

Whurl, *n.* a fawning, cunning child.

Whurl, *v.* to whirl; to wheel. Cf. Whirl.

Whurl-barrow, *n.* a wheelbarrow.

Whurlie-bed, *n.* a truckle-bed.

Whurlie-birlie, *n.* anything that whirls round; any toy that a child spins.

Whurlie-girkie, *n.* a fanciful or untrue tale.

Whurlie-wha, *n.* a useless ornament.—*v.* to gull. Cf. Whirliwha.

Whurligig, *n.* a toy that spins round; a whim. Cf. Whirligig.

Whurly, Whurlie, *n.* a cunning, fawning child. Cf. Whurl.

Whurly, Whurlie, *n.* a truckle-bed; a castor. Cf. Whirly.

Whurr, Whur, *v.* to make a whizzing sound; used of an organ: to sound. Cf. Whirr.

Whurroo, *int.* a cry to draw attention.

Whush, *n.* a rushing noise; a rumour.—*v.* to whiz. Cf. Whish.

Whush, *int.* hush!—*v.* to hush, be silent. Cf. Whish.

Whush, *int.* used to scare away birds. Cf. Whish.

Whusher, *v.* to whisper.—*n.* a whisper.

Whush-hoo, *int.* a cry used to scare away cats or birds.

Whushie, *v.* to soothe, to lull.—*int.* hush! Cf. Whush, Hushie.

Whusker, *n.* a whisker; the hair on one's face.

Whussle, *v.* to rustle.

Whussle, Whustle, Whus'le, *v.* to whistle. Cf. Whistle.

Whussle-wud, *n.* wood used by boys for making whistles. Cf. Whistle-wood.

Whut, *n.* a morning dram; an appetizer.

Whut, *adj.* what.

Whuten, *adj.* what kind of. Cf. Whaten.

Whuther, *v.* to flutter; to bluster; to whiz by. Cf. Whither.

Whuther-spale, *n.* a child's toy for making mimic thunder. Cf. Whither-spale.

Whutter, *n.* the barb of an arrow-head. Cf. Witter.

Whutterick, *n.* a weasel. Cf. Whitrack.

Whutterick-faced, *adj.* having a weasel-like face.

Whutterick-fuffing, *n.* a gathering of weasels.

Whut-throat, *n.* a weasel. Cf. Whitrack.

Whutting, *n.* used of spirits: a small draught.

Whuttle, *n.* a knife; a reaping-hook.—*v.* to sharpen. Cf. Whittle.

Whuttle-grass, *n.* the melilot, a species of trefoil. Cf. King's-claver.

Whuttling, *n.* a whispering; a quickening.

Whuttorock, *n.* a weasel. Cf. Whitrack.

Why, *n.* a reason.

Why, *int.* a call to a cart-horse to keep to the left.

Whyles, *adv.* sometimes. Cf. Whiles.

Whylock, Whyleock, *n.* a little while. Cf. Whilock.

Whynger, *n.* a short sword. Cf. Whinger.

Whyripe, *v.* to whimper, whine; to torment with mourning.

Whyte, *v.* to whittle. Cf. White.

Whyte, *n.* wheat.

Whyten, *n.* the whiting.

Wi', *prep.* with.

Wice, *adj.* wise. Cf. Wise.

Wicht, *n.* a wight, creature, person, fellow; the shrew-mouse.

Wicht, *adj.* strong; stout; brisk, nimble; clever.

Wichtfu', *adj.* strong, vigorous.

Wichtly, *adv.* vigorously; briskly; swiftly.

Wichty, *adj.* powerful.

Wick, *n.* a farmstead.

Wick, Wic, *n.* a creek; a small bay or inlet of the sea; an open bay.

Wick, *n.* a corner, angle; a corner of the eye or mouth.

Wick, *n.* used in curling: a narrow passage in the rink flanked by the stones of previous players; a shot to remove a stone by striking it at an angle.—*v.* to drive a stone through an opening; to 'cannon' a stone.

Wicker, *v.* to whiz through the air; to flutter as a bird. Cf. Whihher.

Wicker, *n.* a pliant twig; a switch; an erection of wicker-work.

Wicker, *n.* in *phr.* 'wicker o' a shower,' a quick, sharp shower.

Wicker, *n.* an old, cross-grained woman.

Wicker, *v.* to twist a thread very tightly; to become knotted from being too tightly twisted.

Wicker, *n.* the barb of a hook.

Wickerton, *n.* an old, cross-grained woman.

Wicket, *adj.* wicked; vicious, savage; angry, bitter.—*adv.* very, exceedingly.

†**Wicket,** *n.* the back-door of a barn; a sparred opening on either side of an old-fashioned barn for the purpose of winnowing.

Wid, *n.* wood. Cf. Wood.

Wid, *v.* would.

Wid, *adj.* mad. Cf. Wood.

Widbin, *n.* woodbine.

Widda, *n.* a widow.

Widden, *ppl.* waded. Cf. Wide.

Widden, *adj.* wooden, stiff.

Widden-dreme, *n.* a wild dream; a state of madness, or confusion; a state of sudden perturbation.

Widder, *n.* weather.

Widder-gaw, -ga, *n.* an abnormally fine day, sometimes portending bad weather to follow. Cf. Weather-gaw.

Widder-gleam, *n.* any cold or exposed place on an eminence.

Widdershins, Widdersins, Widdersones, *adv.* in a direction contrary to the sun's course; unluckily.—*n.* contrariety. Cf. Withershins.

Widdershins-grow, *n.* what grows in a direction contrary to the sun's course.

Widdie, Widdy, *n.* a withy; a hangman's noose, the gallows; a band or hoop of twisted willow; a twig with several smaller shoots branching out from it, which being plaited, it is used as a whip, the single grain serving for a handle; a person who has been hanged or deserves hanging.

Widdie, *n.* in *phr.* 'at the knag and the widdie thegither,' at loggerheads.

Widdie, *n.* a haddock dried without being split.

Widdie-waan, *n.* a willow-wand; a band of twisted willow-twigs.

Widdifow, Widdiefu, *n.* a small, ill-tempered person; a romp; a scamp; a gallows-bird. —*adj.* ill-tempered, wrathful; worthless; deserving to be hanged; romping.

Widdle, Widdil, *v.* to walk slowly about; to waddle; to wriggle; to attain an end by short, noiseless, or apparently feeble but prolonged exertions; to struggle; to deceive, beguile; to introduce by shifting motion, also by circuitous courses.—*n.* a wriggling motion; a contention, a struggle, a bustle; a crowd; the space occupied by a crowd.

Widdle-waddle, *v.* to waddle.

Widdrim, Wid-dreme, *n.* a state of confusion; a sudden perturbation; a wild dream. Cf. Widden-dreme.

Widdy, Widdie, *adj.* woody. Cf. Woody.

Wide, *v.* to wade.

Wide-gab, *n.* the frog-fish.

Wide-waken, *adj.* wide-awake.

Widi, *n.* a withy; a band of twisted willows; the gallows. Cf. Widdie.

Widow, *n.* a widower; a children's singing game.

Widow-body, *n.* a widow.

Widowerhood, *n.* the state of being a widower.

Widow-man, *n.* a widower.

Widow-wife, -woman, *n.* a widow.

Wie, *adj.* small. Cf. Wee.

Wiel, *n.* a pool; an eddy. Cf. Weel.

Wield, *v.* to manage successfully; to exert; to exercise; to possess.

Wieldiness, *n.* easiness of management; nimbleness.

Wieldy, *adj.* manageable; nimble, easy.

Wier, *v.* to guard; to lead, herd. Cf. Wear.

Wierd, *adj.* troublesome; mischievous.

Wierd, *adj.* weird, fateful; put in the way of, destined. Cf. Weird.

Wiers, *n.* in *phr.* 'on wiers,' in danger of; on the point of. Cf. Weirs.

Wife, *n.* a woman; a landlady.

Wife-body, *n.* a woman.

Wife-carle, *n.* a man who takes on himself a woman's household duties.

Wifely, *adj.* womanish, feminine.

Wifie, Wifey, *n.* a term of endearment used to a wife; a little woman; used endearingly, familiarly, or contemptuously of a woman.—*adj.* matronly.

Wifiekie, Wifikie, *n.* a little wife; a little woman; a term of endearment.

Wifie-like, *adj.* like a little wife.

Wiffin, *n.* a moment.

Wifock, Wifockie, *n.* a 'wifiekie.'

Wig, *n.* a piece of paper for holding small groceries, confections, &c., rolled upon the hand and twisted at one end, called also 'sow's-mou'; a sharp stroke; a whim, caprice.—*v.* to beat, strike sharply; to scold severely.

†**Wig, Wyg,** *n.* in *phr.* 'from wig to wa,' from pillar to post.

Wig, Wigg, *n.* whey. Cf. Whig.

Wig, *v.* to go quickly; to drink copiously; to work nimbly. Cf. Whig.

Wig, Wigg, *n.* fine wheaten bread; a small, oblong currant-roll. Cf. Whig.

Wig, Wigg, *v.* to wag, shake; to move.

Wig, *n.* a penny.

Wiggam-tree, *n.* the mountain-ash.

Wiggie, *adj.* loose, shaky, waggly.

Wiggie, Wiggy, *n.* a barber; a name for the devil; any judge who wears a wig on the bench.

Wiggle, *v.* to waggle, shake, move loosely; to swing in walking; to wriggle; to waddle, reel, stagger; to work listlessly and without heart; to trifle.—*n.* a waggle; a shaking motion; a waddling gait; a swing in the gait; a trifle, toy, gimcrack; anything more ornamental than useful.

Wigglety-wagglety, *adj.* swinging from side to side; unstable.—*adv.* used of a rider who does not move with the motion of his horse : from side to side, unsteadily.

Wiggle-waggle, *v.* to shake or move from side to side; to sway; to wriggle.—*n.* waggling, quivering.—*adv.* zigzag.

Wiggle-waggly, *adj.* very unstable.

Wiggly, *adj.* waggling, unstable.

Wiggly-waggly, *adj.* waggling, shaking.

Wiggy, *n.* a small currant-roll. Cf. Wig.

Wight, *n.* the shrew-mouse; a fellow. Cf. Wicht.

Wight, *adj.* stout, mighty; clever. Cf. Wicht.

Wight, *n.* blame; accusation; fault. Cf. Wite.

Wightdom, *n.* weight.

Wightly, *adv.* vigorously, strongly.

Wightman, *n.* a strong man.

Wightness, *n.* power, strength.

Wight-warping, *n.* nimble-throwing at the loom.

Wigle, *v.* to waggle. Cf. Wiggle.

Wigle-wagle, *v.* to move from side to side. Cf. Wiggle-waggle.

Wig-wag, *v.* to swing backwards and forwards. —*n.* vicissitude.

Wig-waggle, *v.* to swing backwards and forwards.

Wig-wag-slow, *adj.* slow as the swing of a pendulum.

Wike, *n.* a corner, angle. Cf. Wick.

Wil, *adj.* wild. Cf. Wild.

Wilcat, Wild-cat, *n.* the polecat; an ill-natured person.—*adj.* wild, stormy, raging. Cf. Wullcat.

Wild, *adj.* mad with anger; cross.—*adv.* extremely.

Wild, *adj.* bewildered; uncertain how to act.— *adv.*—astray. Cf. Will.

Wild-bear, *n.* in *phr.* 'shoein' the wild-bear,' a game, in which a person sits cross-legged on a swinging beam or pole. With a switch he whips the beam as if riding, and if he keeps his balance, he is victor over those who fail to do so.

Wild-birds, *n.* in *phr.* 'all the wild-birds in the air,' a naming and carrying game, in which the person who fails is switched on the back.

Wild-cotton, *n.* the tassel cotton-grass.

Wilder, Wildar, *v.* to lose one's way; to go astray.

Wildering, *ppl. adj.* bewildered; 'wild,' gone astray.

Wildert, Wilderit, *ppl. adj.* 'wild,' gone astray.

Wildfire, *n.* the phosphorescence of decaying vegetation, &c.; summer lightning; erysipelas; a will-o'-the-wisp; the small spearmint; the marsh-marigold; false zeal.

Wildie, *n.* a wild, restless child.

Wild-like, *adj.* wild; used of weather, threatening storm.—*adv.* wildly.

Wild-liquorice, *n.* the sweet milk-vetch.

Wild mustard, *n.* the charlock; the wild radish.

Wild pink, *n.* the maiden pink.

Wildrif, Wildruff, *adj.* wild, boisterous, unruly; wild-looking.

Wile, *n.* an instrument for twisting straw-ropes.

Wile, *v.* to choose, select.—*n.* a choice number. Cf. Wale.

Wile, *adj.* bewildered. Cf. Will.

Wile, *adj.* wild.

Wile, *adj.* vile.

Wilerie, *n.* wiling; seductiveness.

Wilesome, *adj.* wilful.

Wiley-coat, *n.* an under-coat or -vest. Cf. Wyliecoat.

Wil-fire, *n.* erysipelas. Cf. Wildfire.

Wilful, *adj.* willing, eager to work.

Wilk, *n.* a periwinkle, an edible shell-fish.

Will, *adj.* bewildered; lost in error; uncertain how to proceed.—*adv.* astray.—*v.* to lose one's way; to wander about.—*n.* the state of having lost one's way.

Will, *n.* a wish; a desire; inclination; hope; liking for.—*v.* to bequeath; to impose one's will on another.

Will, *v. aux.* to be accustomed to; shall; to be bent upon; to be under necessity; with *be*, indicates the simple present in estimating distances and time.

Willan, *n.* a willow.

Willawackits, *int.* 'well-a-day!'

Will-a-waes, *int.* an excl. of sorrow, 'well-a-day!' Cf. Well-a-day.

Willawaun, *int.* an excl. of sorrow, &c.

Will-a-wins, *int.* an excl. of pity, sorrow, &c. Cf. Weel-a-wins.

Willa-woo, *int.* an excl. of sorrow. Cf. Will-a-waes.

Will-be, *n.* a guess; a conjecture.

Willcorn, *n.* wild oats; oats growing without culture.

Willed, *ppl. adj.* wilful.

Willess, *adj.* aimless, purposeless; mechanical.

Will-gate, *n.* an erroneous course; an improper course.

Will he, nill he, *adv.* perforce; willy-nilly, *nolens volens.*

Willick, *n.* the common guillemot; the puffin; the razor-bill; a young heron.

Willie, *n.* a willow.

Willie-and-the-wisp, *n.* a will-o'-the wisp.

Willie Arnot, *n.* a slang name for good whisky.

Willie Cossar, *n.* a large pin of brass, two or three inches long, for pinning shawls or plaids, called after its maker; an expression of bigness, applied to a turnip, animal, or woman.

Willie-dragel, *adj.* dirty, draggled.

Willie Fisher, *n.* a notorious liar.

Willie fisher, *n.* the common tern ; a water-fowl ; ? the little grebe.

Willie-goat, *n.* a goat, a billy-goat.

Willie-gow, *n.* the herring-gull.

Willie-Jack, *n.* a go-between in a love affair.

Willie-miln, *n.* a door-latch worked by a string.

Willie-muflie, *n.* the willow-warbler.

Willie-o'-the-wisp, *n.* a will-o'-the-wisp, *ignis fatuus.*

Willie-pourit, *n.* the spawn of the frog; a tadpole.

Willie-powret, *n.* a child's name for the seal.

Willie-run-hedge, *n.* the goose-grass.

Willies, *n.* clippings of cloth.

Willie's-wisp, *n.* a will-o'-the-wisp.

Willie-wagtail, *n.* a name given to various species of wagtail ; the pied wagtail.

Williewaick, *n.* a loud shout.—*v.* to shout loudly.

Willie-wanbeard, *n.* the fifteen-spined stickle-back.

Willie-wand, -wain, -wairn, *n.* a wand or twig of willow. Cf. Willow-wand.

Willie-wastell, -wassle, *n.* a children's game. Cf. Wastell.

Willie-waught, -waucht, *n.* a hearty drink of any strong liquor.

Willie-whae, *v.* to make the cry of the curlew.

Willie-whaup, *n.* the curlew.

Willie-whip-the-wind, *n.* the kestrel.

Willie-winkie, *n.* a fondling name for a small child.

Willie-with-a-wisp, *n.* a will-o'-the-wisp.

Willie-wogie, *n.* a small piece of wood burning at one end, which is twirled quickly and continuously round.

Willin-sweert, *adj.* coy ; partly willing, partly unwilling.

Willint, *adj.* willing.

Willintly, *adv.* willingly ; readily.

Williwa, *int.* an excl of sorrow. Cf. Will-a-waes.

Will-kail, *n.* wild mustard or charlock.

Willness, *n.* dizziness.

Willow-boost, *n.* a rustic basket for holding meal, &c.

Willow-wand, *n.* a willow-rod or -twig; a willow-rod, which, when peeled and placed against the door of a Highland house, indicated that the inmates wished no visitors to enter ; a thin, lanky person. Cf. Willie-wand.

Willy, *adj.* wilful ; self-willed.

Willyard, Willyart, *adj.* obstinate ; self-willed. Cf. Wilyart.

Willyart, *adj.* shy, bashful. Cf. Wilyart.

Willy-wa, *v.* to wheedle, flatter. Cf. Whilly-wha.

Willy-wacht, *n.* a deep draught. Cf. Willie-waught.

Willy-wally, *int.* an excl. of sorrow.

Willy-wambles, *n.* a complaint of the bowels attended with a rumbling noise.

Wilshoch, *adj.* perverse ; changeable.—*n.* a timid courter.

Wilsum, Wilsome, *adj.* bewildered, wandering, lonely, dreary.

Wilsum, Willsome, *adj.* wilful.

Wilt, *n.* a blow, a stroke. Cf. Whilt.

Wilt, *v.* to wither, fade.—*n.* a state of feebleness or despondency.

Wiltu, Wilto, *v.* and *pron.* wilt thou ?

Wiltuna, *v.*, *pron.*, and *neg.* wilt thou not ?

Wilyart, Wilyard, *adj.* obstinate ; unmanageable ; self-willed.

Wilyart, *adj.* shy, bashful ; awkward ; bewildered ; lonely ; wild ; shunning human habitations and society.—*n.* a timid, faint-hearted fellow.

Wimble, *n.* a twist.

Wimble-bore, *n.* a hole bored by a wimble ; a defect in the throat causing indistinct speech.

Wime, *n.* the belly. Cf. Wame.

Wimmel, *n.* the windpipe.

Wimmelbree, Wimmelbreis, *n.* a thin soup made of the same constituents as a 'haggis.'

Wimmle, *n.* a wimble.

Wimple, Wimpil, *v.* to wrap, cover ; used of a river, stream : to wind, meander, ripple ; of love : to glance forth shyly from the eye ; to wriggle, squirm, writhe ; used of growing corn : to toss, wave ; of a boat : to move unsteadily, to be top-heavy ; to perplex ; to use circumlocution with intent to deceive.—*n.* a winding ; a curve ; a meandering movement ; a curl ; an intricate turn ; a wile ; a piece of craft ; a fit of perversity ; a sulky temper.

Wimpled, *ppl. adj.* indirect, involved, intricate ; circumlocutory, perplexed.

Wimplefeyst, *n.* a sulky humour.—*adj.* unmanageable, untoward. Cf. Amplefeyst.

Wimpler, *n.* a waving lock of hair.

Win, *v.* to earn ; to quarry stone ; to find and dig out coal ; to attain or reach by effort or with difficulty ; to succeed ; to succeed in reaching a place ; to go ; to come ; to have power or liberty to go ; to arrive at ; to work, labour ; to deliver a blow.—*n.* earnings, wages.

Win, *n.* the quantity of standing corn that a band of reapers could cut ; the group of three reapers, generally a man and two women, who worked on the same 'rig.'

Win, *v.* to dry hay, corn, peat, &c. by exposure to the air ; to dry or season by the heat of the fire ; to winnow.

Win, *v.* to dwell, reside. Cf. Won.

Win, *n.* wind ; a boasting, empty bravado.

Win, *v.* to wind.—*ppl.* wound.

Win aboon, *v.* to get above.

Win about, *v.* to circumvent.

Winach, *v.* to winnow.

Win and loss, *n.* a game at marbles in which marbles are won or lost by the players.

Win awa, *v.* to get away ; to die.

Wince, *v.* used of a horse : to prance, kick out behind.

Winch, *n.* a wench.

Winch, *v.* to wince.—*n.* a wince ; the act of wincing.

Winchancie, *adj.* unlucky. Cf. Unchancy.

Winchie, *n.* a young woman.

Wincock, *n.* a toy windmill ; a person of unstable disposition.

Wind, *n.* talk, foolish talk ; mood, spirits ; a children's singing game.—*v.* to boast ; to talk long and loudly ; to out-talk a person ; to taint ; to become tainted or sour.

Wind, *v.* to enfold a corpse in grave-clothes ; to twist.

Wind, *n.* an alley ; a narrow street. Cf. Wynd.

Wind, Winde, *v.* used of horses, &c.: to turn to the left. Cf. Wynd.

Windasses, *n.* fanners for winnowing grain.

Wind-ba', -ball, *n.* a balloon ; wind broken behind.

Wind-band, *n.* an iron band wound round anything broken or spliced.

Wind-bill, *n.* an accommodation bill.

Wind-broken, *adj.* broken-winded.

Wind-buff't, *adj.* driven and buffeted by wind.

Wind-craw, *n.* a large potato, stuck full of a gull's wing-feathers, which will drive and jump before a strong breeze, and which boys consider it a feat to be able to catch.

Wind-cuffer, *n.* the kestrel.

Winder, *n.* one who deals in the marvellous in story-telling.—*v.* to wonder.

Wind-feed, *n.* occasional showers which increase the force of the wind.

Wind-flaucht, -flaught, *adv.* with impetuous force, as if driven by the wind.

Wind in, *n.* the smallest matter.

Windin', *n.* out-talking ; silencing by loud, long talking.

Winding, *n.* a gathering of tallow rising up against the wick of a candle, deemed an omen of death in the family.

Windings, *n.* what is wound in spinning.

Windisome, *adj.* producing flatulence ; long-winded.

Windle, *n.* a 'bottle' of straw.—*v.* to make up straw in 'bottles.' Cf. Winnel.

Windle, Windles, *n.* an instrument used for winding yarn.

Windle, *v.* to walk wearily in the wind.—*n.* a measure of straw, corn, &c.

Windlen, *n.* a 'bottle' of straw, &c. Cf. Windlin.

Windless, *adj.* breathless ; exhausted.

Windlestrae, *n.* smooth-crested grass ; a stalk of withered grass ; a thin, unhealthy person ; a vacillating fellow ; anything weak and slender ; a trifling obstacle.

Windlin, Windling, *n.* a 'bottle' of straw, hay, &c.

Windock, *n.* a window. Cf. Winnock.

Window, *v.* to winnow.

Window, *n.* any opening in a room other than the door ; a recess in the wall of a room for small articles.

Window-bole, *n.* a small opening in a wall for light and air, covered with a wooden shutter.

Window-brod, *n.* a shutter.

Window-sole, *n.* a window-sill.

Windraw, *n.* a windrow.—*v.* to put hay, peats, &c. into windrows.

Windrem, *n.* confusion ; a wild dream. Cf. Widden-dream.

Windskew, *n.* a broad piece of wood attached to a long handle which is placed within the chimney-top, and is movable with changing winds, to prevent smoke.

Wind-sucker, *n.* a horse that draws air into its stomach by sucking the manger or biting the crib.

Wind-warks, *n.* the lungs.

Wind-waved, *ppl. adj.* used of plants, &c. : having the stem whirled about by the wind, so that the roots become loosened in the earth.

Wind-wecht, *n.* a hoop covered with skin, for winnowing grain.

Windy, *adj.* having plenty of breath ; flatulent ; causing flatulence ; noisy, talkative, garrulous ; boastful ; vain, ostentatious.

Windy Saturday, *n.* a peculiarly windy day, which, like 'Black'- or 'Mirk-Monday,' became a traditional era from which subsequent events were dated.

Windysome, *adj.* causing flatulence ; long-winded.

Windy-wallets, *n.* one given to fibbing or exaggeration ; a person given to break wind behind.

Wine, *v.* to turn ; to wind. Cf. Wynd.

Wine-berry, *n.* the common red-currant.

Wine-tree, *n.* the blackthorn.

Win-free, *v.* to liberate, set free ; to obtain release ; to raise from the ground ; to disentangle.

Wing, *n.* an arm; the side of a cart; in *pl.* the mud-guards of gig-wheels.—*v.* used in curling: to strike the side of an unguarded stone.

Winged-chair, *n.* an easy-chair with projecting sides.

Winged-row, *n.* a halfpenny roll baked with flat sides like wings.

Wingel, *n.* a tumour; a soft blister from walking in tight shoes.

Wingle, *v.* to flutter, wave; to hang or dangle loosely; to flap, wag; to bend and twist; to walk feebly; to wriggle; to carry in a dangling way; to move with difficulty under a load.

Wingle-strae, *n.* a stalk of withered grass. Cf. Windlestrae.

Winglit-looking, *adj.* very slender.

Wink, *n.* a nap; a sleep; a moment.

Winker, *n.* an eye; an eyelash; an eyelid.

Winkie, *n.* the twinkling of an eye; a nursery word for sleep.

Win-kill, *n.* a hollow in a stack of oats, &c., for ventilation and the prevention of heating.

Winkish, *v.* to deceive; to cajole.

Winkit, *ppl. adj.* used of milk: slightly turned.

Winkle, *v.* to sparkle; to twinkle.

Winklot, *n.* a wench; a young woman.

Wink o' a wintle, *n.* a very short time.

Winle, *n.* a 'bottle' of straw. Cf. Windle.

Winless, *adj.* breathless.

Winlin, *n.* a 'bottle' of straw. Cf. Windlin.

Winn, *v.* to winnow. Cf. Win.

Winn, *v.* to earn, win.—*ppl.* won. Cf. Win.

Winna, Winnae, *v. neg.* will not.

Winned, *ppl.* winnowed.

Winnel, Winnle, *n.* a 'bottle' of straw or hay.—*v.* to put up hay or straw in 'bottles.' Cf. Windle.

Winnel-skewed, *adj.* under optical illusion.

Winnel-strae, *n.* a stalk of withered grass. Cf. Windlestrae.

Winner, *v.* to wonder.

Winner, *n.* used in curling: the stone lying nearest the tee, the winning shot.

Winnerfu', *adj.* wonderful; wonderfully well, or recovered from an illness.

Winnes, *n.* misuse; abuse; waste. Cf. Wanuse.

Winnie, *adj.* windy.

Winnie, *n.* a game of marbles in which the stakes are lost and won.

Winning, *n.* earnings; wages.

Winning-ring, *n.* the game of 'winnie.'

Winnister, *n.* a fan for winnowing corn. Cf. Winnowster.

Winnle, *n.* a 'bottle' of straw. Cf. Winnel.

Winnle, Winnles, *n.* an instrument for winding yarn. Cf. Windle.

Winnlen, *n.* a 'bottle' of straw. Cf. Windlen.

Winnle-strae, *n.* a stalk of withered grass; a thin, unhealthy person; a vacillating fellow. Cf. Windiestrae.

Winnock, Winnoc, *n.* a window.

Winnock, *n.* a wind-egg.

Winnock-bole, *n.* a small aperture for a window, generally closed with a wooden shutter instead of with glass.

Winnock-brod, *n.* a window-shutter.

Winnock-bunker, *n.* a window-seat, forming a chest.

Winnock-cheek, -lug, *n.* the side of a window.

Winnock-glass, *n.* window-glass; a glazed window.

Winnock-neuk, *n.* a window-corner.

Winnock-sole, *n.* a window-sill.

Winnow, *v.* to fan; to wave; to wave wings.

Winnow-claith, *n.* a winnowing-sheet.

Winnowster, *n.* a winnowing-fan.

Winny, *adj.* windy.

Winny, *v.* to winnow.

Winraa, Winraw, *v.* to windrow. Cf. Windraw.

Winrame's birds, *n.* in *phr.* 'like Winrame's birds,' used of a tedious tale.

Wins, *suff.* towards; in the direction of.

Win's, *n.* rheumatism.

Winsday, *n.* Wednesday.

Winsome, *adj.* large; comely.

Winsomelie, *adv.* pleasantly; winningly; in an engaging way.

Winsomeness, *n.* cheerfulness.

Wint, *v.* to want; to wish.

Wint, *v.* to befall.

Wint, *n.* a glimpse; an instant; a hint as to the whereabouts of a person or thing. Cf. Waint, Went.

Winter, *n.* a wanter; one seeking a wife. Cf. Wanter.

Winter, *n.* the last load of corn brought home from the harvest-field; the person who brought it; the state of having all the harvest ingathered; the feast of the ingathering, the 'kirn.'—*v.* to keep and feed cattle through the winter.

Winter, *n.* an iron frame or loose bar made to fit on to the bars of a grate to hold anything which has to be heated.

Winter downfall, *n.* the descent of sheep in winter from the hills to lower adjacent ground.

Winter-dykes, *n.* a clothes-horse; a wooden frame for drying clothes out-of-doors.

Winterer, *n.* an animal kept to feed in a particular place during winter; an animal taken to be kept during winter.

Winter-fish, *n.* ling salted for winter use.

Winter-haining, *n.* pasture or common enclosed in winter in order to get hay from it.

Winter-hap, *n.* winter covering.

Winterin, *n.* an ox or cow of one year.

Winterish, *adj.* wintry.

Winterling, *n.* a 'winterin'.

Winter-Saturday, *n.* the last Saturday of October, on which the winter half-year begins.

Winter-shadit, *adj.* sheltered from the north, facing the south.

Winter-slap, *n.* a gap in a fence allowing cattle to roam from field to field in winter.

Winter-sour, *n.* curds and butter mixed and eaten with bread; curds, made of soured milk, mixed with butter.

Winter-Sunday, *n.* the last Sunday in October.

Wintin, *ppl. adj.* defective mentally.—*prep.* without. Cf. Wanting.

Wintle, *v.* to stagger; to reel; to tumble; to struggle; to wriggle; to wave to and fro hanging on a gallows; to writhe; to wind round.—*n.* a staggering motion.

Wintle, *n.* a withered stalk of grass or straw, a 'windlestrae.'

Winton-money, *n.* money given to a herd to induce carefulness of the cattle under his charge while grazing.

Winze, *v.* to curse.—*n.* an oath; a curse.

Winzie, *adj.* winsome, pleasant.

Wi'outen, *prep.* without. Cf. Withouten.

Wip, Wipp, *v.* to wrap or bind round tightly; to overlay with cord, &c.; to tie.—*n.* a tight twist of a rope, &c.; a coil; a wrapping.

Wipe, *v.* to whip, strike, beat.—*n.* a blow, stroke; a sarcastic remark; a large amount, degree, or extent.

Wiper, *n.* a severe blow; a severe taunt or retort.

Wippen, *n.* that with which the handle of a golf-club is overlaid.

Wipple, *v.* to wind, twist; to intertwine; to roll or bundle up.

Wir, *pron.* our.

Wird, *n.* word; news; rumour. Cf. Word.

Wirdie, *n.* a little word; a word or two; a short speech.

Wire, *n.* a knitting-needle.—*v.* to work vigorously.

Wire-scraper, *n.* a fiddler.

Wirk, *v.* to work. Cf. Wark.

Wirl, *n.* a small, rickety child; a small, harsh-featured person; a stunted animal.

Wir lane, Wirlens, *n.* ourselves alone. Cf. Lane.

Wirlie, *n.* a puny, rickety child.

Wirlie, *n.* an eddy. Cf. Whirly.

Wirling, *n.* a puny, feeble child or animal.

Wirly, *adj.* puny; small.

Wirr, *n.* a dog's growl; an angry answer; a fit of bad temper; wrath; roughness;

a crabbed fellow; a diminutive, peevish person.—*v.* to growl as a dog; to fret; to whine.—*int.* a call to dogs, inciting them to fight.

Wirr, *v.* to fly like a startled partridge. Cf. Whirr.

Wirrablaa, *n.* a violent but short exertion.

Wirricow, *n.* a scarecrow; a bogle. Cf. Worricow.

Wirring, *ppl. adj.* crabbed.

Wirry, *v.* to worry; to strangle. Cf. Worry.

Wirry carl, *n.* a bugbear.

Wirrycow, *n.* a bugbear; a scarecrow. Cf. Worricow.

Wirsat, Wirsit, *n.* worsted. Cf. Worset.

Wirsels, *refl. pron.* ourselves.

Wirsle, *v.* to struggle very hard; to be very energetic.—*n.* a hard struggle. Cf. Warsle.

Wirsle-warsle, *n.* a hard, continuous struggle.—*v.* to struggle hard and continuously.

Wirth, *n.* importance, worth.—*adj.* worthy; deserving; of use; of value.

Wis, *v.* to wish. Cf. Wish.

Wis, *v. pret.* knew, wist.

Wisdom, *n.* a wise or prudent action.

Wise, *v.* to direct, guide, lead; to counsel, advise; to be cautious or use policy in reaching one's end; to get by skill or craft; to manœuvre; to entice, lure, persuade; to beguile; to induce; to let out or draw anything so as to prevent it from breaking; to spend; to use; to withdraw, take away; to incline; to slip away.

Wise, *n.* guise.

Wise, *adj.* knowing, well-informed; sane; possessing or pretending to possess powers of magic or witchcraft.

Wisehorn, *n.* the gullet; the gizzard. Cf. Weasan.

Wiselike, *adj.* sagacious; proper; seemly; respectable; becoming, befitting; good- or nice-looking. — *adv.* properly, sensibly; decently; becomingly.

Wise-lóoking, *adj.* prudent; sensible; proper; respectable; seemly.

Wisen, *v.* to dry up; to shrivel. Cf. Wizzen.

Wise-spoken, *adj.* wise or prudent of speech.

Wise-wife, *n.* a witch; a fortune-teller.

Wise-woman, *n.* a woman who professed to cure ailments by skill or by charms; a '.wise-wife.'

Wish, *v.* to hope; to trust.

Wish, *int.* hush!

Wishie, *n.* in *phr.* 'neither hishie nor wishie,' profound silence.

Wisht, *int.* hush! Cf. Whisht.

Wish-wash, *n.* worthless stuff.

Wishy, Wishie, *adj.* delicate; watery, weak.—*v.* to hesitate; to make trifling excuses.

Wishy-washy, *adj.* delicate; of weak constitution.—*n.* any weak, watery drink; in *pl.* shuffling language; prevarications; fanciful evasions; slowness in coming to the point. —*v.* to make trifling excuses.

Wisk, *n.* a bulky, untidy wrapping about the neck.

Wisk, *v.* to give a light brushing stroke with anything pliant; to hurry away. — *n.* a slight brushing stroke with anything pliant. Cf. Whisk.

Wiskar, *n.* a whisker. Cf. Whisker.

Wisle, *v.* to exchange money. Cf. Wissel.

Wislie, *adj.* thin, shrivelled; stunted. Cf. Wuzlie.

Wisn'd, *ppl.* parched; dried up. Cf. Wizzen.

Wisock, *n.* a wise person.

Wisp, *n.* a bunch of twigs; a 'bush,' as a tavern-sign; a candle; the nest of a certain kind of wild bee, made on the surface of the ground.—*v.* to rub down a horse with a wisp of straw, hay, &c.; used of shoes or clogs: to put a wisp of straw in them in order to keep the feet warm and dry.

Wisp, *n.* a wasp; an ill-natured person.

Wiss, *v.* to wish. Cf. Wish.

Wiss, *v.* to lead; to persuade; to lure. Cf. Wise.

Wiss, *n.* the moisture exuding from bark in preparing it for tanning.

Wiss, *v. pret.* knew.

Wissel, Wissle, *n.* used of money: the change. —*v.* to exchange; to change money; with *words:* to talk; to hold discourse; to exchange angry words, to quarrel; to club in payment of drink; to wager, bet.

Wissen, *v.* to wither; to shrivel. Cf. Wizzen.

Wissler, *n.* a money-changer.

Wist, *n.* a wisp.

Wist, *v. pret.* wished.

Wistel, *v.* to wager, stake, bet. Cf. Wissel.

Wister, *v.* to scuffle; to mix in a broil.—*n.* a broil, a noisy scuffle, accompanied by high words.

Wit, *n.* intelligence; information, knowledge; sense; wisdom.

Wit, *v.* to know; to assure.

Witch, *n.* a wizard; a moth.

Witch-bead, *n.* a kind of fossil of the class of *Entrochi.*

Witch-bell, *n.* the harebell.

Witch-book, *n.* a book of spells, charms, &c.

Witch-bracken, *n.* a species of bracken.

Witch-bridle, *n.* an iron collar or frame with prongs fixed on a witch's neck and head, and fastened to a wall.

Witch-cake, *n.* an uncanny and virulent cake prepared for purposes of incantation at witches' meetings.

Witch-carline, *n.* a witch.

Witch-charming, *n.* witchcraft.

Witch-doctor, *n.* one who claims to cure by charming; one who cures the bewitched.

Witchery, *n.* witchcraft; a tale of witchcraft.

Witches, *n.* round, red, clay marbles.

Witches' butterfly, *n.* a large, thick-bodied moth, of drab or light-brown colour.

Witches' hazel, *n.* the mountain ash.

Witches' knots, *n.* a bundle of matted twigs formed on branches of birch and blackthorn, and resembling birds'-nests; a disease supposed to arise from the stoppage of the juices; a sort of charm applied to a woman's hair.

Witches' ride, *n.* a riding of witches at midnight of Hallowe'en.

Witches'-thimmles, -thummles, *n.* the flowers of the foxglove.

Witch-gathering, *n.* a gathering of witches for a 'witches' ride.'

Witch-gowan, *n.* the dandelion.

Witch-hag, *n.* the swallow.

Witching, *n.* witchcraft.

Witching-docken, *n.* an old woman's name for tobacco.

Witch-knots, *n.* a charm applied to a woman's hair. Cf. Witches' knots.

Witch-mark, *n.* a mark supposed to exist on the body of a witch.

Witch-pricker, *n.* a witch-finder who discovered witches by pricking them for the 'witch-mark.'

Witch-Sabbath, *n.* a gathering of all the witches in Scotland on the evening between the first Friday and Saturday in April.

Witch-score, *n.* the mark made with a sharp instrument on the forehead of a supposed witch to render her harmless.

Witch's-milk, *n.* the juice of the 'witch-gowan.'

Witchuk, *n.* the sand-martin.

Witch-wean, *n.* a changeling substituted by fairies, &c., for a new-born child.

Witch-wife, -woman, *n.* a witch.

Witchy, *adj.* witch-like; bewitching.

Wite, *v.* to blame; to accuse; to twit with; to bear the blame.—*n.* blame; accusation; the fault of; the cause of any ill; a wrong; an injury.

Witeless, *adj.* blameless.

Witer, *n.* one who blames; a fault-finder.

Witewordy, *adj.* blameworthy.

With, *prep.* against; upsides with; according to; in agreement with; expressing tolerance of; by; owing to; in consequence of; for; in exchange for; of; to.

Withe, *n.* a rod.

Wither, *v.* to fret; to whine, whimper.

Wither, *n.* weather.

Wither, *pref.* indicating contrary direction.

Wither, *n.* a wether.

Wither, *v.* to tremble; to bluster. Cf. Whither.

Wither, *n.* the barb of an arrow-head, fishing-hook, &c. Cf. Witter.

Wither-gates, *adv.* in a contrary direction; against the sun's course.

Wither-gloom, *n.* the clear sky near the horizon. Cf. Weather-gleam.

Witherips, *n.* the sweet woodruff.

Wither-lands, *adv.* in a contrary direction; against the sun's course.

Wither-lock, *n.* the lock of hair in a horse's mane, grasped by a rider in mounting.

Withershins, Withershines, *adv.* against the sun's course; topsy-turvily; unluckily; contrarily.—*adj.* at enmity with; opposed to.—*n.* contrariness.

Withershins-grow, *n.* anything growing contrary to the sun's course.

Witherspail, *n.* the goose-grass.

Wither-spale, *n.* a notched piece of wood, whirled round at the end of a string, to mimic thunder; a thin, lanky person; a versatile person. Cf. Whither-spale.

Witherty-weep, *n.* the plover.

Wither-wecht, *n.* the weight allowed to counterbalance the paper, vessel, &c. in which the goods are weighed.

Wither-wise, *adv.* against the course of the sun.

With-gate, *n.* the advantage, the better of a person, by overreaching.

Withinside, *prep.* inside, within.

Wi' this, *adv.* hereupon.

Without, *prep.* outside.—*conj.* unless.

Withouten, Withooten, *prep.* without.

Witling, *n.* a simpleton; a fool.

Witness, *n.* a sponsor at a baptism.—*v.* to see; to be present at.

Witrat, *n.* a weasel. Cf. Whitrack.

Witten, Wittan, *n.* knowledge; in *pl.* news.

Witten, *ppl.* waited.

Witter, *n.* the barb of an arrow-head, fish-hook, &c.

Witter, *v.* to be peevish; to growl.—*n.* a peevish person, one always growling.

Witter, *n.* a token, sign; a mark; a tree reserved in cutting timber; a pennon; a standard; used in curling: the tee.—*v.* to inform; to guide; to prognosticate.

Witter, *v.* to struggle for a livelihood; to fight; to fall foul of; to take by the throat. —*n.* the throat.

Wittered, *ppl. adj.* barbed; mixed.

Wittered-heuks, *n.* barbed hooks.

Witterel, *n.* a peevish, waspish person.

Witteret, *n.* a weasel. Cf. Whitrack.

Wittering, *n.* knowledge, information; a hint.

Witter-length, *n.* in curling: as far as the tee.

Witterly, *adv.* wittingly, knowingly.

Witterous, *adj.* barbed.

Witterous, *adj.* crabbed; determined.

Witters, *n.* the throat. Cf. Witter.

Witter-shot, *n.* a curling-stone reaching and resting on the tee.

Witter-stone, *n.* a stone placed as a mark.

Wittert, *ppl. adj.* barbed.

Wittin, Wittins, *n.* knowledge; information; tidings.

Witty, *adj.* wise; knowing; shrewd; well-informed; sensible.—*n.* cleverness; skill.

Wize, Wizz, *v.* to lead; to lure. Cf. Wise.

Wizen, Wizzen, Wizzon, *n.* the gullet. Cf. Weasan.

Wizzards, *n.* couch-grass and other weeds dried, or 'wizzened,' on fallow fields.

Wizzen, *v.* to wither; to shrivel; to become dry, parched; to be wrinkled; to bake.—*adj.* withered, dried up, shrivelled.

Wizzen-faced, *adj.* with withered, pinched, wrinkled features.

Wo, *n.* woe.—*int.* alas! Cf. Wae.

Wo, Woa, *int.* a call to a horse to stand still.

Wob, *n.* a web. Cf. Wab.

Wo-back, *int.* a call to a horse to back.

Wobart, *adj.* weak, feeble; decayed.

Wobart-like, *adj.* used of a faded, withered appearance.

Wobat, *adj.* 'wobart.'

Wobat, *n.* a hairy caterpillar. Cf. Woubit.

Wobble, *v.* to sell drink without a license.

Wobbling-shop, *n.* an unlicensed drinking shop.

Wobster, *n.* a weaver. Cf. Webster.

Wochle, *v.* to stagger; to waddle. Cf. Wauchle.

Wod, *adj.* mad; eager.—*n.* eagerness, keenness. Cf. Wood.

Wod, *n.* a wood.

Wodat, *adj.* weak, feeble, decayed.

Wodder, *pref.* indicating a contrary direction. Cf. Wither.

Woddie, *n.* a withy. Cf. Widdie.

Woddram, *n.* a fit of obstinacy; furious madness. Cf. Woodrum.

Wode, *n.* a corruption of the word 'God,' used as an expletive.

Wode, *adj.* mad. Cf. Wood.

Wodeness, *n.* madness.

Wodensday, *n.* Wednesday.

Wodershins, *adv.* against the sun's course. Cf. Withershins.

Wodge, *v.* to brandish. Cf. Wadge.

Wodroam, Wodrome, *n.* a fit of obstinacy. Cf. Woodrum.

Wodset, *n.* a mortgage. Cf. Wadset.

Wodspur, *n.* a forward, unsettled, fiery person; a 'Hotspur.' Cf. Woodspurs.

Wog, *v.* to wag; to twitch.

Wog, *n.* vogue, a fashion.

Wogh, *adj.* insipid. Cf. Waugh.

Wolron, Wolroun, *n.* a poor, miserable creature.

Wolter, *v.* to welter ; to surge.—*n.* an upset. Cf. Walter.

Woman, *n.* a familiar term of address ; a contemptuous designation ; a maid-servant.

Woman-big, *adj.* grown to womanhood.

Woman-body, *n.* a woman ; a female.

Woman-folk, *n.* women.

Woman-grown, *adj.* grown to womanhood.

Woman-house, *n.* a laundry.

Woman-muckle, *adj.* grown to womanhood.

Woman-scared, *adj.* shy in the presence of women.

Woman-school, *n.* a dame's school.

Woman's wark, *n.* what takes up a woman's whole time.

Woman-wark, *n.* work a woman may do.

Womb, *n.* the belly.

Womble, *v.* to rumble ; to stir uneasily. Cf. Wamble.

Womell, Womill, Wommle, *n.* a wimble.

Wommal, *n.* a warble in the skin of cattle caused by the larva of the gadfly.

Wommle, *v.* to rumble. Cf. Wamble.

Won, *v.* to dwell, reside, live.—*n.* a dwelling ; an abode.

Won, *v.* to dry by exposure to air.—*ppl.* dried. Cf. Win.

Won, *ppl.* quarried ; dug from a mine. Cf. Win.

Won, *v.* to have in one's power. Cf. Win.

Wonding-sheet, *n.* a winding-sheet.

Wone, *v.* to dwell. Cf. Won.

Won'er, *v.* to wonder.

Wonlyne, *n.* a 'bottle' of straw. Cf. Windlin.

Wonna, *v. neg.* will not.

Wonne, *v.* to dwell. Cf. Wone.

Wonnels, *n.* an instrument for winding yarn. Cf. Windle.

Wonner, *v.* to wonder.—*n.* a wonder ; a prodigy ; a term of contempt.—*adv.* wonderfully ; extremely.

Wonnerfu, *adj.* great, large.—*adv.* extremely.

Wonnerfully, *adv.* very, extremely.

Wonnersome, *adv.* wonderfully ; very.

Wonning, *n.* a dwelling ; the chief house on a farm.

Wonning-house, *n.* a dwelling-house.

Wonnles, *n.* an instrument for winding yarn. Cf. Windle.

Wonnle-, Wondle-sheet, *n.* a winding-sheet for the dead.

Wont, *v.* to accustom.

Wont-to-be, *n.* a custom or practice that prevailed in former times.

Woo', *n.* wool.

Wooorool, *n.* a wicker-basket for holding wool.

Wood, *adj.* mad ; furious with rage ; eager ; excited ; keen.—*adv.* madly ; wildly.

Wood, *n.* a blue dye, woad.

Wood-body, *n.* a person of very violent temper.

Wood-doo, *n.* the stock-dove.

Wooden, *adj.* clumsy ; stiff.

Wooden-breeks, -sark, -surtout, -surtoo, *n.* a coffin.

Wooden-turnpike, *n.* the treadmill.

Wooder, *n.* the dust of cotton or flax.

Woodersones, *adv.* against the course of the sun. Cf. Withershins.

Woodie, *n.* a halter ; the gallows. Cf. Widdie.

Woodie, *n.* a mad person or animal.

Woodie-, Woodee-, Woody-carl, *n.* a particular kind of pear.

Wood-ill, *n.* a disease of cattle causing bloody urine, &c.

Woodlins, *adv.* very eagerly. Cf. Wudlins.

Wood-louse, *n.* the book-worm.

Woodly, *adv.* madly.

Woodness, *n.* madness.

Woodpecker, *n.* the tree-creeper, *Certhia.*

Wood-rasp, *n.* the wild raspberry.

Woodrip, *n.* woodruff.

Woodrum, *n.* furious madness, especially causing cattle to run about madly ; a fit of obstinacy or wildness ; a state of confusion unexpectedly created.

Wood-scud, *n.* a mad, romping boy or girl.

Woodspurs, *n.* a fiery, unsettled person ; a 'Hotspur.'

Wood-thrush, *n.* the missel-thrush.

Woodwise, *n.* the dyer's broom, *Genista tinctoria.*

Wood-wrang, *adj.* thoroughly in the wrong.

Wood-wroth, *adj.* madly angry.

Woody, *n.* a halter ; the gallows. Cf. Widdie.

Woody, *n.* a child's wooden plaything.—*adj.* used of vegetables : stringy.

Wooer-bab, *n.* a lover's knot ; the garter-knot below the knee with a couple of knots, formerly worn by sheepish wooers ; a neck-cloth fastened in a lover's knot, so as to show the ends or 'babs.'

Woof, *adj.* crazed ; deranged in mind. Cf. Wowff.

Woof, *n.* the gray gurnard.

Wooin-swabs, *n.* 'cupboard-love' ; a belly-ful.

Wook, *n.* a week. Cf. Ouk.

Wool, *n.* with *the,* blankets ; thistle-down.

Woo'-leddy, *n.* a woman who gathers wool left by sheep on bushes, hedges, &c.

Wool-gather, *v.* to gather wool left by sheep on bushes, &c.

Wool-gleaner, *n.* one who gathers wool left by sheep on bushes, &c.

Woolly, *adj.* used of pasture: thick with sheep feeding.

Woolly-bear, *n.* the 'hairy-oobit.'

Woolly-soft-grass, *n.* the meadow soft-grass.

Wool-shears, *n.* shears for clipping sheep.

Woolster, *n.* a wool-stapler.

Wöon, *adj.* woollen.

Woor, *v. pret.* wore.

Woosh, *v. pret.* washed.

Wooster, *n.* a lover; a wooer.

Wooster-tryst, *n.* a lovers' meeting.

Woo'-wheel, *n.* a large wheel for spinning wool.

Wooy, *adj.* woolly.

Wooze, *v.* to ooze; to distil.

Woozlie, *adj.* thin; shrivelled; stunted; unhealthy-looking. Cf. Wuzlie.

Wop, *v.* to wrap; to bundle up hastily. Cf Wap.

Word, *n.* a saying; a proverb; an order, command; news; a rumour, report; the voice; in *pl.* with *the*, the baptismal formula.—*v.* to be credited with by report; with *over*, to reprove; with *refl. pron.*, to express one's self.

Word, *v.* to become.

Wordle, *n.* the world. Cf. Wardle.

Wordy, *adj.* worthy.

Wore, *ppl. adj.* worn.

Work, *n.* a structure; a stately building; a fuss, disturbance; a religious revival.—*v.* to knit; to net; used of material: to lend itself easily to work; of a pipe: to draw, smoke easily; to manage, influence; to struggle convulsively; used of physic: to purge, operate; to ferment; to irritate, trouble, harass; to sprain. Cf. Wark.

Working body, *n.* an industrious, active person.

Workingsome, *adj.* fit for work; working steadily.

Worl, *n.* an ill-grown child. Cf. Wirl.

Worlin, *n.* a puny, feeble creature. Cf. Urling, Wirling.

Worm, *n.* a serpent; a snake-like dragon; a term of contempt; a gimlet; toothache; the gnawings of hunger; the craving for liquor; sour water from the stomach.

Wormful, *n.* as much whisky as fills a distilling tube.

Worming, *n.* a gnawing pain.

Worm-month, *n.* the month of July; the last half of July and the first half of August.

Worm-web, *n.* a cobweb.

Worn-wab, *n.* a thin or ill-spun web of cloth.

Worping-dinner, *n.* a present of food given to a weaver by those who brought their own yarn. Cf. Warping-dinner.

Worricow, Worriecow, Worrikow, Worry-cow, *n.* a bugbear; a hobgoblin; a frightful object; an awkward-looking person; a scarecrow; with *the*, the devil.

Worriecraw, *n.* a 'worricow.'

Worriganger, *n.* a sturdy beggar.

Worry, *v.* to choke; to strangle; to suffocate; to devour; to eat voraciously; to dispute angrily; to snarl and gibe.—*n.* an altercation, a wrangle.

Worry-baldie, *n.* an artichoke. Cf. Baldie-worrie.

Worry-carl, *n.* a snarling, ill-natured person; a bugbear; a coarse winter pear.

Worry-craw, *n.* a scarecrow, a 'worricow.'

Worser, *adj.* worse.

Worset, Worsat, Worsit, Worsad, *n.* worsted.

Worship, *n.* family prayers.

Worsted, *ppl. adj.* worse off, poorer.

Worst one, *n.* the devil.

Wort, *v.* to waste food.—*n.* in *pl.* refuse. Cf. Ort.

Wort, *v.* to become; to befall; worth (as in 'wae worth').

Worth, *adj.* worthy, deserving; of use; of value.—*n.* importance.

Worthy, *adj.* prudent.

Woslie, *adj.* shrivelled, small-featured, and hard-looking. Cf. Wuzlie.

Woster, *n.* a struggle, a scrimmage.

Wot, *v.* to befall; to become. Cf. Wort.

Wot, *v.* to know; to let know; to assure.—*ppl.* known. Cf. Wat.

Wut, *n.* sense; intelligence; information. Cf. Wit.

Wother, *pref.* indicating contrary direction. Cf. Wither.

Wother-weight, *n.* the weight added to balance the paper or vessel in which goods are sold. Cf. Wither-weight.

Wottin, *ppl.* aware, informed.

Wou', *n.* wool. Cf. Woo', Wool.

Woubit, *n.* a hairy caterpillar. Cf. Oobit, Vowbit.

Wouch, *v.* to bark.—*n.* a dog's bark. Cf. Wouff.

Wouf, *n.* a wolf.

Wouf, *adj.* strayed; disreputable; rakish; shabby. Cf. Waff.

Wouff, Wouf, *v.* to bark as a dog.—*n.* the bark of a dog.

Wough, *v.* to bark like a dog. Cf. Wouch.

Woulder, *n.* one who would. Cf. Walder.

Would I, nould I, *adv.* willy-nilly; perforce.

Woun, *adj.* woollen.

Woundily, *adv.* exceedingly.

Woursum, *n.* pus, purulent matter. Cf. Wursum.

Woust, *v.* to boast.—*n.* a boast. Cf. Voust.

Wouster, *n.* a boaster.

Wouy, *adj.* woolly.

Wow, *v.* to mew as a cat; to howl or bark

as a dog ; to wail as an infant.—*n.* a cat's mew ; a dog's howl ; an infant's wail. Cf. Waw.

Wow, *v.* to wave ; to beckon ; to wag.

Wow, *int.* an excl. of wonder, surprise, grief, or gratification.

Wowbat, *adj.* feeble, weakly. Cf. Wobart.

Wowf, *adj.* somewhat deranged in intellect ; crazed ; disreputable ; melancholy ; shabby ; weak. Cf. Waff.

Wowf, *n.* a wolf.

Wowff, Wowf, *v.* to bark. Cf. Wouff.

Wowfish, *adj.* approaching mental derangement.

Wowfness, *n.* the condition of being somewhat deranged ; madness.

Wowg, *v.* to wave ; to wag. Cf. Wow.

Wowgie, *adj.* vain ; lively ; dashing ; moving so as to draw attention. Cf. Vogie.

†**Wowt,** *n.* an arch ; a deep well, pond, or hole of any kind.—*v.* to arch, vault. Cf. Vout.

Wozlie, *adj.* shrivelled, small-featured, and hard-looking. Cf. Wuzlie.

Wrack, *n.* any kind of rubbish ; field-weeds ; vegetable rubbish found on land ; anything worthless ; a broken-down person or animal ; scum, sediment, sordes ; destruction.—*v.* to break ; to destroy, ruin.

Wrack, *v.* to wreak ; to execute vengeance ; to avenge.

Wrack, *v.* to worry ; to tease ; to torment.

Wrack, *v.* used of the sky : to clear.—*n.* flying clouds. Cf. Rack.

Wrack, *n.* couch-grass. Cf. Rack.

Wrack-boxes, *n.* vesicles or air-bladders found on certain seaweeds.

Wrack's grass, *n.* a kind of rye-grass.

Wrack-ship, *n.* a wrecked ship.

Wrack-wid, *n.* wood cast up by the sea.

Wraik, Wrak, *n.* rubbish ; field-weeds. Cf. Wrack.

Wraith, *n.* an apparition ; the spectral apparition of a living person ; a water-sprite.

Wraith, *n.* a quarter of a year. Cf. Raith.

Wraith, *n.* wrath.

Wraith, *n.* a wreath ; a drift ; a mass of drifted snow. Cf. Wreath.

Wraith-bell, *n.* a bell supposed to sound before a death ; a ghostly, solemn passing-bell.

Wraith-like, *adj.* ghost-like.

Wramp, *v.* to wrench, twist, sprain.—*n.* a wrench, sprain.

Wran, *n.* the wren.

Wrang, *v. pret.* wrung.

Wrang, *adj.* wrong ; injured ; deranged in intellect ; unjust ; injurious.—*n.* a mistake ; a fault ; an untruth.—*v.* to disorder ; to hurt, injure ; with *self*, to be guilty of perjury or falsehood.

Wrang-gaites, *adv.* in a wrong direction ; against the course of the sun.

Wrang-like, *adj.* apparently wrong.

Wrang-nail, *n.* a sore condition of the skin at the base of the finger-nails.

Wrangous, *adj.* wrongful ; unjust ; used of a move at play : bad, false.

Wrangously, *adv.* wrongfully, unjustly.

Wrangwise, *adv.* in a wrong direction ; backwards.

Wrannie, Wrannock, *n.* the wren.

Wrap, *v.* to knock smartly. Cf. Rap.

Wraple, *v.* to entangle ; to warp. Cf. Warple.

Wrapper, *n.* a working apron or overall.

Wrassel, Wrassle, *v.* to wrestle. Cf. Wrastle.

Wrastle, *v.* to wrestle ; to struggle ; to contend.—*n.* a wrestle, struggle, fight. Cf. Warsle.

Wrat, *n.* a wart. Cf. Oorat.

Wratack, *n.* a dwarf.

Wratch, *v.* to overstrain by exertion ; to fatigue one's self. Cf. Ratch.

Wratch, *n.* a wretch ; a niggard, miser ; a covetous person.—*v.* to become niggardly or avaricious.

Wrate, *v. pret.* wrote.

Wrathily, *adv.* angrily.

Wrathsome, *adj.* wrathful ; angry.

Wrathy, *adj.* wrathful ; angry.

Wrattie, *adj.* warty.

Wrattieness, *n.* the condition of being warty.

Wratwel, *n.* a small, sore piece of skin at the side of a finger-nail. Cf. Wartweil.

Wraught, *n.* a wart. Cf. Wrat.

Wraul, *n.* a dwarfish creature. Cf. Wroul.

Wrawt, *n.* a wart. Cf. Wrat.

Wrax, *v.* to stretch, extend ; to overstrain ; to hand.—*n.* a wrench, a sprain. Cf. Rax.

Wray, *adj.* wry.—*v.* to distort ; to writhe. Cf. Wry.

Wread, *n.* a drift of snow in mass.—*v.* used of snow : to drift into a mass. Cf. Wreath.

Wread, *n.* an enclosure for cattle. Cf. Wreath.

Wreat, *v.* to write. Cf. Write.

Wreath, *n.* a drift ; a mass of any substance, especially of snow, drifted together.—*v.* to twist, twine, curl ; used of snow : to drift, eddy, swirl ; to bank up with drift.

Wreath, *n.* an enclosure for cattle.

Wreathe, *v.* to writhe.

Wreck, *n.* rubbish.—*v.* to break. Cf. Wrack.

Wrede, *n.* a snowdrift. Cf. Wreath.

Wree, *v.* to twist ; to writhe. Cf. Wry.

Wree, *v.* to riddle corn. Cf. Ree.

Wregling, *n.* the youngest or smallest of a brood or litter ; the weakest and youngest of a family ; a weakling. Cf. Wrig.

Wreist, *v.* to twist ; to sprain. Cf. Wrest.

Wrek, *n.* rubbish. Cf. Wrack.

Wrest, *v.* to twist; to sprain.—*n.* a sprain; a wrench.

Wrested-thread, *n.* a thread wound round a sprain.

Wresting-string -thread, *n.* a thread wound round a sprain.

Wretch, *n.* a niggard. Cf. Wratch.

Wreuch, *n.* wretchedness.

Wricht, *n.* a wright, a carpenter.—*v.* to follow the trade of a wright.

Wrichtin', *n.* the trade of a carpenter.

Wride, *n.* a snow-'wreath.' Cf. Wreath.

Wridy, *adj.* covered with snow-'wreaths.'

Wrig, *n.* the smallest or weakest of a brood or litter; the youngest or weakest of a family; a weak, puny child.

Wriggle, *v.* to wrestle; to struggle.—*n.* an instrument for preventing smoke, a 'wind-skew.'

Wring, *v.* used of a sword : to cut; to sweep.

Wringit, *v. pret.* wrung.

Wringle, *v.* to writhe; to wriggle.—*n.* a writhing motion.

Wrinkle, *n.* a hint.—*v.* used of paper : to crumple. Cf. Runkle.

Wrinkle-frichtin', *adj.* smoothing or banishing wrinkles.

Wrisk, *n.* a 'brownie.'

Wrist, *v.* to sprain. Cf. Wrest.

Writ, Write, *n.* writing; anything written; handwriting; the size of handwriting; a lawyer, a 'writer.'

Writer, *n.* a lawyer, solicitor, law-agent; an agent or man of business.

Writer-body, *n.* a contemptuous designation of a lawyer.

Writhen, *ppl.* writhed.

Writing, *n.* law-business; the profession of a lawyer; a written agreement; a legal document.

Writing-pen, *n.* a goose-quill.

Wro, *n.* an enclosure in a grass field for penning up cattle at night. Cf. Roo.

Wroch, *adj.* rough; reckless. Cf. Wruch.

Wrocht, *v. pret.* worked, laboured; struggled; with *for*, deserved, earned; with *about*, happened. — *ppl. adj.* knitted; woven; made with the hands; brought about; troubled; annoyed; frightened; sprained.

Wrocht-bane, *n.* a sprained joint.

Wroo, *n.* a 'wro' for cattle.

Wrothily, *adv.* wrathfully, angrily.

Wrothy, *adj.* wrathful, angry. Cf. Wrathy.

Wroucht, *v. pret.* and *ppl.* wrought. Cf. Wrocht.

Wrought, *n.* a manufactory, works.

Wroul, *n.* an ill-grown person; a puny child; a changeling; a dwarf.

Wruch, *adj.* rough; reckless.—*n.* the larger part of anything.

Wrunch, *n.* a winch; a windlass.

Wrunkle, *v.* to wrinkle.—*n.* a wrinkle.

Wry, *v.* to twist; to writhe; to distort.

Wrythe, *n.* a wreath; a snow 'wreath.'

Wub, *n.* a web. Cf. Wab.

Wubbit, *n.* a hairy worm. Cf. Oobit.

Wud, *v. pret.* would.

Wud, Wuddy, *adj.* mad. Cf. Wood.

Wud, *n.* a wood.

Wud, *n.* blue, woad.

Wuddie, *n.* a willow; a band of twisted willows; a halter, the gallows. Cf. Widdie.

Wuddiefu, *adj.* cross-tempered.—*n.* a scamp; a gallows'-bird; a small, ill-tempered person. Cf. Widdifow.

Wuddie-tow, *n.* a hangman's rope.

Wuddle, *v.* to wander about; to wriggle; to struggle. Cf. Widdle.

Wuddrum, *n.* a state of confusion; a wild fit. Cf. Woodrum.

Wuddy, *n.* a mad person. Cf. Woodie.

Wude, *adj.* mad. Cf. Wood.

Wudlins, *adv.* most eagerly. Cf. Woodlins.

Wud-muffled, *adj.* used of sounds, voices, &c. : muffled by woods.

Wudscud, *n.* a mad, romping boy or girl. Cf. Woodscud.

Wudwise, *n.* the dyer's broom. Cf. Woodwise.

Wudy, *n.* a halter; the gallows. Cf. Widdie

Wuff, *n.* a flighty, fiery person.

Wuff, *adj.* strayed; disreputable; shabby. Cf. Waff.

Wuffle, *v.* to turn over anything lightly; to rumple; to knit loosely.

Wuggle, *v.* to waddle; to stagger along.—*n.* a bog, marsh. Cf. Waggle.

Wugrum, *n.* water running down the inside of a wall from leakage about the eaves.

Wuif, *n.* woof, weft.

Wuir, *v. pret.* wore.

Wuish, *v. pret.* washed.

Wuive, *v. pret.* wove.

Wul, *n.* a well.

Wul, *adj.* and *adv.* well. Cf. Weel.

Wul, Wull, *adj.* wild.—*adv.* extremely. Cf. Wild.

Wulbeast, *n.* a maddened horse or ox.

Wulcat, *n.* a wild-cat; in *phr.* to 'tumble the wulcat,' to whirl heels overhead.

Wuld, *adj.* wild.

Wuld, *adj.* bewildered; roving.—*adv.* astray. Cf. Will.

Wulee, *n.* a pool. Cf. Wull-ee.

Wulfire, *n.* erysipelas. Cf. Wildfire.

Wulk, *n.* the periwinkle, edible shell-fish. Cf. Wilk.

Wull, *n.* will, wish; choice. Cf. Will.

Wull, *v. aux.* will.

Wull, *adv.* astray. Cf. Will.

Wull-a-wean, *int.* an excl. of sorrow. Cf. Weel-a-wins.

Wull-a-wins, -wons, -wuns, *int.* 'weel-a-wins!'

Wullcat, *n.* a wild-cat. Cf. Wulcat.

Wull-ee, *n.* the orifice of a well; a spring in a quagmire; a pool. Cf. Well-ee.

†Wullees, *n.* saddle-bags. Cf. Wallise.

Wullet, *n.* a wallet; a budget of news.

Wull-gate, *n.* an erroneous course. Cf. Will-gate.

Wullie-wagtail, *n.* the pied wagtail. Cf. Willie-wagtail.

Wullie-waucht, -waught, *n.* a hearty draught of liquor. Cf. Willie-waught.

Wullin', Wullint, *adj.* willing. Cf. Willint.

Wull-like, *adj.* wild-like.

Wullshoch, Wulshoch, *n.* a timid courter.— *adj.* changeable. Cf. Wilshoch.

Wullsome, *adj.* wild; lonely, dreary. Cf. Wilsum.

Wullyart, *adj.* shy; bewildered; lonely. Cf. Wilyart.

Wully-wambles, -wamles, *n.* a bowel-complaint attended with a rumbling noise. Cf. Willy-wambles.

Wul-wierd, *n.* an evil prediction.

Wumble, *v.* to upset. Cf. Whamble.

Wumble, Wumle, Wummle, *n.* a wimble. Cf. Womill.

Wummilton, Wummilton's mutch, *n.* used in whist: the four of spades.

Wummle, *v.* to rumble; to turn over and over. Cf. Wamble.

Wammle, *v.* to upset. Cf. Whamble.

Wummle-bore, *n.* a hole bored by a wimble.

Wumple, Wumpel, *v.* to wind, meander; to wrap; to rumple. Cf. Wimple.

Wun, *v.* to win.—*v. pret.* won.—*ppl.* won.

Wun, *n.* wind.—*v.* to dry in the wind.

Wun, *v. pret.* did wind, wound.—*ppl.* wound.

Wun, *v.* to dwell. Cf. Won.

Wund, *v.* to wind.

Wund, *n.* wind; boastful talk.

Wund-band, *n.* an iron band round anything weak, broken, or spliced.

Wundy, *adj.* boastful; windy.

Wundy, *n.* a window.

Wungall, *n.* a tumour; a soft blister from walking in tight shoes. Cf. Wingel.

Wunna, *v. neg.* will not. Cf. Winna.

Wunnel, Wunnle, *n.* a 'bottle' of straw. Cf. Windle.

Wunnel-strae, *n.* a stalk of withered grass, &c. Cf. Windlestrae.

Wunner, *v.* to wonder. Cf. Wonner.

Wunnock, *n.* a window. Cf. Winnock.

Wunt, *v.* to want.—*n.* a mental deficiency.

Wuntle, *v.* to writhe with passion; to stagger; to tumble. Cf. Wintle.

Wuntlin, *n.* the writhing in a passion.

Wup, *v.* to bind with cord or thread. Cf. Wip.

Wupple, *v.* to wind, twist; to bundle up. Cf. Wipple.

Wur, *v.* were.

Wurble, *v.* to wriggle; to crawl; to stagger, stumble; to move like a worm.

Wurble, *v.* used in weaving: to tie a broken thread; to twist; to twine with the fingers; to crush by friction between the thumb and finger.—*n.* a twist; a twine; a rub between the thumb and finger.

Wurd, *n.* a word.

Wurdle, *v.* to work hard with little prospect of success.

Wurdy, *adj.* deserving. Cf. Wordy.

Wure, *v. pret.* wore.

Wurf, *n.* an ill-grown, stunted person; a fairy. Cf. Urf.

Wurf-like, *adj.* having a stunted and puny appearance.

Wurgill, *n.* a narrow-minded worldling.

Wurk, *v.* to work. Cf. Wark.

Wurl, *n.* a dwarfish person. Cf. Wirl.

Wurlie, Wurly, *adj.* rough, knotted; wrinkled.

Wurlie, *adj.* puny.—*n.* a puny child; a stunted animal. Cf. Wirly.

Wurlin, *n.* a child or beast that does not thrive. Cf. Wirling.

Wurlyon, *n.* a 'wurlin.'

Wurn, *v.* to be peevish and complaining.

Wurna, *v. neg.* were not.

Wurp, *v.* to be fretful.—*n.* a fretful, peevish person.

Wurpit, *ppl. adj.* fretful, peevish.

Wurr, *v.* to snarl or growl like a dog. Cf. Wirr.

Wurrico, Wurrycow, *n.* a bugbear. Cf. Worricow.

Wurset, *n.* worsted. Cf. Worset.

Wursum, *n.* pus, purulent matter.

Wurtle, *v.* to writhe like a worm.—*n.* a writhe.

Warts, *n.* herbs; worts.

Wush, *v.* to wish.—*n.* a wish.

Wush, *n. pret.* washed.

Washen, *ppl. adj.* washed.

Wusp, *n.* a wisp.

Wuss, *v.* to wish.

Wuss, *n.* juice; moisture.

Wust, *v. pret.* wist, knew.

Wuster, *n.* a struggle; a scrimmage. Cf. Woster.

Wut, *n.* wit; sense; intelligence; information. Cf. Wit.

Wut, *v.* to know. Cf. Wit.

Wutch, *n.* a witch.—*v.* to bewitch.

Wuth, *n.* anger, wrath.

Wutless, *adj.* senseless, thoughtless.

Wutter, *n.* the barb of an arrow-head or fish-hook. Cf. Witter.

Wutter, *n.* a mark; a token; a 'tee.'—*v.* to inform. Cf. Witter.

Wutter, *v.* to be peevish, waspish. Cf. Witter.

Wutterel, *n.* a peevish, waspish person. Cf. Witterel.

Wutterick, *n.* a weasel. Cf. Whitrack.

Wutterin', *n.* a rumour. Cf. Wittering.

Wutter-length, *n.* the distance of the player from the 'tee,' in curling.

Wutter-shot, *n.* a stone played in curling so as to rest on the 'tee.'

Wuzlie, *adj.* thin, shrivelled; dwarfish, stunted; unhealthy-looking. Cf. Woslie.

Wuzlie-like, *adj.* 'wuzlie' in appearance.

W'y, *n.* way.

Wy, *v.* to weigh.

Wybis, *n.* the common ragwort; the tansy. Cf. Weebo.

Wybister, *n.* a weaver. Cf. Webster.

Wyde, *v.* to wade.

Wyde, *n.* a weed.

Wye, *n.* way.

Wye, *v.* to weigh.

Wyelay, *v.* to waylay.

Wyfock, Wyfockie, *n.* a wife; a term of endearment addressed to a wife. Cf. Wifock, Wifockie.

Wyg, *n.* ? a wall. Cf. Wig.

Wyg, *n.* a small, oblong currant-roll. Cf. Whig.

Wyise, *n.* a wisp; a truss of hay or straw. Cf. Waese.

Wyke, *adj.* weak. Cf. Waik.

Wyl, *adj.* bewildered. Cf. Will.

Wylart, *adj.* self-willed. Cf. Wilyart.

Wylart, *adj.* shy, bashful. Cf. Wilyart.

Wyle, *v.* to choose, select. Cf. Wale.

Wyle, *adj.* wicked; vile.

Wyle, *adj.* wild.

Wyle, *n.* an instrument for twisting straw-ropes. Cf. Wile.

Wyle, *v.* to wile, lure.

Wyleoot, *n.* an under-garment. Cf. Wylie-coat.

Wylie, *n.* an instrument for twisting straw-ropes.

Wylie, *n.* a kind of flannel used for vests and petticoats.

Wylie-coat, *n.* an under-vest; an under-petticoat; a flannel shirt; a child's night-dress.

Wylly, *adj.* wily.

Wyme, *n.* the belly; the womb. Cf. Wame.

Wyn, *v.* to win; to earn; to get, reach to. Cf. Win.

Wyn, *v.* to turn to the left.—*int.* a call to horses to do so. Cf. Wynd.

Wynan, *n.* the half of a field.

Wynd, *n.* a narrow lane or street; an alley; a small court.

Wynd, Wyne, *v.* used of horses: to turn to the left.—*int.* a call to a horse or ox to turn to the left.—*n.* the call of 'wyne'; a turn; a winding; an end, a termination.

Wyndel-stray, *n.* a withered stalk of grass, &c. Cf. Windlestrae.

Wyne and on wyne, *adv.* to the right and left; everywhere.

Wyner, *n.* the foremost ox on the right hand in a team of oxen; in *pl.* the foremost pair of oxen.

Wynis, *v.* to decay; to pine away.

Wynish'd, *ppl. adj.* pinched, thin. Cf. Wainisht.

Wynnie, *n.* an alley.

Wynt, *v.* used of milk, butter, &c.: to become tainted or sour. Cf. Wind.

Wyntit, *ppl. adj.* tainted.

Wype, *n.* a blow given accidentally or carelessly; a gibe. Cf. Wipe.

Wyringing, *n.* fretting, carking.

Wyrock, *n.* a corn; a boil or sore on the foot. Cf. Weerock.

Wyse, *v.* to guide; to lead; to entice. Cf. Wise.

Wyse, *adj.* wise.

Wysh, Wyshe, *int.* a call to a horse to turn to the right.—*n.* 'wyshe,' the call.

Wyson, *n.* the gullet. Cf. Weasan.

Wyss, Wysse, *adj.* wise.

Wyster, *v.* to scuffle.—*n.* a broil, struggle. Cf. Wister.

Wyt, *v.* to know. Cf. Wit.

Wyt, *n.* blame. Cf. Wite.

Wyte, *v.* to wait.

Wyte, *v.* to know; to assure. Cf. Wit, Wat.

Wyte, *v.* to blame. Cf. Wite.

Wyteless, *adj.* blameless, innocent.

Wytononfa, *n.* a chill; a fever; an onfall of a 'weed.'

Wyth, *n.* width.

Wyttle, *n.* a big knife. Cf. Whittle.

Wynchlet, *n.* a thin, spare person or thing.

Wyve, *v.* to weave.

Wyven-kwite, *n.* a knitted petticoat.

Wyver, *n.* a weaver; a spider.

Wyvers' wobs, *n.* cobwebs.

Wyze, *v.* to guide; to entice. Cf. Wise.

Wyzeron, *n.* the weasand, gullet. Cf. Wisehorn.

Wyzon, *n.* the weasand, gullet. Cf. Weasan.

Ya, *int.* an excl. of contempt or derision. Cf. Yah.

Ya, Yaa, *adv.* yes.

Yaa, *n.* an eel. Cf. Yaw.

Yaab, *v.* to talk incessantly. Cf. Yab.

Yaaber, *n.* an incessant talker.

Yaad, *n.* an old mare; a jade. Cf. Yad.

Yaag, *v.* to importune incessantly; to nag; to gossip.—*n.* gossip, gossiping; a gossip. Cf. Yag.

Yaager, *n.* one given to gossip.

Yaager, *n.* a pedlar, hawker; a clandestine buyer of things unfairly disposed of. Cf. Jagger.

Yaal, *v.* to howl, cry.

Yaal, *int.* an excl. of defiance, contempt, &c.

Yaalta, *int.* an excl. used to prevent a person from doing a thing. Cf. Yalto.

Yaam, *n.* a potato. Cf. Yam.

Yaap, *v.* to bawl, shout; to talk loudly. Cf. Yap.

Yaar, *n.* a curved enclosure on the seashore for catching salmon. Cf. Yair.

Yaavel, *n.* a second crop of grain after lea. Cf. Yaval.

Yab, *v.* to talk incessantly; to harp on a subject.

Yabble, *v.* to bark rapidly.—*n.* a dog's rapid barking; a wrangling.

Yabble, *v.* to gabble; to scold; to be querulous; to mutter; to speak incoherently.

Yabblock, *n.* a chatterer; a talkative person.

Yabbock, *n.* an incessant talker.

Yable, *adj.* able.

Yachis, *adv.* with violence. Cf. Jossich, Yassich.

Yachle, *v.* to shamble, to shuffle in walking.

Yachlin, *n.* one who shambles.

Yacht, *v.* to own.—*v. pret.* owned, was owner. Cf. Aucht.

Yacht, *n.* a big drink. Cf. Waught.

Yack, *n.* perplexity; perturbation.—*v.* to be in perturbation.

Yack, *v.* to talk thickly.

Yackie, *n.* perturbation. Cf. Yack.

Yackuz, *n.* one who talks thickly.

Yad, *n.* an old mare; a mare; an old cow; a contemptuous term for a slovenly or vicious woman; a jade. Cf. Jad.

Yad, *n.* a piece of bad coal which becomes a white, ashy lump when burned.

Yad, *n.* a thread which, in reeling, has been let over one of the reel-spokes.

Yaddle, *v.* to contend.

Yade, *n.* a mare, horse; a worthless woman. Cf. Yad, Jad.

Yae, *adj.* one.

Yae, *int.* yea? an excl. of interrogatory surprise.

Yae, yae, *adj.* one only.

Yaff, *v.* to bark, as a small dog; to yelp; to scold; to nag.—*n.* the bark of a dog.

Yaff, *v.* to talk nonsense; to prate; to talk pertly.

Yaffing, *n.* the act of barking.

Yag, *v.* to make a noise; to talk angrily; to importune; to irritate; to gossip.—*n.* gossip, a gossiper.

Yagger, *n.* a travelling pedlar, a trader. Cf. Jagger.

Yaghies, *n.* the sound of a soft, heavy body falling. Cf. Yachis.

Yagiment, *n.* a state of great excitement, or anxiety to get at anything.

Yah, *int.* an excl. of contempt, &c.

Yaid, *n.* an old horse; a jade. Cf. Yad.

Yaik, *v.* to ache.

Yaik, *n.* perturbation. Cf. Yack.

Yaike, Yaik, *n.* a stroke, a blow.

Yaikert, *ppl. adj.* used of grain: eared. Cf. Aicherd.

Yail, *int.* an expression of contempt or derision. Cf. Yaal.

Yaip, *adj.* hungry; keen; forward. Cf. Yap.

Yair, *Yaire,* *n.* a small enclosure built in a curve near the shore for catching salmon.

Yaird, *n.* a yard in length, &c.

Yaird, *n.* a garden; an enclosure or court near a house; a churchyard.

Yaird-dyke, *n.* a garden-wall.

Yaird-fit, *n.* the lower end of a garden.

Yaird-heid, *n.* the upper end of a garden.

Yairdin, *n.* a garden.

Yair-fishing, *n.* fishing by 'yairs.'

Yair-haugh, *n.* a 'haugh' on which a 'yair' is built.

Yair-net, *n.* a net extending into the bed of a river, inclining upwards and fixed by poles.

Yald, Yal, *adj.* sprightly; nimble; vigorous; hale. Cf. Yauld.

Yald, *v. pret.* yielded.

Yald, *adj.* niggardly, close-fisted.

Yalder, *v.* to bark noisily and rapidly.—*n.* the noisy barking of a dog in chase, or bringing an animal to bay.

Yaldie, *n.* the yellow-ammer.

Yaldran, Yaldrin, *n.* the yellow-ammer.

Yalla, *adj.* yellow.

Yallackie, *n.* the yellow-ammer. Cf. Yallock.

Yaller, *v.* to bawl, yell; to speak indistinctly through passion.

Yaller, *v.* to bark noisily and rapidly, as a dog in chase. Cf. Yoller.

Yallieckie, *n.* the yellow-ammer.

Yalloch, *v.* to shout; to yell. Cf. Yelloch.

Yallock, *n.* the yellow-ammer.

Yallow, *adj.* yellow.

Yallowchy, *adj.* yellowish.

Yalp, *v.* to yelp. Cf. Yelp.

Yalp-yulp, *v.* to whine.

Yaltie, *adv.* slowly.—*int.* take time! take leisure!

Yalto, Yaltoco, *int.* an expression of surprise or defiance.

Yam, *n.* a large potato.

Yamer, *v.* to lament; to fret. Cf. Yammer.

Yamf, *adj.* hungry. Cf. Yamph.

Yamf, Yamff, *v.* to bark. Cf. Yamph.

Yammer, Yammir, *v.* to lament; to cry aloud fretfully; to fret, complain; to grumble; to make a great outcry, or a loud, disagreeable noise; to talk loudly and continuously; to shout; to utter a shrill cry, as a bird; to sing loudly; to talk or hum indistinctly; to stammer.—*n.* a lamentation, whimpering; continuous loud talking or complaining; a great outcry; a loud, disagreeable noise; loud, incessant, or rambling talk; the cry of a bird.

Yammerer, *n.* a loud, incessant talker.

Yammering, *n.* a continued whining.

Yamner, *v.* to 'yammer.'

Yamour, *n.* a whine; a 'yammer.'

Yamp, *adj.* noisy.

Yamph, *v.* to bark; to yelp; to yap; to rampage; to career.—*n.* a bark; a yelp.

Yamph, *adj.* hungry; ravenous.

Yamps, *n.* the garlic.

Yan, *adj.* small; puny.—*n.* a small thing.

Yance, *adv.* once.

Yane, *adj.* one.

Yank, *v.* to move nimbly and quickly; to push on smartly; to pull suddenly; to jerk; to pass quickly.—*n.* a sudden, severe blow.

Yanker, *n.* a smart stroke, a 'yank'; a great falsehood; a tall, agile girl; a clever girl; an incessant talker.

Yankie, *n.* a sharp, clever, forward woman.

Yanking, *ppl. adj.* active; forward, pushing.

Yanky, *adj.* agile; nimble; active.

Yant, *adj.* small, puny. Cf. Yan.

Yap, *v.* to talk snappishly; to cry, as nestlings for food. Cf. Yaup.

Yap, Yape, *adj.* quick, apt; eager, keen; desirous; forward; very hungry.—*v.* to be hungry.

Yap, *n.* a cant name for an apple.

Yapish, *adj.* somewhat keen; hungry.

Yaply, *adv.* hungrily.

Yapness, *n.* hunger; keenness for food.

Yappish, *adj.* hungry.

Yapps, *n.* apples stolen by boys from a garden.

Yappy, *adj.* hungry-looking; thin.

Yarbin-carblin, *n.* a wordy fight; an ill-natured argument.

Yard, *n.* a garden. Cf. Yaird.

Yard, *n.* a rod, staff; a sceptre; a yard-stick.

Yardie, *n.* a small garden.

Yare, *adj.* desirous, eager; alert, nimble; ready. —*int.* quick!

Yare, *n.* a wire for catching fish; an enclosure for catching salmon. Cf. Yair.

Yare, *n.* yore.

Yarely, *adv.* eagerly; quickly.

Yark, *v.* to jerk; to seize and pull forcibly; to wrench; to throw with a jerk; to throw violently; to dig out smartly; to push; to slam; to strike hard with a cane, to thrash; used of a blacksmith: to hammer smartly; to stab; to chop, split; used of the sun-rays: to beat strongly; to start a tune; to strike up, reel off; to move on quickly; to push on with work; used of beer: to 'work,' ferment; to think hard, cudgel one's brains; to be busy; to get excited; to bind tightly and smartly; to pack tightly; with *on*, to growl incessantly; to ram in full; used of fish: to bite greedily; to drink.—*n.* a smart stroke; a stab; a heavy blow; any quick movement; a long drink; a greedy bite; an indefinite quantity.

Yarker, *n.* a sudden, severe blow; a 'thumper.'

Yarkin, *ppl. adj.* severe.

Yarking, *n.* the side-seam of a shoe. Cf. Yerkin.

Yarking, *n.* continual fault-finding.

Yarking-elshin, -allishen, *n.* an out-seam awl.

Yarlin, *n.* the yellow-ammer. Cf. Yoldrin.

Yarn-beam, *n.* the beam on which the warp is wrapped.

Yarn-clue, *n.* a ball of worsted for knitting.

Yarnets, *n.* an instrument for winding wool.

Yarn-nag, *n.* ? a stock of worsted.

Yarnut, *n.* the pig-nut, earth-nut.

Yarn-washer, *n.* a woman who washes yarn in a dye-house.

Yarn-windles, -winnles, *n.* an instrument for winding yarn.

Yarn-winds, -wins, *n.* a 'yarn-windles.'

Yarp, *v.* to 'harp' fretfully; to grumble; to carp, whine.—*n.* a fretting, a whine; a carping.

Yarr, *n.* spurrey.

Yarr, *v.* to snarl like a dog. Cf. Ylrr, Wurr.

Yarring, *ppl. adj.* snarling; captious; troublesome.

Yarrow, *v.* to earn; to · ain by industry.

Yassich, *adv.* with viole··ce. Cf. Jossich.

Yatch, *n.* a yacht.

Yate, *n.* a gate. Cf. Yett.

Yator, *v.* to fret; to chatter. Cf. Yatter.

Yatter, *v.* to chatter; to speak loudly or angrily; to carp, fret, grumble; to rattle;

to rustle.—*n.* chatter; a chattering sound; noisy or angry talk; brawling, scolding; grumbling; confused talk; an incessant talker.

Yatter, *n.* a confused mass of small objects. Cf. Hatter.

Yattery, *adj.* fretful.

Yattle, *n.* an endeavour; strength of mind. Cf. Ettle.

Yattle, *n.* a quantity of small stones on the land.—*adj.* used of ground: covered with small stones.

Yauchle, *v.* to walk with a shuffling gait. Cf. Yachle.

Yauchle, *n.* a Highlander.

Yaucht, *v.* to owe. Cf. Aucht.

Yaud, *int.* a call to a dog to go after sheep.

Yaud, *n.* an old horse; an old cow; a jade. Cf. Jad.

Yaud, *n.* a thread which, in the act of reeling, has been let over one of the reel-spokes. Cf. Yad.

Yauff, *v.* to bark as a dog; to bark in a suppressed manner.—*n.* a bark. Cf. Youff.

Yaught, *n.* a yacht; a transport, ship.

Yauk, *v.* to ache. Cf. Yaik.

Yaul, *adj.* hale in old age. Cf. Yauld.

Yaul, *n.* in *phr.* 'drunk as a yaul,' dead drunk.

Yaul, *v.* to howl; to bawl.—*n.* a howl. Cf. Yawl.

Yaul-cuted, *adj.* having the ankles formed for quick motion.

Yauld, *adj.* alert, sprightly; nimble, agile; able-bodied; strong, powerful; used of an elderly person: vigorous; sharp, cold, frosty.

Yaumer, Yaummer, Yaumour, *v.* to lament; to cry loudly. Cf. Yammer.

Yaup, *v.* to shout; to cry aloud, bawl; to talk boisterously; to whine; to bark, to yelp; used of birds: to scream, utter cries of distress; to cough.—*n.* a shout, yell; a loud cry; a short, sharp bark; the cry of a sickly or distressed bird; a cough.

Yaup, *n.* the blue titmouse.

Yaup, *adj.* hungry; quick, keen. Cf. Yap.

Yauping, *ppl. adj.* peevish; ill-natured.

Yaupish-looking, *adj.* hungry-looking.

Yaupit, *n.* the blue titmouse.

Yauprie, *n.* the refuse of grain blown away by the wind.

Yaur, *n.* the name given by Newhaven fishermen to a species of fucus, which children use for painting their faces.

Yauvins, *n.* the awns of barley.

Yauw, *n.* the sail of a windmill.

Yauw, *v.* to mew like a cat. Cf. Yaw.

Yaux, *n.* an axe.

Yaval, Yavil, *n.* a second crop of grain after lea. Cf. Awal.

Yave, *v.* to keep in subjection; to impress most earnestly.—*n.* the power of keeping in subjection; the act of impressing very earnestly; awe.

Yavil, Yaval, Yavel, *adj.* prostrate and unable to rise; prone, flat. Cf. Aval.

Yavil-bachelor, *n.* a widower.

Yaw, *n.* a child's name for an eel. Cf. Yaa.

Yaw, *v.* to mew as a cat; to whine.

Yaw, *v.* to yawn.

Yaw, *v.* to own, possess. Cf. Aucht.

Yawd, *n.* an old horse. Cf. Yad.

Yawe, *v.* to own, possess.

Yawfu', *adj.* awful.—*adv.* awfully.

Yawin', *ppl.* owing.

Yawk, Yawck, *v.* to speak quickly and thickly; to shout; to hoot.

Yawkie, *n.* the yellow-ammer.

Yawl, *v.* to howl; to bawl, shout.—*n.* a howl; a cry.

Yawl, *adj.* alert; nimble; strong. Cf. Yauld.

Yawmer, *v.* to cry aloud fretfully. Cf. Yammer.

Yawn, *v.* to own.

Yawp, *adj.* keen; hungry. Cf. Yap.

Yawp, *v.* to yelp.—*n.* the cry of a sickly bird. Cf. Yaup.

Yawpish, *adj.* rather hungry.

Yawr, *v.* the corn-spurrey. Cf. Yarr.

Yaws, *n.* syphilis.

Yaxe, *n.* an axe.

Ye, *pron.* yourself; yourselves.

Yea, *adj.* one.

Yea, *adv.* yes; before a *vb.*, again, again and again.

Yeables, *adv.* perhaps. Cf. Ablins.

Yeadies'-race, -sons, *n.* the human race, Adam's sons.

Yeal, Yeald, *adj.* barren. Cf. Yeld, Eld.

Yealie, *v.* to disappear gradually. Cf. Ely.

Yealins, *n.* equals in age.—*adj.* born in the same year. Cf. Eeldins.

Yealtou, Yealto, *int.* yea, wilt thou? used as an excl. of surprise, and as a *n.* in expletives.

Yean, *int.* a call to a horse.

Yeanling, *adj.* new-born.

Year, *n.* years.

Yearack, *n.* a hen a year old. Cf. Earock.

Year-auld, *n.* an animal a year old.

Yeard, *n.* earth; the grave. Cf. Yerd, Eard.

Yeard, *n.* a garden. Cf. Yard.

Yearl, *n.* an earl.

Yearn, *n.* an errand.

Yearn, *v.* to coagulate; to cause to coagulate. —*n.* rennet. Cf. Earn.

Yearn, *n.* an eagle.

Yearned-milk, *n.* curdled milk; curds.

Yearnin'-bag, *n.* the stomach of a calf, used for curdling milk.

Yearning, *n.* rennet used in cheese-making ; a calf's stomach ; the human stomach. Cf. Earning.

Yearnin'-grass, *n.* the common butterwort.

Yearock, *n.* a hen a year old. Cf. Earock.

Year's bairns, *n.* children born in the same year.

Year's-mate, *n.* a companion of the same age.

Yearth, *n.* earth. Cf. Eard.

Yearthen, *adj.* earthen.

Yeather, *n.* a flexible twig. Cf. Yether, Ether.

Yeattle, *v.* to snarl ; to grumble.

Yeck, *v.* to retch ; to hiccup.

Ye'd, *pron.* and *v.* ye would.

Ye'd, *pron.* and *v.* ye had.

Yed, *v.* to fib ; to exaggerate in narration.— *n.* a fib.

Yed, Yedd, *v.* to contend ; to wrangle.—*n.* strife ; contention.

Yeddle, *adj.* used of water : thick, muddy, putrid.—*n.* dunghill-drainage.

Yeddlie, *adj.* used of water : thick, muddy.

Yede, Yeed, *v. pret.* went.

Yedicate, *v.* to educate.

Yeekie-yakie, *n.* a shoemaker's tool. Cf. Yickie-yawkie.

Yeel, *n.* Christmas, 'Yule.' Cf. Yule.

Yeel, Yeeld, *adj.* used of an animal : barren, ceasing to give milk. Cf. Yeld.

Yeeld, *n.* old age. Cf. Eild.

Yeel-day, *n.* Christmas Day.

Yeelin, Yeelins, *adj.* of the same age, equal in age. Cf. Eeldins.

Yeel-kebbuck, *n.* a kind of cheese eaten at Christmas.

Yeel-mart, *n.* an ox killed at Christmas for home use.

Yeel-play, *n.* Christmas holidays.

Yeel-preens, *n.* pins used for playing with the tee-totum for sweets at Christmas.

Yeenoo, *adv.* even now ; at present. Cf. Eenoo.

Yeerie, Yeery, *adj.* afraid of goblins ; dismal ; weird. Cf. Eerie.

Yeesk, Yeisk, *v.* to retch ; to hiccup. Cf. Yesk.

Yeild, *adj.* barren. Cf. Yeld.

Yeildins, *n.* equals in age. Cf. Eeldins.

Yeld, *adj.* childless ; used of an animal : barren, having aborted, ceasing to have young, not old enough to have young, ceasing to give milk ; of birds : unmated ; of broth : made without meat.—*n.* a barren cow or ewe.— *v.* to keep from breeding.

Yelder-e'ed, *adj.* having evil or unlucky eyes.

Yeld-ewe, *n.* a ewe from which the lamb has been weaned.

Yeld-gimmer, *n.* a ewe once or twice shorn, without having ever been served by a ram.

Yeld-kittiwake, *n.* the kittiwake, *Larus corvus.*

Yeldrick, Yeldrin, Yeldrock, *n.* the yellow ammer.

Ye'll, *pron.* and *v.* you will.

Yell, *v.* to bawl ; to quarrel noisily.—*n.* a shout, roar ; a 'spree' ; a brawl. Cf. Gell.

Yell, *n.* an echo.

Yell, *adj.* childless, barren. Cf. Yeld.

Yell, *int.* yea will ? an expression of defiance. Cf. Yaal.

Yello, *v.* to scream, yell. Cf. Yelloch.

Yelloch, Yellough, *v.* to scream, yell, bawl.— *n.* a yell ; a shrill cry.

Yellop, *v.* to yelp.

Yellow, *n.* a gold guinea.

Yellow-beak, *n.* a 'bejan,' a first year's student at Aberdeen University.

Yellow-boy, *n.* a gold coin.

Yellowch, *v.* to yell.

Yellowchin', *n.* yelling.

Yellow-fin, *n.* a trout with yellow fins.

Yellow-gowan, *n.* various species of buttercup ; the corn-marigold ; the marsh-marigold.

Yellowing-grass, *n.* a grass yielding a yellow dye.

Yellow July-flower, *n.* a double garden variety of the common winter cress.

Yellowman, *n.* a kind of candy.

Yellow plover, *n.* the golden plover.

Yellow queen, *n.* a sovereign of Queen Victoria's reign.

Yellow rattle, *n.* the penny-grass.

Yellow-rocket, *n.* the 'yellow July-flower' ; the dyer's rocket.

Yellow tang, *n.* the knotty fucus, a seaweed.

Yellow wagtail, *n.* the gray wagtail.

Yellow wymed, *adj.* yellow-bellied.

Yellow-yarlin, -yerlin, *n.* the yellow-ammer.

Yellow-yeldering, -yeldrick, -yeldrin, *n.* the yellow-ammer.

Yellow-yite, -yoit, *n.* the yellow-ammer ; the fieldfare.

Yellow-yoldrin, -yorlin, *n.* the yellow-ammer.

Yellow-yout, -yowley, *n.* the yellow-ammer.

Yelly, *int.* yea, will you ? an excl. of defiance. Cf. Yell.

Yelly-hooing, *n.* yelling, screaming.

Yelp, *n.* a buffet ; a blow.

Yelp, *v.* used of a person : to call loudly and shrilly ; to whine.—*n.* a whine.

Yelta, Yeltow, *ints.* excls. of surprise. Cf. Yealtou.

Yence, *adv.* once.

Yenoo, *adv.* just now ; presently.

Yeorling, *n.* the yellow-ammer.

†**Yepie,** *n.* a blow, as with a sword. Cf. Epie.

Yer, *poss. adj. pron.* your.

Yerbs, *n.* herbs.

Yerd, *n.* a yard ; a rod, staff, sceptre.

Yerd, *n.* a garden. Cf. Yaird.

Yerd, *n.* earth ; the grave.—*v.* to bury, inter ;

to cover with earth; to knock violently on the ground.—*ppl. adj.* buried. Cf. Eard, Earth.

Yerd-fast, *adj.* firmly fastened in the ground.

Yerd-hunger, *n.* a keen desire for food sometimes shown by dying persons, and viewed as a presage of the grave; voraciousness.

Yerd-hungry, *adj.* voraciously hungry; having an unnatural appetite before death.

Yerd-meal, *n.* earth-mould; churchyard dust.

Yerd-swine, *n.* a mysterious, dreaded animal supposed to burrow among graves and devour their contents.

Ye're, *v.* and *pron.* you are.

Yere, *v.* to snarl or growl as a dog. Cf. Yirr.

Yerestreue, *n.* the night before last. Cf. Eveyestreen.

Yerk, *v.* to ferment; to work smartly, laboriously, keenly; to beat with the open hand; to strike smartly; to bind tightly; to beat upon powerfully.—*n.* a smart blow; a jerk; a whip. Cf. Yark.

Yerker, *n.* a sudden, severe blow.

Yerkin', Yerking, *n.* the seam by which the hinder-part of the upper of a shoe is joined to the fore-part.

Yerksome, *adj.* irksome.

Yerl, *n.* an earl; in *comb.*, the 'long-necked-yerl,' the red-breasted merganser.

Yerlin, *n.* the yellow-ammer.

Yerm, *v.* to whine, complain; to chirp. Cf. Yirm.

Yern, *v.* to desire, yearn.

Yern, *v.* to curdle. Cf. Yearn.

Yern, *n.* the heron. Cf. Hern.

Yern-bliter, *n.* the snipe. Cf. Ern-bleater.

Yerp, *v.* to yelp; to fret, grumble.—*n.* the act of fretting.

Yerp, *v.* to dwell constantly on one subject; to 'harp.' Cf. Hirp.

Yerran, *n.* an errand.

Yerre, *v.* to snarl. Cf. Yirr.

Yersel', *refl. pron.* yourself.

Yesday, *n.* yesterday.

Ye'se, *pron.* and *v.* you shall.

Yesk, *v.* to hiccup; to retch; to heave at the stomach.—*n.* a hiccup.

Yester, *v.* to discompose; to disturb.

Yestere'en, *n.* last night, yester-even.

Yester-tale, *n.* a thing of yesterday, what happened recently.

Yestreen, *n.* 'yestere'en.'

Yet, *n.* a gate. Cf. Yett.

Yeterie, *adj.* severe, tormenting, excessive. Cf. Eterie.

Yether, Yethar, *n.* a willow; a switch; a wand; a smart blow with a switch, &c.; the mark of tight binding.—*v.* to bind firmly; to flog with a pliant rod, or lash with a whip. Cf. Ether.

Yethering, *n.* a thrashing, whipping.

Yethert, *ppl. adj.* heather-clad.

Yetin, Yeten, *n.* a giant. Cf. Red-etin.

Yetlin, Yetlan, Yetland, *n.* cast-iron; a small pot or 'boiler'; a 'girdle' on which cakes are baked; an iron ball used in games in Fifeshire.—*adj.* made of cast-iron.

Yetrie, *adj.* severe. Cf. Yeterie.

Yett, *v.* to rivet; to fasten in the firmest way.

Yett, *n.* a gate.

Yett-cheek, *n.* the side or post of a gate.

Yetter, *v.* to chatter. Cf. Yatter.

Yettis, *adv.* yet; as yet.

Yettlin-soles, *n.* iron toe-pieces, heel-pieces, &c. for boots, &c.

Yeubit, *n.* the caterpillar of the tiger-moth. Cf. Vowbit.

Yeuk, Yeuck, *v.* to itch.—*n.* the itch; itchiness.

Yeukie-bane, *n.* the 'funny-bone,' the elbow-joint.

Yeukieness, *n.* itchiness; itching.

Yeuky, *adj.* itching.

Yeul, *v.* to howl. Cf. Yowl.

Yeuns, *n.* the refuse of grain blown away by fanners.

Ye've, *pron.* and *v.* you have.

Yevey, *adj.* voracious; clamorous for food. Cf. Every.

Yevrisome, *adj.* having a habitually craving appetite. Cf. Aiverie, Every.

Yewest, *adj.* nearest; most contiguous. Cf. Ewest.

Yewk, *v.* to itch. Cf. Yeuk.

Yewns, *n.* refuse of grain.

Yickie-yawkie, -yakie, *n.* a wooden tool, blunted like a wedge, with which shoemakers polish the edges and bottoms of soles.

Yield, *n.* the influence of the sun on frost.

Yield, *v.* to admit, confess.

Yield, *adj.* barren; ceasing to give milk. Cf. Yeld.

Yieldins, *n.* persons of the same age. Cf. Eeldins.

Yieldy, *adj.* yielding, giving way.

Yield-yow, *n.* a violent pressure of the thumb under the lobe of the ear.

Yiff-yaff, *n.* a small person who talks a great deal to little purpose.

Yill, Yild, *n.* ale.—*v.* to treat to ale.

Yill, *adj.* barren. Cf. Yeld.

Yill-boat, *n.* an ale-barrel; a brewing-tub.

Yill-caup, -cap, *n.* a horn or wooden cup from which ale is drunk.

Yill-caup-een, *n.* large or 'saucer' eyes.

Yill-house, *n.* an ale-house.

Yilloch, *v.* to yell. Cf. Yelloch.

Yill-seasoned, *adj.* seasoned with ale.

Yill-seller, *n.* one who sells ale.

Yill-shop, *n.* an ale-house.

Yill-wife, *n.* the landlady of an ale-house.

Yillyart, *adj.* stubborn; ill-conditioned; froward.

Yim, *n.* a particle, an atom; the smallest portion of anything; a very thin film of fat or of condensed vapour.—*v.* to break into fragments; to become covered with a thin film.

Yimmet, *n.* a lunch, a 'piece.'

Yimost, *adj.* uppermost. Cf. Eemost.

Yin, *num. adj.* one.—*n.* one o'clock.

Yin, *adj.* yon.

Yince, *adv.* once.

Yinst, *adv.* once.

Yinterrup, *v.* to interrupt.

Yip, *n.* a pert, forward girl; a shrew.

Yirbs, *n.* herbs. Cf. Yerbs.

Yirb-wife, *n.* a woman skilled in the virtues of herbs.

Yird, *n.* earth.—*v.* to bury. Cf. Yerd, Eard.

Yird-drift, *n.* snow lifted from the earth and driven by the wind.

Yird-eldin, *n.* fuel of peat or turf.

Yird-fast, *n.* a stone firmly fixed in the ground.

Yirdie-bee, *n.* a bee that burrows in the ground.

Yirdin, *n.* thunder; an earthquake.—*adj.* earthen.

Yirditams, Yirdie-tams, *n.* small heaps of earth spread over a field.

Yird-laigh, *adj.* as low as earth.

Yirdlins, *adv.* to the earth, earthwards. Cf. Earthlins.

Yirdy, *adj.* earthy.

Yirk, *v.* to jerk; to seize forcibly. Cf. Yark.

Yirl, *n.* an earl.

Yirlich, *adj.* wild, unnatural, 'eldritch.'

Yirlichly, *adv.* wildly.

Yirlin, *n.* the yellow-ammer.

Yirlish, *adj.* unearthly. Cf. Eldritch.

Yirlishly, *adv.* wildly.

Yirm, *v.* to whine, complain; to utter low cries; to ask in a querulous tone; to chirp as a bird.—*n.* the rattle in the throat of the dying. Cf. Irm.

Yirmin, *n.* a grumbling, complaining.

Yirms, *n.* small-sized fruit.

Yirn, *v.* to whine; to grumble; to 'girn'; to distort the face; to grimace.—*n.* a complaint, whine.

Yirn, *v.* to twist; to entwine.

Yirn, *n.* an eagle. Cf. Erne.

Yirn, *v.* to curdle. Cf. Yearn.

Yirnin, *n.* rennet; a rennet-bag.

Yirp, *v.* to yelp. Cf. Yerp.

Yirr, *v.* to snarl or growl as a dog; to yell.—*n.* the growl of a dog.

Yirth, *n.* earth. Cf. Yerd, Eard.

Yirze, *adj.* not acquainted.

Yis, Yiss, *adv.* yes.

Yis, *n.* use.

Yisk, *v.* to hiccup. Cf. Yesk.

Yisky, *adj.* given to the hiccup.

Yisless, *adj.* useless.

Yister, *adj.* yester, last, past.

Yistrene, *n.* last night. Cf. Yestreen.

Yit, *adv.* at present.—*conj.* yet.

Yite, *n.* the yellow-ammer.

Yite-hub, -hup, *int.* a call to a horse.

Yite-wo, *int.* a call to a horse.

Yits, *n.* oats.

Yivvering, *ppl. adj.* eager for, hungering. Cf. Aivering.

Ymmer, *v.* to break into fragments.

Yoak, *v.* to look.

Yoam, *n.* steam, vapour; a blast of warm air. —*v.* to blow with a warm, close air. Cf. Oam.

Yochel, Yocho, *n.* a yokel; a stupid, clumsy person.

Yock, *n.* harness; a wooden frame on the shoulders for carrying pails, &c.—*v.* to harness; to join. Cf. Yoke.

Yode, *v. pret.* went. Cf. Yede.

Yof, *v.* to bark. Cf. Youff.

Yoir, *adj.* ready; alert, yare.

Yoit, *n.* the yellow-ammer. Cf. Yite.

Yok, *n.* a yoke. Cf. Yoke.

Yoke, *n.* yolk; the natural grease of wool. Cf. Yolk.

Yoke, *n.* harness; a wooden frame or pole borne on the shoulders for carrying pails, &c.; the quantity of water carried by means of a 'yoke' on the shoulders at a time; the load carried by a cart at a 'yoking'; the time during which ploughmen and carters with their teams work at a stretch; a bout, game; a trial of strength or skill; a grasp; a quarrel.—*v.* to attach a horse to a plough, cart, or gig, &c.; to plough the ridges of a field in pairs; to join, match, marry; to burden; to fasten; to bind down; to oppress; to deal or meddle with; to set to with vigour; to begin; to attack, grip, fight; to tackle with.

Yoke-sticks, *n.* the cross-beams of a plough at right angles to the pole.

Yokie, *adj.* itching. Cf. Yewky.

Yoking, *n.* the period during which a ploughman and his team work at a stretch; any long stretch of work; a fight; a mauling; a bout, turn; in *pl.* harness.

Yoking-time, *n.* the time to begin or resume farm-work.

Yokit-tuilyie, *n.* a winter game in which a group of lads sit on ice, holding each other by their clothes, and are dragged along by two or three others.

Yoldrin, *n.* the yellow-ammer.

Yole, *n.* a yawl.

Yolk, *n.* a pane of glass taken from the thick central parts of cylindrical sheets of glass, with a sort of bull's-eye in the middle; the natural greasiness of wool.

Yolky-stane, *n.* plum-pudding stone.

Yoll, *v.* to strike; to strike with an axe.

Yoller, *v.* to speak in a loud, passionate, and inarticulate manner; to bellow, bawl; to yell discordantly; to bark noisily.

Yollerin, *n.* confused or convulsed noise.

Yolling, *n.* the yellow-ammer.

Yolpin, *n.* an unfledged bird; a child.

Yome, *n.* aroma; steam, vapour; the strong odour of home-brewed ale fermenting in the domestic barrel. Cf. Oam, Youm.

Yomer, *v.* to whine; to complain loudly. Cf. Yammer.

Yomf, *n.* a blow.—*v.* to strike; to thrust.

Yon, *adj.* that; those.—*adv.* thither.

Yond, *adv.* yonder; thither.—*adj.* farther, distant.—*prep.* along. Cf. Yont.

Yonder, *comp. adj.* more distant. Cf. Yonter.

Yondmost, *n.* the uttermost.

Yong, Yongue, *adj.* young.

Yonker, *n.* a youngster, younker.

Yonner, Yon'er, *adv.* yonder; in that place; over there.—*adj.* that; 'yon.'

Yonner-abouts, *adv.* in that place.

Yont, *adv.* yonder; thither; farther; away. —*adj.* distant; removed; that; those.— *prep.* beyond, past; along.

Yonter, *adj.* more distant.

Yontermost, *adj.* most distant.

Yook, *v.* to itch. Cf. Yeuk.

Yool, *v.* to howl.

Yool, *n.* Christmas. Cf. Yule, Yeel.

Yooll, *n.* a yawl; a small coasting-vessel.

Yooloughan, *n.* yelling.

Yoons, *n.* refuse of grain blown away by fanners. Cf. Yeuns.

Yoorn, *v.* to move lazily.

Yoornt, *ppl. adj.* inured; used of a horse: broken in to work; of a postman: going his round easily and without being tired, because seasoned.

Yore, *adj.* ready; alert, yare.

Yorkshire fog, *n.* the meadow soft-grass.

Yorlin, Yorlyn, *n.* the yellow-ammer.

Youch, *v.* to bark.

Youd, *n.* youth.

Youden, *v.* to move; to agitate; to tremble. —*n.* the act of moving; inconvenience; agitation.—*ppl.* yielded.—*ppl. adj.* wearied. Cf. Yowden.

Youden-drift, *n.* snow driven by the wind. Cf. Ewden-drift.

Youdfu', *adj.* youthful.

Youdith, Youdeth, *n.* youth.

Youdlin, *n.* a youth; a stripling.

Youf, Youff, *v.* to strike forcibly.—*n.* a swinging blow. Cf. Yowff.

Youfat, *adj.* puny, diminutive.

Youff, Youf, *v.* to bark as a dog; to bark in a suppressed manner.—*n.* a bark.

Youk, *v.* to itch. Cf. Yeuk.

Youkfit, *n.* the snipe. Cf. Yuckfit.

Youky, *adj.* itching; eager; anxious. Cf. Yeuky.

Youl, Youle, *v.* to howl. Cf. Yowl.

Youldrin, Youlring, *n.* the yellow-ammer.

Youllie, *n.* a policeman. Cf. Yowlie.

Youm, *n.* aroma; steam, vapour; the odour of brewing.—*v.* to smell strongly of drink. Cf. Oam, Yome.

Yound, *adv.* yonder. Cf. Yond.

Young, *adj.* youngest; used of time: early.

Young-fowk, *n.* a newly-married pair.

Young guidman, *n.* a newly-married man.

Young guidwife, *n.* a newly-married wife.

Young laird, *n.* the eldest son or heir of a laird.

Young-like, *adj.* as if young again.

Youngsome, *adj.* youthful.

Young tide, *n.* a tide just beginning to flow.

Younklin, *n.* a youngster; a youngling.—*adj.* young; youthful.

Youp, *v.* to bawl; to scream. Cf. Yaup.

Youph, *v.* to bark. Cf. Youff.

Yourn, *v.* to move about lazily. Cf. Yoorn.

Youst, *v.* to talk idly and loosely, with volubility and noise.—*n.* conversation of this kind.

Yout, *v.* to cry; to roar.—*n.* a cry; a bellow. Cf. Yowt.

Youtheid, Youthied, *n.* the state of youth.

Youther, *n.* a strong, disagreeable smell or odour; the steam or vapour arising from anything boiling or burning; dust; a collection of small particles; the dust of flax; a haze; flickering ground exhalations in heat. Cf. Ewder, Ouder.

Youthhood, *n.* 'youtheid.'

Youthiness, *n.* youthfulness.

Youthir, *n.* the red ashes of peat or turf. Cf. Youther.

Youth-time, *n.* youthful days.

Youth-wort, *n.* the common sun-dew.

Youthy, *adj.* youthful; affecting youthful habits, dress, &c.

Youtt, *v.* to roar. Cf. Yowt.

Yove, *v.* to talk in a free, familiar, and jocular way; to go at a round pace.

Yow, *v.* to caterwaul.

Yow, *n.* a ewe; a larch or pine cone, used as a plaything. Cf. Yowe.

Yowch, *v.* to bark.

Yowden, *v.* to move. Cf. Youden.

Yowden, *ppl. adj.* wearied.

Yowden-drift, *n.* wind-driven snow.

Yowdlin, *ppl. adj.* dilatory; wearied.

Yowe, *pron.* you.

Yowe, *n.* a ewe; a contemptuous term for a man.

Yowe-brose, *n.* ewe-milk brose.

Yowff, Yowf, *n.* a smart, swinging blow.—*v.* to beat; to drive or send forcibly.—*adv.* with a heavy fall.

Yowff, Yowf, *v.* to bark. Cf. Youff.

Yowie, *n.* a little ewe. Cf. Ewie.

Yowl, Yowll, *v.* to howl; to cry loudly or piteously; to yelp as a dog.—*n.* a howl, yell, a loud cry; the sound made in yelling or barking.

Yowl for yowl, *n.* continuous howling.

Yowlie, *n.* a policeman.

Yowm, *n.* steam; vapour. Cf. Oam.

Yown-drift, *n.* 'youden-drift,' wind-driven snow.

Yowp, *v.* to shout, cry aloud. Cf. Yaup.

Yowt, Yowte, *v.* to howl, roar, cry; to scream; to bark; to yelp.—*n.* a cry, yell, bellow.

Yowther, *v.* to push anything heavy; to move by a lever; to walk heavily with a lumbering step.—*n.* a push; a lever; the act of walking heavily; a tall, heavy, awkward person.—*adv.* with a heavy, lumbering step.

Yowther, *n.* a strong, disagreeable smell. Cf. Youther, Ewder.

Yrlin, *n.* a puny, sickly, stunted creature; a dwarf. Cf. Urlin.

Yuck, *v.* to itch. Cf. Yeuk.

Yuckfit, Yucfit, *n.* the snipe.

Yucky, *adj.* itching.

Yudith, *n.* youth. Cf. Youdith.

Yuff, *v.* to bark. Cf. Youff.

Yuik, *v.* to itch. Cf. Yeuk.

Yuill, *n.* ale. Cf. Yill.

Yuke, *v.* to itch. Cf. Yeuk.

Yukie, *adj.* itching, itchy.

Yule, *adj.* barren. Cf. Yeld.

Yule, *v.* to howl. Cf. Yowl.

Yule, *n.* Christmas; Hogmanay, 31st Dec.; an entertainment given by a farmer to his servants on the 31st Dec., and repeated on the first Monday morning of the New Year. —*v.* to keep Christmas. Cf. Yeel.

Yule-blinker, *n.* the Christmas star.

Yule-boys, *n.* Christmas guisers.

Yule-brose, *n.* rich Christmas beef brose in which a ring was placed, the winner of which was to be first married.

Yule candles, *n.* the remains of specially large candles burned at Yule, and extinguished at the close of the day, what was left being carefully preserved and locked away, to be burned at the owner's 'lykewake.'

Yule-day, *n.* Christmas Day.

Yule-e'en, *n.* Christmas Eve.

Yule feast, *n.* a Christmas feast.

Yule guse, *n.* a Christmas goose.

Yule hole, *n.* the last hole to which a man could stretch his belt at a Christmas feast.

Yule-kebbuck, *n.* a special cheese prepared for Christmas.

Yule mairt, *n.* an ox or sheep killed at Christmas for home use.

Yule-morning, *n.* Christmas morning.

Yule-night, *n.* Christmas night, as a merry, festive night.

Yule-pins, *n.* pins for playing at Christmas with the 'tee-totum.'

Yule-play, *n.* the Christmas holidays.

Yule-preens, *n.* 'yule-pins.'

Yule-sowens, *n.* flummery made at Christmas.

Yule-steek, *n.* a very wide stitch in sewing.

Yule-time, *n.* Christmas-time.

Yule-toy, *n.* a Christmas plaything.

Yule-yowe, *n.* a sheep killed and eaten at Christmas.

Yurlin, *n.* a puny, sickly, stunted creature; a dwarf. Cf. Urling.

Yurm, *v.* to whine; to chirp. Cf. Yirm.

Yurn, *v.* to curdle.—*n.* rennet. Cf. Yearn.

Yurn, *v.* to whine; to distort the face. Cf. Yirn.

Yyte, *n.* the yellow-ammer. Cf. Yite.

Zeenty-teenty, *n.* a children's counting-out game.

Zickety, Zickerty, *n.* a children's counting-out game.

Zill, *n.* a child; a 'chield.'

ADDENDA.

A' ane, *n.* everybody ; quite the same thing.
Accrese, *v.* to accrue.
Accudom't, *ppl. adj.* settled down upon.
Ace o' picks, *n.* the ace of spades.
Ach, *int.* an excl. of impatience.
A-clatter, *adv.* in a clattering, chattering way ; noisily.
Adap, *v.* to adapt.
Adderlin, *n.* a young adder.
A' een, *n.* everybody ; quite the same thing, all one.
Aesome, *adj.* used of spouses : living as one and in perfect sympathy.
Aet, *v.* to eat.
Affrichten, *v.* to affright.
A-fit, *adv.* afoot.
Aftwhiles, *adv.* often.
Agane, *adv.* ago.
Agaun, *adv.* agoing.
Aggress, *v.* to assail.
Aicht, *v.* to own. Cf. Aight.
Aiderin, *conj.* and *adv.* either.
Aifter, *adj., adv.,* and *prep.* after.
Aifterhin, *adv.* afterwards.
Aifternune, *n.* afternoon.
Aires, *n.* heirs.
Airm, *n.* an arm.
Airm-cheer, *n.* an arm-chair.
Airn-sauled, *adj.* iron-hearted.
Airt, *n.* an evil or artful design.
Aise-midden, *n.* an ashpit.
'Aith, *n.* faith.—*int.* faith ! Cf. Haith, Heth.
Aiven, *adj.* and *adv.* even.
Aivis, *n.* an unprofitable job.
Alaney, *adj.* alone.
Alelladay, *int.* an excl. of grief.
Alleadgance, *n.* an allegation.
Alse, *conj.* as.
Amains o', *phr.* getting even with one ; getting the advantage or upper hand of one. Cf. Amains o', Mains o'.
Amangs, *prep.* amongst.
†A-maugres, *adv.* in spite of.
Ane-e'ed, *adj.* one-eyed.
Anger, *n.* what causes anger.
Anidder, *adj.* another.

Aquavity-hoose, *n.* a tavern in which spirits are sold.
Arase, *v. pret.* arose.
Arinfrew, *n.* the old name of Renfrew.
Arm-lang, *adj.* as long as the arm ; prolix.
Arns, *n.* a low-lying marsh.
Assyser, *n.* a juryman.
Astride-leg, *adv.* astride.
Ata, *adv.* at all, in the least degree ; used after a *neg.*
Atap, *adv.* atop.
At one's alone, *phr.* by one's self, alone.
A-tune, *adv.* in tune, in harmony.
Aught-pairt, *n.* an eighth.
Aul'-da, *n.* a grandfather.
Auld Coomey, *n.* a name for the devil.
Auld Mischanter, *n.* a name for the devil. Cf. Auld.
Aul'-eel, *n.* Christmas o.s.
Avayle, *v.* to unveil ; to doff.
Awat fu' weel, a *phr.* adding emphasis to what has just been said.
Aw'd, *pron.* with *v.* I would.
Awee, *n.* a little time ; a little of anything.
Aweel-a-wat, *adv.* assuredly.
Aweil, *int.* ah well ! Cf. Aweel.
Aw'll, *pron.* with *v.* I will ; I shall.
Aw'm, *pron.* with *v.* I am.
Aworth, *adj.* used of time : long enough to be worth counting.
Awprile, *n.* April.
Awpron, *n.* an apron.
Aw'se, *pron.* with *v.* I shall.
Aw've, *pron.* with *v.* I have.
A'wye an' athort, *adv.* in every direction.
Awyte, *pron.* with *v.* I wot ; I warrant.—*adv.* assuredly. Cf. Awat.
Ayden, *adj.* diligent, industrious. Cf. Eydent.
Ayehae, *int.* an excl. of approval.
Ayler, *n.* an elder.
Aynoo, *adv.* just now. Cf. E'enow.

B', *prep.* by.
Back, *v.* to move a horse backwards.
Back-a-back, *adv.* back to back.
Back-an-side, *adv.* completely.
Back-answer, *n.* a reply, retort.

Back-fa, *n.* a fall on one's back, a somersault.

Back-fire, *n.* in *phr.* 'to gyang back-fire'; used of grazing cattle : to fall off in condition through the failure of grass.

Back-hand o' the wa', *n.* the other side of a wall ; the outside of a room.

Back-het, *adj.* used of food : twice heated or cooked.

Back-thought, *n.* reflection.

Badderin' breet, *n.* one who delights to tease.

Bagglers, *n.* the fry of trout.

Bain, *n.* a bucket ; a washing-tub. Cf. Boin.

Bairdy, *adj.* belonging to the beard.

Baister, *n.* a boy's challenge to his companions to a daring or difficult feat.

Bait, *n.* a mash of oats, &c., for a horse.

Baivis, *n.* a large fire. Cf. Baivee.

Bake-byoord, *n.* a kneading-board. Cf. Bake-brod.

Ban, *v. pret.* bound.

Bandie, *n.* a stick hooked at one end, used in a boy's game played with a 'nacket.'

Bane-headit, *adj.* used of a staff : having a bone handle.

Bap, *n.* a blow, a thump.

†Barbulie, *v.* to perplex. Cf. Barbulyie.

Bare, *adj.* used of soil : poor.

Bare-naked, *adj.* quite naked.

Barfit, *adj.* barefooted. Cf. Barefit.

Bargain-bide, *v.* to take one's own way, being under no obligation to others, and quite able to act for one's self.

Barley-cream, *n.* whisky.

Barley Jock, *n.* whisky.

Barmkin, *n.* the parapet of a bridge.

Barrel-briestit stays, *n.* corsets for pigeon-breasted women.

Bar-strae, *n.* barley-straw. Cf. Bar.

Barty, *n.* a boy's name for a bartizan.

Bar-yauven, *n.* a spike surrounding barley, thrown off while the grain is being threshed, and very dangerous to the eyes.

Baser, *n.* a bass-singer.

†Bassonet, *n.* a light helmet shaped like a skull. Cf. Basnet.

Ba'-stane, *n.* a testicle.

†Bastel-chamber, *n.* a chamber in a Border fortress.

Bastert, *adj.* bastard, illegitimate.

Bateable Land, *n.* the Debatable Land on the borders of Scotland and England.

Batterification, *n.* battery, assault.

Bauch, *adj.* dull, lustreless. Cf. Bauch.

Baud, *v. pret.* bade.

Bauk, *n.* a weighing-machine ; one hanging from the 'bauks' or rafters ; in *phr.* 'to deal the bauk with one,' to settle a matter with one, come to terms.

Bauk, *n.* a footpath or narrow road through a field ; a 'march' between two estates.

Baulie-loo, *n.* a lullaby. Cf. Balaloo.

Bawd-skin, *n.* a hare's skin

Bawm, *n.* a silly person.

Be, *prep.* by.

Beamy, *adj.* beaming, glittering.

Beardy-land, *n.* the part of the face and throat on which the beard grows.

Bearers, *n.* legs.

Beas', *n.* beasts ; lice.

Beaster, *n.* a challenge to a feat of daring. Cf. Baister.

†Beaufit, *n.* a side-table set apart for wine, glasses, &c., a buffet.

Beaver, *n.* a schoolboy's term for his lunch.

Beck and boo, *v.* to curry favour.

Bed, *v. pret.* stayed, abode.

Be deein', *v.* to have patience, wait.

Bedicht, *v.* to wipe.

Beef-bree, *n.* beef-tea.

Beerial, *n.* a funeral, burial.

Beerly, *adj.* stalwart. Cf. Buirdly.

Beery, *v.* to bury.

Beest, *v.* to have to pay at a card-game.

Beet, *n.* what is given along with an article exchanged for another to equalize the exchange. Cf. Boot.

Beezim, *n.* a besom. Cf. Besom.

Beezim-ticht, *adj.* clean-swept.

Befa', *v.* to befall.

Beff, *n.* fat ; a swelling, as when the face is swollen by a blow.

Beflude, *v.* to flood.

Befreen, *v.* to befriend.

Begging-weed, *n.* a beggar's garb.

Begyke, *v.* to jilt. Cf. Begeck.

Begyte, *v.* to cheat.

Behan, B'han, *adj.* by-hand, over and done.

Beheef, *n.* behoof.

Beheeld, *v. pret.* beheld ; waited to see what would happen. Cf. Behald.

Belaw, *prep.* and *adv.* below.

Bell'd-wadder, *n.* a bell-wether.

Bell-groat, *n.* a bell-man's fee for ringing.

Bell-string, *n.* a bell-rope.

Bell-time, *n.* the time when church-bells begin to toll for service.

Belly-rack, *n.* good things to eat. Cf. Belly-rack.

Ben', *v.* to bend.

Bend up, *v.* to bear-up.

Benicht, *v.* to stay in another's house until after midnight.

Bensel, *n.* used of cloth : tear and wear.

Berje, *v.* to talk boisterously, scold. Cf. Bairge.

Berjer, *n.* a female scold.

Bess, *n.* a boys' school-game with bat and ball ; base-ball.

Bess, *v.* to be a match for, to beat. Cf. Baiss.

Bet, *v. pret.* did bite.

Bettermer, *n.* the better or upper classes.

Betuik, *v. pret.* betook.

Beuch, *n.* a bough.

Beuch, *n.* a limb.

Beukin', *n.* the handing in of banns of marriage for proclamation.

Bewaur, *v.* to beware.

Bewild, *v.* to lead astray. Cf. Bewill.

Beychel, *n.* a small, agile person.

†Beylie, *n.* a bailie. Cf. Bailie.

Bicker, *n.* a mess of porridge or brose in a 'bicker.'

Bicker, *n.* a droll fellow. Cf. Bicker.

Bicker-joy, *n.* the joy of a carouse.

Bile, *n.* the boiling-point. Cf. Bile.

Biler, *n.* a boiler; a kettle.

Bilfert, *n.* an overgrown lad; a stout or fat person.

Bilget, *n.* a billet for a soldier's quarters.

Billie-dawkus, *n.* a leader, chief manager, principal actor, 'boss.'

Bink, *n.* a raised built part, or a large stone, at each side of a fire, with a kind of grate resting on the pair.

Binner, *n.* a state of excitement.

Bin up, *v.* to bind a cow to her stall.

Bious, *adj.* extraordinary. Cf. Byous.

Birl, *n.* the sound of a coin flung on a table.

Birse, Birze, *n.* a push; help in pushing; pecuniary help.

Birth-grun, *n.* one's birthplace.

Bit, *conj.*, *prep.*, and *adv.* but.

Bitch-full, *adj.* used of liquors: filling the containing vessels full.

Bited, *ppl.* bitten.

Bizz, *int.* an excl. of derision; in *phr.* 'to say bizz to one,' to be more than a match for one.

Black, *n.* a contemptuous designation for a puny, insignificant person.

Blackit, *adj.* looking as if stained with blacking.

Black-wamed, *adj.* having a black belly.

Black wood, *n.* ebony.

Blaiker, *n.* a challenge to a feat of daring; a puzzle. Cf. Bleck.

Blainy, *adj.* full of blains; used of a potato-patch in which frequent gaps occur; of seeds that have not germinated. Cf. Blain.

Blairney, *n.* blarney; silly talk.

Blarn, *v.* to employ blarney or flattery.

Blastit, *ppl. adj.* paralysed, having a shock of paralysis.

Blauve, *v.* to blow.

Blauven, *ppl.* blown.

Blawn-win', *n.* broken wind in a horse.

Blazin' chield, *n.* a braggart.

Blease, *v.* to bleach.

Bleather, *n.* nonsense. Cf. Blether.

Bleck, *adj.* black.—*n.* a negro.

Bledder, *n.* a wind-bag, one who talks too much.

Bledderin, *n.* boastful talking.

Bleddin', *ppl.* used of snow-flakes: falling.

Bleeze, *v.* in *phr.* 'to let bleeze at one,' to strike one.

Blench, *v.* to blanch, turn pale.

Blench, *v.* used of milk: to turn sour.

Blewart, *n.* the blue corn-flower. Cf. Blaewort.

Blew-spot, *n.* a blue spot on the body, regarded as a 'witch-mark.'

Blicker, *n.* a boaster, a braggart.

Blin', *n.* a rest, a pause. Cf. Blin'.

Blind-hoy, *v.* used of boys: to exchange articles, such as knives, by 'blin'-hooie.'

Blin'-hooie, *n.* an exchange of two articles by boys, each of whom holds his own concealed in the closed hand until the exchange is made. Cf. Hooie.

Blirtin'-fu', -fow, *adj.* maudlin in drink, 'greetin' fu'.

Blirty, *adj.* rainy and squally. Cf. Blirtie.

Blobb, *n.* a gooseberry.

Bloomy, *adj.* blooming; having many blooms.

Blowt, *n.* an outburst of liquid. Cf. Blowt.

Blue, *n.* quality, condition; a bad state of matters.

Blue-bonnet, *n.* the blue-cap or titmouse.

Blue seams, *n.* an emissary of the law.

Bluidy alley, *n.* a boy's marble, used for pitching, and often painted with blue and red lines.

Bluifs, *n.* clumsy shoes or slippers made of selvedges.

Bluit, *n.* a skate.

Bluter, *n.* a boaster. Cf. Bluiter.

Boardly, *adj.* stalwart. Cf. Buirdly.

Bobs, *n.* loose cash.

Bocht, *v. pret.* in *phr.* 'he bocht aboot him,' he offended another so as to lead to retaliation.

Bode, *v. pret.* abode.

Bodement, *n.* a foreboding.

Bog, *v.* to flow as from a bog; used of pus: to flow or ooze from a festering sore.

Bog-shaivelt, *adj.* knocked out of shape.

Bokin, *n.* a bodkin.

Bole-window, *n.* a small window with one pane of glass; the window of a 'bole' or small recess. Cf. Bole.

Boll, *n.* six bushels of barley or oats; four bushels of wheat, beans, and peas.

Boll-kail, *n.* cabbage. Cf. Bow-kail.

†Bon, *n.* humour, mood.

Bon-companion, *n.* a boon companion.

Bonnack, *n.* a thick, flat, and round cake, a 'bannock.'

Booat, *n.* a hand-lantern. Cf. Bouet.

Booby, *adj.* shy, bashful.

Boof, *n.* a stroke causing a hollow sound. Cf. Bouff.

Boofin, *n.* a clumsy person.

Booled-oars, *n.* oars strengthened with wood towards the handles.

†**Boolyie**, *n.* perplexity.

Boor, Boore, *v. pret.* bore.

Boos, *n.* the shoulders of a horse.

Boose, *int.* an excl. expressing a rushing sound of water, blood, &c. Cf. Boose.

Boosum, *adj.* pliant; blithe.

Boot, *v.* to divide.

Bootikin, *n.* an instrument of torture for crushing the leg.

Booty, *n.* in *phr.* 'to play booty,' to play the cheat.

Boozy, *adj.* fat; thriving. Cf. Bousy.

Borough-laird, *n.* the owner of house-property in a burgh.

†**Borthel**, *n.* a brothel. Cf. Bordel.

Bosh, *v.* to talk nonsense.

Bosom-faulds, *n.* a woman's breasts.

Boss, *adj.* hungry. Cf. Boss.

Bot, *v.* had to. Cf. Boot.

Botany, *n.* Botany Bay.

Botion, *n.* a botch, bungle.

Bouch, *v.* to pilfer in a sneaking way; to plagiarize.

Bougies, *n.* boxes; coffins.

Boules, *n.* boys' marbles. Cf. Bool.

Bouncie, *n.* a slight bounce.

Bount, *v.* to spring.

Bourd, *v.* to meddle with, contend. Cf. Bowrad.

Bournie, *n.* a small bourne.

Boussie, *adj.* fat, plump. Cf. Boozy.

Boustrously, *adv.* boisterously.

Boutent, *ppl. adj.* used of cattle: swollen up after eating wet clover. Cf. Bowden.

Bow-sail, -sele, *n.* a piece of heavy wire or curved iron-rod, going round a cow's neck, and, with the ends clasped together with a piece of iron, attached to a rope or chain, and used for binding her to the stall.

Bowzelly, *v.* to frighten children. Cf. Bowzelly.

Box-kirn, *n.* a box-churn.

Boysteous, *adj.* boisterous; fierce. Cf. Busteous.

Brace-brod, *n.* a chimney-board.

Bracking, *adj.* abounding in brackens.

Braid-letter, *n.* a letter on a broadsheet; a long letter.

Braidsome, *adj.* rather broad.

Braik, *v.* to belch up wind from the stomach.

Braik-fur, *n.* a particular kind of ploughing. Cf. Break-fur.

Brak, *ppl.* broken.

Brakin, *n.* chastisement; a severe whipping.

Bran, *adv.* quite, entirely.

Bran', *n.* a brand.

Bran'er, *n.* a brander.

Branit, *adj.* brindled.

Braucht, *v. pret.* brought.

Braxies, *n.* brown-spotted marbles for playing.

Break, *n.* a defeat.

Bree, *v.* to spring past a person.

Breed, *n.* bread; oat-cake.

Breenje, *v.* to show excitement. Cf. Braindge.

Breid-roller, *n.* a roller for flattening oat-cake or scones in baking.

Briddell, *n.* a wedding. Cf. Brithell.

Bridstell, *n.* the seat occupied by bride and bridegroom before the beginning of the marriage service.

Brisky, *adj.* brisk.

Broadband, *adj.* spread out as a sheaf in the band, openly exposed.

Broad-lipped, *adj.* used of a hat: broad-brimmed.

Broch, *n.* an apron.

Brod, *ppl. adj.* used of the hair: braided.

Brogglie, *adj.* used of a road: awkward and dangerous for a rider.

Broke, *n.* gleanings raked off a harvest-field and made up in bundles. Cf. Brock.

Broodent, *ppl. adj.* used of a child: petted, spoiled; cross. Cf. Browdened.

Brook, *v. pret.* broke.

Broostle, *v.* to perspire. Cf. Broostle.

Brooze, *n.* the race run at country weddings. Cf. Broose.

Brose-fed, *adj.* fed on 'brose.'

Brow, *adj.* gentle; unselfish; loved for such qualities.

Browl, *n.* a gnarled limb of a tree.

Browls, *n.* bits of dry wood gathered for burning.

Browly, *adj.* very well, in good health. Cf. Browlies, Brawly.

Bruize, *v.* to bruise; to squeeze.

Bruk, *n.* a boil, a tumour. Cf. Bruick.

Brunt, *v.* to bear the brunt of.

Brym, *adj.* grim; fierce.

Bucker, *v.* to bother, worry about; to suffer pain.

Buckle, *n.* in *phr.* 'up-i'-the-buckle,' used of one rising in the social scale.

Buckle't, *ppl. adj.* dressed.

Buckling, *n.* a fight; a grappling in a fight.

Bugelet-horn, *n.* a bugle.

Buggin, *ppl.* built.

Buide, *v.* must, had to.

Buik, *v. pret.* curtsied.

Buikie, *n.* a booklet.

Buiksome, *adj.* large.

Buise, *v.* to enclose in a stall. Cf. Buise.

Buist, *n.* a football.

Bukow, *n.* anything that scares.

Bullets, *n.* the game of bowls.

Bullie, *n.* a boys' fight.

Bullie-stick, *n.* a stick used in a 'bullie.'

Bull-reel, *n.* a reel danced by men alone. Cf. Ram-reel.

Bully, *v.* to holla. Cf. Bullie.

Bully-war, *n.* a boys' game in which, from a certain line, they seek to dislodge with pebbles the top stone of a conical heap of stones of a gradually lessening size, without dislodging any of these.

Bumlick, *n.* anything round and full like a turnip.

Bung, *v.* to sulk and refuse to speak ; with *out*, to rush or burst forth.

Bunkert, *n.* a small mound in a field. Cf. Bunker.

Bunn, *v. pret.* and *ppl.* bound.

Buntin, *n.* a bantam.

Bur, *n.* the tongue of a boot or shoe. Cf. Burr.

Burger, *n.* a burgher.

†Burreo-like, *adj.* like an executioner. Cf. Burio.

Burry, *adj.* full of burs.

Burst, *n.* a company or detachment forming part of a moving or mobbing crowd.

Bussy, Buzzy, *adj.* busy.

Butt-a-hoose, *adj.* pertaining to the kitchen-end of a house. Cf. But-a-hoose.

Button-mule, *n.* a mould for a button.

Byauk, *v.* to bake. Cf. Byaak.

Bye-days, *n.* former days.

Caddis, *n.* shoddy. Cf. Caddis.

Cacuana, *n.* ipecacuanha.

Caime, *n.* a comb. Cf. Kaim.

Cairriet, *ppl. adj.* carried ; light-headed ; excited ; flighty ; flirting.

Caker, *n.* a stroke on the palm of the hand with a 'tawse.'

Calsh, *adj.* constantly finding fault ; rough and ill-tempered. Cf. Calshie.

Camaled, *ppl. adj.* used of a scythe : turned on the edge. Cf. Cammelt.

Can, *n.* intuitive knowledge. Cf. Can.

Cangle, *v.* to find fault with, to show displeasure. Cf. Cangle.

Canies, *n.* canvas. Cf. Cannas.

Cap, *v.* to take possession of anything used in play out of season.

Capernodgous, *adj.* discontented. Cf. Capernishious.

Capernuitie, *adj.* under the influence of drink. Cf. Capernoited.

Capper, *n.* a late riser, one who has to make the best of what remains in the 'porridge-cap' at breakfast.

Capper-nosed, *adj.* having a copper-coloured nose.

Carcidge, *n.* a carcass.

†Carknet, *n.* a carcanet, a necklace.

Carn, *v.* to spoil. Cf. Kirn.

Carneed, *n.* a pig. Cf. Curneedy.

Carrick, *n.* a crag.

Catterthraw, *n.* a fit of rebellious ill-temper.

Catter-wurr, *n.* an ill-tempered person. Cf. Catter-wier.

Cauk, *v.* to demand payment of what is due, or is marked as a debt. Cf. Cawk.

Cauppie, *n.* a small wooden drinking-vessel, a small wooden porringer. Cf. Caup.

†Cautionry-bond, *n.* a bond in security. Cf. Cautionry.

Cave, *v.* to live in a cave ; to dwell.

Cawk, *v.* to make one pay dear for.

Cawn soul, *n.* a cunning person.

Ceety-fowk, *n.* citizens, dwellers in a city.

Chacker, *adj.* used of tartans : checked.

Chack-purse, *n.* a sporran.

Chad, *n.* a rough mixture of earth and stones, quarry-refuse.

Chaep, Chaip, *adj.* cheap. Cf. Cheap.

Chaff-blades, *n.* jaw-bones. Cf. Chaft-blades.

Chaise, *v.* to drive fast in a wheeled conveyance.

Chait, *v.* to cheat.

Chalk-heugh, *n.* a chalk-quarry.

Chamber, *v.* to confine, restrain ; to be chary of.

Change, *n.* custom given to a shop.

Change-house-keeper, *n.* a tavern-keeper.

Chantin' thing, *n.* an impertinent young person.

Chappit tatties, *n.* mashed potatoes.

Charter, *v.* to hand down to one's posterity.

Chat-maet, *n.* a little food. Cf. Chat.

Chaumer, *n.* the farm-servants' sleeping-room, formerly above the stable or partitioned off from it.

Cheat, *n.* a cat. Cf. Cheet.

Check, *n.* a door-key.

Cheek-stone, *n.* a curling-stone played so as to lie alongside of another.

Cheekyside, *adv.* aslant. Cf. Cheek-aside.

Cheepers, *n.* creaking shoes.

Cheery-pyke, *n.* anything pleasant to the taste or feeling ; generally with a *neg.*

Cheetie-pussy, *n.* a cat.

Cheritable, *adj.* charitable.

Cherity, *n.* charity.

†Chess, *n.* a strap ; a hawk's jess.

Chiff, *v.* to fray out at the ends of a garment.

Chilp, Chilpie, *adj.* cold and wet. Cf. Chilpy.

Chippey-holey, *n.* a game of marbles in which the 'chippy' was used.

Chippy, *n.* a boy's large, hard marble.

Chirm, *v.* to argue a point that has been settled. Cf. Chirm.

Chit, *n.* a piece of bread.

Chizzy, *n.* a chosen article.

Choup, *n.* in *phr.* 'tak choup for a cheenge,' take a 'dish of want' for a change of diet.

Chucks, *n.* lumps of oatmeal in porridge.

Chue down, *int.* a call to a dog to keep quiet.

Chulpit, *adj.* pinched, starved-looking. Cf. Shilpit.

Chye, *n.* the chaffinch.

Chyne, *n.* a chain.

Cip, *v.* to play truant. Cf. Kip.

Clag, *v.* used of a lubricant : to thicken.

Claiperdin, *n.* a gossip.

Clair, *adj.* used of a lesson : repeated without mistake.

Clairty, *adj.* messy ; sticky ; soiled with mud, filth, &c. Cf. Clarty.

Claithe, *v.* to clothe.

Clangle, *n.* a slight clang.

Clapperdin, *n.* a gossip. Cf. Claiperdin.

Clappit-leukin, *adj.* thin, or twisted in appearance.

Clark-plays, *n.* stage-plays performed on open-air platforms. Cf. Clerk-plays.

Claut-hook, *n.* a gaff or clip for landing salmon.

Claw, *n.* a greatly perplexed, excited, or frenzied state.

Clayey, *n.* a boy's clay marble.

Clean-dakeith for, *adj.* too clever for.

Cleck, *n.* a setting of eggs. Cf. Cleck.

Cleek, *v.* used of tooth and pinion : to click.

Cleet, *n.* a rock in the sea broken off from adjoining rocks on the shore. Cf. Clet.

Cleethe, *v.* to clothe. Cf. Cleed.

Cleipy, *adj.* talkative, with a story to tell. Cf. Clype.

Clied, *v.* to clothe. Cf. Cleed.

Cliftin', *n.* a cleft of a rock.

Clintin', *n.* a cleft of a rock.

Clippy, *n.* a greedy, grasping person.

Clish-ma-clashin', *ppl. adj.* gossiping. Cf. Clish-ma-clash.

Clockin', *n.* a hearty welcome.

Cloik, *v.* to cluck.

Cloo, *n.* a ball of worsted ; a ball of straw-rope.

Clood, *n.* a cloud.

Cloose, *n.* a sluice. Cf. Clouse.

Closhich, *n.* savings. Cf. Closhach.

Cloth-runds, *n.* selvedges of cloth.

Clotterit, Clottert, *ppl.* clotted.

Clouter, *v.* to walk noisily ; to work in a dirty fashion. Cf. Clouter.

Clown, *ppl.* cloven.

Clunkert, *n.* a heavy weight of anything. Cf. Clunkart.

Clyack-dish, *n.* meal and ale, a mixture of home-brewed ale and oatmeal, with a little whisky stirred into it, forming the chief dish at the harvest-home.

Clyack-sheaf, *n.* the last sheaf shorn at harvest.

Clyauk, *v.* to gossip. Cf. Clack.

Clypie-clash-pyet, *n.* a chattering tell-tale.

Clypin' thing, *n.* a tale-bearer.

Cobble, *n.* a watering-place for cattle, usually surrounded by cobble-stones. Cf. Coble.

Cock-my-fud, *n.* rum-shrub.

Cock-shilfa, *n.* the male chaffinch.

Cock-up, *n.* a towering head-dress formerly worn by ladies.

Coffin-cough, *n.* a cough that threatens to end fatally.

Coggling-like, *adj.* looking unsteady.

Cok, *v.* to cock, erect.

Colf, *v.* to stop a leak. Cf. Colf.

Collect, *n.* a collection, an offertory.

Colled, Coled, *ppl. adj.* cut, shaped, fashioned. Cf. Coll.

Combie, *n.* a small comb.

Comely, *n.* a term of endearment applied to a child.

Comitt, *ppl.* committed.

Commy, *n.* a common clay marble.

Compengon, *n.* a companion.

Conceit, *n.* the object of one's particular fancy or love ; a chosen sweetheart.

Cone, *n.* butcher-meat.

Confoondedest, *adj.* most confounded.

Construct, *v.* to construe.

Conter, *n.* the contrary, the opposite.

Contermaushus, *adj.* perverse. Cf. Conter-mashious.

Contra, *v.* to contradict, oppose. Cf. Conter.

Cony, *n.* cognac.

Cooard, *n.* a coward. Cf. Coordie.

Coodie, *adj.* pleasant, kindly. Cf. Couthie.

Cookit, *ppl. adj.* hidden ; secluded. Cf. Cook.

Cool, *n.* a certain quantity of any soft mess, as porridge.

Coolyshangie, *n.* a dog-fight ; a squabble. Cf. Collieshangie.

Coomb, *n.* a tub ; a cistern. Cf. Cuan.

Coomey, *n.* with *Auld*, a name for the devil. Cf. Coomy.

Coonchie, *n.* a hunchback.

Coonjerin, *n.* a drubbing ; a scolding. Cf. Coonjer.

Coonter, *n.* one who does counts ; a shop-counter.

Coosie, *n.* a challenge to a feat of daring, dexterity, or difficulty.

Cordain, *n.* Spanish leather. Cf. Cordowan.

Corn-pipe, *n.* a toy music-pipe made from a corn-stalk.

Corrybuction, *n.* a dense crowd of people moving to and fro, and rendering a passage through difficult.

Coss-, Cost-blade, *n.* the costmary, an aromatic plant with yellow flowers growing in umbels on the top of the stalks.

Cothie, *adj.* kindly ; snug. Cf. Couthie.

Cothie-guckie, -juke, *n.* a snug, cosy shelter.

Cotter, *v.* to live together in fellowship.

Cotton, *n.* a village of cottagers who work on neighbouring farms. Cf. Cottar-town.

Couch, *v.* used of dogs: to be sulky, un-yielding.

Coug, *n.* a boat.

Coulie, *n.* a boy's cap.

Coup, *v.* to catch in a trap. Cf. Coop.

Cour, *v.* to fold.

Courers, *n.* covers.

Coutch, *v.* in *phr.* 'to coutch by cavel,' to divide land by lots. Cf. Coutch, Cavel.

Crack-wittet, *adj.* silly.

Craig's naigie, *n.* the throat.

Craitur, *n.* a creature.

Cranks, *n.* the crooked windings of a river or stream.

Crannie-doodlie, *n.* the little finger.

Crappie, *n.* the crop; the throat.

Creel-house, *n.* a cottage of wattle or wicker-work.

Creepie, *n.* a child at the creeping stage.

Crettur, *n.* a creature.

Crickly, *adj.* small, puny. Cf. Cricklet.

Criv't, *ppl. adj.* used of one who is unable to leave his home for a time. Cf. Criv.

Crochlet, *ppl. adj.* having the limbs twisted by rheumatism, &c. Cf. Crochle.

Croggie, *n.* a small jar. Cf. Crock.

Cronnie, *n.* a crony.

Crooden-doo, *n.* a wood-pigeon.

Crook-yowe, *n.* a ewe too old for breeding.

Croon, *n.* in *phr.* 'to kaim one's croon,' to tear one's hair.

Croonach, *n.* the gray gurnard.

Croonle, *n.* the 'croonach.'

Crootle, *n.* a heap.

Croupit, *ppl. adj.* crabbed.

Crowl, *v.* to crouch, cower. Cf. Crowl.

Crowp, *v.* to growl, grumble. Cf. Croup.

Crow-toe, *n.* the crow-foot; the wild hyacinth. Cf. Craw-tae.

Croze, *v.* to speak with a weak, shaky voice like an aged person.

Cruden, *n.* a crab.

Cruittie, *n.* a measure of beer.

Crynet, *ppl. adj.* stunted in growth. Cf. Crine.

Cudd, *n.* a donkey.

Cuddum o' tait, *n.* the custom of giving a newly-bought horse part of a handful of unthreshed straw as it enters the new stable, and putting the remainder above the stable-door, the idea being that the horse, when at liberty outside, will remember and return to finish the straw.

Cuissen, *ppl.* cast. Cf. Cuisten.

Cuiter, *v.* to work in a trifling way.

Cunjer, *v.* to conquer; to tame a wild animal. Cf. Counger.

Curdie, *n.* a farthing.

Curdooer, *n.* a travelling tinker. Cf. Cur-dower.

Cur doon, *v.* to cower under danger; to lie down in a cramped position.

Curlie-pow, *n.* a curly head; a curly-headed boy.

Curneedy, *n.* a pig.

Curple-gawt, *adj.* used of a horse: galled by the crupper under the tail.

Cutchick, *n.* the fireside. Cf. Cutchack.

Cuttikins, *n.* gaiters. Cf. Cuitikins.

†**Cuve,** *n.* a tub.

Cweef, *n.* a trick, catch.

Cweelie off, *v.* to wheedle out of. Cf. Culyie.

Daak, *adj.* dark and dull.

Dab, *v.* in *phr.* 'to let dab at,' to snatch at.

Dabbich, *v.* to seize; to peck.

Dabble, *v.* to compel one to work in wet weather.

Dabblet, *ppl. adj.* employed at work not conducive to tidiness.

Dabbril, *n.* a woman slovenly at work and heartless in manner.

Dabrich, *adj.* lewd, lustful.

Dachle, *v.* to slow down. Cf. Dackle.

Dachter, *n.* a daughter.

Daggered, *ppl. adj.* used of lightning: forked.

Daicent, *adj.* decent.

Daik, *v.* to deck.

†**Dail,** *n.* grief; evil.

Dainty wheen, *n.* a good many.

Dakker, *v.* to search minutely. Cf. Dacker.

Damp, *n.* low spirits.

Dandy, *n.* a female paramour.

Danglers, *n.* the weights of a clock.

Darden, *n.* a dry, soft wind.

Dargin', *n.* unskilled labour. Cf. Darging.

Dark-benichtit, *adj.* overtaken by darkness.

Dauble, *v.* to dabble.

Daul'd, *ppl. adj.* fagged, worn-out; depressed.

Dauldness, *n.* low spirits, 'the dumps.'

Dauldrums, *n.* 'dauldness.' Cf. Doldrum.

Daverer, *n.* a shuffler.

Dawbrach, Dawbrich, *adj.* lewd. Cf. Dabrich.

Dawtie, *n.* a schoolboy's favourite companion.

Dearsome, *adj.* costly.

Deathful, *adj.* death-dealing.

Deaven, *v.* to deafen; to stun; to worry. Cf. Deave.

†**Debute,** *v.* to make one's début. Cf. Debout.

Deck-buirds, *n.* the bulwarks of a ship.

Decript, *adj.* decrepit.

Deeder, *n.* a doer.

Deed-linnings, *n.* dead-clothes.

Deem, *v.* to doom.

†**Deese,** *n.* a long wooden seat with back and turned ends, and often with a folding-down table fixed to the middle of the back. Cf. Deece, Dais.

Deevilment, *n.* roguery, the spirit of mischief.

Degs, *n.* rags, tatters.

Deid-day, *n.* a calm, dull winter day.

Del', *v.* to dig with a spade, delve.

Delicht, *v.* to delight.

Del'in', *ppl.* delving.

Del't, *v. pret.* delved.

Demauns, *n.* demands for one's services, skill, &c.

Demity, *n.* dimity.

Demous, *adv.* very, exceedingly. Cf. Deemes.

†**Demurr,** *n.* a demurrer.

Dented, *ppl. adj.* tainted by damp.

†**Deray** *v.* to rout, drive away.

Deuk, *n.* a duke.

Deukie, *n.* a duckling.

Dev, *v. aux.* do.

Dew-droukit, *adj.* drenched with dew.

Deyvle, *v.* to use the word 'devil' profanely.

Dial-cock, *n.* the style or gnomon of a sun-dial.

Dibber-dabber, *n.* a confused, purposeless discussion. Cf. Dibber-dabber.

Diddle, *v.* to sing dance-tunes to any jingle, or without words.

Diddle-um-dird, *n.* one who vainly tries to walk neatly and primly.

Dight, *adv.* readily; freely. Cf. Dight.

Dilatour, *n.* what tends to delay procedure. Cf. Dilature.

Dilet, Dylet, *ppl. adj.* used of one whose life is burdensome and miserable from hard work or ill-treatment, or one who has a worn and weary look. Cf. Doilt.

Dilt, *v.* to fondle. Cf. Delt.

Dimirrities, *n.* details, points.

Dimple, *v.* to dibble.—*n.* a dibble. Cf. Dimple.

Dimsome, *adj.* used of colours: somewhat dim.

Din, *ppl.* done.

Dince, *v.* to dance.

Dindee, *n.* noise and fuss. Cf. Dundee.

Dindlin, *n.* a tingling. Cf. Dinle.

Dinnagilt, *ppl.* judged.

Dint, *n.* a fancy or liking for a person or thing. Cf. Dent.

Diploma, *n.* a scolding dismissal.

Dippit, *n.* a tippet.

Dirdum, *n.* a scolding woman. Cf. Dirdum.

Dirdum-kick, *n.* a person who walks with a fanciful or affected gait.

Dirk, *v.* to bungle, blunder.

Dirler, *n.* one who can make things move briskly or 'hum.'

Dirry, *n.* tobacco-ash.

†**Disabeels,** *n.* deshabille. Cf. Disabil.

Disadvise, *v.* to advise against.

Dischanter, *n.* a disenchanter.

Discontent, *adj.* discontented.

Dishealth, *n.* bad health.

Dist, *adv.* just.

Ditty, *v.* to write ditties.

Ditty-gifted, *adj.* having the gift of composing ditties.

Docket, *ppl. adj.* showing an unusually short temper.

Doddit, *ppl. adj.* hornless, deprived of horns. Cf. Dod.

Doe, *n.* a boy's large marble, a 'plunker.'

Dole-day, *n.* the day for serving with doles.

Dong-ding, *adv.* ding-dong.

Doock, *n.* strong, coarse cloth. Cf. Douk.

Dool-ding, *n.* the mournful knell of the passing-bell.

Doolies, *n.* a boy's marbles.

Dooms-earnes't, *adj.* in dead earnest.

Doon-drug, *v.* to pull down.

Doone, *n.* a hill-fort; a mound.

†**Door,** *adj.* hard. Cf. Dour.

Door-stand, *n.* a door-step.

Doosh, *v.* to butt.

Doosht, *n.* a rough shake; a push from side to side. Cf. Doosht.

Dooshtin, *n.* a beating.

Dorn, *n.* diaper. Cf. Dornick.

Dorty, *adj.* ailing, always weak. Cf. Dorty.

Dose, *n.* an allowance of bread.

Dosie, *n.* a small dose.

Doss, *n.* a bow or circular bunch of ribbons. Cf. Doss.

Double-horsed, *adj.* used of a horse: carrying two persons on its back.

Douden, *n.* a dry, soft wind.

Doule, *n.* a fool.

Doun-pouthered, *adj.* reduced to powder.

Douss, *v.* to strike a ball out of play; to extinguish; to pay down. Cf. Douse.

Douthless, *adj.* weak; helpless.

Dow, *n.* the fading of a leaf, &c.

Dowden, *v.* to toss about with the wind.

Dowf-like, *adj.* gloomy-looking.

Dowilie, *adj.* sad; depressing. Cf. Dowiely.

Dozent, *ppl. adj.* sleepy. Cf. Dozent.

Dozing-tap, *n.* a spinning-top.

Dracht, *n.* a draught, load, freight.

†**Dragen,** *n.* sweets, comfits.

Drappings, *n.* droppings.

Drauchtet, *ppl. adj.* used of a horse or ox: trained to draw a plough, &c.

Draw my leg, *n.* one who takes advantage of another, or seeks to make fun of him.

Dream, *n.* in *phr.* 'in a widden dream,' in a dazed condition, under momentary excitement. Cf. Widden-dreme.

Dream-fleyed, *adj.* scared by dreams.

Dreeple, *n.* a small quantity of liquid.

Dreeve, *v. pret.* drove.

Dret, *v.* to excrete.

Dribbs, *n.* dribblings. Cf. Drib.

Driffle, *n.* anything that urges one to action. Cf. Driffle.

Drint, *v.* used of birds: to sing; to chirp.

Drochle, *n.* a short, stout person.

Droddy-bottle, *n.* a private bottle into which the liquor formerly given profusely at funerals, instead of being consumed at the service, could be poured, to be taken home, or at least taken outside.

Drollich, *n.* a short, strange-looking woman.

Droop, *adj.* dripping, dropping; drooping.

Droud, *n.* a herring-hake. Cf. Droud.

Drub, *v.* to scold.

Drubbing, *n.* a scolding.

Druchty, *n.* dry weather. Cf. Druchty.

Drug, *v.* to pull. Cf. Drug.

Druin, *v.* to drone. Cf. Drune.

Drult, *adj.* clumsy. Cf. Drulled.

Drunkilie, *adv.* merrily, as with drink.

Drunyie, *v.* to moan; to complain.—*n.* a moan; a complaint. Cf. Drune.

Drussie, *adj.* drowsy.

Dry-land sailor, *n.* a sham sailor, a tramp professing to be a sailor.

Dry tea, *n.* tea without bread, &c.

Duckie, *n.* a' boys' game with a small stone placed on a large one; the small stone; the boy in charge of the small stone. Cf. Duck.

Duddieheid, *adj.* wearing a short shawl round the head.

Dufe, *n.* a blow with a soft body; a hollow-sounding fall. Cf. Doof.

Dught, *v. pret.* could, was able. Cf. Dought.

Duishin, *ppl.* butting; pushing with horns. Cf. Doosh.

Dule-tree, *n.* a gallows. Cf. Dool-tree.

Dulser-wife, *n.* a dulse-gatherer; an untidy woman.

Dumfootert, *ppl. adj.* speechless; mesmerized. Cf. Dumfoutter.

Dumfouther, *v.* to astonish. Cf. Dumfoutter.

Dump, *v.* to depress the spirits. Cf. Dump.

Dung a-smash, *adj.* beaten to powder.

Durs, *v. pret.* dared.

Dweable, *adj.* pliable; lithe. Cf. Dwable.

Dyow, *n.* dew.

†**Dyper**, *v.* to decorate, adorn; to dress well or beautifully.

'Ear-aul, *n.* a yearling heifer.

Eat, *v.* in *phr.* 'to eat one's self,' to be much vexed.

Eenin, *n.* evening.

Eesefu', *adj.* useful.

Eeseless, *adj.* useless.

Eeset, Eezet, *ppl.* used; accustomed.

Efter an' a', *phr.* after all.

Efter-sting, *n.* the after-sting. Cf. After-stang.

†**Egeall**, *adj.* equal. Cf. Egal.

Eggie, *n.* a small bird's egg.

Eight-part, *n.* an eighth.

Elfin, *n.* Elf-land; Hades.

Elison, *n.* a shoemaker's awl. Cf. Elsin.

Endurement, *n.* endurance.

Enlicht, *v.* to enlighten.

Ereck, *v.* to erect.—*adj.* erect.

Ess, *v.* used by hospital-boys: to save part of one's allowance of bread in order to pay one's debt.

Etten, *ppl. adj.* peevish.

Eul-cruke, -cruik, *n.* an oil-jar. Cf. Uily.

Even-en-ways, *adv.* straight on; continuously.

Evens, *n.* in *phr.* 'at evens wi' the warld,' solvent, paying one's way.

Every, *int.* the call of a boy playing at marbles for liberty to play in any position he chose.

Ew, *n.* a yew.

Ewdroch, *n.* dust. Cf. Ewdroch.

Ewous, *adj.* contiguous.

Exterordinar, *adj.* extraordinary.—*adv.* extraordinarily.

Extree, Extra, *n.* an axle. Cf. Aix-tree.

Eyn, *n.* an oven.

Face-the-clarts, *n.* a low, plausible sneak; a mean, grovelling fellow.

Fae, *n.* faith.

Faggot, *n.* a stout person. Cf. Fagot.

Faimily, *n.* a family.

Faimish, *v.* to famish.

Faist, *adj.* fast. Cf. Fest.

Falloch, *adj.* thick, bulky.

Fallow, *v.* to follow.

Falsary, *n.* a forger. Cf. Falsary.

Fame, *n.* foam; the sea. Cf. Fame.

Fame, *v.* to publish, proclaim.

Fanglet, *ppl. adj.* fashioned.

Fant, *v.* to faint.

†**Fardingale**, *n.* a farthingale; a crinoline.

Fardle, *n.* a quarter of oat-cake. Cf. Farle.

Faust, *ppl. adj.* favoured, featured; mannered.

Fautie, *adj.* a slight fault.

Fear, *n.* a comrade. Cf. Fere.

Fearie, *adj.* sturdy.

Fecklish, *adj.* feeble. Cf. Feckless.

Feem, *n.* an angry flush. Cf. Fame.

Feese, *v. pret.* fetched. Cf. Fess.

Feesic, *n.* physic.

Fengie, *v.* to feign.

Feriat, *adj.* observed as a festival.

Feurd, *n.* a ford.

Feure, *n.* a furrow.

Fewgle, *v.* to manipulate cleverly or artfully. Cf. Fugle.

Fib, *v.* to fight as pugilists.

Fid, *n.* a small wooden chisel for splicing ropes.

Fiddle, *v.* to walk with short, quick steps.

Fidgie, *n.* a 'mealy-pudding.'

Fidjie-fiz, *n.* the crowberry.

Filch, *n.* a bad character; a detested person. Cf. Filsch.

Filsh, *v.* to filch, procure by stealth.

Finger-brod, *n.* the part of a fiddle grasped by the left hand.

Firl, *n.* a ferrule.

Fit, *v.* to please.

Fitchie, *n.* a 'mealy-pudding.' Cf. Fidgie.

Fivvert, *ppl. adj.* fevered. Cf. Fivver.

Flachter-golak, *n.* an earwig.

Flachter-spad, *n.* a spade used for cutting peats. Cf. Flaughter-spade.

Flaggin, *n.* a flogging.

Flaisick, *n.* a spark shot out from burning wood. Cf. Flasicks.

Flaucht, *n.* used of aviation : flight.—*v.* to fly. Cf. Flaught.

Flee-catcher, *n.* a kind of glazed hat or cap.

Fleed, *n.* a flood.

Fleenge, *v.* to plunge; to flounder. Cf. Fling.

Fleesh, *v.* to fleece.—*n.* in *phr.* 'a fleesh o' beasts,' any number of cattle bought or sold at one time by a farmer.

Fleetins, *n.* the small particles floating in whey. Cf. Float-whey.

Flick, *n.* a flitch of bacon.

Flipe-wool, *n.* skin-wool.

Flirdach, *n.* a light and cheery person.

Flirr, *v.* to flare up. Cf. Flirr.

Flitch, *v.* to coax, wheedle. Cf. Fleech.

Fliz, *v.* in *phr.* 'to let fliz,' to let fly at or strike an opponent.

Flone, *v.* to fawn. Cf. Floan.

Flouncing, *ppl.* used of trees in a gale : tossing to and fro ; of a sail : flapping.

Flower-bab, *n.* a bunch of flowers, a bouquet.

Flow-moss, *n.* a moving bog. Cf. Flow-moss.

Flup, *n.* a person of clumsy appearance. Cf. Flup.

Flushy, *adj.* used of ice on the surface of a lake : thawing. Cf. Flush.

Fluthers, *n.* frippery attached to a woman's dress.

Foogie, Foojie, *v.* to play truant. Cf. Fugie.

Foogie-lick, *n.* a blow challenging to a fight. Cf. Fugie-blow.

†Foolyery, *n.* leaved work. Cf. Foolyie.

Fooriochie, *adj.* feeble. Cf. Fooriochie.

Foosht-ye-may-ca . . . , *n.* what do you call (it or him)? Cf. Fousticat.

Foosticate, *n.* what do you call it ? Cf. Fousticat.

Forby, Forbye, *adv.* apart, aside.

Fore-guard, *n.* an advanced guard.

Foreloppen, *adj.* fugitive.

Foreseen, *ppl. adj.* well-known, famous.

Forespent, *adj.* prematurely spent or worn out.

Fore-start, *n.* a start before others.

Fore-wark, *n.* the front-work of a fortified castle.

Fore-winter-nicht, *n.* the early part of a winter night.

Forfowden, *adj.* exhausted.

Forgya, *v. pret.* forgave. Cf. Forgie.

For-lee, *n.* the lee-bow.

Fort, *adj.* fourth.

Forten, *n.* fortune ; a fortune.

Forvoo, *v.* to forsake. Cf. Forhow.

Foul-be-lickit, *n.* absolutely nothing. Cf. Deil-be-lickit.

Foun', *n.* a foundation. Cf. Found.

Fourthen, *adj.* fourth.

Foustie, *n.* a roll split up and eaten with butter or jelly.

Fouthy, *adj.* abundant. Cf. Fouthy.

Fozie, *adj.* soft and hairy like wool. Cf. Fozy.

Fraak, *n.* a whim ; a foolish, superstitious fancy. Cf. Freak.

Fracht, *n.* in *phrs.* 'a fracht o' water,' two buckets of water ; 'a fracht o' corn,' two cartloads of corn. Cf. Fraucht.

Frachty, *adj.* in *phr.* 'gweed frachty,' generous, liberal. Cf. Frauchty.

Fractious, *adj.* troublesome or particular about one's food.

†Fraeca, *n.* a disturbance, fracas.

Fraiday, *n.* Friday.

Fraik, *n.* sulks, fretting. Cf. Freak.

Fraisen, *v.* to flatter. Cf. Fraise.

Fraixie, *adj.* smooth-tongued. Cf. Fraisie.

Fram, *n.* a stranger. Cf. Frem.

Frap, *n.* a jugful, a canful.

Freachy, *adj.* spoiled in the making; faded in colour.

Freely, *adv.* exactly ; in *phr.* 'nae freely,' used with reference to anything that had been asserted, yet was not true.

Freenly, *adj.* friendly.—*adv.* in a friendly way.

Freikit, *adj.* whimsical, odd.

French-pearie, *n.* a humming-top.

Frig, *v.* to be fastidious about trifles.

Frizzing, *n.* the hammer of a gun. Cf. Frizzel.

Frooch, *adj.* unbending.

Froon, *v.* to frown.—*n.* a frown.

Frough, *adj.* brittle.

Fruch, *adj.* brittle ; used of cloth or wood ; rotten. Cf. Frush.

Fucher, *v.* to work aimlessly, carelessly, or awkwardly. Cf. Ficher.

Fudd, *adj.* afraid.

Fugle, *v.* to manage so as to cheat.—*n.* a clever, cunning cheat.

Fugle, *n.* anything crumpled up, and not neatly folded together.

Fuir-nicht, *phr.* late in the night.

Fuist, *n.* rust ; mould. Cf. Fuist.

Fulzie-can, *n.* a slop-pail ; a vessel for holding night-soil.

Funk, *n.* a sulking-fit.

Fup, *v.* to seize, whip up. Cf. Fup.

Furrineerer, *n.* a foreigner.

Fyaach, *v.* to work hard and to little purpose. Cf. Fyaach.

Fyantich, *adj.* fawning, fulsome. Cf. Fyantish.

Fykie, *adj.* very particular; fidgety.

Fyoord, *n.* a ford.

Gad, *int.* an excl. of disgust.

Gade, *n.* a bar; a goad. Cf. Gaud.

Gaffer, *v.* to oversee, act as 'gaffer.'

Gaining, *ppl. adj.* ingratiating.

Gaivin, *adj.* awkward and reckless.

Gale, Gaile, *n.* a state of excitement; anger. Cf. Gale.

Gallows-pin, *n.* the beam or projection of a gallows upon which the hangman's rope could be fastened.

Galsh, *n.* rubbishy talk.

Galshachs, Galshichs, *n.* sweetmeats; any kind of food not in common use. Cf. Galshochs.

Galshin, *ppl.* talking rubbish.

Gamester, *n.* one who plays in a game, not necessarily a gambler.

Ganj, Ganzh, *v.* to speak impertinently. Cf. Gange.

Ganjin, *n.* impudent speaking back.

Garb, *n.* any thin, coarse cloth.

Gare, *n.* that part of the body close to which is the gusset of one's shirt; a strip large enough for a bandage. Cf. Gare.

Gargle, *n.* a cant name for liquor.

Garrer, *n.* one who makes a boy his fag.

Garrie-bee, *n.* the black-and-yellow-striped wild bee. Cf. Gairie.

Garrin'-law, *n.* the system or law of fagging at school or boys' hospital.

Gashin, *ppl.* gesticulating and screwing the open mouth in an ugly way.

Gast, *n.* a surprise. Cf. Gast.

Gathering-bodie, *n.* one who gathers goods or money by industry and thrift.

Gauden, *adj.* golden.

Gaumit, *n.* the gamut.

Gaut, *ppl.* galled. Cf. Gaw.

Geems, *n.* the gums.

Geggie, *n.* the shows and stir of a fair.

Gentle gates, *n.* delicate habits.

Gess, *v.* to play truant. Cf. Gess.

Gess, *n.* a measure by guess.

Gey-geddert, -gethered, *adj.* used of one who is well-off by his own industry or thrift.

Gey loon, *n.* a rather wild young fellow; a scamp, scoundrel.

Geyzenin, *n.* the craving for drink. Cf. Gizzen.

Gid, *v. pret.* went.

Giein', *ppl.* giving.

Giftie, *n.* a gift.—*adj.* used of a crop: large, abundant.

Gigmaleeries, *n.* young people frolicking at a fair.

Gimma, *v.* with *pron.* give to me.

Gin, *n.* the lever of a latch.

Ging, *n.* filth. Cf. Geing.

Gingie, *adj.* filthy.

Glaiket, *ppl. adj.* inattentive to duty. Cf. Glaikit.

Glaiks, *n.* an instrument for twisting straw-ropes.

Glaive, *n.* a glove.

Glamshach, *adj.* greedy, grasping; gluttonous.

Glancy, *adj.* glancing.

Glare, *v.* to cause to glare.

Glaur-hole, *n.* a mud-hole.

Glazen, *adj.* made of glass; used of weak arguments: easily refuted. Cf. Glassen.

Glead, Gleade, *n.* the kite; a kite's feathers used for dressing salmon-hooks.

Glee, *n.* a glove.

Gleg-gabbit, *adj.* sharp-tongued; nimble or fluent of speech.

Gleig, *adj.* clear-sighted; keen. Cf. Gleg.

Gleuve, *n.* a glove.

Gliff, *v.* to evade quickly or suddenly. Cf. Gliff.

Glim, *v.* to light up; to gleam. Cf. Glim.

Gliv, *n.* a glove.

Glogger, *n.* the gurgle of a liquid when poured quickly from a bottle.

Glone, *n.* excitement over some coveted possession. Cf. Gloan.

Glose, *n.* a glow of light. Cf. Glose.

Gloss, *v.* to sleep lightly.

Glourin'-fow, *adj.* at the staring stage of tipsiness.

Glue, *n.* a glove.

Gluff, *v.* to puff and blow after a plunge into cold water.

Glupe, *n.* a great chasm or cavern.

Glut, *n.* phlegm ejected from the throat.

Glut, *v.* to gush.

Gly't, *ppl. adj.* squinting. Cf. Gly.

Gnapper, *n.* in *phr.* 'gnipper nor gnapper,' not the least particle. Cf. Gnipper for gnapper.

Gnap the win', *n.* a disastrous policy; an issue unexpectedly bad.

Gneck-in-the-neck, *n.* a person's manifest peculiarity or weakness.

Gneggum, *n.* the nasty taste or smell of anything. Cf. Kneggum.

Gnyauve, *v.* to gnaw.

Gock-a-hoy, *adj.* silly and childish in speech and behaviour.

Gockit, Gokit, *adj.* silly. Cf. Gowkit.

Goog, *n.* any soft, moist stuff. Cf. Googg.

Google, v. to deceive, juggle.

Googlie, n. a deceptive ball at cricket.

Gooms, n. the gums.

Goor, n. stagnant water full of animal and vegetable life.

†**Goord,** adj. stiff. Cf. Gourd.

Goord, v. to stop running water by earth or ice.

Goordness, n. stiffness.

Goorie, n. the garbage of salmon. Cf. Gouries.

Gooshet, n. a gusset.

Gorglyum, n. a young bird in the nest.

Gouff, Gowf, Gowff, v. to reel off verses, &c., in recitation.

Gounk, n. a disappointment; a jilting. Cf. Gunk.

Gove, Govy, n. a name given to the head-master of a school or hospital.

Gow, v. to persuade by argument. Cf. Gow.

Gowfin, n. a soft, pliable person; a coward. Cf. Gowfin.

Gowk, adj. foolish. Cf. Gowk.

Gowpen, v. used of a wound or sore: to throb. Cf. Goup.

Graapus, n. a mean, greedy fellow. Cf. Grampus.

Graen, v. to groan; to clear the throat.

Graithlie, adv. properly, sufficiently. Cf. Graidly.

Granniedey, n. a grandfather; an old man. Cf. Grandey.

Gray-plaidit, adj. wearing a gray plaid.

Gray thrums n. the purring of a cat.

Greesh, n. a fireplace of clay built against the gable of a cottage.

Grew-dog, n. a greyhound.

†**Grimalder,** n. an ugly person.

Grissel, Grisel, n. a gray horse.

Groofflins, adv. in a grovelling position. Cf. Grouflins.

Groofling, adj. lying close wrapped up.

Grool, v. to growl.

Grootins, n. any dirty, oily thing. Cf. Groot.

Grooze, n. a shivering fit.

Groozy, adj. shivering.

Growthy-tasted, adj. used of potatoes: having a taste peculiar to their beginning to sprout in spring.

Gruif, n. the surface of the stomach. Cf. Grufe.

Gruive, v. pret. graved.

Gryte, adj. great, big.

Gu', n. a seagull.

Guild o' glee, n. a merry group of playmates.

Guilish, adj. guileful; beguiling.

Guillie, n. a big knife. Cf. Gully.

Gully, n. human excrement.

Gun, n. in phr. 'a great gun,' a great friend.

Gurious, adj. grim. Cf. Gruous.

Gurkie, n. a short, stout person. Cf. Gurk.

Gurling, ppl. adj. used of rivulets: gurgling, running noisily. Cf. Gurl.

Gurr, n. courage, bravery.

Gusslin, n. boasting.

Guttam, n. a drop.

Gweed-wully, adj. generous, willing to give. Cf. Gude-willie.

Gyad, int. an excl. of disgust. Cf. Gad.

Gype-like, adj. like a fool or a lout.

Gype-written, adj. written by a fool.

Gypical, adj. characteristic of a fool, foolish.

Gypical-like, adj. 'gype-like.'

Gypit, ppl. made a fool of.

Haar-cluds, n. clouds brought by a raw, cold wind from the east.

Habieshaw, v. to scatter sweets among children to scramble for.

Hag and hash, v. to hack and hew.

Hailzin, n. a rude or angry salutation. Cf. Hailzin.

Hairst-baps, n. large, white rolls given at lunch on the harvest-field.

Hairt, adj. used of clothes, linens, &c. in the open air: partly dry.

Haive, v. to heave.

Hale an' wale, n. health and wealth, given as a toast.

Halend, n. an inner wall. Cf. Hallan.

Hame-hatched, adj. hatched at home.

Hame-rout, n. the homeward way.

Han'-ban', n. a wrist-band.

Hand-canny, adj. handy with tools.

Hand-wealed, adj. picked by hand.

Hank, v. to compress.

Hardlins, adv. hardly, scarcely.

Harlin, adj. slight. Cf. Harlin.

Harl in the throat, n. hoarseness.

Haroosh, n. a noisy clamour. Cf. Huroosh.

Harvest kemp, n. a keen competition on the harvest-field.

Hash, v. to overwork a person.—n. work done at great speed and under great strain. Cf. Hash.

Haummer, v. to walk carelessly. Cf. Hammer.

Heather-wight, n. a Highlander.

Hed, v. pret. hid.

Heesh, v. to scare away birds, &c. Cf. Hish.

Heid an' heels, adv. completely, wholly.

Heid-deester, n. the chief actor in a function.

Heidsteen, n. a headstone.

Helm, n. a noisy crowd. Cf. Hemmil.

Herrying the peer man, n. a boys' game like 'smuggle-the gig.'

Hert-sair, adj. heart-sore.

Hert-stawed, adj. thoroughly surfeited.

Heuch, v. pret. hewed.

Heuch-stone, n. sulphate of copper applied to the inflamed eyes of cattle. Cf. Heuch.

Hew, *v. pret.* hoed.

Hey, *n.* hay.

Hichen, *v.* to heighten; to raise the price of an article.

Hid, *v. pret.* had.

Hielan, *adj.* in *phr.* 'nae sae Hielan,' not so bad.

Himpie, *n.* a half-angry word called by a mother to a child. Cf. Hempy.

Hinder-lins, *n.* the posteriors. Cf. Hinner-lans.

Hinder nicht, *n.* last night. Cf. Hinner nicht.

Hin'-the-han', *n.* anything stored for future use.

Hirpledird, *v.* to walk lamely with a rebounding motion.

Hist, *n.* a great quantity. Cf. Hist.

Hiz, *v.* has.

Hoch-on, *n.* help given to mount on horseback, a leg-up.

Hole, *v.* to stay in a place longer than seems needful. Cf. Hole.

Hood, *n.* the joining of the two parts of a flail, generally of leather, sometimes of eel's skin.

Hoolat, *v.* to henpeck; to look miserable.

Hoozle, *n.* the Sacrament of the Lord's Supper. Cf. Ousel.

Hork, *v.* to grub like a pig.

Horse-orts, *n.* horse-dung.

†Hostee, *n.* the Host.

Hotchin-hippit, *adj.* having hips that cause clumsy walking.

Hotten, *ppl.* hit.

Hotter, *v.* used of the heart: to palpitate; to shake with cold or fear.

Houe, *v.* to hoot; to howl; to scare away.

Hougheneugh, *adj.* but so-so or middling.

Houin, *n.* the cry of the owl in warm weather. Cf. Huam.

Hout, *v.* to pooh-pooh; to flout. Cf. Hoot.

Hoven, *ppl.* swollen.

Howdie-trade, *n.* the practice of midwifery.

Huckerspoke, *adj.* ? showing dignity.

Hue and hair, *n.* main force; every effort or inducement.

Huggerin, *n.* the shaky, creepy feeling caused by intense cold. Cf. Hugger.

Huggermagrillian, *n.* a coarse, slovenly woman.

Huil, *n.* a husk, a shell. Cf. Hool.

Huish, *n.* a lumpish, slovenly woman.

Huistrie, *n.* bad food; trash; the contents of a beggar's wallet. Cf. Houstrie.

Hule, *n.* a hovel.

Hull, *v.* to hurry.

Hulster, *v.* to throw upon back or shoulder; to burden one's self needlessly.—*n.* a load of any kind. Cf. Hulster.

Hummel, *adj.* at a loss. Cf. Hummel.

Hun', *v.* to run about from place to place like a hound.

Hurdie-rickle, *n.* rheumatism.

Hurkle-beens, *n.* the projecting points of the thigh-bones. Cf. Hurkle-bane.

Hurkles, *n.* the hams, the 'hunkers.'

Hurl, *n.* the snoring sound in the chest during a bronchial attack.

Hurley-load, *n.* the load of a hand-cart; a heavy burden.

Hurlmaadie, *n.* an ancient style of head-gear.

Hurry, *v.* to raise a disturbance. Cf. Hurry.

Hyauve-leukin', *adj.* of sallow complexion. Cf. Hyaave.

Hyow, *v.* to hoe.—*n.* a hoe.

Hyppel, *n.* an opprobrious name given to any one. Cf. Hypal.

Hyve, *v.* to heave.

Ice-hill, *n.* an iceberg.

Ice-skid, *n.* a skate.

Id, *v.* would.

Ilky, *adj.* each; every. Cf. Ilka.

Ill-deedly, *adj.* mischievous.

Ill-ee'd, *adj.* having an evil or unfriendly eye.

Ill-hertit, *adj.* easily daunted. Cf. Ill-hairtit.

Ill-set, *adj.* selfish.

Ill-shakken-up, *adj.* used of a person: careless as to personal appearance.

Ill-teen, *n.* a bad humour.

Ill-words, *n.* swear-words.

Immis, *adj.* used of the weather: variable, foggy. Cf. Emmis.

Incastred, *ppl.* incarcerated.

Indy, *n.* a peculiar mode of pitching a boys' marble, by placing the thumb of the left hand on the ground, with the hand held up, placing also the marble in front of the middle finger of that hand, and with the right hand propelling it forward.

Ingle-blink, *n.* the flickering light from the 'ingle.'

Inhaudin', *ppl. adj.* ingratiating. Cf. In hadden.

Iniquious, *adj.* iniquitous. Cf. Iniquous.

Inlat, *n.* an inlet.

Inlucky, *adj.* dirty.

Inpit, *n.* the gaining for some one a footing in favour, or in a company.

Intack, *adj.* intact.

Intak, *v.* to cheat; to lift stitches in knitting.

Intear, *adj.* entirely intimate or dear.

Intenet, *v. pret.* and *ppl.* intended.

Intention, *v.* to intend.

Invitors, *n.* the crops, fencing, &c. paid by the incoming tenant of a farm. Cf. Invitor.

Isdel, *n.* a red-hot cinder. Cf. Aizle, Eysle.

Isle, *n.* an aisle.

Itherwhere, *adv.* elsewhere.

Ivry, *int.* the call of a boy, in playing marbles, for liberty to play in any position he chose. Cf Every.

Jabbit, *ppl. adj.* fatigued, worn out.

Jabbit-leukin', *adj.* looking as if tired.

Jamb o' a hoose, *n.* a badly-built house, cheerless, cold, with the wind whistling through crevices in walls, doors, and windows.

Jammie, *n.* a hovel.

Japandet, *ppl. adj.* japanned.

Jaupit, *ppl. adj.* empty-looking ; thin.

Jaurie, *n.* a boys' common marble.

Jeck, *v.* to go rightly or smoothly.

Jeedge, *v.* to rage and swear. Cf. Jeedge.

†**Jeel o' caul,** *n.* a chill, a cold.

†**Jeel wi' caul,** *v.* to catch cold, get a chill. Cf. Geal.

Jeer, *n.* the seat of the trousers.

Jeestie, *adj.* with *neg.* not safe, 'no joke.' Cf. Jeestie.

Jenk-amang-the-whins, *n* the linnet.

Jibble, *n.* a thin, watery liquid. Cf. Geeble.

Jiff, *n.* a giddy girl.

Jiffer, *n.* a contemptuous name applied to a queer person, a 'jigger.'

Jilpert, *n.* anything too thin, as soup ; milk deficient in fat ; any liquid having little more than water in it.

Jine, *v.* to join.

Jinker, *n.* an immoral fellow. Cf. Jinker.

Jirge, *v.* to churn ; to move violently.

Jirple, *v.* to shake a vessel containing liquid so as to spill some of its contents. Cf. Jirble.

Jivvle, *n.* a house with more space than is needed. Cf. Jivvle.

Jock-Hack, *n.* a farm-servant in his working-clothes.

Jock-strike-the-knock, *n.* the striking-hammer of a clock.

Joco', *adj.* jocose.

Joggle, *v.* to cause oscillation.

John Barley-bree, *n.* malt liquor ; whisky.

Jokelar, *adj.* jocular.

†**Jouf,** *n.* a kind of 'bed-gown'

Jouker, *n.* a dissembler. Cf. Jouker.

Joukrie-pawkrie, *n.* deceit.

Joute, *n.* sour liquor. Cf. Joot.

Jouter, *v.* to saunter. Cf. Jotter.

Judaism, *n.* treachery ; the being two-faced, like a 'Judas.'

Judas, *n.* one who is one thing to your face and another behind your back.

Judas-limmer, -scoundrel, *n.* a 'Judas.'

Juice, *n.* the moisture of the body coming out in perspiration.

Jummle, *v.* to suffer from shock ; to be insane.

Junny, *v.* to irritate one by doing what he forbids ; to provoke to anger. Cf. Junnie.

Keeser, *n.* a strongly-built, muscular person. Cf. Keessar.

Kell, *n.* a scabbed head. Cf. Kell.

Kem, *v.* in *phr.* 'to kem one's croon,' to tear one's hair ; to strike one's head.

Kemp, *v.* to take food hurriedly so as to finish first. Cf. Kemp.

Kenspeck, *adj.* easily recognized, conspicuous. Cf. Kenspeckle.

Keuk, *v.* in *phr.* 'to keuk (cook) one,' to get what one wants of a person.

Keystane, *n.* a masonic symbolical decoration.

Kibble, *adj.* smart at walking.

Kickers, *n.* in *phr.* 'to stand one's kickers,' to withstand one.

Kiddie, *n.* a candle.

Kidgie, *adj.* used of a married couple : comfortable and happy. Cf. Cadgie.

Kigger, *n.* a wet mass. Cf. Kigger.

Kilpin, *n.* a stout, muscular person.

Kiltimmer, *n.* an opprobrious epithet applied to a woman of doubtful character.

Kintramen, *n.* rustics.

Kirk-gaun-claes, *n.* Sunday clothes.

Kissing-kind, *adj.* seemingly, but not really, kind.

Kitching, *n.* a kitchen.

Kitly, *adj.* tickly. Cf. Kittly.

Kitty, *n.* the jack in the game of bowls. Cf. Kitty.

Kivy, *n.* a covey ; a bevy. Cf. Kivin.

Kleckit oot, *ppl. adj.* knocked out.

Klyak, *v.* to gossip.—*n.* a gossip. Cf. Claik.

Knabberie, *n.* gentry. Cf. Knabbry.

Knag, *n.* in *phr.* 'at the knag and widdie thegither,' at loggerheads.

Knaist, Knaisht, *n.* a lump of anything.

Knap, *n.* a knock on the head. Cf. Knap.

Knap-darlichs, *n.* lumps of dung hanging from the hind-legs of cattle.

Knap-grass, *n.* knot-grass.

Knaplich, *n.* a bit broken off.

Knarlich, *n.* an irregularly-shaped lump of anything. Cf. Knorlack.

Knat, *n.* a solid body ; in *phr.* 'a knat o' a littlin,' a child who is solid fat.

Kneef, *adj.* vigorous for one's age ; in thorough intimacy and sympathy. Cf. Kneef.

Knibblach, *n.* the barb of a harpoon.

Knockles, *n.* the knuckles.

Knot, *v.* used of turnips : to suffer from 'finger and toe.'

Knowpert, *n.* the crowberry. Cf. Knauperts.

Knuve, *v.* to converse familiarly. Cf. Knuff.

Knyockles, Knyockels, *n.* the knuckles.

Knyockles of the queets, *n.* the ankle-bones.

Knyte, *n.* a stout person. Cf. Knyte.

Kowe, *n.* what cows one.

Kurchie, *n.* a curtsy.

Kuter, *v.* to cocker, coax ; to talk secretly. Cf. Cuiter.

Kweeger, *n.* a mess, an untidy mixture.

Kweetin, *n.* a coverlet.

Kyaak, Kyak, *n.* a cake; in *pl.* oat-cakes.
Kyard, *n.* a tinker. Cf. Caird.
Kyob, Kyobie, *n.* a bird's crop.

Labbich, *n.* speech, talk; a way of talking. Cf. Llabbach.
Lagin, *n.* the junction of the bottom of a pot or pan with its sides. Cf. Laggen.
Lags, *n.* small tufts of corn left uncut.
Laidle, *n.* a ladle; a box with a long handle for collecting the offertory.
Laik, *v.* to leak.—*n.* a leak.
Lairge, *adj.* large; plentiful. Cf. Large.
Laist, *v.* to last.
Laithfu-like, *adj.* seemingly shy or reluctant.
Lang-gammachy, *n.* a long, rambling speech or story.
Langle, *v.* to hinder; to entangle. Cf. Langel.
Lang-lenth, *n.* in *phr.* 'at lang-lenth,' at last.
Lang-shanks, *n.* Death.
Langure, *n.* longing.
Lapperty, *n.* milk that has stood until it is curdled.
Lard, *int.* an excl. of disgust.
Lass-fond, *adj.* fond of a lass, or of the lasses.
Lat, *v.* in *phr.* 'to lat a raught,' to aim a blow.
Laugin, *ppl. adj.* gossiping. Cf. Laig.
Lawman, *n.* a lawyer, solicitor.
Lay, *v.* in *phr.* 'to lay up one's mittens,' to beat out one's brains.—*n.* a footing.
Leader, *n.* a leaden bullet, sometimes used as a boys' marble.
Lead-stone, *n.* the first stone played on a curling-rink.
Leather-jacket, *n.* a name given to the corn-grub.
Leek-strae, *n.* straw placed under a dead body in a bed.
Leepit thing, *n.* a dog or cat that presses near to a fire.
Leerip, Leerup, *n.* a blow with fist or stick. Cf. Larrup.
Leesh, *n.* a large slice.
Leet, *v.* to let, allow.—*v. pret.* allowed.
Leive, *n.* the palm of the hand. Cf. Loof.
Lems, *n.* broken pieces of crockery. Cf. Lame.
Len', *n.* in *phr.* 'to tak the len' o' a boddy,' to make a fool of one. Cf. Len'.
Lench, *v.* to pay out money unwillingly. Cf. Lainch.
Lerb, *n.* a sip of liquid lapped like a dog.
Lettrin, *n.* a latrine; the channel in a stable for carrying off urine.
Libberlay, *n.* a long, rambling story.
Lien by, *ppl.* refrained from.
Lingle-threeder, *n.* one who uses 'lingles' or shoemakers' threads.
Lingo, *n.* a long story.
Lipp, *n.* the broad brim of a soft hat.
Lithie, *v.* to break the neck.

Lloostre, *n.* sloth; a slothful person.—*v.* to remain slothful.
Lloostrie, *n.* idleness. Cf. Looster.
Lochy, *adj.* having a loch; abounding in lochs.
Lod, *int.* Lord !
Lounie, *n.* a small milking-park. Cf. Loan.
Looffin, *n.* a handful.
Loom-sprung, *adj.* said of those who have risen in the world by the toil of the weavers in their employment.
Loomy, *n.* a small loom.
Loonikie, *n.* a very small boy.
Loop o' the shank, *n.* the knitting of stockings.
Loorach, *n.* rags.
†Loordy, *adj.* lazy. Cf. Lourdy.
Loose, *v.* to lose.
Loosie, *adj.* covered with dandriff. Cf. Loossie.
Looten o', *adj.* esteemed.
Losing one's sel', *phr.* losing care for one's personal appearance.
Loup, *v.* used of a boot or shoe: to open between the upper and the sole.
Louthrick, *n.* a lever; a great stick; a blow with a stick. Cf. Louther.
Love-lichtit, *adj.* used of the eyes: lighted by love.
Lowren-fair, *n.* an Aberdeenshire fair held on St Lawrence-day, Aug 23.
Luck-daddy, *n.* a grandfather. Cf. Lucky-dad.
Luck-minnie, *n.* a grandmother. Cf. Lucky-minnie.
Lue-warm, *adj.* lukewarm.
Luffie, *n.* a stroke on the palm; a flat stone. Cf. Loofie.
Luggerheids, *n.* loggerheads.
Luggie, *n.* a window-like aperture in a room of an old baronial castle, from which could be heard and surveyed by the baron unseen what went on in the room underneath.
Lug-storming, *adj.* assailing or deafening the ears.
Luiffie, *n.* a morning roll.
Lüin, *n.* the red-throated diver.
Lunnie, *n.* a lunatic. Cf. Lunie.
Lunshach, *n.* a large supply of food.
Luppen, *ppl. adj.* used of a boot or shoe: opened between the upper and the sole through stitches giving way; in *phr.* 'luppen a gutter,' escaped some danger.
Lyaag, *v.* to talk, to gossip. Cf. Lyaag.
Lyawger, *n.* gossiping.
Lybbich, *n.* reading, reciting. Cf. Llabbach.
Ly-by, *adj.* standing aside, neutral.
Lyowder, *v.* to amble, or sway from side to side; in walking.

Maggateevish, *adj.* peculiar in temperament; changeable in moods. Cf. Maggative.
Mains o', *n.* the upper hand of; the advantage over; the best of a bargain or argument.

Maitter, *n.* matter; pus.

Maize, *v.* to wonder.

Malygroose, *v.* to maim by accident or disease. Cf. Malagruze.

†**Mank,** *n.* an objection, a complaint; a disturbance. Cf. Mank.

Man-life, *n.* human life; life as a man.

Mappy, *n.* a boys' marble marked with lines like a map.

Marce-Billion, *n.* the feast of the Translation of St Martin, July 4. Cf. Martin-a-bullimus.

Marra, *n.* a match, an equal. Cf. Marrow.

Marshlick, Marshlach, *n.* a collection of things no two of which are alike.—*adj.* untidy.

Mathy, *adj.* warm and misty. Cf. Meeth.

†**Maugre,** *v.* to overpower in spite of. Cf. Magyers.

Maugres o', *adv.* in spite of.

Mauzie, *n.* a knitted woollen undershirt. Cf. Mawsie.

†**Mealie,** *n.* a mob; a mêlée.

†**Meal in wi',** *v.* to share with; to make friends with; to mingle with.

Memmel, *n.* timber from Memel.

†**Mengie,** *n.* a mixed crowd of people; retainers. Cf. Menyie.

Meniment, *n.* amendment. Cf. Mendiment.

†**Menstril,** *n.* a minstrel.

Mewtle, *v.* used of cows and ewes: to cry.

Mid-seas, *adj.* half-tipsy, 'half-seas over.'

Milk-cum, -kim, *n.* a milk-tub.

Mimp, *n.* an affected gait. Cf. Mimp.

Miscomfit, *v.* to displease.

Misfit, *v.* to displease.

Misgien, *ppl.* used of a crop: failed.

Misimproven, *adj.* not improved, wrongly improved.

Misrestit, *adj.* having broken sleep or disturbed rest.

Mis-thrift, *n.* thriftlessness, wastefulness.

Moals, *n.* earth. Cf. Mool.

†**Moen,** *n.* influence; mediation. Cf. Moyen.

Mogan, *n.* a hidden or secret purse. Cf. Moggan.

Moggan, *n.* in *phr.* 'to wet the sma' end o' a moggan,' to find great difficulty.

†**Monshie, Monzie,** *n.* a Frenchman.

Mooching, *n.* a kind of sly begging.

Moodie, *adj.* down-hearted.

Moodie, *adj.* gallant.

Moolating, *n.* whimpering, whining. Cf. Moolet.

Mooligh, *v.* to whimper.

Moonge, *v.* to grumble in a low tone; to munch. Cf. Mounge.

Moose, *n.* the outside fleshy part of a leg of mutton. Cf. Mouse.

Mooth-ruif, *n.* the palate.

†**Morbleu, Morblue,** *n.* a murder-cry.—*adv.* with vigour.

Mouden, *v.* to melt; to clarify. Cf. Mouten.

Moudiwort, *n.* a very slow worker. Cf. Moudiewarp.

Mougart, *n.* mugwort.

Moulter, *v.* to crumble; to take away piecemeal.

Moup, *v.* to fall off in health. Cf. Moup.

Mouze, *v.* to plunder clandestinely.

Muchty, *adj.* close; musty; stale.

Mucklest, *adj.* biggest. Cf. Muckle.

Muis, *n.* heaps; parcels.

Muith, *adj.* cheerful.

Muithly, *adv.* softly.

Mulde, *n.* earth, mould; in *pl.* the grave.

Mulde-meat, *n.* in *phr.* 'to give one his mulde-meat,' to kill him.

†**Mule in,** *v.* in *phr.* 'to mule in with one,' to be familiar, on intimate terms, with one.

Murjin, *n.* a murmur; in *phr.* 'no murjins at a place,' no movement or sign of life about a place. Cf. Murgeon.

Museock, *n.* a familiar or contemptuous name for the Muse.

Mutch-bord, *n.* the border of a woman's cap.

Myowt, *n.* a muttering; a grumble; a peevish utterance.

Nabaler, *n.* a covetous person. Cf. Nabal.

Nabble, *v.* to work fast, to hurry through with one's work.

Nabbler, *n.* a 'nabaler.'

Na be here, *int.* an excl. of surprise or pleasure.

†**Nacket,** *n.* a smart young fellow. Cf. Nacket.

Nae-ho, *adv.* nohow.—*n.* no other way or resource.

Nae idder, *adj.* and *n.* no other.

Nafferel, *adj.* insignificant-looking.

Nail-pinn, *n.* a nail or pin used in boatbuilding.

Na, sirs, *int.* an excl. of surprise.

Naubal, *adj.* crusty; grippy, close-fisted. Cf. Nabal.

Nauborly, *adj.* close-fisted.

Naucht, *n.* naught, nought.

Naup, *n.* a nap, short sleep.

Nax, *n.* a schoolboy's humiliating birching, &c. Cf. Knack.

Neap, *n.* the nape.

Neerder, *adj.* nearer.

Ne'er may care, *adv.* nevertheless.

Neg, *n.* a pony. Cf. Naig.

Newan, *n.* a drubbing. Cf. New.

Nibawa, *adj.* thin, emaciated-looking.

Nick-in-the-neck, *n.* a person's manifest weak point or peculiarity. Cf. Gneck-in-the-neck.

Nickle doon, *v.* to propel a marble with the knuckles touching the ground.

Nickle in, v. to propel a marble with the hand inverted in a strained position, so as to reduce the chance of hitting a marble in the ring.

Nickler, *n.* a boys' marble used as a 'pitcher.'

Nickling, *n.* the act of propelling a marble.

Night-gown, *n.* a dressing-gown.

Nimle, *adj.* nimble.

Nip, *n.* in *phr.* 'to take a nip of one,' to take undue advantage of one. Cf. Nip.

Nit-brown, *adj.* nut-brown.

Nitfu', *n.* used of whisky: a 'thimbleful,' a 'nip.'

Nob, *n.* a swell.

Noddie, *n.* a slight nod.

Non-wordit, *adj.* neglected; counted unworthy or worthless. Cf. Wordy.

Noof, *v.* to be neat. Cf. Noof.

Noonin, *n.* noon.

Noonog, *n.* the cranberry; the heath.

Noop, *n.* a pin.

Noosly, *adv.* snugly. Cf. Noosle.

Noozle, *n.* a squeeze. Cf. Noozle.

Normost, *adj.* northmost.

Nosie-way, *n.* one with little knowledge.

Not-swearer, *n.* a nonjuror.

Noture, *adj.* notorious. Cf. Notour.

Numerosity, *n.* numbers.

Nyarbit, *ppl. adj.* of a peevish, growling disposition. Cf. Nyarb.

Nyauve, *v.* to gnaw. Cf. Gnyauve.

Off-casten, *adj.* cast off; rejected.

Ohoy, *int.* ahoy!

Oncome, *n.* how an affair goes on and issues. Cf. Oncome.

Ook-eyn, *n.* a week-end.

Oolt-leukin', *adj.* looking cowed, terrified. Cf. Ool.

Oon, *n.* an egg without a shell. Cf. Oon-egg.

Oonermine, *v.* to undermine.

Oonless, *conj.* unless.

Oonsizzonable, *adj.* unseasonable.

Oorit, *adj.* with the hair standing on end. Cf. Oorat.

Oorlich, *adj.* raw, damp. Cf. Oorlich.

Oosie, *adj.* having a fine woollen nap. Cf. Ooze.

Ordinary, *n.* what happens in the ordinary course of things. Cf. Ordinar.

Orow, *adj.* odd, occasional. Cf. Orra.

Orts, *n.* horse-dung. Cf. Ort.

Out-edge, *n.* the cutting edge of a knife, sword, &c.

Outshoot, *v.* to outwit, overreach, overshoot.

Outwards, *n.* externals.

Outweel, *adv.* assuredly. Cf. Atweel.

Overdraw, *v.* to over-induce.

Pachty, *adj.* proud, haughty. Cf. Paughty.

Pae-wae, *adj.* woe-begone; out of sorts. Cf. Bae-wae.

Pailie, *n.* a small pail.

Pairis', *n.* a parish.

Palie, *adj.* delicious, palatable.

Pan, *v.* to tie a pan or kettle to a dog's tail.

Pandomie, *n.* pandemonium.

Parliament, *n.* in *phr.* 'a free parliament,' freedom of speech.

Parry, *v.* to fight in play.

Pauchler, *n.* a small farmer who works on his own land. Cf. Pauchle.

Paule, *n.* the half of one's allowance of bread.

Paumer, *v.* to ride rough-shod over things; to move about noisily, as in a dark room, by knocking up against furniture. Cf. Palmer.

Pea-claw, *n.* a name for pea-soup.

Pealings, *n.* 'strippings,' the last milk drawn from a cow.

Peasie, *int.* a call given to calves, pigeons, &c. Cf. Pease.

Peeack, *n.* one with a thin, insignificant voice. Cf. Pëak.

Peek, *v.* to weep, cry. Cf. Pëak.

Peel, *n.* an equal. Cf. Peel.

Peel, *v.* to shear corn with a sickle.

Peelie-waly, *n.* very weak stuff.

†**Peise**, *n.* the weight of a clock. Cf. Paise.

Pell, *n.* a salted hide.

Pepper-quern, *n.* a hand-mill for grinding pepper.

Petts, *n.* projections on the slanting part of a gable, resembling steps. Cf. Corbie-steps.

Peugh, *v.* to breathe shortly and spasmodically.

Peught, *adj.* asthmatical.

Pewel, *n.* a small bite; a whine; a stifled cough. Cf. Peughle, Pewil.

Pewter, *v.* to whine. Cf. Peuter.

Phring, *n.* a wife, a consort.

†**Pincie**, *adj.* neat, tidy; prim. Cf. Pensy.

Pinner, *n.* a heavy drinking-bout.

Pirl, *v.* to move slowly and lazily. Cf. Pirl.

Pirn, *n.* in *phr.* 'wun in a pirn,' entangled beyond easy extrication. Cf. Pirn.

Pitt, *n.* a peat.

Plack and farden, *n.* every penny, the uttermost farthing.

Plaick, *n.* a plaything. Cf. Playock.

Plain, *v.* to play plaintive music.

Plapperdosh, *n.* a tremendous fall. Cf. Plapper.

Plopper, *v.* to bubble like boiling water.

Plopperin', *n.* the noise made by anything boiling in a pot.

Plot, *v.* to be very hot. Cf. Plot.

Plottin', *ppl. adj.* in *phr.* 'plottin' wi' rage,' very angry, boiling with indignation.

Ploudie, Ploudy, *n.* a fat or plump child. Cf. Ploud.

Plump-shower, *n.* a sudden, heavy shower.

Plumy, *adj.* used of birds : feathered.

Plunky, *n.* a game of marbles in which large marbles are used.

Pob, *n.* rope or twine shredded into its original material. Cf. Pob.

Pock and string, *n.* a state of beggary; begging for a livelihood.

†Politick, *n.* policy. Cf. Politique.

Poochle, *adj.* prim ; tidy, neatly dressed.

Pook, *n.* declining health. Cf. Pook.

Poorail, *n.* the poorer people.

Pootch, *v.* to eat with relish.

Pootchin, *ppl. adj.* fond of good things ; big-bellied, corpulent.

Poother, *n.* powder ; gunpowder. Cf. Pouther.

Poother-deelie, *n.* a small cone of moistened gunpowder, used as a firework. Cf. Powder-deil.

Pot, *n.* a name for porridge.

Pouchie, *n.* a child's pocket ; a small pocket.

Pour taties, *v.* to kill by blood-letting.

Pouss, *n.* a kind of cake. Cf. Poos.

†Powstet, *ppl. adj.* exhausted, overcome. Cf. Postit.

Preen-holed, *adj.* pricked by a pin.

Prethy, *int.* prithee !

Prob, *v.* to lance. Cf. Prob.

Prodie, *n.* a trinket. Cf. Prodie.

Proportion, *n.* the district in a parish under the care of an elder for visitation.

Ptrua, Ptruita, *int.* a call to cattle and horses. Cf. Ptru.

Purfling, *ppl. adj.* causing shortness of breath.

Purposedly, *adv.* purposely.

Pussy-nickle, *n.* the method of propelling a marble by placing it in the hollow made by the bent forefinger and the thumb.

Pyke, *n.* a pique. Cf. Pike.

Quaff, *v.* to drink one's health.

Queit, *adj.* quiet.

Quicher, *n.* any needless work in household duties.

Raakin, *v.* to reckon. Cf. Rackon.

Rade, *n.* a rapid journey. Cf. Raid.

Rag-a-tag, *n.* an old horse.

Rancers, *n.* the bars running across the bottom of an open kitchen-dresser, on which bowls, pots, &c. might be placed. Cf. Rance.

†Ran-dan, *n.* a boys' holiday and frolic without leave. Cf. Ran-dan.

Rapper, *n.* the tongue of a bell ; the hammer of a clock.

Ratling, *n.* the death-rattle.

Rat-rythm, *n.* rote. Cf. Rat-rhyme.

†Reable, *v.* to render a bastard legitimate. Cf. Rehable.

Read, *n.* the fourth stomach of a cow. Cf. Reed.

†Rebat, *v.* to draw back ; to prove recalcitrant. Cf. Rebat.

Recant, *v.* to recite or tell over again. Cf. Recant.

Recognosce, *v.* to rejudge.

Red Rab, *n.* the robin.

Remm, *v.* to reiterate the same words. Cf. Rame.

Retard, *v.* to be late ; to fall behind.

Reverie, *n.* delirium. Cf. Ravery.

Rippadeeity, *n.* the loud noise caused by romping children.

Risp, *v.* and *n.* See the NOTE on Tirling-pin.

Rive, *n.* a large quantity of anything. Cf. Rive.

Riv't haet, *n.* absolutely nothing.

Rob, *n.* the robin.

Rook, *v.* a boys' term : to win all one's stock of marbles in playing for stakes.—*n.* a boy's marble.—*int.* in *pl.* a boy's shout when he is to grab the marbles of the other players. Cf. Rook.

Rookitty-coo, *n.* a pigeon's coo. Cf. Rooketty-coo.

Rookitty-cooin', *n.* the act and sound of pigeons cooing.

Rorie, *n.* a big lie. Cf. Rorie.

Round, *v.* to make a loud, hoarse sound in coughing or munching. Cf. Roond.

Roustit, *ppl. adj.* grizzled. Cf. Roustit.

Royter, *v.* to work unskilfully ; to talk foolishly. Cf. Royt.

Rud-hand, *adj.* red-handed.

Ruil, *v.* to romp. Cf. Ruil.

Runk, *n.* a harsh, cruel woman. Cf. Runk.

Rust, *v.* to be restive. Cf. Roost.

Rusty, *adj.* restive. Cf. Roosty.

Ruve, *n.* a rivet. Cf. Ruve.

Saal, *n.* the soul. Cf. Saul.

Sagor, *n.* a wild fellow.

Saint, *v.* to turn saint, become devout.

Sangschaw, *n.* a competitive exhibition of vocal and instrumental music.

Satire, *v.* to satirize.

Saugh-shaded, *adj.* shaded by willows.

Saum, *n.* a psalm.—*v.* to tell a long story.

Saurless, *adj.* limp. Cf. Sarless.

Scaal, *v.* to scold.

Scaal-pyock, *n.* a double chin.

Scaup, *adj.* used of soil : thin, bare, unfertile. Cf. Scaup.

Schuip, *v. pret.* shaped.

Schurling, *n.* the skin of a newly-shorn sheep.

Sclitter, *adj.* uncouth.—*n.* a lazy person.

Scoot-bog, *n.* a term of reproach.

Scoot-laniels, *n.* diarrhœa.

Scotian, *adj.* Scottish.

Scour, *n.* a quick walk ; a run of water. Cf. Scour.

Scour, *v.* to whip off with an article.

Scourie, *v.* to upbraid.

Scouth, *n.* used in playing marbles : ample space or room sufficient for a player to take his shot.

Scry, *n.* an advertisement in a newspaper. Cf. Scry.

Scumming, *ppl.* in *phr.* 'scumming the text,' preaching from a text superficially, ignoring its doctrines, or only touching lightly on them, without pressing them home.

Scutsh, *v.* to dress one's self up.

Several, *n.* a piece of land lying apart from the main portion.

Shaghlie, *adj.* loose-jointed ; bandy-legged. Cf. Shaghle.

Shank, *v.* used of a stream : to join another.

Shankless, *adj.* without a handle or shaft.

Sharplyer, *adv.* more sharply.

Shave, *n.* a sheaf.

Sheded, *ppl.* shed.

Shiffel, *n.* a shovel.

Shim, *n.* a drill-harrow. Cf. Shim.

Shoe-whang, *n.* a shoe-tie.

Shoot, *v.* in *phr.* 'to shoot a shower,' to avoid a shower. Cf. Shoot.

Shot, *ppl.* shoved, thrust.

Shot, *n.* a fabric made of warp and woof threads of different colours. Cf. Shot.

Shot-about weaver, *n.* one who produces a fabric of different colours. Cf. Shot-about.

Shoughie, *n.* a short, bandy-legged person. Cf. Shoughie.

Shoultie, *n.* a pony. Cf. Sheltie.

Shouskie, *n.* a designation of the devil ; a fondling term for a child.—*int.* a call to cattle.

Shukkie-mill, *n.* the 'death-watch,' an omen of death. Cf. Chacky-mill.

Sider, *adj.* hanging down more. Cf. Side.

Signers, *n.* subscribers for a book.

Sinny, *adj.* sunny.

Sinteen, *adj.* seventeen.

Sixty-pence, *n.* a crown-piece.

Skeep, *n.* scope.

Skeut, *adv.* aslant.

Skewl, *v.* to squint. Cf. Skewl.

Skleush, *adv.* with dirty, dragging steps. Cf. Skleush.

Skleut, *adv.* flat ; with heavy step. Cf. Skleut.

Skleuter, *adv.* with a spluttering noise ; with a splashing step.

Skleutrie, *adj.* wet and dirty. Cf. Skleuterie.

Sklitter, *v.* to walk or work in slovenly fashion.

Skug, *v.* to expiate.—*n.* a ghost. Cf. Skug.

Slacked, *ppl.* spent. Cf. Slack.

Slock, *n.* a gully in a rocky coast. Cf. Slock.

Slooter, *v.* to lounge about lazily. Cf. Slooter.

Slopin, *n.* a flight from creditors. Cf. Slope.

Sluit, *n.* a lazy animal. Cf. Sluit.

Slyp, *n.* a sledge ; a whetstone.—*v.* to whet a scythe. Cf. Slype.

Smick-smick-smack, *n.* the sound of continuous kissing.

Smoo, *v.* to sneak off.

Smookie, *n.* a bird of prey.

Smookie, *adj.* pilfering.

Smool, *n.* a scowl, a sulky look. Cf. Smool.

Smooze, *v.* to smoulder.

Smuke, *v.* to suffocate with burning sulphur. —*n.* such suffocation. Cf. Smuik.

Smushter, *n.* dross.

Smyout, *n.* a small child ; a small thing. Cf. Smout.

Snarle, *n.* a ravel, a tangle. Cf. Snorl.

Sneuker, *n.* an irritating smell. Cf. Snooker.

Sneukit, *adj.* artful.

Snoozle, *v.* to nestle into. Cf. Snoozle.

Snuiter, *v.* to move carelessly. Cf. Snuit.

Soday, *n.* a dirty woman ; a gross person.

Soosh, *v.* to work or walk energetically ; to drink off at once ; to keep intoxicated.

Soo-stack, *n.* a rectangular stack. Cf. Soo.

Souf, *adj.* faint ; exhausted. Cf. Souft.

Soule, *n.* a swivel. Cf. Sool.

Spawly, *adj.* having long, thin legs like a race-horse. Cf. Spauly.

Spool, *n.* spoil, booty. Cf. Spoolie.

Sputten, *ppl.* spat.

SS, *n.* the S-shaped openings in a fiddle.

Stapper, *n.* a stopper, anything that stuffs.

Steely, *adj.* steel-tipped.

Stew, *v.* to lop, crop. Cf. Stoo.

Stookie, *n.* stucco.—*adj.* made of stucco.

Stoorock, *n.* a warm drink, gruel. Cf. Stourum.

Stourdie, *n.* a dog.—*int.* a call to a dog.

Stouth, *n.* plenty.

Strow, *n.* bustle. Cf. Strow.

Stuit, *v.* to stutter. Cf. Stute.

Sture, *v.* to be in a bad humour. Cf. Stour.

Suit, *v. pret.* did set.

Suitten, *ppl.* set.

Sulyie, *n.* soil.

Sunblink, *adj.* bright, gleaming at intervals ; having frequent gleams of sunshine.

Suple, *adj.* supple ; nimble. Cf. Souple.

Supplee, *v.* to supply.

Suwarrow, *n.* a kind of yarn or worsted used for knitting petticoats. Cf. Suwaawra-wursit.

Swain, *n.* a shepherd.

Swoo, *n.* a heavy sound ; a whizzing sound.

Swoof, *v.* to faint.

Swuffs, *n.* an implement for winding yarn.

Syllable, *v.* to read very carefully.

Tacket, *n.* a contemptuous name for an old, toothless person. Cf. Tacket.

Tail-pocks, *n.* bags or covers for horses' tails.

Takingest, *adj.* most taking.

Tapet, *ppl.* tapped.

Tawn, *v.* to tan with the sun.

Teuve, *v. pret.* wrought hard. Cf. Tyaave.

Tew-iron, *n.* one of the stones at the bottom of a furnace that receives the metal. Cf. Tew-iron.

Thissilago, *n.* the tussilago or colt's-foot.

Thoor, *poss. adj.* your.

Thraw-cock, *n.* an implement for twisting straw-ropes.

Threeten, *v.* to threaten.

Thrushen, *ppl.* thrashed.

Thummikins, *n.* thumbkins. Cf. Thumbikins.

Tink-wife, *n.* a tinker's wife. Cf. Tinkler-wife.

Tirling-pin, -ring, *n.* the description generally given is properly that of the 'risp and ring.' The real 'tirling-pin' was probably a different device, connected with the latch of a door, which was 'tirled' or rattled to attract attention by the person seeking admittance (NOTE).

Toilman, *n.* a toiler, a labouring man.

Tool, *n.* a towel.

Tooter, *v.* to work in a silly way; to totter.— *n.* working in a silly way; ruin; a tottering walk; a weakling at work. Cf. Tootter.

Tootie, *adj.* putting into disorder; irritable; easily disturbed; subject to frequent ailments. Cf. Toutie.

Toot-mouit, *adj.* having a projecting jaw.

Toppen, *v.* to surpass.

Topperer, *n.* a term of admiration, a 'topper.'

Torr, *n.* the pommel of a saddle. Cf. Tore.

Tort, *adj.* taut.

Tour, *n.* a weed. Cf. Toor.

†Tourbillon, *n.* a whirlwind.

Tree-plate, *n.* a wooden plate or trencher.

Trimmer, *n.* a loose woman. Cf. Trimmer.

Trood, *n.* wood for fences.

Trunchered, *ppl. adj.* borne in a trencher.

Tuir, *v. pret.* tore.

Unlickit, *adj.* unpunished.

Unrigged, *ppl. adj.* unroofed, roofless. Cf. Unrig.

Unscrapit, *adj.* used of the tongue: foul, abusive.

Upmost, *adj.* having the highest score in a game or match.

Up-redd, *adj.* used of doubts, &c.: cleared up.

Vital, *n.* grain. Cf. Victual.

Wad-be, *adj.* would-be.

Waes my craws, *int.* an excl. of sorrow, pity, &c. Cf. Craws.

Waggary, *n.* a wagging movement.

Washing-hoose, *n.* a wash-house.

Wauts, *n.* the harness resting on a pony's hips.

Whanger, *n.* one who wields a lash.

Wharin', *adv.* wherewith.

Wheeoin, *n.* the whistling of a steam-engine.

Wheese, *v.* to coax. Cf. Wheeze.

Whim, *v.* to carry one's point by humouring another's whims.

Whitie, *n.* a name given to a white cow.

Wirdy, *adj.* wordy, full of words.

Wirthless, *adj.* worthless.

Wret, *v. pret.* wrote. Cf. Wrate.

Yeldness, *n.* the cessation of milk in cows.